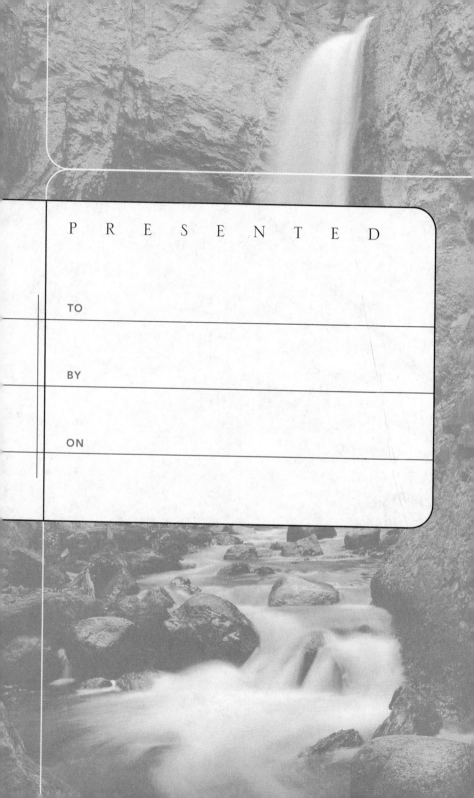

PRESENTED

TO

BY

ON

NEW INTERNATIONAL VERSION

PRAYER
DEVOTIONAL
BIBLE

ZONDERVAN™

GRAND RAPIDS, MICHIGAN 49530 USA

The Holy Bible, New International Version ®
Copyright © 1973, 1978, 1984 by International Bible Society

ZONDERVAN™

Prayer Devotional Bible

Copyright © 2004 by The Zondervan Corporation

Published by Zondervan
Grand Rapids, Michigan 49530, U.S.A.

www.zondervan.com

Library of Congress Catalog Card Number 2003116745

General Editor: Ben Patterson

Printed in the United States of America

04 05 06 07 08 09 10 /❖ DC/ 10 9 8 7 6 5 4 3

You will be pleased to know that a portion of the purchase price of your new NIV Bible has been provided to International Bible Society to help spread the gospel of Jesus Christ around the world!

Wrestling With God

32:11 "SAVE ME, I PRAY."

Jacob had been a wrestler from birth; the second of twins, he came out of his mother's womb grasping his brother Esau's heel—in itself a pretty good wrestling move! His name even means "wrestler," sort of. *Jacob* means "he grasps the heel," or figuratively "he deceives" (see Genesis 25:26). Up to this point Jacob had wrestling experience, but he wasn't a *good* wrestler. He was effective but sneaky, and he used his skills in deception to cheat his older brother Esau out of the firstborn's blessing. Esau's rage resulted in Jacob's escape and exile. But even in his new surroundings, he wrestled with his father-in-law, Laban, who also knew how to put on a few good wrestling moves.

Now in Genesis 32, Jacob is going home, hoping to reconcile with Esau. The day before he meets Esau, he prays, "God of my father Isaac, O LORD, who said to me, 'Go back to your country and your relatives, and I will make you prosper,' I am unworthy of all the kindness and faithfulness you have shown your servant . . . Save me, I pray, from the hand of my brother Esau" (verses 9–11). What lessons Jacob has learned! Before this day, he was a master at manipulating situations for his own good. Now he prays humbly for God's mercy.

But Jacob is not done wrestling; verses 24–30 describe how he wrestles with God for a blessing—and gets it! And God also gives him a new name, *Israel*, which means "he struggles with God."

God loves this kind of wrestling. Not much good comes from wrestling with people: resentment rises and enemies are made. Not much good comes from wrestling with life and work either: sleep becomes elusive and ulcers form. "In vain you rise early and stay up late, toiling for food to eat" (Psalm 127:2). "Toiling" is another word for fruitless wrestling.

Instead of "toiling," take it to the Lord in prayer. Wrestle with him for the blessing, not with people and circumstances. "Resist God, in the sense of rejecting God, and you will not be able to resist any evil. But resist God in the sense of closing with God, cling to him with your strength, not your weakness only . . . and he will give you strength. Cast yourself into his arms not to be caressed but to wrestle with him. He loves that holy war. He may be too many for you, and lift you from your feet. But it will be to lift you from earth, and set you in the heavenly places which are theirs who fight the good fight and lay hold of God as their eternal life."[3]

P R A Y :
My soul clings to you, O God. You alone have the words of life.
I will not let go till you bless me.

————

FOR YOUR NEXT DEVOTIONAL READING, GO TO PAGE 62.

from your flocks. ³⁹I did not bring you animals torn by wild beasts; I bore the loss myself. And you demanded payment from me for whatever was stolen by day or night. ⁴⁰This was my situation: The heat consumed me in the daytime and the cold at night, and sleep fled from my eyes. ⁴¹It was like this for the twenty years I was in your household. I worked for you fourteen years for your two daughters and six years for your flocks, and you changed my wages ten times. ⁴²If the God of my father, the God of Abraham and the Fear of Isaac, had not been with me, you would surely have sent me away empty-handed. But God has seen my hardship and the toil of my hands, and last night he rebuked you."

⁴³Laban answered Jacob, "The women are my daughters, the children are my children, and the flocks are my flocks. All you see is mine. Yet what can I do today about these daughters of mine, or about the children they have borne? ⁴⁴Come now, let's make a covenant, you and I, and let it serve as a witness between us."

⁴⁵So Jacob took a stone and set it up as a pillar. ⁴⁶He said to his relatives, "Gather some stones." So they took stones and piled them in a heap, and they ate there by the heap. ⁴⁷Laban called it Jegar Sahadutha,ᵃ and Jacob called it Galeed.ᵇ

⁴⁸Laban said, "This heap is a witness between you and me today." That is why it was called Galeed. ⁴⁹It was also called Mizpah,ᶜ because he said, "May the LORD keep watch between you and me when we are away from each other. ⁵⁰If you mistreat my daughters or if you take any wives besides my daughters, even though no one is with us, remember that God is a witness between you and me."

> IT WAS also called Mizpah, because he said, "May the LORD keep watch between you and me when we are away from each other."
>
> GENESIS 31:49

⁵¹Laban also said to Jacob, "Here is this heap, and here is this pillar I have set up between you and me. ⁵²This heap is a witness, and this pillar is a witness, that I will not go past this heap to your side to harm you and that you will not go past this heap and pillar to my side to harm me. ⁵³May the God of Abraham and the God of Nahor, the God of their father, judge between us."

So Jacob took an oath in the name of the Fear of his father Isaac. ⁵⁴He offered a sacrifice there in the hill country and invited his relatives to a meal. After they had eaten, they spent the night there.

⁵⁵Early the next morning Laban kissed his grandchildren and his daughters and blessed them. Then he left and returned home.

Jacob Prepares to Meet Esau

32 Jacob also went on his way, and the angels of God met him. ²When Jacob saw them, he said, "This is the camp of God!" So he named that place Mahanaim.ᵈ

³Jacob sent messengers ahead of him to his brother Esau in the land of Seir, the country of Edom. ⁴He instructed them: "This is what you are to say to my master Esau: 'Your servant Jacob says, I have been staying with Laban and have remained there till now. ⁵I have cattle and donkeys, sheep and goats, menservants and maidservants. Now I am sending this message to my lord, that I may find favor in your eyes.'"

⁶When the messengers returned to Jacob, they said, "We went to your brother Esau, and now he is coming to meet you, and four hundred men are with him."

⁷In great fear and distress Jacob divided the people who were with him into two groups,ᵉ and the flocks and herds and camels as well. ⁸He thought, "If Esau comes and attacks one group,ᶠ the groupᶠ that is left may escape."

⁹Then Jacob prayed, "O God of my father Abraham, God of my father Isaac, O LORD, who said to me, 'Go back to your country and your relatives, and I will make you prosper,' ¹⁰I am unworthy of all the kindness and faithfulness you have

---

ᵃ47 The Aramaic Jegar Sahadutha means witness heap.   ᵇ47 The Hebrew Galeed means witness heap.   ᶜ49 Mizpah means watchtower.   ᵈ2 Mahanaim means two camps.   ᵉ7 Or camps; also in verse 10   ᶠ8 Or camp

be your wages,' then all the flocks gave birth to speckled young; and if he said, 'The streaked ones will be your wages,' then all the flocks bore streaked young. ⁹So God has taken away your father's livestock and has given them to me.

¹⁰"In breeding season I once had a dream in which I looked up and saw that the male goats mating with the flock were streaked, speckled or spotted. ¹¹The angel of God said to me in the dream, 'Jacob.' I answered, 'Here I am.' ¹²And he said, 'Look up and see that all the male goats mating with the flock are streaked, speckled or spotted, for I have seen all that Laban has been doing to you. ¹³I am the God of Bethel, where you anointed a pillar and where you made a vow to me. Now leave this land at once and go back to your native land.' "

¹⁴Then Rachel and Leah replied, "Do we still have any share in the inheritance of our father's estate? ¹⁵Does he not regard us as foreigners? Not only has he sold us, but he has used up what was paid for us. ¹⁶Surely all the wealth that God took away from our father belongs to us and our children. So do whatever God has told you."

¹⁷Then Jacob put his children and his wives on camels, ¹⁸and he drove all his livestock ahead of him, along with all the goods he had accumulated in Paddan Aram,ᵃ to go to his father Isaac in the land of Canaan.

¹⁹When Laban had gone to shear his sheep, Rachel stole her father's household gods. ²⁰Moreover, Jacob deceived Laban the Aramean by not telling him he was running away. ²¹So he fled with all he had, and crossing the River,ᵇ he headed for the hill country of Gilead.

Laban Pursues Jacob

²²On the third day Laban was told that Jacob had fled. ²³Taking his relatives with him, he pursued Jacob for seven days and caught up with him in the hill country of Gilead. ²⁴Then God came to Laban the Aramean in a dream at night and said to him, "Be careful not to say anything to Jacob, either good or bad."

²⁵Jacob had pitched his tent in the hill country of Gilead when Laban overtook him, and Laban and his relatives camped there too. ²⁶Then Laban said to Jacob, "What have you done? You've deceived me, and you've carried off my daughters like captives in war. ²⁷Why did you run off secretly and deceive me? Why didn't you tell me, so I could send you away with joy and singing to the music of tambourines and harps? ²⁸You didn't even let me kiss my grandchildren and my daughters good-by. You have done a foolish thing. ²⁹I have the power to harm you; but last night the God of your father said to me, 'Be careful not to say anything to Jacob, either good or bad.' ³⁰Now you have gone off because you longed to return to your father's house. But why did you steal my gods?"

³¹Jacob answered Laban, "I was afraid, because I thought you would take your daughters away from me by force. ³²But if you find anyone who has your gods, he shall not live. In the presence of our relatives, see for yourself whether there is anything of yours here with me; and if so, take it." Now Jacob did not know that Rachel had stolen the gods.

³³So Laban went into Jacob's tent and into Leah's tent and into the tent of the two maidservants, but he found nothing. After he came out of Leah's tent, he entered Rachel's tent. ³⁴Now Rachel had taken the household gods and put them inside her camel's saddle and was sitting on them. Laban searched through everything in the tent but found nothing.

³⁵Rachel said to her father, "Don't be angry, my lord, that I cannot stand up in your presence; I'm having my period." So he searched but could not find the household gods.

³⁶Jacob was angry and took Laban to task. "What is my crime?" he asked Laban. "What sin have I committed that you hunt me down? ³⁷Now that you have searched through all my goods, what have you found that belongs to your household? Put it here in front of your relatives and mine, and let them judge between the two of us.

³⁸"I have been with you for twenty years now. Your sheep and goats have not miscarried, nor have I eaten rams

---

ᵃ18 That is, Northwest Mesopotamia
ᵇ21 That is, the Euphrates

listened to her and opened her womb. ²³She became pregnant and gave birth to a son and said, "God has taken away my disgrace." ²⁴She named him Joseph,ᵃ and said, "May the LORD add to me another son."

Jacob's Flocks Increase

²⁵After Rachel gave birth to Joseph, Jacob said to Laban, "Send me on my way so I can go back to my own homeland. ²⁶Give me my wives and children, for whom I have served you, and I will be on my way. You know how much work I've done for you."

²⁷But Laban said to him, "If I have found favor in your eyes, please stay. I have learned by divination thatᵇ the LORD has blessed me because of you." ²⁸He added, "Name your wages, and I will pay them."

²⁹Jacob said to him, "You know how I have worked for you and how your livestock has fared under my care. ³⁰The little you had before I came has increased greatly, and the LORD has blessed you wherever I have been. But now, when may I do something for my own household?"

³¹"What shall I give you?" he asked.

"Don't give me anything," Jacob replied. "But if you will do this one thing for me, I will go on tending your flocks and watching over them: ³²Let me go through all your flocks today and remove from them every speckled or spotted sheep, every dark-colored lamb and every spotted or speckled goat. They will be my wages. ³³And my honesty will testify for me in the future, whenever you check on the wages you have paid me. Any goat in my possession that is not speckled or spotted, or any lamb that is not dark-colored, will be considered stolen."

³⁴"Agreed," said Laban. "Let it be as you have said." ³⁵That same day he removed all the male goats that were streaked or spotted, and all the speckled or spotted female goats (all that had white on them) and all the dark-colored lambs, and he placed them in the care of his sons. ³⁶Then he put a three-day journey between himself and Jacob, while Jacob continued to tend the rest of Laban's flocks.

³⁷Jacob, however, took fresh-cut branches from poplar, almond and plane trees and made white stripes on them by peeling the bark and exposing the white inner wood of the branches. ³⁸Then he placed the peeled branches in all the watering troughs, so that they would be directly in front of the flocks when they came to drink. When the flocks were in heat and came to drink, ³⁹they mated in front of the branches. And they bore young that were streaked or speckled or spotted. ⁴⁰Jacob set apart the young of the flock by themselves, but made the rest face the streaked and dark-colored animals that belonged to Laban. Thus he made separate flocks for himself and did not put them with Laban's animals. ⁴¹Whenever the stronger females were in heat, Jacob would place the branches in the troughs in front of the animals so they would mate near the branches, ⁴²but if the animals were weak, he would not place them there. So the weak animals went to Laban and the strong ones to Jacob. ⁴³In this way the man grew exceedingly prosperous and came to own large flocks, and maidservants and menservants, and camels and donkeys.

Jacob Flees From Laban

31 Jacob heard that Laban's sons were saying, "Jacob has taken everything our father owned and has gained all this wealth from what belonged to our father." ²And Jacob noticed that Laban's attitude toward him was not what it had been.

³Then the LORD said to Jacob, "Go back to the land of your fathers and to your relatives, and I will be with you."

⁴So Jacob sent word to Rachel and Leah to come out to the fields where his flocks were. ⁵He said to them, "I see that your father's attitude toward me is not what it was before, but the God of my father has been with me. ⁶You know that I've worked for your father with all my strength, ⁷yet your father has cheated me by changing my wages ten times. However, God has not allowed him to harm me. ⁸If he said, 'The speckled ones will

---

ᵃ24 Joseph means may he add.
ᵇ27 Or possibly have become rich and

Jacob's Children

³¹When the LORD saw that Leah was not loved, he opened her womb, but Rachel was barren. ³²Leah became pregnant and gave birth to a son. She named him Reuben,ª for she said, "It is because the LORD has seen my misery. Surely my husband will love me now."

³³She conceived again, and when she gave birth to a son she said, "Because the LORD heard that I am not loved, he gave me this one too." So she named him Simeon.ᵇ

³⁴Again she conceived, and when she gave birth to a son she said, "Now at last my husband will become attached to me, because I have borne him three sons." So he was named Levi.ᶜ

> SHE conceived again, and when she gave birth to a son she said, "This time I will praise the LORD." So she named him Judah.
>
> GENESIS 29:35

³⁵She conceived again, and when she gave birth to a son she said, "This time I will praise the LORD." So she named him Judah.ᵈ Then she stopped having children.

30 When Rachel saw that she was not bearing Jacob any children, she became jealous of her sister. So she said to Jacob, "Give me children, or I'll die!"

²Jacob became angry with her and said, "Am I in the place of God, who has kept you from having children?"

³Then she said, "Here is Bilhah, my maidservant. Sleep with her so that she can bear children for me and that through her I too can build a family."

⁴So she gave him her servant Bilhah as a wife. Jacob slept with her, ⁵and she became pregnant and bore him a son. ⁶Then Rachel said, "God has vindicated me; he has listened to my plea and given me a son." Because of this she named him Dan.ᵉ

⁷Rachel's servant Bilhah conceived again and bore Jacob a second son. ⁸Then Rachel said, "I have had a great struggle with my sister, and I have won." So she named him Naphtali.ᶠ

⁹When Leah saw that she had stopped having children, she took her maidservant Zilpah and gave her to Jacob as a wife. ¹⁰Leah's servant Zilpah bore Jacob a son. ¹¹Then Leah said, "What good fortune!"ᵍ So she named him Gad.ʰ

¹²Leah's servant Zilpah bore Jacob a second son. ¹³Then Leah said, "How happy I am! The women will call me happy." So she named him Asher.ⁱ

¹⁴During wheat harvest, Reuben went out into the fields and found some mandrake plants, which he brought to his mother Leah. Rachel said to Leah, "Please give me some of your son's mandrakes."

¹⁵But she said to her, "Wasn't it enough that you took away my husband? Will you take my son's mandrakes too?"

"Very well," Rachel said, "he can sleep with you tonight in return for your son's mandrakes."

¹⁶So when Jacob came in from the fields that evening, Leah went out to meet him. "You must sleep with me," she said. "I have hired you with my son's mandrakes." So he slept with her that night.

¹⁷God listened to Leah, and she became pregnant and bore Jacob a fifth son. ¹⁸Then Leah said, "God has rewarded me for giving my maidservant to my husband." So she named him Issachar.ʲ

¹⁹Leah conceived again and bore Jacob a sixth son. ²⁰Then Leah said, "God has presented me with a precious gift. This time my husband will treat me with honor, because I have borne him six sons." So she named him Zebulun.ᵏ

²¹Some time later she gave birth to a daughter and named her Dinah.

²²Then God remembered Rachel; he

ª32 *Reuben* sounds like the Hebrew for *he has seen my misery*; the name means *see, a son.*   ᵇ33 *Simeon* probably means *one who hears.*   ᶜ34 *Levi* sounds like and may be derived from the Hebrew for *attached.*   ᵈ35 *Judah* sounds like and may be derived from the Hebrew for *praise.*   ᵉ6 *Dan* here means *he has vindicated.*   ᶠ8 *Naphtali* means *my struggle.*   ᵍ11 Or *"A troop is coming!"*   ʰ11 *Gad* can mean *good fortune* or *a troop.*   ⁱ13 *Asher* means *happy.*   ʲ18 *Issachar* sounds like the Hebrew for *reward.*   ᵏ20 *Zebulun* probably means *honor.*

give me food to eat and clothes to wear ²¹so that I return safely to my father's house, then the LORD*ᵃ* will be my God ²²and*ᵇ* this stone that I have set up as a pillar will be God's house, and of all that you give me I will give you a tenth."

Jacob Arrives in Paddan Aram

29 Then Jacob continued on his journey and came to the land of the eastern peoples. ²There he saw a well in the field, with three flocks of sheep lying near it because the flocks were watered from that well. The stone over the mouth of the well was large. ³When all the flocks were gathered there, the shepherds would roll the stone away from the well's mouth and water the sheep. Then they would return the stone to its place over the mouth of the well.

⁴Jacob asked the shepherds, "My brothers, where are you from?"

"We're from Haran," they replied.

⁵He said to them, "Do you know Laban, Nahor's grandson?"

"Yes, we know him," they answered.

⁶Then Jacob asked them, "Is he well?"

"Yes, he is," they said, "and here comes his daughter Rachel with the sheep."

⁷"Look," he said, "the sun is still high; it is not time for the flocks to be gathered. Water the sheep and take them back to pasture."

⁸"We can't," they replied, "until all the flocks are gathered and the stone has been rolled away from the mouth of the well. Then we will water the sheep."

⁹While he was still talking with them, Rachel came with her father's sheep, for she was a shepherdess. ¹⁰When Jacob saw Rachel daughter of Laban, his mother's brother, and Laban's sheep, he went over and rolled the stone away from the mouth of the well and watered his uncle's sheep. ¹¹Then Jacob kissed Rachel and began to weep aloud. ¹²He had told Rachel that he was a relative of her father and a son of Rebekah. So she ran and told her father.

¹³As soon as Laban heard the news about Jacob, his sister's son, he hurried to meet him. He embraced him and kissed him and brought him to his home, and there Jacob told him all these things.

¹⁴Then Laban said to him, "You are my own flesh and blood."

Jacob Marries Leah and Rachel

After Jacob had stayed with him for a whole month, ¹⁵Laban said to him, "Just because you are a relative of mine, should you work for me for nothing? Tell me what your wages should be."

¹⁶Now Laban had two daughters; the name of the older was Leah, and the name of the younger was Rachel. ¹⁷Leah had weak*ᶜ* eyes, but Rachel was lovely in form, and beautiful. ¹⁸Jacob was in love with Rachel and said, "I'll work for you seven years in return for your younger daughter Rachel."

¹⁹Laban said, "It's better that I give her to you than to some other man. Stay here with me." ²⁰So Jacob served seven years to get Rachel, but they seemed like only a few days to him because of his love for her.

²¹Then Jacob said to Laban, "Give me my wife. My time is completed, and I want to lie with her."

²²So Laban brought together all the people of the place and gave a feast. ²³But when evening came, he took his daughter Leah and gave her to Jacob, and Jacob lay with her. ²⁴And Laban gave his servant girl Zilpah to his daughter as her maidservant.

²⁵When morning came, there was Leah! So Jacob said to Laban, "What is this you have done to me? I served you for Rachel, didn't I? Why have you deceived me?"

²⁶Laban replied, "It is not our custom here to give the younger daughter in marriage before the older one. ²⁷Finish this daughter's bridal week; then we will give you the younger one also, in return for another seven years of work."

²⁸And Jacob did so. He finished the week with Leah, and then Laban gave him his daughter Rachel to be his wife. ²⁹Laban gave his servant girl Bilhah to his daughter Rachel as her maidservant. ³⁰Jacob lay with Rachel also, and he loved Rachel more than Leah. And he worked for Laban another seven years.

ᵃ20,21 Or *Since God… father's house, the* LORD *ᵇ21,22* Or *house, and the* LORD *will be my God,* ²²*then* *ᶜ17* Or *delicate*

him. He said to himself, "The days of mourning for my father are near; then I will kill my brother Jacob."

⁴²When Rebekah was told what her older son Esau had said, she sent for her younger son Jacob and said to him, "Your brother Esau is consoling himself with the thought of killing you. ⁴³Now then, my son, do what I say: Flee at once to my brother Laban in Haran. ⁴⁴Stay with him for a while until your brother's fury subsides. ⁴⁵When your brother is no longer angry with you and forgets what you did to him, I'll send word for you to come back from there. Why should I lose both of you in one day?"

⁴⁶Then Rebekah said to Isaac, "I'm disgusted with living because of these Hittite women. If Jacob takes a wife from among the women of this land, from Hittite women like these, my life will not be worth living."

28 So Isaac called for Jacob and blessed[a] him and commanded him: "Do not marry a Canaanite woman. ²Go at once to Paddan Aram,[b] to the house of your mother's father Bethuel. Take a wife for yourself there, from among the daughters of Laban, your mother's brother. ³May God Almighty[c] bless you and make you fruitful and increase your numbers until you become a community of peoples. ⁴May he give you and your descendants the blessing given

> "MAY God Almighty bless you and make you fruitful and increase your numbers until you become a community of peoples."
>
> GENESIS 28:3

to Abraham, so that you may take possession of the land where you now live as an alien, the land God gave to Abraham." ⁵Then Isaac sent Jacob on his way, and he went to Paddan Aram, to Laban son of Bethuel the Aramean, the brother of Rebekah, who was the mother of Jacob and Esau.

⁶Now Esau learned that Isaac had blessed Jacob and had sent him to Paddan Aram to take a wife from there, and that when he blessed him he command-

ed him, "Do not marry a Canaanite woman," ⁷and that Jacob had obeyed his father and mother and had gone to Paddan Aram. ⁸Esau then realized how displeasing the Canaanite women were to his father Isaac; ⁹so he went to Ishmael and married Mahalath, the sister of Nebaioth and daughter of Ishmael son of Abraham, in addition to the wives he already had.

Jacob's Dream at Bethel

¹⁰Jacob left Beersheba and set out for Haran. ¹¹When he reached a certain place, he stopped for the night because the sun had set. Taking one of the stones there, he put it under his head and lay down to sleep. ¹²He had a dream in which he saw a stairway[d] resting on the earth, with its top reaching to heaven, and the angels of God were ascending and descending on it. ¹³There above it[e] stood the LORD, and he said: "I am the LORD, the God of your father Abraham and the God of Isaac. I will give you and your descendants the land on which you are lying. ¹⁴Your descendants will be like the dust of the earth, and you will spread out to the west and to the east, to the north and to the south. All peoples on earth will be blessed through you and your offspring. ¹⁵I am with you and will watch over you wherever you go, and I will bring you back to this land. I will not leave you until I have done what I have promised you."

¹⁶When Jacob awoke from his sleep, he thought, "Surely the LORD is in this place, and I was not aware of it." ¹⁷He was afraid and said, "How awesome is this place! This is none other than the house of God; this is the gate of heaven."

¹⁸Early the next morning Jacob took the stone he had placed under his head and set it up as a pillar and poured oil on top of it. ¹⁹He called that place Bethel,[f] though the city used to be called Luz.

²⁰Then Jacob made a vow, saying, "If God will be with me and will watch over me on this journey I am taking and will

---

*a1 Or greeted   *b2 That is, Northwest Mesopotamia; also in verses 5, 6 and 7   *c3 Hebrew El-Shaddai   *d12 Or ladder   *e13 Or There beside him   *f19 Bethel means house of God.

ered his hands and the smooth part of his neck with the goatskins. ¹⁷Then she handed to her son Jacob the tasty food and the bread she had made.

¹⁸He went to his father and said, "My father."

"Yes, my son," he answered. "Who is it?"

¹⁹Jacob said to his father, "I am Esau your firstborn. I have done as you told me. Please sit up and eat some of my game so that you may give me your blessing."

²⁰Isaac asked his son, "How did you find it so quickly, my son?"

"The LORD your God gave me success," he replied.

²¹Then Isaac said to Jacob, "Come near so I can touch you, my son, to know whether you really are my son Esau or not."

²²Jacob went close to his father Isaac, who touched him and said, "The voice is the voice of Jacob, but the hands are the hands of Esau." ²³He did not recognize him, for his hands were hairy like those of his brother Esau; so he blessed him. ²⁴"Are you really my son Esau?" he asked.

"I am," he replied.

²⁵Then he said, "My son, bring me some of your game to eat, so that I may give you my blessing."

Jacob brought it to him and he ate; and he brought some wine and he drank. ²⁶Then his father Isaac said to him, "Come here, my son, and kiss me."

²⁷So he went to him and kissed him. When Isaac caught the smell of his clothes, he blessed him and said,

"Ah, the smell of my son
    is like the smell of a field
    that the LORD has blessed.
²⁸May God give you of heaven's dew
    and of earth's richness—
    an abundance of grain and
        new wine.
²⁹May nations serve you
    and peoples bow down to you.
Be lord over your brothers,
    and may the sons of your mother
        bow down to you.
May those who curse you be cursed
    and those who bless you be
        blessed."

³⁰After Isaac finished blessing him and Jacob had scarcely left his father's presence, his brother Esau came in from hunting. ³¹He too prepared some tasty food and brought it to his father. Then he said to him, "My father, sit up and eat some of my game, so that you may give me your blessing."

³²His father Isaac asked him, "Who are you?"

"I am your son," he answered, "your firstborn, Esau."

³³Isaac trembled violently and said, "Who was it, then, that hunted game and brought it to me? I ate it just before you came and I blessed him—and indeed he will be blessed!"

³⁴When Esau heard his father's words, he burst out with a loud and bitter cry and said to his father, "Bless me—me too, my father!"

³⁵But he said, "Your brother came deceitfully and took your blessing."

³⁶Esau said, "Isn't he rightly named Jacob[a]? He has deceived me these two times: He took my birthright, and now he's taken my blessing!" Then he asked, "Haven't you reserved any blessing for me?"

³⁷Isaac answered Esau, "I have made him lord over you and have made all his relatives his servants, and I have sustained him with grain and new wine. So what can I possibly do for you, my son?"

³⁸Esau said to his father, "Do you have only one blessing, my father? Bless me too, my father!" Then Esau wept aloud.

³⁹His father Isaac answered him,

"Your dwelling will be
    away from the earth's richness,
    away from the dew of heaven
        above.
⁴⁰You will live by the sword
    and you will serve your brother.
But when you grow restless,
    you will throw his yoke
    from off your neck."

Jacob Flees to Laban

⁴¹Esau held a grudge against Jacob because of the blessing his father had given

---

[a]36 Jacob means he grasps the heel (figuratively, he deceives).

Abraham, which the Philistines had stopped up after Abraham died, and he gave them the same names his father had given them.

¹⁹Isaac's servants dug in the valley and discovered a well of fresh water there. ²⁰But the herdsmen of Gerar quarreled with Isaac's herdsmen and said, "The water is ours!" So he named the well Esek,ᵃ because they disputed with him. ²¹Then they dug another well, but they quarreled over that one also; so he named it Sitnah.ᵇ ²²He moved on from there and dug another well, and no one quarreled over it. He named it Rehoboth,ᶜ saying, "Now the LORD has given us room and we will flourish in the land."

²³From there he went up to Beersheba. ²⁴That night the LORD appeared to him and said, "I am the God of your father Abraham. Do not be afraid, for I am with you; I will bless you and will increase the number of your descendants for the sake of my servant Abraham."

²⁵Isaac built an altar there and called on the name of the LORD. There he pitched his tent, and there his servants dug a well.

²⁶Meanwhile, Abimelech had come to him from Gerar, with Ahuzzath his personal adviser and Phicol the commander of his forces. ²⁷Isaac asked them, "Why have you come to me, since you were hostile to me and sent me away?"

²⁸They answered, "We saw clearly that the LORD was with you; so we said, 'There ought to be a sworn agreement between us'—between us and you. Let us make a treaty with you ²⁹that you will do us no harm, just as we did not molest you but always treated you well and sent you away in peace. And now you are blessed by the LORD."

³⁰Isaac then made a feast for them, and they ate and drank. ³¹Early the next morning the men swore an oath to each other. Then Isaac sent them on their way, and they left him in peace.

³²That day Isaac's servants came and told him about the well they had dug. They said, "We've found water!" ³³He called it Shibah,ᵈ and to this day the name of the town has been Beersheba.ᵉ

³⁴When Esau was forty years old, he married Judith daughter of Beeri the Hittite, and also Basemath daughter of Elon the Hittite. ³⁵They were a source of grief to Isaac and Rebekah.

Jacob Gets Isaac's Blessing

27 When Isaac was old and his eyes were so weak that he could no longer see, he called for Esau his older son and said to him, "My son."

"Here I am," he answered.

²Isaac said, "I am now an old man and don't know the day of my death. ³Now then, get your weapons—your quiver and bow—and go out to the open country to hunt some wild game for me. ⁴Prepare me the kind of tasty food I like and bring it to me to eat, so that I may give you my blessing before I die."

⁵Now Rebekah was listening as Isaac spoke to his son Esau. When Esau left for the open country to hunt game and bring it back, ⁶Rebekah said to her son Jacob, "Look, I overheard your father say to your brother Esau, ⁷'Bring me some game and prepare me some tasty food to eat, so that I may give you my blessing in the presence of the LORD before I die.' ⁸Now, my son, listen carefully and do what I tell you: ⁹Go out to the flock and bring me two choice young goats, so I can prepare some tasty food for your father, just the way he likes it. ¹⁰Then take it to your father to eat, so that he may give you his blessing before he dies."

¹¹Jacob said to Rebekah his mother, "But my brother Esau is a hairy man, and I'm a man with smooth skin. ¹²What if my father touches me? I would appear to be tricking him and would bring down a curse on myself rather than a blessing."

¹³His mother said to him, "My son, let the curse fall on me. Just do what I say; go and get them for me."

¹⁴So he went and got them and brought them to his mother, and she prepared some tasty food, just the way his father liked it. ¹⁵Then Rebekah took the best clothes of Esau her older son, which she had in the house, and put them on her younger son Jacob. ¹⁶She also cov-

---

ᵃ20 *Esek* means *dispute.* ᵇ21 *Sitnah* means *opposition.* ᶜ22 *Rehoboth* means *room.*
ᵈ33 *Shibah* can mean *oath* or *seven.*
ᵉ33 *Beersheba* can mean *well of the oath* or *well of seven.*

jostled each other within her, and she said, "Why is this happening to me?" So she went to inquire of the LORD.

²³The LORD said to her,

"Two nations are in your womb,
     and two peoples from within you
          will be separated;
one people will be stronger than
          the other,
     and the older will serve the
          younger."

²⁴When the time came for her to give birth, there were twin boys in her womb. ²⁵The first to come out was red, and his whole body was like a hairy garment; so they named him Esau.[a] ²⁶After this, his brother came out, with his hand grasping Esau's heel; so he was named Jacob.[b] Isaac was sixty years old when Rebekah gave birth to them.

²⁷The boys grew up, and Esau became a skillful hunter, a man of the open country, while Jacob was a quiet man, staying among the tents. ²⁸Isaac, who had a taste for wild game, loved Esau, but Rebekah loved Jacob.

²⁹Once when Jacob was cooking some stew, Esau came in from the open country, famished. ³⁰He said to Jacob, "Quick, let me have some of that red stew! I'm famished!" (That is why he was also called Edom.[c])

³¹Jacob replied, "First sell me your birthright."

³²"Look, I am about to die," Esau said. "What good is the birthright to me?"

³³But Jacob said, "Swear to me first." So he swore an oath to him, selling his birthright to Jacob.

³⁴Then Jacob gave Esau some bread and some lentil stew. He ate and drank, and then got up and left.

So Esau despised his birthright.

Isaac and Abimelech

26 Now there was a famine in the land—besides the earlier famine of Abraham's time—and Isaac went to Abimelech king of the Philistines in Gerar. ²The LORD appeared to Isaac and said, "Do not go down to Egypt; live in the land where I tell you to live. ³Stay in this land for a while, and I will be with you and will bless you. For to you and

your descendants I will give all these lands and will confirm the oath I swore to your father Abraham. ⁴I will make your descendants as numerous as the stars in the sky and will give them all these lands, and through your offspring[d] all nations on earth will be blessed, ⁵because Abraham obeyed me and kept my requirements, my commands, my decrees and my laws." ⁶So Isaac stayed in Gerar.

⁷When the men of that place asked him about his wife, he said, "She is my sister," because he was afraid to say, "She is my wife." He thought, "The men of this place might kill me on account of Rebekah, because she is beautiful."

⁸When Isaac had been there a long time, Abimelech king of the Philistines looked down from a window and saw Isaac caressing his wife Rebekah. ⁹So Abimelech summoned Isaac and said, "She is really your wife! Why did you say, 'She is my sister'?"

Isaac answered him, "Because I thought I might lose my life on account of her."

¹⁰Then Abimelech said, "What is this you have done to us? One of the men might well have slept with your wife, and you would have brought guilt upon us."

¹¹So Abimelech gave orders to all the people: "Anyone who molests this man or his wife shall surely be put to death."

¹²Isaac planted crops in that land and the same year reaped a hundredfold, because the LORD blessed him. ¹³The man became rich, and his wealth continued to grow until he became very wealthy. ¹⁴He had so many flocks and herds and servants that the Philistines envied him. ¹⁵So all the wells that his father's servants had dug in the time of his father Abraham, the Philistines stopped up, filling them with earth.

¹⁶Then Abimelech said to Isaac, "Move away from us; you have become too powerful for us."

¹⁷So Isaac moved away from there and encamped in the Valley of Gerar and settled there. ¹⁸Isaac reopened the wells that had been dug in the time of his father

---

[a]25 Esau may mean hairy; he was also called Edom, which means red.   [b]26 Jacob means he grasps the heel (figuratively, he deceives).   [c]30 Edom means red.   [d]4 Or seed

"I will go," she said.

⁵⁹So they sent their sister Rebekah on her way, along with her nurse and Abraham's servant and his men. ⁶⁰And they blessed Rebekah and said to her,

"Our sister, may you increase
  to thousands upon thousands;
may your offspring possess
  the gates of their enemies."

⁶¹Then Rebekah and her maids got ready and mounted their camels and went back with the man. So the servant took Rebekah and left.

⁶²Now Isaac had come from Beer Lahai Roi, for he was living in the Negev. ⁶³He went out to the field one evening to meditate,^a and as he looked up, he saw camels approaching. ⁶⁴Rebekah also looked up and saw Isaac. She got down from her camel ⁶⁵and asked the servant, "Who is that man in the field coming to meet us?"

"He is my master," the servant answered. So she took her veil and covered herself.

⁶⁶Then the servant told Isaac all he had done. ⁶⁷Isaac brought her into the tent of his mother Sarah, and he married Rebekah. So she became his wife, and he loved her; and Isaac was comforted after his mother's death.

The Death of Abraham

25 Abraham took^b another wife, whose name was Keturah. ²She bore him Zimran, Jokshan, Medan, Midian, Ishbak and Shuah. ³Jokshan was the father of Sheba and Dedan; the descendants of Dedan were the Asshurites, the Letushites and the Leummites. ⁴The sons of Midian were Ephah, Epher, Hanoch, Abida and Eldaah. All these were descendants of Keturah.

⁵Abraham left everything he owned to Isaac. ⁶But while he was still living, he gave gifts to the sons of his concubines and sent them away from his son Isaac to the land of the east.

⁷Altogether, Abraham lived a hundred and seventy-five years. ⁸Then Abraham breathed his last and died at a good old age, an old man and full of years; and he was gathered to his people. ⁹His sons Isaac and Ishmael buried him in the cave of Machpelah near Mamre, in the field of Ephron son of Zohar the Hittite, ¹⁰the field Abraham had bought from the Hittites.^c There Abraham was buried with his wife Sarah. ¹¹After Abraham's death, God blessed his son Isaac, who then lived near Beer Lahai Roi.

Ishmael's Sons

¹²This is the account of Abraham's son Ishmael, whom Sarah's maidservant, Hagar the Egyptian, bore to Abraham.

¹³These are the names of the sons of Ishmael, listed in the order of their birth: Nebaioth the firstborn of Ishmael, Kedar, Adbeel, Mibsam, ¹⁴Mishma, Dumah, Massa, ¹⁵Hadad, Tema, Jetur, Naphish and Kedemah. ¹⁶These were the sons of Ishmael, and these are the names of the twelve tribal rulers according to their settlements and camps. ¹⁷Altogether, Ishmael lived a hundred and thirty-seven years. He breathed his last and died, and he was gathered to his people. ¹⁸His descendants settled in the area from Havilah to Shur, near the border of Egypt, as you go toward Asshur. And they lived in hostility toward^d all their brothers.

Jacob and Esau

¹⁹This is the account of Abraham's son Isaac.

Abraham became the father of Isaac, ²⁰and Isaac was forty years old when he married Rebekah daughter of Bethuel the Aramean from Paddan Aram^e and sister of Laban the Aramean.

> ISAAC prayed to the LORD on behalf of his wife, because she was barren. The LORD answered his prayer, and his wife Rebekah became pregnant.
>
> GENESIS 25:21

²¹Isaac prayed to the LORD on behalf of his wife, because she was barren. The LORD answered his prayer, and his wife Rebekah became pregnant. ²²The babies

^a63 The meaning of the Hebrew for this word is uncertain. ^b1 Or had taken ^c10 Or the sons of Heth ^d18 Or lived to the east of ^e20 That is, Northwest Mesopotamia

Rebekah had a brother named Laban, and he hurried out to the man at the spring. ³⁰As soon as he had seen the nose ring, and the bracelets on his sister's arms, and had heard Rebekah tell what the man said to her, he went out to the man and found him standing by the camels near the spring. ³¹"Come, you who are blessed by the LORD," he said. "Why are you standing out here? I have prepared the house and a place for the camels."

³²So the man went to the house, and the camels were unloaded. Straw and fodder were brought for the camels, and water for him and his men to wash their feet. ³³Then food was set before him, but he said, "I will not eat until I have told you what I have to say."

"Then tell us," ⸢Laban⸣ said.

³⁴So he said, "I am Abraham's servant. ³⁵The LORD has blessed my master abundantly, and he has become wealthy. He has given him sheep and cattle, silver and gold, menservants and maidservants, and camels and donkeys. ³⁶My master's wife Sarah has borne him a son in her*ᵃ* old age, and he has given him everything he owns. ³⁷And my master made me swear an oath, and said, 'You must not get a wife for my son from the daughters of the Canaanites, in whose land I live, ³⁸but go to my father's family and to my own clan, and get a wife for my son.'

³⁹"Then I asked my master, 'What if the woman will not come back with me?'

⁴⁰"He replied, 'The LORD, before whom I have walked, will send his angel with you and make your journey a success, so that you can get a wife for my son from my own clan and from my father's family. ⁴¹Then, when you go to my clan, you will be released from my oath even if they refuse to give her to you—you will be released from my oath.'

⁴²"When I came to the spring today, I said, 'O LORD, God of my master Abraham, if you will, please grant success to the journey on which I have come. ⁴³See, I am standing beside this spring; if a maiden comes out to draw water and I say to her, "Please let me drink a little water from your jar," ⁴⁴and if she says to me, "Drink, and I'll draw water for your

camels too," let her be the one the LORD has chosen for my master's son.'

⁴⁵"Before I finished praying in my heart, Rebekah came out, with her jar on her shoulder. She went down to the spring and drew water, and I said to her, 'Please give me a drink.'

⁴⁶"She quickly lowered her jar from her shoulder and said, 'Drink, and I'll water your camels too.' So I drank, and she watered the camels also.

⁴⁷"I asked her, 'Whose daughter are you?'

"She said, 'The daughter of Bethuel son of Nahor, whom Milcah bore to him.'

"Then I put the ring in her nose and the bracelets on her arms, ⁴⁸and I bowed down and worshiped the LORD. I praised the LORD, the God of my master Abraham, who had led me on the right road to get the granddaughter of my master's brother for his son. ⁴⁹Now if you will show kindness and faithfulness to my master, tell me; and if not, tell me, so I may know which way to turn."

⁵⁰Laban and Bethuel answered, "This is from the LORD; we can say nothing to you one way or the other. ⁵¹Here is Rebekah; take her and go, and let her become the wife of your master's son, as the LORD has directed."

⁵²When Abraham's servant heard what they said, he bowed down to the ground before the LORD. ⁵³Then the servant brought out gold and silver jewelry and articles of clothing and gave them to Rebekah; he also gave costly gifts to her brother and to her mother. ⁵⁴Then he and the men who were with him ate and drank and spent the night there.

When they got up the next morning, he said, "Send me on my way to my master."

⁵⁵But her brother and her mother replied, "Let the girl remain with us ten days or so; then you*ᵇ* may go."

⁵⁶But he said to them, "Do not detain me, now that the LORD has granted success to my journey. Send me on my way so I may go to my master."

⁵⁷Then they said, "Let's call the girl and ask her about it." ⁵⁸So they called Rebekah and asked her, "Will you go with this man?"

ᵃ36 Or his   ᵇ55 Or she

weighing a beka[a] and two gold bracelets weighing ten shekels.[b] 23Then he asked, "Whose daughter are you? Please tell me, is there room in your father's house for us to spend the night?"

24She answered him, "I am the daughter of Bethuel, the son that Milcah bore to Nahor." 25And she added, "We have plenty of straw and fodder, as well as room for you to spend the night."

26Then the man bowed down and worshiped the LORD, 27saying, "Praise be to the LORD, the God of my master Abraham, who has not abandoned his kindness and faithfulness to my master. As for me, the LORD has led me on the journey to the house of my master's relatives."

28The girl ran and told her mother's household about these things. 29Now

> THEN the man bowed down and worshiped the LORD.
>
> GENESIS 24:26

[a]22 That is, about 1/5 ounce (about 5.5 grams)
[b]22 That is, about 4 ounces (about 110 grams)

[TUESDAY]

GENESIS 24:12–15

Prayer for Spouses and Masters

24:12 "GIVE ME SUCCESS TODAY, AND SHOW KINDNESS TO MY MASTER ABRAHAM."

You can't fail to be moved by the sweetness of this servant's prayer: "O LORD, God of my master Abraham, give me success today, and show kindness to my master Abraham" (verse 12). It is the most natural thing in the world to ask God for a loving, godly spouse because the God to whom we pray has said, "It is not good for the man to be alone. I will make a helper suitable for him" (Genesis 2:18). Proverbs 18:22 also encourages confidence in this kind of prayer: "He who finds a wife finds what is good and receives favor from the LORD." God even chose the relationship of husband to wife to be the defining metaphor of Christ's relationship to the church (see Ephesians 5:22–33).

The Lord loves to answer our petitions for a spouse with a warm "Yes!" But even when his answer is "No" it is for the sake of a different "Yes." His gracious will for most is not his will for all; but it is no less gracious for those who receive a different gift (see 1 Corinthians 7:7–8 for Paul's advice to those who are single).

The servant's prayer is praiseworthy for another reason: It is a prayer to serve his master faithfully. He understands on a deep level that to serve Abraham well is to serve God well. The Apostle Paul speaks to this type of prayer, too. In Ephesians 6:5–7, he tells slaves to obey their "earthly masters with respect and fear, and with sincerity of heart, just as you would obey Christ. Obey them not only to win their favor when their eye is on you, but like slaves of Christ, doing the will of God from your heart. Serve wholeheartedly, as if you were serving the Lord, not men." Serve your earthly master, or boss, from your heart, and you will find yourself praying for your boss from your heart.

PRAY:
Master of all, tune my heart both to sing your praise, and to praise you with my heartfelt service and prayers for my earthly "master."

FOR YOUR NEXT DEVOTIONAL READING, GO TO PAGE 42.

¹²Again Abraham bowed down before the people of the land ¹³and he said to Ephron in their hearing, "Listen to me, if you will. I will pay the price of the field. Accept it from me so I can bury my dead there."

¹⁴Ephron answered Abraham, ¹⁵"Listen to me, my lord; the land is worth four hundred shekels[a] of silver, but what is that between me and you? Bury your dead."

¹⁶Abraham agreed to Ephron's terms and weighed out for him the price he had named in the hearing of the Hittites: four hundred shekels of silver, according to the weight current among the merchants.

¹⁷So Ephron's field in Machpelah near Mamre—both the field and the cave in it, and all the trees within the borders of the field—was deeded ¹⁸to Abraham as his property in the presence of all the Hittites who had come to the gate of the city. ¹⁹Afterward Abraham buried his wife Sarah in the cave in the field of Machpelah near Mamre (which is at Hebron) in the land of Canaan. ²⁰So the field and the cave in it were deeded to Abraham by the Hittites as a burial site.

Isaac and Rebekah

24 Abraham was now old and well advanced in years, and the LORD had blessed him in every way. ²He said to the chief[b] servant in his household, the one in charge of all that he had, "Put your hand under my thigh. ³I want you to swear by the LORD, the God of heaven and the God of earth, that you will not get a wife for my son from the daughters of the Canaanites, among whom I am living, ⁴but will go to my country and my own relatives and get a wife for my son Isaac."

⁵The servant asked him, "What if the woman is unwilling to come back with me to this land? Shall I then take your son back to the country you came from?"

⁶"Make sure that you do not take my son back there," Abraham said. ⁷"The LORD, the God of heaven, who brought me out of my father's household and my native land and who spoke to me and promised me on oath, saying, 'To your offspring[c] I will give this land'—he will send his angel before you so that you can get a wife for my son from there. ⁸If the woman is unwilling to come back with you, then you will be released from this oath of mine. Only do not take my son back there." ⁹So the servant put his hand under the thigh of his master Abraham and swore an oath to him concerning this matter.

¹⁰Then the servant took ten of his master's camels and left, taking with him all kinds of good things from his master. He set out for Aram Naharaim[d] and made his way to the town of Nahor. ¹¹He had the camels kneel down near the well outside the town; it was toward evening, the time the women go out to draw water.

¹²Then he prayed, "O LORD, God of my master Abraham, give me success today, and show kindness to my master Abraham. ¹³See, I am standing beside this spring, and the daughters of the townspeople are coming out to draw water. ¹⁴May it be that when I say to a girl, 'Please let down your jar that I may have a drink,' and she says, 'Drink, and I'll water your camels too'—let her be the one you have chosen for your servant Isaac. By this I will know that you have shown kindness to my master."

¹⁵Before he had finished praying, Rebekah came out with her jar on her shoulder. She was the daughter of Bethuel son of Milcah, who was the wife of Abraham's brother Nahor. ¹⁶The girl was very beautiful, a virgin; no man had ever lain with her. She went down to the spring, filled her jar and came up again.

¹⁷The servant hurried to meet her and said, "Please give me a little water from your jar."

¹⁸"Drink, my lord," she said, and quickly lowered the jar to her hands and gave him a drink.

¹⁹After she had given him a drink, she said, "I'll draw water for your camels too, until they have finished drinking." ²⁰So she quickly emptied her jar into the trough, ran back to the well to draw more water, and drew enough for all his camels. ²¹Without saying a word, the man watched her closely to learn whether or not the LORD had made his journey successful.

²²When the camels had finished drinking, the man took out a gold nose ring

---

a15 That is, about 10 pounds (about 4.5 kilograms)   *b2* Or *oldest*   *c7* Or *seed*
d10 That is, Northwest Mesopotamia

day Abraham looked up and saw the place in the distance. [5]He said to his servants, "Stay here with the donkey while I and the boy go over there. We will worship and then we will come back to you."

[6]Abraham took the wood for the burnt offering and placed it on his son Isaac, and he himself carried the fire and the knife. As the two of them went on together, [7]Isaac spoke up and said to his father Abraham, "Father?"

"Yes, my son?" Abraham replied.

"The fire and wood are here," Isaac said, "but where is the lamb for the burnt offering?"

[8]Abraham answered, "God himself will provide the lamb for the burnt offering, my son." And the two of them went on together.

[9]When they reached the place God had told him about, Abraham built an altar there and arranged the wood on it. He bound his son Isaac and laid him on the altar, on top of the wood. [10]Then he reached out his hand and took the knife to slay his son. [11]But the angel of the LORD called out to him from heaven, "Abraham! Abraham!"

"Here I am," he replied.

[12]"Do not lay a hand on the boy," he said. "Do not do anything to him. Now I know that you fear God, because you have not withheld from me your son, your only son."

[13]Abraham looked up and there in a thicket he saw a ram[a] caught by its horns. He went over and took the ram and sacrificed it as a burnt offering instead of his son. [14]So Abraham called that place The LORD Will Provide. And to this day it is said, "On the mountain of the LORD it will be provided."

[15]The angel of the LORD called to Abraham from heaven a second time [16]and said, "I swear by myself, declares the LORD, that because you have done this and have not withheld your son, your only son, [17]I will surely bless you and make your descendants as numerous as the stars in the sky and as the sand on the seashore. Your descendants will take possession of the cities of their enemies, [18]and through your offspring[b] all nations on earth will be blessed, because you have obeyed me."

[19]Then Abraham returned to his servants, and they set off together for Beersheba. And Abraham stayed in Beersheba.

Nahor's Sons

[20]Some time later Abraham was told, "Milcah is also a mother; she has borne sons to your brother Nahor: [21]Uz the firstborn, Buz his brother, Kemuel (the father of Aram), [22]Kesed, Hazo, Pildash, Jidlaph and Bethuel." [23]Bethuel became the father of Rebekah. Milcah bore these eight sons to Abraham's brother Nahor. [24]His concubine, whose name was Reumah, also had sons: Tebah, Gaham, Tahash and Maacah.

The Death of Sarah

23 Sarah lived to be a hundred and twenty-seven years old. [2]She died at Kiriath Arba (that is, Hebron) in the land of Canaan, and Abraham went to mourn for Sarah and to weep over her.

[3]Then Abraham rose from beside his dead wife and spoke to the Hittites.[c] He said, [4]"I am an alien and a stranger among you. Sell me some property for a burial site here so I can bury my dead."

[5]The Hittites replied to Abraham, [6]"Sir, listen to us. You are a mighty prince among us. Bury your dead in the choicest of our tombs. None of us will refuse you his tomb for burying your dead."

[7]Then Abraham rose and bowed down before the people of the land, the Hittites. [8]He said to them, "If you are willing to let me bury my dead, then listen to me and intercede with Ephron son of Zohar on my behalf [9]so he will sell me the cave of Machpelah, which belongs to him and is at the end of his field. Ask him to sell it to me for the full price as a burial site among you."

[10]Ephron the Hittite was sitting among his people and he replied to Abraham in the hearing of all the Hittites who had come to the gate of his city. [11]"No, my lord," he said. "Listen to me; I give[d] you the field, and I give[d] you the cave that is in it. I give[d] it to you in the presence of my people. Bury your dead."

---

[a]13 Many manuscripts of the Masoretic Text, Samaritan Pentateuch, Septuagint and Syriac; most manuscripts of the Masoretic Text *a ram behind him.*   [b]18 Or *seed*   [c]3 Or *the sons of Heth*; also in verses 5, 7, 10, 16, 18 and 20   [d]11 Or *sell*

³²After the treaty had been made at Beersheba, Abimelech and Phicol the commander of his forces returned to the land of the Philistines. ³³Abraham planted a tamarisk tree in Beersheba, and there he called upon the name of the LORD, the Eternal God. ³⁴And Abraham stayed in the land of the Philistines for a long time.

Abraham Tested

22 Some time later God tested Abraham. He said to him, "Abraham!"

"Here I am," he replied.

²Then God said, "Take your son, your only son, Isaac, whom you love, and go to the region of Moriah. Sacrifice him there as a burnt offering on one of the mountains I will tell you about."

³Early the next morning Abraham got up and saddled his donkey. He took with him two of his servants and his son Isaac. When he had cut enough wood for the burnt offering, he set out for the place God had told him about. ⁴On the third

---

{ MONDAY }

GENESIS 22:1–19

For Life or Death

22:8 "GOD HIMSELF WILL PROVIDE THE LAMB."

Martin Luther said, "The only saving faith is that which casts itself on God for life or death." Abraham's faith, in this gut-wrenching story, is exhibit "A" of that truth. It has puzzled and inspired both believers and nonbelievers alike for centuries. In his weakness and grief, Abraham's faith was strong, even though it probably didn't feel that way to him. But believing that God's promise to bless the world through his offspring was true, he "reasoned that God could raise the dead" (Hebrews 11:19) if necessary. So he cast himself on God for life or death.

Abraham's faith has come a long way from the finagling and second guessing of the Hagar episode. It is different, though not necessarily better, from the faith that wrestled with God over Sodom and Gomorrah. This time he simply says "Yes," to God's command and explains his actions to a confused son who wants to know where the lamb for the offering is: "God himself will provide the lamb for the burnt offering, my son" (Genesis 22:8). Abraham had learned that the only way to keep his life was to completely trust in God.

How does one get to this kind of faith? By years of walking, and sometimes stumbling, in a faith relationship. The key to a growing faith is the cultivation of a close relationship with God over the long haul. Abraham had grown in intimacy with God by being forced sometimes to have to trust him in ways he didn't understand. But mostly, it was the day-in, day-out choice to walk by faith in the little things that taught him to trust God in the big things. That is why the spiritual disciplines, particularly of prayer and Scripture reading, are so important. By showing us the face of God when we can see it, they help us to trust when we can't see it.

PRAY:

Dear Father, help me to see you today, that I might remember what I saw when I can't see you. Teach me to walk by faith, casting myself on you for life or death.

FOR YOUR NEXT DEVOTIONAL READING, GO TO PAGE 30.

> *NOW the LORD was gracious to Sarah as he had said, and the LORD did for Sarah what he had promised.*
>
> GENESIS 21:1

The Birth of Isaac

21 Now the LORD was gracious to Sarah as he had said, and the LORD did for Sarah what he had promised. ²Sarah became pregnant and bore a son to Abraham in his old age, at the very time God had promised him. ³Abraham gave the name Isaac*ᵃ* to the son Sarah bore him. ⁴When his son Isaac was eight days old, Abraham circumcised him, as God commanded him. ⁵Abraham was a hundred years old when his son Isaac was born to him.

⁶Sarah said, "God has brought me laughter, and everyone who hears about this will laugh with me." ⁷And she added, "Who would have said to Abraham that Sarah would nurse children? Yet I have borne him a son in his old age."

Hagar and Ishmael Sent Away

⁸The child grew and was weaned, and on the day Isaac was weaned Abraham held a great feast. ⁹But Sarah saw that the son whom Hagar the Egyptian had borne to Abraham was mocking, ¹⁰and she said to Abraham, "Get rid of that slave woman and her son, for that slave woman's son will never share in the inheritance with my son Isaac."

¹¹The matter distressed Abraham greatly because it concerned his son. ¹²But God said to him, "Do not be so distressed about the boy and your maidservant. Listen to whatever Sarah tells you, because it is through Isaac that your offspring*ᵇ* will be reckoned. ¹³I will make the son of the maidservant into a nation also, because he is your offspring."

¹⁴Early the next morning Abraham took some food and a skin of water and gave them to Hagar. He set them on her shoulders and then sent her off with the boy. She went on her way and wandered in the desert of Beersheba.

¹⁵When the water in the skin was gone, she put the boy under one of the bushes.

¹⁶Then she went off and sat down nearby, about a bowshot away, for she thought, "I cannot watch the boy die." And as she sat there nearby, she*ᶜ* began to sob.

¹⁷God heard the boy crying, and the angel of God called to Hagar from heaven and said to her, "What is the matter, Hagar? Do not be afraid; God has heard the boy crying as he lies there. ¹⁸Lift the boy up and take him by the hand, for I will make him into a great nation."

¹⁹Then God opened her eyes and she saw a well of water. So she went and filled the skin with water and gave the boy a drink.

²⁰God was with the boy as he grew up. He lived in the desert and became an archer. ²¹While he was living in the Desert of Paran, his mother got a wife for him from Egypt.

The Treaty at Beersheba

²²At that time Abimelech and Phicol the commander of his forces said to Abraham, "God is with you in everything you do. ²³Now swear to me here before God that you will not deal falsely with me or my children or my descendants. Show to me and the country where you are living as an alien the same kindness I have shown to you."

²⁴Abraham said, "I swear it."

²⁵Then Abraham complained to Abimelech about a well of water that Abimelech's servants had seized. ²⁶But Abimelech said, "I don't know who has done this. You did not tell me, and I heard about it only today."

²⁷So Abraham brought sheep and cattle and gave them to Abimelech, and the two men made a treaty. ²⁸Abraham set apart seven ewe lambs from the flock, ²⁹and Abimelech asked Abraham, "What is the meaning of these seven ewe lambs you have set apart by themselves?"

³⁰He replied, "Accept these seven lambs from my hand as a witness that I dug this well."

³¹So that place was called Beersheba,*ᵈ* because the two men swore an oath there.

ᵃ3 Isaac means *he laughs.* *ᵇ12* Or *seed*
ᶜ16 Hebrew; Septuagint *the child*
ᵈ31 Beersheba can mean *well of seven* or *well of the oath.*

a continuous 24 hour, 7 day a week prayer vigil, and sent 2000 missionaries
to the ends of the earth. It was at a Moravian prayer meeting in London that
John Wesley felt his heart "strangely warmed." From that encounter came
the world-shaking Wesleyan revival, the impact of which we feel to this day.

Comenius prayed for God to preserve in Bohemia "a hidden seed to
glorify thy name." From a human perspective, it may have seemed that God
did nothing for a century. But for the next two and a half centuries he went
far beyond anything that little bunch of refugees could have ever
imagined—beyond Bohemia to the world!

God's ways are not our ways. His timing is not our timing. Where are you
in your prayers now? Kneeling with Comenius in the snow? Wondering with
Comenius at the end of his life? Read and reflect on the seed parables of Mark
4. Ask the Holy Spirit to strengthen your praying with mustard seed hope.

PRAY:

Holy Spirit of God! I pray, hoping for things I cannot
now see. Strengthen my little mustard seed faith to wait
for the day when faith becomes sight. Amen.

MEMORIZE:

"What shall we say the kingdom of God is like, or what parable shall
we use to describe it? It is like a mustard seed, which is the smallest
seed you plant in the ground. Yet when planted, it grows and
becomes the largest of all garden plants, with such big branches
that the birds of the air can perch in its shade." MARK 4:30–32

FOR YOUR NEXT DEVOTIONAL READING, GO TO PAGE 27.

Mustard Seed Praying

JESUS SAID the kingdom of God starts small but grows large, quietly and mysteriously, like a tiny seed planted in the soil (see Mark 4:1–20,26–32). It should not surprise us, therefore, that God's answers to prayer often come in the same way. We pray and we wait and wait and wait. We wonder, *Did he hear, does he care, has he refused?*

In the 1620s, John Amos Comenius and a rag tag bunch of his church members knelt in the snow at the Polish border and prayed a wistful but bold mustard seed prayer. Caught in the turmoil of Catholic-Protestant rivalry in The Thirty Years War, they had been forced to leave their beloved Bohemia. As they knelt shivering, they looked back longingly at their homeland, as Comenius asked God to preserve in Bohemia "a hidden seed to glorify thy name." But Comenius never saw his prayer answered. In 1670 he died an expatriate, penniless and homeless. He did, however, leave the world 154 books that were seminal in the formation of modern ideas about Christian education.

Comenius's prayer wasn't answered until 100 years later when a young Count Zinzendorf opened his family estate in Moravia as a refuge for the followers of Comenius. They called their community the *Herrnhut*, or "Lord's Watch." Since they themselves were the fruit of mustard seed praying, they took their name from Isaiah 62:6–7, a great text on mustard seed prayer: "I have posted watchmen on your walls, O Jerusalem; they will never be silent day or night. You who call on the LORD, give yourselves no rest, and give him no rest till he establishes Jerusalem and makes her the praise of the earth."

The Moravian Brethren, as they came to be known, were the pioneers of modern missions. In the first 100 years of their existence, they maintained

and preserve our family line through our father."

³³That night they got their father to drink wine, and the older daughter went in and lay with him. He was not aware of it when she lay down or when she got up.

³⁴The next day the older daughter said to the younger, "Last night I lay with my father. Let's get him to drink wine again tonight, and you go in and lie with him so we can preserve our family line through our father." ³⁵So they got their father to drink wine that night also, and the younger daughter went and lay with him. Again he was not aware of it when she lay down or when she got up.

³⁶So both of Lot's daughters became pregnant by their father. ³⁷The older daughter had a son, and she named him Moab*ᵃ*; he is the father of the Moabites of today. ³⁸The younger daughter also had a son, and she named him Ben-Ammi*ᵇ*; he is the father of the Ammonites of today.

Abraham and Abimelech

20 Now Abraham moved on from there into the region of the Negev and lived between Kadesh and Shur. For a while he stayed in Gerar, ²and there Abraham said of his wife Sarah, "She is my sister." Then Abimelech king of Gerar sent for Sarah and took her.

³But God came to Abimelech in a dream one night and said to him, "You are as good as dead because of the woman you have taken; she is a married woman."

⁴Now Abimelech had not gone near her, so he said, "Lord, will you destroy an innocent nation? ⁵Did he not say to me, 'She is my sister,' and didn't she also say, 'He is my brother'? I have done this with a clear conscience and clean hands."

⁶Then God said to him in the dream, "Yes, I know you did this with a clear conscience, and so I have kept you from sinning against me. That is why I did not let you touch her. ⁷Now return the man's wife, for he is a prophet, and he will pray for you and you will live. But if you do not

return her, you may be sure that you and all yours will die."

⁸Early the next morning Abimelech summoned all his officials, and when he told them all that had happened, they were very much afraid. ⁹Then Abimelech called Abraham in and said, "What have you done to us? How have I wronged you that you have brought such great guilt upon me and my kingdom? You have done things to me that should not be done." ¹⁰And Abimelech asked Abraham, "What was your reason for doing this?"

¹¹Abraham replied, "I said to myself, 'There is surely no fear of God in this place, and they will kill me because of my wife.' ¹²Besides, she really is my sister, the daughter of my father though not of my mother; and she became my wife. ¹³And when God had me wander from my father's household, I said to her, 'This is how you can show your love to me: Everywhere we go, say of me, "He is my brother." ' "

¹⁴Then Abimelech brought sheep and cattle and male and female slaves and gave them to Abraham, and he returned Sarah his wife to him. ¹⁵And Abimelech said, "My land is before you; live wherever you like."

¹⁶To Sarah he said, "I am giving your brother a thousand shekels*ᶜ* of silver. This is to cover the offense against you before all who are with you; you are completely vindicated."

> THEN *Abraham prayed to God, and God healed Abimelech, his wife and his slave girls so they could have children again.*
>
> GENESIS 20:17

¹⁷Then Abraham prayed to God, and God healed Abimelech, his wife and his slave girls so they could have children again, ¹⁸for the LORD had closed up every womb in Abimelech's household because of Abraham's wife Sarah.

ᵃ*37* Moab *sounds like the Hebrew for* from father. ᵇ*38* Ben-Ammi *means* son of my people. ᶜ*16* That is, about 25 pounds (about 11.5 kilograms)

both young and old—surrounded the house. ⁵They called to Lot, "Where are the men who came to you tonight? Bring them out to us so that we can have sex with them."

⁶Lot went outside to meet them and shut the door behind him ⁷and said, "No, my friends. Don't do this wicked thing. ⁸Look, I have two daughters who have never slept with a man. Let me bring them out to you, and you can do what you like with them. But don't do anything to these men, for they have come under the protection of my roof."

⁹"Get out of our way," they replied. And they said, "This fellow came here as an alien, and now he wants to play the judge! We'll treat you worse than them." They kept bringing pressure on Lot and moved forward to break down the door.

¹⁰But the men inside reached out and pulled Lot back into the house and shut the door. ¹¹Then they struck the men who were at the door of the house, young and old, with blindness so that they could not find the door.

¹²The two men said to Lot, "Do you have anyone else here—sons-in-law, sons or daughters, or anyone else in the city who belongs to you? Get them out of here, ¹³because we are going to destroy this place. The outcry to the LORD against its people is so great that he has sent us to destroy it."

¹⁴So Lot went out and spoke to his sons-in-law, who were pledged to marry[a] his daughters. He said, "Hurry and get out of this place, because the LORD is about to destroy the city!" But his sons-in-law thought he was joking.

¹⁵With the coming of dawn, the angels urged Lot, saying, "Hurry! Take your wife and your two daughters who are here, or you will be swept away when the city is punished."

¹⁶When he hesitated, the men grasped his hand and the hands of his wife and of his two daughters and led them safely out of the city, for the LORD was merciful to them. ¹⁷As soon as they had brought them out, one of them said, "Flee for your lives! Don't look back, and don't stop anywhere in the plain! Flee to the mountains or you will be swept away!"

¹⁸But Lot said to them, "No, my lords,[b] please! ¹⁹Your[c] servant has found favor in your[c] eyes, and you[c] have shown great kindness to me in sparing my life. But I can't flee to the mountains; this disaster will overtake me, and I'll die. ²⁰Look, here is a town near enough to run to, and it is small. Let me flee to it—it is very small, isn't it? Then my life will be spared."

²¹He said to him, "Very well, I will grant this request too; I will not overthrow the town you speak of. ²²But flee there quickly, because I cannot do anything until you reach it." (That is why the town was called Zoar.[d])

²³By the time Lot reached Zoar, the sun had risen over the land. ²⁴Then the LORD rained down burning sulfur on Sodom and Gomorrah—from the LORD out of the heavens. ²⁵Thus he overthrew those cities and the entire plain, including all those living in the cities—and also the vegetation in the land. ²⁶But Lot's wife looked back, and she became a pillar of salt.

²⁷Early the next morning Abraham got up and returned to the place where he had stood before the LORD. ²⁸He looked down toward Sodom and Gomorrah, toward all the land of the plain, and he saw dense smoke rising from the land, like smoke from a furnace.

²⁹So when God destroyed the cities of the plain, he remembered Abraham, and he brought Lot out of the catastrophe that overthrew the cities where Lot had lived.

Lot and His Daughters

³⁰Lot and his two daughters left Zoar and settled in the mountains, for he was afraid to stay in Zoar. He and his two daughters lived in a cave. ³¹One day the older daughter said to the younger, "Our father is old, and there is no man around here to lie with us, as is the custom all over the earth. ³²Let's get our father to drink wine and then lie with him

---

[a] 14 Or were married to   [b] 18 Or No, Lord; or No, my lord   [c] 19 The Hebrew is singular.   [d] 22 Zoar means small.

GENESIS 18:16–33

Finding Out About Prayer

18:17 "SHALL I HIDE FROM ABRAHAM WHAT I AM ABOUT TO DO?"

In 1952 a doctoral student at Princeton asked a visiting lecturer, "What is there left in the world for original dissertation research?" The visiting lecturer was Albert Einstein. His answer was, "Find out about prayer. Somebody must find out about prayer." The problem with the question is that it was about science, and prayer doesn't yield its secrets to scientific methods. God won't be put under a microscope.

But God most definitely wants us to learn about prayer. First, he takes the initiative to get us to pray. *Why* he does this with Abraham is fascinating. He asks himself, "Shall I hide from Abraham what I am about to do?" (verse 17). He answers his own question: "Abraham will surely become a great and powerful nation, and all nations on earth will be blessed through him" (verse 18). Since Abraham has a key role to play in God's purposes for the world, God decides therefore to bring him into the conversation about Sodom and Gomorrah. Like a king with his royal advisers, God wants Abraham to intercede for the cities.

Pascal reasoned that one of the reasons God gave us prayer was to give us the dignity of causality. Do you appreciate the extraordinary gift God gives in prayer? He works on us by his grace to get us to work on him by our faith. He grants to prayer a power to which he will graciously condescend to submit.

How God gets us to pray is equally fascinating. As with Abraham, he often uses perplexity to draw us into prayer. Abraham's nephew Lot lives in Sodom and may die if God carries out his plan. Abraham is aghast and remonstrates, "Far be it from you . . . Will not the Judge of all the earth do right?" (verse 25). Sadly, many of us would not pray if we weren't driven to our knees. The result is that when the praying is over, we and Abraham discover God is better than we knew him to be before the perplexity.

We rejoice in testing because it makes faith pure (see James 1:2–4). God himself seems to rejoice in the effects the perplexity has on us. He so wants us to pray that he seems to more than tolerate Abraham's *chutzpah* in verse 25 (see also the devotion on Mark 7:24–30) . He actually seems to enjoy it. In prayer, God calls us to be active partners, not passive spectators.

PRAY:

Great God! You don't need us, but in your wisdom and love,

you call us to this partnership of prayer.

Get me out of the grandstands onto the praying field.

FOR YOUR NEXT DEVOTIONAL READING, GO TO PAGE 24.

and well advanced in years, and Sarah was past the age of childbearing. ¹²So Sarah laughed to herself as she thought, "After I am worn out and my master*a* is old, will I now have this pleasure?"

¹³Then the LORD said to Abraham, "Why did Sarah laugh and say, 'Will I really have a child, now that I am old?' ¹⁴Is anything too hard for the LORD? I will return to you at the appointed time next year and Sarah will have a son."

¹⁵Sarah was afraid, so she lied and said, "I did not laugh."

But he said, "Yes, you did laugh."

Abraham Pleads for Sodom

¹⁶When the men got up to leave, they looked down toward Sodom, and Abraham walked along with them to see them on their way. ¹⁷Then the LORD said, "Shall I hide from Abraham what I am about to do? ¹⁸Abraham will surely become a great and powerful nation, and all nations on earth will be blessed through him. ¹⁹For I have chosen him, so that he will direct his children and his household after him to keep the way of the LORD by doing what is right and just, so that the LORD will bring about for Abraham what he has promised him."

²⁰Then the LORD said, "The outcry against Sodom and Gomorrah is so great and their sin so grievous ²¹that I will go down and see if what they have done is as bad as the outcry that has reached me. If not, I will know."

²²The men turned away and went toward Sodom, but Abraham remained standing before the LORD.*b* ²³Then Abraham approached him and said: "Will you sweep away the righteous with the wicked? ²⁴What if there are fifty righteous people in the city? Will you really sweep it away and not spare*c* the place for the sake of the fifty righteous people in it? ²⁵Far be it from you to do such a thing—to kill the righteous with the wicked, treating the righteous and the wicked alike. Far be it from you! Will not the Judge*d* of all the earth do right?"

²⁶The LORD said, "If I find fifty righteous people in the city of Sodom, I will spare the whole place for their sake."

²⁷Then Abraham spoke up again: "Now that I have been so bold as to speak to the Lord, though I am nothing but dust and ashes, ²⁸what if the number of the righteous is five less than fifty? Will you destroy the whole city because of five people?"

"If I find forty-five there," he said, "I will not destroy it."

²⁹Once again he spoke to him, "What if only forty are found there?"

He said, "For the sake of forty, I will not do it."

³⁰Then he said, "May the Lord not be angry, but let me speak. What if only thirty can be found there?"

He answered, "I will not do it if I find thirty there."

³¹Abraham said, "Now that I have been so bold as to speak to the Lord, what if only twenty can be found there?"

He said, "For the sake of twenty, I will not destroy it."

³²Then he said, "May the Lord not be angry, but let me speak just once more. What if only ten can be found there?"

He answered, "For the sake of ten, I will not destroy it."

³³When the LORD had finished speaking with Abraham, he left, and Abraham returned home.

Sodom and Gomorrah Destroyed

19 The two angels arrived at Sodom in the evening, and Lot was sitting in the gateway of the city. When he saw them, he got up to meet them and bowed down with his face to the ground. ²"My lords," he said, "please turn aside to your servant's house. You can wash your feet and spend the night and then go on your way early in the morning."

"No," they answered, "we will spend the night in the square."

³But he insisted so strongly that they did go with him and entered his house. He prepared a meal for them, baking bread without yeast, and they ate. ⁴Before they had gone to bed, all the men from every part of the city of Sodom—

---

a 12 Or *husband* *b 22* Masoretic Text; an ancient Hebrew scribal tradition *but the LORD remained standing before Abraham*
c 24 Or *forgive*; also in verse 26 *d 25* Or *Ruler*

sion, and it will be the sign of the covenant between me and you. ¹²For the generations to come every male among you who is eight days old must be circumcised, including those born in your household or bought with money from a foreigner—those who are not your offspring. ¹³Whether born in your household or bought with your money, they must be circumcised. My covenant in your flesh is to be an everlasting covenant. ¹⁴Any uncircumcised male, who has not been circumcised in the flesh, will be cut off from his people; he has broken my covenant."

¹⁵God also said to Abraham, "As for Sarai your wife, you are no longer to call her Sarai; her name will be Sarah. ¹⁶I will bless her and will surely give you a son by her. I will bless her so that she will be the mother of nations; kings of peoples will come from her."

¹⁷Abraham fell facedown; he laughed and said to himself, "Will a son be born to a man a hundred years old? Will Sarah bear a child at the age of ninety?" ¹⁸And Abraham said to God, "If only Ishmael might live under your blessing!"

> ABRAHAM said to God, "If only Ishmael might live under your blessing!" Then God said ... as for Ishmael, I have heard you: I will surely bless him.
>
> GENESIS 17:18 – 20

¹⁹Then God said, "Yes, but your wife Sarah will bear you a son, and you will call him Isaac.ᵃ I will establish my covenant with him as an everlasting covenant for his descendants after him. ²⁰And as for Ishmael, I have heard you: I will surely bless him; I will make him fruitful and will greatly increase his numbers. He will be the father of twelve rulers, and I will make him into a great nation. ²¹But my covenant I will establish with Isaac, whom Sarah will bear to you by this time next year." ²²When he had finished speaking with Abraham, God went up from him.

²³On that very day Abraham took his son Ishmael and all those born in his household or bought with his money, every male in his household, and circumcised them, as God told him. ²⁴Abraham was ninety-nine years old when he was circumcised, ²⁵and his son Ishmael was thirteen; ²⁶Abraham and his son Ishmael were both circumcised on that same day. ²⁷And every male in Abraham's household, including those born in his household or bought from a foreigner, was circumcised with him.

The Three Visitors

18 The LORD appeared to Abraham near the great trees of Mamre while he was sitting at the entrance to his tent in the heat of the day. ²Abraham looked up and saw three men standing nearby. When he saw them, he hurried from the entrance of his tent to meet them and bowed low to the ground.

³He said, "If I have found favor in your eyes, my lord,ᵇ do not pass your servant by. ⁴Let a little water be brought, and then you may all wash your feet and rest under this tree. ⁵Let me get you something to eat, so you can be refreshed and then go on your way—now that you have come to your servant."

"Very well," they answered, "do as you say."

⁶So Abraham hurried into the tent to Sarah. "Quick," he said, "get three seahsᶜ of fine flour and knead it and bake some bread."

⁷Then he ran to the herd and selected a choice, tender calf and gave it to a servant, who hurried to prepare it. ⁸He then brought some curds and milk and the calf that had been prepared, and set these before them. While they ate, he stood near them under a tree.

⁹"Where is your wife Sarah?" they asked him.

"There, in the tent," he said.

¹⁰Then the LORDᵈ said, "I will surely return to you about this time next year, and Sarah your wife will have a son."

Now Sarah was listening at the entrance to the tent, which was behind him. ¹¹Abraham and Sarah were already old

---

ᵃ19 Isaac means he laughs.   ᵇ3 Or O Lord
ᶜ6 That is, probably about 20 quarts (about 22 liters)   ᵈ10 Hebrew Then he

the pieces. [18]On that day the LORD made a covenant with Abram and said, "To your descendants I give this land, from the river[a] of Egypt to the great river, the Euphrates— [19]the land of the Kenites, Kenizzites, Kadmonites, [20]Hittites, Perizzites, Rephaites, [21]Amorites, Canaanites, Girgashites and Jebusites."

Hagar and Ishmael

16 Now Sarai, Abram's wife, had borne him no children. But she had an Egyptian maidservant named Hagar; [2]so she said to Abram, "The LORD has kept me from having children. Go, sleep with my maidservant; perhaps I can build a family through her."

Abram agreed to what Sarai said. [3]So after Abram had been living in Canaan ten years, Sarai his wife took her Egyptian maidservant Hagar and gave her to her husband to be his wife. [4]He slept with Hagar, and she conceived.

When she knew she was pregnant, she began to despise her mistress. [5]Then Sarai said to Abram, "You are responsible for the wrong I am suffering. I put my servant in your arms, and now that she knows she is pregnant, she despises me. May the LORD judge between you and me."

[6]"Your servant is in your hands," Abram said. "Do with her whatever you think best." Then Sarai mistreated Hagar; so she fled from her.

[7]The angel of the LORD found Hagar near a spring in the desert; it was the spring that is beside the road to Shur. [8]And he said, "Hagar, servant of Sarai, where have you come from, and where are you going?"

"I'm running away from my mistress Sarai," she answered.

[9]Then the angel of the LORD told her, "Go back to your mistress and submit to her." [10]The angel added, "I will so increase your descendants that they will be too numerous to count."

[11]The angel of the LORD also said to her:

"You are now with child
   and you will have a son.
You shall name him Ishmael,[b]
   for the LORD has heard of your
      misery.

[12]He will be a wild donkey of a man;
   his hand will be against everyone
   and everyone's hand against him,
   and he will live in hostility
      toward[c] all his brothers."

[13]She gave this name to the LORD who spoke to her: "You are the God who sees me," for she said, "I have now seen[d] the One who sees me." [14]That is why the well was called Beer Lahai Roi[e]; it is still there, between Kadesh and Bered.

[15]So Hagar bore Abram a son, and Abram gave the name Ishmael to the son she had borne. [16]Abram was eighty-six years old when Hagar bore him Ishmael.

The Covenant of Circumcision

17 When Abram was ninety-nine years old, the LORD appeared to him and said, "I am God Almighty[f]; walk before me and be blameless. [2]I will confirm my covenant between me and you and will greatly increase your numbers."

[3]Abram fell facedown, and God said to him, [4]"As for me, this is my covenant with you: You will be the father of many nations. [5]No longer will you be called Abram[g]; your name will be Abraham,[h] for I have made you a father of many nations. [6]I will make you very fruitful; I will make nations of you, and kings will come from you. [7]I will establish my covenant as an everlasting covenant between me and you and your descendants after you for the generations to come, to be your God and the God of your descendants after you. [8]The whole land of Canaan, where you are now an alien, I will give as an everlasting possession to you and your descendants after you; and I will be their God."

[9]Then God said to Abraham, "As for you, you must keep my covenant, you and your descendants after you for the generations to come. [10]This is my covenant with you and your descendants after you, the covenant you are to keep: Every male among you shall be circumcised. [11]You are to undergo circumci-

---

[a]18 Or *Wadi*   [b]11 *Ishmael* means *God hears.*   [c]12 Or *live to the east / of*   [d]13 Or *seen the back of*   [e]14 *Beer Lahai Roi* means *well of the Living One who sees me.*   [f]1 Hebrew *El-Shaddai*   [g]5 *Abram* means *exalted father.*   [h]5 *Abraham* means *father of many.*

¹²As the sun was setting, Abram fell into a deep sleep, and a thick and dreadful darkness came over him. ¹³Then the LORD said to him, "Know for certain that your descendants will be strangers in a country not their own, and they will be enslaved and mistreated four hundred years. ¹⁴But I will punish the nation they serve as slaves, and afterward they will come out with great possessions. ¹⁵You, however, will go to your fathers in peace and be buried at a good old age. ¹⁶In the fourth generation your descendants will come back here, for the sin of the Amorites has not yet reached its full measure."

¹⁷When the sun had set and darkness had fallen, a smoking firepot with a blazing torch appeared and passed between

---

GENESIS 15

The Forge

15:6 ABRAM BELIEVED THE LORD, AND HE CREDITED IT TO HIM AS RIGHTEOUSNESS.

This verse is really good news. God knows how bad we are at the thing we most need to be good at: meeting his holy standards. It pleases him to accept us as holy if we trust his promises. Think about it, and you will be astonished by the Good News: "For it is by grace you have been saved, through faith" (Ephesians 2:8).

Now hear the hard part: Faith is forged in delay. A forge is a furnace heated to a high temperature. Metal is thrust into the forge and made white hot; it is then pounded into shape. God's forge for our faith is the gap between the giving of his promise and its fulfillment. Faith is forged in delay, but the temptation in delay is to jump out of the forge. The most common way we do this is by becoming "God's little helpers"—believing we can achieve his ends using our own means.

That's Abram's temptation here. In his day, a childless couple could adopt a slave and make him their heir. For Abram, that man is Eliezer of Damascus. True, God had promised Abram and Sarai a child, but that was when Abram was 75 years old. Time has passed, and they're not getting any younger, so maybe what God wants is for them to practice a little common sense, a little conventional wisdom, and do the prudent thing. But God makes it clear once again that he means to give them their own biological child. Abram believes this and is credited with righteousness. So far, so good. But one chapter later the childless couple will jump out of the forge and try their own methods again with disastrous results.

The hardest thing about prayer is the waiting. Jesus told his disciples a parable about prayer so that they would keep on praying and not lose heart. It ended with the question, "When the Son of Man comes, will he find faith on the earth?" (Luke 18:8). Will we still be in the forge, praying and waiting, our faith being tested and strengthened?

PRAY:

Dear Father, your timing is perfect. You make all things beautiful in your time.
Strengthen me to wait and pray with patience and faith.

FOR YOUR NEXT DEVOTIONAL READING, GO TO PAGE 21.

⁹against Kedorlaomer king of Elam, Tidal king of Goiim, Amraphel king of Shinar and Arioch king of Ellasar—four kings against five. ¹⁰Now the Valley of Siddim was full of tar pits, and when the kings of Sodom and Gomorrah fled, some of the men fell into them and the rest fled to the hills. ¹¹The four kings seized all the goods of Sodom and Gomorrah and all their food; then they went away. ¹²They also carried off Abram's nephew Lot and his possessions, since he was living in Sodom.

¹³One who had escaped came and reported this to Abram the Hebrew. Now Abram was living near the great trees of Mamre the Amorite, a brother*a* of Eshcol and Aner, all of whom were allied with Abram. ¹⁴When Abram heard that his relative had been taken captive, he called out the 318 trained men born in his household and went in pursuit as far as Dan. ¹⁵During the night Abram divided his men to attack them and he routed them, pursuing them as far as Hobah, north of Damascus. ¹⁶He recovered all the goods and brought back his relative Lot and his possessions, together with the women and the other people.

¹⁷After Abram returned from defeating Kedorlaomer and the kings allied with him, the king of Sodom came out to meet him in the Valley of Shaveh (that is, the King's Valley).

¹⁸Then Melchizedek king of Salem*b* brought out bread and wine. He was priest of God Most High, ¹⁹and he blessed Abram, saying,

"Blessed be Abram by God Most
    High,
    Creator*c* of heaven and earth.
²⁰And blessed be*d* God Most High,
    who delivered your enemies into
    your hand."

Then Abram gave him a tenth of everything.

²¹The king of Sodom said to Abram, "Give me the people and keep the goods for yourself."

²²But Abram said to the king of Sodom, "I have raised my hand to the LORD, God Most High, Creator of heaven and earth, and have taken an oath ²³that I will accept nothing belonging to you, not even

a thread or the thong of a sandal, so that you will never be able to say, 'I made Abram rich.' ²⁴I will accept nothing but what my men have eaten and the share that belongs to the men who went with me—to Aner, Eshcol and Mamre. Let them have their share."

God's Covenant With Abram

15 After this, the word of the LORD came to Abram in a vision:

"Do not be afraid, Abram.
    I am your shield,*e*
    your very great reward.*f*"

²But Abram said, "O Sovereign LORD, what can you give me since I remain childless and the one who will inherit*g* my estate is Eliezer of Damascus?" ³And Abram said, "You have given me no children; so a servant in my household will be my heir."

⁴Then the word of the LORD came to him: "This man will not be your heir, but a son coming from your own body will be your heir." ⁵He took him outside and said, "Look up at the heavens and count the stars—if indeed you can count them." Then he said to him, "So shall your offspring be."

⁶Abram believed the LORD, and he credited it to him as righteousness.

⁷He also said to him, "I am the LORD, who brought you out of Ur of the Chaldeans to give you this land to take possession of it."

⁸But Abram said, "O Sovereign LORD, how can I know that I will gain possession of it?"

⁹So the LORD said to him, "Bring me a heifer, a goat and a ram, each three years old, along with a dove and a young pigeon."

¹⁰Abram brought all these to him, cut them in two and arranged the halves opposite each other; the birds, however, he did not cut in half. ¹¹Then birds of prey came down on the carcasses, but Abram drove them away.

---

*a*13 Or *a relative*; or *an ally*   *b*18 That is, Jerusalem   *c*19 Or *Possessor*; also in verse 22   *d*20 Or *And praise be to*   *e*1 Or *sovereign*   *f*1 Or *shield; / your reward will be very great*   *g*2 The meaning of the Hebrew for this phrase is uncertain.

cials saw her, they praised her to Pharaoh, and she was taken into his palace. [16]He treated Abram well for her sake, and Abram acquired sheep and cattle, male and female donkeys, menservants and maidservants, and camels.

[17]But the Lord inflicted serious diseases on Pharaoh and his household because of Abram's wife Sarai. [18]So Pharaoh summoned Abram. "What have you done to me?" he said. "Why didn't you tell me she was your wife? [19]Why did you say, 'She is my sister,' so that I took her to be my wife? Now then, here is your wife. Take her and go!" [20]Then Pharaoh gave orders about Abram to his men, and they sent him on his way, with his wife and everything he had.

Abram and Lot Separate

13 So Abram went up from Egypt to the Negev, with his wife and everything he had, and Lot went with him. [2]Abram had become very wealthy in livestock and in silver and gold.

[3]From the Negev he went from place to place until he came to Bethel, to the place between Bethel and Ai where his tent had been earlier [4]and where he had first built an altar. There Abram called on the name of the Lord.

[5]Now Lot, who was moving about with Abram, also had flocks and herds and tents. [6]But the land could not support them while they stayed together, for their possessions were so great that they were not able to stay together. [7]And quarreling arose between Abram's herdsmen and the herdsmen of Lot. The Canaanites and Perizzites were also living in the land at that time.

[8]So Abram said to Lot, "Let's not have any quarreling between you and me, or between your herdsmen and mine, for we are brothers. [9]Is not the whole land before you? Let's part company. If you go to the left, I'll go to the right; if you go to the right, I'll go to the left."

[10]Lot looked up and saw that the whole plain of the Jordan was well watered, like the garden of the Lord, like the land of Egypt, toward Zoar. (This was before the Lord destroyed Sodom and Gomorrah.) [11]So Lot chose for himself the whole plain of the Jordan and set out toward the east.

The two men parted company: [12]Abram lived in the land of Canaan, while Lot lived among the cities of the plain and pitched his tents near Sodom. [13]Now the men of Sodom were wicked and were sinning greatly against the Lord.

[14]The Lord said to Abram after Lot had parted from him, "Lift up your eyes from where you are and look north and south, east and west. [15]All the land that you see I will give to you and your offspring[a] forever. [16]I will make your offspring like the dust of the earth, so that if anyone could count the dust, then your offspring could be counted. [17]Go, walk through the length and breadth of the land, for I am giving it to you."

[18]So Abram moved his tents and went to live near the great trees of Mamre at Hebron, where he built an altar to the Lord.

Abram Rescues Lot

14 At this time Amraphel king of Shinar,[b] Arioch king of Ellasar, Kedorlaomer king of Elam and Tidal king of Goiim [2]went to war against Bera king of Sodom, Birsha king of Gomorrah, Shinab king of Admah, Shemeber king of Zeboiim, and the king of Bela (that is, Zoar). [3]All these latter kings joined forces in the Valley of Siddim (the Salt Sea[c]). [4]For twelve years they had been subject to Kedorlaomer, but in the thirteenth year they rebelled.

[5]In the fourteenth year, Kedorlaomer and the kings allied with him went out and defeated the Rephaites in Ashteroth Karnaim, the Zuzites in Ham, the Emites in Shaveh Kiriathaim [6]and the Horites in the hill country of Seir, as far as El Paran near the desert. [7]Then they turned back and went to En Mishpat (that is, Kadesh), and they conquered the whole territory of the Amalekites, as well as the Amorites who were living in Hazazon Tamar.

[8]Then the king of Sodom, the king of Gomorrah, the king of Admah, the king of Zeboiim and the king of Bela (that is, Zoar) marched out and drew up their battle lines in the Valley of Siddim

severe. ¹¹As he was about to enter Egypt, he said to his wife Sarai, "I know what a beautiful woman you are. ¹²When the Egyptians see you, they will say, 'This is his wife.' Then they will kill me but will let you live. ¹³Say you are my sister, so that I will be treated well for your sake and my life will be spared because of you."

¹⁴When Abram came to Egypt, the Egyptians saw that she was a very beautiful woman. ¹⁵And when Pharaoh's offi-

---

[WEDNESDAY]

GENESIS 12:1–9; 13:14–18

Living by Unseen Realities

12:2 "I WILL MAKE YOU INTO A GREAT NATION."

"How odd / Of God, / To choose / The Jews." The whole question of why God chooses whom he chooses to do his work in the world is a mystery. Those lines of William Norman Ewer were his way of wondering why. The Bible's answer regarding God's choosing people is, "so that no one may boast before him" (1 Corinthians 1:29). This means that the real story here is about God, not about whom he chooses as his servant. The personal and moral qualities one might look for in a man who was to be the father of millions, and through whom the peoples of earth would be blessed, aren't mentioned in Genesis 12 because they are beside the point. All God looked for in Abram was faith. Would Abram trust God enough to leave what he had known, to travel to something he didn't know? Note: It was not something God *had* shown him; it was what God *would* show him. Abram didn't even get a map; all he got was a promise. His faith was a call to live by unseen realties.

What a worldview of prayer! When we do something on our own with what we can see, who gets the glory? We do. When God answers prayer in ways we can't see, who gets the glory? He does. So now no one can boast.

Wherever Abram went, this man of faith pitched tents and built altars (see 12:7; 13:18). Tents are about the seen, what is ours; altars are about the unseen, what is God's. Abram's place of residence was a passing thing, his hope in the God he prayed to was fixed. If God's people are often odd (see 1 Corinthians 1:25–29), it's only because God's methods are odd too—from the world's perspective. So again, no one can boast.

To pray you must hope in God's good promises more than you do in your own good ideas. When you do this, you are taken places you never dreamed, for you hear God calling you to:

> Leap out from your reedy shallows.
> Dive into the moving water.
> Eyeless, learn to see truly.
> Find in my folly your true sanity.²

PRAY:

God of Abraham, Isaac, Jacob and our Lord Jesus Christ: Teach me to pray, that you may gain great glory, and I might know the joy of communion with you.

FOR YOUR NEXT DEVOTIONAL READING, GO TO PAGE 17.

¹²When Arphaxad had lived 35 years, he became the father of Shelah. ¹³And after he became the father of Shelah, Arphaxad lived 403 years and had other sons and daughters.ᵃ

¹⁴When Shelah had lived 30 years, he became the father of Eber. ¹⁵And after he became the father of Eber, Shelah lived 403 years and had other sons and daughters.

¹⁶When Eber had lived 34 years, he became the father of Peleg. ¹⁷And after he became the father of Peleg, Eber lived 430 years and had other sons and daughters.

¹⁸When Peleg had lived 30 years, he became the father of Reu. ¹⁹And after he became the father of Reu, Peleg lived 209 years and had other sons and daughters.

²⁰When Reu had lived 32 years, he became the father of Serug. ²¹And after he became the father of Serug, Reu lived 207 years and had other sons and daughters.

²²When Serug had lived 30 years, he became the father of Nahor. ²³And after he became the father of Nahor, Serug lived 200 years and had other sons and daughters.

²⁴When Nahor had lived 29 years, he became the father of Terah. ²⁵And after he became the father of Terah, Nahor lived 119 years and had other sons and daughters.

²⁶After Terah had lived 70 years, he became the father of Abram, Nahor and Haran.

²⁷This is the account of Terah.

Terah became the father of Abram, Nahor and Haran. And Haran became the father of Lot. ²⁸While his father Terah was still alive, Haran died in Ur of the Chaldeans, in the land of his birth. ²⁹Abram and Nahor both married. The name of Abram's wife was Sarai, and the name of Nahor's wife was Milcah; she was the daughter of Haran, the father of both Milcah and Iscah. ³⁰Now Sarai was barren; she had no children.

³¹Terah took his son Abram, his grandson Lot son of Haran, and his daughter-in-law Sarai, the wife of his son Abram, and together they set out from Ur of the Chaldeans to go to Canaan. But when they came to Haran, they settled there. ³²Terah lived 205 years, and he died in Haran.

The Call of Abram

12 The LORD had said to Abram, "Leave your country, your people and your father's household and go to the land I will show you.

² "I will make you into a great nation
    and I will bless you;
I will make your name great,
    and you will be a blessing.
³ I will bless those who bless you,
    and whoever curses you I will
        curse;
and all peoples on earth
    will be blessed through you."

⁴So Abram left, as the LORD had told him; and Lot went with him. Abram was seventy-five years old when he set out from Haran. ⁵He took his wife Sarai, his nephew Lot, all the possessions they had accumulated and the people they had acquired in Haran, and they set out for the land of Canaan, and they arrived there.

⁶Abram traveled through the land as far as the site of the great tree of Moreh at Shechem. At that time the Canaanites were in the land. ⁷The LORD appeared to Abram and said, "To your offspringᵇ I will give this land." So he built an altar there to the LORD, who had appeared to him.

⁸From there he went on toward the hills east of Bethel and pitched his tent, with Bethel on the west and Ai on the east. There he built an altar to the LORD and called on the name of the LORD. ⁹Then Abram set out and continued toward the Negev.

Abram in Egypt

¹⁰Now there was a famine in the land, and Abram went down to Egypt to live there for a while because the famine was

ᵃ12,13 Hebrew; Septuagint (see also Luke 3:35, 36 and note at Gen. 10:24) 35 years, he became the father of Cainan. ¹³And after he became the father of Cainan, Arphaxad lived 430 years and had other sons and daughters, and then he died. When Cainan had lived 130 years, he became the father of Shelah. And after he became the father of Shelah, Cainan lived 330 years and had other sons and daughters   ᵇ7 Or seed

were Babylon, Erech, Akkad and Calneh, in[a] Shinar.[b] [11]From that land he
went to Assyria, where he built Nineveh,
Rehoboth Ir,[c] Calah [12]and Resen, which
is between Nineveh and Calah; that is
the great city.

[13]Mizraim was the father of
the Ludites, Anamites, Lehabites,
Naphtuhites, [14]Pathrusites, Casluhites (from whom the Philistines
came) and Caphtorites.
[15]Canaan was the father of
Sidon his firstborn,[d] and of the
Hittites, [16]Jebusites, Amorites, Girgashites, [17]Hivites, Arkites, Sinites, [18]Arvadites, Zemarites and
Hamathites.

Later the Canaanite clans scattered
[19]and the borders of Canaan reached
from Sidon toward Gerar as far as Gaza,
and then toward Sodom, Gomorrah, Admah and Zeboiim, as far as Lasha.

[20]These are the sons of Ham by their
clans and languages, in their territories
and nations.

The Semites

[21]Sons were also born to Shem, whose
older brother was[e] Japheth; Shem was
the ancestor of all the sons of Eber.

[22]The sons of Shem:
Elam, Asshur, Arphaxad, Lud and
Aram.
[23]The sons of Aram:
Uz, Hul, Gether and Meshech.[f]
[24]Arphaxad was the father of[g] Shelah,
and Shelah the father of Eber.
[25]Two sons were born to Eber:
One was named Peleg,[h] because
in his time the earth was divided;
his brother was named Joktan.
[26]Joktan was the father of
Almodad, Sheleph, Hazarmaveth,
Jerah, [27]Hadoram, Uzal, Diklah,
[28]Obal, Abimael, Sheba, [29]Ophir,
Havilah and Jobab. All these were
sons of Joktan.

[30]The region where they lived stretched
from Mesha toward Sephar, in the eastern hill country.

[31]These are the sons of Shem by their
clans and languages, in their territories
and nations.

[32]These are the clans of Noah's sons,
according to their lines of descent, within their nations. From these the nations
spread out over the earth after the flood.

The Tower of Babel

11 Now the whole world had one language and a common speech. [2]As
men moved eastward,[i] they found a plain
in Shinar[j] and settled there.

[3]They said to each other, "Come, let's
make bricks and bake them thoroughly."
They used brick instead of stone, and tar
for mortar. [4]Then they said, "Come, let
us build ourselves a city, with a tower
that reaches to the heavens, so that we
may make a name for ourselves and not
be scattered over the face of the whole
earth."

[5]But the LORD came down to see the
city and the tower that the men were
building. [6]The LORD said, "If as one people speaking the same language they
have begun to do this, then nothing they
plan to do will be impossible for them.
[7]Come, let us go down and confuse their
language so they will not understand
each other."

[8]So the LORD scattered them from
there over all the earth, and they
stopped building the city. [9]That is why
it was called Babel[k]—because there the
LORD confused the language of the
whole world. From there the LORD scattered them over the face of the whole
earth.

From Shem to Abram

[10]This is the account of Shem.

Two years after the flood, when Shem
was 100 years old, he became the father[l]
of Arphaxad. [11]And after he became the
father of Arphaxad, Shem lived 500 years
and had other sons and daughters.

---

[a]10 Or Erech and Akkad—all of them in
[b]10 That is, Babylonia   [c]11 Or Nineveh with
its city squares   [d]15 Or of the Sidonians, the
foremost   [e]21 Or Shem, the older brother of
[f]23 See Septuagint and 1 Chron. 1:17; Hebrew
Mash   [g]24 Hebrew; Septuagint father of
Cainan, and Cainan was the father of
[h]25 Peleg means division.   [i]2 Or from the
east; or in the east   [j]2 That is, Babylonia
[k]9 That is, Babylon; Babel sounds like the Hebrew
for confused.   [l]10 Father may mean ancestor;
also in verses 11–25.

with you: Never again will all life be cut off by the waters of a flood; never again will there be a flood to destroy the earth."

¹²And God said, "This is the sign of the covenant I am making between me and you and every living creature with you, a covenant for all generations to come: ¹³I have set my rainbow in the clouds, and it will be the sign of the covenant between me and the earth. ¹⁴Whenever I bring clouds over the earth and the rainbow appears in the clouds, ¹⁵I will remember my covenant between me and you and all living creatures of every kind. Never again will the waters become a flood to destroy all life. ¹⁶Whenever the rainbow appears in the clouds, I will see it and remember the everlasting covenant between God and all living creatures of every kind on the earth."

¹⁷So God said to Noah, "This is the sign of the covenant I have established between me and all life on the earth."

The Sons of Noah

¹⁸The sons of Noah who came out of the ark were Shem, Ham and Japheth. (Ham was the father of Canaan.) ¹⁹These were the three sons of Noah, and from them came the people who were scattered over the earth.

²⁰Noah, a man of the soil, proceeded^a to plant a vineyard. ²¹When he drank some of its wine, he became drunk and lay uncovered inside his tent. ²²Ham, the father of Canaan, saw his father's nakedness and told his two brothers outside. ²³But Shem and Japheth took a garment and laid it across their shoulders; then they walked in backward and covered their father's nakedness. Their faces were turned the other way so that they would not see their father's nakedness.

²⁴When Noah awoke from his wine and found out what his youngest son had done to him, ²⁵he said,

"Cursed be Canaan!
    The lowest of slaves
    will he be to his brothers."

²⁶He also said,

"Blessed be the LORD, the God
    of Shem!
    May Canaan be the slave of Shem.^{b}

²⁷May God extend the territory
        of Japheth^c;
    may Japheth live in the tents
        of Shem,
    and may Canaan be his^d slave."

²⁸After the flood Noah lived 350 years. ²⁹Altogether, Noah lived 950 years, and then he died.

The Table of Nations

10 This is the account of Shem, Ham and Japheth, Noah's sons, who themselves had sons after the flood.

The Japhethites

²The sons^e of Japheth:
    Gomer, Magog, Madai, Javan, Tubal, Meshech and Tiras.
³The sons of Gomer:
    Ashkenaz, Riphath and Togarmah.
⁴The sons of Javan:
    Elishah, Tarshish, the Kittim and the Rodanim.^{f} ⁵(From these the maritime peoples spread out into their territories by their clans within their nations, each with its own language.)

The Hamites

⁶The sons of Ham:
    Cush, Mizraim,^{g} Put and Canaan.
⁷The sons of Cush:
    Seba, Havilah, Sabtah, Raamah and Sabteca.
The sons of Raamah:
    Sheba and Dedan.

⁸Cush was the father^h of Nimrod, who grew to be a mighty warrior on the earth. ⁹He was a mighty hunter before the LORD; that is why it is said, "Like Nimrod, a mighty hunter before the LORD." ¹⁰The first centers of his kingdom

---

^{a}20 Or soil, was the first ^{b}26 Or be his slave
^{c}27 Japheth sounds like the Hebrew for extend.
^{d}27 Or their ^{e}2 Sons may mean descendants or successors or nations; also in verses 3, 4, 6, 7, 20–23, 29 and 31. ^{f}4 Some manuscripts of the Masoretic Text and Samaritan Pentateuch (see also Septuagint and 1 Chron. 1:7); most manuscripts of the Masoretic Text Dodanim
^{g}6 That is, Egypt; also in verse 13 ^{h}8 Father may mean ancestor or predecessor or founder; also in verses 13, 15, 24 and 26.

had been closed, and the rain had stopped falling from the sky. ³The water receded steadily from the earth. At the end of the hundred and fifty days the water had gone down, ⁴and on the seventeenth day of the seventh month the ark came to rest on the mountains of Ararat. ⁵The waters continued to recede until the tenth month, and on the first day of the tenth month the tops of the mountains became visible.

⁶After forty days Noah opened the window he had made in the ark ⁷and sent out a raven, and it kept flying back and forth until the water had dried up from the earth. ⁸Then he sent out a dove to see if the water had receded from the surface of the ground. ⁹But the dove could find no place to set its feet because there was water over all the surface of the earth; so it returned to Noah in the ark. He reached out his hand and took the dove and brought it back to himself in the ark. ¹⁰He waited seven more days and again sent out the dove from the ark. ¹¹When the dove returned to him in the evening, there in its beak was a freshly plucked olive leaf! Then Noah knew that the water had receded from the earth. ¹²He waited seven more days and sent the dove out again, but this time it did not return to him.

¹³By the first day of the first month of Noah's six hundred and first year, the water had dried up from the earth. Noah then removed the covering from the ark and saw that the surface of the ground was dry. ¹⁴By the twenty-seventh day of the second month the earth was completely dry.

¹⁵Then God said to Noah, ¹⁶"Come out of the ark, you and your wife and your sons and their wives. ¹⁷Bring out every kind of living creature that is with you—the birds, the animals, and all the creatures that move along the ground—so they can multiply on the earth and be fruitful and increase in number upon it."

¹⁸So Noah came out, together with his sons and his wife and his sons' wives. ¹⁹All the animals and all the creatures that move along the ground and all the birds—everything that moves on the earth—came out of the ark, one kind after another.

²⁰Then Noah built an altar to the LORD and, taking some of all the clean animals and clean birds, he sacrificed burnt offerings on it. ²¹The LORD smelled the pleasing aroma and said in his heart: "Never again will I curse the ground because of man, even though[a] every inclination of his heart is evil from childhood. And never again will I destroy all living creatures, as I have done.

²² "As long as the earth endures,
    seedtime and harvest,
    cold and heat,
    summer and winter,
    day and night
    will never cease."

God's Covenant With Noah

9 Then God blessed Noah and his sons, saying to them, "Be fruitful and increase in number and fill the earth. ²The fear and dread of you will fall upon all the beasts of the earth and all the birds of the air, upon every creature that moves along the ground, and upon all the fish of the sea; they are given into your hands. ³Everything that lives and moves will be food for you. Just as I gave you the green plants, I now give you everything.

⁴"But you must not eat meat that has its lifeblood still in it. ⁵And for your lifeblood I will surely demand an accounting. I will demand an accounting from every animal. And from each man, too, I will demand an accounting for the life of his fellow man.

⁶ "Whoever sheds the blood of man,
    by man shall his blood be shed;
    for in the image of God
    has God made man.

⁷As for you, be fruitful and increase in number; multiply on the earth and increase upon it."

⁸Then God said to Noah and to his sons with him: ⁹"I now establish my covenant with you and with your descendants after you ¹⁰and with every living creature that was with you—the birds, the livestock and all the wild animals, all those that came out of the ark with you—every living creature on earth. ¹¹I establish my covenant

---

ᵃ21 Or man, for

is to be 450 feet long, 75 feet wide and 45 feet high.[a] [16]Make a roof for it and finish[b] the ark to within 18 inches[c] of the top. Put a door in the side of the ark and make lower, middle and upper decks. [17]I am going to bring floodwaters on the earth to destroy all life under the heavens, every creature that has the breath of life in it. Everything on earth will perish. [18]But I will establish my covenant with you, and you will enter the ark— you and your sons and your wife and your sons' wives with you. [19]You are to bring into the ark two of all living creatures, male and female, to keep them alive with you. [20]Two of every kind of bird, of every kind of animal and of every kind of creature that moves along the ground will come to you to be kept alive. [21]You are to take every kind of food that is to be eaten and store it away as food for you and for them."

[22]Noah did everything just as God commanded him.

7 The LORD then said to Noah, "Go into the ark, you and your whole family, because I have found you righteous in this generation. [2]Take with you seven[d] of every kind of clean animal, a male and its mate, and two of every kind of unclean animal, a male and its mate, [3]and also seven of every kind of bird, male and female, to keep their various kinds alive throughout the earth. [4]Seven days from now I will send rain on the earth for forty days and forty nights, and I will wipe from the face of the earth every living creature I have made."

[5]And Noah did all that the LORD commanded him.

[6]Noah was six hundred years old when the floodwaters came on the earth. [7]And Noah and his sons and his wife and his sons' wives entered the ark to escape the waters of the flood. [8]Pairs of clean and unclean animals, of birds and of all creatures that move along the ground, [9]male and female, came to Noah and entered the ark, as God had commanded Noah. [10]And after the seven days the floodwaters came on the earth.

[11]In the six hundredth year of Noah's life, on the seventeenth day of the second month—on that day all the springs of the great deep burst forth, and the floodgates of the heavens were opened. [12]And rain fell on the earth forty days and forty nights.

[13]On that very day Noah and his sons, Shem, Ham and Japheth, together with his wife and the wives of his three sons, entered the ark. [14]They had with them every wild animal according to its kind, all livestock according to their kinds, every creature that moves along the ground according to its kind and every bird according to its kind, everything with wings. [15]Pairs of all creatures that have the breath of life in them came to Noah and entered the ark. [16]The animals going in were male and female of every living thing, as God had commanded Noah. Then the LORD shut him in.

[17]For forty days the flood kept coming on the earth, and as the waters increased they lifted the ark high above the earth. [18]The waters rose and increased greatly on the earth, and the ark floated on the surface of the water. [19]They rose greatly on the earth, and all the high mountains under the entire heavens were covered. [20]The waters rose and covered the mountains to a depth of more than twenty feet.[e,f] [21]Every living thing that moved on the earth perished—birds, livestock, wild animals, all the creatures that swarm over the earth, and all mankind. [22]Everything on dry land that had the breath of life in its nostrils died. [23]Every living thing on the face of the earth was wiped out; men and animals and the creatures that move along the ground and the birds of the air were wiped from the earth. Only Noah was left, and those with him in the ark.

[24]The waters flooded the earth for a hundred and fifty days.

8 But God remembered Noah and all the wild animals and the livestock that were with him in the ark, and he sent a wind over the earth, and the waters receded. [2]Now the springs of the deep and the floodgates of the heavens

[a]15 Hebrew 300 cubits long, 50 cubits wide and 30 cubits high (about 140 meters long, 23 meters wide and 13.5 meters high)   [b]16 Or Make an opening for light by finishing   [c]16 Hebrew a cubit (about 0.5 meter)   [d]2 Or seven pairs; also in verse 3   [e]20 Hebrew fifteen cubits (about 6.9 meters)   [f]20 Or rose more than twenty feet, and the mountains were covered

⁶When Seth had lived 105 years, he became the father*a* of Enosh. ⁷And after he became the father of Enosh, Seth lived 807 years and had other sons and daughters. ⁸Altogether, Seth lived 912 years, and then he died.

⁹When Enosh had lived 90 years, he became the father of Kenan. ¹⁰And after he became the father of Kenan, Enosh lived 815 years and had other sons and daughters. ¹¹Altogether, Enosh lived 905 years, and then he died.

¹²When Kenan had lived 70 years, he became the father of Mahalalel. ¹³And after he became the father of Mahalalel, Kenan lived 840 years and had other sons and daughters. ¹⁴Altogether, Kenan lived 910 years, and then he died.

¹⁵When Mahalalel had lived 65 years, he became the father of Jared. ¹⁶And after he became the father of Jared, Mahalalel lived 830 years and had other sons and daughters. ¹⁷Altogether, Mahalalel lived 895 years, and then he died.

¹⁸When Jared had lived 162 years, he became the father of Enoch. ¹⁹And after he became the father of Enoch, Jared lived 800 years and had other sons and daughters. ²⁰Altogether, Jared lived 962 years, and then he died.

²¹When Enoch had lived 65 years, he became the father of Methuselah. ²²And after he became the father of Methuselah, Enoch walked with God 300 years and had other sons and daughters. ²³Altogether, Enoch lived 365 years. ²⁴Enoch walked with God; then he was no more, because God took him away.

²⁵When Methuselah had lived 187 years, he became the father of Lamech. ²⁶And after he became the father of Lamech, Methuselah lived 782 years and had other sons and daughters. ²⁷Altogether, Methuselah lived 969 years, and then he died.

²⁸When Lamech had lived 182 years, he had a son. ²⁹He named him Noah*b* and said, "He will comfort us in the labor and painful toil of our hands caused by the ground the LORD has cursed." ³⁰After Noah was born, Lamech lived 595 years and had other sons and daughters. ³¹Altogether, Lamech lived 777 years, and then he died.

³²After Noah was 500 years old, he became the father of Shem, Ham and Japheth.

The Flood

6 When men began to increase in number on the earth and daughters were born to them, ²the sons of God saw that the daughters of men were beautiful, and they married any of them they chose. ³Then the LORD said, "My Spirit will not contend with*c* man forever, for he is mortal*d*; his days will be a hundred and twenty years."

⁴The Nephilim were on the earth in those days—and also afterward—when the sons of God went to the daughters of men and had children by them. They were the heroes of old, men of renown.

⁵The LORD saw how great man's wickedness on the earth had become, and that every inclination of the thoughts of his heart was only evil all the time. ⁶The LORD was grieved that he had made man on the earth, and his heart was filled with pain. ⁷So the LORD said, "I will wipe mankind, whom I have created, from the face of the earth—men and animals, and creatures that move along the ground, and birds of the air—for I am grieved that I have made them." ⁸But Noah found favor in the eyes of the LORD.

⁹This is the account of Noah.

Noah was a righteous man, blameless among the people of his time, and he walked with God. ¹⁰Noah had three sons: Shem, Ham and Japheth.

¹¹Now the earth was corrupt in God's sight and was full of violence. ¹²God saw how corrupt the earth had become, for all the people on earth had corrupted their ways. ¹³So God said to Noah, "I am going to put an end to all people, for the earth is filled with violence because of them. I am surely going to destroy both them and the earth. ¹⁴So make yourself an ark of cypress*e* wood; make rooms in it and coat it with pitch inside and out. ¹⁵This is how you are to build it: The ark

a6 Father may mean *ancestor*; also in verses 7–26.   *b29 Noah* sounds like the Hebrew for *comfort.*   *c3* Or *My spirit will not remain in*   *d3* Or *corrupt*   *e14* The meaning of the Hebrew for this word is uncertain.

When All Else Fails

> 4:26 AT THAT TIME MEN BEGAN TO CALL ON THE NAME OF THE LORD.

This is the first time prayer is explicitly mentioned in the Bible. What is the significance of "at that time"? Look at all that leads up to "that time." In four brief chapters we read that God created the heavens and earth and pronounced them "good." After he makes humans, the crown of his creation, in his own image, he pronounced all that he had made "*very* good." But like a shattered mirror, God's image is broken when these first people disobey him. The humans, Adam and Eve, have two sons: Cain and Abel. When Cain murders his brother, we see that the first offspring of God's crowning creation is a murderer. It gets worse: Cain's descendants follow in his footsteps. Soon we hear of a certain Lamech who intends to outdo Cain in malice: "If Cain is avenged seven times, then Lamech seventy-seven times" (4:24). Lamech will make Cain's days seem like the good old days. Death and violence increase exponentially. Frederick Buechner observes this about the nature of sin: "The power of sin is centrifugal . . . It tends to push everything out toward the periphery. Bits and pieces go flying off until only the core is left . . . In the end nothing at all is left."[1]

Nevertheless is a great grace word. So nevertheless, in spite of all that is going on in the world, God acts graciously and gives Adam and Eve another child to replace Abel; they call him Seth, which probably means "granted." It's at this time, with the line of Seth, that people begin to call on the name of the Lord.

There's a saying, "When all else fails, read the directions." The impulse to pray is a little like that. So far, taking matters into their own hands has gotten everybody in trouble. Without the guidance of God, the earth becomes filled with violence and strife. People are more apt to see the need to pray when they see how great their needs are, when they run up against the hard edge of their own limitations. There's not much we humans can do in our own name, but "The name of the LORD is a strong tower; the righteous run to it and are safe" (Proverbs 18:10).

There is hope. Centuries (but only a few verses in the Bible) later, we read about a man of prayer named Enoch, who "walked with God" (Genesis 5:21–24). Echoes of what was originally intended for all humankind reverberate in those few words (see Genesis 3:8). In the fullness of time there will come another child of grace, and communion with God will again be what it was supposed to be (see Galatians 4:4–5; Hebrews 4:14–16).

PRAY:

I call on your name, O Lord. Thank you for your
grace that allows me to walk with you. I recognize
how much I need you, Father God.

FOR YOUR NEXT DEVOTIONAL READING, GO TO PAGE 14.

LORD I have brought forth[a] a man." ²Later she gave birth to his brother Abel.

Now Abel kept flocks, and Cain worked the soil. ³In the course of time Cain brought some of the fruits of the soil as an offering to the LORD. ⁴But Abel brought fat portions from some of the firstborn of his flock. The LORD looked with favor on Abel and his offering, ⁵but on Cain and his offering he did not look with favor. So Cain was very angry, and his face was downcast.

⁶Then the LORD said to Cain, "Why are you angry? Why is your face downcast? ⁷If you do what is right, will you not be accepted? But if you do not do what is right, sin is crouching at your door; it desires to have you, but you must master it."

⁸Now Cain said to his brother Abel, "Let's go out to the field."[b] And while they were in the field, Cain attacked his brother Abel and killed him.

⁹Then the LORD said to Cain, "Where is your brother Abel?"

"I don't know," he replied. "Am I my brother's keeper?"

¹⁰The LORD said, "What have you done? Listen! Your brother's blood cries out to me from the ground. ¹¹Now you are under a curse and driven from the ground, which opened its mouth to receive your brother's blood from your hand. ¹²When you work the ground, it will no longer yield its crops for you. You will be a restless wanderer on the earth."

¹³Cain said to the LORD, "My punishment is more than I can bear. ¹⁴Today you are driving me from the land, and I will be hidden from your presence; I will be a restless wanderer on the earth, and whoever finds me will kill me."

¹⁵But the LORD said to him, "Not so[c]; if anyone kills Cain, he will suffer vengeance seven times over." Then the LORD put a mark on Cain so that no one who found him would kill him. ¹⁶So Cain went out from the LORD's presence and lived in the land of Nod,[d] east of Eden.

¹⁷Cain lay with his wife, and she became pregnant and gave birth to Enoch. Cain was then building a city, and he named it after his son Enoch. ¹⁸To Enoch was born Irad, and Irad was the father of Mehujael, and Mehujael was the father of Methushael, and Methushael was the father of Lamech.

¹⁹Lamech married two women, one named Adah and the other Zillah. ²⁰Adah gave birth to Jabal; he was the father of those who live in tents and raise livestock. ²¹His brother's name was Jubal; he was the father of all who play the harp and flute. ²²Zillah also had a son, Tubal-Cain, who forged all kinds of tools out of[e] bronze and iron. Tubal-Cain's sister was Naamah.

²³Lamech said to his wives,

"Adah and Zillah, listen to me;
    wives of Lamech, hear my words.
I have killed[f] a man for wounding
    me,
    a young man for injuring me.
²⁴If Cain is avenged seven times,
    then Lamech seventy-seven times."

²⁵Adam lay with his wife again, and she gave birth to a son and named him Seth,[g] saying, "God has granted me another child in place of Abel, since Cain killed him." ²⁶Seth also had a son, and he named him Enosh.

At that time men began to call on[h] the name of the LORD.

From Adam to Noah

5 This is the written account of Adam's line.

When God created man, he made him in the likeness of God. ²He created them male and female and blessed them. And when they were created, he called them "man.[i]"

³When Adam had lived 130 years, he had a son in his own likeness, in his own image; and he named him Seth. ⁴After Seth was born, Adam lived 800 years and had other sons and daughters. ⁵Altogether, Adam lived 930 years, and then he died.

[a]1 Or have acquired   [b]8 Samaritan Pentateuch, Septuagint, Vulgate and Syriac; Masoretic Text does not have "Let's go out to the field."   [c]15 Septuagint, Vulgate and Syriac; Hebrew Very well   [d]16 Nod means wandering (see verses 12 and 14).   [e]22 Or who instructed all who work in   [f]23 Or I will kill   [g]25 Seth probably means granted.   [h]26 Or to proclaim   [i]2 Hebrew adam

when you eat of it your eyes will be opened, and you will be like God, knowing good and evil."

⁶When the woman saw that the fruit of the tree was good for food and pleasing to the eye, and also desirable for gaining wisdom, she took some and ate it. She also gave some to her husband, who was with her, and he ate it. ⁷Then the eyes of both of them were opened, and they realized they were naked; so they sewed fig leaves together and made coverings for themselves.

⁸Then the man and his wife heard the sound of the LORD God as he was walking in the garden in the cool of the day, and they hid from the LORD God among the trees of the garden. ⁹But the LORD God called to the man, "Where are you?"

¹⁰He answered, "I heard you in the garden, and I was afraid because I was naked; so I hid."

¹¹And he said, "Who told you that you were naked? Have you eaten from the tree that I commanded you not to eat from?"

¹²The man said, "The woman you put here with me—she gave me some fruit from the tree, and I ate it."

¹³Then the LORD God said to the woman, "What is this you have done?"

The woman said, "The serpent deceived me, and I ate."

¹⁴So the LORD God said to the serpent, "Because you have done this,

"Cursed are you above all the
     livestock
   and all the wild animals!
You will crawl on your belly
   and you will eat dust
     all the days of your life.
¹⁵ And I will put enmity
   between you and the woman,
   and between your offspring[a]
     and hers;
he will crush[b] your head,
   and you will strike his heel."

¹⁶To the woman he said,

"I will greatly increase your pains in
   childbearing;
   with pain you will give birth to
     children.
Your desire will be for your husband,
   and he will rule over you."

¹⁷To Adam he said, "Because you listened to your wife and ate from the tree about which I commanded you, 'You must not eat of it,'

"Cursed is the ground because of you;
   through painful toil you will eat
     of it
   all the days of your life.
¹⁸It will produce thorns and thistles
     for you,
   and you will eat the plants of
     the field.
¹⁹By the sweat of your brow
   you will eat your food
until you return to the ground,
   since from it you were taken;
for dust you are
   and to dust you will return."

²⁰Adam[c] named his wife Eve,[d] because she would become the mother of all the living.

²¹The LORD God made garments of skin for Adam and his wife and clothed them. ²²And the LORD God said, "The man has now become like one of us, knowing good and evil. He must not be allowed to reach out his hand and take also from the tree of life and eat, and live forever." ²³So the LORD God banished him from the Garden of Eden to work the ground from which he had been taken. ²⁴After he drove the man out, he placed on the east side[e] of the Garden of Eden cherubim and a flaming sword flashing back and forth to guard the way to the tree of life.

> ADAM *lay with his wife Eve, and she became pregnant and gave birth to Cain. She said, "With the help of the LORD I have brought forth a man."*
>
> GENESIS 4:1

Cain and Abel

4 Adam[c] lay with his wife Eve, and she became pregnant and gave birth to Cain.[f] She said, "With the help of the

---

[a]15 Or *seed*   [b]15 Or *strike*   [c]20, 1 Or *The man*   [d]20 *Eve* probably means *living*.   [e]24 Or *placed in front*   [f]1 *Cain* sounds like the Hebrew for *brought forth* or *acquired*.

2 Thus the heavens and the earth were completed in all their vast array.

²By the seventh day God had finished the work he had been doing; so on the seventh day he rested[a] from all his work. ³And God blessed the seventh day and made it holy, because on it he rested from all the work of creating that he had done.

Adam and Eve

⁴This is the account of the heavens and the earth when they were created.

When the LORD God made the earth and the heavens— ⁵and no shrub of the field had yet appeared on the earth[b] and no plant of the field had yet sprung up, for the LORD God had not sent rain on the earth[c] and there was no man to work the ground, ⁶but streams[d] came up from the earth and watered the whole surface of the ground— ⁷the LORD God formed the man[e] from the dust of the ground and breathed into his nostrils the breath of life, and the man became a living being.

⁸Now the LORD God had planted a garden in the east, in Eden; and there he put the man he had formed. ⁹And the LORD God made all kinds of trees grow out of the ground—trees that were pleasing to the eye and good for food. In the middle of the garden were the tree of life and the tree of the knowledge of good and evil.

¹⁰A river watering the garden flowed from Eden; from there it was separated into four headwaters. ¹¹The name of the first is the Pishon; it winds through the entire land of Havilah, where there is gold. ¹²(The gold of that land is good; aromatic resin[f] and onyx are also there.) ¹³The name of the second river is the Gihon; it winds through the entire land of Cush.[g] ¹⁴The name of the third river is the Tigris; it runs along the east side of Asshur. And the fourth river is the Euphrates.

¹⁵The LORD God took the man and put him in the Garden of Eden to work it and take care of it. ¹⁶And the LORD God commanded the man, "You are free to eat from any tree in the garden; ¹⁷but you must not eat from the tree of the knowledge of good and evil, for when you eat of it you will surely die."

¹⁸The LORD God said, "It is not good for the man to be alone. I will make a helper suitable for him."

¹⁹Now the LORD God had formed out of the ground all the beasts of the field and all the birds of the air. He brought them to the man to see what he would name them; and whatever the man called each living creature, that was its name. ²⁰So the man gave names to all the livestock, the birds of the air and all the beasts of the field.

But for Adam[h] no suitable helper was found. ²¹So the LORD God caused the man to fall into a deep sleep; and while he was sleeping, he took one of the man's ribs[i] and closed up the place with flesh. ²²Then the LORD God made a woman from the rib[j] he had taken out of the man, and he brought her to the man.

²³The man said,

"This is now bone of my bones
   and flesh of my flesh;
she shall be called 'woman,'[k]
   for she was taken out of man."

²⁴For this reason a man will leave his father and mother and be united to his wife, and they will become one flesh.

²⁵The man and his wife were both naked, and they felt no shame.

The Fall of Man

3 Now the serpent was more crafty than any of the wild animals the LORD God had made. He said to the woman, "Did God really say, 'You must not eat from any tree in the garden'?"

²The woman said to the serpent, "We may eat fruit from the trees in the garden, ³but God did say, 'You must not eat fruit from the tree that is in the middle of the garden, and you must not touch it, or you will die.'"

⁴"You will not surely die," the serpent said to the woman. ⁵"For God knows that

[a]2 Or ceased; also in verse 3   [b]5 Or land; also in verse 6   [c]5 Or land; also in verse 6
[d]6 Or mist   [e]7 The Hebrew for man (adam) sounds like and may be related to the Hebrew for ground (adamah); it is also the name Adam (see Gen. 2:20).   [f]12 Or good; pearls
[g]13 Possibly southeast Mesopotamia
[h]20 Or the man   [i]21 Or took part of the man's side   [j]22 Or part   [k]23 The Hebrew for woman sounds like the Hebrew for man.

²⁹Then God said, "I give you every seed-bearing plant on the face of the whole earth and every tree that has fruit with seed in it. They will be yours for food. ³⁰And to all the beasts of the earth and all the birds of the air and all the creatures that move on the ground—everything that has the breath of life in it—I give every green plant for food." And it was so.

³¹God saw all that he had made, and it was very good. And there was evening, and there was morning—the sixth day.

[MONDAY]

GENESIS 1

The Face in Front of the World

1:1 IN THE BEGINNING GOD CREATED THE HEAVENS AND THE EARTH.

The secret of the world, said G. K. Chesterton, is to know that we only see the back of it. We see everything from behind: trees, clouds, planets, stars, oceans, everything. "Cannot you see that everything is stooping and hiding a face? If only we could get round in front." Behold, the face on the front of the world is God's! That's what Genesis 1 is about. When we see just the backside of the creation, we are tempted to think of it only in terms of space and matter. When we see creation from the front, from the face, as the opening chapter in the Bible does, we must sing—we must give praise to the Maker. Whatever else Genesis 1 is, it is a hymn of praise to the God who made it all. You can add your own embellishments, your own verses, to the song by singing of particulars. Doesn't God say the birds, fish and livestock he created are good? You say, as you pray, the crows, dolphins and Hereford cows are good. Make up a tune as you go.

Imagine this chapter as footage from a time-lapse film of the creation. Light bursts forth, waters separate and gather, mountains arise, forests spread, animals appear. Then the film slows down to real time—then slow motion. A man and a woman stand naked and innocent, warm and glistening in the love of God. God's face brightens as he looks at something of his own face gazing back at him. "So God created man in his own image, in the image of God he created him; male and female he created them" (verse 27). Time to sing again. The words of Psalm 8 would be good: "When I consider your heavens, the work of your fingers, the moon and the stars, which you have set in place, what is man that your are mindful of him ... You made him a little lower than the heavenly beings and crowned him with glory and honor" (verses 3–5).

The next time you are perplexed, disappointed and discouraged by another person—or yourself—remember you are seeing things from behind. In front, there is the face of God's Son. And there are also the human faces that he came to transform into his own image (see 2 Corinthians 3:18).

PRAY:

There's not a plant or flower below, but makes Thy glories known;
And clouds arise, and tempests blow, by order from Thy throne;
while all that borrows life from Thee is ever in Thy care. And everywhere
that man can be; Thou, God, art present there. ISAAC WATTS

FOR YOUR NEXT DEVOTIONAL READING, GO TO PAGE 7.

The Beginning

1 In the beginning God created the heavens and the earth. [2]Now the earth was[a] formless and empty, darkness was over the surface of the deep, and the Spirit of God was hovering over the waters.

[3]And God said, "Let there be light," and there was light. [4]God saw that the light was good, and he separated the light from the darkness. [5]God called the light "day," and the darkness he called "night." And there was evening, and there was morning—the first day.

[6]And God said, "Let there be an expanse between the waters to separate water from water." [7]So God made the expanse and separated the water under the expanse from the water above it. And it was so. [8]God called the expanse "sky." And there was evening, and there was morning—the second day.

[9]And God said, "Let the water under the sky be gathered to one place, and let dry ground appear." And it was so. [10]God called the dry ground "land," and the gathered waters he called "seas." And God saw that it was good.

[11]Then God said, "Let the land produce vegetation: seed-bearing plants and trees on the land that bear fruit with seed in it, according to their various kinds." And it was so. [12]The land produced vegetation: plants bearing seed according to their kinds and trees bearing fruit with seed in it according to their kinds. And God saw that it was good. [13]And there was evening, and there was morning—the third day.

[14]And God said, "Let there be lights in the expanse of the sky to separate the day from the night, and let them serve as signs to mark seasons and days and years, [15]and let them be lights in the expanse of the sky to give light on the earth." And it was so. [16]God made two great lights—the greater light to govern the day and the lesser light to govern the night. He also made the stars. [17]God set them in the expanse of the sky to give light on the earth, [18]to govern the day and the night, and to separate light from darkness. And God saw that it was good. [19]And there was evening, and there was morning—the fourth day.

[20]And God said, "Let the water teem with living creatures, and let birds fly above the earth across the expanse of the sky." [21]So God created the great creatures of the sea and every living and moving thing with which the water teems, according to their kinds, and every winged bird according to its kind. And God saw that it was good. [22]God blessed them and said, "Be fruitful and increase in number and fill the water in the seas, and let the birds increase on the earth." [23]And there was evening, and there was morning—the fifth day.

[24]And God said, "Let the land produce living creatures according to their kinds: livestock, creatures that move along the ground, and wild animals, each according to its kind." And it was so. [25]God made the wild animals according to their kinds, the livestock according to their kinds, and all the creatures that move along the ground according to their kinds. And God saw that it was good.

[26]Then God said, "Let us make man in our image, in our likeness, and let them rule over the fish of the sea and the birds of the air, over the livestock, over all the earth,[b] and over all the creatures that move along the ground."

[27]So God created man in his own
image,
    in the image of God he created
    him;
    male and female he created them.

[28]God blessed them and said to them, "Be fruitful and increase in number; fill the earth and subdue it. Rule over the fish of the sea and the birds of the air and over every living creature that moves on the ground."

[a]2 Or possibly *became*   [b]26 Hebrew; Syriac *all the wild animals*

Genesis

THE BOOK of Genesis tells how the world began. It says God spoke the creation into existence, out of nothing, *ex nihilo*; that he was not limited in his creative work by any preexistent material but acted in perfect freedom when he made the heavens and the earth. His only limitation, if one can call it that, was his character. This has enormous significance for prayer. Since God freely created the universe by his Word, out of nothing, we can expect God to continue to act in that way. P. T. Forsyth marveled at God's creativity and called him an "infinite opportunist." The universe is not a closed system of cause and effect; it remains open-ended and responsive to God's Word. Nothing is too hard for the Lord. God answers prayer.

GOD SAW ALL THAT HE HAD MADE, AND IT WAS VERY GOOD. (1:31)

This book also affirms, touchingly, that we were made *for* God because we are made *like* God, in his image. It pleased him, from the beginning, to create humankind to walk with him in the world and share with him in the care of his creation. Intercessory prayer is on the same order as all the other things we do to share with God in his work. What we do when we pray is no different, fundamentally, than what we do when we plow a field or manage a budget. All of these activities are rooted in Genesis 1:26–28 (see weekend study on C. S. Lewis, the Dignity of Causality, page 336).

When sin entered the picture and the image of God was distorted in us, God did not give up on us, but acted to save and restore his broken and beloved creatures. The first explicit mention of prayer in the Bible comes in this context (see Genesis 4:26). When sin broke our fellowship with God, he kept the door open to call on his name and be restored. The communion with God that made the Garden of Eden such a delight remains God's great passion for his creatures, and will be established one day forever. Prayer will once again be as the air we breathe (see Revelation 21:3).

The Old Testament

convey the sense of the Hebrew, namely, "he who is sovereign over all the 'hosts' (powers) in heaven and on earth, especially over the 'hosts' (armies) of Israel." For readers unacquainted with Hebrew this does not make clear the distinction between *Sabaoth* ("hosts" or "Almighty") and *Shaddai* (which can also be translated "Almighty"), but the latter occurs infrequently and is always footnoted. When *Adonai* and *YHWH Sabaoth* occur together, they are rendered "the Lord, the LORD Almighty."

As for other proper nouns, the familiar spellings of the King James Version are generally retained. Names traditionally spelled with "ch," except where it is final, are usually spelled in this translation with "k" or "c," since the biblical languages do not have the sound that "ch" frequently indicates in English—for example, in *chant*. For well-known names such as Zechariah, however, the traditional spelling has been retained. Variation in the spelling of names in the original languages has usually not been indicated. Where a person or place has two or more different names in the Hebrew, Aramaic or Greek texts, the more familiar one has generally been used, with footnotes where needed.

To achieve clarity the translators sometimes supplied words not in the original texts but required by the context. If there was uncertainty about such material, it is enclosed in brackets. Also for the sake of clarity or style, nouns, including some proper nouns, are sometimes substituted for pronouns, and vice versa. And though the Hebrew writers often shifted back and forth between first, second and third personal pronouns without change of antecedent, this translation often makes them uniform, in accordance with English style and without the use of footnotes.

Poetical passages are printed as poetry, that is, with indentation of lines and with separate stanzas. These are generally designed to reflect the structure of Hebrew poetry. This poetry is normally characterized by parallelism in balanced lines. Most of the poetry in the Bible is in the Old Testament, and scholars differ regarding the scansion of Hebrew lines. The translators determined the stanza divisions for the most part by analysis of the subject matter. The stanzas therefore serve as poetic paragraphs.

As an aid to the reader, italicized sectional headings are inserted in most of the books. They are not to be regarded as part of the NIV text, are not for oral reading, and are not intended to dictate the interpretation of the sections they head.

The footnotes in this version are of several kinds, most of which need no explanation. Those giving alternative translations begin with "Or" and generally introduce the alternative with the last word preceding it in the text, except when it is a single-word alternative; in poetry quoted in a footnote a slant mark indicates a line division. Footnotes introduced by "Or" do not have uniform significance. In some cases two possible translations were considered to have about equal validity. In other cases, though the translators were convinced that the translation in the text was correct, they judged that another interpretation was possible and of sufficient importance to be represented in a footnote.

In the New Testament, footnotes that refer to uncertainty regarding the original text are introduced by "Some manuscripts" or similar expressions. In the Old Testament, evidence for the reading chosen is given first and evidence for the alternative is added after a semicolon (for example: Septuagint; Hebrew *father*). In such notes the term "Hebrew" refers to the Masoretic Text.

It should be noted that minerals, flora and fauna, architectural details, articles of clothing and jewelry, musical instruments and other articles cannot always be identified with precision. Also measures of capacity in the biblical period are particularly uncertain (see the table of weights and measures following the text).

Like all translations of the Bible, made as they are by imperfect man, this one undoubtedly falls short of its goals. Yet we are grateful to God for the extent to which he has enabled us to realize these goals and for the strength he has given us and our colleagues to complete our task. We offer this version of the Bible to him in whose name and for whose glory it has been made. We pray that it will lead many into a better understanding of the Holy Scriptures and a fuller knowledge of Jesus Christ the incarnate Word, of whom the Scriptures so faithfully testify.

The Committee on Bible Translation

June 1978
(Revised Aug 1983)

Names of the translators and editors may be secured from the International Bible Society translation sponsors of the New International Version, 1820 Jet Stream Drive, Colorado Springs, Colorado 08921-3696 U.S.A

A sensitive feeling for style does not always accompany scholarship. Accordingly the Committee on Bible Translation submitted the developing version to a number of stylistic consultants. Two of them read every book of both Old and New Testaments twice—once before and once after the last major revision—and made invaluable suggestions. Samples of the translation were tested for clarity and ease of reading by various kinds of people—young and old, highly educated and less well educated, ministers and laymen.

Concern for clear and natural English—that the New International Version should be idiomatic but not idiosyncratic, contemporary but not dated—motivated the translators and consultants. At the same time, they tried to reflect the differing styles of the biblical writers. In view of the international use of English, the translators sought to avoid obvious Americanisms on the one hand and obvious Anglicisms on the other. A British edition reflects the comparatively few differences of significant idiom and of spelling.

As for the traditional pronouns "thou," "thee" and "thine" in reference to the Deity, the translators judged that to use these archaisms (along with the old verb forms such as "doest," "wouldest" and "hadst") would violate accuracy in translation. Neither Hebrew, Aramaic nor Greek uses special pronouns for the persons of the Godhead. A present-day translation is not enhanced by forms that in the time of the King James Version were used in everyday speech, whether referring to God or man.

For the Old Testament the standard Hebrew text, the Masoretic Text as published in the latest editions of *Biblia Hebraica*, was used throughout. The Dead Sea Scrolls contain material bearing on an earlier stage of the Hebrew text. They were consulted, as were the Samaritan Pentateuch and the ancient scribal traditions relating to textual changes. Sometimes a variant Hebrew reading in the margin of the Masoretic Text was followed instead of the text itself. Such instances, being variants within the Masoretic tradition, are not specified by footnotes. In rare cases, words in the consonantal text were divided differently from the way they appear in the Masoretic Text. Footnotes indicate this. The translators also consulted the more important early versions—the Septuagint; Aquila, Symmachus and Theodotion; the Vulgate; the Syriac Peshitta; the Targums; and for the Psalms the *Juxta Hebraica* of Jerome. Readings from these versions were occasionally followed where the Masoretic Text seemed doubtful and where accepted principles of textual criticism showed that one or more of these textual witnesses appeared to provide the correct reading. Such instances are footnoted. Sometimes vowel letters and vowel signs did not, in the judgment of the translators, represent the correct vowels for the original consonantal text. Accordingly some words were read with a different set of vowels. These instances are usually not indicated by footnotes.

The Greek text used in translating the New Testament was an eclectic one. No other piece of ancient literature has such an abundance of manuscript witnesses as does the New Testament. Where existing manuscripts differ, the translators made their choice of readings according to accepted principles of New Testament textual criticism. Footnotes call attention to places where there was uncertainty about what the original text was. The best current printed texts of the Greek New Testament were used.

There is a sense in which the work of translation is never wholly finished. This applies to all great literature and uniquely so to the Bible. In 1973 the New Testament in the New International Version was published. Since then, suggestions for corrections and revisions have been received from various sources. The Committee on Bible Translation carefully considered the suggestions and adopted a number of them. These were incorporated in the first printing of the entire Bible in 1978. Additional revisions were made by the Committee on Bible Translation in 1983 and appear in printings after that date.

As in other ancient documents, the precise meaning of the biblical texts is sometimes uncertain. This is more often the case with the Hebrew and Aramaic texts than with the Greek text. Although archaeological and linguistic discoveries in this century aid in understanding difficult passages, some uncertainties remain. The more significant of these have been called to the reader's attention in the footnotes.

In regard to the divine name YHWH, commonly referred to as the *Tetragrammaton*, the translators adopted the device used in most English versions of rendering that name as "LORD" in capital letters to distinguish it from *Adonai*, another Hebrew word rendered "Lord," for which small letters are used. Wherever the two names stand together in the Old Testament as a compound name of God, they are rendered "Sovereign LORD."

Because for most readers today the phrases "the LORD of hosts" and "God of hosts" have little meaning, this version renders them "the LORD Almighty" and "God Almighty." These renderings

THE NEW INTERNATIONAL VERSION is a completely new translation of the Holy Bible made by over a hundred scholars working directly from the best available Hebrew, Aramaic and Greek texts. It had its beginning in 1965 when, after several years of exploratory study by committees from the Christian Reformed Church and the National Association of Evangelicals, a group of scholars met at Palos Heights, Illinois, and concurred in the need for a new translation of the Bible in contemporary English. This group, though not made up of official church representatives, was transdenominational. Its conclusion was endorsed by a large number of leaders from many denominations who met in Chicago in 1966.

Responsibility for the new version was delegated by the Palos Heights group to a self-governing body of fifteen, the Committee on Bible Translation, composed for the most part of biblical scholars from colleges, universities and seminaries. In 1967 the New York Bible Society (now the International Bible Society) generously undertook the financial sponsorship of the project—a sponsorship that made it possible to enlist the help of many distinguished scholars. The fact that participants from the United States, Great Britain, Canada, Australia and New Zealand worked together gave the project its international scope. That they were from many denominations—including Anglican, Assemblies of God, Baptist, Brethren, Christian Reformed, Church of Christ, Evangelical Free, Lutheran, Mennonite, Methodist, Nazarene, Presbyterian, Wesleyan and other churches—helped to safeguard the translation from sectarian bias.

How it was made helps to give the New International Version its distinctiveness. The translation of each book was assigned to a team of scholars. Next, one of the Intermediate Editorial Committees revised the initial translation, with constant reference to the Hebrew, Aramaic or Greek. Their work then went to one of the General Editorial Committees, which checked it in detail and made another thorough revision. This revision in turn was carefully reviewed by the Committee on Bible Translation, which made further changes and then released the final version for publication. In this way the entire Bible underwent three revisions, during each of which the translation was examined for its faithfulness to the original languages and for its English style.

All this involved many thousands of hours of research and discussion regarding the meaning of the texts and the precise way of putting them into English. It may well be that no other translation has been made by a more thorough process of review and revision from committee to committee than this one.

From the beginning of the project, the Committee on Bible Translation held to certain goals for the New International Version: that it would be an accurate translation and one that would have clarity and literary quality and so prove suitable for public and private reading, teaching, preaching, memorizing and liturgical use. The Committee also sought to preserve some measure of continuity with the long tradition of translating the Scriptures into English.

In working toward these goals, the translators were united in their commitment to the authority and infallibility of the Bible as God's Word in written form. They believe that it contains the divine answer to the deepest needs of humanity, that it sheds unique light on our path in a dark world, and that it sets forth the way to our eternal well-being.

The first concern of the translators has been the accuracy of the translation and its fidelity to the thought of the biblical writers. They have weighed the significance of the lexical and grammatical details of the Hebrew, Aramaic and Greek texts. At the same time, they have striven for more than a word-for-word translation. Because thought patterns and syntax differ from language to language, faithful communication of the meaning of the writers of the Bible demands frequent modifications in sentence structure and constant regard for the contextual meanings of words.

On Saturday or Sunday, you can read a special devotion that focuses on people who've prayed and what prayer has done for their lives. These inspirational stories include a verse for mediation and a reflective prayer.

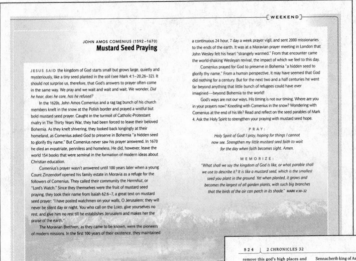

Scripture Call-Outs and Quotes

Throughout this Bible are boxes containing highlighted inspirational or informative verses that relate to prayer. And some boxes contain interesting quotes about prayer.

Special References

Starting on page 1603 are a variety of Bible helps, including a topical index, an index of people mentioned in the devotions, a list of prayers of the Bible and a place for you to record prayer requests.

How to Use This Bible

Book Introductions

Each of the 66 books in this Bible begins with an introduction. The introductions succinctly highlight themes, provide helpful background information or offer insight into prayers in the book.

Devotions

This Bible contains 260 devotional articles and 52 devotionals for each weekend. These devotions follow the days of the week. No matter what day of the week you begin, simply turn to the devotion for that day. For example, if you start on a Tuesday, just turn to the first "Tuesday" devotion in the book of Genesis. To know where to go for the next day, look at the bottom of the devotion for the page number of the next devotion.

At the top of each devotion is a passage of Scripture. The subject of each devotion is tied to this passage. Part of the passage is highlighted in the bar that runs across the top of the devotion.

Ending each devotion is a prayer for you to pray. These prayers relate to the devotion for each day and can help get you started talking with God about what you've just read.

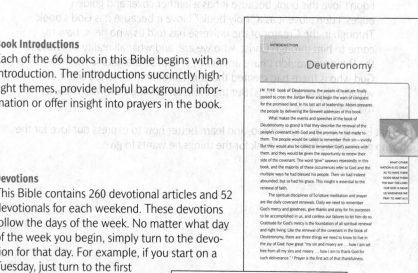

INTRODUCTION

Deuteronomy

IN THE book of Deuteronomy, the people of Israel are finally poised to cross the Jordan River and begin the wars of conquest for the promised land. In his last act of leadership, Moses prepares the people by delivering the farewell addresses of this book.

What makes the events and speeches of the book of Deuteronomy so grand is that they describe the renewal of the people's covenant with God and the promises he had made to them. The people would be called to remember their sin—vividly. But they would also be called to remember God's patience with them, and they would be given the opportunity to renew their side of the covenant. The word "give" appears repeatedly in this book, and the majority of these occurrences refer to God and the multiple ways he had blessed his people. Their sin had indeed abounded, but so had his grace. This insight is essential to the renewal of faith.

The spiritual disciplines of Scripture meditation and prayer are like daily covenant renewals. Daily we need to remember God's mercy and goodness, give thanks and pray for his purposes to be accomplished in us, and confess our failures to let him do so. Gratitude for God's mercy is the foundation of all spiritual renewal and right living. Like the renewal of the covenant in the book of Deuteronomy, there are three things we need to know to live in the joy of God: how great "my sin and misery are . . . how I am set free from all my sins and misery . . . how I am to thank God for such deliverance." [1] Prayer is the first act of that thankfulness.

WHAT OTHER NATION IS SO GREAT AS TO HAVE THEIR GODS NEAR THEM THE WAY THE LORD OUR GOD IS NEAR US WHENEVER WE PRAY TO HIM? (4:7)

MATTHEW 2 | 1141

[7]When King Herod heard this he was disturbed, and all Jerusalem with him. [4]When he had called together all the people's chief priests and teachers of the law, he asked them where the Christ[a] was to be born. [5]"In Bethlehem in Judea," they replied, "for this is what the prophet has written:

[6]" 'But you, Bethlehem, in the land of Judah,
    are by no means least among the rulers of Judah;

for out of you will come a ruler
    who will be the shepherd of my
    people Israel.'[b]"

[7]Then Herod called the Magi secretly and found out from them the exact time the star had appeared. [8]He sent them to Bethlehem and said, "Go and make a careful search for the child. As soon as you find him, report to me, so that I too may go and worship him."

[a] 4 Or Messiah [b] 6 Micah 5:2

MATTHEW 1:1–17

{ MONDAY }

He's Been Waiting for You

1:1 A RECORD OF THE GENEALOGY OF JESUS CHRIST.

This is one of two passages that many people skip over when reading the Gospels. The other is Luke 3:23–38. Both are genealogies, lists of obscure people with hard-to-pronounce names that serve as a kind of family tree or pedigree for Jesus. Both include names of people who can only be described as good, bad, ugly and surprising. Look up the names sometime; it's worth the effort.

When did God start thinking about Jesus? Matthew's list says it began at least with Abraham, 2000 years before Jesus was born. Luke's list goes back even further, to Adam, the first human. Actually, the orthodox and correct answer is, God never started thinking about Jesus. God the Son was always with God the Father.

Maybe a better question is: When did God start thinking about us? The genealogies tell us that God has been thinking about saving us for a very long time. These names are like synapses in the mind of God, leading up to the great name he will speak in Jesus. The names in these genealogies are the connections in God's thoughts about his plan to save the world through his Son. Actually, his thoughts began before these people. "For he chose us in [Christ] before the creation of the world" (Ephesians 1:4).

Before you speak to God today, know that he has been speaking to you. To pray is to enter into the conversation. Jesus said your Father knows what you need before you ask him (see Matthew 6:8). That's because he knew you before you knew him. There is nothing you can say that can possibly surprise him—no sin you might confess, no need you might express. He has been waiting for you to talk with him for a very long time.

PRAY:

Father in Heaven! I come to you today knowing that you've been thinking about me for a long time now. Thank you for making me part of your eternal plan, and that I can join you in your grand purposes as I pray.

FOR YOUR NEXT DEVOTIONAL READING, GO TO PAGE 1146.

Joseph Scriven's old hymn about prayer is true: "What a friend we have in Jesus, all our sins and griefs to bear! What a privilege to carry everything to God in prayer!" But we would know nothing about this wonderful Jesus, and his gift of prayer, were it not for the Bible. What a friend we have in Jesus, and what a gift we have in the Holy Scriptures he has given us. Francis Schaeffer confessed that he would sometimes reach over to the Bible on his nightstand and just pat it as he woke up in the morning. He explained:

> I don't love this book because it has a leather cover and golden edges. I don't love it as a "holy book." I love it because it is God's book. Through it, the Creator of the universe has told us who he is, how to come to him through Christ, who we are, and what all reality is. Without the Bible we wouldn't have anything . . . I am so thankful for it. If the God who is there had created the earth and then remained silent, we wouldn't know who he is. But the Bible reveals the God who is there; that is why I love it.[4]

That is why we may love it too, and learn better how to express our love for the God who gave us his book, and ask for the things he wants to give.

distillation of all the prayers that are to be found in the heart of the Bible. It's all there in the Psalms: prayer that God's name be hallowed, his rule be supreme and his will be done; that our needs be met and our sins forgiven; that we be kept safe from all danger to soul and body.

Paul coined a word to describe the character of Scripture: He said it is "God-breathed" (see 2 Timothy 3:16). The breath of God permeates the Bible. The breath of God is the Holy Spirit, the same Spirit who spoke light into darkness and turned dust into living beings made in the image of God. This is the Spirit who speaks to us in the Bible, making it "useful for teaching, rebuking, correcting and training in righteousness." We need all these things to be able to pray well, for although the need for prayer is natural, the ability is not. We must be taught and trained in prayer, and if need be, rebuked and corrected. Like the first disciples who asked Jesus to teach them to pray, we may go to Scripture with the same intent and ask the Spirit of Jesus to do the teaching.

When the members of his synagogue complained that the words of the liturgy did not express what they felt, Abraham Heschel, the great philosopher of religion replied that the liturgy wasn't supposed to express what they felt; they were supposed to feel what the liturgy expressed. To be taught by the Bible to pray is to learn to pray and feel what the Bible expresses—to say what it means and mean what it says. This Bible is designed to help you listen to the voice of the Spirit in Scripture in such a way that any text can be a text for prayer. Its object is to teach habits of Bible reading that flow into praise and thanks, confession and supplication.

To pray through, in and from Scripture is not only to pray according to God's will, but also according to what philosopher Peter Kreeft calls "the grammar of existence." Grammar has to do with the proper relationship between words in a sentence, the way things like verbs, nouns and adjectives are to be positioned relative to each other. Just as a sentence makes no sense when the grammar is bad, our lives make no sense when we fail to appreciate the elemental grammar of our existence: God is God and we are not. He does not exist for us; we exist for him. Prayer, then, as with everything else in life, is ultimately not about us, but about God. Happy are those who know this! We were made for God, and our hearts are restless until they rest in him.

Learning to pray Scripture can teach this joyous grammar of existence because it gets the focus where it belongs—on God, not us and our perceived needs and feelings. Frankly, our own self-generated prayers can quickly become boring. Biblical prayer raises our desires up to heaven, where they and we are transformed, and our pleasure in prayer is renewed.

The grammar of existence says that God is always there first, ahead of us. We "are" because he first was and is and will be. "We love because he first loved us" (1 John 4:19). And so we pray, for we also speak because he first spoke. "Our prayer is the answer to God's," wrote P. T. Forsyth. "Herein is prayer, not that we prayed him, but that he first prayed us, in giving his Son to be a propitiation for us. The heart of the Atonement is prayer—Christ's great self-offering to God in the Eternal Spirit."[3] Prayer is a dialogue, a conversation initiated by God; he speaks, we respond, he responds to our response, and so it goes forever. To pray is to be lifted up into the eternal fellowship of the community of God—Father, Son and Holy Spirit.

Since God starts the conversation by first speaking his Word to us, what better place to begin to pray than with his Word in the Bible? We begin with Jesus, God's Word incarnate. There would be no conversation at all were it not for his death and resurrection. The dialogue continues and is cultivated with God's written Word.

WELCOME

WHAT IS THE *PRAYER DEVOTIONAL BIBLE*? It is the text of the Old and New Testaments with devotional helps, prompts, historical and biographical sketches and book introductions to help you pray through, in and from Scripture.

But why should such a thing exist?

The easiest answer is that whenever you pray through, in and from Scripture, you never need wonder whether you are praying according to God's will. Prayer is not a means by which we get God to give us what we want. "Prayer is a means God uses to give us what he wants," writes Bingham Hunter.[1] The Bible tells us what God wants. At first that may seem a little deflating, asking God only for what God already wants to give. By this definition, prayer can sound like a noble and lofty exercise, a soul-purifying meditation on platonic ideals—hardly anything to get the heart beating faster.

But look at what God wants to give! Paul's prayer that the Ephesians might be filled to the measure of all the fullness of God and know a love that surpasses knowledge (see Ephesians 3:14–21) is better than the best any of us could possibly have imagined and wished on our own. That's only one example of the things the Bible says God wants to give. To desire what God wants to give and to turn that desire into prayer is to be expanded in spirit. Stated simply, the purpose of the *Prayer Devotional Bible* is to help you notice what God wants to give.

The relationship between the Bible and prayer is profound. Picture it this way: Children have long been told that the best way to find the book of Psalms, the longest book in the Bible, is to put their finger in the middle of the Bible, in its heart, so to speak. What is the book of Psalms? It is a book of prayers. And the longest prayer in this longest book is Psalm 119, a prayer about the Scriptures. Prayer is at the heart of the Bible, and the Bible is in the heart of prayer.

But that's just a picture, an illustration of the relationship. Better is a demonstration—the prayer life of our Lord Jesus Christ. At the end of his life, as he hung dying on the cross, he went to the Scriptures for his prayers. "My God, my God, why have you forsaken me" is a quotation from Psalm 22:1. "Father, into your hands I commit my spirit" comes from Psalm 31:5. At the point of his greatest anguish and extremity, Jesus turned to the Bible for his prayers. Charles Spurgeon urges us to learn from the fact that when he most needed to pray, Jesus the grand original thinker saw no need to be original or extemporaneous. "How instructive is this great truth that the Incarnate Word lived on the Inspired Word! It was food to him, as it is to us; and . . . if Christ thus lived upon the Word of God, should not you and I do the same? . . . I think it well worthy of your constant remembrance that, even in death, our blessed Master showed the ruling passion of his spirit, so that his last words were a quotation from Scripture."[2]

As a devout Jew, Jesus' prayer book was the Psalms. A close look at the Psalms shows the Lord's Prayer, the prayer Jesus taught us to pray, to be a summary and

Foreword

ONE OF THE MOST SIGNIFICANT MOMENTS in Bible history is often overlooked by students of Scripture. What a marvelous day it was when "men began to call on the name of the Lord" (Genesis 4:26). This is the first record of human beings feeling their need of God's help and reaching out to him in sincere prayer. Human history was changed forever when it was discovered that the Creator of the universe was also the compassionate Helper who responded when people called on his name.

The blessings that flowed from this privilege were what separated Abraham's descendants from all the other nations and their lifeless idols. "What other nation is so great as to have their gods near them the way the Lord our God is near us whenever we pray to him?" (Deuteronomy 4:7, italics added). Israel's invincibility in battle was not a result of sophisticated weaponry and superior numbers, but rather a result of their dependence on the Lord expressed through prayer. Confidence in this fact became such a part of the mindset of those devoted to God that David would boldly declare that "the Lord has set apart the godly for himself; the Lord will hear when I call to him" (Psalm 4:3, italics added).

No subsequent teaching of Scripture has ever altered the fact that God still delights in hearing and answering the prayers of his people. The experience of every true believer and two thousand years of church history confirm that the Lord indeed "richly blesses all who call on him" (Romans 10:12). May the reading of this Bible produce more than a mere intellectual exercise concerning truth about God. Rather, let it draw the reader to the throne of God where mercy and grace are always available in the time of need (see Hebrews 4:16).

Jim Cymbala

Foreword

ONE OF THE MOST SIGNIFICANT MOMENTS in Bible history is often overlooked by students of Scripture. What a marvelous day it was when "men began to call on the name of the LORD" (Genesis 4:26)! This is the first record of human beings feeling their need of God's help and reaching out to him in sincere prayer. Human history was changed forever when it was discovered that the Creator of the universe was also the compassionate Helper who responded when people called on his name.

The blessings that flowed from this privilege were what separated Abraham's descendants from all the other nations and their lifeless idols. "What other nation is so great as to have their gods near them the way the LORD our God is near us *whenever we pray to him?*" (Deuteronomy 4:7, italics added). Israel's invincibility in battle was not a result of sophisticated weaponry and superior numbers, but rather a result of their dependence on the Lord expressed through prayer. Confidence in this fact became such a part of the mindset of those devoted to God that David would boldly declare that "the LORD has set apart the godly for himself; *the LORD will hear when I call to him*" (Psalm 4:3, italics added).

No subsequent teaching of Scripture has ever altered the fact that God still delights in hearing and answering the prayers of his people. The experience of every true believer and two thousand years of church history confirm that the Lord indeed "richly blesses all who call on him" (Romans 10:12). May the reading of this Bible produce more than a mere intellectual exercise concerning truth about God. Rather, let it draw the reader to the throne of God where mercy and grace are always available in the time of need (see Hebrews 4:16).

Jim Cymbala

Contents

shown your servant. I had only my staff when I crossed this Jordan, but now I have become two groups. ¹¹Save me, I pray, from the hand of my brother Esau, for I am afraid he will come and attack me, and also the mothers with their children. ¹²But you have said, 'I will surely make you prosper and will make your descendants like the sand of the sea, which cannot be counted.'"

¹³He spent the night there, and from what he had with him he selected a gift for his brother Esau: ¹⁴two hundred female goats and twenty male goats, two hundred ewes and twenty rams, ¹⁵thirty female camels with their young, forty cows and ten bulls, and twenty female donkeys and ten male donkeys. ¹⁶He put them in the care of his servants, each herd by itself, and said to his servants, "Go ahead of me, and keep some space between the herds."

¹⁷He instructed the one in the lead: "When my brother Esau meets you and asks, 'To whom do you belong, and where are you going, and who owns all these animals in front of you?' ¹⁸then you are to say, 'They belong to your servant Jacob. They are a gift sent to my lord Esau, and he is coming behind us.'"

¹⁹He also instructed the second, the third and all the others who followed the herds: "You are to say the same thing to Esau when you meet him. ²⁰And be sure to say, 'Your servant Jacob is coming behind us.'" For he thought, "I will pacify him with these gifts I am sending on ahead; later, when I see him, perhaps he will receive me." ²¹So Jacob's gifts went on ahead of him, but he himself spent the night in the camp.

Jacob Wrestles With God

²²That night Jacob got up and took his two wives, his two maidservants and his eleven sons and crossed the ford of the Jabbok. ²³After he had sent them across the stream, he sent over all his possessions. ²⁴So Jacob was left alone, and a man wrestled with him till daybreak. ²⁵When the man saw that he could not overpower him, he touched the socket of Jacob's hip so that his hip was wrenched as he wrestled with the man. ²⁶Then the man said, "Let me go, for it is daybreak."

But Jacob replied, "I will not let you go unless you bless me."

²⁷The man asked him, "What is your name?"

"Jacob," he answered.

²⁸Then the man said, "Your name will no longer be Jacob, but Israel,ᵃ because you have struggled with God and with men and have overcome."

²⁹Jacob said, "Please tell me your name."

But he replied, "Why do you ask my name?" Then he blessed him there.

³⁰So Jacob called the place Peniel,ᵇ saying, "It is because I saw God face to face, and yet my life was spared."

³¹The sun rose above him as he passed Peniel,ᶜ and he was limping because of his hip. ³²Therefore to this day the Israelites do not eat the tendon attached to the socket of the hip, because the socket of Jacob's hip was touched near the tendon.

Jacob Meets Esau

33 Jacob looked up and there was Esau, coming with his four hundred men; so he divided the children among Leah, Rachel and the two maidservants. ²He put the maidservants and their children in front, Leah and her children next, and Rachel and Joseph in the rear. ³He himself went on ahead and bowed down to the ground seven times as he approached his brother.

⁴But Esau ran to meet Jacob and embraced him; he threw his arms around his neck and kissed him. And they wept. ⁵Then Esau looked up and saw the women and children. "Who are these with you?" he asked.

Jacob answered, "They are the children God has graciously given your servant."

⁶Then the maidservants and their children approached and bowed down. ⁷Next, Leah and her children came and bowed down. Last of all came Joseph and Rachel, and they too bowed down.

⁸Esau asked, "What do you mean by all these droves I met?"

"To find favor in your eyes, my lord," he said.

ᵃ28 Israel means he struggles with God.
ᵇ30 Peniel means face of God.   ᶜ31 Hebrew Penuel, a variant of Peniel

⁹But Esau said, "I already have plenty, my brother. Keep what you have for yourself."

¹⁰"No, please!" said Jacob. "If I have found favor in your eyes, accept this gift from me. For to see your face is like seeing the face of God, now that you have received me favorably. ¹¹Please accept the present that was brought to you, for God has been gracious to me and I have all I need." And because Jacob insisted, Esau accepted it.

¹²Then Esau said, "Let us be on our way; I'll accompany you."

¹³But Jacob said to him, "My lord knows that the children are tender and that I must care for the ewes and cows that are nursing their young. If they are driven hard just one day, all the animals will die. ¹⁴So let my lord go on ahead of his servant, while I move along slowly at the pace of the droves before me and that of the children, until I come to my lord in Seir."

¹⁵Esau said, "Then let me leave some of my men with you."

"But why do that?" Jacob asked. "Just let me find favor in the eyes of my lord."

¹⁶So that day Esau started on his way back to Seir. ¹⁷Jacob, however, went to Succoth, where he built a place for himself and made shelters for his livestock. That is why the place is called Succoth.ᵃ

¹⁸After Jacob came from Paddan Aram,ᵇ he arrived safely at theᶜ city of Shechem in Canaan and camped within sight of the city. ¹⁹For a hundred pieces of silver,ᵈ he bought from the sons of Hamor, the father of Shechem, the plot of ground where he pitched his tent. ²⁰There he set up an altar and called it El Elohe Israel.ᵉ

Dinah and the Shechemites

34 Now Dinah, the daughter Leah had borne to Jacob, went out to visit the women of the land. ²When Shechem son of Hamor the Hivite, the ruler of that area, saw her, he took her and violated her. ³His heart was drawn to Dinah daughter of Jacob, and he loved the girl and spoke tenderly to her. ⁴And Shechem said to his father Hamor, "Get me this girl as my wife."

⁵When Jacob heard that his daughter Dinah had been defiled, his sons were in the fields with his livestock; so he kept quiet about it until they came home.

⁶Then Shechem's father Hamor went out to talk with Jacob. ⁷Now Jacob's sons had come in from the fields as soon as they heard what had happened. They were filled with grief and fury, because Shechem had done a disgraceful thing inᶠ Israel by lying with Jacob's daughter—a thing that should not be done.

⁸But Hamor said to them, "My son Shechem has his heart set on your daughter. Please give her to him as his wife. ⁹Intermarry with us; give us your daughters and take our daughters for yourselves. ¹⁰You can settle among us; the land is open to you. Live in it, tradeᵍ in it, and acquire property in it."

¹¹Then Shechem said to Dinah's father and brothers, "Let me find favor in your eyes, and I will give you whatever you ask. ¹²Make the price for the bride and the gift I am to bring as great as you like, and I'll pay whatever you ask me. Only give me the girl as my wife."

¹³Because their sister Dinah had been defiled, Jacob's sons replied deceitfully as they spoke to Shechem and his father Hamor. ¹⁴They said to them, "We can't do such a thing; we can't give our sister to a man who is not circumcised. That would be a disgrace to us. ¹⁵We will give our consent to you on one condition only: that you become like us by circumcising all your males. ¹⁶Then we will give you our daughters and take your daughters for ourselves. We'll settle among you and become one people with you. ¹⁷But if you will not agree to be circumcised, we'll take our sisterʰ and go."

¹⁸Their proposal seemed good to Hamor and his son Shechem. ¹⁹The young man, who was the most honored of all his father's household, lost no time in doing what they said, because he was de-

ᵃ17 Succoth means shelters.   ᵇ18 That is, Northwest Mesopotamia   ᶜ18 Or arrived at Shalem, a   ᵈ19 Hebrew hundred kesitahs; a kesitah was a unit of money of unknown weight and value.   ᵉ20 El Elohe Israel can mean God, the God of Israel or mighty is the God of Israel.   ᶠ7 Or against   ᵍ10 Or move about freely; also in verse 21   ʰ17 Hebrew daughter

lighted with Jacob's daughter. ²⁰So Hamor and his son Shechem went to the gate of their city to speak to their fellow townsmen. ²¹"These men are friendly toward us," they said. "Let them live in our land and trade in it; the land has plenty of room for them. We can marry their daughters and they can marry ours. ²²But the men will consent to live with us as one people only on the condition that our males be circumcised, as they themselves are. ²³Won't their livestock, their property and all their other animals become ours? So let us give our consent to them, and they will settle among us."

²⁴All the men who went out of the city gate agreed with Hamor and his son Shechem, and every male in the city was circumcised.

²⁵Three days later, while all of them were still in pain, two of Jacob's sons, Simeon and Levi, Dinah's brothers, took their swords and attacked the unsuspecting city, killing every male. ²⁶They put Hamor and his son Shechem to the sword and took Dinah from Shechem's house and left. ²⁷The sons of Jacob came upon the dead bodies and looted the city where^a their sister had been defiled. ²⁸They seized their flocks and herds and donkeys and everything else of theirs in the city and out in the fields. ²⁹They carried off all their wealth and all their women and children, taking as plunder everything in the houses.

³⁰Then Jacob said to Simeon and Levi, "You have brought trouble on me by making me a stench to the Canaanites and Perizzites, the people living in this land. We are few in number, and if they join forces against me and attack me, I and my household will be destroyed."

³¹But they replied, "Should he have treated our sister like a prostitute?"

Jacob Returns to Bethel

35 Then God said to Jacob, "Go up to Bethel and settle there, and build an altar there to God, who appeared to you when you were fleeing from your brother Esau."

²So Jacob said to his household and to all who were with him, "Get rid of the foreign gods you have with you, and purify yourselves and change your clothes.

> "THEN come, let us go up to Bethel, where I will build an altar to God, who answered me in the day of my distress and who has been with me wherever I have gone."
>
> GENESIS 35:3

³Then come, let us go up to Bethel, where I will build an altar to God, who answered me in the day of my distress and who has been with me wherever I have gone." ⁴So they gave Jacob all the foreign gods they had and the rings in their ears, and Jacob buried them under the oak at Shechem. ⁵Then they set out, and the terror of God fell upon the towns all around them so that no one pursued them.

⁶Jacob and all the people with him came to Luz (that is, Bethel) in the land of Canaan. ⁷There he built an altar, and he called the place El Bethel,^b because it was there that God revealed himself to him when he was fleeing from his brother.

⁸Now Deborah, Rebekah's nurse, died and was buried under the oak below Bethel. So it was named Allon Bacuth.^c

⁹After Jacob returned from Paddan Aram,^d God appeared to him again and blessed him. ¹⁰God said to him, "Your name is Jacob,^e but you will no longer be called Jacob; your name will be Israel.^f" So he named him Israel.

¹¹And God said to him, "I am God Almighty^g; be fruitful and increase in number. A nation and a community of nations will come from you, and kings will come from your body. ¹²The land I gave to Abraham and Isaac I also give to you, and I will give this land to your descendants after you." ¹³Then God went up from him at the place where he had talked with him.

¹⁴Jacob set up a stone pillar at the place where God had talked with him, and he poured out a drink offering on it; he also

---

^a27 Or because   ^b7 El Bethel means God of Bethel.   ^c8 Allon Bacuth means oak of weeping.   ^d9 That is, Northwest Mesopotamia; also in verse 26   ^e10 Jacob means he grasps the heel (figuratively, he deceives).   ^f10 Israel means he struggles with God.   ^g11 Hebrew El-Shaddai

poured oil on it. [15]Jacob called the place where God had talked with him Bethel.[a]

The Deaths of Rachel and Isaac

[16]Then they moved on from Bethel. While they were still some distance from Ephrath, Rachel began to give birth and had great difficulty. [17]And as she was having great difficulty in childbirth, the midwife said to her, "Don't be afraid, for you have another son." [18]As she breathed her last—for she was dying—she named her son Ben-Oni.[b] But his father named him Benjamin.[c]

[19]So Rachel died and was buried on the way to Ephrath (that is, Bethlehem). [20]Over her tomb Jacob set up a pillar, and to this day that pillar marks Rachel's tomb. [21]Israel moved on again and pitched his tent beyond Migdal Eder. [22]While Israel was living in that region, Reuben went in and slept with his father's concubine Bilhah, and Israel heard of it.

Jacob had twelve sons:
[23]The sons of Leah:
    Reuben the firstborn of Jacob,
    Simeon, Levi, Judah, Issachar and
    Zebulun.
[24]The sons of Rachel:
    Joseph and Benjamin.
[25]The sons of Rachel's maidservant
    Bilhah:
    Dan and Naphtali.
[26]The sons of Leah's maidservant Zilpah:
    Gad and Asher.
These were the sons of Jacob, who were born to him in Paddan Aram.

[27]Jacob came home to his father Isaac in Mamre, near Kiriath Arba (that is, Hebron), where Abraham and Isaac had stayed. [28]Isaac lived a hundred and eighty years. [29]Then he breathed his last and died and was gathered to his people, old and full of years. And his sons Esau and Jacob buried him.

Esau's Descendants

36 This is the account of Esau (that is, Edom).

[2]Esau took his wives from the women of Canaan: Adah daughter of Elon the Hittite, and Oholibamah daughter of Anah and granddaughter of Zibeon the Hivite— [3]also Basemath daughter of Ishmael and sister of Nebaioth.

[4]Adah bore Eliphaz to Esau, Basemath bore Reuel, [5]and Oholibamah bore Jeush, Jalam and Korah. These were the sons of Esau, who were born to him in Canaan.

[6]Esau took his wives and sons and daughters and all the members of his household, as well as his livestock and all his other animals and all the goods he had acquired in Canaan, and moved to a land some distance from his brother Jacob. [7]Their possessions were too great for them to remain together; the land where they were staying could not support them both because of their livestock. [8]So Esau (that is, Edom) settled in the hill country of Seir.

[9]This is the account of Esau the father of the Edomites in the hill country of Seir.

[10]These are the names of Esau's sons:
    Eliphaz, the son of Esau's wife
    Adah, and Reuel, the son of Esau's
    wife Basemath.
[11]The sons of Eliphaz:
    Teman, Omar, Zepho, Gatam and
    Kenaz.
[12]Esau's son Eliphaz also had a concubine named Timna, who bore him Amalek. These were grandsons of Esau's wife Adah.
[13]The sons of Reuel:
    Nahath, Zerah, Shammah and
    Mizzah. These were grandsons of
    Esau's wife Basemath.
[14]The sons of Esau's wife Oholibamah
    daughter of Anah and granddaughter
    of Zibeon, whom she bore to Esau:
    Jeush, Jalam and Korah.

[15]These were the chiefs among Esau's descendants:
    The sons of Eliphaz the firstborn of
    Esau:
    Chiefs Teman, Omar, Zepho, Kenaz, [16]Korah,[d] Gatam and Amalek.

[a]15 Bethel means house of God.   [b]18 Ben-Oni means son of my trouble.   [c]18 Benjamin means son of my right hand.   [d]16 Masoretic Text; Samaritan Pentateuch (see also Gen. 36:11 and 1 Chron. 1:36) does not have Korah.

These were the chiefs descended from Eliphaz in Edom; they were grandsons of Adah.

¹⁷ The sons of Esau's son Reuel:

Chiefs Nahath, Zerah, Shammah and Mizzah. These were the chiefs descended from Reuel in Edom; they were grandsons of Esau's wife Basemath.

¹⁸ The sons of Esau's wife Oholibamah:

Chiefs Jeush, Jalam and Korah. These were the chiefs descended from Esau's wife Oholibamah daughter of Anah.

¹⁹ These were the sons of Esau (that is, Edom), and these were their chiefs.

²⁰ These were the sons of Seir the Horite, who were living in the region:

Lotan, Shobal, Zibeon, Anah, ²¹ Dishon, Ezer and Dishan. These sons of Seir in Edom were Horite chiefs.

²² The sons of Lotan:

Hori and Homam.ᵃ Timna was Lotan's sister.

²³ The sons of Shobal:

Alvan, Manahath, Ebal, Shepho and Onam.

²⁴ The sons of Zibeon:

Aiah and Anah. This is the Anah who discovered the hot springsᵇ in the desert while he was grazing the donkeys of his father Zibeon.

²⁵ The children of Anah:

Dishon and Oholibamah daughter of Anah.

²⁶ The sons of Dishonᶜ:

Hemdan, Eshban, Ithran and Keran.

²⁷ The sons of Ezer:

Bilhan, Zaavan and Akan.

²⁸ The sons of Dishan:

Uz and Aran.

²⁹ These were the Horite chiefs:

Lotan, Shobal, Zibeon, Anah, ³⁰ Dishon, Ezer and Dishan. These were the Horite chiefs, according to their divisions, in the land of Seir.

The Rulers of Edom

³¹ These were the kings who reigned in Edom before any Israelite king reignedᵈ:

³² Bela son of Beor became king of Edom. His city was named Dinhabah.

³³ When Bela died, Jobab son of Zerah from Bozrah succeeded him as king.

³⁴ When Jobab died, Husham from the land of the Temanites succeeded him as king.

³⁵ When Husham died, Hadad son of Bedad, who defeated Midian in the country of Moab, succeeded him as king. His city was named Avith.

³⁶ When Hadad died, Samlah from Masrekah succeeded him as king.

³⁷ When Samlah died, Shaul from Rehoboth on the riverᵉ succeeded him as king.

³⁸ When Shaul died, Baal-Hanan son of Acbor succeeded him as king.

³⁹ When Baal-Hanan son of Acbor died, Hadadᶠ succeeded him as king. His city was named Pau, and his wife's name was Mehetabel daughter of Matred, the daughter of Me-Zahab.

⁴⁰ These were the chiefs descended from Esau, by name, according to their clans and regions:

Timna, Alvah, Jetheth, ⁴¹ Oholibamah, Elah, Pinon, ⁴² Kenaz, Teman, Mibzar, ⁴³ Magdiel and Iram. These were the chiefs of Edom, according to their settlements in the land they occupied.

This was Esau the father of the Edomites.

Joseph's Dreams

37 Jacob lived in the land where his father had stayed, the land of Canaan.

²This is the account of Jacob.

Joseph, a young man of seventeen, was tending the flocks with his brothers, the sons of Bilhah and the sons of Zilpah, his father's wives, and he brought their father a bad report about them.

ᵃ22 Hebrew *Hemam*, a variant of *Homam* (see 1 Chron. 1:39) ᵇ24 Vulgate; Syriac *discovered water*; the meaning of the Hebrew for this word is uncertain. ᶜ26 Hebrew *Dishan*, a variant of *Dishon* ᵈ31 Or *before an Israelite king reigned over them* ᵉ37 Possibly the Euphrates ᶠ39 Many manuscripts of the Masoretic Text, Samaritan Pentateuch and Syriac (see also 1 Chron. 1:50); most manuscripts of the Masoretic Text *Hadar*

³Now Israel loved Joseph more than any of his other sons, because he had been born to him in his old age; and he made a richly ornamented*a* robe for him. ⁴When his brothers saw that their father loved him more than any of them, they hated him and could not speak a kind word to him.

⁵Joseph had a dream, and when he told it to his brothers, they hated him all the more. ⁶He said to them, "Listen to this dream I had: ⁷We were binding sheaves of grain out in the field when suddenly my sheaf rose and stood upright, while your sheaves gathered around mine and bowed down to it."

⁸His brothers said to him, "Do you intend to reign over us? Will you actually rule us?" And they hated him all the more because of his dream and what he had said.

⁹Then he had another dream, and he told it to his brothers. "Listen," he said, "I had another dream, and this time the sun and moon and eleven stars were bowing down to me."

¹⁰When he told his father as well as his brothers, his father rebuked him and said, "What is this dream you had? Will your mother and I and your brothers actually come and bow down to the ground before you?" ¹¹His brothers were jealous of him, but his father kept the matter in mind.

Joseph Sold by His Brothers

¹²Now his brothers had gone to graze their father's flocks near Shechem, ¹³and Israel said to Joseph, "As you know, your brothers are grazing the flocks near Shechem. Come, I am going to send you to them."

"Very well," he replied.

¹⁴So he said to him, "Go and see if all is well with your brothers and with the flocks, and bring word back to me." Then he sent him off from the Valley of Hebron.

When Joseph arrived at Shechem, ¹⁵a man found him wandering around in the fields and asked him, "What are you looking for?"

¹⁶He replied, "I'm looking for my brothers. Can you tell me where they are grazing their flocks?"

¹⁷"They have moved on from here," the man answered. "I heard them say, 'Let's go to Dothan.'"

So Joseph went after his brothers and found them near Dothan. ¹⁸But they saw him in the distance, and before he reached them, they plotted to kill him.

¹⁹"Here comes that dreamer!" they said to each other. ²⁰"Come now, let's kill him and throw him into one of these cisterns and say that a ferocious animal devoured him. Then we'll see what comes of his dreams."

²¹When Reuben heard this, he tried to rescue him from their hands. "Let's not take his life," he said. ²²"Don't shed any blood. Throw him into this cistern here in the desert, but don't lay a hand on him." Reuben said this to rescue him from them and take him back to his father.

²³So when Joseph came to his brothers, they stripped him of his robe—the richly ornamented robe he was wearing— ²⁴and they took him and threw him into the cistern. Now the cistern was empty; there was no water in it.

²⁵As they sat down to eat their meal, they looked up and saw a caravan of Ishmaelites coming from Gilead. Their camels were loaded with spices, balm and myrrh, and they were on their way to take them down to Egypt.

²⁶Judah said to his brothers, "What will we gain if we kill our brother and cover up his blood? ²⁷Come, let's sell him to the Ishmaelites and not lay our hands on him; after all, he is our brother, our own flesh and blood." His brothers agreed.

²⁸So when the Midianite merchants came by, his brothers pulled Joseph up out of the cistern and sold him for twenty shekels*b* of silver to the Ishmaelites, who took him to Egypt.

²⁹When Reuben returned to the cistern and saw that Joseph was not there, he tore his clothes. ³⁰He went back to his brothers and said, "The boy isn't there! Where can I turn now?"

³¹Then they got Joseph's robe, slaughtered a goat and dipped the robe in the

a 3 The meaning of the Hebrew for *richly ornamented* is uncertain; also in verses 23 and 32. *b 28* That is, about 8 ounces (about 0.2 kilogram)

blood. ³²They took the ornamented robe back to their father and said, "We found this. Examine it to see whether it is your son's robe."

³³He recognized it and said, "It is my son's robe! Some ferocious animal has devoured him. Joseph has surely been torn to pieces."

³⁴Then Jacob tore his clothes, put on sackcloth and mourned for his son many days. ³⁵All his sons and daughters came to comfort him, but he refused to be comforted. "No," he said, "in mourning will I go down to the grave*a* to my son." So his father wept for him.

³⁶Meanwhile, the Midianites*b* sold Joseph in Egypt to Potiphar, one of Pharaoh's officials, the captain of the guard.

Judah and Tamar

38 At that time, Judah left his brothers and went down to stay with a man of Adullam named Hirah. ²There Judah met the daughter of a Canaanite man named Shua. He married her and lay with her; ³she became pregnant and gave birth to a son, who was named Er. ⁴She conceived again and gave birth to a son and named him Onan. ⁵She gave birth to still another son and named him Shelah. It was at Kezib that she gave birth to him.

⁶Judah got a wife for Er, his firstborn, and her name was Tamar. ⁷But Er, Judah's firstborn, was wicked in the LORD's sight; so the LORD put him to death.

⁸Then Judah said to Onan, "Lie with your brother's wife and fulfill your duty to her as a brother-in-law to produce offspring for your brother." ⁹But Onan knew that the offspring would not be his; so whenever he lay with his brother's wife, he spilled his semen on the ground to keep from producing offspring for his brother. ¹⁰What he did was wicked in the LORD's sight; so he put him to death also.

¹¹Judah then said to his daughter-in-law Tamar, "Live as a widow in your father's house until my son Shelah grows up." For he thought, "He may die too, just like his brothers." So Tamar went to live in her father's house.

¹²After a long time Judah's wife, the daughter of Shua, died. When Judah had recovered from his grief, he went up to Timnah, to the men who were shearing his sheep, and his friend Hirah the Adullamite went with him.

¹³When Tamar was told, "Your father-in-law is on his way to Timnah to shear his sheep," ¹⁴she took off her widow's clothes, covered herself with a veil to disguise herself, and then sat down at the entrance to Enaim, which is on the road to Timnah. For she saw that, though Shelah had now grown up, she had not been given to him as his wife.

¹⁵When Judah saw her, he thought she was a prostitute, for she had covered her face. ¹⁶Not realizing that she was his daughter-in-law, he went over to her by the roadside and said, "Come now, let me sleep with you."

"And what will you give me to sleep with you?" she asked.

¹⁷"I'll send you a young goat from my flock," he said.

"Will you give me something as a pledge until you send it?" she asked.

¹⁸He said, "What pledge should I give you?"

"Your seal and its cord, and the staff in your hand," she answered. So he gave them to her and slept with her, and she became pregnant by him. ¹⁹After she left, she took off her veil and put on her widow's clothes again.

²⁰Meanwhile Judah sent the young goat by his friend the Adullamite in order to get his pledge back from the woman, but he did not find her. ²¹He asked the men who lived there, "Where is the shrine prostitute who was beside the road at Enaim?"

"There hasn't been any shrine prostitute here," they said.

²²So he went back to Judah and said, "I didn't find her. Besides, the men who lived there said, 'There hasn't been any shrine prostitute here.'"

²³Then Judah said, "Let her keep what she has, or we will become a laughingstock. After all, I did send her this young goat, but you didn't find her."

²⁴About three months later Judah was told, "Your daughter-in-law Tamar is

a35 Hebrew *Sheol*   *b36* Samaritan Pentateuch, Septuagint, Vulgate and Syriac (see also verse 28); Masoretic Text *Medanites*

guilty of prostitution, and as a result she is now pregnant."

Judah said, "Bring her out and have her burned to death!"

²⁵As she was being brought out, she sent a message to her father-in-law. "I am pregnant by the man who owns these," she said. And she added, "See if you recognize whose seal and cord and staff these are."

²⁶Judah recognized them and said, "She is more righteous than I, since I wouldn't give her to my son Shelah." And he did not sleep with her again.

²⁷When the time came for her to give birth, there were twin boys in her womb. ²⁸As she was giving birth, one of them put out his hand; so the midwife took a scarlet thread and tied it on his wrist and said, "This one came out first." ²⁹But when he drew back his hand, his brother came out, and she said, "So this is how you have broken out!" And he was named Perez.ᵃ ³⁰Then his brother, who had the scarlet thread on his wrist, came out and he was given the name Zerah.ᵇ

Joseph and Potiphar's Wife

39 Now Joseph had been taken down to Egypt. Potiphar, an Egyptian who was one of Pharaoh's officials, the captain of the guard, bought him from the Ishmaelites who had taken him there.

²The LORD was with Joseph and he prospered, and he lived in the house of his Egyptian master. ³When his master saw that the LORD was with him and that the LORD gave him success in everything he did, ⁴Joseph found favor in his eyes and became his attendant. Potiphar put him in charge of his household, and he entrusted to his care everything he owned. ⁵From the time he put him in charge of his household and of all that he owned, the LORD blessed the household of the Egyptian because of Joseph. The blessing of the LORD was on everything Potiphar had, both in the house and in the field. ⁶So he left in Joseph's care everything he had; with Joseph in charge, he did not concern himself with anything except the food he ate.

Now Joseph was well-built and hand-some, ⁷and after a while his master's wife took notice of Joseph and said, "Come to bed with me!"

⁸But he refused. "With me in charge," he told her, "my master does not concern himself with anything in the house; everything he owns he has entrusted to my care. ⁹No one is greater in this house than I am. My master has withheld nothing from me except you, because you are his wife. How then could I do such a wicked thing and sin against God?" ¹⁰And though she spoke to Joseph day after day, he refused to go to bed with her or even be with her.

¹¹One day he went into the house to attend to his duties, and none of the household servants was inside. ¹²She caught him by his cloak and said, "Come to bed with me!" But he left his cloak in her hand and ran out of the house.

¹³When she saw that he had left his cloak in her hand and had run out of the house, ¹⁴she called her household servants. "Look," she said to them, "this Hebrew has been brought to us to make sport of us! He came in here to sleep with me, but I screamed. ¹⁵When he heard me scream for help, he left his cloak beside me and ran out of the house."

¹⁶She kept his cloak beside her until his master came home. ¹⁷Then she told him this story: "That Hebrew slave you brought us came to me to make sport of me. ¹⁸But as soon as I screamed for help, he left his cloak beside me and ran out of the house."

¹⁹When his master heard the story his wife told him, saying, "This is how your slave treated me," he burned with anger. ²⁰Joseph's master took him and put him in prison, the place where the king's prisoners were confined.

But while Joseph was there in the prison, ²¹the LORD was with him; he showed him kindness and granted him favor in the eyes of the prison warden. ²²So the warden put Joseph in charge of all those held in the prison, and he was made responsible for all that was done there. ²³The warden paid no attention to anything under Joseph's care, because the

---

ᵃ29 *Perez* means *breaking out.* ᵇ30 *Zerah* can mean *scarlet* or *brightness.*

LORD was with Joseph and gave him success in whatever he did.

The Cupbearer and the Baker

40 Some time later, the cupbearer and the baker of the king of Egypt offended their master, the king of Egypt. ²Pharaoh was angry with his two officials, the chief cupbearer and the chief baker, ³and put them in custody in the house of the captain of the guard, in the same prison where Joseph was confined. ⁴The captain of the guard assigned them to Joseph, and he attended them.

After they had been in custody for some time, ⁵each of the two men—the cupbearer and the baker of the king of Egypt, who were being held in prison—had a dream the same night, and each dream had a meaning of its own.

⁶When Joseph came to them the next morning, he saw that they were dejected. ⁷So he asked Pharaoh's officials who were in custody with him in his master's house, "Why are your faces so sad today?"

⁸"We both had dreams," they answered, "but there is no one to interpret them."

Then Joseph said to them, "Do not interpretations belong to God? Tell me your dreams."

⁹So the chief cupbearer told Joseph his dream. He said to him, "In my dream I saw a vine in front of me, ¹⁰and on the vine were three branches. As soon as it budded, it blossomed, and its clusters ripened into grapes. ¹¹Pharaoh's cup was in my hand, and I took the grapes, squeezed them into Pharaoh's cup and put the cup in his hand."

¹²"This is what it means," Joseph said to him. "The three branches are three days. ¹³Within three days Pharaoh will lift up your head and restore you to your position, and you will put Pharaoh's cup in his hand, just as you used to do when you were his cupbearer. ¹⁴But when all goes well with you, remember me and show me kindness; mention me to Pharaoh and get me out of this prison. ¹⁵For I was forcibly carried off from the land of the Hebrews, and even here I have done nothing to deserve being put in a dungeon."

¹⁶When the chief baker saw that Joseph had given a favorable interpretation, he said to Joseph, "I too had a dream: On my head were three baskets of bread.ᵃ ¹⁷In the top basket were all kinds of baked goods for Pharaoh, but the birds were eating them out of the basket on my head."

¹⁸"This is what it means," Joseph said. "The three baskets are three days. ¹⁹Within three days Pharaoh will lift off your head and hang you on a tree.ᵇ And the birds will eat away your flesh."

²⁰Now the third day was Pharaoh's birthday, and he gave a feast for all his officials. He lifted up the heads of the chief cupbearer and the chief baker in the presence of his officials: ²¹He restored the chief cupbearer to his position, so that he once again put the cup into Pharaoh's hand, ²²but he hangedᶜ the chief baker, just as Joseph had said to them in his interpretation.

²³The chief cupbearer, however, did not remember Joseph; he forgot him.

Pharaoh's Dreams

41 When two full years had passed, Pharaoh had a dream: He was standing by the Nile, ²when out of the river there came up seven cows, sleek and fat, and they grazed among the reeds. ³After them, seven other cows, ugly and gaunt, came up out of the Nile and stood beside those on the riverbank. ⁴And the cows that were ugly and gaunt ate up the seven sleek, fat cows. Then Pharaoh woke up.

> ❝ In a world of prayer, we are all equal in the sense that each of us is a unique person, with a unique perspective on the world, a member of a class of one. ❞
>
> W.H. AUDEN

⁵He fell asleep again and had a second dream: Seven heads of grain, healthy and good, were growing on a single stalk. ⁶After them, seven other heads of grain sprouted—thin and scorched by the east wind. ⁷The thin heads of grain swallowed up the seven healthy, full heads. Then Pharaoh woke up; it had been a dream.

ᵃ16 Or three wicker baskets   ᵇ19 Or and impale you on a pole   ᶜ22 Or impaled

⁸In the morning his mind was troubled, so he sent for all the magicians and wise men of Egypt. Pharaoh told them his dreams, but no one could interpret them for him.

⁹Then the chief cupbearer said to Pharaoh, "Today I am reminded of my shortcomings. ¹⁰Pharaoh was once angry with his servants, and he imprisoned me and the chief baker in the house of the captain of the guard. ¹¹Each of us had a dream the same night, and each dream had a meaning of its own. ¹²Now a young Hebrew was there with us, a servant of the captain of the guard. We told him our dreams, and he interpreted them for us, giving each man the interpretation of his dream. ¹³And things turned out exactly as he interpreted them to us: I was restored to my position, and the other man was hanged.ᵃ"

¹⁴So Pharaoh sent for Joseph, and he was quickly brought from the dungeon. When he had shaved and changed his clothes, he came before Pharaoh.

¹⁵Pharaoh said to Joseph, "I had a dream, and no one can interpret it. But I have heard it said of you that when you hear a dream you can interpret it."

¹⁶"I cannot do it," Joseph replied to Pharaoh, "but God will give Pharaoh the answer he desires."

¹⁷Then Pharaoh said to Joseph, "In my dream I was standing on the bank of the Nile, ¹⁸when out of the river there came up seven cows, fat and sleek, and they grazed among the reeds. ¹⁹After them, seven other cows came up—scrawny and very ugly and lean. I had never seen such ugly cows in all the land of Egypt. ²⁰The lean, ugly cows ate up the seven fat cows that came up first. ²¹But even after they ate them, no one could tell that they had done so; they looked just as ugly as before. Then I woke up.

²²"In my dreams I also saw seven heads of grain, full and good, growing on a single stalk. ²³After them, seven other heads sprouted—withered and thin and scorched by the east wind. ²⁴The thin heads of grain swallowed up the seven good heads. I told this to the magicians, but none could explain it to me."

²⁵Then Joseph said to Pharaoh, "The dreams of Pharaoh are one and the same. God has revealed to Pharaoh what he is about to do. ²⁶The seven good cows are seven years, and the seven good heads of grain are seven years; it is one and the same dream. ²⁷The seven lean, ugly cows that came up afterward are seven years, and so are the seven worthless heads of grain scorched by the east wind: They are seven years of famine.

²⁸"It is just as I said to Pharaoh: God has shown Pharaoh what he is about to do. ²⁹Seven years of great abundance are coming throughout the land of Egypt, ³⁰but seven years of famine will follow them. Then all the abundance in Egypt will be forgotten, and the famine will ravage the land. ³¹The abundance in the land will not be remembered, because the famine that follows it will be so severe. ³²The reason the dream was given to Pharaoh in two forms is that the matter has been firmly decided by God, and God will do it soon.

³³"And now let Pharaoh look for a discerning and wise man and put him in charge of the land of Egypt. ³⁴Let Pharaoh appoint commissioners over the land to take a fifth of the harvest of Egypt during the seven years of abundance. ³⁵They should collect all the food of these good years that are coming and store up the grain under the authority of Pharaoh, to be kept in the cities for food. ³⁶This food should be held in reserve for the country, to be used during the seven years of famine that will come upon Egypt, so that the country may not be ruined by the famine."

³⁷The plan seemed good to Pharaoh and to all his officials. ³⁸So Pharaoh asked them, "Can we find anyone like this man, one in whom is the spirit of Godᵇ?"

³⁹Then Pharaoh said to Joseph, "Since God has made all this known to you, there is no one so discerning and wise as you. ⁴⁰You shall be in charge of my palace, and all my people are to submit to your orders. Only with respect to the throne will I be greater than you."

ᵃ13 Or *impaled*   ᵇ38 Or *of the gods*

Joseph in Charge of Egypt

[41]So Pharaoh said to Joseph, "I hereby put you in charge of the whole land of Egypt." [42]Then Pharaoh took his signet ring from his finger and put it on Joseph's finger. He dressed him in robes of fine linen and put a gold chain around his neck. [43]He had him ride in a chariot as his second-in-command,[a] and men shouted before him, "Make way[b]!" Thus he put him in charge of the whole land of Egypt.

[44]Then Pharaoh said to Joseph, "I am Pharaoh, but without your word no one will lift hand or foot in all Egypt." [45]Pharaoh gave Joseph the name Zaphenath-Paneah and gave him Asenath daughter of Potiphera, priest of On,[c] to be his wife. And Joseph went throughout the land of Egypt.

[46]Joseph was thirty years old when he entered the service of Pharaoh king of Egypt. And Joseph went out from Pharaoh's presence and traveled throughout Egypt. [47]During the seven years of abundance the land produced plentifully. [48]Joseph collected all the food produced in those seven years of abundance in Egypt and stored it in the cities. In each city he put the food grown in the fields surrounding it. [49]Joseph stored up huge quantities of grain, like the sand of the sea; it was so much that he stopped keeping records because it was beyond measure.

[50]Before the years of famine came, two sons were born to Joseph by Asenath daughter of Potiphera, priest of On. [51]Joseph named his firstborn Manasseh[d] and said, "It is because God has made me forget all my trouble and all my father's household." [52]The second son he named Ephraim[e] and said, "It is because God has made me fruitful in the land of my suffering."

[53]The seven years of abundance in Egypt came to an end, [54]and the seven years of famine began, just as Joseph had said. There was famine in all the other lands, but in the whole land of Egypt there was food. [55]When all Egypt began to feel the famine, the people cried to Pharaoh for food. Then Pharaoh told all the Egyptians, "Go to Joseph and do what he tells you."

[56]When the famine had spread over the whole country, Joseph opened the storehouses and sold grain to the Egyptians, for the famine was severe throughout Egypt. [57]And all the countries came to Egypt to buy grain from Joseph, because the famine was severe in all the world.

Joseph's Brothers Go to Egypt

42 When Jacob learned that there was grain in Egypt, he said to his sons, "Why do you just keep looking at each other?" [2]He continued, "I have heard that there is grain in Egypt. Go down there and buy some for us, so that we may live and not die."

[3]Then ten of Joseph's brothers went down to buy grain from Egypt. [4]But Jacob did not send Benjamin, Joseph's brother, with the others, because he was afraid that harm might come to him. [5]So Israel's sons were among those who went to buy grain, for the famine was in the land of Canaan also.

[6]Now Joseph was the governor of the land, the one who sold grain to all its people. So when Joseph's brothers arrived, they bowed down to him with their faces to the ground. [7]As soon as Joseph saw his brothers, he recognized them, but he pretended to be a stranger and spoke harshly to them. "Where do you come from?" he asked.

"From the land of Canaan," they replied, "to buy food."

[8]Although Joseph recognized his brothers, they did not recognize him. [9]Then he remembered his dreams about them and said to them, "You are spies! You have come to see where our land is unprotected."

[10]"No, my lord," they answered. "Your servants have come to buy food. [11]We are all the sons of one man. Your servants are honest men, not spies."

[12]"No!" he said to them. "You have come to see where our land is unprotected."

[13]But they replied, "Your servants were twelve brothers, the sons of one man,

---

[a]43 Or *in the chariot of his second-in-command;* or *in his second chariot*   [b]43 Or *Bow down*   [c]45 That is, Heliopolis; also in verse 50   [d]51 *Manasseh* sounds like and may be derived from the Hebrew for *forget.*   [e]52 *Ephraim* sounds like the Hebrew for *twice fruitful.*

who lives in the land of Canaan. The youngest is now with our father, and one is no more."

¹⁴Joseph said to them, "It is just as I told you: You are spies! ¹⁵And this is how you will be tested: As surely as Pharaoh lives, you will not leave this place unless your youngest brother comes here. ¹⁶Send one of your number to get your brother; the rest of you will be kept in prison, so that your words may be tested to see if you are telling the truth. If you are not, then as surely as Pharaoh lives, you are spies!" ¹⁷And he put them all in custody for three days.

¹⁸On the third day, Joseph said to them, "Do this and you will live, for I fear God: ¹⁹If you are honest men, let one of your brothers stay here in prison, while the rest of you go and take grain back for your starving households. ²⁰But you must bring your youngest brother to me, so that your words may be verified and that you may not die." This they proceeded to do.

²¹They said to one another, "Surely we are being punished because of our brother. We saw how distressed he was when he pleaded with us for his life, but we would not listen; that's why this distress has come upon us."

²²Reuben replied, "Didn't I tell you not to sin against the boy? But you wouldn't listen! Now we must give an accounting for his blood." ²³They did not realize that Joseph could understand them, since he was using an interpreter.

²⁴He turned away from them and began to weep, but then turned back and spoke to them again. He had Simeon taken from them and bound before their eyes.

²⁵Joseph gave orders to fill their bags with grain, to put each man's silver back in his sack, and to give them provisions for their journey. After this was done for them, ²⁶they loaded their grain on their donkeys and left.

²⁷At the place where they stopped for the night one of them opened his sack to get feed for his donkey, and he saw his silver in the mouth of his sack. ²⁸"My silver has been returned," he said to his brothers. "Here it is in my sack."

Their hearts sank and they turned to each other trembling and said, "What is this that God has done to us?"

²⁹When they came to their father Jacob in the land of Canaan, they told him all that had happened to them. They said, ³⁰"The man who is lord over the land spoke harshly to us and treated us as though we were spying on the land. ³¹But we said to him, 'We are honest men; we are not spies. ³²We were twelve brothers, sons of one father. One is no more, and the youngest is now with our father in Canaan.'

³³"Then the man who is lord over the land said to us, 'This is how I will know whether you are honest men: Leave one of your brothers here with me, and take food for your starving households and go. ³⁴But bring your youngest brother to me so I will know that you are not spies but honest men. Then I will give your brother back to you, and you can trade^a in the land.'"

³⁵As they were emptying their sacks, there in each man's sack was his pouch of silver! When they and their father saw the money pouches, they were frightened. ³⁶Their father Jacob said to them, "You have deprived me of my children. Joseph is no more and Simeon is no more, and now you want to take Benjamin. Everything is against me!"

³⁷Then Reuben said to his father, "You may put both of my sons to death if I do not bring him back to you. Entrust him to my care, and I will bring him back."

³⁸But Jacob said, "My son will not go down there with you; his brother is dead and he is the only one left. If harm comes to him on the journey you are taking, you will bring my gray head down to the grave^b in sorrow."

The Second Journey to Egypt

43 Now the famine was still severe in the land. ²So when they had eaten all the grain they had brought from Egypt, their father said to them, "Go back and buy us a little more food."

³But Judah said to him, "The man warned us solemnly, 'You will not see my face again unless your brother is with you.' ⁴If you will send our brother along with us, we will go down and buy food

---

^{a}34 Or *move about freely* ^{b}38 Hebrew *Sheol*

for you. ⁵But if you will not send him, we will not go down, because the man said to us, 'You will not see my face again unless your brother is with you.'"

⁶Israel asked, "Why did you bring this trouble on me by telling the man you had another brother?"

⁷They replied, "The man questioned us closely about ourselves and our family. 'Is your father still living?' he asked us. 'Do you have another brother?' We simply answered his questions. How were we to know he would say, 'Bring your brother down here'?"

⁸Then Judah said to Israel his father, "Send the boy along with me and we will go at once, so that we and you and our children may live and not die. ⁹I myself will guarantee his safety; you can hold me personally responsible for him. If I do not bring him back to you and set him here before you, I will bear the blame before you all my life. ¹⁰As it is, if we had not delayed, we could have gone and returned twice."

¹¹Then their father Israel said to them, "If it must be, then do this: Put some of the best products of the land in your bags and take them down to the man as a gift—a little balm and a little honey, some spices and myrrh, some pistachio nuts and almonds. ¹²Take double the amount of silver with you, for you must return the silver that was put back into the mouths of your sacks. Perhaps it was a mistake. ¹³Take your brother also and go back to the man at once. ¹⁴And may God Almighty*a* grant you mercy before the man so that he will let your other brother and Benjamin come back with you. As for me, if I am bereaved, I am bereaved."

¹⁵So the men took the gifts and double the amount of silver, and Benjamin also. They hurried down to Egypt and presented themselves to Joseph. ¹⁶When Joseph saw Benjamin with them, he said to the steward of his house, "Take these men to my house, slaughter an animal and prepare dinner; they are to eat with me at noon."

¹⁷The man did as Joseph told him and took the men to Joseph's house. ¹⁸Now the men were frightened when they were taken to his house. They thought, "We were brought here because of the silver that was put back into our sacks the first time. He wants to attack us and overpower us and seize us as slaves and take our donkeys."

¹⁹So they went up to Joseph's steward and spoke to him at the entrance to the house. ²⁰"Please, sir," they said, "we came down here the first time to buy food. ²¹But at the place where we stopped for the night we opened our sacks and each of us found his silver—the exact weight—in the mouth of his sack. So we have brought it back with us. ²²We have also brought additional silver with us to buy food. We don't know who put our silver in our sacks."

²³"It's all right," he said. "Don't be afraid. Your God, the God of your father, has given you treasure in your sacks; I received your silver." Then he brought Simeon out to them.

²⁴The steward took the men into Joseph's house, gave them water to wash their feet and provided fodder for their donkeys. ²⁵They prepared their gifts for Joseph's arrival at noon, because they had heard that they were to eat there.

²⁶When Joseph came home, they presented to him the gifts they had brought into the house, and they bowed down before him to the ground. ²⁷He asked them how they were, and then he said, "How is your aged father you told me about? Is he still living?"

²⁸They replied, "Your servant our father is still alive and well." And they bowed low to pay him honor.

²⁹As he looked about and saw his brother Benjamin, his own mother's son, he asked, "Is this your youngest brother, the one you told me about?" And he said, "God be gracious to you, my son." ³⁰Deeply moved at the sight of his brother, Joseph hurried out and looked for a place to weep. He went into his private room and wept there.

³¹After he had washed his face, he came out and, controlling himself, said, "Serve the food."

³²They served him by himself, the brothers by themselves, and the Egyptians who ate with him by themselves,

*a*14 Hebrew *El-Shaddai*

because Egyptians could not eat with Hebrews, for that is detestable to Egyptians. ³³The men had been seated before him in the order of their ages, from the firstborn to the youngest; and they looked at each other in astonishment. ³⁴When portions were served to them from Joseph's table, Benjamin's portion was five times as much as anyone else's. So they feasted and drank freely with him.

A Silver Cup in a Sack

44 Now Joseph gave these instructions to the steward of his house: "Fill the men's sacks with as much food as they can carry, and put each man's silver in the mouth of his sack. ²Then put my cup, the silver one, in the mouth of the youngest one's sack, along with the silver for his grain." And he did as Joseph said.

³As morning dawned, the men were sent on their way with their donkeys. ⁴They had not gone far from the city when Joseph said to his steward, "Go after those men at once, and when you catch up with them, say to them, 'Why have you repaid good with evil? ⁵Isn't this the cup my master drinks from and also uses for divination? This is a wicked thing you have done.'"

⁶When he caught up with them, he repeated these words to them. ⁷But they said to him, "Why does my lord say such things? Far be it from your servants to do anything like that! ⁸We even brought back to you from the land of Canaan the silver we found inside the mouths of our sacks. So why would we steal silver or gold from your master's house? ⁹If any of your servants is found to have it, he will die; and the rest of us will become my lord's slaves."

¹⁰"Very well, then," he said, "let it be as you say. Whoever is found to have it will become my slave; the rest of you will be free from blame."

¹¹Each of them quickly lowered his sack to the ground and opened it. ¹²Then the steward proceeded to search, beginning with the oldest and ending with the youngest. And the cup was found in Benjamin's sack. ¹³At this, they tore their clothes. Then they all loaded their donkeys and returned to the city.

¹⁴Joseph was still in the house when Judah and his brothers came in, and they threw themselves to the ground before him. ¹⁵Joseph said to them, "What is this you have done? Don't you know that a man like me can find things out by divination?"

¹⁶"What can we say to my lord?" Judah replied. "What can we say? How can we prove our innocence? God has uncovered your servants' guilt. We are now my lord's slaves—we ourselves and the one who was found to have the cup."

¹⁷But Joseph said, "Far be it from me to do such a thing! Only the man who was found to have the cup will become my slave. The rest of you, go back to your father in peace."

¹⁸Then Judah went up to him and said: "Please, my lord, let your servant speak a word to my lord. Do not be angry with your servant, though you are equal to Pharaoh himself. ¹⁹My lord asked his servants, 'Do you have a father or a brother?' ²⁰And we answered, 'We have an aged father, and there is a young son born to him in his old age. His brother is dead, and he is the only one of his mother's sons left, and his father loves him.'

²¹"Then you said to your servants, 'Bring him down to me so I can see him for myself.' ²²And we said to my lord, 'The boy cannot leave his father; if he leaves him, his father will die.' ²³But you told your servants, 'Unless your youngest brother comes down with you, you will not see my face again.' ²⁴When we went back to your servant my father, we told him what my lord had said.

²⁵"Then our father said, 'Go back and buy a little more food.' ²⁶But we said, 'We cannot go down. Only if our youngest brother is with us will we go. We cannot see the man's face unless our youngest brother is with us.'

²⁷"Your servant my father said to us, 'You know that my wife bore me two sons. ²⁸One of them went away from me, and I said, "He has surely been torn to pieces." And I have not seen him since. ²⁹If you take this one from me too and harm comes to him, you will bring my gray head down to the grave^a in misery.'

---

^{a}29 Hebrew *Sheol*; also in verse 31

30 "So now, if the boy is not with us when I go back to your servant my father and if my father, whose life is closely bound up with the boy's life, 31 sees that the boy isn't there, he will die. Your servants will bring the gray head of our father down to the grave in sorrow. 32 Your servant guaranteed the boy's safety to my father. I said, 'If I do not bring him back to you, I will bear the blame before you, my father, all my life!'

33 "Now then, please let your servant remain here as my lord's slave in place of the boy, and let the boy return with his brothers. 34 How can I go back to my father if the boy is not with me? No! Do not let me see the misery that would come upon my father."

Joseph Makes Himself Known

45 Then Joseph could no longer control himself before all his attendants, and he cried out, "Have everyone leave my presence!" So there was no one with Joseph when he made himself known to his brothers. 2 And he wept so loudly that the Egyptians heard him, and Pharaoh's household heard about it.

3 Joseph said to his brothers, "I am Joseph! Is my father still living?" But his brothers were not able to answer him, because they were terrified at his presence.

4 Then Joseph said to his brothers, "Come close to me." When they had done so, he said, "I am your brother Joseph, the one you sold into Egypt! 5 And now, do not be distressed and do not be angry with yourselves for selling me here, because it was to save lives that God sent me ahead of you. 6 For two years now there has been famine in the land, and for the next five years there will not be plowing and reaping. 7 But God sent me ahead of you to preserve for you a remnant on earth and to save your lives by a great deliverance.[a]

8 "So then, it was not you who sent me here, but God. He made me father to Pharaoh, lord of his entire household and ruler of all Egypt. 9 Now hurry back to my father and say to him, 'This is what your son Joseph says: God has made me lord of all Egypt. Come down to me; don't delay. 10 You shall live in the region of Goshen and be near me—you, your chil-

dren and grandchildren, your flocks and herds, and all you have. 11 I will provide for you there, because five years of famine are still to come. Otherwise you and your household and all who belong to you will become destitute.'

12 "You can see for yourselves, and so can my brother Benjamin, that it is really I who am speaking to you. 13 Tell my father about all the honor accorded me in Egypt and about everything you have seen. And bring my father down here quickly."

14 Then he threw his arms around his brother Benjamin and wept, and Benjamin embraced him, weeping. 15 And he kissed all his brothers and wept over them. Afterward his brothers talked with him.

16 When the news reached Pharaoh's palace that Joseph's brothers had come, Pharaoh and all his officials were pleased. 17 Pharaoh said to Joseph, "Tell your brothers, 'Do this: Load your animals and return to the land of Canaan, 18 and bring your father and your families back to me. I will give you the best of the land of Egypt and you can enjoy the fat of the land.'

19 "You are also directed to tell them, 'Do this: Take some carts from Egypt for your children and your wives, and get your father and come. 20 Never mind about your belongings, because the best of all Egypt will be yours.'"

21 So the sons of Israel did this. Joseph gave them carts, as Pharaoh had commanded, and he also gave them provisions for their journey. 22 To each of them he gave new clothing, but to Benjamin he gave three hundred shekels[b] of silver and five sets of clothes. 23 And this is what he sent to his father: ten donkeys loaded with the best things of Egypt, and ten female donkeys loaded with grain and bread and other provisions for his journey. 24 Then he sent his brothers away, and as they were leaving he said to them, "Don't quarrel on the way!"

25 So they went up out of Egypt and came to their father Jacob in the land of Canaan. 26 They told him, "Joseph is still

---

*a7 Or save you as a great band of survivors
b22 That is, about 7 1/2 pounds (about 3.5 kilograms)

alive! In fact, he is ruler of all Egypt." Jacob was stunned; he did not believe them. ²⁷But when they told him everything Joseph had said to them, and when he saw the carts Joseph had sent to carry him back, the spirit of their father Jacob revived. ²⁸And Israel said, "I'm convinced! My son Joseph is still alive. I will go and see him before I die."

Jacob Goes to Egypt

46 So Israel set out with all that was his, and when he reached Beersheba, he offered sacrifices to the God of his father Isaac.

²And God spoke to Israel in a vision at night and said, "Jacob! Jacob!"

"Here I am," he replied.

³"I am God, the God of your father," he said. "Do not be afraid to go down to Egypt, for I will make you into a great nation there. ⁴I will go down to Egypt with you, and I will surely bring you back again. And Joseph's own hand will close your eyes."

⁵Then Jacob left Beersheba, and Israel's sons took their father Jacob and their children and their wives in the carts that Pharaoh had sent to transport him. ⁶They also took with them their livestock and the possessions they had acquired in Canaan, and Jacob and all his offspring went to Egypt. ⁷He took with him to Egypt his sons and grandsons and his daughters and granddaughters—all his offspring.

⁸These are the names of the sons of Israel (Jacob and his descendants) who went to Egypt:

Reuben the firstborn of Jacob.
⁹The sons of Reuben:
Hanoch, Pallu, Hezron and Carmi.
¹⁰The sons of Simeon:
Jemuel, Jamin, Ohad, Jakin, Zohar and Shaul the son of a Canaanite woman.
¹¹The sons of Levi:
Gershon, Kohath and Merari.
¹²The sons of Judah:
Er, Onan, Shelah, Perez and Zerah (but Er and Onan had died in the land of Canaan).
The sons of Perez:
Hezron and Hamul.

¹³The sons of Issachar:
Tola, Puah,ᵃ Jashubᵇ and Shimron.
¹⁴The sons of Zebulun:
Sered, Elon and Jahleel.
¹⁵These were the sons Leah bore to Jacob in Paddan Aram,ᶜ besides his daughter Dinah. These sons and daughters of his were thirty-three in all.

¹⁶The sons of Gad:
Zephon,ᵈ Haggi, Shuni, Ezbon, Eri, Arodi and Areli.
¹⁷The sons of Asher:
Imnah, Ishvah, Ishvi and Beriah.
Their sister was Serah.
The sons of Beriah:
Heber and Malkiel.
¹⁸These were the children born to Jacob by Zilpah, whom Laban had given to his daughter Leah—sixteen in all.

¹⁹The sons of Jacob's wife Rachel:
Joseph and Benjamin. ²⁰In Egypt, Manasseh and Ephraim were born to Joseph by Asenath daughter of Potiphera, priest of On.ᵉ
²¹The sons of Benjamin:
Bela, Beker, Ashbel, Gera, Naaman, Ehi, Rosh, Muppim, Huppim and Ard.
²²These were the sons of Rachel who were born to Jacob—fourteen in all.

²³The son of Dan:
Hushim.
²⁴The sons of Naphtali:
Jahziel, Guni, Jezer and Shillem.
²⁵These were the sons born to Jacob by Bilhah, whom Laban had given to his daughter Rachel—seven in all.

²⁶All those who went to Egypt with Jacob—those who were his direct descendants, not counting his sons' wives—numbered sixty-six persons. ²⁷With the two sonsᶠ who had been born to Joseph in Egypt, the members of

---

ᵃ13 Samaritan Pentateuch and Syriac
(see also 1 Chron. 7:1); Masoretic Text *Puvah*
ᵇ13 Samaritan Pentateuch and some
Septuagint manuscripts (see also Num. 26:24
and 1 Chron. 7:1); Masoretic Text *Iob*
ᶜ15 That is, Northwest Mesopotamia
ᵈ16 Samaritan Pentateuch and Septuagint (see
also Num. 26:15); Masoretic Text *Ziphion*
ᵉ20 That is, Heliopolis   ᶠ27 Hebrew;
Septuagint *the nine children*

Jacob's family, which went to Egypt, were seventy*a* in all.

²⁸Now Jacob sent Judah ahead of him to Joseph to get directions to Goshen. When they arrived in the region of Goshen, ²⁹Joseph had his chariot made ready and went to Goshen to meet his father Israel. As soon as Joseph appeared before him, he threw his arms around his father*b* and wept for a long time.

³⁰Israel said to Joseph, "Now I am ready to die, since I have seen for myself that you are still alive."

³¹Then Joseph said to his brothers and to his father's household, "I will go up and speak to Pharaoh and will say to him, 'My brothers and my father's household, who were living in the land of Canaan, have come to me. ³²The men are shepherds; they tend livestock, and they have brought along their flocks and herds and everything they own.' ³³When Pharaoh calls you in and asks, 'What is your occupation?' ³⁴you should answer, 'Your servants have tended livestock from our boyhood on, just as our fathers did.' Then you will be allowed to settle in the region of Goshen, for all shepherds are detestable to the Egyptians."

47 Joseph went and told Pharaoh, "My father and brothers, with their flocks and herds and everything they own, have come from the land of Canaan and are now in Goshen." ²He chose five of his brothers and presented them before Pharaoh.

³Pharaoh asked the brothers, "What is your occupation?"

"Your servants are shepherds," they replied to Pharaoh, "just as our fathers were." ⁴They also said to him, "We have come to live here awhile, because the famine is severe in Canaan and your servants' flocks have no pasture. So now, please let your servants settle in Goshen."

⁵Pharaoh said to Joseph, "Your father and your brothers have come to you, ⁶and the land of Egypt is before you; settle your father and your brothers in the best part of the land. Let them live in Goshen. And if you know of any among them with special ability, put them in charge of my own livestock."

⁷Then Joseph brought his father Jacob in and presented him before Pharaoh. After Jacob blessed*c* Pharaoh, ⁸Pharaoh asked him, "How old are you?"

⁹And Jacob said to Pharaoh, "The years of my pilgrimage are a hundred and thirty. My years have been few and difficult, and they do not equal the years of the pilgrimage of my fathers." ¹⁰Then Jacob blessed*d* Pharaoh and went out from his presence.

¹¹So Joseph settled his father and his brothers in Egypt and gave them property in the best part of the land, the district of Rameses, as Pharaoh directed. ¹²Joseph also provided his father and his brothers and all his father's household with food, according to the number of their children.

Joseph and the Famine

¹³There was no food, however, in the whole region because the famine was severe; both Egypt and Canaan wasted away because of the famine. ¹⁴Joseph collected all the money that was to be found in Egypt and Canaan in payment for the grain they were buying, and he brought it to Pharaoh's palace. ¹⁵When the money of the people of Egypt and Canaan was gone, all Egypt came to Joseph and said, "Give us food. Why should we die before your eyes? Our money is used up."

¹⁶"Then bring your livestock," said Joseph. "I will sell you food in exchange for your livestock, since your money is gone." ¹⁷So they brought their livestock to Joseph, and he gave them food in exchange for their horses, their sheep and goats, their cattle and donkeys. And he brought them through that year with food in exchange for all their livestock.

¹⁸When that year was over, they came to him the following year and said, "We cannot hide from our lord the fact that since our money is gone and our livestock belongs to you, there is nothing left for our lord except our bodies and our land. ¹⁹Why should we perish before your eyes—we and our land as well? Buy us

---

*a*27 Hebrew (see also Exodus 1:5 and footnote); Septuagint (see also Acts 7:14) *seventy-five*
*b*29 Hebrew *around him*   *c*7 Or *greeted*
*d*10 Or *said farewell to*

and our land in exchange for food, and we with our land will be in bondage to Pharaoh. Give us seed so that we may live and not die, and that the land may not become desolate."

20So Joseph bought all the land in Egypt for Pharaoh. The Egyptians, one and all, sold their fields, because the famine was too severe for them. The land became Pharaoh's, 21and Joseph reduced the people to servitude,a from one end of Egypt to the other. 22However, he did not buy the land of the priests, because they received a regular allotment from Pharaoh and had food enough from the allotment Pharaoh gave them. That is why they did not sell their land.

23Joseph said to the people, "Now that I have bought you and your land today for Pharaoh, here is seed for you so you can plant the ground. 24But when the crop comes in, give a fifth of it to Pharaoh. The other four-fifths you may keep as seed for the fields and as food for yourselves and your households and your children."

25"You have saved our lives," they said. "May we find favor in the eyes of our lord; we will be in bondage to Pharaoh."

26So Joseph established it as a law concerning land in Egypt—still in force today—that a fifth of the produce belongs to Pharaoh. It was only the land of the priests that did not become Pharaoh's.

27Now the Israelites settled in Egypt in the region of Goshen. They acquired property there and were fruitful and increased greatly in number.

28Jacob lived in Egypt seventeen years, and the years of his life were a hundred and forty-seven. 29When the time drew near for Israel to die, he called for his son Joseph and said to him, "If I have found favor in your eyes, put your hand under my thigh and promise that you will show me kindness and faithfulness. Do not bury me in Egypt, 30but when I rest with my fathers, carry me out of Egypt and bury me where they are buried."

"I will do as you say," he said.

31"Swear to me," he said. Then Joseph swore to him, and Israel worshiped as he leaned on the top of his staff.b

Manasseh and Ephraim

48 Some time later Joseph was told, "Your father is ill." So he took his two sons Manasseh and Ephraim along with him. 2When Jacob was told, "Your son Joseph has come to you," Israel rallied his strength and sat up on the bed.

3Jacob said to Joseph, "God Almightyc appeared to me at Luz in the land of Canaan, and there he blessed me 4and said to me, 'I am going to make you fruitful and will increase your numbers. I will make you a community of peoples, and I will give this land as an everlasting possession to your descendants after you.'

5"Now then, your two sons born to you in Egypt before I came to you here will be reckoned as mine; Ephraim and Manasseh will be mine, just as Reuben and Simeon are mine. 6Any children born to you after them will be yours; in the territory they inherit they will be reckoned under the names of their brothers. 7As I was returning from Paddan,d to my sorrow Rachel died in the land of Canaan while we were still on the way, a little distance from Ephrath. So I buried her there beside the road to Ephrath" (that is, Bethlehem).

8When Israel saw the sons of Joseph, he asked, "Who are these?"

9"They are the sons God has given me here," Joseph said to his father.

Then Israel said, "Bring them to me so I may bless them."

10Now Israel's eyes were failing because of old age, and he could hardly see. So Joseph brought his sons close to him, and his father kissed them and embraced them.

11Israel said to Joseph, "I never expected to see your face again, and now God has allowed me to see your children too."

12Then Joseph removed them from Israel's knees and bowed down with his face to the ground. 13And Joseph took both of them, Ephraim on his right toward Israel's left hand and Manasseh on his left

a21 Samaritan Pentateuch and Septuagint (see also Vulgate); Masoretic Text and he moved the people into the cities   b31 Or Israel bowed down at the head of his bed   c3 Hebrew El-Shaddai   d7 That is, Northwest Mesopotamia

toward Israel's right hand, and brought them close to him. [14]But Israel reached out his right hand and put it on Ephraim's head, though he was the younger, and crossing his arms, he put his left hand on Manasseh's head, even though Manasseh was the firstborn.

[15]Then he blessed Joseph and said,

"May the God before whom my
   fathers
   Abraham and Isaac walked,
the God who has been my shepherd
   all my life to this day,
[16] the Angel who has delivered me
      from all harm
   —may he bless these boys.
May they be called by my name
   and the names of my fathers
      Abraham and Isaac,
and may they increase greatly
   upon the earth."

[17]When Joseph saw his father placing his right hand on Ephraim's head he was displeased; so he took hold of his father's hand to move it from Ephraim's head to Manasseh's head. [18]Joseph said to him, "No, my father, this one is the firstborn; put your right hand on his head."

[19]But his father refused and said, "I know, my son, I know. He too will become a people, and he too will become great. Nevertheless, his younger brother will be greater than he, and his descendants will become a group of nations." [20]He blessed them that day and said,

"In your[a] name will Israel pronounce
   this blessing:
   'May God make you like Ephraim
      and Manasseh.'"

So he put Ephraim ahead of Manasseh.

[21]Then Israel said to Joseph, "I am about to die, but God will be with you[b] and take you[b] back to the land of your[b] fathers. [22]And to you, as one who is over your brothers, I give the ridge of land[c] I took from the Amorites with my sword and my bow."

Jacob Blesses His Sons

49 Then Jacob called for his sons and said: "Gather around so I can tell you what will happen to you in days to come.

[2] "Assemble and listen, sons of Jacob;
   listen to your father Israel.

[3] "Reuben, you are my firstborn,
   my might, the first sign of my
      strength,
   excelling in honor, excelling
      in power.
[4]Turbulent as the waters, you will no
      longer excel,
   for you went up onto your
      father's bed,
   onto my couch and defiled it.

[5] "Simeon and Levi are brothers—
   their swords[d] are weapons
      of violence.
[6]Let me not enter their council,
   let me not join their assembly,
   for they have killed men in
      their anger
   and hamstrung oxen as they
      pleased.
[7]Cursed be their anger, so fierce,
   and their fury, so cruel!
   I will scatter them in Jacob
   and disperse them in Israel.

[8] "Judah,[e] your brothers will
      praise you;
   your hand will be on the neck of
      your enemies;
   your father's sons will bow down
      to you.
[9]You are a lion's cub, O Judah;
   you return from the prey, my son.
Like a lion he crouches and lies
      down,
   like a lioness—who dares to
      rouse him?
[10]The scepter will not depart from
      Judah,
   nor the ruler's staff from between
      his feet,
until he comes to whom it belongs[f]
   and the obedience of the nations
      is his.
[11]He will tether his donkey to a vine,
   his colt to the choicest branch;

---

[a]20 The Hebrew is singular.   [b]21 The Hebrew is plural.   [c]22 Or And to you I give one portion more than to your brothers—the portion [d]5 The meaning of the Hebrew for this word is uncertain.   [e]8 Judah sounds like and may be derived from the Hebrew for praise.   [f]10 Or until Shiloh comes; or until he comes to whom tribute belongs

An Elder's Prayer

48:15 THEN HE BLESSED JOSEPH.

The prospect of one's death acutely focuses the mind, but on what? Astonishingly, for some it only intensifies concerns for personal peace and comfort. But for others, it directs their minds toward eternity and the next generation. Jacob is a very old man, near death, and that is his frame of mind as Joseph brings him his two sons, Ephraim and Manasseh, to be blessed by their grandfather. The faith Jacob is remembered for in the New Testament is not the faith that wrestled with God, but the faith that blessed Joseph's sons. The reason for this has much to teach about prayer.

"By faith Jacob, when he was dying, blessed each of Joseph's sons, and worshiped as he leaned on the top of his staff" (Hebrews 11:21). To say Jacob blessed while he was dying is to say that the blessing was something that he himself would not see. That is the faith that so pleases God: "being sure of what we hope for and certain of what we do not see" (Hebrews 11:1). The verse in Hebrews just before Jacob's mention says the same thing about Isaac's faith, and the verse just after about Joseph's faith. Reubem Alves said hope is hearing the music of the future, and faith is to dance to it. Jacob, though old and infirm, is dancing as he prays his blessing.

How should the elderly pray? With a great abandon to faith and a generous love that will bless the next generation. Bodies may slow down, but our prayers shouldn't. Theologian Karl Barth believed the nearness of death should not shrink our faith, but cause the river of responsibility "to flow more torrentially than ever in view of the approaching falls, of the proximity of the coming Judge!"[4]

And David was comforted that God understood his frailty and mortality: "He knows how we are formed, he remembers that we are dust." David's comfort grew as he considered that even though he will die, God's love will continue to the generations to come: "As for man, his days are like grass, he flourishes like a flower of the field; the wind blows over it and it is gone, and its place remembers it no more. But from everlasting to everlasting the LORD's love is with those who fear him, and his righteousness with their children's children" (Psalm 103:15–17). The passion of every generation should be to know the Lord. But the passion of a passing generation should especially be that the next generation will know the Lord—and so to pray that blessing.

P R A Y :

Eternal Father! Give us faith and strength to pray for
those who will come after us; and so to teach the next generation,
even the children yet to be born, and those yet to come
after them, to know you, O Lord.

FOR YOUR NEXT DEVOTIONAL READING, GO TO PAGE 64.

he will wash his garments in wine,
   his robes in the blood of grapes.
[12] His eyes will be darker than wine,
   his teeth whiter than milk.[a]

[13] "Zebulun will live by the seashore
   and become a haven for ships;
   his border will extend toward
      Sidon.

[14] "Issachar is a rawboned[b] donkey
   lying down between two
      saddlebags.[c]
[15] When he sees how good is his resting
      place
   and how pleasant is his land,
he will bend his shoulder to the
      burden
   and submit to forced labor.

[16] "Dan[d] will provide justice for his
      people
   as one of the tribes of Israel.
[17] Dan will be a serpent by the roadside,
   a viper along the path,
that bites the horse's heels
   so that its rider tumbles backward.

[18] "I look for your deliverance, O LORD.

[19] "Gad[e] will be attacked by a band
      of raiders,
   but he will attack them at their
      heels.

[20] "Asher's food will be rich;
   he will provide delicacies fit for
      a king.

[21] "Naphtali is a doe set free
   that bears beautiful fawns.[f]

[22] "Joseph is a fruitful vine,
   a fruitful vine near a spring,
   whose branches climb over
      a wall.[g]
[23] With bitterness archers attacked him;
   they shot at him with hostility.
[24] But his bow remained steady,
   his strong arms stayed[h] limber,
because of the hand of the Mighty
      One of Jacob,
   because of the Shepherd, the Rock
      of Israel,
[25] because of your father's God, who
      helps you,
   because of the Almighty,[i] who
      blesses you
with blessings of the heavens above,

blessings of the deep that lies
      below,
blessings of the breast and womb.
[26] Your father's blessings are greater
   than the blessings of the ancient
      mountains,
   than[j] the bounty of the age-old
      hills.
Let all these rest on the head of
      Joseph,
   on the brow of the prince among[k]
      his brothers.

[27] "Benjamin is a ravenous wolf;
   in the morning he devours
      the prey,
   in the evening he divides the
      plunder."

[28] All these are the twelve tribes of Israel, and this is what their father said to them when he blessed them, giving each the blessing appropriate to him.

The Death of Jacob

[29] Then he gave them these instructions: "I am about to be gathered to my people. Bury me with my fathers in the cave in the field of Ephron the Hittite, [30] the cave in the field of Machpelah, near Mamre in Canaan, which Abraham bought as a burial place from Ephron the Hittite, along with the field. [31] There Abraham and his wife Sarah were buried, there Isaac and his wife Rebekah were buried, and there I buried Leah. [32] The field and the cave in it were bought from the Hittites.[l]"

[33] When Jacob had finished giving instructions to his sons, he drew his feet up into the bed, breathed his last and was gathered to his people.

50 Joseph threw himself upon his father and wept over him and kissed him. [2] Then Joseph directed the physicians in his service to embalm his

---

[a]12 Or will be dull from wine, / his teeth white from milk   [b]14 Or strong   [c]14 Or campfires   [d]16 Dan here means he provides justice.   [e]19 Gad can mean attack and band of raiders.   [f]21 Or free; / he utters beautiful words   [g]22 Or Joseph is a wild colt, / a wild colt near a spring, / a wild donkey on a terraced hill   [h]23,24 Or archers will attack… will shoot… will remain… will stay   [i]25 Hebrew Shaddai   [j]26 Or of my progenitors, / as great as   [k]26 Or the one separated from   [l]32 Or the sons of Heth

GENESIS 50:15 – 21

God Intends It for Good

50:20 "GOD INTENDED IT FOR GOOD."

Of course Joseph's brothers expected him to try to kill them after their father Jacob died. They had it coming to them; years before they had tried callously to murder him. So they were stunned at what Joseph did when he heard of their fears. First he wept, then he said to them, "Don't be afraid. Am I in the place of God? You intended to harm me, but God intended it for good to accomplish what is now being done, the saving of many lives" (verses 19–20). The worldwide famine would have destroyed them and their families had Joseph not been "sent" to Egypt ahead of them.

Over the years Joseph had gained a perspective on life that is priceless. It is wonderfully captured in the sixteenth century Heidelberg Catechism's description of the providence of God: "Providence is the almighty and ever present power of God by which he upholds, as with his hand, heaven and earth and all creatures, and so rules them that leaf and blade, rain and drought, fruitful and lean years, food and drink, health and sickness, prosperity and poverty—all things, in fact, come to us not by chance but from his fatherly hand."

What Joseph had come to see was that the fundamental issue had not been between him and his brothers, but between him and his God. True, his brothers were scoundrels, but ultimately it was God who gave them permission to act as they did—and to use their evil against him to promote God's good for all of them! Over the years his conflict with his brothers had been transformed into his wrestling with God—with a glorious result: He was freed of his bitterness. The Catechism says this perspective will make us "patient when things go against us, thankful when things go well, and for the future we can have good confidence in our faithful God and Father that nothing will separate us from his love."[5] This is the fruit of a lifetime of wrestling with God in prayer over the bad things others have done to us. It doesn't relieve them of their responsibility, but it frees us of our slavery to anger and a victim mentality. Fight them, and the fighting will be endless. Wrestle with God, and you will be free.

PRAY:

Almighty and loving Father, I thank you that all the things
that come to me pass through your great heart of wisdom and love.
Teach me to talk less to others about the wrongs people have
done to me, and talk more to you about the wrongs you have
allowed me to suffer for your name.

FOR YOUR NEXT DEVOTIONAL READING, GO TO PAGE 68.

father Israel. So the physicians embalmed him, ³taking a full forty days, for that was the time required for embalming. And the Egyptians mourned for him seventy days.

⁴When the days of mourning had passed, Joseph said to Pharaoh's court, "If I have found favor in your eyes, speak to Pharaoh for me. Tell him, ⁵'My father made me swear an oath and said, "I am about to die; bury me in the tomb I dug for myself in the land of Canaan." Now let me go up and bury my father; then I will return.'"

⁶Pharaoh said, "Go up and bury your father, as he made you swear to do."

⁷So Joseph went up to bury his father. All Pharaoh's officials accompanied him—the dignitaries of his court and all the dignitaries of Egypt— ⁸besides all the members of Joseph's household and his brothers and those belonging to his father's household. Only their children and their flocks and herds were left in Goshen. ⁹Chariots and horsemen*ᵃ* also went up with him. It was a very large company.

¹⁰When they reached the threshing floor of Atad, near the Jordan, they lamented loudly and bitterly; and there Joseph observed a seven-day period of mourning for his father. ¹¹When the Canaanites who lived there saw the mourning at the threshing floor of Atad, they said, "The Egyptians are holding a solemn ceremony of mourning." That is why that place near the Jordan is called Abel Mizraim.*ᵇ*

¹²So Jacob's sons did as he had commanded them: ¹³They carried him to the land of Canaan and buried him in the cave in the field of Machpelah, near Mamre, which Abraham had bought as a burial place from Ephron the Hittite, along with the field. ¹⁴After burying his father, Joseph returned to Egypt, together with his brothers and all the others who had gone with him to bury his father.

Joseph Reassures His Brothers

¹⁵When Joseph's brothers saw that their father was dead, they said, "What if Joseph holds a grudge against us and pays us back for all the wrongs we did to him?" ¹⁶So they sent word to Joseph, saying, "Your father left these instructions before he died: ¹⁷'This is what you are to say to Joseph: I ask you to forgive your brothers the sins and the wrongs they committed in treating you so badly.' Now please forgive the sins of the servants of the God of your father." When their message came to him, Joseph wept.

¹⁸His brothers then came and threw themselves down before him. "We are your slaves," they said.

¹⁹But Joseph said to them, "Don't be afraid. Am I in the place of God? ²⁰You intended to harm me, but God intended it for good to accomplish what is now being done, the saving of many lives. ²¹So then, don't be afraid. I will provide for you and your children." And he reassured them and spoke kindly to them.

The Death of Joseph

²²Joseph stayed in Egypt, along with all his father's family. He lived a hundred and ten years ²³and saw the third generation of Ephraim's children. Also the children of Makir son of Manasseh were placed at birth on Joseph's knees.*ᶜ*

²⁴Then Joseph said to his brothers, "I am about to die. But God will surely come to your aid and take you up out of this land to the land he promised on oath to Abraham, Isaac and Jacob." ²⁵And Joseph made the sons of Israel swear an oath and said, "God will surely come to your aid, and then you must carry my bones up from this place."

²⁶So Joseph died at the age of a hundred and ten. And after they embalmed him, he was placed in a coffin in Egypt.

ᵃ9 Or charioteers   *ᵇ11 Abel Mizraim means mourning of the Egyptians.*   *ᶜ23 That is, were counted as his*

Exodus

THE STORY of the exodus really gets started when the oppressed people of God begin to pray. God says to Moses, "I have indeed seen the misery of my people in Egypt. I have heard them crying out because of their slave drivers, and I am concerned about their suffering. So I have come down to rescue them … So now, go. I am sending you to Pharaoh to bring my people the Israelites out of Egypt" (3:7–8,10; see also 2:23–25).

It's all here—the building blocks of a theology of prayer. God is a God who hears us, who saves us and who enlists some of us to be his instrument to answer our prayers.

From what we learn later about the Israelites, the people who prayed, their theology was pretty weak and shallow. No doubt they had very little appreciation of the God they prayed to, or even what it meant to pray; but God was so willing to hear that he started with them where they were. All of us who pray should take comfort in God's willingness to work with us in whatever state we find ourselves.

God's desire for communion with his people is what drives him to save us and set us free. Everything that follows in the book of Exodus, from the giving of the law to the building of the tabernacle, springs from the same divine passion to be present with us. The events of Exodus will one day be fulfilled when God's law is written on our hearts (see Jeremiah 31:31–34), and all the saved of the earth will "serve him day and night in his temple [tabernacle]; and he who sits on the throne will spread his tent [tabernacle] over them" (Revelation 7:15). We can learn from this book that prayer is a rehearsal for the future.

MOSES REPLIED, "WHEN I HAVE GONE OUT OF THE CITY, I WILL SPREAD OUT MY HANDS IN PRAYER TO THE LORD." (9:29)

The Israelites Oppressed

1 These are the names of the sons of Israel who went to Egypt with Jacob, each with his family: ²Reuben, Simeon, Levi and Judah; ³Issachar, Zebulun and Benjamin; ⁴Dan and Naphtali; Gad and Asher. ⁵The descendants of Jacob numbered seventy*a* in all; Joseph was already in Egypt.

⁶Now Joseph and all his brothers and all that generation died, ⁷but the Israelites were fruitful and multiplied greatly and became exceedingly numerous, so that the land was filled with them.

⁸Then a new king, who did not know about Joseph, came to power in Egypt. ⁹"Look," he said to his people, "the Israelites have become much too numerous for us. ¹⁰Come, we must deal shrewdly with them or they will become even more numerous and, if war breaks out, will join our enemies, fight against us and leave the country."

¹¹So they put slave masters over them to oppress them with forced labor, and they built Pithom and Rameses as store cities for Pharaoh. ¹²But the more they were oppressed, the more they multiplied and spread; so the Egyptians came to dread the Israelites ¹³and worked them ruthlessly. ¹⁴They made their lives bitter with hard labor in brick and mortar and with all kinds of work in the fields; in all their hard labor the Egyptians used them ruthlessly.

¹⁵The king of Egypt said to the Hebrew midwives, whose names were Shiphrah and Puah, ¹⁶"When you help the Hebrew women in childbirth and observe them on the delivery stool, if it is a boy, kill him; but if it is a girl, let her live." ¹⁷The midwives, however, feared God and did not do what the king of Egypt had told them to do; they let the boys live. ¹⁸Then the king of Egypt summoned the midwives and asked them, "Why have you done this? Why have you let the boys live?"

¹⁹The midwives answered Pharaoh, "Hebrew women are not like Egyptian women; they are vigorous and give birth before the midwives arrive."

²⁰So God was kind to the midwives and the people increased and became even more numerous. ²¹And because the mid-wives feared God, he gave them families of their own.

²²Then Pharaoh gave this order to all his people: "Every boy that is born*b* you must throw into the Nile, but let every girl live."

The Birth of Moses

2 Now a man of the house of Levi married a Levite woman, ²and she became pregnant and gave birth to a son. When she saw that he was a fine child, she hid him for three months. ³But when she could hide him no longer, she got a papyrus basket for him and coated it with tar and pitch. Then she placed the child in it and put it among the reeds along the bank of the Nile. ⁴His sister stood at a distance to see what would happen to him.

⁵Then Pharaoh's daughter went down to the Nile to bathe, and her attendants were walking along the river bank. She saw the basket among the reeds and sent her slave girl to get it. ⁶She opened it and saw the baby. He was crying, and she felt sorry for him. "This is one of the Hebrew babies," she said.

⁷Then his sister asked Pharaoh's daughter, "Shall I go and get one of the Hebrew women to nurse the baby for you?"

⁸"Yes, go," she answered. And the girl went and got the baby's mother. ⁹Pharaoh's daughter said to her, "Take this baby and nurse him for me, and I will pay you." So the woman took the baby and nursed him. ¹⁰When the child grew older, she took him to Pharaoh's daughter and he became her son. She named him Moses,*c* saying, "I drew him out of the water."

Moses Flees to Midian

¹¹One day, after Moses had grown up, he went out to where his own people were and watched them at their hard labor. He saw an Egyptian beating a Hebrew, one of his own people. ¹²Glancing this way and that and seeing no one, he killed the Egyptian and hid him in the

---

a5 Masoretic Text (see also Gen. 46:27); Dead Sea Scrolls and Septuagint (see also Acts 7:14 and note at Gen. 46:27) *seventy-five*
b22 Masoretic Text; Samaritan Pentateuch, Septuagint and Targums *born to the Hebrews*
c10 Moses sounds like the Hebrew for *draw out.*

Night of Fire

BLAISE PASCAL was one of the greatest minds in history. His work on probability, experiments with the vacuum and atmospheric pressure, and invention of the first calculating machine established him as a scientist of the highest order. The elegance of his prose moved Voltaire to proclaim him the finest writer in France. But what he will most be remembered for are his Pensées, a collection of thoughts that, had he lived long enough, were to form the basis of a defense of the Christian faith.

After Pascal's death a piece of parchment was found sewn into his clothing. It is the record of a decisive and ecstatic encounter he had with God on the night of November 23, 1654. What follows is a portion of what he wrote.

Fire

"God of Abraham, God of Isaac, God of Jacob," not of philosophers
and scholars. Certainty, certainty, heartfelt, joy, peace.

God of Jesus Christ.

God of Jesus Christ . . .

Joy, joy, joy, tears of joy . . .

"And this is life eternal, that they might know thee, the only true God,
and Jesus Christ whom thou hast sent."

Jesus Christ.

Jesus Christ . . .

Sweet and total renunciation . . .

Everlasting joy in return for one day's effort on earth.

I will not forget thy word. Amen.

The god of Pascal's times was an abstract noun, merely part of the intellectual and theoretical landscape, a principle to ponder—not the consuming Fire of the Bible, the Father of Jesus Christ (see Hebrews 12:29; John 14:9). The god of "philosophers and scholars" is something one thinks about; the God of Scripture is someone one meets. And this God is much more than interesting and impressive. To meet God face to face is to know "Certainty, certainty, heartfelt, joy, peace . . . Joy, joy, joy, tears of joy."

What Pascal saw of God is breathtakingly lovely and wonderful. But not everyone has Pascal's experience, and one can hardly read of it and not ache with envy. Nevertheless, what Pascal glimpsed that night awaits all who hope in Christ. One day, in heaven, when we see him as he is, we too will be as he is, gloriously so (see 1 John 3:2; Romans 8:18–21). In fact, to see him as he is, *is* heaven. We pray in that hope, knowing that although we don't see him now, we are still filled with "an inexpressible and glorious joy," for we are receiving the goal of our faith, the salvation of our souls (1 Peter 1:8–9).

PRAY:

Father of Joy! I hope in you, for you have made known to me the path of life; you fill me with joy in your presence, with eternal pleasures at your right hand (Psalm 16:11).

MEMORIZE:

Though you have not seen him, you love him; and even though you do not see him now, you believe in him and are filled with an inexpressible and glorious joy, for you are receiving the goal of your faith, the salvation of your souls. 1 PETER 1:8–9

FOR YOUR NEXT DEVOTIONAL READING, GO TO PAGE 71.

sand. ¹³The next day he went out and saw two Hebrews fighting. He asked the one in the wrong, "Why are you hitting your fellow Hebrew?"

¹⁴The man said, "Who made you ruler and judge over us? Are you thinking of killing me as you killed the Egyptian?" Then Moses was afraid and thought, "What I did must have become known."

¹⁵When Pharaoh heard of this, he tried to kill Moses, but Moses fled from Pharaoh and went to live in Midian, where he sat down by a well. ¹⁶Now a priest of Midian had seven daughters, and they came to draw water and fill the troughs to water their father's flock. ¹⁷Some shepherds came along and drove them away, but Moses got up and came to their rescue and watered their flock.

¹⁸When the girls returned to Reuel their father, he asked them, "Why have you returned so early today?"

¹⁹They answered, "An Egyptian rescued us from the shepherds. He even drew water for us and watered the flock."

²⁰"And where is he?" he asked his daughters. "Why did you leave him? Invite him to have something to eat."

²¹Moses agreed to stay with the man, who gave his daughter Zipporah to Moses in marriage. ²²Zipporah gave birth to a son, and Moses named him Gershom,ᵃ saying, "I have become an alien in a foreign land."

²³During that long period, the king of Egypt died. The Israelites groaned in their slavery and cried out, and their cry for help because of their slavery went up to God. ²⁴God heard their groaning and he remembered his covenant with Abraham, with Isaac and with Jacob. ²⁵So God looked on the Israelites and was concerned about them.

> AND their cry for help because of their slavery went up to God.
>
> EXODUS 2:23

Moses and the Burning Bush

3 Now Moses was tending the flock of Jethro his father-in-law, the priest of Midian, and he led the flock to the far side of the desert and came to Horeb, the mountain of God. ²There the angel of the LORD appeared to him in flames of fire from within a bush. Moses saw that though the bush was on fire it did not burn up. ³So Moses thought, "I will go over and see this strange sight—why the bush does not burn up."

⁴When the LORD saw that he had gone over to look, God called to him from within the bush, "Moses! Moses!"

And Moses said, "Here I am."

⁵"Do not come any closer," God said. "Take off your sandals, for the place where you are standing is holy ground." ⁶Then he said, "I am the God of your father, the God of Abraham, the God of Isaac and the God of Jacob." At this, Moses hid his face, because he was afraid to look at God.

⁷The LORD said, "I have indeed seen the misery of my people in Egypt. I have heard them crying out because of their slave drivers, and I am concerned about their suffering. ⁸So I have come down to rescue them from the hand of the Egyptians and to bring them up out of that land into a good and spacious land, a land flowing with milk and honey—the home of the Canaanites, Hittites, Amorites, Perizzites, Hivites and Jebusites. ⁹And now the cry of the Israelites has reached me, and I have seen the way the Egyptians are oppressing them. ¹⁰So now, go. I am sending you to Pharaoh to bring my people the Israelites out of Egypt."

¹¹But Moses said to God, "Who am I, that I should go to Pharaoh and bring the Israelites out of Egypt?"

¹²And God said, "I will be with you. And this will be the sign to you that it is I who have sent you: When you have brought the people out of Egypt, youᵇ will worship God on this mountain."

¹³Moses said to God, "Suppose I go to the Israelites and say to them, 'The God of your fathers has sent me to you,' and they ask me, 'What is his name?' Then what shall I tell them?"

¹⁴God said to Moses, "I AM WHO I AM.ᶜ This is what you are to say to the Israelites: 'I AM has sent me to you.'"

ᵃ22 Gershom sounds like the Hebrew for an alien there. ᵇ12 The Hebrew is plural. ᶜ14 Or I WILL BE WHAT I WILL BE

Prayer As Big As God

3:11 "WHO AM I, THAT I SHOULD GO TO PHARAOH AND BRING THE ISRAELITES OUT OF EGYPT?"

The question "Who am I?" has become one of the most tiresome questions of our age. And by the time Moses finishes asking it of God four or five different ways, in a conversation spanning nearly two chapters, God is fed up with it, too. It starts with surprise and a little humility (3:11); moves on to doubt (3:13); stalls in the "what ifs" (4:1); mumbles in self-deprecation (4:10); and finally stands up and refuses God's command (4:13). The driving force throughout is self-preoccupation.

Prayer is a dialogue with God. Often the dialogue breaks down, not because God won't speak, but because we don't want to hear what he says. Two things keep our ears plugged. One is our tendency to focus on what we believe about ourselves rather than on what we believe about God. After God promises to give Moses miraculous help, Moses still is more concerned about what he can't do than with what God can do. But God's commands and promises are about him, not us—in the same way that our salvation is about his grace, not our works. We're like children holding a parent's hand as we cross a busy street. The question is never how well we hold on, but how well the parent is holding us.

The other thing that keeps us from hearing God's voice is that most of the time we would rather be tending sheep in Midian than freeing the slaves in Egypt. We're often like Moses: We may not like life in Midian all much, but we prefer the comfort of the boring but predictable to the insecurity of the fulfilling but unpredictable.

A host at a dinner party attended by G. K. Chesterton asked the guests what single book they would not want to be without if stranded on a desert island. Books like the Bible and *The Complete Works of Shakespeare* were put forth. When Chesterton's turn came, he said he would want a copy of *Thomas's Guide to Practical Shipbuilding*!

It's dangerous to pray and really listen to God. Well, not really. Actually, the safest place in the world is in the center of God's will. But it may be unsettling, and our fear of that may keep us from hearing God. Thank God that he is merciful and relentless. Moses finally did.

PRAY:

Dear Father, be the center of my life and the circumference
of my hopes. Help me get my mind off myself
and my limitations, that I may see your greatness
and hear what you want to do in and through my life.

FOR YOUR NEXT DEVOTIONAL READING, GO TO PAGE 74.

¹⁵God also said to Moses, "Say to the Israelites, 'The LORD,ᵃ the God of your fathers—the God of Abraham, the God of Isaac and the God of Jacob—has sent me to you.' This is my name forever, the name by which I am to be remembered from generation to generation.

¹⁶"Go, assemble the elders of Israel and say to them, 'The LORD, the God of your fathers—the God of Abraham, Isaac and Jacob—appeared to me and said: I have watched over you and have seen what has been done to you in Egypt. ¹⁷And I have promised to bring you up out of your misery in Egypt into the land of the Canaanites, Hittites, Amorites, Perizzites, Hivites and Jebusites—a land flowing with milk and honey.'

¹⁸"The elders of Israel will listen to you. Then you and the elders are to go to the king of Egypt and say to him, 'The LORD, the God of the Hebrews, has met with us. Let us take a three-day journey into the desert to offer sacrifices to the LORD our God.' ¹⁹But I know that the king of Egypt will not let you go unless a mighty hand compels him. ²⁰So I will stretch out my hand and strike the Egyptians with all the wonders that I will perform among them. After that, he will let you go.

²¹"And I will make the Egyptians favorably disposed toward this people, so that when you leave you will not go empty-handed. ²²Every woman is to ask her neighbor and any woman living in her house for articles of silver and gold and for clothing, which you will put on your sons and daughters. And so you will plunder the Egyptians."

Signs for Moses

4 Moses answered, "What if they do not believe me or listen to me and say, 'The LORD did not appear to you'?"

²Then the LORD said to him, "What is that in your hand?"

"A staff," he replied.

³The LORD said, "Throw it on the ground."

Moses threw it on the ground and it became a snake, and he ran from it. ⁴Then the LORD said to him, "Reach out your hand and take it by the tail." So Moses reached out and took hold of the snake and it turned back into a staff in

his hand. ⁵"This," said the LORD, "is so that they may believe that the LORD, the God of their fathers—the God of Abraham, the God of Isaac and the God of Jacob—has appeared to you."

⁶Then the LORD said, "Put your hand inside your cloak." So Moses put his hand into his cloak, and when he took it out, it was leprous,ᵇ like snow.

⁷"Now put it back into your cloak," he said. So Moses put his hand back into his cloak, and when he took it out, it was restored, like the rest of his flesh.

⁸Then the LORD said, "If they do not believe you or pay attention to the first miraculous sign, they may believe the second. ⁹But if they do not believe these two signs or listen to you, take some water from the Nile and pour it on the dry ground. The water you take from the river will become blood on the ground."

¹⁰Moses said to the LORD, "O Lord, I have never been eloquent, neither in the past nor since you have spoken to your servant. I am slow of speech and tongue."

¹¹The LORD said to him, "Who gave man his mouth? Who makes him deaf or mute? Who gives him sight or makes him blind? Is it not I, the LORD? ¹²Now go; I will help you speak and will teach you what to say."

¹³But Moses said, "O Lord, please send someone else to do it."

¹⁴Then the LORD's anger burned against Moses and he said, "What about your brother, Aaron the Levite? I know he can speak well. He is already on his way to meet you, and his heart will be glad when he sees you. ¹⁵You shall speak to him and put words in his mouth; I will help both of you speak and will teach you what to do. ¹⁶He will speak to the people for you, and it will be as if he were your mouth and as if you were God to him. ¹⁷But take this staff in your hand so you can perform miraculous signs with it."

Moses Returns to Egypt

¹⁸Then Moses went back to Jethro his father-in-law and said to him, "Let me go

---

ᵃ15 The Hebrew for LORD sounds like and may be derived from the Hebrew for I AM in verse 14.
ᵇ6 The Hebrew word was used for various diseases affecting the skin—not necessarily leprosy.

back to my own people in Egypt to see if any of them are still alive."

Jethro said, "Go, and I wish you well."

[19]Now the LORD had said to Moses in Midian, "Go back to Egypt, for all the men who wanted to kill you are dead." [20]So Moses took his wife and sons, put them on a donkey and started back to Egypt. And he took the staff of God in his hand.

[21]The LORD said to Moses, "When you return to Egypt, see that you perform before Pharaoh all the wonders I have given you the power to do. But I will harden his heart so that he will not let the people go. [22]Then say to Pharaoh, 'This is what the LORD says: Israel is my firstborn son, [23]and I told you, "Let my son go, so he may worship me." But you refused to let him go; so I will kill your firstborn son.'"

[24]At a lodging place on the way, the LORD met ˌMoses,[a] and was about to kill him. [25]But Zipporah took a flint knife, cut off her son's foreskin and touched ˌMoses'ˌ feet with it.[b] "Surely you are a bridegroom of blood to me," she said. [26]So the LORD let him alone. (At that time she said "bridegroom of blood," referring to circumcision.)

[27]The LORD said to Aaron, "Go into the desert to meet Moses." So he met Moses at the mountain of God and kissed him. [28]Then Moses told Aaron everything the LORD had sent him to say, and also about all the miraculous signs he had commanded him to perform.

[29]Moses and Aaron brought together all the elders of the Israelites, [30]and Aaron told them everything the LORD had said to Moses. He also performed the signs before the people, [31]and they believed. And when they heard that the LORD was concerned about them and had seen their misery, they bowed down and worshiped.

Bricks Without Straw

5 Afterward Moses and Aaron went to Pharaoh and said, "This is what the LORD, the God of Israel, says: 'Let my people go, so that they may hold a festival to me in the desert.'"

[2]Pharaoh said, "Who is the LORD, that I should obey him and let Israel go? I do not know the LORD and I will not let Israel go."

[3]Then they said, "The God of the Hebrews has met with us. Now let us take a three-day journey into the desert to offer sacrifices to the LORD our God, or he may strike us with plagues or with the sword."

[4]But the king of Egypt said, "Moses and Aaron, why are you taking the people away from their labor? Get back to your work!" [5]Then Pharaoh said, "Look, the people of the land are now numerous, and you are stopping them from working."

[6]That same day Pharaoh gave this order to the slave drivers and foremen in charge of the people: [7]"You are no longer to supply the people with straw for making bricks; let them go and gather their own straw. [8]But require them to make the same number of bricks as before; don't reduce the quota. They are lazy; that is why they are crying out, 'Let us go and sacrifice to our God.' [9]Make the work harder for the men so that they keep working and pay no attention to lies."

[10]Then the slave drivers and the foremen went out and said to the people, "This is what Pharaoh says: 'I will not give you any more straw. [11]Go and get your own straw wherever you can find it, but your work will not be reduced at all.'" [12]So the people scattered all over Egypt to gather stubble to use for straw. [13]The slave drivers kept pressing them, saying, "Complete the work required of you for each day, just as when you had straw." [14]The Israelite foremen appointed by Pharaoh's slave drivers were beaten and were asked, "Why didn't you meet your quota of bricks yesterday or today, as before?"

[15]Then the Israelite foremen went and appealed to Pharaoh: "Why have you treated your servants this way? [16]Your servants are given no straw, yet we are told, 'Make bricks!' Your servants are being beaten, but the fault is with your own people."

[17]Pharaoh said, "Lazy, that's what you are—lazy! That is why you keep saying, 'Let us go and sacrifice to the LORD.' [18]Now get to work. You will not be given any straw, yet you must produce your full quota of bricks."

---

[a]24 Or ˌMoses' sonˌ; Hebrew him drew near ˌMoses'ˌ feet   [b]25 Or and

¹⁹The Israelite foremen realized they were in trouble when they were told, "You are not to reduce the number of bricks required of you for each day." ²⁰When they left Pharaoh, they found Moses and Aaron waiting to meet them, ²¹and they said, "May the LORD look upon you and judge you! You have made us a stench to Pharaoh and his officials and have put a sword in their hand to kill us."

God Promises Deliverance

²²Moses returned to the LORD and said, "O Lord, why have you brought trouble upon this people? Is this why you sent me? ²³Ever since I went to Pharaoh to

---

EXODUS 5:22–23

Honest Complaint and Mere Grumbling

5:22 "O LORD, WHY HAVE YOU BROUGHT TROUBLE UPON THIS PEOPLE?"

Life was pretty bad for the people of Israel before God sent his deliverer, Moses. After Moses arrived, things got really bad. Thus this prayer of Moses. "Moses returned to the LORD and said, 'O Lord, why have you brought trouble upon this people? Is this why you sent me? Ever since I went to Pharaoh to speak in your name, he has brought trouble upon this people, and you have not rescued your people at all'" (5:22–23). Have you ever had the courage, or at least the inclination, to pray to God this way?

First, the inclination: It's not easy to serve God. In the work of his kingdom, things often get worse before they get better. Abraham enters the promised land only to find a famine (see Genesis 12:10). Jesus is crucified before he's raised (see Mark 15–16). It is almost axiomatic that the mark of any true work of God is opposition and difficulty. Don't be surprised by this, and that you struggle. Take it to the Lord.

Second, the courage: Sometimes God doesn't really seem to be in control. Are you comfortable telling God exactly how you feel about how things are going? Or do you feel you need to edit your prayers for theological accuracy? It's important that good theology inform the way we pray. But it's also important to know that a healthy relationship with God (and people) requires the freedom to say what you feel: happy or sad, glad or mad. Read the book of Psalms—these are definitely the prayers of people who had a healthy relationship with God.

But keep in mind the difference between honest complaint and mere grumbling. The difference is in the prepositions: Honest complaint speaks *to* God about the complaint; mere griping talks *about* God. When you speak to God about your concern, you pray. When you complain about your situation to others, you gripe. Honest complaint, like this prayer of Moses, is open-ended and teachable. Behind the prayer is a question mark. Behind mere grumbling is an exclamation point.[1]

PRAY:

Lord, forgive my grumbling. I want to turn it instead to honest complaint.
Take away the fear that love casts out, and free me to speak my heart to you.

FOR YOUR NEXT DEVOTIONAL READING, GO TO PAGE 88.

speak in your name, he has brought trouble upon this people, and you have not rescued your people at all."

6 Then the LORD said to Moses, "Now you will see what I will do to Pharaoh: Because of my mighty hand he will let them go; because of my mighty hand he will drive them out of his country."

[2]God also said to Moses, "I am the LORD. [3]I appeared to Abraham, to Isaac and to Jacob as God Almighty,[a] but by my name the LORD[b] I did not make myself known to them.[c] [4]I also established my covenant with them to give them the land of Canaan, where they lived as aliens. [5]Moreover, I have heard the groaning of the Israelites, whom the Egyptians are enslaving, and I have remembered my covenant.

[6]"Therefore, say to the Israelites: 'I am the LORD, and I will bring you out from under the yoke of the Egyptians. I will free you from being slaves to them, and I will redeem you with an outstretched arm and with mighty acts of judgment. [7]I will take you as my own people, and I will be your God. Then you will know that I am the LORD your God, who brought you out from under the yoke of the Egyptians. [8]And I will bring you to the land I swore with uplifted hand to give to Abraham, to Isaac and to Jacob. I will give it to you as a possession. I am the LORD.' "

[9]Moses reported this to the Israelites, but they did not listen to him because of their discouragement and cruel bondage.

[10]Then the LORD said to Moses, [11]"Go, tell Pharaoh king of Egypt to let the Israelites go out of his country."

[12]But Moses said to the LORD, "If the Israelites will not listen to me, why would Pharaoh listen to me, since I speak with faltering lips[d]?"

Family Record of Moses and Aaron

[13]Now the LORD spoke to Moses and Aaron about the Israelites and Pharaoh king of Egypt, and he commanded them to bring the Israelites out of Egypt.

[14]These were the heads of their families[e]:

The sons of Reuben the firstborn son of Israel were Hanoch and Pallu, Hezron and Carmi. These were the clans of Reuben.

[15]The sons of Simeon were Jemuel, Jamin, Ohad, Jakin, Zohar and Shaul the son of a Canaanite woman. These were the clans of Simeon.

[16]These were the names of the sons of Levi according to their records: Gershon, Kohath and Merari. Levi lived 137 years.

[17]The sons of Gershon, by clans, were Libni and Shimei.

[18]The sons of Kohath were Amram, Izhar, Hebron and Uzziel. Kohath lived 133 years.

[19]The sons of Merari were Mahli and Mushi.

These were the clans of Levi according to their records.

[20]Amram married his father's sister Jochebed, who bore him Aaron and Moses. Amram lived 137 years.

[21]The sons of Izhar were Korah, Nepheg and Zicri.

[22]The sons of Uzziel were Mishael, Elzaphan and Sithri.

[23]Aaron married Elisheba, daughter of Amminadab and sister of Nahshon, and she bore him Nadab and Abihu, Eleazar and Ithamar.

[24]The sons of Korah were Assir, Elkanah and Abiasaph. These were the Korahite clans.

[25]Eleazar son of Aaron married one of the daughters of Putiel, and she bore him Phinehas.

These were the heads of the Levite families, clan by clan.

[26]It was this same Aaron and Moses to whom the LORD said, "Bring the Israelites out of Egypt by their divisions." [27]They were the ones who spoke to Pharaoh king of Egypt about bringing the Israelites out of Egypt. It was the same Moses and Aaron.

Aaron to Speak for Moses

[28]Now when the LORD spoke to Moses in Egypt, [29]he said to him, "I am the LORD.

[a]3 Hebrew El-Shaddai   [b]3 See note at Exodus 3:15.   [c]3 Or Almighty, and by my name the LORD did I not let myself be known to them?
[d]12 Hebrew I am uncircumcised of lips; also in verse 30   [e]14 The Hebrew for families here and in verse 25 refers to units larger than clans.

Tell Pharaoh king of Egypt everything I tell you."

30But Moses said to the LORD, "Since I speak with faltering lips, why would Pharaoh listen to me?"

7 Then the LORD said to Moses, "See, I have made you like God to Pharaoh, and your brother Aaron will be your prophet. 2You are to say everything I command you, and your brother Aaron is to tell Pharaoh to let the Israelites go out of his country. 3But I will harden Pharaoh's heart, and though I multiply my miraculous signs and wonders in Egypt, 4he will not listen to you. Then I will lay my hand on Egypt and with mighty acts of judgment I will bring out my divisions, my people the Israelites. 5And the Egyptians will know that I am the LORD when I stretch out my hand against Egypt and bring the Israelites out of it."

6Moses and Aaron did just as the LORD commanded them. 7Moses was eighty years old and Aaron eighty-three when they spoke to Pharaoh.

Aaron's Staff Becomes a Snake

8The LORD said to Moses and Aaron, 9"When Pharaoh says to you, 'Perform a miracle,' then say to Aaron, 'Take your staff and throw it down before Pharaoh,' and it will become a snake."

10So Moses and Aaron went to Pharaoh and did just as the LORD commanded. Aaron threw his staff down in front of Pharaoh and his officials, and it became a snake. 11Pharaoh then summoned wise men and sorcerers, and the Egyptian magicians also did the same things by their secret arts: 12Each one threw down his staff and it became a snake. But Aaron's staff swallowed up their staffs. 13Yet Pharaoh's heart became hard and he would not listen to them, just as the LORD had said.

The Plague of Blood

14Then the LORD said to Moses, "Pharaoh's heart is unyielding; he refuses to let the people go. 15Go to Pharaoh in the morning as he goes out to the water. Wait on the bank of the Nile to meet him, and take in your hand the staff that was changed into a snake. 16Then say to him, 'The LORD, the God of the Hebrews, has sent me to say to you: Let my people go, so that they may worship me in the desert. But until now you have not listened. 17This is what the LORD says: By this you will know that I am the LORD: With the staff that is in my hand I will strike the water of the Nile, and it will be changed into blood. 18The fish in the Nile will die, and the river will stink; the Egyptians will not be able to drink its water.'"

19The LORD said to Moses, "Tell Aaron, 'Take your staff and stretch out your hand over the waters of Egypt—over the streams and canals, over the ponds and all the reservoirs'—and they will turn to blood. Blood will be everywhere in Egypt, even in the wooden buckets and stone jars."

20Moses and Aaron did just as the LORD had commanded. He raised his staff in the presence of Pharaoh and his officials and struck the water of the Nile, and all the water was changed into blood. 21The fish in the Nile died, and the river smelled so bad that the Egyptians could not drink its water. Blood was everywhere in Egypt.

22But the Egyptian magicians did the same things by their secret arts, and Pharaoh's heart became hard; he would not listen to Moses and Aaron, just as the LORD had said. 23Instead, he turned and went into his palace, and did not take even this to heart. 24And all the Egyptians dug along the Nile to get drinking water, because they could not drink the water of the river.

The Plague of Frogs

25Seven days passed after the LORD struck the Nile. 8 1Then the LORD said to Moses, "Go to Pharaoh and say to him, 'This is what the LORD says: Let my people go, so that they may worship me. 2If you refuse to let them go, I will plague your whole country with frogs. 3The Nile will teem with frogs. They will come up into your palace and your bedroom and onto your bed, into the houses of your officials and on your people, and into your ovens and kneading troughs. 4The frogs will go up on you and your people and all your officials.'"

5Then the LORD said to Moses, "Tell Aaron, 'Stretch out your hand with your staff over the streams and canals and ponds, and make frogs come up on the land of Egypt.'"

⁶So Aaron stretched out his hand over the waters of Egypt, and the frogs came up and covered the land. ⁷But the magicians did the same things by their secret arts; they also made frogs come up on the land of Egypt.

⁸Pharaoh summoned Moses and Aaron and said, "Pray to the LORD to take the frogs away from me and my people, and I will let your people go to offer sacrifices to the LORD."

> PHARAOH *summoned Moses and Aaron and said, "Pray to the LORD to take the frogs away from me and my people, and I will let your people go."*
>
> EXODUS 8:8

⁹Moses said to Pharaoh, "I leave to you the honor of setting the time for me to pray for you and your officials and your people that you and your houses may be rid of the frogs, except for those that remain in the Nile."

¹⁰"Tomorrow," Pharaoh said.

Moses replied, "It will be as you say, so that you may know there is no one like the LORD our God. ¹¹The frogs will leave you and your houses, your officials and your people; they will remain only in the Nile."

¹²After Moses and Aaron left Pharaoh, Moses cried out to the LORD about the frogs he had brought on Pharaoh. ¹³And the LORD did what Moses asked. The frogs died in the houses, in the courtyards and in the fields. ¹⁴They were piled into heaps, and the land reeked of them. ¹⁵But when Pharaoh saw that there was relief, he hardened his heart and would not listen to Moses and Aaron, just as the LORD had said.

The Plague of Gnats

¹⁶Then the LORD said to Moses, "Tell Aaron, 'Stretch out your staff and strike the dust of the ground,' and throughout the land of Egypt the dust will become gnats." ¹⁷They did this, and when Aaron stretched out his hand with the staff and struck the dust of the ground, gnats came upon men and animals. All the dust throughout the land of Egypt became gnats. ¹⁸But when the magicians tried to produce gnats by their secret arts, they could not. And the gnats were on men and animals.

¹⁹The magicians said to Pharaoh, "This is the finger of God." But Pharaoh's heart was hard and he would not listen, just as the LORD had said.

The Plague of Flies

²⁰Then the LORD said to Moses, "Get up early in the morning and confront Pharaoh as he goes to the water and say to him, 'This is what the LORD says: Let my people go, so that they may worship me. ²¹If you do not let my people go, I will send swarms of flies on you and your officials, on your people and into your houses. The houses of the Egyptians will be full of flies, and even the ground where they are.

²²"'But on that day I will deal differently with the land of Goshen, where my people live; no swarms of flies will be there, so that you will know that I, the LORD, am in this land. ²³I will make a distinction[a] between my people and your people. This miraculous sign will occur tomorrow.'"

²⁴And the LORD did this. Dense swarms of flies poured into Pharaoh's palace and into the houses of his officials, and throughout Egypt the land was ruined by the flies.

²⁵Then Pharaoh summoned Moses and Aaron and said, "Go, sacrifice to your God here in the land."

²⁶But Moses said, "That would not be right. The sacrifices we offer the LORD our God would be detestable to the Egyptians. And if we offer sacrifices that are detestable in their eyes, will they not stone us? ²⁷We must take a three-day journey into the desert to offer sacrifices to the LORD our God, as he commands us."

²⁸Pharaoh said, "I will let you go to offer sacrifices to the LORD your God in the desert, but you must not go very far. Now pray for me."

---

a23 Septuagint and Vulgate; Hebrew *will put a deliverance*

²⁹Moses answered, "As soon as I leave you, I will pray to the LORD, and tomorrow the flies will leave Pharaoh and his officials and his people. Only be sure that Pharaoh does not act deceitfully again by not letting the people go to offer sacrifices to the LORD."

³⁰Then Moses left Pharaoh and prayed to the LORD, ³¹and the LORD did what Moses asked: The flies left Pharaoh and his officials and his people; not a fly remained. ³²But this time also Pharaoh hardened his heart and would not let the people go.

> THEN Moses left Pharaoh and prayed to the LORD.
>
> EXODUS 8:30

The Plague on Livestock

9 Then the LORD said to Moses, "Go to Pharaoh and say to him, 'This is what the LORD, the God of the Hebrews, says: "Let my people go, so that they may worship me."' ²If you refuse to let them go and continue to hold them back, ³the hand of the LORD will bring a terrible plague on your livestock in the field—on your horses and donkeys and camels and on your cattle and sheep and goats. ⁴But the LORD will make a distinction between the livestock of Israel and that of Egypt, so that no animal belonging to the Israelites will die.'"

⁵The LORD set a time and said, "Tomorrow the LORD will do this in the land." ⁶And the next day the LORD did it: All the livestock of the Egyptians died, but not one animal belonging to the Israelites died. ⁷Pharaoh sent men to investigate and found that not even one of the animals of the Israelites had died. Yet his heart was unyielding and he would not let the people go.

The Plague of Boils

⁸Then the LORD said to Moses and Aaron, "Take handfuls of soot from a furnace and have Moses toss it into the air in the presence of Pharaoh. ⁹It will become fine dust over the whole land of Egypt, and festering boils will break out on men and animals throughout the land."

¹⁰So they took soot from a furnace and stood before Pharaoh. Moses tossed it into the air, and festering boils broke out on men and animals. ¹¹The magicians could not stand before Moses because of the boils that were on them and on all the Egyptians. ¹²But the LORD hardened Pharaoh's heart and he would not listen to Moses and Aaron, just as the LORD had said to Moses.

The Plague of Hail

¹³Then the LORD said to Moses, "Get up early in the morning, confront Pharaoh and say to him, 'This is what the LORD, the God of the Hebrews, says: Let my people go, so that they may worship me, ¹⁴or this time I will send the full force of my plagues against you and against your officials and your people, so you may know that there is no one like me in all the earth. ¹⁵For by now I could have stretched out my hand and struck you and your people with a plague that would have wiped you off the earth. ¹⁶But I have raised you up[a] for this very purpose, that I might show you my power and that my name might be proclaimed in all the earth. ¹⁷You still set yourself against my people and will not let them go. ¹⁸Therefore, at this time tomorrow I will send the worst hailstorm that has ever fallen on Egypt, from the day it was founded till now. ¹⁹Give an order now to bring your livestock and everything you have in the field to a place of shelter, because the hail will fall on every man and animal that has not been brought in and is still out in the field, and they will die.'"

²⁰Those officials of Pharaoh who feared the word of the LORD hurried to bring their slaves and their livestock inside. ²¹But those who ignored the word of the LORD left their slaves and livestock in the field.

²²Then the LORD said to Moses, "Stretch out your hand toward the sky so that hail will fall all over Egypt—on men and animals and on everything growing in the fields of Egypt." ²³When Moses stretched out his staff toward the sky, the LORD sent thunder and hail, and lightning flashed down to the ground. So the LORD rained

---

[a]16 Or *have spared you*

hail on the land of Egypt; ²⁴hail fell and lightning flashed back and forth. It was the worst storm in all the land of Egypt since it had become a nation. ²⁵Throughout Egypt hail struck everything in the fields—both men and animals; it beat down everything growing in the fields and stripped every tree. ²⁶The only place it did not hail was the land of Goshen, where the Israelites were.

²⁷Then Pharaoh summoned Moses and Aaron. "This time I have sinned," he said to them. "The LORD is in the right, and I and my people are in the wrong. ²⁸Pray to the LORD, for we have had enough thunder and hail. I will let you go; you don't have to stay any longer."

²⁹Moses replied, "When I have gone out of the city, I will spread out my hands in prayer to the LORD. The thunder will stop and there will be no more hail, so you may know that the earth is the LORD's. ³⁰But I know that you and your officials still do not fear the LORD God."

> "WHEN I have gone out of the city, I will spread out my hands in prayer to the LORD."
>
> EXODUS 9:29

³¹(The flax and barley were destroyed, since the barley had headed and the flax was in bloom. ³²The wheat and spelt, however, were not destroyed, because they ripen later.)

³³Then Moses left Pharaoh and went out of the city. He spread out his hands toward the LORD; the thunder and hail stopped, and the rain no longer poured down on the land. ³⁴When Pharaoh saw that the rain and hail and thunder had stopped, he sinned again: He and his officials hardened their hearts. ³⁵So Pharaoh's heart was hard and he would not let the Israelites go, just as the LORD had said through Moses.

The Plague of Locusts

10 Then the LORD said to Moses, "Go to Pharaoh, for I have hardened his heart and the hearts of his officials so that I may perform these miraculous signs of mine among them ²that you may tell your children and grandchildren how I dealt harshly with the Egyptians and how I performed my signs among them, and that you may know that I am the LORD."

³So Moses and Aaron went to Pharaoh and said to him, "This is what the LORD, the God of the Hebrews, says: 'How long will you refuse to humble yourself before me? Let my people go, so that they may worship me. ⁴If you refuse to let them go, I will bring locusts into your country tomorrow. ⁵They will cover the face of the ground so that it cannot be seen. They will devour what little you have left after the hail, including every tree that is growing in your fields. ⁶They will fill your houses and those of all your officials and all the Egyptians—something neither your fathers nor your forefathers have ever seen from the day they settled in this land till now.'" Then Moses turned and left Pharaoh.

⁷Pharaoh's officials said to him, "How long will this man be a snare to us? Let the people go, so that they may worship the LORD their God. Do you not yet realize that Egypt is ruined?"

⁸Then Moses and Aaron were brought back to Pharaoh. "Go, worship the LORD your God," he said. "But just who will be going?"

⁹Moses answered, "We will go with our young and old, with our sons and daughters, and with our flocks and herds, because we are to celebrate a festival to the LORD."

¹⁰Pharaoh said, "The LORD be with you—if I let you go, along with your women and children! Clearly you are bent on evil.ᵃ ¹¹No! Have only the men go; and worship the LORD, since that's what you have been asking for." Then Moses and Aaron were driven out of Pharaoh's presence.

¹²And the LORD said to Moses, "Stretch out your hand over Egypt so that locusts will swarm over the land and devour everything growing in the fields, everything left by the hail."

¹³So Moses stretched out his staff over Egypt, and the LORD made an east wind

ᵃ10 Or Be careful, trouble is in store for you!

blow across the land all that day and all that night. By morning the wind had brought the locusts; ¹⁴they invaded all Egypt and settled down in every area of the country in great numbers. Never before had there been such a plague of locusts, nor will there ever be again. ¹⁵They covered all the ground until it was black. They devoured all that was left after the hail—everything growing in the fields and the fruit on the trees. Nothing green remained on tree or plant in all the land of Egypt.

¹⁶Pharaoh quickly summoned Moses and Aaron and said, "I have sinned against the LORD your God and against you. ¹⁷Now forgive my sin once more and pray to the LORD your God to take this deadly plague away from me."

> "NOW forgive my sin once more and pray to the LORD your God to take this deadly plague away from me."
>
> EXODUS 10:17

¹⁸Moses then left Pharaoh and prayed to the LORD. ¹⁹And the LORD changed the wind to a very strong west wind, which caught up the locusts and carried them into the Red Sea.ᵃ Not a locust was left anywhere in Egypt. ²⁰But the LORD hardened Pharaoh's heart, and he would not let the Israelites go.

The Plague of Darkness

²¹Then the LORD said to Moses, "Stretch out your hand toward the sky so that darkness will spread over Egypt—darkness that can be felt." ²²So Moses stretched out his hand toward the sky, and total darkness covered all Egypt for three days. ²³No one could see anyone else or leave his place for three days. Yet all the Israelites had light in the places where they lived.

²⁴Then Pharaoh summoned Moses and said, "Go, worship the LORD. Even your women and children may go with you; only leave your flocks and herds behind."

²⁵But Moses said, "You must allow us to have sacrifices and burnt offerings to present to the LORD our God. ²⁶Our livestock too must go with us; not a hoof is to be left behind. We have to use some of them in worshiping the LORD our God, and until we get there we will not know what we are to use to worship the LORD."

²⁷But the LORD hardened Pharaoh's heart, and he was not willing to let them go. ²⁸Pharaoh said to Moses, "Get out of my sight! Make sure you do not appear before me again! The day you see my face you will die."

²⁹"Just as you say," Moses replied, "I will never appear before you again."

The Plague on the Firstborn

11 Now the LORD had said to Moses, "I will bring one more plague on Pharaoh and on Egypt. After that, he will let you go from here, and when he does, he will drive you out completely. ²Tell the people that men and women alike are to ask their neighbors for articles of silver and gold." ³(The LORD made the Egyptians favorably disposed toward the people, and Moses himself was highly regarded in Egypt by Pharaoh's officials and by the people.)

⁴So Moses said, "This is what the LORD says: 'About midnight I will go throughout Egypt. ⁵Every firstborn son in Egypt will die, from the firstborn son of Pharaoh, who sits on the throne, to the firstborn son of the slave girl, who is at her hand mill, and all the firstborn of the cattle as well. ⁶There will be loud wailing throughout Egypt—worse than there has ever been or ever will be again. ⁷But among the Israelites not a dog will bark at any man or animal.' Then you will know that the LORD makes a distinction between Egypt and Israel. ⁸All these officials of yours will come to me, bowing down before me and saying, 'Go, you and all the people who follow you!' After that I will leave." Then Moses, hot with anger, left Pharaoh.

⁹The LORD had said to Moses, "Pharaoh will refuse to listen to you—so that my wonders may be multiplied in Egypt." ¹⁰Moses and Aaron performed all these wonders before Pharaoh, but the LORD hardened Pharaoh's heart, and he would not let the Israelites go out of his country.

ᵃ19 Hebrew *Yam Suph*; that is, Sea of Reeds

> *Prayer is less about changing the world than it is about changing ourselves.*
>
> DAVID J. WOLPE

The Passover

12 The LORD said to Moses and Aaron in Egypt, [2]"This month is to be for you the first month, the first month of your year. [3]Tell the whole community of Israel that on the tenth day of this month each man is to take a lamb[a] for his family, one for each household. [4]If any household is too small for a whole lamb, they must share one with their nearest neighbor, having taken into account the number of people there are. You are to determine the amount of lamb needed in accordance with what each person will eat. [5]The animals you choose must be year-old males without defect, and you may take them from the sheep or the goats. [6]Take care of them until the fourteenth day of the month, when all the people of the community of Israel must slaughter them at twilight. [7]Then they are to take some of the blood and put it on the sides and tops of the doorframes of the houses where they eat the lambs. [8]That same night they are to eat the meat roasted over the fire, along with bitter herbs, and bread made without yeast. [9]Do not eat the meat raw or cooked in water, but roast it over the fire—head, legs and inner parts. [10]Do not leave any of it till morning; if some is left till morning, you must burn it. [11]This is how you are to eat it: with your cloak tucked into your belt, your sandals on your feet and your staff in your hand. Eat it in haste; it is the LORD's Passover.

[12]"On that same night I will pass through Egypt and strike down every firstborn—both men and animals—and I will bring judgment on all the gods of Egypt. I am the LORD. [13]The blood will be a sign for you on the houses where you are; and when I see the blood, I will pass over you. No destructive plague will touch you when I strike Egypt.

[14]"This is a day you are to commemorate; for the generations to come you shall celebrate it as a festival to the LORD—a lasting ordinance. [15]For seven days you are to eat bread made without yeast. On the first day remove the yeast from your houses, for whoever eats anything with yeast in it from the first day through the seventh must be cut off from Israel. [16]On the first day hold a sacred assembly, and another one on the seventh day. Do no work at all on these days, except to prepare food for everyone to eat—that is all you may do.

[17]"Celebrate the Feast of Unleavened Bread, because it was on this very day that I brought your divisions out of Egypt. Celebrate this day as a lasting ordinance for the generations to come. [18]In the first month you are to eat bread made without yeast, from the evening of the fourteenth day until the evening of the twenty-first day. [19]For seven days no yeast is to be found in your houses. And whoever eats anything with yeast in it must be cut off from the community of Israel, whether he is an alien or native-born. [20]Eat nothing made with yeast. Wherever you live, you must eat unleavened bread."

[21]Then Moses summoned all the elders of Israel and said to them, "Go at once and select the animals for your families and slaughter the Passover lamb. [22]Take a bunch of hyssop, dip it into the blood in the basin and put some of the blood on the top and on both sides of the doorframe. Not one of you shall go out the door of his house until morning. [23]When the LORD goes through the land to strike down the Egyptians, he will see the blood on the top and sides of the doorframe and will pass over that doorway, and he will not permit the destroyer to enter your houses and strike you down.

[24]"Obey these instructions as a lasting ordinance for you and your descendants. [25]When you enter the land that the LORD will give you as he promised, observe this ceremony. [26]And when your children ask you, 'What does this ceremony mean to you?' [27]then tell them, 'It is the Passover sacrifice to the LORD, who passed over the houses of the Israelites in Egypt and spared our homes when he struck down

---

[a]3 The Hebrew word can mean *lamb* or *kid*; also in verse 4.

the Egyptians.'" Then the people bowed down and worshiped. ²⁸The Israelites did just what the LORD commanded Moses and Aaron.

²⁹At midnight the LORD struck down all the firstborn in Egypt, from the firstborn of Pharaoh, who sat on the throne, to the firstborn of the prisoner, who was in the dungeon, and the firstborn of all the livestock as well. ³⁰Pharaoh and all his officials and all the Egyptians got up during the night, and there was loud wailing in Egypt, for there was not a house without someone dead.

The Exodus

³¹During the night Pharaoh summoned Moses and Aaron and said, "Up! Leave my people, you and the Israelites! Go, worship the LORD as you have requested. ³²Take your flocks and herds, as you have said, and go. And also bless me."

³³The Egyptians urged the people to hurry and leave the country. "For otherwise," they said, "we will all die!" ³⁴So the people took their dough before the yeast was added, and carried it on their shoulders in kneading troughs wrapped in clothing. ³⁵The Israelites did as Moses instructed and asked the Egyptians for articles of silver and gold and for clothing. ³⁶The LORD had made the Egyptians favorably disposed toward the people, and they gave them what they asked for; so they plundered the Egyptians.

³⁷The Israelites journeyed from Rameses to Succoth. There were about six hundred thousand men on foot, besides women and children. ³⁸Many other people went up with them, as well as large droves of livestock, both flocks and herds. ³⁹With the dough they had brought from Egypt, they baked cakes of unleavened bread. The dough was without yeast because they had been driven out of Egypt and did not have time to prepare food for themselves.

⁴⁰Now the length of time the Israelite people lived in Egypt[a] was 430 years. ⁴¹At the end of the 430 years, to the very day, all the LORD's divisions left Egypt. ⁴²Because the LORD kept vigil that night to bring them out of Egypt, on this night all the Israelites are to keep vigil to honor the LORD for the generations to come.

Passover Restrictions

⁴³The LORD said to Moses and Aaron, "These are the regulations for the Passover:

"No foreigner is to eat of it. ⁴⁴Any slave you have bought may eat of it after you have circumcised him, ⁴⁵but a temporary resident and a hired worker may not eat of it.

⁴⁶"It must be eaten inside one house; take none of the meat outside the house. Do not break any of the bones. ⁴⁷The whole community of Israel must celebrate it.

⁴⁸"An alien living among you who wants to celebrate the LORD's Passover must have all the males in his household circumcised; then he may take part like one born in the land. No uncircumcised male may eat of it. ⁴⁹The same law applies to the native-born and to the alien living among you."

⁵⁰All the Israelites did just what the LORD had commanded Moses and Aaron. ⁵¹And on that very day the LORD brought the Israelites out of Egypt by their divisions.

Consecration of the Firstborn

13 The LORD said to Moses, ²"Consecrate to me every firstborn male. The first offspring of every womb among the Israelites belongs to me, whether man or animal."

³Then Moses said to the people, "Commemorate this day, the day you came out of Egypt, out of the land of slavery, because the LORD brought you out of it with a mighty hand. Eat nothing containing yeast. ⁴Today, in the month of Abib, you are leaving. ⁵When the LORD brings you into the land of the Canaanites, Hittites, Amorites, Hivites and Jebusites—the land he swore to your forefathers to give you, a land flowing with milk and honey—you are to observe this ceremony in this month: ⁶For seven days eat bread made without yeast and on the seventh day hold a festival to the LORD. ⁷Eat unleavened bread during those seven days; nothing with yeast in it is to be seen

---

[a]40 Masoretic Text; Samaritan Pentateuch and Septuagint *Egypt and Canaan*

among you, nor shall any yeast be seen anywhere within your borders. ⁸On that day tell your son, 'I do this because of what the Lord did for me when I came out of Egypt.' ⁹This observance will be for you like a sign on your hand and a reminder on your forehead that the law of the Lord is to be on your lips. For the Lord brought you out of Egypt with his mighty hand. ¹⁰You must keep this ordinance at the appointed time year after year.

¹¹"After the Lord brings you into the land of the Canaanites and gives it to you, as he promised on oath to you and your forefathers, ¹²you are to give over to the Lord the first offspring of every womb. All the firstborn males of your livestock belong to the Lord. ¹³Redeem with a lamb every firstborn donkey, but if you do not redeem it, break its neck. Redeem every firstborn among your sons.

¹⁴"In days to come, when your son asks you, 'What does this mean?' say to him, 'With a mighty hand the Lord brought us out of Egypt, out of the land of slavery. ¹⁵When Pharaoh stubbornly refused to let us go, the Lord killed every firstborn in Egypt, both man and animal. This is why I sacrifice to the Lord the first male offspring of every womb and redeem each of my firstborn sons.' ¹⁶And it will be like a sign on your hand and a symbol on your forehead that the Lord brought us out of Egypt with his mighty hand."

Crossing the Sea

¹⁷When Pharaoh let the people go, God did not lead them on the road through the Philistine country, though that was shorter. For God said, "If they face war, they might change their minds and return to Egypt." ¹⁸So God led the people around by the desert road toward the Red Sea.[a] The Israelites went up out of Egypt armed for battle.

¹⁹Moses took the bones of Joseph with him because Joseph had made the sons of Israel swear an oath. He had said, "God will surely come to your aid, and then you must carry my bones up with you from this place."[b]

²⁰After leaving Succoth they camped at Etham on the edge of the desert. ²¹By day the Lord went ahead of them in a pillar of cloud to guide them on their way and by night in a pillar of fire to give them light, so that they could travel by day or night. ²²Neither the pillar of cloud by day nor the pillar of fire by night left its place in front of the people.

14 Then the Lord said to Moses, ²"Tell the Israelites to turn back and encamp near Pi Hahiroth, between Migdol and the sea. They are to encamp by the sea, directly opposite Baal Zephon. ³Pharaoh will think, 'The Israelites are wandering around the land in confusion, hemmed in by the desert.' ⁴And I will harden Pharaoh's heart, and he will pursue them. But I will gain glory for myself through Pharaoh and all his army, and the Egyptians will know that I am the Lord." So the Israelites did this.

⁵When the king of Egypt was told that the people had fled, Pharaoh and his officials changed their minds about them and said, "What have we done? We have let the Israelites go and have lost their services!" ⁶So he had his chariot made ready and took his army with him. ⁷He took six hundred of the best chariots, along with all the other chariots of Egypt, with officers over all of them. ⁸The Lord hardened the heart of Pharaoh king of Egypt, so that he pursued the Israelites, who were marching out boldly. ⁹The Egyptians—all Pharaoh's horses and chariots, horsemen[c] and troops—pursued the Israelites and overtook them as they camped by the sea near Pi Hahiroth, opposite Baal Zephon.

¹⁰As Pharaoh approached, the Israelites looked up, and there were the Egyptians, marching after them. They were terrified and cried out to the Lord. ¹¹They said to Moses, "Was it because there were no graves in Egypt that you brought

> AS PHARAOH approached, the Israelites looked up, and there were the Egyptians, marching after them. They were terrified and cried out to the Lord.
>
> EXODUS 14:10

[a]18 Hebrew Yam Suph; that is, Sea of Reeds [b]19 See Gen. 50:25. [c]9 Or charioteers; also in verses 17, 18, 23, 26 and 28

us to the desert to die? What have you done to us by bringing us out of Egypt? ¹²Didn't we say to you in Egypt, 'Leave us alone; let us serve the Egyptians'? It would have been better for us to serve the Egyptians than to die in the desert!" ¹³Moses answered the people, "Do not be afraid. Stand firm and you will see the deliverance the Lord will bring you today. The Egyptians you see today you will never see again. ¹⁴The Lord will fight for you; you need only to be still."

¹⁵Then the Lord said to Moses, "Why are you crying out to me? Tell the Israelites to move on. ¹⁶Raise your staff and stretch out your hand over the sea to divide the water so that the Israelites can go through the sea on dry ground. ¹⁷I will harden the hearts of the Egyptians so that they will go in after them. And I will gain glory through Pharaoh and all his army, through his chariots and his horsemen. ¹⁸The Egyptians will know that I am the Lord when I gain glory through Pharaoh, his chariots and his horsemen."

¹⁹Then the angel of God, who had been traveling in front of Israel's army, withdrew and went behind them. The pillar of cloud also moved from in front and stood behind them, ²⁰coming between the armies of Egypt and Israel. Throughout the night the cloud brought darkness to the one side and light to the other side; so neither went near the other all night long.

²¹Then Moses stretched out his hand over the sea, and all that night the Lord drove the sea back with a strong east wind and turned it into dry land. The waters were divided, ²²and the Israelites went through the sea on dry ground, with a wall of water on their right and on their left.

²³The Egyptians pursued them, and all Pharaoh's horses and chariots and horsemen followed them into the sea. ²⁴During the last watch of the night the Lord looked down from the pillar of fire and cloud at the Egyptian army and threw it into confusion. ²⁵He made the wheels of their chariots come off[a] so that they had difficulty driving. And the Egyptians said, "Let's get away from the Israelites! The Lord is fighting for them against Egypt."

²⁶Then the Lord said to Moses, "Stretch out your hand over the sea so that the waters may flow back over the Egyptians and their chariots and horsemen." ²⁷Moses stretched out his hand over the sea, and at daybreak the sea went back to its place. The Egyptians were fleeing toward[b] it, and the Lord swept them into the sea. ²⁸The water flowed back and covered the chariots and horsemen—the entire army of Pharaoh that had followed the Israelites into the sea. Not one of them survived.

²⁹But the Israelites went through the sea on dry ground, with a wall of water on their right and on their left. ³⁰That day the Lord saved Israel from the hands of the Egyptians, and Israel saw the Egyptians lying dead on the shore. ³¹And when the Israelites saw the great power the Lord displayed against the Egyptians, the people feared the Lord and put their trust in him and in Moses his servant.

The Song of Moses and Miriam

15 Then Moses and the Israelites sang this song to the Lord:

"I will sing to the Lord,
    for he is highly exalted.
The horse and its rider
    he has hurled into the sea.
²The Lord is my strength and my song;
    he has become my salvation.
He is my God, and I will praise him,
    my father's God, and I will exalt
    him.
³The Lord is a warrior;
    the Lord is his name.
⁴Pharaoh's chariots and his army
    he has hurled into the sea.
The best of Pharaoh's officers
    are drowned in the Red Sea.[c]
⁵The deep waters have covered them;
    they sank to the depths like
    a stone.

⁶"Your right hand, O Lord,
    was majestic in power.
Your right hand, O Lord,
    shattered the enemy.

---

[a]25 Or *He jammed the wheels of their chariots*
(see Samaritan Pentateuch, Septuagint and
Syriac)   [b]27 Or *from*   [c]4 Hebrew *Yam*
Suph; that is, Sea of Reeds; also in verse 22

7In the greatness of your majesty
  you threw down those who
    opposed you.
You unleashed your burning anger;
  it consumed them like stubble.
8By the blast of your nostrils
  the waters piled up.
The surging waters stood firm like
  a wall;
  the deep waters congealed in the
    heart of the sea.

9 "The enemy boasted,
  'I will pursue, I will overtake them.
I will divide the spoils;
  I will gorge myself on them.
I will draw my sword
  and my hand will destroy them.'
10But you blew with your breath,
  and the sea covered them.
They sank like lead
  in the mighty waters.

11 "Who among the gods is like you,
    O LORD?
  Who is like you—
    majestic in holiness,
    awesome in glory,
    working wonders?
12You stretched out your right hand
  and the earth swallowed them.

13 "In your unfailing love you will lead
  the people you have redeemed.
In your strength you will guide
    them
  to your holy dwelling.
14The nations will hear and tremble;
  anguish will grip the people
    of Philistia.
15The chiefs of Edom will be terrified,
  the leaders of Moab will be seized
    with trembling,
  the people*a* of Canaan will melt
    away;
16   terror and dread will fall
    upon them.
By the power of your arm
  they will be as still as a stone—
until your people pass by, O LORD,
  until the people you bought*b*
    pass by.
17You will bring them in and plant
    them
  on the mountain of your
    inheritance—

the place, O LORD, you made for
    your dwelling,
  the sanctuary, O Lord, your hands
    established.
18The LORD will reign
  for ever and ever."

19When Pharaoh's horses, chariots
and horsemen*c* went into the sea, the
LORD brought the waters of the sea back
over them, but the Israelites walked
through the sea on dry ground. 20Then
Miriam the prophetess, Aaron's sister,
took a tambourine in her hand, and all
the women followed her, with tambourines and dancing. 21Miriam sang to
them:

  "Sing to the LORD,
    for he is highly exalted.
  The horse and its rider
    he has hurled into the sea."

The Waters of Marah and Elim

22Then Moses led Israel from the Red
Sea and they went into the Desert of
Shur. For three days they traveled in the
desert without finding water. 23When
they came to Marah, they could not drink
its water because it was bitter. (That is
why the place is called Marah.*d*) 24So the
people grumbled against Moses, saying,
"What are we to drink?"
25Then Moses cried out to the LORD,
and the LORD showed him a piece of
wood. He threw it into the water, and the
water became sweet.

> THEN Moses cried out to the LORD, and
> the LORD showed him a piece of wood. He
> threw it into the water, and the water
> became sweet.
>
> EXODUS 15:25

There the LORD made a decree and a
law for them, and there he tested them.
26He said, "If you listen carefully to the
voice of the LORD your God and do what
is right in his eyes, if you pay attention to
his commands and keep all his decrees, I
will not bring on you any of the diseases

*a*15 Or rulers   *b*16 Or created
*c*19 Or charioteers   *d*23 Marah means bitter.

I brought on the Egyptians, for I am the LORD, who heals you."

²⁷Then they came to Elim, where there were twelve springs and seventy palm trees, and they camped there near the water.

Manna and Quail

16 The whole Israelite community set out from Elim and came to the Desert of Sin, which is between Elim and Sinai, on the fifteenth day of the second month after they had come out of Egypt. ²In the desert the whole community grumbled against Moses and Aaron. ³The Israelites said to them, "If only we had died by the LORD's hand in Egypt! There we sat around pots of meat and ate all the food we wanted, but you have brought us out into this desert to starve this entire assembly to death."

⁴Then the LORD said to Moses, "I will rain down bread from heaven for you. The people are to go out each day and gather enough for that day. In this way I will test them and see whether they will follow my instructions. ⁵On the sixth day they are to prepare what they bring in, and that is to be twice as much as they gather on the other days."

⁶So Moses and Aaron said to all the Israelites, "In the evening you will know that it was the LORD who brought you out of Egypt, ⁷and in the morning you will see the glory of the LORD, because he has heard your grumbling against him. Who are we, that you should grumble against us?" ⁸Moses also said, "You will know that it was the LORD when he gives you meat to eat in the evening and all the bread you want in the morning, because he has heard your grumbling against him. Who are we? You are not grumbling against us, but against the LORD."

⁹Then Moses told Aaron, "Say to the entire Israelite community, 'Come before the LORD, for he has heard your grumbling.'"

¹⁰While Aaron was speaking to the whole Israelite community, they looked toward the desert, and there was the glory of the LORD appearing in the cloud.

¹¹The LORD said to Moses, ¹²"I have heard the grumbling of the Israelites. Tell them, 'At twilight you will eat meat, and in the morning you will be filled with bread. Then you will know that I am the LORD your God.'"

¹³That evening quail came and covered the camp, and in the morning there was a layer of dew around the camp. ¹⁴When the dew was gone, thin flakes like frost on the ground appeared on the desert floor. ¹⁵When the Israelites saw it, they said to each other, "What is it?" For they did not know what it was.

Moses said to them, "It is the bread the LORD has given you to eat. ¹⁶This is what the LORD has commanded: 'Each one is to gather as much as he needs. Take an omer[a] for each person you have in your tent.'"

¹⁷The Israelites did as they were told; some gathered much, some little. ¹⁸And when they measured it by the omer, he who gathered much did not have too much, and he who gathered little did not have too little. Each one gathered as much as he needed.

¹⁹Then Moses said to them, "No one is to keep any of it until morning."

²⁰However, some of them paid no attention to Moses; they kept part of it until morning, but it was full of maggots and began to smell. So Moses was angry with them.

²¹Each morning everyone gathered as much as he needed, and when the sun grew hot, it melted away. ²²On the sixth day, they gathered twice as much—two omers[b] for each person—and the leaders of the community came and reported this to Moses. ²³He said to them, "This is what the LORD commanded: 'Tomorrow is to be a day of rest, a holy Sabbath to the LORD. So bake what you want to bake and boil what you want to boil. Save whatever is left and keep it until morning.'"

²⁴So they saved it until morning, as Moses commanded, and it did not stink or get maggots in it. ²⁵"Eat it today," Moses said, "because today is a Sabbath to the LORD. You will not find any of it on the ground today. ²⁶Six days you are to

---

[a]*16* That is, probably about 2 quarts (about 2 liters); also in verses 18, 32, 33 and 36
[b]*22* That is, probably about 4 quarts (about 4.5 liters)

gather it, but on the seventh day, the Sabbath, there will not be any."

²⁷Nevertheless, some of the people went out on the seventh day to gather it, but they found none. ²⁸Then the LORD said to Moses, "How long will you⁴ refuse to keep my commands and my instructions? ²⁹Bear in mind that the LORD has given you the Sabbath; that is why on the sixth day he gives you bread for two days. Everyone is to stay where he is on the seventh day; no one is to go out." ³⁰So the people rested on the seventh day.

³¹The people of Israel called the bread manna.ᵇ It was white like coriander seed and tasted like wafers made with honey. ³²Moses said, "This is what the LORD has commanded: 'Take an omer of manna and keep it for the generations to come, so they can see the bread I gave you to eat in the desert when I brought you out of Egypt.'"

³³So Moses said to Aaron, "Take a jar and put an omer of manna in it. Then place it before the LORD to be kept for the generations to come."

³⁴As the LORD commanded Moses, Aaron put the manna in front of the Testimony, that it might be kept. ³⁵The Israelites ate manna forty years, until they came to a land that was settled; they ate manna until they reached the border of Canaan.

³⁶(An omer is one tenth of an ephah.)

Water From the Rock

17 The whole Israelite community set out from the Desert of Sin, traveling from place to place as the LORD commanded. They camped at Rephidim, but there was no water for the people to drink. ²So they quarreled with Moses and said, "Give us water to drink."

Moses replied, "Why do you quarrel with me? Why do you put the LORD to the test?"

³But the people were thirsty for water there, and they grumbled against Moses. They said, "Why did you bring us up out of Egypt to make us and our children and livestock die of thirst?"

⁴Then Moses cried out to the LORD, "What am I to do with these people? They are almost ready to stone me."

⁵The LORD answered Moses, "Walk on ahead of the people. Take with you some of the elders of Israel and take in your hand the staff with which you struck the Nile, and go. ⁶I will stand there before you by the rock at Horeb. Strike the rock, and water will come out of it for the people to drink." So Moses did this in the sight of the elders of Israel. ⁷And he called the place Massahᶜ and Meribahᵈ because the Israelites quarreled and because they tested the LORD saying, "Is the LORD among us or not?"

The Amalekites Defeated

⁸The Amalekites came and attacked the Israelites at Rephidim. ⁹Moses said to Joshua, "Choose some of our men and go out to fight the Amalekites. Tomorrow I will stand on top of the hill with the staff of God in my hands."

¹⁰So Joshua fought the Amalekites as Moses had ordered, and Moses, Aaron and Hur went to the top of the hill. ¹¹As long as Moses held up his hands, the Israelites were winning, but whenever he lowered his hands, the Amalekites were winning. ¹²When Moses' hands grew tired, they took a stone and put it under him and he sat on it. Aaron and Hur held his hands up—one on one side, one on the other—so that his hands remained steady till sunset. ¹³So Joshua overcame the Amalekite army with the sword.

¹⁴Then the LORD said to Moses, "Write this on a scroll as something to be remembered and make sure that Joshua hears it, because I will completely blot out the memory of Amalek from under heaven."

¹⁵Moses built an altar and called it The LORD is my Banner. ¹⁶He said, "For hands were lifted up to the throne of the LORD. Theᵉ LORD will be at war against the Amalekites from generation to generation."

Jethro Visits Moses

18 Now Jethro, the priest of Midian and father-in-law of Moses, heard of everything God had done for Moses

---

ᵃ28 The Hebrew is plural.   ᵇ31 *Manna* means *What is it?* (see verse 15).   ᶜ7 *Massah* means *testing.*   ᵈ7 *Meribah* means *quarreling.*
ᵉ16 Or "*Because a hand was against the throne of the LORD, the*

and for his people Israel, and how the LORD had brought Israel out of Egypt. ²After Moses had sent away his wife Zipporah, his father-in-law Jethro received her ³and her two sons. One son was named Gershom,ᵃ for Moses said, "I have become an alien in a foreign land"; ⁴and the other was named Eliezer,ᵇ for he said, "My father's God was my helper; he saved me from the sword of Pharaoh." ⁵Jethro, Moses' father-in-law, together

with Moses' sons and wife, came to him in the desert, where he was camped near the mountain of God. ⁶Jethro had sent word to him, "I, your father-in-law Jethro, am coming to you with your wife and her two sons."

⁷So Moses went out to meet his father-in-law and bowed down and kissed him.

ᵃ3 *Gershom* sounds like the Hebrew for *an alien there.* ᵇ4 *Eliezer* means *my God is helper.*

⸢WEDNESDAY⸣

EXODUS 17:8 – 16

The Battle Is the Lord's

17:16 "FOR HANDS WERE LIFTED UP TO THE THRONE OF THE LORD."

Based on this episode, many "Aaron and Hur Prayer Societies" were formed to pray for pastors and other Christian leaders in the 19ᵗʰ century. It was believed that as the spiritual life of the pastor went, especially in prayer, so went the success of the spiritual battle in the church. So people banded together to uphold their pastor in prayer and to intercede for the health of the church.

The picture in Exodus is vivid: The typical posture of prayer in the Bible is to stand with arms lifted and hands held out. Added to this picture of supplication is Moses' staff, the symbol of divine power and conquest. As Joshua leads the troops in battle against the Amalekites in the valley below, Moses stands on the hill above and holds out his staff over the battle. When his arms are raised and the staff is held out, Joshua's army prevails; when Moses tires and the staff is lowered, the Amalekites prevail. So Aaron and Hur come alongside Moses to provide a rock for him to sit on and to hold up his arms.

The imagery of spiritual warfare in this story is also vivid. The battle always belongs to the Lord; we succeed only as we are "strong in the Lord and in his mighty power" (Ephesians 6:10). Prayer is one way we continue to stay strong in God. Only through an ongoing relationship with the Lord can we stay vigilant and fight the battle (see Ephesians 6:18). And prayer is never a solitary exercise; even when we pray alone, we pray in the fellowship of the church, the body of Christ. Paul urged the believers in Rome, "by our Lord Jesus Christ and by the love of the Spirit, to *join me in my struggle* by praying to God for me" (Romans 15:30, italics added).

Hold up your pastor in prayer. Leaders need protection and encouragement to keep on praying.

PRAY:

God, our great Warrior and Defender! Teach us to pray. Teach our leaders to know their need so they will pray. Teach us to pray together.

FOR YOUR NEXT DEVOTIONAL READING, GO TO PAGE 104.

They greeted each other and then went into the tent. [8]Moses told his father-in-law about everything the LORD had done to Pharaoh and the Egyptians for Israel's sake and about all the hardships they had met along the way and how the LORD had saved them.

[9]Jethro was delighted to hear about all the good things the LORD had done for Israel in rescuing them from the hand of the Egyptians. [10]He said, "Praise be to the LORD, who rescued you from the hand of the Egyptians and of Pharaoh, and who rescued the people from the hand of the Egyptians. [11]Now I know that the LORD is greater than all other gods, for he did this to those who had treated Israel arrogantly." [12]Then Jethro, Moses' father-in-law, brought a burnt offering and other sacrifices to God, and Aaron came with all the elders of Israel to eat bread with Moses' father-in-law in the presence of God.

[13]The next day Moses took his seat to serve as judge for the people, and they stood around him from morning till evening. [14]When his father-in-law saw all that Moses was doing for the people, he said, "What is this you are doing for the people? Why do you alone sit as judge, while all these people stand around you from morning till evening?"

[15]Moses answered him, "Because the people come to me to seek God's will. [16]Whenever they have a dispute, it is brought to me, and I decide between the parties and inform them of God's decrees and laws."

[17]Moses' father-in-law replied, "What you are doing is not good. [18]You and these people who come to you will only wear yourselves out. The work is too heavy for you; you cannot handle it alone. [19]Listen now to me and I will give you some advice, and may God be with you. You must be the people's representative before God and bring their disputes to him. [20]Teach them the decrees and laws, and show them the way to live and the duties they are to perform. [21]But select capable men from all the people—men who fear God, trustworthy men who hate dishonest gain—and appoint them as officials over thousands, hundreds, fifties and tens. [22]Have them serve as judges for the people at all times, but have them bring every difficult case to you; the simple cases they can decide themselves. That will make your load lighter, because they will share it with you. [23]If you do this and God so commands, you will be able to stand the strain, and all these people will go home satisfied."

[24]Moses listened to his father-in-law and did everything he said. [25]He chose capable men from all Israel and made them leaders of the people, officials over thousands, hundreds, fifties and tens. [26]They served as judges for the people at all times. The difficult cases they brought to Moses, but the simple ones they decided themselves.

[27]Then Moses sent his father-in-law on his way, and Jethro returned to his own country.

At Mount Sinai

19 In the third month after the Israelites left Egypt—on the very day—they came to the Desert of Sinai. [2]After they set out from Rephidim, they entered the Desert of Sinai, and Israel camped there in the desert in front of the mountain.

[3]Then Moses went up to God, and the LORD called to him from the mountain and said, "This is what you are to say to the house of Jacob and what you are to tell the people of Israel: [4]'You yourselves have seen what I did to Egypt, and how I carried you on eagles' wings and brought you to myself. [5]Now if you obey me fully and keep my covenant, then out of all nations you will be my treasured possession. Although the whole earth is mine, [6]you[a] will be for me a kingdom of priests and a holy nation.' These are the words you are to speak to the Israelites."

[7]So Moses went back and summoned the elders of the people and set before them all the words the LORD had commanded him to speak. [8]The people all responded together, "We will do everything the LORD has said." So Moses brought their answer back to the LORD.

[9]The LORD said to Moses, "I am going to come to you in a dense cloud, so that

---

[a] 5,6 Or possession, for the whole earth is mine. [6]You

the people will hear me speaking with you and will always put their trust in you." Then Moses told the LORD what the people had said.

¹⁰And the LORD said to Moses, "Go to the people and consecrate them today and tomorrow. Have them wash their clothes ¹¹and be ready by the third day, because on that day the LORD will come down on Mount Sinai in the sight of all the people. ¹²Put limits for the people around the mountain and tell them, 'Be careful that you do not go up the mountain or touch the foot of it. Whoever touches the mountain shall surely be put to death. ¹³He shall surely be stoned or shot with arrows; not a hand is to be laid on him. Whether man or animal, he shall not be permitted to live.' Only when the ram's horn sounds a long blast may they go up to the mountain."

¹⁴After Moses had gone down the mountain to the people, he consecrated them, and they washed their clothes. ¹⁵Then he said to the people, "Prepare yourselves for the third day. Abstain from sexual relations."

¹⁶On the morning of the third day there was thunder and lightning, with a thick cloud over the mountain, and a very loud trumpet blast. Everyone in the camp trembled. ¹⁷Then Moses led the people out of the camp to meet with God, and they stood at the foot of the mountain. ¹⁸Mount Sinai was covered with smoke, because the LORD descended on it in fire. The smoke billowed up from it like smoke from a furnace, the whole mountain*ᵃ* trembled violently, ¹⁹and the sound of the trumpet grew louder and louder. Then Moses spoke and the voice of God answered him.*ᵇ*

> MOSES *spoke and the voice of God answered him.*
>
> EXODUS 19:19

²⁰The LORD descended to the top of Mount Sinai and called Moses to the top of the mountain. So Moses went up ²¹and the LORD said to him, "Go down and warn the people so they do not force their way through to see the LORD and many of them

perish. ²²Even the priests, who approach the LORD, must consecrate themselves, or the LORD will break out against them."

²³Moses said to the LORD, "The people cannot come up Mount Sinai, because you yourself warned us, 'Put limits around the mountain and set it apart as holy.'"

²⁴The LORD replied, "Go down and bring Aaron up with you. But the priests and the people must not force their way through to come up to the LORD, or he will break out against them."

²⁵So Moses went down to the people and told them.

The Ten Commandments

20 And God spoke all these words:

²"I am the LORD your God, who brought you out of Egypt, out of the land of slavery.

³"You shall have no other gods before*ᶜ* me.

⁴"You shall not make for yourself an idol in the form of anything in heaven above or on the earth beneath or in the waters below. ⁵You shall not bow down to them or worship them; for I, the LORD your God, am a jealous God, punishing the children for the sin of the fathers to the third and fourth generation of those who hate me, ⁶but showing love to a thousand ⌞generations⌟ of those who love me and keep my commandments.

⁷"You shall not misuse the name of the LORD your God, for the LORD will not hold anyone guiltless who misuses his name.

⁸"Remember the Sabbath day by keeping it holy. ⁹Six days you shall labor and do all your work, ¹⁰but the seventh day is a Sabbath to the LORD your God. On it you shall not do any work, neither you, nor

---

ᵃ18 Most Hebrew manuscripts; a few Hebrew manuscripts and Septuagint *all the people*
ᵇ19 Or *and God answered him with thunder*
ᶜ3 Or *besides*

your son or daughter, nor your manservant or maidservant, nor your animals, nor the alien within your gates. ¹¹For in six days the LORD made the heavens and the earth, the sea, and all that is in them, but he rested on the seventh day. Therefore the LORD blessed the Sabbath day and made it holy.

¹²"Honor your father and your mother, so that you may live long in the land the LORD your God is giving you.

¹³"You shall not murder.

¹⁴"You shall not commit adultery.

¹⁵"You shall not steal.

¹⁶"You shall not give false testimony against your neighbor.

¹⁷"You shall not covet your neighbor's house. You shall not covet your neighbor's wife, or his manservant or maidservant, his ox or donkey, or anything that belongs to your neighbor."

¹⁸When the people saw the thunder and lightning and heard the trumpet and saw the mountain in smoke, they trembled with fear. They stayed at a distance ¹⁹and said to Moses, "Speak to us yourself and we will listen. But do not have God speak to us or we will die."

²⁰Moses said to the people, "Do not be afraid. God has come to test you, so that the fear of God will be with you to keep you from sinning."

²¹The people remained at a distance, while Moses approached the thick darkness where God was.

Idols and Altars

²²Then the LORD said to Moses, "Tell the Israelites this: 'You have seen for yourselves that I have spoken to you from heaven: ²³Do not make any gods to be alongside me; do not make for yourselves gods of silver or gods of gold.

²⁴" 'Make an altar of earth for me and sacrifice on it your burnt offerings and fellowship offerings,ᵃ your sheep and goats and your cattle. Wherever I cause my name to be honored, I will come to you and bless you. ²⁵If you make an altar of stones for me, do not build it with dressed stones, for you will defile it if you use a tool on it. ²⁶And do not go up to my altar on steps, lest your nakedness be exposed on it.'

21 "These are the laws you are to set before them:

Hebrew Servants

²"If you buy a Hebrew servant, he is to serve you for six years. But in the seventh year, he shall go free, without paying anything. ³If he comes alone, he is to go free alone; but if he has a wife when he comes, she is to go with him. ⁴If his master gives him a wife and she bears him sons or daughters, the woman and her children shall belong to her master, and only the man shall go free.

⁵"But if the servant declares, 'I love my master and my wife and children and do not want to go free,' ⁶then his master must take him before the judges.ᵇ He shall take him to the door or the doorpost and pierce his ear with an awl. Then he will be his servant for life.

⁷"If a man sells his daughter as a servant, she is not to go free as menservants do. ⁸If she does not please the master who has selected her for himself,ᶜ he must let her be redeemed. He has no right to sell her to foreigners, because he has broken faith with her. ⁹If he selects her for his son, he must grant her the rights of a daughter. ¹⁰If he marries another woman, he must not deprive the first one of her food, clothing and marital rights. ¹¹If he does not provide her with these three things, she is to go free, without any payment of money.

Personal Injuries

¹²"Anyone who strikes a man and kills him shall surely be put to death. ¹³However, if he does not do it intentionally, but God lets it happen, he is to flee to a place I will designate. ¹⁴But if a man schemes and kills another man deliberately, take him away from my altar and put him to death.

ᵃ24 Traditionally *peace offerings*   ᵇ6 Or *before God*   ᶜ8 Or *master so that he does not choose her*

¹⁵ "Anyone who attacks^a his father or his mother must be put to death.

¹⁶ "Anyone who kidnaps another and either sells him or still has him when he is caught must be put to death.

¹⁷ "Anyone who curses his father or mother must be put to death.

¹⁸ "If men quarrel and one hits the other with a stone or with his fist^b and he does not die but is confined to bed, ¹⁹the one who struck the blow will not be held responsible if the other gets up and walks around outside with his staff; however, he must pay the injured man for the loss of his time and see that he is completely healed.

²⁰ "If a man beats his male or female slave with a rod and the slave dies as a direct result, he must be punished, ²¹but he is not to be punished if the slave gets up after a day or two, since the slave is his property.

²² "If men who are fighting hit a pregnant woman and she gives birth prematurely^c but there is no serious injury, the offender must be fined whatever the woman's husband demands and the court allows. ²³But if there is serious injury, you are to take life for life, ²⁴eye for eye, tooth for tooth, hand for hand, foot for foot, ²⁵burn for burn, wound for wound, bruise for bruise.

²⁶ "If a man hits a manservant or maidservant in the eye and destroys it, he must let the servant go free to compensate for the eye. ²⁷And if he knocks out the tooth of a manservant or maidservant, he must let the servant go free to compensate for the tooth.

²⁸ "If a bull gores a man or a woman to death, the bull must be stoned to death, and its meat must not be eaten. But the owner of the bull will not be held responsible. ²⁹If, however, the bull has had the habit of goring and the owner has been warned but has not kept it penned up and it kills a man or woman, the bull must be stoned and the owner also must be put to death. ³⁰However, if payment is demanded of him, he may redeem his life by paying whatever is demanded. ³¹This law also applies if the bull gores a son or daughter. ³²If the bull gores a male or female slave, the owner must pay thirty shekels^d of silver to the master of the slave, and the bull must be stoned.

³³ "If a man uncovers a pit or digs one and fails to cover it and an ox or a donkey falls into it, ³⁴the owner of the pit must pay for the loss; he must pay its owner, and the dead animal will be his.

³⁵ "If a man's bull injures the bull of another and it dies, they are to sell the live one and divide both the money and the dead animal equally. ³⁶However, if it was known that the bull had the habit of goring, yet the owner did not keep it penned up, the owner must pay, animal for animal, and the dead animal will be his.

Protection of Property

22 "If a man steals an ox or a sheep and slaughters it or sells it, he must pay back five head of cattle for the ox and four sheep for the sheep.

² "If a thief is caught breaking in and is struck so that he dies, the defender is not guilty of bloodshed; ³but if it happens^e after sunrise, he is guilty of bloodshed.

"A thief must certainly make restitution, but if he has nothing, he must be sold to pay for his theft.

⁴ "If the stolen animal is found alive in his possession—whether ox or donkey or sheep—he must pay back double.

⁵ "If a man grazes his livestock in a field or vineyard and lets them stray and they graze in another man's field, he must make restitution from the best of his own field or vineyard.

⁶ "If a fire breaks out and spreads into thornbushes so that it burns shocks of grain or standing grain or the whole field, the one who started the fire must make restitution.

⁷ "If a man gives his neighbor silver or goods for safekeeping and they are stolen from the neighbor's house, the thief, if he is caught, must pay back double. ⁸But if the thief is not found, the owner of the house must appear before the judges^f to determine whether he has laid his hands on the other man's property. ⁹In all cases of illegal possession of an ox, a

---

^a15 Or kills   ^b18 Or with a tool   ^c22 Or she has a miscarriage   ^d32 That is, about 12 ounces (about 0.3 kilogram)   ^e3 Or if he strikes him   ^f8 Or before God; also in verse 9

donkey, a sheep, a garment, or any other lost property about which somebody says, 'This is mine,' both parties are to bring their cases before the judges. The one whom the judges declare[a] guilty must pay back double to his neighbor.

10 "If a man gives a donkey, an ox, a sheep or any other animal to his neighbor for safekeeping and it dies or is injured or is taken away while no one is looking, 11the issue between them will be settled by the taking of an oath before the LORD that the neighbor did not lay hands on the other person's property. The owner is to accept this, and no restitution is required. 12But if the animal was stolen from the neighbor, he must make restitution to the owner. 13If it was torn to pieces by a wild animal, he shall bring in the remains as evidence and he will not be required to pay for the torn animal.

14 "If a man borrows an animal from his neighbor and it is injured or dies while the owner is not present, he must make restitution. 15But if the owner is with the animal, the borrower will not have to pay. If the animal was hired, the money paid for the hire covers the loss.

Social Responsibility

16 "If a man seduces a virgin who is not pledged to be married and sleeps with her, he must pay the bride-price, and she shall be his wife. 17If her father absolutely refuses to give her to him, he must still pay the bride-price for virgins.

18 "Do not allow a sorceress to live.

19 "Anyone who has sexual relations with an animal must be put to death.

20 "Whoever sacrifices to any god other than the LORD must be destroyed.[b]

21 "Do not mistreat an alien or oppress him, for you were aliens in Egypt.

22 "Do not take advantage of a widow or an orphan. 23If you do and they cry out to me, I will certainly hear their cry. 24My anger will be aroused, and I will kill you with the sword; your wives will become widows and your children fatherless.

25 "If you lend money to one of my people among you who is needy, do not be like a moneylender; charge him no interest.[c] 26If you take your neighbor's cloak as a pledge, return it to him by sunset,

27because his cloak is the only covering he has for his body. What else will he sleep in? When he cries out to me, I will hear, for I am compassionate.

28 "Do not blaspheme God[d] or curse the ruler of your people.

29 "Do not hold back offerings from your granaries or your vats.[e]

"You must give me the firstborn of your sons. 30Do the same with your cattle and your sheep. Let them stay with their mothers for seven days, but give them to me on the eighth day.

31 "You are to be my holy people. So do not eat the meat of an animal torn by wild beasts; throw it to the dogs.

Laws of Justice and Mercy

23 "Do not spread false reports. Do not help a wicked man by being a malicious witness.

2 "Do not follow the crowd in doing wrong. When you give testimony in a lawsuit, do not pervert justice by siding with the crowd, 3and do not show favoritism to a poor man in his lawsuit.

4 "If you come across your enemy's ox or donkey wandering off, be sure to take it back to him. 5If you see the donkey of someone who hates you fallen down under its load, do not leave it there; be sure you help him with it.

6 "Do not deny justice to your poor people in their lawsuits. 7Have nothing to do with a false charge and do not put an innocent or honest person to death, for I will not acquit the guilty.

8 "Do not accept a bribe, for a bribe blinds those who see and twists the words of the righteous.

9 "Do not oppress an alien; you yourselves know how it feels to be aliens, because you were aliens in Egypt.

Sabbath Laws

10 "For six years you are to sow your fields and harvest the crops, 11but during the seventh year let the land lie unplowed and unused. Then the poor among your

---

[a]9 Or whom God declares   [b]20 The Hebrew term refers to the irrevocable giving over of things or persons to the LORD, often by totally destroying them.   [c]25 Or excessive interest   [d]28 Or Do not revile the judges   [e]29 The meaning of the Hebrew for this phrase is uncertain.

people may get food from it, and the wild animals may eat what they leave. Do the same with your vineyard and your olive grove.

¹²"Six days do your work, but on the seventh day do not work, so that your ox and your donkey may rest and the slave born in your household, and the alien as well, may be refreshed.

¹³"Be careful to do everything I have said to you. Do not invoke the names of other gods; do not let them be heard on your lips.

The Three Annual Festivals

¹⁴"Three times a year you are to celebrate a festival to me.

¹⁵"Celebrate the Feast of Unleavened Bread; for seven days eat bread made without yeast, as I commanded you. Do this at the appointed time in the month of Abib, for in that month you came out of Egypt.

"No one is to appear before me empty-handed.

¹⁶"Celebrate the Feast of Harvest with the firstfruits of the crops you sow in your field.

"Celebrate the Feast of Ingathering at the end of the year, when you gather in your crops from the field.

¹⁷"Three times a year all the men are to appear before the Sovereign LORD.

¹⁸"Do not offer the blood of a sacrifice to me along with anything containing yeast.

"The fat of my festival offerings must not be kept until morning.

¹⁹"Bring the best of the firstfruits of your soil to the house of the LORD your God.

"Do not cook a young goat in its mother's milk.

God's Angel to Prepare the Way

²⁰"See, I am sending an angel ahead of you to guard you along the way and to bring you to the place I have prepared. ²¹Pay attention to him and listen to what he says. Do not rebel against him; he will not forgive your rebellion, since my Name is in him. ²²If you listen carefully to what he says and do all that I say, I will be an enemy to your enemies and will oppose those who oppose you. ²³My angel

will go ahead of you and bring you into the land of the Amorites, Hittites, Perizzites, Canaanites, Hivites and Jebusites, and I will wipe them out. ²⁴Do not bow down before their gods or worship them or follow their practices. You must demolish them and break their sacred stones to pieces. ²⁵Worship the LORD your God, and his blessing will be on your food and water. I will take away sickness from among you, ²⁶and none will miscarry or be barren in your land. I will give you a full life span.

> "WORSHIP the LORD your God, and his blessing will be on your food and water."
>
> EXODUS 23:25

²⁷"I will send my terror ahead of you and throw into confusion every nation you encounter. I will make all your enemies turn their backs and run. ²⁸I will send the hornet ahead of you to drive the Hivites, Canaanites and Hittites out of your way. ²⁹But I will not drive them out in a single year, because the land would become desolate and the wild animals too numerous for you. ³⁰Little by little I will drive them out before you, until you have increased enough to take possession of the land.

³¹"I will establish your borders from the Red Sea[a] to the Sea of the Philistines,[b] and from the desert to the River.[c] I will hand over to you the people who live in the land and you will drive them out before you. ³²Do not make a covenant with them or with their gods. ³³Do not let them live in your land, or they will cause you to sin against me, because the worship of their gods will certainly be a snare to you."

The Covenant Confirmed

24 Then he said to Moses, "Come up to the LORD, you and Aaron, Nadab and Abihu, and seventy of the elders of Israel. You are to worship at a distance, ²but Moses alone is to approach

---

a31 Hebrew *Yam Suph*; that is, Sea of Reeds
b31 That is, the Mediterranean   *c31* That is, the Euphrates

the LORD; the others must not come near. And the people may not come up with him."

³When Moses went and told the people all the LORD's words and laws, they responded with one voice, "Everything the LORD has said we will do." ⁴Moses then wrote down everything the LORD had said.

He got up early the next morning and built an altar at the foot of the mountain and set up twelve stone pillars representing the twelve tribes of Israel. ⁵Then he sent young Israelite men, and they offered burnt offerings and sacrificed young bulls as fellowship offerings[a] to the LORD. ⁶Moses took half of the blood and put it in bowls, and the other half he sprinkled on the altar. ⁷Then he took the Book of the Covenant and read it to the people. They responded, "We will do everything the LORD has said; we will obey."

⁸Moses then took the blood, sprinkled it on the people and said, "This is the blood of the covenant that the LORD has made with you in accordance with all these words."

⁹Moses and Aaron, Nadab and Abihu, and the seventy elders of Israel went up ¹⁰and saw the God of Israel. Under his feet was something like a pavement made of sapphire,[b] clear as the sky itself. ¹¹But God did not raise his hand against these leaders of the Israelites; they saw God, and they ate and drank.

¹²The LORD said to Moses, "Come up to me on the mountain and stay here, and I will give you the tablets of stone, with the law and commands I have written for their instruction."

¹³Then Moses set out with Joshua his aide, and Moses went up on the mountain of God. ¹⁴He said to the elders, "Wait here for us until we come back to you. Aaron and Hur are with you, and anyone involved in a dispute can go to them."

¹⁵When Moses went up on the mountain, the cloud covered it, ¹⁶and the glory of the LORD settled on Mount Sinai. For six days the cloud covered the mountain, and on the seventh day the LORD called to Moses from within the cloud. ¹⁷To the Israelites the glory of the LORD looked like a consuming fire on top of the mountain. ¹⁸Then Moses entered the cloud as he went on up the mountain. And he stayed on the mountain forty days and forty nights.

Offerings for the Tabernacle

25 The LORD said to Moses, ²"Tell the Israelites to bring me an offering. You are to receive the offering for me from each man whose heart prompts him to give. ³These are the offerings you are to receive from them: gold, silver and bronze; ⁴blue, purple and scarlet yarn and fine linen; goat hair; ⁵ram skins dyed red and hides of sea cows[c]; acacia wood; ⁶olive oil for the light; spices for the anointing oil and for the fragrant incense; ⁷and onyx stones and other gems to be mounted on the ephod and breastpiece.

⁸"Then have them make a sanctuary for me, and I will dwell among them. ⁹Make this tabernacle and all its furnishings exactly like the pattern I will show you.

The Ark

¹⁰"Have them make a chest of acacia wood—two and a half cubits long, a cubit and a half wide, and a cubit and a half high.[d] ¹¹Overlay it with pure gold, both inside and out, and make a gold molding around it. ¹²Cast four gold rings for it and fasten them to its four feet, with two rings on one side and two rings on the other. ¹³Then make poles of acacia wood and overlay them with gold. ¹⁴Insert the poles into the rings on the sides of the chest to carry it. ¹⁵The poles are to remain in the rings of this ark; they are not to be removed. ¹⁶Then put in the ark the Testimony, which I will give you.

¹⁷"Make an atonement cover[e] of pure gold—two and a half cubits long and a cubit and a half wide.[f] ¹⁸And make two cherubim out of hammered gold at the ends of the cover. ¹⁹Make one cherub on one end and the second cherub on the other; make the cherubim of one piece

---

[a]5 Traditionally *peace offerings*   [b]10 Or *lapis lazuli*   [c]5 That is, dugongs   [d]10 That is, about 3 3/4 feet (about 1.1 meters) long and 2 1/4 feet (about 0.7 meter) wide and high   [e]17 Traditionally *a mercy seat*   [f]17 That is, about 3 3/4 feet (about 1.1 meters) long and 2 1/4 feet (about 0.7 meter) wide

with the cover, at the two ends. ²⁰The cherubim are to have their wings spread upward, overshadowing the cover with them. The cherubim are to face each other, looking toward the cover. ²¹Place the cover on top of the ark and put in the ark the Testimony, which I will give you. ²²There, above the cover between the two cherubim that are over the ark of the Testimony, I will meet with you and give you all my commands for the Israelites.

The Table

²³"Make a table of acacia wood—two cubits long, a cubit wide and a cubit and a half high.ᵃ ²⁴Overlay it with pure gold and make a gold molding around it. ²⁵Also make around it a rim a handbreadthᵇ wide and put a gold molding on the rim. ²⁶Make four gold rings for the table and fasten them to the four corners, where the four legs are. ²⁷The rings are to be close to the rim to hold the poles used in carrying the table. ²⁸Make the poles of acacia wood, overlay them with gold and carry the table with them. ²⁹And make its plates and dishes of pure gold, as well as its pitchers and bowls for the pouring out of offerings. ³⁰Put the bread of the Presence on this table to be before me at all times.

The Lampstand

³¹"Make a lampstand of pure gold and hammer it out, base and shaft; its flowerlike cups, buds and blossoms shall be of one piece with it. ³²Six branches are to extend from the sides of the lampstand—three on one side and three on the other. ³³Three cups shaped like almond flowers with buds and blossoms are to be on one branch, three on the next branch, and the same for all six branches extending from the lampstand. ³⁴And on the lampstand there are to be four cups shaped like almond flowers with buds and blossoms. ³⁵One bud shall be under the first pair of branches extending from the lampstand, a second bud under the second pair, and a third bud under the third pair—six branches in all. ³⁶The buds and branches shall all be of one piece with the lampstand, hammered out of pure gold.

³⁷"Then make its seven lamps and set them up on it so that they light the space

in front of it. ³⁸Its wick trimmers and trays are to be of pure gold. ³⁹A talentᶜ of pure gold is to be used for the lampstand and all these accessories. ⁴⁰See that you make them according to the pattern shown you on the mountain.

The Tabernacle

26 "Make the tabernacle with ten curtains of finely twisted linen and blue, purple and scarlet yarn, with cherubim worked into them by a skilled craftsman. ²All the curtains are to be the same size—twenty-eight cubits long and four cubits wide.ᵈ ³Join five of the curtains together, and do the same with the other five. ⁴Make loops of blue material along the edge of the end curtain in one set, and do the same with the end curtain in the other set. ⁵Make fifty loops on one curtain and fifty loops on the end curtain of the other set, with the loops opposite each other. ⁶Then make fifty gold clasps and use them to fasten the curtains together so that the tabernacle is a unit.

⁷"Make curtains of goat hair for the tent over the tabernacle—eleven altogether. ⁸All eleven curtains are to be the same size—thirty cubits long and four cubits wide.ᵉ ⁹Join five of the curtains together into one set and the other six into another set. Fold the sixth curtain double at the front of the tent. ¹⁰Make fifty loops along the edge of the end curtain in one set and also along the edge of the end curtain in the other set. ¹¹Then make fifty bronze clasps and put them in the loops to fasten the tent together as a unit. ¹²As for the additional length of the tent curtains, the half curtain that is left over is to hang down at the rear of the tabernacle. ¹³The tent curtains will be a cubitᶠ longer on both sides; what is left will hang over the sides of the tabernacle so as to cover it. ¹⁴Make for the tent a cov-

---

ᵃ23 That is, about 3 feet (about 0.9 meter) long and 1 1/2 feet (about 0.5 meter) wide and 2 1/4 feet (about 0.7 meter) high   ᵇ25 That is, about 3 inches (about 8 centimeters)   ᶜ39 That is, about 75 pounds (about 34 kilograms) ᵈ2 That is, about 42 feet (about 12.5 meters) long and 6 feet (about 1.8 meters) wide   ᵉ8 That is, about 45 feet (about 13.5 meters) long and 6 feet (about 1.8 meters) wide   ᶠ13 That is, about 1 1/2 feet (about 0.5 meter)

ering of ram skins dyed red, and over that a covering of hides of sea cows.[a]

15 "Make upright frames of acacia wood for the tabernacle. 16Each frame is to be ten cubits long and a cubit and a half wide,[b] 17with two projections set parallel to each other. Make all the frames of the tabernacle in this way. 18Make twenty frames for the south side of the tabernacle 19and make forty silver bases to go under them—two bases for each frame, one under each projection. 20For the other side, the north side of the tabernacle, make twenty frames 21and forty silver bases—two under each frame. 22Make six frames for the far end, that is, the west end of the tabernacle, 23and make two frames for the corners at the far end. 24At these two corners they must be double from the bottom all the way to the top, and fitted into a single ring; both shall be like that. 25So there will be eight frames and sixteen silver bases—two under each frame.

26 "Also make crossbars of acacia wood: five for the frames on one side of the tabernacle, 27five for those on the other side, and five for the frames on the west, at the far end of the tabernacle. 28The center crossbar is to extend from end to end at the middle of the frames. 29Overlay the frames with gold and make gold rings to hold the crossbars. Also overlay the crossbars with gold.

30 "Set up the tabernacle according to the plan shown you on the mountain.

31 "Make a curtain of blue, purple and scarlet yarn and finely twisted linen, with cherubim worked into it by a skilled craftsman. 32Hang it with gold hooks on four posts of acacia wood overlaid with gold and standing on four silver bases. 33Hang the curtain from the clasps and place the ark of the Testimony behind the curtain. The curtain will separate the Holy Place from the Most Holy Place. 34Put the atonement cover on the ark of the Testimony in the Most Holy Place. 35Place the table outside the curtain on the north side of the tabernacle and put the lampstand opposite it on the south side.

36 "For the entrance to the tent make a curtain of blue, purple and scarlet yarn and finely twisted linen—the work of an embroiderer. 37Make gold hooks for this curtain and five posts of acacia wood overlaid with gold. And cast five bronze bases for them.

The Altar of Burnt Offering

27 "Build an altar of acacia wood, three cubits[c] high; it is to be square, five cubits long and five cubits wide.[d] 2Make a horn at each of the four corners, so that the horns and the altar are of one piece, and overlay the altar with bronze. 3Make all its utensils of bronze—its pots to remove the ashes, and its shovels, sprinkling bowls, meat forks and firepans. 4Make a grating for it, a bronze network, and make a bronze ring at each of the four corners of the network. 5Put it under the ledge of the altar so that it is halfway up the altar. 6Make poles of acacia wood for the altar and overlay them with bronze. 7The poles are to be inserted into the rings so they will be on two sides of the altar when it is carried. 8Make the altar hollow, out of boards. It is to be made just as you were shown on the mountain.

The Courtyard

9 "Make a courtyard for the tabernacle. The south side shall be a hundred cubits[e] long and is to have curtains of finely twisted linen, 10with twenty posts and twenty bronze bases and with silver hooks and bands on the posts. 11The north side shall also be a hundred cubits long and is to have curtains, with twenty posts and twenty bronze bases and with silver hooks and bands on the posts.

12 "The west end of the courtyard shall be fifty cubits[f] wide and have curtains, with ten posts and ten bases. 13On the east end, toward the sunrise, the courtyard shall also be fifty cubits wide. 14Curtains fifteen cubits[g] long are to be on one side of the entrance, with three posts and

---

[a]14 That is, dugongs   [b]16 That is, about 15 feet (about 4.5 meters) long and 2 1/4 feet (about 0.7 meter) wide   [c]1 That is, about 4 1/2 feet (about 1.3 meters)   [d]1 That is, about 7 1/2 feet (about 2.3 meters) long and wide   [e]9 That is, about 150 feet (about 46 meters); also in verse 11   [f]12 That is, about 75 feet (about 23 meters); also in verse 13   [g]14 That is, about 22 1/2 feet (about 6.9 meters); also in verse 15

three bases, 15and curtains fifteen cubits long are to be on the other side, with three posts and three bases.

16"For the entrance to the courtyard, provide a curtain twenty cubits[a] long, of blue, purple and scarlet yarn and finely twisted linen—the work of an embroiderer—with four posts and four bases. 17All the posts around the courtyard are to have silver bands and hooks, and bronze bases. 18The courtyard shall be a hundred cubits long and fifty cubits wide,[b] with curtains of finely twisted linen five cubits[c] high, and with bronze bases. 19All the other articles used in the service of the tabernacle, whatever their function, including all the tent pegs for it and those for the courtyard, are to be of bronze.

Oil for the Lampstand

20"Command the Israelites to bring you clear oil of pressed olives for the light so that the lamps may be kept burning. 21In the Tent of Meeting, outside the curtain that is in front of the Testimony, Aaron

> 66 Prayer is reaching out and after the unseen; fasting, letting go of all that is seen and temporal. Fasting helps express, deepens, confirms the resolution that we are ready to sacrifice anything, even ourselves, to attain what we seek for the kingdom of God. 99
>
> ANDREW MURRAY

and his sons are to keep the lamps burning before the LORD from evening till morning. This is to be a lasting ordinance among the Israelites for the generations to come.

The Priestly Garments

28 "Have Aaron your brother brought to you from among the Israelites, along with his sons Nadab and Abihu, Eleazar and Ithamar, so they may serve me as priests. 2Make sacred garments for your brother Aaron, to give him dignity and honor. 3Tell all the skilled men to whom I have given wisdom in such matters that they are to make garments for Aaron, for his consecration, so he may

serve me as priest. 4These are the garments they are to make: a breastpiece, an ephod, a robe, a woven tunic, a turban and a sash. They are to make these sacred garments for your brother Aaron and his sons, so they may serve me as priests. 5Have them use gold, and blue, purple and scarlet yarn, and fine linen.

The Ephod

6"Make the ephod of gold, and of blue, purple and scarlet yarn, and of finely twisted linen—the work of a skilled craftsman. 7It is to have two shoulder pieces attached to two of its corners, so it can be fastened. 8Its skillfully woven waistband is to be like it—of one piece with the ephod and made with gold, and with blue, purple and scarlet yarn, and with finely twisted linen.

9"Take two onyx stones and engrave on them the names of the sons of Israel 10in the order of their birth—six names on one stone and the remaining six on the other. 11Engrave the names of the sons of Israel on the two stones the way a gem cutter engraves a seal. Then mount the stones in gold filigree settings 12and fasten them on the shoulder pieces of the ephod as memorial stones for the sons of Israel. Aaron is to bear the names on his shoulders as a memorial before the LORD. 13Make gold filigree settings 14and two braided chains of pure gold, like a rope, and attach the chains to the settings.

The Breastpiece

15"Fashion a breastpiece for making decisions—the work of a skilled craftsman. Make it like the ephod: of gold, and of blue, purple and scarlet yarn, and of finely twisted linen. 16It is to be square—a span[d] long and a span wide—and folded double. 17Then mount four rows of precious stones on it. In the first row there shall be a ruby, a topaz and a beryl; 18in the second row a turquoise, a sapphire[e] and an emerald; 19in the third row

---

[a]16 That is, about 30 feet (about 9 meters)
[b]18 That is, about 150 feet (about 46 meters) long and 75 feet (about 23 meters) wide   [c]18 That is, about 7 1/2 feet (about 2.3 meters)
[d]16 That is, about 9 inches (about 22 centimeters)   [e]18 Or lapis lazuli

a jacinth, an agate and an amethyst; [20]in the fourth row a chrysolite, an onyx and a jasper.[a] Mount them in gold filigree settings. [21]There are to be twelve stones, one for each of the names of the sons of Israel, each engraved like a seal with the name of one of the twelve tribes.

[22]"For the breastpiece make braided chains of pure gold, like a rope. [23]Make two gold rings for it and fasten them to two corners of the breastpiece. [24]Fasten the two gold chains to the rings at the corners of the breastpiece, [25]and the other ends of the chains to the two settings, attaching them to the shoulder pieces of the ephod at the front. [26]Make two gold rings and attach them to the other two corners of the breastpiece on the inside edge next to the ephod. [27]Make two more gold rings and attach them to the bottom of the shoulder pieces on the front of the ephod, close to the seam just above the waistband of the ephod. [28]The rings of the breastpiece are to be tied to the rings of the ephod with blue cord, connecting it to the waistband, so that the breastpiece will not swing out from the ephod.

[29]"Whenever Aaron enters the Holy Place, he will bear the names of the sons of Israel over his heart on the breastpiece of decision as a continuing memorial before the LORD. [30]Also put the Urim and the Thummim in the breastpiece, so they may be over Aaron's heart whenever he enters the presence of the LORD. Thus Aaron will always bear the means of making decisions for the Israelites over his heart before the LORD.

Other Priestly Garments

[31]"Make the robe of the ephod entirely of blue cloth, [32]with an opening for the head in its center. There shall be a woven edge like a collar[b] around this opening, so that it will not tear. [33]Make pomegranates of blue, purple and scarlet yarn around the hem of the robe, with gold bells between them. [34]The gold bells and the pomegranates are to alternate around the hem of the robe. [35]Aaron must wear it when he ministers. The sound of the bells will be heard when he enters the Holy Place before the LORD and when he comes out, so that he will not die.

[36]"Make a plate of pure gold and engrave on it as on a seal: HOLY TO THE LORD. [37]Fasten a blue cord to it to attach it to the turban; it is to be on the front of the turban. [38]It will be on Aaron's forehead, and he will bear the guilt involved in the sacred gifts the Israelites consecrate, whatever their gifts may be. It will be on Aaron's forehead continually so that they will be acceptable to the LORD.

[39]"Weave the tunic of fine linen and make the turban of fine linen. The sash is to be the work of an embroiderer. [40]Make tunics, sashes and headbands for Aaron's sons, to give them dignity and honor. [41]After you put these clothes on your brother Aaron and his sons, anoint and ordain them. Consecrate them so they may serve me as priests.

[42]"Make linen undergarments as a covering for the body, reaching from the waist to the thigh. [43]Aaron and his sons must wear them whenever they enter the Tent of Meeting or approach the altar to minister in the Holy Place, so that they will not incur guilt and die.

"This is to be a lasting ordinance for Aaron and his descendants.

Consecration of the Priests

29 "This is what you are to do to consecrate them, so they may serve me as priests: Take a young bull and two rams without defect. [2]And from fine wheat flour, without yeast, make bread, and cakes mixed with oil, and wafers spread with oil. [3]Put them in a basket and present them in it—along with the bull and the two rams. [4]Then bring Aaron and his sons to the entrance to the Tent of Meeting and wash them with water. [5]Take the garments and dress Aaron with the tunic, the robe of the ephod, the ephod itself and the breastpiece. Fasten the ephod on him by its skillfully woven waistband. [6]Put the turban on his head and attach the sacred diadem to the turban. [7]Take the anointing oil and anoint him by pouring it on his head. [8]Bring his sons and dress them in tunics [9]and put headbands on them. Then tie sashes on Aaron and his sons.[c] The priesthood is

---

[a]20 The precise identification of some of these precious stones is uncertain.   [b]32 The meaning of the Hebrew for this word is uncertain.
[c]9 Hebrew; Septuagint *on them*

theirs by a lasting ordinance. In this way you shall ordain Aaron and his sons.

¹⁰"Bring the bull to the front of the Tent of Meeting, and Aaron and his sons shall lay their hands on its head. ¹¹Slaughter it in the Lᴏʀᴅ's presence at the entrance to the Tent of Meeting. ¹²Take some of the bull's blood and put it on the horns of the altar with your finger, and pour out the rest of it at the base of the altar. ¹³Then take all the fat around the inner parts, the covering of the liver, and both kidneys with the fat on them, and burn them on the altar. ¹⁴But burn the bull's flesh and its hide and its offal outside the camp. It is a sin offering.

¹⁵"Take one of the rams, and Aaron and his sons shall lay their hands on its head. ¹⁶Slaughter it and take the blood and sprinkle it against the altar on all sides. ¹⁷Cut the ram into pieces and wash the inner parts and the legs, putting them with the head and the other pieces. ¹⁸Then burn the entire ram on the altar. It is a burnt offering to the Lᴏʀᴅ, a pleasing aroma, an offering made to the Lᴏʀᴅ by fire.

¹⁹"Take the other ram, and Aaron and his sons shall lay their hands on its head. ²⁰Slaughter it, take some of its blood and put it on the lobes of the right ears of Aaron and his sons, on the thumbs of their right hands, and on the big toes of their right feet. Then sprinkle blood against the altar on all sides. ²¹And take some of the blood on the altar and some of the anointing oil and sprinkle it on Aaron and his garments and on his sons and their garments. Then he and his sons and their garments will be consecrated.

²²"Take from this ram the fat, the fat tail, the fat around the inner parts, the covering of the liver, both kidneys with the fat on them, and the right thigh. (This is the ram for the ordination.) ²³From the basket of bread made without yeast, which is before the Lᴏʀᴅ, take a loaf, and a cake made with oil, and a wafer. ²⁴Put all these in the hands of Aaron and his sons and wave them before the Lᴏʀᴅ as a wave offering. ²⁵Then take them from their hands and burn them on the altar along with the burnt offering for a pleasing aroma to the Lᴏʀᴅ, an offering made to the Lᴏʀᴅ by fire. ²⁶After you take the breast of the ram for Aaron's ordination,

wave it before the Lᴏʀᴅ as a wave offering, and it will be your share.

²⁷"Consecrate those parts of the ordination ram that belong to Aaron and his sons: the breast that was waved and the thigh that was presented. ²⁸This is always to be the regular share from the Israelites for Aaron and his sons. It is the contribution the Israelites are to make to the Lᴏʀᴅ from their fellowship offerings.ᵃ

²⁹"Aaron's sacred garments will belong to his descendants so that they can be anointed and ordained in them. ³⁰The son who succeeds him as priest and comes to the Tent of Meeting to minister in the Holy Place is to wear them seven days.

³¹"Take the ram for the ordination and cook the meat in a sacred place. ³²At the entrance to the Tent of Meeting, Aaron and his sons are to eat the meat of the ram and the bread that is in the basket. ³³They are to eat these offerings by which atonement was made for their ordination and consecration. But no one else may eat them, because they are sacred. ³⁴And if any of the meat of the ordination ram or any bread is left over till morning, burn it up. It must not be eaten, because it is sacred.

³⁵"Do for Aaron and his sons everything I have commanded you, taking seven days to ordain them. ³⁶Sacrifice a bull each day as a sin offering to make atonement. Purify the altar by making atonement for it, and anoint it to consecrate it. ³⁷For seven days make atonement for the altar and consecrate it. Then the altar will be most holy, and whatever touches it will be holy.

³⁸"This is what you are to offer on the altar regularly each day: two lambs a year old. ³⁹Offer one in the morning and the other at twilight. ⁴⁰With the first lamb offer a tenth of an ephahᵇ of fine flour mixed with a quarter of a hinᶜ of oil from pressed olives, and a quarter of a hin of wine as a drink offering. ⁴¹Sacrifice the other lamb at twilight with the same grain offering and its drink offering as in the morning—a pleasing aroma, an offering made to the Lᴏʀᴅ by fire.

ᵃ28 Traditionally *peace offerings*   ᵇ40 That is, probably about 2 quarts (about 2 liters)   ᶜ40 That is, probably about 1 quart (about 1 liter)

42"For the generations to come this burnt offering is to be made regularly at the entrance to the Tent of Meeting before the LORD. There I will meet you and speak to you; 43there also I will meet with the Israelites, and the place will be consecrated by my glory.

44"So I will consecrate the Tent of Meeting and the altar and will consecrate Aaron and his sons to serve me as priests. 45Then I will dwell among the Israelites and be their God. 46They will know that I am the LORD their God, who brought them out of Egypt so that I might dwell among them. I am the LORD their God.

The Altar of Incense

30 "Make an altar of acacia wood for burning incense. 2It is to be square, a cubit long and a cubit wide, and two cubits high[a]—its horns of one piece with it. 3Overlay the top and all the sides and the horns with pure gold, and make a gold molding around it. 4Make two gold rings for the altar below the molding—two on opposite sides—to hold the poles used to carry it. 5Make the poles of acacia wood and overlay them with gold. 6Put the altar in front of the curtain that is before the ark of the Testimony—before the atonement cover that is over the Testimony—where I will meet with you.

7"Aaron must burn fragrant incense on the altar every morning when he tends the lamps. 8He must burn incense again when he lights the lamps at twilight so incense will burn regularly before the LORD for the generations to come. 9Do not offer on this altar any other incense or any burnt offering or grain offering, and do not pour a drink offering on it. 10Once a year Aaron shall make atonement on its horns. This annual atonement must be made with the blood of the atoning sin offering for the generations to come. It is most holy to the LORD."

Atonement Money

11Then the LORD said to Moses, 12"When you take a census of the Israelites to count them, each one must pay the LORD a ransom for his life at the time he is counted. Then no plague will come on them when you number them. 13Each one

who crosses over to those already counted is to give a half shekel,[b] according to the sanctuary shekel, which weighs twenty gerahs. This half shekel is an offering to the LORD. 14All who cross over, those twenty years old or more, are to give an offering to the LORD. 15The rich are not to give more than a half shekel and the poor are not to give less when you make the offering to the LORD to atone for your lives. 16Receive the atonement money from the Israelites and use it for the service of the Tent of Meeting. It will be a memorial for the Israelites before the LORD, making atonement for your lives."

Basin for Washing

17Then the LORD said to Moses, 18"Make a bronze basin, with its bronze stand, for washing. Place it between the Tent of Meeting and the altar, and put water in it. 19Aaron and his sons are to wash their hands and feet with water from it. 20Whenever they enter the Tent of Meeting, they shall wash with water so that they will not die. Also, when they approach the altar to minister by presenting an offering made to the LORD by fire, 21they shall wash their hands and feet so that they will not die. This is to be a lasting ordinance for Aaron and his descendants for the generations to come."

Anointing Oil

22Then the LORD said to Moses, 23"Take the following fine spices: 500 shekels[c] of liquid myrrh, half as much (that is, 250 shekels) of fragrant cinnamon, 250 shekels of fragrant cane, 24500 shekels of cassia—all according to the sanctuary shekel—and a hin[d] of olive oil. 25Make these into a sacred anointing oil, a fragrant blend, the work of a perfumer. It will be the sacred anointing oil. 26Then use it to anoint the Tent of Meeting, the ark of the Testimony, 27the table and all its articles, the lampstand and its accessories, the altar of incense, 28the altar of

---

[a]2 That is, about 1 1/2 feet (about 0.5 meter) long and wide and about 3 feet (about 0.9 meter) high
[b]13 That is, about 1/5 ounce (about 6 grams); also in verse 15   [c]23 That is, about 12 1/2 pounds (about 6 kilograms)   [d]24 That is, probably about 4 quarts (about 4 liters)

burnt offering and all its utensils, and the basin with its stand. ²⁹You shall consecrate them so they will be most holy, and whatever touches them will be holy.

³⁰"Anoint Aaron and his sons and consecrate them so they may serve me as priests. ³¹Say to the Israelites, 'This is to be my sacred anointing oil for the generations to come. ³²Do not pour it on men's bodies and do not make any oil with the same formula. It is sacred, and you are to consider it sacred. ³³Whoever makes perfume like it and whoever puts it on anyone other than a priest must be cut off from his people.'"

Incense

³⁴Then the LORD said to Moses, "Take fragrant spices—gum resin, onycha and galbanum—and pure frankincense, all in equal amounts, ³⁵and make a fragrant blend of incense, the work of a perfumer. It is to be salted and pure and sacred. ³⁶Grind some of it to powder and place it in front of the Testimony in the Tent of Meeting, where I will meet with you. It shall be most holy to you. ³⁷Do not make any incense with this formula for yourselves; consider it holy to the LORD. ³⁸Whoever makes any like it to enjoy its fragrance must be cut off from his people."

Bezalel and Oholiab

31 Then the LORD said to Moses, ²"See, I have chosen Bezalel son of Uri, the son of Hur, of the tribe of Judah, ³and I have filled him with the Spirit of God, with skill, ability and knowledge in all kinds of crafts— ⁴to make artistic designs for work in gold, silver and bronze, ⁵to cut and set stones, to work in wood, and to engage in all kinds of craftsmanship. ⁶Moreover, I have appointed Oholiab son of Ahisamach, of the tribe of Dan, to help him. Also I have given skill to all the craftsmen to make everything I have commanded you: ⁷the Tent of Meeting, the ark of the Testimony with the atonement cover on it, and all the other furnishings of the tent— ⁸the table and its articles, the pure gold lampstand and all its accessories, the altar of incense, ⁹the altar of burnt offering and all its utensils, the basin with its stand— ¹⁰and also the

woven garments, both the sacred garments for Aaron the priest and the garments for his sons when they serve as priests, ¹¹and the anointing oil and fragrant incense for the Holy Place. They are to make them just as I commanded you."

The Sabbath

¹²Then the LORD said to Moses, ¹³"Say to the Israelites, 'You must observe my Sabbaths. This will be a sign between me and you for the generations to come, so you may know that I am the LORD, who makes you holy.ᵃ

¹⁴"'Observe the Sabbath, because it is holy to you. Anyone who desecrates it must be put to death; whoever does any work on that day must be cut off from his people. ¹⁵For six days, work is to be done, but the seventh day is a Sabbath of rest, holy to the LORD. Whoever does any work on the Sabbath day must be put to death. ¹⁶The Israelites are to observe the Sabbath, celebrating it for the generations to come as a lasting covenant. ¹⁷It will be a sign between me and the Israelites forever, for in six days the LORD made the heavens and the earth, and on the seventh day he abstained from work and rested.'"

¹⁸When the LORD finished speaking to Moses on Mount Sinai, he gave him the two tablets of the Testimony, the tablets of stone inscribed by the finger of God.

The Golden Calf

32 When the people saw that Moses was so long in coming down from the mountain, they gathered around Aaron and said, "Come, make us godsᵇ who will go before us. As for this fellow Moses who brought us up out of Egypt, we don't know what has happened to him."

²Aaron answered them, "Take off the gold earrings that your wives, your sons and your daughters are wearing, and bring them to me." ³So all the people took off their earrings and brought them to Aaron. ⁴He took what they handed him and made it into an idol cast in the shape of a calf, fashioning it with a tool. Then

---

ᵃ13 Or who sanctifies you; or who sets you apart as holy   ᵇ1 Or a god; also in verses 23 and 31

they said, "These are your gods,ᵃ O Israel, who brought you up out of Egypt."

⁵When Aaron saw this, he built an altar in front of the calf and announced, "Tomorrow there will be a festival to the LORD." ⁶So the next day the people rose early and sacrificed burnt offerings and presented fellowship offerings.ᵇ Afterward they sat down to eat and drink and got up to indulge in revelry.

⁷Then the LORD said to Moses, "Go down, because your people, whom you brought up out of Egypt, have become corrupt. ⁸They have been quick to turn away from what I commanded them and have made themselves an idol cast in the shape of a calf. They have bowed down to it and sacrificed to it and have said, 'These are your gods, O Israel, who brought you up out of Egypt.'

⁹"I have seen these people," the LORD said to Moses, "and they are a stiff-necked people. ¹⁰Now leave me alone so that my anger may burn against them and that I may destroy them. Then I will make you into a great nation."

¹¹But Moses sought the favor of the LORD his God. "O LORD," he said, "why should your anger burn against your people, whom you brought out of Egypt with great power and a mighty hand? ¹²Why should the Egyptians say, 'It was with evil intent that he brought them out, to kill them in the mountains and to wipe them off the face of the earth'? Turn from your fierce anger; relent and do not bring disaster on your people. ¹³Remember your servants Abraham, Isaac and Israel, to whom you swore by your own self: 'I will make your descendants as numerous as the stars in the sky and I will give your descendants all this land I promised them, and it will be their inheritance forever.'" ¹⁴Then the LORD relented and did not bring on his people the disaster he had threatened.

¹⁵Moses turned and went down the mountain with the two tablets of the Testimony in his hands. They were inscribed on both sides, front and back. ¹⁶The tablets were the work of God; the writing was the writing of God, engraved on the tablets.

¹⁷When Joshua heard the noise of the people shouting, he said to Moses, "There is the sound of war in the camp."

¹⁸Moses replied:

"It is not the sound of victory,
   it is not the sound of defeat;
   it is the sound of singing that
      I hear."

¹⁹When Moses approached the camp and saw the calf and the dancing, his anger burned and he threw the tablets out of his hands, breaking them to pieces at the foot of the mountain. ²⁰And he took the calf they had made and burned it in the fire; then he ground it to powder, scattered it on the water and made the Israelites drink it.

²¹He said to Aaron, "What did these people do to you, that you led them into such great sin?"

²²"Do not be angry, my lord," Aaron answered. "You know how prone these people are to evil. ²³They said to me, 'Make us gods who will go before us. As for this fellow Moses who brought us up out of Egypt, we don't know what has happened to him.' ²⁴So I told them, 'Whoever has any gold jewelry, take it off.' Then they gave me the gold, and I threw it into the fire, and out came this calf!"

²⁵Moses saw that the people were running wild and that Aaron had let them get out of control and so become a laughingstock to their enemies. ²⁶So he stood at the entrance to the camp and said, "Whoever is for the LORD, come to me." And all the Levites rallied to him.

²⁷Then he said to them, "This is what the LORD, the God of Israel, says: 'Each man strap a sword to his side. Go back and forth through the camp from one end to the other, each killing his brother and friend and neighbor.'" ²⁸The Levites did as Moses commanded, and that day about three thousand of the people died. ²⁹Then Moses said, "You have been set apart to the LORD today, for you were against your own sons and brothers, and he has blessed you this day."

³⁰The next day Moses said to the people, "You have committed a great sin. But now I will go up to the LORD; perhaps I can make atonement for your sin." ³¹So Moses went back to the LORD and

ᵃ4 Or *This is your god*; also in verse 8
ᵇ6 Traditionally *peace offerings*

The Basis of Intercession

**32:10 "NOW LEAVE ME ALONE SO THAT MY ANGER MAY BURN AGAINST THEM …
THEN I WILL MAKE YOU INTO A GREAT NATION."**

Most people would have stumbled over themselves trying to get out
of God's way. God was angry! And he had every reason to be. The first
commandment God gave to his people was to have no other gods (see
Exodus 20:3). However, the first thing the people did when Moses was out
of the picture was to have a pagan orgy around an idol. But Moses remained
standing before God, interceding for his people. This chapter is the first of
three consecutive chapters in Exodus that give a rich picture of the prayer
life of one of the Bible's greatest men of prayer. They also provide a model
for the prayer life of any follower of Christ.

Moses' intercession was based on three realities. The first was God's
self-chosen relationship with his people. When God spoke to Moses and
called the people "*your* people, whom *you* brought up out of Egypt," Moses
corrected the Lord and called them "*your* people, whom *you* brought out of
Egypt" (32:7,11, italics added). The basis of all prayer is the relationship God
has taken the initiative to form with us. When we pray, we pray in his name,
the name he gave—"Our *Father*."

Moses also prayed on the basis of God's reputation, pleading with
the Lord to consider how he would be thought of by the Egyptians if he
executed his fierce anger: "Why should the Egyptians say, 'It was with evil
intent that he brought them out, to kill them'?" (verse 12). Moses truly
wanted God to get glory in all things. And we can learn from this. As
Jesus taught, we intercede by praying, "Our Father in heaven, hallowed
be your name" (Matthew 6:9).

Finally, Moses prayed for the people on the basis of God's promises:
"Remember your servants Abraham, Isaac and Israel, to whom you swore by
your own self: 'I will make your descendants as numerous as the stars in the
sky'" (verse 13). In his usual picturesque way, Martin Luther describes what
Moses did in this prayer as "throwing the sack of God's promises at [God's]
feet," and he couldn't step over them! It is beyond exhilarating to pray the
promises of God, for they go far beyond the best we could ever think of on
our own.

PRAY:

*Dear God, you told us to call you Father, so we do. You are glorious,
and we pray that you will be glorified. So may all the peoples
on earth praise you. And we remind you to fulfill your
promises to bless your people.*

FOR YOUR NEXT DEVOTIONAL READING, GO TO PAGE 106.

said, "Oh, what a great sin these people have committed! They have made themselves gods of gold. ³²But now, please forgive their sin—but if not, then blot me out of the book you have written."

³³The LORD replied to Moses, "Whoever has sinned against me I will blot out of my book. ³⁴Now go, lead the people to the place I spoke of, and my angel will go before you. However, when the time comes for me to punish, I will punish them for their sin."

³⁵And the LORD struck the people with a plague because of what they did with the calf Aaron had made.

33 Then the LORD said to Moses, "Leave this place, you and the people you brought up out of Egypt, and go up to the land I promised on oath to Abraham, Isaac and Jacob, saying, 'I will give it to your descendants.' ²I will send an angel before you and drive out the Canaanites, Amorites, Hittites, Perizzites, Hivites and Jebusites. ³Go up to the land flowing with milk and honey. But I will not go with you, because you are a stiff-necked people and I might destroy you on the way."

⁴When the people heard these distressing words, they began to mourn and no one put on any ornaments. ⁵For the LORD had said to Moses, "Tell the Israelites, 'You are a stiff-necked people. If I were to go with you even for a moment, I might destroy you. Now take off your ornaments and I will decide what to do with you.'" ⁶So the Israelites stripped off their ornaments at Mount Horeb.

The Tent of Meeting

⁷Now Moses used to take a tent and pitch it outside the camp some distance away, calling it the "tent of meeting." Anyone inquiring of the LORD would go to the tent of meeting outside the camp. ⁸And whenever Moses went out to the tent, all the people rose and stood at the entrances to their tents, watching Moses until he entered the tent. ⁹As Moses went into the tent, the pillar of cloud would come down and stay at the entrance, while the LORD spoke with Moses. ¹⁰Whenever the people saw the pillar of cloud standing at the entrance to the tent, they all stood and worshiped, each at the entrance to his tent.

¹¹The LORD would speak to Moses face to face, as a man speaks with his friend. Then Moses would return to the camp, but his young aide Joshua son of Nun did not leave the tent.

Moses and the Glory of the LORD

¹²Moses said to the LORD, "You have been telling me, 'Lead these people,' but you have not let me know whom you will send with me. You have said, 'I know you by name and you have found favor with me.' ¹³If you are pleased with me, teach me your ways so I may know you and continue to find favor with you. Remember that this nation is your people."

¹⁴The LORD replied, "My Presence will go with you, and I will give you rest."

¹⁵Then Moses said to him, "If your Presence does not go with us, do not send us up from here. ¹⁶How will anyone know that you are pleased with me and with your people unless you go with us? What else will distinguish me and your people from all the other people on the face of the earth?"

¹⁷And the LORD said to Moses, "I will do the very thing you have asked, because I am pleased with you and I know you by name."

¹⁸Then Moses said, "Now show me your glory."

¹⁹And the LORD said, "I will cause all my goodness to pass in front of you, and I will proclaim my name, the LORD, in your presence. I will have mercy on whom I will have mercy, and I will have compassion on whom I will have compassion. ²⁰But," he said, "you cannot see my face, for no one may see me and live."

²¹Then the LORD said, "There is a place near me where you may stand on a rock. ²²When my glory passes by, I will put you in a cleft in the rock and cover you with my hand until I have passed by. ²³Then I will remove my hand and you will see my back; but my face must not be seen."

> THE LORD said to Moses, "I will do the very thing you have asked, because I am pleased with you and I know you by name."
>
> EXODUS 33:17

The New Stone Tablets

34 The LORD said to Moses, "Chisel out two stone tablets like the first ones, and I will write on them the words that were on the first tablets, which you broke. ²Be ready in the morning, and then come up on Mount Sinai. Present yourself to me there on top of the mountain. ³No one is to come with you or be seen anywhere on the mountain; not even the flocks and herds may graze in front of the mountain."

⁴So Moses chiseled out two stone tablets like the first ones and went up

---

EXODUS 33:11–23

{ **FRIDAY** }

The Pure Love of God

33:20 "NO ONE MAY SEE ME AND LIVE."

Sooner or later it comes to this: Conversation with God leads to the desire to see God. To hear the words of life is to want see the Speaker. That is where Moses is in this text. Hymn writer Frederick Faber was thinking thoughts like Moses' when he wrote:

> How wonderful, how beautiful,
> The sight of Thee must be,
> Thine endless wisdom, boundless power,
> And awful purity!

But no one can see God and live. We may see his goodness, but not his face (see 33:19–20). The expression in verse 11—"The LORD would speak to Moses face to face, as a man speaks with his friend"—means that God communicated with Moses directly—but without visually showing his "face."

Moses asked to see God, and God said no. However, there is a sense in which God answered Moses' prayer in a special way hundreds of years later on the Mount of Transfiguration. Jesus was there, and "his face shone like the sun" (Matthew 17:1–5). Moses was able to witness this miraculous display.

St. Augustine preached a sermon he titled, "On the Pure Love of God." In his message, he proposed a Faustian kind of offer from God: You can have everything you want, nothing will be held back from you; there will be no negative consequences for anything you do, and you'll live forever. The price? "You will never see my face." Would you make that exchange: everything—without God? If your answer is "No," you have the pure love of God. Augustine asked, "Did a chill arise in your heart when you heard the words, 'You will never see my face'?" That chill is priceless; it is the pure love of God.[2]

PRAY:
*Glorious God, have you said that no one
can see you and live?
Then let me die.*
FROM A PRAYER ATTRIBUTED TO ST. AUGUSTINE

FOR YOUR NEXT DEVOTIONAL READING, GO TO PAGE 108.

Mount Sinai early in the morning, as the LORD had commanded him; and he carried the two stone tablets in his hands. ⁵Then the LORD came down in the cloud and stood there with him and proclaimed his name, the LORD. ⁶And he passed in front of Moses, proclaiming, "The LORD, the LORD, the compassionate and gracious God, slow to anger, abounding in love and faithfulness, ⁷maintaining love to thousands, and forgiving wickedness, rebellion and sin. Yet he does not leave the guilty unpunished; he punishes the children and their children for the sin of the fathers to the third and fourth generation."

⁸Moses bowed to the ground at once and worshiped. ⁹"O Lord, if I have found favor in your eyes," he said, "then let the Lord go with us. Although this is a stiff-necked people, forgive our wickedness and our sin, and take us as your inheritance."

¹⁰Then the LORD said: "I am making a covenant with you. Before all your people I will do wonders never before done in any nation in all the world. The people you live among will see how awesome is the work that I, the LORD, will do for you. ¹¹Obey what I command you today. I will drive out before you the Amorites, Canaanites, Hittites, Perizzites, Hivites and Jebusites. ¹²Be careful not to make a treaty with those who live in the land where you are going, or they will be a snare among you. ¹³Break down their altars, smash their sacred stones and cut down

> "O LORD, if I have found favor in your eyes," he said, "then let the Lord go with us. Although this is a stiff-necked people, forgive our wickedness and our sin, and take us as your inheritance."
>
> EXODUS 34:9

their Asherah poles.ᵃ ¹⁴Do not worship any other god, for the LORD, whose name is Jealous, is a jealous God.

¹⁵"Be careful not to make a treaty with those who live in the land; for when they prostitute themselves to their gods and sacrifice to them, they will invite you and you will eat their sacrifices. ¹⁶And when you choose some of their daughters as wives for your sons and those daughters prostitute themselves to their gods, they will lead your sons to do the same.

¹⁷"Do not make cast idols.

¹⁸"Celebrate the Feast of Unleavened Bread. For seven days eat bread made without yeast, as I commanded you. Do this at the appointed time in the month of Abib, for in that month you came out of Egypt.

¹⁹"The first offspring of every womb belongs to me, including all the firstborn males of your livestock, whether from herd or flock. ²⁰Redeem the firstborn donkey with a lamb, but if you do not redeem it, break its neck. Redeem all your firstborn sons.

"No one is to appear before me empty-handed.

²¹"Six days you shall labor, but on the seventh day you shall rest; even during the plowing season and harvest you must rest.

²²"Celebrate the Feast of Weeks with the firstfruits of the wheat harvest, and the Feast of Ingathering at the turn of the year.ᵇ ²³Three times a year all your men are to appear before the Sovereign LORD, the God of Israel. ²⁴I will drive out nations before you and enlarge your territory, and no one will covet your land when you go up three times each year to appear before the LORD your God.

²⁵"Do not offer the blood of a sacrifice to me along with anything containing yeast, and do not let any of the sacrifice from the Passover Feast remain until morning.

²⁶"Bring the best of the firstfruits of your soil to the house of the LORD your God.

"Do not cook a young goat in its mother's milk."

²⁷Then the LORD said to Moses, "Write down these words, for in accordance with these words I have made a covenant with you and with Israel." ²⁸Moses was there with the LORD forty days and forty nights without eating bread or drinking water. And he wrote on the tablets the words of the covenant—the Ten Commandments.

ᵃ13 That is, symbols of the goddess Asherah
ᵇ22 That is, in the fall

THOMAS MORE (1478–1535)
Lord, Give Me a Sense of Humor

THOMAS MORE'S long and distinguished career in public service was capped by an appointment to Lord Chancellor of England—one of the highest and most powerful offices in England. That was in 1529. Six years later, in 1535, King Henry VIII, the same man who appointed More to office, had him beheaded. Henry wanted More to declare him as supreme head of the church in England. More refused, explaining on his way to the scaffold, "I die the king's servant, but God's first."

More had long been ready to die if need be. Beneath all the finery of his position, he often wore a hair shirt. This private penance was to impress upon himself the fragility of his life and the emptiness of earthly ambition; each scratch a whispering reminder that though he was in the world, he was not of it. "The worms," he often told his friends, "will one day have it all."

More was also a comic, famous well beyond England for his practical jokes. He even kept in his home a pet monkey and a professional live-in jester. His sense of humor came from the same place as the hair shirt. The pretensions of the world will one day pass away; the only sure hope is in God. Hope kept More encouraged about the future; humor helped him cope with the present. Humor was the lens through which More could see clearly the incongruities and possibilities of this life, the gap between what is and what one day will be.

In a way, More was beheaded because of his sense of humor, or at least because of what it helped him to see. When set against eternity, all the posturings of the most powerful person in England were laughable. Even in death. As he walked up the shaky steps of the scaffold to be beheaded, More said to the executioner, "I pray you, see me safely up, and for my coming down let me shift for myself." When his head was on the block, he asked the executioner to wait while he moved his scraggly beard off the block. He quipped that his beard, after all, had not committed treason.

PRAY:

Pray this prayer of Thomas More: "Lord, grant me a
holy heart that sees always what is fine and pure and is not
frightened at the sight of sin, but creates order wherever it goes.
Grant me a heart that knows nothing of boredom, weeping and
sighing, let me not be too concerned with the bothersome thing
I call 'myself.' Lord, give me a sense of humor, and I will find
happiness in life and profit for others."

MEMORIZE:

The world and its desires pass away, but the man who does
the will of God lives forever. 1 JOHN 2:17

FOR YOUR NEXT DEVOTIONAL READING, GO TO PAGE 110.

The Radiant Face of Moses

²⁹When Moses came down from Mount Sinai with the two tablets of the Testimony in his hands, he was not aware that his face was radiant because he had spoken with the LORD. ³⁰When Aaron and all the Israelites saw Moses, his face was radiant, and they were afraid to come near him. ³¹But Moses called to them; so Aaron and all the leaders of the community came back to him, and he spoke to them. ³²Afterward all the Israelites came near him, and he gave them all the commands the LORD had given him on Mount Sinai.

³³When Moses finished speaking to them, he put a veil over his face. ³⁴But whenever he entered the LORD's presence to speak with him, he removed the veil until he came out. And when he came out and told the Israelites what he had been commanded, ³⁵they saw that his face was radiant. Then Moses would put the veil back over his face until he went in to speak with the LORD.

[MONDAY]

EXODUS 34:29 – 35

What You Become Through Prayer

34:29 HIS FACE WAS RADIANT BECAUSE HE HAD SPOKEN WITH THE LORD.

The best thing you have to give to others is not your education or your gifts. It is what has happened to you in the time you've spent with God. It is not what you know but who you know. At first Moses didn't realize what had happened to him during those long hours in God's presence on Mount Sinai. Even though he couldn't see God's face and his glory (33:18–20), Moses' own face had begun to reflect some of God's glory. The people noticed, though. There is no substitute for the beauty, power and goodness that come upon us when we spend time with God.

But there can be a downside to this radiance. It frightened the people to see Moses' face. The old Latin Vulgate translation of the Bible mistranslated "radiant" as "having horns." That's why many medieval pictures and statues of Moses show little horns on his head, giving him a somewhat evil appearance. There's a parable here: The closer you come to God and become like God, the more likely some may respond to you as though you were the devil.

When the members of the Sanhedrin noticed how bold and articulate Peter and John were and yet "realized that they were unschooled, ordinary men, they were astonished and they took note that these men had been with Jesus" (Acts 4:13). Unfortunately, rather than turning to Christ themselves, these leaders became even more determined to squelch the gospel (Acts 4:18,21). That's the way it is in this world: "This is the verdict: Light has come into the world, but men loved darkness instead of light because their deeds were evil" (John 3:19). There is no greater privilege or joy than to stand in the presence of God, but it will set you apart.

Jesus said he was the light of the world. He said the same thing about his disciples (see John 8:12; Matthew 5:14–16). Prayer is one of the ways we walk in his light and become light.

PRAY:
I draw near to you, Lord Jesus; draw near to me as you promised, that I may become light in the world as you are light in the world.

FOR YOUR NEXT DEVOTIONAL READING, GO TO PAGE 128.

Sabbath Regulations

35 Moses assembled the whole Israelite community and said to them, "These are the things the LORD has commanded you to do: ²For six days, work is to be done, but the seventh day shall be your holy day, a Sabbath of rest to the LORD. Whoever does any work on it must be put to death. ³Do not light a fire in any of your dwellings on the Sabbath day."

Materials for the Tabernacle

⁴Moses said to the whole Israelite community, "This is what the LORD has commanded: ⁵From what you have, take an offering for the LORD. Everyone who is willing is to bring to the LORD an offering of gold, silver and bronze; ⁶blue, purple and scarlet yarn and fine linen; goat hair; ⁷ram skins dyed red and hides of sea cows*a*; acacia wood; ⁸olive oil for the light; spices for the anointing oil and for the fragrant incense; ⁹and onyx stones and other gems to be mounted on the ephod and breastpiece.

¹⁰"All who are skilled among you are to come and make everything the LORD has commanded: ¹¹the tabernacle with its tent and its covering, clasps, frames, crossbars, posts and bases; ¹²the ark with its poles and the atonement cover and the curtain that shields it; ¹³the table with its poles and all its articles and the bread of the Presence; ¹⁴the lampstand that is for light with its accessories, lamps and oil for the light; ¹⁵the altar of incense with its poles, the anointing oil and the fragrant incense; the curtain for the doorway at the entrance to the tabernacle; ¹⁶the altar of burnt offering with its bronze grating, its poles and all its utensils; the bronze basin with its stand; ¹⁷the curtains of the courtyard with its posts and bases, and the curtain for the entrance to the courtyard; ¹⁸the tent pegs for the tabernacle and for the courtyard, and their ropes; ¹⁹the woven garments worn for ministering in the sanctuary—both the sacred garments for Aaron the priest and the garments for his sons when they serve as priests."

²⁰Then the whole Israelite community withdrew from Moses' presence, ²¹and everyone who was willing and whose heart moved him came and brought an offering to the LORD for the work on the Tent of Meeting, for all its service, and for the sacred garments. ²²All who were willing, men and women alike, came and brought gold jewelry of all kinds: brooches, earrings, rings and ornaments. They all presented their gold as a wave offering to the LORD. ²³Everyone who had blue, purple or scarlet yarn or fine linen, or goat hair, ram skins dyed red or hides of sea cows brought them. ²⁴Those presenting an offering of silver or bronze brought it as an offering to the LORD, and everyone who had acacia wood for any part of the work brought it. ²⁵Every skilled woman spun with her hands and brought what she had spun—blue, purple or scarlet yarn or fine linen. ²⁶And all the women who were willing and had the skill spun the goat hair. ²⁷The leaders brought onyx stones and other gems to be mounted on the ephod and breastpiece. ²⁸They also brought spices and olive oil for the light and for the anointing oil and for the fragrant incense. ²⁹All the Israelite men and women who were willing brought to the LORD freewill offerings for all the work the LORD through Moses had commanded them to do.

Bezalel and Oholiab

³⁰Then Moses said to the Israelites, "See, the LORD has chosen Bezalel son of Uri, the son of Hur, of the tribe of Judah, ³¹and he has filled him with the Spirit of God, with skill, ability and knowledge in all kinds of crafts— ³²to make artistic designs for work in gold, silver and bronze, ³³to cut and set stones, to work in wood and to engage in all kinds of artistic craftsmanship. ³⁴And he has given both him and Oholiab son of Ahisamach, of the tribe of Dan, the ability to teach others. ³⁵He has filled them with skill to do all kinds of work as craftsmen, designers, embroiderers in blue, purple and scarlet yarn and fine linen, and weavers—all of them master craftsmen and designers.

36 ¹So Bezalel, Oholiab and every skilled person to whom the LORD has given skill and ability to know how to carry out all the work of constructing

a 7 That is, dugongs; also in verse 23

the sanctuary are to do the work just as the LORD has commanded."

²Then Moses summoned Bezalel and Oholiab and every skilled person to whom the LORD had given ability and who was willing to come and do the work. ³They received from Moses all the offerings the Israelites had brought to carry out the work of constructing the sanctuary. And the people continued to bring freewill offerings morning after morning. ⁴So all the skilled craftsmen who were doing all the work on the sanctuary left their work ⁵and said to Moses, "The people are bringing more than enough for doing the work the LORD commanded to be done."

⁶Then Moses gave an order and they sent this word throughout the camp: "No man or woman is to make anything else as an offering for the sanctuary." And so the people were restrained from bringing more, ⁷because what they already had was more than enough to do all the work.

The Tabernacle

⁸All the skilled men among the workmen made the tabernacle with ten curtains of finely twisted linen and blue, purple and scarlet yarn, with cherubim worked into them by a skilled craftsman. ⁹All the curtains were the same size—twenty-eight cubits long and four cubits wide.ᵃ ¹⁰They joined five of the curtains together and did the same with the other five. ¹¹Then they made loops of blue material along the edge of the end curtain in one set, and the same was done with the end curtain in the other set. ¹²They also made fifty loops on one curtain and fifty loops on the end curtain of the other set, with the loops opposite each other. ¹³Then they made fifty gold clasps and used them to fasten the two sets of curtains together so that the tabernacle was a unit.

¹⁴They made curtains of goat hair for the tent over the tabernacle—eleven altogether. ¹⁵All eleven curtains were the same size—thirty cubits long and four cubits wide.ᵇ ¹⁶They joined five of the curtains into one set and the other six into another set. ¹⁷Then they made fifty loops along the edge of the end curtain

in one set and also along the edge of the end curtain in the other set. ¹⁸They made fifty bronze clasps to fasten the tent together as a unit. ¹⁹Then they made for the tent a covering of ram skins dyed red, and over that a covering of hides of sea cows.ᶜ

²⁰They made upright frames of acacia wood for the tabernacle. ²¹Each frame was ten cubits long and a cubit and a half wide,ᵈ ²²with two projections set parallel to each other. They made all the frames of the tabernacle in this way. ²³They made twenty frames for the south side of the tabernacle ²⁴and made forty silver bases to go under them—two bases for each frame, one under each projection. ²⁵For the other side, the north side of the tabernacle, they made twenty frames ²⁶and forty silver bases—two under each frame. ²⁷They made six frames for the far end, that is, the west end of the tabernacle, ²⁸and two frames were made for the corners of the tabernacle at the far end. ²⁹At these two corners the frames were double from the bottom all the way to the top and fitted into a single ring; both were made alike. ³⁰So there were eight frames and sixteen silver bases—two under each frame.

³¹They also made crossbars of acacia wood: five for the frames on one side of the tabernacle, ³²five for those on the other side, and five for the frames on the west, at the far end of the tabernacle. ³³They made the center crossbar so that it extended from end to end at the middle of the frames. ³⁴They overlaid the frames with gold and made gold rings to hold the crossbars. They also overlaid the crossbars with gold.

³⁵They made the curtain of blue, purple and scarlet yarn and finely twisted linen, with cherubim worked into it by a skilled craftsman. ³⁶They made four posts of acacia wood for it and overlaid them with gold. They made gold hooks for

ᵃ9 That is, about 42 feet (about 12.5 meters) long and 6 feet (about 1.8 meters) wide
ᵇ15 That is, about 45 feet (about 13.5 meters) long and 6 feet (about 1.8 meters) wide
ᶜ19 That is, dugongs   ᵈ21 That is, about 15 feet (about 4.5 meters) long and 2 1/4 feet (about 0.7 meter) wide

them and cast their four silver bases. ³⁷For the entrance to the tent they made a curtain of blue, purple and scarlet yarn and finely twisted linen—the work of an embroiderer; ³⁸and they made five posts with hooks for them. They overlaid the tops of the posts and their bands with gold and made their five bases of bronze.

The Ark

37 Bezalel made the ark of acacia wood—two and a half cubits long, a cubit and a half wide, and a cubit and a half high.ᵃ ²He overlaid it with pure gold, both inside and out, and made a gold molding around it. ³He cast four gold rings for it and fastened them to its four feet, with two rings on one side and two rings on the other. ⁴Then he made poles of acacia wood and overlaid them with gold. ⁵And he inserted the poles into the rings on the sides of the ark to carry it.

⁶He made the atonement cover of pure gold—two and a half cubits long and a cubit and a half wide.ᵇ ⁷Then he made two cherubim out of hammered gold at the ends of the cover. ⁸He made one cherub on one end and the second cherub on the other; at the two ends he made them of one piece with the cover. ⁹The cherubim had their wings spread upward, overshadowing the cover with them. The cherubim faced each other, looking toward the cover.

The Table

¹⁰Theyᶜ made the table of acacia wood—two cubits long, a cubit wide, and a cubit and a half high.ᵈ ¹¹Then they overlaid it with pure gold and made a gold molding around it. ¹²They also made around it a rim a handbreadthᵉ wide and put a gold molding on the rim. ¹³They cast four gold rings for the table and fastened them to the four corners, where the four legs were. ¹⁴The rings were put close to the rim to hold the poles used in carrying the table. ¹⁵The poles for carrying the table were made of acacia wood and were overlaid with gold. ¹⁶And they made from pure gold the articles for the table—its plates and dishes and bowls and its pitchers for the pouring out of drink offerings.

The Lampstand

¹⁷They made the lampstand of pure gold and hammered it out, base and shaft; its flowerlike cups, buds and blossoms were of one piece with it. ¹⁸Six branches extended from the sides of the lampstand—three on one side and three on the other. ¹⁹Three cups shaped like almond flowers with buds and blossoms were on one branch, three on the next branch and the same for all six branches extending from the lampstand. ²⁰And on the lampstand were four cups shaped like almond flowers with buds and blossoms. ²¹One bud was under the first pair of branches extending from the lampstand, a second bud under the second pair, and a third bud under the third pair—six branches in all. ²²The buds and the branches were all of one piece with the lampstand, hammered out of pure gold.

²³They made its seven lamps, as well as its wick trimmers and trays, of pure gold. ²⁴They made the lampstand and all its accessories from one talentᶠ of pure gold.

The Altar of Incense

²⁵They made the altar of incense out of acacia wood. It was square, a cubit long and a cubit wide, and two cubits highᵍ—its horns of one piece with it. ²⁶They overlaid the top and all the sides and the horns with pure gold, and made a gold molding around it. ²⁷They made two gold rings below the molding—two on opposite sides—to hold the poles used to carry it. ²⁸They made the poles of acacia wood and overlaid them with gold.

²⁹They also made the sacred anointing oil and the pure, fragrant incense—the work of a perfumer.

ᵃ1 That is, about 3 3/4 feet (about 1.1 meters) long and 2 1/4 feet (about 0.7 meter) wide and high   ᵇ6 That is, about 3 3/4 feet (about 1.1 meters) long and 2 1/4 feet (about 0.7 meter) wide   ᶜ10 Or He; also in verses 11–29   ᵈ10 That is, about 3 feet (about 0.9 meter) long, 1 1/2 feet (about 0.5 meter) wide, and 2 1/4 feet (about 0.7 meter) high   ᵉ12 That is, about 3 inches (about 8 centimeters)   ᶠ24 That is, about 75 pounds (about 34 kilograms)   ᵍ25 That is, about 1 1/2 feet (about 0.5 meter) long and wide, and about 3 feet (about 0.9 meter) high

The Altar of Burnt Offering

38 They[a] built the altar of burnt offering of acacia wood, three cubits[b] high; it was square, five cubits long and five cubits wide.[c] ²They made a horn at each of the four corners, so that the horns and the altar were of one piece, and they overlaid the altar with bronze. ³They made all its utensils of bronze—its pots, shovels, sprinkling bowls, meat forks and firepans. ⁴They made a grating for the altar, a bronze network, to be under its ledge, halfway up the altar. ⁵They cast bronze rings to hold the poles for the four corners of the bronze grating. ⁶They made the poles of acacia wood and overlaid them with bronze. ⁷They inserted the poles into the rings so they would be on the sides of the altar for carrying it. They made it hollow, out of boards.

Basin for Washing

⁸They made the bronze basin and its bronze stand from the mirrors of the women who served at the entrance to the Tent of Meeting.

The Courtyard

⁹Next they made the courtyard. The south side was a hundred cubits[d] long and had curtains of finely twisted linen, ¹⁰with twenty posts and twenty bronze bases, and with silver hooks and bands on the posts. ¹¹The north side was also a hundred cubits long and had twenty posts and twenty bronze bases, with silver hooks and bands on the posts. ¹²The west end was fifty cubits[e] wide and had curtains, with ten posts and ten bases, with silver hooks and bands on the posts. ¹³The east end, toward the sunrise, was also fifty cubits wide. ¹⁴Curtains fifteen cubits[f] long were on one side of the entrance, with three posts and three bases, ¹⁵and curtains fifteen cubits long were on the other side of the entrance to the courtyard, with three posts and three bases. ¹⁶All the curtains around the courtyard were of finely twisted linen. ¹⁷The bases for the posts were bronze. The hooks and bands on the posts were silver, and their tops were overlaid with silver; so all the posts of the courtyard had silver bands.

¹⁸The curtain for the entrance to the courtyard was of blue, purple and scarlet yarn and finely twisted linen—the work of an embroiderer. It was twenty cubits[g] long and, like the curtains of the courtyard, five cubits[h] high, ¹⁹with four posts and four bronze bases. Their hooks and bands were silver, and their tops were overlaid with silver. ²⁰All the tent pegs of the tabernacle and of the surrounding courtyard were bronze.

The Materials Used

²¹These are the amounts of the materials used for the tabernacle, the tabernacle of the Testimony, which were recorded at Moses' command by the Levites under the direction of Ithamar son of Aaron, the priest. ²²(Bezalel son of Uri, the son of Hur, of the tribe of Judah, made everything the LORD commanded Moses; ²³with him was Oholiab son of Ahisamach, of the tribe of Dan—a craftsman and designer, and an embroiderer in blue, purple and scarlet yarn and fine linen.) ²⁴The total amount of the gold from the wave offering used for all the work on the sanctuary was 29 talents and 730 shekels,[i] according to the sanctuary shekel.

²⁵The silver obtained from those of the community who were counted in the census was 100 talents and 1,775 shekels,[j] according to the sanctuary shekel— ²⁶one beka per person, that is, half a shekel,[k] according to the sanctuary shekel, from everyone who had crossed over to those counted, twenty years old or more, a total of 603,550 men. ²⁷The 100 talents[l] of silver were used to cast the bases for the sanctuary and for the curtain—100 bases from the 100 talents, one talent for each base. ²⁸They used the

---

[a]1 Or He; also in verses 2–9   [b]1 That is, about 4 1/2 feet (about 1.3 meters)   [c]1 That is, about 7 1/2 feet (about 2.3 meters) long and wide
[d]9 That is, about 150 feet (about 46 meters)
[e]12 That is, about 75 feet (about 23 meters)
[f]14 That is, about 22 1/2 feet (about 6.9 meters)
[g]18 That is, about 30 feet (about 9 meters)
[h]18 That is, about 7 1/2 feet (about 2.3 meters)
[i]24 The weight of the gold was a little over one ton (about 1 metric ton).   [j]25 The weight of the silver was a little over 3 3/4 tons (about 3.4 metric tons).   [k]26 That is, about 1/5 ounce (about 5.5 grams)   [l]27 That is, about 3 3/4 tons (about 3.4 metric tons)

1,775 shekels[a] to make the hooks for the posts, to overlay the tops of the posts, and to make their bands.

²⁹The bronze from the wave offering was 70 talents and 2,400 shekels.[b] ³⁰They used it to make the bases for the entrance to the Tent of Meeting, the bronze altar with its bronze grating and all its utensils, ³¹the bases for the surrounding courtyard and those for its entrance and all the tent pegs for the tabernacle and those for the surrounding courtyard.

The Priestly Garments

39 From the blue, purple and scarlet yarn they made woven garments for ministering in the sanctuary. They also made sacred garments for Aaron, as the LORD commanded Moses.

The Ephod

²They[c] made the ephod of gold, and of blue, purple and scarlet yarn, and of finely twisted linen. ³They hammered out thin sheets of gold and cut strands to be worked into the blue, purple and scarlet yarn and fine linen—the work of a skilled craftsman. ⁴They made shoulder pieces for the ephod, which were attached to two of its corners, so it could be fastened. ⁵Its skillfully woven waistband was like it—of one piece with the ephod and made with gold, and with blue, purple and scarlet yarn, and with finely twisted linen, as the LORD commanded Moses.

⁶They mounted the onyx stones in gold filigree settings and engraved them like a seal with the names of the sons of Israel. ⁷Then they fastened them on the shoulder pieces of the ephod as memorial stones for the sons of Israel, as the LORD commanded Moses.

The Breastpiece

⁸They fashioned the breastpiece—the work of a skilled craftsman. They made it like the ephod: of gold, and of blue, purple and scarlet yarn, and of finely twisted linen. ⁹It was square—a span[d] long and a span wide—and folded double. ¹⁰Then they mounted four rows of precious stones on it. In the first row there was a ruby, a topaz and a beryl; ¹¹in the second row a turquoise, a sapphire[e] and an emerald; ¹²in the third row a jacinth, an ag-

ate and an amethyst; ¹³in the fourth row a chrysolite, an onyx and a jasper.[f] They were mounted in gold filigree settings. ¹⁴There were twelve stones, one for each of the names of the sons of Israel, each engraved like a seal with the name of one of the twelve tribes.

¹⁵For the breastpiece they made braided chains of pure gold, like a rope. ¹⁶They made two gold filigree settings and two gold rings, and fastened the rings to two of the corners of the breastpiece. ¹⁷They fastened the two gold chains to the rings at the corners of the breastpiece, ¹⁸and the other ends of the chains to the two settings, attaching them to the shoulder pieces of the ephod at the front. ¹⁹They made two gold rings and attached them to the other two corners of the breastpiece on the inside edge next to the ephod. ²⁰Then they made two more gold rings and attached them to the bottom of the shoulder pieces on the front of the ephod, close to the seam just above the waistband of the ephod. ²¹They tied the rings of the breastpiece to the rings of the ephod with blue cord, connecting it to the waistband so that the breastpiece would not swing out from the ephod—as the LORD commanded Moses.

Other Priestly Garments

²²They made the robe of the ephod entirely of blue cloth—the work of a weaver— ²³with an opening in the center of the robe like the opening of a collar,[g] and a band around this opening, so that it would not tear. ²⁴They made pomegranates of blue, purple and scarlet yarn and finely twisted linen around the hem of the robe. ²⁵And they made bells of pure gold and attached them around the hem between the pomegranates. ²⁶The bells and pomegranates alternated around the hem of the robe to be worn for ministering, as the LORD commanded Moses.

<hr>

a28 That is, about 45 pounds (about 20 kilograms)   *b29* The weight of the bronze was about 2 1/2 tons (about 2.4 metric tons).   *c2* Or *He*; also in verses 7, 8 and 22   *d9* That is, about 9 inches (about 22 centimeters)   *e11* Or *lapis lazuli*   *f13* The precise identification of some of these precious stones is uncertain.   *g23* The meaning of the Hebrew for this word is uncertain.

27For Aaron and his sons, they made tunics of fine linen—the work of a weaver— 28and the turban of fine linen, the linen headbands and the undergarments of finely twisted linen. 29The sash was of finely twisted linen and blue, purple and scarlet yarn—the work of an embroiderer—as the LORD commanded Moses.

30They made the plate, the sacred diadem, out of pure gold and engraved on it, like an inscription on a seal: HOLY TO THE LORD. 31Then they fastened a blue cord to it to attach it to the turban, as the LORD commanded Moses.

Moses Inspects the Tabernacle

32So all the work on the tabernacle, the Tent of Meeting, was completed. The Israelites did everything just as the LORD commanded Moses. 33Then they brought the tabernacle to Moses: the tent and all its furnishings, its clasps, frames, crossbars, posts and bases; 34the covering of ram skins dyed red, the covering of hides of sea cows*a* and the shielding curtain; 35the ark of the Testimony with its poles and the atonement cover; 36the table with all its articles and the bread of the Presence; 37the pure gold lampstand with its row of lamps and all its accessories, and the oil for the light; 38the gold altar, the anointing oil, the fragrant incense, and the curtain for the entrance to the tent; 39the bronze altar with its bronze grating, its poles and all its utensils; the basin with its stand; 40the curtains of the courtyard with its posts and bases, and the curtain for the entrance to the courtyard; the ropes and tent pegs for the courtyard; all the furnishings for the tabernacle, the Tent of Meeting; 41and the woven garments worn for ministering in the sanctuary, both the sacred garments for Aaron the priest and the garments for his sons when serving as priests.

42The Israelites had done all the work just as the LORD had commanded Moses. 43Moses inspected the work and saw that they had done it just as the LORD had commanded. So Moses blessed them.

Setting Up the Tabernacle

40 Then the LORD said to Moses: 2"Set up the tabernacle, the Tent of Meeting, on the first day of the first month. 3Place the ark of the Testimony in it and shield the ark with the curtain. 4Bring in the table and set out what belongs on it. Then bring in the lampstand and set up its lamps. 5Place the gold altar of incense in front of the ark of the Testimony and put the curtain at the entrance to the tabernacle.

6"Place the altar of burnt offering in front of the entrance to the tabernacle, the Tent of Meeting; 7place the basin between the Tent of Meeting and the altar and put water in it. 8Set up the courtyard around it and put the curtain at the entrance to the courtyard.

9"Take the anointing oil and anoint the tabernacle and everything in it; consecrate it and all its furnishings, and it will be holy. 10Then anoint the altar of burnt offering and all its utensils; consecrate the altar, and it will be most holy. 11Anoint the basin and its stand and consecrate them.

12"Bring Aaron and his sons to the entrance to the Tent of Meeting and wash them with water. 13Then dress Aaron in the sacred garments, anoint him and consecrate him so he may serve me as priest. 14Bring his sons and dress them in tunics. 15Anoint them just as you anointed their father, so they may serve me as priests. Their anointing will be to a priesthood that will continue for all generations to come." 16Moses did everything just as the LORD commanded him.

17So the tabernacle was set up on the first day of the first month in the second year. 18When Moses set up the tabernacle, he put the bases in place, erected the frames, inserted the crossbars and set up the posts. 19Then he spread the tent over the tabernacle and put the covering over the tent, as the LORD commanded him.

20He took the Testimony and placed it in the ark, attached the poles to the ark and put the atonement cover over it. 21Then he brought the ark into the tabernacle and hung the shielding curtain and shielded the ark of the Testimony, as the LORD commanded him.

22Moses placed the table in the Tent of Meeting on the north side of the tabernacle outside the curtain 23and set out

a 34 That is, dugongs

the bread on it before the LORD, as the LORD commanded him.

²⁴He placed the lampstand in the Tent of Meeting opposite the table on the south side of the tabernacle ²⁵and set up the lamps before the LORD, as the LORD commanded him.

²⁶Moses placed the gold altar in the Tent of Meeting in front of the curtain ²⁷and burned fragrant incense on it, as the LORD commanded him. ²⁸Then he put up the curtain at the entrance to the tabernacle.

²⁹He set the altar of burnt offering near the entrance to the tabernacle, the Tent of Meeting, and offered on it burnt offerings and grain offerings, as the LORD commanded him.

³⁰He placed the basin between the Tent of Meeting and the altar and put water in it for washing, ³¹and Moses and Aaron and his sons used it to wash their hands and feet. ³²They washed whenever they entered the Tent of Meeting or approached the altar, as the LORD commanded Moses.

³³Then Moses set up the courtyard around the tabernacle and altar and put up the curtain at the entrance to the courtyard. And so Moses finished the work.

The Glory of the LORD

³⁴Then the cloud covered the Tent of Meeting, and the glory of the LORD filled the tabernacle. ³⁵Moses could not enter the Tent of Meeting because the cloud had settled upon it, and the glory of the LORD filled the tabernacle.

³⁶In all the travels of the Israelites, whenever the cloud lifted from above the tabernacle, they would set out; ³⁷but if the cloud did not lift, they did not set out—until the day it lifted. ³⁸So the cloud of the LORD was over the tabernacle by day, and fire was in the cloud by night, in the sight of all the house of Israel during all their travels.

Leviticus

MOSES DID AS THE
LORD COMMANDED
HIM. (8:4)

"YOU ARE to be holy to me because I, the LORD, am holy, and I have set you apart from the nations to be my own" (20:26). This breathtaking command is, in summary, the purpose of the book of Leviticus and the goal of life with God, the premise of prayer. God didn't deliver Israel—and Christ didn't die for our sins—so we could just keep on being who we were before the rescue operation. He saved us from one thing to make us free for something else: to be holy as he is holy, to be with him, to walk with him. He actually wants to make us like he is. This idea is a scandal to the devils in C. S. Lewis's *Screwtape Letters*. They cannot imagine that God would really "want to fill the universe with a lot of loathsome little replicas of himself—creatures whose life, on its miniature scale, will be qualitatively like his own." But that's precisely what God is calling for in this summary command in Leviticus.

How this divine project for the making of holy people is addressed in the book of Leviticus takes some getting used to. The book is a mass of laws and ceremonies that seem remote from our modern sensibilities today. But the purpose of the law was to take a group of people with the haziest notions of what it meant to be set apart for God, and to make that idea concrete in everyday life, in everything they did. The laws didn't actually make anyone holy, but they imbedded deep in the consciousness of the people the dream and desire, the yearning to be set apart. The shadows and signposts that make up the book of Leviticus are fulfilled in the Spirit, the *Holy* Spirit, who calls us to prayer and leads us to cry, "*Abba,* Father" (Romans 8:15).

The Burnt Offering

1 The LORD called to Moses and spoke to him from the Tent of Meeting. He said, ²"Speak to the Israelites and say to them: 'When any of you brings an offering to the LORD, bring as your offering an animal from either the herd or the flock.

³" 'If the offering is a burnt offering from the herd, he is to offer a male without defect. He must present it at the entrance to the Tent of Meeting so that it*a* will be acceptable to the LORD. ⁴He is to lay his hand on the head of the burnt offering, and it will be accepted on his behalf to make atonement for him. ⁵He is to slaughter the young bull before the LORD, and then Aaron's sons the priests shall bring the blood and sprinkle it against the altar on all sides at the entrance to the Tent of Meeting. ⁶He is to skin the burnt offering and cut it into pieces. ⁷The sons of Aaron the priest are to put fire on the altar and arrange wood on the fire. ⁸Then Aaron's sons the priests shall arrange the pieces, including the head and the fat, on the burning wood that is on the altar. ⁹He is to wash the inner parts and the legs with water, and the priest is to burn all of it on the altar. It is a burnt offering, an offering made by fire, an aroma pleasing to the LORD.

¹⁰" 'If the offering is a burnt offering from the flock, from either the sheep or the goats, he is to offer a male without defect. ¹¹He is to slaughter it at the north side of the altar before the LORD, and Aaron's sons the priests shall sprinkle its blood against the altar on all sides. ¹²He is to cut it into pieces, and the priest shall arrange them, including the head and the fat, on the burning wood that is on the altar. ¹³He is to wash the inner parts and the legs with water, and the priest is to bring all of it and burn it on the altar. It is a burnt offering, an offering made by fire, an aroma pleasing to the LORD.

¹⁴" 'If the offering to the LORD is a burnt offering of birds, he is to offer a dove or a young pigeon. ¹⁵The priest shall bring it to the altar, wring off the head and burn it on the altar; its blood shall be drained out on the side of the altar. ¹⁶He is to remove the crop with its contents*b* and throw it to the east side of the altar,

where the ashes are. ¹⁷He shall tear it open by the wings, not severing it completely, and then the priest shall burn it on the wood that is on the fire on the altar. It is a burnt offering, an offering made by fire, an aroma pleasing to the LORD.

The Grain Offering

2 " 'When someone brings a grain offering to the LORD, his offering is to be of fine flour. He is to pour oil on it, put incense on it ²and take it to Aaron's sons the priests. The priest shall take a handful of the fine flour and oil, together with all the incense, and burn this as a memorial portion on the altar, an offering made by fire, an aroma pleasing to the LORD. ³The rest of the grain offering belongs to Aaron and his sons; it is a most holy part of the offerings made to the LORD by fire.

⁴" 'If you bring a grain offering baked in an oven, it is to consist of fine flour: cakes made without yeast and mixed with oil, or*c* wafers made without yeast and spread with oil. ⁵If your grain offering is prepared on a griddle, it is to be

> THE priest shall take a handful of the fine flour and oil, together with all the incense, and burn this as a memorial portion on the altar, an offering made by fire, an aroma pleasing to the LORD.
>
> LEVITICUS 2:2

made of fine flour mixed with oil, and without yeast. ⁶Crumble it and pour oil on it; it is a grain offering. ⁷If your grain offering is cooked in a pan, it is to be made of fine flour and oil. ⁸Bring the grain offering made of these things to the LORD; present it to the priest, who shall take it to the altar. ⁹He shall take out the memorial portion from the grain offering and burn it on the altar as an offering made by fire, an aroma pleasing to the LORD. ¹⁰The rest of the grain offering belongs to Aaron and his sons; it is a most holy part of the offerings made to the LORD by fire.

---

*a*3 Or *he*   *b*16 Or *crop and the feathers*; the meaning of the Hebrew for this word is uncertain. *c*4 Or *and*

¹¹ " 'Every grain offering you bring to the LORD must be made without yeast, for you are not to burn any yeast or honey in an offering made to the LORD by fire. ¹²You may bring them to the LORD as an offering of the firstfruits, but they are not to be offered on the altar as a pleasing aroma. ¹³Season all your grain offerings with salt. Do not leave the salt of the covenant of your God out of your grain offerings; add salt to all your offerings.

¹⁴ " 'If you bring a grain offering of firstfruits to the LORD, offer crushed heads of new grain roasted in the fire. ¹⁵Put oil and incense on it; it is a grain offering. ¹⁶The priest shall burn the memorial portion of the crushed grain and the oil, together with all the incense, as an offering made to the LORD by fire.

The Fellowship Offering

3 " 'If someone's offering is a fellowship offering,ᵃ and he offers an animal from the herd, whether male or female, he is to present before the LORD an animal without defect. ²He is to lay his hand on the head of his offering and slaughter it at the entrance to the Tent of Meeting. Then Aaron's sons the priests shall sprinkle the blood against the altar on all sides. ³From the fellowship offering he is to bring a sacrifice made to the LORD by fire: all the fat that covers the inner parts or is connected to them, ⁴both kidneys with the fat on them near the loins, and the covering of the liver, which he will remove with the kidneys. ⁵Then Aaron's sons are to burn it on the altar on top of the burnt offering that is on the burning wood, as an offering made by fire, an aroma pleasing to the LORD.

⁶ " 'If he offers an animal from the flock as a fellowship offering to the LORD, he is to offer a male or female without defect. ⁷If he offers a lamb, he is to present it before the LORD. ⁸He is to lay his hand on the head of his offering and slaughter it in front of the Tent of Meeting. Then Aaron's sons shall sprinkle its blood against the altar on all sides. ⁹From the fellowship offering he is to bring a sacrifice made to the LORD by fire: its fat, the entire fat tail cut off close to the backbone, all the fat that covers the inner parts or is

connected to them, ¹⁰both kidneys with the fat on them near the loins, and the covering of the liver, which he will remove with the kidneys. ¹¹The priest shall burn them on the altar as food, an offering made to the LORD by fire.

> **❝** Let the first rule of right prayer then be, to have our heart and mind framed as becomes those who are entering into converse with God. **❞**
>
> JOHN CALVIN

¹² " 'If his offering is a goat, he is to present it before the LORD. ¹³He is to lay his hand on its head and slaughter it in front of the Tent of Meeting. Then Aaron's sons shall sprinkle its blood against the altar on all sides. ¹⁴From what he offers he is to make this offering to the LORD by fire: all the fat that covers the inner parts or is connected to them, ¹⁵both kidneys with the fat on them near the loins, and the covering of the liver, which he will remove with the kidneys. ¹⁶The priest shall burn them on the altar as food, an offering made by fire, a pleasing aroma. All the fat is the LORD's.

¹⁷ " 'This is a lasting ordinance for the generations to come, wherever you live: You must not eat any fat or any blood.' "

The Sin Offering

4 The LORD said to Moses, ²"Say to the Israelites: 'When anyone sins unintentionally and does what is forbidden in any of the LORD's commands—

³ " 'If the anointed priest sins, bringing guilt on the people, he must bring to the LORD a young bull without defect as a sin offering for the sin he has committed. ⁴He is to present the bull at the entrance to the Tent of Meeting before the LORD. He is to lay his hand on its head and slaughter it before the LORD. ⁵Then the anointed priest shall take some of the bull's blood and carry it into the Tent of Meeting. ⁶He is to dip his finger into the blood and sprinkle some of it seven times before the LORD, in front of the curtain of

---

ᵃ1 Traditionally *peace offering*; also in verses 3, 6 and 9

the sanctuary. 7The priest shall then put some of the blood on the horns of the altar of fragrant incense that is before the LORD in the Tent of Meeting. The rest of the bull's blood he shall pour out at the base of the altar of burnt offering at the entrance to the Tent of Meeting. 8He shall remove all the fat from the bull of the sin offering—the fat that covers the inner parts or is connected to them, 9both kidneys with the fat on them near the loins, and the covering of the liver, which he will remove with the kidneys— 10just as the fat is removed from the ox*a* sacrificed as a fellowship offering.*b* Then the priest shall burn them on the altar of burnt offering. 11But the hide of the bull and all its flesh, as well as the head and legs, the inner parts and offal— 12that is, all the rest of the bull—he must take outside the camp to a place ceremonially clean, where the ashes are thrown, and burn it in a wood fire on the ash heap.

13 " 'If the whole Israelite community sins unintentionally and does what is forbidden in any of the LORD's commands, even though the community is unaware of the matter, they are guilty. 14When they become aware of the sin they committed, the assembly must bring a young bull as a sin offering and present it before the Tent of Meeting. 15The elders of the community are to lay their hands on the bull's head before the LORD, and the bull shall be slaughtered before the LORD. 16Then the anointed priest is to take some of the bull's blood into the Tent of Meeting. 17He shall dip his finger into the blood and sprinkle it before the LORD seven times in front of the curtain. 18He is to put some of the blood on the horns of the altar that is before the LORD in the Tent of Meeting. The rest of the blood he shall pour out at the base of the altar of burnt offering at the entrance to the Tent of Meeting. 19He shall remove all the fat from it and burn it on the altar, 20and do with this bull just as he did with the bull for the sin offering. In this way the priest will make atonement for them, and they will be forgiven. 21Then he shall take the bull outside the camp and burn it as he burned the first bull. This is the sin offering for the community.

22 " 'When a leader sins unintentionally and does what is forbidden in any of the commands of the LORD his God, he is guilty. 23When he is made aware of the sin he committed, he must bring as his offering a male goat without defect. 24He is to lay his hand on the goat's head and slaughter it at the place where the burnt offering is slaughtered before the LORD. It is a sin offering. 25Then the priest shall take some of the blood of the sin offering with his finger and put it on the horns of the altar of burnt offering and pour out the rest of the blood at the base of the altar. 26He shall burn all the fat on the altar as he burned the fat of the fellowship offering. In this way the priest will make atonement for the man's sin, and he will be forgiven.

27 " 'If a member of the community sins unintentionally and does what is forbidden in any of the LORD's commands, he is guilty. 28When he is made aware of the sin he committed, he must bring as his offering for the sin he committed a female goat without defect. 29He is to lay his hand on the head of the sin offering and slaughter it at the place of the burnt offering. 30Then the priest is to take some of the blood with his finger and put it on the horns of the altar of burnt offering and pour out the rest of the blood at the base of the altar. 31He shall remove all the fat, just as the fat is removed from the fellowship offering, and the priest shall burn it on the altar as an aroma pleasing to the LORD. In this way the priest will make atonement for him, and he will be forgiven.

32 " 'If he brings a lamb as his sin offering, he is to bring a female without defect. 33He is to lay his hand on its head and slaughter it for a sin offering at the place where the burnt offering is slaughtered. 34Then the priest shall take some of the blood of the sin offering with his finger and put it on the horns of the altar of burnt offering and pour out the rest of the blood at the base of the altar. 35He shall remove all the fat, just as the fat is removed from the lamb of the fellowship

*a*10 The Hebrew word can include both male and female.   *b*10 Traditionally *peace offering*; also in verses 26, 31 and 35

offering, and the priest shall burn it on the altar on top of the offerings made to the LORD by fire. In this way the priest will make atonement for him for the sin he has committed, and he will be forgiven.

5 " 'If a person sins because he does not speak up when he hears a public charge to testify regarding something he has seen or learned about, he will be held responsible.

2 " 'Or if a person touches anything ceremonially unclean—whether the carcasses of unclean wild animals or of unclean livestock or of unclean creatures that move along the ground—even though he is unaware of it, he has become unclean and is guilty.

3 " 'Or if he touches human uncleanness—anything that would make him unclean—even though he is unaware of it, when he learns of it he will be guilty.

4 " 'Or if a person thoughtlessly takes an oath to do anything, whether good or evil—in any matter one might carelessly swear about—even though he is unaware of it, in any case when he learns of it he will be guilty.

5 " 'When anyone is guilty in any of these ways, he must confess in what way he has sinned 6and, as a penalty for the sin he has committed, he must bring to the LORD a female lamb or goat from the flock as a sin offering; and the priest shall make atonement for him for his sin.

7 " 'If he cannot afford a lamb, he is to bring two doves or two young pigeons to the LORD as a penalty for his sin—one for a sin offering and the other for a burnt offering. 8He is to bring them to the priest, who shall first offer the one for the sin offering. He is to wring its head from its neck, not severing it completely, 9and is to sprinkle some of the blood of the sin offering against the side of the altar; the rest of the blood must be drained out at the base of the altar. It is a sin offering. 10The priest shall then offer the other as a burnt offering in the prescribed way and make atonement for him for the sin he has committed, and he will be forgiven.

11 " 'If, however, he cannot afford two doves or two young pigeons, he is to bring as an offering for his sin a tenth of an ephah[a] of fine flour for a sin offering.

He must not put oil or incense on it, because it is a sin offering. 12He is to bring it to the priest, who shall take a handful of it as a memorial portion and burn it on the altar on top of the offerings made to the LORD by fire. It is a sin offering. 13In this way the priest will make atonement for him for any of these sins he has committed, and he will be forgiven. The rest of the offering will belong to the priest, as in the case of the grain offering.' "

The Guilt Offering

14The LORD said to Moses: 15"When a person commits a violation and sins unintentionally in regard to any of the LORD's holy things, he is to bring to the LORD as a penalty a ram from the flock, one without defect and of the proper value in silver, according to the sanctuary shekel.[b] It is a guilt offering. 16He must make restitution for what he has failed to do in regard to the holy things, add a fifth of the value to that and give it all to the priest, who will make atonement for him with the ram as a guilt offering, and he will be forgiven.

17"If a person sins and does what is forbidden in any of the LORD's commands, even though he does not know it, he is guilty and will be held responsible. 18He is to bring to the priest as a guilt offering a ram from the flock, one without defect and of the proper value. In this way the priest will make atonement for him for the wrong he has committed unintentionally, and he will be forgiven. 19It is a guilt offering; he has been guilty of[c] wrongdoing against the LORD."

6 The LORD said to Moses: 2"If anyone sins and is unfaithful to the LORD by deceiving his neighbor about something entrusted to him or left in his care or stolen, or if he cheats him, 3or if he finds lost property and lies about it, or if he swears falsely, or if he commits any such sin that people may do— 4when he thus sins and becomes guilty, he must return what he has stolen or taken by extortion, or what was entrusted to him, or the lost property he found, 5or whatever it was he swore

---

a11 That is, probably about 2 quarts (about 2 liters)   b15 That is, about 2/5 ounce (about 11.5 grams)   c19 Or has made full expiation for his

falsely about. He must make restitution in full, add a fifth of the value to it and give it all to the owner on the day he presents his guilt offering. 6And as a penalty he must bring to the priest, that is, to the LORD, his guilt offering, a ram from the flock, one without defect and of the proper value. 7In this way the priest will make atonement for him before the LORD, and he will be forgiven for any of these things he did that made him guilty."

The Burnt Offering

8The LORD said to Moses: 9"Give Aaron and his sons this command: 'These are the regulations for the burnt offering: The burnt offering is to remain on the altar hearth throughout the night, till morning, and the fire must be kept burning on the altar. 10The priest shall then put on his linen clothes, with linen undergarments next to his body, and shall remove the ashes of the burnt offering that the fire has consumed on the altar and place them beside the altar. 11Then he is to take off these clothes and put on others, and carry the ashes outside the camp to a place that is ceremonially clean. 12The fire on the altar must be kept burning; it must not go out. Every morning the priest is to add firewood and arrange the burnt offering on the fire and burn the fat of the fellowship offerings[a] on it. 13The fire must be kept burning on the altar continuously; it must not go out.

The Grain Offering

14" 'These are the regulations for the grain offering: Aaron's sons are to bring it before the LORD, in front of the altar. 15The priest is to take a handful of fine flour and oil, together with all the incense on the grain offering, and burn the memorial portion on the altar as an aroma pleasing to the LORD. 16Aaron and his sons shall eat the rest of it, but it is to be eaten without yeast in a holy place; they are to eat it in the courtyard of the Tent of Meeting. 17It must not be baked with yeast; I have given it as their share of the offerings made to me by fire. Like the sin offering and the guilt offering, it is most holy. 18Any male descendant of Aaron may eat it. It is his regular share of the offerings made to the LORD by fire for the generations to come. Whatever touches them will become holy.[b]' "

19The LORD also said to Moses, 20"This is the offering Aaron and his sons are to bring to the LORD on the day he[c] is anointed: a tenth of an ephah[d] of fine flour as a regular grain offering, half of it in the morning and half in the evening. 21Prepare it with oil on a griddle; bring it well-mixed and present the grain offering broken[e] in pieces as an aroma pleasing to the LORD. 22The son who is to succeed him as anointed priest shall prepare it. It is the LORD's regular share and is to be burned completely. 23Every grain offering of a priest shall be burned completely; it must not be eaten."

The Sin Offering

24The LORD said to Moses, 25"Say to Aaron and his sons: 'These are the regulations for the sin offering: The sin offering is to be slaughtered before the LORD in the place the burnt offering is slaughtered; it is most holy. 26The priest who offers it shall eat it; it is to be eaten in a holy place, in the courtyard of the Tent of Meeting. 27Whatever touches any of the flesh will become holy, and if any of the blood is spattered on a garment, you must wash it in a holy place. 28The clay pot the meat is cooked in must be broken; but if it is cooked in a bronze pot, the pot is to be scoured and rinsed with water. 29Any male in a priest's family may eat it; it is most holy. 30But any sin offering whose blood is brought into the Tent of Meeting to make atonement in the Holy Place must not be eaten; it must be burned.

The Guilt Offering

7 " 'These are the regulations for the guilt offering, which is most holy: 2The guilt offering is to be slaughtered in the place where the burnt offering is slaughtered, and its blood is to be sprinkled against the altar on all sides. 3All its fat shall be offered: the fat tail and the fat

[a]12 Traditionally *peace offerings*
[b]18 Or *Whoever touches them must be holy*; similarly in verse 27   [c]20 Or *each*   [d]20 That is, probably about 2 quarts (about 2 liters)
[e]21 The meaning of the Hebrew for this word is uncertain.

that covers the inner parts, [4]both kidneys with the fat on them near the loins, and the covering of the liver, which is to be removed with the kidneys. [5]The priest shall burn them on the altar as an offering made to the LORD by fire. It is a guilt offering. [6]Any male in a priest's family may eat it, but it must be eaten in a holy place; it is most holy.

[7]"'The same law applies to both the sin offering and the guilt offering: They belong to the priest who makes atonement with them. [8]The priest who offers a burnt offering for anyone may keep its hide for himself. [9]Every grain offering baked in an oven or cooked in a pan or on a griddle belongs to the priest who offers it, [10]and every grain offering, whether mixed with oil or dry, belongs equally to all the sons of Aaron.

The Fellowship Offering

[11]"'These are the regulations for the fellowship offering[a] a person may present to the LORD:

[12]"'If he offers it as an expression of thankfulness, then along with this thank offering he is to offer cakes of bread made without yeast and mixed with oil, wafers made without yeast and spread with oil, and cakes of fine flour well-kneaded and mixed with oil. [13]Along with his fellowship offering of thanksgiving he is to present an offering with cakes of bread made with yeast. [14]He is to bring one of each kind as an offering, a contribution to the LORD; it belongs to the priest who sprinkles the blood of the fellowship offerings. [15]The meat of his fellowship offering of thanksgiving must be eaten on the day it is offered; he must leave none of it till morning.

[16]"'If, however, his offering is the result of a vow or is a freewill offering, the sacrifice shall be eaten on the day he offers it, but anything left over may be eaten on the next day. [17]Any meat of the sacrifice left over till the third day must be burned up. [18]If any meat of the fellowship offering is eaten on the third day, it will not be accepted. It will not be credited to the one who offered it, for it is impure; the person who eats any of it will be held responsible.

[19]"'Meat that touches anything ceremonially unclean must not be eaten; it must be burned up. As for other meat, anyone ceremonially clean may eat it. [20]But if anyone who is unclean eats any meat of the fellowship offering belonging to the LORD, that person must be cut off from his people. [21]If anyone touches something unclean—whether human uncleanness or an unclean animal or any unclean, detestable thing—and then eats any of the meat of the fellowship offering belonging to the LORD, that person must be cut off from his people.'"

Eating Fat and Blood Forbidden

[22]The LORD said to Moses, [23]"Say to the Israelites: 'Do not eat any of the fat of cattle, sheep or goats. [24]The fat of an animal found dead or torn by wild animals may be used for any other purpose, but you must not eat it. [25]Anyone who eats the fat of an animal from which an offering by fire may be[b] made to the LORD must be cut off from his people. [26]And wherever you live, you must not eat the blood of any bird or animal. [27]If anyone eats blood, that person must be cut off from his people.'"

The Priests' Share

[28]The LORD said to Moses, [29]"Say to the Israelites: 'Anyone who brings a fellowship offering to the LORD is to bring part of it as his sacrifice to the LORD. [30]With his own hands he is to bring the offering made to the LORD by fire; he is to bring the fat, together with the breast, and wave the breast before the LORD as a wave offering. [31]The priest shall burn the fat on the altar, but the breast belongs to Aaron and his sons. [32]You are to give the right thigh of your fellowship offerings to the priest as a contribution. [33]The son of Aaron who offers the blood and the fat of the fellowship offering shall have the right thigh as his share. [34]From the fellowship offerings of the Israelites, I have taken the breast that is waved and the thigh that is presented and have given them to Aaron the priest and his sons as their regular share from the Israelites.'"

[35]This is the portion of the offerings made to the LORD by fire that were allot-

---

[a]11 Traditionally *peace offering*; also in verses 13–37   [b]25 Or *fire is*

ted to Aaron and his sons on the day they were presented to serve the LORD as priests. ³⁶On the day they were anointed, the LORD commanded that the Israelites give this to them as their regular share for the generations to come.

³⁷These, then, are the regulations for the burnt offering, the grain offering, the sin offering, the guilt offering, the ordination offering and the fellowship offering, ³⁸which the LORD gave Moses on Mount Sinai on the day he commanded the Israelites to bring their offerings to the LORD, in the Desert of Sinai.

The Ordination of Aaron and His Sons

8 The LORD said to Moses, ²"Bring Aaron and his sons, their garments, the anointing oil, the bull for the sin offering, the two rams and the basket containing bread made without yeast, ³and gather the entire assembly at the entrance to the Tent of Meeting." ⁴Moses did as the LORD commanded him, and the assembly gathered at the entrance to the Tent of Meeting.

> MOSES did as the LORD commanded him.
>
> LEVITICUS 8:4

⁵Moses said to the assembly, "This is what the LORD has commanded to be done." ⁶Then Moses brought Aaron and his sons forward and washed them with water. ⁷He put the tunic on Aaron, tied the sash around him, clothed him with the robe and put the ephod on him. He also tied the ephod to him by its skillfully woven waistband; so it was fastened on him. ⁸He placed the breastpiece on him and put the Urim and Thummim in the breastpiece. ⁹Then he placed the turban on Aaron's head and set the gold plate, the sacred diadem, on the front of it, as the LORD commanded Moses.

¹⁰Then Moses took the anointing oil and anointed the tabernacle and everything in it, and so consecrated them. ¹¹He sprinkled some of the oil on the altar seven times, anointing the altar and all its utensils and the basin with its stand, to consecrate them. ¹²He poured some of the anointing oil on Aaron's head and anointed him to consecrate him. ¹³Then he brought Aaron's sons forward, put tunics on them, tied sashes around them and put headbands on them, as the LORD commanded Moses.

¹⁴He then presented the bull for the sin offering, and Aaron and his sons laid their hands on its head. ¹⁵Moses slaughtered the bull and took some of the blood, and with his finger he put it on all the horns of the altar to purify the altar. He poured out the rest of the blood at the base of the altar. So he consecrated it to make atonement for it. ¹⁶Moses also took all the fat around the inner parts, the covering of the liver, and both kidneys and their fat, and burned it on the altar. ¹⁷But the bull with its hide and its flesh and its offal he burned up outside the camp, as the LORD commanded Moses.

¹⁸He then presented the ram for the burnt offering, and Aaron and his sons laid their hands on its head. ¹⁹Then Moses slaughtered the ram and sprinkled the blood against the altar on all sides. ²⁰He cut the ram into pieces and burned the head, the pieces and the fat. ²¹He washed the inner parts and the legs with water and burned the whole ram on the altar as a burnt offering, a pleasing aroma, an offering made to the LORD by fire, as the LORD commanded Moses.

²²He then presented the other ram, the ram for the ordination, and Aaron and his sons laid their hands on its head. ²³Moses slaughtered the ram and took some of its blood and put it on the lobe of Aaron's right ear, on the thumb of his right hand and on the big toe of his right foot. ²⁴Moses also brought Aaron's sons forward and put some of the blood on the lobes of their right ears, on the thumbs of their right hands and on the big toes of their right feet. Then he sprinkled blood against the altar on all sides. ²⁵He took the fat, the fat tail, all the fat around the inner parts, the covering of the liver, both kidneys and their fat and the right thigh. ²⁶Then from the basket of bread made without yeast, which was before the LORD, he took a cake of bread, and one made with oil, and a wafer; he put these on the fat portions and on the right thigh. ²⁷He put all these in the hands of Aaron

and his sons and waved them before the LORD as a wave offering. ²⁸Then Moses took them from their hands and burned them on the altar on top of the burnt offering as an ordination offering, a pleasing aroma, an offering made to the LORD by fire. ²⁹He also took the breast—Moses' share of the ordination ram—and waved it before the LORD as a wave offering, as the LORD commanded Moses.

³⁰Then Moses took some of the anointing oil and some of the blood from the altar and sprinkled them on Aaron and his garments and on his sons and their garments. So he consecrated Aaron and his garments and his sons and their garments.

³¹Moses then said to Aaron and his sons, "Cook the meat at the entrance to the Tent of Meeting and eat it there with the bread from the basket of ordination offerings, as I commanded, saying,ᵃ 'Aaron and his sons are to eat it.' ³²Then burn up the rest of the meat and the bread. ³³Do not leave the entrance to the Tent of Meeting for seven days, until the days of your ordination are completed, for your ordination will last seven days. ³⁴What has been done today was commanded by the LORD to make atonement for you. ³⁵You must stay at the entrance to the Tent of Meeting day and night for seven days and do what the LORD requires, so you will not die; for that is what I have been commanded." ³⁶So Aaron and his sons did everything the LORD commanded through Moses.

The Priests Begin Their Ministry

9 On the eighth day Moses summoned Aaron and his sons and the elders of Israel. ²He said to Aaron, "Take a bull calf for your sin offering and a ram for

> 66 The influence of prayer on the human mind and body is as demonstrable as that of secreting glands. Its results can be measured in terms of increased physical buoyancy, greater intellectual vigor, moral stamina, and a deeper understanding of the realities underlying human relationships. 99
>
> DR. ALEX CARREL

your burnt offering, both without defect, and present them before the LORD. ³Then say to the Israelites: 'Take a male goat for a sin offering, a calf and a lamb—both a year old and without defect—for a burnt offering, ⁴and an oxᵇ and a ram for a fellowship offeringᶜ to sacrifice before the LORD, together with a grain offering mixed with oil. For today the LORD will appear to you.'"

⁵They took the things Moses commanded to the front of the Tent of Meeting, and the entire assembly came near and stood before the LORD. ⁶Then Moses said, "This is what the LORD has commanded you to do, so that the glory of the LORD may appear to you."

⁷Moses said to Aaron, "Come to the altar and sacrifice your sin offering and your burnt offering and make atonement for yourself and the people; sacrifice the offering that is for the people and make atonement for them, as the LORD has commanded."

⁸So Aaron came to the altar and slaughtered the calf as a sin offering for himself. ⁹His sons brought the blood to him, and he dipped his finger into the blood and put it on the horns of the altar; the rest of the blood he poured out at the base of the altar. ¹⁰On the altar he burned the fat, the kidneys and the covering of the liver from the sin offering, as the LORD commanded Moses; ¹¹the flesh and the hide he burned up outside the camp.

¹²Then he slaughtered the burnt offering. His sons handed him the blood, and he sprinkled it against the altar on all sides. ¹³They handed him the burnt offering piece by piece, including the head, and he burned them on the altar. ¹⁴He washed the inner parts and the legs and burned them on top of the burnt offering on the altar.

¹⁵Aaron then brought the offering that was for the people. He took the goat for the people's sin offering and slaughtered it and offered it for a sin offering as he did with the first one.

¹⁶He brought the burnt offering and offered it in the prescribed way. ¹⁷He also

---

ᵃ31 Or I was commanded: ᵇ4 The Hebrew word can include both male and female; also in verses 18 and 19.   ᶜ4 Traditionally peace offering; also in verses 18 and 22

brought the grain offering, took a handful of it and burned it on the altar in addition to the morning's burnt offering.
¹⁸He slaughtered the ox and the ram as the fellowship offering for the people. His sons handed him the blood, and he sprinkled it against the altar on all sides. ¹⁹But the fat portions of the ox and the ram—the fat tail, the layer of fat, the kidneys and the covering of the liver—²⁰these they laid on the breasts, and then Aaron burned the fat on the altar. ²¹Aaron waved the breasts and the right thigh before the LORD as a wave offering, as Moses commanded.

²²Then Aaron lifted his hands toward the people and blessed them. And having sacrificed the sin offering, the burnt offering and the fellowship offering, he stepped down.

²³Moses and Aaron then went into the Tent of Meeting. When they came out, they blessed the people; and the glory of the LORD appeared to all the people. ²⁴Fire came out from the presence of the LORD and consumed the burnt offering and the fat portions on the altar. And when all the people saw it, they shouted for joy and fell facedown.

The Death of Nadab and Abihu

10 Aaron's sons Nadab and Abihu took their censers, put fire in them and added incense; and they offered unauthorized fire before the LORD, contrary to his command. ²So fire came out from the presence of the LORD and consumed them, and they died before the LORD. ³Moses then said to Aaron, "This is what the LORD spoke of when he said:

" 'Among those who approach me
I will show myself holy;
in the sight of all the people
I will be honored.' "

Aaron remained silent.

⁴Moses summoned Mishael and Elzaphan, sons of Aaron's uncle Uzziel, and said to them, "Come here; carry your cousins outside the camp, away from the front of the sanctuary." ⁵So they came and carried them, still in their tunics, outside the camp, as Moses ordered.

⁶Then Moses said to Aaron and his sons Eleazar and Ithamar, "Do not let your hair become unkempt,ᵃ and do not tear your clothes, or you will die and the LORD will be angry with the whole community. But your relatives, all the house of Israel, may mourn for those the LORD has destroyed by fire. ⁷Do not leave the entrance to the Tent of Meeting or you will die, because the LORD's anointing oil is on you." So they did as Moses said.

⁸Then the LORD said to Aaron, ⁹"You and your sons are not to drink wine or other fermented drink whenever you go into the Tent of Meeting, or you will die. This is a lasting ordinance for the generations to come. ¹⁰You must distinguish between the holy and the common, between the unclean and the clean, ¹¹and you must teach the Israelites all the decrees the LORD has given them through Moses."

¹²Moses said to Aaron and his remaining sons, Eleazar and Ithamar, "Take the grain offering left over from the offerings made to the LORD by fire and eat it prepared without yeast beside the altar, for it is most holy. ¹³Eat it in a holy place, because it is your share and your sons' share of the offerings made to the LORD by fire; for so I have been commanded. ¹⁴But you and your sons and your daughters may eat the breast that was waved and the thigh that was presented. Eat them in a ceremonially clean place; they have been given to you and your children as your share of the Israelites' fellowship offerings.ᵇ ¹⁵The thigh that was presented and the breast that was waved must be brought with the fat portions of the offerings made by fire, to be waved before the LORD as a wave offering. This will be the regular share for you and your children, as the LORD has commanded."

¹⁶When Moses inquired about the goat of the sin offering and found that it had been burned up, he was angry with Eleazar and Ithamar, Aaron's remaining sons, and asked, ¹⁷"Why didn't you eat the sin offering in the sanctuary area? It is most holy; it was given to you to take away the guilt of the community by making atonement for them before the LORD. ¹⁸Since its

---

ᵃ6 Or *Do not uncover your heads*
ᵇ14 Traditionally *peace offerings*

blood was not taken into the Holy Place, you should have eaten the goat in the sanctuary area, as I commanded."

[19]Aaron replied to Moses, "Today they sacrificed their sin offering and their burnt offering before the LORD, but such things as this have happened to me. Would the LORD have been pleased if I had eaten the sin offering today?" [20]When Moses heard this, he was satisfied.

LEVITICUS 10:1–3

Amazing Grace and Prayer

10:2 THEY DIED BEFORE THE LORD.

This story always appears in books about difficult passages in the Bible. But it's mostly a passage that modern readers struggle to grasp. Earlier generations did not have the same horror and repulsion that we feel when reading about the deaths of Nadab and Abihu. Why that is so is the key to understanding the passage and its relevance for prayer.

A cornerstone to justice is that the punishment fit the crime. Parking violations should not result in lethal injection; murder should not be punished by doing community service. The question is, "Was Nadab and Abihu's use of 'unauthorized fire before the LORD' the equivalent of a parking violation or murder?"

The book of Exodus shows us that the priests were given strict orders regarding making sacrifices on the altar (see 30:1–10). Scripture doesn't tell us what Nadab and Abihu's "unauthorized fire" was (cf. Numbers 3:4; 26:61)—giving the impression that the very idea was disgusting. At any rate, these priests surely knew that what they were doing was "contrary to [God's] command" (Leviticus 10:1).

Would violating God's instructions warrant death? How you answer that question depends on how seriously you take God and his holiness. If God is not supremely and inexpressibly good and pure, then this little fire violation is no big deal. But if he is completely holy and set apart, then any violation is cold defiance and treason, profanity of the basest kind. Perhaps you are thinking, "But God doesn't do that kind of thing now, for even worse offenses!" True, but the Scriptures would have us be amazed by that grace—not offended by the justice of what God did to Aaron's sons. The Bible would have us put "amazing" back into "grace."

No person has any right to enter God's presence. In fact, every one of us should tremble at the very thought of sinful people standing before a holy God—the way that Isaiah trembled (see Isaiah 6:5). It is a grace of the highest magnitude that God should allow us access to him through the blood of Jesus (see Hebrews 10:19). Every time we pray, we should tremble with awe and gratitude that we may. Our confidence should be tempered with deep reverence. Speaking the very phrase, "Our Father," should leave us stunned with wonder.

PRAY:

Almighty and holy God, you are the Father of compassion.
I bless you for the grace that allows me to say even this to you.

FOR YOUR NEXT DEVOTIONAL READING, GO TO PAGE 138.

Clean and Unclean Food

11 The LORD said to Moses and Aaron, ²"Say to the Israelites: 'Of all the animals that live on land, these are the ones you may eat: ³You may eat any animal that has a split hoof completely divided and that chews the cud.

⁴"'There are some that only chew the cud or only have a split hoof, but you must not eat them. The camel, though it chews the cud, does not have a split hoof; it is ceremonially unclean for you. ⁵The coney,ᵃ though it chews the cud, does not have a split hoof; it is unclean for you. ⁶The rabbit, though it chews the cud, does not have a split hoof; it is unclean for you. ⁷And the pig, though it has a split hoof completely divided, does not chew the cud; it is unclean for you. ⁸You must not eat their meat or touch their carcasses; they are unclean for you.

⁹"'Of all the creatures living in the water of the seas and the streams, you may eat any that have fins and scales. ¹⁰But all creatures in the seas or streams that do not have fins and scales—whether among all the swarming things or among all the other living creatures in the water—you are to detest. ¹¹And since you are to detest them, you must not eat their meat and you must detest their carcasses. ¹²Anything living in the water that does not have fins and scales is to be detestable to you.

¹³"'These are the birds you are to detest and not eat because they are detestable: the eagle, the vulture, the black vulture, ¹⁴the red kite, any kind of black kite, ¹⁵any kind of raven, ¹⁶the horned owl, the screech owl, the gull, any kind of hawk, ¹⁷the little owl, the cormorant, the great owl, ¹⁸the white owl, the desert owl, the osprey, ¹⁹the stork, any kind of heron, the hoopoe and the bat.ᵇ

²⁰"'All flying insects that walk on all fours are to be detestable to you. ²¹There are, however, some winged creatures that walk on all fours that you may eat: those that have jointed legs for hopping on the ground. ²²Of these you may eat any kind of locust, katydid, cricket or grasshopper. ²³But all other winged creatures that have four legs you are to detest.

²⁴"'You will make yourselves unclean by these; whoever touches their carcasses will be unclean till evening. ²⁵Whoever picks up one of their carcasses must wash his clothes, and he will be unclean till evening.

²⁶"'Every animal that has a split hoof not completely divided or that does not chew the cud is unclean for you; whoever touches ⌞the carcass of⌟ any of them will be unclean. ²⁷Of all the animals that walk on all fours, those that walk on their paws are unclean for you; whoever touches their carcasses will be unclean till evening. ²⁸Anyone who picks up their carcasses must wash his clothes, and he will be unclean till evening. They are unclean for you.

²⁹"'Of the animals that move about on the ground, these are unclean for you: the weasel, the rat, any kind of great lizard, ³⁰the gecko, the monitor lizard, the wall lizard, the skink and the chameleon. ³¹Of all those that move along the ground, these are unclean for you. Whoever touches them when they are dead will be unclean till evening. ³²When one of them dies and falls on something, that article, whatever its use, will be unclean, whether it is made of wood, cloth, hide or sackcloth. Put it in water; it will be unclean till evening, and then it will be clean. ³³If one of them falls into a clay pot, everything in it will be unclean, and you must break the pot. ³⁴Any food that could be eaten but has water on it from such a pot is unclean, and any liquid that could be drunk from it is unclean. ³⁵Anything that one of their carcasses falls on becomes unclean; an oven or cooking pot must be broken up. They are unclean, and you are to regard them as unclean. ³⁶A spring, however, or a cistern for collecting water remains clean, but anyone who touches one of these carcasses is unclean. ³⁷If a carcass falls on any seeds that are to be planted, they remain clean. ³⁸But if water has been put on the seed and a carcass falls on it, it is unclean for you.

³⁹"'If an animal that you are allowed to eat dies, anyone who touches the carcass

---

ᵃ5 That is, the hyrax or rock badger
ᵇ19 The precise identification of some of the birds, insects and animals in this chapter is uncertain.

will be unclean till evening. ⁴⁰Anyone who eats some of the carcass must wash his clothes, and he will be unclean till evening. Anyone who picks up the carcass must wash his clothes, and he will be unclean till evening.

⁴¹“ ‘Every creature that moves about on the ground is detestable; it is not to be eaten. ⁴²You are not to eat any creature that moves about on the ground, whether it moves on its belly or walks on all fours or on many feet; it is detestable. ⁴³Do not defile yourselves by any of these creatures. Do not make yourselves unclean by means of them or be made unclean by them. ⁴⁴I am the LORD your God; consecrate yourselves and be holy, because I am holy. Do not make yourselves unclean by any creature that moves about on the ground. ⁴⁵I am the LORD who brought you up out of Egypt to be your God; therefore be holy, because I am holy.

⁴⁶“ ‘These are the regulations concerning animals, birds, every living thing that moves in the water and every creature that moves about on the ground. ⁴⁷You must distinguish between the unclean and the clean, between living creatures that may be eaten and those that may not be eaten.’ ”

Purification After Childbirth

12 The LORD said to Moses, ²“Say to the Israelites: ‘A woman who becomes pregnant and gives birth to a son will be ceremonially unclean for seven days, just as she is unclean during her monthly period. ³On the eighth day the boy is to be circumcised. ⁴Then the woman must wait thirty-three days to be purified from her bleeding. She must not touch anything sacred or go to the sanctuary until the days of her purification are over. ⁵If she gives birth to a daughter, for two weeks the woman will be unclean, as during her period. Then she must wait sixty-six days to be purified from her bleeding.

⁶“ ‘When the days of her purification for a son or daughter are over, she is to bring to the priest at the entrance to the Tent of Meeting a year-old lamb for a burnt offering and a young pigeon or a dove for a sin offering. ⁷He shall offer them before the LORD to make atonement for her, and then she will be ceremonially clean from her flow of blood.

“ ‘These are the regulations for the woman who gives birth to a boy or a girl. ⁸If she cannot afford a lamb, she is to bring two doves or two young pigeons, one for a burnt offering and the other for a sin offering. In this way the priest will make atonement for her, and she will be clean.’ ”

Regulations About Infectious Skin Diseases

13 The LORD said to Moses and Aaron, ²“When anyone has a swelling or a rash or a bright spot on his skin that may become an infectious skin disease,ᵃ he must be brought to Aaron the priest or to one of his sonsᵇ who is a priest. ³The priest is to examine the sore on his skin, and if the hair in the sore has turned white and the sore appears to be more than skin deep,ᶜ it is an infectious skin disease. When the priest examines him, he shall pronounce him ceremonially unclean. ⁴If the spot on his skin is white but does not appear to be more than skin deep and the hair in it has not turned white, the priest is to put the infected person in isolation for seven days. ⁵On the seventh day the priest is to examine him, and if he sees that the sore is unchanged and has not spread in the skin, he is to keep him in isolation another seven days. ⁶On the seventh day the priest is to examine him again, and if the sore has faded and has not spread in the skin, the priest shall pronounce him clean; it is only a rash. The man must wash his clothes, and he will be clean. ⁷But if the rash does spread in his skin after he has shown himself to the priest to be pronounced clean, he must appear before the priest again. ⁸The priest is to examine him, and if the rash has spread in the skin, he shall pronounce him unclean; it is an infectious disease.

⁹“When anyone has an infectious skin disease, he must be brought to the priest.

ᵃ2 Traditionally *leprosy*; the Hebrew word was used for various diseases affecting the skin—not necessarily leprosy; also elsewhere in this chapter. ᵇ2 Or *descendants* ᶜ3 Or *be lower than the rest of the skin*; also elsewhere in this chapter

¹⁰The priest is to examine him, and if there is a white swelling in the skin that has turned the hair white and if there is raw flesh in the swelling, ¹¹it is a chronic skin disease and the priest shall pronounce him unclean. He is not to put him in isolation, because he is already unclean.

¹²"If the disease breaks out all over his skin and, so far as the priest can see, it covers all the skin of the infected person from head to foot, ¹³the priest is to examine him, and if the disease has covered his whole body, he shall pronounce that person clean. Since it has all turned white, he is clean. ¹⁴But whenever raw flesh appears on him, he will be unclean. ¹⁵When the priest sees the raw flesh, he shall pronounce him unclean. The raw flesh is unclean; he has an infectious disease. ¹⁶Should the raw flesh change and turn white, he must go to the priest. ¹⁷The priest is to examine him, and if the sores have turned white, the priest shall pronounce the infected person clean; then he will be clean.

¹⁸"When someone has a boil on his skin and it heals, ¹⁹and in the place where the boil was, a white swelling or reddish-white spot appears, he must present himself to the priest. ²⁰The priest is to examine it, and if it appears to be more than skin deep and the hair in it has turned white, the priest shall pronounce him unclean. It is an infectious skin disease that has broken out where the boil was. ²¹But if, when the priest examines it, there is no white hair in it and it is not more than skin deep and has faded, then the priest is to put him in isolation for seven days. ²²If it is spreading in the skin, the priest shall pronounce him unclean; it is infectious. ²³But if the spot is unchanged and has not spread, it is only a scar from the boil, and the priest shall pronounce him clean.

²⁴"When someone has a burn on his skin and a reddish-white or white spot appears in the raw flesh of the burn, ²⁵the priest is to examine the spot, and if the hair in it has turned white, and it appears to be more than skin deep, it is an infectious disease that has broken out in the burn. The priest shall pronounce him unclean; it is an infectious skin disease.

²⁶But if the priest examines it and there is no white hair in the spot and if it is not more than skin deep and has faded, then the priest is to put him in isolation for seven days. ²⁷On the seventh day the priest is to examine him, and if it is spreading in the skin, the priest shall pronounce him unclean; it is an infectious skin disease. ²⁸If, however, the spot is unchanged and has not spread in the skin but has faded, it is a swelling from the burn, and the priest shall pronounce him clean; it is only a scar from the burn.

²⁹"If a man or woman has a sore on the head or on the chin, ³⁰the priest is to examine the sore, and if it appears to be more than skin deep and the hair in it is yellow and thin, the priest shall pronounce that person unclean; it is an itch, an infectious disease of the head or chin. ³¹But if, when the priest examines this kind of sore, it does not seem to be more than skin deep and there is no black hair in it, then the priest is to put the infected person in isolation for seven days. ³²On the seventh day the priest is to examine the sore, and if the itch has not spread and there is no yellow hair in it and it does not appear to be more than skin deep, ³³he must be shaved except for the diseased area, and the priest is to keep him in isolation another seven days. ³⁴On the seventh day the priest is to examine the itch, and if it has not spread in the skin and appears to be no more than skin deep, the priest shall pronounce him clean. He must wash his clothes, and he will be clean. ³⁵But if the itch does spread in the skin after he is pronounced clean, ³⁶the priest is to examine him, and if the itch has spread in the skin, the priest does not need to look for yellow hair; the person is unclean. ³⁷If, however, in his judgment it is unchanged and black hair has grown in it, the itch is healed. He is clean, and the priest shall pronounce him clean.

³⁸"When a man or woman has white spots on the skin, ³⁹the priest is to examine them, and if the spots are dull white, it is a harmless rash that has broken out on the skin; that person is clean.

⁴⁰"When a man has lost his hair and is bald, he is clean. ⁴¹If he has lost his hair from the front of his scalp and has a bald

forehead, he is clean. ⁴²But if he has a reddish-white sore on his bald head or forehead, it is an infectious disease breaking out on his head or forehead. ⁴³The priest is to examine him, and if the swollen sore on his head or forehead is reddish-white like an infectious skin disease, ⁴⁴the man is diseased and is unclean. The priest shall pronounce him unclean because of the sore on his head.

⁴⁵"The person with such an infectious disease must wear torn clothes, let his hair be unkempt,ᵃ cover the lower part of his face and cry out, 'Unclean! Unclean!' ⁴⁶As long as he has the infection he remains unclean. He must live alone; he must live outside the camp.

Regulations About Mildew

⁴⁷"If any clothing is contaminated with mildew—any woolen or linen clothing, ⁴⁸any woven or knitted material of linen or wool, any leather or anything made of leather— ⁴⁹and if the contamination in the clothing, or leather, or woven or knitted material, or any leather article, is greenish or reddish, it is a spreading mildew and must be shown to the priest. ⁵⁰The priest is to examine the mildew and isolate the affected article for seven days. ⁵¹On the seventh day he is to examine it, and if the mildew has spread in the clothing, or the woven or knitted material, or the leather, whatever its use, it is a destructive mildew; the article is unclean. ⁵²He must burn up the clothing, or the woven or knitted material of wool or linen, or any leather article that has the contamination in it, because the mildew is destructive; the article must be burned up.

⁵³"But if, when the priest examines it, the mildew has not spread in the clothing, or the woven or knitted material, or the leather article, ⁵⁴he shall order that the contaminated article be washed. Then he is to isolate it for another seven days. ⁵⁵After the affected article has been washed, the priest is to examine it, and if the mildew has not changed its appearance, even though it has not spread, it is unclean. Burn it with fire, whether the mildew has affected one side or the other. ⁵⁶If, when the priest examines it, the mildew has faded after the article has

been washed, he is to tear the contaminated part out of the clothing, or the leather, or the woven or knitted material. ⁵⁷But if it reappears in the clothing, or in the woven or knitted material, or in the leather article, it is spreading, and whatever has the mildew must be burned with fire. ⁵⁸The clothing, or the woven or knitted material, or any leather article that has been washed and is rid of the mildew, must be washed again, and it will be clean."

⁵⁹These are the regulations concerning contamination by mildew in woolen or linen clothing, woven or knitted material, or any leather article, for pronouncing them clean or unclean.

Cleansing From Infectious Skin Diseases

14 The Lord said to Moses, ²"These are the regulations for the diseased person at the time of his ceremonial cleansing, when he is brought to the priest: ³The priest is to go outside the camp and examine him. If the person has been healed of his infectious skin disease,ᵇ ⁴the priest shall order that two live clean birds and some cedar wood, scarlet yarn and hyssop be brought for the one to be cleansed. ⁵Then the priest shall order that one of the birds be killed over fresh water in a clay pot. ⁶He is then to take the live bird and dip it, together with the cedar wood, the scarlet yarn and the hyssop, into the blood of the bird that was killed over the fresh water. ⁷Seven times he shall sprinkle the one to be cleansed of the infectious disease and pronounce him clean. Then he is to release the live bird in the open fields.

⁸"The person to be cleansed must wash his clothes, shave off all his hair and bathe with water; then he will be ceremonially clean. After this he may come into the camp, but he must stay outside his tent for seven days. ⁹On the seventh day he must shave off all his hair; he must shave his head, his beard, his eyebrows and the rest of his hair. He must wash his clothes and bathe himself with water, and he will be clean.

ᵃ45 Or clothes, uncover his head
ᵇ3 Traditionally leprosy; the Hebrew word was used for various diseases affecting the skin—not necessarily leprosy; also elsewhere in this chapter.

10"On the eighth day he must bring two male lambs and one ewe lamb a year old, each without defect, along with three-tenths of an ephah[a] of fine flour mixed with oil for a grain offering, and one log[b] of oil. 11The priest who pronounces him clean shall present both the one to be cleansed and his offerings before the LORD at the entrance to the Tent of Meeting.

12"Then the priest is to take one of the male lambs and offer it as a guilt offering, along with the log of oil; he shall wave them before the LORD as a wave offering. 13He is to slaughter the lamb in the holy place where the sin offering and the burnt offering are slaughtered. Like the sin offering, the guilt offering belongs to the priest; it is most holy. 14The priest is to take some of the blood of the guilt offering and put it on the lobe of the right ear of the one to be cleansed, on the thumb of his right hand and on the big toe of his right foot. 15The priest shall then take some of the log of oil, pour it in the palm of his own left hand, 16dip his right forefinger into the oil in his palm, and with his finger sprinkle some of it before the LORD seven times. 17The priest is to put some of the oil remaining in his palm on the lobe of the right ear of the one to be cleansed, on the thumb of his right hand and on the big toe of his right foot, on top of the blood of the guilt offering. 18The rest of the oil in his palm the priest shall put on the head of the one to be cleansed and make atonement for him before the LORD.

19"Then the priest is to sacrifice the sin offering and make atonement for the one to be cleansed from his uncleanness. After that, the priest shall slaughter the burnt offering 20and offer it on the altar, together with the grain offering, and make atonement for him, and he will be clean.

21"If, however, he is poor and cannot afford these, he must take one male lamb as a guilt offering to be waved to make atonement for him, together with a tenth of an ephah[c] of fine flour mixed with oil for a grain offering, a log of oil, 22and two doves or two young pigeons, which he can afford, one for a sin offering and the other for a burnt offering.

23"On the eighth day he must bring them for his cleansing to the priest at the entrance to the Tent of Meeting, before the LORD. 24The priest is to take the lamb for the guilt offering, together with the log of oil, and wave them before the LORD as a wave offering. 25He shall slaughter the lamb for the guilt offering and take some of its blood and put it on the lobe of the right ear of the one to be cleansed, on the thumb of his right hand and on the big toe of his right foot. 26The priest is to pour some of the oil into the palm of his own left hand, 27and with his right forefinger sprinkle some of the oil from his palm seven times before the LORD. 28Some of the oil in his palm he is to put on the same places he put the blood of the guilt offering—on the lobe of the right ear of the one to be cleansed, on the thumb of his right hand and on the big toe of his right foot. 29The rest of the oil in his palm the priest shall put on the head of the one to be cleansed, to make atonement for him before the LORD. 30Then he shall sacrifice the doves or the young pigeons, which the person can afford, 31one[d] as a sin offering and the other as a burnt offering, together with the grain offering. In this way the priest will make atonement before the LORD on behalf of the one to be cleansed."

32These are the regulations for anyone who has an infectious skin disease and who cannot afford the regular offerings for his cleansing.

Cleansing From Mildew

33The LORD said to Moses and Aaron, 34"When you enter the land of Canaan, which I am giving you as your possession, and I put a spreading mildew in a house in that land, 35the owner of the house must go and tell the priest, 'I have seen something that looks like mildew in my house.' 36The priest is to order the house to be emptied before he goes in to examine the mildew, so that nothing in the house will be pronounced unclean.

a10 That is, probably about 6 quarts (about 6.5 liters)   b10 That is, probably about 2/3 pint (about 0.3 liter); also in verses 12, 15, 21 and 24   c21 That is, probably about 2 quarts (about 2 liters)   d31 Septuagint and Syriac; Hebrew 31such as the person can afford, one

After this the priest is to go in and inspect the house. ³⁷He is to examine the mildew on the walls, and if it has greenish or reddish depressions that appear to be deeper than the surface of the wall, ³⁸the priest shall go out the doorway of the house and close it up for seven days. ³⁹On the seventh day the priest shall return to inspect the house. If the mildew has spread on the walls, ⁴⁰he is to order that the contaminated stones be torn out and thrown into an unclean place outside the town. ⁴¹He must have all the inside walls of the house scraped and the material that is scraped off dumped into an unclean place outside the town. ⁴²Then they are to take other stones to replace these and take new clay and plaster the house.

⁴³"If the mildew reappears in the house after the stones have been torn out and the house scraped and plastered, ⁴⁴the priest is to go and examine it and, if the mildew has spread in the house, it is a destructive mildew; the house is unclean. ⁴⁵It must be torn down—its stones, timbers and all the plaster—and taken out of the town to an unclean place.

⁴⁶"Anyone who goes into the house while it is closed up will be unclean till evening. ⁴⁷Anyone who sleeps or eats in the house must wash his clothes.

⁴⁸"But if the priest comes to examine it and the mildew has not spread after the house has been plastered, he shall pronounce the house clean, because the mildew is gone. ⁴⁹To purify the house he is to take two birds and some cedar wood, scarlet yarn and hyssop. ⁵⁰He shall kill one of the birds over fresh water in a clay pot. ⁵¹Then he is to take the cedar wood, the hyssop, the scarlet yarn and the live bird, dip them into the blood of the dead bird and the fresh water, and sprinkle the house seven times. ⁵²He shall purify the house with the bird's blood, the fresh water, the live bird, the cedar wood, the hyssop and the scarlet yarn. ⁵³Then he is to release the live bird in the open fields outside the town. In this way he will make atonement for the house, and it will be clean."

⁵⁴These are the regulations for any infectious skin disease, for an itch, ⁵⁵for mildew in clothing or in a house, ⁵⁶and

for a swelling, a rash or a bright spot, ⁵⁷to determine when something is clean or unclean.

These are the regulations for infectious skin diseases and mildew.

Discharges Causing Uncleanness

15 The LORD said to Moses and Aaron, ²"Speak to the Israelites and say to them: 'When any man has a bodily discharge, the discharge is unclean. ³Whether it continues flowing from his body or is blocked, it will make him unclean. This is how his discharge will bring about uncleanness:

⁴"'Any bed the man with a discharge lies on will be unclean, and anything he sits on will be unclean. ⁵Anyone who touches his bed must wash his clothes and bathe with water, and he will be unclean till evening. ⁶Whoever sits on anything the man with a discharge sat on must wash his clothes and bathe with water, and he will be unclean till evening.

⁷"'Whoever touches the man who has a discharge must wash his clothes and bathe with water, and he will be unclean till evening.

⁸"'If the man with the discharge spits on someone who is clean, that person must wash his clothes and bathe with water, and he will be unclean till evening.

⁹"'Everything the man sits on when riding will be unclean, ¹⁰and whoever touches any of the things that were under him will be unclean till evening; whoever picks up those things must wash his clothes and bathe with water, and he will be unclean till evening.

¹¹"'Anyone the man with a discharge touches without rinsing his hands with water must wash his clothes and bathe with water, and he will be unclean till evening.

¹²"'A clay pot that the man touches must be broken, and any wooden article is to be rinsed with water.

¹³"'When a man is cleansed from his discharge, he is to count off seven days for his ceremonial cleansing; he must wash his clothes and bathe himself with fresh water, and he will be clean. ¹⁴On the eighth day he must take two doves or

two young pigeons and come before the LORD to the entrance to the Tent of Meeting and give them to the priest. ¹⁵The priest is to sacrifice them, the one for a sin offering and the other for a burnt offering. In this way he will make atonement before the LORD for the man because of his discharge.

¹⁶ " 'When a man has an emission of semen, he must bathe his whole body with water, and he will be unclean till evening. ¹⁷Any clothing or leather that has semen on it must be washed with water, and it will be unclean till evening. ¹⁸When a man lies with a woman and there is an emission of semen, both must bathe with water, and they will be unclean till evening.

¹⁹ " 'When a woman has her regular flow of blood, the impurity of her monthly period will last seven days, and anyone who touches her will be unclean till evening.

²⁰ " 'Anything she lies on during her period will be unclean, and anything she sits on will be unclean. ²¹Whoever touches her bed must wash his clothes and bathe with water, and he will be unclean till evening. ²²Whoever touches anything she sits on must wash his clothes and bathe with water, and he will be unclean till evening. ²³Whether it is the bed or anything she was sitting on, when anyone touches it, he will be unclean till evening.

²⁴ " 'If a man lies with her and her monthly flow touches him, he will be unclean for seven days; any bed he lies on will be unclean.

²⁵ " 'When a woman has a discharge of blood for many days at a time other than her monthly period or has a discharge that continues beyond her period, she will be unclean as long as she has the discharge, just as in the days of her period. ²⁶Any bed she lies on while her discharge continues will be unclean, as is her bed during her monthly period, and anything she sits on will be unclean, as during her period. ²⁷Whoever touches them will be unclean; he must wash his clothes and bathe with water, and he will be unclean till evening.

²⁸ " 'When she is cleansed from her discharge, she must count off seven days, and after that she will be ceremonially clean. ²⁹On the eighth day she must take

two doves or two young pigeons and bring them to the priest at the entrance to the Tent of Meeting. ³⁰The priest is to sacrifice one for a sin offering and the other for a burnt offering. In this way he will make atonement for her before the LORD for the uncleanness of her discharge.

³¹ " 'You must keep the Israelites separate from things that make them unclean, so they will not die in their uncleanness for defiling my dwelling place,ᵃ which is among them.' "

³²These are the regulations for a man with a discharge, for anyone made unclean by an emission of semen, ³³for a woman in her monthly period, for a man or a woman with a discharge, and for a man who lies with a woman who is ceremonially unclean.

The Day of Atonement

16 The LORD spoke to Moses after the death of the two sons of Aaron who died when they approached the LORD. ²The LORD said to Moses: "Tell your brother Aaron not to come whenever he chooses into the Most Holy Place behind the curtain in front of the atonement cover on the ark, or else he will die, because I appear in the cloud over the atonement cover.

³"This is how Aaron is to enter the sanctuary area: with a young bull for a sin offering and a ram for a burnt offering. ⁴He is to put on the sacred linen tunic, with linen undergarments next to his body; he is to tie the linen sash around him and put on the linen turban. These are sacred garments; so he must bathe himself with water before he puts them on. ⁵From the Israelite community he is to take two male goats for a sin offering and a ram for a burnt offering.

⁶"Aaron is to offer the bull for his own sin offering to make atonement for himself and his household. ⁷Then he is to take the two goats and present them before the LORD at the entrance to the Tent of Meeting. ⁸He is to cast lots for the two goats—one lot for the LORD and the other for the scapegoat.ᵇ ⁹Aaron shall bring the goat whose lot falls to the LORD and

---

ᵃ31 Or my tabernacle   ᵇ8 That is, the goat of removal; Hebrew azazel; also in verses 10 and 26

sacrifice it for a sin offering. ¹⁰But the goat chosen by lot as the scapegoat shall be presented alive before the LORD to be used for making atonement by sending it into the desert as a scapegoat.

¹¹"Aaron shall bring the bull for his own sin offering to make atonement for himself and his household, and he is to slaughter the bull for his own sin offering. ¹²He is to take a censer full of burning coals from the altar before the LORD and two handfuls of finely ground fragrant incense and take them behind the curtain. ¹³He is to put the incense on the fire before the LORD, and the smoke of the incense will conceal the atonement cover above the Testimony, so that he will not die. ¹⁴He is to take some of the bull's blood and with his finger sprinkle it on the front of the atonement cover; then he shall sprinkle some of it with his finger seven times before the atonement cover.

¹⁵"He shall then slaughter the goat for the sin offering for the people and take its blood behind the curtain and do with it as he did with the bull's blood: He shall sprinkle it on the atonement cover and in front of it. ¹⁶In this way he will make atonement for the Most Holy Place because of the uncleanness and rebellion of the Israelites, whatever their sins have been. He is to do the same for the Tent of Meeting, which is among them in the midst of their uncleanness. ¹⁷No one is to be in the Tent of Meeting from the time Aaron goes in to make atonement in the Most Holy Place until he comes out, having made atonement for himself, his household and the whole community of Israel.

¹⁸"Then he shall come out to the altar that is before the LORD and make atonement for it. He shall take some of the bull's blood and some of the goat's blood and put it on all the horns of the altar. ¹⁹He shall sprinkle some of the blood on it with his finger seven times to cleanse it and to consecrate it from the uncleanness of the Israelites.

²⁰"When Aaron has finished making atonement for the Most Holy Place, the Tent of Meeting and the altar, he shall bring forward the live goat. ²¹He is to lay both hands on the head of the live goat and confess over it all the wickedness and rebellion of the Israelites—all their sins—and put them on the goat's head. He shall send the goat away into the desert in the care of a man appointed for the task. ²²The goat will carry on itself all their sins to a solitary place; and the man shall release it in the desert.

²³"Then Aaron is to go into the Tent of Meeting and take off the linen garments he put on before he entered the Most Holy Place, and he is to leave them there. ²⁴He shall bathe himself with water in a holy place and put on his regular garments. Then he shall come out and sacrifice the burnt offering for himself and the burnt offering for the people, to make atonement for himself and for the people. ²⁵He shall also burn the fat of the sin offering on the altar.

²⁶"The man who releases the goat as a scapegoat must wash his clothes and bathe himself with water; afterward he may come into the camp. ²⁷The bull and the goat for the sin offerings, whose blood was brought into the Most Holy Place to make atonement, must be taken outside the camp; their hides, flesh and offal are to be burned up. ²⁸The man who burns them must wash his clothes and bathe himself with water; afterward he may come into the camp.

²⁹"This is to be a lasting ordinance for you: On the tenth day of the seventh month you must deny yourselves*ᵃ* and not do any work—whether native-born or an alien living among you— ³⁰because on this day atonement will be made for you, to cleanse you. Then, before the LORD, you will be clean from all your sins. ³¹It is a sabbath of rest, and you must deny yourselves; it is a lasting ordinance. ³²The priest who is anointed and ordained to succeed his father as high priest is to make atonement. He is to put on the sacred linen garments ³³and make atonement for the Most Holy Place, for the Tent of Meeting and the altar, and for the priests and all the people of the community.

³⁴"This is to be a lasting ordinance for you: Atonement is to be made once a year for all the sins of the Israelites."

And it was done, as the LORD commanded Moses.

ᵃ29 Or must fast; also in verse 31

Eating Blood Forbidden

17 The LORD said to Moses, [2]"Speak to Aaron and his sons and to all the Israelites and say to them: 'This is what the LORD has commanded: [3]Any Israelite who sacrifices an ox,[a] a lamb or a goat in the camp or outside of it [4]instead of bringing it to the entrance to the Tent of Meeting to present it as an offering to the LORD in front of the tabernacle of the LORD—that man shall be considered guilty of bloodshed; he has shed blood and must be cut off from his people. [5]This is so the Israelites will bring to the LORD the sacrifices they are now making in the open fields. They must bring them to the priest, that is, to the LORD, at the entrance to the Tent of Meeting and sacrifice them as fellowship offerings.[b] [6]The priest is to sprinkle the blood against the altar of the LORD at the entrance to the Tent of Meeting and burn the fat as an aroma pleasing to the LORD. [7]They must no longer offer any of their sacrifices to the goat idols[c] to whom they prostitute themselves. This is to be a lasting ordinance for them and for the generations to come.'

[8]"Say to them: 'Any Israelite or any alien living among them who offers a burnt offering or sacrifice [9]and does not bring it to the entrance to the Tent of Meeting to sacrifice it to the LORD—that man must be cut off from his people.

[10]"'Any Israelite or any alien living among them who eats any blood—I will set my face against that person who eats blood and will cut him off from his people. [11]For the life of a creature is in the blood, and I have given it to you to make atonement for yourselves on the altar; it is the blood that makes atonement for one's life. [12]Therefore I say to the Israelites, "None of you may eat blood, nor may an alien living among you eat blood."

[13]"'Any Israelite or any alien living among you who hunts any animal or bird that may be eaten must drain out the blood and cover it with earth, [14]because the life of every creature is its blood. That is why I have said to the Israelites, "You must not eat the blood of any creature, because the life of every creature is its blood; anyone who eats it must be cut off."

[15]"'Anyone, whether native-born or alien, who eats anything found dead or torn by wild animals must wash his clothes and bathe with water, and he will be ceremonially unclean till evening; then he will be clean. [16]But if he does not wash his clothes and bathe himself, he will be held responsible.'"

Unlawful Sexual Relations

18 The LORD said to Moses, [2]"Speak to the Israelites and say to them: 'I am the LORD your God. [3]You must not do as they do in Egypt, where you used to live, and you must not do as they do in the land of Canaan, where I am bringing you. Do not follow their practices. [4]You must obey my laws and be careful to follow my decrees. I am the LORD your God. [5]Keep my decrees and laws, for the man who obeys them will live by them. I am the LORD.

[6]"'No one is to approach any close relative to have sexual relations. I am the LORD.

[7]"'Do not dishonor your father by having sexual relations with your mother. She is your mother; do not have relations with her.

[8]"'Do not have sexual relations with your father's wife; that would dishonor your father.

[9]"'Do not have sexual relations with your sister, either your father's daughter or your mother's daughter, whether she was born in the same home or elsewhere.

[10]"'Do not have sexual relations with your son's daughter or your daughter's daughter; that would dishonor you.

[11]"'Do not have sexual relations with the daughter of your father's wife, born to your father; she is your sister.

[12]"'Do not have sexual relations with your father's sister; she is your father's close relative.

[13]"'Do not have sexual relations with your mother's sister, because she is your mother's close relative.

[14]"'Do not dishonor your father's brother by approaching his wife to have sexual relations; she is your aunt.

[15]"'Do not have sexual relations with your daughter-in-law. She is your son's wife; do not have relations with her.

¹⁶ " 'Do not have sexual relations with your brother's wife; that would dishonor your brother.

¹⁷ " 'Do not have sexual relations with both a woman and her daughter. Do not have sexual relations with either her son's daughter or her daughter's daughter; they are her close relatives. That is wickedness.

¹⁸ " 'Do not take your wife's sister as a rival wife and have sexual relations with her while your wife is living.

¹⁹ " 'Do not approach a woman to have sexual relations during the uncleanness of her monthly period.

²⁰ " 'Do not have sexual relations with your neighbor's wife and defile yourself with her.

²¹ " 'Do not give any of your children to be sacrificed[a] to Molech, for you must not profane the name of your God. I am the LORD.

a21 Or to be passed through the fire

LEVITICUS 17:10–11

[WEDNESDAY]

A Bloody Faith

17:11 FOR THE LIFE OF A CREATURE IS IN THE BLOOD.

If you were in Jerusalem in the time of Jesus, what you might have noticed was the presence of smoke in the air, the sounds of bleating sheep and goats, the sight of animals herded to the place of sacrifice, and the smell of burning flesh everywhere, especially near the temple. It may be hard for us to envision, but bulls, lambs and goats were brought daily to the priests and slaughtered. Their blood was smeared on the horns of the altar, the rest poured at its foot, part of the animal burned at the altar, the rest outside the city walls. The clergy had the hands of butchers.

The Bible says Jesus came like those lambs, to offer his life as an atoning sacrifice for sin (see 1 John 4:10). Our faith is inescapably bloody; at its heart it is raw; it is not genteel. "Without the shedding of blood there is no forgiveness" (Hebrews 9:22). Jesus was not a Socrates, drinking hemlock among friends, dying a death of protest. He was not a Buddha, sitting in the lotus position on a mountaintop, dying in deep meditation. He was a lamb slaughtered, a victim bloodied and scourged and impaled on a Roman cross.

The point of sacrifice is not merely death for the sake of death, but life released through death—"the life of a creature is in the blood" (Leviticus 17:11). One life is substituted for the life of another. It is the blood of Christ, the new life released by his death and resurrection, that cleanses and gives us access to God (see Hebrews 10:19–22). At the heart of a bloody faith is access to God. We can pray because we now *may* pray, thanks to his sacrifice.

P R A Y :

"O wondrous love, to bleed and die,
To bear the Cross and shame,
That guilty sinners, such as I,
Might plead Thy gracious Name." ¹

JOHN NEWTON

FOR YOUR NEXT DEVOTIONAL READING, GO TO PAGE 159.

22 " 'Do not lie with a man as one lies with a woman; that is detestable.

23 " 'Do not have sexual relations with an animal and defile yourself with it. A woman must not present herself to an animal to have sexual relations with it; that is a perversion.

24 " 'Do not defile yourselves in any of these ways, because this is how the nations that I am going to drive out before you became defiled. 25Even the land was defiled; so I punished it for its sin, and the land vomited out its inhabitants. 26But you must keep my decrees and my laws. The native-born and the aliens living among you must not do any of these detestable things, 27for all these things were done by the people who lived in the land before you, and the land became defiled. 28And if you defile the land, it will vomit you out as it vomited out the nations that were before you.

29 " 'Everyone who does any of these detestable things—such persons must be cut off from their people. 30Keep my requirements and do not follow any of the detestable customs that were practiced before you came and do not defile yourselves with them. I am the LORD your God.' "

Various Laws

19 The LORD said to Moses, 2"Speak to the entire assembly of Israel and say to them: 'Be holy because I, the LORD your God, am holy.

3 " 'Each of you must respect his mother and father, and you must observe my Sabbaths. I am the LORD your God.

4 " 'Do not turn to idols or make gods of cast metal for yourselves. I am the LORD your God.

5 " 'When you sacrifice a fellowship offering[a] to the LORD, sacrifice it in such a way that it will be accepted on your behalf. 6It shall be eaten on the day you sacrifice it or on the next day; anything left over until the third day must be burned up. 7If any of it is eaten on the third day, it is impure and will not be accepted. 8Whoever eats it will be held responsible because he has desecrated what is holy to the LORD; that person must be cut off from his people.

9 " 'When you reap the harvest of your land, do not reap to the very edges of your field or gather the gleanings of your harvest. 10Do not go over your vineyard a second time or pick up the grapes that have fallen. Leave them for the poor and the alien. I am the LORD your God.

11 " 'Do not steal.

" 'Do not lie.

" 'Do not deceive one another.

12 " 'Do not swear falsely by my name and so profane the name of your God. I am the LORD.

13 " 'Do not defraud your neighbor or rob him.

" 'Do not hold back the wages of a hired man overnight.

14 " 'Do not curse the deaf or put a stumbling block in front of the blind, but fear your God. I am the LORD.

15 " 'Do not pervert justice; do not show partiality to the poor or favoritism to the great, but judge your neighbor fairly.

16 " 'Do not go about spreading slander among your people.

" 'Do not do anything that endangers your neighbor's life. I am the LORD.

17 " 'Do not hate your brother in your heart. Rebuke your neighbor frankly so you will not share in his guilt.

18 " 'Do not seek revenge or bear a grudge against one of your people, but love your neighbor as yourself. I am the LORD.

19 " 'Keep my decrees.

" 'Do not mate different kinds of animals.

" 'Do not plant your field with two kinds of seed.

" 'Do not wear clothing woven of two kinds of material.

20 " 'If a man sleeps with a woman who is a slave girl promised to another man but who has not been ransomed or given her freedom, there must be due punishment. Yet they are not to be put to death, because she had not been freed. 21The man, however, must bring a ram to the entrance to the Tent of Meeting for a guilt offering to the LORD. 22With the ram of the guilt offering the priest is to make atonement for him before the LORD for the sin he has committed, and his sin will be forgiven.

a5 Traditionally *peace offering*

23 " 'When you enter the land and plant any kind of fruit tree, regard its fruit as forbidden.ᵃ For three years you are to consider it forbiddenᵃ; it must not be eaten. 24In the fourth year all its fruit will be holy, an offering of praise to the LORD. 25But in the fifth year you may eat its fruit. In this way your harvest will be increased. I am the LORD your God.

26 " 'Do not eat any meat with the blood still in it.

" 'Do not practice divination or sorcery.

27 " 'Do not cut the hair at the sides of your head or clip off the edges of your beard.

28 " 'Do not cut your bodies for the dead or put tattoo marks on yourselves. I am the LORD.

29 " 'Do not degrade your daughter by making her a prostitute, or the land will turn to prostitution and be filled with wickedness.

30 " 'Observe my Sabbaths and have reverence for my sanctuary. I am the LORD.

31 " 'Do not turn to mediums or seek out spiritists, for you will be defiled by them. I am the LORD your God.

32 " 'Rise in the presence of the aged, show respect for the elderly and revere your God. I am the LORD.

33 " 'When an alien lives with you in your land, do not mistreat him. 34The alien living with you must be treated as one of your native-born. Love him as yourself, for you were aliens in Egypt. I am the LORD your God.

35 " 'Do not use dishonest standards when measuring length, weight or quantity. 36Use honest scales and honest weights, an honest ephahᵇ and an honest hin.ᶜ I am the LORD your God, who brought you out of Egypt.

37 " 'Keep all my decrees and all my laws and follow them. I am the LORD.' "

Punishments for Sin

20 The LORD said to Moses, 2"Say to the Israelites: 'Any Israelite or any alien living in Israel who givesᵈ any of his children to Molech must be put to death. The people of the community are to stone him. 3I will set my face against that man and I will cut him off from his people; for by giving his children to Molech, he has defiled my sanctuary and pro-

faned my holy name. 4If the people of the community close their eyes when that man gives one of his children to Molech and they fail to put him to death, 5I will set my face against that man and his family and will cut off from their people both him and all who follow him in prostituting themselves to Molech.

6 " 'I will set my face against the person who turns to mediums and spiritists to prostitute himself by following them, and I will cut him off from his people.

7 " 'Consecrate yourselves and be holy, because I am the LORD your God. 8Keep my decrees and follow them. I am the LORD, who makes you holy.ᵉ

9 " 'If anyone curses his father or mother, he must be put to death. He has cursed his father or his mother, and his blood will be on his own head.

10 " 'If a man commits adultery with another man's wife—with the wife of his neighbor—both the adulterer and the adulteress must be put to death.

11 " 'If a man sleeps with his father's wife, he has dishonored his father. Both the man and the woman must be put to death; their blood will be on their own heads.

12 " 'If a man sleeps with his daughter-in-law, both of them must be put to death. What they have done is a perversion; their blood will be on their own heads.

13 " 'If a man lies with a man as one lies with a woman, both of them have done what is detestable. They must be put to death; their blood will be on their own heads.

14 " 'If a man marries both a woman and her mother, it is wicked. Both he and they must be burned in the fire, so that no wickedness will be among you.

15 " 'If a man has sexual relations with an animal, he must be put to death, and you must kill the animal.

16 " 'If a woman approaches an animal to have sexual relations with it, kill both the woman and the animal. They must be put to death; their blood will be on their own heads.

ᵃ23 Hebrew uncircumcised   ᵇ36 An ephah was a dry measure.   ᶜ36 A hin was a liquid measure.   ᵈ2 Or sacrifices; also in verses 3 and 4   ᵉ8 Or who sanctifies you; or who sets you apart as holy

¹⁷" 'If a man marries his sister, the daughter of either his father or his mother, and they have sexual relations, it is a disgrace. They must be cut off before the eyes of their people. He has dishonored his sister and will be held responsible.

¹⁸" 'If a man lies with a woman during her monthly period and has sexual relations with her, he has exposed the source of her flow, and she has also uncovered it. Both of them must be cut off from their people.

¹⁹" 'Do not have sexual relations with the sister of either your mother or your father, for that would dishonor a close relative; both of you would be held responsible.

²⁰" 'If a man sleeps with his aunt, he has dishonored his uncle. They will be held responsible; they will die childless.

²¹" 'If a man marries his brother's wife, it is an act of impurity; he has dishonored his brother. They will be childless.

²²" 'Keep all my decrees and laws and follow them, so that the land where I am bringing you to live may not vomit you out. ²³You must not live according to the customs of the nations I am going to drive out before you. Because they did all these things, I abhorred them. ²⁴But I said to you, "You will possess their land; I will give it to you as an inheritance, a land flowing with milk and honey." I am the LORD your God, who has set you apart from the nations.

²⁵" 'You must therefore make a distinction between clean and unclean animals and between unclean and clean birds. Do not defile yourselves by any animal or bird or anything that moves along the ground—those which I have set apart as unclean for you. ²⁶You are to be holy to me*a* because I, the LORD, am holy, and I have set you apart from the nations to be my own.

²⁷" 'A man or woman who is a medium or spiritist among you must be put to death. You are to stone them; their blood will be on their own heads.' "

Rules for Priests

21 The LORD said to Moses, "Speak to the priests, the sons of Aaron, and say to them: 'A priest must not make himself ceremonially unclean for any of his people who die, ²except for a close relative, such as his mother or father, his son or daughter, his brother, ³or an unmarried sister who is dependent on him since she has no husband—for her he may make himself unclean. ⁴He must not make himself unclean for people related to him by marriage,*b* and so defile himself.

⁵" 'Priests must not shave their heads or shave off the edges of their beards or cut their bodies. ⁶They must be holy to their God and must not profane the name of their God. Because they present the offerings made to the LORD by fire, the food of their God, they are to be holy.

⁷" 'They must not marry women defiled by prostitution or divorced from their husbands, because priests are holy to their God. ⁸Regard them as holy, because they offer up the food of your God. Consider them holy, because I the LORD am holy—I who make you holy.*c*

⁹" 'If a priest's daughter defiles herself by becoming a prostitute, she disgraces her father; she must be burned in the fire.

¹⁰" 'The high priest, the one among his brothers who has had the anointing oil poured on his head and who has been ordained to wear the priestly garments, must not let his hair become unkempt*d* or tear his clothes. ¹¹He must not enter a place where there is a dead body. He must not make himself unclean, even for his father or mother, ¹²nor leave the sanctuary of his God or desecrate it, because he has been dedicated by the anointing oil of his God. I am the LORD.

¹³" 'The woman he marries must be a virgin. ¹⁴He must not marry a widow, a divorced woman, or a woman defiled by prostitution, but only a virgin from his own people, ¹⁵so he will not defile his offspring among his people. I am the LORD, who makes him holy.*e* '"

¹⁶The LORD said to Moses, ¹⁷"Say to Aaron: 'For the generations to come none of your descendants who has a defect may come near to offer the food of his God. ¹⁸No man who has any defect may come

---

a26 Or *be my holy ones*   *b4* Or *unclean as a leader among his people*   *c8* Or *who sanctify you; or who set you apart as holy*   *d10* Or *not uncover his head*   *e15* Or *who sanctifies him; or who sets him apart as holy*

near: no man who is blind or lame, disfigured or deformed; [19]no man with a crippled foot or hand, [20]or who is hunchbacked or dwarfed, or who has any eye defect, or who has festering or running sores or damaged testicles. [21]No descendant of Aaron the priest who has any defect is to come near to present the offerings made to the LORD by fire. He has a defect; he must not come near to offer the food of his God. [22]He may eat the most holy food of his God, as well as the holy food; [23]yet because of his defect, he must not go near the curtain or approach the altar, and so desecrate my sanctuary. I am the LORD, who makes them holy.[a]' "

[24]So Moses told this to Aaron and his sons and to all the Israelites.

22 The LORD said to Moses, [2]"Tell Aaron and his sons to treat with respect the sacred offerings the Israelites consecrate to me, so they will not profane my holy name. I am the LORD.

[3]"Say to them: 'For the generations to come, if any of your descendants is ceremonially unclean and yet comes near the sacred offerings that the Israelites consecrate to the LORD, that person must be cut off from my presence. I am the LORD.

[4]" 'If a descendant of Aaron has an infectious skin disease[b] or a bodily discharge, he may not eat the sacred offerings until he is cleansed. He will also be unclean if he touches something defiled by a corpse or by anyone who has an emission of semen, [5]or if he touches any crawling thing that makes him unclean, or any person who makes him unclean, whatever the uncleanness may be. [6]The one who touches any such thing will be unclean till evening. He must not eat any of the sacred offerings unless he has bathed himself with water. [7]When the sun goes down, he will be clean, and after that he may eat the sacred offerings, for they are his food. [8]He must not eat anything found dead or torn by wild animals, and so become unclean through it. I am the LORD.

[9]" 'The priests are to keep my requirements so that they do not become guilty and die for treating them with contempt. I am the LORD, who makes them holy.[c]

[10]" 'No one outside a priest's family may eat the sacred offering, nor may the guest of a priest or his hired worker eat it. [11]But if a priest buys a slave with money, or if a slave is born in his household, that slave may eat his food. [12]If a priest's daughter marries anyone other than a priest, she may not eat any of the sacred contributions. [13]But if a priest's daughter becomes a widow or is divorced, yet has no children, and she returns to live in her father's house as in her youth, she may eat of her father's food. No unauthorized person, however, may eat any of it.

[14]" 'If anyone eats a sacred offering by mistake, he must make restitution to the priest for the offering and add a fifth of the value to it. [15]The priests must not desecrate the sacred offerings the Israelites present to the LORD [16]by allowing them to eat the sacred offerings and so bring upon them guilt requiring payment. I am the LORD, who makes them holy.' "

Unacceptable Sacrifices

[17]The LORD said to Moses, [18]"Speak to Aaron and his sons and to all the Israelites and say to them: 'If any of you—either an Israelite or an alien living in Israel—presents a gift for a burnt offering to the LORD, either to fulfill a vow or as a freewill offering, [19]you must present a male without defect from the cattle, sheep or goats in order that it may be accepted on your behalf. [20]Do not bring anything with a defect, because it will not be accepted on your behalf. [21]When anyone brings from the herd or flock a fellowship offering[d] to the LORD to fulfill a special vow or as a freewill offering, it must be without defect or blemish to be acceptable. [22]Do not offer to the LORD the blind, the injured or the maimed, or anything with warts or festering or running sores. Do not place any of these on the altar as an offering made to the LORD by fire. [23]You may, however, present as a freewill offering an ox[e] or a sheep that is deformed or stunted, but it will not be

---

[a]23 Or *who sanctifies them*; or *who sets them apart as holy* [b]4 Traditionally *leprosy*; the Hebrew word was used for various diseases affecting the skin—not necessarily leprosy.
[c]9 Or *who sanctifies them*; or *who sets them apart as holy*; also in verse 16 [d]21 Traditionally *peace offering* [e]23 The Hebrew word can include both male and female.

accepted in fulfillment of a vow. ²⁴You must not offer to the LORD an animal whose testicles are bruised, crushed, torn or cut. You must not do this in your own land, ²⁵and you must not accept such animals from the hand of a foreigner and offer them as the food of your God. They will not be accepted on your behalf, because they are deformed and have defects.' "

²⁶The LORD said to Moses, ²⁷"When a calf, a lamb or a goat is born, it is to remain with its mother for seven days. From the eighth day on, it will be acceptable as an offering made to the LORD by fire. ²⁸Do not slaughter a cow or a sheep and its young on the same day.

²⁹"When you sacrifice a thank offering to the LORD, sacrifice it in such a way that it will be accepted on your behalf. ³⁰It must be eaten that same day; leave none of it till morning. I am the LORD.

> "WHEN you sacrifice a thank offering to the LORD, sacrifice it in such a way that it will be accepted on your behalf."
>
> LEVITICUS 22:29

³¹"Keep my commands and follow them. I am the LORD. ³²Do not profane my holy name. I must be acknowledged as holy by the Israelites. I am the LORD, who makes*a* you holy*b* ³³and who brought you out of Egypt to be your God. I am the LORD."

23 The LORD said to Moses, ²"Speak to the Israelites and say to them: 'These are my appointed feasts, the appointed feasts of the LORD, which you are to proclaim as sacred assemblies.

The Sabbath

³" 'There are six days when you may work, but the seventh day is a Sabbath of rest, a day of sacred assembly. You are not to do any work; wherever you live, it is a Sabbath to the LORD.

The Passover and Unleavened Bread

⁴" 'These are the LORD's appointed feasts, the sacred assemblies you are to proclaim at their appointed times: ⁵The

LORD's Passover begins at twilight on the fourteenth day of the first month. ⁶On the fifteenth day of that month the LORD's Feast of Unleavened Bread begins; for seven days you must eat bread made without yeast. ⁷On the first day hold a sacred assembly and do no regular work. ⁸For seven days present an offering made to the LORD by fire. And on the seventh day hold a sacred assembly and do no regular work.' "

Firstfruits

⁹The LORD said to Moses, ¹⁰"Speak to the Israelites and say to them: 'When you enter the land I am going to give you and you reap its harvest, bring to the priest a sheaf of the first grain you harvest. ¹¹He is to wave the sheaf before the LORD so it will be accepted on your behalf; the priest is to wave it on the day after the Sabbath. ¹²On the day you wave the sheaf, you must sacrifice as a burnt offering to the LORD a lamb a year old without defect, ¹³together with its grain offering of two-tenths of an ephah*c* of fine flour mixed with oil—an offering made to the LORD by fire, a pleasing aroma—and its drink offering of a quarter of a hin*d* of wine. ¹⁴You must not eat any bread, or roasted or new grain, until the very day you bring this offering to your God. This is to be a lasting ordinance for the generations to come, wherever you live.

Feast of Weeks

¹⁵" 'From the day after the Sabbath, the day you brought the sheaf of the wave offering, count off seven full weeks. ¹⁶Count off fifty days up to the day after the seventh Sabbath, and then present an offering of new grain to the LORD. ¹⁷From wherever you live, bring two loaves made of two-tenths of an ephah of fine flour, baked with yeast, as a wave offering of firstfruits to the LORD. ¹⁸Present with this bread seven male lambs, each a year old and without defect, one young bull and two rams. They will be a burnt offering

a32 Or made   *b32* Or who sanctifies you; or who sets you apart as holy   *c13* That is, probably about 4 quarts (about 4.5 liters); also in verse 17   *d13* That is, probably about 1 quart (about 1 liter)

to the LORD, together with their grain offerings and drink offerings—an offering made by fire, an aroma pleasing to the LORD. [19]Then sacrifice one male goat for a sin offering and two lambs, each a year old, for a fellowship offering.[a] [20]The priest is to wave the two lambs before the LORD as a wave offering, together with the bread of the firstfruits. They are a sacred offering to the LORD for the priest. [21]On that same day you are to proclaim a sacred assembly and do no regular work. This is to be a lasting ordinance for the generations to come, wherever you live.

[22]" 'When you reap the harvest of your land, do not reap to the very edges of your field or gather the gleanings of your harvest. Leave them for the poor and the alien. I am the LORD your God.' "

Feast of Trumpets

[23]The LORD said to Moses, [24]"Say to the Israelites: 'On the first day of the seventh month you are to have a day of rest, a sacred assembly commemorated with trumpet blasts. [25]Do no regular work, but present an offering made to the LORD by fire.' "

Day of Atonement

[26]The LORD said to Moses, [27]"The tenth day of this seventh month is the Day of Atonement. Hold a sacred assembly and deny yourselves,[b] and present an offering made to the LORD by fire. [28]Do no work on that day, because it is the Day of Atonement, when atonement is made for you before the LORD your God. [29]Anyone who does not deny himself on that day must be cut off from his people. [30]I will destroy from among his people anyone who does any work on that day. [31]You shall do no work at all. This is to be a lasting ordinance for the generations to come, wherever you live. [32]It is a sabbath of rest for you, and you must deny yourselves. From the evening of the ninth day of the month until the following evening you are to observe your sabbath."

Feast of Tabernacles

[33]The LORD said to Moses, [34]"Say to the Israelites: 'On the fifteenth day of the seventh month the LORD's Feast of Tabernacles begins, and it lasts for seven days.

[35]The first day is a sacred assembly; do no regular work. [36]For seven days present offerings made to the LORD by fire, and on the eighth day hold a sacred assembly and present an offering made to the LORD by fire. It is the closing assembly; do no regular work.

[37](" 'These are the LORD's appointed feasts, which you are to proclaim as sacred assemblies for bringing offerings made to the LORD by fire—the burnt offerings and grain offerings, sacrifices and drink offerings required for each day. [38]These offerings are in addition to those for the LORD's Sabbaths and[c] in addition to your gifts and whatever you have vowed and all the freewill offerings you give to the LORD.)

[39]" 'So beginning with the fifteenth day of the seventh month, after you have gathered the crops of the land, celebrate the festival to the LORD for seven days; the first day is a day of rest, and the eighth day also is a day of rest. [40]On the first day you are to take choice fruit from the trees, and palm fronds, leafy branches and poplars, and rejoice before the LORD your God for seven days. [41]Celebrate this as a festival to the LORD for seven days each year. This is to be a lasting ordinance for the generations to come; celebrate it in the seventh month. [42]Live in booths for seven days: All native-born Israelites are to live in booths [43]so your descendants will know that I had the Israelites live in booths when I brought them out of Egypt. I am the LORD your God.' "

[44]So Moses announced to the Israelites the appointed feasts of the LORD.

Oil and Bread Set Before the LORD

24 The LORD said to Moses, [2]"Command the Israelites to bring you clear oil of pressed olives for the light so that the lamps may be kept burning continually. [3]Outside the curtain of the Testimony in the Tent of Meeting, Aaron is to tend the lamps before the LORD from evening till morning, continually. This is to be a lasting ordinance for the genera-

---

[a]19 Traditionally *peace offering*   [b]27 Or *and fast*; also in verses 29 and 32   [c]38 Or *These feasts are in addition to the LORD's Sabbaths, and these offerings are*

tions to come. [4]The lamps on the pure gold lampstand before the LORD must be tended continually.

[5]"Take fine flour and bake twelve loaves of bread, using two-tenths of an ephah[a] for each loaf. [6]Set them in two rows, six in each row, on the table of pure gold before the LORD. [7]Along each row put some pure incense as a memorial portion to represent the bread and to be an offering made to the LORD by fire. [8]This bread is to be set out before the LORD regularly, Sabbath after Sabbath, on behalf of the Israelites, as a lasting covenant. [9]It belongs to Aaron and his sons, who are to eat it in a holy place, because it is a most holy part of their regular share of the offerings made to the LORD by fire."

A Blasphemer Stoned

[10]Now the son of an Israelite mother and an Egyptian father went out among the Israelites, and a fight broke out in the camp between him and an Israelite. [11]The son of the Israelite woman blasphemed the Name with a curse; so they brought him to Moses. (His mother's name was Shelomith, the daughter of Dibri the Danite.) [12]They put him in custody until the will of the LORD should be made clear to them.

[13]Then the LORD said to Moses: [14]"Take the blasphemer outside the camp. All those who heard him are to lay their hands on his head, and the entire assembly is to stone him. [15]Say to the Israelites: 'If anyone curses his God, he will be held responsible; [16]anyone who blasphemes the name of the LORD must be put to death. The entire assembly must stone him. Whether an alien or native-born, when he blasphemes the Name, he must be put to death.

[17]"'If anyone takes the life of a human being, he must be put to death. [18]Anyone who takes the life of someone's animal must make restitution—life for life. [19]If anyone injures his neighbor, whatever he has done must be done to him: [20]fracture for fracture, eye for eye, tooth for tooth. As he has injured the other, so he is to be injured. [21]Whoever kills an animal must make restitution, but whoever kills a man must be put to death. [22]You

are to have the same law for the alien and the native-born. I am the LORD your God.'"

[23]Then Moses spoke to the Israelites, and they took the blasphemer outside the camp and stoned him. The Israelites did as the LORD commanded Moses.

The Sabbath Year

25 The LORD said to Moses on Mount Sinai, [2]"Speak to the Israelites and say to them: 'When you enter the land I am going to give you, the land itself must observe a sabbath to the LORD. [3]For six years sow your fields, and for six years prune your vineyards and gather their crops. [4]But in the seventh year the land is to have a sabbath of rest, a sabbath to the LORD. Do not sow your fields or prune your vineyards. [5]Do not reap what grows of itself or harvest the grapes of your untended vines. The land is to have a year of rest. [6]Whatever the land yields during the sabbath year will be food for you—for yourself, your manservant and maidservant, and the hired worker and temporary resident who live among you, [7]as well as for your livestock and the wild animals in your land. Whatever the land produces may be eaten.

The Year of Jubilee

[8]"'Count off seven sabbaths of years—seven times seven years—so that the seven sabbaths of years amount to a period of forty-nine years. [9]Then have the trumpet sounded everywhere on the tenth day of the seventh month; on the Day of Atonement sound the trumpet throughout your land. [10]Consecrate the fiftieth year and proclaim liberty throughout the land to all its inhabitants. It shall be a jubilee for you; each one of you is to return to his family property and each to his own clan. [11]The fiftieth year shall be a jubilee for you; do not sow and do not reap what grows of itself or harvest the untended vines. [12]For it is a jubilee and is to be holy for you; eat only what is taken directly from the fields.

[13]"'In this Year of Jubilee everyone is to return to his own property.

[a]5 That is, probably about 4 quarts (about 4.5 liters)

¹⁴" 'If you sell land to one of your countrymen or buy any from him, do not take advantage of each other. ¹⁵You are to buy from your countryman on the basis of the number of years since the Jubilee. And he is to sell to you on the basis of the number of years left for harvesting crops. ¹⁶When the years are many, you are to increase the price, and when the years are few, you are to decrease the price, because what he is really selling you is the number of crops. ¹⁷Do not take advantage of each other, but fear your God. I am the LORD your God.

¹⁸" 'Follow my decrees and be careful to obey my laws, and you will live safely in the land. ¹⁹Then the land will yield its fruit, and you will eat your fill and live there in safety. ²⁰You may ask, "What will we eat in the seventh year if we do not plant or harvest our crops?" ²¹I will send you such a blessing in the sixth year that the land will yield enough for three years. ²²While you plant during the eighth year, you will eat from the old crop and will continue to eat from it until the harvest of the ninth year comes in.

²³" 'The land must not be sold permanently, because the land is mine and you are but aliens and my tenants. ²⁴Throughout the country that you hold as a possession, you must provide for the redemption of the land.

²⁵" 'If one of your countrymen becomes poor and sells some of his property, his nearest relative is to come and redeem what his countryman has sold. ²⁶If, however, a man has no one to redeem it for him but he himself prospers and acquires sufficient means to redeem it, ²⁷he is to determine the value for the years since he sold it and refund the balance to the man to whom he sold it; he can then go back to his own property. ²⁸But if he does not acquire the means to repay him, what he sold will remain in the possession of the buyer until the Year of Jubilee. It will be returned in the Jubilee, and he can then go back to his property.

²⁹" 'If a man sells a house in a walled city, he retains the right of redemption a full year after its sale. During that time he may redeem it. ³⁰If it is not redeemed before a full year has passed, the house in the walled city shall belong permanently to the buyer and his descendants. It is not to be returned in the Jubilee. ³¹But houses in villages without walls around them are to be considered as open country. They can be redeemed, and they are to be returned in the Jubilee.

³²" 'The Levites always have the right to redeem their houses in the Levitical towns, which they possess. ³³So the property of the Levites is redeemable—that is, a house sold in any town they hold—and is to be returned in the Jubilee, because the houses in the towns of the Levites are their property among the Israelites. ³⁴But the pastureland belonging to their towns must not be sold; it is their permanent possession.

³⁵" 'If one of your countrymen becomes poor and is unable to support himself among you, help him as you would an alien or a temporary resident, so he can continue to live among you. ³⁶Do not take interest of any kind[a] from him, but fear your God, so that your countryman may continue to live among you. ³⁷You must not lend him money at interest or sell him food at a profit. ³⁸I am the LORD your God, who brought you out of Egypt to give you the land of Canaan and to be your God.

³⁹" 'If one of your countrymen becomes poor among you and sells himself to you, do not make him work as a slave. ⁴⁰He is to be treated as a hired worker or a temporary resident among you; he is to work for you until the Year of Jubilee. ⁴¹Then he and his children are to be released, and he will go back to his own clan and to the property of his forefathers. ⁴²Because the Israelites are my servants, whom I brought out of Egypt, they must not be sold as slaves. ⁴³Do not rule over them ruthlessly, but fear your God.

⁴⁴" 'Your male and female slaves are to come from the nations around you; from them you may buy slaves. ⁴⁵You may also buy some of the temporary residents living among you and members of their clans born in your country, and they will become your property. ⁴⁶You can will them to your children as inherited property and can make them slaves for life,

---

[a]36 Or take excessive interest; similarly in verse 37

but you must not rule over your fellow Israelites ruthlessly.

⁴⁷ " 'If an alien or a temporary resident among you becomes rich and one of your countrymen becomes poor and sells himself to the alien living among you or to a member of the alien's clan, ⁴⁸he retains the right of redemption after he has sold himself. One of his relatives may redeem him: ⁴⁹An uncle or a cousin or any blood relative in his clan may redeem him. Or if he prospers, he may redeem himself. ⁵⁰He and his buyer are to count the time from the year he sold himself up to the Year of Jubilee. The price for his release is to be based on the rate paid to a hired man for that number of years. ⁵¹If many years remain, he must pay for his redemption a larger share of the price paid for him. ⁵²If only a few years remain until the Year of Jubilee, he is to compute that and pay for his redemption accordingly. ⁵³He is to be treated as a man hired from year to year; you must see to it that his owner does not rule over him ruthlessly.

⁵⁴ " 'Even if he is not redeemed in any of these ways, he and his children are to be released in the Year of Jubilee, ⁵⁵for the Israelites belong to me as servants. They are my servants, whom I brought out of Egypt. I am the LORD your God.

Reward for Obedience

26 " 'Do not make idols or set up an image or a sacred stone for yourselves, and do not place a carved stone in your land to bow down before it. I am the LORD your God.

² " 'Observe my Sabbaths and have reverence for my sanctuary. I am the LORD.

³ " 'If you follow my decrees and are careful to obey my commands, ⁴I will send you rain in its season, and the ground will yield its crops and the trees of the field their fruit. ⁵Your threshing will continue until grape harvest and the grape harvest will continue until planting, and you will eat all the food you want and live in safety in your land.

⁶ " 'I will grant peace in the land, and you will lie down and no one will make you afraid. I will remove savage beasts from the land, and the sword will not pass through your country. ⁷You will pursue your enemies, and they will fall by the sword before you. ⁸Five of you will chase a hundred, and a hundred of you will chase ten thousand, and your enemies will fall by the sword before you.

⁹ " 'I will look on you with favor and make you fruitful and increase your numbers, and I will keep my covenant with you. ¹⁰You will still be eating last year's harvest when you will have to move it out to make room for the new. ¹¹I will put my dwelling place*ᵃ* among you, and I will not abhor you. ¹²I will walk among you and be your God, and you will be my people. ¹³I am the LORD your God, who brought you out of Egypt so that you would no longer be slaves to the Egyptians; I broke the bars of your yoke and enabled you to walk with heads held high.

Punishment for Disobedience

¹⁴ " 'But if you will not listen to me and carry out all these commands, ¹⁵and if you reject my decrees and abhor my laws and fail to carry out all my commands and so violate my covenant, ¹⁶then I will do this to you: I will bring upon you sudden terror, wasting diseases and fever that will destroy your sight and drain away your life. You will plant seed in vain, because your enemies will eat it. ¹⁷I will set my face against you so that you will be defeated by your enemies; those who hate you will rule over you, and you will flee even when no one is pursuing you.

¹⁸ " 'If after all this you will not listen to me, I will punish you for your sins seven times over. ¹⁹I will break down your stubborn pride and make the sky above you like iron and the ground beneath you like bronze. ²⁰Your strength will be spent in vain, because your soil will not yield its crops, nor will the trees of the land yield their fruit.

²¹ " 'If you remain hostile toward me and refuse to listen to me, I will multiply your afflictions seven times over, as your sins deserve. ²²I will send wild animals against you, and they will rob you of your children, destroy your cattle and make you so few in number that your roads will be deserted.

²³ " 'If in spite of these things you do not accept my correction but continue to be

ᵃ11 Or *my tabernacle*

hostile toward me, ²⁴I myself will be hostile toward you and will afflict you for your sins seven times over. ²⁵And I will bring the sword upon you to avenge the breaking of the covenant. When you withdraw into your cities, I will send a plague among you, and you will be given into enemy hands. ²⁶When I cut off your supply of bread, ten women will be able to bake your bread in one oven, and they will dole out the bread by weight. You will eat, but you will not be satisfied.

²⁷" 'If in spite of this you still do not listen to me but continue to be hostile toward me, ²⁸then in my anger I will be hostile toward you, and I myself will punish you for your sins seven times over. ²⁹You will eat the flesh of your sons and the flesh of your daughters. ³⁰I will destroy your high places, cut down your incense altars and pile your dead bodies on the lifeless forms of your idols, and I will abhor you. ³¹I will turn your cities into ruins and lay waste your sanctuaries, and I will take no delight in the pleasing aroma of your offerings. ³²I will lay waste the land, so that your enemies who live there will be appalled. ³³I will scatter you among the nations and will draw out my sword and pursue you. Your land will be laid waste, and your cities will lie in ruins. ³⁴Then the land will enjoy its sabbath years all the time that it lies desolate and you are in the country of your enemies; then the land will rest and enjoy its sabbaths. ³⁵All the time that it lies desolate, the land will have the rest it did not have during the sabbaths you lived in it.

³⁶" 'As for those of you who are left, I will make their hearts so fearful in the lands of their enemies that the sound of a windblown leaf will put them to flight. They will run as though fleeing from the sword, and they will fall, even though no one is pursuing them. ³⁷They will stumble over one another as though fleeing from the sword, even though no one is pursuing them. So you will not be able to stand before your enemies. ³⁸You will perish among the nations; the land of your enemies will devour you. ³⁹Those of you who are left will waste away in the lands of their enemies because of their sins; also because of their fathers' sins they will waste away.

⁴⁰" 'But if they will confess their sins and the sins of their fathers—their treachery against me and their hostility toward me, ⁴¹which made me hostile toward them so that I sent them into the land of their enemies—then when their uncircumcised hearts are humbled and they pay for their sin, ⁴²I will remember my covenant with Jacob and my covenant with Isaac and my covenant with Abraham, and I will remember the land. ⁴³For the land will be deserted by them and will enjoy its sabbaths while it lies desolate without them. They will pay for their sins because they rejected my laws and abhorred my decrees. ⁴⁴Yet in spite of this, when they are in the land of their enemies, I will not reject them or abhor them so as to destroy them completely, breaking my covenant with them. I am the LORD their God. ⁴⁵But for their sake I will remember the covenant with their ancestors whom I brought out of Egypt in the sight of the nations to be their God. I am the LORD.' "

⁴⁶These are the decrees, the laws and the regulations that the LORD established on Mount Sinai between himself and the Israelites through Moses.

Redeeming What Is the LORD's

27 The LORD said to Moses, ²"Speak to the Israelites and say to them: 'If anyone makes a special vow to dedicate persons to the LORD by giving equivalent values, ³set the value of a male between the ages of twenty and sixty at fifty shekels^a of silver, according to the sanctuary shekel^b; ⁴and if it is a female, set her value at thirty shekels.^c ⁵If it is a person between the ages of five and twenty, set the value of a male at twenty shekels^d and of a female at ten shekels.^e ⁶If it is a person between one month and five years, set the value of a male at five shekels^f of silver and that of a female at three shekels^g of silver. ⁷If it is a person sixty years old or more, set the value of a male at fifteen

---

^a3 That is, about 1 1/4 pounds (about 0.6 kilogram); also in verse 16   ^b3 That is, about 2/5 ounce (about 11.5 grams); also in verse 25   ^c4 That is, about 12 ounces (about 0.3 kilogram)   ^d5 That is, about 8 ounces (about 0.2 kilogram)   ^e5 That is, about 4 ounces (about 110 grams); also in verse 7   ^f6 That is, about 2 ounces (about 55 grams)   ^g6 That is, about 1 1/4 ounces (about 35 grams)

shekels[a] and of a female at ten shekels. [8]If anyone making the vow is too poor to pay the specified amount, he is to present the person to the priest, who will set the value for him according to what the man making the vow can afford.

[9]" 'If what he vowed is an animal that is acceptable as an offering to the LORD, such an animal given to the LORD becomes holy. [10]He must not exchange it or substitute a good one for a bad one, or a bad one for a good one; if he should substitute one animal for another, both it and the substitute become holy. [11]If what he vowed is a ceremonially unclean animal—one that is not acceptable as an offering to the LORD—the animal must be presented to the priest, [12]who will judge its quality as good or bad. Whatever value the priest then sets, that is what it will be. [13]If the owner wishes to redeem the animal, he must add a fifth to its value.

[14]" 'If a man dedicates his house as something holy to the LORD, the priest will judge its quality as good or bad. Whatever value the priest then sets, so it will remain. [15]If the man who dedicates his house redeems it, he must add a fifth to its value, and the house will again become his.

[16]" 'If a man dedicates to the LORD part of his family land, its value is to be set according to the amount of seed required for it—fifty shekels of silver to a homer[b] of barley seed. [17]If he dedicates his field during the Year of Jubilee, the value that has been set remains. [18]But if he dedicates his field after the Jubilee, the priest will determine the value according to the number of years that remain until the next Year of Jubilee, and its set value will be reduced. [19]If the man who dedicates the field wishes to redeem it, he must add a fifth to its value, and the field will again become his. [20]If, however, he does not redeem the field, or if he has sold it to someone else, it can never be redeemed. [21]When the field is released in the Jubilee, it will become holy, like a field devoted to the LORD; it will become the property of the priests.[c]

[22]" 'If a man dedicates to the LORD a field he has bought, which is not part of his family land, [23]the priest will determine its value up to the Year of Jubilee, and the man must pay its value on that day as something holy to the LORD. [24]In the Year of Jubilee the field will revert to the person from whom he bought it, the one whose land it was. [25]Every value is to be set according to the sanctuary shekel, twenty gerahs to the shekel.

[26]" 'No one, however, may dedicate the firstborn of an animal, since the firstborn already belongs to the LORD; whether an ox[d] or a sheep, it is the LORD's. [27]If it is one of the unclean animals, he may buy it back at its set value, adding a fifth of the value to it. If he does not redeem it, it is to be sold at its set value.

[28]" 'But nothing that a man owns and devotes[e] to the LORD—whether man or animal or family land—may be sold or redeemed; everything so devoted is most holy to the LORD.

> "BUT nothing that a man owns and devotes to the LORD—whether man or animal or family land—may be sold or redeemed; everything so devoted is most holy to the LORD."
>
> LEVITICUS 27:28

[29]" 'No person devoted to destruction[f] may be ransomed; he must be put to death.

[30]" 'A tithe of everything from the land, whether grain from the soil or fruit from the trees, belongs to the LORD; it is holy to the LORD. [31]If a man redeems any of his tithe, he must add a fifth of the value to it. [32]The entire tithe of the herd and flock—every tenth animal that passes under the shepherd's rod—will be holy to the LORD. [33]He must not pick out the good from the bad or make any substitution. If he does make a substitution, both the animal and its substitute become holy and cannot be redeemed.' "

[34]These are the commands the LORD gave Moses on Mount Sinai for the Israelites.

[a]7 That is, about 6 ounces (about 170 grams) [b]16 That is, probably about 6 bushels (about 220 liters)   [c]21 Or priest   [d]26 The Hebrew word can include both male and female. [e]28 The Hebrew term refers to the irrevocable giving over of things or persons to the LORD. [f]29 The Hebrew term refers to the irrevocable giving over of things or persons to the LORD, often by totally destroying them.

Numbers

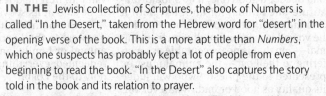

IN THE Jewish collection of Scriptures, the book of Numbers is called "In the Desert," taken from the Hebrew word for "desert" in the opening verse of the book. This is a more apt title than *Numbers*, which one suspects has probably kept a lot of people from even beginning to read the book. "In the Desert" also captures the story told in the book and its relation to prayer.

In his *Confessions*, St. Augustine writes, "For it is one thing to see the land of peace from a wooded ridge . . . and another to tread the road that leads to it."[1] God had promised to lead his rescued people to a land of freedom, flowing with milk and honey (see Exodus 3:8). What a wonderful concept to a group of slaves whose workweek was 24/7, who had no medical and dental coverage, and who had no hope for retirement. They couldn't wait to pack their bags and start the journey. But there was just one problem: They had to cross a desert and to trust God to give them everything they needed as they traveled. They would have to become pilgrims. It is the struggle to be a pilgrim that forms the plot of the book of Numbers or "In the Desert."

The spiritual life is a marathon, not a sprint; it is a "long obedience in the same direction" (Nietzsche), not a weekend getaway. The gift of freedom and peace is just that: a gift, free, gratis. But it is not cheap. The saved still need to put one foot in front of the other, day in and day out. William Carey said his great virtue was that he could "plod." That's more than a virtue; it's essential for this journey. Ninety percent of learning to pray is just showing up—faithfully.

The journey of prayer is full of surprises and challenges, and God has much to teach us along the way. But we won't learn anything unless we come to the school of prayer. From this school the graduates will sing,

> Hitherto Thy love has blest me;
> Thou hast brought me to this place;
> And I know Thy hand will bring me
> Safely home by Thy good grace.
> Jesus sought me when a stranger,
> Wandering from the fold of God;
> He, to rescue me from danger,
> Bought me with His precious blood.[2]

SO MOSES PRAYED FOR THE PEOPLE.
(21:7)

The Census

1 The LORD spoke to Moses in the Tent of Meeting in the Desert of Sinai on the first day of the second month of the second year after the Israelites came out of Egypt. He said: ²"Take a census of the whole Israelite community by their clans and families, listing every man by name, one by one. ³You and Aaron are to number by their divisions all the men in Israel twenty years old or more who are able to serve in the army. ⁴One man from each tribe, each the head of his family, is to help you. ⁵These are the names of the men who are to assist you:

from Reuben, Elizur son of Shedeur;
⁶from Simeon, Shelumiel son of Zurishaddai;
⁷from Judah, Nahshon son of Amminadab;
⁸from Issachar, Nethanel son of Zuar;
⁹from Zebulun, Eliab son of Helon;
¹⁰from the sons of Joseph:
from Ephraim, Elishama son of Ammihud;
from Manasseh, Gamaliel son of Pedahzur;
¹¹from Benjamin, Abidan son of Gideoni;
¹²from Dan, Ahiezer son of Ammishaddai;
¹³from Asher, Pagiel son of Ocran;
¹⁴from Gad, Eliasaph son of Deuel;
¹⁵from Naphtali, Ahira son of Enan."

¹⁶These were the men appointed from the community, the leaders of their ancestral tribes. They were the heads of the clans of Israel. ¹⁷Moses and Aaron took these men whose names had been given, ¹⁸and they called the whole community together on the first day of the second month. The people indicated their ancestry by their clans and families, and the men twenty years old or more were listed by name, one by one, ¹⁹as the LORD commanded Moses. And so he counted them in the Desert of Sinai:

²⁰From the descendants of Reuben the firstborn son of Israel:

All the men twenty years old or more who were able to serve in the army were listed by name, one by one, according to the records of their clans and families. ²¹The number from the tribe of Reuben was 46,500.

²²From the descendants of Simeon:

All the men twenty years old or more who were able to serve in the army were counted and listed by name, one by one, according to the records of their clans and families. ²³The number from the tribe of Simeon was 59,300.

²⁴From the descendants of Gad:

All the men twenty years old or more who were able to serve in the army were listed by name, according to the records of their clans and families. ²⁵The number from the tribe of Gad was 45,650.

²⁶From the descendants of Judah:

All the men twenty years old or more who were able to serve in the army were listed by name, according to the records of their clans and families. ²⁷The number from the tribe of Judah was 74,600.

²⁸From the descendants of Issachar:

All the men twenty years old or more who were able to serve in the army were listed by name, according to the records of their clans and families. ²⁹The number from the tribe of Issachar was 54,400.

³⁰From the descendants of Zebulun:

All the men twenty years old or more who were able to serve in the army were listed by name, according to the records of their clans and families. ³¹The number from the tribe of Zebulun was 57,400.

³²From the sons of Joseph:

From the descendants of Ephraim:

All the men twenty years old or more who were able to serve in the army were listed by name, according to the records of their clans and families. ³³The number from the tribe of Ephraim was 40,500.

34From the descendants of Manasseh: All the men twenty years old or more who were able to serve in the army were listed by name, according to the records of their clans and families. 35The number from the tribe of Manasseh was 32,200.

36From the descendants of Benjamin: All the men twenty years old or more who were able to serve in the army were listed by name, according to the records of their clans and families. 37The number from the tribe of Benjamin was 35,400.

38From the descendants of Dan: All the men twenty years old or more who were able to serve in the army were listed by name, according to the records of their clans and families. 39The number from the tribe of Dan was 62,700.

40From the descendants of Asher: All the men twenty years old or more who were able to serve in the army were listed by name, according to the records of their clans and families. 41The number from the tribe of Asher was 41,500.

42From the descendants of Naphtali: All the men twenty years old or more who were able to serve in the army were listed by name, according to the records of their clans and families. 43The number from the tribe of Naphtali was 53,400.

44These were the men counted by Moses and Aaron and the twelve leaders of Israel, each one representing his family. 45All the Israelites twenty years old or more who were able to serve in Israel's army were counted according to their families. 46The total number was 603,550.

47The families of the tribe of Levi, however, were not counted along with the others. 48The LORD had said to Moses: 49"You must not count the tribe of Levi or include them in the census of the other Israelites. 50Instead, appoint the Levites to

be in charge of the tabernacle of the Testimony—over all its furnishings and everything belonging to it. They are to carry the tabernacle and all its furnishings; they are to take care of it and encamp around it. 51Whenever the tabernacle is to move, the Levites are to take it down, and whenever the tabernacle is to be set up, the Levites shall do it. Anyone else who goes near it shall be put to death. 52The Israelites are to set up their tents by divisions, each man in his own camp under his own standard. 53The Levites, however, are to set up their tents around the tabernacle of the Testimony so that wrath will not fall on the Israelite community. The Levites are to be responsible for the care of the tabernacle of the Testimony."

54The Israelites did all this just as the LORD commanded Moses.

The Arrangement of the Tribal Camps

2 The LORD said to Moses and Aaron: 2"The Israelites are to camp around the Tent of Meeting some distance from it, each man under his standard with the banners of his family."

3On the east, toward the sunrise, the divisions of the camp of Judah are to encamp under their standard. The leader of the people of Judah is Nahshon son of Amminadab. 4His division numbers 74,600.

5The tribe of Issachar will camp next to them. The leader of the people of Issachar is Nethanel son of Zuar. 6His division numbers 54,400. 7The tribe of Zebulun will be next. The leader of the people of Zebulun is Eliab son of Helon. 8His division numbers 57,400.

9All the men assigned to the camp of Judah, according to their divisions, number 186,400. They will set out first.

> *One must learn an inner solitude, where or with whomsoever he may be. He must learn to penetrate things and find God there, to get a strong impression of God firmly fixed on his mind.*
>
> MEISTER ECKART

¹⁰On the south will be the divisions of the camp of Reuben under their standard. The leader of the people of Reuben is Elizur son of Shedeur. ¹¹His division numbers 46,500.

¹²The tribe of Simeon will camp next to them. The leader of the people of Simeon is Shelumiel son of Zurishaddai. ¹³His division numbers 59,300.

¹⁴The tribe of Gad will be next. The leader of the people of Gad is Eliasaph son of Deuel.ᵃ ¹⁵His division numbers 45,650.

¹⁶All the men assigned to the camp of Reuben, according to their divisions, number 151,450. They will set out second.

¹⁷Then the Tent of Meeting and the camp of the Levites will set out in the middle of the camps. They will set out in the same order as they encamp, each in his own place under his standard.

¹⁸On the west will be the divisions of the camp of Ephraim under their standard. The leader of the people of Ephraim is Elishama son of Ammihud. ¹⁹His division numbers 40,500.

²⁰The tribe of Manasseh will be next to them. The leader of the people of Manasseh is Gamaliel son of Pedahzur. ²¹His division numbers 32,200.

²²The tribe of Benjamin will be next. The leader of the people of Benjamin is Abidan son of Gideoni. ²³His division numbers 35,400.

²⁴All the men assigned to the camp of Ephraim, according to their divisions, number 108,100. They will set out third.

²⁵On the north will be the divisions of the camp of Dan, under their standard. The leader of the people of Dan is Ahiezer son of Ammishaddai. ²⁶His division numbers 62,700.

²⁷The tribe of Asher will camp next to them. The leader of the people of Asher is Pagiel son of Ocran. ²⁸His division numbers 41,500.

²⁹The tribe of Naphtali will be next. The leader of the people of Naphtali is Ahira son of Enan. ³⁰His division numbers 53,400.

³¹All the men assigned to the camp of Dan number 157,600. They will set out last, under their standards.

³²These are the Israelites, counted according to their families. All those in the camps, by their divisions, number 603,550. ³³The Levites, however, were not counted along with the other Israelites, as the LORD commanded Moses.

³⁴So the Israelites did everything the LORD commanded Moses; that is the way they encamped under their standards, and that is the way they set out, each with his clan and family.

The Levites

3 This is the account of the family of Aaron and Moses at the time the LORD talked with Moses on Mount Sinai.

²The names of the sons of Aaron were Nadab the firstborn and Abihu, Eleazar and Ithamar. ³Those were the names of Aaron's sons, the anointed priests, who were ordained to serve as priests. ⁴Nadab and Abihu, however, fell dead before the LORD when they made an offering with unauthorized fire before him in the Desert of Sinai. They had no sons; so only Eleazar and Ithamar served as priests during the lifetime of their father Aaron.

⁵The LORD said to Moses, ⁶"Bring the tribe of Levi and present them to Aaron the priest to assist him. ⁷They are to perform duties for him and for the whole community at the Tent of Meeting by doing the work of the tabernacle. ⁸They are to take care of all the furnishings of the Tent of Meeting, fulfilling the obligations of the Israelites by doing the work of the tabernacle. ⁹Give the Levites to Aaron and his sons; they are the Israelites who are to be given wholly to him.ᵇ ¹⁰Appoint

ᵃ14 Many manuscripts of the Masoretic Text, Samaritan Pentateuch and Vulgate (see also Num. 1:14); most manuscripts of the Masoretic Text Reuel   ᵇ9 Most manuscripts of the Masoretic Text; some manuscripts of the Masoretic Text, Samaritan Pentateuch and Septuagint (see also Num. 8:16) to me

Aaron and his sons to serve as priests; anyone else who approaches the sanctuary must be put to death."

[11]The LORD also said to Moses, [12]"I have taken the Levites from among the Israelites in place of the first male offspring of every Israelite woman. The Levites are mine, [13]for all the firstborn are mine. When I struck down all the firstborn in Egypt, I set apart for myself every firstborn in Israel, whether man or animal. They are to be mine. I am the LORD."

[14]The LORD said to Moses in the Desert of Sinai, [15]"Count the Levites by their families and clans. Count every male a month old or more." [16]So Moses counted them, as he was commanded by the word of the LORD.

[17]These were the names of the sons of Levi:

Gershon, Kohath and Merari.

[18]These were the names of the Gershonite clans:

Libni and Shimei.

[19]The Kohathite clans:

Amram, Izhar, Hebron and Uzziel.

[20]The Merarite clans:

Mahli and Mushi.

These were the Levite clans, according to their families.

[21]To Gershon belonged the clans of the Libnites and Shimeites; these were the Gershonite clans. [22]The number of all the males a month old or more who were counted was 7,500. [23]The Gershonite clans were to camp on the west, behind the tabernacle. [24]The leader of the families of the Gershonites was Eliasaph son of Lael. [25]At the Tent of Meeting the Gershonites were responsible for the care of the tabernacle and tent, its coverings, the curtain at the entrance to the Tent of Meeting, [26]the curtains of the courtyard, the curtain at the entrance to the courtyard surrounding the tabernacle and altar, and the ropes—and everything related to their use.

[27]To Kohath belonged the clans of the Amramites, Izharites, Hebronites and Uzzielites; these were the Kohathite clans. [28]The number of all the males a month old or more was 8,600.[a] The Kohathites were responsible for the care of the sanc-

tuary. [29]The Kohathite clans were to camp on the south side of the tabernacle. [30]The leader of the families of the Kohathite clans was Elizaphan son of Uzziel. [31]They were responsible for the care of the ark, the table, the lampstand, the altars, the articles of the sanctuary used in ministering, the curtain, and everything related to their use. [32]The chief leader of the Levites was Eleazar son of Aaron, the priest. He was appointed over those who were responsible for the care of the sanctuary.

[33]To Merari belonged the clans of the Mahlites and the Mushites; these were the Merarite clans. [34]The number of all the males a month old or more who were counted was 6,200. [35]The leader of the families of the Merarite clans was Zuriel son of Abihail; they were to camp on the north side of the tabernacle. [36]The Merarites were appointed to take care of the frames of the tabernacle, its crossbars, posts, bases, all its equipment, and everything related to their use, [37]as well as the posts of the surrounding courtyard with their bases, tent pegs and ropes.

[38]Moses and Aaron and his sons were to camp to the east of the tabernacle, toward the sunrise, in front of the Tent of Meeting. They were responsible for the care of the sanctuary on behalf of the Israelites. Anyone else who approached the sanctuary was to be put to death.

[39]The total number of Levites counted at the LORD's command by Moses and Aaron according to their clans, including every male a month old or more, was 22,000.

[40]The LORD said to Moses, "Count all the firstborn Israelite males who are a month old or more and make a list of their names. [41]Take the Levites for me in place of all the firstborn of the Israelites, and the livestock of the Levites in place of all the firstborn of the livestock of the Israelites. I am the LORD."

[42]So Moses counted all the firstborn of the Israelites, as the LORD commanded

[a]28 Hebrew; some Septuagint manuscripts 8,300

him. [43]The total number of firstborn males a month old or more, listed by name, was 22,273.

[44]The LORD also said to Moses, [45]"Take the Levites in place of all the firstborn of Israel, and the livestock of the Levites in place of their livestock. The Levites are to be mine. I am the LORD. [46]To redeem the 273 firstborn Israelites who exceed the number of the Levites, [47]collect five shekels[a] for each one, according to the sanctuary shekel, which weighs twenty gerahs. [48]Give the money for the redemption of the additional Israelites to Aaron and his sons."

[49]So Moses collected the redemption money from those who exceeded the number redeemed by the Levites. [50]From the firstborn of the Israelites he collected silver weighing 1,365 shekels,[b] according to the sanctuary shekel. [51]Moses gave the redemption money to Aaron and his sons, as he was commanded by the word of the LORD.

The Kohathites

4 The LORD said to Moses and Aaron: [2]"Take a census of the Kohathite branch of the Levites by their clans and families. [3]Count all the men from thirty to fifty years of age who come to serve in the work in the Tent of Meeting.

[4]"This is the work of the Kohathites in the Tent of Meeting: the care of the most holy things. [5]When the camp is to move, Aaron and his sons are to go in and take down the shielding curtain and cover the ark of the Testimony with it. [6]Then they are to cover this with hides of sea cows,[c] spread a cloth of solid blue over that and put the poles in place.

[7]"Over the table of the Presence they are to spread a blue cloth and put on it the plates, dishes and bowls, and the jars for drink offerings; the bread that is continually there is to remain on it. [8]Over these they are to spread a scarlet cloth, cover that with hides of sea cows and put its poles in place.

[9]"They are to take a blue cloth and cover the lampstand that is for light, together with its lamps, its wick trimmers and trays, and all its jars for the oil used to supply it. [10]Then they are to wrap it and all its accessories in a covering of hides of sea cows and put it on a carrying frame.

[11]"Over the gold altar they are to spread a blue cloth and cover that with hides of sea cows and put its poles in place.

[12]"They are to take all the articles used for ministering in the sanctuary, wrap them in a blue cloth, cover that with hides of sea cows and put them on a carrying frame.

[13]"They are to remove the ashes from the bronze altar and spread a purple cloth over it. [14]Then they are to place on it all the utensils used for ministering at the altar, including the firepans, meat forks, shovels and sprinkling bowls. Over it they are to spread a covering of hides of sea cows and put its poles in place.

[15]"After Aaron and his sons have finished covering the holy furnishings and all the holy articles, and when the camp is ready to move, the Kohathites are to come to do the carrying. But they must not touch the holy things or they will die. The Kohathites are to carry those things that are in the Tent of Meeting.

[16]"Eleazar son of Aaron, the priest, is to have charge of the oil for the light, the fragrant incense, the regular grain offering and the anointing oil. He is to be in charge of the entire tabernacle and everything in it, including its holy furnishings and articles."

[17]The LORD said to Moses and Aaron, [18]"See that the Kohathite tribal clans are not cut off from the Levites. [19]So that they may live and not die when they come near the most holy things, do this for them: Aaron and his sons are to go into the sanctuary and assign to each man his work and what he is to carry. [20]But the Kohathites must not go in to look at the holy things, even for a moment, or they will die."

The Gershonites

[21]The LORD said to Moses, [22]"Take a census also of the Gershonites by their families and clans. [23]Count all the men from thirty to fifty years of age who come to serve in the work at the Tent of Meeting.

[a]47 That is, about 2 ounces (about 55 grams)
[b]50 That is, about 35 pounds (about 15.5 kilograms)   [c]6 That is, dugongs; also in verses 8, 10, 11, 12, 14 and 25

24"This is the service of the Gershonite clans as they work and carry burdens: 25They are to carry the curtains of the tabernacle, the Tent of Meeting, its covering and the outer covering of hides of sea cows, the curtains for the entrance to the Tent of Meeting, 26the curtains of the courtyard surrounding the tabernacle and altar, the curtain for the entrance, the ropes and all the equipment used in its service. The Gershonites are to do all that needs to be done with these things. 27All their service, whether carrying or doing other work, is to be done under the direction of Aaron and his sons. You shall assign to them as their responsibility all they are to carry. 28This is the service of the Gershonite clans at the Tent of Meeting. Their duties are to be under the direction of Ithamar son of Aaron, the priest.

The Merarites

29"Count the Merarites by their clans and families. 30Count all the men from thirty to fifty years of age who come to serve in the work at the Tent of Meeting. 31This is their duty as they perform service at the Tent of Meeting: to carry the frames of the tabernacle, its crossbars, posts and bases, 32as well as the posts of the surrounding courtyard with their bases, tent pegs, ropes, all their equipment and everything related to their use. Assign to each man the specific things he is to carry. 33This is the service of the Merarite clans as they work at the Tent of Meeting under the direction of Ithamar son of Aaron, the priest."

The Numbering of the Levite Clans

34Moses, Aaron and the leaders of the community counted the Kohathites by their clans and families. 35All the men from thirty to fifty years of age who came to serve in the work in the Tent of Meeting, 36counted by clans, were 2,750. 37This was the total of all those in the Kohathite clans who served in the Tent of Meeting. Moses and Aaron counted them according to the LORD's command through Moses.

38The Gershonites were counted by their clans and families. 39All the men from thirty to fifty years of age who came

to serve in the work at the Tent of Meeting, 40counted by their clans and families, were 2,630. 41This was the total of those in the Gershonite clans who served at the Tent of Meeting. Moses and Aaron counted them according to the LORD's command.

42The Merarites were counted by their clans and families. 43All the men from thirty to fifty years of age who came to serve in the work at the Tent of Meeting, 44counted by their clans, were 3,200. 45This was the total of those in the Merarite clans. Moses and Aaron counted them according to the LORD's command through Moses.

46So Moses, Aaron and the leaders of Israel counted all the Levites by their clans and families. 47All the men from thirty to fifty years of age who came to do the work of serving and carrying the Tent of Meeting 48numbered 8,580. 49At the LORD's command through Moses, each was assigned his work and told what to carry.

Thus they were counted, as the LORD commanded Moses.

The Purity of the Camp

5 The LORD said to Moses, 2"Command the Israelites to send away from the camp anyone who has an infectious skin disease[a] or a discharge of any kind, or who is ceremonially unclean because of a dead body. 3Send away male and female alike; send them outside the camp so they will not defile their camp, where I dwell among them." 4The Israelites did this; they sent them outside the camp. They did just as the LORD had instructed Moses.

Restitution for Wrongs

5The LORD said to Moses, 6"Say to the Israelites: 'When a man or woman wrongs another in any way[b] and so is unfaithful to the LORD, that person is guilty 7and must confess the sin he has committed. He must make full restitution for his wrong, add one fifth to it and give it all to the person he has wronged. 8But if that

---

[a]2 Traditionally *leprosy*; the Hebrew word was used for various diseases affecting the skin—not necessarily leprosy.   [b]6 Or *woman commits any wrong common to mankind*

person has no close relative to whom restitution can be made for the wrong, the restitution belongs to the LORD and must be given to the priest, along with the ram with which atonement is made for him. [9]All the sacred contributions the Israelites bring to a priest will belong to him. [10]Each man's sacred gifts are his own, but what he gives to the priest will belong to the priest.' "

The Test for an Unfaithful Wife

[11]Then the LORD said to Moses, [12]"Speak to the Israelites and say to them: 'If a man's wife goes astray and is unfaithful to him [13]by sleeping with another man, and this is hidden from her husband and her impurity is undetected (since there is no witness against her and she has not been caught in the act), [14]and if feelings of jealousy come over her husband and he suspects his wife and she is impure—or if he is jealous and suspects her even though she is not impure— [15]then he is to take his wife to the priest. He must also take an offering of a tenth of an ephah[a] of barley flour on her behalf. He must not pour oil on it or put incense on it, because it is a grain offering for jealousy, a reminder offering to draw attention to guilt.

[16]" 'The priest shall bring her and have her stand before the LORD. [17]Then he shall take some holy water in a clay jar and put some dust from the tabernacle floor into the water. [18]After the priest has had the woman stand before the LORD, he shall loosen her hair and place in her hands the reminder offering, the grain offering for jealousy, while he himself holds the bitter water that brings a curse. [19]Then the priest shall put the woman under oath and say to her, "If no other man has slept with you and you have not gone astray and become impure while married to your husband, may this bitter water that brings a curse not harm you. [20]But if you have gone astray while married to your husband and you have defiled yourself by sleeping with a man other than your husband"— [21]here the priest is to put the woman under this curse of the oath—"may the LORD cause your people to curse and denounce you when he causes your thigh to waste away and your abdomen to swell.[b] [22]May this water

that brings a curse enter your body so that your abdomen swells and your thigh wastes away.[c]"

" 'Then the woman is to say, "Amen. So be it."

[23]" 'The priest is to write these curses on a scroll and then wash them off into the bitter water. [24]He shall have the woman drink the bitter water that brings a curse, and this water will enter her and cause bitter suffering. [25]The priest is to take from her hands the grain offering for jealousy, wave it before the LORD and bring it to the altar. [26]The priest is then to take a handful of the grain offering as a memorial offering and burn it on the altar; after that, he is to have the woman drink the water. [27]If she has defiled herself and been unfaithful to her husband, then when she is made to drink the water that brings a curse, it will go into her and cause bitter suffering; her abdomen will swell and her thigh waste away,[d] and she will become accursed among her people. [28]If, however, the woman has not defiled herself and is free from impurity, she will be cleared of guilt and will be able to have children.

[29]" 'This, then, is the law of jealousy when a woman goes astray and defiles herself while married to her husband, [30]or when feelings of jealousy come over a man because he suspects his wife. The priest is to have her stand before the LORD and is to apply this entire law to her. [31]The husband will be innocent of any wrongdoing, but the woman will bear the consequences of her sin.' "

The Nazirite

6 The LORD said to Moses, [2]"Speak to the Israelites and say to them: 'If a man or woman wants to make a special vow, a vow of separation to the LORD as a Nazirite, [3]he must abstain from wine and other fermented drink and must not drink vinegar made from wine or from other fermented drink. He must not drink grape juice or eat grapes or raisins.

---

[a]15 That is, probably about 2 quarts (about 2 liters)   [b]21 Or causes you to have a miscarrying womb and barrenness
[c]22 Or body and cause you to be barren and have a miscarrying womb   [d]27 Or suffering; she will have barrenness and a miscarrying womb

4As long as he is a Nazirite, he must not eat anything that comes from the grapevine, not even the seeds or skins.

5" 'During the entire period of his vow of separation no razor may be used on his head. He must be holy until the period of his separation to the LORD is over; he must let the hair of his head grow long. 6Throughout the period of his separation to the LORD he must not go near a dead body. 7Even if his own father or mother or brother or sister dies, he must not make himself ceremonially unclean on account of them, because the symbol of his separation to God is on his head. 8Throughout the period of his separation he is consecrated to the LORD.

9" 'If someone dies suddenly in his presence, thus defiling the hair he has dedicated, he must shave his head on the day of his cleansing—the seventh day. 10Then on the eighth day he must bring two doves or two young pigeons to the priest at the entrance to the Tent of Meeting. 11The priest is to offer one as a sin offering and the other as a burnt offering to make atonement for him because he sinned by being in the presence of the dead body. That same day he is to consecrate his head. 12He must dedicate himself to the LORD for the period of his separation and must bring a year-old male lamb as a guilt offering. The previous days do not count, because he became defiled during his separation.

13" 'Now this is the law for the Nazirite when the period of his separation is over. He is to be brought to the entrance to the Tent of Meeting. 14There he is to present his offerings to the LORD: a year-old male lamb without defect for a burnt offering, a year-old ewe lamb without defect for a sin offering, a ram without defect for a fellowship offering,*a* 15together with their grain offerings and drink offerings, and a basket of bread made without yeast— cakes of fine flour mixed with oil, and wafers spread with oil.

16" 'The priest is to present them before the LORD and make the sin offering and the burnt offering. 17He is to present the basket of unleavened bread and is to sacrifice the ram as a fellowship offering to the LORD, together with its grain offering and drink offering.

18" 'Then at the entrance to the Tent of Meeting, the Nazirite must shave off the hair that he dedicated. He is to take the hair and put it in the fire that is under the sacrifice of the fellowship offering.

19" 'After the Nazirite has shaved off the hair of his dedication, the priest is to place in his hands a boiled shoulder of the ram, and a cake and a wafer from the basket, both made without yeast. 20The priest shall then wave them before the LORD as a wave offering; they are holy and belong to the priest, together with the breast that was waved and the thigh that was presented. After that, the Nazirite may drink wine.

21" 'This is the law of the Nazirite who vows his offering to the LORD in accordance with his separation, in addition to whatever else he can afford. He must fulfill the vow he has made, according to the law of the Nazirite.' "

The Priestly Blessing

22The LORD said to Moses, 23"Tell Aaron and his sons, 'This is how you are to bless the Israelites. Say to them:

24 " ' "The LORD bless you
  and keep you;
25 the LORD make his face shine
    upon you
  and be gracious to you;
26 the LORD turn his face toward you
  and give you peace." '

27"So they will put my name on the Israelites, and I will bless them."

Offerings at the Dedication of the Tabernacle

7 When Moses finished setting up the tabernacle, he anointed it and consecrated it and all its furnishings. He also anointed and consecrated the altar and all its utensils. 2Then the leaders of Israel, the heads of families who were the tribal leaders in charge of those who were counted, made offerings. 3They brought as their gifts before the LORD six covered carts and twelve oxen—an ox from each leader and a cart from every two. These they presented before the tabernacle.

---

a14 Traditionally *peace offering*; also in verses 17 and 18

4The LORD said to Moses, 5"Accept these from them, that they may be used in the work at the Tent of Meeting. Give them to the Levites as each man's work requires."

6So Moses took the carts and oxen and gave them to the Levites. 7He gave two carts and four oxen to the Gershonites, as their work required, 8and he gave four carts and eight oxen to the Merarites, as their work required. They were all under the direction of Ithamar son of Aaron, the priest. 9But Moses did not give any to the Kohathites, because they were to carry on their shoulders the holy things, for which they were responsible.

10When the altar was anointed, the leaders brought their offerings for its

---

NUMBERS 6:22–27

{THURSDAY}

A Blessing for All Time

6:24 "THE LORD BLESS YOU."

This is a great prayer to say if you don't have a prayer! God prepared this prayer and gave it to Aaron and his sons to say as a blessing over the Israelites. God's people have been repeating it ever since. This prayer of blessing spans the whole Biblical story and taps into the richest sources of Scriptural truth as we pray for others. Take it a line at a time:

"The LORD bless you": A blessing is not a religious way of saying, "Have a nice day." Blessing is a powerful Biblical word. It is expansive, comprehensive, concrete, touching on all aspects of the good life lived under God: health, abundance, a good marriage and a happy family (see Genesis 9:1; 17:6; 28:3).

"and keep you": God is a warrior and a defender of his people—our shield and fortress (see Psalm 18:2; 121:7–8). We pray that he will protect and guide those we pray for.

"the LORD make his face shine upon you . . . the LORD turn his face toward you": A shining face is a beautiful picture of a friend who delights in you, or of a bridegroom with love in his eyes, gazing at his bride. God is looking at us this way—read it in Isaiah 62:5. We pray that he will do what he loves to do.

"and be gracious to you": God is gracious and shows favor to those who don't deserve it (see Exodus 34:5–6). In fact, not deserving it is what makes it gracious, the very condition for grace to be grace! We pray that others will receive the good things they *don't* deserve.

"and give you peace": *Peace* is another word like *blessing*, and often in the New Testament the two are linked: "grace and peace." Peace, God's shalom, is comprehensive well-being, the kind of blessedness that is experienced as inner peace and tranquility.

Memorize this prayer, and you will always be prepared to pray the best for others.

PRAY:
Think of a few other people, and pray this blessing on their behalf.

FOR YOUR NEXT DEVOTIONAL READING, GO TO PAGE 166.

dedication and presented them before the altar. ¹¹For the LORD had said to Moses, "Each day one leader is to bring his offering for the dedication of the altar."

¹²The one who brought his offering on the first day was Nahshon son of Amminadab of the tribe of Judah.

¹³His offering was one silver plate weighing a hundred and thirty shekels,ᵃ and one silver sprinkling bowl weighing seventy shekels,ᵇ both according to the sanctuary shekel, each filled with fine flour mixed with oil as a grain offering; ¹⁴one gold dish weighing ten shekels,ᶜ filled with incense; ¹⁵one young bull, one ram and one male lamb a year old, for a burnt offering; ¹⁶one male goat for a sin offering; ¹⁷and two oxen, five rams, five male goats and five male lambs a year old, to be sacrificed as a fellowship offering.ᵈ This was the offering of Nahshon son of Amminadab.

¹⁸On the second day Nethanel son of Zuar, the leader of Issachar, brought his offering.

¹⁹The offering he brought was one silver plate weighing a hundred and thirty shekels, and one silver sprinkling bowl weighing seventy shekels, both according to the sanctuary shekel, each filled with fine flour mixed with oil as a grain offering; ²⁰one gold dish weighing ten shekels, filled with incense; ²¹one young bull, one ram and one male lamb a year old, for a burnt offering; ²²one male goat for a sin offering; ²³and two oxen, five rams, five male goats and five male lambs a year old, to be sacrificed as a fellowship offering. This was the offering of Nethanel son of Zuar.

²⁴On the third day, Eliab son of Helon, the leader of the people of Zebulun, brought his offering.

²⁵His offering was one silver plate weighing a hundred and thirty shekels, and one silver sprinkling bowl weighing seventy shekels, both according to the sanctuary shekel, each filled with fine flour mixed with

oil as a grain offering; ²⁶one gold dish weighing ten shekels, filled with incense; ²⁷one young bull, one ram and one male lamb a year old, for a burnt offering; ²⁸one male goat for a sin offering; ²⁹and two oxen, five rams, five male goats and five male lambs a year old, to be sacrificed as a fellowship offering. This was the offering of Eliab son of Helon.

³⁰On the fourth day Elizur son of Shedeur, the leader of the people of Reuben, brought his offering.

³¹His offering was one silver plate weighing a hundred and thirty shekels, and one silver sprinkling bowl weighing seventy shekels, both according to the sanctuary shekel, each filled with fine flour mixed with oil as a grain offering; ³²one gold dish weighing ten shekels, filled with incense; ³³one young bull, one ram and one male lamb a year old, for a burnt offering; ³⁴one male goat for a sin offering; ³⁵and two oxen, five rams, five male goats and five male lambs a year old, to be sacrificed as a fellowship offering. This was the offering of Elizur son of Shedeur.

³⁶On the fifth day Shelumiel son of Zurishaddai, the leader of the people of Simeon, brought his offering.

³⁷His offering was one silver plate weighing a hundred and thirty shekels, and one silver sprinkling bowl weighing seventy shekels, both according to the sanctuary shekel, each filled with fine flour mixed with oil as a grain offering; ³⁸one gold dish weighing ten shekels, filled with incense; ³⁹one young bull, one ram and one male lamb a year old, for a burnt offering; ⁴⁰one male goat for a sin offering; ⁴¹and two oxen, five rams, five male goats and five

---

ᵃ13 That is, about 3 1/4 pounds (about 1.5 kilograms); also elsewhere in this chapter
ᵇ13 That is, about 1 3/4 pounds (about 0.8 kilogram); also elsewhere in this chapter
ᶜ14 That is, about 4 ounces (about 110 grams); also elsewhere in this chapter
ᵈ17 Traditionally *peace offering*; also elsewhere in this chapter

male lambs a year old, to be sacrificed as a fellowship offering. This was the offering of Shelumiel son of Zurishaddai.

⁴²On the sixth day Eliasaph son of Deuel, the leader of the people of Gad, brought his offering.

⁴³His offering was one silver plate weighing a hundred and thirty shekels, and one silver sprinkling bowl weighing seventy shekels, both according to the sanctuary shekel, each filled with fine flour mixed with oil as a grain offering; ⁴⁴one gold dish weighing ten shekels, filled with incense; ⁴⁵one young bull, one ram and one male lamb a year old, for a burnt offering; ⁴⁶one male goat for a sin offering; ⁴⁷and two oxen, five rams, five male goats and five male lambs a year old, to be sacrificed as a fellowship offering. This was the offering of Eliasaph son of Deuel.

⁴⁸On the seventh day Elishama son of Ammihud, the leader of the people of Ephraim, brought his offering.

⁴⁹His offering was one silver plate weighing a hundred and thirty shekels, and one silver sprinkling bowl weighing seventy shekels, both according to the sanctuary shekel, each filled with fine flour mixed with oil as a grain offering; ⁵⁰one gold dish weighing ten shekels, filled with incense; ⁵¹one young bull, one ram and one male lamb a year old, for a burnt offering; ⁵²one male goat for a sin offering; ⁵³and two oxen, five rams, five male goats and five male lambs a year old, to be sacrificed as a fellowship offering. This was the offering of Elishama son of Ammihud.

⁵⁴On the eighth day Gamaliel son of Pedahzur, the leader of the people of Manasseh, brought his offering.

⁵⁵His offering was one silver plate weighing a hundred and thirty shekels, and one silver sprinkling bowl weighing seventy shekels, both according to the sanctuary shekel, each filled with fine flour mixed with oil as a grain offering; ⁵⁶one gold dish weighing ten shekels, filled with incense; ⁵⁷one young bull, one ram and one male lamb a year old, for a burnt offering; ⁵⁸one male goat for a sin offering; ⁵⁹and two oxen, five rams, five male goats and five male lambs a year old, to be sacrificed as a fellowship offering. This was the offering of Gamaliel son of Pedahzur.

⁶⁰On the ninth day Abidan son of Gideoni, the leader of the people of Benjamin, brought his offering.

⁶¹His offering was one silver plate weighing a hundred and thirty shekels, and one silver sprinkling bowl weighing seventy shekels, both according to the sanctuary shekel, each filled with fine flour mixed with oil as a grain offering; ⁶²one gold dish weighing ten shekels, filled with incense; ⁶³one young bull, one ram and one male lamb a year old, for a burnt offering; ⁶⁴one male goat for a sin offering; ⁶⁵and two oxen, five rams, five male goats and five male lambs a year old, to be sacrificed as a fellowship offering. This was the offering of Abidan son of Gideoni.

⁶⁶On the tenth day Ahiezer son of Ammishaddai, the leader of the people of Dan, brought his offering.

⁶⁷His offering was one silver plate weighing a hundred and thirty shekels, and one silver sprinkling bowl weighing seventy shekels, both according to the sanctuary shekel, each filled with fine flour mixed with oil as a grain offering; ⁶⁸one gold dish weighing ten shekels, filled with incense; ⁶⁹one young bull, one ram and one male lamb a year old, for a burnt offering; ⁷⁰one male goat for a sin offering; ⁷¹and two oxen, five rams, five male goats and five male lambs a year old, to be sacrificed as a fellowship offering. This was the offering of Ahiezer son of Ammishaddai.

⁷²On the eleventh day Pagiel son of Ocran, the leader of the people of Asher, brought his offering.

⁷³His offering was one silver plate weighing a hundred and thirty shekels, and one silver sprinkling bowl weighing seventy shekels, both according to the sanctuary shekel, each filled with fine flour mixed with oil as a grain offering; ⁷⁴one gold dish weighing ten shekels, filled with incense; ⁷⁵one young bull, one ram and one male lamb a year old, for a burnt offering; ⁷⁶one male goat for a sin offering; ⁷⁷and two oxen, five rams, five male goats and five male lambs a year old, to be sacrificed as a fellowship offering. This was the offering of Pagiel son of Ocran.

⁷⁸On the twelfth day Ahira son of Enan, the leader of the people of Naphtali, brought his offering.

⁷⁹His offering was one silver plate weighing a hundred and thirty shekels, and one silver sprinkling bowl weighing seventy shekels, both according to the sanctuary shekel, each filled with fine flour mixed with oil as a grain offering; ⁸⁰one gold dish weighing ten shekels, filled with incense; ⁸¹one young bull, one ram and one male lamb a year old, for a burnt offering; ⁸²one male goat for a sin offering; ⁸³and two oxen, five rams, five male goats and five male lambs a year old, to be sacrificed as a fellowship offering. This was the offering of Ahira son of Enan.

⁸⁴These were the offerings of the Israelite leaders for the dedication of the altar when it was anointed: twelve silver plates, twelve silver sprinkling bowls and twelve gold dishes. ⁸⁵Each silver plate weighed a hundred and thirty shekels, and each sprinkling bowl seventy shekels. Altogether, the silver dishes weighed two thousand four hundred shekels,ᵃ according to the sanctuary shekel. ⁸⁶The twelve gold dishes filled with incense weighed ten shekels each, according to the sanctuary shekel. Altogether, the gold dishes weighed a hundred and twenty shekels.ᵇ ⁸⁷The total number of animals for the burnt offering came to twelve young bulls, twelve rams and twelve male lambs a year old, together with their grain offering. Twelve male goats were used for the sin offering. ⁸⁸The total number of animals for the sacrifice of the fellowship offering came to twenty-four oxen, sixty rams, sixty male goats and sixty male lambs a year old. These were the offerings for the dedication of the altar after it was anointed.

⁸⁹When Moses entered the Tent of Meeting to speak with the LORD, he heard the voice speaking to him from between the two cherubim above the atonement cover on the ark of the Testimony. And he spoke with him.

Setting Up the Lamps

8 The LORD said to Moses, ²"Speak to Aaron and say to him, 'When you set up the seven lamps, they are to light the area in front of the lampstand.'"

³Aaron did so; he set up the lamps so that they faced forward on the lampstand, just as the LORD commanded Moses. ⁴This is how the lampstand was made: It was made of hammered gold— from its base to its blossoms. The lampstand was made exactly like the pattern the LORD had shown Moses.

The Setting Apart of the Levites

⁵The LORD said to Moses: ⁶"Take the Levites from among the other Israelites and make them ceremonially clean. ⁷To purify them, do this: Sprinkle the water of cleansing on them; then have them shave their whole bodies and wash their clothes, and so purify themselves. ⁸Have them take a young bull with its grain offering of fine flour mixed with oil; then you are to take a second young bull for a sin offering. ⁹Bring the Levites to the front of the Tent of Meeting and assemble the whole Israelite community. ¹⁰You are to bring the Levites before the LORD, and the Israelites are to lay their hands on them. ¹¹Aaron is to present the Levites before the LORD as a wave offering from the Israelites, so that they may be ready to do the work of the LORD.

¹²"After the Levites lay their hands on the heads of the bulls, use the one for a sin offering to the LORD and the other for a burnt offering, to make atonement for

ᵃ85 That is, about 60 pounds (about 28 kilograms)   ᵇ86 That is, about 3 pounds (about 1.4 kilograms)

the Levites. ¹³Have the Levites stand in front of Aaron and his sons and then present them as a wave offering to the LORD. ¹⁴In this way you are to set the Levites apart from the other Israelites, and the Levites will be mine.

¹⁵"After you have purified the Levites and presented them as a wave offering, they are to come to do their work at the Tent of Meeting. ¹⁶They are the Israelites who are to be given wholly to me. I have taken them as my own in place of the firstborn, the first male offspring from every Israelite woman. ¹⁷Every firstborn male in Israel, whether man or animal, is mine. When I struck down all the first-born in Egypt, I set them apart for myself. ¹⁸And I have taken the Levites in place of all the firstborn sons in Israel. ¹⁹Of all the Israelites, I have given the Levites as gifts to Aaron and his sons to do the work at the Tent of Meeting on behalf of the Israelites and to make atonement for them so that no plague will strike the Israelites when they go near the sanctuary."

²⁰Moses, Aaron and the whole Israelite community did with the Levites just as the LORD commanded Moses. ²¹The Levites purified themselves and washed their clothes. Then Aaron presented them as a wave offering before the LORD and made atonement for them to purify them. ²²After that, the Levites came to do their work at the Tent of Meeting under the supervision of Aaron and his sons. They did with the Levites just as the LORD commanded Moses.

²³The LORD said to Moses, ²⁴"This applies to the Levites: Men twenty-five years old or more shall come to take part in the work at the Tent of Meeting, ²⁵but at the age of fifty, they must retire from their regular service and work no longer. ²⁶They may assist their brothers in performing their duties at the Tent of Meeting, but they themselves must not do the work. This, then, is how you are to assign the responsibilities of the Levites."

The Passover

9 The LORD spoke to Moses in the Desert of Sinai in the first month of the second year after they came out of Egypt. He said, ²"Have the Israelites cele-brate the Passover at the appointed time. ³Celebrate it at the appointed time, at twilight on the fourteenth day of this month, in accordance with all its rules and regulations."

⁴So Moses told the Israelites to cele-brate the Passover, ⁵and they did so in the Desert of Sinai at twilight on the four-teenth day of the first month. The Israel-ites did everything just as the LORD commanded Moses.

⁶But some of them could not celebrate the Passover on that day because they were ceremonially unclean on account of a dead body. So they came to Moses and Aaron that same day ⁷and said to Moses, "We have become unclean because of a dead body, but why should we be kept from presenting the LORD's offering with the other Israelites at the appointed time?"

⁸Moses answered them, "Wait until I find out what the LORD commands concerning you."

⁹Then the LORD said to Moses, ¹⁰"Tell the Israelites: 'When any of you or your descendants are unclean because of a dead body or are away on a journey, they may still celebrate the LORD's Passover. ¹¹They are to celebrate it on the four-teenth day of the second month at twilight. They are to eat the lamb, together with unleavened bread and bitter herbs. ¹²They must not leave any of it till morning or break any of its bones. When they celebrate the Passover, they must follow all the regulations. ¹³But if a man who is ceremonially clean and not on a journey fails to celebrate the Passover, that person must be cut off from his people because he did not present the LORD's offering at the appointed time. That man will bear the consequences of his sin. ¹⁴"'An alien living among you who wants to celebrate the LORD's Passover must do so in accordance with its rules and regulations. You must have the same regulations for the alien and the native-born.'"

The Cloud Above the Tabernacle

¹⁵On the day the tabernacle, the Tent of the Testimony, was set up, the cloud covered it. From evening till morning the cloud above the tabernacle looked like fire. ¹⁶That is how it continued to be; the

cloud covered it, and at night it looked like fire. ¹⁷Whenever the cloud lifted from above the Tent, the Israelites set out; wherever the cloud settled, the Israelites encamped. ¹⁸At the LORD's command the Israelites set out, and at his command they encamped. As long as the cloud stayed over the tabernacle, they remained in camp. ¹⁹When the cloud remained over the tabernacle a long time, the Israelites obeyed the LORD's order and did not set out. ²⁰Sometimes the cloud was over the tabernacle only a few days; at the LORD's command they would encamp, and then at his command they would set out. ²¹Sometimes the cloud stayed only from evening till morning, and when it lifted in the morning, they set out. Whether by day or by night, whenever the cloud lifted, they set out. ²²Whether the cloud stayed over the tabernacle for two days or a month or a year, the Israelites would remain in camp and not set out; but when it lifted, they would set out. ²³At the LORD's command they encamped, and at the LORD's command they set out. They obeyed the LORD's order, in accordance with his command through Moses.

The Silver Trumpets

10 The LORD said to Moses: ²"Make two trumpets of hammered silver, and use them for calling the community together and for having the camps set out. ³When both are sounded, the whole community is to assemble before you at the entrance to the Tent of Meeting. ⁴If only one is sounded, the leaders—the heads of the clans of Israel—are to assemble before you. ⁵When a trumpet blast is sounded, the tribes camping on the east are to set out. ⁶At the sounding of a second blast, the camps on the south are to set out. The blast will be the signal for setting out. ⁷To gather the assembly, blow the trumpets, but not with the same signal.

⁸"The sons of Aaron, the priests, are to blow the trumpets. This is to be a lasting ordinance for you and the generations to come. ⁹When you go into battle in your own land against an enemy who is oppressing you, sound a blast on the trumpets. Then you will be remembered by the LORD your God and rescued from your enemies. ¹⁰Also at your times of rejoicing—your appointed feasts and New Moon festivals—you are to sound the trumpets over your burnt offerings and fellowship offerings,ᵃ and they will be a memorial for you before your God. I am the LORD your God."

The Israelites Leave Sinai

¹¹On the twentieth day of the second month of the second year, the cloud lifted from above the tabernacle of the Testimony. ¹²Then the Israelites set out from the Desert of Sinai and traveled from place to place until the cloud came to rest in the Desert of Paran. ¹³They set out, this first time, at the LORD's command through Moses.

¹⁴The divisions of the camp of Judah went first, under their standard. Nahshon son of Amminadab was in command. ¹⁵Nethanel son of Zuar was over the division of the tribe of Issachar, ¹⁶and Eliab son of Helon was over the division of the tribe of Zebulun. ¹⁷Then the tabernacle was taken down, and the Gershonites and Merarites, who carried it, set out.

¹⁸The divisions of the camp of Reuben went next, under their standard. Elizur son of Shedeur was in command. ¹⁹Shelumiel son of Zurishaddai was over the division of the tribe of Simeon, ²⁰and Eliasaph son of Deuel was over the division of the tribe of Gad. ²¹Then the Kohathites set out, carrying the holy things. The tabernacle was to be set up before they arrived.

²²The divisions of the camp of Ephraim went next, under their standard. Elishama son of Ammihud was in command. ²³Gamaliel son of Pedahzur was over the division of the tribe of Manasseh, ²⁴and Abidan son of Gideoni was over the division of the tribe of Benjamin.

²⁵Finally, as the rear guard for all the units, the divisions of the camp of Dan set out, under their standard. Ahiezer son of Ammishaddai was in command. ²⁶Pagiel son of Ocran was over the division of the tribe of Asher, ²⁷and Ahira son of Enan was over the division of the tribe of Naphtali. ²⁸This was the order of march for the Israelite divisions as they set out.

ᵃ10 Traditionally *peace offerings*

²⁹Now Moses said to Hobab son of Reuel the Midianite, Moses' father-in-law, "We are setting out for the place about which the LORD said, 'I will give it to you.' Come with us and we will treat you well, for the LORD has promised good things to Israel."

³⁰He answered, "No, I will not go; I am going back to my own land and my own people."

³¹But Moses said, "Please do not leave us. You know where we should camp in the desert, and you can be our eyes. ³²If you come with us, we will share with you whatever good things the LORD gives us."

³³So they set out from the mountain of the LORD and traveled for three days. The ark of the covenant of the LORD went before them during those three days to find them a place to rest. ³⁴The cloud of the LORD was over them by day when they set out from the camp.

³⁵Whenever the ark set out, Moses said,

"Rise up, O LORD!
    May your enemies be scattered;
    may your foes flee before you."

³⁶Whenever it came to rest, he said,

"Return, O LORD,
    to the countless thousands
        of Israel."

Fire From the LORD

11 Now the people complained about their hardships in the hearing of the LORD, and when he heard them his anger was aroused. Then fire from the LORD burned among them and consumed some of the outskirts of the camp. ²When the people cried out to Moses, he prayed to the LORD and the fire died down. ³So that place was called Taberah,ᵃ because fire from the LORD had burned among them.

> WHEN the people cried out to Moses, he prayed to the LORD and the fire died down.
>
> NUMBERS 11:2

Quail From the LORD

⁴The rabble with them began to crave other food, and again the Israelites start-ed wailing and said, "If only we had meat to eat! ⁵We remember the fish we ate in Egypt at no cost—also the cucumbers, melons, leeks, onions and garlic. ⁶But now we have lost our appetite; we never see anything but this manna!"

⁷The manna was like coriander seed and looked like resin. ⁸The people went around gathering it, and then ground it in a handmill or crushed it in a mortar. They cooked it in a pot or made it into cakes. And it tasted like something made with olive oil. ⁹When the dew settled on the camp at night, the manna also came down.

¹⁰Moses heard the people of every family wailing, each at the entrance to his tent. The LORD became exceedingly angry, and Moses was troubled. ¹¹He asked the LORD, "Why have you brought this trouble on your servant? What have I done to displease you that you put the burden of all these people on me? ¹²Did I conceive all these people? Did I give them birth? Why do you tell me to carry them in my arms, as a nurse carries an infant, to the land you promised on oath to their forefathers? ¹³Where can I get meat for all these people? They keep wailing to me, 'Give us meat to eat!' ¹⁴I cannot carry all these people by myself; the burden is too heavy for me. ¹⁵If this is how you are going to treat me, put me to death right now—if I have found favor in your eyes—and do not let me face my own ruin."

¹⁶The LORD said to Moses: "Bring me seventy of Israel's elders who are known to you as leaders and officials among the people. Have them come to the Tent of Meeting, that they may stand there with you. ¹⁷I will come down and speak with you there, and I will take of the Spirit that is on you and put the Spirit on them. They will help you carry the burden of the people so that you will not have to carry it alone.

¹⁸"Tell the people: 'Consecrate yourselves in preparation for tomorrow, when you will eat meat. The LORD heard you when you wailed, "If only we had meat to eat! We were better off in Egypt!" Now the LORD will give you meat, and you

---

ᵃ3 Taberah means burning.

NUMBERS 11:10–34

A Mirror of Prayer

11:11 "WHY HAVE YOU BROUGHT THIS TROUBLE ON YOUR SERVANT?"

Like its leading characters, the Bible has many models of prayer—prayers to emulate. And like its leading characters, it also has many mirrors of prayer—prayers prayed by flawed people like us, not prescribed but allowed. This prayer is a mirror of prayer. Moses is fed up with God's people and maybe a little fed up with God, too. Why else would he say, "Why have you brought this trouble on your servant? What have I done to displease you that you put the burden of all these people on me? Did I conceive all these people? Did I give them birth?" (11:11–12). Moses is engaged in a little reversal of the appeal he made to God in Exodus 32, where God called the Israelites "your people."

Part of the comfort of this prayer is the fact that we may pray a prayer like this at all. Venting our feelings isn't usually the catharsis we think it is. There is no healing inherent in merely spouting off; sometimes it makes things worse, reinforcing negative feelings by the negative feedback of what we hear ourselves say. The healing isn't in the venting but in the one to whom we vent—God. To know he hears with mercy and without censure is of enormous comfort and encouragement.

But God also answers our "venting prayers." He showed mercy to Moses by giving him men to share the responsibility that so weighed him down (see Numbers 11:16–18). He also punished the people; and while there really isn't a lot of comfort in seeing God punish people who have made life miserable for us, there is a sense of justice being done (see verses 31–34).

The best part of God's answer to Moses' prayer is the reminder that our struggles really aren't about us but about God. He tells Moses to tell the people, "you have rejected the LORD, who is among you" (verse 20). It's never ultimately about us; it's always about God. Life's burdens are heavy enough without the added burden of narcissism and self-pity. God's response relieves us of that load—and yet gives us the dignity of knowing that our struggles bring us into the fellowship of God's sufferings (see also Philippians 3:10; Colossians 1:24).

P R A Y :

*Thank you, Lord, that I can be real in my prayers, that I can
vent my feelings to you—and then watch you work
by changing my attitude and by helping me through
other people. I really want to know you,
even if it means sharing in your sufferings.*

FOR YOUR NEXT DEVOTIONAL READING, GO TO PAGE 168.

will eat it. [19]You will not eat it for just one day, or two days, or five, ten or twenty days, [20]but for a whole month—until it comes out of your nostrils and you loathe it—because you have rejected the Lord, who is among you, and have wailed before him, saying, "Why did we ever leave Egypt?" ' "

[21]But Moses said, "Here I am among six hundred thousand men on foot, and you say, 'I will give them meat to eat for a whole month!' [22]Would they have enough if flocks and herds were slaughtered for them? Would they have enough if all the fish in the sea were caught for them?"

[23]The Lord answered Moses, "Is the Lord's arm too short? You will now see whether or not what I say will come true for you."

[24]So Moses went out and told the people what the Lord had said. He brought together seventy of their elders and had them stand around the Tent. [25]Then the Lord came down in the cloud and spoke with him, and he took of the Spirit that was on him and put the Spirit on the seventy elders. When the Spirit rested on them, they prophesied, but they did not do so again.[a]

[26]However, two men, whose names were Eldad and Medad, had remained in the camp. They were listed among the elders, but did not go out to the Tent. Yet the Spirit also rested on them, and they prophesied in the camp. [27]A young man ran and told Moses, "Eldad and Medad are prophesying in the camp."

[28]Joshua son of Nun, who had been Moses' aide since youth, spoke up and said, "Moses, my lord, stop them!"

[29]But Moses replied, "Are you jealous for my sake? I wish that all the Lord's people were prophets and that the Lord would put his Spirit on them!" [30]Then Moses and the elders of Israel returned to the camp.

[31]Now a wind went out from the Lord and drove quail in from the sea. It brought them[b] down all around the camp to about three feet[c] above the ground, as far as a day's walk in any direction. [32]All that day and night and all the next day the people went out and gathered quail. No one gathered less than ten homers.[d] Then they spread them out all around the camp. [33]But while the meat was still between their teeth and before it could be consumed, the anger of the Lord burned against the people, and he struck them with a severe plague. [34]Therefore the place was named Kibroth Hattaavah,[e] because there they buried the people who had craved other food.

[35]From Kibroth Hattaavah the people traveled to Hazeroth and stayed there.

Miriam and Aaron Oppose Moses

12 Miriam and Aaron began to talk against Moses because of his Cushite wife, for he had married a Cushite. [2]"Has the Lord spoken only through Moses?" they asked. "Hasn't he also spoken through us?" And the Lord heard this.

[3](Now Moses was a very humble man, more humble than anyone else on the face of the earth.)

[4]At once the Lord said to Moses, Aaron and Miriam, "Come out to the Tent of Meeting, all three of you." So the three of them came out. [5]Then the Lord came down in a pillar of cloud; he stood at the entrance to the Tent and summoned Aaron and Miriam. When both of them stepped forward, [6]he said, "Listen to my words:

"When a prophet of the Lord is
  among you,
 I reveal myself to him in visions,
 I speak to him in dreams.
[7]But this is not true of my servant
  Moses;
 he is faithful in all my house.
[8]With him I speak face to face,
 clearly and not in riddles;
 he sees the form of the Lord.
Why then were you not afraid
 to speak against my servant
  Moses?"

[9]The anger of the Lord burned against them, and he left them.

[10]When the cloud lifted from above the Tent, there stood Miriam—leprous,[f] like snow. Aaron turned toward her and saw

[a]25 Or prophesied and continued to do so
[b]31 Or They flew   [c]31 Hebrew two cubits (about 1 meter)   [d]32 That is, probably about 60 bushels (about 2.2 kiloliters)   [e]34 Kibroth Hattaavah means graves of craving.   [f]10 The Hebrew word was used for various diseases affecting the skin—not necessarily leprosy.

Outrageous Grace

THE FOLLOWING lines were found on the body of a dead American soldier, killed in North Africa in World War II in 1944. His name is not known.

Look, God, I have never spoken to you,
And now I want to say, "How do you do?"
And see, God, they told me you did not exist,
And I, like a fool, believed all this.
Last night, from a shell-hole, I saw your sky,
I figured that they had told me a lie.
Had I taken time before to see things you had made,
I'd sure have known they weren't calling a spade a spade.
I wonder, God, if you would shake my poor hand?
Somehow I feel you would understand.
Strange I had to come to this hellish place
Before I had time to see your face.
Well, I guess, there isn't much more to say,
But I'm glad, God, that I met you today.
The zero hour will soon be here,
But I'm not afraid to know that you're near.
The signal has come—I shall soon have to go,
I like you lots—this I want you to know.
I'm sure this will be a horrible fight;
Who knows? I may come to your house tonight.
Though I wasn't friendly to you before,
I wonder, God, if you'd wait at your door?
Look, I'm shedding tears—*me* shedding tears!
Oh! I wish I'd known you these long, long years.
Well, I have to go now, dear God. Good bye,
But now that I've met you I'm not scared to die.[3]

Jesus met a man like this soldier. He too asked for mercy very late in life. Perhaps he would have written some lines like these, but his hands were occupied. They were nailed to a cross, for he was being executed next to Jesus (see Luke 23:39–43).

Jesus also told a parable about God's attitude toward people like this man on the cross. It's about a landowner who hired day laborers early one morning and then others throughout the day: mid-morning, noon, mid-afternoon and late afternoon. When the workday was over, the man paid all the workers the same wage—including those who worked all day and those who worked only one hour. When the laborers who had worked all day protested what they believed to be the injustice of this, the man said, "Don't I have the right to do what I want with my own money? Or are you envious because I am generous?" (Matthew 20:15).

Generous indeed! We have no idea how generous God is. The only thing worse than the sin that keeps us away from God is the fear that he will spurn our cry for mercy, that we have run out of time and our sin has exceeded the strength of his will to forgive. Then the Enemy of our souls will have won a double victory: He will have kept us from the God who loves us first by our sin and then by our fear. It's never too late to pray.

PRAY:

"Into your hands I commit my spirit; redeem me,
O LORD, the God of truth" (Psalm 31:5).

MEMORIZE:

But because of his great love for us, God, who is rich in mercy,
made us alive with Christ even when we were dead in
transgressions—it is by grace you have been saved. EPHESIANS 2:4–5

FOR YOUR NEXT DEVOTIONAL READING, GO TO PAGE 172.

that she had leprosy; ¹¹and he said to Moses, "Please, my lord, do not hold against us the sin we have so foolishly committed. ¹²Do not let her be like a stillborn infant coming from its mother's womb with its flesh half eaten away."

¹³So Moses cried out to the Lord, "O God, please heal her!"

> SO MOSES cried out to the Lord, "O God,
> please heal her!"
>
> NUMBERS 12:13

¹⁴The Lord replied to Moses, "If her father had spit in her face, would she not have been in disgrace for seven days? Confine her outside the camp for seven days; after that she can be brought back." ¹⁵So Miriam was confined outside the camp for seven days, and the people did not move on till she was brought back.

¹⁶After that, the people left Hazeroth and encamped in the Desert of Paran.

Exploring Canaan

13 The Lord said to Moses, ²"Send some men to explore the land of Canaan, which I am giving to the Israelites. From each ancestral tribe send one of its leaders."

³So at the Lord's command Moses sent them out from the Desert of Paran. All of them were leaders of the Israelites. ⁴These are their names:

from the tribe of Reuben, Shammua son of Zaccur;
⁵from the tribe of Simeon, Shaphat son of Hori;
⁶from the tribe of Judah, Caleb son of Jephunneh;
⁷from the tribe of Issachar, Igal son of Joseph;
⁸from the tribe of Ephraim, Hoshea son of Nun;
⁹from the tribe of Benjamin, Palti son of Raphu;
¹⁰from the tribe of Zebulun, Gaddiel son of Sodi;
¹¹from the tribe of Manasseh (a tribe of Joseph), Gaddi son of Susi;
¹²from the tribe of Dan, Ammiel son of Gemalli;

¹³from the tribe of Asher, Sethur son of Michael;
¹⁴from the tribe of Naphtali, Nahbi son of Vophsi;
¹⁵from the tribe of Gad, Geuel son of Maki.

¹⁶These are the names of the men Moses sent to explore the land. (Moses gave Hoshea son of Nun the name Joshua.)

¹⁷When Moses sent them to explore Canaan, he said, "Go up through the Negev and on into the hill country. ¹⁸See what the land is like and whether the people who live there are strong or weak, few or many. ¹⁹What kind of land do they live in? Is it good or bad? What kind of towns do they live in? Are they unwalled or fortified? ²⁰How is the soil? Is it fertile or poor? Are there trees on it or not? Do your best to bring back some of the fruit of the land." (It was the season for the first ripe grapes.)

²¹So they went up and explored the land from the Desert of Zin as far as Rehob, toward Leboᵃ Hamath. ²²They went up through the Negev and came to Hebron, where Ahiman, Sheshai and Talmai, the descendants of Anak, lived. (Hebron had been built seven years before Zoan in Egypt.) ²³When they reached the Valley of Eshcol,ᵇ they cut off a branch bearing a single cluster of grapes. Two of them carried it on a pole between them, along with some pomegranates and figs. ²⁴That place was called the Valley of Eshcol because of the cluster of grapes the Israelites cut off there. ²⁵At the end of forty days they returned from exploring the land.

Report on the Exploration

²⁶They came back to Moses and Aaron and the whole Israelite community at Kadesh in the Desert of Paran. There they reported to them and to the whole assembly and showed them the fruit of the land. ²⁷They gave Moses this account: "We went into the land to which you sent us, and it does flow with milk and honey! Here is its fruit. ²⁸But the people who live there are powerful, and the cities are fortified and very large. We even saw de-

ᵃ21 Or toward the entrance to   ᵇ23 Eshcol means cluster; also in verse 24.

scendants of Anak there. ²⁹The Amalekites live in the Negev; the Hittites, Jebusites and Amorites live in the hill country; and the Canaanites live near the sea and along the Jordan."

³⁰Then Caleb silenced the people before Moses and said, "We should go up and take possession of the land, for we can certainly do it."

³¹But the men who had gone up with him said, "We can't attack those people; they are stronger than we are." ³²And they spread among the Israelites a bad report about the land they had explored. They said, "The land we explored devours those living in it. All the people we saw there are of great size. ³³We saw the Nephilim there (the descendants of Anak come from the Nephilim). We seemed like grasshoppers in our own eyes, and we looked the same to them."

The People Rebel

14 That night all the people of the community raised their voices and wept aloud. ²All the Israelites grumbled against Moses and Aaron, and the whole assembly said to them, "If only we had died in Egypt! Or in this desert! ³Why is the LORD bringing us to this land only to let us fall by the sword? Our wives and children will be taken as plunder. Wouldn't it be better for us to go back to Egypt?" ⁴And they said to each other, "We should choose a leader and go back to Egypt."

⁵Then Moses and Aaron fell facedown in front of the whole Israelite assembly gathered there. ⁶Joshua son of Nun and Caleb son of Jephunneh, who were among those who had explored the land, tore their clothes ⁷and said to the entire Israelite assembly, "The land we passed through and explored is exceedingly good. ⁸If the LORD is pleased with us, he will lead us into that land, a land flowing with milk and honey, and will give it to us. ⁹Only do not rebel against the LORD. And do not be afraid of the people of the land, because we will swallow them up. Their protection is gone, but the LORD is with us. Do not be afraid of them."

¹⁰But the whole assembly talked about stoning them. Then the glory of the LORD appeared at the Tent of Meeting to all the Israelites. ¹¹The LORD said to Moses, "How long will these people treat me with contempt? How long will they refuse to believe in me, in spite of all the miraculous signs I have performed among them? ¹²I will strike them down with a plague and destroy them, but I will make you into a nation greater and stronger than they."

¹³Moses said to the LORD, "Then the Egyptians will hear about it! By your power you brought these people up from among them. ¹⁴And they will tell the inhabitants of this land about it. They have already heard that you, O LORD, are with these people and that you, O LORD, have been seen face to face, and that your cloud stays over them, and that you go before them in a pillar of cloud by day and a pillar of fire by night. ¹⁵If you put these people to death all at one time, the nations who have heard this report about you will say, ¹⁶'The LORD was not able to bring these people into the land he promised them on oath; so he slaughtered them in the desert.'

¹⁷"Now may the Lord's strength be displayed, just as you have declared: ¹⁸'The LORD is slow to anger, abounding in love and forgiving sin and rebellion. Yet he does not leave the guilty unpunished; he punishes the children for the sin of the fathers to the third and fourth generation.' ¹⁹In accordance with your great love, forgive the sin of these people, just as you have pardoned them from the time they left Egypt until now."

²⁰The LORD replied, "I have forgiven them, as you asked. ²¹Nevertheless, as surely as I live and as surely as the glory of the LORD fills the whole earth, ²²not one of the men who saw my glory and the miraculous signs I performed in Egypt and in the desert but who disobeyed me and tested me ten times— ²³not one of them will ever see the land I promised on oath to their forefathers. No one who has treated me with contempt will ever see it. ²⁴But because my servant Caleb has a different spirit and follows me wholeheartedly, I will bring him into the land he went to, and his descendants will inherit it. ²⁵Since the Amalekites and Canaanites are living in the

NUMBERS 14:1–23

Praying for the Hard to Pray For

14:18 "THE LORD IS SLOW TO ANGER."

Some people are easier to pray for than others. At the top of our lists are close friends and family, those who are ill, missionaries. Harder to pray for are thieves or drug dealers; but still, pity and a passion to see the power of God at work can motivate us to pray for such people. But at the bottom of our lists are the cravenly ungrateful, the gripers and bellyachers—like the people in this text. Earlier they complained about the food God gave to keep them alive in the desert: "Not enough variety," they moaned (see 11:4–6). Now they're complaining about the dangers of entering the promised land, a land flowing with milk, honey and some very large grapes (see 13:23,27).

God finds the people's grumbling ingratitude particularly offensive, and he decides then and there that this generation of gripers will never enter the good land (see 14:22–23). God's actions may seem extreme, but basically, he is being accused of mismanagement. It's as though his people are dissatisfied customers in a poorly run hotel—his! The Israelites seem to think God exists for their sake. Beneath the attitude of ingratitude is more than spiritual boorishness; it is blatant disrespect of God. "How long will these people treat me with contempt?" asks God with good reason (verse 11).

These are the people Moses prays for in this passage. Significantly, he prays for mercy and justice: "Now may the Lord's strength be displayed, just as you have declared: 'The LORD is slow to anger, abounding in love and forgiving sin and rebellion. Yet he does not leave the guilty unpunished'" (verses 17–18). Mercy and justice are not opposites, for God is both merciful and just. His mercy tempers his justice but does not eliminate it. The writer of the book of Lamentations reminds us: "I remember my affliction and my wandering . . . Yet this I call to mind and therefore I have hope: Because of the LORD's great love we are not consumed, for his compassions never fail" (3:19,21–22).

Christ died and rose again to make the loveless lovely. So we must pray for those caught in this particularly gross lovelessness. And by cultivating grateful prayer and praise to God, we can be sure that we also do not fall into the trap of ungratefulness ourselves.

PRAY:

Open our eyes to your mercies, Lord. Forgive our ingratitude
as we pray for the ungrateful—that their eyes too may be opened.

———

FOR YOUR NEXT DEVOTIONAL READING, GO TO PAGE 204.

valleys, turn back tomorrow and set out toward the desert along the route to the Red Sea.*"

²⁶The LORD said to Moses and Aaron: ²⁷"How long will this wicked community grumble against me? I have heard the complaints of these grumbling Israelites. ²⁸So tell them, 'As surely as I live, declares the LORD, I will do to you the very things I heard you say: ²⁹In this desert your bodies will fall—every one of you twenty years old or more who was counted in the census and who has grumbled against me. ³⁰Not one of you will enter the land I swore with uplifted hand to make your home, except Caleb son of Jephunneh and Joshua son of Nun. ³¹As for your children that you said would be taken as plunder, I will bring them in to enjoy the land you have rejected. ³²But you—your bodies will fall in this desert. ³³Your children will be shepherds here for forty years, suffering for your unfaithfulness, until the last of your bodies lies in the desert. ³⁴For forty years—one year for each of the forty days you explored the land—you will suffer for your sins and know what it is like to have me against you.' ³⁵I, the LORD, have spoken, and I will surely do these things to this whole wicked community, which has banded together against me. They will meet their end in this desert; here they will die."

³⁶So the men Moses had sent to explore the land, who returned and made the whole community grumble against him by spreading a bad report about it— ³⁷these men responsible for spreading the bad report about the land were struck down and died of a plague before the LORD. ³⁸Of the men who went to explore the land, only Joshua son of Nun and Caleb son of Jephunneh survived.

³⁹When Moses reported this to all the Israelites, they mourned bitterly. ⁴⁰Early the next morning they went up toward the high hill country. "We have sinned," they said. "We will go up to the place the LORD promised."

⁴¹But Moses said, "Why are you disobeying the LORD's command? This will not succeed! ⁴²Do not go up, because the LORD is not with you. You will be defeated by your enemies, ⁴³for the Amalekites

and Canaanites will face you there. Because you have turned away from the LORD, he will not be with you and you will fall by the sword."

⁴⁴Nevertheless, in their presumption they went up toward the high hill country, though neither Moses nor the ark of the LORD's covenant moved from the camp. ⁴⁵Then the Amalekites and Canaanites who lived in that hill country came down and attacked them and beat them down all the way to Hormah.

Supplementary Offerings

15 The LORD said to Moses, ²"Speak to the Israelites and say to them: 'After you enter the land I am giving you as a home ³and you present to the LORD offerings made by fire, from the herd or the flock, as an aroma pleasing to the LORD— whether burnt offerings or sacrifices, for special vows or freewill offerings or festival offerings— ⁴then the one who brings his offering shall present to the LORD a grain offering of a tenth of an ephah*ᵇ* of fine flour mixed with a quarter of a hin*ᶜ* of oil. ⁵With each lamb for the burnt offering or the sacrifice, prepare a quarter of a hin of wine as a drink offering.

⁶" 'With a ram prepare a grain offering of two-tenths of an ephah*ᵈ* of fine flour mixed with a third of a hin*ᵉ* of oil, ⁷and a third of a hin of wine as a drink offering. Offer it as an aroma pleasing to the LORD.

⁸" 'When you prepare a young bull as a burnt offering or sacrifice, for a special vow or a fellowship offering*ᶠ* to the LORD, ⁹bring with the bull a grain offering of three-tenths of an ephah*ᵍ* of fine flour mixed with half a hin*ʰ* of oil. ¹⁰Also bring half a hin of wine as a drink offering. It will be an offering made by fire, an aroma pleasing to the LORD. ¹¹Each bull or ram, each lamb or young goat, is to be prepared in this manner. ¹²Do this for each one, for as many as you prepare.

---

*ᵃ*25 Hebrew *Yam Suph*; that is, Sea of Reeds
*ᵇ*4 That is, probably about 2 quarts (about 2 liters)
*ᶜ*4 That is, probably about 1 quart (about 1 liter); also in verse 5   *ᵈ* 6 That is, probably about 4 (about 4.5 liters)   *ᵉ*6 That is, probably about 1 1/4 quarts (about 1.2 liters); also in verse 7
*ᶠ*8 Traditionally *peace offering*   *ᵍ*9 That is, probably about 6 quarts (about 6.5 liters)
ʰ 9 That is, probably about 2 quarts (about 2 liters); also in verse 10

[13] " 'Everyone who is native-born must do these things in this way when he brings an offering made by fire as an aroma pleasing to the LORD. [14]For the generations to come, whenever an alien or anyone else living among you presents an offering made by fire as an aroma pleasing to the LORD, he must do exactly as you do. [15]The community is to have the same rules for you and for the alien living among you; this is a lasting ordinance for the generations to come. You and the alien shall be the same before the LORD: [16]The same laws and regulations will apply both to you and to the alien living among you.' "

[17]The LORD said to Moses, [18]"Speak to the Israelites and say to them: 'When you enter the land to which I am taking you [19]and you eat the food of the land, present a portion as an offering to the LORD. [20]Present a cake from the first of your ground meal and present it as an offering from the threshing floor. [21]Throughout the generations to come you are to give this offering to the LORD from the first of your ground meal.

Offerings for Unintentional Sins

[22]" 'Now if you unintentionally fail to keep any of these commands the LORD gave Moses— [23]any of the LORD's commands to you through him, from the day the LORD gave them and continuing through the generations to come— [24]and if this is done unintentionally without the community being aware of it, then the whole community is to offer a young bull for a burnt offering as an aroma pleasing to the LORD, along with its prescribed grain offering and drink offering, and a male goat for a sin offering. [25]The priest is to make atonement for the whole Israelite community, and they will be forgiven, for it was not intentional and they have brought to the LORD for their wrong an offering made by fire and a sin offering. [26]The whole Israelite community and the aliens living among them will be forgiven, because all the people were involved in the unintentional wrong.

[27]" 'But if just one person sins unintentionally, he must bring a year-old female goat for a sin offering. [28]The priest is to make atonement before the LORD for the one who erred by sinning unintentionally, and when atonement has been made for him, he will be forgiven. [29]One and the same law applies to everyone who sins unintentionally, whether he is a native-born Israelite or an alien.

[30]" 'But anyone who sins defiantly, whether native-born or alien, blasphemes the LORD, and that person must be cut off from his people. [31]Because he has despised the LORD's word and broken his commands, that person must surely be cut off; his guilt remains on him.' "

The Sabbath-Breaker Put to Death

[32]While the Israelites were in the desert, a man was found gathering wood on the Sabbath day. [33]Those who found him gathering wood brought him to Moses and Aaron and the whole assembly, [34]and they kept him in custody, because it was not clear what should be done to him. [35]Then the LORD said to Moses, "The man must die. The whole assembly must stone him outside the camp." [36]So the assembly took him outside the camp and stoned him to death, as the LORD commanded Moses.

Tassels on Garments

[37]The LORD said to Moses, [38]"Speak to the Israelites and say to them: 'Throughout the generations to come you are to make tassels on the corners of your garments, with a blue cord on each tassel. [39]You will have these tassels to look at and so you will remember all the commands of the LORD, that you may obey them and not prostitute yourselves by going after the lusts of your own hearts and eyes. [40]Then you will remember to obey all my commands and will be consecrated to your God. [41]I am the LORD your God, who brought you out of Egypt to be your God. I am the LORD your God.' "

Korah, Dathan and Abiram

16 Korah son of Izhar, the son of Kohath, the son of Levi, and certain Reubenites—Dathan and Abiram, sons of Eliab, and On son of Peleth—became insolent[a] [2]and rose up against Moses. With them were 250 Israelite men, well-

---

[a]1 Or Peleth—took ˌmen˛

known community leaders who had been appointed members of the council. ³They came as a group to oppose Moses and Aaron and said to them, "You have gone too far! The whole community is holy, every one of them, and the LORD is with them. Why then do you set yourselves above the LORD's assembly?"

⁴When Moses heard this, he fell facedown. ⁵Then he said to Korah and all his followers: "In the morning the LORD will show who belongs to him and who is holy, and he will have that person come near him. The man he chooses he will cause to come near him. ⁶You, Korah, and all your followers are to do this: Take censers ⁷and tomorrow put fire and incense in them before the LORD. The man the LORD chooses will be the one who is holy. You Levites have gone too far!"

⁸Moses also said to Korah, "Now listen, you Levites! ⁹Isn't it enough for you that the God of Israel has separated you from the rest of the Israelite community and brought you near himself to do the work at the LORD's tabernacle and to stand before the community and minister to them? ¹⁰He has brought you and all your fellow Levites near himself, but now you are trying to get the priesthood too. ¹¹It is against the LORD that you and all your followers have banded together. Who is Aaron that you should grumble against him?"

¹²Then Moses summoned Dathan and Abiram, the sons of Eliab. But they said, "We will not come! ¹³Isn't it enough that you have brought us up out of a land flowing with milk and honey to kill us in the desert? And now you also want to lord it over us? ¹⁴Moreover, you haven't brought us into a land flowing with milk and honey or given us an inheritance of fields and vineyards. Will you gouge out the eyes of ᵃ these men? No, we will not come!"

¹⁵Then Moses became very angry and said to the LORD, "Do not accept their offering. I have not taken so much as a donkey from them, nor have I wronged any of them."

¹⁶Moses said to Korah, "You and all your followers are to appear before the LORD tomorrow—you and they and Aaron. ¹⁷Each man is to take his censer and put incense in it—250 censers in all—

and present it before the LORD. You and Aaron are to present your censers also." ¹⁸So each man took his censer, put fire and incense in it, and stood with Moses and Aaron at the entrance to the Tent of Meeting. ¹⁹When Korah had gathered all his followers in opposition to them at the entrance to the Tent of Meeting, the glory of the LORD appeared to the entire assembly. ²⁰The LORD said to Moses and Aaron, ²¹"Separate yourselves from this assembly so I can put an end to them at once."

²²But Moses and Aaron fell facedown and cried out, "O God, God of the spirits of all mankind, will you be angry with the entire assembly when only one man sins?"

> BUT MOSES and Aaron fell facedown and cried out, "O God, God of the spirits of all mankind, will you be angry with the entire assembly when only one man sins?"
>
> NUMBERS 16:22

²³Then the LORD said to Moses, ²⁴"Say to the assembly, 'Move away from the tents of Korah, Dathan and Abiram.'"

²⁵Moses got up and went to Dathan and Abiram, and the elders of Israel followed him. ²⁶He warned the assembly, "Move back from the tents of these wicked men! Do not touch anything belonging to them, or you will be swept away because of all their sins." ²⁷So they moved away from the tents of Korah, Dathan and Abiram. Dathan and Abiram had come out and were standing with their wives, children and little ones at the entrances to their tents.

²⁸Then Moses said, "This is how you will know that the LORD has sent me to do all these things and that it was not my idea: ²⁹If these men die a natural death and experience only what usually happens to men, then the LORD has not sent me. ³⁰But if the LORD brings about something totally new, and the earth opens its mouth and swallows them, with everything that belongs to them, and they go down alive into the grave,ᵇ then you will

ᵃ14 Or *you make slaves of*; or *you deceive*
ᵇ30 Hebrew *Sheol*; also in verse 33

know that these men have treated the LORD with contempt."

³¹As soon as he finished saying all this, the ground under them split apart ³²and the earth opened its mouth and swallowed them, with their households and all Korah's men and all their possessions. ³³They went down alive into the grave, with everything they owned; the earth closed over them, and they perished and were gone from the community. ³⁴At their cries, all the Israelites around them fled, shouting, "The earth is going to swallow us too!"

³⁵And fire came out from the LORD and consumed the 250 men who were offering the incense.

³⁶The LORD said to Moses, ³⁷"Tell Eleazar son of Aaron, the priest, to take the censers out of the smoldering remains and scatter the coals some distance away, for the censers are holy— ³⁸the censers of the men who sinned at the cost of their lives. Hammer the censers into sheets to overlay the altar, for they were presented before the LORD and have become holy. Let them be a sign to the Israelites."

³⁹So Eleazar the priest collected the bronze censers brought by those who had been burned up, and he had them hammered out to overlay the altar, ⁴⁰as the LORD directed him through Moses. This was to remind the Israelites that no one except a descendant of Aaron should come to burn incense before the LORD, or he would become like Korah and his followers.

⁴¹The next day the whole Israelite community grumbled against Moses and Aaron. "You have killed the LORD's people," they said.

⁴²But when the assembly gathered in opposition to Moses and Aaron and turned toward the Tent of Meeting, suddenly the cloud covered it and the glory of the LORD appeared. ⁴³Then Moses and Aaron went to the front of the Tent of Meeting, ⁴⁴and the LORD said to Moses, ⁴⁵"Get away from this assembly so I can put an end to them at once." And they fell facedown.

⁴⁶Then Moses said to Aaron, "Take your censer and put incense in it, along with fire from the altar, and hurry to the assembly to make atonement for them. Wrath has come out from the LORD; the plague has started." ⁴⁷So Aaron did as Moses said, and ran into the midst of the assembly. The plague had already started among the people, but Aaron offered the incense and made atonement for them. ⁴⁸He stood between the living and the dead, and the plague stopped. ⁴⁹But 14,700 people died from the plague, in addition to those who had died because of Korah. ⁵⁰Then Aaron returned to Moses at the entrance to the Tent of Meeting, for the plague had stopped.

The Budding of Aaron's Staff

17 The LORD said to Moses, ²"Speak to the Israelites and get twelve staffs from them, one from the leader of each of their ancestral tribes. Write the name of each man on his staff. ³On the staff of Levi write Aaron's name, for there must be one staff for the head of each ancestral tribe. ⁴Place them in the Tent of Meeting in front of the Testimony, where I meet with you. ⁵The staff belonging to the man I choose will sprout, and I will rid myself of this constant grumbling against you by the Israelites."

⁶So Moses spoke to the Israelites, and their leaders gave him twelve staffs, one for the leader of each of their ancestral tribes, and Aaron's staff was among them. ⁷Moses placed the staffs before the LORD in the Tent of the Testimony.

⁸The next day Moses entered the Tent of the Testimony and saw that Aaron's staff, which represented the house of Levi, had not only sprouted but had budded, blossomed and produced almonds. ⁹Then Moses brought out all the staffs from the LORD's presence to all the Israelites. They looked at them, and each man took his own staff.

¹⁰The LORD said to Moses, "Put back Aaron's staff in front of the Testimony, to be kept as a sign to the rebellious. This will put an end to their grumbling against me, so that they will not die." ¹¹Moses did just as the LORD commanded him.

¹²The Israelites said to Moses, "We will die! We are lost, we are all lost! ¹³Anyone who even comes near the tabernacle of the LORD will die. Are we all going to die?"

Duties of Priests and Levites

18 The LORD said to Aaron, "You, your sons and your father's family are to bear the responsibility for offenses against the sanctuary, and you and your sons alone are to bear the responsibility for offenses against the priesthood. [2]Bring your fellow Levites from your ancestral tribe to join you and assist you when you and your sons minister before the Tent of the Testimony. [3]They are to be responsible to you and are to perform all the duties of the Tent, but they must not go near the furnishings of the sanctuary or the altar, or both they and you will die. [4]They are to join you and be responsible for the care of the Tent of Meeting—all the work at the Tent—and no one else may come near where you are.

[5]"You are to be responsible for the care of the sanctuary and the altar, so that wrath will not fall on the Israelites again. [6]I myself have selected your fellow Levites from among the Israelites as a gift to you, dedicated to the LORD to do the work at the Tent of Meeting. [7]But only you and your sons may serve as priests in connection with everything at the altar and inside the curtain. I am giving you the service of the priesthood as a gift. Anyone else who comes near the sanctuary must be put to death."

Offerings for Priests and Levites

[8]Then the LORD said to Aaron, "I myself have put you in charge of the offerings presented to me; all the holy offerings the Israelites give me I give to you and your sons as your portion and regular share. [9]You are to have the part of the most holy offerings that is kept from the fire. From all the gifts they bring me as most holy offerings, whether grain or sin or guilt offerings, that part belongs to you and your sons. [10]Eat it as something most holy; every male shall eat it. You must regard it as holy.

[11]"This also is yours: whatever is set aside from the gifts of all the wave offerings of the Israelites. I give this to you and your sons and daughters as your regular share. Everyone in your household who is ceremonially clean may eat it.

[12]"I give you all the finest olive oil and all the finest new wine and grain they give the LORD as the firstfruits of their harvest. [13]All the land's firstfruits that they bring to the LORD will be yours. Everyone in your household who is ceremonially clean may eat it.

[14]"Everything in Israel that is devoted[a] to the LORD is yours. [15]The first offspring of every womb, both man and animal, that is offered to the LORD is yours. But you must redeem every firstborn son and every firstborn male of unclean animals. [16]When they are a month old, you must redeem them at the redemption price set at five shekels[b] of silver, according to the sanctuary shekel, which weighs twenty gerahs.

[17]"But you must not redeem the firstborn of an ox, a sheep or a goat; they are holy. Sprinkle their blood on the altar and burn their fat as an offering made by fire, an aroma pleasing to the LORD. [18]Their meat is to be yours, just as the breast of the wave offering and the right thigh are yours. [19]Whatever is set aside from the holy offerings the Israelites present to the LORD I give to you and your sons and daughters as your regular share. It is an everlasting covenant of salt before the LORD for both you and your offspring."

[20]The LORD said to Aaron, "You will have no inheritance in their land, nor will you have any share among them; I am your share and your inheritance among the Israelites.

[21]"I give to the Levites all the tithes in Israel as their inheritance in return for the work they do while serving at the Tent of Meeting. [22]From now on the Israelites must not go near the Tent of Meeting, or they will bear the consequences of their sin and will die. [23]It is the Levites who are to do the work at the Tent of Meeting and bear the responsibility for offenses against it. This is a lasting ordinance for the generations to come. They will receive no inheritance among the Israelites. [24]Instead, I give to the Levites as their inheritance the tithes that the Israelites present as an offering to the LORD.

---

[a]14 The Hebrew term refers to the irrevocable giving over of things or persons to the LORD.
[b]16 That is, about 2 ounces (about 55 grams)

That is why I said concerning them: 'They will have no inheritance among the Israelites.' "

²⁵The LORD said to Moses, ²⁶"Speak to the Levites and say to them: 'When you receive from the Israelites the tithe I give you as your inheritance, you must present a tenth of that tithe as the LORD's offering. ²⁷Your offering will be reckoned to you as grain from the threshing floor or juice from the winepress. ²⁸In this way you also will present an offering to the LORD from all the tithes you receive from the Israelites. From these tithes you must give the LORD's portion to Aaron the priest. ²⁹You must present as the LORD's portion the best and holiest part of everything given to you.'

³⁰"Say to the Levites: 'When you present the best part, it will be reckoned to you as the product of the threshing floor or the winepress. ³¹You and your households may eat the rest of it anywhere, for it is your wages for your work at the Tent of Meeting. ³²By presenting the best part of it you will not be guilty in this matter; then you will not defile the holy offerings of the Israelites, and you will not die.' "

The Water of Cleansing

19 The LORD said to Moses and Aaron: ²"This is a requirement of the law that the LORD has commanded: Tell the Israelites to bring you a red heifer without defect or blemish and that has never been under a yoke. ³Give it to Eleazar the priest; it is to be taken outside the camp and slaughtered in his presence. ⁴Then Eleazar the priest is to take some of its blood on his finger and sprinkle it seven times toward the front of the Tent of Meeting. ⁵While he watches, the heifer is to be burned—its hide, flesh, blood and offal. ⁶The priest is to take some cedar wood, hyssop and scarlet wool and throw them onto the burning heifer. ⁷After that, the priest must wash his clothes and bathe himself with water. He may then come into the camp, but he will be ceremonially unclean till evening. ⁸The man who burns it must also wash his clothes and bathe with water, and he too will be unclean till evening.

⁹"A man who is clean shall gather up the ashes of the heifer and put them in a ceremonially clean place outside the camp. They shall be kept by the Israelite community for use in the water of cleansing; it is for purification from sin. ¹⁰The man who gathers up the ashes of the heifer must also wash his clothes, and he too will be unclean till evening. This will be a lasting ordinance both for the Israelites and for the aliens living among them.

¹¹"Whoever touches the dead body of anyone will be unclean for seven days. ¹²He must purify himself with the water on the third day and on the seventh day; then he will be clean. But if he does not purify himself on the third and seventh days, he will not be clean. ¹³Whoever touches the dead body of anyone and fails to purify himself defiles the LORD's tabernacle. That person must be cut off from Israel. Because the water of cleansing has not been sprinkled on him, he is unclean; his uncleanness remains on him.

¹⁴"This is the law that applies when a person dies in a tent: Anyone who enters the tent and anyone who is in it will be unclean for seven days, ¹⁵and every open container without a lid fastened on it will be unclean.

¹⁶"Anyone out in the open who touches someone who has been killed with a sword or someone who has died a natural death, or anyone who touches a human bone or a grave, will be unclean for seven days.

¹⁷"For the unclean person, put some ashes from the burned purification offering into a jar and pour fresh water over them. ¹⁸Then a man who is ceremonially clean is to take some hyssop, dip it in the water and sprinkle the tent and all the furnishings and the people who were there. He must also sprinkle anyone who has touched a human bone or a grave or someone who has been killed or someone who has died a natural death. ¹⁹The man who is clean is to sprinkle the unclean person on the third and seventh days, and on the seventh day he is to purify him. The person being cleansed must wash his clothes and bathe with water, and that evening he will be clean. ²⁰But if a person who is unclean does not purify himself, he must be cut off from the community, because he has defiled

the sanctuary of the LORD. The water of cleansing has not been sprinkled on him, and he is unclean. ²¹This is a lasting ordinance for them.

"The man who sprinkles the water of cleansing must also wash his clothes, and anyone who touches the water of cleansing will be unclean till evening. ²²Anything that an unclean person touches becomes unclean, and anyone who touches it becomes unclean till evening."

Water From the Rock

20 In the first month the whole Israelite community arrived at the Desert of Zin, and they stayed at Kadesh. There Miriam died and was buried.

²Now there was no water for the community, and the people gathered in opposition to Moses and Aaron. ³They quarreled with Moses and said, "If only we had died when our brothers fell dead before the LORD! ⁴Why did you bring the LORD's community into this desert, that we and our livestock should die here? ⁵Why did you bring us up out of Egypt to this terrible place? It has no grain or figs, grapevines or pomegranates. And there is no water to drink!"

⁶Moses and Aaron went from the assembly to the entrance to the Tent of Meeting and fell facedown, and the glory of the LORD appeared to them. ⁷The LORD said to Moses, ⁸"Take the staff, and you and your brother Aaron gather the assembly together. Speak to that rock before their eyes and it will pour out its water. You will bring water out of the rock for the community so they and their livestock can drink."

⁹So Moses took the staff from the LORD's presence, just as he commanded him. ¹⁰He and Aaron gathered the assembly together in front of the rock and Moses said to them, "Listen, you rebels, must we bring you water out of this rock?" ¹¹Then Moses raised his arm and struck the rock twice with his staff. Water gushed out, and the community and their livestock drank.

¹²But the LORD said to Moses and Aaron, "Because you did not trust in me enough to honor me as holy in the sight of the Israelites, you will not bring this community into the land I give them."

¹³These were the waters of Meribah,ª where the Israelites quarreled with the LORD and where he showed himself holy among them.

Edom Denies Israel Passage

¹⁴Moses sent messengers from Kadesh to the king of Edom, saying:

"This is what your brother Israel says: You know about all the hardships that have come upon us. ¹⁵Our forefathers went down into Egypt, and we lived there many years. The Egyptians mistreated us and our fathers, ¹⁶but when we cried out to the LORD, he heard our cry and sent an angel and brought us out of Egypt.

"Now we are here at Kadesh, a town on the edge of your territory. ¹⁷Please let us pass through your country. We will not go through any field or vineyard, or drink water from any well. We will travel along the king's highway and not turn to the right or to the left until we have passed through your territory."

¹⁸But Edom answered:

"You may not pass through here; if you try, we will march out and attack you with the sword."

¹⁹The Israelites replied:

"We will go along the main road, and if we or our livestock drink any of your water, we will pay for it. We only want to pass through on foot— nothing else."

²⁰Again they answered:

"You may not pass through."

Then Edom came out against them with a large and powerful army. ²¹Since Edom refused to let them go through their territory, Israel turned away from them.

The Death of Aaron

²²The whole Israelite community set out from Kadesh and came to Mount Hor. ²³At Mount Hor, near the border of Edom, the LORD said to Moses and Aaron,

ª13 Meribah means quarreling.

[24]"Aaron will be gathered to his people. He will not enter the land I give the Israelites, because both of you rebelled against my command at the waters of Meribah. [25]Get Aaron and his son Eleazar and take them up Mount Hor. [26]Remove Aaron's garments and put them on his son Eleazar, for Aaron will be gathered to his people; he will die there."

[27]Moses did as the LORD commanded: They went up Mount Hor in the sight of the whole community. [28]Moses removed Aaron's garments and put them on his son Eleazar. And Aaron died there on top of the mountain. Then Moses and Eleazar came down from the mountain, [29]and when the whole community learned that Aaron had died, the entire house of Israel mourned for him thirty days.

Arad Destroyed

21 When the Canaanite king of Arad, who lived in the Negev, heard that Israel was coming along the road to Atharim, he attacked the Israelites and captured some of them. [2]Then Israel made this vow to the LORD: "If you will deliver these people into our hands, we will totally destroy[a] their cities." [3]The LORD listened to Israel's plea and gave the Canaanites over to them. They completely destroyed them and their towns; so the place was named Hormah.[b]

The Bronze Snake

[4]They traveled from Mount Hor along the route to the Red Sea,[c] to go around Edom. But the people grew impatient on the way; [5]they spoke against God and against Moses, and said, "Why have you brought us up out of Egypt to die in the desert? There is no bread! There is no water! And we detest this miserable food!"

[6]Then the LORD sent venomous snakes among them; they bit the people and many Israelites died. [7]The people came to Moses and said, "We sinned when we spoke against the LORD and against you. Pray that the LORD will take the snakes away from us." So Moses prayed for the people.

[8]The LORD said to Moses, "Make a snake and put it up on a pole; anyone who is bitten can look at it and live." [9]So Moses made a bronze snake and put it up on a pole. Then when anyone was bitten by a snake and looked at the bronze snake, he lived.

> THE people came to Moses and said, "We sinned when we spoke against the LORD and against you. Pray that the LORD will take the snakes away from us." So Moses prayed for the people.
>
> NUMBERS 21:7

The Journey to Moab

[10]The Israelites moved on and camped at Oboth. [11]Then they set out from Oboth and camped in Iye Abarim, in the desert that faces Moab toward the sunrise. [12]From there they moved on and camped in the Zered Valley. [13]They set out from there and camped alongside the Arnon, which is in the desert extending into Amorite territory. The Arnon is the border of Moab, between Moab and the Amorites. [14]That is why the Book of the Wars of the LORD says:

"... Waheb in Suphah[d] and the
    ravines,
  the Arnon [15]and[e] the slopes of
    the ravines
that lead to the site of Ar
  and lie along the border of Moab."

[16]From there they continued on to Beer, the well where the LORD said to Moses, "Gather the people together and I will give them water."

[17]Then Israel sang this song:

"Spring up, O well!
  Sing about it,
[18]about the well that the princes dug,
  that the nobles of the people
    sank—
  the nobles with scepters
    and staffs."

---

[a]2 The Hebrew term refers to the irrevocable giving over of things or persons to the LORD, often by totally destroying them; also in verse 3.
[b]3 *Hormah* means *destruction.*   [c]4 Hebrew *Yam Suph*; that is, Sea of Reeds   [d]14 The meaning of the Hebrew for this phrase is uncertain.   [e]14,15 Or *"I have been given from Suphah and the ravines / of the Arnon* [15]*to*

Then they went from the desert to Mattanah, [19]from Mattanah to Nahaliel, from Nahaliel to Bamoth, [20]and from Bamoth to the valley in Moab where the top of Pisgah overlooks the wasteland.

Defeat of Sihon and Og

[21]Israel sent messengers to say to Sihon king of the Amorites:

[22]"Let us pass through your country. We will not turn aside into any field or vineyard, or drink water from any well. We will travel along the king's highway until we have passed through your territory."

[23]But Sihon would not let Israel pass through his territory. He mustered his entire army and marched out into the desert against Israel. When he reached Jahaz, he fought with Israel. [24]Israel, however, put him to the sword and took over his land from the Arnon to the Jabbok, but only as far as the Ammonites, because their border was fortified. [25]Israel captured all the cities of the Amorites and occupied them, including Heshbon and all its surrounding settlements. [26]Heshbon was the city of Sihon king of the Amorites, who had fought against the former king of Moab and had taken from him all his land as far as the Arnon.

[27]That is why the poets say:

"Come to Heshbon and let it
    be rebuilt;
    let Sihon's city be restored.

[28] "Fire went out from Heshbon,
    a blaze from the city of Sihon.
It consumed Ar of Moab,
    the citizens of Arnon's heights.
[29]Woe to you, O Moab!
    You are destroyed, O people
        of Chemosh!
He has given up his sons as fugitives
    and his daughters as captives
    to Sihon king of the Amorites.

[30] "But we have overthrown them;
    Heshbon is destroyed all the way
        to Dibon.
We have demolished them as far as
        Nophah,
    which extends to Medeba."

[31]So Israel settled in the land of the Amorites.

[32]After Moses had sent spies to Jazer, the Israelites captured its surrounding settlements and drove out the Amorites who were there. [33]Then they turned and went up along the road toward Bashan, and Og king of Bashan and his whole army marched out to meet them in battle at Edrei.

[34]The LORD said to Moses, "Do not be afraid of him, for I have handed him over to you, with his whole army and his land. Do to him what you did to Sihon king of the Amorites, who reigned in Heshbon." [35]So they struck him down, together with his sons and his whole army, leaving them no survivors. And they took possession of his land.

Balak Summons Balaam

22 Then the Israelites traveled to the plains of Moab and camped along the Jordan across from Jericho.[a]

[2]Now Balak son of Zippor saw all that Israel had done to the Amorites, [3]and Moab was terrified because there were so many people. Indeed, Moab was filled with dread because of the Israelites.

[4]The Moabites said to the elders of Midian, "This horde is going to lick up everything around us, as an ox licks up the grass of the field."

So Balak son of Zippor, who was king of Moab at that time, [5]sent messengers to summon Balaam son of Beor, who was at Pethor, near the River,[b] in his native land. Balak said:

"A people has come out of Egypt; they cover the face of the land and have settled next to me. [6]Now come and put a curse on these people, because they are too powerful for me. Perhaps then I will be able to defeat them and drive them out of the country. For I know that those you bless are blessed, and those you curse are cursed."

[7]The elders of Moab and Midian left, taking with them the fee for divination.

[a]1 Hebrew *Jordan of Jericho*; possibly an ancient name for the Jordan River   [b]5 That is, the Euphrates

When they came to Balaam, they told him what Balak had said.

⁸"Spend the night here," Balaam said to them, "and I will bring you back the answer the Lord gives me." So the Moabite princes stayed with him.

⁹God came to Balaam and asked, "Who are these men with you?"

¹⁰Balaam said to God, "Balak son of Zippor, king of Moab, sent me this message: ¹¹'A people that has come out of Egypt covers the face of the land. Now come and put a curse on them for me. Perhaps then I will be able to fight them and drive them away.'"

¹²But God said to Balaam, "Do not go with them. You must not put a curse on those people, because they are blessed."

¹³The next morning Balaam got up and said to Balak's princes, "Go back to your own country, for the Lord has refused to let me go with you."

¹⁴So the Moabite princes returned to Balak and said, "Balaam refused to come with us."

¹⁵Then Balak sent other princes, more numerous and more distinguished than the first. ¹⁶They came to Balaam and said:

"This is what Balak son of Zippor says: Do not let anything keep you from coming to me, ¹⁷because I will reward you handsomely and do whatever you say. Come and put a curse on these people for me."

¹⁸But Balaam answered them, "Even if Balak gave me his palace filled with silver and gold, I could not do anything great or small to go beyond the command of the Lord my God. ¹⁹Now stay here tonight as the others did, and I will find out what else the Lord will tell me."

²⁰That night God came to Balaam and said, "Since these men have come to summon you, go with them, but do only what I tell you."

Balaam's Donkey

²¹Balaam got up in the morning, saddled his donkey and went with the princes of Moab. ²²But God was very angry when he went, and the angel of the Lord stood in the road to oppose him. Balaam was riding on his donkey, and his two servants were with him. ²³When the donkey saw the angel of the Lord standing in the road with a drawn sword in his hand, she turned off the road into a field. Balaam beat her to get her back on the road.

²⁴Then the angel of the Lord stood in a narrow path between two vineyards, with walls on both sides. ²⁵When the donkey saw the angel of the Lord, she pressed close to the wall, crushing Balaam's foot against it. So he beat her again.

²⁶Then the angel of the Lord moved on ahead and stood in a narrow place where there was no room to turn, either to the right or to the left. ²⁷When the donkey saw the angel of the Lord, she lay down under Balaam, and he was angry and beat her with his staff. ²⁸Then the Lord opened the donkey's mouth, and she said to Balaam, "What have I done to you to make you beat me these three times?"

²⁹Balaam answered the donkey, "You have made a fool of me! If I had a sword in my hand, I would kill you right now."

³⁰The donkey said to Balaam, "Am I not your own donkey, which you have always ridden, to this day? Have I been in the habit of doing this to you?"

"No," he said.

³¹Then the Lord opened Balaam's eyes, and he saw the angel of the Lord standing in the road with his sword drawn. So he bowed low and fell facedown.

³²The angel of the Lord asked him, "Why have you beaten your donkey these three times? I have come here to oppose you because your path is a reckless one before me.ᵃ ³³The donkey saw me and turned away from me these three times. If she had not turned away, I would certainly have killed you by now, but I would have spared her."

³⁴Balaam said to the angel of the Lord, "I have sinned. I did not realize you were standing in the road to oppose me. Now if you are displeased, I will go back."

³⁵The angel of the Lord said to Balaam, "Go with the men, but speak only what I tell you." So Balaam went with the princes of Balak.

³⁶When Balak heard that Balaam was coming, he went out to meet him at the Moabite town on the Arnon border, at

ᵃ32 The meaning of the Hebrew for this clause is uncertain.

the edge of his territory. ³⁷Balak said to Balaam, "Did I not send you an urgent summons? Why didn't you come to me? Am I really not able to reward you?"

³⁸"Well, I have come to you now," Balaam replied. "But can I say just anything? I must speak only what God puts in my mouth."

³⁹Then Balaam went with Balak to Kiriath Huzoth. ⁴⁰Balak sacrificed cattle and sheep, and gave some to Balaam and the princes who were with him. ⁴¹The next morning Balak took Balaam up to Bamoth Baal, and from there he saw part of the people.

Balaam's First Oracle

23 Balaam said, "Build me seven altars here, and prepare seven bulls and seven rams for me." ²Balak did as Balaam said, and the two of them offered a bull and a ram on each altar.

³Then Balaam said to Balak, "Stay here beside your offering while I go aside. Perhaps the LORD will come to meet with me. Whatever he reveals to me I will tell you." Then he went off to a barren height.

⁴God met with him, and Balaam said, "I have prepared seven altars, and on each altar I have offered a bull and a ram."

⁵The LORD put a message in Balaam's mouth and said, "Go back to Balak and give him this message."

⁶So he went back to him and found him standing beside his offering, with all the princes of Moab. ⁷Then Balaam uttered his oracle:

"Balak brought me from Aram,
    the king of Moab from the eastern mountains.
'Come,' he said, 'curse Jacob for me;
    come, denounce Israel.'
⁸How can I curse
    those whom God has not cursed?
How can I denounce
    those whom the LORD has not denounced?
⁹From the rocky peaks I see them,
    from the heights I view them.
I see a people who live apart
    and do not consider themselves
    one of the nations.

¹⁰Who can count the dust of Jacob
    or number the fourth part of Israel?
Let me die the death of the righteous,
    and may my end be like theirs!"

¹¹Balak said to Balaam, "What have you done to me? I brought you to curse my enemies, but you have done nothing but bless them!"

¹²He answered, "Must I not speak what the LORD puts in my mouth?"

Balaam's Second Oracle

¹³Then Balak said to him, "Come with me to another place where you can see them; you will see only a part but not all of them. And from there, curse them for me." ¹⁴So he took him to the field of Zophim on the top of Pisgah, and there he built seven altars and offered a bull and a ram on each altar.

¹⁵Balaam said to Balak, "Stay here beside your offering while I meet with him over there."

¹⁶The LORD met with Balaam and put a message in his mouth and said, "Go back to Balak and give him this message."

¹⁷So he went to him and found him standing beside his offering, with the princes of Moab. Balak asked him, "What did the LORD say?"

¹⁸Then he uttered his oracle:

"Arise, Balak, and listen;
    hear me, son of Zippor.
¹⁹God is not a man, that he should lie,
    nor a son of man, that he should
    change his mind.
Does he speak and then not act?
    Does he promise and not fulfill?
²⁰I have received a command to bless;
    he has blessed, and I cannot
    change it.

²¹"No misfortune is seen in Jacob,
    no misery observed in Israel.ᵃ
The LORD their God is with them;
    the shout of the King is among
    them.
²²God brought them out of Egypt;
    they have the strength of a wild ox.
²³There is no sorcery against Jacob,
    no divination against Israel.

─────────
ᵃ21 Or *He has not looked on Jacob's offenses / or on the wrongs found in Israel.*

It will now be said of Jacob
and of Israel, 'See what God
has done!'
24 The people rise like a lioness;
they rouse themselves like a lion
that does not rest till he devours
his prey
and drinks the blood of his
victims."

25 Then Balak said to Balaam, "Neither
curse them at all nor bless them at all!"
26 Balaam answered, "Did I not tell you
I must do whatever the LORD says?"

Balaam's Third Oracle

27 Then Balak said to Balaam, "Come,
let me take you to another place. Perhaps it will please God to let you curse
them for me from there." 28 And Balak
took Balaam to the top of Peor, overlooking the wasteland.
29 Balaam said, "Build me seven altars
here, and prepare seven bulls and seven
rams for me." 30 Balak did as Balaam had
said, and offered a bull and a ram on
each altar.

24 Now when Balaam saw that it
pleased the LORD to bless Israel,
he did not resort to sorcery as at other
times, but turned his face toward the
desert. 2 When Balaam looked out and
saw Israel encamped tribe by tribe, the
Spirit of God came upon him 3 and he uttered his oracle:

"The oracle of Balaam son of Beor,
the oracle of one whose eye sees
clearly,
4 the oracle of one who hears the
words of God,
who sees a vision from the
Almighty,[a]
who falls prostrate, and whose
eyes are opened:

5 "How beautiful are your tents,
O Jacob,
your dwelling places, O Israel!

6 "Like valleys they spread out,
like gardens beside a river,
like aloes planted by the LORD,
like cedars beside the waters.
7 Water will flow from their buckets;
their seed will have abundant
water.

"Their king will be greater
than Agag;
their kingdom will be exalted.

8 "God brought them out of Egypt;
they have the strength of a
wild ox.
They devour hostile nations
and break their bones in pieces;
with their arrows they pierce
them.
9 Like a lion they crouch and lie down,
like a lioness—who dares to
rouse them?

"May those who bless you be blessed
and those who curse you be
cursed!"

10 Then Balak's anger burned against
Balaam. He struck his hands together
and said to him, "I summoned you to
curse my enemies, but you have blessed
them these three times. 11 Now leave at
once and go home! I said I would reward
you handsomely, but the LORD has kept
you from being rewarded."

12 Balaam answered Balak, "Did I not
tell the messengers you sent me, 13 Even
if Balak gave me his palace filled with silver and gold, I could not do anything of
my own accord, good or bad, to go beyond the command of the LORD—and I
must say only what the LORD says'? 14 Now
I am going back to my people, but come,
let me warn you of what this people will
do to your people in days to come."

Balaam's Fourth Oracle

15 Then he uttered his oracle:

"The oracle of Balaam son of Beor,
the oracle of one whose eye sees
clearly,
16 the oracle of one who hears the
words of God,
who has knowledge from the Most
High,
who sees a vision from the Almighty,
who falls prostrate, and whose eyes
are opened:

17 "I see him, but not now;
I behold him, but not near.
A star will come out of Jacob;
a scepter will rise out of Israel.

---

a 4 Hebrew *Shaddai;* also in verse 16

He will crush the foreheads of Moab,
    the skulls[a] of[b] all the sons
      of Sheth.[c]
18 Edom will be conquered;
    Seir, his enemy, will be conquered,
    but Israel will grow strong.
19 A ruler will come out of Jacob
    and destroy the survivors of
      the city."

Balaam's Final Oracles

20Then Balaam saw Amalek and uttered his oracle:

"Amalek was first among the nations,
    but he will come to ruin at last."

21Then he saw the Kenites and uttered his oracle:

"Your dwelling place is secure,
    your nest is set in a rock;
22 yet you Kenites will be destroyed
    when Asshur takes you captive."

23Then he uttered his oracle:

"Ah, who can live when God
    does this?[d]
24   Ships will come from the shores
      of Kittim;
    they will subdue Asshur and Eber,
    but they too will come to ruin."

25Then Balaam got up and returned home and Balak went his own way.

Moab Seduces Israel

25 While Israel was staying in Shittim, the men began to indulge in sexual immorality with Moabite women, 2who invited them to the sacrifices to their gods. The people ate and bowed down before these gods. 3So Israel joined in worshiping the Baal of Peor. And the LORD's anger burned against them.

4The LORD said to Moses, "Take all the leaders of these people, kill them and expose them in broad daylight before the LORD, so that the LORD's fierce anger may turn away from Israel."

5So Moses said to Israel's judges, "Each of you must put to death those of your men who have joined in worshiping the Baal of Peor."

6Then an Israelite man brought to his family a Midianite woman right before the eyes of Moses and the whole assembly of Israel while they were weeping at the entrance to the Tent of Meeting. 7When Phinehas son of Eleazar, the son of Aaron, the priest, saw this, he left the assembly, took a spear in his hand 8and followed the Israelite into the tent. He drove the spear through both of them—through the Israelite and into the woman's body. Then the plague against the Israelites was stopped; 9but those who died in the plague numbered 24,000.

10The LORD said to Moses, 11"Phinehas son of Eleazar, the son of Aaron, the priest, has turned my anger away from the Israelites; for he was as zealous as I am for my honor among them, so that in my zeal I did not put an end to them. 12Therefore tell him I am making my covenant of peace with him. 13He and his descendants will have a covenant of a lasting priesthood, because he was zealous for the honor of his God and made atonement for the Israelites."

14The name of the Israelite who was killed with the Midianite woman was Zimri son of Salu, the leader of a Simeonite family. 15And the name of the Midianite woman who was put to death was Cozbi daughter of Zur, a tribal chief of a Midianite family.

16The LORD said to Moses, 17"Treat the Midianites as enemies and kill them, 18because they treated you as enemies when they deceived you in the affair of Peor and their sister Cozbi, the daughter of a Midianite leader, the woman who was killed when the plague came as a result of Peor."

The Second Census

26 After the plague the LORD said to Moses and Eleazar son of Aaron, the priest, 2"Take a census of the whole Israelite community by families—all those twenty years old or more who are able to serve in the army of Israel." 3So on the plains of Moab by the Jordan across from Jericho,[e] Moses and Eleazar

a17 Samaritan Pentateuch (see also Jer. 48:45); the meaning of the word in the Masoretic Text is uncertain.   b17 Or possibly Moab, / batter   c17 Or all the noisy boasters   d23 Masoretic Text; with a different word division of the Hebrew A people will gather from the north.   e3 Hebrew Jordan of Jericho; possibly an ancient name for the Jordan River; also in verse 63

the priest spoke with them and said, [4]"Take a census of the men twenty years old or more, as the LORD commanded Moses."

These were the Israelites who came out of Egypt:

[5]The descendants of Reuben, the firstborn son of Israel, were:

through Hanoch, the Hanochite clan;
through Pallu, the Palluite clan;
[6]through Hezron, the Hezronite clan;
through Carmi, the Carmite clan.

[7]These were the clans of Reuben; those numbered were 43,730.

[8]The son of Pallu was Eliab, [9]and the sons of Eliab were Nemuel, Dathan and Abiram. The same Dathan and Abiram were the community officials who rebelled against Moses and Aaron and were among Korah's followers when they rebelled against the LORD. [10]The earth opened its mouth and swallowed them along with Korah, whose followers died when the fire devoured the 250 men. And they served as a warning sign. [11]The line of Korah, however, did not die out.

[12]The descendants of Simeon by their clans were:

through Nemuel, the Nemuelite clan;
through Jamin, the Jaminite clan;
through Jakin, the Jakinite clan;
[13]through Zerah, the Zerahite clan;
through Shaul, the Shaulite clan.

[14]These were the clans of Simeon; there were 22,200 men.

[15]The descendants of Gad by their clans were:

through Zephon, the Zephonite clan;
through Haggi, the Haggite clan;
through Shuni, the Shunite clan;
[16]through Ozni, the Oznite clan;
through Eri, the Erite clan;
[17]through Arodi,[a] the Arodite clan;
through Areli, the Arelite clan.

[18]These were the clans of Gad; those numbered were 40,500.

[19]Er and Onan were sons of Judah, but they died in Canaan.

[20]The descendants of Judah by their clans were:

through Shelah, the Shelanite clan;
through Perez, the Perezite clan;
through Zerah, the Zerahite clan.
[21]The descendants of Perez were:
through Hezron, the Hezronite clan;
through Hamul, the Hamulite clan.

[22]These were the clans of Judah; those numbered were 76,500.

[23]The descendants of Issachar by their clans were:

through Tola, the Tolaite clan;
through Puah, the Puite[b] clan;
[24]through Jashub, the Jashubite clan;
through Shimron, the Shimronite clan.

[25]These were the clans of Issachar; those numbered were 64,300.

[26]The descendants of Zebulun by their clans were:

through Sered, the Seredite clan;
through Elon, the Elonite clan;
through Jahleel, the Jahleelite clan.

[27]These were the clans of Zebulun; those numbered were 60,500.

[28]The descendants of Joseph by their clans through Manasseh and Ephraim were:

[29]The descendants of Manasseh:
through Makir, the Makirite clan (Makir was the father of Gilead);
through Gilead, the Gileadite clan.
[30]These were the descendants of Gilead:
through Iezer, the Iezerite clan;
through Helek, the Helekite clan;
[31]through Asriel, the Asrielite clan;
through Shechem, the Shechemite clan;
[32]through Shemida, the Shemidaite clan;
through Hepher, the Hepherite clan.
[33](Zelophehad son of Hepher had no sons; he had only daughters,

[a]17 Samaritan Pentateuch and Syriac (see also Gen. 46:16); Masoretic Text *Arod*
[b]23 Samaritan Pentateuch, Septuagint, Vulgate and Syriac (see also 1 Chron. 7:1); Masoretic Text *through Puvah, the Punite*

whose names were Mahlah, Noah, Hoglah, Milcah and Tirzah.)
³⁴These were the clans of Manasseh; those numbered were 52,700.

³⁵These were the descendants of Ephraim by their clans:
through Shuthelah, the Shuthelahite clan;
through Beker, the Bekerite clan;
through Tahan, the Tahanite clan.
³⁶ These were the descendants of Shuthelah:
through Eran, the Eranite clan.
³⁷These were the clans of Ephraim; those numbered were 32,500.

These were the descendants of Joseph by their clans.

³⁸The descendants of Benjamin by their clans were:
through Bela, the Belaite clan;
through Ashbel, the Ashbelite clan;
through Ahiram, the Ahiramite clan;
³⁹ through Shupham,ᵃ the Shuphamite clan;
through Hupham, the Huphamite clan.
⁴⁰ The descendants of Bela through Ard and Naaman were:
through Ard,ᵇ the Ardite clan;
through Naaman, the Naamite clan.
⁴¹These were the clans of Benjamin; those numbered were 45,600.

⁴²These were the descendants of Dan by their clans:
through Shuham, the Shuhamite clan.
These were the clans of Dan: ⁴³All of them were Shuhamite clans; and those numbered were 64,400.

⁴⁴The descendants of Asher by their clans were:
through Imnah, the Imnite clan;
through Ishvi, the Ishvite clan;
through Beriah, the Beriite clan;
⁴⁵ and through the descendants of Beriah:
through Heber, the Heberite clan;
through Malkiel, the Malkielite clan.
⁴⁶(Asher had a daughter named Serah.)

⁴⁷These were the clans of Asher; those numbered were 53,400.

⁴⁸The descendants of Naphtali by their clans were:
through Jahzeel, the Jahzeelite clan;
through Guni, the Gunite clan;
⁴⁹ through Jezer, the Jezerite clan;
through Shillem, the Shillemite clan.
⁵⁰These were the clans of Naphtali; those numbered were 45,400.

⁵¹The total number of the men of Israel was 601,730.

⁵²The LORD said to Moses, ⁵³"The land is to be allotted to them as an inheritance based on the number of names. ⁵⁴To a larger group give a larger inheritance, and to a smaller group a smaller one; each is to receive its inheritance according to the number of those listed. ⁵⁵Be sure that the land is distributed by lot. What each group inherits will be according to the names for its ancestral tribe. ⁵⁶Each inheritance is to be distributed by lot among the larger and smaller groups."

⁵⁷These were the Levites who were counted by their clans:
through Gershon, the Gershonite clan;
through Kohath, the Kohathite clan;
through Merari, the Merarite clan.
⁵⁸ These also were Levite clans:
the Libnite clan,
the Hebronite clan,
the Mahlite clan,
the Mushite clan,
the Korahite clan.
(Kohath was the forefather of Amram; ⁵⁹the name of Amram's wife was Jochebed, a descendant of Levi, who was born to the Levitesᶜ in Egypt. To Amram she bore Aaron, Moses and their sister Miriam. ⁶⁰Aaron was the father of Nadab and

ᵃ39 A few manuscripts of the Masoretic Text, Samaritan Pentateuch, Vulgate and Syriac (see also Septuagint); most manuscripts of the Masoretic Text Shephupham   ᵇ40 Samaritan Pentateuch and Vulgate (see also Septuagint); Masoretic Text does not have through Ard.   ᶜ59 Or Jochebed, a daughter of Levi, who was born to Levi

Abihu, Eleazar and Ithamar. ⁶¹But Nadab and Abihu died when they made an offering before the LORD with unauthorized fire.)

⁶²All the male Levites a month old or more numbered 23,000. They were not counted along with the other Israelites because they received no inheritance among them.

⁶³These are the ones counted by Moses and Eleazar the priest when they counted the Israelites on the plains of Moab by the Jordan across from Jericho. ⁶⁴Not one of them was among those counted by Moses and Aaron the priest when they counted the Israelites in the Desert of Sinai. ⁶⁵For the LORD had told those Israelites they would surely die in the desert, and not one of them was left except Caleb son of Jephunneh and Joshua son of Nun.

Zelophehad's Daughters

27 The daughters of Zelophehad son of Hepher, the son of Gilead, the son of Makir, the son of Manasseh, belonged to the clans of Manasseh son of Joseph. The names of the daughters were Mahlah, Noah, Hoglah, Milcah and Tirzah. They approached ²the entrance to the Tent of Meeting and stood before Moses, Eleazar the priest, the leaders and the whole assembly, and said, ³"Our father died in the desert. He was not among Korah's followers, who banded together against the LORD, but he died for his own sin and left no sons. ⁴Why should our father's name disappear from his clan because he had no son? Give us property among our father's relatives."

⁵So Moses brought their case before the LORD ⁶and the LORD said to him, ⁷"What Zelophehad's daughters are saying is right. You must certainly give them property as an inheritance among their father's relatives and turn their father's inheritance over to them.

⁸"Say to the Israelites, 'If a man dies and leaves no son, turn his inheritance over to his daughter. ⁹If he has no daughter, give his inheritance to his brothers. ¹⁰If he has no brothers, give his inheritance to his father's brothers. ¹¹If his fa-

ther had no brothers, give his inheritance to the nearest relative in his clan, that he may possess it. This is to be a legal requirement for the Israelites, as the LORD commanded Moses.'"

Joshua to Succeed Moses

¹²Then the LORD said to Moses, "Go up this mountain in the Abarim range and see the land I have given the Israelites. ¹³After you have seen it, you too will be gathered to your people, as your brother Aaron was, ¹⁴for when the community rebelled at the waters in the Desert of Zin, both of you disobeyed my command to honor me as holy before their eyes." (These were the waters of Meribah Kadesh, in the Desert of Zin.)

¹⁵Moses said to the LORD, ¹⁶"May the LORD, the God of the spirits of all mankind, appoint a man over this community ¹⁷to go out and come in before them, one who will lead them out and bring them in, so the LORD's people will not be like sheep without a shepherd."

> "MAY the LORD, the God of the spirits of all mankind, appoint a man over this community."
>
> NUMBERS 27:16

¹⁸So the LORD said to Moses, "Take Joshua son of Nun, a man in whom is the spirit,ᵃ and lay your hand on him. ¹⁹Have him stand before Eleazar the priest and the entire assembly and commission him in their presence. ²⁰Give him some of your authority so the whole Israelite community will obey him. ²¹He is to stand before Eleazar the priest, who will obtain decisions for him by inquiring of the Urim before the LORD. At his command he and the entire community of the Israelites will go out, and at his command they will come in."

²²Moses did as the LORD commanded him. He took Joshua and had him stand before Eleazar the priest and the whole assembly. ²³Then he laid his hands on him and commissioned him, as the LORD instructed through Moses.

ᵃ18 Or Spirit

Daily Offerings

28 The LORD said to Moses, [2] "Give this command to the Israelites and say to them: 'See that you present to me at the appointed time the food for my offerings made by fire, as an aroma pleasing to me.' [3]Say to them: 'This is the offering made by fire that you are to present to the LORD: two lambs a year old without defect, as a regular burnt offering each day. [4]Prepare one lamb in the morning and the other at twilight, [5]together with a grain offering of a tenth of an ephah[a] of fine flour mixed with a quarter of a hin[b] of oil from pressed olives. [6]This is the regular burnt offering instituted at Mount Sinai as a pleasing aroma, an offering made to the LORD by fire. [7]The accompanying drink offering is to be a quarter of a hin of fermented drink with each lamb. Pour out the drink offering to the LORD at the sanctuary. [8]Prepare the second lamb at twilight, along with the same kind of grain offering and drink offering that you prepare in the morning. This is an offering made by fire, an aroma pleasing to the LORD.

Sabbath Offerings

[9] "'On the Sabbath day, make an offering of two lambs a year old without defect, together with its drink offering and a grain offering of two-tenths of an ephah[c] of fine flour mixed with oil. [10]This is the burnt offering for every Sabbath, in addition to the regular burnt offering and its drink offering.

Monthly Offerings

[11] "'On the first of every month, present to the LORD a burnt offering of two young bulls, one ram and seven male lambs a year old, all without defect. [12]With each bull there is to be a grain offering of three-tenths of an ephah[d] of fine flour mixed with oil; with the ram, a grain offering of two-tenths of an ephah of fine flour mixed with oil; [13]and with each lamb, a grain offering of a tenth of an ephah of fine flour mixed with oil. This is for a burnt offering, a pleasing aroma, an offering made to the LORD by fire. [14]With each bull there is to be a drink offering of half a hin[e] of wine; with the ram, a third

of a hin[f]; and with each lamb, a quarter of a hin. This is the monthly burnt offering to be made at each new moon during the year. [15]Besides the regular burnt offering with its drink offering, one male goat is to be presented to the LORD as a sin offering.

The Passover

[16] "'On the fourteenth day of the first month the LORD's Passover is to be held. [17]On the fifteenth day of this month there is to be a festival; for seven days eat bread made without yeast. [18]On the first day hold a sacred assembly and do no regular work. [19]Present to the LORD an offering made by fire, a burnt offering of two young bulls, one ram and seven male lambs a year old, all without defect. [20]With each bull prepare a grain offering of three-tenths of an ephah of fine flour mixed with oil; with the ram, two-tenths; [21]and with each of the seven lambs, one-tenth. [22]Include one male goat as a sin offering to make atonement for you. [23]Prepare these in addition to the regular morning burnt offering. [24]In this way prepare the food for the offering made by fire every day for seven days as an aroma pleasing to the LORD; it is to be prepared in addition to the regular burnt offering and its drink offering. [25]On the seventh day hold a sacred assembly and do no regular work.

Feast of Weeks

[26] "'On the day of firstfruits, when you present to the LORD an offering of new grain during the Feast of Weeks, hold a sacred assembly and do no regular work. [27]Present a burnt offering of two young bulls, one ram and seven male lambs a year old as an aroma pleasing to the LORD. [28]With each bull there is to be a grain offering of three-tenths of an ephah of fine flour mixed with oil; with the ram,

[a]5 That is, probably about 2 quarts (about 2 liters); also in verses 13, 21 and 29   [b]5 That is, probably about 1 quart (about 1 liter); also in verses 7 and 14   [c]9 That is, probably about 4 quarts (about 4.5 liters); also in verses 12, 20 and 28   [d]12 That is, probably about 6 quarts (about 6.5 liters); also in verses 20 and 28   [e]14 That is, probably about 2 quarts (about 2 liters)   [f]14 That is, probably about 1 1/4 quarts (about 1.2 liters)

two-tenths; [29]and with each of the seven lambs, one-tenth. [30]Include one male goat to make atonement for you. [31]Prepare these together with their drink offerings, in addition to the regular burnt offering and its grain offering. Be sure the animals are without defect.

Feast of Trumpets

29 "'On the first day of the seventh month hold a sacred assembly and do no regular work. It is a day for you to sound the trumpets. [2]As an aroma pleasing to the LORD, prepare a burnt offering of one young bull, one ram and seven male lambs a year old, all without defect. [3]With the bull prepare a grain offering of three-tenths of an ephah[a] of fine flour mixed with oil; with the ram, two-tenths[b]; [4]and with each of the seven lambs, one-tenth.[c] [5]Include one male goat as a sin offering to make atonement for you. [6]These are in addition to the monthly and daily burnt offerings with their grain offerings and drink offerings as specified. They are offerings made to the LORD by fire—a pleasing aroma.

Day of Atonement

[7]"'On the tenth day of this seventh month hold a sacred assembly. You must deny yourselves[d] and do no work. [8]Present as an aroma pleasing to the LORD a burnt offering of one young bull, one ram and seven male lambs a year old, all without defect. [9]With the bull prepare a grain offering of three-tenths of an ephah of fine flour mixed with oil; with the ram, two-tenths; [10]and with each of the seven lambs, one-tenth. [11]Include one male goat as a sin offering, in addition to the sin offering for atonement and the regular burnt offering with its grain offering, and their drink offerings.

Feast of Tabernacles

[12]"'On the fifteenth day of the seventh month, hold a sacred assembly and do no regular work. Celebrate a festival to the LORD for seven days. [13]Present an offering made by fire as an aroma pleasing to the LORD, a burnt offering of thirteen young bulls, two rams and fourteen male lambs a year old, all without defect. [14]With each of the thirteen bulls prepare

a grain offering of three-tenths of an ephah of fine flour mixed with oil; with each of the two rams, two-tenths; [15]and with each of the fourteen lambs, one-tenth. [16]Include one male goat as a sin offering, in addition to the regular burnt offering with its grain offering and drink offering.

[17]"'On the second day prepare twelve young bulls, two rams and fourteen male lambs a year old, all without defect. [18]With the bulls, rams and lambs, prepare their grain offerings and drink offerings according to the number specified. [19]Include one male goat as a sin offering, in addition to the regular burnt offering with its grain offering, and their drink offerings.

[20]"'On the third day prepare eleven bulls, two rams and fourteen male lambs a year old, all without defect. [21]With the bulls, rams and lambs, prepare their grain offerings and drink offerings according to the number specified. [22]Include one male goat as a sin offering, in addition to the regular burnt offering with its grain offering and drink offering.

[23]"'On the fourth day prepare ten bulls, two rams and fourteen male lambs a year old, all without defect. [24]With the bulls, rams and lambs, prepare their grain offerings and drink offerings according to the number specified. [25]Include one male goat as a sin offering, in addition to the regular burnt offering with its grain offering and drink offering.

[26]"'On the fifth day prepare nine bulls, two rams and fourteen male lambs a year old, all without defect. [27]With the bulls, rams and lambs, prepare their grain offerings and drink offerings according to the number specified. [28]Include one male goat as a sin offering, in addition to the regular burnt offering with its grain offering and drink offering.

[29]"'On the sixth day prepare eight bulls, two rams and fourteen male lambs a year old, all without defect. [30]With the bulls, rams and lambs, prepare their grain offerings and drink offerings ac-

---

[a]3 That is, probably about 6 quarts (about 6.5 liters); also in verses 9 and 14   [b]3 That is, probably about 4 quarts (about 4.5 liters); also in verses 9 and 14   [c]4 That is, probably about 2 quarts (about 2 liters); also in verses 10 and 15   [d]7 Or *must fast*

cording to the number specified. ³¹Include one male goat as a sin offering, in addition to the regular burnt offering with its grain offering and drink offering.

³²" 'On the seventh day prepare seven bulls, two rams and fourteen male lambs a year old, all without defect. ³³With the bulls, rams and lambs, prepare their grain offerings and drink offerings according to the number specified. ³⁴Include one male goat as a sin offering, in addition to the regular burnt offering with its grain offering and drink offering.

³⁵" 'On the eighth day hold an assembly and do no regular work. ³⁶Present an offering made by fire as an aroma pleasing to the Lord, a burnt offering of one bull, one ram and seven male lambs a year old, all without defect. ³⁷With the bull, the ram and the lambs, prepare their grain offerings and drink offerings according to the number specified. ³⁸Include one male goat as a sin offering, in addition to the regular burnt offering with its grain offering and drink offering.

³⁹" 'In addition to what you vow and your freewill offerings, prepare these for the Lord at your appointed feasts: your burnt offerings, grain offerings, drink offerings and fellowship offerings.ᵃ' "

⁴⁰Moses told the Israelites all that the Lord commanded him.

Vows

30 Moses said to the heads of the tribes of Israel: "This is what the Lord commands: ²When a man makes a vow to the Lord or takes an oath to obligate himself by a pledge, he must not break his word but must do everything he said.

³"When a young woman still living in her father's house makes a vow to the Lord or obligates herself by a pledge ⁴and her father hears about her vow or pledge but says nothing to her, then all her vows and every pledge by which she obligated herself will stand. ⁵But if her father forbids her when he hears about it, none of her vows or the pledges by which she obligated herself will stand; the Lord will release her because her father has forbidden her.

⁶"If she marries after she makes a vow or after her lips utter a rash promise by which she obligates herself ⁷and her husband hears about it but says nothing to her, then her vows or the pledges by which she obligated herself will stand. ⁸But if her husband forbids her when he hears about it, he nullifies the vow that obligates her or the rash promise by which she obligates herself, and the Lord will release her.

⁹"Any vow or obligation taken by a widow or divorced woman will be binding on her.

¹⁰"If a woman living with her husband makes a vow or obligates herself by a pledge under oath ¹¹and her husband hears about it but says nothing to her and does not forbid her, then all her vows or the pledges by which she obligated herself will stand. ¹²But if her husband nullifies them when he hears about them, then none of the vows or pledges that came from her lips will stand. Her husband has nullified them, and the Lord will release her. ¹³Her husband may confirm or nullify any vow she makes or any sworn pledge to deny herself. ¹⁴But if her husband says nothing to her about it from day to day, then he confirms all her vows or the pledges binding on her. He confirms them by saying nothing to her when he hears about them. ¹⁵If, however, he nullifies them some time after he hears about them, then he is responsible for her guilt."

¹⁶These are the regulations the Lord gave Moses concerning relationships between a man and his wife, and between a father and his young daughter still living in his house.

> ❝ Where does love begin? In our own homes. When does it begin? When we pray together. ❞
>
> MOTHER TERESA

Vengeance on the Midianites

31 The Lord said to Moses, ²"Take vengeance on the Midianites for the Israelites. After that, you will be gathered to your people."

ᵃ39 Traditionally *peace offerings*

³So Moses said to the people, "Arm some of your men to go to war against the Midianites and to carry out the LORD's vengeance on them. ⁴Send into battle a thousand men from each of the tribes of Israel." ⁵So twelve thousand men armed for battle, a thousand from each tribe, were supplied from the clans of Israel. ⁶Moses sent them into battle, a thousand from each tribe, along with Phinehas son of Eleazar, the priest, who took with him articles from the sanctuary and the trumpets for signaling.

⁷They fought against Midian, as the LORD commanded Moses, and killed every man. ⁸Among their victims were Evi, Rekem, Zur, Hur and Reba—the five kings of Midian. They also killed Balaam son of Beor with the sword. ⁹The Israelites captured the Midianite women and children and took all the Midianite herds, flocks and goods as plunder. ¹⁰They burned all the towns where the Midianites had settled, as well as all their camps. ¹¹They took all the plunder and spoils, including the people and animals, ¹²and brought the captives, spoils and plunder to Moses and Eleazar the priest and the Israelite assembly at their camp on the plains of Moab, by the Jordan across from Jericho.ᵃ

¹³Moses, Eleazar the priest and all the leaders of the community went to meet them outside the camp. ¹⁴Moses was angry with the officers of the army—the commanders of thousands and commanders of hundreds—who returned from the battle.

¹⁵"Have you allowed all the women to live?" he asked them. ¹⁶"They were the ones who followed Balaam's advice and were the means of turning the Israelites away from the LORD in what happened at Peor, so that a plague struck the LORD's people. ¹⁷Now kill all the boys. And kill every woman who has slept with a man, ¹⁸but save for yourselves every girl who has never slept with a man.

¹⁹"All of you who have killed anyone or touched anyone who was killed must stay outside the camp seven days. On the third and seventh days you must purify yourselves and your captives. ²⁰Purify every garment as well as everything made of leather, goat hair or wood."

²¹Then Eleazar the priest said to the soldiers who had gone into battle, "This is the requirement of the law that the LORD gave Moses: ²²Gold, silver, bronze, iron, tin, lead ²³and anything else that can withstand fire must be put through the fire, and then it will be clean. But it must also be purified with the water of cleansing. And whatever cannot withstand fire must be put through that water. ²⁴On the seventh day wash your clothes and you will be clean. Then you may come into the camp."

Dividing the Spoils

²⁵The LORD said to Moses, ²⁶"You and Eleazar the priest and the family heads of the community are to count all the people and animals that were captured. ²⁷Divide the spoils between the soldiers who took part in the battle and the rest of the community. ²⁸From the soldiers who fought in the battle, set apart as tribute for the LORD one out of every five hundred, whether persons, cattle, donkeys, sheep or goats. ²⁹Take this tribute from their half share and give it to Eleazar the priest as the LORD's part. ³⁰From the Israelites' half, select one out of every fifty, whether persons, cattle, donkeys, sheep, goats or other animals. Give them to the Levites, who are responsible for the care of the LORD's tabernacle." ³¹So Moses and Eleazar the priest did as the LORD commanded Moses.

³²The plunder remaining from the spoils that the soldiers took was 675,000 sheep, ³³72,000 cattle, ³⁴61,000 donkeys ³⁵and 32,000 women who had never slept with a man.

³⁶The half share of those who fought in the battle was:

337,500 sheep, ³⁷of which the tribute for the LORD was 675;
³⁸ 36,000 cattle, of which the tribute for the LORD was 72;
³⁹ 30,500 donkeys, of which the tribute for the LORD was 61;
⁴⁰ 16,000 people, of which the tribute for the LORD was 32.

ᵃ12 Hebrew *Jordan of Jericho*; possibly an ancient name for the Jordan River

⁴¹Moses gave the tribute to Eleazar the priest as the LORD's part, as the LORD commanded Moses.

⁴²The half belonging to the Israelites, which Moses set apart from that of the fighting men— ⁴³the community's half—was 337,500 sheep, ⁴⁴36,000 cattle, ⁴⁵30,500 donkeys ⁴⁶and 16,000 people. ⁴⁷From the Israelites' half, Moses selected one out of every fifty persons and animals, as the LORD commanded him, and gave them to the Levites, who were responsible for the care of the LORD's tabernacle.

⁴⁸Then the officers who were over the units of the army—the commanders of thousands and commanders of hundreds—went to Moses ⁴⁹and said to him, "Your servants have counted the soldiers under our command, and not one is missing. ⁵⁰So we have brought as an offering to the LORD the gold articles each of us acquired—armlets, bracelets, signet rings, earrings and necklaces—to make atonement for ourselves before the LORD."

⁵¹Moses and Eleazar the priest accepted from them the gold—all the crafted articles. ⁵²All the gold from the commanders of thousands and commanders of hundreds that Moses and Eleazar presented as a gift to the LORD weighed 16,750 shekels.ᵃ ⁵³Each soldier had taken plunder for himself. ⁵⁴Moses and Eleazar the priest accepted the gold from the commanders of thousands and commanders of hundreds and brought it into the Tent of Meeting as a memorial for the Israelites before the LORD.

The Transjordan Tribes

32 The Reubenites and Gadites, who had very large herds and flocks, saw that the lands of Jazer and Gilead were suitable for livestock. ²So they came to Moses and Eleazar the priest and to the leaders of the community, and said, ³"Ataroth, Dibon, Jazer, Nimrah, Heshbon, Elealeh, Sebam, Nebo and Beon— ⁴the land the LORD subdued before the people of Israel—are suitable for livestock, and your servants have livestock. ⁵If we have found favor in your eyes," they said, "let this land be given to your servants as our possession. Do not make us cross the Jordan."

⁶Moses said to the Gadites and Reubenites, "Shall your countrymen go to war while you sit here? ⁷Why do you discourage the Israelites from going over into the land the LORD has given them? ⁸This is what your fathers did when I sent them from Kadesh Barnea to look over the land. ⁹After they went up to the Valley of Eshcol and viewed the land, they discouraged the Israelites from entering the land the LORD had given them. ¹⁰The LORD's anger was aroused that day and he swore this oath: ¹¹'Because they have not followed me wholeheartedly, not one of the men twenty years old or more who came up out of Egypt will see the land I promised on oath to Abraham, Isaac and Jacob— ¹²not one except Caleb son of Jephunneh the Kenizzite and Joshua son of Nun, for they followed the LORD wholeheartedly.' ¹³The LORD's anger burned against Israel and he made them wander in the desert forty years, until the whole generation of those who had done evil in his sight was gone.

¹⁴"And here you are, a brood of sinners, standing in the place of your fathers and making the LORD even more angry with Israel. ¹⁵If you turn away from following him, he will again leave all this people in the desert, and you will be the cause of their destruction."

¹⁶Then they came up to him and said, "We would like to build pens here for our livestock and cities for our women and children. ¹⁷But we are ready to arm ourselves and go ahead of the Israelites until we have brought them to their place. Meanwhile our women and children will live in fortified cities, for protection from the inhabitants of the land. ¹⁸We will not return to our homes until every Israelite has received his inheritance. ¹⁹We will not receive any inheritance with them on the other side of the Jordan, because our inheritance has come to us on the east side of the Jordan."

²⁰Then Moses said to them, "If you will do this—if you will arm yourselves before the LORD for battle, ²¹and if all of you will go armed over the Jordan before the LORD until he has driven his enemies out

ᵃ52 That is, about 420 pounds (about 190 kilograms)

before him— ²²then when the land is subdued before the LORD, you may return and be free from your obligation to the LORD and to Israel. And this land will be your possession before the LORD.

²³"But if you fail to do this, you will be sinning against the LORD; and you may be sure that your sin will find you out. ²⁴Build cities for your women and children, and pens for your flocks, but do what you have promised."

²⁵The Gadites and Reubenites said to Moses, "We your servants will do as our lord commands. ²⁶Our children and wives, our flocks and herds will remain here in the cities of Gilead. ²⁷But your servants, every man armed for battle, will cross over to fight before the LORD, just as our lord says."

²⁸Then Moses gave orders about them to Eleazar the priest and Joshua son of Nun and to the family heads of the Israelite tribes. ²⁹He said to them, "If the Gadites and Reubenites, every man armed for battle, cross over the Jordan with you before the LORD, then when the land is subdued before you, give them the land of Gilead as their possession. ³⁰But if they do not cross over with you armed, they must accept their possession with you in Canaan."

³¹The Gadites and Reubenites answered, "Your servants will do what the LORD has said. ³²We will cross over before the LORD into Canaan armed, but the property we inherit will be on this side of the Jordan."

³³Then Moses gave to the Gadites, the Reubenites and the half-tribe of Manasseh son of Joseph the kingdom of Sihon king of the Amorites and the kingdom of Og king of Bashan—the whole land with its cities and the territory around them.

³⁴The Gadites built up Dibon, Ataroth, Aroer, ³⁵Atroth Shophan, Jazer, Jogbehah, ³⁶Beth Nimrah and Beth Haran as fortified cities, and built pens for their flocks. ³⁷And the Reubenites rebuilt Heshbon, Elealeh and Kiriathaim, ³⁸as well as Nebo and Baal Meon (these names were changed) and Sibmah. They gave names to the cities they rebuilt.

³⁹The descendants of Makir son of Manasseh went to Gilead, captured it and drove out the Amorites who were there.

⁴⁰So Moses gave Gilead to the Makirites, the descendants of Manasseh, and they settled there. ⁴¹Jair, a descendant of Manasseh, captured their settlements and called them Havvoth Jair.ᵃ ⁴²And Nobah captured Kenath and its surrounding settlements and called it Nobah after himself.

Stages in Israel's Journey

33 Here are the stages in the journey of the Israelites when they came out of Egypt by divisions under the leadership of Moses and Aaron. ²At the LORD's command Moses recorded the stages in their journey. This is their journey by stages:

³The Israelites set out from Rameses on the fifteenth day of the first month, the day after the Passover. They marched out boldly in full view of all the Egyptians, ⁴who were burying all their firstborn, whom the LORD had struck down among them; for the LORD had brought judgment on their gods.

⁵The Israelites left Rameses and camped at Succoth.

⁶They left Succoth and camped at Etham, on the edge of the desert.

⁷They left Etham, turned back to Pi Hahiroth, to the east of Baal Zephon, and camped near Migdol.

⁸They left Pi Hahirothᵇ and passed through the sea into the desert, and when they had traveled for three days in the Desert of Etham, they camped at Marah.

⁹They left Marah and went to Elim, where there were twelve springs and seventy palm trees, and they camped there.

¹⁰They left Elim and camped by the Red Sea.ᶜ

¹¹They left the Red Sea and camped in the Desert of Sin.

¹²They left the Desert of Sin and camped at Dophkah.

¹³They left Dophkah and camped at Alush.

ᵃ41 Or them the settlements of Jair   ᵇ8 Many manuscripts of the Masoretic Text, Samaritan Pentateuch and Vulgate; most manuscripts of the Masoretic Text left from before Hahiroth
ᶜ10 Hebrew Yam Suph; that is, Sea of Reeds; also in verse 11

¹⁴They left Alush and camped at Rephidim, where there was no water for the people to drink.

¹⁵They left Rephidim and camped in the Desert of Sinai.

¹⁶They left the Desert of Sinai and camped at Kibroth Hattaavah.

¹⁷They left Kibroth Hattaavah and camped at Hazeroth.

¹⁸They left Hazeroth and camped at Rithmah.

¹⁹They left Rithmah and camped at Rimmon Perez.

²⁰They left Rimmon Perez and camped at Libnah.

²¹They left Libnah and camped at Rissah.

²²They left Rissah and camped at Kehelathah.

²³They left Kehelathah and camped at Mount Shepher.

²⁴They left Mount Shepher and camped at Haradah.

²⁵They left Haradah and camped at Makheloth.

²⁶They left Makheloth and camped at Tahath.

²⁷They left Tahath and camped at Terah.

²⁸They left Terah and camped at Mithcah.

²⁹They left Mithcah and camped at Hashmonah.

³⁰They left Hashmonah and camped at Moseroth.

³¹They left Moseroth and camped at Bene Jaakan.

³²They left Bene Jaakan and camped at Hor Haggidgad.

³³They left Hor Haggidgad and camped at Jotbathah.

³⁴They left Jotbathah and camped at Abronah.

³⁵They left Abronah and camped at Ezion Geber.

³⁶They left Ezion Geber and camped at Kadesh, in the Desert of Zin.

³⁷They left Kadesh and camped at Mount Hor, on the border of Edom.

³⁸At the LORD's command Aaron the priest went up Mount Hor, where he died on the first day of the fifth month of the fortieth year after the Israelites came out of Egypt. ³⁹Aaron was a hundred and twenty-three years old when he died on Mount Hor.

⁴⁰The Canaanite king of Arad, who lived in the Negev of Canaan, heard that the Israelites were coming.

⁴¹They left Mount Hor and camped at Zalmonah.

⁴²They left Zalmonah and camped at Punon.

⁴³They left Punon and camped at Oboth.

⁴⁴They left Oboth and camped at Iye Abarim, on the border of Moab.

⁴⁵They left Iyim^a and camped at Dibon Gad.

⁴⁶They left Dibon Gad and camped at Almon Diblathaim.

⁴⁷They left Almon Diblathaim and camped in the mountains of Abarim, near Nebo.

⁴⁸They left the mountains of Abarim and camped on the plains of Moab by the Jordan across from Jericho.^b ⁴⁹There on the plains of Moab they camped along the Jordan from Beth Jeshimoth to Abel Shittim.

⁵⁰On the plains of Moab by the Jordan across from Jericho the LORD said to Moses, ⁵¹"Speak to the Israelites and say to them: 'When you cross the Jordan into Canaan, ⁵²drive out all the inhabitants of the land before you. Destroy all their carved images and their cast idols, and demolish all their high places. ⁵³Take possession of the land and settle in it, for I have given you the land to possess. ⁵⁴Distribute the land by lot, according to your clans. To a larger group give a larger inheritance, and to a smaller group a smaller one. Whatever falls to them by lot will be theirs. Distribute it according to your ancestral tribes.

⁵⁵" 'But if you do not drive out the inhabitants of the land, those you allow to remain will become barbs in your eyes and thorns in your sides. They will give you trouble in the land where you will live. ⁵⁶And then I will do to you what I plan to do to them.' "

---

^a45 That is, Iye Abarim ^b48 Hebrew *Jordan of Jericho*; possibly an ancient name for the Jordan River; also in verse 50

Boundaries of Canaan

34 The LORD said to Moses, ²"Command the Israelites and say to them: 'When you enter Canaan, the land that will be allotted to you as an inheritance will have these boundaries:

³ "'Your southern side will include some of the Desert of Zin along the border of Edom. On the east, your southern boundary will start from the end of the Salt Sea,ᵃ ⁴cross south of Scorpionᵇ Pass, continue on to Zin and go south of Kadesh Barnea. Then it will go to Hazar Addar and over to Azmon, ⁵where it will turn, join the Wadi of Egypt and end at the Sea.ᶜ

⁶ "'Your western boundary will be the coast of the Great Sea. This will be your boundary on the west.

⁷ "'For your northern boundary, run a line from the Great Sea to Mount Hor ⁸and from Mount Hor to Leboᵈ Hamath. Then the boundary will go to Zedad, ⁹continue to Ziphron and end at Hazar Enan. This will be your boundary on the north.

¹⁰ "'For your eastern boundary, run a line from Hazar Enan to Shepham. ¹¹The boundary will go down from Shepham to Riblah on the east side of Ain and continue along the slopes east of the Sea of Kinnereth.ᵉ ¹²Then the boundary will go down along the Jordan and end at the Salt Sea.

"'This will be your land, with its boundaries on every side.'"

¹³Moses commanded the Israelites: "Assign this land by lot as an inheritance. The LORD has ordered that it be given to the nine and a half tribes, ¹⁴because the families of the tribe of Reuben, the tribe of Gad and the half-tribe of Manasseh have received their inheritance. ¹⁵These two and a half tribes have received their inheritance on the east side of the Jordan of Jericho,ᶠ toward the sunrise."

¹⁶The LORD said to Moses, ¹⁷"These are the names of the men who are to assign the land for you as an inheritance: Eleazar the priest and Joshua son of Nun. ¹⁸And appoint one leader from each tribe to help assign the land. ¹⁹These are their names:

Caleb son of Jephunneh,
from the tribe of Judah;
²⁰Shemuel son of Ammihud,
from the tribe of Simeon;
²¹Elidad son of Kislon,
from the tribe of Benjamin;
²²Bukki son of Jogli,
the leader from the tribe of Dan;
²³Hanniel son of Ephod,
the leader from the tribe of Manasseh son of Joseph;
²⁴Kemuel son of Shiphtan,
the leader from the tribe of Ephraim son of Joseph;
²⁵Elizaphan son of Parnach,
the leader from the tribe of Zebulun;
²⁶Paltiel son of Azzan,
the leader from the tribe of Issachar;
²⁷Ahihud son of Shelomi,
the leader from the tribe of Asher;
²⁸Pedahel son of Ammihud,
the leader from the tribe of Naphtali."

²⁹These are the men the LORD commanded to assign the inheritance to the Israelites in the land of Canaan.

Towns for the Levites

35 On the plains of Moab by the Jordan across from Jericho,ᵍ the LORD said to Moses, ²"Command the Israelites to give the Levites towns to live in from the inheritance the Israelites will possess. And give them pasturelands around the towns. ³Then they will have towns to live in and pasturelands for their cattle, flocks and all their other livestock.

⁴"The pasturelands around the towns that you give the Levites will extend out fifteen hundred feetʰ from the town wall. ⁵Outside the town, measure three thousand feetⁱ on the east side, three thousand on the south side, three thousand on the west and three thousand on the

---

ᵃ3 That is, the Dead Sea; also in verse 12
ᵇ4 Hebrew *Akrabbim*   ᶜ5 That is, the
Mediterranean; also in verses 6 and 7   ᵈ8 Or *to
the entrance to*   ᵉ11 That is, Galilee
ᶠ15 *Jordan of Jericho* was possibly an ancient
name for the Jordan River.   ᵍ1 Hebrew *Jordan
of Jericho*; possibly an ancient name for the Jordan
River   ʰ4 Hebrew *a thousand cubits* (about
450 meters)   ⁱ5 Hebrew *two thousand cubits*
(about 900 meters)

north, with the town in the center. They will have this area as pastureland for the towns.

Cities of Refuge

6 "Six of the towns you give the Levites will be cities of refuge, to which a person who has killed someone may flee. In addition, give them forty-two other towns. 7 In all you must give the Levites forty-eight towns, together with their pasturelands. 8 The towns you give the Levites from the land the Israelites possess are to be given in proportion to the inheritance of each tribe: Take many towns from a tribe that has many, but few from one that has few."

9 Then the LORD said to Moses: 10 "Speak to the Israelites and say to them: 'When you cross the Jordan into Canaan, 11 select some towns to be your cities of refuge, to which a person who has killed someone accidentally may flee. 12 They will be places of refuge from the avenger, so that a person accused of murder may not die before he stands trial before the assembly. 13 These six towns you give will be your cities of refuge. 14 Give three on this side of the Jordan and three in Canaan as cities of refuge. 15 These six towns will be a place of refuge for Israelites, aliens and any other people living among them, so that anyone who has killed another accidentally can flee there.

16 "'If a man strikes someone with an iron object so that he dies, he is a murderer; the murderer shall be put to death. 17 Or if anyone has a stone in his hand that could kill, and he strikes someone so that he dies, he is a murderer; the murderer shall be put to death. 18 Or if anyone has a wooden object in his hand that could kill, and he hits someone so that he dies, he is a murderer; the murderer shall be put to death. 19 The avenger of blood shall put the murderer to death; when he meets him, he shall put him to death. 20 If anyone with malice aforethought shoves another or throws something at him intentionally so that he dies 21 or if in hostility he hits him with his fist so that he dies, that person shall be put to death; he is a murderer. The avenger of blood shall put the murderer to death when he meets him.

22 "'But if without hostility someone suddenly shoves another or throws something at him unintentionally 23 or, without seeing him, drops a stone on him that could kill him, and he dies, then since he was not his enemy and he did not intend to harm him, 24 the assembly must judge between him and the avenger of blood according to these regulations. 25 The assembly must protect the one accused of murder from the avenger of blood and send him back to the city of refuge to which he fled. He must stay there until the death of the high priest, who was anointed with the holy oil.

26 "'But if the accused ever goes outside the limits of the city of refuge to which he has fled 27 and the avenger of blood finds him outside the city, the avenger of blood may kill the accused without being guilty of murder. 28 The accused must stay in his city of refuge until the death of the high priest; only after the death of the high priest may he return to his own property.

29 "'These are to be legal requirements for you throughout the generations to come, wherever you live.

30 "'Anyone who kills a person is to be put to death as a murderer only on the testimony of witnesses. But no one is to be put to death on the testimony of only one witness.

31 "'Do not accept a ransom for the life of a murderer, who deserves to die. He must surely be put to death.

32 "'Do not accept a ransom for anyone who has fled to a city of refuge and so allow him to go back and live on his own land before the death of the high priest.

33 "'Do not pollute the land where you are. Bloodshed pollutes the land, and atonement cannot be made for the land on which blood has been shed, except by the blood of the one who shed it. 34 Do not defile the land where you live and where I dwell, for I, the LORD, dwell among the Israelites.'"

Inheritance of Zelophehad's Daughters

36 The family heads of the clan of Gilead son of Makir, the son of Manasseh, who were from the clans of the descendants of Joseph, came and spoke before Moses and the leaders, the heads

of the Israelite families. ²They said, "When the LORD commanded my lord to give the land as an inheritance to the Israelites by lot, he ordered you to give the inheritance of our brother Zelophehad to his daughters. ³Now suppose they marry men from other Israelite tribes; then their inheritance will be taken from our ancestral inheritance and added to that of the tribe they marry into. And so part of the inheritance allotted to us will be taken away. ⁴When the Year of Jubilee for the Israelites comes, their inheritance will be added to that of the tribe into which they marry, and their property will be taken from the tribal inheritance of our forefathers."

⁵Then at the LORD's command Moses gave this order to the Israelites: "What the tribe of the descendants of Joseph is saying is right. ⁶This is what the LORD commands for Zelophehad's daughters: They may marry anyone they please as long as they marry within the tribal clan of their father. ⁷No inheritance in Israel is to pass from tribe to tribe, for every Israelite shall keep the tribal land inherited from his forefathers. ⁸Every daughter who inherits land in any Israelite tribe must marry someone in her father's tribal clan, so that every Israelite will possess the inheritance of his fathers. ⁹No inheritance may pass from tribe to tribe, for each Israelite tribe is to keep the land it inherits."

¹⁰So Zelophehad's daughters did as the LORD commanded Moses. ¹¹Zelophehad's daughters—Mahlah, Tirzah, Hoglah, Milcah and Noah—married their cousins on their father's side. ¹²They married within the clans of the descendants of Manasseh son of Joseph, and their inheritance remained in their father's clan and tribe.

¹³These are the commands and regulations the LORD gave through Moses to the Israelites on the plains of Moab by the Jordan across from Jericho.ᵃ

ᵃ13 Hebrew *Jordan of Jericho*; possibly an ancient name for the Jordan River

Deuteronomy

IN THE book of Deuteronomy, the people of Israel are finally poised to cross the Jordan River and begin the wars of conquest for the promised land. In his last act of leadership, Moses prepares the people by delivering the farewell addresses of this book.

What makes the events and speeches of the book of Deuteronomy so grand is that they describe the renewal of the people's covenant with God and the promises he had made to them. The people would be called to remember their sin—vividly. But they would also be called to remember God's patience with them, and they would be given the opportunity to renew their side of the covenant. The word "give" appears repeatedly in this book, and the majority of these occurrences refer to God and the multiple ways he had blessed his people. Their sin had indeed abounded, but so had his grace. This insight is essential to the renewal of faith.

The spiritual disciplines of Scripture meditation and prayer are like daily covenant renewals. Daily we need to remember God's mercy and goodness, give thanks and pray for his purposes to be accomplished in us, and confess our failures to let him do so. Gratitude for God's mercy is the foundation of all spiritual renewal and right living. Like the renewal of the covenant in the book of Deuteronomy, there are three things we need to know to live in the joy of God: how great "my sin and misery are . . . how I am set free from all my sins and misery . . . how I am to thank God for such deliverance." [1] Prayer is the first act of that thankfulness.

WHAT OTHER NATION IS SO GREAT AS TO HAVE THEIR GODS NEAR THEM THE WAY THE LORD OUR GOD IS NEAR US WHENEVER WE PRAY TO HIM? (4:7)

The Command to Leave Horeb

1 These are the words Moses spoke to all Israel in the desert east of the Jordan—that is, in the Arabah—opposite Suph, between Paran and Tophel, Laban, Hazeroth and Dizahab. ²(It takes eleven days to go from Horeb to Kadesh Barnea by the Mount Seir road.)

³In the fortieth year, on the first day of the eleventh month, Moses proclaimed to the Israelites all that the LORD had commanded him concerning them. ⁴This was after he had defeated Sihon king of the Amorites, who reigned in Heshbon, and at Edrei had defeated Og king of Bashan, who reigned in Ashtaroth.

⁵East of the Jordan in the territory of Moab, Moses began to expound this law, saying:

⁶The LORD our God said to us at Horeb, "You have stayed long enough at this mountain. ⁷Break camp and advance into the hill country of the Amorites; go to all the neighboring peoples in the Arabah, in the mountains, in the western foothills, in the Negev and along the coast, to the land of the Canaanites and to Lebanon, as far as the great river, the Euphrates. ⁸See, I have given you this land. Go in and take possession of the land that the LORD swore he would give to your fathers—to Abraham, Isaac and Jacob—and to their descendants after them."

The Appointment of Leaders

⁹At that time I said to you, "You are too heavy a burden for me to carry alone. ¹⁰The LORD your God has increased your numbers so that today you are as many as the stars in the sky. ¹¹May the LORD, the God of your fathers, increase you a thousand times and bless you as he has promised! ¹²But how can I bear your problems and your burdens and your disputes all by myself? ¹³Choose some wise, understanding and respected men from each of your tribes, and I will set them over you."

¹⁴You answered me, "What you propose to do is good."

¹⁵So I took the leading men of your tribes, wise and respected men, and appointed them to have authority over you—as commanders of thousands, of hundreds, of fifties and of tens and as tribal officials. ¹⁶And I charged your judges at that time: Hear the disputes between your brothers and judge fairly,

> "MAY the LORD, the God of your fathers, increase you a thousand times and bless you as he has promised!"
>
> DEUTERONOMY 1:11

whether the case is between brother Israelites or between one of them and an alien. ¹⁷Do not show partiality in judging; hear both small and great alike. Do not be afraid of any man, for judgment belongs to God. Bring me any case too hard for you, and I will hear it. ¹⁸And at that time I told you everything you were to do.

Spies Sent Out

¹⁹Then, as the LORD our God commanded us, we set out from Horeb and went toward the hill country of the Amorites through all that vast and dreadful desert that you have seen, and so we reached Kadesh Barnea. ²⁰Then I said to you, "You have reached the hill country of the Amorites, which the LORD our God is giving us. ²¹See, the LORD your God has given you the land. Go up and take possession of it as the LORD, the God of your fathers, told you. Do not be afraid; do not be discouraged."

²²Then all of you came to me and said, "Let us send men ahead to spy out the land for us and bring back a report about the route we are to take and the towns we will come to."

²³The idea seemed good to me; so I selected twelve of you, one man from each tribe. ²⁴They left and went up into the hill country, and came to the Valley of Eshcol and explored it. ²⁵Taking with them some of the fruit of the land, they brought it down to us and reported, "It is a good land that the LORD our God is giving us."

Rebellion Against the LORD

²⁶But you were unwilling to go up; you rebelled against the command of the LORD your God. ²⁷You grumbled in your tents and said, "The LORD hates us; so

he brought us out of Egypt to deliver us into the hands of the Amorites to destroy us. ²⁸Where can we go? Our brothers have made us lose heart. They say, 'The people are stronger and taller than we are; the cities are large, with walls up to the sky. We even saw the Anakites there.'"

²⁹Then I said to you, "Do not be terrified; do not be afraid of them. ³⁰The LORD your God, who is going before you, will fight for you, as he did for you in Egypt, before your very eyes, ³¹and in the desert. There you saw how the LORD your God carried you, as a father carries his son, all the way you went until you reached this place."

³²In spite of this, you did not trust in the LORD your God, ³³who went ahead of you on your journey, in fire by night and in a cloud by day, to search out places for you to camp and to show you the way you should go.

³⁴When the LORD heard what you said, he was angry and solemnly swore: ³⁵"Not a man of this evil generation shall see the good land I swore to give your forefathers, ³⁶except Caleb son of Jephunneh. He will see it, and I will give him and his descendants the land he set his feet on, because he followed the LORD wholeheartedly."

³⁷Because of you the LORD became angry with me also and said, "You shall not enter it, either. ³⁸But your assistant, Joshua son of Nun, will enter it. Encourage him, because he will lead Israel to inherit it. ³⁹And the little ones that you said would be taken captive, your children who do not yet know good from bad—they will enter the land. I will give it to them and they will take possession of it. ⁴⁰But as for you, turn around and set out toward the desert along the route to the Red Sea.ᵃ"

⁴¹Then you replied, "We have sinned against the LORD. We will go up and fight, as the LORD our God commanded us." So every one of you put on his weapons, thinking it easy to go up into the hill country.

⁴²But the LORD said to me, "Tell them, 'Do not go up and fight, because I will not be with you. You will be defeated by your enemies.'"

⁴³So I told you, but you would not listen. You rebelled against the LORD's command and in your arrogance you marched up into the hill country. ⁴⁴The Amorites who lived in those hills came out against you; they chased you like a swarm of bees and beat you down from Seir all the way to Hormah. ⁴⁵You came back and wept before the LORD, but he paid no attention to your weeping and turned a deaf ear to you. ⁴⁶And so you stayed in Kadesh many days—all the time you spent there.

Wanderings in the Desert

2 Then we turned back and set out toward the desert along the route to the Red Sea,ᵃ as the LORD had directed me. For a long time we made our way around the hill country of Seir.

²Then the LORD said to me, ³"You have made your way around this hill country long enough; now turn north. ⁴Give the people these orders: 'You are about to pass through the territory of your brothers the descendants of Esau, who live in Seir. They will be afraid of you, but be very careful. ⁵Do not provoke them to war, for I will not give you any of their land, not even enough to put your foot on. I have given Esau the hill country of Seir as his own. ⁶You are to pay them in silver for the food you eat and the water you drink.'"

⁷The LORD your God has blessed you in all the work of your hands. He has watched over your journey through this vast desert. These forty years the LORD your God has been with you, and you have not lacked anything.

⁸So we went on past our brothers the descendants of Esau, who live in Seir. We turned from the Arabah road, which comes up from Elath and Ezion Geber, and traveled along the desert road of Moab.

⁹Then the LORD said to me, "Do not harass the Moabites or provoke them to war, for I will not give you any part of their land. I have given Ar to the descendants of Lot as a possession."

¹⁰(The Emites used to live there—a people strong and numerous, and as tall

ᵃ40,1 Hebrew *Yam Suph*; that is, Sea of Reeds

as the Anakites. ¹¹Like the Anakites, they too were considered Rephaites, but the Moabites called them Emites. ¹²Horites used to live in Seir, but the descendants of Esau drove them out. They destroyed the Horites from before them and settled in their place, just as Israel did in the land the LORD gave them as their possession.)

¹³And the LORD said, "Now get up and cross the Zered Valley." So we crossed the valley.

¹⁴Thirty-eight years passed from the time we left Kadesh Barnea until we crossed the Zered Valley. By then, that entire generation of fighting men had perished from the camp, as the LORD had sworn to them. ¹⁵The LORD's hand was against them until he had completely eliminated them from the camp.

¹⁶Now when the last of these fighting men among the people had died, ¹⁷the LORD said to me, ¹⁸"Today you are to pass by the region of Moab at Ar. ¹⁹When you come to the Ammonites, do not harass them or provoke them to war, for I will not give you possession of any land belonging to the Ammonites. I have given it as a possession to the descendants of Lot."

²⁰(That too was considered a land of the Rephaites, who used to live there; but the Ammonites called them Zamzummites. ²¹They were a people strong and numerous, and as tall as the Anakites. The LORD destroyed them from before the Ammonites, who drove them out and settled in their place. ²²The LORD had done the same for the descendants of Esau, who lived in Seir, when he destroyed the Horites from before them. They drove them out and have lived in their place to this day. ²³And as for the Avvites who lived in villages as far as Gaza, the Caphtorites coming out from Caphtorᵃ destroyed them and settled in their place.)

Defeat of Sihon King of Heshbon

²⁴"Set out now and cross the Arnon Gorge. See, I have given into your hand Sihon the Amorite, king of Heshbon, and his country. Begin to take possession of it and engage him in battle. ²⁵This very day I will begin to put the terror and fear of you on all the nations under heaven. They will hear reports of you and will tremble and be in anguish because of you."

²⁶From the desert of Kedemoth I sent messengers to Sihon king of Heshbon offering peace and saying, ²⁷"Let us pass through your country. We will stay on the main road; we will not turn aside to the right or to the left. ²⁸Sell us food to eat and water to drink for their price in silver. Only let us pass through on foot— ²⁹as the descendants of Esau, who live in Seir, and the Moabites, who live in Ar, did for us—until we cross the Jordan into the land the LORD our God is giving us." ³⁰But Sihon king of Heshbon refused to let us pass through. For the LORD your God had made his spirit stubborn and his heart obstinate in order to give him into your hands, as he has now done.

³¹The LORD said to me, "See, I have begun to deliver Sihon and his country over to you. Now begin to conquer and possess his land."

³²When Sihon and all his army came out to meet us in battle at Jahaz, ³³the LORD our God delivered him over to us and we struck him down, together with his sons and his whole army. ³⁴At that time we took all his towns and completely destroyedᵇ them—men, women and children. We left no survivors. ³⁵But the livestock and the plunder from the towns we had captured we carried off for ourselves. ³⁶From Aroer on the rim of the Arnon Gorge, and from the town in the gorge, even as far as Gilead, not one town was too strong for us. The LORD our God gave us all of them. ³⁷But in accordance with the command of the LORD our God, you did not encroach on any of the land of the Ammonites, neither the land along the course of the Jabbok nor that around the towns in the hills.

Defeat of Og King of Bashan

3 Next we turned and went up along the road toward Bashan, and Og king of Bashan with his whole army marched out to meet us in battle at Edrei. ²The LORD said to me, "Do not be afraid of him, for I have handed him over to you with

---

ᵃ23 That is, Crete   ᵇ34 The Hebrew term refers to the irrevocable giving over of things or persons to the LORD, often by totally destroying them.

his whole army and his land. Do to him what you did to Sihon king of the Amorites, who reigned in Heshbon."

³So the LORD our God also gave into our hands Og king of Bashan and all his army. We struck them down, leaving no survivors. ⁴At that time we took all his cities. There was not one of the sixty cities that we did not take from them—the whole region of Argob, Og's kingdom in Bashan. ⁵All these cities were fortified with high walls and with gates and bars, and there were also a great many unwalled villages. ⁶We completely destroyed*a* them, as we had done with Sihon king of Heshbon, destroying*a* every city—men, women and children. ⁷But all the livestock and the plunder from their cities we carried off for ourselves.

⁸So at that time we took from these two kings of the Amorites the territory east of the Jordan, from the Arnon Gorge as far as Mount Hermon. ⁹(Hermon is called Sirion by the Sidonians; the Amorites call it Senir.) ¹⁰We took all the towns on the plateau, and all Gilead, and all Bashan as far as Salecah and Edrei, towns of Og's kingdom in Bashan. ¹¹(Only Og king of Bashan was left of the remnant of the Rephaites. His bed*b* was made of iron and was more than thirteen feet long and six feet wide.*c* It is still in Rabbah of the Ammonites.)

Division of the Land

¹²Of the land that we took over at that time, I gave the Reubenites and the Gadites the territory north of Aroer by the Arnon Gorge, including half the hill country of Gilead, together with its towns. ¹³The rest of Gilead and also all of Bashan, the kingdom of Og, I gave to the half-tribe of Manasseh. (The whole region of Argob in Bashan used to be known as a land of the Rephaites. ¹⁴Jair, a descendant of Manasseh, took the whole region of Argob as far as the border of the Geshurites and the Maacathites; it was named after him, so that to this day Bashan is called Havvoth Jair.*d*) ¹⁵And I gave Gilead to Makir. ¹⁶But to the Reubenites and the Gadites I gave the territory extending from Gilead down to the Arnon Gorge (the middle of the gorge being the border) and out to the Jabbok River, which is the border of the Ammonites. ¹⁷Its western border was the Jordan in the Arabah, from Kinnereth to the Sea of the Arabah (the Salt Sea*e*), below the slopes of Pisgah.

¹⁸I commanded you at that time: "The LORD your God has given you this land to take possession of it. But all your able-bodied men, armed for battle, must cross over ahead of your brother Israelites. ¹⁹However, your wives, your children and your livestock (I know you have much livestock) may stay in the towns I have given you, ²⁰until the LORD gives rest to your brothers as he has to you, and they too have taken over the land that the LORD your God is giving them, across the Jordan. After that, each of you may go back to the possession I have given you."

Moses Forbidden to Cross the Jordan

²¹At that time I commanded Joshua: "You have seen with your own eyes all that the LORD your God has done to these two kings. The LORD will do the same to all the kingdoms over there where you are going. ²²Do not be afraid of them; the LORD your God himself will fight for you."

²³At that time I pleaded with the LORD: ²⁴"O Sovereign LORD, you have begun to show to your servant your greatness and your strong hand. For what god is there in heaven or on earth who can do the deeds and mighty works you do? ²⁵Let me go over and see the good land beyond the Jordan—that fine hill country and Lebanon."

²⁶But because of you the LORD was angry with me and would not listen to me. "That is enough," the LORD said. "Do not speak to me anymore about this matter. ²⁷Go up to the top of Pisgah and look west and north and south and east. Look at the land with your own eyes, since you are not going to cross this Jordan. ²⁸But commission Joshua, and encourage and strengthen him, for he will lead this people across and will cause them to inherit the land that you will see." ²⁹So we stayed in the valley near Beth Peor.

a6 The Hebrew term refers to the irrevocable giving over of things or persons to the LORD, often by totally destroying them.   *b11* Or *sarcophagus*   *c11* Hebrew *nine cubits long and four cubits wide* (about 4 meters long and 1.8 meters wide)   *d14* Or *called the settlements of Jair*   *e17* That is, the Dead Sea

DEUTERONOMY 3:23–29

When God Says No

3:23 AT THAT TIME I PLEADED WITH THE LORD.

Sometimes we can tell more from someone's tone of voice than from their words. When God refused Moses' prayer, Moses must have listened attentively to God's tone. The words were straightforward: "'That is enough,' the LORD said, 'Do not speak to me anymore about this matter'" (3:26).

Moses could hardly be surprised by the Lord's response. Not long before this, as recorded in Numbers 20, Moses and the Israelites had returned to Kadesh—the scene of their tragic rebellion nearly 40 years earlier. Just like their parents, the next generation rose up against Moses and his brother Aaron, crying out in despair when they had no water. God told Moses to speak to a rock, which would then pour out water for the people and their livestock. But Moses disobeyed the Lord's directions and struck the rock twice with his staff—likely the expression of the pent up frustration and anger from the last 40 years. Although God still provided water from the rock, his rebuke of Moses and Aaron was swift and stern: "But the LORD said to Moses and Aaron, 'Because you did not trust in me enough to honor me as holy in the sight of the Israelites, you will not bring this community into the land I give them'" (Numbers 20:12).

Since then, God had also told Moses that he would be allowed to go up on a mountain to see the promised land before dying (see Numbers 27:12–14).

Moses and the Lord had been through a lot together. Moses was a man the Lord spoke with "face to face, as a man speaks with his friend" (Exodus 33:11). God later hinted to Jeremiah that, along with Samuel, Moses was one of the two greatest intercessors who had ever lived (see Jeremiah 15:1). We might wonder if it grieved the Lord to refuse his friend's request. But just as a good parent follows through with declarations of discipline, God stood firm in regard to his stated consequences.

We do know this: Even though Moses wanted to enter Canaan so bad he could taste it, God was giving him heaven. And someday, long after Moses went up on the mountain to die, he would appear on another mountain, with Elijah, and speak with God's own Son, the Savior of the world (see Matthew 17:1–8).

We also know that God is good—no matter if the answer is yes or no.

P R A Y :

Dear Friend, I will love you when you say yes
and when you say no. I will trust you when you give me what
I want and when you don't. All you do is good.

FOR YOUR NEXT DEVOTIONAL READING, GO TO PAGE 226.

Obedience Commanded

4 Hear now, O Israel, the decrees and laws I am about to teach you. Follow them so that you may live and may go in and take possession of the land that the LORD, the God of your fathers, is giving you. ²Do not add to what I command you and do not subtract from it, but keep the commands of the LORD your God that I give you.

³You saw with your own eyes what the LORD did at Baal Peor. The LORD your God destroyed from among you everyone who followed the Baal of Peor, ⁴but all of you who held fast to the LORD your God are still alive today.

⁵See, I have taught you decrees and laws as the LORD my God commanded me, so that you may follow them in the land you are entering to take possession of it. ⁶Observe them carefully, for this will show your wisdom and understanding to the nations, who will hear about all these decrees and say, "Surely this great nation is a wise and understanding people." ⁷What other nation is so great as to have their gods near them the way the LORD our God is near us whenever we pray to him? ⁸And what other nation is so great as to have such righteous decrees and laws as this body of laws I am setting before you today?

> WHAT other nation is so great as to have their gods near them the way the LORD our God is near us whenever we pray to him?
>
> DEUTERONOMY 4:7

⁹Only be careful, and watch yourselves closely so that you do not forget the things your eyes have seen or let them slip from your heart as long as you live. Teach them to your children and to their children after them. ¹⁰Remember the day you stood before the LORD your God at Horeb, when he said to me, "Assemble the people before me to hear my words so that they may learn to revere me as long as they live in the land and may teach them to their children." ¹¹You came near and stood at the foot of the moun-tain while it blazed with fire to the very heavens, with black clouds and deep darkness. ¹²Then the LORD spoke to you out of the fire. You heard the sound of words but saw no form; there was only a voice. ¹³He declared to you his covenant, the Ten Commandments, which he com-manded you to follow and then wrote them on two stone tablets. ¹⁴And the LORD directed me at that time to teach you the decrees and laws you are to fol-low in the land that you are crossing the Jordan to possess.

Idolatry Forbidden

¹⁵You saw no form of any kind the day the LORD spoke to you at Horeb out of the fire. Therefore watch yourselves very carefully, ¹⁶so that you do not become corrupt and make for yourselves an idol, an image of any shape, whether formed like a man or a woman, ¹⁷or like any ani-mal on earth or any bird that flies in the air, ¹⁸or like any creature that moves along the ground or any fish in the wa-ters below. ¹⁹And when you look up to the sky and see the sun, the moon and the stars—all the heavenly array—do not be enticed into bowing down to them and worshiping things the LORD your God has apportioned to all the nations under heaven. ²⁰But as for you, the LORD took you and brought you out of the iron-smelting furnace, out of Egypt, to be the people of his inheritance, as you now are.

²¹The LORD was angry with me because of you, and he solemnly swore that I would not cross the Jordan and enter the good land the LORD your God is giving you as your inheritance. ²²I will die in this land; I will not cross the Jordan; but you are about to cross over and take posses-sion of that good land. ²³Be careful not to forget the covenant of the LORD your God that he made with you; do not make for yourselves an idol in the form of anything the LORD your God has forbidden. ²⁴For the LORD your God is a consuming fire, a jealous God.

²⁵After you have had children and grandchildren and have lived in the land a long time—if you then become corrupt and make any kind of idol, doing evil in the eyes of the LORD your God and provok-ing him to anger, ²⁶I call heaven and earth

as witnesses against you this day that you will quickly perish from the land that you are crossing the Jordan to possess. You will not live there long but will certainly be destroyed. ²⁷The LORD will scatter you among the peoples, and only a few of you will survive among the nations to which the LORD will drive you. ²⁸There you will worship man-made gods of wood and stone, which cannot see or hear or eat or smell. ²⁹But if from there you seek the LORD your God, you will find him if you look for him with all your heart and with all your soul. ³⁰When you are in distress

> BUT *if from there you seek the LORD your God, you will find him if you look for him with all your heart and with all your soul.*
>
> DEUTERONOMY 4:29

and all these things have happened to you, then in later days you will return to the LORD your God and obey him. ³¹For the LORD your God is a merciful God; he will not abandon or destroy you or forget the covenant with your forefathers, which he confirmed to them by oath.

The LORD Is God

³²Ask now about the former days, long before your time, from the day God created man on the earth; ask from one end of the heavens to the other. Has anything so great as this ever happened, or has anything like it ever been heard of? ³³Has any other people heard the voice of God^a speaking out of fire, as you have, and lived? ³⁴Has any god ever tried to take for himself one nation out of another nation, by testings, by miraculous signs and wonders, by war, by a mighty hand and an outstretched arm, or by great and awesome deeds, like all the things the LORD your God did for you in Egypt before your very eyes?

³⁵You were shown these things so that you might know that the LORD is God; besides him there is no other. ³⁶From heaven he made you hear his voice to discipline you. On earth he showed you his great fire, and you heard his words from out of the fire. ³⁷Because he loved your forefathers and chose their descen-

dants after them, he brought you out of Egypt by his Presence and his great strength, ³⁸to drive out before you nations greater and stronger than you and to bring you into their land to give it to you for your inheritance, as it is today.

³⁹Acknowledge and take to heart this day that the LORD is God in heaven above and on the earth below. There is no other. ⁴⁰Keep his decrees and commands, which I am giving you today, so that it may go well with you and your children after you and that you may live long in the land the LORD your God gives you for all time.

Cities of Refuge

⁴¹Then Moses set aside three cities east of the Jordan, ⁴²to which anyone who had killed a person could flee if he had unintentionally killed his neighbor without malice aforethought. He could flee into one of these cities and save his life. ⁴³The cities were these: Bezer in the desert plateau, for the Reubenites; Ramoth in Gilead, for the Gadites; and Golan in Bashan, for the Manassites.

Introduction to the Law

⁴⁴This is the law Moses set before the Israelites. ⁴⁵These are the stipulations, decrees and laws Moses gave them when they came out of Egypt ⁴⁶and were in the valley near Beth Peor east of the Jordan, in the land of Sihon king of the Amorites, who reigned in Heshbon and was defeated by Moses and the Israelites as they came out of Egypt. ⁴⁷They took possession of his land and the land of Og king of Bashan, the two Amorite kings east of the Jordan. ⁴⁸This land extended from Aroer on the rim of the Arnon Gorge to Mount Siyon^b (that is, Hermon), ⁴⁹and included all the Arabah east of the Jordan, as far as the Sea of the Arabah,^c below the slopes of Pisgah.

The Ten Commandments

5 Moses summoned all Israel and said: Hear, O Israel, the decrees and laws I declare in your hearing today. Learn them and be sure to follow them. ²The

---

^a33 Or *of a god* ^b48 Hebrew; Syriac (see also Deut. 3:9) *Sirion* ^c49 That is, the Dead Sea

LORD our God made a covenant with us at Horeb. ³It was not with our fathers that the LORD made this covenant, but with us, with all of us who are alive here today. ⁴The LORD spoke to you face to face out of the fire on the mountain. ⁵(At that time I stood between the LORD and you to declare to you the word of the LORD, because you were afraid of the fire and did not go up the mountain.) And he said:

> ⁶"I am the LORD your God, who brought you out of Egypt, out of the land of slavery.
>
> ⁷"You shall have no other gods before*a* me.
>
> ⁸"You shall not make for yourself an idol in the form of anything in heaven above or on the earth beneath or in the waters below. ⁹You shall not bow down to them or worship them; for I, the LORD your God, am a jealous God, punishing the children for the sin of the fathers to the third and fourth generation of those who hate me, ¹⁰but showing love to a thousand ⸤generations⸣ of those who love me and keep my commandments.
>
> ¹¹"You shall not misuse the name of the LORD your God, for the LORD will not hold anyone guiltless who misuses his name.
>
> ¹²"Observe the Sabbath day by keeping it holy, as the LORD your God has commanded you. ¹³Six days you shall labor and do all your work, ¹⁴but the seventh day is a Sabbath to the LORD your God. On it you shall not do any work, neither you, nor your son or daughter, nor your manservant or maidservant, nor your ox, your donkey or any of your animals, nor the alien within your gates, so that your manservant and maidservant may rest, as you do. ¹⁵Remember that you were slaves in Egypt and that the LORD your God brought you

out of there with a mighty hand and an outstretched arm. Therefore the LORD your God has commanded you to observe the Sabbath day.

> ¹⁶"Honor your father and your mother, as the LORD your God has commanded you, so that you may live long and that it may go well with you in the land the LORD your God is giving you.
>
> ¹⁷"You shall not murder.
>
> ¹⁸"You shall not commit adultery.
>
> ¹⁹"You shall not steal.
>
> ²⁰"You shall not give false testimony against your neighbor.
>
> ²¹"You shall not covet your neighbor's wife. You shall not set your desire on your neighbor's house or land, his manservant or maidservant, his ox or donkey, or anything that belongs to your neighbor."

²²These are the commandments the LORD proclaimed in a loud voice to your whole assembly there on the mountain from out of the fire, the cloud and the deep darkness; and he added nothing more. Then he wrote them on two stone tablets and gave them to me.

²³When you heard the voice out of the darkness, while the mountain was ablaze with fire, all the leading men of your tribes and your elders came to me. ²⁴And you said, "The LORD our God has shown us his glory and his majesty, and we have heard his voice from the fire. Today we have seen that a man can live even if God speaks with him. ²⁵But now, why should we die? This great fire will consume us, and we will die if we hear the voice of the LORD our God any longer. ²⁶For what mortal man has ever heard the voice of the living God speaking out of fire, as we have, and survived? ²⁷Go near and listen to all that the LORD our God says. Then tell us whatever the LORD our God tells you. We will listen and obey."

²⁸The LORD heard you when you spoke to me and the LORD said to me, "I have heard what this people said to you. Everything they said was good. ²⁹Oh, that

a 7 Or besides

their hearts would be inclined to fear me and keep all my commands always, so that it might go well with them and their children forever!

³⁰"Go, tell them to return to their tents. ³¹But you stay here with me so that I may give you all the commands, decrees and laws you are to teach them to follow in the land I am giving them to possess."

³²So be careful to do what the LORD your God has commanded you; do not turn aside to the right or to the left. ³³Walk in all the way that the LORD your God has commanded you, so that you may live and prosper and prolong your days in the land that you will possess.

Love the LORD Your God

6 These are the commands, decrees and laws the LORD your God directed me to teach you to observe in the land that you are crossing the Jordan to possess, ²so that you, your children and their children after them may fear the LORD your God as long as you live by keeping all his decrees and commands that I give you, and so that you may enjoy long life. ³Hear, O Israel, and be careful to obey so that it may go well with you and that you may increase greatly in a land flowing with milk and honey, just as the LORD, the God of your fathers, promised you.

⁴Hear, O Israel: The LORD our God, the LORD is one.ᵃ ⁵Love the LORD your God with all your heart and with all your soul and with all your strength. ⁶These commandments that I give you today are to be upon your hearts. ⁷Impress them on your children. Talk about them when you sit at home and when you walk along the road, when you lie down and when you get up. ⁸Tie them as symbols on your hands and bind them on your foreheads. ⁹Write them on the doorframes of your houses and on your gates.

¹⁰When the LORD your God brings you into the land he swore to your fathers, to Abraham, Isaac and Jacob, to give you— a land with large, flourishing cities you did not build, ¹¹houses filled with all kinds of good things you did not provide, wells you did not dig, and vineyards and olive groves you did not plant—then when you eat and are satisfied, ¹²be care-

ful that you do not forget the LORD, who brought you out of Egypt, out of the land of slavery.

¹³Fear the LORD your God, serve him only and take your oaths in his name. ¹⁴Do not follow other gods, the gods of the peoples around you; ¹⁵for the LORD your God, who is among you, is a jealous God and his anger will burn against you, and he will destroy you from the face of the land. ¹⁶Do not test the LORD your God as you did at Massah. ¹⁷Be sure to keep the commands of the LORD your God and the stipulations and decrees he has given you. ¹⁸Do what is right and good in the LORD's sight, so that it may go well with you and you may go in and take over the good land that the LORD promised on oath to your forefathers, ¹⁹thrusting out all your enemies before you, as the LORD said.

²⁰In the future, when your son asks you, "What is the meaning of the stipulations, decrees and laws the LORD our God has commanded you?" ²¹tell him: "We were slaves of Pharaoh in Egypt, but the LORD brought us out of Egypt with a mighty hand. ²²Before our eyes the LORD sent miraculous signs and wonders— great and terrible—upon Egypt and Pharaoh and his whole household. ²³But he brought us out from there to bring us in and give us the land that he promised on oath to our forefathers. ²⁴The LORD commanded us to obey all these decrees and to fear the LORD our God, so that we might always prosper and be kept alive, as is the case today. ²⁵And if we are careful to obey all this law before the LORD our God, as he has commanded us, that will be our righteousness."

Driving Out the Nations

7 When the LORD your God brings you into the land you are entering to possess and drives out before you many nations—the Hittites, Girgashites, Amorites, Canaanites, Perizzites, Hivites and Jebusites, seven nations larger and stronger than you— ²and when the LORD your God has delivered them over to you and you

ᵃ4 Or *The LORD our God is one LORD*; or *The LORD is our God, the LORD is one*; or *The LORD is our God, the LORD alone* have defeated them, then you must destroy them totally.[a] Make no treaty with them, and show them no mercy. [3]Do not intermarry with them. Do not give your daughters to their sons or take their daughters for your sons, [4]for they will turn your sons away from following me to serve other gods, and the LORD's anger will burn against you and will quickly destroy you. [5]This is what you are to do to them: Break down their altars, smash their sacred stones, cut down their Asherah poles[b] and burn their idols in the fire. [6]For you are a people holy to the LORD your God. The LORD your God has chosen you out of all the peoples on the face of the earth to be his people, his treasured possession.

[7]The LORD did not set his affection on you and choose you because you were more numerous than other peoples, for you were the fewest of all peoples. [8]But it was because the LORD loved you and kept the oath he swore to your forefathers that he brought you out with a mighty hand and redeemed you from the land of slavery, from the power of Pharaoh king of Egypt. [9]Know therefore that the LORD your God is God; he is the faithful God, keeping his covenant of love to a thousand generations of those who love him and keep his commands. [10]But

those who hate him he will repay to
     their face by destruction;
he will not be slow to repay to their
     face those who hate him.

[11]Therefore, take care to follow the commands, decrees and laws I give you today. [12]If you pay attention to these laws and are careful to follow them, then the LORD your God will keep his covenant of love with you, as he swore to your forefathers. [13]He will love you and bless you and increase your numbers. He will bless the fruit of your womb, the crops of your land—your grain, new wine and oil—the calves of your herds and the lambs of your flocks in the land that he swore to your forefathers to give you. [14]You will be blessed more than any other people; none of your men or women will be childless, nor any of your livestock without young. [15]The LORD will keep you free from every disease. He will not inflict on you the hor-

rible diseases you knew in Egypt, but he will inflict them on all who hate you. [16]You must destroy all the peoples the LORD your God gives over to you. Do not look on them with pity and do not serve their gods, for that will be a snare to you.

[17]You may say to yourselves, "These nations are stronger than we are. How can we drive them out?" [18]But do not be afraid of them; remember well what the LORD your God did to Pharaoh and to all Egypt. [19]You saw with your own eyes the great trials, the miraculous signs and wonders, the mighty hand and outstretched arm, with which the LORD your God brought you out. The LORD your God will do the same to all the peoples you now fear. [20]Moreover, the LORD your God will send the hornet among them until even the survivors who hide from you have perished. [21]Do not be terrified by them, for the LORD your God, who is among you, is a great and awesome God. [22]The LORD your God will drive out those nations before you, little by little. You will not be allowed to eliminate them all at once, or the wild animals will multiply around you. [23]But the LORD your God will deliver them over to you, throwing them into great confusion until they are destroyed. [24]He will give their kings into your hand, and you will wipe out their names from under heaven. No one will be able to stand up against you; you will destroy them. [25]The images of their gods you are to burn in the fire. Do not covet the silver and gold on them, and do not take it for yourselves, or you will be ensnared by it, for it is detestable to the LORD your God. [26]Do not bring a detestable thing into your house or you, like it, will be set apart for destruction. Utterly abhor and detest it, for it is set apart for destruction.

Do Not Forget the LORD

8 Be careful to follow every command I am giving you today, so that you may live and increase and may enter and possess the land that the LORD promised on

---

[a]2 The Hebrew term refers to the irrevocable giving over of things or persons to the LORD, often by totally destroying them; also in verse 26.
[b]5 That is, symbols of the goddess Asherah; here and elsewhere in Deuteronomy

oath to your forefathers. ²Remember how the LORD your God led you all the way in the desert these forty years, to humble you and to test you in order to know what was in your heart, whether or not you would keep his commands. ³He humbled you, causing you to hunger and then feeding you with manna, which neither you nor your fathers had known, to teach you that man does not live on bread alone but on every word that comes from the mouth of the LORD. ⁴Your clothes did not wear out and your feet did not swell during these forty years. ⁵Know then in your heart that as a man disciplines his son, so the LORD your God disciplines you.

⁶Observe the commands of the LORD your God, walking in his ways and revering him. ⁷For the LORD your God is bringing you into a good land—a land with streams and pools of water, with springs flowing in the valleys and hills; ⁸a land with wheat and barley, vines and fig trees, pomegranates, olive oil and honey; ⁹a land where bread will not be scarce and you will lack nothing; a land where the rocks are iron and you can dig copper out of the hills.

¹⁰When you have eaten and are satisfied, praise the LORD your God for the good land he has given you. ¹¹Be careful that you do not forget the LORD your God, failing to observe his commands, his

> WHEN you have eaten and are satisfied, praise the LORD your God for the good land he has given you.
>
> DEUTERONOMY 8:10

laws and his decrees that I am giving you this day. ¹²Otherwise, when you eat and are satisfied, when you build fine houses and settle down, ¹³and when your herds and flocks grow large and your silver and gold increase and all you have is multiplied, ¹⁴then your heart will become proud and you will forget the LORD your God, who brought you out of Egypt, out of the land of slavery. ¹⁵He led you through the vast and dreadful desert, that thirsty and waterless land, with its venomous snakes and scorpions. He

brought you water out of hard rock. ¹⁶He gave you manna to eat in the desert, something your fathers had never known, to humble and to test you so that in the end it might go well with you. ¹⁷You may say to yourself, "My power and the strength of my hands have produced this wealth for me." ¹⁸But remember the LORD your God, for it is he who gives you the ability to produce wealth, and so confirms his covenant, which he swore to your forefathers, as it is today.

¹⁹If you ever forget the LORD your God and follow other gods and worship and bow down to them, I testify against you today that you will surely be destroyed. ²⁰Like the nations the LORD destroyed before you, so you will be destroyed for not obeying the LORD your God.

Not Because of Israel's Righteousness

9 Hear, O Israel. You are now about to cross the Jordan to go in and dispossess nations greater and stronger than you, with large cities that have walls up to the sky. ²The people are strong and tall—Anakites! You know about them and have heard it said: "Who can stand up against the Anakites?" ³But be assured today that the LORD your God is the one who goes across ahead of you like a devouring fire. He will destroy them; he will subdue them before you. And you will drive them out and annihilate them quickly, as the LORD has promised you.

⁴After the LORD your God has driven them out before you, do not say to yourself, "The LORD has brought me here to take possession of this land because of my righteousness." No, it is on account of the wickedness of these nations that the LORD is going to drive them out before you. ⁵It is not because of your righteousness or your integrity that you are going in to take possession of their land; but on account of the wickedness of these nations, the LORD your God will drive them out before you, to accomplish what he swore to your fathers, to Abraham, Isaac and Jacob. ⁶Understand, then, that it is not because of your righteousness that the LORD your God is giving you this good land to possess, for you are a stiff-necked people.

The Golden Calf

7Remember this and never forget how you provoked the LORD your God to anger in the desert. From the day you left Egypt until you arrived here, you have been rebellious against the LORD. 8At Horeb you aroused the LORD's wrath so that he was angry enough to destroy you. 9When I went up on the mountain to receive the tablets of stone, the tablets of the covenant that the LORD had made with you, I stayed on the mountain forty days and forty nights; I ate no bread and drank no water. 10The LORD gave me two stone tablets inscribed by the finger of God. On them were all the commandments the LORD proclaimed to you on the mountain out of the fire, on the day of the assembly.

11At the end of the forty days and forty nights, the LORD gave me the two stone tablets, the tablets of the covenant. 12Then the LORD told me, "Go down from here at once, because your people whom you brought out of Egypt have become corrupt. They have turned away quickly from what I commanded them and have made a cast idol for themselves."

13And the LORD said to me, "I have seen this people, and they are a stiff-necked people indeed! 14Let me alone, so that I may destroy them and blot out their name from under heaven. And I will make you into a nation stronger and more numerous than they."

15So I turned and went down from the mountain while it was ablaze with fire. And the two tablets of the covenant were in my hands.a 16When I looked, I saw that you had sinned against the LORD your God; you had made for yourselves an idol cast in the shape of a calf. You had turned aside quickly from the way that the LORD had commanded you. 17So I took the two tablets and threw them out of my hands, breaking them to pieces before your eyes.

18Then once again I fell prostrate before the LORD for forty days and forty nights; I ate no bread and drank no water, because of all the sin you had committed, doing what was evil in the LORD's sight and so provoking him to anger. 19I feared the anger and wrath of the LORD, for he was angry enough with you to destroy you. But again the LORD listened to me. 20And the LORD was angry enough with Aaron to destroy him, but at that time I prayed for Aaron too. 21Also I took that sinful thing of yours, the calf you had made, and burned it in the fire. Then I crushed it and ground it to powder as fine as dust and threw the dust into a stream that flowed down the mountain.

22You also made the LORD angry at Taberah, at Massah and at Kibroth Hattaavah.

23And when the LORD sent you out from Kadesh Barnea, he said, "Go up and take possession of the land I have given you." But you rebelled against the command of the LORD your God. You did not trust him or obey him. 24You have been rebellious against the LORD ever since I have known you.

25I lay prostrate before the LORD those forty days and forty nights because the LORD had said he would destroy you. 26I prayed to the LORD and said, "O Sovereign LORD, do not destroy your people, your own inheritance that you redeemed by your great power and brought out of Egypt with a mighty hand. 27Remember your servants Abraham, Isaac and Jacob.

> I PRAYED to the LORD and said,
> "O Sovereign LORD, do not destroy
> your people, your own inheritance that
> you redeemed by your great power and
> brought out of Egypt with a mighty
> hand."
>
> DEUTERONOMY 9:26

Overlook the stubbornness of this people, their wickedness and their sin. 28Otherwise, the country from which you brought us will say, 'Because the LORD was not able to take them into the land he had promised them, and because he hated them, he brought them out to put them to death in the desert.' 29But they are your people, your inheritance that you brought out by your great power and your outstretched arm."

a15 Or And I had the two tablets of the covenant with me, one in each hand

Tablets Like the First Ones

10 At that time the LORD said to me, "Chisel out two stone tablets like the first ones and come up to me on the mountain. Also make a wooden chest.*ᵃ* ²I will write on the tablets the words that were on the first tablets, which you broke. Then you are to put them in the chest."

³So I made the ark out of acacia wood and chiseled out two stone tablets like the first ones, and I went up on the mountain with the two tablets in my hands. ⁴The LORD wrote on these tablets what he had written before, the Ten Commandments he had proclaimed to you on the mountain, out of the fire, on the day of the assembly. And the LORD gave them to me. ⁵Then I came back down the mountain and put the tablets in the ark I had made, as the LORD commanded me, and they are there now.

⁶(The Israelites traveled from the wells of the Jaakanites to Moserah. There Aaron died and was buried, and Eleazar his son succeeded him as priest. ⁷From there they traveled to Gudgodah and on to Jotbathah, a land with streams of water. ⁸At that time the LORD set apart the tribe of Levi to carry the ark of the covenant of the LORD, to stand before the LORD to minister and to pronounce blessings in his name, as they still do today. ⁹That is why the Levites have no share or inheritance among their brothers; the LORD is their inheritance, as the LORD your God told them.)

¹⁰Now I had stayed on the mountain forty days and nights, as I did the first time, and the LORD listened to me at this time also. It was not his will to destroy you. ¹¹"Go," the LORD said to me, "and lead the people on their way, so that they may enter and possess the land that I swore to their fathers to give them."

Fear the LORD

¹²And now, O Israel, what does the LORD your God ask of you but to fear the LORD your God, to walk in all his ways, to love him, to serve the LORD your God with all your heart and with all your soul, ¹³and to observe the LORD's commands and decrees that I am giving you today for your own good?

> *WHAT* does the LORD your God ask of you but to fear the LORD your God, to walk in all his ways, to love him, to serve the LORD your God with all your heart and with all your soul, and to observe the LORD's commands and decrees?
>
> DEUTERONOMY 10:12 – 13

¹⁴To the LORD your God belong the heavens, even the highest heavens, the earth and everything in it. ¹⁵Yet the LORD set his affection on your forefathers and loved them, and he chose you, their descendants, above all the nations, as it is today. ¹⁶Circumcise your hearts, therefore, and do not be stiff-necked any longer. ¹⁷For the LORD your God is God of gods and Lord of lords, the great God, mighty and awesome, who shows no partiality and accepts no bribes. ¹⁸He defends the cause of the fatherless and the widow, and loves the alien, giving him food and clothing. ¹⁹And you are to love those who are aliens, for you yourselves were aliens in Egypt. ²⁰Fear the LORD your God and serve him. Hold fast to him and take your oaths in his name. ²¹He is your praise; he is your God, who performed for you those great and awesome wonders you saw with your own eyes. ²²Your forefathers who went down into Egypt were seventy in all, and now the LORD your God has made you as numerous as the stars in the sky.

Love and Obey the LORD

11 Love the LORD your God and keep his requirements, his decrees, his laws and his commands always. ²Remember today that your children were not the ones who saw and experienced the discipline of the LORD your God: his majesty, his mighty hand, his outstretched arm; ³the signs he performed and the things he did in the heart of Egypt, both to Pharaoh king of Egypt and to his whole country; ⁴what he did to the Egyptian army, to its horses and chariots, how he overwhelmed them with the waters of the Red Sea*ᵇ* as they were pur-

---

ᵃ1 That is, an ark   *ᵇ4* Hebrew *Yam Suph*; that is, Sea of Reeds

suing you, and how the LORD brought lasting ruin on them. ⁵It was not your children who saw what he did for you in the desert until you arrived at this place, ⁶and what he did to Dathan and Abiram, sons of Eliab the Reubenite, when the earth opened its mouth right in the middle of all Israel and swallowed them up with their households, their tents and every living thing that belonged to them. ⁷But it was your own eyes that saw all these great things the LORD has done.

⁸Observe therefore all the commands I am giving you today, so that you may have the strength to go in and take over the land that you are crossing the Jordan to possess, ⁹and so that you may live long in the land that the LORD swore to your forefathers to give to them and their descendants, a land flowing with milk and honey. ¹⁰The land you are entering to take over is not like the land of Egypt, from which you have come, where you planted your seed and irrigated it by foot as in a vegetable garden. ¹¹But the land you are crossing the Jordan to take possession of is a land of mountains and valleys that drinks rain from heaven. ¹²It is a land the LORD your God cares for; the eyes of the LORD your God are continually on it from the beginning of the year to its end.

¹³So if you faithfully obey the commands I am giving you today—to love the LORD your God and to serve him with all your heart and with all your soul— ¹⁴then I will send rain on your land in its season, both autumn and spring rains, so that you may gather in your grain, new wine and oil. ¹⁵I will provide grass in the fields for your cattle, and you will eat and be satisfied.

¹⁶Be careful, or you will be enticed to turn away and worship other gods and bow down to them. ¹⁷Then the LORD's anger will burn against you, and he will shut the heavens so that it will not rain and the ground will yield no produce, and you will soon perish from the good land the LORD is giving you. ¹⁸Fix these words of mine in your hearts and minds; tie them as symbols on your hands and bind them on your foreheads. ¹⁹Teach them to your children, talking about them when you sit at home and when

you walk along the road, when you lie down and when you get up. ²⁰Write them on the doorframes of your houses and on your gates, ²¹so that your days and the days of your children may be many in the land that the LORD swore to give your forefathers, as many as the days that the heavens are above the earth.

²²If you carefully observe all these commands I am giving you to follow—to love the LORD your God, to walk in all his ways and to hold fast to him— ²³then the LORD will drive out all these nations before you, and you will dispossess nations larger and stronger than you. ²⁴Every place where you set your foot will be yours: Your territory will extend from the desert to Lebanon, and from the Euphrates River to the western sea.ᵃ ²⁵No man will be able to stand against you. The LORD your God, as he promised you, will put the terror and fear of you on the whole land, wherever you go.

²⁶See, I am setting before you today a blessing and a curse— ²⁷the blessing if you obey the commands of the LORD your God that I am giving you today; ²⁸the curse if you disobey the commands of the LORD your God and turn from the way that I command you today by following other gods, which you have not known. ²⁹When the LORD your God has brought you into the land you are entering to possess, you are to proclaim on Mount Gerizim the blessings, and on Mount Ebal the curses. ³⁰As you know, these mountains are across the Jordan, west of the road,ᵇ toward the setting sun, near the great trees of Moreh, in the territory of those Canaanites living in the Arabah in the vicinity of Gilgal. ³¹You are about to cross the Jordan to enter and take possession of the land the LORD your God is giving you. When you have taken it over and are living there, ³²be sure that you obey all the decrees and laws I am setting before you today.

The One Place of Worship

12 These are the decrees and laws you must be careful to follow in the land that the LORD, the God of your fathers,

ᵃ24 That is, the Mediterranean
ᵇ30 Or Jordan, westward

has given you to possess—as long as you live in the land. ²Destroy completely all the places on the high mountains and on the hills and under every spreading tree where the nations you are dispossessing worship their gods. ³Break down their altars, smash their sacred stones and burn their Asherah poles in the fire; cut down the idols of their gods and wipe out their names from those places.

⁴You must not worship the LORD your God in their way. ⁵But you are to seek the place the LORD your God will choose from among all your tribes to put his Name there for his dwelling. To that place you must go; ⁶there bring your burnt offerings and sacrifices, your tithes and special gifts, what you have vowed to give and your freewill offerings, and the firstborn of your herds and flocks. ⁷There, in the presence of the LORD your God, you and your families shall eat and shall rejoice in everything you have put your hand to, because the LORD your God has blessed you.

⁸You are not to do as we do here today, everyone as he sees fit, ⁹since you have not yet reached the resting place and the inheritance the LORD your God is giving you. ¹⁰But you will cross the Jordan and settle in the land the LORD your God is giving you as an inheritance, and he will give you rest from all your enemies around you so that you will live in safety. ¹¹Then to the place the LORD your God will choose as a dwelling for his Name— there you are to bring everything I command you: your burnt offerings and sacrifices, your tithes and special gifts, and all the choice possessions you have vowed to the LORD. ¹²And there rejoice before the LORD your God, you, your sons and daughters, your menservants and maidservants, and the Levites from your towns, who have no allotment or inheritance of their own. ¹³Be careful not to sacrifice your burnt offerings anywhere you please. ¹⁴Offer them only at the place the LORD will choose in one of your tribes, and there observe everything I command you.

¹⁵Nevertheless, you may slaughter your animals in any of your towns and eat as much of the meat as you want, as if it were gazelle or deer, according to the blessing the LORD your God gives you. Both the ceremonially unclean and the clean may eat it. ¹⁶But you must not eat the blood; pour it out on the ground like water. ¹⁷You must not eat in your own towns the tithe of your grain and new wine and oil, or the firstborn of your herds and flocks, or whatever you have vowed to give, or your freewill offerings or special gifts. ¹⁸Instead, you are to eat them in the presence of the LORD your God at the place the LORD your God will choose—you, your sons and daughters, your menservants and maidservants, and the Levites from your towns—and you are to rejoice before the LORD your God in everything you put your hand to. ¹⁹Be careful not to neglect the Levites as long as you live in your land.

> ❝ Perhaps you will have to spend hours on your knees or upon your face before the throne. Never mind. Wait. God will do great things for you if you will wait for him. Yield to him. Cooperate with him. ❞
>
> JOHN SMITH

²⁰When the LORD your God has enlarged your territory as he promised you, and you crave meat and say, "I would like some meat," then you may eat as much of it as you want. ²¹If the place where the LORD your God chooses to put his Name is too far away from you, you may slaughter animals from the herds and flocks the LORD has given you, as I have commanded you, and in your own towns you may eat as much of them as you want. ²²Eat them as you would gazelle or deer. Both the ceremonially unclean and the clean may eat. ²³But be sure you do not eat the blood, because the blood is the life, and you must not eat the life with the meat. ²⁴You must not eat the blood; pour it out on the ground like water. ²⁵Do not eat it, so that it may go well with you and your children after you, because you will be doing what is right in the eyes of the LORD.

²⁶But take your consecrated things and whatever you have vowed to give, and go to the place the LORD will choose. ²⁷Pre-

sent your burnt offerings on the altar of the LORD your God, both the meat and the blood. The blood of your sacrifices must be poured beside the altar of the LORD your God, but you may eat the meat. ²⁸Be careful to obey all these regulations I am giving you, so that it may always go well with you and your children after you, because you will be doing what is good and right in the eyes of the LORD your God.

²⁹The LORD your God will cut off before you the nations you are about to invade and dispossess. But when you have driven them out and settled in their land, ³⁰and after they have been destroyed before you, be careful not to be ensnared by inquiring about their gods, saying, "How do these nations serve their gods? We will do the same." ³¹You must not worship the LORD your God in their way, because in worshiping their gods, they do all kinds of detestable things the LORD hates. They even burn their sons and daughters in the fire as sacrifices to their gods.

³²See that you do all I command you; do not add to it or take away from it.

Worshiping Other Gods

13 If a prophet, or one who foretells by dreams, appears among you and announces to you a miraculous sign or wonder, ²and if the sign or wonder of which he has spoken takes place, and he says, "Let us follow other gods" (gods you have not known) "and let us worship them," ³you must not listen to the words of that prophet or dreamer. The LORD your God is testing you to find out whether you love him with all your heart and with all your soul. ⁴It is the LORD your God you must follow, and him you must revere. Keep his commands and obey him; serve him and hold fast to him. ⁵That prophet or dreamer must be put to death, because he preached rebellion against the LORD your God, who brought you out of Egypt and redeemed you from the land of slavery; he has tried to turn you from the way the LORD your God commanded you to follow. You must purge the evil from among you.

⁶If your very own brother, or your son or daughter, or the wife you love, or your closest friend secretly entices you, say-

ing, "Let us go and worship other gods" (gods that neither you nor your fathers have known, ⁷gods of the peoples around you, whether near or far, from one end of the land to the other), ⁸do not yield to him or listen to him. Show him no pity. Do not spare him or shield him. ⁹You must certainly put him to death. Your hand must be the first in putting him to death, and then the hands of all the people. ¹⁰Stone him to death, because he tried to turn you away from the LORD your God, who brought you out of Egypt, out of the land of slavery. ¹¹Then all Israel will hear and be afraid, and no one among you will do such an evil thing again.

¹²If you hear it said about one of the towns the LORD your God is giving you to live in ¹³that wicked men have arisen among you and have led the people of their town astray, saying, "Let us go and worship other gods" (gods you have not known), ¹⁴then you must inquire, probe and investigate it thoroughly. And if it is true and it has been proved that this detestable thing has been done among you, ¹⁵you must certainly put to the sword all who live in that town. Destroy it completely,ᵃ both its people and its livestock. ¹⁶Gather all the plunder of the town into the middle of the public square and completely burn the town and all its plunder as a whole burnt offering to the LORD your God. It is to remain a ruin forever, never to be rebuilt. ¹⁷None of those condemned thingsᵃ shall be found in your hands, so that the LORD will turn from his fierce anger; he will show you mercy, have compassion on you, and increase your numbers, as he promised on oath to your forefathers, ¹⁸because you obey the LORD your God, keeping all his commands that I am giving you today and doing what is right in his eyes.

Clean and Unclean Food

14 You are the children of the LORD your God. Do not cut yourselves or shave the front of your heads for the dead, ²for you are a people holy to the LORD your God. Out of all the peoples on

ᵃ15,17 The Hebrew term refers to the irrevocable giving over of things or persons to the LORD, often by totally destroying them.

the face of the earth, the LORD has chosen you to be his treasured possession.

³Do not eat any detestable thing. ⁴These are the animals you may eat: the ox, the sheep, the goat, ⁵the deer, the gazelle, the roe deer, the wild goat, the ibex, the antelope and the mountain sheep.ᵃ ⁶You may eat any animal that has a split hoof divided in two and that chews the cud. ⁷However, of those that chew the cud or that have a split hoof completely divided you may not eat the camel, the rabbit or the coney.ᵇ Although they chew the cud, they do not have a split hoof; they are ceremonially unclean for you. ⁸The pig is also unclean; although it has a split hoof, it does not chew the cud. You are not to eat their meat or touch their carcasses.

⁹Of all the creatures living in the water, you may eat any that has fins and scales. ¹⁰But anything that does not have fins and scales you may not eat; for you it is unclean.

¹¹You may eat any clean bird. ¹²But these you may not eat: the eagle, the vulture, the black vulture, ¹³the red kite, the black kite, any kind of falcon, ¹⁴any kind of raven, ¹⁵the horned owl, the screech owl, the gull, any kind of hawk, ¹⁶the little owl, the great owl, the white owl, ¹⁷the desert owl, the osprey, the cormorant, ¹⁸the stork, any kind of heron, the hoopoe and the bat.

¹⁹All flying insects that swarm are unclean to you; do not eat them. ²⁰But any winged creature that is clean you may eat.

²¹Do not eat anything you find already dead. You may give it to an alien living in any of your towns, and he may eat it, or you may sell it to a foreigner. But you are a people holy to the LORD your God.

Do not cook a young goat in its mother's milk.

Tithes

²²Be sure to set aside a tenth of all that your fields produce each year. ²³Eat the tithe of your grain, new wine and oil, and the firstborn of your herds and flocks in the presence of the LORD your God at the place he will choose as a dwelling for his Name, so that you may learn to revere the LORD your God al-

ways. ²⁴But if that place is too distant and you have been blessed by the LORD your God and cannot carry your tithe (because the place where the LORD will choose to put his Name is so far away), ²⁵then exchange your tithe for silver, and take the silver with you and go to the place the LORD your God will choose. ²⁶Use the silver to buy whatever you like: cattle, sheep, wine or other fermented drink, or anything you wish. Then you and your household shall eat there in the presence of the LORD your God and rejoice. ²⁷And do not neglect the Levites living in your towns, for they have no allotment or inheritance of their own.

²⁸At the end of every three years, bring all the tithes of that year's produce and store it in your towns, ²⁹so that the Levites (who have no allotment or inheritance of their own) and the aliens, the fatherless and the widows who live in your towns may come and eat and be satisfied, and so that the LORD your God may bless you in all the work of your hands.

The Year for Canceling Debts

15 At the end of every seven years you must cancel debts. ²This is how it is to be done: Every creditor shall cancel the loan he has made to his fellow Israelite. He shall not require payment from his fellow Israelite or brother, because the LORD's time for canceling debts has been proclaimed. ³You may require payment from a foreigner, but you must cancel any debt your brother owes you. ⁴However, there should be no poor among you, for in the land the LORD your God is giving you to possess as your inheritance, he will richly bless you, ⁵if only you fully obey the LORD your God and are careful to follow all these commands I am giving you today. ⁶For the LORD your God will bless you as he has promised, and you will lend to many nations but will borrow from none. You will rule over many nations but none will rule over you.

⁷If there is a poor man among your brothers in any of the towns of the land that the LORD your God is giving you, do

---

ᵃ5 The precise identification of some of the birds and animals in this chapter is uncertain.
ᵇ7 That is, the hyrax or rock badger

not be hardhearted or tightfisted toward your poor brother. ⁸Rather be openhanded and freely lend him whatever he needs. ⁹Be careful not to harbor this wicked thought: "The seventh year, the year for canceling debts, is near," so that you do not show ill will toward your needy brother and give him nothing. He may then appeal to the LORD against you, and you will be found guilty of sin. ¹⁰Give generously to him and do so without a grudging heart; then because of this the LORD your God will bless you in all your work and in everything you put your hand to. ¹¹There will always be poor people in the land. Therefore I command you to be openhanded toward your brothers and toward the poor and needy in your land.

Freeing Servants

¹²If a fellow Hebrew, a man or a woman, sells himself to you and serves you six years, in the seventh year you must let him go free. ¹³And when you release him, do not send him away empty-handed. ¹⁴Supply him liberally from your flock, your threshing floor and your winepress. Give to him as the LORD your God has blessed you. ¹⁵Remember that you were slaves in Egypt and the LORD your God redeemed you. That is why I give you this command today.

¹⁶But if your servant says to you, "I do not want to leave you," because he loves you and your family and is well off with you, ¹⁷then take an awl and push it through his ear lobe into the door, and he will become your servant for life. Do the same for your maidservant.

¹⁸Do not consider it a hardship to set your servant free, because his service to you these six years has been worth twice as much as that of a hired hand. And the LORD your God will bless you in everything you do.

The Firstborn Animals

¹⁹Set apart for the LORD your God every firstborn male of your herds and flocks. Do not put the firstborn of your oxen to work, and do not shear the firstborn of your sheep. ²⁰Each year you and your family are to eat them in the presence of the LORD your God at the place he will choose. ²¹If an animal has a defect, is lame or blind, or has any serious flaw, you must not sacrifice it to the LORD your God. ²²You are to eat it in your own towns. Both the ceremonially unclean and the clean may eat it, as if it were gazelle or deer. ²³But you must not eat the blood; pour it out on the ground like water.

Passover

16 Observe the month of Abib and celebrate the Passover of the LORD your God, because in the month of Abib he brought you out of Egypt by night. ²Sacrifice as the Passover to the LORD your God an animal from your flock or herd at the place the LORD will choose as a dwelling for his Name. ³Do not eat it with bread made with yeast, but for seven days eat unleavened bread, the bread of affliction, because you left Egypt in haste—so that all the days of your life you may remember the time of your departure from Egypt. ⁴Let no yeast be found in your possession in all your land for seven days. Do not let any of the meat you sacrifice on the evening of the first day remain until morning.

⁵You must not sacrifice the Passover in any town the LORD your God gives you ⁶except in the place he will choose as a dwelling for his Name. There you must sacrifice the Passover in the evening, when the sun goes down, on the anniversary*a* of your departure from Egypt. ⁷Roast it and eat it at the place the LORD your God will choose. Then in the morning return to your tents. ⁸For six days eat unleavened bread and on the seventh day hold an assembly to the LORD your God and do no work.

Feast of Weeks

⁹Count off seven weeks from the time you begin to put the sickle to the standing grain. ¹⁰Then celebrate the Feast of Weeks to the LORD your God by giving a freewill offering in proportion to the blessings the LORD your God has given you. ¹¹And rejoice before the LORD your God at the place he will choose as a dwelling for his Name—you, your sons and daughters, your menservants and

a 6 Or down, at the time of day

maidservants, the Levites in your towns, and the aliens, the fatherless and the widows living among you. ¹²Remember that you were slaves in Egypt, and follow carefully these decrees.

Feast of Tabernacles

¹³Celebrate the Feast of Tabernacles for seven days after you have gathered the produce of your threshing floor and your winepress. ¹⁴Be joyful at your Feast—you, your sons and daughters, your menservants and maidservants, and the Levites, the aliens, the fatherless and the widows who live in your towns. ¹⁵For seven days celebrate the Feast to the LORD your God at the place the LORD will choose. For the LORD your God will bless you in all your harvest and in all the work of your hands, and your joy will be complete.

¹⁶Three times a year all your men must appear before the LORD your God at the place he will choose: at the Feast of Unleavened Bread, the Feast of Weeks and the Feast of Tabernacles. No man should appear before the LORD empty-handed: ¹⁷Each of you must bring a gift in proportion to the way the LORD your God has blessed you.

Judges

¹⁸Appoint judges and officials for each of your tribes in every town the LORD your God is giving you, and they shall judge the people fairly. ¹⁹Do not pervert justice or show partiality. Do not accept a bribe, for a bribe blinds the eyes of the wise and twists the words of the righteous. ²⁰Follow justice and justice alone, so that you may live and possess the land the LORD your God is giving you.

Worshiping Other Gods

²¹Do not set up any wooden Asherah poleᵃ beside the altar you build to the LORD your God, ²²and do not erect a sacred stone, for these the LORD your God hates.

17 Do not sacrifice to the LORD your God an ox or a sheep that has any defect or flaw in it, for that would be detestable to him.

²If a man or woman living among you in one of the towns the LORD gives you is found doing evil in the eyes of the LORD your God in violation of his covenant, ³and contrary to my command has worshiped other gods, bowing down to them or to the sun or the moon or the stars of the sky, ⁴and this has been brought to your attention, then you must investigate it thoroughly. If it is true and it has been proved that this detestable thing has been done in Israel, ⁵take the man or woman who has done this evil deed to your city gate and stone that person to death. ⁶On the testimony of two or three witnesses a man shall be put to death, but no one shall be put to death on the testimony of only one witness. ⁷The hands of the witnesses must be the first in putting him to death, and then the hands of all the people. You must purge the evil from among you.

Law Courts

⁸If cases come before your courts that are too difficult for you to judge—whether bloodshed, lawsuits or assaults—take them to the place the LORD your God will choose. ⁹Go to the priests, who are Levites, and to the judge who is in office at that time. Inquire of them and they will give you the verdict. ¹⁰You must act according to the decisions they give you at the place the LORD will choose. Be careful to do everything they direct you to do. ¹¹Act according to the law they teach you and the decisions they give you. Do not turn aside from what they tell you, to the right or to the left. ¹²The man who shows contempt for the judge or for the priest who stands ministering there to the LORD your God must be put to death. You must purge the evil from Israel. ¹³All the people will hear and be afraid, and will not be contemptuous again.

The King

¹⁴When you enter the land the LORD your God is giving you and have taken possession of it and settled in it, and you say, "Let us set a king over us like all the nations around us," ¹⁵be sure to appoint over you the king the LORD your God chooses. He must be from among your

ᵃ21 Or *Do not plant any tree dedicated to Asherah*

own brothers. Do not place a foreigner over you, one who is not a brother Israelite. [16]The king, moreover, must not acquire great numbers of horses for himself or make the people return to Egypt to get more of them, for the LORD has told you, "You are not to go back that way again." [17]He must not take many wives, or his heart will be led astray. He must not accumulate large amounts of silver and gold.

[18]When he takes the throne of his kingdom, he is to write for himself on a scroll a copy of this law, taken from that of the priests, who are Levites. [19]It is to be with him, and he is to read it all the days of his life so that he may learn to revere the LORD his God and follow carefully all the words of this law and these decrees [20]and not consider himself better than his brothers and turn from the law to the right or to the left. Then he and his descendants will reign a long time over his kingdom in Israel.

Offerings for Priests and Levites

18 The priests, who are Levites—indeed the whole tribe of Levi—are to have no allotment or inheritance with Israel. They shall live on the offerings made to the LORD by fire, for that is their inheritance. [2]They shall have no inheritance among their brothers; the LORD is their inheritance, as he promised them.

[3]This is the share due the priests from the people who sacrifice a bull or a sheep: the shoulder, the jowls and the inner parts. [4]You are to give them the firstfruits of your grain, new wine and oil, and the first wool from the shearing of your sheep, [5]for the LORD your God has chosen them and their descendants out of all your tribes to stand and minister in the LORD's name always.

[6]If a Levite moves from one of your towns anywhere in Israel where he is living, and comes in all earnestness to the place the LORD will choose, [7]he may minister in the name of the LORD his God like all his fellow Levites who serve there in the presence of the LORD. [8]He is to share equally in their benefits, even though he has received money from the sale of family possessions.

Detestable Practices

[9]When you enter the land the LORD your God is giving you, do not learn to imitate the detestable ways of the nations there. [10]Let no one be found among

> *None can believe how powerful prayer is, and what it is able to effect, but those who have learned it by experience. It is a great matter when in extreme need to take hold on prayer. I know, whenever I have prayed earnestly, that I have been amply heard, and have obtained more than I prayed for. God indeed sometimes delayed, but at last he came.*
>
> MARTIN LUTHER

you who sacrifices his son or daughter in[a] the fire, who practices divination or sorcery, interprets omens, engages in witchcraft, [11]or casts spells, or who is a medium or spiritist or who consults the dead. [12]Anyone who does these things is detestable to the LORD, and because of these detestable practices the LORD your God will drive out those nations before you. [13]You must be blameless before the LORD your God.

The Prophet

[14]The nations you will dispossess listen to those who practice sorcery or divination. But as for you, the LORD your God has not permitted you to do so. [15]The LORD your God will raise up for you a prophet like me from among your own brothers. You must listen to him. [16]For this is what you asked of the LORD your God at Horeb on the day of the assembly when you said, "Let us not hear the voice of the LORD our God nor see this great fire anymore, or we will die."

[17]The LORD said to me: "What they say is good. [18]I will raise up for them a prophet like you from among their brothers; I will put my words in his mouth, and he will tell them everything I command him. [19]If anyone does not listen to my words that the prophet speaks in my name, I

[a]10 Or *who makes his son or daughter pass through*

myself will call him to account. ²⁰But a prophet who presumes to speak in my name anything I have not commanded him to say, or a prophet who speaks in the name of other gods, must be put to death."

²¹You may say to yourselves, "How can we know when a message has not been spoken by the LORD?" ²²If what a prophet proclaims in the name of the LORD does not take place or come true, that is a message the LORD has not spoken. That prophet has spoken presumptuously. Do not be afraid of him.

Cities of Refuge

19 When the LORD your God has destroyed the nations whose land he is giving you, and when you have driven them out and settled in their towns and houses, ²then set aside for yourselves three cities centrally located in the land the LORD your God is giving you to possess. ³Build roads to them and divide into three parts the land the LORD your God is giving you as an inheritance, so that anyone who kills a man may flee there.

⁴This is the rule concerning the man who kills another and flees there to save his life—one who kills his neighbor unintentionally, without malice aforethought. ⁵For instance, a man may go into the forest with his neighbor to cut wood, and as he swings his ax to fell a tree, the head may fly off and hit his neighbor and kill him. That man may flee to one of these cities and save his life. ⁶Otherwise, the avenger of blood might pursue him in a rage, overtake him if the distance is too great, and kill him even though he is not deserving of death, since he did it to his neighbor without malice aforethought. ⁷This is why I command you to set aside for yourselves three cities.

⁸If the LORD your God enlarges your territory, as he promised on oath to your forefathers, and gives you the whole land he promised them, ⁹because you carefully follow all these laws I command you today—to love the LORD your God and to walk always in his ways—then you are to set aside three more cities. ¹⁰Do this so that innocent blood will not be shed in your land, which the LORD your God is giving you as your inheritance, and so that you will not be guilty of bloodshed.

¹¹But if a man hates his neighbor and lies in wait for him, assaults and kills him, and then flees to one of these cities, ¹²the elders of his town shall send for him, bring him back from the city, and hand him over to the avenger of blood to die. ¹³Show him no pity. You must purge from Israel the guilt of shedding innocent blood, so that it may go well with you.

¹⁴Do not move your neighbor's boundary stone set up by your predecessors in the inheritance you receive in the land the LORD your God is giving you to possess.

Witnesses

¹⁵One witness is not enough to convict a man accused of any crime or offense he may have committed. A matter must be established by the testimony of two or three witnesses.

¹⁶If a malicious witness takes the stand to accuse a man of a crime, ¹⁷the two men involved in the dispute must stand in the presence of the LORD before the priests and the judges who are in office at the time. ¹⁸The judges must make a thorough investigation, and if the witness proves to be a liar, giving false testimony against his brother, ¹⁹then do to him as he intended to do to his brother. You must purge the evil from among you. ²⁰The rest of the people will hear of this and be afraid, and never again will such an evil thing be done among you. ²¹Show no pity: life for life, eye for eye, tooth for tooth, hand for hand, foot for foot.

Going to War

20 When you go to war against your enemies and see horses and chariots and an army greater than yours, do not be afraid of them, because the LORD your God, who brought you up out of Egypt, will be with you. ²When you are about to go into battle, the priest shall

> *We must not sit still and look for miracles; up and doing, and the Lord will be with thee. Prayer and pains, through faith in Christ Jesus, will do anything.*
>
> GEORGE ELIOT

come forward and address the army. ³He shall say: "Hear, O Israel, today you are going into battle against your enemies. Do not be fainthearted or afraid; do not be terrified or give way to panic before them. ⁴For the LORD your God is the one who goes with you to fight for you against your enemies to give you victory."

⁵The officers shall say to the army: "Has anyone built a new house and not dedicated it? Let him go home, or he may die in battle and someone else may dedicate it. ⁶Has anyone planted a vineyard and not begun to enjoy it? Let him go home, or he may die in battle and someone else enjoy it. ⁷Has anyone become pledged to a woman and not married her? Let him go home, or he may die in battle and someone else marry her." ⁸Then the officers shall add, "Is any man afraid or fainthearted? Let him go home so that his brothers will not become disheartened too." ⁹When the officers have finished speaking to the army, they shall appoint commanders over it.

¹⁰When you march up to attack a city, make its people an offer of peace. ¹¹If they accept and open their gates, all the people in it shall be subject to forced labor and shall work for you. ¹²If they refuse to make peace and they engage you in battle, lay siege to that city. ¹³When the LORD your God delivers it into your hand, put to the sword all the men in it. ¹⁴As for the women, the children, the livestock and everything else in the city, you may take these as plunder for yourselves. And you may use the plunder the LORD your God gives you from your enemies. ¹⁵This is how you are to treat all the cities that are at a distance from you and do not belong to the nations nearby.

¹⁶However, in the cities of the nations the LORD your God is giving you as an inheritance, do not leave alive anything that breathes. ¹⁷Completely destroy[a] them—the Hittites, Amorites, Canaanites, Perizzites, Hivites and Jebusites—as the LORD your God has commanded you. ¹⁸Otherwise, they will teach you to follow all the detestable things they do in worshiping their gods, and you will sin against the LORD your God.

¹⁹When you lay siege to a city for a long time, fighting against it to capture it, do not destroy its trees by putting an ax to them, because you can eat their fruit. Do not cut them down. Are the trees of the field people, that you should besiege them?[b] ²⁰However, you may cut down trees that you know are not fruit trees and use them to build siege works until the city at war with you falls.

Atonement for an Unsolved Murder

21 If a man is found slain, lying in a field in the land the LORD your God is giving you to possess, and it is not known who killed him, ²your elders and judges shall go out and measure the distance from the body to the neighboring towns. ³Then the elders of the town nearest the body shall take a heifer that has never been worked and has never worn a yoke ⁴and lead her down to a valley that has not been plowed or planted and where there is a flowing stream. There in the valley they are to break the heifer's neck. ⁵The priests, the sons of Levi, shall step forward, for the LORD your God has chosen them to minister and to pronounce blessings in the name of the LORD and to decide all cases of dispute and assault. ⁶Then all the elders of the town nearest the body shall wash their hands over the heifer whose neck was broken in the valley, ⁷and they shall declare: "Our hands did not shed this blood, nor did our eyes see it done. ⁸Accept this atonement for your people Israel, whom you have redeemed, O LORD, and do not hold your people guilty of the blood of an innocent man." And the bloodshed will be atoned for. ⁹So you will purge from yourselves the guilt of shedding innocent blood, since you have done what is right in the eyes of the LORD.

Marrying a Captive Woman

¹⁰When you go to war against your enemies and the LORD your God delivers them into your hands and you take captives, ¹¹if you notice among the captives a beautiful woman and are attracted to her, you may take her as your wife. ¹²Bring her into

---

[a]17 The Hebrew term refers to the irrevocable giving over of things or persons to the LORD, often by totally destroying them.   [b]19 Or down to use in the siege, for the fruit trees are for the benefit of man.

your home and have her shave her head, trim her nails ¹³and put aside the clothes she was wearing when captured. After she has lived in your house and mourned her father and mother for a full month, then you may go to her and be her husband and she shall be your wife. ¹⁴If you are not pleased with her, let her go wherever she wishes. You must not sell her or treat her as a slave, since you have dishonored her.

The Right of the Firstborn

¹⁵If a man has two wives, and he loves one but not the other, and both bear him sons but the firstborn is the son of the wife he does not love, ¹⁶when he wills his property to his sons, he must not give the rights of the firstborn to the son of the wife he loves in preference to his actual firstborn, the son of the wife he does not love. ¹⁷He must acknowledge the son of his unloved wife as the firstborn by giving him a double share of all he has. That son is the first sign of his father's strength. The right of the firstborn belongs to him.

A Rebellious Son

¹⁸If a man has a stubborn and rebellious son who does not obey his father and mother and will not listen to them when they discipline him, ¹⁹his father and mother shall take hold of him and bring him to the elders at the gate of his town. ²⁰They shall say to the elders, "This son of ours is stubborn and rebellious. He will not obey us. He is a profligate and a drunkard." ²¹Then all the men of his town shall stone him to death. You must purge the evil from among you. All Israel will hear of it and be afraid.

Various Laws

²²If a man guilty of a capital offense is put to death and his body is hung on a tree, ²³you must not leave his body on the tree overnight. Be sure to bury him that same day, because anyone who is hung on a tree is under God's curse. You must not desecrate the land the LORD your God is giving you as an inheritance.

22 If you see your brother's ox or sheep straying, do not ignore it but be sure to take it back to him. ²If the brother does not live near you or if you do not know who he is, take it home with you and keep it until he comes looking for it. Then give it back to him. ³Do the same if you find your brother's donkey or his cloak or anything he loses. Do not ignore it.

⁴If you see your brother's donkey or his ox fallen on the road, do not ignore it. Help him get it to its feet.

⁵A woman must not wear men's clothing, nor a man wear women's clothing, for the LORD your God detests anyone who does this.

⁶If you come across a bird's nest beside the road, either in a tree or on the ground, and the mother is sitting on the young or on the eggs, do not take the mother with the young. ⁷You may take the young, but be sure to let the mother go, so that it may go well with you and you may have a long life.

⁸When you build a new house, make a parapet around your roof so that you may not bring the guilt of bloodshed on your house if someone falls from the roof.

⁹Do not plant two kinds of seed in your vineyard; if you do, not only the crops you plant but also the fruit of the vineyard will be defiled.[a]

¹⁰Do not plow with an ox and a donkey yoked together.

¹¹Do not wear clothes of wool and linen woven together.

¹²Make tassels on the four corners of the cloak you wear.

Marriage Violations

¹³If a man takes a wife and, after lying with her, dislikes her ¹⁴and slanders her and gives her a bad name, saying, "I married this woman, but when I approached her, I did not find proof of her virginity," ¹⁵then the girl's father and mother shall bring proof that she was a virgin to the town elders at the gate. ¹⁶The girl's father will say to the elders, "I gave my daughter in marriage to this man, but he dislikes her. ¹⁷Now he has slandered her and said, 'I did not find your daughter to be a virgin.' But here is the proof of my daughter's virginity." Then her parents shall display the cloth before the elders of the town, ¹⁸and the elders shall take the man

---

a9 Or be forfeited to the sanctuary

and punish him. [19]They shall fine him a hundred shekels of silver[a] and give them to the girl's father, because this man has given an Israelite virgin a bad name. She shall continue to be his wife; he must not divorce her as long as he lives.

[20]If, however, the charge is true and no proof of the girl's virginity can be found, [21]she shall be brought to the door of her father's house and there the men of her town shall stone her to death. She has done a disgraceful thing in Israel by being promiscuous while still in her father's house. You must purge the evil from among you.

[22]If a man is found sleeping with another man's wife, both the man who slept with her and the woman must die. You must purge the evil from Israel.

[23]If a man happens to meet in a town a virgin pledged to be married and he sleeps with her, [24]you shall take both of them to the gate of that town and stone them to death—the girl because she was in a town and did not scream for help, and the man because he violated another man's wife. You must purge the evil from among you.

[25]But if out in the country a man happens to meet a girl pledged to be married and rapes her, only the man who has done this shall die. [26]Do nothing to the girl; she has committed no sin deserving death. This case is like that of someone who attacks and murders his neighbor, [27]for the man found the girl out in the country, and though the betrothed girl screamed, there was no one to rescue her.

[28]If a man happens to meet a virgin who is not pledged to be married and rapes her and they are discovered, [29]he shall pay the girl's father fifty shekels of silver.[b] He must marry the girl, for he has violated her. He can never divorce her as long as he lives.

[30]A man is not to marry his father's wife; he must not dishonor his father's bed.

Exclusion From the Assembly

23 No one who has been emasculated by crushing or cutting may enter the assembly of the LORD.

[2]No one born of a forbidden marriage[c] nor any of his descendants may enter the assembly of the LORD, even down to the tenth generation.

[3]No Ammonite or Moabite or any of his descendants may enter the assembly of the LORD, even down to the tenth generation. [4]For they did not come to meet you with bread and water on your way when you came out of Egypt, and they hired Balaam son of Beor from Pethor in Aram Naharaim[d] to pronounce a curse on you. [5]However, the LORD your God would not listen to Balaam but turned the curse into a blessing for you, because the LORD your God loves you. [6]Do not seek a treaty of friendship with them as long as you live.

[7]Do not abhor an Edomite, for he is your brother. Do not abhor an Egyptian, because you lived as an alien in his country. [8]The third generation of children born to them may enter the assembly of the LORD.

Uncleanness in the Camp

[9]When you are encamped against your enemies, keep away from everything impure. [10]If one of your men is unclean because of a nocturnal emission, he is to go outside the camp and stay there. [11]But as evening approaches he is to wash himself, and at sunset he may return to the camp.

[12]Designate a place outside the camp where you can go to relieve yourself. [13]As part of your equipment have something to dig with, and when you relieve yourself, dig a hole and cover up your excrement. [14]For the LORD your God moves about in your camp to protect you and to deliver your enemies to you. Your camp must be holy, so that he will not see among you anything indecent and turn away from you.

Miscellaneous Laws

[15]If a slave has taken refuge with you, do not hand him over to his master. [16]Let him live among you wherever he likes and in whatever town he chooses. Do not oppress him.

[17]No Israelite man or woman is to become a shrine prostitute. [18]You must not bring the earnings of a female prostitute or

---

[a]19 That is, about 2 1/2 pounds (about 1 kilogram)   [b]29 That is, about 1 1/4 pounds (about 0.6 kilogram)   [c]2 Or one of illegitimate birth   [d]4 That is, Northwest Mesopotamia

of a male prostitute[a] into the house of the LORD your God to pay any vow, because the LORD your God detests them both.

19Do not charge your brother interest, whether on money or food or anything else that may earn interest. 20You may charge a foreigner interest, but not a brother Israelite, so that the LORD your God may bless you in everything you put your hand to in the land you are entering to possess.

21If you make a vow to the LORD your God, do not be slow to pay it, for the LORD your God will certainly demand it of you and you will be guilty of sin. 22But if you refrain from making a vow, you will not be guilty. 23Whatever your lips utter you must be sure to do, because you made your vow freely to the LORD your God with your own mouth.

24If you enter your neighbor's vineyard, you may eat all the grapes you want, but do not put any in your basket. 25If you enter your neighbor's grainfield, you may pick kernels with your hands, but you must not put a sickle to his standing grain.

24 If a man marries a woman who becomes displeasing to him because he finds something indecent about her, and he writes her a certificate of divorce, gives it to her and sends her from his house, 2and if after she leaves his house she becomes the wife of another man, 3and her second husband dislikes her and writes her a certificate of divorce, gives it to her and sends her from his house, or if he dies, 4then her first husband, who divorced her, is not allowed to marry her again after she has been defiled. That would be detestable in the eyes of the LORD. Do not bring sin upon the land the LORD your God is giving you as an inheritance.

5If a man has recently married, he must not be sent to war or have any other duty laid on him. For one year he is to be free to stay at home and bring happiness to the wife he has married.

6Do not take a pair of millstones—not even the upper one—as security for a debt, because that would be taking a man's livelihood as security.

7If a man is caught kidnapping one of his brother Israelites and treats him as a slave or sells him, the kidnapper must die. You must purge the evil from among you.

8In cases of leprous[b] diseases be very careful to do exactly as the priests, who are Levites, instruct you. You must follow carefully what I have commanded them. 9Remember what the LORD your God did to Miriam along the way after you came out of Egypt.

10When you make a loan of any kind to your neighbor, do not go into his house to get what he is offering as a pledge. 11Stay outside and let the man to whom you are making the loan bring the pledge out to you. 12If the man is poor, do not go to sleep with his pledge in your possession. 13Return his cloak to him by sunset so that he may sleep in it. Then he will thank you, and it will be regarded as a righteous act in the sight of the LORD your God.

14Do not take advantage of a hired man who is poor and needy, whether he is a brother Israelite or an alien living in one of your towns. 15Pay him his wages each day before sunset, because he is poor and is counting on it. Otherwise he may cry to the LORD against you, and you will be guilty of sin.

16Fathers shall not be put to death for their children, nor children put to death for their fathers; each is to die for his own sin.

17Do not deprive the alien or the fatherless of justice, or take the cloak of the widow as a pledge. 18Remember that you were slaves in Egypt and the LORD your God redeemed you from there. That is why I command you to do this.

19When you are harvesting in your field and you overlook a sheaf, do not go back to get it. Leave it for the alien, the fatherless and the widow, so that the LORD your God may bless you in all the work of your hands. 20When you beat the olives from your trees, do not go over the branches a second time. Leave what remains for the alien, the fatherless and the widow. 21When you harvest the grapes in your vineyard, do not go over the vines again. Leave what remains for the alien, the fatherless and the widow. 22Remember that you were slaves in Egypt. That is why I command you to do this.

---

[a]18 Hebrew *of a dog*   [b]8 The Hebrew word was used for various diseases affecting the skin—not necessarily leprosy.

25 When men have a dispute, they are to take it to court and the judges will decide the case, acquitting the innocent and condemning the guilty. ²If the guilty man deserves to be beaten, the judge shall make him lie down and have him flogged in his presence with the number of lashes his crime deserves, ³but he must not give him more than forty lashes. If he is flogged more than that, your brother will be degraded in your eyes.

⁴Do not muzzle an ox while it is treading out the grain.

⁵If brothers are living together and one of them dies without a son, his widow must not marry outside the family. Her husband's brother shall take her and marry her and fulfill the duty of a brother-in-law to her. ⁶The first son she bears shall carry on the name of the dead brother so that his name will not be blotted out from Israel.

⁷However, if a man does not want to marry his brother's wife, she shall go to the elders at the town gate and say, "My husband's brother refuses to carry on his brother's name in Israel. He will not fulfill the duty of a brother-in-law to me." ⁸Then the elders of his town shall summon him and talk to him. If he persists in saying, "I do not want to marry her," ⁹his brother's widow shall go up to him in the presence of the elders, take off one of his sandals, spit in his face and say, "This is what is done to the man who will not build up his brother's family line." ¹⁰That man's line shall be known in Israel as The Family of the Unsandaled.

¹¹If two men are fighting and the wife of one of them comes to rescue her husband from his assailant, and she reaches out and seizes him by his private parts, ¹²you shall cut off her hand. Show her no pity.

¹³Do not have two differing weights in your bag—one heavy, one light. ¹⁴Do not have two differing measures in your house—one large, one small. ¹⁵You must have accurate and honest weights and measures, so that you may live long in the land the LORD your God is giving you. ¹⁶For the LORD your God detests anyone who does these things, anyone who deals dishonestly.

¹⁷Remember what the Amalekites did to you along the way when you came out of Egypt. ¹⁸When you were weary and worn out, they met you on your journey and cut off all who were lagging behind; they had no fear of God. ¹⁹When the LORD your God gives you rest from all the enemies around you in the land he is giving you to possess as an inheritance, you shall blot out the memory of Amalek from under heaven. Do not forget!

Firstfruits and Tithes

26 When you have entered the land the LORD your God is giving you as an inheritance and have taken possession of it and settled in it, ²take some of the firstfruits of all that you produce from the soil of the land the LORD your God is giving you and put them in a basket. Then go to the place the LORD your God will choose as a dwelling for his Name ³and say to the priest in office at the time, "I declare today to the LORD your God that I have come to the land the LORD swore to our forefathers to give us." ⁴The priest shall take the basket from your hands and set it down in front of the altar of the LORD your God. ⁵Then you shall declare before the LORD your God: "My father was a wandering Aramean, and he went down into Egypt with a few people and lived there and became a great nation, powerful and numerous. ⁶But the Egyptians mistreated us and made us suffer, putting us to hard labor. ⁷Then we cried out to the LORD, the God of our fathers, and the LORD heard our voice and saw our misery, toil and oppression.

> "*WE CRIED* out to the LORD, the God of our fathers, and the LORD heard our voice and saw our misery, toil and oppression."
>
> DEUTERONOMY 26:7

⁸So the LORD brought us out of Egypt with a mighty hand and an outstretched arm, with great terror and with miraculous signs and wonders. ⁹He brought us to this place and gave us this land, a land flowing with milk and honey; ¹⁰and now I bring the firstfruits of the soil that you, O LORD, have given me." Place the basket before the LORD your God and bow down

before him. ¹¹And you and the Levites and the aliens among you shall rejoice in all the good things the LORD your God has given to you and your household.

¹²When you have finished setting aside a tenth of all your produce in the third year, the year of the tithe, you shall give it to the Levite, the alien, the fatherless and the widow, so that they may eat in your towns and be satisfied. ¹³Then say to the LORD your God: "I have removed from my house the sacred portion and have given

---

DEUTERONOMY 26:1–11

Creed and Prayer

26:5 THEN YOU SHALL DECLARE BEFORE THE LORD YOUR GOD . . .

Martin Luther's morning and evening prayers typically included saying the Apostles' Creed and the Lord's Prayer, followed by a prayer of thanksgiving. For many of us, the Lord's Prayer and the thanksgiving make perfect sense—but the Creed? It's a nice thing to do, but is it necessary to do it daily? Luther's sequence was thoroughly and anciently Biblical, and it followed the pattern of the liturgy in this text: Confess your faith and pray; pray and confess your faith.

Moses is giving instructions for when the Israelites take possession of the promised land. After the people are settled in the land, each family leader is to take some of the first produce to offer to the Lord. When bringing the offering to the priest, the worshiper is first to confess his faith and say this creed: "My father was a wandering Aramean, and he went down into Egypt . . . But the Egyptians mistreated us and made us suffer . . . So the LORD brought us out of Egypt with a mighty hand and an outstretched arm" (26:5–6,8). Then the person was to place the offering before the Lord and bow in prayer to "rejoice in all the good things the LORD your God has given to you and your household" (verse 11).

Prayer is coupled with creed because prayer is a relationship, not a technique. Techniques are about what we can do in and through ourselves. Prayer is about who we are in God and who he is to us—and that is what creeds are about, like the one in this text and the great creeds of Christian history. In retelling and summarizing the story of our redemption, they describe the terms of the engagement we call prayer. They help us talk to the true and living God, not just to ourselves.

Creeds have great power to enrich our prayer lives. Take the first line of the Apostles' Creed and think of what it can mean for the enjoyment of prayer: "I believe in God, the Father Almighty, creator of heaven and earth." This first line expresses the belief that the God we address as Father is the very one who spoke the universe into existence and continues to sustain it by his word. He is more than able to care for us because he is almighty. He is more than willing because he is our Father!

Learn a creed like the Apostles' Creed; it will help you enter the relationship of prayer more thoughtfully and joyfully.

P R A Y :

Father in Heaven! Teach me to apply my mind more fully to our relationship by deepening my understanding of the propositions and creeds of Christian faith.

FOR YOUR NEXT DEVOTIONAL READING, GO TO PAGE 234.

it to the Levite, the alien, the fatherless and the widow, according to all you commanded. I have not turned aside from your commands nor have I forgotten any of them. ¹⁴I have not eaten any of the sacred portion while I was in mourning, nor have I removed any of it while I was unclean, nor have I offered any of it to the dead. I have obeyed the LORD my God; I have done everything you commanded me. ¹⁵Look down from heaven, your holy dwelling place, and bless your people Israel and the land you have given us as you promised on oath to our forefathers, a land flowing with milk and honey."

Follow the LORD's Commands

¹⁶The LORD your God commands you this day to follow these decrees and laws; carefully observe them with all your heart and with all your soul. ¹⁷You have declared this day that the LORD is your God and that you will walk in his ways, that you will keep his decrees, commands and laws, and that you will obey him. ¹⁸And the LORD has declared this day that you are his people, his treasured possession as he promised, and that you are to keep all his commands. ¹⁹He has declared that he will set you in praise, fame and honor high above all the nations he has made and that you will be a people holy to the LORD your God, as he promised.

The Altar on Mount Ebal

27 Moses and the elders of Israel commanded the people: "Keep all these commands that I give you today. ²When you have crossed the Jordan into the land the LORD your God is giving you, set up some large stones and coat them with plaster. ³Write on them all the words of this law when you have crossed over to enter the land the LORD your God is giving you, a land flowing with milk and honey, just as the LORD, the God of your fathers, promised you. ⁴And when you have crossed the Jordan, set up these stones on Mount Ebal, as I command you today, and coat them with plaster. ⁵Build there an altar to the LORD your God, an altar of stones. Do not use any iron tool upon them. ⁶Build the altar of the LORD your God with fieldstones and offer burnt offerings on it to the LORD your God. ⁷Sac-

rifice fellowship offerings[a] there, eating them and rejoicing in the presence of the LORD your God. ⁸And you shall write very clearly all the words of this law on these stones you have set up."

Curses From Mount Ebal

⁹Then Moses and the priests, who are Levites, said to all Israel, "Be silent, O Israel, and listen! You have now become the people of the LORD your God. ¹⁰Obey the LORD your God and follow his commands and decrees that I give you today."

¹¹On the same day Moses commanded the people:

¹²When you have crossed the Jordan, these tribes shall stand on Mount Gerizim to bless the people: Simeon, Levi, Judah, Issachar, Joseph and Benjamin. ¹³And these tribes shall stand on Mount Ebal to pronounce curses: Reuben, Gad, Asher, Zebulun, Dan and Naphtali.

¹⁴The Levites shall recite to all the people of Israel in a loud voice:

¹⁵"Cursed is the man who carves an image or casts an idol—a thing detestable to the LORD, the work of the craftsman's hands—and sets it up in secret."

Then all the people shall say, "Amen!"

¹⁶"Cursed is the man who dishonors his father or his mother."

Then all the people shall say, "Amen!"

¹⁷"Cursed is the man who moves his neighbor's boundary stone."

Then all the people shall say, "Amen!"

¹⁸"Cursed is the man who leads the blind astray on the road."

Then all the people shall say, "Amen!"

¹⁹"Cursed is the man who withholds justice from the alien, the fatherless or the widow."

Then all the people shall say, "Amen!"

²⁰"Cursed is the man who sleeps with his father's wife, for he dishonors his father's bed."

Then all the people shall say, "Amen!"

---

a 7 Traditionally *peace offerings*

21"Cursed is the man who has sexual relations with any animal."

Then all the people shall say, "Amen!"

22"Cursed is the man who sleeps with his sister, the daughter of his father or the daughter of his mother."

Then all the people shall say, "Amen!"

23"Cursed is the man who sleeps with his mother-in-law."

Then all the people shall say, "Amen!"

24"Cursed is the man who kills his neighbor secretly."

Then all the people shall say, "Amen!"

25"Cursed is the man who accepts a bribe to kill an innocent person."

Then all the people shall say, "Amen!"

26"Cursed is the man who does not uphold the words of this law by carrying them out."

Then all the people shall say, "Amen!"

Blessings for Obedience

28 If you fully obey the LORD your God and carefully follow all his commands I give you today, the LORD your God will set you high above all the nations on earth. 2All these blessings will come upon you and accompany you if you obey the LORD your God:

3You will be blessed in the city and blessed in the country.

4The fruit of your womb will be blessed, and the crops of your land and the young of your livestock— the calves of your herds and the lambs of your flocks.

5Your basket and your kneading trough will be blessed.

6You will be blessed when you come in and blessed when you go out.

7The LORD will grant that the enemies who rise up against you will be defeated before you. They will come at you from one direction but flee from you in seven.

8The LORD will send a blessing on your barns and on everything you put your hand to. The LORD your God will bless you in the land he is giving you.

9The LORD will establish you as his holy people, as he promised you on oath, if you keep the commands of the LORD your God and walk in his ways. 10Then all the peoples on earth will see that you are called by the name of the LORD, and they will fear you. 11The LORD will grant you abundant prosperity—in the fruit of your womb, the young of your livestock and the crops of your ground—in the land he swore to your forefathers to give you.

12The LORD will open the heavens, the storehouse of his bounty, to send rain on your land in season and to bless all the work of your hands. You will lend to many nations but will borrow from none. 13The LORD will make you the head, not the tail. If you pay attention to the commands of the LORD your God that I give you this day and carefully follow them, you will always be at the top, never at the bottom. 14Do not turn aside from any of the commands I give you today, to the right or to the left, following other gods and serving them.

Curses for Disobedience

15However, if you do not obey the LORD your God and do not carefully follow all his commands and decrees I am giving you today, all these curses will come upon you and overtake you:

16You will be cursed in the city and cursed in the country.

17Your basket and your kneading trough will be cursed.

18The fruit of your womb will be cursed, and the crops of your land, and the calves of your herds and the lambs of your flocks.

19You will be cursed when you come in and cursed when you go out.

20The LORD will send on you curses, confusion and rebuke in everything you put your hand to, until you are destroyed and come to sudden ruin because of the evil you have done in forsaking him.ᵃ 21The LORD will plague you with diseases until he has destroyed you from the land

ᵃ20 Hebrew me

you are entering to possess. ²²The LORD will strike you with wasting disease, with fever and inflammation, with scorching heat and drought, with blight and mildew, which will plague you until you perish. ²³The sky over your head will be bronze, the ground beneath you iron. ²⁴The LORD will turn the rain of your country into dust and powder; it will come down from the skies until you are destroyed.

²⁵The LORD will cause you to be defeated before your enemies. You will come at them from one direction but flee from them in seven, and you will become a thing of horror to all the kingdoms on earth. ²⁶Your carcasses will be food for all the birds of the air and the beasts of the earth, and there will be no one to frighten them away. ²⁷The LORD will afflict you with the boils of Egypt and with tumors, festering sores and the itch, from which you cannot be cured. ²⁸The LORD will afflict you with madness, blindness and confusion of mind. ²⁹At midday you will grope about like a blind man in the dark. You will be unsuccessful in everything you do; day after day you will be oppressed and robbed, with no one to rescue you.

³⁰You will be pledged to be married to a woman, but another will take her and ravish her. You will build a house, but you will not live in it. You will plant a vineyard, but you will not even begin to enjoy its fruit. ³¹Your ox will be slaughtered before your eyes, but you will eat none of it. Your donkey will be forcibly taken from you and will not be returned. Your sheep will be given to your enemies, and no one will rescue them. ³²Your sons and daughters will be given to another nation, and you will wear out your eyes watching for them day after day, powerless to lift a hand. ³³A people that you do not know will eat what your land and labor produce, and you will have nothing but cruel oppression all your days. ³⁴The sights you see will drive you mad. ³⁵The LORD will afflict your knees and legs with painful boils that cannot be cured, spreading from the soles of your feet to the top of your head.

³⁶The LORD will drive you and the king you set over you to a nation unknown to you or your fathers. There you will worship other gods, gods of wood and stone. ³⁷You will become a thing of horror and an object of scorn and ridicule to all the nations where the LORD will drive you.

³⁸You will sow much seed in the field but you will harvest little, because locusts will devour it. ³⁹You will plant vineyards and cultivate them but you will not drink the wine or gather the grapes, because worms will eat them. ⁴⁰You will have olive trees throughout your country but you will not use the oil, because the olives will drop off. ⁴¹You will have sons and daughters but you will not keep them, because they will go into captivity. ⁴²Swarms of locusts will take over all your trees and the crops of your land.

⁴³The alien who lives among you will rise above you higher and higher, but you will sink lower and lower. ⁴⁴He will lend to you, but you will not lend to him. He will be the head, but you will be the tail.

⁴⁵All these curses will come upon you. They will pursue you and overtake you until you are destroyed, because you did not obey the LORD your God and observe the commands and decrees he gave you. ⁴⁶They will be a sign and a wonder to you and your descendants forever. ⁴⁷Because you did not serve the LORD your God joyfully and gladly in the time of prosperity, ⁴⁸therefore in hunger and thirst, in nakedness and dire poverty, you will serve the enemies the LORD sends against you. He will put an iron yoke on your neck until he has destroyed you.

⁴⁹The LORD will bring a nation against you from far away, from the ends of the earth, like an eagle swooping down, a nation whose language you will not understand, ⁵⁰a fierce-looking nation without respect for the old or pity for the young. ⁵¹They will devour the young of your livestock and the crops of your land until you are destroyed. They will leave you no grain, new wine or oil, nor any calves of your herds or lambs of your flocks until you are ruined. ⁵²They will lay siege to all the cities throughout your land until the high fortified walls in which you trust fall down. They will besiege all the cities throughout the land the LORD your God is giving you.

⁵³Because of the suffering that your enemy will inflict on you during the siege, you will eat the fruit of the womb, the flesh of the sons and daughters the LORD your God has given you. ⁵⁴Even the most gentle and sensitive man among you will have no compassion on his own brother or the wife he loves or his surviving children, ⁵⁵and he will not give to one of them any of the flesh of his children that he is eating. It will be all he has left because of the suffering your enemy will inflict on you during the siege of all your cities. ⁵⁶The most gentle and sensitive woman among you—so sensitive and gentle that she would not venture to touch the ground with the sole of her foot—will begrudge the husband she loves and her own son or daughter ⁵⁷the afterbirth from her womb and the children she bears. For she intends to eat them secretly during the siege and in the distress that your enemy will inflict on you in your cities.

⁵⁸If you do not carefully follow all the words of this law, which are written in this book, and do not revere this glorious and awesome name—the LORD your God— ⁵⁹the LORD will send fearful plagues on you and your descendants, harsh and prolonged disasters, and severe and lingering illnesses. ⁶⁰He will bring upon you all the diseases of Egypt that you dreaded, and they will cling to you. ⁶¹The LORD will also bring on you every kind of sickness and disaster not recorded in this Book of the Law, until you are destroyed. ⁶²You who were as numerous as the stars in the sky will be left but few in number, because you did not obey the LORD your God. ⁶³Just as it pleased the LORD to make you prosper and increase in number, so it will please him to ruin and destroy you. You will be uprooted from the land you are entering to possess.

⁶⁴Then the LORD will scatter you among all nations, from one end of the earth to the other. There you will worship other gods—gods of wood and stone, which neither you nor your fathers have known. ⁶⁵Among those nations you will find no repose, no resting place for the sole of your foot. There the LORD will give you an anxious mind, eyes weary with longing, and a despairing heart. ⁶⁶You will live in constant suspense, filled with dread both night and day, never sure of your life. ⁶⁷In the morning you will say, "If only it were evening!" and in the evening, "If only it were morning!"—because of the terror that will fill your hearts and the sights that your eyes will see. ⁶⁸The LORD will send you back in ships to Egypt on a journey I said you should never make again. There you will offer yourselves for sale to your enemies as male and female slaves, but no one will buy you.

Renewal of the Covenant

29 These are the terms of the covenant the LORD commanded Moses to make with the Israelites in Moab, in addition to the covenant he had made with them at Horeb.

²Moses summoned all the Israelites and said to them:

Your eyes have seen all that the LORD did in Egypt to Pharaoh, to all his officials and to all his land. ³With your own eyes you saw those great trials, those miraculous signs and great wonders. ⁴But to this day the LORD has not given you a mind that understands or eyes that see or ears that hear. ⁵During the forty years that I led you through the desert, your clothes did not wear out, nor did the sandals on your feet. ⁶You ate no bread and drank no wine or other fermented drink. I did this so that you might know that I am the LORD your God.

⁷When you reached this place, Sihon king of Heshbon and Og king of Bashan came out to fight against us, but we defeated them. ⁸We took their land and gave it as an inheritance to the Reubenites, the Gadites and the half-tribe of Manasseh.

⁹Carefully follow the terms of this covenant, so that you may prosper in everything you do. ¹⁰All of you are standing today in the presence of the LORD your God—your leaders and chief men, your elders and officials, and all the other men of Israel, ¹¹together with your children and your wives, and the aliens living in your camps who chop your wood and carry your water. ¹²You are standing here in order to enter into a covenant with the LORD your God, a covenant the LORD is

making with you this day and sealing with you an oath, [13]to confirm you this day as his people, that he may be your God as he promised you and as he swore to your fathers, Abraham, Isaac and Jacob. [14]I am making this covenant, with its oath, not only with you [15]who are standing here with us today in the presence of the LORD our God but also with those who are not here today.

[16]You yourselves know how we lived in Egypt and how we passed through the countries on the way here. [17]You saw among them their detestable images and idols of wood and stone, of silver and gold. [18]Make sure there is no man or woman, clan or tribe among you today whose heart turns away from the LORD our God to go and worship the gods of those nations; make sure there is no root among you that produces such bitter poison.

[19]When such a person hears the words of this oath, he invokes a blessing on himself and therefore thinks, "I will be safe, even though I persist in going my own way." This will bring disaster on the watered land as well as the dry.[a] [20]The LORD will never be willing to forgive him; his wrath and zeal will burn against that man. All the curses written in this book will fall upon him, and the LORD will blot out his name from under heaven. [21]The LORD will single him out from all the tribes of Israel for disaster, according to all the curses of the covenant written in this Book of the Law.

[22]Your children who follow you in later generations and foreigners who come from distant lands will see the calamities that have fallen on the land and the diseases with which the LORD has afflicted it. [23]The whole land will be a burning waste of salt and sulfur—nothing planted, nothing sprouting, no vegetation growing on it. It will be like the destruction of Sodom and Gomorrah, Admah and Zeboiim, which the LORD overthrew in fierce anger. [24]All the nations will ask: "Why has the LORD done this to this land? Why this fierce, burning anger?"

[25]And the answer will be: "It is because this people abandoned the covenant of the LORD, the God of their fathers, the covenant he made with them when he brought them out of Egypt. [26]They went off and worshiped other gods and bowed down to them, gods they did not know, gods he had not given them. [27]Therefore the LORD's anger burned against this land, so that he brought on it all the curses written in this book. [28]In furious anger and in great wrath the LORD uprooted them from their land and thrust them into another land, as it is now."

[29]The secret things belong to the LORD our God, but the things revealed belong to us and to our children forever, that we may follow all the words of this law.

Prosperity After Turning to the LORD

30 When all these blessings and curses I have set before you come upon you and you take them to heart wherever the LORD your God disperses you among the nations, [2]and when you and your children return to the LORD your God and obey him with all your heart and with all your soul according to everything I command you today, [3]then the LORD your God will restore your fortunes[b] and have compassion on you and gather you again from all the nations where he scattered you. [4]Even if you have been banished to the most distant land under the heavens, from there the LORD your God will gather you and bring you back. [5]He will bring you to the land that belonged to your fathers, and you will take possession of it. He will make you more prosperous and numerous than your fathers. [6]The LORD your God will circumcise your hearts and the hearts of your descendants, so that you may love him with all your heart and with all your soul, and live. [7]The LORD your God will put all these curses on your enemies who hate and persecute you. [8]You will again obey the LORD and follow all his commands I am giving you today. [9]Then the LORD your God will make you most prosperous in all the work of your hands and in the fruit of your womb, the young of your livestock and the crops of your land. The LORD will again delight in you and make you prosperous, just as he delighted in your fathers, [10]if you obey the LORD your God and keep his commands and decrees

[a]19 Or way, in order to add drunkenness to thirst."   [b]3 Or will bring you back from captivity

that are written in this Book of the Law and turn to the LORD your God with all your heart and with all your soul.

The Offer of Life or Death

11Now what I am commanding you today is not too difficult for you or beyond your reach. 12It is not up in heaven, so that you have to ask, "Who will ascend into heaven to get it and proclaim it to us so we may obey it?" 13Nor is it beyond the sea, so that you have to ask, "Who will cross the sea to get it and proclaim it to us so we may obey it?" 14No, the word is very near you; it is in your mouth and in your heart so you may obey it.

15See, I set before you today life and prosperity, death and destruction. 16For I command you today to love the LORD your God, to walk in his ways, and to keep his commands, decrees and laws; then you will live and increase, and the LORD your God will bless you in the land you are entering to possess.

17But if your heart turns away and you are not obedient, and if you are drawn away to bow down to other gods and worship them, 18I declare to you this day that you will certainly be destroyed. You will not live long in the land you are crossing the Jordan to enter and possess.

19This day I call heaven and earth as witnesses against you that I have set before you life and death, blessings and curses. Now choose life, so that you and your children may live 20and that you may love the LORD your God, listen to his voice, and hold fast to him. For the LORD is your life, and he will give you many years in the land he swore to give to your fathers, Abraham, Isaac and Jacob.

Joshua to Succeed Moses

31 Then Moses went out and spoke these words to all Israel: 2"I am now a hundred and twenty years old and I am no longer able to lead you. The LORD has said to me, 'You shall not cross the Jordan.' 3The LORD your God himself will cross over ahead of you. He will destroy these nations before you, and you will take possession of their land. Joshua also will cross over ahead of you, as the LORD said. 4And the LORD will do to them what he did to Sihon and Og, the kings of the Amorites, whom he destroyed along with their land. 5The LORD will deliver them to you, and you must do to them all that I have commanded you. 6Be strong and courageous. Do not be afraid or terrified because of them, for the LORD your God goes with you; he will never leave you nor forsake you."

7Then Moses summoned Joshua and said to him in the presence of all Israel, "Be strong and courageous, for you must go with this people into the land that the LORD swore to their forefathers to give them, and you must divide it among them as their inheritance. 8The LORD himself goes before you and will be with you; he will never leave you nor forsake you. Do not be afraid; do not be discouraged."

The Reading of the Law

9So Moses wrote down this law and gave it to the priests, the sons of Levi, who carried the ark of the covenant of the LORD, and to all the elders of Israel. 10Then Moses commanded them: "At the end of every seven years, in the year for canceling debts, during the Feast of Tabernacles, 11when all Israel comes to appear before the LORD your God at the place he will choose, you shall read this law before them in their hearing. 12Assemble the people—men, women and children, and the aliens living in your towns—so they can listen and learn to fear the LORD your God and follow carefully all the words of this law. 13Their children, who do not know this law, must hear it and learn to fear the LORD your God as long as you live in the land you are crossing the Jordan to possess."

Israel's Rebellion Predicted

14The LORD said to Moses, "Now the day of your death is near. Call Joshua and present yourselves at the Tent of Meeting, where I will commission him." So Moses and Joshua came and presented themselves at the Tent of Meeting.

15Then the LORD appeared at the Tent in a pillar of cloud, and the cloud stood over the entrance to the Tent. 16And the LORD said to Moses: "You are going to rest with your fathers, and these people will soon prostitute themselves to the foreign gods of the land they are entering. They will forsake me and break the covenant I made with them. ¹⁷On that day I will become angry with them and forsake them; I will hide my face from them, and they will be destroyed. Many disasters and difficulties will come upon them, and on that day they will ask, 'Have not these disasters come upon us because our God is not with us?' ¹⁸And I will certainly hide my face on that day because of all their wickedness in turning to other gods.

¹⁹"Now write down for yourselves this song and teach it to the Israelites and have them sing it, so that it may be a witness for me against them. ²⁰When I have brought them into the land flowing with milk and honey, the land I promised on oath to their forefathers, and when they eat their fill and thrive, they will turn to other gods and worship them, rejecting me and breaking my covenant. ²¹And when many disasters and difficulties come upon them, this song will testify against them, because it will not be forgotten by their descendants. I know what they are disposed to do, even before I bring them into the land I promised them on oath." ²²So Moses wrote down this song that day and taught it to the Israelites.

²³The LORD gave this command to Joshua son of Nun: "Be strong and courageous, for you will bring the Israelites into the land I promised them on oath, and I myself will be with you."

²⁴After Moses finished writing in a book the words of this law from beginning to end, ²⁵he gave this command to the Levites who carried the ark of the covenant of the LORD: ²⁶"Take this Book of the Law and place it beside the ark of the covenant of the LORD your God. There it will remain as a witness against you. ²⁷For I know how rebellious and stiff-necked you are. If you have been rebellious against the LORD while I am still alive and with you, how much more will you rebel after I die! ²⁸Assemble before me all the elders of your tribes and all your officials, so that I can speak these words in their hearing and call heaven and earth to testify against them. ²⁹For I know that after my death you are sure to become utterly corrupt and to turn from the way I have commanded you. In days

to come, disaster will fall upon you because you will do evil in the sight of the LORD and provoke him to anger by what your hands have made."

The Song of Moses

³⁰And Moses recited the words of this song from beginning to end in the hearing of the whole assembly of Israel:

32 Listen, O heavens, and I will speak;
 hear, O earth, the words of my mouth.
² Let my teaching fall like rain
 and my words descend like dew,
 like showers on new grass,
 like abundant rain on tender plants.

³ I will proclaim the name of the LORD.
 Oh, praise the greatness of our God!
⁴ He is the Rock, his works are perfect,
 and all his ways are just.
 A faithful God who does no wrong,
 upright and just is he.

⁵ They have acted corruptly toward him;
 to their shame they are no longer his children,
 but a warped and crooked generation.ᵃ
⁶ Is this the way you repay the LORD,
 O foolish and unwise people?
 Is he not your Father, your Creator,ᵇ
 who made you and formed you?

⁷ Remember the days of old;
 consider the generations long past.
 Ask your father and he will tell you,
 your elders, and they will explain to you.
⁸ When the Most High gave the nations their inheritance,
 when he divided all mankind,
 he set up boundaries for the peoples
 according to the number of the sons of Israel.ᶜ
⁹ For the LORD's portion is his people,
 Jacob his allotted inheritance.

ᵃ5 Or *Corrupt are they and not his children, / a generation warped and twisted to their shame* ᵇ6 Or *Father, who bought you* ᶜ8 Masoretic Text; Dead Sea Scrolls (see also Septuagint) *sons of God*

Whatever It Takes

31:30 AND MOSES RECITED THE WORDS OF THIS SONG.

What makes this song so remarkable are two things. One is the audience. It is sung before the whole assembly of Israel, and much of it is sharply critical of how ungrateful the Israelites have been over the last 40 years. God has been inexpressibly good, and the thanks he gets are rebellion and faithlessness from the very people he has been so generous to. The song is a combination of praise and indictment: "I will proclaim the name of the LORD. Oh, praise the greatness of our God! He is the Rock, his works are perfect, and all his ways are just. A faithful God who does no wrong, upright and just is he. They have acted corruptly toward him; to their shame they are no longer his children, but a warped and crooked generation." (32:3–5). This theme is repeated many times. The people were probably not humming along as Moses sang.

The second remarkable thing about this song is the subject, God, and the extraordinary variety of ways he dealt with the people he came to save. Two stand out, very different from each other. On the one hand, God "shielded [Israel] and cared for him; he guarded him as the apple of his eye" (verse 10). The word translated "apple" is literally "little man of his eye." The "little man" is the pupil, the delicate and vulnerable inner part of the eye that we reflexively protect. God has protected and shielded his people with the gentle and solicitous care we give our own eyes.

On the other hand, God has been "like an eagle that stirs up its nest and hovers over its young, that spreads its wings to catch them and carries them on its pinions" (verse 11). Mother eagles teach their young to fly by stirring up and essentially destroying the nest their little eaglets have been so comfortable in. Not a pleasant process, but the young won't leave home without such a disruption. Then the eagle takes each eaglet upon her back, throws them off and lets them fall, to force them to use their wings. Against their will, the young learn to fly. Again, not a pleasant process, but the only way to make a lazy little eaglet—or child of God—fly.

God's dealings with us run the gamut from gentle to rough, tender to tough, teaching to terror (32:2,25); whatever it takes. We are unworthy of his love and often ungrateful for it, but he continues to love anyway. And for that, we may sing along with Moses.

PRAY:

Spirit of the living God, fall afresh on me.
Break me, mold me, fill me, use me.
Spirit of the living God, fall afresh on me.[2]

FOR YOUR NEXT DEVOTIONAL READING, GO TO PAGE 244.

¹⁰ In a desert land he found him,
  in a barren and howling waste.
He shielded him and cared for him;
  he guarded him as the apple of
    his eye,
¹¹ like an eagle that stirs up its nest
  and hovers over its young,
that spreads its wings to catch them
  and carries them on its pinions.
¹² The LORD alone led him;
  no foreign god was with him.

¹³ He made him ride on the heights
    of the land
  and fed him with the fruit of the
    fields.
He nourished him with honey from
    the rock,
  and with oil from the flinty crag,
¹⁴ with curds and milk from herd
    and flock
  and with fattened lambs and
    goats,
with choice rams of Bashan
  and the finest kernels of wheat.
You drank the foaming blood of
    the grape.

¹⁵ Jeshurun*a* grew fat and kicked;
  filled with food, he became heavy
    and sleek.
He abandoned the God who made
    him
  and rejected the Rock his Savior.
¹⁶ They made him jealous with their
    foreign gods
  and angered him with their
    detestable idols.
¹⁷ They sacrificed to demons, which
    are not God—
  gods they had not known,
  gods that recently appeared,
  gods your fathers did not fear.
¹⁸ You deserted the Rock, who
    fathered you;
  you forgot the God who gave you
    birth.

¹⁹ The LORD saw this and rejected them
  because he was angered by his
    sons and daughters.
²⁰ "I will hide my face from them,"
    he said,
  "and see what their end will be;
for they are a perverse generation,
  children who are unfaithful.

²¹ They made me jealous by what is
    no god
  and angered me with their
    worthless idols.
I will make them envious by those
  who are not a people;
  I will make them angry by a nation
    that has no understanding.
²² For a fire has been kindled by my
    wrath,
  one that burns to the realm of
    death*b* below.
It will devour the earth and its
    harvests
  and set afire the foundations of
    the mountains.

²³ "I will heap calamities upon them
  and spend my arrows against them.
²⁴ I will send wasting famine against
    them,
  consuming pestilence and deadly
    plague;
I will send against them the fangs of
    wild beasts,
  the venom of vipers that glide in
    the dust.
²⁵ In the street the sword will make
    them childless;
  in their homes terror will reign.
Young men and young women
  will perish,
  infants and gray-haired men.
²⁶ I said I would scatter them
  and blot out their memory from
    mankind,
²⁷ but I dreaded the taunt of the enemy,
  lest the adversary misunderstand
and say, 'Our hand has triumphed;
  the LORD has not done all this.'"

²⁸ They are a nation without sense,
  there is no discernment in them.
²⁹ If only they were wise and would
    understand this
  and discern what their end will be!
³⁰ How could one man chase a
    thousand,
  or two put ten thousand to flight,
unless their Rock had sold them,
  unless the LORD had given them up?
³¹ For their rock is not like our Rock,
  as even our enemies concede.

---

*a*15 *Jeshurun* means *the upright one*, that is,
Israel.   *b*22 Hebrew *to Sheol*

32 Their vine comes from the vine of
Sodom
and from the fields of Gomorrah.
Their grapes are filled with poison,
and their clusters with bitterness.
33 Their wine is the venom of serpents,
the deadly poison of cobras.

34 "Have I not kept this in reserve
and sealed it in my vaults?
35 It is mine to avenge; I will repay.
In due time their foot will slip;
their day of disaster is near
and their doom rushes upon them."

36 The LORD will judge his people
and have compassion on his
servants
when he sees their strength is gone
and no one is left, slave or free.
37 He will say: "Now where are
their gods,
the rock they took refuge in,
38 the gods who ate the fat of their
sacrifices
and drank the wine of their drink
offerings?
Let them rise up to help you!
Let them give you shelter!

39 "See now that I myself am He!
There is no god besides me.
I put to death and I bring to life,
I have wounded and I will heal,
and no one can deliver out of
my hand.
40 I lift my hand to heaven and declare:
As surely as I live forever,
41 when I sharpen my flashing sword
and my hand grasps it in judgment,
I will take vengeance on my
adversaries
and repay those who hate me.
42 I will make my arrows drunk with
blood,
while my sword devours flesh:
the blood of the slain and the
captives,
the heads of the enemy leaders."

43 Rejoice, O nations, with his people,[a,b]
for he will avenge the blood of his
servants;
he will take vengeance on his
enemies
and make atonement for his land
and people.

44 Moses came with Joshua[c] son of Nun
and spoke all the words of this song in
the hearing of the people. 45 When Moses finished reciting all these words to
all Israel, 46 he said to them, "Take to
heart all the words I have solemnly declared to you this day, so that you may
command your children to obey carefully all the words of this law. 47 They are
not just idle words for you—they are
your life. By them you will live long in
the land you are crossing the Jordan to
possess."

Moses to Die on Mount Nebo

48 On that same day the LORD told Moses, 49 "Go up into the Abarim Range to
Mount Nebo in Moab, across from Jericho, and view Canaan, the land I am giving the Israelites as their own possession.
50 There on the mountain that you have
climbed you will die and be gathered to
your people, just as your brother Aaron
died on Mount Hor and was gathered to
his people. 51 This is because both of you
broke faith with me in the presence of
the Israelites at the waters of Meribah
Kadesh in the Desert of Zin and because
you did not uphold my holiness among
the Israelites. 52 Therefore, you will see
the land only from a distance; you will
not enter the land I am giving to the people of Israel."

Moses Blesses the Tribes

33 This is the blessing that Moses the
man of God pronounced on the Israelites before his death. 2 He said:

"The LORD came from Sinai
and dawned over them from Seir;
he shone forth from Mount Paran.
He came with[d] myriads of holy ones
from the south, from his mountain
slopes.[e]
3 Surely it is you who love the people;
all the holy ones are in your hand.
At your feet they all bow down,
and from you receive instruction,

---

[a]43 Or *Make his people rejoice, O nations*
[b]43 Masoretic Text; Dead Sea Scrolls (see also
Septuagint) *people, / and let all the angels
worship him /*   [c]44 Hebrew *Hoshea*, a variant
of *Joshua*   [d]2 Or *from*   [e]2 The meaning of
the Hebrew for this phrase is uncertain.

⁴the law that Moses gave us,
  the possession of the assembly
    of Jacob.
⁵He was king over Jeshurun*ᵃ*
  when the leaders of the people
    assembled,
  along with the tribes of Israel.

⁶"Let Reuben live and not die,
  nor*ᵇ* his men be few."

⁷And this he said about Judah:

"Hear, O Lᴏʀᴅ, the cry of Judah;
  bring him to his people.
With his own hands he defends
    his cause.
  Oh, be his help against his foes!"

⁸About Levi he said:

"Your Thummim and Urim belong
  to the man you favored.
You tested him at Massah;
  you contended with him at the
    waters of Meribah.
⁹He said of his father and mother,
  'I have no regard for them.'
He did not recognize his brothers
  or acknowledge his own
    children,
but he watched over your word
  and guarded your covenant.
¹⁰He teaches your precepts to Jacob
  and your law to Israel.
He offers incense before you
  and whole burnt offerings on
    your altar.
¹¹Bless all his skills, O Lᴏʀᴅ,
  and be pleased with the work of
    his hands.
Smite the loins of those who rise up
    against him;
  strike his foes till they rise no
    more."

¹²About Benjamin he said:

"Let the beloved of the Lᴏʀᴅ rest
    secure in him,
  for he shields him all day long,
  and the one the Lᴏʀᴅ loves rests
    between his shoulders."

¹³About Joseph he said:

"May the Lᴏʀᴅ bless his land
  with the precious dew from heaven
    above

and with the deep waters that
    lie below;
¹⁴with the best the sun brings forth
  and the finest the moon can yield;
¹⁵with the choicest gifts of the ancient
    mountains
  and the fruitfulness of the
    everlasting hills;
¹⁶with the best gifts of the earth and its
    fullness
  and the favor of him who dwelt in
    the burning bush.
Let all these rest on the head of
    Joseph,
  on the brow of the prince among*ᶜ*
    his brothers.
¹⁷In majesty he is like a firstborn bull;
  his horns are the horns of a
    wild ox.
With them he will gore the nations,
  even those at the ends of the earth.
Such are the ten thousands of
    Ephraim;
  such are the thousands of
    Manasseh."

¹⁸About Zebulun he said:

"Rejoice, Zebulun, in your going out,
  and you, Issachar, in your tents.
¹⁹They will summon peoples to the
    mountain
  and there offer sacrifices of
    righteousness;
they will feast on the abundance of
    the seas,
  on the treasures hidden in
    the sand."

²⁰About Gad he said:

"Blessed is he who enlarges Gad's
    domain!
Gad lives there like a lion,
  tearing at arm or head.
²¹He chose the best land for himself;
  the leader's portion was kept for
    him.
When the heads of the people
    assembled,
  he carried out the Lᴏʀᴅ's righteous
    will,
  and his judgments concerning
    Israel."

ᵃ5 Jeshurun means *the upright one,* that is, Israel;
also in verse 26. *ᵇ6* Or *but let* *ᶜ16* Or *of
the one separated from*

> "*THE eternal God is your refuge, and underneath are the everlasting arms. He will drive out your enemy before you, saying, 'Destroy him!'*"
>
> DEUTERONOMY 33:27

22About Dan he said:

"Dan is a lion's cub,
 springing out of Bashan."

23About Naphtali he said:

"Naphtali is abounding with the favor
   of the LORD
 and is full of his blessing;
 he will inherit southward to
   the lake."

24About Asher he said:

"Most blessed of sons is Asher;
 let him be favored by his brothers,
 and let him bathe his feet in oil.
25 The bolts of your gates will be iron
     and bronze,
 and your strength will equal
     your days.

26 "There is no one like the God of
     Jeshurun,
 who rides on the heavens to
     help you
 and on the clouds in his majesty.
27 The eternal God is your refuge,
 and underneath are the everlasting
     arms.
 He will drive out your enemy
     before you,
 saying, 'Destroy him!'
28 So Israel will live in safety alone;
 Jacob's spring is secure
 in a land of grain and new wine,
 where the heavens drop dew.
29 Blessed are you, O Israel!
 Who is like you,
 a people saved by the LORD?
 He is your shield and helper
 and your glorious sword.

Your enemies will cower before you,
 and you will trample down their
   high places.*a*"

The Death of Moses

34 Then Moses climbed Mount Nebo from the plains of Moab to the top of Pisgah, across from Jericho. There the LORD showed him the whole land—from Gilead to Dan, 2all of Naphtali, the territory of Ephraim and Manasseh, all the land of Judah as far as the western sea,*b* 3the Negev and the whole region from the Valley of Jericho, the City of Palms, as far as Zoar. 4Then the LORD said to him, "This is the land I promised on oath to Abraham, Isaac and Jacob when I said, 'I will give it to your descendants.' I have let you see it with your eyes, but you will not cross over into it."

5And Moses the servant of the LORD died there in Moab, as the LORD had said. 6He buried him*c* in Moab, in the valley opposite Beth Peor, but to this day no one knows where his grave is. 7Moses was a hundred and twenty years old when he died, yet his eyes were not weak nor his strength gone. 8The Israelites grieved for Moses in the plains of Moab thirty days, until the time of weeping and mourning was over.

9Now Joshua son of Nun was filled with the spirit*d* of wisdom because Moses had laid his hands on him. So the Israelites listened to him and did what the LORD had commanded Moses.

10Since then, no prophet has risen in Israel like Moses, whom the LORD knew face to face, 11who did all those miraculous signs and wonders the LORD sent him to do in Egypt—to Pharaoh and to all his officials and to his whole land. 12For no one has ever shown the mighty power or performed the awesome deeds that Moses did in the sight of all Israel.

a29 Or *will tread upon their bodies*   *b2* That is, the Mediterranean   *c6* Or *He was buried*   *d9* Or *Spirit*

Joshua

A YOUNG pastor asked a wise mentor, an older pastor, what his best advice was for someone beginning in Christian ministry. Without hesitation, the older pastor answered, "Don't take it personally."

"Don't take what personally?" the younger pastor asked.

"Don't take it personally when the work of God seems like fighting a battle," the mentor replied. "It isn't about you; it's about God."

The young pastor thought about it. Of course, a soldier doesn't get his feelings hurt when the enemy shoots at him. He doesn't look over the top of his foxhole and shout, "Was it something I said?" It's a war, and getting shot at goes with the territory.

More than any other book of the Bible, we owe the war imagery of the Christian life to the book of Joshua. The story of Joshua is the story of holy war. It was Joshua's calling to lead the people of Israel in battle for the land that was their inheritance.

> "BUT AS FOR ME AND MY HOUSEHOLD, WE WILL SERVE THE LORD." (24:15)

In the Greek language of the New Testament period, the name *Joshua* is rendered "Jesus." Jesus is a "Joshua" but greater than Joshua. The inheritance he secured is greater than anything Joshua accomplished (see 1 Peter 1:3–5). And the battle we fight is different from the battles Israel fought. "For though we live in the world, we do not wage war as the world does. The weapons we fight with are not the weapons of the world. On the contrary, they have divine power to demolish strongholds. We demolish arguments and every pretension that sets itself up against the knowledge of God, and we take captive every thought to make it obedient to Christ" (2 Corinthians 10:3–5).

The qualities of faith and character necessary for fighting the good fight remain the same as they were when Joshua and the army of Israel began their assault on Canaan: "Be strong and very courageous ... Do not let this Book of the Law depart from your mouth; meditate on it day and night, so that you may be careful to do everything written in it. Then you will be prosperous and successful" (Joshua 1:7–8). Our greatest weapons are the courage to pray and to proclaim the Word of God.

The LORD Commands Joshua

1 After the death of Moses the servant of the LORD, the LORD said to Joshua son of Nun, Moses' aide: ²"Moses my servant is dead. Now then, you and all these people, get ready to cross the Jordan River into the land I am about to give to them—to the Israelites. ³I will give you every place where you set your foot, as I promised Moses. ⁴Your territory will extend from the desert to Lebanon, and from the great river, the Euphrates—all the Hittite country—to the Great Sea[a] on the west. ⁵No one will be able to stand up against you all the days of your life. As I was with Moses, so I will be with you; I will never leave you nor forsake you.

⁶"Be strong and courageous, because you will lead these people to inherit the land I swore to their forefathers to give them. ⁷Be strong and very courageous. Be careful to obey all the law my servant Moses gave you; do not turn from it to the right or to the left, that you may be successful wherever you go. ⁸Do not let this Book of the Law depart from your mouth; meditate on it day and night, so that you may be careful to do everything written in it. Then you will be prosperous and successful. ⁹Have I not commanded you? Be strong and courageous. Do not be terrified; do not be discouraged, for the LORD your God will be with you wherever you go."

¹⁰So Joshua ordered the officers of the people: ¹¹"Go through the camp and tell the people, 'Get your supplies ready. Three days from now you will cross the Jordan here to go in and take possession of the land the LORD your God is giving you for your own.'"

¹²But to the Reubenites, the Gadites and the half-tribe of Manasseh, Joshua said, ¹³"Remember the command that Moses the servant of the LORD gave you: 'The LORD your God is giving you rest and has granted you this land.' ¹⁴Your wives, your children and your livestock may stay in the land that Moses gave you east of the Jordan, but all your fighting men, fully armed, must cross over ahead of your brothers. You are to help your brothers ¹⁵until the LORD gives them rest, as he has done for you, and until they too

have taken possession of the land that the LORD your God is giving them. After that, you may go back and occupy your own land, which Moses the servant of the LORD gave you east of the Jordan toward the sunrise."

¹⁶Then they answered Joshua, "Whatever you have commanded us we will do, and wherever you send us we will go. ¹⁷Just as we fully obeyed Moses, so we will obey you. Only may the LORD your God be with you as he was with Moses. ¹⁸Whoever rebels against your word and does not obey your words, whatever you may command them, will be put to death. Only be strong and courageous!"

Rahab and the Spies

2 Then Joshua son of Nun secretly sent two spies from Shittim. "Go, look over the land," he said, "especially Jericho." So they went and entered the house of a prostitute[b] named Rahab and stayed there.

> *You know the value of prayer: It is precious beyond all price. Never, never neglect it.*
>
> SIR THOMAS BUXTON

²The king of Jericho was told, "Look! Some of the Israelites have come here tonight to spy out the land." ³So the king of Jericho sent this message to Rahab: "Bring out the men who came to you and entered your house, because they have come to spy out the whole land."

⁴But the woman had taken the two men and hidden them. She said, "Yes, the men came to me, but I did not know where they had come from. ⁵At dusk, when it was time to close the city gate, the men left. I don't know which way they went. Go after them quickly. You may catch up with them." ⁶(But she had taken them up to the roof and hidden them under the stalks of flax she had laid out on the roof.) ⁷So the men set out in pursuit of the spies on the road that leads to the fords of the Jordan, and as

---

[a] 4 That is, the Mediterranean   [b] 1 Or possibly an innkeeper

soon as the pursuers had gone out, the gate was shut.

⁸Before the spies lay down for the night, she went up on the roof ⁹and said to them, "I know that the LORD has given this land to you and that a great fear of you has fallen on us, so that all who live in this country are melting in fear because of you. ¹⁰We have heard how the LORD dried up the water of the Red Sea*ᵃ* for you when you came out of Egypt, and what you did to Sihon and Og, the two kings of the Amorites east of the Jordan, whom you completely destroyed.*ᵇ* ¹¹When we heard of it, our hearts melted and everyone's courage failed because of you, for the LORD your God is God in heaven above and on the earth below. ¹²Now then, please swear to me by the LORD that you will show kindness to my family, because I have shown kindness to you. Give me a sure sign ¹³that you will spare the lives of my father and mother, my brothers and sisters, and all who belong to them, and that you will save us from death."

¹⁴"Our lives for your lives!" the men assured her. "If you don't tell what we are doing, we will treat you kindly and faithfully when the LORD gives us the land."

¹⁵So she let them down by a rope through the window, for the house she lived in was part of the city wall. ¹⁶Now she had said to them, "Go to the hills so the pursuers will not find you. Hide yourselves there three days until they return, and then go on your way."

¹⁷The men said to her, "This oath you made us swear will not be binding on us ¹⁸unless, when we enter the land, you have tied this scarlet cord in the window through which you let us down, and unless you have brought your father and mother, your brothers and all your family into your house. ¹⁹If anyone goes outside your house into the street, his blood will be on his own head; we will not be responsible. As for anyone who is in the house with you, his blood will be on our head if a hand is laid on him. ²⁰But if you tell what we are doing, we will be released from the oath you made us swear."

²¹"Agreed," she replied. "Let it be as you say." So she sent them away and they departed. And she tied the scarlet cord in the window.

²²When they left, they went into the hills and stayed there three days, until the pursuers had searched all along the road and returned without finding them. ²³Then the two men started back. They went down out of the hills, forded the river and came to Joshua son of Nun and told him everything that had happened to them. ²⁴They said to Joshua, "The LORD has surely given the whole land into our hands; all the people are melting in fear because of us."

Crossing the Jordan

3 Early in the morning Joshua and all the Israelites set out from Shittim and went to the Jordan, where they camped before crossing over. ²After three days the officers went throughout the camp, ³giving orders to the people: "When you see the ark of the covenant of the LORD your God, and the priests, who are Levites, carrying it, you are to move out from your positions and follow it. ⁴Then you will know which way to go, since you have never been this way before. But keep a distance of about a thousand yards*ᶜ* between you and the ark; do not go near it."

⁵Joshua told the people, "Consecrate yourselves, for tomorrow the LORD will do amazing things among you."

⁶Joshua said to the priests, "Take up the ark of the covenant and pass on ahead of the people." So they took it up and went ahead of them.

⁷And the LORD said to Joshua, "Today I will begin to exalt you in the eyes of all Israel, so they may know that I am with you as I was with Moses. ⁸Tell the priests who carry the ark of the covenant: 'When you reach the edge of the Jordan's waters, go and stand in the river.'"

⁹Joshua said to the Israelites, "Come here and listen to the words of the LORD your God. ¹⁰This is how you will know that the living God is among you and that he will certainly drive out before you the Canaanites, Hittites, Hivites, Perizzites, Girgashites, Amorites and Jebusites. ¹¹See, the ark of the covenant of the Lord

ᵃ10 Hebrew *Yam Suph*; that is, Sea of Reeds
ᵇ10 The Hebrew term refers to the irrevocable giving over of things or persons to the LORD, often by totally destroying them.   *ᶜ4* Hebrew *about two thousand cubits* (about 900 meters)

of all the earth will go into the Jordan ahead of you. ¹²Now then, choose twelve men from the tribes of Israel, one from each tribe. ¹³And as soon as the priests who carry the ark of the LORD—the Lord of all the earth—set foot in the Jordan, its waters flowing downstream will be cut off and stand up in a heap."

¹⁴So when the people broke camp to cross the Jordan, the priests carrying the ark of the covenant went ahead of them. ¹⁵Now the Jordan is at flood stage all during harvest. Yet as soon as the priests who carried the ark reached the Jordan and their feet touched the water's edge, ¹⁶the water from upstream stopped flowing. It piled up in a heap a great distance away, at a town called Adam in the vicinity of Zarethan, while the water flowing down to the Sea of the Arabah (the Salt Seaᵃ) was completely cut off. So the people crossed over opposite Jericho. ¹⁷The priests who carried the ark of the covenant of the LORD stood firm on dry ground in the middle of the Jordan, while all Israel passed by until the whole nation had completed the crossing on dry ground.

4 When the whole nation had finished crossing the Jordan, the LORD said to Joshua, ²"Choose twelve men from among the people, one from each tribe, ³and tell them to take up twelve stones from the middle of the Jordan from right where the priests stood and to carry them over with you and put them down at the place where you stay tonight."

⁴So Joshua called together the twelve men he had appointed from the Israelites, one from each tribe, ⁵and said to them, "Go over before the ark of the LORD your God into the middle of the Jordan. Each of you is to take up a stone on his shoulder, according to the number of the tribes of the Israelites, ⁶to serve as a sign among you. In the future, when your children ask you, 'What do these stones mean?' ⁷tell them that the flow of the Jordan was cut off before the ark of the covenant of the LORD. When it crossed the Jordan, the waters of the Jordan were cut off. These stones are to be a memorial to the people of Israel forever."

⁸So the Israelites did as Joshua commanded them. They took twelve stones from the middle of the Jordan, according to the number of the tribes of the Israelites, as the LORD had told Joshua; and they carried them over with them to their camp, where they put them down. ⁹Joshua set up the twelve stones that had beenᵇ in the middle of the Jordan at the spot where the priests who carried the ark of the covenant had stood. And they are there to this day.

¹⁰Now the priests who carried the ark remained standing in the middle of the Jordan until everything the LORD had commanded Joshua was done by the people, just as Moses had directed Joshua. The people hurried over, ¹¹and as soon as all of them had crossed, the ark of the LORD and the priests came to the other side while the people watched. ¹²The men of Reuben, Gad and the half-tribe of Manasseh crossed over, armed, in front of the Israelites, as Moses had directed them. ¹³About forty thousand armed for battle crossed over before the LORD to the plains of Jericho for war.

¹⁴That day the LORD exalted Joshua in the sight of all Israel; and they revered him all the days of his life, just as they had revered Moses.

¹⁵Then the LORD said to Joshua, ¹⁶"Command the priests carrying the ark of the Testimony to come up out of the Jordan."

¹⁷So Joshua commanded the priests, "Come up out of the Jordan."

¹⁸And the priests came up out of the river carrying the ark of the covenant of the LORD. No sooner had they set their feet on the dry ground than the waters of the Jordan returned to their place and ran at flood stage as before.

¹⁹On the tenth day of the first month the people went up from the Jordan and camped at Gilgal on the eastern border of Jericho. ²⁰And Joshua set up at Gilgal the twelve stones they had taken out of the Jordan. ²¹He said to the Israelites, "In the future when your descendants ask their fathers, 'What do these stones mean?' ²²tell them, 'Israel crossed the Jordan on dry ground.' ²³For the LORD your God dried up the Jordan before you until you had crossed over. The LORD your God did to the Jordan just what he

---

ᵃ16 That is, the Dead Sea   ᵇ9 Or Joshua also set up twelve stones

had done to the Red Sea[a] when he dried it up before us until we had crossed over. [24]He did this so that all the peoples of the earth might know that the hand of the LORD is powerful and so that you might always fear the LORD your God."

Circumcision at Gilgal

5 Now when all the Amorite kings west of the Jordan and all the Canaanite kings along the coast heard how the LORD had dried up the Jordan before the Israelites until we had crossed over, their hearts melted and they no longer had the courage to face the Israelites.

[2]At that time the LORD said to Joshua, "Make flint knives and circumcise the Israelites again." [3]So Joshua made flint knives and circumcised the Israelites at Gibeath Haaraloth.[b]

[4]Now this is why he did so: All those who came out of Egypt—all the men of military age—died in the desert on the way after leaving Egypt. [5]All the people that came out had been circumcised, but all the people born in the desert during the journey from Egypt had not. [6]The Israelites had moved about in the desert forty years until all the men who were of military age when they left Egypt had died, since they had not obeyed the LORD. For the LORD had sworn to them that they would not see the land that he had solemnly promised their fathers to give us, a land flowing with milk and honey. [7]So he raised up their sons in their place, and these were the ones Joshua circumcised. They were still uncircumcised because they had not been circumcised on the way. [8]And after the whole nation had been circumcised, they remained where they were in camp until they were healed.

[9]Then the LORD said to Joshua, "Today I have rolled away the reproach of Egypt from you." So the place has been called Gilgal[c] to this day.

[10]On the evening of the fourteenth day of the month, while camped at Gilgal on the plains of Jericho, the Israelites celebrated the Passover. [11]The day after the Passover, that very day, they ate some of the produce of the land: unleavened bread and roasted grain. [12]The manna stopped the day after[d] they ate this food from the land; there was no longer any

manna for the Israelites, but that year they ate of the produce of Canaan.

The Fall of Jericho

[13]Now when Joshua was near Jericho, he looked up and saw a man standing in front of him with a drawn sword in his hand. Joshua went up to him and asked, "Are you for us or for our enemies?"

[14]"Neither," he replied, "but as commander of the army of the LORD I have now come." Then Joshua fell facedown to the ground in reverence, and asked him, "What message does my Lord[e] have for his servant?"

[15]The commander of the LORD's army replied, "Take off your sandals, for the place where you are standing is holy." And Joshua did so.

6 Now Jericho was tightly shut up because of the Israelites. No one went out and no one came in.

[2]Then the LORD said to Joshua, "See, I have delivered Jericho into your hands, along with its king and its fighting men. [3]March around the city once with all the armed men. Do this for six days. [4]Have seven priests carry trumpets of rams' horns in front of the ark. On the seventh day, march around the city seven times, with the priests blowing the trumpets. [5]When you hear them sound a long blast on the trumpets, have all the people give a loud shout; then the wall of the city will collapse and the people will go up, every man straight in."

[6]So Joshua son of Nun called the priests and said to them, "Take up the ark of the covenant of the LORD and have seven priests carry trumpets in front of it." [7]And he ordered the people, "Advance! March around the city, with the armed guard going ahead of the ark of the LORD."

[8]When Joshua had spoken to the people, the seven priests carrying the seven trumpets before the LORD went forward, blowing their trumpets, and the ark of the LORD's covenant followed them. [9]The armed guard marched ahead of the priests who blew the trumpets, and the rear guard followed the ark. All this time the

[a]23 Hebrew *Yam Suph*; that is, Sea of Reeds
[b]3 *Gibeath Haaraloth* means *hill of foreskins*.
[c]9 *Gilgal* sounds like the Hebrew for *roll*.
[d]12 Or *the day* [e]14 Or *lord*

trumpets were sounding. ¹⁰But Joshua had commanded the people, "Do not give a war cry, do not raise your voices, do not say a word until the day I tell you to shout. Then shout!" ¹¹So he had the ark of the LORD carried around the city, circling it once. Then the people returned to camp and spent the night there.

¹²Joshua got up early the next morning and the priests took up the ark of the LORD. ¹³The seven priests carrying the seven trumpets went forward, marching before the ark of the LORD and blowing the trumpets. The armed men went ahead of them and the rear guard followed the ark of the LORD, while the trumpets kept sounding. ¹⁴So on the second day they marched around the city once and returned to the camp. They did this for six days.

¹⁵On the seventh day, they got up at daybreak and marched around the city seven times in the same manner, except that on that day they circled the city seven times. ¹⁶The seventh time around, when the priests sounded the trumpet blast, Joshua commanded the people, "Shout! For the LORD has given you the city! ¹⁷The city and all that is in it are to be devoted*ᵃ* to the LORD. Only Rahab the prostitute*ᵇ* and all who are with her in her house shall be spared, because she hid the spies we sent. ¹⁸But keep away from the devoted things, so that you will

ᵃ17 The Hebrew term refers to the irrevocable giving over of things or persons to the LORD, often by totally destroying them; also in verses 18 and 21. *ᵇ17* Or possibly *innkeeper*; also in verses 22 and 25

JOSHUA 5:13–15

[**FRIDAY**]

Pray to Be on God's Side

5:13: "ARE YOU FOR US OR FOR OUR ENEMIES?"

"Pray not that God is on our side, but that we are on God's side." That saying, attributed to Abraham Lincoln, is the point of this story. Joshua is put in his place when he challenges the warrior standing in the road with a drawn sword, "Are you for us or for our enemies?" He wasn't expecting to hear, "Neither . . . but as commander of the army of the LORD I have now come." Joshua is the one who should be answering the question.

What Joshua hears is humbling, but it is also heartening. God is involved in Israel's war—actually, the war is God's, and Israel is involved in God's war. What a relief for Joshua, the rookie commander of the army. "Then Joshua fell facedown to the ground in reverence, and asked him, 'What message does my Lord have for his servant?'" Joshua may not be sure of his battle plan, but he can have absolute confidence in God. What a relief to not have to figure things out ourselves, but to submit to God in humble reverence and do his will. That's what prayer is: not asking God to do what we want, but doing what he wants. Then he lets us be a part of his great plan. God's plan will blow Joshua's mind and topple the walls of Jericho. Do you have a "Jericho" to face? Be humbled, be heartened, be prayerful.

P R A Y :

Father in heaven, rather than asking you to be on "my side,"
I commit myself to be on "your side." Help me to listen and obey
your message regarding the challenges ahead of me.

FOR YOUR NEXT DEVOTIONAL READING, GO TO PAGE 246.

THE seventh time around, when the priests sounded the trumpet blast, Joshua commanded the people, "Shout! For the LORD has given you the city!"

JOSHUA 6:16

not bring about your own destruction by taking any of them. Otherwise you will make the camp of Israel liable to destruction and bring trouble on it. ¹⁹All the silver and gold and the articles of bronze and iron are sacred to the LORD and must go into his treasury."

²⁰When the trumpets sounded, the people shouted, and at the sound of the trumpet, when the people gave a loud shout, the wall collapsed; so every man charged straight in, and they took the city. ²¹They devoted the city to the LORD and destroyed with the sword every living thing in it—men and women, young and old, cattle, sheep and donkeys.

²²Joshua said to the two men who had spied out the land, "Go into the prostitute's house and bring her out and all who belong to her, in accordance with your oath to her." ²³So the young men who had done the spying went in and brought out Rahab, her father and mother and brothers and all who belonged to her. They brought out her entire family and put them in a place outside the camp of Israel.

²⁴Then they burned the whole city and everything in it, but they put the silver and gold and the articles of bronze and iron into the treasury of the LORD's house. ²⁵But Joshua spared Rahab the prostitute, with her family and all who belonged to her, because she hid the men Joshua had sent as spies to Jericho—and she lives among the Israelites to this day.

²⁶At that time Joshua pronounced this solemn oath: "Cursed before the LORD is the man who undertakes to rebuild this city, Jericho:

"At the cost of his firstborn son
   will he lay its foundations;
at the cost of his youngest
   will he set up its gates."

²⁷So the LORD was with Joshua, and his fame spread throughout the land.

Achan's Sin

7 But the Israelites acted unfaithfully in regard to the devoted things[a]; Achan son of Carmi, the son of Zimri,[b] the son of Zerah, of the tribe of Judah, took some of them. So the LORD's anger burned against Israel.

²Now Joshua sent men from Jericho to Ai, which is near Beth Aven to the east of Bethel, and told them, "Go up and spy out the region." So the men went up and spied out Ai.

³When they returned to Joshua, they said, "Not all the people will have to go up against Ai. Send two or three thousand men to take it and do not weary all the people, for only a few men are there." ⁴So about three thousand men went up; but they were routed by the men of Ai, ⁵who killed about thirty-six of them. They chased the Israelites from the city gate as far as the stone quarries[c] and struck them down on the slopes. At this the hearts of the people melted and became like water.

⁶Then Joshua tore his clothes and fell facedown to the ground before the ark of the LORD, remaining there till evening. The elders of Israel did the same, and sprinkled dust on their heads. ⁷And Joshua said, "Ah, Sovereign LORD, why did you ever bring this people across the Jordan to deliver us into the hands of the Amorites to destroy us? If only we had been content to stay on the other side of the Jordan! ⁸O Lord, what can I say, now that Israel has been routed by its enemies? ⁹The Canaanites and the other people of the country will hear about this and they will surround us and wipe out our name from the earth. What then will you do for your own great name?"

¹⁰The LORD said to Joshua, "Stand up! What are you doing down on your face? ¹¹Israel has sinned; they have violated my covenant, which I commanded them to

---

[a]1 The Hebrew term refers to the irrevocable giving over of things or persons to the LORD, often by totally destroying them; also in verses 11, 12, 13 and 15.   [b]1 See Septuagint and 1 Chron. 2:6; Hebrew Zabdi; also in verses 17 and 18.   [c]5 Or as far as Shebarim

From Social Butterfly to Saint

"**NOTHING WAS** more easy to me now than to practice prayer. Hours passed away like moments, while I could hardly do anything else but pray. The fervency of my love allowed me no intermission … So strong, almost insatiable, was my desire for communion with God that I arose at four o'clock to pray."[1]

These are not words one would have expected to hear from the young woman who grew up to become the saintly mystic we know as Madame Guyon. Born into the pleasure-seeking class in France during the reign of Louis XIV, Mademoiselle de La Mothe (Jeanne Marie Bourvieres) possessed unusual beauty. As her mother lavished upon her clothes, jewelry and the things of the world, Jeanne read romance novels and spent hours looking at herself in the mirror. When she was 15, the La Mothe family moved near Paris where Jeanne continued to climb the social ladder.

Amid the social whirl of Paris, Jeanne married M. Jacques Guyon, a wealthy invalid 23 years her senior. The marriage was unhappy from the beginning, and thus Madame Guyon began to finally seek her true happiness in God. She was rewarded with a deep sense of God's salvation and presence, and after a mystical experience while walking the river Seine, she wrote, "From this day, this hour, if it be possible, I will be wholly the Lord's. The world shall have no portion in me." In the years that followed, trouble mounted for Madame Guyon: She went through what St. John of the Cross called the "dark night of the soul," her husband and young son died, a severe case of small pox left her face disfigured, and she was persecuted and imprisoned in the Bastille by the clergy for what they believed to be her heretical religious views. Through all this, Jeanne Guyon prayed with Job, "The Lord gave and the Lord hath taken away. Blessed be his name." Her contribution to devotional literature was prodigious during those years. The poems, hymns and books she authored have touched thousands down to the present day, including Watchman Nee, Francois Fenelon, Hudson Taylor and John Wesley. The shallow social butterfly had become a woman of great spiritual substance by the time she died in 1717.

Guyon outlined her method of praying Scripture in her book, *Experiencing the Depths of Jesus Christ*, also known as *A Short and Very Easy Method of Prayer*. She recommended the practice of reading the Bible very slowly, tasting and digesting each verse, a line at a time, moving on only after extracting the essence of the passage. The end result of this practice: "The Lord's chief desire is to reveal himself to you and, in order for him to do that, he gives you abundant grace. The Lord gives you the experience of enjoying his presence. He touches you, and his touch is so delightful that, more than ever, you are drawn inwardly to him."[2]

PRAY:

Pray this prayer of Madame Guyon's: "To me remains no place nor time; my country is in every clime; I can be calm and free from care on any shore since God is there."[3]

MEMORIZE:

I have been crucified with Christ and I no longer live, but Christ lives in me. The life I live in the body, I live by faith in the Son of God, who loved me and gave himself for me. GALATIANS 2:20

FOR YOUR NEXT DEVOTIONAL READING, GO TO PAGE 248.

keep. They have taken some of the devoted things; they have stolen, they have lied, they have put them with their own possessions. ¹²That is why the Israelites cannot stand against their enemies; they turn their backs and run because they have been made liable to destruction. I will not be with you anymore unless you destroy whatever among you is devoted to destruction.

¹³"Go, consecrate the people. Tell them, 'Consecrate yourselves in preparation for tomorrow; for this is what the LORD, the God of Israel, says: That which

[MONDAY]

JOSHUA 7

One for All, All for One

7:11 "ISRAEL HAS SINNED."

The individualism of Western culture can make this story hard for us to understand. We think: This man sinned; let him be punished for his sin. Don't punish the whole community. Thirty-six good men (7:5), plus Achan's children (verse 24), died because of one man's disobedience. We might be willing to be our brother's keeper, but we certainly don't like the idea of being our brother's victim, especially if we were as ignorant of his sin as the Israelites were of Achan's.

God disagrees with our Western mindset. The people of God are not a group; they are a body. The church is not an organization; it's an organism, the body of Christ. You can be a member of a group and have a life outside the group. But you can't be a member of a body and have a life outside the body. An eye or a lung is distinct, wonderfully different within the body, but outside the body each part is dead: no more than dull, lifeless flesh. True individuality happens only in the community of the body of Christ. You are never less an individual than you are in the church or more an individual than you are in the church. Likewise, the actions and health of every member of a body directly affect the actions and health of every other member. Witness what happens to the rest of the body when the eyes go blind or the lungs become diseased. Witness what happened with Achan and the nation of Israel.

What tremendous implications, not only for things like morality and church discipline, but for *prayer*. On the level of individuals, the prayerlessness of one hurts the whole body; just as the prayerfulness of one helps it. On the level of the whole body, what would it mean if all the members were praying together in concerted agreement for the things the head of the body wants for his church? It would be, on a spiritual level, what a body is when all of its members are functioning harmoniously under the direction of the head. It would be for the work of the kingdom what a great team is to a game, or a great orchestra is to a symphony. It is a beautiful thing when the church acts as one and prays as one (see Matthew 18:19–20; John 17:23).

PRAY:

Jesus, you are the great head of the church, your body. I repent of my individualism, and ask that you teach us to pray—together.

FOR YOUR NEXT DEVOTIONAL READING, GO TO PAGE 251.

is devoted is among you, O Israel. You cannot stand against your enemies until you remove it.

14 " 'In the morning, present yourselves tribe by tribe. The tribe that the LORD takes shall come forward clan by clan; the clan that the LORD takes shall come forward family by family; and the family that the LORD takes shall come forward man by man. 15He who is caught with the devoted things shall be destroyed by fire, along with all that belongs to him. He has violated the covenant of the LORD and has done a disgraceful thing in Israel!' "

16Early the next morning Joshua had Israel come forward by tribes, and Judah was taken. 17The clans of Judah came forward, and he took the Zerahites. He had the clan of the Zerahites come forward by families, and Zimri was taken. 18Joshua had his family come forward man by man, and Achan son of Carmi, the son of Zimri, the son of Zerah, of the tribe of Judah, was taken.

19Then Joshua said to Achan, "My son, give glory to the LORD,[a] the God of Israel, and give him the praise.[b] Tell me what you have done; do not hide it from me."

20Achan replied, "It is true! I have sinned against the LORD, the God of Israel. This is what I have done: 21When I saw in the plunder a beautiful robe from Babylonia,[c] two hundred shekels[d] of silver and a wedge of gold weighing fifty shekels,[e] I coveted them and took them. They are hidden in the ground inside my tent, with the silver underneath."

22So Joshua sent messengers, and they ran to the tent, and there it was, hidden in his tent, with the silver underneath. 23They took the things from the tent, brought them to Joshua and all the Israelites and spread them out before the LORD.

24Then Joshua, together with all Israel, took Achan son of Zerah, the silver, the robe, the gold wedge, his sons and daughters, his cattle, donkeys and sheep, his tent and all that he had, to the Valley of Achor. 25Joshua said, "Why have you brought this trouble on us? The LORD will bring trouble on you today."

Then all Israel stoned him, and after they had stoned the rest, they burned them. 26Over Achan they heaped up a large pile of rocks, which remains to this day. Then the LORD turned from his fierce anger. Therefore that place has been called the Valley of Achor[f] ever since.

Ai Destroyed

8 Then the LORD said to Joshua, "Do not be afraid; do not be discouraged. Take the whole army with you, and go up and attack Ai. For I have delivered into your hands the king of Ai, his people, his city and his land. 2You shall do to Ai and its king as you did to Jericho and its king, except that you may carry off their plunder and livestock for yourselves. Set an ambush behind the city."

3So Joshua and the whole army moved out to attack Ai. He chose thirty thousand of his best fighting men and sent them out at night 4with these orders: "Listen carefully. You are to set an ambush behind the city. Don't go very far from it. All of you be on the alert. 5I and all those with me will advance on the city, and when the men come out against us, as they did before, we will flee from them. 6They will pursue us until we have lured them away from the city, for they will say, 'They are running away from us as they did before.' So when we flee from them, 7you are to rise up from ambush and take the city. The LORD your God will give it into your hand. 8When you have taken the city, set it on fire. Do what the LORD has commanded. See to it; you have my orders."

9Then Joshua sent them off, and they went to the place of ambush and lay in wait between Bethel and Ai, to the west of Ai—but Joshua spent that night with the people.

10Early the next morning Joshua mustered his men, and he and the leaders of Israel marched before them to Ai. 11The entire force that was with him marched up and approached the city and arrived in front of it. They set up camp north of Ai, with the valley between them and the city. 12Joshua had taken about five thousand men and set them in ambush between

---

[a]19 A solemn charge to tell the truth
[b]19 Or *and confess to him*   [c]21 Hebrew *Shinar*
[d]21 That is, about 5 pounds (about 2.3 kilograms)
[e]21 That is, about 1 1/4 pounds (about 0.6 kilogram)   [f]26 *Achor* means *trouble.*

Bethel and Ai, to the west of the city. [13]They had the soldiers take up their positions—all those in the camp to the north of the city and the ambush to the west of it. That night Joshua went into the valley. [14]When the king of Ai saw this, he and all the men of the city hurried out early in the morning to meet Israel in battle at a certain place overlooking the Arabah. But he did not know that an ambush had been set against him behind the city. [15]Joshua and all Israel let themselves be driven back before them, and they fled toward the desert. [16]All the men of Ai were called to pursue them, and they pursued Joshua and were lured away from the city. [17]Not a man remained in Ai or Bethel who did not go after Israel. They left the city open and went in pursuit of Israel.

[18]Then the LORD said to Joshua, "Hold out toward Ai the javelin that is in your hand, for into your hand I will deliver the city." So Joshua held out his javelin toward Ai. [19]As soon as he did this, the men in the ambush rose quickly from their position and rushed forward. They entered the city and captured it and quickly set it on fire.

[20]The men of Ai looked back and saw the smoke of the city rising against the sky, but they had no chance to escape in any direction, for the Israelites who had been fleeing toward the desert had turned back against their pursuers. [21]For when Joshua and all Israel saw that the ambush had taken the city and that smoke was going up from the city, they turned around and attacked the men of Ai. [22]The men of the ambush also came out of the city against them, so that they were caught in the middle, with Israelites on both sides. Israel cut them down, leaving them neither survivors nor fugitives. [23]But they took the king of Ai alive and brought him to Joshua.

[24]When Israel had finished killing all the men of Ai in the fields and in the desert where they had chased them, and when every one of them had been put to the sword, all the Israelites returned to Ai and killed those who were in it. [25]Twelve thousand men and women fell that day—all the people of Ai. [26]For Joshua did not draw back the hand that held out his jav-

elin until he had destroyed[a] all who lived in Ai. [27]But Israel did carry off for themselves the livestock and plunder of this city, as the LORD had instructed Joshua.

[28]So Joshua burned Ai and made it a permanent heap of ruins, a desolate place to this day. [29]He hung the king of Ai on a tree and left him there until evening. At sunset, Joshua ordered them to take his body from the tree and throw it down at the entrance of the city gate. And they raised a large pile of rocks over it, which remains to this day.

The Covenant Renewed at Mount Ebal

[30]Then Joshua built on Mount Ebal an altar to the LORD, the God of Israel, [31]as Moses the servant of the LORD had commanded the Israelites. He built it according to what is written in the Book of the Law of Moses—an altar of uncut stones, on which no iron tool had been used. On it they offered to the LORD burnt offerings and sacrificed fellowship offerings.[b] [32]There, in the presence of the Israelites, Joshua copied on stones the law of Moses, which he had written. [33]All Israel, aliens and citizens alike, with their elders, officials and judges, were standing on both sides of the ark of the covenant of the LORD, facing those who carried it— the priests, who were Levites. Half of the people stood in front of Mount Gerizim and half of them in front of Mount Ebal, as Moses the servant of the LORD had formerly commanded when he gave instructions to bless the people of Israel.

[34]Afterward, Joshua read all the words of the law—the blessings and the curses—just as it is written in the Book of the Law. [35]There was not a word of all that Moses had commanded that Joshua did not read to the whole assembly of Israel, including the women and children, and the aliens who lived among them.

The Gibeonite Deception

9 Now when all the kings west of the Jordan heard about these things— those in the hill country, in the western foothills, and along the entire coast of

---

[a]26 The Hebrew term refers to the irrevocable giving over of things or persons to the LORD, often by totally destroying them.   [b]31 Traditionally *peace offerings*

the Great Sea[a] as far as Lebanon (the kings of the Hittites, Amorites, Canaanites, Perizzites, Hivites and Jebusites)— [2]they came together to make war against Joshua and Israel.

[3]However, when the people of Gibeon heard what Joshua had done to Jericho and Ai, [4]they resorted to a ruse: They went as a delegation whose donkeys were loaded[b] with worn-out sacks and old wineskins, cracked and mended. [5]The men put worn and patched sandals on their feet and wore old clothes. All the bread of their food supply was dry and moldy. [6]Then they went to Joshua in the camp at Gilgal and said to him and the

[a]1 That is, the Mediterranean   [b]4 Most Hebrew manuscripts; some Hebrew manuscripts, Vulgate and Syriac (see also Septuagint) *They prepared provisions and loaded their donkeys*

JOSHUA 9

{ TUESDAY }

The Flimflam Men

9:14: THE MEN OF ISRAEL SAMPLED THEIR PROVISIONS BUT DID NOT INQUIRE OF THE LORD.

There are a lot of ways to describe what happened to the Israelites when they met the Gibeonites: flimflammed, snookered, duped, deceived. Having heard what the Israelites did to Jericho and Ai, the Gibeonites knew they needed something more than an army to survive the Israelite military machine; they needed a *plan*. Their plan was to trick the Israelites into a treaty by making them think they weren't part of the peoples Israel was commanded by God to subdue. So they made their clothes and food look old and stale, like they had come from a great distance, and they proposed a treaty. The Israelites bought the story: They sampled their provisions, but they did not "inquire of the LORD." Full of themselves after consecutive victories, they were so confident about what they thought that they didn't bother to ask the Lord what he thought. The treaty was ratified.

If only the Israelites would have prayed about the Gibeonites and their proposal, this story would have turned out better for God's people. "Would've, could've, should've" are the words of regrets. Taking the time to pray uses up time in the short run, but it saves time in the long run. When was the last time you thought you were too busy to pray? This morning, perhaps? The Gibeonites were whispering deception in your ear. The lesson of this story is the title of a book on prayer by Bill Hybels: The truth of the matter was that you were *Too Busy Not to Pray*.

There is another lesson in the story of the Gibeonite deception: Simply pursuing God's goals is not enough. We need to use God's means, too. God's will covers not only what we are to do, but how; and in the case of the Gibeonites, it covers *who* we are to do it with. Pray until you hear the Lord speak, and don't stop praying until he stops speaking. "In all your ways acknowledge him, and he will make your paths straight" (Proverbs 3:6).

PRAY:
God of all knowledge and truth, help me avoid the deceptive idea that says I don't need to pray. I recognize my constant need to hear from you.

FOR YOUR NEXT DEVOTIONAL READING, GO TO PAGE 272.

men of Israel, "We have come from a distant country; make a treaty with us."

7The men of Israel said to the Hivites, "But perhaps you live near us. How then can we make a treaty with you?"

8"We are your servants," they said to Joshua.

But Joshua asked, "Who are you and where do you come from?"

9They answered: "Your servants have come from a very distant country because of the fame of the LORD your God. For we have heard reports of him: all that he did in Egypt, 10and all that he did to the two kings of the Amorites east of the Jordan—Sihon king of Heshbon, and Og king of Bashan, who reigned in Ashtaroth. 11And our elders and all those living in our country said to us, 'Take provisions for your journey; go and meet them and say to them, "We are your servants; make a treaty with us." ' 12This bread of ours was warm when we packed it at home on the day we left to come to you. But now see how dry and moldy it is. 13And these wineskins that we filled were new, but see how cracked they are. And our clothes and sandals are worn out by the very long journey."

14The men of Israel sampled their provisions but did not inquire of the LORD. 15Then Joshua made a treaty of peace with them to let them live, and the leaders of the assembly ratified it by oath.

16Three days after they made the treaty with the Gibeonites, the Israelites heard that they were neighbors, living near them. 17So the Israelites set out and on the third day came to their cities: Gibeon, Kephirah, Beeroth and Kiriath Jearim. 18But the Israelites did not attack them, because the leaders of the assembly had sworn an oath to them by the LORD, the God of Israel.

The whole assembly grumbled against the leaders, 19but all the leaders answered, "We have given them our oath by the LORD, the God of Israel, and we cannot touch them now. 20This is what we will do to them: We will let them live, so that wrath will not fall on us for breaking the oath we swore to them." 21They continued, "Let them live, but let them be woodcutters and water carriers for the entire community." So the leaders' promise to them was kept.

22Then Joshua summoned the Gibeonites and said, "Why did you deceive us by saying, 'We live a long way from you,' while actually you live near us? 23You are now under a curse: You will never cease to serve as woodcutters and water carriers for the house of my God."

24They answered Joshua, "Your servants were clearly told how the LORD your God had commanded his servant Moses to give you the whole land and to wipe out all its inhabitants from before you. So we feared for our lives because of you, and that is why we did this. 25We are now in your hands. Do to us whatever seems good and right to you."

26So Joshua saved them from the Israelites, and they did not kill them. 27That day he made the Gibeonites woodcutters and water carriers for the community and for the altar of the LORD at the place the LORD would choose. And that is what they are to this day.

The Sun Stands Still

10 Now Adoni-Zedek king of Jerusalem heard that Joshua had taken Ai and totally destroyed[a] it, doing to Ai and its king as he had done to Jericho and its king, and that the people of Gibeon had made a treaty of peace with Israel and were living near them. 2He and his people were very much alarmed at this, because Gibeon was an important city, like one of the royal cities; it was larger than Ai, and all its men were good fighters. 3So Adoni-Zedek king of Jerusalem appealed to Hoham king of Hebron, Piram king of Jarmuth, Japhia king of Lachish and Debir king of Eglon. 4"Come up and help me attack Gibeon," he said, "because it has made peace with Joshua and the Israelites."

5Then the five kings of the Amorites—the kings of Jerusalem, Hebron, Jarmuth, Lachish and Eglon—joined forces. They moved up with all their troops and took up positions against Gibeon and attacked it.

a1 The Hebrew term refers to the irrevocable giving over of things or persons to the LORD, often by totally destroying them; also in verses 28, 35, 37, 39 and 40.

⁶The Gibeonites then sent word to Joshua in the camp at Gilgal: "Do not abandon your servants. Come up to us quickly and save us! Help us, because all the Amorite kings from the hill country have joined forces against us."

⁷So Joshua marched up from Gilgal with his entire army, including all the best fighting men. ⁸The LORD said to Joshua, "Do not be afraid of them; I have given them into your hand. Not one of them will be able to withstand you."

⁹After an all-night march from Gilgal, Joshua took them by surprise. ¹⁰The LORD threw them into confusion before Israel, who defeated them in a great victory at Gibeon. Israel pursued them along the road going up to Beth Horon and cut them down all the way to Azekah and Makkedah. ¹¹As they fled before Israel on the road down from Beth Horon to Azekah, the LORD hurled large hailstones down on them from the sky, and more of them died from the hailstones than were killed by the swords of the Israelites.

¹²On the day the LORD gave the Amorites over to Israel, Joshua said to the LORD in the presence of Israel:

"O sun, stand still over Gibeon,
    O moon, over the Valley of
        Aijalon."
¹³ So the sun stood still,
    and the moon stopped,
    till the nation avenged itself on[a]
        its enemies,

as it is written in the Book of Jashar.

The sun stopped in the middle of the sky and delayed going down about a full day. ¹⁴There has never been a day like it before or since, a day when the LORD listened to a man. Surely the LORD was fighting for Israel!

¹⁵Then Joshua returned with all Israel to the camp at Gilgal.

Five Amorite Kings Killed

¹⁶Now the five kings had fled and hidden in the cave at Makkedah. ¹⁷When Joshua was told that the five kings had been found hiding in the cave at Makkedah, ¹⁸he said, "Roll large rocks up to the mouth of the cave, and post some men there to guard it. ¹⁹But don't stop! Pursue your enemies, attack them from the rear

and don't let them reach their cities, for the LORD your God has given them into your hand."

²⁰So Joshua and the Israelites destroyed them completely—almost to a man—but the few who were left reached their fortified cities. ²¹The whole army then returned safely to Joshua in the camp at Makkedah, and no one uttered a word against the Israelites.

²²Joshua said, "Open the mouth of the cave and bring those five kings out to me." ²³So they brought the five kings out of the cave—the kings of Jerusalem, Hebron, Jarmuth, Lachish and Eglon. ²⁴When they had brought these kings to Joshua, he summoned all the men of Israel and said to the army commanders who had come with him, "Come here and put your feet on the necks of these kings." So they came forward and placed their feet on their necks.

²⁵Joshua said to them, "Do not be afraid; do not be discouraged. Be strong and courageous. This is what the LORD will do to all the enemies you are going to fight." ²⁶Then Joshua struck and killed the kings and hung them on five trees, and they were left hanging on the trees until evening.

²⁷At sunset Joshua gave the order and they took them down from the trees and threw them into the cave where they had been hiding. At the mouth of the cave they placed large rocks, which are there to this day.

²⁸That day Joshua took Makkedah. He put the city and its king to the sword and totally destroyed everyone in it. He left no survivors. And he did to the king of Makkedah as he had done to the king of Jericho.

Southern Cities Conquered

²⁹Then Joshua and all Israel with him moved on from Makkedah to Libnah and attacked it. ³⁰The LORD also gave that city and its king into Israel's hand. The city and everyone in it Joshua put to the sword. He left no survivors there. And he did to its king as he had done to the king of Jericho.

³¹Then Joshua and all Israel with him moved on from Libnah to Lachish; he

---

[a]13 Or nation triumphed over

took up positions against it and attacked it. ³²The LORD handed Lachish over to Israel, and Joshua took it on the second day. The city and everyone in it he put to the sword, just as he had done to Libnah. ³³Meanwhile, Horam king of Gezer had come up to help Lachish, but Joshua defeated him and his army—until no survivors were left.

³⁴Then Joshua and all Israel with him moved on from Lachish to Eglon; they took up positions against it and attacked it. ³⁵They captured it that same day and put it to the sword and totally destroyed everyone in it, just as they had done to Lachish.

³⁶Then Joshua and all Israel with him went up from Eglon to Hebron and attacked it. ³⁷They took the city and put it to the sword, together with its king, its villages and everyone in it. They left no survivors. Just as at Eglon, they totally destroyed it and everyone in it.

³⁸Then Joshua and all Israel with him turned around and attacked Debir. ³⁹They took the city, its king and its villages, and put them to the sword. Everyone in it they totally destroyed. They left no survivors. They did to Debir and its king as they had done to Libnah and its king and to Hebron.

⁴⁰So Joshua subdued the whole region, including the hill country, the Negev, the western foothills and the mountain slopes, together with all their kings. He left no survivors. He totally destroyed all who breathed, just as the LORD, the God of Israel, had commanded. ⁴¹Joshua subdued them from Kadesh Barnea to Gaza and from the whole region of Goshen to Gibeon. ⁴²All these kings and their lands Joshua conquered in one campaign, because the LORD, the God of Israel, fought for Israel.

⁴³Then Joshua returned with all Israel to the camp at Gilgal.

Northern Kings Defeated

11 When Jabin king of Hazor heard of this, he sent word to Jobab king of Madon, to the kings of Shimron and Acshaph, ²and to the northern kings who were in the mountains, in the Arabah south of Kinnereth, in the western foothills and in Naphoth Dor*a* on the west; ³to the Canaanites in the east and west;

to the Amorites, Hittites, Perizzites and Jebusites in the hill country; and to the Hivites below Hermon in the region of Mizpah. ⁴They came out with all their troops and a large number of horses and chariots—a huge army, as numerous as the sand on the seashore. ⁵All these kings joined forces and made camp together at the Waters of Merom, to fight against Israel.

⁶The LORD said to Joshua, "Do not be afraid of them, because by this time tomorrow I will hand all of them over to Israel, slain. You are to hamstring their horses and burn their chariots."

⁷So Joshua and his whole army came against them suddenly at the Waters of Merom and attacked them, ⁸and the LORD gave them into the hand of Israel. They defeated them and pursued them all the way to Greater Sidon, to Misrephoth Maim, and to the Valley of Mizpah on the east, until no survivors were left. ⁹Joshua did to them as the LORD had directed: He hamstrung their horses and burned their chariots.

¹⁰At that time Joshua turned back and captured Hazor and put its king to the sword. (Hazor had been the head of all these kingdoms.) ¹¹Everyone in it they put to the sword. They totally destroyed*b* them, not sparing anything that breathed, and he burned up Hazor itself.

¹²Joshua took all these royal cities and their kings and put them to the sword. He totally destroyed them, as Moses the servant of the LORD had commanded. ¹³Yet Israel did not burn any of the cities built on their mounds—except Hazor, which Joshua burned. ¹⁴The Israelites carried off for themselves all the plunder and livestock of these cities, but all the people they put to the sword until they completely destroyed them, not sparing anyone that breathed. ¹⁵As the LORD commanded his servant Moses, so Moses commanded Joshua, and Joshua did it; he left nothing undone of all that the LORD commanded Moses.

¹⁶So Joshua took this entire land: the hill country, all the Negev, the whole

---

*a*2 Or *in the heights of Dor*   *b*11 The Hebrew term refers to the irrevocable giving over of things or persons to the LORD, often by totally destroying them; also in verses 12, 20 and 21.

region of Goshen, the western foothills, the Arabah and the mountains of Israel with their foothills, [17]from Mount Halak, which rises toward Seir, to Baal Gad in the Valley of Lebanon below Mount Hermon. He captured all their kings and struck them down, putting them to death. [18]Joshua waged war against all these kings for a long time. [19]Except for the Hivites living in Gibeon, not one city made a treaty of peace with the Israelites, who took them all in battle. [20]For it was the LORD himself who hardened their hearts to wage war against Israel, so that he might destroy them totally, exterminating them without mercy, as the LORD had commanded Moses.

[21]At that time Joshua went and destroyed the Anakites from the hill country: from Hebron, Debir and Anab, from all the hill country of Judah, and from all the hill country of Israel. Joshua totally destroyed them and their towns. [22]No Anakites were left in Israelite territory; only in Gaza, Gath and Ashdod did any survive. [23]So Joshua took the entire land, just as the LORD had directed Moses, and he gave it as an inheritance to Israel according to their tribal divisions.

Then the land had rest from war.

List of Defeated Kings

12 These are the kings of the land whom the Israelites had defeated and whose territory they took over east of the Jordan, from the Arnon Gorge to Mount Hermon, including all the eastern side of the Arabah:

[2]Sihon king of the Amorites,
who reigned in Heshbon. He ruled from Aroer on the rim of the Arnon Gorge—from the middle of the gorge—to the Jabbok River, which is the border of the Ammonites. This included half of Gilead. [3]He also ruled over the eastern Arabah from the Sea of Kinnereth[a] to the Sea of the Arabah (the Salt Sea[b]), to Beth Jeshimoth, and then southward below the slopes of Pisgah.

[4]And the territory of Og king of Bashan, one of the last of the Rephaites, who reigned in Ashtaroth and Edrei. [5]He ruled over Mount Hermon, Salecah, all of Bashan to the border of the people of Geshur and Maacah, and half of Gilead to the border of Sihon king of Heshbon.

[6]Moses, the servant of the LORD, and the Israelites conquered them. And Moses the servant of the LORD gave their land to the Reubenites, the Gadites and the half-tribe of Manasseh to be their possession.

[7]These are the kings of the land that Joshua and the Israelites conquered on the west side of the Jordan, from Baal Gad in the Valley of Lebanon to Mount Halak, which rises toward Seir (their lands Joshua gave as an inheritance to the tribes of Israel according to their tribal divisions— [8]the hill country, the western foothills, the Arabah, the mountain slopes, the desert and the Negev—the lands of the Hittites, Amorites, Canaanites, Perizzites, Hivites and Jebusites):

[9]the king of Jericho	one
the king of Ai (near Bethel)	one
[10]the king of Jerusalem	one
the king of Hebron	one
[11]the king of Jarmuth	one
the king of Lachish	one
[12]the king of Eglon	one
the king of Gezer	one
[13]the king of Debir	one
the king of Geder	one
[14]the king of Hormah	one
the king of Arad	one
[15]the king of Libnah	one
the king of Adullam	one
[16]the king of Makkedah	one
the king of Bethel	one
[17]the king of Tappuah	one
the king of Hepher	one
[18]the king of Aphek	one
the king of Lasharon	one
[19]the king of Madon	one
the king of Hazor	one
[20]the king of Shimron Meron	one
the king of Acshaph	one
[21]the king of Taanach	one
the king of Megiddo	one
[22]the king of Kedesh	one
the king of Jokneam in Carmel	one

[a]3 That is, Galilee   [b]3 That is, the Dead Sea

23 the king of Dor (in Naphoth Dor[a])   one
   the king of Goyim in Gilgal   one
24 the king of Tirzah   one
thirty-one kings in all.

Land Still to Be Taken

13 When Joshua was old and well advanced in years, the LORD said to him, "You are very old, and there are still very large areas of land to be taken over.

2 "This is the land that remains: all the regions of the Philistines and Geshurites: 3 from the Shihor River on the east of Egypt to the territory of Ekron on the north, all of it counted as Canaanite (the territory of the five Philistine rulers in Gaza, Ashdod, Ashkelon, Gath and Ekron—that of the Avvites); 4 from the south, all the land of the Canaanites, from Arah of the Sidonians as far as Aphek, the region of the Amorites, 5 the area of the Gebalites[b]; and all Lebanon to the east, from Baal Gad below Mount Hermon to Lebo[c] Hamath.

6 "As for all the inhabitants of the mountain regions from Lebanon to Misrephoth Maim, that is, all the Sidonians, I myself will drive them out before the Israelites. Be sure to allocate this land to Israel for an inheritance, as I have instructed you, 7 and divide it as an inheritance among the nine tribes and half of the tribe of Manasseh."

Division of the Land East of the Jordan

8 The other half of Manasseh,[d] the Reubenites and the Gadites had received the inheritance that Moses had given them east of the Jordan, as he, the servant of the LORD, had assigned it to them.

9 It extended from Aroer on the rim of the Arnon Gorge, and from the town in the middle of the gorge, and included the whole plateau of Medeba as far as Dibon, 10 and all the towns of Sihon king of the Amorites, who ruled in Heshbon, out to the border of the Ammonites. 11 It also included Gilead, the territory of the people of Geshur and Maacah, all of Mount Hermon and all Bashan as

far as Salecah— 12 that is, the whole kingdom of Og in Bashan, who had reigned in Ashtaroth and Edrei and had survived as one of the last of the Rephaites. Moses had defeated them and taken over their land. 13 But the Israelites did not drive out the people of Geshur and Maacah, so they continue to live among the Israelites to this day.

14 But to the tribe of Levi he gave no inheritance, since the offerings made by fire to the LORD, the God of Israel, are their inheritance, as he promised them.

15 This is what Moses had given to the tribe of Reuben, clan by clan:

16 The territory from Aroer on the rim of the Arnon Gorge, and from the town in the middle of the gorge, and the whole plateau past Medeba 17 to Heshbon and all its towns on the plateau, including Dibon, Bamoth Baal, Beth Baal Meon, 18 Jahaz, Kedemoth, Mephaath, 19 Kiriathaim, Sibmah, Zereth Shahar on the hill in the valley, 20 Beth Peor, the slopes of Pisgah, and Beth Jeshimoth 21 —all the towns on the plateau and the entire realm of Sihon king of the Amorites, who ruled at Heshbon. Moses had defeated him and the Midianite chiefs, Evi, Rekem, Zur, Hur and Reba—princes allied with Sihon— who lived in that country. 22 In addition to those slain in battle, the Israelites had put to the sword Balaam son of Beor, who practiced divination. 23 The boundary of the Reubenites was the bank of the Jordan. These towns and their villages were the inheritance of the Reubenites, clan by clan.

24 This is what Moses had given to the tribe of Gad, clan by clan:

25 The territory of Jazer, all the towns of Gilead and half the Ammonite country as far as Aroer, near Rabbah; 26 and from Heshbon to Ramath

---

[a]23 Or in the heights of Dor   [b]5 That is, the area of Byblos   [c]5 Or to the entrance to
[d]8 Hebrew With it (that is, with the other half of Manasseh)

Mizpah and Betonim, and from Mahanaim to the territory of Debir; [27]and in the valley, Beth Haram, Beth Nimrah, Succoth and Zaphon with the rest of the realm of Sihon king of Heshbon (the east side of the Jordan, the territory up to the end of the Sea of Kinnereth[a]). [28]These towns and their villages were the inheritance of the Gadites, clan by clan.

[29]This is what Moses had given to the half-tribe of Manasseh, that is, to half the family of the descendants of Manasseh, clan by clan:

[30]The territory extending from Mahanaim and including all of Bashan, the entire realm of Og king of Bashan—all the settlements of Jair in Bashan, sixty towns, [31]half of Gilead, and Ashtaroth and Edrei (the royal cities of Og in Bashan). This was for the descendants of Makir son of Manasseh—for half of the sons of Makir, clan by clan.

[32]This is the inheritance Moses had given when he was in the plains of Moab across the Jordan east of Jericho. [33]But to the tribe of Levi, Moses had given no inheritance; the LORD, the God of Israel, is their inheritance, as he promised them.

Division of the Land West of the Jordan

14 Now these are the areas the Israelites received as an inheritance in the land of Canaan, which Eleazar the priest, Joshua son of Nun and the heads of the tribal clans of Israel allotted to them. [2]Their inheritances were assigned by lot to the nine-and-a-half tribes, as the LORD had commanded through Moses. [3]Moses had granted the two-and-a-half tribes their inheritance east of the Jordan but had not granted the Levites an inheritance among the rest, [4]for the sons of Joseph had become two tribes—Manasseh and Ephraim. The Levites received no share of the land but only towns to live in, with pasturelands for their flocks and herds. [5]So the Israelites divided the land, just as the LORD had commanded Moses.

Hebron Given to Caleb

[6]Now the men of Judah approached Joshua at Gilgal, and Caleb son of Jephunneh the Kenizzite said to him, "You know what the LORD said to Moses the man of God at Kadesh Barnea about you and me. [7]I was forty years old when Moses the servant of the LORD sent me from Kadesh Barnea to explore the land. And I brought him back a report according to my convictions, [8]but my brothers who went up with me made the hearts of the people melt with fear. I, however, followed the LORD my God wholeheartedly. [9]So on that day Moses swore to me, 'The land on which your feet have walked will be your inheritance and that of your children forever, because you have followed the LORD my God wholeheartedly.'[b]

[10]"Now then, just as the LORD promised, he has kept me alive for forty-five years since the time he said this to Moses, while Israel moved about in the desert. So here I am today, eighty-five years old! [11]I am still as strong today as the day Moses sent me out; I'm just as vigorous to go out to battle now as I was then. [12]Now give me this hill country that the LORD promised me that day. You yourself heard then that the Anakites were there and their cities were large and fortified, but, the LORD helping me, I will drive them out just as he said."

[13]Then Joshua blessed Caleb son of Jephunneh and gave him Hebron as his inheritance. [14]So Hebron has belonged to Caleb son of Jephunneh the Kenizzite ever since, because he followed the LORD, the God of Israel, wholeheartedly. [15](Hebron used to be called Kiriath Arba after Arba, who was the greatest man among the Anakites.)

Then the land had rest from war.

Allotment for Judah

15 The allotment for the tribe of Judah, clan by clan, extended down to the territory of Edom, to the Desert of Zin in the extreme south.

[2]Their southern boundary started from the bay at the southern end of the Salt Sea,[c] [3]crossed south of Scorpion[d] Pass, continued on to Zin and went over to the south of Kadesh Barnea. Then it ran past Hezron up

<hr>

[a]27 That is, Galilee   [b]9 Deut. 1:36   [c]2 That is, the Dead Sea; also in verse 5   [d]3 Hebrew Akrabbim

to Addar and curved around to Karka. [4]It then passed along to Azmon and joined the Wadi of Egypt, ending at the sea. This is their[a] southern boundary.

[5]The eastern boundary is the Salt Sea as far as the mouth of the Jordan.

The northern boundary started from the bay of the sea at the mouth of the Jordan, [6]went up to Beth Hoglah and continued north of Beth Arabah to the Stone of Bohan son of Reuben. [7]The boundary then went up to Debir from the Valley of Achor and turned north to Gilgal, which faces the Pass of Adummim south of the gorge. It continued along to the waters of En Shemesh and came out at En Rogel. [8]Then it ran up the Valley of Ben Hinnom along the southern slope of the Jebusite city (that is, Jerusalem). From there it climbed to the top of the hill west of the Hinnom Valley at the northern end of the Valley of Rephaim. [9]From the hilltop the boundary headed toward the spring of the waters of Nephtoah, came out at the towns of Mount Ephron and went down toward Baalah (that is, Kiriath Jearim). [10]Then it curved westward from Baalah to Mount Seir, ran along the northern slope of Mount Jearim (that is, Kesalon), continued down to Beth Shemesh and crossed to Timnah. [11]It went to the northern slope of Ekron, turned toward Shikkeron, passed along to Mount Baalah and reached Jabneel. The boundary ended at the sea.

[12]The western boundary is the coastline of the Great Sea.[b] These are the boundaries around the people of Judah by their clans.

[13]In accordance with the LORD's command to him, Joshua gave to Caleb son of Jephunneh a portion in Judah—Kiriath Arba, that is, Hebron. (Arba was the forefather of Anak.) [14]From Hebron Caleb drove out the three Anakites—Sheshai, Ahiman and Talmai—descendants of Anak. [15]From there he marched against the people living in Debir (formerly called Kiriath Sepher). [16]And Caleb said, "I will give my daughter Acsah in marriage to the man who attacks and captures Kiriath Sepher." [17]Othniel son of Kenaz, Caleb's brother, took it; so Caleb gave his daughter Acsah to him in marriage.

[18]One day when she came to Othniel, she urged him[c] to ask her father for a field. When she got off her donkey, Caleb asked her, "What can I do for you?"

[19]She replied, "Do me a special favor. Since you have given me land in the Negev, give me also springs of water." So Caleb gave her the upper and lower springs.

[20]This is the inheritance of the tribe of Judah, clan by clan:

[21]The southernmost towns of the tribe of Judah in the Negev toward the boundary of Edom were:

Kabzeel, Eder, Jagur, [22]Kinah, Dimonah, Adadah, [23]Kedesh, Hazor, Ithnan, [24]Ziph, Telem, Bealoth, [25]Hazor Hadattah, Kerioth Hezron (that is, Hazor), [26]Amam, Shema, Moladah, [27]Hazar Gaddah, Heshmon, Beth Pelet, [28]Hazar Shual, Beersheba, Biziothiah, [29]Baalah, Iim, Ezem, [30]Eltolad, Kesil, Hormah, [31]Ziklag, Madmannah, Sansannah, [32]Lebaoth, Shilhim, Ain and Rimmon—a total of twenty-nine towns and their villages.

[33]In the western foothills:

Eshtaol, Zorah, Ashnah, [34]Zanoah, En Gannim, Tappuah, Enam, [35]Jarmuth, Adullam, Socoh, Azekah, [36]Shaaraim, Adithaim and Gederah (or Gederothaim)[d]—fourteen towns and their villages.

[37]Zenan, Hadashah, Migdal Gad, [38]Dilean, Mizpah, Joktheel, [39]Lachish, Bozkath, Eglon, [40]Cabbon, Lahmas, Kitlish, [41]Gederoth, Beth Dagon, Naamah and Makkedah—sixteen towns and their villages.

[42]Libnah, Ether, Ashan, [43]Iphtah, Ashnah, Nezib, [44]Keilah, Aczib and Mareshah—nine towns and their villages.

[a]4 Hebrew your   [b]12 That is, the Mediterranean; also in verse 47   [c]18 Hebrew and some Septuagint manuscripts; other Septuagint manuscripts (see also note at Judges 1:14) Othniel, he urged her   [d]36 Or Gederah and Gederothaim

⁴⁵Ekron, with its surrounding settlements and villages; ⁴⁶west of Ekron, all that were in the vicinity of Ashdod, together with their villages; ⁴⁷Ashdod, its surrounding settlements and villages; and Gaza, its settlements and villages, as far as the Wadi of Egypt and the coastline of the Great Sea.

⁴⁸In the hill country:

Shamir, Jattir, Socoh, ⁴⁹Dannah, Kiriath Sannah (that is, Debir), ⁵⁰Anab, Eshtemoh, Anim, ⁵¹Goshen, Holon and Giloh—eleven towns and their villages.

⁵²Arab, Dumah, Eshan, ⁵³Janim, Beth Tappuah, Aphekah, ⁵⁴Humtah, Kiriath Arba (that is, Hebron) and Zior—nine towns and their villages.

⁵⁵Maon, Carmel, Ziph, Juttah, ⁵⁶Jezreel, Jokdeam, Zanoah, ⁵⁷Kain, Gibeah and Timnah—ten towns and their villages.

⁵⁸Halhul, Beth Zur, Gedor, ⁵⁹Maarath, Beth Anoth and Eltekon—six towns and their villages.

⁶⁰Kiriath Baal (that is, Kiriath Jearim) and Rabbah—two towns and their villages.

⁶¹In the desert:

Beth Arabah, Middin, Secacah, ⁶²Nibshan, the City of Salt and En Gedi—six towns and their villages.

⁶³Judah could not dislodge the Jebusites, who were living in Jerusalem; to this day the Jebusites live there with the people of Judah.

Allotment for Ephraim and Manasseh

16 The allotment for Joseph began at the Jordan of Jericho,[a] east of the waters of Jericho, and went up from there through the desert into the hill country of Bethel. ²It went on from Bethel (that is, Luz),[b] crossed over to the territory of the Arkites in Ataroth, ³descended westward to the territory of the Japhletites as far as the region of Lower Beth Horon and on to Gezer, ending at the sea.

⁴So Manasseh and Ephraim, the descendants of Joseph, received their inheritance.

⁵This was the territory of Ephraim, clan by clan:

The boundary of their inheritance went from Ataroth Addar in the east to Upper Beth Horon ⁶and continued to the sea. From Micmethath on the north it curved eastward to Taanath Shiloh, passing by it to Janoah on the east. ⁷Then it went down from Janoah to Ataroth and Naarah, touched Jericho and came out at the Jordan. ⁸From Tappuah the border went west to the Kanah Ravine and ended at the sea. This was the inheritance of the tribe of the Ephraimites, clan by clan. ⁹It also included all the towns and their villages that were set aside for the Ephraimites within the inheritance of the Manassites.

¹⁰They did not dislodge the Canaanites living in Gezer; to this day the Canaanites live among the people of Ephraim but are required to do forced labor.

17 This was the allotment for the tribe of Manasseh as Joseph's firstborn, that is, for Makir, Manasseh's firstborn. Makir was the ancestor of the Gileadites, who had received Gilead and Bashan because the Makirites were great soldiers. ²So this allotment was for the rest of the people of Manasseh—the clans of Abiezer, Helek, Asriel, Shechem, Hepher and Shemida. These are the other male descendants of Manasseh son of Joseph by their clans.

> God is waiting eagerly to respond with new strength to each little act of self-control, small disciplines of prayer, feeble searching after him. And his children shall be filled if they will only hunger and thirst after what he offers.
>
> RICHARD HOLLOWAY

³Now Zelophehad son of Hepher, the son of Gilead, the son of Makir, the son of Manasseh, had no sons but only daughters, whose names were Mahlah,

---

[a]1 *Jordan of Jericho* was possibly an ancient name for the Jordan River.   [b]2 Septuagint; Hebrew *Bethel to Luz*

Noah, Hoglah, Milcah and Tirzah. ⁴They went to Eleazar the priest, Joshua son of Nun, and the leaders and said, "The LORD commanded Moses to give us an inheritance among our brothers." So Joshua gave them an inheritance along with the brothers of their father, according to the LORD's command. ⁵Manasseh's share consisted of ten tracts of land besides Gilead and Bashan east of the Jordan, ⁶because the daughters of the tribe of Manasseh received an inheritance among the sons. The land of Gilead belonged to the rest of the descendants of Manasseh.

⁷The territory of Manasseh extended from Asher to Micmethath east of Shechem. The boundary ran southward from there to include the people living at En Tappuah. ⁸(Manasseh had the land of Tappuah, but Tappuah itself, on the boundary of Manasseh, belonged to the Ephraimites.) ⁹Then the boundary continued south to the Kanah Ravine. There were towns belonging to Ephraim lying among the towns of Manasseh, but the boundary of Manasseh was the northern side of the ravine and ended at the sea. ¹⁰On the south the land belonged to Ephraim, on the north to Manasseh. The territory of Manasseh reached the sea and bordered Asher on the north and Issachar on the east. ¹¹Within Issachar and Asher, Manasseh also had Beth Shan, Ibleam and the people of Dor, Endor, Taanach and Megiddo, together with their surrounding settlements (the third in the list is Naphoth*a*).

¹²Yet the Manassites were not able to occupy these towns, for the Canaanites were determined to live in that region. ¹³However, when the Israelites grew stronger, they subjected the Canaanites to forced labor but did not drive them out completely.

¹⁴The people of Joseph said to Joshua, "Why have you given us only one allotment and one portion for an inheritance? We are a numerous people and the LORD has blessed us abundantly."

¹⁵"If you are so numerous," Joshua answered, "and if the hill country of Ephraim is too small for you, go up into the forest and clear land for yourselves there in the land of the Perizzites and Rephaites."

¹⁶The people of Joseph replied, "The hill country is not enough for us, and all the Canaanites who live in the plain have iron chariots, both those in Beth Shan and its settlements and those in the Valley of Jezreel."

¹⁷But Joshua said to the house of Joseph—to Ephraim and Manasseh—"You are numerous and very powerful. You will have not only one allotment ¹⁸but the forested hill country as well. Clear it, and its farthest limits will be yours; though the Canaanites have iron chariots and though they are strong, you can drive them out."

Division of the Rest of the Land

18 The whole assembly of the Israelites gathered at Shiloh and set up the Tent of Meeting there. The country was brought under their control, ²but there were still seven Israelite tribes who had not yet received their inheritance.

³So Joshua said to the Israelites: "How long will you wait before you begin to take possession of the land that the LORD, the God of your fathers, has given you? ⁴Appoint three men from each tribe. I will send them out to make a survey of the land and to write a description of it, according to the inheritance of each. Then they will return to me. ⁵You are to divide the land into seven parts. Judah is to remain in its territory on the south and the house of Joseph in its territory on the north. ⁶After you have written descriptions of the seven parts of the land, bring them here to me and I will cast lots for you in the presence of the LORD our God. ⁷The Levites, however, do not get a portion among you, because the priestly service of the LORD is their inheritance. And Gad, Reuben and the half-tribe of Manasseh have already received their inheritance on the east side of the Jordan. Moses the servant of the LORD gave it to them."

⁸As the men started on their way to map out the land, Joshua instructed them, "Go and make a survey of the land and write a description of it. Then return

a11 That is, Naphoth Dor

to me, and I will cast lots for you here at Shiloh in the presence of the LORD." [9]So the men left and went through the land. They wrote its description on a scroll, town by town, in seven parts, and returned to Joshua in the camp at Shiloh. [10]Joshua then cast lots for them in Shiloh in the presence of the LORD, and there he distributed the land to the Israelites according to their tribal divisions.

Allotment for Benjamin

[11]The lot came up for the tribe of Benjamin, clan by clan. Their allotted territory lay between the tribes of Judah and Joseph:

[12]On the north side their boundary began at the Jordan, passed the northern slope of Jericho and headed west into the hill country, coming out at the desert of Beth Aven. [13]From there it crossed to the south slope of Luz (that is, Bethel) and went down to Ataroth Addar on the hill south of Lower Beth Horon.

[14]From the hill facing Beth Horon on the south the boundary turned south along the western side and came out at Kiriath Baal (that is, Kiriath Jearim), a town of the people of Judah. This was the western side.

[15]The southern side began at the outskirts of Kiriath Jearim on the west, and the boundary came out at the spring of the waters of Nephtoah. [16]The boundary went down to the foot of the hill facing the Valley of Ben Hinnom, north of the Valley of Rephaim. It continued down the Hinnom Valley along the southern slope of the Jebusite city and so to En Rogel. [17]It then curved north, went to En Shemesh, continued to Geliloth, which faces the Pass of Adummim, and ran down to the Stone of Bohan son of Reuben. [18]It continued to the northern slope of Beth Arabah[a] and on down into the Arabah. [19]It then went to the northern slope of Beth Hoglah and came out at the northern bay of the Salt Sea,[b] at the mouth of the Jordan in the south. This was the southern boundary.

[20]The Jordan formed the boundary on the eastern side.

These were the boundaries that marked out the inheritance of the clans of Benjamin on all sides.

[21]The tribe of Benjamin, clan by clan, had the following cities:

Jericho, Beth Hoglah, Emek Keziz, [22]Beth Arabah, Zemaraim, Bethel, [23]Avvim, Parah, Ophrah, [24]Kephar Ammoni, Ophni and Geba—twelve towns and their villages.

[25]Gibeon, Ramah, Beeroth, [26]Mizpah, Kephirah, Mozah, [27]Rekem, Irpeel, Taralah, [28]Zelah, Haeleph, the Jebusite city (that is, Jerusalem), Gibeah and Kiriath—fourteen towns and their villages.

This was the inheritance of Benjamin for its clans.

Allotment for Simeon

19 The second lot came out for the tribe of Simeon, clan by clan. Their inheritance lay within the territory of Judah. [2]It included:

Beersheba (or Sheba),[c] Moladah, [3]Hazar Shual, Balah, Ezem, [4]Eltolad, Bethul, Hormah, [5]Ziklag, Beth Marcaboth, Hazar Susah, [6]Beth Lebaoth and Sharuhen—thirteen towns and their villages;

[7]Ain, Rimmon, Ether and Ashan—four towns and their villages— [8]and all the villages around these towns as far as Baalath Beer (Ramah in the Negev).

This was the inheritance of the tribe of the Simeonites, clan by clan. [9]The inheritance of the Simeonites was taken from the share of Judah, because Judah's portion was more than they needed. So the Simeonites received their inheritance within the territory of Judah.

Allotment for Zebulun

[10]The third lot came up for Zebulun, clan by clan:

The boundary of their inheritance went as far as Sarid. [11]Going west it ran to Maralah, touched Dabbesheth, and extended to the ravine near Jokneam. [12]It turned east from

[a]18 Septuagint; Hebrew *slope facing the Arabah*
[b]19 That is, the Dead Sea   [c]2 Or *Beersheba, Sheba*; 1 Chron. 4:28 does not have *Sheba*.

Sarid toward the sunrise to the territory of Kisloth Tabor and went on to Daberath and up to Japhia. ¹³Then it continued eastward to Gath Hepher and Eth Kazin; it came out at Rimmon and turned toward Neah. ¹⁴There the boundary went around on the north to Hannathon and ended at the Valley of Iphtah El. ¹⁵Included were Kattath, Nahalal, Shimron, Idalah and Bethlehem. There were twelve towns and their villages.

¹⁶These towns and their villages were the inheritance of Zebulun, clan by clan.

Allotment for Issachar

¹⁷The fourth lot came out for Issachar, clan by clan. ¹⁸Their territory included:

Jezreel, Kesulloth, Shunem, ¹⁹Hapharaim, Shion, Anaharath, ²⁰Rabbith, Kishion, Ebez, ²¹Remeth, En Gannim, En Haddah and Beth Pazzez. ²²The boundary touched Tabor, Shahazumah and Beth Shemesh, and ended at the Jordan. There were sixteen towns and their villages.

²³These towns and their villages were the inheritance of the tribe of Issachar, clan by clan.

Allotment for Asher

²⁴The fifth lot came out for the tribe of Asher, clan by clan. ²⁵Their territory included:

Helkath, Hali, Beten, Acshaph, ²⁶Allammelech, Amad and Mishal. On the west the boundary touched Carmel and Shihor Libnath. ²⁷It then turned east toward Beth Dagon, touched Zebulun and the Valley of Iphtah El, and went north to Beth Emek and Neiel, passing Cabul on the left. ²⁸It went to Abdon,ᵃ Rehob, Hammon and Kanah, as far as Greater Sidon. ²⁹The boundary then turned back toward Ramah and went to the fortified city of Tyre, turned toward Hosah and came out at the sea in the region of Aczib, ³⁰Ummah, Aphek and Rehob. There were twenty-two towns and their villages.

³¹These towns and their villages were the inheritance of the tribe of Asher, clan by clan.

Allotment for Naphtali

³²The sixth lot came out for Naphtali, clan by clan:

³³Their boundary went from Heleph and the large tree in Zaanannim, passing Adami Nekeb and Jabneel to Lakkum and ending at the Jordan. ³⁴The boundary ran west through Aznoth Tabor and came out at Hukkok. It touched Zebulun on the south, Asher on the west and the Jordanᵇ on the east. ³⁵The fortified cities were Ziddim, Zer, Hammath, Rakkath, Kinnereth, ³⁶Adamah, Ramah, Hazor, ³⁷Kedesh, Edrei, En Hazor, ³⁸Iron, Migdal El, Horem, Beth Anath and Beth Shemesh. There were nineteen towns and their villages.

³⁹These towns and their villages were the inheritance of the tribe of Naphtali, clan by clan.

Allotment for Dan

⁴⁰The seventh lot came out for the tribe of Dan, clan by clan. ⁴¹The territory of their inheritance included:

Zorah, Eshtaol, Ir Shemesh, ⁴²Shaalabbin, Aijalon, Ithlah, ⁴³Elon, Timnah, Ekron, ⁴⁴Eltekeh, Gibbethon, Baalath, ⁴⁵Jehud, Bene Berak, Gath Rimmon, ⁴⁶Me Jarkon and Rakkon, with the area facing Joppa.

⁴⁷(But the Danites had difficulty taking possession of their territory, so they went up and attacked Leshem, took it, put it to the sword and occupied it. They settled in Leshem and named it Dan after their forefather.)

⁴⁸These towns and their villages were the inheritance of the tribe of Dan, clan by clan.

Allotment for Joshua

⁴⁹When they had finished dividing the land into its allotted portions, the Israelites gave Joshua son of Nun an inheritance among them, ⁵⁰as the LORD had commanded. They gave him the town he asked for—Timnath Serahᶜ in the hill

---

ᵃ28 Some Hebrew manuscripts (see also Joshua 21:30); most Hebrew manuscripts Ebron
ᵇ34 Septuagint; Hebrew west, and Judah, the Jordan,   ᶜ50 Also known as Timnath Heres (see Judges 2:9)

country of Ephraim. And he built up the town and settled there.

⁵¹These are the territories that Eleazar the priest, Joshua son of Nun and the heads of the tribal clans of Israel assigned by lot at Shiloh in the presence of the LORD at the entrance to the Tent of Meeting. And so they finished dividing the land.

Cities of Refuge

20 Then the LORD said to Joshua: ²"Tell the Israelites to designate the cities of refuge, as I instructed you through Moses, ³so that anyone who kills a person accidentally and unintentionally may flee there and find protection from the avenger of blood.

> If we would pray aright, the first thing we should do is to see to it that we really get an audience with God, that we really get into his very presence. Before a word of petition is offered, we should have the definite consciousness that we are talking to God, and should believe that he is listening and is going to grant the thing that we ask of him.
>
> DR. R. A. TORREY

⁴"When he flees to one of these cities, he is to stand in the entrance of the city gate and state his case before the elders of that city. Then they are to admit him into their city and give him a place to live with them. ⁵If the avenger of blood pursues him, they must not surrender the one accused, because he killed his neighbor unintentionally and without malice aforethought. ⁶He is to stay in that city until he has stood trial before the assembly and until the death of the high priest who is serving at that time. Then he may go back to his own home in the town from which he fled."

⁷So they set apart Kedesh in Galilee in the hill country of Naphtali, Shechem in the hill country of Ephraim, and Kiriath Arba (that is, Hebron) in the hill country of Judah. ⁸On the east side of the Jordan of Jericho*ᵃ* they designated Bezer in the desert on the plateau in the tribe of Reuben, Ramoth in Gilead in the tribe of Gad, and Golan in Bashan in the tribe of Manasseh. ⁹Any of the Israelites or any alien living among them who killed someone accidentally could flee to these designated cities and not be killed by the avenger of blood prior to standing trial before the assembly.

Towns for the Levites

21 Now the family heads of the Levites approached Eleazar the priest, Joshua son of Nun, and the heads of the other tribal families of Israel ²at Shiloh in Canaan and said to them, "The LORD commanded through Moses that you give us towns to live in, with pasturelands for our livestock." ³So, as the LORD had commanded, the Israelites gave the Levites the following towns and pasturelands out of their own inheritance:

⁴The first lot came out for the Kohathites, clan by clan. The Levites who were descendants of Aaron the priest were allotted thirteen towns from the tribes of Judah, Simeon and Benjamin. ⁵The rest of Kohath's descendants were allotted ten towns from the clans of the tribes of Ephraim, Dan and half of Manasseh.

⁶The descendants of Gershon were allotted thirteen towns from the clans of the tribes of Issachar, Asher, Naphtali and the half-tribe of Manasseh in Bashan.

⁷The descendants of Merari, clan by clan, received twelve towns from the tribes of Reuben, Gad and Zebulun.

⁸So the Israelites allotted to the Levites these towns and their pasturelands, as the LORD had commanded through Moses.

⁹From the tribes of Judah and Simeon they allotted the following towns by name ¹⁰(these towns were assigned to the descendants of Aaron who were from the Kohathite clans of the Levites, because the first lot fell to them):

¹¹They gave them Kiriath Arba (that is, Hebron), with its surrounding pastureland, in the hill country of Judah. (Arba was the forefather of Anak.) ¹²But the fields and villages around the city they had given to Caleb son of Jephunneh as his possession.

ᵃ8 Jordan of Jericho was possibly an ancient name for the Jordan River.

¹³So to the descendants of Aaron the priest they gave Hebron (a city of refuge for one accused of murder), Libnah, ¹⁴Jattir, Eshtemoa, ¹⁵Holon, Debir, ¹⁶Ain, Juttah and Beth Shemesh, together with their pasturelands—nine towns from these two tribes.

¹⁷And from the tribe of Benjamin they gave them Gibeon, Geba, ¹⁸Anathoth and Almon, together with their pasturelands—four towns.

¹⁹All the towns for the priests, the descendants of Aaron, were thirteen, together with their pasturelands.

²⁰The rest of the Kohathite clans of the Levites were allotted towns from the tribe of Ephraim:

²¹In the hill country of Ephraim they were given Shechem (a city of refuge for one accused of murder) and Gezer, ²²Kibzaim and Beth Horon, together with their pasturelands—four towns.

²³Also from the tribe of Dan they received Eltekeh, Gibbethon, ²⁴Aijalon and Gath Rimmon, together with their pasturelands—four towns.

²⁵From half the tribe of Manasseh they received Taanach and Gath Rimmon, together with their pasturelands—two towns.

²⁶All these ten towns and their pasturelands were given to the rest of the Kohathite clans.

²⁷The Levite clans of the Gershonites were given:

from the half-tribe of Manasseh,
Golan in Bashan (a city of refuge for one accused of murder) and Be Eshtarah, together with their pasturelands—two towns;
²⁸from the tribe of Issachar,
Kishion, Daberath, ²⁹Jarmuth and En Gannim, together with their pasturelands—four towns;
³⁰from the tribe of Asher,
Mishal, Abdon, ³¹Helkath and Rehob, together with their pasturelands—four towns;
³²from the tribe of Naphtali,
Kedesh in Galilee (a city of refuge for one accused of murder), Hammoth Dor and Kartan, together with their pasturelands—three towns.

³³All the towns of the Gershonite clans were thirteen, together with their pasturelands.

³⁴The Merarite clans (the rest of the Levites) were given:

from the tribe of Zebulun,
Jokneam, Kartah, ³⁵Dimnah and Nahalal, together with their pasturelands—four towns;
³⁶from the tribe of Reuben,
Bezer, Jahaz, ³⁷Kedemoth and Mephaath, together with their pasturelands—four towns;
³⁸from the tribe of Gad,
Ramoth in Gilead (a city of refuge for one accused of murder), Mahanaim, ³⁹Heshbon and Jazer, together with their pasturelands—four towns in all.

⁴⁰All the towns allotted to the Merarite clans, who were the rest of the Levites, were twelve.

⁴¹The towns of the Levites in the territory held by the Israelites were forty-eight in all, together with their pasturelands. ⁴²Each of these towns had pasturelands surrounding it; this was true for all these towns.

⁴³So the LORD gave Israel all the land he had sworn to give their forefathers, and they took possession of it and settled there. ⁴⁴The LORD gave them rest on every side, just as he had sworn to their forefathers. Not one of their enemies withstood them; the LORD handed all their enemies over to them. ⁴⁵Not one of all the LORD's good promises to the house of Israel failed; every one was fulfilled.

Eastern Tribes Return Home

22 Then Joshua summoned the Reubenites, the Gadites and the half-tribe of Manasseh ²and said to them, "You have done all that Moses the servant of the LORD commanded, and you have obeyed me in everything I commanded. ³For a long time now—to this very day—you have not deserted your brothers but have carried out the mission the LORD your God gave you. ⁴Now that the LORD your God has given your brothers rest as he promised, return to your homes in the land that Moses the servant of the LORD gave you on the other

side of the Jordan. ⁵But be very careful to keep the commandment and the law that Moses the servant of the LORD gave you: to love the LORD your God, to walk in all his ways, to obey his commands, to hold fast to him and to serve him with all your heart and all your soul."

⁶Then Joshua blessed them and sent them away, and they went to their homes. ⁷(To the half-tribe of Manasseh Moses had given land in Bashan, and to the other half of the tribe Joshua gave land on the west side of the Jordan with their brothers.) When Joshua sent them home, he blessed them, ⁸saying, "Return to your homes with your great wealth—with large herds of livestock, with silver, gold, bronze and iron, and a great quantity of clothing—and divide with your brothers the plunder from your enemies."

⁹So the Reubenites, the Gadites and the half-tribe of Manasseh left the Israelites at Shiloh in Canaan to return to Gilead, their own land, which they had acquired in accordance with the command of the LORD through Moses.

¹⁰When they came to Geliloth near the Jordan in the land of Canaan, the Reubenites, the Gadites and the half-tribe of Manasseh built an imposing altar there by the Jordan. ¹¹And when the Israelites heard that they had built the altar on the border of Canaan at Geliloth near the Jordan on the Israelite side, ¹²the whole assembly of Israel gathered at Shiloh to go to war against them.

¹³So the Israelites sent Phinehas son of Eleazar, the priest, to the land of Gilead—to Reuben, Gad and the half-tribe of Manasseh. ¹⁴With him they sent ten of the chief men, one for each of the tribes of Israel, each the head of a family division among the Israelite clans.

¹⁵When they went to Gilead—to Reuben, Gad and the half-tribe of Manasseh—they said to them: ¹⁶"The whole assembly of the LORD says: 'How could you break faith with the God of Israel like this? How could you turn away from the LORD and build yourselves an altar in rebellion against him now? ¹⁷Was not the sin of Peor enough for us? Up to this very day we have not cleansed ourselves from that sin, even though a plague fell on the

community of the LORD! ¹⁸And are you now turning away from the LORD?

"'If you rebel against the LORD today, tomorrow he will be angry with the whole community of Israel. ¹⁹If the land you possess is defiled, come over to the LORD's land, where the LORD's tabernacle stands, and share the land with us. But do not rebel against the LORD or against us by building an altar for yourselves, other than the altar of the LORD our God. ²⁰When Achan son of Zerah acted unfaithfully regarding the devoted things,ᵃ did not wrath come upon the whole community of Israel? He was not the only one who died for his sin.'"

²¹Then Reuben, Gad and the half-tribe of Manasseh replied to the heads of the clans of Israel: ²²"The Mighty One, God, the LORD! The Mighty One, God, the LORD! He knows! And let Israel know! If this has been in rebellion or disobedience to the LORD, do not spare us this day. ²³If we have built our own altar to turn away from the LORD and to offer burnt offerings and grain offerings, or to sacrifice fellowship offeringsᵇ on it, may the LORD himself call us to account.

²⁴"No! We did it for fear that some day your descendants might say to ours, 'What do you have to do with the LORD, the God of Israel? ²⁵The LORD has made the Jordan a boundary between us and you—you Reubenites and Gadites! You have no share in the LORD.' So your descendants might cause ours to stop fearing the LORD.

²⁶"That is why we said, 'Let us get ready and build an altar—but not for burnt offerings or sacrifices.' ²⁷On the contrary, it is to be a witness between us and you and the generations that follow, that we will worship the LORD at his sanctuary with our burnt offerings, sacrifices and fellowship offerings. Then in the future your descendants will not be able to say to ours, 'You have no share in the LORD.'

²⁸"And we said, 'If they ever say this to us, or to our descendants, we will answer: Look at the replica of the LORD's

---

ᵃ20 The Hebrew term refers to the irrevocable giving over of things or persons to the LORD, often by totally destroying them.   ᵇ23 Traditionally peace offerings; also in verse 27

altar, which our fathers built, not for burnt offerings and sacrifices, but as a witness between us and you.'

29"Far be it from us to rebel against the LORD and turn away from him today by building an altar for burnt offerings, grain offerings and sacrifices, other than the altar of the LORD our God that stands before his tabernacle."

30When Phinehas the priest and the leaders of the community—the heads of the clans of the Israelites—heard what Reuben, Gad and Manasseh had to say, they were pleased. 31And Phinehas son of Eleazar, the priest, said to Reuben, Gad and Manasseh, "Today we know that the LORD is with us, because you have not acted unfaithfully toward the LORD in this matter. Now you have rescued the Israelites from the LORD's hand."

32Then Phinehas son of Eleazar, the priest, and the leaders returned to Canaan from their meeting with the Reubenites and Gadites in Gilead and reported to the Israelites. 33They were glad to hear the report and praised God. And they talked no more about going to war against them to devastate the country where the Reubenites and the Gadites lived.

> THEY were glad to hear the report and praised God.
>
> JOSHUA 22:33

34And the Reubenites and the Gadites gave the altar this name: A Witness Between Us that the LORD is God.

Joshua's Farewell to the Leaders

23 After a long time had passed and the LORD had given Israel rest from all their enemies around them, Joshua, by then old and well advanced in years, 2summoned all Israel—their elders, leaders, judges and officials—and said to them: "I am old and well advanced in years. 3You yourselves have seen everything the LORD your God has done to all these nations for your sake; it was the LORD your God who fought for you. 4Remember how I have allotted as an inheritance for your tribes all the land of the nations that remain—the nations I conquered—between the Jordan and the Great Sea*a* in the west. 5The LORD your God himself will drive them out of your way. He will push them out before you, and you will take possession of their land, as the LORD your God promised you.

6"Be very strong; be careful to obey all that is written in the Book of the Law of Moses, without turning aside to the right or to the left. 7Do not associate with these nations that remain among you; do not invoke the names of their gods or swear by them. You must not serve them or bow down to them. 8But you are to hold fast to the LORD your God, as you have done until now.

9"The LORD has driven out before you great and powerful nations; to this day no one has been able to withstand you. 10One of you routs a thousand, because the LORD your God fights for you, just as he promised. 11So be very careful to love the LORD your God.

12"But if you turn away and ally yourselves with the survivors of these nations that remain among you and if you intermarry with them and associate with them, 13then you may be sure that the LORD your God will no longer drive out these nations before you. Instead, they will become snares and traps for you, whips on your backs and thorns in your eyes, until you perish from this good land, which the LORD your God has given you.

14"Now I am about to go the way of all the earth. You know with all your heart and soul that not one of all the good promises the LORD your God gave you has failed. Every promise has been fulfilled; not one has failed. 15But just as every good promise of the LORD your God has come true, so the LORD will bring on you all the evil he has threatened, until he has destroyed you from this good land he has given you. 16If you violate the covenant of the LORD your God, which he commanded you, and go and serve other gods and bow down to them, the LORD's anger will burn against you, and you will quickly perish from the good land he has given you."

a4 That is, the Mediterranean

The Covenant Renewed at Shechem

24 Then Joshua assembled all the tribes of Israel at Shechem. He summoned the elders, leaders, judges and officials of Israel, and they presented themselves before God.

²Joshua said to all the people, "This is what the LORD, the God of Israel, says: 'Long ago your forefathers, including Terah the father of Abraham and Nahor, lived beyond the River[a] and worshiped other gods. ³But I took your father Abraham from the land beyond the River and led him throughout Canaan and gave him many descendants. I gave him Isaac, ⁴and to Isaac I gave Jacob and Esau. I assigned the hill country of Seir to Esau, but Jacob and his sons went down to Egypt.

⁵ "Then I sent Moses and Aaron, and I afflicted the Egyptians by what I did there, and I brought you out. ⁶When I brought your fathers out of Egypt, you came to the sea, and the Egyptians pursued them with chariots and horsemen[b] as far as the Red Sea.[c] ⁷But they cried to the LORD for help, and he put darkness between you and the Egyptians; he brought the sea over them and covered them. You saw with your own eyes what I did to the Egyptians. Then you lived in the desert for a long time.

⁸ "'I brought you to the land of the Amorites who lived east of the Jordan. They fought against you, but I gave them into your hands. I destroyed them from before you, and you took possession of their land. ⁹When Balak son of Zippor, the king of Moab, prepared to fight against Israel, he sent for Balaam son of Beor to put a curse on you. ¹⁰But I would not listen to Balaam, so he blessed you again and again, and I delivered you out of his hand.

¹¹ "'Then you crossed the Jordan and came to Jericho. The citizens of Jericho fought against you, as did also the Amorites, Perizzites, Canaanites, Hittites, Girgashites, Hivites and Jebusites, but I gave them into your hands. ¹²I sent the hornet ahead of you, which drove them out before you—also the two Amorite kings. You did not do it with your own sword and bow. ¹³So I gave you a land on which you did not toil and cities you did not build; and you live in them and eat from vineyards and olive groves that you did not plant.'

¹⁴"Now fear the LORD and serve him with all faithfulness. Throw away the gods your forefathers worshiped beyond the River and in Egypt, and serve the LORD. ¹⁵But if serving the LORD seems undesirable to you, then choose for yourselves this day whom you will serve, whether the gods your forefathers served beyond the River, or the gods of the Amorites, in whose land you are living. But as for me and my household, we will serve the LORD."

> "BUT as for me and my household, we will serve the LORD."
>
> JOSHUA 24:15

¹⁶Then the people answered, "Far be it from us to forsake the LORD to serve other gods! ¹⁷It was the LORD our God himself who brought us and our fathers up out of Egypt, from that land of slavery, and performed those great signs before our eyes. He protected us on our entire journey and among all the nations through which we traveled. ¹⁸And the LORD drove out before us all the nations, including the Amorites, who lived in the land. We too will serve the LORD, because he is our God."

¹⁹Joshua said to the people, "You are not able to serve the LORD. He is a holy God; he is a jealous God. He will not forgive your rebellion and your sins. ²⁰If you forsake the LORD and serve foreign gods, he will turn and bring disaster on you and make an end of you, after he has been good to you."

²¹But the people said to Joshua, "No! We will serve the LORD."

²²Then Joshua said, "You are witnesses against yourselves that you have chosen to serve the LORD."

"Yes, we are witnesses," they replied.

²³"Now then," said Joshua, "throw away the foreign gods that are among

[a]2 That is, the Euphrates; also in verses 3, 14 and 15   [b]6 Or charioteers   [c]6 Hebrew Yam Suph; that is, Sea of Reeds

you and yield your hearts to the LORD, the God of Israel."

²⁴And the people said to Joshua, "We will serve the LORD our God and obey him."

²⁵On that day Joshua made a covenant for the people, and there at Shechem he drew up for them decrees and laws. ²⁶And Joshua recorded these things in the Book of the Law of God. Then he took a large stone and set it up there under the oak near the holy place of the LORD.

²⁷"See!" he said to all the people. "This stone will be a witness against us. It has heard all the words the LORD has said to us. It will be a witness against you if you are untrue to your God."

Buried in the Promised Land

²⁸Then Joshua sent the people away, each to his own inheritance.

²⁹After these things, Joshua son of Nun, the servant of the LORD, died at the age of a hundred and ten. ³⁰And they buried him in the land of his inheritance, at Timnath Serah[a] in the hill country of Ephraim, north of Mount Gaash.

³¹Israel served the LORD throughout the lifetime of Joshua and of the elders who outlived him and who had experienced everything the LORD had done for Israel.

³²And Joseph's bones, which the Israelites had brought up from Egypt, were buried at Shechem in the tract of land that Jacob bought for a hundred pieces of silver[b] from the sons of Hamor, the father of Shechem. This became the inheritance of Joseph's descendants.

³³And Eleazar son of Aaron died and was buried at Gibeah, which had been allotted to his son Phinehas in the hill country of Ephraim.

---

[a]30 Also known as *Timnath Heres* (see Judges 2:9)   [b]32 Hebrew *hundred kesitahs*; a kesitah was a unit of money of unknown weight and value.

Judges

"**THE CHURCH** is in need of perennial revival because of recurrent spiritual decline," wrote church historian Earle Cairns.[1] The second generation of Israelites pictured in Judges 2:7,10–13 is a case in point. "They *forsook* the LORD, the God of their fathers" (verse 12, italics added) because they had not known the power and reality of the Lord as their parents had.

Jeremiah's favorite word for Israel's spiritual decline is *forsook*: "They have forsaken me, the spring of living water" (Jeremiah 2:13; cf. 5:7,19; 9:13). Later, John tells the church at Ephesus that they are in spiritual danger because they have "forsaken [their] first love" (Revelation 2:4). The pattern of spiritual decline, crisis and revival has repeated itself too many times in Biblical and church history to be dismissed as an anomaly. It keeps happening because the enemies of God keep attacking the people of God. If left unchecked, the devil, the world and our own flesh will destroy the church from the inside by false teaching and immorality, and from the outside by persecution. We seem to be terminally drawn to forsakenness.

"O GOD, PLEASE STRENGTHEN ME JUST ONCE MORE." (16:28)

The book of Judges is a kind of cautionary tale about the dangers of not paying attention to this insidious cycle, of the need to be vigilant and prayerful for the purity of the faith. This book demonstrates that if we do not have God over us to rule us, we will succumb to whatever is around us.

But the book of Judges is also a story of hope. God's patience is matched only by his creativity in the odds and ends of people he will use to restore his people. What are we to make of the likes of Othniel, Ehud, Barak, Gideon, Jephthah and Samson? They fit as easily in a menagerie or a police lineup as they do in the hall of fame of faith (see Hebrews 11:32–34). But they encourage more than they amaze and amuse: "God chose the foolish things of the world to shame the wise; God chose the weak things of the world to shame the strong" (1 Corinthians 1:27). There's hope for us all!

Israel Fights the Remaining Canaanites

1 After the death of Joshua, the Israelites asked the LORD, "Who will be the first to go up and fight for us against the Canaanites?"

²The LORD answered, "Judah is to go; I have given the land into their hands."

³Then the men of Judah said to the Simeonites their brothers, "Come up with us into the territory allotted to us, to fight against the Canaanites. We in turn will go with you into yours." So the Simeonites went with them.

⁴When Judah attacked, the LORD gave the Canaanites and Perizzites into their hands and they struck down ten thousand men at Bezek. ⁵It was there that they found Adoni-Bezek and fought against him, putting to rout the Canaanites and Perizzites. ⁶Adoni-Bezek fled, but they chased him and caught him, and cut off his thumbs and big toes.

⁷Then Adoni-Bezek said, "Seventy kings with their thumbs and big toes cut off have picked up scraps under my table. Now God has paid me back for what I did to them." They brought him to Jerusalem, and he died there.

⁸The men of Judah attacked Jerusalem also and took it. They put the city to the sword and set it on fire.

⁹After that, the men of Judah went down to fight against the Canaanites living in the hill country, the Negev and the western foothills. ¹⁰They advanced against the Canaanites living in Hebron (formerly called Kiriath Arba) and defeated Sheshai, Ahiman and Talmai.

¹¹From there they advanced against the people living in Debir (formerly called Kiriath Sepher). ¹²And Caleb said, "I will give my daughter Acsah in marriage to the man who attacks and captures Kiriath Sepher." ¹³Othniel son of Kenaz, Caleb's younger brother, took it; so Caleb gave his daughter Acsah to him in marriage.

¹⁴One day when she came to Othniel, she urged him*ᵃ* to ask her father for a field. When she got off her donkey, Caleb asked her, "What can I do for you?"

¹⁵She replied, "Do me a special favor. Since you have given me land in the Negev, give me also springs of water." Then Caleb gave her the upper and lower springs.

¹⁶The descendants of Moses' father-in-law, the Kenite, went up from the City of Palms*ᵇ* with the men of Judah to live among the people of the Desert of Judah in the Negev near Arad.

¹⁷Then the men of Judah went with the Simeonites their brothers and attacked the Canaanites living in Zephath, and they totally destroyed*ᶜ* the city. Therefore it was called Hormah.*ᵈ* ¹⁸The men of Judah also took*ᵉ* Gaza, Ashkelon and Ekron—each city with its territory.

¹⁹The LORD was with the men of Judah. They took possession of the hill country, but they were unable to drive the people from the plains, because they had iron chariots. ²⁰As Moses had promised, Hebron was given to Caleb, who drove from it the three sons of Anak. ²¹The Benjamites, however, failed to dislodge the Jebusites, who were living in Jerusalem; to this day the Jebusites live there with the Benjamites.

²²Now the house of Joseph attacked Bethel, and the LORD was with them. ²³When they sent men to spy out Bethel (formerly called Luz), ²⁴the spies saw a man coming out of the city and they said to him, "Show us how to get into the city and we will see that you are treated well." ²⁵So he showed them, and they put the city to the sword but spared the man and his whole family. ²⁶He then went to the land of the Hittites, where he built a city and called it Luz, which is its name to this day.

²⁷But Manasseh did not drive out the people of Beth Shan or Taanach or Dor or Ibleam or Megiddo and their surrounding settlements, for the Canaanites were determined to live in that land. ²⁸When Israel became strong, they pressed the Canaanites into forced labor but never drove them out completely. ²⁹Nor did Ephraim drive out the Canaanites living in Gezer, but the Canaanites continued to live there among them. ³⁰Neither did Zebulun drive out the Canaanites living in

---

ᵃ14 Hebrew; Septuagint and Vulgate *Othniel, he urged her*   *ᵇ16* That is, Jericho
ᶜ17 The Hebrew term refers to the irrevocable giving over of things or persons to the LORD, often by totally destroying them.   *ᵈ17 Hormah* means *destruction.*   *ᵉ18* Hebrew; Septuagint *Judah did not take*

Kitron or Nahalol, who remained among them; but they did subject them to forced labor. ³¹Nor did Asher drive out those living in Acco or Sidon or Ahlab or Aczib or Helbah or Aphek or Rehob, ³²and because of this the people of Asher lived among the Canaanite inhabitants of the land. ³³Neither did Naphtali drive out those living in Beth Shemesh or Beth Anath; but the Naphtalites too lived among the Canaanite inhabitants of the land, and those living in Beth Shemesh and Beth Anath became forced laborers for them. ³⁴The Amorites confined the Danites to the hill country, not allowing them to come down into the plain. ³⁵And the Amorites were determined also to hold out in Mount Heres, Aijalon and Shaalbim, but when the power of the house of Joseph increased, they too were pressed into forced labor. ³⁶The boundary of the Amorites was from Scorpion[a] Pass to Sela and beyond.

The Angel of the LORD at Bokim

2 The angel of the LORD went up from Gilgal to Bokim and said, "I brought you up out of Egypt and led you into the land that I swore to give to your forefathers. I said, 'I will never break my covenant with you, ²and you shall not make a covenant with the people of this land, but you shall break down their altars.' Yet you have disobeyed me. Why have you done this? ³Now therefore I tell you that I will not drive them out before you; they will be ⌞thorns⌟ in your sides and their gods will be a snare to you."

⁴When the angel of the LORD had spoken these things to all the Israelites, the people wept aloud, ⁵and they called that place Bokim.[b] There they offered sacrifices to the LORD.

Disobedience and Defeat

⁶After Joshua had dismissed the Israelites, they went to take possession of the land, each to his own inheritance. ⁷The people served the LORD throughout the lifetime of Joshua and of the elders who outlived him and who had seen all the great things the LORD had done for Israel. ⁸Joshua son of Nun, the servant of the LORD, died at the age of a hundred and ten. ⁹And they buried him in the land of his inheritance, at Timnath Heres[c] in the hill country of Ephraim, north of Mount Gaash.

¹⁰After that whole generation had been gathered to their fathers, another generation grew up, who knew neither the LORD nor what he had done for Israel. ¹¹Then the Israelites did evil in the eyes of the LORD and served the Baals. ¹²They forsook the LORD, the God of their fathers, who had brought them out of Egypt. They followed and worshiped various gods of the peoples around them. They provoked the LORD to anger ¹³because they forsook him and served Baal and the Ashtoreths. ¹⁴In his anger against Israel the LORD handed them over to raiders who plundered them. He sold them to their enemies all around, whom they were no longer able to resist. ¹⁵Whenever Israel went out to fight, the hand of the LORD was against them to defeat them, just as he had sworn to them. They were in great distress.

¹⁶Then the LORD raised up judges,[d] who saved them out of the hands of these raiders. ¹⁷Yet they would not listen to their judges but prostituted themselves to other gods and worshiped them. Unlike their fathers, they quickly turned from the way in which their fathers had walked, the way of obedience to the LORD's commands. ¹⁸Whenever the LORD raised up a judge for them, he was with the judge and saved them out of the hands of their enemies as long as the judge lived; for the LORD had compassion on them as they groaned under those who oppressed and afflicted them. ¹⁹But when the judge died, the people returned to ways even more corrupt than those of their fathers, following other gods and serving and worshiping them. They refused to give up their evil practices and stubborn ways.

²⁰Therefore the LORD was very angry with Israel and said, "Because this nation has violated the covenant that I laid down for their forefathers and has not listened to me, ²¹I will no longer drive out before them any of the nations Joshua left when he died. ²²I will use them to test

---

[a]36 Hebrew *Akrabbim*   [b]5 *Bokim* means *weepers.*   [c]9 Also known as *Timnath Serah* (see Joshua 19:50 and 24:30)   [d]16 Or *leaders*; similarly in verses 17–19

Israel and see whether they will keep the way of the LORD and walk in it as their forefathers did." ²³The LORD had allowed those nations to remain; he did not drive them out at once by giving them into the hands of Joshua.

3 These are the nations the LORD left to test all those Israelites who had not experienced any of the wars in Canaan ²(he did this only to teach warfare to the descendants of the Israelites who had not had previous battle experience): ³the five rulers of the Philistines, all the Canaanites, the Sidonians, and the Hivites living in the Lebanon mountains from Mount Baal Hermon to Lebo*a* Hamath. ⁴They were left to test the Israelites to see whether they would obey the LORD's

a3 Or to the entrance to

JUDGES 2:6–15

Praying for the Next Generation

2:10 ANOTHER GENERATION GREW UP, WHO KNEW NEITHER THE LORD NOR WHAT HE HAD DONE FOR ISRAEL.

Judges 2:10 reads like an epitaph on the graves of those who should have been teaching the next generation about the Lord. And it puts a chill in the heart of all parents and grandparents who love their children: What if those who come after us don't know the goodness of God?

This passage is a call to pray for generations that will come after us. What could be more important than to pray that those who follow us will follow the Lord, too—only with more passion and fervor? What greater tragedy, even indictment, is there than that those who know us best, our families and children, know the Lord least? Psalm 78 is a call to arms and to prayer for the next generation: "We will tell the next generation the praiseworthy deeds of the LORD, his power, and the wonders he has done. He decreed statutes for Jacob and established the law in Israel, which he commanded our forefathers to teach their children, so the next generation would know them, even the children yet to be born, and they in turn would tell their children. Then they would put their trust in God and would not forget his deeds but would keep his commands" (verses 4–7).

The ministry Moms in Touch has seen God quietly change school campuses and students' lives as it has summoned moms to "pour out your heart like water in the presence of the Lord. Lift up your hands to him for the lives of your children" (Lamentations 2:19). Who is more passionate for the faith of children than mothers? History abounds with the stories of women like Susanna Wesley (the mother of John and Charles Wesley) and Monica (the mother of Augustine) who prevailed in prayer for their children. And history is different because of their commitment.

P R A Y :

Dear Father, from whom your whole family in heaven and earth derives its name, empower me to be a faithful teacher of the Good News and faithful in prayer for the next generation. Put your Spirit in the hearts of those who come after me, so that they would put their trust in you and no other.

FOR YOUR NEXT DEVOTIONAL READING, GO TO PAGE 278.

commands, which he had given their forefathers through Moses.

⁵The Israelites lived among the Canaanites, Hittites, Amorites, Perizzites, Hivites and Jebusites. ⁶They took their daughters in marriage and gave their own daughters to their sons, and served their gods.

Othniel

⁷The Israelites did evil in the eyes of the LORD; they forgot the LORD their God and served the Baals and the Asherahs. ⁸The anger of the LORD burned against Israel so that he sold them into the hands of Cushan-Rishathaim king of Aram Naharaim,ᵃ to whom the Israelites were subject for eight years. ⁹But when they cried out to the LORD, he raised up for them a deliverer, Othniel son of Kenaz, Caleb's younger brother, who saved them. ¹⁰The Spirit of the LORD came upon him, so that he became Israel's judgeᵇ

> BUT when they cried out to the LORD, he raised up for them a deliverer, Othniel son of Kenaz, Caleb's younger brother, who saved them.
>
> JUDGES 3:9

and went to war. The LORD gave Cushan-Rishathaim king of Aram into the hands of Othniel, who overpowered him. ¹¹So the land had peace for forty years, until Othniel son of Kenaz died.

Ehud

¹²Once again the Israelites did evil in the eyes of the LORD, and because they did this evil the LORD gave Eglon king of Moab power over Israel. ¹³Getting the Ammonites and Amalekites to join him, Eglon came and attacked Israel, and they took possession of the City of Palms.ᶜ ¹⁴The Israelites were subject to Eglon king of Moab for eighteen years.

¹⁵Again the Israelites cried out to the LORD, and he gave them a deliverer—Ehud, a left-handed man, the son of Gera the Benjamite. The Israelites sent him with tribute to Eglon king of Moab. ¹⁶Now Ehud had made a double-edged sword about a foot and a halfᵈ long, which he strapped to his right thigh under his

clothing. ¹⁷He presented the tribute to Eglon king of Moab, who was a very fat man. ¹⁸After Ehud had presented the tribute, he sent on their way the men who had carried it. ¹⁹At the idolsᵉ near Gilgal he himself turned back and said, "I have a secret message for you, O king."

The king said, "Quiet!" And all his attendants left him.

²⁰Ehud then approached him while he was sitting alone in the upper room of his summer palaceᶠ and said, "I have a message from God for you." As the king rose from his seat, ²¹Ehud reached with his left hand, drew the sword from his right thigh and plunged it into the king's belly. ²²Even the handle sank in after the blade, which came out his back. Ehud did not pull the sword out, and the fat closed in over it. ²³Then Ehud went out to the porchᵍ; he shut the doors of the upper room behind him and locked them.

²⁴After he had gone, the servants came and found the doors of the upper room locked. They said, "He must be relieving himself in the inner room of the house." ²⁵They waited to the point of embarrassment, but when he did not open the doors of the room, they took a key and unlocked them. There they saw their lord fallen to the floor, dead.

²⁶While they waited, Ehud got away. He passed by the idols and escaped to Seirah. ²⁷When he arrived there, he blew a trumpet in the hill country of Ephraim, and the Israelites went down with him from the hills, with him leading them.

²⁸"Follow me," he ordered, "for the LORD has given Moab, your enemy, into your hands." So they followed him down and, taking possession of the fords of the Jordan that led to Moab, they allowed no one to cross over. ²⁹At that time they struck down about ten thousand Moabites, all vigorous and strong; not a man escaped. ³⁰That day Moab was made subject to Israel, and the land had peace for eighty years.

ᵃ8 That is, Northwest Mesopotamia
ᵇ10 Or *leader*   ᶜ13 That is, Jericho
ᵈ16 Hebrew *a cubit* (about 0.5 meter)
ᵉ19 Or *the stone quarries*; also in verse 26
ᶠ20 The meaning of the Hebrew for this phrase is uncertain.   ᵍ23 The meaning of the Hebrew for this word is uncertain.

Shamgar

31After Ehud came Shamgar son of Anath, who struck down six hundred Philistines with an oxgoad. He too saved Israel.

Deborah

4 After Ehud died, the Israelites once again did evil in the eyes of the LORD. **2**So the LORD sold them into the hands of Jabin, a king of Canaan, who reigned in Hazor. The commander of his army was Sisera, who lived in Harosheth Haggoyim. **3**Because he had nine hundred iron chariots and had cruelly oppressed the Israelites for twenty years, they cried to the LORD for help.

> BECAUSE *[Sisera] had nine hundred iron chariots and had cruelly oppressed the Israelites for twenty years, they cried to the LORD for help.*
>
> JUDGES 4:3

4Deborah, a prophetess, the wife of Lappidoth, was leading*a* Israel at that time. **5**She held court under the Palm of Deborah between Ramah and Bethel in the hill country of Ephraim, and the Israelites came to her to have their disputes decided. **6**She sent for Barak son of Abinoam from Kedesh in Naphtali and said to him, "The LORD, the God of Israel, commands you: 'Go, take with you ten thousand men of Naphtali and Zebulun and lead the way to Mount Tabor. **7**I will lure Sisera, the commander of Jabin's army, with his chariots and his troops to the Kishon River and give him into your hands.'"

8Barak said to her, "If you go with me, I will go; but if you don't go with me, I won't go."

9"Very well," Deborah said, "I will go with you. But because of the way you are going about this,*b* the honor will not be yours, for the LORD will hand Sisera over to a woman." So Deborah went with Barak to Kedesh, **10**where he summoned Zebulun and Naphtali. Ten thousand men followed him, and Deborah also went with him.

11Now Heber the Kenite had left the other Kenites, the descendants of Hobab, Moses' brother-in-law,*c* and pitched his tent by the great tree in Zaanannim near Kedesh.

12When they told Sisera that Barak son of Abinoam had gone up to Mount Tabor, **13**Sisera gathered together his nine hundred iron chariots and all the men with him, from Harosheth Haggoyim to the Kishon River.

14Then Deborah said to Barak, "Go! This is the day the LORD has given Sisera into your hands. Has not the LORD gone ahead of you?" So Barak went down Mount Tabor, followed by ten thousand men. **15**At Barak's advance, the LORD routed Sisera and all his chariots and army by the sword, and Sisera abandoned his chariot and fled on foot. **16**But Barak pursued the chariots and army as far as Harosheth Haggoyim. All the troops of Sisera fell by the sword; not a man was left.

17Sisera, however, fled on foot to the tent of Jael, the wife of Heber the Kenite, because there were friendly relations between Jabin king of Hazor and the clan of Heber the Kenite.

18Jael went out to meet Sisera and said to him, "Come, my lord, come right in. Don't be afraid." So he entered her tent, and she put a covering over him.

19"I'm thirsty," he said. "Please give me some water." She opened a skin of milk, gave him a drink, and covered him up.

20"Stand in the doorway of the tent," he told her. "If someone comes by and asks you, 'Is anyone here?' say 'No.'"

21But Jael, Heber's wife, picked up a tent peg and a hammer and went quietly to him while he lay fast asleep, exhausted. She drove the peg through his temple into the ground, and he died.

22Barak came by in pursuit of Sisera, and Jael went out to meet him. "Come," she said, "I will show you the man you're looking for." So he went in with her, and there lay Sisera with the tent peg through his temple—dead.

23On that day God subdued Jabin, the Canaanite king, before the Israelites.

---

a4 Traditionally *judging* *b9* Or *But on the expedition you are undertaking* *c11* Or *father-in-law*

²⁴And the hand of the Israelites grew stronger and stronger against Jabin, the Canaanite king, until they destroyed him.

The Song of Deborah

5 On that day Deborah and Barak son of Abinoam sang this song:

² "When the princes in Israel take the lead,
when the people willingly offer themselves—
praise the LORD!

³ "Hear this, you kings! Listen, you rulers!
I will sing to*ᵃ* the LORD, I will sing;
I will make music to*ᵇ* the LORD, the God of Israel.

⁴ "O LORD, when you went out from Seir,
when you marched from the land of Edom,
the earth shook, the heavens poured,
the clouds poured down water.
⁵ The mountains quaked before the LORD, the One of Sinai,
before the LORD, the God of Israel.

⁶ "In the days of Shamgar son of Anath,
in the days of Jael, the roads were abandoned;
travelers took to winding paths.
⁷ Village life*ᶜ* in Israel ceased,
ceased until I,*ᵈ* Deborah, arose,
arose a mother in Israel.
⁸ When they chose new gods,
war came to the city gates,
and not a shield or spear was seen among forty thousand in Israel.
⁹ My heart is with Israel's princes,
with the willing volunteers among the people.
Praise the LORD!

¹⁰ "You who ride on white donkeys,
sitting on your saddle blankets,
and you who walk along the road,
consider ¹¹the voice of the singers*ᵉ* at the watering places.
They recite the righteous acts of the LORD,
the righteous acts of his warriors*ᶠ* in Israel.

"Then the people of the LORD went down to the city gates.
¹² 'Wake up, wake up, Deborah!
Wake up, wake up, break out in song!
Arise, O Barak!
Take captive your captives, O son of Abinoam.'

¹³ "Then the men who were left came down to the nobles;
the people of the LORD came to me with the mighty.
¹⁴ Some came from Ephraim, whose roots were in Amalek;
Benjamin was with the people who followed you.
From Makir captains came down,
from Zebulun those who bear a commander's staff.
¹⁵ The princes of Issachar were with Deborah;
yes, Issachar was with Barak,
rushing after him into the valley.
In the districts of Reuben there was much searching of heart.
¹⁶ Why did you stay among the campfires*ᵍ*
to hear the whistling for the flocks?
In the districts of Reuben there was much searching of heart.
¹⁷ Gilead stayed beyond the Jordan.
And Dan, why did he linger by the ships?
Asher remained on the coast and stayed in his coves.
¹⁸ The people of Zebulun risked their very lives;
so did Naphtali on the heights of the field.

¹⁹ "Kings came, they fought;
the kings of Canaan fought

ᵃ3 Or *of*   *ᵇ3* Or *I with song I will praise*
ᶜ7 Or *Warriors*   *ᵈ7* Or *you*   *ᵉ11* Or *archers*; the meaning of the Hebrew for this word is uncertain.   *ᶠ11* Or *villagers*
ᵍ16 Or *saddlebags*

at Taanach by the waters of Megiddo,
but they carried off no silver, no
plunder.
20 From the heavens the stars fought,
from their courses they fought
against Sisera.
21 The river Kishon swept them away,
the age-old river, the river Kishon.
March on, my soul; be strong!
22 Then thundered the horses' hoofs—
galloping, galloping go his mighty
steeds.
23 'Curse Meroz,' said the angel of the
LORD.
'Curse its people bitterly,
because they did not come to help
the LORD,
to help the LORD against the
mighty.'

24 "Most blessed of women be Jael,
the wife of Heber the Kenite,
most blessed of tent-dwelling
women.
25 He asked for water, and she gave
him milk;
in a bowl fit for nobles she brought
him curdled milk.
26 Her hand reached for the tent peg,
her right hand for the workman's
hammer.
She struck Sisera, she crushed his
head,
she shattered and pierced his
temple.
27 At her feet he sank,
he fell; there he lay.
At her feet he sank, he fell;
where he sank, there he fell—
dead.

28 "Through the window peered Sisera's
mother;
behind the lattice she cried out,
'Why is his chariot so long in coming?
Why is the clatter of his chariots
delayed?'
29 The wisest of her ladies answer her;
indeed, she keeps saying to herself,
30 'Are they not finding and dividing
the spoils:
a girl or two for each man,
colorful garments as plunder for
Sisera,
colorful garments embroidered,

highly embroidered garments for
my neck—
all this as plunder?'

31 "So may all your enemies perish,
O LORD!
But may they who love you be like
the sun
when it rises in its strength."

Then the land had peace forty years.

Gideon

6 Again the Israelites did evil in the
eyes of the LORD, and for seven years
he gave them into the hands of the Midianites. 2Because the power of Midian
was so oppressive, the Israelites prepared shelters for themselves in mountain clefts, caves and strongholds.
3Whenever the Israelites planted their
crops, the Midianites, Amalekites and
other eastern peoples invaded the country. 4They camped on the land and ruined
the crops all the way to Gaza and did not
spare a living thing for Israel, neither
sheep nor cattle nor donkeys. 5They
came up with their livestock and their
tents like swarms of locusts. It was impossible to count the men and their camels; they invaded the land to ravage it.
6Midian so impoverished the Israelites
that they cried out to the LORD for help.

7When the Israelites cried to the LORD
because of Midian, 8he sent them a prophet, who said, "This is what the LORD, the
God of Israel, says: I brought you up out of
Egypt, out of the land of slavery. 9I
snatched you from the power of Egypt and
from the hand of all your oppressors. I
drove them from before you and gave you
their land. 10I said to you, 'I am the LORD
your God; do not worship the gods of the
Amorites, in whose land you live.' But you
have not listened to me."

11The angel of the LORD came and sat
down under the oak in Ophrah that belonged to Joash the Abiezrite, where his
son Gideon was threshing wheat in a
winepress to keep it from the Midianites.
12When the angel of the LORD appeared
to Gideon, he said, "The LORD is with you,
mighty warrior."

13"But sir," Gideon replied, "if the LORD
is with us, why has all this happened to

us? Where are all his wonders that our fathers told us about when they said, 'Did not the LORD bring us up out of Egypt?' But now the LORD has abandoned us and put us into the hand of Midian."

¹⁴The LORD turned to him and said, "Go in the strength you have and save Israel out of Midian's hand. Am I not sending you?"

¹⁵"But Lord,ᵃ" Gideon asked, "how can I save Israel? My clan is the weakest in Manasseh, and I am the least in my family."

¹⁶The LORD answered, "I will be with you, and you will strike down all the Midianites together."

¹⁷Gideon replied, "If now I have found favor in your eyes, give me a sign that it is really you talking to me. ¹⁸Please do not go away until I come back and bring my offering and set it before you."

And the LORD said, "I will wait until you return."

¹⁹Gideon went in, prepared a young goat, and from an ephahᵇ of flour he made bread without yeast. Putting the meat in a basket and its broth in a pot, he brought them out and offered them to him under the oak.

²⁰The angel of God said to him, "Take the meat and the unleavened bread, place them on this rock, and pour out the broth." And Gideon did so. ²¹With the tip of the staff that was in his hand, the angel of the LORD touched the meat and the unleavened bread. Fire flared from the rock, consuming the meat and the bread. And the angel of the LORD disappeared. ²²When Gideon realized that it was the angel of the LORD, he exclaimed, "Ah, Sovereign LORD! I have seen the angel of the LORD face to face!"

²³But the LORD said to him, "Peace! Do not be afraid. You are not going to die."

²⁴So Gideon built an altar to the LORD there and called it The LORD is Peace. To this day it stands in Ophrah of the Abiezrites.

²⁵That same night the LORD said to him, "Take the second bull from your father's herd, the one seven years old.ᶜ Tear down your father's altar to Baal and cut down the Asherah poleᵈ beside it. ²⁶Then build a proper kind ofᵉ altar to the LORD your God on the top of this height. Using

the wood of the Asherah pole that you cut down, offer the secondᶠ bull as a burnt offering."

²⁷So Gideon took ten of his servants and did as the LORD told him. But because he was afraid of his family and the men of the town, he did it at night rather than in the daytime.

²⁸In the morning when the men of the town got up, there was Baal's altar, demolished, with the Asherah pole beside it cut down and the second bull sacrificed on the newly built altar!

²⁹They asked each other, "Who did this?"

When they carefully investigated, they were told, "Gideon son of Joash did it."

³⁰The men of the town demanded of Joash, "Bring out your son. He must die, because he has broken down Baal's altar and cut down the Asherah pole beside it."

³¹But Joash replied to the hostile crowd around him, "Are you going to plead Baal's cause? Are you trying to save him? Whoever fights for him shall be put to death by morning! If Baal really is a god, he can defend himself when someone breaks down his altar." ³²So that day they called Gideon "Jerub-Baal,ᵍ" saying, "Let Baal contend with him," because he broke down Baal's altar.

³³Now all the Midianites, Amalekites and other eastern peoples joined forces and crossed over the Jordan and camped in the Valley of Jezreel. ³⁴Then the Spirit of the LORD came upon Gideon, and he blew a trumpet, summoning the Abiezrites to follow him. ³⁵He sent messengers throughout Manasseh, calling them to arms, and also into Asher, Zebulun and Naphtali, so that they too went up to meet them.

³⁶Gideon said to God, "If you will save Israel by my hand as you have promised— ³⁷look, I will place a wool fleece on the threshing floor. If there is dew only on

---

ᵃ15 Or sir   ᵇ19 That is, probably about 3/5 bushel (about 22 liters)   ᶜ25 Or Take a full-grown, mature bull from your father's herd   ᵈ25 That is, a symbol of the goddess Asherah; here and elsewhere in Judges   ᵉ26 Or build with layers of stone an   ᶠ26 Or full-grown; also in verse 28   ᵍ32 Jerub-Baal means let Baal contend.

the fleece and all the ground is dry, then I will know that you will save Israel by my hand, as you said." ³⁸And that is what happened. Gideon rose early the next day; he squeezed the fleece and wrung out the dew—a bowlful of water.

³⁹Then Gideon said to God, "Do not be angry with me. Let me make just one more request. Allow me one more test with the fleece. This time make the fleece dry and

the ground covered with dew." ⁴⁰That night God did so. Only the fleece was dry; all the ground was covered with dew.

Gideon Defeats the Midianites

7 Early in the morning, Jerub-Baal (that is, Gideon) and all his men camped at the spring of Harod. The camp of Midian was north of them in the valley near the hill of Moreh. ²The Lord said to Gid-

---

[**THURSDAY**]

JUDGES 6:36–40

Forget Fleeces!

6:36 "I WILL PLACE A WOOL FLEECE ON THE THRESHING FLOOR ... "

John White's advice regarding using Gideon's method of "fleece" praying may seem a little blunt, but his point is clear: "Forget about fleeces. If you've never used them, don't start. If you have, then quit."² His reasoning is compelling.

One: Gideon was a semi-pagan, thinking and acting like a semi-pagan, and God was simply being patient and condescending to accommodate Gideon's primitive prayer the way he did. It isn't becoming of a Christian to behave like Gideon, who was ignorant of God's ways. God uses all kinds of people, some of whom we rightly see as unworthy, like Gideon. He does this to show his sovereign grace. But it is a kind of trafficking in the grace of God to conclude that you can forego the serious study of Scripture and waiting on God and instead give God a few binary choices to show you what to do.

Two: Putting out a "fleece" for God to show us what to do doesn't satisfy our need to know the will of God. It didn't really do it for Gideon, either. The first time he tried the fleece thing and saw it get wet when there was no dew, he still wasn't sure. Maybe there was another hypothesis to explain it; maybe fleeces sometimes do get wet when there is no dew. This kind of crude application of the scientific method always leaves room for more doubt. There is always one more "test" to try, one more avoidance of making a decision. Eventually we all have to learn to walk by faith and not by sight.

Those are White's reasons, but there is one more: The use of "fleeces" circumvents the trying and difficult process of waiting on God and trusting him with less than all the information we want. God is more concerned about who we are than what we do in most situations. Our concerns are often the opposite, and we are drawn to fleeces instead of spiritual maturity. At least as important as what we wait for in prayer is what happens to our character as we wait.

P R A Y :
Father, you promised that those who hope in you and wait
will be strengthened (see Isaiah 40:31). I am hoping and waiting.
Keep me from the temptation to take shortcuts.

———

FOR YOUR NEXT DEVOTIONAL READING, GO TO PAGE 285.

eon, "You have too many men for me to deliver Midian into their hands. In order that Israel may not boast against me that her own strength has saved her, ³announce now to the people, 'Anyone who trembles with fear may turn back and leave Mount Gilead.'" So twenty-two thousand men left, while ten thousand remained.

⁴But the LORD said to Gideon, "There are still too many men. Take them down to the water, and I will sift them for you there. If I say, 'This one shall go with you,' he shall go; but if I say, 'This one shall not go with you,' he shall not go."

⁵So Gideon took the men down to the water. There the LORD told him, "Separate those who lap the water with their tongues like a dog from those who kneel down to drink." ⁶Three hundred men lapped with their hands to their mouths. All the rest got down on their knees to drink.

⁷The LORD said to Gideon, "With the three hundred men that lapped I will save you and give the Midianites into your hands. Let all the other men go, each to his own place." ⁸So Gideon sent the rest of the Israelites to their tents but kept the three hundred, who took over the provisions and trumpets of the others.

Now the camp of Midian lay below him in the valley. ⁹During that night the LORD said to Gideon, "Get up, go down against the camp, because I am going to give it into your hands. ¹⁰If you are afraid to attack, go down to the camp with your servant Purah ¹¹and listen to what they are saying. Afterward, you will be encouraged to attack the camp." So he and Purah his servant went down to the outposts of the camp. ¹²The Midianites, the Amalekites and all the other eastern peoples had settled in the valley, thick as locusts. Their camels could no more be counted than the sand on the seashore.

¹³Gideon arrived just as a man was telling a friend his dream. "I had a dream," he was saying. "A round loaf of barley bread came tumbling into the Midianite camp. It struck the tent with such force that the tent overturned and collapsed."

¹⁴His friend responded, "This can be nothing other than the sword of Gideon son of Joash, the Israelite. God has given the Midianites and the whole camp into his hands."

¹⁵When Gideon heard the dream and its interpretation, he worshiped God. He returned to the camp of Israel and called out, "Get up! The LORD has given the Midianite camp into your hands." ¹⁶Dividing the three hundred men into three companies, he placed trumpets and empty jars in the hands of all of them, with torches inside.

¹⁷"Watch me," he told them. "Follow my lead. When I get to the edge of the camp, do exactly as I do. ¹⁸When I and all who are with me blow our trumpets, then from all around the camp blow yours and shout, 'For the LORD and for Gideon.'"

¹⁹Gideon and the hundred men with him reached the edge of the camp at the beginning of the middle watch, just after they had changed the guard. They blew their trumpets and broke the jars that were in their hands. ²⁰The three companies blew the trumpets and smashed the jars. Grasping the torches in their left hands and holding in their right hands the trumpets they were to blow, they shouted, "A sword for the LORD and for Gideon!" ²¹While each man held his position around the camp, all the Midianites ran, crying out as they fled.

²²When the three hundred trumpets sounded, the LORD caused the men throughout the camp to turn on each other with their swords. The army fled to Beth Shittah toward Zererah as far as the border of Abel Meholah near Tabbath. ²³Israelites from Naphtali, Asher and all Manasseh were called out, and they pursued the Midianites. ²⁴Gideon sent messengers throughout the hill country of Ephraim, saying, "Come down against the Midianites and seize the waters of the Jordan ahead of them as far as Beth Barah."

So all the men of Ephraim were called out and they took the waters of the Jordan as far as Beth Barah. ²⁵They also captured two of the Midianite leaders, Oreb and Zeeb. They killed Oreb at the rock of Oreb, and Zeeb at the winepress of Zeeb. They pursued the Midianites and brought the heads of Oreb and Zeeb to Gideon, who was by the Jordan.

Zebah and Zalmunna

8 Now the Ephraimites asked Gideon, "Why have you treated us like this? Why didn't you call us when you went to fight Midian?" And they criticized him sharply.

²But he answered them, "What have I accomplished compared to you? Aren't the gleanings of Ephraim's grapes better than the full grape harvest of Abiezer? ³God gave Oreb and Zeeb, the Midianite leaders, into your hands. What was I able to do compared to you?" At this, their resentment against him subsided.

⁴Gideon and his three hundred men, exhausted yet keeping up the pursuit, came to the Jordan and crossed it. ⁵He said to the men of Succoth, "Give my troops some bread; they are worn out, and I am still pursuing Zebah and Zalmunna, the kings of Midian."

⁶But the officials of Succoth said, "Do you already have the hands of Zebah and Zalmunna in your possession? Why should we give bread to your troops?"

> 66 We must move from asking God to take care of the things that are breaking our hearts, to praying about the things that are breaking his heart. 99
>
> MARGARET GIBB

⁷Then Gideon replied, "Just for that, when the LORD has given Zebah and Zalmunna into my hand, I will tear your flesh with desert thorns and briers."

⁸From there he went up to Peniel*a* and made the same request of them, but they answered as the men of Succoth had. ⁹So he said to the men of Peniel, "When I return in triumph, I will tear down this tower."

¹⁰Now Zebah and Zalmunna were in Karkor with a force of about fifteen thousand men, all that were left of the armies of the eastern peoples; a hundred and twenty thousand swordsmen had fallen. ¹¹Gideon went up by the route of the nomads east of Nobah and Jogbehah and fell upon the unsuspecting army. ¹²Zebah and Zalmunna, the two kings of Midian, fled, but he pur-

sued them and captured them, routing their entire army.

¹³Gideon son of Joash then returned from the battle by the Pass of Heres. ¹⁴He caught a young man of Succoth and questioned him, and the young man wrote down for him the names of the seventy-seven officials of Succoth, the elders of the town. ¹⁵Then Gideon came and said to the men of Succoth, "Here are Zebah and Zalmunna, about whom you taunted me by saying, 'Do you already have the hands of Zebah and Zalmunna in your possession? Why should we give bread to your exhausted men?'" ¹⁶He took the elders of the town and taught the men of Succoth a lesson by punishing them with desert thorns and briers. ¹⁷He also pulled down the tower of Peniel and killed the men of the town.

¹⁸Then he asked Zebah and Zalmunna, "What kind of men did you kill at Tabor?"

"Men like you," they answered, "each one with the bearing of a prince."

¹⁹Gideon replied, "Those were my brothers, the sons of my own mother. As surely as the LORD lives, if you had spared their lives, I would not kill you." ²⁰Turning to Jether, his oldest son, he said, "Kill them!" But Jether did not draw his sword, because he was only a boy and was afraid.

²¹Zebah and Zalmunna said, "Come, do it yourself. 'As is the man, so is his strength.'" So Gideon stepped forward and killed them, and took the ornaments off their camels' necks.

Gideon's Ephod

²²The Israelites said to Gideon, "Rule over us—you, your son and your grandson—because you have saved us out of the hand of Midian."

²³But Gideon told them, "I will not rule over you, nor will my son rule over you. The LORD will rule over you." ²⁴And he said, "I do have one request, that each of you give me an earring from your share of the plunder." (It was the custom of the Ishmaelites to wear gold earrings.)

²⁵They answered, "We'll be glad to give them." So they spread out a garment,

---

a8 Hebrew *Penuel,* a variant of *Peniel*; also in verses 9 and 17

and each man threw a ring from his plunder onto it. ²⁶The weight of the gold rings he asked for came to seventeen hundred shekels,ᵃ not counting the ornaments, the pendants and the purple garments worn by the kings of Midian or the chains that were on their camels' necks. ²⁷Gideon made the gold into an ephod, which he placed in Ophrah, his town. All Israel prostituted themselves by worshiping it there, and it became a snare to Gideon and his family.

Gideon's Death

²⁸Thus Midian was subdued before the Israelites and did not raise its head again. During Gideon's lifetime, the land enjoyed peace forty years.

²⁹Jerub-Baal son of Joash went back home to live. ³⁰He had seventy sons of his own, for he had many wives. ³¹His concubine, who lived in Shechem, also bore him a son, whom he named Abimelech. ³²Gideon son of Joash died at a good old age and was buried in the tomb of his father Joash in Ophrah of the Abiezrites.

³³No sooner had Gideon died than the Israelites again prostituted themselves to the Baals. They set up Baal-Berith as their god and ³⁴did not remember the LORD their God, who had rescued them from the hands of all their enemies on every side. ³⁵They also failed to show kindness to the family of Jerub-Baal (that is, Gideon) for all the good things he had done for them.

Abimelech

9 Abimelech son of Jerub-Baal went to his mother's brothers in Shechem and said to them and to all his mother's clan, ²"Ask all the citizens of Shechem, 'Which is better for you: to have all seventy of Jerub-Baal's sons rule over you, or just one man?' Remember, I am your flesh and blood."

³When the brothers repeated all this to the citizens of Shechem, they were inclined to follow Abimelech, for they said, "He is our brother." ⁴They gave him seventy shekelsᵇ of silver from the temple of Baal-Berith, and Abimelech used it to hire reckless adventurers, who became his followers. ⁵He went to his father's home in Ophrah and on one stone murdered his seventy brothers, the sons of Jerub-Baal. But Jotham, the youngest son of Jerub-Baal, escaped by hiding. ⁶Then all the citizens of Shechem and Beth Millo gathered beside the great tree at the pillar in Shechem to crown Abimelech king.

⁷When Jotham was told about this, he climbed up on the top of Mount Gerizim and shouted to them, "Listen to me, citizens of Shechem, so that God may listen to you. ⁸One day the trees went out to anoint a king for themselves. They said to the olive tree, 'Be our king.'

⁹"But the olive tree answered, 'Should I give up my oil, by which both gods and men are honored, to hold sway over the trees?'

¹⁰"Next, the trees said to the fig tree, 'Come and be our king.'

¹¹"But the fig tree replied, 'Should I give up my fruit, so good and sweet, to hold sway over the trees?'

¹²"Then the trees said to the vine, 'Come and be our king.'

¹³"But the vine answered, 'Should I give up my wine, which cheers both gods and men, to hold sway over the trees?'

¹⁴"Finally all the trees said to the thornbush, 'Come and be our king.'

¹⁵"The thornbush said to the trees, 'If you really want to anoint me king over you, come and take refuge in my shade; but if not, then let fire come out of the thornbush and consume the cedars of Lebanon!'

¹⁶"Now if you have acted honorably and in good faith when you made Abimelech king, and if you have been fair to Jerub-Baal and his family, and if you have treated him as he deserves— ¹⁷and to think that my father fought for you, risked his life to rescue you from the hand of Midian ¹⁸(but today you have revolted against my father's family, murdered his seventy sons on a single stone, and made Abimelech, the son of his slave girl, king over the citizens of Shechem because he is your brother)— ¹⁹if then you have acted honorably and in good faith toward Jerub-Baal and his family

---

ᵃ26 That is, about 43 pounds (about 19.5 kilograms)   ᵇ4 That is, about 1 3/4 pounds (about 0.8 kilogram)

today, may Abimelech be your joy, and may you be his, too! ²⁰But if you have not, let fire come out from Abimelech and consume you, citizens of Shechem and Beth Millo, and let fire come out from you, citizens of Shechem and Beth Millo, and consume Abimelech!"

²¹Then Jotham fled, escaping to Beer, and he lived there because he was afraid of his brother Abimelech.

²²After Abimelech had governed Israel three years, ²³God sent an evil spirit between Abimelech and the citizens of Shechem, who acted treacherously against Abimelech. ²⁴God did this in order that the crime against Jerub-Baal's seventy sons, the shedding of their blood, might be avenged on their brother Abimelech and on the citizens of Shechem, who had helped him murder his brothers. ²⁵In opposition to him these citizens of Shechem set men on the hilltops to ambush and rob everyone who passed by, and this was reported to Abimelech.

²⁶Now Gaal son of Ebed moved with his brothers into Shechem, and its citizens put their confidence in him. ²⁷After they had gone out into the fields and gathered the grapes and trodden them, they held a festival in the temple of their god. While they were eating and drinking, they cursed Abimelech. ²⁸Then Gaal son of Ebed said, "Who is Abimelech, and who is Shechem, that we should be subject to him? Isn't he Jerub-Baal's son, and isn't Zebul his deputy? Serve the men of Hamor, Shechem's father! Why should we serve Abimelech? ²⁹If only this people were under my command! Then I would get rid of him. I would say to Abimelech, 'Call out your whole army!' "ᵃ

³⁰When Zebul the governor of the city heard what Gaal son of Ebed said, he was very angry. ³¹Under cover he sent messengers to Abimelech, saying, "Gaal son of Ebed and his brothers have come to Shechem and are stirring up the city against you. ³²Now then, during the night you and your men should come and lie in wait in the fields. ³³In the morning at sunrise, advance against the city. When Gaal and his men come out against you, do whatever your hand finds to do."

³⁴So Abimelech and all his troops set out by night and took up concealed positions near Shechem in four companies. ³⁵Now Gaal son of Ebed had gone out and was standing at the entrance to the city gate just as Abimelech and his soldiers came out from their hiding place.

³⁶When Gaal saw them, he said to Zebul, "Look, people are coming down from the tops of the mountains!"

Zebul replied, "You mistake the shadows of the mountains for men."

³⁷But Gaal spoke up again: "Look, people are coming down from the center of the land, and a company is coming from the direction of the soothsayers' tree."

³⁸Then Zebul said to him, "Where is your big talk now, you who said, 'Who is Abimelech that we should be subject to him?' Aren't these the men you ridiculed? Go out and fight them!"

³⁹So Gaal led outᵇ the citizens of Shechem and fought Abimelech. ⁴⁰Abimelech chased him, and many fell wounded in the flight—all the way to the entrance to the gate. ⁴¹Abimelech stayed in Arumah, and Zebul drove Gaal and his brothers out of Shechem.

⁴²The next day the people of Shechem went out to the fields, and this was reported to Abimelech. ⁴³So he took his men, divided them into three companies and set an ambush in the fields. When he saw the people coming out of the city, he rose to attack them. ⁴⁴Abimelech and the companies with him rushed forward to a position at the entrance to the city gate. Then two companies rushed upon those in the fields and struck them down. ⁴⁵All that day Abimelech pressed his attack against the city until he had captured it and killed its people. Then he destroyed the city and scattered salt over it.

⁴⁶On hearing this, the citizens in the tower of Shechem went into the stronghold of the temple of El-Berith. ⁴⁷When Abimelech heard that they had assembled there, ⁴⁸he and all his men went up Mount Zalmon. He took an ax and cut off some branches, which he lifted to his shoulders. He ordered the men with him, "Quick! Do what you have seen me do!" ⁴⁹So all the men cut branches and

---

ᵃ29 Septuagint; Hebrew *him.*" Then he said to Abimelech, "Call out your whole army!"
ᵇ39 Or *Gaal went out in the sight of*

followed Abimelech. They piled them against the stronghold and set it on fire over the people inside. So all the people in the tower of Shechem, about a thousand men and women, also died.

⁵⁰Next Abimelech went to Thebez and besieged it and captured it. ⁵¹Inside the city, however, was a strong tower, to which all the men and women—all the people of the city—fled. They locked themselves in and climbed up on the tower roof. ⁵²Abimelech went to the tower and stormed it. But as he approached the entrance to the tower to set it on fire, ⁵³a woman dropped an upper millstone on his head and cracked his skull.

⁵⁴Hurriedly he called to his armorbearer, "Draw your sword and kill me, so that they can't say, 'A woman killed him.'" So his servant ran him through, and he died. ⁵⁵When the Israelites saw that Abimelech was dead, they went home.

⁵⁶Thus God repaid the wickedness that Abimelech had done to his father by murdering his seventy brothers. ⁵⁷God also made the men of Shechem pay for all their wickedness. The curse of Jotham son of Jerub-Baal came on them.

Tola

10 After the time of Abimelech a man of Issachar, Tola son of Puah, the son of Dodo, rose to save Israel. He lived in Shamir, in the hill country of Ephraim. ²He led[a] Israel twenty-three years; then he died, and was buried in Shamir.

Jair

³He was followed by Jair of Gilead, who led Israel twenty-two years. ⁴He had thirty sons, who rode thirty donkeys. They controlled thirty towns in Gilead, which to this day are called Havvoth Jair.[b] ⁵When Jair died, he was buried in Kamon.

Jephthah

⁶Again the Israelites did evil in the eyes of the LORD. They served the Baals and the Ashtoreths, and the gods of Aram, the gods of Sidon, the gods of Moab, the gods of the Ammonites and the gods of the Philistines. And because the Israelites forsook the LORD and no longer

served him, ⁷he became angry with them. He sold them into the hands of the Philistines and the Ammonites, ⁸who that year shattered and crushed them. For eighteen years they oppressed all the Israelites on the east side of the Jordan in Gilead, the land of the Amorites. ⁹The Ammonites also crossed the Jordan to fight against Judah, Benjamin and the house of Ephraim; and Israel was in great distress. ¹⁰Then the Israelites cried out to the LORD, "We have sinned against you, forsaking our God and serving the Baals."

¹¹The LORD replied, "When the Egyptians, the Amorites, the Ammonites, the Philistines, ¹²the Sidonians, the Amalekites and the Maonites[c] oppressed you and you cried to me for help, did I not save you from their hands? ¹³But you have forsaken me and served other gods, so I will no longer save you. ¹⁴Go and cry out to the gods you have chosen. Let them save you when you are in trouble!"

¹⁵But the Israelites said to the LORD, "We have sinned. Do with us whatever you think best, but please rescue us now." ¹⁶Then they got rid of the foreign gods among them and served the LORD. And he could bear Israel's misery no longer.

¹⁷When the Ammonites were called to arms and camped in Gilead, the Israelites assembled and camped at Mizpah. ¹⁸The leaders of the people of Gilead said to each other, "Whoever will launch the attack against the Ammonites will be the head of all those living in Gilead."

11 Jephthah the Gileadite was a mighty warrior. His father was Gilead; his mother was a prostitute. ²Gilead's wife also bore him sons, and when they were grown up, they drove Jephthah away. "You are not going to get any inheritance in our family," they said, "because you are the son of another woman." ³So Jephthah fled from his brothers and settled in the land of Tob, where a group of adventurers gathered around him and followed him.

⁴Some time later, when the Ammonites made war on Israel, ⁵the elders of Gilead

---

a2 Traditionally judged; also in verse 3
b4 Or called the settlements of Jair
c12 Hebrew; some Septuagint manuscripts Midianites

went to get Jephthah from the land of Tob. 6"Come," they said, "be our commander, so we can fight the Ammonites."

7Jephthah said to them, "Didn't you hate me and drive me from my father's house? Why do you come to me now, when you're in trouble?"

8The elders of Gilead said to him, "Nevertheless, we are turning to you now; come with us to fight the Ammonites, and you will be our head over all who live in Gilead."

9Jephthah answered, "Suppose you take me back to fight the Ammonites and the LORD gives them to me—will I really be your head?"

10The elders of Gilead replied, "The LORD is our witness; we will certainly do as you say." 11So Jephthah went with the elders of Gilead, and the people made him head and commander over them. And he repeated all his words before the LORD in Mizpah.

12Then Jephthah sent messengers to the Ammonite king with the question: "What do you have against us that you have attacked our country?"

13The king of the Ammonites answered Jephthah's messengers, "When Israel came up out of Egypt, they took away my land from the Arnon to the Jabbok, all the way to the Jordan. Now give it back peaceably."

14Jephthah sent back messengers to the Ammonite king, 15saying:

"This is what Jephthah says: Israel did not take the land of Moab or the land of the Ammonites. 16But when they came up out of Egypt, Israel went through the desert to the Red Sea*a* and on to Kadesh. 17Then Israel sent messengers to the king of Edom, saying, 'Give us permission to go through your country,' but the king of Edom would not listen. They sent also to the king of Moab, and he refused. So Israel stayed at Kadesh.

18"Next they traveled through the desert, skirted the lands of Edom and Moab, passed along the eastern side of the country of Moab, and camped on the other side of the Arnon. They did not enter the territory of Moab, for the Arnon was its border.

19"Then Israel sent messengers to Sihon king of the Amorites, who ruled in Heshbon, and said to him, 'Let us pass through your country to our own place.' 20Sihon, however, did not trust Israel*b* to pass through his territory. He mustered all his men and encamped at Jahaz and fought with Israel.

21"Then the LORD, the God of Israel, gave Sihon and all his men into Israel's hands, and they defeated them. Israel took over all the land of the Amorites who lived in that country, 22capturing all of it from the Arnon to the Jabbok and from the desert to the Jordan.

23"Now since the LORD, the God of Israel, has driven the Amorites out before his people Israel, what right have you to take it over? 24Will you not take what your god Chemosh gives you? Likewise, whatever the LORD our God has given us, we will possess. 25Are you better than Balak son of Zippor, king of Moab? Did he ever quarrel with Israel or fight with them? 26For three hundred years Israel occupied Heshbon, Aroer, the surrounding settlements and all the towns along the Arnon. Why didn't you retake them during that time? 27I have not wronged you, but you are doing me wrong by waging war against me. Let the LORD, the Judge,*c* decide the dispute this day between the Israelites and the Ammonites."

28The king of Ammon, however, paid no attention to the message Jephthah sent him.

29Then the Spirit of the LORD came upon Jephthah. He crossed Gilead and Manasseh, passed through Mizpah of Gilead, and from there he advanced against the Ammonites. 30And Jephthah made a vow to the LORD: "If you give the Ammonites into my hands, 31whatever comes out of the door of my house to meet me when I return in triumph from the Ammonites will be the LORD's, and I will sacrifice it as a burnt offering."

a16 Hebrew *Yam Suph*; that is, Sea of Reeds
b20 Or *however, would not make an agreement for Israel*   *c27* Or *Ruler*

³²Then Jephthah went over to fight the Ammonites, and the LORD gave them into his hands. ³³He devastated twenty towns from Aroer to the vicinity of Minnith, as far as Abel Keramim. Thus Israel subdued Ammon.

³⁴When Jephthah returned to his home in Mizpah, who should come out to meet him but his daughter, dancing to the sound of tambourines! She was an only child. Except for her he had neither son nor daughter. ³⁵When he saw her, he tore his clothes and cried, "Oh! My daughter! You have made me miserable and wretched, because I have made a vow to the LORD that I cannot break."

³⁶"My father," she replied, "you have given your word to the LORD. Do to me

[FRIDAY]

JUDGES 11:29–40

Watch What You Pray

11:30 AND JEPHTHAH MADE A VOW TO THE LORD.

This story of Jephthah's rash and foolish vow leaves us unsure whether to weep, scream or simply walk away in confusion. He wins a battle for the Lord, yet his beloved daughter becomes a senseless human sacrifice. What on earth does this story have to teach us about prayer?

One lesson is that we must be careful with our vows. The obvious caution is to never make a vow we would hate to have to keep if our prayers were answered. The deeper insight is to know our own hearts well enough to know why we're making the vow in the first place. Some vows, like Jephthah's, are really attempts to cut a deal with the Lord—subtle efforts at raising the stakes if he does what we want. They come from anxiety and doubt that the Lord really loves us, that we can't trust him to do the right thing unless he gets something from us. That motive is what seems to be behind Jephthah's vow.

The second lesson is to always pray and act according to the best knowledge we have. Jephthah, like Gideon, was probably semi-pagan in his understanding of the Lord God. His knowledge of the Law of Moses perhaps did not include the prohibitions against child sacrifice (see Deuteronomy 12:29–31; 18:9–10). But he did know something about the importance of keeping his word. Out of ignorance, he unfortunately cancelled one law of God with another.

The third lesson is the reason for this Bible: how critically important it is that we know Scripture well enough to pray from the Word of God, according to the will of God! That, in essence, is what Jesus meant about giving us whatever we ask for in his name, according to his character.

PRAY:

Dear Lord, may I be able to present myself to you, approved as a person of prayer, who does not need to be ashamed and who correctly prays the word of truth (see 2 Timothy 2:15).

FOR YOUR NEXT DEVOTIONAL READING, GO TO PAGE 290.

just as you promised, now that the LORD has avenged you of your enemies, the Ammonites. ³⁷But grant me this one request," she said. "Give me two months to roam the hills and weep with my friends, because I will never marry."

³⁸"You may go," he said. And he let her go for two months. She and the girls went into the hills and wept because she would never marry. ³⁹After the two months, she returned to her father and he did to her as he had vowed. And she was a virgin.

From this comes the Israelite custom ⁴⁰that each year the young women of Israel go out for four days to commemorate the daughter of Jephthah the Gileadite.

Jephthah and Ephraim

12 The men of Ephraim called out their forces, crossed over to Zaphon and said to Jephthah, "Why did you go to fight the Ammonites without calling us to go with you? We're going to burn down your house over your head."

²Jephthah answered, "I and my people were engaged in a great struggle with the Ammonites, and although I called, you didn't save me out of their hands. ³When I saw that you wouldn't help, I took my life in my hands and crossed over to fight the Ammonites, and the LORD gave me the victory over them. Now why have you come up today to fight me?"

⁴Jephthah then called together the men of Gilead and fought against Ephraim. The Gileadites struck them down because the Ephraimites had said, "You Gileadites are renegades from Ephraim and Manasseh." ⁵The Gileadites captured the fords of the Jordan leading to Ephraim, and whenever a survivor of Ephraim said, "Let me cross over," the men of Gilead asked him, "Are you an Ephraimite?" If he replied, "No," ⁶they said, "All right, say 'Shibboleth.'" If he said, "Sibboleth," because he could not pronounce the word correctly, they seized him and killed him at the fords of the Jordan. Forty-two thousand Ephraimites were killed at that time.

⁷Jephthah led*ᵃ* Israel six years. Then Jephthah the Gileadite died, and was buried in a town in Gilead.

Ibzan, Elon and Abdon

⁸After him, Ibzan of Bethlehem led Israel. ⁹He had thirty sons and thirty daughters. He gave his daughters away in marriage to those outside his clan, and for his sons he brought in thirty young women as wives from outside his clan. Ibzan led Israel seven years. ¹⁰Then Ibzan died, and was buried in Bethlehem.

¹¹After him, Elon the Zebulunite led Israel ten years. ¹²Then Elon died, and was buried in Aijalon in the land of Zebulun.

¹³After him, Abdon son of Hillel, from Pirathon, led Israel. ¹⁴He had forty sons and thirty grandsons, who rode on seventy donkeys. He led Israel eight years. ¹⁵Then Abdon son of Hillel died, and was buried at Pirathon in Ephraim, in the hill country of the Amalekites.

The Birth of Samson

13 Again the Israelites did evil in the eyes of the LORD, so the LORD delivered them into the hands of the Philistines for forty years.

²A certain man of Zorah, named Manoah, from the clan of the Danites, had a wife who was sterile and remained childless. ³The angel of the LORD appeared to her and said, "You are sterile and childless, but you are going to conceive and have a son. ⁴Now see to it that you drink no wine or other fermented drink and that you do not eat anything unclean, ⁵because you will conceive and give birth to a son. No razor may be used on his head, because the boy is to be a Nazirite, set apart to God from birth, and he will begin the deliverance of Israel from the hands of the Philistines."

⁶Then the woman went to her husband and told him, "A man of God came to me. He looked like an angel of God, very awesome. I didn't ask him where he came from, and he didn't tell me his name. ⁷But he said to me, 'You will conceive and give birth to a son. Now then, drink no wine or other fermented drink and do not eat anything unclean, because the boy will be a Nazirite of God from birth until the day of his death.'"

⁸Then Manoah prayed to the LORD: "O Lord, I beg you, let the man of God

---

ᵃ 7 Traditionally judged; also in verses 8–14

you sent to us come again to teach us how to bring up the boy who is to be born."

⁹God heard Manoah, and the angel of God came again to the woman while she was out in the field; but her husband Manoah was not with her. ¹⁰The woman hurried to tell her husband, "He's here! The man who appeared to me the other day!"

> MANOAH prayed to the LORD: "O Lord, I beg you, let the man of God you sent to us come again to teach us how to bring up the boy who is to be born."
>
> JUDGES 13:8

¹¹Manoah got up and followed his wife. When he came to the man, he said, "Are you the one who talked to my wife?"

"I am," he said.

¹²So Manoah asked him, "When your words are fulfilled, what is to be the rule for the boy's life and work?"

¹³The angel of the LORD answered, "Your wife must do all that I have told her. ¹⁴She must not eat anything that comes from the grapevine, nor drink any wine or other fermented drink nor eat anything unclean. She must do everything I have commanded her."

¹⁵Manoah said to the angel of the LORD, "We would like you to stay until we prepare a young goat for you."

¹⁶The angel of the LORD replied, "Even though you detain me, I will not eat any of your food. But if you prepare a burnt offering, offer it to the LORD." (Manoah did not realize that it was the angel of the LORD.)

¹⁷Then Manoah inquired of the angel of the LORD, "What is your name, so that we may honor you when your word comes true?"

¹⁸He replied, "Why do you ask my name? It is beyond understanding.ᵃ"

¹⁹Then Manoah took a young goat, together with the grain offering, and sacrificed it on a rock to the LORD. And the LORD did an amazing thing while Manoah and his wife watched: ²⁰As the flame blazed up from the altar toward heaven, the angel of the LORD ascended in the flame. Seeing this, Manoah and his wife

fell with their faces to the ground. ²¹When the angel of the LORD did not show himself again to Manoah and his wife, Manoah realized that it was the angel of the LORD.

²²"We are doomed to die!" he said to his wife. "We have seen God!"

²³But his wife answered, "If the LORD had meant to kill us, he would not have accepted a burnt offering and grain offering from our hands, nor shown us all these things or now told us this."

²⁴The woman gave birth to a boy and named him Samson. He grew and the LORD blessed him, ²⁵and the Spirit of the LORD began to stir him while he was in Mahaneh Dan, between Zorah and Eshtaol.

Samson's Marriage

14 Samson went down to Timnah and saw there a young Philistine woman. ²When he returned, he said to his father and mother, "I have seen a Philistine woman in Timnah; now get her for me as my wife."

³His father and mother replied, "Isn't there an acceptable woman among your relatives or among all our people? Must you go to the uncircumcised Philistines to get a wife?"

But Samson said to his father, "Get her for me. She's the right one for me." ⁴(His parents did not know that this was from the LORD, who was seeking an occasion to confront the Philistines; for at that time they were ruling over Israel.) ⁵Samson went down to Timnah together with his father and mother. As they approached the vineyards of Timnah, suddenly a young lion came roaring toward him. ⁶The Spirit of the LORD came upon him in power so that he tore the lion apart with his bare hands as he might have torn a young goat. But he told neither his father nor his mother what he had done. ⁷Then he went down and talked with the woman, and he liked her.

⁸Some time later, when he went back to marry her, he turned aside to look at the lion's carcass. In it was a swarm of bees and some honey, ⁹which he scooped out with his hands and ate as he went along. When he rejoined his parents, he

ᵃ18 Or is wonderful

gave them some, and they too ate it. But he did not tell them that he had taken the honey from the lion's carcass.

[10]Now his father went down to see the woman. And Samson made a feast there, as was customary for bridegrooms. [11]When he appeared, he was given thirty companions.

[12]"Let me tell you a riddle," Samson said to them. "If you can give me the answer within the seven days of the feast, I will give you thirty linen garments and thirty sets of clothes. [13]If you can't tell me the answer, you must give me thirty linen garments and thirty sets of clothes."

"Tell us your riddle," they said. "Let's hear it."

[14]He replied,

"Out of the eater, something to eat;
    out of the strong, something
        sweet."

For three days they could not give the answer.

[15]On the fourth[a] day, they said to Samson's wife, "Coax your husband into explaining the riddle for us, or we will burn you and your father's household to death. Did you invite us here to rob us?"

[16]Then Samson's wife threw herself on him, sobbing, "You hate me! You don't really love me. You've given my people a riddle, but you haven't told me the answer."

"I haven't even explained it to my father or mother," he replied, "so why should I explain it to you?" [17]She cried the whole seven days of the feast. So on the seventh day he finally told her, because she continued to press him. She in turn explained the riddle to her people.

[18]Before sunset on the seventh day the men of the town said to him,

"What is sweeter than honey?
    What is stronger than a lion?"

Samson said to them,

"If you had not plowed with
        my heifer,
    you would not have solved my
        riddle."

[19]Then the Spirit of the LORD came upon him in power. He went down to Ashkelon, struck down thirty of their men, stripped them of their belongings and gave their clothes to those who had explained the riddle. Burning with anger, he went up to his father's house. [20]And Samson's wife was given to the friend who had attended him at his wedding.

Samson's Vengeance on the Philistines

15 Later on, at the time of wheat harvest, Samson took a young goat and went to visit his wife. He said, "I'm going to my wife's room." But her father would not let him go in.

[2]"I was so sure you thoroughly hated her," he said, "that I gave her to your friend. Isn't her younger sister more attractive? Take her instead."

[3]Samson said to them, "This time I have a right to get even with the Philistines; I will really harm them." [4]So he went out and caught three hundred foxes and tied them tail to tail in pairs. He then fastened a torch to every pair of tails, [5]lit the torches and let the foxes loose in the standing grain of the Philistines. He burned up the shocks and standing grain, together with the vineyards and olive groves.

[6]When the Philistines asked, "Who did this?" they were told, "Samson, the Timnite's son-in-law, because his wife was given to his friend."

So the Philistines went up and burned her and her father to death. [7]Samson said to them, "Since you've acted like this, I won't stop until I get my revenge on you." [8]He attacked them viciously and slaughtered many of them. Then he went down and stayed in a cave in the rock of Etam.

[9]The Philistines went up and camped in Judah, spreading out near Lehi. [10]The men of Judah asked, "Why have you come to fight us?"

"We have come to take Samson prisoner," they answered, "to do to him as he did to us."

[11]Then three thousand men from Judah went down to the cave in the rock of Etam and said to Samson, "Don't you realize that the Philistines are rulers over us? What have you done to us?"

---

[a]15 Some Septuagint manuscripts and Syriac; Hebrew *seventh*

He answered, "I merely did to them what they did to me."

¹²They said to him, "We've come to tie you up and hand you over to the Philistines."

Samson said, "Swear to me that you won't kill me yourselves."

¹³"Agreed," they answered. "We will only tie you up and hand you over to them. We will not kill you." So they bound him with two new ropes and led him up from the rock. ¹⁴As he approached Lehi, the Philistines came toward him shouting. The Spirit of the LORD came upon him in power. The ropes on his arms became like charred flax, and the bindings dropped from his hands. ¹⁵Finding a fresh jawbone of a donkey, he grabbed it and struck down a thousand men.

¹⁶Then Samson said,

"With a donkey's jawbone
   I have made donkeys of them.ᵃ
With a donkey's jawbone
   I have killed a thousand men."

¹⁷When he finished speaking, he threw away the jawbone; and the place was called Ramath Lehi.ᵇ

¹⁸Because he was very thirsty, he cried out to the LORD, "You have given your servant this great victory. Must I now die of thirst and fall into the hands of the uncircumcised?" ¹⁹Then God opened up the hollow place in Lehi, and water came out of it. When Samson drank, his strength returned and he revived. So the spring was called En Hakkore,ᶜ and it is still there in Lehi.

²⁰Samson ledᵈ Israel for twenty years in the days of the Philistines.

Samson and Delilah

16 One day Samson went to Gaza, where he saw a prostitute. He went in to spend the night with her. ²The people of Gaza were told, "Samson is here!" So they surrounded the place and lay in wait for him all night at the city gate. They made no move during the night, saying, "At dawn we'll kill him."

³But Samson lay there only until the middle of the night. Then he got up and took hold of the doors of the city gate, together with the two posts, and tore them loose, bar and all. He lifted them to his shoulders and carried them to the top of the hill that faces Hebron.

⁴Some time later, he fell in love with a woman in the Valley of Sorek whose name was Delilah. ⁵The rulers of the Philistines went to her and said, "See if you can lure him into showing you the secret of his great strength and how we can overpower him so we may tie him up and subdue him. Each one of us will give you eleven hundred shekelsᵉ of silver."

⁶So Delilah said to Samson, "Tell me the secret of your great strength and how you can be tied up and subdued."

⁷Samson answered her, "If anyone ties me with seven fresh thongsᶠ that have not been dried, I'll become as weak as any other man."

⁸Then the rulers of the Philistines brought her seven fresh thongs that had not been dried, and she tied him with them. ⁹With men hidden in the room, she called to him, "Samson, the Philistines are upon you!" But he snapped the thongs as easily as a piece of string snaps when it comes close to a flame. So the secret of his strength was not discovered.

¹⁰Then Delilah said to Samson, "You have made a fool of me; you lied to me. Come now, tell me how you can be tied."

¹¹He said, "If anyone ties me securely with new ropes that have never been used, I'll become as weak as any other man."

¹²So Delilah took new ropes and tied him with them. Then, with men hidden in the room, she called to him, "Samson, the Philistines are upon you!" But he snapped the ropes off his arms as if they were threads.

¹³Delilah then said to Samson, "Until now, you have been making a fool of me and lying to me. Tell me how you can be tied."

He replied, "If you weave the seven braids of my head into the fabric ⌊on the loom⌋ and tighten it with the pin, I'll become as weak as any other man." So while he was sleeping, Delilah took the seven

---

ᵃ16 Or made a heap or two; the Hebrew for donkey sounds like the Hebrew for heap.
ᵇ17 Ramath Lehi means jawbone hill.
ᶜ19 En Hakkore means caller's spring.
ᵈ20 Traditionally judged   ᵉ5 That is, about 28 pounds (about 13 kilograms)
ᶠ7 Or bowstrings; also in verses 8 and 9

Father, Make of Me a Crisis Man

IN THE FALL of 1955, five young men went deep into the rain forest of Ecuador to deliver an invitation. Their names were Nate Saint, Jim Elliot, Roger Youderian, Ed McCully and Peter Fleming. Their mission was to invite an obscure and warlike people to bring an offering into the courts of the living God and sit down with all the other peoples of the earth to feast in his presence (see Psalm 96:7–10; Luke 13:29–30; Revelation 21:22–26). This group called themselves the *Huaorani*, meaning simply, "the people." Everyone who knew of them called them the *Auca*, meaning "savages." Their culture was literally a culture of death: Babies were thrown into the river, children were buried alive with dying family members, and friends and enemies alike were speared with appalling regularity. But one of the missionaries, Peter Fleming, spoke for them all when he said, "I would gladly give my life for [the Aucas] if only to see those proud, clever, smart people gathering around a table to honor the Son." Many of the Huaorani now gather to honor the Son, but those five missionaries first had to die to make that happen. The Aucas murdered them on January 8, 1956.

Jim Elliot's wife, Elisabeth Elliot, has preserved many of his prayers and thoughts on prayer and Christian discipleship. Most of them come out of his student years at Wheaton College. They are remarkable for their depth and passion.

"That saint who advances on his knees never retreats."

"Father, make of me a crisis man. Bring those I contact to decision. Let me not be a milepost on a single road; make me a fork, that men must turn one way or another on facing Christ in me."

"He is no fool who gives what he cannot keep to gain what he cannot lose."

"One treasure, a single eye, and a sole master."

"God, I pray thee, light these idle sticks of my life and may I burn for thee. Consume my life, my God, for it is thine. I seek not a long life, but a full one, like you, Lord Jesus."

"Father, take my life, yea, my blood if thou wilt, and consume it with thine enveloping fire. I would not save it, for it is not mine to save. Have it, Lord, have it all. Pour out my life as an oblation to the world. Blood is only of value as it flows from thine altar."

"Saturate me with the oil of the Spirit that I may be aflame. But flame is often short-lived. Canst thou bear this, my soul? Short life? In me there dwells the spirit of the Great Short-Lived, whose zeal for God's house consumed him. 'Make me thy fuel, Flame of God.'"

"The will of God is always a bigger thing than we bargain for."

"Give me a faith that will take sufficient quiver out of me so that I may sing. Over the Aucas, Father, I want to sing!"[3]

PRAY:

Pray one of Jim Elliot's prayers as your own.

MEMORIZE:

However, I consider my life worth nothing to me, if only I may finish the race and complete the task the Lord Jesus has given me—the task of testifying to the gospel of God's grace. ACTS 20:24

FOR YOUR NEXT DEVOTIONAL READING, GO TO PAGE 301.

braids of his head, wove them into the fabric ¹⁴and*ᵃ* tightened it with the pin.

Again she called to him, "Samson, the Philistines are upon you!" He awoke from his sleep and pulled up the pin and the loom, with the fabric.

¹⁵Then she said to him, "How can you say, 'I love you,' when you won't confide in me? This is the third time you have made a fool of me and haven't told me the secret of your great strength." ¹⁶With such nagging she prodded him day after day until he was tired to death.

¹⁷So he told her everything. "No razor has ever been used on my head," he said, "because I have been a Nazirite set apart to God since birth. If my head were shaved, my strength would leave me, and I would become as weak as any other man."

¹⁸When Delilah saw that he had told her everything, she sent word to the rulers of the Philistines, "Come back once more; he has told me everything." So the rulers of the Philistines returned with the silver in their hands. ¹⁹Having put him to sleep on her lap, she called a man to shave off the seven braids of his hair, and so began to subdue him.*ᵇ* And his strength left him.

²⁰Then she called, "Samson, the Philistines are upon you!"

He awoke from his sleep and thought, "I'll go out as before and shake myself free." But he did not know that the LORD had left him.

²¹Then the Philistines seized him, gouged out his eyes and took him down to Gaza. Binding him with bronze shackles, they set him to grinding in the prison. ²²But the hair on his head began to grow again after it had been shaved.

The Death of Samson

²³Now the rulers of the Philistines assembled to offer a great sacrifice to Dagon their god and to celebrate, saying, "Our god has delivered Samson, our enemy, into our hands."

²⁴When the people saw him, they praised their god, saying,

"Our god has delivered our enemy
  into our hands,
the one who laid waste our land
  and multiplied our slain."

²⁵While they were in high spirits, they shouted, "Bring out Samson to entertain us." So they called Samson out of the prison, and he performed for them.

When they stood him among the pillars, ²⁶Samson said to the servant who held his hand, "Put me where I can feel the pillars that support the temple, so that I may lean against them." ²⁷Now the temple was crowded with men and women; all the rulers of the Philistines were there, and on the roof were about three thousand men and women watching Samson perform. ²⁸Then Samson prayed to the LORD, "O Sovereign LORD, remember me. O God, please strengthen me just once more, and let me with one blow get revenge on the Philistines for my two eyes." ²⁹Then Samson reached toward the two central pillars on which the temple stood. Bracing himself against them, his right hand on the one and his left hand on the other, ³⁰Samson said, "Let me die with the Philistines!" Then he pushed with all his might, and down came the temple on the rulers and all the people in it. Thus he killed many more when he died than while he lived.

> SAMSON *prayed to the LORD,*
> "O Sovereign LORD, remember me. O God,
> please strengthen me just once more, and
> let me with one blow get revenge on the
> Philistines for my two eyes."
>
> JUDGES 16:28

³¹Then his brothers and his father's whole family went down to get him. They brought him back and buried him between Zorah and Eshtaol in the tomb of Manoah his father. He had led*ᶜ* Israel twenty years.

Micah's Idols

17 Now a man named Micah from the hill country of Ephraim ²said to his mother, "The eleven hundred shekels*ᵈ* of

---

ᵃ13,14 Some Septuagint manuscripts; Hebrew "*I can, if you weave the seven braids of my head into the fabric, on the loom.*" *¹⁴So she*   *ᵇ19* Hebrew; some Septuagint manuscripts *and he began to weaken*   *ᶜ31* Traditionally *judged*   *ᵈ2* That is, about 28 pounds (about 13 kilograms)

silver that were taken from you and about which I heard you utter a curse—I have that silver with me; I took it."

Then his mother said, "The LORD bless you, my son!"

3When he returned the eleven hundred shekels of silver to his mother, she said, "I solemnly consecrate my silver to the LORD for my son to make a carved image and a cast idol. I will give it back to you."

4So he returned the silver to his mother, and she took two hundred shekels[a] of silver and gave them to a silversmith, who made them into the image and the idol. And they were put in Micah's house.

5Now this man Micah had a shrine, and he made an ephod and some idols and installed one of his sons as his priest. 6In those days Israel had no king; everyone did as he saw fit.

7A young Levite from Bethlehem in Judah, who had been living within the clan of Judah, 8left that town in search of some other place to stay. On his way[b] he came to Micah's house in the hill country of Ephraim.

9Micah asked him, "Where are you from?"

"I'm a Levite from Bethlehem in Judah," he said, "and I'm looking for a place to stay."

10Then Micah said to him, "Live with me and be my father and priest, and I'll give you ten shekels[c] of silver a year, your clothes and your food." 11So the Levite agreed to live with him, and the young man was to him like one of his sons. 12Then Micah installed the Levite, and the young man became his priest and lived in his house. 13And Micah said, "Now I know that the LORD will be good to me, since this Levite has become my priest."

Danites Settle in Laish

18 In those days Israel had no king.

And in those days the tribe of the Danites was seeking a place of their own where they might settle, because they had not yet come into an inheritance among the tribes of Israel. 2So the Danites sent five warriors from Zorah and Eshtaol to spy out the land and explore it. These men represented all their clans. They told them, "Go, explore the land."

The men entered the hill country of Ephraim and came to the house of Micah, where they spent the night. 3When they were near Micah's house, they recognized the voice of the young Levite; so they turned in there and asked him, "Who brought you here? What are you doing in this place? Why are you here?"

4He told them what Micah had done for him, and said, "He has hired me and I am his priest."

5Then they said to him, "Please inquire of God to learn whether our journey will be successful."

6The priest answered them, "Go in peace. Your journey has the LORD's approval."

7So the five men left and came to Laish, where they saw that the people were living in safety, like the Sidonians, unsuspecting and secure. And since their land lacked nothing, they were prosperous.[d] Also, they lived a long way from the Sidonians and had no relationship with anyone else.[e]

8When they returned to Zorah and Eshtaol, their brothers asked them, "How did you find things?"

> Grace and gratitude belong together like heaven and earth. Gratitude evokes grace like the voice and echo. Gratitude follows grace as thunder follows lightning.
>
> KARL BARTH

9They answered, "Come on, let's attack them! We have seen that the land is very good. Aren't you going to do something? Don't hesitate to go there and take it over. 10When you get there, you will find an unsuspecting people and a spacious land that God has put into your hands, a land that lacks nothing whatever."

11Then six hundred men from the clan of the Danites, armed for battle, set out

[a]4 That is, about 5 pounds (about 2.3 kilograms)   [b]8 Or To carry on his profession   [c]10 That is, about 4 ounces (about 110 grams)   [d]7 The meaning of the Hebrew for this clause is uncertain.   [e]7 Hebrew; some Septuagint manuscripts with the Arameans

from Zorah and Eshtaol. ¹²On their way they set up camp near Kiriath Jearim in Judah. This is why the place west of Kiriath Jearim is called Mahaneh Dan*ᵃ* to this day. ¹³From there they went on to the hill country of Ephraim and came to Micah's house.

¹⁴Then the five men who had spied out the land of Laish said to their brothers, "Do you know that one of these houses has an ephod, other household gods, a carved image and a cast idol? Now you know what to do." ¹⁵So they turned in there and went to the house of the young Levite at Micah's place and greeted him. ¹⁶The six hundred Danites, armed for battle, stood at the entrance to the gate. ¹⁷The five men who had spied out the land went inside and took the carved image, the ephod, the other household gods and the cast idol while the priest and the six hundred armed men stood at the entrance to the gate.

¹⁸When these men went into Micah's house and took the carved image, the ephod, the other household gods and the cast idol, the priest said to them, "What are you doing?"

¹⁹They answered him, "Be quiet! Don't say a word. Come with us, and be our father and priest. Isn't it better that you serve a tribe and clan in Israel as priest rather than just one man's household?" ²⁰Then the priest was glad. He took the ephod, the other household gods and the carved image and went along with the people. ²¹Putting their little children, their livestock and their possessions in front of them, they turned away and left.

²²When they had gone some distance from Micah's house, the men who lived near Micah were called together and overtook the Danites. ²³As they shouted after them, the Danites turned and said to Micah, "What's the matter with you that you called out your men to fight?"

²⁴He replied, "You took the gods I made, and my priest, and went away. What else do I have? How can you ask, 'What's the matter with you?'"

²⁵The Danites answered, "Don't argue with us, or some hot-tempered men will attack you, and you and your family will lose your lives." ²⁶So the Danites went their way, and Micah, seeing that they

were too strong for him, turned around and went back home.

²⁷Then they took what Micah had made, and his priest, and went on to Laish, against a peaceful and unsuspecting people. They attacked them with the sword and burned down their city. ²⁸There was no one to rescue them because they lived a long way from Sidon and had no relationship with anyone else. The city was in a valley near Beth Rehob.

The Danites rebuilt the city and settled there. ²⁹They named it Dan after their forefather Dan, who was born to Israel—though the city used to be called Laish. ³⁰There the Danites set up for themselves the idols, and Jonathan son of Gershom, the son of Moses,*ᵇ* and his sons were priests for the tribe of Dan until the time of the captivity of the land. ³¹They continued to use the idols Micah had made, all the time the house of God was in Shiloh.

A Levite and His Concubine

19 In those days Israel had no king.
Now a Levite who lived in a remote area in the hill country of Ephraim took a concubine from Bethlehem in Judah. ²But she was unfaithful to him. She left him and went back to her father's house in Bethlehem, Judah. After she had been there four months, ³her husband went to her to persuade her to return. He had with him his servant and two donkeys. She took him into her father's house, and when her father saw him, he gladly welcomed him. ⁴His father-in-law, the girl's father, prevailed upon him to stay; so he remained with him three days, eating and drinking, and sleeping there.

⁵On the fourth day they got up early and he prepared to leave, but the girl's father said to his son-in-law, "Refresh yourself with something to eat; then you can go." ⁶So the two of them sat down to eat and drink together. Afterward the girl's father said, "Please stay tonight and enjoy yourself." ⁷And when the man got up to go, his father-in-law persuaded him, so he stayed there that night. ⁸On the morning of the fifth day, when he

---

ᵃ12 Mahaneh Dan means Dan's camp.
ᵇ30 An ancient Hebrew scribal tradition, some Septuagint manuscripts and Vulgate; Masoretic Text Manasseh

rose to go, the girl's father said, "Refresh yourself. Wait till afternoon!" So the two of them ate together.

⁹Then when the man, with his concubine and his servant, got up to leave, his father-in-law, the girl's father, said, "Now look, it's almost evening. Spend the night here; the day is nearly over. Stay and enjoy yourself. Early tomorrow morning you can get up and be on your way home." ¹⁰But, unwilling to stay another night, the man left and went toward Jebus (that is, Jerusalem), with his two saddled donkeys and his concubine.

¹¹When they were near Jebus and the day was almost gone, the servant said to his master, "Come, let's stop at this city of the Jebusites and spend the night."

¹²His master replied, "No. We won't go into an alien city, whose people are not Israelites. We will go on to Gibeah." ¹³He added, "Come, let's try to reach Gibeah or Ramah and spend the night in one of those places." ¹⁴So they went on, and the sun set as they neared Gibeah in Benjamin. ¹⁵There they stopped to spend the night. They went and sat in the city square, but no one took them into his home for the night.

¹⁶That evening an old man from the hill country of Ephraim, who was living in Gibeah (the men of the place were Benjamites), came in from his work in the fields. ¹⁷When he looked and saw the traveler in the city square, the old man asked, "Where are you going? Where did you come from?"

¹⁸He answered, "We are on our way from Bethlehem in Judah to a remote area in the hill country of Ephraim where I live. I have been to Bethlehem in Judah and now I am going to the house of the LORD. No one has taken me into his house. ¹⁹We have both straw and fodder for our donkeys and bread and wine for ourselves your servants—me, your maidservant, and the young man with us. We don't need anything."

²⁰"You are welcome at my house," the old man said. "Let me supply whatever you need. Only don't spend the night in the square." ²¹So he took him into his house and fed his donkeys. After they had washed their feet, they had something to eat and drink.

²²While they were enjoying themselves, some of the wicked men of the city surrounded the house. Pounding on the door, they shouted to the old man who owned the house, "Bring out the man who came to your house so we can have sex with him."

²³The owner of the house went outside and said to them, "No, my friends, don't be so vile. Since this man is my guest, don't do this disgraceful thing. ²⁴Look, here is my virgin daughter, and his concubine. I will bring them out to you now, and you can use them and do to them whatever you wish. But to this man, don't do such a disgraceful thing." ²⁵But the men would not listen to him. So the man took his concubine and sent her outside to them, and they raped her and abused her throughout the night, and at dawn they let her go. ²⁶At daybreak the woman went back to the house where her master was staying, fell down at the door and lay there until daylight.

²⁷When her master got up in the morning and opened the door of the house and stepped out to continue on his way, there lay his concubine, fallen in the doorway of the house, with her hands on the threshold. ²⁸He said to her, "Get up; let's go." But there was no answer. Then the man put her on his donkey and set out for home.

²⁹When he reached home, he took a knife and cut up his concubine, limb by limb, into twelve parts and sent them into all the areas of Israel. ³⁰Everyone who saw it said, "Such a thing has never been seen or done, not since the day the Israelites came up out of Egypt. Think about it! Consider it! Tell us what to do!"

Israelites Fight the Benjamites

20 Then all the Israelites from Dan to Beersheba and from the land of Gilead came out as one man and assembled before the LORD in Mizpah. ²The leaders of all the people of the tribes of Israel took their places in the assembly of the people of God, four hundred thousand soldiers armed with swords. ³(The Benjamites heard that the Israelites had gone up to Mizpah.) Then the Israelites said, "Tell us how this awful thing happened."

⁴So the Levite, the husband of the murdered woman, said, "I and my concubine came to Gibeah in Benjamin to spend the night. ⁵During the night the men of Gibeah came after me and surrounded the house, intending to kill me. They raped my concubine, and she died. ⁶I took my concubine, cut her into pieces and sent one piece to each region of Israel's inheritance, because they committed this lewd and disgraceful act in Israel. ⁷Now, all you Israelites, speak up and give your verdict."

⁸All the people rose as one man, saying, "None of us will go home. No, not one of us will return to his house. ⁹But now this is what we'll do to Gibeah: We'll go up against it as the lot directs. ¹⁰We'll take ten men out of every hundred from all the tribes of Israel, and a hundred from a thousand, and a thousand from ten thousand, to get provisions for the army. Then, when the army arrives at Gibeah*ᵃ* in Benjamin, it can give them what they deserve for all this vileness done in Israel." ¹¹So all the men of Israel got together and united as one man against the city.

¹²The tribes of Israel sent men throughout the tribe of Benjamin, saying, "What about this awful crime that was committed among you? ¹³Now surrender those wicked men of Gibeah so that we may put them to death and purge the evil from Israel."

But the Benjamites would not listen to their fellow Israelites. ¹⁴From their towns they came together at Gibeah to fight against the Israelites. ¹⁵At once the Benjamites mobilized twenty-six thousand swordsmen from their towns, in addition to seven hundred chosen men from those living in Gibeah. ¹⁶Among all these soldiers there were seven hundred chosen men who were left-handed, each of whom could sling a stone at a hair and not miss.

¹⁷Israel, apart from Benjamin, mustered four hundred thousand swordsmen, all of them fighting men.

¹⁸The Israelites went up to Bethel*ᵇ* and inquired of God. They said, "Who of us shall go first to fight against the Benjamites?"

The LORD replied, "Judah shall go first."

¹⁹The next morning the Israelites got up and pitched camp near Gibeah. ²⁰The men of Israel went out to fight the Benjamites and took up battle positions against them at Gibeah. ²¹The Benjamites came out of Gibeah and cut down twenty-two thousand Israelites on the battlefield that day. ²²But the men of Israel encouraged one another and again took up their positions where they had stationed themselves the first day. ²³The Israelites went up and wept before the LORD until evening, and they inquired of the LORD. They said, "Shall we go up again to battle against the Benjamites, our brothers?"

The LORD answered, "Go up against them."

²⁴Then the Israelites drew near to Benjamin the second day. ²⁵This time, when the Benjamites came out from Gibeah to oppose them, they cut down another eighteen thousand Israelites, all of them armed with swords.

²⁶Then the Israelites, all the people, went up to Bethel, and there they sat weeping before the LORD. They fasted that day until evening and presented burnt offerings and fellowship offerings*ᶜ* to the LORD. ²⁷And the Israelites inquired of the LORD. (In those days the ark of the covenant of God was there, ²⁸with Phinehas son of Eleazar, the son of Aaron, ministering before it.) They asked, "Shall we go up again to battle with Benjamin our brother, or not?"

The LORD responded, "Go, for tomorrow I will give them into your hands."

²⁹Then Israel set an ambush around Gibeah. ³⁰They went up against the Benjamites on the third day and took up positions against Gibeah as they had done before. ³¹The Benjamites came out to meet them and were drawn away from the city. They began to inflict casualties on the Israelites as before, so that about thirty men fell in the open field and on the roads—the one leading to Bethel and the other to Gibeah.

³²While the Benjamites were saying, "We are defeating them as before," the

---

ᵃ10 One Hebrew manuscript; most Hebrew manuscripts *Geba*, a variant of *Gibeah*
ᵇ18 Or *to the house of God*; also in verse 26
ᶜ26 Traditionally *peace offerings*

Israelites were saying, "Let's retreat and draw them away from the city to the roads."

³³All the men of Israel moved from their places and took up positions at Baal Tamar, and the Israelite ambush charged out of its place on the west[a] of Gibeah.[b] ³⁴Then ten thousand of Israel's finest men made a frontal attack on Gibeah. The fighting was so heavy that the Benjamites did not realize how near disaster was. ³⁵The LORD defeated Benjamin before Israel, and on that day the Israelites struck down 25,100 Benjamites, all armed with swords. ³⁶Then the Benjamites saw that they were beaten.

Now the men of Israel had given way before Benjamin, because they relied on the ambush they had set near Gibeah. ³⁷The men who had been in ambush made a sudden dash into Gibeah, spread out and put the whole city to the sword. ³⁸The men of Israel had arranged with the ambush that they should send up a great cloud of smoke from the city, ³⁹and then the men of Israel would turn in the battle.

The Benjamites had begun to inflict casualties on the men of Israel (about thirty), and they said, "We are defeating them as in the first battle." ⁴⁰But when the column of smoke began to rise from the city, the Benjamites turned and saw the smoke of the whole city going up into the sky. ⁴¹Then the men of Israel turned on them, and the men of Benjamin were terrified, because they realized that disaster had come upon them. ⁴²So they fled before the Israelites in the direction of the desert, but they could not escape the battle. And the men of Israel who came out of the towns cut them down there. ⁴³They surrounded the Benjamites, chased them and easily[c] overran them in the vicinity of Gibeah on the east. ⁴⁴Eighteen thousand Benjamites fell, all of them valiant fighters. ⁴⁵As they turned and fled toward the desert to the rock of Rimmon, the Israelites cut down five thousand men along the roads. They kept pressing after the Benjamites as far as Gidom and struck down two thousand more.

⁴⁶On that day twenty-five thousand Benjamite swordsmen fell, all of them valiant fighters. ⁴⁷But six hundred men turned and fled into the desert to the rock of Rimmon, where they stayed four months. ⁴⁸The men of Israel went back to Benjamin and put all the towns to the sword, including the animals and everything else they found. All the towns they came across they set on fire.

Wives for the Benjamites

21 The men of Israel had taken an oath at Mizpah: "Not one of us will give his daughter in marriage to a Benjamite."

²The people went to Bethel,[d] where they sat before God until evening, raising their voices and weeping bitterly. ³"O LORD, the God of Israel," they cried, "why has this happened to Israel? Why should one tribe be missing from Israel today?"

⁴Early the next day the people built an altar and presented burnt offerings and fellowship offerings.[e]

⁵Then the Israelites asked, "Who from all the tribes of Israel has failed to assemble before the LORD?" For they had taken a solemn oath that anyone who failed to assemble before the LORD at Mizpah should certainly be put to death.

⁶Now the Israelites grieved for their brothers, the Benjamites. "Today one tribe is cut off from Israel," they said. ⁷"How can we provide wives for those who are left, since we have taken an oath by the LORD not to give them any of our daughters in marriage?" ⁸Then they asked, "Which one of the tribes of Israel failed to assemble before the LORD at Mizpah?" They discovered that no one from Jabesh Gilead had come to the camp for the assembly. ⁹For when they counted the people, they found that none of the people of Jabesh Gilead were there.

¹⁰So the assembly sent twelve thousand fighting men with instructions to go to Jabesh Gilead and put to the sword those living there, including the women and children. ¹¹"This is what you are to do," they said. "Kill every male and every

ᵃ33 Some Septuagint manuscripts and Vulgate; the meaning of the Hebrew for this word is uncertain.   ᵇ33 Hebrew Geba, a variant of Gibeah   ᶜ43 The meaning of the Hebrew for this word is uncertain.   ᵈ2 Or to the house of God   ᵉ4 Traditionally peace offerings

woman who is not a virgin." ¹²They found among the people living in Jabesh Gilead four hundred young women who had never slept with a man, and they took them to the camp at Shiloh in Canaan.

¹³Then the whole assembly sent an offer of peace to the Benjamites at the rock of Rimmon. ¹⁴So the Benjamites returned at that time and were given the women of Jabesh Gilead who had been spared. But there were not enough for all of them.

¹⁵The people grieved for Benjamin, because the LORD had made a gap in the tribes of Israel. ¹⁶And the elders of the assembly said, "With the women of Benjamin destroyed, how shall we provide wives for the men who are left? ¹⁷The Benjamite survivors must have heirs," they said, "so that a tribe of Israel will not be wiped out. ¹⁸We can't give them our daughters as wives, since we Israelites have taken this oath: 'Cursed be anyone who gives a wife to a Benjamite.' ¹⁹But look, there is the annual festival of the LORD in Shiloh, to the north of Bethel, and east of the road that goes from Bethel to Shechem, and to the south of Lebonah."

²⁰So they instructed the Benjamites, saying, "Go and hide in the vineyards ²¹and watch. When the girls of Shiloh come out to join in the dancing, then rush from the vineyards and each of you seize a wife from the girls of Shiloh and go to the land of Benjamin. ²²When their fathers or brothers complain to us, we will say to them, 'Do us a kindness by helping them, because we did not get wives for them during the war, and you are innocent, since you did not give your daughters to them.' "

²³So that is what the Benjamites did. While the girls were dancing, each man caught one and carried her off to be his wife. Then they returned to their inheritance and rebuilt the towns and settled in them.

²⁴At that time the Israelites left that place and went home to their tribes and clans, each to his own inheritance.

²⁵In those days Israel had no king; everyone did as he saw fit.

Ruth

WEDDING CEREMONIES are services of worship on the occasion of a marriage. The event itself is a microcosm of grand and universal realities and points to themes far bigger than itself. The account of Ruth works in the same way and delivers a powerful message of redemption in the context of a love story. Forms of the Hebrew word for redemption appear 23 times in this short story, all woven into the fabric of the tale of how two broken and desolate women find hope and a purpose far beyond their greatest dreams. Ruth will become the bride of Boaz, the great-grandmother of David, Israel's greatest king, and one of the ancestors of the King of kings, the "son of David" (Matthew 1:1,5–6).

    The backdrop of the story is the time of the judges—which is to say it was a time like Thomas Hobbes's state of nature, in which the life of the Israelites was usually "solitary, poor, nasty, brutish and short." Apostasy was grievous, and the wars were bloody. Ethnic hatreds burned, with the antipathy of the Hebrews and Moabites primarily among them. But the story of Ruth, a Moabite woman, was the best of times in these worst of times, like the light that shone in Bethlehem's dark streets centuries later. Bethlehem is where the story of Ruth unfolds, and it teaches a lesson of God's tender willingness to answer prayer in the most intimate and happiest of human relations—and to go far beyond what we ask or even imagine (see Ephesians 3:20–21).

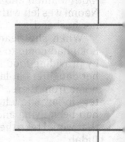

"MAY YOU BE RICHLY REWARDED BY THE LORD, THE GOD OF ISRAEL, UNDER WHOSE WINGS YOU HAVE COME TO TAKE REFUGE." (2:12)

Naomi and Ruth

1 In the days when the judges ruled,[a] there was a famine in the land, and a man from Bethlehem in Judah, together with his wife and two sons, went to live for a while in the country of Moab. [2]The man's name was Elimelech, his wife's name Naomi, and the names of his two sons were Mahlon and Kilion. They were Ephrathites from Bethlehem, Judah. And they went to Moab and lived there.

[3]Now Elimelech, Naomi's husband, died, and she was left with her two sons. [4]They married Moabite women, one named Orpah and the other Ruth. After they had lived there about ten years, [5]both Mahlon and Kilion also died, and Naomi was left without her two sons and her husband.

[6]When she heard in Moab that the LORD had come to the aid of his people by providing food for them, Naomi and her daughters-in-law prepared to return home from there. [7]With her two daughters-in-law she left the place where she had been living and set out on the road that would take them back to the land of Judah.

[8]Then Naomi said to her two daughters-in-law, "Go back, each of you, to your mother's home. May the LORD show kindness to you, as you have shown to your dead and to me. [9]May the LORD grant that each of you will find rest in the home of another husband."

Then she kissed them and they wept aloud [10]and said to her, "We will go back with you to your people."

[11]But Naomi said, "Return home, my daughters. Why would you come with me? Am I going to have any more sons, who could become your husbands? [12]Return home, my daughters; I am too old to have another husband. Even if I thought there was still hope for me— even if I had a husband tonight and then gave birth to sons— [13]would you wait until they grew up? Would you remain unmarried for them? No, my daughters. It is more bitter for me than for you, because the LORD's hand has gone out against me!"

[14]At this they wept again. Then Orpah kissed her mother-in-law good-by, but Ruth clung to her.

[15]"Look," said Naomi, "your sister-in-law is going back to her people and her gods. Go back with her."

[16]But Ruth replied, "Don't urge me to leave you or to turn back from you. Where you go I will go, and where you stay I will stay. Your people will be my people and your God my God. [17]Where you die I will die, and there I will be buried. May the LORD deal with me, be it ever so severely, if anything but death separates you and me." [18]When Naomi realized that Ruth was determined to go with her, she stopped urging her.

[19]So the two women went on until they came to Bethlehem. When they arrived in Bethlehem, the whole town was stirred because of them, and the women exclaimed, "Can this be Naomi?"

[20]"Don't call me Naomi,[b]" she told them. "Call me Mara,[c] because the Almighty[d] has made my life very bitter. [21]I went away full, but the LORD has brought me back empty. Why call me Naomi? The LORD has afflicted[e] me; the Almighty has brought misfortune upon me."

[22]So Naomi returned from Moab accompanied by Ruth the Moabitess, her daughter-in-law, arriving in Bethlehem as the barley harvest was beginning.

Ruth Meets Boaz

2 Now Naomi had a relative on her husband's side, from the clan of Elimelech, a man of standing, whose name was Boaz.

[2]And Ruth the Moabitess said to Naomi, "Let me go to the fields and pick up the leftover grain behind anyone in whose eyes I find favor."

Naomi said to her, "Go ahead, my daughter." [3]So she went out and began to glean in the fields behind the harvesters. As it turned out, she found herself working in a field belonging to Boaz, who was from the clan of Elimelech.

[4]Just then Boaz arrived from Bethlehem and greeted the harvesters, "The LORD be with you!"

"The LORD bless you!" they called back.

---

[a]1 Traditionally *judged*   [b]20 *Naomi* means *pleasant*; also in verse 21.   [c]20 *Mara* means *bitter*.   [d]20 Hebrew *Shaddai*; also in verse 21   [e]21 Or *has testified against*

⁵Boaz asked the foreman of his harvesters, "Whose young woman is that?"

⁶The foreman replied, "She is the Moabitess who came back from Moab with Naomi. ⁷She said, 'Please let me glean and gather among the sheaves behind the harvesters.' She went into the field and has worked steadily from morning till now, except for a short rest in the shelter."

⁸So Boaz said to Ruth, "My daughter, listen to me. Don't go and glean in another field and don't go away from here. Stay here with my servant girls. ⁹Watch the field where the men are harvesting, and

---

RUTH 2:11–12

Prayer Changes Things

2:12 "MAY YOU BE RICHLY REWARDED BY THE LORD . . . UNDER WHOSE WINGS YOU HAVE COME TO TAKE REFUGE."

"Awful things happen to people who pray," writes Virginia Owens. "Their plans are frequently disrupted. They end up in strange places. Abraham went out, not knowing where he was to go—hardly the picture of someone who has struck it rich on a brand new power source. After Mary's magnificent prayer at the annunciation, she finds herself the pariah of Nazareth society. The well-worn phrase, 'Prayer changes things,' often meant to comfort, is as tricky as any Greek oracle."[1]

What happened to Boaz after he prayed for Ruth wasn't awful; in fact it was thrilling—but it sure disrupted the plans of this middle-aged Bethlehem elder. What followed was an unexpected wedding, with he and his young bride becoming the great-grandparents of the great king David. Boaz prayed a blessing for Ruth, that God, "under whose wings you have come to take refuge" (2:12), would be to her like a mother hen that covers her weak and defenseless young with her wings (see Psalm 17:8; 36:7; 63:7).

God honored Boaz's prayer by letting Boaz be the mother hen! He was awakened one night with the beautiful woman he blessed lying at his feet. When he asked who she was, she answered, "I am your servant Ruth . . . Spread the corner of your garment over me, since you are a kinsman-redeemer" (3:9). These words accomplished two things: They amounted to a Middle Eastern proposal of marriage ("Spread the corner of your garment over me"), and they were a play on the word "wings." The Hebrew word for the corner of a garment is literally "wings." Boaz had prayed that God's wings would cover Ruth; now she asked that the "wings" of his garment be her cover.

The lesson isn't, "Don't pray for single people unless you plan to marry them." The lesson is, "Always be ready to be part of God's answer to your prayers." Asking God to help others is not merely a way of putting the responsibility on his shoulders, but of shouldering the responsibility with him. When we pray for others, we pray not only *to* God, but also *with* Christ who always intercedes for us (see Hebrews 7:25).

PRAY:

Father, as I pray for your will for others, make my will one with yours.
I want to be willing to combine action with my prayers for them.

FOR YOUR NEXT DEVOTIONAL READING, GO TO PAGE 306.

follow along after the girls. I have told the men not to touch you. And whenever you are thirsty, go and get a drink from the water jars the men have filled."

¹⁰At this, she bowed down with her face to the ground. She exclaimed, "Why have I found such favor in your eyes that you notice me—a foreigner?"

¹¹Boaz replied, "I've been told all about what you have done for your mother-in-law since the death of your husband—how you left your father and mother and your homeland and came to live with a people you did not know before. ¹²May the LORD repay you for what you have done. May you be richly rewarded by the LORD, the God of Israel, under whose wings you have come to take refuge."

> "MAY the LORD repay you for what you have done. May you be richly rewarded by the LORD, the God of Israel, under whose wings you have come to take refuge."
>
> RUTH 2:12

¹³"May I continue to find favor in your eyes, my lord," she said. "You have given me comfort and have spoken kindly to your servant—though I do not have the standing of one of your servant girls."

¹⁴At mealtime Boaz said to her, "Come over here. Have some bread and dip it in the wine vinegar."

When she sat down with the harvesters, he offered her some roasted grain. She ate all she wanted and had some left over. ¹⁵As she got up to glean, Boaz gave orders to his men, "Even if she gathers among the sheaves, don't embarrass her. ¹⁶Rather, pull out some stalks for her from the bundles and leave them for her to pick up, and don't rebuke her."

¹⁷So Ruth gleaned in the field until evening. Then she threshed the barley she had gathered, and it amounted to about an ephah.ᵃ ¹⁸She carried it back to town, and her mother-in-law saw how much she had gathered. Ruth also brought out and gave her what she had left over after she had eaten enough.

¹⁹Her mother-in-law asked her, "Where did you glean today? Where did you work? Blessed be the man who took notice of you!"

Then Ruth told her mother-in-law about the one at whose place she had been working. "The name of the man I worked with today is Boaz," she said.

²⁰"The LORD bless him!" Naomi said to her daughter-in-law. "He has not stopped showing his kindness to the living and the dead." She added, "That man is our close relative; he is one of our kinsman-redeemers."

²¹Then Ruth the Moabitess said, "He even said to me, 'Stay with my workers until they finish harvesting all my grain.'"

²²Naomi said to Ruth her daughter-in-law, "It will be good for you, my daughter, to go with his girls, because in someone else's field you might be harmed."

²³So Ruth stayed close to the servant girls of Boaz to glean until the barley and wheat harvests were finished. And she lived with her mother-in-law.

Ruth and Boaz at the Threshing Floor

3 One day Naomi her mother-in-law said to her, "My daughter, should I not try to find a homeᵇ for you, where you will be well provided for? ²Is not Boaz, with whose servant girls you have been, a kinsman of ours? Tonight he will be winnowing barley on the threshing floor. ³Wash and perfume yourself, and put on your best clothes. Then go down to the threshing floor, but don't let him know you are there until he has finished eating and drinking. ⁴When he lies down, note the place where he is lying. Then go and uncover his feet and lie down. He will tell you what to do."

⁵"I will do whatever you say," Ruth answered. ⁶So she went down to the threshing floor and did everything her mother-in-law told her to do.

⁷When Boaz had finished eating and drinking and was in good spirits, he went over to lie down at the far end of the grain pile. Ruth approached quietly, uncovered his feet and lay down. ⁸In the middle of the night something startled

ᵃ17 That is, probably about 3/5 bushel (about 22 liters) ᵇ1 Hebrew *find rest* (see Ruth 1:9)

the man, and he turned and discovered a woman lying at his feet.

⁹"Who are you?" he asked.

"I am your servant Ruth," she said. "Spread the corner of your garment over me, since you are a kinsman-redeemer."

¹⁰"The LORD bless you, my daughter," he replied. "This kindness is greater than that which you showed earlier: You have not run after the younger men, whether rich or poor. ¹¹And now, my daughter, don't be afraid. I will do for you all you ask. All my fellow townsmen know that you are a woman of noble character. ¹²Although it is true that I am near of kin, there is a kinsman-redeemer nearer than I. ¹³Stay here for the night, and in the morning if he wants to redeem, good; let him redeem. But if he is not willing, as surely as the LORD lives I will do it. Lie here until morning."

¹⁴So she lay at his feet until morning, but got up before anyone could be recognized; and he said, "Don't let it be known that a woman came to the threshing floor."

¹⁵He also said, "Bring me the shawl you are wearing and hold it out." When she did so, he poured into it six measures of barley and put it on her. Then he*ᵃ* went back to town.

¹⁶When Ruth came to her mother-in-law, Naomi asked, "How did it go, my daughter?"

Then she told her everything Boaz had done for her ¹⁷and added, "He gave me these six measures of barley, saying, 'Don't go back to your mother-in-law empty-handed.'"

¹⁸Then Naomi said, "Wait, my daughter, until you find out what happens. For the man will not rest until the matter is settled today."

Boaz Marries Ruth

4 Meanwhile Boaz went up to the town gate and sat there. When the kinsman-redeemer he had mentioned came along, Boaz said, "Come over here, my friend, and sit down." So he went over and sat down. ²Boaz took ten of the elders of the town and said, "Sit here," and they did so. ³Then he said to the kinsman-redeemer, "Naomi, who has come back from Moab, is sell-

ing the piece of land that belonged to our brother Elimelech. ⁴I thought I should bring the matter to your attention and suggest that you buy it in the presence of these seated here and in the presence of the elders of my people. If you will redeem it, do so. But if you*ᵇ* will not, tell me, so I will know. For no one has the right to do it except you, and I am next in line."

"I will redeem it," he said.

⁵Then Boaz said, "On the day you buy the land from Naomi and from Ruth the Moabitess, you acquire*ᶜ* the dead man's widow, in order to maintain the name of the dead with his property."

⁶At this, the kinsman-redeemer said, "Then I cannot redeem it because I might endanger my own estate. You redeem it yourself. I cannot do it."

⁷(Now in earlier times in Israel, for the redemption and transfer of property to become final, one party took off his sandal and gave it to the other. This was the method of legalizing transactions in Israel.)

⁸So the kinsman-redeemer said to Boaz, "Buy it yourself." And he removed his sandal.

⁹Then Boaz announced to the elders and all the people, "Today you are witnesses that I have bought from Naomi all the property of Elimelech, Kilion and Mahlon. ¹⁰I have also acquired Ruth the Moabitess, Mahlon's widow, as my wife, in order to maintain the name of the dead with his property, so that his name will not disappear from among his family or from the town records. Today you are witnesses!"

¹¹Then the elders and all those at the gate said, "We are witnesses. May the LORD make the woman who is coming into your home like Rachel and Leah, who together built up the house of Israel. May you have standing in Ephrathah and be famous in Bethlehem. ¹²Through the offspring the LORD gives you by this young woman, may your family be like that of Perez, whom Tamar bore to Judah."

*ᵃ*15 Most Hebrew manuscripts; many Hebrew manuscripts, Vulgate and Syriac *she*   *ᵇ*4 Many Hebrew manuscripts, Septuagint, Vulgate and Syriac; most Hebrew manuscripts *he*
*ᶜ*5 Hebrew; Vulgate and Syriac *Naomi, you acquire Ruth the Moabitess,*

The Genealogy of David

¹³So Boaz took Ruth and she became
his wife. Then he went to her, and the
LORD enabled her to conceive, and she
gave birth to a son. ¹⁴The women said
to Naomi: "Praise be to the LORD, who
this day has not left you without a kinsman-redeemer. May he become famous
throughout Israel! ¹⁵He will renew your
life and sustain you in your old age. For
your daughter-in-law, who loves you
and who is better to you than seven
sons, has given him birth."

¹⁶Then Naomi took the child, laid him
in her lap and cared for him. ¹⁷The wom-
en living there said, "Naomi has a son."
And they named him Obed. He was the
father of Jesse, the father of David.

¹⁸This, then, is the family line of Perez:

Perez was the father of Hezron,
¹⁹ Hezron the father of Ram,
Ram the father of Amminadab,
²⁰ Amminadab the father of Nahshon,
Nahshon the father of Salmon,ᵃ
²¹ Salmon the father of Boaz,
Boaz the father of Obed,
²² Obed the father of Jesse,
and Jesse the father of David.

ᵃ20 A few Hebrew manuscripts, some Septuagint
manuscripts and Vulgate (see also verse 21 and
Septuagint of 1 Chron. 2:11); most Hebrew
manuscripts Salma

1 Samuel

IN THE BOOK of 1 Samuel, we read about the very beginnings of the monarchy of Israel, and we read much about Samuel, who was considered one of the greatest intercessors in the Old Testament. When God wanted Jeremiah to know how determined he was to execute judgment on Judah, he implied that Moses and Samuel were intercessors who made a difference: "Even if Moses and Samuel were to stand before me, my heart would not go out to this people" (Jeremiah 15:1; see also Psalm 99:6).

The opening chapters of 1 Samuel tell how Samuel was a child who was prayed for and set apart by his mother Hannah. In a real sense, Samuel was birthed in prayer, and his training and ministry were rooted in prayer.

This alone makes Samuel a worthy study in the ministry of intercessory prayer. But his role as a prophet, which came at a critical time in Israel's history, adds even greater significance to his calling as a man of prayer. Samuel is the bridge between the time when Israel was a loose collection of tribes, a theocracy united by a common faith and sometimes little more, and the time when Israel became a monarchy. It was a perilous move, ambiguous at best, based on questionable motives. The people explain their desire to have a king in this way: "Then we will be like all the other nations, with a king to lead us and to go out before us and fight our battles" (1 Samuel 8:20).

"DO NOT STOP CRYING OUT TO THE LORD OUR GOD FOR US." (7:8)

God ended up allowing the Israelites their king even though he knew it was a rejection of him (see 8:7). There is a profound lesson in this: at a moment of tumultuous change in a nation's history, God's choice of a leader was a man who was both a prophet and an intercessor. The man of the hour was one who would speak about God to the people and who would speak to God about the people. He embodied P. T. Forsyth's dictum that a leader must be much with the people to know their problems, and much with God to know how to solve them.

The Birth of Samuel

1 There was a certain man from Rama-thaim, a Zuphite[a] from the hill country of Ephraim, whose name was Elkanah son of Jeroham, the son of Elihu, the son of Tohu, the son of Zuph, an Ephraimite. ²He had two wives; one was called Hannah and the other Peninnah. Peninnah had children, but Hannah had none.

³Year after year this man went up from his town to worship and sacrifice to the LORD Almighty at Shiloh, where Hophni and Phinehas, the two sons of Eli, were priests of the LORD. ⁴Whenever the day came for Elkanah to sacrifice, he would give portions of the meat to his wife Peninnah and to all her sons and daughters. ⁵But to Hannah he gave a double portion because he loved her, and the LORD had closed her womb. ⁶And be-

---

a 1 Or from Ramathaim Zuphim

---

1 SAMUEL 1

Answers Bigger Than Our Prayers

1:15 "I WAS POURING OUT MY SOUL TO THE LORD."

In her culture, the term used to describe Hannah's condition was "barren." Childlessness was thought to be punishment for sin, and since Hannah could not have children, she was considered cursed. Hannah was hollow at the point in her life where it was most important that she be fruitful and filled. And Peninnah made sure she didn't forget it. Though Hannah was her husband's delight, his encouragement didn't comfort her and he couldn't take away her pain: "Hannah, why are you weeping? Why don't you eat? Why are you downhearted? Don't I mean more to you than ten sons?" (1:8).

Hannah had no place to go but to the Lord. He heard her prayer and gave her a son and more: Her child became a great prophet in Israel. The answer to Hannah's prayer was bigger than her prayer. The place where she prayed was bigger too, like the address Emily gave herself in Thornton Wilder's *Our Town*: "temple, nation of Israel, planet earth, solar system, Milky Way galaxy, Universe, Mind of God." God heard Hannah's prayer from his throne in heaven where he controls history. All Hannah saw was a baby and the relief of her misery. God saw that too, but he also saw his people and their destiny to be a great nation through whom he would bless the whole earth (see Genesis 12:1–3). God is a master of efficiency: He could bless Hannah beyond her greatest hopes and bless a people beyond theirs.

Hannah told Eli the priest that she was pouring out her soul to the Lord (1 Samuel 1:15). When we pray for the things we care for most deeply, we, too, pour out our souls. But our souls are small, and they are poured out into the great heart of God, who answers better than we can ask or even think (see Ephesians 3:20–21).

PRAY:

Father, I trust you to do better with my requests,
even my biggest requests, than I can ever hope. "Your love,
O LORD, reaches to the heavens" (Psalm 36:5).

FOR YOUR NEXT DEVOTIONAL READING, GO TO PAGE 310.

cause the LORD had closed her womb, her rival kept provoking her in order to irritate her. ⁷This went on year after year. Whenever Hannah went up to the house of the LORD, her rival provoked her till she wept and would not eat. ⁸Elkanah her husband would say to her, "Hannah, why are you weeping? Why don't you eat? Why are you downhearted? Don't I mean more to you than ten sons?"

⁹Once when they had finished eating and drinking in Shiloh, Hannah stood up. Now Eli the priest was sitting on a chair by the doorpost of the LORD's temple.ᵃ ¹⁰In bitterness of soul Hannah wept much and prayed to the LORD. ¹¹And she made a vow, saying, "O LORD Almighty, if you will only look upon your servant's misery and remember me, and not forget your servant but give her a son, then I will give him to the LORD for all the days of his life, and no razor will ever be used on his head."

¹²As she kept on praying to the LORD, Eli observed her mouth. ¹³Hannah was praying in her heart, and her lips were moving but her voice was not heard. Eli thought she was drunk ¹⁴and said to her, "How long will you keep on getting drunk? Get rid of your wine."

¹⁵"Not so, my lord," Hannah replied, "I am a woman who is deeply troubled. I have not been drinking wine or beer; I was pouring out my soul to the LORD. ¹⁶Do not take your servant for a wicked woman; I have been praying here out of my great anguish and grief."

¹⁷Eli answered, "Go in peace, and may the God of Israel grant you what you have asked of him."

¹⁸She said, "May your servant find favor in your eyes." Then she went her way and ate something, and her face was no longer downcast.

¹⁹Early the next morning they arose and worshiped before the LORD and then went back to their home at Ramah. Elkanah lay with Hannah his wife, and the LORD remembered her. ²⁰So in the course of time Hannah conceived and gave birth to a son. She named him Samuel,ᵇ saying, "Because I asked the LORD for him."

Hannah Dedicates Samuel

²¹When the man Elkanah went up with all his family to offer the annual sacrifice to the LORD and to fulfill his vow, ²²Hannah did not go. She said to her husband, "After the boy is weaned, I will take him and present him before the LORD, and he will live there always."

²³"Do what seems best to you," Elkanah her husband told her. "Stay here until you have weaned him; only may the LORD make good hisᶜ word." So the woman stayed at home and nursed her son until she had weaned him.

²⁴After he was weaned, she took the boy with her, young as he was, along with a three-year-old bull,ᵈ an ephahᵉ of flour and a skin of wine, and brought him to the house of the LORD at Shiloh. ²⁵When they had slaughtered the bull, they brought the boy to Eli, ²⁶and she said to him, "As surely as you live, my lord, I am the woman who stood here beside you praying to the LORD. ²⁷I prayed for this child, and the LORD has granted me what I asked of him. ²⁸So now I give him to the LORD. For his whole life he will be given over to the LORD." And he worshiped the LORD there.

> "I PRAYED for this child, and the LORD has granted me what I asked of him."
>
> 1 SAMUEL 1:27

Hannah's Prayer

2 Then Hannah prayed and said:

"My heart rejoices in the LORD;
  in the LORD my hornᶠ is lifted high.
My mouth boasts over my enemies,
  for I delight in your deliverance.

² "There is no one holyᵍ like the LORD;
  there is no one besides you;
  there is no Rock like our God.

³ "Do not keep talking so proudly
  or let your mouth speak such
    arrogance,

ᵃ9 That is, tabernacle   ᵇ20 Samuel sounds like the Hebrew for heard of God.   ᶜ23 Masoretic Text; Dead Sea Scrolls, Septuagint and Syriac your   ᵈ24 Dead Sea Scrolls, Septuagint and Syriac; Masoretic Text with three bulls   ᵉ24 That is, probably about 3/5 bushel (about 22 liters)   ᶠ1 Horn here symbolizes strength; also in verse 10.   ᵍ2 Or no Holy One

> *THEN Hannah prayed and said:*
> *"My heart rejoices in the Lord;*
>   *in the Lord my horn is lifted high.*
> *My mouth boasts over my enemies,*
>   *for I delight in your deliverance."*
>
> 1 SAMUEL 2:1

for the Lord is a God who knows,
  and by him deeds are weighed.

4 "The bows of the warriors are broken,
  but those who stumbled are armed
    with strength.
5 Those who were full hire themselves
    out for food,
  but those who were hungry hunger
    no more.
She who was barren has borne seven
    children,
  but she who has had many sons
    pines away.

6 "The Lord brings death and makes
    alive;
  he brings down to the grave[a] and
    raises up.
7 The Lord sends poverty and wealth;
  he humbles and he exalts.
8 He raises the poor from the dust
  and lifts the needy from the
    ash heap;
  he seats them with princes
  and has them inherit a throne
    of honor.

"For the foundations of the earth are
    the Lord's;
  upon them he has set the world.
9 He will guard the feet of his saints,
  but the wicked will be silenced in
    darkness.

"It is not by strength that one
    prevails;
10   those who oppose the Lord will be
    shattered.
He will thunder against them from
    heaven;
  the Lord will judge the ends of the
    earth.

"He will give strength to his king
  and exalt the horn of his anointed."

11 Then Elkanah went home to Ramah,
but the boy ministered before the Lord
under Eli the priest.

Eli's Wicked Sons

12 Eli's sons were wicked men; they
had no regard for the Lord. 13 Now it was
the practice of the priests with the people that whenever anyone offered a sacrifice and while the meat was being
boiled, the servant of the priest would
come with a three-pronged fork in his
hand. 14 He would plunge it into the pan
or kettle or caldron or pot, and the
priest would take for himself whatever
the fork brought up. This is how they
treated all the Israelites who came to
Shiloh. 15 But even before the fat was
burned, the servant of the priest would
come and say to the man who was sacrificing, "Give the priest some meat to
roast; he won't accept boiled meat from
you, but only raw."

16 If the man said to him, "Let the fat be
burned up first, and then take whatever
you want," the servant would then answer, "No, hand it over now; if you don't,
I'll take it by force."

17 This sin of the young men was very
great in the Lord's sight, for they[b] were
treating the Lord's offering with contempt.

18 But Samuel was ministering before
the Lord—a boy wearing a linen ephod.
19 Each year his mother made him a little
robe and took it to him when she went
up with her husband to offer the annual
sacrifice. 20 Eli would bless Elkanah and
his wife, saying, "May the Lord give you
children by this woman to take the place
of the one she prayed for and gave to the
Lord." Then they would go home. 21 And
the Lord was gracious to Hannah; she
conceived and gave birth to three sons
and two daughters. Meanwhile, the boy
Samuel grew up in the presence of the
Lord.

> *"MAY the Lord give you children by this*
> *woman to take the place of the one she*
> *prayed for and gave to the Lord."*
>
> 1 SAMUEL 2:20

22 Now Eli, who was very old, heard
about everything his sons were doing to
all Israel and how they slept with the
women who served at the entrance to the

---

[a]6 Hebrew *Sheol*   [b]17 Or *men*

Tent of Meeting. ²³So he said to them, "Why do you do such things? I hear from all the people about these wicked deeds of yours. ²⁴No, my sons; it is not a good report that I hear spreading among the LORD's people. ²⁵If a man sins against another man, God*a* may mediate for him; but if a man sins against the LORD, who will intercede for him?" His sons, however, did not listen to their father's rebuke, for it was the LORD's will to put them to death.

²⁶And the boy Samuel continued to grow in stature and in favor with the LORD and with men.

Prophecy Against the House of Eli

²⁷Now a man of God came to Eli and said to him, "This is what the LORD says: 'Did I not clearly reveal myself to your father's house when they were in Egypt under Pharaoh? ²⁸I chose your father out of all the tribes of Israel to be my priest, to go up to my altar, to burn incense, and to wear an ephod in my presence. I also gave your father's house all the offerings made with fire by the Israelites. ²⁹Why do you*b* scorn my sacrifice and offering that I prescribed for my dwelling? Why do you honor your sons more than me by fattening yourselves on the choice parts of every offering made by my people Israel?'

³⁰"Therefore the LORD, the God of Israel, declares: 'I promised that your house and your father's house would minister before me forever.' But now the LORD declares: 'Far be it from me! Those who honor me I will honor, but those who despise me will be disdained. ³¹The time is coming when I will cut short your strength and the strength of your father's house, so that there will not be an old man in your family line ³²and you will see distress in my dwelling. Although good will be done to Israel, in your family line there will never be an old man. ³³Every one of you that I do not cut off from my altar will be spared only to blind your eyes with tears and to grieve your heart, and all your descendants will die in the prime of life.

³⁴"'And what happens to your two sons, Hophni and Phinehas, will be a sign to you—they will both die on the same day. ³⁵I will raise up for myself a faithful priest, who will do according to what is in my heart and mind. I will firmly establish his house, and he will minister before my anointed one always. ³⁶Then everyone left in your family line will come and bow down before him for a piece of silver and a crust of bread and plead, "Appoint me to some priestly office so I can have food to eat."'"

The LORD Calls Samuel

3 The boy Samuel ministered before the LORD under Eli. In those days the word of the LORD was rare; there were not many visions.

²One night Eli, whose eyes were becoming so weak that he could barely see, was lying down in his usual place. ³The lamp of God had not yet gone out, and Samuel was lying down in the temple*c* of the LORD, where the ark of God was. ⁴Then the LORD called Samuel.

Samuel answered, "Here I am." ⁵And he ran to Eli and said, "Here I am; you called me."

But Eli said, "I did not call; go back and lie down." So he went and lay down.

⁶Again the LORD called, "Samuel!" And Samuel got up and went to Eli and said, "Here I am; you called me."

"My son," Eli said, "I did not call; go back and lie down."

⁷Now Samuel did not yet know the LORD: The word of the LORD had not yet been revealed to him.

⁸The LORD called Samuel a third time, and Samuel got up and went to Eli and said, "Here I am; you called me."

Then Eli realized that the LORD was calling the boy. ⁹So Eli told Samuel, "Go and lie down, and if he calls you, say, 'Speak, LORD, for your servant is listening.'" So Samuel went and lay down in his place.

¹⁰The LORD came and stood there, calling as at the other times, "Samuel! Samuel!"

Then Samuel said, "Speak, for your servant is listening."

¹¹And the LORD said to Samuel: "See, I am about to do something in Israel that will make the ears of everyone who hears of it tingle. ¹²At that time I will carry out

---

*a*25 Or *the judges*   *b*29 The Hebrew is plural.
*c*3 That is, tabernacle

against Eli everything I spoke against his family—from beginning to end. ¹³For I told him that I would judge his family forever because of the sin he knew about; his sons made themselves contemptible,ᵃ and he failed to restrain them. ¹⁴Therefore, I swore to the house of Eli, 'The guilt of Eli's house will never be atoned for by sacrifice or offering.'"

¹⁵Samuel lay down until morning and then opened the doors of the house of the LORD. He was afraid to tell Eli the vision, ¹⁶but Eli called him and said, "Samuel, my son."

Samuel answered, "Here I am."

ᵃ13 Masoretic Text; an ancient Hebrew scribal tradition and Septuagint *sons blasphemed God*

---

1 SAMUEL 3

[WEDNESDAY]

Ready to Listen

3:10 THEN SAMUEL SAID, "SPEAK, FOR YOUR SERVANT IS LISTENING."

The fact that the Lord is speaking and young Samuel is listening is remarkable on two counts. One: "In those days the word of the LORD was rare" (3:1). Two: The people who should have been listening had stopped a long time ago. And now—as Eli snored away, and his sons no doubt caroused (see 2:22)—God was speaking again.

But why now, why Samuel? God has his reasons, which he usually keeps to himself, but some educated guesses—or better, musings—can be made. Certainly God always acts wisely and sovereignly, quite apart from the good things we have done. It would be a mistake to look for qualities in Samuel that moved God to start speaking again. A better approach is to marvel and be thankful that he had decided to speak, and that he had raised up a person who would listen.

It's understanding the act of listening that can help us most. Samuel was lying down at night when he heard God. This doesn't mean that we only hear God at night, but it is a picture of how we hear God best, which is when we are quiet. In the book, *The Pilgrim's Progress*, John Bunyan's character Eargate couldn't hear because his hearing was stopped up with filth. The filth of modern life usually comes in the form of noise. Though he sometimes uses them, God doesn't often resort to megaphones. "In quietness and trust is your strength" (Isaiah 30:15).

Samuel's response to God, though coached by Eli, says a lot too: He says, "Speak, for your servant is listening." God is more apt to speak to those who listen than to those who don't. It's not that God is shy, but that he waits to speak until he sees the submission and obedience inherent in the willingness to listen. Obedience opens eyes and ears. Jesus said, "If anyone chooses to do God's will, he will find out whether my teaching comes from God or whether I speak on my own" (John 7:17).

God won't speak until he's ready—and we are ready. The way to get ready is to get quiet and to resolve to obey what we hear when we hear it.

PRAY:
Speak, Lord, for I am listening.

FOR YOUR NEXT DEVOTIONAL READING, GO TO PAGE 315.

[17]"What was it he said to you?" Eli asked. "Do not hide it from me. May God deal with you, be it ever so severely, if you hide from me anything he told you." [18]So Samuel told him everything, hiding nothing from him. Then Eli said, "He is the LORD; let him do what is good in his eyes."

[19]The LORD was with Samuel as he grew up, and he let none of his words fall to the ground. [20]And all Israel from Dan to Beersheba recognized that Samuel was attested as a prophet of the LORD. [21]The LORD continued to appear at Shiloh, and there he revealed himself to Samuel through his word.

4 And Samuel's word came to all Israel.

The Philistines Capture the Ark

Now the Israelites went out to fight against the Philistines. The Israelites camped at Ebenezer, and the Philistines at Aphek. [2]The Philistines deployed their forces to meet Israel, and as the battle spread, Israel was defeated by the Philistines, who killed about four thousand of them on the battlefield. [3]When the soldiers returned to camp, the elders of Israel asked, "Why did the LORD bring defeat upon us today before the Philistines? Let us bring the ark of the LORD's covenant from Shiloh, so that it[a] may go with us and save us from the hand of our enemies."

[4]So the people sent men to Shiloh, and they brought back the ark of the covenant of the LORD Almighty, who is enthroned between the cherubim. And Eli's two sons, Hophni and Phinehas, were there with the ark of the covenant of God.

[5]When the ark of the LORD's covenant came into the camp, all Israel raised such a great shout that the ground shook. [6]Hearing the uproar, the Philistines asked, "What's all this shouting in the Hebrew camp?"

When they learned that the ark of the LORD had come into the camp, [7]the Philistines were afraid. "A god has come into the camp," they said. "We're in trouble! Nothing like this has happened before. [8]Woe to us! Who will deliver us from the hand of these mighty gods? They are the gods who struck the Egyptians with all kinds of plagues in the desert. [9]Be strong, Philistines! Be men, or you will be subject to the Hebrews, as they have been to you. Be men, and fight!"

[10]So the Philistines fought, and the Israelites were defeated and every man fled to his tent. The slaughter was very great; Israel lost thirty thousand foot soldiers. [11]The ark of God was captured, and Eli's two sons, Hophni and Phinehas, died.

Death of Eli

[12]That same day a Benjamite ran from the battle line and went to Shiloh, his clothes torn and dust on his head. [13]When he arrived, there was Eli sitting on his chair by the side of the road, watching, because his heart feared for the ark of God. When the man entered the town and told what had happened, the whole town sent up a cry.

[14]Eli heard the outcry and asked, "What is the meaning of this uproar?"

The man hurried over to Eli, [15]who was ninety-eight years old and whose eyes were set so that he could not see. [16]He told Eli, "I have just come from the battle line; I fled from it this very day."

Eli asked, "What happened, my son?"

[17]The man who brought the news replied, "Israel fled before the Philistines, and the army has suffered heavy losses. Also your two sons, Hophni and Phinehas, are dead, and the ark of God has been captured."

[18]When he mentioned the ark of God, Eli fell backward off his chair by the side of the gate. His neck was broken and he died, for he was an old man and heavy. He had led[b] Israel forty years.

[19]His daughter-in-law, the wife of Phinehas, was pregnant and near the time of delivery. When she heard the news that the ark of God had been captured and that her father-in-law and her husband were dead, she went into labor and gave birth, but was overcome by her labor pains. [20]As she was dying, the women attending her said, "Don't despair; you have given birth to a son." But she did not respond or pay any attention.

[21]She named the boy Ichabod,[c] saying, "The glory has departed from Israel"—

---

[a]3 Or he   [b]18 Traditionally judged
[c]21 Ichabod means no glory.

because of the capture of the ark of God and the deaths of her father-in-law and her husband. ²²She said, "The glory has departed from Israel, for the ark of God has been captured."

The Ark in Ashdod and Ekron

5 After the Philistines had captured the ark of God, they took it from Ebenezer to Ashdod. ²Then they carried the ark into Dagon's temple and set it beside Dagon. ³When the people of Ashdod rose early the next day, there was Dagon, fallen on his face on the ground before the ark of the LORD! They took Dagon and put him back in his place. ⁴But the following morning when they rose, there was Dagon, fallen on his face on the ground before the ark of the LORD! His head and hands had been broken off and were lying on the threshold; only his body remained. ⁵That is why to this day neither the priests of Dagon nor any others who enter Dagon's temple at Ashdod step on the threshold.

⁶The LORD's hand was heavy upon the people of Ashdod and its vicinity; he brought devastation upon them and afflicted them with tumors.ᵃ ⁷When the men of Ashdod saw what was happening, they said, "The ark of the god of Israel must not stay here with us, because his hand is heavy upon us and upon Dagon our god." ⁸So they called together all the rulers of the Philistines and asked them, "What shall we do with the ark of the god of Israel?"

They answered, "Have the ark of the god of Israel moved to Gath." So they moved the ark of the God of Israel.

⁹But after they had moved it, the LORD's hand was against that city, throwing it into a great panic. He afflicted the people of the city, both young and old, with an outbreak of tumors.ᵇ ¹⁰So they sent the ark of God to Ekron.

As the ark of God was entering Ekron, the people of Ekron cried out, "They have brought the ark of the god of Israel around to us to kill us and our people." ¹¹So they called together all the rulers of the Philistines and said, "Send the ark of the god of Israel away; let it go back to its own place, or itᶜ will kill us and our people." For death had filled the city with panic; God's hand was very heavy upon it. ¹²Those who did not die were afflicted with tumors, and the outcry of the city went up to heaven.

The Ark Returned to Israel

6 When the ark of the LORD had been in Philistine territory seven months, ²the Philistines called for the priests and the diviners and said, "What shall we do with the ark of the LORD? Tell us how we should send it back to its place."

³They answered, "If you return the ark of the god of Israel, do not send it away empty, but by all means send a guilt offering to him. Then you will be healed, and you will know why his hand has not been lifted from you."

⁴The Philistines asked, "What guilt offering should we send to him?"

They replied, "Five gold tumors and five gold rats, according to the number of the Philistine rulers, because the same plague has struck both you and your rulers. ⁵Make models of the tumors and of the rats that are destroying the country, and pay honor to Israel's god. Perhaps he will lift his hand from you and your gods and your land. ⁶Why do you harden your hearts as the Egyptians and Pharaoh did? When heᵈ treated them harshly, did they not send the Israelites out so they could go on their way?

⁷"Now then, get a new cart ready, with two cows that have calved and have never been yoked. Hitch the cows to the cart, but take their calves away and pen them up. ⁸Take the ark of the LORD and put it on the cart, and in a chest beside it put the gold objects you are sending back to him as a guilt offering. Send it on its way, ⁹but keep watching it. If it goes up to its own territory, toward Beth Shemesh, then the LORD has brought this great disaster on us. But if it does not, then we will know that it was not his hand that struck us and that it happened to us by chance."

¹⁰So they did this. They took two such cows and hitched them to the cart and penned up their calves. ¹¹They placed the

ᵃ6 Hebrew; Septuagint and Vulgate *tumors. And rats appeared in their land, and death and destruction were throughout the city*
ᵇ9 Or *with tumors in the groin* (see Septuagint)
ᶜ11 Or *he*   ᵈ6 That is, God

ark of the LORD on the cart and along with it the chest containing the gold rats and the models of the tumors. ¹²Then the cows went straight up toward Beth Shemesh, keeping on the road and lowing all the way; they did not turn to the right or to the left. The rulers of the Philistines followed them as far as the border of Beth Shemesh.

¹³Now the people of Beth Shemesh were harvesting their wheat in the valley, and when they looked up and saw the ark, they rejoiced at the sight. ¹⁴The cart came to the field of Joshua of Beth Shemesh, and there it stopped beside a large rock. The people chopped up the wood of the cart and sacrificed the cows as a burnt offering to the LORD. ¹⁵The Levites took down the ark of the LORD, together with the chest containing the gold objects, and placed them on the large rock. On that day the people of Beth Shemesh offered burnt offerings and made sacrifices to the LORD. ¹⁶The five rulers of the Philistines saw all this and then returned that same day to Ekron.

¹⁷These are the gold tumors the Philistines sent as a guilt offering to the LORD—one each for Ashdod, Gaza, Ashkelon, Gath and Ekron. ¹⁸And the number of the gold rats was according to the number of Philistine towns belonging to the five rulers—the fortified towns with their country villages. The large rock, on which*a* they set the ark of the LORD, is a witness to this day in the field of Joshua of Beth Shemesh.

¹⁹But God struck down some of the men of Beth Shemesh, putting seventy*b* of them to death because they had looked into the ark of the LORD. The people mourned because of the heavy blow the LORD had dealt them, ²⁰and the men of Beth Shemesh asked, "Who can stand in the presence of the LORD, this holy God? To whom will the ark go up from here?"

²¹Then they sent messengers to the people of Kiriath Jearim, saying, "The Philistines have returned the ark of the LORD. Come down and take it up to your place." 7 ¹So the men of Kiriath Jearim came and took up the ark of the LORD. They took it to Abinadab's house on the hill and consecrated Eleazar his son to guard the ark of the LORD.

Samuel Subdues the Philistines at Mizpah

²It was a long time, twenty years in all, that the ark remained at Kiriath Jearim, and all the people of Israel mourned and sought after the LORD. ³And Samuel said to the whole house of Israel, "If you are returning to the LORD with all your hearts, then rid yourselves of the foreign gods and the Ashtoreths and commit yourselves to the LORD and serve him only, and he will deliver you out of the hand of the Philistines." ⁴So the Israelites put away their Baals and Ashtoreths, and served the LORD only.

⁵Then Samuel said, "Assemble all Israel at Mizpah and I will intercede with the LORD for you." ⁶When they had assembled at Mizpah, they drew water and poured it out before the LORD. On that day they fasted and there they confessed, "We have sinned against the LORD." And Samuel was leader*c* of Israel at Mizpah.

⁷When the Philistines heard that Israel had assembled at Mizpah, the rulers of the Philistines came up to attack them. And when the Israelites heard of it, they were afraid because of the Philistines. ⁸They said to Samuel, "Do not stop crying out to the LORD our God for us, that he may rescue us from the hand of the Philistines." ⁹Then Samuel took a suckling lamb and offered it up as a whole burnt offering to the LORD. He cried out to the LORD on Israel's behalf, and the LORD answered him.

> "DO NOT stop crying out to the LORD our God for us, that he may rescue us from the hand of the Philistines."
>
> 1 SAMUEL 7:8

¹⁰While Samuel was sacrificing the burnt offering, the Philistines drew near to engage Israel in battle. But that day the LORD thundered with loud thunder against the Philistines and threw them into such a panic that they were routed

a18 A few Hebrew manuscripts (see also Septuagint); most Hebrew manuscripts *villages as far as Greater Abel, where*   *b19* A few Hebrew manuscripts; most Hebrew manuscripts and Septuagint *50,070*   *c6* Traditionally *judge*

before the Israelites. ¹¹The men of Israel rushed out of Mizpah and pursued the Philistines, slaughtering them along the way to a point below Beth Car.

¹²Then Samuel took a stone and set it up between Mizpah and Shen. He named it Ebenezer,ᵃ saying, "Thus far has the LORD helped us." ¹³So the Philistines were subdued and did not invade Israelite territory again.

Throughout Samuel's lifetime, the hand of the LORD was against the Philistines. ¹⁴The towns from Ekron to Gath that the Philistines had captured from Israel were restored to her, and Israel delivered the neighboring territory from the power of the Philistines. And there was peace between Israel and the Amorites.

¹⁵Samuel continued as judge over Israel all the days of his life. ¹⁶From year to year he went on a circuit from Bethel to Gilgal to Mizpah, judging Israel in all those places. ¹⁷But he always went back to Ramah, where his home was, and there he also judged Israel. And he built an altar there to the LORD.

Israel Asks for a King

8 When Samuel grew old, he appointed his sons as judges for Israel. ²The name of his firstborn was Joel and the name of his second was Abijah, and they served at Beersheba. ³But his sons did not walk in his ways. They turned aside after dishonest gain and accepted bribes and perverted justice.

⁴So all the elders of Israel gathered together and came to Samuel at Ramah. ⁵They said to him, "You are old, and your sons do not walk in your ways; now appoint a king to leadᵇ us, such as all the other nations have."

⁶But when they said, "Give us a king to lead us," this displeased Samuel; so he prayed to the LORD. ⁷And the LORD told him: "Listen to all that the people are saying to you; it is not you they have rejected, but they have rejected me as their king. ⁸As they have done from the day I brought them up out of Egypt until this day, forsaking me and serving other gods, so they are doing to you. ⁹Now listen to them; but warn them solemnly and let them know what the king who will reign over them will do."

¹⁰Samuel told all the words of the LORD to the people who were asking him for a king. ¹¹He said, "This is what the king who will reign over you will do: He will take your sons and make them serve with his chariots and horses, and they will run in front of his chariots. ¹²Some he will assign to be commanders of thousands and commanders of fifties, and others to plow his ground and reap his harvest, and still others to make weapons of war and equipment for his chariots. ¹³He will take your daughters to be perfumers and cooks and bakers. ¹⁴He will take the best of your fields and vineyards and olive groves and give them to his attendants. ¹⁵He will take a tenth of your grain and of your vintage and give it to his officials and attendants. ¹⁶Your menservants and maidservants and the best of your cattleᶜ and donkeys he will take for his own use. ¹⁷He will take a tenth of your flocks, and you yourselves will become his slaves. ¹⁸When that day comes, you will cry out for relief from the king you have chosen, and the LORD will not answer you in that day."

¹⁹But the people refused to listen to Samuel. "No!" they said. "We want a king over us. ²⁰Then we will be like all the other nations, with a king to lead us and to go out before us and fight our battles."

²¹When Samuel heard all that the people said, he repeated it before the LORD. ²²The LORD answered, "Listen to them and give them a king."

Then Samuel said to the men of Israel, "Everyone go back to his town."

Samuel Anoints Saul

9 There was a Benjamite, a man of standing, whose name was Kish son of Abiel, the son of Zeror, the son of Becorath, the son of Aphiah of Benjamin. ²He had a son named Saul, an impressive young man without equal among the Israelites—a head taller than any of the others.

³Now the donkeys belonging to Saul's father Kish were lost, and Kish said to his son Saul, "Take one of the servants with

---

ᵃ12 *Ebenezer* means *stone of help.*
ᵇ5 Traditionally *judge*; also in verses 6 and 20
ᶜ16 Septuagint; Hebrew *young men*

1 SAMUEL 8

Work With Them

8:7 "IT IS NOT YOU THEY HAVE REJECTED, BUT THEY HAVE REJECTED ME AS THEIR KING."

What the people wanted displeased the Lord as much as it displeased Samuel, so the Lord told Samuel not to take it personally: "It is not you they have rejected, but they have rejected me as their king" (8:7). The Lord reminded Samuel that the people had been rejecting him from the beginning. But when Samuel surely thought the Lord would send him back to the people with a firm "No" to their desire, God surprised Samuel with this: "Now listen to them; but warn them solemnly and let them know what the king who will reign over them will do" (verse 9).

Samuel did as he was told and described the kind of oppression any despot would engage in. The implicit question is: Is this what you want? The people are sure and reply, "We want a king over us. Then we will be like all the other nations" (verses 19–20). When Samuel told the Lord the answer from the people, God responded, "Listen to them and give them a king" (verse 22), much to Samuel's even greater surprise, no doubt.

What's going on here? The Lord has many ways to answer our prayers. He can answer with a yes, or no, or wait, or yes and no, or yes, but (see devotion on Romans 15:30–33). Or in this case, he can answer with what is, in effect, "Work with them on this." The Lord wants to give the people a king, but not the kind of king they think they want. The people want a strong man, a typical autonomous tyrant who can conduct successful military campaigns against their enemies. The people want the right thing for the wrong reasons. The kingship God will give will be unlike any in the world. Israel's king will rule, not as a tyrant, but under the law of God (see 10:25), as God's chosen instrument, and ultimately as a type, or forerunner, of the King of all kings.

Some of our most misguided and selfish desires can be redeemed. They may have come from God originally, but through our sinful nature they have become corrupted and distorted. For instance, the legitimate need for love can mutate into lust, or more subtly, an ill-advised relationship or marriage. God works with us on these things. He knows how we are formed; he knows our weaknesses; and instead of cutting off our desires, he satisfies us with good things (see Psalm 103:5,13–14).

PRAY:

Father, you have compassion on your children.
Satisfy my desires, not with the things I think I need,
but with the better things only you can give.

FOR YOUR NEXT DEVOTIONAL READING, GO TO PAGE 319.

you and go and look for the donkeys." ⁴So he passed through the hill country of Ephraim and through the area around Shalisha, but they did not find them. They went on into the district of Shaalim, but the donkeys were not there. Then he passed through the territory of Benjamin, but they did not find them.

⁵When they reached the district of Zuph, Saul said to the servant who was with him, "Come, let's go back, or my father will stop thinking about the donkeys and start worrying about us."

⁶But the servant replied, "Look, in this town there is a man of God; he is highly respected, and everything he says comes true. Let's go there now. Perhaps he will tell us what way to take."

⁷Saul said to his servant, "If we go, what can we give the man? The food in our sacks is gone. We have no gift to take to the man of God. What do we have?"

⁸The servant answered him again. "Look," he said, "I have a quarter of a shekel*a* of silver. I will give it to the man of God so that he will tell us what way to take." ⁹(Formerly in Israel, if a man went to inquire of God, he would say, "Come, let us go to the seer," because the prophet of today used to be called a seer.)

¹⁰"Good," Saul said to his servant. "Come, let's go." So they set out for the town where the man of God was.

¹¹As they were going up the hill to the town, they met some girls coming out to draw water, and they asked them, "Is the seer here?"

¹²"He is," they answered. "He's ahead of you. Hurry now; he has just come to our town today, for the people have a sacrifice at the high place. ¹³As soon as you enter the town, you will find him before he goes up to the high place to eat. The people will not begin eating until he comes, because he must bless the sacrifice; afterward, those who are invited will eat. Go up now; you should find him about this time."

¹⁴They went up to the town, and as they were entering it, there was Samuel, coming toward them on his way up to the high place.

¹⁵Now the day before Saul came, the LORD had revealed this to Samuel: ¹⁶"About this time tomorrow I will send you a man from the land of Benjamin. Anoint him leader over my people Israel; he will deliver my people from the hand of the Philistines. I have looked upon my people, for their cry has reached me."

¹⁷When Samuel caught sight of Saul, the LORD said to him, "This is the man I spoke to you about; he will govern my people."

¹⁸Saul approached Samuel in the gateway and asked, "Would you please tell me where the seer's house is?"

¹⁹"I am the seer," Samuel replied. "Go up ahead of me to the high place, for today you are to eat with me, and in the morning I will let you go and will tell you all that is in your heart. ²⁰As for the donkeys you lost three days ago, do not worry about them; they have been found. And to whom is all the desire of Israel turned, if not to you and all your father's family?"

²¹Saul answered, "But am I not a Benjamite, from the smallest tribe of Israel, and is not my clan the least of all the clans of the tribe of Benjamin? Why do you say such a thing to me?"

²²Then Samuel brought Saul and his servant into the hall and seated them at the head of those who were invited—about thirty in number. ²³Samuel said to the cook, "Bring the piece of meat I gave you, the one I told you to lay aside."

²⁴So the cook took up the leg with what was on it and set it in front of Saul. Samuel said, "Here is what has been kept for you. Eat, because it was set aside for you for this occasion, from the time I said, 'I have invited guests.'" And Saul dined with Samuel that day.

²⁵After they came down from the high place to the town, Samuel talked with Saul on the roof of his house. ²⁶They rose about daybreak and Samuel called to Saul on the roof, "Get ready, and I will send you on your way." When Saul got ready, he and Samuel went outside together. ²⁷As they were going down to the edge of the town, Samuel said to Saul, "Tell the servant to go on ahead of us"—and the servant did so—"but you stay here awhile, so that I may give you a message from God."

---

a8 That is, about 1/10 ounce (about 3 grams)

10 Then Samuel took a flask of oil and poured it on Saul's head and kissed him, saying, "Has not the LORD anointed you leader over his inheritance?[a] 2When you leave me today, you will meet two men near Rachel's tomb, at Zelzah on the border of Benjamin. They will say to you, 'The donkeys you set out to look for have been found. And now your father has stopped thinking about them and is worried about you. He is asking, "What shall I do about my son?"'

3"Then you will go on from there until you reach the great tree of Tabor. Three men going up to God at Bethel will meet you there. One will be carrying three young goats, another three loaves of bread, and another a skin of wine. 4They will greet you and offer you two loaves of bread, which you will accept from them.

5"After that you will go to Gibeah of God, where there is a Philistine outpost. As you approach the town, you will meet a procession of prophets coming down from the high place with lyres, tambourines, flutes and harps being played before them, and they will be prophesying. 6The Spirit of the LORD will come upon you in power, and you will prophesy with them; and you will be changed into a different person. 7Once these signs are fulfilled, do whatever your hand finds to do, for God is with you.

8"Go down ahead of me to Gilgal. I will surely come down to you to sacrifice burnt offerings and fellowship offerings,[b] but you must wait seven days until I come to you and tell you what you are to do."

Saul Made King

9As Saul turned to leave Samuel, God changed Saul's heart, and all these signs were fulfilled that day. 10When they arrived at Gibeah, a procession of prophets met him; the Spirit of God came upon him in power, and he joined in their prophesying. 11When all those who had formerly known him saw him prophesying with the prophets, they asked each other, "What is this that has happened to the son of Kish? Is Saul also among the prophets?"

12A man who lived there answered, "And who is their father?" So it became a saying: "Is Saul also among the proph-

ets?" 13After Saul stopped prophesying, he went to the high place.

14Now Saul's uncle asked him and his servant, "Where have you been?"

"Looking for the donkeys," he said. "But when we saw they were not to be found, we went to Samuel."

15Saul's uncle said, "Tell me what Samuel said to you."

16Saul replied, "He assured us that the donkeys had been found." But he did not tell his uncle what Samuel had said about the kingship.

17Samuel summoned the people of Israel to the LORD at Mizpah 18and said to them, "This is what the LORD, the God of Israel, says: 'I brought Israel up out of Egypt, and I delivered you from the power of Egypt and all the kingdoms that oppressed you.' 19But you have now rejected your God, who saves you out of all your calamities and distresses. And you have said, 'No, set a king over us.' So now present yourselves before the LORD by your tribes and clans."

20When Samuel brought all the tribes of Israel near, the tribe of Benjamin was chosen. 21Then he brought forward the tribe of Benjamin, clan by clan, and Matri's clan was chosen. Finally Saul son of Kish was chosen. But when they looked for him, he was not to be found. 22So they inquired further of the LORD, "Has the man come here yet?"

And the LORD said, "Yes, he has hidden himself among the baggage."

23They ran and brought him out, and as he stood among the people he was a head taller than any of the others. 24Samuel said to all the people, "Do you see the man the LORD has chosen? There is no one like him among all the people."

Then the people shouted, "Long live the king!"

25Samuel explained to the people the regulations of the kingship. He wrote them down on a scroll and deposited it before the LORD. Then Samuel dismissed the people, each to his own home.

[a]1 Hebrew; Septuagint and Vulgate over his people Israel? You will reign over the LORD's people and save them from the power of their enemies round about. And this will be a sign to you that the LORD has anointed you leader over his inheritance: [b]8 Traditionally peace offerings

²⁶Saul also went to his home in Gibeah, accompanied by valiant men whose hearts God had touched. ²⁷But some troublemakers said, "How can this fellow save us?" They despised him and brought him no gifts. But Saul kept silent.

Saul Rescues the City of Jabesh

11 Nahash the Ammonite went up and besieged Jabesh Gilead. And all the men of Jabesh said to him, "Make a treaty with us, and we will be subject to you."

²But Nahash the Ammonite replied, "I will make a treaty with you only on the condition that I gouge out the right eye of every one of you and so bring disgrace on all Israel."

³The elders of Jabesh said to him, "Give us seven days so we can send messengers throughout Israel; if no one comes to rescue us, we will surrender to you."

⁴When the messengers came to Gibeah of Saul and reported these terms to the people, they all wept aloud. ⁵Just then Saul was returning from the fields, behind his oxen, and he asked, "What is wrong with the people? Why are they weeping?" Then they repeated to him what the men of Jabesh had said.

⁶When Saul heard their words, the Spirit of God came upon him in power, and he burned with anger. ⁷He took a pair of oxen, cut them into pieces, and sent the pieces by messengers throughout Israel, proclaiming, "This is what will be done to the oxen of anyone who does not follow Saul and Samuel." Then the terror of the LORD fell on the people, and they turned out as one man. ⁸When Saul mustered them at Bezek, the men of Israel numbered three hundred thousand and the men of Judah thirty thousand.

⁹They told the messengers who had come, "Say to the men of Jabesh Gilead, 'By the time the sun is hot tomorrow, you will be delivered.'" When the messengers went and reported this to the men of Jabesh, they were elated. ¹⁰They said to the Ammonites, "Tomorrow we will surrender to you, and you can do to us whatever seems good to you."

¹¹The next day Saul separated his men into three divisions; during the last watch of the night they broke into the camp of the Ammonites and slaughtered them until the heat of the day. Those who survived were scattered, so that no two of them were left together.

Saul Confirmed as King

¹²The people then said to Samuel, "Who was it that asked, 'Shall Saul reign over us?' Bring these men to us and we will put them to death."

¹³But Saul said, "No one shall be put to death today, for this day the LORD has rescued Israel."

¹⁴Then Samuel said to the people, "Come, let us go to Gilgal and there reaffirm the kingship." ¹⁵So all the people went to Gilgal and confirmed Saul as king in the presence of the LORD. There they sacrificed fellowship offeringsᵃ before the LORD, and Saul and all the Israelites held a great celebration.

Samuel's Farewell Speech

12 Samuel said to all Israel, "I have listened to everything you said to me and have set a king over you. ²Now you have a king as your leader. As for me, I am old and gray, and my sons are here with you. I have been your leader from my youth until this day. ³Here I stand. Testify against me in the presence of the LORD and his anointed. Whose ox have I taken? Whose donkey have I taken? Whom have I cheated? Whom have I oppressed? From whose hand have I accepted a bribe to make me shut my eyes? If I have done any of these, I will make it right."

⁴"You have not cheated or oppressed us," they replied. "You have not taken anything from anyone's hand."

⁵Samuel said to them, "The LORD is witness against you, and also his anointed is witness this day, that you have not found anything in my hand."

> "AFTER Jacob entered Egypt, they cried to the LORD for help, and the LORD sent Moses and Aaron, who brought your forefathers out of Egypt and settled them in this place."
>
> 1 SAMUEL 12:8

ᵃ15 Traditionally *peace offerings*

"He is witness," they said.

⁶Then Samuel said to the people, "It is the LORD who appointed Moses and Aaron and brought your forefathers up out of Egypt. ⁷Now then, stand here, because I am going to confront you with evidence before the LORD as to all the righteous acts performed by the LORD for you and your fathers.

⁸"After Jacob entered Egypt, they cried to the LORD for help, and the LORD sent Moses and Aaron, who brought your forefathers out of Egypt and settled them in this place.

---

1 SAMUEL 12

{ FRIDAY }

Far Be It From Me

12:23 "AS FOR ME, FAR BE IT FROM ME THAT I SHOULD SIN AGAINST THE LORD BY FAILING TO PRAY FOR YOU."

The last thing Samuel said he would do for them was the first thing he did. He would keep on praying for the people. Prayer wasn't a last resort; it was a first *and* last resort. Samuel's intercession didn't begin when all his other options ran out, as in, "All we can do now is pray"; other options could come and go, but prayer would remain.

At the high point of his ministry, Samuel could not only be seen praying, but also seen leading by prayer (see 7:2–11). After the Israelites had been oppressed by the Philistines for many years, they finally saw the light, sought the Lord and repented of their sins. Samuel promised that the Lord would liberate them from the Philistines, and to seal it he promised to intercede for them. The nation gathered at Mizpah for a service of recommitment. What happened that day is a vivid picture of a people at prayer, led by a man of prayer. As they fasted and prayed, they filled jars with water and poured them out before the Lord, probably as a symbol of their hearts poured out in prayer (see 1:15; Psalm 62:8; Lamentations 2:19). Then word came that the Philistine army was approaching for attack. The Israelites said to Samuel, "'Do not stop crying out to the LORD our God for us, that he may rescue us from the hand of the Philistines.' Then Samuel . . . cried out to the LORD on Israel's behalf, and the LORD answered him" (1 Samuel 7:8–9). The Philistine army was defeated.

Samuel also prayed at the low points of his life. When confronted by the sins of his wicked sons and the Israelites' desire for a king, he turned again to prayer (see 1 Samuel 8:1–6). When time had run out for Saul, and God had rejected him completely, what did Samuel do? He prayed for Saul: "Samuel was troubled, and he cried out to the LORD all that night" (15:11).

Happy or sad, in good times or in bad, Samuel knew he had to give an accounting to God for how he did his work. That's why he prayed. Do you see your responsibilities in the same light? Far be it from you that you should do otherwise!

PRAY:

Blessed Master, give me Samuel's spiritual vision, strength and perseverance so that I will not fail to pray for those you have given me to care and pray for.

FOR YOUR NEXT DEVOTIONAL READING, GO TO PAGE 336.

⁹"But they forgot the LORD their God; so he sold them into the hand of Sisera, the commander of the army of Hazor, and into the hands of the Philistines and the king of Moab, who fought against them. ¹⁰They cried out to the LORD and said, 'We have sinned; we have forsaken the LORD and served the Baals and the Ashtoreths. But now deliver us from the hands of our enemies, and we will serve you.' ¹¹Then the LORD sent Jerub-Baal,ᵃ Barak,ᵇ Jephthah and Samuel,ᶜ and he delivered you from the hands of your enemies on every side, so that you lived securely.

¹²"But when you saw that Nahash king of the Ammonites was moving against you, you said to me, 'No, we want a king to rule over us'—even though the LORD your God was your king. ¹³Now here is the king you have chosen, the one you asked for; see, the LORD has set a king over you. ¹⁴If you fear the LORD and serve and obey him and do not rebel against his commands, and if both you and the king who reigns over you follow the LORD your God—good! ¹⁵But if you do not obey the LORD, and if you rebel against his commands, his hand will be against you, as it was against your fathers.

¹⁶"Now then, stand still and see this great thing the LORD is about to do before your eyes! ¹⁷Is it not wheat harvest now? I will call upon the LORD to send thunder and rain. And you will realize what an evil thing you did in the eyes of the LORD when you asked for a king."

¹⁸Then Samuel called upon the LORD, and that same day the LORD sent thunder and rain. So all the people stood in awe of the LORD and of Samuel.

¹⁹The people all said to Samuel, "Pray to the LORD your God for your servants so that we will not die, for we have added to all our other sins the evil of asking for a king."

²⁰"Do not be afraid," Samuel replied. "You have done all this evil; yet do not turn away from the LORD, but serve the LORD with all your heart. ²¹Do not turn away after useless idols. They can do you no good, nor can they rescue you, because they are useless. ²²For the sake of his great name the LORD will not reject his people, because the LORD was pleased to make you his own. ²³As for me, far be

> "AS FOR ME, far be it from me that I should sin against the LORD by failing to pray for you. And I will teach you the way that is good and right."
>
> 1 SAMUEL 12:23

it from me that I should sin against the LORD by failing to pray for you. And I will teach you the way that is good and right. ²⁴But be sure to fear the LORD and serve him faithfully with all your heart; consider what great things he has done for you. ²⁵Yet if you persist in doing evil, both you and your king will be swept away."

Samuel Rebukes Saul

13 Saul was ⌊thirty,ᵈ years old when he became king, and he reigned over Israel ⌊forty-⌋ᵉ two years.

²Saulᶠ chose three thousand men from Israel; two thousand were with him at Micmash and in the hill country of Bethel, and a thousand were with Jonathan at Gibeah in Benjamin. The rest of the men he sent back to their homes.

³Jonathan attacked the Philistine outpost at Geba, and the Philistines heard about it. Then Saul had the trumpet blown throughout the land and said, "Let the Hebrews hear!" ⁴So all Israel heard the news: "Saul has attacked the Philistine outpost, and now Israel has become a stench to the Philistines." And the people were summoned to join Saul at Gilgal.

⁵The Philistines assembled to fight Israel, with three thousandᵍ chariots, six thousand charioteers, and soldiers as numerous as the sand on the seashore. They went up and camped at Micmash, east of Beth Aven. ⁶When the men of Israel saw that their situation was critical and that their army was hard pressed, they hid in caves and thickets, among the

---

ᵃ11 Also called *Gideon*   ᵇ11 Some Septuagint manuscripts and Syriac; Hebrew *Bedan*
ᶜ11 Hebrew; some Septuagint manuscripts and Syriac *Samson*   ᵈ1 A few late manuscripts of the Septuagint; Hebrew does not have *thirty*.
ᵉ1 See the round number in Acts 13:21; Hebrew does not have *forty-*.   ᶠ1,2 Or *and when he had reigned over Israel two years,* ²*he*
ᵍ5 Some Septuagint manuscripts and Syriac; Hebrew *thirty thousand*

rocks, and in pits and cisterns. [7]Some Hebrews even crossed the Jordan to the land of Gad and Gilead.

Saul remained at Gilgal, and all the troops with him were quaking with fear. [8]He waited seven days, the time set by Samuel; but Samuel did not come to Gilgal, and Saul's men began to scatter. [9]So he said, "Bring me the burnt offering and the fellowship offerings.[a]" And Saul offered up the burnt offering. [10]Just as he finished making the offering, Samuel arrived, and Saul went out to greet him.

[11]"What have you done?" asked Samuel.

Saul replied, "When I saw that the men were scattering, and that you did not come at the set time, and that the Philistines were assembling at Micmash, [12]I thought, 'Now the Philistines will come down against me at Gilgal, and I have not sought the LORD's favor.' So I felt compelled to offer the burnt offering."

[13]"You acted foolishly," Samuel said. "You have not kept the command the LORD your God gave you; if you had, he would have established your kingdom over Israel for all time. [14]But now your kingdom will not endure; the LORD has sought out a man after his own heart and appointed him leader of his people, because you have not kept the LORD's command."

[15]Then Samuel left Gilgal[b] and went up to Gibeah in Benjamin, and Saul counted the men who were with him. They numbered about six hundred.

Israel Without Weapons

[16]Saul and his son Jonathan and the men with them were staying in Gibeah[c] in Benjamin, while the Philistines camped at Micmash. [17]Raiding parties went out from the Philistine camp in three detachments. One turned toward Ophrah in the vicinity of Shual, [18]another toward Beth Horon, and the third toward the borderland overlooking the Valley of Zeboim facing the desert.

[19]Not a blacksmith could be found in the whole land of Israel, because the Philistines had said, "Otherwise the Hebrews will make swords or spears!" [20]So all Israel went down to the Philistines to have their plowshares, mattocks, axes and sickles[d] sharpened. [21]The price was two thirds of a shekel[e] for sharpening plowshares and mattocks, and a third of a shekel[f] for sharpening forks and axes and for repointing goads.

[22]So on the day of the battle not a soldier with Saul and Jonathan had a sword or spear in his hand; only Saul and his son Jonathan had them.

Jonathan Attacks the Philistines

[23]Now a detachment of Philistines had gone out to the pass at Micmash. 14 [1]One day Jonathan son of Saul said to the young man bearing his armor, "Come, let's go over to the Philistine outpost on the other side." But he did not tell his father.

[2]Saul was staying on the outskirts of Gibeah under a pomegranate tree in Migron. With him were about six hundred men, [3]among whom was Ahijah, who was wearing an ephod. He was a son of Ichabod's brother Ahitub son of Phinehas, the son of Eli, the LORD's priest in Shiloh. No one was aware that Jonathan had left.

[4]On each side of the pass that Jonathan intended to cross to reach the Philistine outpost was a cliff; one was called Bozez, and the other Seneh. [5]One cliff stood to the north toward Micmash, the other to the south toward Geba.

[6]Jonathan said to his young armorbearer, "Come, let's go over to the outpost of those uncircumcised fellows. Perhaps the LORD will act in our behalf. Nothing can hinder the LORD from saving, whether by many or by few."

[7]"Do all that you have in mind," his armor-bearer said. "Go ahead; I am with you heart and soul."

[8]Jonathan said, "Come, then; we will cross over toward the men and let them see us. [9]If they say to us, 'Wait there until we come to you,' we will stay where we are and not go up to them. [10]But if

[a]9 Traditionally *peace offerings*   [b]15 Hebrew; Septuagint *Gilgal and went his way; the rest of the people went after Saul to meet the army, and they went out of Gilgal*   [c]16 Two Hebrew manuscripts; most Hebrew manuscripts *Geba,* a variant of *Gibeah*   [d]20 Septuagint; Hebrew *plowshares*   [e]21 Hebrew *pim;* that is, about 1/4 ounce (about 8 grams)   [f]21 That is, about 1/8 ounce (about 4 grams)

they say, 'Come up to us,' we will climb up, because that will be our sign that the LORD has given them into our hands."

¹¹So both of them showed themselves to the Philistine outpost. "Look!" said the Philistines. "The Hebrews are crawling out of the holes they were hiding in." ¹²The men of the outpost shouted to Jonathan and his armor-bearer, "Come up to us and we'll teach you a lesson."

So Jonathan said to his armor-bearer, "Climb up after me; the LORD has given them into the hand of Israel."

¹³Jonathan climbed up, using his hands and feet, with his armor-bearer right behind him. The Philistines fell before Jonathan, and his armor-bearer followed and killed behind him. ¹⁴In that first attack Jonathan and his armor-bearer killed some twenty men in an area of about half an acre.ᵃ

Israel Routs the Philistines

¹⁵Then panic struck the whole army—those in the camp and field, and those in the outposts and raiding parties—and the ground shook. It was a panic sent by God.ᵇ

¹⁶Saul's lookouts at Gibeah in Benjamin saw the army melting away in all directions. ¹⁷Then Saul said to the men who were with him, "Muster the forces and see who has left us." When they did, it was Jonathan and his armor-bearer who were not there.

¹⁸Saul said to Ahijah, "Bring the ark of God." (At that time it was with the Israelites.)ᶜ ¹⁹While Saul was talking to the priest, the tumult in the Philistine camp increased more and more. So Saul said to the priest, "Withdraw your hand."

²⁰Then Saul and all his men assembled and went to the battle. They found the Philistines in total confusion, striking each other with their swords. ²¹Those Hebrews who had previously been with the Philistines and had gone up with them to their camp went over to the Israelites who were with Saul and Jonathan. ²²When all the Israelites who had hidden in the hill country of Ephraim heard that the Philistines were on the run, they joined the battle in hot pursuit. ²³So the LORD rescued Israel that day, and the battle moved on beyond Beth Aven.

Jonathan Eats Honey

²⁴Now the men of Israel were in distress that day, because Saul had bound the people under an oath, saying, "Cursed be any man who eats food before evening comes, before I have avenged myself on my enemies!" So none of the troops tasted food.

²⁵The entire armyᵈ entered the woods, and there was honey on the ground. ²⁶When they went into the woods, they saw the honey oozing out, yet no one put his hand to his mouth, because they feared the oath. ²⁷But Jonathan had not heard that his father had bound the people with the oath, so he reached out the end of the staff that was in his hand and dipped it into the honeycomb. He raised his hand to his mouth, and his eyes brightened.ᵉ ²⁸Then one of the soldiers told him, "Your father bound the army under a strict oath, saying, 'Cursed be any man who eats food today!' That is why the men are faint."

²⁹Jonathan said, "My father has made trouble for the country. See how my eyes brightenedᶠ when I tasted a little of this honey. ³⁰How much better it would have been if the men had eaten today some of the plunder they took from their enemies. Would not the slaughter of the Philistines have been even greater?"

³¹That day, after the Israelites had struck down the Philistines from Micmash to Aijalon, they were exhausted. ³²They pounced on the plunder and, taking sheep, cattle and calves, they butchered them on the ground and ate them, together with the blood. ³³Then someone said to Saul, "Look, the men are sinning against the LORD by eating meat that has blood in it."

"You have broken faith," he said. "Roll a large stone over here at once." ³⁴Then he said, "Go out among the men and tell them, 'Each of you bring me your cattle and sheep, and slaughter them here and

---

ᵃ14 Hebrew *half a yoke*; a "yoke" was the land plowed by a yoke of oxen in one day.
ᵇ15 Or *a terrible panic*   ᶜ18 Hebrew; Septuagint *"Bring the ephod." (At that time he wore the ephod before the Israelites.)*
ᵈ25 Or *Now all the people of the land*
ᵉ27 Or *his strength was renewed*   ᶠ29 Or *my strength was renewed*

eat them. Do not sin against the LORD by eating meat with blood still in it.'"

So everyone brought his ox that night and slaughtered it there. ³⁵Then Saul built an altar to the LORD; it was the first time he had done this.

³⁶Saul said, "Let us go down after the Philistines by night and plunder them till dawn, and let us not leave one of them alive."

"Do whatever seems best to you," they replied.

But the priest said, "Let us inquire of God here."

³⁷So Saul asked God, "Shall I go down after the Philistines? Will you give them into Israel's hand?" But God did not answer him that day.

³⁸Saul therefore said, "Come here, all you who are leaders of the army, and let us find out what sin has been committed today. ³⁹As surely as the LORD who rescues Israel lives, even if it lies with my son Jonathan, he must die." But not one of the men said a word.

⁴⁰Saul then said to all the Israelites, "You stand over there; I and Jonathan my son will stand over here."

"Do what seems best to you," the men replied.

⁴¹Then Saul prayed to the LORD, the God of Israel, "Give me the right answer."ᵃ And Jonathan and Saul were taken by lot, and the men were cleared. ⁴²Saul said, "Cast the lot between me and Jonathan my son." And Jonathan was taken.

> THEN Saul prayed to the LORD, the God of Israel, "Give me the right answer."
>
> 1 SAMUEL 14:41

⁴³Then Saul said to Jonathan, "Tell me what you have done."

So Jonathan told him, "I merely tasted a little honey with the end of my staff. And now must I die?"

⁴⁴Saul said, "May God deal with me, be it ever so severely, if you do not die, Jonathan."

⁴⁵But the men said to Saul, "Should Jonathan die—he who has brought about this great deliverance in Israel? Never! As surely as the LORD lives, not a hair of his head will fall to the ground, for he did this today with God's help." So the men rescued Jonathan, and he was not put to death.

⁴⁶Then Saul stopped pursuing the Philistines, and they withdrew to their own land.

⁴⁷After Saul had assumed rule over Israel, he fought against their enemies on every side: Moab, the Ammonites, Edom, the kingsᵇ of Zobah, and the Philistines. Wherever he turned, he inflicted punishment on them.ᶜ ⁴⁸He fought valiantly and defeated the Amalekites, delivering Israel from the hands of those who had plundered them.

Saul's Family

⁴⁹Saul's sons were Jonathan, Ishvi and Malki-Shua. The name of his older daughter was Merab, and that of the younger was Michal. ⁵⁰His wife's name was Ahinoam daughter of Ahimaaz. The name of the commander of Saul's army was Abner son of Ner, and Ner was Saul's uncle. ⁵¹Saul's father Kish and Abner's father Ner were sons of Abiel.

⁵²All the days of Saul there was bitter war with the Philistines, and whenever Saul saw a mighty or brave man, he took him into his service.

The LORD Rejects Saul as King

15 Samuel said to Saul, "I am the one the LORD sent to anoint you king over his people Israel; so listen now to the message from the LORD. ²This is what the LORD Almighty says: 'I will punish the Amalekites for what they did to Israel when they waylaid them as they came up from Egypt. ³Now go, attack the Amalekites and totally destroyᵈ everything that belongs to them. Do not spare them; put to death men and women, children and infants, cattle and sheep, camels and donkeys.'"

ᵃ41 Hebrew; Septuagint "Why have you not answered your servant today? If the fault is in me or my son Jonathan, respond with Urim, but if the men of Israel are at fault, respond with Thummim."   ᵇ47 Masoretic Text; Dead Sea Scrolls and Septuagint king   ᶜ47 Hebrew; Septuagint he was victorious   ᵈ3 The Hebrew term refers to the irrevocable giving over of things or persons to the LORD, often by totally destroying them; also in verses 8, 9, 15, 18, 20 and 21.

⁴So Saul summoned the men and mustered them at Telaim—two hundred thousand foot soldiers and ten thousand men from Judah. ⁵Saul went to the city of Amalek and set an ambush in the ravine. ⁶Then he said to the Kenites, "Go away, leave the Amalekites so that I do not destroy you along with them; for you showed kindness to all the Israelites when they came up out of Egypt." So the Kenites moved away from the Amalekites.

⁷Then Saul attacked the Amalekites all the way from Havilah to Shur, to the east of Egypt. ⁸He took Agag king of the Amalekites alive, and all his people he totally destroyed with the sword. ⁹But Saul and the army spared Agag and the best of the sheep and cattle, the fat calves*ᵃ* and lambs—everything that was good. These they were unwilling to destroy completely, but everything that was despised and weak they totally destroyed.

¹⁰Then the word of the LORD came to Samuel: ¹¹"I am grieved that I have made Saul king, because he has turned away from me and has not carried out my instructions." Samuel was troubled, and he cried out to the LORD all that night.

> SAMUEL *was troubled, and he cried out to the* LORD *all that night.*
>
> 1 SAMUEL 15:11

¹²Early in the morning Samuel got up and went to meet Saul, but he was told, "Saul has gone to Carmel. There he has set up a monument in his own honor and has turned and gone on down to Gilgal."

¹³When Samuel reached him, Saul said, "The LORD bless you! I have carried out the LORD's instructions."

¹⁴But Samuel said, "What then is this bleating of sheep in my ears? What is this lowing of cattle that I hear?"

¹⁵Saul answered, "The soldiers brought them from the Amalekites; they spared the best of the sheep and cattle to sacrifice to the LORD your God, but we totally destroyed the rest."

¹⁶"Stop!" Samuel said to Saul. "Let me tell you what the LORD said to me last night."

"Tell me," Saul replied.

¹⁷Samuel said, "Although you were once small in your own eyes, did you not become the head of the tribes of Israel? The LORD anointed you king over Israel. ¹⁸And he sent you on a mission, saying, 'Go and completely destroy those wicked people, the Amalekites; make war on them until you have wiped them out.' ¹⁹Why did you not obey the LORD? Why did you pounce on the plunder and do evil in the eyes of the LORD?"

²⁰"But I did obey the LORD," Saul said. "I went on the mission the LORD assigned me. I completely destroyed the Amalekites and brought back Agag their king. ²¹The soldiers took sheep and cattle from the plunder, the best of what was devoted to God, in order to sacrifice them to the LORD your God at Gilgal."

²²But Samuel replied:

"Does the LORD delight in burnt
        offerings and sacrifices
    as much as in obeying the voice
        of the LORD?
To obey is better than sacrifice,
    and to heed is better than the fat
        of rams.
²³ For rebellion is like the sin of
        divination,
    and arrogance like the evil of
        idolatry.
Because you have rejected the word
        of the LORD,
    he has rejected you as king."

²⁴Then Saul said to Samuel, "I have sinned. I violated the LORD's command and your instructions. I was afraid of the people and so I gave in to them. ²⁵Now I beg you, forgive my sin and come back with me, so that I may worship the LORD."

²⁶But Samuel said to him, "I will not go back with you. You have rejected the word of the LORD, and the LORD has rejected you as king over Israel!"

²⁷As Samuel turned to leave, Saul caught hold of the hem of his robe, and it tore. ²⁸Samuel said to him, "The LORD has torn the kingdom of Israel from you today and has given it to one of your neighbors—to one better than you. ²⁹He who is the Glory of Israel does not lie or

---

ᵃ9 Or *the grown bulls*; the meaning of the Hebrew for this phrase is uncertain.

change his mind; for he is not a man, that he should change his mind."

³⁰Saul replied, "I have sinned. But please honor me before the elders of my people and before Israel; come back with me, so that I may worship the LORD your God." ³¹So Samuel went back with Saul, and Saul worshiped the LORD.

³²Then Samuel said, "Bring me Agag king of the Amalekites."

Agag came to him confidently,ᵃ thinking, "Surely the bitterness of death is past."

³³But Samuel said,

"As your sword has made women childless,
    so will your mother be childless among women."

And Samuel put Agag to death before the LORD at Gilgal.

³⁴Then Samuel left for Ramah, but Saul went up to his home in Gibeah of Saul. ³⁵Until the day Samuel died, he did not go to see Saul again, though Samuel mourned for him. And the LORD was grieved that he had made Saul king over Israel.

Samuel Anoints David

16 The LORD said to Samuel, "How long will you mourn for Saul, since I have rejected him as king over Israel? Fill your horn with oil and be on your way; I am sending you to Jesse of Bethlehem. I have chosen one of his sons to be king."

²But Samuel said, "How can I go? Saul will hear about it and kill me."

The LORD said, "Take a heifer with you and say, 'I have come to sacrifice to the LORD.' ³Invite Jesse to the sacrifice, and I will show you what to do. You are to anoint for me the one I indicate."

⁴Samuel did what the LORD said. When he arrived at Bethlehem, the elders of the town trembled when they met him. They asked, "Do you come in peace?"

⁵Samuel replied, "Yes, in peace; I have come to sacrifice to the LORD. Consecrate yourselves and come to the sacrifice with me." Then he consecrated Jesse and his sons and invited them to the sacrifice.

⁶When they arrived, Samuel saw Eliab and thought, "Surely the LORD's anointed stands here before the LORD."

⁷But the LORD said to Samuel, "Do not consider his appearance or his height, for I have rejected him. The LORD does not look at the things man looks at. Man looks at the outward appearance, but the LORD looks at the heart."

⁸Then Jesse called Abinadab and had him pass in front of Samuel. But Samuel said, "The LORD has not chosen this one either." ⁹Jesse then had Shammah pass by, but Samuel said, "Nor has the LORD chosen this one." ¹⁰Jesse had seven of his sons pass before Samuel, but Samuel said to him, "The LORD has not chosen these." ¹¹So he asked Jesse, "Are these all the sons you have?"

"There is still the youngest," Jesse answered, "but he is tending the sheep."

Samuel said, "Send for him; we will not sit downᵇ until he arrives."

¹²So he sent and had him brought in. He was ruddy, with a fine appearance and handsome features.

Then the LORD said, "Rise and anoint him; he is the one."

¹³So Samuel took the horn of oil and anointed him in the presence of his brothers, and from that day on the Spirit of the LORD came upon David in power. Samuel then went to Ramah.

David in Saul's Service

¹⁴Now the Spirit of the LORD had departed from Saul, and an evilᶜ spirit from the LORD tormented him.

¹⁵Saul's attendants said to him, "See, an evil spirit from God is tormenting you. ¹⁶Let our lord command his servants here to search for someone who can play the harp. He will play when the evil spirit from God comes upon you, and you will feel better."

¹⁷So Saul said to his attendants, "Find someone who plays well and bring him to me."

¹⁸One of the servants answered, "I have seen a son of Jesse of Bethlehem who knows how to play the harp. He is a brave man and a warrior. He speaks well and is a fine-looking man. And the LORD is with him."

ᵃ32 Or him trembling, yet   ᵇ11 Some Septuagint manuscripts; Hebrew not gather around   ᶜ14 Or injurious; also in verses 15, 16 and 23

¹⁹Then Saul sent messengers to Jesse and said, "Send me your son David, who is with the sheep." ²⁰So Jesse took a donkey loaded with bread, a skin of wine and a young goat and sent them with his son David to Saul.

²¹David came to Saul and entered his service. Saul liked him very much, and David became one of his armor-bearers. ²²Then Saul sent word to Jesse, saying, "Allow David to remain in my service, for I am pleased with him."

²³Whenever the spirit from God came upon Saul, David would take his harp and play. Then relief would come to Saul; he would feel better, and the evil spirit would leave him.

David and Goliath

17 Now the Philistines gathered their forces for war and assembled at Socoh in Judah. They pitched camp at Ephes Dammim, between Socoh and Azekah. ²Saul and the Israelites assembled and camped in the Valley of Elah and drew up their battle line to meet the Philistines. ³The Philistines occupied one hill and the Israelites another, with the valley between them.

⁴A champion named Goliath, who was from Gath, came out of the Philistine camp. He was over nine feet[a] tall. ⁵He had a bronze helmet on his head and wore a coat of scale armor of bronze weighing five thousand shekels[b]; ⁶on his legs he wore bronze greaves, and a bronze javelin was slung on his back. ⁷His spear shaft was like a weaver's rod, and its iron point weighed six hundred shekels.[c] His shield bearer went ahead of him.

⁸Goliath stood and shouted to the ranks of Israel, "Why do you come out and line up for battle? Am I not a Philistine, and are you not the servants of Saul? Choose a man and have him come down to me. ⁹If he is able to fight and kill me, we will become your subjects; but if I overcome him and kill him, you will become our subjects and serve us." ¹⁰Then the Philistine said, "This day I defy the ranks of Israel! Give me a man and let us fight each other." ¹¹On hearing the Philistine's words, Saul and all the Israelites were dismayed and terrified.

¹²Now David was the son of an Ephrathite named Jesse, who was from Bethlehem in Judah. Jesse had eight sons, and in Saul's time he was old and well advanced in years. ¹³Jesse's three oldest sons had followed Saul to the war: The firstborn was Eliab; the second, Abinadab; and the third, Shammah. ¹⁴David was the youngest. The three oldest followed Saul, ¹⁵but David went back and forth from Saul to tend his father's sheep at Bethlehem.

¹⁶For forty days the Philistine came forward every morning and evening and took his stand.

¹⁷Now Jesse said to his son David, "Take this ephah[d] of roasted grain and these ten loaves of bread for your brothers and hurry to their camp. ¹⁸Take along these ten cheeses to the commander of their unit.[e] See how your brothers are and bring back some assurance[f] from them. ¹⁹They are with Saul and all the men of Israel in the Valley of Elah, fighting against the Philistines."

²⁰Early in the morning David left the flock with a shepherd, loaded up and set out, as Jesse had directed. He reached the camp as the army was going out to its battle positions, shouting the war cry. ²¹Israel and the Philistines were drawing up their lines facing each other. ²²David left his things with the keeper of supplies, ran to the battle lines and greeted his brothers. ²³As he was talking with them, Goliath, the Philistine champion from Gath, stepped out from his lines and shouted his usual defiance, and David heard it. ²⁴When the Israelites saw the man, they all ran from him in great fear.

²⁵Now the Israelites had been saying, "Do you see how this man keeps coming out? He comes out to defy Israel. The king will give great wealth to the man who kills him. He will also give him his daughter in marriage and will exempt his father's family from taxes in Israel."

---

a4 Hebrew *was six cubits and a span* (about 3 meters)   *b5* That is, about 125 pounds (about 57 kilograms)   *c7* That is, about 15 pounds (about 7 kilograms)   *d17* That is, probably about 3/5 bushel (about 22 liters)   *e18* Hebrew *thousand*   *f18* Or *some token*; or *some pledge of spoils*

²⁶David asked the men standing near him, "What will be done for the man who kills this Philistine and removes this disgrace from Israel? Who is this uncircumcised Philistine that he should defy the armies of the living God?"

²⁷They repeated to him what they had been saying and told him, "This is what will be done for the man who kills him."

²⁸When Eliab, David's oldest brother, heard him speaking with the men, he burned with anger at him and asked, "Why have you come down here? And with whom did you leave those few sheep in the desert? I know how conceited you are and how wicked your heart is; you came down only to watch the battle."

²⁹"Now what have I done?" said David. "Can't I even speak?" ³⁰He then turned away to someone else and brought up the same matter, and the men answered him as before. ³¹What David said was overheard and reported to Saul, and Saul sent for him.

³²David said to Saul, "Let no one lose heart on account of this Philistine; your servant will go and fight him."

³³Saul replied, "You are not able to go out against this Philistine and fight him; you are only a boy, and he has been a fighting man from his youth."

³⁴But David said to Saul, "Your servant has been keeping his father's sheep. When a lion or a bear came and carried off a sheep from the flock, ³⁵I went after it, struck it and rescued the sheep from its mouth. When it turned on me, I seized it by its hair, struck it and killed it. ³⁶Your servant has killed both the lion and the bear; this uncircumcised Philistine will be like one of them, because he has defied the armies of the living God. ³⁷The LORD who delivered me from the paw of the lion and the paw of the bear will deliver me from the hand of this Philistine."

Saul said to David, "Go, and the LORD be with you."

³⁸Then Saul dressed David in his own tunic. He put a coat of armor on him and a bronze helmet on his head. ³⁹David fastened on his sword over the tunic and tried walking around, because he was not used to them.

"I cannot go in these," he said to Saul, "because I am not used to them." So he took them off. ⁴⁰Then he took his staff in his hand, chose five smooth stones from the stream, put them in the pouch of his shepherd's bag and, with his sling in his hand, approached the Philistine.

⁴¹Meanwhile, the Philistine, with his shield bearer in front of him, kept coming closer to David. ⁴²He looked David over and saw that he was only a boy, ruddy and handsome, and he despised him. ⁴³He said to David, "Am I a dog, that you come at me with sticks?" And the Philistine cursed David by his gods. ⁴⁴"Come here," he said, "and I'll give your flesh to the birds of the air and the beasts of the field!"

⁴⁵David said to the Philistine, "You come against me with sword and spear and javelin, but I come against you in the name of the LORD Almighty, the God of the armies of Israel, whom you have defied. ⁴⁶This day the LORD will hand you over to me, and I'll strike you down and cut off your head. Today I will give the carcasses of the Philistine army to the birds of the air and the beasts of the earth, and the whole world will know that there is a God in Israel. ⁴⁷All those gathered here will know that it is not by sword or spear that the LORD saves; for the battle is the LORD's, and he will give all of you into our hands."

⁴⁸As the Philistine moved closer to attack him, David ran quickly toward the battle line to meet him. ⁴⁹Reaching into his bag and taking out a stone, he slung it and struck the Philistine on the forehead. The stone sank into his forehead, and he fell facedown on the ground.

⁵⁰So David triumphed over the Philistine with a sling and a stone; without a sword in his hand he struck down the Philistine and killed him.

⁵¹David ran and stood over him. He took hold of the Philistine's sword and drew it from the scabbard. After he killed him, he cut off his head with the sword.

When the Philistines saw that their hero was dead, they turned and ran. ⁵²Then the men of Israel and Judah surged forward with a shout and pursued the Philistines to the entrance of Gath*a*

a52 Some Septuagint manuscripts; Hebrew *a valley*

and to the gates of Ekron. Their dead were strewn along the Shaaraim road to Gath and Ekron. [53]When the Israelites returned from chasing the Philistines, they plundered their camp. [54]David took the Philistine's head and brought it to Jerusalem, and he put the Philistine's weapons in his own tent.

[55]As Saul watched David going out to meet the Philistine, he said to Abner, commander of the army, "Abner, whose son is that young man?"

Abner replied, "As surely as you live, O king, I don't know."

[56]The king said, "Find out whose son this young man is."

[57]As soon as David returned from killing the Philistine, Abner took him and brought him before Saul, with David still holding the Philistine's head.

[58]"Whose son are you, young man?" Saul asked him.

David said, "I am the son of your servant Jesse of Bethlehem."

Saul's Jealousy of David

18 After David had finished talking with Saul, Jonathan became one in spirit with David, and he loved him as himself. [2]From that day Saul kept David with him and did not let him return to his father's house. [3]And Jonathan made a covenant with David because he loved him as himself. [4]Jonathan took off the robe he was wearing and gave it to David, along with his tunic, and even his sword, his bow and his belt.

[5]Whatever Saul sent him to do, David did it so successfully[a] that Saul gave him a high rank in the army. This pleased all the people, and Saul's officers as well.

[6]When the men were returning home after David had killed the Philistine, the women came out from all the towns of Israel to meet King Saul with singing and dancing, with joyful songs and with tambourines and lutes. [7]As they danced, they sang:

"Saul has slain his thousands,
    and David his tens of thousands."

[8]Saul was very angry; this refrain galled him. "They have credited David with tens of thousands," he thought, "but me with only thousands. What more

can he get but the kingdom?" [9]And from that time on Saul kept a jealous eye on David.

[10]The next day an evil[b] spirit from God came forcefully upon Saul. He was prophesying in his house, while David was playing the harp, as he usually did. Saul had a spear in his hand [11]and he hurled it, saying to himself, "I'll pin David to the wall." But David eluded him twice.

[12]Saul was afraid of David, because the LORD was with David but had left Saul. [13]So he sent David away from him and gave him command over a thousand men, and David led the troops in their campaigns. [14]In everything he did he had great success,[c] because the LORD was with him. [15]When Saul saw how successful[d] he was, he was afraid of him. [16]But all Israel and Judah loved David, because he led them in their campaigns.

[17]Saul said to David, "Here is my older daughter Merab. I will give her to you in marriage; only serve me bravely and fight the battles of the LORD." For Saul said to himself, "I will not raise a hand against him. Let the Philistines do that!"

[18]But David said to Saul, "Who am I, and what is my family or my father's clan in Israel, that I should become the king's son-in-law?" [19]So[e] when the time came for Merab, Saul's daughter, to be given to David, she was given in marriage to Adriel of Meholah.

[20]Now Saul's daughter Michal was in love with David, and when they told Saul about it, he was pleased. [21]"I will give her to him," he thought, "so that she may be a snare to him and so that the hand of the Philistines may be against him." So Saul said to David, "Now you have a second opportunity to become my son-in-law."

[22]Then Saul ordered his attendants: "Speak to David privately and say, 'Look, the king is pleased with you, and his attendants all like you; now become his son-in-law.'"

[23]They repeated these words to David. But David said, "Do you think it is a small matter to become the king's son-in-law? I'm only a poor man and little known."

---

[a]5 Or *wisely*   [b]10 Or *injurious*   [c]14 Or *he was very wise*   [d]15 Or *wise*   [e]19 Or *However,*

²⁴When Saul's servants told him what David had said, ²⁵Saul replied, "Say to David, 'The king wants no other price for the bride than a hundred Philistine foreskins, to take revenge on his enemies.' " Saul's plan was to have David fall by the hands of the Philistines.

²⁶When the attendants told David these things, he was pleased to become the king's son-in-law. So before the allotted time elapsed, ²⁷David and his men went out and killed two hundred Philistines. He brought their foreskins and presented the full number to the king so that he might become the king's son-in-law. Then Saul gave him his daughter Michal in marriage.

²⁸When Saul realized that the LORD was with David and that his daughter Michal loved David, ²⁹Saul became still more afraid of him, and he remained his enemy the rest of his days.

³⁰The Philistine commanders continued to go out to battle, and as often as they did, David met with more success^a than the rest of Saul's officers, and his name became well known.

Saul Tries to Kill David

19 Saul told his son Jonathan and all the attendants to kill David. But Jonathan was very fond of David ²and warned him, "My father Saul is looking for a chance to kill you. Be on your guard tomorrow morning; go into hiding and stay there. ³I will go out and stand with my father in the field where you are. I'll speak to him about you and will tell you what I find out."

⁴Jonathan spoke well of David to Saul his father and said to him, "Let not the king do wrong to his servant David; he has not wronged you, and what he has done has benefited you greatly. ⁵He took his life in his hands when he killed the Philistine. The LORD won a great victory for all Israel, and you saw it and were glad. Why then would you do wrong to an innocent man like David by killing him for no reason?"

⁶Saul listened to Jonathan and took this oath: "As surely as the LORD lives, David will not be put to death."

⁷So Jonathan called David and told him the whole conversation. He brought him to Saul, and David was with Saul as before.

⁸Once more war broke out, and David went out and fought the Philistines. He struck them with such force that they fled before him.

⁹But an evil^b spirit from the LORD came upon Saul as he was sitting in his house with his spear in his hand. While David was playing the harp, ¹⁰Saul tried to pin him to the wall with his spear, but David eluded him as Saul drove the spear into the wall. That night David made good his escape.

¹¹Saul sent men to David's house to watch it and to kill him in the morning. But Michal, David's wife, warned him, "If you don't run for your life tonight, tomorrow you'll be killed." ¹²So Michal let David down through a window, and he fled and escaped. ¹³Then Michal took an idol^c and laid it on the bed, covering it with a garment and putting some goats' hair at the head.

¹⁴When Saul sent the men to capture David, Michal said, "He is ill."

¹⁵Then Saul sent the men back to see David and told them, "Bring him up to me in his bed so that I may kill him." ¹⁶But when the men entered, there was the idol in the bed, and at the head was some goats' hair.

¹⁷Saul said to Michal, "Why did you deceive me like this and send my enemy away so that he escaped?"

Michal told him, "He said to me, 'Let me get away. Why should I kill you?' "

¹⁸When David had fled and made his escape, he went to Samuel at Ramah and told him all that Saul had done to him. Then he and Samuel went to Naioth and stayed there. ¹⁹Word came to Saul: "David is in Naioth at Ramah"; ²⁰so he sent men to capture him. But when they saw a group of prophets prophesying, with Samuel standing there as their leader, the Spirit of God came upon Saul's men and they also prophesied. ²¹Saul was told about it, and he sent more men, and they prophesied too. Saul sent men a third time, and they also

---

^a30 Or *David acted more wisely*
^b9 Or *injurious*   ^c13 Hebrew *teraphim*; also in verse 16

prophesied. ²²Finally, he himself left for Ramah and went to the great cistern at Secu. And he asked, "Where are Samuel and David?"

"Over in Naioth at Ramah," they said. ²³So Saul went to Naioth at Ramah. But the Spirit of God came even upon him, and he walked along prophesying until he came to Naioth. ²⁴He stripped off his robes and also prophesied in Samuel's presence. He lay that way all that day and night. This is why people say, "Is Saul also among the prophets?"

> ❝ God has editing rights over our prayers. He will . . . edit them, correct them, bring them in line with his will and then hand them back to us to be resubmitted. ❞
>
> STEPHEN CROTTS

David and Jonathan

20 Then David fled from Naioth at Ramah and went to Jonathan and asked, "What have I done? What is my crime? How have I wronged your father, that he is trying to take my life?"

²"Never!" Jonathan replied. "You are not going to die! Look, my father doesn't do anything, great or small, without confiding in me. Why would he hide this from me? It's not so!"

³But David took an oath and said, "Your father knows very well that I have found favor in your eyes, and he has said to himself, 'Jonathan must not know this or he will be grieved.' Yet as surely as the LORD lives and as you live, there is only a step between me and death."

⁴Jonathan said to David, "Whatever you want me to do, I'll do for you."

⁵So David said, "Look, tomorrow is the New Moon festival, and I am supposed to dine with the king; but let me go and hide in the field until the evening of the day after tomorrow. ⁶If your father misses me at all, tell him, 'David earnestly asked my permission to hurry to Bethlehem, his hometown, because an annual sacrifice is being made there for his whole clan.' ⁷If he says, 'Very well,' then your servant is safe. But if he loses his temper, you can be sure that he is determined to harm me. ⁸As for you, show kindness to your servant, for you have brought him into a covenant with you before the LORD. If I am guilty, then kill me yourself! Why hand me over to your father?"

⁹"Never!" Jonathan said. "If I had the least inkling that my father was determined to harm you, wouldn't I tell you?"

¹⁰David asked, "Who will tell me if your father answers you harshly?"

¹¹"Come," Jonathan said, "let's go out into the field." So they went there together.

¹²Then Jonathan said to David: "By the LORD, the God of Israel, I will surely sound out my father by this time the day after tomorrow! If he is favorably disposed toward you, will I not send you word and let you know? ¹³But if my father is inclined to harm you, may the LORD deal with me, be it ever so severely, if I do not let you know and send you away safely. May the LORD be with you as he has been with my father. ¹⁴But show me unfailing kindness like that of the LORD as long as I live, so that I may not be killed, ¹⁵and do not ever cut off your kindness from my family—not even when the LORD has cut off every one of David's enemies from the face of the earth."

¹⁶So Jonathan made a covenant with the house of David, saying, "May the LORD call David's enemies to account." ¹⁷And Jonathan had David reaffirm his oath out of love for him, because he loved him as he loved himself.

¹⁸Then Jonathan said to David: "Tomorrow is the New Moon festival. You will be missed, because your seat will be empty. ¹⁹The day after tomorrow, toward evening, go to the place where you hid when this trouble began, and wait by the stone Ezel. ²⁰I will shoot three arrows to the side of it, as though I were shooting at a target. ²¹Then I will send a boy and say, 'Go, find the arrows.' If I say to him, 'Look, the arrows are on this side of you; bring them here,' then come, because, as surely as the LORD lives, you are safe; there is no danger. ²²But if I say to the boy, 'Look, the arrows are beyond you,' then you must go, because the LORD has sent you away. ²³And about the matter you and I dis-

cussed—remember, the LORD is witness between you and me forever."

²⁴So David hid in the field, and when the New Moon festival came, the king sat down to eat. ²⁵He sat in his customary place by the wall, opposite Jonathan,ᵃ and Abner sat next to Saul, but David's place was empty. ²⁶Saul said nothing that day, for he thought, "Something must have happened to David to make him ceremonially unclean—surely he is unclean." ²⁷But the next day, the second day of the month, David's place was empty again. Then Saul said to his son Jonathan, "Why hasn't the son of Jesse come to the meal, either yesterday or today?"

²⁸Jonathan answered, "David earnestly asked me for permission to go to Bethlehem. ²⁹He said, 'Let me go, because our family is observing a sacrifice in the town and my brother has ordered me to be there. If I have found favor in your eyes, let me get away to see my brothers.' That is why he has not come to the king's table."

³⁰Saul's anger flared up at Jonathan and he said to him, "You son of a perverse and rebellious woman! Don't I know that you have sided with the son of Jesse to your own shame and to the shame of the mother who bore you? ³¹As long as the son of Jesse lives on this earth, neither you nor your kingdom will be established. Now send and bring him to me, for he must die!"

³²"Why should he be put to death? What has he done?" Jonathan asked his father. ³³But Saul hurled his spear at him to kill him. Then Jonathan knew that his father intended to kill David.

³⁴Jonathan got up from the table in fierce anger; on that second day of the month he did not eat, because he was grieved at his father's shameful treatment of David.

³⁵In the morning Jonathan went out to the field for his meeting with David. He had a small boy with him, ³⁶and he said to the boy, "Run and find the arrows I shoot." As the boy ran, he shot an arrow beyond him. ³⁷When the boy came to the place where Jonathan's arrow had fallen, Jonathan called out after him, "Isn't the arrow beyond you?" ³⁸Then he shouted, "Hurry! Go quickly! Don't stop!" The boy picked up the arrow and returned to his master. ³⁹(The boy knew nothing of all this; only Jonathan and David knew.) ⁴⁰Then Jonathan gave his weapons to the boy and said, "Go, carry them back to town."

⁴¹After the boy had gone, David got up from the south side ˌof the stone˩ and bowed down before Jonathan three times, with his face to the ground. Then they kissed each other and wept together—but David wept the most.

⁴²Jonathan said to David, "Go in peace, for we have sworn friendship with each other in the name of the LORD, saying, 'The LORD is witness between you and me, and between your descendants and my descendants forever.'" Then David left, and Jonathan went back to the town.

David at Nob

21 David went to Nob, to Ahimelech the priest. Ahimelech trembled when he met him, and asked, "Why are you alone? Why is no one with you?"

²David answered Ahimelech the priest, "The king charged me with a certain matter and said to me, 'No one is to know anything about your mission and your instructions.' As for my men, I have told them to meet me at a certain place. ³Now then, what do you have on hand? Give me five loaves of bread, or whatever you can find."

⁴But the priest answered David, "I don't have any ordinary bread on hand; however, there is some consecrated bread here—provided the men have kept themselves from women."

⁵David replied, "Indeed women have been kept from us, as usual wheneverᵇ I set out. The men's thingsᶜ are holy even on missions that are not holy. How much more so today!" ⁶So the priest gave him the consecrated bread, since there was no bread there except the bread of the Presence that had been removed from before the LORD and replaced by hot bread on the day it was taken away.

⁷Now one of Saul's servants was there that day, detained before the LORD; he was Doeg the Edomite, Saul's head shepherd.

ᵃ25 Septuagint; Hebrew wall. Jonathan arose
ᵇ5 Or from us in the past few days since
ᶜ5 Or bodies

[8]David asked Ahimelech, "Don't you have a spear or a sword here? I haven't brought my sword or any other weapon, because the king's business was urgent."

[9]The priest replied, "The sword of Goliath the Philistine, whom you killed in the Valley of Elah, is here; it is wrapped in a cloth behind the ephod. If you want it, take it; there is no sword here but that one."

David said, "There is none like it; give it to me."

David at Gath

[10]That day David fled from Saul and went to Achish king of Gath. [11]But the servants of Achish said to him, "Isn't this David, the king of the land? Isn't he the one they sing about in their dances:

> " 'Saul has slain his thousands,
> and David his tens of thousands'?"

[12]David took these words to heart and was very much afraid of Achish king of Gath. [13]So he pretended to be insane in their presence; and while he was in their hands he acted like a madman, making marks on the doors of the gate and letting saliva run down his beard.

[14]Achish said to his servants, "Look at the man! He is insane! Why bring him to me? [15]Am I so short of madmen that you have to bring this fellow here to carry on like this in front of me? Must this man come into my house?"

David at Adullam and Mizpah

22 David left Gath and escaped to the cave of Adullam. When his brothers and his father's household heard about it, they went down to him there. [2]All those who were in distress or in debt or discontented gathered around him, and he became their leader. About four hundred men were with him.

[3]From there David went to Mizpah in Moab and said to the king of Moab, "Would you let my father and mother come and stay with you until I learn what God will do for me?" [4]So he left them with the king of Moab, and they stayed with him as long as David was in the stronghold.

[5]But the prophet Gad said to David, "Do not stay in the stronghold. Go into the land of Judah." So David left and went to the forest of Hereth.

Saul Kills the Priests of Nob

[6]Now Saul heard that David and his men had been discovered. And Saul, spear in hand, was seated on the tamarisk tree on the hill at Gibeah, with all his officials standing around him. [7]Saul said to them, "Listen, men of Benjamin! Will the son of Jesse give all of you fields and vineyards? Will he make all of you commanders of thousands and commanders of hundreds? [8]Is that why you have all conspired against me? No one tells me when my son makes a covenant with the son of Jesse. None of you is concerned about me or tells me that my son has incited my servant to lie in wait for me, as he does today."

[9]But Doeg the Edomite, who was standing with Saul's officials, said, "I saw the son of Jesse come to Ahimelech son of Ahitub at Nob. [10]Ahimelech inquired of the LORD for him; he also gave him provisions and the sword of Goliath the Philistine."

[11]Then the king sent for the priest Ahimelech son of Ahitub and his father's whole family, who were the priests at Nob, and they all came to the king. [12]Saul said, "Listen now, son of Ahitub."

"Yes, my lord," he answered.

[13]Saul said to him, "Why have you conspired against me, you and the son of Jesse, giving him bread and a sword and inquiring of God for him, so that he has rebelled against me and lies in wait for me, as he does today?"

[14]Ahimelech answered the king, "Who of all your servants is as loyal as David, the king's son-in-law, captain of your bodyguard and highly respected in your household? [15]Was that day the first time I inquired of God for him? Of course not! Let not the king accuse your servant or any of his father's family, for your servant knows nothing at all about this whole affair."

[16]But the king said, "You will surely die, Ahimelech, you and your father's whole family."

[17]Then the king ordered the guards at his side: "Turn and kill the priests of the LORD, because they too have sided with

David. They knew he was fleeing, yet they did not tell me."

But the king's officials were not willing to raise a hand to strike the priests of the LORD.

¹⁸The king then ordered Doeg, "You turn and strike down the priests." So Doeg the Edomite turned and struck them down. That day he killed eighty-five men who wore the linen ephod. ¹⁹He also put to the sword Nob, the town of the priests, with its men and women, its children and infants, and its cattle, donkeys and sheep.

²⁰But Abiathar, a son of Ahimelech son of Ahitub, escaped and fled to join David. ²¹He told David that Saul had killed the priests of the LORD. ²²Then David said to Abiathar: "That day, when Doeg the Edomite was there, I knew he would be sure to tell Saul. I am responsible for the death of your father's whole family. ²³Stay with me; don't be afraid; the man who is seeking your life is seeking mine also. You will be safe with me."

David Saves Keilah

23 When David was told, "Look, the Philistines are fighting against Keilah and are looting the threshing floors," ²he inquired of the LORD, saying, "Shall I go and attack these Philistines?"

The LORD answered him, "Go, attack the Philistines and save Keilah."

³But David's men said to him, "Here in Judah we are afraid. How much more, then, if we go to Keilah against the Philistine forces!"

⁴Once again David inquired of the LORD, and the LORD answered him, "Go down to Keilah, for I am going to give the Philistines into your hand." ⁵So David and his men went to Keilah, fought the Philistines and carried off their livestock. He inflicted heavy losses on the Philistines and saved the people of Keilah. ⁶(Now Abiathar son of Ahimelech had brought the ephod down with him when he fled to David at Keilah.)

Saul Pursues David

⁷Saul was told that David had gone to Keilah, and he said, "God has handed him over to me, for David has imprisoned himself by entering a town with gates

and bars." ⁸And Saul called up all his forces for battle, to go down to Keilah to besiege David and his men.

⁹When David learned that Saul was plotting against him, he said to Abiathar the priest, "Bring the ephod." ¹⁰David said, "O LORD, God of Israel, your servant has heard definitely that Saul plans to come to Keilah and destroy the town on account of me. ¹¹Will the citizens of Keilah surrender me to him? Will Saul come down, as your servant has heard? O LORD, God of Israel, tell your servant."

And the LORD said, "He will."

¹²Again David asked, "Will the citizens of Keilah surrender me and my men to Saul?"

And the LORD said, "They will."

¹³So David and his men, about six hundred in number, left Keilah and kept moving from place to place. When Saul was told that David had escaped from Keilah, he did not go there.

¹⁴David stayed in the desert strongholds and in the hills of the Desert of Ziph. Day after day Saul searched for him, but God did not give David into his hands.

¹⁵While David was at Horesh in the Desert of Ziph, he learned that Saul had come out to take his life. ¹⁶And Saul's son Jonathan went to David at Horesh and helped him find strength in God. ¹⁷"Don't be afraid," he said. "My father Saul will not lay a hand on you. You will be king over Israel, and I will be second to you. Even my father Saul knows this." ¹⁸The two of them made a covenant before the LORD. Then Jonathan went home, but David remained at Horesh.

¹⁹The Ziphites went up to Saul at Gibeah and said, "Is not David hiding among us in the strongholds at Horesh, on the hill of Hakilah, south of Jeshimon? ²⁰Now, O king, come down whenever it pleases you to do so, and we will be responsible for handing him over to the king."

²¹Saul replied, "The LORD bless you for your concern for me. ²²Go and make further preparation. Find out where David usually goes and who has seen him there. They tell me he is very crafty. ²³Find out about all the hiding places he uses and come back to me with definite

information.[a] Then I will go with you; if he is in the area, I will track him down among all the clans of Judah."

[24]So they set out and went to Ziph ahead of Saul. Now David and his men were in the Desert of Maon, in the Arabah south of Jeshimon. [25]Saul and his men began the search, and when David was told about it, he went down to the rock and stayed in the Desert of Maon. When Saul heard this, he went into the Desert of Maon in pursuit of David.

[26]Saul was going along one side of the mountain, and David and his men were on the other side, hurrying to get away from Saul. As Saul and his forces were closing in on David and his men to capture them, [27]a messenger came to Saul, saying, "Come quickly! The Philistines are raiding the land." [28]Then Saul broke off his pursuit of David and went to meet the Philistines. That is why they call this place Sela Hammahlekoth.[b] [29]And David went up from there and lived in the strongholds of En Gedi.

David Spares Saul's Life

24 After Saul returned from pursuing the Philistines, he was told, "David is in the Desert of En Gedi." [2]So Saul took three thousand chosen men from all Israel and set out to look for David and his men near the Crags of the Wild Goats.

[3]He came to the sheep pens along the way; a cave was there, and Saul went in to relieve himself. David and his men were far back in the cave. [4]The men said, "This is the day the LORD spoke of when he said[c] to you, 'I will give your enemy into your hands for you to deal with as you wish.'" Then David crept up unnoticed and cut off a corner of Saul's robe.

[5]Afterward, David was conscience-stricken for having cut off a corner of his robe. [6]He said to his men, "The LORD forbid that I should do such a thing to my master, the LORD's anointed, or lift my hand against him; for he is the anointed of the LORD." [7]With these words David rebuked his men and did not allow them to attack Saul. And Saul left the cave and went his way.

[8]Then David went out of the cave and called out to Saul, "My lord the king!" When Saul looked behind him, David bowed down and prostrated himself with his face to the ground. [9]He said to Saul, "Why do you listen when men say, 'David is bent on harming you'? [10]This day you have seen with your own eyes how the LORD delivered you into my hands in the cave. Some urged me to kill you, but I spared you; I said, 'I will not lift my hand against my master, because he is the LORD's anointed.' [11]See, my father, look at this piece of your robe in my hand! I cut off the corner of your robe but did not kill you. Now understand and recognize that I am not guilty of wrongdoing or rebellion. I have not wronged you, but you are hunting me down to take my life. [12]May the LORD judge between you and me. And may the LORD avenge the wrongs you have done to me, but my hand will not touch you. [13]As the old saying goes, 'From evildoers come evil deeds,' so my hand will not touch you.

[14]"Against whom has the king of Israel come out? Whom are you pursuing? A dead dog? A flea? [15]May the LORD be our judge and decide between us. May he consider my cause and uphold it; may he vindicate me by delivering me from your hand."

[16]When David finished saying this, Saul asked, "Is that your voice, David my son?" And he wept aloud. [17]"You are more righteous than I," he said. "You have treated me well, but I have treated you badly. [18]You have just now told me of the good you did to me; the LORD delivered me into your hands, but you did not kill me. [19]When a man finds his enemy, does he let him get away unharmed? May the LORD reward you well for the way you treated me today. [20]I know that you will surely be king and that the kingdom of Israel will be established in your hands. [21]Now swear to me by the LORD that you will not cut off my descendants or wipe out my name from my father's family."

[22]So David gave his oath to Saul. Then Saul returned home, but David and his men went up to the stronghold.

---

[a]23 Or *me at Nacon*   [b]28 *Sela Hammahlekoth* means *rock of parting.*   [c]4 Or "*Today the* LORD *is saying*

David, Nabal and Abigail

25 Now Samuel died, and all Israel assembled and mourned for him; and they buried him at his home in Ramah.

Then David moved down into the Desert of Maon.[a] 2A certain man in Maon, who had property there at Carmel, was very wealthy. He had a thousand goats and three thousand sheep, which he was shearing in Carmel. 3His name was Nabal and his wife's name was Abigail. She was an intelligent and beautiful woman, but her husband, a Calebite, was surly and mean in his dealings.

4While David was in the desert, he heard that Nabal was shearing sheep. 5So he sent ten young men and said to them, "Go up to Nabal at Carmel and greet him in my name. 6Say to him: 'Long life to you! Good health to you and your household! And good health to all that is yours!

7" 'Now I hear that it is sheep-shearing time. When your shepherds were with us, we did not mistreat them, and the whole time they were at Carmel nothing of theirs was missing. 8Ask your own servants and they will tell you. Therefore be favorable toward my young men, since we come at a festive time. Please give your servants and your son David whatever you can find for them.' "

9When David's men arrived, they gave Nabal this message in David's name. Then they waited.

10Nabal answered David's servants, "Who is this David? Who is this son of Jesse? Many servants are breaking away from their masters these days. 11Why should I take my bread and water, and the meat I have slaughtered for my shearers, and give it to men coming from who knows where?"

12David's men turned around and went back. When they arrived, they reported every word. 13David said to his men, "Put on your swords!" So they put on their swords, and David put on his. About four hundred men went up with David, while two hundred stayed with the supplies.

14One of the servants told Nabal's wife Abigail: "David sent messengers from the desert to give our master his greetings, but he hurled insults at them. 15Yet these men were very good to us. They did not mistreat us, and the whole time we were out in the fields near them nothing was missing. 16Night and day they were a wall around us all the time we were herding our sheep near them. 17Now think it over and see what you can do, because disaster is hanging over our master and his whole household. He is such a wicked man that no one can talk to him."

18Abigail lost no time. She took two hundred loaves of bread, two skins of wine, five dressed sheep, five seahs[b] of roasted grain, a hundred cakes of raisins and two hundred cakes of pressed figs, and loaded them on donkeys. 19Then she told her servants, "Go on ahead; I'll follow you." But she did not tell her husband Nabal.

20As she came riding her donkey into a mountain ravine, there were David and his men descending toward her, and she met them. 21David had just said, "It's been useless—all my watching over this fellow's property in the desert so that nothing of his was missing. He has paid me back evil for good. 22May God deal with David,[c] be it ever so severely, if by morning I leave alive one male of all who belong to him!"

23When Abigail saw David, she quickly got off her donkey and bowed down before David with her face to the ground. 24She fell at his feet and said: "My lord, let the blame be on me alone. Please let your servant speak to you; hear what your servant has to say. 25May my lord pay no attention to that wicked man Nabal. He is just like his name—his name is Fool, and folly goes with him. But as for me, your servant, I did not see the men my master sent.

26"Now since the LORD has kept you, my master, from bloodshed and from avenging yourself with your own hands, as surely as the LORD lives and as you live, may your enemies and all who intend to harm my master be like Nabal. 27And let this gift, which your servant has brought to my master, be given to the men who follow you. 28Please forgive your servant's offense, for the LORD will certainly make a lasting dynasty for my master, because he

<hr>

[a]1 Some Septuagint manuscripts; Hebrew *Paran*
[b]18 That is, probably about a bushel (about 37 liters)   [c]22 Some Septuagint manuscripts; Hebrew *with David's enemies*

The Dignity of Causality

C. S. LEWIS described himself at his conversion as "the most dejected convert in all England." Years later, he would look back on that event and muse, "I did not then see what is now the most shining and obvious thing; the Divine humility which will accept a convert even on such terms . . . Who can fully adore that Love which will open the high gates to a prodigal who is brought in kicking, struggling, resentful, and darting his eyes in every direction for a chance of escape?"[1]

But that's how it began for the man who became the foremost apologist for Christian orthodoxy in the 20th century. Lewis brought a capacious and razor-sharp mind to a variety of themes and problems of the faith, with results that have delighted and instructed readers for decades. Interestingly, he may have written more on the subject of prayer than any other topic. In an essay in *God in the Dock*,[2] he addressed the difficult question, "If God is all-wise and all-knowing, he will always do what is best. Why then should our prayers make any difference?"

The answer lies in what can be called God's human project. In his wisdom, God has chosen to work with humans in the unfolding of history, "like a play in which the scene and the general outline of the story is fixed by the author, but certain minor details are left for the actors to improvise." Citing Blaise Pascal, Lewis believed God wants to give humans the "dignity of causality" by granting to us the outcome of minor details in the drama. In a sense, prayer is like work, and no more mysterious: Both are ways God allows us to affect the world.

So why, then, is our work almost guaranteed to have some kind of result, but not our prayers? Lewis' answer is surprising: "This is not because prayer is the weaker kind of causality," as we may often feel when we pray and wait for an answer, "but because it is a stronger kind." If God were to grant to our prayers the kind of immediate results we expect from our work, the results would be catastrophic. Imagine how disastrous it would be if every prayer we prayed selfishly or foolishly or in anger were automatically granted by God. A single yes from God could be far more horrible than any number of his refusals. Otherwise, prayer would be "an activity too dangerous for man and we should have the horrible state of things envisaged by Roman satirist Juvenal: 'Enormous prayers which Heaven in anger grants.'" So in prayer, "God has retained a discretionary power of granting or refusing it"—not because prayer is weak, but because it is so powerful.

When we pray, we should regard God's silences to be at least as meaningful as his voice. His silences are always the silences of his higher designs, his superior sense of timing and his grand purpose in making our wills one with his.

PRAY:

Thank you, Lord, for allowing us the dignity and
privilege of affecting the world through our
"powerful and effective" prayers (see James 5:16).

MEMORIZE:

"So I say to you: Ask and it will be given to you; seek and
you will find; knock and the door will be opened to you.

For everyone who asks receives; he who seeks finds;
and to him who knocks, the door will be opened." LUKE 11:9–10

FOR YOUR NEXT DEVOTIONAL READING, GO TO PAGE 349.

fights the LORD's battles. Let no wrongdoing be found in you as long as you live. [29]Even though someone is pursuing you to take your life, the life of my master will be bound securely in the bundle of the living by the LORD your God. But the lives of your enemies he will hurl away as from the pocket of a sling. [30]When the LORD has done for my master every good thing he promised concerning him and has appointed him leader over Israel, [31]my master will not have on his conscience the staggering burden of needless bloodshed or of having avenged himself. And when the LORD has brought my master success, remember your servant."

[32]David said to Abigail, "Praise be to the LORD, the God of Israel, who has sent you today to meet me. [33]May you be blessed for your good judgment and for keeping me from bloodshed this day and from avenging myself with my own hands. [34]Otherwise, as surely as the LORD, the God of Israel, lives, who has kept me from harming you, if you had not come quickly to meet me, not one male belonging to Nabal would have been left alive by daybreak."

[35]Then David accepted from her hand what she had brought him and said, "Go home in peace. I have heard your words and granted your request."

[36]When Abigail went to Nabal, he was in the house holding a banquet like that of a king. He was in high spirits and very drunk. So she told him nothing until daybreak. [37]Then in the morning, when Nabal was sober, his wife told him all these things, and his heart failed him and he became like a stone. [38]About ten days later, the LORD struck Nabal and he died.

[39]When David heard that Nabal was dead, he said, "Praise be to the LORD, who has upheld my cause against Nabal for treating me with contempt. He has kept his servant from doing wrong and has brought Nabal's wrongdoing down on his own head."

Then David sent word to Abigail, asking her to become his wife. [40]His servants went to Carmel and said to Abigail, "David has sent us to you to take you to become his wife."

[41]She bowed down with her face to the ground and said, "Here is your maidservant, ready to serve you and wash the feet of my master's servants." [42]Abigail quickly got on a donkey and, attended by her five maids, went with David's messengers and became his wife. [43]David had also married Ahinoam of Jezreel, and they both were his wives. [44]But Saul had given his daughter Michal, David's wife, to Paltiel[a] son of Laish, who was from Gallim.

David Again Spares Saul's Life

26 The Ziphites went to Saul at Gibeah and said, "Is not David hiding on the hill of Hakilah, which faces Jeshimon?"

[2]So Saul went down to the Desert of Ziph, with his three thousand chosen men of Israel, to search there for David. [3]Saul made his camp beside the road on the hill of Hakilah facing Jeshimon, but David stayed in the desert. When he saw that Saul had followed him there, [4]he sent out scouts and learned that Saul had definitely arrived.[b]

[5]Then David set out and went to the place where Saul had camped. He saw where Saul and Abner son of Ner, the commander of the army, had lain down. Saul was lying inside the camp, with the army encamped around him.

[6]David then asked Ahimelech the Hittite and Abishai son of Zeruiah, Joab's brother, "Who will go down into the camp with me to Saul?"

"I'll go with you," said Abishai.

[7]So David and Abishai went to the army by night, and there was Saul, lying asleep inside the camp with his spear stuck in the ground near his head. Abner and the soldiers were lying around him.

[8]Abishai said to David, "Today God has delivered your enemy into your hands. Now let me pin him to the ground with one thrust of my spear; I won't strike him twice."

[9]But David said to Abishai, "Don't destroy him! Who can lay a hand on the LORD's anointed and be guiltless? [10]As surely as the LORD lives," he said, "the LORD himself will strike him; either his time will come and he will die, or he will go into battle and perish. [11]But the LORD

---

[a]44 Hebrew *Palti*, a variant of *Paltiel*
[b]4 Or *had come to Nacon*

forbid that I should lay a hand on the LORD's anointed. Now get the spear and water jug that are near his head, and let's go."

¹²So David took the spear and water jug near Saul's head, and they left. No one saw or knew about it, nor did anyone wake up. They were all sleeping, because the LORD had put them into a deep sleep.

¹³Then David crossed over to the other side and stood on top of the hill some distance away; there was a wide space between them. ¹⁴He called out to the army and to Abner son of Ner, "Aren't you going to answer me, Abner?"

Abner replied, "Who are you who calls to the king?"

¹⁵David said, "You're a man, aren't you? And who is like you in Israel? Why didn't you guard your lord the king? Someone came to destroy your lord the king. ¹⁶What you have done is not good. As surely as the LORD lives, you and your men deserve to die, because you did not guard your master, the LORD's anointed. Look around you. Where are the king's spear and water jug that were near his head?"

¹⁷Saul recognized David's voice and said, "Is that your voice, David my son?"

David replied, "Yes it is, my lord the king." ¹⁸And he added, "Why is my lord pursuing his servant? What have I done, and what wrong am I guilty of? ¹⁹Now let my lord the king listen to his servant's words. If the LORD has incited you against me, then may he accept an offering. If, however, men have done it, may they be cursed before the LORD! They have now driven me from my share in the LORD's inheritance and have said, 'Go, serve other gods.' ²⁰Now do not let my blood fall to the ground far from the presence of the LORD. The king of Israel has come out to look for a flea—as one hunts a partridge in the mountains."

²¹Then Saul said, "I have sinned. Come back, David my son. Because you considered my life precious today, I will not try to harm you again. Surely I have acted like a fool and have erred greatly."

²²"Here is the king's spear," David answered. "Let one of your young men come over and get it. ²³The LORD rewards every man for his righteousness and

faithfulness. The LORD delivered you into my hands today, but I would not lay a hand on the LORD's anointed. ²⁴As surely as I valued your life today, so may the LORD value my life and deliver me from all trouble."

²⁵Then Saul said to David, "May you be blessed, my son David; you will do great things and surely triumph."

So David went on his way, and Saul returned home.

David Among the Philistines

27 But David thought to himself, "One of these days I will be destroyed by the hand of Saul. The best thing I can do is to escape to the land of the Philistines. Then Saul will give up searching for me anywhere in Israel, and I will slip out of his hand."

²So David and the six hundred men with him left and went over to Achish son of Maoch king of Gath. ³David and his men settled in Gath with Achish. Each man had his family with him, and David had his two wives: Ahinoam of Jezreel and Abigail of Carmel, the widow of Nabal. ⁴When Saul was told that David had fled to Gath, he no longer searched for him.

⁵Then David said to Achish, "If I have found favor in your eyes, let a place be assigned to me in one of the country towns, that I may live there. Why should your servant live in the royal city with you?"

⁶So on that day Achish gave him Ziklag, and it has belonged to the kings of Judah ever since. ⁷David lived in Philistine territory a year and four months.

⁸Now David and his men went up and raided the Geshurites, the Girzites and the Amalekites. (From ancient times these peoples had lived in the land extending to Shur and Egypt.) ⁹Whenever David attacked an area, he did not leave a man or woman alive, but took sheep and cattle, donkeys and camels, and clothes. Then he returned to Achish.

¹⁰When Achish asked, "Where did you go raiding today?" David would say, "Against the Negev of Judah" or "Against the Negev of Jerahmeel" or "Against the Negev of the Kenites." ¹¹He did not leave a man or woman alive to be brought to Gath, for he thought, "They might inform on us and say, 'This is what David

did.'" And such was his practice as long as he lived in Philistine territory. [12]Achish trusted David and said to himself, "He has become so odious to his people, the Israelites, that he will be my servant forever."

Saul and the Witch of Endor

28 In those days the Philistines gathered their forces to fight against Israel. Achish said to David, "You must understand that you and your men will accompany me in the army."

[2]David said, "Then you will see for yourself what your servant can do."

Achish replied, "Very well, I will make you my bodyguard for life."

[3]Now Samuel was dead, and all Israel had mourned for him and buried him in his own town of Ramah. Saul had expelled the mediums and spiritists from the land.

[4]The Philistines assembled and came and set up camp at Shunem, while Saul gathered all the Israelites and set up camp at Gilboa. [5]When Saul saw the Philistine army, he was afraid; terror filled his heart. [6]He inquired of the LORD, but the LORD did not answer him by dreams or Urim or prophets. [7]Saul then said to his attendants, "Find me a woman who is a medium, so I may go and inquire of her."

"There is one in Endor," they said.

[8]So Saul disguised himself, putting on other clothes, and at night he and two men went to the woman. "Consult a spirit for me," he said, "and bring up for me the one I name."

[9]But the woman said to him, "Surely you know what Saul has done. He has cut off the mediums and spiritists from the land. Why have you set a trap for my life to bring about my death?"

[10]Saul swore to her by the LORD, "As surely as the LORD lives, you will not be punished for this."

[11]Then the woman asked, "Whom shall I bring up for you?"

"Bring up Samuel," he said.

[12]When the woman saw Samuel, she cried out at the top of her voice and said to Saul, "Why have you deceived me? You are Saul!"

[13]The king said to her, "Don't be afraid. What do you see?"

The woman said, "I see a spirit[a] coming up out of the ground."

[14]"What does he look like?" he asked.

"An old man wearing a robe is coming up," she said.

Then Saul knew it was Samuel, and he bowed down and prostrated himself with his face to the ground.

[15]Samuel said to Saul, "Why have you disturbed me by bringing me up?"

"I am in great distress," Saul said. "The Philistines are fighting against me, and God has turned away from me. He no longer answers me, either by prophets or by dreams. So I have called on you to tell me what to do."

[16]Samuel said, "Why do you consult me, now that the LORD has turned away from you and become your enemy? [17]The LORD has done what he predicted through me. The LORD has torn the kingdom out of your hands and given it to one of your neighbors—to David. [18]Because you did not obey the LORD or carry out his fierce wrath against the Amalekites, the LORD has done this to you today. [19]The LORD will hand over both Israel and you to the Philistines, and tomorrow you and your sons will be with me. The LORD will also hand over the army of Israel to the Philistines."

[20]Immediately Saul fell full length on the ground, filled with fear because of Samuel's words. His strength was gone, for he had eaten nothing all that day and night.

[21]When the woman came to Saul and saw that he was greatly shaken, she said, "Look, your maidservant has obeyed you. I took my life in my hands and did what you told me to do. [22]Now please listen to your servant and let me give you some food so you may eat and have the strength to go on your way."

[23]He refused and said, "I will not eat."

But his men joined the woman in urging him, and he listened to them. He got up from the ground and sat on the couch.

[24]The woman had a fattened calf at the house, which she butchered at once. She took some flour, kneaded it and baked bread without yeast. [25]Then she set it before Saul and his men, and they ate. That same night they got up and left.

[a]13 Or see spirits; or see gods

Achish Sends David Back to Ziklag

29 The Philistines gathered all their forces at Aphek, and Israel camped by the spring in Jezreel. ²As the Philistine rulers marched with their units of hundreds and thousands, David and his men were marching at the rear with Achish. ³The commanders of the Philistines asked, "What about these Hebrews?"

Achish replied, "Is this not David, who was an officer of Saul king of Israel? He has already been with me for over a year, and from the day he left Saul until now, I have found no fault in him."

⁴But the Philistine commanders were angry with him and said, "Send the man back, that he may return to the place you assigned him. He must not go with us into battle, or he will turn against us during the fighting. How better could he regain his master's favor than by taking the heads of our own men? ⁵Isn't this the David they sang about in their dances:

" 'Saul has slain his thousands,
   and David his tens of thousands'?"

⁶So Achish called David and said to him, "As surely as the LORD lives, you have been reliable, and I would be pleased to have you serve with me in the army. From the day you came to me until now, I have found no fault in you, but the rulers don't approve of you. ⁷Turn back and go in peace; do nothing to displease the Philistine rulers."

⁸"But what have I done?" asked David. "What have you found against your servant from the day I came to you until now? Why can't I go and fight against the enemies of my lord the king?"

⁹Achish answered, "I know that you have been as pleasing in my eyes as an angel of God; nevertheless, the Philistine commanders have said, 'He must not go up with us into battle.' ¹⁰Now get up early, along with your master's servants who have come with you, and leave in the morning as soon as it is light."

¹¹So David and his men got up early in the morning to go back to the land of the Philistines, and the Philistines went up to Jezreel.

David Destroys the Amalekites

30 David and his men reached Ziklag on the third day. Now the Amalekites had raided the Negev and Ziklag. They had attacked Ziklag and burned it, ²and had taken captive the women and all who were in it, both young and old. They killed none of them, but carried them off as they went on their way.

³When David and his men came to Ziklag, they found it destroyed by fire and their wives and sons and daughters taken captive. ⁴So David and his men wept aloud until they had no strength left to weep. ⁵David's two wives had been captured—Ahinoam of Jezreel and Abigail, the widow of Nabal of Carmel. ⁶David was greatly distressed because the men were talking of stoning him; each one was bitter in spirit because of his sons and daughters. But David found strength in the LORD his God.

⁷Then David said to Abiathar the priest, the son of Ahimelech, "Bring me the ephod." Abiathar brought it to him, ⁸and David inquired of the LORD, "Shall I pursue this raiding party? Will I overtake them?"

"Pursue them," he answered. "You will certainly overtake them and succeed in the rescue."

⁹David and the six hundred men with him came to the Besor Ravine, where some stayed behind, ¹⁰for two hundred men were too exhausted to cross the ravine. But David and four hundred men continued the pursuit.

¹¹They found an Egyptian in a field and brought him to David. They gave him water to drink and food to eat— ¹²part of a cake of pressed figs and two cakes of raisins. He ate and was revived, for he had not eaten any food or drunk any water for three days and three nights.

¹³David asked him, "To whom do you belong, and where do you come from?"

He said, "I am an Egyptian, the slave of an Amalekite. My master abandoned me when I became ill three days ago. ¹⁴We raided the Negev of the Kerethites and

> Who rises from prayer a better man,
> his prayer is answered.
>
> GEORGE MEREDITH

the territory belonging to Judah and the Negev of Caleb. And we burned Ziklag."

¹⁵David asked him, "Can you lead me down to this raiding party?"

He answered, "Swear to me before God that you will not kill me or hand me over to my master, and I will take you down to them."

¹⁶He led David down, and there they were, scattered over the countryside, eating, drinking and reveling because of the great amount of plunder they had taken from the land of the Philistines and from Judah. ¹⁷David fought them from dusk until the evening of the next day, and none of them got away, except four hundred young men who rode off on camels and fled. ¹⁸David recovered everything the Amalekites had taken, including his two wives. ¹⁹Nothing was missing: young or old, boy or girl, plunder or anything else they had taken. David brought everything back. ²⁰He took all the flocks and herds, and his men drove them ahead of the other livestock, saying, "This is David's plunder."

²¹Then David came to the two hundred men who had been too exhausted to follow him and who were left behind at the Besor Ravine. They came out to meet David and the people with him. As David and his men approached, he greeted them. ²²But all the evil men and troublemakers among David's followers said, "Because they did not go out with us, we will not share with them the plunder we recovered. However, each man may take his wife and children and go."

²³David replied, "No, my brothers, you must not do that with what the LORD has given us. He has protected us and handed over to us the forces that came against us. ²⁴Who will listen to what you say? The share of the man who stayed with the supplies is to be the same as that of him who went down to the battle. All will share alike." ²⁵David made this a statute and ordinance for Israel from that day to this.

²⁶When David arrived in Ziklag, he sent some of the plunder to the elders of Judah, who were his friends, saying, "Here is a present for you from the plunder of the LORD's enemies."

²⁷He sent it to those who were in Bethel, Ramoth Negev and Jattir; ²⁸to those in Aroer, Siphmoth, Eshtemoa ²⁹and Racal; to those in the towns of the Jerahmeelites and the Kenites; ³⁰to those in Hormah, Bor Ashan, Athach ³¹and Hebron; and to those in all the other places where David and his men had roamed.

Saul Takes His Life

31 Now the Philistines fought against Israel; the Israelites fled before them, and many fell slain on Mount Gilboa. ²The Philistines pressed hard after Saul and his sons, and they killed his sons Jonathan, Abinadab and Malki-Shua. ³The fighting grew fierce around Saul, and when the archers overtook him, they wounded him critically.

⁴Saul said to his armor-bearer, "Draw your sword and run me through, or these uncircumcised fellows will come and run me through and abuse me."

But his armor-bearer was terrified and would not do it; so Saul took his own sword and fell on it. ⁵When the armor-bearer saw that Saul was dead, he too fell on his sword and died with him. ⁶So Saul and his three sons and his armor-bearer and all his men died together that same day.

⁷When the Israelites along the valley and those across the Jordan saw that the Israelite army had fled and that Saul and his sons had died, they abandoned their towns and fled. And the Philistines came and occupied them.

⁸The next day, when the Philistines came to strip the dead, they found Saul and his three sons fallen on Mount Gilboa. ⁹They cut off his head and stripped off his armor, and they sent messengers throughout the land of the Philistines to proclaim the news in the temple of their idols and among their people. ¹⁰They put his armor in the temple of the Ashtoreths and fastened his body to the wall of Beth Shan.

¹¹When the people of Jabesh Gilead heard of what the Philistines had done to Saul, ¹²all their valiant men journeyed through the night to Beth Shan. They took down the bodies of Saul and his sons from the wall of Beth Shan and went to Jabesh, where they burned them. ¹³Then they took their bones and buried them under a tamarisk tree at Jabesh, and they fasted seven days.

2 Samuel

THE BOOK of 2 Samuel continues the story of Israel's monarchy. The story of 1 Samuel ends with the death of King Saul, and now 2 Samuel begins the account of King David's reign.

Although one might think that Saul was a mistake in God's plan, it's better to think of him as an illustration of the very things Samuel warned the people would happen if they got their king (see 1 Samuel 8:11; 14:52). Saul brought war and strife to the nation.

The next king for Israel is considered their greatest human king. David, though flawed, was yet a "man after [God's] own heart" who desired to walk in God's ways with an "undivided heart" (see 1 Samuel 13:14; Psalm 86:11). David was a man of prayer and the principle author of a collection of prayers, the Psalms.

THEY ANOINTED DAVID KING OVER THE HOUSE OF JUDAH. (2:4)

Psalms is the longest book in the Bible, and the heart God so loved is often laid bare in these prayers. David was "God's anointed," or *messiah*, the precursor of the righteous King who would one day rule and make everything right, not only for Israel, but for the world. The first messiah, like the ultimate Messiah, was a man of prayer.

As we saw with Samuel in the book of 1 Samuel, God's choice of a leader was a man of prayer and worship.

David Hears of Saul's Death

1 After the death of Saul, David returned from defeating the Amalekites and stayed in Ziklag two days. ²On the third day a man arrived from Saul's camp, with his clothes torn and with dust on his head. When he came to David, he fell to the ground to pay him honor.

³"Where have you come from?" David asked him.

He answered, "I have escaped from the Israelite camp."

⁴"What happened?" David asked. "Tell me."

He said, "The men fled from the battle. Many of them fell and died. And Saul and his son Jonathan are dead."

⁵Then David said to the young man who brought him the report, "How do you know that Saul and his son Jonathan are dead?"

⁶"I happened to be on Mount Gilboa," the young man said, "and there was Saul, leaning on his spear, with the chariots and riders almost upon him. ⁷When he turned around and saw me, he called out to me, and I said, 'What can I do?'

⁸"He asked me, 'Who are you?'

"'An Amalekite,' I answered.

⁹"Then he said to me, 'Stand over me and kill me! I am in the throes of death, but I'm still alive.'

¹⁰"So I stood over him and killed him, because I knew that after he had fallen he could not survive. And I took the crown that was on his head and the band on his arm and have brought them here to my lord."

¹¹Then David and all the men with him took hold of their clothes and tore them. ¹²They mourned and wept and fasted till evening for Saul and his son Jonathan, and for the army of the LORD and the house of Israel, because they had fallen by the sword.

¹³David said to the young man who brought him the report, "Where are you from?"

"I am the son of an alien, an Amalekite," he answered.

¹⁴David asked him, "Why were you not afraid to lift your hand to destroy the LORD's anointed?"

¹⁵Then David called one of his men and said, "Go, strike him down!" So he struck him down, and he died. ¹⁶For David had said to him, "Your blood be on your own head. Your own mouth testified against you when you said, 'I killed the LORD's anointed.'"

David's Lament for Saul and Jonathan

¹⁷David took up this lament concerning Saul and his son Jonathan, ¹⁸and ordered that the men of Judah be taught this lament of the bow (it is written in the Book of Jashar):

¹⁹ "Your glory, O Israel, lies slain on
       your heights.
   How the mighty have fallen!

²⁰ "Tell it not in Gath,
       proclaim it not in the streets of
          Ashkelon,
   lest the daughters of the Philistines
       be glad,
       lest the daughters of the
          uncircumcised rejoice.

²¹ "O mountains of Gilboa,
       may you have neither dew nor rain,
       nor fields that yield offerings
          ⌊of grain⌋.
   For there the shield of the mighty was
          defiled,
       the shield of Saul—no longer
          rubbed with oil.

²² From the blood of the slain,
       from the flesh of the mighty,
   the bow of Jonathan did not
          turn back,
       the sword of Saul did not return
          unsatisfied.

²³ "Saul and Jonathan—
       in life they were loved and
          gracious,
       and in death they were not parted.
   They were swifter than eagles,
       they were stronger than lions.

²⁴ "O daughters of Israel,
       weep for Saul,
   who clothed you in scarlet and finery,
       who adorned your garments with
          ornaments of gold.

²⁵ "How the mighty have fallen in
          battle!
   Jonathan lies slain on your heights.
²⁶ I grieve for you, Jonathan my brother;
       you were very dear to me.

Your love for me was wonderful,
more wonderful than that
of women.

[27] "How the mighty have fallen!
The weapons of war have
perished!"

David Anointed King Over Judah

2 In the course of time, David inquired of the LORD. "Shall I go up to one of the towns of Judah?" he asked.

The LORD said, "Go up."

David asked, "Where shall I go?"

"To Hebron," the LORD answered.

[2]So David went up there with his two wives, Ahinoam of Jezreel and Abigail, the widow of Nabal of Carmel. [3]David also took the men who were with him, each with his family, and they settled in Hebron and its towns. [4]Then the men of Judah came to Hebron and there they anointed David king over the house of Judah.

When David was told that it was the men of Jabesh Gilead who had buried Saul, [5]he sent messengers to the men of Jabesh Gilead to say to them, "The LORD bless you for showing this kindness to Saul your master by burying him. [6]May the LORD now show you kindness and faithfulness, and I too will show you the same favor because you have done this. [7]Now then, be strong and brave, for Saul your master is dead, and the house of Judah has anointed me king over them."

> "MAY THE LORD now show you kindness
> and faithfulness, and I too will show you
> the same favor because you have done
> this."
>
> 2 SAMUEL 2:6

War Between the Houses of David and Saul

[8]Meanwhile, Abner son of Ner, the commander of Saul's army, had taken Ish-Bosheth son of Saul and brought him over to Mahanaim. [9]He made him king over Gilead, Ashuri[a] and Jezreel, and also over Ephraim, Benjamin and all Israel.

[10]Ish-Bosheth son of Saul was forty years old when he became king over Israel, and he reigned two years. The

house of Judah, however, followed David. [11]The length of time David was king in Hebron over the house of Judah was seven years and six months.

[12]Abner son of Ner, together with the men of Ish-Bosheth son of Saul, left Mahanaim and went to Gibeon. [13]Joab son of Zeruiah and David's men went out and met them at the pool of Gibeon. One group sat down on one side of the pool and one group on the other side.

[14]Then Abner said to Joab, "Let's have some of the young men get up and fight hand to hand in front of us."

"All right, let them do it," Joab said.

[15]So they stood up and were counted off—twelve men for Benjamin and Ish-Bosheth son of Saul, and twelve for David. [16]Then each man grabbed his opponent by the head and thrust his dagger into his opponent's side, and they fell down together. So that place in Gibeon was called Helkath Hazzurim.[b]

[17]The battle that day was very fierce, and Abner and the men of Israel were defeated by David's men.

[18]The three sons of Zeruiah were there: Joab, Abishai and Asahel. Now Asahel was as fleet-footed as a wild gazelle. [19]He chased Abner, turning neither to the right nor to the left as he pursued him. [20]Abner looked behind him and asked, "Is that you, Asahel?"

"It is," he answered.

[21]Then Abner said to him, "Turn aside to the right or to the left; take on one of the young men and strip him of his weapons." But Asahel would not stop chasing him.

[22]Again Abner warned Asahel, "Stop chasing me! Why should I strike you down? How could I look your brother Joab in the face?"

[23]But Asahel refused to give up the pursuit; so Abner thrust the butt of his spear into Asahel's stomach, and the spear came out through his back. He fell there and died on the spot. And every man stopped when he came to the place where Asahel had fallen and died.

[24]But Joab and Abishai pursued Abner, and as the sun was setting, they came to the hill of Ammah, near Giah on the way

---

[a]9 Or Asher   [b]16 Helkath Hazzurim means
field of daggers or field of hostilities.

to the wasteland of Gibeon. [25]Then the men of Benjamin rallied behind Abner. They formed themselves into a group and took their stand on top of a hill.

[26]Abner called out to Joab, "Must the sword devour forever? Don't you realize that this will end in bitterness? How long before you order your men to stop pursuing their brothers?"

[27]Joab answered, "As surely as God lives, if you had not spoken, the men would have continued the pursuit of their brothers until morning.[a]"

[28]So Joab blew the trumpet, and all the men came to a halt; they no longer pursued Israel, nor did they fight anymore.

[29]All that night Abner and his men marched through the Arabah. They crossed the Jordan, continued through the whole Bithron[b] and came to Mahanaim.

[30]Then Joab returned from pursuing Abner and assembled all his men. Besides Asahel, nineteen of David's men were found missing. [31]But David's men had killed three hundred and sixty Benjamites who were with Abner. [32]They took Asahel and buried him in his father's tomb at Bethlehem. Then Joab and his men marched all night and arrived at Hebron by daybreak.

3 The war between the house of Saul and the house of David lasted a long time. David grew stronger and stronger, while the house of Saul grew weaker and weaker.

[2]Sons were born to David in Hebron:
His firstborn was Amnon the son of Ahinoam of Jezreel;
[3]his second, Kileab the son of Abigail the widow of Nabal of Carmel;
the third, Absalom the son of Maacah daughter of Talmai king of Geshur;
[4]the fourth, Adonijah the son of Haggith;
the fifth, Shephatiah the son of Abital;
[5]and the sixth, Ithream the son of David's wife Eglah.
These were born to David in Hebron.

Abner Goes Over to David

[6]During the war between the house of Saul and the house of David, Abner had been strengthening his own position in the house of Saul. [7]Now Saul had had a concubine named Rizpah daughter of Aiah. And Ish-Bosheth said to Abner, "Why did you sleep with my father's concubine?"

[8]Abner was very angry because of what Ish-Bosheth said and he answered, "Am I a dog's head—on Judah's side? This very day I am loyal to the house of your father Saul and to his family and friends. I haven't handed you over to David. Yet now you accuse me of an offense involving this woman! [9]May God deal with Abner, be it ever so severely, if I do not do for David what the LORD promised him on oath [10]and transfer the kingdom from the house of Saul and establish David's throne over Israel and Judah from Dan to Beersheba." [11]Ish-Bosheth did not dare to say another word to Abner, because he was afraid of him.

[12]Then Abner sent messengers on his behalf to say to David, "Whose land is it? Make an agreement with me, and I will help you bring all Israel over to you."

[13]"Good," said David. "I will make an agreement with you. But I demand one thing of you: Do not come into my presence unless you bring Michal daughter of Saul when you come to see me." [14]Then David sent messengers to Ish-Bosheth son of Saul, demanding, "Give me my wife Michal, whom I betrothed to myself for the price of a hundred Philistine foreskins."

[15]So Ish-Bosheth gave orders and had her taken away from her husband Paltiel son of Laish. [16]Her husband, however, went with her, weeping behind her all the way to Bahurim. Then Abner said to him, "Go back home!" So he went back.

[17]Abner conferred with the elders of Israel and said, "For some time you have wanted to make David your king. [18]Now do it! For the LORD promised David, 'By my servant David I will rescue my people Israel from the hand of the Philistines and from the hand of all their enemies.'"

---

[a]27 Or *spoken this morning, the men would not have taken up the pursuit of their brothers;* or *spoken, the men would have given up the pursuit of their brothers by morning*   [b]29 Or *morning;* or *ravine;* the meaning of the Hebrew for this word is uncertain.

[19]Abner also spoke to the Benjamites in person. Then he went to Hebron to tell David everything that Israel and the whole house of Benjamin wanted to do. [20]When Abner, who had twenty men with him, came to David at Hebron, David prepared a feast for him and his men. [21]Then Abner said to David, "Let me go at once and assemble all Israel for my lord the king, so that they may make a compact with you, and that you may rule over all that your heart desires." So David sent Abner away, and he went in peace.

Joab Murders Abner

[22]Just then David's men and Joab returned from a raid and brought with them a great deal of plunder. But Abner was no longer with David in Hebron, because David had sent him away, and he had gone in peace. [23]When Joab and all the soldiers with him arrived, he was told that Abner son of Ner had come to the king and that the king had sent him away and that he had gone in peace.

[24]So Joab went to the king and said, "What have you done? Look, Abner came to you. Why did you let him go? Now he is gone! [25]You know Abner son of Ner; he came to deceive you and observe your movements and find out everything you are doing."

[26]Joab then left David and sent messengers after Abner, and they brought him back from the well of Sirah. But David did not know it. [27]Now when Abner returned to Hebron, Joab took him aside into the gateway, as though to speak with him privately. And there, to avenge the blood of his brother Asahel, Joab stabbed him in the stomach, and he died.

[28]Later, when David heard about this, he said, "I and my kingdom are forever innocent before the LORD concerning the blood of Abner son of Ner. [29]May his blood fall upon the head of Joab and upon all his father's house! May Joab's house never be without someone who has a running sore or leprosy[a] or who leans on a crutch or who falls by the sword or who lacks food."

[30](Joab and his brother Abishai murdered Abner because he had killed their brother Asahel in the battle at Gibeon.)

[31]Then David said to Joab and all the people with him, "Tear your clothes and put on sackcloth and walk in mourning in front of Abner." King David himself walked behind the bier. [32]They buried Abner in Hebron, and the king wept aloud at Abner's tomb. All the people wept also.

[33]The king sang this lament for Abner:

"Should Abner have died as the
    lawless die?
[34]   Your hands were not bound,
    your feet were not fettered.
You fell as one falls before wicked
    men."

And all the people wept over him again.

[35]Then they all came and urged David to eat something while it was still day; but David took an oath, saying, "May God deal with me, be it ever so severely, if I taste bread or anything else before the sun sets!"

[36]All the people took note and were pleased; indeed, everything the king did pleased them. [37]So on that day all the people and all Israel knew that the king had no part in the murder of Abner son of Ner.

[38]Then the king said to his men, "Do you not realize that a prince and a great man has fallen in Israel this day? [39]And today, though I am the anointed king, I am weak, and these sons of Zeruiah are too strong for me. May the LORD repay the evildoer according to his evil deeds!"

Ish-Bosheth Murdered

4 When Ish-Bosheth son of Saul heard that Abner had died in Hebron, he lost courage, and all Israel became alarmed. [2]Now Saul's son had two men who were leaders of raiding bands. One was named Baanah and the other Recab; they were sons of Rimmon the Beerothite from the tribe of Benjamin—Beeroth is considered part of Benjamin, [3]because the people of Beeroth fled to Gittaim and have lived there as aliens to this day.

[4](Jonathan son of Saul had a son who was lame in both feet. He was five years

---

[a]29 The Hebrew word was used for various diseases affecting the skin—not necessarily leprosy.

old when the news about Saul and Jonathan came from Jezreel. His nurse picked him up and fled, but as she hurried to leave, he fell and became crippled. His name was Mephibosheth.)

⁵Now Recab and Baanah, the sons of Rimmon the Beerothite, set out for the house of Ish-Bosheth, and they arrived there in the heat of the day while he was taking his noonday rest. ⁶They went into the inner part of the house as if to get some wheat, and they stabbed him in the stomach. Then Recab and his brother Baanah slipped away.

⁷They had gone into the house while he was lying on the bed in his bedroom. After they stabbed and killed him, they cut off his head. Taking it with them, they traveled all night by way of the Arabah. ⁸They brought the head of Ish-Bosheth to David at Hebron and said to the king, "Here is the head of Ish-Bosheth son of Saul, your enemy, who tried to take your life. This day the LORD has avenged my lord the king against Saul and his offspring."

⁹David answered Recab and his brother Baanah, the sons of Rimmon the Beerothite, "As surely as the LORD lives, who has delivered me out of all trouble, ¹⁰when a man told me, 'Saul is dead,' and thought he was bringing good news, I seized him and put him to death in Ziklag. That was the reward I gave him for his news! ¹¹How much more—when wicked men have killed an innocent man in his own house and on his own bed—should I not now demand his blood from your hand and rid the earth of you!"

¹²So David gave an order to his men, and they killed them. They cut off their hands and feet and hung the bodies by the pool in Hebron. But they took the head of Ish-Bosheth and buried it in Abner's tomb at Hebron.

David Becomes King Over Israel

5 All the tribes of Israel came to David at Hebron and said, "We are your own flesh and blood. ²In the past, while Saul was king over us, you were the one who led Israel on their military campaigns. And the LORD said to you, 'You will shepherd my people Israel, and you will become their ruler.'"

³When all the elders of Israel had come to King David at Hebron, the king made a compact with them at Hebron before the LORD, and they anointed David king over Israel.

⁴David was thirty years old when he became king, and he reigned forty years. ⁵In Hebron he reigned over Judah seven years and six months, and in Jerusalem he reigned over all Israel and Judah thirty-three years.

David Conquers Jerusalem

⁶The king and his men marched to Jerusalem to attack the Jebusites, who lived there. The Jebusites said to David, "You will not get in here; even the blind and the lame can ward you off." They thought, "David cannot get in here." ⁷Nevertheless, David captured the fortress of Zion, the City of David.

⁸On that day, David said, "Anyone who conquers the Jebusites will have to use the water shaft*ᵃ* to reach those 'lame and blind' who are David's enemies.*ᵇ*" That is why they say, "The 'blind and lame' will not enter the palace."

⁹David then took up residence in the fortress and called it the City of David. He built up the area around it, from the supporting terraces*ᶜ* inward. ¹⁰And he became more and more powerful, because the LORD God Almighty was with him.

¹¹Now Hiram king of Tyre sent messengers to David, along with cedar logs and carpenters and stonemasons, and they built a palace for David. ¹²And David knew that the LORD had established him as king over Israel and had exalted his kingdom for the sake of his people Israel.

¹³After he left Hebron, David took more concubines and wives in Jerusalem, and more sons and daughters were born to him. ¹⁴These are the names of the children born to him there: Shammua, Shobab, Nathan, Solomon, ¹⁵Ibhar, Elishua, Nepheg, Japhia, ¹⁶Elishama, Eliada and Eliphelet.

David Defeats the Philistines

¹⁷When the Philistines heard that David had been anointed king over Israel, they went up in full force to search for

---

ᵃ8 Or *use scaling hooks*   *ᵇ8* Or *are hated by David*   *ᶜ9* Or *the Millo* him, but David heard about it and went down to the stronghold. [18]Now the Philistines had come and spread out in the Valley of Rephaim; [19]so David inquired of the LORD, "Shall I go and attack the Philistines? Will you hand them over to me?"

The LORD answered him, "Go, for I will surely hand the Philistines over to you."

[20]So David went to Baal Perazim, and there he defeated them. He said, "As waters break out, the LORD has broken out against my enemies before me." So that place was called Baal Perazim.[a] [21]The Philistines abandoned their idols there, and David and his men carried them off.

[22]Once more the Philistines came up and spread out in the Valley of Rephaim;

[a]20 Baal Perazim means the lord who breaks out.

━━{ MONDAY }━

2 SAMUEL 5:17–25

Frozen Experience

5:23 SO DAVID INQUIRED OF THE LORD.

When you pray for guidance in any situation, you wait on God until you know what he wants, then do it. The next time you face the same situation, you repeat what the Lord told you the first time. Right? Wrong. Had David operated on this principle, the second time he met the Philistine army he would have been defeated. The Lord's directive for the first encounter was to attack immediately. For the second encounter, it was to circle around behind the Philistines and hold off the attack until he heard "the sound of marching in the tops of the balsam trees . . . because that will mean the LORD has gone out in front of you to strike the Philistine army" (5:24).

Has God met your needs dramatically in the past like he met David's needs in the first Philistine confrontation? It was a wonderful experience, but was it so wonderful that you have been tempted to freeze that experience and make it the norm for every other experience to come? Frozen experience will keep you from hearing God's voice. Has God been able to speak to you freshly in the present, or has he been shackled to his past dealings with you?

What we should learn from the past guidance is that God is faithful, not that he always has the same way of dealing with the same situation every time. The fact is, no situation is ever exactly like its predecessor. Besides, even if the situation were to be the same, we are now different. The permutations could go on and on. Things change; we change; only God doesn't change. But he is infinitely able to address every change that occurs in our lives.

What we need to know in every situation is what God promised David: "The LORD has gone out in front of you." That's what guidance is; it's not a map to read—it's a leader to stay close to and follow. Then we not only get to where we need to be, but we enjoy the pleasure of his company.

PRAY:

Dear Father, if you aren't in front of me, I don't want to go!
Help me to hear a fresh word from you.

———

FOR YOUR NEXT DEVOTIONAL READING, GO TO PAGE 352.

²³so David inquired of the LORD, and he answered, "Do not go straight up, but circle around behind them and attack them in front of the balsam trees. ²⁴As soon as you hear the sound of marching in the tops of the balsam trees, move quickly, because that will mean the LORD has gone out in front of you to strike the Philistine army." ²⁵So David did as the LORD commanded him, and he struck down the Philistines all the way from Gibeon*a* to Gezer.

The Ark Brought to Jerusalem

6 David again brought together out of Israel chosen men, thirty thousand in all. ²He and all his men set out from Baalah of Judah*b* to bring up from there the ark of God, which is called by the Name,*c* the name of the LORD Almighty, who is enthroned between the cherubim that are on the ark. ³They set the ark of God on a new cart and brought it from the house of Abinadab, which was on the hill. Uzzah and Ahio, sons of Abinadab, were guiding the new cart ⁴with the ark of God on it,*d* and Ahio was walking in front of it. ⁵David and the whole house of Israel were celebrating with all their might before the LORD, with songs*e* and with harps, lyres, tambourines, sistrums and cymbals.

⁶When they came to the threshing floor of Nacon, Uzzah reached out and took hold of the ark of God, because the oxen stumbled. ⁷The LORD's anger burned against Uzzah because of his irreverent act; therefore God struck him down and he died there beside the ark of God.

⁸Then David was angry because the LORD's wrath had broken out against Uzzah, and to this day that place is called Perez Uzzah.*f*

⁹David was afraid of the LORD that day and said, "How can the ark of the LORD ever come to me?" ¹⁰He was not willing to take the ark of the LORD to be with him in the City of David. Instead, he took it aside to the house of Obed-Edom the Gittite. ¹¹The ark of the LORD remained in the house of Obed-Edom the Gittite for three months, and the LORD blessed him and his entire household.

¹²Now King David was told, "The LORD has blessed the household of Obed-Edom and everything he has, because of the ark of God." So David went down and brought up the ark of God from the house of Obed-Edom to the City of David with rejoicing. ¹³When those who were carrying the ark of the LORD had taken six steps, he sacrificed a bull and a fattened calf. ¹⁴David, wearing a linen ephod, danced before the LORD with all his might, ¹⁵while he and the entire house of Israel brought up the ark of the LORD with shouts and the sound of trumpets.

¹⁶As the ark of the LORD was entering the City of David, Michal daughter of Saul watched from a window. And when she saw King David leaping and dancing before the LORD, she despised him in her heart.

¹⁷They brought the ark of the LORD and set it in its place inside the tent that David had pitched for it, and David sacrificed burnt offerings and fellowship offerings*g* before the LORD. ¹⁸After he had finished sacrificing the burnt offerings and fellowship offerings, he blessed the people in the name of the LORD Almighty. ¹⁹Then he gave a loaf of bread, a cake of dates and a cake of raisins to each person in the whole crowd of Israelites, both men and women. And all the people went to their homes.

²⁰When David returned home to bless his household, Michal daughter of Saul came out to meet him and said, "How the king of Israel has distinguished himself today, disrobing in the sight of the slave girls of his servants as any vulgar fellow would!"

²¹David said to Michal, "It was before the LORD, who chose me rather than your father or anyone from his house when he appointed me ruler over the LORD's people Israel—I will celebrate before the

---

a25 Septuagint (see also 1 Chron. 14:16); Hebrew *Geba*   *b2* That is, Kiriath Jearim; Hebrew *Baale Judah*, a variant of *Baalah of Judah*
c2 Hebrew; Septuagint and Vulgate do not have the *Name*.   *d3,4* Dead Sea Scrolls and some Septuagint manuscripts; Masoretic Text *cart* *4and they brought it with the ark of God from the house of Abinadab, which was on the hill*
e5 See Dead Sea Scrolls, Septuagint and 1 Chronicles 13:8; Masoretic Text *celebrating before the LORD with all kinds of instruments made of pine.*   *18 Perez Uzzah* means *outbreak against Uzzah.*   *g17* Traditionally *peace offerings*; also in verse 18

LORD. 22I will become even more undignified than this, and I will be humiliated in my own eyes. But by these slave girls you spoke of, I will be held in honor."

23And Michal daughter of Saul had no children to the day of her death.

God's Promise to David

7 After the king was settled in his palace and the LORD had given him rest from all his enemies around him, 2he said to Nathan the prophet, "Here I am, living in a palace of cedar, while the ark of God remains in a tent."

3Nathan replied to the king, "Whatever you have in mind, go ahead and do it, for the LORD is with you."

4That night the word of the LORD came to Nathan, saying:

5"Go and tell my servant David, 'This is what the LORD says: Are you the one to build me a house to dwell in? 6I have not dwelt in a house from the day I brought the Israelites up out of Egypt to this day. I have been moving from place to place with a tent as my dwelling. 7Wherever I have moved with all the Israelites, did I ever say to any of their rulers whom I commanded to shepherd my people Israel, "Why have you not built me a house of cedar?"'

8"Now then, tell my servant David, 'This is what the LORD Almighty says: I took you from the pasture and from following the flock to be ruler over my people Israel. 9I have been with you wherever you have gone, and I have cut off all your enemies from before you. Now I will make your name great, like the names of the greatest men of the earth. 10And I will provide a place for my people Israel and will plant them so that they can have a home of their own and no longer be disturbed. Wicked people will not oppress them anymore, as they did at the beginning 11and have done ever since the time I appointed leaders[a] over my people Israel. I will also give you rest from all your enemies.

"'The LORD declares to you that the LORD himself will establish a house for you: 12When your days are over and you rest with your fathers, I will raise up your offspring to succeed you, who will come from your own body, and I will establish his kingdom. 13He is the one who will build a house for my Name, and I will establish the throne of his kingdom forever. 14I will be his father, and he will be my son. When he does wrong, I will punish him with the rod of men, with floggings inflicted by men. 15But my love will never be taken away from him, as I took it away from Saul, whom I removed from before you. 16Your house and your kingdom will endure forever before me[b]; your throne will be established forever.'"

17Nathan reported to David all the words of this entire revelation.

David's Prayer

18Then King David went in and sat before the LORD, and he said:

"Who am I, O Sovereign LORD, and what is my family, that you have brought me this far? 19And as if this were not enough in your sight, O Sovereign LORD, you have also spoken about the future of the house of your servant. Is this your usual way of dealing with man, O Sovereign LORD?

20"What more can David say to you? For you know your servant, O Sovereign LORD. 21For the sake of your word and according to your will, you have done this great thing and made it known to your servant.

22"How great you are, O Sovereign LORD! There is no one like you, and there is no God but you, as we have heard with our own ears. 23And who is like your people Israel—the one nation on earth that God went out to redeem as a people for himself, and to make a name for himself, and to perform great and awesome wonders by driving out nations and their gods from before your people, whom

[a]11 Traditionally *judges*   [b]16 Some Hebrew manuscripts and Septuagint; most Hebrew manuscripts *you*

you redeemed from Egypt?[a] 24You have established your people Israel as your very own forever, and you, O Lord, have become their God.

25"And now, Lord God, keep forever the promise you have made concerning your servant and his house. Do as you promised, 26so that your name will be great forever. Then men will say, 'The Lord Almighty is God over Israel!' And the house of your servant David will be established before you.

27"O Lord Almighty, God of Israel, you have revealed this to your servant, saying, 'I will build a house for you.' So your servant has found courage to offer you this prayer. 28O Sovereign Lord, you are God! Your words are trustworthy, and you have promised these good things to your servant. 29Now be pleased to

[a]23 See Septuagint and 1 Chron. 17:21; Hebrew *wonders for your land and before your people, whom you redeemed from Egypt, from the nations and their gods.*

---

2 SAMUEL 7:18–29

[**TUESDAY**]

Open My Eyes, Lord

7:18 "WHO AM I ... THAT YOU HAVE BROUGHT ME THIS FAR?"

Open your eyes to God's goodness, and if you cannot say, "Who am I ... that you have brought me this far?" then open them wider. Or pray God will make you aware of his mercies. Surely this is what Jesus had in mind when he said we must become like children to enter the kingdom of God. Annie Dillard writes:

> An infant who has just learned to hold his head up has a frank and forthright way of gazing about him in bewilderment. He hasn't the faintest clue where he is, and he aims to learn. In a couple of years, what he will have learned instead is how to fake it: He'll have the cocksure air of a squatter who has come to feel he owns the place. Some unwonted, taught pride diverts us from our original intent, which is to explore the neighborhood, view the landscape, to discover where it is we have been so startlingly set down, if we can't learn why.[1]

"Who am I?" Don't fake it. Be startled. Can you hear the surprise in the question? "It didn't have to be this good, in fact it wasn't and shouldn't have been this good. But it is. I blush at the extravagance of what you have given me, Lord." David will be a king with an eternal dynasty. So will you, only better. If you are in Christ, your sins are forgiven, and he promised, "To him who overcomes and does my will to the end, I will give authority over the nations ... To him who overcomes, I will give the right to sit with me on my throne" (Revelation 2:26; 3:21). Are you surprised at that? Good! Can you say it now? "Who am I?"

PRAY:

Open the eyes of my heart, Lord. I want to see you, and myself, that I may rejoice with wonder and surprise.

FOR YOUR NEXT DEVOTIONAL READING, GO TO PAGE 357.

bless the house of your servant, that it may continue forever in your sight; for you, O Sovereign LORD, have spoken, and with your blessing the house of your servant will be blessed forever."

David's Victories

8 In the course of time, David defeated the Philistines and subdued them, and he took Metheg Ammah from the control of the Philistines.

²David also defeated the Moabites. He made them lie down on the ground and measured them off with a length of cord. Every two lengths of them were put to death, and the third length was allowed to live. So the Moabites became subject to David and brought tribute.

³Moreover, David fought Hadadezer son of Rehob, king of Zobah, when he went to restore his control along the Euphrates River. ⁴David captured a thousand of his chariots, seven thousand charioteers[a] and twenty thousand foot soldiers. He hamstrung all but a hundred of the chariot horses.

⁵When the Arameans of Damascus came to help Hadadezer king of Zobah, David struck down twenty-two thousand of them. ⁶He put garrisons in the Aramean kingdom of Damascus, and the Arameans became subject to him and brought tribute. The LORD gave David victory wherever he went.

⁷David took the gold shields that belonged to the officers of Hadadezer and brought them to Jerusalem. ⁸From Tebah[b] and Berothai, towns that belonged to Hadadezer, King David took a great quantity of bronze.

⁹When Tou[c] king of Hamath heard that David had defeated the entire army of Hadadezer, ¹⁰he sent his son Joram[d] to King David to greet him and congratulate him on his victory in battle over Hadadezer, who had been at war with Tou. Joram brought with him articles of silver and gold and bronze.

¹¹King David dedicated these articles to the LORD, as he had done with the silver and gold from all the nations he had subdued: ¹²Edom[e] and Moab, the Ammonites and the Philistines, and Amalek. He also dedicated the plunder taken

from Hadadezer son of Rehob, king of Zobah.

¹³And David became famous after he returned from striking down eighteen thousand Edomites[f] in the Valley of Salt.

¹⁴He put garrisons throughout Edom, and all the Edomites became subject to David. The LORD gave David victory wherever he went.

David's Officials

¹⁵David reigned over all Israel, doing what was just and right for all his people. ¹⁶Joab son of Zeruiah was over the army; Jehoshaphat son of Ahilud was recorder; ¹⁷Zadok son of Ahitub and Ahimelech son of Abiathar were priests; Seraiah was secretary; ¹⁸Benaiah son of Jehoiada was over the Kerethites and Pelethites; and David's sons were royal advisers.[g]

David and Mephibosheth

9 David asked, "Is there anyone still left of the house of Saul to whom I can show kindness for Jonathan's sake?"

²Now there was a servant of Saul's household named Ziba. They called him to appear before David, and the king said to him, "Are you Ziba?"

"Your servant," he replied.

³The king asked, "Is there no one still left of the house of Saul to whom I can show God's kindness?"

Ziba answered the king, "There is still a son of Jonathan; he is crippled in both feet."

⁴"Where is he?" the king asked.

Ziba answered, "He is at the house of Makir son of Ammiel in Lo Debar."

⁵So King David had him brought from Lo Debar, from the house of Makir son of Ammiel.

⁶When Mephibosheth son of Jonathan, the son of Saul, came to David, he bowed down to pay him honor.

---

[a]4 Septuagint (see also Dead Sea Scrolls and 1 Chron. 18:4); Masoretic Text *captured seventeen hundred of his charioteers*   [b]8 See some Septuagint manuscripts (see also 1 Chron. 18:8); Hebrew *Betah*.   [c]9 Hebrew *Toi*, a variant of *Tou*; also in verse 10   [d]10 A variant of *Hadoram*   [e]12 Some Hebrew manuscripts, Septuagint and Syriac (see also 1 Chron. 18:11); most Hebrew manuscripts *Aram*   [f]13 A few Hebrew manuscripts, Septuagint and Syriac (see also 1 Chron. 18:12); most Hebrew manuscripts *Aram* (that is, Arameans)   [g]18 Or *were priests*

David said, "Mephibosheth!"

"Your servant," he replied.

⁷"Don't be afraid," David said to him, "for I will surely show you kindness for the sake of your father Jonathan. I will restore to you all the land that belonged to your grandfather Saul, and you will always eat at my table."

⁸Mephibosheth bowed down and said, "What is your servant, that you should notice a dead dog like me?"

⁹Then the king summoned Ziba, Saul's servant, and said to him, "I have given your master's grandson everything that belonged to Saul and his family. ¹⁰You and your sons and your servants are to farm the land for him and bring in the crops, so that your master's grandson may be provided for. And Mephibosheth, grandson of your master, will always eat at my table." (Now Ziba had fifteen sons and twenty servants.)

¹¹Then Ziba said to the king, "Your servant will do whatever my lord the king commands his servant to do." So Mephibosheth ate at David's*ᵃ* table like one of the king's sons.

¹²Mephibosheth had a young son named Mica, and all the members of Ziba's household were servants of Mephibosheth. ¹³And Mephibosheth lived in Jerusalem, because he always ate at the king's table, and he was crippled in both feet.

David Defeats the Ammonites

10 In the course of time, the king of the Ammonites died, and his son Hanun succeeded him as king. ²David thought, "I will show kindness to Hanun son of Nahash, just as his father showed kindness to me." So David sent a delegation to express his sympathy to Hanun concerning his father.

When David's men came to the land of the Ammonites, ³the Ammonite nobles said to Hanun their lord, "Do you think David is honoring your father by sending men to you to express sympathy? Hasn't David sent them to you to explore the city and spy it out and overthrow it?" ⁴So Hanun seized David's men, shaved off half of each man's beard, cut off their garments in the middle at the buttocks, and sent them away.

⁵When David was told about this, he sent messengers to meet the men, for they were greatly humiliated. The king said, "Stay at Jericho till your beards have grown, and then come back."

⁶When the Ammonites realized that they had become a stench in David's nostrils, they hired twenty thousand Aramean foot soldiers from Beth Rehob and Zobah, as well as the king of Maacah with a thousand men, and also twelve thousand men from Tob.

⁷On hearing this, David sent Joab out with the entire army of fighting men. ⁸The Ammonites came out and drew up in battle formation at the entrance to their city gate, while the Arameans of Zobah and Rehob and the men of Tob and Maacah were by themselves in the open country.

⁹Joab saw that there were battle lines in front of him and behind him; so he selected some of the best troops in Israel and deployed them against the Arameans. ¹⁰He put the rest of the men under the command of Abishai his brother and deployed them against the Ammonites. ¹¹Joab said, "If the Arameans are too strong for me, then you are to come to my rescue; but if the Ammonites are too strong for you, then I will come to rescue you. ¹²Be strong and let us fight bravely for our people and the cities of our God. The LORD will do what is good in his sight."

¹³Then Joab and the troops with him advanced to fight the Arameans, and they fled before him. ¹⁴When the Ammonites saw that the Arameans were fleeing, they fled before Abishai and went inside the city. So Joab returned from fighting the Ammonites and came to Jerusalem.

¹⁵After the Arameans saw that they had been routed by Israel, they regrouped. ¹⁶Hadadezer had Arameans brought from beyond the River*ᵇ*; they went to Helam, with Shobach the commander of Hadadezer's army leading them.

¹⁷When David was told of this, he gathered all Israel, crossed the Jordan and

ᵃ11 Septuagint; Hebrew *my*   *ᵇ16* That is, the Euphrates

went to Helam. The Arameans formed their battle lines to meet David and fought against him. [18]But they fled before Israel, and David killed seven hundred of their charioteers and forty thousand of their foot soldiers.[a] He also struck down Shobach the commander of their army, and he died there. [19]When all the kings who were vassals of Hadadezer saw that they had been defeated by Israel, they made peace with the Israelites and became subject to them.

So the Arameans were afraid to help the Ammonites anymore.

David and Bathsheba

11 In the spring, at the time when kings go off to war, David sent Joab out with the king's men and the whole Israelite army. They destroyed the Ammonites and besieged Rabbah. But David remained in Jerusalem.

[2]One evening David got up from his bed and walked around on the roof of the palace. From the roof he saw a woman bathing. The woman was very beautiful, [3]and David sent someone to find out about her. The man said, "Isn't this Bathsheba, the daughter of Eliam and the wife of Uriah the Hittite?" [4]Then David sent messengers to get her. She came to him, and he slept with her. (She had purified herself from her uncleanness.) Then[b] she went back home. [5]The woman conceived and sent word to David, saying, "I am pregnant."

[6]So David sent this word to Joab: "Send me Uriah the Hittite." And Joab sent him to David. [7]When Uriah came to him, David asked him how Joab was, how the soldiers were and how the war was going. [8]Then David said to Uriah, "Go down to your house and wash your feet." So Uriah left the palace, and a gift from the king was sent after him. [9]But Uriah slept at the entrance to the palace with all his master's servants and did not go down to his house.

[10]When David was told, "Uriah did not go home," he asked him, "Haven't you just come from a distance? Why didn't you go home?"

[11]Uriah said to David, "The ark and Israel and Judah are staying in tents, and my master Joab and my lord's men are camped in the open fields. How could I go to my house to eat and drink and lie with my wife? As surely as you live, I will not do such a thing!"

[12]Then David said to him, "Stay here one more day, and tomorrow I will send you back." So Uriah remained in Jerusalem that day and the next. [13]At David's invitation, he ate and drank with him, and David made him drunk. But in the evening Uriah went out to sleep on his mat among his master's servants; he did not go home.

[14]In the morning David wrote a letter to Joab and sent it with Uriah. [15]In it he wrote, "Put Uriah in the front line where the fighting is fiercest. Then withdraw from him so he will be struck down and die."

[16]So while Joab had the city under siege, he put Uriah at a place where he knew the strongest defenders were. [17]When the men of the city came out and fought against Joab, some of the men in David's army fell; moreover, Uriah the Hittite died.

[18]Joab sent David a full account of the battle. [19]He instructed the messenger: "When you have finished giving the king this account of the battle, [20]the king's anger may flare up, and he may ask you, 'Why did you get so close to the city to fight? Didn't you know they would shoot arrows from the wall? [21]Who killed Abimelech son of Jerub-Besheth[c]? Didn't a woman throw an upper millstone on him from the wall, so that he died in Thebez? Why did you get so close to the wall?' If he asks you this, then say to him, 'Also, your servant Uriah the Hittite is dead.'"

[22]The messenger set out, and when he arrived he told David everything Joab had sent him to say. [23]The messenger said to David, "The men overpowered us and came out against us in the open, but we drove them back to the entrance to the city gate. [24]Then the archers shot arrows at your servants from the wall, and some of the king's men died. Moreover, your servant Uriah the Hittite is dead."

---

[a]18 Some Septuagint manuscripts (see also 1 Chron. 19:18); Hebrew *horsemen*   [b]4 Or *with her. When she purified herself from her uncleanness,*   [c]21 Also known as *Jerub-Baal* (that is, Gideon)

25David told the messenger, "Say this to Joab: 'Don't let this upset you; the sword devours one as well as another. Press the attack against the city and destroy it.' Say this to encourage Joab." 26When Uriah's wife heard that her husband was dead, she mourned for him. 27After the time of mourning was over, David had her brought to his house, and she became his wife and bore him a son. But the thing David had done displeased the LORD.

Nathan Rebukes David

12 The LORD sent Nathan to David. When he came to him, he said, "There were two men in a certain town, one rich and the other poor. 2The rich man had a very large number of sheep and cattle, 3but the poor man had nothing except one little ewe lamb he had bought. He raised it, and it grew up with him and his children. It shared his food, drank from his cup and even slept in his arms. It was like a daughter to him.

4"Now a traveler came to the rich man, but the rich man refrained from taking one of his own sheep or cattle to prepare a meal for the traveler who had come to him. Instead, he took the ewe lamb that belonged to the poor man and prepared it for the one who had come to him."

5David burned with anger against the man and said to Nathan, "As surely as the LORD lives, the man who did this deserves to die! 6He must pay for that lamb four times over, because he did such a thing and had no pity."

7Then Nathan said to David, "You are the man! This is what the LORD, the God of Israel, says: 'I anointed you king over Israel, and I delivered you from the hand of Saul. 8I gave your master's house to you, and your master's wives into your arms. I gave you the house of Israel and Judah. And if all this had been too little, I would have given you even more. 9Why did you despise the word of the LORD by doing what is evil in his eyes? You struck down Uriah the Hittite with the sword and took his wife to be your own. You killed him with the sword of the Ammonites. 10Now, therefore, the sword will never depart from your house, because you despised me and took the wife of Uriah the Hittite to be your own.'

11"This is what the LORD says: 'Out of your own household I am going to bring calamity upon you. Before your very eyes I will take your wives and give them to one who is close to you, and he will lie with your wives in broad daylight. 12You did it in secret, but I will do this thing in broad daylight before all Israel.'"

13Then David said to Nathan, "I have sinned against the LORD."

Nathan replied, "The LORD has taken away your sin. You are not going to die. 14But because by doing this you have made the enemies of the LORD show utter contempt,a the son born to you will die."

15After Nathan had gone home, the LORD struck the child that Uriah's wife had borne to David, and he became ill. 16David pleaded with God for the child. He fasted and went into his house and spent the nights lying on the ground. 17The elders of his household stood beside him to get him up from the ground, but he refused, and he would not eat any food with them.

> DAVID pleaded with God for the child. He fasted and went into his house and spent the nights lying on the ground.
>
> 2 SAMUEL 12:16

18On the seventh day the child died. David's servants were afraid to tell him that the child was dead, for they thought, "While the child was still living, we spoke to David but he would not listen to us. How can we tell him the child is dead? He may do something desperate."

19David noticed that his servants were whispering among themselves and he realized the child was dead. "Is the child dead?" he asked.

"Yes," they replied, "he is dead."

20Then David got up from the ground. After he had washed, put on lotions and changed his clothes, he went into the

---

a14 Masoretic Text; an ancient Hebrew scribal tradition *this you have shown utter contempt for the LORD*

house of the LORD and worshiped. Then he went to his own house, and at his request they served him food, and he ate. ²¹His servants asked him, "Why are you acting this way? While the child was alive, you fasted and wept, but now that the child is dead, you get up and eat!"

²²He answered, "While the child was still alive, I fasted and wept. I thought, 'Who knows? The LORD may be gracious to me and let the child live.' ²³But now that he is dead, why should I fast? Can I bring him back again? I will go to him, but he will not return to me."

---

2 SAMUEL 12

When Our Eyes Are Opened

12:13 "I HAVE SINNED AGAINST THE LORD."

A Russian proverb states: "Nothing ages faster than gratitude." David has aged considerably in the time that elapsed between his grateful prayer in chapter 7 and the prayer he prays in chapter 12: "I have sinned against the LORD" (verse 13). The man who slept with another man's wife and connived to murder him (see chapter 11) is hardly grateful at this point.

Blindness to God's mercies will blind us to our sin. "We have two sets of names for vices," said the British preacher Alexander Maclaren, "one set which rather mitigates and excuses them, and another set which puts them in their real hideousness." We use the mitigating vocabulary for our sin, the hideous vocabulary for other people's sin. Nathan had to enrage David about "another man's sin" to make David see the gravity of his own. True repentance comes only when our eyes are opened, as David's were. Though the route to his sight was indirect, the effect was powerful.

What did David see? He saw his sin as detestable and mean. A rich man with everything had plundered a poor man with little. He saw what he deserved for his sin: death. He even pronounced his own sentence when he said, "As surely as the LORD lives, the man who did this deserves to die" (verse 5)! Greatest of all, he saw the evil of his sin against God against the backdrop of God's goodness toward him: "This is what the LORD, the God of Israel, says: 'I anointed you king over Israel, and I delivered you from the hand of Saul. I gave you your master's house to you, and your master's wives into your arms. I gave you the house of Israel and Judah. And if all this had been too little, I would have given you even more. Why did you despise the word of the LORD by doing what is evil in his eyes?'" (verses 7–9). God said he would have done even more for David if David had only asked. David's sin was many things, but perhaps worst of all it was cold ingratitude.

"All have sinned and fall short of the glory of God" (Romans 3:23). We would profit to see what David saw regarding our own sin. There is only one way to reverse the ingratitude that leads to sin: It is to be grateful for the great mercy that forgives great sin.

PRAY:

Merciful God, though the thought is terrifying, let me see the greatness of my sin, that I may praise you for the greatness of your forgiveness.

FOR YOUR NEXT DEVOTIONAL READING, GO TO PAGE 371.

²⁴Then David comforted his wife Bathsheba, and he went to her and lay with her. She gave birth to a son, and they named him Solomon. The LORD loved him; ²⁵and because the LORD loved him, he sent word through Nathan the prophet to name him Jedidiah.ᵃ

²⁶Meanwhile Joab fought against Rabbah of the Ammonites and captured the royal citadel. ²⁷Joab then sent messengers to David, saying, "I have fought against Rabbah and taken its water supply. ²⁸Now muster the rest of the troops and besiege the city and capture it. Otherwise I will take the city, and it will be named after me."

²⁹So David mustered the entire army and went to Rabbah, and attacked and captured it. ³⁰He took the crown from the head of their kingᵇ—its weight was a talentᶜ of gold, and it was set with precious stones—and it was placed on David's head. He took a great quantity of plunder from the city ³¹and brought out the people who were there, consigning them to labor with saws and with iron picks and axes, and he made them work at brickmaking.ᵈ He did this to all the Ammonite towns. Then David and his entire army returned to Jerusalem.

Amnon and Tamar

13 In the course of time, Amnon son of David fell in love with Tamar, the beautiful sister of Absalom son of David.

²Amnon became frustrated to the point of illness on account of his sister Tamar, for she was a virgin, and it seemed impossible for him to do anything to her.

³Now Amnon had a friend named Jonadab son of Shimeah, David's brother. Jonadab was a very shrewd man. ⁴He asked Amnon, "Why do you, the king's son, look so haggard morning after morning? Won't you tell me?"

Amnon said to him, "I'm in love with Tamar, my brother Absalom's sister."

⁵"Go to bed and pretend to be ill," Jonadab said. "When your father comes to see you, say to him, 'I would like my sister Tamar to come and give me something to eat. Let her prepare the food in my sight so I may watch her and then eat it from her hand.'"

⁶So Amnon lay down and pretended to be ill. When the king came to see him, Amnon said to him, "I would like my sister Tamar to come and make some special bread in my sight, so I may eat from her hand."

⁷David sent word to Tamar at the palace: "Go to the house of your brother Amnon and prepare some food for him." ⁸So Tamar went to the house of her brother Amnon, who was lying down. She took some dough, kneaded it, made the bread in his sight and baked it. ⁹Then she took the pan and served him the bread, but he refused to eat.

"Send everyone out of here," Amnon said. So everyone left him. ¹⁰Then Amnon said to Tamar, "Bring the food here into my bedroom so I may eat from your hand." And Tamar took the bread she had prepared and brought it to her brother Amnon in his bedroom. ¹¹But when she took it to him to eat, he grabbed her and said, "Come to bed with me, my sister."

¹²"Don't, my brother!" she said to him. "Don't force me. Such a thing should not be done in Israel! Don't do this wicked thing. ¹³What about me? Where could I get rid of my disgrace? And what about you? You would be like one of the wicked fools in Israel. Please speak to the king; he will not keep me from being married to you." ¹⁴But he refused to listen to her, and since he was stronger than she, he raped her.

¹⁵Then Amnon hated her with intense hatred. In fact, he hated her more than he had loved her. Amnon said to her, "Get up and get out!"

¹⁶"No!" she said to him. "Sending me away would be a greater wrong than what you have already done to me."

But he refused to listen to her. ¹⁷He called his personal servant and said, "Get this woman out of here and bolt the door after her." ¹⁸So his servant put her out and bolted the door after her. She was wearing a richly ornamentedᵉ robe, for this was the kind of garment the vir-

---

ᵃ25 *Jedidiah* means *loved by the* LORD.
ᵇ30 Or *of Milcom* (that is, Molech)   ᶜ30 That is, about 75 pounds (about 34 kilograms)
ᵈ31 The meaning of the Hebrew for this clause is uncertain.   ᵉ18 The meaning of the Hebrew for this phrase is uncertain.

gin daughters of the king wore. [19]Tamar put ashes on her head and tore the ornamented[a] robe she was wearing. She put her hand on her head and went away, weeping aloud as she went.

[20]Her brother Absalom said to her, "Has that Amnon, your brother, been with you? Be quiet now, my sister; he is your brother. Don't take this thing to heart." And Tamar lived in her brother Absalom's house, a desolate woman.

[21]When King David heard all this, he was furious. [22]Absalom never said a word to Amnon, either good or bad; he hated Amnon because he had disgraced his sister Tamar.

Absalom Kills Amnon

[23]Two years later, when Absalom's sheepshearers were at Baal Hazor near the border of Ephraim, he invited all the king's sons to come there. [24]Absalom went to the king and said, "Your servant has had shearers come. Will the king and his officials please join me?"

[25]"No, my son," the king replied. "All of us should not go; we would only be a burden to you." Although Absalom urged him, he still refused to go, but gave him his blessing.

[26]Then Absalom said, "If not, please let my brother Amnon come with us."

The king asked him, "Why should he go with you?" [27]But Absalom urged him, so he sent with him Amnon and the rest of the king's sons.

[28]Absalom ordered his men, "Listen! When Amnon is in high spirits from drinking wine and I say to you, 'Strike Amnon down,' then kill him. Don't be afraid. Have not I given you this order? Be strong and brave." [29]So Absalom's men did to Amnon what Absalom had ordered. Then all the king's sons got up, mounted their mules and fled.

[30]While they were on their way, the report came to David: "Absalom has struck down all the king's sons; not one of them is left." [31]The king stood up, tore his clothes and lay down on the ground; and all his servants stood by with their clothes torn.

[32]But Jonadab son of Shimeah, David's brother, said, "My lord should not think that they killed all the princes; only Am-non is dead. This has been Absalom's expressed intention ever since the day Amnon raped his sister Tamar. [33]My lord the king should not be concerned about the report that all the king's sons are dead. Only Amnon is dead."

[34]Meanwhile, Absalom had fled.

Now the man standing watch looked up and saw many people on the road west of him, coming down the side of the hill. The watchman went and told the king, "I see men in the direction of Horonaim, on the side of the hill."[b]

[35]Jonadab said to the king, "See, the king's sons are here; it has happened just as your servant said."

[36]As he finished speaking, the king's sons came in, wailing loudly. The king, too, and all his servants wept very bitterly.

[37]Absalom fled and went to Talmai son of Ammihud, the king of Geshur. But King David mourned for his son every day.

[38]After Absalom fled and went to Geshur, he stayed there three years. [39]And the spirit of the king[c] longed to go to Absalom, for he was consoled concerning Amnon's death.

Absalom Returns to Jerusalem

14 Joab son of Zeruiah knew that the king's heart longed for Absalom. [2]So Joab sent someone to Tekoa and had a wise woman brought from there. He said to her, "Pretend you are in mourning. Dress in mourning clothes, and don't use any cosmetic lotions. Act like a woman who has spent many days grieving for the dead. [3]Then go to the king and speak these words to him." And Joab put the words in her mouth.

[4]When the woman from Tekoa went[d] to the king, she fell with her face to the ground to pay him honor, and she said, "Help me, O king!"

[5]The king asked her, "What is troubling you?"

---

[a]19 The meaning of the Hebrew for this word is uncertain.   [b]34 Septuagint; Hebrew does not have this sentence.   [c]39 Dead Sea Scrolls and some Septuagint manuscripts; Masoretic Text *But the spirit of, David the king*   [d]4 Many Hebrew manuscripts, Septuagint, Vulgate and Syriac; most Hebrew manuscripts *spoke*

She said, "I am indeed a widow; my husband is dead. 6I your servant had two sons. They got into a fight with each other in the field, and no one was there to separate them. One struck the other and killed him. 7Now the whole clan has risen up against your servant; they say, 'Hand over the one who struck his brother down, so that we may put him to death for the life of his brother whom he killed; then we will get rid of the heir as well.' They would put out the only burning coal I have left, leaving my husband neither name nor descendant on the face of the earth."

8The king said to the woman, "Go home, and I will issue an order in your behalf."

9But the woman from Tekoa said to him, "My lord the king, let the blame rest on me and on my father's family, and let the king and his throne be without guilt."

10The king replied, "If anyone says anything to you, bring him to me, and he will not bother you again."

11She said, "Then let the king invoke the LORD his God to prevent the avenger of blood from adding to the destruction, so that my son will not be destroyed."

"As surely as the LORD lives," he said, "not one hair of your son's head will fall to the ground."

12Then the woman said, "Let your servant speak a word to my lord the king."

"Speak," he replied.

13The woman said, "Why then have you devised a thing like this against the people of God? When the king says this, does he not convict himself, for the king has not brought back his banished son? 14Like water spilled on the ground, which cannot be recovered, so we must die. But God does not take away life; instead, he devises ways so that a banished person may not remain estranged from him.

15"And now I have come to say this to my lord the king because the people have made me afraid. Your servant thought, 'I will speak to the king; perhaps he will do what his servant asks. 16Perhaps the king will agree to deliver his servant from the hand of the man who is trying to cut off both me and my son from the inheritance God gave us.'

17"And now your servant says, 'May the word of my lord the king bring me rest, for my lord the king is like an angel of God in discerning good and evil. May the LORD your God be with you.'"

18Then the king said to the woman, "Do not keep from me the answer to what I am going to ask you."

"Let my lord the king speak," the woman said.

19The king asked, "Isn't the hand of Joab with you in all this?"

The woman answered, "As surely as you live, my lord the king, no one can turn to the right or to the left from anything my lord the king says. Yes, it was your servant Joab who instructed me to do this and who put all these words into the mouth of your servant. 20Your servant Joab did this to change the present situation. My lord has wisdom like that of an angel of God—he knows everything that happens in the land."

21The king said to Joab, "Very well, I will do it. Go, bring back the young man Absalom."

22Joab fell with his face to the ground to pay him honor, and he blessed the king. Joab said, "Today your servant knows that he has found favor in your eyes, my lord the king, because the king has granted his servant's request."

23Then Joab went to Geshur and brought Absalom back to Jerusalem. 24But the king said, "He must go to his own house; he must not see my face." So Absalom went to his own house and did not see the face of the king.

25In all Israel there was not a man so highly praised for his handsome appearance as Absalom. From the top of his head to the sole of his foot there was no blemish in him. 26Whenever he cut the hair of his head—he used to cut his hair from time to time when it became too heavy for him—he would weigh it, and its weight was two hundred shekels[a] by the royal standard.

²⁷Three sons and a daughter were born to Absalom. The daughter's name was Tamar, and she became a beautiful woman.

²⁸Absalom lived two years in Jerusalem without seeing the king's face. ²⁹Then Absalom sent for Joab in order to send him to the king, but Joab refused to come to him. So he sent a second time, but he refused to come. ³⁰Then he said to his servants, "Look, Joab's field is next to mine, and he has barley there. Go and set it on fire." So Absalom's servants set the field on fire.

³¹Then Joab did go to Absalom's house and he said to him, "Why have your servants set my field on fire?"

³²Absalom said to Joab, "Look, I sent word to you and said, 'Come here so I can send you to the king to ask, "Why have I come from Geshur? It would be better for me if I were still there!"' Now then, I want to see the king's face, and if I am guilty of anything, let him put me to death."

³³So Joab went to the king and told him this. Then the king summoned Absalom, and he came in and bowed down with his face to the ground before the king. And the king kissed Absalom.

Absalom's Conspiracy

15 In the course of time, Absalom provided himself with a chariot and horses and with fifty men to run ahead of him. ²He would get up early and stand by the side of the road leading to the city gate. Whenever anyone came with a complaint to be placed before the king for a decision, Absalom would call out to him, "What town are you from?" He would answer, "Your servant is from one of the tribes of Israel." ³Then Absalom would say to him, "Look, your claims are valid and proper, but there is no representative of the king to hear you." ⁴And Absalom would add, "If only I were appointed judge in the land! Then everyone who has a complaint or case could come to me and I would see that he gets justice."

⁵Also, whenever anyone approached him to bow down before him, Absalom would reach out his hand, take hold of

him and kiss him. ⁶Absalom behaved in this way toward all the Israelites who came to the king asking for justice, and so he stole the hearts of the men of Israel.

⁷At the end of four[b] years, Absalom said to the king, "Let me go to Hebron and fulfill a vow I made to the Lord. ⁸While your servant was living at Geshur in Aram, I made this vow: 'If the Lord takes me back to Jerusalem, I will worship the Lord in Hebron.[c]'"

⁹The king said to him, "Go in peace." So he went to Hebron.

¹⁰Then Absalom sent secret messengers throughout the tribes of Israel to say, "As soon as you hear the sound of the trumpets, then say, 'Absalom is king in Hebron.'" ¹¹Two hundred men from Jerusalem had accompanied Absalom. They had been invited as guests and went quite innocently, knowing nothing about the matter. ¹²While Absalom was offering sacrifices, he also sent for Ahithophel the Gilonite, David's counselor, to come from Giloh, his hometown. And so the conspiracy gained strength, and Absalom's following kept on increasing.

David Flees

¹³A messenger came and told David, "The hearts of the men of Israel are with Absalom."

¹⁴Then David said to all his officials who were with him in Jerusalem, "Come! We must flee, or none of us will escape from Absalom. We must leave immediately, or he will move quickly to overtake us and bring ruin upon us and put the city to the sword."

¹⁵The king's officials answered him, "Your servants are ready to do whatever our lord the king chooses."

¹⁶The king set out, with his entire household following him; but he left ten concubines to take care of the palace. ¹⁷So the king set out, with all the people following him, and they halted at a place some distance away. ¹⁸All his men marched past him, along with all the Kerethites and Pelethites; and all the six

---

[a]26 That is, about 5 pounds (about 2.3 kilograms)
[b]7 Some Septuagint manuscripts, Syriac and Josephus; Hebrew forty [c]8 Some Septuagint manuscripts; Hebrew does not have in Hebron.

hundred Gittites who had accompanied him from Gath marched before the king. [19]The king said to Ittai the Gittite, "Why should you come along with us? Go back and stay with King Absalom. You are a foreigner, an exile from your homeland. [20]You came only yesterday. And today shall I make you wander about with us, when I do not know where I am going? Go back, and take your countrymen. May kindness and faithfulness be with you."

[21]But Ittai replied to the king, "As surely as the LORD lives, and as my lord the king lives, wherever my lord the king may be, whether it means life or death, there will your servant be." [22]David said to Ittai, "Go ahead, march on." So Ittai the Gittite marched on with all his men and the families that were with him.

[23]The whole countryside wept aloud as all the people passed by. The king also crossed the Kidron Valley, and all the people moved on toward the desert. [24]Zadok was there, too, and all the Levites who were with him were carrying the ark of the covenant of God. They set down the ark of God, and Abiathar offered sacrifices[a] until all the people had finished leaving the city.

[25]Then the king said to Zadok, "Take the ark of God back into the city. If I find favor in the LORD's eyes, he will bring me back and let me see it and his dwelling place again. [26]But if he says, 'I am not pleased with you,' then I am ready; let him do to me whatever seems good to him." [27]The king also said to Zadok the priest, "Aren't you a seer? Go back to the city in peace, with your son Ahimaaz and Jonathan son of Abiathar. You and Abiathar take your two sons with you. [28]I will wait at the fords in the desert until word comes from you to inform me." [29]So Zadok and Abiathar took the ark of God back to Jerusalem and stayed there.

[30]But David continued up the Mount of Olives, weeping as he went; his head was covered and he was barefoot. All the people with him covered their heads too and were weeping as they went up. [31]Now David had been told, "Ahithophel is among the conspirators with Absalom." So David prayed, "O LORD, turn Ahithophel's counsel into foolishness."

[32]When David arrived at the summit, where people used to worship God, Hushai the Arkite was there to meet him, his robe torn and dust on his head. [33]David said to him, "If you go with me, you will be a burden to me. [34]But if you return to the city and say to Absalom, 'I will be your servant, O king; I was your father's servant in the past, but now I will be your servant,' then you can help me by frustrating Ahithophel's advice. [35]Won't the priests Zadok and Abiathar be there with you? Tell them anything you hear in the king's palace. [36]Their two sons, Ahimaaz son of Zadok and Jonathan son of Abiathar, are there with them. Send them to me with anything you hear."

[37]So David's friend Hushai arrived at Jerusalem as Absalom was entering the city.

David and Ziba

16 When David had gone a short distance beyond the summit, there was Ziba, the steward of Mephibosheth, waiting to meet him. He had a string of donkeys saddled and loaded with two hundred loaves of bread, a hundred cakes of raisins, a hundred cakes of figs and a skin of wine.

[2]The king asked Ziba, "Why have you brought these?"

Ziba answered, "The donkeys are for the king's household to ride on, the bread and fruit are for the men to eat, and the wine is to refresh those who become exhausted in the desert."

[3]The king then asked, "Where is your master's grandson?"

Ziba said to him, "He is staying in Jerusalem, because he thinks, 'Today the house of Israel will give me back my grandfather's kingdom.'"

[4]Then the king said to Ziba, "All that belonged to Mephibosheth is now yours."

"I humbly bow," Ziba said. "May I find favor in your eyes, my lord the king."

Shimei Curses David

[5]As King David approached Bahurim, a man from the same clan as Saul's family came out from there. His name was Shimei son of Gera, and he cursed as he

[a]24 Or *Abiathar went up*

came out. [6]He pelted David and all the king's officials with stones, though all the troops and the special guard were on David's right and left. [7]As he cursed, Shimei said, "Get out, get out, you man of blood, you scoundrel! [8]The LORD has repaid you for all the blood you shed in the household of Saul, in whose place you have reigned. The LORD has handed the kingdom over to your son Absalom. You have come to ruin because you are a man of blood!"

[9]Then Abishai son of Zeruiah said to the king, "Why should this dead dog curse my lord the king? Let me go over and cut off his head."

[10]But the king said, "What do you and I have in common, you sons of Zeruiah? If he is cursing because the LORD said to him, 'Curse David,' who can ask, 'Why do you do this?'"

[11]David then said to Abishai and all his officials, "My son, who is of my own flesh, is trying to take my life. How much more, then, this Benjamite! Leave him alone; let him curse, for the LORD has told him to. [12]It may be that the LORD will see my distress and repay me with good for the cursing I am receiving today."

[13]So David and his men continued along the road while Shimei was going along the hillside opposite him, cursing as he went and throwing stones at him and showering him with dirt. [14]The king and all the people with him arrived at their destination exhausted. And there he refreshed himself.

The Advice of Ahithophel and Hushai

[15]Meanwhile, Absalom and all the men of Israel came to Jerusalem, and Ahithophel was with him. [16]Then Hushai the Arkite, David's friend, went to Absalom and said to him, "Long live the king! Long live the king!"

[17]Absalom asked Hushai, "Is this the love you show your friend? Why didn't you go with your friend?"

[18]Hushai said to Absalom, "No, the one chosen by the LORD, by these people, and by all the men of Israel—his I will be, and I will remain with him. [19]Furthermore, whom should I serve? Should I not serve the son? Just as I served your father, so I will serve you."

[20]Absalom said to Ahithophel, "Give us your advice. What should we do?"

[21]Ahithophel answered, "Lie with your father's concubines whom he left to take care of the palace. Then all Israel will hear that you have made yourself a stench in your father's nostrils, and the hands of everyone with you will be strengthened." [22]So they pitched a tent for Absalom on the roof, and he lay with his father's concubines in the sight of all Israel.

[23]Now in those days the advice Ahithophel gave was like that of one who inquires of God. That was how both David and Absalom regarded all of Ahithophel's advice.

17 Ahithophel said to Absalom, "I would[a] choose twelve thousand men and set out tonight in pursuit of David. [2]I would[b] attack him while he is weary and weak. I would[b] strike him with terror, and then all the people with him will flee. I would[b] strike down only the king [3]and bring all the people back to you. The death of the man you seek will mean the return of all; all the people will be unharmed." [4]This plan seemed good to Absalom and to all the elders of Israel.

[5]But Absalom said, "Summon also Hushai the Arkite, so we can hear what he has to say." [6]When Hushai came to him, Absalom said, "Ahithophel has given this advice. Should we do what he says? If not, give us your opinion."

[7]Hushai replied to Absalom, "The advice Ahithophel has given is not good this time. [8]You know your father and his men; they are fighters, and as fierce as a wild bear robbed of her cubs. Besides, your father is an experienced fighter; he will not spend the night with the troops. [9]Even now, he is hidden in a cave or some other place. If he should attack your troops first,[c] whoever hears about it will say, 'There has been a slaughter among the troops who follow Absalom.' [10]Then even the bravest soldier, whose heart is like the heart of a lion, will melt with fear, for all Israel knows that your father is a fighter and that those with him are brave.

[11]"So I advise you: Let all Israel, from Dan to Beersheba—as numerous as the

---

[a]1 Or *Let me*   [b]2 Or *will*   [c]9 Or *When some of the men fall at the first attack*

sand on the seashore—be gathered to you, with you yourself leading them into battle. [12]Then we will attack him wherever he may be found, and we will fall on him as dew settles on the ground. Neither he nor any of his men will be left alive. [13]If he withdraws into a city, then all Israel will bring ropes to that city, and we will drag it down to the valley until not even a piece of it can be found."

[14]Absalom and all the men of Israel said, "The advice of Hushai the Arkite is better than that of Ahithophel." For the LORD had determined to frustrate the good advice of Ahithophel in order to bring disaster on Absalom.

[15]Hushai told Zadok and Abiathar, the priests, "Ahithophel has advised Absalom and the elders of Israel to do such and such, but I have advised them to do so and so. [16]Now send a message immediately and tell David, 'Do not spend the night at the fords in the desert; cross over without fail, or the king and all the people with him will be swallowed up.'"

[17]Jonathan and Ahimaaz were staying at En Rogel. A servant girl was to go and inform them, and they were to go and tell King David, for they could not risk being seen entering the city. [18]But a young man saw them and told Absalom. So the two of them left quickly and went to the house of a man in Bahurim. He had a well in his courtyard, and they climbed down into it. [19]His wife took a covering and spread it out over the opening of the well and scattered grain over it. No one knew anything about it.

[20]When Absalom's men came to the woman at the house, they asked, "Where are Ahimaaz and Jonathan?"

The woman answered them, "They crossed over the brook."[a] The men searched but found no one, so they returned to Jerusalem.

[21]After the men had gone, the two climbed out of the well and went to inform King David. They said to him, "Set out and cross the river at once; Ahithophel has advised such and such against you." [22]So David and all the people with him set out and crossed the Jordan. By daybreak, no one was left who had not crossed the Jordan.

[23]When Ahithophel saw that his advice had not been followed, he saddled his donkey and set out for his house in his hometown. He put his house in order and then hanged himself. So he died and was buried in his father's tomb.

[24]David went to Mahanaim, and Absalom crossed the Jordan with all the men of Israel. [25]Absalom had appointed Amasa over the army in place of Joab. Amasa was the son of a man named Jether,[b] an Israelite[c] who had married Abigail,[d] the daughter of Nahash and sister of Zeruiah the mother of Joab. [26]The Israelites and Absalom camped in the land of Gilead.

[27]When David came to Mahanaim, Shobi son of Nahash from Rabbah of the Ammonites, and Makir son of Ammiel from Lo Debar, and Barzillai the Gileadite from Rogelim [28]brought bedding and bowls and articles of pottery. They also brought wheat and barley, flour and roasted grain, beans and lentils,[e] [29]honey and curds, sheep, and cheese from cows' milk for David and his people to eat. For they said, "The people have become hungry and tired and thirsty in the desert."

Absalom's Death

18 David mustered the men who were with him and appointed over them commanders of thousands and commanders of hundreds. [2]David sent the troops out—a third under the command of Joab, a third under Joab's brother Abishai son of Zeruiah, and a third under Ittai the Gittite. The king told the troops, "I myself will surely march out with you."

[3]But the men said, "You must not go out; if we are forced to flee, they won't care about us. Even if half of us die, they won't care; but you are worth ten thousand of us.[f] It would be better now for you to give us support from the city."

---

[a]20 Or "They passed by the sheep pen toward the water."   [b]25 Hebrew Ithra, a variant of Jether   [c]25 Hebrew and some Septuagint manuscripts; other Septuagint manuscripts (see also 1 Chron. 2:17) Ishmaelite or Jezreelite   [d]25 Hebrew Abigal, a variant of Abigail   [e]28 Most Septuagint manuscripts and Syriac; Hebrew lentils, and roasted grain   [f]3 Two Hebrew manuscripts, some Septuagint manuscripts and Vulgate; most Hebrew manuscripts care; for now there are ten thousand like us

⁴The king answered, "I will do whatever seems best to you."

So the king stood beside the gate while all the men marched out in units of hundreds and of thousands. ⁵The king commanded Joab, Abishai and Ittai, "Be gentle with the young man Absalom for my sake." And all the troops heard the king giving orders concerning Absalom to each of the commanders.

⁶The army marched into the field to fight Israel, and the battle took place in the forest of Ephraim. ⁷There the army of Israel was defeated by David's men, and the casualties that day were great—twenty thousand men. ⁸The battle spread out over the whole countryside, and the forest claimed more lives that day than the sword.

⁹Now Absalom happened to meet David's men. He was riding his mule, and as the mule went under the thick branches of a large oak, Absalom's head got caught in the tree. He was left hanging in midair, while the mule he was riding kept on going.

¹⁰When one of the men saw this, he told Joab, "I just saw Absalom hanging in an oak tree."

¹¹Joab said to the man who had told him this, "What! You saw him? Why didn't you strike him to the ground right there? Then I would have had to give you ten shekels*a* of silver and a warrior's belt."

¹²But the man replied, "Even if a thousand shekels*b* were weighed out into my hands, I would not lift my hand against the king's son. In our hearing the king commanded you and Abishai and Ittai, 'Protect the young man Absalom for my sake.'*c* ¹³And if I had put my life in jeopardy*d*—and nothing is hidden from the king—you would have kept your distance from me."

¹⁴Joab said, "I'm not going to wait like this for you." So he took three javelins in his hand and plunged them into Absalom's heart while Absalom was still alive in the oak tree. ¹⁵And ten of Joab's armor-bearers surrounded Absalom, struck him and killed him.

¹⁶Then Joab sounded the trumpet, and the troops stopped pursuing Israel, for Joab halted them. ¹⁷They took Absalom, threw him into a big pit in the forest and piled up a large heap of rocks over him. Meanwhile, all the Israelites fled to their homes.

¹⁸During his lifetime Absalom had taken a pillar and erected it in the King's Valley as a monument to himself, for he thought, "I have no son to carry on the memory of my name." He named the pillar after himself, and it is called Absalom's Monument to this day.

David Mourns

¹⁹Now Ahimaaz son of Zadok said, "Let me run and take the news to the king that the LORD has delivered him from the hand of his enemies."

²⁰"You are not the one to take the news today," Joab told him. "You may take the news another time, but you must not do so today, because the king's son is dead."

²¹Then Joab said to a Cushite, "Go, tell the king what you have seen." The Cushite bowed down before Joab and ran off.

²²Ahimaaz son of Zadok again said to Joab, "Come what may, please let me run behind the Cushite."

But Joab replied, "My son, why do you want to go? You don't have any news that will bring you a reward."

²³He said, "Come what may, I want to run."

So Joab said, "Run!" Then Ahimaaz ran by way of the plain*e* and outran the Cushite.

²⁴While David was sitting between the inner and outer gates, the watchman went up to the roof of the gateway by the wall. As he looked out, he saw a man running alone. ²⁵The watchman called out to the king and reported it.

The king said, "If he is alone, he must have good news." And the man came closer and closer.

²⁶Then the watchman saw another man running, and he called down to the gatekeeper, "Look, another man running alone!"

a11 That is, about 4 ounces (about 115 grams)
b12 That is, about 25 pounds (about 11 kilograms)   *c12* A few Hebrew manuscripts, Septuagint, Vulgate and Syriac; most Hebrew manuscripts may be translated *Absalom, whoever you may be.*   *d13* Or *Otherwise, if I had acted treacherously toward him*   *e23* That is, the plain of the Jordan

The king said, "He must be bringing good news, too."

²⁷The watchman said, "It seems to me that the first one runs like Ahimaaz son of Zadok."

"He's a good man," the king said. "He comes with good news."

²⁸Then Ahimaaz called out to the king, "All is well!" He bowed down before the king with his face to the ground and said, "Praise be to the LORD your God! He has delivered up the men who lifted their hands against my lord the king."

²⁹The king asked, "Is the young man Absalom safe?"

Ahimaaz answered, "I saw great confusion just as Joab was about to send the king's servant and me, your servant, but I don't know what it was."

³⁰The king said, "Stand aside and wait here." So he stepped aside and stood there.

³¹Then the Cushite arrived and said, "My lord the king, hear the good news! The LORD has delivered you today from all who rose up against you."

³²The king asked the Cushite, "Is the young man Absalom safe?"

The Cushite replied, "May the enemies of my lord the king and all who rise up to harm you be like that young man."

³³The king was shaken. He went up to the room over the gateway and wept. As he went, he said: "O my son Absalom! My son, my son Absalom! If only I had died instead of you—O Absalom, my son, my son!"

19 Joab was told, "The king is weeping and mourning for Absalom." ²And for the whole army the victory that day was turned into mourning, because on that day the troops heard it said, "The king is grieving for his son." ³The men stole into the city that day as men steal in who are ashamed when they flee from battle. ⁴The king covered his face and cried aloud, "O my son Absalom! O Absalom, my son, my son!"

⁵Then Joab went into the house to the king and said, "Today you have humiliated all your men, who have just saved your life and the lives of your sons and daughters and the lives of your wives and concubines. ⁶You love those who hate you and hate those who love you. You have made it clear today that the commanders and their men mean nothing to you. I see that you would be pleased if Absalom were alive today and all of us were dead. ⁷Now go out and encourage your men. I swear by the LORD that if you don't go out, not a man will be left with you by nightfall. This will be worse for you than all the calamities that have come upon you from your youth till now."

⁸So the king got up and took his seat in the gateway. When the men were told, "The king is sitting in the gateway," they all came before him.

David Returns to Jerusalem

Meanwhile, the Israelites had fled to their homes. ⁹Throughout the tribes of Israel, the people were all arguing with each other, saying, "The king delivered us from the hand of our enemies; he is the one who rescued us from the hand of the Philistines. But now he has fled the country because of Absalom; ¹⁰and Absalom, whom we anointed to rule over us, has died in battle. So why do you say nothing about bringing the king back?"

¹¹King David sent this message to Zadok and Abiathar, the priests: "Ask the elders of Judah, 'Why should you be the last to bring the king back to his palace, since what is being said throughout Israel has reached the king at his quarters? ¹²You are my brothers, my own flesh and blood. So why should you be the last to bring back the king?' ¹³And say to Amasa, 'Are you not my own flesh and blood? May God deal with me, be it ever so severely, if from now on you are not the commander of my army in place of Joab.'"

¹⁴He won over the hearts of all the men of Judah as though they were one man. They sent word to the king, "Return, you and all your men." ¹⁵Then the king returned and went as far as the Jordan.

Now the men of Judah had come to Gilgal to go out and meet the king and bring him across the Jordan. ¹⁶Shimei son of Gera, the Benjamite from Bahurim, hurried down with the men of Judah to meet King David. ¹⁷With him were a thousand Benjamites, along with Ziba, the steward of Saul's household, and his fifteen sons and twenty servants. They rushed to the Jordan, where the king was. [18]They crossed at the ford to take the king's household over and to do whatever he wished.

When Shimei son of Gera crossed the Jordan, he fell prostrate before the king [19]and said to him, "May my lord not hold me guilty. Do not remember how your servant did wrong on the day my lord the king left Jerusalem. May the king put it out of his mind. [20]For I your servant know that I have sinned, but today I have come here as the first of the whole house of Joseph to come down and meet my lord the king."

[21]Then Abishai son of Zeruiah said, "Shouldn't Shimei be put to death for this? He cursed the Lord's anointed."

[22]David replied, "What do you and I have in common, you sons of Zeruiah? This day you have become my adversaries! Should anyone be put to death in Israel today? Do I not know that today I am king over Israel?" [23]So the king said to Shimei, "You shall not die." And the king promised him on oath.

[24]Mephibosheth, Saul's grandson, also went down to meet the king. He had not taken care of his feet or trimmed his mustache or washed his clothes from the day the king left until the day he returned safely. [25]When he came from Jerusalem to meet the king, the king asked him, "Why didn't you go with me, Mephibosheth?"

[26]He said, "My lord the king, since I your servant am lame, I said, 'I will have my donkey saddled and will ride on it, so I can go with the king.' But Ziba my servant betrayed me. [27]And he has slandered your servant to my lord the king. My lord the king is like an angel of God; so do whatever pleases you. [28]All my grandfather's descendants deserved nothing but death from my lord the king, but you gave your servant a place among those who eat at your table. So what right do I have to make any more appeals to the king?"

[29]The king said to him, "Why say more? I order you and Ziba to divide the fields."

[30]Mephibosheth said to the king, "Let him take everything, now that my lord the king has arrived home safely."

[31]Barzillai the Gileadite also came down from Rogelim to cross the Jordan with the king and to send him on his way from there. [32]Now Barzillai was a very old man, eighty years of age. He had provided for the king during his stay in Mahanaim, for he was a very wealthy man. [33]The king said to Barzillai, "Cross over with me and stay with me in Jerusalem, and I will provide for you."

[34]But Barzillai answered the king, "How many more years will I live, that I should go up to Jerusalem with the king? [35]I am now eighty years old. Can I tell the difference between what is good and what is not? Can your servant taste what he eats and drinks? Can I still hear the voices of men and women singers? Why should your servant be an added burden to my lord the king? [36]Your servant will cross over the Jordan with the king for a short distance, but why should the king reward me in this way? [37]Let your servant return, that I may die in my own town near the tomb of my father and mother. But here is your servant Kimham. Let him cross over with my lord the king. Do for him whatever pleases you."

[38]The king said, "Kimham shall cross over with me, and I will do for him whatever pleases you. And anything you desire from me I will do for you."

[39]So all the people crossed the Jordan, and then the king crossed over. The king kissed Barzillai and gave him his blessing, and Barzillai returned to his home.

[40]When the king crossed over to Gilgal, Kimham crossed with him. All the troops of Judah and half the troops of Israel had taken the king over.

[41]Soon all the men of Israel were coming to the king and saying to him, "Why did our brothers, the men of Judah, steal the king away and bring him and his household across the Jordan, together with all his men?"

[42]All the men of Judah answered the men of Israel, "We did this because the king is closely related to us. Why are you angry about it? Have we eaten any of the king's provisions? Have we taken anything for ourselves?"

[43]Then the men of Israel answered the men of Judah, "We have ten shares in the king; and besides, we have a greater claim on David than you have. So why do you treat us with contempt? Were we not the first to speak of bringing back our king?"

But the men of Judah responded even more harshly than the men of Israel.

Sheba Rebels Against David

20 Now a troublemaker named Sheba son of Bicri, a Benjamite, happened to be there. He sounded the trumpet and shouted,

"We have no share in David,
no part in Jesse's son!
Every man to his tent, O Israel!"

²So all the men of Israel deserted David to follow Sheba son of Bicri. But the men of Judah stayed by their king all the way from the Jordan to Jerusalem.

³When David returned to his palace in Jerusalem, he took the ten concubines he had left to take care of the palace and put them in a house under guard. He provided for them, but did not lie with them. They were kept in confinement till the day of their death, living as widows.

⁴Then the king said to Amasa, "Summon the men of Judah to come to me within three days, and be here yourself." ⁵But when Amasa went to summon Judah, he took longer than the time the king had set for him.

⁶David said to Abishai, "Now Sheba son of Bicri will do us more harm than Absalom did. Take your master's men and pursue him, or he will find fortified cities and escape from us." ⁷So Joab's men and the Kerethites and Pelethites and all the mighty warriors went out under the command of Abishai. They marched out from Jerusalem to pursue Sheba son of Bicri.

⁸While they were at the great rock in Gibeon, Amasa came to meet them. Joab was wearing his military tunic, and strapped over it at his waist was a belt with a dagger in its sheath. As he stepped forward, it dropped out of its sheath.

⁹Joab said to Amasa, "How are you, my brother?" Then Joab took Amasa by the beard with his right hand to kiss him. ¹⁰Amasa was not on his guard against the dagger in Joab's hand, and Joab plunged it into his belly, and his intestines spilled out on the ground. Without being stabbed again, Amasa died. Then Joab and his brother Abishai pursued Sheba son of Bicri.

¹¹One of Joab's men stood beside Amasa and said, "Whoever favors Joab, and whoever is for David, let him follow Joab!" ¹²Amasa lay wallowing in his blood in the middle of the road, and the man saw that all the troops came to a halt there. When he realized that everyone who came up to Amasa stopped, he dragged him from the road into a field and threw a garment over him. ¹³After Amasa had been removed from the road, all the men went on with Joab to pursue Sheba son of Bicri.

¹⁴Sheba passed through all the tribes of Israel to Abel Beth Maacah*ᵃ* and through the entire region of the Berites, who gathered together and followed him. ¹⁵All the troops with Joab came and besieged Sheba in Abel Beth Maacah. They built a siege ramp up to the city, and it stood against the outer fortifications. While they were battering the wall to bring it down, ¹⁶a wise woman called from the city, "Listen! Listen! Tell Joab to come here so I can speak to him." ¹⁷He went toward her, and she asked, "Are you Joab?"

"I am," he answered.

She said, "Listen to what your servant has to say."

"I'm listening," he said.

¹⁸She continued, "Long ago they used to say, 'Get your answer at Abel,' and that settled it. ¹⁹We are the peaceful and faithful in Israel. You are trying to destroy a city that is a mother in Israel. Why do you want to swallow up the Lord's inheritance?"

²⁰"Far be it from me!" Joab replied, "Far be it from me to swallow up or destroy! ²¹That is not the case. A man named Sheba son of Bicri, from the hill country of Ephraim, has lifted up his hand against the king, against David. Hand over this one man, and I'll withdraw from the city."

The woman said to Joab, "His head will be thrown to you from the wall."

²²Then the woman went to all the people with her wise advice, and they cut off the head of Sheba son of Bicri and threw it to Joab. So he sounded the trumpet, and his men dispersed from the city,

---

ᵃ14 Or *Abel, even Beth Maacah;* also in verse 15

each returning to his home. And Joab went back to the king in Jerusalem.

²³Joab was over Israel's entire army; Benaiah son of Jehoiada was over the Kerethites and Pelethites; ²⁴Adoniram*a* was in charge of forced labor; Jehoshaphat son of Ahilud was recorder; ²⁵Sheva was secretary; Zadok and Abiathar were priests; ²⁶and Ira the Jairite was David's priest.

The Gibeonites Avenged

21 During the reign of David, there was a famine for three successive years; so David sought the face of the LORD. The LORD said, "It is on account of Saul and his blood-stained house; it is because he put the Gibeonites to death."

²The king summoned the Gibeonites and spoke to them. (Now the Gibeonites were not a part of Israel but were survivors of the Amorites; the Israelites had sworn to ⌊spare⌋ them, but Saul in his zeal for Israel and Judah had tried to annihilate them.) ³David asked the Gibeonites, "What shall I do for you? How shall I make amends so that you will bless the LORD's inheritance?"

⁴The Gibeonites answered him, "We have no right to demand silver or gold from Saul or his family, nor do we have the right to put anyone in Israel to death."

"What do you want me to do for you?" David asked.

⁵They answered the king, "As for the man who destroyed us and plotted against us so that we have been decimated and have no place anywhere in Israel, ⁶let seven of his male descendants be given to us to be killed and exposed before the LORD at Gibeah of Saul—the LORD's chosen one."

So the king said, "I will give them to you."

⁷The king spared Mephibosheth son of Jonathan, the son of Saul, because of the oath before the LORD between David and Jonathan son of Saul. ⁸But the king took Armoni and Mephibosheth, the two sons of Aiah's daughter Rizpah, whom she had borne to Saul, together with the five sons of Saul's daughter Merab,*b* whom she had borne to Adriel son of Barzillai the Meholathite. ⁹He handed them over

to the Gibeonites, who killed and exposed them on a hill before the LORD. All seven of them fell together; they were put to death during the first days of the harvest, just as the barley harvest was beginning.

¹⁰Rizpah daughter of Aiah took sackcloth and spread it out for herself on a rock. From the beginning of the harvest till the rain poured down from the heavens on the bodies, she did not let the birds of the air touch them by day or the wild animals by night. ¹¹When David was told what Aiah's daughter Rizpah, Saul's concubine, had done, ¹²he went and took the bones of Saul and his son Jonathan from the citizens of Jabesh Gilead. (They had taken them secretly from the public square at Beth Shan, where the Philistines had hung them after they struck Saul down on Gilboa.) ¹³David brought the bones of Saul and his son Jonathan from there, and the bones of those who had been killed and exposed were gathered up.

¹⁴They buried the bones of Saul and his son Jonathan in the tomb of Saul's father Kish, at Zela in Benjamin, and did everything the king commanded. After that, God answered prayer in behalf of the land.

> THEY buried the bones of Saul and his son Jonathan in the tomb of Saul's father Kish, at Zela in Benjamin, and did everything the king commanded. After that, God answered prayer in behalf of the land.
>
> 2 SAMUEL 21:14

Wars Against the Philistines

¹⁵Once again there was a battle between the Philistines and Israel. David went down with his men to fight against the Philistines, and he became exhausted. ¹⁶And Ishbi-Benob, one of the descendants of Rapha, whose bronze spearhead

---

a24 Some Septuagint manuscripts (see also 1 Kings 4:6 and 5:14); Hebrew *Adoram*
b8 Two Hebrew manuscripts, some Septuagint manuscripts and Syriac (see also 1 Samuel 18:19); most Hebrew and Septuagint manuscripts *Michal*

weighed three hundred shekels[a] and who was armed with a new ˌswordˌ, said he would kill David. [17]But Abishai son of Zeruiah came to David's rescue; he struck the Philistine down and killed him. Then David's men swore to him, saying, "Never again will you go out with us to battle, so that the lamp of Israel will not be extinguished."

[18]In the course of time, there was another battle with the Philistines, at Gob. At that time Sibbecai the Hushathite killed Saph, one of the descendants of Rapha.

[19]In another battle with the Philistines at Gob, Elhanan son of Jaare-Oregim[b] the Bethlehemite killed Goliath[c] the Gittite, who had a spear with a shaft like a weaver's rod.

[20]In still another battle, which took place at Gath, there was a huge man with six fingers on each hand and six toes on each foot—twenty-four in all. He also was descended from Rapha. [21]When he taunted Israel, Jonathan son of Shimeah, David's brother, killed him.

[22]These four were descendants of Rapha in Gath, and they fell at the hands of David and his men.

David's Song of Praise

22 David sang to the LORD the words of this song when the LORD delivered him from the hand of all his enemies and from the hand of Saul. [2]He said:

"The LORD is my rock, my fortress and
 my deliverer;
[3] my God is my rock, in whom I take
  refuge,
 my shield and the horn[d] of my
  salvation.
He is my stronghold, my refuge and
 my savior—
 from violent men you save me.
[4]I call to the LORD, who is worthy
 of praise,
 and I am saved from my enemies.

[5] "The waves of death swirled
  about me;
 the torrents of destruction
  overwhelmed me.
[6]The cords of the grave[e] coiled
  around me;
 the snares of death confronted me.

[7]In my distress I called to the LORD;
 I called out to my God.
From his temple he heard my voice;
 my cry came to his ears.

[8] "The earth trembled and quaked,
 the foundations of the heavens[f]
  shook;
 they trembled because he
  was angry.
[9]Smoke rose from his nostrils;
 consuming fire came from
  his mouth,
 burning coals blazed out of it.
[10]He parted the heavens and came
  down;
 dark clouds were under his feet.
[11]He mounted the cherubim and flew;
 he soared[g] on the wings of
  the wind.
[12]He made darkness his canopy
  around him—
 the dark[h] rain clouds of the sky.
[13]Out of the brightness of his presence
 bolts of lightning blazed forth.
[14]The LORD thundered from heaven;
 the voice of the Most High
  resounded.
[15]He shot arrows and scattered
 ˌthe enemiesˌ,
 bolts of lightning and routed them.
[16]The valleys of the sea were exposed
 and the foundations of the earth
  laid bare
at the rebuke of the LORD,
 at the blast of breath from his
  nostrils.

[17] "He reached down from on high and
  took hold of me;
 he drew me out of deep waters.
[18]He rescued me from my powerful
  enemy,
 from my foes, who were too strong
  for me.
[19]They confronted me in the day of
  my disaster,
 but the LORD was my support.

---

[a]16 That is, about 7 1/2 pounds (about 3.5 kilograms) [b]19 Or son of Jair the weaver
[c]19 Hebrew and Septuagint; 1 Chron. 20:5 son of Jair killed Lahmi the brother of Goliath
[d]3 Horn here symbolizes strength. [e]6 Hebrew Sheol [f]8 Hebrew; Vulgate and Syriac (see also Psalm 18:7) mountains [g]11 Many Hebrew manuscripts (see also Psalm 18:10); most Hebrew manuscripts appeared [h]12 Septuagint and Vulgate (see also Psalm 18:11); Hebrew massed

2 SAMUEL 22

Seeing Through

22:2 "THE LORD IS MY ROCK."

Whatever David's failures at gratitude were, he will be remembered for his prayers of thanks and praise in the Psalms. He is the great lyricist of praise. This prayer in chapter 22 sums up much of his life and is virtually the same as Psalm 18. It is a superb example of a perspective that makes thanks and praise possible; call it the capacity to "see through" things.

Look at some of the metaphors David uses for God in this song: rock, fortress, deliverer, shield and stronghold. Then look at the things God gave David and trained him for: He armed David with strength (verse 33), made his feet like a deer's (verse 34), trained his hands for battle (verse 35), and so on. Every one of the things David says about God describes literal, physical things he needed and experienced in fighting battles. David really did stand on a rock, hide in a fortress, use a shield and shoot arrows. He was no doubt trained by a real human being to fight with a sword and shield. He certainly spent many hours practicing the skills he would need to fight well. Yet all these things he attributes to God—from God and through God.

David knew the difference between primary causes and secondary causes. The secondary causes were his tutor in hand-to-hand combat, the fortress he hid in, the strength of his feet on a mountain path. But the primary cause was God: "For from him and through him and to him are all things. To him be the glory forever! Amen" (Romans 11:36). All these secondary causes were from and through and to God, so to him be the praise forever!

If there is a secret to being grateful, it is this: seeing through secondary things to the primary One. Poet George Herbert wrote,

> A man that looks on glass,
> On it may stay his eye;
> Or if he pleaseth, through it pass,
> And then the heav'n espy.[2]

The secret of a grateful heart is an eye that will see through the surface to what lies behind it all. Be sure to thank the people in your life who are secondary causes, conduits from the primary giver. Be thankful for things. But do not forget to see through it all to thank the God who is before and in and after all things.

PRAY:

*I thank you, God, for who you are and for everything
and everyone you have given me.*

___

FOR YOUR NEXT DEVOTIONAL READING, GO TO PAGE 375.

²⁰ He brought me out into a spacious
   place;
   he rescued me because he
   delighted in me.

²¹ "The LORD has dealt with me
   according to my
   righteousness;
   according to the cleanness of my
   hands he has rewarded me.
²² For I have kept the ways of the LORD;
   I have not done evil by turning
   from my God.
²³ All his laws are before me;
   I have not turned away from his
   decrees.
²⁴ I have been blameless before him
   and have kept myself from sin.
²⁵ The LORD has rewarded me according
   to my righteousness,
   according to my cleanness*a* in
   his sight.

²⁶ "To the faithful you show yourself
   faithful,
   to the blameless you show yourself
   blameless,
²⁷ to the pure you show yourself pure,
   but to the crooked you show
   yourself shrewd.
²⁸ You save the humble,
   but your eyes are on the haughty to
   bring them low.
²⁹ You are my lamp, O LORD;
   the LORD turns my darkness into
   light.
³⁰ With your help I can advance against
   a troop*b*;
   with my God I can scale a wall.

³¹ "As for God, his way is perfect;
   the word of the LORD is flawless.
   He is a shield
   for all who take refuge in him.
³² For who is God besides the LORD?
   And who is the Rock except
   our God?
³³ It is God who arms me with
   strength*c*
   and makes my way perfect.
³⁴ He makes my feet like the feet of
   a deer;
   he enables me to stand on the
   heights.
³⁵ He trains my hands for battle;
   my arms can bend a bow of bronze.

³⁶ You give me your shield of victory;
   you stoop down to make me great.
³⁷ You broaden the path beneath me,
   so that my ankles do not turn.

³⁸ "I pursued my enemies and crushed
   them;
   I did not turn back till they were
   destroyed.
³⁹ I crushed them completely, and they
   could not rise;
   they fell beneath my feet.
⁴⁰ You armed me with strength
   for battle;
   you made my adversaries bow
   at my feet.
⁴¹ You made my enemies turn their
   backs in flight,
   and I destroyed my foes.
⁴² They cried for help, but there was no
   one to save them—
   to the LORD, but he did not answer.
⁴³ I beat them as fine as the dust of
   the earth;
   I pounded and trampled them like
   mud in the streets.

⁴⁴ "You have delivered me from the
   attacks of my people;
   you have preserved me as the head
   of nations.
   People I did not know are subject
   to me,
⁴⁵ and foreigners come cringing
   to me;
   as soon as they hear me, they
   obey me.
⁴⁶ They all lose heart;
   they come trembling*d* from their
   strongholds.

⁴⁷ "The LORD lives! Praise be to
   my Rock!
   Exalted be God, the Rock,
   my Savior!
⁴⁸ He is the God who avenges me,
   who puts the nations under me,
⁴⁹ who sets me free from my enemies.

a25 Hebrew; Septuagint and Vulgate (see also
Psalm 18:24) *to the cleanness of my hands*
b30 Or *can run through a barricade*   *c33* Dead
Sea Scrolls, some Septuagint manuscripts,
Vulgate and Syriac (see also Psalm 18:32);
Masoretic Text *who is my strong refuge*
d46 Some Septuagint manuscripts and Vulgate
(see also Psalm 18:45); Masoretic Text *they arm
themselves.*

"*THE LORD lives! Praise be to my Rock!
Exalted be God, the Rock, my Savior!*"

2 SAMUEL 22:47

You exalted me above my foes;
  from violent men you
    rescued me.
50 Therefore I will praise you, O LORD,
    among the nations;
  I will sing praises to your name.
51 He gives his king great victories;
  he shows unfailing kindness to
    his anointed,
  to David and his descendants
    forever."

The Last Words of David

23 These are the last words of David:

"The oracle of David son of Jesse,
  the oracle of the man exalted by
    the Most High,
the man anointed by the God
    of Jacob,
  Israel's singer of songs[a]:

2 "The Spirit of the LORD spoke
    through me;
  his word was on my tongue.
3 The God of Israel spoke,
  the Rock of Israel said to me:
'When one rules over men in
    righteousness,
  when he rules in the fear
    of God,
4 he is like the light of morning at
    sunrise
  on a cloudless morning,
like the brightness after rain
  that brings the grass from
    the earth.'

5 "Is not my house right with God?
  Has he not made with me an
    everlasting covenant,
  arranged and secured in
    every part?
Will he not bring to fruition my
    salvation
  and grant me my every desire?
6 But evil men are all to be cast aside
    like thorns,
  which are not gathered with
    the hand.

7 Whoever touches thorns
  uses a tool of iron or the shaft
    of a spear;
  they are burned up where they lie."

David's Mighty Men

8 These are the names of David's mighty
men:

Josheb-Basshebeth,[b] a Tahkemonite,[c]
was chief of the Three; he raised his
spear against eight hundred men, whom
he killed[d] in one encounter.

9 Next to him was Eleazar son of Dodai
the Ahohite. As one of the three mighty
men, he was with David when they
taunted the Philistines gathered ⌊at Pas
Dammim⌋[e] for battle. Then the men of Israel retreated, 10 but he stood his ground
and struck down the Philistines till his
hand grew tired and froze to the sword.
The LORD brought about a great victory
that day. The troops returned to Eleazar,
but only to strip the dead.

11 Next to him was Shammah son of Agee
the Hararite. When the Philistines banded together at a place where there was a
field full of lentils, Israel's troops fled from
them. 12 But Shammah took his stand in
the middle of the field. He defended it and
struck the Philistines down, and the LORD
brought about a great victory.

13 During harvest time, three of the thirty chief men came down to David at the
cave of Adullam, while a band of Philistines was encamped in the Valley of
Rephaim. 14 At that time David was in the
stronghold, and the Philistine garrison
was at Bethlehem. 15 David longed for water and said, "Oh, that someone would
get me a drink of water from the well
near the gate of Bethlehem!" 16 So the
three mighty men broke through the Philistine lines, drew water from the well
near the gate of Bethlehem and carried it
back to David. But he refused to drink it;
instead, he poured it out before the LORD.
17 "Far be it from me, O LORD, to do this!"

---

a 1 Or *Israel's beloved singer*   *b 8* Hebrew; some
Septuagint manuscripts suggest *Ish-Bosheth,* that
is, *Esh-Baal* (see also 1 Chron. 11:11 *Jashobeam*).
c 8 Probably a variant of *Hacmonite* (see 1 Chron.
11:11)   *d 8* Some Septuagint manuscripts (see
also 1 Chron. 11:11); Hebrew and other
Septuagint manuscripts *Three; it was Adino the
Eznite who killed eight hundred men*
e 9 See 1 Chron. 11:13; Hebrew *gathered there.*

he said. "Is it not the blood of men who went at the risk of their lives?" And David would not drink it.

Such were the exploits of the three mighty men.

¹⁸Abishai the brother of Joab son of Zeruiah was chief of the Three.ᵃ He raised his spear against three hundred men, whom he killed, and so he became as famous as the Three. ¹⁹Was he not held in greater honor than the Three? He became their commander, even though he was not included among them.

²⁰Benaiah son of Jehoiada was a valiant fighter from Kabzeel, who performed great exploits. He struck down two of Moab's best men. He also went down into a pit on a snowy day and killed a lion. ²¹And he struck down a huge Egyptian. Although the Egyptian had a spear in his hand, Benaiah went against him with a club. He snatched the spear from the Egyptian's hand and killed him with his own spear. ²²Such were the exploits of Benaiah son of Jehoiada; he too was as famous as the three mighty men. ²³He was held in greater honor than any of the Thirty, but he was not included among the Three. And David put him in charge of his bodyguard.

²⁴Among the Thirty were:
Asahel the brother of Joab,
Elhanan son of Dodo from Bethlehem,
²⁵Shammah the Harodite,
Elika the Harodite,
²⁶Helez the Paltite,
Ira son of Ikkesh from Tekoa,
²⁷Abiezer from Anathoth,
Mebunnaiᵇ the Hushathite,
²⁸Zalmon the Ahohite,
Maharai the Netophathite,
²⁹Heledᶜ son of Baanah the Netophathite,
Ithai son of Ribai from Gibeah in Benjamin,
³⁰Benaiah the Pirathonite,
Hiddaiᵈ from the ravines of Gaash,
³¹Abi-Albon the Arbathite,
Azmaveth the Barhumite,
³²Eliahba the Shaalbonite,
the sons of Jashen,
Jonathan ³³son ofᵉ Shammah the Hararite,
Ahiam son of Shararᶠ the Hararite,

³⁴Eliphelet son of Ahasbai the Maacathite,
Eliam son of Ahithophel the Gilonite,
³⁵Hezro the Carmelite,
Paarai the Arbite,
³⁶Igal son of Nathan from Zobah,
the son of Hagri,ᵍ
³⁷Zelek the Ammonite,
Naharai the Beerothite, the armorbearer of Joab son of Zeruiah,
³⁸Ira the Ithrite,
Gareb the Ithrite
³⁹and Uriah the Hittite.
There were thirty-seven in all.

David Counts the Fighting Men

24 Again the anger of the Lord burned against Israel, and he incited David against them, saying, "Go and take a census of Israel and Judah."

²So the king said to Joab and the army commandersʰ with him, "Go throughout the tribes of Israel from Dan to Beersheba and enroll the fighting men, so that I may know how many there are."

³But Joab replied to the king, "May the Lord your God multiply the troops a hundred times over, and may the eyes of my lord the king see it. But why does my lord the king want to do such a thing?"

⁴The king's word, however, overruled Joab and the army commanders; so they left the presence of the king to enroll the fighting men of Israel.

⁵After crossing the Jordan, they camped near Aroer, south of the town in the gorge, and then went through Gad and on to Jazer. ⁶They went to Gilead and the region of Tahtim Hodshi, and on to Dan Jaan and around toward Sidon. ⁷Then they went toward the fortress of Tyre and

---

ᵃ18 Most Hebrew manuscripts (see also 1 Chron. 11:20); two Hebrew manuscripts and Syriac *Thirty* ᵇ27 Hebrew; some Septuagint manuscripts (see also 1 Chron. 11:29) *Sibbecai* ᶜ29 Some Hebrew manuscripts and Vulgate (see also 1 Chron. 11:30); most Hebrew manuscripts *Heleb* ᵈ30 Hebrew; some Septuagint manuscripts (see also 1 Chron. 11:32) *Hurai* ᵉ33 Some Septuagint manuscripts (see also 1 Chron. 11:34); Hebrew does not have *son of.* ᶠ33 Hebrew; some Septuagint manuscripts (see also 1 Chron. 11:35) *Sacar* ᵍ36 Some Septuagint manuscripts (see also 1 Chron. 11:38); Hebrew *Haggadi* ʰ2 Septuagint (see also verse 4 and 1 Chron. 21:2); Hebrew *Joab the army commander*

all the towns of the Hivites and Canaanites. Finally, they went on to Beersheba in the Negev of Judah.

⁸After they had gone through the entire land, they came back to Jerusalem at the end of nine months and twenty days.

⁹Joab reported the number of the fighting men to the king: In Israel there were eight hundred thousand able-bodied men who could handle a sword, and in Judah five hundred thousand.

¹⁰David was conscience-stricken after

---

2 SAMUEL 24

[FRIDAY]

Deadly Pride

24:10 DAVID WAS CONSCIENCE-STRICKEN AFTER HE HAD COUNTED THE FIGHTING MEN.

Kings and governments take censuses all the time; it's what they do. The nation of Israel had taken a census before without any guilt (see Numbers 1:2–3; 26:2–4). Sometimes a census is needed as part of preparation for battle or for making wise public policy. The problem with David's census was that there was apparently no real reason for it other than highlighting David's pride in what he had and a desire to brag a little about his power as a king. God took a dim view of this pride and wreaked a terrible judgment on his people. What is wrong with a little pride, a little bragging? What's wrong with it is that it is the root of every other sin. It is, as C. S. Lewis put it, "the complete anti-God state of mind."

He explains why:

In God you come up against something which is in every respect immeasurably superior to yourself. Unless you know God as that— and, therefore, know yourself as nothing in comparison—you do not know God at all. As long as you are proud you cannot know God. A proud man is always looking down on things and people, and, of course, as long as you are looking down, you cannot see something that is above you.[3]

Lewis says this raises a terrible question. Some people can appear to be very religious and pious but are consumed with pride. For such people, the God they worship is an imaginary God to whom they pay a penny's worth of false humility to get a dollar's worth of pride toward others. Lewis proposed a test for pride that we should apply to our devotional and prayer lives:

Whenever we find that our religious life is making us feel that we are good—above all, that we are better than someone else—I think we may be sure that we are being acted on, not by God, but by the devil. The real test of being in the presence of God is that you forget about yourself altogether or see yourself as a small, dirty object. It is better to forget about yourself altogether.[4]

PRAY:

Lord, teach me to be so absorbed in thanks and
praise that I forget about myself altogether.

FOR YOUR NEXT DEVOTIONAL READING, GO TO PAGE 380.

he had counted the fighting men, and he said to the LORD, "I have sinned greatly in what I have done. Now, O LORD, I beg you, take away the guilt of your servant. I have done a very foolish thing."

[11]Before David got up the next morning, the word of the LORD had come to Gad the prophet, David's seer: [12]"Go and tell David, 'This is what the LORD says: I am giving you three options. Choose one of them for me to carry out against you.'"

[13]So Gad went to David and said to him, "Shall there come upon you three[a] years of famine in your land? Or three months of fleeing from your enemies while they pursue you? Or three days of plague in your land? Now then, think it over and decide how I should answer the one who sent me."

[14]David said to Gad, "I am in deep distress. Let us fall into the hands of the LORD, for his mercy is great; but do not let me fall into the hands of men."

[15]So the LORD sent a plague on Israel from that morning until the end of the time designated, and seventy thousand of the people from Dan to Beersheba died. [16]When the angel stretched out his hand to destroy Jerusalem, the LORD was grieved because of the calamity and said to the angel who was afflicting the people, "Enough! Withdraw your hand." The angel of the LORD was then at the threshing floor of Araunah the Jebusite.

[17]When David saw the angel who was striking down the people, he said to the LORD, "I am the one who has sinned and done wrong. These are but sheep. What have they done? Let your hand fall upon me and my family."

David Builds an Altar

[18]On that day Gad went to David and said to him, "Go up and build an altar to the LORD on the threshing floor of Arau-

nah the Jebusite." [19]So David went up, as the LORD had commanded through Gad. [20]When Araunah looked and saw the king and his men coming toward him, he went out and bowed down before the king with his face to the ground.

[21]Araunah said, "Why has my lord the king come to his servant?"

"To buy your threshing floor," David answered, "so I can build an altar to the LORD, that the plague on the people may be stopped."

[22]Araunah said to David, "Let my lord the king take whatever pleases him and offer it up. Here are oxen for the burnt offering, and here are threshing sledges and ox yokes for the wood. [23]O king, Araunah gives all this to the king." Araunah also said to him, "May the LORD your God accept you."

[24]But the king replied to Araunah, "No, I insist on paying you for it. I will not sacrifice to the LORD my God burnt offerings that cost me nothing."

> DAVID built an altar to the LORD there and sacrificed burnt offerings and fellowship offerings. Then the LORD answered prayer in behalf of the land, and the plague on Israel was stopped.
>
> 2 SAMUEL 24:25

So David bought the threshing floor and the oxen and paid fifty shekels[b] of silver for them. [25]David built an altar to the LORD there and sacrificed burnt offerings and fellowship offerings.[c] Then the LORD answered prayer in behalf of the land, and the plague on Israel was stopped.

[a]13 Septuagint (see also 1 Chron. 21:12); Hebrew *seven*   [b]24 That is, about 1 1/4 pounds (about 0.6 kilogram)   [c]25 Traditionally *peace offerings*

1 Kings

"**IF MEN** could but learn from history, what lessons it might teach us! But passion and party blind our eyes, and the light which experience gives is a lantern on the stern, which shines only on the waves behind us!" These words by Samuel Taylor Coleridge are the reason the author of the books of 1 and 2 Kings took the trouble to write them. It may be arguable that history repeats itself exactly, but the *mistakes* of history do so with alarming and deadening regularity. The books of 1 and 2 Kings aim to identify the mistakes, so they won't be repeated.

The book of 1 Kings gives the account of the breakup of the united kingdom of Israel. The results of sin are compounded in this case, as King Solomon makes poor choices to seek gods other than the true God (see 11:1–13). Solomon's son Rehoboam succeeds the throne and continues a pattern of poor choices (see 12:1–24). The glorious kingdom of David is lost as the kingdom divides into Israel and Judah with Rehoboam as king in Judah and Jeroboam as king in Israel.

What can we learn from the history of the broken kingdom? We can see by the light of the lantern that God is still seeking his people. He offered a choice to Jeroboam: "If you do whatever I command you and walk in my ways . . . I will be with you" (11:38). God's offer to Jeroboam extends throughout history to his people today. Will we follow him? He is seeking a relationship with us.

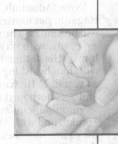

"GIVE ATTENTION TO YOUR SERVANT'S PRAYER." (8:28)

Adonijah Sets Himself Up as King

1 When King David was old and well advanced in years, he could not keep warm even when they put covers over him. ²So his servants said to him, "Let us look for a young virgin to attend the king and take care of him. She can lie beside him so that our lord the king may keep warm."

³Then they searched throughout Israel for a beautiful girl and found Abishag, a Shunammite, and brought her to the king. ⁴The girl was very beautiful; she took care of the king and waited on him, but the king had no intimate relations with her.

⁵Now Adonijah, whose mother was Haggith, put himself forward and said, "I will be king." So he got chariots and horses*a* ready, with fifty men to run ahead of him. ⁶(His father had never interfered with him by asking, "Why do you behave as you do?" He was also very handsome and was born next after Absalom.)

⁷Adonijah conferred with Joab son of Zeruiah and with Abiathar the priest, and they gave him their support. ⁸But Zadok the priest, Benaiah son of Jehoiada, Nathan the prophet, Shimei and Rei*b* and David's special guard did not join Adonijah.

⁹Adonijah then sacrificed sheep, cattle and fattened calves at the Stone of Zoheleth near En Rogel. He invited all his brothers, the king's sons, and all the men of Judah who were royal officials, ¹⁰but he did not invite Nathan the prophet or Benaiah or the special guard or his brother Solomon.

¹¹Then Nathan asked Bathsheba, Solomon's mother, "Have you not heard that Adonijah, the son of Haggith, has become king without our lord David's knowing it? ¹²Now then, let me advise you how you can save your own life and the life of your son Solomon. ¹³Go in to King David and say to him, 'My lord the king, did you not swear to me your servant: "Surely Solomon your son shall be king after me, and he will sit on my throne"? Why then has Adonijah become king?' ¹⁴While you are still there talking to the king, I will come in and confirm what you have said."

¹⁵So Bathsheba went to see the aged king in his room, where Abishag the Shu-

nammite was attending him. ¹⁶Bathsheba bowed low and knelt before the king.

"What is it you want?" the king asked.

¹⁷She said to him, "My lord, you yourself swore to me your servant by the LORD your God: 'Solomon your son shall be king after me, and he will sit on my throne.' ¹⁸But now Adonijah has become king, and you, my lord the king, do not know about it. ¹⁹He has sacrificed great numbers of cattle, fattened calves, and sheep, and has invited all the king's sons, Abiathar the priest and Joab the commander of the army, but he has not invited Solomon your servant. ²⁰My lord the king, the eyes of all Israel are on you, to learn from you who will sit on the throne of my lord the king after him. ²¹Otherwise, as soon as my lord the king is laid to rest with his fathers, I and my son Solomon will be treated as criminals."

²²While she was still speaking with the king, Nathan the prophet arrived. ²³And they told the king, "Nathan the prophet is here." So he went before the king and bowed with his face to the ground.

²⁴Nathan said, "Have you, my lord the king, declared that Adonijah shall be king after you, and that he will sit on your throne? ²⁵Today he has gone down and sacrificed great numbers of cattle, fattened calves, and sheep. He has invited all the king's sons, the commanders of the army and Abiathar the priest. Right now they are eating and drinking with him and saying, 'Long live King Adonijah!' ²⁶But me your servant, and Zadok the priest, and Benaiah son of Jehoiada, and your servant Solomon he did not invite. ²⁷Is this something my lord the king has done without letting his servants know who should sit on the throne of my lord the king after him?"

David Makes Solomon King

²⁸Then King David said, "Call in Bathsheba." So she came into the king's presence and stood before him. ²⁹The king then took an oath: "As surely as the LORD lives, who has delivered me out of every trouble, ³⁰I will surely carry out today what I swore to you by the LORD, the God of Israel: Solomon your

a5 Or charioteers   *b8 Or and his friends*

son shall be king after me, and he will sit on my throne in my place."

³¹Then Bathsheba bowed low with her face to the ground and, kneeling before the king, said, "May my lord King David live forever!"

³²King David said, "Call in Zadok the priest, Nathan the prophet and Benaiah son of Jehoiada." When they came before the king, ³³he said to them: "Take your lord's servants with you and set Solomon my son on my own mule and take him down to Gihon. ³⁴There have Zadok the priest and Nathan the prophet anoint him king over Israel. Blow the trumpet and shout, 'Long live King Solomon!' ³⁵Then you are to go up with him, and he is to come and sit on my throne and reign in my place. I have appointed him ruler over Israel and Judah."

³⁶Benaiah son of Jehoiada answered the king, "Amen! May the LORD, the God of my lord the king, so declare it. ³⁷As the LORD was with my lord the king, so may he be with Solomon to make his throne even greater than the throne of my lord King David!"

³⁸So Zadok the priest, Nathan the prophet, Benaiah son of Jehoiada, the Kerethites and the Pelethites went down and put Solomon on King David's mule and escorted him to Gihon. ³⁹Zadok the priest took the horn of oil from the sacred tent and anointed Solomon. Then they sounded the trumpet and all the people shouted, "Long live King Solomon!" ⁴⁰And all the people went up after him, playing flutes and rejoicing greatly, so that the ground shook with the sound.

⁴¹Adonijah and all the guests who were with him heard it as they were finishing their feast. On hearing the sound of the trumpet, Joab asked, "What's the meaning of all the noise in the city?"

⁴²Even as he was speaking, Jonathan son of Abiathar the priest arrived. Adonijah said, "Come in. A worthy man like you must be bringing good news."

⁴³"Not at all!" Jonathan answered. "Our lord King David has made Solomon king. ⁴⁴The king has sent with him Zadok the priest, Nathan the prophet, Benaiah son of Jehoiada, the Kerethites and the Pelethites, and they have put him on the king's mule, ⁴⁵and Zadok the priest and Nathan the prophet have anointed him king at Gihon. From there they have gone up cheering, and the city resounds with it. That's the noise you hear. ⁴⁶Moreover, Solomon has taken his seat on the royal throne. ⁴⁷Also, the royal officials have come to congratulate our lord King David, saying, 'May your God make Solomon's name more famous than yours and his throne greater than yours!' And the king bowed in worship on his bed ⁴⁸and said, 'Praise be to the LORD, the God of Israel, who has allowed my eyes to see a successor on my throne today.'"

⁴⁹At this, all Adonijah's guests rose in alarm and dispersed. ⁵⁰But Adonijah, in fear of Solomon, went and took hold of the horns of the altar. ⁵¹Then Solomon was told, "Adonijah is afraid of King Solomon and is clinging to the horns of the altar. He says, 'Let King Solomon swear to me today that he will not put his servant to death with the sword.'"

⁵²Solomon replied, "If he shows himself to be a worthy man, not a hair of his head will fall to the ground; but if evil is found in him, he will die." ⁵³Then King Solomon sent men, and they brought him down from the altar. And Adonijah came and bowed down to King Solomon, and Solomon said, "Go to your home."

David's Charge to Solomon

2 When the time drew near for David to die, he gave a charge to Solomon his son.

²"I am about to go the way of all the earth," he said. "So be strong, show yourself a man, ³and observe what the LORD your God requires: Walk in his ways, and keep his decrees and commands, his laws and requirements, as written in the Law of Moses, so that you may prosper in all you do and wherever you go, ⁴and that the LORD may keep his promise to me: 'If your descendants watch how they live, and if they walk faithfully before me with all their heart and soul, you will never fail to have a man on the throne of Israel.'

⁵"Now you yourself know what Joab son of Zeruiah did to me—what he did to the two commanders of Israel's armies, Abner son of Ner and Amasa son of Jether. He killed them, shedding their

SUSANNA WESLEY (1670–1742)

No Higher Calling

NO ONE is busier than a mother with ten children—unless the ten are the survivors of the nineteen she gave birth to—unless her husband is a clergyman who is often absent from the home for weeks and months at a time and is imprisoned for unpaid debts, leaving her to manage both household and parish—unless she also had to suffer the loss of almost everything she owned in fires that twice swept through her home.

Susanna Wesley was a very busy woman. Her family teetered on the brink of starvation so many times that she came to almost dislike the very thought of bread because she had to work so hard to get it. "Strictly speaking, I never did want bread; but then I had so much care to get it before it was eaten, and to pay for it after, as has often made it very unpleasant to me. And I think to have bread on such terms is the next degree of wretchedness to having none at all."[1]

Yet for all that demanded her attention, Wesley knew the real battle was spiritual: not against flesh and blood, numerous and needy children with hungry stomachs, or unpaid debts. The way to victory was through obedience and a willingness to suffer: through times spent in spiritual reading, worship, Scriptural meditation, self-examination and prayer. Her famous son, clergyman John Wesley said of her, "For many years my mother was employed in abundance of temporal business. Yet she never suffered anything to break in upon her stated hours of retirement [prayer times], which she sacredly observed from the age of 17 or 18 to 72."[2] To use a phrase from Bill Hybels, "Where some would find themselves too busy to pray, Wesley knew that she was too busy not to pray."

Susanna Wesley was also animated by a keen sense of the high calling of raising children in the knowledge of God. Though gifted intellectually, and remembered by many as a woman of unusual beauty, charm and intelligence, she felt the most strategic use of her life and gifts was to pour herself into her family. She said, "I desire nothing in this world so much as to have my children well instructed in the principles of religion, that they may walk in the narrow way which alone leads to happiness."[3] The world would later feel the impact of her single-minded sense of vocation through the work of her sons John and Charles.

But her choices were not easy ones, and she often longed for quiet and uninterrupted time with God. She prayed,

> O God, I find it difficult to preserve a devout and serious temper of mind in the midst of much worldly business. Were I permitted to choose a state of life, or positively ask of thee anything in this world, I would humbly choose and beg that I might be placed in such a station wherein I might have daily bread with moderate care and that I may have more leisure to retire from the world without injuring those dependent on me.
>
> Yet I do not know whether such a state of life would really be the best for me; nor am I assured that if I had more leisure I should be more zealously devoted to thee and serve thee better than now. Therefore, O Lord, show me that it is undoubtedly best to keep my mind in habitual submission and resignation to thee.[4]

PRAY:

"O Lord, show me that it is undoubtedly best to keep my mind in habitual submission and resignation to thee."

MEMORIZE:

I know what it is to be in need, and I know what it is to have plenty. I have learned the secret of being content in any and every situation, whether well fed or hungry, whether living in plenty or in want. I can do everything through him who gives me strength. PHILIPPIANS 4:12–13

FOR YOUR NEXT DEVOTIONAL READING, GO TO PAGE 384.

blood in peacetime as if in battle, and with that blood stained the belt around his waist and the sandals on his feet. [6]Deal with him according to your wisdom, but do not let his gray head go down to the grave[a] in peace.

[7]"But show kindness to the sons of Barzillai of Gilead and let them be among those who eat at your table. They stood by me when I fled from your brother Absalom.

[8]"And remember, you have with you Shimei son of Gera, the Benjamite from Bahurim, who called down bitter curses on me the day I went to Mahanaim. When he came down to meet me at the Jordan, I swore to him by the LORD: 'I will not put you to death by the sword.' [9]But now, do not consider him innocent. You are a man of wisdom; you will know what to do to him. Bring his gray head down to the grave in blood."

[10]Then David rested with his fathers and was buried in the City of David. [11]He had reigned forty years over Israel—seven years in Hebron and thirty-three in Jerusalem. [12]So Solomon sat on the throne of his father David, and his rule was firmly established.

Solomon's Throne Established

[13]Now Adonijah, the son of Haggith, went to Bathsheba, Solomon's mother. Bathsheba asked him, "Do you come peacefully?"

He answered, "Yes, peacefully." [14]Then he added, "I have something to say to you."

"You may say it," she replied.

[15]"As you know," he said, "the kingdom was mine. All Israel looked to me as their king. But things changed, and the kingdom has gone to my brother; for it has come to him from the LORD. [16]Now I have one request to make of you. Do not refuse me."

"You may make it," she said.

[17]So he continued, "Please ask King Solomon—he will not refuse you—to give me Abishag the Shunammite as my wife."

[18]"Very well," Bathsheba replied, "I will speak to the king for you."

[19]When Bathsheba went to King Solomon to speak to him for Adonijah, the king stood up to meet her, bowed down to her and sat down on his throne. He had a throne brought for the king's mother, and she sat down at his right hand.

[20]"I have one small request to make of you," she said. "Do not refuse me."

The king replied, "Make it, my mother; I will not refuse you."

[21]So she said, "Let Abishag the Shunammite be given in marriage to your brother Adonijah."

[22]King Solomon answered his mother, "Why do you request Abishag the Shunammite for Adonijah? You might as well request the kingdom for him—after all, he is my older brother—yes, for him and for Abiathar the priest and Joab son of Zeruiah!"

[23]Then King Solomon swore by the LORD: "May God deal with me, be it ever so severely, if Adonijah does not pay with his life for this request! [24]And now, as surely as the LORD lives—he who has established me securely on the throne of my father David and has founded a dynasty for me as he promised—Adonijah shall be put to death today!" [25]So King Solomon gave orders to Benaiah son of Jehoiada, and he struck down Adonijah and he died.

[26]To Abiathar the priest the king said, "Go back to your fields in Anathoth. You deserve to die, but I will not put you to death now, because you carried the ark of the Sovereign LORD before my father David and shared all my father's hardships." [27]So Solomon removed Abiathar from the priesthood of the LORD, fulfilling the word the LORD had spoken at Shiloh about the house of Eli.

[28]When the news reached Joab, who had conspired with Adonijah though not with Absalom, he fled to the tent of the LORD and took hold of the horns of the altar. [29]King Solomon was told that Joab had fled to the tent of the LORD and was beside the altar. Then Solomon ordered Benaiah son of Jehoiada, "Go, strike him down!"

[30]So Benaiah entered the tent of the LORD and said to Joab, "The king says, 'Come out!'"

But he answered, "No, I will die here."

[a]6 Hebrew *Sheol*; also in verse 9

Benaiah reported to the king, "This is how Joab answered me."

³¹Then the king commanded Benaiah, "Do as he says. Strike him down and bury him, and so clear me and my father's house of the guilt of the innocent blood that Joab shed. ³²The LORD will repay him for the blood he shed, because without the knowledge of my father David he attacked two men and killed them with the sword. Both of them—Abner son of Ner, commander of Israel's army, and Amasa son of Jether, commander of Judah's army—were better men and more upright than he. ³³May the guilt of their blood rest on the head of Joab and his descendants forever. But on David and his descendants, his house and his throne, may there be the LORD's peace forever."

³⁴So Benaiah son of Jehoiada went up and struck down Joab and killed him, and he was buried on his own land*a* in the desert. ³⁵The king put Benaiah son of Jehoiada over the army in Joab's position and replaced Abiathar with Zadok the priest.

³⁶Then the king sent for Shimei and said to him, "Build yourself a house in Jerusalem and live there, but do not go anywhere else. ³⁷The day you leave and cross the Kidron Valley, you can be sure you will die; your blood will be on your own head."

³⁸Shimei answered the king, "What you say is good. Your servant will do as my lord the king has said." And Shimei stayed in Jerusalem for a long time.

³⁹But three years later, two of Shimei's slaves ran off to Achish son of Maacah, king of Gath, and Shimei was told, "Your slaves are in Gath." ⁴⁰At this, he saddled his donkey and went to Achish at Gath in search of his slaves. So Shimei went away and brought the slaves back from Gath.

⁴¹When Solomon was told that Shimei had gone from Jerusalem to Gath and had returned, ⁴²the king summoned Shimei and said to him, "Did I not make you swear by the LORD and warn you, 'On the day you leave to go anywhere else, you can be sure you will die'? At that time you said to me, 'What you say is good. I will obey.' ⁴³Why then did you not keep your oath to the LORD and obey the command I gave you?"

⁴⁴The king also said to Shimei, "You know in your heart all the wrong you did to my father David. Now the LORD will repay you for your wrongdoing. ⁴⁵But King Solomon will be blessed, and David's throne will remain secure before the LORD forever."

⁴⁶Then the king gave the order to Benaiah son of Jehoiada, and he went out and struck Shimei down and killed him.

The kingdom was now firmly established in Solomon's hands.

Solomon Asks for Wisdom

3 Solomon made an alliance with Pharaoh king of Egypt and married his daughter. He brought her to the City of David until he finished building his palace and the temple of the LORD, and the wall around Jerusalem. ²The people, however, were still sacrificing at the high places, because a temple had not yet been built for the Name of the LORD. ³Solomon showed his love for the LORD by walking according to the statutes of his father David, except that he offered sacrifices and burned incense on the high places.

⁴The king went to Gibeon to offer sacrifices, for that was the most important high place, and Solomon offered a thousand burnt offerings on that altar. ⁵At Gibeon the LORD appeared to Solomon during the night in a dream, and God said, "Ask for whatever you want me to give you."

⁶Solomon answered, "You have shown great kindness to your servant, my father David, because he was faithful to you and righteous and upright in heart. You have continued this great kindness to him and have given him a son to sit on his throne this very day.

⁷"Now, O LORD my God, you have made your servant king in place of my father David. But I am only a little child and do not know how to carry out my duties. ⁸Your servant is here among the people you have chosen, a great people, too numerous to count or number. ⁹So give your servant a discerning heart to govern your

a34 Or *buried in his tomb*

people and to distinguish between right and wrong. For who is able to govern this great people of yours?"

¹⁰The Lord was pleased that Solomon had asked for this. ¹¹So God said to him, "Since you have asked for this and not for long life or wealth for yourself, nor have asked for the death of your enemies but for discernment in administering justice, ¹²I will do what you have asked. I will give you a wise and discerning heart, so that there will never have been anyone like you, nor will there ever be. ¹³Moreover, I will give you what you have not asked for—both riches and honor—so that in your lifetime you will have no equal among kings. ¹⁴And if you walk in my ways and obey my statutes and commands as David your father did, I will give you a long life." ¹⁵Then Solomon awoke—and he realized it had been a dream.

[MONDAY]

1 KINGS 3:1–15

Whatever You Want

3:5 "GOD SAID, 'ASK FOR WHATEVER YOU WANT ME TO GIVE YOU.'"

The way you respond to an unlimited offer will say a lot about who you are inside. God says, "You can have anything you want, go ahead and ask, and it shall be yours," and adds, implicitly, "and what you ask will reveal you." Is that why Jesus said, "You may ask me for anything in my name, and I will do it" (John 14:14)? The sky's the limit—if you ask in his name. But what you ask will reveal what you know about his name, how congruent your heart is with the heart of God. Your desires say much about you.

Solomon's response could not have been better; being recently established as Israel's king, he asked for a discerning heart to govern the people. When he asked for wisdom, he got all the other things he might have asked for as well. Had he asked only for a good thing, he would have gotten the good thing and nothing more. Asking for the best got him the best and the good as well. It's like seeking first the kingdom of God and his righteousness; when you do "all these things will be given to you as well" (Matthew 6:33).

Merely good things are the red herrings of life. In mystery novels, red herrings are false clues meant to lead the detective down a wrong path. They get their name from the practice of criminals in the 19ᵗʰ century, who dragged smoked herring down a false path to mislead police bloodhounds. The enemy of God's best is not the worst, but the less than the best, the good things.

God's complaint is that we want too little, not too much. C. S. Lewis said: "We are half-hearted creatures, fooling about with drink and sex and ambition when infinite joy is offered us, like an ignorant child who wants to go on making mud pies in a slum because he cannot imagine what is meant by the offer of a holiday at the sea. We are far too easily pleased."⁵ Let your prayers be big—as big as the great and wise God we worship.

PRAY:

Father in heaven, teach me to know you and cause me to so love you that I ask for precisely what you want me to ask for.

FOR YOUR NEXT DEVOTIONAL READING, GO TO PAGE 405.

He returned to Jerusalem, stood before the ark of the Lord's covenant and sacrificed burnt offerings and fellowship offerings.[a] Then he gave a feast for all his court.

A Wise Ruling

[16]Now two prostitutes came to the king and stood before him. [17]One of them said, "My lord, this woman and I live in the same house. I had a baby while she was there with me. [18]The third day after my child was born, this woman also had a baby. We were alone; there was no one in the house but the two of us.

[19]"During the night this woman's son died because she lay on him. [20]So she got up in the middle of the night and took my son from my side while I your servant was asleep. She put him by her breast and put her dead son by my breast. [21]The next morning, I got up to nurse my son—and he was dead! But when I looked at him closely in the morning light, I saw that it wasn't the son I had borne."

[22]The other woman said, "No! The living one is my son; the dead one is yours."

But the first one insisted, "No! The dead one is yours; the living one is mine." And so they argued before the king.

[23]The king said, "This one says, 'My son is alive and your son is dead,' while that one says, 'No! Your son is dead and mine is alive.'"

[24]Then the king said, "Bring me a sword." So they brought a sword for the king. [25]He then gave an order: "Cut the living child in two and give half to one and half to the other."

[26]The woman whose son was alive was filled with compassion for her son and said to the king, "Please, my lord, give her the living baby! Don't kill him!"

But the other said, "Neither I nor you shall have him. Cut him in two!"

[27]Then the king gave his ruling: "Give the living baby to the first woman. Do not kill him; she is his mother."

[28]When all Israel heard the verdict the king had given, they held the king in awe, because they saw that he had wisdom from God to administer justice.

Solomon's Officials and Governors

4 So King Solomon ruled over all Israel. [2]And these were his chief officials:

Azariah son of Zadok—the priest;

[3]Elihoreph and Ahijah, sons of Shisha—secretaries;

Jehoshaphat son of Ahilud—recorder;

[4]Benaiah son of Jehoiada—commander in chief;

Zadok and Abiathar—priests;

[5]Azariah son of Nathan—in charge of the district officers;

Zabud son of Nathan—a priest and personal adviser to the king;

[6]Ahishar—in charge of the palace;

Adoniram son of Abda—in charge of forced labor.

[7]Solomon also had twelve district governors over all Israel, who supplied provisions for the king and the royal household. Each one had to provide supplies for one month in the year. [8]These are their names:

Ben-Hur—in the hill country of Ephraim;

[9]Ben-Deker—in Makaz, Shaalbim, Beth Shemesh and Elon Bethhanan;

[10]Ben-Hesed—in Arubboth (Socoh and all the land of Hepher were his);

[11]Ben-Abinadab—in Naphoth Dor[b] (he was married to Taphath daughter of Solomon);

[12]Baana son of Ahilud—in Taanach and Megiddo, and in all of Beth Shan next to Zarethan below Jezreel, from Beth Shan to Abel Meholah across to Jokmeam;

[13]Ben-Geber—in Ramoth Gilead (the settlements of Jair son of Manasseh in Gilead were his, as well as the district of Argob in Bashan and its sixty large walled cities with bronze gate bars);

[14]Ahinadab son of Iddo—in Mahanaim;

[15]Ahimaaz—in Naphtali (he had married Basemath daughter of Solomon);

[16]Baana son of Hushai—in Asher and in Aloth;

[17]Jehoshaphat son of Paruah—in Issachar;

---

[a]15 Traditionally *peace offerings*   [b]11 Or *in the heights of Dor*

¹⁸Shimei son of Ela—in Benjamin;
¹⁹Geber son of Uri—in Gilead (the country of Sihon king of the Amorites and the country of Og king of Bashan). He was the only governor over the district.

Solomon's Daily Provisions

²⁰The people of Judah and Israel were as numerous as the sand on the seashore; they ate, they drank and they were happy. ²¹And Solomon ruled over all the kingdoms from the River[a] to the land of the Philistines, as far as the border of Egypt. These countries brought tribute and were Solomon's subjects all his life.

²²Solomon's daily provisions were thirty cors[b] of fine flour and sixty cors[c] of meal, ²³ten head of stall-fed cattle, twenty of pasture-fed cattle and a hundred sheep and goats, as well as deer, gazelles, roebucks and choice fowl. ²⁴For he ruled over all the kingdoms west of the River, from Tiphsah to Gaza, and had peace on all sides. ²⁵During Solomon's lifetime Judah and Israel, from Dan to Beersheba, lived in safety, each man under his own vine and fig tree.

²⁶Solomon had four[d] thousand stalls for chariot horses, and twelve thousand horses.[e]

²⁷The district officers, each in his month, supplied provisions for King Solomon and all who came to the king's table. They saw to it that nothing was lacking. ²⁸They also brought to the proper place their quotas of barley and straw for the chariot horses and the other horses.

Solomon's Wisdom

²⁹God gave Solomon wisdom and very great insight, and a breadth of understanding as measureless as the sand on the seashore. ³⁰Solomon's wisdom was greater than the wisdom of all the men of the East, and greater than all the wisdom of Egypt. ³¹He was wiser than any other man, including Ethan the Ezrahite—wiser than Heman, Calcol and Darda, the sons of Mahol. And his fame spread to all the surrounding nations. ³²He spoke three thousand proverbs and his songs numbered a thousand and five. ³³He described plant life, from the cedar

of Lebanon to the hyssop that grows out of walls. He also taught about animals and birds, reptiles and fish. ³⁴Men of all nations came to listen to Solomon's wisdom, sent by all the kings of the world, who had heard of his wisdom.

Preparations for Building the Temple

5 When Hiram king of Tyre heard that Solomon had been anointed king to succeed his father David, he sent his envoys to Solomon, because he had always been on friendly terms with David. ²Solomon sent back this message to Hiram:

³"You know that because of the wars waged against my father David from all sides, he could not build a temple for the Name of the LORD his God until the LORD put his enemies under his feet. ⁴But now the LORD my God has given me rest on every side, and there is no adversary or disaster. ⁵I intend, therefore, to build a temple for the Name of the LORD my God, as the LORD told my father David, when he said, 'Your son whom I will put on the throne in your place will build the temple for my Name.'

⁶"So give orders that cedars of Lebanon be cut for me. My men will work with yours, and I will pay you for your men whatever wages you set. You know that we have no one so skilled in felling timber as the Sidonians."

⁷When Hiram heard Solomon's message, he was greatly pleased and said, "Praise be to the LORD today, for he has given David a wise son to rule over this great nation."

⁸So Hiram sent word to Solomon:

"I have received the message you sent me and will do all you want in providing the cedar and pine logs. ⁹My men will haul them down from Lebanon to the sea, and I will float them in rafts by sea to the place you specify. There I will separate them

---

[a]21 That is, the Euphrates; also in verse 24
[b]22 That is, probably about 185 bushels (about 6.6 kiloliters)   [c]22 That is, probably about 375 bushels (about 13.2 kiloliters)   [d]26 Some Septuagint manuscripts (see also 2 Chron. 9:25); Hebrew forty   [e]26 Or charioteers

and you can take them away. And you are to grant my wish by providing food for my royal household."

[10]In this way Hiram kept Solomon supplied with all the cedar and pine logs he wanted, [11]and Solomon gave Hiram twenty thousand cors[a] of wheat as food for his household, in addition to twenty thousand baths[b,c] of pressed olive oil. Solomon continued to do this for Hiram year after year. [12]The LORD gave Solomon wisdom, just as he had promised him. There were peaceful relations between Hiram and Solomon, and the two of them made a treaty.

[13]King Solomon conscripted laborers from all Israel—thirty thousand men. [14]He sent them off to Lebanon in shifts of ten thousand a month, so that they spent one month in Lebanon and two months at home. Adoniram was in charge of the forced labor. [15]Solomon had seventy thousand carriers and eighty thousand stonecutters in the hills, [16]as well as thirty-three hundred[d] foremen who supervised the project and directed the workmen. [17]At the king's command they removed from the quarry large blocks of quality stone to provide a foundation of dressed stone for the temple. [18]The craftsmen of Solomon and Hiram and the men of Gebal[e] cut and prepared the timber and stone for the building of the temple.

Solomon Builds the Temple

6 In the four hundred and eightieth[f] year after the Israelites had come out of Egypt, in the fourth year of Solomon's reign over Israel, in the month of Ziv, the second month, he began to build the temple of the LORD.

[2]The temple that King Solomon built for the LORD was sixty cubits long, twenty wide and thirty high.[g] [3]The portico at the front of the main hall of the temple extended the width of the temple, that is twenty cubits,[h] and projected ten cubits[i] from the front of the temple. [4]He made narrow clerestory windows in the temple. [5]Against the walls of the main hall and inner sanctuary he built a structure around the building, in which there were side rooms. [6]The lowest floor was five cu-

bits[j] wide, the middle floor six cubits[k] and the third floor seven.[l] He made offset ledges around the outside of the temple so that nothing would be inserted into the temple walls.

[7]In building the temple, only blocks dressed at the quarry were used, and no hammer, chisel or any other iron tool was heard at the temple site while it was being built.

[8]The entrance to the lowest[m] floor was on the south side of the temple; a stairway led up to the middle level and from there to the third. [9]So he built the temple and completed it, roofing it with beams and cedar planks. [10]And he built the side rooms all along the temple. The height of each was five cubits, and they were attached to the temple by beams of cedar.

[11]The word of the LORD came to Solomon: [12]"As for this temple you are building, if you follow my decrees, carry out my regulations and keep all my commands and obey them, I will fulfill through you the promise I gave to David your father. [13]And I will live among the Israelites and will not abandon my people Israel."

[14]So Solomon built the temple and completed it. [15]He lined its interior walls with cedar boards, paneling them from the floor of the temple to the ceiling, and covered the floor of the temple with planks of pine. [16]He partitioned off twenty cubits[h] at the rear of the temple with cedar boards from floor to ceiling to form within the temple an inner sanctuary, the Most Holy Place. [17]The main hall in front of this room was forty cubits[n] long. [18]The

---

[a]11 That is, probably about 125,000 bushels (about 4,400 kiloliters)   [b]11 Septuagint (see also 2 Chron. 2:10); Hebrew *twenty cors*   [c]11 That is, about 115,000 gallons (about 440 kiloliters)   [d]16 Hebrew; some Septuagint manuscripts (see also 2 Chron. 2:2,18) *thirty-six hundred*   [e]18 That is, Byblos   [f]1 Hebrew; Septuagint *four hundred and fortieth*   [g]2 That is, about 90 feet (about 27 meters) long and 30 feet (about 9 meters) wide and 45 feet (about 13.5 meters) high   [h]3,16 That is, about 30 feet (about 9 meters)   [i]3 That is, about 15 feet (about 4.5 meters)   [j]6 That is, about 7 1/2 feet (about 2.3 meters); also in verses 10 and 24   [k]6 That is, about 9 feet (about 2.7 meters)   [l]6 That is, about 10 1/2 feet (about 3.1 meters)   [m]8 Septuagint; Hebrew *middle*   [n]17 That is, about 60 feet (about 18 meters)

inside of the temple was cedar, carved with gourds and open flowers. Everything was cedar; no stone was to be seen.

¹⁹He prepared the inner sanctuary within the temple to set the ark of the covenant of the LORD there. ²⁰The inner sanctuary was twenty cubits long, twenty wide and twenty high.ᵃ He overlaid the inside with pure gold, and he also overlaid the altar of cedar. ²¹Solomon covered the inside of the temple with pure gold, and he extended gold chains across the front of the inner sanctuary, which was overlaid with gold. ²²So he overlaid the whole interior with gold. He also overlaid with gold the altar that belonged to the inner sanctuary.

²³In the inner sanctuary he made a pair of cherubim of olive wood, each ten cubitsᵇ high. ²⁴One wing of the first cherub was five cubits long, and the other wing five cubits—ten cubits from wing tip to wing tip. ²⁵The second cherub also measured ten cubits, for the two cherubim were identical in size and shape. ²⁶The height of each cherub was ten cubits. ²⁷He placed the cherubim inside the innermost room of the temple, with their wings spread out. The wing of one cherub touched one wall, while the wing of the other touched the other wall, and their wings touched each other in the middle of the room. ²⁸He overlaid the cherubim with gold.

²⁹On the walls all around the temple, in both the inner and outer rooms, he carved cherubim, palm trees and open flowers. ³⁰He also covered the floors of both the inner and outer rooms of the temple with gold.

³¹For the entrance of the inner sanctuary he made doors of olive wood with five-sided jambs. ³²And on the two olive wood doors he carved cherubim, palm trees and open flowers, and overlaid the cherubim and palm trees with beaten gold. ³³In the same way he made four-sided jambs of olive wood for the entrance to the main hall. ³⁴He also made two pine doors, each having two leaves that turned in sockets. ³⁵He carved cherubim, palm trees and open flowers on them and overlaid them with gold hammered evenly over the carvings.

³⁶And he built the inner courtyard of three courses of dressed stone and one course of trimmed cedar beams.

³⁷The foundation of the temple of the LORD was laid in the fourth year, in the month of Ziv. ³⁸In the eleventh year in the month of Bul, the eighth month, the temple was finished in all its details according to its specifications. He had spent seven years building it.

Solomon Builds His Palace

7 It took Solomon thirteen years, however, to complete the construction of his palace. ²He built the Palace of the Forest of Lebanon a hundred cubits long, fifty wide and thirty high,ᶜ with four rows of cedar columns supporting trimmed cedar beams. ³It was roofed with cedar above the beams that rested on the columns—forty-five beams, fifteen to a row. ⁴Its windows were placed high in sets of three, facing each other. ⁵All the doorways had rectangular frames; they were in the front part in sets of three, facing each other.ᵈ

⁶He made a colonnade fifty cubits long and thirty wide.ᵉ In front of it was a portico, and in front of that were pillars and an overhanging roof.

⁷He built the throne hall, the Hall of Justice, where he was to judge, and he covered it with cedar from floor to ceiling.ᶠ ⁸And the palace in which he was to live, set farther back, was similar in design. Solomon also made a palace like this hall for Pharaoh's daughter, whom he had married.

⁹All these structures, from the outside to the great courtyard and from foundation to eaves, were made of blocks of high-grade stone cut to size and trimmed with a saw on their inner and outer faces. ¹⁰The foundations were laid with large stones of good quality, some measuring ten cubitsᵍ and some eight.ʰ ¹¹Above were

---

ᵃ20 That is, about 30 feet (about 9 meters) long, wide and high   ᵇ23 That is, about 15 feet (about 4.5 meters)   ᶜ2 That is, about 150 feet (about 46 meters) long, 75 feet (about 23 meters) wide and 45 feet (about 13.5 meters) high
ᵈ5 The meaning of the Hebrew for this verse is uncertain.   ᵉ6 That is, about 75 feet (about 23 meters) long and 45 feet (about 13.5 meters) wide   ᶠ7 Vulgate and Syriac; Hebrew *floor*   ᵍ10 That is, about 15 feet (about 4.5 meters)   ʰ10 That is, about 12 feet (about 3.6 meters)

high-grade stones, cut to size, and cedar beams. ¹²The great courtyard was surrounded by a wall of three courses of dressed stone and one course of trimmed cedar beams, as was the inner courtyard of the temple of the LORD with its portico.

The Temple's Furnishings

¹³King Solomon sent to Tyre and brought Huram,ᵃ ¹⁴whose mother was a widow from the tribe of Naphtali and whose father was a man of Tyre and a craftsman in bronze. Huram was highly skilled and experienced in all kinds of bronze work. He came to King Solomon and did all the work assigned to him.

¹⁵He cast two bronze pillars, each eighteen cubits high and twelve cubits around,ᵇ by line. ¹⁶He also made two capitals of cast bronze to set on the tops of the pillars; each capital was five cubitsᶜ high. ¹⁷A network of interwoven chains festooned the capitals on top of the pillars, seven for each capital. ¹⁸He made pomegranates in two rowsᵈ encircling each network to decorate the capitals on top of the pillars.ᵉ He did the same for each capital. ¹⁹The capitals on top of the pillars in the portico were in the shape of lilies, four cubitsᶠ high. ²⁰On the capitals of both pillars, above the bowl-shaped part next to the network, were the two hundred pomegranates in rows all around. ²¹He erected the pillars at the portico of the temple. The pillar to the south he named Jakinᵍ and the one to the north Boaz.ʰ ²²The capitals on top were in the shape of lilies. And so the work on the pillars was completed.

²³He made the Sea of cast metal, circular in shape, measuring ten cubitsⁱ from rim to rim and five cubits high. It took a line of thirty cubitsʲ to measure around it. ²⁴Below the rim, gourds encircled it— ten to a cubit. The gourds were cast in two rows in one piece with the Sea.

²⁵The Sea stood on twelve bulls, three facing north, three facing west, three facing south and three facing east. The Sea rested on top of them, and their hindquarters were toward the center. ²⁶It was a handbreadthᵏ in thickness, and its rim was like the rim of a cup, like a lily blossom. It held two thousand baths.ˡ

²⁷He also made ten movable stands of bronze; each was four cubits long, four wide and three high.ᵐ ²⁸This is how the stands were made: They had side panels attached to uprights. ²⁹On the panels between the uprights were lions, bulls and cherubim—and on the uprights as well. Above and below the lions and bulls were wreaths of hammered work. ³⁰Each stand had four bronze wheels with bronze axles, and each had a basin resting on four supports, cast with wreaths on each side. ³¹On the inside of the stand there was an opening that had a circular frame one cubitⁿ deep. This opening was round, and with its basework it measured a cubit and a half.ᵒ Around its opening there was engraving. The panels of the stands were square, not round. ³²The four wheels were under the panels, and the axles of the wheels were attached to the stand. The diameter of each wheel was a cubit and a half. ³³The wheels were made like chariot wheels; the axles, rims, spokes and hubs were all of cast metal.

³⁴Each stand had four handles, one on each corner, projecting from the stand. ³⁵At the top of the stand there was a circular band half a cubitᵖ deep. The supports and panels were attached to the top of the stand. ³⁶He engraved cherubim, lions and palm trees on the surfaces of the supports and on the panels, in every available space, with wreaths all around. ³⁷This is the way he made the ten stands.

ᵃ13 Hebrew *Hiram*, a variant of *Huram*; also in verses 40 and 45   ᵇ15 That is, about 27 feet (about 8.1 meters) high and 18 feet (about 5.4 meters) around   ᶜ16 That is, about 7 1/2 feet (about 2.3 meters); also in verse 23   ᵈ18 Two Hebrew manuscripts and Septuagint; most Hebrew manuscripts *made the pillars, and there were two rows*   ᵉ18 Many Hebrew manuscripts and Syriac; most Hebrew manuscripts *pomegranates*   ᶠ19 That is, about 6 feet (about 1.8 meters); also in verse 38   ᵍ21 *Jakin* probably means *he establishes.*   ʰ21 *Boaz* probably means *in him is strength.*   ⁱ23 That is, about 15 feet (about 4.5 meters)   ʲ23 That is, about 45 feet (about 13.5 meters)   ᵏ26 That is, about 3 inches (about 8 centimeters)   ˡ26 That is, probably about 11,500 gallons (about 44 kiloliters); the Septuagint does not have this sentence.   ᵐ27 That is, about 6 feet (about 1.8 meters) long and wide and about 4 1/2 feet (about 1.3 meters) high   ⁿ31 That is, about 1 1/2 feet (about 0.5 meter)   ᵒ31 That is, about 2 1/4 feet (about 0.7 meter); also in verse 32   ᵖ35 That is, about 3/4 foot (about 0.2 meter)

They were all cast in the same molds and were identical in size and shape.

38He then made ten bronze basins, each holding forty baths[a] and measuring four cubits across, one basin to go on each of the ten stands. 39He placed five of the stands on the south side of the temple and five on the north. He placed the Sea on the south side, at the southeast corner of the temple. 40He also made the basins and shovels and sprinkling bowls.

So Huram finished all the work he had undertaken for King Solomon in the temple of the LORD:

41 the two pillars;
the two bowl-shaped capitals on top of the pillars;
the two sets of network decorating the two bowl-shaped capitals on top of the pillars;
42 the four hundred pomegranates for the two sets of network (two rows of pomegranates for each network, decorating the bowl-shaped capitals on top of the pillars);
43 the ten stands with their ten basins;
44 the Sea and the twelve bulls under it;
45 the pots, shovels and sprinkling bowls.

All these objects that Huram made for King Solomon for the temple of the LORD were of burnished bronze. 46The king had them cast in clay molds in the plain of the Jordan between Succoth and Zarethan. 47Solomon left all these things unweighed, because there were so many; the weight of the bronze was not determined.

48Solomon also made all the furnishings that were in the LORD's temple:

the golden altar;
the golden table on which was the bread of the Presence;
49 the lampstands of pure gold (five on the right and five on the left, in front of the inner sanctuary);
the gold floral work and lamps and tongs;
50 the pure gold basins, wick trimmers, sprinkling bowls, dishes and censers;
and the gold sockets for the doors of the innermost room, the Most Holy Place, and also for the doors of the main hall of the temple.

51When all the work King Solomon had done for the temple of the LORD was finished, he brought in the things his father David had dedicated—the silver and gold and the furnishings—and he placed them in the treasuries of the LORD's temple.

The Ark Brought to the Temple

8 Then King Solomon summoned into his presence at Jerusalem the elders of Israel, all the heads of the tribes and the chiefs of the Israelite families, to bring up the ark of the LORD's covenant from Zion, the City of David. 2All the men of Israel came together to King Solomon at the time of the festival in the month of Ethanim, the seventh month.

3When all the elders of Israel had arrived, the priests took up the ark, 4and they brought up the ark of the LORD and the Tent of Meeting and all the sacred furnishings in it. The priests and Levites carried them up, 5and King Solomon and the entire assembly of Israel that had gathered about him were before the ark, sacrificing so many sheep and cattle that they could not be recorded or counted.

6The priests then brought the ark of the LORD's covenant to its place in the inner sanctuary of the temple, the Most Holy Place, and put it beneath the wings of the cherubim. 7The cherubim spread their wings over the place of the ark and overshadowed the ark and its carrying poles. 8These poles were so long that their ends could be seen from the Holy Place in front of the inner sanctuary, but not from outside the Holy Place; and they are still there today. 9There was nothing in the ark except the two stone tablets that Moses had placed in it at Horeb, where the LORD made a covenant with the Israelites after they came out of Egypt.

10When the priests withdrew from the Holy Place, the cloud filled the temple of the LORD. 11And the priests could not perform their service because of the cloud, for the glory of the LORD filled his temple.

12Then Solomon said, "The LORD has said that he would dwell in a dark cloud; 13I have indeed built a magnificent temple for you, a place for you to dwell forever."

---

a38 That is, about 230 gallons (about 880 liters)

¹⁴While the whole assembly of Israel was standing there, the king turned around and blessed them. ¹⁵Then he said:

"Praise be to the LORD, the God of Israel, who with his own hand has fulfilled what he promised with his own mouth to my father David. For he said, ¹⁶'Since the day I brought my people Israel out of Egypt, I have not chosen a city in any tribe of Israel to have a temple built for my Name to be there, but I have chosen David to rule my people Israel.'

¹⁷"My father David had it in his heart to build a temple for the Name of the LORD, the God of Israel. ¹⁸But the LORD said to my father David, 'Because it was in your heart to build a temple for my Name, you did well to have this in your heart. ¹⁹Nevertheless, you are not the one to build the temple, but your son, who is your own flesh and blood—he is the one who will build the temple for my Name.'

²⁰"The LORD has kept the promise he made: I have succeeded David my father and now I sit on the throne of Israel, just as the LORD promised, and I have built the temple for the Name of the LORD, the God of Israel. ²¹I have provided a place there for the ark, in which is the covenant of the LORD that he made with our fathers when he brought them out of Egypt."

Solomon's Prayer of Dedication

²²Then Solomon stood before the altar of the LORD in front of the whole assembly of Israel, spread out his hands toward heaven ²³and said:

"O LORD, God of Israel, there is no God like you in heaven above or on earth below—you who keep your covenant of love with your servants who continue wholeheartedly in your way. ²⁴You have kept your promise to your servant David my father; with your mouth you have promised and with your hand you have fulfilled it—as it is today.

²⁵"Now LORD, God of Israel, keep for your servant David my father the promises you made to him when you said, 'You shall never fail to have a man to sit before me on the throne of Israel, if only your sons are careful in all they do to walk before me as you have done.' ²⁶And now, O God of Israel, let your word that you promised your servant David my father come true.

²⁷"But will God really dwell on earth? The heavens, even the highest heaven, cannot contain you. How much less this temple I have built! ²⁸Yet give attention to your servant's prayer and his plea for mercy, O LORD my God. Hear the cry and the prayer that your servant is praying in your presence this day. ²⁹May your eyes be open toward this temple night and day, this place of which you said, 'My Name shall be there,' so that you will hear the prayer your servant prays toward this place. ³⁰Hear the supplication of your servant and of your people Israel when they pray toward this place. Hear from heaven, your dwelling place, and when you hear, forgive.

> "GIVE attention to your servant's prayer and his plea for mercy, O LORD my God. Hear the cry and the prayer that your servant is praying in your presence this day."
>
> 1 KINGS 8:28

³¹"When a man wrongs his neighbor and is required to take an oath and he comes and swears the oath before your altar in this temple, ³²then hear from heaven and act. Judge between your servants, condemning the guilty and bringing down on his own head what he has done. Declare the innocent not guilty, and so establish his innocence.

³³"When your people Israel have been defeated by an enemy because they have sinned against you, and when they turn back to you and confess your name, praying and making supplication to you in this temple,

³⁴then hear from heaven and forgive the sin of your people Israel and bring them back to the land you gave to their fathers.

³⁵"When the heavens are shut up and there is no rain because your people have sinned against you, and when they pray toward this place and confess your name and turn from their sin because you have afflicted them, ³⁶then hear from heaven and forgive the sin of your servants, your people Israel. Teach them the right way to live, and send rain on the land you gave your people for an inheritance.

³⁷"When famine or plague comes to the land, or blight or mildew, locusts or grasshoppers, or when an enemy besieges them in any of their cities, whatever disaster or disease may come, ³⁸and when a prayer or plea is made by any of your people Israel—each one aware of the afflictions of his own heart, and spreading out his hands toward this temple— ³⁹then hear from heaven, your dwelling place. Forgive and act; deal with each man according to all he does, since you know his heart (for you alone know the hearts of all men), ⁴⁰so that they will fear you all the time they live in the land you gave our fathers.

⁴¹"As for the foreigner who does not belong to your people Israel but has come from a distant land because of your name— ⁴²for men will hear of your great name and your mighty hand and your outstretched arm—when he comes and prays toward this temple, ⁴³then hear from heaven, your dwelling place, and do whatever the foreigner asks of you, so that all the peoples of the earth may know your name and fear you, as do your own people Israel, and may know that this house I have built bears your Name.

⁴⁴"When your people go to war against their enemies, wherever you send them, and when they pray to the LORD toward the city you have chosen and the temple I have built for your Name, ⁴⁵then hear from heaven their prayer and their plea, and uphold their cause.

⁴⁶"When they sin against you—for there is no one who does not sin— and you become angry with them and give them over to the enemy, who takes them captive to his own land, far away or near; ⁴⁷and if they have a change of heart in the land where they are held captive, and repent and plead with you in the land of their conquerors and say, 'We have sinned, we have done wrong, we have acted wickedly'; ⁴⁸and if they turn back to you with all their heart and soul in the land of their enemies who took them captive, and pray to you toward the land you gave their fathers, toward the city you have chosen and the temple I have built for your Name; ⁴⁹then from heaven, your dwelling place, hear their prayer and their plea, and uphold their cause. ⁵⁰And forgive your people, who have sinned against you; forgive all the offenses they have committed against you, and cause their conquerors to show them mercy; ⁵¹for they are your people and your inheritance, whom you brought out of Egypt, out of that iron-smelting furnace.

⁵²"May your eyes be open to your servant's plea and to the plea of your people Israel, and may you listen to them whenever they cry out to you. ⁵³For you singled them out from all the nations of the world to be your own inheritance, just as you declared through your servant Moses when you, O Sovereign LORD, brought our fathers out of Egypt."

⁵⁴When Solomon had finished all these prayers and supplications to the LORD, he rose from before the altar of the LORD, where he had been kneeling with his hands spread out toward heaven. ⁵⁵He

> "MAY your eyes be open to your servant's plea and to the plea of your people Israel, and may you listen to them whenever they cry out to you."
>
> 1 KINGS 8:52

stood and blessed the whole assembly of Israel in a loud voice, saying:

⁵⁶"Praise be to the LORD, who has given rest to his people Israel just as he promised. Not one word has failed of all the good promises he gave through his servant Moses. ⁵⁷May the LORD our God be with us as he was with our fathers; may he never leave us nor forsake us. ⁵⁸May he turn our hearts to him, to walk in all his ways and to keep the commands, decrees and regulations he gave our fathers. ⁵⁹And may these words of mine, which I have prayed before the LORD, be near to the LORD our God day and night, that he may uphold the cause of his servant and the cause of his people Israel according to each day's need, ⁶⁰so that all the peoples of the earth may know that the LORD is God and that there is no other. ⁶¹But your hearts must be fully committed to the LORD our God, to live by his decrees and obey his commands, as at this time."

The Dedication of the Temple

⁶²Then the king and all Israel with him offered sacrifices before the LORD. ⁶³Solomon offered a sacrifice of fellowship offerings[a] to the LORD: twenty-two thousand cattle and a hundred and twenty thousand sheep and goats. So the king and all the Israelites dedicated the temple of the LORD.

⁶⁴On that same day the king consecrated the middle part of the courtyard in front of the temple of the LORD, and there he offered burnt offerings, grain offerings and the fat of the fellowship offerings, because the bronze altar before the LORD was too small to hold the burnt offerings, the grain offerings and the fat of the fellowship offerings.

⁶⁵So Solomon observed the festival at that time, and all Israel with him—a vast assembly, people from Lebo[b] Hamath to the Wadi of Egypt. They celebrated it before the LORD our God for seven days and seven days more, fourteen days in all. ⁶⁶On the following day he sent the people away. They blessed the king and then went home, joyful and glad in heart for all the good things the LORD had done for his servant David and his people Israel.

The LORD Appears to Solomon

9 When Solomon had finished building the temple of the LORD and the royal palace, and had achieved all he had desired to do, ²the LORD appeared to him a second time, as he had appeared to him at Gibeon. ³The LORD said to him:

"I have heard the prayer and plea you have made before me; I have consecrated this temple, which you have built, by putting my Name there forever. My eyes and my heart will always be there.

⁴"As for you, if you walk before me in integrity of heart and uprightness, as David your father did, and do all I command and observe my decrees and laws, ⁵I will establish your royal throne over Israel forever, as I promised David your father when I said, 'You shall never fail to have a man on the throne of Israel.'

⁶"But if you[c] or your sons turn away from me and do not observe the commands and decrees I have given you[c] and go off to serve other gods and worship them, ⁷then I will cut off Israel from the land I have given them and will reject this temple I have consecrated for my Name. Israel will then become a byword and an object of ridicule among all peoples. ⁸And though this temple is now imposing, all who pass by will be appalled and will scoff and say, 'Why has the LORD done such a thing to this land and to this temple?' ⁹People will answer, 'Because they have forsaken the LORD their God, who brought their fathers out of Egypt, and have embraced other gods, worshiping and serving them—that is why the LORD brought all this disaster on them.'"

Solomon's Other Activities

¹⁰At the end of twenty years, during which Solomon built these two buildings—the temple of the LORD and the royal palace— ¹¹King Solomon gave twenty towns in Galilee to Hiram king of

---

a63 Traditionally *peace offerings*; also in verse 64 *b65* Or *from the entrance to* *c6* The Hebrew is plural.

Tyre, because Hiram had supplied him with all the cedar and pine and gold he wanted. ¹²But when Hiram went from Tyre to see the towns that Solomon had given him, he was not pleased with them. ¹³"What kind of towns are these you have given me, my brother?" he asked. And he called them the Land of Cabul,ᵃ a name they have to this day. ¹⁴Now Hiram had sent to the king 120 talentsᵇ of gold.

¹⁵Here is the account of the forced labor King Solomon conscripted to build the LORD's temple, his own palace, the supporting terraces,ᶜ the wall of Jerusalem, and Hazor, Megiddo and Gezer. ¹⁶(Pharaoh king of Egypt had attacked and captured Gezer. He had set it on fire. He killed its Canaanite inhabitants and then gave it as a wedding gift to his daughter, Solomon's wife. ¹⁷And Solomon rebuilt Gezer.) He built up Lower Beth Horon, ¹⁸Baalath, and Tadmorᵈ in the desert, within his land, ¹⁹as well as all his store cities and the towns for his chariots and for his horsesᵉ—whatever he desired to build in Jerusalem, in Lebanon and throughout all the territory he ruled.

²⁰All the people left from the Amorites, Hittites, Perizzites, Hivites and Jebusites (these peoples were not Israelites), ²¹that is, their descendants remaining in the land, whom the Israelites could not exterminateᶠ—these Solomon conscripted for his slave labor force, as it is to this day. ²²But Solomon did not make slaves of any of the Israelites; they were his fighting men, his government officials, his officers, his captains, and the commanders of his chariots and charioteers. ²³They were also the chief officials in charge of Solomon's projects—550 officials supervising the men who did the work.

²⁴After Pharaoh's daughter had come up from the City of David to the palace Solomon had built for her, he constructed the supporting terraces.

²⁵Three times a year Solomon sacrificed burnt offerings and fellowship offeringsᵍ on the altar he had built for the LORD, burning incense before the LORD along with them, and so fulfilled the temple obligations.

²⁶King Solomon also built ships at Ezion Geber, which is near Elath in Edom, on the shore of the Red Sea.ʰ ²⁷And Hiram sent his men—sailors who knew the sea—to serve in the fleet with Solomon's men. ²⁸They sailed to Ophir and brought back 420 talentsⁱ of gold, which they delivered to King Solomon.

The Queen of Sheba Visits Solomon

10 When the queen of Sheba heard about the fame of Solomon and his relation to the name of the LORD, she came to test him with hard questions. ²Arriving at Jerusalem with a very great caravan—with camels carrying spices, large quantities of gold, and precious stones—she came to Solomon and talked with him about all that she had on her mind. ³Solomon answered all her questions; nothing was too hard for the king to explain to her. ⁴When the queen of Sheba saw all the wisdom of Solomon and the palace he had built, ⁵the food on his table, the seating of his officials, the attending servants in their robes, his cupbearers, and the burnt offerings he made atʲ the temple of the LORD, she was overwhelmed.

⁶She said to the king, "The report I heard in my own country about your achievements and your wisdom is true. ⁷But I did not believe these things until I came and saw with my own eyes. Indeed, not even half was told me; in wisdom and wealth you have far exceeded the report I heard. ⁸How happy your men must be! How happy your officials, who continually stand before you and hear your wisdom! ⁹Praise be to the LORD your God, who has delighted in you and placed you on the throne of Israel. Because of the LORD's eternal love for Israel, he has made you king, to maintain justice and righteousness."

ᵃ13 *Cabul* sounds like the Hebrew for *good-for-nothing.*   ᵇ14 That is, about 4 1/2 tons (about 4 metric tons)   ᶜ15 Or *the Millo*; also in verse 24   ᵈ18 The Hebrew may also be read *Tamar.*   ᵉ19 Or *charioteers*   ᶠ21 The Hebrew term refers to the irrevocable giving over of things or persons to the LORD, often by totally destroying them.   ᵍ25 Traditionally *peace offerings*   ʰ26 Hebrew *Yam Suph*; that is, Sea of Reeds   ⁱ28 That is, about 16 tons (about 14.5 metric tons)   ʲ5 Or *the ascent by which he went up to*

[10]And she gave the king 120 talents[a] of gold, large quantities of spices, and precious stones. Never again were so many spices brought in as those the queen of Sheba gave to King Solomon.

[11](Hiram's ships brought gold from Ophir; and from there they brought great cargoes of almugwood[b] and precious stones. [12]The king used the almugwood to make supports for the temple of the LORD and for the royal palace, and to make harps and lyres for the musicians. So much almugwood has never been imported or seen since that day.)

[13]King Solomon gave the queen of Sheba all she desired and asked for, besides what he had given her out of his royal bounty. Then she left and returned with her retinue to her own country.

Solomon's Splendor

[14]The weight of the gold that Solomon received yearly was 666 talents,[c] [15]not including the revenues from merchants and traders and from all the Arabian kings and the governors of the land.

[16]King Solomon made two hundred large shields of hammered gold; six hundred bekas[d] of gold went into each shield. [17]He also made three hundred small shields of hammered gold, with three minas[e] of gold in each shield. The king put them in the Palace of the Forest of Lebanon.

[18]Then the king made a great throne inlaid with ivory and overlaid with fine gold. [19]The throne had six steps, and its back had a rounded top. On both sides of the seat were armrests, with a lion standing beside each of them. [20]Twelve lions stood on the six steps, one at either end of each step. Nothing like it had ever been made for any other kingdom. [21]All King Solomon's goblets were gold, and all the household articles in the Palace of the Forest of Lebanon were pure gold. Nothing was made of silver, because silver was considered of little value in Solomon's days. [22]The king had a fleet of trading ships[f] at sea along with the ships of Hiram. Once every three years it returned, carrying gold, silver and ivory, and apes and baboons.

[23]King Solomon was greater in riches and wisdom than all the other kings of the earth. [24]The whole world sought audience with Solomon to hear the wisdom God had put in his heart. [25]Year after year, everyone who came brought a gift—articles of silver and gold, robes, weapons and spices, and horses and mules.

[26]Solomon accumulated chariots and horses; he had fourteen hundred chariots and twelve thousand horses,[g] which he kept in the chariot cities and also with him in Jerusalem. [27]The king made silver as common in Jerusalem as stones, and cedar as plentiful as sycamore-fig trees in the foothills. [28]Solomon's horses were imported from Egypt[h] and from Kue[i]—the royal merchants purchased them from Kue. [29]They imported a chariot from Egypt for six hundred shekels[j] of silver, and a horse for a hundred and fifty.[k] They also exported them to all the kings of the Hittites and of the Arameans.

Solomon's Wives

11 King Solomon, however, loved many foreign women besides Pharaoh's daughter—Moabites, Ammonites, Edomites, Sidonians and Hittites. [2]They were from nations about which the LORD had told the Israelites, "You must not intermarry with them, because they will surely turn your hearts after their gods." Nevertheless, Solomon held fast to them in love. [3]He had seven hundred wives of royal birth and three hundred concubines, and his wives led him astray. [4]As Solomon grew old, his wives turned his heart after other gods, and his heart was not fully devoted to the LORD his God, as the heart of David his father had been. [5]He followed Ashtoreth the goddess of the Sidonians, and Molech[l] the detestable god of the Ammonites. [6]So Solomon did evil in the eyes of the LORD; he did not

---

[a]10 That is, about 4 1/2 tons (about 4 metric tons) [b]11 Probably a variant of algumwood; also in verse 12 [c]14 That is, about 25 tons (about 23 metric tons) [d]16 That is, about 7 1/2 pounds (about 3.5 kilograms) [e]17 That is, about 3 3/4 pounds (about 1.7 kilograms) [f]22 Hebrew of ships of Tarshish [g]26 Or charioteers [h]28 Or possibly Muzur, a region in Cilicia; also in verse 29 [i]28 Probably Cilicia [j]29 That is, about 15 pounds (about 7 kilograms) [k]29 That is, about 3 3/4 pounds (about 1.7 kilograms) [l]5 Hebrew Milcom; also in verse 33

follow the LORD completely, as David his father had done.

⁷On a hill east of Jerusalem, Solomon built a high place for Chemosh the detestable god of Moab, and for Molech the detestable god of the Ammonites. ⁸He did the same for all his foreign wives, who burned incense and offered sacrifices to their gods.

⁹The LORD became angry with Solomon because his heart had turned away from the LORD, the God of Israel, who had appeared to him twice. ¹⁰Although he had forbidden Solomon to follow other gods, Solomon did not keep the LORD's command. ¹¹So the LORD said to Solomon, "Since this is your attitude and you have not kept my covenant and my decrees, which I commanded you, I will most certainly tear the kingdom away from you and give it to one of your subordinates. ¹²Nevertheless, for the sake of David your father, I will not do it during your lifetime. I will tear it out of the hand of your son. ¹³Yet I will not tear the whole kingdom from him, but will give him one tribe for the sake of David my servant and for the sake of Jerusalem, which I have chosen."

Solomon's Adversaries

¹⁴Then the LORD raised up against Solomon an adversary, Hadad the Edomite, from the royal line of Edom. ¹⁵Earlier when David was fighting with Edom, Joab the commander of the army, who had gone up to bury the dead, had struck down all the men in Edom. ¹⁶Joab and all the Israelites stayed there for six months, until they had destroyed all the men in Edom. ¹⁷But Hadad, still only a boy, fled to Egypt with some Edomite officials who had served his father. ¹⁸They set out from Midian and went to Paran. Then taking men from Paran with them, they went to Egypt, to Pharaoh king of Egypt, who gave Hadad a house and land and provided him with food.

¹⁹Pharaoh was so pleased with Hadad that he gave him a sister of his own wife, Queen Tahpenes, in marriage. ²⁰The sister of Tahpenes bore him a son named Genubath, whom Tahpenes brought up in the royal palace. There Genubath lived with Pharaoh's own children.

²¹While he was in Egypt, Hadad heard that David rested with his fathers and that Joab the commander of the army was also dead. Then Hadad said to Pharaoh, "Let me go, that I may return to my own country."

²²"What have you lacked here that you want to go back to your own country?" Pharaoh asked.

"Nothing," Hadad replied, "but do let me go!"

²³And God raised up against Solomon another adversary, Rezon son of Eliada, who had fled from his master, Hadadezer king of Zobah. ²⁴He gathered men around him and became the leader of a band of rebels when David destroyed the forces ^{a} of Zobah; the rebels went to Damascus, where they settled and took control. ²⁵Rezon was Israel's adversary as long as Solomon lived, adding to the trouble caused by Hadad. So Rezon ruled in Aram and was hostile toward Israel.

Jeroboam Rebels Against Solomon

²⁶Also, Jeroboam son of Nebat rebelled against the king. He was one of Solomon's officials, an Ephraimite from Zeredah, and his mother was a widow named Zeruah.

²⁷Here is the account of how he rebelled against the king: Solomon had built the supporting terraces ^{b} and had filled in the gap in the wall of the city of David his father. ²⁸Now Jeroboam was a man of standing, and when Solomon saw how well the young man did his work, he put him in charge of the whole labor force of the house of Joseph.

²⁹About that time Jeroboam was going out of Jerusalem, and Ahijah the prophet of Shiloh met him on the way, wearing a new cloak. The two of them were alone out in the country, ³⁰and Ahijah took hold of the new cloak he was wearing and tore it into twelve pieces. ³¹Then he said to Jeroboam, "Take ten pieces for yourself, for this is what the LORD, the God of Israel, says: 'See, I am going to tear the kingdom out of Solomon's hand and give you ten tribes. ³²But for the sake of my servant David and the city of Jeru-

^{a}24 Hebrew destroyed them ^{b}27 Or the Millo

salem, which I have chosen out of all the tribes of Israel, he will have one tribe. ³³I will do this because they have[a] forsaken me and worshiped Ashtoreth the goddess of the Sidonians, Chemosh the god of the Moabites, and Molech the god of the Ammonites, and have not walked in my ways, nor done what is right in my eyes, nor kept my statutes and laws as David, Solomon's father, did.

³⁴"But I will not take the whole kingdom out of Solomon's hand; I have made him ruler all the days of his life for the sake of David my servant, whom I chose and who observed my commands and statutes. ³⁵I will take the kingdom from his son's hands and give you ten tribes. ³⁶I will give one tribe to his son so that David my servant may always have a lamp before me in Jerusalem, the city where I chose to put my Name. ³⁷However, as for you, I will take you, and you will rule over all that your heart desires; you will be king over Israel. ³⁸If you do whatever I command you and walk in my ways and do what is right in my eyes by keeping my statutes and commands, as David my servant did, I will be with you. I will build you a dynasty as enduring as the one I built for David and will give Israel to you. ³⁹I will humble David's descendants because of this, but not forever.'"

⁴⁰Solomon tried to kill Jeroboam, but Jeroboam fled to Egypt, to Shishak the king, and stayed there until Solomon's death.

Solomon's Death

⁴¹As for the other events of Solomon's reign—all he did and the wisdom he displayed—are they not written in the book of the annals of Solomon? ⁴²Solomon reigned in Jerusalem over all Israel forty years. ⁴³Then he rested with his fathers and was buried in the city of David his father. And Rehoboam his son succeeded him as king.

Israel Rebels Against Rehoboam

12 Rehoboam went to Shechem, for all the Israelites had gone there to make him king. ²When Jeroboam son of Nebat heard this (he was still in Egypt, where he had fled from King Solomon), he returned from[b] Egypt. ³So they sent for Jeroboam, and he and the whole assembly of Israel went to Rehoboam and said to him: ⁴"Your father put a heavy yoke on us, but now lighten the harsh labor and the heavy yoke he put on us, and we will serve you."

⁵Rehoboam answered, "Go away for three days and then come back to me." So the people went away.

⁶Then King Rehoboam consulted the elders who had served his father Solomon during his lifetime. "How would you advise me to answer these people?" he asked.

⁷They replied, "If today you will be a servant to these people and serve them and give them a favorable answer, they will always be your servants."

⁸But Rehoboam rejected the advice the elders gave him and consulted the young men who had grown up with him and were serving him. ⁹He asked them, "What is your advice? How should we answer these people who say to me, 'Lighten the yoke your father put on us'?"

¹⁰The young men who had grown up with him replied, "Tell these people who have said to you, 'Your father put a heavy yoke on us, but make our yoke lighter'—tell them, 'My little finger is thicker than my father's waist. ¹¹My father laid on you a heavy yoke; I will make it even heavier. My father scourged you with whips; I will scourge you with scorpions.'"

¹²Three days later Jeroboam and all the people returned to Rehoboam, as the king had said, "Come back to me in three days." ¹³The king answered the people harshly. Rejecting the advice given him by the elders, ¹⁴he followed the advice of the young men and said, "My father made your yoke heavy; I will make it even heavier. My father scourged you with whips; I will scourge you with scorpions." ¹⁵So the king did not listen to the people, for this turn of events was from the LORD, to fulfill the word the LORD had spoken to Jeroboam son of Nebat through Ahijah the Shilonite.

¹⁶When all Israel saw that the king refused to listen to them, they answered the king:

---

[a]33 Hebrew; Septuagint, Vulgate and Syriac because he has   [b]2 Or he remained in

"What share do we have in David,
    what part in Jesse's son?
To your tents, O Israel!
    Look after your own house,
        O David!"

So the Israelites went home. ¹⁷But as for the Israelites who were living in the towns of Judah, Rehoboam still ruled over them.

¹⁸King Rehoboam sent out Adoniram,[a] who was in charge of forced labor, but all Israel stoned him to death. King Rehoboam, however, managed to get into his chariot and escape to Jerusalem. ¹⁹So Israel has been in rebellion against the house of David to this day.

²⁰When all the Israelites heard that Jeroboam had returned, they sent and called him to the assembly and made him king over all Israel. Only the tribe of Judah remained loyal to the house of David.

²¹When Rehoboam arrived in Jerusalem, he mustered the whole house of Judah and the tribe of Benjamin—a hundred and eighty thousand fighting men—to make war against the house of Israel and to regain the kingdom for Rehoboam son of Solomon.

²²But this word of God came to Shemaiah the man of God: ²³"Say to Rehoboam son of Solomon king of Judah, to the whole house of Judah and Benjamin, and to the rest of the people, ²⁴'This is what the LORD says: Do not go up to fight against your brothers, the Israelites. Go home, every one of you, for this is my doing.'" So they obeyed the word of the LORD and went home again, as the LORD had ordered.

Golden Calves at Bethel and Dan

²⁵Then Jeroboam fortified Shechem in the hill country of Ephraim and lived there. From there he went out and built up Peniel.[b]

²⁶Jeroboam thought to himself, "The kingdom will now likely revert to the house of David. ²⁷If these people go up to offer sacrifices at the temple of the LORD in Jerusalem, they will again give their allegiance to their lord, Rehoboam king of Judah. They will kill me and return to King Rehoboam."

²⁸After seeking advice, the king made two golden calves. He said to the people,

"It is too much for you to go up to Jerusalem. Here are your gods, O Israel, who brought you up out of Egypt." ²⁹One he set up in Bethel, and the other in Dan. ³⁰And this thing became a sin; the people went even as far as Dan to worship the one there.

³¹Jeroboam built shrines on high places and appointed priests from all sorts of people, even though they were not Levites. ³²He instituted a festival on the fifteenth day of the eighth month, like the festival held in Judah, and offered sacrifices on the altar. This he did in Bethel, sacrificing to the calves he had made. And at Bethel he also installed priests at the high places he had made. ³³On the fifteenth day of the eighth month, a month of his own choosing, he offered sacrifices on the altar he had built at Bethel. So he instituted the festival for the Israelites and went up to the altar to make offerings.

The Man of God From Judah

13 By the word of the LORD a man of God came from Judah to Bethel, as Jeroboam was standing by the altar to make an offering. ²He cried out against the altar by the word of the LORD: "O altar, altar! This is what the LORD says: 'A son named Josiah will be born to the house of David. On you he will sacrifice the priests of the high places who now make offerings here, and human bones will be burned on you.'" ³That same day the man of God gave a sign: "This is the sign the LORD has declared: The altar will be split apart and the ashes on it will be poured out."

⁴When King Jeroboam heard what the man of God cried out against the altar at Bethel, he stretched out his hand from the altar and said, "Seize him!" But the hand he stretched out toward the man shriveled up, so that he could not pull it back. ⁵Also, the altar was split apart and its ashes poured out according to the sign given by the man of God by the word of the LORD.

⁶Then the king said to the man of God, "Intercede with the LORD your God and

---

[a]18 Some Septuagint manuscripts and Syriac (see also 1 Kings 4:6 and 5:14); Hebrew *Adoram*
[b]25 Hebrew *Penuel,* a variant of *Peniel*

pray for me that my hand may be restored." So the man of God interceded with the LORD, and the king's hand was restored and became as it was before.

THEN the king said to the man of God, "Intercede with the LORD your God and pray for me that my hand may be restored." So the man of God interceded with the LORD, and the king's hand was restored and became as it was before.

1 KINGS 13:6

⁷The king said to the man of God, "Come home with me and have something to eat, and I will give you a gift."

⁸But the man of God answered the king, "Even if you were to give me half your possessions, I would not go with you, nor would I eat bread or drink water here. ⁹For I was commanded by the word of the LORD: 'You must not eat bread or drink water or return by the way you came.'" ¹⁰So he took another road and did not return by the way he had come to Bethel.

¹¹Now there was a certain old prophet living in Bethel, whose sons came and told him all that the man of God had done there that day. They also told their father what he had said to the king. ¹²Their father asked them, "Which way did he go?" And his sons showed him which road the man of God from Judah had taken. ¹³So he said to his sons, "Saddle the donkey for me." And when they had saddled the donkey for him, he mounted it ¹⁴and rode after the man of God. He found him sitting under an oak tree and asked, "Are you the man of God who came from Judah?"

"I am," he replied.

¹⁵So the prophet said to him, "Come home with me and eat."

¹⁶The man of God said, "I cannot turn back and go with you, nor can I eat bread or drink water with you in this place. ¹⁷I have been told by the word of the LORD: 'You must not eat bread or drink water there or return by the way you came.'"

¹⁸The old prophet answered, "I too am a prophet, as you are. And an angel said to me by the word of the LORD: 'Bring him

back with you to your house so that he may eat bread and drink water.'" (But he was lying to him.) ¹⁹So the man of God returned with him and ate and drank in his house.

²⁰While they were sitting at the table, the word of the LORD came to the old prophet who had brought him back. ²¹He cried out to the man of God who had come from Judah, "This is what the LORD says: 'You have defied the word of the LORD and have not kept the command the LORD your God gave you. ²²You came back and ate bread and drank water in the place where he told you not to eat or drink. Therefore your body will not be buried in the tomb of your fathers.'"

²³When the man of God had finished eating and drinking, the prophet who had brought him back saddled his donkey for him. ²⁴As he went on his way, a lion met him on the road and killed him, and his body was thrown down on the road, with both the donkey and the lion standing beside it. ²⁵Some people who passed by saw the body thrown down there, with the lion standing beside the body, and they went and reported it in the city where the old prophet lived.

²⁶When the prophet who had brought him back from his journey heard of it, he said, "It is the man of God who defied the word of the LORD. The LORD has given him over to the lion, which has mauled him and killed him, as the word of the LORD had warned him."

²⁷The prophet said to his sons, "Saddle the donkey for me," and they did so. ²⁸Then he went out and found the body thrown down on the road, with the donkey and the lion standing beside it. The lion had neither eaten the body nor mauled the donkey. ²⁹So the prophet picked up the body of the man of God, laid it on the donkey, and brought it back to his own city to mourn for him and bury him. ³⁰Then he laid the body in his own tomb, and they mourned over him and said, "Oh, my brother!"

³¹After burying him, he said to his sons, "When I die, bury me in the grave where the man of God is buried; lay my bones beside his bones. ³²For the message he declared by the word of the LORD against the altar in Bethel and against all the

shrines on the high places in the towns of Samaria will certainly come true."

³³Even after this, Jeroboam did not change his evil ways, but once more appointed priests for the high places from all sorts of people. Anyone who wanted to become a priest he consecrated for the high places. ³⁴This was the sin of the house of Jeroboam that led to its downfall and to its destruction from the face of the earth.

Ahijah's Prophecy Against Jeroboam

14 At that time Abijah son of Jeroboam became ill, ²and Jeroboam said to his wife, "Go, disguise yourself, so you won't be recognized as the wife of Jeroboam. Then go to Shiloh. Ahijah the prophet is there—the one who told me I would be king over this people. ³Take ten loaves of bread with you, some cakes and a jar of honey, and go to him. He will tell you what will happen to the boy." ⁴So Jeroboam's wife did what he said and went to Ahijah's house in Shiloh.

Now Ahijah could not see; his sight was gone because of his age. ⁵But the LORD had told Ahijah, "Jeroboam's wife is coming to ask you about her son, for he is ill, and you are to give her such and such an answer. When she arrives, she will pretend to be someone else."

⁶So when Ahijah heard the sound of her footsteps at the door, he said, "Come in, wife of Jeroboam. Why this pretense? I have been sent to you with bad news. ⁷Go, tell Jeroboam that this is what the LORD, the God of Israel, says: 'I raised you up from among the people and made you a leader over my people Israel. ⁸I tore the kingdom away from the house of David and gave it to you, but you have not been like my servant David, who kept my commands and followed me with all his heart, doing only what was right in my eyes. ⁹You have done more evil than all who lived before you. You have made for yourself other gods, idols made of metal; you have provoked me to anger and thrust me behind your back.

¹⁰" 'Because of this, I am going to bring disaster on the house of Jeroboam. I will cut off from Jeroboam every last male in Israel—slave or free. I will burn up the house of Jeroboam as one burns dung, until it is all gone. ¹¹Dogs will eat those belonging to Jeroboam who die in the city, and the birds of the air will feed on those who die in the country. The LORD has spoken!'

¹²"As for you, go back home. When you set foot in your city, the boy will die. ¹³All Israel will mourn for him and bury him. He is the only one belonging to Jeroboam who will be buried, because he is the only one in the house of Jeroboam in whom the LORD, the God of Israel, has found anything good.

¹⁴"The LORD will raise up for himself a king over Israel who will cut off the family of Jeroboam. This is the day! What? Yes, even now.ᵃ ¹⁵And the LORD will strike Israel, so that it will be like a reed swaying in the water. He will uproot Israel from this good land that he gave to their forefathers and scatter them beyond the River,ᵇ because they provoked the LORD to anger by making Asherah poles.ᶜ ¹⁶And he will give Israel up because of the sins Jeroboam has committed and has caused Israel to commit."

¹⁷Then Jeroboam's wife got up and left and went to Tirzah. As soon as she stepped over the threshold of the house, the boy died. ¹⁸They buried him, and all Israel mourned for him, as the LORD had said through his servant the prophet Ahijah.

¹⁹The other events of Jeroboam's reign, his wars and how he ruled, are written in the book of the annals of the kings of Israel. ²⁰He reigned for twenty-two years and then rested with his fathers. And Nadab his son succeeded him as king.

Rehoboam King of Judah

²¹Rehoboam son of Solomon was king in Judah. He was forty-one years old when he became king, and he reigned seventeen years in Jerusalem, the city the LORD had chosen out of all the tribes of Israel in which to put his Name. His mother's name was Naamah; she was an Ammonite.

²²Judah did evil in the eyes of the LORD. By the sins they committed they stirred up his jealous anger more than their

---

ᵃ14 The meaning of the Hebrew for this sentence is uncertain.   ᵇ15 That is, the Euphrates
ᶜ15 That is, symbols of the goddess Asherah; here and elsewhere in 1 Kings

fathers had done. 23They also set up for themselves high places, sacred stones and Asherah poles on every high hill and under every spreading tree. 24There were even male shrine prostitutes in the land; the people engaged in all the detestable practices of the nations the LORD had driven out before the Israelites.

25In the fifth year of King Rehoboam, Shishak king of Egypt attacked Jerusalem. 26He carried off the treasures of the temple of the LORD and the treasures of the royal palace. He took everything, including all the gold shields Solomon had made. 27So King Rehoboam made bronze shields to replace them and assigned these to the commanders of the guard on duty at the entrance to the royal palace. 28Whenever the king went to the LORD's temple, the guards bore the shields, and afterward they returned them to the guardroom.

29As for the other events of Rehoboam's reign, and all he did, are they not written in the book of the annals of the kings of Judah? 30There was continual warfare between Rehoboam and Jeroboam. 31And Rehoboam rested with his fathers and was buried with them in the City of David. His mother's name was Naamah; she was an Ammonite. And Abijah*a* his son succeeded him as king.

Abijah King of Judah

15 In the eighteenth year of the reign of Jeroboam son of Nebat, Abijah*b* became king of Judah, 2and he reigned in Jerusalem three years. His mother's name was Maacah daughter of Abishalom.*c*

3He committed all the sins his father had done before him; his heart was not fully devoted to the LORD his God, as the heart of David his forefather had been. 4Nevertheless, for David's sake the LORD his God gave him a lamp in Jerusalem by raising up a son to succeed him and by making Jerusalem strong. 5For David had done what was right in the eyes of the LORD and had not failed to keep any of the LORD's commands all the days of his life—except in the case of Uriah the Hittite.

6There was war between Rehoboam*d* and Jeroboam throughout Abijah's lifetime. 7As for the other events of Abijah's reign, and all he did, are they not written

in the book of the annals of the kings of Judah? There was war between Abijah and Jeroboam. 8And Abijah rested with his fathers and was buried in the City of David. And Asa his son succeeded him as king.

Asa King of Judah

9In the twentieth year of Jeroboam king of Israel, Asa became king of Judah, 10and he reigned in Jerusalem forty-one years. His grandmother's name was Maacah daughter of Abishalom.

11Asa did what was right in the eyes of the LORD, as his father David had done. 12He expelled the male shrine prostitutes from the land and got rid of all the idols his fathers had made. 13He even deposed his grandmother Maacah from her position as queen mother, because she had made a repulsive Asherah pole. Asa cut the pole down and burned it in the Kidron Valley. 14Although he did not remove the high places, Asa's heart was fully committed to the LORD all his life. 15He brought into the temple of the LORD the silver and gold and the articles that he and his father had dedicated.

16There was war between Asa and Baasha king of Israel throughout their reigns. 17Baasha king of Israel went up against Judah and fortified Ramah to prevent anyone from leaving or entering the territory of Asa king of Judah.

18Asa then took all the silver and gold that was left in the treasuries of the LORD's temple and of his own palace. He entrusted it to his officials and sent them to Ben-Hadad son of Tabrimmon, the son of Hezion, the king of Aram, who was ruling in Damascus. 19"Let there be a treaty between me and you," he said, "as there was between my father and your father. See, I am sending you a gift of silver and gold. Now break your treaty with Baasha king of Israel so he will withdraw from me."

20Ben-Hadad agreed with King Asa and sent the commanders of his forces against

a31 Some Hebrew manuscripts and Septuagint (see also 2 Chron. 12:16); most Hebrew manuscripts *Abijam*   *b1* Some Hebrew manuscripts and Septuagint (see also 2 Chron. 12:16); most Hebrew manuscripts *Abijam*; also in verses 7 and 8   *c2* A variant of *Absalom*; also in verse 10   *d6* Most Hebrew manuscripts; some Hebrew manuscripts and Syriac *Abijam* (that is, Abijah)

the towns of Israel. He conquered Ijon, Dan, Abel Beth Maacah and all Kinnereth in addition to Naphtali. ²¹When Baasha heard this, he stopped building Ramah and withdrew to Tirzah. ²²Then King Asa issued an order to all Judah—no one was exempt—and they carried away from Ramah the stones and timber Baasha had been using there. With them King Asa built up Geba in Benjamin, and also Mizpah.

²³As for all the other events of Asa's reign, all his achievements, all he did and the cities he built, are they not written in the book of the annals of the kings of Judah? In his old age, however, his feet became diseased. ²⁴Then Asa rested with his fathers and was buried with them in the city of his father David. And Jehoshaphat his son succeeded him as king.

Nadab King of Israel

²⁵Nadab son of Jeroboam became king of Israel in the second year of Asa king of Judah, and he reigned over Israel two years. ²⁶He did evil in the eyes of the LORD, walking in the ways of his father and in his sin, which he had caused Israel to commit.

²⁷Baasha son of Ahijah of the house of Issachar plotted against him, and he struck him down at Gibbethon, a Philistine town, while Nadab and all Israel were besieging it. ²⁸Baasha killed Nadab in the third year of Asa king of Judah and succeeded him as king.

²⁹As soon as he began to reign, he killed Jeroboam's whole family. He did not leave Jeroboam anyone that breathed, but destroyed them all, according to the word of the LORD given through his servant Ahijah the Shilonite— ³⁰because of the sins Jeroboam had committed and had caused Israel to commit, and because he provoked the LORD, the God of Israel, to anger.

³¹As for the other events of Nadab's reign, and all he did, are they not written in the book of the annals of the kings of Israel? ³²There was war between Asa and Baasha king of Israel throughout their reigns.

Baasha King of Israel

³³In the third year of Asa king of Judah, Baasha son of Ahijah became king of all Israel in Tirzah, and he reigned twenty-four years. ³⁴He did evil in the eyes of the LORD, walking in the ways of Jeroboam and in his sin, which he had caused Israel to commit.

16 Then the word of the LORD came to Jehu son of Hanani against Baasha: ²"I lifted you up from the dust and made you leader of my people Israel, but you walked in the ways of Jeroboam and caused my people Israel to sin and to provoke me to anger by their sins. ³So I am about to consume Baasha and his house, and I will make your house like that of Jeroboam son of Nebat. ⁴Dogs will eat those belonging to Baasha who die in the city, and the birds of the air will feed on those who die in the country."

⁵As for the other events of Baasha's reign, what he did and his achievements, are they not written in the book of the annals of the kings of Israel? ⁶Baasha rested with his fathers and was buried in Tirzah. And Elah his son succeeded him as king.

⁷Moreover, the word of the LORD came through the prophet Jehu son of Hanani to Baasha and his house, because of all the evil he had done in the eyes of the LORD, provoking him to anger by the things he did, and becoming like the house of Jeroboam—and also because he destroyed it.

Elah King of Israel

⁸In the twenty-sixth year of Asa king of Judah, Elah son of Baasha became king of Israel, and he reigned in Tirzah two years.

⁹Zimri, one of his officials, who had command of half his chariots, plotted against him. Elah was in Tirzah at the time, getting drunk in the home of Arza, the man in charge of the palace at Tirzah. ¹⁰Zimri came in, struck him down and killed him in the twenty-seventh year of Asa king of Judah. Then he succeeded him as king.

¹¹As soon as he began to reign and was seated on the throne, he killed off Baasha's whole family. He did not spare a single male, whether relative or friend. ¹²So Zimri destroyed the whole family of Baasha, in accordance with the word of the LORD spoken against Baasha through the prophet Jehu— ¹³because of all the sins

Baasha and his son Elah had committed and had caused Israel to commit, so that they provoked the LORD, the God of Israel, to anger by their worthless idols. ¹⁴As for the other events of Elah's reign, and all he did, are they not written in the book of the annals of the kings of Israel?

Zimri King of Israel

¹⁵In the twenty-seventh year of Asa king of Judah, Zimri reigned in Tirzah seven days. The army was encamped near Gibbethon, a Philistine town. ¹⁶When the Israelites in the camp heard that Zimri had plotted against the king and murdered him, they proclaimed Omri, the commander of the army, king over Israel that very day there in the camp. ¹⁷Then Omri and all the Israelites with him withdrew from Gibbethon and laid siege to Tirzah. ¹⁸When Zimri saw that the city was taken, he went into the citadel of the royal palace and set the palace on fire around him. So he died, ¹⁹because of the sins he had committed, doing evil in the eyes of the LORD and walking in the ways of Jeroboam and in the sin he had committed and had caused Israel to commit.

²⁰As for the other events of Zimri's reign, and the rebellion he carried out, are they not written in the book of the annals of the kings of Israel?

Omri King of Israel

²¹Then the people of Israel were split into two factions; half supported Tibni son of Ginath for king, and the other half supported Omri. ²²But Omri's followers proved stronger than those of Tibni son of Ginath. So Tibni died and Omri became king.

²³In the thirty-first year of Asa king of Judah, Omri became king of Israel, and he reigned twelve years, six of them in Tirzah. ²⁴He bought the hill of Samaria from Shemer for two talents^a of silver and built a city on the hill, calling it Samaria, after Shemer, the name of the former owner of the hill.

²⁵But Omri did evil in the eyes of the LORD and sinned more than all those before him. ²⁶He walked in all the ways of Jeroboam son of Nebat and in his sin, which he had caused Israel to commit, so that they provoked the LORD, the God of Israel, to anger by their worthless idols.

²⁷As for the other events of Omri's reign, what he did and the things he achieved, are they not written in the book of the annals of the kings of Israel? ²⁸Omri rested with his fathers and was buried in Samaria. And Ahab his son succeeded him as king.

Ahab Becomes King of Israel

²⁹In the thirty-eighth year of Asa king of Judah, Ahab son of Omri became king of Israel, and he reigned in Samaria over Israel twenty-two years. ³⁰Ahab son of Omri did more evil in the eyes of the LORD than any of those before him. ³¹He not only considered it trivial to commit the sins of Jeroboam son of Nebat, but he also married Jezebel daughter of Ethbaal king of the Sidonians, and began to serve Baal and worship him. ³²He set up an altar for Baal in the temple of Baal that he built in Samaria. ³³Ahab also made an Asherah pole and did more to provoke the LORD, the God of Israel, to anger than did all the kings of Israel before him.

³⁴In Ahab's time, Hiel of Bethel rebuilt Jericho. He laid its foundations at the cost of his firstborn son Abiram, and he set up its gates at the cost of his youngest son Segub, in accordance with the word of the LORD spoken by Joshua son of Nun.

Elijah Fed by Ravens

17 Now Elijah the Tishbite, from Tishbe^b in Gilead, said to Ahab, "As the LORD, the God of Israel, lives, whom I serve, there will be neither dew nor rain in the next few years except at my word."

²Then the word of the LORD came to Elijah: ³"Leave here, turn eastward and hide in the Kerith Ravine, east of the Jordan. ⁴You will drink from the brook, and I have ordered the ravens to feed you there."

⁵So he did what the LORD had told him. He went to the Kerith Ravine, east of the Jordan, and stayed there. ⁶The ravens brought him bread and meat in the morning and bread and meat in the evening, and he drank from the brook.

^{a}24 That is, about 150 pounds (about 70 kilograms) ^{b}1 Or Tishbite, of the settlers

The Widow at Zarephath

7Some time later the brook dried up because there had been no rain in the land. 8Then the word of the Lord came to him: 9"Go at once to Zarephath of Sidon and stay there. I have commanded a widow in that place to supply you with food." 10So he went to Zarephath. When he came to the town gate, a widow was there gathering sticks. He called to her and asked, "Would you bring me a little water in a jar so I may have a drink?" 11As she was going to get it, he called, "And bring me, please, a piece of bread."

12"As surely as the Lord your God lives," she replied, "I don't have any bread—only a handful of flour in a jar and a little oil in a jug. I am gathering a few sticks to take home and make a meal for myself and my son, that we may eat it—and die."

13Elijah said to her, "Don't be afraid. Go home and do as you have said. But first make a small cake of bread for me from what you have and bring it to me, and then make something for yourself and your son. 14For this is what the Lord, the God of Israel, says: 'The jar of flour will not be used up and the jug of oil will not run dry until the day the Lord gives rain on the land.'"

15She went away and did as Elijah had told her. So there was food every day for Elijah and for the woman and her family. 16For the jar of flour was not used up and the jug of oil did not run dry, in keeping with the word of the Lord spoken by Elijah.

17Some time later the son of the woman who owned the house became ill. He grew worse and worse, and finally stopped breathing. 18She said to Elijah, "What do you have against me, man of God? Did you come to remind me of my sin and kill my son?"

19"Give me your son," Elijah replied. He took him from her arms, carried him to the upper room where he was staying, and laid him on his bed. 20Then he cried out to the Lord, "O Lord my God, have you brought tragedy also upon this widow I am staying with, by causing her son to die?" 21Then he stretched himself out on the boy three times and cried to the Lord, "O Lord my God, let this boy's life return to him!"

22The Lord heard Elijah's cry, and the boy's life returned to him, and he lived. 23Elijah picked up the child and carried him down from the room into the house. He gave him to his mother and said, "Look, your son is alive!"

24Then the woman said to Elijah, "Now I know that you are a man of God and that the word of the Lord from your mouth is the truth."

Elijah and Obadiah

18 After a long time, in the third year, the word of the Lord came to Elijah: "Go and present yourself to Ahab, and I will send rain on the land." 2So Elijah went to present himself to Ahab.

Now the famine was severe in Samaria, 3and Ahab had summoned Obadiah, who was in charge of his palace. (Obadiah was a devout believer in the Lord. 4While Jezebel was killing off the Lord's prophets, Obadiah had taken a hundred prophets and hidden them in two caves, fifty in each, and had supplied them with food and water.) 5Ahab had said to Obadiah, "Go through the land to all the springs and valleys. Maybe we can find some grass to keep the horses and mules alive so we will not have to kill any of our animals." 6So they divided the land they were to cover, Ahab going in one direction and Obadiah in another.

7As Obadiah was walking along, Elijah met him. Obadiah recognized him, bowed down to the ground, and said, "Is it really you, my lord Elijah?"

8"Yes," he replied. "Go tell your master, 'Elijah is here.'"

9"What have I done wrong," asked Obadiah, "that you are handing your servant over to Ahab to be put to death? 10As surely as the Lord your God lives, there is not a nation or kingdom where my master has not sent someone to look for you. And whenever a nation or kingdom claimed you were not there, he made them swear they could not find you. 11But now you tell me to go to my master and say, 'Elijah is here.' 12I don't know where the Spirit of the Lord may carry you when I leave you. If I go and tell Ahab and he doesn't find you, he will kill me.

Yet I your servant have worshiped the LORD since my youth. ¹³Haven't you heard, my lord, what I did while Jezebel was killing the prophets of the LORD? I hid a hundred of the LORD's prophets in two caves, fifty in each, and supplied them with food and water. ¹⁴And now you tell me to go to my master and say, 'Elijah is here.' He will kill me!"

¹⁵Elijah said, "As the LORD Almighty lives, whom I serve, I will surely present myself to Ahab today."

Elijah on Mount Carmel

¹⁶So Obadiah went to meet Ahab and told him, and Ahab went to meet Elijah. ¹⁷When he saw Elijah, he said to him, "Is that you, you troubler of Israel?"

---

1 KINGS 17 – 18

Just Like Us

17:22 THE LORD HEARD ELIJAH'S CRY.

Frankly, most people cannot relate to James's description of Elijah as "a man just like us" (James 5:17). Elijah was fed miraculously by ravens (see 1 Kings 17:4–6) and by bottomless jars of oil and flour (see verses 7–16). He raised a boy from the dead (see verses 17–24), and totally shut down the prophets of Baal and Asherah in a display of pyrotechnics that kept Israel talking for centuries (see 18:16–40). Oh, and it didn't rain for three and a half years because he said so, and the rain started again when he said the time was right (see 17:1; 18:41–46). If our being able to relate to a man like Elijah is supposed to encourage us to pray, we have a lot of thinking to do about Elijah.

Maybe we're not supposed to identify first with Elijah himself, and therefore his prayer life. Maybe we're supposed to understand what prayer is, and therefore identify with Elijah. Maybe Elijah was indeed a man just like us, whose experience of prayer shows us that people just like us can see great and wonderful things when we pray. That's the point of James's commentary on these chapters from 1 Kings (see James 5:16–18).

James says prayer is "powerful and effective" (5:16). With both adjectives, the sense is of inherent power and effectiveness, of potency and strength just beneath the surface, waiting to be summoned. "Beneath the surface" is usually the way the power and effectiveness of prayer looks: not too impressive on the outside. Do we really believe that people with their eyes shut and hands folded are moving heaven and earth? It's a stretch of the imagination, but that is exactly what is happening. Read Revelation 8:1–5.

There's one more problem about James's exposition of our texts in 1 Kings: What about the prayers of a "righteous man" being answered? Do any of us qualify? By faith in Christ, we are credited as righteous. And in the context of James, Elijah's prayers were his faith in action (see James 2:22–23). What holds you back from praying with the confidence of Elijah? He really was just like you, and he saw God's glory because he prayed to see God's glory.

PRAY:

Almighty God, nothing is too hard for you: weather, food supply and miraculous signs are easy for you. So take my little faith and grow it!

FOR YOUR NEXT DEVOTIONAL READING, GO TO PAGE 408.

[18] "I have not made trouble for Israel," Elijah replied. "But you and your father's family have. You have abandoned the LORD's commands and have followed the Baals. [19] Now summon the people from all over Israel to meet me on Mount Carmel. And bring the four hundred and fifty prophets of Baal and the four hundred prophets of Asherah, who eat at Jezebel's table."

[20] So Ahab sent word throughout all Israel and assembled the prophets on Mount Carmel. [21] Elijah went before the people and said, "How long will you waver between two opinions? If the LORD is God, follow him; but if Baal is God, follow him."

But the people said nothing.

[22] Then Elijah said to them, "I am the only one of the LORD's prophets left, but Baal has four hundred and fifty prophets. [23] Get two bulls for us. Let them choose one for themselves, and let them cut it into pieces and put it on the wood but not set fire to it. I will prepare the other bull and put it on the wood but not set fire to it. [24] Then you call on the name of your god, and I will call on the name of the LORD. The god who answers by fire— he is God."

Then all the people said, "What you say is good."

[25] Elijah said to the prophets of Baal, "Choose one of the bulls and prepare it first, since there are so many of you. Call on the name of your god, but do not light the fire." [26] So they took the bull given them and prepared it.

Then they called on the name of Baal from morning till noon. "O Baal, answer us!" they shouted. But there was no response; no one answered. And they danced around the altar they had made.

[27] At noon Elijah began to taunt them. "Shout louder!" he said. "Surely he is a god! Perhaps he is deep in thought, or busy, or traveling. Maybe he is sleeping and must be awakened." [28] So they shouted louder and slashed themselves with swords and spears, as was their custom, until their blood flowed. [29] Midday passed, and they continued their frantic prophesying until the time for the evening sacrifice. But there was no response, no one answered, no one paid attention.

[30] Then Elijah said to all the people, "Come here to me." They came to him, and he repaired the altar of the LORD, which was in ruins. [31] Elijah took twelve stones, one for each of the tribes descended from Jacob, to whom the word of the LORD had come, saying, "Your name shall be Israel." [32] With the stones he built an altar in the name of the LORD, and he dug a trench around it large enough to hold two seahs[a] of seed. [33] He arranged the wood, cut the bull into pieces and laid it on the wood. Then he said to them, "Fill four large jars with water and pour it on the offering and on the wood."

[34] "Do it again," he said, and they did it again.

"Do it a third time," he ordered, and they did it the third time. [35] The water ran down around the altar and even filled the trench.

[36] At the time of sacrifice, the prophet Elijah stepped forward and prayed: "O LORD, God of Abraham, Isaac and Israel, let it be known today that you are God in Israel and that I am your servant and have done all these things at your command. [37] Answer me, O LORD, answer me, so these people will know that you, O LORD, are God, and that you are turning their hearts back again."

> "ANSWER me, O LORD, answer me, so these people will know that you, O LORD, are God, and that you are turning their hearts back again."
>
> 1 KINGS 18:37

[38] Then the fire of the LORD fell and burned up the sacrifice, the wood, the stones and the soil, and also licked up the water in the trench.

[39] When all the people saw this, they fell prostrate and cried, "The LORD—he is God! The LORD—he is God!"

[40] Then Elijah commanded them, "Seize the prophets of Baal. Don't let anyone get away!" They seized them, and Elijah had them brought down to the Kishon Valley and slaughtered there.

[a] 32 That is, probably about 13 quarts (about 15 liters)

⁴¹And Elijah said to Ahab, "Go, eat and drink, for there is the sound of a heavy rain." ⁴²So Ahab went off to eat and drink, but Elijah climbed to the top of Carmel, bent down to the ground and put his face between his knees.

⁴³"Go and look toward the sea," he told his servant. And he went up and looked.

"There is nothing there," he said.

Seven times Elijah said, "Go back."

⁴⁴The seventh time the servant reported, "A cloud as small as a man's hand is rising from the sea."

So Elijah said, "Go and tell Ahab, 'Hitch up your chariot and go down before the rain stops you.'"

⁴⁵Meanwhile, the sky grew black with clouds, the wind rose, a heavy rain came on and Ahab rode off to Jezreel. ⁴⁶The power of the LORD came upon Elijah and, tucking his cloak into his belt, he ran ahead of Ahab all the way to Jezreel.

Elijah Flees to Horeb

19 Now Ahab told Jezebel everything Elijah had done and how he had killed all the prophets with the sword. ²So Jezebel sent a messenger to Elijah to say, "May the gods deal with me, be it ever so severely, if by this time tomorrow I do not make your life like that of one of them."

³Elijah was afraid*ᵃ* and ran for his life. When he came to Beersheba in Judah, he left his servant there, ⁴while he himself went a day's journey into the desert. He came to a broom tree, sat down under it and prayed that he might die. "I have had enough, LORD," he said. "Take my life; I am no better than my ancestors." ⁵Then he lay down under the tree and fell asleep.

All at once an angel touched him and said, "Get up and eat." ⁶He looked around, and there by his head was a cake of bread baked over hot coals, and a jar of water. He ate and drank and then lay down again.

⁷The angel of the LORD came back a second time and touched him and said, "Get up and eat, for the journey is too much for you." ⁸So he got up and ate and drank. Strengthened by that food, he traveled forty days and forty nights until he reached Horeb, the mountain of God. ⁹There he went into a cave and spent the night.

The LORD Appears to Elijah

And the word of the LORD came to him: "What are you doing here, Elijah?"

¹⁰He replied, "I have been very zealous for the LORD God Almighty. The Israelites have rejected your covenant, broken down your altars, and put your prophets to death with the sword. I am the only one left, and now they are trying to kill me too."

¹¹The LORD said, "Go out and stand on the mountain in the presence of the LORD, for the LORD is about to pass by."

Then a great and powerful wind tore the mountains apart and shattered the rocks before the LORD, but the LORD was not in the wind. After the wind there was an earthquake, but the LORD was not in the earthquake. ¹²After the earthquake came a fire, but the LORD was not in the fire. And after the fire came a gentle whisper. ¹³When Elijah heard it, he pulled his cloak over his face and went out and stood at the mouth of the cave.

Then a voice said to him, "What are you doing here, Elijah?"

¹⁴He replied, "I have been very zealous for the LORD God Almighty. The Israelites have rejected your covenant, broken down your altars, and put your prophets to death with the sword. I am the only one left, and now they are trying to kill me too."

¹⁵The LORD said to him, "Go back the way you came, and go to the Desert of Damascus. When you get there, anoint Hazael king over Aram. ¹⁶Also, anoint Jehu son of Nimshi king over Israel, and anoint Elisha son of Shaphat from Abel Meholah to succeed you as prophet. ¹⁷Jehu will put to death any who escape the sword of Hazael, and Elisha will put to death any who escape the sword of Jehu. ¹⁸Yet I reserve seven thousand in Israel—all whose knees have not bowed down to Baal and all whose mouths have not kissed him."

The Call of Elisha

¹⁹So Elijah went from there and found Elisha son of Shaphat. He was plowing with twelve yoke of oxen, and he himself was driving the twelfth pair. Elijah went up to him and threw his cloak around

ᵃ3 Or Elijah saw

him. ²⁰Elisha then left his oxen and ran after Elijah. "Let me kiss my father and mother good-by," he said, "and then I will come with you."

"Go back," Elijah replied. "What have I done to you?"

²¹So Elisha left him and went back. He took his yoke of oxen and slaughtered them. He burned the plowing equipment to cook the meat and gave it to the people, and they ate. Then he set out to follow Elijah and became his attendant.

---

1 KINGS 19:1–18

When You Want to Give Up

19:4 "'I HAVE HAD ENOUGH, LORD,' HE SAID. 'TAKE MY LIFE; I AM NO BETTER THAN MY ANCESTORS.'"

This kind of thing can happen to the best of us—and often does! It's what we feel when it seems our best isn't enough. Elijah was in the middle of a struggle that pitted the God of Abraham, Isaac and Jacob against the religion of Baal and Asherah. It was not an interdenominational squabble, like Calvinists and Arminians, Baptists and Methodists. These were two distinct religions with irreconcilable differences; Israel's future as the people of God hung in the balance. And Elijah had expended much in the struggle. His efforts culminated in a victory on Mount Carmel, or so he thought (see 1 Kings 18:16–46). But now the evil Jezebel had a contract out on his life, and he wanted to give up. After the experience on Mount Carmel, Elijah had been riding high; but after Jezebel's murderous pledge, he came down hard (see 19:1–4). Elijah was so despondent that he prayed that God would take his life.

God's answer to Elijah's prayer is a model of the way God cares for his servants. The most priceless encouragement is the revelation of his character. God sent a mighty wind, then an earthquake and then fire. But each time it is said that the Lord was not in any of these. When the Lord did arrive, it was in a gentle whisper. The message to Elijah is that the way he wanted the Lord to speak—in power and judgment—is not the way the Lord will come this time. He will speak softly. More than his wrath, it is his kindness that leads to repentance (see Romans 2:4).

Did Elijah's anger at evil get the best of him? It's likely. Twice he told the Lord that he had been very zealous for the Lord and that he was the only one amid a nation of apostates! That was manifestly not the case, as the Lord reminded him (see 1 Kings 19:10,14,18). Excessive anger distorts the facts and makes people feel victimized. The next step is depression, the flip side of anger. Are you weary and despondent? Look into your heart; is it full of anger? Then look to the Lord and his love.

PRAY:

Dear Father, lest I grow weary and despondent in your service,
show me your love for me and for those you have called me to love.

FOR YOUR NEXT DEVOTIONAL READING, GO TO PAGE 419.

Ben-Hadad Attacks Samaria

20 Now Ben-Hadad king of Aram mustered his entire army. Accompanied by thirty-two kings with their horses and chariots, he went up and besieged Samaria and attacked it. ²He sent messengers into the city to Ahab king of Israel, saying, "This is what Ben-Hadad says: ³'Your silver and gold are mine, and the best of your wives and children are mine.'"

⁴The king of Israel answered, "Just as you say, my lord the king. I and all I have are yours."

⁵The messengers came again and said, "This is what Ben-Hadad says: 'I sent to demand your silver and gold, your wives and your children. ⁶But about this time tomorrow I am going to send my officials to search your palace and the houses of your officials. They will seize everything you value and carry it away.'"

⁷The king of Israel summoned all the elders of the land and said to them, "See how this man is looking for trouble! When he sent for my wives and my children, my silver and my gold, I did not refuse him."

⁸The elders and the people all answered, "Don't listen to him or agree to his demands."

⁹So he replied to Ben-Hadad's messengers, "Tell my lord the king, 'Your servant will do all you demanded the first time, but this demand I cannot meet.'" They left and took the answer back to Ben-Hadad.

¹⁰Then Ben-Hadad sent another message to Ahab: "May the gods deal with me, be it ever so severely, if enough dust remains in Samaria to give each of my men a handful."

¹¹The king of Israel answered, "Tell him: 'One who puts on his armor should not boast like one who takes it off.'"

¹²Ben-Hadad heard this message while he and the kings were drinking in their tents,ᵃ and he ordered his men: "Prepare to attack." So they prepared to attack the city.

Ahab Defeats Ben-Hadad

¹³Meanwhile a prophet came to Ahab king of Israel and announced, "This is what the LORD says: 'Do you see this vast army? I will give it into your hand today, and then you will know that I am the LORD.'"

¹⁴"But who will do this?" asked Ahab.

The prophet replied, "This is what the LORD says: 'The young officers of the provincial commanders will do it.'"

"And who will start the battle?" he asked.

The prophet answered, "You will."

¹⁵So Ahab summoned the young officers of the provincial commanders, 232 men. Then he assembled the rest of the Israelites, 7,000 in all. ¹⁶They set out at noon while Ben-Hadad and the 32 kings allied with him were in their tents getting drunk. ¹⁷The young officers of the provincial commanders went out first.

Now Ben-Hadad had dispatched scouts, who reported, "Men are advancing from Samaria."

¹⁸He said, "If they have come out for peace, take them alive; if they have come out for war, take them alive."

¹⁹The young officers of the provincial commanders marched out of the city with the army behind them ²⁰and each one struck down his opponent. At that, the Arameans fled, with the Israelites in pursuit. But Ben-Hadad king of Aram escaped on horseback with some of his horsemen. ²¹The king of Israel advanced and overpowered the horses and chariots and inflicted heavy losses on the Arameans.

²²Afterward, the prophet came to the king of Israel and said, "Strengthen your position and see what must be done, because next spring the king of Aram will attack you again."

²³Meanwhile, the officials of the king of Aram advised him, "Their gods are gods of the hills. That is why they were too strong for us. But if we fight them on the plains, surely we will be stronger than they. ²⁴Do this: Remove all the kings from their commands and replace them with other officers. ²⁵You must also raise an army like the one you lost—horse for horse and chariot for chariot—so we can fight Israel on the plains. Then surely we will be stronger than they." He agreed with them and acted accordingly.

ᵃ12 Or in Succoth; also in verse 16

²⁶The next spring Ben-Hadad mustered the Arameans and went up to Aphek to fight against Israel. ²⁷When the Israelites were also mustered and given provisions, they marched out to meet them. The Israelites camped opposite them like two small flocks of goats, while the Arameans covered the countryside.

²⁸The man of God came up and told the king of Israel, "This is what the LORD says: 'Because the Arameans think the LORD is a god of the hills and not a god of the valleys, I will deliver this vast army into your hands, and you will know that I am the LORD.'"

²⁹For seven days they camped opposite each other, and on the seventh day the battle was joined. The Israelites inflicted a hundred thousand casualties on the Aramean foot soldiers in one day. ³⁰The rest of them escaped to the city of Aphek, where the wall collapsed on twenty-seven thousand of them. And Ben-Hadad fled to the city and hid in an inner room.

³¹His officials said to him, "Look, we have heard that the kings of the house of Israel are merciful. Let us go to the king of Israel with sackcloth around our waists and ropes around our heads. Perhaps he will spare your life."

³²Wearing sackcloth around their waists and ropes around their heads, they went to the king of Israel and said, "Your servant Ben-Hadad says: 'Please let me live.'"

The king answered, "Is he still alive? He is my brother."

³³The men took this as a good sign and were quick to pick up his word. "Yes, your brother Ben-Hadad!" they said.

"Go and get him," the king said. When Ben-Hadad came out, Ahab had him come up into his chariot.

³⁴"I will return the cities my father took from your father," Ben-Hadad offered. "You may set up your own market areas in Damascus, as my father did in Samaria."

⌊Ahab said,⌋ "On the basis of a treaty I will set you free." So he made a treaty with him, and let him go.

A Prophet Condemns Ahab

³⁵By the word of the LORD one of the sons of the prophets said to his compan-

ion, "Strike me with your weapon," but the man refused.

³⁶So the prophet said, "Because you have not obeyed the LORD, as soon as you leave me a lion will kill you." And after the man went away, a lion found him and killed him.

³⁷The prophet found another man and said, "Strike me, please." So the man struck him and wounded him. ³⁸Then the prophet went and stood by the road waiting for the king. He disguised himself with his headband down over his eyes. ³⁹As the king passed by, the prophet called out to him, "Your servant went into the thick of the battle, and someone came to me with a captive and said, 'Guard this man. If he is missing, it will be your life for his life, or you must pay a talent[a] of silver.' ⁴⁰While your servant was busy here and there, the man disappeared."

"That is your sentence," the king of Israel said. "You have pronounced it yourself."

⁴¹Then the prophet quickly removed the headband from his eyes, and the king of Israel recognized him as one of the prophets. ⁴²He said to the king, "This is what the LORD says: 'You have set free a man I had determined should die.[b] Therefore it is your life for his life, your people for his people.'" ⁴³Sullen and angry, the king of Israel went to his palace in Samaria.

Naboth's Vineyard

21 Some time later there was an incident involving a vineyard belonging to Naboth the Jezreelite. The vineyard was in Jezreel, close to the palace of Ahab king of Samaria. ²Ahab said to Naboth, "Let me have your vineyard to use for a vegetable garden, since it is close to my palace. In exchange I will give you a better vineyard or, if you prefer, I will pay you whatever it is worth."

³But Naboth replied, "The LORD forbid that I should give you the inheritance of my fathers."

⁴So Ahab went home, sullen and angry because Naboth the Jezreelite had said,

---

[a]39 That is, about 75 pounds (about 34 kilograms)   [b]42 The Hebrew term refers to the irrevocable giving over of things or persons to the LORD, often by totally destroying them.

"I will not give you the inheritance of my fathers." He lay on his bed sulking and refused to eat.

⁵His wife Jezebel came in and asked him, "Why are you so sullen? Why won't you eat?"

⁶He answered her, "Because I said to Naboth the Jezreelite, 'Sell me your vineyard; or if you prefer, I will give you another vineyard in its place.' But he said, 'I will not give you my vineyard.'"

⁷Jezebel his wife said, "Is this how you act as king over Israel? Get up and eat! Cheer up. I'll get you the vineyard of Naboth the Jezreelite."

⁸So she wrote letters in Ahab's name, placed his seal on them, and sent them to the elders and nobles who lived in Naboth's city with him. ⁹In those letters she wrote:

> "Proclaim a day of fasting and seat Naboth in a prominent place among the people. ¹⁰But seat two scoundrels opposite him and have them testify that he has cursed both God and the king. Then take him out and stone him to death."

¹¹So the elders and nobles who lived in Naboth's city did as Jezebel directed in the letters she had written to them. ¹²They proclaimed a fast and seated Naboth in a prominent place among the people. ¹³Then two scoundrels came and sat opposite him and brought charges against Naboth before the people, saying, "Naboth has cursed both God and the king." So they took him outside the city and stoned him to death. ¹⁴Then they sent word to Jezebel: "Naboth has been stoned and is dead."

¹⁵As soon as Jezebel heard that Naboth had been stoned to death, she said to Ahab, "Get up and take possession of the vineyard of Naboth the Jezreelite that he refused to sell you. He is no longer alive, but dead." ¹⁶When Ahab heard that Naboth was dead, he got up and went down to take possession of Naboth's vineyard.

¹⁷Then the word of the LORD came to Elijah the Tishbite: ¹⁸"Go down to meet Ahab king of Israel, who rules in Samaria. He is now in Naboth's vineyard, where he has gone to take possession of it. ¹⁹Say to him, 'This is what the LORD

says: Have you not murdered a man and seized his property?' Then say to him, 'This is what the LORD says: In the place where dogs licked up Naboth's blood, dogs will lick up your blood—yes, yours!'"

²⁰Ahab said to Elijah, "So you have found me, my enemy!"

"I have found you," he answered, "because you have sold yourself to do evil in the eyes of the LORD. ²¹'I am going to bring disaster on you. I will consume your descendants and cut off from Ahab every last male in Israel—slave or free. ²²I will make your house like that of Jeroboam son of Nebat and that of Baasha son of Ahijah, because you have provoked me to anger and have caused Israel to sin.'

²³"And also concerning Jezebel the LORD says: 'Dogs will devour Jezebel by the wall of* Jezreel.'

²⁴"Dogs will eat those belonging to Ahab who die in the city, and the birds of the air will feed on those who die in the country."

²⁵(There was never a man like Ahab, who sold himself to do evil in the eyes of the LORD, urged on by Jezebel his wife. ²⁶He behaved in the vilest manner by going after idols, like the Amorites the LORD drove out before Israel.)

²⁷When Ahab heard these words, he tore his clothes, put on sackcloth and fasted. He lay in sackcloth and went around meekly.

²⁸Then the word of the LORD came to Elijah the Tishbite: ²⁹"Have you noticed how Ahab has humbled himself before me? Because he has humbled himself, I will not bring this disaster in his day, but I will bring it on his house in the days of his son."

Micaiah Prophesies Against Ahab

22 For three years there was no war between Aram and Israel. ²But in the third year Jehoshaphat king of Judah went down to see the king of Israel. ³The king of Israel had said to his officials, "Don't you know that Ramoth Gilead

---

*a23 Most Hebrew manuscripts; a few Hebrew manuscripts, Vulgate and Syriac (see also 2 Kings 9:26) *the plot of ground at*

belongs to us and yet we are doing nothing to retake it from the king of Aram?"

⁴So he asked Jehoshaphat, "Will you go with me to fight against Ramoth Gilead?"

Jehoshaphat replied to the king of Israel, "I am as you are, my people as your people, my horses as your horses." ⁵But Jehoshaphat also said to the king of Israel, "First seek the counsel of the Lᴏʀᴅ."

⁶So the king of Israel brought together the prophets—about four hundred men—and asked them, "Shall I go to war against Ramoth Gilead, or shall I refrain?"

"Go," they answered, "for the Lord will give it into the king's hand."

⁷But Jehoshaphat asked, "Is there not a prophet of the Lᴏʀᴅ here whom we can inquire of?"

⁸The king of Israel answered Jehoshaphat, "There is still one man through whom we can inquire of the Lᴏʀᴅ, but I hate him because he never prophesies anything good about me, but always bad. He is Micaiah son of Imlah."

"The king should not say that," Jehoshaphat replied.

⁹So the king of Israel called one of his officials and said, "Bring Micaiah son of Imlah at once."

¹⁰Dressed in their royal robes, the king of Israel and Jehoshaphat king of Judah were sitting on their thrones at the threshing floor by the entrance of the gate of Samaria, with all the prophets prophesying before them. ¹¹Now Zedekiah son of Kenaanah had made iron horns and he declared, "This is what the Lᴏʀᴅ says: 'With these you will gore the Arameans until they are destroyed.'"

¹²All the other prophets were prophesying the same thing. "Attack Ramoth Gilead and be victorious," they said, "for the Lᴏʀᴅ will give it into the king's hand."

¹³The messenger who had gone to summon Micaiah said to him, "Look, as one man the other prophets are predicting success for the king. Let your word agree with theirs, and speak favorably."

¹⁴But Micaiah said, "As surely as the Lᴏʀᴅ lives, I can tell him only what the Lᴏʀᴅ tells me."

¹⁵When he arrived, the king asked him, "Micaiah, shall we go to war against Ramoth Gilead, or shall I refrain?"

"Attack and be victorious," he answered, "for the Lᴏʀᴅ will give it into the king's hand."

¹⁶The king said to him, "How many times must I make you swear to tell me nothing but the truth in the name of the Lᴏʀᴅ?"

¹⁷Then Micaiah answered, "I saw all Israel scattered on the hills like sheep without a shepherd, and the Lᴏʀᴅ said, 'These people have no master. Let each one go home in peace.'"

¹⁸The king of Israel said to Jehoshaphat, "Didn't I tell you that he never prophesies anything good about me, but only bad?"

¹⁹Micaiah continued, "Therefore hear the word of the Lᴏʀᴅ: I saw the Lᴏʀᴅ sitting on his throne with all the host of heaven standing around him on his right and on his left. ²⁰And the Lᴏʀᴅ said, 'Who will entice Ahab into attacking Ramoth Gilead and going to his death there?'

"One suggested this, and another that. ²¹Finally, a spirit came forward, stood before the Lᴏʀᴅ and said, 'I will entice him.'

²²"'By what means?' the Lᴏʀᴅ asked.

"'I will go out and be a lying spirit in the mouths of all his prophets,' he said.

"'You will succeed in enticing him,' said the Lᴏʀᴅ. 'Go and do it.'

²³"So now the Lᴏʀᴅ has put a lying spirit in the mouths of all these prophets of yours. The Lᴏʀᴅ has decreed disaster for you."

²⁴Then Zedekiah son of Kenaanah went up and slapped Micaiah in the face. "Which way did the spirit from[a] the Lᴏʀᴅ go when he went from me to speak to you?" he asked.

²⁵Micaiah replied, "You will find out on the day you go to hide in an inner room."

²⁶The king of Israel then ordered, "Take Micaiah and send him back to Amon the ruler of the city and to Joash the king's son ²⁷and say, 'This is what the king says: Put this fellow in prison and give him nothing but bread and water until I return safely.'"

²⁸Micaiah declared, "If you ever return safely, the Lᴏʀᴅ has not spoken through me." Then he added, "Mark my words, all you people!"

ᵃ24 Or Spirit of

Ahab Killed at Ramoth Gilead

²⁹So the king of Israel and Jehoshaphat king of Judah went up to Ramoth Gilead. ³⁰The king of Israel said to Jehoshaphat, "I will enter the battle in disguise, but you wear your royal robes." So the king of Israel disguised himself and went into battle.

³¹Now the king of Aram had ordered his thirty-two chariot commanders, "Do not fight with anyone, small or great, except the king of Israel." ³²When the chariot commanders saw Jehoshaphat, they thought, "Surely this is the king of Israel." So they turned to attack him, but when Jehoshaphat cried out, ³³the chariot commanders saw that he was not the king of Israel and stopped pursuing him.

³⁴But someone drew his bow at random and hit the king of Israel between the sections of his armor. The king told his chariot driver, "Wheel around and get me out of the fighting. I've been wounded." ³⁵All day long the battle raged, and the king was propped up in his chariot facing the Arameans. The blood from his wound ran onto the floor of the chariot, and that evening he died. ³⁶As the sun was setting, a cry spread through the army: "Every man to his town; everyone to his land!"

³⁷So the king died and was brought to Samaria, and they buried him there. ³⁸They washed the chariot at a pool in Samaria (where the prostitutes bathed),ᵃ and the dogs licked up his blood, as the word of the LORD had declared.

³⁹As for the other events of Ahab's reign, including all he did, the palace he built and inlaid with ivory, and the cities he fortified, are they not written in the book of the annals of the kings of Israel? ⁴⁰Ahab rested with his fathers. And Ahaziah his son succeeded him as king.

Jehoshaphat King of Judah

⁴¹Jehoshaphat son of Asa became king of Judah in the fourth year of Ahab king of Israel. ⁴²Jehoshaphat was thirty-five years old when he became king, and he reigned in Jerusalem twenty-five years. His mother's name was Azubah daughter of Shilhi. ⁴³In everything he walked in the ways of his father Asa and did not stray from them; he did what was right in the eyes of the LORD. The high places, however, were not removed, and the people continued to offer sacrifices and burn incense there. ⁴⁴Jehoshaphat was also at peace with the king of Israel.

⁴⁵As for the other events of Jehoshaphat's reign, the things he achieved and his military exploits, are they not written in the book of the annals of the kings of Judah? ⁴⁶He rid the land of the rest of the male shrine prostitutes who remained there even after the reign of his father Asa. ⁴⁷There was then no king in Edom; a deputy ruled.

⁴⁸Now Jehoshaphat built a fleet of trading shipsᵇ to go to Ophir for gold, but they never set sail—they were wrecked at Ezion Geber. ⁴⁹At that time Ahaziah son of Ahab said to Jehoshaphat, "Let my men sail with your men," but Jehoshaphat refused.

⁵⁰Then Jehoshaphat rested with his fathers and was buried with them in the city of David his father. And Jehoram his son succeeded him.

Ahaziah King of Israel

⁵¹Ahaziah son of Ahab became king of Israel in Samaria in the seventeenth year of Jehoshaphat king of Judah, and he reigned over Israel two years. ⁵²He did evil in the eyes of the LORD, because he walked in the ways of his father and mother and in the ways of Jeroboam son of Nebat, who caused Israel to sin. ⁵³He served and worshiped Baal and provoked the LORD, the God of Israel, to anger, just as his father had done.

ᵃ38 Or *Samaria and cleaned the weapons*
ᵇ48 Hebrew *of ships of Tarshish*

2 Kings

"THE LORD WILL DO
WHAT HE HAS
PROMISED." (20:9)

THE BOOK of 2 Kings continues the history lesson that was
started in 1 Kings. Here we witness the demise of the nations of
Israel and Judah at the hands of the Assyrians and Babylonians,
respectively. This raises a burning theological question: Did the
gods of the pagan nations defeat Israel's God when Israel was
defeated? The common assumption of the times was that when
one nation defeated another nation, the winner's gods beat the
loser's gods. Military defeat brought on a spiritual crisis. The books
of 1 and 2 Kings address this issue by demonstrating how time
and again God's people were defeated not because their God had
failed them, but because they had failed their God. This is a key
truth that these books of history reveal to us.

The Israelite's failure was idolatry, the worship of gods other
than the true and living God. It wasn't that the people of Israel
and Judah ever stopped believing in the Lord. It was just that they
wanted the Lord *plus* all the benefits the other gods might offer.
Their Canaanite neighbors worshiped gods of fertility and agricul-
ture. Since those were departments vital to everyone's life, it
seemed reasonable that the Lord's people should get a little help
from some of the "specialists." They wanted to have God *and* the
gods. The appeal of "God-plus" was overwhelming.

Jesus said all great prayer begins with three great petitions:
that God's name be revered, that his kingdom come, and that his
will, and no other's, be done on earth as it is in heaven (see
Matthew 6:9–10). Such a prayer is the opposite of "God-plus." To
pray the Lord's Prayer is to learn the lessons of Israel's history.

The LORD's Judgment on Ahaziah

1 After Ahab's death, Moab rebelled against Israel. ²Now Ahaziah had fallen through the lattice of his upper room in Samaria and injured himself. So he sent messengers, saying to them, "Go and consult Baal-Zebub, the god of Ekron, to see if I will recover from this injury."

³But the angel of the LORD said to Elijah the Tishbite, "Go up and meet the messengers of the king of Samaria and ask them, 'Is it because there is no God in Israel that you are going off to consult Baal-Zebub, the god of Ekron?' ⁴Therefore this is what the LORD says: 'You will not leave the bed you are lying on. You will certainly die!'" So Elijah went.

⁵When the messengers returned to the king, he asked them, "Why have you come back?"

⁶"A man came to meet us," they replied. "And he said to us, 'Go back to the king who sent you and tell him, "This is what the LORD says: Is it because there is no God in Israel that you are sending men to consult Baal-Zebub, the god of Ekron? Therefore you will not leave the bed you are lying on. You will certainly die!"'"

⁷The king asked them, "What kind of man was it who came to meet you and told you this?"

⁸They replied, "He was a man with a garment of hair and with a leather belt around his waist."

The king said, "That was Elijah the Tishbite."

⁹Then he sent to Elijah a captain with his company of fifty men. The captain went up to Elijah, who was sitting on the top of a hill, and said to him, "Man of God, the king says, 'Come down!'"

¹⁰Elijah answered the captain, "If I am a man of God, may fire come down from heaven and consume you and your fifty men!" Then fire fell from heaven and consumed the captain and his men.

¹¹At this the king sent to Elijah another captain with his fifty men. The captain said to him, "Man of God, this is what the king says, 'Come down at once!'"

¹²"If I am a man of God," Elijah replied, "may fire come down from heaven and consume you and your fifty men!" Then the fire of God fell from heaven and consumed him and his fifty men.

¹³So the king sent a third captain with his fifty men. This third captain went up and fell on his knees before Elijah. "Man of God," he begged, "please have respect for my life and the lives of these fifty men, your servants! ¹⁴See, fire has fallen from heaven and consumed the first two captains and all their men. But now have respect for my life!"

¹⁵The angel of the LORD said to Elijah, "Go down with him; do not be afraid of him." So Elijah got up and went down with him to the king.

¹⁶He told the king, "This is what the LORD says: Is it because there is no God in Israel for you to consult that you have sent messengers to consult Baal-Zebub, the god of Ekron? Because you have done this, you will never leave the bed you are lying on. You will certainly die!" ¹⁷So he died, according to the word of the LORD that Elijah had spoken.

Because Ahaziah had no son, Joram*a* succeeded him as king in the second year of Jehoram son of Jehoshaphat king of Judah. ¹⁸As for all the other events of Ahaziah's reign, and what he did, are they not written in the book of the annals of the kings of Israel?

Elijah Taken Up to Heaven

2 When the LORD was about to take Elijah up to heaven in a whirlwind, Elijah and Elisha were on their way from Gilgal. ²Elijah said to Elisha, "Stay here; the LORD has sent me to Bethel."

But Elisha said, "As surely as the LORD lives and as you live, I will not leave you." So they went down to Bethel.

³The company of the prophets at Bethel came out to Elisha and asked, "Do you know that the LORD is going to take your master from you today?"

"Yes, I know," Elisha replied, "but do not speak of it."

⁴Then Elijah said to him, "Stay here, Elisha; the LORD has sent me to Jericho."

And he replied, "As surely as the LORD lives and as you live, I will not leave you." So they went to Jericho.

⁵The company of the prophets at Jericho

a 17 Hebrew Jehoram, a variant of Joram

went up to Elisha and asked him, "Do you know that the LORD is going to take your master from you today?"

"Yes, I know," he replied, "but do not speak of it."

⁶Then Elijah said to him, "Stay here; the LORD has sent me to the Jordan."

And he replied, "As surely as the LORD lives and as you live, I will not leave you." So the two of them walked on.

⁷Fifty men of the company of the prophets went and stood at a distance, facing the place where Elijah and Elisha had stopped at the Jordan. ⁸Elijah took his cloak, rolled it up and struck the water with it. The water divided to the right and to the left, and the two of them crossed over on dry ground.

⁹When they had crossed, Elijah said to Elisha, "Tell me, what can I do for you before I am taken from you?"

"Let me inherit a double portion of your spirit," Elisha replied.

¹⁰"You have asked a difficult thing," Elijah said, "yet if you see me when I am taken from you, it will be yours—otherwise not."

¹¹As they were walking along and talking together, suddenly a chariot of fire and horses of fire appeared and separated the two of them, and Elijah went up to heaven in a whirlwind. ¹²Elisha saw this and cried out, "My father! My father! The chariots and horsemen of Israel!" And Elisha saw him no more. Then he took hold of his own clothes and tore them apart.

¹³He picked up the cloak that had fallen from Elijah and went back and stood on the bank of the Jordan. ¹⁴Then he took the cloak that had fallen from him and struck the water with it. "Where now is the LORD, the God of Elijah?" he asked. When he struck the water, it divided to the right and to the left, and he crossed over.

¹⁵The company of the prophets from Jericho, who were watching, said, "The spirit of Elijah is resting on Elisha." And they went to meet him and bowed to the ground before him. ¹⁶"Look," they said, "we your servants have fifty able men. Let them go and look for your master. Perhaps the Spirit of the LORD has picked him up and set him down on some mountain or in some valley."

"No," Elisha replied, "do not send them."

¹⁷But they persisted until he was too ashamed to refuse. So he said, "Send them." And they sent fifty men, who searched for three days but did not find him. ¹⁸When they returned to Elisha, who was staying in Jericho, he said to them, "Didn't I tell you not to go?"

Healing of the Water

¹⁹The men of the city said to Elisha, "Look, our lord, this town is well situated, as you can see, but the water is bad and the land is unproductive."

²⁰"Bring me a new bowl," he said, "and put salt in it." So they brought it to him.

²¹Then he went out to the spring and threw the salt into it, saying, "This is what the LORD says: 'I have healed this water. Never again will it cause death or make the land unproductive.'" ²²And the water has remained wholesome to this day, according to the word Elisha had spoken.

Elisha Is Jeered

²³From there Elisha went up to Bethel. As he was walking along the road, some youths came out of the town and jeered at him. "Go on up, you baldhead!" they said. "Go on up, you baldhead!" ²⁴He turned around, looked at them and called down a curse on them in the name of the LORD. Then two bears came out of the woods and mauled forty-two of the youths. ²⁵And he went on to Mount Carmel and from there returned to Samaria.

Moab Revolts

3 Joram^a son of Ahab became king of Israel in Samaria in the eighteenth year of Jehoshaphat king of Judah, and he reigned twelve years. ²He did evil in the eyes of the LORD, but not as his father and mother had done. He got rid of the sacred stone of Baal that his father had made. ³Nevertheless he clung to the sins of Jeroboam son of Nebat, which he had caused Israel to commit; he did not turn away from them.

⁴Now Mesha king of Moab raised sheep, and he had to supply the king of

---

^{a}1 Hebrew *Jehoram*, a variant of *Joram*; also in verse 6

Israel with a hundred thousand lambs and with the wool of a hundred thousand rams. ⁵But after Ahab died, the king of Moab rebelled against the king of Israel. ⁶So at that time King Joram set out from Samaria and mobilized all Israel. ⁷He also sent this message to Jehoshaphat king of Judah: "The king of Moab has rebelled against me. Will you go with me to fight against Moab?"

"I will go with you," he replied. "I am as you are, my people as your people, my horses as your horses."

⁸"By what route shall we attack?" he asked.

"Through the Desert of Edom," he answered.

⁹So the king of Israel set out with the king of Judah and the king of Edom. After a roundabout march of seven days, the army had no more water for themselves or for the animals with them.

¹⁰"What!" exclaimed the king of Israel. "Has the LORD called us three kings together only to hand us over to Moab?"

¹¹But Jehoshaphat asked, "Is there no prophet of the LORD here, that we may inquire of the LORD through him?"

An officer of the king of Israel answered, "Elisha son of Shaphat is here. He used to pour water on the hands of Elijah.ᵃ"

¹²Jehoshaphat said, "The word of the LORD is with him." So the king of Israel and Jehoshaphat and the king of Edom went down to him.

¹³Elisha said to the king of Israel, "What do we have to do with each other? Go to the prophets of your father and the prophets of your mother."

"No," the king of Israel answered, "because it was the LORD who called us three kings together to hand us over to Moab."

¹⁴Elisha said, "As surely as the LORD Almighty lives, whom I serve, if I did not have respect for the presence of Jehoshaphat king of Judah, I would not look at you or even notice you. ¹⁵But now bring me a harpist."

While the harpist was playing, the hand of the LORD came upon Elisha ¹⁶and he said, "This is what the LORD says: Make this valley full of ditches. ¹⁷For this is what the LORD says: You will see neither wind nor rain, yet this valley will be filled with water, and you, your cattle and your other animals will drink. ¹⁸This is an easy thing in the eyes of the LORD; he will also hand Moab over to you. ¹⁹You will overthrow every fortified city and every major town. You will cut down every good tree, stop up all the springs, and ruin every good field with stones."

²⁰The next morning, about the time for offering the sacrifice, there it was—water flowing from the direction of Edom! And the land was filled with water.

²¹Now all the Moabites had heard that the kings had come to fight against them; so every man, young and old, who could bear arms was called up and stationed on the border. ²²When they got up early in the morning, the sun was shining on the water. To the Moabites across the way, the water looked red—like blood. ²³"That's blood!" they said. "Those kings must have fought and slaughtered each other. Now to the plunder, Moab!"

²⁴But when the Moabites came to the camp of Israel, the Israelites rose up and fought them until they fled. And the Israelites invaded the land and slaughtered the Moabites. ²⁵They destroyed the towns, and each man threw a stone on every good field until it was covered. They stopped up all the springs and cut down every good tree. Only Kir Hareseth was left with its stones in place, but men armed with slings surrounded it and attacked it as well.

²⁶When the king of Moab saw that the battle had gone against him, he took with him seven hundred swordsmen to break through to the king of Edom, but they failed. ²⁷Then he took his firstborn son, who was to succeed him as king, and offered him as a sacrifice on the city wall. The fury against Israel was great; they withdrew and returned to their own land.

The Widow's Oil

4 The wife of a man from the company of the prophets cried out to Elisha, "Your servant my husband is dead, and you know that he revered the LORD. But now his creditor is coming to take my two boys as his slaves."

ᵃ11 That is, he was Elijah's personal servant.

²Elisha replied to her, "How can I help you? Tell me, what do you have in your house?"

"Your servant has nothing there at all," she said, "except a little oil."

³Elisha said, "Go around and ask all your neighbors for empty jars. Don't ask for just a few. ⁴Then go inside and shut the door behind you and your sons. Pour oil into all the jars, and as each is filled, put it to one side."

⁵She left him and afterward shut the door behind her and her sons. They brought the jars to her and she kept pouring. ⁶When all the jars were full, she said to her son, "Bring me another one."

But he replied, "There is not a jar left." Then the oil stopped flowing.

⁷She went and told the man of God, and he said, "Go, sell the oil and pay your debts. You and your sons can live on what is left."

The Shunammite's Son Restored to Life

⁸One day Elisha went to Shunem. And a well-to-do woman was there, who urged him to stay for a meal. So whenever he came by, he stopped there to eat. ⁹She said to her husband, "I know that this man who often comes our way is a holy man of God. ¹⁰Let's make a small room on the roof and put in it a bed and a table, a chair and a lamp for him. Then he can stay there whenever he comes to us."

¹¹One day when Elisha came, he went up to his room and lay down there. ¹²He said to his servant Gehazi, "Call the Shunammite." So he called her, and she stood before him. ¹³Elisha said to him, "Tell her, 'You have gone to all this trouble for us. Now what can be done for you? Can we speak on your behalf to the king or the commander of the army?'"

She replied, "I have a home among my own people."

¹⁴"What can be done for her?" Elisha asked.

Gehazi said, "Well, she has no son and her husband is old."

¹⁵Then Elisha said, "Call her." So he called her, and she stood in the doorway. ¹⁶"About this time next year," Elisha said, "you will hold a son in your arms."

"No, my lord," she objected. "Don't mislead your servant, O man of God!"

¹⁷But the woman became pregnant, and the next year about that same time she gave birth to a son, just as Elisha had told her.

¹⁸The child grew, and one day he went out to his father, who was with the reapers. ¹⁹"My head! My head!" he said to his father.

His father told a servant, "Carry him to his mother." ²⁰After the servant had lifted him up and carried him to his mother, the boy sat on her lap until noon, and then he died. ²¹She went up and laid him on the bed of the man of God, then shut the door and went out.

²²She called her husband and said, "Please send me one of the servants and a donkey so I can go to the man of God quickly and return."

²³"Why go to him today?" he asked. "It's not the New Moon or the Sabbath."

"It's all right," she said.

²⁴She saddled the donkey and said to her servant, "Lead on; don't slow down for me unless I tell you." ²⁵So she set out and came to the man of God at Mount Carmel.

When he saw her in the distance, the man of God said to his servant Gehazi, "Look! There's the Shunammite! ²⁶Run to meet her and ask her, 'Are you all right? Is your husband all right? Is your child all right?'"

"Everything is all right," she said.

²⁷When she reached the man of God at the mountain, she took hold of his feet. Gehazi came over to push her away, but the man of God said, "Leave her alone! She is in bitter distress, but the LORD has hidden it from me and has not told me why."

²⁸"Did I ask you for a son, my lord?" she said. "Didn't I tell you, 'Don't raise my hopes'?"

²⁹Elisha said to Gehazi, "Tuck your cloak into your belt, take my staff in your hand and run. If you meet anyone, do not greet him, and if anyone greets you, do not answer. Lay my staff on the boy's face."

HE WENT IN, shut the door on the two of them and prayed to the LORD.

2 KINGS 4:33

³⁰But the child's mother said, "As surely as the LORD lives and as you live, I will not leave you." So he got up and followed her.

³¹Gehazi went on ahead and laid the staff on the boy's face, but there was no sound or response. So Gehazi went back to meet Elisha and told him, "The boy has not awakened."

³²When Elisha reached the house, there was the boy lying dead on his couch. ³³He went in, shut the door on the two of them and prayed to the LORD. ³⁴Then he got on the bed and lay upon

---

[THURSDAY]

2 KINGS 4:8 – 37

Breathe on Them, Breath of God

4:33 HE WENT IN, SHUT THE DOOR ON THE TWO OF THEM AND PRAYED TO THE LORD.

No one knows for sure why Elisha stretched his body over the dead boy's body, mouth to mouth, eyes to eyes, hands to hands (see 4:34–35). It certainly wasn't ancient CPR! Depending upon one's sensibilities, the action can seem sweet or strange. But it was what the prophet did—after he prayed to the Lord for the boy to be raised (see verse 33). Elijah did the same thing, with the same result (see 1 Kings 17:21).

Maybe what this story of prayer and healing shows us is not so much a teaching on a particular kind of prayer, but a picture of prayer of a particular kind. Perhaps its intent is to move our compassion more than to add to our prayer repertoire. Sometimes prayer for others is a laying down of our lives for them. All intercessory prayer is an act of love, but there are times when we wrestle with God for the life of another, pouring out our hearts in tears and loud cries (see Lamentations 2:19; Hebrews 5:7). When Jesus went about healing the sick and those tormented by demons, Matthew says it was the fulfillment of Isaiah 53:4: "He took up our infirmities and carried our diseases" (Matthew 8:17). A close look at Isaiah 53 shows that this bearing of pain was intimately connected with Jesus' ministry of intercession: "For he bore the sin of many, and made intercession for the transgressors" (Isaiah 53:12). In his prayers for the deliverance of others, he took their pain upon himself. His prayers were more than mere words; they were a further incarnation of God's redeeming love.

Poet George Herbert described prayer as "God's breath in man returning to his birth." Like the story of Elisha, that line isn't about the mechanics of prayer, but the heart of prayer. When God breathed his breath into Adam, Adam became a "living being" (Genesis 2:7). When we pray to the one who gave us breath, our breath, in a sense, goes back to the one who gave it. Does something like that happen in prayer—not mechanically and literally, but spiritually? God breathes his life in us. "Come, Holy Spirit," we breathe back in the prayer of faith; and something of his breath is breathed on others. Intercessory prayer is a miraculous kind of CPR.

PRAY:

*Breathe on me, Breath of God, and then use my prayers
to transmit your Spirit to those I intercede for.*

FOR YOUR NEXT DEVOTIONAL READING, GO TO PAGE 423.

the boy, mouth to mouth, eyes to eyes, hands to hands. As he stretched himself out upon him, the boy's body grew warm. [35]Elisha turned away and walked back and forth in the room and then got on the bed and stretched out upon him once more. The boy sneezed seven times and opened his eyes.

[36]Elisha summoned Gehazi and said, "Call the Shunammite." And he did. When she came, he said, "Take your son." [37]She came in, fell at his feet and bowed to the ground. Then she took her son and went out.

Death in the Pot

[38]Elisha returned to Gilgal and there was a famine in that region. While the company of the prophets was meeting with him, he said to his servant, "Put on the large pot and cook some stew for these men."

[39]One of them went out into the fields to gather herbs and found a wild vine. He gathered some of its gourds and filled the fold of his cloak. When he returned, he cut them up into the pot of stew, though no one knew what they were. [40]The stew was poured out for the men, but as they began to eat it, they cried out, "O man of God, there is death in the pot!" And they could not eat it.

[41]Elisha said, "Get some flour." He put it into the pot and said, "Serve it to the people to eat." And there was nothing harmful in the pot.

Feeding of a Hundred

[42]A man came from Baal Shalishah, bringing the man of God twenty loaves of barley bread baked from the first ripe grain, along with some heads of new grain. "Give it to the people to eat," Elisha said.

[43]"How can I set this before a hundred men?" his servant asked.

But Elisha answered, "Give it to the people to eat. For this is what the LORD says: 'They will eat and have some left over.'" [44]Then he set it before them, and they ate and had some left over, according to the word of the LORD.

Naaman Healed of Leprosy

5 Now Naaman was commander of the army of the king of Aram. He was a great man in the sight of his master and highly regarded, because through him the LORD had given victory to Aram. He was a valiant soldier, but he had leprosy.[a]

[2]Now bands from Aram had gone out and had taken captive a young girl from Israel, and she served Naaman's wife. [3]She said to her mistress, "If only my master would see the prophet who is in Samaria! He would cure him of his leprosy."

[4]Naaman went to his master and told him what the girl from Israel had said. [5]"By all means, go," the king of Aram replied. "I will send a letter to the king of Israel." So Naaman left, taking with him ten talents[b] of silver, six thousand shekels[c] of gold and ten sets of clothing. [6]The letter that he took to the king of Israel read: "With this letter I am sending my servant Naaman to you so that you may cure him of his leprosy."

[7]As soon as the king of Israel read the letter, he tore his robes and said, "Am I God? Can I kill and bring back to life? Why does this fellow send someone to me to be cured of his leprosy? See how he is trying to pick a quarrel with me!"

[8]When Elisha the man of God heard that the king of Israel had torn his robes, he sent him this message: "Why have you torn your robes? Have the man come to me and he will know that there is a prophet in Israel." [9]So Naaman went with his horses and chariots and stopped at the door of Elisha's house. [10]Elisha sent a messenger to say to him, "Go, wash yourself seven times in the Jordan, and your flesh will be restored and you will be cleansed."

[11]But Naaman went away angry and said, "I thought that he would surely come out to me and stand and call on the name of the LORD his God, wave his hand over the spot and cure me of my leprosy. [12]Are not Abana and Pharpar, the rivers of Damascus, better than any of the waters of Israel? Couldn't I wash in them and be cleansed?" So he turned and went off in a rage.

[a]1 The Hebrew word was used for various diseases affecting the skin—not necessarily leprosy; also in verses 3, 6, 7, 11 and 27.
[b]5 That is, about 750 pounds (about 340 kilograms)   [c]5 That is, about 150 pounds (about 70 kilograms)

[13]Naaman's servants went to him and said, "My father, if the prophet had told you to do some great thing, would you not have done it? How much more, then, when he tells you, 'Wash and be cleansed'!" [14]So he went down and dipped himself in the Jordan seven times, as the man of God had told him, and his flesh was restored and became clean like that of a young boy.

[15]Then Naaman and all his attendants went back to the man of God. He stood before him and said, "Now I know that there is no God in all the world except in Israel. Please accept now a gift from your servant."

[16]The prophet answered, "As surely as the LORD lives, whom I serve, I will not accept a thing." And even though Naaman urged him, he refused.

[17]"If you will not," said Naaman, "please let me, your servant, be given as much earth as a pair of mules can carry, for your servant will never again make burnt offerings and sacrifices to any other god but the LORD. [18]But may the LORD forgive your servant for this one thing: When my master enters the temple of Rimmon to bow down and he is leaning on my arm and I bow there also—when I bow down in the temple of Rimmon, may the LORD forgive your servant for this."

[19]"Go in peace," Elisha said.

After Naaman had traveled some distance, [20]Gehazi, the servant of Elisha the man of God, said to himself, "My master was too easy on Naaman, this Aramean, by not accepting from him what he brought. As surely as the LORD lives, I will run after him and get something from him."

[21]So Gehazi hurried after Naaman. When Naaman saw him running toward him, he got down from the chariot to meet him. "Is everything all right?" he asked.

[22]"Everything is all right," Gehazi answered. "My master sent me to say, 'Two young men from the company of the prophets have just come to me from the hill country of Ephraim. Please give them a talent[a] of silver and two sets of clothing.'"

[23]"By all means, take two talents," said Naaman. He urged Gehazi to accept them, and then tied up the two talents of silver in two bags, with two sets of clothing. He gave them to two of his servants, and they carried them ahead of Gehazi. [24]When Gehazi came to the hill, he took the things from the servants and put them away in the house. He sent the men away and they left. [25]Then he went in and stood before his master Elisha.

"Where have you been, Gehazi?" Elisha asked.

"Your servant didn't go anywhere," Gehazi answered.

[26]But Elisha said to him, "Was not my spirit with you when the man got down from his chariot to meet you? Is this the time to take money, or to accept clothes, olive groves, vineyards, flocks, herds, or menservants and maidservants? [27]Naaman's leprosy will cling to you and to your descendants forever." Then Gehazi went from Elisha's presence and he was leprous, as white as snow.

An Axhead Floats

6 The company of the prophets said to Elisha, "Look, the place where we meet with you is too small for us. [2]Let us go to the Jordan, where each of us can get a pole; and let us build a place there for us to live."

And he said, "Go."

[3]Then one of them said, "Won't you please come with your servants?"

"I will," Elisha replied. [4]And he went with them.

They went to the Jordan and began to cut down trees. [5]As one of them was cutting down a tree, the iron axhead fell into the water. "Oh, my lord," he cried out, "it was borrowed!"

[6]The man of God asked, "Where did it fall?" When he showed him the place, Elisha cut a stick and threw it there, and made the iron float. [7]"Lift it out," he said. Then the man reached out his hand and took it.

Elisha Traps Blinded Arameans

[8]Now the king of Aram was at war with Israel. After conferring with his officers, he said, "I will set up my camp in such and such a place."

[a]22 That is, about 75 pounds (about 34 kilograms)

[9]The man of God sent word to the king of Israel: "Beware of passing that place, because the Arameans are going down there." [10]So the king of Israel checked on the place indicated by the man of God. Time and again Elisha warned the king, so that he was on his guard in such places.

[11]This enraged the king of Aram. He summoned his officers and demanded of them, "Will you not tell me which of us is on the side of the king of Israel?"

[12]"None of us, my lord the king," said one of his officers, "but Elisha, the prophet who is in Israel, tells the king of Israel the very words you speak in your bedroom."

[13]"Go, find out where he is," the king ordered, "so I can send men and capture him." The report came back: "He is in Dothan." [14]Then he sent horses and chariots and a strong force there. They went by night and surrounded the city.

[15]When the servant of the man of God got up and went out early the next morning, an army with horses and chariots had surrounded the city. "Oh, my lord, what shall we do?" the servant asked.

[16]"Don't be afraid," the prophet answered. "Those who are with us are more than those who are with them."

[17]And Elisha prayed, "O LORD, open his eyes so he may see." Then the LORD opened the servant's eyes, and he looked and saw the hills full of horses and chariots of fire all around Elisha.

[18]As the enemy came down toward him, Elisha prayed to the LORD, "Strike these people with blindness." So he struck them with blindness, as Elisha had asked.

[19]Elisha told them, "This is not the road and this is not the city. Follow me, and I will lead you to the man you are looking for." And he led them to Samaria.

[20]After they entered the city, Elisha said, "LORD, open the eyes of these men so they can see." Then the LORD opened their eyes and they looked, and there they were, inside Samaria.

[21]When the king of Israel saw them, he asked Elisha, "Shall I kill them, my father? Shall I kill them?"

[22]"Do not kill them," he answered. "Would you kill men you have captured with your own sword or bow? Set food and water before them so that they may eat and drink and then go back to their master." [23]So he prepared a great feast for them, and after they had finished eating and drinking, he sent them away, and they returned to their master. So the bands from Aram stopped raiding Israel's territory.

Famine in Besieged Samaria

[24]Some time later, Ben-Hadad king of Aram mobilized his entire army and marched up and laid siege to Samaria. [25]There was a great famine in the city; the siege lasted so long that a donkey's head sold for eighty shekels[a] of silver, and a quarter of a cab[b] of seed pods[c] for five shekels.[d]

[26]As the king of Israel was passing by on the wall, a woman cried to him, "Help me, my lord the king!"

[27]The king replied, "If the LORD does not help you, where can I get help for you? From the threshing floor? From the winepress?" [28]Then he asked her, "What's the matter?"

She answered, "This woman said to me, 'Give up your son so we may eat him today, and tomorrow we'll eat my son.' [29]So we cooked my son and ate him. The next day I said to her, 'Give up your son so we may eat him,' but she had hidden him."

[30]When the king heard the woman's words, he tore his robes. As he went along the wall, the people looked, and there, underneath, he had sackcloth on his body. [31]He said, "May God deal with me, be it ever so severely, if the head of Elisha son of Shaphat remains on his shoulders today!"

[32]Now Elisha was sitting in his house, and the elders were sitting with him. The king sent a messenger ahead, but before he arrived, Elisha said to the elders, "Don't you see how this murderer is sending someone to cut off my head? Look, when the messenger comes, shut the door and hold it shut against him. Is not the sound of his master's footsteps behind him?"

---

[a]25 That is, about 2 pounds (about 1 kilogram)   [b]25 That is, probably about 1/2 pint (about 0.3 liter)   [c]25 Or *of doves' dung*   [d]25 That is, about 2 ounces (about 55 grams)

³³While he was still talking to them, the messenger came down to him. And ˌthe kingˌ said, "This disaster is from the LORD. Why should I wait for the LORD any longer?"

7 Elisha said, "Hear the word of the LORD. This is what the LORD says: About this time tomorrow, a seah*a* of flour will sell for a shekel*b* and two seahs*c* of barley for a shekel at the gate of Samaria."

²The officer on whose arm the king was leaning said to the man of God, "Look, even if the LORD should open the floodgates of the heavens, could this happen?"

a1 That is, probably about 7 quarts (about 7.3 liters); also in verses 16 and 18   *b1* That is, about 2/5 ounce (about 11 grams); also in verses 16 and 18   *c1* That is, probably about 13 quarts (about 15 liters); also in verses 16 and 18

[FRIDAY]

2 KINGS 6:8 – 23

Creatures from the World Next Door

6:17 ELISHA PRAYED, "O LORD, OPEN HIS EYES SO HE MAY SEE."

There's a world next door, just around the corner. It's full of marvelous creatures, closer than you think, and yet a universe away. In fairy tales, it's the place Alice gets to through the looking glass; or the land the Pevensie children enter through an old wardrobe. Elisha's servant saw it when the prophet prayed, "'O Lord, open his eyes so he may see.' Then the LORD opened the servant's eyes, and he looked and saw the hills full of horses and chariots of fire all around Elisha" (6:17). If there were some kind of spiritual eyeglasses we could put on to see the world next door, all around us, we would be as astonished as that servant was. We would know that no matter who or how many our enemies may be, "Those who are with us are more than those who are with them" (verse 16).

"For he will command his angels concerning you to guard you in all your ways; they will lift you up in their hands, so that you will not strike your foot against a stone" (Psalm 91:11–12). This is not a metaphor; it is literally true. "Are not all angels ministering spirits sent to serve those who will inherit salvation?" (Hebrews 1:14). This passage sounds like fairy tale talk, except this fairy tale is true. If we could see the times these marvelous creatures have served God by protecting us, we would be—what would we be, besides amazed?

We are never alone. Jesus was so confident of the presence of these beings in the world next door that when the mob came for him, he told his disciples, "Do you think I cannot call on my Father, and he will at once put at my disposal more than twelve legions of angels?" (Matthew 26:53).

It is God's business, not ours, to call on the angels to come to our side. Like all his servants, human and otherwise, they are not to be worshiped or prayed to. But they are to encourage us in the spiritual battle we are embroiled in till Christ returns.

PRAY:
O Lord, open my spiritual eyes so that I may see and appreciate
the vast heavenly host that is with me.

FOR YOUR NEXT DEVOTIONAL READING, GO TO PAGE 434.

"You will see it with your own eyes," answered Elisha, "but you will not eat any of it!"

The Siege Lifted

³Now there were four men with leprosy[a] at the entrance of the city gate. They said to each other, "Why stay here until we die? ⁴If we say, 'We'll go into the city'—the famine is there, and we will die. And if we stay here, we will die. So let's go over to the camp of the Arameans and surrender. If they spare us, we live; if they kill us, then we die."

⁵At dusk they got up and went to the camp of the Arameans. When they reached the edge of the camp, not a man was there, ⁶for the Lord had caused the Arameans to hear the sound of chariots and horses and a great army, so that they said to one another, "Look, the king of Israel has hired the Hittite and Egyptian kings to attack us!" ⁷So they got up and fled in the dusk and abandoned their tents and their horses and donkeys. They left the camp as it was and ran for their lives.

⁸The men who had leprosy reached the edge of the camp and entered one of the tents. They ate and drank, and carried away silver, gold and clothes, and went off and hid them. They returned and entered another tent and took some things from it and hid them also.

⁹Then they said to each other, "We're not doing right. This is a day of good news and we are keeping it to ourselves. If we wait until daylight, punishment will overtake us. Let's go at once and report this to the royal palace."

¹⁰So they went and called out to the city gatekeepers and told them, "We went into the Aramean camp and not a man was there—not a sound of anyone—only tethered horses and donkeys, and the tents left just as they were." ¹¹The gatekeepers shouted the news, and it was reported within the palace.

¹²The king got up in the night and said to his officers, "I will tell you what the Arameans have done to us. They know we are starving; so they have left the camp to hide in the countryside, thinking, 'They will surely come out, and then we will take them alive and get into the city.'"

¹³One of his officers answered, "Have some men take five of the horses that are left in the city. Their plight will be like that of all the Israelites left here—yes, they will only be like all these Israelites who are doomed. So let us send them to find out what happened."

¹⁴So they selected two chariots with their horses, and the king sent them after the Aramean army. He commanded the drivers, "Go and find out what has happened." ¹⁵They followed them as far as the Jordan, and they found the whole road strewn with the clothing and equipment the Arameans had thrown away in their headlong flight. So the messengers returned and reported to the king. ¹⁶Then the people went out and plundered the camp of the Arameans. So a seah of flour sold for a shekel, and two seahs of barley sold for a shekel, as the Lord had said.

¹⁷Now the king had put the officer on whose arm he leaned in charge of the gate, and the people trampled him in the gateway, and he died, just as the man of God had foretold when the king came down to his house. ¹⁸It happened as the man of God had said to the king: "About this time tomorrow, a seah of flour will sell for a shekel and two seahs of barley for a shekel at the gate of Samaria."

¹⁹The officer had said to the man of God, "Look, even if the Lord should open the floodgates of the heavens, could this happen?" The man of God had replied, "You will see it with your own eyes, but you will not eat any of it!" ²⁰And that is exactly what happened to him, for the people trampled him in the gateway, and he died.

The Shunammite's Land Restored

8 Now Elisha had said to the woman whose son he had restored to life, "Go away with your family and stay for a while wherever you can, because the Lord has decreed a famine in the land that will last seven years." ²The woman proceeded to do as the man of God said. She and her family went away and stayed in the land of the Philistines seven years.

---

[a] 3 The Hebrew word is used for various diseases affecting the skin—not necessarily leprosy; also in verse 8.

[3]At the end of the seven years she came back from the land of the Philistines and went to the king to beg for her house and land. [4]The king was talking to Gehazi, the servant of the man of God, and had said, "Tell me about all the great things Elisha has done." [5]Just as Gehazi was telling the king how Elisha had restored the dead to life, the woman whose son Elisha had brought back to life came to beg the king for her house and land. Gehazi said, "This is the woman, my lord the king, and this is her son whom Elisha restored to life." [6]The king asked the woman about it, and she told him.

Then he assigned an official to her case and said to him, "Give back everything that belonged to her, including all the income from her land from the day she left the country until now."

Hazael Murders Ben-Hadad

[7]Elisha went to Damascus, and Ben-Hadad king of Aram was ill. When the king was told, "The man of God has come all the way up here," [8]he said to Hazael, "Take a gift with you and go to meet the man of God. Consult the LORD through him; ask him, 'Will I recover from this illness?'"

[9]Hazael went to meet Elisha, taking with him as a gift forty camel-loads of all the finest wares of Damascus. He went in and stood before him, and said, "Your son Ben-Hadad king of Aram has sent me to ask, 'Will I recover from this illness?'"

[10]Elisha answered, "Go and say to him, 'You will certainly recover'; but[a] the LORD has revealed to me that he will in fact die." [11]He stared at him with a fixed gaze until Hazael felt ashamed. Then the man of God began to weep.

[12]"Why is my lord weeping?" asked Hazael.

"Because I know the harm you will do to the Israelites," he answered. "You will set fire to their fortified places, kill their young men with the sword, dash their little children to the ground, and rip open their pregnant women." [13]Hazael said, "How could your servant, a mere dog, accomplish such a feat?"

"The LORD has shown me that you will become king of Aram," answered Elisha.

[14]Then Hazael left Elisha and returned to his master. When Ben-Hadad asked, "What did Elisha say to you?" Hazael replied, "He told me that you would certainly recover." [15]But the next day he took a thick cloth, soaked it in water and spread it over the king's face, so that he died. Then Hazael succeeded him as king.

Jehoram King of Judah

[16]In the fifth year of Joram son of Ahab king of Israel, when Jehoshaphat was king of Judah, Jehoram son of Jehoshaphat began his reign as king of Judah. [17]He was thirty-two years old when he became king, and he reigned in Jerusalem eight years. [18]He walked in the ways of the kings of Israel, as the house of Ahab had done, for he married a daughter of Ahab. He did evil in the eyes of the LORD. [19]Nevertheless, for the sake of his servant David, the LORD was not willing to destroy Judah. He had promised to maintain a lamp for David and his descendants forever.

[20]In the time of Jehoram, Edom rebelled against Judah and set up its own king. [21]So Jehoram[b] went to Zair with all his chariots. The Edomites surrounded him and his chariot commanders, but he rose up and broke through by night; his army, however, fled back home. [22]To this day Edom has been in rebellion against Judah. Libnah revolted at the same time.

[23]As for the other events of Jehoram's reign, and all he did, are they not written in the book of the annals of the kings of Judah? [24]Jehoram rested with his fathers and was buried with them in the City of David. And Ahaziah his son succeeded him as king.

Ahaziah King of Judah

[25]In the twelfth year of Joram son of Ahab king of Israel, Ahaziah son of Jehoram king of Judah began to reign. [26]Ahaziah was twenty-two years old when he became king, and he reigned in Jerusalem one year. His mother's name was Athaliah, a granddaughter of Omri king

[a]10 The Hebrew may also be read Go and say, 'You will certainly not recover,' for.
[b]21 Hebrew Joram, a variant of Jehoram; also in verses 23 and 24

of Israel. ²⁷He walked in the ways of the house of Ahab and did evil in the eyes of the LORD, as the house of Ahab had done, for he was related by marriage to Ahab's family.

²⁸Ahaziah went with Joram son of Ahab to war against Hazael king of Aram at Ramoth Gilead. The Arameans wounded Joram; ²⁹so King Joram returned to Jezreel to recover from the wounds the Arameans had inflicted on him at Ramoth*ᵃ* in his battle with Hazael king of Aram.

Then Ahaziah son of Jehoram king of Judah went down to Jezreel to see Joram son of Ahab, because he had been wounded.

Jehu Anointed King of Israel

9 The prophet Elisha summoned a man from the company of the prophets and said to him, "Tuck your cloak into your belt, take this flask of oil with you and go to Ramoth Gilead. ²When you get there, look for Jehu son of Jehoshaphat, the son of Nimshi. Go to him, get him away from his companions and take him into an inner room. ³Then take the flask and pour the oil on his head and declare, 'This is what the LORD says: I anoint you king over Israel.' Then open the door and run; don't delay!"

⁴So the young man, the prophet, went to Ramoth Gilead. ⁵When he arrived, he found the army officers sitting together. "I have a message for you, commander," he said.

"For which of us?" asked Jehu.

"For you, commander," he replied.

⁶Jehu got up and went into the house. Then the prophet poured the oil on Jehu's head and declared, "This is what the LORD, the God of Israel, says: 'I anoint you king over the LORD's people Israel. ⁷You are to destroy the house of Ahab your master, and I will avenge the blood of my servants the prophets and the blood of all the LORD's servants shed by Jezebel. ⁸The whole house of Ahab will perish. I will cut off from Ahab every last male in Israel—slave or free. ⁹I will make the house of Ahab like the house of Jeroboam son of Nebat and like the house of Baasha son of Ahijah. ¹⁰As for Jezebel, dogs will devour her on the plot of ground at Jezreel, and no one will bury her.' " Then he opened the door and ran.

¹¹When Jehu went out to his fellow officers, one of them asked him, "Is everything all right? Why did this madman come to you?"

"You know the man and the sort of things he says," Jehu replied.

¹²"That's not true!" they said. "Tell us."

Jehu said, "Here is what he told me: 'This is what the LORD says: I anoint you king over Israel.' "

¹³They hurried and took their cloaks and spread them under him on the bare steps. Then they blew the trumpet and shouted, "Jehu is king!"

Jehu Kills Joram and Ahaziah

¹⁴So Jehu son of Jehoshaphat, the son of Nimshi, conspired against Joram. (Now Joram and all Israel had been defending Ramoth Gilead against Hazael king of Aram, ¹⁵but King Joram*ᵇ* had returned to Jezreel to recover from the wounds the Arameans had inflicted on him in the battle with Hazael king of Aram.) Jehu said, "If this is the way you feel, don't let anyone slip out of the city to go and tell the news in Jezreel." ¹⁶Then he got into his chariot and rode to Jezreel, because Joram was resting there and Ahaziah king of Judah had gone down to see him.

¹⁷When the lookout standing on the tower in Jezreel saw Jehu's troops approaching, he called out, "I see some troops coming."

"Get a horseman," Joram ordered. "Send him to meet them and ask, 'Do you come in peace?' "

¹⁸The horseman rode off to meet Jehu and said, "This is what the king says: 'Do you come in peace?' "

"What do you have to do with peace?" Jehu replied. "Fall in behind me."

The lookout reported, "The messenger has reached them, but he isn't coming back."

¹⁹So the king sent out a second horseman. When he came to them he said, "This is what the king says: 'Do you come in peace?' "

Jehu replied, "What do you have to do with peace? Fall in behind me."

---

*ᵃ*29 Hebrew *Ramah*, a variant of *Ramoth*
*ᵇ*15 Hebrew *Jehoram*, a variant of *Joram*; also in verses 17 and 21–24

²⁰The lookout reported, "He has reached them, but he isn't coming back either. The driving is like that of Jehu son of Nimshi—he drives like a madman."

²¹"Hitch up my chariot," Joram ordered. And when it was hitched up, Joram king of Israel and Ahaziah king of Judah rode out, each in his own chariot, to meet Jehu. They met him at the plot of ground that had belonged to Naboth the Jezreelite. ²²When Joram saw Jehu he asked, "Have you come in peace, Jehu?"

"How can there be peace," Jehu replied, "as long as all the idolatry and witchcraft of your mother Jezebel abound?"

²³Joram turned about and fled, calling out to Ahaziah, "Treachery, Ahaziah!"

²⁴Then Jehu drew his bow and shot Joram between the shoulders. The arrow pierced his heart and he slumped down in his chariot. ²⁵Jehu said to Bidkar, his chariot officer, "Pick him up and throw him on the field that belonged to Naboth the Jezreelite. Remember how you and I were riding together in chariots behind Ahab his father when the LORD made this prophecy about him: ²⁶'Yesterday I saw the blood of Naboth and the blood of his sons, declares the LORD, and I will surely make you pay for it on this plot of ground, declares the LORD.'ᵃ Now then, pick him up and throw him on that plot, in accordance with the word of the LORD."

²⁷When Ahaziah king of Judah saw what had happened, he fled up the road to Beth Haggan.ᵇ Jehu chased him, shouting, "Kill him too!" They wounded him in his chariot on the way up to Gur near Ibleam, but he escaped to Megiddo and died there. ²⁸His servants took him by chariot to Jerusalem and buried him with his fathers in his tomb in the City of David. ²⁹(In the eleventh year of Joram son of Ahab, Ahaziah had become king of Judah.)

Jezebel Killed

³⁰Then Jehu went to Jezreel. When Jezebel heard about it, she painted her eyes, arranged her hair and looked out of a window. ³¹As Jehu entered the gate, she asked, "Have you come in peace, Zimri, you murderer of your master?"ᶜ

³²He looked up at the window and called out, "Who is on my side? Who?"

Two or three eunuchs looked down at him. ³³"Throw her down!" Jehu said. So they threw her down, and some of her blood spattered the wall and the horses as they trampled her underfoot.

³⁴Jehu went in and ate and drank. "Take care of that cursed woman," he said, "and bury her, for she was a king's daughter." ³⁵But when they went out to bury her, they found nothing except her skull, her feet and her hands. ³⁶They went back and told Jehu, who said, "This is the word of the LORD that he spoke through his servant Elijah the Tishbite: On the plot of ground at Jezreel dogs will devour Jezebel's flesh.ᵈ ³⁷Jezebel's body will be like refuse on the ground in the plot at Jezreel, so that no one will be able to say, 'This is Jezebel.' "

Ahab's Family Killed

10 Now there were in Samaria seventy sons of the house of Ahab. So Jehu wrote letters and sent them to Samaria: to the officials of Jezreel,ᵉ to the elders and to the guardians of Ahab's children. He said, ²"As soon as this letter reaches you, since your master's sons are with you and you have chariots and horses, a fortified city and weapons, ³choose the best and most worthy of your master's sons and set him on his father's throne. Then fight for your master's house."

⁴But they were terrified and said, "If two kings could not resist him, how can we?"

⁵So the palace administrator, the city governor, the elders and the guardians sent this message to Jehu: "We are your servants and we will do anything you say. We will not appoint anyone as king; you do whatever you think best."

⁶Then Jehu wrote them a second letter, saying, "If you are on my side and will obey me, take the heads of your master's sons and come to me in Jezreel by this time tomorrow."

Now the royal princes, seventy of them, were with the leading men of the

---

ᵃ26 See 1 Kings 21:19. ᵇ27 Or fled by way of the garden house   ᶜ31 Or "Did Zimri have peace, who murdered his master?"
ᵈ36 See 1 Kings 21:23.   ᵉ1 Hebrew; some Septuagint manuscripts and Vulgate of the city

city, who were rearing them. 7When the letter arrived, these men took the princes and slaughtered all seventy of them. They put their heads in baskets and sent them to Jehu in Jezreel. 8When the messenger arrived, he told Jehu, "They have brought the heads of the princes."

Then Jehu ordered, "Put them in two piles at the entrance of the city gate until morning."

9The next morning Jehu went out. He stood before all the people and said, "You are innocent. It was I who conspired against my master and killed him, but who killed all these? 10Know then, that not a word the LORD has spoken against the house of Ahab will fail. The LORD has done what he promised through his servant Elijah." 11So Jehu killed everyone in Jezreel who remained of the house of Ahab, as well as all his chief men, his close friends and his priests, leaving him no survivor.

12Jehu then set out and went toward Samaria. At Beth Eked of the Shepherds, 13he met some relatives of Ahaziah king of Judah and asked, "Who are you?"

They said, "We are relatives of Ahaziah, and we have come down to greet the families of the king and of the queen mother."

14"Take them alive!" he ordered. So they took them alive and slaughtered them by the well of Beth Eked—forty-two men. He left no survivor.

15After he left there, he came upon Jehonadab son of Recab, who was on his way to meet him. Jehu greeted him and said, "Are you in accord with me, as I am with you?"

"I am," Jehonadab answered.

"If so," said Jehu, "give me your hand." So he did, and Jehu helped him up into the chariot. 16Jehu said, "Come with me and see my zeal for the LORD." Then he had him ride along in his chariot.

17When Jehu came to Samaria, he killed all who were left there of Ahab's family; he destroyed them, according to the word of the LORD spoken to Elijah.

Ministers of Baal Killed

18Then Jehu brought all the people together and said to them, "Ahab served Baal a little; Jehu will serve him much.

19Now summon all the prophets of Baal, all his ministers and all his priests. See that no one is missing, because I am going to hold a great sacrifice for Baal. Anyone who fails to come will no longer live." But Jehu was acting deceptively in order to destroy the ministers of Baal. 20Jehu said, "Call an assembly in honor of Baal." So they proclaimed it. 21Then he sent word throughout Israel, and all the ministers of Baal came; not one stayed away. They crowded into the temple of Baal until it was full from one end to the other. 22And Jehu said to the keeper of the wardrobe, "Bring robes for all the ministers of Baal." So he brought out robes for them.

23Then Jehu and Jehonadab son of Recab went into the temple of Baal. Jehu said to the ministers of Baal, "Look around and see that no servants of the LORD are here with you—only ministers of Baal." 24So they went in to make sacrifices and burnt offerings. Now Jehu had posted eighty men outside with this warning: "If one of you lets any of the men I am placing in your hands escape, it will be your life for his life."

25As soon as Jehu finished making the burnt offering, he ordered the guards and officers: "Go in and kill them; let no one escape." So they cut them down with the sword. The guards and officers threw the bodies out and then entered the inner shrine of the temple of Baal. 26They brought the sacred stone out of the temple of Baal and burned it. 27They demolished the sacred stone of Baal and tore down the temple of Baal, and people have used it for a latrine to this day.

28So Jehu destroyed Baal worship in Israel. 29However, he did not turn away from the sins of Jeroboam son of Nebat, which he had caused Israel to commit—the worship of the golden calves at Bethel and Dan.

30The LORD said to Jehu, "Because you have done well in accomplishing what is right in my eyes and have done to the house of Ahab all I had in mind to do, your descendants will sit on the throne of Israel to the fourth generation." 31Yet Jehu was not careful to keep the law of the LORD, the God of Israel, with all his heart. He did not turn away from the sins of Jeroboam, which he had caused Israel to commit.

³²In those days the LORD began to reduce the size of Israel. Hazael overpowered the Israelites throughout their territory ³³east of the Jordan in all the land of Gilead (the region of Gad, Reuben and Manasseh), from Aroer by the Arnon Gorge through Gilead to Bashan.

³⁴As for the other events of Jehu's reign, all he did, and all his achievements, are they not written in the book of the annals of the kings of Israel? ³⁵Jehu rested with his fathers and was buried in Samaria. And Jehoahaz his son succeeded him as king. ³⁶The time that Jehu reigned over Israel in Samaria was twenty-eight years.

Athaliah and Joash

11 When Athaliah the mother of Ahaziah saw that her son was dead, she proceeded to destroy the whole royal family. ²But Jehosheba, the daughter of King Jehoram*ᵃ* and sister of Ahaziah, took Joash son of Ahaziah and stole him away from among the royal princes, who were about to be murdered. She put him and his nurse in a bedroom to hide him from Athaliah; so he was not killed. ³He remained hidden with his nurse at the temple of the LORD for six years while Athaliah ruled the land.

⁴In the seventh year Jehoiada sent for the commanders of units of a hundred, the Carites and the guards and had them brought to him at the temple of the LORD. He made a covenant with them and put them under oath at the temple of the LORD. Then he showed them the king's son. ⁵He commanded them, saying, "This is what you are to do: You who are in the three companies that are going on duty on the Sabbath—a third of you guarding the royal palace, ⁶a third at the Sur Gate, and a third at the gate behind the guard, who take turns guarding the temple— ⁷and you who are in the other two companies that normally go off Sabbath duty are all to guard the temple for the king. ⁸Station yourselves around the king, each man with his weapon in his hand. Anyone who approaches your ranksᵇ must be put to death. Stay close to the king wherever he goes."

⁹The commanders of units of a hundred did just as Jehoiada the priest ordered. Each one took his men—those who were going on duty on the Sabbath and those who were going off duty—and came to Jehoiada the priest. ¹⁰Then he gave the commanders the spears and shields that had belonged to King David and that were in the temple of the LORD. ¹¹The guards, each with his weapon in his hand, stationed themselves around the king—near the altar and the temple, from the south side to the north side of the temple.

¹²Jehoiada brought out the king's son and put the crown on him; he presented him with a copy of the covenant and proclaimed him king. They anointed him, and the people clapped their hands and shouted, "Long live the king!"

¹³When Athaliah heard the noise made by the guards and the people, she went to the people at the temple of the LORD. ¹⁴She looked and there was the king, standing by the pillar, as the custom was. The officers and the trumpeters were beside the king, and all the people of the land were rejoicing and blowing trumpets. Then Athaliah tore her robes and called out, "Treason! Treason!"

> God speaks in the silence of the heart. Listening is the beginning of prayer. 99
>
> MOTHER TERESA

¹⁵Jehoiada the priest ordered the commanders of units of a hundred, who were in charge of the troops: "Bring her out between the ranksᶜ and put to the sword anyone who follows her." For the priest had said, "She must not be put to death in the temple of the LORD." ¹⁶So they seized her as she reached the place where the horses enter the palace grounds, and there she was put to death.

¹⁷Jehoiada then made a covenant between the LORD and the king and people

---

ᵃ2 Hebrew *Joram,* a variant of *Jehoram*
ᵇ8 Or *approaches the precincts*   ᶜ15 Or *out from the precincts*

that they would be the Lord's people. He also made a covenant between the king and the people. ¹⁸All the people of the land went to the temple of Baal and tore it down. They smashed the altars and idols to pieces and killed Mattan the priest of Baal in front of the altars.

Then Jehoiada the priest posted guards at the temple of the Lord. ¹⁹He took with him the commanders of hundreds, the Carites, the guards and all the people of the land, and together they brought the king down from the temple of the Lord and went into the palace, entering by way of the gate of the guards. The king then took his place on the royal throne, ²⁰and all the people of the land rejoiced. And the city was quiet, because Athaliah had been slain with the sword at the palace.

²¹Joash[a] was seven years old when he began to reign.

Joash Repairs the Temple

12 In the seventh year of Jehu, Joash[b] became king, and he reigned in Jerusalem forty years. His mother's name was Zibiah; she was from Beersheba. ²Joash did what was right in the eyes of the Lord all the years Jehoiada the priest instructed him. ³The high places, however, were not removed; the people continued to offer sacrifices and burn incense there.

⁴Joash said to the priests, "Collect all the money that is brought as sacred offerings to the temple of the Lord—the money collected in the census, the money received from personal vows and the money brought voluntarily to the temple. ⁵Let every priest receive the money from one of the treasurers, and let it be used to repair whatever damage is found in the temple."

⁶But by the twenty-third year of King Joash the priests still had not repaired the temple. ⁷Therefore King Joash summoned Jehoiada the priest and the other priests and asked them, "Why aren't you repairing the damage done to the temple? Take no more money from your treasurers, but hand it over for repairing the temple." ⁸The priests agreed that they would not collect any more money from the people and that they would not repair the temple themselves.

⁹Jehoiada the priest took a chest and bored a hole in its lid. He placed it beside the altar, on the right side as one enters the temple of the Lord. The priests who guarded the entrance put into the chest all the money that was brought to the temple of the Lord. ¹⁰Whenever they saw that there was a large amount of money in the chest, the royal secretary and the high priest came, counted the money that had been brought into the temple of the Lord and put it into bags. ¹¹When the amount had been determined, they gave the money to the men appointed to supervise the work on the temple. With it they paid those who worked on the temple of the Lord—the carpenters and builders, ¹²the masons and stonecutters. They purchased timber and dressed stone for the repair of the temple of the Lord, and met all the other expenses of restoring the temple.

¹³The money brought into the temple was not spent for making silver basins, wick trimmers, sprinkling bowls, trumpets or any other articles of gold or silver for the temple of the Lord; ¹⁴it was paid to the workmen, who used it to repair the temple. ¹⁵They did not require an accounting from those to whom they gave the money to pay the workers, because they acted with complete honesty. ¹⁶The money from the guilt offerings and sin offerings was not brought into the temple of the Lord; it belonged to the priests.

¹⁷About this time Hazael king of Aram went up and attacked Gath and captured it. Then he turned to attack Jerusalem. ¹⁸But Joash king of Judah took all the sacred objects dedicated by his fathers—Jehoshaphat, Jehoram and Ahaziah, the kings of Judah—and the gifts he himself had dedicated and all the gold found in the treasuries of the temple of the Lord and of the royal palace, and he sent them to Hazael king of Aram, who then withdrew from Jerusalem.

¹⁹As for the other events of the reign of Joash, and all he did, are they not written in the book of the annals of the kings of

---

[a]21 Hebrew *Jehoash,* a variant of *Joash*
[b]1 Hebrew *Jehoash,* a variant of *Joash*; also in verses 2, 4, 6, 7 and 18

Judah? 20His officials conspired against him and assassinated him at Beth Millo, on the road down to Silla. 21The officials who murdered him were Jozabad son of Shimeath and Jehozabad son of Shomer. He died and was buried with his fathers in the City of David. And Amaziah his son succeeded him as king.

Jehoahaz King of Israel

13 In the twenty-third year of Joash son of Ahaziah king of Judah, Jehoahaz son of Jehu became king of Israel in Samaria, and he reigned seventeen years. 2He did evil in the eyes of the LORD by following the sins of Jeroboam son of Nebat, which he had caused Israel to commit, and he did not turn away from them. 3So the LORD's anger burned against Israel, and for a long time he kept them under the power of Hazael king of Aram and Ben-Hadad his son.

> JEHOAHAZ sought the LORD's favor, and the LORD listened to him, for he saw how severely the king of Aram was oppressing Israel.
>
> 2 KINGS 13:4

4Then Jehoahaz sought the LORD's favor, and the LORD listened to him, for he saw how severely the king of Aram was oppressing Israel. 5The LORD provided a deliverer for Israel, and they escaped from the power of Aram. So the Israelites lived in their own homes as they had before. 6But they did not turn away from the sins of the house of Jeroboam, which he had caused Israel to commit; they continued in them. Also, the Asherah pole*a* remained standing in Samaria.

7Nothing had been left of the army of Jehoahaz except fifty horsemen, ten chariots and ten thousand foot soldiers, for the king of Aram had destroyed the rest and made them like the dust at threshing time.

8As for the other events of the reign of Jehoahaz, all he did and his achievements, are they not written in the book of the annals of the kings of Israel? 9Jehoahaz rested with his fathers and was bur-

ied in Samaria. And Jehoash*b* his son succeeded him as king.

Jehoash King of Israel

10In the thirty-seventh year of Joash king of Judah, Jehoash son of Jehoahaz became king of Israel in Samaria, and he reigned sixteen years. 11He did evil in the eyes of the LORD and did not turn away from any of the sins of Jeroboam son of Nebat, which he had caused Israel to commit; he continued in them.

12As for the other events of the reign of Jehoash, all he did and his achievements, including his war against Amaziah king of Judah, are they not written in the book of the annals of the kings of Israel? 13Jehoash rested with his fathers, and Jeroboam succeeded him on the throne. Jehoash was buried in Samaria with the kings of Israel.

14Now Elisha was suffering from the illness from which he died. Jehoash king of Israel went down to see him and wept over him. "My father! My father!" he cried. "The chariots and horsemen of Israel!"

15Elisha said, "Get a bow and some arrows," and he did so. 16"Take the bow in your hands," he said to the king of Israel. When he had taken it, Elisha put his hands on the king's hands.

17"Open the east window," he said, and he opened it. "Shoot!" Elisha said, and he shot. "The LORD's arrow of victory, the arrow of victory over Aram!" Elisha declared. "You will completely destroy the Arameans at Aphek."

18Then he said, "Take the arrows," and the king took them. Elisha told him, "Strike the ground." He struck it three times and stopped. 19The man of God was angry with him and said, "You should have struck the ground five or six times; then you would have defeated Aram and completely destroyed it. But now you will defeat it only three times."

20Elisha died and was buried.

Now Moabite raiders used to enter the country every spring. 21Once while some

---

a6 That is, a symbol of the goddess Asherah; here and elsewhere in 2 Kings   *b9* Hebrew *Joash*, a variant of *Jehoash*; also in verses 12–14 and 25

Israelites were burying a man, suddenly they saw a band of raiders; so they threw the man's body into Elisha's tomb. When the body touched Elisha's bones, the man came to life and stood up on his feet.

²²Hazael king of Aram oppressed Israel throughout the reign of Jehoahaz. ²³But the LORD was gracious to them and had compassion and showed concern for them because of his covenant with Abraham, Isaac and Jacob. To this day he has been unwilling to destroy them or banish them from his presence.

²⁴Hazael king of Aram died, and Ben-Hadad his son succeeded him as king. ²⁵Then Jehoash son of Jehoahaz recaptured from Ben-Hadad son of Hazael the towns he had taken in battle from his father Jehoahaz. Three times Jehoash defeated him, and so he recovered the Israelite towns.

Amaziah King of Judah

14 In the second year of Jehoash[a] son of Jehoahaz king of Israel, Amaziah son of Joash king of Judah began to reign. ²He was twenty-five years old when he became king, and he reigned in Jerusalem twenty-nine years. His mother's name was Jehoaddin; she was from Jerusalem. ³He did what was right in the eyes of the LORD, but not as his father David had done. In everything he followed the example of his father Joash. ⁴The high places, however, were not removed; the people continued to offer sacrifices and burn incense there.

⁵After the kingdom was firmly in his grasp, he executed the officials who had murdered his father the king. ⁶Yet he did not put the sons of the assassins to death, in accordance with what is written in the Book of the Law of Moses where the LORD commanded: "Fathers shall not be put to death for their children, nor children put to death for their fathers; each is to die for his own sins."[b]

⁷He was the one who defeated ten thousand Edomites in the Valley of Salt and captured Sela in battle, calling it Joktheel, the name it has to this day.

⁸Then Amaziah sent messengers to Jehoash son of Jehoahaz, the son of Jehu, king of Israel, with the challenge: "Come, meet me face to face."

⁹But Jehoash king of Israel replied to Amaziah king of Judah: "A thistle in Lebanon sent a message to a cedar in Lebanon, 'Give your daughter to my son in marriage.' Then a wild beast in Lebanon came along and trampled the thistle underfoot. ¹⁰You have indeed defeated Edom and now you are arrogant. Glory in your victory, but stay at home! Why ask for trouble and cause your own downfall and that of Judah also?"

¹¹Amaziah, however, would not listen, so Jehoash king of Israel attacked. He and Amaziah king of Judah faced each other at Beth Shemesh in Judah. ¹²Judah was routed by Israel, and every man fled to his home. ¹³Jehoash king of Israel captured Amaziah king of Judah, the son of Joash, the son of Ahaziah, at Beth Shemesh. Then Jehoash went to Jerusalem and broke down the wall of Jerusalem from the Ephraim Gate to the Corner Gate—a section about six hundred feet long.[c] ¹⁴He took all the gold and silver and all the articles found in the temple of the LORD and in the treasuries of the royal palace. He also took hostages and returned to Samaria.

¹⁵As for the other events of the reign of Jehoash, what he did and his achievements, including his war against Amaziah king of Judah, are they not written in the book of the annals of the kings of Israel? ¹⁶Jehoash rested with his fathers and was buried in Samaria with the kings of Israel. And Jeroboam his son succeeded him as king.

¹⁷Amaziah son of Joash king of Judah lived for fifteen years after the death of Jehoash son of Jehoahaz king of Israel. ¹⁸As for the other events of Amaziah's reign, are they not written in the book of the annals of the kings of Judah?

¹⁹They conspired against him in Jerusalem, and he fled to Lachish, but they sent men after him to Lachish and killed him there. ²⁰He was brought back by horse and was buried in Jerusalem with his fathers, in the City of David.

²¹Then all the people of Judah took

[a]1 Hebrew *Joash*, a variant of *Jehoash*; also in verses 13, 23 and 27   [b]6 Deut. 24:16
[c]13 Hebrew *four hundred cubits* (about 180 meters)

Azariah,[a] who was sixteen years old, and made him king in place of his father Amaziah. [22]He was the one who rebuilt Elath and restored it to Judah after Amaziah rested with his fathers.

Jeroboam II King of Israel

[23]In the fifteenth year of Amaziah son of Joash king of Judah, Jeroboam son of Jehoash king of Israel became king in Samaria, and he reigned forty-one years. [24]He did evil in the eyes of the LORD and did not turn away from any of the sins of Jeroboam son of Nebat, which he had caused Israel to commit. [25]He was the one who restored the boundaries of Israel from Lebo[b] Hamath to the Sea of the Arabah,[c] in accordance with the word of the LORD, the God of Israel, spoken through his servant Jonah son of Amittai, the prophet from Gath Hepher. [26]The LORD had seen how bitterly everyone in Israel, whether slave or free, was suffering; there was no one to help them. [27]And since the LORD had not said he would blot out the name of Israel from under heaven, he saved them by the hand of Jeroboam son of Jehoash.

[28]As for the other events of Jeroboam's reign, all he did, and his military achievements, including how he recovered for Israel both Damascus and Hamath, which had belonged to Yaudi,[d] are they not written in the book of the annals of the kings of Israel? [29]Jeroboam rested with his fathers, the kings of Israel. And Zechariah his son succeeded him as king.

Azariah King of Judah

15 In the twenty-seventh year of Jeroboam king of Israel, Azariah son of Amaziah king of Judah began to reign. [2]He was sixteen years old when he became king, and he reigned in Jerusalem fifty-two years. His mother's name was Jecoliah; she was from Jerusalem. [3]He did what was right in the eyes of the LORD, just as his father Amaziah had done. [4]The high places, however, were not removed; the people continued to offer sacrifices and burn incense there.

[5]The LORD afflicted the king with leprosy[e] until the day he died, and he lived in a separate house.[f] Jotham the king's son had charge of the palace and governed the people of the land.

[6]As for the other events of Azariah's reign, and all he did, are they not written in the book of the annals of the kings of Judah? [7]Azariah rested with his fathers and was buried near them in the City of David. And Jotham his son succeeded him as king.

Zechariah King of Israel

[8]In the thirty-eighth year of Azariah king of Judah, Zechariah son of Jeroboam became king of Israel in Samaria, and he reigned six months. [9]He did evil in the eyes of the LORD, as his fathers had done. He did not turn away from the sins of Jeroboam son of Nebat, which he had caused Israel to commit.

[10]Shallum son of Jabesh conspired against Zechariah. He attacked him in front of the people,[g] assassinated him and succeeded him as king. [11]The other events of Zechariah's reign are written in the book of the annals of the kings of Israel. [12]So the word of the LORD spoken to Jehu was fulfilled: "Your descendants will sit on the throne of Israel to the fourth generation."[h]

Shallum King of Israel

[13]Shallum son of Jabesh became king in the thirty-ninth year of Uzziah king of Judah, and he reigned in Samaria one month. [14]Then Menahem son of Gadi went from Tirzah up to Samaria. He attacked Shallum son of Jabesh in Samaria, assassinated him and succeeded him as king.

[15]The other events of Shallum's reign, and the conspiracy he led, are written in the book of the annals of the kings of Israel.

[16]At that time Menahem, starting out from Tirzah, attacked Tiphsah and everyone in the city and its vicinity, because they refused to open their gates. He sacked Tiphsah and ripped open all the pregnant women.

---

[a]21 Also called *Uzziah*   [b]25 Or *from the entrance to*   [c]25 That is, the Dead Sea   [d]28 Or *Judah*   [e]5 The Hebrew word was used for various diseases affecting the skin—not necessarily leprosy.   [f]5 Or *in a house where he was relieved of responsibility*   [g]10 Hebrew; some Septuagint manuscripts *in Ibleam*   [h]12 2 Kings 10:30

The 7.5 Million Dollar Man

THE ORPHANS sat in silence as George Mueller rose to pray for their daily bread. The tables were set for breakfast, but there was no food. Just then, there was a knock on the door; it was the local baker. "Mr. Mueller," he explained, "I couldn't sleep last night. Somehow I felt you didn't have bread for breakfast, so I got up at 2:00 A.M. and baked some fresh bread." Minutes later, another man knocked at the door; this time it was the milkman. His cart had broken down right in front of the orphanage. He needed to empty his cart to repair it, and he wanted to give away all his milk. Breakfast was served.[1]

This kind of thing happened to George Mueller over and over again in a ministry that spanned 57 years. Mueller believed the only one he should ever speak to about his personal needs and the needs of his orphans was God—no one else. Mueller trusted God for every detail. At the end of his life, George Mueller could say that God had provided for over 10,000 orphaned children, answered 50,000 specific prayers, and brought in 1,453,153 pounds ($7,500,000 by the days' standards) in contributions, all in response to simple faith and tenacious prayer. Once he explained his unusual "fund-raising techniques" to an incredulous businessman, who exclaimed unapprovingly, "Why, you live from hand to mouth!" Mueller agreed, saying, "Yes, it's God's hand and my mouth."

He writes, "When I first began to allow God to deal with me, relying on Him, taking Him at His Word, and set out fifty years ago simply relying on

Him for myself, family, taxes, traveling expenses and every other need, I rested on the simple promises I found in the sixth chapter of Matthew, 'I say unto you, take no thought for your life, what ye shall eat, or what ye shall drink; nor yet for your body, what ye shall put on ... for your heavenly Father knoweth that ye have need of all these things. But seek ye first the kingdom of God and His righteousness; and all these things shall be added unto you.' I believed the Word, I rested on it and practiced it. I took God at His Word."[2]

Despite his amazing experiences, the task of trusting in God for everything was not always easy for Mueller. "I have had my trials and difficulties, and my purse empty ... there will always be difficulties, always trials. But God has sustained me out of them and the work has gone on." Mueller also shrugged off any claims of greatness. "No, this is not, as some have said, because I am a man of great mental power, or endowed with energy and perseverance—these are not the reasons. *It is because I have confided in God* ... The great point is to never give up until the answer comes."[3]

PRAY:

Nothing is too hard for you, my dear Father. You are completely willing and able to care for me and those I love. I commit us, and our needs, into your hands.

MEMORIZE:

But seek first his kingdom and his righteousness, and all these things will be given to you as well. MATTHEW 6:33

FOR YOUR NEXT DEVOTIONAL READING, GO TO PAGE 442.

Menahem King of Israel

[17]In the thirty-ninth year of Azariah king of Judah, Menahem son of Gadi became king of Israel, and he reigned in Samaria ten years. [18]He did evil in the eyes of the LORD. During his entire reign he did not turn away from the sins of Jeroboam son of Nebat, which he had caused Israel to commit.

[19]Then Pul[a] king of Assyria invaded the land, and Menahem gave him a thousand talents[b] of silver to gain his support and strengthen his own hold on the kingdom. [20]Menahem exacted this money from Israel. Every wealthy man had to contribute fifty shekels[c] of silver to be given to the king of Assyria. So the king of Assyria withdrew and stayed in the land no longer.

[21]As for the other events of Menahem's reign, and all he did, are they not written in the book of the annals of the kings of Israel? [22]Menahem rested with his fathers. And Pekahiah his son succeeded him as king.

Pekahiah King of Israel

[23]In the fiftieth year of Azariah king of Judah, Pekahiah son of Menahem became king of Israel in Samaria, and he reigned two years. [24]Pekahiah did evil in the eyes of the LORD. He did not turn away from the sins of Jeroboam son of Nebat, which he had caused Israel to commit. [25]One of his chief officers, Pekah son of Remaliah, conspired against him. Taking fifty men of Gilead with him, he assassinated Pekahiah, along with Argob and Arieh, in the citadel of the royal palace at Samaria. So Pekah killed Pekahiah and succeeded him as king.

[26]The other events of Pekahiah's reign, and all he did, are written in the book of the annals of the kings of Israel.

Pekah King of Israel

[27]In the fifty-second year of Azariah king of Judah, Pekah son of Remaliah became king of Israel in Samaria, and he reigned twenty years. [28]He did evil in the eyes of the LORD. He did not turn away from the sins of Jeroboam son of Nebat, which he had caused Israel to commit.

[29]In the time of Pekah king of Israel, Tiglath-Pileser king of Assyria came and took Ijon, Abel Beth Maacah, Janoah, Kedesh and Hazor. He took Gilead and Galilee, including all the land of Naphtali, and deported the people to Assyria. [30]Then Hoshea son of Elah conspired against Pekah son of Remaliah. He attacked and assassinated him, and then succeeded him as king in the twentieth year of Jotham son of Uzziah.

[31]As for the other events of Pekah's reign, and all he did, are they not written in the book of the annals of the kings of Israel?

Jotham King of Judah

[32]In the second year of Pekah son of Remaliah king of Israel, Jotham son of Uzziah king of Judah began to reign. [33]He was twenty-five years old when he became king, and he reigned in Jerusalem sixteen years. His mother's name was Jerusha daughter of Zadok. [34]He did what was right in the eyes of the LORD, just as his father Uzziah had done. [35]The high places, however, were not removed; the people continued to offer sacrifices and burn incense there. Jotham rebuilt the Upper Gate of the temple of the LORD.

[36]As for the other events of Jotham's reign, and what he did, are they not written in the book of the annals of the kings of Judah? [37](In those days the LORD began to send Rezin king of Aram and Pekah son of Remaliah against Judah.) [38]Jotham rested with his fathers and was buried with them in the City of David, the city of his father. And Ahaz his son succeeded him as king.

Ahaz King of Judah

16 In the seventeenth year of Pekah son of Remaliah, Ahaz son of Jotham king of Judah began to reign. [2]Ahaz was twenty years old when he became king, and he reigned in Jerusalem sixteen years. Unlike David his father, he did not do what was right in the eyes of the LORD his God. [3]He walked in the ways of the kings of Israel and even sacrificed his son in[d] the fire, following the detestable ways

---

[a]19 Also called Tiglath-Pileser   [b]19 That is, about 37 tons (about 34 metric tons)   [c]20 That is, about 1 1/4 pounds (about 0.6 kilogram)
[d]3 Or even made his son pass through

of the nations the LORD had driven out before the Israelites. [4]He offered sacrifices and burned incense at the high places, on the hilltops and under every spreading tree.

[5]Then Rezin king of Aram and Pekah son of Remaliah king of Israel marched up to fight against Jerusalem and besieged Ahaz, but they could not overpower him. [6]At that time, Rezin king of Aram recovered Elath for Aram by driving out the men of Judah. Edomites then moved into Elath and have lived there to this day.

[7]Ahaz sent messengers to say to Tiglath-Pileser king of Assyria, "I am your servant and vassal. Come up and save me out of the hand of the king of Aram and of the king of Israel, who are attacking me." [8]And Ahaz took the silver and gold found in the temple of the LORD and in the treasuries of the royal palace and sent it as a gift to the king of Assyria. [9]The king of Assyria complied by attacking Damascus and capturing it. He deported its inhabitants to Kir and put Rezin to death.

[10]Then King Ahaz went to Damascus to meet Tiglath-Pileser king of Assyria. He saw an altar in Damascus and sent to Uriah the priest a sketch of the altar, with detailed plans for its construction. [11]So Uriah the priest built an altar in accordance with all the plans that King Ahaz had sent from Damascus and finished it before King Ahaz returned. [12]When the king came back from Damascus and saw the altar, he approached it and presented offerings[a] on it. [13]He offered up his burnt offering and grain offering, poured out his drink offering, and sprinkled the blood of his fellowship offerings[b] on the altar. [14]The bronze altar that stood before the LORD he brought from the front of the temple—from between the new altar and the temple of the LORD—and put it on the north side of the new altar.

[15]King Ahaz then gave these orders to Uriah the priest: "On the large new altar, offer the morning burnt offering and the evening grain offering, the king's burnt offering and his grain offering, and the burnt offering of all the people of the land, and their grain offering and their drink offering. Sprinkle on the altar all the blood of the burnt offerings and sacrifices. But I will use the bronze altar for seeking guidance." [16]And Uriah the priest did just as King Ahaz had ordered.

[17]King Ahaz took away the side panels and removed the basins from the movable stands. He removed the Sea from the bronze bulls that supported it and set it on a stone base. [18]He took away the Sabbath canopy[c] that had been built at the temple and removed the royal entryway outside the temple of the LORD, in deference to the king of Assyria.

[19]As for the other events of the reign of Ahaz, and what he did, are they not written in the book of the annals of the kings of Judah? [20]Ahaz rested with his fathers and was buried with them in the City of David. And Hezekiah his son succeeded him as king.

Hoshea Last King of Israel

17 In the twelfth year of Ahaz king of Judah, Hoshea son of Elah became king of Israel in Samaria, and he reigned nine years. [2]He did evil in the eyes of the LORD, but not like the kings of Israel who preceded him.

[3]Shalmaneser king of Assyria came up to attack Hoshea, who had been Shalmaneser's vassal and had paid him tribute. [4]But the king of Assyria discovered that Hoshea was a traitor, for he had sent envoys to So[d] king of Egypt, and he no longer paid tribute to the king of Assyria, as he had done year by year. Therefore Shalmaneser seized him and put him in prison. [5]The king of Assyria invaded the entire land, marched against Samaria and laid siege to it for three years. [6]In the ninth year of Hoshea, the king of Assyria captured Samaria and deported the Israelites to Assyria. He settled them in Halah, in Gozan on the Habor River and in the towns of the Medes.

Israel Exiled Because of Sin

[7]All this took place because the Israelites had sinned against the LORD their God, who had brought them up out of

---

[a]12 Or and went up   [b]13 Traditionally peace offerings   [c]18 Or the dais of his throne (see Septuagint)   [d]4 Or to Sais, to the; So is possibly an abbreviation for Osorkon.

Egypt from under the power of Pharaoh king of Egypt. They worshiped other gods [8]and followed the practices of the nations the LORD had driven out before them, as well as the practices that the kings of Israel had introduced. [9]The Israelites secretly did things against the LORD their God that were not right. From watchtower to fortified city they built themselves high places in all their towns. [10]They set up sacred stones and Asherah poles on every high hill and under every spreading tree. [11]At every high place they burned incense, as the nations whom the LORD had driven out before them had done. They did wicked things that provoked the LORD to anger. [12]They worshiped idols, though the LORD had said, "You shall not do this."[a] [13]The LORD warned Israel and Judah through all his prophets and seers: "Turn from your evil ways. Observe my commands and decrees, in accordance with the entire Law that I commanded your fathers to obey and that I delivered to you through my servants the prophets."

[14]But they would not listen and were as stiff-necked as their fathers, who did not trust in the LORD their God. [15]They rejected his decrees and the covenant he had made with their fathers and the warnings he had given them. They followed worthless idols and themselves became worthless. They imitated the nations around them although the LORD had ordered them, "Do not do as they do," and they did the things the LORD had forbidden them to do.

[16]They forsook all the commands of the LORD their God and made for themselves two idols cast in the shape of calves, and an Asherah pole. They bowed down to all the starry hosts, and they worshiped Baal. [17]They sacrificed their sons and daughters in[b] the fire. They practiced divination and sorcery and sold themselves to do evil in the eyes of the LORD, provoking him to anger.

[18]So the LORD was very angry with Israel and removed them from his presence. Only the tribe of Judah was left, [19]and even Judah did not keep the commands of the LORD their God. They followed the practices Israel had introduced. [20]Therefore the LORD rejected all the people of Israel; he afflicted them and gave them into the hands of plunderers, until he thrust them from his presence.

[21]When he tore Israel away from the house of David, they made Jeroboam son of Nebat their king. Jeroboam enticed Israel away from following the LORD and caused them to commit a great sin. [22]The Israelites persisted in all the sins of Jeroboam and did not turn away from them [23]until the LORD removed them from his presence, as he had warned through all his servants the prophets. So the people of Israel were taken from their homeland into exile in Assyria, and they are still there.

Samaria Resettled

[24]The king of Assyria brought people from Babylon, Cuthah, Avva, Hamath and Sepharvaim and settled them in the towns of Samaria to replace the Israelites. They took over Samaria and lived in its towns. [25]When they first lived there, they did not worship the LORD; so he sent lions among them and they killed some of the people. [26]It was reported to the king of Assyria: "The people you deported and resettled in the towns of Samaria do not know what the god of that country requires. He has sent lions among them, which are killing them off, because the people do not know what he requires." [27]Then the king of Assyria gave this order: "Have one of the priests you took captive from Samaria go back to live there and teach the people what the god of the land requires." [28]So one of the priests who had been exiled from Samaria came to live in Bethel and taught them how to worship the LORD.

[29]Nevertheless, each national group made its own gods in the several towns where they settled, and set them up in the shrines the people of Samaria had made at the high places. [30]The men from Babylon made Succoth Benoth, the men from Cuthah made Nergal, and the men from Hamath made Ashima; [31]the Avvites made Nibhaz and Tartak, and the Sepharvites burned their children in the fire as sacrifices to Adrammelech and

---

[a]12 Exodus 20:4,5   [b]17 Or *They made their sons and daughters pass through*

Anammelech, the gods of Sepharvaim. ³²They worshiped the LORD, but they also appointed all sorts of their own people to officiate for them as priests in the shrines at the high places. ³³They worshiped the LORD, but they also served their own gods in accordance with the customs of the nations from which they had been brought.

³⁴To this day they persist in their former practices. They neither worship the LORD nor adhere to the decrees and ordinances, the laws and commands that the LORD gave the descendants of Jacob, whom he named Israel. ³⁵When the LORD made a covenant with the Israelites, he commanded them: "Do not worship any other gods or bow down to them, serve them or sacrifice to them. ³⁶But the LORD, who brought you up out of Egypt with mighty power and outstretched arm, is the one you must worship. To him you shall bow down and to him offer sacrifices. ³⁷You must always be careful to keep the decrees and ordinances, the laws and commands he wrote for you. Do not worship other gods. ³⁸Do not forget the covenant I have made with you, and do not worship other gods. ³⁹Rather, worship the LORD your God; it is he who will deliver you from the hand of all your enemies."

⁴⁰They would not listen, however, but persisted in their former practices. ⁴¹Even while these people were worshiping the LORD, they were serving their idols. To this day their children and grandchildren continue to do as their fathers did.

Hezekiah King of Judah

18 In the third year of Hoshea son of Elah king of Israel, Hezekiah son of Ahaz king of Judah began to reign. ²He was twenty-five years old when he became king, and he reigned in Jerusalem twenty-nine years. His mother's name was Abijah[a] daughter of Zechariah. ³He did what was right in the eyes of the LORD, just as his father David had done. ⁴He removed the high places, smashed the sacred stones and cut down the Asherah poles. He broke into pieces the bronze snake Moses had made, for up to that time the Israelites had been burning incense to it. (It was called[b] Nehushtan.[c])

⁵Hezekiah trusted in the LORD, the God of Israel. There was no one like him among all the kings of Judah, either before him or after him. ⁶He held fast to the LORD and did not cease to follow him; he kept the commands the LORD had given Moses. ⁷And the LORD was with him; he was successful in whatever he undertook. He rebelled against the king of Assyria and did not serve him. ⁸From watchtower to fortified city, he defeated the Philistines, as far as Gaza and its territory.

⁹In King Hezekiah's fourth year, which was the seventh year of Hoshea son of Elah king of Israel, Shalmaneser king of Assyria marched against Samaria and laid siege to it. ¹⁰At the end of three years the Assyrians took it. So Samaria was captured in Hezekiah's sixth year, which was the ninth year of Hoshea king of Israel. ¹¹The king of Assyria deported Israel to Assyria and settled them in Halah, in Gozan on the Habor River and in towns of the Medes. ¹²This happened because they had not obeyed the LORD their God, but had violated his covenant—all that Moses the servant of the LORD commanded. They neither listened to the commands nor carried them out.

¹³In the fourteenth year of King Hezekiah's reign, Sennacherib king of Assyria attacked all the fortified cities of Judah and captured them. ¹⁴So Hezekiah king of Judah sent this message to the king of Assyria at Lachish: "I have done wrong. Withdraw from me, and I will pay whatever you demand of me." The king of Assyria exacted from Hezekiah king of Judah three hundred talents[d] of silver and thirty talents[e] of gold. ¹⁵So Hezekiah gave him all the silver that was found in the temple of the LORD and in the treasuries of the royal palace.

¹⁶At this time Hezekiah king of Judah stripped off the gold with which he had covered the doors and doorposts of the temple of the LORD, and gave it to the king of Assyria.

---

[a]2 Hebrew Abi, a variant of Abijah   [b]4 Or He called it   [c]4 Nehushtan sounds like the Hebrew for bronze and snake and unclean thing.   [d]14 That is, about 11 tons (about 10 metric tons)   [e]14 That is, about 1 ton (about 1 metric ton)

Sennacherib Threatens Jerusalem

¹⁷The king of Assyria sent his supreme commander, his chief officer and his field commander with a large army, from Lachish to King Hezekiah at Jerusalem. They came up to Jerusalem and stopped at the aqueduct of the Upper Pool, on the road to the Washerman's Field. ¹⁸They called for the king; and Eliakim son of Hilkiah the palace administrator, Shebna the secretary, and Joah son of Asaph the recorder went out to them.

¹⁹The field commander said to them, "Tell Hezekiah:

"'This is what the great king, the king of Assyria, says: On what are you basing this confidence of yours? ²⁰You say you have strategy and military strength—but you speak only empty words. On whom are you depending, that you rebel against me? ²¹Look now, you are depending on Egypt, that splintered reed of a staff, which pierces a man's hand and wounds him if he leans on it! Such is Pharaoh king of Egypt to all who depend on him. ²²And if you say to me, "We are depending on the LORD our God"—isn't he the one whose high places and altars Hezekiah removed, saying to Judah and Jerusalem, "You must worship before this altar in Jerusalem"?

²³"'Come now, make a bargain with my master, the king of Assyria: I will give you two thousand horses—if you can put riders on them! ²⁴How can you repulse one officer of the least of my master's officials, even though you are depending on Egypt for chariots and horsemen*ᵃ*? ²⁵Furthermore, have I come to attack and destroy this place without word from the LORD? The LORD himself told me to march against this country and destroy it.'"

²⁶Then Eliakim son of Hilkiah, and Shebna and Joah said to the field commander, "Please speak to your servants in Aramaic, since we understand it. Don't speak to us in Hebrew in the hearing of the people on the wall."

²⁷But the commander replied, "Was it only to your master and you that my master sent me to say these things, and not to the men sitting on the wall—who, like you, will have to eat their own filth and drink their own urine?"

²⁸Then the commander stood and called out in Hebrew: "Hear the word of the great king, the king of Assyria! ²⁹This is what the king says: Do not let Hezekiah deceive you. He cannot deliver you from my hand. ³⁰Do not let Hezekiah persuade you to trust in the LORD when he says, 'The LORD will surely deliver us; this city will not be given into the hand of the king of Assyria.'

³¹"Do not listen to Hezekiah. This is what the king of Assyria says: Make peace with me and come out to me. Then every one of you will eat from his own vine and fig tree and drink water from his own cistern, ³²until I come and take you to a land like your own, a land of grain and new wine, a land of bread and vineyards, a land of olive trees and honey. Choose life and not death!

"Do not listen to Hezekiah, for he is misleading you when he says, 'The LORD will deliver us.' ³³Has the god of any nation ever delivered his land from the hand of the king of Assyria? ³⁴Where are the gods of Hamath and Arpad? Where are the gods of Sepharvaim, Hena and Ivvah? Have they rescued Samaria from my hand? ³⁵Who of all the gods of these countries has been able to save his land from me? How then can the LORD deliver Jerusalem from my hand?"

³⁶But the people remained silent and said nothing in reply, because the king had commanded, "Do not answer him."

³⁷Then Eliakim son of Hilkiah the palace administrator, Shebna the secretary and Joah son of Asaph the recorder went to Hezekiah, with their clothes torn, and told him what the field commander had said.

Jerusalem's Deliverance Foretold

19 When King Hezekiah heard this, he tore his clothes and put on sackcloth and went into the temple of the LORD. ²He sent Eliakim the palace administrator, Shebna the secretary and the leading priests, all wearing sackcloth, to

ᵃ24 Or charioteers

the prophet Isaiah son of Amoz. ³They told him, "This is what Hezekiah says: This day is a day of distress and rebuke and disgrace, as when children come to the point of birth and there is no strength to deliver them. ⁴It may be that the LORD your God will hear all the words of the field commander, whom his master, the king of Assyria, has sent to ridicule the living God, and that he will rebuke him for the words the LORD your God has heard. Therefore pray for the remnant that still survives."

⁵When King Hezekiah's officials came to Isaiah, ⁶Isaiah said to them, "Tell your master, 'This is what the LORD says: Do not be afraid of what you have heard—those words with which the underlings of the king of Assyria have blasphemed me. ⁷Listen! I am going to put such a spirit in him that when he hears a certain report, he will return to his own country, and there I will have him cut down with the sword.'"

⁸When the field commander heard that the king of Assyria had left Lachish, he withdrew and found the king fighting against Libnah.

⁹Now Sennacherib received a report that Tirhakah, the Cushite*ᵃ* king of Egypt, was marching out to fight against him. So he again sent messengers to Hezekiah with this word: ¹⁰"Say to Hezekiah king of Judah: Do not let the god you depend on deceive you when he says, 'Jerusalem will not be handed over to the king of Assyria.' ¹¹Surely you have heard what the kings of Assyria have done to all the countries, destroying them completely. And will you be delivered? ¹²Did the gods of the nations that were destroyed by my forefathers deliver them: the gods of Gozan, Haran, Rezeph and the people of Eden who were in Tel Assar? ¹³Where is the king of Hamath, the king of Arpad, the king of the city of Sepharvaim, or of Hena or Ivvah?"

Hezekiah's Prayer

¹⁴Hezekiah received the letter from the messengers and read it. Then he went up to the temple of the LORD and spread it out before the LORD. ¹⁵And Hezekiah prayed to the LORD: "O LORD, God of Israel, enthroned between the cherubim,

you alone are God over all the kingdoms of the earth. You have made heaven and earth. ¹⁶Give ear, O LORD, and hear; open your eyes, O LORD, and see; listen to the words Sennacherib has sent to insult the living God.

¹⁷"It is true, O LORD, that the Assyrian kings have laid waste these nations and their lands. ¹⁸They have thrown their gods into the fire and destroyed them, for they were not gods but only wood and stone, fashioned by men's hands. ¹⁹Now, O LORD our God, deliver us from his hand, so that all kingdoms on earth may know that you alone, O LORD, are God."

Isaiah Prophesies Sennacherib's Fall

²⁰Then Isaiah son of Amoz sent a message to Hezekiah: "This is what the LORD, the God of Israel, says: I have heard your prayer concerning Sennacherib king of Assyria. ²¹This is the word that the LORD has spoken against him:

" 'The Virgin Daughter of Zion
    despises you and mocks you.
The Daughter of Jerusalem
    tosses her head as you flee.
²²Who is it you have insulted and
        blasphemed?
    Against whom have you raised
        your voice
and lifted your eyes in pride?
    Against the Holy One of Israel!
²³By your messengers
    you have heaped insults on
        the Lord.
And you have said,
    "With my many chariots
I have ascended the heights of
        the mountains,
    the utmost heights of Lebanon.
I have cut down its tallest cedars,
    the choicest of its pines.
I have reached its remotest parts,
    the finest of its forests.
²⁴I have dug wells in foreign lands
    and drunk the water there.
With the soles of my feet
    I have dried up all the streams
        of Egypt."
²⁵" 'Have you not heard?
    Long ago I ordained it.

ᵃ9 That is, from the upper Nile region

Spread It Out Before the Lord

19:14 HEZEKIAH RECEIVED THE LETTER ... AND SPREAD IT OUT BEFORE THE LORD.

A dictionary could well define the word *insolence* this way: "See Sennacherib, 2 Kings 19:9–13." Any sane person would be terrified to say what he said to Hezekiah about God: "Do not let the god you depend on deceive you when he says, 'Jerusalem will not be handed over to the king of the Assyria.' Surely you have heard what the kings of Assyria have done to all the countries, destroying them completely. And will you be delivered? Did the gods of the nations that were destroyed by my forefathers deliver them?" (19:10–12). This is insolence that defies a reply. Hezekiah did the only wise thing that could be done. He took the letter "up to the temple of the LORD and spread it out before the LORD. And Hezekiah prayed to the LORD" (verses 14–15).

Sennacherib's letter may have reached the limits of insolence, but today's newspaper headlines can be just as terrible in their own way. Things like child abuse, murders, kidnappings, acts of terrorism, rape, robbery and mayhem can defy human reply. They can so stupefy as to leave us mute with outrage and grief. Have you ever felt that way? Spread the newspaper out before the Lord and pray as Hezekiah did! Really. Open the page filled with the outrage, lay it on a table or desk and read it aloud to the Lord as part of a prayer. Begin as Hezekiah did by remembering God's greatness and sovereignty over the affairs of nations; read verse 15 in this text, or read a psalm such as Psalm 9. Then read the newspaper article aloud to God, beginning with something like, "Almighty God, you know that . . ." Fill in the details. Then declare God's truth regarding the situation, as Hezekiah did in verse 18. End by asking God to do what only he can do: to bring salvation and to make the kingdom of this world the kingdom of God (see 2 Kings 19:19). Read Revelation 11:15. Then say a hearty "Amen" to what you have prayed. Nothing is too hard for the Lord. One hundred eighty-five thousand Assyrian troops died as a result of Hezekiah's prayer; and Sennacherib's own sons assassinated him while he was worshiping his god (see 2 Kings 19:35–37).

PRAY:

"Arise, O LORD, let not man triumph;
let the nations be judged in your presence.
Strike them with terror, O LORD;
let the nations know they are but men"
(Psalm 9:19–20).

FOR YOUR NEXT DEVOTIONAL READING, GO TO PAGE 457.

In days of old I planned it;
  now I have brought it to pass,
that you have turned fortified cities
  into piles of stone.
²⁶Their people, drained of power,
  are dismayed and put to shame.
They are like plants in the field,
  like tender green shoots,
like grass sprouting on the roof,
  scorched before it grows up.

²⁷ " 'But I know where you stay
  and when you come and go
  and how you rage against me.
²⁸Because you rage against me
  and your insolence has reached
    my ears,
I will put my hook in your nose
  and my bit in your mouth,
and I will make you return
  by the way you came.'

²⁹"This will be the sign for you, O Hezekiah:

"This year you will eat what grows
    by itself,
  and the second year what springs
    from that.
But in the third year sow and reap,
  plant vineyards and eat their fruit.
³⁰Once more a remnant of the house
    of Judah
  will take root below and bear
    fruit above.
³¹For out of Jerusalem will come a
    remnant,
  and out of Mount Zion a band
    of survivors.

The zeal of the LORD Almighty will accomplish this.

³²"Therefore this is what the LORD says concerning the king of Assyria:

"He will not enter this city
  or shoot an arrow here.
He will not come before it with shield
  or build a siege ramp against it.
³³By the way that he came he
    will return;
  he will not enter this city,
            declares the LORD.
³⁴I will defend this city and save it,
  for my sake and for the sake
    of David my servant."

³⁵That night the angel of the LORD went out and put to death a hundred and eighty-five thousand men in the Assyrian camp. When the people got up the next morning—there were all the dead bodies! ³⁶So Sennacherib king of Assyria broke camp and withdrew. He returned to Nineveh and stayed there.

³⁷One day, while he was worshiping in the temple of his god Nisroch, his sons Adrammelech and Sharezer cut him down with the sword, and they escaped to the land of Ararat. And Esarhaddon his son succeeded him as king.

Hezekiah's Illness

20 In those days Hezekiah became ill and was at the point of death. The prophet Isaiah son of Amoz went to him and said, "This is what the LORD says: Put your house in order, because you are going to die; you will not recover."

²Hezekiah turned his face to the wall and prayed to the LORD, ³"Remember, O LORD, how I have walked before you faithfully and with wholehearted devotion and have done what is good in your eyes." And Hezekiah wept bitterly.

> HEZEKIAH turned his face to the wall
> and prayed to the LORD.
>
> 2 KINGS 20:2

⁴Before Isaiah had left the middle court, the word of the LORD came to him: ⁵"Go back and tell Hezekiah, the leader of my people, 'This is what the LORD, the God of your father David, says: I have heard your prayer and seen your tears; I will heal you. On the third day from now you will go up to the temple of the LORD. ⁶I will add fifteen years to your life. And I will deliver you and this city from the hand of the king of Assyria. I will defend this city for my sake and for the sake of my servant David.' "

⁷Then Isaiah said, "Prepare a poultice of figs." They did so and applied it to the boil, and he recovered.

⁸Hezekiah had asked Isaiah, "What will be the sign that the LORD will heal me and that I will go up to the temple of the LORD on the third day from now?"

⁹Isaiah answered, "This is the LORD's sign to you that the LORD will do what he has promised: Shall the shadow go forward ten steps, or shall it go back ten steps?"

¹⁰"It is a simple matter for the shadow to go forward ten steps," said Hezekiah. "Rather, have it go back ten steps."

¹¹Then the prophet Isaiah called upon the LORD, and the LORD made the shadow go back the ten steps it had gone down on the stairway of Ahaz.

Envoys From Babylon

¹²At that time Merodach-Baladan son of Baladan king of Babylon sent Hezekiah letters and a gift, because he had heard of Hezekiah's illness. ¹³Hezekiah received the messengers and showed them all that was in his storehouses—the silver, the gold, the spices and the fine oil—his armory and everything found among his treasures. There was nothing in his palace or in all his kingdom that Hezekiah did not show them.

¹⁴Then Isaiah the prophet went to King Hezekiah and asked, "What did those men say, and where did they come from?"

"From a distant land," Hezekiah replied. "They came from Babylon."

¹⁵The prophet asked, "What did they see in your palace?"

"They saw everything in my palace," Hezekiah said. "There is nothing among my treasures that I did not show them."

¹⁶Then Isaiah said to Hezekiah, "Hear the word of the LORD: ¹⁷The time will surely come when everything in your palace, and all that your fathers have stored up until this day, will be carried off to Babylon. Nothing will be left, says the LORD. ¹⁸And some of your descendants, your own flesh and blood, that will be born to you, will be taken away, and they will become eunuchs in the palace of the king of Babylon."

¹⁹"The word of the LORD you have spoken is good," Hezekiah replied. For he thought, "Will there not be peace and security in my lifetime?"

²⁰As for the other events of Hezekiah's reign, all his achievements and how he made the pool and the tunnel by which he brought water into the city, are they not written in the book of the annals of the kings of Judah? ²¹Hezekiah rested with his fathers. And Manasseh his son succeeded him as king.

Manasseh King of Judah

21 Manasseh was twelve years old when he became king, and he reigned in Jerusalem fifty-five years. His mother's name was Hephzibah. ²He did evil in the eyes of the LORD, following the detestable practices of the nations the LORD had driven out before the Israelites. ³He rebuilt the high places his father Hezekiah had destroyed; he also erected altars to Baal and made an Asherah pole, as Ahab king of Israel had done. He bowed down to all the starry hosts and worshiped them. ⁴He built altars in the temple of the LORD, of which the LORD had said, "In Jerusalem I will put my Name." ⁵In both courts of the temple of the LORD, he built altars to all the starry hosts. ⁶He sacrificed his own son in[a] the fire, practiced sorcery and divination, and consulted mediums and spiritists. He did much evil in the eyes of the LORD, provoking him to anger.

⁷He took the carved Asherah pole he had made and put it in the temple, of which the LORD had said to David and to his son Solomon, "In this temple and in Jerusalem, which I have chosen out of all the tribes of Israel, I will put my Name forever. ⁸I will not again make the feet of the Israelites wander from the land I gave their forefathers, if only they will be careful to do everything I commanded them and will keep the whole Law that my servant Moses gave them." ⁹But the people did not listen. Manasseh led them astray, so that they did more evil than the nations the LORD had destroyed before the Israelites.

¹⁰The LORD said through his servants the prophets: ¹¹"Manasseh king of Judah has committed these detestable sins. He has done more evil than the Amorites who preceded him and has led Judah into sin with his idols. ¹²Therefore this is what the LORD, the God of Israel, says: I am going to bring such disaster on Jerusalem and Judah that the ears of everyone who hears of it will tingle. ¹³I will stretch out

---

[a] 6 Or *He made his own son pass through*

over Jerusalem the measuring line used against Samaria and the plumb line used against the house of Ahab. I will wipe out Jerusalem as one wipes a dish, wiping it and turning it upside down. ¹⁴I will forsake the remnant of my inheritance and hand them over to their enemies. They will be looted and plundered by all their foes, ¹⁵because they have done evil in my eyes and have provoked me to anger from the day their forefathers came out of Egypt until this day."

¹⁶Moreover, Manasseh also shed so much innocent blood that he filled Jerusalem from end to end—besides the sin that he had caused Judah to commit, so that they did evil in the eyes of the LORD.

¹⁷As for the other events of Manasseh's reign, and all he did, including the sin he committed, are they not written in the book of the annals of the kings of Judah? ¹⁸Manasseh rested with his fathers and was buried in his palace garden, the garden of Uzza. And Amon his son succeeded him as king.

Amon King of Judah

¹⁹Amon was twenty-two years old when he became king, and he reigned in Jerusalem two years. His mother's name was Meshullemeth daughter of Haruz; she was from Jotbah. ²⁰He did evil in the eyes of the LORD, as his father Manasseh had done. ²¹He walked in all the ways of his father; he worshiped the idols his father had worshiped, and bowed down to them. ²²He forsook the LORD, the God of his fathers, and did not walk in the way of the LORD.

²³Amon's officials conspired against him and assassinated the king in his palace. ²⁴Then the people of the land killed all who had plotted against King Amon, and they made Josiah his son king in his place.

²⁵As for the other events of Amon's reign, and what he did, are they not written in the book of the annals of the kings of Judah? ²⁶He was buried in his grave in the garden of Uzza. And Josiah his son succeeded him as king.

The Book of the Law Found

22 Josiah was eight years old when he became king, and he reigned in Jerusalem thirty-one years. His mother's name was Jedidah daughter of Adaiah;

she was from Bozkath. ²He did what was right in the eyes of the LORD and walked in all the ways of his father David, not turning aside to the right or to the left.

³In the eighteenth year of his reign, King Josiah sent the secretary, Shaphan son of Azaliah, the son of Meshullam, to the temple of the LORD. He said: ⁴"Go up to Hilkiah the high priest and have him get ready the money that has been brought into the temple of the LORD, which the doorkeepers have collected from the people. ⁵Have them entrust it to the men appointed to supervise the work on the temple. And have these men pay the workers who repair the temple of the LORD— ⁶the carpenters, the builders and the masons. Also have them purchase timber and dressed stone to repair the temple. ⁷But they need not account for the money entrusted to them, because they are acting faithfully."

⁸Hilkiah the high priest said to Shaphan the secretary, "I have found the Book of the Law in the temple of the LORD." He gave it to Shaphan, who read it. ⁹Then Shaphan the secretary went to the king and reported to him: "Your officials have paid out the money that was in the temple of the LORD and have entrusted it to the workers and supervisors at the temple." ¹⁰Then Shaphan the secretary informed the king, "Hilkiah the priest has given me a book." And Shaphan read from it in the presence of the king.

¹¹When the king heard the words of the Book of the Law, he tore his robes. ¹²He gave these orders to Hilkiah the priest, Ahikam son of Shaphan, Acbor son of Micaiah, Shaphan the secretary and Asaiah the king's attendant: ¹³"Go and inquire of the LORD for me and for the people and for all Judah about what is written in this book that has been found. Great is the LORD's anger that burns against us because our fathers have not obeyed the words of this book; they have not acted in accordance with all that is written there concerning us."

¹⁴Hilkiah the priest, Ahikam, Acbor, Shaphan and Asaiah went to speak to the prophetess Huldah, who was the wife of Shallum son of Tikvah, the son of Harhas, keeper of the wardrobe. She lived in Jerusalem, in the Second District.

¹⁵She said to them, "This is what the LORD, the God of Israel, says: Tell the man who sent you to me, ¹⁶'This is what the LORD says: I am going to bring disaster on this place and its people, according to everything written in the book the king of Judah has read. ¹⁷Because they have forsaken me and burned incense to other gods and provoked me to anger by all the idols their hands have made,ᵃ my anger will burn against this place and will not be quenched.' ¹⁸Tell the king of Judah, who sent you to inquire of the LORD, 'This is what the LORD, the God of Israel, says concerning the words you heard: ¹⁹Because your heart was responsive and you humbled yourself before the LORD when you heard what I have spoken against this place and its people, that they would become accursed and laid waste, and because you tore your robes and wept in my presence, I have heard you, declares the LORD. ²⁰Therefore I will gather you to your fathers, and you will be buried in peace. Your eyes will not see all the disaster I am going to bring on this place.' "

So they took her answer back to the king.

Josiah Renews the Covenant

23 Then the king called together all the elders of Judah and Jerusalem. ²He went up to the temple of the LORD with the men of Judah, the people of Jerusalem, the priests and the prophets—all the people from the least to the greatest. He read in their hearing all the words of the Book of the Covenant, which had been found in the temple of the LORD. ³The king stood by the pillar and renewed the covenant in the presence of the LORD—to follow the LORD and keep his commands, regulations and decrees with all his heart and all his soul, thus confirming the words of the covenant written in this book. Then all the people pledged themselves to the covenant.

⁴The king ordered Hilkiah the high priest, the priests next in rank and the doorkeepers to remove from the temple of the LORD all the articles made for Baal and Asherah and all the starry hosts. He burned them outside Jerusalem in the fields of the Kidron Valley and took the ashes to Bethel. ⁵He did away with the pagan priests appointed by the kings of Judah to burn incense on the high places of the towns of Judah and on those around Jerusalem—those who burned incense to Baal, to the sun and moon, to the constellations and to all the starry hosts. ⁶He took the Asherah pole from the temple of the LORD to the Kidron Valley outside Jerusalem and burned it there. He ground it to powder and scattered the dust over the graves of the common people. ⁷He also tore down the quarters of the male shrine prostitutes, which were in the temple of the LORD and where women did weaving for Asherah.

⁸Josiah brought all the priests from the towns of Judah and desecrated the high places, from Geba to Beersheba, where the priests had burned incense. He broke down the shrinesᵇ at the gates—at the entrance to the Gate of Joshua, the city governor, which is on the left of the city gate. ⁹Although the priests of the high places did not serve at the altar of the LORD in Jerusalem, they ate unleavened bread with their fellow priests.

¹⁰He desecrated Topheth, which was in the Valley of Ben Hinnom, so no one could use it to sacrifice his son or daughter inᶜ the fire to Molech. ¹¹He removed from the entrance to the temple of the LORD the horses that the kings of Judah had dedicated to the sun. They were in the court near the room of an official named Nathan-Melech. Josiah then burned the chariots dedicated to the sun.

¹²He pulled down the altars the kings of Judah had erected on the roof near the upper room of Ahaz, and the altars Manasseh had built in the two courts of the temple of the LORD. He removed them from there, smashed them to pieces and threw the rubble into the Kidron Valley. ¹³The king also desecrated the high places that were east of Jerusalem on the south of the Hill of Corruption—the ones Solomon king of Israel had built for Ashtoreth the vile goddess of the Sidonians, for Chemosh the vile god of Moab, and for Molechᵈ the detestable god of the

---

ᵃ17 Or by everything they have done
ᵇ8 Or high places   ᶜ10 Or to make his son or daughter pass through   ᵈ13 Hebrew Milcom

people of Ammon. ¹⁴Josiah smashed the sacred stones and cut down the Asherah poles and covered the sites with human bones.

¹⁵Even the altar at Bethel, the high place made by Jeroboam son of Nebat, who had caused Israel to sin—even that altar and high place he demolished. He burned the high place and ground it to powder, and burned the Asherah pole also. ¹⁶Then Josiah looked around, and when he saw the tombs that were there on the hillside, he had the bones removed from them and burned on the altar to defile it, in accordance with the word of the LORD proclaimed by the man of God who foretold these things.

¹⁷The king asked, "What is that tombstone I see?"

The men of the city said, "It marks the tomb of the man of God who came from Judah and pronounced against the altar of Bethel the very things you have done to it."

¹⁸"Leave it alone," he said. "Don't let anyone disturb his bones." So they spared his bones and those of the prophet who had come from Samaria.

¹⁹Just as he had done at Bethel, Josiah removed and defiled all the shrines at the high places that the kings of Israel had built in the towns of Samaria that had provoked the LORD to anger. ²⁰Josiah slaughtered all the priests of those high places on the altars and burned human bones on them. Then he went back to Jerusalem.

²¹The king gave this order to all the people: "Celebrate the Passover to the LORD your God, as it is written in this Book of the Covenant." ²²Not since the days of the judges who led Israel, nor throughout the days of the kings of Israel and the kings of Judah, had any such Passover been observed. ²³But in the eighteenth year of King Josiah, this Passover was celebrated to the LORD in Jerusalem.

²⁴Furthermore, Josiah got rid of the mediums and spiritists, the household gods, the idols and all the other detestable things seen in Judah and Jerusalem. This he did to fulfill the requirements of the law written in the book that Hilkiah the priest had discovered in the temple of the LORD. ²⁵Neither before nor after Josiah was there a king like him who turned to the LORD as he did—with all his heart and with all his soul and with all his strength, in accordance with all the Law of Moses.

²⁶Nevertheless, the LORD did not turn away from the heat of his fierce anger, which burned against Judah because of all that Manasseh had done to provoke him to anger. ²⁷So the LORD said, "I will remove Judah also from my presence as I removed Israel, and I will reject Jerusalem, the city I chose, and this temple, about which I said, 'There shall my Name be.'ᵃ"

²⁸As for the other events of Josiah's reign, and all he did, are they not written in the book of the annals of the kings of Judah?

²⁹While Josiah was king, Pharaoh Neco king of Egypt went up to the Euphrates River to help the king of Assyria. King Josiah marched out to meet him in battle, but Neco faced him and killed him at Megiddo. ³⁰Josiah's servants brought his body in a chariot from Megiddo to Jerusalem and buried him in his own tomb. And the people of the land took Jehoahaz son of Josiah and anointed him and made him king in place of his father.

> ❝ Sinning and praying agree not well together. If a man be constant in the duty of secret prayer, it will tend to restrain him from willful sinning. ❞
>
> JONATHAN EDWARDS

Jehoahaz King of Judah

³¹Jehoahaz was twenty-three years old when he became king, and he reigned in Jerusalem three months. His mother's name was Hamutal daughter of Jeremiah; she was from Libnah. ³²He did evil in the eyes of the LORD, just as his fathers had done. ³³Pharaoh Neco put him in chains at Riblah in the land of Hamathᵇ so that he might not reign in Jerusalem, and he imposed on Judah a levy of a hun-

---

ᵃ27 1 Kings 8:29   ᵇ33 Hebrew; Septuagint (see also 2 Chron. 36:3) *Neco at Riblah in Hamath removed him*

dred talents*a* of silver and a talent*b* of gold. ³⁴Pharaoh Neco made Eliakim son of Josiah king in place of his father Josiah and changed Eliakim's name to Jehoiakim. But he took Jehoahaz and carried him off to Egypt, and there he died. ³⁵Jehoiakim paid Pharaoh Neco the silver and gold he demanded. In order to do so, he taxed the land and exacted the silver and gold from the people of the land according to their assessments.

Jehoiakim King of Judah

³⁶Jehoiakim was twenty-five years old when he became king, and he reigned in Jerusalem eleven years. His mother's name was Zebidah daughter of Pedaiah; she was from Rumah. ³⁷And he did evil in the eyes of the LORD, just as his fathers had done.

24 During Jehoiakim's reign, Nebuchadnezzar king of Babylon invaded the land, and Jehoiakim became his vassal for three years. But then he changed his mind and rebelled against Nebuchadnezzar. ²The LORD sent Babylonian,*c* Aramean, Moabite and Ammonite raiders against him. He sent them to destroy Judah, in accordance with the word of the LORD proclaimed by his servants the prophets. ³Surely these things happened to Judah according to the LORD's command, in order to remove them from his presence because of the sins of Manasseh and all he had done, ⁴including the shedding of innocent blood. For he had filled Jerusalem with innocent blood, and the LORD was not willing to forgive.

⁵As for the other events of Jehoiakim's reign, and all he did, are they not written in the book of the annals of the kings of Judah? ⁶Jehoiakim rested with his fathers. And Jehoiachin his son succeeded him as king.

⁷The king of Egypt did not march out from his own country again, because the king of Babylon had taken all his territory, from the Wadi of Egypt to the Euphrates River.

Jehoiachin King of Judah

⁸Jehoiachin was eighteen years old when he became king, and he reigned in Jerusalem three months. His mother's name was Nehushta daughter of Elnathan; she was from Jerusalem. ⁹He did evil in the eyes of the LORD, just as his father had done.

¹⁰At that time the officers of Nebuchadnezzar king of Babylon advanced on Jerusalem and laid siege to it, ¹¹and Nebuchadnezzar himself came up to the city while his officers were besieging it. ¹²Jehoiachin king of Judah, his mother, his attendants, his nobles and his officials all surrendered to him.

In the eighth year of the reign of the king of Babylon, he took Jehoiachin prisoner. ¹³As the LORD had declared, Nebuchadnezzar removed all the treasures from the temple of the LORD and from the royal palace, and took away all the gold articles that Solomon king of Israel had made for the temple of the LORD. ¹⁴He carried into exile all Jerusalem: all the officers and fighting men, and all the craftsmen and artisans—a total of ten thousand. Only the poorest people of the land were left.

¹⁵Nebuchadnezzar took Jehoiachin captive to Babylon. He also took from Jerusalem to Babylon the king's mother, his wives, his officials and the leading men of the land. ¹⁶The king of Babylon also deported to Babylon the entire force of seven thousand fighting men, strong and fit for war, and a thousand craftsmen and artisans. ¹⁷He made Mattaniah, Jehoiachin's uncle, king in his place and changed his name to Zedekiah.

Zedekiah King of Judah

¹⁸Zedekiah was twenty-one years old when he became king, and he reigned in Jerusalem eleven years. His mother's name was Hamutal daughter of Jeremiah; she was from Libnah. ¹⁹He did evil in the eyes of the LORD, just as Jehoiakim had done. ²⁰It was because of the LORD's anger that all this happened to Jerusalem and Judah, and in the end he thrust them from his presence.

The Fall of Jerusalem

Now Zedekiah rebelled against the king of Babylon.

---

a33 That is, about 3 3/4 tons (about 3.4 metric tons)   *b33* That is, about 75 pounds (about 34 kilograms)   *c2* Or *Chaldean*

25 So in the ninth year of Zedekiah's reign, on the tenth day of the tenth month, Nebuchadnezzar king of Babylon marched against Jerusalem with his whole army. He encamped outside the city and built siege works all around it. ²The city was kept under siege until the eleventh year of King Zedekiah. ³By the ninth day of the ̦fourth̦ᵃ month the famine in the city had become so severe that there was no food for the people to eat. ⁴Then the city wall was broken through, and the whole army fled at night through the gate between the two walls near the king's garden, though the Babyloniansᵇ were surrounding the city. They fled toward the Arabah,ᶜ ⁵but the Babylonianᵈ army pursued the king and overtook him in the plains of Jericho. All his soldiers were separated from him and scattered, ⁶and he was captured. He was taken to the king of Babylon at Riblah, where sentence was pronounced on him. ⁷They killed the sons of Zedekiah before his eyes. Then they put out his eyes, bound him with bronze shackles and took him to Babylon.

⁸On the seventh day of the fifth month, in the nineteenth year of Nebuchadnezzar king of Babylon, Nebuzaradan commander of the imperial guard, an official of the king of Babylon, came to Jerusalem. ⁹He set fire to the temple of the LORD, the royal palace and all the houses of Jerusalem. Every important building he burned down. ¹⁰The whole Babylonian army, under the commander of the imperial guard, broke down the walls around Jerusalem. ¹¹Nebuzaradan the commander of the guard carried into exile the people who remained in the city, along with the rest of the populace and those who had gone over to the king of Babylon. ¹²But the commander left behind some of the poorest people of the land to work the vineyards and fields.

¹³The Babylonians broke up the bronze pillars, the movable stands and the bronze Sea that were at the temple of the LORD and they carried the bronze to Babylon. ¹⁴They also took away the pots, shovels, wick trimmers, dishes and all the bronze articles used in the temple service. ¹⁵The commander of the imperial guard took away the censers and sprinkling bowls—all that were made of pure gold or silver.

¹⁶The bronze from the two pillars, the Sea and the movable stands, which Solomon had made for the temple of the LORD, was more than could be weighed. ¹⁷Each pillar was twenty-seven feetᵉ high. The bronze capital on top of one pillar was four and a half feetᶠ high and was decorated with a network and pomegranates of bronze all around. The other pillar, with its network, was similar.

¹⁸The commander of the guard took as prisoners Seraiah the chief priest, Zephaniah the priest next in rank and the three doorkeepers. ¹⁹Of those still in the city, he took the officer in charge of the fighting men and five royal advisers. He also took the secretary who was chief officer in charge of conscripting the people of the land and sixty of his men who were found in the city. ²⁰Nebuzaradan the commander took them all and brought them to the king of Babylon at Riblah. ²¹There at Riblah, in the land of Hamath, the king had them executed.

So Judah went into captivity, away from her land.

²²Nebuchadnezzar king of Babylon appointed Gedaliah son of Ahikam, the son of Shaphan, to be over the people he had left behind in Judah. ²³When all the army officers and their men heard that the king of Babylon had appointed Gedaliah as governor, they came to Gedaliah at Mizpah—Ishmael son of Nethaniah, Johanan son of Kareah, Seraiah son of Tanhumeth the Netophathite, Jaazaniah the son of the Maacathite, and their men. ²⁴Gedaliah took an oath to reassure them and their men. "Do not be afraid of the Babylonian officials," he said. "Settle down in the land and serve the king of Babylon, and it will go well with you."

²⁵In the seventh month, however, Ishmael son of Nethaniah, the son of Elishama, who was of royal blood, came with ten men and assassinated Gedaliah and also the men of Judah and the Babylonians who were with him at Mizpah. ²⁶At

ᵃ3 See Jer. 52:6.   ᵇ4 Or Chaldeans; also in verses 13, 25 and 26   ᶜ4 Or the Jordan Valley
ᵈ5 Or Chaldean; also in verses 10 and 24
ᵉ17 Hebrew eighteen cubits (about 8.1 meters)
ᶠ17 Hebrew three cubits (about 1.3 meters)

this, all the people from the least to the greatest, together with the army officers, fled to Egypt for fear of the Babylonians.

Jehoiachin Released

27In the thirty-seventh year of the exile of Jehoiachin king of Judah, in the year Evil-Merodach*a* became king of Babylon, he released Jehoiachin from prison on the twenty-seventh day of the twelfth month. 28He spoke kindly to him and gave him a seat of honor higher than those of the other kings who were with him in Babylon. 29So Jehoiachin put aside his prison clothes and for the rest of his life ate regularly at the king's table. 30Day by day the king gave Jehoiachin a regular allowance as long as he lived.

a27 Also called *Amel-Marduk*

1 Chronicles

THE BOOKS of 1 and 2 Chronicles were written for the exiles who had returned to Israel after the Babylonian captivity. The books of 1 and 2 Kings describe the end of the two kingdoms and how the people were conquered and deported into slavery. Now some of the Israelites have returned from captivity to rebuild their land.

For these exiles, if 1 and 2 Kings are the pathology report, then 1 and 2 Chronicles are the prognosis and treatment. The books of 1 and 2 Kings explain to the Jews how the disaster happened and why: It wasn't because the gods of the Assyrians and Babylonians had defeated the Lord; it was because the people of Israel had abandoned God.

HE ANSWERED THEIR
PRAYERS, BECAUSE
THEY TRUSTED
IN HIM. (5:20)

Now, as the people return to their land, they need to know that God was as involved in their slavery in exile as he was when he delivered them from slavery in Egypt. The first time the people were delivered, it was an act of redemption for their salvation; the second time it was an act of discipline for their sanctification. But the people aren't so sure of this. Does God still want them back? Is there still a future and a hope for them? Is their illness terminal? The books of 1 and 2 Chronicles say there is hope. God has never stopped loving his people and wanting them to be a blessing to the world.

Historical Records From Adam to Abraham

To Noah's Sons

1 Adam, Seth, Enosh, ²Kenan, Mahalalel, Jared, ³Enoch, Methuselah, Lamech, Noah.

⁴The sons of Noah:ᵃ
Shem, Ham and Japheth.

The Japhethites

⁵The sonsᵇ of Japheth:
Gomer, Magog, Madai, Javan, Tubal, Meshech and Tiras.
⁶The sons of Gomer:
Ashkenaz, Riphathᶜ and Togarmah.
⁷The sons of Javan:
Elishah, Tarshish, the Kittim and the Rodanim.

The Hamites

⁸The sons of Ham:
Cush, Mizraim,ᵈ Put and Canaan.
⁹The sons of Cush:
Seba, Havilah, Sabta, Raamah and Sabteca.
The sons of Raamah:
Sheba and Dedan.
¹⁰Cush was the fatherᵉ of
Nimrod, who grew to be a mighty warrior on earth.
¹¹Mizraim was the father of
the Ludites, Anamites, Lehabites, Naphtuhites, ¹²Pathrusites, Casluhites (from whom the Philistines came) and Caphtorites.
¹³Canaan was the father of
Sidon his firstborn,ᶠ and of the Hittites, ¹⁴Jebusites, Amorites, Girgashites, ¹⁵Hivites, Arkites, Sinites, ¹⁶Arvadites, Zemarites and Hamathites.

The Semites

¹⁷The sons of Shem:
Elam, Asshur, Arphaxad, Lud and Aram.
The sons of Aram:ᵍ
Uz, Hul, Gether and Meshech.
¹⁸Arphaxad was the father of Shelah, and Shelah the father of Eber.
¹⁹Two sons were born to Eber:
One was named Peleg,ʰ because in his time the earth was divided; his brother was named Joktan.

²⁰Joktan was the father of
Almodad, Sheleph, Hazarmaveth, Jerah, ²¹Hadoram, Uzal, Diklah, ²²Obal,ⁱ Abimael, Sheba, ²³Ophir, Havilah and Jobab. All these were sons of Joktan.

²⁴Shem, Arphaxad,ʲ Shelah,
²⁵Eber, Peleg, Reu,
²⁶Serug, Nahor, Terah
²⁷and Abram (that is, Abraham).

The Family of Abraham

²⁸The sons of Abraham:
Isaac and Ishmael.

Descendants of Hagar

²⁹These were their descendants:
Nebaioth the firstborn of Ishmael, Kedar, Adbeel, Mibsam, ³⁰Mishma, Dumah, Massa, Hadad, Tema, ³¹Jetur, Naphish and Kedemah. These were the sons of Ishmael.

Descendants of Keturah

³²The sons born to Keturah, Abraham's concubine:
Zimran, Jokshan, Medan, Midian, Ishbak and Shuah.
The sons of Jokshan:
Sheba and Dedan.
³³The sons of Midian:
Ephah, Epher, Hanoch, Abida and Eldaah.
All these were descendants of Keturah.

Descendants of Sarah

³⁴Abraham was the father of Isaac.
The sons of Isaac:
Esau and Israel.

ᵃ4 Septuagint; Hebrew does not have this line.
ᵇ5 Sons may mean descendants or successors or nations; also in verses 6–10, 17 and 20.
ᶜ6 Many Hebrew manuscripts and Vulgate (see also Septuagint and Gen. 10:3); most Hebrew manuscripts Diphath   ᵈ8 That is, Egypt; also in verse 11   ᵉ10 Father may mean ancestor or predecessor or founder; also in verses 11, 13, 18 and 20.   ᶠ13 Or of the Sidonians, the foremost
ᵍ17 One Hebrew manuscript and some Septuagint manuscripts (see also Gen. 10:23); most Hebrew manuscripts do not have this line.
ʰ19 Peleg means division.   ⁱ22 Some Hebrew manuscripts and Syriac (see also Gen. 10:28); most Hebrew manuscripts Ebal   ʲ24 Hebrew; some Septuagint manuscripts Arphaxad, Cainan (see also note at Gen. 11:10)

Esau's Sons

35 The sons of Esau:

Eliphaz, Reuel, Jeush, Jalam and Korah.

36 The sons of Eliphaz:

Teman, Omar, Zepho,[a] Gatam and Kenaz;

by Timna: Amalek.[b]

37 The sons of Reuel:

Nahath, Zerah, Shammah and Mizzah.

The People of Seir in Edom

38 The sons of Seir:

Lotan, Shobal, Zibeon, Anah, Dishon, Ezer and Dishan.

39 The sons of Lotan:

Hori and Homam. Timna was Lotan's sister.

40 The sons of Shobal:

Alvan,[c] Manahath, Ebal, Shepho and Onam.

The sons of Zibeon:

Aiah and Anah.

41 The son of Anah:

Dishon.

The sons of Dishon:

Hemdan,[d] Eshban, Ithran and Keran.

42 The sons of Ezer:

Bilhan, Zaavan and Akan.[e]

The sons of Dishan[f]:

Uz and Aran.

The Rulers of Edom

43 These were the kings who reigned in Edom before any Israelite king reigned[g]:

Bela son of Beor, whose city was named Dinhabah.

44 When Bela died, Jobab son of Zerah from Bozrah succeeded him as king.

45 When Jobab died, Husham from the land of the Temanites succeeded him as king.

46 When Husham died, Hadad son of Bedad, who defeated Midian in the country of Moab, succeeded him as king. His city was named Avith.

47 When Hadad died, Samlah from Masrekah succeeded him as king.

48 When Samlah died, Shaul from Rehoboth on the river[h] succeeded him as king.

49 When Shaul died, Baal-Hanan son of Acbor succeeded him as king.

50 When Baal-Hanan died, Hadad succeeded him as king. His city was named Pau,[i] and his wife's name was Mehetabel daughter of Matred, the daughter of Me-Zahab.

51 Hadad also died.

The chiefs of Edom were:

Timna, Alvah, Jetheth, 52 Oholibamah, Elah, Pinon, 53 Kenaz, Teman, Mibzar, 54 Magdiel and Iram. These were the chiefs of Edom.

Israel's Sons

2 These were the sons of Israel:

Reuben, Simeon, Levi, Judah, Issachar, Zebulun, 2 Dan, Joseph, Benjamin, Naphtali, Gad and Asher.

Judah

To Hezron's Sons

3 The sons of Judah:

Er, Onan and Shelah. These three were born to him by a Canaanite woman, the daughter of Shua. Er, Judah's firstborn, was wicked in the LORD's sight; so the LORD put him to death. 4 Tamar, Judah's daughter-in-law, bore him Perez and Zerah. Judah had five sons in all.

5 The sons of Perez:

Hezron and Hamul.

6 The sons of Zerah:

Zimri, Ethan, Heman, Calcol and Darda[j]—five in all.

[a] 36 Many Hebrew manuscripts, some Septuagint manuscripts and Syriac (see also Gen. 36:11); most Hebrew manuscripts *Zephi*   [b] 36 Some Septuagint manuscripts (see also Gen. 36:12); Hebrew *Gatam, Kenaz, Timna and Amalek*   [c] 40 Many Hebrew manuscripts and some Septuagint manuscripts (see also Gen. 36:23); most Hebrew manuscripts *Alian*   [d] 41 Many Hebrew manuscripts and some Septuagint manuscripts (see also Gen. 36:26); most Hebrew manuscripts *Hamran*   [e] 42 Many Hebrew and Septuagint manuscripts (see also Gen. 36:27); most Hebrew manuscripts *Zaavan, Jaakan*   [f] 42 Hebrew *Dishon*, a variant of *Dishan*   [g] 43 Or *before an Israelite king reigned over them*   [h] 48 Possibly the Euphrates   [i] 50 Many Hebrew manuscripts, some Septuagint manuscripts, Vulgate and Syriac (see also Gen. 36:39); most Hebrew manuscripts *Pai*   [j] 6 Many Hebrew manuscripts, some Septuagint manuscripts and Syriac (see also 1 Kings 4:31); most Hebrew manuscripts *Dara*

7 The son of Carmi:
Achar,[a] who brought trouble on Israel by violating the ban on taking devoted things.[b]
8 The son of Ethan:
Azariah.
9 The sons born to Hezron were:
Jerahmeel, Ram and Caleb.[c]

> *Prayer is not a substitute for work, thinking, watching, suffering, or giving; prayer is a support for all other efforts.*
>
> GEORGE BUTTRICK

From Ram Son of Hezron

10 Ram was the father of
Amminadab, and Amminadab the father of Nahshon, the leader of the people of Judah. 11 Nahshon was the father of Salmon,[d] Salmon the father of Boaz, 12 Boaz the father of Obed and Obed the father of Jesse.
13 Jesse was the father of
Eliab his firstborn; the second son was Abinadab, the third Shimea, 14 the fourth Nethanel, the fifth Raddai, 15 the sixth Ozem and the seventh David. 16 Their sisters were Zeruiah and Abigail. Zeruiah's three sons were Abishai, Joab and Asahel. 17 Abigail was the mother of Amasa, whose father was Jether the Ishmaelite.

Caleb Son of Hezron

18 Caleb son of Hezron had children by his wife Azubah (and by Jerioth). These were her sons: Jesher, Shobab and Ardon. 19 When Azubah died, Caleb married Ephrath, who bore him Hur. 20 Hur was the father of Uri, and Uri the father of Bezalel.
21 Later, Hezron lay with the daughter of Makir the father of Gilead (he had married her when he was sixty years old), and she bore him Segub. 22 Segub was the father of Jair, who controlled twenty-three towns in Gilead. 23 (But Geshur and Aram captured Havvoth Jair,[e] as well as Kenath with its surrounding settlements—sixty towns.) All these were descendants of Makir the father of Gilead.

24 After Hezron died in Caleb Ephrathah, Abijah the wife of Hezron bore him Ashhur the father[f] of Tekoa.

Jerahmeel Son of Hezron

25 The sons of Jerahmeel the firstborn of Hezron:
Ram his firstborn, Bunah, Oren, Ozem and[g] Ahijah. 26 Jerahmeel had another wife, whose name was Atarah; she was the mother of Onam.
27 The sons of Ram the firstborn of Jerahmeel:
Maaz, Jamin and Eker.
28 The sons of Onam:
Shammai and Jada.
The sons of Shammai:
Nadab and Abishur.
29 Abishur's wife was named Abihail, who bore him Ahban and Molid.
30 The sons of Nadab:
Seled and Appaim. Seled died without children.
31 The son of Appaim:
Ishi, who was the father of Sheshan.
Sheshan was the father of Ahlai.
32 The sons of Jada, Shammai's brother:
Jether and Jonathan. Jether died without children.
33 The sons of Jonathan:
Peleth and Zaza.
These were the descendants of Jerahmeel.
34 Sheshan had no sons—only daughters.
He had an Egyptian servant named Jarha. 35 Sheshan gave his daughter in marriage to his servant Jarha, and she bore him Attai.

---

[a] 7 *Achar* means *trouble*; *Achar* is called *Achan* in Joshua.   [b] 7 The Hebrew term refers to the irrevocable giving over of things or persons to the Lord, often by totally destroying them.
[c] 9 Hebrew *Kelubai*, a variant of *Caleb*
[d] 11 Septuagint (see also Ruth 4:21); Hebrew *Salma*   [e] 23 Or *captured the settlements of Jair*   [f] 24 *Father* may mean *civic leader* or *military leader*; also in verses 42, 45, 49–52 and possibly elsewhere.   [g] 25 Or *Oren and Ozem, by*

³⁶ Attai was the father of Nathan,
Nathan the father of Zabad,
³⁷ Zabad the father of Ephlal,
Ephlal the father of Obed,
³⁸ Obed the father of Jehu,
Jehu the father of Azariah,
³⁹ Azariah the father of Helez,
Helez the father of Eleasah,
⁴⁰ Eleasah the father of Sismai,
Sismai the father of Shallum,
⁴¹ Shallum the father of Jekamiah,
and Jekamiah the father of Elishama.

The Clans of Caleb

⁴² The sons of Caleb the brother of Jerahmeel:
Mesha his firstborn, who was the father of Ziph, and his son Mareshah,ᵃ who was the father of Hebron.
⁴³ The sons of Hebron:
Korah, Tappuah, Rekem and Shema. ⁴⁴Shema was the father of Raham, and Raham the father of Jorkeam. Rekem was the father of Shammai. ⁴⁵The son of Shammai was Maon, and Maon was the father of Beth Zur.
⁴⁶ Caleb's concubine Ephah was the mother of Haran, Moza and Gazez. Haran was the father of Gazez.
⁴⁷ The sons of Jahdai:
Regem, Jotham, Geshan, Pelet, Ephah and Shaaph.
⁴⁸ Caleb's concubine Maacah was the mother of Sheber and Tirhanah.
⁴⁹ She also gave birth to Shaaph the father of Madmannah and to Sheva the father of Macbenah and Gibea. Caleb's daughter was Acsah. ⁵⁰These were the descendants of Caleb.

The sons of Hur the firstborn of Ephrathah:
Shobal the father of Kiriath Jearim, ⁵¹Salma the father of Bethlehem, and Hareph the father of Beth Gader.
⁵² The descendants of Shobal the father of Kiriath Jearim were:
Haroeh, half the Manahathites, ⁵³and the clans of Kiriath Jearim:

the Ithrites, Puthites, Shumathites and Mishraites. From these descended the Zorathites and Eshtaolites.
⁵⁴ The descendants of Salma:
Bethlehem, the Netophathites, Atroth Beth Joab, half the Manahathites, the Zorites, ⁵⁵and the clans of scribesᵇ who lived at Jabez: the Tirathites, Shimeathites and Sucathites. These are the Kenites who came from Hammath, the father of the house of Recab.ᶜ

The Sons of David

3 These were the sons of David born to him in Hebron:
The firstborn was Amnon the son of Ahinoam of Jezreel;
the second, Daniel the son of Abigail of Carmel;
² the third, Absalom the son of Maacah daughter of Talmai king of Geshur;
the fourth, Adonijah the son of Haggith;
³ the fifth, Shephatiah the son of Abital;
and the sixth, Ithream, by his wife Eglah.
⁴ These six were born to David in Hebron, where he reigned seven years and six months.
David reigned in Jerusalem thirty-three years, ⁵and these were the children born to him there:
Shammua,ᵈ Shobab, Nathan and Solomon. These four were by Bathshebaᵉ daughter of Ammiel.
⁶There were also Ibhar, Elishua,ᶠ Eliphelet, ⁷Nogah, Nepheg, Japhia, ⁸Elishama, Eliada and Eliphelet—nine in all. ⁹All these were the sons of David, besides his sons by his concubines. And Tamar was their sister.

ᵃ42 The meaning of the Hebrew for this phrase is uncertain.   ᵇ55 Or of the Sopherites   ᶜ55 Or father of Beth Recab   ᵈ5 Hebrew Shimea, a variant of Shammua   ᵉ5 One Hebrew manuscript and Vulgate (see also Septuagint and 2 Samuel 11:3); most Hebrew manuscripts Bathshua   ᶠ6 Two Hebrew manuscripts (see also 2 Samuel 5:15 and 1 Chron. 14:5); most Hebrew manuscripts Elishama

The Kings of Judah

10 Solomon's son was Rehoboam,
Abijah his son,
Asa his son,
Jehoshaphat his son,
11 Jehoram[a] his son,
Ahaziah his son,
Joash his son,
12 Amaziah his son,
Azariah his son,
Jotham his son,
13 Ahaz his son,
Hezekiah his son,
Manasseh his son,
14 Amon his son,
Josiah his son,
15 The sons of Josiah:
Johanan the firstborn,
Jehoiakim the second son,
Zedekiah the third,
Shallum the fourth.
16 The successors of Jehoiakim:
Jehoiachin[b] his son,
and Zedekiah.

The Royal Line After the Exile

17 The descendants of Jehoiachin the captive:
Shealtiel his son, 18 Malkiram, Pedaiah, Shenazzar, Jekamiah, Hoshama and Nedabiah.
19 The sons of Pedaiah:
Zerubbabel and Shimei.
The sons of Zerubbabel:
Meshullam and Hananiah.
Shelomith was their sister.
20 There were also five others:
Hashubah, Ohel, Berekiah, Hasadiah and Jushab-Hesed.
21 The descendants of Hananiah:
Pelatiah and Jeshaiah, and the sons of Rephaiah, of Arnan, of Obadiah and of Shecaniah.
22 The descendants of Shecaniah:
Shemaiah and his sons:
Hattush, Igal, Bariah, Neariah and Shaphat—six in all.
23 The sons of Neariah:
Elioenai, Hizkiah and Azrikam—three in all.
24 The sons of Elioenai:
Hodaviah, Eliashib, Pelaiah, Akkub, Johanan, Delaiah and Anani—seven in all.

Other Clans of Judah

4 The descendants of Judah:
Perez, Hezron, Carmi, Hur and Shobal.
2 Reaiah son of Shobal was the father of Jahath, and Jahath the father of Ahumai and Lahad. These were the clans of the Zorathites.
3 These were the sons[c] of Etam:
Jezreel, Ishma and Idbash. Their sister was named Hazzelelponi.
4 Penuel was the father of Gedor, and Ezer the father of Hushah.
These were the descendants of Hur, the firstborn of Ephrathah and father[d] of Bethlehem.
5 Ashhur the father of Tekoa had two wives, Helah and Naarah.
6 Naarah bore him Ahuzzam, Hepher, Temeni and Haahashtari. These were the descendants of Naarah.
7 The sons of Helah:
Zereth, Zohar, Ethnan, 8 and Koz, who was the father of Anub and Hazzobebah and of the clans of Aharhel son of Harum.

> JABEZ cried out to the God of Israel,
> "Oh, that you would bless me and
> enlarge my territory! Let your hand be
> with me, and keep me from harm so that
> I will be free from pain." And God
> granted his request.
>
> 1 CHRONICLES 4:10

9 Jabez was more honorable than his brothers. His mother had named him Jabez,[e] saying, "I gave birth to him in pain." 10 Jabez cried out to the God of Israel, "Oh, that you would bless me and enlarge my territory! Let your hand be with me, and keep me from harm so that I will be free from pain." And God granted his request.

---

[a] 11 Hebrew Joram, a variant of Jehoram
[b] 16 Hebrew Jeconiah, a variant of Jehoiachin; also in verse 17   [c] 3 Some Septuagint manuscripts (see also Vulgate); Hebrew father
[d] 4 Father may mean civic leader or military leader; also in verses 12, 14, 17, 18 and possibly elsewhere.   [e] 9 Jabez sounds like the Hebrew for pain.

1 CHRONICLES 4:9–10

Doing God's Will by Resisting God's Will

4:9 HIS MOTHER HAD NAMED HIM JABEZ, SAYING, "I GAVE BIRTH TO HIM IN PAIN."

It was a terrible name to be saddled with from birth. *Jabez* sounds like the Hebrew word for "pain," and that's how Jabez's mother remembered him. Since she had a painful delivery, she decided he would have a painful identity. Names tell us who we are in a powerfully subliminal way. Before Jabez was able to reflect on his name, he must have, at some level, believed what his name said about him: discomfort, sadness, sorrow. We don't know when or how he decided to pray what was essentially a prayer of rebellion against his mother's intent: "Oh, that you would bless me and enlarge my territory" (4:10). But something deep inside us is very glad he did.

We live in a fallen world. Because of the sinfulness of humanity, God willed that the whole creation be subjected to frustration and futility (see Genesis 3:17–19; Romans 8:19–21). Though these things were not part of God's original will in creation, and are not part of his ultimate will in redemption, they are, for the time being, part of his temporary will in judgment. For instance, like Jabez, many people are born into harsh and unjust situations—by God's will, in this temporary sense. Should they therefore passively acquiesce to their state? Not at all. Shouldn't they resist them as Jabez did, in the name of the God who permissively willed them? Sometimes, to resist God's temporary, lower will is to embrace his higher, redemptive purposes. That's the kind of prayer Jabez prayed. His mother gave him a bad name; but God wanted better for him, even though he willed that she be Jabez's mother.

What difficulty are you facing now? It may be recent, or it may be longstanding. How should you pray about it? For patience, certainly; surely for endurance too, and for a grateful heart and the trust to accept God's decision. But it may also be his perfect will that you resist his permissive will, to grasp his higher and better will. We may obey God as much when we push our case and plead our cause, as we do when we accept our state.

PRAY:

"Oh Lord, that you would bless me and enlarge
my territory! Let your hand be with me,
and keep me from harm so that I will be free from pain."

FOR YOUR NEXT DEVOTIONAL READING, GO TO PAGE 480.

[11]Kelub, Shuhah's brother, was the father of Mehir, who was the father of Eshton. [12]Eshton was the father of Beth Rapha, Paseah and Tehinnah the father of Ir Nahash.[a] These were the men of Recah.

[13]The sons of Kenaz:
Othniel and Seraiah.
The sons of Othniel:
Hathath and Meonothai.[b] [14]Meonothai was the father of Ophrah.
Seraiah was the father of Joab,
the father of Ge Harashim.[c] It was called this because its people were craftsmen.
[15]The sons of Caleb son of Jephunneh:
Iru, Elah and Naam.
The son of Elah:
Kenaz.
[16]The sons of Jehallelel:
Ziph, Ziphah, Tiria and Asarel.
[17]The sons of Ezrah:
Jether, Mered, Epher and Jalon. One of Mered's wives gave birth to Miriam, Shammai and Ishbah the father of Eshtemoa. [18](His Judean wife gave birth to Jered the father of Gedor, Heber the father of Soco, and Jekuthiel the father of Zanoah.) These were the children of Pharaoh's daughter Bithiah, whom Mered had married.
[19]The sons of Hodiah's wife, the sister of Naham:
the father of Keilah the Garmite, and Eshtemoa the Maacathite.
[20]The sons of Shimon:
Amnon, Rinnah, Ben-Hanan and Tilon.
The descendants of Ishi:
Zoheth and Ben-Zoheth.
[21]The sons of Shelah son of Judah:
Er the father of Lecah, Laadah the father of Mareshah and the clans of the linen workers at Beth Ashbea, [22]Jokim, the men of Cozeba, and Joash and Saraph, who ruled in Moab and Jashubi Lehem. (These records are from ancient times.) [23]They were the potters who lived at Netaim and Gederah; they stayed there and worked for the king.

Simeon

[24]The descendants of Simeon:
Nemuel, Jamin, Jarib, Zerah and Shaul;
[25]Shallum was Shaul's son, Mibsam his son and Mishma his son.
[26]The descendants of Mishma:
Hammuel his son, Zaccur his son and Shimei his son.
[27]Shimei had sixteen sons and six daughters, but his brothers did not have many children; so their entire clan did not become as numerous as the people of Judah. [28]They lived in Beersheba, Moladah, Hazar Shual, [29]Bilhah, Ezem, Tolad, [30]Bethuel, Hormah, Ziklag, [31]Beth Marcaboth, Hazar Susim, Beth Biri and Shaaraim. These were their towns until the reign of David. [32]Their surrounding villages were Etam, Ain, Rimmon, Token and Ashan—five towns— [33]and all the villages around these towns as far as Baalath.[d] These were their settlements. And they kept a genealogical record.

[34]Meshobab, Jamlech, Joshah son of Amaziah, [35]Joel, Jehu son of Joshibiah, the son of Seraiah, the son of Asiel, [36]also Elioenai, Jaakobah, Jeshohaiah, Asaiah, Adiel, Jesimiel, Benaiah, [37]and Ziza son of Shiphi, the son of Allon, the son of Jedaiah, the son of Shimri, the son of Shemaiah.

[38]The men listed above by name were leaders of their clans. Their families increased greatly, [39]and they went to the outskirts of Gedor to the east of the valley in search of pasture for their flocks. [40]They found rich, good pasture, and the land was spacious, peaceful and quiet. Some Hamites had lived there formerly.

[41]The men whose names were listed came in the days of Hezekiah king of Judah. They attacked the Hamites in their dwellings and also the Meunites who were there and completely destroyed[e]

---

[a]12 Or of the city of Nahash   [b]13 Some Septuagint manuscripts and Vulgate; Hebrew does not have and Meonothai.   [c]14 Ge Harashim means valley of craftsmen.   [d]33 Some Septuagint manuscripts (see also Joshua 19:8); Hebrew Baal   [e]41 The Hebrew term refers to the irrevocable giving over of things or persons to the LORD, often by totally destroying them.

them, as is evident to this day. Then they settled in their place, because there was pasture for their flocks. ⁴²And five hundred of these Simeonites, led by Pelatiah, Neariah, Rephaiah and Uzziel, the sons of Ishi, invaded the hill country of Seir. ⁴³They killed the remaining Amalekites who had escaped, and they have lived there to this day.

Reuben

5 The sons of Reuben the firstborn of Israel (he was the firstborn, but when he defiled his father's marriage bed, his rights as firstborn were given to the sons of Joseph son of Israel; so he could not be listed in the genealogical record in accordance with his birthright, ²and though Judah was the strongest of his brothers and a ruler came from him, the rights of the firstborn belonged to Joseph)— ³the sons of Reuben the firstborn of Israel:

Hanoch, Pallu, Hezron and Carmi.
⁴ The descendants of Joel:
    Shemaiah his son, Gog his son, Shimei his son, ⁵Micah his son, Reaiah his son, Baal his son, ⁶and Beerah his son, whom Tiglath-Pileserᵃ king of Assyria took into exile. Beerah was a leader of the Reubenites.
⁷ Their relatives by clans, listed according to their genealogical records:
    Jeiel the chief, Zechariah, ⁸and Bela son of Azaz, the son of Shema, the son of Joel. They settled in the area from Aroer to Nebo and Baal Meon. ⁹To the east they occupied the land up to the edge of the desert that extends to the Euphrates River, because their livestock had increased in Gilead.
¹⁰During Saul's reign they waged war against the Hagrites, who were defeated at their hands; they occupied the dwellings of the Hagrites throughout the entire region east of Gilead.

Gad

¹¹ The Gadites lived next to them in Bashan, as far as Salecah:
¹²Joel was the chief, Shapham the second, then Janai and Shaphat, in Bashan.

¹³Their relatives, by families, were:
    Michael, Meshullam, Sheba, Jorai, Jacan, Zia and Eber—seven in all.
¹⁴These were the sons of Abihail son of Huri, the son of Jaroah, the son of Gilead, the son of Michael, the son of Jeshishai, the son of Jahdo, the son of Buz.
¹⁵Ahi son of Abdiel, the son of Guni, was head of their family.
¹⁶The Gadites lived in Gilead, in Bashan and its outlying villages, and on all the pasturelands of Sharon as far as they extended.

¹⁷All these were entered in the genealogical records during the reigns of Jotham king of Judah and Jeroboam king of Israel.

¹⁸The Reubenites, the Gadites and the half-tribe of Manasseh had 44,760 men ready for military service—able-bodied men who could handle shield and sword, who could use a bow, and who were trained for battle. ¹⁹They waged war against the Hagrites, Jetur, Naphish and Nodab. ²⁰They were helped in fighting them, and God handed the Hagrites and all their allies over to them, because they cried out to him during the battle. He answered their prayers, because they trusted in him. ²¹They seized the livestock of the Hagrites—fifty thousand camels, two hundred fifty thousand sheep and two thousand donkeys. They also took one hundred thousand people captive, ²²and many others fell slain, because the battle was God's. And they occupied the land until the exile.

> HE answered their prayers, because they trusted in him.
>
> 1 CHRONICLES 5:20

The Half-Tribe of Manasseh

²³The people of the half-tribe of Manasseh were numerous; they settled in the land from Bashan to Baal Hermon, that is, to Senir (Mount Hermon).

ᵃ6 Hebrew *Tilgath-Pilneser*, a variant of *Tiglath-Pileser*; also in verse 26

²⁴These were the heads of their families: Epher, Ishi, Eliel, Azriel, Jeremiah, Hodaviah and Jahdiel. They were brave warriors, famous men, and heads of their families. ²⁵But they were unfaithful to the God of their fathers and prostituted themselves to the gods of the peoples of the land, whom God had destroyed before them. ²⁶So the God of Israel stirred up the spirit of Pul king of Assyria (that is, Tiglath-Pileser king of Assyria), who took the Reubenites, the Gadites and the half-tribe of Manasseh into exile. He took them to Halah, Habor, Hara and the river of Gozan, where they are to this day.

Levi

6 The sons of Levi:
Gershon, Kohath and Merari.

² The sons of Kohath:
Amram, Izhar, Hebron and Uzziel.

³ The children of Amram:
Aaron, Moses and Miriam.

The sons of Aaron:
Nadab, Abihu, Eleazar and Ithamar.

⁴ Eleazar was the father of Phinehas,
Phinehas the father of Abishua,

⁵ Abishua the father of Bukki,
Bukki the father of Uzzi,

⁶ Uzzi the father of Zerahiah,
Zerahiah the father of Meraioth,

⁷ Meraioth the father of Amariah,
Amariah the father of Ahitub,

⁸ Ahitub the father of Zadok,
Zadok the father of Ahimaaz,

⁹ Ahimaaz the father of Azariah,
Azariah the father of Johanan,

¹⁰ Johanan the father of Azariah (it was he who served as priest in the temple Solomon built in Jerusalem),

¹¹ Azariah the father of Amariah,
Amariah the father of Ahitub,

¹² Ahitub the father of Zadok,
Zadok the father of Shallum,

¹³ Shallum the father of Hilkiah,
Hilkiah the father of Azariah,

¹⁴ Azariah the father of Seraiah,
and Seraiah the father of Jehozadak.

¹⁵ Jehozadak was deported when the LORD sent Judah and Jerusalem into exile by the hand of Nebuchadnezzar.

¹⁶ The sons of Levi:
Gershon,ᵃ Kohath and Merari.

¹⁷ These are the names of the sons of Gershon:
Libni and Shimei.

¹⁸ The sons of Kohath:
Amram, Izhar, Hebron and Uzziel.

¹⁹ The sons of Merari:
Mahli and Mushi.

These are the clans of the Levites listed according to their fathers:

²⁰ Of Gershon:
Libni his son, Jehath his son,
Zimmah his son, ²¹Joah his son,
Iddo his son, Zerah his son
and Jeatherai his son.

²² The descendants of Kohath:
Amminadab his son, Korah his son,
Assir his son, ²³Elkanah his son,
Ebiasaph his son, Assir his son,
²⁴Tahath his son, Uriel his son,
Uzziah his son and Shaul his son.

²⁵ The descendants of Elkanah:
Amasai, Ahimoth,
²⁶Elkanah his son,ᵇ Zophai his son,
Nahath his son, ²⁷Eliab his son,
Jeroham his son, Elkanah his son
and Samuel his son.ᶜ

²⁸ The sons of Samuel:
Joelᵈ the firstborn
and Abijah the second son.

²⁹ The descendants of Merari:
Mahli, Libni his son,
Shimei his son, Uzzah his son,
³⁰Shimea his son, Haggiah his son
and Asaiah his son.

The Temple Musicians

³¹These are the men David put in charge of the music in the house of the LORD after the ark came to rest there. ³²They ministered with music before the tabernacle, the Tent of Meeting, until Solomon built the temple of the LORD in Jerusalem. They performed their duties

---

ᵃ16 Hebrew Gershom, a variant of Gershon; also in verses 17, 20, 43, 62 and 71   ᵇ26 Some Hebrew manuscripts, Septuagint and Syriac; most Hebrew manuscripts Ahimoth ²⁶and Elkanah. The sons of Elkanah: ᶜ27 Some Septuagint manuscripts (see also 1 Samuel 1:19,20 and 1 Chron. 6:33,34); Hebrew does not have and Samuel his son.   ᵈ28 Some Septuagint manuscripts and Syriac (see also 1 Samuel 8:2 and 1 Chron. 6:33); Hebrew does not have Joel.

according to the regulations laid down for them.

[33] Here are the men who served, together with their sons:

From the Kohathites:

Heman, the musician,
the son of Joel, the son of Samuel,
[34] the son of Elkanah, the son of Jeroham,
the son of Eliel, the son of Toah,
[35] the son of Zuph, the son of Elkanah,
the son of Mahath, the son of Amasai,
[36] the son of Elkanah, the son of Joel,
the son of Azariah, the son of Zephaniah,
[37] the son of Tahath, the son of Assir,
the son of Ebiasaph, the son of Korah,
[38] the son of Izhar, the son of Kohath,
the son of Levi, the son of Israel;
[39] and Heman's associate Asaph, who served at his right hand:

Asaph son of Berekiah, the son of Shimea,
[40] the son of Michael, the son of Baaseiah,[a]
the son of Malkijah, [41] the son of Ethni,
the son of Zerah, the son of Adaiah,
[42] the son of Ethan, the son of Zimmah,
the son of Shimei, [43] the son of Jahath,
the son of Gershon, the son of Levi;
[44] and from their associates, the Merarites, at his left hand:

Ethan son of Kishi, the son of Abdi,
the son of Malluch, [45] the son of Hashabiah,
the son of Amaziah, the son of Hilkiah,
[46] the son of Amzi, the son of Bani,
the son of Shemer, [47] the son of Mahli,
the son of Mushi, the son of Merari,
the son of Levi.

[48] Their fellow Levites were assigned to all the other duties of the tabernacle, the house of God. [49] But Aaron and his descendants were the ones who presented offerings on the altar of burnt offering and on the altar of incense in connection with all that was done in the Most Holy Place, making atonement for Israel, in accordance with all that Moses the servant of God had commanded.

[50] These were the descendants of Aaron:

Eleazar his son, Phinehas his son, Abishua his son, [51] Bukki his son, Uzzi his son, Zerahiah his son, [52] Meraioth his son, Amariah his son, Ahitub his son, [53] Zadok his son and Ahimaaz his son.

[54] These were the locations of their settlements allotted as their territory (they were assigned to the descendants of Aaron who were from the Kohathite clan, because the first lot was for them):

[55] They were given Hebron in Judah with its surrounding pasturelands. [56] But the fields and villages around the city were given to Caleb son of Jephunneh.

[57] So the descendants of Aaron were given Hebron (a city of refuge), and Libnah,[b] Jattir, Eshtemoa, [58] Hilen, Debir, [59] Ashan, Juttah[c] and Beth Shemesh, together with their pasturelands. [60] And from the tribe of Benjamin they were given Gibeon,[d] Geba, Alemeth and Anathoth, together with their pasturelands.

These towns, which were distributed among the Kohathite clans, were thirteen in all.

[61] The rest of Kohath's descendants were allotted ten towns from the clans of half the tribe of Manasseh.

[62] The descendants of Gershon, clan by clan, were allotted thirteen towns from the tribes of Issachar, Asher and Naphtali, and from the part of the tribe of Manasseh that is in Bashan.

[63] The descendants of Merari, clan by clan, were allotted twelve towns from the tribes of Reuben, Gad and Zebulun.

---

[a]40 Most Hebrew manuscripts; some Hebrew manuscripts, one Septuagint manuscript and Syriac *Maaseiah*   [b]57 See Joshua 21:13; Hebrew *given the cities of refuge: Hebron, Libnah.* [c]59 Syriac (see also Septuagint and Joshua 21:16); Hebrew does not have *Juttah.* [d]60 See Joshua 21:17; Hebrew does not have *Gibeon.*

⁶⁴So the Israelites gave the Levites these towns and their pasturelands. ⁶⁵From the tribes of Judah, Simeon and Benjamin they allotted the previously named towns.

⁶⁶Some of the Kohathite clans were given as their territory towns from the tribe of Ephraim.

⁶⁷In the hill country of Ephraim they were given Shechem (a city of refuge), and Gezer,ᵃ ⁶⁸Jokmeam, Beth Horon, ⁶⁹Aijalon and Gath Rimmon, together with their pasturelands.

⁷⁰And from half the tribe of Manasseh the Israelites gave Aner and Bileam, together with their pasturelands, to the rest of the Kohathite clans.

⁷¹ The Gershonites received the following:
From the clan of the half-tribe of Manasseh
they received Golan in Bashan and also Ashtaroth, together with their pasturelands;
⁷² from the tribe of Issachar
they received Kedesh, Daberath, ⁷³Ramoth and Anem, together with their pasturelands;
⁷⁴ from the tribe of Asher
they received Mashal, Abdon, ⁷⁵Hukok and Rehob, together with their pasturelands;
⁷⁶ and from the tribe of Naphtali
they received Kedesh in Galilee, Hammon and Kiriathaim, together with their pasturelands.

⁷⁷The Merarites (the rest of the Levites) received the following:
From the tribe of Zebulun
they received Jokneam, Kartah,ᵇ Rimmono and Tabor, together with their pasturelands;
⁷⁸ from the tribe of Reuben across the Jordan east of Jericho
they received Bezer in the desert, Jahzah, ⁷⁹Kedemoth and Mephaath, together with their pasturelands;
⁸⁰ and from the tribe of Gad
they received Ramoth in Gilead, Mahanaim, ⁸¹Heshbon and Jazer, together with their pasturelands.

Issachar

7 The sons of Issachar:
Tola, Puah, Jashub and Shimron—four in all.
² The sons of Tola:
Uzzi, Rephaiah, Jeriel, Jahmai, Ibsam and Samuel—heads of their families. During the reign of David, the descendants of Tola listed as fighting men in their genealogy numbered 22,600.
³ The son of Uzzi:
Izrahiah.
The sons of Izrahiah:
Michael, Obadiah, Joel and Isshiah. All five of them were chiefs.
⁴According to their family genealogy, they had 36,000 men ready for battle, for they had many wives and children.
⁵ The relatives who were fighting men belonging to all the clans of Issachar, as listed in their genealogy, were 87,000 in all.

Benjamin

⁶ Three sons of Benjamin:
Bela, Beker and Jediael.
⁷ The sons of Bela:
Ezbon, Uzzi, Uzziel, Jerimoth and Iri, heads of families—five in all. Their genealogical record listed 22,034 fighting men.
⁸ The sons of Beker:
Zemirah, Joash, Eliezer, Elioenai, Omri, Jeremoth, Abijah, Anathoth and Alemeth. All these were the sons of Beker. ⁹Their genealogical record listed the heads of families and 20,200 fighting men.
¹⁰The son of Jediael:
Bilhan.
The sons of Bilhan:
Jeush, Benjamin, Ehud, Kenaanah, Zethan, Tarshish and Ahishahar. ¹¹All these sons of Jediael were heads of families. There were 17,200 fighting men ready to go out to war.
¹²The Shuppites and Huppites were the descendants of Ir, and the Hushites the descendants of Aher.

ᵃ67 See Joshua 21:21; Hebrew *given the cities of refuge: Shechem, Gezer.*   ᵇ77 See Septuagint and Joshua 21:34; Hebrew does not have *Jokneam, Kartah.*

Naphtali

13 The sons of Naphtali:
Jahziel, Guni, Jezer and Shillem[a]—
the descendants of Bilhah.

Manasseh

14 The descendants of Manasseh:
Asriel was his descendant through his Aramean concubine. She gave birth to Makir the father of Gilead. 15 Makir took a wife from among the Huppites and Shuppites. His sister's name was Maacah.

Another descendant was named Zelophehad, who had only daughters.

16 Makir's wife Maacah gave birth to a son and named him Peresh. His brother was named Sheresh, and his sons were Ulam and Rakem.

17 The son of Ulam:
Bedan.

These were the sons of Gilead son of Makir, the son of Manasseh. 18 His sister Hammoleketh gave birth to Ishhod, Abiezer and Mahlah.

19 The sons of Shemida were:
Ahian, Shechem, Likhi and Aniam.

Ephraim

20 The descendants of Ephraim:
Shuthelah, Bered his son,
Tahath his son, Eleadah his son,
Tahath his son, 21 Zabad his son
and Shuthelah his son.

Ezer and Elead were killed by the native-born men of Gath, when they went down to seize their livestock. 22 Their father Ephraim mourned for them many days, and his relatives came to comfort him. 23 Then he lay with his wife again, and she became pregnant and gave birth to a son. He named him Beriah,[b] because there had been misfortune in his family. 24 His daughter was Sheerah, who built Lower and Upper Beth Horon as well as Uzzen Sheerah.

25 Rephah was his son, Resheph his son,[c]
Telah his son, Tahan his son,
26 Ladan his son, Ammihud his son,
Elishama his son, 27 Nun his son
and Joshua his son.

28 Their lands and settlements included Bethel and its surrounding villages, Naaran to the east, Gezer and its villages to the west, and Shechem and its villages all the way to Ayyah and its villages. 29 Along the borders of Manasseh were Beth Shan, Taanach, Megiddo and Dor, together with their villages. The descendants of Joseph son of Israel lived in these towns.

Asher

30 The sons of Asher:
Imnah, Ishvah, Ishvi and Beriah.
Their sister was Serah.

31 The sons of Beriah:
Heber and Malkiel, who was the father of Birzaith.

32 Heber was the father of Japhlet, Shomer and Hotham and of their sister Shua.

33 The sons of Japhlet:
Pasach, Bimhal and Ashvath.
These were Japhlet's sons.

34 The sons of Shomer:
Ahi, Rohgah,[d] Hubbah and Aram.

35 The sons of his brother Helem:
Zophah, Imna, Shelesh and Amal.

36 The sons of Zophah:
Suah, Harnepher, Shual, Beri, Imrah, 37 Bezer, Hod, Shamma, Shilshah, Ithran[e] and Beera.

38 The sons of Jether:
Jephunneh, Pispah and Ara.

39 The sons of Ulla:
Arah, Hanniel and Rizia.

40 All these were descendants of Asher—heads of families, choice men, brave warriors and outstanding leaders. The number of men ready for battle, as listed in their genealogy, was 26,000.

The Genealogy of Saul the Benjamite

8 Benjamin was the father of Bela his firstborn,
Ashbel the second son, Aharah the third,
2 Nohah the fourth and Rapha the fifth.

---

[a]13 Some Hebrew and Septuagint manuscripts (see also Gen. 46:24 and Num. 26:49); most Hebrew manuscripts *Shallum*   [b]23 *Beriah* sounds like the Hebrew for *misfortune.*
[c]25 Some Septuagint manuscripts; Hebrew does not have *his son.*   [d]34 Or *of his brother Shomer: Rohgah*   [e]37 Possibly a variant of *Jether*

³The sons of Bela were:

Addar, Gera, Abihud,ᵃ ⁴Abishua, Naaman, Ahoah, ⁵Gera, Shephuphan and Huram.

⁶These were the descendants of Ehud, who were heads of families of those living in Geba and were deported to Manahath:

⁷Naaman, Ahijah, and Gera, who deported them and who was the father of Uzza and Ahihud.

⁸Sons were born to Shaharaim in Moab after he had divorced his wives Hushim and Baara. ⁹By his wife Hodesh he had Jobab, Zibia, Mesha, Malcam, ¹⁰Jeuz, Sakia and Mirmah. These were his sons, heads of families. ¹¹By Hushim he had Abitub and Elpaal.

¹²The sons of Elpaal:

Eber, Misham, Shemed (who built Ono and Lod with its surrounding villages), ¹³and Beriah and Shema, who were heads of families of those living in Aijalon and who drove out the inhabitants of Gath.

¹⁴Ahio, Shashak, Jeremoth, ¹⁵Zebadiah, Arad, Eder, ¹⁶Michael, Ishpah and Joha were the sons of Beriah.

¹⁷Zebadiah, Meshullam, Hizki, Heber, ¹⁸Ishmerai, Izliah and Jobab were the sons of Elpaal.

¹⁹Jakim, Zicri, Zabdi, ²⁰Elienai, Zillethai, Eliel, ²¹Adaiah, Beraiah and Shimrath were the sons of Shimei.

²²Ishpan, Eber, Eliel, ²³Abdon, Zicri, Hanan, ²⁴Hananiah, Elam, Anthothijah, ²⁵Iphdeiah and Penuel were the sons of Shashak.

²⁶Shamsherai, Shehariah, Athaliah, ²⁷Jaareshiah, Elijah and Zicri were the sons of Jeroham.

²⁸All these were heads of families, chiefs as listed in their genealogy, and they lived in Jerusalem.

²⁹Jeielᵇ the fatherᶜ of Gibeon lived in Gibeon.

His wife's name was Maacah, ³⁰and his firstborn son was Abdon, followed by Zur, Kish, Baal, Ner,ᵈ Nadab, ³¹Gedor, Ahio, Zeker ³²and Mikloth, who was the father of Shimeah. They too lived near their relatives in Jerusalem.

³³Ner was the father of Kish, Kish the father of Saul, and Saul the father of Jonathan, Malki-Shua, Abinadab and Esh-Baal.ᵉ

³⁴The son of Jonathan:

Merib-Baal,ᶠ who was the father of Micah.

³⁵The sons of Micah:

Pithon, Melech, Tarea and Ahaz.

³⁶Ahaz was the father of Jehoaddah, Jehoaddah was the father of Alemeth, Azmaveth and Zimri, and Zimri was the father of Moza. ³⁷Moza was the father of Binea; Raphah was his son, Eleasah his son and Azel his son.

³⁸Azel had six sons, and these were their names:

Azrikam, Bokeru, Ishmael, Sheariah, Obadiah and Hanan. All these were the sons of Azel.

³⁹The sons of his brother Eshek:

Ulam his firstborn, Jeush the second son and Eliphelet the third. ⁴⁰The sons of Ulam were brave warriors who could handle the bow. They had many sons and grandsons—150 in all.

All these were the descendants of Benjamin.

9 All Israel was listed in the genealogies recorded in the book of the kings of Israel.

The People in Jerusalem

The people of Judah were taken captive to Babylon because of their unfaithfulness. ²Now the first to resettle on their own property in their own towns were some Israelites, priests, Levites and temple servants.

³Those from Judah, from Benjamin, and from Ephraim and Manasseh who lived in Jerusalem were:

⁴Uthai son of Ammihud, the son of Omri, the son of Imri, the son of Bani, a descendant of Perez son of Judah.

ᵃ3 Or Gera the father of Ehud   ᵇ29 Some Septuagint manuscripts (see also 1 Chron. 9:35); Hebrew does not have Jeiel.   ᶜ29 Father may mean civic leader or military leader.
ᵈ30 Some Septuagint manuscripts (see also 1 Chron. 9:36); Hebrew does not have Ner.
ᵉ33 Also known as Ish-Bosheth   ᶠ34 Also known as Mephibosheth

⁵Of the Shilonites:
Asaiah the firstborn and his sons.
⁶Of the Zerahites:
Jeuel.

The people from Judah numbered 690.

⁷Of the Benjamites:
Sallu son of Meshullam, the son of Hodaviah, the son of Hassenuah;
⁸Ibneiah son of Jeroham; Elah son of Uzzi, the son of Micri; and Meshullam son of Shephatiah, the son of Reuel, the son of Ibnijah.
⁹The people from Benjamin, as listed in their genealogy, numbered 956. All these men were heads of their families.

¹⁰Of the priests:
Jedaiah; Jehoiarib; Jakin;
¹¹Azariah son of Hilkiah, the son of Meshullam, the son of Zadok, the son of Meraioth, the son of Ahitub, the official in charge of the house of God;
¹²Adaiah son of Jeroham, the son of Pashhur, the son of Malkijah; and Maasai son of Adiel, the son of Jahzerah, the son of Meshullam, the son of Meshillemith, the son of Immer.
¹³The priests, who were heads of families, numbered 1,760. They were able men, responsible for ministering in the house of God.

¹⁴Of the Levites:
Shemaiah son of Hasshub, the son of Azrikam, the son of Hashabiah, a Merarite; ¹⁵Bakbakkar, Heresh, Galal and Mattaniah son of Mica, the son of Zicri, the son of Asaph; ¹⁶Obadiah son of Shemaiah, the son of Galal, the son of Jeduthun; and Berekiah son of Asa, the son of Elkanah, who lived in the villages of the Netophathites.

¹⁷The gatekeepers:
Shallum, Akkub, Talmon, Ahiman and their brothers, Shallum their chief ¹⁸being stationed at the King's Gate on the east, up to the present time. These were the gatekeepers belonging to the camp of the Levites. ¹⁹Shallum son of Kore, the son of Ebiasaph, the son of Korah, and his fellow gatekeepers from his family (the Korahites) were responsible for guarding the thresholds of the Tent[a] just as their fathers had been responsible for guarding the entrance to the dwelling of the LORD. ²⁰In earlier times Phinehas son of Eleazar was in charge of the gatekeepers, and the LORD was with him. ²¹Zechariah son of Meshelemiah was the gatekeeper at the entrance to the Tent of Meeting.

²²Altogether, those chosen to be gatekeepers at the thresholds numbered 212. They were registered by genealogy in their villages. The gatekeepers had been assigned to their positions of trust by David and Samuel the seer. ²³They and their descendants were in charge of guarding the gates of the house of the LORD—the house called the Tent. ²⁴The gatekeepers were on the four sides: east, west, north and south. ²⁵Their brothers in their villages had to come from time to time and share their duties for seven-day periods. ²⁶But the four principal gatekeepers, who were Levites, were entrusted with the responsibility for the rooms and treasuries in the house of God. ²⁷They would spend the night stationed around the house of God, because they had to guard it; and they had charge of the key for opening it each morning.

²⁸Some of them were in charge of the articles used in the temple service; they counted them when they were brought in and when they were taken out. ²⁹Others were assigned to take care of the furnishings and all the other articles of the sanctuary, as well as the flour and wine, and the oil, incense and spices. ³⁰But some of the priests took care of mixing the spices. ³¹A Levite named Mattithiah, the firstborn son of Shallum the Korahite, was entrusted with the responsibility for baking the offering bread. ³²Some of their Kohathite brothers were in charge of preparing for every Sabbath the bread set out on the table.

³³Those who were musicians, heads of Levite families, stayed in the rooms of the temple and were exempt from other

---

a19 That is, the temple; also in verses 21 and 23

duties because they were responsible for the work day and night.

³⁴All these were heads of Levite families, chiefs as listed in their genealogy, and they lived in Jerusalem.

The Genealogy of Saul

³⁵Jeiel the father*ª* of Gibeon lived in Gibeon.

His wife's name was Maacah, ³⁶and his firstborn son was Abdon, followed by Zur, Kish, Baal, Ner, Nadab, ³⁷Gedor, Ahio, Zechariah and Mikloth. ³⁸Mikloth was the father of Shimeam. They too lived near their relatives in Jerusalem.

³⁹Ner was the father of Kish, Kish the father of Saul, and Saul the father of Jonathan, Malki-Shua, Abinadab and Esh-Baal.*ᵇ*

⁴⁰The son of Jonathan:

Merib-Baal,*ᶜ* who was the father of Micah.

⁴¹The sons of Micah:

Pithon, Melech, Tahrea and Ahaz.*ᵈ*

⁴²Ahaz was the father of Jadah, Jadah*ᵉ* was the father of Alemeth, Azmaveth and Zimri, and Zimri was the father of Moza. ⁴³Moza was the father of Binea; Rephaiah was his son, Eleasah his son and Azel his son.

⁴⁴Azel had six sons, and these were their names:

Azrikam, Bokeru, Ishmael, Sheariah, Obadiah and Hanan. These were the sons of Azel.

Saul Takes His Life

10 Now the Philistines fought against Israel; the Israelites fled before them, and many fell slain on Mount Gilboa. ²The Philistines pressed hard after Saul and his sons, and they killed his sons Jonathan, Abinadab and Malki-Shua. ³The fighting grew fierce around Saul, and when the archers overtook him, they wounded him.

⁴Saul said to his armor-bearer, "Draw your sword and run me through, or these uncircumcised fellows will come and abuse me."

But his armor-bearer was terrified and would not do it; so Saul took his own sword and fell on it. ⁵When the armor-bearer saw that Saul was dead, he too fell on his sword and died. ⁶So Saul and his three sons died, and all his house died together.

⁷When all the Israelites in the valley saw that the army had fled and that Saul and his sons had died, they abandoned their towns and fled. And the Philistines came and occupied them.

⁸The next day, when the Philistines came to strip the dead, they found Saul and his sons fallen on Mount Gilboa. ⁹They stripped him and took his head and his armor, and sent messengers throughout the land of the Philistines to proclaim the news among their idols and their people. ¹⁰They put his armor in the temple of their gods and hung up his head in the temple of Dagon.

¹¹When all the inhabitants of Jabesh Gilead heard of everything the Philistines had done to Saul, ¹²all their valiant men went and took the bodies of Saul and his sons and brought them to Jabesh. Then they buried their bones under the great tree in Jabesh, and they fasted seven days.

¹³Saul died because he was unfaithful to the LORD; he did not keep the word of the LORD and even consulted a medium for guidance, ¹⁴and did not inquire of the LORD. So the LORD put him to death and turned the kingdom over to David son of Jesse.

David Becomes King Over Israel

11 All Israel came together to David at Hebron and said, "We are your own flesh and blood. ²In the past, even while Saul was king, you were the one who led Israel on their military campaigns. And the LORD your God said to you, 'You will shepherd my people Israel, and you will become their ruler.'"

³When all the elders of Israel had come to King David at Hebron, he made a compact with them at Hebron before the

---

ª35 Father *may mean* civic leader *or* military leader.   *ᵇ39* Also known as Ish-Bosheth
ᶜ40 Also known as Mephibosheth
ᵈ41 Vulgate and Syriac (see also Septuagint and 1 Chron. 8:35); Hebrew does not have *and Ahaz.*
ᵉ42 Some Hebrew manuscripts and Septuagint (see also 1 Chron. 8:36); most Hebrew manuscripts *Jarah, Jarah*

LORD, and they anointed David king over Israel, as the LORD had promised through Samuel.

David Conquers Jerusalem

4David and all the Israelites marched to Jerusalem (that is, Jebus). The Jebusites who lived there 5said to David, "You will not get in here." Nevertheless, David captured the fortress of Zion, the City of David.

6David had said, "Whoever leads the attack on the Jebusites will become commander-in-chief." Joab son of Zeruiah went up first, and so he received the command.

7David then took up residence in the fortress, and so it was called the City of David. 8He built up the city around it, from the supporting terraces*a* to the surrounding wall, while Joab restored the rest of the city. 9And David became more and more powerful, because the LORD Almighty was with him.

> 66 I must often be glad that certain past prayers of my own were not granted. 99
>
> C. S. LEWIS

David's Mighty Men

10These were the chiefs of David's mighty men—they, together with all Israel, gave his kingship strong support to extend it over the whole land, as the LORD had promised— 11this is the list of David's mighty men:

Jashobeam,*b* a Hacmonite, was chief of the officers*c*; he raised his spear against three hundred men, whom he killed in one encounter.

12Next to him was Eleazar son of Dodai the Ahohite, one of the three mighty men. 13He was with David at Pas Dammim when the Philistines gathered there for battle. At a place where there was a field full of barley, the troops fled from the Philistines. 14But they took their stand in the middle of the field. They defended it and struck the Philistines down, and the LORD brought about a great victory.

15Three of the thirty chiefs came down to David to the rock at the cave of Adullam, while a band of Philistines was encamped in the Valley of Rephaim. 16At that time David was in the stronghold, and the Philistine garrison was at Bethlehem. 17David longed for water and said, "Oh, that someone would get me a drink of water from the well near the gate of Bethlehem!" 18So the Three broke through the Philistine lines, drew water from the well near the gate of Bethlehem and carried it back to David. But he refused to drink it; instead, he poured it out before the LORD. 19"God forbid that I should do this!" he said. "Should I drink the blood of these men who went at the risk of their lives?" Because they risked their lives to bring it back, David would not drink it.

Such were the exploits of the three mighty men.

20Abishai the brother of Joab was chief of the Three. He raised his spear against three hundred men, whom he killed, and so he became as famous as the Three. 21He was doubly honored above the Three and became their commander, even though he was not included among them.

22Benaiah son of Jehoiada was a valiant fighter from Kabzeel, who performed great exploits. He struck down two of Moab's best men. He also went down into a pit on a snowy day and killed a lion. 23And he struck down an Egyptian who was seven and a half feet*d* tall. Although the Egyptian had a spear like a weaver's rod in his hand, Benaiah went against him with a club. He snatched the spear from the Egyptian's hand and killed him with his own spear. 24Such were the exploits of Benaiah son of Jehoiada; he too was as famous as the three mighty men. 25He was held in greater honor than any of the Thirty, but he was not included among the Three. And David put him in charge of his bodyguard.

26The mighty men were:
Asahel the brother of Joab,
Elhanan son of Dodo from Bethlehem,

---

*a*8 Or *the Millo*   *b*11 Possibly a variant of *Jashob-Baal*   *c*11 Or *Thirty*; some Septuagint manuscripts *Three* (see also 2 Samuel 23:8)
*d*23 Hebrew *five cubits* (about 2.3 meters)

27 Shammoth the Harorite,
Helez the Pelonite,
28 Ira son of Ikkesh from Tekoa,
Abiezer from Anathoth,
29 Sibbecai the Hushathite,
Ilai the Ahohite,
30 Maharai the Netophathite,
Heled son of Baanah the Netophathite,
31 Ithai son of Ribai from Gibeah in Benjamin,
Benaiah the Pirathonite,
32 Hurai from the ravines of Gaash,
Abiel the Arbathite,
33 Azmaveth the Baharumite,
Eliahba the Shaalbonite,
34 the sons of Hashem the Gizonite,
Jonathan son of Shagee the Hararite,
35 Ahiam son of Sacar the Hararite,
Eliphal son of Ur,
36 Hepher the Mekerathite,
Ahijah the Pelonite,
37 Hezro the Carmelite,
Naarai son of Ezbai,
38 Joel the brother of Nathan,
Mibhar son of Hagri,
39 Zelek the Ammonite,
Naharai the Berothite, the armorbearer of Joab son of Zeruiah,
40 Ira the Ithrite,
Gareb the Ithrite,
41 Uriah the Hittite,
Zabad son of Ahlai,
42 Adina son of Shiza the Reubenite, who was chief of the Reubenites, and the thirty with him,
43 Hanan son of Maacah,
Joshaphat the Mithnite,
44 Uzzia the Ashterathite,
Shama and Jeiel the sons of Hotham the Aroerite,
45 Jediael son of Shimri,
his brother Joha the Tizite,
46 Eliel the Mahavite,
Jeribai and Joshaviah the sons of Elnaam,
Ithmah the Moabite,
47 Eliel, Obed and Jaasiel the Mezobaite.

Warriors Join David

12 These were the men who came to David at Ziklag, while he was banished from the presence of Saul son of Kish (they were among the warriors who helped him in battle; 2they were armed with bows and were able to shoot arrows or to sling stones right-handed or left-handed; they were kinsmen of Saul from the tribe of Benjamin):

3Ahiezer their chief and Joash the sons of Shemaah the Gibeathite; Jeziel and Pelet the sons of Azmaveth; Beracah, Jehu the Anathothite, 4and Ishmaiah the Gibeonite, a mighty man among the Thirty, who was a leader of the Thirty; Jeremiah, Jahaziel, Johanan, Jozabad the Gederathite, 5Eluzai, Jerimoth, Bealiah, Shemariah and Shephatiah the Haruphite; 6Elkanah, Isshiah, Azarel, Joezer and Jashobeam the Korahites; 7and Joelah and Zebadiah the sons of Jeroham from Gedor.

8Some Gadites defected to David at his stronghold in the desert. They were brave warriors, ready for battle and able to handle the shield and spear. Their faces were the faces of lions, and they were as swift as gazelles in the mountains.

9Ezer was the chief,
Obadiah the second in command,
Eliab the third,
10Mishmannah the fourth, Jeremiah the fifth,
11Attai the sixth, Eliel the seventh,
12Johanan the eighth, Elzabad the ninth,
13Jeremiah the tenth and Macbannai the eleventh.

14These Gadites were army commanders; the least was a match for a hundred, and the greatest for a thousand. 15It was they who crossed the Jordan in the first month when it was overflowing all its banks, and they put to flight everyone living in the valleys, to the east and to the west.

16Other Benjamites and some men from Judah also came to David in his stronghold. 17David went out to meet them and said to them, "If you have come to me in peace, to help me, I am ready to have you unite with me. But if you have come to betray me to my enemies when my hands are free from violence, may the God of our fathers see it and judge you."

[18]Then the Spirit came upon Amasai, chief of the Thirty, and he said:

"We are yours, O David!
We are with you, O son of Jesse!
Success, success to you,
    and success to those who help you,
    for your God will help you."

So David received them and made them leaders of his raiding bands.

[19]Some of the men of Manasseh defected to David when he went with the Philistines to fight against Saul. (He and his men did not help the Philistines because, after consultation, their rulers sent him away. They said, "It will cost us our heads if he deserts to his master Saul.") [20]When David went to Ziklag, these were the men of Manasseh who defected to him: Adnah, Jozabad, Jediael, Michael, Jozabad, Elihu and Zillethai, leaders of units of a thousand in Manasseh. [21]They helped David against raiding bands, for all of them were brave warriors, and they were commanders in his army. [22]Day after day men came to help David, until he had a great army, like the army of God.[a]

Others Join David at Hebron

[23]These are the numbers of the men armed for battle who came to David at Hebron to turn Saul's kingdom over to him, as the LORD had said:

[24]men of Judah, carrying shield and spear—6,800 armed for battle;
[25]men of Simeon, warriors ready for battle—7,100;
[26]men of Levi—4,600, [27]including Jehoiada, leader of the family of Aaron, with 3,700 men, [28]and Zadok, a brave young warrior, with 22 officers from his family;
[29]men of Benjamin, Saul's kinsmen—3,000, most of whom had remained loyal to Saul's house until then;
[30]men of Ephraim, brave warriors, famous in their own clans—20,800;
[31]men of half the tribe of Manasseh, designated by name to come and make David king—18,000;
[32]men of Issachar, who understood the times and knew what Israel should do—200 chiefs, with all their relatives under their command;

[33]men of Zebulun, experienced soldiers prepared for battle with every type of weapon, to help David with undivided loyalty—50,000;
[34]men of Naphtali—1,000 officers, together with 37,000 men carrying shields and spears;
[35]men of Dan, ready for battle—28,600;
[36]men of Asher, experienced soldiers prepared for battle—40,000;
[37]and from east of the Jordan, men of Reuben, Gad and the half-tribe of Manasseh, armed with every type of weapon—120,000.

[38]All these were fighting men who volunteered to serve in the ranks. They came to Hebron fully determined to make David king over all Israel. All the rest of the Israelites were also of one mind to make David king. [39]The men spent three days there with David, eating and drinking, for their families had supplied provisions for them. [40]Also, their neighbors from as far away as Issachar, Zebulun and Naphtali came bringing food on donkeys, camels, mules and oxen. There were plentiful supplies of flour, fig cakes, raisin cakes, wine, oil, cattle and sheep, for there was joy in Israel.

Bringing Back the Ark

13 David conferred with each of his officers, the commanders of thousands and commanders of hundreds. [2]He then said to the whole assembly of Israel, "If it seems good to you and if it is the will of the LORD our God, let us send word far and wide to the rest of our brothers throughout the territories of Israel, and also to the priests and Levites who are with them in their towns and pasturelands, to come and join us. [3]Let us bring the ark of our God back to us, for we did not inquire of[b] it[c] during the reign of Saul." [4]The whole assembly agreed to do this, because it seemed right to all the people.

[5]So David assembled all the Israelites, from the Shihor River in Egypt to Lebo[d] Hamath, to bring the ark of God from

[a]22 Or a great and mighty army   [b]3 Or we neglected   [c]3 Or him   [d]5 Or to the entrance to

Kiriath Jearim. [6]David and all the Israelites with him went to Baalah of Judah (Kiriath Jearim) to bring up from there the ark of God the LORD, who is enthroned between the cherubim—the ark that is called by the Name.

[7]They moved the ark of God from Abinadab's house on a new cart, with Uzzah and Ahio guiding it. [8]David and all the Israelites were celebrating with all their might before God, with songs and with harps, lyres, tambourines, cymbals and trumpets.

[9]When they came to the threshing floor of Kidon, Uzzah reached out his hand to steady the ark, because the oxen stumbled. [10]The LORD's anger burned against Uzzah, and he struck him down because he had put his hand on the ark. So he died there before God.

[11]Then David was angry because the LORD's wrath had broken out against Uzzah, and to this day that place is called Perez Uzzah.[a]

[12]David was afraid of God that day and asked, "How can I ever bring the ark of God to me?" [13]He did not take the ark to be with him in the City of David. Instead, he took it aside to the house of Obed-Edom the Gittite. [14]The ark of God remained with the family of Obed-Edom in his house for three months, and the LORD blessed his household and everything he had.

David's House and Family

14 Now Hiram king of Tyre sent messengers to David, along with cedar logs, stonemasons and carpenters to build a palace for him. [2]And David knew that the LORD had established him as king over Israel and that his kingdom had been highly exalted for the sake of his people Israel.

[3]In Jerusalem David took more wives and became the father of more sons and daughters. [4]These are the names of the children born to him there: Shammua, Shobab, Nathan, Solomon, [5]Ibhar, Elishua, Elpelet, [6]Nogah, Nepheg, Japhia, [7]Elishama, Beeliada[b] and Eliphelet.

David Defeats the Philistines

[8]When the Philistines heard that David had been anointed king over all Israel, they went up in full force to search for him, but David heard about it and went out to meet them. [9]Now the Philistines had come and raided the Valley of Rephaim; [10]so David inquired of God: "Shall I go and attack the Philistines? Will you hand them over to me?"

The LORD answered him, "Go, I will hand them over to you."

[11]So David and his men went up to Baal Perazim, and there he defeated them. He said, "As waters break out, God has broken out against my enemies by my hand." So that place was called Baal Perazim.[c] [12]The Philistines had abandoned their gods there, and David gave orders to burn them in the fire.

[13]Once more the Philistines raided the valley; [14]so David inquired of God again, and God answered him, "Do not go straight up, but circle around them and attack them in front of the balsam trees. [15]As soon as you hear the sound of marching in the tops of the balsam trees, move out to battle, because that will mean God has gone out in front of you to strike the Philistine army." [16]So David did as God commanded him, and they struck down the Philistine army, all the way from Gibeon to Gezer.

[17]So David's fame spread throughout every land, and the LORD made all the nations fear him.

The Ark Brought to Jerusalem

15 After David had constructed buildings for himself in the City of David, he prepared a place for the ark of God and pitched a tent for it. [2]Then David said, "No one but the Levites may carry the ark of God, because the LORD chose them to carry the ark of the LORD and to minister before him forever."

[3]David assembled all Israel in Jerusalem to bring up the ark of the LORD to the place he had prepared for it. [4]He called together the descendants of Aaron and the Levites:

[5]From the descendants of Kohath,
   Uriel the leader and 120 relatives;
[6]from the descendants of Merari,
   Asaiah the leader and 220 relatives;

---

[a]11 Perez Uzzah means outbreak against Uzzah.
[b]7 A variant of Eliada   [c]11 Baal Perazim means the lord who breaks out.

[7]from the descendants of Gershon,[a]
Joel the leader and 130 relatives;
[8]from the descendants of Elizaphan,
Shemaiah the leader and 200 relatives;
[9]from the descendants of Hebron,
Eliel the leader and 80 relatives;
[10]from the descendants of Uzziel,
Amminadab the leader and 112 relatives.

[11]Then David summoned Zadok and Abiathar the priests, and Uriel, Asaiah, Joel, Shemaiah, Eliel and Amminadab the Levites. [12]He said to them, "You are the heads of the Levitical families; you and your fellow Levites are to consecrate yourselves and bring up the ark of the Lord, the God of Israel, to the place I have prepared for it. [13]It was because you, the Levites, did not bring it up the first time that the Lord our God broke out in anger against us. We did not inquire of him about how to do it in the prescribed way." [14]So the priests and Levites consecrated themselves in order to bring up the ark of the Lord, the God of Israel. [15]And the Levites carried the ark of God with the poles on their shoulders, as Moses had commanded in accordance with the word of the Lord.

[16]David told the leaders of the Levites to appoint their brothers as singers to sing joyful songs, accompanied by musical instruments: lyres, harps and cymbals.

[17]So the Levites appointed Heman son of Joel; from his brothers, Asaph son of Berekiah; and from their brothers the Merarites, Ethan son of Kushaiah; [18]and with them their brothers next in rank: Zechariah,[b] Jaaziel, Shemiramoth, Jehiel, Unni, Eliab, Benaiah, Maaseiah, Mattithiah, Eliphelehu, Mikneiah, Obed-Edom and Jeiel,[c] the gatekeepers. [19]The musicians Heman, Asaph and Ethan were to sound the bronze cymbals; [20]Zechariah, Aziel, Shemiramoth, Jehiel, Unni, Eliab, Maaseiah and Benaiah were to play the lyres according to alamoth,[d] [21]and Mattithiah, Eliphelehu, Mikneiah, Obed-Edom, Jeiel and Azaziah were to play the harps, directing according to sheminith.[d] [22]Kenaniah the head Levite was in charge of the singing; that was his responsibility because he was skillful at it. [23]Berekiah and Elkanah were to be doorkeepers for the ark. [24]Shebaniah, Joshaphat, Nethanel, Amasai, Zechariah, Benaiah and Eliezer the priests were to blow trumpets before the ark of God. Obed-Edom and Jehiah were also to be doorkeepers for the ark.

[25]So David and the elders of Israel and the commanders of units of a thousand went to bring up the ark of the covenant of the Lord from the house of Obed-Edom, with rejoicing. [26]Because God had helped the Levites who were carrying the ark of the covenant of the Lord, seven bulls and seven rams were sacrificed. [27]Now David was clothed in a robe of fine linen, as were all the Levites who were carrying the ark, and as were the singers, and Kenaniah, who was in charge of the singing of the choirs. David also wore a linen ephod. [28]So all Israel brought up the ark of the covenant of the Lord with shouts, with the sounding of rams' horns and trumpets, and of cymbals, and the playing of lyres and harps.

[29]As the ark of the covenant of the Lord was entering the City of David, Michal daughter of Saul watched from a window. And when she saw King David dancing and celebrating, she despised him in her heart.

16 They brought the ark of God and set it inside the tent that David had pitched for it, and they presented burnt offerings and fellowship offerings[e] before God. [2]After David had finished sacrificing the burnt offerings and fellowship offerings, he blessed the people in the name of the Lord. [3]Then he gave a loaf of bread, a cake of dates and a cake of raisins to each Israelite man and woman.

[4]He appointed some of the Levites to minister before the ark of the Lord, to make petition, to give thanks, and to praise the Lord, the God of Israel: [5]Asaph was the chief, Zechariah second, then Jeiel, Shemiramoth, Jehiel, Mattithiah, Eliab, Benaiah, Obed-Edom and Jeiel. They were to play the lyres and harps, Asaph was to sound the cymbals, [6]and

---

[a]7 Hebrew Gershom, a variant of Gershon
[b]18 Three Hebrew manuscripts and most Septuagint manuscripts (see also verse 20 and 1 Chron. 16:5); most Hebrew manuscripts Zechariah son and or Zechariah, Ben and
[c]18 Hebrew; Septuagint (see also verse 21) Jeiel and Azaziah   [d]20,21 Probably a musical term
[e]1 Traditionally peace offerings; also in verse 2

> HE appointed some of the Levites to minister before the ark of the LORD, to make petition, to give thanks, and to praise the LORD, the God of Israel.
>
> 1 CHRONICLES 16:4

Benaiah and Jahaziel the priests were to blow the trumpets regularly before the ark of the covenant of God.

David's Psalm of Thanks

⁷That day David first committed to Asaph and his associates this psalm of thanks to the LORD:

⁸Give thanks to the LORD, call on
    his name;
  make known among the nations
    what he has done.
⁹Sing to him, sing praise to him;
  tell of all his wonderful acts.
¹⁰Glory in his holy name;
  let the hearts of those who seek the
    LORD rejoice.
¹¹Look to the LORD and his strength;
  seek his face always.
¹²Remember the wonders he has
    done,
  his miracles, and the judgments
    he pronounced,
¹³O descendants of Israel his servant,
  O sons of Jacob, his chosen ones.

¹⁴He is the LORD our God;
  his judgments are in all the earth.
¹⁵He remembers[a] his covenant
    forever,
  the word he commanded, for a
    thousand generations,
¹⁶the covenant he made with Abraham,
  the oath he swore to Isaac.
¹⁷He confirmed it to Jacob as a decree,
  to Israel as an everlasting
    covenant:
¹⁸"To you I will give the land of Canaan
  as the portion you will inherit."

¹⁹When they were but few in number,
  few indeed, and strangers in it,
²⁰they[b] wandered from nation to
    nation,
  from one kingdom to another.
²¹He allowed no man to oppress them;
  for their sake he rebuked kings:

²²"Do not touch my anointed ones;
  do my prophets no harm."

²³Sing to the LORD, all the earth;
  proclaim his salvation day
    after day.
²⁴Declare his glory among the nations,
  his marvelous deeds among all
    peoples.

²⁵For great is the LORD and most worthy
    of praise;
  he is to be feared above all gods.
²⁶For all the gods of the nations are
    idols,
  but the LORD made the heavens.
²⁷Splendor and majesty are before him;
  strength and joy in his dwelling
    place.

²⁸Ascribe to the LORD, O families
    of nations,
  ascribe to the LORD glory and
    strength,
²⁹ ascribe to the LORD the glory due
    his name.
  Bring an offering and come
    before him;
  worship the LORD in the splendor
    of his[c] holiness.
³⁰Tremble before him, all the earth!
  The world is firmly established; it
    cannot be moved.

³¹Let the heavens rejoice, let the earth
    be glad;
  let them say among the nations,
    "The LORD reigns!"
³²Let the sea resound, and all that is
    in it;
  let the fields be jubilant, and
    everything in them!
³³Then the trees of the forest will sing,
  they will sing for joy before
    the LORD,
  for he comes to judge the earth.

³⁴Give thanks to the LORD, for he
    is good;
  his love endures forever.

³⁵Cry out, "Save us, O God our Savior;
  gather us and deliver us from
    the nations,

---

[a]15 Some Septuagint manuscripts (see also Psalm 105:8); Hebrew *Remember*   [b]18–20 One Hebrew manuscript, Septuagint and Vulgate (see also Psalm 105:12); most Hebrew manuscripts *inherit, /*[19]*though you are but few in number, / few indeed, and strangers in it." /*[20]*They*   [c]29 Or *LORD with the splendor of*

that we may give thanks to your
holy name,
that we may glory in your praise."
36 Praise be to the LORD, the God
of Israel,
from everlasting to everlasting.

Then all the people said "Amen" and
"Praise the LORD."

37 David left Asaph and his associates
before the ark of the covenant of the
LORD to minister there regularly, according to each day's requirements. 38 He also
left Obed-Edom and his sixty-eight associates to minister with them. Obed-Edom
son of Jeduthun, and also Hosah, were
gatekeepers.

39 David left Zadok the priest and his
fellow priests before the tabernacle of
the LORD at the high place in Gibeon 40 to
present burnt offerings to the LORD on
the altar of burnt offering regularly,
morning and evening, in accordance
with everything written in the Law of the
LORD, which he had given Israel. 41 With
them were Heman and Jeduthun and the
rest of those chosen and designated by
name to give thanks to the LORD, "for his
love endures forever." 42 Heman and Jeduthun were responsible for the sounding of the trumpets and cymbals and for
the playing of the other instruments for
sacred song. The sons of Jeduthun were
stationed at the gate.

43 Then all the people left, each for his
own home, and David returned home to
bless his family.

God's Promise to David

17 After David was settled in his palace, he said to Nathan the prophet,
"Here I am, living in a palace of cedar,
while the ark of the covenant of the LORD
is under a tent."

2 Nathan replied to David, "Whatever
you have in mind, do it, for God is with
you."

3 That night the word of God came to
Nathan, saying:

4 "Go and tell my servant David,
'This is what the LORD says: You are
not the one to build me a house to
dwell in. 5 I have not dwelt in a house
from the day I brought Israel up out

of Egypt to this day. I have moved
from one tent site to another, from
one dwelling place to another.
6 Wherever I have moved with all the
Israelites, did I ever say to any of
their leaders[a] whom I commanded
to shepherd my people, "Why have
you not built me a house of cedar?"'

7 "Now then, tell my servant David,
'This is what the LORD Almighty says:
I took you from the pasture and from
following the flock, to be ruler over
my people Israel. 8 I have been with
you wherever you have gone, and I
have cut off all your enemies from
before you. Now I will make your
name like the names of the greatest
men of the earth. 9 And I will provide
a place for my people Israel and will
plant them so that they can have a
home of their own and no longer be
disturbed. Wicked people will not
oppress them anymore, as they did
at the beginning 10 and have done
ever since the time I appointed leaders over my people Israel. I will also
subdue all your enemies.

" 'I declare to you that the LORD
will build a house for you: 11 When
your days are over and you go to be
with your fathers, I will raise up your
offspring to succeed you, one of your
own sons, and I will establish his
kingdom. 12 He is the one who will
build a house for me, and I will establish his throne forever. 13 I will be
his father, and he will be my son. I
will never take my love away from
him, as I took it away from your predecessor. 14 I will set him over my
house and my kingdom forever; his
throne will be established forever.' "

15 Nathan reported to David all the
words of this entire revelation.

David's Prayer

16 Then King David went in and sat before the LORD, and he said:

"Who am I, O LORD God, and what
is my family, that you have brought
me this far? 17 And as if this were not
enough in your sight, O God, you

---

[a] 6 Traditionally judges; also in verse 10

have spoken about the future of the house of your servant. You have looked on me as though I were the most exalted of men, O Lord God.

18 "What more can David say to you for honoring your servant? For you know your servant, 19O Lord. For the sake of your servant and according to your will, you have done this great thing and made known all these great promises.

20 "There is no one like you, O Lord, and there is no God but you, as we have heard with our own ears. 21And who is like your people Israel—the one nation on earth whose God went out to redeem a people for himself, and to make a name for yourself, and to perform great and awesome wonders by driving out nations from before your people, whom you redeemed from Egypt? 22You made your people Israel your very own forever, and you, O Lord, have become their God.

23 "And now, Lord, let the promise you have made concerning your servant and his house be established forever. Do as you promised, 24so that it will be established and that your name will be great forever. Then men will say, 'The Lord Almighty, the God over Israel, is Israel's God!' And the house of your servant David will be established before you.

25 "You, my God, have revealed to your servant that you will build a house for him. So your servant has found courage to pray to you. 26O Lord, you are God! You have promised these good things to your servant. 27Now you have been pleased to bless the house of your servant, that it may continue forever in your sight; for you, O Lord, have blessed it, and it will be blessed forever."

David's Victories

18 In the course of time, David defeated the Philistines and subdued them, and he took Gath and its surrounding villages from the control of the Philistines.

2David also defeated the Moabites, and they became subject to him and brought tribute.

3Moreover, David fought Hadadezer king of Zobah, as far as Hamath, when he went to establish his control along the Euphrates River. 4David captured a thousand of his chariots, seven thousand charioteers and twenty thousand foot soldiers. He hamstrung all but a hundred of the chariot horses.

5When the Arameans of Damascus came to help Hadadezer king of Zobah, David struck down twenty-two thousand of them. 6He put garrisons in the Aramean kingdom of Damascus, and the Arameans became subject to him and brought tribute. The Lord gave David victory everywhere he went.

7David took the gold shields carried by the officers of Hadadezer and brought them to Jerusalem. 8From Tebah[a] and Cun, towns that belonged to Hadadezer, David took a great quantity of bronze, which Solomon used to make the bronze Sea, the pillars and various bronze articles.

9When Tou king of Hamath heard that David had defeated the entire army of Hadadezer king of Zobah, 10he sent his son Hadoram to King David to greet him and congratulate him on his victory in battle over Hadadezer, who had been at war with Tou. Hadoram brought all kinds of articles of gold and silver and bronze.

11King David dedicated these articles to the Lord, as he had done with the silver and gold he had taken from all these nations: Edom and Moab, the Ammonites and the Philistines, and Amalek.

12Abishai son of Zeruiah struck down eighteen thousand Edomites in the Valley of Salt. 13He put garrisons in Edom, and all the Edomites became subject to David. The Lord gave David victory everywhere he went.

David's Officials

14David reigned over all Israel, doing what was just and right for all his people. 15Joab son of Zeruiah was over the army; Jehoshaphat son of Ahilud was recorder;

---

a8 Hebrew *Tibhath,* a variant of *Tebah*

¹⁶Zadok son of Ahitub and Ahimelech*a* son of Abiathar were priests; Shavsha was secretary; ¹⁷Benaiah son of Jehoiada was over the Kerethites and Pelethites; and David's sons were chief officials at the king's side.

The Battle Against the Ammonites

19 In the course of time, Nahash king of the Ammonites died, and his son succeeded him as king. ²David thought, "I will show kindness to Hanun son of Nahash, because his father showed kindness to me." So David sent a delegation to express his sympathy to Hanun concerning his father.

When David's men came to Hanun in the land of the Ammonites to express sympathy to him, ³the Ammonite nobles said to Hanun, "Do you think David is honoring your father by sending men to you to express sympathy? Haven't his men come to you to explore and spy out the country and overthrow it?" ⁴So Hanun seized David's men, shaved them, cut off their garments in the middle at the buttocks, and sent them away.

⁵When someone came and told David about the men, he sent messengers to meet them, for they were greatly humiliated. The king said, "Stay at Jericho till your beards have grown, and then come back."

⁶When the Ammonites realized that they had become a stench in David's nostrils, Hanun and the Ammonites sent a thousand talents*b* of silver to hire chariots and charioteers from Aram Naharaim,*c* Aram Maacah and Zobah. ⁷They hired thirty-two thousand chariots and charioteers, as well as the king of Maacah with his troops, who came and camped near Medeba, while the Ammonites were mustered from their towns and moved out for battle.

⁸On hearing this, David sent Joab out with the entire army of fighting men. ⁹The Ammonites came out and drew up in battle formation at the entrance to their city, while the kings who had come were by themselves in the open country.

¹⁰Joab saw that there were battle lines in front of him and behind him; so he selected some of the best troops in Israel and deployed them against the Arame-ans. ¹¹He put the rest of the men under the command of Abishai his brother, and they were deployed against the Ammonites. ¹²Joab said, "If the Arameans are too strong for me, then you are to rescue me; but if the Ammonites are too strong for you, then I will rescue you. ¹³Be strong and let us fight bravely for our people and the cities of our God. The Lord will do what is good in his sight."

¹⁴Then Joab and the troops with him advanced to fight the Arameans, and they fled before him. ¹⁵When the Ammonites saw that the Arameans were fleeing, they too fled before his brother Abishai and went inside the city. So Joab went back to Jerusalem.

¹⁶After the Arameans saw that they had been routed by Israel, they sent messengers and had Arameans brought from beyond the River,*d* with Shophach the commander of Hadadezer's army leading them.

¹⁷When David was told of this, he gathered all Israel and crossed the Jordan; he advanced against them and formed his battle lines opposite them. David formed his lines to meet the Arameans in battle, and they fought against him. ¹⁸But they fled before Israel, and David killed seven thousand of their charioteers and forty thousand of their foot soldiers. He also killed Shophach the commander of their army.

¹⁹When the vassals of Hadadezer saw that they had been defeated by Israel, they made peace with David and became subject to him.

So the Arameans were not willing to help the Ammonites anymore.

The Capture of Rabbah

20 In the spring, at the time when kings go off to war, Joab led out the armed forces. He laid waste the land of the Ammonites and went to Rabbah and besieged it, but David remained in Jerusalem. Joab attacked Rabbah and left it in ruins. ²David took the crown

---

a16 Some Hebrew manuscripts, Vulgate and Syriac (see also 2 Samuel 8:17); most Hebrew manuscripts *Abimelech*   *b6* That is, about 37 tons (about 34 metric tons)   *c6* That is, Northwest Mesopotamia   *d16* That is, the Euphrates

from the head of their king[a]—its weight was found to be a talent[b] of gold, and it was set with precious stones—and it was placed on David's head. He took a great quantity of plunder from the city ³and brought out the people who were there, consigning them to labor with saws and with iron picks and axes. David did this to all the Ammonite towns. Then David and his entire army returned to Jerusalem.

War With the Philistines

⁴In the course of time, war broke out with the Philistines, at Gezer. At that time Sibbecai the Hushathite killed Sippai, one of the descendants of the Rephaites, and the Philistines were subjugated.

⁵In another battle with the Philistines, Elhanan son of Jair killed Lahmi the brother of Goliath the Gittite, who had a spear with a shaft like a weaver's rod.

⁶In still another battle, which took place at Gath, there was a huge man with six fingers on each hand and six toes on each foot—twenty-four in all. He also was descended from Rapha. ⁷When he taunted Israel, Jonathan son of Shimea, David's brother, killed him.

⁸These were descendants of Rapha in Gath, and they fell at the hands of David and his men.

David Numbers the Fighting Men

21 Satan rose up against Israel and incited David to take a census of Israel. ²So David said to Joab and the commanders of the troops, "Go and count the Israelites from Beersheba to Dan. Then report back to me so that I may know how many there are."

³But Joab replied, "May the LORD multiply his troops a hundred times over. My lord the king, are they not all my lord's subjects? Why does my lord want to do this? Why should he bring guilt on Israel?"

⁴The king's word, however, overruled Joab; so Joab left and went throughout Israel and then came back to Jerusalem. ⁵Joab reported the number of the fighting men to David: In all Israel there were one million one hundred thousand men who could handle a sword, including four hundred and seventy thousand in Judah.

⁶But Joab did not include Levi and Benjamin in the numbering, because the king's command was repulsive to him. ⁷This command was also evil in the sight of God; so he punished Israel.

⁸Then David said to God, "I have sinned greatly by doing this. Now, I beg you, take away the guilt of your servant. I have done a very foolish thing."

⁹The LORD said to Gad, David's seer, ¹⁰"Go and tell David, 'This is what the LORD says: I am giving you three options. Choose one of them for me to carry out against you.'"

¹¹So Gad went to David and said to him, "This is what the LORD says: 'Take your choice: ¹²three years of famine, three months of being swept away[c] before your enemies, with their swords overtaking you, or three days of the sword of the LORD—days of plague in the land, with the angel of the LORD ravaging every part of Israel.' Now then, decide how I should answer the one who sent me."

¹³David said to Gad, "I am in deep distress. Let me fall into the hands of the LORD, for his mercy is very great; but do not let me fall into the hands of men."

¹⁴So the LORD sent a plague on Israel, and seventy thousand men of Israel fell dead. ¹⁵And God sent an angel to destroy Jerusalem. But as the angel was doing so, the LORD saw it and was grieved because of the calamity and said to the angel who was destroying the people, "Enough! Withdraw your hand." The angel of the LORD was then standing at the threshing floor of Araunah[d] the Jebusite.

¹⁶David looked up and saw the angel of the LORD standing between heaven and earth, with a drawn sword in his hand extended over Jerusalem. Then David and the elders, clothed in sackcloth, fell facedown.

¹⁷David said to God, "Was it not I who ordered the fighting men to be counted? I am the one who has sinned and done wrong. These are but sheep. What have they done? O LORD my God, let

---

[a]2 Or of Milcom, that is, Molech   [b]2 That is, about 75 pounds (about 34 kilograms)
[c]12 Hebrew; Septuagint and Vulgate (see also 2 Samuel 24:13) of fleeing   [d]15 Hebrew Ornan, a variant of Araunah; also in verses 18–28

your hand fall upon me and my family, but do not let this plague remain on your people."

¹⁸Then the angel of the LORD ordered Gad to tell David to go up and build an altar to the LORD on the threshing floor of Araunah the Jebusite. ¹⁹So David went up in obedience to the word that Gad had spoken in the name of the LORD.

²⁰While Araunah was threshing wheat, he turned and saw the angel; his four sons who were with him hid themselves. ²¹Then David approached, and when Araunah looked and saw him, he left the threshing floor and bowed down before David with his face to the ground.

²²David said to him, "Let me have the site of your threshing floor so I can build an altar to the LORD, that the plague on the people may be stopped. Sell it to me at the full price."

²³Araunah said to David, "Take it! Let my lord the king do whatever pleases him. Look, I will give the oxen for the burnt offerings, the threshing sledges for the wood, and the wheat for the grain offering. I will give all this."

²⁴But King David replied to Araunah, "No, I insist on paying the full price. I will not take for the LORD what is yours, or sacrifice a burnt offering that costs me nothing."

²⁵So David paid Araunah six hundred shekels*a* of gold for the site. ²⁶David built an altar to the LORD there and sacrificed burnt offerings and fellowship offerings.*b* He called on the LORD, and the LORD answered him with fire from heaven on the altar of burnt offering.

²⁷Then the LORD spoke to the angel, and he put his sword back into its sheath. ²⁸At that time, when David saw that the LORD had answered him on the threshing floor of Araunah the Jebusite, he offered sacrifices there. ²⁹The tabernacle of the LORD, which Moses had made in the desert, and the altar of burnt offering were at that time on the high place at Gibeon. ³⁰But David could not go before it to inquire of God, because he was afraid of the sword of the angel of the LORD.

22 Then David said, "The house of the LORD God is to be here, and also the altar of burnt offering for Israel."

Preparations for the Temple

²So David gave orders to assemble the aliens living in Israel, and from among them he appointed stonecutters to prepare dressed stone for building the house of God. ³He provided a large amount of iron to make nails for the doors of the gateways and for the fittings, and more bronze than could be weighed. ⁴He also provided more cedar logs than could be counted, for the Sidonians and Tyrians had brought large numbers of them to David.

⁵David said, "My son Solomon is young and inexperienced, and the house to be built for the LORD should be of great magnificence and fame and splendor in the sight of all the nations. Therefore I will make preparations for it." So David made extensive preparations before his death.

⁶Then he called for his son Solomon and charged him to build a house for the LORD, the God of Israel. ⁷David said to Solomon: "My son, I had it in my heart to build a house for the Name of the LORD my God. ⁸But this word of the LORD came to me: 'You have shed much blood and have fought many wars. You are not to build a house for my Name, because you have shed much blood on the earth in my sight. ⁹But you will have a son who will be a man of peace and rest, and I will give him rest from all his enemies on every side. His name will be Solomon,*c* and I will grant Israel peace and quiet during his reign. ¹⁰He is the one who will build a house for my Name. He will be my son, and I will be his father. And I will establish the throne of his kingdom over Israel forever.'

¹¹"Now, my son, the LORD be with you, and may you have success and build the house of the LORD your God, as he said you would. ¹²May the LORD give you discretion and understanding when he puts you in command over Israel, so that you may keep the law of the LORD your God. ¹³Then you will have success if you are

---

a25 That is, about 15 pounds (about 7 kilograms)
b26 Traditionally *peace offerings*   *c9* *Solomon* sounds like and may be derived from the Hebrew for *peace.*

careful to observe the decrees and laws that the LORD gave Moses for Israel. Be strong and courageous. Do not be afraid or discouraged.

¹⁴"I have taken great pains to provide for the temple of the LORD a hundred thousand talents*ᵃ* of gold, a million talents*ᵇ* of silver, quantities of bronze and iron too great to be weighed, and wood and stone. And you may add to them. ¹⁵You have many workmen: stonecutters, masons and carpenters, as well as men skilled in every kind of work ¹⁶in gold and silver, bronze and iron—craftsmen beyond number. Now begin the work, and the LORD be with you."

¹⁷Then David ordered all the leaders of Israel to help his son Solomon. ¹⁸He said to them, "Is not the LORD your God with you? And has he not granted you rest on every side? For he has handed the inhabitants of the land over to me, and the land is subject to the LORD and to his people. ¹⁹Now devote your heart and soul to seeking the LORD your God. Begin to build the sanctuary of the LORD God, so that you may bring the ark of the covenant of the LORD and the sacred articles belonging to God into the temple that will be built for the Name of the LORD."

The Levites

23 When David was old and full of years, he made his son Solomon king over Israel.

²He also gathered together all the leaders of Israel, as well as the priests and Levites. ³The Levites thirty years old or more were counted, and the total number of men was thirty-eight thousand. ⁴David said, "Of these, twenty-four thousand are to supervise the work of the temple of the LORD and six thousand are to be officials and judges. ⁵Four thousand are to be gatekeepers and four thousand are to praise the LORD with the musical instruments I have provided for that purpose."

⁶David divided the Levites into groups corresponding to the sons of Levi: Gershon, Kohath and Merari.

Gershonites

⁷Belonging to the Gershonites:
Ladan and Shimei.

⁸The sons of Ladan:
Jehiel the first, Zetham and Joel—three in all.
⁹The sons of Shimei:
Shelomoth, Haziel and Haran—three in all.
These were the heads of the families of Ladan.
¹⁰And the sons of Shimei:
Jahath, Ziza,*ᶜ* Jeush and Beriah.
These were the sons of Shimei—four in all.
¹¹Jahath was the first and Ziza the second, but Jeush and Beriah did not have many sons; so they were counted as one family with one assignment.

Kohathites

¹²The sons of Kohath:
Amram, Izhar, Hebron and Uzziel—four in all.
¹³The sons of Amram:
Aaron and Moses.

Aaron was set apart, he and his descendants forever, to consecrate the most holy things, to offer sacrifices before the LORD, to minister before him and to pronounce blessings in his name forever. ¹⁴The sons of Moses the man of God were counted as part of the tribe of Levi.
¹⁵The sons of Moses:
Gershom and Eliezer.
¹⁶The descendants of Gershom:
Shubael was the first.
¹⁷The descendants of Eliezer:
Rehabiah was the first.
Eliezer had no other sons, but the sons of Rehabiah were very numerous.
¹⁸The sons of Izhar:
Shelomith was the first.
¹⁹The sons of Hebron:
Jeriah the first, Amariah the second, Jahaziel the third and Jekameam the fourth.
²⁰The sons of Uzziel:
Micah the first and Isshiah the second.

ᵃ14 That is, about 3,750 tons (about 3,450 metric tons)   ᵇ14 That is, about 37,500 tons (about 34,500 metric tons)   ᶜ10 One Hebrew manuscript, Septuagint and Vulgate (see also verse 11); most Hebrew manuscripts Zina

Merarites

²¹The sons of Merari:
Mahli and Mushi.
The sons of Mahli:
Eleazar and Kish.
²²Eleazar died without having sons:
he had only daughters. Their
cousins, the sons of Kish, married
them.
²³The sons of Mushi:
Mahli, Eder and Jerimoth—three
in all.

²⁴These were the descendants of Levi
by their families—the heads of families
as they were registered under their
names and counted individually, that is,
the workers twenty years old or more
who served in the temple of the LORD.
²⁵For David had said, "Since the LORD, the
God of Israel, has granted rest to his people and has come to dwell in Jerusalem
forever, ²⁶the Levites no longer need to
carry the tabernacle or any of the articles
used in its service." ²⁷According to the
last instructions of David, the Levites
were counted from those twenty years
old or more.

²⁸The duty of the Levites was to help
Aaron's descendants in the service of the
temple of the LORD: to be in charge of the
courtyards, the side rooms, the purification of all sacred things and the performance of other duties at the house of
God. ²⁹They were in charge of the bread
set out on the table, the flour for the
grain offerings, the unleavened wafers,
the baking and the mixing, and all measurements of quantity and size. ³⁰They
were also to stand every morning to
thank and praise the LORD. They were to
do the same in the evening ³¹and whenever burnt offerings were presented to
the LORD on Sabbaths and at New Moon
festivals and at appointed feasts. They
were to serve before the LORD regularly
in the proper number and in the way prescribed for them.

> THEY were also to stand every morning
> to thank and praise the LORD. They were
> to do the same in the evening.
>
> 1 CHRONICLES 23:30

³²And so the Levites carried out their
responsibilities for the Tent of Meeting,
for the Holy Place and, under their brothers the descendants of Aaron, for the service of the temple of the LORD.

The Divisions of Priests

24 These were the divisions of the
sons of Aaron:
The sons of Aaron were Nadab, Abihu,
Eleazar and Ithamar. ²But Nadab and
Abihu died before their father did, and
they had no sons; so Eleazar and Ithamar
served as the priests. ³With the help of Zadok a descendant of Eleazar and Ahimelech a descendant of Ithamar, David
separated them into divisions for their
appointed order of ministering. ⁴A larger
number of leaders were found among Eleazar's descendants than among Ithamar's, and they were divided accordingly:
sixteen heads of families from Eleazar's
descendants and eight heads of families
from Ithamar's descendants. ⁵They divided them impartially by drawing lots, for
there were officials of the sanctuary and
officials of God among the descendants
of both Eleazar and Ithamar.

⁶The scribe Shemaiah son of Nethanel,
a Levite, recorded their names in the
presence of the king and of the officials:
Zadok the priest, Ahimelech son of Abiathar and the heads of families of the
priests and of the Levites—one family
being taken from Eleazar and then one
from Ithamar.

⁷The first lot fell to Jehoiarib,
the second to Jedaiah,
⁸the third to Harim,
the fourth to Seorim,
⁹the fifth to Malkijah,
the sixth to Mijamin,
¹⁰the seventh to Hakkoz,
the eighth to Abijah,
¹¹the ninth to Jeshua,
the tenth to Shecaniah,
¹²the eleventh to Eliashib,
the twelfth to Jakim,
¹³the thirteenth to Huppah,
the fourteenth to Jeshebeab,
¹⁴the fifteenth to Bilgah,
the sixteenth to Immer,
¹⁵the seventeenth to Hezir,
the eighteenth to Happizzez,

¹⁶ the nineteenth to Pethahiah,
the twentieth to Jehezkel,
¹⁷ the twenty-first to Jakin,
the twenty-second to Gamul,
¹⁸ the twenty-third to Delaiah
and the twenty-fourth to Maaziah.

¹⁹ This was their appointed order of ministering when they entered the temple of the LORD, according to the regulations prescribed for them by their forefather Aaron, as the LORD, the God of Israel, had commanded him.

[**WEDNESDAY**]

Indiscriminate Thanks

23:30 THEY WERE ALSO TO STAND EVERY MORNING TO THANK AND PRAISE THE LORD. THEY WERE TO DO THE SAME IN THE EVENING.

Try to get your mind around the sheer numbers involved in the exercise of thanksgiving in the temple. Thirty-eight thousand Levites are involved. They work in shifts, morning and evening. Four thousand of them play in the band (see 23:1–5). The care and attention given to thanksgiving are extravagant and indiscriminate compared to modern Christian standards, or just about any standards for that matter. Thanksgiving was formalized, to be done twice daily, regardless of how anyone felt that day. No committee was convened to discuss whether they had sufficient reasons to be thankful; God commanded that they do it because he believed they always had sufficient reasons. God's mind hasn't changed on this subject.

"Thanksgiving is not a task to be undertaken lightly," writes Virginia Stem Owens. "It is not for dilettantes or aesthetes. One does not dabble in praise for one's own amusement, nor train the intellect and develop perceptual skills to add to his repertoire. We're not talking about the world as a free course in art appreciation. No. *Thanksgiving is not a result of perception; thanksgiving is the access to perception*"[1] [italics added]. We think we need to see something in order to be thankful. But it works the other way: We need to give thanks so we can see. If we wait until we see it, we will never see it. That's why Paul said to always be joyful, to pray continually and to give thanks in all circumstances (see 1 Thessalonians 5:16–18).

But we need help. We must give thanks so that we may be thankful, and we pray for hearts willing to do that. George Herbert prayed a prayer we may all pray:

> Thou that hast given so much to me,
> Give one thing more, a grateful heart . . .
> Not thankful when it pleaseth me,
> As if Thy blessings had spare days;
> But such a heart whose pulse may be
> Thy praise.[2]

PRAY:
Pray George Herbert's prayer.

FOR YOUR NEXT DEVOTIONAL READING, GO TO PAGE 487.

The Rest of the Levites

20 As for the rest of the descendants of Levi:
from the sons of Amram: Shubael;
from the sons of Shubael: Jehdeiah.
21 As for Rehabiah, from his sons:
Isshiah was the first.
22 From the Izharites: Shelomoth;
from the sons of Shelomoth: Jahath.
23 The sons of Hebron: Jeriah the first,[a]
Amariah the second, Jahaziel the third and Jekameam the fourth.
24 The son of Uzziel: Micah;
from the sons of Micah: Shamir.
25 The brother of Micah: Isshiah;
from the sons of Isshiah: Zechariah.
26 The sons of Merari: Mahli and Mushi.
The son of Jaaziah: Beno.
27 The sons of Merari:
from Jaaziah: Beno, Shoham, Zaccur and Ibri.
28 From Mahli: Eleazar, who had no sons.
29 From Kish: the son of Kish:
Jerahmeel.
30 And the sons of Mushi: Mahli, Eder and Jerimoth.

These were the Levites, according to their families. 31 They also cast lots, just as their brothers the descendants of Aaron did, in the presence of King David and of Zadok, Ahimelech, and the heads of families of the priests and of the Levites. The families of the oldest brother were treated the same as those of the youngest.

The Singers

25 David, together with the commanders of the army, set apart some of the sons of Asaph, Heman and Jeduthun for the ministry of prophesying, accompanied by harps, lyres and cymbals. Here is the list of the men who performed this service:

2 From the sons of Asaph:
Zaccur, Joseph, Nethaniah and Asarelah. The sons of Asaph were under the supervision of Asaph, who prophesied under the king's supervision.

3 As for Jeduthun, from his sons:
Gedaliah, Zeri, Jeshaiah, Shimei,[b] Hashabiah and Mattithiah, six in all, under the supervision of their father Jeduthun, who prophesied, using the harp in thanking and praising the LORD.
4 As for Heman, from his sons:
Bukkiah, Mattaniah, Uzziel, Shubael and Jerimoth; Hananiah, Hanani, Eliathah, Giddalti and Romamti-Ezer; Joshbekashah, Mallothi, Hothir and Mahazioth. 5 All these were sons of Heman the king's seer. They were given him through the promises of God to exalt him.[c] God gave Heman fourteen sons and three daughters.

6 All these men were under the supervision of their fathers for the music of the temple of the LORD, with cymbals, lyres and harps, for the ministry at the house of God. Asaph, Jeduthun and Heman were under the supervision of the king. 7 Along with their relatives—all of them trained and skilled in music for the LORD—they numbered 288. 8 Young and old alike, teacher as well as student, cast lots for their duties.

9 The first lot, which was for
Asaph, fell to Joseph,
his sons and relatives,[d]   12[e]
the second to Gedaliah,
he and his relatives
and sons,   12
10 the third to Zaccur,
his sons and relatives,   12
11 the fourth to Izri,[f]
his sons and relatives,   12
12 the fifth to Nethaniah,
his sons and relatives,   12
13 the sixth to Bukkiah,
his sons and relatives,   12
14 the seventh to Jesarelah,[g]
his sons and relatives,   12

---

[a]23 Two Hebrew manuscripts and some Septuagint manuscripts (see also 1 Chron. 23:19); most Hebrew manuscripts *The sons of Jeriah:*
[b]3 One Hebrew manuscript and some Septuagint manuscripts (see also verse 17); most Hebrew manuscripts do not have *Shimei.*   [c]5 Hebrew *exalt the horn*   [d]9 See Septuagint; Hebrew does not have *his sons and relatives.*   [e]9 See the total in verse 7; Hebrew does not have *twelve.*
[f]11 A variant of *Zeri*   [g]14 A variant of *Asarelah*

¹⁵the eighth to Jeshaiah,
   his sons and relatives,   12
¹⁶the ninth to Mattaniah,
   his sons and relatives,   12
¹⁷the tenth to Shimei,
   his sons and relatives,   12
¹⁸the eleventh to Azarel,ᵃ
   his sons and relatives,   12
¹⁹the twelfth to Hashabiah,
   his sons and relatives,   12
²⁰the thirteenth to Shubael,
   his sons and relatives,   12
²¹the fourteenth to Mattithiah,
   his sons and relatives,   12
²²the fifteenth to Jerimoth,
   his sons and relatives,   12
²³the sixteenth to Hananiah,
   his sons and relatives,   12
²⁴the seventeenth to
   Joshbekashah,
   his sons and relatives,   12
²⁵the eighteenth to Hanani,
   his sons and relatives,   12
²⁶the nineteenth to Mallothi,
   his sons and relatives,   12
²⁷the twentieth to Eliathah,
   his sons and relatives,   12
²⁸the twenty-first to Hothir,
   his sons and relatives,   12
²⁹the twenty-second to Giddalti,
   his sons and relatives,   12
³⁰the twenty-third to Mahazioth,
   his sons and relatives,   12
³¹the twenty-fourth to
   Romamti-Ezer,
   his sons and relatives,   12

The Gatekeepers

26 The divisions of the gatekeepers:

From the Korahites: Meshelemiah son of Kore, one of the sons of Asaph.
²Meshelemiah had sons:
   Zechariah the firstborn,
   Jediael the second,
   Zebadiah the third,
   Jathniel the fourth,
 ³Elam the fifth,
   Jehohanan the sixth
   and Eliehoenai the seventh.
⁴Obed-Edom also had sons:
   Shemaiah the firstborn,
   Jehozabad the second,
   Joah the third,

   Sacar the fourth,
   Nethanel the fifth,
 ⁵Ammiel the sixth,
   Issachar the seventh
   and Peullethai the eighth.
   (For God had blessed Obed-Edom.)

⁶His son Shemaiah also had sons, who were leaders in their father's family because they were very capable men. ⁷The sons of Shemaiah: Othni, Rephael, Obed and Elzabad; his relatives Elihu and Semakiah were also able men. ⁸All these were descendants of Obed-Edom; they and their sons and their relatives were capable men with the strength to do the work—descendants of Obed-Edom, 62 in all.

⁹Meshelemiah had sons and relatives, who were able men—18 in all.

¹⁰Hosah the Merarite had sons: Shimri the first (although he was not the firstborn, his father had appointed him the first), ¹¹Hilkiah the second, Tabaliah the third and Zechariah the fourth. The sons and relatives of Hosah were 13 in all.

¹²These divisions of the gatekeepers, through their chief men, had duties for ministering in the temple of the LORD, just as their relatives had. ¹³Lots were cast for each gate, according to their families, young and old alike.

¹⁴The lot for the East Gate fell to Shelemiah.ᵇ Then lots were cast for his son Zechariah, a wise counselor, and the lot for the North Gate fell to him. ¹⁵The lot for the South Gate fell to Obed-Edom, and the lot for the storehouse fell to his sons. ¹⁶The lots for the West Gate and the Shalleketh Gate on the upper road fell to Shuppim and Hosah.

Guard was alongside of guard: ¹⁷There were six Levites a day on the east, four a day on the north, four a day on the south and two at a time at the storehouse. ¹⁸As for the court to the west, there were four at the road and two at the court itself.

ᵃ18 A variant of *Uzziel*   ᵇ14 A variant of *Meshelemiah*

¹⁹These were the divisions of the gate-keepers who were descendants of Korah and Merari.

The Treasurers and Other Officials

²⁰Their fellow Levites were*a* in charge of the treasuries of the house of God and the treasuries for the dedicated things.

²¹The descendants of Ladan, who were Gershonites through Ladan and who were heads of families belonging to Ladan the Gershonite, were Jehieli, ²²the sons of Jehieli, Zetham and his brother Joel. They were in charge of the treasuries of the temple of the LORD.

²³From the Amramites, the Izharites, the Hebronites and the Uzzielites:

²⁴Shubael, a descendant of Gershom son of Moses, was the officer in charge of the treasuries. ²⁵His relatives through Eliezer: Rehabiah his son, Jeshaiah his son, Joram his son, Zicri his son and Shelomith his son. ²⁶Shelomith and his relatives were in charge of all the treasuries for the things dedicated by King David, by the heads of families who were the commanders of thousands and commanders of hundreds, and by the other army commanders. ²⁷Some of the plunder taken in battle they dedicated for the repair of the temple of the LORD. ²⁸And everything dedicated by Samuel the seer and by Saul son of Kish, Abner son of Ner and Joab son of Zeruiah, and all the other dedicated things were in the care of Shelomith and his relatives.

²⁹From the Izharites: Kenaniah and his sons were assigned duties away from the temple, as officials and judges over Israel.

³⁰From the Hebronites: Hashabiah and his relatives—seventeen hundred able men—were responsible in Israel west of the Jordan for all the work of the LORD and for the king's service. ³¹As for the Hebronites, Jeriah was their chief according to the genealogical records of their families. In the fortieth year of David's reign a search was made in the records, and capable men among the Hebronites were found at Jazer in Gilead. ³²Jeriah had twenty-seven hundred relatives, who were able men and heads of families, and King David put them in charge of the Reubenites, the Gadites and the half-tribe of Manasseh for every matter pertaining to God and for the affairs of the king.

Army Divisions

27 This is the list of the Israelites— heads of families, commanders of thousands and commanders of hundreds, and their officers, who served the king in all that concerned the army divisions that were on duty month by month throughout the year. Each division consisted of 24,000 men.

²In charge of the first division, for the first month, was Jashobeam son of Zabdiel. There were 24,000 men in his division. ³He was a descendant of Perez and chief of all the army officers for the first month.

⁴In charge of the division for the second month was Dodai the Ahohite; Mikloth was the leader of his division. There were 24,000 men in his division.

⁵The third army commander, for the third month, was Benaiah son of Jehoiada the priest. He was chief and there were 24,000 men in his division. ⁶This was the Benaiah who was a mighty man among the Thirty and was over the Thirty. His son Ammizabad was in charge of his division.

⁷The fourth, for the fourth month, was Asahel the brother of Joab; his son Zebadiah was his successor. There were 24,000 men in his division.

⁸The fifth, for the fifth month, was the commander Shamhuth the Izrahite. There were 24,000 men in his division.

⁹The sixth, for the sixth month, was Ira the son of Ikkesh the Tekoite. There were 24,000 men in his division.

a20 Septuagint; Hebrew As for the Levites, Ahijah was

¹⁰The seventh, for the seventh month, was Helez the Pelonite, an Ephraimite. There were 24,000 men in his division.

¹¹The eighth, for the eighth month, was Sibbecai the Hushathite, a Zerahite. There were 24,000 men in his division.

¹²The ninth, for the ninth month, was Abiezer the Anathothite, a Benjamite. There were 24,000 men in his division.

¹³The tenth, for the tenth month, was Maharai the Netophathite, a Zerahite. There were 24,000 men in his division.

¹⁴The eleventh, for the eleventh month, was Benaiah the Pirathonite, an Ephraimite. There were 24,000 men in his division.

¹⁵The twelfth, for the twelfth month, was Heldai the Netophathite, from the family of Othniel. There were 24,000 men in his division.

Officers of the Tribes

¹⁶The officers over the tribes of Israel:

over the Reubenites: Eliezer son of Zicri;

over the Simeonites: Shephatiah son of Maacah;

¹⁷over Levi: Hashabiah son of Kemuel;

over Aaron: Zadok;

¹⁸over Judah: Elihu, a brother of David;

over Issachar: Omri son of Michael;

¹⁹over Zebulun: Ishmaiah son of Obadiah;

over Naphtali: Jerimoth son of Azriel;

²⁰over the Ephraimites: Hoshea son of Azaziah;

over half the tribe of Manasseh: Joel son of Pedaiah;

²¹over the half-tribe of Manasseh in Gilead: Iddo son of Zechariah;

over Benjamin: Jaasiel son of Abner;

²²over Dan: Azarel son of Jeroham.

These were the officers over the tribes of Israel.

²³David did not take the number of the men twenty years old or less, because the LORD had promised to make Israel as numerous as the stars in the sky. ²⁴Joab son of Zeruiah began to count the men but did not finish. Wrath came on Israel on account of this numbering, and the number was not entered in the book[a] of the annals of King David.

The King's Overseers

²⁵Azmaveth son of Adiel was in charge of the royal storehouses.

Jonathan son of Uzziah was in charge of the storehouses in the outlying districts, in the towns, the villages and the watchtowers.

²⁶Ezri son of Kelub was in charge of the field workers who farmed the land.

²⁷Shimei the Ramathite was in charge of the vineyards.

Zabdi the Shiphmite was in charge of the produce of the vineyards for the wine vats.

²⁸Baal-Hanan the Gederite was in charge of the olive and sycamore-fig trees in the western foothills.

Joash was in charge of the supplies of olive oil.

²⁹Shitrai the Sharonite was in charge of the herds grazing in Sharon.

Shaphat son of Adlai was in charge of the herds in the valleys.

³⁰Obil the Ishmaelite was in charge of the camels.

Jehdeiah the Meronothite was in charge of the donkeys.

³¹Jaziz the Hagrite was in charge of the flocks.

All these were the officials in charge of King David's property.

³²Jonathan, David's uncle, was a counselor, a man of insight and a scribe. Jehiel son of Hacmoni took care of the king's sons.

³³Ahithophel was the king's counselor. Hushai the Arkite was the king's friend. ³⁴Ahithophel was succeeded by Jehoiada son of Benaiah and by Abiathar.

Joab was the commander of the royal army.

David's Plans for the Temple

28 David summoned all the officials of Israel to assemble at Jerusalem: the officers over the tribes, the commanders of the divisions in the service of the king, the commanders of thou-

[a] 24 Septuagint; Hebrew *number*

sands and commanders of hundreds, and the officials in charge of all the property and livestock belonging to the king and his sons, together with the palace officials, the mighty men and all the brave warriors.

²King David rose to his feet and said: "Listen to me, my brothers and my people. I had it in my heart to build a house as a place of rest for the ark of the covenant of the LORD, for the footstool of our God, and I made plans to build it. ³But God said to me, 'You are not to build a house for my Name, because you are a warrior and have shed blood.'

⁴"Yet the LORD, the God of Israel, chose me from my whole family to be king over Israel forever. He chose Judah as leader, and from the house of Judah he chose my family, and from my father's sons he was pleased to make me king over all Israel. ⁵Of all my sons—and the LORD has given me many—he has chosen my son Solomon to sit on the throne of the kingdom of the LORD over Israel. ⁶He said to me: 'Solomon your son is the one who will build my house and my courts, for I have chosen him to be my son, and I will be his father. ⁷I will establish his kingdom forever if he is unswerving in carrying out my commands and laws, as is being done at this time.'

⁸"So now I charge you in the sight of all Israel and of the assembly of the LORD, and in the hearing of our God: Be careful to follow all the commands of the LORD your God, that you may possess this good land and pass it on as an inheritance to your descendants forever.

⁹"And you, my son Solomon, acknowledge the God of your father, and serve him with wholehearted devotion and with a willing mind, for the LORD searches every heart and understands every motive behind the thoughts. If you seek him, he will be found by you; but if you forsake him, he will reject you forever. ¹⁰Consider now, for the LORD has chosen you to build a temple as a sanctuary. Be strong and do the work."

¹¹Then David gave his son Solomon the plans for the portico of the temple, its buildings, its storerooms, its upper parts, its inner rooms and the place of atonement. ¹²He gave him the plans of all that the Spirit had put in his mind for the courts of the temple of the LORD and all the surrounding rooms, for the treasuries of the temple of God and for the treasuries for the dedicated things. ¹³He gave him instructions for the divisions of the priests and Levites, and for all the work of serving in the temple of the LORD, as well as for all the articles to be used in its service. ¹⁴He designated the weight of gold for all the gold articles to be used in various kinds of service, and the weight of silver for all the silver articles to be used in various kinds of service: ¹⁵the weight of gold for the gold lampstands and their lamps, with the weight for each lampstand and its lamps; and the weight of silver for each silver lampstand and its lamps, according to the use of each lampstand; ¹⁶the weight of gold for each table for consecrated bread; the weight of silver for the silver tables; ¹⁷the weight of pure gold for the forks, sprinkling bowls and pitchers; the weight of gold for each gold dish; the weight of silver for each silver dish; ¹⁸and the weight of the refined gold for the altar of incense. He also gave him the plan for the chariot, that is, the cherubim of gold that spread their wings and shelter the ark of the covenant of the LORD.

¹⁹"All this," David said, "I have in writing from the hand of the LORD upon me, and he gave me understanding in all the details of the plan."

²⁰David also said to Solomon his son, "Be strong and courageous, and do the work. Do not be afraid or discouraged, for the LORD God, my God, is with you. He will not fail you or forsake you until all the work for the service of the temple of the LORD is finished. ²¹The divisions of the priests and Levites are ready for all the work on the temple of God, and every willing man skilled in any craft will help you in all the work. The officials and all the people will obey your every command."

Gifts for Building the Temple

29 Then King David said to the whole assembly: "My son Solomon, the one whom God has chosen, is young and inexperienced. The task is great, because this palatial structure is not for man but

for the LORD God. ²With all my resources I have provided for the temple of my God—gold for the gold work, silver for the silver, bronze for the bronze, iron for the iron and wood for the wood, as well as onyx for the settings, turquoise,*ᵃ* stones of various colors, and all kinds of fine stone and marble—all of these in large quantities. ³Besides, in my devotion to the temple of my God I now give my personal treasures of gold and silver for the temple of my God, over and above everything I have provided for this holy temple: ⁴three thousand talents*ᵇ* of gold (gold of Ophir) and seven thousand talents*ᶜ* of refined silver, for the overlaying of the walls of the buildings, ⁵for the gold work and the silver work, and for all the work to be done by the craftsmen. Now, who is willing to consecrate himself today to the LORD?"

⁶Then the leaders of families, the officers of the tribes of Israel, the commanders of thousands and commanders of hundreds, and the officials in charge of the king's work gave willingly. ⁷They gave toward the work on the temple of God five thousand talents*ᵈ* and ten thousand darics*ᵉ* of gold, ten thousand talents*ᶠ* of silver, eighteen thousand talents*ᵍ* of bronze and a hundred thousand talents*ʰ* of iron. ⁸Any who had precious stones gave them to the treasury of the temple of the LORD in the custody of Jehiel the Gershonite. ⁹The people rejoiced at the willing response of their leaders, for they had given freely and wholeheartedly to the LORD. David the king also rejoiced greatly.

David's Prayer

¹⁰David praised the LORD in the presence of the whole assembly, saying,

"Praise be to you, O LORD,
   God of our father Israel,
   from everlasting to everlasting.
¹¹ Yours, O LORD, is the greatness and
      the power
   and the glory and the majesty and
      the splendor,
   for everything in heaven and earth
      is yours.
Yours, O LORD, is the kingdom;
   you are exalted as head over all.

¹²Wealth and honor come from you;
   you are the ruler of all things.
In your hands are strength and power
   to exalt and give strength to all.
¹³Now, our God, we give you thanks,
   and praise your glorious name.

¹⁴"But who am I, and who are my people, that we should be able to give as generously as this? Everything comes from you, and we have given you only what comes from your hand. ¹⁵We are aliens and strangers in your sight, as were all our forefathers. Our days on earth are like a shadow, without hope. ¹⁶O LORD our God, as for all this abundance that we have provided for building you a temple for your Holy Name, it comes from your hand, and all of it belongs to you. ¹⁷I know, my God, that you test the heart and are pleased with integrity. All these things have I given willingly and with honest intent. And now I have seen with joy how willingly your people who are here have given to you. ¹⁸O LORD, God of our fathers Abraham, Isaac and Israel, keep this desire in the hearts of your people forever, and keep their hearts loyal to you. ¹⁹And give my son Solomon the wholehearted devotion to keep your commands, requirements and decrees and to do everything to build the palatial structure for which I have provided."

²⁰Then David said to the whole assembly, "Praise the LORD your God." So they all praised the LORD, the God of their fathers; they bowed low and fell prostrate before the LORD and the king.

Solomon Acknowledged as King

²¹The next day they made sacrifices to the LORD and presented burnt offerings to him: a thousand bulls, a thousand rams and a thousand male lambs, together with their drink offerings, and

---

ᵃ2 The meaning of the Hebrew for this word is uncertain.   *ᵇ4* That is, about 110 tons (about 100 metric tons)   *ᶜ4* That is, about 260 tons (about 240 metric tons)   *ᵈ7* That is, about 190 tons (about 170 metric tons)   *ᵉ7* That is, about 185 pounds (about 84 kilograms)   *ᶠ7* That is, about 375 tons (about 345 metric tons)   *ᵍ7* That is, about 675 tons (about 610 metric tons)   *ʰ7* That is, about 3,750 tons (about 3,450 metric tons)

other sacrifices in abundance for all Israel. ²²They ate and drank with great joy in the presence of the LORD that day.

Then they acknowledged Solomon son of David as king a second time, anointing him before the LORD to be ruler and Zadok to be priest. ²³So Solomon sat on the throne of the LORD as king in place of his father David. He prospered and all Israel obeyed him. ²⁴All the officers and mighty men, as well as all of King David's sons, pledged their submission to King Solomon.

²⁵The LORD highly exalted Solomon in the sight of all Israel and bestowed on him royal splendor such as no king over Israel ever had before.

[THURSDAY]

1 CHRONICLES 29:10–20

Keep Drawing Water

29:10 DAVID PRAISED THE LORD.

David's prayer in verses 10–13 is a prayer to memorize, like Aaron's blessing on the Israelites (see Numbers 6:24–26). That's because David is to thanks and praise what Andres Segovia is to a guitar, or Arthur Rubinstein to a piano. These people deserve to be imitated. David had spent a lifetime in earnest and vital prayer. In this passage we see the Grand Master at his best, at the end of his life, leading the nation in prayer. We can never thank God too much or in too many different ways, for thanksgiving is an organ of perception; the more we give thanks, the more we see to give thanks for (see previous devotion).

David's prayer is a real eye-opener; or a real well-opener. Jack Sanford tells of an old well his family used during summer vacations in rural New Hampshire. It was just outside the 150-year-old farmhouse they stayed in. Even in the worst droughts, the old well yielded cold, pure water. Over the years, the family remodeled the farmhouse and made improvements, like indoor plumbing. Since the well was no longer needed, it was covered in order to have a reserve should the need arise in the future.

One day, years later, Sanford got a hankering for the well's wonderful water. So he took off the cover, lowered a bucket and was shocked to discover that the well had gone bone dry. He asked around in the village for an explanation. He learned that wells like that well were fed by hundreds of tiny underground rivulets. When water is drawn from the well, more water flows through the rivulets. When water is not drawn, sediments collect, and the rivulets are stopped up. The more water flows out, the more water flows in.

Our hearts are that way too. The more we give thanks, the more we are able to give thanks. We learn to pray by praying. Sometimes the best way to learn is to learn the prayer of a master, like David.

PRAY:

Pray David's great prayer aloud, until you can pray it by heart.

FOR YOUR NEXT DEVOTIONAL READING, GO TO PAGE 497.

The Death of David

²⁶David son of Jesse was king over all Israel. ²⁷He ruled over Israel forty years— seven in Hebron and thirty-three in Jerusalem. ²⁸He died at a good old age, having enjoyed long life, wealth and honor. His son Solomon succeeded him as king. ²⁹As for the events of King David's reign, from beginning to end, they are written in the records of Samuel the seer, the records of Nathan the prophet and the records of Gad the seer, ³⁰together with the details of his reign and power, and the circumstances that surrounded him and Israel and the kingdoms of all the other lands.

2 Chronicles

WE SAW the pathology report in 1 and 2 Kings. We saw the prognosis in 1 Chronicles. (See the Introductions to those books.) Now, in 2 Chronicles, we see the treatment. It is simply: "If my people, who are called by my name, will humble themselves and pray and seek my face and turn from their wicked ways, then will I hear from heaven and will forgive their sin and will heal their land" (7:14). Within the book of 2 Chronicles, there are illustrations of this formula from Israel's history. Read about Abijah who sought the Lord's help and won a great battle (chapter 13). Or read the account of Jehoshaphat, who followed God in his early years, and as a result, "The LORD established the kingdom under his control" (17:3–5).

GOD HEARD THEM, FOR THEIR PRAYER REACHED HEAVEN, HIS HOLY DWELLING PLACE. (30:27)

The message of Chronicles can give great encouragement to prayer, especially prayers of repentance and sorrow for sin. If the promise of 2 Chronicles 7:14 is true (as all of God's promises are), we may be confident that God has a good future for us, no matter how dark and sordid our past. The words of the prophet Hosea are the message of 1 and 2 Chronicles: "Come, let us return to the LORD. He has torn us to pieces but he will heal us; he has injured us but he will bind up our wounds" (Hosea 6:1).

Solomon Asks for Wisdom

1 Solomon son of David established himself firmly over his kingdom, for the LORD his God was with him and made him exceedingly great.

2 Then Solomon spoke to all Israel—to the commanders of thousands and commanders of hundreds, to the judges and to all the leaders in Israel, the heads of families— 3 and Solomon and the whole assembly went to the high place at Gibeon, for God's Tent of Meeting was there, which Moses the LORD's servant had made in the desert. 4 Now David had brought up the ark of God from Kiriath Jearim to the place he had prepared for it, because he had pitched a tent for it in Jerusalem. 5 But the bronze altar that Bezalel son of Uri, the son of Hur, had made was in Gibeon in front of the tabernacle of the LORD; so Solomon and the assembly inquired of him there. 6 Solomon went up to the bronze altar before the LORD in the Tent of Meeting and offered a thousand burnt offerings on it.

7 That night God appeared to Solomon and said to him, "Ask for whatever you want me to give you."

> THAT night God appeared to Solomon and said to him, "Ask for whatever you want me to give you."
>
> 2 CHRONICLES 1:7

8 Solomon answered God, "You have shown great kindness to David my father and have made me king in his place. 9 Now, LORD God, let your promise to my father David be confirmed, for you have made me king over a people who are as numerous as the dust of the earth. 10 Give me wisdom and knowledge, that I may lead this people, for who is able to govern this great people of yours?"

11 God said to Solomon, "Since this is your heart's desire and you have not asked for wealth, riches or honor, nor for the death of your enemies, and since you have not asked for a long life but for wisdom and knowledge to govern my people over whom I have made you king, 12 therefore wisdom and knowledge will be given you. And I will also give you wealth, riches and honor, such as no king who was before you ever had and none after you will have."

13 Then Solomon went to Jerusalem from the high place at Gibeon, from before the Tent of Meeting. And he reigned over Israel.

14 Solomon accumulated chariots and horses; he had fourteen hundred chariots and twelve thousand horses,[a] which he kept in the chariot cities and also with him in Jerusalem. 15 The king made silver and gold as common in Jerusalem as stones, and cedar as plentiful as sycamore-fig trees in the foothills. 16 Solomon's horses were imported from Egypt[b] and from Kue[c]—the royal merchants purchased them from Kue. 17 They imported a chariot from Egypt for six hundred shekels[d] of silver, and a horse for a hundred and fifty.[e] They also exported them to all the kings of the Hittites and of the Arameans.

Preparations for Building the Temple

2 Solomon gave orders to build a temple for the Name of the LORD and a royal palace for himself. 2 He conscripted seventy thousand men as carriers and eighty thousand as stonecutters in the hills and thirty-six hundred as foremen over them.

3 Solomon sent this message to Hiram[f] king of Tyre:

"Send me cedar logs as you did for my father David when you sent him cedar to build a palace to live in. 4 Now I am about to build a temple for the Name of the LORD my God and to dedicate it to him for burning fragrant incense before him, for setting out the consecrated bread regularly, and for making burnt offerings every morning and evening and on Sabbaths and New Moons and at the appointed feasts of the LORD our God. This is a lasting ordinance for Israel.

---

a14 Or charioteers   b16 Or possibly Muzur, a region in Cilicia; also in verse 17   c16 Probably Cilicia   d17 That is, about 15 pounds (about 7 kilograms)   e17 That is, about 3 3/4 pounds (about 1.7 kilograms)   f3 Hebrew Huram, a variant of Hiram; also in verses 11 and 12

5"The temple I am going to build will be great, because our God is greater than all other gods. 6But who is able to build a temple for him, since the heavens, even the highest heavens, cannot contain him? Who then am I to build a temple for him, except as a place to burn sacrifices before him?

7"Send me, therefore, a man skilled to work in gold and silver, bronze and iron, and in purple, crimson and blue yarn, and experienced in the art of engraving, to work in Judah and Jerusalem with my skilled craftsmen, whom my father David provided.

8"Send me also cedar, pine and algum*a* logs from Lebanon, for I know that your men are skilled in cutting timber there. My men will work with yours 9to provide me with plenty of lumber, because the temple I build must be large and magnificent. 10I will give your servants, the woodsmen who cut the timber, twenty thousand cors*b* of ground wheat, twenty thousand cors of barley, twenty thousand baths*c* of wine and twenty thousand baths of olive oil."

11Hiram king of Tyre replied by letter to Solomon:

"Because the LORD loves his people, he has made you their king."

12And Hiram added:

"Praise be to the LORD, the God of Israel, who made heaven and earth! He has given King David a wise son, endowed with intelligence and discernment, who will build a temple for the LORD and a palace for himself.

13"I am sending you Huram-Abi, a man of great skill, 14whose mother was from Dan and whose father was from Tyre. He is trained to work in gold and silver, bronze and iron, stone and wood, and with purple and blue and crimson yarn and fine linen. He is experienced in all kinds of engraving and can execute any design given to him. He will work with your craftsmen and with those of my lord, David your father.

15"Now let my lord send his servants the wheat and barley and the olive oil and wine he promised, 16and we will cut all the logs from Lebanon that you need and will float them in rafts by sea down to Joppa. You can then take them up to Jerusalem."

17Solomon took a census of all the aliens who were in Israel, after the census his father David had taken; and they were found to be 153,600. 18He assigned 70,000 of them to be carriers and 80,000 to be stonecutters in the hills, with 3,600 foremen over them to keep the people working.

Solomon Builds the Temple

3 Then Solomon began to build the temple of the LORD in Jerusalem on Mount Moriah, where the LORD had appeared to his father David. It was on the threshing floor of Araunah*d* the Jebusite, the place provided by David. 2He began building on the second day of the second month in the fourth year of his reign.

3The foundation Solomon laid for building the temple of God was sixty cubits long and twenty cubits wide*e* (using the cubit of the old standard). 4The portico at the front of the temple was twenty cubits*f* long across the width of the building and twenty cubits*g* high.

He overlaid the inside with pure gold. 5He paneled the main hall with pine and covered it with fine gold and decorated it with palm tree and chain designs. 6He adorned the temple with precious stones. And the gold he used was gold of Parvaim. 7He overlaid the ceiling beams, doorframes, walls and doors of the temple with gold, and he carved cherubim on the walls.

8He built the Most Holy Place, its length corresponding to the width of the temple—twenty cubits long and twenty

---

a8 Probably a variant of *almug*; possibly juniper
b10 That is, probably about 125,000 bushels (about 4,400 kiloliters)   *c10* That is, probably about 115,000 gallons (about 440 kiloliters)
d1 Hebrew *Ornan*, a variant of *Araunah*
e3 That is, about 90 feet (about 27 meters) long and 30 feet (about 9 meters) wide   *f4* That is, about 30 feet (about 9 meters); also in verses 8, 11 and 13   *g4* Some Septuagint and Syriac manuscripts; Hebrew *and a hundred and twenty*

cubits wide. He overlaid the inside with six hundred talents[a] of fine gold. [9]The gold nails weighed fifty shekels.[b] He also overlaid the upper parts with gold.

[10]In the Most Holy Place he made a pair of sculptured cherubim and overlaid them with gold. [11]The total wingspan of the cherubim was twenty cubits. One wing of the first cherub was five cubits[c] long and touched the temple wall, while its other wing, also five cubits long, touched the wing of the other cherub. [12]Similarly one wing of the second cherub was five cubits long and touched the other temple wall, and its other wing, also five cubits long, touched the wing of the first cherub. [13]The wings of these cherubim extended twenty cubits. They stood on their feet, facing the main hall.[d]

[14]He made the curtain of blue, purple and crimson yarn and fine linen, with cherubim worked into it.

[15]In the front of the temple he made two pillars, which together were thirty-five cubits[e] long, each with a capital on top measuring five cubits. [16]He made interwoven chains[f] and put them on top of the pillars. He also made a hundred pomegranates and attached them to the chains. [17]He erected the pillars in the front of the temple, one to the south and one to the north. The one to the south he named Jakin[g] and the one to the north Boaz.[h]

The Temple's Furnishings

4 He made a bronze altar twenty cubits long, twenty cubits wide and ten cubits high.[i] [2]He made the Sea of cast metal, circular in shape, measuring ten cubits from rim to rim and five cubits[j] high. It took a line of thirty cubits[k] to measure around it. [3]Below the rim, figures of bulls encircled it—ten to a cubit.[l] The bulls were cast in two rows in one piece with the Sea.

[4]The Sea stood on twelve bulls, three facing north, three facing west, three facing south and three facing east. The Sea rested on top of them, and their hindquarters were toward the center. [5]It was a handbreadth[m] in thickness, and its rim was like the rim of a cup, like a lily blossom. It held three thousand baths.[n]

[6]He then made ten basins for washing and placed five on the south side and five on the north. In them the things to be used for the burnt offerings were rinsed, but the Sea was to be used by the priests for washing.

[7]He made ten gold lampstands according to the specifications for them and placed them in the temple, five on the south side and five on the north.

[8]He made ten tables and placed them in the temple, five on the south side and five on the north. He also made a hundred gold sprinkling bowls.

[9]He made the courtyard of the priests, and the large court and the doors for the court, and overlaid the doors with bronze. [10]He placed the Sea on the south side, at the southeast corner.

[11]He also made the pots and shovels and sprinkling bowls.

So Huram finished the work he had undertaken for King Solomon in the temple of God:

[12] the two pillars;
    the two bowl-shaped capitals on top
        of the pillars;
    the two sets of network decorating
        the two bowl-shaped capitals on
        top of the pillars;
[13] the four hundred pomegranates for
        the two sets of network (two rows
        of pomegranates for each network,
        decorating the bowl-shaped
        capitals on top of the pillars);
[14] the stands with their basins;
[15] the Sea and the twelve bulls under it;
[16] the pots, shovels, meat forks and all
        related articles.

All the objects that Huram-Abi made for King Solomon for the temple of the

---

[a]8 That is, about 23 tons (about 21 metric tons)   [b]9 That is, about 1 1/4 pounds (about 0.6 kilogram)   [c]11 That is, about 7 1/2 feet (about 2.3 meters); also in verse 15   [d]13 Or facing inward   [e]15 That is, about 52 feet (about 16 meters)   [f]16 Or possibly made chains in the inner sanctuary; the meaning of the Hebrew for this phrase is uncertain.   [g]17 Jakin probably means he establishes.   [h]17 Boaz probably means in him is strength.   [i]1 That is, about 30 feet (about 9 meters) long and wide, and about 15 feet (about 4.5 meters) high   [j]2 That is, about 7 1/2 feet (about 2.3 meters)   [k]2 That is, about 45 feet (about 13.5 meters)   [l]3 That is, about 1 1/2 feet (about 0.5 meter)   [m]5 That is, about 3 inches (about 8 centimeters)   [n]5 That is, about 17,500 gallons (about 66 kiloliters)

LORD were of polished bronze. ¹⁷The king had them cast in clay molds in the plain of the Jordan between Succoth and Zarethan.ᵃ ¹⁸All these things that Solomon made amounted to so much that the weight of the bronze was not determined.

¹⁹Solomon also made all the furnishings that were in God's temple:

the golden altar;
the tables on which was the bread of the Presence;
²⁰the lampstands of pure gold with their lamps, to burn in front of the inner sanctuary as prescribed;
²¹the gold floral work and lamps and tongs (they were solid gold);
²²the pure gold wick trimmers, sprinkling bowls, dishes and censers; and the gold doors of the temple: the inner doors to the Most Holy Place and the doors of the main hall.

5 When all the work Solomon had done for the temple of the LORD was finished, he brought in the things his father David had dedicated—the silver and gold and all the furnishings—and he placed them in the treasuries of God's temple.

The Ark Brought to the Temple

²Then Solomon summoned to Jerusalem the elders of Israel, all the heads of the tribes and the chiefs of the Israelite families, to bring up the ark of the LORD's covenant from Zion, the City of David. ³And all the men of Israel came together to the king at the time of the festival in the seventh month.

⁴When all the elders of Israel had arrived, the Levites took up the ark, ⁵and they brought up the ark and the Tent of Meeting and all the sacred furnishings in it. The priests, who were Levites, carried them up; ⁶and King Solomon and the entire assembly of Israel that had gathered about him were before the ark, sacrificing so many sheep and cattle that they could not be recorded or counted.

⁷The priests then brought the ark of the LORD's covenant to its place in the inner sanctuary of the temple, the Most Holy Place, and put it beneath the wings of the cherubim. ⁸The cherubim spread their wings over the place of the ark and covered the ark and its carrying poles. ⁹These poles were so long that their ends, extending from the ark, could be seen from in front of the inner sanctuary, but not from outside the Holy Place; and they are still there today. ¹⁰There was nothing in the ark except the two tablets that Moses had placed in it at Horeb, where the LORD made a covenant with the Israelites after they came out of Egypt.

¹¹The priests then withdrew from the Holy Place. All the priests who were there had consecrated themselves, regardless of their divisions. ¹²All the Levites who were musicians—Asaph, Heman, Jeduthun and their sons and relatives—stood on the east side of the altar, dressed in fine linen and playing cymbals, harps and lyres. They were accompanied by 120 priests sounding trumpets. ¹³The trumpeters and singers joined in unison, as with one voice, to give praise and thanks to the LORD. Accompanied by trumpets, cymbals and other instruments, they raised their voices in praise to the LORD and sang:

"He is good;
his love endures forever."

Then the temple of the LORD was filled with a cloud, ¹⁴and the priests could not perform their service because of the cloud, for the glory of the LORD filled the temple of God.

6 Then Solomon said, "The LORD has said that he would dwell in a dark cloud; ²I have built a magnificent temple for you, a place for you to dwell forever."

³While the whole assembly of Israel was standing there, the king turned around and blessed them. ⁴Then he said:

"Praise be to the LORD, the God of Israel, who with his hands has fulfilled what he promised with his mouth to my father David. For he said, ⁵'Since the day I brought my people out of Egypt, I have not chosen a city in any tribe of Israel to have a temple built for my Name to be

ᵃ17 Hebrew Zeredatha, a variant of Zarethan

there, nor have I chosen anyone to be the leader over my people Israel. [6]But now I have chosen Jerusalem for my Name to be there, and I have chosen David to rule my people Israel.'

[7]"My father David had it in his heart to build a temple for the Name of the LORD, the God of Israel. [8]But the LORD said to my father David, 'Because it was in your heart to build a temple for my Name, you did well to have this in your heart. [9]Nevertheless, you are not the one to build the temple, but your son, who is your own flesh and blood—he is the one who will build the temple for my Name.'

[10]"The LORD has kept the promise he made. I have succeeded David my father and now I sit on the throne of Israel, just as the LORD promised, and I have built the temple for the Name of the LORD, the God of Israel. [11]There I have placed the ark, in which is the covenant of the LORD that he made with the people of Israel."

Solomon's Prayer of Dedication

[12]Then Solomon stood before the altar of the LORD in front of the whole assembly of Israel and spread out his hands. [13]Now he had made a bronze platform, five cubits[a] long, five cubits wide and three cubits[b] high, and had placed it in the center of the outer court. He stood on the platform and then knelt down before the whole assembly of Israel and spread out his hands toward heaven. [14]He said:

"O LORD, God of Israel, there is no God like you in heaven or on earth—you who keep your covenant of love with your servants who continue wholeheartedly in your way. [15]You have kept your promise to your servant David my father; with your mouth you have promised and with your hand you have fulfilled it—as it is today.

[16]"Now LORD, God of Israel, keep for your servant David my father the promises you made to him when you said, 'You shall never fail to have a man to sit before me on the throne of Israel, if only your sons are careful

in all they do to walk before me according to my law, as you have done.' [17]And now, O LORD, God of Israel, let your word that you promised your servant David come true.

[18]"But will God really dwell on earth with men? The heavens, even the highest heavens, cannot contain you. How much less this temple I have built! [19]Yet give attention to your servant's prayer and his plea for mercy, O LORD my God. Hear the cry and the prayer that your servant is praying in your presence. [20]May your eyes be open toward this temple day and night, this place of which you said you would put your Name there. May you hear the prayer your servant prays toward this place. [21]Hear the supplications of your servant and of your people Israel when they pray toward this place. Hear from heaven, your dwelling place; and when you hear, forgive.

> "YET give attention to your servant's prayer and his plea for mercy, O LORD my God. Hear the cry and the prayer that your servant is praying in your presence."
>
> 2 CHRONICLES 6:19

[22]"When a man wrongs his neighbor and is required to take an oath and he comes and swears the oath before your altar in this temple, [23]then hear from heaven and act. Judge between your servants, repaying the guilty by bringing down on his own head what he has done. Declare the innocent not guilty and so establish his innocence.

[24]"When your people Israel have been defeated by an enemy because they have sinned against you and when they turn back and confess your name, praying and making supplication before you in this temple, [25]then hear from heaven and forgive the sin of your people Israel and bring them back to the land you gave to them and their fathers.

[a]13 That is, about 7 1/2 feet (about 2.3 meters)
[b]13 That is, about 4 1/2 feet (about 1.3 meters)

26"When the heavens are shut up and there is no rain because your people have sinned against you, and when they pray toward this place and confess your name and turn from their sin because you have afflicted them, 27then hear from heaven and forgive the sin of your servants, your people Israel. Teach them the right way to live, and send rain on the land you gave your people for an inheritance.

28"When famine or plague comes to the land, or blight or mildew, locusts or grasshoppers, or when enemies besiege them in any of their cities, whatever disaster or disease may come, 29and when a prayer or plea is made by any of your people Israel—each one aware of his afflictions and pains, and spreading out his hands toward this temple— 30then hear from heaven, your dwelling place. Forgive, and deal with each man according to all he does, since you know his heart (for you alone know the hearts of men), 31so that they will fear you and walk in your ways all the time they live in the land you gave our fathers.

32"As for the foreigner who does not belong to your people Israel but has come from a distant land because of your great name and your mighty hand and your outstretched arm—when he comes and prays toward this temple, 33then hear from heaven, your dwelling place, and do whatever the foreigner asks of you, so that all the peoples of the earth may know your name and fear you, as do your own people Israel, and may know that this house I have built bears your Name.

34"When your people go to war against their enemies, wherever you send them, and when they pray to you toward this city you have chosen and the temple I have built for your Name, 35then hear from heaven their prayer and their plea, and uphold their cause.

36"When they sin against you—for there is no one who does not sin—and you become angry with them and give them over to the enemy, who takes them captive to a land far away or near; 37and if they have a change of heart in the land where they are held captive, and repent and plead with you in the land of their captivity and say, 'We have sinned, we have done wrong and acted wickedly'; 38and if they turn back to you with all their heart and soul in the land of their captivity where they were taken, and pray toward the land you gave their fathers, toward the city you have chosen and toward the temple I have built for your Name; 39then from heaven, your dwelling place, hear their prayer and their pleas, and uphold their cause. And forgive your people, who have sinned against you.

40"Now, my God, may your eyes be open and your ears attentive to the prayers offered in this place.

41 "Now arise, O LORD God, and
come to your resting
place,
you and the ark of your might.
May your priests, O LORD God, be
clothed with salvation,
may your saints rejoice in your
goodness.
42 O LORD God, do not reject your
anointed one.
Remember the great love
promised to David your
servant."

> "NOW, my God, may your eyes be open and your ears attentive to the prayers offered in this place."
>
> 2 CHRONICLES 6:40

The Dedication of the Temple

7 When Solomon finished praying, fire came down from heaven and consumed the burnt offering and the sacrifices, and the glory of the LORD filled the temple. 2The priests could not enter the temple of the LORD because the glory of the LORD filled it. 3When all the Israelites saw the fire coming down and the glory of the LORD above the temple, they knelt

on the pavement with their faces to the ground, and they worshiped and gave thanks to the LORD, saying,

"He is good;
his love endures forever."

⁴Then the king and all the people offered sacrifices before the LORD. ⁵And King Solomon offered a sacrifice of twenty-two thousand head of cattle and a hundred and twenty thousand sheep and goats. So the king and all the people dedicated the temple of God. ⁶The priests took their positions, as did the Levites with the LORD's musical instruments, which King David had made for praising the LORD and which were used when he gave thanks, saying, "His love endures forever." Opposite the Levites, the priests blew their trumpets, and all the Israelites were standing.

⁷Solomon consecrated the middle part of the courtyard in front of the temple of the LORD, and there he offered burnt offerings and the fat of the fellowship offerings,ᵃ because the bronze altar he had made could not hold the burnt offerings, the grain offerings and the fat portions.

⁸So Solomon observed the festival at that time for seven days, and all Israel with him—a vast assembly, people from Leboᵇ Hamath to the Wadi of Egypt. ⁹On the eighth day they held an assembly, for they had celebrated the dedication of the altar for seven days and the festival for seven days more. ¹⁰On the twenty-third day of the seventh month he sent the people to their homes, joyful and glad in heart for the good things the LORD had done for David and Solomon and for his people Israel.

The LORD Appears to Solomon

¹¹When Solomon had finished the temple of the LORD and the royal palace, and had succeeded in carrying out all he had in mind to do in the temple of the LORD and in his own palace, ¹²the LORD appeared to him at night and said:

"I have heard your prayer and have chosen this place for myself as a temple for sacrifices.

¹³"When I shut up the heavens so that there is no rain, or command locusts to devour the land or send a plague among my people, ¹⁴if my people, who are called by my name, will humble themselves and pray and seek my face and turn from their wicked ways, then will I hear from heaven and will forgive their sin and will heal their land. ¹⁵Now my eyes will be open and my ears attentive to the prayers offered in this place. ¹⁶I have chosen and consecrated this temple so that my Name may be there forever. My eyes and my heart will always be there.

¹⁷"As for you, if you walk before me as David your father did, and do all I command, and observe my decrees and laws, ¹⁸I will establish your royal throne, as I covenanted with David your father when I said, 'You shall never fail to have a man to rule over Israel.'

¹⁹"But if youᶜ turn away and forsake the decrees and commands I have given youᶜ and go off to serve other gods and worship them, ²⁰then I will uproot Israel from my land, which I have given them, and will reject this temple I have consecrated for my Name. I will make it a byword and an object of ridicule among all peoples. ²¹And though this temple is now so imposing, all who pass by will be appalled and say, 'Why has the LORD done such a thing to this land and to this temple?' ²²People will answer, 'Because they have forsaken the LORD, the God of their fathers, who brought them out of Egypt, and have embraced other gods, worshiping and serving them—that is why he brought all this disaster on them.'"

Solomon's Other Activities

8 At the end of twenty years, during which Solomon built the temple of the LORD and his own palace, ²Solomon rebuilt the villages that Hiramᵈ had given him, and settled Israelites in them. ³Solomon then went to Hamath Zobah and captured it. ⁴He also built up Tadmor in

---

ᵃ7 Traditionally *peace offerings* ᵇ8 Or *from the entrance to* ᶜ19 The Hebrew is plural.
ᵈ2 Hebrew *Huram*, a variant of *Hiram*; also in verse 18

2 CHRONICLES 7:14

Prescription for Revival

7:14 "IF MY PEOPLE, WHO ARE CALLED BY MY NAME ..."

For centuries Christians have viewed this ancient prayer-promise, first given to Israel, as a kind of prescription for revival in the church. What is a revival? There are a lot of ways to think of it, but let this be a picture: Have you seen the photo booths at carnivals where people can put their heads in holes over paintings of the bodies of muscle men and princesses and cowboys? The result is usually funny. You see Grandma's face on the body of a muscle man, your bookish Uncle Fred's face over the body of a pirate. The humor is in the incongruity. Sometimes the actual faces of the people who make up the church, the body of Christ, seem incongruous in the extreme, but the result isn't funny. Our faces, which is a way the Bible talks about our inner selves, don't look like they belong on Christ's body. Revival is what happens when spiritual vitality is restored in such a way that the faces and the Body match again.

The prayer-promise says there are four things that must happen for God to revive his people:

1. We must humble ourselves; renounce pride and self-sufficiency.

2. We must pray. Genuine prayer comes only from humility. Think of the classic postures of prayer: hands folded, head bowed; hands open and raised toward heaven; face down, prostrate—all are postures of humility and deep dependence on God.

3. We must seek God's face. God's face is his inner self, or his heart. He shows it only to those who want to know God as a person knows a friend or a lover. To seek God's face is to have your first love restored.

4. We must turn from our wicked ways. The word is *repent*. We cannot seek God's face if we have been seeking something else.

The word *prescription* really isn't a good word to use for this revival prayer-promise. It smacks too much of the mechanical and automatic. But if it helps to underline the certainty we have that God will keep his promise, then keep the word, for he said, "then will I hear from heaven and will forgive their sin and will heal their land."

PRAY:

"Restore us again, O God our Savior ...
Will you not revive us again,
that your people may rejoice in you?" (Psalm 85:4,6).

FOR YOUR NEXT DEVOTIONAL READING, GO TO PAGE 500.

the desert and all the store cities he had built in Hamath. ⁵He rebuilt Upper Beth Horon and Lower Beth Horon as fortified cities, with walls and with gates and bars, ⁶as well as Baalath and all his store cities, and all the cities for his chariots and for his horses*ᵃ*—whatever he desired to build in Jerusalem, in Lebanon and throughout all the territory he ruled.

⁷All the people left from the Hittites, Amorites, Perizzites, Hivites and Jebusites (these peoples were not Israelites), ⁸that is, their descendants remaining in the land, whom the Israelites had not destroyed—these Solomon conscripted for his slave labor force, as it is to this day. ⁹But Solomon did not make slaves of the Israelites for his work; they were his fighting men, commanders of his captains, and commanders of his chariots and charioteers. ¹⁰They were also King Solomon's chief officials—two hundred and fifty officials supervising the men.

¹¹Solomon brought Pharaoh's daughter up from the City of David to the palace he had built for her, for he said, "My wife must not live in the palace of David king of Israel, because the places the ark of the LORD has entered are holy."

¹²On the altar of the LORD that he had built in front of the portico, Solomon sacrificed burnt offerings to the LORD, ¹³according to the daily requirement for offerings commanded by Moses for Sabbaths, New Moons and the three annual feasts—the Feast of Unleavened Bread, the Feast of Weeks and the Feast of Tabernacles. ¹⁴In keeping with the ordinance of his father David, he appointed the divisions of the priests for their duties, and the Levites to lead the praise and to assist the priests according to each day's requirement. He also appointed the gatekeepers by divisions for the various gates, because this was what David the man of God had ordered. ¹⁵They did not deviate from the king's commands to the priests or to the Levites in any matter, including that of the treasuries.

¹⁶All Solomon's work was carried out, from the day the foundation of the temple of the LORD was laid until its completion. So the temple of the LORD was finished.

¹⁷Then Solomon went to Ezion Geber and Elath on the coast of Edom. ¹⁸And Hiram sent him ships commanded by his own officers, men who knew the sea. These, with Solomon's men, sailed to Ophir and brought back four hundred and fifty talents*ᵇ* of gold, which they delivered to King Solomon.

The Queen of Sheba Visits Solomon

9 When the queen of Sheba heard of Solomon's fame, she came to Jerusalem to test him with hard questions. Arriving with a very great caravan—with camels carrying spices, large quantities of gold, and precious stones—she came to Solomon and talked with him about all she had on her mind. ²Solomon answered all her questions; nothing was too hard for him to explain to her. ³When the queen of Sheba saw the wisdom of Solomon, as well as the palace he had built, ⁴the food on his table, the seating of his officials, the attending servants in their robes, the cupbearers in their robes and the burnt offerings he made at*ᶜ* the temple of the LORD, she was overwhelmed.

⁵She said to the king, "The report I heard in my own country about your achievements and your wisdom is true. ⁶But I did not believe what they said until I came and saw with my own eyes. Indeed, not even half the greatness of your wisdom was told me; you have far exceeded the report I heard. ⁷How happy your men must be! How happy your officials, who continually stand before you and hear your wisdom! ⁸Praise be to the LORD your God, who has delighted in you and placed you on his throne as king to rule for the LORD your God. Because of the love of your God for Israel and his desire to uphold them forever, he has made you king over them, to maintain justice and righteousness."

⁹Then she gave the king 120 talents*ᵈ* of gold, large quantities of spices, and precious stones. There had never been such spices as those the queen of Sheba gave to King Solomon.

¹⁰(The men of Hiram and the men of Solomon brought gold from Ophir; they

---

ᵃ6 Or *charioteers*   *ᵇ18* That is, about 17 tons (about 16 metric tons)   *ᶜ4* Or *the ascent by which he went up*   *ᵈ9* That is, about 4 1/2 tons (about 4 metric tons)

also brought algumwood[a] and precious stones. [11]The king used the algumwood to make steps for the temple of the LORD and for the royal palace, and to make harps and lyres for the musicians. Nothing like them had ever been seen in Judah.)

[12]King Solomon gave the queen of Sheba all she desired and asked for; he gave her more than she had brought to him. Then she left and returned with her retinue to her own country.

Solomon's Splendor

[13]The weight of the gold that Solomon received yearly was 666 talents,[b] [14]not including the revenues brought in by merchants and traders. Also all the kings of Arabia and the governors of the land brought gold and silver to Solomon.

[15]King Solomon made two hundred large shields of hammered gold; six hundred bekas[c] of hammered gold went into each shield. [16]He also made three hundred small shields of hammered gold, with three hundred bekas[d] of gold in each shield. The king put them in the Palace of the Forest of Lebanon.

[17]Then the king made a great throne inlaid with ivory and overlaid with pure gold. [18]The throne had six steps, and a footstool of gold was attached to it. On both sides of the seat were armrests, with a lion standing beside each of them. [19]Twelve lions stood on the six steps, one at either end of each step. Nothing like it had ever been made for any other kingdom. [20]All King Solomon's goblets were gold, and all the household articles in the Palace of the Forest of Lebanon were pure gold. Nothing was made of silver, because silver was considered of little value in Solomon's day. [21]The king had a fleet of trading ships[e] manned by Hiram's[f] men. Once every three years it returned, carrying gold, silver and ivory, and apes and baboons.

[22]King Solomon was greater in riches and wisdom than all the other kings of the earth. [23]All the kings of the earth sought audience with Solomon to hear the wisdom God had put in his heart. [24]Year after year, everyone who came brought a gift—articles of silver and gold, and robes, weapons and spices, and horses and mules.

[25]Solomon had four thousand stalls for horses and chariots, and twelve thousand horses,[g] which he kept in the chariot cities and also with him in Jerusalem. [26]He ruled over all the kings from the River[h] to the land of the Philistines, as far as the border of Egypt. [27]The king made silver as common in Jerusalem as stones, and cedar as plentiful as sycamore-fig trees in the foothills. [28]Solomon's horses were imported from Egypt[i] and from all other countries.

Solomon's Death

[29]As for the other events of Solomon's reign, from beginning to end, are they not written in the records of Nathan the prophet, in the prophecy of Ahijah the Shilonite and in the visions of Iddo the seer concerning Jeroboam son of Nebat? [30]Solomon reigned in Jerusalem over all Israel forty years. [31]Then he rested with his fathers and was buried in the city of David his father. And Rehoboam his son succeeded him as king.

Israel Rebels Against Rehoboam

10 Rehoboam went to Shechem, for all the Israelites had gone there to make him king. [2]When Jeroboam son of Nebat heard this (he was in Egypt, where he had fled from King Solomon), he returned from Egypt. [3]So they sent for Jeroboam, and he and all Israel went to Rehoboam and said to him: [4]"Your father put a heavy yoke on us, but now lighten the harsh labor and the heavy yoke he put on us, and we will serve you."

[5]Rehoboam answered, "Come back to me in three days." So the people went away.

[6]Then King Rehoboam consulted the elders who had served his father Solomon during his lifetime. "How would you advise me to answer these people?" he asked.

---

[a]10 Probably a variant of *almugwood*
[b]13 That is, about 25 tons (about 23 metric tons)
[c]15 That is, about 7 1/2 pounds (about 3.5 kilograms)   [d]16 That is, about 3 3/4 pounds (about 1.7 kilograms)   [e]21 Hebrew *of ships that could go to Tarshish*   [f]21 Hebrew *Huram,* a variant of *Hiram*   [g]25 Or *charioteers*
[h]26 That is, the Euphrates   [i]28 Or possibly *Muzur,* a region in Cilicia

Intercessor

REES HOWELLS had seen Will Battery before, a homeless drunk who smelled bad and slept in the boiler room of the local tin mill: an outcast. Still, Howells was drawn to the man, strongly convinced that God wanted to restore him to sanity and salvation. So Howells spent all his Sundays with Will, taking genuine joy in his company and enduring the stares of the townsfolk as they walked side by side. For three years Rees prayed for Will, sharing his money and resources until Will finally was converted. "In this way," Howells later commented, "I started at the bottom and loved just one, and if you love one, you can love many; and if many, you can love all."[1]

Such was the work of God in the life of Rees Howells, a simple praying man whose name became synonymous with *intercessor*; he became a lightning rod for revival, a missionary to South Africa and founder of the Bible College of Wales.

Believing prayer was the single most important act he could perform for the future of the world, Howells called college-wide prayer meetings throughout World War II to cry out to God for the defeat of Hitler and freedom of the gospel in Europe. He was troubled and burdened greatly for the Allied troops, saying, "If they suffer more than we suffer for them, it will be our lifelong shame ... Lord, don't allow us to pray any differently from what we could if we were on the front line."[2]

In September 1943, the Allied troops attempted to capture a beachhead in Salerno, Italy—a major foothold in the southern approach to Rome. The Bible College was meeting for prayer when Rees suddenly said in a trembling voice, "The Lord has burdened me ... with the invasion of Salerno. I believe our men are in great difficulties, and the Lord has told me that unless we can pray them through, they are in danger of losing their hold." The college prayed fervently until exactly 11:00 P.M., when everyone spontaneously began praising God, believing that the victory had been won.

A few days later the news came with the headline, "The Miracle of Salerno." It told how enemy artillery was advancing and that unless a miracle happened the beachhead would be lost. "Suddenly," an eyewitness said, "for no accountable reason, the firing ceased and the Nazi artillery stopped its advance. A deathly stillness settled on the scene. We waited in breathless anticipation, but nothing happened. I looked at my watch—*it was eleven o'clock at night*. Still we waited, but still nothing happened; and nothing happened all that night, but those hours made all the difference to the invasion. By the morning the beachhead was established."[3]

During the war God had called the college to pray for the world, just as Howells had been called to pray for the soul of Will Battery. In both were embodied what Howells believed to be the main principle of intercession, that "man's extremity is God's opportunity."

PRAY:

Lord, lead me into the depths of intercession. Make me to see the world as you do, and to join your Son in passionate intercession for the world (see Hebrews 7:25).

MEMORIZE:

Some trust in chariots and some in horses, but we trust in the name of the LORD our God. **PSALM 20:7**

FOR YOUR NEXT DEVOTIONAL READING, GO TO PAGE 505.

⁷They replied, "If you will be kind to these people and please them and give them a favorable answer, they will always be your servants."

⁸But Rehoboam rejected the advice the elders gave him and consulted the young men who had grown up with him and were serving him. ⁹He asked them, "What is your advice? How should we answer these people who say to me, 'Lighten the yoke your father put on us'?"

¹⁰The young men who had grown up with him replied, "Tell the people who have said to you, 'Your father put a heavy yoke on us, but make our yoke lighter'— tell them, 'My little finger is thicker than my father's waist. ¹¹My father laid on you a heavy yoke; I will make it even heavier. My father scourged you with whips; I will scourge you with scorpions.'"

¹²Three days later Jeroboam and all the people returned to Rehoboam, as the king had said, "Come back to me in three days." ¹³The king answered them harshly. Rejecting the advice of the elders, ¹⁴he followed the advice of the young men and said, "My father made your yoke heavy; I will make it even heavier. My father scourged you with whips; I will scourge you with scorpions." ¹⁵So the king did not listen to the people, for this turn of events was from God, to fulfill the word the LORD had spoken to Jeroboam son of Nebat through Ahijah the Shilonite.

¹⁶When all Israel saw that the king refused to listen to them, they answered the king:

"What share do we have in David,
    what part in Jesse's son?
To your tents, O Israel!
    Look after your own house,
        O David!"

So all the Israelites went home. ¹⁷But as for the Israelites who were living in the towns of Judah, Rehoboam still ruled over them.

¹⁸King Rehoboam sent out Adoniram,ᵃ who was in charge of forced labor, but the Israelites stoned him to death. King Rehoboam, however, managed to get into his chariot and escape to Jerusalem. ¹⁹So Israel has been in rebellion against the house of David to this day.

11 When Rehoboam arrived in Jerusalem, he mustered the house of Judah and Benjamin—a hundred and eighty thousand fighting men—to make war against Israel and to regain the kingdom for Rehoboam.

²But this word of the LORD came to Shemaiah the man of God: ³"Say to Rehoboam son of Solomon king of Judah and to all the Israelites in Judah and Benjamin, ⁴'This is what the LORD says: Do not go up to fight against your brothers. Go home, every one of you, for this is my doing.'" So they obeyed the words of the LORD and turned back from marching against Jeroboam.

Rehoboam Fortifies Judah

⁵Rehoboam lived in Jerusalem and built up towns for defense in Judah: ⁶Bethlehem, Etam, Tekoa, ⁷Beth Zur, Soco, Adullam, ⁸Gath, Mareshah, Ziph, ⁹Adoraim, Lachish, Azekah, ¹⁰Zorah, Aijalon and Hebron. These were fortified cities in Judah and Benjamin. ¹¹He strengthened their defenses and put commanders in them, with supplies of food, olive oil and wine. ¹²He put shields and spears in all the cities, and made them very strong. So Judah and Benjamin were his.

¹³The priests and Levites from all their districts throughout Israel sided with him. ¹⁴The Levites even abandoned their pasturelands and property, and came to Judah and Jerusalem because Jeroboam and his sons had rejected them as priests of the LORD. ¹⁵And he appointed his own priests for the high places and for the goat and calf idols he had made. ¹⁶Those from every tribe of Israel who set their hearts on seeking the LORD, the God of Israel, followed the Levites to Jerusalem to offer sacrifices to the LORD, the God of their fathers. ¹⁷They strengthened the kingdom of Judah and supported Rehoboam son of Solomon three years, walking in the ways of David and Solomon during this time.

Rehoboam's Family

¹⁸Rehoboam married Mahalath, who was the daughter of David's son Jerimoth

---

ᵃ18 Hebrew *Hadoram*, a variant of *Adoniram*

and of Abihail, the daughter of Jesse's son Eliab. ¹⁹She bore him sons: Jeush, Shemariah and Zaham. ²⁰Then he married Maacah daughter of Absalom, who bore him Abijah, Attai, Ziza and Shelomith. ²¹Rehoboam loved Maacah daughter of Absalom more than any of his other wives and concubines. In all, he had eighteen wives and sixty concubines, twenty-eight sons and sixty daughters.

²²Rehoboam appointed Abijah son of Maacah to be the chief prince among his brothers, in order to make him king. ²³He acted wisely, dispersing some of his sons throughout the districts of Judah and Benjamin, and to all the fortified cities. He gave them abundant provisions and took many wives for them.

Shishak Attacks Jerusalem

12 After Rehoboam's position as king was established and he had become strong, he and all Israel*ᵃ* with him abandoned the law of the LORD. ²Because they had been unfaithful to the LORD, Shishak king of Egypt attacked Jerusalem in the fifth year of King Rehoboam. ³With twelve hundred chariots and sixty thousand horsemen and the innumerable troops of Libyans, Sukkites and Cushites*ᵇ* that came with him from Egypt, ⁴he captured the fortified cities of Judah and came as far as Jerusalem.

⁵Then the prophet Shemaiah came to Rehoboam and to the leaders of Judah who had assembled in Jerusalem for fear of Shishak, and he said to them, "This is what the LORD says, 'You have abandoned me; therefore, I now abandon you to Shishak.'"

⁶The leaders of Israel and the king humbled themselves and said, "The LORD is just."

⁷When the LORD saw that they humbled themselves, this word of the LORD came to Shemaiah: "Since they have humbled themselves, I will not destroy them but will soon give them deliverance. My wrath will not be poured out on Jerusalem through Shishak. ⁸They will, however, become subject to him, so that they may learn the difference between serving me and serving the kings of other lands."

⁹When Shishak king of Egypt attacked Jerusalem, he carried off the treasures of the temple of the LORD and the treasures of the royal palace. He took everything, including the gold shields Solomon had made. ¹⁰So King Rehoboam made bronze shields to replace them and assigned these to the commanders of the guard on duty at the entrance to the royal palace. ¹¹Whenever the king went to the LORD's temple, the guards went with him, bearing the shields, and afterward they returned them to the guardroom.

¹²Because Rehoboam humbled himself, the LORD's anger turned from him, and he was not totally destroyed. Indeed, there was some good in Judah.

¹³King Rehoboam established himself firmly in Jerusalem and continued as king. He was forty-one years old when he became king, and he reigned seventeen years in Jerusalem, the city the LORD had chosen out of all the tribes of Israel in which to put his Name. His mother's name was Naamah; she was an Ammonite. ¹⁴He did evil because he had not set his heart on seeking the LORD.

¹⁵As for the events of Rehoboam's reign, from beginning to end, are they not written in the records of Shemaiah the prophet and of Iddo the seer that deal with genealogies? There was continual warfare between Rehoboam and Jeroboam. ¹⁶Rehoboam rested with his fathers and was buried in the City of David. And Abijah his son succeeded him as king.

Abijah King of Judah

13 In the eighteenth year of the reign of Jeroboam, Abijah became king of Judah, ²and he reigned in Jerusalem three years. His mother's name was Maacah,*ᶜ* a daughter*ᵈ* of Uriel of Gibeah.

There was war between Abijah and Jeroboam. ³Abijah went into battle with a force of four hundred thousand able fighting men, and Jeroboam drew up a battle line against him with eight hundred thousand able troops.

⁴Abijah stood on Mount Zemaraim, in the hill country of Ephraim, and said,

---

ᵃ1 That is, Judah, as frequently in 2 Chronicles
ᵇ3 That is, people from the upper Nile region
ᶜ2 Most Septuagint manuscripts and Syriac (see also 2 Chron. 11:20 and 1 Kings 15:2); Hebrew *Micaiah*   *ᵈ2* Or *granddaughter*

"Jeroboam and all Israel, listen to me! [5]Don't you know that the LORD, the God of Israel, has given the kingship of Israel to David and his descendants forever by a covenant of salt? [6]Yet Jeroboam son of Nebat, an official of Solomon son of David, rebelled against his master. [7]Some worthless scoundrels gathered around him and opposed Rehoboam son of Solomon when he was young and indecisive and not strong enough to resist them.

[8]"And now you plan to resist the kingdom of the LORD, which is in the hands of David's descendants. You are indeed a vast army and have with you the golden calves that Jeroboam made to be your gods. [9]But didn't you drive out the priests of the LORD, the sons of Aaron, and the Levites, and make priests of your own as the peoples of other lands do? Whoever comes to consecrate himself with a young bull and seven rams may become a priest of what are not gods.

[10]"As for us, the LORD is our God, and we have not forsaken him. The priests who serve the LORD are sons of Aaron, and the Levites assist them. [11]Every morning and evening they present burnt offerings and fragrant incense to the LORD. They set out the bread on the ceremonially clean table and light the lamps on the gold lampstand every evening. We are observing the requirements of the LORD our God. But you have forsaken him. [12]God is with us; he is our leader. His priests with their trumpets will sound the battle cry against you. Men of Israel, do not fight against the LORD, the God of your fathers, for you will not succeed."

[13]Now Jeroboam had sent troops around to the rear, so that while he was in front of Judah the ambush was behind them. [14]Judah turned and saw that they were being attacked at both front and rear. Then they cried out to the LORD. The priests blew their trumpets [15]and the men of Judah raised the battle cry. At the sound of their battle cry, God routed Jeroboam and all Israel before Abijah and Judah. [16]The Israelites fled before Judah, and God delivered them into their hands. [17]Abijah and his men inflicted heavy losses on them, so that there were five hundred thousand casualties among Israel's able men. [18]The men of Israel were subdued on that occasion, and the men of Judah were victorious because they relied on the LORD, the God of their fathers.

> JUDAH *turned and saw that they were being attacked at both front and rear. Then they cried out to the LORD.*
>
> 2 CHRONICLES 13:14

[19]Abijah pursued Jeroboam and took from him the towns of Bethel, Jeshanah and Ephron, with their surrounding villages. [20]Jeroboam did not regain power during the time of Abijah. And the LORD struck him down and he died.

[21]But Abijah grew in strength. He married fourteen wives and had twenty-two sons and sixteen daughters.

[22]The other events of Abijah's reign, what he did and what he said, are written in the annotations of the prophet Iddo.

14 And Abijah rested with his fathers and was buried in the City of David. Asa his son succeeded him as king, and in his days the country was at peace for ten years.

Asa King of Judah

[2]Asa did what was good and right in the eyes of the LORD his God. [3]He removed the foreign altars and the high places, smashed the sacred stones and cut down the Asherah poles.[a] [4]He commanded Judah to seek the LORD, the God of their fathers, and to obey his laws and commands. [5]He removed the high places and incense altars in every town in Judah, and the kingdom was at peace under him. [6]He built up the fortified cities of Judah, since the land was at peace. No one was at war with him during those years, for the LORD gave him rest.

[7]"Let us build up these towns," he said to Judah, "and put walls around them, with towers, gates and bars. The land is still ours, because we have sought the LORD our God; we sought him and he has given us rest on every side." So they built and prospered.

[8]Asa had an army of three hundred

---

[a]3 That is, symbols of the goddess Asherah; here and elsewhere in 2 Chronicles

thousand men from Judah, equipped with large shields and with spears, and two hundred and eighty thousand from Benjamin, armed with small shields and with bows. All these were brave fighting men. ⁹Zerah the Cushite marched out against them with a vast army*ᵃ* and three hundred chariots, and came as far as Mareshah. ¹⁰Asa went out to meet him, and they took up battle positions in the Valley of Zephathah near Mareshah. ¹¹Then Asa called to the LORD his God and said, "LORD, there is no one like you

ᵃ9 Hebrew *with an army of a thousand thousands* or *with an army of thousands upon thousands*

---

2 CHRONICLES 14:2-15

[M O N D A Y]

The Best Posture for Prayer

14:11 "LORD, THERE IS NO ONE LIKE YOU TO HELP THE POWERLESS AGAINST THE MIGHTY."

"Then Asa called to the LORD his God and said, 'LORD, there is no one like you to help the powerless against the mighty. Help us, O LORD our God, for we rely on you, and in your name we have come against this vast army'" (14:11).

As a telephone repairman worked on the pastor's telephone, he listened to the pastor and two colleagues discuss the best posture for prayer. One said, "I still think the best way to pray is head bowed, hands folded." Another said, "That's fine if it helps you, but I prefer standing with hands open and raised to heaven. It helps me feel my need." The last pastor agreed with the first two, but added, "Both of those have their advantages, but I'm discovering the value of laying face down on the floor. It helps me be humble." Then the telephone repairman spoke up: "I think the best posture for prayer is upside down. I was working on a telephone pole, 20 feet in the air, and fell. My harness held me, but I was hanging upside down until I got help."

Asa would have agreed with the telephone repairman—desperate is the best posture for prayer. When Asa looked at Zerah the Cushite's vast army, he knew there was no hope, except in God. When people become acutely conscious of their weaknesses, it does one of two things to them: It either so unnerves them that they panic, or it drives them to their knees in prayer. Blessed are those who pray when there is no hope. God created the universe out of nothing. He can just as easily save us when we come to nothing. He not only can, but it delights him to do so. His eyes even roam the earth looking for people like Asa (see 16:9).

It's too bad this lesson is not one that can be learned once-for-all. Asa got it right once, but he later forgot (see 16:1-12). It may take many times to get it right, but each time you learn to trust God a little bit, he will teach you to trust him a little bit more.

P R A Y :

Make Asa's prayer your own the next time you are faced with an impossible situation: "Lord, there is no one like you to help the powerless against the mighty. Help me, O Lord my God, for I rely on you."

FOR YOUR NEXT DEVOTIONAL READING, GO TO PAGE 511.

to help the powerless against the mighty. Help us, O LORD our God, for we rely on you, and in your name we have come against this vast army. O LORD, you are our God; do not let man prevail against you."

¹²The LORD struck down the Cushites before Asa and Judah. The Cushites fled, ¹³and Asa and his army pursued them as far as Gerar. Such a great number of Cushites fell that they could not recover; they were crushed before the LORD and his forces. The men of Judah carried off a large amount of plunder. ¹⁴They destroyed all the villages around Gerar, for the terror of the LORD had fallen upon them. They plundered all these villages, since there was much booty there. ¹⁵They also attacked the camps of the herdsmen and carried off droves of sheep and goats and camels. Then they returned to Jerusalem.

Asa's Reform

15 The Spirit of God came upon Azariah son of Oded. ²He went out to meet Asa and said to him, "Listen to me, Asa and all Judah and Benjamin. The LORD is with you when you are with him. If you seek him, he will be found by you, but if you forsake him, he will forsake you. ³For a long time Israel was without the true God, without a priest to teach and without the law. ⁴But in their distress they turned to the LORD, the God of Israel, and sought him, and he was found by them. ⁵In those days it was not safe to travel about, for all the inhabitants of the lands were in great turmoil. ⁶One nation was being crushed by another and one city by another, because God was troubling them with every kind of distress. ⁷But as for you, be strong and do not give up, for your work will be rewarded."

⁸When Asa heard these words and the prophecy of Azariah son of[a] Oded the prophet, he took courage. He removed the detestable idols from the whole land of Judah and Benjamin and from the towns he had captured in the hills of Ephraim. He repaired the altar of the LORD that was in front of the portico of the LORD's temple.

⁹Then he assembled all Judah and Benjamin and the people from Ephraim, Manasseh and Simeon who had settled among them, for large numbers had come over to him from Israel when they saw that the LORD his God was with him. ¹⁰They assembled at Jerusalem in the third month of the fifteenth year of Asa's reign. ¹¹At that time they sacrificed to the LORD seven hundred head of cattle and seven thousand sheep and goats from the plunder they had brought back. ¹²They entered into a covenant to seek the LORD, the God of their fathers, with all their heart and soul. ¹³All who would not seek the LORD, the God of Israel, were to be put to death, whether small or great, man or woman. ¹⁴They took an oath to the LORD with loud acclamation, with shouting and with trumpets and horns. ¹⁵All Judah rejoiced about the oath because they had sworn it wholeheartedly. They sought God eagerly, and he was found by them. So the LORD gave them rest on every side.

¹⁶King Asa also deposed his grandmother Maacah from her position as queen mother, because she had made a repulsive Asherah pole. Asa cut the pole down, broke it up and burned it in the Kidron Valley. ¹⁷Although he did not remove the high places from Israel, Asa's heart was fully committed ⌊to the LORD⌋ all his life. ¹⁸He brought into the temple of God the silver and gold and the articles that he and his father had dedicated.

¹⁹There was no more war until the thirty-fifth year of Asa's reign.

Asa's Last Years

16 In the thirty-sixth year of Asa's reign Baasha king of Israel went up against Judah and fortified Ramah to prevent anyone from leaving or entering the territory of Asa king of Judah.

²Asa then took the silver and gold out of the treasuries of the LORD's temple and of his own palace and sent it to Ben-Hadad king of Aram, who was ruling in Damascus. ³"Let there be a treaty between me and you," he said, "as there was between my father and your father. See, I am sending you silver and gold. Now break your treaty with Baasha king of Israel so he will withdraw from me."

---

a8 Vulgate and Syriac (see also Septuagint and verse 1); Hebrew does not have *Azariah son of.*

⁴Ben-Hadad agreed with King Asa and sent the commanders of his forces against the towns of Israel. They conquered Ijon, Dan, Abel Maim*ᵃ* and all the store cities of Naphtali. ⁵When Baasha heard this, he stopped building Ramah and abandoned his work. ⁶Then King Asa brought all the men of Judah, and they carried away from Ramah the stones and timber Baasha had been using. With them he built up Geba and Mizpah.

⁷At that time Hanani the seer came to Asa king of Judah and said to him: "Because you relied on the king of Aram and not on the LORD your God, the army of the king of Aram has escaped from your hand. ⁸Were not the Cushites*ᵇ* and Libyans a mighty army with great numbers of chariots and horsemen*ᶜ*? Yet when you relied on the LORD, he delivered them into your hand. ⁹For the eyes of the LORD range throughout the earth to strengthen those whose hearts are fully committed to him. You have done a foolish thing, and from now on you will be at war."

¹⁰Asa was angry with the seer because of this; he was so enraged that he put him in prison. At the same time Asa brutally oppressed some of the people.

¹¹The events of Asa's reign, from beginning to end, are written in the book of the kings of Judah and Israel. ¹²In the thirty-ninth year of his reign Asa was afflicted with a disease in his feet. Though his disease was severe, even in his illness he did not seek help from the LORD, but only from the physicians. ¹³Then in the forty-first year of his reign Asa died and rested with his fathers. ¹⁴They buried him in the tomb that he had cut out for himself in the City of David. They laid him on a bier covered with spices and various blended perfumes, and they made a huge fire in his honor.

Jehoshaphat King of Judah

17 Jehoshaphat his son succeeded him as king and strengthened himself against Israel. ²He stationed troops in all the fortified cities of Judah and put garrisons in Judah and in the towns of Ephraim that his father Asa had captured.

³The LORD was with Jehoshaphat because in his early years he walked in the ways his father David had followed. He did not consult the Baals ⁴but sought the God of his father and followed his commands rather than the practices of Israel. ⁵The LORD established the kingdom under his control; and all Judah brought gifts to Jehoshaphat, so that he had great wealth and honor. ⁶His heart was devoted to the ways of the LORD; furthermore, he removed the high places and the Asherah poles from Judah.

⁷In the third year of his reign he sent his officials Ben-Hail, Obadiah, Zechariah, Nethanel and Micaiah to teach in the towns of Judah. ⁸With them were certain Levites—Shemaiah, Nethaniah, Zebadiah, Asahel, Shemiramoth, Jehonathan, Adonijah, Tobijah and Tob-Adonijah—and the priests Elishama and Jehoram. ⁹They taught throughout Judah, taking with them the Book of the Law of the LORD; they went around to all the towns of Judah and taught the people.

¹⁰The fear of the LORD fell on all the kingdoms of the lands surrounding Judah, so that they did not make war with Jehoshaphat. ¹¹Some Philistines brought Jehoshaphat gifts and silver as tribute, and the Arabs brought him flocks: seven thousand seven hundred rams and seven thousand seven hundred goats.

¹²Jehoshaphat became more and more powerful; he built forts and store cities in Judah ¹³and had large supplies in the towns of Judah. He also kept experienced fighting men in Jerusalem. ¹⁴Their enrollment by families was as follows:

From Judah, commanders of units of 1,000:
Adnah the commander, with 300,000 fighting men;
¹⁵next, Jehohanan the commander, with 280,000;
¹⁶next, Amasiah son of Zicri, who volunteered himself for the service of the LORD, with 200,000.
¹⁷From Benjamin:
Eliada, a valiant soldier, with 200,000 men armed with bows and shields;
¹⁸next, Jehozabad, with 180,000 men armed for battle.

ᵃ4 Also known as *Abel Beth Maacah*
ᵇ8 That is, people from the upper Nile region
ᶜ8 Or *charioteers*

¹⁹These were the men who served the king, besides those he stationed in the fortified cities throughout Judah.

Micaiah Prophesies Against Ahab

18 Now Jehoshaphat had great wealth and honor, and he allied himself with Ahab by marriage. ²Some years later he went down to visit Ahab in Samaria. Ahab slaughtered many sheep and cattle for him and the people with him and urged him to attack Ramoth Gilead. ³Ahab king of Israel asked Jehoshaphat king of Judah, "Will you go with me against Ramoth Gilead?"

Jehoshaphat replied, "I am as you are, and my people as your people; we will join you in the war." ⁴But Jehoshaphat also said to the king of Israel, "First seek the counsel of the LORD."

⁵So the king of Israel brought together the prophets—four hundred men—and asked them, "Shall we go to war against Ramoth Gilead, or shall I refrain?"

"Go," they answered, "for God will give it into the king's hand."

⁶But Jehoshaphat asked, "Is there not a prophet of the LORD here whom we can inquire of?"

⁷The king of Israel answered Jehoshaphat, "There is still one man through whom we can inquire of the LORD, but I hate him because he never prophesies anything good about me, but always bad. He is Micaiah son of Imlah."

"The king should not say that," Jehoshaphat replied.

⁸So the king of Israel called one of his officials and said, "Bring Micaiah son of Imlah at once."

⁹Dressed in their royal robes, the king of Israel and Jehoshaphat king of Judah were sitting on their thrones at the threshing floor by the entrance to the gate of Samaria, with all the prophets prophesying before them. ¹⁰Now Zedekiah son of Kenaanah had made iron horns, and he declared, "This is what the LORD says: 'With these you will gore the Arameans until they are destroyed.'"

¹¹All the other prophets were prophesying the same thing. "Attack Ramoth Gilead and be victorious," they said, "for the LORD will give it into the king's hand."

¹²The messenger who had gone to summon Micaiah said to him, "Look, as one man the other prophets are predicting success for the king. Let your word agree with theirs, and speak favorably."

¹³But Micaiah said, "As surely as the LORD lives, I can tell him only what my God says."

¹⁴When he arrived, the king asked him, "Micaiah, shall we go to war against Ramoth Gilead, or shall I refrain?"

"Attack and be victorious," he answered, "for they will be given into your hand."

¹⁵The king said to him, "How many times must I make you swear to tell me nothing but the truth in the name of the LORD?"

¹⁶Then Micaiah answered, "I saw all Israel scattered on the hills like sheep without a shepherd, and the LORD said, 'These people have no master. Let each one go home in peace.'"

¹⁷The king of Israel said to Jehoshaphat, "Didn't I tell you that he never prophesies anything good about me, but only bad?"

¹⁸Micaiah continued, "Therefore hear the word of the LORD: I saw the LORD sitting on his throne with all the host of heaven standing on his right and on his left. ¹⁹And the LORD said, 'Who will entice Ahab king of Israel into attacking Ramoth Gilead and going to his death there?'

"One suggested this, and another that. ²⁰Finally, a spirit came forward, stood before the LORD and said, 'I will entice him.'

"'By what means?' the LORD asked.

²¹"'I will go and be a lying spirit in the mouths of all his prophets,' he said.

"'You will succeed in enticing him,' said the LORD. 'Go and do it.'

²²"So now the LORD has put a lying spirit in the mouths of these prophets of yours. The LORD has decreed disaster for you."

²³Then Zedekiah son of Kenaanah went up and slapped Micaiah in the face. "Which way did the spirit from*ᵃ* the LORD go when he went from me to speak to you?" he asked.

²⁴Micaiah replied, "You will find out on the day you go to hide in an inner room."

ᵃ23 Or *Spirit of*

²⁵The king of Israel then ordered, "Take Micaiah and send him back to Amon the ruler of the city and to Joash the king's son, ²⁶and say, 'This is what the king says: Put this fellow in prison and give him nothing but bread and water until I return safely.'"

²⁷Micaiah declared, "If you ever return safely, the LORD has not spoken through me." Then he added, "Mark my words, all you people!"

Ahab Killed at Ramoth Gilead

²⁸So the king of Israel and Jehoshaphat king of Judah went up to Ramoth Gilead. ²⁹The king of Israel said to Jehoshaphat, "I will enter the battle in disguise, but you wear your royal robes." So the king of Israel disguised himself and went into battle.

³⁰Now the king of Aram had ordered his chariot commanders, "Do not fight with anyone, small or great, except the king of Israel." ³¹When the chariot commanders saw Jehoshaphat, they thought, "This is the king of Israel." So they turned to attack him, but Jehoshaphat cried out, and the LORD helped him. God drew them away from him, ³²for when the chariot commanders saw that he was not the king of Israel, they stopped pursuing him.

³³But someone drew his bow at random and hit the king of Israel between the sections of his armor. The king told the chariot driver, "Wheel around and get me out of the fighting. I've been wounded." ³⁴All day long the battle raged, and the king of Israel propped himself up in his chariot facing the Arameans until evening. Then at sunset he died.

19 When Jehoshaphat king of Judah returned safely to his palace in Jerusalem, ²Jehu the seer, the son of Hanani, went out to meet him and said to the king, "Should you help the wicked and loveᵃ those who hate the LORD? Because of this, the wrath of the LORD is upon you. ³There is, however, some good in you, for you have rid the land of the Asherah poles and have set your heart on seeking God."

Jehoshaphat Appoints Judges

⁴Jehoshaphat lived in Jerusalem, and he went out again among the people from Beersheba to the hill country of Ephraim and turned them back to the LORD, the God of their fathers. ⁵He appointed judges in the land, in each of the fortified cities of Judah. ⁶He told them, "Consider carefully what you do, because you are not judging for man but for the LORD, who is with you whenever you give a verdict. ⁷Now let the fear of the LORD be upon you. Judge carefully, for with the LORD our God there is no injustice or partiality or bribery."

⁸In Jerusalem also, Jehoshaphat appointed some of the Levites, priests and heads of Israelite families to administer the law of the LORD and to settle disputes. And they lived in Jerusalem. ⁹He gave them these orders: "You must serve faithfully and wholeheartedly in the fear of the LORD. ¹⁰In every case that comes before you from your fellow countrymen who live in the cities—whether bloodshed or other concerns of the law, commands, decrees or ordinances—you are to warn them not to sin against the LORD; otherwise his wrath will come on you and your brothers. Do this, and you will not sin.

¹¹"Amariah the chief priest will be over you in any matter concerning the LORD, and Zebadiah son of Ishmael, the leader of the tribe of Judah, will be over you in any matter concerning the king, and the Levites will serve as officials before you. Act with courage, and may the LORD be with those who do well."

Jehoshaphat Defeats Moab and Ammon

20 After this, the Moabites and Ammonites with some of the Meunitesᵇ came to make war on Jehoshaphat.

²Some men came and told Jehoshaphat, "A vast army is coming against you from Edom,ᶜ from the other side of the Sea.ᵈ It is already in Hazazon Tamar" (that is, En Gedi). ³Alarmed, Jehoshaphat resolved to inquire of the LORD, and he proclaimed a fast for all Judah. ⁴The people of Judah came together to seek help from the LORD; indeed, they came from every town in Judah to seek him.

ᵃ2 Or and make alliances with   ᵇ1 Some Septuagint manuscripts; Hebrew Ammonites
ᶜ2 One Hebrew manuscript; most Hebrew manuscripts, Septuagint and Vulgate Aram
ᵈ2 That is, the Dead Sea

THE *people of Judah came together to seek help from the* LORD; *indeed, they came from every town in Judah to seek him.*

2 CHRONICLES 20:4

⁵Then Jehoshaphat stood up in the assembly of Judah and Jerusalem at the temple of the LORD in the front of the new courtyard ⁶and said:

"O LORD, God of our fathers, are you not the God who is in heaven? You rule over all the kingdoms of the nations. Power and might are in your hand, and no one can withstand you. ⁷O our God, did you not drive out the inhabitants of this land before your people Israel and give it forever to the descendants of Abraham your friend? ⁸They have lived in it and have built in it a sanctuary for your Name, saying, ⁹'If calamity comes upon us, whether the sword of judgment, or plague or famine, we will stand in your presence before this temple that bears your Name and will cry out to you in our distress, and you will hear us and save us.'

¹⁰"But now here are men from Ammon, Moab and Mount Seir, whose territory you would not allow Israel to invade when they came from Egypt; so they turned away from them and did not destroy them. ¹¹See how they are repaying us by coming to drive us out of the possession you gave us as an inheritance. ¹²O our God, will you not judge them? For we have no power to face this vast army that is attacking us. We do not know what to do, but our eyes are upon you."

¹³All the men of Judah, with their wives and children and little ones, stood there before the LORD.

¹⁴Then the Spirit of the LORD came upon Jahaziel son of Zechariah, the son of Benaiah, the son of Jeiel, the son of Mattaniah, a Levite and descendant of Asaph, as he stood in the assembly. ¹⁵He said: "Listen, King Jehoshaphat

and all who live in Judah and Jerusalem! This is what the LORD says to you: 'Do not be afraid or discouraged because of this vast army. For the battle is not yours, but God's. ¹⁶Tomorrow march down against them. They will be climbing up by the Pass of Ziz, and you will find them at the end of the gorge in the Desert of Jeruel. ¹⁷You will not have to fight this battle. Take up your positions; stand firm and see the deliverance the LORD will give you, O Judah and Jerusalem. Do not be afraid; do not be discouraged. Go out to face them tomorrow, and the LORD will be with you.'"

¹⁸Jehoshaphat bowed with his face to the ground, and all the people of Judah and Jerusalem fell down in worship before the LORD. ¹⁹Then some Levites from the Kohathites and Korahites stood up and praised the LORD, the God of Israel, with a very loud voice.

²⁰Early in the morning they left for the Desert of Tekoa. As they set out, Jehoshaphat stood and said, "Listen to me, Judah and people of Jerusalem! Have faith in the LORD your God and you will be upheld; have faith in his prophets and you will be successful." ²¹After consulting the people, Jehoshaphat appointed men to sing to the LORD and to praise him for the splendor of his*ᵃ* holiness as they went out at the head of the army, saying:

"Give thanks to the LORD,
    for his love endures forever."

²²As they began to sing and praise, the LORD set ambushes against the men of Ammon and Moab and Mount Seir who were invading Judah, and they were defeated. ²³The men of Ammon and Moab rose up against the men from Mount Seir to destroy and annihilate them. After they finished slaughtering the men from Seir, they helped to destroy one another.

²⁴When the men of Judah came to the place that overlooks the desert and looked toward the vast army, they saw only dead bodies lying on the ground; no one had escaped. ²⁵So Jehoshaphat and his men went to carry off their plunder, and they found among them a great

ᵃ*21* Or *him with the splendor of*

amount of equipment and clothing[a] and also articles of value—more than they could take away. There was so much plunder that it took three days to collect it. ²⁶On the fourth day they assembled in the Valley of Beracah, where they praised the LORD. This is why it is called the Valley of Beracah[b] to this day.

²⁷Then, led by Jehoshaphat, all the men of Judah and Jerusalem returned joyfully to Jerusalem, for the LORD had given them cause to rejoice over their enemies. ²⁸They entered Jerusalem and went to the temple of the LORD with harps and lutes and trumpets.

[a]25 Some Hebrew manuscripts and Vulgate; most Hebrew manuscripts *corpses* [b]26 *Beracah* means *praise.*

{ TUESDAY }

2 CHRONICLES 20:1 – 30

Leading With Praise

20:12 "WE DO NOT KNOW WHAT TO DO, BUT OUR EYES ARE UPON YOU."

Jehoshaphat started in the same prayer posture as Asa (see previous devotion). He was desperate, but perhaps there was a twist in his desperation; the phrase, "we do not know what to do" sounds like something he might have said after expending a lot of time and sweat trying to figure out what to do. It sounds like the kind of thing one says after reading and rereading the spreadsheets and budget reports, and everything still points to disaster. In any case, Jehoshaphat is where he needs to be—desperate—and his eyes are on God.

The pattern of Jehoshaphat's prayer for help is classic and is repeated again and again in the Bible. It bears repeating and underlining: First, he praises God for who he is and what he has promised; that is, Jehoshaphat remembers to whom he is talking (20:6–9). Second, he briefly describes the situation (verses 10–11); and third, he asks God to intervene (verse 12). Take note of the relative weight he gives to these three sections of his prayer: He spends a lot of time praising God, and then, in descending order of time, describes the situation and asks for help. There is a lesson here we need to learn, for so often our prayers reflect a reversed order of priorities: A lot of time is given to weeping and wailing and advising God on what he should do, and very little time is spent thanking him for what he can do!

The prayer meeting ends with a prophetic word from Jahaziel that so encourages the people that they go into battle with the singers leading! That is an amazing picture of prayer. Jehoshaphat's prayer is led by praise and so is his army. They go to meet their enemies singing, "Give thanks to the LORD, for his love endures forever" (verse 21). But when the people get to their enemies, their enemies are all dead. How pleasing it was to thank God for the victory before seeing it. It was pleasing to them and pleasing to God. Let praise and thanksgiving be your banner in prayer of all kinds and especially your prayers of desperation.

PRAY:

Jehoshaphat's prayer is another good prayer to make your own:
"I do not know what to do, but my eyes are upon you."

FOR YOUR NEXT DEVOTIONAL READING, GO TO PAGE 540.

²⁹The fear of God came upon all the kingdoms of the countries when they heard how the LORD had fought against the enemies of Israel. ³⁰And the kingdom of Jehoshaphat was at peace, for his God had given him rest on every side.

The End of Jehoshaphat's Reign

³¹So Jehoshaphat reigned over Judah. He was thirty-five years old when he became king of Judah, and he reigned in Jerusalem twenty-five years. His mother's name was Azubah daughter of Shilhi. ³²He walked in the ways of his father Asa and did not stray from them; he did what was right in the eyes of the LORD. ³³The high places, however, were not removed, and the people still had not set their hearts on the God of their fathers.

³⁴The other events of Jehoshaphat's reign, from beginning to end, are written in the annals of Jehu son of Hanani, which are recorded in the book of the kings of Israel.

³⁵Later, Jehoshaphat king of Judah made an alliance with Ahaziah king of Israel, who was guilty of wickedness. ³⁶He agreed with him to construct a fleet of trading ships.ᵃ After these were built at Ezion Geber, ³⁷Eliezer son of Dodavahu of Mareshah prophesied against Jehoshaphat, saying, "Because you have made an alliance with Ahaziah, the LORD will destroy what you have made." The ships were wrecked and were not able to set sail to trade.ᵇ

21 Then Jehoshaphat rested with his fathers and was buried with them in the City of David. And Jehoram his son succeeded him as king. ²Jehoram's brothers, the sons of Jehoshaphat, were Azariah, Jehiel, Zechariah, Azariahu, Michael and Shephatiah. All these were sons of Jehoshaphat king of Israel.ᶜ ³Their father had given them many gifts of silver and gold and articles of value, as well as fortified cities in Judah, but he had given the kingdom to Jehoram because he was his firstborn son.

Jehoram King of Judah

⁴When Jehoram established himself firmly over his father's kingdom, he put all his brothers to the sword along with some of the princes of Israel. ⁵Jehoram was thirty-two years old when he became king, and he reigned in Jerusalem eight years. ⁶He walked in the ways of the kings of Israel, as the house of Ahab had done, for he married a daughter of Ahab. He did evil in the eyes of the LORD. ⁷Nevertheless, because of the covenant the LORD had made with David, the LORD was not willing to destroy the house of David. He had promised to maintain a lamp for him and his descendants forever.

⁸In the time of Jehoram, Edom rebelled against Judah and set up its own king. ⁹So Jehoram went there with his officers and all his chariots. The Edomites surrounded him and his chariot commanders, but he rose up and broke through by night. ¹⁰To this day Edom has been in rebellion against Judah.

Libnah revolted at the same time, because Jehoram had forsaken the LORD, the God of his fathers. ¹¹He had also built high places on the hills of Judah and had caused the people of Jerusalem to prostitute themselves and had led Judah astray.

¹²Jehoram received a letter from Elijah the prophet, which said:

"This is what the LORD, the God of your father David, says: 'You have not walked in the ways of your father Jehoshaphat or of Asa king of Judah. ¹³But you have walked in the ways of the kings of Israel, and you have led Judah and the people of Jerusalem to prostitute themselves, just as the house of Ahab did. You have also murdered your own brothers, members of your father's house, men who were better than you. ¹⁴So now the LORD is about to strike your people, your sons, your wives and everything that is yours, with a heavy blow. ¹⁵You yourself will be very ill with a lingering disease of the bowels, until the disease causes your bowels to come out.'"

¹⁶The LORD aroused against Jehoram the hostility of the Philistines and of the Arabs who lived near the Cushites. ¹⁷They

---

ᵃ36 Hebrew *of ships that could go to Tarshish*
ᵇ37 Hebrew *sail for Tarshish*   ᶜ2 That is, Judah, as frequently in 2 Chronicles

attacked Judah, invaded it and carried off all the goods found in the king's palace, together with his sons and wives. Not a son was left to him except Ahaziah,[a] the youngest.

[18]After all this, the LORD afflicted Jehoram with an incurable disease of the bowels. [19]In the course of time, at the end of the second year, his bowels came out because of the disease, and he died in great pain. His people made no fire in his honor, as they had for his fathers.

[20]Jehoram was thirty-two years old when he became king, and he reigned in Jerusalem eight years. He passed away, to no one's regret, and was buried in the City of David, but not in the tombs of the kings.

Ahaziah King of Judah

22 The people of Jerusalem made Ahaziah, Jehoram's youngest son, king in his place, since the raiders, who came with the Arabs into the camp, had killed all the older sons. So Ahaziah son of Jehoram king of Judah began to reign.

[2]Ahaziah was twenty-two[b] years old when he became king, and he reigned in Jerusalem one year. His mother's name was Athaliah, a granddaughter of Omri.

[3]He too walked in the ways of the house of Ahab, for his mother encouraged him in doing wrong. [4]He did evil in the eyes of the LORD, as the house of Ahab had done, for after his father's death they became his advisers, to his undoing. [5]He also followed their counsel when he went with Joram[c] son of Ahab king of Israel to war against Hazael king of Aram at Ramoth Gilead. The Arameans wounded Joram; [6]so he returned to Jezreel to recover from the wounds they had inflicted on him at Ramoth[d] in his battle with Hazael king of Aram.

Then Ahaziah[e] son of Jehoram king of Judah went down to Jezreel to see Joram son of Ahab because he had been wounded.

[7]Through Ahaziah's visit to Joram, God brought about Ahaziah's downfall. When Ahaziah arrived, he went out with Joram to meet Jehu son of Nimshi, whom the LORD had anointed to destroy the house of Ahab. [8]While Jehu was executing judgment on the house of Ahab, he found the princes of Judah and the sons of Ahaziah's relatives, who had been attending Ahaziah, and he killed them. [9]He then went in search of Ahaziah, and his men captured him while he was hiding in Samaria. He was brought to Jehu and put to death. They buried him, for they said, "He was a son of Jehoshaphat, who sought the LORD with all his heart." So there was no one in the house of Ahaziah powerful enough to retain the kingdom.

Athaliah and Joash

[10]When Athaliah the mother of Ahaziah saw that her son was dead, she proceeded to destroy the whole royal family of the house of Judah. [11]But Jehosheba,[f] the daughter of King Jehoram, took Joash son of Ahaziah and stole him away from among the royal princes who were about to be murdered and put him and his nurse in a bedroom. Because Jehosheba,[f] the daughter of King Jehoram and wife of the priest Jehoiada, was Ahaziah's sister, she hid the child from Athaliah so she could not kill him. [12]He remained hidden with them at the temple of God for six years while Athaliah ruled the land.

23 In the seventh year Jehoiada showed his strength. He made a covenant with the commanders of units of a hundred: Azariah son of Jeroham, Ishmael son of Jehohanan, Azariah son of Obed, Maaseiah son of Adaiah, and Elishaphat son of Zicri. [2]They went throughout Judah and gathered the Levites and the heads of Israelite families from all the towns. When they came to Jerusalem, [3]the whole assembly made a covenant with the king at the temple of God.

Jehoiada said to them, "The king's son shall reign, as the LORD promised concerning the descendants of David. [4]Now this is what you are to do: A third of you priests and Levites who are going on

---

[a]17 Hebrew *Jehoahaz*, a variant of *Ahaziah*
[b]2 Some Septuagint manuscripts and Syriac (see also 2 Kings 8:26); Hebrew *forty-two*
[c]5 Hebrew *Jehoram*, a variant of *Joram*; also in verses 6 and 7   [d]6 Hebrew *Ramah*, a variant of *Ramoth*   [e]6 Some Hebrew manuscripts, Septuagint, Vulgate and Syriac (see also 2 Kings 8:29); most Hebrew manuscripts *Azariah*
[f]11 Hebrew *Jehoshabeath*, a variant of *Jehosheba*

duty on the Sabbath are to keep watch at the doors, ⁵a third of you at the royal palace and a third at the Foundation Gate, and all the other men are to be in the courtyards of the temple of the LORD. ⁶No one is to enter the temple of the LORD except the priests and Levites on duty; they may enter because they are consecrated, but all the other men are to guard what the LORD has assigned to them.ᵃ ⁷The Levites are to station themselves around the king, each man with his weapons in his hand. Anyone who enters the temple must be put to death. Stay close to the king wherever he goes."

⁸The Levites and all the men of Judah did just as Jehoiada the priest ordered. Each one took his men—those who were going on duty on the Sabbath and those who were going off duty—for Jehoiada the priest had not released any of the divisions. ⁹Then he gave the commanders of units of a hundred the spears and the large and small shields that had belonged to King David and that were in the temple of God. ¹⁰He stationed all the men, each with his weapon in his hand, around the king—near the altar and the temple, from the south side to the north side of the temple.

¹¹Jehoiada and his sons brought out the king's son and put the crown on him; they presented him with a copy of the covenant and proclaimed him king. They anointed him and shouted, "Long live the king!"

¹²When Athaliah heard the noise of the people running and cheering the king, she went to them at the temple of the LORD. ¹³She looked, and there was the king, standing by his pillar at the entrance. The officers and the trumpeters were beside the king, and all the people of the land were rejoicing and blowing trumpets, and singers with musical instruments were leading the praises. Then Athaliah tore her robes and shouted, "Treason! Treason!"

¹⁴Jehoiada the priest sent out the commanders of units of a hundred, who were in charge of the troops, and said to them: "Bring her out between the ranksᵇ and put to the sword anyone who follows her." For the priest had said, "Do not put her to death at the temple of the LORD."

¹⁵So they seized her as she reached the entrance of the Horse Gate on the palace grounds, and there they put her to death.

¹⁶Jehoiada then made a covenant that he and the people and the kingᶜ would be the LORD's people. ¹⁷All the people went to the temple of Baal and tore it down. They smashed the altars and idols and killed Mattan the priest of Baal in front of the altars.

¹⁸Then Jehoiada placed the oversight of the temple of the LORD in the hands of the priests, who were Levites, to whom David had made assignments in the temple, to present the burnt offerings of the LORD as written in the Law of Moses, with rejoicing and singing, as David had ordered. ¹⁹He also stationed doorkeepers at the gates of the LORD's temple so that no one who was in any way unclean might enter.

²⁰He took with him the commanders of hundreds, the nobles, the rulers of the people and all the people of the land and brought the king down from the temple of the LORD. They went into the palace through the Upper Gate and seated the king on the royal throne, ²¹and all the people of the land rejoiced. And the city was quiet, because Athaliah had been slain with the sword.

Joash Repairs the Temple

24 Joash was seven years old when he became king, and he reigned in Jerusalem forty years. His mother's name was Zibiah; she was from Beersheba. ²Joash did what was right in the eyes of the LORD all the years of Jehoiada the priest. ³Jehoiada chose two wives for him, and he had sons and daughters.

⁴Some time later Joash decided to restore the temple of the LORD. ⁵He called together the priests and Levites and said to them, "Go to the towns of Judah and collect the money due annually from all Israel, to repair the temple of your God. Do it now." But the Levites did not act at once.

⁶Therefore the king summoned Jehoiada the chief priest and said to him, "Why haven't you required the Levites to bring

ᵃ6 Or to observe the LORD's command ˌnot to enterˌ   ᵇ14 Or out from the precincts
ᶜ16 Or covenant between ˌthe LORDˌ and the people and the king that they (see 2 Kings 11:17)

in from Judah and Jerusalem the tax imposed by Moses the servant of the LORD and by the assembly of Israel for the Tent of the Testimony?"

[7]Now the sons of that wicked woman Athaliah had broken into the temple of God and had used even its sacred objects for the Baals.

[8]At the king's command, a chest was made and placed outside, at the gate of the temple of the LORD. [9]A proclamation was then issued in Judah and Jerusalem that they should bring to the LORD the tax that Moses the servant of God had required of Israel in the desert. [10]All the officials and all the people brought their contributions gladly, dropping them into the chest until it was full. [11]Whenever the chest was brought in by the Levites to the king's officials and they saw that there was a large amount of money, the royal secretary and the officer of the chief priest would come and empty the chest and carry it back to its place. They did this regularly and collected a great amount of money. [12]The king and Jehoiada gave it to the men who carried out the work required for the temple of the LORD. They hired masons and carpenters to restore the LORD's temple, and also workers in iron and bronze to repair the temple.

[13]The men in charge of the work were diligent, and the repairs progressed under them. They rebuilt the temple of God according to its original design and reinforced it. [14]When they had finished, they brought the rest of the money to the king and Jehoiada, and with it were made articles for the LORD's temple: articles for the service and for the burnt offerings, and also dishes and other objects of gold and silver. As long as Jehoiada lived, burnt offerings were presented continually in the temple of the LORD.

[15]Now Jehoiada was old and full of years, and he died at the age of a hundred and thirty. [16]He was buried with the kings in the City of David, because of the good he had done in Israel for God and his temple.

The Wickedness of Joash

[17]After the death of Jehoiada, the officials of Judah came and paid homage to the king, and he listened to them. [18]They abandoned the temple of the LORD, the God of their fathers, and worshiped Asherah poles and idols. Because of their guilt, God's anger came upon Judah and Jerusalem. [19]Although the LORD sent prophets to the people to bring them back to him, and though they testified against them, they would not listen.

[20]Then the Spirit of God came upon Zechariah son of Jehoiada the priest. He stood before the people and said, "This is what God says: 'Why do you disobey the LORD's commands? You will not prosper. Because you have forsaken the LORD, he has forsaken you.'"

[21]But they plotted against him, and by order of the king they stoned him to death in the courtyard of the LORD's temple. [22]King Joash did not remember the kindness Zechariah's father Jehoiada had shown him but killed his son, who said as he lay dying, "May the LORD see this and call you to account."

[23]At the turn of the year,[a] the army of Aram marched against Joash; it invaded Judah and Jerusalem and killed all the leaders of the people. They sent all the plunder to their king in Damascus. [24]Although the Aramean army had come with only a few men, the LORD delivered into their hands a much larger army. Because Judah had forsaken the LORD, the God of their fathers, judgment was executed on Joash. [25]When the Arameans withdrew, they left Joash severely wounded. His officials conspired against him for murdering the son of Jehoiada the priest, and they killed him in his bed. So he died and was buried in the City of David, but not in the tombs of the kings.

[26]Those who conspired against him were Zabad,[b] son of Shimeath an Ammonite woman, and Jehozabad, son of Shimrith[c] a Moabite woman. [27]The account of his sons, the many prophecies about him, and the record of the restoration of the temple of God are written in the annotations on the book of the kings. And Amaziah his son succeeded him as king.

[a]23 Probably in the spring   [b]26 A variant of Jozabad   [c]26 A variant of Shomer

Amaziah King of Judah

25 Amaziah was twenty-five years old when he became king, and he reigned in Jerusalem twenty-nine years. His mother's name was Jehoaddin[a]; she was from Jerusalem. ²He did what was right in the eyes of the Lord, but not wholeheartedly. ³After the kingdom was firmly in his control, he executed the officials who had murdered his father the king. ⁴Yet he did not put their sons to death, but acted in accordance with what is written in the Law, in the Book of Moses, where the Lord commanded: "Fathers shall not be put to death for their children, nor children put to death for their fathers; each is to die for his own sins."[b]

⁵Amaziah called the people of Judah together and assigned them according to their families to commanders of thousands and commanders of hundreds for all Judah and Benjamin. He then mustered those twenty years old or more and found that there were three hundred thousand men ready for military service, able to handle the spear and shield. ⁶He also hired a hundred thousand fighting men from Israel for a hundred talents[c] of silver.

⁷But a man of God came to him and said, "O king, these troops from Israel must not march with you, for the Lord is not with Israel—not with any of the people of Ephraim. ⁸Even if you go and fight courageously in battle, God will overthrow you before the enemy, for God has the power to help or to overthrow."

⁹Amaziah asked the man of God, "But what about the hundred talents I paid for these Israelite troops?"

The man of God replied, "The Lord can give you much more than that."

¹⁰So Amaziah dismissed the troops who had come to him from Ephraim and sent them home. They were furious with Judah and left for home in a great rage.

¹¹Amaziah then marshaled his strength and led his army to the Valley of Salt, where he killed ten thousand men of Seir. ¹²The army of Judah also captured ten thousand men alive, took them to the top of a cliff and threw them down so that all were dashed to pieces.

¹³Meanwhile the troops that Amaziah had sent back and had not allowed to take part in the war raided Judean towns from Samaria to Beth Horon. They killed three thousand people and carried off great quantities of plunder.

¹⁴When Amaziah returned from slaughtering the Edomites, he brought back the gods of the people of Seir. He set them up as his own gods, bowed down to them and burned sacrifices to them. ¹⁵The anger of the Lord burned against Amaziah, and he sent a prophet to him, who said, "Why do you consult this people's gods, which could not save their own people from your hand?"

¹⁶While he was still speaking, the king said to him, "Have we appointed you an adviser to the king? Stop! Why be struck down?"

So the prophet stopped but said, "I know that God has determined to destroy you, because you have done this and have not listened to my counsel."

¹⁷After Amaziah king of Judah consulted his advisers, he sent this challenge to Jehoash[d] son of Jehoahaz, the son of Jehu, king of Israel: "Come, meet me face to face."

¹⁸But Jehoash king of Israel replied to Amaziah king of Judah: "A thistle in Lebanon sent a message to a cedar in Lebanon, 'Give your daughter to my son in marriage.' Then a wild beast in Lebanon came along and trampled the thistle underfoot. ¹⁹You say to yourself that you have defeated Edom, and now you are arrogant and proud. But stay at home! Why ask for trouble and cause your own downfall and that of Judah also?"

²⁰Amaziah, however, would not listen, for God so worked that he might hand them over to ₍Jehoash₎, because they sought the gods of Edom. ²¹So Jehoash king of Israel attacked. He and Amaziah king of Judah faced each other at Beth Shemesh in Judah. ²²Judah was routed by Israel, and every man fled to his home. ²³Jehoash king of Israel captured Amaziah king of Judah, the son of Joash, the

---

a 1 Hebrew *Jehoaddan,* a variant of *Jehoaddin*
b 4 Deut. 24:16   *c 6* That is, about 3 3/4 tons (about 3.4 metric tons); also in verse 9
d 17 Hebrew *Joash,* a variant of *Jehoash;* also in verses 18, 21, 23 and 25

son of Ahaziah,[a] at Beth Shemesh. Then Jehoash brought him to Jerusalem and broke down the wall of Jerusalem from the Ephraim Gate to the Corner Gate—a section about six hundred feet[b] long. 24He took all the gold and silver and all the articles found in the temple of God that had been in the care of Obed-Edom, together with the palace treasures and the hostages, and returned to Samaria.

25Amaziah son of Joash king of Judah lived for fifteen years after the death of Jehoash son of Jehoahaz king of Israel. 26As for the other events of Amaziah's reign, from beginning to end, are they not written in the book of the kings of Judah and Israel? 27From the time that Amaziah turned away from following the LORD, they conspired against him in Jerusalem and he fled to Lachish, but they sent men after him to Lachish and killed him there. 28He was brought back by horse and was buried with his fathers in the City of Judah.

Uzziah King of Judah

26 Then all the people of Judah took Uzziah,[c] who was sixteen years old, and made him king in place of his father Amaziah. 2He was the one who rebuilt Elath and restored it to Judah after Amaziah rested with his fathers.

3Uzziah was sixteen years old when he became king, and he reigned in Jerusalem fifty-two years. His mother's name was Jecoliah; she was from Jerusalem. 4He did what was right in the eyes of the LORD, just as his father Amaziah had done. 5He sought God during the days of Zechariah, who instructed him in the fear[d] of God. As long as he sought the LORD, God gave him success.

6He went to war against the Philistines and broke down the walls of Gath, Jabneh and Ashdod. He then rebuilt towns near Ashdod and elsewhere among the Philistines. 7God helped him against the Philistines and against the Arabs who lived in Gur Baal and against the Meunites. 8The Ammonites brought tribute to Uzziah, and his fame spread as far as the border of Egypt, because he had become very powerful.

9Uzziah built towers in Jerusalem at the Corner Gate, at the Valley Gate and at the angle of the wall, and he fortified them. 10He also built towers in the desert and dug many cisterns, because he had much livestock in the foothills and in the plain. He had people working his fields and vineyards in the hills and in the fertile lands, for he loved the soil.

11Uzziah had a well-trained army, ready to go out by divisions according to their numbers as mustered by Jeiel the secretary and Maaseiah the officer under the direction of Hananiah, one of the royal officials. 12The total number of family leaders over the fighting men was 2,600. 13Under their command was an army of 307,500 men trained for war, a powerful force to support the king against his enemies. 14Uzziah provided shields, spears, helmets, coats of armor, bows and slingstones for the entire army. 15In Jerusalem he made machines designed by skillful men for use on the towers and on the corner defenses to shoot arrows and hurl large stones. His fame spread far and wide, for he was greatly helped until he became powerful.

16But after Uzziah became powerful, his pride led to his downfall. He was unfaithful to the LORD his God, and entered the temple of the LORD to burn incense on the altar of incense. 17Azariah the priest with eighty other courageous priests of the LORD followed him in. 18They confronted him and said, "It is not right for you, Uzziah, to burn incense to the LORD. That is for the priests, the descendants of Aaron, who have been consecrated to burn incense. Leave the sanctuary, for you have been unfaithful; and you will not be honored by the LORD God."

19Uzziah, who had a censer in his hand ready to burn incense, became angry. While he was raging at the priests in their presence before the incense altar in the LORD's temple, leprosy[e] broke out on his forehead. 20When Azariah the chief

---

a23 Hebrew *Jehoahaz,* a variant of *Ahaziah*
b23 Hebrew *four hundred cubits* (about 180 meters)   *c1* Also called *Azariah*   *d5* Many Hebrew manuscripts, Septuagint and Syriac; other Hebrew manuscripts *vision*   *e19* The Hebrew word was used for various diseases affecting the skin—not necessarily leprosy; also in verses 20, 21 and 23.

priest and all the other priests looked at him, they saw that he had leprosy on his forehead, so they hurried him out. Indeed, he himself was eager to leave, because the LORD had afflicted him.

²¹King Uzziah had leprosy until the day he died. He lived in a separate house*—leprous, and excluded from the temple of the LORD. Jotham his son had charge of the palace and governed the people of the land.

²²The other events of Uzziah's reign, from beginning to end, are recorded by the prophet Isaiah son of Amoz. ²³Uzziah rested with his fathers and was buried near them in a field for burial that belonged to the kings, for people said, "He had leprosy." And Jotham his son succeeded him as king.

Jotham King of Judah

27 Jotham was twenty-five years old when he became king, and he reigned in Jerusalem sixteen years. His mother's name was Jerusha daughter of Zadok. ²He did what was right in the eyes of the LORD, just as his father Uzziah had done, but unlike him he did not enter the temple of the LORD. The people, however, continued their corrupt practices. ³Jotham rebuilt the Upper Gate of the temple of the LORD and did extensive work on the wall at the hill of Ophel. ⁴He built towns in the Judean hills and forts and towers in the wooded areas.

⁵Jotham made war on the king of the Ammonites and conquered them. That year the Ammonites paid him a hundred talents*b* of silver, ten thousand cors*c* of wheat and ten thousand cors of barley. The Ammonites brought him the same amount also in the second and third years.

⁶Jotham grew powerful because he walked steadfastly before the LORD his God.

⁷The other events in Jotham's reign, including all his wars and the other things he did, are written in the book of the kings of Israel and Judah. ⁸He was twenty-five years old when he became king, and he reigned in Jerusalem sixteen years. ⁹Jotham rested with his fathers and was buried in the City of David. And Ahaz his son succeeded him as king.

> *Prayer is the first thing, the second thing, the third thing necessary to a minister. Pray, then, my dear brother: pray, pray, pray.*
>
> EDWARD PAYSON

Ahaz King of Judah

28 Ahaz was twenty years old when he became king, and he reigned in Jerusalem sixteen years. Unlike David his father, he did not do what was right in the eyes of the LORD. ²He walked in the ways of the kings of Israel and also made cast idols for worshiping the Baals. ³He burned sacrifices in the Valley of Ben Hinnom and sacrificed his sons in the fire, following the detestable ways of the nations the LORD had driven out before the Israelites. ⁴He offered sacrifices and burned incense at the high places, on the hilltops and under every spreading tree.

⁵Therefore the LORD his God handed him over to the king of Aram. The Arameans defeated him and took many of his people as prisoners and brought them to Damascus.

He was also given into the hands of the king of Israel, who inflicted heavy casualties on him. ⁶In one day Pekah son of Remaliah killed a hundred and twenty thousand soldiers in Judah—because Judah had forsaken the LORD, the God of their fathers. ⁷Zicri, an Ephraimite warrior, killed Maaseiah the king's son, Azrikam the officer in charge of the palace, and Elkanah, second to the king. ⁸The Israelites took captive from their kinsmen two hundred thousand wives, sons and daughters. They also took a great deal of plunder, which they carried back to Samaria.

⁹But a prophet of the LORD named Oded was there, and he went out to meet the army when it returned to Samaria. He said to them, "Because the LORD, the God of your fathers, was angry with Judah, he gave them into your hand. But you have slaughtered them in a rage that

---

a 21 Or in a house where he was relieved of responsibilities   *b 5 That is, about 3 3/4 tons (about 3.4 metric tons)*   *c 5 That is, probably about 62,000 bushels (about 2,200 kiloliters)*

reaches to heaven. ¹⁰And now you intend to make the men and women of Judah and Jerusalem your slaves. But aren't you also guilty of sins against the LORD your God? ¹¹Now listen to me! Send back your fellow countrymen you have taken as prisoners, for the LORD's fierce anger rests on you."

¹²Then some of the leaders in Ephraim—Azariah son of Jehohanan, Berekiah son of Meshillemoth, Jehizkiah son of Shallum, and Amasa son of Hadlai—confronted those who were arriving from the war. ¹³"You must not bring those prisoners here," they said, "or we will be guilty before the LORD. Do you intend to add to our sin and guilt? For our guilt is already great, and his fierce anger rests on Israel."

¹⁴So the soldiers gave up the prisoners and plunder in the presence of the officials and all the assembly. ¹⁵The men designated by name took the prisoners, and from the plunder they clothed all who were naked. They provided them with clothes and sandals, food and drink, and healing balm. All those who were weak they put on donkeys. So they took them back to their fellow countrymen at Jericho, the City of Palms, and returned to Samaria.

¹⁶At that time King Ahaz sent to the king[a] of Assyria for help. ¹⁷The Edomites had again come and attacked Judah and carried away prisoners, ¹⁸while the Philistines had raided towns in the foothills and in the Negev of Judah. They captured and occupied Beth Shemesh, Aijalon and Gederoth, as well as Soco, Timnah and Gimzo, with their surrounding villages. ¹⁹The LORD had humbled Judah because of Ahaz king of Israel,[b] for he had promoted wickedness in Judah and had been most unfaithful to the LORD. ²⁰Tiglath-Pileser[c] king of Assyria came to him, but he gave him trouble instead of help. ²¹Ahaz took some of the things from the temple of the LORD and from the royal palace and from the princes and presented them to the king of Assyria, but that did not help him.

²²In his time of trouble King Ahaz became even more unfaithful to the LORD. ²³He offered sacrifices to the gods of Damascus, who had defeated him; for he thought, "Since the gods of the kings of Aram have helped them, I will sacrifice to them so they will help me." But they were his downfall and the downfall of all Israel.

²⁴Ahaz gathered together the furnishings from the temple of God and took them away.[d] He shut the doors of the LORD's temple and set up altars at every street corner in Jerusalem. ²⁵In every town in Judah he built high places to burn sacrifices to other gods and provoked the LORD, the God of his fathers, to anger.

²⁶The other events of his reign and all his ways, from beginning to end, are written in the book of the kings of Judah and Israel. ²⁷Ahaz rested with his fathers and was buried in the city of Jerusalem, but he was not placed in the tombs of the kings of Israel. And Hezekiah his son succeeded him as king.

Hezekiah Purifies the Temple

29 Hezekiah was twenty-five years old when he became king, and he reigned in Jerusalem twenty-nine years. His mother's name was Abijah daughter of Zechariah. ²He did what was right in the eyes of the LORD, just as his father David had done.

³In the first month of the first year of his reign, he opened the doors of the temple of the LORD and repaired them. ⁴He brought in the priests and the Levites, assembled them in the square on the east side ⁵and said: "Listen to me, Levites! Consecrate yourselves now and consecrate the temple of the LORD, the God of your fathers. Remove all defilement from the sanctuary. ⁶Our fathers were unfaithful; they did evil in the eyes of the LORD our God and forsook him. They turned their faces away from the LORD's dwelling place and turned their backs on him. ⁷They also shut the doors of the portico and put out the lamps. They did not burn incense or present any burnt offerings at the sanctuary to the

a16 One Hebrew manuscript, Septuagint and Vulgate (see also 2 Kings 16:7); most Hebrew manuscripts *kings*   *b19* That is, Judah, as frequently in 2 Chronicles   *c20* Hebrew *Tilgath-Pilneser,* a variant of *Tiglath-Pileser*   *d24* Or *and cut them up*

God of Israel. [8]Therefore, the anger of the LORD has fallen on Judah and Jerusalem; he has made them an object of dread and horror and scorn, as you can see with your own eyes. [9]This is why our fathers have fallen by the sword and why our sons and daughters and our wives are in captivity. [10]Now I intend to make a covenant with the LORD, the God of Israel, so that his fierce anger will turn away from us. [11]My sons, do not be negligent now, for the LORD has chosen you to stand before him and serve him, to minister before him and to burn incense."

[12]Then these Levites set to work:

from the Kohathites,
   Mahath son of Amasai and Joel son of Azariah;
from the Merarites,
   Kish son of Abdi and Azariah son of Jehallelel;
from the Gershonites,
   Joah son of Zimmah and Eden son of Joah;
[13]from the descendants of Elizaphan,
   Shimri and Jeiel;
from the descendants of Asaph,
   Zechariah and Mattaniah;
[14]from the descendants of Heman,
   Jehiel and Shimei;
from the descendants of Jeduthun,
   Shemaiah and Uzziel.

[15]When they had assembled their brothers and consecrated themselves, they went in to purify the temple of the LORD, as the king had ordered, following the word of the LORD. [16]The priests went into the sanctuary of the LORD to purify it. They brought out to the courtyard of the LORD's temple everything unclean that they found in the temple of the LORD. The Levites took it and carried it out to the Kidron Valley. [17]They began the consecration on the first day of the first month, and by the eighth day of the month they reached the portico of the LORD. For eight more days they consecrated the temple of the LORD itself, finishing on the sixteenth day of the first month.

[18]Then they went in to King Hezekiah and reported: "We have purified the entire temple of the LORD, the altar of burnt offering with all its utensils, and the table for setting out the consecrated bread, with all its articles. [19]We have prepared and consecrated all the articles that King Ahaz removed in his unfaithfulness while he was king. They are now in front of the LORD's altar."

[20]Early the next morning King Hezekiah gathered the city officials together and went up to the temple of the LORD. [21]They brought seven bulls, seven rams, seven male lambs and seven male goats as a sin offering for the kingdom, for the sanctuary and for Judah. The king commanded the priests, the descendants of Aaron, to offer these on the altar of the LORD. [22]So they slaughtered the bulls, and the priests took the blood and sprinkled it on the altar; next they slaughtered the rams and sprinkled their blood on the altar; then they slaughtered the lambs and sprinkled their blood on the altar. [23]The goats for the sin offering were brought before the king and the assembly, and they laid their hands on them. [24]The priests then slaughtered the goats and presented their blood on the altar for a sin offering to atone for all Israel, because the king had ordered the burnt offering and the sin offering for all Israel.

[25]He stationed the Levites in the temple of the LORD with cymbals, harps and lyres in the way prescribed by David and Gad the king's seer and Nathan the prophet; this was commanded by the LORD through his prophets. [26]So the Levites stood ready with David's instruments, and the priests with their trumpets.

[27]Hezekiah gave the order to sacrifice the burnt offering on the altar. As the offering began, singing to the LORD began also, accompanied by trumpets and the instruments of David king of Israel. [28]The whole assembly bowed in worship, while the singers sang and the trumpeters played. All this continued until the sacrifice of the burnt offering was completed.

[29]When the offerings were finished, the king and everyone present with him knelt down and worshiped. [30]King Hezekiah and his officials ordered the Levites to praise the LORD with the words of David and of Asaph the seer. So they sang praises with gladness and bowed their heads and worshiped.

[31]Then Hezekiah said, "You have now dedicated yourselves to the LORD. Come

and bring sacrifices and thank offerings to the temple of the LORD." So the assembly brought sacrifices and thank offerings, and all whose hearts were willing brought burnt offerings.

³²The number of burnt offerings the assembly brought was seventy bulls, a hundred rams and two hundred male lambs—all of them for burnt offerings to the LORD. ³³The animals consecrated as sacrifices amounted to six hundred bulls and three thousand sheep and goats. ³⁴The priests, however, were too few to skin all the burnt offerings; so their kinsmen the Levites helped them until the task was finished and until other priests had been consecrated, for the Levites had been more conscientious in consecrating themselves than the priests had been. ³⁵There were burnt offerings in abundance, together with the fat of the fellowship offerings[a] and the drink offerings that accompanied the burnt offerings.

So the service of the temple of the LORD was reestablished. ³⁶Hezekiah and all the people rejoiced at what God had brought about for his people, because it was done so quickly.

Hezekiah Celebrates the Passover

30 Hezekiah sent word to all Israel and Judah and also wrote letters to Ephraim and Manasseh, inviting them to come to the temple of the LORD in Jerusalem and celebrate the Passover to the LORD, the God of Israel. ²The king and his officials and the whole assembly in Jerusalem decided to celebrate the Passover in the second month. ³They had not been able to celebrate it at the regular time because not enough priests had consecrated themselves and the people had not assembled in Jerusalem. ⁴The plan seemed right both to the king and to the whole assembly. ⁵They decided to send a proclamation throughout Israel, from Beersheba to Dan, calling the people to come to Jerusalem and celebrate the Passover to the LORD, the God of Israel. It had not been celebrated in large numbers according to what was written.

⁶At the king's command, couriers went throughout Israel and Judah with letters from the king and from his officials, which read:

"People of Israel, return to the LORD, the God of Abraham, Isaac and Israel, that he may return to you who are left, who have escaped from the hand of the kings of Assyria. ⁷Do not be like your fathers and brothers, who were unfaithful to the LORD, the God of their fathers, so that he made them an object of horror, as you see. ⁸Do not be stiff-necked, as your fathers were; submit to the LORD. Come to the sanctuary, which he has consecrated forever. Serve the LORD your God, so that his fierce anger will turn away from you. ⁹If you return to the LORD, then your brothers and your children will be shown compassion by their captors and will come back to this land, for the LORD your God is gracious and compassionate. He will not turn his face from you if you return to him."

¹⁰The couriers went from town to town in Ephraim and Manasseh, as far as Zebulun, but the people scorned and ridiculed them. ¹¹Nevertheless, some men of Asher, Manasseh and Zebulun humbled themselves and went to Jerusalem. ¹²Also in Judah the hand of God was on the people to give them unity of mind to carry out what the king and his officials had ordered, following the word of the LORD.

¹³A very large crowd of people assembled in Jerusalem to celebrate the Feast of Unleavened Bread in the second month. ¹⁴They removed the altars in Jerusalem and cleared away the incense altars and threw them into the Kidron Valley.

¹⁵They slaughtered the Passover lamb on the fourteenth day of the second month. The priests and the Levites were ashamed and consecrated themselves and brought burnt offerings to the temple of the LORD. ¹⁶Then they took up their regular positions as prescribed in the Law of Moses the man of God. The priests sprinkled the blood handed to them by the Levites. ¹⁷Since many in the crowd had not consecrated themselves, the Levites had to kill the Passover lambs for all those who were not ceremonially

[a]35 Traditionally *peace offerings*

clean and could not consecrate ⌊their lambs⌋ to the Lord. [18]Although most of the many people who came from Ephraim, Manasseh, Issachar and Zebulun had not purified themselves, yet they ate the Passover, contrary to what was written. But Hezekiah prayed for them, saying, "May the Lord, who is good, pardon everyone [19]who sets his heart on seeking God—the Lord, the God of his fathers— even if he is not clean according to the rules of the sanctuary." [20]And the Lord heard Hezekiah and healed the people.

[21]The Israelites who were present in Jerusalem celebrated the Feast of Unleavened Bread for seven days with great rejoicing, while the Levites and priests sang to the Lord every day, accompanied by the Lord's instruments of praise.[a]

[22]Hezekiah spoke encouragingly to all the Levites, who showed good understanding of the service of the Lord. For the seven days they ate their assigned portion and offered fellowship offerings[b] and praised the Lord, the God of their fathers.

[23]The whole assembly then agreed to celebrate the festival seven more days; so for another seven days they celebrated joyfully. [24]Hezekiah king of Judah provided a thousand bulls and seven thousand sheep and goats for the assembly, and the officials provided them with a thousand bulls and ten thousand sheep and goats. A great number of priests consecrated themselves. [25]The entire assembly of Judah rejoiced, along with the priests and Levites and all who had assembled from Israel, including the aliens who had come from Israel and those who lived in Judah. [26]There was great joy in Jerusalem, for since the days of Solomon son of David king of Israel there had been nothing like this in Jerusalem. [27]The priests and the Levites stood to bless the people, and God heard them, for their prayer reached heaven, his holy dwelling place.

> THE priests and the Levites stood to bless the people, and God heard them, for their prayer reached heaven, his holy dwelling place.
>
> 2 CHRONICLES 30:27

31 When all this had ended, the Israelites who were there went out to the towns of Judah, smashed the sacred stones and cut down the Asherah poles. They destroyed the high places and the altars throughout Judah and Benjamin and in Ephraim and Manasseh. After they had destroyed all of them, the Israelites returned to their own towns and to their own property.

Contributions for Worship

[2]Hezekiah assigned the priests and Levites to divisions—each of them according to their duties as priests or Levites—to offer burnt offerings and fellowship offerings,[b] to minister, to give thanks and to sing praises at the gates of the Lord's dwelling. [3]The king contributed from his own possessions for the morning and evening burnt offerings and for the burnt offerings on the Sabbaths, New Moons and appointed feasts as written in the Law of the Lord. [4]He ordered the people living in Jerusalem to give the portion due the priests and Levites so they could devote themselves to the Law of the Lord. [5]As soon as the order went out, the Israelites generously gave the firstfruits of their grain, new wine, oil and honey and all that the fields produced. They brought a great amount, a tithe of everything. [6]The men of Israel and Judah who lived in the towns of Judah also brought a tithe of their herds and flocks and a tithe of the holy things dedicated to the Lord their God, and they piled them in heaps. [7]They began doing this in the third month and finished in the seventh month. [8]When Hezekiah and his officials came and saw the heaps, they praised the Lord and blessed his people Israel.

[9]Hezekiah asked the priests and Levites about the heaps; [10]and Azariah the chief priest, from the family of Zadok, answered, "Since the people began to bring their contributions to the temple of the Lord, we have had enough to eat and plenty to spare, because the Lord has blessed his people, and this great amount is left over."

---

[a]21 Or *priests praised the Lord every day with resounding instruments belonging to the Lord*
[b]22,2 Traditionally *peace offerings*

[11]Hezekiah gave orders to prepare storerooms in the temple of the LORD, and this was done. [12]Then they faithfully brought in the contributions, tithes and dedicated gifts. Conaniah, a Levite, was in charge of these things, and his brother Shimei was next in rank. [13]Jehiel, Azaziah, Nahath, Asahel, Jerimoth, Jozabad, Eliel, Ismakiah, Mahath and Benaiah were supervisors under Conaniah and Shimei his brother, by appointment of King Hezekiah and Azariah the official in charge of the temple of God.

[14]Kore son of Imnah the Levite, keeper of the East Gate, was in charge of the freewill offerings given to God, distributing the contributions made to the LORD and also the consecrated gifts. [15]Eden, Miniamin, Jeshua, Shemaiah, Amariah and Shecaniah assisted him faithfully in the towns of the priests, distributing to their fellow priests according to their divisions, old and young alike.

[16]In addition, they distributed to the males three years old or more whose names were in the genealogical records—all who would enter the temple of the LORD to perform the daily duties of their various tasks, according to their responsibilities and their divisions. [17]And they distributed to the priests enrolled by their families in the genealogical records and likewise to the Levites twenty years old or more, according to their responsibilities and their divisions. [18]They included all the little ones, the wives, and the sons and daughters of the whole community listed in these genealogical records. For they were faithful in consecrating themselves.

[19]As for the priests, the descendants of Aaron, who lived on the farm lands around their towns or in any other towns, men were designated by name to distribute portions to every male among them and to all who were recorded in the genealogies of the Levites.

[20]This is what Hezekiah did throughout Judah, doing what was good and right and faithful before the LORD his God. [21]In everything that he undertook in the service of God's temple and in obedience to the law and the commands, he sought his God and worked wholeheartedly. And so he prospered.

Sennacherib Threatens Jerusalem

32 After all that Hezekiah had so faithfully done, Sennacherib king of Assyria came and invaded Judah. He laid siege to the fortified cities, thinking to conquer them for himself. [2]When Hezekiah saw that Sennacherib had come and that he intended to make war on Jerusalem, [3]he consulted with his officials and military staff about blocking off the water from the springs outside the city, and they helped him. [4]A large force of men assembled, and they blocked all the springs and the stream that flowed through the land. "Why should the kings[a] of Assyria come and find plenty of water?" they said. [5]Then he worked hard repairing all the broken sections of the wall and building towers on it. He built another wall outside that one and reinforced the supporting terraces[b] of the City of David. He also made large numbers of weapons and shields.

[6]He appointed military officers over the people and assembled them before him in the square at the city gate and encouraged them with these words: [7]"Be strong and courageous. Do not be afraid or discouraged because of the king of Assyria and the vast army with him, for there is a greater power with us than with him. [8]With him is only the arm of flesh, but with us is the LORD our God to help us and to fight our battles." And the people gained confidence from what Hezekiah the king of Judah said.

[9]Later, when Sennacherib king of Assyria and all his forces were laying siege to Lachish, he sent his officers to Jerusalem with this message for Hezekiah king of Judah and for all the people of Judah who were there:

[10]"This is what Sennacherib king of Assyria says: On what are you basing your confidence, that you remain in Jerusalem under siege? [11]When Hezekiah says, 'The LORD our God will save us from the hand of the king of Assyria,' he is misleading you, to let you die of hunger and thirst. [12]Did not Hezekiah himself

---

[a]4 Hebrew; Septuagint and Syriac *king*
[b]5 Or *the Millo*

remove this god's high places and altars, saying to Judah and Jerusalem, 'You must worship before one altar and burn sacrifices on it'?

[13] "Do you not know what I and my fathers have done to all the peoples of the other lands? Were the gods of those nations ever able to deliver their land from my hand? [14]Who of all the gods of these nations that my fathers destroyed has been able to save his people from me? How then can your god deliver you from my hand? [15]Now do not let Hezekiah deceive you and mislead you like this. Do not believe him, for no god of any nation or kingdom has been able to deliver his people from my hand or the hand of my fathers. How much less will your god deliver you from my hand!"

[16]Sennacherib's officers spoke further against the LORD God and against his servant Hezekiah. [17]The king also wrote letters insulting the LORD, the God of Israel, and saying this against him: "Just as the gods of the peoples of the other lands did not rescue their people from my hand, so the god of Hezekiah will not rescue his people from my hand." [18]Then they called out in Hebrew to the people of Jerusalem who were on the wall, to terrify them and make them afraid in order to capture the city. [19]They spoke about the God of Jerusalem as they did about the gods of the other peoples of the world—the work of men's hands.

> KING Hezekiah and the prophet Isaiah son of Amoz cried out in prayer to heaven about this.
>
> 2 CHRONICLES 32:20

[20]King Hezekiah and the prophet Isaiah son of Amoz cried out in prayer to heaven about this. [21]And the LORD sent an angel, who annihilated all the fighting men and the leaders and officers in the camp of the Assyrian king. So he withdrew to his own land in disgrace. And when he went into the temple of his god, some of his sons cut him down with the sword.

[22]So the LORD saved Hezekiah and the people of Jerusalem from the hand of Sennacherib king of Assyria and from the hand of all others. He took care of them[a] on every side. [23]Many brought offerings to Jerusalem for the LORD and valuable gifts for Hezekiah king of Judah. From then on he was highly regarded by all the nations.

Hezekiah's Pride, Success and Death

[24]In those days Hezekiah became ill and was at the point of death. He prayed to the LORD, who answered him and gave him a miraculous sign. [25]But Hezekiah's heart was proud and he did not respond to the kindness shown him; therefore the LORD's wrath was on him and on Judah and Jerusalem. [26]Then Hezekiah repented of the pride of his heart, as did the people of Jerusalem; therefore the LORD's wrath did not come upon them during the days of Hezekiah.

> IN those days Hezekiah became ill and was at the point of death. He prayed to the LORD, who answered him and gave him a miraculous sign.
>
> 2 CHRONICLES 32:24

[27]Hezekiah had very great riches and honor, and he made treasuries for his silver and gold and for his precious stones, spices, shields and all kinds of valuables. [28]He also made buildings to store the harvest of grain, new wine and oil; and he made stalls for various kinds of cattle, and pens for the flocks. [29]He built villages and acquired great numbers of flocks and herds, for God had given him very great riches.

[30]It was Hezekiah who blocked the upper outlet of the Gihon spring and channeled the water down to the west side of the City of David. He succeeded in everything he undertook. [31]But when envoys were sent by the rulers of Babylon to ask him about the miraculous sign that had occurred in the land, God left him to test him and to know everything that was in his heart.

[32]The other events of Hezekiah's reign and his acts of devotion are written in the

a22 Hebrew; Septuagint and Vulgate *He gave them rest*

vision of the prophet Isaiah son of Amoz in the book of the kings of Judah and Israel. [33]Hezekiah rested with his fathers and was buried on the hill where the tombs of David's descendants are. All Judah and the people of Jerusalem honored him when he died. And Manasseh his son succeeded him as king.

Manasseh King of Judah

33 Manasseh was twelve years old when he became king, and he reigned in Jerusalem fifty-five years. [2]He did evil in the eyes of the LORD, following the detestable practices of the nations the LORD had driven out before the Israelites. [3]He rebuilt the high places his father Hezekiah had demolished; he also erected altars to the Baals and made Asherah poles. He bowed down to all the starry hosts and worshiped them. [4]He built altars in the temple of the LORD, of which the LORD had said, "My Name will remain in Jerusalem forever." [5]In both courts of the temple of the LORD, he built altars to all the starry hosts. [6]He sacrificed his sons in[a] the fire in the Valley of Ben Hinnom, practiced sorcery, divination and witchcraft, and consulted mediums and spiritists. He did much evil in the eyes of the LORD, provoking him to anger.

[7]He took the carved image he had made and put it in God's temple, of which God had said to David and to his son Solomon, "In this temple and in Jerusalem, which I have chosen out of all the tribes of Israel, I will put my Name forever. [8]I will not again make the feet of the Israelites leave the land I assigned to your forefathers, if only they will be careful to do everything I commanded them concerning all the laws, decrees and ordinances given through Moses." [9]But Manasseh led Judah and the people of Jerusalem astray, so that they did more evil than the nations the LORD had destroyed before the Israelites.

[10]The LORD spoke to Manasseh and his people, but they paid no attention. [11]So the LORD brought against them the army commanders of the king of Assyria, who took Manasseh prisoner, put a hook in his nose, bound him with bronze shackles and took him to Babylon. [12]In his distress he sought the favor of the LORD his God and humbled himself greatly before the God of his fathers. [13]And when he prayed to him, the LORD was moved by his entreaty and listened to his plea; so he brought him back to Jerusalem and to his kingdom. Then Manasseh knew that the LORD is God.

[14]Afterward he rebuilt the outer wall of the City of David, west of the Gihon spring in the valley, as far as the entrance of the Fish Gate and encircling the hill of Ophel; he also made it much higher. He stationed military commanders in all the fortified cities in Judah.

[15]He got rid of the foreign gods and removed the image from the temple of the LORD, as well as all the altars he had built on the temple hill and in Jerusalem; and he threw them out of the city. [16]Then he restored the altar of the LORD and sacrificed fellowship offerings[b] and thank offerings on it, and told Judah to serve the LORD, the God of Israel. [17]The people, however, continued to sacrifice at the high places, but only to the LORD their God.

[18]The other events of Manasseh's reign, including his prayer to his God and the words the seers spoke to him in the name of the LORD, the God of Israel, are written in the annals of the kings of Israel.[c] [19]His prayer and how God was moved by his entreaty, as well as all his sins and unfaithfulness, and the sites where he built high places and set up Asherah poles and idols before he humbled himself—all are written in the records of the seers.[d] [20]Manasseh rested with his fathers and was buried in his palace. And Amon his son succeeded him as king.

Amon King of Judah

[21]Amon was twenty-two years old when he became king, and he reigned in Jerusalem two years. [22]He did evil in the eyes of the LORD, as his father Manasseh had done. Amon worshiped and offered sacrifices to all the idols Manasseh had made. [23]But unlike his father Manasseh, he did not humble himself before the LORD; Amon increased his guilt.

a 6 Or *He made his sons pass through*
b 16 Traditionally *peace offerings*   *c 18* That is, Judah, as frequently in 2 Chronicles
d 19 One Hebrew manuscript and Septuagint; most Hebrew manuscripts *of Hozai*

²⁴Amon's officials conspired against him and assassinated him in his palace. ²⁵Then the people of the land killed all who had plotted against King Amon, and they made Josiah his son king in his place.

Josiah's Reforms

34 Josiah was eight years old when he became king, and he reigned in Jerusalem thirty-one years. ²He did what was right in the eyes of the LORD and walked in the ways of his father David, not turning aside to the right or to the left.

³In the eighth year of his reign, while he was still young, he began to seek the God of his father David. In his twelfth year he began to purge Judah and Jerusalem of high places, Asherah poles, carved idols and cast images. ⁴Under his direction the altars of the Baals were torn down; he cut to pieces the incense altars that were above them, and smashed the Asherah poles, the idols and the images. These he broke to pieces and scattered over the graves of those who had sacrificed to them. ⁵He burned the bones of the priests on their altars, and so he purged Judah and Jerusalem. ⁶In the towns of Manasseh, Ephraim and Simeon, as far as Naphtali, and in the ruins around them, ⁷he tore down the altars and the Asherah poles and crushed the idols to powder and cut to pieces all the incense altars throughout Israel. Then he went back to Jerusalem.

> 66 God does nothing but by prayer, and everything with it. 99
>
> JOHN WESLEY

⁸In the eighteenth year of Josiah's reign, to purify the land and the temple, he sent Shaphan son of Azaliah and Maaseiah the ruler of the city, with Joah son of Joahaz, the recorder, to repair the temple of the LORD his God.

⁹They went to Hilkiah the high priest and gave him the money that had been brought into the temple of God, which the Levites who were the doorkeepers had collected from the people of Manasseh, Ephraim and the entire remnant of Israel and from all the people of Judah and Benjamin and the inhabitants of Jerusalem. ¹⁰Then they entrusted it to the men appointed to supervise the work on the LORD's temple. These men paid the workers who repaired and restored the temple. ¹¹They also gave money to the carpenters and builders to purchase dressed stone, and timber for joists and beams for the buildings that the kings of Judah had allowed to fall into ruin.

¹²The men did the work faithfully. Over them to direct them were Jahath and Obadiah, Levites descended from Merari, and Zechariah and Meshullam, descended from Kohath. The Levites—all who were skilled in playing musical instruments— ¹³had charge of the laborers and supervised all the workers from job to job. Some of the Levites were secretaries, scribes and doorkeepers.

The Book of the Law Found

¹⁴While they were bringing out the money that had been taken into the temple of the LORD, Hilkiah the priest found the Book of the Law of the LORD that had been given through Moses. ¹⁵Hilkiah said to Shaphan the secretary, "I have found the Book of the Law in the temple of the LORD." He gave it to Shaphan. ¹⁶Then Shaphan took the book to the king and reported to him: "Your officials are doing everything that has been committed to them. ¹⁷They have paid out the money that was in the temple of the LORD and have entrusted it to the supervisors and workers." ¹⁸Then Shaphan the secretary informed the king, "Hilkiah the priest has given me a book." And Shaphan read from it in the presence of the king.

¹⁹When the king heard the words of the Law, he tore his robes. ²⁰He gave these orders to Hilkiah, Ahikam son of Shaphan, Abdon son of Micah,ᵃ Shaphan the secretary and Asaiah the king's attendant: ²¹"Go and inquire of the LORD for me and for the remnant in Israel and Judah about what is written in this book that has been found. Great is the LORD's anger that is poured out on us because our fathers have not kept the word of the

ᵃ20 Also called Acbor son of Micaiah

LORD; they have not acted in accordance with all that is written in this book."

²²Hilkiah and those the king had sent with him[a] went to speak to the prophetess Huldah, who was the wife of Shallum son of Tokhath,[b] the son of Hasrah,[c] keeper of the wardrobe. She lived in Jerusalem, in the Second District.

²³She said to them, "This is what the LORD, the God of Israel, says: Tell the man who sent you to me, ²⁴'This is what the LORD says: I am going to bring disaster on this place and its people—all the curses written in the book that has been read in the presence of the king of Judah. ²⁵Because they have forsaken me and burned incense to other gods and provoked me to anger by all that their hands have made,[d] my anger will be poured out on this place and will not be quenched.' ²⁶Tell the king of Judah, who sent you to inquire of the LORD, 'This is what the LORD, the God of Israel, says concerning the words you heard: ²⁷Because your heart was responsive and you humbled yourself before God when you heard what he spoke against this place and its people, and because you humbled yourself before me and tore your robes and wept in my presence, I have heard you, declares the LORD. ²⁸Now I will gather you to your fathers, and you will be buried in peace. Your eyes will not see all the disaster I am going to bring on this place and on those who live here.' "

So they took her answer back to the king.

²⁹Then the king called together all the elders of Judah and Jerusalem. ³⁰He went up to the temple of the LORD with the men of Judah, the people of Jerusalem, the priests and the Levites—all the people from the least to the greatest. He read in their hearing all the words of the Book of the Covenant, which had been found in the temple of the LORD. ³¹The king stood by his pillar and renewed the covenant in the presence of the LORD—to follow the LORD and keep his commands, regulations and decrees with all his heart and all his soul, and to obey the words of the covenant written in this book. ³²Then he had everyone in Jerusalem and Benjamin pledge themselves to it;

the people of Jerusalem did this in accordance with the covenant of God, the God of their fathers.

³³Josiah removed all the detestable idols from all the territory belonging to the Israelites, and he had all who were present in Israel serve the LORD their God. As long as he lived, they did not fail to follow the LORD, the God of their fathers.

Josiah Celebrates the Passover

35 Josiah celebrated the Passover to the LORD in Jerusalem, and the Passover lamb was slaughtered on the fourteenth day of the first month. ²He appointed the priests to their duties and encouraged them in the service of the LORD's temple. ³He said to the Levites, who instructed all Israel and who had been consecrated to the LORD: "Put the sacred ark in the temple that Solomon son of David king of Israel built. It is not to be carried about on your shoulders. Now serve the LORD your God and his people Israel. ⁴Prepare yourselves by families in your divisions, according to the directions written by David king of Israel and by his son Solomon.

⁵"Stand in the holy place with a group of Levites for each subdivision of the families of your fellow countrymen, the lay people. ⁶Slaughter the Passover lambs, consecrate yourselves and prepare ⌊the lambs⌋ for your fellow countrymen, doing what the LORD commanded through Moses."

⁷Josiah provided for all the lay people who were there a total of thirty thousand sheep and goats for the Passover offerings, and also three thousand cattle—all from the king's own possessions.

⁸His officials also contributed voluntarily to the people and the priests and Levites. Hilkiah, Zechariah and Jehiel, the administrators of God's temple, gave the priests twenty-six hundred Passover offerings and three hundred cattle. ⁹Also Conaniah along with Shemaiah and Nethanel, his brothers, and Hashabiah, Jeiel and Jozabad, the leaders of the Levites,

---

[a]22 One Hebrew manuscript, Vulgate and Syriac; most Hebrew manuscripts do not have *had sent with him*.   [b]22 Also called *Tikvah*   [c]22 Also called *Harhas*   [d]25 Or *by everything they have done*

provided five thousand Passover offerings and five hundred head of cattle for the Levites.

[10]The service was arranged and the priests stood in their places with the Levites in their divisions as the king had ordered. [11]The Passover lambs were slaughtered, and the priests sprinkled the blood handed to them, while the Levites skinned the animals. [12]They set aside the burnt offerings to give them to the subdivisions of the families of the people to offer to the LORD, as is written in the Book of Moses. They did the same with the cattle. [13]They roasted the Passover animals over the fire as prescribed, and boiled the holy offerings in pots, caldrons and pans and served them quickly to all the people. [14]After this, they made preparations for themselves and for the priests, because the priests, the descendants of Aaron, were sacrificing the burnt offerings and the fat portions until nightfall. So the Levites made preparations for themselves and for the Aaronic priests.

[15]The musicians, the descendants of Asaph, were in the places prescribed by David, Asaph, Heman and Jeduthun the king's seer. The gatekeepers at each gate did not need to leave their posts, because their fellow Levites made the preparations for them.

[16]So at that time the entire service of the LORD was carried out for the celebration of the Passover and the offering of burnt offerings on the altar of the LORD, as King Josiah had ordered. [17]The Israelites who were present celebrated the Passover at that time and observed the Feast of Unleavened Bread for seven days. [18]The Passover had not been observed like this in Israel since the days of the prophet Samuel; and none of the kings of Israel had ever celebrated such a Passover as did Josiah, with the priests, the Levites and all Judah and Israel who were there with the people of Jerusalem. [19]This Passover was celebrated in the eighteenth year of Josiah's reign.

The Death of Josiah

[20]After all this, when Josiah had set the temple in order, Neco king of Egypt went up to fight at Carchemish on the Euphrates, and Josiah marched out to meet him in battle. [21]But Neco sent messengers to him, saying, "What quarrel is there between you and me, O king of Judah? It is not you I am attacking at this time, but the house with which I am at war. God has told me to hurry; so stop opposing God, who is with me, or he will destroy you."

[22]Josiah, however, would not turn away from him, but disguised himself to engage him in battle. He would not listen to what Neco had said at God's command but went to fight him on the plain of Megiddo.

[23]Archers shot King Josiah, and he told his officers, "Take me away; I am badly wounded." [24]So they took him out of his chariot, put him in the other chariot he had and brought him to Jerusalem, where he died. He was buried in the tombs of his fathers, and all Judah and Jerusalem mourned for him.

[25]Jeremiah composed laments for Josiah, and to this day all the men and women singers commemorate Josiah in the laments. These became a tradition in Israel and are written in the Laments.

[26]The other events of Josiah's reign and his acts of devotion, according to what is written in the Law of the LORD— [27]all the events, from beginning to end, are written in the book of the kings of Israel and
36 Judah. [1]And the people of the land took Jehoahaz son of Josiah and made him king in Jerusalem in place of his father.

Jehoahaz King of Judah

[2]Jehoahaz[a] was twenty-three years old when he became king, and he reigned in Jerusalem three months. [3]The king of Egypt dethroned him in Jerusalem and imposed on Judah a levy of a hundred talents[b] of silver and a talent[c] of gold. [4]The king of Egypt made Eliakim, a brother of Jehoahaz, king over Judah and Jerusalem and changed Eliakim's name to Jehoiakim. But Neco took Eliakim's brother Jehoahaz and carried him off to Egypt.

[a]2 Hebrew *Joahaz*, a variant of *Jehoahaz*; also in verse 4   [b]3 That is, about 3 3/4 tons (about 3.4 metric tons)   [c]3 That is, about 75 pounds (about 34 kilograms)

Jehoiakim King of Judah

[5]Jehoiakim was twenty-five years old when he became king, and he reigned in Jerusalem eleven years. He did evil in the eyes of the LORD his God. [6]Nebuchadnezzar king of Babylon attacked him and bound him with bronze shackles to take him to Babylon. [7]Nebuchadnezzar also took to Babylon articles from the temple of the LORD and put them in his temple[a] there.

[8]The other events of Jehoiakim's reign, the detestable things he did and all that was found against him, are written in the book of the kings of Israel and Judah. And Jehoiachin his son succeeded him as king.

Jehoiachin King of Judah

[9]Jehoiachin was eighteen[b] years old when he became king, and he reigned in Jerusalem three months and ten days. He did evil in the eyes of the LORD. [10]In the spring, King Nebuchadnezzar sent for him and brought him to Babylon, together with articles of value from the temple of the LORD, and he made Jehoiachin's uncle,[c] Zedekiah, king over Judah and Jerusalem.

Zedekiah King of Judah

[11]Zedekiah was twenty-one years old when he became king, and he reigned in Jerusalem eleven years. [12]He did evil in the eyes of the LORD his God and did not humble himself before Jeremiah the prophet, who spoke the word of the LORD. [13]He also rebelled against King Nebuchadnezzar, who had made him take an oath in God's name. He became stiff-necked and hardened his heart and would not turn to the LORD, the God of Israel. [14]Furthermore, all the leaders of the priests and the people became more and more unfaithful, following all the detestable practices of the nations and defiling the temple of the LORD, which he had consecrated in Jerusalem.

The Fall of Jerusalem

[15]The LORD, the God of their fathers, sent word to them through his messengers again and again, because he had pity on his people and on his dwelling place. [16]But they mocked God's messengers, despised his words and scoffed at his prophets until the wrath of the LORD was aroused against his people and there was no remedy. [17]He brought up against them the king of the Babylonians,[d] who killed their young men with the sword in the sanctuary, and spared neither young man nor young woman, old man or aged. God handed all of them over to Nebuchadnezzar. [18]He carried to Babylon all the articles from the temple of God, both large and small, and the treasures of the LORD's temple and the treasures of the king and his officials. [19]They set fire to God's temple and broke down the wall of Jerusalem; they burned all the palaces and destroyed everything of value there.

[20]He carried into exile to Babylon the remnant, who escaped from the sword, and they became servants to him and his sons until the kingdom of Persia came to power. [21]The land enjoyed its sabbath rests; all the time of its desolation it rested, until the seventy years were completed in fulfillment of the word of the LORD spoken by Jeremiah.

[22]In the first year of Cyrus king of Persia, in order to fulfill the word of the LORD spoken by Jeremiah, the LORD moved the heart of Cyrus king of Persia to make a proclamation throughout his realm and to put it in writing:

[23]"This is what Cyrus king of Persia says:

" 'The LORD, the God of heaven, has given me all the kingdoms of the earth and he has appointed me to build a temple for him at Jerusalem in Judah. Anyone of his people among you—may the LORD his God be with him, and let him go up.' "

---

[a]7 Or *palace*   [b]9 One Hebrew manuscript, some Septuagint manuscripts and Syriac (see also 2 Kings 24:8); most Hebrew manuscripts *eight*   [c]10 Hebrew *brother*, that is, relative (see 2 Kings 24:17)   [d]17 Or *Chaldeans*

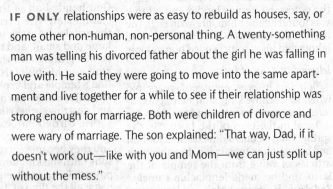

Ezra

HE ANSWERED OUR
PRAYER. (8:23)

IF ONLY relationships were as easy to rebuild as houses, say, or some other non-human, non-personal thing. A twenty-something man was telling his divorced father about the girl he was falling in love with. He said they were going to move into the same apartment and live together for a while to see if their relationship was strong enough for marriage. Both were children of divorce and were wary of marriage. The son explained: "That way, Dad, if it doesn't work out—like with you and Mom—we can just split up without the mess."

Pain clouded his father's eyes. He answered, "Rocks split, son; people tear."

The return of the exiles from Babylon to Jerusalem was more like rebuilding a relationship than rebuilding a city. The people had felt divorced and abandoned by God when in exile. It had not been an amicable parting of the ways. But they had come to learn that it was they, not the Lord, who had walked away from the relationship. They had moved back in, so to speak, but there were a lot of issues to work through—like their infidelity to God, which still was a sore temptation for them. A pattern of philandering doesn't change overnight. Plus, there were the enemies of God who absolutely did not want a renewed Israel.

God sent two brave and prayerful men to lead this renewal: Ezra and Nehemiah. They were skilled and wise pioneers and administrators. But it was their ministry of intercession that stands out, not alongside of their wisdom and courage, but as the source. Like so many great and godly rebuilders, they knew that unless the Lord did the building, their work was futile (see Psalm 127:1).

Cyrus Helps the Exiles to Return

1 In the first year of Cyrus king of Persia, in order to fulfill the word of the LORD spoken by Jeremiah, the LORD moved the heart of Cyrus king of Persia to make a proclamation throughout his realm and to put it in writing:

2 "This is what Cyrus king of Persia says:

" 'The LORD, the God of heaven, has given me all the kingdoms of the earth and he has appointed me to build a temple for him at Jerusalem in Judah. 3 Anyone of his people among you—may his God be with him, and let him go up to Jerusalem in Judah and build the temple of the LORD, the God of Israel, the God who is in Jerusalem. 4 And the people of any place where survivors may now be living are to provide him with silver and gold, with goods and livestock, and with freewill offerings for the temple of God in Jerusalem.' "

5 Then the family heads of Judah and Benjamin, and the priests and Levites—everyone whose heart God had moved—prepared to go up and build the house of the LORD in Jerusalem. 6 All their neighbors assisted them with articles of silver and gold, with goods and livestock, and with valuable gifts, in addition to all the freewill offerings. 7 Moreover, King Cyrus brought out the articles belonging to the temple of the LORD, which Nebuchadnezzar had carried away from Jerusalem and had placed in the temple of his god.[a] 8 Cyrus king of Persia had them brought by Mithredath the treasurer, who counted them out to Sheshbazzar the prince of Judah.

9 This was the inventory:

gold dishes	30
silver dishes	1,000
silver pans[b]	29
10 gold bowls	30
matching silver bowls	410
other articles	1,000

11 In all, there were 5,400 articles of gold and of silver. Sheshbazzar brought all these along when the exiles came up from Babylon to Jerusalem.

The List of the Exiles Who Returned

2 Now these are the people of the province who came up from the captivity of the exiles, whom Nebuchadnezzar king of Babylon had taken captive to Babylon (they returned to Jerusalem and Judah, each to his own town, 2 in company with Zerubbabel, Jeshua, Nehemiah, Seraiah, Reelaiah, Mordecai, Bilshan, Mispar, Bigvai, Rehum and Baanah):

The list of the men of the people of Israel:

3 the descendants of Parosh	2,172
4 of Shephatiah	372
5 of Arah	775
6 of Pahath-Moab (through the line of Jeshua and Joab)	2,812
7 of Elam	1,254
8 of Zattu	945
9 of Zaccai	760
10 of Bani	642
11 of Bebai	623
12 of Azgad	1,222
13 of Adonikam	666
14 of Bigvai	2,056
15 of Adin	454
16 of Ater (through Hezekiah)	98
17 of Bezai	323
18 of Jorah	112
19 of Hashum	223
20 of Gibbar	95
21 the men of Bethlehem	123
22 of Netophah	56
23 of Anathoth	128
24 of Azmaveth	42
25 of Kiriath Jearim,[c] Kephirah and Beeroth	743
26 of Ramah and Geba	621
27 of Micmash	122
28 of Bethel and Ai	223
29 of Nebo	52
30 of Magbish	156
31 of the other Elam	1,254
32 of Harim	320
33 of Lod, Hadid and Ono	725
34 of Jericho	345
35 of Senaah	3,630

---

[a] 7 Or gods   [b] 9 The meaning of the Hebrew for this word is uncertain.   [c] 25 See Septuagint (see also Neh. 7:29); Hebrew Kiriath Arim.

³⁶The priests:

the descendants of Jedaiah
(through the family
of Jeshua) 973
³⁷of Immer 1,052
³⁸of Pashhur 1,247
³⁹of Harim 1,017

⁴⁰The Levites:

the descendants of Jeshua
and Kadmiel (through
the line of Hodaviah) 74

⁴¹The singers:

the descendants of Asaph 128

⁴²The gatekeepers of the temple:

the descendants of
Shallum, Ater, Talmon,
Akkub, Hatita and Shobai 139

⁴³The temple servants:

the descendants of
Ziha, Hasupha, Tabbaoth,
⁴⁴Keros, Siaha, Padon,
⁴⁵Lebanah, Hagabah, Akkub,
⁴⁶Hagab, Shalmai, Hanan,
⁴⁷Giddel, Gahar, Reaiah,
⁴⁸Rezin, Nekoda, Gazzam,
⁴⁹Uzza, Paseah, Besai,
⁵⁰Asnah, Meunim, Nephusim,
⁵¹Bakbuk, Hakupha, Harhur,
⁵²Bazluth, Mehida, Harsha,
⁵³Barkos, Sisera, Temah,
⁵⁴Neziah and Hatipha

⁵⁵The descendants of the servants of
Solomon:

the descendants of
Sotai, Hassophereth, Peruda,
⁵⁶Jaala, Darkon, Giddel,
⁵⁷Shephatiah, Hattil,
Pokereth-Hazzebaim and Ami

⁵⁸The temple servants and
the descendants of the
servants of Solomon 392

⁵⁹The following came up from the
towns of Tel Melah, Tel Harsha, Ke-
rub, Addon and Immer, but they
could not show that their families
were descended from Israel:

⁶⁰The descendants of
Delaiah, Tobiah and
Nekoda 652

⁶¹And from among the priests:

The descendants of
Hobaiah, Hakkoz and Barzillai
(a man who had married a
daughter of Barzillai the
Gileadite and was called by
that name).

⁶²These searched for their family
records, but they could not find
them and so were excluded from the
priesthood as unclean. ⁶³The governor ordered them not to eat any of
the most sacred food until there was
a priest ministering with the Urim
and Thummim.

⁶⁴The whole company numbered
42,360, ⁶⁵besides their 7,337 menservants and maidservants; and
they also had 200 men and women
singers. ⁶⁶They had 736 horses,
245 mules, ⁶⁷435 camels and 6,720
donkeys.

⁶⁸When they arrived at the house of the
LORD in Jerusalem, some of the heads of
the families gave freewill offerings toward the rebuilding of the house of God
on its site. ⁶⁹According to their ability
they gave to the treasury for this work
61,000 drachmas*ᵃ* of gold, 5,000 minas*ᵇ*
of silver and 100 priestly garments.

⁷⁰The priests, the Levites, the singers,
the gatekeepers and the temple servants
settled in their own towns, along with
some of the other people, and the rest of
the Israelites settled in their towns.

Rebuilding the Altar

3 When the seventh month came and
the Israelites had settled in their
towns, the people assembled as one man
in Jerusalem. ²Then Jeshua son of Jozadak and his fellow priests and Zerubbabel son of Shealtiel and his associates
began to build the altar of the God of Israel to sacrifice burnt offerings on it, in
accordance with what is written in the
Law of Moses the man of God. ³Despite
their fear of the peoples around them,
they built the altar on its foundation and
sacrificed burnt offerings on it to the

ᵃ69 That is, about 1,100 pounds (about 500
kilograms)   *ᵇ69* That is, about 3 tons (about
2.9 metric tons)

LORD, both the morning and evening sacrifices. [4]Then in accordance with what is written, they celebrated the Feast of Tabernacles with the required number of burnt offerings prescribed for each day. [5]After that, they presented the regular burnt offerings, the New Moon sacrifices and the sacrifices for all the appointed sacred feasts of the LORD, as well as those brought as freewill offerings to the LORD. [6]On the first day of the seventh month they began to offer burnt offerings to the LORD, though the foundation of the LORD's temple had not yet been laid.

Rebuilding the Temple

[7]Then they gave money to the masons and carpenters, and gave food and drink and oil to the people of Sidon and Tyre, so that they would bring cedar logs by sea from Lebanon to Joppa, as authorized by Cyrus king of Persia.

[8]In the second month of the second year after their arrival at the house of God in Jerusalem, Zerubbabel son of Shealtiel, Jeshua son of Jozadak and the rest of their brothers (the priests and the Levites and all who had returned from the captivity to Jerusalem) began the work, appointing Levites twenty years of age and older to supervise the building of the house of the LORD. [9]Jeshua and his sons and brothers and Kadmiel and his sons (descendants of Hodaviah[a]) and the sons of Henadad and their sons and brothers—all Levites—joined together in supervising those working on the house of God.

[10]When the builders laid the foundation of the temple of the LORD, the priests in their vestments and with trumpets, and the Levites (the sons of Asaph) with cymbals, took their places to praise the LORD, as prescribed by David king of Israel. [11]With praise and thanksgiving they sang to the LORD:

"He is good;
    his love to Israel endures forever."

And all the people gave a great shout of praise to the LORD, because the foundation of the house of the LORD was laid. [12]But many of the older priests and Levites and family heads, who had seen the former temple, wept aloud when they

saw the foundation of this temple being laid, while many others shouted for joy. [13]No one could distinguish the sound of the shouts of joy from the sound of weeping, because the people made so much noise. And the sound was heard far away.

Opposition to the Rebuilding

4 When the enemies of Judah and Benjamin heard that the exiles were building a temple for the LORD, the God of Israel, [2]they came to Zerubbabel and to the heads of the families and said, "Let us help you build because, like you, we seek your God and have been sacrificing to him since the time of Esarhaddon king of Assyria, who brought us here."

[3]But Zerubbabel, Jeshua and the rest of the heads of the families of Israel answered, "You have no part with us in building a temple to our God. We alone will build it for the LORD, the God of Israel, as King Cyrus, the king of Persia, commanded us."

[4]Then the peoples around them set out to discourage the people of Judah and make them afraid to go on building.[b] [5]They hired counselors to work against them and frustrate their plans during the entire reign of Cyrus king of Persia and down to the reign of Darius king of Persia.

Later Opposition Under Xerxes and Artaxerxes

[6]At the beginning of the reign of Xerxes,[c] they lodged an accusation against the people of Judah and Jerusalem.

[7]And in the days of Artaxerxes king of Persia, Bishlam, Mithredath, Tabeel and the rest of his associates wrote a letter to Artaxerxes. The letter was written in

[a]9 Hebrew *Yehudah*, probably a variant of Hodaviah   [b]4 Or *and troubled them as they built*   [c]6 Hebrew *Ahasuerus*, a variant of Xerxes' Persian name

Aramaic script and in the Aramaic language.[a,b]

[8]Rehum the commanding officer and Shimshai the secretary wrote a letter against Jerusalem to Artaxerxes the king as follows:

[9]Rehum the commanding officer and Shimshai the secretary, together with the rest of their associates—the judges and officials over the men from Tripolis, Persia,[c] Erech and Babylon, the Elamites of Susa, [10]and the other people whom the great and honorable Ashurbanipal[d] deported and settled in the city of Samaria and elsewhere in Trans-Euphrates.

[11](This is a copy of the letter they sent him.)

To King Artaxerxes,

From your servants, the men of Trans-Euphrates:

[12]The king should know that the Jews who came up to us from you have gone to Jerusalem and are rebuilding that rebellious and wicked city. They are restoring the walls and repairing the foundations.

[13]Furthermore, the king should know that if this city is built and its walls are restored, no more taxes, tribute or duty will be paid, and the royal revenues will suffer. [14]Now since we are under obligation to the palace and it is not proper for us to see the king dishonored, we are sending this message to inform the king, [15]so that a search may be made in the archives of your predecessors. In these records you will find that this city is a rebellious city, troublesome to kings and provinces, a place of rebellion from ancient times. That is why this city was destroyed. [16]We inform the king that if this city is built and its walls are restored, you will be left with nothing in Trans-Euphrates.

[17]The king sent this reply:

To Rehum the commanding officer, Shimshai the secretary and the rest of their associates living in Samaria and elsewhere in Trans-Euphrates:

Greetings.

[18]The letter you sent us has been read and translated in my presence. [19]I issued an order and a search was made, and it was found that this city has a long history of revolt against kings and has been a place of rebellion and sedition. [20]Jerusalem has had powerful kings ruling over the whole of Trans-Euphrates, and taxes, tribute and duty were paid to them. [21]Now issue an order to these men to stop work, so that this city will not be rebuilt until I so order. [22]Be careful not to neglect this matter. Why let this threat grow, to the detriment of the royal interests?

[23]As soon as the copy of the letter of King Artaxerxes was read to Rehum and Shimshai the secretary and their associates, they went immediately to the Jews in Jerusalem and compelled them by force to stop.

[24]Thus the work on the house of God in Jerusalem came to a standstill until the second year of the reign of Darius king of Persia.

Tattenai's Letter to Darius

5 Now Haggai the prophet and Zechariah the prophet, a descendant of Iddo, prophesied to the Jews in Judah and Jerusalem in the name of the God of Israel, who was over them. [2]Then Zerubbabel son of Shealtiel and Jeshua son of Jozadak set to work to rebuild the house of God in Jerusalem. And the prophets of God were with them, helping them.

[3]At that time Tattenai, governor of Trans-Euphrates, and Shethar-Bozenai and their associates went to them and asked, "Who authorized you to rebuild this temple and restore this structure?" [4]They also asked, "What are the names of the men constructing this building?"[e] [5]But the eye of their God was watching

---

[a]7 Or *written in Aramaic and translated*
[b]7 The text of Ezra 4:8—6:18 is in Aramaic.
[c]9 Or *officials, magistrates and governors over the men from*   [d]10 Aramaic *Osnappar*, a variant of *Ashurbanipal*   [e]4 See Septuagint; Aramaic *We told them the names of the men constructing this building*.

over the elders of the Jews, and they were not stopped until a report could go to Darius and his written reply be received.

⁶This is a copy of the letter that Tattenai, governor of Trans-Euphrates, and Shethar-Bozenai and their associates, the officials of Trans-Euphrates, sent to King Darius. ⁷The report they sent him read as follows:

To King Darius:

Cordial greetings.

⁸The king should know that we went to the district of Judah, to the temple of the great God. The people are building it with large stones and placing the timbers in the walls. The work is being carried on with diligence and is making rapid progress under their direction.

⁹We questioned the elders and asked them, "Who authorized you to rebuild this temple and restore this structure?" ¹⁰We also asked them their names, so that we could write down the names of their leaders for your information.

¹¹This is the answer they gave us:

"We are the servants of the God of heaven and earth, and we are rebuilding the temple that was built many years ago, one that a great king of Israel built and finished. ¹²But because our fathers angered the God of heaven, he handed them over to Nebuchadnezzar the Chaldean, king of Babylon, who destroyed this temple and deported the people to Babylon.

¹³"However, in the first year of Cyrus king of Babylon, King Cyrus issued a decree to rebuild this house of God. ¹⁴He even removed from the temple^a of Babylon the gold and silver articles of the house of God, which Nebuchadnezzar had taken from the temple in Jerusalem and brought to the temple^a in Babylon.

"Then King Cyrus gave them to a man named Sheshbazzar, whom he had appointed governor, ¹⁵and he told him, 'Take these articles and go and deposit them in the temple in Jerusalem. And rebuild the house of

God on its site.' ¹⁶So this Sheshbazzar came and laid the foundations of the house of God in Jerusalem. From that day to the present it has been under construction but is not yet finished."

¹⁷Now if it pleases the king, let a search be made in the royal archives of Babylon to see if King Cyrus did in fact issue a decree to rebuild this house of God in Jerusalem. Then let the king send us his decision in this matter.

The Decree of Darius

6 King Darius then issued an order, and they searched in the archives stored in the treasury at Babylon. ²A scroll was found in the citadel of Ecbatana in the province of Media, and this was written on it:

Memorandum:

³In the first year of King Cyrus, the king issued a decree concerning the temple of God in Jerusalem:

Let the temple be rebuilt as a place to present sacrifices, and let its foundations be laid. It is to be ninety feet^b high and ninety feet wide, ⁴with three courses of large stones and one of timbers. The costs are to be paid by the royal treasury. ⁵Also, the gold and silver articles of the house of God, which Nebuchadnezzar took from the temple in Jerusalem and brought to Babylon, are to be returned to their places in the temple in Jerusalem; they are to be deposited in the house of God.

⁶Now then, Tattenai, governor of Trans-Euphrates, and Shethar-Bozenai and you, their fellow officials of that province, stay away from there. ⁷Do not interfere with the work on this temple of God. Let the governor of the Jews and the Jewish elders rebuild this house of God on its site.

⁸Moreover, I hereby decree what you are to do for these elders of the Jews in the construction of this house of God:

---

^{a}14 Or palace ^{b}3 Aramaic sixty cubits (about 27 meters)

The expenses of these men are to be fully paid out of the royal treasury, from the revenues of Trans-Euphrates, so that the work will not stop. [9]Whatever is needed—young bulls, rams, male lambs for burnt offerings to the God of heaven, and wheat, salt, wine and oil, as requested by the priests in Jerusalem—must be given them daily without fail, [10]so that they may offer sacrifices pleasing to the God of heaven and pray for the well-being of the king and his sons.

[11]Furthermore, I decree that if anyone changes this edict, a beam is to be pulled from his house and he is to be lifted up and impaled on it. And for this crime his house is to be made a pile of rubble. [12]May God, who has caused his Name to dwell there, overthrow any king or people who lifts a hand to change this decree or to destroy this temple in Jerusalem.

I Darius have decreed it. Let it be carried out with diligence.

Completion and Dedication of the Temple

[13]Then, because of the decree King Darius had sent, Tattenai, governor of Trans-Euphrates, and Shethar-Bozenai and their associates carried it out with diligence. [14]So the elders of the Jews continued to build and prosper under the preaching of Haggai the prophet and Zechariah, a descendant of Iddo. They finished building the temple according to the command of the God of Israel and the decrees of Cyrus, Darius and Artaxerxes, kings of Persia. [15]The temple was completed on the third day of the month Adar, in the sixth year of the reign of King Darius.

> The value of consistent prayer is not that he will hear us, but that we will hear him.
>
> WILLIAM MCGILL

[16]Then the people of Israel—the priests, the Levites and the rest of the exiles—celebrated the dedication of the house of God with joy. [17]For the dedication of this house of God they offered a hundred bulls, two hundred rams, four hundred male lambs and, as a sin offering for all Israel, twelve male goats, one for each of the tribes of Israel. [18]And they installed the priests in their divisions and the Levites in their groups for the service of God at Jerusalem, according to what is written in the Book of Moses.

The Passover

[19]On the fourteenth day of the first month, the exiles celebrated the Passover. [20]The priests and Levites had purified themselves and were all ceremonially clean. The Levites slaughtered the Passover lamb for all the exiles, for their brothers the priests and for themselves. [21]So the Israelites who had returned from the exile ate it, together with all who had separated themselves from the unclean practices of their Gentile neighbors in order to seek the LORD, the God of Israel. [22]For seven days they celebrated with joy the Feast of Unleavened Bread, because the LORD had filled them with joy by changing the attitude of the king of Assyria, so that he assisted them in the work on the house of God, the God of Israel.

Ezra Comes to Jerusalem

7 After these things, during the reign of Artaxerxes king of Persia, Ezra son of Seraiah, the son of Azariah, the son of Hilkiah, [2]the son of Shallum, the son of Zadok, the son of Ahitub, [3]the son of Amariah, the son of Azariah, the son of Meraioth, [4]the son of Zerahiah, the son of Uzzi, the son of Bukki, [5]the son of Abishua, the son of Phinehas, the son of Eleazar, the son of Aaron the chief priest— [6]this Ezra came up from Babylon. He was a teacher well versed in the Law of Moses, which the LORD, the God of Israel, had given. The king had granted him everything he asked, for the hand of the LORD his God was on him. [7]Some of the Israelites, including priests, Levites, singers, gatekeepers and temple servants, also came up to Jerusalem in the seventh year of King Artaxerxes.

[8]Ezra arrived in Jerusalem in the fifth month of the seventh year of the king. [9]He had begun his journey from Babylon

on the first day of the first month, and he arrived in Jerusalem on the first day of the fifth month, for the gracious hand of his God was on him. [10]For Ezra had devoted himself to the study and observance of the Law of the LORD, and to teaching its decrees and laws in Israel.

King Artaxerxes' Letter to Ezra

[11]This is a copy of the letter King Artaxerxes had given to Ezra the priest and teacher, a man learned in matters concerning the commands and decrees of the LORD for Israel:

[12a] Artaxerxes, king of kings,

To Ezra the priest, a teacher of the Law of the God of heaven:

Greetings.

[13]Now I decree that any of the Israelites in my kingdom, including priests and Levites, who wish to go to Jerusalem with you, may go. [14]You are sent by the king and his seven advisers to inquire about Judah and Jerusalem with regard to the Law of your God, which is in your hand. [15]Moreover, you are to take with you the silver and gold that the king and his advisers have freely given to the God of Israel, whose dwelling is in Jerusalem, [16]together with all the silver and gold you may obtain from the province of Babylon, as well as the freewill offerings of the people and priests for the temple of their God in Jerusalem. [17]With this money be sure to buy bulls, rams and male lambs, together with their grain offerings and drink offerings, and sacrifice them on the altar of the temple of your God in Jerusalem.

[18]You and your brother Jews may then do whatever seems best with the rest of the silver and gold, in accordance with the will of your God. [19]Deliver to the God of Jerusalem all the articles entrusted to you for worship in the temple of your God. [20]And anything else needed for the temple of your God that you may have occasion to supply, you may provide from the royal treasury.

[21]Now I, King Artaxerxes, order all the treasurers of Trans-Euphrates to provide with diligence whatever Ezra the priest, a teacher of the Law of the God of heaven, may ask of you— [22]up to a hundred talents[b] of silver, a hundred cors[c] of wheat, a hundred baths[d] of wine, a hundred baths[d] of olive oil, and salt without limit. [23]Whatever the God of heaven has prescribed, let it be done with diligence for the temple of the God of heaven. Why should there be wrath against the realm of the king and of his sons? [24]You are also to know that you have no authority to impose taxes, tribute or duty on any of the priests, Levites, singers, gatekeepers, temple servants or other workers at this house of God.

[25]And you, Ezra, in accordance with the wisdom of your God, which you possess, appoint magistrates and judges to administer justice to all the people of Trans-Euphrates— all who know the laws of your God. And you are to teach any who do not know them. [26]Whoever does not obey the law of your God and the law of the king must surely be punished by death, banishment, confiscation of property, or imprisonment.

[27]Praise be to the LORD, the God of our fathers, who has put it into the king's heart to bring honor to the house of the LORD in Jerusalem in this way [28]and who has extended his good favor to me before the king and his advisers and all the king's powerful officials. Because the hand of the LORD my God was on me, I took courage and gathered leading men from Israel to go up with me.

List of the Family Heads Returning With Ezra

8 These are the family heads and those registered with them who came up with me from Babylon during the reign of King Artaxerxes:

---

[a]12 The text of Ezra 7:12–26 is in Aramaic.
[b]22 That is, about 3 3/4 tons (about 3.4 metric tons)   [c]22 That is, probably about 600 bushels (about 22 kiloliters)   [d]22 That is, probably about 600 gallons (about 2.2 kiloliters)

²of the descendants of Phinehas, Gershom;
of the descendants of Ithamar, Daniel;
of the descendants of David, Hattush ³of the descendants of Shecaniah;

of the descendants of Parosh, Zechariah, and with him were registered 150 men;
⁴of the descendants of Pahath-Moab, Eliehoenai son of Zerahiah, and with him 200 men;
⁵of the descendants of Zattu,ᵃ Shecaniah son of Jahaziel, and with him 300 men;
⁶of the descendants of Adin, Ebed son of Jonathan, and with him 50 men;
⁷of the descendants of Elam, Jeshaiah son of Athaliah, and with him 70 men;
⁸of the descendants of Shephatiah, Zebadiah son of Michael, and with him 80 men;
⁹of the descendants of Joab, Obadiah son of Jehiel, and with him 218 men;
¹⁰of the descendants of Bani,ᵇ Shelomith son of Josiphiah, and with him 160 men;
¹¹of the descendants of Bebai, Zechariah son of Bebai, and with him 28 men;
¹²of the descendants of Azgad, Johanan son of Hakkatan, and with him 110 men;
¹³of the descendants of Adonikam, the last ones, whose names were Eliphelet, Jeuel and Shemaiah, and with them 60 men;
¹⁴of the descendants of Bigvai, Uthai and Zaccur, and with them 70 men.

The Return to Jerusalem

¹⁵I assembled them at the canal that flows toward Ahava, and we camped there three days. When I checked among the people and the priests, I found no Levites there. ¹⁶So I summoned Eliezer, Ariel, Shemaiah, Elnathan, Jarib, Elnathan, Nathan, Zechariah and Meshullam, who were leaders, and Joiarib and Elnathan, who were men of learning, ¹⁷and I sent them to Iddo, the leader in Casiphia. I told them what to say to Iddo and his kinsmen, the temple servants in Casiphia, so that they might bring attendants to us for the house of our God. ¹⁸Because the gracious hand of our God was on us, they brought us Sherebiah, a capable man, from the descendants of Mahli son of Levi, the son of Israel, and Sherebiah's sons and brothers, 18 men; ¹⁹and Hashabiah, together with Jeshaiah from the descendants of Merari, and his brothers and nephews, 20 men. ²⁰They also brought 220 of the temple servants—a body that David and the officials had established to assist the Levites. All were registered by name.

²¹There, by the Ahava Canal, I proclaimed a fast, so that we might humble ourselves before our God and ask him for a safe journey for us and our children, with all our possessions. ²²I was ashamed to ask the king for soldiers and horsemen to protect us from enemies on the road, because we had told the king, "The gracious hand of our God is on everyone who looks to him, but his great anger is against all who forsake him." ²³So we fasted and petitioned our God about this, and he answered our prayer.

> SO WE fasted and petitioned our God about this, and he answered our prayer.
>
> EZRA 8:23

²⁴Then I set apart twelve of the leading priests, together with Sherebiah, Hashabiah and ten of their brothers, ²⁵and I weighed out to them the offering of silver and gold and the articles that the king, his advisers, his officials and all Israel present there had donated for the house of our God. ²⁶I weighed out to them 650 talentsᶜ of silver, silver articles weighing 100 talents,ᵈ 100 talentsᵈ of gold, ²⁷20 bowls of gold valued at 1,000

ᵃ5 Some Septuagint manuscripts (also
1 Esdras 8:32); Hebrew does not have *Zattu*.
ᵇ10 Some Septuagint manuscripts (also 1 Esdras
8:36); Hebrew does not have *Bani*. ᶜ26 That
is, about 25 tons (about 22 metric tons)
ᵈ26 That is, about 3 3/4 tons (about 3.4 metric
tons)

darics,ᵃ and two fine articles of polished bronze, as precious as gold.

²⁸I said to them, "You as well as these articles are consecrated to the LORD. The silver and gold are a freewill offering to the LORD, the God of your fathers. ²⁹Guard them carefully until you weigh them out in the chambers of the house of the LORD in Jerusalem before the leading priests and the Levites and the family heads of Israel." ³⁰Then the priests and Levites received the silver and gold and sacred articles that had been weighed out to be taken to the house of our God in Jerusalem.

³¹On the twelfth day of the first month we set out from the Ahava Canal to go to Jerusalem. The hand of our God was on us, and he protected us from enemies and bandits along the way. ³²So we arrived in Jerusalem, where we rested three days.

³³On the fourth day, in the house of our God, we weighed out the silver and gold and the sacred articles into the hands of Meremoth son of Uriah, the priest. Eleazar son of Phinehas was with him, and so were the Levites Jozabad son of Jeshua and Noadiah son of Binnui. ³⁴Everything was accounted for by number and weight, and the entire weight was recorded at that time.

³⁵Then the exiles who had returned from captivity sacrificed burnt offerings to the God of Israel: twelve bulls for all Israel, ninety-six rams, seventy-seven male lambs and, as a sin offering, twelve male goats. All this was a burnt offering to the LORD. ³⁶They also delivered the king's orders to the royal satraps and to the governors of Trans-Euphrates, who then gave assistance to the people and to the house of God.

Ezra's Prayer About Intermarriage

9 After these things had been done, the leaders came to me and said, "The people of Israel, including the priests and the Levites, have not kept themselves separate from the neighboring peoples with their detestable practices, like those of the Canaanites, Hittites, Perizzites, Jebusites, Ammonites, Moabites, Egyptians and Amorites. ²They have taken some of their daughters as wives for themselves and their sons, and have mingled the holy race with the peoples around them. And the leaders and officials have led the way in this unfaithfulness."

³When I heard this, I tore my tunic and cloak, pulled hair from my head and beard and sat down appalled. ⁴Then everyone who trembled at the words of the God of Israel gathered around me because of this unfaithfulness of the exiles. And I sat there appalled until the evening sacrifice.

> *I ROSE from my self-abasement, with my tunic and cloak torn, and fell on my knees with my hands spread out to the LORD my God and prayed:*
>
> *"O my God, I am too ashamed and disgraced to lift up my face to you, my God, because our sins are higher than our heads and our guilt has reached to the heavens."*
>
> EZRA 9:5–6

⁵Then, at the evening sacrifice, I rose from my self-abasement, with my tunic and cloak torn, and fell on my knees with my hands spread out to the LORD my God ⁶and prayed:

"O my God, I am too ashamed and disgraced to lift up my face to you, my God, because our sins are higher than our heads and our guilt has reached to the heavens. ⁷From the days of our forefathers until now, our guilt has been great. Because of our sins, we and our kings and our priests have been subjected to the sword and captivity, to pillage and humiliation at the hand of foreign kings, as it is today.

⁸"But now, for a brief moment, the LORD our God has been gracious in leaving us a remnant and giving us a firm place in his sanctuary, and so our God gives light to our eyes and a little relief in our bondage. ⁹Though we are slaves, our God has not deserted us in our bondage. He has shown us kindness in the sight of

ᵃ27 That is, about 19 pounds (about 8.5 kilograms)

the kings of Persia: He has granted us new life to rebuild the house of our God and repair its ruins, and he has given us a wall of protection in Judah and Jerusalem.

¹⁰"But now, O our God, what can we say after this? For we have disregarded the commands ¹¹you gave through your servants the prophets when you said: 'The land you are entering to possess is a land polluted by the corruption of its peoples. By their detestable practices they have filled it with their impurity from one end to the other. ¹²Therefore, do not give your daughters in marriage to

---

[**WEDNESDAY**]

EZRA 9:1 – 15

Be a We Instead of a Me

9:6 "OUR SINS ARE HIGHER THAN OUR HEADS AND OUR GUILT HAS REACHED TO THE HEAVENS."

Two things set this prayer apart from the prayers of many modern Christians in the Western world. The first, and easier to understand, is the frequency of words like *our* and *we* and *us*; as opposed to words like *I* and *me*. Clearly, Ezra's chief identity is his Jewishness. He is a "we" before he is an "I." Scholars call this way of thinking "corporate solidarity." The individualism of Western culture has a hard time getting its mind around this point of view. There is far too much "me and Jesus" in our thinking and praying. There should be a lot more "we and Jesus."

The second thing that sets this prayer apart is the really hard part: Ezra repents of the sins of others as though they were his own. This act takes his "corporate solidarity" to an even deeper level. But this isn't something peculiar to Ezra; it is the view of Scripture. God's people are members of a body, not an organization. A member of an organization can exist outside the organization; a member of a body is dead outside the body. And the body stretches out not only in space, but in time. Read the end of Hebrews 11 and the beginning of Hebrews 12. Hebrews 12:1 says that a great cloud of witnesses—the heroes of the faith who came before us, mentioned in chapter 11—are waiting for us to finish the race. "God had planned something better for us so that only *together with us would they be made perfect*" (Hebrews 11:40, italics added).

We are linked to one another in ways we must understand if we are to give to intercessory prayer the urgency it deserves. What I do for another, or fail to do for another, has profound implications for that person's well-being. Ezra is stricken over the effect others' sins have had on the whole people— so much so that he repents as one of them. In the final analysis, this kind of praying is not about "corporate solidarity"; it is about love. Ask God to expand your sense of your self, so you can pray for others as you would for yourself. In this way, you love your neighbor as yourself.

PRAY:

Father, teach me when I pray to think "we" and "our"
more than I think "me" and "I."

FOR YOUR NEXT DEVOTIONAL READING, GO TO PAGE 545.

their sons or take their daughters for your sons. Do not seek a treaty of friendship with them at any time, that you may be strong and eat the good things of the land and leave it to your children as an everlasting inheritance.'

¹³"What has happened to us is a result of our evil deeds and our great guilt, and yet, our God, you have punished us less than our sins have deserved and have given us a remnant like this. ¹⁴Shall we again break your commands and intermarry with the peoples who commit such detestable practices? Would you not be angry enough with us to destroy us, leaving us no remnant or survivor? ¹⁵O Lord, God of Israel, you are righteous! We are left this day as a remnant. Here we are before you in our guilt, though because of it not one of us can stand in your presence."

The People's Confession of Sin

10 While Ezra was praying and confessing, weeping and throwing himself down before the house of God, a large crowd of Israelites—men, women and children—gathered around him. They too wept bitterly. ²Then Shecaniah son of Jehiel, one of the descendants of Elam, said to Ezra, "We have been unfaithful to our God by marrying foreign women from the peoples around us. But in spite of this, there is still hope for Israel. ³Now let us make a covenant before our God to send away all these women and their children, in accordance with the counsel of my lord and of those who fear the commands of our God. Let it be done according to the Law. ⁴Rise up; this matter is in your hands. We will support you, so take courage and do it."

⁵So Ezra rose up and put the leading priests and Levites and all Israel under oath to do what had been suggested. And they took the oath. ⁶Then Ezra withdrew from before the house of God and went to the room of Jehohanan son of Eliashib. While he was there, he ate no food and drank no water, because he continued to mourn over the unfaithfulness of the exiles.

⁷A proclamation was then issued throughout Judah and Jerusalem for all the exiles to assemble in Jerusalem. ⁸Anyone who failed to appear within three days would forfeit all his property, in accordance with the decision of the officials and elders, and would himself be expelled from the assembly of the exiles.

⁹Within the three days, all the men of Judah and Benjamin had gathered in Jerusalem. And on the twentieth day of the ninth month, all the people were sitting in the square before the house of God, greatly distressed by the occasion and because of the rain. ¹⁰Then Ezra the priest stood up and said to them, "You have been unfaithful; you have married foreign women, adding to Israel's guilt. ¹¹Now make confession to the Lord, the God of your fathers, and do his will. Separate yourselves from the peoples around you and from your foreign wives."

¹²The whole assembly responded with a loud voice: "You are right! We must do as you say. ¹³But there are many people here and it is the rainy season; so we cannot stand outside. Besides, this matter cannot be taken care of in a day or two, because we have sinned greatly in this thing. ¹⁴Let our officials act for the whole assembly. Then let everyone in our towns who has married a foreign woman come at a set time, along with the elders and judges of each town, until the fierce anger of our God in this matter is turned away from us." ¹⁵Only Jonathan son of Asahel and Jahzeiah son of Tikvah, supported by Meshullam and Shabbethai the Levite, opposed this.

¹⁶So the exiles did as was proposed. Ezra the priest selected men who were family heads, one from each family division, and all of them designated by name. On the first day of the tenth month they sat down to investigate the cases, ¹⁷and by the first day of the first month they finished dealing with all the men who had married foreign women.

Those Guilty of Intermarriage

¹⁸Among the descendants of the priests, the following had married foreign women:

From the descendants of Jeshua son of Jozadak, and his brothers: Maaseiah, Eliezer, Jarib and Gedaliah. ¹⁹(They all gave their hands in pledge to put away their wives, and for their guilt they each presented a ram from the flock as a guilt offering.)

²⁰ From the descendants of Immer:
Hanani and Zebadiah.

²¹ From the descendants of Harim:
Maaseiah, Elijah, Shemaiah, Jehiel and Uzziah.

²² From the descendants of Pashhur:
Elioenai, Maaseiah, Ishmael, Nethanel, Jozabad and Elasah.

²³ Among the Levites:

Jozabad, Shimei, Kelaiah (that is, Kelita), Pethahiah, Judah and Eliezer.

²⁴ From the singers:
Eliashib.

From the gatekeepers:
Shallum, Telem and Uri.

²⁵ And among the other Israelites:

From the descendants of Parosh:
Ramiah, Izziah, Malkijah, Mijamin, Eleazar, Malkijah and Benaiah.

²⁶ From the descendants of Elam:
Mattaniah, Zechariah, Jehiel, Abdi, Jeremoth and Elijah.

²⁷ From the descendants of Zattu:
Elioenai, Eliashib, Mattaniah, Jeremoth, Zabad and Aziza.

²⁸ From the descendants of Bebai:
Jehohanan, Hananiah, Zabbai and Athlai.

²⁹ From the descendants of Bani:
Meshullam, Malluch, Adaiah, Jashub, Sheal and Jeremoth.

³⁰ From the descendants of Pahath-Moab:
Adna, Kelal, Benaiah, Maaseiah, Mattaniah, Bezalel, Binnui and Manasseh.

³¹ From the descendants of Harim:
Eliezer, Ishijah, Malkijah, Shemaiah, Shimeon, ³²Benjamin, Malluch and Shemariah.

³³ From the descendants of Hashum:
Mattenai, Mattattah, Zabad, Eliphelet, Jeremai, Manasseh and Shimei.

³⁴ From the descendants of Bani:
Maadai, Amram, Uel, ³⁵Benaiah, Bedeiah, Keluhi, ³⁶Vaniah, Meremoth, Eliashib, ³⁷Mattaniah, Mattenai and Jaasu.

³⁸ From the descendants of Binnui:[a]
Shimei, ³⁹Shelemiah, Nathan, Adaiah, ⁴⁰Macnadebai, Shashai, Sharai, ⁴¹Azarel, Shelemiah, Shemariah, ⁴²Shallum, Amariah and Joseph.

⁴³ From the descendants of Nebo:
Jeiel, Mattithiah, Zabad, Zebina, Jaddai, Joel and Benaiah.

⁴⁴ All these had married foreign women, and some of them had children by these wives.[b]

---

[a] *37,38* See Septuagint (also 1 Esdras 9:34); Hebrew *Jaasu* *38and Bani and Binnui,*
[b] *44* Or *and they sent them away with their children*

Nehemiah

GOD CHOSE two men to assist in leading the exiled Jews from captivity back to their home. Both Ezra and Nehemiah were men who had firm relationships with God. The book of Nehemiah gives many descriptions of the importance of prayer in Nehemiah's life. The very first chapter gives the account of Nehemiah learning tragic news about his people back in Jerusalem. And who does Nehemiah turn to? God! Later, when Nehemiah approaches the king with a request for his people, he again looks to God for help (2:4).

Throughout the chapters of this book, no matter what the situation, Nehemiah continues his conversation with God.

Nehemiah supervised a great work for God, but he never shouldered the burden alone. It was a partnership with heaven from beginning to end. What an example he was to the people he was chosen to lead. And what an example for us today!

> THEN I PRAYED
> TO THE GOD
> OF HEAVEN. (2:4)

Nehemiah's Prayer

1 The words of Nehemiah son of Hacaliah:

In the month of Kislev in the twentieth year, while I was in the citadel of Susa, [2]Hanani, one of my brothers, came from Judah with some other men, and I questioned them about the Jewish remnant that survived the exile, and also about Jerusalem.

[3]They said to me, "Those who survived the exile and are back in the province are in great trouble and disgrace. The wall of Jerusalem is broken down, and its gates have been burned with fire."

> *WHEN I heard these things, I sat down and wept. For some days I mourned and fasted and prayed before the God of heaven.*
>
> NEHEMIAH 1:4

[4]When I heard these things, I sat down and wept. For some days I mourned and fasted and prayed before the God of heaven. [5]Then I said:

"O LORD, God of heaven, the great and awesome God, who keeps his covenant of love with those who love him and obey his commands, [6]let your ear be attentive and your eyes open to hear the prayer your servant is praying before you day and night for your servants, the people of Israel. I confess the sins we Israelites, including myself and my father's house, have committed against you. [7]We have acted very wickedly toward you. We have not obeyed the commands, decrees and laws you gave your servant Moses.

[8]"Remember the instruction you gave your servant Moses, saying, 'If you are unfaithful, I will scatter you among the nations, [9]but if you return to me and obey my commands, then even if your exiled people are at the farthest horizon, I will gather them from there and bring them to the place I have chosen as a dwelling for my Name.'

[10]"They are your servants and your people, whom you redeemed by your great strength and your mighty hand. [11]O Lord, let your ear be attentive to the prayer of this your servant and to the prayer of your servants who delight in revering your name. Give your servant success today by granting him favor in the presence of this man."

I was cupbearer to the king.

Artaxerxes Sends Nehemiah to Jerusalem

2 In the month of Nisan in the twentieth year of King Artaxerxes, when wine was brought for him, I took the wine and gave it to the king. I had not been sad in his presence before; [2]so the king asked me, "Why does your face look so sad when you are not ill? This can be nothing but sadness of heart."

I was very much afraid, [3]but I said to the king, "May the king live forever! Why should my face not look sad when the city where my fathers are buried lies in ruins, and its gates have been destroyed by fire?"

[4]The king said to me, "What is it you want?"

Then I prayed to the God of heaven, [5]and I answered the king, "If it pleases the king and if your servant has found favor in his sight, let him send me to the city in Judah where my fathers are buried so that I can rebuild it."

> *THEN I prayed to the God of heaven.*
>
> NEHEMIAH 2:4

[6]Then the king, with the queen sitting beside him, asked me, "How long will your journey take, and when will you get back?" It pleased the king to send me; so I set a time.

[7]I also said to him, "If it pleases the king, may I have letters to the governors of Trans-Euphrates, so that they will provide me safe-conduct until I arrive in Judah? [8]And may I have a letter to Asaph, keeper of the king's forest, so he will give me timber to make beams for the gates of the citadel by the temple and for the city wall and for the residence I will occupy?" And because the gracious hand of my

God was upon me, the king granted my requests. 9So I went to the governors of Trans-Euphrates and gave them the king's letters. The king had also sent army officers and cavalry with me.

10When Sanballat the Horonite and Tobiah the Ammonite official heard about this, they were very much disturbed that someone had come to promote the welfare of the Israelites.

Nehemiah Inspects Jerusalem's Walls

11I went to Jerusalem, and after staying there three days 12I set out during the night with a few men. I had not told anyone what my God had put in my heart to

---

NEHEMIAH 1

No One Is an Island

1:10 "THEY ARE YOUR SERVANTS AND YOUR PEOPLE, WHOM YOU REDEEMED BY YOUR GREAT STRENGTH."

This is the second of three prayers by Ezra and Nehemiah that we will look at in these devotions. All three prayers are exemplars of the mind of an intercessor—that deep sense of solidarity with a people, treating their sins as one's own and pleading for God's mercy for "us," not "them." John Donne's famous meditation captures the perspective of these great men of prayer:

> No man is an Island, entire of itself; every man is a piece of the Continent, a part of the main; if a clod be washed away by the sea, Europe is the less, as well as if a promontory were, as well as if a manor of thy friends or of thine own were; any man's death diminishes me, because I am involved in Mankind; And therefore never send to know for whom the bell tolls; It tolls for thee.[1]

Only love can cause us to see others this way. Paul told husbands to love their wives as they love their own bodies, for that is how Christ loves the church—as his own body (see Ephesians 5:25–33). Ezra and Nehemiah love the people of God the way Christ loves the church.

In this prayer, Nehemiah draws on a text from Moses' intercession and puts himself in the same place Moses was when he pleaded with God for the life of the nation. Nehemiah prays, "They are your servants and your people, whom you redeemed" (Nehemiah 1:10). The first time that kind of prayer was prayed, the Israelites were close to extinction following the incident with the golden calf (see Deuteronomy 9:25–29). So Moses did a daring and provocative thing: He "stood in the breach before [God] to keep his wrath from destroying" the nation (Psalm 106:23). Now Nehemiah does the same.

What would happen to your personal prayer life, and the prayers of your church, if these were the perspectives you brought to prayer: a deep sense of solidarity with the people you pray for and the courage to stand in the breach between them and destruction? It would be harder to get drowsy and trivial when you pray.

P R A Y :

Holy God, my heart is narrow! Expand it with your holy presence,
that I might make room for others in my prayers.

FOR YOUR NEXT DEVOTIONAL READING, GO TO PAGE 554.

do for Jerusalem. There were no mounts with me except the one I was riding on.

¹³By night I went out through the Valley Gate toward the Jackal*ᵃ* Well and the Dung Gate, examining the walls of Jerusalem, which had been broken down, and its gates, which had been destroyed by fire. ¹⁴Then I moved on toward the Fountain Gate and the King's Pool, but there was not enough room for my mount to get through; ¹⁵so I went up the valley by night, examining the wall. Finally, I turned back and reentered through the Valley Gate. ¹⁶The officials did not know where I had gone or what I was doing, because as yet I had said nothing to the Jews or the priests or nobles or officials or any others who would be doing the work.

¹⁷Then I said to them, "You see the trouble we are in: Jerusalem lies in ruins, and its gates have been burned with fire. Come, let us rebuild the wall of Jerusalem, and we will no longer be in disgrace." ¹⁸I also told them about the gracious hand of my God upon me and what the king had said to me.

They replied, "Let us start rebuilding." So they began this good work.

¹⁹But when Sanballat the Horonite, Tobiah the Ammonite official and Geshem the Arab heard about it, they mocked and ridiculed us. "What is this you are doing?" they asked. "Are you rebelling against the king?"

²⁰I answered them by saying, "The God of heaven will give us success. We his servants will start rebuilding, but as for you, you have no share in Jerusalem or any claim or historic right to it."

Builders of the Wall

3 Eliashib the high priest and his fellow priests went to work and rebuilt the Sheep Gate. They dedicated it and set its doors in place, building as far as the Tower of the Hundred, which they dedicated, and as far as the Tower of Hananel. ²The men of Jericho built the adjoining section, and Zaccur son of Imri built next to them.

³The Fish Gate was rebuilt by the sons of Hassenaah. They laid its beams and put its doors and bolts and bars in place.

⁴Meremoth son of Uriah, the son of Hakkoz, repaired the next section. Next to him Meshullam son of Berekiah, the son of Meshezabel, made repairs, and next to him Zadok son of Baana also made repairs. ⁵The next section was repaired by the men of Tekoa, but their nobles would not put their shoulders to the work under their supervisors.*ᵇ*

⁶The Jeshanah*ᶜ* Gate was repaired by Joiada son of Paseah and Meshullam son of Besodeiah. They laid its beams and put its doors and bolts and bars in place. ⁷Next to them, repairs were made by men from Gibeon and Mizpah—Melatiah of Gibeon and Jadon of Meronoth—places under the authority of the governor of Trans-Euphrates. ⁸Uzziel son of Harhaiah, one of the goldsmiths, repaired the next section; and Hananiah, one of the perfume-makers, made repairs next to that. They restored*ᵈ* Jerusalem as far as the Broad Wall. ⁹Rephaiah son of Hur, ruler of a half-district of Jerusalem, repaired the next section. ¹⁰Adjoining this, Jedaiah son of Harumaph made repairs opposite his house, and Hattush son of Hashabneiah made repairs next to him. ¹¹Malkijah son of Harim and Hasshub son of Pahath-Moab repaired another section and the Tower of the Ovens. ¹²Shallum son of Hallohesh, ruler of a half-district of Jerusalem, repaired the next section with the help of his daughters.

¹³The Valley Gate was repaired by Hanun and the residents of Zanoah. They rebuilt it and put its doors and bolts and bars in place. They also repaired five hundred yards*ᵉ* of the wall as far as the Dung Gate.

¹⁴The Dung Gate was repaired by Malkijah son of Recab, ruler of the district of Beth Hakkerem. He rebuilt it and put its doors and bolts and bars in place.

¹⁵The Fountain Gate was repaired by Shallun son of Col-Hozeh, ruler of the district of Mizpah. He rebuilt it, roofing it over and putting its doors and bolts and bars in place. He also repaired the wall

ᵃ13 Or *Serpent* or *Fig*   *ᵇ5* Or *their Lord* or *the governor*   *ᶜ6* Or *Old*   *ᵈ8* Or *They left out part of*   *ᵉ13* Hebrew *a thousand cubits* (about 450 meters)

of the Pool of Siloam,[a] by the King's Garden, as far as the steps going down from the City of David. [16]Beyond him, Nehemiah son of Azbuk, ruler of a half-district of Beth Zur, made repairs up to a point opposite the tombs[b] of David, as far as the artificial pool and the House of the Heroes.

[17]Next to him, the repairs were made by the Levites under Rehum son of Bani. Beside him, Hashabiah, ruler of half the district of Keilah, carried out repairs for his district. [18]Next to him, the repairs were made by their countrymen under Binnui[c] son of Henadad, ruler of the other half-district of Keilah. [19]Next to him, Ezer son of Jeshua, ruler of Mizpah, repaired another section, from a point facing the ascent to the armory as far as the angle. [20]Next to him, Baruch son of Zabbai zealously repaired another section, from the angle to the entrance of the house of Eliashib the high priest. [21]Next to him, Meremoth son of Uriah, the son of Hakkoz, repaired another section, from the entrance of Eliashib's house to the end of it.

[22]The repairs next to him were made by the priests from the surrounding region. [23]Beyond them, Benjamin and Hasshub made repairs in front of their house; and next to them, Azariah son of Maaseiah, the son of Ananiah, made repairs beside his house. [24]Next to him, Binnui son of Henadad repaired another section, from Azariah's house to the angle and the corner, [25]and Palal son of Uzai worked opposite the angle and the tower projecting from the upper palace near the court of the guard. Next to him, Pedaiah son of Parosh [26]and the temple servants living on the hill of Ophel made repairs up to a point opposite the Water Gate toward the east and the projecting tower. [27]Next to them, the men of Tekoa repaired another section, from the great projecting tower to the wall of Ophel.

[28]Above the Horse Gate, the priests made repairs, each in front of his own house. [29]Next to them, Zadok son of Immer made repairs opposite his house. Next to him, Shemaiah son of Shecaniah, the guard at the East Gate, made re-

pairs. [30]Next to him, Hananiah son of Shelemiah, and Hanun, the sixth son of Zalaph, repaired another section. Next to them, Meshullam son of Berekiah made repairs opposite his living quarters. [31]Next to him, Malkijah, one of the goldsmiths, made repairs as far as the house of the temple servants and the merchants, opposite the Inspection Gate, and as far as the room above the corner; [32]and between the room above the corner and the Sheep Gate the goldsmiths and merchants made repairs.

Opposition to the Rebuilding

4 When Sanballat heard that we were rebuilding the wall, he became angry and was greatly incensed. He ridiculed the Jews, [2]and in the presence of his associates and the army of Samaria, he said, "What are those feeble Jews doing? Will they restore their wall? Will they offer sacrifices? Will they finish in a day? Can they bring the stones back to life from those heaps of rubble—burned as they are?"

[3]Tobiah the Ammonite, who was at his side, said, "What they are building—if even a fox climbed up on it, he would break down their wall of stones!"

[4]Hear us, O our God, for we are despised. Turn their insults back on their own heads. Give them over as plunder in a land of captivity. [5]Do not cover up their guilt or blot out their sins from your sight, for they have thrown insults in the face of[d] the builders.

[6]So we rebuilt the wall till all of it reached half its height, for the people worked with all their heart.

[7]But when Sanballat, Tobiah, the Arabs, the Ammonites and the men of Ashdod heard that the repairs to Jerusalem's walls had gone ahead and that the gaps were being closed, they were very angry. [8]They all plotted together to come and fight against Jerusalem and stir up trouble against it. [9]But we prayed to our

[a]15 Hebrew *Shelah,* a variant of *Shiloah,* that is, Siloam   [b]16 Hebrew; Septuagint, some Vulgate manuscripts and Syriac *tomb*   [c]18 Two Hebrew manuscripts and Syriac (see also Septuagint and verse 24); most Hebrew manuscripts *Bavvai*   [d]5 Or *have provoked you to anger before*

God and posted a guard day and night to meet this threat.

[10]Meanwhile, the people in Judah said, "The strength of the laborers is giving out, and there is so much rubble that we cannot rebuild the wall."

[11]Also our enemies said, "Before they know it or see us, we will be right there among them and will kill them and put an end to the work."

[12]Then the Jews who lived near them came and told us ten times over, "Wherever you turn, they will attack us."

[13]Therefore I stationed some of the people behind the lowest points of the wall at the exposed places, posting them by families, with their swords, spears and bows. [14]After I looked things over, I stood up and said to the nobles, the officials and the rest of the people, "Don't be afraid of them. Remember the Lord, who is great and awesome, and fight for your brothers, your sons and your daughters, your wives and your homes."

[15]When our enemies heard that we were aware of their plot and that God had frustrated it, we all returned to the wall, each to his own work.

[16]From that day on, half of my men did the work, while the other half were equipped with spears, shields, bows and armor. The officers posted themselves behind all the people of Judah [17]who were building the wall. Those who carried materials did their work with one hand and held a weapon in the other, [18]and each of the builders wore his sword at his side as he worked. But the man who sounded the trumpet stayed with me.

[19]Then I said to the nobles, the officials and the rest of the people, "The work is extensive and spread out, and we are widely separated from each other along the wall. [20]Wherever you hear the sound of the trumpet, join us there. Our God will fight for us!"

[21]So we continued the work with half the men holding spears, from the first light of dawn till the stars came out. [22]At that time I also said to the people, "Have every man and his helper stay inside Jerusalem at night, so they can serve us as guards by night and workmen by day." [23]Neither I nor my brothers nor my men nor the guards with me took off our clothes; each had his weapon, even when he went for water.[a]

Nehemiah Helps the Poor

5 Now the men and their wives raised a great outcry against their Jewish brothers. [2]Some were saying, "We and our sons and daughters are numerous; in order for us to eat and stay alive, we must get grain."

[3]Others were saying, "We are mortgaging our fields, our vineyards and our homes to get grain during the famine."

[4]Still others were saying, "We have had to borrow money to pay the king's tax on our fields and vineyards. [5]Although we are of the same flesh and blood as our countrymen and though our sons are as good as theirs, yet we have to subject our sons and daughters to slavery. Some of our daughters have already been enslaved, but we are powerless, because our fields and our vineyards belong to others."

[6]When I heard their outcry and these charges, I was very angry. [7]I pondered them in my mind and then accused the nobles and officials. I told them, "You are exacting usury from your own countrymen!" So I called together a large meeting to deal with them [8]and said: "As far as possible, we have bought back our Jewish brothers who were sold to the Gentiles. Now you are selling your brothers, only for them to be sold back to us!" They kept quiet, because they could find nothing to say.

[9]So I continued, "What you are doing is not right. Shouldn't you walk in the fear of our God to avoid the reproach of our Gentile enemies? [10]I and my brothers and my men are also lending the people money and grain. But let the exacting of usury stop! [11]Give back to them immediately their fields, vineyards, olive groves and houses, and also the usury you are charging them—the hundredth part of the money, grain, new wine and oil."

[12]"We will give it back," they said. "And we will not demand anything more from them. We will do as you say."

[a]23 The meaning of the Hebrew for this clause is uncertain.

Then I summoned the priests and made the nobles and officials take an oath to do what they had promised. [13]I also shook out the folds of my robe and said, "In this way may God shake out of his house and possessions every man who does not keep this promise. So may such a man be shaken out and emptied!"

At this the whole assembly said, "Amen," and praised the LORD. And the people did as they had promised.

[14]Moreover, from the twentieth year of King Artaxerxes, when I was appointed to be their governor in the land of Judah, until his thirty-second year—twelve years—neither I nor my brothers ate the food allotted to the governor. [15]But the earlier governors—those preceding me—placed a heavy burden on the people and took forty shekels[a] of silver from them in addition to food and wine. Their assistants also lorded it over the people. But out of reverence for God I did not act like that. [16]Instead, I devoted myself to the work on this wall. All my men were assembled there for the work; we[b] did not acquire any land.

[17]Furthermore, a hundred and fifty Jews and officials ate at my table, as well as those who came to us from the surrounding nations. [18]Each day one ox, six choice sheep and some poultry were prepared for me, and every ten days an abundant supply of wine of all kinds. In spite of all this, I never demanded the food allotted to the governor, because the demands were heavy on these people.

[19]Remember me with favor, O my God, for all I have done for these people.

> REMEMBER me with favor, O my God,
> for all I have done for these people.
>
> NEHEMIAH 5:19

Further Opposition to the Rebuilding

6 When word came to Sanballat, Tobiah, Geshem the Arab and the rest of our enemies that I had rebuilt the wall and not a gap was left in it—though up to that time I had not set the doors in the gates—[2]Sanballat and Geshem sent me this message: "Come, let us meet together in one of the villages[c] on the plain of Ono."

But they were scheming to harm me; [3]so I sent messengers to them with this reply: "I am carrying on a great project and cannot go down. Why should the work stop while I leave it and go down to you?" [4]Four times they sent me the same message, and each time I gave them the same answer.

[5]Then, the fifth time, Sanballat sent his aide to me with the same message, and in his hand was an unsealed letter [6]in which was written:

"It is reported among the nations—and Geshem[d] says it is true—that you and the Jews are plotting to revolt, and therefore you are building the wall. Moreover, according to these reports you are about to become their king [7]and have even appointed prophets to make this proclamation about you in Jerusalem: 'There is a king in Judah!' Now this report will get back to the king; so come, let us confer together."

[8]I sent him this reply: "Nothing like what you are saying is happening; you are just making it up out of your head."

[9]They were all trying to frighten us, thinking, "Their hands will get too weak for the work, and it will not be completed."

⌊But I prayed,⌋ "Now strengthen my hands."

[10]One day I went to the house of Shemaiah son of Delaiah, the son of Mehetabel, who was shut in at his home. He said, "Let us meet in the house of God, inside the temple, and let us close the temple doors, because men are coming to kill you—by night they are coming to kill you."

[11]But I said, "Should a man like me run away? Or should one like me go into the temple to save his life? I will not go!" [12]I realized that God had not sent him, but that he had prophesied against me because Tobiah and Sanballat had hired him. [13]He had been hired to intimidate me so that I would commit a sin by doing this, and then they would give me a bad name to discredit me.

[a]15 That is, about 1 pound (about 0.5 kilogram)   [b]16 Most Hebrew manuscripts; some Hebrew manuscripts, Septuagint, Vulgate and Syriac *I*   [c]2 Or *in Kephirim*   [d]6 Hebrew *Gashmu,* a variant of *Geshem*

[14]Remember Tobiah and Sanballat, O my God, because of what they have done; remember also the prophetess Noadiah and the rest of the prophets who have been trying to intimidate me.

The Completion of the Wall

[15]So the wall was completed on the twenty-fifth of Elul, in fifty-two days. [16]When all our enemies heard about this, all the surrounding nations were afraid and lost their self-confidence, because they realized that this work had been done with the help of our God.

[17]Also, in those days the nobles of Judah were sending many letters to Tobiah, and replies from Tobiah kept coming to them. [18]For many in Judah were under oath to him, since he was son-in-law to Shecaniah son of Arah, and his son Jehohanan had married the daughter of Meshullam son of Berekiah. [19]Moreover, they kept reporting to me his good deeds and then telling him what I said. And Tobiah sent letters to intimidate me.

7 After the wall had been rebuilt and I had set the doors in place, the gatekeepers and the singers and the Levites were appointed. [2]I put in charge of Jerusalem my brother Hanani, along with[a] Hananiah the commander of the citadel, because he was a man of integrity and feared God more than most men do. [3]I said to them, "The gates of Jerusalem are not to be opened until the sun is hot. While the gatekeepers are still on duty, have them shut the doors and bar them. Also appoint residents of Jerusalem as guards, some at their posts and some near their own houses."

The List of the Exiles Who Returned

[4]Now the city was large and spacious, but there were few people in it, and the houses had not yet been rebuilt. [5]So my God put it into my heart to assemble the nobles, the officials and the common people for registration by families. I found the genealogical record of those who had been the first to return. This is what I found written there:

[6]These are the people of the province who came up from the captivity of the exiles whom Nebuchadnezzar king of Babylon had taken captive (they returned to Jerusalem and Judah, each to his own town, [7]in company with Zerubbabel, Jeshua, Nehemiah, Azariah, Raamiah, Nahamani, Mordecai, Bilshan, Mispereth, Bigvai, Nehum and Baanah):

The list of the men of Israel:

[8]the descendants of Parosh	2,172
[9]of Shephatiah	372
[10]of Arah	652
[11]of Pahath-Moab (through the line of Jeshua and Joab)	2,818
[12]of Elam	1,254
[13]of Zattu	845
[14]of Zaccai	760
[15]of Binnui	648
[16]of Bebai	628
[17]of Azgad	2,322
[18]of Adonikam	667
[19]of Bigvai	2,067
[20]of Adin	655
[21]of Ater (through Hezekiah)	98
[22]of Hashum	328
[23]of Bezai	324
[24]of Hariph	112
[25]of Gibeon	95
[26]the men of Bethlehem and Netophah	188
[27]of Anathoth	128
[28]of Beth Azmaveth	42
[29]of Kiriath Jearim, Kephirah and Beeroth	743
[30]of Ramah and Geba	621
[31]of Micmash	122
[32]of Bethel and Ai	123
[33]of the other Nebo	52
[34]of the other Elam	1,254
[35]of Harim	320
[36]of Jericho	345
[37]of Lod, Hadid and Ono	721
[38]of Senaah	3,930

[39]The priests:

the descendants of Jedaiah (through the family of Jeshua)	973
[40]of Immer	1,052
[41]of Pashhur	1,247
[42]of Harim	1,017

[a]2 Or *Hanani, that is,*

⁴³The Levites:

the descendants of Jeshua
(through Kadmiel through
the line of Hodaviah)   74

⁴⁴The singers:

the descendants of Asaph   148

⁴⁵The gatekeepers:

the descendants of
Shallum, Ater, Talmon,
Akkub, Hatita and
Shobai   138

⁴⁶The temple servants:

the descendants of
Ziha, Hasupha, Tabbaoth,
⁴⁷Keros, Sia, Padon,
⁴⁸Lebana, Hagaba, Shalmai,
⁴⁹Hanan, Giddel, Gahar,
⁵⁰Reaiah, Rezin, Nekoda,
⁵¹Gazzam, Uzza, Paseah,
⁵²Besai, Meunim, Nephusim,
⁵³Bakbuk, Hakupha, Harhur,
⁵⁴Bazluth, Mehida, Harsha,
⁵⁵Barkos, Sisera, Temah,
⁵⁶Neziah and Hatipha

⁵⁷The descendants of the servants of
Solomon:

the descendants of
Sotai, Sophereth, Perida,
⁵⁸Jaala, Darkon, Giddel,
⁵⁹Shephatiah, Hattil,
Pokereth-Hazzebaim and
Amon

⁶⁰The temple servants and the
descendants of the servants
of Solomon   392

⁶¹The following came up from the
towns of Tel Melah, Tel Harsha, Ke-
rub, Addon and Immer, but they
could not show that their families
were descended from Israel:

⁶²the descendants of
Delaiah, Tobiah and
Nekoda   642

⁶³And from among the priests:

the descendants of
Hobaiah, Hakkoz and Barzillai
(a man who had married a
daughter of Barzillai the
Gileadite and was called by
that name).

⁶⁴These searched for their family
records, but they could not find
them and so were excluded from the
priesthood as unclean. ⁶⁵The governor, therefore, ordered them not to
eat any of the most sacred food until there should be a priest ministering with the Urim and Thummim.

⁶⁶The whole company numbered
42,360, ⁶⁷besides their 7,337 menservants and maidservants; and
they also had 245 men and women
singers. ⁶⁸There were 736 horses,
245 mules,^a ⁶⁹435 camels and 6,720
donkeys.

⁷⁰Some of the heads of the fami-
lies contributed to the work. The
governor gave to the treasury 1,000
drachmas^b of gold, 50 bowls and
530 garments for priests. ⁷¹Some of
the heads of the families gave to the
treasury for the work 20,000 drach-
mas^c of gold and 2,200 minas^d of silver. ⁷²The total given by the rest of
the people was 20,000 drachmas of
gold, 2,000 minas^e of silver and 67
garments for priests.

⁷³The priests, the Levites, the
gatekeepers, the singers and the
temple servants, along with certain
of the people and the rest of the Israelites, settled in their own towns.

Ezra Reads the Law

When the seventh month came and
the Israelites had settled in their towns,
8 ¹all the people assembled as one
man in the square before the Water
Gate. They told Ezra the scribe to bring
out the Book of the Law of Moses, which
the LORD had commanded for Israel.

²So on the first day of the seventh
month Ezra the priest brought the Law
before the assembly, which was made
up of men and women and all who were
able to understand. ³He read it aloud

---

^a68 Some Hebrew manuscripts (see also Ezra
2:66); most Hebrew manuscripts do not have this
verse.   ^b70 That is, about 19 pounds (about
8.5 kilograms)   ^c71 That is, about 375 pounds
(about 170 kilograms); also in verse 72
^d71 That is, about 1 1/3 tons (about 1.2 metric
tons)   ^e72 That is, about 1 1/4 tons (about 1.1
metric tons)

from daybreak till noon as he faced the square before the Water Gate in the presence of the men, women and others who could understand. And all the people listened attentively to the Book of the Law.

[4]Ezra the scribe stood on a high wooden platform built for the occasion. Beside him on his right stood Mattithiah, Shema, Anaiah, Uriah, Hilkiah and Maaseiah; and on his left were Pedaiah, Mishael, Malkijah, Hashum, Hashbaddanah, Zechariah and Meshullam.

[5]Ezra opened the book. All the people could see him because he was standing above them; and as he opened it, the people all stood up. [6]Ezra praised the LORD, the great God; and all the people lifted their hands and responded, "Amen! Amen!" Then they bowed down and worshiped the LORD with their faces to the ground.

[7]The Levites—Jeshua, Bani, Sherebiah, Jamin, Akkub, Shabbethai, Hodiah, Maaseiah, Kelita, Azariah, Jozabad, Hanan and Pelaiah—instructed the people in the Law while the people were standing there. [8]They read from the Book of the Law of God, making it clear[a] and giving the meaning so that the people could understand what was being read.

[9]Then Nehemiah the governor, Ezra the priest and scribe, and the Levites who were instructing the people said to them all, "This day is sacred to the LORD your God. Do not mourn or weep." For all the people had been weeping as they listened to the words of the Law.

[10]Nehemiah said, "Go and enjoy choice food and sweet drinks, and send some to those who have nothing prepared. This day is sacred to our Lord. Do not grieve, for the joy of the LORD is your strength."

[11]The Levites calmed all the people, saying, "Be still, for this is a sacred day. Do not grieve."

[12]Then all the people went away to eat and drink, to send portions of food and to celebrate with great joy, because they now understood the words that had been made known to them.

[13]On the second day of the month, the heads of all the families, along with the priests and the Levites, gathered around Ezra the scribe to give attention to the words of the Law. [14]They found written in the Law, which the LORD had commanded through Moses, that the Israelites were to live in booths during the feast of the seventh month [15]and that they should proclaim this word and spread it throughout their towns and in Jerusalem: "Go out into the hill country and bring back branches from olive and wild olive trees, and from myrtles, palms and shade trees, to make booths"—as it is written.[b]

[16]So the people went out and brought back branches and built themselves booths on their own roofs, in their courtyards, in the courts of the house of God and in the square by the Water Gate and the one by the Gate of Ephraim. [17]The whole company that had returned from exile built booths and lived in them. From the days of Joshua son of Nun until that day, the Israelites had not celebrated it like this. And their joy was very great.

[18]Day after day, from the first day to the last, Ezra read from the Book of the Law of God. They celebrated the feast for seven days, and on the eighth day, in accordance with the regulation, there was an assembly.

The Israelites Confess Their Sins

9 On the twenty-fourth day of the same month, the Israelites gathered together, fasting and wearing sackcloth and having dust on their heads. [2]Those of Israelite descent had separated themselves from all foreigners. They stood in their places and confessed their sins and the wickedness of their fathers. [3]They stood where they were and read from the Book of the Law of the LORD their God for a quarter of the day, and spent another quarter in confession and in worshiping the LORD their God. [4]Standing on the stairs were the Levites—Jeshua, Bani, Kadmiel, Shebaniah, Bunni, Sherebiah, Bani and Kenani—who called with loud voices to the LORD their God. [5]And the Levites—Jeshua, Kadmiel, Bani, Hashabneiah, Sherebiah, Hodiah, Shebaniah

---

[a]8 Or God, translating it   [b]15 See Lev. 23:37–40.

and Pethahiah—said: "Stand up and praise the LORD your God, who is from everlasting to everlasting.*"

"Blessed be your glorious name, and may it be exalted above all blessing and praise. 6You alone are the LORD. You made the heavens, even the highest heavens, and all their starry host, the earth and all that is on it, the seas and all that is in them. You give life to everything, and the multitudes of heaven worship you.

7"You are the LORD God, who chose Abram and brought him out of Ur of the Chaldeans and named him Abraham. 8You found his heart faithful to you, and you made a covenant with him to give to his descendants the land of the Canaanites, Hittites, Amorites, Perizzites, Jebusites and Girgashites. You have kept your promise because you are righteous.

9"You saw the suffering of our forefathers in Egypt; you heard their cry at the Red Sea.*b 10You sent miraculous signs and wonders against Pharaoh, against all his officials and all the people of his land, for you knew how arrogantly the Egyptians treated them. You made a name for yourself, which remains to this day. 11You divided the sea before them, so that they passed through it on dry ground, but you hurled their pursuers into the depths, like a stone into mighty waters. 12By day you led them with a pillar of cloud, and by night with a pillar of fire to give them light on the way they were to take.

13"You came down on Mount Sinai; you spoke to them from heaven. You gave them regulations and laws that are just and right, and decrees and commands that are good. 14You made known to them your holy Sabbath and gave them commands, decrees and laws through your servant Moses. 15In their hunger you gave them bread from heaven and in their thirst you brought them water from the rock; you told them to go in and take possession of the land

you had sworn with uplifted hand to give them.

16"But they, our forefathers, became arrogant and stiff-necked, and did not obey your commands. 17They refused to listen and failed to remember the miracles you performed among them. They became stiff-necked and in their rebellion appointed a leader in order to return to their slavery. But you are a forgiving God, gracious and compassionate, slow to anger and abounding in love. Therefore you did not desert them, 18even when they cast for themselves an image of a calf and said, 'This is your god, who brought you up out of Egypt,' or when they committed awful blasphemies.

19"Because of your great compassion you did not abandon them in the desert. By day the pillar of cloud did not cease to guide them on their path, nor the pillar of fire by night to shine on the way they were to take. 20You gave your good Spirit to instruct them. You did not withhold your manna from their mouths, and you gave them water for their thirst. 21For forty years you sustained them in the desert; they lacked nothing, their clothes did not wear out nor did their feet become swollen.

22"You gave them kingdoms and nations, allotting to them even the remotest frontiers. They took over the country of Sihon*c king of Heshbon and the country of Og king of Bashan. 23You made their sons as numerous as the stars in the sky, and you brought them into the land that you told their fathers to enter and possess. 24Their sons went in and took possession of the land. You subdued before them the Canaanites, who lived in the land; you handed the Canaanites over to them, along with their kings and the peoples of the land, to deal with

*a*5 Or *God for ever and ever*   *b*9 Hebrew *Yam Suph*; that is, Sea of Reeds   *c*22 One Hebrew manuscript and Septuagint; most Hebrew manuscripts *Sihon, that is, the country of the*

Love to Tell the Story

9:5 "STAND UP AND PRAISE THE LORD YOUR GOD, WHO IS FROM EVERLASTING TO EVERLASTING."

It has been said that history is "His Story," God's story. If life is a story, and God is the author, then everything depends on understanding where we are in the plot line. The happiness or sadness of any moment is meaningful only in the context of the whole narrative. Given the enormous and daunting difficulty of rebuilding a shattered nation, it's a good thing that Nehemiah knows the story well.

In his prayer for Israel in this chapter, Nehemiah touchingly retells the story of the Israelites, making his case—from the story God has been writing himself—for God to continue to rescue his people despite their sin. He starts with creation, moves to Abraham and then to the rescue from captivity in Egypt, the giving of the law on Sinai, the rebelliousness of the people in the wilderness, the conquest of Canaan, and the national apostasy that has gotten them where they are now. At every turn in the story, the theme has been God's amazing grace. In the creation: "You give life to everything" (9:6). With Abraham: "You have kept your promise because you are righteous" (verse 8). In the deliverance from slavery: "You sent miraculous signs and wonders" (verse 10). In the subsequent ingratitude and rebelliousness of the people in the wilderness, Nehemiah recounted how the Lord is "a forgiving God, gracious and compassionate, slow to anger and abounding in love" (verse 17). In the apostasy of the years of the kings of Israel and Judah, it was the same as it had always been: "But in your great mercy you did not put an end to them or abandon them, for you are a gracious and merciful God" (verse 31).

All this retelling of the story brings Nehemiah up to the present and the prayer for God to keep writing the story the way he always has: "Now therefore, O our God, the great, mighty and awesome God, who keeps his covenant of love, do not let all this hardship seem trifling in your eyes" (verse 32). In other words, it's been bad for us before, and it's just as bad now. Please save us.

This kind of praying does three things for us: It keeps us clear on what we may expect from God; our reflections on who God is get longer and our petitions get shorter; and it's fun. It pleases the Lord when his people start thinking the way he always has.

P R A Y :

"I love to tell the story—
'tis pleasant to repeat.
What seems each time I tell it,
more wonderfully sweet."
CATHARINE HANKEY

FOR YOUR NEXT DEVOTIONAL READING, GO TO PAGE 560.

them as they pleased. ²⁵They captured fortified cities and fertile land; they took possession of houses filled with all kinds of good things, wells already dug, vineyards, olive groves and fruit trees in abundance. They ate to the full and were well-nourished; they reveled in your great goodness.

²⁶"But they were disobedient and rebelled against you; they put your law behind their backs. They killed your prophets, who had admonished them in order to turn them back to you; they committed awful blasphemies. ²⁷So you handed them over to their enemies, who oppressed them. But when they were oppressed they cried out to you. From heaven you heard them, and in your great compassion you gave them deliverers, who rescued them from the hand of their enemies.

²⁸"But as soon as they were at rest, they again did what was evil in your sight. Then you abandoned them to the hand of their enemies so that they ruled over them. And when they cried out to you again, you heard from heaven, and in your compassion you delivered them time after time.

²⁹"You warned them to return to your law, but they became arrogant and disobeyed your commands. They sinned against your ordinances, by which a man will live if he obeys them. Stubbornly they turned their backs on you, became stiff-necked and refused to listen. ³⁰For many years you were patient with them. By your Spirit you admonished them through your prophets. Yet they paid no attention, so you handed them over to the neighboring peoples. ³¹But in your great mercy you did not put an end to them or abandon them, for you are a gracious and merciful God.

³²"Now therefore, O our God, the great, mighty and awesome God, who keeps his covenant of love, do not let all this hardship seem trifling in your eyes—the hardship that has come upon us, upon our kings and leaders, upon our priests and prophets, upon our fathers and all your people, from the days of the kings of Assyria until today. ³³In all that has happened to us, you have been just; you have acted faithfully, while we did wrong. ³⁴Our kings, our leaders, our priests and our fathers did not follow your law; they did not pay attention to your commands or the warnings you gave them. ³⁵Even while they were in their kingdom, enjoying your great goodness to them in the spacious and fertile land you gave them, they did not serve you or turn from their evil ways.

³⁶"But see, we are slaves today, slaves in the land you gave our forefathers so they could eat its fruit and the other good things it produces. ³⁷Because of our sins, its abundant harvest goes to the kings you have placed over us. They rule over our bodies and our cattle as they please. We are in great distress.

The Agreement of the People

³⁸"In view of all this, we are making a binding agreement, putting it in writing, and our leaders, our Levites and our priests are affixing their seals to it."

10 Those who sealed it were:

Nehemiah the governor, the son of Hacaliah.

Zedekiah, ²Seraiah, Azariah, Jeremiah,
³Pashhur, Amariah, Malkijah,
⁴Hattush, Shebaniah, Malluch,
⁵Harim, Meremoth, Obadiah,
⁶Daniel, Ginnethon, Baruch,
⁷Meshullam, Abijah, Mijamin,
⁸Maaziah, Bilgai and Shemaiah.
These were the priests.

⁹The Levites:

Jeshua son of Azaniah, Binnui of the sons of Henadad, Kadmiel,
¹⁰and their associates: Shebaniah, Hodiah, Kelita, Pelaiah, Hanan,
¹¹Mica, Rehob, Hashabiah,
¹²Zaccur, Sherebiah, Shebaniah,
¹³Hodiah, Bani and Beninu.

¹⁴The leaders of the people:

> Parosh, Pahath-Moab, Elam, Zattu, Bani,
> ¹⁵Bunni, Azgad, Bebai,
> ¹⁶Adonijah, Bigvai, Adin,
> ¹⁷Ater, Hezekiah, Azzur,
> ¹⁸Hodiah, Hashum, Bezai,
> ¹⁹Hariph, Anathoth, Nebai,
> ²⁰Magpiash, Meshullam, Hezir,
> ²¹Meshezabel, Zadok, Jaddua,
> ²²Pelatiah, Hanan, Anaiah,
> ²³Hoshea, Hananiah, Hasshub,
> ²⁴Hallohesh, Pilha, Shobek,
> ²⁵Rehum, Hashabnah, Maaseiah,
> ²⁶Ahiah, Hanan, Anan,
> ²⁷Malluch, Harim and Baanah.

²⁸"The rest of the people—priests, Levites, gatekeepers, singers, temple servants and all who separated themselves from the neighboring peoples for the sake of the Law of God, together with their wives and all their sons and daughters who are able to understand— ²⁹all these now join their brothers the nobles, and bind themselves with a curse and an oath to follow the Law of God given through Moses the servant of God and to obey carefully all the commands, regulations and decrees of the Lord our Lord.

³⁰"We promise not to give our daughters in marriage to the peoples around us or take their daughters for our sons.

³¹"When the neighboring peoples bring merchandise or grain to sell on the Sabbath, we will not buy from them on the Sabbath or on any holy day. Every seventh year we will forgo working the land and will cancel all debts.

³²"We assume the responsibility for carrying out the commands to give a third of a shekel*ᵃ* each year for the service of the house of our God: ³³for the bread set out on the table; for the regular grain offerings and burnt offerings; for the offerings on the Sabbaths, New Moon festivals and appointed feasts; for the holy offerings; for sin offerings to make atonement for Israel; and for all the duties of the house of our God.

³⁴"We—the priests, the Levites and the people—have cast lots to determine when each of our families is to bring to the house of our God at set times each year a contribution of wood to burn on the altar of the Lord our God, as it is written in the Law.

³⁵"We also assume responsibility for bringing to the house of the Lord each year the firstfruits of our crops and of every fruit tree.

³⁶"As it is also written in the Law, we will bring the firstborn of our sons and of our cattle, of our herds and of our flocks to the house of our God, to the priests ministering there.

³⁷"Moreover, we will bring to the storerooms of the house of our God, to the priests, the first of our ground meal, of our ⌊grain⌋ offerings, of the fruit of all our trees and of our new wine and oil. And we will bring a tithe of our crops to the Levites, for it is the Levites who collect the tithes in all the towns where we work. ³⁸A priest descended from Aaron is to accompany the Levites when they receive the tithes, and the Levites are to bring a tenth of the tithes up to the house of our God, to the storerooms of the treasury. ³⁹The people of Israel, including the Levites, are to bring their contributions of grain, new wine and oil to the storerooms where the articles for the sanctuary are kept and where the ministering priests, the gatekeepers and the singers stay.

"We will not neglect the house of our God."

The New Residents of Jerusalem

11 Now the leaders of the people settled in Jerusalem, and the rest of the people cast lots to bring one out of every ten to live in Jerusalem, the holy city, while the remaining nine were to stay in their own towns. ²The people commended all the men who volunteered to live in Jerusalem.

³These are the provincial leaders who settled in Jerusalem (now some Israel-

ᵃ32 That is, about 1/8 ounce (about 4 grams)

ites, priests, Levites, temple servants and descendants of Solomon's servants lived in the towns of Judah, each on his own property in the various towns, [4]while other people from both Judah and Benjamin lived in Jerusalem):

From the descendants of Judah:

Athaiah son of Uzziah, the son of Zechariah, the son of Amariah, the son of Shephatiah, the son of Mahalalel, a descendant of Perez; [5]and Maaseiah son of Baruch, the son of Col-Hozeh, the son of Hazaiah, the son of Adaiah, the son of Joiarib, the son of Zechariah, a descendant of Shelah. [6]The descendants of Perez who lived in Jerusalem totaled 468 able men.

[7]From the descendants of Benjamin:

Sallu son of Meshullam, the son of Joed, the son of Pedaiah, the son of Kolaiah, the son of Maaseiah, the son of Ithiel, the son of Jeshaiah, [8]and his followers, Gabbai and Sallai—928 men. [9]Joel son of Zicri was their chief officer, and Judah son of Hassenuah was over the Second District of the city.

[10]From the priests:

Jedaiah; the son of Joiarib; Jakin; [11]Seraiah son of Hilkiah, the son of Meshullam, the son of Zadok, the son of Meraioth, the son of Ahitub, supervisor in the house of God, [12]and their associates, who carried on work for the temple—822 men; Adaiah son of Jeroham, the son of Pelaliah, the son of Amzi, the son of Zechariah, the son of Pashhur, the son of Malkijah, [13]and his associates, who were heads of families—242 men; Amashsai son of Azarel, the son of Ahzai, the son of Meshillemoth, the son of Immer, [14]and his[a] associates, who were able men— 128. Their chief officer was Zabdiel son of Haggedolim.

[15]From the Levites:

Shemaiah son of Hasshub, the son of Azrikam, the son of Hashabiah, the son of Bunni; [16]Shabbethai and Jozabad, two of the heads of the Levites, who had charge of the outside work of the house of God; [17]Mattaniah son of Mica, the son of Zabdi, the son of Asaph, the director who led in thanksgiving and prayer; Bakbukiah, second among his associates; and Abda son of Shammua, the son of Galal, the son of Jeduthun. [18]The Levites in the holy city totaled 284.

[19]The gatekeepers:

Akkub, Talmon and their associates, who kept watch at the gates—172 men.

[20]The rest of the Israelites, with the priests and Levites, were in all the towns of Judah, each on his ancestral property. [21]The temple servants lived on the hill of Ophel, and Ziha and Gishpa were in charge of them.

[22]The chief officer of the Levites in Jerusalem was Uzzi son of Bani, the son of Hashabiah, the son of Mattaniah, the son of Mica. Uzzi was one of Asaph's descendants, who were the singers responsible for the service of the house of God. [23]The singers were under the king's orders, which regulated their daily activity.

[24]Pethahiah son of Meshezabel, one of the descendants of Zerah son of Judah, was the king's agent in all affairs relating to the people.

[25]As for the villages with their fields, some of the people of Judah lived in Kiriath Arba and its surrounding settlements, in Dibon and its settlements, in Jekabzeel and its villages, [26]in Jeshua, in Moladah, in Beth Pelet, [27]in Hazar Shual, in Beersheba and its settlements, [28]in Ziklag, in Meconah and its settlements, [29]in En Rimmon, in Zorah, in Jarmuth, [30]Zanoah, Adullam and their villages, in Lachish and its fields, and in Azekah and its settlements. So they were living all the way from Beersheba to the Valley of Hinnom.

[31]The descendants of the Benjamites from Geba lived in Micmash, Aija, Bethel and its settlements, [32]in Anathoth, Nob and Ananiah, [33]in Hazor, Ramah and Gittaim, [34]in Hadid, Zeboim and Neballat,

[a]14 Most Septuagint manuscripts; Hebrew *their*

35in Lod and Ono, and in the Valley of the Craftsmen. 36Some of the divisions of the Levites of Judah settled in Benjamin.

Priests and Levites

12 These were the priests and Levites who returned with Zerubbabel son of Shealtiel and with Jeshua:

Seraiah, Jeremiah, Ezra,
2 Amariah, Malluch, Hattush,
3 Shecaniah, Rehum, Meremoth,
4 Iddo, Ginnethon,*a* Abijah,
5 Mijamin,*b* Moadiah, Bilgah,
6 Shemaiah, Joiarib, Jedaiah,
7 Sallu, Amok, Hilkiah and Jedaiah.

These were the leaders of the priests and their associates in the days of Jeshua.

8The Levites were Jeshua, Binnui, Kadmiel, Sherebiah, Judah, and also Mattaniah, who, together with his associates, was in charge of the songs of thanksgiving. 9Bakbukiah and Unni, their associates, stood opposite them in the services.

10Jeshua was the father of Joiakim, Joiakim the father of Eliashib, Eliashib the father of Joiada, 11Joiada the father of Jonathan, and Jonathan the father of Jaddua.

12In the days of Joiakim, these were the heads of the priestly families:

of Seraiah's family, Meraiah;
of Jeremiah's, Hananiah;
13 of Ezra's, Meshullam;
of Amariah's, Jehohanan;
14 of Malluch's, Jonathan;
of Shecaniah's,*c* Joseph;
15 of Harim's, Adna;
of Meremoth's,*d* Helkai;
16 of Iddo's, Zechariah;
of Ginnethon's, Meshullam;
17 of Abijah's, Zicri;
of Miniamin's and of Moadiah's, Piltai;
18 of Bilgah's, Shammua;
of Shemaiah's, Jehonathan;
19 of Joiarib's, Mattenai;
of Jedaiah's, Uzzi;
20 of Sallu's, Kallai;
of Amok's, Eber;
21 of Hilkiah's, Hashabiah;
of Jedaiah's, Nethanel.

22The family heads of the Levites in the days of Eliashib, Joiada, Johanan and Jaddua, as well as those of the priests, were recorded in the reign of Darius the Persian. 23The family heads among the descendants of Levi up to the time of Johanan son of Eliashib were recorded in the book of the annals. 24And the leaders of the Levites were Hashabiah, Sherebiah, Jeshua son of Kadmiel, and their associates, who stood opposite them to give praise and thanksgiving, one section responding to the other, as prescribed by David the man of God.

25Mattaniah, Bakbukiah, Obadiah, Meshullam, Talmon and Akkub were gatekeepers who guarded the storerooms at the gates. 26They served in the days of Joiakim son of Jeshua, the son of Jozadak, and in the days of Nehemiah the governor and of Ezra the priest and scribe.

Dedication of the Wall of Jerusalem

27At the dedication of the wall of Jerusalem, the Levites were sought out from where they lived and were brought to Jerusalem to celebrate joyfully the dedication with songs of thanksgiving and with the music of cymbals, harps and lyres. 28The singers also were brought together from the region around Jerusalem—from the villages of the Netophathites, 29from Beth Gilgal, and from the area of Geba and Azmaveth, for the singers had built villages for themselves around Jerusalem. 30When the priests and Levites had purified themselves ceremonially, they purified the people, the gates and the wall.

31I had the leaders of Judah go up on top*e* of the wall. I also assigned two large choirs to give thanks. One was to proceed on top*f* of the wall to the right, toward the Dung Gate. 32Hoshaiah and half the leaders of Judah followed them, 33along with Azariah, Ezra, Meshullam, 34Judah, Benjamin, Shemaiah, Jeremiah, 35as well as some priests with trumpets, and also Zechariah son of Jonathan, the son of Shemaiah, the son of Mattaniah,

---

a4 Many Hebrew manuscripts and Vulgate (see also Neh. 12:16); most Hebrew manuscripts *Ginnethoi* *b5* A variant of *Miniamin* *c14* Very many Hebrew manuscripts, some Septuagint manuscripts and Syriac (see also Neh. 12:3); most Hebrew manuscripts *Shebaniah's* *d15* Some Septuagint manuscripts (see also Neh. 12:3); Hebrew *Meraioth's* *e31* Or *go alongside* *f31* Or *proceed alongside*

the son of Micaiah, the son of Zaccur, the son of Asaph, ³⁶and his associates—Shemaiah, Azarel, Milalai, Gilalai, Maai, Nethanel, Judah and Hanani—with musical instruments ⌐prescribed by⌐ David the man of God. Ezra the scribe led the procession. ³⁷At the Fountain Gate they continued directly up the steps of the City of David on the ascent to the wall and passed above the house of David to the Water Gate on the east.

³⁸The second choir proceeded in the opposite direction. I followed them on top*a* of the wall, together with half the people—past the Tower of the Ovens to the Broad Wall, ³⁹over the Gate of Ephraim, the Jeshanah*b* Gate, the Fish Gate, the Tower of Hananel and the Tower of the Hundred, as far as the Sheep Gate. At the Gate of the Guard they stopped.

⁴⁰The two choirs that gave thanks then took their places in the house of God; so did I, together with half the officials, ⁴¹as well as the priests—Eliakim, Maaseiah, Miniamin, Micaiah, Elioenai, Zechariah and Hananiah with their trumpets— ⁴²and also Maaseiah, Shemaiah, Eleazar, Uzzi, Jehohanan, Malkijah, Elam and Ezer. The choirs sang under the direction of Jezrahiah. ⁴³And on that day they offered great sacrifices, rejoicing because God had given them great joy. The women and children also rejoiced. The sound of rejoicing in Jerusalem could be heard far away.

⁴⁴At that time men were appointed to be in charge of the storerooms for the contributions, firstfruits and tithes. From the fields around the towns they were to bring into the storerooms the portions required by the Law for the priests and the Levites, for Judah was pleased with the ministering priests and Levites. ⁴⁵They performed the service of their God and the service of purification, as did also the singers and gatekeepers, according to the commands of David and his son Solomon. ⁴⁶For long ago, in the days of David and Asaph, there had been directors for the singers and for the songs of praise and thanksgiving to God. ⁴⁷So in the days of Zerubbabel and of Nehemiah, all Israel contributed the daily portions for the singers and gatekeepers. They also set aside the portion for the

other Levites, and the Levites set aside the portion for the descendants of Aaron.

Nehemiah's Final Reforms

13 On that day the Book of Moses was read aloud in the hearing of the people and there it was found written that no Ammonite or Moabite should ever be admitted into the assembly of God, ²because they had not met the Israelites with food and water but had hired Balaam to call a curse down on them. (Our God, however, turned the curse into a blessing.) ³When the people heard this law, they excluded from Israel all who were of foreign descent.

⁴Before this, Eliashib the priest had been put in charge of the storerooms of the house of our God. He was closely associated with Tobiah, ⁵and he had provided him with a large room formerly used to store the grain offerings and incense and temple articles, and also the tithes of grain, new wine and oil prescribed for the Levites, singers and gatekeepers, as well as the contributions for the priests.

⁶But while all this was going on, I was not in Jerusalem, for in the thirty-second year of Artaxerxes king of Babylon I had returned to the king. Some time later I asked his permission ⁷and came back to Jerusalem. Here I learned about the evil thing Eliashib had done in providing Tobiah a room in the courts of the house of God. ⁸I was greatly displeased and threw all Tobiah's household goods out of the room. ⁹I gave orders to purify the rooms, and then I put back into them the equipment of the house of God, with the grain offerings and the incense.

¹⁰I also learned that the portions assigned to the Levites had not been given to them, and that all the Levites and singers responsible for the service had gone back to their own fields. ¹¹So I rebuked the officials and asked them, "Why is the house of God neglected?" Then I called them together and stationed them at their posts.

¹²All Judah brought the tithes of grain, new wine and oil into the storerooms. ¹³I put Shelemiah the priest, Zadok the

a38 Or them alongside   b39 Or Old

The Sacrament of Geometry

IN 1938, while at the Benedictine abbey of Solesmes, France, Simone Weil had a mystical encounter with God. As she read a poem by George Herbert, "Christ came down and seized me," she later wrote to a friend. Although Weil was never baptized or formally joined a denomination, she continued to have an intense interest in Christianity during the few remaining years of her life. She died in England in 1943 of starvation and pulmonary tuberculosis after refusing to eat in order to show solidarity with the French under Nazi occupation.

Weil's early years were impassioned and restless. Born into an agnostic Jewish family in Paris in 1909, she obtained her undergraduate degree with honors at age 15 and spent her young adulthood teaching philosophy and involving herself in causes of social reform. As a writer, she contributed to several communist and socialist publications. As an activist, she became an advocate for the unemployed and the lower class worker, even taking a job in an automobile factory to better understand the workers' plight. But it was in her writings as a fervent, though somewhat unorthodox, Christian that she made her most enduring contributions.

Her essay, "Reflections on the Right Use of School Studies with a View to the Love of God," has inspired many Christian students to see their studies as more than mere academic pursuits—instead understanding them to be a means to a higher end. This higher end is the love of God and is achieved through a rigorous discipline Weil calls "the faculty of attention." The concept is simple: All academic pursuits train the mind to focus its full attention on the problem or the task at hand. Weil believed this focus of attention is the very substance of prayer in which God is the subject. In this way, learning has value in and of itself, as a lower means. But it also trains one to give the necessary attention to the higher end: loving God in prayer.

"The solution of a geometry problem does not in itself constitute a precious gift," wrote Weil, "but the same law applies to it because it is the image of something precious. Being a little fragment of particular truth, it is a pure image of the unique, eternal, and living Truth, the very Truth that once in a human voice declared: 'I am the Truth.' Every school exercise, thought of in this way, is like a sacrament."[2]

But Weil warned against approaching learning (and prayer) with the stoic drudgery of a homework assignment. "Contrary to the usual belief, ... the type of will power that makes us set our teeth and endure suffering ... has practically no place in study. The intelligence can only be led by desire. For there to be desire, there must be pleasure and joy in the work. The intelligence only grows and bears fruit in joy. The joy of learning [and praying!] is as indispensable as breathing is to running."[3]

PRAY:

"Teach me, my God and King/In all things thee to see
And what I do in any thing/To do it as for thee."

GEORGE HERBERT

MEMORIZE:

Whatever you do, work at it with all your heart, as working for
the Lord, not for men, since you know that you will
receive an inheritance from the Lord as a reward.
It is the Lord Christ you are serving. COLOSSIANS 3:23–24

FOR YOUR NEXT DEVOTIONAL READING, GO TO PAGE 567.

scribe, and a Levite named Pedaiah in charge of the storerooms and made Hanan son of Zaccur, the son of Mattaniah, their assistant, because these men were considered trustworthy. They were made responsible for distributing the supplies to their brothers.

¹⁴Remember me for this, O my God, and do not blot out what I have so faithfully done for the house of my God and its services.

¹⁵In those days I saw men in Judah treading winepresses on the Sabbath and bringing in grain and loading it on donkeys, together with wine, grapes, figs and all other kinds of loads. And they were bringing all this into Jerusalem on the Sabbath. Therefore I warned them against selling food on that day. ¹⁶Men from Tyre who lived in Jerusalem were bringing in fish and all kinds of merchandise and selling them in Jerusalem on the Sabbath to the people of Judah. ¹⁷I rebuked the nobles of Judah and said to them, "What is this wicked thing you are doing—desecrating the Sabbath day? ¹⁸Didn't your forefathers do the same things, so that our God brought all this calamity upon us and upon this city? Now you are stirring up more wrath against Israel by desecrating the Sabbath."

¹⁹When evening shadows fell on the gates of Jerusalem before the Sabbath, I ordered the doors to be shut and not opened until the Sabbath was over. I stationed some of my own men at the gates so that no load could be brought in on the Sabbath day. ²⁰Once or twice the merchants and sellers of all kinds of goods spent the night outside Jerusalem. ²¹But I warned them and said, "Why do you spend the night by the wall? If you do this again, I will lay hands on you." From that time on they no longer came on the Sabbath. ²²Then I commanded the Levites to purify themselves and go and guard the gates in order to keep the Sabbath day holy.

Remember me for this also, O my God, and show mercy to me according to your great love.

²³Moreover, in those days I saw men of Judah who had married women from Ashdod, Ammon and Moab. ²⁴Half of their children spoke the language of Ashdod or the language of one of the other peoples, and did not know how to speak the language of Judah. ²⁵I rebuked them and called curses down on them. I beat some of the men and pulled out their hair. I made them take an oath in God's name and said: "You are not to give your daughters in marriage to their sons, nor are you to take their daughters in marriage for your sons or for yourselves. ²⁶Was it not because of marriages like these that Solomon king of Israel sinned? Among the many nations there was no king like him. He was loved by his God, and God made him king over all Israel, but even he was led into sin by foreign women. ²⁷Must we hear now that you too are doing all this terrible wickedness and are being unfaithful to our God by marrying foreign women?"

²⁸One of the sons of Joiada son of Eliashib the high priest was son-in-law to Sanballat the Horonite. And I drove him away from me.

²⁹Remember them, O my God, because they defiled the priestly office and the covenant of the priesthood and of the Levites.

³⁰So I purified the priests and the Levites of everything foreign, and assigned them duties, each to his own task. ³¹I also made provision for contributions of wood at designated times, and for the firstfruits.

Remember me with favor, O my God.

Esther

WHAT ARE we to make of a book in the Bible that doesn't even
mention God? Sometimes actions speak louder than words.

Though threatened with genocide, the Jews seem to be the
luckiest people on earth when the story is over. How lucky for
them that Esther was so beautiful. How fortunate that she won
the Bride-for-Xerxes competition. How lucky for them that Mordecai just happened to overhear an assassination plot. Coincidences
collect, one upon another, and Lo! the evil Haman ends up falling
into the pit he dug for others.[1]

But maybe the Jews are just a little too lucky, like the suspi-
cious character who keeps beating the house in roulette. Maybe
there is some manipulation of the game going on somewhere. To
use a line by songwriter David Wilcox, there is a choreography in
these coincidences. That is the point of a story in which the main
character, God, isn't mentioned. That is the way he seems to carry
out so much of his governance of the world: incognito, choreog-
raphing coincidences, working quietly behind the scenes. Or
maybe it's the other way around; as G. K. Chesterton suggested,
maybe we are the ones behind the scenes. Maybe we are looking
at the world from behind, and if we could get in front we would
meet, face-to-face, the smiling Providence who seems so quiet.[2]
One would think that Esther would agree and would encourage us
to not lose heart when our prayers seem to fall into a silent abyss.

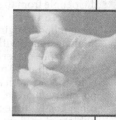

GATHER TOGETHER
ALL THE JEWS WHO
ARE IN SUSA, AND
FAST FOR ME. (4:16)

Queen Vashti Deposed

1 This is what happened during the time of Xerxes,[a] the Xerxes who ruled over 127 provinces stretching from India to Cush[b]: ²At that time King Xerxes reigned from his royal throne in the citadel of Susa, ³and in the third year of his reign he gave a banquet for all his nobles and officials. The military leaders of Persia and Media, the princes, and the nobles of the provinces were present.

⁴For a full 180 days he displayed the vast wealth of his kingdom and the splendor and glory of his majesty. ⁵When these days were over, the king gave a banquet, lasting seven days, in the enclosed garden of the king's palace, for all the people from the least to the greatest, who were in the citadel of Susa. ⁶The garden had hangings of white and blue linen, fastened with cords of white linen and purple material to silver rings on marble pillars. There were couches of gold and silver on a mosaic pavement of porphyry, marble, mother-of-pearl and other costly stones. ⁷Wine was served in goblets of gold, each one different from the other, and the royal wine was abundant, in keeping with the king's liberality. ⁸By the king's command each guest was allowed to drink in his own way, for the king instructed all the wine stewards to serve each man what he wished.

⁹Queen Vashti also gave a banquet for the women in the royal palace of King Xerxes.

¹⁰On the seventh day, when King Xerxes was in high spirits from wine, he commanded the seven eunuchs who served him—Mehuman, Biztha, Harbona, Bigtha, Abagtha, Zethar and Carcas— ¹¹to bring before him Queen Vashti, wearing her royal crown, in order to display her beauty to the people and nobles, for she was lovely to look at. ¹²But when the attendants delivered the king's command, Queen Vashti refused to come. Then the king became furious and burned with anger.

¹³Since it was customary for the king to consult experts in matters of law and justice, he spoke with the wise men who understood the times ¹⁴and were closest to the king—Carshena, Shethar, Admatha, Tarshish, Meres, Marsena and Memucan, the seven nobles of Persia and Media who had special access to the king and were highest in the kingdom.

¹⁵"According to law, what must be done to Queen Vashti?" he asked. "She has not obeyed the command of King Xerxes that the eunuchs have taken to her."

¹⁶Then Memucan replied in the presence of the king and the nobles, "Queen Vashti has done wrong, not only against the king but also against all the nobles and the peoples of all the provinces of King Xerxes. ¹⁷For the queen's conduct will become known to all the women, and so they will despise their husbands and say, 'King Xerxes commanded Queen Vashti to be brought before him, but she would not come.' ¹⁸This very day the Persian and Median women of the nobility who have heard about the queen's conduct will respond to all the king's nobles in the same way. There will be no end of disrespect and discord.

¹⁹"Therefore, if it pleases the king, let him issue a royal decree and let it be written in the laws of Persia and Media, which cannot be repealed, that Vashti is never again to enter the presence of King Xerxes. Also let the king give her royal position to someone else who is better than she. ²⁰Then when the king's edict is proclaimed throughout all his vast realm, all the women will respect their husbands, from the least to the greatest."

²¹The king and his nobles were pleased with this advice, so the king did as Memucan proposed. ²²He sent dispatches to all parts of the kingdom, to each province in its own script and to each people in its own language, proclaiming in each people's tongue that every man should be ruler over his own household.

Esther Made Queen

2 Later when the anger of King Xerxes had subsided, he remembered Vashti and what she had done and what he had decreed about her. ²Then the king's personal attendants proposed, "Let a

---

[a] 1 Hebrew *Ahasuerus*, a variant of Xerxes' Persian name; here and throughout Esther
[b] 1 That is, the upper Nile region

search be made for beautiful young virgins for the king. [3]Let the king appoint commissioners in every province of his realm to bring all these beautiful girls into the harem at the citadel of Susa. Let them be placed under the care of Hegai, the king's eunuch, who is in charge of the women; and let beauty treatments be given to them. [4]Then let the girl who pleases the king be queen instead of Vashti." This advice appealed to the king, and he followed it.

[5]Now there was in the citadel of Susa a Jew of the tribe of Benjamin, named Mordecai son of Jair, the son of Shimei, the son of Kish, [6]who had been carried into exile from Jerusalem by Nebuchadnezzar king of Babylon, among those taken captive with Jehoiachin[a] king of Judah. [7]Mordecai had a cousin named Hadassah, whom he had brought up because she had neither father nor mother. This girl, who was also known as Esther, was lovely in form and features, and Mordecai had taken her as his own daughter when her father and mother died.

[8]When the king's order and edict had been proclaimed, many girls were brought to the citadel of Susa and put under the care of Hegai. Esther also was taken to the king's palace and entrusted to Hegai, who had charge of the harem. [9]The girl pleased him and won his favor. Immediately he provided her with her beauty treatments and special food. He assigned to her seven maids selected from the king's palace and moved her and her maids into the best place in the harem.

[10]Esther had not revealed her nationality and family background, because Mordecai had forbidden her to do so. [11]Every day he walked back and forth near the courtyard of the harem to find out how Esther was and what was happening to her.

[12]Before a girl's turn came to go in to King Xerxes, she had to complete twelve months of beauty treatments prescribed for the women, six months with oil of myrrh and six with perfumes and cosmetics. [13]And this is how she would go to the king: Anything she wanted was given her to take with her from the harem to the king's palace. [14]In the evening she would go there and in the morning return to another part of the harem to the care of Shaashgaz, the king's eunuch who was in charge of the concubines. She would not return to the king unless he was pleased with her and summoned her by name.

[15]When the turn came for Esther (the girl Mordecai had adopted, the daughter of his uncle Abihail) to go to the king, she asked for nothing other than what Hegai, the king's eunuch who was in charge of the harem, suggested. And Esther won the favor of everyone who saw her. [16]She was taken to King Xerxes in the royal residence in the tenth month, the month of Tebeth, in the seventh year of his reign.

[17]Now the king was attracted to Esther more than to any of the other women, and she won his favor and approval more than any of the other virgins. So he set a royal crown on her head and made her queen instead of Vashti. [18]And the king gave a great banquet, Esther's banquet, for all his nobles and officials. He proclaimed a holiday throughout the provinces and distributed gifts with royal liberality.

Mordecai Uncovers a Conspiracy

[19]When the virgins were assembled a second time, Mordecai was sitting at the king's gate. [20]But Esther had kept secret her family background and nationality just as Mordecai had told her to do, for she continued to follow Mordecai's instructions as she had done when he was bringing her up.

[21]During the time Mordecai was sitting at the king's gate, Bigthana[b] and Teresh, two of the king's officers who guarded the doorway, became angry and conspired to assassinate King Xerxes. [22]But Mordecai found out about the plot and told Queen Esther, who in turn reported it to the king, giving credit to Mordecai. [23]And when the report was investigated and found to be true, the two officials were hanged on a gallows.[c] All this was recorded in the book of the annals in the presence of the king.

[a]6 Hebrew Jeconiah, a variant of Jehoiachin
[b]21 Hebrew Bigthan, a variant of Bigthana
[c]23 Or were hung (or impaled) on poles; similarly elsewhere in Esther

Haman's Plot to Destroy the Jews

3 After these events, King Xerxes honored Haman son of Hammedatha, the Agagite, elevating him and giving him a seat of honor higher than that of all the other nobles. ²All the royal officials at the king's gate knelt down and paid honor to Haman, for the king had commanded this concerning him. But Mordecai would not kneel down or pay him honor.

³Then the royal officials at the king's gate asked Mordecai, "Why do you disobey the king's command?" ⁴Day after day they spoke to him but he refused to comply. Therefore they told Haman about it to see whether Mordecai's behavior would be tolerated, for he had told them he was a Jew.

⁵When Haman saw that Mordecai would not kneel down or pay him honor, he was enraged. ⁶Yet having learned who Mordecai's people were, he scorned the idea of killing only Mordecai. Instead Haman looked for a way to destroy all Mordecai's people, the Jews, throughout the whole kingdom of Xerxes.

⁷In the twelfth year of King Xerxes, in the first month, the month of Nisan, they cast the *pur* (that is, the lot) in the presence of Haman to select a day and month. And the lot fell on*ᵃ* the twelfth month, the month of Adar.

⁸Then Haman said to King Xerxes, "There is a certain people dispersed and scattered among the peoples in all the provinces of your kingdom whose customs are different from those of all other people and who do not obey the king's laws; it is not in the king's best interest to tolerate them. ⁹If it pleases the king, let a decree be issued to destroy them, and I will put ten thousand talents*ᵇ* of silver into the royal treasury for the men who carry out this business."

¹⁰So the king took his signet ring from his finger and gave it to Haman son of Hammedatha, the Agagite, the enemy of the Jews. ¹¹"Keep the money," the king said to Haman, "and do with the people as you please."

¹²Then on the thirteenth day of the first month the royal secretaries were summoned. They wrote out in the script of each province and in the language of each people all Haman's orders to the king's satraps, the governors of the various provinces and the nobles of the various peoples. These were written in the name of King Xerxes himself and sealed

> *It is for us to pray not for tasks equal to our powers, but for powers equal to our tasks, to go forward with a great desire forever beating at the door of our hearts as we travel toward our distant goal.*
>
> HELEN KELLER

with his own ring. ¹³Dispatches were sent by couriers to all the king's provinces with the order to destroy, kill and annihilate all the Jews—young and old, women and little children—on a single day, the thirteenth day of the twelfth month, the month of Adar, and to plunder their goods. ¹⁴A copy of the text of the edict was to be issued as law in every province and made known to the people of every nationality so they would be ready for that day.

¹⁵Spurred on by the king's command, the couriers went out, and the edict was issued in the citadel of Susa. The king and Haman sat down to drink, but the city of Susa was bewildered.

Mordecai Persuades Esther to Help

4 When Mordecai learned of all that had been done, he tore his clothes, put on sackcloth and ashes, and went out into the city, wailing loudly and bitterly. ²But he went only as far as the king's gate, because no one clothed in sackcloth was allowed to enter it. ³In every province to which the edict and order of the king came, there was great mourning among the Jews, with fasting, weeping and wailing. Many lay in sackcloth and ashes.

⁴When Esther's maids and eunuchs came and told her about Mordecai, she was in great distress. She sent clothes for him to put on instead of his sackcloth,

---

ᵃ7 Septuagint; Hebrew does not have *And the lot fell on.* *ᵇ9* That is, about 375 tons (about 345 metric tons)

ESTHER 4

For Such a Time As This

4:14 "AND WHO KNOWS BUT THAT YOU HAVE COME TO ROYAL POSITION FOR SUCH A TIME AS THIS?"

The stakes could not have been higher: The very existence of an entire people hung in the balance. If Haman, the ancient Hitler, had his way there would be genocide, and the Jews would cease to exist in Persia. Everything now seemed to vector in on the lovely Esther. She was the only hope, if there was any hope. What she did with the opportunity before her, how she seized the day, would affect generations to come. Her cousin, and surrogate father, Mordecai urged her to act: "Who knows but that you have come to royal position for such a time as this?" (4:14).

Socrates said the heart of wisdom is to "Know Yourself." The Bible says it is to "Know Your Time." In the Greek language of the New Testament, "time" is spoken of in two ways: *chronos* and *kairos. Chronos* is time as a concrete measurement, like on a clock. *Kairos* is time as a season, a moment; it is about meaning, not measurement. *Kairos* is what the Bible is interested in. Jesus was sometimes irritated when people didn't know their *kairos* (see Matthew 16:2–3). Other times he was heartbroken, as when he wept over Jerusalem, "because you did not recognize the time (*kairos*) of God's coming to you" (Luke 19:44).

One of the ways the Bible speaks of prayer is in the language of watchfulness and alertness (see Isaiah 62:6–7; Ephesians 6:18; 1 Peter 5:8). To pray is by definition to be alert to the moment, to know what time it is, because prayer is birthed in an awareness of God's *kairos:* "I tell you, now is the time (*kairos*) of God's favor, now is the day of salvation" (2 Corinthians 6:2). For this very reason, Jesus was grieved and frustrated because his disciples would not "keep watch" with him in Gethsemane (Matthew 26:38–40). By "keep watch" he meant stay awake and pray, for to pray was to *be* awake. He said, "The spirit is willing, but the body is weak" (Matthew 26:41). Prayer would keep the disciples from falling into temptation. But the disciples couldn't stay awake because they didn't know what time it was.

Getting up in the morning to pray, or setting aside time in the evening to pray, is about much more than the clock and your schedule. It is understanding that whenever you come to pray, you do so "for such a time as this." Who knows what your prayers may mean for the world?

PRAY:

Holy Spirit: Remind me of what time it is!
Awaken me each day to the time of my life.
Teach me that it is always time to pray.

FOR YOUR NEXT DEVOTIONAL READING, GO TO PAGE 575.

but he would not accept them. ⁵Then Esther summoned Hathach, one of the king's eunuchs assigned to attend her, and ordered him to find out what was troubling Mordecai and why.

⁶So Hathach went out to Mordecai in the open square of the city in front of the king's gate. ⁷Mordecai told him everything that had happened to him, including the exact amount of money Haman had promised to pay into the royal treasury for the destruction of the Jews. ⁸He also gave him a copy of the text of the edict for their annihilation, which had been published in Susa, to show to Esther and explain it to her, and he told him to urge her to go into the king's presence to beg for mercy and plead with him for her people.

⁹Hathach went back and reported to Esther what Mordecai had said. ¹⁰Then she instructed him to say to Mordecai, ¹¹"All the king's officials and the people of the royal provinces know that for any man or woman who approaches the king in the inner court without being summoned the king has but one law: that he be put to death. The only exception to this is for the king to extend the gold scepter to him and spare his life. But thirty days have passed since I was called to go to the king."

¹²When Esther's words were reported to Mordecai, ¹³he sent back this answer: "Do not think that because you are in the king's house you alone of all the Jews will escape. ¹⁴For if you remain silent at this time, relief and deliverance for the Jews will arise from another place, but you and your father's family will perish. And who knows but that you have come to royal position for such a time as this?"

¹⁵Then Esther sent this reply to Mordecai: ¹⁶"Go, gather together all the Jews who are in Susa, and fast for me. Do not

eat or drink for three days, night or day. I and my maids will fast as you do. When this is done, I will go to the king, even though it is against the law. And if I perish, I perish."

¹⁷So Mordecai went away and carried out all of Esther's instructions.

Esther's Request to the King

5 On the third day Esther put on her royal robes and stood in the inner court of the palace, in front of the king's hall. The king was sitting on his royal throne in the hall, facing the entrance. ²When he saw Queen Esther standing in the court, he was pleased with her and held out to her the gold scepter that was in his hand. So Esther approached and touched the tip of the scepter.

³Then the king asked, "What is it, Queen Esther? What is your request? Even up to half the kingdom, it will be given you."

⁴"If it pleases the king," replied Esther, "let the king, together with Haman, come today to a banquet I have prepared for him."

⁵"Bring Haman at once," the king said, "so that we may do what Esther asks."

So the king and Haman went to the banquet Esther had prepared. ⁶As they were drinking wine, the king again asked Esther, "Now what is your petition? It will be given you. And what is your request? Even up to half the kingdom, it will be granted."

⁷Esther replied, "My petition and my request is this: ⁸If the king regards me with favor and if it pleases the king to grant my petition and fulfill my request, let the king and Haman come tomorrow to the banquet I will prepare for them. Then I will answer the king's question."

Haman's Rage Against Mordecai

⁹Haman went out that day happy and in high spirits. But when he saw Mordecai at the king's gate and observed that he neither rose nor showed fear in his presence, he was filled with rage against Mordecai. ¹⁰Nevertheless, Haman restrained himself and went home.

Calling together his friends and Zeresh, his wife, ¹¹Haman boasted to them about his vast wealth, his many sons,

> "FOR IF you remain silent at this time, relief and deliverance for the Jews will arise from another place, but you and your father's family will perish. And who knows but that you have come to royal position for such a time as this?"
>
> ESTHER 4:14

and all the ways the king had honored him and how he had elevated him above the other nobles and officials. ¹²"And that's not all," Haman added. "I'm the only person Queen Esther invited to accompany the king to the banquet she gave. And she has invited me along with the king tomorrow. ¹³But all this gives me no satisfaction as long as I see that Jew Mordecai sitting at the king's gate."

¹⁴His wife Zeresh and all his friends said to him, "Have a gallows built, seventy-five feet*a* high, and ask the king in the morning to have Mordecai hanged on it. Then go with the king to the dinner and be happy." This suggestion delighted Haman, and he had the gallows built.

Mordecai Honored

6 That night the king could not sleep; so he ordered the book of the chronicles, the record of his reign, to be brought in and read to him. ²It was found recorded there that Mordecai had exposed Bigthana and Teresh, two of the king's officers who guarded the doorway, who had conspired to assassinate King Xerxes.

³"What honor and recognition has Mordecai received for this?" the king asked.

"Nothing has been done for him," his attendants answered.

⁴The king said, "Who is in the court?" Now Haman had just entered the outer court of the palace to speak to the king about hanging Mordecai on the gallows he had erected for him.

⁵His attendants answered, "Haman is standing in the court."

"Bring him in," the king ordered.

⁶When Haman entered, the king asked him, "What should be done for the man the king delights to honor?"

Now Haman thought to himself, "Who is there that the king would rather honor than me?" ⁷So he answered the king, "For the man the king delights to honor, ⁸have them bring a royal robe the king has worn and a horse the king has ridden, one with a royal crest placed on its head. ⁹Then let the robe and horse be entrusted to one of the king's most noble princes. Let them robe the man the king delights to honor, and lead him on the horse through the city streets, proclaiming before him, 'This is what is done for the man the king delights to honor!'"

¹⁰"Go at once," the king commanded Haman. "Get the robe and the horse and do just as you have suggested for Mordecai the Jew, who sits at the king's gate. Do not neglect anything you have recommended."

¹¹So Haman got the robe and the horse. He robed Mordecai, and led him on horseback through the city streets, proclaiming before him, "This is what is done for the man the king delights to honor!"

¹²Afterward Mordecai returned to the king's gate. But Haman rushed home, with his head covered in grief, ¹³and told Zeresh his wife and all his friends everything that had happened to him.

His advisers and his wife Zeresh said to him, "Since Mordecai, before whom your downfall has started, is of Jewish origin, you cannot stand against him—you will surely come to ruin!" ¹⁴While they were still talking with him, the king's eunuchs arrived and hurried Haman away to the banquet Esther had prepared.

Haman Hanged

7 So the king and Haman went to dine with Queen Esther, ²and as they were drinking wine on that second day, the king again asked, "Queen Esther, what is your petition? It will be given you. What is your request? Even up to half the kingdom, it will be granted."

³Then Queen Esther answered, "If I have found favor with you, O king, and if it pleases your majesty, grant me my life—this is my petition. And spare my people—this is my request. ⁴For I and my people have been sold for destruction and slaughter and annihilation. If we had merely been sold as male and female slaves, I would have kept quiet, because no such distress would justify disturbing the king.*b*"

⁵King Xerxes asked Queen Esther, "Who is he? Where is the man who has dared to do such a thing?"

a14 Hebrew *fifty cubits* (about 23 meters)
b4 Or *quiet, but the compensation our adversary offers cannot be compared with the loss the king would suffer*

⁶Esther said, "The adversary and enemy is this vile Haman."

Then Haman was terrified before the king and queen. ⁷The king got up in a rage, left his wine and went out into the palace garden. But Haman, realizing that the king had already decided his fate, stayed behind to beg Queen Esther for his life.

⁸Just as the king returned from the palace garden to the banquet hall, Haman was falling on the couch where Esther was reclining.

The king exclaimed, "Will he even molest the queen while she is with me in the house?"

As soon as the word left the king's mouth, they covered Haman's face. ⁹Then Harbona, one of the eunuchs attending the king, said, "A gallows seventy-five feet[a] high stands by Haman's house. He had it made for Mordecai, who spoke up to help the king."

The king said, "Hang him on it!" ¹⁰So they hanged Haman on the gallows he had prepared for Mordecai. Then the king's fury subsided.

The King's Edict in Behalf of the Jews

8 That same day King Xerxes gave Queen Esther the estate of Haman, the enemy of the Jews. And Mordecai came into the presence of the king, for Esther had told how he was related to her. ²The king took off his signet ring, which he had reclaimed from Haman, and presented it to Mordecai. And Esther appointed him over Haman's estate.

³Esther again pleaded with the king, falling at his feet and weeping. She begged him to put an end to the evil plan of Haman the Agagite, which he had devised against the Jews. ⁴Then the king extended the gold scepter to Esther and she arose and stood before him.

⁵"If it pleases the king," she said, "and if he regards me with favor and thinks it the right thing to do, and if he is pleased with me, let an order be written overruling the dispatches that Haman son of Hammedatha, the Agagite, devised and wrote to destroy the Jews in all the king's provinces. ⁶For how can I bear to see disaster fall on my people? How can I bear to see the destruction of my family?"

⁷King Xerxes replied to Queen Esther and to Mordecai the Jew, "Because Haman attacked the Jews, I have given his estate to Esther, and they have hanged him on the gallows. ⁸Now write another decree in the king's name in behalf of the Jews as seems best to you, and seal it with the king's signet ring—for no document written in the king's name and sealed with his ring can be revoked."

⁹At once the royal secretaries were summoned—on the twenty-third day of the third month, the month of Sivan. They wrote out all Mordecai's orders to the Jews, and to the satraps, governors and nobles of the 127 provinces stretching from India to Cush.[b] These orders were written in the script of each province and the language of each people and also to the Jews in their own script and language. ¹⁰Mordecai wrote in the name of King Xerxes, sealed the dispatches with the king's signet ring, and sent them by mounted couriers, who rode fast horses especially bred for the king.

¹¹The king's edict granted the Jews in every city the right to assemble and protect themselves; to destroy, kill and annihilate any armed force of any nationality or province that might attack them and their women and children; and to plunder the property of their enemies. ¹²The day appointed for the Jews to do this in all the provinces of King Xerxes was the thirteenth day of the twelfth month, the month of Adar. ¹³A copy of the text of the edict was to be issued as law in every province and made known to the people of every nationality so that the Jews would be ready on that day to avenge themselves on their enemies.

¹⁴The couriers, riding the royal horses, raced out, spurred on by the king's command. And the edict was also issued in the citadel of Susa.

¹⁵Mordecai left the king's presence wearing royal garments of blue and white, a large crown of gold and a purple robe of fine linen. And the city of Susa held a joyous celebration. ¹⁶For the Jews it was a time of happiness and joy, gladness and honor. ¹⁷In every province and

---

*a*9 Hebrew *fifty cubits* (about 23 meters)
*b*9 That is, the upper Nile region

in every city, wherever the edict of the king went, there was joy and gladness among the Jews, with feasting and celebrating. And many people of other nationalities became Jews because fear of the Jews had seized them.

Triumph of the Jews

9 On the thirteenth day of the twelfth month, the month of Adar, the edict commanded by the king was to be carried out. On this day the enemies of the Jews had hoped to overpower them, but now the tables were turned and the Jews got the upper hand over those who hated them. ²The Jews assembled in their cities in all the provinces of King Xerxes to attack those seeking their destruction. No one could stand against them, because the people of all the other nationalities were afraid of them. ³And all the nobles of the provinces, the satraps, the governors and the king's administrators helped the Jews, because fear of Mordecai had seized them. ⁴Mordecai was prominent in the palace; his reputation spread throughout the provinces, and he became more and more powerful.

⁵The Jews struck down all their enemies with the sword, killing and destroying them, and they did what they pleased to those who hated them. ⁶In the citadel of Susa, the Jews killed and destroyed five hundred men. ⁷They also killed Parshandatha, Dalphon, Aspatha, ⁸Poratha, Adalia, Aridatha, ⁹Parmashta, Arisai, Aridai and Vaizatha, ¹⁰the ten sons of Haman son of Hammedatha, the enemy of the Jews. But they did not lay their hands on the plunder.

¹¹The number of those slain in the citadel of Susa was reported to the king that same day. ¹²The king said to Queen Esther, "The Jews have killed and destroyed five hundred men and the ten sons of Haman in the citadel of Susa. What have they done in the rest of the king's provinces? Now what is your petition? It will be given you. What is your request? It will also be granted."

¹³"If it pleases the king," Esther answered, "give the Jews in Susa permission to carry out this day's edict tomorrow also, and let Haman's ten sons be hanged on gallows."

¹⁴So the king commanded that this be done. An edict was issued in Susa, and they hanged the ten sons of Haman. ¹⁵The Jews in Susa came together on the fourteenth day of the month of Adar, and they put to death in Susa three hundred men, but they did not lay their hands on the plunder.

¹⁶Meanwhile, the remainder of the Jews who were in the king's provinces also assembled to protect themselves and get relief from their enemies. They killed seventy-five thousand of them but did not lay their hands on the plunder. ¹⁷This happened on the thirteenth day of the month of Adar, and on the fourteenth they rested and made it a day of feasting and joy.

Purim Celebrated

¹⁸The Jews in Susa, however, had assembled on the thirteenth and fourteenth, and then on the fifteenth they rested and made it a day of feasting and joy.

¹⁹That is why rural Jews—those living in villages—observe the fourteenth of the month of Adar as a day of joy and feasting, a day for giving presents to each other.

²⁰Mordecai recorded these events, and he sent letters to all the Jews throughout the provinces of King Xerxes, near and far, ²¹to have them celebrate annually the fourteenth and fifteenth days of the month of Adar ²²as the time when the Jews got relief from their enemies, and as the month when their sorrow was turned into joy and their mourning into a day of celebration. He wrote them to observe the days as days of feasting and joy and giving presents of food to one another and gifts to the poor.

²³So the Jews agreed to continue the celebration they had begun, doing what Mordecai had written to them. ²⁴For Haman son of Hammedatha, the Agagite, the enemy of all the Jews, had plotted against the Jews to destroy them and had cast the *pur* (that is, the lot) for their ruin and destruction. ²⁵But when the plot came to the king's attention,ᵃ he issued written orders that the evil scheme

ᵃ25 Or *when Esther came before the king*

Haman had devised against the Jews should come back onto his own head, and that he and his sons should be hanged on the gallows. 26(Therefore these days were called Purim, from the word *pur.*) Because of everything written in this letter and because of what they had seen and what had happened to them, 27the Jews took it upon themselves to establish the custom that they and their descendants and all who join them should without fail observe these two days every year, in the way prescribed and at the time appointed. 28These days should be remembered and observed in every generation by every family, and in every province and in every city. And these days of Purim should never cease to be celebrated by the Jews, nor should the memory of them die out among their descendants.

29So Queen Esther, daughter of Abihail, along with Mordecai the Jew, wrote with full authority to confirm this second letter concerning Purim. 30And Mordecai sent letters to all the Jews in the 127 provinces of the kingdom of Xerxes—words of goodwill and assurance— 31to establish these days of Purim at their designated times, as Mordecai the Jew and Queen Esther had decreed for them, and as they had established for themselves and their descendants in regard to their times of fasting and lamentation. 32Esther's decree confirmed these regulations about Purim, and it was written down in the records.

The Greatness of Mordecai

10 King Xerxes imposed tribute throughout the empire, to its distant shores. 2And all his acts of power and might, together with a full account of the greatness of Mordecai to which the king had raised him, are they not written in the book of the annals of the kings of Media and Persia? 3Mordecai the Jew was second in rank to King Xerxes, preeminent among the Jews, and held in high esteem by his many fellow Jews, because he worked for the good of his people and spoke up for the welfare of all the Jews.

Job

IF GOD is God, he can't be good. If God is good, he can't be God. That is the way Archibald MacLeish sums up the conundrum of Job in his modern retelling of the story in his play, *J.B.* It's also a pithy way of stating what for Christians and Jews is the problem of evil: How could a God who is infinitely powerful, wise and good allow a world in which the innocent suffer?

On the one hand, if God is God, infinitely powerful and wise, can he also be good? On the other hand, if God is good, can he also be what God is supposed to be: infinitely powerful and wise? Surely God's power and wisdom must in some way be limited.

The book of Job raises the question of evil, but does not answer it—at least in the way we pose the problem. But it does something better. It gives us a vision of God's grandeur and mystery that is more satisfying than any answer could ever be. Besides, answers are overrated. For the philosopher in all of us, one answer always leads to many more questions, which when answered, pose yet more questions, *ad infinitum*.

This book also encourages us to pray, and if need be, wrestle with God through our suffering. For when read through the lens of the life, death and resurrection of our Lord Jesus Christ—the ultimate innocent sufferer—we are assured that we need no longer wonder whether God cares. We pray to a sympathetic High Priest who suffered as we have (see Hebrews 4:14–16).

"MY EARS HAD HEARD OF YOU BUT NOW MY EYES HAVE SEEN YOU." (42:5)

Prologue

1 In the land of Uz there lived a man whose name was Job. This man was blameless and upright; he feared God and shunned evil. ²He had seven sons and three daughters, ³and he owned seven thousand sheep, three thousand camels, five hundred yoke of oxen and five hundred donkeys, and had a large number of servants. He was the greatest man among all the people of the East.

⁴His sons used to take turns holding feasts in their homes, and they would invite their three sisters to eat and drink with them. ⁵When a period of feasting had run its course, Job would send and have them purified. Early in the morning he would sacrifice a burnt offering for each of them, thinking, "Perhaps my children have sinned and cursed God in their hearts." This was Job's regular custom.

Job's First Test

⁶One day the angels[a] came to present themselves before the LORD, and Satan[b] also came with them. ⁷The LORD said to Satan, "Where have you come from?"

Satan answered the LORD, "From roaming through the earth and going back and forth in it."

⁸Then the LORD said to Satan, "Have you considered my servant Job? There is no one on earth like him; he is blameless and upright, a man who fears God and shuns evil."

⁹"Does Job fear God for nothing?" Satan replied. ¹⁰"Have you not put a hedge around him and his household and everything he has? You have blessed the work of his hands, so that his flocks and herds are spread throughout the land. ¹¹But stretch out your hand and strike everything he has, and he will surely curse you to your face."

¹²The LORD said to Satan, "Very well, then, everything he has is in your hands, but on the man himself do not lay a finger."

Then Satan went out from the presence of the LORD.

¹³One day when Job's sons and daughters were feasting and drinking wine at the oldest brother's house, ¹⁴a messenger came to Job and said, "The oxen were plowing and the donkeys were grazing nearby, ¹⁵and the Sabeans attacked and carried them off. They put the servants to the sword, and I am the only one who has escaped to tell you!"

¹⁶While he was still speaking, another messenger came and said, "The fire of God fell from the sky and burned up the sheep and the servants, and I am the only one who has escaped to tell you!"

¹⁷While he was still speaking, another messenger came and said, "The Chaldeans formed three raiding parties and swept down on your camels and carried them off. They put the servants to the sword, and I am the only one who has escaped to tell you!"

¹⁸While he was still speaking, yet another messenger came and said, "Your sons and daughters were feasting and drinking wine at the oldest brother's house, ¹⁹when suddenly a mighty wind swept in from the desert and struck the four corners of the house. It collapsed on them and they are dead, and I am the only one who has escaped to tell you!"

²⁰At this, Job got up and tore his robe and shaved his head. Then he fell to the ground in worship ²¹and said:

"Naked I came from my mother's
    womb,
    and naked I will depart.[c]
The LORD gave and the LORD has
        taken away;
    may the name of the LORD
        be praised."

²²In all this, Job did not sin by charging God with wrongdoing.

Job's Second Test

2 On another day the angels[a] came to present themselves before the LORD, and Satan also came with them to present himself before him. ²And the LORD said to Satan, "Where have you come from?"

Satan answered the LORD, "From roaming through the earth and going back and forth in it."

³Then the LORD said to Satan, "Have you considered my servant Job? There is no one on earth like him; he is blameless and upright, a man who fears God and shuns evil. And he still maintains his

---

^a6,1 Hebrew *the sons of God*   ^b6 *Satan* means *accuser.*   ^c21 Or *will return there*

integrity, though you incited me against him to ruin him without any reason."

⁴"Skin for skin!" Satan replied. "A man will give all he has for his own life. ⁵But stretch out your hand and strike his flesh and bones, and he will surely curse you to your face."

⁶The LORD said to Satan, "Very well, then, he is in your hands; but you must spare his life."

⁷So Satan went out from the presence of the LORD and afflicted Job with painful sores from the soles of his feet to the top of his head. ⁸Then Job took a piece of

---

{ TUESDAY }

JOB 1

A Humble and Grateful Guide

1:21 "THE LORD GAVE AND THE LORD HAS TAKEN AWAY; MAY THE NAME OF THE LORD BE PRAISED."

God was proud of his servant Job (see 1:8), and Job's prayer in verse 21 shows why. First there is his remarkable humility. He had known all along that everything came from God. Naked he arrived in this world; naked he would depart. Second, even though Job had just learned that he had lost the people and things most precious to him, he utters an amazing expression of gratitude. His attitude wasn't "God took what was *mine!*" Job acknowledged that everything is the Lord's. Everything he had was his by gift, not by right. Humility and gratitude are the irreducible minimums of prayer. The grateful are humble or they wouldn't be grateful. God dwells only with the humble (see Isaiah 57:15; 1 Peter 5:5). Until we know we have no ground to stand on before God, we have no ground to stand on before God.

Job's humility and gratitude will be even more severely tested. He will be pushed out to the very edge of humanity, and return holier and happier. Søren Kierkegaard pictured Job as standing at an outpost from which he could lead the rest of us through the dark wilds of suffering. Job is a guide; he gives us hope; he reassures us that what we thought isn't possible *is* possible. When Job's story ends, "the terror is endured, the horror experienced, the battle of despair waged, to the honor of God, to his own salvation, to the profit and happiness of others. In joyful days, in fortunate times, Job walks by the side of the race and guarantees it its happiness, combats the apprehensive dream that some horror may suddenly befall a man and have power to destroy his soul as its certain prey."[1]

Job is a great prayer partner. His prayers aren't necessarily tidy, because his life isn't always tidy. Because of this, he teaches prayer, but mainly he encourages us to pray just as we are. He is one of the original, "Just as I am" pray-ers.

PRAY:

"Just as I am, tho' tossed about
With many a conflict, many a doubt,
Fightings within, and fears without,
O Lamb of God, I come!"
CHARLOTTE ELLIOTT

FOR YOUR NEXT DEVOTIONAL READING, GO TO PAGE 576.

broken pottery and scraped himself with it as he sat among the ashes.

⁹His wife said to him, "Are you still holding on to your integrity? Curse God and die!"

¹⁰He replied, "You are talking like a foolish*a* woman. Shall we accept good from God, and not trouble?"

In all this, Job did not sin in what he said.

Job's Three Friends

¹¹When Job's three friends, Eliphaz the Temanite, Bildad the Shuhite and Zophar the Naamathite, heard about all the troubles that had come upon him, they set out from their homes and met together by agreement to go and sympathize

*a*10 The Hebrew word rendered *foolish* denotes moral deficiency.

JOB 2:11–13

The Ministry of Silence and Prayer

2:13 THEN THEY SAT ON THE GROUND WITH HIM FOR SEVEN DAYS.

When Job's friends arrived on the scene and saw Job's suffering, they sat on the ground and were silent for seven days and nights. The moment they opened their mouths (starting in chapter 4), Job's suffering got a lot worse. Job hadn't yet asked why he was suffering, but in case he did, his friends wanted him to know why. The reason was, to their way of thinking, simple. Good things happen to good people, and bad things happen to bad people. The universe is morally ordered by a God who punishes evil and rewards good. Bad things had happened to Job, exceedingly bad things; Job must therefore have done some exceedingly bad things. But Job's friends were wrong. Job knew they were, and God eventually said they were (see 42:7).

Job's friends' errors can be put this way: They were superficially right but fundamentally wrong. God does punish evil and reward good—the Bible says so. But when it comes to the timing in this world, there are exceptions and mysteries. Job's friends were following the letter of the law: They looked at Job's symptoms, checked their listing in the index, read the appropriate pages, and drew their conclusions. The problem is that God's Word isn't an owner's manual because God isn't a mechanism. Job isn't either. Both are persons. The moment we forget that axiomatic truth, we make ourselves the god of God. We elevate our theology, what we think about God, to the level of God.

How much better it would have been if Job's friends were slow to speak and quick to listen (see James 1:19). How much better it would have been if, when they spoke, it was to ask questions and listen to Job, and then pray with him. Especially pray with him. A ministry of silence and prayer would have been healing to Job and honoring to God. The Spirit who moves us to pray is the *Paraclete*, the Spirit of encouragement, who comes from the God of all comfort (see John 14:16; Romans 8:15–16; 2 Corinthians 1:3–4). Consider how quiet his ministry is, and do likewise.

PRAY:

Holy Spirit of God, great comforter and friend!
Teach me to listen and pray with those who suffer.

FOR YOUR NEXT DEVOTIONAL READING, GO TO PAGE 606.

with him and comfort him. ¹²When they saw him from a distance, they could hardly recognize him; they began to weep aloud, and they tore their robes and sprinkled dust on their heads. ¹³Then they sat on the ground with him for seven days and seven nights. No one said a word to him, because they saw how great his suffering was.

Job Speaks

3 After this, Job opened his mouth and cursed the day of his birth. ²He said:

³ "May the day of my birth perish,
   and the night it was said, 'A boy
      is born!'
⁴ That day—may it turn to darkness;
   may God above not care about it;
   may no light shine upon it.
⁵ May darkness and deep shadow*ᵃ*
      claim it once more;
   may a cloud settle over it;
   may blackness overwhelm its light.
⁶ That night—may thick darkness
      seize it;
   may it not be included among the
      days of the year
   nor be entered in any of the
      months.
⁷ May that night be barren;
   may no shout of joy be heard in it.
⁸ May those who curse days*ᵇ* curse
      that day,
   those who are ready to rouse
      Leviathan.
⁹ May its morning stars become dark;
   may it wait for daylight in vain
   and not see the first rays of dawn,
¹⁰ for it did not shut the doors of the
      womb on me
   to hide trouble from my eyes.

¹¹ "Why did I not perish at birth,
   and die as I came from the womb?
¹² Why were there knees to receive me
   and breasts that I might be nursed?
¹³ For now I would be lying down
      in peace;
   I would be asleep and at rest
¹⁴ with kings and counselors of
      the earth,
   who built for themselves places
      now lying in ruins,
¹⁵ with rulers who had gold,
   who filled their houses with silver.

¹⁶ Or why was I not hidden in the
      ground like a stillborn child,
   like an infant who never saw the
      light of day?
¹⁷ There the wicked cease from turmoil,
   and there the weary are at rest.
¹⁸ Captives also enjoy their ease;
   they no longer hear the slave
      driver's shout.
¹⁹ The small and the great are there,
   and the slave is freed from
      his master.

²⁰ "Why is light given to those in misery,
   and life to the bitter of soul,
²¹ to those who long for death that does
      not come,
   who search for it more than for
      hidden treasure,
²² who are filled with gladness
   and rejoice when they reach
      the grave?
²³ Why is life given to a man
   whose way is hidden,
   whom God has hedged in?
²⁴ For sighing comes to me instead
      of food;
   my groans pour out like water.
²⁵ What I feared has come upon me;
   what I dreaded has happened to me.
²⁶ I have no peace, no quietness;
   I have no rest, but only turmoil."

Eliphaz

4 Then Eliphaz the Temanite replied:

² "If someone ventures a word with
      you, will you be impatient?
   But who can keep from speaking?
³ Think how you have instructed many,
   how you have strengthened feeble
      hands.
⁴ Your words have supported those
      who stumbled;
   you have strengthened faltering
      knees.
⁵ But now trouble comes to you, and
      you are discouraged;
   it strikes you, and you are
      dismayed.
⁶ Should not your piety be your
      confidence
   and your blameless ways your
      hope?

ᵃ5 Or *and the shadow of death*   *ᵇ8* Or *the sea*

7 "Consider now: Who, being innocent,
    has ever perished?
Where were the upright ever
    destroyed?
8 As I have observed, those who
    plow evil
    and those who sow trouble reap it.
9 At the breath of God they are
    destroyed;
    at the blast of his anger they
      perish.
10 The lions may roar and growl,
    yet the teeth of the great lions
      are broken.
11 The lion perishes for lack of prey,
    and the cubs of the lioness are
      scattered.

12 "A word was secretly brought to me,
    my ears caught a whisper of it.
13 Amid disquieting dreams in the
    night,
    when deep sleep falls on men,
14 fear and trembling seized me
    and made all my bones shake.
15 A spirit glided past my face,
    and the hair on my body stood
      on end.
16 It stopped,
    but I could not tell what it was.
    A form stood before my eyes,
    and I heard a hushed voice:
17 'Can a mortal be more righteous
    than God?
    Can a man be more pure than
      his Maker?
18 If God places no trust in his servants,
    if he charges his angels with error,
19 how much more those who live in
    houses of clay,
    whose foundations are in the dust,
    who are crushed more readily than
      a moth!
20 Between dawn and dusk they are
    broken to pieces;
    unnoticed, they perish forever.
21 Are not the cords of their tent
    pulled up,
    so that they die without wisdom?'*a*

5 "Call if you will, but who will
    answer you?
    To which of the holy ones will you
      turn?
2 Resentment kills a fool,
    and envy slays the simple.

3 I myself have seen a fool taking root,
    but suddenly his house was
      cursed.
4 His children are far from safety,
    crushed in court without a
      defender.
5 The hungry consume his harvest,
    taking it even from among
      thorns,
    and the thirsty pant after his
      wealth.
6 For hardship does not spring from
    the soil,
    nor does trouble sprout from
      the ground.
7 Yet man is born to trouble
    as surely as sparks fly upward.

8 "But if it were I, I would appeal
    to God;
    I would lay my cause before him.
9 He performs wonders that cannot be
    fathomed,
    miracles that cannot be counted.
10 He bestows rain on the earth;
    he sends water upon the
      countryside.
11 The lowly he sets on high,
    and those who mourn are lifted
      to safety.
12 He thwarts the plans of the crafty,
    so that their hands achieve
      no success.
13 He catches the wise in their
    craftiness,
    and the schemes of the wily are
      swept away.
14 Darkness comes upon them in
    the daytime;
    at noon they grope as in the night.
15 He saves the needy from the sword
    in their mouth;
    he saves them from the clutches
      of the powerful.
16 So the poor have hope,
    and injustice shuts its mouth.

17 "Blessed is the man whom God
    corrects;
    so do not despise the discipline of
      the Almighty.*b*
18 For he wounds, but he also binds up;
    he injures, but his hands also heal.

a21 Some interpreters end the quotation after
verse 17.   *b17* Hebrew *Shaddai*; here and
throughout Job

¹⁹ From six calamities he will
rescue you;
in seven no harm will befall you.
²⁰ In famine he will ransom you from
death,
and in battle from the stroke of
the sword.
²¹ You will be protected from the lash of
the tongue,
and need not fear when
destruction comes.
²² You will laugh at destruction and
famine,
and need not fear the beasts of
the earth.
²³ For you will have a covenant with the
stones of the field,
and the wild animals will be at
peace with you.
²⁴ You will know that your tent
is secure;
you will take stock of your property
and find nothing missing.
²⁵ You will know that your children
will be many,
and your descendants like the
grass of the earth.
²⁶ You will come to the grave in
full vigor,
like sheaves gathered in season.

²⁷ "We have examined this, and it
is true.
So hear it and apply it to yourself."

Job

6 Then Job replied:

² "If only my anguish could be weighed
and all my misery be placed on the
scales!
³ It would surely outweigh the sand of
the seas—
no wonder my words have been
impetuous.
⁴ The arrows of the Almighty are in me,
my spirit drinks in their poison;
God's terrors are marshaled
against me.
⁵ Does a wild donkey bray when it
has grass,
or an ox bellow when it has fodder?
⁶ Is tasteless food eaten without salt,
or is there flavor in the white of
an egg^a?

⁷ I refuse to touch it;
such food makes me ill.

⁸ "Oh, that I might have my request,
that God would grant what
I hope for,
⁹ that God would be willing to
crush me,
to let loose his hand and cut
me off!
¹⁰ Then I would still have this
consolation—
my joy in unrelenting pain—
that I had not denied the words of
the Holy One.

> "*OH*, that I might have my request,
> that God would grant what I hope for."
>
> JOB 6:8

¹¹ "What strength do I have, that I
should still hope?
What prospects, that I should
be patient?
¹² Do I have the strength of stone?
Is my flesh bronze?
¹³ Do I have any power to help
myself,
now that success has been
driven from me?

¹⁴ "A despairing man should have the
devotion of his friends,
even though he forsakes the fear
of the Almighty.
¹⁵ But my brothers are as undependable
as intermittent streams,
as the streams that overflow
¹⁶ when darkened by thawing ice
and swollen with melting
snow,
¹⁷ but that cease to flow in the
dry season,
and in the heat vanish from their
channels.
¹⁸ Caravans turn aside from their
routes;
they go up into the wasteland
and perish.
¹⁹ The caravans of Tema look for water,
the traveling merchants of Sheba
look in hope.

^{a}6 The meaning of the Hebrew for this phrase is
uncertain.

20 They are distressed, because they
had been confident;
they arrive there, only to be
disappointed.
21 Now you too have proved to be of
no help;
you see something dreadful and
are afraid.
22 Have I ever said, 'Give something on
my behalf,
pay a ransom for me from your
wealth,
23 deliver me from the hand of
the enemy,
ransom me from the clutches of the
ruthless'?

24 "Teach me, and I will be quiet;
show me where I have been wrong.
25 How painful are honest words!
But what do your arguments
prove?
26 Do you mean to correct what I say,
and treat the words of a despairing
man as wind?
27 You would even cast lots for the
fatherless
and barter away your friend.

28 "But now be so kind as to look at me.
Would I lie to your face?
29 Relent, do not be unjust;
reconsider, for my integrity is
at stake.ᵃ
30 Is there any wickedness on my lips?
Can my mouth not discern malice?

7 "Does not man have hard service
on earth?
Are not his days like those of a
hired man?
2 Like a slave longing for the evening
shadows,
or a hired man waiting eagerly for
his wages,
3 so I have been allotted months of
futility,
and nights of misery have been
assigned to me.
4 When I lie down I think, 'How long
before I get up?'
The night drags on, and I toss till
dawn.
5 My body is clothed with worms
and scabs,
my skin is broken and festering.

6 "My days are swifter than a weaver's
shuttle,
and they come to an end without
hope.
7 Remember, O God, that my life is but
a breath;
my eyes will never see happiness
again.
8 The eye that now sees me will see
me no longer;
you will look for me, but I will be
no more.
9 As a cloud vanishes and is gone,
so he who goes down to the graveᵇ
does not return.
10 He will never come to his house
again;
his place will know him
no more.

11 "Therefore I will not keep silent;
I will speak out in the anguish of
my spirit,
I will complain in the bitterness of
my soul.
12 Am I the sea, or the monster of
the deep,
that you put me under guard?
13 When I think my bed will comfort me
and my couch will ease my
complaint,
14 even then you frighten me with
dreams
and terrify me with visions,
15 so that I prefer strangling and
death,
rather than this body of mine.
16 I despise my life; I would not live
forever.
Let me alone; my days have no
meaning.

17 "What is man that you make so much
of him,
that you give him so much
attention,
18 that you examine him every morning
and test him every moment?
19 Will you never look away from me,
or let me alone even for an instant?
20 If I have sinned, what have I done
to you,
O watcher of men?

ᵃ29 Or *my righteousness still stands*
ᵇ9 Hebrew *Sheol*

Why have you made me your target?
Have I become a burden to you?[a]
21 Why do you not pardon my offenses
and forgive my sins?
For I will soon lie down in the dust;
you will search for me, but I will be
no more."

Bildad

8 Then Bildad the Shuhite replied:

2 "How long will you say such things?
Your words are a blustering wind.
3 Does God pervert justice?
Does the Almighty pervert what
is right?
4 When your children sinned against
him,
he gave them over to the penalty
of their sin.
5 But if you will look to God
and plead with the Almighty,
6 if you are pure and upright,
even now he will rouse himself
on your behalf
and restore you to your rightful
place.
7 Your beginnings will seem humble,
so prosperous will your future be.

8 "Ask the former generations
and find out what their fathers
learned,
9 for we were born only yesterday and
know nothing,
and our days on earth are but
a shadow.
10 Will they not instruct you and
tell you?
Will they not bring forth words
from their understanding?
11 Can papyrus grow tall where there
is no marsh?
Can reeds thrive without water?
12 While still growing and uncut,
they wither more quickly than
grass.
13 Such is the destiny of all who
forget God;
so perishes the hope of the
godless.
14 What he trusts in is fragile[b];
what he relies on is a spider's web.
15 He leans on his web, but it gives way;
he clings to it, but it does not hold.

16 He is like a well-watered plant in the
sunshine,
spreading its shoots over the
garden;
17 it entwines its roots around a pile
of rocks
and looks for a place among the
stones.
18 But when it is torn from its spot,
that place disowns it and says,
'I never saw you.'
19 Surely its life withers away,
and[c] from the soil other plants
grow.

20 "Surely God does not reject a
blameless man
or strengthen the hands of
evildoers.
21 He will yet fill your mouth with
laughter
and your lips with shouts of joy.
22 Your enemies will be clothed
in shame,
and the tents of the wicked will
be no more."

Job

9 Then Job replied:

2 "Indeed, I know that this is true.
But how can a mortal be righteous
before God?
3 Though one wished to dispute
with him,
he could not answer him one time
out of a thousand.
4 His wisdom is profound, his power
is vast.
Who has resisted him and come
out unscathed?
5 He moves mountains without their
knowing it
and overturns them in his anger.
6 He shakes the earth from its place
and makes its pillars tremble.
7 He speaks to the sun and it does
not shine;
he seals off the light of the stars.

[a]20 A few manuscripts of the Masoretic Text, an
ancient Hebrew scribal tradition and Septuagint;
most manuscripts of the Masoretic Text *I have
become a burden to myself.*   [b]14 The meaning
of the Hebrew for this word is uncertain.
[c]19 Or *Surely all the joy it has / is that*

⁸ He alone stretches out the heavens
and treads on the waves of the sea.
⁹ He is the Maker of the Bear and
Orion,
the Pleiades and the constellations
of the south.
¹⁰ He performs wonders that cannot be
fathomed,
miracles that cannot be counted.
¹¹ When he passes me, I cannot
see him;
when he goes by, I cannot
perceive him.
¹² If he snatches away, who can
stop him?
Who can say to him, 'What are
you doing?'
¹³ God does not restrain his anger;
even the cohorts of Rahab cowered
at his feet.

¹⁴ "How then can I dispute with him?
How can I find words to argue
with him?
¹⁵ Though I were innocent, I could not
answer him;
I could only plead with my Judge
for mercy.
¹⁶ Even if I summoned him and he
responded,
I do not believe he would give me
a hearing.
¹⁷ He would crush me with a storm
and multiply my wounds for
no reason.
¹⁸ He would not let me regain my breath
but would overwhelm me with
misery.
¹⁹ If it is a matter of strength, he
is mighty!
And if it is a matter of justice, who
will summon him[a]?
²⁰ Even if I were innocent, my mouth
would condemn me;
if I were blameless, it would
pronounce me guilty.

²¹ "Although I am blameless,
I have no concern for myself;
I despise my own life.
²² It is all the same; that is why I say,
'He destroys both the blameless
and the wicked.'
²³ When a scourge brings sudden death,
he mocks the despair of the
innocent.

> 66 *The prayer that prevails is not the
> work of lips and fingertips. It is the cry of
> a broken heart and the travail of a
> stricken soul.* 99
>
> SAMUEL CHADWICK

²⁴ When a land falls into the hands of
the wicked,
he blindfolds its judges.
If it is not he, then who is it?

²⁵ "My days are swifter than a runner;
they fly away without a glimpse
of joy.
²⁶ They skim past like boats of papyrus,
like eagles swooping down on
their prey.
²⁷ If I say, 'I will forget my complaint,
I will change my expression, and
smile,'
²⁸ I still dread all my sufferings,
for I know you will not hold me
innocent.
²⁹ Since I am already found guilty,
why should I struggle in vain?
³⁰ Even if I washed myself with soap[b]
and my hands with washing soda,
³¹ you would plunge me into a slime pit
so that even my clothes would
detest me.

³² "He is not a man like me that I might
answer him,
that we might confront each other
in court.
³³ If only there were someone to
arbitrate between us,
to lay his hand upon us both,
³⁴ someone to remove God's rod
from me,
so that his terror would frighten
me no more.
³⁵ Then I would speak up without fear
of him,
but as it now stands with me,
I cannot.

10 "I loathe my very life;
therefore I will give free rein to
my complaint
and speak out in the bitterness of
my soul.

[a]19 See Septuagint; Hebrew *me*.   [b]30 Or *snow*

² I will say to God: Do not condemn me,
  but tell me what charges you have
  against me.
³ Does it please you to oppress me,
  to spurn the work of your hands,
  while you smile on the schemes of
  the wicked?
⁴ Do you have eyes of flesh?
  Do you see as a mortal sees?
⁵ Are your days like those of a mortal
  or your years like those of a man,
⁶ that you must search out my faults
  and probe after my sin—
⁷ though you know that I am not guilty
  and that no one can rescue me
  from your hand?

⁸ "Your hands shaped me and
  made me.
  Will you now turn and destroy me?
⁹ Remember that you molded me
  like clay.
  Will you now turn me to dust
  again?
¹⁰ Did you not pour me out like milk
  and curdle me like cheese,
¹¹ clothe me with skin and flesh
  and knit me together with bones
  and sinews?
¹² You gave me life and showed me
  kindness,
  and in your providence watched
  over my spirit.

¹³ "But this is what you concealed in
  your heart,
  and I know that this was in your
  mind:
¹⁴ If I sinned, you would be watching
  me
  and would not let my offense go
  unpunished.
¹⁵ If I am guilty—woe to me!
  Even if I am innocent, I cannot lift
  my head,
  for I am full of shame
  and drowned in[a] my affliction.
¹⁶ If I hold my head high, you stalk me
  like a lion
  and again display your awesome
  power against me.
¹⁷ You bring new witnesses against me
  and increase your anger toward
  me;
  your forces come against me wave
  upon wave.

¹⁸ "Why then did you bring me out of
  the womb?
  I wish I had died before any eye
  saw me.
¹⁹ If only I had never come into being,
  or had been carried straight from
  the womb to the grave!
²⁰ Are not my few days almost over?
  Turn away from me so I can have a
  moment's joy
²¹ before I go to the place of no
  return,
  to the land of gloom and deep
  shadow,[b]
²² to the land of deepest night,
  of deep shadow and disorder,
  where even the light is like
  darkness."

Zophar

11 Then Zophar the Naamathite replied:

² "Are all these words to go
  unanswered?
  Is this talker to be vindicated?
³ Will your idle talk reduce men
  to silence?
  Will no one rebuke you when
  you mock?
⁴ You say to God, 'My beliefs are
  flawless
  and I am pure in your sight.'
⁵ Oh, how I wish that God would
  speak,
  that he would open his lips
  against you
⁶ and disclose to you the secrets
  of wisdom,
  for true wisdom has two sides.
  Know this: God has even forgotten
  some of your sin.

⁷ "Can you fathom the mysteries
  of God?
  Can you probe the limits of the
  Almighty?
⁸ They are higher than the heavens—
  what can you do?
  They are deeper than the depths
  of the grave[c]—what can you
  know?

[a]15 Or and aware of   [b]21 Or and the shadow
of death; also in verse 22   [c]8 Hebrew than
Sheol

9 Their measure is longer than
the earth
and wider than the sea.

10 "If he comes along and confines you
in prison
and convenes a court, who can
oppose him?
11 Surely he recognizes deceitful men;
and when he sees evil, does he not
take note?
12 But a witless man can no more
become wise
than a wild donkey's colt can be
born a man.*a*

13 "Yet if you devote your heart to him
and stretch out your hands to him,
14 if you put away the sin that is in
your hand
and allow no evil to dwell in
your tent,
15 then you will lift up your face without
shame;
you will stand firm and without
fear.
16 You will surely forget your trouble,
recalling it only as waters gone by.
17 Life will be brighter than noonday,
and darkness will become like
morning.
18 You will be secure, because there
is hope;
you will look about you and take
your rest in safety.
19 You will lie down, with no one to
make you afraid,
and many will court your favor.
20 But the eyes of the wicked will fail,
and escape will elude them;
their hope will become a dying
gasp."

Job

12 Then Job replied:

2 "Doubtless you are the people,
and wisdom will die with you!
3 But I have a mind as well as you;
I am not inferior to you.
Who does not know all these
things?

4 "I have become a laughingstock to
my friends,
though I called upon God and he
answered—

a mere laughingstock, though
righteous and blameless!
5 Men at ease have contempt for
misfortune
as the fate of those whose feet are
slipping.
6 The tents of marauders are
undisturbed,
and those who provoke God are
secure—
those who carry their god in their
hands.*b*

7 "But ask the animals, and they will
teach you,
or the birds of the air, and they will
tell you;
8 or speak to the earth, and it will
teach you,
or let the fish of the sea inform you.
9 Which of all these does not know
that the hand of the LORD has
done this?
10 In his hand is the life of every
creature
and the breath of all mankind.
11 Does not the ear test words
as the tongue tastes food?
12 Is not wisdom found among
the aged?
Does not long life bring
understanding?

13 "To God belong wisdom and power;
counsel and understanding
are his.
14 What he tears down cannot be
rebuilt;
the man he imprisons cannot be
released.
15 If he holds back the waters, there is
drought;
if he lets them loose, they devastate
the land.
16 To him belong strength and victory;
both deceived and deceiver
are his.
17 He leads counselors away stripped
and makes fools of judges.
18 He takes off the shackles put on
by kings
and ties a loincloth*c* around
their waist.

a 12 Or *wild donkey can be born tame*
b 6 Or *secure / in what God's hand brings them*
c 18 Or *shackles of kings / and ties a belt*

¹⁹ He leads priests away stripped
    and overthrows men long
      established.
²⁰ He silences the lips of trusted
    advisers
    and takes away the discernment
      of elders.
²¹ He pours contempt on nobles
    and disarms the mighty.
²² He reveals the deep things of
    darkness
    and brings deep shadows into
      the light.
²³ He makes nations great, and destroys
    them;
    he enlarges nations, and disperses
      them.
²⁴ He deprives the leaders of the earth
    of their reason;
    he sends them wandering through
      a trackless waste.
²⁵ They grope in darkness with no light;
    he makes them stagger like
      drunkards.

*I DESIRE to speak to the Almighty and to
argue my case with God.*

JOB 13:3

13 "My eyes have seen all this,
    my ears have heard and
      understood it.
² What you know, I also know;
    I am not inferior to you.
³ But I desire to speak to the Almighty
    and to argue my case with God.
⁴ You, however, smear me with lies;
    you are worthless physicians,
      all of you!
⁵ If only you would be altogether
    silent!
    For you, that would be wisdom.
⁶ Hear now my argument;
    listen to the plea of my lips.
⁷ Will you speak wickedly on God's
    behalf?
    Will you speak deceitfully for him?
⁸ Will you show him partiality?
    Will you argue the case for God?
⁹ Would it turn out well if he examined
    you?
    Could you deceive him as you
      might deceive men?

¹⁰ He would surely rebuke you
    if you secretly showed partiality.
¹¹ Would not his splendor terrify you?
    Would not the dread of him fall
      on you?
¹² Your maxims are proverbs of ashes;
    your defenses are defenses of clay.
¹³ "Keep silent and let me speak;
    then let come to me what may.
¹⁴ Why do I put myself in jeopardy
    and take my life in my hands?
¹⁵ Though he slay me, yet will I hope
    in him;
    I will surely*ᵃ* defend my ways to
      his face.
¹⁶ Indeed, this will turn out for my
    deliverance,
    for no godless man would dare
      come before him!
¹⁷ Listen carefully to my words;
    let your ears take in what I say.
¹⁸ Now that I have prepared my case,
    I know I will be vindicated.
¹⁹ Can anyone bring charges
    against me?
    If so, I will be silent and die.
²⁰ "Only grant me these two things,
    O God,
    and then I will not hide
      from you:
²¹ Withdraw your hand far from me,
    and stop frightening me with
      your terrors.
²² Then summon me and I will
    answer,
    or let me speak, and you reply.
²³ How many wrongs and sins have
    I committed?
    Show me my offense and my sin.
²⁴ Why do you hide your face
    and consider me your enemy?
²⁵ Will you torment a windblown leaf?
    Will you chase after dry chaff?
²⁶ For you write down bitter things
    against me
    and make me inherit the sins of
      my youth.
²⁷ You fasten my feet in shackles;
    you keep close watch on all
      my paths
    by putting marks on the soles
      of my feet.

*ᵃ15 Or He will surely slay me; I have no
hope — / yet I will*

²⁸ "So man wastes away like something
  rotten,
  like a garment eaten by moths.

14 "Man born of woman
  is of few days and full of trouble.
² He springs up like a flower and
  withers away;
  like a fleeting shadow, he does
  not endure.
³ Do you fix your eye on such a one?
  Will you bring him^a before you for
  judgment?
⁴ Who can bring what is pure from
  the impure?
  No one!
⁵ Man's days are determined;
  you have decreed the number of
  his months
  and have set limits he cannot
  exceed.
⁶ So look away from him and let him
  alone,
  till he has put in his time like a
  hired man.

⁷ "At least there is hope for a tree:
  If it is cut down, it will sprout
  again,
  and its new shoots will not fail.
⁸ Its roots may grow old in the ground
  and its stump die in the soil,
⁹ yet at the scent of water it will bud
  and put forth shoots like a plant.
¹⁰ But man dies and is laid low;
  he breathes his last and is no more.
¹¹ As water disappears from the sea
  or a riverbed becomes parched
  and dry,
¹² so man lies down and does not rise;
  till the heavens are no more, men
  will not awake
  or be roused from their sleep.

¹³ "If only you would hide me in
  the grave^b
  and conceal me till your anger
  has passed!
  If only you would set me a time
  and then remember me!
¹⁴ If a man dies, will he live again?
  All the days of my hard service
  I will wait for my renewal^c to come.
¹⁵ You will call and I will answer you;
  you will long for the creature your
  hands have made.

¹⁶ Surely then you will count my steps
  but not keep track of my sin.
¹⁷ My offenses will be sealed up in
  a bag;
  you will cover over my sin.

¹⁸ "But as a mountain erodes and
  crumbles
  and as a rock is moved from its
  place,
¹⁹ as water wears away stones
  and torrents wash away the soil,
  so you destroy man's hope.
²⁰ You overpower him once for all, and
  he is gone;
  you change his countenance and
  send him away.
²¹ If his sons are honored, he does not
  know it;
  if they are brought low, he does not
  see it.
²² He feels but the pain of his own body
  and mourns only for himself."

Eliphaz

15 Then Eliphaz the Temanite replied:

² "Would a wise man answer with
  empty notions
  or fill his belly with the hot east
  wind?
³ Would he argue with useless words,
  with speeches that have no value?
⁴ But you even undermine piety
  and hinder devotion to God.
⁵ Your sin prompts your mouth;
  you adopt the tongue of the crafty.
⁶ Your own mouth condemns you,
  not mine;
  your own lips testify against you.

⁷ "Are you the first man ever born?
  Were you brought forth before
  the hills?
⁸ Do you listen in on God's council?
  Do you limit wisdom to yourself?
⁹ What do you know that we do not
  know?
  What insights do you have that we
  do not have?
¹⁰ The gray-haired and the aged are on
  our side,
  men even older than your father.

^a3 Septuagint, Vulgate and Syriac; Hebrew *me*
^b13 Hebrew *Sheol*   ^c14 Or *release*

11 Are God's consolations not enough
for you,
words spoken gently to you?
12 Why has your heart carried you away,
and why do your eyes flash,
13 so that you vent your rage against
God
and pour out such words from
your mouth?

14 "What is man, that he could
be pure,
or one born of woman, that he
could be righteous?
15 If God places no trust in his holy
ones,
if even the heavens are not pure in
his eyes,
16 how much less man, who is vile and
corrupt,
who drinks up evil like water!

17 "Listen to me and I will explain
to you;
let me tell you what I have seen,
18 what wise men have declared,
hiding nothing received from their
fathers
19 (to whom alone the land was given
when no alien passed among
them):
20 All his days the wicked man suffers
torment,
the ruthless through all the years
stored up for him.
21 Terrifying sounds fill his ears;
when all seems well, marauders
attack him.
22 He despairs of escaping the darkness;
he is marked for the sword.
23 He wanders about—food for
vultures*;
he knows the day of darkness is
at hand.
24 Distress and anguish fill him with
terror;
they overwhelm him, like a king
poised to attack,
25 because he shakes his fist at God
and vaunts himself against the
Almighty,
26 defiantly charging against him
with a thick, strong shield.

27 "Though his face is covered with fat
and his waist bulges with flesh,

28 he will inhabit ruined towns
and houses where no one lives,
houses crumbling to rubble.
29 He will no longer be rich and his
wealth will not endure,
nor will his possessions spread
over the land.
30 He will not escape the darkness;
a flame will wither his shoots,
and the breath of God's mouth will
carry him away.
31 Let him not deceive himself by
trusting what is worthless,
for he will get nothing in return.
32 Before his time he will be paid in full,
and his branches will not flourish.
33 He will be like a vine stripped of its
unripe grapes,
like an olive tree shedding its
blossoms.
34 For the company of the godless will
be barren,
and fire will consume the tents of
those who love bribes.
35 They conceive trouble and give birth
to evil;
their womb fashions deceit."

Job

16 Then Job replied:

2 "I have heard many things like these;
miserable comforters are you all!
3 Will your long-winded speeches
never end?
What ails you that you keep on
arguing?
4 I also could speak like you,
if you were in my place;
I could make fine speeches against
you
and shake my head at you.
5 But my mouth would encourage you;
comfort from my lips would bring
you relief.

6 "Yet if I speak, my pain is not
relieved;
and if I refrain, it does not go away.
7 Surely, O God, you have worn me out;
you have devastated my entire
household.
8 You have bound me—and it has
become a witness;

a 23 Or *about, looking for food*

my gauntness rises up and testifies
against me.
⁹ God assails me and tears me in his
anger
and gnashes his teeth at me;
my opponent fastens on me his
piercing eyes.
¹⁰ Men open their mouths to jeer
at me;
they strike my cheek in scorn
and unite together against me.
¹¹ God has turned me over to evil men
and thrown me into the clutches of
the wicked.
¹² All was well with me, but he
shattered me;
he seized me by the neck and
crushed me.
He has made me his target;
¹³   his archers surround me.
Without pity, he pierces my kidneys
and spills my gall on the ground.
¹⁴ Again and again he bursts upon me;
he rushes at me like a warrior.

¹⁵ "I have sewed sackcloth over my skin
and buried my brow in the dust.
¹⁶ My face is red with weeping,
deep shadows ring my eyes;
¹⁷ yet my hands have been free of
violence
and my prayer is pure.

¹⁸ "O earth, do not cover my blood;
may my cry never be laid to rest!
¹⁹ Even now my witness is in heaven;
my advocate is on high.
²⁰ My intercessor is my friend[a]
as my eyes pour out tears to God;
²¹ on behalf of a man he pleads
with God
as a man pleads for his friend.

²² "Only a few years will pass
before I go on the journey of no
return.

17 ¹ My spirit is broken,
my days are cut short,
the grave awaits me.
² Surely mockers surround me;
my eyes must dwell on their
hostility.

³ "Give me, O God, the pledge you
demand.
Who else will put up security
for me?

⁴ You have closed their minds to
understanding;
therefore you will not let them
triumph.
⁵ If a man denounces his friends for
reward,
the eyes of his children will fail.

⁶ "God has made me a byword to
everyone,
a man in whose face people spit.
⁷ My eyes have grown dim with grief;
my whole frame is but a shadow.
⁸ Upright men are appalled at this;
the innocent are aroused against
the ungodly.
⁹ Nevertheless, the righteous will hold
to their ways,
and those with clean hands will
grow stronger.

¹⁰ "But come on, all of you, try again!
I will not find a wise man among
you.
¹¹ My days have passed, my plans are
shattered,
and so are the desires of my heart.
¹² These men turn night into day;
in the face of darkness they say,
'Light is near.'
¹³ If the only home I hope for is
the grave,[b]
if I spread out my bed in darkness,
¹⁴ if I say to corruption, 'You are my
father,'
and to the worm, 'My mother' or
'My sister,'
¹⁵ where then is my hope?
Who can see any hope for me?
¹⁶ Will it go down to the gates of death[b]?
Will we descend together into
the dust?"

Bildad

18 Then Bildad the Shuhite replied:

² "When will you end these speeches?
Be sensible, and then we can talk.
³ Why are we regarded as cattle
and considered stupid in your
sight?
⁴ You who tear yourself to pieces in
your anger,

---

a20 Or *My friends treat me with scorn*
b13,16 Hebrew *Sheol*

is the earth to be abandoned for
your sake?
Or must the rocks be moved from
their place?

5 "The lamp of the wicked is
snuffed out;
the flame of his fire stops
burning.
6 The light in his tent becomes dark;
the lamp beside him goes out.
7 The vigor of his step is weakened;
his own schemes throw him
down.
8 His feet thrust him into a net
and he wanders into its mesh.
9 A trap seizes him by the heel;
a snare holds him fast.
10 A noose is hidden for him on the
ground;
a trap lies in his path.
11 Terrors startle him on every side
and dog his every step.
12 Calamity is hungry for him;
disaster is ready for him when
he falls.
13 It eats away parts of his skin;
death's firstborn devours his limbs.
14 He is torn from the security of his tent
and marched off to the king
of terrors.
15 Fire resides*a* in his tent;
burning sulfur is scattered over
his dwelling.
16 His roots dry up below
and his branches wither above.
17 The memory of him perishes from
the earth;
he has no name in the land.
18 He is driven from light into darkness
and is banished from the world.

19 He has no offspring or descendants
among his people,
no survivor where once he lived.
20 Men of the west are appalled at his
fate;
men of the east are seized with
horror.
21 Surely such is the dwelling of an
evil man;
such is the place of one who knows
not God."

Job

19

Then Job replied:

2 "How long will you torment me
and crush me with words?
3 Ten times now you have reproached
me;
shamelessly you attack me.
4 If it is true that I have gone astray,
my error remains my concern
alone.
5 If indeed you would exalt yourselves
above me
and use my humiliation against
me,
6 then know that God has wronged me
and drawn his net around me.

7 "Though I cry, 'I've been wronged!'
I get no response;
though I call for help, there is
no justice.
8 He has blocked my way so I cannot
pass;
he has shrouded my paths in
darkness.
9 He has stripped me of my honor
and removed the crown from
my head.
10 He tears me down on every side till I
am gone;
he uproots my hope like a tree.
11 His anger burns against me;
he counts me among his enemies.
12 His troops advance in force;
they build a siege ramp against me
and encamp around my tent.

13 "He has alienated my brothers
from me;
my acquaintances are completely
estranged from me.

a15 Or *Nothing he had remains*

¹⁴ My kinsmen have gone away;
  my friends have forgotten me.
¹⁵ My guests and my maidservants
     count me a stranger;
  they look upon me as an alien.
¹⁶ I summon my servant, but he does
     not answer,
  though I beg him with my own
     mouth.
¹⁷ My breath is offensive to my wife;
  I am loathsome to my own
     brothers.
¹⁸ Even the little boys scorn me;
  when I appear, they ridicule me.
¹⁹ All my intimate friends detest me;
  those I love have turned against
     me.
²⁰ I am nothing but skin and bones;
  I have escaped with only the skin
     of my teeth.ᵃ

²¹ "Have pity on me, my friends,
     have pity,
  for the hand of God has
     struck me.
²² Why do you pursue me as God
     does?
  Will you never get enough of
     my flesh?

²³ "Oh, that my words were recorded,
  that they were written on
     a scroll,
²⁴ that they were inscribed with an iron
     tool onᵇ lead,
  or engraved in rock forever!
²⁵ I know that my Redeemerᶜ lives,
  and that in the end he will stand
     upon the earth.ᵈ
²⁶ And after my skin has been
     destroyed,
  yetᵉ inᶠ my flesh I will see
     God;
²⁷ I myself will see him
  with my own eyes—I, and not
     another.
  How my heart yearns within me!

²⁸ "If you say, 'How we will hound him,
  since the root of the trouble lies
     in him,ᵍ'
²⁹ you should fear the sword yourselves;
  for wrath will bring punishment by
     the sword,
  and then you will know that there
     is judgment.ʰ"

Zophar

20 Then Zophar the Naamathite replied:

² "My troubled thoughts prompt me to
     answer
  because I am greatly disturbed.
³ I hear a rebuke that dishonors me,
  and my understanding inspires me
     to reply.

⁴ "Surely you know how it has been
     from of old,
  ever since manⁱ was placed on
     the earth,
⁵ that the mirth of the wicked is brief,
  the joy of the godless lasts but a
     moment.
⁶ Though his pride reaches to the
     heavens
  and his head touches the clouds,
⁷ he will perish forever, like his own
     dung;
  those who have seen him will say,
     'Where is he?'
⁸ Like a dream he flies away, no more
     to be found,
  banished like a vision of the night.
⁹ The eye that saw him will not see
     him again;
  his place will look on him no more.
¹⁰ His children must make amends to
     the poor;
  his own hands must give back his
     wealth.
¹¹ The youthful vigor that fills his bones
  will lie with him in the dust.

¹² "Though evil is sweet in his mouth
  and he hides it under his tongue,
¹³ though he cannot bear to let it go
  and keeps it in his mouth,
¹⁴ yet his food will turn sour in his
     stomach;
  it will become the venom of
     serpents within him.
¹⁵ He will spit out the riches he
     swallowed;

ᵃ20 Or only my gums   ᵇ24 Or and
ᶜ25 Or defender   ᵈ25 Or upon my grave
ᵉ26 Or And after I awake, / though this body has
been destroyed, / then   ᶠ26 Or / apart from
ᵍ28 Many Hebrew manuscripts, Septuagint and
Vulgate; most Hebrew manuscripts me
ʰ29 Or / that you may come to know the Almighty
ⁱ4 Or Adam

God will make his stomach vomit
them up.
¹⁶ He will suck the poison of serpents;
the fangs of an adder will kill him.
¹⁷ He will not enjoy the streams,
the rivers flowing with honey and
cream.
¹⁸ What he toiled for he must give back
uneaten;
he will not enjoy the profit from his
trading.
¹⁹ For he has oppressed the poor and
left them destitute;
he has seized houses he did not
build.

²⁰ "Surely he will have no respite from
his craving;
he cannot save himself by his
treasure.
²¹ Nothing is left for him to devour;
his prosperity will not endure.
²² In the midst of his plenty, distress will
overtake him;
the full force of misery will come
upon him.
²³ When he has filled his belly,
God will vent his burning anger
against him
and rain down his blows upon him.
²⁴ Though he flees from an iron
weapon,
a bronze-tipped arrow pierces him.
²⁵ He pulls it out of his back,
the gleaming point out of his liver.
Terrors will come over him;
²⁶   total darkness lies in wait for his
treasures.
A fire unfanned will consume him
and devour what is left in his tent.
²⁷ The heavens will expose his guilt;
the earth will rise up against him.
²⁸ A flood will carry off his house,
rushing waters^a on the day of God's
wrath.
²⁹ Such is the fate God allots the
wicked,
the heritage appointed for them
by God."

Job

21

Then Job replied:

² "Listen carefully to my words;
let this be the consolation you
give me.

³ Bear with me while I speak,
and after I have spoken, mock on.

⁴ "Is my complaint directed to man?
Why should I not be impatient?
⁵ Look at me and be astonished;
clap your hand over your mouth.
⁶ When I think about this, I am
terrified;
trembling seizes my body.
⁷ Why do the wicked live on,
growing old and increasing in
power?
⁸ They see their children established
around them,
their offspring before their eyes.
⁹ Their homes are safe and free from
fear;
the rod of God is not upon them.
¹⁰ Their bulls never fail to breed;
their cows calve and do not
miscarry.
¹¹ They send forth their children as
a flock;
their little ones dance about.
¹² They sing to the music of tambourine
and harp;
they make merry to the sound of
the flute.
¹³ They spend their years in prosperity
and go down to the grave^b in
peace.^c
¹⁴ Yet they say to God, 'Leave us alone!
We have no desire to know your
ways.
¹⁵ Who is the Almighty, that we should
serve him?
What would we gain by praying
to him?'
¹⁶ But their prosperity is not in their
own hands,
so I stand aloof from the counsel
of the wicked.

¹⁷ "Yet how often is the lamp of the
wicked snuffed out?
How often does calamity come
upon them,
the fate God allots in his anger?
¹⁸ How often are they like straw before
the wind,
like chaff swept away by a gale?

---

^a28 Or *The possessions in his house will be
carried off, / washed away*   ^b13 Hebrew *Sheol*
^c13 Or *in an instant*

¹⁹ It is said, 'God stores up a man's
     punishment for his sons.'
  Let him repay the man himself, so
     that he will know it!
²⁰ Let his own eyes see his destruction;
     let him drink of the wrath of the
     Almighty.ᵃ
²¹ For what does he care about the
     family he leaves behind
  when his allotted months come
     to an end?

²² "Can anyone teach knowledge
     to God,
  since he judges even the highest?
²³ One man dies in full vigor,
     completely secure and at ease,
²⁴ his bodyᵇ well nourished,
     his bones rich with marrow.
²⁵ Another man dies in bitterness
     of soul,
  never having enjoyed anything
     good.
²⁶ Side by side they lie in the dust,
  and worms cover them both.

²⁷ "I know full well what you are
     thinking,
  the schemes by which you would
     wrong me.
²⁸ You say, 'Where now is the great
     man's house,
  the tents where wicked men lived?'
²⁹ Have you never questioned those
     who travel?
  Have you paid no regard to their
     accounts—
³⁰ that the evil man is spared from the
     day of calamity,
  that he is delivered fromᶜ the day
     of wrath?
³¹ Who denounces his conduct to
     his face?
  Who repays him for what he has
     done?
³² He is carried to the grave,
  and watch is kept over his tomb.
³³ The soil in the valley is sweet to him;
     all men follow after him,
  and a countless throng goesᵈ
     before him.

³⁴ "So how can you console me with
     your nonsense?
  Nothing is left of your answers but
     falsehood!"

Eliphaz

22 Then Eliphaz the Temanite re-
    plied:

² "Can a man be of benefit to God?
  Can even a wise man benefit him?
³ What pleasure would it give the
     Almighty if you were
     righteous?
  What would he gain if your ways
     were blameless?

⁴ "Is it for your piety that he rebukes
     you
  and brings charges against you?
⁵ Is not your wickedness great?
  Are not your sins endless?
⁶ You demanded security from your
     brothers for no reason;
  you stripped men of their clothing,
     leaving them naked.
⁷ You gave no water to the weary
  and you withheld food from
     the hungry,
⁸ though you were a powerful man,
     owning land—
  an honored man, living on it.
⁹ And you sent widows away empty-
     handed
  and broke the strength of the
     fatherless.
¹⁰ That is why snares are all around
     you,
  why sudden peril terrifies you,
¹¹ why it is so dark you cannot see,
  and why a flood of water
     covers you.

¹² "Is not God in the heights of heaven?
  And see how lofty are the highest
     stars!
¹³ Yet you say, 'What does God know?
  Does he judge through such
     darkness?
¹⁴ Thick clouds veil him, so he does not
     see us
  as he goes about in the vaulted
     heavens.'
¹⁵ Will you keep to the old path
  that evil men have trod?

ᵃ 17–20 Verses 17 and 18 may be taken as
exclamations and 19 and 20 as declarations.
ᵇ 24 The meaning of the Hebrew for this word is
uncertain.   ᶜ 30 Or *man is reserved for the day
of calamity, / that he is brought forth to*
ᵈ 33 Or / *as a countless throng went*

¹⁶They were carried off before their
time,
their foundations washed away by
a flood.
¹⁷They said to God, 'Leave us
alone!
What can the Almighty do to us?'
¹⁸Yet it was he who filled their houses
with good things,
so I stand aloof from the counsel
of the wicked.

¹⁹"The righteous see their ruin
and rejoice;
the innocent mock them, saying,
²⁰'Surely our foes are destroyed,
and fire devours their wealth.'

²¹"Submit to God and be at peace
with him;
in this way prosperity will come
to you.
²²Accept instruction from his mouth
and lay up his words in your
heart.
²³If you return to the Almighty, you
will be restored:
If you remove wickedness far from
your tent
²⁴and assign your nuggets to the dust,
your gold of Ophir to the rocks in
the ravines,
²⁵then the Almighty will be your gold,
the choicest silver for you.
²⁶Surely then you will find delight in
the Almighty
and will lift up your face to God.
²⁷You will pray to him, and he will
hear you,
and you will fulfill your vows.
²⁸What you decide on will be done,
and light will shine on your ways.
²⁹When men are brought low and you
say, 'Lift them up!'
then he will save the downcast.
³⁰He will deliver even one who is not
innocent,
who will be delivered through the
cleanness of your hands."

> "YOU will pray to him, and he will
> hear you,
> and you will fulfill your vows."
>
> JOB 22:27

Job

23

Then Job replied:

²"Even today my complaint is bitter;
his hand*a* is heavy in spite of*b*
my groaning.
³If only I knew where to find him;
if only I could go to his dwelling!
⁴I would state my case before him
and fill my mouth with
arguments.
⁵I would find out what he would
answer me,
and consider what he would say.
⁶Would he oppose me with great
power?
No, he would not press charges
against me.
⁷There an upright man could present
his case before him,
and I would be delivered forever
from my judge.

⁸"But if I go to the east, he is not
there;
if I go to the west, I do not find him.
⁹When he is at work in the north, I do
not see him;
when he turns to the south, I catch
no glimpse of him.
¹⁰But he knows the way that I take;
when he has tested me, I will come
forth as gold.
¹¹My feet have closely followed his
steps;
I have kept to his way without
turning aside.
¹²I have not departed from the
commands of his lips;
I have treasured the words of his
mouth more than my daily
bread.

¹³"But he stands alone, and who can
oppose him?
He does whatever he pleases.
¹⁴He carries out his decree against me,
and many such plans he still has
in store.
¹⁵That is why I am terrified before him;
when I think of all this, I fear him.
¹⁶God has made my heart faint;
the Almighty has terrified me.

---

a2 Septuagint and Syriac; Hebrew / *the hand
on me*   *b2* Or *heavy on me in*

17 Yet I am not silenced by the darkness,
 by the thick darkness that covers
 my face.

24 "Why does the Almighty not set
 times for judgment?
 Why must those who know him
 look in vain for such days?
2 Men move boundary stones;
 they pasture flocks they
 have stolen.
3 They drive away the orphan's
 donkey
 and take the widow's ox
 in pledge.
4 They thrust the needy from the path
 and force all the poor of the land
 into hiding.
5 Like wild donkeys in the desert,
 the poor go about their labor of
 foraging food;
 the wasteland provides food for
 their children.
6 They gather fodder in the fields
 and glean in the vineyards of
 the wicked.
7 Lacking clothes, they spend the
 night naked;
 they have nothing to cover
 themselves in the cold.
8 They are drenched by mountain rains
 and hug the rocks for lack of
 shelter.
9 The fatherless child is snatched from
 the breast;
 the infant of the poor is seized
 for a debt.
10 Lacking clothes, they go about
 naked;
 they carry the sheaves, but still
 go hungry.
11 They crush olives among the
 terraces[a];
 they tread the winepresses, yet
 suffer thirst.
12 The groans of the dying rise from
 the city,
 and the souls of the wounded cry
 out for help.
 But God charges no one with
 wrongdoing.

13 "There are those who rebel against
 the light,
 who do not know its ways
 or stay in its paths.
14 When daylight is gone, the murderer
 rises up
 and kills the poor and needy;
 in the night he steals forth like
 a thief.
15 The eye of the adulterer watches
 for dusk;
 he thinks, 'No eye will see me,'
 and he keeps his face concealed.
16 In the dark, men break into houses,
 but by day they shut themselves in;
 they want nothing to do with
 the light.
17 For all of them, deep darkness is their
 morning[b];
 they make friends with the terrors
 of darkness.[c]

18 "Yet they are foam on the surface of
 the water;
 their portion of the land is cursed,
 so that no one goes to the
 vineyards.
19 As heat and drought snatch away the
 melted snow,
 so the grave[d] snatches away those
 who have sinned.
20 The womb forgets them,
 the worm feasts on them;
 evil men are no longer remembered
 but are broken like a tree.
21 They prey on the barren and childless
 woman,
 and to the widow show no
 kindness.
22 But God drags away the mighty by his
 power;
 though they become established,
 they have no assurance of life.
23 He may let them rest in a feeling of
 security,
 but his eyes are on their ways.
24 For a little while they are exalted, and
 then they are gone;
 they are brought low and gathered
 up like all others;
 they are cut off like heads of grain.

25 "If this is not so, who can prove
 me false
 and reduce my words to nothing?"

---

a 11 Or olives between the millstones; the
meaning of the Hebrew for this word is uncertain.
b 17 Or them, their morning is like the shadow of
death   c 17 Or of the shadow of death
d 19 Hebrew Sheol

Bildad

25 Then Bildad the Shuhite replied:

2 "Dominion and awe belong to God;
  he establishes order in the heights
    of heaven.
3 Can his forces be numbered?
  Upon whom does his light
    not rise?
4 How then can a man be righteous
    before God?
  How can one born of woman be
    pure?
5 If even the moon is not bright
  and the stars are not pure in
    his eyes,
6 how much less man, who is but a
    maggot—
  a son of man, who is only a worm!"

Job

26 Then Job replied:

2 "How you have helped the powerless!
  How you have saved the arm that
    is feeble!
3 What advice you have offered to one
    without wisdom!
  And what great insight you have
    displayed!
4 Who has helped you utter these
    words?
  And whose spirit spoke from your
    mouth?

5 "The dead are in deep anguish,
  those beneath the waters and all
    that live in them.
6 Death[a] is naked before God;
  Destruction[b] lies uncovered.
7 He spreads out the northern ⸤skies⸥
    over empty space;
  he suspends the earth over
    nothing.
8 He wraps up the waters in his clouds,
  yet the clouds do not burst under
    their weight.
9 He covers the face of the full moon,
  spreading his clouds over it.
10 He marks out the horizon on the face
    of the waters
  for a boundary between light and
    darkness.
11 The pillars of the heavens quake,
  aghast at his rebuke.

12 By his power he churned up the sea;
  by his wisdom he cut Rahab
    to pieces.
13 By his breath the skies became fair;
  his hand pierced the gliding
    serpent.
14 And these are but the outer fringe
    of his works;
  how faint the whisper we hear of
    him!
  Who then can understand the
    thunder of his power?"

27 And Job continued his discourse:

2 "As surely as God lives, who has
    denied me justice,
  the Almighty, who has made me
    taste bitterness of soul,
3 as long as I have life within me,
  the breath of God in my nostrils,
4 my lips will not speak wickedness,
  and my tongue will utter no deceit.
5 I will never admit you are in the
    right;
  till I die, I will not deny my
    integrity.
6 I will maintain my righteousness and
    never let go of it;
  my conscience will not reproach
    me as long as I live.

7 "May my enemies be like the wicked,
  my adversaries like the unjust!
8 For what hope has the godless when
    he is cut off,
  when God takes away his life?
9 Does God listen to his cry
  when distress comes upon him?
10 Will he find delight in the Almighty?
  Will he call upon God at all times?

11 "I will teach you about the power
    of God;
  the ways of the Almighty I will not
    conceal.
12 You have all seen this yourselves.
  Why then this meaningless talk?

13 "Here is the fate God allots to the
    wicked,
  the heritage a ruthless man
    receives from the Almighty:
14 However many his children, their fate
    is the sword;

a6 Hebrew *Sheol*   *b6* Hebrew *Abaddon*

his offspring will never have
enough to eat.
¹⁵ The plague will bury those who
survive him,
and their widows will not weep
for them.
¹⁶ Though he heaps up silver like dust
and clothes like piles of clay,
¹⁷ what he lays up the righteous will
wear,
and the innocent will divide his
silver.
¹⁸ The house he builds is like a moth's
cocoon,
like a hut made by a watchman.
¹⁹ He lies down wealthy, but will do so
no more;
when he opens his eyes, all is gone.
²⁰ Terrors overtake him like a flood;
a tempest snatches him away in
the night.
²¹ The east wind carries him off, and he
is gone;
it sweeps him out of his place.
²² It hurls itself against him without
mercy
as he flees headlong from its
power.
²³ It claps its hands in derision
and hisses him out of his place.

28

¹ "There is a mine for silver
and a place where gold is refined.
² Iron is taken from the earth,
and copper is smelted from ore.
³ Man puts an end to the darkness;
he searches the farthest recesses
for ore in the blackest darkness.
⁴ Far from where people dwell he cuts
a shaft,
in places forgotten by the foot
of man;
far from men he dangles and
sways.
⁵ The earth, from which food comes,
is transformed below as
by fire;
⁶ sapphires*a* come from its rocks,
and its dust contains nuggets
of gold.
⁷ No bird of prey knows that hidden
path,
no falcon's eye has seen it.
⁸ Proud beasts do not set foot on it,
and no lion prowls there.

⁹ Man's hand assaults the flinty rock
and lays bare the roots of the
mountains.
¹⁰ He tunnels through the rock;
his eyes see all its treasures.
¹¹ He searches*b* the sources of
the rivers
and brings hidden things to light.

¹² "But where can wisdom be found?
Where does understanding dwell?
¹³ Man does not comprehend its worth;
it cannot be found in the land of
the living.
¹⁴ The deep says, 'It is not in me';
the sea says, 'It is not with me.'
¹⁵ It cannot be bought with the finest
gold,
nor can its price be weighed
in silver.
¹⁶ It cannot be bought with the gold
of Ophir,
with precious onyx or sapphires.
¹⁷ Neither gold nor crystal can compare
with it,
nor can it be had for jewels of gold.
¹⁸ Coral and jasper are not worthy
of mention;
the price of wisdom is beyond
rubies.
¹⁹ The topaz of Cush cannot compare
with it;
it cannot be bought with pure gold.

²⁰ "Where then does wisdom come
from?
Where does understanding dwell?
²¹ It is hidden from the eyes of every
living thing,
concealed even from the birds
of the air.
²² Destruction*c* and Death say,
'Only a rumor of it has reached
our ears.'
²³ God understands the way to it
and he alone knows where it
dwells,
²⁴ for he views the ends of the earth
and sees everything under the
heavens.
²⁵ When he established the force of
the wind
and measured out the waters,

---

a6 Or *lapis lazuli;* also in verse 16
b11 Septuagint, Aquila and Vulgate; Hebrew *He
dams up*   *c22* Hebrew *Abaddon*

²⁶when he made a decree for the rain
and a path for the thunder
storm,
²⁷then he looked at wisdom and
appraised it;
he confirmed it and tested it.
²⁸And he said to man,
'The fear of the Lord—that is
wisdom,
and to shun evil is
understanding.' "

29 Job continued his discourse:

²"How I long for the months gone by,
for the days when God watched
over me,
³when his lamp shone upon my head
and by his light I walked through
darkness!
⁴Oh, for the days when I was in
my prime,
when God's intimate friendship
blessed my house,
⁵when the Almighty was still with me
and my children were around me,
⁶when my path was drenched with
cream
and the rock poured out for me
streams of olive oil.

⁷"When I went to the gate of the city
and took my seat in the public
square,
⁸the young men saw me and stepped
aside
and the old men rose to their feet;
⁹the chief men refrained from
speaking
and covered their mouths with
their hands;
¹⁰the voices of the nobles were hushed,
and their tongues stuck to the roof
of their mouths.
¹¹Whoever heard me spoke well of me,
and those who saw me
commended me,
¹²because I rescued the poor who cried
for help,
and the fatherless who had none to
assist him.
¹³The man who was dying blessed me;
I made the widow's heart sing.
¹⁴I put on righteousness as my
clothing;
justice was my robe and my turban.

¹⁵I was eyes to the blind
and feet to the lame.
¹⁶I was a father to the needy;
I took up the case of the stranger.
¹⁷I broke the fangs of the wicked
and snatched the victims from
their teeth.

¹⁸"I thought, 'I will die in my own
house,
my days as numerous as the grains
of sand.
¹⁹My roots will reach to the water,
and the dew will lie all night on
my branches.
²⁰My glory will remain fresh in me,
the bow ever new in my hand.'

²¹"Men listened to me expectantly,
waiting in silence for my counsel.
²²After I had spoken, they spoke
no more;
my words fell gently on their ears.
²³They waited for me as for showers
and drank in my words as the
spring rain.
²⁴When I smiled at them, they scarcely
believed it;
the light of my face was precious
to them.ᵃ
²⁵I chose the way for them and sat as
their chief;
I dwelt as a king among his troops;
I was like one who comforts
mourners.

30 "But now they mock me,
men younger than I,
whose fathers I would have disdained
to put with my sheep dogs.
²Of what use was the strength of their
hands to me,
since their vigor had gone from
them?
³Haggard from want and hunger,
they roamedᵇ the parched land
in desolate wastelands at night.
⁴In the brush they gathered salt
herbs,
and their foodᶜ was the root of the
broom tree.
⁵They were banished from their
fellow men,
shouted at as if they were thieves.

ᵃ24 The meaning of the Hebrew for this clause is
uncertain. ᵇ3 Or gnawed ᶜ4 Or fuel

⁶They were forced to live in the dry
stream beds,
among the rocks and in holes in
the ground.
⁷They brayed among the bushes
and huddled in the undergrowth.
⁸A base and nameless brood,
they were driven out of the land.

⁹"And now their sons mock me
in song;
I have become a byword among
them.
¹⁰They detest me and keep their
distance;
they do not hesitate to spit in
my face.
¹¹Now that God has unstrung my bow
and afflicted me,
they throw off restraint in my
presence.
¹²On my right the tribe[a] attacks;
they lay snares for my feet,
they build their siege ramps
against me.
¹³They break up my road;
they succeed in destroying me—
without anyone's helping them.[b]
¹⁴They advance as through a gaping
breach;
amid the ruins they come
rolling in.
¹⁵Terrors overwhelm me;
my dignity is driven away as by
the wind,
my safety vanishes like a cloud.

¹⁶"And now my life ebbs away;
days of suffering grip me.
¹⁷Night pierces my bones;
my gnawing pains never rest.
¹⁸In his great power ⌊God⌋ becomes
like clothing to me[c];
he binds me like the neck of my
garment.
¹⁹He throws me into the mud,
and I am reduced to dust
and ashes.

²⁰"I cry out to you, O God, but you
do not answer;
I stand up, but you merely look
at me.
²¹You turn on me ruthlessly;
with the might of your hand you
attack me.

²²You snatch me up and drive me
before the wind;
you toss me about in the storm.
²³I know you will bring me down
to death,
to the place appointed for all the
living.

²⁴"Surely no one lays a hand on a
broken man
when he cries for help in his
distress.
²⁵Have I not wept for those in trouble?
Has not my soul grieved for the
poor?
²⁶Yet when I hoped for good, evil came;
when I looked for light, then came
darkness.
²⁷The churning inside me never stops;
days of suffering confront me.
²⁸I go about blackened, but not by
the sun;
I stand up in the assembly and cry
for help.
²⁹I have become a brother of jackals,
a companion of owls.
³⁰My skin grows black and peels;
my body burns with fever.
³¹My harp is tuned to mourning,
and my flute to the sound of
wailing.

31 "I made a covenant with my eyes
not to look lustfully at a girl.
²For what is man's lot from God
above,
his heritage from the Almighty
on high?
³Is it not ruin for the wicked,
disaster for those who do wrong?
⁴Does he not see my ways
and count my every step?

⁵"If I have walked in falsehood
or my foot has hurried after
deceit—
⁶let God weigh me in honest scales
and he will know that I am
blameless—
⁷if my steps have turned from the path,
if my heart has been led by my eyes,
or if my hands have been defiled,

---

[a]12 The meaning of the Hebrew for this word is
uncertain.   [b]13 Or me. / 'No one can help him,'
⌊they say⌋.   [c]18 Hebrew; Septuagint ⌊God⌋
grasps my clothing

⁸then may others eat what I have
sown,
and may my crops be uprooted.

⁹ "If my heart has been enticed by a
woman,
or if I have lurked at my neighbor's
door,
¹⁰then may my wife grind another
man's grain,
and may other men sleep with her.
¹¹ For that would have been shameful,
a sin to be judged.
¹² It is a fire that burns to Destruction[a];
it would have uprooted my harvest.

¹³ "If I have denied justice to my
menservants and
maidservants
when they had a grievance
against me,
¹⁴what will I do when God confronts
me?
What will I answer when called
to account?
¹⁵ Did not he who made me in the
womb make them?
Did not the same one form us both
within our mothers?

¹⁶ "If I have denied the desires of
the poor
or let the eyes of the widow grow
weary,
¹⁷ if I have kept my bread to myself,
not sharing it with the fatherless—
¹⁸ but from my youth I reared him as
would a father,
and from my birth I guided the
widow—
¹⁹ if I have seen anyone perishing for
lack of clothing,
or a needy man without a garment,
²⁰ and his heart did not bless me
for warming him with the fleece
from my sheep,
²¹ if I have raised my hand against the
fatherless,
knowing that I had influence
in court,
²² then let my arm fall from the
shoulder,
let it be broken off at the joint.
²³ For I dreaded destruction from God,
and for fear of his splendor I could
not do such things.

²⁴ "If I have put my trust in gold
or said to pure gold, 'You are my
security,'
²⁵ if I have rejoiced over my great
wealth,
the fortune my hands had gained,
²⁶ if I have regarded the sun in its
radiance
or the moon moving in splendor,
²⁷ so that my heart was secretly enticed
and my hand offered them a kiss of
homage,
²⁸ then these also would be sins to be
judged,
for I would have been unfaithful to
God on high.

²⁹ "If I have rejoiced at my enemy's
misfortune
or gloated over the trouble that
came to him—
³⁰ I have not allowed my mouth to sin
by invoking a curse against his
life—
³¹ if the men of my household have
never said,
'Who has not had his fill of Job's
meat?'—
³² but no stranger had to spend the
night in the street,
for my door was always open to the
traveler—
³³ if I have concealed my sin as
men do,[b]
by hiding my guilt in my heart
³⁴ because I so feared the crowd
and so dreaded the contempt of
the clans
that I kept silent and would not go
outside—

³⁵ ("Oh, that I had someone to
hear me!
I sign now my defense—let the
Almighty answer me;
let my accuser put his indictment
in writing.
³⁶ Surely I would wear it on my
shoulder,
I would put it on like a crown.
³⁷ I would give him an account of my
every step;
like a prince I would approach
him.)—

----

[a]12 Hebrew *Abaddon*   [b]33 Or *as Adam did*

38 "if my land cries out against me
 and all its furrows are wet
  with tears,
39 if I have devoured its yield without
  payment
 or broken the spirit of its tenants,
40 then let briers come up instead
  of wheat
 and weeds instead of barley."

The words of Job are ended.

Elihu

32 So these three men stopped answering Job, because he was righteous in his own eyes. ²But Elihu son of Barakel the Buzite, of the family of Ram, became very angry with Job for justifying himself rather than God. ³He was also angry with the three friends, because they had found no way to refute Job, and yet had condemned him.ᵃ ⁴Now Elihu had waited before speaking to Job because they were older than he. ⁵But when he saw that the three men had nothing more to say, his anger was aroused.

⁶So Elihu son of Barakel the Buzite said:

"I am young in years,
 and you are old;
that is why I was fearful,
 not daring to tell you what I know.
⁷ I thought, 'Age should speak;
 advanced years should teach
  wisdom.'
⁸ But it is the spiritᵇ in a man,
 the breath of the Almighty, that
  gives him understanding.
⁹ It is not only the oldᶜ who are wise,
 not only the aged who understand
  what is right.

¹⁰ "Therefore I say: Listen to me;
 I too will tell you what I know.
¹¹ I waited while you spoke,
 I listened to your reasoning;
while you were searching for words,
¹² I gave you my full attention.
But not one of you has proved
  Job wrong;
 none of you has answered his
  arguments.
¹³ Do not say, 'We have found wisdom;
 let God refute him, not man.'

¹⁴ But Job has not marshaled his words
  against me,
 and I will not answer him with your
  arguments.

¹⁵ "They are dismayed and have no
  more to say;
 words have failed them.
¹⁶ Must I wait, now that they are silent,
 now that they stand there with no
  reply?
¹⁷ I too will have my say;
 I too will tell what I know.
¹⁸ For I am full of words,
 and the spirit within me compels
  me;
¹⁹ inside I am like bottled-up wine,
 like new wineskins ready to burst.
²⁰ I must speak and find relief;
 I must open my lips and reply.
²¹ I will show partiality to no one,
 nor will I flatter any man;
²² for if I were skilled in flattery,
 my Maker would soon take
  me away.

33 "But now, Job, listen to my
  words;
 pay attention to everything I say.
² I am about to open my mouth;
 my words are on the tip of my
  tongue.
³ My words come from an upright heart;
 my lips sincerely speak what I
  know.
⁴ The Spirit of God has made me;
 the breath of the Almighty gives
  me life.
⁵ Answer me then, if you can;
 prepare yourself and confront me.
⁶ I am just like you before God;
 I too have been taken from clay.
⁷ No fear of me should alarm you,
 nor should my hand be heavy
  upon you.

⁸ "But you have said in my hearing—
 I heard the very words—
⁹ 'I am pure and without sin;
 I am clean and free from guilt.
¹⁰ Yet God has found fault with me;
 he considers me his enemy.

ᵃ3 Masoretic Text; an ancient Hebrew scribal tradition *Job, and so had condemned God*   ᵇ8 Or *Spirit*; also in verse 18   ᶜ9 Or *many*; or *great*

> *We are all weak, finite, simple human beings, standing in the need of prayer. None need it so much as those who think they are strong, those who know it not, but are deluded by self-sufficiency.*

HAROLD C. PHILLIPS

¹¹ He fastens my feet in shackles;
  he keeps close watch on all my
    paths.'

¹² "But I tell you, in this you are
    not right,
  for God is greater than man.

¹³ Why do you complain to him
  that he answers none of man's
    words[a]?

¹⁴ For God does speak—now one way,
    now another—
  though man may not perceive it.

¹⁵ In a dream, in a vision of the night,
  when deep sleep falls on men
  as they slumber in their beds,

¹⁶ he may speak in their ears
  and terrify them with warnings,

¹⁷ to turn man from wrongdoing
  and keep him from pride,

¹⁸ to preserve his soul from the pit,[b]
  his life from perishing by the
    sword.[c]

¹⁹ Or a man may be chastened on a
    bed of pain
  with constant distress in his bones,

²⁰ so that his very being finds food
    repulsive
  and his soul loathes the choicest
    meal.

²¹ His flesh wastes away to nothing,
  and his bones, once hidden, now
    stick out.

²² His soul draws near to the pit,[d]
  and his life to the messengers
    of death.[e]

²³ "Yet if there is an angel on his side
    as a mediator, one out of a
    thousand,
  to tell a man what is right for him,

²⁴ to be gracious to him and say,
  'Spare him from going down to
    the pit[f];
  I have found a ransom for him'—

²⁵ then his flesh is renewed like a
    child's;

it is restored as in the days of his
    youth.

²⁶ He prays to God and finds favor with
    him,
  he sees God's face and shouts for
    joy;
  he is restored by God to his
    righteous state.

²⁷ Then he comes to men and says,
  'I sinned, and perverted what was
    right,
  but I did not get what I deserved.

²⁸ He redeemed my soul from going
    down to the pit,[g]
  and I will live to enjoy the light.'

²⁹ "God does all these things to a man—
    twice, even three times—

³⁰ to turn back his soul from the pit,[h]
  that the light of life may shine
    on him.

³¹ "Pay attention, Job, and listen to me;
  be silent, and I will speak.

³² If you have anything to say, answer me;
  speak up, for I want you to be
    cleared.

³³ But if not, then listen to me;
  be silent, and I will teach you
    wisdom."

> *"HE prays to God and finds favor
>   with him,
> he sees God's face and shouts for joy;
> he is restored by God to his righteous
>   state."*

JOB 33:26

34

Then Elihu said:

² "Hear my words, you wise men;
  listen to me, you men of learning.

³ For the ear tests words
  as the tongue tastes food.

⁴ Let us discern for ourselves what
    is right;
  let us learn together what is good.

---

[a]13 Or *that he does not answer for any of his actions*   [b]18 Or *preserve him from the grave*   [c]18 Or *from crossing the River*   [d]22 Or *He draws near to the grave*   [e]22 Or *to the dead*   [f]24 Or *grave*   [g]28 Or *redeemed me from going down to the grave*   [h]30 Or *turn him back from the grave*

⁵ "Job says, 'I am innocent,
  but God denies me justice.
⁶ Although I am right,
  I am considered a liar;
  although I am guiltless,
    his arrow inflicts an incurable
      wound.'
⁷ What man is like Job,
  who drinks scorn like water?
⁸ He keeps company with evildoers;
  he associates with wicked men.
⁹ For he says, 'It profits a man
    nothing
  when he tries to please God.'

¹⁰ "So listen to me, you men of
    understanding.
  Far be it from God to do evil,
  from the Almighty to do wrong.
¹¹ He repays a man for what he has
    done;
  he brings upon him what his
    conduct deserves.
¹² It is unthinkable that God would
    do wrong,
  that the Almighty would pervert
    justice.
¹³ Who appointed him over the earth?
  Who put him in charge of the
    whole world?
¹⁴ If it were his intention
  and he withdrew his spirit*ᵃ* and
    breath,
¹⁵ all mankind would perish together
  and man would return to the dust.

¹⁶ "If you have understanding, hear
    this;
  listen to what I say.
¹⁷ Can he who hates justice govern?
  Will you condemn the just and
    mighty One?
¹⁸ Is he not the One who says to kings,
    'You are worthless,'
  and to nobles, 'You are wicked,'
¹⁹ who shows no partiality to princes
  and does not favor the rich over
    the poor,
  for they are all the work of his
    hands?
²⁰ They die in an instant, in the middle
    of the night;
  the people are shaken and they
    pass away;
  the mighty are removed without
    human hand.

²¹ "His eyes are on the ways of men;
  he sees their every step.
²² There is no dark place, no deep
    shadow,
  where evildoers can hide.
²³ God has no need to examine men
    further,
  that they should come before him
    for judgment.
²⁴ Without inquiry he shatters the
    mighty
  and sets up others in their place.
²⁵ Because he takes note of their
    deeds,
  he overthrows them in the night
    and they are crushed.
²⁶ He punishes them for their
    wickedness
  where everyone can see them,
²⁷ because they turned from following
    him
  and had no regard for any of
    his ways.
²⁸ They caused the cry of the poor to
    come before him,
  so that he heard the cry of
    the needy.
²⁹ But if he remains silent, who can
    condemn him?
  If he hides his face, who can
    see him?
  Yet he is over man and nation alike,
³⁰ to keep a godless man from ruling,
  from laying snares for the people.

³¹ "Suppose a man says to God,
    'I am guilty but will offend
    no more.
³² Teach me what I cannot see;
  if I have done wrong, I will not do
    so again.'
³³ Should God then reward you on your
    terms,
  when you refuse to repent?
  You must decide, not I;
  so tell me what you know.

³⁴ "Men of understanding declare,
  wise men who hear me say to me,
³⁵ 'Job speaks without knowledge;
  his words lack insight.'
³⁶ Oh, that Job might be tested to
    the utmost
  for answering like a wicked man!

ᵃ14 Or *Spirit*

37 To his sin he adds rebellion;
    scornfully he claps his hands
        among us
    and multiplies his words against
        God."

35 Then Elihu said:

2 "Do you think this is just?
    You say, 'I will be cleared
        by God.ᵃ'
3 Yet you ask him, 'What profit is it
        to me,ᵇ
    and what do I gain by not sinning?'

4 "I would like to reply to you
    and to your friends with you.
5 Look up at the heavens and see;
    gaze at the clouds so high above
        you.
6 If you sin, how does that affect him?
    If your sins are many, what does
        that do to him?
7 If you are righteous, what do you
        give to him,
    or what does he receive from your
        hand?
8 Your wickedness affects only a man
        like yourself,
    and your righteousness only the
        sons of men.

9 "Men cry out under a load of
        oppression;
    they plead for relief from the arm of
        the powerful.
10 But no one says, 'Where is God my
        Maker,
    who gives songs in the night,
11 who teaches more to us than toᶜ the
        beasts of the earth
    and makes us wiser thanᵈ the birds
        of the air?'
12 He does not answer when men
        cry out
    because of the arrogance of the
        wicked.
13 Indeed, God does not listen to their
        empty plea;
    the Almighty pays no attention
        to it.
14 How much less, then, will he listen
    when you say that you do not
        see him,
    that your case is before him
    and you must wait for him,

15 and further, that his anger never
        punishes
    and he does not take the least
        notice of wickedness.ᵉ
16 So Job opens his mouth with empty
        talk;
    without knowledge he multiplies
        words."

36 Elihu continued:

2 "Bear with me a little longer and I
        will show you
    that there is more to be said in
        God's behalf.
3 I get my knowledge from afar;
    I will ascribe justice to my
        Maker.
4 Be assured that my words are not
        false;
    one perfect in knowledge is with you.

5 "God is mighty, but does not despise
        men;
    he is mighty, and firm in his
        purpose.
6 He does not keep the wicked alive
    but gives the afflicted their rights.
7 He does not take his eyes off the
        righteous;
    he enthrones them with kings
    and exalts them forever.
8 But if men are bound in chains,
    held fast by cords of affliction,
9 he tells them what they have done—
    that they have sinned arrogantly.
10 He makes them listen to correction
    and commands them to repent
        of their evil.
11 If they obey and serve him,
    they will spend the rest of their
        days in prosperity
    and their years in contentment.
12 But if they do not listen,
    they will perish by the swordᶠ
    and die without knowledge.

13 "The godless in heart harbor
        resentment;
    even when he fetters them, they do
        not cry for help.

ᵃ2 Or My righteousness is more than God's
ᵇ3 Or you   ᶜ11 Or teaches us by   ᵈ11 Or us
wise by   ᵉ15 Symmachus, Theodotion and
Vulgate; the meaning of the Hebrew for this word
is uncertain.   ᶠ12 Or will cross the River

14 They die in their youth,
among male prostitutes of the
shrines.
15 But those who suffer he delivers in
their suffering;
he speaks to them in their
affliction.

16 "He is wooing you from the jaws of
distress
to a spacious place free from
restriction,
to the comfort of your table laden
with choice food.
17 But now you are laden with the
judgment due the wicked;
judgment and justice have taken
hold of you.
18 Be careful that no one entices you by
riches;
do not let a large bribe turn
you aside.
19 Would your wealth
or even all your mighty efforts
sustain you so you would not be in
distress?
20 Do not long for the night,
to drag people away from their
homes.[a]
21 Beware of turning to evil,
which you seem to prefer to
affliction.

22 "God is exalted in his power.
Who is a teacher like him?
23 Who has prescribed his ways for him,
or said to him, 'You have done
wrong'?
24 Remember to extol his work,
which men have praised in song.
25 All mankind has seen it;
men gaze on it from afar.
26 How great is God—beyond our
understanding!
The number of his years is past
finding out.

27 "He draws up the drops of water,
which distill as rain to the
streams[b];
28 the clouds pour down their moisture
and abundant showers fall on
mankind.
29 Who can understand how he spreads
out the clouds,
how he thunders from his pavilion?

30 See how he scatters his lightning
about him,
bathing the depths of the sea.
31 This is the way he governs[c] the
nations
and provides food in abundance.
32 He fills his hands with lightning
and commands it to strike its mark.
33 His thunder announces the coming
storm;
even the cattle make known its
approach.[d]

37 "At this my heart pounds
and leaps from its place.
2 Listen! Listen to the roar of his voice,
to the rumbling that comes from
his mouth.
3 He unleashes his lightning beneath
the whole heaven
and sends it to the ends of
the earth.
4 After that comes the sound of his
roar;
he thunders with his majestic voice.
When his voice resounds,
he holds nothing back.
5 God's voice thunders in marvelous
ways;
he does great things beyond our
understanding.
6 He says to the snow, 'Fall on the
earth,'
and to the rain shower, 'Be a
mighty downpour.'
7 So that all men he has made may
know his work,
he stops every man from his
labor.[e]
8 The animals take cover;
they remain in their dens.
9 The tempest comes out from its
chamber,
the cold from the driving winds.
10 The breath of God produces ice,
and the broad waters become
frozen.
11 He loads the clouds with moisture;
he scatters his lightning through
them.

---

a20 The meaning of the Hebrew for verses 18–20
is uncertain.   *b27* Or *distill from the mist as
rain*   *c31* Or *nourishes*   *d33* Or *announces
his coming— / the One zealous against evil*
e7 Or / *he fills all men with fear by his power*

¹²At his direction they swirl around
over the face of the whole earth
to do whatever he commands
them.
¹³He brings the clouds to punish men,
or to water his earth* and show
his love.

¹⁴"Listen to this, Job;
stop and consider God's wonders.
¹⁵Do you know how God controls the
clouds
and makes his lightning flash?
¹⁶Do you know how the clouds hang
poised,
those wonders of him who is
perfect in knowledge?
¹⁷You who swelter in your clothes
when the land lies hushed under
the south wind,
¹⁸can you join him in spreading out
the skies,
hard as a mirror of cast bronze?

¹⁹"Tell us what we should say to him;
we cannot draw up our case
because of our darkness.
²⁰Should he be told that I want to
speak?
Would any man ask to be
swallowed up?
²¹Now no one can look at the sun,
bright as it is in the skies
after the wind has swept them
clean.
²²Out of the north he comes in golden
splendor;
God comes in awesome majesty.
²³The Almighty is beyond our reach
and exalted in power;
in his justice and great
righteousness, he does not
oppress.
²⁴Therefore, men revere him,
for does he not have regard for all
the wise in heart?*"

The LORD Speaks

38 Then the LORD answered Job out of
the storm. He said:

²"Who is this that darkens my counsel
with words without knowledge?
³Brace yourself like a man;
I will question you,
and you shall answer me.

THEN the LORD answered Job out of the
storm.

JOB 38:1

⁴"Where were you when I laid the
earth's foundation?
Tell me, if you understand.
⁵Who marked off its dimensions?
Surely you know!
Who stretched a measuring line
across it?
⁶On what were its footings set,
or who laid its cornerstone—
⁷while the morning stars sang
together
and all the angels* shouted
for joy?

⁸"Who shut up the sea behind doors
when it burst forth from the womb,
⁹when I made the clouds its garment
and wrapped it in thick darkness,
¹⁰when I fixed limits for it
and set its doors and bars in place,
¹¹when I said, 'This far you may come
and no farther;
here is where your proud waves
halt'?

¹²"Have you ever given orders to the
morning,
or shown the dawn its place,
¹³that it might take the earth by the
edges
and shake the wicked out of it?
¹⁴The earth takes shape like clay under
a seal;
its features stand out like those of
a garment.
¹⁵The wicked are denied their light,
and their upraised arm is broken.

¹⁶"Have you journeyed to the springs
of the sea
or walked in the recesses of the
deep?
¹⁷Have the gates of death been shown
to you?
Have you seen the gates of the
shadow of death*?

*13 Or to favor them   *24 Or for he does not
have regard for any who think they are wise.
*7 Hebrew the sons of God   *17 Or gates of
deep shadows

¹⁸ Have you comprehended the vast
    expanses of the earth?
  Tell me, if you know all this.

¹⁹ "What is the way to the abode of light?
  And where does darkness reside?
²⁰ Can you take them to their places?
  Do you know the paths to their
    dwellings?

²¹ Surely you know, for you were
    already born!
  You have lived so many years!

²² "Have you entered the storehouses of
    the snow
  or seen the storehouses of the hail,
²³ which I reserve for times of trouble,
  for days of war and battle?

JOB 38

{ **THURSDAY** }

God's Questions

38:1 THEN THE LORD ANSWERED JOB OUT OF THE STORM.

God answers Job's questions with a question of his own: "Who is this that darkens my counsel with words without knowledge?" (38:2). God's "counsel" is his design, his purpose and plan in the world. Job has been questioning God's fairness in his management of the world. God's question is mostly rhetorical, "Who is this?" as in, "Who do you think you are?" Then he follows up with a barrage of questions, spanning chapters 38–41, all of which add up to a huge, "Who do you think you are?"

The point is not lost on Job. When God is finished with his questions, Job is finished with his. "I know that you can do all things; no plan of yours can be thwarted. You asked, 'Who is this that obscures my counsel without knowledge?' Surely I spoke of things I did not understand, things too wonderful for me to know" (42:2–3). Note that God did not even make an attempt to answer any of Job's questions. He barely acknowledged them. All he did was confront Job with two things: Job's smallness and God's greatness. And that was sufficient for Job; he received it as an answer. God basically said, "This is as far as your intellect can go. The universe I made and manage is wilder and bigger and more terrifying than you can ever understand."

The effect of great pain is claustrophobic. Our pain can become the whole world to us. Suffering makes egotists of us all. God's treatment of Job, though harsh, relieved him of the burden Job and his friends created. It is burden enough to suffer in a world we don't understand; it is too heavy a burden to believe that our suffering, not God, is what was and is and ever will be, world without end. Job's humility was chastened and deepened.

The greatest of innocent sufferers was Jesus. When he prayed in Gethsemane, he was very clear about the lesson of Job. His world was big and his humility deep. So he prayed, "*Abba*, Father, everything is possible for you. Take this cup from me. Yet not what I will, but what you will" (Mark 14:36). We can learn to pray the same way too, from the heart.

PRAY:

*Abba, Father, thank you that I don't have to understand everything
to trust you completely. No matter what—I know that you love me
and that you are in control of this, your world.*

FOR YOUR NEXT DEVOTIONAL READING, GO TO PAGE 610.

24 What is the way to the place where
the lightning is dispersed,
or the place where the east winds
are scattered over the earth?
25 Who cuts a channel for the torrents
of rain,
and a path for the thunderstorm,
26 to water a land where no man lives,
a desert with no one in it,
27 to satisfy a desolate wasteland
and make it sprout with grass?
28 Does the rain have a father?
Who fathers the drops of dew?
29 From whose womb comes the ice?
Who gives birth to the frost from
the heavens
30 when the waters become hard
as stone,
when the surface of the deep is
frozen?

31 "Can you bind the beautiful*a*
Pleiades?
Can you loose the cords of Orion?
32 Can you bring forth the constellations
in their seasons*b*
or lead out the Bear*c* with its cubs?
33 Do you know the laws of the
heavens?
Can you set up ⌊God's*d*⌋ dominion
over the earth?

34 "Can you raise your voice to the
clouds
and cover yourself with a flood
of water?
35 Do you send the lightning bolts on
their way?
Do they report to you, 'Here
we are'?
36 Who endowed the heart*e* with
wisdom
or gave understanding to the
mind*e*?
37 Who has the wisdom to count the
clouds?
Who can tip over the water jars of
the heavens
38 when the dust becomes hard
and the clods of earth stick
together?

39 "Do you hunt the prey for the lioness
and satisfy the hunger of the lions
40 when they crouch in their dens
or lie in wait in a thicket?

41 Who provides food for the raven
when its young cry out to God
and wander about for lack of food?

39 "Do you know when the
mountain goats give birth?
Do you watch when the doe bears
her fawn?
2 Do you count the months till they
bear?
Do you know the time they
give birth?
3 They crouch down and bring forth
their young;
their labor pains are ended.
4 Their young thrive and grow strong in
the wilds;
they leave and do not return.

5 "Who let the wild donkey go free?
Who untied his ropes?
6 I gave him the wasteland as his
home,
the salt flats as his habitat.
7 He laughs at the commotion in
the town;
he does not hear a driver's shout.
8 He ranges the hills for his pasture
and searches for any green thing.

9 "Will the wild ox consent to
serve you?
Will he stay by your manger
at night?
10 Can you hold him to the furrow with
a harness?
Will he till the valleys behind you?
11 Will you rely on him for his great
strength?
Will you leave your heavy work
to him?
12 Can you trust him to bring in
your grain
and gather it to your threshing
floor?

13 "The wings of the ostrich flap joyfully,
but they cannot compare with the
pinions and feathers of the
stork.
14 She lays her eggs on the ground
and lets them warm in the sand,

a31 Or *the twinkling*; or *the chains of the*
b32 Or *the morning star in its season*
c32 Or *out Leo*   *d33* Or *his*; or *their*
e36 The meaning of the Hebrew for this word is
uncertain.

¹⁵ unmindful that a foot may crush
them,
that some wild animal may trample
them.

¹⁶ She treats her young harshly, as if
they were not hers;
she cares not that her labor was
in vain,

¹⁷ for God did not endow her with
wisdom
or give her a share of good
sense.

¹⁸ Yet when she spreads her feathers
to run,
she laughs at horse and rider.

¹⁹ "Do you give the horse his strength
or clothe his neck with a flowing
mane?

²⁰ Do you make him leap like a locust,
striking terror with his proud
snorting?

²¹ He paws fiercely, rejoicing in his
strength,
and charges into the fray.

²² He laughs at fear, afraid of nothing;
he does not shy away from
the sword.

²³ The quiver rattles against his side,
along with the flashing spear
and lance.

²⁴ In frenzied excitement he eats up
the ground;
he cannot stand still when the
trumpet sounds.

²⁵ At the blast of the trumpet he snorts,
'Aha!'
He catches the scent of battle
from afar,
the shout of commanders and the
battle cry.

²⁶ "Does the hawk take flight by your
wisdom
and spread his wings toward the
south?

²⁷ Does the eagle soar at your command
and build his nest on high?

²⁸ He dwells on a cliff and stays there
at night;
a rocky crag is his stronghold.

²⁹ From there he seeks out his food;
his eyes detect it from afar.

³⁰ His young ones feast on blood,
and where the slain are, there
is he."

40 The LORD said to Job:

² "Will the one who contends with the
Almighty correct him?
Let him who accuses God answer
him!"

³ Then Job answered the LORD:

⁴ "I am unworthy—how can I reply
to you?
I put my hand over my mouth.

⁵ I spoke once, but I have no answer—
twice, but I will say no more."

⁶ Then the LORD spoke to Job out of the
storm:

⁷ "Brace yourself like a man;
I will question you,
and you shall answer me.

⁸ "Would you discredit my justice?
Would you condemn me to justify
yourself?

⁹ Do you have an arm like God's,
and can your voice thunder
like his?

¹⁰ Then adorn yourself with glory and
splendor,
and clothe yourself in honor and
majesty.

¹¹ Unleash the fury of your wrath,
look at every proud man and bring
him low,

¹² look at every proud man and humble
him,
crush the wicked where they
stand.

¹³ Bury them all in the dust together;
shroud their faces in the grave.

¹⁴ Then I myself will admit to you
that your own right hand can
save you.

¹⁵ "Look at the behemoth,ᵃ
which I made along with you
and which feeds on grass like
an ox.

¹⁶ What strength he has in his loins,
what power in the muscles of
his belly!

¹⁷ His tailᵇ sways like a cedar;
the sinews of his thighs are
close-knit.

ᵃ15 Possibly the hippopotamus or the elephant
ᵇ17 Possibly trunk

¹⁸ His bones are tubes of bronze,
   his limbs like rods of iron.
¹⁹ He ranks first among the works
      of God,
   yet his Maker can approach him
      with his sword.
²⁰ The hills bring him their produce,
   and all the wild animals play
      nearby.
²¹ Under the lotus plants he lies,
   hidden among the reeds in
      the marsh.
²² The lotuses conceal him in their
      shadow;
   the poplars by the stream
      surround him.
²³ When the river rages, he is not
      alarmed;
   he is secure, though the Jordan
      should surge against his
      mouth.
²⁴ Can anyone capture him by
      the eyes,ᵃ
   or trap him and pierce his nose?

41 "Can you pull in the leviathanᵇ
      with a fishhook
   or tie down his tongue with a rope?
² Can you put a cord through his nose
   or pierce his jaw with a hook?
³ Will he keep begging you for mercy?
   Will he speak to you with gentle
      words?
⁴ Will he make an agreement with you
   for you to take him as your slave
      for life?
⁵ Can you make a pet of him like a bird
   or put him on a leash for your girls?
⁶ Will traders barter for him?
   Will they divide him up among the
      merchants?
⁷ Can you fill his hide with harpoons
   or his head with fishing spears?
⁸ If you lay a hand on him,
   you will remember the struggle and
      never do it again!
⁹ Any hope of subduing him is false;
   the mere sight of him is
      overpowering.
¹⁰ No one is fierce enough to rouse him.
   Who then is able to stand against
      me?
¹¹ Who has a claim against me that
      I must pay?
   Everything under heaven belongs
      to me.

¹² "I will not fail to speak of his limbs,
   his strength and his graceful
      form.
¹³ Who can strip off his outer coat?
   Who would approach him with a
      bridle?
¹⁴ Who dares open the doors of his
      mouth,
   ringed about with his fearsome
      teeth?
¹⁵ His back hasᶜ rows of shields
   tightly sealed together;
¹⁶ each is so close to the next
   that no air can pass between.
¹⁷ They are joined fast to one another;
   they cling together and cannot
      be parted.
¹⁸ His snorting throws out flashes of
      light;
   his eyes are like the rays of dawn.
¹⁹ Firebrands stream from his mouth;
   sparks of fire shoot out.
²⁰ Smoke pours from his nostrils
   as from a boiling pot over a fire
      of reeds.
²¹ His breath sets coals ablaze,
   and flames dart from his mouth.
²² Strength resides in his neck;
   dismay goes before him.
²³ The folds of his flesh are tightly
      joined;
   they are firm and immovable.
²⁴ His chest is hard as rock,
   hard as a lower millstone.
²⁵ When he rises up, the mighty are
      terrified;
   they retreat before his thrashing.
²⁶ The sword that reaches him has
      no effect,
   nor does the spear or the dart or
      the javelin.
²⁷ Iron he treats like straw
   and bronze like rotten wood.
²⁸ Arrows do not make him flee;
   slingstones are like chaff to him.
²⁹ A club seems to him but a piece
      of straw;
   he laughs at the rattling of the
      lance.
³⁰ His undersides are jagged potsherds,
   leaving a trail in the mud like a
      threshing sledge.

ᵃ24 Or by a water hole   ᵇ1 Possibly the
crocodile   ᶜ15 Or His pride is his

³¹ He makes the depths churn like a
boiling caldron
and stirs up the sea like a pot of
ointment.
³² Behind him he leaves a glistening
wake;
one would think the deep had
white hair.
³³ Nothing on earth is his equal—
a creature without fear.

³⁴ He looks down on all that are
haughty;
he is king over all that are
proud."

Job

42 Then Job replied to the LORD:

² "I know that you can do all things;
no plan of yours can be thwarted.

JOB 42

The Answerer Is Better Than Answers

42:5 NOW MY EYES HAVE SEEN YOU.

When Job is confronted with all of God's questions, he is crushed. He says,
"Therefore I despise myself and repent in dust and ashes" (42:6). Our English word *despise* isn't strong enough. The Hebrew word is literally "to melt,"
"to flow."

For what does Job despise himself? It certainly wasn't for any sin his
friends were sure he had committed. Instead, it was for the monstrous spiritual crime of putting God on the judgment stand. Now Job is embarrassed
and revolted at himself. He is terrified by what he has done.

But he is satisfied. God answered none of Job's questions; he only asked
his own. Yet Job is satisfied because he has seen something of the Answerer:
"My ears had heard of you but now my eyes have seen you" (verse 5). That is
enough. Job is like the resistance fighter in English philospher Basil Mitchell's
parable. His country is captive to an evil army of occupation. One night he
meets a stranger who makes a deep impression on him. The stranger tells
him that he is leader of the resistance and urges him to trust him no matter
what he sees later. When the night is past, and they part company, the resistance fighter is completely confident that this stranger is who he said he is.
They never meet again, although the resistance fighter personally sees the
stranger often. Sometimes he sees him helping his friends in the resistance,
and they say, "Look, he is on our side, he is helping us." Other times he sees
him dressed in the uniform of the army of occupation, handing over patriots
to the firing squad. Then his friends curse the stranger. But the fighter insists,
"He is still on our side; the stranger knows best."

Nothing could be more important to spiritual health in a seemingly
chaotic world than to know the Lord, to seek his face in his Word and in prayer.
Do you know him, or have you just heard about him? Until you know him personally, all the truth you may know about him cannot sustain you in a crisis.

PRAY:

"My heart says of you, 'Seek his face!'
Your face, LORD, I will seek" (Psalm 27:8).

FOR YOUR NEXT DEVOTIONAL READING, GO TO PAGE 612.

³ˌYou asked,ˌ 'Who is this that
  obscures my counsel without
  knowledge?'
Surely I spoke of things I did not
  understand,
  things too wonderful for me to
  know.
⁴ˌ "You said,ˌ 'Listen now, and I will
  speak;
  I will question you,
  and you shall answer me.'
⁵ My ears had heard of you
  but now my eyes have seen you.
⁶ Therefore I despise myself
  and repent in dust and ashes.'"

Epilogue

⁷After the LORD had said these things to Job, he said to Eliphaz the Temanite, "I am angry with you and your two friends, because you have not spoken of me what is right, as my servant Job has. ⁸So now take seven bulls and seven rams and go to my servant Job and sacrifice a burnt offering for yourselves. My servant Job will pray for you, and I will accept his prayer and not deal with you according to your folly. You have not spoken of me what is right, as my servant Job has." ⁹So Eliphaz the Temanite, Bildad the Shuhite and Zophar the Naamathite did what the LORD told them; and the LORD accepted Job's prayer.

¹⁰After Job had prayed for his friends, the LORD made him prosperous again and gave him twice as much as he had before. ¹¹All his brothers and sisters and everyone who had known him before came and ate with him in his house. They comforted and consoled him over all the trouble the LORD had brought upon him, and each one gave him a piece of silver*ᵃ* and a gold ring. ¹²The LORD blessed the latter part of Job's life more than the first. He had fourteen thousand sheep, six thousand camels, a thousand yoke of oxen and a thousand donkeys. ¹³And he also had seven sons and three daughters. ¹⁴The first daughter he named Jemimah, the second Keziah and the third Keren-Happuch. ¹⁵Nowhere in all the land were there found women as beautiful as Job's daughters, and their father granted them an inheritance along with their brothers.

¹⁶After this, Job lived a hundred and forty years; he saw his children and their children to the fourth generation. ¹⁷And so he died, old and full of years.

ᵃ11 Hebrew *him a kesitah*; a kesitah was a unit of money of unknown weight and value.

POLYCARP (69–155)

Little Left to Lose

POLYCARP, the bishop of Smyrna, was a very old man when he was ordered to stand before the proconsul. At age 86, with his body weak and his life nearly over, it seemed that his options were few, like the choice the proconsul gave him: either renounce Christ or die. But there's a freedom in having little to lose. When the proconsul demanded he renounce his faith in Christ, he answered, "I have served him for 80 years, and he has never done me wrong: How can I blaspheme my King who saved me?"

"I have wild beasts," said the proconsul.

"Call them," replied Polycarp.

"If you make light of the beasts," retorted the governor, "I'll have you destroyed by fire."

Polycarp answered, "The fire you threaten burns for a time and is soon extinguished: There is a fire you know nothing about—the fire of the judgment to come and of eternal punishment, the fire reserved for the ungodly. But why do you hesitate? Do what you want."[2]

The crowd quickly gathered wood and built a pyre. After Polycarp said a prayer, the men in charge lit the fire, a great flame shot up, and one of the last individuals to have personally known one of the apostles was gone. Polycarp's predecessor in Smyrna had been John. The year was A.D. 155.

Theologian Karl Barth said the approach at the end of life should be like the approach of a waterfall, where "the river of responsibility should flow more torrentially than ever in view of the ... proximity of the coming Judge!"[3] Just as a river speeds up its pace as it nears the precipice of the falls, so old age should be a time to follow Christ with more abandon than ever before. Why hold back and play it safe when the time is so short? Polycarp didn't. He knew the choice was not whether to die, but when—and that made him a free and courageous man. There really is a freedom in having little left to lose.

PRAY:

Consider Polycarp's prayer on the day of his death: "O Father of thy beloved and blessed Son, Jesus Christ, through whom we have come to know thee, the God of angels and powers and all creation, and of the whole family of the righteous who live in thy presence; I bless thee for counting me worthy of this day and hour, that in the number of the martyrs I may partake of Christ's cup, to the resurrection of eternal life of both soul and body in the imperishability that is the gift of the Holy Spirit."[4]

MEMORIZE:

They overcame him by the blood of the Lamb and by the word of their testimony; they did not love their lives so much as to shrink from death. REVELATION 12:11

FOR YOUR NEXT DEVOTIONAL READING, GO TO PAGE 615.

Psalms

THE PSALMS are easy to find in the Bible. Just put your finger somewhere near the middle of your Bible, open it there and you will probably find the book of Psalms. These are not quite the heart of Scripture—Jesus is—but they are all about what it means to have a relationship with him. The Psalms, a book of prayers, also make up the longest book in the Bible. That should tell us how important prayer is to a vital relationship with God.

The phrase "divine-human encounter" is a favorite among Bible scholars. It is another way of describing what the Psalms help us do: have a relationship with God; to meet with him like Moses did, as a friend would meet a friend, as a child would relate to a parent or as a husband and wife would communicate. God is amazingly concrete and personal in the Psalms, definitely not the "god" of some philosophers. He goes far beyond Alfred North Whitehead's "principle of concretion," Henry Nelson Wieman's "integrating factor in experience" or Paul Tillich's "ground of all being." These gods are for contemplation and discussion—not for communication and relationship. "The field of second-rate religion is strewn with the corpses of abstract nouns," wrote George Buttrick. The book of Psalms is no book of second-rate religion; it is a book of prayer. And it sets the stage for us to encounter God in the most intimate way, the way Jesus taught: to call him "Abba"—dear Father.

The Psalms are unique for another reason—whom we pray *with* as we pray them. When we pray them, we pray with God's people who have come before us, from ancient Israel to the modern church. We enter a mystical fellowship stretching back in time, known as the "communion of saints." We are never less alone than when we pray the Psalms. And, more wondrously, we pray *to* and *with* our Lord Jesus, who prayed them. The Psalms even anticipated his coming (see Luke 24:44). The same prayers and laments Jesus prayed, we may pray to him—the second being of the Trinity, the fulfillment of Israel's hope, who lives to intercede for us (see Hebrews 7:25).

THE LORD HAS HEARD MY CRY FOR MERCY; THE LORD ACCEPTS MY PRAYER. (6:9)

BOOK I

Psalms 1–41

Psalm 1

¹Blessed is the man
   who does not walk in the counsel
      of the wicked
   or stand in the way of sinners
      or sit in the seat of mockers.
²But his delight is in the law of the Lord,
   and on his law he meditates
      day and night.
³He is like a tree planted by streams
      of water,
which yields its fruit in season
   and whose leaf does not
      wither.
   Whatever he does prospers.

⁴Not so the wicked!
   They are like chaff
      that the wind blows away.
⁵Therefore the wicked will not stand
      in the judgment,
   nor sinners in the assembly of
      the righteous.

⁶For the Lord watches over the way
      of the righteous,
   but the way of the wicked will
      perish.

PSALM 1

[MONDAY]

The Blessed Life

1:3 HE IS LIKE A TREE PLANTED BY STREAMS OF WATER, WHICH YIELDS ITS FRUIT IN SEASON AND WHOSE LEAF DOES NOT WITHER.

"Life isn't a supermarket" is one way to paraphrase this psalm. Contrary to modern popular religious tastes, there aren't many varieties of truth, like the varieties of food in a supermarket. We like to customize faith, like mixing and matching items in a big store. There are many ways to be nourished spiritually, right?

Wrong. There are only two choices: One way leads to blessedness and life; the other way leads to death. One way plants you; the other uproots you. Both ways progress in opposite directions: The blessed way delights and meditates on God's law, and brings health and fruitfulness. The way of death descends from thinking to doing to promoting sin ("counsel of the wicked . . . way of sinners . . . seat of mockers"). Those who follow it end up rootless and dead.

There is only one way to have life, but the ways life shows itself are nearly endless, like the varieties of fruit in the world: raspberries, mangoes, kiwis, apples, bananas, papayas—the list would fill pages. There is a rich variety to the ways life expresses itself in the people who are planted in it. God is the author of life; he revels in originals. Look around at his creation. He is not a cookie-cutter God.

We are planted in life by delighting and meditating on God's truth in Scripture. Scriptural meditation is like a dialogue or conversation. We listen carefully to what God says and then talk to him about what we hear; by praise, confession, petition, questions, weeping, laughing, longing. Then we listen some more and say some more. Bible reading and prayer go together the way listening and speaking go together in good conversation. Both lead to delight in the dialogue.

PRAY:

*Father in heaven! Deepen my life in you as I deepen
my conversation with you through your word and prayer.*

FOR YOUR NEXT DEVOTIONAL READING, GO TO PAGE 619.

Psalm 2

[1] Why do the nations conspire[a]
and the peoples plot in vain?
[2] The kings of the earth take their
stand
and the rulers gather together
against the LORD
and against his Anointed One.[b]
[3] "Let us break their chains," they say,
"and throw off their fetters."

[4] The One enthroned in heaven laughs;
the Lord scoffs at them.
[5] Then he rebukes them in his anger
and terrifies them in his wrath,
saying,
[6] "I have installed my King[c]
on Zion, my holy hill."

[7] I will proclaim the decree of the LORD:

He said to me, "You are my Son[d];
today I have become your Father.[e]
[8] Ask of me,
and I will make the nations your
inheritance,
the ends of the earth your
possession.
[9] You will rule them with an iron
scepter[f];
you will dash them to pieces
like pottery."

[10] Therefore, you kings, be wise;
be warned, you rulers of the earth.
[11] Serve the LORD with fear
and rejoice with trembling.
[12] Kiss the Son, lest he be angry
and you be destroyed in your way,
for his wrath can flare up in a
moment.
Blessed are all who take refuge
in him.

Psalm 3

*A psalm of David. When he fled from
his son Absalom.*

[1] O LORD, how many are my foes!
How many rise up against me!
[2] Many are saying of me,
"God will not deliver him." *Selah*[g]

[3] But you are a shield around me,
O LORD;
you bestow glory on me and lift[h] up
my head.

[4] To the LORD I cry aloud,
and he answers me from his
holy hill. *Selah*

[5] I lie down and sleep;
I wake again, because the LORD
sustains me.
[6] I will not fear the tens of thousands
drawn up against me on every side.

[7] Arise, O LORD!
Deliver me, O my God!
Strike all my enemies on the jaw;
break the teeth of the wicked.

[8] From the LORD comes deliverance.
May your blessing be on your
people. *Selah*

Psalm 4

*For the director of music. With stringed
instruments. A psalm of David.*

[1] Answer me when I call to you,
O my righteous God.
Give me relief from my distress;
be merciful to me and hear my
prayer.

[2] How long, O men, will you turn
my glory into shame[i]?
How long will you love delusions
and seek false gods[j]? *Selah*
[3] Know that the LORD has set apart
the godly for himself;
the LORD will hear when I call
to him.

[4] In your anger do not sin;
when you are on your beds,
search your hearts and be
silent. *Selah*

> ANSWER *me when I call to you,*
> O my righteous God.
> Give me relief from my distress;
> be merciful to me and hear my prayer.
>
> PSALM 4:1

[a] *1* Hebrew; Septuagint *rage*   [b] *2* Or *anointed
one*   [c] *6* Or *king*   [d] *7* Or *son*; also in verse 12
[e] *7* Or *have begotten you*   [f] *9* Or *will break
them with a rod of iron*   [g] *2* A word of
uncertain meaning, occurring frequently in the
Psalms; possibly a musical term   [h] *3* Or LORD, /
my Glorious One, who lifts   [i] *2* Or *you dishonor
my Glorious One*   [j] *2* Or *seek lies*

⁵Offer right sacrifices
and trust in the LORD.

⁶Many are asking, "Who can show us
any good?"
Let the light of your face shine
upon us, O LORD.
⁷You have filled my heart with greater
joy
than when their grain and new
wine abound.
⁸I will lie down and sleep in peace,
for you alone, O LORD,
make me dwell in safety.

Psalm 5

For the director of music. For flutes.
A psalm of David.

¹Give ear to my words, O LORD,
consider my sighing.
²Listen to my cry for help,
my King and my God,
for to you I pray.
³In the morning, O LORD, you hear
my voice;
in the morning I lay my requests
before you
and wait in expectation.

> IN THE morning, O LORD, you hear
> my voice;
> in the morning I lay my requests
> before you
> and wait in expectation.
>
> PSALM 5:3

⁴You are not a God who takes
pleasure in evil;
with you the wicked cannot
dwell.
⁵The arrogant cannot stand in your
presence;
you hate all who do wrong.
⁶You destroy those who tell lies;
bloodthirsty and deceitful men
the LORD abhors.
⁷But I, by your great mercy,
will come into your house;
in reverence will I bow down
toward your holy temple.
⁸Lead me, O LORD, in your
righteousness

because of my enemies—
make straight your way before me.
⁹Not a word from their mouth can be
trusted;
their heart is filled with
destruction.
Their throat is an open grave;
with their tongue they speak
deceit.
¹⁰Declare them guilty, O God!
Let their intrigues be their
downfall.
Banish them for their many sins,
for they have rebelled against you.
¹¹But let all who take refuge in you be
glad;
let them ever sing for joy.
Spread your protection over them,
that those who love your name may
rejoice in you.
¹²For surely, O LORD, you bless the
righteous;
you surround them with your favor
as with a shield.

Psalm 6

For the director of music. With
stringed instruments. According to
sheminith.ᵃ A psalm of David.

¹O LORD, do not rebuke me in your
anger
or discipline me in your wrath.
²Be merciful to me, LORD, for I am
faint;
O LORD, heal me, for my bones
are in agony.
³My soul is in anguish.
How long, O LORD, how long?

⁴Turn, O LORD, and deliver me;
save me because of your unfailing
love.
⁵No one remembers you when he is
dead.
Who praises you from the graveᵇ?

⁶I am worn out from groaning;
all night long I flood my bed with
weeping
and drench my couch with tears.
⁷My eyes grow weak with sorrow;
they fail because of all my foes.

ᵃTitle: Probably a musical term   ᵇ5 Hebrew
Sheol

8 Away from me, all you who do
   evil,
   for the LORD has heard my
      weeping.
9 The LORD has heard my cry for mercy;
   the LORD accepts my prayer.
10 All my enemies will be ashamed and
      dismayed;
   they will turn back in sudden
      disgrace.

> THE LORD has heard my cry for mercy;
> the LORD accepts my prayer.
>
> PSALM 6:9

Psalm 7

A *shiggaion*[a] of David, which he sang
to the LORD concerning Cush,
a Benjamite.

1 O LORD my God, I take refuge in you;
   save and deliver me from all who
      pursue me,
2 or they will tear me like a lion
   and rip me to pieces with no one
      to rescue me.

3 O LORD my God, if I have done this
   and there is guilt on my hands—
4 if I have done evil to him who is at
      peace with me
   or without cause have robbed
      my foe—
5 then let my enemy pursue and
      overtake me;
   let him trample my life to the
      ground
   and make me sleep in the dust.
                                    Selah

6 Arise, O LORD, in your anger;
   rise up against the rage of my
      enemies.
   Awake, my God; decree justice.
7 Let the assembled peoples gather
      around you.
   Rule over them from on high;
8   let the LORD judge the peoples.
   Judge me, O LORD, according to my
      righteousness,
   according to my integrity,
      O Most High.
9 O righteous God,
   who searches minds and hearts,

bring to an end the violence of the
      wicked
   and make the righteous secure.
10 My shield[b] is God Most High,
   who saves the upright in heart.
11 God is a righteous judge,
   a God who expresses his wrath
      every day.
12 If he does not relent,
   he[c] will sharpen his sword;
   he will bend and string his bow.
13 He has prepared his deadly weapons;
   he makes ready his flaming arrows.

14 He who is pregnant with evil
   and conceives trouble gives birth to
      disillusionment.
15 He who digs a hole and scoops it out
   falls into the pit he has made.
16 The trouble he causes recoils on
      himself;
   his violence comes down on his
      own head.

17 I will give thanks to the LORD because
      of his righteousness
   and will sing praise to the name
      of the LORD Most High.

Psalm 8

For the director of music. According
to *gittith*.[d] A psalm of David.

1 O LORD, our Lord,
   how majestic is your name in
      all the earth!

   You have set your glory
      above the heavens.
2 From the lips of children and infants
      you have ordained praise[e]
   because of your enemies,
   to silence the foe and the avenger.

3 When I consider your heavens,
   the work of your fingers,
   the moon and the stars,
   which you have set in place,
4 what is man that you are mindful of
      him,
   the son of man that you care for
      him?

---

[a]Title: Probably a literary or musical term
[b]10 Or *sovereign*   [c]12 Or *If a man does not
repent, / God*   [d]Title: Probably a musical term
[e]2 Or *strength*

PSALM 8

What Does It Mean to Be a Human Being?

8:4 WHAT IS MAN THAT YOU ARE MINDFUL OF HIM?

How do you begin your work each day? Enthusiastically, like the seven dwarves in the Disney classic, *Snow White*? "Hi ho, hi ho, it's off to work we go!" Or resignedly, like the bumper sticker, "I owe, I owe, it's off to work I go"? Try this: Go to work with this psalm on your lips, and take with it a profound sense of wonder and gratitude for the place God has given you and your work in his creation.

Begin the way the psalmist begins. Consider first the majesty of God and the magnificence of his creation: "O LORD, our Lord, how majestic is your name in all the earth! You have set your glory above the heavens . . . When I consider your heavens . . . what is man that you are mindful of him?" (see 8:1–4). That question can be asked humbly and straightforwardly (see Psalm 144:3–4); or desperately, as a plea for mercy (see Job 7:17–18); or in astonishment, the way it is asked here. What can we be in a universe so large that its center is everywhere, its circumference nowhere? What can we be to a God so great that this massive universe is but the work of his fingers (see Psalm 8:3), his "needlepoint," so to speak?

What we are to God is "a little lower than the heavenly beings and crowned . . . with glory and honor" (Psalm 8:5). We are made in his image (see Genesis 1:26–31), and appointed as "ruler over the works of [his] hands" (Psalm 8:6).

That's where your work comes in. No matter how small and insignificant it may seem to you, if your work is worth doing at all, it is a piece of God's world to be cared for in his majestic name. That amounts to nothing less than glory and honor.

So frame your day's work in worship. Begin with praise—the way a child praises God (see Psalm 8:2), surrendering yourself simply and unquestioningly to his greatness. Affirm, with humble thankfulness, your place in God's great world (see Psalm 8:5–8). Then work as though you believed it were true, learning from Christ, who shows us how to work with gentleness and humility (see Matthew 11:25–30).

P R A Y :

Thank you for the work you have given me to do,
and for the dignity of working. Sustain me
in my work with a vision of the glory and honor
you give your servants in the world.

———

FOR YOUR NEXT DEVOTIONAL READING, GO TO PAGE 624.

5 You made him a little lower than
the heavenly beings[a]
and crowned him with glory
and honor.

6 You made him ruler over the works
of your hands;
you put everything under his feet:
7 all flocks and herds,
and the beasts of the field,
8 the birds of the air,
and the fish of the sea,
all that swim the paths of the
seas.

9 O LORD, our Lord,
how majestic is your name in all
the earth!

Psalm 9[b]

*For the director of music. To the tune of
"The Death of the Son." A psalm of David.*

1 I will praise you, O LORD, with all
my heart;
I will tell of all your wonders.
2 I will be glad and rejoice in you;
I will sing praise to your name,
O Most High.

3 My enemies turn back;
they stumble and perish
before you.
4 For you have upheld my right and
my cause;
you have sat on your throne,
judging righteously.
5 You have rebuked the nations and
destroyed the wicked;
you have blotted out their name for
ever and ever.
6 Endless ruin has overtaken the
enemy,
you have uprooted their cities;
even the memory of them has
perished.

7 The LORD reigns forever;
he has established his throne
for judgment.
8 He will judge the world in
righteousness;
he will govern the peoples with
justice.
9 The LORD is a refuge for the
oppressed,
a stronghold in times of trouble.

10 Those who know your name will trust
in you,
for you, LORD, have never forsaken
those who seek you.

11 Sing praises to the LORD, enthroned
in Zion;
proclaim among the nations what
he has done.
12 For he who avenges blood
remembers;
he does not ignore the cry of the
afflicted.

13 O LORD, see how my enemies
persecute me!
Have mercy and lift me up from the
gates of death,
14 that I may declare your praises
in the gates of the Daughter of
Zion
and there rejoice in your salvation.

15 The nations have fallen into the pit
they have dug;
their feet are caught in the net they
have hidden.
16 The LORD is known by his justice;
the wicked are ensnared by the
work of their hands.
Higgaion.[c] Selah

17 The wicked return to the grave,[d]
all the nations that forget God.
18 But the needy will not always be
forgotten,
nor the hope of the afflicted ever
perish.

19 Arise, O LORD, let not man triumph;
let the nations be judged in your
presence.
20 Strike them with terror, O LORD;
let the nations know they
are but men. *Selah*

Psalm 10[b]

1 Why, O LORD, do you stand far off?
Why do you hide yourself in times
of trouble?

---

*a5 Or than God bPsalms 9 and 10 may
have been originally a single acrostic poem,
the stanzas of which begin with the successive
letters of the Hebrew alphabet. In the
Septuagint they constitute one psalm.
c16 Or Meditation; possibly a musical notation
d17 Hebrew Sheol*

2 In his arrogance the wicked man
  hunts down the weak,
who are caught in the schemes he
  devises.
3 He boasts of the cravings of his heart;
  he blesses the greedy and reviles
  the LORD.
4 In his pride the wicked does not
  seek him;
in all his thoughts there is no room
  for God.
5 His ways are always prosperous;
  he is haughty and your laws are far
  from him;
  he sneers at all his enemies.
6 He says to himself, "Nothing will
  shake me;
I'll always be happy and never have
  trouble."
7 His mouth is full of curses and lies
  and threats;
  trouble and evil are under his
  tongue.
8 He lies in wait near the villages;
from ambush he murders the
  innocent,
  watching in secret for his victims.
9 He lies in wait like a lion in cover;
he lies in wait to catch the helpless;
he catches the helpless and drags
  them off in his net.
10 His victims are crushed, they collapse;
  they fall under his strength.
11 He says to himself, "God has
  forgotten;
  he covers his face and never sees."

12 Arise, LORD! Lift up your hand, O God.
  Do not forget the helpless.
13 Why does the wicked man revile God?
  Why does he say to himself,
  "He won't call me to account"?
14 But you, O God, do see trouble and
  grief;
  you consider it to take it in hand.
The victim commits himself to you;
  you are the helper of the fatherless.
15 Break the arm of the wicked and
  evil man;
  call him to account for his
  wickedness
  that would not be found out.

16 The LORD is King for ever and ever;
  the nations will perish from his
  land.

17 You hear, O LORD, the desire of the
  afflicted;
  you encourage them, and you
  listen to their cry,
18 defending the fatherless and the
  oppressed,
  in order that man, who is of the
  earth, may terrify no more.

> YOU hear, O LORD, the desire of the
> afflicted;
> you encourage them, and you
> listen to their cry
>
> PSALM 10:17

Psalm 11

For the director of music.
Of David.

1 In the LORD I take refuge.
  How then can you say to me:
  "Flee like a bird to your mountain.
2 For look, the wicked bend their
  bows;
they set their arrows against the
  strings
to shoot from the shadows
  at the upright in heart.
3 When the foundations are being
  destroyed,
  what can the righteous do*a*?"

4 The LORD is in his holy temple;
  the LORD is on his heavenly
  throne.
He observes the sons of men;
  his eyes examine them.
5 The LORD examines the righteous,
  but the wicked*b* and those who
  love violence
  his soul hates.
6 On the wicked he will rain
  fiery coals and burning sulfur;
  a scorching wind will be their
  lot.

7 For the LORD is righteous,
  he loves justice;
  upright men will see his face.

a 3 Or *what is the Righteous One doing*
b 5 Or *The LORD, the Righteous One, examines the
wicked, /*

Psalm 12

For the director of music.
According to *sheminith*.[a]
A psalm of David.

[1] Help, LORD, for the godly are no more;
the faithful have vanished from
among men.
[2] Everyone lies to his neighbor;
their flattering lips speak with
deception.

[3] May the LORD cut off all flattering lips
and every boastful tongue
[4] that says, "We will triumph with our
tongues;
we own our lips[b]—who is our
master?"

[5] "Because of the oppression of the
weak
and the groaning of the needy,
I will now arise," says the LORD.
"I will protect them from those who
malign them."
[6] And the words of the LORD are
flawless,
like silver refined in a furnace of
clay,
purified seven times.

[7] O LORD, you will keep us safe
and protect us from such people
forever.
[8] The wicked freely strut about
when what is vile is honored
among men.

Psalm 13

For the director of music.
A psalm of David.

[1] How long, O LORD? Will you forget
me forever?
How long will you hide your face
from me?
[2] How long must I wrestle with my
thoughts
and every day have sorrow in my
heart?
How long will my enemy triumph
over me?

[3] Look on me and answer, O LORD my
God.
Give light to my eyes, or I will sleep
in death;

[4] my enemy will say, "I have overcome
him,"
and my foes will rejoice when I fall.

[5] But I trust in your unfailing love;
my heart rejoices in your salvation.
[6] I will sing to the LORD,
for he has been good to me.

Psalm 14

For the director of music. Of David.

[1] The fool[c] says in his heart,
"There is no God."
They are corrupt, their deeds are vile;
there is no one who does good.

[2] The LORD looks down from heaven
on the sons of men
to see if there are any who
understand,
any who seek God.
[3] All have turned aside,
they have together become
corrupt;
there is no one who does good,
not even one.

[4] Will evildoers never learn—
those who devour my people as
men eat bread
and who do not call on the LORD?
[5] There they are, overwhelmed with
dread,
for God is present in the company
of the righteous.
[6] You evildoers frustrate the plans of
the poor,
but the LORD is their refuge.

[7] Oh, that salvation for Israel would
come out of Zion!
When the LORD restores the
fortunes of his people,
let Jacob rejoice and Israel be glad!

Psalm 15

A psalm of David.

[1] LORD, who may dwell in your
sanctuary?
Who may live on your holy hill?

---

*a*Title: Probably a musical term   *b*4 Or / *our lips
are our plowshares*   *c*1 The Hebrew words
rendered *fool* in Psalms denote one who is morally
deficient.

2 He whose walk is blameless
and who does what is righteous,
who speaks the truth from his heart
3 and has no slander on his tongue,
who does his neighbor no wrong
and casts no slur on his fellowman,
4 who despises a vile man
but honors those who fear the
Lord,
who keeps his oath
even when it hurts,
5 who lends his money without usury
and does not accept a bribe against
the innocent.

He who does these things
will never be shaken.

Psalm 16

A *miktam*[a] of David.

1 Keep me safe, O God,
for in you I take refuge.

2 I said to the Lord, "You are my Lord;
apart from you I have no good
thing."
3 As for the saints who are in the land,
they are the glorious ones in whom
is all my delight.[b]
4 The sorrows of those will increase
who run after other gods.
I will not pour out their libations of
blood
or take up their names on my lips.

5 Lord, you have assigned me my
portion and my cup;
you have made my lot secure.
6 The boundary lines have fallen for me
in pleasant places;
surely I have a delightful
inheritance.

7 I will praise the Lord, who counsels
me;
even at night my heart instructs
me.
8 I have set the Lord always before me.
Because he is at my right hand,
I will not be shaken.

9 Therefore my heart is glad and my
tongue rejoices;
my body also will rest secure,
10 because you will not abandon me to
the grave,[c]

nor will you let your Holy One[d]
see decay.
11 You have made[e] known to me the
path of life;
you will fill me with joy in your
presence,
with eternal pleasures at your
right hand.

Psalm 17

A prayer of David.

1 Hear, O Lord, my righteous plea;
listen to my cry.
Give ear to my prayer—
it does not rise from deceitful lips.
2 May my vindication come from you;
may your eyes see what is right.

3 Though you probe my heart and
examine me at night,
though you test me, you will find
nothing;
I have resolved that my mouth will
not sin.
4 As for the deeds of men—
by the word of your lips
I have kept myself
from the ways of the violent.
5 My steps have held to your paths;
my feet have not slipped.

6 I call on you, O God, for you will
answer me;
give ear to me and hear my prayer.
7 Show the wonder of your great love,
you who save by your right hand
those who take refuge in you from
their foes.
8 Keep me as the apple of your eye;
hide me in the shadow of your wings
9 from the wicked who assail me,
from my mortal enemies who
surround me.

> I CALL on you, O God, for you will
> answer me;
> give ear to me and hear my prayer.
>
> PSALM 17:6

[a] Title: Probably a literary or musical term
[b] 3 Or *As for the pagan priests who are in the land
/ and the nobles in whom all delight, I said:*
[c] 10 Hebrew *Sheol*   [d] 10 Or *your faithful one*
[e] 11 Or *You will make*

PSALM 16

The Pleasure of God's Company

16:11 YOU WILL FILL ME WITH JOY IN YOUR PRESENCE, WITH ETERNAL PLEASURES AT YOUR RIGHT HAND.

Jonathan Edwards, the leading preacher of early America's Great Awakening, thought of God the way David thought of God in this psalm. It was for "sweet delight in God" that Edwards gave himself to God. He writes:

"The first instance I remember of that sort of inward, sweet delight in God and in divine things, that I have lived much in since, was on reading these words, 1 Timothy 1:17: 'Now unto the King eternal, immortal, invisible, the only wise God, be honor and glory for ever and ever. Amen' [KJV]. As I read the words, there came into my soul, and was as it were, diffused through it, a sense of the glory of the Divine Being; a new sense, quite different from anything I ever experienced before. Never any words of Scripture seemed to me as these did. I thought with myself, *how excellent a Being that was, and how happy I should be, if I might enjoy that God*, and be rapt up to Him in Heaven, and be, as it were, swallowed up in Him forever" (italics added).[1]

Edwards's words are a variation on the theme of Psalm 16:11: "You have made known to me the path of life; you will fill me with joy in your presence, with eternal pleasures at your right hand."

A modern myth has it that the way to happiness and freedom is broad and filled with many choices. The more we can do when we want to do it, the freer and happier we think we will be. The Bible takes the opposite point of view. The way of joy is narrow and singular (see Matthew 7:13–14; see also the devotion on Psalm 1). It is like getting married: faithfulness to one partner for life radically narrows one kind of choice, but opens a universe of other glorious possibilities. Those who want to keep their options open are the ones who are trapped. This psalm is the prayer of a single-minded man who knows that apart from God he has no good thing (see 16:2). God has assigned him his portion and his cup (verse 5), and the psalmist has set the Lord always before him (verse 8). The pleasure of God's company is the only path of freedom and life.

PRAY:

Gracious God: You have made known to me
the path of life; you will fill me with joy
in your presence, with eternal pleasures at your
right hand. Praise your holy name!

FOR YOUR NEXT DEVOTIONAL READING, GO TO PAGE 628.

¹⁰ They close up their callous hearts,
and their mouths speak with
arrogance.
¹¹ They have tracked me down, they
now surround me,
with eyes alert, to throw me to
the ground.
¹² They are like a lion hungry for prey,
like a great lion crouching in cover.

¹³ Rise up, O LORD, confront them, bring
them down;
rescue me from the wicked by
your sword.
¹⁴ O LORD, by your hand save me from
such men,
from men of this world whose
reward is in this life.

You still the hunger of those you
cherish;
their sons have plenty,
and they store up wealth for their
children.
¹⁵ And I—in righteousness I will see
your face;
when I awake, I will be satisfied
with seeing your likeness.

Psalm 18

For the director of music. Of David
the servant of the LORD. He sang to
the LORD the words of this song
when the LORD delivered him from the
hand of all his enemies and from the
hand of Saul. He said:

¹ I love you, O LORD, my strength.

² The LORD is my rock, my fortress and
my deliverer;
my God is my rock, in whom I take
refuge.
He is my shield and the horn[a] of
my salvation, my stronghold.
³ I call to the LORD, who is worthy of
praise,
and I am saved from my enemies.

⁴ The cords of death entangled me;
the torrents of destruction
overwhelmed me.
⁵ The cords of the grave[b] coiled
around me;
the snares of death confronted me.
⁶ In my distress I called to the LORD;
I cried to my God for help.

> IN MY distress I called to the LORD;
> I cried to my God for help.
> From his temple he heard my voice;
> my cry came before him, into his ears.
>
> PSALM 18:6

From his temple he heard my voice;
my cry came before him, into his
ears.

⁷ The earth trembled and quaked,
and the foundations of the
mountains shook;
they trembled because he was
angry.
⁸ Smoke rose from his nostrils;
consuming fire came from his
mouth,
burning coals blazed out of it.
⁹ He parted the heavens and came
down;
dark clouds were under his feet.
¹⁰ He mounted the cherubim and flew;
he soared on the wings of the
wind.
¹¹ He made darkness his covering, his
canopy around him—
the dark rain clouds of the sky.
¹² Out of the brightness of his presence
clouds advanced,
with hailstones and bolts of
lightning.
¹³ The LORD thundered from heaven;
the voice of the Most High
resounded.[c]
¹⁴ He shot his arrows and scattered
ˌthe enemies„
great bolts of lightning and routed
them.
¹⁵ The valleys of the sea were exposed
and the foundations of the earth
laid bare
at your rebuke, O LORD,
at the blast of breath from your
nostrils.

¹⁶ He reached down from on high and
took hold of me;
he drew me out of deep waters.

---

[a]2 Horn here symbolizes strength.   [b]5 Hebrew
Sheol   [c]13 Some Hebrew manuscripts and
Septuagint (see also 2 Samuel 22:14); most
Hebrew manuscripts resounded, / amid hailstones
and bolts of lightning

17 He rescued me from my powerful
    enemy,
  from my foes, who were too strong
    for me.
18 They confronted me in the day of my
    disaster,
  but the LORD was my support.
19 He brought me out into a spacious
    place;
  he rescued me because he
    delighted in me.

20 The LORD has dealt with me according
    to my righteousness;
  according to the cleanness of my
    hands he has rewarded me.
21 For I have kept the ways of the LORD;
  I have not done evil by turning
    from my God.
22 All his laws are before me;
  I have not turned away from his
    decrees.
23 I have been blameless before him
  and have kept myself from sin.
24 The LORD has rewarded me according
    to my righteousness,
  according to the cleanness of my
    hands in his sight.

25 To the faithful you show yourself
    faithful,
  to the blameless you show yourself
    blameless,
26 to the pure you show yourself pure,
  but to the crooked you show
    yourself shrewd.
27 You save the humble
  but bring low those whose eyes
    are haughty.
28 You, O LORD, keep my lamp burning;
  my God turns my darkness into
    light.
29 With your help I can advance against
    a troop[a];
  with my God I can scale a wall.

30 As for God, his way is perfect;
  the word of the LORD is flawless.
He is a shield
  for all who take refuge in him.
31 For who is God besides the LORD?
  And who is the Rock except our
    God?
32 It is God who arms me with
    strength
  and makes my way perfect.

33 He makes my feet like the feet of a
    deer;
  he enables me to stand on the
    heights.
34 He trains my hands for battle;
  my arms can bend a bow of
    bronze.
35 You give me your shield of victory,
  and your right hand sustains me;
  you stoop down to make me great.
36 You broaden the path beneath me,
  so that my ankles do not turn.

37 I pursued my enemies and overtook
    them;
  I did not turn back till they were
    destroyed.
38 I crushed them so that they could not
    rise;
  they fell beneath my feet.
39 You armed me with strength for
    battle;
  you made my adversaries bow at
    my feet.
40 You made my enemies turn their
    backs in flight,
  and I destroyed my foes.
41 They cried for help, but there was no
    one to save them—
  to the LORD, but he did not answer.
42 I beat them as fine as dust borne on
    the wind;
  I poured them out like mud in the
    streets.

43 You have delivered me from the
    attacks of the people;
  you have made me the head of
    nations;
  people I did not know are subject
    to me.
44 As soon as they hear me, they
    obey me;
  foreigners cringe before me.
45 They all lose heart;
  they come trembling from their
    strongholds.

46 The LORD lives! Praise be to my Rock!
  Exalted be God my Savior!
47 He is the God who avenges me,
  who subdues nations under me,
48   who saves me from my enemies.
You exalted me above my foes;
  from violent men you rescued me.

[a] 29 Or *can run through a barricade*

⁴⁹ Therefore I will praise you among the
nations, O LORD;
I will sing praises to your name.
⁵⁰ He gives his king great victories;
he shows unfailing kindness to his
anointed,
to David and his descendants
forever.

Psalm 19

For the director of music. A psalm of David.

¹ The heavens declare the glory of God;
the skies proclaim the work of his
hands.
² Day after day they pour forth speech;
night after night they display
knowledge.
³ There is no speech or language
where their voice is not heard.ᵃ
⁴ Their voiceᵇ goes out into all the
earth,
their words to the ends of the
world.

In the heavens he has pitched a tent
for the sun,
⁵ which is like a bridegroom coming
forth from his pavilion,
like a champion rejoicing to run his
course.
⁶ It rises at one end of the heavens
and makes its circuit to the other;
nothing is hidden from its heat.

⁷ The law of the LORD is perfect,
reviving the soul.
The statutes of the LORD are
trustworthy,
making wise the simple.
⁸ The precepts of the LORD are right,
giving joy to the heart.
The commands of the LORD are
radiant,
giving light to the eyes.
⁹ The fear of the LORD is pure,
enduring forever.
The ordinances of the LORD are sure
and altogether righteous.
¹⁰ They are more precious than gold,
than much pure gold;
they are sweeter than honey,
than honey from the comb.
¹¹ By them is your servant warned;
in keeping them there is great
reward.

¹² Who can discern his errors?
Forgive my hidden faults.
¹³ Keep your servant also from willful
sins;
may they not rule over me.
Then will I be blameless,
innocent of great transgression.

¹⁴ May the words of my mouth and the
meditation of my heart
be pleasing in your sight,
O LORD, my Rock and my
Redeemer.

Psalm 20

For the director of music.
A psalm of David.

¹ May the LORD answer you when you
are in distress;
may the name of the God of Jacob
protect you.
² May he send you help from the
sanctuary
and grant you support from Zion.
³ May he remember all your sacrifices
and accept your burnt offerings.
Selah
⁴ May he give you the desire of your
heart
and make all your plans succeed.
⁵ We will shout for joy when you are
victorious
and will lift up our banners in the
name of our God.
May the LORD grant all your requests.

⁶ Now I know that the LORD saves his
anointed;
he answers him from his holy
heaven
with the saving power of his right
hand.

WE WILL shout for joy when you are
victorious
and will lift up our banners in the
name of our God.
May the LORD grant all your requests.

PSALM 20:5

ᵃ 3 Or *They have no speech, there are no words; /
no sound is heard from them*   ᵇ 4 Septuagint,
Jerome and Syriac; Hebrew *line*

PSALM 19

The Glory and Power of God's Revelation

19:1,7 THE HEAVENS DECLARE THE GLORY OF GOD ... THE LAW OF THE LORD IS PERFECT.

In all of the Bible, there is no greater celebration of God's revelation than this psalm. What does David think of when he looks at the sun and the other stars? He sees them as evidence of the glorious reality and revelation of God (see verses 1–6). Then David proceeds to rejoice in God's revealed law (see verses 7–11). Poet Gerard Manley Hopkins wrote, "The world is charged with the grandeur of God. It will flame out like shining light from shook foil." David might add, "It will flame out like light from the Scriptures, too." The medieval church thought Galileo a heretic when he asserted that God had two books, the creation and the Bible. But David was a "heretic" thousands of years before when he praised the God who speaks both in the skies and in the Scriptures.

Do you consider the Bible difficult to read? Dry? Uninteresting? Don't worry, you're in good company. Martin Luther said, "Sometimes there has been more in a line of Scripture than I could bear to stand under. Other times, the Bible has been to me as dry as a stick." You shouldn't worry, but you shouldn't be blasé, either. Remember, the Bible is a critical part of the dialogue we call prayer, the chief part of God's side of the conversation.

There are some things you can do to help your understanding and enjoyment of God's Word. Practice the lesser-known spiritual discipline of imaginative association; connect in your imagination the wonder and beauty you see in a night sky with the contents of this book. Look at the Milky Way, and think, "The Bible reveals that God is like that—vast and awesome and glorious." Also ask yourself, "Do I really expect or want to meet God when I read the Bible?" "It's not what I don't understand in the Bible that worries me," wrote Mark Twain. "It's what I do understand." Maybe your apathy toward the Bible is a smokescreen to hide your fear of exposure (note verses 12–13). Finally, ask yourself, "How would I act if I believed there is treasure hidden in the Bible?" If you had in your hands a map showing where you could find great material treasure, wouldn't you apply yourself diligently to crack any code or language, and overcome any mountain, weather or foe, to find the treasure? What is to be found in Scripture is "more precious than gold, than much pure gold" (verse 10).

PRAY:

Father in heaven! Open my eyes to see wonderful
things in your creation and in your Word; and
open my mouth to sing your praise.

FOR YOUR NEXT DEVOTIONAL READING, GO TO PAGE 631.

⁷Some trust in chariots and some in
 horses,
 but we trust in the name of the
 LORD our God.
⁸They are brought to their knees and
 fall,
 but we rise up and stand firm.

⁹O LORD, save the king!
 Answer*ᵃ* us when we call!

Psalm 21

For the director of music.
A psalm of David.

¹O LORD, the king rejoices in your
 strength.
 How great is his joy in the victories
 you give!
²You have granted him the desire of
 his heart
 and have not withheld the request
 of his lips.   *Selah*
³You welcomed him with rich
 blessings
 and placed a crown of pure gold on
 his head.
⁴He asked you for life, and you gave it
 to him—
 length of days, for ever and ever.
⁵Through the victories you gave, his
 glory is great;
 you have bestowed on him
 splendor and majesty.
⁶Surely you have granted him eternal
 blessings
 and made him glad with the joy of
 your presence.
⁷For the king trusts in the LORD;
 through the unfailing love of the
 Most High
 he will not be shaken.

⁸Your hand will lay hold on all your
 enemies;
 your right hand will seize your foes.
⁹At the time of your appearing
 you will make them like a fiery
 furnace.
 In his wrath the LORD will swallow
 them up,
 and his fire will consume them.
¹⁰You will destroy their descendants
 from the earth,
 their posterity from mankind.
¹¹Though they plot evil against you

and devise wicked schemes, they
 cannot succeed;
¹²for you will make them turn their
 backs
 when you aim at them with drawn
 bow.

¹³Be exalted, O LORD, in your strength;
 we will sing and praise your might.

Psalm 22

For the director of music.
To ˌthe tune ofˌ "The Doe of the Morning."
A psalm of David.

¹My God, my God, why have you
 forsaken me?
 Why are you so far from saving me,
 so far from the words of my
 groaning?
²O my God, I cry out by day, but you
 do not answer,
 by night, and am not silent.

³Yet you are enthroned as the Holy
 One;
 you are the praise of Israel.*ᵇ*
⁴In you our fathers put their trust;
 they trusted and you delivered
 them.
⁵They cried to you and were saved;
 in you they trusted and were not
 disappointed.

⁶But I am a worm and not a man,
 scorned by men and despised by
 the people.
⁷All who see me mock me;
 they hurl insults, shaking their
 heads:
⁸"He trusts in the LORD;
 let the LORD rescue him.
 Let him deliver him,
 since he delights in him."

⁹Yet you brought me out of the womb;
 you made me trust in you
 even at my mother's breast.
¹⁰From birth I was cast upon you;
 from my mother's womb you have
 been my God.
¹¹Do not be far from me,
 for trouble is near
 and there is no one to help.

ᵃ9 Or *save! / O King, answer*   *ᵇ3* Or *Yet you are
holy, / enthroned on the praises of Israel*

¹²Many bulls surround me;
    strong bulls of Bashan encircle me.
¹³Roaring lions tearing their prey
    open their mouths wide against
        me.
¹⁴I am poured out like water,
    and all my bones are out of joint.
My heart has turned to wax;
    it has melted away within me.
¹⁵My strength is dried up like a
        potsherd,
    and my tongue sticks to the roof
        of my mouth;
    you lay me*ᵃ* in the dust of death.
¹⁶Dogs have surrounded me;
    a band of evil men has encircled me,
    they have pierced*ᵇ* my hands and
        my feet.
¹⁷I can count all my bones;
    people stare and gloat over me.
¹⁸They divide my garments among
        them
    and cast lots for my clothing.

¹⁹But you, O LORD, be not far off;
    O my Strength, come quickly to
        help me.
²⁰Deliver my life from the sword,
    my precious life from the power
        of the dogs.
²¹Rescue me from the mouth of
        the lions;
    save*ᶜ* me from the horns of the
        wild oxen.

²²I will declare your name to my
        brothers;
    in the congregation I will praise
        you.
²³You who fear the LORD, praise him!
    All you descendants of Jacob,
        honor him!
    Revere him, all you descendants
        of Israel!
²⁴For he has not despised or disdained
    the suffering of the afflicted one;
he has not hidden his face from him
    but has listened to his cry for help.

²⁵From you comes the theme of my
        praise in the great assembly;
    before those who fear you*ᵈ* will I
        fulfill my vows.
²⁶The poor will eat and be satisfied;
    they who seek the LORD will praise
        him—
    may your hearts live forever!

²⁷All the ends of the earth
    will remember and turn to the
        LORD,
and all the families of the nations
    will bow down before him,
²⁸for dominion belongs to the LORD
    and he rules over the nations.

²⁹All the rich of the earth will feast and
        worship;
    all who go down to the dust will
        kneel before him—
    those who cannot keep themselves
        alive.
³⁰Posterity will serve him;
    future generations will be told
        about the Lord.
³¹They will proclaim his righteousness
    to a people yet unborn—
    for he has done it.

Psalm 23

A psalm of David.

¹The LORD is my shepherd, I shall
        not be in want.
²   He makes me lie down in green
        pastures,
    he leads me beside quiet waters,
³   he restores my soul.
He guides me in paths of
        righteousness
    for his name's sake.
⁴Even though I walk
    through the valley of the shadow
        of death,*ᵉ*
I will fear no evil,
    for you are with me;
your rod and your staff,
    they comfort me.

⁵You prepare a table before me
    in the presence of my enemies.
You anoint my head with oil;
    my cup overflows.
⁶Surely goodness and love will follow
        me
    all the days of my life,
and I will dwell in the house of the
        LORD
    forever.

ᵃ15 Or */I am laid*   *ᵇ16* Some Hebrew
manuscripts, Septuagint and Syriac; most Hebrew
manuscripts */like the lion,*   *ᶜ21* Or */ you have
heard*   *ᵈ25* Hebrew *him*   *ᵉ4* Or *through the
darkest valley*

PSALM 23

The Good Shepherd

23:1 THE LORD IS MY SHEPHERD.

The idea of God being a shepherd to his people is not unique to this psalm. The picture appears many other places (see Psalms 28:9; 79:13; 80:1; 95:7; 100:3). The analogy was also widely used in the ancient Near East, as well in the Bible, as a metaphor for a king. It worked well. Most people knew what shepherds did to protect and care for their flocks.

What makes this psalm so special is how personal it is. For God to be a shepherd to his flock or his people, the nation of Israel, is one thing; but for God to be David's personal shepherd is something else, something quite wonderful. Read this psalm aloud, and take in the staggering message that God makes *you* lie down in green pastures, leads *you* beside quiet waters and restores *your* soul. If God is not really this kind of shepherd toward each of us personally, then to pray this psalm is to engage in an act of almost criminal narcissism. But Jesus assured us that God knows even the number of hairs on our heads (see Matthew 10:29–31), and that Jesus himself is our good shepherd, who even laid down his life for us (see John 10:11–15). Let these truths sink in as you pray this psalm. There is great joy in the comfort it brings.

There is also a great awe as we read this psalm. An astronomer, who was also a Christian, had lectured at a university on the immensity of the universe. During the question and answer session that followed, a student who was not a believer asked the astronomer a provocative question: "How can a God big enough to manage the cosmos you just described possibly be involved in the personal lives of his followers—as you believe he is?" The scientist answered quietly, "The God I believe in is bigger than you think." God's love and wisdom are immeasurable, both in the extent he goes into space, and the depth he enters into our hearts. A truly big God can do both.

PRAY:

Savior, like a shepherd lead us,
Much we need Thy tender care;
In thy pleasant pastures feed us,
For our use Thy folds prepare:
Blessed Jesus, blessed Jesus,
Thou hast bought us, Thine we are;
Blessed Jesus, blessed Jesus,
Thou hast bought us, Thine we are.
ATTRIBUTED TO DOROTHY A. THRUPP

FOR YOUR NEXT DEVOTIONAL READING, GO TO PAGE 632.

Just as I Am

IT WAS a bad time for Dr. Malan to ask Charlotte the question. In pain and emotionally depressed, she didn't want to be asked if she felt the peace of God in spite of her circumstances. So she ended the conversation abruptly. A debilitating sickness had afflicted her in her 30's and had left her in pain and frequently bedridden until the end of her life. She had been ill-tempered and melancholy ever since.

But Dr. Malan's question pricked her conscience. She had been raised in a Christian home—her grandfather was the famous preacher Henry Venn, and her father and brothers were also ministers. But she knew little of Christ's peace. She sought Malan out. "I am miserable," she admitted to him. "I want to be saved; I want to come to Jesus, but I don't know how." Malan's reply was destined to affect millions. He said, "Come to him just as you are."[2]

Charlotte Elliot's health didn't improve, but from that moment on she lived in the peace of Christ, "a man of sorrows, and familiar with suffering" (Isaiah 53:3). Homebound, Elliot wrote hymns to be sung in church, penning nearly 150 before her death on September 22, 1871.

One day Elliot was feeling especially sick. Again she wondered despairingly how she could serve God as an invalid. Feeling dejected and useless, she began to write. The words flowed out of her, echoing the words of Dr. Malan years before:

> Just as I am, without one plea
> But that Thy blood was shed for me,
> And that Thou bidd'st me come to Thee,
> O Lamb of God, I come! I come!

Elliot sent the hymn anonymously to a Christian publication and forgot about it. Years later, one of her doctors handed her a poem inside a tract, hoping it would console her. Inside, Elliot was amazed to find her own poem! "Just as I Am" had become so popular that it had circulated across England and found its way back to her bedside.

"Just as I Am" continued to touch lives across the world. After her death, more than 1000 letters were found among Elliot's belongings, thanking her for writing the hymn. Years later, in 1934, a skeptical young man attended a revival meeting in South Carolina. As the choir sang "Just as I Am," he made his way forward and gave his life to Christ. The young man's name was Billy Graham. Only heaven knows how many millions of lost and dejected souls have been found to the tune of that hymn as it has been sung at Billy Graham evangelistic meetings around the world.

PRAY:

Just as I am—though tossed about
With many a conflict, many a doubt
Fightings and fears within, without—
O Lamb of God, I come, I come
Just as I am—Thou wilt receive,
Wilt welcome, pardon, cleanse, relieve,
Because Thy promise I believe—
O Lamb of God, I come, I come.

MEMORIZE:

But he said to me, "My grace is sufficient for you, for my
power is made perfect in weakness." Therefore I will boast
all the more gladly about my weaknesses, so that
Christ's power may rest on me   2 CORINTHIANS 12:9

FOR YOUR NEXT DEVOTIONAL READING, GO TO PAGE 636.

Psalm 24

Of David. A psalm.

¹ The earth is the LORD's, and
everything in it,
the world, and all who live in it;
² for he founded it upon the seas
and established it upon the waters.

³ Who may ascend the hill of the LORD?
Who may stand in his holy place?
⁴ He who has clean hands and a pure
heart,
who does not lift up his soul to an
idol
or swear by what is false.ᵃ
⁵ He will receive blessing from the
LORD
and vindication from God his
Savior.
⁶ Such is the generation of those who
seek him,
who seek your face, O God of
Jacob.ᵇ   *Selah*

⁷ Lift up your heads, O you gates;
be lifted up, you ancient doors,
that the King of glory may
come in.
⁸ Who is this King of glory?
The LORD strong and mighty,
the LORD mighty in battle.
⁹ Lift up your heads, O you gates;
lift them up, you ancient doors,
that the King of glory may
come in.
¹⁰ Who is he, this King of glory?
The LORD Almighty—
he is the King of glory.   *Selah*

Psalm 25ᶜ

Of David.

¹ To you, O LORD, I lift up my soul;
²   in you I trust, O my God.
Do not let me be put to shame,
nor let my enemies triumph
over me.
³ No one whose hope is in you
will ever be put to shame,
but they will be put to shame
who are treacherous without
excuse.

⁴ Show me your ways, O LORD,
teach me your paths;

⁵ guide me in your truth and teach me,
for you are God my Savior,
and my hope is in you all day
long.
⁶ Remember, O LORD, your great mercy
and love,
for they are from of old.
⁷ Remember not the sins of my youth
and my rebellious ways;
according to your love remember me,
for you are good, O LORD.

⁸ Good and upright is the LORD;
therefore he instructs sinners in
his ways.
⁹ He guides the humble in what is right
and teaches them his way.
¹⁰ All the ways of the LORD are loving
and faithful
for those who keep the demands
of his covenant.
¹¹ For the sake of your name, O LORD,
forgive my iniquity, though it is
great.
¹² Who, then, is the man that fears
the LORD?
He will instruct him in the way
chosen for him.
¹³ He will spend his days in prosperity,
and his descendants will inherit
the land.
¹⁴ The LORD confides in those who
fear him;
he makes his covenant known to
them.
¹⁵ My eyes are ever on the LORD,
for only he will release my feet from
the snare.

¹⁶ Turn to me and be gracious to me,
for I am lonely and afflicted.
¹⁷ The troubles of my heart have
multiplied;
free me from my anguish.
¹⁸ Look upon my affliction and my
distress
and take away all my sins.
¹⁹ See how my enemies have
increased
and how fiercely they hate me!

ᵃ4 Or *swear falsely*   ᵇ6 Two Hebrew
manuscripts and Syriac (see also Septuagint);
most Hebrew manuscripts *face, Jacob*   ᶜThis
psalm is an acrostic poem, the verses of which
begin with the successive letters of the Hebrew
alphabet.

20 Guard my life and rescue me;
  let me not be put to shame,
  for I take refuge in you.
21 May integrity and uprightness
    protect me,
  because my hope is in you.

22 Redeem Israel, O God,
  from all their troubles!

Psalm 26

Of David.

1 Vindicate me, O LORD,
  for I have led a blameless life;
  I have trusted in the LORD
  without wavering.
2 Test me, O LORD, and try me,
  examine my heart and my mind;
3 for your love is ever before me,
  and I walk continually in your
    truth.
4 I do not sit with deceitful men,
  nor do I consort with hypocrites;
5 I abhor the assembly of evildoers
  and refuse to sit with the wicked.
6 I wash my hands in innocence,
  and go about your altar, O LORD,
7 proclaiming aloud your praise
  and telling of all your wonderful
    deeds.
8 I love the house where you live,
  O LORD,
  the place where your glory dwells.

9 Do not take away my soul along with
    sinners,
  my life with bloodthirsty men,
10 in whose hands are wicked schemes,
  whose right hands are full of
    bribes.
11 But I lead a blameless life;
  redeem me and be merciful to me.

12 My feet stand on level ground;
  in the great assembly I will praise
  the LORD.

Psalm 27

Of David.

1 The LORD is my light and my
    salvation—
  whom shall I fear?
The LORD is the stronghold of my
    life—
  of whom shall I be afraid?

2 When evil men advance against me
  to devour my flesh,[a]
  when my enemies and my foes
    attack me,
  they will stumble and fall.
3 Though an army besiege me,
  my heart will not fear;
  though war break out against me,
  even then will I be confident.

4 One thing I ask of the LORD,
  this is what I seek:
  that I may dwell in the house of the
    LORD
  all the days of my life,
  to gaze upon the beauty of the LORD
  and to seek him in his temple.
5 For in the day of trouble
  he will keep me safe in his
    dwelling;
  he will hide me in the shelter of his
    tabernacle
  and set me high upon a rock.
6 Then my head will be exalted
  above the enemies who surround
    me;
  at his tabernacle will I sacrifice with
    shouts of joy;
  I will sing and make music to the
    LORD.

7 Hear my voice when I call, O LORD;
  be merciful to me and answer me.
8 My heart says of you, "Seek his[b]
    face!"
  Your face, LORD, I will seek.
9 Do not hide your face from me,
  do not turn your servant away in
    anger;
  you have been my helper.
Do not reject me or forsake me,
  O God my Savior.
10 Though my father and mother
    forsake me,
  the LORD will receive me.
11 Teach me your way, O LORD;
  lead me in a straight path
  because of my oppressors.
12 Do not turn me over to the desire of
    my foes,
  for false witnesses rise up against
    me,
  breathing out violence.

a 2 Or to slander me   b 8 Or To you, O my heart,
he has said, "Seek my

¹³ I am still confident of this:
    I will see the goodness of the LORD
    in the land of the living.
¹⁴ Wait for the LORD;
    be strong and take heart
    and wait for the LORD.

Psalm 28

Of David.

¹ To you I call, O LORD my Rock;
    do not turn a deaf ear to me.

For if you remain silent,
    I will be like those who have gone
      down to the pit.
² Hear my cry for mercy
    as I call to you for help,
    as I lift up my hands
    toward your Most Holy Place.

³ Do not drag me away with the wicked,
    with those who do evil,
who speak cordially with their
    neighbors
    but harbor malice in their hearts.

[MONDAY]

PSALM 27

Safety in God's Presence

27:4 ONE THING I ASK OF THE LORD, THIS IS WHAT I SEEK: THAT I MAY DWELL IN THE HOUSE OF THE LORD ALL THE DAYS OF MY LIFE.

What do you need most when your enemies surround you? A safe place to escape to, a fortress, a hiding place. This is what David yearns for: "One thing I ask of the LORD, this is what I seek: that I may dwell in the house of the LORD all the days of my life, to gaze upon the beauty of the LORD and to seek him in his temple" (27:4).

But it would be a serious misreading of this prayer to conclude that David wanted to exchange public life for the life of a priest. David knew that no one was allowed to live in the temple (or tabernacle); what he wanted was to enjoy daily and forever what the temple stood for—the presence of God. God's house is the whole world (see Psalm 36:8); what David wanted was the pleasure and protection of unbroken communion with God. That was what entering a human house stood for in the ancient Near East: It was a place of fellowship and safety. So strong was this concept that if even your mortal enemy was able to enter your house, you were bound to protect that person!

It's not where you are, but whom you're with, that makes all the difference. Threats, fear and worry cannot touch you in God's presence. Not even disaster and death can separate you from his love (see Romans 8:31–39). The endless distractions and demands of life are unified and ordered in God's presence. The one thing needed (see Luke 10:38–42) is "to gaze upon the beauty of the LORD and to seek him in his temple." What David prays for is the breakdown of the wall between the sacred and the secular. So must we. There are no compartments, no inside and outside to God. He sees our thoughts and motives as clearly as he sees our actions. "The earth is the LORD's, and everything in it" (Psalm 24:1). If this is true, then everything we do is done in his temple and falls under the heading "sacred."

PRAY:

Lord, one thing I ask of you, this is what I seek: that where I work and where
I study, where I think and where I eat, in my car and in my home—
that I may dwell in your presence, gaze upon your beauty and seek you.

FOR YOUR NEXT DEVOTIONAL READING, GO TO PAGE 643.

4 Repay them for their deeds
and for their evil work;
repay them for what their hands have
done
and bring back upon them what
they deserve.
5 Since they show no regard for the
works of the LORD
and what his hands have done,
he will tear them down
and never build them up again.

6 Praise be to the LORD,
for he has heard my cry for mercy.
7 The LORD is my strength and my
shield;
my heart trusts in him, and I am
helped.
My heart leaps for joy
and I will give thanks to him
in song.

8 The LORD is the strength of his
people,
a fortress of salvation for his
anointed one.
9 Save your people and bless your
inheritance;
be their shepherd and carry them
forever.

Psalm 29

A psalm of David.

1 Ascribe to the LORD, O mighty ones,
ascribe to the LORD glory and
strength.
2 Ascribe to the LORD the glory due
his name;
worship the LORD in the splendor
of his*a* holiness.

3 The voice of the LORD is over the
waters;
the God of glory thunders,
the LORD thunders over the mighty
waters.
4 The voice of the LORD is powerful;
the voice of the LORD is majestic.
5 The voice of the LORD breaks the
cedars;
the LORD breaks in pieces the
cedars of Lebanon.
6 He makes Lebanon skip like a calf,
Sirion*b* like a young wild ox.
7 The voice of the LORD strikes
with flashes of lightning.

8 The voice of the LORD shakes the
desert;
the LORD shakes the Desert of
Kadesh.
9 The voice of the LORD twists the
oaks*c*
and strips the forests bare.
And in his temple all cry, "Glory!"
10 The LORD sits*d* enthroned over the
flood;
the LORD is enthroned as King
forever.
11 The LORD gives strength to his people;
the LORD blesses his people with
peace.

Psalm 30

*A psalm. A song. For the dedication
of the temple.*e* Of David.*

1 I will exalt you, O LORD,
for you lifted me out of the depths
and did not let my enemies gloat
over me.
2 O LORD my God, I called to you for help
and you healed me.
3 O LORD, you brought me up from the
grave*f*;
you spared me from going down
into the pit.
4 Sing to the LORD, you saints of his;
praise his holy name.
5 For his anger lasts only a moment,
but his favor lasts a lifetime;
weeping may remain for a night,
but rejoicing comes in the
morning.

> *O LORD my God, I called to you for help
> and you healed me.*
>
> PSALM 30:2

6 When I felt secure, I said,
"I will never be shaken."
7 O LORD, when you favored me,
you made my mountain*g* stand firm;
but when you hid your face,
I was dismayed.

*a2 Or LORD with the splendor of   b6 That is,
Mount Hermon   c9 Or LORD makes the deer
give birth   d10 Or sat   eTitle: Or palace
f3 Hebrew Sheol   g7 Or hill country*

8 To you, O LORD, I called;
    to the Lord I cried for mercy:
9 "What gain is there in my
        destruction,[a]
    in my going down into the pit?
    Will the dust praise you?
    Will it proclaim your faithfulness?
10 Hear, O LORD, and be merciful to me;
    O LORD, be my help."

11 You turned my wailing into dancing;
    you removed my sackcloth and
        clothed me with joy,
12 that my heart may sing to you and
        not be silent.
    O LORD my God, I will give you
        thanks forever.

Psalm 31

For the director of music.
A psalm of David.

1 In you, O LORD, I have taken refuge;
    let me never be put to shame;
    deliver me in your righteousness.
2 Turn your ear to me,
    come quickly to my rescue;
    be my rock of refuge,
    a strong fortress to save me.
3 Since you are my rock and my
        fortress,
    for the sake of your name lead
        and guide me.
4 Free me from the trap that is set
        for me,
    for you are my refuge.
5 Into your hands I commit my spirit;
    redeem me, O LORD, the God of
        truth.

6 I hate those who cling to worthless
        idols;
    I trust in the LORD.
7 I will be glad and rejoice in your love,
    for you saw my affliction
    and knew the anguish of my soul.
8 You have not handed me over to
        the enemy
    but have set my feet in a spacious
        place.

9 Be merciful to me, O LORD, for I am
        in distress;
    my eyes grow weak with sorrow,
    my soul and my body with grief.
10 My life is consumed by anguish
    and my years by groaning;

my strength fails because of my
        affliction,[b]
    and my bones grow weak.
11 Because of all my enemies,
    I am the utter contempt of my
        neighbors;
    I am a dread to my friends—
    those who see me on the street flee
        from me.
12 I am forgotten by them as though
        I were dead;
    I have become like broken pottery.
13 For I hear the slander of many;
    there is terror on every side;
    they conspire against me
    and plot to take my life.

14 But I trust in you, O LORD;
    I say, "You are my God."
15 My times are in your hands;
    deliver me from my enemies
    and from those who pursue me.
16 Let your face shine on your
        servant;
    save me in your unfailing love.
17 Let me not be put to shame,
        O LORD,
    for I have cried out to you;
    but let the wicked be put to shame
    and lie silent in the grave.[c]
18 Let their lying lips be silenced,
    for with pride and contempt
    they speak arrogantly against
        the righteous.

19 How great is your goodness,
    which you have stored up for those
        who fear you,
    which you bestow in the sight of men
    on those who take refuge in you.
20 In the shelter of your presence you
        hide them
    from the intrigues of men;
    in your dwelling you keep them safe
    from accusing tongues.

21 Praise be to the LORD,
    for he showed his wonderful love
        to me
    when I was in a besieged city.
22 In my alarm I said,
    "I am cut off from your sight!"
    Yet you heard my cry for mercy
    when I called to you for help.

---

[a]9 Or *there if I am silenced*   [b]10 Or *guilt*
[c]17 Hebrew *Sheol*

²³ Love the Lord, all his saints!
  The Lord preserves the faithful,
    but the proud he pays back in full.
²⁴ Be strong and take heart,
  all you who hope in the Lord.

> ❝ Prayer begins where human capacity ends. ❞
>
> MARIAN ANDERSON

Psalm 32

Of David. A *maskil*.[a]

¹ Blessed is he
  whose transgressions are forgiven,
  whose sins are covered.
² Blessed is the man
  whose sin the Lord does not count
    against him
  and in whose spirit is no deceit.

³ When I kept silent,
  my bones wasted away
    through my groaning all day long.
⁴ For day and night
  your hand was heavy upon me;
  my strength was sapped
    as in the heat of summer.   *Selah*
⁵ Then I acknowledged my sin to you
  and did not cover up my iniquity.
  I said, "I will confess
  my transgressions to the Lord"—
  and you forgave
    the guilt of my sin.   *Selah*

⁶ Therefore let everyone who is godly
    pray to you
  while you may be found;
  surely when the mighty waters rise,
    they will not reach him.
⁷ You are my hiding place;
  you will protect me from trouble
  and surround me with songs of
    deliverance.   *Selah*

⁸ I will instruct you and teach you in
    the way you should go;
  I will counsel you and watch over
    you.
⁹ Do not be like the horse or the mule,
  which have no understanding
  but must be controlled by bit and
    bridle
  or they will not come to you.

¹⁰ Many are the woes of the wicked,
  but the Lord's unfailing love
  surrounds the man who trusts in
    him.
¹¹ Rejoice in the Lord and be glad, you
    righteous;
  sing, all you who are upright in
    heart!

Psalm 33

¹ Sing joyfully to the Lord, you
    righteous;
  it is fitting for the upright to
    praise him.
² Praise the Lord with the harp;
  make music to him on the
    ten-stringed lyre.
³ Sing to him a new song;
  play skillfully, and shout for joy.

⁴ For the word of the Lord is right
    and true;
  he is faithful in all he does.
⁵ The Lord loves righteousness and
    justice;
  the earth is full of his unfailing
    love.

⁶ By the word of the Lord were the
    heavens made,
  their starry host by the breath
    of his mouth.
⁷ He gathers the waters of the sea
    into jars[b];
  he puts the deep into storehouses.
⁸ Let all the earth fear the Lord;
  let all the people of the world
    revere him.
⁹ For he spoke, and it came to be;
  he commanded, and it stood firm.
¹⁰ The Lord foils the plans of the
    nations;
  he thwarts the purposes of the
    peoples.
¹¹ But the plans of the Lord stand
    firm forever,
  the purposes of his heart through
    all generations.

¹² Blessed is the nation whose God is
    the Lord,
  the people he chose for his
    inheritance.

---

[a] Title: Probably a literary or musical term
[b] 7 Or *sea as into a heap*

13 From heaven the Lord looks down
and sees all mankind;
14 from his dwelling place he watches
all who live on earth—
15 he who forms the hearts of all,
who considers everything they do.
16 No king is saved by the size of his
army;
no warrior escapes by his great
strength.
17 A horse is a vain hope for
deliverance;
despite all its great strength it
cannot save.
18 But the eyes of the Lord are on those
who fear him,
on those whose hope is in his
unfailing love,
19 to deliver them from death
and keep them alive in famine.

20 We wait in hope for the Lord;
he is our help and our shield.
21 In him our hearts rejoice,
for we trust in his holy name.
22 May your unfailing love rest upon us,
O Lord,
even as we put our hope in you.

Psalm 34[a]

Of David. When he pretended
to be insane before Abimelech,
who drove him away, and he left.

1 I will extol the Lord at all times;
his praise will always be on my lips.
2 My soul will boast in the Lord;
let the afflicted hear and rejoice.
3 Glorify the Lord with me;
let us exalt his name together.

4 I sought the Lord, and he answered
me;
he delivered me from all my fears.
5 Those who look to him are radiant;
their faces are never covered with
shame.
6 This poor man called, and the Lord
heard him;
he saved him out of all his troubles.

> I SOUGHT the Lord, and he answered me;
> he delivered me from all my fears.
>
> PSALM 34:4

7 The angel of the Lord encamps
around those who fear him,
and he delivers them.

8 Taste and see that the Lord is good;
blessed is the man who takes
refuge in him.
9 Fear the Lord, you his saints,
for those who fear him lack
nothing.
10 The lions may grow weak and
hungry,
but those who seek the Lord lack
no good thing.

11 Come, my children, listen to me;
I will teach you the fear of the Lord.
12 Whoever of you loves life
and desires to see many good days,
13 keep your tongue from evil
and your lips from speaking lies.
14 Turn from evil and do good;
seek peace and pursue it.

15 The eyes of the Lord are on the
righteous
and his ears are attentive to
their cry;
16 the face of the Lord is against those
who do evil,
to cut off the memory of them from
the earth.

17 The righteous cry out, and the Lord
hears them;
he delivers them from all their
troubles.
18 The Lord is close to the
brokenhearted
and saves those who are crushed
in spirit.

19 A righteous man may have many
troubles,
but the Lord delivers him from
them all;
20 he protects all his bones,
not one of them will be broken.

21 Evil will slay the wicked;
the foes of the righteous will be
condemned.
22 The Lord redeems his servants;
no one will be condemned who
takes refuge in him.

[a] This psalm is an acrostic poem, the verses of
which begin with the successive letters of the
Hebrew alphabet.

Psalm 35

Of David.

¹ Contend, O LORD, with those who
   contend with me;
   fight against those who fight
   against me.
² Take up shield and buckler;
   arise and come to my aid.
³ Brandish spear and javelin[a]
   against those who pursue me.
   Say to my soul,
   "I am your salvation."

⁴ May those who seek my life
   be disgraced and put to shame;
   may those who plot my ruin
   be turned back in dismay.
⁵ May they be like chaff before the
   wind,
   with the angel of the LORD driving
   them away;
⁶ may their path be dark and slippery,
   with the angel of the LORD pursuing
   them.
⁷ Since they hid their net for me
   without cause
   and without cause dug a pit
   for me,
⁸ may ruin overtake them by
   surprise—
   may the net they hid entangle
   them,
   may they fall into the pit, to
   their ruin.
⁹ Then my soul will rejoice in the LORD
   and delight in his salvation.
¹⁰ My whole being will exclaim,
   "Who is like you, O LORD?
   You rescue the poor from those too
   strong for them,
   the poor and needy from those
   who rob them."

¹¹ Ruthless witnesses come forward;
   they question me on things I know
   nothing about.
¹² They repay me evil for good
   and leave my soul forlorn.
¹³ Yet when they were ill, I put on
   sackcloth
   and humbled myself with fasting.
   When my prayers returned to me
   unanswered,
¹⁴   I went about mourning
   as though for my friend or brother.

   I bowed my head in grief
   as though weeping for my mother.
¹⁵ But when I stumbled, they gathered
   in glee;
   attackers gathered against me
   when I was unaware.
   They slandered me without
   ceasing.
¹⁶ Like the ungodly they maliciously
   mocked[b];
   they gnashed their teeth at me.
¹⁷ O Lord, how long will you look on?
   Rescue my life from their ravages,
   my precious life from these lions.
¹⁸ I will give you thanks in the great
   assembly;
   among throngs of people I will
   praise you.

¹⁹ Let not those gloat over me
   who are my enemies without
   cause;
   let not those who hate me without
   reason
   maliciously wink the eye.
²⁰ They do not speak peaceably,
   but devise false accusations
   against those who live quietly in
   the land.
²¹ They gape at me and say, "Aha! Aha!
   With our own eyes we have
   seen it."

²² O LORD, you have seen this; be not
   silent.
   Do not be far from me, O Lord.
²³ Awake, and rise to my defense!
   Contend for me, my God and Lord.
²⁴ Vindicate me in your righteousness,
   O LORD my God;
   do not let them gloat over me.
²⁵ Do not let them think, "Aha, just
   what we wanted!"
   or say, "We have swallowed him
   up."

²⁶ May all who gloat over my distress
   be put to shame and confusion;
   may all who exalt themselves over me
   be clothed with shame and
   disgrace.
²⁷ May those who delight in my
   vindication
   shout for joy and gladness;

---

a 3 Or *and block the way*   *b 16* Septuagint;
Hebrew may mean *ungodly circle of mockers.*

may they always say, "The LORD be
exalted,
  who delights in the well-being of
his servant."
28 My tongue will speak of your
righteousness
  and of your praises all day long.

Psalm 36

For the director of music.
Of David the servant of the LORD.

1 An oracle is within my heart
  concerning the sinfulness of the
wicked:*a*
There is no fear of God
  before his eyes.
2 For in his own eyes he flatters himself
  too much to detect or hate his sin.
3 The words of his mouth are wicked
  and deceitful;
  he has ceased to be wise and to do
good.
4 Even on his bed he plots evil;
  he commits himself to a sinful
course
  and does not reject what is wrong.

5 Your love, O LORD, reaches to the
heavens,
  your faithfulness to the skies.
6 Your righteousness is like the mighty
mountains,
  your justice like the great deep.
O LORD, you preserve both man
  and beast.
7   How priceless is your unfailing
love!
Both high and low among men
  find*b* refuge in the shadow of
your wings.
8 They feast on the abundance of
your house;
  you give them drink from your river
of delights.
9 For with you is the fountain of life;
  in your light we see light.

10 Continue your love to those who
know you,
  your righteousness to the upright
in heart.
11 May the foot of the proud not come
against me,
  nor the hand of the wicked drive
me away.

12 See how the evildoers lie fallen—
  thrown down, not able to rise!

Psalm 37*c*

Of David.

1 Do not fret because of evil men
  or be envious of those who do
wrong;
2 for like the grass they will soon
wither,
  like green plants they will soon die
away.

3 Trust in the LORD and do good;
  dwell in the land and enjoy safe
pasture.
4 Delight yourself in the LORD
  and he will give you the desires of
your heart.

5 Commit your way to the LORD;
  trust in him and he will do this:
6 He will make your righteousness
shine like the dawn,
  the justice of your cause like the
noonday sun.

7 Be still before the LORD and wait
patiently for him;
  do not fret when men succeed in
their ways,
  when they carry out their wicked
schemes.

8 Refrain from anger and turn from
wrath;
  do not fret—it leads only to evil.
9 For evil men will be cut off,
  but those who hope in the LORD will
inherit the land.

10 A little while, and the wicked will be
no more;
  though you look for them, they will
not be found.
11 But the meek will inherit the land
  and enjoy great peace.

12 The wicked plot against the righteous
  and gnash their teeth at them;
13 but the Lord laughs at the wicked,
  for he knows their day is coming.

a 1 Or *heart: / Sin proceeds from the wicked.*
b 7 Or *love, O God! / Men find*; or *love! / Both
heavenly beings and men / find*   *c*This psalm is
an acrostic poem, the stanzas of which begin with
the successive letters of the Hebrew alphabet.

PSALM 36

The Inexhaustible God

36:5 YOUR LOVE, O LORD, REACHES TO THE HEAVENS.

Go outside, look up to the heavens and stretch your imagination: In August of 1989 the unmanned spacecraft, Voyager 2, flew over the polar ice cap of the planet Neptune, 2.8 billion miles away from Earth, on the edge of our solar system. It transmitted astonishing photographs of a strange and stormy world, a planet covered by a thick haze of helium and hydrogen, with 1,500 mile-per-hour winds pushing great frozen clouds of methane across its surface. In its southern hemisphere Voyager 2 discovered a tremendous storm system, a continuing counter-cyclone that is as big across as the earth. Traveling at speeds in excess of 60,000 miles per hour, it took Voyager 2 twelve years just to get to the outer rim of our solar system. Long after it has ceased to send signals back to Earth, it will still be traveling through space. In the year 40,176 it will likely pass within 1.7 light years of the star Ross 248, and in the year 296,036 it will perhaps come within 4.3 light years of the star Sirius!

Now read verse 5: "Your love, O LORD, reaches to the heavens, your faithfulness to the skies." God's love is there; it reaches that far and farther; it is that unsearchable. You could perform other such exercises of the imagination to get your mind around this text: His righteousness is as unshakable as the Himalayas (see verse 6a); his justice is as profound as the Pacific Ocean (see verse 6b). But you get the idea.

God's love and justice are that big, and this small and intimate: "O LORD, you preserve both man and beast. How priceless is your unfailing love! Both high and low among men find refuge in the shadow of your wings. They feast on the abundance of your house; you give them drink from your river of delights. For with you is the fountain of life; in your light we see light" (verses 6–9). Like a gracious host, the inexhaustible God stands at the door and welcomes us into the bounty of his house. He bids us drink from his delightful river and gives us his light, truth, life and wisdom to appreciate and enjoy his world—and the world to come (see Revelation 22:1–2). Be thankful and rejoice!

P R A Y :

"We pray, give us such an awareness of your mercies,
that our hearts may be sincerely thankful,
and that we may show forth your praise
not only with our lips, but in our lives."

FROM THE BOOK OF COMMON PRAYER

FOR YOUR NEXT DEVOTIONAL READING, GO TO PAGE 647.

¹⁴ The wicked draw the sword
    and bend the bow
to bring down the poor and needy,
    to slay those whose ways are
        upright.
¹⁵ But their swords will pierce their
    own hearts,
    and their bows will be broken.

¹⁶ Better the little that the righteous have
    than the wealth of many wicked;
¹⁷ for the power of the wicked will be
    broken,
    but the LORD upholds the righteous.

¹⁸ The days of the blameless are known
    to the LORD,
    and their inheritance will endure
        forever.
¹⁹ In times of disaster they will not
    wither;
    in days of famine they will enjoy
        plenty.

²⁰ But the wicked will perish:
    The LORD's enemies will be like the
        beauty of the fields,
    they will vanish—vanish like
        smoke.

²¹ The wicked borrow and do not repay,
    but the righteous give generously;
²² those the LORD blesses will inherit
    the land,
    but those he curses will be cut off.

²³ If the LORD delights in a man's way,
    he makes his steps firm;
²⁴ though he stumble, he will not fall,
    for the LORD upholds him with his
        hand.

²⁵ I was young and now I am old,
    yet I have never seen the righteous
        forsaken
    or their children begging bread.
²⁶ They are always generous and lend
    freely;
    their children will be blessed.

²⁷ Turn from evil and do good;
    then you will dwell in the land
        forever.
²⁸ For the LORD loves the just
    and will not forsake his faithful ones.

They will be protected forever,
    but the offspring of the wicked will
        be cut off;

²⁹ the righteous will inherit the land
    and dwell in it forever.

³⁰ The mouth of the righteous man
    utters wisdom,
    and his tongue speaks what is just.
³¹ The law of his God is in his heart;
    his feet do not slip.

³² The wicked lie in wait for the
    righteous,
    seeking their very lives;
³³ but the LORD will not leave them in
    their power
    or let them be condemned when
        brought to trial.

³⁴ Wait for the LORD
    and keep his way.
He will exalt you to inherit the land;
    when the wicked are cut off, you
        will see it.

³⁵ I have seen a wicked and ruthless
    man
    flourishing like a green tree in its
        native soil,
³⁶ but he soon passed away and was no
    more;
    though I looked for him, he could
        not be found.

³⁷ Consider the blameless, observe the
    upright;
    there is a futureᵃ for the man of
        peace.
³⁸ But all sinners will be destroyed;
    the futureᵇ of the wicked will be cut
        off.

³⁹ The salvation of the righteous comes
    from the LORD;
    he is their stronghold in time of
        trouble.
⁴⁰ The LORD helps them and delivers
    them;
    he delivers them from the wicked
    and saves them,
    because they take refuge in him.

Psalm 38

A psalm of David. A petition.

¹ O LORD, do not rebuke me in your
    anger
    or discipline me in your wrath.

ᵃ37 Or there will be posterity   ᵇ38 Or posterity

² For your arrows have pierced me,
and your hand has come down
upon me.
³ Because of your wrath there is no
health in my body;
my bones have no soundness
because of my sin.
⁴ My guilt has overwhelmed me
like a burden too heavy to bear.

⁵ My wounds fester and are loathsome
because of my sinful folly.
⁶ I am bowed down and brought very
low;
all day long I go about mourning.
⁷ My back is filled with searing pain;
there is no health in my body.
⁸ I am feeble and utterly crushed;
I groan in anguish of heart.

⁹ All my longings lie open before you,
O Lord;
my sighing is not hidden from you.
¹⁰ My heart pounds, my strength fails
me;
even the light has gone from my
eyes.
¹¹ My friends and companions avoid me
because of my wounds;
my neighbors stay far away.
¹² Those who seek my life set their
traps,
those who would harm me talk of
my ruin;
all day long they plot deception.

¹³ I am like a deaf man, who cannot
hear,
like a mute, who cannot open his
mouth;
¹⁴ I have become like a man who does
not hear,
whose mouth can offer no reply.
¹⁵ I wait for you, O LORD;
you will answer, O Lord my God.
¹⁶ For I said, "Do not let them gloat
or exalt themselves over me when
my foot slips."

¹⁷ For I am about to fall,
and my pain is ever with me.
¹⁸ I confess my iniquity;
I am troubled by my sin.
¹⁹ Many are those who are my vigorous
enemies;
those who hate me without reason
are numerous.

²⁰ Those who repay my good with evil
slander me when I pursue what is
good.

²¹ O LORD, do not forsake me;
be not far from me, O my God.
²² Come quickly to help me,
O Lord my Savior.

Psalm 39

For the director of music. For Jeduthun.
A psalm of David.

¹ I said, "I will watch my ways
and keep my tongue from sin;
I will put a muzzle on my mouth
as long as the wicked are in my
presence."
² But when I was silent and still,
not even saying anything good,
my anguish increased.
³ My heart grew hot within me,
and as I meditated, the fire burned;
then I spoke with my tongue:

⁴ "Show me, O LORD, my life's end
and the number of my days;
let me know how fleeting is my life.
⁵ You have made my days a mere
handbreadth;
the span of my years is as nothing
before you.
Each man's life is but a breath.
                                    Selah
⁶ Man is a mere phantom as he goes to
and fro:
He bustles about, but only in vain;
he heaps up wealth, not knowing
who will get it.

⁷ "But now, Lord, what do I look for?
My hope is in you.
⁸ Save me from all my transgressions;
do not make me the scorn of fools.
⁹ I was silent; I would not open my
mouth,
for you are the one who has done
this.
¹⁰ Remove your scourge from me;
I am overcome by the blow of
your hand.
¹¹ You rebuke and discipline men for
their sin;
you consume their wealth like
a moth—
each man is but a breath.   *Selah*

12 "Hear my prayer, O LORD,
   listen to my cry for help;
   be not deaf to my weeping.
For I dwell with you as an alien,
   a stranger, as all my fathers were.
13 Look away from me, that I may
      rejoice again
   before I depart and am no more."

> "HEAR my prayer, O LORD,
>   listen to my cry for help."
>
> PSALM 39:12

Psalm 40

For the director of music.
Of David. A psalm.

1 I waited patiently for the LORD;
   he turned to me and heard my cry.
2 He lifted me out of the slimy pit,
   out of the mud and mire;
   he set my feet on a rock
      and gave me a firm place to stand.
3 He put a new song in my mouth,
   a hymn of praise to our God.
Many will see and fear
   and put their trust in the LORD.

4 Blessed is the man
   who makes the LORD his trust,
who does not look to the proud,
   to those who turn aside to false
      gods.[a]
5 Many, O LORD my God,
   are the wonders you have done.
The things you planned for us
   no one can recount to you;
were I to speak and tell of them,
   they would be too many to declare.

6 Sacrifice and offering you did not
      desire,
   but my ears you have pierced[b,c];
burnt offerings and sin offerings
   you did not require.
7 Then I said, "Here I am, I have
      come—
   it is written about me in the scroll.[d]
8 I desire to do your will, O my God;
   your law is within my heart."

9 I proclaim righteousness in the great
      assembly;
   I do not seal my lips,
   as you know, O LORD.

10 I do not hide your righteousness in
      my heart;
   I speak of your faithfulness and
      salvation.
I do not conceal your love and your
      truth
   from the great assembly.
11 Do not withhold your mercy from me,
      O LORD;
   may your love and your truth
      always protect me.
12 For troubles without number
      surround me;
   my sins have overtaken me, and I
      cannot see.
They are more than the hairs of my
      head,
   and my heart fails within me.

13 Be pleased, O LORD, to save me;
   O LORD, come quickly to help me.
14 May all who seek to take my life
   be put to shame and confusion;
may all who desire my ruin
   be turned back in disgrace.
15 May those who say to me, "Aha! Aha!"
   be appalled at their own shame.
16 But may all who seek you
   rejoice and be glad in you;
may those who love your salvation
      always say,
   "The LORD be exalted!"

17 Yet I am poor and needy;
   may the Lord think of me.
You are my help and my deliverer;
   O my God, do not delay.

Psalm 41

For the director of music.
A psalm of David.

1 Blessed is he who has regard for the
      weak;
   the LORD delivers him in times of
      trouble.
2 The LORD will protect him and
      preserve his life;
   he will bless him in the land
   and not surrender him to the desire
      of his foes.

---

[a]4 Or *to falsehood*   [b]6 Hebrew; Septuagint *but
a body you have prepared for me* (see also
Symmachus and Theodotion)   [c]6 Or *opened*
[d]7 Or *come / with the scroll written for me*

Saved to Serve

40:8 I DESIRE TO DO YOUR WILL, O MY GOD.

In his great hymn, "When I Survey the Wondrous Cross," Isaac Watts wrote an excellent paraphrase of the first eight verses of this psalm: "Love so amazing, so divine, demands my soul, my life, my all." The flow of the hymn matches the flow of the psalm. A great love has saved a great sinner; the only appropriate response is a great offering—one's very self in love and gratitude. Watts' hymn and David's psalm should be read as the spiritual autobiography of every Christian.

David was in a terrible mess before God acted on his behalf. He was stuck in a "slimy pit," but God lifted him "out of the mud and mire" and set his "feet on a rock" (40:2). David must declare God's goodness, but how? Offering praise with his lips is one way (see verse 3). But the most fitting declaration is his whole life offered as a sacrifice. David's description of this sacrifice is striking. Mere ritual sacrifices are not what God wants; David knows that full well, having seen the emptiness of his predecessor Saul's superficial observance (see 1 Samuel 15:22–23). So he, David, will be the sacrifice—a living sacrifice! "Sacrifice and offering you did not desire, but my ears you have pierced" (Psalm 40:6).

The Hebrew word for pierced is literally "dug." Translators wrangle over whether the "digging" spoken of here refers to the practice of piercing a slave's ear when he offers himself to his master for life (see Exodus 21:6), or whether it means simply "opened" as in ears opened to hear and obey God's Word (see Isaiah 50:4–5). Both options paint a picture of the response fitting a total salvation and anticipate the perfect sacrifice made by Christ for our salvation (see Hebrews 10:5–10).

Having made of his life a living sacrifice, God's Word takes on new meaning for David. Now he can say, "Here I am, I have come—it is written about me in the scroll. I desire to do your will, O my God; your law is within my heart" (Psalm 40:7–8). The scroll is the Word of God, and David sees it no longer as a collection of abstract rules, but as his Savior's loving will, written to him and about him. In fact, God's will is even written on his heart!

David's story is your story if you name Christ as your Savior. Pray that your response will be as appropriate as David's was (see Romans 12:1–2).

PRAY:
Here I am, Lord, I am yours.
I desire to do your will, O my God;
your law is within my heart.

FOR YOUR NEXT DEVOTIONAL READING, GO TO PAGE 649.

³The LORD will sustain him on his
    sickbed
    and restore him from his bed of
      illness.

⁴I said, "O LORD, have mercy on me;
    heal me, for I have sinned against
      you."
⁵My enemies say of me in malice,
    "When will he die and his name
      perish?"
⁶Whenever one comes to see me,
    he speaks falsely, while his heart
      gathers slander;
    then he goes out and spreads it
      abroad.

⁷All my enemies whisper together
    against me;
    they imagine the worst for me,
      saying,
⁸"A vile disease has beset him;
    he will never get up from the place
      where he lies."
⁹Even my close friend, whom I trusted,
    he who shared my bread,
    has lifted up his heel against me.

¹⁰But you, O LORD, have mercy on me;
    raise me up, that I may repay them.
¹¹I know that you are pleased with me,
    for my enemy does not triumph
      over me.
¹²In my integrity you uphold me
    and set me in your presence forever.

¹³Praise be to the LORD, the God of
    Israel,
    from everlasting to everlasting.
      Amen and Amen.

BOOK II

Psalms 42–72

Psalm 42ᵃ

For the director of music.
A *maskil*ᵇ of the Sons of Korah.

¹As the deer pants for streams of
    water,
    so my soul pants for you, O God.
²My soul thirsts for God, for the
    living God.
    When can I go and meet with God?
³My tears have been my food
    day and night,

while men say to me all day long,
    "Where is your God?"
⁴These things I remember
    as I pour out my soul:
how I used to go with the multitude,
    leading the procession to the house
      of God,
with shouts of joy and thanksgiving
    among the festive throng.

⁵Why are you downcast, O my soul?
    Why so disturbed within me?
Put your hope in God,
    for I will yet praise him,
    my Savior and ⁶my God.

Myᶜ soul is downcast within me;
    therefore I will remember you
from the land of the Jordan,
    the heights of Hermon—from
      Mount Mizar.
⁷Deep calls to deep
    in the roar of your waterfalls;
all your waves and breakers
    have swept over me.

⁸By day the LORD directs his love,
    at night his song is with me—
    a prayer to the God of my life.

⁹I say to God my Rock,
    "Why have you forgotten me?
Why must I go about mourning,
    oppressed by the enemy?"
¹⁰My bones suffer mortal agony
    as my foes taunt me,
saying to me all day long,
    "Where is your God?"

¹¹Why are you downcast, O my soul?
    Why so disturbed within me?
Put your hope in God,
    for I will yet praise him,
    my Savior and my God.

Psalm 43ᵃ

¹Vindicate me, O God,
    and plead my cause against an
      ungodly nation;
    rescue me from deceitful and
      wicked men.

ᵃIn many Hebrew manuscripts Psalms 42 and 43
constitute one psalm.   ᵇTitle: Probably a
literary or musical term   ᶜ5,6 A few Hebrew
manuscripts, Septuagint and Syriac; most Hebrew
manuscripts *praise him for his saving help.* /
⁶O my God, my

² You are God my stronghold.
    Why have you rejected me?
Why must I go about mourning,
    oppressed by the enemy?
³ Send forth your light and your
        truth,
    let them guide me;

let them bring me to your holy
        mountain,
    to the place where you dwell.
⁴ Then will I go to the altar of God,
    to God, my joy and my delight.
I will praise you with the harp,
    O God, my God.

[THURSDAY]

PSALMS 42–43

Prayer and Depression

42:5–6 PUT YOUR HOPE IN GOD, FOR I WILL YET PRAISE HIM, MY SAVIOR AND MY GOD.

Not all depressions are the same. Some are circumstantial, the result of loss or disappointment or fatigue; some are clinical and more complex. But whatever their nature or source, their symptoms are very similar: the numbing dread that the darkness and grief are impenetrable and immovable; the lie that what is passing is really eternal. These two psalms give some very helpful clues as to how to deal with depression.

The first is to talk to God about your depression. That is what these psalms are: addresses to God about how the psalmist feels. You can be brutally honest—the psalmist certainly is: "I say to God my Rock, 'Why have you forgotten me? Why must I go about mourning, oppressed by the enemy?' My bones suffer mortal agony as my foes taunt me, saying to me all day long, 'Where is your God?'" (42:9–10). It's always better to talk to God about how you feel about God than to talk to others about how you feel about God. The most destructive aspect of any depression is the sense of abandonment by God. So talk to him about that! Prayer can turn the chasm into a bridge.

Talk to yourself about your depression too. Three times the psalmist says, "Why are you downcast, O my soul? Why so disturbed within me? Put your hope in God, for I will yet praise him, my Savior and my God" (42:5,11; 43:5). Feelings can be like unruly children; and, like unruly children, they must not be allowed to have the last word. Let them sound off, but also let them know about what is true. It may seem a little strange at first to talk to yourself this way, but the power of depression is schizoid; it splits you off from what is true. It takes a piece of the picture and makes it the whole picture. Talk back to yourself and affirm the truth and your intent: "I will yet praise him, my Savior and my God." Let your faith speak to your faith.

Remind yourself what your deepest need is, whether you are depressed or not: God. Depression can be a reminder that we are not whole without God, no matter how well we may feel.

PRAY:

By day, O Lord, you direct your love toward me, at night your
song is with me—a prayer to the God of my life (see 42:8).
Why are you downcast, O my soul? Put your hope in God,
for I will yet praise him, my Savior and my God.

FOR YOUR NEXT DEVOTIONAL READING, GO TO PAGE 652.

⁵Why are you downcast, O my soul?
Why so disturbed within me?
Put your hope in God,
for I will yet praise him,
my Savior and my God.

Psalm 44

For the director of music. Of the Sons
of Korah. A *maskil.*ᵃ

¹We have heard with our ears, O God;
our fathers have told us
what you did in their days,
in days long ago.
²With your hand you drove out the
nations
and planted our fathers;
you crushed the peoples
and made our fathers flourish.
³It was not by their sword that they
won the land,
nor did their arm bring them
victory;
it was your right hand, your arm,
and the light of your face, for you
loved them.

⁴You are my King and my God,
who decreesᵇ victories for Jacob.
⁵Through you we push back our
enemies;
through your name we trample
our foes.
⁶I do not trust in my bow,
my sword does not bring me
victory;
⁷but you give us victory over our
enemies,
you put our adversaries to shame.
⁸In God we make our boast all day
long,
and we will praise your name
forever.   *Selah*

⁹But now you have rejected and
humbled us;
you no longer go out with our
armies.
¹⁰You made us retreat before the
enemy,
and our adversaries have
plundered us.
¹¹You gave us up to be devoured like
sheep
and have scattered us among the
nations.

¹²You sold your people for a pittance,
gaining nothing from their sale.
¹³You have made us a reproach to our
neighbors,
the scorn and derision of those
around us.
¹⁴You have made us a byword among
the nations;
the peoples shake their heads at
us.
¹⁵My disgrace is before me all day long,
and my face is covered with shame
¹⁶at the taunts of those who reproach
and revile me,
because of the enemy, who is bent
on revenge.

¹⁷All this happened to us,
though we had not forgotten you
or been false to your covenant.
¹⁸Our hearts had not turned back;
our feet had not strayed from
your path.
¹⁹But you crushed us and made us a
haunt for jackals
and covered us over with deep
darkness.

²⁰If we had forgotten the name of our
God
or spread out our hands to a
foreign god,
²¹would not God have discovered it,
since he knows the secrets of the
heart?
²²Yet for your sake we face death all
day long;
we are considered as sheep to be
slaughtered.

²³Awake, O Lord! Why do you sleep?
Rouse yourself! Do not reject us
forever.
²⁴Why do you hide your face
and forget our misery and
oppression?
²⁵We are brought down to the
dust;
our bodies cling to the ground.
²⁶Rise up and help us;
redeem us because of your
unfailing love.

ᵃTitle: Probably a literary or musical term
ᵇ4 Septuagint, Aquila and Syriac; Hebrew *King,
O God; / command*

Psalm 45

For the director of music. To the tune of
"Lilies." Of the Sons of Korah. A *maskil.*[a]
A wedding song.

[1] My heart is stirred by a noble theme
as I recite my verses for the king;
my tongue is the pen of a skillful
writer.

[2] You are the most excellent of men
and your lips have been anointed
with grace,
since God has blessed you forever.
[3] Gird your sword upon your side,
O mighty one;
clothe yourself with splendor and
majesty.
[4] In your majesty ride forth victoriously
in behalf of truth, humility and
righteousness;
let your right hand display
awesome deeds.
[5] Let your sharp arrows pierce the
hearts of the king's enemies;
let the nations fall beneath your
feet.
[6] Your throne, O God, will last for ever
and ever;
a scepter of justice will be the
scepter of your kingdom.
[7] You love righteousness and hate
wickedness;
therefore God, your God, has set
you above your companions
by anointing you with the oil of joy.
[8] All your robes are fragrant with
myrrh and aloes and cassia;
from palaces adorned with ivory
the music of the strings makes
you glad.
[9] Daughters of kings are among your
honored women;
at your right hand is the royal bride
in gold of Ophir.

[10] Listen, O daughter, consider and
give ear:
Forget your people and your
father's house.
[11] The king is enthralled by your
beauty;
honor him, for he is your lord.
[12] The Daughter of Tyre will come with
a gift,[b]
men of wealth will seek your favor.

[13] All glorious is the princess within
her chamber;
her gown is interwoven with gold.
[14] In embroidered garments she is led
to the king;
her virgin companions follow her
and are brought to you.
[15] They are led in with joy and
gladness;
they enter the palace of the king.

[16] Your sons will take the place of
your fathers;
you will make them princes
throughout the land.
[17] I will perpetuate your memory
through all generations;
therefore the nations will praise
you for ever and ever.

Psalm 46

For the director of music.
Of the Sons of Korah. According
to *alamoth.*[c] A song.

[1] God is our refuge and strength,
an ever-present help in trouble.
[2] Therefore we will not fear, though
the earth give way
and the mountains fall into the
heart of the sea,
[3] though its waters roar and foam
and the mountains quake with
their surging. *Selah*

[4] There is a river whose streams make
glad the city of God,
the holy place where the
Most High dwells.
[5] God is within her, she will not fall;
God will help her at break of
day.
[6] Nations are in uproar, kingdoms fall;
he lifts his voice, the earth melts.

[7] The LORD Almighty is with us;
the God of Jacob is our fortress.
Selah

[8] Come and see the works of the LORD,
the desolations he has brought on
the earth.
[9] He makes wars cease to the ends of
the earth;

[a] Title: Probably a literary or musical term
[b] 12 Or *A Tyrian robe is among the gifts* [c] Title:
Probably a musical term

he breaks the bow and shatters
the spear,
he burns the shields[a] with fire.
¹⁰ "Be still, and know that I am God;
I will be exalted among the
nations,
I will be exalted in the earth."

¹¹ The LORD Almighty is with us;
the God of Jacob is our
fortress.   *Selah*

Psalm 47

For the director of music. Of the Sons
of Korah. A psalm.

¹ Clap your hands, all you nations;
shout to God with cries of joy.
² How awesome is the LORD Most High,
the great King over all the
earth!

^a9 Or *chariots*

PSALM 46

Bring it On!

46:1 GOD IS OUR REFUGE AND STRENGTH, AN EVER-PRESENT HELP IN TROUBLE.

Let the worst come, the psalmist says. Bring it on! We can handle whatever comes because "God is our refuge and strength, an ever-present help in trouble" (46:1). Then he conjures up the worst, what we might today describe in terms of nuclear holocaust: "Though the earth give way and the mountains fall into the heart of the sea, though its waters roar and foam and the mountains quake with their surging" (verses 2–3). There are other bad things that can happen and do happen: Enemies may attack us, and nations continually fight amongst themselves (verse 6). But God is God, and they are not, so we will not fear.

One of the most famous verses in the Bible is verse 10: "Be still, and know that I am God." It is often read in a tone of calm assurance and comfort, or as a call to be still and peaceful in one's soul. While that is good advice, it is probably not the tone of the verse. The Hebrew is more like, "Hush!" or "Enough!" Since it is spoken to warring and violent peoples, we should read it as a stern rebuke; God gets in the face of arrogant and angry nations and says, "Stop! Right now!" The closest New Testament parallel are the words Jesus shouted to the storm, "Quiet! Be still!" (Mark 4:39). That's how God speaks to our enemies.

How he usually speaks to us is quite different. The psalmist describes it this way: "There is a river whose streams make glad the city of God, the holy place where the Most High dwells" (verse 4). Jerusalem is the city spoken of here, but Jerusalem had no river, like her powerful enemies. Egypt had the Nile; Babylon had the Tigris and Euphrates; but Jerusalem had only a little creek at most. The river *who* makes the city glad was the presence of God. God's people can drink to their deepest satisfaction from the "river of delights" (see Psalm 36:8)! God's word to the nations is "Hush!" His word to us is, "The LORD Almighty is with us" (Psalm 46:7). Believe this, and let God rebuke your enemies and calm your fears.

PRAY:
You are my refuge and strength, O Lord, an ever-present help in trouble.
I will not be afraid of anything.

FOR YOUR NEXT DEVOTIONAL READING, GO TO PAGE 654.

3 He subdued nations under us,
   peoples under our feet.
4 He chose our inheritance for us,
   the pride of Jacob, whom he loved.
                                        Selah

5 God has ascended amid shouts of
   joy,
   the LORD amid the sounding
   of trumpets.
6 Sing praises to God, sing praises;
   sing praises to our King, sing
   praises.

7 For God is the King of all the earth;
   sing to him a psalm*a* of praise.
8 God reigns over the nations;
   God is seated on his holy throne.
9 The nobles of the nations assemble
   as the people of the God of
   Abraham,
for the kings*b* of the earth belong to
   God;
   he is greatly exalted.

Psalm 48

A song. A psalm of the Sons of Korah.

1 Great is the LORD, and most worthy of
   praise,
   in the city of our God, his holy
   mountain.
2 It is beautiful in its loftiness,
   the joy of the whole earth.
Like the utmost heights of Zaphon*c*
   is Mount Zion,
   the*d* city of the Great King.
3 God is in her citadels;
   he has shown himself to be her
   fortress.

4 When the kings joined forces,
   when they advanced together,
5 they saw her, and were astounded;
   they fled in terror.
6 Trembling seized them there,
   pain like that of a woman in labor.
7 You destroyed them like ships of
   Tarshish
   shattered by an east wind.

8 As we have heard,
   so have we seen
in the city of the LORD Almighty,
   in the city of our God:
   God makes her secure forever.
                                        Selah

9 Within your temple, O God,
   we meditate on your unfailing love.
10 Like your name, O God,
   your praise reaches to the ends of
   the earth;
   your right hand is filled with
   righteousness.
11 Mount Zion rejoices,
   the villages of Judah are glad
   because of your judgments.

12 Walk about Zion, go around her,
   count her towers,
13 consider well her ramparts,
   view her citadels,
   that you may tell of them to the
   next generation.

14 For this God is our God for ever
   and ever;
   he will be our guide even to
   the end.

Psalm 49

For the director of music. Of the Sons
   of Korah. A psalm.

1 Hear this, all you peoples;
   listen, all who live in this world,
2 both low and high,
   rich and poor alike:
3 My mouth will speak words of
   wisdom;
   the utterance from my heart will
   give understanding.
4 I will turn my ear to a proverb;
   with the harp I will expound
   my riddle:

5 Why should I fear when evil days
   come,
   when wicked deceivers surround
   me—
6 those who trust in their wealth
   and boast of their great riches?
7 No man can redeem the life of
   another
   or give to God a ransom for him—
8 the ransom for a life is costly,
   no payment is ever enough—
9 that he should live on forever
   and not see decay.

a7 Or *a maskil* (probably a literary or musical
term)   *b9* Or *shields*   *c2* *Zaphon* can refer
to a sacred mountain or the direction north.
d2 Or *earth, / Mount Zion, on the northern side /
of the*

THOMAS CRANMER (1489–1556)
If Your Right Hand Offends You

IT'S NOT too much of an exaggeration to say Thomas Cranmer, the compiler of the *Book of Common Prayer*, the Anglican prayer book, was the man who taught England to pray. It may therefore come as a surprise to learn that he was also a man who had a reputation for political maneuvering. In many ways Cranmer's life was a microcosm of his era. Sixteenth century England was a time of revolution, passion and intrigue, which saw King Henry VIII wade his way through six wives and the kingdom totter uncertainly between Protestantism and Catholicism.

Cranmer had been a brilliant student at Cambridge. His excellent scholarship earned him the status of fellow of Jesus College, where he eventually became a lecturer and authority on original Biblical texts. Then Cranmer became Archbishop of Canterbury—almost by fluke. One night he and his friends were in a tavern discussing how Henry might be able to secure a divorce from an unwilling Pope and be allowed to marry his mistress Anne Boleyn. Cranmer came up with a clever legal loophole that could enable this to happen; word got back to a delighted king, and Cranmer was eventually appointed archbishop.

In the years that followed, Cranmer used his influence to shepherd the Reformation of the Church of England. His greatest work was the *Book of Common Prayer*, which expressed the Protestant faith in the vernacular of the people instead of Latin. Also, with the support of Anne Boleyn, Cranmer helped translate the Bible into English. Soon every church had an English Bible chained to a pillar.

When the ardent Catholic "Bloody Mary" became queen, however, Cranmer was stripped of his position and imprisoned. He was forced to watch his friends Ridley and Latimer burned at the stake; he was then tortured and brainwashed until he signed a recantation of his Protestant beliefs. Wanting to make a public spectacle of Cranmer, the queen scheduled a public ceremony in which Cranmer would read his recantation.

On March 21, 1556, a huge crowd gathered in the Church of Great Saint Mary in Oxford. Cranmer mounted the stage and prayed a prayer that rocked the crowd:

> "O Lord, Whose property is always to have mercy . . . Now I come to the Great Thing that troubleth my conscience more than any other thing that I ever said or did in my life; and that is the setting abroad of writings contrary to the truth . . . writ for fear of death and to save my life . . . And forasmuch as my hand offended in writing contrary to my heart, therefore my hand shall first be punished . . . it shall first be burned."[3]

He had recanted his recantation! Livid, his enemies hurried him to the place of execution, where he was chained to the stake. As the flames rose around him, he thrust his right hand into the fire, the same hand that had signed the recantation, crying, "This hand hath offended!"[4] Within a short time Cranmer was dead. But the prayers he wrote have been prayed for centuries.

PRAY:

"O Lord, who hast taught us that all our doings without love
are worth nothing; send thy Holy Ghost, and pour into our hearts
that most excellent gift of love, the very bond of peace and all
virtues, without which whosoever liveth is counted dead before thee;
grant us this for thy Son Jesus Christ's sake."[5] THOMAS CRANMER

MEMORIZE:

"Whoever acknowledges me before men, I will also acknowledge him
before my Father in heaven. But whoever disowns me before men, I
will disown him before my Father in heaven." MATTHEW 10:32–33

FOR YOUR NEXT DEVOTIONAL READING, GO TO PAGE 658.

¹⁰For all can see that wise men die;
the foolish and the senseless alike
perish
and leave their wealth to others.
¹¹Their tombs will remain their
houses*ᵃ* forever,
their dwellings for endless
generations,
though they had*ᵇ* named lands
after themselves.
¹²But man, despite his riches, does not
endure;
he is*ᶜ* like the beasts that perish.

¹³This is the fate of those who trust in
themselves,
and of their followers, who approve
their sayings. *Selah*
¹⁴Like sheep they are destined for the
grave,*ᵈ*
and death will feed on them.
The upright will rule over them in the
morning;
their forms will decay in the
grave,*ᵈ*
far from their princely mansions.
¹⁵But God will redeem my life*ᵉ* from
the grave;
he will surely take me to himself.
Selah

¹⁶Do not be overawed when a man
grows rich,
when the splendor of his house
increases;
¹⁷for he will take nothing with him
when he dies,
his splendor will not descend
with him.
¹⁸Though while he lived he counted
himself blessed—
and men praise you when you
prosper—
¹⁹he will join the generation of his
fathers,
who will never see the light ˌof lifeˌ.

²⁰A man who has riches without
understanding
is like the beasts that perish.

Psalm 50

A psalm of Asaph.

¹The Mighty One, God, the LORD,
speaks and summons the earth

from the rising of the sun to the
place where it sets.
²From Zion, perfect in beauty,
God shines forth.
³Our God comes and will not be
silent;
a fire devours before him,
and around him a tempest
rages.
⁴He summons the heavens above,
and the earth, that he may judge
his people:
⁵"Gather to me my consecrated ones,
who made a covenant with me by
sacrifice."
⁶And the heavens proclaim his
righteousness,
for God himself is judge. *Selah*

⁷"Hear, O my people, and I will speak,
O Israel, and I will testify against
you:
I am God, your God.
⁸I do not rebuke you for your sacrifices
or your burnt offerings, which are
ever before me.
⁹I have no need of a bull from your
stall
or of goats from your pens,
¹⁰for every animal of the forest is mine,
and the cattle on a thousand hills.
¹¹I know every bird in the mountains,
and the creatures of the field are
mine.
¹²If I were hungry I would not tell you,
for the world is mine, and all that
is in it.
¹³Do I eat the flesh of bulls
or drink the blood of goats?
¹⁴Sacrifice thank offerings to God,
fulfill your vows to the Most High,
¹⁵and call upon me in the day of
trouble;
I will deliver you, and you will
honor me."

¹⁶But to the wicked, God says:

"What right have you to recite my
laws
or take my covenant on your lips?

ᵃ11 Septuagint and Syriac; Hebrew *In their
thoughts their houses will remain* *ᵇ11* Or */for
they have* *ᶜ12* Hebrew; Septuagint and Syriac
read verse 12 the same as verse 20. *ᵈ14* Hebrew
Sheol; also in verse 15 *ᵉ15* Or *soul*

¹⁷ You hate my instruction
    and cast my words behind you.
¹⁸ When you see a thief, you join
        with him;
    you throw in your lot with
        adulterers.
¹⁹ You use your mouth for evil
    and harness your tongue to deceit.
²⁰ You speak continually against
        your brother
    and slander your own mother's
        son.
²¹ These things you have done and
        I kept silent;
    you thought I was altogether[a]
        like you.
    But I will rebuke you
    and accuse you to your face.

²² "Consider this, you who forget God,
    or I will tear you to pieces, with
        none to rescue:
²³ He who sacrifices thank offerings
        honors me,
    and he prepares the way
    so that I may show him[b] the
        salvation of God."

Psalm 51

For the director of music. A psalm of
David. When the prophet Nathan came
to him after David had committed
adultery with Bathsheba.

¹ Have mercy on me, O God,
    according to your unfailing
        love;
    according to your great compassion
    blot out my transgressions.
² Wash away all my iniquity
    and cleanse me from my sin.

³ For I know my transgressions,
    and my sin is always before me.
⁴ Against you, you only, have I
        sinned
    and done what is evil in your sight,
    so that you are proved right when
        you speak
    and justified when you judge.
⁵ Surely I was sinful at birth,
    sinful from the time my mother
        conceived me.
⁶ Surely you desire truth in the inner
    parts[c];

you teach[d] me wisdom in the
    inmost place.

⁷ Cleanse me with hyssop, and I will be
        clean;
    wash me, and I will be whiter than
        snow.
⁸ Let me hear joy and gladness;
    let the bones you have crushed
        rejoice.
⁹ Hide your face from my sins
    and blot out all my iniquity.

¹⁰ Create in me a pure heart, O God,
    and renew a steadfast spirit
        within me.
¹¹ Do not cast me from your presence
    or take your Holy Spirit from me.
¹² Restore to me the joy of your
        salvation
    and grant me a willing spirit, to
        sustain me.

¹³ Then I will teach transgressors your
        ways,
    and sinners will turn back to you.
¹⁴ Save me from bloodguilt, O God,
    the God who saves me,
    and my tongue will sing of your
        righteousness.
¹⁵ O Lord, open my lips,
    and my mouth will declare your
        praise.
¹⁶ You do not delight in sacrifice, or
        I would bring it;
    you do not take pleasure in burnt
        offerings.
¹⁷ The sacrifices of God are[e] a broken
        spirit;
    a broken and contrite heart,
    O God, you will not despise.

¹⁸ In your good pleasure make Zion
        prosper;
    build up the walls of Jerusalem.
¹⁹ Then there will be righteous
        sacrifices,
    whole burnt offerings to delight
        you;
    then bulls will be offered on your
        altar.

---

[a]21 Or *thought the 'I AM' was*   [b]23 Or *and
to him who considers his way / I will show*
[c]6 The meaning of the Hebrew for this phrase is
uncertain.   [d]6 Or *you desired…; / you taught*
[e]17 Or *My sacrifice, O God, is*

PSALM 51

The Bible Is an Adult Book

51:4 AGAINST YOU, YOU ONLY, HAVE I SINNED.

Churches ought to put a neon sign outside the entrance to their buildings, shaped like an arrow, pointing inside, and reading, "ADULT BOOKS." When curious "adults" walked in the door, they would find inside a stack of Bibles. In the truest sense of the word, the Bible is an adult book. To teach it to children we must often delete some portions and dilute others. Portions of the Bible, if made into a film, might get an R rating. The story of sin that lies behind this great psalm of David is one such portion. It is a story of adultery and murder as lurid as anything Hollywood has ever filmed. You can read the story in 2 Samuel 11 and 12.

Uriah, were he able, might have argued with David's confession that it was against God and God alone that he had sinned (see Psalm 51:4). David had, after all, murdered Uriah to cover up his adultery with Uriah's wife, Bathsheba. But this psalm of confession is a radical prayer. The word *radical* comes from the Latin *radix*, which means root. David has thought long and hard about the roots of this sin against Uriah and sees that it began with his disregard of God. In this, he predates Paul's searching analysis in Romans 1:21: "For although they knew God, they neither glorified him as God nor gave thanks to him, but their thinking became futile and their foolish hearts were darkened." From this fundamental futility and darkness comes every other transgression and iniquity against others. Uriah would never have been killed if David had attended to his relationship with God.

David's radical approach extends deep into his own heart, as he acknowledges that God isn't interested in superficial obedience, but inward purity: "Surely you desire truth in the inner parts; you teach me wisdom in the inmost place" (Psalm 51:6). So David prays for a radical cure for a radical sin: "Create in me a pure heart, O God, and renew a steadfast spirit within me. Do not cast me from your presence or take your Holy Spirit from me. Restore to me the joy of your salvation and grant me a willing spirit, to sustain me" (verses 10–12).

Confess your sins as David did. Your sin may not have the consequences his did, but it is no less radical in its origin and requires no less radical a cure.

P R A Y :

Lord, I have sinned against you, and only you. Forgive me,
for Christ's sake, and restore to me the joy of your salvation.

———

FOR YOUR NEXT DEVOTIONAL READING, GO TO PAGE 665.

Psalm 52

For the director of music. A *maskil*[a]
of David. When Doeg the Edomite had
gone to Saul and told him: "David has
gone to the house of Ahimelech."

[1] Why do you boast of evil, you
  mighty man?
  Why do you boast all day long,
  you who are a disgrace in the
  eyes of God?
[2] Your tongue plots destruction;
  it is like a sharpened razor,
  you who practice deceit.
[3] You love evil rather than good,
  falsehood rather than speaking
  the truth.   *Selah*
[4] You love every harmful word,
  O you deceitful tongue!

[5] Surely God will bring you down to
  everlasting ruin:
  He will snatch you up and tear you
  from your tent;
  he will uproot you from the
  land of the living.   *Selah*
[6] The righteous will see and fear;
  they will laugh at him, saying,
[7] "Here now is the man
  who did not make God his
  stronghold
  but trusted in his great wealth
  and grew strong by destroying
  others!"

[8] But I am like an olive tree
  flourishing in the house of God;
  I trust in God's unfailing love
  for ever and ever.
[9] I will praise you forever for what you
  have done;
  in your name I will hope, for your
  name is good.
  I will praise you in the presence
  of your saints.

Psalm 53

For the director of music.
According to *mahalath*.[b] A *maskil*[a]
of David.

[1] The fool says in his heart,
  "There is no God."
They are corrupt, and their ways
  are vile;
  there is no one who does good.

[2] God looks down from heaven
  on the sons of men
to see if there are any who
  understand,
  any who seek God.
[3] Everyone has turned away,
  they have together become
  corrupt;
there is no one who does good,
  not even one.

[4] Will the evildoers never learn—
  those who devour my people as
  men eat bread
  and who do not call on God?
[5] There they were, overwhelmed with
  dread,
  where there was nothing to dread.
God scattered the bones of those who
  attacked you;
  you put them to shame, for God
  despised them.

[6] Oh, that salvation for Israel would
  come out of Zion!
  When God restores the fortunes of
  his people,
  let Jacob rejoice and Israel be glad!

Psalm 54

For the director of music. With stringed
instruments. A *maskil*[a] of David. When
the Ziphites had gone to Saul and said,
"Is not David hiding among us?"

[1] Save me, O God, by your name;
  vindicate me by your might.
[2] Hear my prayer, O God;
  listen to the words of my mouth.

[3] Strangers are attacking me;
  ruthless men seek my life—
  men without regard for God.   *Selah*

[4] Surely God is my help;
  the Lord is the one who sustains
  me.

[5] Let evil recoil on those who slander
  me;
  in your faithfulness destroy them.

[6] I will sacrifice a freewill offering to
  you;
  I will praise your name, O LORD,
  for it is good.

[a]Title: Probably a literary or musical term
[b]Title: Probably a musical term

7 For he has delivered me from all my
   troubles,
   and my eyes have looked in
      triumph on my foes.

Psalm 55

For the director of music. With stringed
instruments. A *maskil*[a] of David.

1 Listen to my prayer, O God,
   do not ignore my plea;
2   hear me and answer me.
My thoughts trouble me and I am
      distraught
3   at the voice of the enemy,
   at the stares of the wicked;
for they bring down suffering
      upon me
   and revile me in their anger.

4 My heart is in anguish within me;
   the terrors of death assail me.
5 Fear and trembling have beset me;
   horror has overwhelmed me.
6 I said, "Oh, that I had the wings of
      a dove!
   I would fly away and be at rest—
7 I would flee far away
   and stay in the desert;   *Selah*
8 I would hurry to my place of shelter,
   far from the tempest and storm."

9 Confuse the wicked, O Lord,
      confound their speech,
   for I see violence and strife in
      the city.
10 Day and night they prowl about on
      its walls;
   malice and abuse are within it.
11 Destructive forces are at work in
      the city;
   threats and lies never leave its
      streets.

12 If an enemy were insulting me,
   I could endure it;
if a foe were raising himself against
      me,
   I could hide from him.
13 But it is you, a man like myself,
   my companion, my close friend,
14 with whom I once enjoyed sweet
      fellowship
   as we walked with the throng at
      the house of God.

15 Let death take my enemies by
      surprise;

let them go down alive to the grave,[b]
   for evil finds lodging among them.

16 But I call to God,
   and the LORD saves me.
17 Evening, morning and noon
   I cry out in distress,
   and he hears my voice.
18 He ransoms me unharmed
   from the battle waged against me,
   even though many oppose me.
19 God, who is enthroned forever,
   will hear them and afflict
      them—   *Selah*
men who never change their ways
   and have no fear of God.

20 My companion attacks his friends;
   he violates his covenant.
21 His speech is smooth as butter,
   yet war is in his heart;
his words are more soothing than oil,
   yet they are drawn swords.

22 Cast your cares on the LORD
   and he will sustain you;
   he will never let the righteous fall.
23 But you, O God, will bring down the
      wicked
   into the pit of corruption;
bloodthirsty and deceitful men
   will not live out half their days.

But as for me, I trust in you.

---

*EVENING, morning and noon
I cry out in distress,
and he hears my voice.*

PSALM 55:17

Psalm 56

For the director of music. To ⌊the tune of⌋
"A Dove on Distant Oaks." Of David.
A *miktam*.[a] When the Philistines
had seized him in Gath.

1 Be merciful to me, O God, for men
      hotly pursue me;
   all day long they press their attack.
2 My slanderers pursue me all day
      long;
   many are attacking me in their
      pride.

---

[a] Title: Probably a literary or musical term
[b] 15 Hebrew *Sheol*

³ When I am afraid,
  I will trust in you.
⁴ In God, whose word I praise,
  in God I trust; I will not be
    afraid.
  What can mortal man do to me?

⁵ All day long they twist my words;
  they are always plotting to harm
    me.
⁶ They conspire, they lurk,
  they watch my steps,
  eager to take my life.
⁷ On no account let them escape;
  in your anger, O God, bring down
    the nations.
⁸ Record my lament;
  list my tears on your scroll[a]—
  are they not in your record?

⁹ Then my enemies will turn back
  when I call for help.
  By this I will know that God is
    for me.
¹⁰ In God, whose word I praise,
  in the LORD, whose word I
    praise—
¹¹ in God I trust; I will not be afraid.
  What can man do to me?

¹² I am under vows to you, O God;
  I will present my thank offerings
    to you.
¹³ For you have delivered me[b] from
    death
  and my feet from stumbling,
  that I may walk before God
  in the light of life.[c]

Psalm 57

For the director of music. To the
tune of "Do Not Destroy." Of David.
A *miktam*.[d] When he had fled from
Saul into the cave.

¹ Have mercy on me, O God, have
    mercy on me,
  for in you my soul takes refuge.
  I will take refuge in the shadow
    of your wings
  until the disaster has passed.

² I cry out to God Most High,
  to God, who fulfills his purpose
    for me.
³ He sends from heaven and
    saves me,

rebuking those who hotly
    pursue me;   *Selah*
  God sends his love and his
    faithfulness.

⁴ I am in the midst of lions;
  I lie among ravenous beasts—
  men whose teeth are spears and
    arrows,
  whose tongues are sharp swords.

⁵ Be exalted, O God, above the
    heavens;
  let your glory be over all the earth.

⁶ They spread a net for my feet—
  I was bowed down in distress.
  They dug a pit in my path—
  but they have fallen into it
    themselves.   *Selah*

⁷ My heart is steadfast, O God,
  my heart is steadfast;
  I will sing and make music.
⁸ Awake, my soul!
  Awake, harp and lyre!
  I will awaken the dawn.

⁹ I will praise you, O Lord, among the
    nations;
  I will sing of you among the
    peoples.
¹⁰ For great is your love, reaching to
    the heavens;
  your faithfulness reaches to the
    skies.

¹¹ Be exalted, O God, above the
    heavens;
  let your glory be over all the earth.

Psalm 58

For the director of music. To the
tune of "Do Not Destroy." Of David.
A *miktam*.[d]

¹ Do you rulers indeed speak justly?
  Do you judge uprightly among
    men?
² No, in your heart you devise injustice,
  and your hands mete out violence
    on the earth.
³ Even from birth the wicked go astray;
  from the womb they are wayward
    and speak lies.

---

[a]8 Or / put my tears in your wineskin
[b]13 Or my soul   [c]13 Or the land of the living
[d]Title: Probably a literary or musical term

4 Their venom is like the venom of
a snake,
like that of a cobra that has
stopped its ears,
5 that will not heed the tune of the
charmer,
however skillful the enchanter
may be.

6 Break the teeth in their mouths,
O God;
tear out, O LORD, the fangs of the
lions!
7 Let them vanish like water that
flows away;
when they draw the bow, let their
arrows be blunted.
8 Like a slug melting away as it moves
along,
like a stillborn child, may they not
see the sun.

9 Before your pots can feel ⌊the heat of⌋
the thorns—
whether they be green or dry—the
wicked will be swept away.[a]
10 The righteous will be glad when they
are avenged,
when they bathe their feet in the
blood of the wicked.
11 Then men will say,
"Surely the righteous still are
rewarded;
surely there is a God who judges
the earth."

Psalm 59

For the director of music. ⌊To the tune of⌋
"Do Not Destroy." Of David. A *miktam*.[b]
When Saul had sent men to watch
David's house in order to kill him.

1 Deliver me from my enemies,
O God;
protect me from those who rise up
against me.
2 Deliver me from evildoers
and save me from bloodthirsty
men.

3 See how they lie in wait for me!
Fierce men conspire against me
for no offense or sin of mine,
O LORD.
4 I have done no wrong, yet they are
ready to attack me.
Arise to help me; look on my plight!

5 O LORD God Almighty, the God of
Israel,
rouse yourself to punish all the
nations;
show no mercy to wicked traitors.
Selah

6 They return at evening,
snarling like dogs,
and prowl about the city.
7 See what they spew from their
mouths—
they spew out swords from
their lips,
and they say, "Who can hear us?"
8 But you, O LORD, laugh at them;
you scoff at all those nations.

9 O my Strength, I watch for you;
you, O God, are my fortress, 10 my
loving God.

God will go before me
and will let me gloat over those
who slander me.
11 But do not kill them, O Lord our
shield,[c]
or my people will forget.
In your might make them wander
about,
and bring them down.
12 For the sins of their mouths,
for the words of their lips,
let them be caught in their
pride.
For the curses and lies they utter,
13   consume them in wrath,
consume them till they are no
more.
Then it will be known to the ends of
the earth
that God rules over Jacob. *Selah*

14 They return at evening,
snarling like dogs,
and prowl about the city.
15 They wander about for food
and howl if not satisfied.
16 But I will sing of your strength,
in the morning I will sing of your
love;
for you are my fortress,
my refuge in times of trouble.

---

[a]9 The meaning of the Hebrew for this verse
is uncertain.   [b]Title: Probably a literary or
musical term   [c]11 Or *sovereign*

[17] O my Strength, I sing praise to you;
    you, O God, are my fortress, my
      loving God.

Psalm 60

For the director of music. To ˻the tune of˼
"The Lily of the Covenant." A *miktam*[a]
of David. For teaching. When he fought
Aram Naharaim[b] and Aram Zobah,[c]
and when Joab returned and struck
down twelve thousand Edomites in
the Valley of Salt.

[1] You have rejected us, O God, and
    burst forth upon us;
    you have been angry—now
      restore us!
[2] You have shaken the land and torn
    it open;
    mend its fractures, for it is
      quaking.
[3] You have shown your people
    desperate times;
    you have given us wine that makes
      us stagger.

[4] But for those who fear you, you have
    raised a banner
    to be unfurled against the bow.
               Selah

[5] Save us and help us with your right
    hand,
    that those you love may be
      delivered.
[6] God has spoken from his sanctuary:
    "In triumph I will parcel out
      Shechem
    and measure off the Valley of
      Succoth.
[7] Gilead is mine, and Manasseh is
    mine;
    Ephraim is my helmet,
    Judah my scepter.
[8] Moab is my washbasin,
    upon Edom I toss my sandal;
    over Philistia I shout in triumph."

[9] Who will bring me to the fortified
    city?
    Who will lead me to Edom?
[10] Is it not you, O God, you who have
    rejected us
    and no longer go out with our
      armies?
[11] Give us aid against the enemy,
    for the help of man is worthless.

[12] With God we will gain the victory,
    and he will trample down our
      enemies.

Psalm 61

For the director of music. With stringed
instruments. Of David.

[1] Hear my cry, O God;
    listen to my prayer.

[2] From the ends of the earth I call to
    you,
    I call as my heart grows faint;
    lead me to the rock that is higher
      than I.
[3] For you have been my refuge,
    a strong tower against the foe.

[4] I long to dwell in your tent forever
    and take refuge in the shelter
      of your wings.   *Selah*
[5] For you have heard my vows,
    O God;
    you have given me the heritage of
      those who fear your name.

[6] Increase the days of the king's life,
    his years for many generations.
[7] May he be enthroned in God's
    presence forever;
    appoint your love and faithfulness
      to protect him.

[8] Then will I ever sing praise to your
    name
    and fulfill my vows day after day.

> HEAR my cry, O God;
> listen to my prayer.
>
> PSALM 61:1

Psalm 62

For the director of music. For Jeduthun.
A psalm of David.

[1] My soul finds rest in God alone;
    my salvation comes from him.
[2] He alone is my rock and my salvation;
    he is my fortress, I will never be
      shaken.

[a] Title: Probably a literary or musical term
[b] Title: That is, Arameans of Northwest
Mesopotamia   [c] Title: That is, Arameans of
central Syria

³ How long will you assault a man?
  Would all of you throw him
    down—
  this leaning wall, this tottering
    fence?
⁴ They fully intend to topple him
  from his lofty place;
  they take delight in lies.
  With their mouths they bless,
    but in their hearts they
      curse.   *Selah*

⁵ Find rest, O my soul, in God alone;
  my hope comes from him.
⁶ He alone is my rock and my salvation;
  he is my fortress, I will not be
    shaken.
⁷ My salvation and my honor depend
    on God*ᵃ*;
  he is my mighty rock, my refuge.
⁸ Trust in him at all times, O people;
  pour out your hearts to him,
  for God is our refuge.   *Selah*

⁹ Lowborn men are but a breath,
  the highborn are but a lie;
  if weighed on a balance, they are
    nothing;
  together they are only a breath.
¹⁰ Do not trust in extortion
  or take pride in stolen goods;
  though your riches increase,
  do not set your heart on them.

¹¹ One thing God has spoken,
  two things have I heard:
  that you, O God, are strong,
¹²   and that you, O Lord, are loving.
  Surely you will reward each person
  according to what he has done.

Psalm 63

*A psalm of David. When he was
in the Desert of Judah.*

¹ O God, you are my God,
  earnestly I seek you;
  my soul thirsts for you,
  my body longs for you,
  in a dry and weary land
  where there is no water.

² I have seen you in the sanctuary
  and beheld your power and your
    glory.
³ Because your love is better than life,
  my lips will glorify you.

⁴ I will praise you as long as I live,
  and in your name I will lift up my
    hands.
⁵ My soul will be satisfied as with the
    richest of foods;
  with singing lips my mouth will
    praise you.

⁶ On my bed I remember you;
  I think of you through the watches
    of the night.
⁷ Because you are my help,
  I sing in the shadow of your wings.
⁸ My soul clings to you;
  your right hand upholds me.

⁹ They who seek my life will be
    destroyed;
  they will go down to the depths of
    the earth.
¹⁰ They will be given over to the sword
  and become food for jackals.

¹¹ But the king will rejoice in God;
  all who swear by God's name will
    praise him,
  while the mouths of liars will be
    silenced.

Psalm 64

*For the director of music.
A psalm of David.*

¹ Hear me, O God, as I voice my
    complaint;
  protect my life from the threat of
    the enemy.
² Hide me from the conspiracy of the
    wicked,
  from that noisy crowd of evildoers.

³ They sharpen their tongues like
    swords
  and aim their words like deadly
    arrows.
⁴ They shoot from ambush at the
    innocent man;
  they shoot at him suddenly,
    without fear.

⁵ They encourage each other in evil
    plans,
  they talk about hiding their
    snares;
  they say, "Who will see them*ᵇ*?"

*ᵃ7 Or / God Most High is my salvation and my
honor   ᵇ5 Or us*

PSALM 63

Hunger for God

63:1 MY SOUL THIRSTS FOR YOU, MY BODY LONGS FOR YOU.

David was literally and physically hungry and thirsty when he wrote this psalm in the desolate wilderness of Judah. But he saw in the longings of his body a deeper meaning; his hunger and thirst were signposts to his need of God. That brought a dignity to his cravings. He was more than his belly; he was made for God. Hungry and thirsty in the same wilderness, Jesus did the same thing with his bodily yearnings when he rebuked Satan: "It is written, 'Man does not live on bread alone, but on every word that comes from the mouth of God'" (see Matthew 4:4; Deuteronomy 8:3).

Here is a great way to pray: Turn your longings and hungers toward God. Do not pray only that they be removed. Pray that they become reminders and parables of your need for God. Pain and suffering, frustration and anxiety, can become sacramental experiences if you let them lead you to their deeper meaning in God.

Poet George Herbert painted a vivid picture of the meaning of the empty places in our lives. He pictured God, having made a kind of empty husk of a human, pouring good things into the person, filling him with strength, beauty, wisdom, honor and pleasure. But God stops pouring with one thing left—satisfaction. He decides it would hurt the human to have this last gift.

> For if I should (said he)
> Bestow this jewel on my creature,
> He would adore his gifts instead of me,
> And rest in Nature, not the God of Nature.
> So both should losers be.
> Yet let him keep the rest,
> But keep them with repining restlessness:
> Let him be rich and weary, that at least,
> If goodness lead him not, yet weariness
> May toss him to my breast.[6]

Thank God for your emptiness, and let it lead you to him. God fills up only empty hearts.

PRAY:

Thank you, Father, for the emptiness I sometimes feel.

Let it point me to your Son, the Bread of Life.

FOR YOUR NEXT DEVOTIONAL READING, GO TO PAGE 673.

⁶ They plot injustice and say,
  "We have devised a perfect plan!"
 Surely the mind and heart of man
  are cunning.

⁷ But God will shoot them with arrows;
  suddenly they will be struck down.
⁸ He will turn their own tongues
  against them
 and bring them to ruin;
  all who see them will shake their
  heads in scorn.

⁹ All mankind will fear;
  they will proclaim the works of God
  and ponder what he has done.
¹⁰ Let the righteous rejoice in the LORD
  and take refuge in him;
 let all the upright in heart praise
  him!

Psalm 65

For the director of music. A psalm
of David. A song.

¹ Praise awaits*ᵃ* you, O God, in Zion;
  to you our vows will be fulfilled.
² O you who hear prayer,
  to you all men will come.
³ When we were overwhelmed by
  sins,
  you forgave*ᵇ* our transgressions.
⁴ Blessed are those you choose
  and bring near to live in your
  courts!
 We are filled with the good things of
  your house,
  of your holy temple.

⁵ You answer us with awesome deeds
  of righteousness,
  O God our Savior,
 the hope of all the ends of the earth
  and of the farthest seas,
⁶ who formed the mountains by your
  power,
  having armed yourself with
  strength,
⁷ who stilled the roaring of the seas,
  the roaring of their waves,
  and the turmoil of the nations.
⁸ Those living far away fear your
  wonders;
  where morning dawns and evening
  fades
 you call forth songs of joy.

⁹ You care for the land and water it;
  you enrich it abundantly.
 The streams of God are filled with
  water
  to provide the people with grain,
  for so you have ordained it.*ᶜ*
¹⁰ You drench its furrows
  and level its ridges;
 you soften it with showers
  and bless its crops.
¹¹ You crown the year with your bounty,
  and your carts overflow with
  abundance.
¹² The grasslands of the desert overflow;
  the hills are clothed with gladness.
¹³ The meadows are covered with flocks
  and the valleys are mantled with
  grain;
  they shout for joy and sing.

Psalm 66

For the director of music.
A song. A psalm.

¹ Shout with joy to God, all the earth!
² Sing the glory of his name;
  make his praise glorious!
³ Say to God, "How awesome are your
  deeds!
 So great is your power
  that your enemies cringe before
  you.
⁴ All the earth bows down to you;
  they sing praise to you,
  they sing praise to your name."
                                   Selah

⁵ Come and see what God has done,
  how awesome his works in man's
  behalf!
⁶ He turned the sea into dry land,
  they passed through the waters
  on foot—
  come, let us rejoice in him.
⁷ He rules forever by his power,
  his eyes watch the nations—
  let not the rebellious rise up
  against him.   *Selah*

⁸ Praise our God, O peoples,
  let the sound of his praise be
  heard;

ᵃ1 Or *befits*; the meaning of the Hebrew for
this word is uncertain.   *ᵇ3* Or *made
atonement for*   *ᶜ9* Or *for that is how you
prepare the land*

9 he has preserved our lives
   and kept our feet from slipping.
10 For you, O God, tested us;
   you refined us like silver.
11 You brought us into prison
   and laid burdens on our backs.
12 You let men ride over our heads;
   we went through fire and water,
   but you brought us to a place of
   abundance.

13 I will come to your temple with
   burnt offerings
   and fulfill my vows to you—
14 vows my lips promised and my
   mouth spoke
   when I was in trouble.
15 I will sacrifice fat animals to you
   and an offering of rams;
   I will offer bulls and goats.   *Selah*

16 Come and listen, all you who fear
   God;
   let me tell you what he has done
   for me.
17 I cried out to him with my mouth;
   his praise was on my tongue.
18 If I had cherished sin in my heart,
   the Lord would not have listened;
19 but God has surely listened
   and heard my voice in prayer.
20 Praise be to God,
   who has not rejected my prayer
   or withheld his love from me!

> *PRAISE be to God,*
> *who has not rejected my prayer*
> *or withheld his love from me!*
>
> PSALM 66:20

Psalm 67

For the director of music. With stringed
instruments. A psalm. A song.

1 May God be gracious to us and
   bless us
   and make his face shine upon us,
                                   Selah
2 that your ways may be known on
   earth,
   your salvation among all nations.

3 May the peoples praise you, O God;
   may all the peoples praise you.

4 May the nations be glad and sing for
   joy,
   for you rule the peoples justly
   and guide the nations of the
   earth.   *Selah*
5 May the peoples praise you, O God;
   may all the peoples praise you.

6 Then the land will yield its harvest,
   and God, our God, will bless us.
7 God will bless us,
   and all the ends of the earth will
   fear him.

Psalm 68

For the director of music. Of David.
A psalm. A song.

1 May God arise, may his enemies be
   scattered;
   may his foes flee before him.
2 As smoke is blown away by the wind,
   may you blow them away;
   as wax melts before the fire,
   may the wicked perish before God.
3 But may the righteous be glad
   and rejoice before God;
   may they be happy and joyful.

4 Sing to God, sing praise to his name,
   extol him who rides on the clouds[a]—
   his name is the LORD—
   and rejoice before him.
5 A father to the fatherless, a defender
   of widows,
   is God in his holy dwelling.
6 God sets the lonely in families,[b]
   he leads forth the prisoners with
   singing;
   but the rebellious live in a
   sun-scorched land.

7 When you went out before your
   people, O God,
   when you marched through the
   wasteland,   *Selah*
8 the earth shook,
   the heavens poured down rain,
   before God, the One of Sinai,
   before God, the God of Israel.
9 You gave abundant showers, O God;
   you refreshed your weary
   inheritance.

---

[a]4 Or / prepare the way for him who rides
through the deserts   [b]6 Or the desolate in a
homeland

¹⁰ Your people settled in it,
　　and from your bounty, O God, you
　　　provided for the poor.

¹¹ The Lord announced the word,
　　and great was the company of
　　　those who proclaimed it:
¹² "Kings and armies flee in haste;
　　in the camps men divide the
　　　plunder.
¹³ Even while you sleep among the
　　campfires,ᵃ
　　the wings of ⌞my⌟ dove are
　　　sheathed with silver,
　　its feathers with shining gold."
¹⁴ When the Almightyᵇ scattered the
　　kings in the land,
　　it was like snow fallen on Zalmon.

¹⁵ The mountains of Bashan are
　　majestic mountains;
　　rugged are the mountains of
　　　Bashan.
¹⁶ Why gaze in envy, O rugged
　　mountains,
　　at the mountain where God
　　　chooses to reign,
　　where the Lord himself will dwell
　　　forever?
¹⁷ The chariots of God are tens of
　　thousands
　　and thousands of thousands;
　　the Lord ⌞has come⌟ from Sinai into
　　　his sanctuary.
¹⁸ When you ascended on high,
　　you led captives in your train;
　　you received gifts from men,
　　even fromᶜ the rebellious—
　　that you,ᵈ O Lord God, might
　　　dwell there.

¹⁹ Praise be to the Lord, to God our
　　Savior,
　　who daily bears our burdens.
　　　　　　　　　　　　　Selah
²⁰ Our God is a God who saves;
　　from the Sovereign Lord comes
　　　escape from death.

²¹ Surely God will crush the heads of
　　his enemies,
　　the hairy crowns of those who go
　　　on in their sins.
²² The Lord says, "I will bring them from
　　Bashan;
　　I will bring them from the depths
　　　of the sea,

²³ that you may plunge your feet in the
　　blood of your foes,
　　while the tongues of your dogs
　　　have their share."

²⁴ Your procession has come into view,
　　O God,
　　the procession of my God and King
　　　into the sanctuary.
²⁵ In front are the singers, after them
　　the musicians;
　　with them are the maidens playing
　　　tambourines.
²⁶ Praise God in the great congregation;
　　praise the Lord in the assembly of
　　　Israel.
²⁷ There is the little tribe of Benjamin,
　　leading them,
　　there the great throng of Judah's
　　　princes,
　　and there the princes of Zebulun
　　　and of Naphtali.

²⁸ Summon your power, O Godᵉ;
　　show us your strength, O God, as
　　　you have done before.
²⁹ Because of your temple at Jerusalem
　　kings will bring you gifts.
³⁰ Rebuke the beast among the reeds,
　　the herd of bulls among the calves
　　　of the nations.
　　Humbled, may it bring bars of silver.
　　Scatter the nations who delight in
　　　war.
³¹ Envoys will come from Egypt;
　　Cushᶠ will submit herself to God.

³² Sing to God, O kingdoms of the earth,
　　sing praise to the Lord,　　　*Selah*
³³ to him who rides the ancient skies
　　above,
　　who thunders with mighty voice.
³⁴ Proclaim the power of God,
　　whose majesty is over Israel,
　　whose power is in the skies.
³⁵ You are awesome, O God, in your
　　sanctuary;
　　the God of Israel gives power and
　　　strength to his people.

　　Praise be to God!

ᵃ 13 Or *saddlebags*　　ᵇ 14 Hebrew *Shaddai*
ᶜ 18 Or *gifts for men, / even*　　ᵈ 18 Or *they*
ᵉ 28 Many Hebrew manuscripts, Septuagint and
Syriac; most Hebrew manuscripts *Your God has
summoned power for you*　　ᶠ 31 That is, the
upper Nile region

Psalm 69

For the director of music. To ⌊the tune of⌋ "Lilies." Of David.

¹ Save me, O God,
for the waters have come up to
my neck.
² I sink in the miry depths,
where there is no foothold.
I have come into the deep waters;
the floods engulf me.
³ I am worn out calling for help;
my throat is parched.
My eyes fail,
looking for my God.
⁴ Those who hate me without reason
outnumber the hairs of my head;
many are my enemies without cause,
those who seek to destroy me.
I am forced to restore
what I did not steal.

⁵ You know my folly, O God;
my guilt is not hidden from you.

⁶ May those who hope in you
not be disgraced because of me,
O Lord, the LORD Almighty;
may those who seek you
not be put to shame because of me,
O God of Israel.
⁷ For I endure scorn for your sake,
and shame covers my face.
⁸ I am a stranger to my brothers,
an alien to my own mother's sons;
⁹ for zeal for your house consumes me,
and the insults of those who insult
you fall on me.
¹⁰ When I weep and fast,
I must endure scorn;
¹¹ when I put on sackcloth,
people make sport of me.
¹² Those who sit at the gate mock me,
and I am the song of the
drunkards.

¹³ But I pray to you, O LORD,
in the time of your favor;
in your great love, O God,
answer me with your sure
salvation.

> **BUT** *I pray to you, O LORD,*
> *in the time of your favor;*
> *in your great love, O God,*
> *answer me with your sure salvation.*
>
> PSALM 69:13

¹⁴ Rescue me from the mire,
do not let me sink;
deliver me from those who hate me,
from the deep waters.
¹⁵ Do not let the floodwaters engulf me
or the depths swallow me up
or the pit close its mouth over
me.
¹⁶ Answer me, O LORD, out of the
goodness of your love;
in your great mercy turn to me.
¹⁷ Do not hide your face from your
servant;
answer me quickly, for I am in
trouble.
¹⁸ Come near and rescue me;
redeem me because of my foes.

¹⁹ You know how I am scorned,
disgraced and shamed;
all my enemies are before you.
²⁰ Scorn has broken my heart
and has left me helpless;
I looked for sympathy, but there was
none,
for comforters, but I found none.
²¹ They put gall in my food
and gave me vinegar for my thirst.

²² May the table set before them
become a snare;
may it become retribution and*ᵃ* a
trap.
²³ May their eyes be darkened so they
cannot see,
and their backs be bent forever.
²⁴ Pour out your wrath on them;
let your fierce anger overtake
them.
²⁵ May their place be deserted;
let there be no one to dwell in
their tents.
²⁶ For they persecute those you
wound
and talk about the pain of those
you hurt.

ᵃ22 Or snare / and their fellowship become

> 66 *Prayer is the language of a man*
> *burdened with a sense of need.* 99
>
> E. M. BOUNDS

27 Charge them with crime upon crime;
    do not let them share in your
        salvation.
28 May they be blotted out of the book
        of life
    and not be listed with the
        righteous.

29 I am in pain and distress;
    may your salvation, O God,
        protect me.

30 I will praise God's name in song
    and glorify him with thanksgiving.
31 This will please the Lord more than
        an ox,
    more than a bull with its horns
        and hoofs.
32 The poor will see and be glad—
    you who seek God, may your
        hearts live!
33 The Lord hears the needy
    and does not despise his captive
        people.

34 Let heaven and earth praise him,
    the seas and all that move in them,
35 for God will save Zion
    and rebuild the cities of Judah.
    Then people will settle there and
        possess it;
36   the children of his servants will
        inherit it,
    and those who love his name will
        dwell there.

Psalm 70

For the director of music.
Of David. A petition.

1 Hasten, O God, to save me;
    O Lord, come quickly to help me.
2 May those who seek my life
    be put to shame and confusion;
    may all who desire my ruin
        be turned back in disgrace.
3 May those who say to me,
        "Aha! Aha!"
    turn back because of their
        shame.
4 But may all who seek you
    rejoice and be glad in you;
    may those who love your salvation
        always say,
        "Let God be exalted!"

5 Yet I am poor and needy;
    come quickly to me, O God.
You are my help and my deliverer;
    O Lord, do not delay.

> YOU are my help and my deliverer;
>   O Lord, do not delay.
>
> PSALM 70:5

Psalm 71

1 In you, O Lord, I have taken refuge;
    let me never be put to shame.
2 Rescue me and deliver me in your
        righteousness;
    turn your ear to me and save me.
3 Be my rock of refuge,
    to which I can always go;
    give the command to save me,
    for you are my rock and my
        fortress.
4 Deliver me, O my God, from the hand
        of the wicked,
    from the grasp of evil and cruel
        men.

5 For you have been my hope,
    O Sovereign Lord,
    my confidence since my youth.
6 From birth I have relied on you;
    you brought me forth from my
        mother's womb.
    I will ever praise you.
7 I have become like a portent to many,
    but you are my strong refuge.
8 My mouth is filled with your praise,
    declaring your splendor all day
        long.

9 Do not cast me away when I am old;
    do not forsake me when my
        strength is gone.
10 For my enemies speak against me;
    those who wait to kill me conspire
        together.
11 They say, "God has forsaken him;
    pursue him and seize him,
    for no one will rescue him."
12 Be not far from me, O God;
    come quickly, O my God, to help
        me.
13 May my accusers perish in shame;
    may those who want to harm me
        be covered with scorn and disgrace.

¹⁴ But as for me, I will always have
hope;
I will praise you more and
more.
¹⁵ My mouth will tell of your
righteousness,
of your salvation all day long,
though I know not its measure.
¹⁶ I will come and proclaim your mighty
acts, O Sovereign LORD;
I will proclaim your righteousness,
yours alone.
¹⁷ Since my youth, O God, you have
taught me,
and to this day I declare your
marvelous deeds.
¹⁸ Even when I am old and gray,
do not forsake me, O God,
till I declare your power to the next
generation,
your might to all who are to come.

¹⁹ Your righteousness reaches to
the skies, O God,
you who have done great things.
Who, O God, is like you?
²⁰ Though you have made me see
troubles, many and bitter,
you will restore my life again;
from the depths of the earth
you will again bring me up.
²¹ You will increase my honor
and comfort me once again.

²² I will praise you with the harp
for your faithfulness, O my God;
I will sing praise to you with the lyre,
O Holy One of Israel.
²³ My lips will shout for joy
when I sing praise to you—
I, whom you have redeemed.
²⁴ My tongue will tell of your righteous
acts
all day long,
for those who wanted to harm me
have been put to shame and
confusion.

Psalm 72

Of Solomon.

¹ Endow the king with your justice,
O God,
the royal son with your
righteousness.

² He will*a* judge your people in
righteousness,
your afflicted ones with justice.
³ The mountains will bring prosperity
to the people,
the hills the fruit of righteousness.
⁴ He will defend the afflicted among
the people
and save the children of the needy;
he will crush the oppressor.

⁵ He will endure*b* as long as the sun,
as long as the moon, through all
generations.
⁶ He will be like rain falling on a
mown field,
like showers watering the earth.
⁷ In his days the righteous will flourish;
prosperity will abound till the
moon is no more.

⁸ He will rule from sea to sea
and from the River*c* to the ends of
the earth.*d*
⁹ The desert tribes will bow before him
and his enemies will lick the dust.
¹⁰ The kings of Tarshish and of distant
shores
will bring tribute to him;
the kings of Sheba and Seba
will present him gifts.
¹¹ All kings will bow down to him
and all nations will serve him.

¹² For he will deliver the needy who
cry out,
the afflicted who have no one to
help.
¹³ He will take pity on the weak and
the needy
and save the needy from death.
¹⁴ He will rescue them from oppression
and violence,
for precious is their blood in his
sight.

¹⁵ Long may he live!
May gold from Sheba be given him.
May people ever pray for him
and bless him all day long.
¹⁶ Let grain abound throughout the
land;
on the tops of the hills may it sway.

---

*a*2 Or *May he*; similarly in verses 3–11 and 17
*b*5 Septuagint; Hebrew *You will be feared*
*c*8 That is, the Euphrates   *d*8 Or *the end of
the land*

Let its fruit flourish like Lebanon;
   let it thrive like the grass of the
   field.
¹⁷ May his name endure forever;
   may it continue as long as the sun.

All nations will be blessed through
   him,
   and they will call him blessed.

¹⁸ Praise be to the LORD God, the God
   of Israel,
   who alone does marvelous deeds.
¹⁹ Praise be to his glorious name
   forever;
   may the whole earth be filled with
   his glory.
   Amen and Amen.

²⁰ This concludes the prayers of David
   son of Jesse.

BOOK III

Psalms 73–89

Psalm 73

A psalm of Asaph.

¹ Surely God is good to Israel,
   to those who are pure in heart.

² But as for me, my feet had almost
   slipped;
   I had nearly lost my foothold.
³ For I envied the arrogant
   when I saw the prosperity of the
   wicked.

⁴ They have no struggles;
   their bodies are healthy and
   strong.ᵃ
⁵ They are free from the burdens
   common to man;
   they are not plagued by
   human ills.
⁶ Therefore pride is their necklace;
   they clothe themselves with
   violence.
⁷ From their callous hearts comes
   iniquityᵇ;
   the evil conceits of their minds
   know no limits.
⁸ They scoff, and speak with malice;
   in their arrogance they threaten
   oppression.

⁹ Their mouths lay claim to heaven,
   and their tongues take possession
   of the earth.
¹⁰ Therefore their people turn to them
   and drink up waters in abundance.ᶜ
¹¹ They say, "How can God know?
   Does the Most High have
   knowledge?"

¹² This is what the wicked are like—
   always carefree, they increase in
   wealth.

¹³ Surely in vain have I kept my heart
   pure;
   in vain have I washed my hands in
   innocence.
¹⁴ All day long I have been plagued;
   I have been punished every
   morning.

¹⁵ If I had said, "I will speak thus,"
   I would have betrayed your
   children.
¹⁶ When I tried to understand all this,
   it was oppressive to me
¹⁷ till I entered the sanctuary of God;
   then I understood their final
   destiny.

¹⁸ Surely you place them on slippery
   ground;
   you cast them down to ruin.
¹⁹ How suddenly are they destroyed,
   completely swept away by terrors!
²⁰ As a dream when one awakes,
   so when you arise, O Lord,
   you will despise them as fantasies.

²¹ When my heart was grieved
   and my spirit embittered,
²² I was senseless and ignorant;
   I was a brute beast before you.

²³ Yet I am always with you;
   you hold me by my right hand.
²⁴ You guide me with your counsel,
   and afterward you will take me
   into glory.
²⁵ Whom have I in heaven but you?
   And earth has nothing I desire
   besides you.

ᵃ4 With a different word division of the Hebrew;
Masoretic Text *struggles at their death; / their
bodies are healthy*   ᵇ7 Syriac (see also
Septuagint); Hebrew *Their eyes bulge with fat*
ᶜ10 The meaning of the Hebrew for this verse is
uncertain.

Whom Have I in Heaven but You?

73:26 GOD IS THE STRENGTH OF MY HEART AND MY PORTION FOREVER.

"Of the Seven Deadly Sins, anger is possibly the most fun," writes Frederick Buechner. "To lick your wounds, to smack your lips over grievances long past, to roll over your tongue the prospect of bitter confrontations still to come, to savor to the last toothsome morsel both the pain you are given and the pain you are giving back—in many ways it is a feast fit for a king. The chief drawback is that what you are wolfing down is yourself. The skeleton at the feast is you."[7]

The writer of this psalm looks back on how things were for him at one time and admits that he was being consumed by bitterness and anger. He was full of envy for what seemed to be the unchecked arrogance and rapaciousness of the wicked. Not only were they getting away with violence and theft, they were prospering. God seemed worse than an absentee landlord; he appeared unfazed and uninterested. The psalmist almost began complaining about God and the uselessness of living a good life. He's glad he didn't (see 73:15). In retrospect, he says to God, "When my heart was grieved and my spirit embittered, I was senseless and ignorant; I was a brute beast before you" (verses 21–22).

What changed things for the psalmist was one day entering the sanctuary and gaining a refreshed vision of God's love and justice. In worship he remembers that a holy God will not let sin go unpunished (see verses 16–20). Even better, in worship he remembers the sweetness of God's love. He prays some of the sweetest words of friendship with God in all of Scripture:

Yet I am always with you; you hold me by my right hand. You guide me with your counsel, and afterward you will take me into glory. Whom have I in heaven but you? And earth has nothing I desire besides you. My flesh and my heart may fail, but God is the strength of my heart and my portion forever (verses 23–26).

Let the wicked enjoy their temporary successes! The psalmist now knows that "the man that has everything minus God is a pauper; and the other who has God minus everything is 'rich to all the intents of bliss.'"[8] The cure for anger, envy and bitterness is gratitude for the goodness of God's friendship.

P R A Y :

Whom have I in heaven but you?
And earth has nothing I desire besides you.
Lord God, you are the strength of my heart
and my portion forever!

FOR YOUR NEXT DEVOTIONAL READING, GO TO PAGE 683.

26 My flesh and my heart may fail,
   but God is the strength of my heart
   and my portion forever.

27 Those who are far from you will
      perish;
   you destroy all who are unfaithful
      to you.
28 But as for me, it is good to be near
      God.
   I have made the Sovereign LORD
      my refuge;
   I will tell of all your deeds.

Psalm 74

A maskil[a] *of Asaph.*

1 Why have you rejected us forever,
      O God?
   Why does your anger smolder
      against the sheep of your
      pasture?
2 Remember the people you purchased
      of old,
   the tribe of your inheritance, whom
      you redeemed—
   Mount Zion, where you dwelt.
3 Turn your steps toward these
      everlasting ruins,
   all this destruction the enemy has
      brought on the sanctuary.

4 Your foes roared in the place where
      you met with us;
   they set up their standards as
      signs.
5 They behaved like men wielding axes
      to cut through a thicket of trees.
6 They smashed all the carved paneling
      with their axes and hatchets.
7 They burned your sanctuary to the
      ground;
   they defiled the dwelling place of
      your Name.
8 They said in their hearts, "We will
      crush them completely!"
   They burned every place where
      God was worshiped in the
      land.
9 We are given no miraculous signs;
      no prophets are left,
   and none of us knows how long
      this will be.

10 How long will the enemy mock you,
      O God?
   Will the foe revile your name
      forever?
11 Why do you hold back your hand,
      your right hand?
   Take it from the folds of your
      garment and destroy them!

12 But you, O God, are my king from
      of old;
   you bring salvation upon the earth.
13 It was you who split open the sea by
      your power;
   you broke the heads of the monster
      in the waters.
14 It was you who crushed the heads of
      Leviathan
   and gave him as food to the
      creatures of the desert.
15 It was you who opened up springs
      and streams;
   you dried up the ever flowing
      rivers.
16 The day is yours, and yours also
      the night;
   you established the sun and moon.
17 It was you who set all the boundaries
      of the earth;
   you made both summer and
      winter.

18 Remember how the enemy has
      mocked you, O LORD,
   how foolish people have reviled
      your name.
19 Do not hand over the life of your dove
      to wild beasts;
   do not forget the lives of your
      afflicted people forever.
20 Have regard for your covenant,
   because haunts of violence fill the
      dark places of the land.
21 Do not let the oppressed retreat in
      disgrace;
   may the poor and needy praise
      your name.

22 Rise up, O God, and defend your
      cause;
   remember how fools mock you all
      day long.
23 Do not ignore the clamor of your
      adversaries,
   the uproar of your enemies, which
      rises continually.

---

*a*Title: Probably a literary or musical term

Psalm 75

For the director of music.
⌊To the tune of⌋ "Do Not Destroy."
A psalm of Asaph. A song.

[1] We give thanks to you, O God,
  we give thanks, for your Name is
   near;
  men tell of your wonderful deeds.

[2] You say, "I choose the appointed
   time;
  it is I who judge uprightly.
[3] When the earth and all its people
   quake,
  it is I who hold its pillars firm. *Selah*
[4] To the arrogant I say, 'Boast no
   more,'
  and to the wicked, 'Do not lift up
   your horns.
[5] Do not lift your horns against
   heaven;
  do not speak with outstretched
   neck.' "

[6] No one from the east or the west
  or from the desert can exalt a man.
[7] But it is God who judges:
  He brings one down, he exalts
   another.
[8] In the hand of the LORD is a cup
  full of foaming wine mixed with
   spices;
  he pours it out, and all the wicked
   of the earth
  drink it down to its very dregs.

[9] As for me, I will declare this forever;
  I will sing praise to the God of
   Jacob.
[10] I will cut off the horns of all the
   wicked,
  but the horns of the righteous will
   be lifted up.

Psalm 76

For the director of music.
With stringed instruments.
A psalm of Asaph. A song.

[1] In Judah God is known;
  his name is great in Israel.
[2] His tent is in Salem,
  his dwelling place in Zion.
[3] There he broke the flashing arrows,
  the shields and the swords, the
  weapons of war. *Selah*

[4] You are resplendent with light,
  more majestic than mountains rich
   with game.
[5] Valiant men lie plundered,
  they sleep their last sleep;
  not one of the warriors
  can lift his hands.
[6] At your rebuke, O God of Jacob,
  both horse and chariot lie still.
[7] You alone are to be feared.
  Who can stand before you when
   you are angry?
[8] From heaven you pronounced
   judgment,
  and the land feared and was
   quiet—
[9] when you, O God, rose up to judge,
  to save all the afflicted of the land.
   Selah
[10] Surely your wrath against men brings
   you praise,
  and the survivors of your wrath are
   restrained.[a]

[11] Make vows to the LORD your God and
   fulfill them;
  let all the neighboring lands
  bring gifts to the One to be feared.
[12] He breaks the spirit of rulers;
  he is feared by the kings of the
   earth.

Psalm 77

For the director of music. For Jeduthun.
Of Asaph. A psalm.

[1] I cried out to God for help;
  I cried out to God to hear me.
[2] When I was in distress, I sought the
   Lord;
  at night I stretched out untiring
   hands
  and my soul refused to be
   comforted.

[3] I remembered you, O God, and I
   groaned;
  I mused, and my spirit grew faint.
   Selah
[4] You kept my eyes from closing;
  I was too troubled to speak.
[5] I thought about the former days,
  the years of long ago;

---

[a] *10 Or* Surely the wrath of men brings you praise,
/ and with the remainder of wrath you arm
yourself

6 I remembered my songs in the night.
My heart mused and my spirit
inquired:

7 "Will the Lord reject forever?
Will he never show his favor again?
8 Has his unfailing love vanished
forever?
Has his promise failed for all time?
9 Has God forgotten to be merciful?
Has he in anger withheld his
compassion?" *Selah*

10 Then I thought, "To this I will appeal:
the years of the right hand of the
Most High."
11 I will remember the deeds of the
LORD;
yes, I will remember your miracles
of long ago.
12 I will meditate on all your works
and consider all your mighty deeds.

13 Your ways, O God, are holy.
What god is so great as our God?
14 You are the God who performs
miracles;
you display your power among
the peoples.
15 With your mighty arm you redeemed
your people,
the descendants of Jacob and
Joseph. *Selah*

16 The waters saw you, O God,
the waters saw you and writhed;
the very depths were convulsed.
17 The clouds poured down water,
the skies resounded with thunder;
your arrows flashed back and forth.
18 Your thunder was heard in the
whirlwind,
your lightning lit up the world;
the earth trembled and quaked.
19 Your path led through the sea,
your way through the mighty
waters,
though your footprints were not
seen.
20 You led your people like a flock
by the hand of Moses and Aaron.

Psalm 78

A *maskil*[a] of Asaph.

1 O my people, hear my teaching;
listen to the words of my mouth.

2 I will open my mouth in parables,
I will utter hidden things, things
from of old—
3 what we have heard and known,
what our fathers have told us.
4 We will not hide them from their
children;
we will tell the next generation
the praiseworthy deeds of the LORD,
his power, and the wonders he
has done.
5 He decreed statutes for Jacob
and established the law in Israel,
which he commanded our forefathers
to teach their children,
6 so the next generation would know
them,
even the children yet to be born,
and they in turn would tell their
children.
7 Then they would put their trust in
God
and would not forget his deeds
but would keep his commands.
8 They would not be like their
forefathers—
a stubborn and rebellious
generation,
whose hearts were not loyal to God,
whose spirits were not faithful to
him.

9 The men of Ephraim, though armed
with bows,
turned back on the day of battle;
10 they did not keep God's covenant
and refused to live by his law.
11 They forgot what he had done,
the wonders he had shown them.
12 He did miracles in the sight of their
fathers
in the land of Egypt, in the region
of Zoan.
13 He divided the sea and led them
through;
he made the water stand firm like
a wall.
14 He guided them with the cloud by
day
and with light from the fire all
night.
15 He split the rocks in the desert
and gave them water as abundant
as the seas;

---

[a] Title: Probably a literary or musical term

16 he brought streams out of a rocky
       crag
   and made water flow down like
       rivers.
17 But they continued to sin against
       him,
   rebelling in the desert against the
       Most High.
18 They willfully put God to the test
   by demanding the food they
       craved.
19 They spoke against God, saying,
   "Can God spread a table in the
       desert?
20 When he struck the rock, water
       gushed out,
   and streams flowed abundantly.
   But can he also give us food?
   Can he supply meat for his
       people?"
21 When the LORD heard them, he was
       very angry;
   his fire broke out against Jacob,
   and his wrath rose against Israel,
22 for they did not believe in God
   or trust in his deliverance.
23 Yet he gave a command to the skies
       above
   and opened the doors of the
       heavens;
24 he rained down manna for the people
       to eat,
   he gave them the grain of heaven.
25 Men ate the bread of angels;
   he sent them all the food they
       could eat.
26 He let loose the east wind from the
       heavens
   and led forth the south wind by his
       power.
27 He rained meat down on them like
       dust,
   flying birds like sand on the
       seashore.
28 He made them come down inside
       their camp,
   all around their tents.
29 They ate till they had more than
       enough,
   for he had given them what they
       craved.
30 But before they turned from the food
       they craved,
   even while it was still in their
       mouths,

31 God's anger rose against them;
   he put to death the sturdiest
       among them,
   cutting down the young men of
       Israel.
32 In spite of all this, they kept on
       sinning;
   in spite of his wonders, they did
       not believe.
33 So he ended their days in futility
   and their years in terror.
34 Whenever God slew them, they would
       seek him;
   they eagerly turned to him again.
35 They remembered that God was their
       Rock,
   that God Most High was their
       Redeemer.
36 But then they would flatter him with
       their mouths,
   lying to him with their tongues;
37 their hearts were not loyal to him,
   they were not faithful to his
       covenant.
38 Yet he was merciful;
   he forgave their iniquities
   and did not destroy them.
   Time after time he restrained his anger
   and did not stir up his full wrath.
39 He remembered that they were but
       flesh,
   a passing breeze that does not
       return.

40 How often they rebelled against him
       in the desert
   and grieved him in the wasteland!
41 Again and again they put God to
       the test;
   they vexed the Holy One of Israel.
42 They did not remember his power—
   the day he redeemed them from
       the oppressor,
43 the day he displayed his miraculous
       signs in Egypt,
   his wonders in the region of Zoan.
44 He turned their rivers to blood;
   they could not drink from their
       streams.
45 He sent swarms of flies that devoured
       them,
   and frogs that devastated them.
46 He gave their crops to the
       grasshopper,
   their produce to the locust.

47 He destroyed their vines with hail
and their sycamore-figs with
sleet.
48 He gave over their cattle to the hail,
their livestock to bolts of lightning.
49 He unleashed against them his hot
anger,
his wrath, indignation and
hostility—
a band of destroying angels.
50 He prepared a path for his anger;
he did not spare them from death
but gave them over to the plague.
51 He struck down all the firstborn of
Egypt,
the firstfruits of manhood in the
tents of Ham.
52 But he brought his people out like
a flock;
he led them like sheep through
the desert.
53 He guided them safely, so they were
unafraid;
but the sea engulfed their enemies.
54 Thus he brought them to the border
of his holy land,
to the hill country his right hand
had taken.
55 He drove out nations before them
and allotted their lands to them as
an inheritance;
he settled the tribes of Israel in
their homes.

56 But they put God to the test
and rebelled against the Most
High;
they did not keep his statutes.
57 Like their fathers they were disloyal
and faithless,
as unreliable as a faulty bow.
58 They angered him with their high
places;
they aroused his jealousy with
their idols.
59 When God heard them, he was very
angry;
he rejected Israel completely.
60 He abandoned the tabernacle of
Shiloh,
the tent he had set up among men.
61 He sent ˌthe ark ofˌ his might into
captivity,
his splendor into the hands of the
enemy.

62 He gave his people over to the
sword;
he was very angry with his
inheritance.
63 Fire consumed their young men,
and their maidens had no
wedding songs;
64 their priests were put to the
sword,
and their widows could not
weep.

65 Then the Lord awoke as from sleep,
as a man wakes from the stupor of
wine.
66 He beat back his enemies;
he put them to everlasting shame.
67 Then he rejected the tents of Joseph,
he did not choose the tribe of
Ephraim;
68 but he chose the tribe of Judah,
Mount Zion, which he loved.
69 He built his sanctuary like the
heights,
like the earth that he established
forever.
70 He chose David his servant
and took him from the sheep pens;
71 from tending the sheep he brought
him
to be the shepherd of his people
Jacob,
of Israel his inheritance.
72 And David shepherded them with
integrity of heart;
with skillful hands he led them.

Psalm 79

A psalm of Asaph.

1 O God, the nations have invaded your
inheritance;
they have defiled your holy temple,
they have reduced Jerusalem to
rubble.
2 They have given the dead bodies of
your servants
as food to the birds of the air,
the flesh of your saints to the
beasts of the earth.
3 They have poured out blood like
water
all around Jerusalem,
and there is no one to bury the
dead.

⁴We are objects of reproach to our
neighbors,
of scorn and derision to those
around us.
⁵How long, O LORD? Will you be angry
forever?
How long will your jealousy burn
like fire?
⁶Pour out your wrath on the nations
that do not acknowledge you,
on the kingdoms
that do not call on your name;
⁷for they have devoured Jacob
and destroyed his homeland.
⁸Do not hold against us the sins of
the fathers;
may your mercy come quickly to
meet us,
for we are in desperate need.

⁹Help us, O God our Savior,
for the glory of your name;
deliver us and forgive our sins
for your name's sake.
¹⁰Why should the nations say,
"Where is their God?"
Before our eyes, make known among
the nations
that you avenge the outpoured
blood of your servants.
¹¹May the groans of the prisoners come
before you;
by the strength of your arm
preserve those condemned to die.

¹²Pay back into the laps of our
neighbors seven times
the reproach they have hurled at
you, O Lord.
¹³Then we your people, the sheep of
your pasture,
will praise you forever;
from generation to generation
we will recount your praise.

Psalm 80

For the director of music.
To the tune of "The Lilies of
the Covenant." Of Asaph. A psalm.

¹Hear us, O Shepherd of Israel,
you who lead Joseph like a flock;
you who sit enthroned between the
cherubim, shine forth
²   before Ephraim, Benjamin and
Manasseh.

Awaken your might;
come and save us.
³Restore us, O God;
make your face shine upon us,
that we may be saved.

⁴O LORD God Almighty,
how long will your anger smolder
against the prayers of your people?
⁵You have fed them with the bread of
tears;
you have made them drink tears by
the bowlful.
⁶You have made us a source of
contention to our neighbors,
and our enemies mock us.

⁷Restore us, O God Almighty;
make your face shine upon us,
that we may be saved.

⁸You brought a vine out of Egypt;
you drove out the nations and
planted it.
⁹You cleared the ground for it,
and it took root and filled the land.
¹⁰The mountains were covered with
its shade,
the mighty cedars with its
branches.
¹¹It sent out its boughs to the Sea,ᵃ
its shoots as far as the River.ᵇ

¹²Why have you broken down its walls
so that all who pass by pick its
grapes?
¹³Boars from the forest ravage it
and the creatures of the field feed
on it.
¹⁴Return to us, O God Almighty!
Look down from heaven and see!
Watch over this vine,
¹⁵   the root your right hand has
planted,
the sonᶜ you have raised up for
yourself.

¹⁶Your vine is cut down, it is burned
with fire;
at your rebuke your people perish.
¹⁷Let your hand rest on the man at your
right hand,
the son of man you have raised up
for yourself.

ᵃ11 Probably the Mediterranean   ᵇ11 That is,
the Euphrates   ᶜ15 Or branch

18 Then we will not turn away from you;
  revive us, and we will call on your
  name.

19 Restore us, O LORD God Almighty;
  make your face shine upon us,
  that we may be saved.

Psalm 81

For the director of music. According
to *gittith.*[a] Of Asaph.

1 Sing for joy to God our strength;
  shout aloud to the God of Jacob!
2 Begin the music, strike the
  tambourine,
  play the melodious harp and lyre.

3 Sound the ram's horn at the New
  Moon,
  and when the moon is full, on the
  day of our Feast;
4 this is a decree for Israel,
  an ordinance of the God of Jacob.
5 He established it as a statute for
  Joseph
  when he went out against Egypt,
  where we heard a language we did
  not understand.[b]

6 He says, "I removed the burden from
  their shoulders;
  their hands were set free from the
  basket.
7 In your distress you called and I
  rescued you,
  I answered you out of a
  thundercloud;
  I tested you at the waters of
  Meribah.   *Selah*
8 "Hear, O my people, and I will warn
  you—
  if you would but listen to me,
  O Israel!
9 You shall have no foreign god among
  you;
  you shall not bow down to an
  alien god.
10 I am the LORD your God,
  who brought you up out of Egypt.
  Open wide your mouth and I will
  fill it.

11 "But my people would not listen to
  me;
  Israel would not submit to me.

12 So I gave them over to their
  stubborn hearts
  to follow their own devices.

13 "If my people would but listen to
  me,
  if Israel would follow my ways,
14 how quickly would I subdue their
  enemies
  and turn my hand against their
  foes!
15 Those who hate the LORD would
  cringe before him,
  and their punishment would last
  forever.
16 But you would be fed with the finest
  of wheat;
  with honey from the rock I would
  satisfy you."

Psalm 82

A psalm of Asaph.

1 God presides in the great assembly;
  he gives judgment among the
  "gods":

2 "How long will you[c] defend the
  unjust
  and show partiality to the
  wicked?   *Selah*
3 Defend the cause of the weak
  and fatherless;
  maintain the rights of the poor
  and oppressed.
4 Rescue the weak and needy;
  deliver them from the hand of the
  wicked.

5 "They know nothing, they
  understand nothing.
  They walk about in darkness;
  all the foundations of the earth
  are shaken.

6 "I said, 'You are "gods";
  you are all sons of the Most High.'
7 But you will die like mere men;
  you will fall like every other
  ruler."

8 Rise up, O God, judge the earth,
  for all the nations are your
  inheritance.

[a]Title: Probably a musical term   [b]5 Or / *and
we heard a voice we had not known*   [c]2 The
Hebrew is plural.

Psalm 83

A song. A psalm of Asaph.

¹ O God, do not keep silent;
  be not quiet, O God, be not still.
² See how your enemies are astir,
  how your foes rear their heads.
³ With cunning they conspire against
    your people;
  they plot against those you cherish.
⁴ "Come," they say, "let us destroy
    them as a nation,
  that the name of Israel be
    remembered no more."

⁵ With one mind they plot together;
  they form an alliance against you—
⁶ the tents of Edom and the
    Ishmaelites,
  of Moab and the Hagrites,
⁷ Gebal,*a* Ammon and Amalek,
  Philistia, with the people of Tyre.
⁸ Even Assyria has joined them
  to lend strength to the descendants
    of Lot.   *Selah*

⁹ Do to them as you did to Midian,
  as you did to Sisera and Jabin at
    the river Kishon,
¹⁰ who perished at Endor
  and became like refuse on the
    ground.
¹¹ Make their nobles like Oreb and Zeeb,
  all their princes like Zebah and
    Zalmunna,
¹² who said, "Let us take possession
  of the pasturelands of God."

¹³ Make them like tumbleweed,
    O my God,
  like chaff before the wind.
¹⁴ As fire consumes the forest
  or a flame sets the mountains
    ablaze,
¹⁵ so pursue them with your tempest
  and terrify them with your storm.
¹⁶ Cover their faces with shame
  so that men will seek your name,
    O LORD.

¹⁷ May they ever be ashamed and
    dismayed;
  may they perish in disgrace.
¹⁸ Let them know that you, whose name
    is the LORD—
  that you alone are the Most High
    over all the earth.

Psalm 84

*For the director of music. According to
gittith.*b* Of the Sons of Korah. A psalm.*

¹ How lovely is your dwelling place,
    O LORD Almighty!
² My soul yearns, even faints,
  for the courts of the LORD;
  my heart and my flesh cry out
    for the living God.

³ Even the sparrow has found a home,
  and the swallow a nest for herself,
  where she may have her young—
  a place near your altar,
    O LORD Almighty, my King and my
      God.
⁴ Blessed are those who dwell in your
    house;
  they are ever praising you.   *Selah*

⁵ Blessed are those whose strength is
    in you,
  who have set their hearts on
    pilgrimage.
⁶ As they pass through the Valley of
    Baca,
  they make it a place of springs;
  the autumn rains also cover it with
    pools.*c*
⁷ They go from strength to strength,
  till each appears before God in
    Zion.

⁸ Hear my prayer, O LORD God
    Almighty;
  listen to me, O God of Jacob.   *Selah*
⁹ Look upon our shield,*d* O God;
  look with favor on your anointed
    one.

¹⁰ Better is one day in your courts
  than a thousand elsewhere;
  I would rather be a doorkeeper in the
    house of my God
  than dwell in the tents of the
    wicked.
¹¹ For the LORD God is a sun and shield;
  the LORD bestows favor and honor;
  no good thing does he withhold
    from those whose walk is
      blameless.

¹² O LORD Almighty,
  blessed is the man who trusts in you.

*a7 That is, Byblos   b Title: Probably a musical
term   c6 Or blessings   d9 Or sovereign*

Psalm 85

For the director of music. Of the Sons
of Korah. A psalm.

¹ You showed favor to your land,
    O LORD;
    you restored the fortunes of Jacob.
² You forgave the iniquity of your
    people
    and covered all their sins.   *Selah*
³ You set aside all your wrath
    and turned from your fierce anger.

⁴ Restore us again, O God our Savior,
    and put away your displeasure
        toward us.
⁵ Will you be angry with us forever?
    Will you prolong your anger
    through all generations?
⁶ Will you not revive us again,
    that your people may rejoice in
        you?
⁷ Show us your unfailing love, O LORD,
    and grant us your salvation.

⁸ I will listen to what God the LORD
    will say;
    he promises peace to his people,
        his saints—
    but let them not return to folly.
⁹ Surely his salvation is near those who
        fear him,
    that his glory may dwell in our
        land.

¹⁰ Love and faithfulness meet together;
    righteousness and peace kiss each
        other.
¹¹ Faithfulness springs forth from the
        earth,
    and righteousness looks down
        from heaven.
¹² The LORD will indeed give what is
        good,
    and our land will yield its harvest.
¹³ Righteousness goes before him
    and prepares the way for his steps.

Psalm 86

A prayer of David.

¹ Hear, O LORD, and answer me,
    for I am poor and needy.
² Guard my life, for I am devoted to
        you.
    You are my God; save your servant
    who trusts in you.

³ Have mercy on me, O Lord,
    for I call to you all day long.
⁴ Bring joy to your servant,
    for to you, O Lord,
    I lift up my soul.

⁵ You are forgiving and good, O Lord,
    abounding in love to all who call to
        you.
⁶ Hear my prayer, O LORD;
    listen to my cry for mercy.
⁷ In the day of my trouble I will call
        to you,
    for you will answer me.

⁸ Among the gods there is none like
        you, O Lord;
    no deeds can compare with yours.
⁹ All the nations you have made
    will come and worship before you,
        O Lord;
    they will bring glory to your name.
¹⁰ For you are great and do marvelous
        deeds;
    you alone are God.

¹¹ Teach me your way, O LORD,
    and I will walk in your truth;
    give me an undivided heart,
    that I may fear your name.
¹² I will praise you, O Lord my God, with
        all my heart;
    I will glorify your name forever.
¹³ For great is your love toward me;
    you have delivered me from the
        depths of the grave.ᵃ

¹⁴ The arrogant are attacking me,
        O God;
    a band of ruthless men seeks my
        life—
    men without regard for you.
¹⁵ But you, O Lord, are a compassionate
        and gracious God,
    slow to anger, abounding in love
        and faithfulness.
¹⁶ Turn to me and have mercy on me;
    grant your strength to your servant
    and save the son of your
        maidservant.ᵇ
¹⁷ Give me a sign of your goodness,
    that my enemies may see it and be
        put to shame,
    for you, O LORD, have helped me
    and comforted me.

ᵃ13 Hebrew Sheol   *ᵇ16 Or save your faithful son*

Psalm 87

Of the Sons of Korah. A psalm. A song.

¹ He has set his foundation on the holy
mountain;
² the LORD loves the gates of Zion
more than all the dwellings of Jacob.

³ Glorious things are said of you,
O city of God: *Selah*
⁴ "I will record Rahab*ᵃ* and Babylon
among those who acknowledge
me—

ᵃ4 A poetic name for Egypt

PSALM 85

{THURSDAY}

Revive Us Again

85:6 WILL YOU NOT REVIVE US AGAIN, THAT YOUR PEOPLE MAY REJOICE IN YOU?

It happens in marriages and between friends, in families and in churches. Love grows cold and passion fades, and what once was personal and intimate becomes rote and formal. But if even the memory of what once was remains, it can be enough to spur renewal, or revival. This is especially the case with God's people. The risen Christ urged the Ephesian church to remember and be revived: "You have forsaken your first love. Remember the height from which you have fallen! Repent and do the things you did at first" (Revelation 2:4–5). In the same way, this psalm of the Sons of Korah remembers what once was (verses 1–3) and prays for the revival of God's people: "Will you not revive us again, that your people may rejoice in you?" (verse 6).

What is revival? The prayer itself provides the definition and the goal: "that your people may rejoice in you." As in a marriage, to be revived in faith is to be renewed in love and joy. To have a powerful faith that can move mountains and a courage that will be willingly consumed by fire, but to have no love, is to have a dead religion (see 1 Corinthians 13:1–3). Far from being honored by mere empty obedience, God is insulted. No, as John Piper says, God is glorified in us only as we are satisfied in him.

This psalm provides a lovely picture of revival, very much in keeping with its definition: "Love and faithfulness meet together; righteousness and peace kiss each other" (verse 10). Could anyone wish for anything more? The quality of life takes on a kind of marital bliss, and heaven and earth meet, as "Faithfulness springs forth from the earth, and righteousness looks down from heaven" (verse 11). A clearer picture comes from the first chapter of John's Gospel: "The Word became flesh and made his dwelling among us. We have seen his glory, the glory of the One and Only, who came from the Father, full of grace and truth" (1:14). Revival is the presence of Christ, dwelling among us in love, in our hearts (see Ephesians 3:17).

The history of God's people seems to be a history of recurrent spiritual decline (see Judges 2:10–19). That's the bad news. The good news is that God is always ready to hear his people pray, "Will you not revive us again, that your people may rejoice in you?"

PRAY:

Dear Father, our love has grown cold, our faith is weak. May Christ dwell
fully in our hearts; revive us again that we might rejoice in you!

FOR YOUR NEXT DEVOTIONAL READING, GO TO PAGE 690.

Philistia too, and Tyre, along with
Cush[a]—
and will say, 'This[b] one was born in
Zion.' "

5 Indeed, of Zion it will be said,
"This one and that one were born
in her,
and the Most High himself will
establish her."
6 The LORD will write in the register of
the peoples:
"This one was born in Zion." *Selah*
7 As they make music they will sing,
"All my fountains are in you."

Psalm 88

A song. A psalm of the Sons of Korah.
For the director of music. According
to *mahalath leannoth*.[c] A *maskil*[d]
of Heman the Ezrahite.

1 O LORD, the God who saves me,
day and night I cry out before you.
2 May my prayer come before you;
turn your ear to my cry.

3 For my soul is full of trouble
and my life draws near the grave.[e]
4 I am counted among those who go
down to the pit;
I am like a man without strength.
5 I am set apart with the dead,
like the slain who lie in the grave,
whom you remember no more,
who are cut off from your care.

6 You have put me in the lowest pit,
in the darkest depths.
7 Your wrath lies heavily upon me;
you have overwhelmed me with
all your waves. *Selah*
8 You have taken from me my closest
friends
and have made me repulsive to
them.
I am confined and cannot escape;
9 my eyes are dim with grief.

I call to you, O LORD, every day;
I spread out my hands to you.
10 Do you show your wonders to the
dead?
Do those who are dead rise up
and praise you? *Selah*
11 Is your love declared in the grave,
your faithfulness in Destruction[f]?

12 Are your wonders known in the place
of darkness,
or your righteous deeds in the land
of oblivion?
13 But I cry to you for help, O LORD;
in the morning my prayer comes
before you.
14 Why, O LORD, do you reject me
and hide your face from me?

15 From my youth I have been afflicted
and close to death;
I have suffered your terrors and am
in despair.
16 Your wrath has swept over me;
your terrors have destroyed me.
17 All day long they surround me like a
flood;
they have completely engulfed me.
18 You have taken my companions and
loved ones from me;
the darkness is my closest friend.

> BUT *I cry to you for help, O LORD;*
> *in the morning my prayer comes*
> *before you.*
>
> PSALM 88:13

Psalm 89

A *maskil*[d] of Ethan the Ezrahite.

1 I will sing of the LORD's great love
forever;
with my mouth I will make your
faithfulness known through all
generations.
2 I will declare that your love stands
firm forever,
that you established your
faithfulness in heaven itself.
3 You said, "I have made a covenant
with my chosen one,
I have sworn to David my servant,
4 'I will establish your line forever
and make your throne firm through
all generations.' " *Selah*

---

a4 That is, the upper Nile region   *b4* Or "O
*Rahab and Babylon, / Philistia, Tyre and Cush, /
I will record concerning those who acknowledge
me: / 'This*   *c*Title: Possibly a tune, "The
Suffering of Affliction"   *d*Title: Probably a
literary or musical term   *e3* Hebrew *Sheol*
f11 Hebrew *Abaddon*

⁵The heavens praise your wonders,
 O LORD,
  your faithfulness too, in the
   assembly of the holy ones.
⁶For who in the skies above can
   compare with the LORD?
  Who is like the LORD among the
   heavenly beings?
⁷In the council of the holy ones God is
   greatly feared;
  he is more awesome than all who
   surround him.
⁸O LORD God Almighty, who is like
   you?
  You are mighty, O LORD, and your
   faithfulness surrounds you.

⁹You rule over the surging sea;
  when its waves mount up, you still
   them.
¹⁰You crushed Rahab like one of the
   slain;
  with your strong arm you scattered
   your enemies.
¹¹The heavens are yours, and yours
   also the earth;
  you founded the world and all that
   is in it.
¹²You created the north and the south;
  Tabor and Hermon sing for joy at
   your name.
¹³Your arm is endued with power;
  your hand is strong, your right
   hand exalted.

¹⁴Righteousness and justice are the
   foundation of your throne;
  love and faithfulness go before you.
¹⁵Blessed are those who have learned
   to acclaim you,
  who walk in the light of your
   presence, O LORD.
¹⁶They rejoice in your name all day
   long;
  they exult in your righteousness.
¹⁷For you are their glory and strength,
  and by your favor you exalt our
   horn.ᵃ
¹⁸Indeed, our shieldᵇ belongs to the
   LORD,
  our king to the Holy One of Israel.

¹⁹Once you spoke in a vision,
  to your faithful people you said:
 "I have bestowed strength on a
   warrior;

I have exalted a young man from
   among the people.
²⁰I have found David my servant;
  with my sacred oil I have anointed
   him.
²¹My hand will sustain him;
  surely my arm will strengthen him.
²²No enemy will subject him to
   tribute;
  no wicked man will oppress him.
²³I will crush his foes before him
  and strike down his adversaries.
²⁴My faithful love will be with him,
  and through my name his hornᶜ
   will be exalted.
²⁵I will set his hand over the sea,
  his right hand over the rivers.
²⁶He will call out to me, 'You are my
   Father,
  my God, the Rock my Savior.'
²⁷I will also appoint him my firstborn,
  the most exalted of the kings of
   the earth.
²⁸I will maintain my love to him
   forever,
  and my covenant with him will
   never fail.
²⁹I will establish his line forever,
  his throne as long as the heavens
   endure.

³⁰"If his sons forsake my law
  and do not follow my statutes,
³¹if they violate my decrees
  and fail to keep my commands,
³²I will punish their sin with the rod,
  their iniquity with flogging;
³³but I will not take my love from him,
  nor will I ever betray my
   faithfulness.
³⁴I will not violate my covenant
  or alter what my lips have uttered.
³⁵Once for all, I have sworn by my
   holiness—
  and I will not lie to David—
³⁶that his line will continue forever
  and his throne endure before me
   like the sun;
³⁷it will be established forever like
   the moon,
  the faithful witness in the sky."

Selah

ᵃ17 *Horn* here symbolizes strong one.
ᵇ18 Or *sovereign*   ᶜ24 *Horn* here symbolizes
strength.

38 But you have rejected, you have
 spurned,
 you have been very angry with your
  anointed one.
39 You have renounced the covenant
  with your servant
 and have defiled his crown in the
  dust.
40 You have broken through all his walls
 and reduced his strongholds to
  ruins.
41 All who pass by have plundered him;
 he has become the scorn of his
  neighbors.
42 You have exalted the right hand of
  his foes;
 you have made all his enemies
  rejoice.
43 You have turned back the edge of
  his sword
 and have not supported him in
  battle.
44 You have put an end to his splendor
 and cast his throne to the ground.
45 You have cut short the days of his
  youth;
 you have covered him with a
  mantle of shame.   *Selah*

46 How long, O LORD? Will you hide
  yourself forever?
 How long will your wrath burn
  like fire?
47 Remember how fleeting is my life.
 For what futility you have created
  all men!
48 What man can live and not see death,
 or save himself from the power of
  the grave[a]?   *Selah*
49 O Lord, where is your former great
  love,
 which in your faithfulness you
  swore to David?
50 Remember, Lord, how your servant
  has[b] been mocked,
 how I bear in my heart the taunts
  of all the nations,
51 the taunts with which your enemies
  have mocked, O LORD,

PRAISE be to the LORD forever!
Amen and Amen.

with which they have mocked every
 step of your anointed one.

52 Praise be to the LORD forever!
 Amen and Amen.

BOOK IV

Psalms 90–106

Psalm 90

A prayer of Moses the man of God.

1 Lord, you have been our dwelling
  place
 throughout all generations.
2 Before the mountains were born
 or you brought forth the earth and
  the world,
 from everlasting to everlasting you
  are God.

3 You turn men back to dust,
 saying, "Return to dust, O sons of
  men."
4 For a thousand years in your sight
 are like a day that has just gone by,
 or like a watch in the night.
5 You sweep men away in the sleep of
  death;
 they are like the new grass of the
  morning—
6 though in the morning it springs up
  new,
 by evening it is dry and withered.

7 We are consumed by your anger
 and terrified by your indignation.
8 You have set our iniquities before
  you,
 our secret sins in the light of
  your presence.
9 All our days pass away under your
  wrath;
 we finish our years with a moan.
10 The length of our days is seventy
  years—
 or eighty, if we have the strength;
 yet their span[c] is but trouble and
  sorrow,
 for they quickly pass, and we fly
  away.

[a]48 Hebrew *Sheol*   [b]50 Or *your servants have*
[c]10 Or *yet the best of them*

11 Who knows the power of your anger?
    For your wrath is as great as the
      fear that is due you.
12 Teach us to number our days aright,
    that we may gain a heart of
      wisdom.
13 Relent, O LORD! How long will it be?
    Have compassion on your
      servants.
14 Satisfy us in the morning with your
      unfailing love,
    that we may sing for joy and be
      glad all our days.
15 Make us glad for as many days as you
      have afflicted us,
    for as many years as we have seen
      trouble.
16 May your deeds be shown to your
      servants,
    your splendor to their children.

17 May the favor*a* of the Lord our God
      rest upon us;
    establish the work of our hands
      for us—
    yes, establish the work of our
      hands.

Psalm 91

1 He who dwells in the shelter of the
      Most High
    will rest in the shadow of the
      Almighty.*b*
2 I will say*c* of the LORD, "He is my
      refuge and my fortress,
    my God, in whom I trust."

3 Surely he will save you from the
      fowler's snare
    and from the deadly pestilence.
4 He will cover you with his feathers,
    and under his wings you will find
      refuge;
    his faithfulness will be your shield
      and rampart.
5 You will not fear the terror of night,
    nor the arrow that flies by day,
6 nor the pestilence that stalks in the
      darkness,
    nor the plague that destroys at
      midday.
7 A thousand may fall at your side,
    ten thousand at your right hand,
    but it will not come near you.

8 You will only observe with your eyes
    and see the punishment of the
      wicked.

9 If you make the Most High your
      dwelling—
    even the LORD, who is my refuge—
10 then no harm will befall you,
    no disaster will come near your tent.
11 For he will command his angels
      concerning you
    to guard you in all your ways;
12 they will lift you up in their hands,
    so that you will not strike your foot
      against a stone.
13 You will tread upon the lion and the
      cobra;
    you will trample the great lion and
      the serpent.

14 "Because he loves me," says the LORD,
    "I will rescue him;
    I will protect him, for he
      acknowledges my name.
15 He will call upon me, and I will
      answer him;
    I will be with him in trouble,
    I will deliver him and honor him.
16 With long life will I satisfy him
    and show him my salvation."

Psalm 92

A psalm. A song. For the Sabbath day.

1 It is good to praise the LORD
    and make music to your name,
      O Most High,
2 to proclaim your love in the morning
    and your faithfulness at night,
3 to the music of the ten-stringed lyre
    and the melody of the harp.

4 For you make me glad by your deeds,
      O LORD;
    I sing for joy at the works of your
      hands.
5 How great are your works, O LORD,
    how profound your thoughts!
6 The senseless man does not know,
    fools do not understand,
7 that though the wicked spring up
      like grass
    and all evildoers flourish,
    they will be forever destroyed.

a17 Or *beauty*   *b1* Hebrew *Shaddai*
c2 Or *He says*

8 But you, O LORD, are exalted forever.

9 For surely your enemies, O LORD,
   surely your enemies will perish;
   all evildoers will be scattered.
10 You have exalted my horn[a] like that
   of a wild ox;
   fine oils have been poured upon
   me.
11 My eyes have seen the defeat of my
   adversaries;
   my ears have heard the rout of
   my wicked foes.

12 The righteous will flourish like a
   palm tree,
   they will grow like a cedar of
   Lebanon;
13 planted in the house of the LORD,
   they will flourish in the courts
   of our God.
14 They will still bear fruit in old age,
   they will stay fresh and green,
15 proclaiming, "The LORD is upright;
   he is my Rock, and there is no
   wickedness in him."

Psalm 93

1 The LORD reigns, he is robed in
   majesty;
   the LORD is robed in majesty
   and is armed with strength.
   The world is firmly established;
   it cannot be moved.
2 Your throne was established long
   ago;
   you are from all eternity.

3 The seas have lifted up, O LORD,
   the seas have lifted up their voice;
   the seas have lifted up their
   pounding waves.
4 Mightier than the thunder of the
   great waters,
   mightier than the breakers of
   the sea—
   the LORD on high is mighty.

5 Your statutes stand firm;
   holiness adorns your house
   for endless days, O LORD.

Psalm 94

1 O LORD, the God who avenges,
   O God who avenges, shine forth.

2 Rise up, O Judge of the earth;
   pay back to the proud what they
   deserve.
3 How long will the wicked, O LORD,
   how long will the wicked be
   jubilant?

4 They pour out arrogant words;
   all the evildoers are full of
   boasting.
5 They crush your people, O LORD;
   they oppress your inheritance.
6 They slay the widow and the alien;
   they murder the fatherless.
7 They say, "The LORD does not see;
   the God of Jacob pays no heed."

8 Take heed, you senseless ones among
   the people;
   you fools, when will you become
   wise?
9 Does he who implanted the ear not
   hear?
   Does he who formed the eye not
   see?
10 Does he who disciplines nations not
   punish?
   Does he who teaches man lack
   knowledge?
11 The LORD knows the thoughts of
   man;
   he knows that they are futile.

12 Blessed is the man you discipline,
   O LORD,
   the man you teach from your law;
13 you grant him relief from days of
   trouble,
   till a pit is dug for the wicked.
14 For the LORD will not reject his
   people;
   he will never forsake his
   inheritance.
15 Judgment will again be founded on
   righteousness,
   and all the upright in heart will
   follow it.

16 Who will rise up for me against the
   wicked?
   Who will take a stand for me
   against evildoers?
17 Unless the LORD had given me help,
   I would soon have dwelt in the
   silence of death.

[a]10 *Horn* here symbolizes strength.

18 When I said, "My foot is slipping,"
   your love, O LORD, supported me.
19 When anxiety was great within me,
   your consolation brought joy to
      my soul.

20 Can a corrupt throne be allied with
      you—
   one that brings on misery by its
      decrees?
21 They band together against the
      righteous
   and condemn the innocent to
      death.
22 But the LORD has become my fortress,
   and my God the rock in whom I
      take refuge.
23 He will repay them for their sins
   and destroy them for their
      wickedness;
   the LORD our God will destroy them.

Psalm 95

1 Come, let us sing for joy to the LORD;
   let us shout aloud to the Rock of
      our salvation.
2 Let us come before him with
      thanksgiving
   and extol him with music and song.

3 For the LORD is the great God,
   the great King above all gods.
4 In his hand are the depths of the
      earth,
   and the mountain peaks belong
      to him.
5 The sea is his, for he made it,
   and his hands formed the dry land.

6 Come, let us bow down in worship,
   let us kneel before the LORD our
      Maker;
7 for he is our God
   and we are the people of his pasture,
   the flock under his care.

   Today, if you hear his voice,
8   do not harden your hearts as you
      did at Meribah,ᵃ

> COME, let us sing for joy to the LORD;
> let us shout aloud to the Rock of
>   our salvation.
>
> PSALM 95:1

as you did that day at Massahᵇ in
   the desert,
9 where your fathers tested and tried
   me,
   though they had seen what I did.
10 For forty years I was angry with that
      generation;
   I said, "They are a people whose
      hearts go astray,
   and they have not known my ways."
11 So I declared on oath in my anger,
   "They shall never enter my rest."

Psalm 96

1 Sing to the LORD a new song;
   sing to the LORD, all the earth.
2 Sing to the LORD, praise his
      name;
   proclaim his salvation day after day.
3 Declare his glory among the nations,
   his marvelous deeds among all
      peoples.

4 For great is the LORD and most worthy
      of praise;
   he is to be feared above all gods.
5 For all the gods of the nations are
      idols,
   but the LORD made the heavens.
6 Splendor and majesty are before him;
   strength and glory are in his
      sanctuary.

7 Ascribe to the LORD, O families of
      nations,
   ascribe to the LORD glory and
      strength.
8 Ascribe to the LORD the glory due his
      name;
   bring an offering and come into
      his courts.
9 Worship the LORD in the splendor of
      hisᶜ holiness;
   tremble before him, all the earth.
10 Say among the nations, "The LORD
      reigns."
   The world is firmly established,
      it cannot be moved;
   he will judge the peoples with
      equity.
11 Let the heavens rejoice, let the earth
      be glad;

ᵃ8 Meribah means quarreling. ᵇ8 Massah
means testing. ᶜ9 Or LORD with the splendor of

let the sea resound, and all that is
in it;
12 let the fields be jubilant, and
everything in them.
Then all the trees of the forest will
sing for joy;

13 they will sing before the LORD, for
he comes,
he comes to judge the earth.
He will judge the world in
righteousness
and the peoples in his truth.

PSALM 96

Praying With Imagination

96:1 SING TO THE LORD, ALL THE EARTH.

This psalm marvelously engages the praying imagination. The peoples of the earth are summoned to "ascribe to the LORD the glory due his name" by bringing an offering into his courts (96:8). What might that offering be? The vision in Revelation gives a clue: Kings and peoples will bring their glory, honor and splendor into the heavenly city (see 21:24,26). Surely this offering must relate to who each nationality is as a people. Imagine the breadth of differences in culture between Masai, French, Chinese and Mexican—their music and dance, their food and stories! See them carry trays of tacos and fried rice and honey to the sounds of drums, accordions, flutes and tubas. They are wearing straw hats and sarongs, cowboy boots and sandals! Try it for yourself. Imagine what the glory and honor and splendor of the nations would look like offered to God in worship.

And what about the natural world? This psalm describes trees singing for joy, fields jubilant and the creatures of the sea resounding at the coming of the Lord (see Psalm 96:11–12). Again, this is a wonderful opportunity for imaginative prayer. Think of the variety of creatures in the natural world. Imagine pines, myrtle and barley; whales and anemones celebrating together in ways appropriate to the way God made them.

When the Lord comes in glory, we will witness the nations and all creatures on earth celebrating the Lord. For now, we have a unique role to play in the world. The poet George Herbert wrote that when we use human language to praise God, we act as "the world's high Priest" presenting "the sacrifice for all" the rest. For us to refrain from praise is not to refrain unto ourselves alone, but for the rest of creation, and to "commit a world of sin in one."[9] Until that great day when all creation rejoices, let us not sin, but with all our senses and faculties and imaginations "sing to the LORD a new song."

PRAY:

"May the peoples praise you, O God; may all the peoples praise you.
May the nations be glad and sing for joy, for you rule the peoples justly
and guide the nations of the earth" (Psalm 67:3–4).

FOR YOUR NEXT DEVOTIONAL READING, GO TO PAGE 692.

Psalm 97

[1] The LORD reigns, let the earth be glad;
  let the distant shores rejoice.

[2] Clouds and thick darkness surround
    him;
  righteousness and justice are the
    foundation of his throne.
[3] Fire goes before him
  and consumes his foes on every
    side.
[4] His lightning lights up the world;
  the earth sees and trembles.
[5] The mountains melt like wax before
    the LORD,
  before the Lord of all the earth.
[6] The heavens proclaim his
    righteousness,
  and all the peoples see his glory.

[7] All who worship images are put to
    shame,
  those who boast in idols—
  worship him, all you gods!

[8] Zion hears and rejoices
  and the villages of Judah are glad
  because of your judgments,
    O LORD.
[9] For you, O LORD, are the Most High
    over all the earth;
  you are exalted far above all gods.

[10] Let those who love the LORD hate evil,
  for he guards the lives of his
    faithful ones
  and delivers them from the hand
    of the wicked.
[11] Light is shed upon the righteous
  and joy on the upright in heart.
[12] Rejoice in the LORD, you who are
    righteous,
  and praise his holy name.

Psalm 98

A psalm.

[1] Sing to the LORD a new song,
  for he has done marvelous things;
  his right hand and his holy arm
  have worked salvation for him.
[2] The LORD has made his salvation
    known
  and revealed his righteousness to
    the nations.
[3] He has remembered his love

and his faithfulness to the house
    of Israel;
  all the ends of the earth have seen
    the salvation of our God.

[4] Shout for joy to the LORD, all the
    earth,
  burst into jubilant song with
    music;
[5] make music to the LORD with the
    harp,
  with the harp and the sound of
    singing,
[6] with trumpets and the blast of the
    ram's horn—
  shout for joy before the LORD,
    the King.

[7] Let the sea resound, and everything
    in it,
  the world, and all who live in it.
[8] Let the rivers clap their hands,
  let the mountains sing together for
    joy;
[9] let them sing before the LORD,
  for he comes to judge the earth.
He will judge the world in
    righteousness
  and the peoples with equity.

Psalm 99

[1] The LORD reigns,
  let the nations tremble;
he sits enthroned between the
    cherubim,
  let the earth shake.
[2] Great is the LORD in Zion;
  he is exalted over all the nations.
[3] Let them praise your great and
    awesome name—
  he is holy.

[4] The King is mighty, he loves justice—
  you have established equity;
in Jacob you have done
  what is just and right.
[5] Exalt the LORD our God
  and worship at his footstool;
  he is holy.

[6] Moses and Aaron were among his
    priests,
  Samuel was among those who
    called on his name;
they called on the LORD
  and he answered them.

The Son of These Tears

A CLASSIC scenario: a godly, faithful mother; an ungodly, faithless child. What's a mother to do? Pray. The time is the fourth century A.D.; the mother is Monica. The son is the brilliant, egotistical, heretical and licentious Augustine. Mother and son have wills of steel; her will the irresistible force, his the immovable object.

Monica visited the local priest to make a modest request: Would he do her a favor and have a talk with her son? Would he refute Augustine's errors, drive out the evil in him and replace it with good? Put simply, could this priest do everything she, Augustine's mother, had not been able to do? The priest was not the first or the last to hear such an unreasonable request from a distraught parent. He answered wisely, and he graciously refused her request. Augustine later wrote: "He told her that I was still unripe for instruction because, as she had told him, I was brimming over with the novelty of the heresy and had already upset a great many simple people with my casuistry."

In other words, Monica's son was having too much fun being a fool to be persuaded to do otherwise. There was but one thing to do: pray. "Leave him alone," the priest counseled. "Just pray to God for him. From his own reading he will discover his mistakes and the depth of his profanity."

The priest then gave a personal testimony of how he had once been right where Augustine was, but he had been brought to the truth even though his mother was herself a heretic. His point seemed to be that nothing is too hard for God. Human extremity is God's opportunity. You can't fix him; I can't fix him; only God can fix him, so trust in God.

Monica didn't like that answer, so she pressed her case and pestered the priest, this time with tears. The priest had enough. He answered, "Leave me and go in peace. It cannot be that the son of these tears should be lost."

Augustine wrote: "In later years, as we talked together, she used to say that she accepted these words as a message from heaven."[10] A message from heaven they were. Monica prayed, and the son of her tears became Saint Augustine, one of the most powerful voices the Christian church has ever had, the author of the monumental *City of God* and the matchless *Confessions*. Jesus taught that we should always pray and not give up (see Luke 18:1). Thank God that Monica did not give up. The faith of millions has been enriched through the faithful prayers of this tenacious woman.

PRAY:

Eternal God,
the light of the minds that know thee,
the life of the souls that love thee,
the strength of the wills that serve thee;
help us so to know thee that we may truly love thee,
so to love thee that we may fully serve thee,
whom to serve is perfect freedom.[11]

MEMORIZE:

Immediately the boy's father exclaimed, "I do believe;
help me overcome my unbelief!" MARK 9:24

FOR YOUR NEXT DEVOTIONAL READING, GO TO PAGE 696.

7 He spoke to them from the pillar of
cloud;
they kept his statutes and the
decrees he gave them.

8 O LORD our God,
you answered them;
you were to Israel[a] a forgiving God,
though you punished their
misdeeds.[b]
9 Exalt the LORD our God
and worship at his holy mountain,
for the LORD our God is holy.

Psalm 100

A psalm. For giving thanks.

1 Shout for joy to the LORD, all the
earth.
2   Worship the LORD with gladness;
come before him with joyful songs.
3 Know that the LORD is God.
It is he who made us, and we are
his[c];
we are his people, the sheep of his
pasture.

4 Enter his gates with thanksgiving
and his courts with praise;
give thanks to him and praise his
name.
5 For the LORD is good and his love
endures forever;
his faithfulness continues through
all generations.

> SHOUT for joy to the LORD, all the earth.
>
> PSALM 100:1

Psalm 101

Of David. A psalm.

1 I will sing of your love and justice;
to you, O LORD, I will sing praise.
2 I will be careful to lead a blameless
life—
when will you come to me?

I will walk in my house
with blameless heart.
3 I will set before my eyes
no vile thing.

The deeds of faithless men I hate;
they will not cling to me.

4 Men of perverse heart shall be far
from me;
I will have nothing to do with evil.

5 Whoever slanders his neighbor in
secret,
him will I put to silence;
whoever has haughty eyes and a
proud heart,
him will I not endure.

6 My eyes will be on the faithful in the
land,
that they may dwell with me;
he whose walk is blameless
will minister to me.

7 No one who practices deceit
will dwell in my house;
no one who speaks falsely
will stand in my presence.

8 Every morning I will put to silence
all the wicked in the land;
I will cut off every evildoer
from the city of the LORD.

Psalm 102

A prayer of an afflicted man. When he is
faint and pours out his lament
before the LORD.

1 Hear my prayer, O LORD;
let my cry for help come to you.
2 Do not hide your face from me
when I am in distress.
Turn your ear to me;
when I call, answer me quickly.

3 For my days vanish like smoke;
my bones burn like glowing
embers.
4 My heart is blighted and withered
like grass;
I forget to eat my food.
5 Because of my loud groaning
I am reduced to skin and bones.
6 I am like a desert owl,
like an owl among the ruins.
7 I lie awake; I have become
like a bird alone on a roof.
8 All day long my enemies taunt me;
those who rail against me use my
name as a curse.

a8 Hebrew them   b8 Or / an avenger of the
wrongs done to them   c3 Or and not we
ourselves

⁹For I eat ashes as my food
and mingle my drink with tears
¹⁰because of your great wrath,
for you have taken me up and
thrown me aside.
¹¹My days are like the evening shadow;
I wither away like grass.

¹²But you, O Lord, sit enthroned
forever;
your renown endures through all
generations.
¹³You will arise and have compassion
on Zion,
for it is time to show favor to her;
the appointed time has come.
¹⁴For her stones are dear to your
servants;
her very dust moves them to pity.
¹⁵The nations will fear the name of
the Lord,
all the kings of the earth will revere
your glory.
¹⁶For the Lord will rebuild Zion
and appear in his glory.
¹⁷He will respond to the prayer of the
destitute;
he will not despise their plea.

¹⁸Let this be written for a future
generation,
that a people not yet created may
praise the Lord:
¹⁹"The Lord looked down from his
sanctuary on high,
from heaven he viewed the earth,
²⁰to hear the groans of the prisoners
and release those condemned to
death."
²¹So the name of the Lord will be
declared in Zion
and his praise in Jerusalem
²²when the peoples and the kingdoms
assemble to worship the Lord.

²³In the course of my life[a] he broke my
strength;
he cut short my days.
²⁴So I said:
"Do not take me away, O my God,
in the midst of my days;
your years go on through all
generations.
²⁵In the beginning you laid the
foundations of the earth,
and the heavens are the work of
your hands.

²⁶They will perish, but you remain;
they will all wear out like a
garment.
Like clothing you will change them
and they will be discarded.
²⁷But you remain the same,
and your years will never end.
²⁸The children of your servants will live
in your presence;
their descendants will be
established before you."

> PRAISE the Lord, O my soul;
> all my inmost being, praise his
> holy name.
>
> PSALM 103:1

Psalm 103
Of David.

¹Praise the Lord, O my soul;
all my inmost being, praise his
holy name.
²Praise the Lord, O my soul,
and forget not all his benefits—
³who forgives all your sins
and heals all your diseases,
⁴who redeems your life from the pit
and crowns you with love and
compassion,
⁵who satisfies your desires with
good things
so that your youth is renewed like
the eagle's.

⁶The Lord works righteousness
and justice for all the oppressed.

⁷He made known his ways to
Moses,
his deeds to the people of Israel:
⁸The Lord is compassionate and
gracious,
slow to anger, abounding in love.
⁹He will not always accuse,
nor will he harbor his anger
forever;
¹⁰he does not treat us as our sins
deserve
or repay us according to our
iniquities.

---

a 23 Or *By his power*

PSALM 103

Praise the Lord!

103:22 PRAISE THE LORD, O MY SOUL.

Frederick Lehman's hymn to the love of God expresses beautifully the impossibility of ever adequately describing the love of God:

> Could we with ink the ocean fill,
> And were the skies of parchment made;
> Were every stalk on earth a quill,
> And every man a scribe by trade;
> To write the love of God above,
> Would drain the ocean dry,
> Nor could the scroll contain the whole,
> Though stretched from sky to sky.
> O love of God, how rich and pure!
> How measureless and strong!
> It shall forevermore endure
> The saints' and angels' song.[12]

Yet unfathomable as God's love is, we must keep trying to sing of it. Psalm 103 offers one of the best ways to try. Using its words and structure as a guide, pray through four stages.

1. Praise him for what he has done for you personally (verses 1–5): What has God been to you? He forgives, heals, redeems, crowns and satisfies. List the ways you have known him to do this. Praise him that he loves you from youth to old age, even renewing your youth like the eagle's (see also Isaiah 40:30–31; Psalm 92:14).

2. Praise him for his patient love for his people (verses 6–14): Maybe you've never thought to do this before, but it will greatly deepen your appreciation of the love of God. Use what you know of Biblical history, or church history, and do what David does: Think of God's patience with a people who have never distinguished themselves by their faithfulness—and of a God who nevertheless has. Their story is our story too.

3. Praise God for his faithfulness in life and death (verses 15–18): Remember that life is short, and your only firm hope is in the eternal Father who made you and sympathizes with your frailty. The idea here is not to be somber, but sober enough to understand freshly your hope in God's love.

4. Praise God with the whole created order (verses 19–22): Tell the angels to praise God. Tell all of God's "works," his creatures and plants and mountains and bodies of water, to praise the Lord! David did. So did St. Francis. Address them by name: "Azaleas and whales, Gobi Desert and Lake Michigan—praise the Lord!"

P R A Y :
Praise the Lord, O my soul!
All that is within me, praise his holy name!

FOR YOUR NEXT DEVOTIONAL READING, GO TO PAGE 709.

¹¹ For as high as the heavens are above
the earth,
so great is his love for those who
fear him;
¹² as far as the east is from the west,
so far has he removed our
transgressions from us.
¹³ As a father has compassion on his
children,
so the LORD has compassion on
those who fear him;
¹⁴ for he knows how we are formed,
he remembers that we are dust.
¹⁵ As for man, his days are like grass,
he flourishes like a flower of the
field;
¹⁶ the wind blows over it and it is gone,
and its place remembers it no
more.
¹⁷ But from everlasting to everlasting
the LORD's love is with those who
fear him,
and his righteousness with their
children's children—
¹⁸ with those who keep his covenant
and remember to obey his
precepts.

¹⁹ The LORD has established his throne
in heaven,
and his kingdom rules over all.

²⁰ Praise the LORD, you his angels,
you mighty ones who do his
bidding,
who obey his word.
²¹ Praise the LORD, all his heavenly
hosts,
you his servants who do his will.
²² Praise the LORD, all his works
everywhere in his dominion.

Praise the LORD, O my soul.

Psalm 104

¹ Praise the LORD, O my soul.

O LORD my God, you are very great;
you are clothed with splendor and
majesty.
² He wraps himself in light as with a
garment;
he stretches out the heavens like
a tent
³   and lays the beams of his upper
chambers on their waters.

He makes the clouds his chariot
and rides on the wings of the wind.
⁴ He makes winds his messengers,ᵃ
flames of fire his servants.

⁵ He set the earth on its foundations;
it can never be moved.
⁶ You covered it with the deep as with
a garment;
the waters stood above the
mountains.
⁷ But at your rebuke the waters fled,
at the sound of your thunder they
took to flight;
⁸ they flowed over the mountains,
they went down into the valleys,
to the place you assigned for them.
⁹ You set a boundary they cannot
cross;
never again will they cover the
earth.

¹⁰ He makes springs pour water into the
ravines;
it flows between the mountains.
¹¹ They give water to all the beasts of
the field;
the wild donkeys quench their
thirst.
¹² The birds of the air nest by the
waters;
they sing among the branches.
¹³ He waters the mountains from his
upper chambers;
the earth is satisfied by the fruit
of his work.
¹⁴ He makes grass grow for the cattle,
and plants for man to cultivate—
bringing forth food from the earth:
¹⁵ wine that gladdens the heart of man,
oil to make his face shine,
and bread that sustains his heart.
¹⁶ The trees of the LORD are well
watered,
the cedars of Lebanon that he
planted.
¹⁷ There the birds make their nests;
the stork has its home in the pine
trees.
¹⁸ The high mountains belong to the
wild goats;
the crags are a refuge for the
coneys.ᵇ

ᵃ4 Or angels   ᵇ18 That is, the hyrax or rock
badger

¹⁹ The moon marks off the seasons,
and the sun knows when to go
down.
²⁰ You bring darkness, it becomes night,
and all the beasts of the forest
prowl.
²¹ The lions roar for their prey
and seek their food from God.
²² The sun rises, and they steal away;
they return and lie down in their
dens.
²³ Then man goes out to his work,
to his labor until evening.

²⁴ How many are your works,
O LORD!
In wisdom you made them all;
the earth is full of your creatures.
²⁵ There is the sea, vast and spacious,
teeming with creatures beyond
number—
living things both large and
small.
²⁶ There the ships go to and fro,
and the leviathan, which you
formed to frolic there.

²⁷ These all look to you
to give them their food at the
proper time.
²⁸ When you give it to them,
they gather it up;
when you open your hand,
they are satisfied with good things.
²⁹ When you hide your face,
they are terrified;
when you take away their breath,
they die and return to the dust.
³⁰ When you send your Spirit,
they are created,
and you renew the face of the
earth.

³¹ May the glory of the LORD endure
forever;
may the LORD rejoice in his works—
³² he who looks at the earth, and it
trembles,
who touches the mountains, and
they smoke.

³³ I will sing to the LORD all my life;
I will sing praise to my God as long
as I live.
³⁴ May my meditation be pleasing
to him,
as I rejoice in the LORD.

³⁵ But may sinners vanish from the
earth
and the wicked be no more.

Praise the LORD, O my soul.

Praise the LORD.*ᵃ*

Psalm 105

¹ Give thanks to the LORD, call on his
name;
make known among the nations
what he has done.
² Sing to him, sing praise to him;
tell of all his wonderful acts.
³ Glory in his holy name;
let the hearts of those who seek the
LORD rejoice.
⁴ Look to the LORD and his strength;
seek his face always.

⁵ Remember the wonders he has done,
his miracles, and the judgments he
pronounced,
⁶ O descendants of Abraham his
servant,
O sons of Jacob, his chosen ones.
⁷ He is the LORD our God;
his judgments are in all the earth.

⁸ He remembers his covenant forever,
the word he commanded, for a
thousand generations,
⁹ the covenant he made with Abraham,
the oath he swore to Isaac.
¹⁰ He confirmed it to Jacob as a decree,
to Israel as an everlasting
covenant:
¹¹ "To you I will give the land of Canaan
as the portion you will inherit."

¹² When they were but few in number,
few indeed, and strangers in it,
¹³ they wandered from nation to nation,
from one kingdom to another.
¹⁴ He allowed no one to oppress them;
for their sake he rebuked kings:
¹⁵ "Do not touch my anointed ones;
do my prophets no harm."

¹⁶ He called down famine on the land
and destroyed all their supplies of
food;
¹⁷ and he sent a man before them—
Joseph, sold as a slave.

ᵃ35 Hebrew *Hallelu Yah*; in the Septuagint this
line stands at the beginning of Psalm 105.

18 They bruised his feet with shackles,
   his neck was put in irons,
19 till what he foretold came to pass,
   till the word of the LORD proved
      him true.
20 The king sent and released him,
   the ruler of peoples set him free.
21 He made him master of his
      household,
   ruler over all he possessed,
22 to instruct his princes as he pleased
   and teach his elders wisdom.

23 Then Israel entered Egypt;
   Jacob lived as an alien in the land
      of Ham.
24 The LORD made his people very
      fruitful;
   he made them too numerous for
      their foes,
25 whose hearts he turned to hate his
      people,
   to conspire against his servants.
26 He sent Moses his servant,
   and Aaron, whom he had chosen.
27 They performed his miraculous signs
      among them,
   his wonders in the land of Ham.
28 He sent darkness and made the
      land dark—
   for had they not rebelled against
      his words?
29 He turned their waters into blood,
   causing their fish to die.
30 Their land teemed with frogs,
   which went up into the bedrooms
      of their rulers.
31 He spoke, and there came swarms
      of flies,
   and gnats throughout their
      country.
32 He turned their rain into hail,
   with lightning throughout their
      land;
33 he struck down their vines and
      fig trees
   and shattered the trees of their
      country.
34 He spoke, and the locusts came,
   grasshoppers without number;
35 they ate up every green thing in
      their land,
   ate up the produce of their soil.
36 Then he struck down all the firstborn
      in their land,
   the firstfruits of all their manhood.

37 He brought out Israel, laden with
      silver and gold,
   and from among their tribes no
      one faltered.
38 Egypt was glad when they left,
   because dread of Israel had fallen
      on them.
39 He spread out a cloud as a covering,
   and a fire to give light at night.
40 They asked, and he brought them
      quail
   and satisfied them with the bread
      of heaven.
41 He opened the rock, and water
      gushed out;
   like a river it flowed in the desert.

42 For he remembered his holy promise
   given to his servant Abraham.
43 He brought out his people with
      rejoicing,
   his chosen ones with shouts of joy;
44 he gave them the lands of the
      nations,
   and they fell heir to what others
      had toiled for—
45 that they might keep his precepts
   and observe his laws.

Praise the LORD.[a]

Psalm 106

1 Praise the LORD.[b]

Give thanks to the LORD, for he is
      good;
   his love endures forever.
2 Who can proclaim the mighty acts of
      the LORD
   or fully declare his praise?
3 Blessed are they who maintain
      justice,
   who constantly do what is right.
4 Remember me, O LORD, when you
      show favor to your people,
   come to my aid when you save
      them,
5 that I may enjoy the prosperity of
      your chosen ones,
   that I may share in the joy of your
      nation
   and join your inheritance in giving
      praise.

a45 Hebrew *Hallelu Yah*   b1 Hebrew *Hallelu Yah*; also in verse 48

⁶We have sinned, even as our
  fathers did;
  we have done wrong and acted
    wickedly.
⁷When our fathers were in Egypt,
  they gave no thought to your
    miracles;
  they did not remember your many
    kindnesses,
  and they rebelled by the sea, the
    Red Sea.ᵃ
⁸Yet he saved them for his name's
    sake,
  to make his mighty power known.
⁹He rebuked the Red Sea, and it
    dried up;
  he led them through the depths as
    through a desert.
¹⁰He saved them from the hand of
    the foe;
  from the hand of the enemy he
    redeemed them.
¹¹The waters covered their adversaries;
  not one of them survived.
¹²Then they believed his promises
  and sang his praise.

¹³But they soon forgot what he had
    done
  and did not wait for his counsel.
¹⁴In the desert they gave in to their
    craving;
  in the wasteland they put God to
    the test.
¹⁵So he gave them what they asked for,
  but sent a wasting disease upon
    them.

¹⁶In the camp they grew envious of
    Moses
  and of Aaron, who was consecrated
    to the LORD.
¹⁷The earth opened up and swallowed
    Dathan;
  it buried the company of Abiram.
¹⁸Fire blazed among their followers;
  a flame consumed the wicked.

¹⁹At Horeb they made a calf
  and worshiped an idol cast from
    metal.
²⁰They exchanged their Glory
  for an image of a bull, which
    eats grass.
²¹They forgot the God who saved them,
  who had done great things in
    Egypt,

²²miracles in the land of Ham
  and awesome deeds by the Red
    Sea.
²³So he said he would destroy them—
  had not Moses, his chosen one,
  stood in the breach before him
  to keep his wrath from destroying
    them.

²⁴Then they despised the pleasant land;
  they did not believe his promise.
²⁵They grumbled in their tents
  and did not obey the LORD.
²⁶So he swore to them with uplifted
    hand
  that he would make them fall in
    the desert,
²⁷make their descendants fall among
    the nations
  and scatter them throughout the
    lands.

²⁸They yoked themselves to the Baal
    of Peor
  and ate sacrifices offered to
    lifeless gods;
²⁹they provoked the LORD to anger by
    their wicked deeds,
  and a plague broke out among
    them.
³⁰But Phinehas stood up and
    intervened,
  and the plague was checked.
³¹This was credited to him as
    righteousness
  for endless generations to come.

³²By the waters of Meribah they
    angered the LORD,
  and trouble came to Moses
    because of them;
³³for they rebelled against the Spirit of
    God,
  and rash words came from
    Moses' lips.ᵇ

³⁴They did not destroy the peoples
  as the LORD had commanded them,
³⁵but they mingled with the nations
  and adopted their customs.
³⁶They worshiped their idols,
  which became a snare to them.
³⁷They sacrificed their sons
  and their daughters to demons.

ᵃ7 Hebrew *Yam Suph*; that is, Sea of Reeds; also
in verses 9 and 22   ᵇ33 Or *against his spirit, /
and rash words came from his lips*

38 They shed innocent blood,
the blood of their sons and
daughters,
whom they sacrificed to the idols
of Canaan,
and the land was desecrated by
their blood.
39 They defiled themselves by what
they did;
by their deeds they prostituted
themselves.

40 Therefore the LORD was angry with
his people
and abhorred his inheritance.
41 He handed them over to the nations,
and their foes ruled over them.
42 Their enemies oppressed them
and subjected them to their power.
43 Many times he delivered them,
but they were bent on rebellion
and they wasted away in their sin.

44 But he took note of their distress
when he heard their cry;
45 for their sake he remembered his
covenant
and out of his great love he relented.
46 He caused them to be pitied
by all who held them captive.

47 Save us, O LORD our God,
and gather us from the nations,
that we may give thanks to your
holy name
and glory in your praise.

48 Praise be to the LORD, the God of Israel,
from everlasting to everlasting.
Let all the people say, "Amen!"

Praise the LORD.

BOOK V

Psalms 107–150

Psalm 107

1 Give thanks to the LORD, for he
is good;
his love endures forever.
2 Let the redeemed of the LORD say
this—
those he redeemed from the hand
of the foe,
3 those he gathered from the lands,
from east and west, from north
and south.*a*

> GIVE thanks to the LORD, for he is good;
> his love endures forever.
>
> PSALM 107:1

4 Some wandered in desert wastelands,
finding no way to a city where they
could settle.
5 They were hungry and thirsty,
and their lives ebbed away.
6 Then they cried out to the LORD in
their trouble,
and he delivered them from their
distress.
7 He led them by a straight way
to a city where they could settle.
8 Let them give thanks to the LORD for
his unfailing love
and his wonderful deeds for men,
9 for he satisfies the thirsty
and fills the hungry with good
things.

10 Some sat in darkness and the deepest
gloom,
prisoners suffering in iron chains,
11 for they had rebelled against the
words of God
and despised the counsel of the
Most High.
12 So he subjected them to bitter labor;
they stumbled, and there was no
one to help.
13 Then they cried to the LORD in their
trouble,
and he saved them from their
distress.
14 He brought them out of darkness and
the deepest gloom
and broke away their chains.
15 Let them give thanks to the LORD for
his unfailing love
and his wonderful deeds for men,
16 for he breaks down gates of bronze
and cuts through bars of iron.

17 Some became fools through their
rebellious ways
and suffered affliction because of
their iniquities.
18 They loathed all food
and drew near the gates of
death.

a3 Hebrew *north and the sea*

19 Then they cried to the LORD in their
trouble,
and he saved them from their
distress.
20 He sent forth his word and healed
them;
he rescued them from the grave.
21 Let them give thanks to the LORD for
his unfailing love
and his wonderful deeds for men.
22 Let them sacrifice thank offerings
and tell of his works with songs
of joy.

23 Others went out on the sea in ships;
they were merchants on the mighty
waters.
24 They saw the works of the LORD,
his wonderful deeds in the deep.
25 For he spoke and stirred up a tempest
that lifted high the waves.
26 They mounted up to the heavens and
went down to the depths;
in their peril their courage melted
away.
27 They reeled and staggered like
drunken men;
they were at their wits' end.
28 Then they cried out to the LORD in
their trouble,
and he brought them out of their
distress.
29 He stilled the storm to a whisper;
the waves of the sea were hushed.
30 They were glad when it grew calm,
and he guided them to their
desired haven.
31 Let them give thanks to the LORD for
his unfailing love
and his wonderful deeds for men.
32 Let them exalt him in the assembly
of the people
and praise him in the council of
the elders.

33 He turned rivers into a desert,
flowing springs into thirsty ground,
34 and fruitful land into a salt waste,
because of the wickedness of those
who lived there.
35 He turned the desert into pools of
water
and the parched ground into
flowing springs;
36 there he brought the hungry to live,

and they founded a city where
they could settle.
37 They sowed fields and planted
vineyards
that yielded a fruitful harvest;
38 he blessed them, and their numbers
greatly increased,
and he did not let their herds
diminish.

39 Then their numbers decreased, and
they were humbled
by oppression, calamity and
sorrow;
40 he who pours contempt on nobles
made them wander in a trackless
waste.
41 But he lifted the needy out of their
affliction
and increased their families like
flocks.
42 The upright see and rejoice,
but all the wicked shut their
mouths.

43 Whoever is wise, let him heed these
things
and consider the great love of
the LORD.

Psalm 108

A song. A psalm of David.

1 My heart is steadfast, O God;
I will sing and make music with all
my soul.
2 Awake, harp and lyre!
I will awaken the dawn.
3 I will praise you, O LORD, among the
nations;
I will sing of you among the
peoples.
4 For great is your love, higher than the
heavens;
your faithfulness reaches to the
skies.

> 66 Beware in your prayers, above
> everything else, of limiting God, not only
> by unbelief, but by fancying that you
> know what he can do. Expect unexpected
> things 'above all that we ask or think.' 99
>
> ANDREW MURRAY

⁵Be exalted, O God, above the heavens,
  and let your glory be over all the
    earth.

⁶Save us and help us with your right
    hand,
  that those you love may be
    delivered.
⁷God has spoken from his sanctuary:
  "In triumph I will parcel out
    Shechem
  and measure off the Valley of
    Succoth.
⁸Gilead is mine, Manasseh is mine;
  Ephraim is my helmet,
    Judah my scepter.
⁹Moab is my washbasin,
  upon Edom I toss my sandal;
  over Philistia I shout in triumph."

¹⁰Who will bring me to the fortified
    city?
  Who will lead me to Edom?
¹¹Is it not you, O God, you who have
    rejected us
  and no longer go out with our
    armies?
¹²Give us aid against the enemy,
  for the help of man is worthless.
¹³With God we will gain the victory,
  and he will trample down our
    enemies.

Psalm 109

For the director of music.
Of David. A psalm.

¹O God, whom I praise,
  do not remain silent,
²for wicked and deceitful men
  have opened their mouths
    against me;
  they have spoken against me
    with lying tongues.
³With words of hatred they surround
    me;
  they attack me without cause.
⁴In return for my friendship they
    accuse me,
  but I am a man of prayer.
⁵They repay me evil for good,
  and hatred for my friendship.

⁶Appoint*a* an evil man*b* to oppose him;
  let an accuser*c* stand at his right
    hand.

⁷When he is tried, let him be found
    guilty,
  and may his prayers condemn him.
⁸May his days be few;
  may another take his place of
    leadership.
⁹May his children be fatherless
  and his wife a widow.
¹⁰May his children be wandering
    beggars;
  may they be driven*d* from their
    ruined homes.
¹¹May a creditor seize all he has;
  may strangers plunder the fruits
    of his labor.
¹²May no one extend kindness to him
  or take pity on his fatherless
    children.
¹³May his descendants be cut off,
  their names blotted out from the
    next generation.
¹⁴May the iniquity of his fathers be
  remembered before the LORD;
  may the sin of his mother never be
    blotted out.
¹⁵May their sins always remain before
    the LORD,
  that he may cut off the memory of
    them from the earth.

¹⁶For he never thought of doing a
    kindness,
  but hounded to death the poor
  and the needy and the
    brokenhearted.
¹⁷He loved to pronounce a curse—
  may it*e* come on him;
  he found no pleasure in
    blessing—
  may it be*f* far from him.
¹⁸He wore cursing as his garment;
  it entered into his body like
    water,
  into his bones like oil.
¹⁹May it be like a cloak wrapped
    about him,
  like a belt tied forever around him.
²⁰May this be the LORD's payment to
    my accusers,
  to those who speak evil of me.

---

a6 Or *They say:* "*Appoint* (with quotation marks
at the end of verse 19)   *b6* Or *the Evil One*
c6 Or *let Satan*   *d10* Septuagint; Hebrew
sought   *e17* Or *curse, / and it has*
f17 Or *blessing, / and it is*

21 But you, O Sovereign LORD,
   deal well with me for your name's
      sake;
   out of the goodness of your love,
      deliver me.
22 For I am poor and needy,
   and my heart is wounded within me.
23 I fade away like an evening shadow;
   I am shaken off like a locust.
24 My knees give way from fasting;
   my body is thin and gaunt.
25 I am an object of scorn to my accusers;
   when they see me, they shake
      their heads.

26 Help me, O LORD my God;
   save me in accordance with your
      love.
27 Let them know that it is your hand,
   that you, O LORD, have done it.
28 They may curse, but you will bless;
   when they attack they will be put
      to shame,
   but your servant will rejoice.
29 My accusers will be clothed with
      disgrace
   and wrapped in shame as in a
      cloak.

30 With my mouth I will greatly extol
      the LORD;
   in the great throng I will praise
      him.
31 For he stands at the right hand of the
      needy one,
   to save his life from those who
      condemn him.

Psalm 110

Of David. A psalm.

1 The LORD says to my Lord:
   "Sit at my right hand
until I make your enemies
   a footstool for your feet."

2 The LORD will extend your mighty
      scepter from Zion;
   you will rule in the midst of your
      enemies.
3 Your troops will be willing
   on your day of battle.
Arrayed in holy majesty,
   from the womb of the dawn
   you will receive the dew of your
      youth.[a]

4 The LORD has sworn
   and will not change his mind:
"You are a priest forever,
   in the order of Melchizedek."

5 The Lord is at your right hand;
   he will crush kings on the day of
      his wrath.
6 He will judge the nations, heaping
      up the dead
   and crushing the rulers of the
      whole earth.
7 He will drink from a brook beside
      the way[b];
   therefore he will lift up his head.

Psalm 111[c]

1 Praise the LORD.[d]

I will extol the LORD with all my heart
   in the council of the upright and in
      the assembly.

2 Great are the works of the LORD;
   they are pondered by all who
      delight in them.
3 Glorious and majestic are his deeds,
   and his righteousness endures
      forever.
4 He has caused his wonders to be
      remembered;
   the LORD is gracious and
      compassionate.
5 He provides food for those who
      fear him;
   he remembers his covenant forever.
6 He has shown his people the power
      of his works,
   giving them the lands of other
      nations.
7 The works of his hands are faithful
      and just;
   all his precepts are trustworthy.
8 They are steadfast for ever and ever,
   done in faithfulness and
      uprightness.
9 He provided redemption for his
      people;
   he ordained his covenant forever—
   holy and awesome is his name.

---

a 3 Or / *your young men will come to you like the*
dew   *b 7* Or / *The One who grants succession*
will set him in authority   *c*This psalm is an
acrostic poem, the lines of which begin with the
successive letters of the Hebrew alphabet.
d 1 Hebrew *Hallelu Yah*

> *If the only prayer you said in your whole life was "thank you," that would suffice.*
>
> MEISTER ECKART

[10] The fear of the LORD is the beginning of wisdom;
all who follow his precepts have good understanding.
To him belongs eternal praise.

Psalm 112[a]

[1] Praise the LORD.[b]

Blessed is the man who fears the LORD,
who finds great delight in his commands.

[2] His children will be mighty in the land;
the generation of the upright will be blessed.

[3] Wealth and riches are in his house,
and his righteousness endures forever.

[4] Even in darkness light dawns for the upright,
for the gracious and compassionate and righteous man.[c]

[5] Good will come to him who is generous and lends freely,
who conducts his affairs with justice.

[6] Surely he will never be shaken;
a righteous man will be remembered forever.

[7] He will have no fear of bad news;
his heart is steadfast, trusting in the LORD.

[8] His heart is secure, he will have no fear;
in the end he will look in triumph on his foes.

[9] He has scattered abroad his gifts to the poor,
his righteousness endures forever;
his horn[d] will be lifted high in honor.

[10] The wicked man will see and be vexed,

he will gnash his teeth and waste away;
the longings of the wicked will come to nothing.

Psalm 113

[1] Praise the LORD.[e]

Praise, O servants of the LORD,
praise the name of the LORD.

[2] Let the name of the LORD be praised,
both now and forevermore.

[3] From the rising of the sun to the place where it sets,
the name of the LORD is to be praised.

[4] The LORD is exalted over all the nations,
his glory above the heavens.

[5] Who is like the LORD our God,
the One who sits enthroned on high,

[6] who stoops down to look
on the heavens and the earth?

[7] He raises the poor from the dust
and lifts the needy from the ash heap;

[8] he seats them with princes,
with the princes of their people.

[9] He settles the barren woman in her home
as a happy mother of children.

Praise the LORD.

Psalm 114

[1] When Israel came out of Egypt,
the house of Jacob from a people of foreign tongue,

[2] Judah became God's sanctuary,
Israel his dominion.

[3] The sea looked and fled,
the Jordan turned back;

[4] the mountains skipped like rams,
the hills like lambs.

[5] Why was it, O sea, that you fled,
O Jordan, that you turned back,

---

[a] This psalm is an acrostic poem, the lines of which begin with the successive letters of the Hebrew alphabet.   [b] 1 Hebrew *Hallelu Yah*   [c] 4 Or / for the LORD, is gracious and compassionate and righteous   [d] 9 *Horn* here symbolizes dignity.
[e] 1 Hebrew *Hallelu Yah*; also in verse 9

⁶you mountains, that you skipped
  like rams,
    you hills, like lambs?

⁷Tremble, O earth, at the presence
    of the Lord,
  at the presence of the God of Jacob,
⁸who turned the rock into a pool,
    the hard rock into springs of water.

Psalm 115

¹Not to us, O LORD, not to us
  but to your name be the glory,
    because of your love and
      faithfulness.

²Why do the nations say,
    "Where is their God?"
³Our God is in heaven;
    he does whatever pleases him.
⁴But their idols are silver and gold,
    made by the hands of men.
⁵They have mouths, but cannot speak,
    eyes, but they cannot see;
⁶they have ears, but cannot hear,
    noses, but they cannot smell;
⁷they have hands, but cannot feel,
    feet, but they cannot walk;
  nor can they utter a sound with
      their throats.
⁸Those who make them will be like
      them,
  and so will all who trust in them.

⁹O house of Israel, trust in the LORD—
    he is their help and shield.
¹⁰O house of Aaron, trust in the LORD—
    he is their help and shield.
¹¹You who fear him, trust in the LORD—
    he is their help and shield.

¹²The LORD remembers us and will
      bless us:
  He will bless the house of Israel,
  he will bless the house of Aaron,
¹³he will bless those who fear the
      LORD—
    small and great alike.

¹⁴May the LORD make you increase,
    both you and your children.
¹⁵May you be blessed by the LORD,
    the Maker of heaven and earth.

¹⁶The highest heavens belong to
      the LORD,
  but the earth he has given to man.

¹⁷It is not the dead who praise the LORD,
    those who go down to silence;
¹⁸it is we who extol the LORD,
    both now and forevermore.

Praise the LORD.ᵃ

Psalm 116

¹I love the LORD, for he heard my voice;
    he heard my cry for mercy.
²Because he turned his ear to me,
    I will call on him as long as I live.

³The cords of death entangled me,
    the anguish of the graveᵇ came
      upon me;
  I was overcome by trouble and
      sorrow.
⁴Then I called on the name of the
      LORD:
    "O LORD, save me!"

⁵The LORD is gracious and righteous;
    our God is full of compassion.
⁶The LORD protects the simplehearted;
    when I was in great need, he
      saved me.

⁷Be at rest once more, O my soul,
    for the LORD has been good to you.

⁸For you, O LORD, have delivered my
      soul from death,
  my eyes from tears,
  my feet from stumbling,
⁹that I may walk before the LORD
    in the land of the living.
¹⁰I believed; thereforeᶜ I said,
    "I am greatly afflicted."
¹¹And in my dismay I said,
    "All men are liars."

¹²How can I repay the LORD
    for all his goodness to me?
¹³I will lift up the cup of salvation
    and call on the name of the LORD.
¹⁴I will fulfill my vows to the LORD
    in the presence of all his people.

¹⁵Precious in the sight of the LORD
    is the death of his saints.
¹⁶O LORD, truly I am your servant;
  I am your servant, the son of your
      maidservantᵈ;
  you have freed me from my chains.

ᵃ18 Hebrew *Hallelu Yah*   ᵇ3 Hebrew *Sheol*
ᶜ10 Or *believed even when*   ᵈ16 Or *servant,*
your faithful son

¹⁷ I will sacrifice a thank offering to you
and call on the name of the LORD.
¹⁸ I will fulfill my vows to the LORD
in the presence of all his people,
¹⁹ in the courts of the house of the
LORD—
in your midst, O Jerusalem.

Praise the LORD.ᵃ

> I WILL sacrifice a thank offering to you
> And call on the name of the LORD.
>
> PSALM 116:17

Psalm 117

¹ Praise the LORD, all you nations;
extol him, all you peoples.
² For great is his love toward us,
and the faithfulness of the LORD
endures forever.

Praise the LORD.ᵃ

Psalm 118

¹ Give thanks to the LORD, for he is
good;
his love endures forever.

² Let Israel say:
"His love endures forever."
³ Let the house of Aaron say:
"His love endures forever."
⁴ Let those who fear the LORD say:
"His love endures forever."

⁵ In my anguish I cried to the LORD,
and he answered by setting me free.
⁶ The LORD is with me; I will not be
afraid.
What can man do to me?
⁷ The LORD is with me; he is my helper.
I will look in triumph on my
enemies.

⁸ It is better to take refuge in the LORD
than to trust in man.
⁹ It is better to take refuge in the LORD
than to trust in princes.

> IN MY anguish I cried to the LORD,
> and he answered by setting me free.
>
> PSALM 118:5

¹⁰ All the nations surrounded me,
but in the name of the LORD I cut
them off.
¹¹ They surrounded me on every side,
but in the name of the LORD I cut
them off.
¹² They swarmed around me like bees,
but they died out as quickly as
burning thorns;
in the name of the LORD I cut
them off.

¹³ I was pushed back and about to fall,
but the LORD helped me.
¹⁴ The LORD is my strength and my
song;
he has become my salvation.

¹⁵ Shouts of joy and victory
resound in the tents of the
righteous:
"The LORD's right hand has done
mighty things!
¹⁶   The LORD's right hand is lifted
high;
the LORD's right hand has done
mighty things!"

¹⁷ I will not die but live,
and will proclaim what the LORD
has done.
¹⁸ The LORD has chastened me severely,
but he has not given me over to
death.

¹⁹ Open for me the gates of
righteousness;
I will enter and give thanks to the
LORD.
²⁰ This is the gate of the LORD
through which the righteous may
enter.
²¹ I will give you thanks, for you
answered me;
you have become my salvation.

²² The stone the builders rejected
has become the capstone;
²³ the LORD has done this,
and it is marvelous in our eyes.
²⁴ This is the day the LORD has made;
let us rejoice and be glad in it.

²⁵ O LORD, save us;
O LORD, grant us success.

ᵃ 19,2 Hebrew *Hallelu Yah*

²⁶ Blessed is he who comes in the name
of the LORD.
From the house of the LORD we
bless you.*a*
²⁷ The LORD is God,
and he has made his light shine
upon us.
With boughs in hand, join in the
festal procession
up*b* to the horns of the altar.

²⁸ You are my God, and I will give
you thanks;
you are my God, and I will
exalt you.

²⁹ Give thanks to the LORD, for he
is good;
his love endures forever.

Psalm 119*c*

א Aleph

¹ Blessed are they whose ways are
blameless,
who walk according to the law
of the LORD.
² Blessed are they who keep his
statutes
and seek him with all their heart.
³ They do nothing wrong;
they walk in his ways.
⁴ You have laid down precepts
that are to be fully obeyed.
⁵ Oh, that my ways were steadfast
in obeying your decrees!
⁶ Then I would not be put to shame
when I consider all your
commands.
⁷ I will praise you with an upright heart
as I learn your righteous laws.
⁸ I will obey your decrees;
do not utterly forsake me.

ב Beth

⁹ How can a young man keep his
way pure?
By living according to your word.
¹⁰ I seek you with all my heart;
do not let me stray from your
commands.
¹¹ I have hidden your word in my heart
that I might not sin against you.
¹² Praise be to you, O LORD;
teach me your decrees.

¹³ With my lips I recount
all the laws that come from your
mouth.
¹⁴ I rejoice in following your statutes
as one rejoices in great riches.
¹⁵ I meditate on your precepts
and consider your ways.
¹⁶ I delight in your decrees;
I will not neglect your word.

ג Gimel

¹⁷ Do good to your servant, and I will
live;
I will obey your word.
¹⁸ Open my eyes that I may see
wonderful things in your law.
¹⁹ I am a stranger on earth;
do not hide your commands from
me.
²⁰ My soul is consumed with longing
for your laws at all times.
²¹ You rebuke the arrogant, who are
cursed
and who stray from your
commands.
²² Remove from me scorn and
contempt,
for I keep your statutes.
²³ Though rulers sit together and
slander me,
your servant will meditate on your
decrees.
²⁴ Your statutes are my delight;
they are my counselors.

ד Daleth

²⁵ I am laid low in the dust;
preserve my life according to
your word.
²⁶ I recounted my ways and you
answered me;
teach me your decrees.
²⁷ Let me understand the teaching of
your precepts;
then I will meditate on your
wonders.
²⁸ My soul is weary with sorrow;
strengthen me according to your
word.

---

a 26 The Hebrew is plural.   *b 27* Or *Bind the
festal sacrifice with ropes / and take it*   *c*This
psalm is an acrostic poem; the verses of each stanza
begin with the same letter of the Hebrew alphabet.

PSALM 119

The Bible and Prayer

119:1 BLESSED ARE THEY ... WHO WALK ACCORDING TO THE LAW OF THE LORD.

The longest book in the Bible, Psalms, is a book of prayer. The longest psalm in this book of prayer is a psalm celebrating the law, the Word of God. There is a strong, though implicit, message in this fact: In the heart of the Bible is a book about the life of prayer, and Scripture is critical to the life of prayer.

There are two reasons Scripture is so important to prayer. One, Scripture emphasizes God's side of the prayer conversation. It is not the only way God speaks, but it is the norm by which we know he is speaking. God speaks through his Spirit into our hearts, for example. But if what we think we hear the Spirit saying conflicts with Scripture, we can be sure it is not the Spirit speaking. Two, Scripture teaches us how to better hold up our end of the prayer conversation. The psalms, for instance, may not always express what we feel, nor should they. But more often than not, they are models of prayer.

What follows are some highlights from this psalm of the Word of God. Use them as material for praise, confession and petition.

1. Don't worship the book, but the God of the book. By reading the book, "I seek [God] with all my heart" (verse 10).

2. The Word of God will keep you from sin. "I have hidden your word in my heart that I might not sin against you" (verse 11).

3. Pray that the Holy Spirit will give you understanding when you read. "Open my eyes that I may see wonderful things in your law" (verse 18).

4. The Word of God shows the way of freedom. "I run in the path of your commands, for you have set my heart free ... I will walk about in freedom, for I have sought out your precepts" (verses 32,45).

5. The Word of God provides wisdom and develops character. "I gain understanding from your precepts; therefore I hate every wrong path" (verse 104).

6. The Word of God gives guidance in life. "Your word is a lamp to my feet and a light for my path" (verse 105).

7. The Word of God is absolutely faithful. "Your promises have been thoroughly tested, and your servant loves them" (verse 140).

PRAY:

Open my eyes that I may see wonderful things in your Word.
And set my heart free, that I may run in the path of your commands!

FOR YOUR NEXT DEVOTIONAL READING, GO TO PAGE 716.

²⁹ Keep me from deceitful ways;
  be gracious to me through
    your law.
³⁰ I have chosen the way of truth;
  I have set my heart on your laws.
³¹ I hold fast to your statutes, O LORD;
  do not let me be put to shame.
³² I run in the path of your commands,
  for you have set my heart free.

ה He

³³ Teach me, O LORD, to follow your
    decrees;
  then I will keep them to the end.
³⁴ Give me understanding, and I will
    keep your law
  and obey it with all my heart.
³⁵ Direct me in the path of your
    commands,
  for there I find delight.
³⁶ Turn my heart toward your statutes
  and not toward selfish gain.
³⁷ Turn my eyes away from worthless
    things;
  preserve my life according to
    your word.ᵃ
³⁸ Fulfill your promise to your servant,
  so that you may be feared.
³⁹ Take away the disgrace I dread,
  for your laws are good.
⁴⁰ How I long for your precepts!
  Preserve my life in your
    righteousness.

ו Waw

⁴¹ May your unfailing love come to me,
    O LORD,
  your salvation according to your
    promise;
⁴² then I will answer the one who
    taunts me,
  for I trust in your word.
⁴³ Do not snatch the word of truth from
    my mouth,
  for I have put my hope in your
    laws.
⁴⁴ I will always obey your law,
  for ever and ever.
⁴⁵ I will walk about in freedom,
  for I have sought out your precepts.
⁴⁶ I will speak of your statutes before
    kings
  and will not be put to shame,

⁴⁷ for I delight in your commands
  because I love them.
⁴⁸ I lift up my hands toᵇ your
    commands, which I love,
  and I meditate on your decrees.

ז Zayin

⁴⁹ Remember your word to your
    servant,
  for you have given me hope.
⁵⁰ My comfort in my suffering is this:
  Your promise preserves my life.
⁵¹ The arrogant mock me without
    restraint,
  but I do not turn from your law.
⁵² I remember your ancient laws,
    O LORD,
  and I find comfort in them.
⁵³ Indignation grips me because of the
    wicked,
  who have forsaken your law.
⁵⁴ Your decrees are the theme of my
    song
  wherever I lodge.
⁵⁵ In the night I remember your name,
    O LORD,
  and I will keep your law.
⁵⁶ This has been my practice:
  I obey your precepts.

ח Heth

⁵⁷ You are my portion, O LORD;
  I have promised to obey your
    words.
⁵⁸ I have sought your face with all my
    heart;
  be gracious to me according to
    your promise.
⁵⁹ I have considered my ways
  and have turned my steps to your
    statutes.
⁶⁰ I will hasten and not delay
  to obey your commands.
⁶¹ Though the wicked bind me with
    ropes,
  I will not forget your law.
⁶² At midnight I rise to give you thanks
  for your righteous laws.
⁶³ I am a friend to all who fear you,
  to all who follow your precepts.

ᵃ37 Two manuscripts of the Masoretic Text and
Dead Sea Scrolls; most manuscripts of the
Masoretic Text *life in your way*   ᵇ48 Or *for*

⁶⁴ The earth is filled with your love,
O Lord;
teach me your decrees.

ט Teth

⁶⁵ Do good to your servant
according to your word,
O Lord.
⁶⁶ Teach me knowledge and good
judgment,
for I believe in your commands.
⁶⁷ Before I was afflicted I went astray,
but now I obey your word.
⁶⁸ You are good, and what you do is
good;
teach me your decrees.
⁶⁹ Though the arrogant have smeared
me with lies,
I keep your precepts with all
my heart.
⁷⁰ Their hearts are callous and
unfeeling,
but I delight in your law.
⁷¹ It was good for me to be afflicted
so that I might learn your decrees.
⁷² The law from your mouth is more
precious to me
than thousands of pieces of silver
and gold.

י Yodh

⁷³ Your hands made me and formed me;
give me understanding to learn
your commands.
⁷⁴ May those who fear you rejoice when
they see me,
for I have put my hope in your
word.
⁷⁵ I know, O Lord, that your laws are
righteous,
and in faithfulness you have
afflicted me.
⁷⁶ May your unfailing love be my
comfort,
according to your promise to your
servant.
⁷⁷ Let your compassion come to me that
I may live,
for your law is my delight.
⁷⁸ May the arrogant be put to shame for
wronging me without cause;
but I will meditate on your
precepts.

⁷⁹ May those who fear you turn to me,
those who understand your
statutes.
⁸⁰ May my heart be blameless toward
your decrees,
that I may not be put to shame.

כ Kaph

⁸¹ My soul faints with longing for your
salvation,
but I have put my hope in your
word.
⁸² My eyes fail, looking for your
promise;
I say, "When will you comfort me?"
⁸³ Though I am like a wineskin in
the smoke,
I do not forget your decrees.
⁸⁴ How long must your servant wait?
When will you punish my
persecutors?
⁸⁵ The arrogant dig pitfalls for me,
contrary to your law.
⁸⁶ All your commands are trustworthy;
help me, for men persecute me
without cause.
⁸⁷ They almost wiped me from the
earth,
but I have not forsaken your
precepts.
⁸⁸ Preserve my life according to your
love,
and I will obey the statutes of
your mouth.

ל Lamedh

⁸⁹ Your word, O Lord, is eternal;
it stands firm in the heavens.
⁹⁰ Your faithfulness continues through
all generations;
you established the earth, and
it endures.
⁹¹ Your laws endure to this day,
for all things serve you.
⁹² If your law had not been my
delight,
I would have perished in my
affliction.
⁹³ I will never forget your precepts,
for by them you have preserved
my life.
⁹⁴ Save me, for I am yours;
I have sought out your precepts.

⁹⁵ The wicked are waiting to destroy me,
  but I will ponder your statutes.
⁹⁶ To all perfection I see a limit;
  but your commands are boundless.

מ Mem

⁹⁷ Oh, how I love your law!
  I meditate on it all day long.
⁹⁸ Your commands make me wiser than
  my enemies,
  for they are ever with me.
⁹⁹ I have more insight than all my
  teachers,
  for I meditate on your statutes.
¹⁰⁰ I have more understanding than the
  elders,
  for I obey your precepts.
¹⁰¹ I have kept my feet from every evil
  path
  so that I might obey your word.
¹⁰² I have not departed from your laws,
  for you yourself have taught me.
¹⁰³ How sweet are your words to my
  taste,
  sweeter than honey to my mouth!
¹⁰⁴ I gain understanding from your
  precepts;
  therefore I hate every wrong path.

נ Nun

¹⁰⁵ Your word is a lamp to my feet
  and a light for my path.
¹⁰⁶ I have taken an oath and
  confirmed it,
  that I will follow your righteous
  laws.
¹⁰⁷ I have suffered much;
  preserve my life, O LORD, according
  to your word.
¹⁰⁸ Accept, O LORD, the willing praise of
  my mouth,
  and teach me your laws.
¹⁰⁹ Though I constantly take my life in
  my hands,
  I will not forget your law.
¹¹⁰ The wicked have set a snare for me,
  but I have not strayed from your
  precepts.
¹¹¹ Your statutes are my heritage forever;
  they are the joy of my heart.
¹¹² My heart is set on keeping your
  decrees
  to the very end.

ס Samekh

¹¹³ I hate double-minded men,
  but I love your law.
¹¹⁴ You are my refuge and my shield;
  I have put my hope in your word.
¹¹⁵ Away from me, you evildoers,
  that I may keep the commands of
  my God!
¹¹⁶ Sustain me according to your
  promise, and I will live;
  do not let my hopes be dashed.
¹¹⁷ Uphold me, and I will be delivered;
  I will always have regard for your
  decrees.
¹¹⁸ You reject all who stray from your
  decrees,
  for their deceitfulness is in vain.
¹¹⁹ All the wicked of the earth you
  discard like dross;
  therefore I love your statutes.
¹²⁰ My flesh trembles in fear of you;
  I stand in awe of your laws.

ע Ayin

¹²¹ I have done what is righteous and
  just;
  do not leave me to my oppressors.
¹²² Ensure your servant's well-being;
  let not the arrogant oppress me.
¹²³ My eyes fail, looking for your
  salvation,
  looking for your righteous promise.
¹²⁴ Deal with your servant according to
  your love
  and teach me your decrees.
¹²⁵ I am your servant; give me
  discernment
  that I may understand your
  statutes.
¹²⁶ It is time for you to act, O LORD;
  your law is being broken.
¹²⁷ Because I love your commands
  more than gold, more than pure
  gold,
¹²⁸ and because I consider all your
  precepts right,
  I hate every wrong path.

פ Pe

¹²⁹ Your statutes are wonderful;
  therefore I obey them.
¹³⁰ The unfolding of your words gives
  light;

it gives understanding to the
  simple.
131 I open my mouth and pant,
  longing for your commands.
132 Turn to me and have mercy on me,
  as you always do to those who love
    your name.
133 Direct my footsteps according to your
    word;
  let no sin rule over me.
134 Redeem me from the oppression
    of men,
  that I may obey your precepts.
135 Make your face shine upon your
    servant
  and teach me your decrees.
136 Streams of tears flow from my eyes,
  for your law is not obeyed.

צ Tsadhe

137 Righteous are you, O LORD,
  and your laws are right.
138 The statutes you have laid down are
    righteous;
  they are fully trustworthy.
139 My zeal wears me out,
  for my enemies ignore your words.
140 Your promises have been thoroughly
    tested,
  and your servant loves them.
141 Though I am lowly and despised,
  I do not forget your precepts.
142 Your righteousness is everlasting
  and your law is true.
143 Trouble and distress have come
    upon me,
  but your commands are my delight.
144 Your statutes are forever right;
  give me understanding that I may
    live.

ק Qoph

145 I call with all my heart; answer me,
    O LORD,
  and I will obey your decrees.
146 I call out to you; save me
  and I will keep your statutes.
147 I rise before dawn and cry for help;
  I have put my hope in your word.
148 My eyes stay open through the
    watches of the night,
  that I may meditate on your
    promises.

> *I RISE before dawn and cry for help;*
> *I have put my hope in your word.*
>
> PSALM 119:147

149 Hear my voice in accordance with
    your love;
  preserve my life, O LORD, according
    to your laws.
150 Those who devise wicked schemes
    are near,
  but they are far from your law.
151 Yet you are near, O LORD,
  and all your commands are true.
152 Long ago I learned from your
    statutes
  that you established them to last
    forever.

ר Resh

153 Look upon my suffering and
    deliver me,
  for I have not forgotten your law.
154 Defend my cause and redeem me;
  preserve my life according to your
    promise.
155 Salvation is far from the wicked,
  for they do not seek out your
    decrees.
156 Your compassion is great, O LORD;
  preserve my life according to your
    laws.
157 Many are the foes who persecute me,
  but I have not turned from your
    statutes.
158 I look on the faithless with loathing,
  for they do not obey your word.
159 See how I love your precepts;
  preserve my life, O LORD, according
    to your love.
160 All your words are true;
  all your righteous laws are
    eternal.

ש Sin and Shin

161 Rulers persecute me without cause,
  but my heart trembles at your
    word.
162 I rejoice in your promise
  like one who finds great spoil.
163 I hate and abhor falsehood
  but I love your law.

¹⁶⁴ Seven times a day I praise you
    for your righteous laws.
¹⁶⁵ Great peace have they who love
      your law,
    and nothing can make them
      stumble.
¹⁶⁶ I wait for your salvation, O LORD,
    and I follow your commands.
¹⁶⁷ I obey your statutes,
    for I love them greatly.
¹⁶⁸ I obey your precepts and your
      statutes,
    for all my ways are known to you.

ת Taw

¹⁶⁹ May my cry come before you, O LORD;
    give me understanding according
      to your word.
¹⁷⁰ May my supplication come
      before you;
    deliver me according to your
      promise.
¹⁷¹ May my lips overflow with praise,
    for you teach me your decrees.
¹⁷² May my tongue sing of your word,
    for all your commands are
      righteous.
¹⁷³ May your hand be ready to help me,
    for I have chosen your precepts.
¹⁷⁴ I long for your salvation, O LORD,
    and your law is my delight.
¹⁷⁵ Let me live that I may praise you,
    and may your laws sustain me.
¹⁷⁶ I have strayed like a lost sheep.
    Seek your servant,
    for I have not forgotten your
      commands.

> *I CALL on the LORD in my distress,
> and he answers me.*
>
> PSALM 120:1

Psalm 120

A song of ascents.

¹ I call on the LORD in my distress,
    and he answers me.
² Save me, O LORD, from lying lips
    and from deceitful tongues.

³ What will he do to you,
    and what more besides, O deceitful
      tongue?

⁴ He will punish you with a warrior's
      sharp arrows,
    with burning coals of the broom
      tree.

⁵ Woe to me that I dwell in Meshech,
    that I live among the tents of
      Kedar!
⁶ Too long have I lived
    among those who hate peace.
⁷ I am a man of peace;
    but when I speak, they are for war.

Psalm 121

A song of ascents.

¹ I lift up my eyes to the hills—
    where does my help come from?
² My help comes from the LORD,
    the Maker of heaven and earth.

³ He will not let your foot slip—
    he who watches over you will not
      slumber;
⁴ indeed, he who watches over Israel
    will neither slumber nor sleep.

⁵ The LORD watches over you—
    the LORD is your shade at your
      right hand;
⁶ the sun will not harm you by day,
    nor the moon by night.

⁷ The LORD will keep you from all
      harm—
    he will watch over your life;
⁸ the LORD will watch over your coming
      and going
    both now and forevermore.

Psalm 122

A song of ascents. Of David.

¹ I rejoiced with those who said to me,
    "Let us go to the house of the
      LORD."
² Our feet are standing
    in your gates, O Jerusalem.

³ Jerusalem is built like a city
    that is closely compacted together.
⁴ That is where the tribes go up,
    the tribes of the LORD,
    to praise the name of the LORD
    according to the statute given to
      Israel.

⁵There the thrones for judgment
stand,
the thrones of the house of David.

⁶Pray for the peace of Jerusalem:
"May those who love you be
secure.
⁷May there be peace within your walls
and security within your citadels."
⁸For the sake of my brothers and
friends,
I will say, "Peace be within you."
⁹For the sake of the house of the LORD
our God,
I will seek your prosperity.

Psalm 123

A song of ascents.

¹I lift up my eyes to you,
to you whose throne is in heaven.
²As the eyes of slaves look to the hand
of their master,
as the eyes of a maid look to the
hand of her mistress,
so our eyes look to the LORD our God,
till he shows us his mercy.

³Have mercy on us, O LORD, have
mercy on us,
for we have endured much
contempt.
⁴We have endured much ridicule from
the proud,
much contempt from the arrogant.

Psalm 124

A song of ascents. Of David.

¹If the LORD had not been on our
side—
let Israel say—
²if the LORD had not been on our side
when men attacked us,
³when their anger flared against us,
they would have swallowed us
alive;
⁴the flood would have engulfed us,
the torrent would have swept
over us,
⁵the raging waters
would have swept us away.

⁶Praise be to the LORD,
who has not let us be torn by their
teeth.

> " There come times when I have
> nothing more to tell God. If I were to
> continue to pray in words, I would have
> to repeat what I have already said. At
> such times it is wonderful to say to God,
> "May I be in Thy presence, Lord? I have
> nothing more to say to Thee, but I do
> love to be in Thy presence." "
>
> O. HALLESBY

⁷We have escaped like a bird
out of the fowler's snare;
the snare has been broken,
and we have escaped.
⁸Our help is in the name of the LORD,
the Maker of heaven and earth.

Psalm 125

A song of ascents.

¹Those who trust in the LORD are like
Mount Zion,
which cannot be shaken but
endures forever.
²As the mountains surround
Jerusalem,
so the LORD surrounds his people
both now and forevermore.

³The scepter of the wicked will not
remain
over the land allotted to the
righteous,
for then the righteous might use
their hands to do evil.

⁴Do good, O LORD, to those who are
good,
to those who are upright in heart.
⁵But those who turn to crooked ways
the LORD will banish with the
evildoers.

Peace be upon Israel.

Psalm 126

A song of ascents.

¹When the LORD brought back the
captives to*a* Zion,
we were like men who dreamed.*b*

a 1 Or LORD *restored the fortunes of*   *b 1* Or *men
restored to health*

Road Songs

120 A SONG OF ASCENTS.

Psalms 120 to 134 known as the "Psalms of Ascent." They were likely sung by Jewish pilgrims on their way to Jerusalem to celebrate festivals. Jerusalem was at a higher elevation than the area around it, so the journey was literally an "ascending" trip.

For centuries, the church has also prayed these "road songs" as metaphors for the Christian journey of discipleship, the pilgrimage toward our upward calling in Christ (see Philippians 3:14). The roots of this notion go deep in the soil of the Bible. Abraham, the father of all who believe (see Romans 4:11–12), was a traveler and a pilgrim, who was "called to go to a place he would later receive as his inheritance ... By faith he made his home in the promised land like a stranger in a foreign country ... For he was looking forward to the city with foundations, whose architect and builder is God" (see Hebrews 11:8–10). His son, Isaac, lived the same way, as did his children and their children's children—for more than 400 years in Egypt, until they were again called out to continue to go to the land God had promised Abraham.

The Hebrew word for the congregation of Israel, *qahal*, means "the called out ones." In the Old Testament, the people of God were those called out to go to the land God would show them. Today Christians are also called to live as pilgrims, "as aliens and strangers in the world" (1 Peter 2:11). Not surprisingly, the church is also the *ekklesia*, from the Greek *ek*, "out," and *klesis*, "calling."

Pilgrims need a map to guide them. The psalms of ascent are like a map, dealing with the essentials of discipleship—the perspectives, skills and disciplines necessary for the journey. The themes are easy to detect, and you may make them your own as you learn to pray them as road songs for your journey.[13]

120—Repentance: "Woe to me that I dwell in Meshech" (verse 5).
121—Providence: "The LORD will keep you from all harm" (verse 7).
122—Worship: "Let us go to the house of the LORD" (verse 1).
123—Service: "Our eyes look to the LORD our God" (verse 2).
124—Help: "Our help is in the name of the LORD" (verse 8).
125—Security: "The LORD surrounds his people" (verse 2).
126—Joy: "Our mouths were filled with laughter" (verse 2).
127—Work: "Unless the LORD builds the house" (verse 1).
128—Happiness: "Thus is the man blessed who fears the LORD" (verse 4).
129—Perseverance: "They have not gained the victory over me" (verse 2).
130—Hope: "I wait for the LORD, my soul waits" (verse 5).
131—Humility: "My eyes are not haughty" (verse 1).
132—Obedience: "He swore an oath to the LORD" (verse 2).
133—Community: "Like precious oil poured on the head" (verse 2).
134—Blessing: "Lift up your hands" (verse 2).

P R A Y :

"Guide me, O Thou great Jehovah, / Pilgrim through this barren land;
I am weak, but Thou art mighty; / Hold me with Thy powerful hand.
Bread of heaven, Bread of heaven, / Feed me till I want no more."

WILLIAM WILLIAMS

FOR YOUR NEXT DEVOTIONAL READING, GO TO PAGE 719.

² Our mouths were filled with laughter,
  our tongues with songs of joy.
Then it was said among the nations,
  "The Lord has done great things
    for them."
³ The Lord has done great things for
    us,
  and we are filled with joy.

⁴ Restore our fortunes,ᵃ O Lord,
  like streams in the Negev.
⁵ Those who sow in tears
  will reap with songs of joy.
⁶ He who goes out weeping,
  carrying seed to sow,
will return with songs of joy,
  carrying sheaves with him.

Psalm 127

A song of ascents. Of Solomon.

¹ Unless the Lord builds the house,
  its builders labor in vain.
Unless the Lord watches over the
    city,
  the watchmen stand guard in vain.
² In vain you rise early
  and stay up late,
toiling for food to eat—
  for he grants sleep toᵇ those he
    loves.

³ Sons are a heritage from the Lord,
  children a reward from him.
⁴ Like arrows in the hands of a warrior
  are sons born in one's youth.
⁵ Blessed is the man
  whose quiver is full of them.
They will not be put to shame
  when they contend with their
    enemies in the gate.

Psalm 128

A song of ascents.

¹ Blessed are all who fear the Lord,
  who walk in his ways.
² You will eat the fruit of your labor;
  blessings and prosperity will be
    yours.
³ Your wife will be like a fruitful vine
  within your house;
your sons will be like olive shoots
  around your table.
⁴ Thus is the man blessed
  who fears the Lord.

⁵ May the Lord bless you from Zion
  all the days of your life;
may you see the prosperity of
    Jerusalem,
⁶   and may you live to see your
    children's children.

Peace be upon Israel.

Psalm 129

A song of ascents.

¹ They have greatly oppressed me from
    my youth—
  let Israel say—
² they have greatly oppressed me from
    my youth,
  but they have not gained the
    victory over me.
³ Plowmen have plowed my back
  and made their furrows long.
⁴ But the Lord is righteous;
  he has cut me free from the cords
    of the wicked.

⁵ May all who hate Zion
  be turned back in shame.
⁶ May they be like grass on the roof,
  which withers before it can grow;
⁷ with it the reaper cannot fill his
    hands,
  nor the one who gathers fill his
    arms.
⁸ May those who pass by not say,
  "The blessing of the Lord be upon
    you;
we bless you in the name of the
    Lord."

Psalm 130

A song of ascents.

¹ Out of the depths I cry to you, O Lord;
²   O Lord, hear my voice.
Let your ears be attentive
  to my cry for mercy.

> O Lord, hear my voice.
> Let your ears be attentive
> to my cry for mercy.
>
> PSALM 130:2

ᵃ4 Or *Bring back our captives*   ᵇ2 Or *eat— /
for while they sleep he provides for*

³ If you, O LORD, kept a record of sins,
O Lord, who could stand?
⁴ But with you there is forgiveness;
therefore you are feared.

⁵ I wait for the LORD, my soul waits,
and in his word I put my hope.
⁶ My soul waits for the Lord
more than watchmen wait for
the morning,
more than watchmen wait for
the morning.

⁷ O Israel, put your hope in the LORD,
for with the LORD is unfailing love
and with him is full redemption.
⁸ He himself will redeem Israel
from all their sins.

Psalm 131

A song of ascents. Of David.

¹ My heart is not proud, O LORD,
my eyes are not haughty;
I do not concern myself with great
matters
or things too wonderful for me.
² But I have stilled and quieted my
soul;
like a weaned child with its
mother,
like a weaned child is my soul
within me.

³ O Israel, put your hope in the LORD
both now and forevermore.

Psalm 132

A song of ascents.

¹ O LORD, remember David
and all the hardships he endured.

² He swore an oath to the LORD
and made a vow to the Mighty One
of Jacob:
³ "I will not enter my house
or go to my bed—
⁴ I will allow no sleep to my eyes,
no slumber to my eyelids,
⁵ till I find a place for the LORD,
a dwelling for the Mighty One
of Jacob."

⁶ We heard it in Ephrathah,
we came upon it in the fields of
Jaarᵃˑᵇ

⁷ "Let us go to his dwelling place;
let us worship at his footstool—
⁸ arise, O LORD, and come to your
resting place,
you and the ark of your might.
⁹ May your priests be clothed with
righteousness;
may your saints sing for joy."

¹⁰ For the sake of David your
servant,
do not reject your anointed
one.

¹¹ The LORD swore an oath to David,
a sure oath that he will not revoke:
"One of your own descendants
I will place on your throne—
¹² if your sons keep my covenant
and the statutes I teach them,
then their sons will sit
on your throne for ever and ever."

¹³ For the LORD has chosen Zion,
he has desired it for his dwelling:
¹⁴ "This is my resting place for ever
and ever;
here I will sit enthroned, for I have
desired it—
¹⁵ I will bless her with abundant
provisions;
her poor will I satisfy with food.
¹⁶ I will clothe her priests with
salvation,
and her saints will ever sing for joy.

¹⁷ "Here I will make a hornᶜ grow for
David
and set up a lamp for my anointed
one.
¹⁸ I will clothe his enemies with shame,
but the crown on his head will be
resplendent."

Psalm 133

A song of ascents. Of David.

¹ How good and pleasant it is
when brothers live together in
unity!
² It is like precious oil poured on the
head,
running down on the beard,

ᵃ6 That is, Kiriath Jearim   ᵇ6 Or *heard of it in
Ephrathah, / we found it in the fields of Jaar.* (And
no quotes around verses 7–9)   ᶜ17 *Horn* here
symbolizes strong one, that is, king.

running down on Aaron's beard,
　down upon the collar of his robes.
³ It is as if the dew of Hermon
　were falling on Mount Zion.
For there the LORD bestows his
　blessing,
　even life forevermore.

Psalm 134

A song of ascents.

¹ Praise the LORD, all you servants of
　the LORD
　who minister by night in the house
　of the LORD.

PSALM 133

How Good and Pleasant

133:1 HOW GOOD AND PLEASANT IT IS WHEN BROTHERS LIVE TOGETHER IN UNITY!

Some things are good, but not pleasant; and some things are pleasant, but not good. You can probably think immediately of things that fit the "good, but not pleasant" category: any number of medical and dental procedures, for instance. Maybe you can think of many more things that qualify as pleasant, but not good, as in good for you—most of them probably having to do with food.

But not everything qualifies as both good *and* pleasant. This psalm says unity among God's people is definitely one of these blessings. It's fun and it's good for you! It is as though the priestly oil that anointd and consecrated Aaron is poured down on God's people, consecrating them in the same way. It is like the dew from Mount Hermon that refreshes and fructifies the promised land. It is a very, very good thing when God's people get along with each other. God is glorified, and people flourish and are joyful. "For there the LORD bestows his blessing, even life forevermore" (verse 3).

Jesus might have had this psalm in mind when he prayed that his church would be one, as he and his Father are one: "That they be one as we are one: I in them and you in me. May they be brought to complete unity to let the world know that you sent me and have loved them even as you have loved me" (John 17:22–23). Jesus believed that unity in the church would be such a powerful demonstration of the presence of God in the church, "precious oil poured on the head," that it would make believers of nonbelievers. This is because God is a good and pleasant fellowship of Father, Son and Holy Spirit, the one in three, the three as one. God is a loving community. For the Christian community to be one is for them to be a little bit of heaven on earth. Pray Psalm 133 for your church. When you do, you pray with Jesus himself, and it's good for you.

PRAY:

Father, Son and Holy Spirit—may we be one as you are one;
that the world may know that Jesus is the Son of God
and that we are beloved of the Father.

FOR YOUR NEXT DEVOTIONAL READING, GO TO PAGE 723.

2 Lift up your hands in the sanctuary
    and praise the LORD.

3 May the LORD, the Maker of heaven
        and earth,
    bless you from Zion.

Psalm 135

1 Praise the LORD.[a]

Praise the name of the LORD;
    praise him, you servants of
        the LORD,
2 you who minister in the house of
        the LORD,
    in the courts of the house of
        our God.

3 Praise the LORD, for the LORD is good;
    sing praise to his name, for that
        is pleasant.
4 For the LORD has chosen Jacob to be
        his own,
    Israel to be his treasured
        possession.

5 I know that the LORD is great,
    that our Lord is greater than
        all gods.
6 The LORD does whatever pleases him,
    in the heavens and on the earth,
    in the seas and all their depths.
7 He makes clouds rise from the ends
        of the earth;
    he sends lightning with the rain
    and brings out the wind from his
        storehouses.

8 He struck down the firstborn of
        Egypt,
    the firstborn of men and animals.
9 He sent his signs and wonders into
        your midst, O Egypt,
    against Pharaoh and all his
        servants.
10 He struck down many nations
    and killed mighty kings—
11 Sihon king of the Amorites,
    Og king of Bashan
    and all the kings of Canaan—
12 and he gave their land as an
        inheritance,
    an inheritance to his people Israel.

13 Your name, O LORD, endures forever,
    your renown, O LORD, through all
        generations.

> *There are many things that are essential to arriving at true peace of mind, and one of the most important is faith, which cannot be acquired without prayer.* 99
>
> JOHN WOODEN

14 For the LORD will vindicate his people
    and have compassion on his
        servants.

15 The idols of the nations are silver
        and gold,
    made by the hands of men.
16 They have mouths, but cannot speak,
    eyes, but they cannot see;
17 they have ears, but cannot hear,
    nor is there breath in their mouths.
18 Those who make them will be like
        them,
    and so will all who trust in them.

19 O house of Israel, praise the LORD;
    O house of Aaron, praise the LORD;
20 O house of Levi, praise the LORD;
    you who fear him, praise the LORD.
21 Praise be to the LORD from Zion,
    to him who dwells in Jerusalem.

    Praise the LORD.

Psalm 136

1 Give thanks to the LORD, for he is good.
        His love endures forever.
2 Give thanks to the God of gods.
        His love endures forever.
3 Give thanks to the Lord of lords:
        His love endures forever.

4 to him who alone does great
        wonders,
        His love endures forever.
5 who by his understanding made the
        heavens,
        His love endures forever.
6 who spread out the earth upon the
        waters,
        His love endures forever.
7 who made the great lights—
        His love endures forever.
8 the sun to govern the day,
        His love endures forever.

a 1 Hebrew *Hallelu Yah*; also in verses 3 and 21

⁹the moon and stars to govern the
night;
His love endures forever.
¹⁰to him who struck down the firstborn
of Egypt
His love endures forever.
¹¹and brought Israel out from among
them
His love endures forever.
¹²with a mighty hand and outstretched
arm;
His love endures forever.
¹³to him who divided the Red Sea*ᵃ*
asunder
His love endures forever.
¹⁴and brought Israel through the midst
of it,
His love endures forever.
¹⁵but swept Pharaoh and his army into
the Red Sea;
His love endures forever.
¹⁶to him who led his people through
the desert,
His love endures forever.
¹⁷who struck down great kings,
His love endures forever.
¹⁸and killed mighty kings—
His love endures forever.
¹⁹Sihon king of the Amorites
His love endures forever.
²⁰and Og king of Bashan—
His love endures forever.
²¹and gave their land as an inheritance,
His love endures forever.
²²an inheritance to his servant Israel;
His love endures forever.
²³to the One who remembered us in
our low estate
His love endures forever.
²⁴and freed us from our enemies,
His love endures forever.
²⁵and who gives food to every creature.
His love endures forever.
²⁶Give thanks to the God of heaven.
His love endures forever.

Psalm 137

¹By the rivers of Babylon we sat
and wept
when we remembered Zion.
²There on the poplars
we hung our harps,

³for there our captors asked us for
songs,
our tormentors demanded songs
of joy;
they said, "Sing us one of the songs
of Zion!"
⁴How can we sing the songs of
the LORD
while in a foreign land?
⁵If I forget you, O Jerusalem,
may my right hand forget ⸤its skill⸥.
⁶May my tongue cling to the roof of
my mouth
if I do not remember you,
if I do not consider Jerusalem
my highest joy.

⁷Remember, O LORD, what the
Edomites did
on the day Jerusalem fell.
"Tear it down," they cried,
"tear it down to its foundations!"
⁸O Daughter of Babylon, doomed to
destruction,
happy is he who repays you
for what you have done to us—
⁹he who seizes your infants
and dashes them against the rocks.

> WHEN I called, you answered me;
> you made me bold and stouthearted.
>
> PSALM 138:3

Psalm 138

Of David.

¹I will praise you, O LORD, with all my
heart;
before the "gods" I will sing your
praise.
²I will bow down toward your holy
temple
and will praise your name
for your love and your faithfulness,
for you have exalted above all things
your name and your word.
³When I called, you answered me;
you made me bold and
stouthearted.

ᵃ13 Hebrew *Yam Suph*; that is, Sea of Reeds; also
in verse 15

4 May all the kings of the earth praise
    you, O LORD,
    when they hear the words of your
    mouth.
5 May they sing of the ways of the LORD,
    for the glory of the LORD is great.

6 Though the LORD is on high, he looks
    upon the lowly,
    but the proud he knows from afar.
7 Though I walk in the midst of trouble,
    you preserve my life;
    you stretch out your hand against the
    anger of my foes,
    with your right hand you save me.
8 The LORD will fulfill ⌊his purpose⌋
    for me;
    your love, O LORD, endures
    forever—
    do not abandon the works of your
    hands.

Psalm 139

For the director of music.
Of David. A psalm.

1 O LORD, you have searched me
    and you know me.
2 You know when I sit and when I rise;
    you perceive my thoughts from
    afar.
3 You discern my going out and my
    lying down;
    you are familiar with all my ways.
4 Before a word is on my tongue
    you know it completely, O LORD.

5 You hem me in—behind and before;
    you have laid your hand upon me.
6 Such knowledge is too wonderful
    for me,
    too lofty for me to attain.

7 Where can I go from your Spirit?
    Where can I flee from your
    presence?
8 If I go up to the heavens, you are
    there;
    if I make my bed in the depths,[a]
    you are there.
9 If I rise on the wings of the dawn,
    if I settle on the far side of the sea,
10 even there your hand will guide me,
    your right hand will hold me fast.

11 If I say, "Surely the darkness will
    hide me

and the light become night
    around me,"
12 even the darkness will not be dark
    to you;
    the night will shine like the day,
    for darkness is as light to you.

13 For you created my inmost being;
    you knit me together in my
    mother's womb.
14 I praise you because I am fearfully
    and wonderfully made;
    your works are wonderful,
    I know that full well.
15 My frame was not hidden from you
    when I was made in the secret
    place.
    When I was woven together in the
    depths of the earth,
16   your eyes saw my unformed
    body.
    All the days ordained for me
    were written in your book
    before one of them came to be.

17 How precious to[b] me are your
    thoughts, O God!
    How vast is the sum of them!
18 Were I to count them,
    they would outnumber the grains
    of sand.
    When I awake,
    I am still with you.

19 If only you would slay the wicked,
    O God!
    Away from me, you bloodthirsty
    men!
20 They speak of you with evil intent;
    your adversaries misuse your
    name.
21 Do I not hate those who hate you,
    O LORD,
    and abhor those who rise up
    against you?
22 I have nothing but hatred for them;
    I count them my enemies.

23 Search me, O God, and know my
    heart;
    test me and know my anxious
    thoughts.
24 See if there is any offensive way in
    me,
    and lead me in the way everlasting.

---

[a]8 Hebrew *Sheol*   [b]17 Or *concerning*

You Know Me!

139:1 O LORD, YOU HAVE SEARCHED ME AND YOU KNOW ME.

At the Museum of Modern Art in New York City, there is a sculpture of a hand by the French sculptor Auguste Rodin. Two clay figures of a man and a woman appear to be emerging out of its palm. It was one of Rodin's favorites; he called it "The Hand of God." Picture that hand and know this: Before you cared, one way or another, and whether or not you ever do, God has held you by his hand. That is the message of this psalm.

It's significant that the Scripture says he has held you by his hand, not his intellect. Surely his intellect, if one can call it that, comprehends us completely. But there is small comfort in the idea of a giant mind knowing all there is to know about us. It's even scary, like the idea of a "Big Brother" type of mind control, as described in George Orwell's book *1984*. God's knowledge of us is not the knowledge of someone who wants to control us, but of someone who wants to love us. "O LORD, you have searched me and you know me . . . you have laid your hand upon me. Such knowledge is too wonderful for me" (139:1,5–6).

God's hand has held you not only by his knowledge of you, but also by his presence with you (see verse 7). There is no place you can go and not find God there with you, ahead of you (see verses 8–12). A child was asked how she knew there was only one God. She answered, "Because he's so big there isn't room for anyone else." There is room for you, however. He is everywhere present, not just as a fact of his deity, but because of his love. Further, his hand has done more than hold you; he has shaped you by creating you, even knitting you together in your mother's womb. You are a marvel (see verses 13–16).

The wonderful result of all this is that God knows what you need before you ask (see Matthew 6:8). If you bring some great and troubling situation to him, you need not worry that he will say, "Really?! Oh that's terrible! I had no idea. Let me think about what to do." He is master of the situation before you pray about it. In fact, you are praying about it because he has moved you to pray. So be at peace.

PRAY:

*Lord and Giver of life: Thank you that you have
made me fearfully and wonderfully! Search me and know me; show me
if there is anything in me that offends you.*

———

FOR YOUR NEXT DEVOTIONAL READING, GO TO PAGE 726.

Psalm 140

For the director of music.
A psalm of David.

[1] Rescue me, O LORD, from evil men;
  protect me from men of violence,
[2] who devise evil plans in their
    hearts
  and stir up war every day.
[3] They make their tongues as sharp
    as a serpent's;
  the poison of vipers is on their lips.
                              Selah

[4] Keep me, O LORD, from the hands of
    the wicked;
  protect me from men of violence
  who plan to trip my feet.
[5] Proud men have hidden a snare
    for me;
  they have spread out the cords
    of their net
  and have set traps for me along my
    path.   *Selah*

[6] O LORD, I say to you, "You are my
    God."
  Hear, O LORD, my cry for mercy.
[7] O Sovereign LORD, my strong
    deliverer,
  who shields my head in the day
    of battle—
[8] do not grant the wicked their desires,
    O LORD;
  do not let their plans succeed,
  or they will become proud. *Selah*

[9] Let the heads of those who
    surround me
  be covered with the trouble their
    lips have caused.
[10] Let burning coals fall upon them;
  may they be thrown into the fire,
  into miry pits, never to rise.
[11] Let slanderers not be established in
    the land;
  may disaster hunt down men of
    violence.

[12] I know that the LORD secures justice
    for the poor
  and upholds the cause of the
    needy.
[13] Surely the righteous will praise
    your name
  and the upright will live before
    you.

Psalm 141

A psalm of David.

[1] O LORD, I call to you; come quickly
    to me.
  Hear my voice when I call to you.
[2] May my prayer be set before you like
    incense;
  may the lifting up of my hands be
    like the evening sacrifice.

[3] Set a guard over my mouth, O LORD;
  keep watch over the door of my
    lips.
[4] Let not my heart be drawn to what
    is evil,
  to take part in wicked deeds
  with men who are evildoers;
  let me not eat of their delicacies.

[5] Let a righteous man[a] strike me—it is
    a kindness;
  let him rebuke me—it is oil on my
    head.
  My head will not refuse it.

Yet my prayer is ever against the
    deeds of evildoers;
[6]   their rulers will be thrown down
    from the cliffs,
  and the wicked will learn that my
    words were well spoken.
[7] They will say, "As one plows and
    breaks up the earth,
  so our bones have been scattered
    at the mouth of the grave.[b]"

[8] But my eyes are fixed on you,
    O Sovereign LORD;
  in you I take refuge—do not give
    me over to death.
[9] Keep me from the snares they have
    laid for me,
  from the traps set by evildoers.
[10] Let the wicked fall into their own
    nets,
  while I pass by in safety.

Psalm 142

A *maskil*[c] of David. When he was
    in the cave. A prayer.

[1] I cry aloud to the LORD;
  I lift up my voice to the LORD for
    mercy.

[a]5 Or *Let the Righteous One*   [b]7 Hebrew *Sheol*
[c]Title: Probably a literary or musical term

²I pour out my complaint before
     him;
     before him I tell my trouble.

³When my spirit grows faint within
     me,
     it is you who know my way.
In the path where I walk
     men have hidden a snare for me.
⁴Look to my right and see;
     no one is concerned for me.
I have no refuge;
     no one cares for my life.

⁵I cry to you, O LORD;
     I say, "You are my refuge,
     my portion in the land of the
          living."
⁶Listen to my cry,
     for I am in desperate need;
rescue me from those who pursue
     me,
     for they are too strong for me.
⁷Set me free from my prison,
     that I may praise your name.
Then the righteous will gather
     about me
     because of your goodness to me.

Psalm 143

A psalm of David.

¹O LORD, hear my prayer,
     listen to my cry for mercy;
in your faithfulness and
     righteousness
     come to my relief.
²Do not bring your servant into
     judgment,
     for no one living is righteous
          before you.

³The enemy pursues me,
     he crushes me to the ground;
he makes me dwell in darkness
     like those long dead.
⁴So my spirit grows faint within me;
     my heart within me is dismayed.
⁵I remember the days of long ago;
     I meditate on all your works
     and consider what your hands
          have done.
⁶I spread out my hands to you;
     my soul thirsts for you like a
          parched land.   *Selah*

⁷Answer me quickly, O LORD;
     my spirit fails.
Do not hide your face from me
     or I will be like those who go down
          to the pit.
⁸Let the morning bring me word of
     your unfailing love,
     for I have put my trust in you.
Show me the way I should go,
     for to you I lift up my soul.
⁹Rescue me from my enemies,
     O LORD,
     for I hide myself in you.
¹⁰Teach me to do your will,
     for you are my God;
may your good Spirit
     lead me on level ground.

¹¹For your name's sake, O LORD,
     preserve my life;
in your righteousness, bring me
     out of trouble.
¹²In your unfailing love, silence my
     enemies;
     destroy all my foes,
     for I am your servant.

Psalm 144

Of David.

¹Praise be to the LORD my Rock,
     who trains my hands for war,
     my fingers for battle.
²He is my loving God and my fortress,
     my stronghold and my deliverer,
my shield, in whom I take refuge,
     who subdues peoples*ᵃ* under me.

³O LORD, what is man that you care
     for him,
     the son of man that you think of
          him?
⁴Man is like a breath;
     his days are like a fleeting shadow.

⁵Part your heavens, O LORD, and
     come down;
     touch the mountains, so that they
          smoke.
⁶Send forth lightning and scatter
     ˌthe enemiesˌ;
     shoot your arrows and rout them.

ᵃ2 Many manuscripts of the Masoretic Text, Dead
Sea Scrolls, Aquila, Jerome and Syriac; most
manuscripts of the Masoretic Text *subdues my
people*

Saying No to Say Yes

DESPITE HER tearful prayers, Monica's son Augustine had not yet become a Christian. She had been assured by a wise priest to pray with hope, believing, "It cannot be that the son of these tears should be lost." But if anything, since that time things seemed to be getting worse: Now Augustine wanted to leave his mother and his home in Carthage to sail to Rome to pursue his profession as a teacher of rhetoric. Carthage in the fourth century A.D. was a conservative North African town in what was the "Bible Belt" of the Roman Empire. Rome was cosmopolitan and immoral, filled with the temptations of flesh and mind. Monica knew how susceptible Augustine was to both. A trip to Rome would seal his doom—she was sure of it! "She wept bitterly to see me go," Augustine wrote, "and followed me to the water's edge, clinging to me with all her strength in the hope that I would either come home or take her with me." What a scene it must have been to see this brilliant young adult and his frantic mother struggling and arguing at the docks! Again, it was the irresistible force versus the immovable object.

Augustine decided the only way out was to lie. He told his mother he wouldn't be leaving after all, at least for a while. He said he needed to wait for the wind to rise and wanted to visit a friend before departure. But that night he secretly sailed away. The next day Monica was "wild with grief, pouring her sighs and sorrows" out to God, sure he had not listened to her prayers.

But it was in Rome, the last place his mother wanted him to go, that Augustine found what she most wanted him to have. For it was there he met his intellectual equal, Ambrose, the Christian bishop, and was converted. Through the painful breach between mother and son, God in his sovereign love did something wonderful for both. Augustine thanked God for "letting my own desires carry me away on a journey that was to put an end to those desires." What looked like running away from God had really been running to God. In much the same way, Monica, against her will, actually got what she most wanted in a way she least expected. In his *Confessions*, Augustine wrote that in refusing her, God, "in the depth of [his] wisdom . . . granted the wish that was closest to her heart."[14]

God is the master of all things, even the wills that resist his. He always reserves the right to be God and answer our prayers not our way, but his way. A bitter lesson for some, but ultimately one of the sweetest lessons of all. When he says no it often means he has planned a greater yes.

PRAY:
Father, before I even ask, you know better than I do what I need and what those I love need. Your will alone is good. Do for me what you see best.

MEMORIZE:
"In the same way, I tell you, there is rejoicing in the presence of the angels of God over one sinner who repents." LUKE 15:10

FOR YOUR NEXT DEVOTIONAL READING, GO TO PAGE 734.

7 Reach down your hand from on high;
   deliver me and rescue me
from the mighty waters,
   from the hands of foreigners
8 whose mouths are full of lies,
   whose right hands are deceitful.

9 I will sing a new song to you, O God;
   on the ten-stringed lyre I will make
      music to you,
10 to the One who gives victory to kings,
   who delivers his servant David
      from the deadly sword.

11 Deliver me and rescue me
   from the hands of foreigners
whose mouths are full of lies,
   whose right hands are deceitful.

12 Then our sons in their youth
   will be like well-nurtured plants,
and our daughters will be like pillars
   carved to adorn a palace.
13 Our barns will be filled
   with every kind of provision.
Our sheep will increase by
      thousands,
   by tens of thousands in our fields;
14   our oxen will draw heavy loads.*a*
There will be no breaching of walls,
   no going into captivity,
   no cry of distress in our streets.

15 Blessed are the people of whom this
      is true;
   blessed are the people whose God
      is the LORD.

Psalm 145*b*

A psalm of praise. Of David.

1 I will exalt you, my God the King;
   I will praise your name for ever
      and ever.
2 Every day I will praise you
   and extol your name for ever
      and ever.

3 Great is the LORD and most worthy
      of praise;
   his greatness no one can fathom.
4 One generation will commend your
      works to another;
   they will tell of your mighty acts.
5 They will speak of the glorious
      splendor of your majesty,
   and I will meditate on your
      wonderful works.*c*

6 They will tell of the power of your
      awesome works,
   and I will proclaim your great
      deeds.
7 They will celebrate your abundant
      goodness
   and joyfully sing of your
      righteousness.

8 The LORD is gracious and
      compassionate,
   slow to anger and rich in love.
9 The LORD is good to all;
   he has compassion on all he has
      made.

10 All you have made will praise you,
      O LORD;
   your saints will extol you.
11 They will tell of the glory of your
      kingdom
   and speak of your might,
12 so that all men may know of your
      mighty acts
   and the glorious splendor of your
      kingdom.
13 Your kingdom is an everlasting
      kingdom,
   and your dominion endures
      through all generations.

The LORD is faithful to all his
      promises
   and loving toward all he has
      made.*d*
14 The LORD upholds all those who fall
   and lifts up all who are bowed
      down.
15 The eyes of all look to you,
   and you give them their food at the
      proper time.
16 You open your hand
   and satisfy the desires of every
      living thing.

17 The LORD is righteous in all his ways
   and loving toward all he has made.

a 14 Or *our chieftains will be firmly established*
b This psalm is an acrostic poem, the verses of
which (including verse 13b) begin with the
successive letters of the Hebrew alphabet.
c 5 Dead Sea Scrolls and Syriac (see also
Septuagint); Masoretic Text *On the glorious
splendor of your majesty / and on your wonderful
works I will meditate*   *d 13* One manuscript of
the Masoretic Text, Dead Sea Scrolls and Syriac
(see also Septuagint); most manuscripts of the
Masoretic Text do not have the last two lines of
verse 13.

¹⁸ The LORD is near to all who call
    on him,
    to all who call on him in truth.
¹⁹ He fulfills the desires of those who
    fear him;
    he hears their cry and saves them.
²⁰ The LORD watches over all who love
    him,
    but all the wicked he will destroy.

²¹ My mouth will speak in praise of
    the LORD.
    Let every creature praise his
    holy name
    for ever and ever.

> *HE fulfills the desires of those who*
> *fear him;*
> *he hears their cry and saves them.*
>
> PSALM 145:19

Psalm 146

¹ Praise the LORD.ᵃ

Praise the LORD, O my soul.
²   I will praise the LORD all my life;
    I will sing praise to my God as long
    as I live.

³ Do not put your trust in princes,
    in mortal men, who cannot save.
⁴ When their spirit departs, they return
    to the ground;
    on that very day their plans come
    to nothing.

⁵ Blessed is he whose help is the God
    of Jacob,
    whose hope is in the LORD his God,
⁶ the Maker of heaven and earth,
    the sea, and everything in them—
    the LORD, who remains faithful
    forever.
⁷ He upholds the cause of the
    oppressed
    and gives food to the hungry.
    The LORD sets prisoners free,
⁸   the LORD gives sight to the blind,
    the LORD lifts up those who are bowed
    down,
    the LORD loves the righteous.
⁹ The LORD watches over the alien
    and sustains the fatherless and the
    widow,

but he frustrates the ways of the
    wicked.

¹⁰ The LORD reigns forever,
    your God, O Zion, for all
    generations.

Praise the LORD.

Psalm 147

¹ Praise the LORD.ᵇ

How good it is to sing praises to our
    God,
    how pleasant and fitting to praise
    him!

² The LORD builds up Jerusalem;
    he gathers the exiles of Israel.
³ He heals the brokenhearted
    and binds up their wounds.
⁴ He determines the number of the stars
    and calls them each by name.
⁵ Great is our Lord and mighty in
    power;
    his understanding has no limit.
⁶ The LORD sustains the humble
    but casts the wicked to the ground.

⁷ Sing to the LORD with thanksgiving;
    make music to our God on the
    harp.
⁸ He covers the sky with clouds;
    he supplies the earth with rain
    and makes grass grow on the hills.
⁹ He provides food for the cattle
    and for the young ravens when
    they call.

¹⁰ His pleasure is not in the strength of
    the horse,
    nor his delight in the legs of a man;
¹¹ the LORD delights in those who fear
    him,
    who put their hope in his unfailing
    love.

¹² Extol the LORD, O Jerusalem;
    praise your God, O Zion,
¹³ for he strengthens the bars of your
    gates
    and blesses your people within you.
¹⁴ He grants peace to your borders
    and satisfies you with the finest
    of wheat.

ᵃ1 Hebrew *Hallelu Yah*; also in verse 10
ᵇ1 Hebrew *Hallelu Yah*; also in verse 20

¹⁵ He sends his command to the earth;
　his word runs swiftly.
¹⁶ He spreads the snow like wool
　and scatters the frost like ashes.
¹⁷ He hurls down his hail like pebbles.
　Who can withstand his icy blast?
¹⁸ He sends his word and melts them;
　he stirs up his breezes, and the
　　waters flow.

¹⁹ He has revealed his word to Jacob,
　his laws and decrees to Israel.
²⁰ He has done this for no other
　nation;
　they do not know his laws.

　Praise the LORD.

Psalm 148

¹ Praise the LORD.ᵃ

Praise the LORD from the heavens,
　praise him in the heights above.
² Praise him, all his angels,
　praise him, all his heavenly hosts.
³ Praise him, sun and moon,
　praise him, all you shining stars.
⁴ Praise him, you highest heavens
　and you waters above the skies.

⁵ Let them praise the name of the LORD,
　for he commanded and they were
　　created.
⁶ He set them in place for ever and
　ever;
　he gave a decree that will never
　　pass away.

⁷ Praise the LORD from the earth,
　you great sea creatures and all
　　ocean depths,
⁸ lightning and hail, snow and clouds,
　stormy winds that do his bidding,
⁹ you mountains and all hills,
　fruit trees and all cedars,
¹⁰ wild animals and all cattle,
　small creatures and flying birds,
¹¹ kings of the earth and all nations,
　you princes and all rulers on earth,
¹² young men and maidens,
　old men and children.

¹³ Let them praise the name of the LORD,
　for his name alone is exalted;
　his splendor is above the earth and
　　the heavens.
¹⁴ He has raised up for his people a
　horn,ᵇ

the praise of all his saints,
　of Israel, the people close to his
　　heart.

Praise the LORD.

Psalm 149

¹ Praise the LORD.ᶜ

Sing to the LORD a new song,
　his praise in the assembly of the
　　saints.

² Let Israel rejoice in their Maker;
　let the people of Zion be glad in
　　their King.
³ Let them praise his name with dancing
　and make music to him with
　　tambourine and harp.
⁴ For the LORD takes delight in his
　people;
　he crowns the humble with
　　salvation.
⁵ Let the saints rejoice in this honor
　and sing for joy on their beds.

⁶ May the praise of God be in their
　mouths
　and a double-edged sword in their
　　hands,
⁷ to inflict vengeance on the nations
　and punishment on the peoples,
⁸ to bind their kings with fetters,
　their nobles with shackles of iron,
⁹ to carry out the sentence written
　against them.
　This is the glory of all his saints.

Praise the LORD.

Psalm 150

¹ Praise the LORD.ᵈ

Praise God in his sanctuary;
　praise him in his mighty heavens.
² Praise him for his acts of power;

> *LET everything that has breath praise
> 　the LORD.*
> *Praise the LORD.*
>
> PSALM 150:6

ᵃ1 Hebrew *Hallelu Yah*; also in verse 14
ᵇ14 *Horn* here symbolizes strong one, that is,
king.　　ᶜ1 Hebrew *Hallelu Yah*; also in verse 9
ᵈ1 Hebrew *Hallelu Yah*; also in verse 6

praise him for his surpassing
greatness.
3 Praise him with the sounding of the
trumpet,
praise him with the harp and lyre,
4 praise him with tambourine and
dancing,
praise him with the strings and flute,

5 praise him with the clash of
cymbals,
praise him with resounding
cymbals.

6 Let everything that has breath
praise the LORD.

Praise the LORD.

Proverbs

WHAT IS wisdom? Knowing what it is *not* will help you to understand it. Wisdom is not genius or intelligence. Mere intelligence without wisdom is like a fast runner on the wrong road. The advantage of speed is really a disadvantage, for all it does is take the runner further from her destination. To be smart but not wise is to be capable of inventing even more ways to be foolish. The race does not always belong to the swift. Having wisdom is knowing on which path to run. It is the moral insight that shows us how to be good so we can live well. "I run in the path of your commands, for you have set my heart free" (Psalms 119:32).

Our Lord Jesus made the same point with a different metaphor when he said, "Therefore everyone who hears these words of mine and puts them into practice is like a wise man who built his house on the rock. The rain came down, the streams rose, and the winds blew and beat against that house; yet it did not fall, because it had its foundation on the rock" (Matthew 7:24–25). The foolish man, Jesus went on to say, built his house on sand, and when the rains came, the house fell. In other words, if his life were a house, the second man in the parable could have built something worthy of the cover of *Architectural Digest*, but it would be worthless after the first sprinkle. What a tragedy to have a high IQ and a great education, but a fool's outlook.

The book of Proverbs is filled with things even a child can understand, yet it also includes things those who refuse to humble themselves will never understand. It is a great book to read on your knees, humbly and prayerfully. "At that time Jesus, full of joy through the Holy Spirit, said, 'I praise you, Father, Lord of heaven and earth, because you have hidden these things from the wise and learned, and revealed them to little children. Yes, Father, for this was your good pleasure'" (Luke 10:21).

THE LORD IS FAR FROM THE WICKED BUT HE HEARS THE PRAYER OF THE RIGHTEOUS. (15:29)

Prologue: Purpose and Theme

1 The proverbs of Solomon son of David, king of Israel:

2 for attaining wisdom and discipline;
  for understanding words of insight;
3 for acquiring a disciplined and
    prudent life,
  doing what is right and just and
    fair;
4 for giving prudence to the simple,
  knowledge and discretion to
    the young—
5 let the wise listen and add to their
    learning,
  and let the discerning get
    guidance—
6 for understanding proverbs and
    parables,
  the sayings and riddles of the wise.

7 The fear of the LORD is the beginning
    of knowledge,
  but fools[a] despise wisdom and
    discipline.

> Prayer requires more of the heart than of the tongue.
>
> ADAM CLARKE

Exhortations to Embrace Wisdom

Warning Against Enticement

8 Listen, my son, to your father's
    instruction
  and do not forsake your mother's
    teaching.
9 They will be a garland to grace
    your head
  and a chain to adorn your neck.

10 My son, if sinners entice you,
  do not give in to them.
11 If they say, "Come along with us;
  let's lie in wait for someone's
    blood,
  let's waylay some harmless soul;
12 let's swallow them alive, like the
    grave,[b]
  and whole, like those who go down
    to the pit;
13 we will get all sorts of valuable things
  and fill our houses with plunder;

14 throw in your lot with us,
  and we will share a common
    purse"—
15 my son, do not go along with
    them,
  do not set foot on their paths;
16 for their feet rush into sin,
  they are swift to shed blood.
17 How useless to spread a net
  in full view of all the birds!
18 These men lie in wait for their
    own blood;
  they waylay only themselves!
19 Such is the end of all who go after
    ill-gotten gain;
  it takes away the lives of those
    who get it.

Warning Against Rejecting Wisdom

20 Wisdom calls aloud in the street,
  she raises her voice in the public
    squares;
21 at the head of the noisy streets[c]
    she cries out,
  in the gateways of the city she
    makes her speech:

22 "How long will you simple ones[d] love
    your simple ways?
  How long will mockers delight in
    mockery
  and fools hate knowledge?
23 If you had responded to my rebuke,
  I would have poured out my heart
    to you
  and made my thoughts known
    to you.
24 But since you rejected me when
    I called
  and no one gave heed when
    I stretched out my hand,
25 since you ignored all my advice
  and would not accept my rebuke,
26 I in turn will laugh at your disaster;
  I will mock when calamity
    overtakes you—
27 when calamity overtakes you like
    a storm,

---

[a]7 The Hebrew words rendered *fool* in Proverbs, and often elsewhere in the Old Testament, denote one who is morally deficient.   [b]12 Hebrew *Sheol*   [c]21 Hebrew; Septuagint / *on the tops of the walls*   [d]22 The Hebrew word rendered *simple* in Proverbs generally denotes one without moral direction and inclined to evil.

PROVERBS 1:7; 9:10; 14:26–27

The Lighthouse

1:7 THE FEAR OF THE LORD IS THE BEGINNING OF KNOWLEDGE.

A large battleship was coursing through the North Atlantic Ocean in a heavy fog when the captain saw a light ahead. Since his ship appeared to be on a collision course with whatever the light was, he radioed immediately, "Alter your course ten degrees south." The message came back, "Alter your course ten degrees south." Irritated, the captain, radioed, "This is Captain Dillard. I repeat: Alter your course ten degrees south." The message came back, "This is Ensign Collins. I repeat: Alter your course ten degrees south." The situation was approaching a crisis. The captain bellowed, "This is a battleship, you idiot! Alter your course ten degrees south!" The message came back, "This is a lighthouse, sir. Alter your course ten degrees south."

The topic sentence of the book of Proverbs is like a lighthouse: "The fear of the LORD is the beginning of knowledge, but fools despise wisdom and discipline" (1:7). You may be clear about a lot of other things such as your name and the kind of ship you're on, but if you are not clear on this fundamental truth, you are headed for disaster. Money, intelligence and good looks will just be part of the wreckage.

The greatest commandment, according to Jesus, is that we love God with our whole being (see Matthew 22:37). If loving God is the greatest thing we can do, and fearing him is the beginning of everything else, how do the two fit together? Can we both love God and fear him? Doesn't one cancel out the other? Some translations render the word "fear" in Proverbs as *reverence*. While accurate, they miss the strength of the word, which is literally "fear" in the Hebrew text. What Jesus is getting at in the Matthew passage is that our love for God should be like fear in its intensity. The sight of something you fear focuses your mind. It blocks out everything else. In this sense then, you can truly love only whom you truly fear. There can be no deep love without a corresponding deep reverence.

When you pray, whether you use the words or not, let your "Father" always be "Father in heaven." For God is both closer than a friend and higher than the greatest king, a lighthouse guiding you home or a rock upon which you are broken (see Luke 20:17–18).

PRAY:

"O, how I fear Thee, living God,
With deepest, tend'rest fears,
And worship Thee with trembling hope
And penitential tears!
Yet I may love Thee too, O Lord,
Almighty as Thou art,
For Thou hast stooped to ask of me
The love of my poor heart!"

FREDERICK FABER

FOR YOUR NEXT DEVOTIONAL READING, GO TO PAGE 736.

when disaster sweeps over you like
a whirlwind,
when distress and trouble
overwhelm you.
28 "Then they will call to me but I will
not answer;
they will look for me but will
not find me.
29 Since they hated knowledge
and did not choose to fear the LORD,
30 since they would not accept my
advice
and spurned my rebuke,
31 they will eat the fruit of their ways
and be filled with the fruit of their
schemes.
32 For the waywardness of the simple
will kill them,
and the complacency of fools will
destroy them;
33 but whoever listens to me will live
in safety
and be at ease, without fear
of harm."

Moral Benefits of Wisdom

2 My son, if you accept my words
and store up my commands
within you,
2 turning your ear to wisdom
and applying your heart to
understanding,
3 and if you call out for insight
and cry aloud for understanding,
4 and if you look for it as for silver
and search for it as for hidden
treasure,
5 then you will understand the fear of
the LORD
and find the knowledge of God.
6 For the LORD gives wisdom,
and from his mouth come
knowledge and
understanding.
7 He holds victory in store for the
upright,
he is a shield to those whose walk
is blameless,
8 for he guards the course of the just
and protects the way of his faithful
ones.
9 Then you will understand what is
right and just
and fair—every good path.

10 For wisdom will enter your heart,
and knowledge will be pleasant to
your soul.
11 Discretion will protect you,
and understanding will guard you.
12 Wisdom will save you from the ways
of wicked men,
from men whose words are
perverse,
13 who leave the straight paths
to walk in dark ways,
14 who delight in doing wrong
and rejoice in the perverseness
of evil,
15 whose paths are crooked
and who are devious in their ways.

16 It will save you also from the
adulteress,
from the wayward wife with her
seductive words,
17 who has left the partner of her youth
and ignored the covenant she
made before God.[a]
18 For her house leads down to death
and her paths to the spirits of
the dead.
19 None who go to her return
or attain the paths of life.

20 Thus you will walk in the ways of
good men
and keep to the paths of the
righteous.
21 For the upright will live in the land,
and the blameless will remain in it;
22 but the wicked will be cut off from the
land,
and the unfaithful will be torn
from it.

Further Benefits of Wisdom

3 My son, do not forget my teaching,
but keep my commands in your
heart,
2 for they will prolong your life many
years
and bring you prosperity.

3 Let love and faithfulness never
leave you;
bind them around your neck,
write them on the tablet of your
heart.

a 17 Or covenant of her God

⁴Then you will win favor and a good name
in the sight of God and man.

⁵Trust in the LORD with all your heart
and lean not on your own understanding;
⁶in all your ways acknowledge him,
and he will make your paths straight.ᵃ

⁷Do not be wise in your own eyes;
fear the LORD and shun evil.
⁸This will bring health to your body
and nourishment to your bones.

⁹Honor the LORD with your wealth,
with the firstfruits of all your crops;

ᵃ6 Or *will direct your paths*

{ **TUESDAY** }

PROVERBS 3:5–6

Straight Paths and Mature People

3:6 HE WILL MAKE YOUR PATHS STRAIGHT.

This isn't a promise for an easy, obstacle-free life. Proverbs 3:6 says God will *make your paths straight*. There are rugged mountains to climb and deserts to cross, rivers to ford and jungles to traverse. That's where wisdom comes in.

There is a bonus in this straightening process; for in the straightening of our paths, we too are made straight. "Consider it pure joy, my brothers, whenever you face trials of many kinds, because you know that the testing of your faith develops perseverance. Perseverance must finish its work so that you may be mature and complete, not lacking anything" (James 1:2–4). Struggles can be good for us if we have the wisdom to handle them. So, "if any of you lacks wisdom, he should ask God" (James 1:5). There you have it: As paths are made straight, people are made mature.

"In all your ways acknowledge him" (Proverbs 3:6). What does it mean to acknowledge the Lord in all our ways? It means to live by his Word in every circumstance, in every place we find ourselves.

A father and a son were traveling to a city in a far country. The journey would take several days. As they walked over mountain passes and through forests, the boy wanted to explore things. They would enter a meadow, and the boy would want to run to the other side. If they passed a rock outcropping, the boy would beg his dad to let him climb it. The boy got bolder and bolder as they journeyed. One day he wanted to go a greater distance off the road than he had yet ventured. The father agreed that he could, but as the boy started off, he felt a tinge of fear. He asked, "How can I know if I've wandered too far away, Father?"

The father smiled and answered, "I'll call your name every few minutes, and you answer. You call my name every few minutes, and I'll answer. If you get to a place where you can't hear my voice very well, you've wandered too far."

That's what it looks like to acknowledge the Lord in all our ways. It is a picture of prayer and the Word of God—his voice calling to us, and our voice calling to him.

P R A Y :

O dear Father! Speak, for I am listening. And hear me when I pray.
Make my paths straight and my life mature.

FOR YOUR NEXT DEVOTIONAL READING, GO TO PAGE 738.

¹⁰ then your barns will be filled to
overflowing,
and your vats will brim over with
new wine.

¹¹ My son, do not despise the LORD's
discipline
and do not resent his rebuke,
¹² because the LORD disciplines those
he loves,
as a father[a] the son he delights in.

¹³ Blessed is the man who finds wisdom,
the man who gains understanding,
¹⁴ for she is more profitable than silver
and yields better returns than gold.
¹⁵ She is more precious than rubies;
nothing you desire can compare
with her.
¹⁶ Long life is in her right hand;
in her left hand are riches and honor.
¹⁷ Her ways are pleasant ways,
and all her paths are peace.
¹⁸ She is a tree of life to those who
embrace her;
those who lay hold of her will
be blessed.

¹⁹ By wisdom the LORD laid the earth's
foundations,
by understanding he set the
heavens in place;
²⁰ by his knowledge the deeps were
divided,
and the clouds let drop the dew.

²¹ My son, preserve sound judgment
and discernment,
do not let them out of your sight;
²² they will be life for you,
an ornament to grace your neck.
²³ Then you will go on your way
in safety,
and your foot will not stumble;
²⁴ when you lie down, you will not be
afraid;
when you lie down, your sleep
will be sweet.
²⁵ Have no fear of sudden disaster
or of the ruin that overtakes the
wicked,
²⁶ for the LORD will be your confidence
and will keep your foot from being
snared.

²⁷ Do not withhold good from those who
deserve it,
when it is in your power to act.

²⁸ Do not say to your neighbor,
"Come back later; I'll give it
tomorrow"—
when you now have it with you.

²⁹ Do not plot harm against your
neighbor,
who lives trustfully near you.
³⁰ Do not accuse a man for no reason—
when he has done you no harm.

³¹ Do not envy a violent man
or choose any of his ways,
³² for the LORD detests a perverse man
but takes the upright into his
confidence.

³³ The LORD's curse is on the house
of the wicked,
but he blesses the home of the
righteous.
³⁴ He mocks proud mockers
but gives grace to the humble.
³⁵ The wise inherit honor,
but fools he holds up to shame.

Wisdom Is Supreme

4 Listen, my sons, to a father's
instruction;
pay attention and gain
understanding.
² I give you sound learning,
so do not forsake my teaching.
³ When I was a boy in my father's
house,
still tender, and an only child of
my mother,
⁴ he taught me and said,
"Lay hold of my words with all
your heart;
keep my commands and you
will live.
⁵ Get wisdom, get understanding;
do not forget my words or swerve
from them.
⁶ Do not forsake wisdom, and she will
protect you;
love her, and she will watch over
you.
⁷ Wisdom is supreme; therefore get
wisdom.
Though it cost all you have,[b] get
understanding.

ᵃ12 Hebrew; Septuagint / and he punishes
ᵇ7 Or Whatever else you get

8 Esteem her, and she will exalt you;
  embrace her, and she will honor
  you.
9 She will set a garland of grace on
  your head
  and present you with a crown
  of splendor."

10 Listen, my son, accept what I say,
  and the years of your life will be
  many.
11 I guide you in the way of wisdom
  and lead you along straight paths.

12 When you walk, your steps will not be
  hampered;
  when you run, you will not
  stumble.
13 Hold on to instruction, do not let it
  go;
  guard it well, for it is your life.
14 Do not set foot on the path of the
  wicked
  or walk in the way of evil men.
15 Avoid it, do not travel on it;
  turn from it and go on your way.

{WEDNESDAY}

PROVERBS 4:1–9

Wisdom Is Supreme

4:7 "THOUGH IT COST YOU ALL YOU HAVE, GET UNDERSTANDING."

"Whatever else you get" is an alternate way to translate, "Though it cost you all you have" (4:7). The image is of a marketplace with so many things to buy—some good, some cheap, only a few excellent. "Whatever else you get in this marketplace of goods and wares, make sure you get wisdom because wisdom is supreme." The truth is, there are a lot of things you could buy, but it's hard to know what is worthwhile. Archbishop William Temple said the world is like a jewelry store in which vandals have switched the price tags around. There are things that are priced highly but are worthless, and there are things that are precious but are shoved to the back of the shelf and are priced cheaply. Wisdom is one of them.

Sometimes we forget where to look for wisdom. "Where is the Life we have lost in living?" wrote T. S. Eliot. "Where is the wisdom we have lost in knowledge? Where is the knowledge we have lost in information?"

To pray for wisdom is to ask for eyes to pick out what is wise amid the marketplace of wisdom substitutes. "And this is my prayer: that your love may abound more and more in knowledge and depth of insight, so that you may be able to discern what is best" (Philippians 1:9–10). To pray for wisdom is also to ask for God to bring a change in your heart to *want* wisdom more than anything. Though it cost you all you have, get wisdom. Wisdom, like the God of wisdom and the kingdom of God, is given only to those who treasure her and seek her with all their heart. Anything less will yield something less. Anyone who comes looking for God "must believe that he exists and that he rewards those who earnestly seek him" (Hebrews 11:6). Those who seek the kingdom must be willing to part with everything they have for the joy of securing it (see Matthew 13:44–46).

PRAY:

Open my eyes that I might see what is wise.
Open my heart that I might want what is wise.

FOR YOUR NEXT DEVOTIONAL READING, GO TO PAGE 750.

¹⁶ For they cannot sleep till they do evil;
they are robbed of slumber till they
make someone fall.
¹⁷ They eat the bread of wickedness
and drink the wine of violence.

¹⁸ The path of the righteous is like the
first gleam of dawn,
shining ever brighter till the full
light of day.
¹⁹ But the way of the wicked is like deep
darkness;
they do not know what makes
them stumble.

²⁰ My son, pay attention to what I say;
listen closely to my words.
²¹ Do not let them out of your sight,
keep them within your heart;
²² for they are life to those who find
them
and health to a man's whole body.
²³ Above all else, guard your heart,
for it is the wellspring of life.
²⁴ Put away perversity from your mouth;
keep corrupt talk far from your lips.
²⁵ Let your eyes look straight ahead,
fix your gaze directly before you.
²⁶ Make level*a* paths for your feet
and take only ways that are firm.
²⁷ Do not swerve to the right or the left;
keep your foot from evil.

Warning Against Adultery

5 My son, pay attention to my
wisdom,
listen well to my words of insight,
² that you may maintain discretion
and your lips may preserve
knowledge.
³ For the lips of an adulteress drip
honey,
and her speech is smoother
than oil;
⁴ but in the end she is bitter as gall,
sharp as a double-edged sword.
⁵ Her feet go down to death;
her steps lead straight to the
grave.*b*
⁶ She gives no thought to the way
of life;
her paths are crooked, but she
knows it not.

⁷ Now then, my sons, listen to me;
do not turn aside from what I say.

⁸ Keep to a path far from her,
do not go near the door of her
house,
⁹ lest you give your best strength to
others
and your years to one who is cruel,
¹⁰ lest strangers feast on your wealth
and your toil enrich another man's
house.
¹¹ At the end of your life you will groan,
when your flesh and body are
spent.
¹² You will say, "How I hated discipline!
How my heart spurned correction!
¹³ I would not obey my teachers
or listen to my instructors.
¹⁴ I have come to the brink of utter ruin
in the midst of the whole
assembly."

¹⁵ Drink water from your own cistern,
running water from your own well.
¹⁶ Should your springs overflow in the
streets,
your streams of water in the public
squares?
¹⁷ Let them be yours alone,
never to be shared with strangers.
¹⁸ May your fountain be blessed,
and may you rejoice in the wife of
your youth.
¹⁹ A loving doe, a graceful deer—
may her breasts satisfy you always,
may you ever be captivated by
her love.
²⁰ Why be captivated, my son, by an
adulteress?
Why embrace the bosom of
another man's wife?

²¹ For a man's ways are in full view of
the Lord,
and he examines all his paths.
²² The evil deeds of a wicked man
ensnare him;
the cords of his sin hold him fast.
²³ He will die for lack of discipline,
led astray by his own great folly.

Warnings Against Folly

6 My son, if you have put up security
for your neighbor,
if you have struck hands in pledge
for another,

a 26 Or *Consider the*   *b 5* Hebrew *Sheol*

2 if you have been trapped by what
you said,
ensnared by the words of your
mouth,
3 then do this, my son, to free yourself,
since you have fallen into your
neighbor's hands:
Go and humble yourself;
press your plea with your neighbor!
4 Allow no sleep to your eyes,
no slumber to your eyelids.
5 Free yourself, like a gazelle from the
hand of the hunter,
like a bird from the snare of the
fowler.

6 Go to the ant, you sluggard;
consider its ways and be wise!
7 It has no commander,
no overseer or ruler,
8 yet it stores its provisions in summer
and gathers its food at harvest.

9 How long will you lie there, you
sluggard?
When will you get up from your
sleep?
10 A little sleep, a little slumber,
a little folding of the hands
to rest—
11 and poverty will come on you like a
bandit
and scarcity like an armed man.[a]

12 A scoundrel and villain,
who goes about with a corrupt
mouth,
13 who winks with his eye,
signals with his feet
and motions with his fingers,
14 who plots evil with deceit in
his heart—
he always stirs up dissension.
15 Therefore disaster will overtake him
in an instant;
he will suddenly be destroyed—
without remedy.

16 There are six things the LORD hates,
seven that are detestable to him:
17 haughty eyes,
a lying tongue,
hands that shed innocent blood,
18 a heart that devises wicked
schemes,
feet that are quick to rush into
evil,

19 a false witness who pours out lies
and a man who stirs up
dissension among brothers.

Warning Against Adultery

20 My son, keep your father's
commands
and do not forsake your mother's
teaching.
21 Bind them upon your heart forever;
fasten them around your neck.
22 When you walk, they will guide you;
when you sleep, they will watch
over you;
when you awake, they will speak
to you.
23 For these commands are a lamp,
this teaching is a light,
and the corrections of discipline
are the way to life,
24 keeping you from the immoral
woman,
from the smooth tongue of the
wayward wife.
25 Do not lust in your heart after her
beauty
or let her captivate you with her
eyes,
26 for the prostitute reduces you to a
loaf of bread,
and the adulteress preys upon your
very life.
27 Can a man scoop fire into his lap
without his clothes being burned?
28 Can a man walk on hot coals
without his feet being scorched?
29 So is he who sleeps with another
man's wife;
no one who touches her will go
unpunished.

30 Men do not despise a thief if he
steals
to satisfy his hunger when he is
starving.
31 Yet if he is caught, he must pay
sevenfold,
though it costs him all the wealth
of his house.
32 But a man who commits adultery
lacks judgment;
whoever does so destroys
himself.

---

a 11 Or *like a vagrant / and scarcity like a beggar*

[33] Blows and disgrace are his lot,
and his shame will never be wiped
away;
[34] for jealousy arouses a husband's fury,
and he will show no mercy when
he takes revenge.
[35] He will not accept any compensation;
he will refuse the bribe, however
great it is.

Warning Against the Adulteress

7 My son, keep my words
and store up my commands within
you.
[2] Keep my commands and you will live;
guard my teachings as the apple of
your eye.
[3] Bind them on your fingers;
write them on the tablet of your
heart.
[4] Say to wisdom, "You are my sister,"
and call understanding your
kinsman;
[5] they will keep you from the
adulteress,
from the wayward wife with her
seductive words.

[6] At the window of my house
I looked out through the lattice.
[7] I saw among the simple,
I noticed among the young men,
a youth who lacked judgment.
[8] He was going down the street near
her corner,
walking along in the direction of
her house
[9] at twilight, as the day was fading,
as the dark of night set in.
[10] Then out came a woman to meet him,
dressed like a prostitute and with
crafty intent.
[11] (She is loud and defiant,
her feet never stay at home;
[12] now in the street, now in the squares,
at every corner she lurks.)
[13] She took hold of him and kissed him
and with a brazen face she said:
[14] "I have fellowship offerings[a] at
home;
today I fulfilled my vows.
[15] So I came out to meet you;
I looked for you and have found
you!

[16] I have covered my bed
with colored linens from Egypt.
[17] I have perfumed my bed
with myrrh, aloes and cinnamon.
[18] Come, let's drink deep of love till
morning;
let's enjoy ourselves with love!
[19] My husband is not at home;
he has gone on a long journey.
[20] He took his purse filled with
money
and will not be home till full
moon."

[21] With persuasive words she led him
astray;
she seduced him with her smooth
talk.
[22] All at once he followed her
like an ox going to the slaughter,
like a deer[b] stepping into a noose[c]
[23] till an arrow pierces his liver,
like a bird darting into a snare,
little knowing it will cost him
his life.

[24] Now then, my sons, listen to me;
pay attention to what I say.
[25] Do not let your heart turn to her ways
or stray into her paths.
[26] Many are the victims she has brought
down;
her slain are a mighty throng.
[27] Her house is a highway to the grave,[d]
leading down to the chambers of
death.

Wisdom's Call

8 Does not wisdom call out?
Does not understanding raise
her voice?
[2] On the heights along the way,
where the paths meet, she takes
her stand;
[3] beside the gates leading into the city,
at the entrances, she cries aloud:
[4] "To you, O men, I call out;
I raise my voice to all mankind.
[5] You who are simple, gain prudence;
you who are foolish, gain
understanding.

---

[a]14 Traditionally *peace offerings*   [b]22 Syriac
(see also Septuagint); Hebrew *fool*
[c]22 The meaning of the Hebrew for this line
is uncertain.   [d]27 Hebrew *Sheol*

⁶ Listen, for I have worthy things
    to say;
   I open my lips to speak what
    is right.
⁷ My mouth speaks what is true,
   for my lips detest wickedness.
⁸ All the words of my mouth are just;
   none of them is crooked or
    perverse.
⁹ To the discerning all of them
    are right;
   they are faultless to those who
    have knowledge.
¹⁰ Choose my instruction instead
    of silver,
   knowledge rather than choice gold,
¹¹ for wisdom is more precious than
    rubies,
   and nothing you desire can
    compare with her.

¹² "I, wisdom, dwell together with
    prudence;
   I possess knowledge and
    discretion.
¹³ To fear the LORD is to hate evil;
   I hate pride and arrogance,
    evil behavior and perverse speech.
¹⁴ Counsel and sound judgment are
    mine;
   I have understanding and power.
¹⁵ By me kings reign
   and rulers make laws that are just;
¹⁶ by me princes govern,
   and all nobles who rule on earth.ᵃ
¹⁷ I love those who love me,
   and those who seek me find me.
¹⁸ With me are riches and honor,
   enduring wealth and prosperity.
¹⁹ My fruit is better than fine gold;
   what I yield surpasses choice
    silver.
²⁰ I walk in the way of righteousness,
   along the paths of justice,
²¹ bestowing wealth on those who
    love me
   and making their treasuries full.

²² "The LORD brought me forth as the
    first of his works,ᵇ,ᶜ
   before his deeds of old;
²³ I was appointedᵈ from eternity,
   from the beginning, before the
    world began.
²⁴ When there were no oceans, I was
    given birth,

when there were no springs
    abounding with water;
²⁵ before the mountains were settled in
    place,
   before the hills, I was given birth,
²⁶ before he made the earth or its fields
   or any of the dust of the world.
²⁷ I was there when he set the heavens
    in place,
   when he marked out the horizon
    on the face of the deep,
²⁸ when he established the clouds
    above
   and fixed securely the fountains
    of the deep,
²⁹ when he gave the sea its boundary
   so the waters would not overstep
    his command,
   and when he marked out the
    foundations of the earth.
³⁰   Then I was the craftsman at his
    side.
   I was filled with delight day after
    day,
   rejoicing always in his presence,
³¹ rejoicing in his whole world
   and delighting in mankind.

³² "Now then, my sons, listen to me;
   blessed are those who keep my
    ways.
³³ Listen to my instruction and be wise;
   do not ignore it.
³⁴ Blessed is the man who listens
    to me,
   watching daily at my doors,
   waiting at my doorway.
³⁵ For whoever finds me finds life
   and receives favor from the LORD.
³⁶ But whoever fails to find me harms
    himself;
   all who hate me love death."

Invitations of Wisdom and of Folly

9 Wisdom has built her house;
   she has hewn out its seven pillars.
² She has prepared her meat and
    mixed her wine;
   she has also set her table.

ᵃ*16* Many Hebrew manuscripts and Septuagint;
most Hebrew manuscripts *and nobles—all
righteous rulers*   ᵇ*22* Or *way;* or *dominion*
ᶜ*22* Or *The LORD possessed me at the beginning of
his work;* or *The LORD brought me forth at the
beginning of his work*   ᵈ*23* Or *fashioned*

³She has sent out her maids, and
she calls
from the highest point of the city.
⁴ "Let all who are simple come in
here!"
she says to those who lack
judgment.
⁵ "Come, eat my food
and drink the wine I have mixed.
⁶Leave your simple ways and you
will live;
walk in the way of understanding.

⁷ "Whoever corrects a mocker invites
insult;
whoever rebukes a wicked man
incurs abuse.
⁸Do not rebuke a mocker or he will
hate you;
rebuke a wise man and he will
love you.
⁹Instruct a wise man and he will be
wiser still;
teach a righteous man and he will
add to his learning.

¹⁰ "The fear of the LORD is the beginning
of wisdom,
and knowledge of the Holy One is
understanding.
¹¹ For through me your days will be
many,
and years will be added to your life.
¹² If you are wise, your wisdom will
reward you;
if you are a mocker, you alone will
suffer."

¹³ The woman Folly is loud;
she is undisciplined and without
knowledge.
¹⁴ She sits at the door of her house,
on a seat at the highest point of
the city,
¹⁵ calling out to those who pass by,
who go straight on their way.
¹⁶ "Let all who are simple come in
here!"
she says to those who lack
judgment.
¹⁷ "Stolen water is sweet;
food eaten in secret is delicious!"
¹⁸ But little do they know that the dead
are there,
that her guests are in the depths
of the grave.ᵃ

Proverbs of Solomon

10 The proverbs of Solomon:

A wise son brings joy to his father,
but a foolish son grief to his
mother.

² Ill-gotten treasures are of no value,
but righteousness delivers from
death.

³ The LORD does not let the righteous
go hungry
but he thwarts the craving of the
wicked.

⁴Lazy hands make a man poor,
but diligent hands bring wealth.

⁵ He who gathers crops in summer is
a wise son,
but he who sleeps during harvest is
a disgraceful son.

⁶Blessings crown the head of the
righteous,
but violence overwhelms the
mouth of the wicked.ᵇ

⁷ The memory of the righteous will be
a blessing,
but the name of the wicked will rot.

⁸ The wise in heart accept commands,
but a chattering fool comes
to ruin.

⁹ The man of integrity walks securely,
but he who takes crooked paths
will be found out.

¹⁰ He who winks maliciously causes
grief,
and a chattering fool comes
to ruin.

¹¹ The mouth of the righteous is a
fountain of life,
but violence overwhelms the
mouth of the wicked.

¹² Hatred stirs up dissension,
but love covers over all wrongs.

¹³ Wisdom is found on the lips of the
discerning,
but a rod is for the back of him who
lacks judgment.

ᵃ18 Hebrew Sheol   ᵇ6 Or but the mouth of the
wicked conceals violence; also in verse 11

14 Wise men store up knowledge,
    but the mouth of a fool invites ruin.

15 The wealth of the rich is their fortified
        city,
    but poverty is the ruin of the poor.

16 The wages of the righteous bring
        them life,
    but the income of the wicked
        brings them punishment.

17 He who heeds discipline shows the
        way to life,
    but whoever ignores correction
        leads others astray.

18 He who conceals his hatred has lying
        lips,
    and whoever spreads slander is
        a fool.

19 When words are many, sin is not
        absent,
    but he who holds his tongue
        is wise.

20 The tongue of the righteous is choice
        silver,
    but the heart of the wicked is of
        little value.

21 The lips of the righteous nourish
        many,
    but fools die for lack of judgment.

22 The blessing of the LORD brings
        wealth,
    and he adds no trouble to it.

23 A fool finds pleasure in evil conduct,
    but a man of understanding
        delights in wisdom.

24 What the wicked dreads will overtake
        him;
    what the righteous desire will be
        granted.

25 When the storm has swept by, the
        wicked are gone,
    but the righteous stand firm
        forever.

WHAT *the wicked dreads will*
    overtake him;
what the righteous desire will be
    granted.

PROVERBS 10:24

26 As vinegar to the teeth and smoke to
        the eyes,
    so is a sluggard to those who send
        him.

27 The fear of the LORD adds length
        to life,
    but the years of the wicked are cut
        short.

28 The prospect of the righteous is joy,
    but the hopes of the wicked come
        to nothing.

29 The way of the LORD is a refuge for
        the righteous,
    but it is the ruin of those who
        do evil.

30 The righteous will never be
        uprooted,
    but the wicked will not remain
        in the land.

31 The mouth of the righteous brings
        forth wisdom,
    but a perverse tongue will be
        cut out.

32 The lips of the righteous know what
        is fitting,
    but the mouth of the wicked only
        what is perverse.

11 The LORD abhors dishonest scales,
    but accurate weights are his
        delight.

2 When pride comes, then comes
        disgrace,
    but with humility comes wisdom.

3 The integrity of the upright guides
        them,
    but the unfaithful are destroyed
        by their duplicity.

4 Wealth is worthless in the day
        of wrath,
    but righteousness delivers from
        death.

5 The righteousness of the blameless
        makes a straight way for them,
    but the wicked are brought down
        by their own wickedness.

6 The righteousness of the upright
        delivers them,
    but the unfaithful are trapped by
        evil desires.

7 When a wicked man dies, his hope
    perishes;
  all he expected from his power
    comes to nothing.

8 The righteous man is rescued from
    trouble,
  and it comes on the wicked
    instead.

9 With his mouth the godless destroys
    his neighbor,
  but through knowledge the
    righteous escape.

10 When the righteous prosper, the city
    rejoices;
  when the wicked perish, there are
    shouts of joy.

11 Through the blessing of the upright a
    city is exalted,
  but by the mouth of the wicked it is
    destroyed.

12 A man who lacks judgment derides
    his neighbor,
  but a man of understanding holds
    his tongue.

13 A gossip betrays a confidence,
  but a trustworthy man keeps
    a secret.

14 For lack of guidance a nation falls,
  but many advisers make victory
    sure.

15 He who puts up security for another
    will surely suffer,
  but whoever refuses to strike hands
    in pledge is safe.

16 A kindhearted woman gains respect,
  but ruthless men gain only wealth.

17 A kind man benefits himself,
  but a cruel man brings trouble on
    himself.

18 The wicked man earns deceptive
    wages,
  but he who sows righteousness
    reaps a sure reward.

19 The truly righteous man attains life,
  but he who pursues evil goes to his
    death.

20 The LORD detests men of perverse
    heart

but he delights in those whose
    ways are blameless.

21 Be sure of this: The wicked will not go
    unpunished,
  but those who are righteous will
    go free.

22 Like a gold ring in a pig's snout
  is a beautiful woman who shows no
    discretion.

23 The desire of the righteous ends only
    in good,
  but the hope of the wicked only
    in wrath.

24 One man gives freely, yet gains even
    more;
  another withholds unduly, but
    comes to poverty.

25 A generous man will prosper;
  he who refreshes others will
    himself be refreshed.

26 People curse the man who hoards
    grain,
  but blessing crowns him who is
    willing to sell.

27 He who seeks good finds goodwill,
  but evil comes to him who searches
    for it.

28 Whoever trusts in his riches will fall,
  but the righteous will thrive like a
    green leaf.

29 He who brings trouble on his family
    will inherit only wind,
  and the fool will be servant to
    the wise.

30 The fruit of the righteous is a tree
    of life,
  and he who wins souls is wise.

31 If the righteous receive their due on
    earth,
  how much more the ungodly and
    the sinner!

12 Whoever loves discipline loves
    knowledge,
  but he who hates correction is
    stupid.

2 A good man obtains favor from
    the LORD,
  but the LORD condemns a crafty
    man.

> A GOOD man obtains favor from
> the LORD.
>
> PROVERBS 12:2

³ A man cannot be established through
   wickedness,
   but the righteous cannot be
   uprooted.

⁴ A wife of noble character is her
   husband's crown,
   but a disgraceful wife is like decay
   in his bones.

⁵ The plans of the righteous are just,
   but the advice of the wicked is
   deceitful.

⁶ The words of the wicked lie in wait
   for blood,
   but the speech of the upright
   rescues them.

⁷ Wicked men are overthrown and are
   no more,
   but the house of the righteous
   stands firm.

⁸ A man is praised according to his
   wisdom,
   but men with warped minds are
   despised.

⁹ Better to be a nobody and yet have
   a servant
   than pretend to be somebody and
   have no food.

¹⁰ A righteous man cares for the needs
   of his animal,
   but the kindest acts of the wicked
   are cruel.

¹¹ He who works his land will have
   abundant food,
   but he who chases fantasies lacks
   judgment.

¹² The wicked desire the plunder of evil
   men,
   but the root of the righteous
   flourishes.

¹³ An evil man is trapped by his sinful
   talk,
   but a righteous man escapes
   trouble.

¹⁴ From the fruit of his lips a man is
   filled with good things
   as surely as the work of his hands
   rewards him.

¹⁵ The way of a fool seems right to him,
   but a wise man listens to advice.

¹⁶ A fool shows his annoyance at once,
   but a prudent man overlooks an
   insult.

¹⁷ A truthful witness gives honest
   testimony,
   but a false witness tells lies.

¹⁸ Reckless words pierce like a sword,
   but the tongue of the wise brings
   healing.

¹⁹ Truthful lips endure forever,
   but a lying tongue lasts only a
   moment.

²⁰ There is deceit in the hearts of those
   who plot evil,
   but joy for those who promote
   peace.

²¹ No harm befalls the righteous,
   but the wicked have their fill of
   trouble.

²² The LORD detests lying lips,
   but he delights in men who are
   truthful.

²³ A prudent man keeps his knowledge
   to himself,
   but the heart of fools blurts out
   folly.

²⁴ Diligent hands will rule,
   but laziness ends in slave labor.

²⁵ An anxious heart weighs a man
   down,
   but a kind word cheers him up.

²⁶ A righteous man is cautious in
   friendship,ᵃ
   but the way of the wicked leads
   them astray.

²⁷ The lazy man does not roastᵇ his
   game,
   but the diligent man prizes his
   possessions.

ᵃ26 Or *man is a guide to his neighbor*
ᵇ27 The meaning of the Hebrew for this word is
uncertain.

28 In the way of righteousness there is
life;
along that path is immortality.

13 A wise son heeds his father's
instruction,
but a mocker does not listen to
rebuke.

2 From the fruit of his lips a man enjoys
good things,
but the unfaithful have a craving
for violence.

3 He who guards his lips guards his life,
but he who speaks rashly will come
to ruin.

4 The sluggard craves and gets
nothing,
but the desires of the diligent are
fully satisfied.

5 The righteous hate what is false,
but the wicked bring shame and
disgrace.

6 Righteousness guards the man of
integrity,
but wickedness overthrows
the sinner.

7 One man pretends to be rich, yet
has nothing;
another pretends to be poor, yet
has great wealth.

8 A man's riches may ransom his life,
but a poor man hears no threat.

9 The light of the righteous shines
brightly,
but the lamp of the wicked is
snuffed out.

10 Pride only breeds quarrels,
but wisdom is found in those who
take advice.

11 Dishonest money dwindles away,
but he who gathers money little by
little makes it grow.

12 Hope deferred makes the heart sick,
but a longing fulfilled is a tree
of life.

13 He who scorns instruction will pay
for it,
but he who respects a command is
rewarded.

14 The teaching of the wise is a fountain
of life,
turning a man from the snares
of death.

15 Good understanding wins favor,
but the way of the unfaithful is
hard.^a

16 Every prudent man acts out of
knowledge,
but a fool exposes his folly.

17 A wicked messenger falls into trouble,
but a trustworthy envoy brings
healing.

18 He who ignores discipline comes to
poverty and shame,
but whoever heeds correction is
honored.

19 A longing fulfilled is sweet to the soul,
but fools detest turning from evil.

20 He who walks with the wise grows
wise,
but a companion of fools suffers
harm.

21 Misfortune pursues the sinner,
but prosperity is the reward of the
righteous.

22 A good man leaves an inheritance for
his children's children,
but a sinner's wealth is stored up
for the righteous.

23 A poor man's field may produce
abundant food,
but injustice sweeps it away.

24 He who spares the rod hates his son,
but he who loves him is careful to
discipline him.

25 The righteous eat to their hearts'
content,
but the stomach of the wicked goes
hungry.

14 The wise woman builds her house,
but with her own hands the
foolish one tears hers down.

2 He whose walk is upright fears the
LORD,
but he whose ways are devious
despises him.

a15 Or *unfaithful does not endure*

3 A fool's talk brings a rod to his back,
but the lips of the wise protect
them.

4 Where there are no oxen, the manger
is empty,
but from the strength of an ox
comes an abundant harvest.

5 A truthful witness does not deceive,
but a false witness pours out lies.

6 The mocker seeks wisdom and finds
none,
but knowledge comes easily to the
discerning.

7 Stay away from a foolish man,
for you will not find knowledge on
his lips.

8 The wisdom of the prudent is to give
thought to their ways,
but the folly of fools is deception.

9 Fools mock at making amends
for sin,
but goodwill is found among
the upright.

10 Each heart knows its own bitterness,
and no one else can share its joy.

11 The house of the wicked will be
destroyed,
but the tent of the upright will
flourish.

12 There is a way that seems right to a
man,
but in the end it leads to death.

13 Even in laughter the heart may ache,
and joy may end in grief.

14 The faithless will be fully repaid for
their ways,
and the good man rewarded for
his.

15 A simple man believes anything,
but a prudent man gives thought to
his steps.

16 A wise man fears the LORD and shuns
evil,
but a fool is hotheaded and
reckless.

17 A quick-tempered man does foolish
things,
and a crafty man is hated.

18 The simple inherit folly,
but the prudent are crowned with
knowledge.

19 Evil men will bow down in the
presence of the good,
and the wicked at the gates of the
righteous.

20 The poor are shunned even by their
neighbors,
but the rich have many friends.

21 He who despises his neighbor sins,
but blessed is he who is kind to the
needy.

22 Do not those who plot evil go astray?
But those who plan what is good
find*a* love and faithfulness.

23 All hard work brings a profit,
but mere talk leads only to poverty.

24 The wealth of the wise is their crown,
but the folly of fools yields folly.

25 A truthful witness saves lives,
but a false witness is deceitful.

26 He who fears the LORD has a secure
fortress,
and for his children it will be
a refuge.

27 The fear of the LORD is a fountain of
life,
turning a man from the snares
of death.

28 A large population is a king's glory,
but without subjects a prince is
ruined.

29 A patient man has great
understanding,
but a quick-tempered man
displays folly.

30 A heart at peace gives life to the
body,
but envy rots the bones.

31 He who oppresses the poor shows
contempt for their Maker,
but whoever is kind to the needy
honors God.

32 When calamity comes, the wicked are
brought down,

a22 Or show

but even in death the righteous
have a refuge.

33 Wisdom reposes in the heart of the
discerning
and even among fools she lets
herself be known.[a]

34 Righteousness exalts a nation,
but sin is a disgrace to any people.

35 A king delights in a wise servant,
but a shameful servant incurs
his wrath.

15 A gentle answer turns away wrath,
but a harsh word stirs up anger.

2 The tongue of the wise commends
knowledge,
but the mouth of the fool gushes
folly.

3 The eyes of the LORD are everywhere,
keeping watch on the wicked and
the good.

4 The tongue that brings healing is a
tree of life,
but a deceitful tongue crushes
the spirit.

5 A fool spurns his father's discipline,
but whoever heeds correction
shows prudence.

6 The house of the righteous contains
great treasure,
but the income of the wicked
brings them trouble.

7 The lips of the wise spread
knowledge;
not so the hearts of fools.

8 The LORD detests the sacrifice of the
wicked,
but the prayer of the upright
pleases him.

9 The LORD detests the way of the
wicked
but he loves those who pursue
righteousness.

10 Stern discipline awaits him who
leaves the path;
he who hates correction will die.

11 Death and Destruction[b] lie open
before the LORD—
how much more the hearts of men!

12 A mocker resents correction;
he will not consult the wise.

13 A happy heart makes the face
cheerful,
but heartache crushes the spirit.

14 The discerning heart seeks
knowledge,
but the mouth of a fool feeds on
folly.

15 All the days of the oppressed are
wretched,
but the cheerful heart has a
continual feast.

16 Better a little with the fear of the LORD
than great wealth with turmoil.

17 Better a meal of vegetables where
there is love
than a fattened calf with hatred.

18 A hot-tempered man stirs up
dissension,
but a patient man calms a quarrel.

19 The way of the sluggard is blocked
with thorns,
but the path of the upright is a
highway.

20 A wise son brings joy to his father,
but a foolish man despises his
mother.

21 Folly delights a man who lacks
judgment,
but a man of understanding keeps
a straight course.

22 Plans fail for lack of counsel,
but with many advisers they
succeed.

23 A man finds joy in giving an apt reply—
and how good is a timely word!

24 The path of life leads upward for the
wise
to keep him from going down to
the grave.[c]

25 The LORD tears down the proud man's
house
but he keeps the widow's
boundaries intact.

---

[a]33 Hebrew; Septuagint and Syriac / but in the
heart of fools she is not known   [b]11 Hebrew
Sheol and Abaddon   [c]24 Hebrew Sheol

²⁶ The Lord detests the thoughts of the wicked,
but those of the pure are pleasing to him.

²⁷ A greedy man brings trouble to his family,
but he who hates bribes will live.

²⁸ The heart of the righteous weighs its answers,
but the mouth of the wicked gushes evil.

²⁹ The Lord is far from the wicked
but he hears the prayer of the righteous.

³⁰ A cheerful look brings joy to the heart,
and good news gives health to the bones.

{ THURSDAY }

PROVERBS 15:8,29

Lips and Lives

15:8 BUT THE PRAYER OF THE UPRIGHT PLEASES HIM.

This is the kind of prayer and pray-er God delights in: one whose life and prayers match up. What we ask for and who we are should point to the same life-goals and the same internal focus. When David understood God's will for his prayer life, it revolutionized his worship. In Psalm 40:6–8, he gushes, "Sacrifice and offering you did not desire . . . burnt offerings and sin offerings you did not require. Then I said, 'Here I am, I have come— . . . I desire to do your will, O my God; your law is within my heart.'" God takes this kind of pray-er into his confidence and grants this person the joy of no longer being only a servant, but an intimate friend (see Genesis 18:17–19; Exodus 33:11; Job 29:4; Psalm 25:14; John 15:14–15). What could be better than that?

But what could be worse than this: "The Lord detests the sacrifice of the wicked" (Proverbs 15:8)? This is the person whose prayers and life conflict. Prayer and deed are two distinct and separate categories. God hates this kind of praying for the obvious reason: It betrays and mocks God to ask him to do what you won't do, or to praise him with lips but not your life. It's doubly galling to God because he always sees us comprehensively; he knows exactly what we've done as we pray. It's not that he's let down after he has heard us pray, but he is disappointed as he hears us pray.

The Great Thanksgiving in the *Book of Common Prayer* frames the matter neatly when it says, "Give us such an awareness of your mercies, that our hearts may be sincerely thankful, and that we may show forth your praise not only with our lips, but in our lives, by giving up ourselves to your service, and by walking before you in holiness and righteousness all our days." Lips and lives: that's the kind of prayer and pray-er that pleases God.

PRAY:

Dear Lord, "Give us such an awareness of your mercies, that our hearts may be sincerely thankful, and that we may show forth your praise not only with our lips, but in our lives, by giving up ourselves to your service, and by walking before you in holiness and righteousness all our days."

FOR YOUR NEXT DEVOTIONAL READING, GO TO PAGE 754.

> THE LORD is far from the wicked
> but he hears the prayer of the righteous.
>
> PROVERBS 15:29

³¹ He who listens to a life-giving rebuke
will be at home among the wise.

³² He who ignores discipline despises
himself,
but whoever heeds correction
gains understanding.

³³ The fear of the LORD teaches a man
wisdom,ᵃ
and humility comes before honor.

16 To man belong the plans of the
heart,
but from the LORD comes the reply
of the tongue.

² All a man's ways seem innocent to
him,
but motives are weighed by the
LORD.

³ Commit to the LORD whatever you do,
and your plans will succeed.

⁴ The LORD works out everything for his
own ends—
even the wicked for a day of
disaster.

⁵ The LORD detests all the proud of
heart.
Be sure of this: They will not go
unpunished.

⁶ Through love and faithfulness sin is
atoned for;
through the fear of the LORD a man
avoids evil.

⁷ When a man's ways are pleasing to
the LORD,
he makes even his enemies live at
peace with him.

⁸ Better a little with righteousness
than much gain with injustice.

⁹ In his heart a man plans his course,
but the LORD determines his steps.

¹⁰ The lips of a king speak as an oracle,
and his mouth should not betray
justice.

¹¹ Honest scales and balances are from
the LORD;
all the weights in the bag are of his
making.

¹² Kings detest wrongdoing,
for a throne is established through
righteousness.

¹³ Kings take pleasure in honest lips;
they value a man who speaks the
truth.

¹⁴ A king's wrath is a messenger of
death,
but a wise man will appease it.

¹⁵ When a king's face brightens, it
means life;
his favor is like a rain cloud in
spring.

¹⁶ How much better to get wisdom than
gold,
to choose understanding rather
than silver!

¹⁷ The highway of the upright avoids
evil;
he who guards his way guards
his life.

¹⁸ Pride goes before destruction,
a haughty spirit before a fall.

¹⁹ Better to be lowly in spirit and among
the oppressed
than to share plunder with the
proud.

²⁰ Whoever gives heed to instruction
prospers,
and blessed is he who trusts in
the LORD.

²¹ The wise in heart are called
discerning,
and pleasant words promote
instruction.ᵇ

²² Understanding is a fountain of life to
those who have it,
but folly brings punishment to
fools.

²³ A wise man's heart guides his mouth,
and his lips promote instruction.ᶜ

ᵃ33 Or *Wisdom teaches the fear of the LORD*
ᵇ21 Or *words make a man persuasive*
ᶜ23 Or *mouth / and makes his lips persuasive*

²⁴ Pleasant words are a honeycomb,
 sweet to the soul and healing to
  the bones.

²⁵ There is a way that seems right to
  a man,
 but in the end it leads to death.

²⁶ The laborer's appetite works for him;
 his hunger drives him on.

²⁷ A scoundrel plots evil,
 and his speech is like a scorching
  fire.

²⁸ A perverse man stirs up dissension,
 and a gossip separates close
  friends.

²⁹ A violent man entices his neighbor
 and leads him down a path that is
  not good.

³⁰ He who winks with his eye is plotting
  perversity;
 he who purses his lips is bent
  on evil.

³¹ Gray hair is a crown of splendor;
 it is attained by a righteous life.

³² Better a patient man than a
  warrior,
 a man who controls his temper
  than one who takes a city.

³³ The lot is cast into the lap,
 but its every decision is from
  the LORD.

17 Better a dry crust with peace
  and quiet
 than a house full of feasting,[a]
  with strife.

² A wise servant will rule over a
  disgraceful son,
 and will share the inheritance as
  one of the brothers.

³ The crucible for silver and the
  furnace for gold,
 but the LORD tests the heart.

⁴ A wicked man listens to evil lips;
 a liar pays attention to a malicious
  tongue.

⁵ He who mocks the poor shows
  contempt for their Maker;
 whoever gloats over disaster will
  not go unpunished.

⁶ Children's children are a crown to
  the aged,
 and parents are the pride of their
  children.

⁷ Arrogant[b] lips are unsuited to
  a fool—
 how much worse lying lips to
  a ruler!

⁸ A bribe is a charm to the one who
  gives it;
 wherever he turns, he succeeds.

⁹ He who covers over an offense
  promotes love,
 but whoever repeats the matter
  separates close friends.

¹⁰ A rebuke impresses a man of
  discernment
 more than a hundred lashes
  a fool.

¹¹ An evil man is bent only on rebellion;
 a merciless official will be sent
  against him.

¹² Better to meet a bear robbed of
  her cubs
 than a fool in his folly.

¹³ If a man pays back evil for good,
 evil will never leave his house.

¹⁴ Starting a quarrel is like breaching
  a dam;
 so drop the matter before a dispute
  breaks out.

¹⁵ Acquitting the guilty and
  condemning the innocent—
 the LORD detests them both.

¹⁶ Of what use is money in the hand of
  a fool,
 since he has no desire to get
  wisdom?

¹⁷ A friend loves at all times,
 and a brother is born for adversity.

¹⁸ A man lacking in judgment strikes
  hands in pledge
 and puts up security for his
  neighbor.

¹⁹ He who loves a quarrel loves sin;
 he who builds a high gate invites
  destruction.

---

a1 Hebrew *sacrifices* *b7* Or *Eloquent*

²⁰ A man of perverse heart does not
prosper;
he whose tongue is deceitful falls
into trouble.

²¹ To have a fool for a son brings grief;
there is no joy for the father of
a fool.

²² A cheerful heart is good medicine,
but a crushed spirit dries up
the bones.

²³ A wicked man accepts a bribe in
secret
to pervert the course of justice.

²⁴ A discerning man keeps wisdom
in view,
but a fool's eyes wander to the
ends of the earth.

²⁵ A foolish son brings grief to his father
and bitterness to the one who
bore him.

²⁶ It is not good to punish an innocent
man,
or to flog officials for their integrity.

²⁷ A man of knowledge uses words with
restraint,
and a man of understanding is
even-tempered.

²⁸ Even a fool is thought wise if he
keeps silent,
and discerning if he holds his
tongue.

18 An unfriendly man pursues selfish
ends;
he defies all sound judgment.

² A fool finds no pleasure in
understanding
but delights in airing his own
opinions.

³ When wickedness comes, so does
contempt,
and with shame comes disgrace.

⁴ The words of a man's mouth are
deep waters,
but the fountain of wisdom is a
bubbling brook.

⁵ It is not good to be partial to the
wicked
or to deprive the innocent of
justice.

⁶ A fool's lips bring him strife,
and his mouth invites a beating.

⁷ A fool's mouth is his undoing,
and his lips are a snare to his soul.

⁸ The words of a gossip are like choice
morsels;
they go down to a man's inmost
parts.

⁹ One who is slack in his work
is brother to one who destroys.

¹⁰ The name of the LORD is a strong
tower;
the righteous run to it and are safe.

¹¹ The wealth of the rich is their fortified
city;
they imagine it an unscalable wall.

¹² Before his downfall a man's heart is
proud,
but humility comes before honor.

¹³ He who answers before listening—
that is his folly and his shame.

¹⁴ A man's spirit sustains him in
sickness,
but a crushed spirit who can bear?

¹⁵ The heart of the discerning acquires
knowledge;
the ears of the wise seek it out.

¹⁶ A gift opens the way for the giver
and ushers him into the presence
of the great.

¹⁷ The first to present his case seems
right,
till another comes forward and
questions him.

¹⁸ Casting the lot settles disputes
and keeps strong opponents apart.

¹⁹ An offended brother is more
unyielding than a fortified city,
and disputes are like the barred
gates of a citadel.

²⁰ From the fruit of his mouth a man's
stomach is filled;
with the harvest from his lips he is
satisfied.

²¹ The tongue has the power of life and
death,
and those who love it will eat its
fruit.

PROVERBS 18:10–11

The Two Towers

18:10–11 THE NAME OF THE LORD IS A STRONG TOWER ... THE WEALTH OF THE RICH IS THEIR FORTIFIED CITY.

There are two towers spoken of here: One is unseen and impregnable, the other seen but wholly imaginary. The imaginary tower, or fortified city, is "the wealth of the rich"; and "they imagine it an unscalable wall" (18:11). The imaginary tower stands for all human efforts for salvation and security. In their heart of hearts those who trust in this tower must know that if it isn't scaled by an army, what they've kept in it will be swallowed up in death. So it takes a great deal of imagination and diversion to prop up this tower.

Mathematician Blaise Pascal tried to shock the people of his day into seeing this. He wrote, "Imagine a number of men in chains, all under the sentence of death, some of whom are butchered in the sight of others; those remaining see their own condition in that of their fellows, and looking at each other with grief and despair await their turn. This is an image of the human condition." Knowing that all mortals will die and lose everything, how can anyone possibly keep trying to hide in that tower? Pascal's answer was, "Being unable to cure death, wretchedness and ignorance, men have decided, in order to be happy, not to think about such things."[1]

The impregnable tower, though unseen, is none other than the name of the Lord. God's name is his character, expressed in his Word and in his mighty deeds to save. Because he is unchanging, his Word is unchanging. Heaven and earth will pass away, but his Word is the strongest of towers and will not (see Matthew 24:35). His pleasure is in those who trust him in every-thing. Nothing else impresses him: not strength, beauty or intelligence. Why should they? He is God!

Nothing can separate us from his love if we're in this strong tower (see Romans 8:37–39). But note: You have to run to this tower. You must seek the Lord and trust the Lord with your whole heart. Imagination requires no effort, but faith does.

P R A Y :

"A mighty fortress is our God,
A Bulwark never failing;
Our Helper He amid the flood
Of mortal ills prevailing."

MARTIN LUTHER

FOR YOUR NEXT DEVOTIONAL READING, GO TO PAGE 758.

22 He who finds a wife finds what
is good
and receives favor from
the LORD.

23 A poor man pleads for mercy,
but a rich man answers harshly.

24 A man of many companions may
come to ruin,
but there is a friend who sticks
closer than a brother.

19 Better a poor man whose walk
is blameless
than a fool whose lips are
perverse.

2 It is not good to have zeal without
knowledge,
nor to be hasty and miss the way.

3 A man's own folly ruins his life,
yet his heart rages against
the LORD.

4 Wealth brings many friends,
but a poor man's friend deserts
him.

5 A false witness will not go
unpunished,
and he who pours out lies will
not go free.

6 Many curry favor with a ruler,
and everyone is the friend of a man
who gives gifts.

7 A poor man is shunned by all his
relatives—
how much more do his friends
avoid him!
Though he pursues them with
pleading,
they are nowhere to be found.[a]

8 He who gets wisdom loves his
own soul;
he who cherishes understanding
prospers.

9 A false witness will not go
unpunished,
and he who pours out lies will
perish.

10 It is not fitting for a fool to live in
luxury—
how much worse for a slave to rule
over princes!

11 A man's wisdom gives him patience;
it is to his glory to overlook an
offense.

12 A king's rage is like the roar of a lion,
but his favor is like dew on the
grass.

13 A foolish son is his father's ruin,
and a quarrelsome wife is like a
constant dripping.

14 Houses and wealth are inherited from
parents,
but a prudent wife is from the LORD.

15 Laziness brings on deep sleep,
and the shiftless man goes hungry.

16 He who obeys instructions guards
his life,
but he who is contemptuous of his
ways will die.

17 He who is kind to the poor lends to
the LORD,
and he will reward him for what
he has done.

18 Discipline your son, for in that there
is hope;
do not be a willing party to his
death.

19 A hot-tempered man must pay the
penalty;
if you rescue him, you will have to
do it again.

20 Listen to advice and accept
instruction,
and in the end you will be wise.

21 Many are the plans in a man's heart,
but it is the LORD's purpose that
prevails.

22 What a man desires is unfailing
love[b];
better to be poor than a liar.

23 The fear of the LORD leads to life:
Then one rests content, untouched
by trouble.

24 The sluggard buries his hand in
the dish;
he will not even bring it back to his
mouth!

[a]7 The meaning of the Hebrew for this sentence is
uncertain.   [b]22 Or *A man's greed is his shame*

²⁵ Flog a mocker, and the simple will
learn prudence;
rebuke a discerning man, and he
will gain knowledge.

²⁶ He who robs his father and drives out
his mother
is a son who brings shame and
disgrace.

²⁷ Stop listening to instruction, my son,
and you will stray from the words
of knowledge.

²⁸ A corrupt witness mocks at justice,
and the mouth of the wicked gulps
down evil.

²⁹ Penalties are prepared for mockers,
and beatings for the backs of fools.

20 Wine is a mocker and beer a
brawler;
whoever is led astray by them is
not wise.

² A king's wrath is like the roar of
a lion;
he who angers him forfeits his life.

³ It is to a man's honor to avoid strife,
but every fool is quick to quarrel.

⁴ A sluggard does not plow in season;
so at harvest time he looks but
finds nothing.

⁵ The purposes of a man's heart are
deep waters,
but a man of understanding draws
them out.

⁶ Many a man claims to have unfailing
love,
but a faithful man who can find?

⁷ The righteous man leads a blameless
life;
blessed are his children after him.

⁸ When a king sits on his throne
to judge,
he winnows out all evil with his
eyes.

⁹ Who can say, "I have kept my heart
pure;
I am clean and without sin"?

¹⁰ Differing weights and differing
measures—
the LORD detests them both.

¹¹ Even a child is known by his
actions,
by whether his conduct is pure
and right.

¹² Ears that hear and eyes that see—
the LORD has made them both.

¹³ Do not love sleep or you will grow
poor;
stay awake and you will have food
to spare.

¹⁴ "It's no good, it's no good!" says
the buyer;
then off he goes and boasts about
his purchase.

¹⁵ Gold there is, and rubies in
abundance,
but lips that speak knowledge are
a rare jewel.

¹⁶ Take the garment of one who puts
up security for a stranger;
hold it in pledge if he does it for a
wayward woman.

¹⁷ Food gained by fraud tastes sweet
to a man,
but he ends up with a mouth full
of gravel.

¹⁸ Make plans by seeking advice;
if you wage war, obtain guidance.

¹⁹ A gossip betrays a confidence;
so avoid a man who talks too
much.

²⁰ If a man curses his father or mother,
his lamp will be snuffed out in
pitch darkness.

²¹ An inheritance quickly gained at the
beginning
will not be blessed at the end.

²² Do not say, "I'll pay you back for this
wrong!"
Wait for the LORD, and he will
deliver you.

²³ The LORD detests differing weights,
and dishonest scales do not please
him.

²⁴ A man's steps are directed by the
LORD.
How then can anyone understand
his own way?

²⁵ It is a trap for a man to dedicate
   something rashly
   and only later to consider his vows.

²⁶ A wise king winnows out the wicked;
   he drives the threshing wheel over
   them.

²⁷ The lamp of the LORD searches the
   spirit of a man[a];
   it searches out his inmost being.

²⁸ Love and faithfulness keep a king
   safe;
   through love his throne is made
   secure.

²⁹ The glory of young men is their
   strength,
   gray hair the splendor of the old.

³⁰ Blows and wounds cleanse away evil,
   and beatings purge the inmost
   being.

21 The king's heart is in the hand of
   the LORD;
   he directs it like a watercourse
   wherever he pleases.

² All a man's ways seem right to him,
   but the LORD weighs the heart.

³ To do what is right and just
   is more acceptable to the LORD than
   sacrifice.

⁴ Haughty eyes and a proud heart,
   the lamp of the wicked, are sin!

⁵ The plans of the diligent lead to profit
   as surely as haste leads to poverty.

⁶ A fortune made by a lying tongue
   is a fleeting vapor and a deadly
   snare.[b]

⁷ The violence of the wicked will drag
   them away,
   for they refuse to do what is right.

⁸ The way of the guilty is devious,
   but the conduct of the innocent is
   upright.

⁹ Better to live on a corner of the roof
   than share a house with a
   quarrelsome wife.

¹⁰ The wicked man craves evil;
   his neighbor gets no mercy from
   him.

¹¹ When a mocker is punished, the
   simple gain wisdom;
   when a wise man is instructed, he
   gets knowledge.

¹² The Righteous One[c] takes note of the
   house of the wicked
   and brings the wicked to ruin.

¹³ If a man shuts his ears to the cry of
   the poor,
   he too will cry out and not be
   answered.

¹⁴ A gift given in secret soothes anger,
   and a bribe concealed in the cloak
   pacifies great wrath.

¹⁵ When justice is done, it brings joy to
   the righteous
   but terror to evildoers.

¹⁶ A man who strays from the path of
   understanding
   comes to rest in the company of
   the dead.

¹⁷ He who loves pleasure will become
   poor;
   whoever loves wine and oil will
   never be rich.

¹⁸ The wicked become a ransom for
   the righteous,
   and the unfaithful for the upright.

¹⁹ Better to live in a desert
   than with a quarrelsome and
   ill-tempered wife.

²⁰ In the house of the wise are stores of
   choice food and oil,
   but a foolish man devours all he has.

²¹ He who pursues righteousness
   and love
   finds life, prosperity[d] and honor.

²² A wise man attacks the city of the
   mighty
   and pulls down the stronghold
   in which they trust.

²³ He who guards his mouth and his
   tongue
   keeps himself from calamity.

---

[a]27 Or *The spirit of man is the LORD's lamp*
[b]6 Some Hebrew manuscripts, Septuagint and
Vulgate; most Hebrew manuscripts *vapor for
those who seek death*   [c]12 Or *The righteous
man*   [d]21 Or *righteousness*

Sink or Swim

ONE OF the saddest chapters in the history of American Christianity is what happened to the churches of New England in the 100 years from the middle of the 18th century to the middle of the 19th century. During that time, church after church and seminary after seminary moved from historic Christian faith to apostasy, as one by one they embraced the heresies of Unitarianism and Universalism. It was as if a flood of spiritual darkness engulfed the Northeast. But there were some heroic exceptions to this decline, notably four churches in the rustic town of Ipswich, tucked along Cape Anne, Massachusetts.

In 1760, John Cleaveland became pastor of the Second Church of Ipswich. When he arrived, he sensed immediately the spiritual malaise in his congregation and called his people to engage in a "Concert of Prayer"— a cross-denominational prayer strategy based on the writings of Jonathan Edwards and a group of pastors from Northern Scotland. The plan was to pray for two things: the revival of religion in the church and the spread of the kingdom of God in the world. The church members were to do this every two weeks, either in small groups or privately, and then to meet quarterly in an all-church prayer meeting. For the next twenty years, the people faithfully followed Cleaveland's plan. Within three years Cleaveland's church began to experience a revival of love for God and a wave of conversions. Little by little, the revival spread throughout the region.

In 1780 Cleaveland invited three other Congregational churches in Ipswich to join in the "Concert of Prayer." The churches agreed. Quarterly prayer meetings were rotated among the four churches, and in the following years each of the churches enjoyed periodic revivals. This "Concert of

Prayer" continued uninterrupted for 100 years, celebrating its centennial celebration on December 31, 1859. Remarkably, for the 100 years they were involved in the Concert of Prayer, the four churches remained true to the historic Christian faith. While most of New England's Protestant churches were drowning in a sea of spiritual darkness, they had learned to swim.

The century of prayer ended with the outbreak of the Civil War. Within five years all four churches sank into the very apostasy they had avoided for so long. Published sermons from this period "show a decidedly nonevangelical bent," writes Robert Bakke. "Several of the sermons reflect upon the town's Puritan past as one might chuckle over the memories of one's grandmother who refused to wear makeup, wore her hair in a bun, and trusted in cod liver oil for every ailment . . . There hasn't been a significant work of revival throughout Cape Anne in nearly 150 years."[2] The churches in Ipswich had forgotten how to swim.

For a church to choose to pray or not to pray is not to decide whether to engage in a nice spiritual discipline. It is to choose between life and death.

PRAY:
Great God! Eternity hangs in the balance.
Teach us to pray as though we realize this for our church,
our city, our nation and the world.

MEMORIZE:
"Again, I tell you that if two of you on earth agree about
anything you ask for, it will be done for you by my
Father in heaven. For where two or three come together in
my name, there am I with them." MATTHEW 18:19–20

FOR YOUR NEXT DEVOTIONAL READING, GO TO PAGE 767.

24 The proud and arrogant man—
"Mocker" is his name;
  he behaves with overweening
  pride.

25 The sluggard's craving will be the
  death of him,
  because his hands refuse to work.

26 All day long he craves for more,
  but the righteous give without
  sparing.

27 The sacrifice of the wicked is
  detestable—
  how much more so when brought
  with evil intent!

28 A false witness will perish,
  and whoever listens to him will be
  destroyed forever.ᵃ

29 A wicked man puts up a bold front,
  but an upright man gives thought
  to his ways.

30 There is no wisdom, no insight,
  no plan
  that can succeed against the LORD.

31 The horse is made ready for the day of
  battle,
  but victory rests with the LORD.

22 A good name is more desirable
  than great riches;
  to be esteemed is better than silver
  or gold.

2 Rich and poor have this in common:
  The LORD is the Maker of them all.

3 A prudent man sees danger and
  takes refuge,
  but the simple keep going and
  suffer for it.

4 Humility and the fear of the LORD
  bring wealth and honor and life.

5 In the paths of the wicked lie thorns
  and snares,
  but he who guards his soul stays far
  from them.

6 Trainᵇ a child in the way he should go,
  and when he is old he will not turn
  from it.

7 The rich rule over the poor,
  and the borrower is servant to the
  lender.

8 He who sows wickedness reaps
  trouble,
  and the rod of his fury will be
  destroyed.

9 A generous man will himself be
  blessed,
  for he shares his food with the poor.

10 Drive out the mocker, and out
  goes strife;
  quarrels and insults are ended.

11 He who loves a pure heart and whose
  speech is gracious
  will have the king for his friend.

12 The eyes of the LORD keep watch over
  knowledge,
  but he frustrates the words of the
  unfaithful.

13 The sluggard says, "There is a lion
  outside!"
  or, "I will be murdered in the
  streets!"

14 The mouth of an adulteress is a
  deep pit;
  he who is under the LORD's wrath
  will fall into it.

15 Folly is bound up in the heart of
  a child,
  but the rod of discipline will drive
  it far from him.

16 He who oppresses the poor to
  increase his wealth
  and he who gives gifts to the rich—
  both come to poverty.

Sayings of the Wise

17 Pay attention and listen to the
  sayings of the wise;
  apply your heart to what I teach,

18 for it is pleasing when you keep them
  in your heart
  and have all of them ready on
  your lips.

19 So that your trust may be in the LORD,
  I teach you today, even you.

20 Have I not written thirtyᶜ sayings
  for you,
  sayings of counsel and knowledge,

ᵃ28 Or / but the words of an obedient man will
live on ᵇ6 Or Start ᶜ20 Or not formerly
written; or not written excellent

21 teaching you true and reliable words,
    so that you can give sound
       answers
    to him who sent you?
22 Do not exploit the poor because they
       are poor
    and do not crush the needy in
       court,
23 for the LORD will take up their case
    and will plunder those who
       plunder them.

24 Do not make friends with a
       hot-tempered man,
    do not associate with one easily
       angered,
25 or you may learn his ways
    and get yourself ensnared.

26 Do not be a man who strikes hands
       in pledge
    or puts up security for debts;
27 if you lack the means to pay,
    your very bed will be snatched from
       under you.

28 Do not move an ancient boundary
       stone
    set up by your forefathers.

29 Do you see a man skilled in his work?
    He will serve before kings;
    he will not serve before obscure
       men.

23 When you sit to dine with a ruler,
    note well what*a* is before you,
2 and put a knife to your throat
    if you are given to gluttony.
3 Do not crave his delicacies,
    for that food is deceptive.

4 Do not wear yourself out to get rich;
    have the wisdom to show restraint.
5 Cast but a glance at riches, and they
       are gone,
    for they will surely sprout wings
    and fly off to the sky like an eagle.

6 Do not eat the food of a stingy man,
    do not crave his delicacies;
7 for he is the kind of man
    who is always thinking about
       the cost.*b*
    "Eat and drink," he says to you,
    but his heart is not with you.
8 You will vomit up the little you have
       eaten

and will have wasted your
    compliments.
9 Do not speak to a fool,
    for he will scorn the wisdom of
       your words.

10 Do not move an ancient boundary
       stone
    or encroach on the fields of the
       fatherless,
11 for their Defender is strong;
    he will take up their case against
       you.

12 Apply your heart to instruction
    and your ears to words of
       knowledge.

13 Do not withhold discipline from a
       child;
    if you punish him with the rod,
    he will not die.
14 Punish him with the rod
    and save his soul from death.*c*

15 My son, if your heart is wise,
    then my heart will be glad;
16 my inmost being will rejoice
    when your lips speak what is right.

17 Do not let your heart envy sinners,
    but always be zealous for the fear
       of the LORD.
18 There is surely a future hope for you,
    and your hope will not be cut off.

19 Listen, my son, and be wise,
    and keep your heart on the
       right path.
20 Do not join those who drink too
       much wine
    or gorge themselves on meat,
21 for drunkards and gluttons become
       poor,
    and drowsiness clothes them
       in rags.

22 Listen to your father, who gave
       you life,
    and do not despise your mother
       when she is old.
23 Buy the truth and do not sell it;
    get wisdom, discipline and
       understanding.

a1 Or *who*   *b7* Or *for as he thinks within
himself, / so he is*; or *for as he puts on a feast, /
so he is*   *c14* Hebrew *Sheol*

²⁴The father of a righteous man has
    great joy;
  he who has a wise son delights
    in him.
²⁵May your father and mother be glad;
  may she who gave you birth
    rejoice!

²⁶My son, give me your heart
  and let your eyes keep to my ways,
²⁷for a prostitute is a deep pit
  and a wayward wife is a narrow
    well.
²⁸Like a bandit she lies in wait,
  and multiplies the unfaithful
    among men.

²⁹Who has woe? Who has sorrow?
  Who has strife? Who has
    complaints?
  Who has needless bruises? Who
    has bloodshot eyes?
³⁰Those who linger over wine,
  who go to sample bowls of mixed
    wine.
³¹Do not gaze at wine when it is red,
  when it sparkles in the cup,
  when it goes down smoothly!
³²In the end it bites like a snake
  and poisons like a viper.
³³Your eyes will see strange sights
  and your mind imagine confusing
    things.
³⁴You will be like one sleeping on the
    high seas,
  lying on top of the rigging.
³⁵"They hit me," you will say, "but I'm
    not hurt!
  They beat me, but I don't feel it!
  When will I wake up
    so I can find another drink?"

24 Do not envy wicked men,
    do not desire their company;
²for their hearts plot violence,
  and their lips talk about making
    trouble.

³By wisdom a house is built,
  and through understanding it is
    established;
⁴through knowledge its rooms are
    filled
  with rare and beautiful treasures.

⁵A wise man has great power,
  and a man of knowledge increases
    strength;

⁶for waging war you need guidance,
  and for victory many advisers.

⁷Wisdom is too high for a fool;
  in the assembly at the gate he has
    nothing to say.

⁸He who plots evil
  will be known as a schemer.
⁹The schemes of folly are sin,
  and men detest a mocker.

¹⁰If you falter in times of trouble,
  how small is your strength!
¹¹Rescue those being led away to
    death;
  hold back those staggering toward
    slaughter.
¹²If you say, "But we knew nothing
    about this,"
  does not he who weighs the heart
    perceive it?
  Does not he who guards your life
    know it?
  Will he not repay each person
    according to what he has
    done?

¹³Eat honey, my son, for it is good;
  honey from the comb is sweet to
    your taste.
¹⁴Know also that wisdom is sweet to
    your soul;
  if you find it, there is a future hope
    for you,
  and your hope will not be cut off.

¹⁵Do not lie in wait like an outlaw
    against a righteous man's
    house,
  do not raid his dwelling place;
¹⁶for though a righteous man falls
    seven times, he rises again,
  but the wicked are brought down
    by calamity.

¹⁷Do not gloat when your enemy falls;
  when he stumbles, do not let your
    heart rejoice,
¹⁸or the LORD will see and disapprove
  and turn his wrath away from
    him.

¹⁹Do not fret because of evil men
  or be envious of the wicked,
²⁰for the evil man has no future hope,
  and the lamp of the wicked will be
    snuffed out.

21 Fear the LORD and the king, my son,
and do not join with the
rebellious,
22 for those two will send sudden
destruction upon them,
and who knows what calamities
they can bring?

Further Sayings of the Wise

23 These also are sayings of the wise:

To show partiality in judging is
not good:
24 Whoever says to the guilty, "You are
innocent"—
peoples will curse him and nations
denounce him.
25 But it will go well with those who
convict the guilty,
and rich blessing will come upon
them.

26 An honest answer
is like a kiss on the lips.

27 Finish your outdoor work
and get your fields ready;
after that, build your house.

28 Do not testify against your neighbor
without cause,
or use your lips to deceive.
29 Do not say, "I'll do to him as he has
done to me;
I'll pay that man back for what
he did."

30 I went past the field of the sluggard,
past the vineyard of the man who
lacks judgment;
31 thorns had come up everywhere,
the ground was covered with
weeds,
and the stone wall was in ruins.

> *Prayer is request. The essence of
> request, as distinct from compulsion, is
> that it may or may not be granted. And
> if an infinitely wise Being listens to the
> requests of finite and foolish creatures,
> of course he will sometimes grant and
> sometimes refuse them.*
>
> C. S. LEWIS

32 I applied my heart to what I
observed
and learned a lesson from
what I saw:
33 A little sleep, a little slumber,
a little folding of the hands to
rest—
34 and poverty will come on you like a
bandit
and scarcity like an armed man.[a]

More Proverbs of Solomon

25 These are more proverbs of Solomon, copied by the men of Hezekiah king of Judah:

2 It is the glory of God to conceal
a matter;
to search out a matter is the glory
of kings.

3 As the heavens are high and the
earth is deep,
so the hearts of kings are
unsearchable.

4 Remove the dross from the silver,
and out comes material for[b] the
silversmith;
5 remove the wicked from the king's
presence,
and his throne will be established
through righteousness.

6 Do not exalt yourself in the king's
presence,
and do not claim a place among
great men;
7 it is better for him to say to you,
"Come up here,"
than for him to humiliate you
before a nobleman.

What you have seen with your eyes
8 do not bring[c] hastily to court,
for what will you do in the end
if your neighbor puts you to
shame?

9 If you argue your case with a
neighbor,
do not betray another man's
confidence,

a 34 Or *like a vagrant / and scarcity like a beggar*
b 4 Or *comes a vessel from*   c 7,8 Or *nobleman /
on whom you had set your eyes. / 8 Do not go*

¹⁰ or he who hears it may shame you
  and you will never lose your bad
  reputation.

¹¹ A word aptly spoken
  is like apples of gold in settings
  of silver.

¹² Like an earring of gold or an
  ornament of fine gold
  is a wise man's rebuke to a
  listening ear.

¹³ Like the coolness of snow at harvest
  time
  is a trustworthy messenger to those
  who send him;
  he refreshes the spirit of his
  masters.

¹⁴ Like clouds and wind without rain
  is a man who boasts of gifts he
  does not give.

¹⁵ Through patience a ruler can be
  persuaded,
  and a gentle tongue can break a
  bone.

¹⁶ If you find honey, eat just enough—
  too much of it, and you will vomit.
¹⁷ Seldom set foot in your neighbor's
  house—
  too much of you, and he will
  hate you.

¹⁸ Like a club or a sword or a sharp
  arrow
  is the man who gives false
  testimony against his
  neighbor.

¹⁹ Like a bad tooth or a lame foot
  is reliance on the unfaithful in
  times of trouble.

²⁰ Like one who takes away a garment
  on a cold day,
  or like vinegar poured on soda,
  is one who sings songs to a heavy
  heart.

²¹ If your enemy is hungry, give him
  food to eat;
  if he is thirsty, give him water to
  drink.
²² In doing this, you will heap burning
  coals on his head,
  and the LORD will reward you.

²³ As a north wind brings rain,
  so a sly tongue brings angry looks.

²⁴ Better to live on a corner of the roof
  than share a house with a
  quarrelsome wife.

²⁵ Like cold water to a weary soul
  is good news from a distant land.

²⁶ Like a muddied spring or a polluted
  well
  is a righteous man who gives way
  to the wicked.

²⁷ It is not good to eat too much honey,
  nor is it honorable to seek one's
  own honor.

²⁸ Like a city whose walls are broken
  down
  is a man who lacks self-control.

26 Like snow in summer or rain in
  harvest,
  honor is not fitting for a fool.

² Like a fluttering sparrow or a darting
  swallow,
  an undeserved curse does not
  come to rest.

³ A whip for the horse, a halter for the
  donkey,
  and a rod for the backs of fools!

⁴ Do not answer a fool according to
  his folly,
  or you will be like him yourself.

⁵ Answer a fool according to his folly,
  or he will be wise in his own eyes.

⁶ Like cutting off one's feet or drinking
  violence
  is the sending of a message by the
  hand of a fool.

⁷ Like a lame man's legs that hang limp
  is a proverb in the mouth of a fool.

⁸ Like tying a stone in a sling
  is the giving of honor to a fool.

⁹ Like a thornbush in a drunkard's
  hand
  is a proverb in the mouth of a fool.

¹⁰ Like an archer who wounds at
  random
  is he who hires a fool or any
  passer-by.

¹¹ As a dog returns to its vomit,
  so a fool repeats his folly.

¹² Do you see a man wise in his own
    eyes?
  There is more hope for a fool than
    for him.

¹³ The sluggard says, "There is a lion in
    the road,
  a fierce lion roaming the streets!"

¹⁴ As a door turns on its hinges,
  so a sluggard turns on his bed.

¹⁵ The sluggard buries his hand in
    the dish;
  he is too lazy to bring it back to
    his mouth.

¹⁶ The sluggard is wiser in his own eyes
  than seven men who answer
    discreetly.

¹⁷ Like one who seizes a dog by the ears
  is a passer-by who meddles in a
    quarrel not his own.

¹⁸ Like a madman shooting
    firebrands or deadly arrows
¹⁹ is a man who deceives his neighbor
  and says, "I was only joking!"

²⁰ Without wood a fire goes out;
  without gossip a quarrel dies down.

²¹ As charcoal to embers and as wood
    to fire,
  so is a quarrelsome man for
    kindling strife.

²² The words of a gossip are like choice
    morsels;
  they go down to a man's inmost
    parts.

²³ Like a coating of glaze[a] over
    earthenware
  are fervent lips with an evil heart.

²⁴ A malicious man disguises himself
    with his lips,
  but in his heart he harbors deceit.
²⁵ Though his speech is charming, do
    not believe him,
  for seven abominations fill his
    heart.
²⁶ His malice may be concealed by
    deception,
  but his wickedness will be exposed
    in the assembly.

²⁷ If a man digs a pit, he will fall into it;
  if a man rolls a stone, it will roll
    back on him.

²⁸ A lying tongue hates those it hurts,
  and a flattering mouth works ruin.

27 Do not boast about tomorrow,
  for you do not know what a day
    may bring forth.

² Let another praise you, and not your
    own mouth;
  someone else, and not your own lips.

³ Stone is heavy and sand a burden,
  but provocation by a fool is heavier
    than both.

⁴ Anger is cruel and fury
    overwhelming,
  but who can stand before jealousy?

⁵ Better is open rebuke
  than hidden love.

⁶ Wounds from a friend can be trusted,
  but an enemy multiplies kisses.

⁷ He who is full loathes honey,
  but to the hungry even what is
    bitter tastes sweet.

⁸ Like a bird that strays from its nest
  is a man who strays from his home.

⁹ Perfume and incense bring joy to
    the heart,
  and the pleasantness of one's
    friend springs from his earnest
    counsel.

¹⁰ Do not forsake your friend and the
    friend of your father,
  and do not go to your brother's
    house when disaster strikes
    you—
  better a neighbor nearby than a
    brother far away.

¹¹ Be wise, my son, and bring joy to my
    heart;
  then I can answer anyone who
    treats me with contempt.

¹² The prudent see danger and take
    refuge,
  but the simple keep going and
    suffer for it.

[a]23 With a different word division of the Hebrew;
Masoretic Text of silver dross

13 Take the garment of one who puts up
   security for a stranger;
   hold it in pledge if he does it for a
   wayward woman.

14 If a man loudly blesses his neighbor
   early in the morning,
   it will be taken as a curse.

15 A quarrelsome wife is like
   a constant dripping on a rainy day;
16 restraining her is like restraining the
   wind
   or grasping oil with the hand.

17 As iron sharpens iron,
   so one man sharpens another.

18 He who tends a fig tree will eat its
   fruit,
   and he who looks after his master
   will be honored.

19 As water reflects a face,
   so a man's heart reflects the man.

20 Death and Destruction[a] are never
   satisfied,
   and neither are the eyes of man.

21 The crucible for silver and the
   furnace for gold,
   but man is tested by the praise he
   receives.

22 Though you grind a fool in a mortar,
   grinding him like grain with a
   pestle,
   you will not remove his folly from
   him.

23 Be sure you know the condition of
   your flocks,
   give careful attention to your
   herds;
24 for riches do not endure forever,
   and a crown is not secure for all
   generations.
25 When the hay is removed and new
   growth appears
   and the grass from the hills is
   gathered in,
26 the lambs will provide you with
   clothing,
   and the goats with the price of a
   field.
27 You will have plenty of goats' milk
   to feed you and your family
   and to nourish your servant girls.

28 The wicked man flees though no
   one pursues,
   but the righteous are as bold as a
   lion.

2 When a country is rebellious, it has
   many rulers,
   but a man of understanding and
   knowledge maintains order.

3 A ruler[b] who oppresses the poor
   is like a driving rain that leaves no
   crops.

4 Those who forsake the law praise the
   wicked,
   but those who keep the law resist
   them.

5 Evil men do not understand justice,
   but those who seek the Lord
   understand it fully.

6 Better a poor man whose walk is
   blameless
   than a rich man whose ways are
   perverse.

7 He who keeps the law is a discerning
   son,
   but a companion of gluttons
   disgraces his father.

8 He who increases his wealth by
   exorbitant interest
   amasses it for another, who will be
   kind to the poor.

9 If anyone turns a deaf ear to the law,
   even his prayers are detestable.

> IF ANYONE *turns a deaf ear to the law,*
> *even his prayers are detestable.*
>
> PROVERBS 28:9

10 He who leads the upright along an
   evil path
   will fall into his own trap,
   but the blameless will receive a
   good inheritance.

11 A rich man may be wise in his own
   eyes,
   but a poor man who has
   discernment sees through him.

---

[a]20 Hebrew *Sheol and Abaddon*   [b]3 Or *A poor man*

¹²When the righteous triumph, there is
great elation;
but when the wicked rise to power,
men go into hiding.

¹³He who conceals his sins does not
prosper,

but whoever confesses and
renounces them finds mercy.

¹⁴Blessed is the man who always fears
the LORD,
but he who hardens his heart falls
into trouble.

PROVERBS 28:13

{ MONDAY }

Bring It into the Light

28:13 HE WHO CONCEALS HIS SINS DOES NOT PROSPER.

G. K. Chesterton said the only Christian doctrine that is empirically verifiable is the doctrine of original sin. We see its devastation all around us. It is possible that the first line of this proverb also meets the empirical test: "He who conceals his sins does not prosper." According to David, lack of prosperity is something of an understatement: "When I kept silent, my bones wasted away through my groaning all day long" (Psalm 32:3). Guilt works like a corrosive agent on our souls, and often on our bodies. The greater power of sin is not necessarily in the act, but in the concealment of the act. Studies of addictions show that in secrecy that they gain control of a person's life. Sin is birthed in darkness and flourishes in darkness. Bring it into the light and it withers.

"He who conceals his sins does not prosper, but whoever confesses and renounces them finds mercy" (Proverbs 28:13). The first step is *confession*. To confess your sin is not to tell God what he doesn't already know; it is to agree with what he already knows. When that happens, a miracle takes place: What came between you and God now connects you. The second step is *renunciation*: Simply to confess your sin is not to bring it into the light—it must be renounced as it is confessed. There is a kind of fellowship of sin that revels in self-disclosure. Have you ever overheard people roll their eyes and laugh as they regale each other with tales of drunkenness and sexual indulgence? Some quip, "I don't want to go to heaven because I'll have no friends up there." The lightweight virtues of sincerity and frankness often outweigh the heavier virtues of chastity, temperance and integrity. "At least he's honest," we will say. But what we need is mercy, not reassurance and social acceptance. We are dying for lack of forgiveness, not for low self-esteem.

David knew how bad it felt to keep his sin hidden. He also knew how great it felt to confess and renounce it: "Blessed is he whose transgressions are forgiven, whose sins are covered. Blessed is the man whose sin the LORD does not count against him and in whose spirit is no deceit" (Psalm 32:1–2).

PRAY:

Merciful God: Thank you for the gift of forgiveness. Thank you that when I confess and renounce my sins you are faithful and just and will forgive my sins and purify me from all unrighteousness (1 John 1:9).

FOR YOUR NEXT DEVOTIONAL READING, GO TO PAGE 770.

15 Like a roaring lion or a charging
      bear
  is a wicked man ruling over a
      helpless people.

16 A tyrannical ruler lacks judgment,
  but he who hates ill-gotten gain
      will enjoy a long life.

17 A man tormented by the guilt of
      murder
  will be a fugitive till death;
  let no one support him.

18 He whose walk is blameless is kept
      safe,
  but he whose ways are perverse
      will suddenly fall.

19 He who works his land will have
      abundant food,
  but the one who chases fantasies
      will have his fill of poverty.

20 A faithful man will be richly blessed,
  but one eager to get rich will not go
      unpunished.

21 To show partiality is not good—
  yet a man will do wrong for a piece
      of bread.

22 A stingy man is eager to get rich
  and is unaware that poverty awaits
      him.

23 He who rebukes a man will in the end
      gain more favor
  than he who has a flattering
      tongue.

24 He who robs his father or mother
  and says, "It's not wrong"—
  he is partner to him who destroys.

25 A greedy man stirs up dissension,
  but he who trusts in the LORD
      will prosper.

26 He who trusts in himself is a fool,
  but he who walks in wisdom is
      kept safe.

27 He who gives to the poor will lack
      nothing,
  but he who closes his eyes to them
      receives many curses.

28 When the wicked rise to power,
      people go into hiding;
  but when the wicked perish, the
      righteous thrive.

29 A man who remains stiff-necked
      after many rebukes
  will suddenly be destroyed—
      without remedy.

2 When the righteous thrive, the
      people rejoice;
  when the wicked rule, the people
      groan.

3 A man who loves wisdom brings joy
      to his father,
  but a companion of prostitutes
      squanders his wealth.

4 By justice a king gives a country
      stability,
  but one who is greedy for bribes
      tears it down.

5 Whoever flatters his neighbor
  is spreading a net for his feet.

6 An evil man is snared by his own sin,
  but a righteous one can sing and
      be glad.

7 The righteous care about justice for
      the poor,
  but the wicked have no such
      concern.

8 Mockers stir up a city,
  but wise men turn away anger.

9 If a wise man goes to court with
      a fool,
  the fool rages and scoffs, and there
      is no peace.

10 Bloodthirsty men hate a man of
      integrity
  and seek to kill the upright.

11 A fool gives full vent to his anger,
  but a wise man keeps himself
      under control.

12 If a ruler listens to lies,
  all his officials become wicked.

13 The poor man and the oppressor
      have this in common:
  The LORD gives sight to the eyes of
      both.

14 If a king judges the poor with
      fairness,
  his throne will always be secure.

15 The rod of correction imparts
      wisdom,

but a child left to himself disgraces his mother.

¹⁶ When the wicked thrive, so does sin,
but the righteous will see their downfall.

¹⁷ Discipline your son, and he will give you peace;
he will bring delight to your soul.

¹⁸ Where there is no revelation, the people cast off restraint;
but blessed is he who keeps the law.

¹⁹ A servant cannot be corrected by mere words;
though he understands, he will not respond.

²⁰ Do you see a man who speaks in haste?
There is more hope for a fool than for him.

²¹ If a man pampers his servant from youth,
he will bring grief[a] in the end.

²² An angry man stirs up dissension,
and a hot-tempered one commits many sins.

²³ A man's pride brings him low,
but a man of lowly spirit gains honor.

²⁴ The accomplice of a thief is his own enemy;
he is put under oath and dare not testify.

²⁵ Fear of man will prove to be a snare,
but whoever trusts in the LORD is kept safe.

²⁶ Many seek an audience with a ruler,
but it is from the LORD that man gets justice.

²⁷ The righteous detest the dishonest;
the wicked detest the upright.

Sayings of Agur

30 The sayings of Agur son of Jakeh—an oracle[b]:

This man declared to Ithiel,
to Ithiel and to Ucal:[c]

² "I am the most ignorant of men;
I do not have a man's understanding.

³ I have not learned wisdom,
nor have I knowledge of the Holy One.

⁴ Who has gone up to heaven and come down?
Who has gathered up the wind in the hollow of his hands?
Who has wrapped up the waters in his cloak?
Who has established all the ends of the earth?
What is his name, and the name of his son?
Tell me if you know!

⁵ "Every word of God is flawless;
he is a shield to those who take refuge in him.

⁶ Do not add to his words,
or he will rebuke you and prove you a liar.

⁷ "Two things I ask of you, O LORD;
do not refuse me before I die:

⁸ Keep falsehood and lies far from me;
give me neither poverty nor riches,
but give me only my daily bread.

⁹ Otherwise, I may have too much and disown you
and say, 'Who is the LORD?'
Or I may become poor and steal,
and so dishonor the name of my God.

¹⁰ "Do not slander a servant to his master,
or he will curse you, and you will pay for it.

¹¹ "There are those who curse their fathers
and do not bless their mothers;

¹² those who are pure in their own eyes
and yet are not cleansed of their filth;

¹³ those whose eyes are ever so haughty,
whose glances are so disdainful;

---

a21 The meaning of the Hebrew for this word is uncertain.   *b1* Or *Jakeh of Massa*
c1 Masoretic Text; with a different word division of the Hebrew *declared,* "I am weary, O God; / I am weary, O God, and faint."

PROVERBS 30:7–9

Just Two

30:7 "TWO THINGS I ASK OF YOU, O LORD; DO NOT REFUSE ME BEFORE I DIE."

This prayer is either a gross oversimplification or a masterful distillation. Only two things—is that all?

But these two things cover a lot of territory. They address us both spiritually and physically. Agur's first request is, "Keep falsehood and lies far from me" (30:8). This speaks to our spiritual capability to process and act upon truth—or untruth. Agur's second request is, "Give me neither poverty nor riches, but give me only my daily bread" (verse 8). This speaks to our bodies, our physicality. Between those two requests, pretty much all we are is covered.

Sin is a lie, *the* lie. Jesus said the enemy of our souls is "a liar and the father of lies" (John 8:44). One of the most persistent temptations we face is to live on the level of our physical appetites. The appetites aren't bad—because God made our bodies good. But the lie of sin will convince us that we are no more than our bodies. When Jesus told Satan the liar, "Man does not live on bread alone, but on every word that comes from the mouth of God" (Matthew 4:4), he gave two gifts to our humanity: On the one hand he affirmed our physicality, that God made us to need bread. On the other hand he affirmed our spirituality, that God made us more than our stomachs.

Yet there's more to this prayer. The proverb explains the reason for these two requests: "Otherwise, I may have too much and disown you and say, 'Who is the LORD?' Or I may become poor and steal, and so dishonor the name of my God" (verse 9). This prayer is a prayer to avoid temptation. It is the prayer of one who knows his weakness and asks God to protect him from it. It is a humble prayer. The Bible never encourages us to pray to be tempted so that we can show how strong we are. Rather, Jesus said to pray that we not be tempted (Matthew 6:13). True, we should expect to be tempted, and when it happens we should pray for strength and endurance—but never that we be tempted.

All that, in a simple prayer for two things. Actually, it may not be so simple after all, since Jesus said only one thing is needed (see Luke 10:38–42). But it's a good place to start.

PRAY:

"Two things I ask of you,
O LORD; do not refuse me before I die:
Keep falsehood and lies far from me;
give me neither poverty nor riches,
but give me only my daily bread" (Psalm 30:7–8).

———

FOR YOUR NEXT DEVOTIONAL READING, GO TO PAGE 772.

14 those whose teeth are swords
and whose jaws are set with knives
to devour the poor from the earth,
the needy from among mankind.

15 "The leech has two daughters.
'Give! Give!' they cry.

"There are three things that are never
satisfied,
four that never say, 'Enough!':
16 the grave,*a* the barren womb,
land, which is never satisfied with
water,
and fire, which never says,
'Enough!'

17 "The eye that mocks a father,
that scorns obedience to a mother,
will be pecked out by the ravens of
the valley,
will be eaten by the vultures.

18 "There are three things that are too
amazing for me,
four that I do not understand:
19 the way of an eagle in the sky,
the way of a snake on a rock,
the way of a ship on the high seas,
and the way of a man with a
maiden.

20 "This is the way of an adulteress:
She eats and wipes her mouth
and says, 'I've done nothing
wrong.'

21 "Under three things the earth
trembles,
under four it cannot bear up:
22 a servant who becomes king,
a fool who is full of food,
23 an unloved woman who is married,
and a maidservant who displaces
her mistress.

24 "Four things on earth are small,
yet they are extremely wise:
25 Ants are creatures of little strength,
yet they store up their food in the
summer;
26 coneys*b* are creatures of little power,
yet they make their home in the
crags;
27 locusts have no king,
yet they advance together in ranks;
28 a lizard can be caught with the hand,
yet it is found in kings' palaces.

29 "There are three things that are
stately in their stride,
four that move with stately
bearing:
30 a lion, mighty among beasts,
who retreats before nothing;
31 a strutting rooster, a he-goat,
and a king with his army around
him.*c*

32 "If you have played the fool and
exalted yourself,
or if you have planned evil,
clap your hand over your mouth!
33 For as churning the milk produces
butter,
and as twisting the nose produces
blood,
so stirring up anger produces
strife."

Sayings of King Lemuel

31 The sayings of King Lemuel—an
oracle*d* his mother taught him:

2 "O my son, O son of my womb,
O son of my vows,*e*
3 do not spend your strength on women,
your vigor on those who ruin kings.

4 "It is not for kings, O Lemuel—
not for kings to drink wine,
not for rulers to crave beer,
5 lest they drink and forget what the
law decrees,
and deprive all the oppressed of
their rights.
6 Give beer to those who are perishing,
wine to those who are in anguish;
7 let them drink and forget their
poverty
and remember their misery
no more.

8 "Speak up for those who cannot
speak for themselves,
for the rights of all who are
destitute.
9 Speak up and judge fairly;
defend the rights of the poor
and needy."

a16 Hebrew *Sheol*   *b26* That is, the hyrax or
rock badger   *c31* Or *king secure against revolt*
d1 Or *of Lemuel king of Massa, which*   *e2* Or /
the answer to my prayers

Epilogue:
The Wife of Noble Character

10 [a] A wife of noble character who
  can find?
    She is worth far more than rubies.
11 Her husband has full confidence
  in her
    and lacks nothing of value.
12 She brings him good, not harm,
    all the days of her life.
13 She selects wool and flax
    and works with eager hands.
14 She is like the merchant ships,
    bringing her food from afar.
15 She gets up while it is still dark;
    she provides food for her family
    and portions for her servant girls.

16 She considers a field and buys it;
    out of her earnings she plants a
    vineyard.
17 She sets about her work vigorously;
    her arms are strong for her tasks.
18 She sees that her trading is
  profitable,
    and her lamp does not go out at
    night.
19 In her hand she holds the distaff
    and grasps the spindle with her
    fingers.
20 She opens her arms to the poor
    and extends her hands to the
    needy.

[a] 10 Verses 10–31 are an acrostic, each
verse beginning with a successive letter of the
Hebrew alphabet.

[WEDNESDAY]

PROVERBS 31:10–31

The "Proverbs 31 Woman"

31:10 A WIFE OF NOBLE CHARACTER WHO CAN FIND? SHE IS WORTH FAR MORE THAN RUBIES.

There was actually an ad in the "Personals" section of a newspaper for the kind of woman praised in this proverb. It was headlined: "Are You My Proverbs 31 Woman?" The description the man who ran the ad gave of himself made one doubt that a woman of the wisdom and discretion described in Proverbs 31 would be interested. But the ad was a kind of prayer, and it is a worthy prayer for anyone to pray for a loyal, honest, loving spouse.

The question that begs to be answered is: Why isn't there a "Proverbs 31 Man" described somewhere in the book of Proverbs? Any answer to that question would be purely speculative. One thing is certain, however; the Bible is full of commands for qualities of character that apply equally to both sexes. All of the qualities praised in the "Proverbs 31 Woman" can be found elsewhere in Scripture in contexts that apply to both men and women. Further, Paul's instructions for husbands call men to a level of love and sacrifice unmatched in religious literature of any kind (see Ephesians 5:25–33).

The best thing to do with the beautiful, poetic portrait of a wife described in Proverbs 31 is to thank God for women who strive to follow God's call. And to thank God that his Word treasures women. We can pray for the women in our lives—our wives, mothers, daughters, sisters and friends—to grow in the grace and knowledge of God.

PRAY:

Father in Heaven! We turn our eyes away from the false images
of womanhood promoted by the commercial interests of our culture.
May we prize the kind of woman you prize.

FOR YOUR NEXT DEVOTIONAL READING, GO TO PAGE 776.

21 When it snows, she has no fear for
her household;
for all of them are clothed in
scarlet.
22 She makes coverings for her bed;
she is clothed in fine linen and
purple.
23 Her husband is respected at the city
gate,
where he takes his seat among the
elders of the land.
24 She makes linen garments and sells
them,
and supplies the merchants with
sashes.
25 She is clothed with strength and
dignity;
she can laugh at the days to come.
26 She speaks with wisdom,

and faithful instruction is on her
tongue.
27 She watches over the affairs of her
household
and does not eat the bread of
idleness.
28 Her children arise and call her
blessed;
her husband also, and he praises
her:
29 "Many women do noble things,
but you surpass them all."
30 Charm is deceptive, and beauty is
fleeting;
but a woman who fears the LORD is
to be praised.
31 Give her the reward she has earned,
and let her works bring her praise
at the city gate.

Ecclesiastes

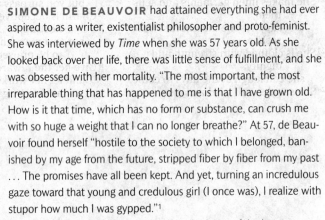

SIMONE DE BEAUVOIR had attained everything she had ever aspired to as a writer, existentialist philosopher and proto-feminist. She was interviewed by *Time* when she was 57 years old. As she looked back over her life, there was little sense of fulfillment, and she was obsessed with her mortality. "The most important, the most irreparable thing that has happened to me is that I have grown old. How is it that time, which has no form or substance, can crush me with so huge a weight that I can no longer breathe?" At 57, de Beauvoir found herself "hostile to the society to which I belonged, banished by my age from the future, stripped fiber by fiber from my past ... The promises have all been kept. And yet, turning an incredulous gaze toward that young and credulous girl (I once was), I realize with stupor how much I was gypped."[1]

De Beauvoir's disillusionment is at the heart of the issues explored by this remarkable book of Ecclesiastes. Professor Peter Kreeft says that whenever he is called upon to teach the Bible in a college classroom, he begins with Ecclesiastes, not with Genesis; for Ecclesiastes raises all the critical questions the rest of the Bible answers. One by one, the writer of this book looks at the ways humans have attempted to find meaning apart from God, and one by one he finds them inadequate. The pursuit of wisdom leads only to frustration and pain. The pursuit of pleasure leads only to disappointment.

After the ascription, the first word of the book is "Meaningless!" The last words are, "Now all has been heard; here is the conclusion of the matter: Fear God and keep his commandments, for this is the whole duty of man. For God will bring every deed into judgment, including every hidden thing, whether it is good or evil" (12:13–14). The journey from the beginning to the end is provocative, puzzling and sobering. But it is worth reading to discover yet again that only in God can there be fulfillment. Apart from the God who hears and answers prayer, the alternative is a gloomy and sour pursuit of earthly satisfactions. To pray the themes of Ecclesiastes is to feel often an acute sense of gratitude and relief that, because of Christ, life is not meaningless!

Everything Is Meaningless

1 The words of the Teacher,[a] son of David, king in Jerusalem:

2 "Meaningless! Meaningless!"
    says the Teacher.
  "Utterly meaningless!
    Everything is meaningless."

3 What does man gain from all his
      labor
    at which he toils under the sun?
4 Generations come and generations
      go,
    but the earth remains forever.
5 The sun rises and the sun sets,
    and hurries back to where it rises.
6 The wind blows to the south
    and turns to the north;
  round and round it goes,
    ever returning on its course.
7 All streams flow into the sea,
    yet the sea is never full.
  To the place the streams come from,
    there they return again.
8 All things are wearisome,
    more than one can say.
  The eye never has enough of seeing,
    nor the ear its fill of hearing.
9 What has been will be again,
    what has been done will be done
      again;
  there is nothing new under the
      sun.
10 Is there anything of which one can
      say,
    "Look! This is something new"?
  It was here already, long ago;
    it was here before our time.
11 There is no remembrance of men
      of old,
    and even those who are yet
      to come
  will not be remembered
    by those who follow.

Wisdom Is Meaningless

12 I, the Teacher, was king over Israel in Jerusalem. 13 I devoted myself to study and to explore by wisdom all that is done under heaven. What a heavy burden God has laid on men! 14 I have seen all the things that are done under the sun; all of them are meaningless, a chasing after the wind.

15 What is twisted cannot be
      straightened;
    what is lacking cannot be counted.

16 I thought to myself, "Look, I have grown and increased in wisdom more than anyone who has ruled over Jerusalem before me; I have experienced much of wisdom and knowledge." 17 Then I applied myself to the understanding of wisdom, and also of madness and folly, but I learned that this, too, is a chasing after the wind.

18 For with much wisdom comes
      much sorrow;
    the more knowledge, the more grief.

Pleasures Are Meaningless

2 I thought in my heart, "Come now, I will test you with pleasure to find out what is good." But that also proved to be meaningless. 2 "Laughter," I said, "is foolish. And what does pleasure accomplish?" 3 I tried cheering myself with wine, and embracing folly—my mind still guiding me with wisdom. I wanted to see what was worthwhile for men to do under heaven during the few days of their lives.

4 I undertook great projects: I built houses for myself and planted vineyards. 5 I made gardens and parks and planted all kinds of fruit trees in them. 6 I made reservoirs to water groves of flourishing trees. 7 I bought male and female slaves and had other slaves who were born in my house. I also owned more herds and flocks than anyone in Jerusalem before me. 8 I amassed silver and gold for myself, and the treasure of kings and provinces. I acquired men and women singers, and a harem[b] as well—the delights of the heart of man. 9 I became greater by far than anyone in Jerusalem before me. In all this my wisdom stayed with me.

10 I denied myself nothing my eyes
      desired;
    I refused my heart no pleasure.
  My heart took delight in all my work,
    and this was the reward for all my
      labor.

---

[a]1 Or *leader of the assembly*; also in verses 2 and 12   [b]8 The meaning of the Hebrew for this phrase is uncertain.

11 Yet when I surveyed all that my
   hands had done
and what I had toiled to achieve,
   everything was meaningless, a
   chasing after the wind;
   nothing was gained under the sun.

Wisdom and Folly Are Meaningless

12 Then I turned my thoughts to
   consider wisdom,

and also madness and folly.
   What more can the king's successor
   do
   than what has already been done?
13 I saw that wisdom is better than
   folly,
   just as light is better than darkness.
14 The wise man has eyes in his head,
   while the fool walks in the
   darkness;

[**THURSDAY**]

ECCLESIASTES 2:24–26

The Blessings of this Life

2:24 A MAN CAN DO NOTHING BETTER THAN TO EAT AND DRINK AND FIND SATISFACTION IN HIS WORK.

The writer of Ecclesiastes misses no folly or foible of the human condition. But even amid all the meaninglessness, he sees that there are certain things God has given humans that are very good and satisfying. Two are mentioned here: good work and good food (compare 3:13; 3:22; 5:18–20; 8:15; 9:7); and a third elsewhere: a good marriage (see 9:9). The whole world may seem askew, but with these earthly pleasures, life can still be good. But there are two provisos: First that God blesses them and enables us to enjoy them (see 5:19), and second that we know they are gifts from God, not our own doing (see 3:13).

There is an important theology of pleasure implicit in these verses. Two things stand out: One, God's good gifts in creation are good. Food, work and marriage are inherently worthwhile. The world is the Lord's manor, his estate, and in his Word he magnanimously encourages us to enjoy being his guests. "Both high and low among men find refuge in the shadow of your wings. They feast on the abundance of your house; you give them drink from your river of delights. For with you is the fountain of life; in your light we see light" (Psalm 36:7b–9). Two, apart from God our earthly joys are too confined, too narrow. They are good in themselves because God made them, but because they are not God, they can't satisfy the way only God can. Many earthly joys will diminish as we age and our senses dwindle (see Ecclesiastes 12:1–8). In order for the gifts to be all they can be, we need the Giver with the gift.

It is common for Christians to pray before meals. Some call the prayer "giving thanks," others "saying grace." Either wording is appropriate. Of course we should be thankful, and our gratitude is enhanced to the degree that we see the grace. But it would also be appropriate to call these prayers "pleasure prayers." The only way to improve on the pleasure of mashed potatoes and gravy, or a joyous evening of family laughter, is to say "Thank you."

PRAY:

Thank you, gracious and generous Father for all the blessings of this life.
"For with you is the fountain of life; in your light we see light" (Psalm 36:9).

FOR YOUR NEXT DEVOTIONAL READING, GO TO PAGE 778.

but I came to realize
that the same fate overtakes
them both. [15]Then I thought in my heart,

"The fate of the fool will overtake
me also.
What then do I gain by being wise?"
I said in my heart,
"This too is meaningless."
[16]For the wise man, like the fool, will
not be long remembered;
in days to come both will be
forgotten.
Like the fool, the wise man too
must die!

Toil Is Meaningless

[17]So I hated life, because the work that is done under the sun was grievous to me. All of it is meaningless, a chasing after the wind. [18]I hated all the things I had toiled for under the sun, because I must leave them to the one who comes after me. [19]And who knows whether he will be a wise man or a fool? Yet he will have control over all the work into which I have poured my effort and skill under the sun. This too is meaningless. [20]So my heart began to despair over all my toilsome labor under the sun. [21]For a man may do his work with wisdom, knowledge and skill, and then he must leave all he owns to someone who has not worked for it. This too is meaningless and a great misfortune. [22]What does a man get for all the toil and anxious striving with which he labors under the sun? [23]All his days his work is pain and grief; even at night his mind does not rest. This too is meaningless.

[24]A man can do nothing better than to eat and drink and find satisfaction in his work. This too, I see, is from the hand of God, [25]for without him, who can eat or find enjoyment? [26]To the man who pleases him, God gives wisdom, knowledge and happiness, but to the sinner he gives the task of gathering and storing up wealth to hand it over to the one who pleases God. This too is meaningless, a chasing after the wind.

A Time for Everything

3 There is a time for everything,
and a season for every activity
under heaven:

[2] a time to be born and a time to die,
a time to plant and a time to
uproot,
[3] a time to kill and a time to heal,
a time to tear down and a time to
build,
[4] a time to weep and a time to laugh,
a time to mourn and a time to
dance,
[5] a time to scatter stones and a time
to gather them,
a time to embrace and a time to
refrain,
[6] a time to search and a time to give
up,
a time to keep and a time to throw
away,
[7] a time to tear and a time to mend,
a time to be silent and a time to
speak,
[8] a time to love and a time to hate,
a time for war and a time for peace.

[9]What does the worker gain from his toil? [10]I have seen the burden God has laid on men. [11]He has made everything beautiful in its time. He has also set eternity in the hearts of men; yet they cannot fathom what God has done from beginning to end. [12]I know that there is nothing better for men than to be happy and do good while they live. [13]That everyone may eat and drink, and find satisfaction in all his toil—this is the gift of God. [14]I know that everything God does will endure forever; nothing can be added to it and nothing taken from it. God does it so that men will revere him.

[15]Whatever is has already been,
and what will be has been before;
and God will call the past to
account.[a]

[16]And I saw something else under the sun:

In the place of judgment—
wickedness was there,
in the place of justice—wickedness
was there.

[17]I thought in my heart,

"God will bring to judgment
both the righteous and the wicked,

[a]15 Or *God calls back the past*

for there will be a time for every
activity,
a time for every deed."

¹⁸I also thought, "As for men, God tests them so that they may see that they are like the animals. ¹⁹Man's fate is like that of the animals; the same fate awaits them both: As one dies, so dies the other. All have the same breath*ᵃ*; man has no advantage over the animal. Everything is meaningless. ²⁰All go to the same place; all come from dust, and to dust all return. ²¹Who knows if the spirit of man rises upward and if the spirit of the animal*ᵇ* goes down into the earth?"

²²So I saw that there is nothing better for a man than to enjoy his work, be-

ᵃ19 Or *spirit*   *ᵇ21* Or *Who knows the spirit of man, which rises upward, or the spirit of the animal, which*

{ FRIDAY }

ECCLESIASTES 3:1–22

Too Much, But Not Enough

3:1 THERE IS A TIME FOR EVERYTHING.

The world is too much for us. We are dwarfed by its glorious and inexorable movements and seasons. For instance: "There is a time for everything, and a season for every activity under heaven: a time to be born and a time to die" (3:1–2). There you have it. Our birth and our death, the two most important events of our life, are things we have absolutely no control over. Do we have control of anything? Eternity rules time and all who move through it. Times and seasons come and go, and only God knows when, why or how. This unsettling knowledge can make us wise, as in the fear of God (see Proverbs 1:7), which is what the writer of Ecclesiastes says it's supposed to do: "I know that everything God does will endure forever; nothing can be added to it and nothing taken from it. God does it so that men will revere him" (3:14).

Yet, dwarfed as we are by the world, the world is not enough for us. We were made for more than the world can give. Moving through times we cannot control, we long for more. God made us that way: "He has made everything beautiful in its time. He has also set eternity in the hearts of men; yet they cannot fathom what God has done from beginning to end" (3:11). The world may dwarf us and the weight of time eventually crush us, but we are greater than both. "Man is but a reed, the most feeble thing in nature; but he is a thinking reed," wrote Blaise Pascal. "If the universe were to crush him, man would still be more noble than that which killed him, because he knows that he dies and the advantage which the universe has over him; the universe knows nothing of this." Pascal believed our greatness is that of a deposed king; we were made for more, we lost it, and now we want it back.

Thoughts like these both humble and ennoble us. We are wretched when seen only against the backdrop of the universe. But God made us for himself, and we are restless until we find rest in him, said Augustine. Only deposed royalty who have been humbled can find their way back.

PRAY:
You made me for yourself, Lord. My heart is restless for you; I hunger and thirst for you as in a desert. Satisfy me with your love.

FOR YOUR NEXT DEVOTIONAL READING, GO TO PAGE 780.

cause that is his lot. For who can bring him to see what will happen after him?

Oppression, Toil, Friendlessness

4 Again I looked and saw all the oppression that was taking place under the sun:

I saw the tears of the oppressed—
and they have no comforter;
power was on the side of their
oppressors—
and they have no comforter.
2 And I declared that the dead,
who had already died,
are happier than the living,
who are still alive.
3 But better than both
is he who has not yet been,
who has not seen the evil
that is done under the sun.

4 And I saw that all labor and all achievement spring from man's envy of his neighbor. This too is meaningless, a chasing after the wind.

5 The fool folds his hands
and ruins himself.
6 Better one handful with tranquillity
than two handfuls with toil
and chasing after the wind.

7 Again I saw something meaningless under the sun:

8 There was a man all alone;
he had neither son nor brother.
There was no end to his toil,
yet his eyes were not content with
his wealth.
"For whom am I toiling," he asked,
"and why am I depriving myself of
enjoyment?"
This too is meaningless—
a miserable business!

9 Two are better than one,
because they have a good return
for their work:
10 If one falls down,
his friend can help him up.
But pity the man who falls
and has no one to help him up!
11 Also, if two lie down together, they
will keep warm.
But how can one keep warm
alone?

12 Though one may be overpowered,
two can defend themselves.
A cord of three strands is not quickly
broken.

Advancement Is Meaningless

13 Better a poor but wise youth than an old but foolish king who no longer knows how to take warning. 14 The youth may have come from prison to the kingship, or he may have been born in poverty within his kingdom. 15 I saw that all who lived and walked under the sun followed the youth, the king's successor. 16 There was no end to all the people who were before them. But those who came later were not pleased with the successor. This too is meaningless, a chasing after the wind.

Stand in Awe of God

5 Guard your steps when you go to the house of God. Go near to listen rather than to offer the sacrifice of fools, who do not know that they do wrong.

2 Do not be quick with your mouth,
do not be hasty in your heart
to utter anything before God.
God is in heaven
and you are on earth,
so let your words be few.
3 As a dream comes when there are
many cares,
so the speech of a fool when there
are many words.

4 When you make a vow to God, do not delay in fulfilling it. He has no pleasure in fools; fulfill your vow. 5 It is better not to vow than to make a vow and not fulfill it. 6 Do not let your mouth lead you into sin. And do not protest to the ⌊temple⌋ messenger, "My vow was a mistake." Why should God be angry at what you say and destroy the work of your hands? 7 Much dreaming and many words are meaningless. Therefore stand in awe of God.

Riches Are Meaningless

8 If you see the poor oppressed in a district, and justice and rights denied, do not be surprised at such things; for one official is eyed by a higher one, and over them both are others higher still. 9 The increase from the land is taken by all; the king himself profits from the fields.

The Praying Activist

ARE YOU too busy to pray—or to pray very much? Don't answer that question until you consider the prayer life of a very busy real-life activist— the apostle Paul. His great ambition in life was to preach the gospel where it had never before been preached, no matter the cost (see Romans 15:20; Acts 20:22–24). That he did, vigorously and unstintingly, traveling from Syria to Rome, through deserts and over mountain passes, on foot and by sea. You can read about some of his experiences in 2 Corinthians 11:22–29. They included multiple imprisonments and floggings, several brushes with death, three beatings with rods, one stoning, three shipwrecks, regular harassment and humiliation, sleepless nights, hunger, thirst, cold, nakedness and the daily pressure of his concern for all the churches.

Yet Paul describes himself as a man who prays constantly (see Romans 1:9–10; Colossians 1:9; 2 Thessalonians 1:11; 2 Timothy 1:3). Instead of causing him to pray less, his busy schedule drove him to pray more. The more there was to do, the more there was to pray about. This is because Paul knew the real issue in life was not the "to-do list" but the spiritual significance of the list. The real struggle was not about what needed to be done but the spiritual realities behind what needed to be done. So this man of action prayed—constantly (see Ephesians 6:11,18–20).

Perhaps the root of our problem with prayer and busy-ness is in how we see reality. Paul knew the real battle was spiritual. Sometimes we don't see this. Christians today have often been secularized, a process by which "religious" things like prayer lose their practical social significance. It's not that we think spiritual reality does not exist; it's just that on some level we come to believe that it doesn't make a lot of difference in how things get done on earth. Nothing could be farther from the truth!

Dr. A. J. Gordon described perfectly the relationship between prayer and work when he wrote, "You can do more than pray, after you have prayed; but you can never do more than pray until you have prayed."[2] There are a lot of important things to do besides pray, but we won't get to them until we pray. In the same vein, Andrew Murray laid out a fundamental principle of Christian priorities: "Our true aim must not be to work a great deal and pray just enough to keep the work right. We should pray a great deal and then work enough for the power and blessing obtained in prayer to find its way through us to men."[3]

PRAY:
Father, forgive my prayerlessness.
Let my working flow out of my praying.

MEMORIZE:
And pray in the Spirit on all occasions with all kinds of
prayers and requests. With this in mind, be alert and always
keep on praying for all the saints. EPHESIANS 6:18

FOR YOUR NEXT DEVOTIONAL READING, GO TO PAGE 782.

¹⁰Whoever loves money never has
  money enough;
 whoever loves wealth is never
  satisfied with his income.
 This too is meaningless.

¹¹As goods increase,
  so do those who consume them.
 And what benefit are they to the
  owner
 except to feast his eyes on them?

¹²The sleep of a laborer is sweet,
  whether he eats little or much,
 but the abundance of a rich man
  permits him no sleep.

¹³I have seen a grievous evil under the
  sun:

 wealth hoarded to the harm of
  its owner,
¹⁴ or wealth lost through some
   misfortune,
 so that when he has a son
  there is nothing left for him.
¹⁵Naked a man comes from his
  mother's womb,
 and as he comes, so he
  departs.
 He takes nothing from his labor
  that he can carry in his hand.

{ MONDAY }

ECCLESIASTES 5:1–7

Sacrifice of Fools

5:7 THEREFORE STAND IN AWE OF GOD.

This passage is to prayer and worship what Proverbs 1:7 is to wisdom: "The fear of the LORD is the beginning of knowledge." Actually this passage is a sub-set of it: "Guard your steps when you go to the house of God" (Ecclesiastes 5:1). When you approach God, pay attention to what you are there for and who you are there to honor. The promise of the New Testament still holds: You may enter the holy place with confidence (see Hebrews 4:16), but not care-lessness. We come into God's presence by the grace of his Son, but grace never gives us license to be irreverent. The most essential and appropriate response to grace is gratitude, and gratitude is never casual. The greater the grace, the greater the gratitude and reverence.

The worst kind of irreverence is mindless worship, according to this pas-sage. It is the sacrifice of fools who don't think about what they are doing, who speak before they think, and make empty promises to God. Their words and prayers are like the mumblings and ramblings of someone in a troubled sleep. The only thing worse than a silent fool is a talkative fool.

How do your prayers and the worship you offer God stand in the light of this text? On the continuum between garrulousness and awe, where does the worship of your church fall? Remember, God is the center of worship, not you and your feelings and opinions. Feelings and opinions matter, and are properly brought before the light of God for their sanctification. But when they, not God, become the center, you know how serious an offense that is. The Bible calls it idolatry. "God is in heaven and you are on earth, so let your words be few" (Ecclesiastes 5:2). It doesn't say, "Let your words be eloquent or theologi-cally profound." Sometimes the greatest eloquence and profundity is in simple, listening silence.

PRAY:
*Holy God, teach me the discipline and grace of silence. I shut my mouth
and open my ears. Speak, so I may speak well of you.*

FOR YOUR NEXT DEVOTIONAL READING, GO TO PAGE 788.

¹⁶This too is a grievous evil:

As a man comes, so he departs,
and what does he gain,
since he toils for the wind?
¹⁷All his days he eats in darkness,
with great frustration, affliction
and anger.

¹⁸Then I realized that it is good and proper for a man to eat and drink, and to find satisfaction in his toilsome labor under the sun during the few days of life God has given him—for this is his lot. ¹⁹Moreover, when God gives any man wealth and possessions, and enables him to enjoy them, to accept his lot and be happy in his work—this is a gift of God. ²⁰He seldom reflects on the days of his life, because God keeps him occupied with gladness of heart.

6 I have seen another evil under the sun, and it weighs heavily on men: ²God gives a man wealth, possessions and honor, so that he lacks nothing his heart desires, but God does not enable him to enjoy them, and a stranger enjoys them instead. This is meaningless, a grievous evil.

³A man may have a hundred children and live many years; yet no matter how long he lives, if he cannot enjoy his prosperity and does not receive proper burial, I say that a stillborn child is better off than he. ⁴It comes without meaning, it departs in darkness, and in darkness its name is shrouded. ⁵Though it never saw the sun or knew anything, it has more rest than does that man— ⁶even if he lives a thousand years twice over but fails to enjoy his prosperity. Do not all go to the same place?

⁷All man's efforts are for his mouth,
yet his appetite is never satisfied.
⁸What advantage has a wise man
over a fool?
What does a poor man gain
by knowing how to conduct himself
before others?
⁹Better what the eye sees
than the roving of the appetite.
This too is meaningless,
a chasing after the wind.

¹⁰Whatever exists has already been
named,
and what man is has been known;
no man can contend
with one who is stronger than he.
¹¹The more the words,
the less the meaning,
and how does that profit anyone?

¹²For who knows what is good for a man in life, during the few and meaningless days he passes through like a shadow? Who can tell him what will happen under the sun after he is gone?

Wisdom

7 A good name is better than fine
perfume,
and the day of death better than
the day of birth.
²It is better to go to a house of
mourning
than to go to a house of feasting,
for death is the destiny of every man;
the living should take this to heart.
³Sorrow is better than laughter,
because a sad face is good for the
heart.
⁴The heart of the wise is in the house
of mourning,
but the heart of fools is in the
house of pleasure.
⁵It is better to heed a wise man's
rebuke
than to listen to the song of fools.
⁶Like the crackling of thorns under
the pot,
so is the laughter of fools.
This too is meaningless.

⁷Extortion turns a wise man into
a fool,
and a bribe corrupts the heart.
⁸The end of a matter is better than its
beginning,
and patience is better than pride.
⁹Do not be quickly provoked in
your spirit,
for anger resides in the lap of fools.
¹⁰Do not say, "Why were the old days
better than these?"
For it is not wise to ask such
questions.
¹¹Wisdom, like an inheritance, is a
good thing
and benefits those who see the sun.

12 Wisdom is a shelter
  as money is a shelter,
  but the advantage of knowledge
    is this:
    that wisdom preserves the life of
      its possessor.

13 Consider what God has done:

  Who can straighten
    what he has made crooked?
14 When times are good, be happy;
    but when times are bad, consider:
  God has made the one
    as well as the other.
  Therefore, a man cannot discover
    anything about his future.

15 In this meaningless life of mine I have
seen both of these:

  a righteous man perishing in his
    righteousness,
    and a wicked man living long in
      his wickedness.
16 Do not be overrighteous,
    neither be overwise—
    why destroy yourself?
17 Do not be overwicked,
    and do not be a fool—
    why die before your time?
18 It is good to grasp the one
    and not let go of the other.
  The man who fears God will avoid
    all extremes.*a*

19 Wisdom makes one wise man more
    powerful
    than ten rulers in a city.

20 There is not a righteous man on earth
    who does what is right and never
    sins.

21 Do not pay attention to every word
    people say,
    or you may hear your servant
      cursing you—
22 for you know in your heart
    that many times you yourself have
    cursed others.

23 All this I tested by wisdom and I said,

  "I am determined to be wise"—
    but this was beyond me.
24 Whatever wisdom may be,
    it is far off and most profound—
    who can discover it?

25 So I turned my mind to understand,
    to investigate and to search out
      wisdom and the scheme of
      things
  and to understand the stupidity of
    wickedness
    and the madness of folly.

26 I find more bitter than death
    the woman who is a snare,
  whose heart is a trap
    and whose hands are chains.
  The man who pleases God will
    escape her,
    but the sinner she will ensnare.

27 "Look," says the Teacher,*b* "this is
what I have discovered:

  "Adding one thing to another to
    discover the scheme of
    things—
28   while I was still searching
    but not finding—
  I found one upright man among a
    thousand,
    but not one upright woman
    among them all.
29 This only have I found:
  God made mankind upright,
    but men have gone in search of
    many schemes."

8 Who is like the wise man?
  Who knows the explanation of
    things?
  Wisdom brightens a man's face
    and changes its hard appearance.

Obey the King

2 Obey the king's command, I say, because you took an oath before God. 3 Do
not be in a hurry to leave the king's presence. Do not stand up for a bad cause,
for he will do whatever he pleases. 4 Since
a king's word is supreme, who can say to
him, "What are you doing?"

5 Whoever obeys his command will
    come to no harm,
    and the wise heart will know the
    proper time and procedure.
6 For there is a proper time and
    procedure for every matter,

*a18 Or will follow them both   b27 Or leader of
the assembly*

though a man's misery weighs heavily upon him.

⁷Since no man knows the future,
who can tell him what is to come?
⁸No man has power over the wind to
contain it[a];
so no one has power over the day
of his death.
As no one is discharged in time of war,
so wickedness will not release
those who practice it.

⁹All this I saw, as I applied my mind to everything done under the sun. There is a time when a man lords it over others to his own[b] hurt. ¹⁰Then too, I saw the wicked buried—those who used to come and go from the holy place and receive praise[c] in the city where they did this. This too is meaningless.

¹¹When the sentence for a crime is not quickly carried out, the hearts of the people are filled with schemes to do wrong. ¹²Although a wicked man commits a hundred crimes and still lives a long time, I know that it will go better with God-fearing men, who are reverent before God. ¹³Yet because the wicked do not fear God, it will not go well with them, and their days will not lengthen like a shadow.

¹⁴There is something else meaningless that occurs on earth: righteous men who get what the wicked deserve, and wicked men who get what the righteous deserve. This too, I say, is meaningless. ¹⁵So I commend the enjoyment of life, because nothing is better for a man under the sun than to eat and drink and be glad. Then joy will accompany him in his work all the days of the life God has given him under the sun.

¹⁶When I applied my mind to know wisdom and to observe man's labor on earth—his eyes not seeing sleep day or night— ¹⁷then I saw all that God has done. No one can comprehend what goes on under the sun. Despite all his efforts to search it out, man cannot discover its meaning. Even if a wise man claims he knows, he cannot really comprehend it.

A Common Destiny for All

9 So I reflected on all this and concluded that the righteous and the wise and what they do are in God's hands, but no man knows whether love or hate awaits him. ²All share a common destiny—the righteous and the wicked, the good and the bad,[d] the clean and the unclean, those who offer sacrifices and those who do not.

As it is with the good man,
so with the sinner;
as it is with those who take oaths,
so with those who are afraid to
take them.

> THE righteous and the wise and what they do are in God's hands.
>
> ECCLESIASTES 9:1

³This is the evil in everything that happens under the sun: The same destiny overtakes all. The hearts of men, moreover, are full of evil and there is madness in their hearts while they live, and afterward they join the dead. ⁴Anyone who is among the living has hope[e]—even a live dog is better off than a dead lion!

⁵For the living know that they will die,
but the dead know nothing;
they have no further reward,
and even the memory of them is
forgotten.
⁶Their love, their hate
and their jealousy have long since
vanished;
never again will they have a part
in anything that happens under
the sun.

⁷Go, eat your food with gladness, and drink your wine with a joyful heart, for it is now that God favors what you do. ⁸Always be clothed in white, and always anoint your head with oil. ⁹Enjoy life with your wife, whom you love, all the days of this meaningless life that God has given you under the sun—all your meaningless days. For this is your lot in life and in your toilsome labor under the sun. ¹⁰Whatever your hand finds to do, do it with all your might, for in the grave,[f] where you are

---

[a]8 Or over his spirit to retain it   [b]9 Or to their
[c]10 Some Hebrew manuscripts and Septuagint (Aquila); most Hebrew manuscripts and are forgotten   [d]2 Septuagint (Aquila), Vulgate and Syriac; Hebrew does not have and the bad.
[e]4 Or What then is to be chosen? With all who live, there is hope   [f]10 Hebrew Sheol

going, there is neither working nor planning nor knowledge nor wisdom.

11 I have seen something else under the sun:

> The race is not to the swift
> or the battle to the strong,
> nor does food come to the wise
> or wealth to the brilliant
> or favor to the learned;
> but time and chance happen to
> them all.

12 Moreover, no man knows when his hour will come:

> As fish are caught in a cruel net,
> or birds are taken in a snare,
> so men are trapped by evil times
> that fall unexpectedly upon them.

Wisdom Better Than Folly

13 I also saw under the sun this example of wisdom that greatly impressed me: 14 There was once a small city with only a few people in it. And a powerful king came against it, surrounded it and built huge siegeworks against it. 15 Now there lived in that city a man poor but wise, and he saved the city by his wisdom. But nobody remembered that poor man. 16 So I said, "Wisdom is better than strength." But the poor man's wisdom is despised, and his words are no longer heeded.

17 The quiet words of the wise are more
> to be heeded
> than the shouts of a ruler of fools.
18 Wisdom is better than weapons of war,
> but one sinner destroys much
> good.

10 As dead flies give perfume a bad
> smell,
> so a little folly outweighs wisdom
> and honor.
2 The heart of the wise inclines to
> the right,
> but the heart of the fool to the left.
3 Even as he walks along the road,
> the fool lacks sense
> and shows everyone how stupid
> he is.
4 If a ruler's anger rises against you,
> do not leave your post;
> calmness can lay great errors
> to rest.

5 There is an evil I have seen under
> the sun,
> the sort of error that arises from
> a ruler:
6 Fools are put in many high positions,
> while the rich occupy the low ones.
7 I have seen slaves on horseback,
> while princes go on foot like slaves.

8 Whoever digs a pit may fall into it;
> whoever breaks through a wall
> may be bitten by a snake.
9 Whoever quarries stones may be
> injured by them;
> whoever splits logs may be
> endangered by them.

10 If the ax is dull
> and its edge unsharpened,
> more strength is needed
> but skill will bring success.

11 If a snake bites before it is charmed,
> there is no profit for the charmer.

12 Words from a wise man's mouth
> are gracious,
> but a fool is consumed by his
> own lips.
13 At the beginning his words are folly;
> at the end they are wicked
> madness—
14 and the fool multiplies words.

> No one knows what is coming—
> who can tell him what will happen
> after him?

15 A fool's work wearies him;
> he does not know the way to town.

16 Woe to you, O land whose king was a
> servant[a]
> and whose princes feast in the
> morning.
17 Blessed are you, O land whose king is
> of noble birth
> and whose princes eat at a proper
> time—
> for strength and not for
> drunkenness.
18 If a man is lazy, the rafters sag;
> if his hands are idle, the house
> leaks.
19 A feast is made for laughter,
> and wine makes life merry,

---

a 16 Or *king is a child*

but money is the answer for
everything.

²⁰ Do not revile the king even in your
thoughts,
  or curse the rich in your bedroom,
because a bird of the air may carry
  your words,
  and a bird on the wing may report
    what you say.

Bread Upon the Waters

11 Cast your bread upon the waters,
  for after many days you will find
    it again.
² Give portions to seven, yes to eight,
  for you do not know what disaster
    may come upon the land.

³ If clouds are full of water,
  they pour rain upon the earth.
Whether a tree falls to the south or to
    the north,
  in the place where it falls, there
    will it lie.
⁴ Whoever watches the wind will
    not plant;
  whoever looks at the clouds
    will not reap.

⁵ As you do not know the path of the
    wind,
  or how the body is formed^a in a
    mother's womb,
so you cannot understand the work
    of God,
  the Maker of all things.

⁶ Sow your seed in the morning,
  and at evening let not your hands
    be idle,
for you do not know which will
    succeed,
  whether this or that,
  or whether both will do equally
    well.

Remember Your Creator While Young

⁷ Light is sweet,
  and it pleases the eyes to see
    the sun.
⁸ However many years a man may live,
  let him enjoy them all.
But let him remember the days of
    darkness,
  for they will be many.
Everything to come is meaningless.

⁹ Be happy, young man, while you
    are young,
  and let your heart give you joy in
    the days of your youth.
Follow the ways of your heart
  and whatever your eyes see,
but know that for all these things
  God will bring you to judgment.
¹⁰ So then, banish anxiety from your
    heart
  and cast off the troubles of your
    body,
  for youth and vigor are meaningless.

12 Remember your Creator
  in the days of your youth,
before the days of trouble come
  and the years approach when you
    will say,
  "I find no pleasure in them"—
² before the sun and the light
  and the moon and the stars
    grow dark,
  and the clouds return after the
    rain;
³ when the keepers of the house
    tremble,
  and the strong men stoop,
when the grinders cease because
    they are few,
  and those looking through the
    windows grow dim;
⁴ when the doors to the street are
    closed
  and the sound of grinding fades;
when men rise up at the sound of
    birds,
  but all their songs grow faint;
⁵ when men are afraid of heights
  and of dangers in the streets;
when the almond tree blossoms
  and the grasshopper drags himself
    along
  and desire no longer is stirred.
Then man goes to his eternal home
  and mourners go about the streets.

⁶ Remember him—before the silver
    cord is severed,
  or the golden bowl is broken;
before the pitcher is shattered at the
    spring,
  or the wheel broken at the well,

^a5 Or *know how life* (or *the spirit*) / *enters the
body being formed*

⁷and the dust returns to the ground it
came from,
and the spirit returns to God who
gave it.

⁸"Meaningless! Meaningless!" says the
Teacher.ᵃ
"Everything is meaningless!"

The Conclusion of the Matter

⁹Not only was the Teacher wise, but
also he imparted knowledge to the people. He pondered and searched out and
set in order many proverbs. ¹⁰The Teach-

ᵃ8 Or *the leader of the assembly*; also in verses 9
and 10

{ TUESDAY }

ECCLESIASTES 11:7 — 12:8

A Good Youth and a Good Death

11:9 BE HAPPY, YOUNG MAN, WHILE YOU ARE YOUNG, AND LET YOUR HEART GIVE YOU
JOY IN THE DAYS OF YOUR YOUTH.

In many collections of famous photographs there is a picture of two
women peering at each other from opposites sides of a giant redwood
tree. One is youthful, full of life and promise. The other is very old and
somewhat shrunken. Both are smiling faintly at what they see. They seem
amused. Youth looks at old age, and old age looks back, like this fascinating meditation.

It's good to be young, but youth is wasted on the young if they don't
know that. The young also waste their youth if they are not reflective and
sober about their state. Be joyful, yes, but also be aware that your youth is a
temporary gift from God that you will have to give an account for someday.
"Know that for all these things God will bring you to judgment" (11:9). Don't
let the passions of youth make you nearsighted; keep the long view before
you. "Remember your Creator in the days of your youth, before the days of
trouble come and the years approach when you will say, 'I find no pleasure
in them'" (12:1).

To state the obvious, for as long as we can remember, we've all been
alive. It's hard to imagine being dead, not to mention that it's an unpleasant
thought. Even the very old can look at their aging selves with incredulity.
Generations before us weren't this squeamish about the subject, and they
used to pray regularly that God would grant them a good death. Peter
Kreeft has written movingly on how all prayer is a preparation for a good
death. "Prayer is a rehearsal for death; prayer is a little death. For to pray is
to enter God's presence, and to enter God's presence we must die ... This is
a blessed death; we die to our own presence, our own I AM. We stop being
our own God and let God be God ... Prayer is the preparation for the last
turning to God ... because in it we are not only taken out of ourselves but
also into the presence of God. Prayer is heaven on earth."⁴ Remember your
Creator not only in your youth but also in your old age when you pray.

PRAY:

*Lord, "Teach us to number our days aright, that we may
gain a heart of wisdom" (Psalm 90:12).*

FOR YOUR NEXT DEVOTIONAL READING, GO TO PAGE 789.

er searched to find just the right words, and what he wrote was upright and true.

¹¹The words of the wise are like goads, their collected sayings like firmly embedded nails—given by one Shepherd. ¹²Be warned, my son, of anything in addition to them.

Of making many books there is no end, and much study wearies the body.

¹³Now all has been heard;
here is the conclusion of the matter:
Fear God and keep his commandments,
for this is the whole ⌊duty⌋ of man.
¹⁴For God will bring every deed into judgment,
including every hidden thing, whether it is good or evil.

[WEDNESDAY]

ECCLESIASTES 12:9–14

Part of the Permanent

12:13 FEAR GOD AND KEEP HIS COMMANDMENTS, FOR THIS IS THE WHOLE DUTY OF MAN.

J. B. Phillips' paraphrase of 1 John 2:15–17 is also a good New Testament paraphrase of the ending of Ecclesiastes.

"Never give your hearts to this world or to any of the things in it. A man cannot love the Father and love the world at the same time. For the whole world-system, based as it is on men's primitive desires, their greedy ambitions and the glamour of all they think splendid, is not derived from the Father at all, but from the world itself. The world and all its passionate desires will one day disappear. *But the man who is following God's will is part of the permanent and cannot die*"(italics added).⁵

Only God lasts. We won't. The things that attract us won't. The rational choice then, the realistic decision, is to do God's will. So much in life is really beyond our control, "a chasing after the wind" to use a phrase from the author of Ecclesiastes (1:14; 2:11). Here is one thing we can build on and bank on, the one real choice we have to do something of eternal consequence: the will of God. Nothing else we can do can make us "part of the permanent."

The resurrection of Jesus Christ from the dead proves it. It is the final answer to the cry, "Meaningless! Meaningless! . . . Everything is meaningless!" (12:8). "When the perishable has been clothed with the imperishable, and the mortal with immortality, then the saying that is written will come true: 'Death has been swallowed up in victory.' 'Where, O death, is your victory? Where, O death, is your sting?' . . . Therefore, my dear brothers, stand firm. Let nothing move you. Always give yourselves fully to the work of the Lord, because you know that your labor in the Lord is not in vain" (1 Corinthians 15:54–55,58).

PRAY:

"Grant, O Lord, that we may live in thy fear, die in thy favor, rest in thy peace, rise in thy power, reign in thy glory; for thine own beloved Son's sake, Jesus Christ our Lord." WILLIAM LAUD⁶

FOR YOUR NEXT DEVOTIONAL READING, GO TO PAGE 793.

Song of Songs

"AS A BRIDEGROOM rejoices over his bride, so will your God rejoice over you" (Isaiah 62:5). If you have never thought of God looking at you this way, you should—because he does. "The Bible is about marriage," wrote David Hubbard.[1] In the very beginning there is a wedding, the union of the first man and first woman, naked but not ashamed (see Genesis 2:23–25). At the end, when history is consummated, there is a huge wedding feast (see Revelation 19:7–9). In between, God's relationship with his people is underlined with marriage metaphors (see Isaiah 54:5; Jeremiah 3). Hosea must faithfully love and stay married to the prostitute Gomer as a picture of what God must endure with Israel (see Hosea 1–3). Marriage is a primary New Testament metaphor for God's relationship to his church (see Ephesians 5:21–33; 2 Corinthians 11:2).

WE REJOICE AND DELIGHT IN YOU; WE WILL PRAISE YOUR LOVE MORE THAN WINE. (1:4)

In the middle of the Bible, nestled between the Law and the Prophets, is a little book that does nothing but celebrate the pleasure, joy, communion and ecstasy of sexual love in marriage. Other parts of the Bible have much to say about the seriousness of the marriage covenant. Song of Songs says marriage is fun—in great, playful detail. Some of its images and metaphors are not suitable for children. It contains no hymns, liturgy, oracles or visions—just love songs.

Song of Songs is lighthearted, but not lightheaded. It makes us yearn and blush and smile, but it also makes us meditate on the love of the God who created marriage. To pray its themes is to be opened up to new dimensions of what it means to be in the church, the bride of Christ. These themes point to the center of the faith we confess, that the love that went to the cross "is as strong as death, its jealousy unyielding as the grave. It burns like blazing fire, like a mighty flame" (8:6).

1

Solomon's Song of Songs.

Beloved[a]

²Let him kiss me with the kisses of his
    mouth—
  for your love is more delightful
    than wine.
³Pleasing is the fragrance of your
    perfumes;
  your name is like perfume poured
    out.
  No wonder the maidens love you!
⁴Take me away with you—let us
    hurry!
  Let the king bring me into his
    chambers.

Friends

We rejoice and delight in you[b];
  we will praise your love more than
    wine.

Beloved

How right they are to adore you!

⁵Dark am I, yet lovely,
  O daughters of Jerusalem,
  dark like the tents of Kedar,
  like the tent curtains of Solomon.[c]
⁶Do not stare at me because I
    am dark,
  because I am darkened by the sun.
My mother's sons were angry with me
  and made me take care of the
    vineyards;
  my own vineyard I have neglected.
⁷Tell me, you whom I love, where you
    graze your flock
  and where you rest your sheep at
    midday.
Why should I be like a veiled woman
  beside the flocks of your friends?

Friends

⁸If you do not know, most beautiful of
    women,
  follow the tracks of the sheep
  and graze your young goats
    by the tents of the shepherds.

Lover

⁹I liken you, my darling, to a mare
  harnessed to one of the chariots of
    Pharaoh.

¹⁰Your cheeks are beautiful with
    earrings,
  your neck with strings of jewels.
¹¹We will make you earrings of gold,
  studded with silver.

Beloved

¹²While the king was at his table,
  my perfume spread its fragrance.
¹³My lover is to me a sachet of myrrh
  resting between my breasts.
¹⁴My lover is to me a cluster of henna
    blossoms
  from the vineyards of En Gedi.

Lover

¹⁵How beautiful you are, my darling!
  Oh, how beautiful!
  Your eyes are doves.

Beloved

¹⁶How handsome you are, my lover!
  Oh, how charming!
  And our bed is verdant.

Lover

¹⁷The beams of our house are cedars;
  our rafters are firs.

Beloved[d]

2

I am a rose[e] of Sharon,
  a lily of the valleys.

Lover

²Like a lily among thorns
  is my darling among the maidens.

Beloved

³Like an apple tree among the trees of
    the forest
  is my lover among the young men.
I delight to sit in his shade,
  and his fruit is sweet to my taste.
⁴He has taken me to the banquet hall,
  and his banner over me is love.

---

[a]Primarily on the basis of the gender of the
Hebrew pronouns used, male and female speakers
are indicated in the margins by the captions *Lover*
and *Beloved* respectively. The words of others are
marked *Friends*. In some instances the divisions
and their captions are debatable.
[b]4 The Hebrew is masculine singular.
[c]5 Or *Salma*   [d]1 Or *Lover*   [e]1 Possibly a
member of the crocus family

5 Strengthen me with raisins,
  refresh me with apples,
  for I am faint with love.
6 His left arm is under my head,
  and his right arm embraces me.
7 Daughters of Jerusalem, I charge you
  by the gazelles and by the does of
    the field:
  Do not arouse or awaken love
  until it so desires.

8 Listen! My lover!
  Look! Here he comes,
leaping across the mountains,
  bounding over the hills.
9 My lover is like a gazelle or a young
    stag.
  Look! There he stands behind our
    wall,
gazing through the windows,
  peering through the lattice.
10 My lover spoke and said to me,
  "Arise, my darling,
  my beautiful one, and come
    with me.
11 See! The winter is past;
  the rains are over and gone.
12 Flowers appear on the earth;
  the season of singing has come,
  the cooing of doves
  is heard in our land.
13 The fig tree forms its early fruit;
  the blossoming vines spread their
    fragrance.
  Arise, come, my darling;
  my beautiful one, come with me."

Lover

14 My dove in the clefts of the rock,
  in the hiding places on the
    mountainside,
show me your face,
  let me hear your voice;
  for your voice is sweet,
  and your face is lovely.
15 Catch for us the foxes,
  the little foxes
that ruin the vineyards,
  our vineyards that are in bloom.

Beloved

16 My lover is mine and I am his;
  he browses among the lilies.
17 Until the day breaks
  and the shadows flee,

turn, my lover,
  and be like a gazelle
or like a young stag
  on the rugged hills.ᵃ

3 All night long on my bed
  I looked for the one my heart loves;
  I looked for him but did not find
    him.
2 I will get up now and go about the
    city,
  through its streets and squares;
I will search for the one my heart
    loves.
  So I looked for him but did not find
    him.
3 The watchmen found me
  as they made their rounds in the
    city.
  "Have you seen the one my heart
    loves?"
4 Scarcely had I passed them
  when I found the one my heart
    loves.
  I held him and would not let him go
  till I had brought him to my
    mother's house,
  to the room of the one who
    conceived me.
5 Daughters of Jerusalem, I charge you
  by the gazelles and by the does of
    the field:
  Do not arouse or awaken love
  until it so desires.

6 Who is this coming up from the
    desert
  like a column of smoke,
perfumed with myrrh and incense
  made from all the spices of the
    merchant?
7 Look! It is Solomon's carriage,
  escorted by sixty warriors,
  the noblest of Israel,
8 all of them wearing the sword,
  all experienced in battle,
each with his sword at his side,
  prepared for the terrors of the
    night.
9 King Solomon made for himself the
    carriage;
  he made it of wood from Lebanon.
10 Its posts he made of silver,
  its base of gold.

ᵃ17 Or *the hills of Bether*

SONG OF SONGS 2:7

Passion and Restraint

2:7 DO NOT AROUSE OR AWAKEN LOVE UNTIL IT SO DESIRES.

Three times this plea for restraint appears in Song of Songs (3:5; 8:4), and each time it is preceded by language of intense sexual excitement and longing. Space doesn't allow for exposition of the many images used throughout the Song, but two will illustrate. First, the man says his beloved is like "a mare harnessed to one of the chariots of Pharaoh" (1:9). A mare is a female horse, and Pharaoh's army didn't use mares to pull their chariots; all the horses were male. Anyone familiar with animal husbandry knows the effect the presence of a female horse has on stallions. It can be nothing short of pandemonium. While we may puzzle over such a comparison, the lover's compliment in this poem is vivid and definite. His beloved not only looks good to him, but to others also!

For the Beloved, her Lover is like "a sachet of myrrh resting between my breasts" (1:13). Her image is a little more genteel than his but no less vivid. The sachet is sweet-smelling and pleasing. And this is what the lover is to her and what she wants him to be, literally.

These metaphors of love are but two of many images of sexual excitement and longing found in the book of Song of Songs. Unmarried couples who feel strong love and passion for each other like the Lover and Beloved in this book may learn from the call to restraint also included. The experience of lovemaking is too powerful, too consuming, to begin until the lovers are ready; and no couple is ready until they have made the lifelong covenant of fidelity and love we call marriage. The call for restraint is for the sake of sexual joy. In 2:7, the couple is charged by a solemn oath "by the gazelles and by the does of the field" to hold back. These creatures are symbols of passion (see 4:5; 7:3). The point is this: for the sake of all you desire sexually, be restrained.

Our prayers for the unmarried must be fed by this perspective. So should our encouragements for them to be pure. Also, a good way to pray for sexual purity is to pray with thanksgiving for the gift of sex and praise for the God who gave it.

PRAY:

Dear Father, our sexuality was your good idea;
may we always be thankful and respectful of what you gave.
And may we show our thanks by living lives of purity and holiness—so that
love may be aroused and awakened only when the time is right.

FOR YOUR NEXT DEVOTIONAL READING, GO TO PAGE 797.

Its seat was upholstered with purple,
its interior lovingly inlaid
by[a] the daughters of Jerusalem.
[11] Come out, you daughters of Zion,
and look at King Solomon wearing
the crown,
the crown with which his mother
crowned him
on the day of his wedding,
the day his heart rejoiced.

Lover

4 How beautiful you are, my darling!
Oh, how beautiful!
Your eyes behind your veil are
doves.
Your hair is like a flock of goats
descending from Mount Gilead.
[2] Your teeth are like a flock of sheep
just shorn,
coming up from the washing.
Each has its twin;
not one of them is alone.
[3] Your lips are like a scarlet ribbon;
your mouth is lovely.
Your temples behind your veil
are like the halves of a
pomegranate.
[4] Your neck is like the tower of David,
built with elegance[b];
on it hang a thousand shields,
all of them shields of warriors.
[5] Your two breasts are like two
fawns,
like twin fawns of a gazelle
that browse among the lilies.
[6] Until the day breaks
and the shadows flee,
I will go to the mountain of myrrh
and to the hill of incense.
[7] All beautiful you are, my darling;
there is no flaw in you.

[8] Come with me from Lebanon,
my bride,
come with me from Lebanon.
Descend from the crest of Amana,
from the top of Senir, the summit
of Hermon,
from the lions' dens
and the mountain haunts of the
leopards.
[9] You have stolen my heart, my sister,
my bride;
you have stolen my heart

with one glance of your eyes,
with one jewel of your necklace.
[10] How delightful is your love, my sister,
my bride!
How much more pleasing is your
love than wine,
and the fragrance of your perfume
than any spice!
[11] Your lips drop sweetness as the
honeycomb, my bride;
milk and honey are under your
tongue.
The fragrance of your garments is
like that of Lebanon.
[12] You are a garden locked up, my
sister, my bride;
you are a spring enclosed, a sealed
fountain.
[13] Your plants are an orchard of
pomegranates
with choice fruits,
with henna and nard,
[14] nard and saffron,
calamus and cinnamon,
with every kind of incense tree,
with myrrh and aloes
and all the finest spices.
[15] You are[c] a garden fountain,
a well of flowing water
streaming down from Lebanon.

Beloved

[16] Awake, north wind,
and come, south wind!
Blow on my garden,
that its fragrance may spread
abroad.
Let my lover come into his
garden
and taste its choice fruits.

Lover

5 I have come into my garden,
my sister, my bride;
I have gathered my myrrh with
my spice.
I have eaten my honeycomb and
my honey;
I have drunk my wine and
my milk.

---

[a]10 Or *its inlaid interior a gift of love / from*
[b]4 The meaning of the Hebrew for this word is
uncertain.   [c]15 Or *I am* (spoken by the
Beloved)

Friends

Eat, O friends, and drink;
 drink your fill, O lovers.

Beloved

²I slept but my heart was awake.
 Listen! My lover is knocking:
"Open to me, my sister, my darling,
 my dove, my flawless one.
My head is drenched with dew,
 my hair with the dampness of
 the night."
³I have taken off my robe—
 must I put it on again?
I have washed my feet—
 must I soil them again?
⁴My lover thrust his hand through the
 latch-opening;
 my heart began to pound for him.
⁵I arose to open for my lover,
 and my hands dripped with myrrh,
 my fingers with flowing myrrh,
 on the handles of the lock.
⁶I opened for my lover,
 but my lover had left; he was gone.
 My heart sank at his departure.ª
I looked for him but did not find him.
 I called him but he did not answer.
⁷The watchmen found me
 as they made their rounds in
 the city.
They beat me, they bruised me;
 they took away my cloak,
 those watchmen of the walls!
⁸O daughters of Jerusalem, I charge
 you—
 if you find my lover,
what will you tell him?
 Tell him I am faint with love.

Friends

⁹How is your beloved better than
 others,
 most beautiful of women?
How is your beloved better than
 others,
 that you charge us so?

Beloved

¹⁰My lover is radiant and ruddy,
 outstanding among ten thousand.
¹¹His head is purest gold;
 his hair is wavy
 and black as a raven.

¹²His eyes are like doves
 by the water streams,
washed in milk,
 mounted like jewels.
¹³His cheeks are like beds of spice
 yielding perfume.
His lips are like lilies
 dripping with myrrh.
¹⁴His arms are rods of gold
 set with chrysolite.
His body is like polished ivory
 decorated with sapphires.ᵇ
¹⁵His legs are pillars of marble
 set on bases of pure gold.
His appearance is like Lebanon,
 choice as its cedars.
¹⁶His mouth is sweetness itself;
 he is altogether lovely.
This is my lover, this my friend,
 O daughters of Jerusalem.

Friends

6 Where has your lover gone,
 most beautiful of women?
Which way did your lover turn,
 that we may look for him with you?

Beloved

²My lover has gone down to his
 garden,
 to the beds of spices,
to browse in the gardens
 and to gather lilies.
³I am my lover's and my lover is mine;
 he browses among the lilies.

Lover

⁴You are beautiful, my darling, as
 Tirzah,
lovely as Jerusalem,
 majestic as troops with banners.
⁵Turn your eyes from me;
 they overwhelm me.
Your hair is like a flock of goats
 descending from Gilead.
⁶Your teeth are like a flock of sheep
 coming up from the washing.
Each has its twin,
 not one of them is alone.
⁷Your temples behind your veil
 are like the halves of a
 pomegranate.

ª6 Or *heart had gone out to him when he spoke*
ᵇ14 Or *lapis lazuli*

⁸Sixty queens there may be,
  and eighty concubines,
  and virgins beyond number;
⁹but my dove, my perfect one, is
    unique,
  the only daughter of her mother,
  the favorite of the one who
    bore her.
The maidens saw her and called
    her blessed;
  the queens and concubines
    praised her.

Friends

¹⁰Who is this that appears like the
    dawn,
  fair as the moon, bright as the sun,
  majestic as the stars in procession?

Lover

¹¹I went down to the grove of nut trees
  to look at the new growth in
    the valley,
  to see if the vines had budded
  or the pomegranates were in
    bloom.
¹²Before I realized it,
  my desire set me among the royal
    chariots of my people.[a]

Friends

¹³Come back, come back,
  O Shulammite;
  come back, come back, that we
    may gaze on you!

Lover

Why would you gaze on the
    Shulammite
  as on the dance of Mahanaim?

7 How beautiful your sandaled feet,
    O prince's daughter!
Your graceful legs are like jewels,
  the work of a craftsman's hands.
²Your navel is a rounded goblet
  that never lacks blended wine.
Your waist is a mound of wheat
  encircled by lilies.
³Your breasts are like two fawns,
  twins of a gazelle.
⁴Your neck is like an ivory tower.
Your eyes are the pools of Heshbon
  by the gate of Bath Rabbim.

Your nose is like the tower of
    Lebanon
  looking toward Damascus.
⁵Your head crowns you like Mount
    Carmel.
Your hair is like royal tapestry;
  the king is held captive by its
    tresses.
⁶How beautiful you are and how
    pleasing,
  O love, with your delights!
⁷Your stature is like that of the palm,
  and your breasts like clusters of
    fruit.
⁸I said, "I will climb the palm tree;
  I will take hold of its fruit."
May your breasts be like the clusters
    of the vine,
  the fragrance of your breath like
    apples,
⁹   and your mouth like the best wine.

Beloved

May the wine go straight to my lover,
  flowing gently over lips and teeth.[b]
¹⁰I belong to my lover,
  and his desire is for me.
¹¹Come, my lover, let us go to the
    countryside,
  let us spend the night in the
    villages.[c]
¹²Let us go early to the vineyards
  to see if the vines have budded,
  if their blossoms have opened,
  and if the pomegranates are in
    bloom—
  there I will give you my love.
¹³The mandrakes send out their
    fragrance,
  and at our door is every delicacy,
both new and old,
  that I have stored up for you, my
    lover.

8 If only you were to me like a
    brother,
  who was nursed at my mother's
    breasts!
Then, if I found you outside,
  I would kiss you,
  and no one would despise me.

---

[a]12 Or *among the chariots of Amminadab*; or
among the chariots of the people of the prince
[b]9 Septuagint, Aquila, Vulgate and Syriac;
Hebrew *lips of sleepers*   [c]11 Or *henna bushes*

The Power of Love

8:6 PLACE ME LIKE A SEAL OVER YOUR HEART.

Lovers sometimes ask each other, "How much do you love me?" The greatest answer is, "I love you enough to marry you." Song of Songs 8:6–7 speaks of marital love as the most powerful and indomitable of all human affections. It asks to be placed "like a seal over your heart." A seal was a personal stamp, the image pressed by a signet ring into the wax that sealed and guaranteed the contents of the scroll to be the owner's. "Let me be pressed into your heart that way," is what marital love asks.

To love someone enough to marry that person is to commit to a kind of love that "is as strong as death." Death is total—one can't be a little bit dead or mostly dead; either you're dead or you're not. Death is final—the dead have no further plans for themselves, no more options. Death is irreversible—there is no turning back. Death is permanent, and so is love, for "Love never fails . . . And now these three remain: faith, hope and love. But the greatest of these is love" (1 Corinthians 13:8,13).

A poplular story tells of a person asking Jesus, "How much do you love me?" He replies, "This much," and then he stretched out his arms and died. Other kinds of human love are compared to the love of Christ, friendship being one of them (see John 15:12–14). But marital love has special status as the most characteristic of God's love for his church (see Ephesians 5:22–33). The Bible is indeed a book about marriage.

Our text doesn't mention that the arena in which this powerful love is lived out is often mundane. It's easy to see love in dreams about a future spent together; it's harder to see love amid diapers, packed schedules, sickness, disappointment and misunderstanding. But this is where prayer becomes so important because prayer is mundane too. Like marital love, so much of it is just being there, showing up day by day; it too is a daily kind of dying to the kingdom of self.

PRAY:

My dear Savior, you have set me like a seal over your heart.

Your love for me is even stronger than death.

All praise and honor be to your holy name!

Strengthen me to love others this way.

FOR YOUR NEXT DEVOTIONAL READING, GO TO PAGE 804.

² I would lead you
  and bring you to my mother's
    house—
  she who has taught me.
  I would give you spiced wine to drink,
    the nectar of my pomegranates.
³ His left arm is under my head
  and his right arm embraces me.
⁴ Daughters of Jerusalem, I charge you:
  Do not arouse or awaken love
    until it so desires.

Friends

⁵ Who is this coming up from the
    desert
  leaning on her lover?

Beloved

  Under the apple tree I roused you;
    there your mother conceived
      you,
    there she who was in labor gave
      you birth.
⁶ Place me like a seal over your heart,
    like a seal on your arm;
  for love is as strong as death,
    its jealousy*a* unyielding as the
      grave.*b*
  It burns like blazing fire,
    like a mighty flame.*c*
⁷ Many waters cannot quench love;
    rivers cannot wash it away.
  If one were to give
    all the wealth of his house for love,
    it*d* would be utterly scorned.

Friends

⁸ We have a young sister,
    and her breasts are not yet grown.
  What shall we do for our sister
    for the day she is spoken for?
⁹ If she is a wall,
    we will build towers of silver on her.
  If she is a door,
    we will enclose her with panels of
      cedar.

Beloved

¹⁰ I am a wall,
    and my breasts are like towers.
  Thus I have become in his eyes
    like one bringing contentment.
¹¹ Solomon had a vineyard in Baal
      Hamon;
  he let out his vineyard to tenants.
  Each was to bring for its fruit
    a thousand shekels*e* of silver.
¹² But my own vineyard is mine to give;
    the thousand shekels are for you,
      O Solomon,
  and two hundred*f* are for those
    who tend its fruit.

Lover

¹³ You who dwell in the gardens
    with friends in attendance,
  let me hear your voice!

Beloved

¹⁴ Come away, my lover,
    and be like a gazelle
  or like a young stag
    on the spice-laden mountains.

---

*a*6 Or *ardor*   *b*6 Hebrew *Sheol*   *c*6 Or / like
the very flame of the Lord   *d*7 Or *he*
*e*11 That is, about 25 pounds (about 11.5
kilograms); also in verse 12   *f*12 That is, about
5 pounds (about 2.3 kilograms)

Isaiah

LORD KENNETH CLARK, narrator of television's *Civilization*, once told a reporter, "I still go to the Chartres Cathedral each year and to the Parthenon every three years. Very good. Keeps your standards high." What is true of Chartres and the Parthenon is true of God. To gaze steadily and lovingly at the God of Scripture is to raise the standards of what is true, good and lovely. Our standards will never be higher than our view of God. Nor will our lives.

The prophet Isaiah has been called the theologian of the Old Testament because of his exalted descriptions of God. His call came out of a stunning and profoundly unsettling vision of God's holiness (see Isaiah 6). And Isaiah 40 is one of the greatest proclamations of the grandeur of God in all of prophetic literature. But with his apprehension of God's greatness, Isaiah is still a pastor-theologian, able to see the practical implications of serving such a God. Many have found hope and encouragement in passages from this book. To renew the sense of his calling, a dispirited pastor once hiked through the Grand Canyon, memorizing and praying Isaiah 40. He was never the same after that time.

"FOR MY HOUSE WILL BE CALLED A HOUSE OF PRAYER FOR ALL NATIONS." (56:7)

Isaiah's consciousness, like that of all the prophets, placed him in a universe dominated by God's presence. In this sense, the prophets were the most blessedly unbalanced of people. They were like magnifying glasses held at just the right angle to focus sunlight intensely on one spot. They were spiritual arsonists, starting fires when they spoke. Their prophecies ignited the people and culture of their day, and do so even now. Read and pray the prophets at your own risk; it doesn't take much exposure to catch fire.

1 The vision concerning Judah and Jerusalem that Isaiah son of Amoz saw during the reigns of Uzziah, Jotham, Ahaz and Hezekiah, kings of Judah.

A Rebellious Nation

2 Hear, O heavens! Listen, O earth!
   For the LORD has spoken:
"I reared children and brought
      them up,
   but they have rebelled
      against me.
3 The ox knows his master,
   the donkey his owner's manger,
but Israel does not know,
   my people do not understand."

4 Ah, sinful nation,
   a people loaded with guilt,
a brood of evildoers,
   children given to corruption!
They have forsaken the LORD;
   they have spurned the Holy One
      of Israel
   and turned their backs on him.

5 Why should you be beaten anymore?
   Why do you persist in rebellion?
Your whole head is injured,
   your whole heart afflicted.
6 From the sole of your foot to the top
      of your head
   there is no soundness—
only wounds and welts
   and open sores,
not cleansed or bandaged
   or soothed with oil.

> 66 Trouble and perplexity drive me to
> prayer, and prayer drives away perplexity
> and trouble. 99
>
> PHILIP MELANCHTHEN

7 Your country is desolate,
   your cities burned with fire;
your fields are being stripped by
      foreigners
   right before you,
   laid waste as when overthrown by
      strangers.
8 The Daughter of Zion is left
   like a shelter in a vineyard,
like a hut in a field of melons,
   like a city under siege.

9 Unless the LORD Almighty
      had left us some survivors,
   we would have become like Sodom,
   we would have been like
      Gomorrah.

10 Hear the word of the LORD,
   you rulers of Sodom;
listen to the law of our God,
   you people of Gomorrah!
11 "The multitude of your sacrifices—
   what are they to me?" says the
      LORD.
"I have more than enough of burnt
      offerings,
   of rams and the fat of fattened
      animals;
I have no pleasure
   in the blood of bulls and lambs
      and goats.
12 When you come to appear before
      me,
   who has asked this of you,
   this trampling of my courts?
13 Stop bringing meaningless offerings!
   Your incense is detestable to me.
New Moons, Sabbaths and
      convocations—
   I cannot bear your evil assemblies.
14 Your New Moon festivals and your
      appointed feasts
   my soul hates.
They have become a burden to me;
   I am weary of bearing them.
15 When you spread out your hands in
      prayer,
   I will hide my eyes from you;
even if you offer many prayers,
   I will not listen.
Your hands are full of blood;
16 wash and make yourselves clean.
Take your evil deeds
   out of my sight!
Stop doing wrong,
17 learn to do right!
Seek justice,
   encourage the oppressed.[a]
Defend the cause of the fatherless,
   plead the case of the widow.
18 "Come now, let us reason together,"
   says the LORD.
"Though your sins are like scarlet,
   they shall be as white as snow;

a 17 Or / rebuke the oppressor

though they are red as crimson,
they shall be like wool.
¹⁹ If you are willing and obedient,
you will eat the best from the land;
²⁰ but if you resist and rebel,
you will be devoured by the sword."
For the mouth of the LORD
has spoken.

²¹ See how the faithful city
has become a harlot!
She once was full of justice;
righteousness used to dwell
in her—
but now murderers!
²² Your silver has become dross,
your choice wine is diluted with
water.
²³ Your rulers are rebels,
companions of thieves;
they all love bribes
and chase after gifts.
They do not defend the cause of the
fatherless;
the widow's case does not come
before them.
²⁴ Therefore the Lord, the LORD
Almighty,
the Mighty One of Israel, declares:
"Ah, I will get relief from my foes
and avenge myself on my enemies.
²⁵ I will turn my hand against you;
I will thoroughly purge away
your dross
and remove all your impurities.
²⁶ I will restore your judges as in days
of old,
your counselors as at the
beginning.
Afterward you will be called
the City of Righteousness,
the Faithful City."

²⁷ Zion will be redeemed with justice,
her penitent ones with
righteousness.
²⁸ But rebels and sinners will both be
broken,
and those who forsake the LORD
will perish.

²⁹ "You will be ashamed because of the
sacred oaks
in which you have delighted;
you will be disgraced because of the
gardens
that you have chosen.

³⁰ You will be like an oak with fading
leaves,
like a garden without water.
³¹ The mighty man will become
tinder
and his work a spark;
both will burn together,
with no one to quench the fire."

The Mountain of the LORD

2 This is what Isaiah son of Amoz saw
concerning Judah and Jerusalem:

² In the last days

the mountain of the LORD's temple
will be established
as chief among the mountains;
it will be raised above the hills,
and all nations will stream to it.

³ Many peoples will come and say,

"Come, let us go up to the mountain
of the LORD,
to the house of the God of Jacob.
He will teach us his ways,
so that we may walk in his paths."
The law will go out from Zion,
the word of the LORD from
Jerusalem.
⁴ He will judge between the nations
and will settle disputes for many
peoples.
They will beat their swords into
plowshares
and their spears into pruning
hooks.
Nation will not take up sword against
nation,
nor will they train for war anymore.

⁵ Come, O house of Jacob,
let us walk in the light of the LORD.

The Day of the LORD

⁶ You have abandoned your people,
the house of Jacob.
They are full of superstitions from
the East;
they practice divination like the
Philistines
and clasp hands with pagans.
⁷ Their land is full of silver and gold;
there is no end to their treasures.
Their land is full of horses;
there is no end to their chariots.

⁸Their land is full of idols;
they bow down to the work of their
hands,
to what their fingers have made.
⁹So man will be brought low
and mankind humbled—
do not forgive them.ª

¹⁰Go into the rocks,
hide in the ground
from dread of the LORD
and the splendor of his majesty!
¹¹The eyes of the arrogant man will be
humbled
and the pride of men brought low;
the LORD alone will be exalted in
that day.

¹²The LORD Almighty has a day in store
for all the proud and lofty,
for all that is exalted
(and they will be humbled),
¹³for all the cedars of Lebanon, tall and
lofty,
and all the oaks of Bashan,
¹⁴for all the towering mountains
and all the high hills,
¹⁵for every lofty tower
and every fortified wall,
¹⁶for every trading shipᵇ
and every stately vessel.
¹⁷The arrogance of man will be
brought low
and the pride of men humbled;
the LORD alone will be exalted in that
day,
¹⁸ and the idols will totally disappear.

¹⁹Men will flee to caves in the rocks
and to holes in the ground
from dread of the LORD
and the splendor of his majesty,
when he rises to shake the earth.
²⁰In that day men will throw away
to the rodents and bats
their idols of silver and idols of gold,
which they made to worship.
²¹They will flee to caverns in the rocks
and to the overhanging crags
from dread of the LORD
and the splendor of his majesty,
when he rises to shake the earth.

²²Stop trusting in man,
who has but a breath in his
nostrils.
Of what account is he?

Judgment on Jerusalem and Judah

3 See now, the Lord,
the LORD Almighty,
is about to take from Jerusalem and
Judah
both supply and support:
all supplies of food and all supplies
of water,
²   the hero and warrior,
the judge and prophet,
the soothsayer and elder,
³the captain of fifty and man of rank,
the counselor, skilled craftsman
and clever enchanter.

⁴I will make boys their officials;
mere children will govern them.
⁵People will oppress each other—
man against man, neighbor against
neighbor.
The young will rise up against the
old,
the base against the honorable.

⁶A man will seize one of his brothers
at his father's home, and say,
"You have a cloak, you be our leader;
take charge of this heap of ruins!"
⁷But in that day he will cry out,
"I have no remedy.
I have no food or clothing in my
house;
do not make me the leader of the
people."

⁸Jerusalem staggers,
Judah is falling;
their words and deeds are against
the LORD,
defying his glorious presence.
⁹The look on their faces testifies
against them;
they parade their sin like Sodom;
they do not hide it.
Woe to them!
They have brought disaster upon
themselves.

¹⁰Tell the righteous it will be well
with them,
for they will enjoy the fruit of
their deeds.
¹¹Woe to the wicked! Disaster is upon
them!

ª9 Or *not raise them up*   ᵇ16 Hebrew *every
ship of Tarshish*

They will be paid back for what their
hands have done.
12 Youths oppress my people,
women rule over them.
O my people, your guides lead you
astray;
they turn you from the path.
13 The LORD takes his place in court;
he rises to judge the people.
14 The LORD enters into judgment
against the elders and leaders of
his people:
"It is you who have ruined my
vineyard;
the plunder from the poor is in
your houses.
15 What do you mean by crushing
my people
and grinding the faces of the
poor?"
declares the Lord,
the LORD Almighty.

16 The LORD says,
"The women of Zion are haughty,
walking along with outstretched
necks,
flirting with their eyes,
tripping along with mincing steps,
with ornaments jingling on their
ankles.
17 Therefore the Lord will bring sores
on the heads of the women
of Zion;
the LORD will make their scalps
bald."

18 In that day the Lord will snatch away
their finery: the bangles and headbands
and crescent necklaces, 19 the earrings
and bracelets and veils, 20 the headdress-
es and ankle chains and sashes, the perfume bottles and charms, 21 the signet
rings and nose rings, 22 the fine robes and
the capes and cloaks, the purses 23 and
mirrors, and the linen garments and ti-
aras and shawls.

24 Instead of fragrance there will be
a stench;
instead of a sash, a rope;
instead of well-dressed hair,
baldness;
instead of fine clothing, sackcloth;
instead of beauty, branding.

25 Your men will fall by the sword,
your warriors in battle.
26 The gates of Zion will lament and
mourn;
destitute, she will sit on the
ground.

4 In that day seven women
will take hold of one man
and say, "We will eat our own food
and provide our own clothes;
only let us be called by your name.
Take away our disgrace!"

The Branch of the LORD

2 In that day the Branch of the LORD will
be beautiful and glorious, and the fruit
of the land will be the pride and glory of
the survivors in Israel. 3 Those who are
left in Zion, who remain in Jerusalem,
will be called holy, all who are recorded
among the living in Jerusalem. 4 The Lord
will wash away the filth of the women of
Zion; he will cleanse the bloodstains
from Jerusalem by a spirit[a] of judgment
and a spirit[a] of fire. 5 Then the LORD will
create over all of Mount Zion and over
those who assemble there a cloud of
smoke by day and a glow of flaming fire
by night; over all the glory will be a canopy. 6 It will be a shelter and shade from
the heat of the day, and a refuge and hiding place from the storm and rain.

The Song of the Vineyard

5 I will sing for the one I love
a song about his vineyard:
My loved one had a vineyard
on a fertile hillside.
2 He dug it up and cleared it of stones
and planted it with the choicest
vines.
He built a watchtower in it
and cut out a winepress as well.
Then he looked for a crop of good
grapes,
but it yielded only bad fruit.

3 "Now you dwellers in Jerusalem and
men of Judah,
judge between me and my vineyard.
4 What more could have been done for
my vineyard
than I have done for it?

a4 Or the Spirit

ANDREW MURRAY (1828–1917)

Take the Time

AS A YOUNG MAN, Andrew Murray spent a lot of time on horseback, riding for weeks of uninterrupted ministry in the sun-baked South African territory of Bloemfontein, an area covering 50,000 square miles. Boers (Dutch-speaking South African farmers) traveled great distances to hear the famous Murray preach. Barely into his 20s and with a frail frame, Murray earned the nickname "the boy preacher." One Dutch farmer, upon seeing Murray for the first time, was overheard saying, "Why, they have lent us a girl to preach to us."[1]

Murray grew up in South Africa, the child of a Dutch Reformed preacher. When he was ten years old, he left home and traveled to Scotland for schooling. His interest in theology and revival prompted him to seek further education in Holland and Germany before returning to South Africa to begin his career as a preacher.

People flocked to hear him speak. He saw conversions at nearly every service. Because of his evangelistic successes, he felt a growing conflict with "pride and self complacency . . . in my heart." Soon Murray found himself too sick to travel or to preach. Hours spent traveling were replaced by hours of quiet waiting on God. Murray's daughter later wrote of this period in his life: "It was after this 'time of silence' when God came so near to [Murray] and he saw more clearly the meaning of a life of full surrender and simple faith. He began to show in all relationships that constant tenderness and unruffled lovingkindness and unselfish thought for others which increasingly characterized his life from that point. At the same time he lost nothing of his strength and determination."

The years that followed were richly productive. Revival came to his church, which led to an invitation to speak at the Keswick and Northfield Conventions. His involvement with these movements led eventually to a prayer movement for worldwide revival. The Welsh revivals of the early 1900s traced their roots back to the Keswick Convention. Missionaries such as James Hudson Taylor, A. T. Pierson and Samuel Zwemer considered the Keswick Convention to be "hunting grounds" for the new generation of missionary recruits.

But Andrew Murray never forgot the lessons of quiet waiting in his youth. His life was sustained by a perpetual hunger for God's presence. His cry was a constant call back to that still place where the soul meets the Word of God: "Take time to read his Word as in his presence, that from it you may know what he asks of you and what he promises you. Let the Word create around you, create within you a holy atmosphere, a holy heavenly light, in which your soul will be refreshed and strengthened for the work of daily life."[2]

P R A Y :

Pray this prayer of Andrew Murray: "May not a single moment
of my life be spent outside the light, love and joy of God's presence
and may not a moment be without the entire surrender of my self
as a vessel for him to fill full of his Spirit and his love."[3]

M E M O R I Z E :

Epaphras, who is one of you and a servant of Christ Jesus,
sends greetings. He is always wrestling in prayer for you,
that you may stand firm in all the will of God, mature
and fully assured. COLOSSIANS 4:12

FOR YOUR NEXT DEVOTIONAL READING, GO TO PAGE 808.

When I looked for good grapes,
  why did it yield only bad?
⁵ Now I will tell you
  what I am going to do to my
    vineyard:
I will take away its hedge,
  and it will be destroyed;
I will break down its wall,
  and it will be trampled.
⁶ I will make it a wasteland,
  neither pruned nor cultivated,
  and briers and thorns will grow
    there.
I will command the clouds
  not to rain on it."

⁷ The vineyard of the LORD Almighty
  is the house of Israel,
and the men of Judah
  are the garden of his delight.
And he looked for justice, but saw
    bloodshed;
  for righteousness, but heard cries
    of distress.

Woes and Judgments

⁸ Woe to you who add house to house
  and join field to field
till no space is left
  and you live alone in the land.

⁹ The LORD Almighty has declared in my
hearing:

"Surely the great houses will become
    desolate,
  the fine mansions left without
    occupants.
¹⁰ A ten-acre*a* vineyard will produce
    only a bath*b* of wine,
  a homer*c* of seed only an ephah*d*
    of grain."

¹¹ Woe to those who rise early in the
    morning
  to run after their drinks,
who stay up late at night
  till they are inflamed with wine.
¹² They have harps and lyres at their
    banquets,
  tambourines and flutes and wine,
but they have no regard for the deeds
    of the LORD,
  no respect for the work of his
    hands.
¹³ Therefore my people will go into exile
  for lack of understanding;

their men of rank will die of hunger
  and their masses will be parched
    with thirst.
¹⁴ Therefore the grave*e* enlarges its
    appetite
  and opens its mouth without limit;
into it will descend their nobles and
    masses
  with all their brawlers and revelers.
¹⁵ So man will be brought low
  and mankind humbled,
  the eyes of the arrogant humbled.
¹⁶ But the LORD Almighty will be exalted
    by his justice,
  and the holy God will show himself
    holy by his righteousness.
¹⁷ Then sheep will graze as in their own
    pasture;
  lambs will feed*f* among the ruins
    of the rich.

¹⁸ Woe to those who draw sin along
    with cords of deceit,
  and wickedness as with cart ropes,
¹⁹ to those who say, "Let God hurry,
  let him hasten his work
    so we may see it.
Let it approach,
  let the plan of the Holy One of
    Israel come,
    so we may know it."

²⁰ Woe to those who call evil good
    and good evil,
who put darkness for light
    and light for darkness,
who put bitter for sweet
    and sweet for bitter.

²¹ Woe to those who are wise in their
    own eyes
  and clever in their own sight.

²² Woe to those who are heroes at
    drinking wine
  and champions at mixing drinks,
²³ who acquit the guilty for a bribe,
  but deny justice to the innocent.
²⁴ Therefore, as tongues of fire lick
    up straw

---

a 10 Hebrew *ten-yoke,* that is, the land plowed by
10 yoke of oxen in one day   *b 10* That is,
probably about 6 gallons (about 22 liters)
c 10 That is, probably about 6 bushels (about 220
liters)   *d 10* That is, probably about 3/5 bushel
(about 22 liters)   *e 14* Hebrew *Sheol*
f 17 Septuagint; Hebrew / *strangers will eat*

and as dry grass sinks down in the
flames,
so their roots will decay
and their flowers blow away like
dust;
for they have rejected the law of the
LORD Almighty
and spurned the word of the Holy
One of Israel.
²⁵ Therefore the LORD's anger burns
against his people;
his hand is raised and he strikes
them down.
The mountains shake,
and the dead bodies are like refuse
in the streets.

Yet for all this, his anger is not turned
away,
his hand is still upraised.

²⁶ He lifts up a banner for the distant
nations,
he whistles for those at the ends of
the earth.
Here they come,
swiftly and speedily!
²⁷ Not one of them grows tired or
stumbles,
not one slumbers or sleeps;
not a belt is loosened at the waist,
not a sandal thong is broken.
²⁸ Their arrows are sharp,
all their bows are strung;
their horses' hoofs seem like flint,
their chariot wheels like a
whirlwind.
²⁹ Their roar is like that of the lion,
they roar like young lions;
they growl as they seize their prey
and carry it off with no one to
rescue.
³⁰ In that day they will roar over it
like the roaring of the sea.
And if one looks at the land,
he will see darkness and distress;
even the light will be darkened by
the clouds.

Isaiah's Commission

6 In the year that King Uzziah died, I
saw the Lord seated on a throne,
high and exalted, and the train of his
robe filled the temple. ²Above him were
seraphs, each with six wings: With two
wings they covered their faces, with two

they covered their feet, and with two
they were flying. ³And they were calling
to one another:

"Holy, holy, holy is the LORD
Almighty;
the whole earth is full of his glory."

⁴At the sound of their voices the doorposts and thresholds shook and the temple was filled with smoke.
⁵"Woe to me!" I cried. "I am ruined!
For I am a man of unclean lips, and I
live among a people of unclean lips,
and my eyes have seen the King, the
LORD Almighty."
⁶Then one of the seraphs flew to me
with a live coal in his hand, which he had
taken with tongs from the altar. ⁷With it
he touched my mouth and said, "See,
this has touched your lips; your guilt is
taken away and your sin atoned for."
⁸Then I heard the voice of the Lord saying, "Whom shall I send? And who will
go for us?"
And I said, "Here am I. Send me!"
⁹He said, "Go and tell this people:

" 'Be ever hearing, but never
understanding;
be ever seeing, but never
perceiving.'
¹⁰ Make the heart of this people
calloused;
make their ears dull
and close their eyes.ᵃ
Otherwise they might see with their
eyes,
hear with their ears,
understand with their hearts,
and turn and be healed."

¹¹Then I said, "For how long, O Lord?"
And he answered:

"Until the cities lie ruined
and without inhabitant,
until the houses are left deserted
and the fields ruined and ravaged,
¹² until the LORD has sent everyone far
away
and the land is utterly forsaken.

ᵃ9,10 Hebrew; Septuagint 'You will be ever
hearing, but never understanding; / you will be
ever seeing, but never perceiving.' / ¹⁰This
people's heart has become calloused; / they hardly
hear with their ears, / and they have closed their
eyes

¹³ And though a tenth remains in the
   land,
   it will again be laid waste.
But as the terebinth and oak
   leave stumps when they are cut
   down,
   so the holy seed will be the stump
   in the land."

The Sign of Immanuel

7 When Ahaz son of Jotham, the son of
Uzziah, was king of Judah, King Rezin of Aram and Pekah son of Remaliah
king of Israel marched up to fight
against Jerusalem, but they could not
overpower it.

²Now the house of David was told,

[MONDAY]

Holy Terror

6:1 I SAW THE LORD.

Why should Isaiah's awe-filled experience with God's holiness matter to us?
First, God's holiness is his most essential quality, more essential than even
his love and justice. *Holy* is the word that modifies everything else about
God: His love is a holy love, his justice is holy justice. We cannot understand
God's love until we understand his holiness.

Second, Jesus said the first thing we should pray for is that we and others would know and honor God's holiness. "This, then, is how you should
pray: 'Our Father in heaven, hallowed be your name'" (Matthew 6:9). "Hallowed" is another word for *holy*. "Hallowed be your name" means, "May
your name be held as holy, regarded and spoken and worshiped as holy."

Third, holiness is not only God's essential quality but is also our calling.
"Just as he who called you is holy, so be holy in all you do; for it is written:
'Be holy, because I am holy'" (1 Peter 1:15–16). Our calling to be holy
should create a tension in us that is both terrifying and thrilling. The terrifying part is that we are not holy, as Isaiah so shatteringly realized. But we are
called to be what we, by virtue of our fallen nature, are not! Yet that is the
thrilling part, for just as the seraphs flew to Isaiah with a live coal from the
altar and touched it to his lips, so God wills to make us holy. The saying that
"God loves us just as we are, but too much to let us stay the way we are" is
exactly true. "To ask that God's love should be content with us as we are is
to ask that God should cease to be God: because he is what he is, his love
must, in the nature of things, be impeded and repelled by certain strains in
our present character, and because he already loves us he must labor to
make us lovable . . . Love may forgive all infirmities and love still in spite of
them: but Love cannot cease to will their removal. Love is more sensitive
than hatred itself to every blemish of the beloved . . . Of all powers he forgives most, but he condones least: he is pleased with little, but demands all"
(C. S. Lewis).⁴

P R A Y :

Holy Father! You have called me to be holy because I belong to you.
May it be so; you have my trembling permission to make me so.

FOR YOUR NEXT DEVOTIONAL READING, GO TO PAGE 810.

"Aram has allied itself with[a] Ephraim"; so the hearts of Ahaz and his people were shaken, as the trees of the forest are shaken by the wind.

[3]Then the LORD said to Isaiah, "Go out, you and your son Shear-Jashub,[b] to meet Ahaz at the end of the aqueduct of the Upper Pool, on the road to the Washerman's Field. [4]Say to him, 'Be careful, keep calm and don't be afraid. Do not lose heart because of these two smoldering stubs of firewood—because of the fierce anger of Rezin and Aram and of the son of Remaliah. [5]Aram, Ephraim and Remaliah's son have plotted your ruin, saying, [6]"Let us invade Judah; let us tear it apart and divide it among ourselves, and make the son of Tabeel king over it." [7]Yet this is what the Sovereign LORD says:

" 'It will not take place,
    it will not happen,
[8]for the head of Aram is Damascus,
    and the head of Damascus is only
      Rezin.
Within sixty-five years
    Ephraim will be too shattered to
      be a people.
[9]The head of Ephraim is Samaria,
    and the head of Samaria is only
      Remaliah's son.
If you do not stand firm in your
      faith,
    you will not stand at all.' "

[10]Again the LORD spoke to Ahaz, [11]"Ask the LORD your God for a sign, whether in the deepest depths or in the highest heights."

[12]But Ahaz said, "I will not ask; I will not put the LORD to the test."

[13]Then Isaiah said, "Hear now, you house of David! Is it not enough to try the patience of men? Will you try the patience of my God also? [14]Therefore the Lord himself will give you[c] a sign: The virgin will be with child and will give birth to a son, and[d] will call him Immanuel.[e] [15]He will eat curds and honey when he knows enough to reject the wrong and choose the right. [16]But before the boy knows enough to reject the wrong and choose the right, the land of the two kings you dread will be laid waste. [17]The LORD will bring on you and on your peo-

ple and on the house of your father a time unlike any since Ephraim broke away from Judah—he will bring the king of Assyria."

[18]In that day the LORD will whistle for flies from the distant streams of Egypt and for bees from the land of Assyria. [19]They will all come and settle in the steep ravines and in the crevices in the rocks, on all the thornbushes and at all the water holes. [20]In that day the Lord will use a razor hired from beyond the River[f]—the king of Assyria—to shave your head and the hair of your legs, and to take off your beards also. [21]In that day, a man will keep alive a young cow and two goats. [22]And because of the abundance of the milk they give, he will have curds to eat. All who remain in the land will eat curds and honey. [23]In that day, in every place where there were a thousand vines worth a thousand silver shekels,[g] there will be only briers and thorns. [24]Men will go there with bow and arrow, for the land will be covered with briers and thorns. [25]As for all the hills once cultivated by the hoe, you will no longer go there for fear of the briers and thorns; they will become places where cattle are turned loose and where sheep run.

Assyria, the LORD's Instrument

8 The LORD said to me, "Take a large scroll and write on it with an ordinary pen: Maher-Shalal-Hash-Baz.[h] [2]And I will call in Uriah the priest and Zechariah son of Jeberekiah as reliable witnesses for me."

[3]Then I went to the prophetess, and she conceived and gave birth to a son. And the LORD said to me, "Name him Maher-Shalal-Hash-Baz. [4]Before the boy knows how to say 'My father' or 'My mother,' the wealth of Damascus and the plunder of Samaria will be carried off by the king of Assyria."

[a]2 Or has set up camp in   [b]3 Shear-Jashub means a remnant will return.   [c]14 The Hebrew is plural.   [d]14 Masoretic Text; Dead Sea Scrolls and he or and they   [e]14 Immanuel means God with us.   [f]20 That is, the Euphrates   [g]23 That is, about 25 pounds (about 11.5 kilograms)   [h]1 Maher-Shalal-Hash-Baz means quick to the plunder, swift to the spoil; also in verse 3.

⁵The LORD spoke to me again:

⁶ "Because this people has rejected
the gently flowing waters of
Shiloah
and rejoices over Rezin
and the son of Remaliah,

⁷therefore the Lord is about to bring
against them
the mighty floodwaters of the
River*—
the king of Assyria with all his pomp.

*7 That is, the Euphrates

ISAIAH 7:10–17

Testing God's Goodness

7:12 "I WILL NOT PUT THE LORD TO THE TEST."

There are two ways to put God to the test. The first way is to say to God: "I won't trust you until you show you can be trusted." This is what happened when the Israelites were traveling in the desert. They needed to trust God to provide water for them (see Exodus 17:1). The Israelites had learned previously that God was trustworthy. He had miraculously delivered them by bringing ten plagues upon their oppressors, the Egyptians. He had wondrously parted the Red Sea. He had provided them with daily manna. And he had supernaturally provided water for them once before—when he had Moses turn bitter water into sweet by throwing a piece of wood into it (see Exodus 15:22–25). The Lord had tested his people (see Exodus 15:25; 16:4); but now the Israelites flunked the test by putting God to the test (see Exodus 17:2–7). They grumbled and complained so much that their sin was memorialized in two psalms (see Psalm 81:7–8; 95:8–9). Their sin was unbelief.

The second way to put the Lord to the test is to do what Ahaz did in this text. God wanted to give Ahaz a sign of his love. So Ahaz could ask for anything, and God would stop at nothing to give it, "whether in the deepest depths or in the highest heights" (Isaiah 7:11). But Ahaz refused the offer, piously so it seemed: "I will not ask; I will not put the LORD to the test" (verse 12). But Ahaz's actions were, in fact, testing God. Isaiah was disgusted: "Is it not enough to try the patience of men? Will you try the patience of my God also?" (verse 13). If Ahaz were to take God up on his offer, it would mean he would have to change his evil ways. The man was a scoundrel (cf. 2 Kings 16), and for him to trust God in this would be a kind of submission which would lead to submitting to God in other things. His sin, like Israel's at Massah, was also unbelief.

The question of testing God is always in the forefront of prayer. We can test him by refusing to believe his promises. We can test him by a mouth that says one thing and a heart that wants another. Ask yourself: What would I do, how would I be different, if I fully experienced God's goodness to me? Could I keep living the way I have been?

PRAY:

Gracious God! May I not test you through unbelief.
Help me to trust you—and your goodness—completely.

FOR YOUR NEXT DEVOTIONAL READING, GO TO PAGE 816.

It will overflow all its channels,
run over all its banks
⁸and sweep on into Judah, swirling
over it,
passing through it and reaching
up to the neck.
Its outspread wings will cover the
breadth of your land,
O Immanuel*ᵃ!"

⁹Raise the war cry,ᵇ you nations, and
be shattered!
Listen, all you distant lands.
Prepare for battle, and be shattered!
Prepare for battle, and be
shattered!
¹⁰Devise your strategy, but it will be
thwarted;
propose your plan, but it will not
stand,
for God is with us.ᶜ

Fear God

¹¹The LORD spoke to me with his strong
hand upon me, warning me not to follow
the way of this people. He said:

¹² "Do not call conspiracy
everything that these people call
conspiracyᵈ;
do not fear what they fear,
and do not dread it.
¹³The LORD Almighty is the one you
are to regard as holy,
he is the one you are to fear,
he is the one you are to dread,
¹⁴and he will be a sanctuary;
but for both houses of Israel he
will be
a stone that causes men to stumble
and a rock that makes them fall.
And for the people of Jerusalem he
will be
a trap and a snare.
¹⁵Many of them will stumble;
they will fall and be broken,
they will be snared and
captured."

¹⁶Bind up the testimony
and seal up the law among my
disciples.
¹⁷I will wait for the LORD,
who is hiding his face from the
house of Jacob.
I will put my trust in him.

¹⁸Here am I, and the children the LORD
has given me. We are signs and symbols
in Israel from the LORD Almighty, who
dwells on Mount Zion.

¹⁹When men tell you to consult mediums and spiritists, who whisper and
mutter, should not a people inquire of
their God? Why consult the dead on behalf of the living? ²⁰To the law and to the
testimony! If they do not speak according to this word, they have no light of
dawn. ²¹Distressed and hungry, they will
roam through the land; when they are
famished, they will become enraged and,
looking upward, will curse their king and
their God. ²²Then they will look toward
the earth and see only distress and darkness and fearful gloom, and they will be
thrust into utter darkness.

To Us a Child Is Born

9 Nevertheless, there will be no more
gloom for those who were in distress. In the past he humbled the land of
Zebulun and the land of Naphtali, but in
the future he will honor Galilee of the
Gentiles, by the way of the sea, along the
Jordan—

²The people walking in darkness
have seen a great light;
on those living in the land of the
shadow of deathᵉ
a light has dawned.
³You have enlarged the nation
and increased their joy;
they rejoice before you
as people rejoice at the harvest,
as men rejoice
when dividing the plunder.
⁴For as in the day of Midian's defeat,
you have shattered
the yoke that burdens them,
the bar across their shoulders,
the rod of their oppressor.
⁵Every warrior's boot used in battle
and every garment rolled in blood
will be destined for burning,
will be fuel for the fire.
⁶For to us a child is born,
to us a son is given,

ᵃ8 Immanuel means God with us.   ᵇ9 Or Do
your worst   ᶜ10 Hebrew Immanuel
ᵈ12 Or Do not call for a treaty / every time these
people call for a treaty   ᵉ2 Or land of darkness

and the government will be on his
shoulders.
And he will be called
Wonderful Counselor,[a] Mighty God,
Everlasting Father, Prince of
Peace.
⁷Of the increase of his government
and peace
there will be no end.
He will reign on David's throne
and over his kingdom,
establishing and upholding it
with justice and righteousness
from that time on and forever.
The zeal of the LORD Almighty
will accomplish this.

The LORD's Anger Against Israel

⁸The Lord has sent a message against
Jacob;
it will fall on Israel.
⁹All the people will know it—
Ephraim and the inhabitants of
Samaria—
who say with pride
and arrogance of heart,
¹⁰ "The bricks have fallen down,
but we will rebuild with dressed
stone;
the fig trees have been felled,
but we will replace them with
cedars."
¹¹ But the LORD has strengthened
Rezin's foes against them
and has spurred their enemies on.
¹² Arameans from the east and
Philistines from the west
have devoured Israel with open
mouth.

Yet for all this, his anger is not
turned away,
his hand is still upraised.

¹³ But the people have not returned to
him who struck them,
nor have they sought the LORD
Almighty.
¹⁴ So the LORD will cut off from Israel
both head and tail,
both palm branch and reed in a
single day;
¹⁵ the elders and prominent men are
the head,
the prophets who teach lies are
the tail.

¹⁶ Those who guide this people mislead
them,
and those who are guided are
led astray.
¹⁷ Therefore the Lord will take no
pleasure in the young men,
nor will he pity the fatherless and
widows,
for everyone is ungodly and wicked,
every mouth speaks vileness.

Yet for all this, his anger is not turned
away,
his hand is still upraised.

¹⁸ Surely wickedness burns like a fire;
it consumes briers and thorns,
it sets the forest thickets ablaze,
so that it rolls upward in a column
of smoke.
¹⁹ By the wrath of the LORD Almighty
the land will be scorched
and the people will be fuel for the
fire;
no one will spare his brother.
²⁰ On the right they will devour,
but still be hungry;
on the left they will eat,
but not be satisfied.
Each will feed on the flesh of his own
offspring[b]:
²¹ Manasseh will feed on Ephraim,
and Ephraim on Manasseh;
together they will turn against
Judah.

Yet for all this, his anger is not turned
away,
his hand is still upraised.

10 Woe to those who make unjust
laws,
to those who issue oppressive
decrees,
²to deprive the poor of their rights
and withhold justice from the
oppressed of my people,
making widows their prey
and robbing the fatherless.
³What will you do on the day of
reckoning,
when disaster comes from afar?
To whom will you run for help?
Where will you leave your
riches?

---

*a*6 Or *Wonderful, Counselor*   *b*20 Or *arm*

⁴Nothing will remain but to cringe
among the captives
or fall among the slain.

Yet for all this, his anger is not turned
away,
his hand is still upraised.

God's Judgment on Assyria

⁵"Woe to the Assyrian, the rod of
my anger,
in whose hand is the club of my
wrath!
⁶I send him against a godless nation,
I dispatch him against a people
who anger me,
to seize loot and snatch plunder,
and to trample them down like
mud in the streets.
⁷But this is not what he intends,
this is not what he has in mind;
his purpose is to destroy,
to put an end to many nations.
⁸'Are not my commanders all kings?'
he says.
⁹ 'Has not Calno fared like
Carchemish?
Is not Hamath like Arpad,
and Samaria like Damascus?
¹⁰As my hand seized the kingdoms of
the idols,
kingdoms whose images excelled
those of Jerusalem and
Samaria—
¹¹shall I not deal with Jerusalem and
her images
as I dealt with Samaria and her
idols?' "

¹²When the Lord has finished all his
work against Mount Zion and Jerusalem,
he will say, "I will punish the king of Assyria for the willful pride of his heart and
the haughty look in his eyes. ¹³For he says:

" 'By the strength of my hand I have
done this,
and by my wisdom, because I have
understanding.
I removed the boundaries of nations,
I plundered their treasures;
like a mighty one I subdued*ᵃ* their
kings.
¹⁴As one reaches into a nest,
so my hand reached for the wealth
of the nations;

as men gather abandoned eggs,
so I gathered all the countries;
not one flapped a wing,
or opened its mouth to chirp.' "

¹⁵Does the ax raise itself above him
who swings it,
or the saw boast against him
who uses it?
As if a rod were to wield him who
lifts it up,
or a club brandish him who is not
wood!
¹⁶Therefore, the Lord, the LORD
Almighty,
will send a wasting disease upon
his sturdy warriors;
under his pomp a fire will be
kindled
like a blazing flame.
¹⁷The Light of Israel will become
a fire,
their Holy One a flame;
in a single day it will burn and
consume
his thorns and his briers.
¹⁸The splendor of his forests and fertile
fields
it will completely destroy,
as when a sick man wastes away.
¹⁹And the remaining trees of his forests
will be so few
that a child could write them down.

The Remnant of Israel

²⁰In that day the remnant of Israel,
the survivors of the house of Jacob,
will no longer rely on him
who struck them down
but will truly rely on the LORD,
the Holy One of Israel.
²¹A remnant will return,ᵇ a remnant
of Jacob
will return to the Mighty God.
²²Though your people, O Israel, be like
the sand by the sea,
only a remnant will return.
Destruction has been decreed,
overwhelming and righteous.
²³The Lord, the LORD Almighty, will
carry out
the destruction decreed upon the
whole land.

ᵃ13 Or / I subdued the mighty,   ᵇ21 Hebrew
shear-jashub; also in verse 22

²⁴Therefore, this is what the Lord, the
LORD Almighty, says:

"O my people who live in Zion,
  do not be afraid of the Assyrians,
who beat you with a rod
  and lift up a club against you, as
    Egypt did.
²⁵Very soon my anger against you
    will end
  and my wrath will be directed to
    their destruction."

²⁶The LORD Almighty will lash them
    with a whip,
  as when he struck down Midian at
    the rock of Oreb;
and he will raise his staff over the
    waters,
  as he did in Egypt.
²⁷In that day their burden will be lifted
    from your shoulders,
  their yoke from your neck;
the yoke will be broken
  because you have grown so fat.ᵃ

²⁸They enter Aiath;
  they pass through Migron;
  they store supplies at Micmash.
²⁹They go over the pass, and say,
  "We will camp overnight at Geba."
Ramah trembles;
  Gibeah of Saul flees.
³⁰Cry out, O Daughter of Gallim!
  Listen, O Laishah!
  Poor Anathoth!
³¹Madmenah is in flight;
  the people of Gebim take cover.
³²This day they will halt at Nob;
  they will shake their fist
at the mount of the Daughter of Zion,
  at the hill of Jerusalem.

³³See, the Lord, the LORD Almighty,
  will lop off the boughs with great
    power.
The lofty trees will be felled,
  the tall ones will be brought low.
³⁴He will cut down the forest thickets
    with an ax;
  Lebanon will fall before the Mighty
    One.

The Branch From Jesse

11 A shoot will come up from the
    stump of Jesse;
  from his roots a Branch will bear
    fruit.

²The Spirit of the LORD will rest
  on him—
the Spirit of wisdom and of
    understanding,
the Spirit of counsel and of
    power,
the Spirit of knowledge and of
    the fear of the LORD—
³and he will delight in the fear of
    the LORD.

He will not judge by what he sees
    with his eyes,
  or decide by what he hears with his
    ears;
⁴but with righteousness he will judge
    the needy,
  with justice he will give decisions
    for the poor of the earth.
He will strike the earth with the rod
    of his mouth;
  with the breath of his lips he will
    slay the wicked.
⁵Righteousness will be his belt
  and faithfulness the sash around
    his waist.

⁶The wolf will live with the lamb,
  the leopard will lie down with
    the goat,
the calf and the lion and the yearlingᵇ
    together;
  and a little child will lead them.
⁷The cow will feed with the bear,
  their young will lie down together,
  and the lion will eat straw like
    the ox.
⁸The infant will play near the hole of
    the cobra,
  and the young child put his hand
    into the viper's nest.
⁹They will neither harm nor destroy
  on all my holy mountain,
for the earth will be full of the
    knowledge of the LORD
  as the waters cover the sea.

¹⁰In that day the Root of Jesse will
stand as a banner for the peoples; the nations will rally to him, and his place of
rest will be glorious. ¹¹In that day the
Lord will reach out his hand a second
time to reclaim the remnant that is left
of his people from Assyria, from Lower

ᵃ27 Hebrew; Septuagint *broken / from your
shoulders*   ᵇ6 Hebrew; Septuagint *lion will feed*

Egypt, from Upper Egypt,[a] from Cush,[b] from Elam, from Babylonia,[c] from Hamath and from the islands of the sea.

¹²He will raise a banner for the nations
   and gather the exiles of Israel;
he will assemble the scattered people
   of Judah
from the four quarters of the earth.
¹³Ephraim's jealousy will vanish,
   and Judah's enemies[d] will be cut
      off;
Ephraim will not be jealous of Judah,
   nor Judah hostile toward Ephraim.
¹⁴They will swoop down on the slopes
   of Philistia to the west;
together they will plunder the
   people to the east.
They will lay hands on Edom and
   Moab,
   and the Ammonites will be subject
      to them.
¹⁵The LORD will dry up
   the gulf of the Egyptian sea;
with a scorching wind he will sweep
   his hand
over the Euphrates River.[e]
He will break it up into seven streams
   so that men can cross over in
      sandals.
¹⁶There will be a highway for the
   remnant of his people
that is left from Assyria,
as there was for Israel
   when they came up from Egypt.

> ALTHOUGH you were angry with me,
> your anger has turned away
>   and you have comforted me."
>
> ISAIAH 12:1

Songs of Praise

12 In that day you will say:

"I will praise you, O LORD.
   Although you were angry with me,
your anger has turned away
   and you have comforted me.
²Surely God is my salvation;
   I will trust and not be afraid.
The LORD, the LORD, is my strength
   and my song;
he has become my salvation."

³With joy you will draw water
   from the wells of salvation.

⁴In that day you will say:

"Give thanks to the LORD, call on
   his name;
make known among the nations
   what he has done,
and proclaim that his name is
   exalted.
⁵Sing to the LORD, for he has done
   glorious things;
   let this be known to all the world.
⁶Shout aloud and sing for joy, people
   of Zion,
   for great is the Holy One of Israel
      among you."

A Prophecy Against Babylon

13 An oracle concerning Babylon that Isaiah son of Amoz saw:

²Raise a banner on a bare hilltop,
   shout to them;
beckon to them
   to enter the gates of the nobles.
³I have commanded my holy ones;
   I have summoned my warriors to
      carry out my wrath—
   those who rejoice in my triumph.

⁴Listen, a noise on the mountains,
   like that of a great multitude!
Listen, an uproar among the
   kingdoms,
   like nations massing together!
The LORD Almighty is mustering
   an army for war.
⁵They come from faraway lands,
   from the ends of the heavens—
the LORD and the weapons of his
   wrath—
   to destroy the whole country.

⁶Wail, for the day of the LORD is near;
   it will come like destruction from
      the Almighty.[f]
⁷Because of this, all hands will go limp,
   every man's heart will melt.
⁸Terror will seize them,
   pain and anguish will grip them;
   they will writhe like a woman in
      labor.

---

[a]11 Hebrew from Pathros   [b]11 That is, the upper Nile region   [c]11 Hebrew Shinar
[d]13 Or hostility   [e]15 Hebrew the River
[f]6 Hebrew Shaddai

They will look aghast at each other,
their faces aflame.

⁹See, the day of the LORD is coming
—a cruel day, with wrath and
fierce anger—
to make the land desolate
and destroy the sinners within it.

¹⁰The stars of heaven and their
constellations
will not show their light.
The rising sun will be darkened
and the moon will not give its light.
¹¹I will punish the world for its evil,
the wicked for their sins.

{ WEDNESDAY }

ISAIAH 12

Drink, Thank, Pray and Proclaim

12:1 IN THAT DAY YOU WILL SAY: ...

There are four things we need to do in response to this song. The first is simply to drink from the well of salvation (12:3). It's a promise by none other than Jesus himself, that whoever believes in him will drink living water, and the water will become a spring of water welling up inside (see John 4:10,13–14). What an extraordinary offer! Are you thirsty for something deeper and more satisfying than you have ever drunk? Drink of Jesus. The leader of no other world religion makes this offer; Jesus alone says *he* is the way, not a law or a code of morals. He desires to be so much a part of you that he is like water in your body—every cell nourished and refreshed.

The second thing we need to do is give thanks for the water. The language and means we use should be exuberant: "Give thanks ... Sing to the LORD ... Shout aloud and sing for joy" (Isaiah 12:4–6). Karl Barth said grace elicits gratitude like the sound of an echo; that gratitude follows grace like thunder follows lightning. The bigger the lightning, the louder the thunder; the greater the grace, the greater the thanks.

Third, we should "call on his name" (verse 4). This is Biblical language for prayer and worship, but especially prayer—not that the two are easily separated. God so loved the world that he gave his only Son that we might have eternal life. Eternal life is more than interminable life. If that were all it were, such life would be horrible to contemplate. Eternal life is the life of God, which does last forever, but it's so much more. It is the quality of life with God, in God. It is communion in the holy and loving fellowship of the Trinity. That is prayer in all its glory!

Finally, we should proclaim our worship of God among the nations: "Make known among the nations what he has done ... let this be known to all the world" (verses 4–5). All our worship of the God who saves and satisfies us should point to reaching others. As John Piper puts it, "Worship is the fuel and goal in missions." The goal of missions "is the gladness of the peoples in the greatness of God." But worship also fuels zeal for evangelism: "Passion for God in worship precedes the offer of God in preaching. You can't commend what you don't cherish."⁵

PRAY:

*Using this passage as a guide, write your own paraphrase as a prayer
along these four themes: drink, thank, pray and proclaim.*

———

FOR YOUR NEXT DEVOTIONAL READING, GO TO PAGE 828.

I will put an end to the arrogance
  of the haughty
and will humble the pride of
  the ruthless.
[12] I will make man scarcer than
  pure gold,
more rare than the gold of Ophir.
[13] Therefore I will make the heavens
  tremble;
and the earth will shake from
  its place
at the wrath of the LORD Almighty,
  in the day of his burning anger.

[14] Like a hunted gazelle,
  like sheep without a shepherd,
each will return to his own people,
  each will flee to his native land.
[15] Whoever is captured will be thrust
  through;
all who are caught will fall by the
  sword.
[16] Their infants will be dashed to pieces
  before their eyes;
their houses will be looted and
  their wives ravished.

[17] See, I will stir up against them
  the Medes,
who do not care for silver
  and have no delight in gold.
[18] Their bows will strike down the
  young men;
they will have no mercy on
  infants
nor will they look with compassion
  on children.
[19] Babylon, the jewel of kingdoms,
  the glory of the Babylonians'[a]
  pride,
will be overthrown by God
  like Sodom and Gomorrah.
[20] She will never be inhabited
  or lived in through all generations;
no Arab will pitch his tent there,
  no shepherd will rest his flocks
  there.
[21] But desert creatures will lie there,
  jackals will fill her houses;
there the owls will dwell,
  and there the wild goats will
  leap about.
[22] Hyenas will howl in her strongholds,
  jackals in her luxurious palaces.
Her time is at hand,
  and her days will not be prolonged.

14 The LORD will have compassion
  on Jacob;
once again he will choose
  Israel
and will settle them in their
  own land.
Aliens will join them
  and unite with the house of Jacob.
[2] Nations will take them
  and bring them to their own place.
And the house of Israel will possess
  the nations
as menservants and maidservants
  in the LORD's land.
They will make captives of their
  captors
and rule over their oppressors.

[3] On the day the LORD gives you relief
from suffering and turmoil and cruel
bondage, [4] you will take up this taunt
against the king of Babylon:

How the oppressor has come to
  an end!
How his fury[b] has ended!
[5] The LORD has broken the rod of the
  wicked,
  the scepter of the rulers,
[6] which in anger struck down peoples
  with unceasing blows,
and in fury subdued nations
  with relentless aggression.
[7] All the lands are at rest and at peace;
  they break into singing.
[8] Even the pine trees and the cedars
  of Lebanon
exult over you and say,
"Now that you have been laid low,
  no woodsman comes to cut us
  down."

[9] The grave[c] below is all astir
  to meet you at your coming;
it rouses the spirits of the departed
  to greet you—
all those who were leaders in the
  world;
it makes them rise from their
  thrones—
all those who were kings over
  the nations.

---

[a]19 Or *Chaldeans'*   [b]4 Dead Sea Scrolls,
Septuagint and Syriac; the meaning of the word in
the Masoretic Text is uncertain.   [c]9 Hebrew
Sheol; also in verses 11 and 15

¹⁰ They will all respond,
they will say to you,
"You also have become weak,
as we are;
you have become like us."
¹¹ All your pomp has been brought
down to the grave,
along with the noise of your harps;
maggots are spread out beneath you
and worms cover you.

¹² How you have fallen from heaven,
O morning star, son of the dawn!
You have been cast down to the earth,
you who once laid low the nations!
¹³ You said in your heart,
"I will ascend to heaven;
I will raise my throne
above the stars of God;
I will sit enthroned on the mount of
assembly,
on the utmost heights of the sacred
mountain.ᵃ
¹⁴ I will ascend above the tops of
the clouds;
I will make myself like the
Most High."
¹⁵ But you are brought down to
the grave,
to the depths of the pit.

¹⁶ Those who see you stare at you,
they ponder your fate:
"Is this the man who shook the earth
and made kingdoms tremble,
¹⁷ the man who made the world a
desert,
who overthrew its cities
and would not let his captives
go home?"

¹⁸ All the kings of the nations lie in
state,
each in his own tomb.
¹⁹ But you are cast out of your tomb
like a rejected branch;
you are covered with the slain,
with those pierced by the sword,
those who descend to the stones
of the pit.
Like a corpse trampled underfoot,
²⁰ you will not join them in burial,
for you have destroyed your land
and killed your people.

The offspring of the wicked
will never be mentioned again.

²¹ Prepare a place to slaughter his sons
for the sins of their forefathers;
they are not to rise to inherit the land
and cover the earth with their
cities.

²² "I will rise up against them,"
declares the LORD Almighty.
"I will cut off from Babylon her name
and survivors,
her offspring and descendants,"
declares the LORD.
²³ "I will turn her into a place for owls
and into swampland;
I will sweep her with the broom of
destruction,"
declares the LORD Almighty.

> ❝ Do not pray for easy lives. Pray to be
> stronger men! Do not pray for tasks
> equal to your powers. Pray for power
> equal to your tasks. ❞
>
> PHILIP BROOKS

A Prophecy Against Assyria

²⁴ The LORD Almighty has sworn,

"Surely, as I have planned, so it
will be,
and as I have purposed, so it
will stand.
²⁵ I will crush the Assyrian in my land;
on my mountains I will trample
him down.
His yoke will be taken from my
people,
and his burden removed from their
shoulders."

²⁶ This is the plan determined for the
whole world;
this is the hand stretched out over
all nations.
²⁷ For the LORD Almighty has purposed,
and who can thwart him?
His hand is stretched out, and who
can turn it back?

A Prophecy Against the Philistines

²⁸ This oracle came in the year King
Ahaz died:

ᵃ13 Or *the north*; Hebrew *Zaphon*

29 Do not rejoice, all you Philistines,
 that the rod that struck you is
 broken;
from the root of that snake will spring
 up a viper,
 its fruit will be a darting, venomous
 serpent.
30 The poorest of the poor will find
 pasture,
 and the needy will lie down
 in safety.
But your root I will destroy by famine;
 it will slay your survivors.
31 Wail, O gate! Howl, O city!
 Melt away, all you Philistines!
A cloud of smoke comes from
 the north,
 and there is not a straggler in
 its ranks.
32 What answer shall be given
 to the envoys of that nation?
"The LORD has established Zion,
 and in her his afflicted people will
 find refuge."

A Prophecy Against Moab

15 An oracle concerning Moab:

Ar in Moab is ruined,
 destroyed in a night!
Kir in Moab is ruined,
 destroyed in a night!
2 Dibon goes up to its temple,
 to its high places to weep;
Moab wails over Nebo and
 Medeba.
Every head is shaved
 and every beard cut off.
3 In the streets they wear sackcloth;
 on the roofs and in the public
 squares
they all wail,
 prostrate with weeping.
4 Heshbon and Elealeh cry out,
 their voices are heard all the way
 to Jahaz.
Therefore the armed men of Moab
 cry out,
 and their hearts are faint.
5 My heart cries out over Moab;
 her fugitives flee as far as Zoar,
 as far as Eglath Shelishiyah.
They go up the way to Luhith,
 weeping as they go;

on the road to Horonaim
 they lament their destruction.
6 The waters of Nimrim are dried up
 and the grass is withered;
the vegetation is gone
 and nothing green is left.
7 So the wealth they have acquired and
 stored up
they carry away over the Ravine of
 the Poplars.
8 Their outcry echoes along the border
 of Moab;
their wailing reaches as far as
 Eglaim,
 their lamentation as far as Beer
 Elim.
9 Dimon's*a* waters are full of blood,
 but I will bring still more upon
 Dimon*a*—
a lion upon the fugitives of Moab
 and upon those who remain in
 the land.

16 Send lambs as tribute
 to the ruler of the land,
from Sela, across the desert,
 to the mount of the Daughter
 of Zion.
2 Like fluttering birds
 pushed from the nest,
so are the women of Moab
 at the fords of the Arnon.

3 "Give us counsel,
 render a decision.
Make your shadow like night—
 at high noon.
Hide the fugitives,
 do not betray the refugees.
4 Let the Moabite fugitives stay
 with you;
 be their shelter from the destroyer."

The oppressor will come to an end,
 and destruction will cease;
 the aggressor will vanish from
 the land.
5 In love a throne will be established;
 in faithfulness a man will sit on it—
 one from the house*b* of David—
one who in judging seeks justice
 and speeds the cause of
 righteousness.

---

*a*9 Masoretic Text; Dead Sea Scrolls, some
Septuagint manuscripts and Vulgate *Dibon*
*b*5 Hebrew *tent*

⁶ We have heard of Moab's pride—
  her overweening pride and conceit,
  her pride and her insolence—
  but her boasts are empty.
⁷ Therefore the Moabites wail,
  they wail together for Moab.
Lament and grieve
  for the men*ᵃ* of Kir Hareseth.
⁸ The fields of Heshbon wither,
  the vines of Sibmah also.
The rulers of the nations
  have trampled down the choicest
    vines,
  which once reached Jazer
  and spread toward the desert.
Their shoots spread out
  and went as far as the sea.
⁹ So I weep, as Jazer weeps,
  for the vines of Sibmah.
O Heshbon, O Elealeh,
  I drench you with tears!
The shouts of joy over your ripened
    fruit
  and over your harvests have been
    stilled.
¹⁰ Joy and gladness are taken away from
    the orchards;
  no one sings or shouts in the
    vineyards;
  no one treads out wine at the presses,
  for I have put an end to the
    shouting.
¹¹ My heart laments for Moab like
    a harp,
  my inmost being for Kir Hareseth.
¹² When Moab appears at her high
    place,
  she only wears herself out;
  when she goes to her shrine to pray,
    it is to no avail.

¹³ This is the word the LORD has already
spoken concerning Moab. ¹⁴ But now the
LORD says: "Within three years, as a servant bound by contract would count
them, Moab's splendor and all her many
people will be despised, and her survivors will be very few and feeble."

An Oracle Against Damascus

17 An oracle concerning Damascus:

"See, Damascus will no longer be
    a city
  but will become a heap of ruins.
² The cities of Aroer will be deserted
  and left to flocks, which will lie
    down,
  with no one to make them afraid.
³ The fortified city will disappear from
    Ephraim,
  and royal power from Damascus;
  the remnant of Aram will be
  like the glory of the Israelites,"
    declares the LORD Almighty.

⁴ "In that day the glory of Jacob will
    fade;
  the fat of his body will waste away.
⁵ It will be as when a reaper gathers
    the standing grain
  and harvests the grain with his
    arm—
  as when a man gleans heads of grain
  in the Valley of Rephaim.
⁶ Yet some gleanings will remain,
  as when an olive tree is beaten,
  leaving two or three olives on the
    topmost branches,
  four or five on the fruitful boughs,"
    declares the LORD, the God
      of Israel.

⁷ In that day men will look to their
    Maker
  and turn their eyes to the Holy One
    of Israel.
⁸ They will not look to the altars,
  the work of their hands,
  and they will have no regard for the
    Asherah poles*ᵇ*
  and the incense altars their fingers
    have made.

⁹ In that day their strong cities, which
they left because of the Israelites, will be
like places abandoned to thickets and
undergrowth. And all will be desolation.

¹⁰ You have forgotten God your Savior;
  you have not remembered the
    Rock, your fortress.
Therefore, though you set out the
    finest plants
  and plant imported vines,
¹¹ though on the day you set them out,
  you make them grow,
  and on the morning when you plant
    them, you bring them to bud,

ᵃ7 Or "*raisin cakes,*" a wordplay   *ᵇ8* That is,
symbols of the goddess Asherah

yet the harvest will be as nothing
 in the day of disease and incurable
 pain.

¹²Oh, the raging of many nations—
 they rage like the raging sea!
Oh, the uproar of the peoples—
 they roar like the roaring of great
 waters!
¹³Although the peoples roar like the
 roar of surging waters,
 when he rebukes them they flee
 far away,
 driven before the wind like chaff on
 the hills,
 like tumbleweed before a gale.
¹⁴In the evening, sudden terror!
 Before the morning, they are gone!
This is the portion of those who
 loot us,
 the lot of those who plunder us.

A Prophecy Against Cush

18 Woe to the land of whirring wings[a]
 along the rivers of Cush,[b]
²which sends envoys by sea
 in papyrus boats over the water.

Go, swift messengers,
to a people tall and smooth-skinned,
 to a people feared far and wide,
an aggressive nation of strange
 speech,
 whose land is divided by rivers.

³All you people of the world,
 you who live on the earth,
when a banner is raised on the
 mountains,
 you will see it,
and when a trumpet sounds,
 you will hear it.
⁴This is what the LORD says to me:
 "I will remain quiet and will look
 on from my dwelling place,
like shimmering heat in the sunshine,
 like a cloud of dew in the heat of
 harvest."
⁵For, before the harvest, when the
 blossom is gone
 and the flower becomes a ripening
 grape,
he will cut off the shoots with
 pruning knives,
 and cut down and take away the
 spreading branches.

⁶They will all be left to the mountain
 birds of prey
 and to the wild animals;
the birds will feed on them all
 summer,
 the wild animals all winter.

⁷At that time gifts will be brought to
the LORD Almighty

from a people tall and smooth-
 skinned,
 from a people feared far and wide,
an aggressive nation of strange
 speech,
 whose land is divided by rivers—

the gifts will be brought to Mount Zion,
the place of the Name of the LORD Almighty.

A Prophecy About Egypt

19 An oracle concerning Egypt:

See, the LORD rides on a swift cloud
 and is coming to Egypt.
The idols of Egypt tremble before
 him,
 and the hearts of the Egyptians
 melt within them.

²"I will stir up Egyptian against
 Egyptian—
 brother will fight against brother,
 neighbor against neighbor,
 city against city,
 kingdom against kingdom.
³The Egyptians will lose heart,
 and I will bring their plans to
 nothing;
they will consult the idols and the
 spirits of the dead,
 the mediums and the spiritists.
⁴I will hand the Egyptians over
 to the power of a cruel master,
and a fierce king will rule over them,"
 declares the Lord, the LORD
 Almighty.

⁵The waters of the river will dry up,
 and the riverbed will be parched
 and dry.
⁶The canals will stink;
 the streams of Egypt will dwindle
 and dry up.

---

[a]1 Or of locusts   [b]1 That is, the upper Nile
region

The reeds and rushes will wither,
7   also the plants along the Nile,
     at the mouth of the river.
Every sown field along the Nile
     will become parched, will blow
        away and be no more.
⁸ The fishermen will groan and lament,
     all who cast hooks into the Nile;
     those who throw nets on the water
        will pine away.
⁹ Those who work with combed flax
        will despair,
     the weavers of fine linen will lose
        hope.
¹⁰ The workers in cloth will be dejected,
     and all the wage earners will be
        sick at heart.

¹¹ The officials of Zoan are nothing but
        fools;
     the wise counselors of Pharaoh
        give senseless advice.
How can you say to Pharaoh,
     "I am one of the wise men,
     a disciple of the ancient kings"?

¹² Where are your wise men now?
     Let them show you and make
        known
what the LORD Almighty
     has planned against Egypt.
¹³ The officials of Zoan have become
        fools,
     the leaders of Memphis*ᵃ* are
        deceived;
     the cornerstones of her peoples
        have led Egypt astray.
¹⁴ The LORD has poured into them
     a spirit of dizziness;
     they make Egypt stagger in all that
        she does,
     as a drunkard staggers around in
        his vomit.
¹⁵ There is nothing Egypt can do—
     head or tail, palm branch or reed.

¹⁶ In that day the Egyptians will be like
women. They will shudder with fear at
the uplifted hand that the LORD Almighty
raises against them. ¹⁷ And the land of
Judah will bring terror to the Egyptians;
everyone to whom Judah is mentioned
will be terrified, because of what the LORD
Almighty is planning against them.

¹⁸ In that day five cities in Egypt will speak
the language of Canaan and swear allegiance to the LORD Almighty. One of them
will be called the City of Destruction.*ᵇ*

¹⁹ In that day there will be an altar to the
LORD in the heart of Egypt, and a monument to the LORD at its border. ²⁰ It will be
a sign and witness to the LORD Almighty
in the land of Egypt. When they cry out to
the LORD because of their oppressors, he
will send them a savior and defender, and
he will rescue them. ²¹ So the LORD will
make himself known to the Egyptians,
and in that day they will acknowledge the
LORD. They will worship with sacrifices
and grain offerings; they will make vows
to the LORD and keep them. ²² The LORD
will strike Egypt with a plague; he will
strike them and heal them. They will turn
to the LORD, and he will respond to their
pleas and heal them.

> WHEN they cry out to the LORD because
> of their oppressors, he will send them a
> savior and defender, and he will rescue
> them.
>
> ISAIAH 19:20

²³ In that day there will be a highway
from Egypt to Assyria. The Assyrians will
go to Egypt and the Egyptians to Assyria.
The Egyptians and Assyrians will worship together. ²⁴ In that day Israel will be
the third, along with Egypt and Assyria, a
blessing on the earth. ²⁵ The LORD Almighty will bless them, saying, "Blessed
be Egypt my people, Assyria my handi-
work, and Israel my inheritance."

A Prophecy Against Egypt and Cush

20   In the year that the supreme com-
      mander, sent by Sargon king of
Assyria, came to Ashdod and attacked
and captured it— ²at that time the LORD
spoke through Isaiah son of Amoz. He
said to him, "Take off the sackcloth from
your body and the sandals from your
feet." And he did so, going around
stripped and barefoot.

³ Then the LORD said, "Just as my servant Isaiah has gone stripped and bare-

---

ᵃ13 Hebrew *Noph*   *ᵇ18* Most manuscripts of
the Masoretic Text; some manuscripts of the
Masoretic Text, Dead Sea Scrolls and Vulgate *City
of the Sun* (that is, Heliopolis)

foot for three years, as a sign and portent against Egypt and Cush,*a* *4*so the king of Assyria will lead away stripped and barefoot the Egyptian captives and Cushite exiles, young and old, with buttocks bared—to Egypt's shame. *5*Those who trusted in Cush and boasted in Egypt will be afraid and put to shame. *6*In that day the people who live on this coast will say, 'See what has happened to those we relied on, those we fled to for help and deliverance from the king of Assyria! How then can we escape?' "

A Prophecy Against Babylon

21 An oracle concerning the Desert by the Sea:

Like whirlwinds sweeping through
the southland,
an invader comes from the desert,
from a land of terror.

2 A dire vision has been shown
to me:
The traitor betrays, the looter
takes loot.
Elam, attack! Media, lay siege!
I will bring to an end all the
groaning she caused.

3 At this my body is racked with pain,
pangs seize me, like those of a
woman in labor;
I am staggered by what I hear,
I am bewildered by what I see.
4 My heart falters,
fear makes me tremble;
the twilight I longed for
has become a horror to me.

5 They set the tables,
they spread the rugs,
they eat, they drink!
Get up, you officers,
oil the shields!

6 This is what the Lord says to me:

"Go, post a lookout
and have him report what he sees.
7 When he sees chariots
with teams of horses,
riders on donkeys
or riders on camels,
let him be alert,
fully alert."

8 And the lookout*b* shouted,

"Day after day, my lord, I stand
on the watchtower;
every night I stay at my post.
9 Look, here comes a man in a
chariot
with a team of horses.
And he gives back the answer:
'Babylon has fallen, has fallen!
All the images of its gods
lie shattered on the ground!' "

10 O my people, crushed on the
threshing floor,
I tell you what I have heard
from the Lord Almighty,
from the God of Israel.

A Prophecy Against Edom

11 An oracle concerning Dumah*c*:

Someone calls to me from Seir,
"Watchman, what is left of the
night?
Watchman, what is left of the
night?"
12 The watchman replies,
"Morning is coming, but also
the night.
If you would ask, then ask;
and come back yet again."

A Prophecy Against Arabia

13 An oracle concerning Arabia:

You caravans of Dedanites,
who camp in the thickets of Arabia,
14   bring water for the thirsty;
you who live in Tema,
bring food for the fugitives.
15 They flee from the sword,
from the drawn sword,
from the bent bow
and from the heat of battle.

16 This is what the Lord says to me: "Within one year, as a servant bound by contract would count it, all the pomp of Kedar will come to an end. *17*The survivors of the bowmen, the warriors of Kedar, will be few." The Lord, the God of Israel, has spoken.

---

a3 That is, the upper Nile region; also in verse 5
b8 Dead Sea Scrolls and Syriac; Masoretic Text *A lion*   *c11* *Dumah* means *silence* or *stillness*, a wordplay on *Edom*.

A Prophecy About Jerusalem

22 An oracle concerning the Valley of Vision:

What troubles you now,
    that you have all gone up on
    the roofs,
²O town full of commotion,
    O city of tumult and revelry?
Your slain were not killed by the
    sword,
    nor did they die in battle.
³All your leaders have fled together;
    they have been captured without
    using the bow.
All you who were caught were taken
    prisoner together,
    having fled while the enemy was
    still far away.
⁴Therefore I said, "Turn away from
    me;
    let me weep bitterly.
Do not try to console me
    over the destruction of my people."

⁵The Lord, the LORD Almighty, has
    a day
    of tumult and trampling and terror
    in the Valley of Vision,
a day of battering down walls
    and of crying out to the mountains.
⁶Elam takes up the quiver,
    with her charioteers and horses;
    Kir uncovers the shield.
⁷Your choicest valleys are full of
    chariots,
    and horsemen are posted at the
    city gates;
⁸   the defenses of Judah are stripped
    away.

And you looked in that day
    to the weapons in the Palace of the
    Forest;
⁹you saw that the City of David
    had many breaches in its defenses;

you stored up water
    in the Lower Pool.
¹⁰You counted the buildings in
    Jerusalem
    and tore down houses to
    strengthen the wall.
¹¹You built a reservoir between the
    two walls
    for the water of the Old Pool,
but you did not look to the One who
    made it,
    or have regard for the One who
    planned it long ago.

¹²The Lord, the LORD Almighty,
    called you on that day
to weep and to wail,
    to tear out your hair and put on
    sackcloth.
¹³But see, there is joy and revelry,
    slaughtering of cattle and killing
    of sheep,
    eating of meat and drinking of wine!
"Let us eat and drink," you say,
    "for tomorrow we die!"

¹⁴The LORD Almighty has revealed this in my hearing: "Till your dying day this sin will not be atoned for," says the Lord, the LORD Almighty.

¹⁵This is what the Lord, the LORD Almighty, says:

"Go, say to this steward,
    to Shebna, who is in charge of the
    palace:
¹⁶What are you doing here and who
    gave you permission
    to cut out a grave for yourself here,
hewing your grave on the height
    and chiseling your resting place in
    the rock?

¹⁷"Beware, the LORD is about to take
    firm hold of you
    and hurl you away, O you mighty
    man.
¹⁸He will roll you up tightly like a ball
    and throw you into a large country.
There you will die
    and there your splendid chariots
    will remain—
    you disgrace to your master's
    house!
¹⁹I will depose you from your office,
    and you will be ousted from your
    position.

²⁰"In that day I will summon my servant, Eliakim son of Hilkiah. ²¹I will clothe him with your robe and fasten your sash around him and hand your authority over to him. He will be a father to those who live in Jerusalem and to the house of Judah. ²²I will place on his shoulder the key to the house of David; what he opens no one can shut, and what he shuts no one can open. ²³I will drive him like a peg into a firm place; he will be a seat[a] of honor for the house of his father. ²⁴All the glory of his family will hang on him: its offspring and offshoots—all its lesser vessels, from the bowls to all the jars.

²⁵"In that day," declares the LORD Almighty, "the peg driven into the firm place will give way; it will be sheared off and will fall, and the load hanging on it will be cut down." The LORD has spoken.

A Prophecy About Tyre

23 An oracle concerning Tyre:

Wail, O ships of Tarshish!
  For Tyre is destroyed
  and left without house or harbor.
From the land of Cyprus[b]
  word has come to them.

² Be silent, you people of the island
  and you merchants of Sidon,
  whom the seafarers have enriched.
³ On the great waters
  came the grain of the Shihor;
the harvest of the Nile[c] was the
    revenue of Tyre,
  and she became the marketplace of
    the nations.

⁴ Be ashamed, O Sidon, and you,
  O fortress of the sea,
  for the sea has spoken:
"I have neither been in labor nor
    given birth;
  I have neither reared sons nor
    brought up daughters."
⁵ When word comes to Egypt,
  they will be in anguish at the report
    from Tyre.

⁶ Cross over to Tarshish;
  wail, you people of the island.
⁷ Is this your city of revelry,
  the old, old city,

whose feet have taken her
  to settle in far-off lands?
⁸ Who planned this against Tyre,
  the bestower of crowns,
whose merchants are princes,
  whose traders are renowned in
    the earth?
⁹ The LORD Almighty planned it,
  to bring low the pride of all glory
  and to humble all who are
    renowned on the earth.

¹⁰ Till[d] your land as along the Nile,
  O Daughter of Tarshish,
  for you no longer have a harbor.
¹¹ The LORD has stretched out his hand
    over the sea
  and made its kingdoms tremble.
He has given an order concerning
    Phoenicia[e]
  that her fortresses be destroyed.
¹² He said, "No more of your reveling,
  O Virgin Daughter of Sidon, now
    crushed!

"Up, cross over to Cyprus[b];
  even there you will find no rest."
¹³ Look at the land of the Babylonians,[f]
  this people that is now of no
    account!
The Assyrians have made it
  a place for desert creatures;
they raised up their siege towers,
  they stripped its fortresses bare
  and turned it into a ruin.

¹⁴ Wail, you ships of Tarshish;
  your fortress is destroyed!

¹⁵ At that time Tyre will be forgotten for seventy years, the span of a king's life. But at the end of these seventy years, it will happen to Tyre as in the song of the prostitute:

¹⁶ "Take up a harp, walk through
    the city,
  O prostitute forgotten;
play the harp well, sing many a song,
  so that you will be remembered."

---

a23 Or *throne* *b1,12* Hebrew *Kittim*
c2,3 Masoretic Text; one Dead Sea Scroll *Sidon, /
who cross over the sea; / your envoys* ³*are on the
great waters. / The grain of the Shihor, / the
harvest of the Nile,* *d10* Dead Sea Scrolls and
some Septuagint manuscripts; Masoretic Text *Go
through* *e11* Hebrew *Canaan* *f13* Or
Chaldeans

¹⁷At the end of seventy years, the LORD will deal with Tyre. She will return to her hire as a prostitute and will ply her trade with all the kingdoms on the face of the earth. ¹⁸Yet her profit and her earnings will be set apart for the LORD; they will not be stored up or hoarded. Her profits will go to those who live before the LORD, for abundant food and fine clothes.

The LORD's Devastation of the Earth

24 See, the LORD is going to lay waste
the earth
and devastate it;
he will ruin its face
and scatter its inhabitants—
² it will be the same
for priest as for people,
for master as for servant,
for mistress as for maid,
for seller as for buyer,
for borrower as for lender,
for debtor as for creditor.
³ The earth will be completely laid waste
and totally plundered.
The LORD has spoken
this word.

⁴ The earth dries up and withers,
the world languishes and withers,
the exalted of the earth languish.
⁵ The earth is defiled by its people;
they have disobeyed the laws,
violated the statutes
and broken the everlasting
covenant.
⁶ Therefore a curse consumes the earth;
its people must bear their guilt.
Therefore earth's inhabitants are
burned up,
and very few are left.
⁷ The new wine dries up and the vine
withers;
all the merrymakers groan.
⁸ The gaiety of the tambourines is
stilled,
the noise of the revelers has
stopped,
the joyful harp is silent.
⁹ No longer do they drink wine with a
song;
the beer is bitter to its drinkers.
¹⁰ The ruined city lies desolate;
the entrance to every house is
barred.

¹¹ In the streets they cry out for wine;
all joy turns to gloom,
all gaiety is banished from the earth.
¹² The city is left in ruins,
its gate is battered to pieces.
¹³ So will it be on the earth
and among the nations,
as when an olive tree is beaten,
or as when gleanings are left after
the grape harvest.

¹⁴ They raise their voices, they shout
for joy;
from the west they acclaim the
LORD's majesty.
¹⁵ Therefore in the east give glory to
the LORD;
exalt the name of the LORD, the God
of Israel,
in the islands of the sea.
¹⁶ From the ends of the earth we hear
singing:
"Glory to the Righteous One."

But I said, "I waste away, I waste
away!
Woe to me!
The treacherous betray!
With treachery the treacherous
betray!"
¹⁷ Terror and pit and snare await you,
O people of the earth.
¹⁸ Whoever flees at the sound of terror
will fall into a pit;
whoever climbs out of the pit
will be caught in a snare.

The floodgates of the heavens are
opened,
the foundations of the earth shake.
¹⁹ The earth is broken up,
the earth is split asunder,
the earth is thoroughly shaken.
²⁰ The earth reels like a drunkard,
it sways like a hut in the wind;
so heavy upon it is the guilt of its
rebellion
that it falls—never to rise again.

²¹ In that day the LORD will punish
the powers in the heavens above
and the kings on the earth below.
²² They will be herded together
like prisoners bound in a dungeon;
they will be shut up in prison
and be punished[a] after many days.

---

[a] 22 Or *released*

²³ The moon will be abashed, the sun
ashamed;
for the LORD Almighty will reign
on Mount Zion and in Jerusalem,
and before its elders, gloriously.

Praise to the LORD

25 O LORD, you are my God;
I will exalt you and praise
your name,
for in perfect faithfulness
you have done marvelous things,
things planned long ago.
² You have made the city a heap of
rubble,
the fortified town a ruin,
the foreigners' stronghold a city
no more;
it will never be rebuilt.
³ Therefore strong peoples will
honor you;
cities of ruthless nations will
revere you.
⁴ You have been a refuge for the poor,
a refuge for the needy in his
distress,
a shelter from the storm
and a shade from the heat.
For the breath of the ruthless
is like a storm driving against
a wall
⁵   and like the heat of the desert.
You silence the uproar of foreigners;
as heat is reduced by the shadow
of a cloud,
so the song of the ruthless is
stilled.

⁶ On this mountain the LORD Almighty
will prepare
a feast of rich food for all peoples,
a banquet of aged wine—
the best of meats and the finest
of wines.
⁷ On this mountain he will destroy
the shroud that enfolds all peoples,
the sheet that covers all nations;
⁸   he will swallow up death forever.
The Sovereign LORD will wipe away
the tears
from all faces;
he will remove the disgrace of his
people
from all the earth.
The LORD has spoken.

⁹ In that day they will say,

"Surely this is our God;
we trusted in him, and he saved us.
This is the LORD, we trusted in him;
let us rejoice and be glad in his
salvation."

¹⁰ The hand of the LORD will rest on
this mountain;
but Moab will be trampled under
him
as straw is trampled down in
the manure.
¹¹ They will spread out their hands in it,
as a swimmer spreads out his
hands to swim.
God will bring down their pride
despite the cleverness[a] of their
hands.
¹² He will bring down your high fortified
walls
and lay them low;
he will bring them down to the
ground,
to the very dust.

A Song of Praise

26 In that day this song will be sung
in the land of Judah:

We have a strong city;
God makes salvation
its walls and ramparts.
² Open the gates
that the righteous nation may
enter,
the nation that keeps faith.
³ You will keep in perfect peace
him whose mind is steadfast,
because he trusts in you.
⁴ Trust in the LORD forever,
for the LORD, the LORD, is the Rock
eternal.
⁵ He humbles those who dwell on high,
he lays the lofty city low;
he levels it to the ground
and casts it down to the dust.
⁶ Feet trample it down—
the feet of the oppressed,
the footsteps of the poor.

⁷ The path of the righteous is level;
O upright One, you make the way
of the righteous smooth.

*a 11 The meaning of the Hebrew for this word is
uncertain.*

⁸Yes, Lᴏʀᴅ, walking in the way of
    your laws,ᵃ
  we wait for you;
  your name and renown
    are the desire of our hearts.
⁹My soul yearns for you in the night;
  in the morning my spirit longs
    for you.

When your judgments come upon
    the earth,
  the people of the world learn
    righteousness.
¹⁰Though grace is shown to the wicked,
  they do not learn righteousness;

ᵃ8 Or judgments

[THURSDAY]

ISAIAH 25:6–9

On This Mountain

25:6 THE LORD ALMIGHTY WILL PREPARE A FEAST OF RICH FOOD FOR ALL PEOPLES.

There is so much to hope for in these lines—and so much to pray for. If prayer is the means God has provided to give us what he wants, this vision of God's good future makes prayer the most joyous of activities. We may pray for the day when God will serve us at a great feast: "On this mountain the Lᴏʀᴅ Almighty will prepare a feast of rich food" (25:6). It is God's pleasure to serve us! The Son of Man did not come to be served, but to serve (see Mark 10:45)—because his Father has served from the beginning and will serve in the end. Amazing. If we won't let him serve us, we can have no part of him (see John 13:8).

We may pray that the whole world will enjoy God's blessings. The feast is "for all peoples" on this mountain. This is underlined by the use of "peoples" (ethnicities), "nations" (political groupings), and "faces" (individuals). What began with a childless couple in the ancient Middle East will culminate in a blessing for the whole world (see Genesis 12:1–3). God's house was to be a house of prayer for all nations, as Jesus said (see Mark 11:17). And no matter how his people have failed to grasp that in the past, in the future it will be so.

We may pray for the end of death. God wills to "destroy the shroud that enfolds all peoples, the sheet that covers all nations; he will swallow up death forever" (Isaiah 25:7–8). Death is now the Great Swallower (see Isaiah 5:14), but proud death will be swallowed up! Paul partially quotes Isaiah 25:8 in his resurrection manifesto in 1 Corinthians 15:54. It no doubt inspired poet John Donne to write some of his most famous lines:

> Death be not proud, though some have called thee
> Mighty and dreadful, for thou art not so ...
> One short sleep past, we wake eternally,
> And death shall be no more; *death, thou shalt die.*⁶

PRAY:

*Come, Lord, and call your people from east and west and
north and south (see Luke 13:29)! Set the table, and we
will feast with you and each other forever.*

FOR YOUR NEXT DEVOTIONAL READING, GO TO PAGE 829.

even in a land of uprightness they go
  on doing evil
and regard not the majesty of the
  LORD.
¹¹ O LORD, your hand is lifted high,
  but they do not see it.
Let them see your zeal for your
  people and be put to shame;
  let the fire reserved for your
  enemies consume them.

¹² LORD, you establish peace for us;
  all that we have accomplished you
  have done for us.

¹³ O LORD, our God, other lords besides
  you have ruled over us,
  but your name alone do we honor.
¹⁴ They are now dead, they live no more;
  those departed spirits do not rise.
You punished them and brought
  them to ruin;
  you wiped out all memory of them.
¹⁵ You have enlarged the nation,
  O LORD;
  you have enlarged the nation.
You have gained glory for yourself;
  you have extended all the borders
  of the land.

[FRIDAY]

ISAIAH 26:3 – 4

Because He Trusts in You

26:4 TRUST IN THE LORD FOREVER.

A great Gospel counterpart and illustration of these two verses is recounted in Mark 4:35–41. Jesus and his disciples were crossing a lake in a boat and were caught in a furious storm. The boat was being swamped with water, and the disciples were frantic. But "Jesus was in the stern, sleeping on a cushion." There you have it: perfect peace. And for the disciples—perfectly destroyed peace: "Teacher, don't you care if we drown?" You probably know the rest: Jesus was soundly asleep because he trusted his Father's power.

How can anyone be calm when everything and everyone are unraveling? Isaiah's explanation is, "You will keep in perfect peace him whose mind is steadfast, *because he trusts in you*" (Isaiah 26:3, italics added). Trust is at once the easiest and hardest thing to do. It's not complicated because even—or especially—children get it. It is simply relinquishing your hold on things and letting God hold them. He is holding them anyway! That's why *not* trusting God is so exhausting; it is our effort to control what can't be controlled. C. S. Lewis said his coming to faith was like diving into a pool of water; it wasn't so much something he did as something he stopped doing—holding on and holding back.

A little boy was trapped on the second floor of a house on fire. He stood at the window, surrounded by smoke and flames, crying for help. He heard his father's voice below, yelling for him to jump into his arms. "But I can't see you, Daddy," the child cried. His father shouted back, "That's OK, I can see you, so jump." We walk by faith, not by sight, do we not? Beneath us are the everlasting arms (see Deuteronomy 33:27). We need not fear what we see, because the one we cannot see has everything under control.

PRAY:

*Almighty God! You are the Rock eternal. You are the one worthy
of all my confidence and trust. I believe; help me when I don't.*

FOR YOUR NEXT DEVOTIONAL READING, GO TO PAGE 832.

16 LORD, they came to you in their
distress;
when you disciplined them,
they could barely whisper a prayer.^a
17 As a woman with child and about to
give birth
writhes and cries out in her pain,
so were we in your presence,
O LORD.
18 We were with child, we writhed
in pain,
but we gave birth to wind.
We have not brought salvation to
the earth;
we have not given birth to people
of the world.

19 But your dead will live;
their bodies will rise.
You who dwell in the dust,
wake up and shout for joy.
Your dew is like the dew of the
morning;
the earth will give birth to her
dead.

20 Go, my people, enter your rooms
and shut the doors behind you;
hide yourselves for a little while
until his wrath has passed by.
21 See, the LORD is coming out of his
dwelling
to punish the people of the earth
for their sins.
The earth will disclose the blood shed
upon her;
she will conceal her slain no
longer.

Deliverance of Israel

27 In that day,

the LORD will punish with his sword,
his fierce, great and powerful
sword,
Leviathan the gliding serpent,
Leviathan the coiling serpent;
he will slay the monster of the sea.

2 In that day—

"Sing about a fruitful vineyard:
3   I, the LORD, watch over it;
I water it continually.
I guard it day and night
so that no one may harm it.
4   I am not angry.

If only there were briers and thorns
confronting me!
I would march against them in
battle;
I would set them all on fire.
5 Or else let them come to me for
refuge;
let them make peace with me,
yes, let them make peace with me."

6 In days to come Jacob will take root,
Israel will bud and blossom
and fill all the world with fruit.

7 Has ⌊the LORD⌋ struck her
as he struck down those who
struck her?
Has she been killed
as those were killed who killed her?
8 By warfare^b and exile you contend
with her—
with his fierce blast he drives her
out,
as on a day the east wind blows.
9 By this, then, will Jacob's guilt be
atoned for,
and this will be the full fruitage of
the removal of his sin:
When he makes all the altar stones
to be like chalk stones crushed to
pieces,
no Asherah poles^c or incense altars
will be left standing.
10 The fortified city stands desolate,
an abandoned settlement, forsaken
like the desert;
there the calves graze,
there they lie down;
they strip its branches bare.
11 When its twigs are dry, they are
broken off
and women come and make fires
with them.
For this is a people without
understanding;
so their Maker has no compassion
on them,
and their Creator shows them
no favor.

12 In that day the LORD will thresh from
the flowing Euphrates^d to the Wadi of

---

^a16 The meaning of the Hebrew for this clause
is uncertain.   ^b8 See Septuagint; the meaning
of the Hebrew for this word is uncertain.
^c9 That is, symbols of the goddess Asherah
^d12 Hebrew *River*

Egypt, and you, O Israelites, will be gathered up one by one. [13]And in that day a great trumpet will sound. Those who were perishing in Assyria and those who were exiled in Egypt will come and worship the LORD on the holy mountain in Jerusalem.

Woe to Ephraim

28 Woe to that wreath, the pride of Ephraim's drunkards,
to the fading flower, his glorious beauty,
set on the head of a fertile valley—
to that city, the pride of those laid low by wine!
[2]See, the Lord has one who is powerful and strong.
Like a hailstorm and a destructive wind,
like a driving rain and a flooding downpour,
he will throw it forcefully to the ground.
[3]That wreath, the pride of Ephraim's drunkards,
will be trampled underfoot.
[4]That fading flower, his glorious beauty,
set on the head of a fertile valley,
will be like a fig ripe before harvest—
as soon as someone sees it and takes it in his hand,
he swallows it.

[5]In that day the LORD Almighty
will be a glorious crown,
a beautiful wreath
for the remnant of his people.
[6]He will be a spirit of justice
to him who sits in judgment,
a source of strength
to those who turn back the battle at the gate.

[7]And these also stagger from wine
and reel from beer:
Priests and prophets stagger from beer
and are befuddled with wine;
they reel from beer,
they stagger when seeing visions,
they stumble when rendering decisions.
[8]All the tables are covered with vomit
and there is not a spot without filth.

[9]"Who is it he is trying to teach?
To whom is he explaining his message?
To children weaned from their milk,
to those just taken from the breast?
[10]For it is:
Do and do, do and do,
rule on rule, rule on rule[a];
a little here, a little there."

[11]Very well then, with foreign lips and strange tongues
God will speak to this people,
[12]to whom he said,
"This is the resting place, let the weary rest";
and, "This is the place of repose"—
but they would not listen.
[13]So then, the word of the LORD to them will become:
Do and do, do and do,
rule on rule, rule on rule;
a little here, a little there—
so that they will go and fall backward,
be injured and snared and captured.

[14]Therefore hear the word of the LORD, you scoffers
who rule this people in Jerusalem.
[15]You boast, "We have entered into a covenant with death,
with the grave[b] we have made an agreement.
When an overwhelming scourge sweeps by,
it cannot touch us,
for we have made a lie our refuge
and falsehood[c] our hiding place."

[16]So this is what the Sovereign LORD says:

"See, I lay a stone in Zion,
a tested stone,
a precious cornerstone for a sure foundation;
the one who trusts will never be dismayed.
[17]I will make justice the measuring line
and righteousness the plumb line;

---

a 10 Hebrew / *sav lasav sav lasav / kav lakav kav lakav* (possibly meaningless sounds; perhaps a mimicking of the prophet's words); also in verse 13   *b 15* Hebrew *Sheol*; also in verse 18   *c 15* Or *false gods*

God Guides

MARY GEEGH was a missionary in India. She faced many difficult circumstances and situations, but whatever she faced, she took to God in prayer.

Once there was a conflict between Geegh and a colleague. The woman had ten children and was often sick and couldn't carry out her work. Geegh was critical because this woman was trying to hold onto her job when she wasn't able to keep up with her responsibilities. One morning Geegh was praying about the conflict, and God told her to take the woman one fresh egg. She writes: "A dozen fresh eggs might be reasonable—but one! That might insult my colleague. So I wrote it off and gave up for that morning. At noon when I came home, there was a chicken in a large armchair in my living room! The hen flew down and started to cackle, and there was an egg, freshly laid."

Geegh still argued with God: "She'll laugh at me."

God said, "Results are not your business. Your business is obedience."

So she took the egg to the woman's house. The woman's son was outside, and Geegh gave the egg to the boy and left quickly.

That evening the woman came to Geegh's house and asked, "How did you happen to bring that egg? It was so fresh and good."

Geegh answered, "I was praying and God told me to."

"Oh that's just like God!" said the colleague. "He knew I had nothing to eat this day. There wasn't enough food for all, so I went without. Then you brought the egg for me. When I ate it, I felt so satisfied and strengthened."

And that was the beginning of healing between Mary and her colleague.[7]

Mary Geegh first learned about communicating with God and following his guidance from another missionary, Dr. L. R. Scudder. After seeing the remarkable way Scudder was led by the Holy Spirit in his ministry, she asked him, "How do I begin to have the power of the Holy Spirit to help people?" He replied: "The first step is to 'wait' … 'be still' … 'listen.' Then be *definite* about your sins—daily; with notebook and pencil, write down the things the Holy Spirit speaks to your mind; determine to obey. Then share with others who come to you for help how the power of Christ changes you."[8]

Mary Geegh practiced quiet listening and obedience for the rest of her life until she died at the age of 101. Many of her experiences of guidance are recorded in a little book she titled simply *God Guides*. The stories are informative, astonishing and wise; and all are vivid demonstrations of how God delights to sweetly lead a humble servant who will listen and obey.

P R A Y :

"Speak, for your servant is listening" (1 Samuel 3:10).

M E M O R I Z E :

Show me your ways, O Lord, teach me your paths;
guide me in your truth and teach me, for you are God my Savior,
and my hope is in you all day long. PSALM 25:4–5

FOR YOUR NEXT DEVOTIONAL READING, GO TO PAGE 837.

hail will sweep away your refuge,
the lie,
and water will overflow your hiding
place.
18 Your covenant with death will be
annulled;
your agreement with the grave will
not stand.
When the overwhelming scourge
sweeps by,
you will be beaten down by it.
19 As often as it comes it will carry you
away;
morning after morning, by day and
by night,
it will sweep through."

The understanding of this message
will bring sheer terror.
20 The bed is too short to stretch out on,
the blanket too narrow to wrap
around you.
21 The LORD will rise up as he did at
Mount Perazim,
he will rouse himself as in the
Valley of Gibeon—
to do his work, his strange work,
and perform his task, his alien task.
22 Now stop your mocking,
or your chains will become heavier;
the Lord, the LORD Almighty, has
told me
of the destruction decreed against
the whole land.

23 Listen and hear my voice;
pay attention and hear what I say.
24 When a farmer plows for planting,
does he plow continually?
Does he keep on breaking up and
harrowing the soil?
25 When he has leveled the surface,
does he not sow caraway and
scatter cummin?
Does he not plant wheat in its place,[a]
barley in its plot,[a]
and spelt in its field?
26 His God instructs him
and teaches him the right way.

27 Caraway is not threshed with a
sledge,
nor is a cartwheel rolled over
cummin;
caraway is beaten out with a rod,
and cummin with a stick.

28 Grain must be ground to make bread;
so one does not go on threshing it
forever.
Though he drives the wheels of his
threshing cart over it,
his horses do not grind it.
29 All this also comes from the LORD
Almighty,
wonderful in counsel and
magnificent in wisdom.

Woe to David's City

29 Woe to you, Ariel, Ariel,
the city where David settled!
Add year to year
and let your cycle of festivals go on.
2 Yet I will besiege Ariel;
she will mourn and lament,
she will be to me like an altar
hearth.[b]
3 I will encamp against you all around;
I will encircle you with towers
and set up my siege works against
you.
4 Brought low, you will speak from
the ground;
your speech will mumble out of
the dust.
Your voice will come ghostlike from
the earth;
out of the dust your speech will
whisper.

5 But your many enemies will become
like fine dust,
the ruthless hordes like blown chaff.
Suddenly, in an instant,
6 the LORD Almighty will come
with thunder and earthquake and
great noise,
with windstorm and tempest and
flames of a devouring fire.
7 Then the hordes of all the nations
that fight against Ariel,
that attack her and her fortress and
besiege her,
will be as it is with a dream,
with a vision in the night—
8 as when a hungry man dreams that
he is eating,
but he awakens, and his hunger
remains;

a25 The meaning of the Hebrew for this word is
uncertain.   b2 The Hebrew for *altar hearth*
sounds like the Hebrew for *Ariel*.

as when a thirsty man dreams that he
is drinking,
but he awakens faint, with his
thirst unquenched.
So will it be with the hordes of all
the nations
that fight against Mount Zion.

⁹ Be stunned and amazed,
blind yourselves and be sightless;
be drunk, but not from wine,
stagger, but not from beer.
¹⁰ The LORD has brought over you a
deep sleep:
He has sealed your eyes (the
prophets);
he has covered your heads (the
seers).

¹¹ For you this whole vision is nothing
but words sealed in a scroll. And if you
give the scroll to someone who can read,
and say to him, "Read this, please," he
will answer, "I can't; it is sealed." ¹² Or if
you give the scroll to someone who cannot read, and say, "Read this, please," he
will answer, "I don't know how to read."

¹³ The Lord says:

"These people come near to me with
their mouth
and honor me with their lips,
but their hearts are far from me.
Their worship of me
is made up only of rules taught
by men.ᵃ
¹⁴ Therefore once more I will astound
these people
with wonder upon wonder;
the wisdom of the wise will perish,
the intelligence of the intelligent
will vanish."
¹⁵ Woe to those who go to great depths
to hide their plans from the
LORD,
who do their work in darkness
and think,
"Who sees us? Who will know?"
¹⁶ You turn things upside down,
as if the potter were thought to
be like the clay!
Shall what is formed say to him who
formed it,
"He did not make me"?
Can the pot say of the potter,
"He knows nothing"?

¹⁷ In a very short time, will not Lebanon
be turned into a fertile field
and the fertile field seem like a
forest?
¹⁸ In that day the deaf will hear the
words of the scroll,
and out of gloom and darkness
the eyes of the blind will see.
¹⁹ Once more the humble will rejoice in
the LORD;
the needy will rejoice in the Holy
One of Israel.
²⁰ The ruthless will vanish,
the mockers will disappear,
and all who have an eye for evil will
be cut down—
²¹ those who with a word make a man
out to be guilty,
who ensnare the defender in court
and with false testimony deprive
the innocent of justice.

²² Therefore this is what the LORD, who
redeemed Abraham, says to the house of
Jacob:

"No longer will Jacob be ashamed;
no longer will their faces grow pale.
²³ When they see among them their
children,
the work of my hands,
they will keep my name holy;
they will acknowledge the holiness
of the Holy One of Jacob,
and will stand in awe of the God
of Israel.
²⁴ Those who are wayward in spirit will
gain understanding;
those who complain will accept
instruction."

Woe to the Obstinate Nation

30 "Woe to the obstinate children,"
declares the LORD,
"to those who carry out plans that
are not mine,
forming an alliance, but not by
my Spirit,
heaping sin upon sin;
² who go down to Egypt
without consulting me;
who look for help to Pharaoh's
protection,
to Egypt's shade for refuge.

ᵃ 13 Hebrew; Septuagint *They worship me in
vain; / their teachings are but rules taught by men*

³ But Pharaoh's protection will be to
your shame,
Egypt's shade will bring you
disgrace.
⁴ Though they have officials in Zoan
and their envoys have arrived
in Hanes,
⁵ everyone will be put to shame
because of a people useless to
them,
who bring neither help nor
advantage,
but only shame and disgrace."

⁶ An oracle concerning the animals of
the Negev:

Through a land of hardship and
distress,
of lions and lionesses,
of adders and darting snakes,
the envoys carry their riches on
donkeys' backs,
their treasures on the humps
of camels,
to that unprofitable nation,
⁷ to Egypt, whose help is utterly
useless.
Therefore I call her
Rahab the Do-Nothing.

⁸ Go now, write it on a tablet for them,
inscribe it on a scroll,
that for the days to come
it may be an everlasting witness.
⁹ These are rebellious people, deceitful
children,
children unwilling to listen to the
LORD's instruction.
¹⁰ They say to the seers,
"See no more visions!"
and to the prophets,
"Give us no more visions of what
is right!
Tell us pleasant things,
prophesy illusions.
¹¹ Leave this way,
get off this path,
and stop confronting us
with the Holy One of Israel!"

¹² Therefore, this is what the Holy One
of Israel says:

"Because you have rejected this
message,
relied on oppression
and depended on deceit,

¹³ this sin will become for you
like a high wall, cracked and
bulging,
that collapses suddenly, in an
instant.
¹⁴ It will break in pieces like pottery,
shattered so mercilessly
that among its pieces not a fragment
will be found
for taking coals from a hearth
or scooping water out of a
cistern."

¹⁵ This is what the Sovereign LORD, the
Holy One of Israel, says:

"In repentance and rest is your
salvation,
in quietness and trust is your
strength,
but you would have none of it.
¹⁶ You said, 'No, we will flee on horses.'
Therefore you will flee!
You said, 'We will ride off on swift
horses.'
Therefore your pursuers will
be swift!
¹⁷ A thousand will flee
at the threat of one;
at the threat of five
you will all flee away,
till you are left
like a flagstaff on a mountaintop,
like a banner on a hill."

¹⁸ Yet the LORD longs to be gracious
to you;
he rises to show you compassion.
For the LORD is a God of justice.
Blessed are all who wait for him!

¹⁹ O people of Zion, who live in Jerusalem, you will weep no more. How gracious
he will be when you cry for help! As soon
as he hears, he will answer you. ²⁰ Although the Lord gives you the bread of adversity and the water of affliction, your
teachers will be hidden no more; with your
own eyes you will see them. ²¹ Whether you

> O PEOPLE of Zion, who live in
> Jerusalem, you will weep no more. How
> gracious he will be when you cry for help!
> As soon as he hears, he will answer you.
>
> ISAIAH 30:19

turn to the right or to the left, your ears will hear a voice behind you, saying, "This is the way; walk in it." ²²Then you will defile your idols overlaid with silver and your images covered with gold; you will throw them away like a menstrual cloth and say to them, "Away with you!"

²³He will also send you rain for the seed you sow in the ground, and the food that comes from the land will be rich and plentiful. In that day your cattle will graze in broad meadows. ²⁴The oxen and donkeys that work the soil will eat fodder and mash, spread out with fork and shovel. ²⁵In the day of great slaughter, when the towers fall, streams of water will flow on every high mountain and every lofty hill. ²⁶The moon will shine like the sun, and the sunlight will be seven times brighter, like the light of seven full days, when the LORD binds up the bruises of his people and heals the wounds he inflicted.

ISAIAH 30:15–18

[**MONDAY**]

Don't Just Do Something

30:15 "IN REPENTANCE AND REST IS YOUR SALVATION."

So often the things God tells us to do seem counter-intuitive to our worldly minds. Here is one example: Judah is in a highly charged military crisis, something that seems clearly to call for alliances, armaments and fast horses (see Isaiah 30:1–2; 31:1). God describes with dead-on accuracy what this mentality will result in: the faster they run, the faster their enemies will run (see 30:16). You know that's true, don't you? Have you ever experienced work and demands on your time that seemed only to increase the harder you worked? Have you lived out your own version of the Greek myth of Sisyphus? He was the man cursed by the gods to spend an eternity toiling and straining to push a giant boulder to the top of a hill, only to have it roll back to the bottom when he got to the top—he had to repeat this torturous work over and over and over again, forever.

The Lord says there is a better way: "In repentance and rest is your salvation, in quietness and trust is your strength" (verse 15). The Hebrew word for "strength" is literally "warrior strength." The best way to be strong like a warrior is to stop trying to be strong the way a warrior gets strong. Let the Lord be your strength, for "the LORD longs to be gracious to you; he rises to show you compassion" (verse 18). God is not only more than able to help you, he is more than willing to help you. Even as you move in his direction, you will see him rising to meet you—like the waiting father in Jesus' parable of the prodigal son (see Luke 15:20).

We live in a culture that prizes activity. We believe that no one should just stand there; people should always be doing something, anything. But very often God's approach is the opposite: Don't just do something, stand there and "call to me and I will answer you and tell you great and unsearchable things you do not know" (Jeremiah 33:3).

PRAY:

In repentance and rest is my salvation; in quietness and trust is my strength. Thank you, Lord.

FOR YOUR NEXT DEVOTIONAL READING, GO TO PAGE 849.

²⁷See, the Name of the LORD comes
from afar,
with burning anger and dense
clouds of smoke;
his lips are full of wrath,
and his tongue is a consuming
fire.
²⁸His breath is like a rushing torrent,
rising up to the neck.
He shakes the nations in the sieve of
destruction;
he places in the jaws of the peoples
a bit that leads them astray.
²⁹And you will sing
as on the night you celebrate a
holy festival;
your hearts will rejoice
as when people go up with flutes
to the mountain of the LORD,
to the Rock of Israel.
³⁰The LORD will cause men to hear his
majestic voice
and will make them see his arm
coming down
with raging anger and consuming
fire,
with cloudburst, thunderstorm
and hail.
³¹The voice of the LORD will shatter
Assyria;
with his scepter he will strike
them down.
³²Every stroke the LORD lays on them
with his punishing rod
will be to the music of tambourines
and harps,
as he fights them in battle with the
blows of his arm.
³³Topheth has long been prepared;
it has been made ready for the
king.
Its fire pit has been made deep
and wide,
with an abundance of fire and
wood;
the breath of the LORD,
like a stream of burning sulfur,
sets it ablaze.

Woe to Those Who Rely on Egypt

31 Woe to those who go down to
Egypt for help,
who rely on horses,
who trust in the multitude of their
chariots

and in the great strength of their
horsemen,
but do not look to the Holy One
of Israel,
or seek help from the LORD.
²Yet he too is wise and can bring
disaster;
he does not take back his words.
He will rise up against the house of
the wicked,
against those who help
evildoers.
³But the Egyptians are men and not
God;
their horses are flesh and not spirit.
When the LORD stretches out his
hand,
he who helps will stumble,
he who is helped will fall;
both will perish together.

⁴This is what the LORD says to me:

"As a lion growls,
a great lion over his prey—
and though a whole band of
shepherds
is called together against him,
he is not frightened by their shouts
or disturbed by their clamor—
so the LORD Almighty will come down
to do battle on Mount Zion and on
its heights.
⁵Like birds hovering overhead,
the LORD Almighty will shield
Jerusalem;
he will shield it and deliver it,
he will 'pass over' it and will
rescue it."

⁶Return to him you have so greatly re-
volted against, O Israelites. ⁷For in that
day every one of you will reject the idols
of silver and gold your sinful hands have
made.

⁸"Assyria will fall by a sword that is
not of man;
a sword, not of mortals, will
devour them.
They will flee before the sword
and their young men will be put to
forced labor.
⁹Their stronghold will fall because of
terror;
at sight of the battle standard their
commanders will panic,"

declares the LORD,
whose fire is in Zion,
whose furnace is in Jerusalem.

The Kingdom of Righteousness

32 See, a king will reign in
righteousness
and rulers will rule with justice.
2 Each man will be like a shelter from
the wind
and a refuge from the storm,
like streams of water in the desert
and the shadow of a great rock in a
thirsty land.

3 Then the eyes of those who see will
no longer be closed,
and the ears of those who hear
will listen.
4 The mind of the rash will know and
understand,
and the stammering tongue will be
fluent and clear.
5 No longer will the fool be called noble
nor the scoundrel be highly
respected.
6 For the fool speaks folly,
his mind is busy with evil:
He practices ungodliness
and spreads error concerning
the LORD;
the hungry he leaves empty
and from the thirsty he withholds
water.
7 The scoundrel's methods are wicked,
he makes up evil schemes
to destroy the poor with lies,
even when the plea of the needy
is just.
8 But the noble man makes noble
plans,
and by noble deeds he stands.

The Women of Jerusalem

9 You women who are so complacent,
rise up and listen to me;
you daughters who feel secure,
hear what I have to say!
10 In little more than a year
you who feel secure will tremble;
the grape harvest will fail,
and the harvest of fruit will not
come.
11 Tremble, you complacent women;
shudder, you daughters who feel
secure!

Strip off your clothes,
put sackcloth around your waists.
12 Beat your breasts for the pleasant
fields,
for the fruitful vines
13 and for the land of my people,
a land overgrown with thorns and
briers—
yes, mourn for all houses of
merriment
and for this city of revelry.
14 The fortress will be abandoned,
the noisy city deserted;
citadel and watchtower will become a
wasteland forever,
the delight of donkeys, a pasture
for flocks,
15 till the Spirit is poured upon us from
on high,
and the desert becomes a fertile
field,
and the fertile field seems like
a forest.
16 Justice will dwell in the desert
and righteousness live in the fertile
field.
17 The fruit of righteousness will be
peace;
the effect of righteousness will be
quietness and confidence
forever.
18 My people will live in peaceful
dwelling places,
in secure homes,
in undisturbed places of rest.
19 Though hail flattens the forest
and the city is leveled completely,
20 how blessed you will be,
sowing your seed by every stream,
and letting your cattle and donkeys
range free.

Distress and Help

33 Woe to you, O destroyer,
you who have not been
destroyed!
Woe to you, O traitor,
you who have not been betrayed!
When you stop destroying,
you will be destroyed;
when you stop betraying,
you will be betrayed.

2 O LORD, be gracious to us;
we long for you.

Be our strength every morning,
our salvation in time of distress.
³ At the thunder of your voice, the
peoples flee;
when you rise up, the nations
scatter.
⁴ Your plunder, O nations, is harvested
as by young locusts;
like a swarm of locusts men pounce
on it.

⁵ The Lord is exalted, for he dwells on
high;
he will fill Zion with justice and
righteousness.
⁶ He will be the sure foundation for
your times,
a rich store of salvation and
wisdom and knowledge;
the fear of the Lord is the key to
this treasure.ª

> ❝ It is not enough to begin to pray,
> nor to pray aright; nor is it enough to
> continue for a time to pray; but we must
> patiently, believingly, continue in prayer
> until we obtain an answer; and further
> we have not only to continue in prayer
> unto the end, but we have also to believe
> that God does hear us, and will answer
> our prayers. Most frequently we fail in
> not continuing in prayer until the
> blessing is obtained, and in not expecting
> the blessing. ❞
>
> GEORGE MUELLER

⁷ Look, their brave men cry aloud in
the streets;
the envoys of peace weep bitterly.
⁸ The highways are deserted,
no travelers are on the roads.
The treaty is broken,
its witnessesᵇ are despised,
no one is respected.
⁹ The land mournsᶜ and wastes away,
Lebanon is ashamed and withers;
Sharon is like the Arabah,
and Bashan and Carmel drop their
leaves.

¹⁰ "Now will I arise," says the Lord.
"Now will I be exalted;
now will I be lifted up.

¹¹ You conceive chaff,
you give birth to straw;
your breath is a fire that consumes
you.
¹² The peoples will be burned as if to
lime;
like cut thornbushes they will be
set ablaze."

¹³ You who are far away, hear what I
have done;
you who are near, acknowledge
my power!
¹⁴ The sinners in Zion are terrified;
trembling grips the godless:
"Who of us can dwell with the
consuming fire?
Who of us can dwell with
everlasting burning?"
¹⁵ He who walks righteously
and speaks what is right,
who rejects gain from extortion
and keeps his hand from accepting
bribes,
who stops his ears against plots of
murder
and shuts his eyes against
contemplating evil—
¹⁶ this is the man who will dwell on the
heights,
whose refuge will be the mountain
fortress.
His bread will be supplied,
and water will not fail him.

¹⁷ Your eyes will see the king in his
beauty
and view a land that stretches afar.
¹⁸ In your thoughts you will ponder the
former terror:
"Where is that chief officer?
Where is the one who took the
revenue?
Where is the officer in charge of the
towers?"
¹⁹ You will see those arrogant people
no more,
those people of an obscure speech,
with their strange,
incomprehensible tongue.

²⁰ Look upon Zion, the city of our
festivals;
your eyes will see Jerusalem,

ª6 Or *is a treasure from him*   ᵇ8 Dead Sea
Scrolls; Masoretic Text / *the cities*   ᶜ9 Or *dries up*

a peaceful abode, a tent that will
  not be moved;
its stakes will never be pulled up,
  nor any of its ropes broken.
²¹ There the LORD will be our Mighty
  One.
It will be like a place of broad rivers
  and streams.
No galley with oars will ride them,
  no mighty ship will sail them.
²² For the LORD is our judge,
  the LORD is our lawgiver,
  the LORD is our king;
  it is he who will save us.

²³ Your rigging hangs loose:
  The mast is not held secure,
  the sail is not spread.
Then an abundance of spoils will be
  divided
  and even the lame will carry off
  plunder.
²⁴ No one living in Zion will say,
  "I am ill";
  and the sins of those who dwell
  there will be forgiven.

Judgment Against the Nations

34 Come near, you nations, and
  listen;
  pay attention, you peoples!
Let the earth hear, and all that is
  in it,
  the world, and all that comes
  out of it!
² The LORD is angry with all nations;
  his wrath is upon all their armies.
He will totally destroy[a] them,
  he will give them over to slaughter.
³ Their slain will be thrown out,
  their dead bodies will send up a
  stench;
  the mountains will be soaked with
  their blood.
⁴ All the stars of the heavens will be
  dissolved
  and the sky rolled up like a scroll;
all the starry host will fall
  like withered leaves from the vine,
  like shriveled figs from the fig tree.

⁵ My sword has drunk its fill in the
  heavens;
  see, it descends in judgment
  on Edom,
  the people I have totally destroyed.

⁶ The sword of the LORD is bathed
  in blood,
  it is covered with fat—
the blood of lambs and goats,
  fat from the kidneys of rams.
For the LORD has a sacrifice in Bozrah
  and a great slaughter in Edom.
⁷ And the wild oxen will fall with them,
  the bull calves and the great bulls.
Their land will be drenched with
  blood,
  and the dust will be soaked with
  fat.

⁸ For the LORD has a day of vengeance,
  a year of retribution, to uphold
  Zion's cause.
⁹ Edom's streams will be turned into
  pitch,
  her dust into burning sulfur;
  her land will become blazing pitch!
¹⁰ It will not be quenched night and
  day;
  its smoke will rise forever.
From generation to generation it will
  lie desolate;
  no one will ever pass through it
  again.
¹¹ The desert owl[b] and screech owl[b] will
  possess it;
  the great owl[b] and the raven will
  nest there.
God will stretch out over Edom
  the measuring line of chaos
  and the plumb line of desolation.
¹² Her nobles will have nothing there to
  be called a kingdom,
  all her princes will vanish away.
¹³ Thorns will overrun her citadels,
  nettles and brambles her
  strongholds.
She will become a haunt for jackals,
  a home for owls.
¹⁴ Desert creatures will meet with
  hyenas,
  and wild goats will bleat to each
  other;
  there the night creatures will
  also repose
  and find for themselves places
  of rest.

[a]2 The Hebrew term refers to the irrevocable
giving over of things or persons to the LORD, often
by totally destroying them; also in verse 5.
[b]11 The precise identification of these birds is
uncertain.

15 The owl will nest there and lay eggs,
    she will hatch them, and care for
       her young under the shadow
       of her wings;
there also the falcons will gather,
    each with its mate.

16 Look in the scroll of the LORD and
read:

None of these will be missing,
    not one will lack her mate.
For it is his mouth that has given
       the order,
    and his Spirit will gather them
       together.
17 He allots their portions;
    his hand distributes them by
       measure.
They will possess it forever
    and dwell there from generation to
       generation.

Joy of the Redeemed

35 The desert and the parched land
    will be glad;
    the wilderness will rejoice and
       blossom.
Like the crocus, 2 it will burst into
       bloom;
    it will rejoice greatly and shout
       for joy.
The glory of Lebanon will be given
       to it,
    the splendor of Carmel and
       Sharon;
they will see the glory of the LORD,
    the splendor of our God.

3 Strengthen the feeble hands,
    steady the knees that give way;
4 say to those with fearful hearts,
    "Be strong, do not fear;
your God will come,
    he will come with vengeance;
with divine retribution
    he will come to save you."

5 Then will the eyes of the blind be
       opened
    and the ears of the deaf unstopped.
6 Then will the lame leap like a deer,
    and the mute tongue shout for joy.
Water will gush forth in the
       wilderness
    and streams in the desert.

7 The burning sand will become a pool,
    the thirsty ground bubbling
       springs.
In the haunts where jackals once lay,
    grass and reeds and papyrus will
       grow.

8 And a highway will be there;
    it will be called the Way of
       Holiness.
The unclean will not journey on it;
    it will be for those who walk in that
       Way;
    wicked fools will not go about
       on it.[a]
9 No lion will be there,
    nor will any ferocious beast get up
       on it;
    they will not be found there.
But only the redeemed will walk
       there,
10   and the ransomed of the LORD will
       return.
They will enter Zion with singing;
    everlasting joy will crown their
       heads.
Gladness and joy will overtake them,
    and sorrow and sighing will flee
       away.

Sennacherib Threatens Jerusalem

36 In the fourteenth year of King Hezekiah's reign, Sennacherib king of Assyria attacked all the fortified cities of Judah and captured them. 2 Then the king of Assyria sent his field commander with a large army from Lachish to King Hezekiah at Jerusalem. When the commander stopped at the aqueduct of the Upper Pool, on the road to the Washerman's Field, 3 Eliakim son of Hilkiah the palace administrator, Shebna the secretary, and Joah son of Asaph the recorder went out to him.

4 The field commander said to them, "Tell Hezekiah,

"'This is what the great king, the king of Assyria, says: On what are you basing this confidence of yours? 5 You say you have strategy and military strength—but you speak only empty words. On whom are you depending, that you rebel against me?

a 8 Or / the simple will not stray from it

⁶Look now, you are depending on Egypt, that splintered reed of a staff, which pierces a man's hand and wounds him if he leans on it! Such is Pharaoh king of Egypt to all who depend on him. ⁷And if you say to me, "We are depending on the LORD our God"—isn't he the one whose high places and altars Hezekiah removed, saying to Judah and Jerusalem, "You must worship before this altar"?

⁸" 'Come now, make a bargain with my master, the king of Assyria: I will give you two thousand horses—if you can put riders on them! ⁹How then can you repulse one officer of the least of my master's officials, even though you are depending on Egypt for chariots and horsemen? ¹⁰Furthermore, have I come to attack and destroy this land without the LORD? The LORD himself told me to march against this country and destroy it.' "

¹¹Then Eliakim, Shebna and Joah said to the field commander, "Please speak to your servants in Aramaic, since we understand it. Don't speak to us in Hebrew in the hearing of the people on the wall."

¹²But the commander replied, "Was it only to your master and you that my master sent me to say these things, and not to the men sitting on the wall—who, like you, will have to eat their own filth and drink their own urine?"

¹³Then the commander stood and called out in Hebrew, "Hear the words of the great king, the king of Assyria! ¹⁴This is what the king says: Do not let Hezekiah deceive you. He cannot deliver you! ¹⁵Do not let Hezekiah persuade you to trust in the LORD when he says, 'The LORD will surely deliver us; this city will not be given into the hand of the king of Assyria.' ¹⁶Do not listen to Hezekiah. This is what the king of Assyria says: Make peace with me and come out to me. Then every one of you will eat from his own vine and fig tree and drink water from his own cistern, ¹⁷until I come and take you to a land like your own—a land of grain and new wine, a land of bread and vineyards.

¹⁸"Do not let Hezekiah mislead you when he says, 'The LORD will deliver us.' Has the god of any nation ever delivered his land from the hand of the king of Assyria? ¹⁹Where are the gods of Hamath and Arpad? Where are the gods of Sepharvaim? Have they rescued Samaria from my hand? ²⁰Who of all the gods of these countries has been able to save his land from me? How then can the LORD deliver Jerusalem from my hand?"

²¹But the people remained silent and said nothing in reply, because the king had commanded, "Do not answer him."

²²Then Eliakim son of Hilkiah the palace administrator, Shebna the secretary, and Joah son of Asaph the recorder went to Hezekiah, with their clothes torn, and told him what the field commander had said.

Jerusalem's Deliverance Foretold

37 When King Hezekiah heard this, he tore his clothes and put on sackcloth and went into the temple of the LORD. ²He sent Eliakim the palace administrator, Shebna the secretary, and the leading priests, all wearing sackcloth, to the prophet Isaiah son of Amoz. ³They told him, "This is what Hezekiah says: This day is a day of distress and rebuke and disgrace, as when children come to the point of birth and there is no strength to deliver them. ⁴It may be that the LORD your God will hear the words of the field commander, whom his master, the king of Assyria, has sent to ridicule the living God, and that he will rebuke him for the words the LORD your God has heard. Therefore pray for the remnant that still survives."

⁵When King Hezekiah's officials came to Isaiah, ⁶Isaiah said to them, "Tell your master, 'This is what the LORD says: Do not be afraid of what you have heard—those words with which the underlings of the king of Assyria have blasphemed me. ⁷Listen! I am going to put a spirit in him so that when he hears a certain report, he will return to his own country, and there I will have him cut down with the sword.' "

⁸When the field commander heard that the king of Assyria had left Lachish, he withdrew and found the king fighting against Libnah.

[9]Now Sennacherib received a report that Tirhakah, the Cushite[a] king of Egypt, was marching out to fight against him. When he heard it, he sent messengers to Hezekiah with this word: [10]"Say to Hezekiah king of Judah: Do not let the god you depend on deceive you when he says, 'Jerusalem will not be handed over to the king of Assyria.' [11]Surely you have heard what the kings of Assyria have done to all the countries, destroying them completely. And will you be delivered? [12]Did the gods of the nations that were destroyed by my forefathers deliver them—the gods of Gozan, Haran, Rezeph and the people of Eden who were in Tel Assar? [13]Where is the king of Hamath, the king of Arpad, the king of the city of Sepharvaim, or of Hena or Ivvah?"

Hezekiah's Prayer

[14]Hezekiah received the letter from the messengers and read it. Then he went up to the temple of the LORD and spread it out before the LORD. [15]And Hezekiah prayed to the LORD: [16]"O LORD Almighty, God of Israel, enthroned between the cherubim, you alone are God over all the kingdoms of the earth. You have made heaven and earth. [17]Give ear, O LORD, and hear; open your eyes, O LORD, and see; listen to all the words Sennacherib has sent to insult the living God.

> AND Hezekiah prayed to the LORD.
>
> ISAIAH 37:15

[18]"It is true, O LORD, that the Assyrian kings have laid waste all these peoples and their lands. [19]They have thrown their gods into the fire and destroyed them, for they were not gods but only wood and stone, fashioned by human hands. [20]Now, O LORD our God, deliver us from his hand, so that all kingdoms on earth may know that you alone, O LORD, are God.[b]"

Sennacherib's Fall

[21]Then Isaiah son of Amoz sent a message to Hezekiah: "This is what the LORD, the God of Israel, says: Because you have prayed to me concerning Sennacherib king of Assyria, [22]this is the word the LORD has spoken against him:

"The Virgin Daughter of Zion
    despises and mocks you.
The Daughter of Jerusalem
    tosses her head as you flee.
[23]Who is it you have insulted and
        blasphemed?
    Against whom have you raised
        your voice
and lifted your eyes in pride?
    Against the Holy One of Israel!
[24]By your messengers
    you have heaped insults on
        the Lord.
And you have said,
    'With my many chariots
I have ascended the heights of the
        mountains,
    the utmost heights of Lebanon.
I have cut down its tallest cedars,
    the choicest of its pines.
I have reached its remotest
        heights,
    the finest of its forests.
[25]I have dug wells in foreign lands[c]
    and drunk the water there.
With the soles of my feet
    I have dried up all the streams
        of Egypt.'

[26]"Have you not heard?
    Long ago I ordained it.
In days of old I planned it;
    now I have brought it to pass,
that you have turned fortified cities
    into piles of stone.
[27]Their people, drained of power,
    are dismayed and put to shame.
They are like plants in the field,
    like tender green shoots,
like grass sprouting on the roof,
    scorched[d] before it grows up.

[28]"But I know where you stay
    and when you come and go
    and how you rage against me.

---

[a]9 That is, from the upper Nile region
[b]20 Dead Sea Scrolls (see also 2 Kings 19:19); Masoretic Text *alone are the LORD*   [c]25 Dead Sea Scrolls (see also 2 Kings 19:24); Masoretic Text does not have *in foreign lands*.   [d]27 Some manuscripts of the Masoretic Text, Dead Sea Scrolls and some Septuagint manuscripts (see also 2 Kings 19:26); most manuscripts of the Masoretic Text *roof / and terraced fields*

²⁹Because you rage against me
and because your insolence has
reached my ears,
I will put my hook in your nose
and my bit in your mouth,
and I will make you return
by the way you came.

³⁰"This will be the sign for you, O Hezekiah:

"This year you will eat what grows
by itself,
and the second year what springs
from that.
But in the third year sow and reap,
plant vineyards and eat their fruit.
³¹Once more a remnant of the house
of Judah
will take root below and bear fruit
above.
³²For out of Jerusalem will come a
remnant,
and out of Mount Zion a band of
survivors.
The zeal of the LORD Almighty
will accomplish this.

³³"Therefore this is what the LORD says
concerning the king of Assyria:

"He will not enter this city
or shoot an arrow here.
He will not come before it with shield
or build a siege ramp against it.
³⁴By the way that he came he will
return;
he will not enter this city,"
declares the LORD.
³⁵"I will defend this city and save it,
for my sake and for the sake of
David my servant!"

³⁶Then the angel of the LORD went out
and put to death a hundred and eighty-
five thousand men in the Assyrian camp.
When the people got up the next morning—there were all the dead bodies! ³⁷So
Sennacherib king of Assyria broke camp
and withdrew. He returned to Nineveh
and stayed there.

³⁸One day, while he was worshiping in
the temple of his god Nisroch, his sons
Adrammelech and Sharezer cut him
down with the sword, and they escaped
to the land of Ararat. And Esarhaddon
his son succeeded him as king.

Hezekiah's Illness

38 In those days Hezekiah became ill
and was at the point of death. The
prophet Isaiah son of Amoz went to him
and said, "This is what the LORD says: Put
your house in order, because you are going to die; you will not recover."

> **HEZEKIAH** turned his face to the wall and
> prayed to the LORD, "Remember, O LORD,
> how I have walked before you faithfully
> and with wholehearted devotion and have
> done what is good in your eyes."
>
> ISAIAH 38:2-3

²Hezekiah turned his face to the wall
and prayed to the LORD, ³"Remember,
O LORD, how I have walked before you
faithfully and with wholehearted devotion and have done what is good in your
eyes." And Hezekiah wept bitterly.

⁴Then the word of the LORD came to
Isaiah: ⁵"Go and tell Hezekiah, 'This is
what the LORD, the God of your father

> "**I HAVE** heard your prayer and seen your
> tears."
>
> ISAIAH 38:5

David, says: I have heard your prayer and
seen your tears; I will add fifteen years to
your life. ⁶And I will deliver you and this
city from the hand of the king of Assyria.
I will defend this city.

⁷"'This is the LORD's sign to you that
the LORD will do what he has promised: ⁸I
will make the shadow cast by the sun go
back the ten steps it has gone down on
the stairway of Ahaz.'" So the sunlight
went back the ten steps it had gone
down.

⁹A writing of Hezekiah king of Judah
after his illness and recovery:

¹⁰I said, "In the prime of my life
must I go through the gates of
death*a*
and be robbed of the rest of my
years?"

a10 Hebrew Sheol

11 I said, "I will not again see the LORD,
  the LORD, in the land of the living;
no longer will I look on mankind,
  or be with those who now dwell in
    this world.[a]
12 Like a shepherd's tent my house
  has been pulled down and taken
    from me.
Like a weaver I have rolled up
  my life,
and he has cut me off from
  the loom;
day and night you made an end
  of me.
13 I waited patiently till dawn,
  but like a lion he broke all my
    bones;
day and night you made an end
  of me.
14 I cried like a swift or thrush,
  I moaned like a mourning dove.
My eyes grew weak as I looked to the
  heavens.
I am troubled; O Lord, come to
  my aid!"

15 But what can I say?
  He has spoken to me, and he
    himself has done this.
I will walk humbly all my years
  because of this anguish of
    my soul.
16 Lord, by such things men live;
  and my spirit finds life in
    them too.
You restored me to health
  and let me live.
17 Surely it was for my benefit
  that I suffered such anguish.
In your love you kept me
  from the pit of destruction;
you have put all my sins
  behind your back.
18 For the grave[b] cannot praise you,
  death cannot sing your praise;
those who go down to the pit
  cannot hope for your faithfulness.
19 The living, the living—they praise
  you,
  as I am doing today;
fathers tell their children
  about your faithfulness.

20 The LORD will save me,
  and we will sing with stringed
    instruments

all the days of our lives
  in the temple of the LORD.

21 Isaiah had said, "Prepare a poultice of figs and apply it to the boil, and he will recover."

22 Hezekiah had asked, "What will be the sign that I will go up to the temple of the LORD?"

Envoys From Babylon

39 At that time Merodach-Baladan son of Baladan king of Babylon sent Hezekiah letters and a gift, because he had heard of his illness and recovery. 2 Hezekiah received the envoys gladly and showed them what was in his storehouses—the silver, the gold, the spices, the fine oil, his entire armory and everything found among his treasures. There was nothing in his palace or in all his kingdom that Hezekiah did not show them.

3 Then Isaiah the prophet went to King Hezekiah and asked, "What did those men say, and where did they come from?"

"From a distant land," Hezekiah replied. "They came to me from Babylon."

4 The prophet asked, "What did they see in your palace?"

"They saw everything in my palace," Hezekiah said. "There is nothing among my treasures that I did not show them."

5 Then Isaiah said to Hezekiah, "Hear the word of the LORD Almighty: 6 The time will surely come when everything in your palace, and all that your fathers have stored up until this day, will be carried off to Babylon. Nothing will be left, says the LORD. 7 And some of your descendants, your own flesh and blood who will be born to you, will be taken away, and they will become eunuchs in the palace of the king of Babylon."

8 "The word of the LORD you have spoken is good," Hezekiah replied. For he thought, "There will be peace and security in my lifetime."

Comfort for God's People

40 Comfort, comfort my people,
  says your God.
2 Speak tenderly to Jerusalem,
  and proclaim to her

<hr>

a 11 A few Hebrew manuscripts; most Hebrew manuscripts in the place of cessation
b 18 Hebrew Sheol

that her hard service has been
completed,
that her sin has been paid for,
that she has received from the
Lord's hand
double for all her sins.

³ A voice of one calling:
"In the desert prepare
the way for the Lord*a*;
make straight in the wilderness
a highway for our God.*b*
⁴ Every valley shall be raised up,
every mountain and hill made low;
the rough ground shall become level,
the rugged places a plain.
⁵ And the glory of the Lord will be
revealed,
and all mankind together will see it.
For the mouth of the Lord
has spoken."

⁶ A voice says, "Cry out."
And I said, "What shall I cry?"

"All men are like grass,
and all their glory is like the
flowers of the field.
⁷ The grass withers and the flowers
fall,
because the breath of the Lord
blows on them.
Surely the people are grass.
⁸ The grass withers and the flowers
fall,
but the word of our God stands
forever."

⁹ You who bring good tidings to Zion,
go up on a high mountain.
You who bring good tidings to
Jerusalem,*c*
lift up your voice with a shout,
lift it up, do not be afraid;
say to the towns of Judah,
"Here is your God!"
¹⁰ See, the Sovereign Lord comes with
power,
and his arm rules for him.
See, his reward is with him,
and his recompense accompanies
him.
¹¹ He tends his flock like a shepherd:
He gathers the lambs in his arms
and carries them close to his heart;
he gently leads those that have
young.

¹² Who has measured the waters in the
hollow of his hand,
or with the breadth of his hand
marked off the heavens?
Who has held the dust of the earth in
a basket,
or weighed the mountains on the
scales
and the hills in a balance?
¹³ Who has understood the mind*d* of
the Lord,
or instructed him as his counselor?
¹⁴ Whom did the Lord consult to
enlighten him,
and who taught him the right way?
Who was it that taught him
knowledge
or showed him the path of
understanding?

¹⁵ Surely the nations are like a drop in
a bucket;
they are regarded as dust on
the scales;
he weighs the islands as though
they were fine dust.
¹⁶ Lebanon is not sufficient for altar
fires,
nor its animals enough for burnt
offerings.
¹⁷ Before him all the nations are as
nothing;
they are regarded by him as
worthless
and less than nothing.

¹⁸ To whom, then, will you compare
God?
What image will you compare
him to?
¹⁹ As for an idol, a craftsman casts it,
and a goldsmith overlays it with
gold
and fashions silver chains for it.
²⁰ A man too poor to present such an
offering
selects wood that will not rot.
He looks for a skilled craftsman
to set up an idol that will not
topple.

a3 Or *A voice of one calling in the desert: /
"Prepare the way for the Lord* *b3* Hebrew;
Septuagint *make straight the paths of our God*
c9 Or *O Zion, bringer of good tidings, / go up on a
high mountain. / O Jerusalem, bringer of good
tidings* *d13* Or *Spirit;* or *spirit*

21 Do you not know?
  Have you not heard?
Has it not been told you from the
    beginning?
Have you not understood since the
    earth was founded?
22 He sits enthroned above the circle of
    the earth,
  and its people are like
    grasshoppers.
He stretches out the heavens like a
    canopy,
  and spreads them out like a tent to
    live in.
23 He brings princes to naught
  and reduces the rulers of this world
    to nothing.
24 No sooner are they planted,
  no sooner are they sown,
  no sooner do they take root in the
    ground,
than he blows on them and they
    wither,
  and a whirlwind sweeps them away
    like chaff.

25 "To whom will you compare me?
  Or who is my equal?" says the
    Holy One.
26 Lift your eyes and look to the
    heavens:
  Who created all these?
He who brings out the starry host
    one by one,
  and calls them each by name.
Because of his great power and
    mighty strength,
  not one of them is missing.

27 Why do you say, O Jacob,
  and complain, O Israel,
"My way is hidden from the LORD;
  my cause is disregarded by my
    God"?
28 Do you not know?
  Have you not heard?
The LORD is the everlasting God,
  the Creator of the ends of the earth.
He will not grow tired or weary,
  and his understanding no one can
    fathom.
29 He gives strength to the weary
  and increases the power of the
    weak.
30 Even youths grow tired and weary,
  and young men stumble and fall;

31 but those who hope in the LORD
  will renew their strength.
They will soar on wings like eagles;
  they will run and not grow weary,
  they will walk and not be faint.

The Helper of Israel

41 "Be silent before me, you islands!
    Let the nations renew their
    strength!
Let them come forward and speak;
  let us meet together at the place of
    judgment.

2 "Who has stirred up one from
    the east,
  calling him in righteousness to
    his service[a]?
He hands nations over to him
  and subdues kings before him.
He turns them to dust with his sword,
  to windblown chaff with his bow.
3 He pursues them and moves on
    unscathed,
  by a path his feet have not traveled
    before.
4 Who has done this and carried it
    through,
  calling forth the generations from
    the beginning?
I, the LORD—with the first of them
  and with the last—I am he."

5 The islands have seen it and fear;
  the ends of the earth tremble.
They approach and come forward;
6   each helps the other
  and says to his brother, "Be
    strong!"
7 The craftsman encourages the
    goldsmith,
  and he who smooths with the
    hammer
  spurs on him who strikes the anvil.
He says of the welding, "It is good."
  He nails down the idol so it will
    not topple.

8 "But you, O Israel, my servant,
  Jacob, whom I have chosen,
  you descendants of Abraham my
    friend,
9 I took you from the ends of the earth,
  from its farthest corners I called
    you.

a2 Or / whom victory meets at every step

I said, 'You are my servant';
I have chosen you and have not
rejected you.
[10] So do not fear, for I am with you;
do not be dismayed, for I am your
God.
I will strengthen you and help you;
I will uphold you with my righteous
right hand.
[11] "All who rage against you
will surely be ashamed and
disgraced;

those who oppose you
will be as nothing and perish.
[12] Though you search for your enemies,
you will not find them.
Those who wage war against you
will be as nothing at all.
[13] For I am the LORD, your God,
who takes hold of your right hand
and says to you, Do not fear;
I will help you.
[14] Do not be afraid, O worm Jacob,
O little Israel,

ISAIAH 40:30–31

[TUESDAY]

Like an Eagle

40:31 THEY WILL SOAR ON WINGS LIKE EAGLES.

Isaiah must have watched eagles closely to see the way they soar. As birds go, eagles' wings are big, but the muscles that make them flap aren't. Pound for pound, an eagle's strength is no match for the strength of a humming-bird. The strength of eagles is not in their flapping but in their soaring. An eagle will perch high atop a canyon wall and wait for the thermals—warm wind currents that rise up from the canyon below. When the rising wind is just right, the eagle will fold its wings to its sides, literally cast itself into the chasm and plummet into the abyss. Isaiah would not have known this in his day, but God has equipped eagles with tiny sensors in their beaks to let the birds know when they have reached the optimal speed. When this happens, the bird will spread its wings, catch the thermals, rise up into the sky and soar. Isaiah didn't know the mechanism, but he could see the effect.

This is a great picture of hoping in God. Through no strength of our own, we cast ourselves upon God, fall into his mercy and soar on his promises. Our strength comes from trusting and soaring, not flapping and working.

To fully appreciate the power of this verse, read the entire chapter. The key sentence is, "To whom, then, will you compare God?" (40:18). Isaiah's method is to use negative contrast to show God's incomparable majesty. He takes the things we already think to be great—the earth, the seas, nations and the starry heavens—and shows them to be nothing compared to God. God has measured the waters in the hollow of his hand, held the dust of the earth in a basket; before him all the nations are like a drop in a bucket, and the stars march out before him like obedient troops on the parade ground. This is the God into whose power we cast ourselves and soar, like eagles!

P R A Y :

*I hope in you, O Lord. Nothing can compare to you! In you I will trust
and be strengthened and renewed. For you have promised this,
and I believe your promise to be worthy of all my trust.*

FOR YOUR NEXT DEVOTIONAL READING, GO TO PAGE 867.

for I myself will help you," declares
the LORD,
your Redeemer, the Holy One of
Israel.
15 "See, I will make you into a threshing
sledge,
new and sharp, with many teeth.
You will thresh the mountains and
crush them,
and reduce the hills to chaff.
16 You will winnow them, the wind will
pick them up,
and a gale will blow them away.
But you will rejoice in the LORD
and glory in the Holy One of
Israel.

17 "The poor and needy search for
water,
but there is none;
their tongues are parched with
thirst.
But I the LORD will answer them;
I, the God of Israel, will not forsake
them.
18 I will make rivers flow on barren
heights,
and springs within the valleys.
I will turn the desert into pools of
water,
and the parched ground into
springs.
19 I will put in the desert
the cedar and the acacia, the
myrtle and the olive.
I will set pines in the wasteland,
the fir and the cypress together,
20 so that people may see and know,
may consider and understand,
that the hand of the LORD has
done this,
that the Holy One of Israel has
created it.

21 "Present your case," says the LORD.
"Set forth your arguments," says
Jacob's King.
22 "Bring in ˻your idols˼ to tell us
what is going to happen.
Tell us what the former things were,
so that we may consider them
and know their final outcome.
Or declare to us the things to come,
23   tell us what the future holds,
so we may know that you
are gods.

Do something, whether good or bad,
so that we will be dismayed and
filled with fear.
24 But you are less than nothing
and your works are utterly
worthless;
he who chooses you is detestable.

25 "I have stirred up one from the north,
and he comes—
one from the rising sun who calls
on my name.
He treads on rulers as if they were
mortar,
as if he were a potter treading the
clay.
26 Who told of this from the beginning,
so we could know,
or beforehand, so we could say,
'He was right'?
No one told of this,
no one foretold it,
no one heard any words from you.
27 I was the first to tell Zion, 'Look, here
they are!'
I gave to Jerusalem a messenger of
good tidings.
28 I look but there is no one—
no one among them to give
counsel,
no one to give answer when I ask
them.
29 See, they are all false!
Their deeds amount to nothing;
their images are but wind and
confusion.

The Servant of the LORD

42 "Here is my servant, whom
I uphold,
my chosen one in whom I delight;
I will put my Spirit on him
and he will bring justice to the
nations.
2 He will not shout or cry out,
or raise his voice in the streets.
3 A bruised reed he will not break,
and a smoldering wick he will not
snuff out.
In faithfulness he will bring forth
justice;
4   he will not falter or be discouraged
till he establishes justice on earth.
In his law the islands will put
their hope."

5 This is what God the Lord says—
  he who created the heavens and
    stretched them out,
  who spread out the earth and all
    that comes out of it,
  who gives breath to its people,
  and life to those who walk on it:
6 "I, the Lord, have called you in
    righteousness;
  I will take hold of your hand.
  I will keep you and will make you
    to be a covenant for the people
    and a light for the Gentiles,
7 to open eyes that are blind,
  to free captives from prison
  and to release from the dungeon
    those who sit in darkness.

8 "I am the Lord; that is my name!
  I will not give my glory to
    another
  or my praise to idols.
9 See, the former things have taken
    place,
  and new things I declare;
  before they spring into being
  I announce them to you."

> SING to the Lord a new song,
>   his praise from the ends of the earth,
> you who go down to the sea, and all
>   that is in it,
>   you islands, and all who live in them.
>
> ISAIAH 42:10

Song of Praise to the Lord
10 Sing to the Lord a new song,
  his praise from the ends of the
    earth,
  you who go down to the sea, and all
    that is in it,
  you islands, and all who live
    in them.
11 Let the desert and its towns raise
    their voices;
  let the settlements where Kedar
    lives rejoice.
  Let the people of Sela sing for joy;
  let them shout from the
    mountaintops.
12 Let them give glory to the Lord
  and proclaim his praise in the
    islands.

13 The Lord will march out like a
    mighty man,
  like a warrior he will stir up
    his zeal;
  with a shout he will raise the battle
    cry
  and will triumph over his enemies.

14 "For a long time I have kept silent,
  I have been quiet and held myself
    back.
  But now, like a woman in childbirth,
  I cry out, I gasp and pant.
15 I will lay waste the mountains and
    hills
  and dry up all their vegetation;
  I will turn rivers into islands
  and dry up the pools.
16 I will lead the blind by ways they have
    not known,
  along unfamiliar paths I will guide
    them;
  I will turn the darkness into light
    before them
  and make the rough places
    smooth.
  These are the things I will do;
  I will not forsake them.
17 But those who trust in idols,
  who say to images, 'You are our
    gods,'
  will be turned back in utter shame.

Israel Blind and Deaf
18 "Hear, you deaf;
  look, you blind, and see!
19 Who is blind but my servant,
  and deaf like the messenger
    I send?
  Who is blind like the one committed
    to me,
  blind like the servant of the Lord?
20 You have seen many things, but have
    paid no attention;
  your ears are open, but you hear
    nothing."
21 It pleased the Lord
  for the sake of his righteousness
  to make his law great and glorious.
22 But this is a people plundered and
    looted,
  all of them trapped in pits
  or hidden away in prisons.
  They have become plunder,
  with no one to rescue them;

they have been made loot,
with no one to say, "Send them
back."

23 Which of you will listen to this
or pay close attention in time
to come?
24 Who handed Jacob over to become
loot,
and Israel to the plunderers?
Was it not the LORD,
against whom we have sinned?
For they would not follow his ways;
they did not obey his law.
25 So he poured out on them his
burning anger,
the violence of war.
It enveloped them in flames, yet they
did not understand;
it consumed them, but they did
not take it to heart.

Israel's Only Savior

43 But now, this is what the LORD
says—
he who created you, O Jacob,
he who formed you, O Israel:
"Fear not, for I have redeemed you;
I have summoned you by name;
you are mine.
2 When you pass through the waters,
I will be with you;
and when you pass through the
rivers,
they will not sweep over you.
When you walk through the fire,
you will not be burned;
the flames will not set you ablaze.
3 For I am the LORD, your God,
the Holy One of Israel, your Savior;
I give Egypt for your ransom,
Cush[a] and Seba in your stead.
4 Since you are precious and honored
in my sight,
and because I love you,
I will give men in exchange for you,
and people in exchange for your
life.
5 Do not be afraid, for I am with you;
I will bring your children from the
east
and gather you from the west.
6 I will say to the north, 'Give them up!'
and to the south, 'Do not hold
them back.'

Bring my sons from afar
and my daughters from the ends
of the earth—
7 everyone who is called by my name,
whom I created for my glory,
whom I formed and made."

8 Lead out those who have eyes but
are blind,
who have ears but are deaf.
9 All the nations gather together
and the peoples assemble.
Which of them foretold this
and proclaimed to us the former
things?
Let them bring in their witnesses to
prove they were right,
so that others may hear and say,
"It is true."
10 "You are my witnesses," declares
the LORD,
"and my servant whom I have
chosen,
so that you may know and believe me
and understand that I am he.
Before me no god was formed,
nor will there be one after me.
11 I, even I, am the LORD,
and apart from me there is no
savior.
12 I have revealed and saved and
proclaimed—
I, and not some foreign god among
you.
You are my witnesses," declares the
LORD, "that I am God.
13 Yes, and from ancient days I
am he.
No one can deliver out of my hand.
When I act, who can reverse it?"

God's Mercy and Israel's Unfaithfulness

14 This is what the LORD says—
your Redeemer, the Holy One of
Israel:
"For your sake I will send to Babylon
and bring down as fugitives all the
Babylonians,[b]
in the ships in which they took
pride.
15 I am the LORD, your Holy One,
Israel's Creator, your King."

a 3 That is, the upper Nile region
b 14 Or Chaldeans

16 This is what the LORD says—
　　he who made a way through
　　　the sea,
　　a path through the mighty waters,
17 who drew out the chariots and
　　　horses,
　　the army and reinforcements
　　　together,
　　and they lay there, never to rise
　　　again,
　　extinguished, snuffed out like
　　　a wick:
18 "Forget the former things;
　　do not dwell on the past.
19 See, I am doing a new thing!
　　Now it springs up; do you not
　　　perceive it?
　　I am making a way in the desert
　　and streams in the wasteland.
20 The wild animals honor me,
　　the jackals and the owls,
　　because I provide water in the
　　　desert
　　and streams in the wasteland,
　　to give drink to my people, my
　　　chosen,
21 　the people I formed for myself
　　that they may proclaim my praise.

22 "Yet you have not called upon me,
　　　O Jacob,
　　you have not wearied yourselves
　　　for me, O Israel.
23 You have not brought me sheep for
　　　burnt offerings,
　　nor honored me with your
　　　sacrifices.
　　I have not burdened you with grain
　　　offerings
　　nor wearied you with demands
　　　for incense.
24 You have not bought any fragrant
　　　calamus for me,
　　or lavished on me the fat of your
　　　sacrifices.
　　But you have burdened me with
　　　your sins
　　and wearied me with your offenses.

25 "I, even I, am he who blots out
　　your transgressions, for my own
　　　sake,
　　and remembers your sins no more.
26 Review the past for me,
　　let us argue the matter together;
　　state the case for your innocence.

27 Your first father sinned;
　　your spokesmen rebelled against
　　　me.
28 So I will disgrace the dignitaries of
　　　your temple,
　　and I will consign Jacob to
　　　destruction[a]
　　and Israel to scorn.

Israel the Chosen

44 "But now listen, O Jacob, my
　　servant,
　　Israel, whom I have chosen.
2 This is what the LORD says—
　　he who made you, who formed you
　　　in the womb,
　　and who will help you:
　　Do not be afraid, O Jacob, my servant,
　　Jeshurun, whom I have chosen.
3 For I will pour water on the thirsty
　　　land,
　　and streams on the dry ground;
　　I will pour out my Spirit on your
　　　offspring,
　　and my blessing on your
　　　descendants.
4 They will spring up like grass in a
　　　meadow,
　　like poplar trees by flowing
　　　streams.
5 One will say, 'I belong to the LORD';
　　another will call himself by the
　　　name of Jacob;
　　still another will write on his hand,
　　　'The LORD's,'
　　and will take the name Israel.

The LORD, Not Idols

6 "This is what the LORD says—
　　Israel's King and Redeemer, the
　　　LORD Almighty:
　　I am the first and I am the last;
　　apart from me there is no God.
7 Who then is like me? Let him
　　　proclaim it.
　　Let him declare and lay out before
　　　me
　　what has happened since I
　　　established my ancient people,
　　and what is yet to come—
　　yes, let him foretell what will come.

a28 The Hebrew term refers to the irrevocable
giving over of things or persons to the LORD, often
by totally destroying them.

8 Do not tremble, do not be afraid.
  Did I not proclaim this and foretell
    it long ago?
  You are my witnesses. Is there any
    God besides me?
  No, there is no other Rock; I know
    not one."

9 All who make idols are nothing,
    and the things they treasure are
      worthless.
  Those who would speak up for them
    are blind;
    they are ignorant, to their own
      shame.
10 Who shapes a god and casts an
      idol,
    which can profit him nothing?
11 He and his kind will be put to shame;
    craftsmen are nothing but men.
  Let them all come together and take
    their stand;
    they will be brought down to terror
      and infamy.

12 The blacksmith takes a tool
    and works with it in the coals;
  he shapes an idol with hammers,
    he forges it with the might of his
      arm.
  He gets hungry and loses his
    strength;
    he drinks no water and grows faint.
13 The carpenter measures with a line
    and makes an outline with a
      marker;
  he roughs it out with chisels
    and marks it with compasses.
  He shapes it in the form of man,
    of man in all his glory,
    that it may dwell in a shrine.
14 He cut down cedars,
    or perhaps took a cypress or oak.
  He let it grow among the trees of the
    forest,
    or planted a pine, and the rain
      made it grow.

15 It is man's fuel for burning;
    some of it he takes and warms
      himself,
  he kindles a fire and bakes bread.
  But he also fashions a god and
    worships it;
    he makes an idol and bows down
      to it.
16 Half of the wood he burns in the fire;
    over it he prepares his meal,
  he roasts his meat and eats his fill.
  He also warms himself and says,
    "Ah! I am warm; I see the fire."
17 From the rest he makes a god, his idol;
    he bows down to it and worships.
  He prays to it and says,
    "Save me; you are my god."
18 They know nothing, they understand
      nothing;
    their eyes are plastered over so
      they cannot see,
    and their minds closed so they
      cannot understand.
19 No one stops to think,
    no one has the knowledge or
      understanding to say,
  "Half of it I used for fuel;
    I even baked bread over its coals,
    I roasted meat and I ate.
  Shall I make a detestable thing from
    what is left?
    Shall I bow down to a block of
      wood?"
20 He feeds on ashes, a deluded heart
      misleads him;
    he cannot save himself, or say,
    "Is not this thing in my right hand a
      lie?"

21 "Remember these things, O Jacob,
    for you are my servant, O Israel.
  I have made you, you are my servant;
    O Israel, I will not forget you.
22 I have swept away your offenses like
    a cloud,
    your sins like the morning mist.
  Return to me,
    for I have redeemed you."

23 Sing for joy, O heavens, for the LORD
    has done this;
    shout aloud, O earth beneath.
  Burst into song, you mountains,
    you forests and all your trees,
  for the LORD has redeemed Jacob,
    he displays his glory in Israel.

Jerusalem to Be Inhabited

24 "This is what the LORD says—
    your Redeemer, who formed you in
        the womb:

I am the LORD,
    who has made all things,
    who alone stretched out the heavens,
    who spread out the earth by myself,

25 who foils the signs of false prophets
        and makes fools of diviners,
    who overthrows the learning of the
        wise
        and turns it into nonsense,
26 who carries out the words of his
        servants
        and fulfills the predictions of his
            messengers,

who says of Jerusalem, 'It shall be
        inhabited,'
    of the towns of Judah, 'They shall
        be built,'
    and of their ruins, 'I will restore
        them,'
27 who says to the watery deep, 'Be dry,
        and I will dry up your streams,'
28 who says of Cyrus, 'He is my
        shepherd
        and will accomplish all that I
            please;
    he will say of Jerusalem, "Let it
        be rebuilt,"
    and of the temple, "Let its
        foundations be laid." '

45 "This is what the LORD says to his
        anointed,
    to Cyrus, whose right hand I take
        hold of
    to subdue nations before him
        and to strip kings of their armor,
    to open doors before him
        so that gates will not be shut:
2 I will go before you
        and will level the mountains[a];
    I will break down gates of bronze
        and cut through bars of iron.
3 I will give you the treasures of
        darkness,
        riches stored in secret places,
    so that you may know that I am
        the LORD,
        the God of Israel, who summons
            you by name.

4 For the sake of Jacob my servant,
        of Israel my chosen,
    I summon you by name
        and bestow on you a title of honor,
        though you do not acknowledge
            me.
5 I am the LORD, and there is no other;
        apart from me there is no God.
    I will strengthen you,
        though you have not
            acknowledged me,
6 so that from the rising of the sun
        to the place of its setting
    men may know there is none besides
        me.
    I am the LORD, and there is no
        other.
7 I form the light and create darkness,
    I bring prosperity and create
        disaster;
    I, the LORD, do all these things.

8 "You heavens above, rain down
        righteousness;
    let the clouds shower it down.
Let the earth open wide,
    let salvation spring up,
    let righteousness grow with it;
    I, the LORD, have created it.

9 "Woe to him who quarrels with
        his Maker,
    to him who is but a potsherd
        among the potsherds on
            the ground.
Does the clay say to the potter,
    'What are you making?'
Does your work say,
    'He has no hands'?
10 Woe to him who says to his father,
    'What have you begotten?'
    or to his mother,
    'What have you brought to birth?'

11 "This is what the LORD says—
        the Holy One of Israel, and its
            Maker:
Concerning things to come,
    do you question me about my
        children,
    or give me orders about the work of
        my hands?
12 It is I who made the earth
    and created mankind upon it.

a2 Dead Sea Scrolls and Septuagint; the meaning
of the word in the Masoretic Text is uncertain.

My own hands stretched out the
    heavens;
  I marshaled their starry hosts.
[13] I will raise up Cyrus[a] in my
    righteousness:
  I will make all his ways straight.
He will rebuild my city
  and set my exiles free,
but not for a price or reward,
  says the LORD Almighty."

[14] This is what the LORD says:

"The products of Egypt and the
    merchandise of Cush,[b]
  and those tall Sabeans—
they will come over to you
  and will be yours;
they will trudge behind you,
  coming over to you in chains.
They will bow down before you
  and plead with you, saying,
'Surely God is with you, and there is
    no other;
  there is no other god.'"

[15] Truly you are a God who hides
    himself,
  O God and Savior of Israel.
[16] All the makers of idols will be put to
    shame and disgraced;
  they will go off into disgrace
    together.
[17] But Israel will be saved by the LORD
  with an everlasting salvation;
you will never be put to shame or
    disgraced,
  to ages everlasting.

[18] For this is what the LORD says—
he who created the heavens,
  he is God;
he who fashioned and made the earth,
  he founded it;
he did not create it to be empty,
  but formed it to be inhabited—
he says:
"I am the LORD,
  and there is no other.
[19] I have not spoken in secret,
  from somewhere in a land of
    darkness;
I have not said to Jacob's
    descendants,
  'Seek me in vain.'
I, the LORD, speak the truth;
  I declare what is right.

[20] "Gather together and come;
  assemble, you fugitives from the
    nations.
Ignorant are those who carry about
    idols of wood,
  who pray to gods that cannot save.
[21] Declare what is to be, present it—
  let them take counsel together.
Who foretold this long ago,
  who declared it from the distant
    past?
Was it not I, the LORD?
  And there is no God apart from me,
a righteous God and a Savior;
  there is none but me.

[22] "Turn to me and be saved,
  all you ends of the earth;
  for I am God, and there is no other.
[23] By myself I have sworn,
  my mouth has uttered in all
    integrity
a word that will not be revoked:
Before me every knee will bow;
  by me every tongue will swear.
[24] They will say of me, 'In the LORD
    alone
are righteousness and strength.'"
All who have raged against him
  will come to him and be put to
    shame.
[25] But in the LORD all the descendants
    of Israel
  will be found righteous and will
    exult.

Gods of Babylon

46 Bel bows down, Nebo stoops low;
  their idols are borne by beasts
    of burden.[c]
The images that are carried about are
    burdensome,
  a burden for the weary.
[2] They stoop and bow down together;
  unable to rescue the burden,
  they themselves go off into captivity.

[3] "Listen to me, O house of Jacob,
  all you who remain of the house
    of Israel,
you whom I have upheld since you
    were conceived,
  and have carried since your birth.

---

[a]13 Hebrew *him*   [b]14 That is, the upper Nile
region   [c]1 Or *are but beasts and cattle*

⁴Even to your old age and gray hairs
  I am he, I am he who will sustain
    you.
I have made you and I will carry you;
  I will sustain you and I will rescue
    you.

⁵ "To whom will you compare me or
    count me equal?
  To whom will you liken me that we
    may be compared?
⁶ Some pour out gold from their bags
    and weigh out silver on the
    scales;
  they hire a goldsmith to make it into
    a god,
  and they bow down and worship it.
⁷ They lift it to their shoulders and
    carry it;
  they set it up in its place, and there
    it stands.
  From that spot it cannot move.
  Though one cries out to it, it does not
    answer;
  it cannot save him from his
    troubles.

⁸ "Remember this, fix it in mind,
  take it to heart, you rebels.
⁹ Remember the former things, those
    of long ago;
  I am God, and there is no other;
  I am God, and there is none like
    me.
¹⁰ I make known the end from the
    beginning,
  from ancient times, what is still
    to come.
  I say: My purpose will stand,
  and I will do all that I please.
¹¹ From the east I summon a bird of
    prey;
  from a far-off land, a man to fulfill
    my purpose.
  What I have said, that will I bring
    about;
  what I have planned, that will I do.
¹² Listen to me, you stubborn-hearted,
  you who are far from
    righteousness.
¹³ I am bringing my righteousness near,
  it is not far away;
  and my salvation will not be
    delayed.
  I will grant salvation to Zion,
  my splendor to Israel.

The Fall of Babylon

47 "Go down, sit in the dust,
    Virgin Daughter of Babylon;
  sit on the ground without a throne,
    Daughter of the Babylonians.ᵃ
  No more will you be called
    tender or delicate.
² Take millstones and grind flour;
    take off your veil.
  Lift up your skirts, bare your legs,
    and wade through the streams.
³ Your nakedness will be exposed
    and your shame uncovered.
  I will take vengeance;
    I will spare no one."

⁴ Our Redeemer—the LORD Almighty
    is his name—
  is the Holy One of Israel.

⁵ "Sit in silence, go into darkness,
    Daughter of the Babylonians;
  no more will you be called
    queen of kingdoms.
⁶ I was angry with my people
    and desecrated my inheritance;
  I gave them into your hand,
    and you showed them no mercy.
  Even on the aged
    you laid a very heavy yoke.
⁷ You said, 'I will continue forever—
    the eternal queen!'
  But you did not consider these things
    or reflect on what might happen.

⁸ "Now then, listen, you wanton
    creature,
  lounging in your security
  and saying to yourself,
    'I am, and there is none besides
    me.
  I will never be a widow
    or suffer the loss of children.'
⁹ Both of these will overtake you
    in a moment, on a single day:
  loss of children and widowhood.
  They will come upon you in full
    measure,
    in spite of your many sorceries
    and all your potent spells.
¹⁰ You have trusted in your wickedness
    and have said, 'No one sees me.'
  Your wisdom and knowledge
    mislead you

ᵃ1 Or *Chaldeans*; also in verse 5

when you say to yourself,
'I am, and there is none besides
me.'
¹¹ Disaster will come upon you,
and you will not know how to
conjure it away.
A calamity will fall upon you
that you cannot ward off with a
ransom;
a catastrophe you cannot foresee
will suddenly come upon you.

¹² "Keep on, then, with your magic
spells
and with your many sorceries,
which you have labored at since
childhood.
Perhaps you will succeed,
perhaps you will cause terror.
¹³ All the counsel you have received has
only worn you out!
Let your astrologers come forward,
those stargazers who make
predictions month by month,
let them save you from what is
coming upon you.
¹⁴ Surely they are like stubble;
the fire will burn them up.
They cannot even save themselves
from the power of the flame.
Here are no coals to warm anyone;
here is no fire to sit by.
¹⁵ That is all they can do for you—
these you have labored with
and trafficked with since
childhood.
Each of them goes on in his error;
there is not one that can save you.

Stubborn Israel

48 "Listen to this, O house of Jacob,
you who are called by the name
of Israel
and come from the line of Judah,
you who take oaths in the name of
the Lord
and invoke the God of Israel—
but not in truth or righteousness—
² you who call yourselves citizens of
the holy city
and rely on the God of Israel—
the Lord Almighty is his name:
³ I foretold the former things long ago,
my mouth announced them and I
made them known;

then suddenly I acted, and they
came to pass.
⁴ For I knew how stubborn you were;
the sinews of your neck were iron,
your forehead was bronze.
⁵ Therefore I told you these things long
ago;
before they happened I announced
them to you
so that you could not say,
'My idols did them;
my wooden image and metal god
ordained them.'
⁶ You have heard these things; look
at them all.
Will you not admit them?

"From now on I will tell you of
new things,
of hidden things unknown to you.
⁷ They are created now, and not long
ago;
you have not heard of them before
today.
So you cannot say,
'Yes, I knew of them.'
⁸ You have neither heard nor
understood;
from of old your ear has not been
open.
Well do I know how treacherous
you are;
you were called a rebel from birth.
⁹ For my own name's sake I delay my
wrath;
for the sake of my praise I hold it
back from you,
so as not to cut you off.
¹⁰ See, I have refined you, though not as
silver;
I have tested you in the furnace of
affliction.
¹¹ For my own sake, for my own sake,
I do this.
How can I let myself be defamed?
I will not yield my glory to another.

Israel Freed

¹² "Listen to me, O Jacob,
Israel, whom I have called:
I am he;
I am the first and I am the last.
¹³ My own hand laid the foundations of
the earth,
and my right hand spread out the
heavens;

when I summon them,
they all stand up together.

14 "Come together, all of you, and listen:
Which of ˻the idols˼ has foretold
these things?
The LORD's chosen ally
will carry out his purpose against
Babylon;
his arm will be against the
Babylonians.ᵃ

15 I, even I, have spoken;
yes, I have called him.
I will bring him,
and he will succeed in his mission.

16 "Come near me and listen to this:

"From the first announcement I have
not spoken in secret;
at the time it happens, I am there."

And now the Sovereign LORD has
sent me,
with his Spirit.

17 This is what the LORD says—
your Redeemer, the Holy One of
Israel:
"I am the LORD your God,
who teaches you what is best
for you,
who directs you in the way you
should go.
18 If only you had paid attention to my
commands,
your peace would have been like
a river,
your righteousness like the waves
of the sea.
19 Your descendants would have been
like the sand,
your children like its numberless
grains;
their name would never be cut off
nor destroyed from before me."

20 Leave Babylon,
flee from the Babylonians!
Announce this with shouts of joy
and proclaim it.
Send it out to the ends of the earth;
say, "The LORD has redeemed his
servant Jacob."
21 They did not thirst when he led them
through the deserts;
he made water flow for them from
the rock;

he split the rock
and water gushed out.

22 "There is no peace," says the LORD,
"for the wicked."

The Servant of the LORD

49 Listen to me, you islands;
hear this, you distant nations:
Before I was born the LORD called me;
from my birth he has made
mention of my name.
2 He made my mouth like a sharpened
sword,
in the shadow of his hand he hid
me;
he made me into a polished arrow
and concealed me in his quiver.
3 He said to me, "You are my servant,
Israel, in whom I will display my
splendor."
4 But I said, "I have labored to no
purpose;
I have spent my strength in vain
and for nothing.
Yet what is due me is in the LORD's
hand,
and my reward is with my God."

5 And now the LORD says—
he who formed me in the womb to
be his servant
to bring Jacob back to him
and gather Israel to himself,
for I am honored in the eyes of the
LORD
and my God has been my
strength—
6 he says:
"It is too small a thing for you to
be my servant
to restore the tribes of Jacob
and bring back those of Israel I
have kept.
I will also make you a light for the
Gentiles,
that you may bring my salvation to
the ends of the earth."

7 This is what the LORD says—
the Redeemer and Holy One of
Israel—
to him who was despised and
abhorred by the nation,
to the servant of rulers:

ᵃ 14 Or *Chaldeans*; also in verse 20

"Kings will see you and rise up,
  princes will see and bow down,
because of the LORD, who is faithful,
  the Holy One of Israel, who has
    chosen you."

Restoration of Israel

⁸This is what the LORD says:

"In the time of my favor I will answer
    you,
  and in the day of salvation I will
    help you;
I will keep you and will make you
  to be a covenant for the people,
to restore the land
  and to reassign its desolate
    inheritances,
⁹to say to the captives, 'Come out,'
  and to those in darkness, 'Be free!'

"They will feed beside the roads
  and find pasture on every barren
    hill.
¹⁰They will neither hunger nor thirst,
  nor will the desert heat or the sun
    beat upon them.
He who has compassion on them will
    guide them
  and lead them beside springs
    of water.
¹¹I will turn all my mountains into
    roads,
  and my highways will be raised up.
¹²See, they will come from afar—
  some from the north, some from
    the west,
  some from the region of Aswan.ᵃ"

¹³Shout for joy, O heavens;
  rejoice, O earth;
  burst into song, O mountains!
For the LORD comforts his people
  and will have compassion on his
    afflicted ones.

SHOUT for joy, O heavens;
  rejoice, O earth;
  burst into song, O mountains!
For the LORD comforts his people
  and will have compassion on his
    afflicted ones.

ISAIAH 49:13

---

¹⁴But Zion said, "The LORD has
    forsaken me,
  the Lord has forgotten me."
¹⁵"Can a mother forget the baby at
    her breast
  and have no compassion on the
    child she has borne?
Though she may forget,
  I will not forget you!
¹⁶See, I have engraved you on the
    palms of my hands;
  your walls are ever before me.
¹⁷Your sons hasten back,
  and those who laid you waste
    depart from you.
¹⁸Lift up your eyes and look around;
  all your sons gather and come to
    you.
As surely as I live," declares the LORD,
  "you will wear them all as
    ornaments;
  you will put them on, like
    a bride.

¹⁹"Though you were ruined and
    made desolate
  and your land laid waste,
now you will be too small for your
    people,
  and those who devoured you will
    be far away.
²⁰The children born during your
    bereavement
  will yet say in your hearing,
'This place is too small for us;
  give us more space to live in.'
²¹Then you will say in your heart,
'Who bore me these?
I was bereaved and barren;
  I was exiled and rejected.
Who brought these up?
I was left all alone,
  but these—where have they come
    from?'"

²²This is what the Sovereign LORD says:

"See, I will beckon to the Gentiles,
  I will lift up my banner to the
    peoples;
they will bring your sons in their
    arms
  and carry your daughters on their
    shoulders.

ᵃ12 Dead Sea Scrolls; Masoretic Text Sinim

²³Kings will be your foster fathers,
and their queens your nursing
mothers.
They will bow down before you with
their faces to the ground;
they will lick the dust at your feet.
Then you will know that I am the
LORD;
those who hope in me will not be
disappointed."

²⁴Can plunder be taken from warriors,
or captives rescued from the
fierce[a]?

²⁵But this is what the LORD says:

"Yes, captives will be taken from
warriors,
and plunder retrieved from the
fierce;
I will contend with those who
contend with you,
and your children I will save.
²⁶I will make your oppressors eat their
own flesh;
they will be drunk on their own
blood, as with wine.
Then all mankind will know
that I, the LORD, am your Savior,
your Redeemer, the Mighty One
of Jacob."

Israel's Sin and the Servant's Obedience

50 This is what the LORD says:

"Where is your mother's certificate
of divorce
with which I sent her away?
Or to which of my creditors
did I sell you?
Because of your sins you were sold;
because of your transgressions
your mother was sent away.
²When I came, why was there
no one?
When I called, why was there no
one to answer?
Was my arm too short to ransom
you?
Do I lack the strength to rescue
you?
By a mere rebuke I dry up the sea,
I turn rivers into a desert;
their fish rot for lack of water
and die of thirst.

³I clothe the sky with darkness
and make sackcloth its covering."

⁴The Sovereign LORD has given me an
instructed tongue,
to know the word that sustains
the weary.
He wakens me morning by morning,
wakens my ear to listen like one
being taught.
⁵The Sovereign LORD has opened
my ears,
and I have not been rebellious;
I have not drawn back.
⁶I offered my back to those who
beat me,
my cheeks to those who pulled out
my beard;
I did not hide my face
from mocking and spitting.
⁷Because the Sovereign LORD helps
me,
I will not be disgraced.
Therefore have I set my face like flint,
and I know I will not be put to
shame.
⁸He who vindicates me is near.
Who then will bring charges
against me?
Let us face each other!
Who is my accuser?
Let him confront me!
⁹It is the Sovereign LORD who helps
me.
Who is he that will condemn me?
They will all wear out like a garment;
the moths will eat them up.

¹⁰Who among you fears the LORD
and obeys the word of his servant?
Let him who walks in the dark,
who has no light,
trust in the name of the LORD
and rely on his God.
¹¹But now, all you who light fires
and provide yourselves with
flaming torches,
go, walk in the light of your fires
and of the torches you have set
ablaze.
This is what you shall receive from
my hand:
You will lie down in torment.

[a]24 Dead Sea Scrolls, Vulgate and Syriac (see also
Septuagint and verse 25); Masoretic Text
righteous

Everlasting Salvation for Zion

51 "Listen to me, you who pursue righteousness
and who seek the LORD:
Look to the rock from which you
were cut
and to the quarry from which you
were hewn;
² look to Abraham, your father,
and to Sarah, who gave you birth.
When I called him he was but one,
and I blessed him and made him
many.
³ The LORD will surely comfort Zion
and will look with compassion on
all her ruins;
he will make her deserts like Eden,
her wastelands like the garden of
the LORD.
Joy and gladness will be found in her,
thanksgiving and the sound of
singing.

⁴ "Listen to me, my people;
hear me, my nation:
The law will go out from me;
my justice will become a light
to the nations.
⁵ My righteousness draws near
speedily,
my salvation is on the way,
and my arm will bring justice to
the nations.
The islands will look to me
and wait in hope for my arm.
⁶ Lift up your eyes to the heavens,
look at the earth beneath;
the heavens will vanish like smoke,
the earth will wear out like a
garment
and its inhabitants die like flies.
But my salvation will last forever,
my righteousness will never fail.

⁷ "Hear me, you who know what is
right,
you people who have my law in
your hearts:
Do not fear the reproach of men
or be terrified by their insults.
⁸ For the moth will eat them up like
a garment;
the worm will devour them like
wool.
But my righteousness will last forever,

my salvation through all
generations."

⁹ Awake, awake! Clothe yourself with
strength,
O arm of the LORD;
awake, as in days gone by,
as in generations of old.
Was it not you who cut Rahab to
pieces,
who pierced that monster through?
¹⁰ Was it not you who dried up the sea,
the waters of the great deep,
who made a road in the depths of
the sea
so that the redeemed might cross
over?
¹¹ The ransomed of the LORD will return.
They will enter Zion with singing;
everlasting joy will crown their
heads.
Gladness and joy will overtake them,
and sorrow and sighing will flee
away.

¹² "I, even I, am he who comforts you.
Who are you that you fear mortal
men,
the sons of men, who are but grass,
¹³ that you forget the LORD your Maker,
who stretched out the heavens
and laid the foundations of the
earth,
that you live in constant terror
every day
because of the wrath of the
oppressor,
who is bent on destruction?
For where is the wrath of the
oppressor?
¹⁴ The cowering prisoners will soon
be set free;
they will not die in their dungeon,
nor will they lack bread.
¹⁵ For I am the LORD your God,
who churns up the sea so that its
waves roar—
the LORD Almighty is his name.
¹⁶ I have put my words in your mouth
and covered you with the shadow
of my hand—
I who set the heavens in place,
who laid the foundations of the
earth,
and who say to Zion, 'You are my
people.'"

The Cup of the LORD's Wrath

17 Awake, awake!
  Rise up, O Jerusalem,
you who have drunk from the hand
    of the LORD
  the cup of his wrath,
you who have drained to its dregs
    the goblet that makes men stagger.
18 Of all the sons she bore
    there was none to guide her;
  of all the sons she reared
    there was none to take her by the
      hand.
19 These double calamities have come
      upon you—
    who can comfort you?—
  ruin and destruction, famine and
      sword—
    who can[a] console you?
20 Your sons have fainted;
    they lie at the head of every street,
    like antelope caught in a net.
  They are filled with the wrath of
      the LORD
    and the rebuke of your God.

21 Therefore hear this, you afflicted one,
    made drunk, but not with wine.
22 This is what your Sovereign LORD says,
    your God, who defends his people:
  "See, I have taken out of your hand
    the cup that made you stagger;
  from that cup, the goblet of my
      wrath,
    you will never drink again.
23 I will put it into the hands of your
      tormentors,
    who said to you,
  'Fall prostrate that we may walk
      over you.'
  And you made your back like the
      ground,
    like a street to be walked over."

52 Awake, awake, O Zion,
    clothe yourself with strength.
  Put on your garments of splendor,
    O Jerusalem, the holy city.
  The uncircumcised and defiled
    will not enter you again.
2 Shake off your dust;
    rise up, sit enthroned, O Jerusalem.
  Free yourself from the chains on your
      neck,
    O captive Daughter of Zion.

3 For this is what the LORD says:

  "You were sold for nothing,
    and without money you will be
      redeemed."

4 For this is what the Sovereign LORD
says:

  "At first my people went down to
      Egypt to live;
    lately, Assyria has oppressed them.

5 "And now what do I have here?" declares the LORD.

  "For my people have been taken
      away for nothing,
    and those who rule them mock,[b]"
      declares the LORD.
  "And all day long
    my name is constantly
      blasphemed.
6 Therefore my people will know my
      name;
    therefore in that day they will
      know
  that it is I who foretold it.
    Yes, it is I."

7 How beautiful on the mountains
    are the feet of those who bring
      good news,
  who proclaim peace,
    who bring good tidings,
    who proclaim salvation,
  who say to Zion,
    "Your God reigns!"
8 Listen! Your watchmen lift up their
      voices;
    together they shout for joy.
  When the LORD returns to Zion,
    they will see it with their own eyes.
9 Burst into songs of joy together,
    you ruins of Jerusalem,
  for the LORD has comforted his
      people,
    he has redeemed Jerusalem.
10 The LORD will lay bare his holy arm
    in the sight of all the nations,
  and all the ends of the earth will see
    the salvation of our God.

11 Depart, depart, go out from there!
    Touch no unclean thing!

---

[a] 19 Dead Sea Scrolls, Septuagint, Vulgate and
Syriac; Masoretic Text / how can I   [b] 5 Dead
Sea Scrolls and Vulgate; Masoretic Text wail

Come out from it and be pure,
  you who carry the vessels of the
    LORD.
[12] But you will not leave in haste
  or go in flight;
for the LORD will go before you,
  the God of Israel will be your rear
    guard.

The Suffering and Glory of the Servant

[13] See, my servant will act wisely[a];
  he will be raised and lifted up and
    highly exalted.
[14] Just as there were many who were
    appalled at him[b]—
  his appearance was so disfigured
    beyond that of any man
  and his form marred beyond
    human likeness—
[15] so will he sprinkle many nations,[c]
  and kings will shut their mouths
    because of him.
For what they were not told, they
    will see,
  and what they have not heard, they
    will understand.

53 Who has believed our message
  and to whom has the arm of the
    LORD been revealed?
[2] He grew up before him like a tender
    shoot,
  and like a root out of dry ground.
He had no beauty or majesty to
    attract us to him,
  nothing in his appearance that we
    should desire him.
[3] He was despised and rejected by men,
  a man of sorrows, and familiar
    with suffering.
Like one from whom men hide their
    faces
  he was despised, and we esteemed
    him not.

[4] Surely he took up our infirmities
  and carried our sorrows,
yet we considered him stricken
    by God,
  smitten by him, and afflicted.
[5] But he was pierced for our
    transgressions,
  he was crushed for our iniquities;
the punishment that brought us
    peace was upon him,
  and by his wounds we are healed.

[6] We all, like sheep, have gone astray,
  each of us has turned to his own
    way;
and the LORD has laid on him
  the iniquity of us all.

[7] He was oppressed and afflicted,
  yet he did not open his mouth;
he was led like a lamb to the
    slaughter,
  and as a sheep before her shearers
    is silent,
so he did not open his mouth.
[8] By oppression[d] and judgment he was
    taken away.
  And who can speak of his
    descendants?
For he was cut off from the land of
    the living;
  for the transgression of my people
    he was stricken.[e]
[9] He was assigned a grave with the
    wicked,
  and with the rich in his death,
though he had done no violence,
  nor was any deceit in his mouth.

[10] Yet it was the LORD's will to crush him
    and cause him to suffer,
  and though the LORD makes[f] his
    life a guilt offering,
he will see his offspring and prolong
    his days,
  and the will of the LORD will
    prosper in his hand.
[11] After the suffering of his soul,
  he will see the light ˌof lifeˌ[g] and
    be satisfied[h];
by his knowledge[i] my righteous
    servant will justify many,
  and he will bear their iniquities.
[12] Therefore I will give him a portion
    among the great,[j]
  and he will divide the spoils with
    the strong,[k]

---

[a]13 Or *will prosper*   [b]14 Hebrew *you*
[c]15 Hebrew; Septuagint *so will many nations
marvel at him*   [d]8 Or *From arrest*
[e]8 Or *away. / Yet who of his generation
considered / that he was cut off from the land of
the living / for the transgression of my people, / to
whom the blow was due?*   [f]10 Hebrew *though
you make*   [g]11 Dead Sea Scrolls (see also
Septuagint); Masoretic Text does not have *the
light of life*.   [h]11 Or (with Masoretic Text)
[11]*He will see the result of the suffering of his soul /
and be satisfied*   [i]11 Or *by knowledge of him*
[j]12 Or *many*   [k]12 Or *numerous*

because he poured out his life unto
death,
and was numbered with the
transgressors.
For he bore the sin of many,
and made intercession for the
transgressors.

The Future Glory of Zion

54 "Sing, O barren woman,
you who never bore a child;
burst into song, shout for joy,
you who were never in labor;
because more are the children of the
desolate woman
than of her who has a husband,"
says the LORD.
2 "Enlarge the place of your tent,
stretch your tent curtains wide,
do not hold back;
lengthen your cords,
strengthen your stakes.
3 For you will spread out to the right
and to the left;
your descendants will dispossess
nations
and settle in their desolate cities.

4 "Do not be afraid; you will not suffer
shame.
Do not fear disgrace; you will not
be humiliated.
You will forget the shame of your
youth
and remember no more the
reproach of your widowhood.
5 For your Maker is your husband—
the LORD Almighty is his name—
the Holy One of Israel is your
Redeemer;
he is called the God of all the earth.
6 The LORD will call you back
as if you were a wife deserted and
distressed in spirit—
a wife who married young,
only to be rejected," says your God.
7 "For a brief moment I abandoned you,
but with deep compassion I will
bring you back.
8 In a surge of anger
I hid my face from you for a
moment,
but with everlasting kindness
I will have compassion on you,"
says the LORD your Redeemer.

9 "To me this is like the days of
Noah,
when I swore that the waters of
Noah would never again cover
the earth.
So now I have sworn not to be angry
with you,
never to rebuke you again.
10 Though the mountains be shaken
and the hills be removed,
yet my unfailing love for you will not
be shaken
nor my covenant of peace be
removed,"
says the LORD, who has compassion
on you.

11 "O afflicted city, lashed by storms
and not comforted,
I will build you with stones of
turquoise,[a]
your foundations with sapphires.[b]
12 I will make your battlements of
rubies,
your gates of sparkling jewels,
and all your walls of precious
stones.
13 All your sons will be taught by the
LORD,
and great will be your children's
peace.
14 In righteousness you will be
established:
Tyranny will be far from you;
you will have nothing to fear.
Terror will be far removed;
it will not come near you.
15 If anyone does attack you, it will not
be my doing;
whoever attacks you will surrender
to you.

16 "See, it is I who created the
blacksmith
who fans the coals into flame
and forges a weapon fit for its
work.
And it is I who have created the
destroyer to work havoc;
17 no weapon forged against you
will prevail,
and you will refute every tongue
that accuses you.

---

a 11 The meaning of the Hebrew for this word is
uncertain. *b 11* Or *lapis lazuli*

This is the heritage of the servants
of the LORD,
and this is their vindication
from me,"
declares the LORD.

Invitation to the Thirsty

55 "Come, all you who are thirsty,
come to the waters;
and you who have no money,
come, buy and eat!
Come, buy wine and milk
without money and without
cost.
² Why spend money on what is not
bread,
and your labor on what does not
satisfy?
Listen, listen to me, and eat what is
good,
and your soul will delight in the
richest of fare.
³ Give ear and come to me;
hear me, that your soul may live.
I will make an everlasting covenant
with you,
my faithful love promised to David.
⁴ See, I have made him a witness to
the peoples,
a leader and commander of the
peoples.
⁵ Surely you will summon nations you
know not,
and nations that do not know you
will hasten to you,
because of the LORD your God,
the Holy One of Israel,
for he has endowed you with
splendor."

⁶ Seek the LORD while he may be
found;
call on him while he is near.
⁷ Let the wicked forsake his way
and the evil man his thoughts.
Let him turn to the LORD, and he will
have mercy on him,
and to our God, for he will freely
pardon.

⁸ "For my thoughts are not your
thoughts,
neither are your ways my ways,"
declares the LORD.
⁹ "As the heavens are higher than
the earth,

so are my ways higher than
your ways
and my thoughts than your
thoughts.
¹⁰ As the rain and the snow
come down from heaven,
and do not return to it
without watering the earth
and making it bud and flourish,
so that it yields seed for the sower
and bread for the eater,
¹¹ so is my word that goes out from my
mouth:
It will not return to me empty,
but will accomplish what I desire
and achieve the purpose for which
I sent it.
¹² You will go out in joy
and be led forth in peace;
the mountains and hills
will burst into song before you,
and all the trees of the field
will clap their hands.
¹³ Instead of the thornbush will grow
the pine tree,
and instead of briers the myrtle will
grow.
This will be for the LORD's renown,
for an everlasting sign,
which will not be destroyed."

Salvation for Others

56 This is what the LORD says:

"Maintain justice
and do what is right,
for my salvation is close at hand
and my righteousness will soon be
revealed.
² Blessed is the man who does this,
the man who holds it fast,
who keeps the Sabbath without
desecrating it,
and keeps his hand from doing any
evil."

³ Let no foreigner who has bound
himself to the LORD say,
"The LORD will surely exclude me
from his people."
And let not any eunuch complain,
"I am only a dry tree."

⁴ For this is what the LORD says:

"To the eunuchs who keep my
Sabbaths,

who choose what pleases me
and hold fast to my covenant—
⁵ to them I will give within my temple
and its walls
a memorial and a name
better than sons and daughters;
I will give them an everlasting name
that will not be cut off.

⁶ And foreigners who bind themselves
to the LORD
to serve him,
to love the name of the LORD,
and to worship him,
all who keep the Sabbath without
desecrating it
and who hold fast to my covenant—

{WEDNESDAY}

ISAIAH 55

Carpe Diem

55:6 SEEK THE LORD WHILE HE MAY BE FOUND; CALL ON HIM WHILE HE IS NEAR.

Could there ever be a time when you would call on the Lord and find he is not near to you? No and yes. God's mercy is greater and wiser than we can ever imagine (so the answer is no), but God's mercy is not infinite or indefinite (so the answer is yes). No one should presume to know when God's mercy has reached its limit; nor should anyone presume to say that it hasn't. Let God be God and the rest of us liars (see Romans 3:3–4); and let that make us humble and breathless with gratitude for the mercy we have known.

In this passage, Isaiah looked many years ahead and addressed the exiles from the Babylonian captivity who would be called to return to the land and to the Lord. This would be a great moment in Judah's history, a window of opportunity, a *kairos* moment (see devotion on Esther 4). This opportunity would come to them as an invitation to a banquet of gourmet food, something not to be missed (see Isaiah 55:1–2). But the people might miss it if they don't seize the moment and RSVP the invitation. That's one way to think of prayer: an RSVP. The meaning of the moment comes down to two words: *carpe diem* (Latin for "pluck—or seize—the day"). So "seek the LORD while he may be found; call on him while he is near" (verse 6).

For us who live between the times, in the *kairos* between the resurrection of Christ and the consummation of history, the message is the same: *carpe diem*. Call on the Lord while he may be found. "Now is the time of God's favor, now is the day of salvation" (2 Corinthians 6:2). The great and gracious day will pass, and with it our opportunity. Perhaps more to the point, our day will certainly pass too, our span of life, our moment to choose our eternity. Death will come, and we may die before we really live; our hearts may grow so dull and cold that we have all but missed the moment to choose God.

Prayer keeps us alive to the moment, God's moment for us. Calling on the Lord is not a one-time event but an ongoing way of life. It is truly living in the moment, in the best sense of that phrase.

PRAY:
Blessed Savior, thank you that this day and this season is the time of your favor. I rejoice in your grace and call on you. Hallowed be your name.

FOR YOUR NEXT DEVOTIONAL READING, GO TO PAGE 871.

> *"THESE I will bring to my holy mountain*
> *and give them joy in my house*
> *of prayer.*
> *Their burnt offerings and sacrifices*
> *will be accepted on my altar;*
> *for my house will be called*
> *a house of prayer for all nations."*
>
> ISAIAH 56:7

⁷ these I will bring to my holy
        mountain
    and give them joy in my house
        of prayer.
Their burnt offerings and sacrifices
    will be accepted on my altar;
for my house will be called
    a house of prayer for all nations."
⁸ The Sovereign LORD declares—
    he who gathers the exiles of
        Israel:
"I will gather still others to them
    besides those already gathered."

God's Accusation Against the Wicked

⁹ Come, all you beasts of the field,
    come and devour, all you beasts
        of the forest!
¹⁰ Israel's watchmen are blind,
    they all lack knowledge;
they are all mute dogs,
    they cannot bark;
they lie around and dream,
    they love to sleep.
¹¹ They are dogs with mighty appetites;
    they never have enough.
They are shepherds who lack
        understanding;
    they all turn to their own way,
        each seeks his own gain.
¹² "Come," each one cries, "let me
        get wine!
    Let us drink our fill of beer!
And tomorrow will be like today,
    or even far better."

57 The righteous perish,
        and no one ponders it in his
            heart;
    devout men are taken away,
        and no one understands
    that the righteous are taken away
        to be spared from evil.

² Those who walk uprightly
    enter into peace;
they find rest as they lie in death.

³ "But you—come here, you sons of a
        sorceress,
    you offspring of adulterers and
        prostitutes!
⁴ Whom are you mocking?
    At whom do you sneer
        and stick out your tongue?
Are you not a brood of rebels,
    the offspring of liars?
⁵ You burn with lust among the oaks
    and under every spreading tree;
you sacrifice your children in the
        ravines
    and under the overhanging crags.
⁶ The idols among the smooth stones
        of the ravines are your portion;
    they, they are your lot.
Yes, to them you have poured out
        drink offerings
    and offered grain offerings.
In the light of these things, should I
        relent?
⁷ You have made your bed on a high
        and lofty hill;
    there you went up to offer your
        sacrifices.
⁸ Behind your doors and your
        doorposts
    you have put your pagan symbols.
Forsaking me, you uncovered your
        bed,
    you climbed into it and opened it
        wide;
you made a pact with those whose
        beds you love,
    and you looked on their nakedness.
⁹ You went to Molech[a] with olive oil
    and increased your perfumes.
You sent your ambassadors[b] far away;
    you descended to the grave[c] itself!
¹⁰ You were wearied by all your ways,
    but you would not say, 'It is
        hopeless.'
You found renewal of your strength,
    and so you did not faint.

¹¹ "Whom have you so dreaded and
        feared
    that you have been false to me,

ᵃ9 Or *to the king*   ᵇ9 Or *idols*   ᶜ9 Hebrew
Sheol

and have neither remembered me
nor pondered this in your hearts?
Is it not because I have long been
silent
that you do not fear me?
¹²I will expose your righteousness and
your works,
and they will not benefit you.
¹³When you cry out for help,
let your collection ⸤of idols⸥
save you!
The wind will carry all of them off,
a mere breath will blow them
away.
But the man who makes me his
refuge
will inherit the land
and possess my holy mountain."

Comfort for the Contrite

¹⁴And it will be said:

"Build up, build up, prepare the
road!
Remove the obstacles out of
the way of my people."
¹⁵For this is what the high and lofty
One says—
he who lives forever, whose name
is holy:
"I live in a high and holy place,
but also with him who is contrite
and lowly in spirit,
to revive the spirit of the lowly
and to revive the heart of the
contrite.
¹⁶I will not accuse forever,
nor will I always be angry,
for then the spirit of man would grow
faint before me—
the breath of man that I have
created.
¹⁷I was enraged by his sinful greed;
I punished him, and hid my face
in anger,
yet he kept on in his willful ways.
¹⁸I have seen his ways, but I will heal
him;
I will guide him and restore
comfort to him,
¹⁹   creating praise on the lips of the
mourners in Israel.
Peace, peace, to those far and near,"
says the LORD. "And I will heal
them."

²⁰But the wicked are like the tossing
sea,
which cannot rest,
whose waves cast up mire and
mud.
²¹"There is no peace," says my God,
"for the wicked."

True Fasting

58 "Shout it aloud, do not hold
back.
Raise your voice like a trumpet.
Declare to my people their rebellion
and to the house of Jacob their
sins.
²For day after day they seek me out;
they seem eager to know my
ways,
as if they were a nation that does
what is right
and has not forsaken the
commands of its God.
They ask me for just decisions
and seem eager for God to come
near them.
³'Why have we fasted,' they say,
'and you have not seen it?
Why have we humbled ourselves,
and you have not noticed?'

"Yet on the day of your fasting, you
do as you please
and exploit all your workers.
⁴Your fasting ends in quarreling and
strife,
and in striking each other with
wicked fists.
You cannot fast as you do today
and expect your voice to be heard
on high.
⁵Is this the kind of fast I have chosen,
only a day for a man to humble
himself?
Is it only for bowing one's head like
a reed
and for lying on sackcloth and
ashes?
Is that what you call a fast,
a day acceptable to the LORD?

⁶"Is not this the kind of fasting I have
chosen:
to loose the chains of injustice
and untie the cords of the yoke,
to set the oppressed free
and break every yoke?

7 Is it not to share your food with the hungry
and to provide the poor wanderer with shelter—
when you see the naked, to clothe him,
and not to turn away from your own flesh and blood?
8 Then your light will break forth like the dawn,
and your healing will quickly appear;
then your righteousness[a] will go before you,
and the glory of the LORD will be your rear guard.
9 Then you will call, and the LORD will answer;
you will cry for help, and he will say: Here am I.

"If you do away with the yoke of oppression,
with the pointing finger and malicious talk,
10 and if you spend yourselves in behalf of the hungry
and satisfy the needs of the oppressed,
then your light will rise in the darkness,
and your night will become like the noonday.
11 The LORD will guide you always;
he will satisfy your needs in a sun-scorched land
and will strengthen your frame.
You will be like a well-watered garden,
like a spring whose waters never fail.
12 Your people will rebuild the ancient ruins
and will raise up the age-old foundations;
you will be called Repairer of Broken Walls,
Restorer of Streets with Dwellings.

13 "If you keep your feet from breaking the Sabbath
and from doing as you please on my holy day,
if you call the Sabbath a delight
and the LORD's holy day honorable,
and if you honor it by not going your own way
and not doing as you please or speaking idle words,
14 then you will find your joy in the LORD,
and I will cause you to ride on the heights of the land
and to feast on the inheritance of your father Jacob."
The mouth of the LORD has spoken.

Sin, Confession and Redemption

59 Surely the arm of the LORD is not too short to save,
nor his ear too dull to hear.
2 But your iniquities have separated you from your God;
your sins have hidden his face from you,
so that he will not hear.
3 For your hands are stained with blood,
your fingers with guilt.
Your lips have spoken lies,
and your tongue mutters wicked things.
4 No one calls for justice;
no one pleads his case with integrity.
They rely on empty arguments and speak lies;
they conceive trouble and give birth to evil.
5 They hatch the eggs of vipers
and spin a spider's web.
Whoever eats their eggs will die,
and when one is broken, an adder is hatched.
6 Their cobwebs are useless for clothing;
they cannot cover themselves with what they make.
Their deeds are evil deeds,
and acts of violence are in their hands.
7 Their feet rush into sin;
they are swift to shed innocent blood.
Their thoughts are evil thoughts;
ruin and destruction mark their ways.

---

[a] 8 Or *your righteous One*

8 The way of peace they do not know;
  there is no justice in their paths.
They have turned them into crooked
  roads;
  no one who walks in them will
    know peace.

9 So justice is far from us,
  and righteousness does not reach
    us.
We look for light, but all is darkness;
  for brightness, but we walk in deep
    shadows.

[THURSDAY]

ISAIAH 59:1–2

He Will Not Hear

59:2 YOUR SINS HAVE HIDDEN HIS FACE FROM YOU, SO THAT HE WILL NOT HEAR.

"He can hear you, but he's not listening," is the way modern idiom might
express this statement. The people have complained that God isn't answering their prayers. Isaiah responds: "Surely the arm of the LORD is not too
short to save, nor his ear too dull to hear. But your iniquities have separated
you from your God" (59:1–2a). God has heard everything the people have to
say, and he can do anything he wants, but he is refusing to act because of
the people's lifestyles.

Later on in chapter 59, Isaiah nearly exhausts the Hebrew theological
vocabulary to describe the people's sin (see verse 12). There are "offenses."
These are acts of rebellion, what the Hebrews sometimes called "sins of the
high hand." Such sins are deliberate, "in your face" kinds of sin. Next in the
verse are simply "sins." These are all the ways the people have fallen short
and missed the mark: sins of weakness and sloth. Last are "iniquities." These
are wanton distortions and perversions of the true and the good, evil inver-
sions, where black becomes white, and upside down becomes right side up.
Together these three words make up a devastating indictment: The people
have become so adept at all the ways of evil that they are masters at sinning, experts in the art of living badly.

Therefore, when the people speak to God, he turns and looks the
other way. "Your sins have hidden his face from you" (verse 2b). It is said
that God hates the sin and loves the sinner. That is true, but with this important proviso: God loves the sinner, but hates the sin so much that he is
offended by the sinner too. God's displeasure with sin goes beyond the grief
that his beloved child is doing bad, self-destructive things. It includes grief,
but it also includes a holy anger at anything that is repugnant to a holy God.
His creature has committed treason; someone he made in his image has
defiled his image. God is angry with the sinner.

What an unbearably depressing concept were it not for God's eagerness to forgive those who confess and repent of their sins. "Christ died for
sinners" means God turned his face from his Son, that he might once again
turn his face toward us (see 2 Corinthians 5:20–21).

PRAY:
*I have sinned against you, Holy Father. For the sake of your Son,
turn your face back toward me. Forgive me and heal me, for Jesus' sake.*

FOR YOUR NEXT DEVOTIONAL READING, GO TO PAGE 875.

[10] Like the blind we grope along
the wall,
feeling our way like men without
eyes.
At midday we stumble as if it were
twilight;
among the strong, we are like
the dead.
[11] We all growl like bears;
we moan mournfully like doves.
We look for justice, but find none;
for deliverance, but it is far away.

[12] For our offenses are many in your
sight,
and our sins testify against us.
Our offenses are ever with us,
and we acknowledge our iniquities:
[13] rebellion and treachery against
the LORD,
turning our backs on our God,
fomenting oppression and revolt,
uttering lies our hearts have
conceived.
[14] So justice is driven back,
and righteousness stands at a
distance;
truth has stumbled in the streets,
honesty cannot enter.
[15] Truth is nowhere to be found,
and whoever shuns evil becomes
a prey.

The LORD looked and was displeased
that there was no justice.
[16] He saw that there was no one,
he was appalled that there was no
one to intervene;
so his own arm worked salvation
for him,
and his own righteousness
sustained him.
[17] He put on righteousness as his
breastplate,
and the helmet of salvation on
his head;
he put on the garments of vengeance
and wrapped himself in zeal as in
a cloak.
[18] According to what they have done,
so will he repay
wrath to his enemies
and retribution to his foes;
he will repay the islands their due.
[19] From the west, men will fear the
name of the LORD,

and from the rising of the sun, they
will revere his glory.
For he will come like a pent-up flood
that the breath of the LORD drives
along.[a]

[20] "The Redeemer will come to Zion,
to those in Jacob who repent of
their sins,"

declares the LORD.

[21] "As for me, this is my covenant with
them," says the LORD. "My Spirit, who is
on you, and my words that I have put in
your mouth will not depart from your
mouth, or from the mouths of your children, or from the mouths of their descendants from this time on and forever,"
says the LORD.

The Glory of Zion

60 "Arise, shine, for your light
has come,
and the glory of the LORD rises
upon you.
[2] See, darkness covers the earth
and thick darkness is over the
peoples,
but the LORD rises upon you
and his glory appears over you.
[3] Nations will come to your light,
and kings to the brightness of
your dawn.

[4] "Lift up your eyes and look about
you:
All assemble and come to you;
your sons come from afar,
and your daughters are carried on
the arm.
[5] Then you will look and be radiant,
your heart will throb and swell
with joy;
the wealth on the seas will be
brought to you,
to you the riches of the nations
will come.
[6] Herds of camels will cover your land,
young camels of Midian and
Ephah.
And all from Sheba will come,
bearing gold and incense
and proclaiming the praise of
the LORD.

[a]19 Or *When the enemy comes in like a flood, /
the Spirit of the LORD will put him to flight*

7 All Kedar's flocks will be gathered
  to you,
  the rams of Nebaioth will serve
  you;
they will be accepted as offerings on
  my altar,
  and I will adorn my glorious
  temple.

8 "Who are these that fly along like
  clouds,
  like doves to their nests?
9 Surely the islands look to me;
  in the lead are the ships of
  Tarshish,ᵃ
bringing your sons from afar,
  with their silver and gold,
to the honor of the LORD your God,
  the Holy One of Israel,
  for he has endowed you with
  splendor.

10 "Foreigners will rebuild your walls,
  and their kings will serve you.
Though in anger I struck you,
  in favor I will show you
  compassion.
11 Your gates will always stand open,
  they will never be shut, day or
  night,
so that men may bring you the wealth
  of the nations—
  their kings led in triumphal
  procession.
12 For the nation or kingdom that will
  not serve you will perish;
  it will be utterly ruined.

13 "The glory of Lebanon will come
  to you,
  the pine, the fir and the cypress
  together,
to adorn the place of my sanctuary;
  and I will glorify the place of my
  feet.
14 The sons of your oppressors will
  come bowing before you;
  all who despise you will bow down
  at your feet
and will call you the City of the LORD,
  Zion of the Holy One of Israel.

15 "Although you have been forsaken
  and hated,
  with no one traveling through,
I will make you the everlasting pride
  and the joy of all generations.

16 You will drink the milk of nations
  and be nursed at royal breasts.
Then you will know that I, the LORD,
  am your Savior,
  your Redeemer, the Mighty One
  of Jacob.
17 Instead of bronze I will bring you
  gold,
  and silver in place of iron.
Instead of wood I will bring you
  bronze,
  and iron in place of stones.
I will make peace your governor
  and righteousness your ruler.
18 No longer will violence be heard in
  your land,
  nor ruin or destruction within your
  borders,
but you will call your walls Salvation
  and your gates Praise.
19 The sun will no more be your light
  by day,
  nor will the brightness of the moon
  shine on you,
for the LORD will be your everlasting
  light,
  and your God will be your glory.
20 Your sun will never set again,
  and your moon will wane no more;
the LORD will be your everlasting
  light,
  and your days of sorrow will end.
21 Then will all your people be righteous
  and they will possess the land
  forever.
They are the shoot I have planted,
  the work of my hands,
  for the display of my splendor.
22 The least of you will become a
  thousand,
  the smallest a mighty nation.
I am the LORD;
  in its time I will do this swiftly."

The Year of the LORD's Favor

61 The Spirit of the Sovereign LORD
  is on me,
  because the LORD has anointed me
  to preach good news to the poor.
He has sent me to bind up the
  brokenhearted,
  to proclaim freedom for the
  captives

ᵃ9 Or *the trading ships*

and release from darkness for the
    prisoners,*[a]*
[2] to proclaim the year of the LORD's
    favor
  and the day of vengeance of
    our God,
to comfort all who mourn,
[3]   and provide for those who grieve
    in Zion—
to bestow on them a crown of beauty
    instead of ashes,
the oil of gladness
    instead of mourning,
and a garment of praise
    instead of a spirit of despair.
They will be called oaks of
    righteousness,
  a planting of the LORD
  for the display of his splendor.

[4] They will rebuild the ancient ruins
    and restore the places long
      devastated;
they will renew the ruined cities
    that have been devastated for
      generations.
[5] Aliens will shepherd your flocks;
    foreigners will work your fields and
      vineyards.
[6] And you will be called priests of the
    LORD,
  you will be named ministers of
    our God.
You will feed on the wealth of
    nations,
  and in their riches you will boast.

[7] Instead of their shame
    my people will receive a double
      portion,
and instead of disgrace
    they will rejoice in their
      inheritance;
and so they will inherit a double
    portion in their land,
  and everlasting joy will be theirs.

[8] "For I, the LORD, love justice;
  I hate robbery and iniquity.
In my faithfulness I will reward them
  and make an everlasting covenant
    with them.
[9] Their descendants will be known
    among the nations
  and their offspring among the
    peoples.

All who see them will acknowledge
    that they are a people the LORD has
    blessed."
[10] I delight greatly in the LORD;
  my soul rejoices in my God.
For he has clothed me with garments
    of salvation
  and arrayed me in a robe of
    righteousness,
as a bridegroom adorns his head like
    a priest,
  and as a bride adorns herself with
    her jewels.
[11] For as the soil makes the sprout
    come up
  and a garden causes seeds to grow,
so the Sovereign LORD will make
    righteousness and praise
spring up before all nations.

Zion's New Name

62 For Zion's sake I will not keep
    silent,
  for Jerusalem's sake I will not
    remain quiet,
till her righteousness shines out like
    the dawn,
  her salvation like a blazing torch.
[2] The nations will see your
    righteousness,
  and all kings your glory;
you will be called by a new name
    that the mouth of the LORD will
      bestow.
[3] You will be a crown of splendor in
    the LORD's hand,
  a royal diadem in the hand of
    your God.
[4] No longer will they call you Deserted,
    or name your land Desolate.
But you will be called Hephzibah,*[b]*
  and your land Beulah*[c]*;
for the LORD will take delight in you,
  and your land will be married.
[5] As a young man marries a maiden,
    so will your sons*[d]* marry you;
as a bridegroom rejoices over his
    bride,
  so will your God rejoice over you.

[6] I have posted watchmen on your
    walls, O Jerusalem;

a1 Hebrew; Septuagint *the blind*
b4 Hephzibah means *my delight is in her.*
c4 Beulah means *married.*   *d5* Or *Builder*

they will never be silent day or night.
You who call on the LORD,
  give yourselves no rest,
⁷and give him no rest till he
    establishes Jerusalem
and makes her the praise of the
    earth.

⁸The LORD has sworn by his right hand
  and by his mighty arm:
"Never again will I give your grain
  as food for your enemies,
and never again will foreigners drink
  the new wine
  for which you have toiled;

{ FRIDAY }

ISAIAH 62:6–7

The Lord's Watch

62:6 | I HAVE POSTED WATCHMEN ON YOUR WALLS, O JERUSALEM.

In prayer, God works on us by his grace and allows us to work on him by our faith.⁹ That he would give us this "dignity of causality"¹⁰ is a mystery to make us rejoice, and above all, pray. These verses add to the mystery—God has posted watchmen on the walls of Jerusalem: "They will never be silent day or night. You who call on the LORD, give yourselves no rest, and give him no rest till he establishes Jerusalem and makes her the praise of the earth" (verses 6–7).

The 18ᵗʰ-century Moravians took these verses very seriously and established what they called "The Lord's Watch," or *Herrnhut*, in German. This community included a twenty-four hour, seven-day-a-week prayer vigil that lasted without interruption for 100 years. During that time, this relatively small Christian fellowship sent out 2,000 missionaries around the globe. It was at a Moravian prayer meeting that John Wesley felt his heart "strangely warmed" and came to know that he really belonged to Christ. The Wesleyan revivals owe a great deal to persistent watchmen determined to pester God.

Beginning in the same century, a group of churches in Ipswich, Massachusetts, also prayed without interruption for a century. It wasn't continuous around-the-clock praying, but it was a regular rhythm of weekly, monthly and quarterly prayer meetings. During that period, most of New England's churches and seminaries became Unitarian. Although under great spiritual pressure, the Ipswich churches remained faithful to the historic Christian faith and experienced periodic revivals. Their vigil ended during the Civil War. Less than five years later, they all lost their grip on the faith.

We are at war; the battle is spiritual. Not to choose sides is to choose a side—the wrong side. We fight this war together, on our knees. Edmund Burke's statement was about politics, but it applies to the Lord's watch, too: "When bad men combine, the good must associate; else they will fall, one by one." God has posted us on the wall, has he not?

PRAY:
Stir us to pray, Lord! Stir me, but stir us, especially us,
to give ourselves and you no rest until your kingdom comes
and your name is revered in all the earth.

FOR YOUR NEXT DEVOTIONAL READING, GO TO PAGE 876.

ROBERT MURRAY McCHEYNE (1813–1843)
A Candle Burning Brightly

ALL HIS life Robert Murray McCheyne seemed to move at an accelerated pace. At age four he taught himself to read and write the Greek alphabet. He began high school at age eight. At fourteen he was admitted to Edinburgh University.

In college McCheyne was "of a lively turn," spending all of his free time in dancing and card playing. It took the death of his beloved older brother to prompt him to think about eternal things. McCheyne later wrote, "This day eleven years ago, I lost my loved and loving brother, and began to seek a Brother who cannot die."[11]

McCheyne re-directed his energies towards knowing God and entered divinity school. At age 23 he answered the call to be a pastor at St. Peter's Church in Dundee, Scotland, "an honour to which I cannot name an equal." He involved himself in the lives of the 4,000 souls of Dundee: preaching, writing, teaching, and above all, praying for revival.

McCheyne believed the primary concern of a minister of God—or any Christian—was first their own soul. "Above all things, cultivate your own spirit," he wrote. "Your own soul is your first and greatest care . . . A word spoken by you when your conscience is clear, and your heart full of God's Spirit, is worth ten thousand words spoken in unbelief and sin . . . A holy minister is an awful weapon in the hand of God."[12]

But how can Christians cultivate their own spirits? McCheyne believed that the answer was found in simple, unhurried communion with God. "The dew comes down when all nature is at rest—when every leaf is still," remarked McCheyne. "A calm hour with God is worth a whole lifetime with man . . . The work of God would flourish by us, if it flourished more richly in us." In a personal journal entry he wrote, "February 23. Sabbath. Rose early to seek God, and found him whom my soul loveth. Who would not rise early to meet such company?"

Throughout his ministerial career, McCheyne continued in intense study of the Scriptures. His overwork contributed to ill health, which included "violent heart palpitations" and subsequent weakness. Nevertheless, he continued his pastoral visits and evangelistic tours through rain and snow. As his health deteriorated, McCheyne saw in his physical condition a parable of the human condition. He told his congregation, "Every day that passes is drawing you nearer to the judgment-seat. Not one of you is standing still." He became more urgent in his preaching, longing for a "deep, pure, widespread, and permanent work of God in Scotland."[13]

In the spring of 1843, McCheyne caught a fever. Many gathered outside St. Peter's Church as he lay dying, and on March 25, 1843, he passed away. McCheyne was only 29 years old—"the candle that burns brightest burns shortest." But the impact of his calm hours with God is felt to this day.

PRAY:

Almighty God, let me be "an awful weapon" in your hand.
May all I do and say flow out of my communion with you.

MEMORIZE:

I eagerly expect and hope that I will in no way be ashamed,
but will have sufficient courage so that now as always Christ will
be exalted in my body, whether by life or by death. For to me,
to live is Christ and to die is gain. PHILIPPIANS 1:20–21

FOR YOUR NEXT DEVOTIONAL READING, GO TO PAGE 880.

9 but those who harvest it will eat it
and praise the LORD,
and those who gather the grapes
will drink it
in the courts of my sanctuary."

10 Pass through, pass through the gates!
Prepare the way for the people.
Build up, build up the highway!
Remove the stones.
Raise a banner for the nations.

11 The LORD has made proclamation
to the ends of the earth:
"Say to the Daughter of Zion,
'See, your Savior comes!
See, his reward is with him,
and his recompense accompanies
him.' "

12 They will be called the Holy People,
the Redeemed of the LORD;
and you will be called Sought After,
the City No Longer Deserted.

God's Day of Vengeance and Redemption

63 Who is this coming from Edom,
from Bozrah, with his garments
stained crimson?
Who is this, robed in splendor,
striding forward in the greatness of
his strength?

"It is I, speaking in righteousness,
mighty to save."

2 Why are your garments red,
like those of one treading the
winepress?

3 "I have trodden the winepress alone;
from the nations no one was
with me.
I trampled them in my anger
and trod them down in my wrath;
their blood spattered my garments,
and I stained all my clothing.
4 For the day of vengeance was in
my heart,
and the year of my redemption
has come.
5 I looked, but there was no one to
help,
I was appalled that no one gave
support;
so my own arm worked salvation
for me,
and my own wrath sustained me.

6 I trampled the nations in my anger;
in my wrath I made them drunk
and poured their blood on the
ground."

Praise and Prayer

7 I will tell of the kindnesses of the
LORD,
the deeds for which he is to be
praised,
according to all the LORD has done
for us—
yes, the many good things he has
done
for the house of Israel,
according to his compassion and
many kindnesses.
8 He said, "Surely they are my people,
sons who will not be false to me";
and so he became their Savior.
9 In all their distress he too was
distressed,
and the angel of his presence saved
them.
In his love and mercy he redeemed
them;
he lifted them up and carried them
all the days of old.
10 Yet they rebelled
and grieved his Holy Spirit.
So he turned and became their
enemy
and he himself fought against
them.

11 Then his people recalled[a] the days
of old,
the days of Moses and his people—
where is he who brought them
through the sea,
with the shepherd of his flock?
Where is he who set
his Holy Spirit among them,
12 who sent his glorious arm of power
to be at Moses' right hand,
who divided the waters before them,
to gain for himself everlasting
renown,
13 who led them through the depths?
Like a horse in open country,
they did not stumble;
14 like cattle that go down to the plain,
they were given rest by the Spirit
of the LORD.

a 11 Or *But may he recall*

This is how you guided your people
to make for yourself a glorious
name.

15 Look down from heaven and see
from your lofty throne, holy and
glorious.
Where are your zeal and your might?
Your tenderness and compassion
are withheld from us.

16 But you are our Father,
though Abraham does not know us
or Israel acknowledge us;
you, O Lord, are our Father,
our Redeemer from of old is your
name.

17 Why, O Lord, do you make us wander
from your ways
and harden our hearts so we
do not revere you?
Return for the sake of your
servants,
the tribes that are your
inheritance.

18 For a little while your people
possessed your holy place,
but now our enemies have
trampled down your
sanctuary.

19 We are yours from of old;
but you have not ruled over them,
they have not been called by your
name.[a]

64 Oh, that you would rend the
heavens and come down,
that the mountains would tremble
before you!

2 As when fire sets twigs ablaze
and causes water to boil,
come down to make your name
known to your enemies
and cause the nations to quake
before you!

3 For when you did awesome things
that we did not expect,
you came down, and the
mountains trembled before
you.

4 Since ancient times no one has
heard,
no ear has perceived,
no eye has seen any God besides you,
who acts on behalf of those who
wait for him.

5 You come to the help of those who
gladly do right,
who remember your ways.
But when we continued to sin
against them,
you were angry.
How then can we be saved?

6 All of us have become like one who
is unclean,
and all our righteous acts are like
filthy rags;
we all shrivel up like a leaf,
and like the wind our sins sweep
us away.

7 No one calls on your name
or strives to lay hold of you;
for you have hidden your face
from us
and made us waste away because
of our sins.

8 Yet, O Lord, you are our Father.
We are the clay, you are the
potter;
we are all the work of your hand.

9 Do not be angry beyond measure,
O Lord;
do not remember our sins
forever.
Oh, look upon us, we pray,
for we are all your people.

10 Your sacred cities have become
a desert;
even Zion is a desert, Jerusalem
a desolation.

11 Our holy and glorious temple, where
our fathers praised you,
has been burned with fire,
and all that we treasured lies
in ruins.

12 After all this, O Lord, will you hold
yourself back?
Will you keep silent and punish
us beyond measure?

Judgment and Salvation

65 "I revealed myself to those who
did not ask for me;
I was found by those who did not
seek me.
To a nation that did not call on
my name,
I said, 'Here am I, here am I.'

a 19 Or *We are like those you have never ruled, /*
like those never called by your name

ISAIAH 64

Come Down, Lord!

64:1 OH, THAT YOU WOULD REND THE HEAVENS AND COME DOWN.

"We're in a terrible mess; it's all our fault, and we're getting exactly what we deserve. But please, Lord, come down and save us." That's the gist of this prayer. It's a kind of prayer that appears many times in Scripture, perhaps also in your life. It's not that bad things are happening to good people, but that bad things are happening to bad people. Why even ask God to lighten up? We're bankrupt morally; we don't have a leg to stand on. So why not just get into a stoic groove until the storm passes?

Isaiah doesn't do that. He does even more than ask God to lighten up; he prays, "Oh, that you would rend the heavens and come down" (64:1). And that's not all; Isaiah makes a strong case for why God should act, the people's guilt notwithstanding. Reason number one is that God has acted before: "Since ancient times no one has heard, no ear has perceived, no eye has seen any God besides you, who acts on behalf of those who wait for him" (verse 4). This may not seem a compelling reason for God to save the people, except what God did in the past was his self-chosen way of showing his people the kind of God he is. Reason number two is that they are his people, in a very intimate sense: "Yet, O LORD, you are our Father. We are the clay, you are the potter; we are all the work of your hand . . . Oh, look upon us, we pray, for we are all your people" (verses 8–9). Again, as in reason number one, Isaiah is doing nothing more than reminding God of his self-chosen relationship to his people: Father and potter. If God's people are ever to be good, it will be because God has shown the mercy of a father and the skill of a potter.

And very important: note that Isaiah's case for mercy has nothing to do with his or his people's good qualities or inner beauty. It is entirely about God's good qualities. Isaiah doesn't ask God to find the spark of good in the people and to fan it into flame because there isn't any spark. The entire appeal is to God's goodness. It may seem a little audacious, but it is exactly the way God wants to be addressed: through prayer in his name, according to his character.

PRAY:

*"We do not make requests of you because
we are righteous, but because of your
great mercy. O Lord, listen! O Lord, forgive!
O Lord, hear and act! For your sake, O my God,
do not delay, because your city and your people
bear your Name" (Daniel 9:18–19).*

FOR YOUR NEXT DEVOTIONAL READING, GO TO PAGE 886.

> "*I REVEALED* myself to those who
>   did not ask for me;
> I was found by those who did not
>   seek me.
> To a nation that did not call on
>   my name,
> I said, 'Here am I, here am I.'"
>
> ISAIAH 65:1

2 All day long I have held out my hands
    to an obstinate people,
who walk in ways not good,
    pursuing their own imaginations—
3 a people who continually provoke me
    to my very face,
offering sacrifices in gardens
    and burning incense on altars of
        brick;
4 who sit among the graves
    and spend their nights keeping
        secret vigil;
who eat the flesh of pigs,
    and whose pots hold broth of
        unclean meat;
5 who say, 'Keep away; don't come
        near me,
    for I am too sacred for you!'
Such people are smoke in my nostrils,
    a fire that keeps burning all day.

6 "See, it stands written before me:
    I will not keep silent but will pay
        back in full;
    I will pay it back into their laps—
7 both your sins and the sins of your
        fathers,"
    says the LORD.
"Because they burned sacrifices on
        the mountains
    and defied me on the hills,
I will measure into their laps
    the full payment for their former
        deeds."

8 This is what the LORD says:

"As when juice is still found in a
        cluster of grapes
    and men say, 'Don't destroy it,
        there is yet some good in it,'
so will I do in behalf of my servants;
    I will not destroy them all.
9 I will bring forth descendants from
        Jacob,

and from Judah those who will
        possess my mountains;
my chosen people will inherit them,
    and there will my servants live.
10 Sharon will become a pasture for
        flocks,
    and the Valley of Achor a resting
        place for herds,
for my people who seek me.

11 "But as for you who forsake the LORD
    and forget my holy mountain,
who spread a table for Fortune
    and fill bowls of mixed wine
        for Destiny,
12 I will destine you for the sword,
    and you will all bend down for the
        slaughter;
for I called but you did not answer,
    I spoke but you did not listen.
You did evil in my sight
    and chose what displeases me."

13 Therefore this is what the Sovereign
LORD says:

"My servants will eat,
    but you will go hungry;
my servants will drink,
    but you will go thirsty;
my servants will rejoice,
    but you will be put to shame.
14 My servants will sing
    out of the joy of their hearts,
but you will cry out
    from anguish of heart
    and wail in brokenness of spirit.
15 You will leave your name
    to my chosen ones as a curse;
the Sovereign LORD will put you to
        death,
    but to his servants he will give
        another name.
16 Whoever invokes a blessing in the
        land
    will do so by the God of truth;
he who takes an oath in the land
    will swear by the God of truth.
For the past troubles will be forgotten
    and hidden from my eyes.

New Heavens and a New Earth

17 "Behold, I will create
    new heavens and a new earth.
The former things will not be
        remembered,
    nor will they come to mind.

18 But be glad and rejoice forever
  in what I will create,
for I will create Jerusalem to be
    a delight
  and its people a joy.
19 I will rejoice over Jerusalem
  and take delight in my people;
the sound of weeping and of
    crying
  will be heard in it no more.

20 "Never again will there be in it
  an infant who lives but a few days,
  or an old man who does not live
    out his years;
he who dies at a hundred
  will be thought a mere youth;
he who fails to reach*a* a hundred
  will be considered accursed.
21 They will build houses and dwell
    in them;
  they will plant vineyards and eat
    their fruit.
22 No longer will they build houses and
    others live in them,
  or plant and others eat.
For as the days of a tree,
  so will be the days of my people;
my chosen ones will long enjoy
  the works of their hands.
23 They will not toil in vain
  or bear children doomed to
    misfortune;
for they will be a people blessed
    by the LORD,
  they and their descendants
    with them.

> "*BEFORE* they call I will answer;
> while they are still speaking I
>   will hear."
>
> ISAIAH 65:24

24 Before they call I will answer;
  while they are still speaking I
    will hear.
25 The wolf and the lamb will feed
    together,
  and the lion will eat straw like
    the ox,
  but dust will be the serpent's food.
They will neither harm nor destroy
  on all my holy mountain,"
    says the LORD.

Judgment and Hope

66 This is what the LORD says:

"Heaven is my throne,
  and the earth is my footstool.
Where is the house you will build
    for me?
  Where will my resting place be?
2 Has not my hand made all these
    things,
  and so they came into being?"
    declares the LORD.

"This is the one I esteem:
  he who is humble and contrite
    in spirit,
  and trembles at my word.
3 But whoever sacrifices a bull
  is like one who kills a man,
and whoever offers a lamb,
  like one who breaks a dog's neck;
whoever makes a grain offering
  is like one who presents pig's
    blood,
and whoever burns memorial
    incense,
  like one who worships an idol.
They have chosen their own ways,
  and their souls delight in their
    abominations;
4 so I also will choose harsh treatment
    for them
  and will bring upon them what
    they dread.
For when I called, no one answered,
  when I spoke, no one listened.
They did evil in my sight
  and chose what displeases me."

5 Hear the word of the LORD,
  you who tremble at his word:
"Your brothers who hate you,
  and exclude you because of my
    name, have said,
'Let the LORD be glorified,
  that we may see your joy!'
  Yet they will be put to shame.
6 Hear that uproar from the city,
  hear that noise from the temple!
It is the sound of the LORD
  repaying his enemies all they
    deserve.

7 "Before she goes into labor,
  she gives birth;

a20 Or / *the sinner who reaches*

before the pains come upon her,
she delivers a son.
[8] Who has ever heard of such a thing?
Who has ever seen such things?
Can a country be born in a day
or a nation be brought forth in a
moment?
Yet no sooner is Zion in labor
than she gives birth to her children.
[9] Do I bring to the moment of birth
and not give delivery?" says the
LORD.
"Do I close up the womb
when I bring to delivery?" says
your God.
[10] "Rejoice with Jerusalem and be glad
for her,
all you who love her;
rejoice greatly with her,
all you who mourn over her.
[11] For you will nurse and be satisfied
at her comforting breasts;
you will drink deeply
and delight in her overflowing
abundance."

[12] For this is what the LORD says:

"I will extend peace to her like a river,
and the wealth of nations like a
flooding stream;
you will nurse and be carried on
her arm
and dandled on her knees.
[13] As a mother comforts her child,
so will I comfort you;
and you will be comforted over
Jerusalem."

[14] When you see this, your heart will
rejoice
and you will flourish like grass;
the hand of the LORD will be made
known to his servants,
but his fury will be shown to his
foes.
[15] See, the LORD is coming with fire,
and his chariots are like a
whirlwind;
he will bring down his anger
with fury,
and his rebuke with flames of fire.

[16] For with fire and with his sword
the LORD will execute judgment
upon all men,
and many will be those slain by
the LORD.

[17] "Those who consecrate and purify
themselves to go into the gardens, following the one in the midst of[a] those who
eat the flesh of pigs and rats and other
abominable things—they will meet their
end together," declares the LORD.

[18] "And I, because of their actions and
their imaginations, am about to come[b]
and gather all nations and tongues, and
they will come and see my glory.

[19] "I will set a sign among them, and I
will send some of those who survive to
the nations—to Tarshish, to the Libyans[c]
and Lydians (famous as archers), to Tubal and Greece, and to the distant islands that have not heard of my fame or
seen my glory. They will proclaim my glory among the nations. [20] And they will
bring all your brothers, from all the nations, to my holy mountain in Jerusalem
as an offering to the LORD—on horses, in
chariots and wagons, and on mules and
camels," says the LORD. "They will bring
them, as the Israelites bring their grain
offerings, to the temple of the LORD in
ceremonially clean vessels. [21] And I will
select some of them also to be priests
and Levites," says the LORD.

[22] "As the new heavens and the new
earth that I make will endure before me,"
declares the LORD, "so will your name
and descendants endure. [23] From one
New Moon to another and from one Sabbath to another, all mankind will come
and bow down before me," says the LORD.
[24] "And they will go out and look upon the
dead bodies of those who rebelled
against me; their worm will not die, nor
will their fire be quenched, and they will
be loathsome to all mankind."

---

[a]17 Or gardens behind one of your temples, and
[b]18 The meaning of the Hebrew for this clause is
uncertain.   [c]19 Some Septuagint manuscripts
Put (Libyans); Hebrew Pul

Jeremiah

JEWISH TRADITION says that Jeremiah was stoned to death in Egypt. If he was, it could not have been a more fitting end to his career as a prophet: killed by his own people in a place he didn't want to be. From the beginning, Jeremiah struggled with his call to be a prophet, even accusing God of bullying and seducing him into service (see 20:7). He was rejected by his own people in every way: from mockery, ridicule and slander to death threats and false imprisonment. Even his own family plotted against him (see 12:6). God's words to him, "Before you were born I set you apart" (1:5), were true in every way. Jeremiah lived and died lonely and set apart.

> **"WHY IS MY PAIN UNENDING AND MY WOUND GRIEVOUS AND INCURABLE?"** (15:18)

Jeremiah was not like Jesus, who embraced his Father's will all the way to the cross without bitterness and complaint. But Jeremiah suffered in ways similar to Jesus. Jesus was familiar with suffering; he was one from whom others hid their faces (see Isaiah 53:3). He was also rejected by his own people and dishonored by members of his own household (see Mark 6:1–6). He was threatened with death by the priests of Jerusalem and led to the cross as a lamb to the slaughter. But through it all he knew how to weep and pray and cling to God (see Matthew 26:36–44; Hebrews 5:7). Jesus is our model of prayer in extreme situations, and Jeremiah is our mirror. We can pray like Jesus when in trouble, but the truth is we often pray like Jeremiah: angry, despondent and despairing. In his own way, Jeremiah gives us hope; he shows us that God takes reluctant and morose people and does great things with them, even though sometimes they can't see those things for themselves. Best of all, he hears our prayers.

1 The words of Jeremiah son of Hilkiah, one of the priests at Anathoth in the territory of Benjamin. ²The word of the LORD came to him in the thirteenth year of the reign of Josiah son of Amon king of Judah, ³and through the reign of Jehoiakim son of Josiah king of Judah, down to the fifth month of the eleventh year of Zedekiah son of Josiah king of Judah, when the people of Jerusalem went into exile.

The Call of Jeremiah

⁴The word of the LORD came to me, saying,

⁵ "Before I formed you in the womb
        I knew*a* you,
    before you were born I set you
        apart;
    I appointed you as a prophet to
        the nations."

⁶"Ah, Sovereign LORD," I said, "I do not know how to speak; I am only a child."

⁷But the LORD said to me, "Do not say, 'I am only a child.' You must go to everyone I send you to and say whatever I command you. ⁸Do not be afraid of them, for I am with you and will rescue you," declares the LORD.

⁹Then the LORD reached out his hand and touched my mouth and said to me, "Now, I have put my words in your mouth. ¹⁰See, today I appoint you over nations and kingdoms to uproot and tear down, to destroy and overthrow, to build and to plant."

¹¹The word of the LORD came to me: "What do you see, Jeremiah?"

"I see the branch of an almond tree," I replied.

¹²The LORD said to me, "You have seen correctly, for I am watching*b* to see that my word is fulfilled."

¹³The word of the LORD came to me again: "What do you see?"

"I see a boiling pot, tilting away from the north," I answered.

¹⁴The LORD said to me, "From the north disaster will be poured out on all who live in the land. ¹⁵I am about to summon all the peoples of the northern kingdoms," declares the LORD.

"Their kings will come and set up
        their thrones

in the entrance of the gates
        of Jerusalem;
    they will come against all her
        surrounding walls
    and against all the towns of Judah.
¹⁶I will pronounce my judgments on
        my people
    because of their wickedness in
        forsaking me,
    in burning incense to other gods
    and in worshiping what their
        hands have made.

¹⁷"Get yourself ready! Stand up and say to them whatever I command you. Do not be terrified by them, or I will terrify you before them. ¹⁸Today I have made you a fortified city, an iron pillar and a bronze wall to stand against the whole land—against the kings of Judah, its officials, its priests and the people of the land. ¹⁹They will fight against you but will not overcome you, for I am with you and will rescue you," declares the LORD.

Israel Forsakes God

2 The word of the LORD came to me: ²"Go and proclaim in the hearing of Jerusalem:

" 'I remember the devotion of your
        youth,
    how as a bride you loved me
    and followed me through the desert,
        through a land not sown.
³Israel was holy to the LORD,
    the firstfruits of his harvest;
all who devoured her were held
        guilty,
    and disaster overtook them,' "
                    declares the LORD.

⁴Hear the word of the LORD, O house
        of Jacob,
    all you clans of the house of Israel.

⁵This is what the LORD says:

"What fault did your fathers find
        in me,
    that they strayed so far from me?
They followed worthless idols
    and became worthless themselves.
⁶They did not ask, 'Where is the LORD,
    who brought us up out of Egypt

---

*a*5 Or *chose*   *b*12 The Hebrew for *watching* sounds like the Hebrew for *almond tree*.

and led us through the barren
   wilderness,
through a land of deserts and
   rifts,
a land of drought and darkness,*ᵃ*
   a land where no one travels and
   no one lives?'

⁷I brought you into a fertile land
   to eat its fruit and rich produce.
But you came and defiled my land
   and made my inheritance
   detestable.

ᵃ6 Or and the shadow of death

JEREMIAH 1

Divine Constraint

1:4 THE WORD OF THE LORD CAME TO ME.

Jeremiah did not look back on the day he was called to be a prophet with warm sentiment, the way we might keep a photo from the day of our baptism. Sometimes he wished it had never happened: "O LORD, you deceived me, and I was deceived; you overpowered me and prevailed . . . the word of the LORD has brought me insult and reproach all day long" (20:7–8). Jeremiah's call to be a prophet was not the culmination of a career path he had been on since he began school. It was, as were other prophets' callings, a matter of divine constraint.

Jeremiah's call wasn't his idea; it was God's, even before Jeremiah was born. God formed him in his mother's womb to be a prophet, and this calling was intensely personal. God reached out and put his words into Jeremiah's mouth (1:5–9). Jeremiah was a receiver, like we all must be. Medieval artists often portrayed the impregnating Spirit entering the Virgin Mary through her ear. It wasn't that they were naïve about the way women became pregnant; rather, they were saying that the entrance of God into a human heart always comes through hearing the Word. Just as it was with Jeremiah and Mary, so it is with us. Once the Word goes in, it must come out. Jeremiah had to speak what he heard, even when it made his life miserable. He couldn't hold it in even when he tried. Jeremiah describes God's Word in this way: "His word is in my heart like a fire, a fire shut up in my bones. I am weary of holding it in; indeed, I cannot" (20:9).

At times, God seemed to bully Jeremiah, but Jeremiah knew better. God was like the lion Aslan in C. S. Lewis's *The Chronicles of Narnia*. When Lucy first hears of Aslan from Mr. and Mrs. Beaver, she wants to know if he is safe. "'Safe?' said Mr. Beaver. Who said anything about safe? 'Course he isn't safe. But he's good. He's the King, I tell you.'"[1] To enter the communion of prayer with a God like this may sometimes be a soothing thought. But it may also be an upsetting one. Like Jeremiah, we may not always like what we hear. God isn't safe, but he is good, and everything he does is good.

PRAY:

*Lord, I am not my own, for I was purchased by the
precious blood of Christ. When I can't understand your commands,
help me trust your love anyway.*

FOR YOUR NEXT DEVOTIONAL READING, GO TO PAGE 896.

8 The priests did not ask,
'Where is the LORD?'
Those who deal with the law did not
know me;
the leaders rebelled against me.
The prophets prophesied by Baal,
following worthless idols.

9 "Therefore I bring charges against
you again,"
declares the LORD.
"And I will bring charges against
your children's children.

10 Cross over to the coasts of Kittim[a]
and look,
send to Kedar[b] and observe closely;
see if there has ever been anything
like this:

11 Has a nation ever changed its gods?
(Yet they are not gods at all.)
But my people have exchanged
their[c] Glory
for worthless idols.

12 Be appalled at this, O heavens,
and shudder with great horror,"
declares the LORD.

13 "My people have committed
two sins:
They have forsaken me,
the spring of living water,
and have dug their own cisterns,
broken cisterns that cannot hold
water.

14 Is Israel a servant, a slave by birth?
Why then has he become plunder?

15 Lions have roared;
they have growled at him.
They have laid waste his land;
his towns are burned and deserted.

16 Also, the men of Memphis[d] and
Tahpanhes
have shaved the crown of your
head.[e]

17 Have you not brought this on
yourselves
by forsaking the LORD your God
when he led you in the way?

18 Now why go to Egypt
to drink water from the Shihor[f]?
And why go to Assyria
to drink water from the River[g]?

19 Your wickedness will punish you;
your backsliding will rebuke you.
Consider then and realize
how evil and bitter it is for you

when you forsake the LORD your God
and have no awe of me,"
declares the Lord,
the LORD Almighty.

20 "Long ago you broke off your yoke
and tore off your bonds;
you said, 'I will not serve you!'
Indeed, on every high hill
and under every spreading tree
you lay down as a prostitute.

21 I had planted you like a choice vine
of sound and reliable stock.
How then did you turn against me
into a corrupt, wild vine?

22 Although you wash yourself with
soda
and use an abundance of soap,
the stain of your guilt is still before
me,"
declares the Sovereign LORD.

23 "How can you say, 'I am not defiled;
I have not run after the Baals'?
See how you behaved in the valley;
consider what you have done.
You are a swift she-camel
running here and there,

24 a wild donkey accustomed to the
desert,
sniffing the wind in her craving—
in her heat who can restrain her?
Any males that pursue her need not
tire themselves;
at mating time they will find her.

25 Do not run until your feet are bare
and your throat is dry.
But you said, 'It's no use!
I love foreign gods,
and I must go after them.'

26 "As a thief is disgraced when he is
caught,
so the house of Israel is
disgraced—
they, their kings and their officials,
their priests and their prophets.

27 They say to wood, 'You are my
father,'
and to stone, 'You gave me birth.'

---

[a]10 That is, Cyprus and western coastlands
[b]10 The home of Bedouin tribes in the Syro-
Arabian desert   [c]11 Masoretic Text; an ancient
Hebrew scribal tradition *my*   [d]16 Hebrew
Noph   [e]16 Or *have cracked your skull*
[f]18 That is, a branch of the Nile   [g]18 That is,
the Euphrates

They have turned their backs to me
  and not their faces;
yet when they are in trouble, they
  say,
'Come and save us!'
²⁸ Where then are the gods you made
  for yourselves?
Let them come if they can save you
  when you are in trouble!
For you have as many gods
  as you have towns, O Judah.

²⁹ "Why do you bring charges against
  me?
You have all rebelled against me,"
            declares the LORD.
³⁰ "In vain I punished your people;
  they did not respond to correction.
Your sword has devoured your
  prophets
  like a ravening lion.

³¹ "You of this generation, consider the
word of the LORD:

"Have I been a desert to Israel
  or a land of great darkness?
Why do my people say, 'We are free
  to roam;
  we will come to you no more'?
³² Does a maiden forget her jewelry,
  a bride her wedding ornaments?
Yet my people have forgotten me,
  days without number.
³³ How skilled you are at pursuing love!
  Even the worst of women can learn
  from your ways.
³⁴ On your clothes men find
  the lifeblood of the innocent poor,
  though you did not catch them
  breaking in.
Yet in spite of all this
³⁵ you say, 'I am innocent;
  he is not angry with me.'
But I will pass judgment on you
  because you say, 'I have not
  sinned.'
³⁶ Why do you go about so much,
  changing your ways?
You will be disappointed by Egypt
  as you were by Assyria.
³⁷ You will also leave that place
  with your hands on your head,
for the LORD has rejected those you
  trust;
  you will not be helped by them.

3 "If a man divorces his wife
  and she leaves him and marries
  another man,
should he return to her again?
Would not the land be completely
  defiled?
But you have lived as a prostitute
  with many lovers—
  would you now return to me?"
            declares the LORD.
² "Look up to the barren heights and
  see.
Is there any place where you have
  not been ravished?
By the roadside you sat waiting for
  lovers,
  sat like a nomad*a* in the desert.
You have defiled the land
  with your prostitution and
  wickedness.
³ Therefore the showers have been
  withheld,
  and no spring rains have fallen.
Yet you have the brazen look of a
  prostitute;
  you refuse to blush with shame.
⁴ Have you not just called to me:
'My Father, my friend from my
  youth,
⁵ will you always be angry?
Will your wrath continue forever?'
This is how you talk,
  but you do all the evil you can."

> ❝ We have to pray with our eyes on
> God, not on the difficulties. ❞
>
> OSWALD CHAMBERS

Unfaithful Israel

⁶During the reign of King Josiah, the
LORD said to me, "Have you seen what
faithless Israel has done? She has gone
up on every high hill and under every
spreading tree and has committed adultery there. ⁷I thought that after she had
done all this she would return to me but
she did not, and her unfaithful sister Judah saw it. ⁸I gave faithless Israel her certificate of divorce and sent her away
because of all her adulteries. Yet I saw
that her unfaithful sister Judah had no

a2 Or an Arab

fear; she also went out and committed adultery. [9]Because Israel's immorality mattered so little to her, she defiled the land and committed adultery with stone and wood. [10]In spite of all this, her unfaithful sister Judah did not return to me with all her heart, but only in pretense," declares the LORD.

[11]The LORD said to me, "Faithless Israel is more righteous than unfaithful Judah. [12]Go, proclaim this message toward the north:

"'Return, faithless Israel,' declares
    the LORD,
  'I will frown on you no longer,
for I am merciful,' declares the LORD,
  'I will not be angry forever.
[13]Only acknowledge your guilt—
    you have rebelled against the LORD
    your God,
  you have scattered your favors to
    foreign gods
  under every spreading tree,
    and have not obeyed me,'"
            declares the LORD.

[14]"Return, faithless people," declares the LORD, "for I am your husband. I will choose you—one from a town and two from a clan—and bring you to Zion. [15]Then I will give you shepherds after my own heart, who will lead you with knowledge and understanding. [16]In those days, when your numbers have increased greatly in the land," declares the LORD, "men will no longer say, 'The ark of the covenant of the LORD.' It will never enter their minds or be remembered; it will not be missed, nor will another one be made. [17]At that time they will call Jerusalem The Throne of the LORD, and all nations will gather in Jerusalem to honor the name of the LORD. No longer will they follow the stubbornness of their evil hearts. [18]In those days the house of Judah will join the house of Israel, and together they will come from a northern land to the land I gave your forefathers as an inheritance.

[19]"I myself said,

"'How gladly would I treat you
    like sons
  and give you a desirable land,
    the most beautiful inheritance of
    any nation.'

I thought you would call me 'Father'
    and not turn away from following
    me.
[20]But like a woman unfaithful to her
    husband,
  so you have been unfaithful to me,
    O house of Israel,"
            declares the LORD.

[21]A cry is heard on the barren
    heights,
  the weeping and pleading of the
    people of Israel,
because they have perverted their
    ways
  and have forgotten the LORD
    their God.

[22]"Return, faithless people;
  I will cure you of backsliding."

"Yes, we will come to you,
  for you are the LORD our God.
[23]Surely the ⌐idolatrous┐ commotion
    on the hills
  and mountains is a deception;
surely in the LORD our God
  is the salvation of Israel.
[24]From our youth shameful gods
    have consumed
  the fruits of our fathers'
    labor—
  their flocks and herds,
    their sons and daughters.
[25]Let us lie down in our shame,
  and let our disgrace cover us.
We have sinned against the LORD
    our God,
  both we and our fathers;
from our youth till this day
  we have not obeyed the LORD
    our God."

4 "If you will return, O Israel,
    return to me,"
            declares the LORD.
"If you put your detestable idols out
    of my sight
  and no longer go astray,
[2]and if in a truthful, just and
    righteous way
  you swear, 'As surely as the
    LORD lives,'
then the nations will be blessed
    by him
  and in him they will glory."

³This is what the LORD says to the men of Judah and to Jerusalem:

"Break up your unplowed ground
  and do not sow among thorns.
⁴Circumcise yourselves to the LORD,
  circumcise your hearts,
  you men of Judah and people of
    Jerusalem,
or my wrath will break out and burn
    like fire
because of the evil you have done—
  burn with no one to quench it.

Disaster From the North

⁵ "Announce in Judah and proclaim in
    Jerusalem and say:
  'Sound the trumpet throughout
    the land!'
  Cry aloud and say:
  'Gather together!
  Let us flee to the fortified cities!'
⁶Raise the signal to go to Zion!
  Flee for safety without delay!
  For I am bringing disaster from the
    north,
    even terrible destruction."

⁷A lion has come out of his lair;
  a destroyer of nations has set out.
  He has left his place
    to lay waste your land.
  Your towns will lie in ruins
    without inhabitant.
⁸So put on sackcloth,
  lament and wail,
  for the fierce anger of the LORD
    has not turned away from us.

⁹ "In that day," declares the LORD,
  "the king and the officials will lose
    heart,
  the priests will be horrified,
    and the prophets will be appalled."

¹⁰Then I said, "Ah, Sovereign LORD, how completely you have deceived this people and Jerusalem by saying, 'You will have peace,' when the sword is at our throats."

¹¹At that time this people and Jerusalem will be told, "A scorching wind from the barren heights in the desert blows toward my people, but not to winnow or cleanse; ¹²a wind too strong for that comes from me.ᵃ Now I pronounce my judgments against them."

¹³Look! He advances like the clouds,
  his chariots come like a whirlwind,
  his horses are swifter than eagles.
  Woe to us! We are ruined!
¹⁴O Jerusalem, wash the evil from your
    heart and be saved.
  How long will you harbor wicked
    thoughts?
¹⁵A voice is announcing from Dan,
  proclaiming disaster from the hills
    of Ephraim.
¹⁶ "Tell this to the nations,
  proclaim it to Jerusalem:
  'A besieging army is coming from a
    distant land,
  raising a war cry against the cities
    of Judah.
¹⁷They surround her like men guarding
    a field,
  because she has rebelled against
    me,' "
                  declares the LORD.
¹⁸ "Your own conduct and actions
    have brought this upon you.
  This is your punishment.
    How bitter it is!
    How it pierces to the heart!"

¹⁹Oh, my anguish, my anguish!
    I writhe in pain.
  Oh, the agony of my heart!
    My heart pounds within me,
    I cannot keep silent.
  For I have heard the sound of the
    trumpet;
    I have heard the battle cry.
²⁰Disaster follows disaster;
  the whole land lies in ruins.
  In an instant my tents are destroyed,
    my shelter in a moment.
²¹How long must I see the battle
    standard
  and hear the sound of the trumpet?

²² "My people are fools;
    they do not know me.
  They are senseless children;
    they have no understanding.
  They are skilled in doing evil;
    they know not how to do good."

²³I looked at the earth,
    and it was formless and empty;
  and at the heavens,
    and their light was gone.

ᵃ12 Or *comes at my command*

²⁴ I looked at the mountains,
and they were quaking;
all the hills were swaying.
²⁵ I looked, and there were no people;
every bird in the sky had flown
away.
²⁶ I looked, and the fruitful land was
a desert;
all its towns lay in ruins
before the LORD, before his fierce
anger.

²⁷This is what the LORD says:

"The whole land will be ruined,
though I will not destroy it
completely.
²⁸ Therefore the earth will mourn
and the heavens above grow
dark,
because I have spoken and will
not relent,
I have decided and will not turn
back."

²⁹ At the sound of horsemen and
archers
every town takes to flight.
Some go into the thickets;
some climb up among the rocks.
All the towns are deserted;
no one lives in them.

³⁰ What are you doing, O devastated
one?
Why dress yourself in scarlet
and put on jewels of gold?
Why shade your eyes with paint?
You adorn yourself in vain.
Your lovers despise you;
they seek your life.

³¹ I hear a cry as of a woman in labor,
a groan as of one bearing her first
child—
the cry of the Daughter of Zion
gasping for breath,
stretching out her hands and
saying,
"Alas! I am fainting;
my life is given over to murderers."

Not One Is Upright

5 "Go up and down the streets of
Jerusalem,
look around and consider,
search through her squares.
If you can find but one person
who deals honestly and seeks the
truth,
I will forgive this city.
² Although they say, 'As surely as the
LORD lives,'
still they are swearing falsely."

³ O LORD, do not your eyes look for
truth?
You struck them, but they felt no
pain;
you crushed them, but they refused
correction.
They made their faces harder than
stone
and refused to repent.
⁴ I thought, "These are only the poor;
they are foolish,
for they do not know the way of the
LORD,
the requirements of their God.
⁵ So I will go to the leaders
and speak to them;
surely they know the way of the
LORD,
the requirements of their God."
But with one accord they too had
broken off the yoke
and torn off the bonds.
⁶ Therefore a lion from the forest will
attack them,
a wolf from the desert will ravage
them,
a leopard will lie in wait near their
towns
to tear to pieces any who venture
out,
for their rebellion is great
and their backslidings many.

⁷ "Why should I forgive you?
Your children have forsaken me
and sworn by gods that are not
gods.
I supplied all their needs,
yet they committed adultery
and thronged to the houses of
prostitutes.
⁸ They are well-fed, lusty stallions,
each neighing for another man's
wife.
⁹ Should I not punish them for this?"
declares the LORD.
"Should I not avenge myself
on such a nation as this?

¹⁰ "Go through her vineyards and
    ravage them,
  but do not destroy them
    completely.
Strip off her branches,
  for these people do not belong to
    the LORD.
¹¹ The house of Israel and the house
    of Judah
  have been utterly unfaithful
    to me,"
            declares the LORD.

¹² They have lied about the LORD;
  they said, "He will do nothing!
No harm will come to us;
  we will never see sword or famine.
¹³ The prophets are but wind
  and the word is not in them;
so let what they say be done to
    them."

¹⁴ Therefore this is what the LORD God
Almighty says:

"Because the people have spoken
    these words,
  I will make my words in your
    mouth a fire
  and these people the wood it
    consumes.
¹⁵ O house of Israel," declares the LORD,
"I am bringing a distant nation
    against you—
an ancient and enduring nation,
  a people whose language you do
    not know,
  whose speech you do not
    understand.
¹⁶ Their quivers are like an open grave;
  all of them are mighty warriors.
¹⁷ They will devour your harvests and
    food,
  devour your sons and daughters;
they will devour your flocks and
    herds,
  devour your vines and fig trees.
With the sword they will destroy
  the fortified cities in which
    you trust.

¹⁸ "Yet even in those days," declares the
LORD, "I will not destroy you completely.
¹⁹ And when the people ask, 'Why has the
LORD our God done all this to us?' you will
tell them, 'As you have forsaken me and
served foreign gods in your own land, so
now you will serve foreigners in a land
not your own.'

²⁰ "Announce this to the house of Jacob
    and proclaim it in Judah:
²¹ Hear this, you foolish and senseless
    people,
  who have eyes but do not see,
  who have ears but do not hear:
²² Should you not fear me?" declares
    the LORD.
"Should you not tremble in my
    presence?
I made the sand a boundary for the
    sea,
  an everlasting barrier it cannot
    cross.
The waves may roll, but they cannot
    prevail;
  they may roar, but they cannot
    cross it.
²³ But these people have stubborn and
    rebellious hearts;
  they have turned aside and gone
    away.
²⁴ They do not say to themselves,
  'Let us fear the LORD our God,
who gives autumn and spring rains
    in season,
who assures us of the regular
    weeks of harvest.'
²⁵ Your wrongdoings have kept these
    away;
  your sins have deprived you of
    good.

²⁶ "Among my people are wicked men
  who lie in wait like men who snare
    birds
  and like those who set traps to
    catch men.
²⁷ Like cages full of birds,
  their houses are full of deceit;
they have become rich and powerful
²⁸   and have grown fat and sleek.
Their evil deeds have no limit;
  they do not plead the case of the
    fatherless to win it,
  they do not defend the rights of
    the poor.
²⁹ Should I not punish them for this?"
    declares the LORD.
"Should I not avenge myself
  on such a nation as this?

³⁰ "A horrible and shocking thing
  has happened in the land:

³¹ The prophets prophesy lies,
  the priests rule by their own
    authority,
and my people love it this way.
  But what will you do in the
    end?

Jerusalem Under Siege

6 "Flee for safety, people of
    Benjamin!
  Flee from Jerusalem!
Sound the trumpet in Tekoa!
  Raise the signal over Beth
    Hakkerem!
For disaster looms out of the north,
  even terrible destruction.
² I will destroy the Daughter of Zion,
  so beautiful and delicate.
³ Shepherds with their flocks will
    come against her;
  they will pitch their tents around
    her,
  each tending his own portion."

⁴ "Prepare for battle against her!
  Arise, let us attack at noon!
But, alas, the daylight is fading,
  and the shadows of evening grow
    long.
⁵ So arise, let us attack at night
  and destroy her fortresses!"

⁶ This is what the Lord Almighty says:

"Cut down the trees
  and build siege ramps against
    Jerusalem.
This city must be punished;
  it is filled with oppression.
⁷ As a well pours out its water,
  so she pours out her wickedness.
Violence and destruction resound
    in her;
  her sickness and wounds are ever
    before me.
⁸ Take warning, O Jerusalem,
  or I will turn away from you
and make your land desolate
  so no one can live in it."

⁹ This is what the Lord Almighty says:

"Let them glean the remnant of Israel
  as thoroughly as a vine;
pass your hand over the branches
    again,
  like one gathering grapes."

¹⁰ To whom can I speak and give
    warning?
  Who will listen to me?
Their ears are closed^a
  so they cannot hear.
The word of the Lord is offensive
    to them;
  they find no pleasure in it.
¹¹ But I am full of the wrath of the
    Lord,
  and I cannot hold it in.

"Pour it out on the children in the
    street
  and on the young men gathered
    together;
both husband and wife will be caught
    in it,
  and the old, those weighed down
    with years.
¹² Their houses will be turned over to
    others,
  together with their fields and their
    wives,
when I stretch out my hand
  against those who live in the
    land,"
                    declares the Lord.
¹³ "From the least to the greatest,
  all are greedy for gain;
prophets and priests alike,
  all practice deceit.
¹⁴ They dress the wound of my people
  as though it were not serious.
'Peace, peace,' they say,
  when there is no peace.
¹⁵ Are they ashamed of their loathsome
    conduct?
  No, they have no shame at all;
  they do not even know how to
    blush.
So they will fall among the fallen;
  they will be brought down when I
    punish them,"
                    says the Lord.

¹⁶ This is what the Lord says:

"Stand at the crossroads and look;
  ask for the ancient paths,
ask where the good way is, and walk
    in it,
  and you will find rest for your souls.
  But you said, 'We will not walk
    in it.'

^a 10 Hebrew uncircumcised

> STAND *at the crossroads and look;*
> *ask for the ancient paths,*
> *ask where the good way is, and walk in it,*
> *and you will find rest for your souls.*
>
> JEREMIAH 6:16

17 I appointed watchmen over you
and said,
'Listen to the sound of the
trumpet!'
But you said, 'We will not listen.'
18 Therefore hear, O nations;
observe, O witnesses,
what will happen to them.
19 Hear, O earth:
I am bringing disaster on this
people,
the fruit of their schemes,
because they have not listened to my
words
and have rejected my law.
20 What do I care about incense from
Sheba
or sweet calamus from a distant
land?
Your burnt offerings are not
acceptable;
your sacrifices do not please me."

21 Therefore this is what the LORD says:

"I will put obstacles before this
people.
Fathers and sons alike will stumble
over them;
neighbors and friends will perish."

22 This is what the LORD says:

"Look, an army is coming
from the land of the north;
a great nation is being stirred up
from the ends of the earth.
23 They are armed with bow and spear;
they are cruel and show no mercy.
They sound like the roaring sea
as they ride on their horses;
they come like men in battle
formation
to attack you, O Daughter of Zion."

24 We have heard reports about them,
and our hands hang limp.
Anguish has gripped us,
pain like that of a woman in labor.

25 Do not go out to the fields
or walk on the roads,
for the enemy has a sword,
and there is terror on every side.
26 O my people, put on sackcloth
and roll in ashes;
mourn with bitter wailing
as for an only son,
for suddenly the destroyer
will come upon us.

27 "I have made you a tester of metals
and my people the ore,
that you may observe
and test their ways.
28 They are all hardened rebels,
going about to slander.
They are bronze and iron;
they all act corruptly.
29 The bellows blow fiercely
to burn away the lead with fire,
but the refining goes on in vain;
the wicked are not purged out.
30 They are called rejected silver,
because the LORD has rejected
them."

False Religion Worthless

7 This is the word that came to Jeremiah from the LORD: 2 "Stand at the gate of the LORD's house and there proclaim this message:
" 'Hear the word of the LORD, all you people of Judah who come through these gates to worship the LORD. 3 This is what the LORD Almighty, the God of Israel, says: Reform your ways and your actions, and I will let you live in this place. 4 Do not trust in deceptive words and say, "This is the temple of the LORD, the temple of the LORD, the temple of the LORD!" 5 If you really change your ways and your actions and deal with each other justly, 6 if you do not oppress the alien, the fatherless or the widow and do not shed innocent blood in this place, and if you do not follow other gods to your own harm, 7 then I will let you live in this place, in the land I gave your forefathers for ever and ever. 8 But look, you are trusting in deceptive words that are worthless.
9 " 'Will you steal and murder, commit adultery and perjury,*a* burn incense to Baal and follow other gods you have not

*a*9 Or *and swear by false gods*

known, [10]and then come and stand before me in this house, which bears my Name, and say, "We are safe"—safe to do all these detestable things? [11]Has this house, which bears my Name, become a den of robbers to you? But I have been watching! declares the LORD.

[12]" 'Go now to the place in Shiloh where I first made a dwelling for my Name, and see what I did to it because of the wickedness of my people Israel. [13]While you were doing all these things, declares the LORD, I spoke to you again and again, but you did not listen; I called you, but you did not answer. [14]Therefore, what I did to Shiloh I will now do to the house that bears my Name, the temple you trust in, the place I gave to you and your fathers. [15]I will thrust you from my presence, just as I did all your brothers, the people of Ephraim.'

[16]"So do not pray for this people nor offer any plea or petition for them; do not plead with me, for I will not listen to you. [17]Do you not see what they are doing in the towns of Judah and in the streets of Jerusalem? [18]The children gather wood, the fathers light the fire, and the women knead the dough and make cakes of bread for the Queen of Heaven. They pour out drink offerings to other gods to provoke me to anger. [19]But am I the one they are provoking? declares the LORD. Are they not rather harming themselves, to their own shame?

[20]" 'Therefore this is what the Sovereign LORD says: My anger and my wrath will be poured out on this place, on man and beast, on the trees of the field and on the fruit of the ground, and it will burn and not be quenched.

[21]" 'This is what the LORD Almighty, the God of Israel, says: Go ahead, add your burnt offerings to your other sacrifices and eat the meat yourselves! [22]For when I brought your forefathers out of Egypt and spoke to them, I did not just give them commands about burnt offerings and sacrifices, [23]but I gave them this command: Obey me, and I will be your God and you will be my people. Walk in all the ways I command you, that it may go well with you. [24]But they did not listen or pay attention; instead, they followed the stubborn inclinations of their evil hearts. They went backward and not forward. [25]From the time your forefathers left Egypt until now, day after day, again and again I sent you my servants the prophets. [26]But they did not listen to me or pay attention. They were stiff-necked and did more evil than their forefathers.'

[27]"When you tell them all this, they will not listen to you; when you call to them, they will not answer. [28]Therefore say to them, 'This is the nation that has not obeyed the LORD its God or responded to correction. Truth has perished; it has vanished from their lips. [29]Cut off your hair and throw it away; take up a lament on the barren heights, for the LORD has rejected and abandoned this generation that is under his wrath.

The Valley of Slaughter

[30]" 'The people of Judah have done evil in my eyes, declares the LORD. They have set up their detestable idols in the house that bears my Name and have defiled it. [31]They have built the high places of Topheth in the Valley of Ben Hinnom to burn their sons and daughters in the fire—something I did not command, nor did it enter my mind. [32]So beware, the days are coming, declares the LORD, when people will no longer call it Topheth or the Valley of Ben Hinnom, but the Valley of Slaughter, for they will bury the dead in Topheth until there is no more room. [33]Then the carcasses of this people will become food for the birds of the air and the beasts of the earth, and there will be no one to frighten them away. [34]I will bring an end to the sounds of joy and gladness and to the voices of bride and bridegroom in the towns of Judah and the streets of Jerusalem, for the land will become desolate.

8 " 'At that time, declares the LORD, the bones of the kings and officials of Judah, the bones of the priests and prophets, and the bones of the people of Jerusalem will be removed from their graves. [2]They will be exposed to the sun and the moon and all the stars of the heavens, which they have loved and served and which they have followed and consulted and worshiped. They will not be gathered up or buried, but will be like refuse lying on the ground. [3]Wherever

Don't Pray for the People?

7:16 "SO DO NOT PRAY FOR THIS PEOPLE NOR OFFER ANY PLEA OR PETITION FOR THEM; DO NOT PLEAD WITH ME, FOR I WILL NOT LISTEN TO YOU."

Sometimes television ads for automobiles will show cars being driven recklessly through mountain passes and busy city streets to demonstrate what marvels of modern engineering they are in speed and handling. A caption will appear at the bottom of the screen indicating that the cars are driven by professional drivers. The message is that we shouldn't try to drive our cars this way. Only the experts, under carefully controlled situations, may do so. This text is like that. What are we to make of God forbidding Jeremiah to pray for the people, not once, but four times (see 7:16; 11:14; 14:11; 15:1)? Obviously, we should not carelessly and simplistically apply this command in our own lives.

Whenever we meet particularly vile and headstrong sinners, we might be tempted to write them off and never pray for them. But the probable meaning of the command was for Jeremiah to stop praying that the people be spared the Babylonian onslaught. The Israelites were too far gone, and God had made up his mind about their punishment. No doubt Jeremiah could pray for other things, like the fulfillment of God's promise that his people one day be restored under a new covenant (see 31:31−34).

What does this mean for us? God may reveal to us that we are to stop praying for something we have been asking for. Maybe our prayer has been for healing that God has not granted. However, we should be very cautious about things like this. Is God really speaking to us, or are we being too impatient to wait for an answer? Far too many prayers are cut short by impatience and lack of faith. The greater lesson is that prayer should not be an attempt to make God do what we want, but rather it is the method he allows us to use in order that he may give us what he wants. Most of what Jesus has to say about prayer is to persist and believe that God will accomplish his divine will. We're not to adopt the attitude that we might as well stop praying since God's going to do what he wants anyway! Usually we won't know what God's will is unless we persist.

P R A Y :

Father, your will alone is good; may your good will be done.

It is your will that I persist in prayer (see Luke 18:1−8).

Help me keep on praying until you say otherwise.

FOR YOUR NEXT DEVOTIONAL READING, GO TO PAGE 901.

I banish them, all the survivors of this evil nation will prefer death to life, declares the LORD Almighty.'

Sin and Punishment

4 "Say to them, 'This is what the LORD says:

"'When men fall down, do they not
    get up?
  When a man turns away, does he
    not return?
5 Why then have these people turned
    away?
  Why does Jerusalem always turn
    away?
  They cling to deceit;
    they refuse to return.
6 I have listened attentively,
    but they do not say what is right.
  No one repents of his wickedness,
    saying, "What have I done?"
  Each pursues his own course
    like a horse charging into battle.
7 Even the stork in the sky
    knows her appointed seasons,
  and the dove, the swift and the
    thrush
      observe the time of their
        migration.
  But my people do not know
    the requirements of the LORD.

8 "'How can you say, "We are wise,
    for we have the law of the LORD,"
  when actually the lying pen of the
    scribes
      has handled it falsely?
9 The wise will be put to shame;
    they will be dismayed and trapped.
  Since they have rejected the word of
    the LORD,
      what kind of wisdom do they have?
10 Therefore I will give their wives to
    other men
  and their fields to new owners.
  From the least to the greatest,
    all are greedy for gain;
  prophets and priests alike,
    all practice deceit.
11 They dress the wound of my people
    as though it were not serious.
  "Peace, peace," they say,
    when there is no peace.
12 Are they ashamed of their loathsome
    conduct?

No, they have no shame at all;
    they do not even know how to
      blush.
  So they will fall among the fallen;
    they will be brought down when
      they are punished,
                        says the LORD.

13 "'I will take away their harvest,
                    declares the LORD.
  There will be no grapes on the vine.
  There will be no figs on the tree,
    and their leaves will wither.
  What I have given them
    will be taken from them.ᵃ'"

14 "Why are we sitting here?
    Gather together!
  Let us flee to the fortified cities
    and perish there!
  For the LORD our God has doomed
    us to perish
  and given us poisoned water to
    drink,
  because we have sinned against
    him.
15 We hoped for peace
    but no good has come,
  for a time of healing
    but there was only terror.
16 The snorting of the enemy's horses
    is heard from Dan;
  at the neighing of their stallions
    the whole land trembles.
  They have come to devour
    the land and everything in it,
    the city and all who live there."

17 "See, I will send venomous snakes
    among you,
  vipers that cannot be charmed,
    and they will bite you,"
                    declares the LORD.

18 O my Comforterᵇ in sorrow,
    my heart is faint within me.
19 Listen to the cry of my people
    from a land far away:
  "Is the LORD not in Zion?
    Is her King no longer there?"

  "Why have they provoked me to
    anger with their images,
  with their worthless foreign idols?"

ᵃ13 The meaning of the Hebrew for this sentence is uncertain.   ᵇ18 The meaning of the Hebrew for this word is uncertain.

20 "The harvest is past,
   the summer has ended,
   and we are not saved."

21 Since my people are crushed, I am
      crushed;
   I mourn, and horror grips me.
22 Is there no balm in Gilead?
   Is there no physician there?
   Why then is there no healing
   for the wound of my people?

9 ¹Oh, that my head were a spring
      of water
   and my eyes a fountain of tears!
   I would weep day and night
   for the slain of my people.
² Oh, that I had in the desert
   a lodging place for travelers,
   so that I might leave my people
   and go away from them;
   for they are all adulterers,
   a crowd of unfaithful people.

3 "They make ready their tongue
   like a bow, to shoot lies;
   it is not by truth
   that they triumph[a] in the land.
   They go from one sin to another;
   they do not acknowledge me,"
                        declares the LORD.
4 "Beware of your friends;
   do not trust your brothers.
   For every brother is a deceiver,[b]
   and every friend a slanderer.
5 Friend deceives friend,
   and no one speaks the truth.
   They have taught their tongues
      to lie;
   they weary themselves with
      sinning.
6 You[c] live in the midst of deception;
   in their deceit they refuse to
      acknowledge me,"
                        declares the LORD.

7 Therefore this is what the LORD Almighty says:

   "See, I will refine and test them,
   for what else can I do
   because of the sin of my people?
8 Their tongue is a deadly arrow;
   it speaks with deceit.
   With his mouth each speaks cordially
      to his neighbor,
   but in his heart he sets a trap for
      him.

9 Should I not punish them for this?"
      declares the LORD.
   "Should I not avenge myself
   on such a nation as this?"

10 I will weep and wail for the
      mountains
   and take up a lament concerning
      the desert pastures.
   They are desolate and untraveled,
   and the lowing of cattle is not
      heard.
   The birds of the air have fled
   and the animals are gone.

11 "I will make Jerusalem a heap of
      ruins,
   a haunt of jackals;
   and I will lay waste the towns of
      Judah
   so no one can live there."

12 What man is wise enough to understand this? Who has been instructed by
the LORD and can explain it? Why has the
land been ruined and laid waste like a
desert that no one can cross?

13 The LORD said, "It is because they
have forsaken my law, which I set before them; they have not obeyed me or
followed my law. 14 Instead, they have
followed the stubbornness of their
hearts; they have followed the Baals, as
their fathers taught them." 15 Therefore,
this is what the LORD Almighty, the God
of Israel, says: "See, I will make this
people eat bitter food and drink poisoned water. 16 I will scatter them among
nations that neither they nor their fathers have known, and I will pursue
them with the sword until I have destroyed them."

17 This is what the LORD Almighty says:

   "Consider now! Call for the wailing
      women to come;
   send for the most skillful of
      them.
18 Let them come quickly
   and wail over us
   till our eyes overflow with tears
   and water streams from our
      eyelids.

---

[a]3 Or lies; / they are not valiant for truth
[b]4 Or a deceiving Jacob   [c]6 That is, Jeremiah
(the Hebrew is singular)

19 The sound of wailing is heard
        from Zion:
    'How ruined we are!
    How great is our shame!
    We must leave our land
    because our houses are in ruins.' "

20 Now, O women, hear the word of the
        LORD;
    open your ears to the words of his
        mouth.
    Teach your daughters how to wail;
    teach one another a lament.
21 Death has climbed in through our
        windows
    and has entered our fortresses;
    it has cut off the children from the
        streets
    and the young men from the public
        squares.

22 Say, "This is what the LORD declares:

    " 'The dead bodies of men will lie
    like refuse on the open field,
    like cut grain behind the reaper,
    with no one to gather them.' "

23 This is what the LORD says:

    "Let not the wise man boast of his
        wisdom
    or the strong man boast of his
        strength
    or the rich man boast of his riches,
24 but let him who boasts boast about
        this:
    that he understands and knows
        me,
    that I am the LORD, who exercises
        kindness,
    justice and righteousness on earth,
    for in these I delight,"
                    declares the LORD.

> "I AM the LORD, who exercises kindness,
> justice and righteousness on earth,
> for in these I delight."
>
> JEREMIAH 9:24

25 "The days are coming," declares the
LORD, "when I will punish all who are circumcised only in the flesh— 26 Egypt, Judah, Edom, Ammon, Moab and all who
live in the desert in distant places.ᵃ For
all these nations are really uncircumcised, and even the whole house of Israel is uncircumcised in heart."

God and Idols

10 Hear what the LORD says to you,
    O house of Israel. 2 This is what the
LORD says:

    "Do not learn the ways of the nations
    or be terrified by signs in the sky,
    though the nations are terrified
        by them.
3 For the customs of the peoples are
        worthless;
    they cut a tree out of the forest,
    and a craftsman shapes it with his
        chisel.
4 They adorn it with silver and gold;
    they fasten it with hammer and
        nails
    so it will not totter.
5 Like a scarecrow in a melon patch,
    their idols cannot speak;
    they must be carried
    because they cannot walk.
    Do not fear them;
    they can do no harm
    nor can they do any good."

6 No one is like you, O LORD;
    you are great,
    and your name is mighty in power.
7 Who should not revere you,
    O King of the nations?
    This is your due.
    Among all the wise men of the
        nations
    and in all their kingdoms,
    there is no one like you.
8 They are all senseless and foolish;
    they are taught by worthless
        wooden idols.
9 Hammered silver is brought from
        Tarshish
    and gold from Uphaz.
    What the craftsman and goldsmith
        have made
    is then dressed in blue and purple—
    all made by skilled workers.
10 But the LORD is the true God;
    he is the living God, the eternal
        King.

ᵃ26 Or desert and who clip the hair by their
foreheads

When he is angry, the earth trembles;
 the nations cannot endure his
 wrath.

¹¹ "Tell them this: 'These gods, who did
not make the heavens and the earth, will
perish from the earth and from under the
heavens.' "ᵃ

¹² But God made the earth by his
 power;
 he founded the world by his
 wisdom
 and stretched out the heavens by
 his understanding.
¹³ When he thunders, the waters in the
 heavens roar;
 he makes clouds rise from the ends
 of the earth.
 He sends lightning with the rain
 and brings out the wind from his
 storehouses.

¹⁴ Everyone is senseless and without
 knowledge;
 every goldsmith is shamed by
 his idols.
 His images are a fraud;
 they have no breath in them.
¹⁵ They are worthless, the objects of
 mockery;
 when their judgment comes, they
 will perish.
¹⁶ He who is the Portion of Jacob is not
 like these,
 for he is the Maker of all things,
 including Israel, the tribe of his
 inheritance—
 the LORD Almighty is his name.

Coming Destruction

¹⁷ Gather up your belongings to leave
 the land,
 you who live under siege.
¹⁸ For this is what the LORD says:
 "At this time I will hurl out
 those who live in this land;
 I will bring distress on them
 so that they may be captured."

¹⁹ Woe to me because of my injury!
 My wound is incurable!
 Yet I said to myself,
 "This is my sickness, and I must
 endure it."
²⁰ My tent is destroyed;
 all its ropes are snapped.

My sons are gone from me and are
 no more;
 no one is left now to pitch my tent
 or to set up my shelter.
²¹ The shepherds are senseless
 and do not inquire of the LORD;
 so they do not prosper
 and all their flock is scattered.
²² Listen! The report is coming—
 a great commotion from the land of
 the north!
 It will make the towns of Judah
 desolate,
 a haunt of jackals.

Jeremiah's Prayer

²³ I know, O LORD, that a man's life is
 not his own;
 it is not for man to direct his steps.
²⁴ Correct me, LORD, but only with
 justice—
 not in your anger,
 lest you reduce me to nothing.
²⁵ Pour out your wrath on the nations
 that do not acknowledge you,
 on the peoples who do not call on
 your name.
 For they have devoured Jacob;
 they have devoured him completely
 and destroyed his homeland.

The Covenant Is Broken

11 This is the word that came to Jeremiah from the LORD: ²"Listen to the
terms of this covenant and tell them to
the people of Judah and to those who live
in Jerusalem. ³Tell them that this is what
the LORD, the God of Israel, says: 'Cursed
is the man who does not obey the terms
of this covenant— ⁴the terms I commanded your forefathers when I brought
them out of Egypt, out of the iron-smelting furnace.' I said, 'Obey me and do everything I command you, and you will be
my people, and I will be your God. ⁵Then
I will fulfill the oath I swore to your forefathers, to give them a land flowing with
milk and honey'—the land you possess
today."

 I answered, "Amen, LORD."
 ⁶The LORD said to me, "Proclaim all
these words in the towns of Judah and in
the streets of Jerusalem: 'Listen to the

ᵃ11 The text of this verse is in Aramaic.

terms of this covenant and follow them. ⁷From the time I brought your forefathers up from Egypt until today, I warned them again and again, saying, "Obey me." ⁸But they did not listen or pay attention; instead, they followed the stubbornness of their evil hearts. So I brought on them all the curses of the covenant I had commanded them to follow but that they did not keep.'"

⁹Then the LORD said to me, "There is a conspiracy among the people of Judah and those who live in Jerusalem. ¹⁰They have returned to the sins of their forefathers, who refused to listen to my words. They have followed other gods to serve them. Both the house of Israel and the house of Judah have broken the covenant I made with their forefathers. ¹¹Therefore this is what the LORD says: 'I will bring on them a disaster they cannot escape. Although they cry out to me, I will not listen to them. ¹²The towns of Judah and the people of Jerusalem will go and cry out to the gods to whom they burn incense, but they will not help them

---

JEREMIAH 10:23–25

{THURSDAY}

Correct Me, Lord

10:24 CORRECT ME, LORD, BUT ONLY WITH JUSTICE.

These verses contain a prayer that Jeremiah prayed on behalf of his people. He said "me," but he meant "us." That's a good way to pray for other believers when they have sinned. Ezra did this, as did many others in the Old Testament (see devotion on Ezra 9). Our sins and needs may not always be similar, but we all belong to each other as members of Christ's body. Praying this way reminds us of that solidarity. It is a concrete way to carry each other's burdens and fulfill the law of Christ (see Galatians 6:2). If we pray corporately in this manner, it will keep our prayers from condescension and pride. And who knows? We may need the very things we pray that others would receive.

We should also pray submissively. "I know, O LORD, that a man's life is not his own; it is not for man to direct his steps" (Jeremiah 10:23). This is a way of remembering that the people we pray for are the Lord's. Not a hair can fall from their heads apart from his will. We go astray if we act as though we are the ones directing our own lives. The first step in being set straight is to let God be in charge of our direction (see Psalm 25:4–5).

We must then submit to God's choice of direction. Jeremiah's prayer is sweet—he wants the Lord's correction—he really does—but he prays that it won't be too harsh to bear: "Correct me, LORD, but only with justice—not in your anger, lest you reduce me to nothing" (verse 24). This type of prayer isn't trying to get God to be kinder than had we not prayed. We are learning to pray in God's name, according to his character. God always tempers his justice with mercy and wounds us only in order to heal. He is delighted when we pray for each other.

PRAY:

Father, forgive us our debts as we forgive our debtors. We do not live only unto ourselves, but unto you, and each other.

FOR YOUR NEXT DEVOTIONAL READING, GO TO PAGE 903.

at all when disaster strikes. [13]You have as many gods as you have towns, O Judah; and the altars you have set up to burn incense to that shameful god Baal are as many as the streets of Jerusalem.'

[14]"Do not pray for this people nor offer any plea or petition for them, because I will not listen when they call to me in the time of their distress.

[15] "What is my beloved doing in my
temple
as she works out her evil schemes
with many?
Can consecrated meat avert ⌐your
punishment⌐?
When you engage in your wickedness,
then you rejoice.[a]"

[16]The LORD called you a thriving olive
tree
with fruit beautiful in form.
But with the roar of a mighty storm
he will set it on fire,
and its branches will be broken.

[17]The LORD Almighty, who planted you, has decreed disaster for you, because the house of Israel and the house of Judah have done evil and provoked me to anger by burning incense to Baal.

Plot Against Jeremiah

[18]Because the LORD revealed their plot to me, I knew it, for at that time he showed me what they were doing. [19]I had been like a gentle lamb led to the slaughter; I did not realize that they had plotted against me, saying,

"Let us destroy the tree and its fruit;
let us cut him off from the land of
the living,
that his name be remembered no
more."

[20]But, O LORD Almighty, you who judge
righteously
and test the heart and mind,
let me see your vengeance upon
them,
for to you I have committed my
cause.

[21]"Therefore this is what the LORD says about the men of Anathoth who are seeking your life and saying, 'Do not prophesy in the name of the LORD or you will die by our hands'— [22]therefore this is what the LORD Almighty says: 'I will punish them. Their young men will die by the sword, their sons and daughters by famine. [23]Not even a remnant will be left to them, because I will bring disaster on the men of Anathoth in the year of their punishment.'"

Jeremiah's Complaint

12 You are always righteous, O LORD,
when I bring a case before you.
Yet I would speak with you about
your justice:
Why does the way of the wicked
prosper?
Why do all the faithless live at
ease?
[2]You have planted them, and they
have taken root;
they grow and bear fruit.
You are always on their lips
but far from their hearts.
[3]Yet you know me, O LORD;
you see me and test my thoughts
about you.
Drag them off like sheep to be
butchered!
Set them apart for the day of
slaughter!
[4]How long will the land lie parched[b]
and the grass in every field be
withered?
Because those who live in it are
wicked,
the animals and birds have
perished.
Moreover, the people are saying,
"He will not see what happens
to us."

God's Answer

[5] "If you have raced with men on foot
and they have worn you out,
how can you compete with horses?
If you stumble in safe country,[c]
how will you manage in the
thickets by[d] the Jordan?
[6]Your brothers, your own family—
even they have betrayed you;
they have raised a loud cry
against you.

---

[a]15 Or *Could consecrated meat avert your
punishment? / Then you would rejoice*
[b]4 Or *land mourn*   [c]5 Or *If you put your trust
in a land of safety*   [d]5 Or *the flooding of*

JEREMIAH 12

Run With the Horses

12:1 WHY DOES THE WAY OF THE WICKED PROSPER?

A paraphrase of Jeremiah's prayer in 12:1–4 might go like this: "You're good, God; after all, you are God. So don't get me wrong. But I know about goodness too, and there are some things I think you need to explain—like the way you seem to have blessed those scoundrels and let me, your servant, suffer." Poet Gerard Manley Hopkins paraphrased Jeremiah's prayer this way:

> Wert thou mine enemy, O thou my friend,
> How wouldst thou worse, I wonder, than thou dost
> Defeat, thwart me?[2]

Essentially, Hopkins says, "With friends like you, who needs enemies?"

The glory of the gift of prayer is that God lets us speak to him honestly! But this gift also includes the privilege of hearing him answer what we say. Prayer is a two-way conversation. God's not-so-gentle answer to Jeremiah's complaint is to put it in perspective. The first perspective is, "You think this is bad? You haven't seen anything yet!" God says, "If you have raced with men on foot and they have worn you out, how can you compete with horses?" (verse 5). The message is that Jeremiah had better brace himself for more of what he doesn't like. He will need the next two perspectives to do that.

The second perspective is of God's own pain in the mess. "I will give the one I love into the hands of her enemies. My inheritance has become to me like a lion in the forest. She roars at me; therefore I hate her" (verses 7–8). God's suffering is always greater and truer than ours because his love is. The purer the love, the keener the pain when the beloved goes astray. Jeremiah's suffering is only a part of God's suffering. But if he chooses, Jeremiah's suffering can make him a participant, a partner with God (see Philippians 3:10).

The final perspective is the perspective of hope. "But after I uproot them, I will again have compassion and will bring each of them back to his own inheritance and his own country" (Jeremiah 12:15). Things will get worse before they get better, but the bad is not worth comparing to the better (see Romans 8:18). Our prayers are surrounded by hope.

God's words to Jeremiah call us to a "muscular" faith, a race against the horses. But they also remind us of who we run with and where we are running to.

PRAY:
Thank you, Lord, for listening to our complaints,
but not caving in to them. Strengthen us to run with the horses.

FOR YOUR NEXT DEVOTIONAL READING, GO TO PAGE 908.

Do not trust them,
though they speak well of you.

7 "I will forsake my house,
abandon my inheritance;
I will give the one I love
into the hands of her enemies.
8 My inheritance has become to me
like a lion in the forest.
She roars at me;
therefore I hate her.
9 Has not my inheritance become to me
like a speckled bird of prey
that other birds of prey surround
and attack?
Go and gather all the wild beasts;
bring them to devour.
10 Many shepherds will ruin my
vineyard
and trample down my field;
they will turn my pleasant field
into a desolate wasteland.
11 It will be made a wasteland,
parched and desolate before me;
the whole land will be laid waste
because there is no one who cares.
12 Over all the barren heights in the
desert
destroyers will swarm,
for the sword of the LORD will devour
from one end of the land to the
other;
no one will be safe.
13 They will sow wheat but reap thorns;
they will wear themselves out but
gain nothing.
So bear the shame of your harvest
because of the LORD's fierce anger."

14 This is what the LORD says: "As for all
my wicked neighbors who seize the inheritance I gave my people Israel, I will
uproot them from their lands and I will
uproot the house of Judah from among
them. 15 But after I uproot them, I will
again have compassion and will bring
each of them back to his own inheritance
and his own country. 16 And if they learn
well the ways of my people and swear by
my name, saying, 'As surely as the LORD
lives'—even as they once taught my people to swear by Baal—then they will be
established among my people. 17 But if
any nation does not listen, I will completely uproot and destroy it," declares
the LORD.

A Linen Belt

13 This is what the LORD said to me:
"Go and buy a linen belt and put it
around your waist, but do not let it touch
water." 2 So I bought a belt, as the LORD
directed, and put it around my waist.

3 Then the word of the LORD came to
me a second time: 4 "Take the belt you
bought and are wearing around your
waist, and go now to Perath[a] and hide it
there in a crevice in the rocks." 5 So I
went and hid it at Perath, as the LORD
told me.

6 Many days later the LORD said to me,
"Go now to Perath and get the belt I told
you to hide there." 7 So I went to Perath
and dug up the belt and took it from the
place where I had hidden it, but now it
was ruined and completely useless.

8 Then the word of the LORD came to
me: 9 "This is what the LORD says: 'In the
same way I will ruin the pride of Judah
and the great pride of Jerusalem. 10 These
wicked people, who refuse to listen to my
words, who follow the stubbornness of
their hearts and go after other gods to
serve and worship them, will be like this
belt—completely useless! 11 For as a belt
is bound around a man's waist, so I
bound the whole house of Israel and the
whole house of Judah to me,' declares
the LORD, 'to be my people for my renown
and praise and honor. But they have not
listened.'

Wineskins

12 "Say to them: 'This is what the LORD,
the God of Israel, says: Every wineskin
should be filled with wine.' And if they
say to you, 'Don't we know that every
wineskin should be filled with wine?'
13 then tell them, 'This is what the LORD
says: I am going to fill with drunkenness
all who live in this land, including the
kings who sit on David's throne, the
priests, the prophets and all those living
in Jerusalem. 14 I will smash them one
against the other, fathers and sons alike,
declares the LORD. I will allow no pity or
mercy or compassion to keep me from
destroying them.' "

---

[a]4 Or possibly *the Euphrates*; also in verses 5–7

Threat of Captivity

15 Hear and pay attention,
  do not be arrogant,
  for the LORD has spoken.
16 Give glory to the LORD your God
  before he brings the darkness,
  before your feet stumble
  on the darkening hills.
  You hope for light,
  but he will turn it to thick
    darkness
  and change it to deep gloom.
17 But if you do not listen,
  I will weep in secret
  because of your pride;
  my eyes will weep bitterly,
  overflowing with tears,
  because the LORD's flock will be
    taken captive.

18 Say to the king and to the queen
    mother,
  "Come down from your thrones,
  for your glorious crowns
  will fall from your heads."
19 The cities in the Negev will be
    shut up,
  and there will be no one to open
    them.
  All Judah will be carried into exile,
  carried completely away.

20 Lift up your eyes and see
  those who are coming from the
    north.
  Where is the flock that was entrusted
    to you,
  the sheep of which you boasted?
21 What will you say when the LORD
    sets over you
  those you cultivated as your special
    allies?
  Will not pain grip you
  like that of a woman in labor?
22 And if you ask yourself,
  "Why has this happened to me?"—
  it is because of your many sins
  that your skirts have been torn off
  and your body mistreated.
23 Can the Ethiopian[a] change his skin
  or the leopard its spots?
  Neither can you do good
  who are accustomed to doing evil.

24 "I will scatter you like chaff
  driven by the desert wind.

25 This is your lot,
  the portion I have decreed for you,"
    declares the LORD,
  "because you have forgotten me
  and trusted in false gods.
26 I will pull up your skirts over your
    face
  that your shame may be seen—
27 your adulteries and lustful neighings,
  your shameless prostitution!
  I have seen your detestable acts
  on the hills and in the fields.
  Woe to you, O Jerusalem!
  How long will you be unclean?"

> "JUDAH mourns,
>   her cities languish;
> they wail for the land,
>   and a cry goes up from Jerusalem."
>
> JEREMIAH 14:2

Drought, Famine, Sword

14 This is the word of the LORD to Jeremiah concerning the drought:

2 "Judah mourns,
  her cities languish;
  they wail for the land,
  and a cry goes up from Jerusalem.
3 The nobles send their servants for
    water;
  they go to the cisterns
  but find no water.
  They return with their jars unfilled;
  dismayed and despairing,
  they cover their heads.
4 The ground is cracked
  because there is no rain in the
    land;
  the farmers are dismayed
  and cover their heads.
5 Even the doe in the field
  deserts her newborn fawn
  because there is no grass.
6 Wild donkeys stand on the barren
    heights
  and pant like jackals;
  their eyesight fails
  for lack of pasture."

a23 Hebrew Cushite (probably a person from the
upper Nile region)

7 Although our sins testify against us,
   O Lord, do something for the sake
      of your name.
For our backsliding is great;
   we have sinned against you.
8 O Hope of Israel,
   its Savior in times of distress,
why are you like a stranger in the
      land,
   like a traveler who stays only
      a night?
9 Why are you like a man taken by
      surprise,
   like a warrior powerless to save?
You are among us, O Lord,
   and we bear your name;
   do not forsake us!

10 This is what the Lord says about this
people:

"They greatly love to wander;
   they do not restrain their feet.
So the Lord does not accept them;
   he will now remember their
      wickedness
   and punish them for their sins."

11 Then the Lord said to me, "Do not
pray for the well-being of this people.
12 Although they fast, I will not listen to
their cry; though they offer burnt offerings and grain offerings, I will not accept
them. Instead, I will destroy them with
the sword, famine and plague."

13 But I said, "Ah, Sovereign Lord, the
prophets keep telling them, 'You will not
see the sword or suffer famine. Indeed, I
will give you lasting peace in this place.'"

14 Then the Lord said to me, "The
prophets are prophesying lies in my
name. I have not sent them or appointed
them or spoken to them. They are
prophesying to you false visions, divinations, idolatries*a* and the delusions of
their own minds. 15 Therefore, this is
what the Lord says about the prophets
who are prophesying in my name: I did
not send them, yet they are saying, 'No
sword or famine will touch this land.'
Those same prophets will perish by
sword and famine. 16 And the people they
are prophesying to will be thrown out
into the streets of Jerusalem because of
the famine and sword. There will be no
one to bury them or their wives, their
sons or their daughters. I will pour out
on them the calamity they deserve.

17 "Speak this word to them:

" 'Let my eyes overflow with tears
      night and day without ceasing;
for my virgin daughter—my people—
   has suffered a grievous wound,
      a crushing blow.
18 If I go into the country,
   I see those slain by the sword;
if I go into the city,
   I see the ravages of famine.
Both prophet and priest
   have gone to a land they know
      not.' "

19 Have you rejected Judah completely?
   Do you despise Zion?
Why have you afflicted us
   so that we cannot be healed?
We hoped for peace
   but no good has come,
for a time of healing
   but there is only terror.
20 O Lord, we acknowledge our
      wickedness
   and the guilt of our fathers;
   we have indeed sinned against you.
21 For the sake of your name do not
      despise us;
   do not dishonor your glorious
      throne.
Remember your covenant with us
   and do not break it.
22 Do any of the worthless idols of the
      nations bring rain?
   Do the skies themselves send down
      showers?
No, it is you, O Lord our God.
   Therefore our hope is in you,
   for you are the one who does all this.

15 Then the Lord said to me: "Even if
   Moses and Samuel were to stand
before me, my heart would not go out to
this people. Send them away from my
presence! Let them go! 2 And if they ask
you, 'Where shall we go?' tell them, 'This
is what the Lord says:

" 'Those destined for death, to death;
those for the sword, to the sword;
those for starvation, to starvation;
those for captivity, to captivity.'

a 14 Or visions, worthless divinations

3 "I will send four kinds of destroyers against them," declares the LORD, "the sword to kill and the dogs to drag away and the birds of the air and the beasts of the earth to devour and destroy. 4 I will make them abhorrent to all the kingdoms of the earth because of what Manasseh son of Hezekiah king of Judah did in Jerusalem.

5 "Who will have pity on you,
   O Jerusalem?
   Who will mourn for you?
   Who will stop to ask how you are?
6 You have rejected me," declares
      the LORD.
   "You keep on backsliding.
   So I will lay hands on you and
      destroy you;
   I can no longer show compassion.
7 I will winnow them with a winnowing
      fork
   at the city gates of the land.
   I will bring bereavement and
      destruction on my people,
   for they have not changed their
      ways.
8 I will make their widows more
      numerous
   than the sand of the sea.
   At midday I will bring a destroyer
      against the mothers of their
      young men;
   suddenly I will bring down on them
      anguish and terror.
9 The mother of seven will grow
      faint
   and breathe her last.
   Her sun will set while it is still day;
   she will be disgraced and
      humiliated.
   I will put the survivors to the sword
   before their enemies,"
            declares the LORD.

10 Alas, my mother, that you gave me
      birth,
   a man with whom the whole land
      strives and contends!
   I have neither lent nor borrowed,
   yet everyone curses me.

11 The LORD said,

"Surely I will deliver you for a good
      purpose;

surely I will make your enemies
      plead with you
   in times of disaster and times
      of distress.

12 "Can a man break iron—
   iron from the north—or bronze?
13 Your wealth and your treasures
   I will give as plunder, without
      charge,
   because of all your sins
      throughout your country.
14 I will enslave you to your enemies
   in^a a land you do not know,
   for my anger will kindle a fire
      that will burn against you."

15 You understand, O LORD;
   remember me and care for me.
   Avenge me on my persecutors.
   You are long-suffering—do not take
      me away;
   think of how I suffer reproach for
      your sake.
16 When your words came, I ate
      them;
   they were my joy and my
      heart's delight,
   for I bear your name,
   O LORD God Almighty.
17 I never sat in the company of
      revelers,
   never made merry with them;
   I sat alone because your hand was
      on me
   and you had filled me with
      indignation.
18 Why is my pain unending
   and my wound grievous and
      incurable?
   Will you be to me like a deceptive
      brook,
   like a spring that fails?

19 Therefore this is what the LORD says:

"If you repent, I will restore you
   that you may serve me;
if you utter worthy, not worthless,
      words,
   you will be my spokesman.
Let this people turn to you,
   but you must not turn to them.

a 14 Some Hebrew manuscripts, Septuagint and Syriac (see also Jer. 17:4); most Hebrew manuscripts I will cause your enemies to bring you / into

Nothing You Ask, All You Hope

THINK OF some of the ways God can answer our prayers.

Sometimes his answers are clear and unambiguous, a simple *yes* or a flat *no*. More often his answers are less clear but more inventive. For example, he can respond with, *yes, but*, as when he answered Paul's prayer that Paul be allowed to go to Rome—but Paul was taken there as a prisoner. Or God can say *yes and no*, as when Paul prayed for protection in Jerusalem but got arrested, tried and imprisoned—yet he was rescued from a lynching, a flogging, and an assassination attempt.[3]

Some of God's most creative answers to our prayers are when he says, "*No—because I want you to look deeper.*" The following prayer is a great example of this kind of answer. Its origin is unknown, though it is often attributed to a Confederate soldier in the Civil War.

He asked for strength that he might achieve;
he was made weak that he might obey.
He asked for health that he might do greater things;
he was given infirmity that he might do better things.
He asked for riches that he might be happy;
he was given poverty that he might be wise.
He asked for power that he might have the praise of men;
he was given weakness that he might feel the need of God.
He asked for all things that he might enjoy life;
he was given life that he might enjoy all things.
He has received nothing that he asked for, all that he hoped for.
His prayer is answered.[4]

These are the kinds of answers God gives when he intends to give us more than we ask for—by appearing to give us less. The Puritan Richard Sibbes said God sometimes "heals not by healing, and leaves infirmities to cure enormities."[5] Similarly, Martin Luther wrote, "We pray for silver, but God often gives gold instead."[6] The "gold" is the people we are becoming in prayer (see 1 Peter 1:6–7). This is why Mary Magdalene de'Pazzi, an Italian Carmelite nun, sometimes thanked God that her prayers were not answered because it meant that God's will, not hers, was being done.[7]

God always has a better idea than we do when he answers our prayers. He always looks beyond the surface of our requests to the deeper cry of our heart, and he speaks out of his infinite depth into our depth.

PRAY:

"O Lord, whose way is perfect, help us always to
trust in thy goodness; that walking with thee and following
thee in all simplicity, we may possess quiet and contented minds,
and may cast all our care on thee who carest for us; for
thy dear Son's sake, Jesus Christ."[8]

MEMORIZE:

"For my thoughts are not your thoughts, neither are your
ways my ways," declares the LORD. "As the heavens are higher
than the earth, so are my ways higher than your ways and
my thoughts than your thoughts." ISAIAH 55:8–9

FOR YOUR NEXT DEVOTIONAL READING, GO TO PAGE 911.

²⁰ I will make you a wall to this
people,
a fortified wall of bronze;
they will fight against you
but will not overcome you,
for I am with you
to rescue and save you,"
declares the LORD.
²¹ "I will save you from the hands of
the wicked
and redeem you from the grasp
of the cruel."

Day of Disaster

16 Then the word of the LORD came to me: ²"You must not marry and have sons or daughters in this place." ³For this is what the LORD says about the sons and daughters born in this land and about the women who are their mothers and the men who are their fathers: ⁴"They will die of deadly diseases. They will not be mourned or buried but will be like refuse lying on the ground. They will perish by sword and famine, and their dead bodies will become food for the birds of the air and the beasts of the earth."

⁵For this is what the LORD says: "Do not enter a house where there is a funeral meal; do not go to mourn or show sympathy, because I have withdrawn my blessing, my love and my pity from this people," declares the LORD. ⁶"Both high and low will die in this land. They will not be buried or mourned, and no one will cut himself or shave his head for them. ⁷No one will offer food to comfort those who mourn for the dead—not even for a father or a mother—nor will anyone give them a drink to console them.

⁸"And do not enter a house where there is feasting and sit down to eat and drink. ⁹For this is what the LORD Almighty, the God of Israel, says: Before your eyes and in your days I will bring an end to the sounds of joy and gladness and to the voices of bride and bridegroom in this place.

¹⁰"When you tell these people all this and they ask you, 'Why has the LORD decreed such a great disaster against us? What wrong have we done? What sin have we committed against the LORD our God?' ¹¹then say to them, 'It is because your fathers forsook me,' declares the LORD, 'and followed other gods and served and worshiped them. They forsook me and did not keep my law. ¹²But you have behaved more wickedly than your fathers. See how each of you is following the stubbornness of his evil heart instead of obeying me. ¹³So I will throw you out of this land into a land neither you nor your fathers have known, and there you will serve other gods day and night, for I will show you no favor.'

¹⁴"However, the days are coming," declares the LORD, "when men will no longer say, 'As surely as the LORD lives, who brought the Israelites up out of Egypt,' ¹⁵but they will say, 'As surely as the LORD lives, who brought the Israelites up out of the land of the north and out of all the countries where he had banished them.' For I will restore them to the land I gave their forefathers.

¹⁶"But now I will send for many fishermen," declares the LORD, "and they will catch them. After that I will send for many hunters, and they will hunt them down on every mountain and hill and from the crevices of the rocks. ¹⁷My eyes are on all their ways; they are not hidden from me, nor is their sin concealed from my eyes. ¹⁸I will repay them double for their wickedness and their sin, because they have defiled my land with the lifeless forms of their vile images and have filled my inheritance with their detestable idols."

¹⁹ O LORD, my strength and my
fortress,
my refuge in time of distress,
to you the nations will come
from the ends of the earth and
say,
"Our fathers possessed nothing but
false gods,
worthless idols that did them no
good.
²⁰ Do men make their own gods?
Yes, but they are not gods!"

²¹ "Therefore I will teach them—
this time I will teach them
my power and might.
Then they will know
that my name is the LORD.

The Divine Amen

16:21 "THEN THEY WILL KNOW THAT MY NAME IS THE LORD."

This is a different kind of prayer than the one Jeremiah prayed in chapter 12, and Jeremiah receives a different kind of answer from God. Jeremiah's prayer life is full of stops and starts, ups and downs. Prayer, like faith, is not a quiet, placid retreat into a quiet little happy place in your heart. It can be quiet and it can be happy, but it is first a relationship of trust that is forged amid the pressure of a struggle against relentless enemies: the devil, the world and our own sinfulness. Prayer is ever the same yet ever changing.

Jeremiah continues to suffer under the hatred and rejection of his own people. Nothing has changed. His generation is doomed to destruction. But he is encouraged by two great things: One, he knows God is his only hope, "my strength and my fortress, my refuge in time of distress" (16:19a). Two, he has a bigger vision of God's purposes—and an older vision: "To you the nations will come from the ends of the earth and say, 'Our fathers possessed nothing but false gods, worthless idols that did them no good'" (verse 19b). As bad as things were for Jeremiah, he knew there would be a glorious future in which all nations and peoples of the earth would repent of their idolatry and come to the Lord. God's chosen people are now just like the nations—idolaters doomed to destruction. But God's promise to Abraham to make his descendants a blessing to the world will come true (see Genesis 12:1–3). In his prayer, Jeremiah is thinking God's thoughts after him.

And again, God comes right back at Jeremiah as he did in chapter 12, but not with a rebuke. God says a kind of divine "Amen!" The Lord so thoroughly agrees with Jeremiah's hope that he says, "Therefore I will teach them—this time I will teach them my power and might. Then they will know that my name is the LORD" (16:21). This kind of praying is deeply satisfying: To hope in the Lord, to pray this hope, and to feel the divine "Amen" is a joy unparalleled and all too rare in prayer. God wants us to want what he wants. He wants us to ask for what we want; and he loves to say, "Yes! It shall be done."

PRAY:

Great God, Almighty Savior! You are all I need,
and "your kingdom come" is all I want.
May your people be renewed and may
the nations know that you are the Lord.

———

FOR YOUR NEXT DEVOTIONAL READING, GO TO PAGE 916.

17 "Judah's sin is engraved with an
 iron tool,
 inscribed with a flint point,
on the tablets of their hearts
 and on the horns of their altars.
² Even their children remember
 their altars and Asherah poles*a*
beside the spreading trees
 and on the high hills.
³ My mountain in the land
 and your*b* wealth and all your
 treasures
I will give away as plunder,
 together with your high places,
 because of sin throughout your
 country.
⁴ Through your own fault you will
 lose
 the inheritance I gave you.
I will enslave you to your enemies
 in a land you do not know,
for you have kindled my anger,
 and it will burn forever."

⁵ This is what the LORD says:

"Cursed is the one who trusts in man,
 who depends on flesh for his
 strength
 and whose heart turns away from
 the LORD.
⁶ He will be like a bush in the
 wastelands;
 he will not see prosperity when it
 comes.
He will dwell in the parched places of
 the desert,
 in a salt land where no one lives.

⁷ "But blessed is the man who trusts in
 the LORD,
 whose confidence is in him.
⁸ He will be like a tree planted by the
 water
 that sends out its roots by the
 stream.
It does not fear when heat comes;
 its leaves are always green.
It has no worries in a year of drought
 and never fails to bear fruit."

⁹ The heart is deceitful above all things
 and beyond cure.
 Who can understand it?

¹⁰ "I the LORD search the heart
 and examine the mind,
to reward a man according to his
 conduct,
 according to what his deeds
 deserve."

¹¹ Like a partridge that hatches eggs it
 did not lay
 is the man who gains riches by
 unjust means.
When his life is half gone, they will
 desert him,
 and in the end he will prove to be
 a fool.

¹² A glorious throne, exalted from the
 beginning,
 is the place of our sanctuary.
¹³ O LORD, the hope of Israel,
 all who forsake you will be put
 to shame.
Those who turn away from you will
 be written in the dust
because they have forsaken
 the LORD,
 the spring of living water.

¹⁴ Heal me, O LORD, and I will be healed;
 save me and I will be saved,
 for you are the one I praise.
¹⁵ They keep saying to me,
 "Where is the word of the LORD?
 Let it now be fulfilled!"
¹⁶ I have not run away from being your
 shepherd;
 you know I have not desired the
 day of despair.
 What passes my lips is open before
 you.
¹⁷ Do not be a terror to me;
 you are my refuge in the day of
 disaster.
¹⁸ Let my persecutors be put to shame,
 but keep me from shame;
let them be terrified,
 but keep me from terror.
Bring on them the day of disaster;
 destroy them with double
 destruction.

Keeping the Sabbath Holy

¹⁹ This is what the LORD said to me: "Go
and stand at the gate of the people,
through which the kings of Judah go in

---

a 2 That is, symbols of the goddess Asherah
b 2,3 Or *hills / 3and the mountains of the land. /
Your*

and out; stand also at all the other gates of Jerusalem. ²⁰Say to them, 'Hear the word of the LORD, O kings of Judah and all people of Judah and everyone living in Jerusalem who come through these gates. ²¹This is what the LORD says: Be careful not to carry a load on the Sabbath day or bring it through the gates of Jerusalem. ²²Do not bring a load out of your houses or do any work on the Sabbath, but keep the Sabbath day holy, as I commanded your forefathers. ²³Yet they did not listen or pay attention; they were stiff-necked and would not listen or respond to discipline. ²⁴But if you are careful to obey me, declares the LORD, and bring no load through the gates of this city on the Sabbath, but keep the Sabbath day holy by not doing any work on it, ²⁵then kings who sit on David's throne will come through the gates of this city with their officials. They and their officials will come riding in chariots and on horses, accompanied by the men of Judah and those living in Jerusalem, and this city will be inhabited forever. ²⁶People will come from the towns of Judah and the villages around Jerusalem, from the territory of Benjamin and the western foothills, from the hill country and the Negev, bringing burnt offerings and sacrifices, grain offerings, incense and thank offerings to the house of the LORD. ²⁷But if you do not obey me to keep the Sabbath day holy by not carrying any load as you come through the gates of Jerusalem on the Sabbath day, then I will kindle an unquenchable fire in the gates of Jerusalem that will consume her fortresses.'"

At the Potter's House

18 This is the word that came to Jeremiah from the LORD: ²"Go down to the potter's house, and there I will give you my message." ³So I went down to the potter's house, and I saw him working at the wheel. ⁴But the pot he was shaping from the clay was marred in his hands; so the potter formed it into another pot, shaping it as seemed best to him.

⁵Then the word of the LORD came to me: ⁶"O house of Israel, can I not do with you as this potter does?" declares the LORD. "Like clay in the hand of the potter,

so are you in my hand, O house of Israel. ⁷If at any time I announce that a nation or kingdom is to be uprooted, torn down and destroyed, ⁸and if that nation I warned repents of its evil, then I will relent and not inflict on it the disaster I had planned. ⁹And if at another time I announce that a nation or kingdom is to be built up and planted, ¹⁰and if it does evil in my sight and does not obey me, then I will reconsider the good I had intended to do for it.

¹¹"Now therefore say to the people of Judah and those living in Jerusalem, 'This is what the LORD says: Look! I am preparing a disaster for you and devising a plan against you. So turn from your evil ways, each one of you, and reform your ways and your actions.' ¹²But they will reply, 'It's no use. We will continue with our own plans; each of us will follow the stubbornness of his evil heart.'"

¹³Therefore this is what the LORD says:

"Inquire among the nations:
 Who has ever heard anything like
   this?
A most horrible thing has been done
   by Virgin Israel.
¹⁴Does the snow of Lebanon
   ever vanish from its rocky slopes?
Do its cool waters from distant
   sources
   ever cease to flow?ᵃ
¹⁵Yet my people have forgotten me;
   they burn incense to worthless
     idols,
which made them stumble in their
   ways
   and in the ancient paths.
They made them walk in bypaths
   and on roads not built up.
¹⁶Their land will be laid waste,
   an object of lasting scorn;
all who pass by will be appalled
   and will shake their heads.
¹⁷Like a wind from the east,
   I will scatter them before their
     enemies;
I will show them my back and not
     my face
   in the day of their disaster."

ᵃ14 The meaning of the Hebrew for this sentence is uncertain.

¹⁸They said, "Come, let's make plans against Jeremiah; for the teaching of the law by the priest will not be lost, nor will counsel from the wise, nor the word from the prophets. So come, let's attack him with our tongues and pay no attention to anything he says."

¹⁹Listen to me, O LORD;
  hear what my accusers are saying!
²⁰Should good be repaid with evil?
  Yet they have dug a pit for me.
Remember that I stood before you
  and spoke in their behalf
  to turn your wrath away from them.
²¹So give their children over to famine;
  hand them over to the power of the sword.
Let their wives be made childless
  and widows;
  let their men be put to death,
  their young men slain by the sword in battle.
²²Let a cry be heard from their houses
  when you suddenly bring invaders against them,
for they have dug a pit to capture me
  and have hidden snares for my feet.
²³But you know, O LORD,
  all their plots to kill me.
Do not forgive their crimes
  or blot out their sins from your sight.
Let them be overthrown before you;
  deal with them in the time of your anger.

19 This is what the LORD says: "Go and buy a clay jar from a potter. Take along some of the elders of the people and of the priests ²and go out to the Valley of Ben Hinnom, near the entrance of the Potsherd Gate. There proclaim the words I tell you, ³and say, 'Hear the word of the LORD, O kings of Judah and people of Jerusalem. This is what the LORD Almighty, the God of Israel, says: Listen! I am going to bring a disaster on this place that will make the ears of everyone who hears of it tingle. ⁴For they have forsaken me and made this a place of foreign gods; they have burned sacrifices in it to gods that neither they nor their fathers nor the kings of Judah ever knew, and they have filled this place with the blood of the innocent. ⁵They have built the high places of Baal to burn their sons in the fire as offerings to Baal—something

I did not command or mention, nor did it enter my mind. ⁶So beware, the days are coming, declares the LORD, when people will no longer call this place Topheth or the Valley of Ben Hinnom, but the Valley of Slaughter.

⁷"'In this place I will ruinᵃ the plans of Judah and Jerusalem. I will make them fall by the sword before their enemies, at the hands of those who seek their lives, and I will give their carcasses as food to the birds of the air and the beasts of the earth. ⁸I will devastate this city and make it an object of scorn; all who pass by will be appalled and will scoff because of all its wounds. ⁹I will make them eat the flesh of their sons and daughters, and they will eat one another's flesh during the stress of the siege imposed on them by the enemies who seek their lives.'

¹⁰"Then break the jar while those who go with you are watching, ¹¹and say to them, 'This is what the LORD Almighty says: I will smash this nation and this city just as this potter's jar is smashed and cannot be repaired. They will bury the dead in Topheth until there is no more room. ¹²This is what I will do to this place and to those who live here, declares the LORD. I will make this city like Topheth. ¹³The houses in Jerusalem and those of the kings of Judah will be defiled like this place, Topheth—all the houses where they burned incense on the roofs to all the starry hosts and poured out drink offerings to other gods.'"

¹⁴Jeremiah then returned from Topheth, where the LORD had sent him to prophesy, and stood in the court of the LORD's temple and said to all the people, ¹⁵"This is what the LORD Almighty, the God of Israel, says: 'Listen! I am going to bring on this city and the villages around it every disaster I pronounced against them, because they were stiff-necked and would not listen to my words.'"

Jeremiah and Pashhur

20 When the priest Pashhur son of Immer, the chief officer in the temple of the LORD, heard Jeremiah prophesying these things, ²he had Jere-

---

ᵃ7 The Hebrew for *ruin* sounds like the Hebrew for *jar* (see verses 1 and 10).

miah the prophet beaten and put in the stocks at the Upper Gate of Benjamin at the LORD's temple. ³The next day, when Pashhur released him from the stocks, Jeremiah said to him, "The LORD's name for you is not Pashhur, but Magor-Missabib.ᵃ ⁴For this is what the LORD says: 'I will make you a terror to yourself and to all your friends; with your own eyes you will see them fall by the sword of their enemies. I will hand all Judah over to the king of Babylon, who will carry them away to Babylon or put them to the sword. ⁵I will hand over to their enemies all the wealth of this city—all its products, all its valuables and all the treasures of the kings of Judah. They will take it away as plunder and carry it off to Babylon. ⁶And you, Pashhur, and all who live in your house will go into exile to Babylon. There you will die and be buried, you and all your friends to whom you have prophesied lies.'"

Jeremiah's Complaint

⁷O LORD, you deceivedᵇ me, and I was
    deceivedᵇ;
  you overpowered me and
    prevailed.
I am ridiculed all day long;
  everyone mocks me.
⁸Whenever I speak, I cry out
  proclaiming violence and
    destruction.
So the word of the LORD has brought
    me
  insult and reproach all day long.
⁹But if I say, "I will not mention him
  or speak any more in his name,"
his word is in my heart like a fire,
  a fire shut up in my bones.
I am weary of holding it in;
  indeed, I cannot.
¹⁰I hear many whispering,
  "Terror on every side!
  Report him! Let's report him!"
All my friends
  are waiting for me to slip, saying,
"Perhaps he will be deceived;
  then we will prevail over him
  and take our revenge on him."

¹¹But the LORD is with me like a mighty
    warrior;
  so my persecutors will stumble and
    not prevail.

They will fail and be thoroughly
    disgraced;
  their dishonor will never be
    forgotten.
¹²O LORD Almighty, you who examine
    the righteous
  and probe the heart and mind,
let me see your vengeance upon them,
  for to you I have committed my
    cause.

¹³Sing to the LORD!
  Give praise to the LORD!
He rescues the life of the needy
  from the hands of the wicked.

¹⁴Cursed be the day I was born!
  May the day my mother bore me
    not be blessed!
¹⁵Cursed be the man who brought my
    father the news,
  who made him very glad, saying,
  "A child is born to you—a son!"
¹⁶May that man be like the towns
    the LORD overthrew without pity.
  May he hear wailing in the morning,
    a battle cry at noon.
¹⁷For he did not kill me in the womb,
  with my mother as my grave,
  her womb enlarged forever.
¹⁸Why did I ever come out of the womb
  to see trouble and sorrow
  and to end my days in shame?

God Rejects Zedekiah's Request

21 The word came to Jeremiah from the LORD when King Zedekiah sent to him Pashhur son of Malkijah and the priest Zephaniah son of Maaseiah. They said: ²"Inquire now of the LORD for us because Nebuchadnezzarᶜ king of Babylon is attacking us. Perhaps the LORD will perform wonders for us as in times past so that he will withdraw from us."

³But Jeremiah answered them, "Tell Zedekiah, ⁴'This is what the LORD, the God of Israel, says: I am about to turn against you the weapons of war that are in your hands, which you are using to fight the king of Babylon and the Babyloniansᵈ who

---

ᵃ3 *Magor-Missabib* means *terror on every side.*
ᵇ7 Or *persuaded*   ᶜ2 Hebrew *Nebuchadrezzar,*
of which *Nebuchadnezzar* is a variant; here and
often in Jeremiah and Ezekiel   ᵈ4 Or
Chaldeans; also in verse 9

JEREMIAH 20:7–18

You Deceived Me, Lord

20:7 O LORD, YOU DECEIVED ME, AND I WAS DECEIVED; YOU OVERPOWERED ME AND PREVAILED.

Have you ever expressed anger and frustration to God this way? Have you been tempted to but backed down for fear of being struck by lightning?! The verb "deceived" literally means *seduced* or *enticed*. Today Jeremiah might have complained that he got "railroaded" into being a prophet by undue pressure from God.

Looking back at Jeremiah's call to be a prophet, God was quite frank with him. He said it would be a difficult task and Jeremiah would have to stand against the whole nation, but God would make him strong enough to withstand the pressure (see 1:17–19). There were no false pretenses there. Maybe what took Jeremiah by surprise was how it felt to stand against the people. Maybe he wasn't ready for the ridicule and mockery (see 20:7–8). It's one thing to suffer great hardship and to be thought of as brave and heroic; it's another thing to be considered a fool and made the butt of jokes. Jeremiah was ready to be hated as a warrior, but not laughed at as a buffoon. Whatever the reasons, Jeremiah felt this was not what he signed up for, and he wanted out. But he couldn't get out. "But if I say, 'I will not mention him or speak any more in his name,' his word is in my heart like a fire, a fire shut up in my bones. I am weary of holding it in; indeed, I cannot" (verse 9).

What are we to make of this prayer? One thing that stands out is how little God seems to be offended by it. At the very least, it must be permissible to speak to God with complete honesty. Jeremiah is wrong about the circumstances of his calling, but he is right about how he feels, and that is reason enough to speak. What matters most to God is not that we address him "correctly," but that we speak honestly. It's our relationship to him that matters to Almighty God. The worst that can happen is that we go silent and cold with the Lord. He can handle our anger, and when he deems the time to be right, he can set us straight. Look at what he did with Job (see Job 38:1–7; 40:1–14). Speak your mind to God, but hang in there and know that he will not turn you away, even if you think he has.

PRAY:

Dear Father, sometimes the things I feel about you
aren't nice or right, but I feel them anyway.
Thank you that I matter enough to you for you
to allow me to say what I feel.
Thank you that you put up with me,
even when I don't deserve it.

FOR YOUR NEXT DEVOTIONAL READING, GO TO PAGE 932.

are outside the wall besieging you. And I will gather them inside this city. ⁵I myself will fight against you with an outstretched hand and a mighty arm in anger and fury and great wrath. ⁶I will strike down those who live in this city—both men and animals—and they will die of a terrible plague. ⁷After that, declares the LORD, I will hand over Zedekiah king of Judah, his officials and the people in this city who survive the plague, sword and famine, to Nebuchadnezzar king of Babylon and to their enemies who seek their lives. He will put them to the sword; he will show them no mercy or pity or compassion.'

⁸"Furthermore, tell the people, 'This is what the LORD says: See, I am setting before you the way of life and the way of death. ⁹Whoever stays in this city will die by the sword, famine or plague. But whoever goes out and surrenders to the Babylonians who are besieging you will live; he will escape with his life. ¹⁰I have determined to do this city harm and not good, declares the LORD. It will be given into the hands of the king of Babylon, and he will destroy it with fire.'

¹¹"Moreover, say to the royal house of Judah, 'Hear the word of the LORD; ¹²O house of David, this is what the LORD says:

" 'Administer justice every morning;
    rescue from the hand of his
        oppressor
    the one who has been robbed,
or my wrath will break out and burn
        like fire
because of the evil you have
        done—
    burn with no one to quench it.
¹³I am against you, Jerusalem,
    you who live above this valley
    on the rocky plateau,
                    declares the LORD—
you who say, "Who can come
        against us?
    Who can enter our refuge?"
¹⁴I will punish you as your deeds
        deserve,
                    declares the LORD.
I will kindle a fire in your forests
    that will consume everything
        around you.' "

Judgment Against Evil Kings

22 This is what the LORD says: "Go down to the palace of the king of Judah and proclaim this message there: ²'Hear the word of the LORD, O king of Judah, you who sit on David's throne—you, your officials and your people who come through these gates. ³This is what the LORD says: Do what is just and right. Rescue from the hand of his oppressor the one who has been robbed. Do no wrong or violence to the alien, the fatherless or the widow, and do not shed innocent blood in this place. ⁴For if you are careful to carry out these commands, then kings who sit on David's throne will come through the gates of this palace, riding in chariots and on horses, accompanied by their officials and their people. ⁵But if you do not obey these commands, declares the LORD, I swear by myself that this palace will become a ruin.' "

⁶For this is what the LORD says about the palace of the king of Judah:

"Though you are like Gilead to me,
    like the summit of Lebanon,
I will surely make you like a desert,
    like towns not inhabited.
⁷I will send destroyers against you,
    each man with his weapons,
and they will cut up your fine cedar
        beams
    and throw them into the fire.

⁸"People from many nations will pass by this city and will ask one another, 'Why has the LORD done such a thing to this great city?' ⁹And the answer will be: 'Because they have forsaken the covenant of the LORD their God and have worshiped and served other gods.' "

¹⁰Do not weep for the dead ˌkingˌ or
        mourn his loss;
rather, weep bitterly for him who
        is exiled,
because he will never return
    nor see his native land again.

¹¹For this is what the LORD says about Shallumᵃ son of Josiah, who succeeded his father as king of Judah but has gone from this place: "He will never return. ¹²He will die in the place where they have

ᵃ 11 Also called Jehoahaz

led him captive; he will not see this land again."

13 "Woe to him who builds his palace by unrighteousness,
  his upper rooms by injustice,
making his countrymen work for nothing,
  not paying them for their labor.
14 He says, 'I will build myself a great palace
  with spacious upper rooms.'
So he makes large windows in it,
  panels it with cedar
  and decorates it in red.

15 "Does it make you a king
  to have more and more cedar?
Did not your father have food and drink?
  He did what was right and just,
  so all went well with him.
16 He defended the cause of the poor and needy,
  and so all went well.
Is that not what it means to know me?"
  declares the LORD.
17 "But your eyes and your heart
  are set only on dishonest gain,
on shedding innocent blood
  and on oppression and extortion."

18 Therefore this is what the LORD says about Jehoiakim son of Josiah king of Judah:

"They will not mourn for him:
  'Alas, my brother! Alas, my sister!'
They will not mourn for him:
  'Alas, my master! Alas, his splendor!'
19 He will have the burial of a donkey—
  dragged away and thrown
  outside the gates of Jerusalem."

20 "Go up to Lebanon and cry out,
  let your voice be heard in Bashan,
cry out from Abarim,
  for all your allies are crushed.
21 I warned you when you felt secure,
  but you said, 'I will not listen!'
This has been your way from your youth;
  you have not obeyed me.
22 The wind will drive all your shepherds away,
  and your allies will go into exile.

Then you will be ashamed and disgraced
  because of all your wickedness.
23 You who live in 'Lebanon,'*a*'
  who are nestled in cedar buildings,
how you will groan when pangs come upon you,
  pain like that of a woman in labor!

24 "As surely as I live," declares the LORD, "even if you, Jehoiachin*b* son of Jehoiakim king of Judah, were a signet ring on my right hand, I would still pull you off. 25 I will hand you over to those who seek your life, those you fear—to Nebuchadnezzar king of Babylon and to the Babylonians.*c* 26 I will hurl you and the mother who gave you birth into another country, where neither of you was born, and there you both will die. 27 You will never come back to the land you long to return to."

28 Is this man Jehoiachin a despised, broken pot,
  an object no one wants?
Why will he and his children be hurled out,
  cast into a land they do not know?
29 O land, land, land,
  hear the word of the LORD!
30 This is what the LORD says:
  "Record this man as if childless,
  a man who will not prosper in his lifetime,
for none of his offspring will prosper,
  none will sit on the throne of David
  or rule anymore in Judah."

The Righteous Branch

23 "Woe to the shepherds who are destroying and scattering the sheep of my pasture!" declares the LORD. 2 Therefore this is what the LORD, the God of Israel, says to the shepherds who tend my people: "Because you have scattered my flock and driven them away and have not bestowed care on them, I will bestow punishment on you for the evil you have done," declares the LORD. 3 "I myself will gather the remnant of my flock out of all

---

a23 That is, the palace in Jerusalem (see 1 Kings 7:2)   *b24* Hebrew *Coniah*, a variant of *Jehoiachin*; also in verse 28   *c25* Or *Chaldeans*

the countries where I have driven them and will bring them back to their pasture, where they will be fruitful and increase in number. ⁴I will place shepherds over them who will tend them, and they will no longer be afraid or terrified, nor will any be missing," declares the LORD.

⁵ "The days are coming," declares the LORD,
"when I will raise up to David*ᵃ*
a righteous Branch,
a King who will reign wisely
and do what is just and right in the land.
⁶ In his days Judah will be saved
and Israel will live in safety.
This is the name by which he will be called:
The LORD Our Righteousness.

⁷ "So then, the days are coming," declares the LORD, "when people will no longer say, 'As surely as the LORD lives, who brought the Israelites up out of Egypt,' ⁸but they will say, 'As surely as the LORD lives, who brought the descendants of Israel up out of the land of the north and out of all the countries where he had banished them.' Then they will live in their own land."

Lying Prophets

⁹Concerning the prophets:

My heart is broken within me;
all my bones tremble.
I am like a drunken man,
like a man overcome by wine,
because of the LORD
and his holy words.
¹⁰The land is full of adulterers;
because of the curse*ᵇ* the land lies parched*ᶜ*
and the pastures in the desert are withered.
The ⌐prophets⌐ follow an evil course
and use their power unjustly.

¹¹ "Both prophet and priest are godless;
even in my temple I find their wickedness,"

declares the LORD.
¹² "Therefore their path will become slippery;
they will be banished to darkness
and there they will fall.

I will bring disaster on them
in the year they are punished,"
declares the LORD.

¹³ "Among the prophets of Samaria
I saw this repulsive thing:
They prophesied by Baal
and led my people Israel astray.
¹⁴And among the prophets of Jerusalem
I have seen something horrible:
They commit adultery and live a lie.
They strengthen the hands of evildoers,
so that no one turns from his wickedness.
They are all like Sodom to me;
the people of Jerusalem are like Gomorrah."

¹⁵Therefore, this is what the LORD Almighty says concerning the prophets:

"I will make them eat bitter food
and drink poisoned water,
because from the prophets of Jerusalem
ungodliness has spread throughout the land."

¹⁶This is what the LORD Almighty says:

"Do not listen to what the prophets
are prophesying to you;
they fill you with false hopes.
They speak visions from their own minds,
not from the mouth of the LORD.
¹⁷They keep saying to those who despise me,
'The LORD says: You will have peace.'
And to all who follow the stubbornness of their hearts
they say, 'No harm will come to you.'
¹⁸But which of them has stood in the council of the LORD
to see or to hear his word?
Who has listened and heard his word?
¹⁹See, the storm of the LORD
will burst out in wrath,
a whirlwind swirling down
on the heads of the wicked.

ᵃ5 Or *up from David's line*   *ᵇ10* Or *because of these things*   *ᶜ10* Or *land mourns*

20 The anger of the LORD will not turn
back
until he fully accomplishes
the purposes of his heart.
In days to come
you will understand it clearly.
21 I did not send these prophets,
yet they have run with their
message;
I did not speak to them,
yet they have prophesied.
22 But if they had stood in my council,
they would have proclaimed my
words to my people
and would have turned them from
their evil ways
and from their evil deeds.

23 "Am I only a God nearby,"
declares the LORD,
"and not a God far away?
24 Can anyone hide in secret places
so that I cannot see him?"
declares the LORD.
"Do not I fill heaven and earth?"
declares the LORD.

25 "I have heard what the prophets say
who prophesy lies in my name. They say,
'I had a dream! I had a dream!' 26 How
long will this continue in the hearts of
these lying prophets, who prophesy the
delusions of their own minds? 27 They
think the dreams they tell one another
will make my people forget my name,
just as their fathers forgot my name
through Baal worship. 28 Let the prophet
who has a dream tell his dream, but let
the one who has my word speak it faithfully. For what has straw to do with
grain?" declares the LORD. 29 "Is not my
word like fire," declares the LORD, "and
like a hammer that breaks a rock in
pieces?

30 "Therefore," declares the LORD, "I am
against the prophets who steal from one
another words supposedly from me.
31 Yes," declares the LORD, "I am against
the prophets who wag their own tongues
and yet declare, 'The LORD declares.' 32 Indeed, I am against those who prophesy
false dreams," declares the LORD. "They
tell them and lead my people astray with
their reckless lies, yet I did not send or
appoint them. They do not benefit these
people in the least," declares the LORD.

> Prayers not felt by us are seldom
> heard by God.
>
> PHILIP HENRY

False Oracles and False Prophets

33 "When these people, or a prophet or
a priest, ask you, 'What is the oracle[a] of
the LORD?' say to them, 'What oracle?[b] I
will forsake you, declares the LORD.' 34 If
a prophet or a priest or anyone else
claims, 'This is the oracle of the LORD,' I
will punish that man and his household.
35 This is what each of you keeps on saying to his friend or relative: 'What is the
LORD's answer?' or 'What has the LORD
spoken?' 36 But you must not mention 'the
oracle of the LORD' again, because every
man's own word becomes his oracle and
so you distort the words of the living
God, the LORD Almighty, our God. 37 This
is what you keep saying to a prophet:
'What is the LORD's answer to you?' or
'What has the LORD spoken?' 38 Although
you claim, 'This is the oracle of the LORD,'
this is what the LORD says: You used the
words, 'This is the oracle of the LORD,'
even though I told you that you must not
claim, 'This is the oracle of the LORD.'
39 Therefore, I will surely forget you and
cast you out of my presence along with
the city I gave to you and your fathers. 40 I
will bring upon you everlasting disgrace—everlasting shame that will not
be forgotten."

Two Baskets of Figs

24 After Jehoiachin[c] son of Jehoiakim
king of Judah and the officials, the
craftsmen and the artisans of Judah were
carried into exile from Jerusalem to Babylon by Nebuchadnezzar king of Babylon, the LORD showed me two baskets of
figs placed in front of the temple of the
LORD. 2 One basket had very good figs, like
those that ripen early; the other basket
had very poor figs, so bad they could not
be eaten.

---

[a]33 Or burden (see Septuagint and Vulgate)
[b]33 Hebrew; Septuagint and Vulgate 'You are the
burden. (The Hebrew for oracle and burden is the
same.)   [c]1 Hebrew Jeconiah, a variant of
Jehoiachin

³Then the LORD asked me, "What do you see, Jeremiah?"

"Figs," I answered. "The good ones are very good, but the poor ones are so bad they cannot be eaten."

⁴Then the word of the LORD came to me: ⁵"This is what the LORD, the God of Israel, says: 'Like these good figs, I regard as good the exiles from Judah, whom I sent away from this place to the land of the Babylonians.ᵃ ⁶My eyes will watch over them for their good, and I will bring them back to this land. I will build them up and not tear them down; I will plant them and not uproot them. ⁷I will give them a heart to know me, that I am the LORD. They will be my people, and I will be their God, for they will return to me with all their heart.

⁸" 'But like the poor figs, which are so bad they cannot be eaten,' says the LORD, 'so will I deal with Zedekiah king of Judah, his officials and the survivors from Jerusalem, whether they remain in this land or live in Egypt. ⁹I will make them abhorrent and an offense to all the kingdoms of the earth, a reproach and a byword, an object of ridicule and cursing, wherever I banish them. ¹⁰I will send the sword, famine and plague against them until they are destroyed from the land I gave to them and their fathers.' "

Seventy Years of Captivity

25 The word came to Jeremiah concerning all the people of Judah in the fourth year of Jehoiakim son of Josiah king of Judah, which was the first year of Nebuchadnezzar king of Babylon. ²So Jeremiah the prophet said to all the people of Judah and to all those living in Jerusalem: ³For twenty-three years—from the thirteenth year of Josiah son of Amon king of Judah until this very day—the word of the LORD has come to me and I have spoken to you again and again, but you have not listened.

⁴And though the LORD has sent all his servants the prophets to you again and again, you have not listened or paid any attention. ⁵They said, "Turn now, each of you, from your evil ways and your evil practices, and you can stay in the land the LORD gave to you and your fathers for ever and ever. ⁶Do not follow other gods to serve and worship them; do not provoke me to anger with what your hands have made. Then I will not harm you."

⁷"But you did not listen to me," declares the LORD, "and you have provoked me with what your hands have made, and you have brought harm to yourselves."

⁸Therefore the LORD Almighty says this: "Because you have not listened to my words, ⁹I will summon all the peoples of the north and my servant Nebuchadnezzar king of Babylon," declares the LORD, "and I will bring them against this land and its inhabitants and against all the surrounding nations. I will completely destroyᵇ them and make them an object of horror and scorn, and an everlasting ruin. ¹⁰I will banish from them the sounds of joy and gladness, the voices of bride and bridegroom, the sound of millstones and the light of the lamp. ¹¹This whole country will become a desolate wasteland, and these nations will serve the king of Babylon seventy years.

¹²"But when the seventy years are fulfilled, I will punish the king of Babylon and his nation, the land of the Babylonians,ᵃ for their guilt," declares the LORD, "and will make it desolate forever. ¹³I will bring upon that land all the things I have spoken against it, all that are written in this book and prophesied by Jeremiah against all the nations. ¹⁴They themselves will be enslaved by many nations and great kings; I will repay them according to their deeds and the work of their hands."

The Cup of God's Wrath

¹⁵This is what the LORD, the God of Israel, said to me: "Take from my hand this cup filled with the wine of my wrath and make all the nations to whom I send you drink it. ¹⁶When they drink it, they will stagger and go mad because of the sword I will send among them."

¹⁷So I took the cup from the LORD's hand and made all the nations to whom he sent me drink it: ¹⁸Jerusalem and the towns of Judah, its kings and officials, to

ᵃ5,12 Or Chaldeans   ᵇ9 The Hebrew term refers to the irrevocable giving over of things or persons to the LORD, often by totally destroying them.

make them a ruin and an object of horror and scorn and cursing, as they are today; ¹⁹Pharaoh king of Egypt, his attendants, his officials and all his people, ²⁰and all the foreign people there; all the kings of Uz; all the kings of the Philistines (those of Ashkelon, Gaza, Ekron, and the people left at Ashdod); ²¹Edom, Moab and Ammon; ²²all the kings of Tyre and Sidon; the kings of the coastlands across the sea; ²³Dedan, Tema, Buz and all who are in distant places*a*; ²⁴all the kings of Arabia and all the kings of the foreign people who live in the desert; ²⁵all the kings of Zimri, Elam and Media; ²⁶and all the kings of the north, near and far, one after the other—all the kingdoms on the face of the earth. And after all of them, the king of Sheshach*b* will drink it too.

²⁷"Then tell them, 'This is what the LORD Almighty, the God of Israel, says: Drink, get drunk and vomit, and fall to rise no more because of the sword I will send among you.' ²⁸But if they refuse to take the cup from your hand and drink, tell them, 'This is what the LORD Almighty says: You must drink it! ²⁹See, I am beginning to bring disaster on the city that bears my Name, and will you indeed go unpunished? You will not go unpunished, for I am calling down a sword upon all who live on the earth, declares the LORD Almighty.'

³⁰"Now prophesy all these words against them and say to them:

"'The LORD will roar from on high;
    he will thunder from his holy
        dwelling
    and roar mightily against his land.
He will shout like those who tread the
        grapes,
    shout against all who live on
        earth.
³¹ The tumult will resound to the ends
        of the earth,
    for the LORD will bring charges
        against the nations;
    he will bring judgment on all
        mankind
    and put the wicked to the sword,'"
            declares the LORD.

³²This is what the LORD Almighty says:

"Look! Disaster is spreading
    from nation to nation;

a mighty storm is rising
    from the ends of the earth."

³³At that time those slain by the LORD will be everywhere—from one end of the earth to the other. They will not be mourned or gathered up or buried, but will be like refuse lying on the ground.

³⁴ Weep and wail, you shepherds;
    roll in the dust, you leaders of
        the flock.
For your time to be slaughtered
        has come;
    you will fall and be shattered like
        fine pottery.
³⁵ The shepherds will have nowhere
        to flee,
    the leaders of the flock no place to
        escape.
³⁶ Hear the cry of the shepherds,
    the wailing of the leaders of the
        flock,
    for the LORD is destroying their
        pasture.
³⁷ The peaceful meadows will be laid
        waste
    because of the fierce anger of the
        LORD.
³⁸ Like a lion he will leave his lair,
    and their land will become
        desolate
because of the sword*c* of the
        oppressor
    and because of the LORD's fierce
        anger.

Jeremiah Threatened With Death

26 Early in the reign of Jehoiakim son of Josiah king of Judah, this word came from the LORD: ²"This is what the LORD says: Stand in the courtyard of the LORD's house and speak to all the people of the towns of Judah who come to worship in the house of the LORD. Tell them everything I command you; do not omit a word. ³Perhaps they will listen and each will turn from his evil way. Then I will relent and not bring on them the disaster I was planning because of the evil they have done. ⁴Say to them, 'This is what

a23 Or *who clip the hair by their foreheads*
b26 Sheshach is a cryptogram for Babylon.
c38 Some Hebrew manuscripts and Septuagint (see also Jer. 46:16 and 50:16); most Hebrew manuscripts *anger*

the Lord says: If you do not listen to me and follow my law, which I have set before you, [5]and if you do not listen to the words of my servants the prophets, whom I have sent to you again and again (though you have not listened), [6]then I will make this house like Shiloh and this city an object of cursing among all the nations of the earth.'"

[7]The priests, the prophets and all the people heard Jeremiah speak these words in the house of the Lord. [8]But as soon as Jeremiah finished telling all the people everything the Lord had commanded him to say, the priests, the prophets and all the people seized him and said, "You must die! [9]Why do you prophesy in the Lord's name that this house will be like Shiloh and this city will be desolate and deserted?" And all the people crowded around Jeremiah in the house of the Lord.

[10]When the officials of Judah heard about these things, they went up from the royal palace to the house of the Lord and took their places at the entrance of the New Gate of the Lord's house. [11]Then the priests and the prophets said to the officials and all the people, "This man should be sentenced to death because he has prophesied against this city. You have heard it with your own ears!"

> If you can't pray a door open, don't pry it open.
>
> LYELL RADER

[12]Then Jeremiah said to all the officials and all the people: "The Lord sent me to prophesy against this house and this city all the things you have heard. [13]Now reform your ways and your actions and obey the Lord your God. Then the Lord will relent and not bring the disaster he has pronounced against you. [14]As for me, I am in your hands; do with me whatever you think is good and right. [15]Be assured, however, that if you put me to death, you will bring the guilt of innocent blood on yourselves and on this city and on those who live in it, for in truth the Lord has sent me to you to speak all these words in your hearing."

[16]Then the officials and all the people said to the priests and the prophets, "This man should not be sentenced to death! He has spoken to us in the name of the Lord our God."

[17]Some of the elders of the land stepped forward and said to the entire assembly of people, [18]"Micah of Moresheth prophesied in the days of Hezekiah king of Judah. He told all the people of Judah, 'This is what the Lord Almighty says:

> " 'Zion will be plowed like a field,
> Jerusalem will become a heap of rubble,
> the temple hill a mound overgrown with thickets.'[a]

[19]"Did Hezekiah king of Judah or anyone else in Judah put him to death? Did not Hezekiah fear the Lord and seek his favor? And did not the Lord relent, so that he did not bring the disaster he pronounced against them? We are about to bring a terrible disaster on ourselves!"

[20](Now Uriah son of Shemaiah from Kiriath Jearim was another man who prophesied in the name of the Lord; he prophesied the same things against this city and this land as Jeremiah did. [21]When King Jehoiakim and all his officers and officials heard his words, the king sought to put him to death. But Uriah heard of it and fled in fear to Egypt. [22]King Jehoiakim, however, sent Elnathan son of Acbor to Egypt, along with some other men. [23]They brought Uriah out of Egypt and took him to King Jehoiakim, who had him struck down with a sword and his body thrown into the burial place of the common people.)

[24]Furthermore, Ahikam son of Shaphan supported Jeremiah, and so he was not handed over to the people to be put to death.

Judah to Serve Nebuchadnezzar

27 Early in the reign of Zedekiah[b] son of Josiah king of Judah, this word came to Jeremiah from the Lord: [2]This is what the Lord said to me: "Make a yoke

---

[a]18 Micah 3:12   [b]1 A few Hebrew manuscripts and Syriac (see also Jer. 27:3, 12 and 28:1); most Hebrew manuscripts *Jehoiakim* (Most Septuagint manuscripts do not have this verse.)

out of straps and crossbars and put it on your neck. ³Then send word to the kings of Edom, Moab, Ammon, Tyre and Sidon through the envoys who have come to Jerusalem to Zedekiah king of Judah. ⁴Give them a message for their masters and say, 'This is what the LORD Almighty, the God of Israel, says: "Tell this to your masters: ⁵With my great power and outstretched arm I made the earth and its people and the animals that are on it, and I give it to anyone I please. ⁶Now I will hand all your countries over to my servant Nebuchadnezzar king of Babylon; I will make even the wild animals subject to him. ⁷All nations will serve him and his son and his grandson until the time for his land comes; then many nations and great kings will subjugate him.

⁸" ' "If, however, any nation or kingdom will not serve Nebuchadnezzar king of Babylon or bow its neck under his yoke, I will punish that nation with the sword, famine and plague, declares the LORD, until I destroy it by his hand. ⁹So do not listen to your prophets, your diviners, your interpreters of dreams, your mediums or your sorcerers who tell you, 'You will not serve the king of Babylon.' ¹⁰They prophesy lies to you that will only serve to remove you far from your lands; I will banish you and you will perish. ¹¹But if any nation will bow its neck under the yoke of the king of Babylon and serve him, I will let that nation remain in its own land to till it and to live there, declares the LORD." ' "

¹²I gave the same message to Zedekiah king of Judah. I said, "Bow your neck under the yoke of the king of Babylon; serve him and his people, and you will live. ¹³Why will you and your people die by the sword, famine and plague with which the LORD has threatened any nation that will not serve the king of Babylon? ¹⁴Do not listen to the words of the prophets who say to you, 'You will not serve the king of Babylon,' for they are prophesying lies to you. ¹⁵'I have not sent them,' declares the LORD. 'They are prophesying lies in my name. Therefore, I will banish you and you will perish, both you and the prophets who prophesy to you.' "

¹⁶Then I said to the priests and all these people, "This is what the LORD says: Do not listen to the prophets who say, 'Very soon now the articles from the LORD's house will be brought back from Babylon.' They are prophesying lies to you. ¹⁷Do not listen to them. Serve the king of Babylon, and you will live. Why should this city become a ruin? ¹⁸If they are prophets and have the word of the LORD, let them plead with the LORD Almighty that the furnishings remaining in the house of the LORD and in the palace of the king of Judah and in Jerusalem not be taken to Babylon. ¹⁹For this is what the LORD Almighty says about the pillars, the Sea, the movable stands and the other furnishings that are left in this city, ²⁰which Nebuchadnezzar king of Babylon did not take away when he carried Jehoiachin[a] son of Jehoiakim king of Judah into exile from Jerusalem to Babylon, along with all the nobles of Judah and Jerusalem— ²¹yes, this is what the LORD Almighty, the God of Israel, says about the things that are left in the house of the LORD and in the palace of the king of Judah and in Jerusalem: ²²'They will be taken to Babylon and there they will remain until the day I come for them,' declares the LORD. 'Then I will bring them back and restore them to this place.' "

The False Prophet Hananiah

28 In the fifth month of that same year, the fourth year, early in the reign of Zedekiah king of Judah, the prophet Hananiah son of Azzur, who was from Gibeon, said to me in the house of the LORD in the presence of the priests and all the people: ²"This is what the LORD Almighty, the God of Israel, says: 'I will break the yoke of the king of Babylon. ³Within two years I will bring back to this place all the articles of the LORD's house that Nebuchadnezzar king of Babylon removed from here and took to Babylon. ⁴I will also bring back to this place Jehoiachin[a] son of Jehoiakim king of Judah and all the other exiles from Judah who went to Babylon,' declares the LORD, 'for I will break the yoke of the king of Babylon.' "

---

[a] 20,4 Hebrew *Jeconiah*, a variant of *Jehoiachin*

⁵Then the prophet Jeremiah replied to the prophet Hananiah before the priests and all the people who were standing in the house of the LORD. ⁶He said, "Amen! May the LORD do so! May the LORD fulfill the words you have prophesied by bringing the articles of the LORD's house and all the exiles back to this place from Babylon. ⁷Nevertheless, listen to what I have to say in your hearing and in the hearing of all the people: ⁸From early times the prophets who preceded you and me have prophesied war, disaster and plague against many countries and great kingdoms. ⁹But the prophet who prophesies peace will be recognized as one truly sent by the LORD only if his prediction comes true."

¹⁰Then the prophet Hananiah took the yoke off the neck of the prophet Jeremiah and broke it, ¹¹and he said before all the people, "This is what the LORD says: 'In the same way will I break the yoke of Nebuchadnezzar king of Babylon off the neck of all the nations within two years.' " At this, the prophet Jeremiah went on his way.

¹²Shortly after the prophet Hananiah had broken the yoke off the neck of the prophet Jeremiah, the word of the LORD came to Jeremiah: ¹³"Go and tell Hananiah, 'This is what the LORD says: You have broken a wooden yoke, but in its place you will get a yoke of iron. ¹⁴This is what the LORD Almighty, the God of Israel, says: I will put an iron yoke on the necks of all these nations to make them serve Nebuchadnezzar king of Babylon, and they will serve him. I will even give him control over the wild animals.' "

¹⁵Then the prophet Jeremiah said to Hananiah the prophet, "Listen, Hananiah! The LORD has not sent you, yet you have persuaded this nation to trust in lies. ¹⁶Therefore, this is what the LORD says: 'I am about to remove you from the face of the earth. This very year you are going to die, because you have preached rebellion against the LORD.' "

¹⁷In the seventh month of that same year, Hananiah the prophet died.

A Letter to the Exiles

29 This is the text of the letter that the prophet Jeremiah sent from Jerusalem to the surviving elders among the exiles and to the priests, the prophets and all the other people Nebuchadnezzar had carried into exile from Jerusalem to Babylon. ²(This was after King Jehoiachin*a* and the queen mother, the court officials and the leaders of Judah and Jerusalem, the craftsmen and the artisans had gone into exile from Jerusalem.) ³He entrusted the letter to Elasah son of Shaphan and to Gemariah son of Hilkiah, whom Zedekiah king of Judah sent to King Nebuchadnezzar in Babylon. It said:

⁴This is what the LORD Almighty, the God of Israel, says to all those I carried into exile from Jerusalem to Babylon: ⁵"Build houses and settle down; plant gardens and eat what they produce. ⁶Marry and have sons and daughters; find wives for your sons and give your daughters in marriage, so that they too may have sons and daughters. Increase in number there; do not decrease. ⁷Also, seek the peace and prosperity of the city to which I have carried you into exile. Pray to the LORD for it, because if it prospers, you too will prosper." ⁸Yes, this is what the LORD Almighty, the God of Israel, says: "Do not let the prophets and diviners among you deceive you. Do not listen to the dreams you encourage them to have. ⁹They are prophesying lies to you in my name. I have not sent them," declares the LORD.

¹⁰This is what the LORD says: "When seventy years are completed for Babylon, I will come to you and fulfill my gracious promise to bring you back to this place. ¹¹For I know the plans I have for you," declares the LORD, "plans to prosper you and not to harm you, plans to give you hope and a future. ¹²Then you will call upon me and come and pray to me, and I will listen to you. ¹³You

> *"THEN you will call upon me and come and pray to me, and I will listen to you."*
>
> JEREMIAH 29:12

*a*2 Hebrew *Jeconiah*, a variant of *Jehoiachin*

will seek me and find me when you seek me with all your heart. ¹⁴I will be found by you," declares the LORD, "and will bring you back from captivity.ª I will gather you from all the nations and places where I have banished you," declares the LORD, "and will bring you back to the place from which I carried you into exile."

¹⁵You may say, "The LORD has raised up prophets for us in Babylon," ¹⁶but this is what the LORD says about the king who sits on David's throne and all the people who remain in this city, your countrymen who did not go with you into exile— ¹⁷yes, this is what the LORD Almighty says: "I will send the sword, famine and plague against them and I will make them like poor figs that are so bad they cannot be eaten. ¹⁸I will pursue them with the sword, famine and plague and will make them abhorrent to all the kingdoms of the earth and an object of cursing and horror, of scorn and reproach, among all the nations where I drive them. ¹⁹For they have not listened to my words," declares the LORD, "words that I sent to them again and again by my servants the prophets. And you exiles have not listened either," declares the LORD.

²⁰Therefore, hear the word of the LORD, all you exiles whom I have sent away from Jerusalem to Babylon. ²¹This is what the LORD Almighty, the God of Israel, says about Ahab son of Kolaiah and Zedekiah son of Maaseiah, who are prophesying lies to you in my name: "I will hand them over to Nebuchadnezzar king of Babylon, and he will put them to death before your very eyes. ²²Because of them, all the exiles from Judah who are in Babylon will use this curse: 'The LORD treat you like Zedekiah and Ahab, whom the king of Babylon burned in the fire.' ²³For they have done outrageous things in Israel; they have committed adultery with their neighbors' wives and in my name have spoken lies, which I did not tell them to do.

I know it and am a witness to it," declares the LORD.

Message to Shemaiah

²⁴Tell Shemaiah the Nehelamite, ²⁵"This is what the LORD Almighty, the God of Israel, says: You sent letters in your own name to all the people in Jerusalem, to Zephaniah son of Maaseiah the priest, and to all the other priests. You said to Zephaniah, ²⁶'The LORD has appointed you priest in place of Jehoiada to be in charge of the house of the LORD; you should put any madman who acts like a prophet into the stocks and neck-irons. ²⁷So why have you not reprimanded Jeremiah from Anathoth, who poses as a prophet among you? ²⁸He has sent this message to us in Babylon: It will be a long time. Therefore build houses and settle down; plant gardens and eat what they produce.'"

²⁹Zephaniah the priest, however, read the letter to Jeremiah the prophet. ³⁰Then the word of the LORD came to Jeremiah: ³¹"Send this message to all the exiles: 'This is what the LORD says about Shemaiah the Nehelamite: Because Shemaiah has prophesied to you, even though I did not send him, and has led you to believe a lie, ³²this is what the LORD says: I will surely punish Shemaiah the Nehelamite and his descendants. He will have no one left among this people, nor will he see the good things I will do for my people, declares the LORD, because he has preached rebellion against me.'"

Restoration of Israel

30 This is the word that came to Jeremiah from the LORD: ²"This is what the LORD, the God of Israel, says: 'Write in a book all the words I have spoken to you. ³The days are coming,' declares the LORD, 'when I will bring my people Israel and Judah back from captivityᵇ and restore them to the land I gave their forefathers to possess,' says the LORD."

⁴These are the words the LORD spoke concerning Israel and Judah: ⁵"This is what the LORD says:

ª14 Or *will restore your fortunes*   ᵇ3 Or *will restore the fortunes of my people Israel and Judah*

" 'Cries of fear are heard—
terror, not peace.
⁶ Ask and see:
Can a man bear children?
Then why do I see every strong man
with his hands on his stomach like
a woman in labor,
every face turned deathly pale?
⁷ How awful that day will be!
None will be like it.
It will be a time of trouble for Jacob,
but he will be saved out of it.

⁸ " 'In that day,' declares the LORD
Almighty,
'I will break the yoke off their necks
and will tear off their bonds;
no longer will foreigners enslave
them.
⁹ Instead, they will serve the LORD
their God
and David their king,
whom I will raise up for them.

¹⁰ " 'So do not fear, O Jacob my servant;
do not be dismayed, O Israel,'
declares the LORD.
'I will surely save you out of a
distant place,
your descendants from the land of
their exile.
Jacob will again have peace and
security,
and no one will make him afraid.
¹¹ I am with you and will save you,'
declares the LORD.
'Though I completely destroy all the
nations
among which I scatter you,
I will not completely destroy you.
I will discipline you but only with
justice;
I will not let you go entirely
unpunished.'

¹² "This is what the LORD says:

" 'Your wound is incurable,
your injury beyond healing.
¹³ There is no one to plead your cause,
no remedy for your sore,
no healing for you.
¹⁴ All your allies have forgotten you;
they care nothing for you.
I have struck you as an enemy would
and punished you as would the
cruel,

because your guilt is so great
and your sins so many.
¹⁵ Why do you cry out over your
wound,
your pain that has no cure?
Because of your great guilt and
many sins
I have done these things to you.

¹⁶ " 'But all who devour you will be
devoured;
all your enemies will go into exile.
Those who plunder you will be
plundered;
all who make spoil of you I will
despoil.
¹⁷ But I will restore you to health
and heal your wounds,'
declares the LORD,
'because you are called an outcast,
Zion for whom no one cares.'

¹⁸ "This is what the LORD says:

" 'I will restore the fortunes of
Jacob's tents
and have compassion on his
dwellings;
the city will be rebuilt on her ruins,
and the palace will stand in its
proper place.
¹⁹ From them will come songs of
thanksgiving
and the sound of rejoicing.
I will add to their numbers,
and they will not be decreased;
I will bring them honor,
and they will not be disdained.
²⁰ Their children will be as in days
of old,
and their community will be
established before me;
I will punish all who oppress them.
²¹ Their leader will be one of their own;
their ruler will arise from among
them.
I will bring him near and he will come
close to me,
for who is he who will devote
himself
to be close to me?'
declares the LORD.
²² " 'So you will be my people,
and I will be your God.' "

²³ See, the storm of the LORD
will burst out in wrath,

a driving wind swirling down
on the heads of the wicked.
24 The fierce anger of the LORD will not
turn back
until he fully accomplishes
the purposes of his heart.
In days to come
you will understand this.

31 "At that time," declares the LORD,
"I will be the God of all the clans of
Israel, and they will be my people."

2 This is what the LORD says:

"The people who survive the sword
will find favor in the desert;
I will come to give rest to Israel."

3 The LORD appeared to us in the past,[a]
saying:

"I have loved you with an everlasting
love;
I have drawn you with
loving-kindness.
4 I will build you up again
and you will be rebuilt, O Virgin
Israel.
Again you will take up your
tambourines
and go out to dance with the joyful.
5 Again you will plant vineyards
on the hills of Samaria;
the farmers will plant them
and enjoy their fruit.
6 There will be a day when watchmen
cry out
on the hills of Ephraim,
'Come, let us go up to Zion,
to the LORD our God.'"

7 This is what the LORD says:

"Sing with joy for Jacob;
shout for the foremost of the
nations.
Make your praises heard, and say,
'O LORD, save your people,
the remnant of Israel.'
8 See, I will bring them from the land of
the north
and gather them from the ends of
the earth.
Among them will be the blind and the
lame,
expectant mothers and women in
labor;

a great throng will return.
9 They will come with weeping;
they will pray as I bring them back.
I will lead them beside streams of
water
on a level path where they will not
stumble,
because I am Israel's father,
and Ephraim is my firstborn son.

> "THEY will come with weeping;
> they will pray as I bring them back.
> I will lead them beside streams of water
> on a level path where they will not
> stumble."
>
> JEREMIAH 31:9

10 "Hear the word of the LORD,
O nations;
proclaim it in distant coastlands:
'He who scattered Israel will gather
them
and will watch over his flock like a
shepherd.'
11 For the LORD will ransom Jacob
and redeem them from the hand of
those stronger than they.
12 They will come and shout for joy on
the heights of Zion;
they will rejoice in the bounty of
the LORD—
the grain, the new wine and the oil,
the young of the flocks and herds.
They will be like a well-watered
garden,
and they will sorrow no more.
13 Then maidens will dance and be glad,
young men and old as well.
I will turn their mourning into
gladness;
I will give them comfort and joy
instead of sorrow.
14 I will satisfy the priests with
abundance,
and my people will be filled with
my bounty,"
declares the LORD.

15 This is what the LORD says:

"A voice is heard in Ramah,
mourning and great weeping,

a 3 Or LORD has appeared to us from afar

Rachel weeping for her children
and refusing to be comforted,
because her children are no more."

[16]This is what the LORD says:

"Restrain your voice from weeping
and your eyes from tears,
for your work will be rewarded,"
declares the LORD.
"They will return from the land of
the enemy.
[17]So there is hope for your future,"
declares the LORD.
"Your children will return to their
own land.

[18]"I have surely heard Ephraim's
moaning:
'You disciplined me like an unruly
calf,
and I have been disciplined.
Restore me, and I will return,
because you are the LORD my God.
[19]After I strayed,
I repented;
after I came to understand,
I beat my breast.
I was ashamed and humiliated
because I bore the disgrace of my
youth.'
[20]Is not Ephraim my dear son,
the child in whom I delight?
Though I often speak against him,
I still remember him.
Therefore my heart yearns for him;
I have great compassion for him,"
declares the LORD.

[21]"Set up road signs;
put up guideposts.
Take note of the highway,
the road that you take.
Return, O Virgin Israel,
return to your towns.
[22]How long will you wander,
O unfaithful daughter?
The LORD will create a new thing
on earth—
a woman will surround[a] a man."

[23]This is what the LORD Almighty, the
God of Israel, says: "When I bring them
back from captivity,[b] the people in the
land of Judah and in its towns will once
again use these words: 'The LORD bless
you, O righteous dwelling, O sacred
mountain.' [24]People will live together in
Judah and all its towns—farmers and
those who move about with their flocks.
[25]I will refresh the weary and satisfy the
faint."

[26]At this I awoke and looked around.
My sleep had been pleasant to me.

[27]"The days are coming," declares the
LORD, "when I will plant the house of Israel and the house of Judah with the offspring of men and of animals. [28]Just as I
watched over them to uproot and tear
down, and to overthrow, destroy and
bring disaster, so I will watch over them
to build and to plant," declares the LORD.
[29]"In those days people will no longer say,

'The fathers have eaten sour grapes,
and the children's teeth are set on
edge.'

[30]Instead, everyone will die for his own
sin; whoever eats sour grapes—his own
teeth will be set on edge.

[31]"The time is coming," declares the
LORD,
"when I will make a new covenant
with the house of Israel
and with the house of Judah.
[32]It will not be like the covenant
I made with their forefathers
when I took them by the hand
to lead them out of Egypt,
because they broke my covenant,
though I was a husband to[c]
them,[d]"
declares the LORD.
[33]"This is the covenant I will make with
the house of Israel
after that time," declares the LORD.
"I will put my law in their minds
and write it on their hearts.
I will be their God,
and they will be my people.
[34]No longer will a man teach his
neighbor,
or a man his brother, saying,
'Know the LORD,'
because they will all know me,
from the least of them to the
greatest,"
declares the LORD.

[a]22 Or will go about seeking; or will protect
[b]23 Or I restore their fortunes   [c]32 Hebrew;
Septuagint and Syriac / and I turned away from
[d]32 Or was their master

"For I will forgive their wickedness
and will remember their sins no
more."

35This is what the LORD says,

he who appoints the sun
to shine by day,
who decrees the moon and stars
to shine by night,
who stirs up the sea
so that its waves roar—
the LORD Almighty is his name:
36 "Only if these decrees vanish from
my sight,"
declares the LORD,
"will the descendants of Israel ever
cease
to be a nation before me."

37This is what the LORD says:

"Only if the heavens above can be
measured
and the foundations of the earth
below be searched out
will I reject all the descendants
of Israel
because of all they have done,"
declares the LORD.

38"The days are coming," declares the
LORD, "when this city will be rebuilt for
me from the Tower of Hananel to the
Corner Gate. 39The measuring line will
stretch from there straight to the hill of
Gareb and then turn to Goah. 40The
whole valley where dead bodies and ashes are thrown, and all the terraces out to
the Kidron Valley on the east as far as the
corner of the Horse Gate, will be holy to
the LORD. The city will never again be uprooted or demolished."

Jeremiah Buys a Field

32 This is the word that came to Jeremiah from the LORD in the tenth
year of Zedekiah king of Judah, which
was the eighteenth year of Nebuchadnezzar. 2The army of the king of Babylon
was then besieging Jerusalem, and Jeremiah the prophet was confined in the
courtyard of the guard in the royal palace of Judah.

3Now Zedekiah king of Judah had imprisoned him there, saying, "Why do you
prophesy as you do? You say, 'This is

what the LORD says: I am about to hand
this city over to the king of Babylon, and
he will capture it. 4Zedekiah king of Judah will not escape out of the hands of
the Babylonians[a] but will certainly be
handed over to the king of Babylon, and
will speak with him face to face and see
him with his own eyes. 5He will take Zedekiah to Babylon, where he will remain
until I deal with him, declares the LORD. If
you fight against the Babylonians, you
will not succeed.' "

6Jeremiah said, "The word of the LORD
came to me: 7Hanamel son of Shallum
your uncle is going to come to you and
say, 'Buy my field at Anathoth, because
as nearest relative it is your right and
duty to buy it.'

8"Then, just as the LORD had said, my
cousin Hanamel came to me in the courtyard of the guard and said, 'Buy my field
at Anathoth in the territory of Benjamin.
Since it is your right to redeem it and
possess it, buy it for yourself.'

"I knew that this was the word of the
LORD; 9so I bought the field at Anathoth
from my cousin Hanamel and weighed
out for him seventeen shekels[b] of silver.
10I signed and sealed the deed, had it witnessed, and weighed out the silver on the
scales. 11I took the deed of purchase—the
sealed copy containing the terms and
conditions, as well as the unsealed
copy— 12and I gave this deed to Baruch
son of Neriah, the son of Mahseiah, in
the presence of my cousin Hanamel and
of the witnesses who had signed the
deed and of all the Jews sitting in the
courtyard of the guard.

13"In their presence I gave Baruch
these instructions: 14'This is what the
LORD Almighty, the God of Israel, says:
Take these documents, both the sealed
and unsealed copies of the deed of purchase, and put them in a clay jar so they
will last a long time. 15For this is what the
LORD Almighty, the God of Israel, says:
Houses, fields and vineyards will again
be bought in this land.'

16"After I had given the deed of purchase to Baruch son of Neriah, I prayed
to the LORD:

a4 Or *Chaldeans*; also in verses 5, 24, 25, 28, 29
and 43   b9 That is, about 7 ounces (about 200
grams)

17"Ah, Sovereign LORD, you have made the heavens and the earth by your great power and outstretched arm. Nothing is too hard for you. 18You show love to thousands but bring the punishment for the fathers' sins into the laps of their children after them. O great and powerful God, whose name is the LORD Almighty, 19great are your purposes and mighty are your deeds. Your eyes are open to all the ways of men; you reward everyone according to his conduct and as his deeds deserve. 20You performed miraculous signs and wonders in Egypt and have continued them to this day, both in Israel and among all mankind, and have gained the renown that is still yours. 21You brought your people Israel out of Egypt with signs and wonders, by a mighty hand and an outstretched arm and with great terror. 22You gave them this land you had sworn to give their forefathers, a land flowing with milk and honey. 23They came in and took possession of it, but they did not obey you or follow your law; they did not do what you commanded them to do. So you brought all this disaster upon them.

24"See how the siege ramps are built up to take the city. Because of the sword, famine and plague, the city will be handed over to the Babylonians who are attacking it. What you said has happened, as you now see. 25And though the city will be handed over to the Babylonians, you, O Sovereign LORD, say to me, 'Buy the field with silver and have the transaction witnessed.'"

26Then the word of the LORD came to Jeremiah: 27"I am the LORD, the God of all mankind. Is anything too hard for me? 28Therefore, this is what the LORD says: I am about to hand this city over to the Babylonians and to Nebuchadnezzar king of Babylon, who will capture it. 29The Babylonians who are attacking this city will come in and set it on fire; they will burn it down, along with the houses where the people provoked me to anger by burning incense on the roofs to Baal and by pouring out drink offerings to other gods.

30"The people of Israel and Judah have done nothing but evil in my sight from their youth; indeed, the people of Israel have done nothing but provoke me with what their hands have made, declares the LORD. 31From the day it was built until now, this city has so aroused my anger and wrath that I must remove it from my sight. 32The people of Israel and Judah have provoked me by all the evil they have done—they, their kings and officials, their priests and prophets, the men of Judah and the people of Jerusalem. 33They turned their backs to me and not their faces; though I taught them again and again, they would not listen or respond to discipline. 34They set up their abominable idols in the house that bears my Name and defiled it. 35They built high places for Baal in the Valley of Ben Hinnom to sacrifice their sons and daughters[a] to Molech, though I never commanded, nor did it enter my mind, that they should do such a detestable thing and so make Judah sin.

36"You are saying about this city, 'By the sword, famine and plague it will be handed over to the king of Babylon'; but this is what the LORD, the God of Israel, says: 37I will surely gather them from all the lands where I banish them in my furious anger and great wrath; I will bring them back to this place and let them live in safety. 38They will be my people, and I will be their God. 39I will give them singleness of heart and action, so that they will always fear me for their own good and the good of their children after them. 40I will make an everlasting covenant with them: I will never stop doing good to them, and I will inspire them to fear me, so that they will never turn away from me. 41I will rejoice in doing them good and will assuredly plant them in this land with all my heart and soul.

42"This is what the LORD says: As I have brought all this great calamity on this people, so I will give them all the prosperity I have promised them. 43Once more fields will be bought in this land of which you say, 'It is a desolate waste, without men or animals, for it has been handed over to the Babylonians.' 44Fields

---

a35 Or to make their sons and daughters pass through the fire

Nothing Is Too Hard for You

32:16 "AFTER I HAD GIVEN THE DEED OF PURCHASE TO BARUCH . . . I PRAYED TO THE LORD."

"Buy low, sell high" is a good rule of thumb for investors in stocks and real estate. The more you can make, the less you may lose—that's the object of any wise purchase. Something like this is in the back of Hanamel's mind as he approaches Jeremiah with an offer that Jeremiah really can't refuse. According to ancient Israelite law (see Leviticus 25:25), Jeremiah, as the nearest relative, must buy the property Hanamel wants to unload. Perhaps the fact that Jerusalem is under siege (see Jeremiah 32:2) has made real estate values drop, and Hanamel wants to liquidate his assets before values go even lower. Whatever his reason, for Hanamel to put this kind of pressure on his cousin while Jeremiah is imprisoned is not the nicest thing to do.

But what Hanamel means for evil, God means for good. The Lord reveals to Jeremiah what Hanamel is going to do. He tells Jeremiah to buy the property, sign and seal the deed, and put the documents in a clay jar so they will last a long time. This will be a sign of hope, says the Lord; for even though Jerusalem will be destroyed in judgment, the day will come when "Houses, fields and vineyards will again be bought in this land" (verse 15). Although Jeremiah surely has some doubts (see verses 24–25), he obeys and then prays. "Ah, Sovereign LORD, you have made the heavens and the earth by your great power and outstretched arm. Nothing is too hard for you" (verse 17). God agrees and answers with a rhetorical question, "I am the LORD, the God of all mankind. Is anything too hard for me?" (verses 26–27). In this situation, Jeremiah turns out to be the wiser investor. For a pittance of faith and a few shekels, he has purchased a goldmine of hope (see 1 Peter 1:3–7).

"Nothing is too hard for you." The next time we read this phrase in Scripture will be centuries later when the angel Gabriel appears to a teenage girl to announce that she is about to have a very unusual pregnancy (see Luke 1:26–38). She will give birth to the Savior, yet remain a virgin. When she wants to know how such a thing can possibly happen, the angel responds, "Nothing is impossible with God" (Luke 1:37). Just like Mary, Jeremiah learns that the only way to have hope is to know that nothing is too hard for God.

PRAY:

What are you facing today that cries out for hope?
Pray about it the way Jeremiah prayed: "Sovereign LORD,
you have made the heavens and the earth by your great power
and outstretched arm. Nothing is too hard for you."

FOR YOUR NEXT DEVOTIONAL READING, GO TO PAGE 964.

will be bought for silver, and deeds will be signed, sealed and witnessed in the territory of Benjamin, in the villages around Jerusalem, in the towns of Judah and in the towns of the hill country, of the western foothills and of the Negev, because I will restore their fortunes,[a] declares the LORD."

Promise of Restoration

33 While Jeremiah was still confined in the courtyard of the guard, the word of the LORD came to him a second time: [2]"This is what the LORD says, he who made the earth, the LORD who formed it and established it—the LORD is his name: [3]'Call to me and I will answer you and tell you great and unsearchable things you do not know.' [4]For this is what the LORD, the God of Israel, says about the houses in this city and the royal palaces of Judah that have been torn down to be used against the siege ramps and the sword [5]in the fight with the Babylonians[b]: 'They will be filled with the dead bodies of the men I will slay in my anger and wrath. I will hide my face from this city because of all its wickedness.

> "CALL to me and I will answer you and tell you great and unsearchable things you do not know."
>
> JEREMIAH 33:3

[6]"'Nevertheless, I will bring health and healing to it; I will heal my people and will let them enjoy abundant peace and security. [7]I will bring Judah and Israel back from captivity[c] and will rebuild them as they were before. [8]I will cleanse them from all the sin they have committed against me and will forgive all their sins of rebellion against me. [9]Then this city will bring me renown, joy, praise and honor before all nations on earth that hear of all the good things I do for it; and they will be in awe and will tremble at the abundant prosperity and peace I provide for it.'

[10]"This is what the LORD says: 'You say about this place, "It is a desolate waste, without men or animals." Yet in the towns of Judah and the streets of Jerusalem that are deserted, inhabited by neither men nor animals, there will be heard once more [11]the sounds of joy and gladness, the voices of bride and bridegroom, and the voices of those who bring thank offerings to the house of the LORD, saying,

"Give thanks to the LORD Almighty,
    for the LORD is good;
    his love endures forever."

For I will restore the fortunes of the land as they were before,' says the LORD.

[12]"This is what the LORD Almighty says: 'In this place, desolate and without men or animals—in all its towns there will again be pastures for shepherds to rest their flocks. [13]In the towns of the hill country, of the western foothills and of the Negev, in the territory of Benjamin, in the villages around Jerusalem and in the towns of Judah, flocks will again pass under the hand of the one who counts them,' says the LORD.

[14]"'The days are coming,' declares the LORD, 'when I will fulfill the gracious promise I made to the house of Israel and to the house of Judah.

[15]"'In those days and at that time
    I will make a righteous Branch
        sprout from David's line;
    he will do what is just and right in
        the land.
[16]In those days Judah will be saved
    and Jerusalem will live in safety.
This is the name by which it[d] will be
        called:
    The LORD Our Righteousness.'

[17]For this is what the LORD says: 'David will never fail to have a man to sit on the throne of the house of Israel, [18]nor will the priests, who are Levites, ever fail to have a man to stand before me continually to offer burnt offerings, to burn grain offerings and to present sacrifices.'"

[19]The word of the LORD came to Jeremiah: [20]"This is what the LORD says: 'If you can break my covenant with the day and my covenant with the night, so that day and night no longer come at their appointed time, [21]then my covenant

[a]44 Or will bring them back from captivity
[b]5 Or Chaldeans   [c]7 Or will restore the fortunes of Judah and Israel   [d]16 Or he

with David my servant—and my covenant with the Levites who are priests ministering before me—can be broken and David will no longer have a descendant to reign on his throne. ²²I will make the descendants of David my servant and the Levites who minister before me as countless as the stars of the sky and as measureless as the sand on the seashore.'"

²³The word of the LORD came to Jeremiah: ²⁴"Have you not noticed that these people are saying, 'The LORD has rejected the two kingdoms[a] he chose'? So they despise my people and no longer regard them as a nation. ²⁵This is what the LORD says: 'If I have not established my covenant with day and night and the fixed laws of heaven and earth, ²⁶then I will reject the descendants of Jacob and David my servant and will not choose one of his sons to rule over the descendants of Abraham, Isaac and Jacob. For I will restore their fortunes[b] and have compassion on them.'"

Warning to Zedekiah

34 While Nebuchadnezzar king of Babylon and all his army and all the kingdoms and peoples in the empire he ruled were fighting against Jerusalem and all its surrounding towns, this word came to Jeremiah from the LORD: ²"This is what the LORD, the God of Israel, says: Go to Zedekiah king of Judah and tell him, 'This is what the LORD says: I am about to hand this city over to the king of Babylon, and he will burn it down. ³You will not escape from his grasp but will surely be captured and handed over to him. You will see the king of Babylon with your own eyes, and he will speak with you face to face. And you will go to Babylon.

⁴"'Yet hear the promise of the LORD, O Zedekiah king of Judah. This is what the LORD says concerning you: You will not die by the sword; ⁵you will die peacefully. As people made a funeral fire in honor of your fathers, the former kings who preceded you, so they will make a fire in your honor and lament, "Alas, O master!" I myself make this promise, declares the LORD.'"

⁶Then Jeremiah the prophet told all this to Zedekiah king of Judah, in Jerusalem, ⁷while the army of the king of Babylon was fighting against Jerusalem and the other cities of Judah that were still holding out—Lachish and Azekah. These were the only fortified cities left in Judah.

Freedom for Slaves

⁸The word came to Jeremiah from the LORD after King Zedekiah had made a covenant with all the people in Jerusalem to proclaim freedom for the slaves. ⁹Everyone was to free his Hebrew slaves, both male and female; no one was to hold a fellow Jew in bondage. ¹⁰So all the officials and people who entered into this covenant agreed that they would free their male and female slaves and no longer hold them in bondage. They agreed, and set them free. ¹¹But afterward they changed their minds and took back the slaves they had freed and enslaved them again.

¹²Then the word of the LORD came to Jeremiah: ¹³"This is what the LORD, the God of Israel, says: I made a covenant with your forefathers when I brought them out of Egypt, out of the land of slavery. I said, ¹⁴'Every seventh year each of you must free any fellow Hebrew who has sold himself to you. After he has served you six years, you must let him go free.'[c] Your fathers, however, did not listen to me or pay attention to me. ¹⁵Recently you repented and did what is right in my sight: Each of you proclaimed freedom to his countrymen. You even made a covenant before me in the house that bears my Name. ¹⁶But now you have turned around and profaned my name; each of you has taken back the male and female slaves you had set free to go where they wished. You have forced them to become your slaves again.

¹⁷"Therefore, this is what the LORD says: You have not obeyed me; you have not proclaimed freedom for your fellow countrymen. So I now proclaim 'freedom' for you, declares the LORD—'freedom' to fall by the sword, plague and famine. I will make you abhorrent to all

---

[a]24 Or *families* [b]26 Or *will bring them back from captivity* [c]14 Deut. 15:12

the kingdoms of the earth. [18]The men who have violated my covenant and have not fulfilled the terms of the covenant they made before me, I will treat like the calf they cut in two and then walked between its pieces. [19]The leaders of Judah and Jerusalem, the court officials, the priests and all the people of the land who walked between the pieces of the calf, [20]I will hand over to their enemies who seek their lives. Their dead bodies will become food for the birds of the air and the beasts of the earth.

[21]"I will hand Zedekiah king of Judah and his officials over to their enemies who seek their lives, to the army of the king of Babylon, which has withdrawn from you. [22]I am going to give the order, declares the LORD, and I will bring them back to this city. They will fight against it, take it and burn it down. And I will lay waste the towns of Judah so no one can live there."

The Recabites

35 This is the word that came to Jeremiah from the LORD during the reign of Jehoiakim son of Josiah king of Judah: [2]"Go to the Recabite family and invite them to come to one of the side rooms of the house of the LORD and give them wine to drink."

[3]So I went to get Jaazaniah son of Jeremiah, the son of Habazziniah, and his brothers and all his sons—the whole family of the Recabites. [4]I brought them into the house of the LORD, into the room of the sons of Hanan son of Igdaliah the man of God. It was next to the room of the officials, which was over that of Maaseiah son of Shallum the doorkeeper. [5]Then I set bowls full of wine and some cups before the men of the Recabite family and said to them, "Drink some wine."

[6]But they replied, "We do not drink wine, because our forefather Jonadab son of Recab gave us this command: 'Neither you nor your descendants must ever drink wine. [7]Also you must never build houses, sow seed or plant vineyards; you must never have any of these things, but must always live in tents. Then you will live a long time in the land where you are nomads.' [8]We have obeyed everything our forefather Jona-

dab son of Recab commanded us. Neither we nor our wives nor our sons and daughters have ever drunk wine [9]or built houses to live in or had vineyards, fields or crops. [10]We have lived in tents and have fully obeyed everything our forefather Jonadab commanded us. [11]But when Nebuchadnezzar king of Babylon invaded this land, we said, 'Come, we must go to Jerusalem to escape the Babylonian[a] and Aramean armies.' So we have remained in Jerusalem."

[12]Then the word of the LORD came to Jeremiah, saying: [13]"This is what the LORD Almighty, the God of Israel, says: Go and tell the men of Judah and the people of Jerusalem, 'Will you not learn a lesson and obey my words?' declares the LORD. [14]'Jonadab son of Recab ordered his sons not to drink wine and this command has been kept. To this day they do not drink wine, because they obey their forefather's command. But I have spoken to you again and again, yet you have not obeyed me. [15]Again and again I sent all my servants the prophets to you. They said, "Each of you must turn from your wicked ways and reform your actions; do not follow other gods to serve them. Then you will live in the land I have given to you and your fathers." But you have not paid attention or listened to me. [16]The descendants of Jonadab son of Recab have carried out the command their forefather gave them, but these people have not obeyed me.'

[17]"Therefore, this is what the LORD God Almighty, the God of Israel, says: 'Listen! I am going to bring on Judah and on everyone living in Jerusalem every disaster I pronounced against them. I spoke to them, but they did not listen; I called to them, but they did not answer.'"

[18]Then Jeremiah said to the family of the Recabites, "This is what the LORD Almighty, the God of Israel, says: 'You have obeyed the command of your forefather Jonadab and have followed all his instructions and have done everything he ordered.' [19]Therefore, this is what the LORD Almighty, the God of Israel, says: 'Jonadab son of Recab will never fail to have a man to serve me.'"

[a]11 Or Chaldean

Jehoiakim Burns Jeremiah's Scroll

36 In the fourth year of Jehoiakim son of Josiah king of Judah, this word came to Jeremiah from the LORD: ²"Take a scroll and write on it all the words I have spoken to you concerning Israel, Judah and all the other nations from the time I began speaking to you in the reign of Josiah till now. ³Perhaps when the people of Judah hear about every disaster I plan to inflict on them, each of them will turn from his wicked way; then I will forgive their wickedness and their sin."

⁴So Jeremiah called Baruch son of Neriah, and while Jeremiah dictated all the words the LORD had spoken to him, Baruch wrote them on the scroll. ⁵Then Jeremiah told Baruch, "I am restricted; I cannot go to the LORD's temple. ⁶So you go to the house of the LORD on a day of fasting and read to the people from the scroll the words of the LORD that you wrote as I dictated. Read them to all the people of Judah who come in from their towns. ⁷Perhaps they will bring their petition before the LORD, and each will turn from his wicked ways, for the anger and wrath pronounced against this people by the LORD are great."

⁸Baruch son of Neriah did everything Jeremiah the prophet told him to do; at the LORD's temple he read the words of the LORD from the scroll. ⁹In the ninth month of the fifth year of Jehoiakim son of Josiah king of Judah, a time of fasting before the LORD was proclaimed for all the people in Jerusalem and those who had come from the towns of Judah. ¹⁰From the room of Gemariah son of Shaphan the secretary, which was in the upper courtyard at the entrance of the New Gate of the temple, Baruch read to all the people at the LORD's temple the words of Jeremiah from the scroll.

¹¹When Micaiah son of Gemariah, the son of Shaphan, heard all the words of the LORD from the scroll, ¹²he went down to the secretary's room in the royal palace, where all the officials were sitting: Elishama the secretary, Delaiah son of Shemaiah, Elnathan son of Acbor, Gemariah son of Shaphan, Zedekiah son of Hananiah, and all the other officials.

¹³After Micaiah told them everything he had heard Baruch read to the people from the scroll, ¹⁴all the officials sent Jehudi son of Nethaniah, the son of Shelemiah, the son of Cushi, to say to Baruch, "Bring the scroll from which you have read to the people and come." So Baruch son of Neriah went to them with the scroll in his hand. ¹⁵They said to him, "Sit down, please, and read it to us."

So Baruch read it to them. ¹⁶When they heard all these words, they looked at each other in fear and said to Baruch, "We must report all these words to the king." ¹⁷Then they asked Baruch, "Tell us, how did you come to write all this? Did Jeremiah dictate it?"

¹⁸"Yes," Baruch replied, "he dictated all these words to me, and I wrote them in ink on the scroll."

¹⁹Then the officials said to Baruch, "You and Jeremiah, go and hide. Don't let anyone know where you are."

²⁰After they put the scroll in the room of Elishama the secretary, they went to the king in the courtyard and reported everything to him. ²¹The king sent Jehudi to get the scroll, and Jehudi brought it from the room of Elishama the secretary and read it to the king and all the officials standing beside him. ²²It was the ninth month and the king was sitting in the winter apartment, with a fire burning in the firepot in front of him. ²³Whenever Jehudi had read three or four columns of the scroll, the king cut them off with a scribe's knife and threw them into the firepot, until the entire scroll was burned in the fire. ²⁴The king and all his attendants who heard all these words showed no fear, nor did they tear their clothes. ²⁵Even though Elnathan, Delaiah and Gemariah urged the king not to burn the scroll, he would not listen to them. ²⁶Instead, the king commanded Jerahmeel, a son of the king, Seraiah son of Azriel and Shelemiah son of Abdeel to arrest Baruch the scribe and Jeremiah the prophet. But the LORD had hidden them.

²⁷After the king burned the scroll containing the words that Baruch had written at Jeremiah's dictation, the word of the LORD came to Jeremiah: ²⁸"Take another scroll and write on it all the words

that were on the first scroll, which Jehoiakim king of Judah burned up. ²⁹Also tell Jehoiakim king of Judah, 'This is what the LORD says: You burned that scroll and said, "Why did you write on it that the king of Babylon would certainly come and destroy this land and cut off both men and animals from it?" ³⁰Therefore, this is what the LORD says about Jehoiakim king of Judah: He will have no one to sit on the throne of David; his body will be thrown out and exposed to the heat by day and the frost by night. ³¹I will punish him and his children and his attendants for their wickedness; I will bring on them and those living in Jerusalem and the people of Judah every disaster I pronounced against them, because they have not listened.'"

³²So Jeremiah took another scroll and gave it to the scribe Baruch son of Neriah, and as Jeremiah dictated, Baruch wrote on it all the words of the scroll that Jehoiakim king of Judah had burned in the fire. And many similar words were added to them.

Jeremiah in Prison

37 Zedekiah son of Josiah was made king of Judah by Nebuchadnezzar king of Babylon; he reigned in place of Jehoiachin*ᵃ* son of Jehoiakim. ²Neither he nor his attendants nor the people of the land paid any attention to the words the LORD had spoken through Jeremiah the prophet.

³King Zedekiah, however, sent Jehucal son of Shelemiah with the priest Zephaniah son of Maaseiah to Jeremiah the prophet with this message: "Please pray to the LORD our God for us."

⁴Now Jeremiah was free to come and go among the people, for he had not yet been put in prison. ⁵Pharaoh's army had marched out of Egypt, and when the Babylonians*ᵇ* who were besieging Jerusalem heard the report about them, they withdrew from Jerusalem.

⁶Then the word of the LORD came to Jeremiah the prophet: ⁷"This is what the LORD, the God of Israel, says: Tell the king of Judah, who sent you to inquire of me, 'Pharaoh's army, which has marched out to support you, will go back to its own land, to Egypt. ⁸Then the Babylonians

will return and attack this city; they will capture it and burn it down.'

⁹"This is what the LORD says: Do not deceive yourselves, thinking, 'The Babylonians will surely leave us.' They will not! ¹⁰Even if you were to defeat the entire Babylonian*ᶜ* army that is attacking you and only wounded men were left in their tents, they would come out and burn this city down."

¹¹After the Babylonian army had withdrawn from Jerusalem because of Pharaoh's army, ¹²Jeremiah started to leave the city to go to the territory of Benjamin to get his share of the property among the people there. ¹³But when he reached the Benjamin Gate, the captain of the guard, whose name was Irijah son of Shelemiah, the son of Hananiah, arrested him and said, "You are deserting to the Babylonians!"

¹⁴"That's not true!" Jeremiah said. "I am not deserting to the Babylonians." But Irijah would not listen to him; instead, he arrested Jeremiah and brought him to the officials. ¹⁵They were angry with Jeremiah and had him beaten and imprisoned in the house of Jonathan the secretary, which they had made into a prison.

¹⁶Jeremiah was put into a vaulted cell in a dungeon, where he remained a long time. ¹⁷Then King Zedekiah sent for him and had him brought to the palace, where he asked him privately, "Is there any word from the LORD?"

"Yes," Jeremiah replied, "you will be handed over to the king of Babylon."

¹⁸Then Jeremiah said to King Zedekiah, "What crime have I committed against you or your officials or this people, that you have put me in prison? ¹⁹Where are your prophets who prophesied to you, 'The king of Babylon will not attack you or this land'? ²⁰But now, my lord the king, please listen. Let me bring my petition before you: Do not send me back to the house of Jonathan the secretary, or I will die there."

²¹King Zedekiah then gave orders for Jeremiah to be placed in the courtyard of the guard and given bread from the

ᵃ*1* Hebrew *Coniah,* a variant of *Jehoiachin*
ᵇ*5* Or *Chaldeans*; also in verses 8, 9, 13 and 14
ᶜ*10* Or *Chaldean*; also in verse 11

street of the bakers each day until all the bread in the city was gone. So Jeremiah remained in the courtyard of the guard.

Jeremiah Thrown Into a Cistern

38 Shephatiah son of Mattan, Gedaliah son of Pashhur, Jehucal[a] son of Shelemiah, and Pashhur son of Malkijah heard what Jeremiah was telling all the people when he said, ²"This is what the LORD says: 'Whoever stays in this city will die by the sword, famine or plague, but whoever goes over to the Babylonians[b] will live. He will escape with his life; he will live.' ³And this is what the LORD says: 'This city will certainly be handed over to the army of the king of Babylon, who will capture it.'"

⁴Then the officials said to the king, "This man should be put to death. He is discouraging the soldiers who are left in this city, as well as all the people, by the things he is saying to them. This man is not seeking the good of these people but their ruin."

⁵"He is in your hands," King Zedekiah answered. "The king can do nothing to oppose you."

⁶So they took Jeremiah and put him into the cistern of Malkijah, the king's son, which was in the courtyard of the guard. They lowered Jeremiah by ropes into the cistern; it had no water in it, only mud, and Jeremiah sank down into the mud.

> 66 *A godly man is a praying man. As soon as grace is poured in, prayer is poured out. Prayer is the soul's traffic with Heaven; God comes down to us by his Spirit, and we go up to him by prayer.* 99
>
> T. WATSON

⁷But Ebed-Melech, a Cushite,[c] an official[d] in the royal palace, heard that they had put Jeremiah into the cistern. While the king was sitting in the Benjamin Gate, ⁸Ebed-Melech went out of the palace and said to him, ⁹"My lord the king, these men have acted wickedly in all they have done to Jeremiah the prophet. They have thrown him into a cistern, where he will starve to death when there is no longer any bread in the city."

¹⁰Then the king commanded Ebed-Melech the Cushite, "Take thirty men from here with you and lift Jeremiah the prophet out of the cistern before he dies."

¹¹So Ebed-Melech took the men with him and went to a room under the treasury in the palace. He took some old rags and worn-out clothes from there and let them down with ropes to Jeremiah in the cistern. ¹²Ebed-Melech the Cushite said to Jeremiah, "Put these old rags and worn-out clothes under your arms to pad the ropes." Jeremiah did so, ¹³and they pulled him up with the ropes and lifted him out of the cistern. And Jeremiah remained in the courtyard of the guard.

Zedekiah Questions Jeremiah Again

¹⁴Then King Zedekiah sent for Jeremiah the prophet and had him brought to the third entrance to the temple of the LORD. "I am going to ask you something," the king said to Jeremiah. "Do not hide anything from me."

¹⁵Jeremiah said to Zedekiah, "If I give you an answer, will you not kill me? Even if I did give you counsel, you would not listen to me."

¹⁶But King Zedekiah swore this oath secretly to Jeremiah: "As surely as the LORD lives, who has given us breath, I will neither kill you nor hand you over to those who are seeking your life."

¹⁷Then Jeremiah said to Zedekiah, "This is what the LORD God Almighty, the God of Israel, says: 'If you surrender to the officers of the king of Babylon, your life will be spared and this city will not be burned down; you and your family will live. ¹⁸But if you will not surrender to the officers of the king of Babylon, this city will be handed over to the Babylonians and they will burn it down; you yourself will not escape from their hands.'"

¹⁹King Zedekiah said to Jeremiah, "I am afraid of the Jews who have gone over to the Babylonians, for the Babylonians may hand me over to them and they will mistreat me."

---

[a] 1 Hebrew *Jucal*, a variant of *Jehucal*
[b] 2 Or *Chaldeans*; also in verses 18, 19 and 23
[c] 7 Probably from the upper Nile region
[d] 7 Or *a eunuch*

20"They will not hand you over," Jeremiah replied. "Obey the LORD by doing what I tell you. Then it will go well with you, and your life will be spared. 21But if you refuse to surrender, this is what the LORD has revealed to me: 22All the women left in the palace of the king of Judah will be brought out to the officials of the king of Babylon. Those women will say to you:

" 'They misled you and overcame
    you—
  those trusted friends of yours.
Your feet are sunk in the mud;
  your friends have deserted you.'

23"All your wives and children will be brought out to the Babylonians. You yourself will not escape from their hands but will be captured by the king of Babylon; and this city will*a* be burned down."

24Then Zedekiah said to Jeremiah, "Do not let anyone know about this conversation, or you may die. 25If the officials hear that I talked with you, and they come to you and say, 'Tell us what you said to the king and what the king said to you; do not hide it from us or we will kill you,' 26then tell them, 'I was pleading with the king not to send me back to Jonathan's house to die there.' "

27All the officials did come to Jeremiah and question him, and he told them everything the king had ordered him to say. So they said no more to him, for no one had heard his conversation with the king.

28And Jeremiah remained in the courtyard of the guard until the day Jerusalem was captured.

The Fall of Jerusalem

39 This is how Jerusalem was taken: 1In the ninth year of Zedekiah king of Judah, in the tenth month, Nebuchadnezzar king of Babylon marched against Jerusalem with his whole army and laid siege to it. 2And on the ninth day of the fourth month of Zedekiah's eleventh year, the city wall was broken through. 3Then all the officials of the king of Babylon came and took seats in the Middle Gate: Nergal-Sharezer of Samgar, Nebo-Sarsekim*b* a chief officer, Nergal-Sharezer a high official and all the other officials of the king of Babylon. 4When

Zedekiah king of Judah and all the soldiers saw them, they fled; they left the city at night by way of the king's garden, through the gate between the two walls, and headed toward the Arabah.*c*

5But the Babylonian*d* army pursued them and overtook Zedekiah in the plains of Jericho. They captured him and took him to Nebuchadnezzar king of Babylon at Riblah in the land of Hamath, where he pronounced sentence on him. 6There at Riblah the king of Babylon slaughtered the sons of Zedekiah before his eyes and also killed all the nobles of Judah. 7Then he put out Zedekiah's eyes and bound him with bronze shackles to take him to Babylon.

8The Babylonians*e* set fire to the royal palace and the houses of the people and broke down the walls of Jerusalem. 9Nebuzaradan commander of the imperial guard carried into exile to Babylon the people who remained in the city, along with those who had gone over to him, and the rest of the people. 10But Nebuzaradan the commander of the guard left behind in the land of Judah some of the poor people, who owned nothing; and at that time he gave them vineyards and fields.

11Now Nebuchadnezzar king of Babylon had given these orders about Jeremiah through Nebuzaradan commander of the imperial guard: 12"Take him and look after him; don't harm him but do for him whatever he asks." 13So Nebuzaradan the commander of the guard, Nebushazban a chief officer, Nergal-Sharezer a high official and all the other officers of the king of Babylon 14sent and had Jeremiah taken out of the courtyard of the guard. They turned him over to Gedaliah son of Ahikam, the son of Shaphan, to take him back to his home. So he remained among his own people.

15While Jeremiah had been confined in the courtyard of the guard, the word of the LORD came to him: 16"Go and tell Ebed-Melech the Cushite, 'This is what the LORD Almighty, the God of Israel, says: I am about to fulfill my words against this

a23 Or *and you will cause this city to*
b3 Or *Nergal-Sharezer, Samgar-Nebo, Sarsekim*
c4 Or *the Jordan Valley*   *d5* Or *Chaldean*
e8 Or *Chaldeans*

city through disaster, not prosperity. At that time they will be fulfilled before your eyes. ¹⁷But I will rescue you on that day, declares the LORD; you will not be handed over to those you fear. ¹⁸I will save you; you will not fall by the sword but will escape with your life, because you trust in me, declares the LORD.'"

Jeremiah Freed

40 The word came to Jeremiah from the LORD after Nebuzaradan commander of the imperial guard had released him at Ramah. He had found Jeremiah bound in chains among all the captives from Jerusalem and Judah who were being carried into exile to Babylon. ²When the commander of the guard found Jeremiah, he said to him, "The LORD your God decreed this disaster for this place. ³And now the LORD has brought it about; he has done just as he said he would. All this happened because you people sinned against the LORD and did not obey him. ⁴But today I am freeing you from the chains on your wrists. Come

> THE LORD has brought it about; he has done just as he said he would.
>
> JEREMIAH 40:3

with me to Babylon, if you like, and I will look after you; but if you do not want to, then don't come. Look, the whole country lies before you; go wherever you please." ⁵However, before Jeremiah turned to go,ᵃ Nebuzaradan added, "Go back to Gedaliah son of Ahikam, the son of Shaphan, whom the king of Babylon has appointed over the towns of Judah, and live with him among the people, or go anywhere else you please."

Then the commander gave him provisions and a present and let him go. ⁶So Jeremiah went to Gedaliah son of Ahikam at Mizpah and stayed with him among the people who were left behind in the land.

Gedaliah Assassinated

⁷When all the army officers and their men who were still in the open country heard that the king of Babylon had ap-

pointed Gedaliah son of Ahikam as governor over the land and had put him in charge of the men, women and children who were the poorest in the land and who had not been carried into exile to Babylon, ⁸they came to Gedaliah at Mizpah—Ishmael son of Nethaniah, Johanan and Jonathan the sons of Kareah, Seraiah son of Tanhumeth, the sons of Ephai the Netophathite, and Jaazaniahᵇ the son of the Maacathite, and their men. ⁹Gedaliah son of Ahikam, the son of Shaphan, took an oath to reassure them and their men. "Do not be afraid to serve the Babylonians,ᶜ" he said. "Settle down in the land and serve the king of Babylon, and it will go well with you. ¹⁰I myself will stay at Mizpah to represent you before the Babylonians who come to us, but you are to harvest the wine, summer fruit and oil, and put them in your storage jars, and live in the towns you have taken over."

¹¹When all the Jews in Moab, Ammon, Edom and all the other countries heard that the king of Babylon had left a remnant in Judah and had appointed Gedaliah son of Ahikam, the son of Shaphan, as governor over them, ¹²they all came back to the land of Judah, to Gedaliah at Mizpah, from all the countries where they had been scattered. And they harvested an abundance of wine and summer fruit.

¹³Johanan son of Kareah and all the army officers still in the open country came to Gedaliah at Mizpah ¹⁴and said to him, "Don't you know that Baalis king of the Ammonites has sent Ishmael son of Nethaniah to take your life?" But Gedaliah son of Ahikam did not believe them.

¹⁵Then Johanan son of Kareah said privately to Gedaliah in Mizpah, "Let me go and kill Ishmael son of Nethaniah, and no one will know it. Why should he take your life and cause all the Jews who are gathered around you to be scattered and the remnant of Judah to perish?"

¹⁶But Gedaliah son of Ahikam said to Johanan son of Kareah, "Don't do such a thing! What you are saying about Ishmael is not true."

ᵃ5 Or *Jeremiah answered*   ᵇ8 Hebrew *Jezaniah,* a variant of *Jaazaniah*   ᶜ9 Or *Chaldeans;* also in verse 10

41 In the seventh month Ishmael son of Nethaniah, the son of Elishama, who was of royal blood and had been one of the king's officers, came with ten men to Gedaliah son of Ahikam at Mizpah. While they were eating together there, ²Ishmael son of Nethaniah and the ten men who were with him got up and struck down Gedaliah son of Ahikam, the son of Shaphan, with the sword, killing the one whom the king of Babylon had appointed as governor over the land. ³Ishmael also killed all the Jews who were with Gedaliah at Mizpah, as well as the Babylonian[a] soldiers who were there.

⁴The day after Gedaliah's assassination, before anyone knew about it, ⁵eighty men who had shaved off their beards, torn their clothes and cut themselves came from Shechem, Shiloh and Samaria, bringing grain offerings and incense with them to the house of the Lord. ⁶Ishmael son of Nethaniah went out from Mizpah to meet them, weeping as he went. When he met them, he said, "Come to Gedaliah son of Ahikam." ⁷When they went into the city, Ishmael son of Nethaniah and the men who were with him slaughtered them and threw them into a cistern. ⁸But ten of them said to Ishmael, "Don't kill us! We have wheat and barley, oil and honey, hidden in a field." So he let them alone and did not kill them with the others. ⁹Now the cistern where he threw all the bodies of the men he had killed along with Gedaliah was the one King Asa had made as part of his defense against Baasha king of Israel. Ishmael son of Nethaniah filled it with the dead.

¹⁰Ishmael made captives of all the rest of the people who were in Mizpah—the king's daughters along with all the others who were left there, over whom Nebuzaradan commander of the imperial guard had appointed Gedaliah son of Ahikam. Ishmael son of Nethaniah took them captive and set out to cross over to the Ammonites.

¹¹When Johanan son of Kareah and all the army officers who were with him heard about all the crimes Ishmael son of Nethaniah had committed, ¹²they took all their men and went to fight Ishmael son of Nethaniah. They caught up with him near the great pool in Gibeon. ¹³When all the people Ishmael had with him saw Johanan son of Kareah and the army officers who were with him, they were glad. ¹⁴All the people Ishmael had taken captive at Mizpah turned and went over to Johanan son of Kareah. ¹⁵But Ishmael son of Nethaniah and eight of his men escaped from Johanan and fled to the Ammonites.

Flight to Egypt

¹⁶Then Johanan son of Kareah and all the army officers who were with him led away all the survivors from Mizpah whom he had recovered from Ishmael son of Nethaniah after he had assassinated Gedaliah son of Ahikam: the soldiers, women, children and court officials he had brought from Gibeon. ¹⁷And they went on, stopping at Geruth Kimham near Bethlehem on their way to Egypt ¹⁸to escape the Babylonians.[b] They were afraid of them because Ishmael son of Nethaniah had killed Gedaliah son of Ahikam, whom the king of Babylon had appointed as governor over the land.

42 Then all the army officers, including Johanan son of Kareah and Jezaniah[c] son of Hoshaiah, and all the people from the least to the greatest approached ²Jeremiah the prophet and said to him, "Please hear our petition and pray to the Lord your God for this entire remnant. For as you now see, though we were once many, now only a few are left. ³Pray that the Lord your God will tell us where we should go and what we should do."

⁴"I have heard you," replied Jeremiah the prophet. "I will certainly pray to the Lord your God as you have requested; I will tell you everything the Lord says and will keep nothing back from you."

⁵Then they said to Jeremiah, "May the Lord be a true and faithful witness against us if we do not act in accordance with everything the Lord your God sends you to tell us. ⁶Whether it is favorable or unfavorable, we will obey the Lord our God, to whom we are sending you, so that it will go well with us, for we will obey the Lord our God."

---

[a]3 Or *Chaldean*   [b]18 Or *Chaldeans*
[c]1 Hebrew; Septuagint (see also 43:2) *Azariah*

⁷Ten days later the word of the LORD came to Jeremiah. ⁸So he called together Johanan son of Kareah and all the army officers who were with him and all the people from the least to the greatest. ⁹He said to them, "This is what the LORD, the God of Israel, to whom you sent me to present your petition, says: ¹⁰'If you stay in this land, I will build you up and not tear you down; I will plant you and not uproot you, for I am grieved over the disaster I have inflicted on you. ¹¹Do not be afraid of the king of Babylon, whom you now fear. Do not be afraid of him, declares the LORD, for I am with you and will save you and deliver you from his hands. ¹²I will show you compassion so that he will have compassion on you and restore you to your land.'

¹³"However, if you say, 'We will not stay in this land,' and so disobey the LORD your God, ¹⁴and if you say, 'No, we will go and live in Egypt, where we will not see war or hear the trumpet or be hungry for bread,' ¹⁵then hear the word of the LORD, O remnant of Judah. This is what the LORD Almighty, the God of Israel, says: 'If you are determined to go to Egypt and you do go to settle there, ¹⁶then the sword you fear will overtake you there, and the famine you dread will follow you into Egypt, and there you will die. ¹⁷Indeed, all who are determined to go to Egypt to settle there will die by the sword, famine and plague; not one of them will survive or escape the disaster I will bring on them.' ¹⁸This is what the LORD Almighty, the God of Israel, says: 'As my anger and wrath have been poured out on those who lived in Jerusalem, so will my wrath be poured out on you when you go to Egypt. You will be an object of cursing and horror, of condemnation and reproach; you will never see this place again.'

¹⁹"O remnant of Judah, the LORD has told you, 'Do not go to Egypt.' Be sure of this: I warn you today ²⁰that you made a fatal mistake[a] when you sent me to the LORD your God and said, 'Pray to the LORD our God for us; tell us everything he says and we will do it.' ²¹I have told you today, but you still have not obeyed the LORD your God in all he sent me to tell you. ²²So now, be sure of this: You will die by the sword, famine and plague in the place where you want to go to settle."

43 When Jeremiah finished telling the people all the words of the LORD their God—everything the LORD had sent him to tell them— ²Azariah son of Hoshaiah and Johanan son of Kareah and all the arrogant men said to Jeremiah, "You are lying! The LORD our God has not sent you to say, 'You must not go to Egypt to settle there.' ³But Baruch son of Neriah is inciting you against us to hand us over to the Babylonians,[b] so they may kill us or carry us into exile to Babylon."

⁴So Johanan son of Kareah and all the army officers and all the people disobeyed the LORD's command to stay in the land of Judah. ⁵Instead, Johanan son of Kareah and all the army officers led away all the remnant of Judah who had come back to live in the land of Judah from all the nations where they had been scattered. ⁶They also led away all the men, women and children and the king's daughters whom Nebuzaradan commander of the imperial guard had left with Gedaliah son of Ahikam, the son of Shaphan, and Jeremiah the prophet and Baruch son of Neriah. ⁷So they entered Egypt in disobedience to the LORD and went as far as Tahpanhes.

⁸In Tahpanhes the word of the LORD came to Jeremiah: ⁹"While the Jews are watching, take some large stones with you and bury them in clay in the brick pavement at the entrance to Pharaoh's palace in Tahpanhes. ¹⁰Then say to them, 'This is what the LORD Almighty, the God of Israel, says: I will send for my servant Nebuchadnezzar king of Babylon, and I will set his throne over these stones I have buried here; he will spread his royal canopy above them. ¹¹He will come and attack Egypt, bringing death to those destined for death, captivity to those destined for captivity, and the sword to those destined for the sword. ¹²He[c] will set fire to the temples of the gods of Egypt; he will burn their temples and take their gods captive. As a shepherd wraps his garment around him, so will he wrap Egypt around himself and

---

[a]20 Or *you erred in your hearts*   [b]3 Or *Chaldeans*   [c]12 Or *I*

depart from there unscathed. [13]There in the temple of the sun[a] in Egypt he will demolish the sacred pillars and will burn down the temples of the gods of Egypt.'"

Disaster Because of Idolatry

44 This word came to Jeremiah concerning all the Jews living in Lower Egypt—in Migdol, Tahpanhes and Memphis[b]—and in Upper Egypt[c]: [2]"This is what the LORD Almighty, the God of Israel, says: You saw the great disaster I brought on Jerusalem and on all the towns of Judah. Today they lie deserted and in ruins [3]because of the evil they have done. They provoked me to anger by burning incense and by worshiping other gods that neither they nor you nor your fathers ever knew. [4]Again and again I sent my servants the prophets, who said, 'Do not do this detestable thing that I hate!' [5]But they did not listen or pay attention; they did not turn from their wickedness or stop burning incense to other gods. [6]Therefore, my fierce anger was poured out; it raged against the towns of Judah and the streets of Jerusalem and made them the desolate ruins they are today.

[7]"Now this is what the LORD God Almighty, the God of Israel, says: Why bring such great disaster on yourselves by cutting off from Judah the men and women, the children and infants, and so leave yourselves without a remnant? [8]Why provoke me to anger with what your hands have made, burning incense to other gods in Egypt, where you have come to live? You will destroy yourselves and make yourselves an object of cursing and reproach among all the nations on earth. [9]Have you forgotten the wickedness committed by your fathers and by the kings and queens of Judah and the wickedness committed by you and your wives in the land of Judah and the streets of Jerusalem? [10]To this day they have not humbled themselves or shown reverence, nor have they followed my law and the decrees I set before you and your fathers.

[11]"Therefore, this is what the LORD Almighty, the God of Israel, says: I am determined to bring disaster on you and to destroy all Judah. [12]I will take away the remnant of Judah who were determined to go to Egypt to settle there. They will all perish in Egypt; they will fall by the sword or die from famine. From the least to the greatest, they will die by sword or famine. They will become an object of cursing and horror, of condemnation and reproach. [13]I will punish those who live in Egypt with the sword, famine and plague, as I punished Jerusalem. [14]None of the remnant of Judah who have gone to live in Egypt will escape or survive to return to the land of Judah, to which they long to return and live; none will return except a few fugitives."

[15]Then all the men who knew that their wives were burning incense to other gods, along with all the women who were present—a large assembly—and all the people living in Lower and Upper Egypt,[d] said to Jeremiah, [16]"We will not listen to the message you have spoken to us in the name of the LORD! [17]We will certainly do everything we said we would: We will burn incense to the Queen of Heaven and will pour out drink offerings to her just as we and our fathers, our kings and our officials did in the towns of Judah and in the streets of Jerusalem. At that time we had plenty of food and were well off and suffered no harm. [18]But ever since we stopped burning incense to the Queen of Heaven and pouring out drink offerings to her, we have had nothing and have been perishing by sword and famine."

[19]The women added, "When we burned incense to the Queen of Heaven and poured out drink offerings to her, did not our husbands know that we were making cakes like her image and pouring out drink offerings to her?"

[20]Then Jeremiah said to all the people, both men and women, who were answering him, [21]"Did not the LORD remember and think about the incense burned in the towns of Judah and the streets of Jerusalem by you and your fathers, your kings and your officials and the people of the land? [22]When the LORD could no longer endure your wicked actions and the detestable things you did, your land became an object of cursing and a desolate waste

---

[a]13 Or in Heliopolis [b]1 Hebrew Noph
[c]1 Hebrew in Pathros [d]15 Hebrew in Egypt and Pathros

without inhabitants, as it is today. ²³Because you have burned incense and have sinned against the LORD and have not obeyed him or followed his law or his decrees or his stipulations, this disaster has come upon you, as you now see."

²⁴Then Jeremiah said to all the people, including the women, "Hear the word of the LORD, all you people of Judah in Egypt. ²⁵This is what the LORD Almighty, the God of Israel, says: You and your wives have shown by your actions what you promised when you said, 'We will certainly carry out the vows we made to burn incense and pour out drink offerings to the Queen of Heaven.'

"Go ahead then, do what you promised! Keep your vows! ²⁶But hear the word of the LORD, all Jews living in Egypt: 'I swear by my great name,' says the LORD, 'that no one from Judah living anywhere in Egypt will ever again invoke my name or swear, "As surely as the Sovereign LORD lives." ²⁷For I am watching over them for harm, not for good; the Jews in Egypt will perish by sword and famine until they are all destroyed. ²⁸Those who escape the sword and return to the land of Judah from Egypt will be very few. Then the whole remnant of Judah who came to live in Egypt will know whose word will stand—mine or theirs.

²⁹" 'This will be the sign to you that I will punish you in this place,' declares the LORD, 'so that you will know that my threats of harm against you will surely stand.' ³⁰This is what the LORD says: 'I am going to hand Pharaoh Hophra king of Egypt over to his enemies who seek his life, just as I handed Zedekiah king of Judah over to Nebuchadnezzar king of Babylon, the enemy who was seeking his life.' "

A Message to Baruch

45 This is what Jeremiah the prophet told Baruch son of Neriah in the fourth year of Jehoiakim son of Josiah king of Judah, after Baruch had written on a scroll the words Jeremiah was then dictating: ²"This is what the LORD, the God of Israel, says to you, Baruch: ³You said, 'Woe to me! The LORD has added sorrow to my pain; I am worn out with groaning and find no rest.' "

⁴The LORD said, "Say this to him: 'This is what the LORD says: I will overthrow what I have built and uproot what I have planted, throughout the land. ⁵Should you then seek great things for yourself? Seek them not. For I will bring disaster on all people, declares the LORD, but wherever you go I will let you escape with your life.' "

A Message About Egypt

46 This is the word of the LORD that came to Jeremiah the prophet concerning the nations:

²Concerning Egypt:

This is the message against the army of Pharaoh Neco king of Egypt, which was defeated at Carchemish on the Euphrates River by Nebuchadnezzar king of Babylon in the fourth year of Jehoiakim son of Josiah king of Judah:

³ "Prepare your shields, both large
        and small,
    and march out for battle!
⁴Harness the horses,
        mount the steeds!
Take your positions
        with helmets on!
Polish your spears,
        put on your armor!
⁵What do I see?
    They are terrified,
    they are retreating,
        their warriors are defeated.
They flee in haste
        without looking back,
    and there is terror on every side,"
                declares the LORD.
⁶ "The swift cannot flee
        nor the strong escape.
In the north by the River Euphrates
        they stumble and fall.

⁷ "Who is this that rises like the Nile,
        like rivers of surging waters?
⁸Egypt rises like the Nile,
        like rivers of surging waters.
    She says, 'I will rise and cover the
        earth;
    I will destroy cities and their
        people.'
⁹Charge, O horses!
    Drive furiously, O charioteers!

March on, O warriors—
   men of Cush[a] and Put who carry
      shields,
   men of Lydia who draw the bow.
10 But that day belongs to the Lord, the
      LORD Almighty—
   a day of vengeance, for vengeance
      on his foes.
The sword will devour till it is
      satisfied,
   till it has quenched its thirst with
      blood.
For the Lord, the LORD Almighty,
   will offer sacrifice
in the land of the north by the
      River Euphrates.

11 "Go up to Gilead and get balm,
   O Virgin Daughter of Egypt.
But you multiply remedies in vain;
   there is no healing for you.
12 The nations will hear of your shame;
   your cries will fill the earth.
One warrior will stumble over
      another;
   both will fall down together."

13 This is the message the LORD spoke to
Jeremiah the prophet about the coming
of Nebuchadnezzar king of Babylon to attack Egypt:

14 "Announce this in Egypt, and
      proclaim it in Migdol;
   proclaim it also in Memphis[b] and
      Tahpanhes:
'Take your positions and get ready,
   for the sword devours those around
      you.'
15 Why will your warriors be laid low?
   They cannot stand, for the LORD
      will push them down.
16 They will stumble repeatedly;
   they will fall over each other.
They will say, 'Get up, let us go back
   to our own people and our native
      lands,
   away from the sword of the
      oppressor.'
17 There they will exclaim,
   'Pharaoh king of Egypt is only a
      loud noise;
   he has missed his opportunity.'
18 "As surely as I live," declares the
      King,
   whose name is the LORD Almighty,

"one will come who is like Tabor
   among the mountains,
   like Carmel by the sea.
19 Pack your belongings for exile,
   you who live in Egypt,
for Memphis will be laid waste
   and lie in ruins without inhabitant.

20 "Egypt is a beautiful heifer,
   but a gadfly is coming
      against her from the north.
21 The mercenaries in her ranks
   are like fattened calves.
They too will turn and flee together,
   they will not stand their ground,
for the day of disaster is coming
      upon them,
   the time for them to be punished.
22 Egypt will hiss like a fleeing serpent
   as the enemy advances in force;
they will come against her with
      axes,
   like men who cut down trees.
23 They will chop down her forest,"
                  declares the LORD,
   "dense though it be.
They are more numerous than
      locusts,
   they cannot be counted.
24 The Daughter of Egypt will be put
      to shame,
   handed over to the people of the
      north."

25 The LORD Almighty, the God of Israel,
says: "I am about to bring punishment on
Amon god of Thebes,[c] on Pharaoh, on
Egypt and her gods and her kings, and
on those who rely on Pharaoh. 26 I will
hand them over to those who seek their
lives, to Nebuchadnezzar king of Babylon
and his officers. Later, however, Egypt
will be inhabited as in times past," declares the LORD.

27 "Do not fear, O Jacob my servant;
   do not be dismayed, O Israel.
I will surely save you out of a distant
      place,
   your descendants from the land of
      their exile.
Jacob will again have peace and
      security,
   and no one will make him afraid.

---

[a]9 That is, the upper Nile region   [b]14 Hebrew
Noph; also in verse 19   [c]25 Hebrew *No*

> DO NOT fear, O Jacob, my servant,
> for I am with you.
>
> JEREMIAH 46:28

28 Do not fear, O Jacob my servant,
for I am with you," declares the
LORD.
"Though I completely destroy all
the nations
among which I scatter you,
I will not completely destroy you.
I will discipline you but only with
justice;
I will not let you go entirely
unpunished."

A Message About the Philistines

47 This is the word of the LORD that
came to Jeremiah the prophet concerning the Philistines before Pharaoh
attacked Gaza:

2 This is what the LORD says:

"See how the waters are rising in the
north;
they will become an overflowing
torrent.
They will overflow the land and
everything in it,
the towns and those who live in
them.
The people will cry out;
all who dwell in the land will wail
3 at the sound of the hoofs of galloping
steeds,
at the noise of enemy chariots
and the rumble of their wheels.
Fathers will not turn to help their
children;
their hands will hang limp.
4 For the day has come
to destroy all the Philistines
and to cut off all survivors
who could help Tyre and Sidon.
The LORD is about to destroy the
Philistines,
the remnant from the coasts of
Caphtor.a
5 Gaza will shave her head in
mourning;
Ashkelon will be silenced.
O remnant on the plain,
how long will you cut yourselves?

6 " 'Ah, sword of the LORD,' ⸢you cry,⸣
'how long till you rest?
Return to your scabbard;
cease and be still.'
7 But how can it rest
when the LORD has commanded it,
when he has ordered it
to attack Ashkelon and the coast?"

> ❝ I have had prayers answered—most
> strangely so sometimes—but I think our
> heavenly Father's loving-kindness has
> been even more evident in what he has
> refused me. ❞
>
> LEWIS CARROLL

A Message About Moab

48 Concerning Moab:

This is what the LORD Almighty, the
God of Israel, says:

"Woe to Nebo, for it will be ruined.
Kiriathaim will be disgraced and
captured;
the strongholdb will be disgraced
and shattered.
2 Moab will be praised no more;
in Heshbonc men will plot her
downfall:
'Come, let us put an end to that
nation.'
You too, O Madmen,d will be
silenced;
the sword will pursue you.
3 Listen to the cries from Horonaim,
cries of great havoc and
destruction.
4 Moab will be broken;
her little ones will cry out.e
5 They go up the way to Luhith,
weeping bitterly as they go;
on the road down to Horonaim
anguished cries over the
destruction are heard.
6 Flee! Run for your lives;
become like a bushf in the desert.

a4 That is, Crete   b1 Or /Misgab
c2 The Hebrew for Heshbon sounds like the
Hebrew for plot.   d2 The name of the Moabite
town Madmen sounds like the Hebrew for be
silenced.   e4 Hebrew; Septuagint /proclaim it
to Zoar   f6 Or like Aroer

7 Since you trust in your deeds and
  riches,
    you too will be taken captive,
and Chemosh will go into exile,
    together with his priests and
    officials.
8 The destroyer will come against
  every town,
    and not a town will escape.
The valley will be ruined
    and the plateau destroyed,
  because the LORD has spoken.
9 Put salt on Moab,
    for she will be laid waste[a];
  her towns will become desolate,
    with no one to live in them.

10 "A curse on him who is lax in doing
  the LORD's work!
    A curse on him who keeps his
    sword from bloodshed!

11 "Moab has been at rest from youth,
    like wine left on its dregs,
  not poured from one jar to another—
    she has not gone into exile.
So she tastes as she did,
    and her aroma is unchanged.
12 But days are coming,"
    declares the LORD,
  "when I will send men who pour
    from jars,
    and they will pour her out;
  they will empty her jars
    and smash her jugs.
13 Then Moab will be ashamed of
  Chemosh,
    as the house of Israel was ashamed
    when they trusted in Bethel.

14 "How can you say, 'We are warriors,
    men valiant in battle'?
15 Moab will be destroyed and her
  towns invaded;
    her finest young men will go down
    in the slaughter,"
  declares the King, whose name is
    the LORD Almighty.
16 "The fall of Moab is at hand;
    her calamity will come quickly.
17 Mourn for her, all who live around
  her,
    all who know her fame;
  say, 'How broken is the mighty
    scepter,
    how broken the glorious staff!'

18 "Come down from your glory
    and sit on the parched ground,
  O inhabitants of the Daughter
    of Dibon,
for he who destroys Moab
    will come up against you
  and ruin your fortified cities.
19 Stand by the road and watch,
    you who live in Aroer.
Ask the man fleeing and the woman
    escaping,
  ask them, 'What has happened?'
20 Moab is disgraced, for she is
  shattered.
    Wail and cry out!
  Announce by the Arnon
    that Moab is destroyed.
21 Judgment has come to the plateau—
    to Holon, Jahzah and Mephaath,
22   to Dibon, Nebo and Beth
    Diblathaim,
23   to Kiriathaim, Beth Gamul and
    Beth Meon,
24   to Kerioth and Bozrah—
  to all the towns of Moab, far and
    near.
25 Moab's horn[b] is cut off;
    her arm is broken,"
              declares the LORD.

26 "Make her drunk,
    for she has defied the LORD.
Let Moab wallow in her vomit;
    let her be an object of ridicule.
27 Was not Israel the object of your
  ridicule?
Was she caught among thieves,
    that you shake your head in scorn
  whenever you speak of her?
28 Abandon your towns and dwell
    among the rocks,
    you who live in Moab.
Be like a dove that makes its nest
    at the mouth of a cave.

29 "We have heard of Moab's pride—
    her overweening pride and conceit,
  her pride and arrogance
    and the haughtiness of her heart.
30 I know her insolence but it is futile,"
              declares the LORD,
  "and her boasts accomplish
    nothing.

[a]9 Or Give wings to Moab, / for she will fly away
[b]25 Horn here symbolizes strength.

³¹ Therefore I wail over Moab,
   for all Moab I cry out,
   I moan for the men of Kir Haraseth.
³² I weep for you, as Jazer weeps,
   O vines of Sibmah.
   Your branches spread as far as
      the sea;
   they reached as far as the sea
      of Jazer.
   The destroyer has fallen
      on your ripened fruit and grapes.
³³ Joy and gladness are gone
   from the orchards and fields
      of Moab.
   I have stopped the flow of wine from
      the presses;
   no one treads them with shouts
      of joy.
   Although there are shouts,
      they are not shouts of joy.

³⁴ "The sound of their cry rises
   from Heshbon to Elealeh and
      Jahaz,
   from Zoar as far as Horonaim and
      Eglath Shelishiyah,
   for even the waters of Nimrim are
      dried up.
³⁵ In Moab I will put an end
   to those who make offerings on the
      high places
   and burn incense to their gods,"
      declares the LORD.
³⁶ "So my heart laments for Moab like
      a flute;
   it laments like a flute for the men
      of Kir Haraseth.
   The wealth they acquired is gone.
³⁷ Every head is shaved
   and every beard cut off;
   every hand is slashed
   and every waist is covered with
      sackcloth.
³⁸ On all the roofs in Moab
   and in the public squares
   there is nothing but mourning,
   for I have broken Moab
   like a jar that no one wants,"
      declares the LORD.

³⁹ "How shattered she is! How they wail!
   How Moab turns her back in
      shame!
   Moab has become an object of
      ridicule,
   an object of horror to all those
      around her."

⁴⁰ This is what the LORD says:

   "Look! An eagle is swooping down,
   spreading its wings over Moab.
⁴¹ Kerioth[a] will be captured
   and the strongholds taken.
   In that day the hearts of Moab's
      warriors
   will be like the heart of a woman
      in labor.
⁴² Moab will be destroyed as a nation
   because she defied the LORD.
⁴³ Terror and pit and snare await you,
   O people of Moab,"
      declares the LORD.
⁴⁴ "Whoever flees from the terror
   will fall into a pit,
   whoever climbs out of the pit
   will be caught in a snare;
   for I will bring upon Moab
   the year of her punishment,"
      declares the LORD.
⁴⁵ "In the shadow of Heshbon
   the fugitives stand helpless,
   for a fire has gone out from Heshbon,
   a blaze from the midst of Sihon;
   it burns the foreheads of Moab,
   the skulls of the noisy boasters.
⁴⁶ Woe to you, O Moab!
   The people of Chemosh are
      destroyed;
   your sons are taken into exile
   and your daughters into captivity.

⁴⁷ "Yet I will restore the fortunes of Moab
   in days to come,"
      declares the LORD.

Here ends the judgment on Moab.

A Message About Ammon

49 Concerning the Ammonites:

This is what the LORD says:

   "Has Israel no sons?
   Has she no heirs?

> 66 A day without prayer is a day
> without blessing, and a life without
> prayer is a life without power. 99
>
> EDWIN HARVEY

ᵃ41 Or The cities

Why then has Molech*ᵃ* taken
possession of Gad?
Why do his people live in its towns?
² But the days are coming,"
declares the LORD,
"when I will sound the battle cry
against Rabbah of the Ammonites;
it will become a mound of ruins,
and its surrounding villages will be
set on fire.
Then Israel will drive out
those who drove her out,"
says the LORD.
³ "Wail, O Heshbon, for Ai is
destroyed!
Cry out, O inhabitants of Rabbah!
Put on sackcloth and mourn;
rush here and there inside the
walls,
for Molech will go into exile,
together with his priests and
officials.
⁴ Why do you boast of your valleys,
boast of your valleys so fruitful?
O unfaithful daughter,
you trust in your riches and say,
'Who will attack me?'
⁵ I will bring terror on you
from all those around you,"
declares the Lord,
the LORD Almighty.
"Every one of you will be driven away,
and no one will gather the fugitives.

⁶ "Yet afterward, I will restore the
fortunes of the Ammonites,"
declares the LORD.

A Message About Edom

⁷ Concerning Edom:

This is what the LORD Almighty says:

"Is there no longer wisdom in
Teman?
Has counsel perished from the
prudent?
Has their wisdom decayed?
⁸ Turn and flee, hide in deep caves,
you who live in Dedan,
for I will bring disaster on Esau
at the time I punish him.
⁹ If grape pickers came to you,
would they not leave a few grapes?
If thieves came during the night,
would they not steal only as much
as they wanted?

¹⁰ But I will strip Esau bare;
I will uncover his hiding places,
so that he cannot conceal himself.
His children, relatives and neighbors
will perish,
and he will be no more.
¹¹ Leave your orphans; I will protect
their lives.
Your widows too can trust in me."

¹² This is what the LORD says: "If those
who do not deserve to drink the cup
must drink it, why should you go unpunished? You will not go unpunished, but
must drink it. ¹³ I swear by myself," declares the LORD, "that Bozrah will become a ruin and an object of horror, of
reproach and of cursing; and all its towns
will be in ruins forever."

¹⁴ I have heard a message from the
LORD:
An envoy was sent to the nations
to say,
"Assemble yourselves to attack it!
Rise up for battle!"
¹⁵ "Now I will make you small among
the nations,
despised among men.
¹⁶ The terror you inspire
and the pride of your heart have
deceived you,
you who live in the clefts of the rocks,
who occupy the heights of the hill.
Though you build your nest as high
as the eagle's,
from there I will bring you down,"
declares the LORD.
¹⁷ "Edom will become an object of
horror;
all who pass by will be appalled
and will scoff
because of all its wounds.
¹⁸ As Sodom and Gomorrah were
overthrown,
along with their neighboring
towns,"
says the LORD,
"so no one will live there;
no man will dwell in it.

¹⁹ "Like a lion coming up from Jordan's
thickets
to a rich pastureland,

ᵃ1 Or *their king*; Hebrew *malcam*; also in verse 3

I will chase Edom from its land in
an instant.
Who is the chosen one I will
appoint for this?
Who is like me and who can
challenge me?
And what shepherd can stand
against me?"
20 Therefore, hear what the LORD has
planned against Edom,
what he has purposed against
those who live in Teman:
The young of the flock will be
dragged away;
he will completely destroy their
pasture because of them.
21 At the sound of their fall the earth
will tremble;
their cry will resound to the
Red Sea.*a*
22 Look! An eagle will soar and swoop
down,
spreading its wings over Bozrah.
In that day the hearts of Edom's
warriors
will be like the heart of a woman
in labor.

A Message About Damascus

23 Concerning Damascus:

"Hamath and Arpad are dismayed,
for they have heard bad news.
They are disheartened,
troubled like*b* the restless sea.
24 Damascus has become feeble,
she has turned to flee
and panic has gripped her;
anguish and pain have seized her,
pain like that of a woman in labor.
25 Why has the city of renown not been
abandoned,
the town in which I delight?
26 Surely, her young men will fall in the
streets;
all her soldiers will be silenced in
that day,"
declares the LORD Almighty.
27 "I will set fire to the walls of Damascus;
it will consume the fortresses of
Ben-Hadad."

A Message About Kedar and Hazor

28 Concerning Kedar and the kingdoms
of Hazor, which Nebuchadnezzar king of
Babylon attacked:

This is what the LORD says:

"Arise, and attack Kedar
and destroy the people of the East.
29 Their tents and their flocks will be
taken;
their shelters will be carried off
with all their goods and camels.
Men will shout to them,
'Terror on every side!'
30 "Flee quickly away!
Stay in deep caves, you who live
in Hazor,"
declares the LORD.
"Nebuchadnezzar king of Babylon
has plotted against you;
he has devised a plan against you.
31 "Arise and attack a nation at ease,
which lives in confidence,"
declares the LORD,
"a nation that has neither gates
nor bars;
its people live alone.
32 Their camels will become plunder,
and their large herds will be booty.
I will scatter to the winds those who
are in distant places*c*
and will bring disaster on them
from every side,"
declares the LORD.
33 "Hazor will become a haunt of jackals,
a desolate place forever.
No one will live there;
no man will dwell in it."

A Message About Elam

34 This is the word of the LORD that
came to Jeremiah the prophet concerning Elam, early in the reign of Zedekiah
king of Judah:

35 This is what the LORD Almighty says:

"See, I will break the bow of Elam,
the mainstay of their might.
36 I will bring against Elam the four
winds
from the four quarters of the
heavens;
I will scatter them to the four winds,
and there will not be a nation
where Elam's exiles do not go.

---

a21 Hebrew *Yam Suph*; that is, Sea of Reeds
b23 Hebrew *on* or *by*   *c32* Or *who clip the hair
by their foreheads*

³⁷ I will shatter Elam before their foes,
      before those who seek their lives;
   I will bring disaster upon them,
      even my fierce anger,"
            declares the LORD.
   "I will pursue them with the sword
      until I have made an end of them.
³⁸ I will set my throne in Elam
      and destroy her king and officials,"
            declares the LORD.
³⁹ "Yet I will restore the fortunes of Elam
      in days to come,"
            declares the LORD.

A Message About Babylon

50 This is the word the LORD spoke
   through Jeremiah the prophet
concerning Babylon and the land of the
Babylonians[a]:

² "Announce and proclaim among
         the nations,
      lift up a banner and proclaim it;
      keep nothing back, but say,
   'Babylon will be captured;
      Bel will be put to shame,
      Marduk filled with terror.
   Her images will be put to shame
      and her idols filled with terror.'
³ A nation from the north will attack her
      and lay waste her land.
   No one will live in it;
      both men and animals will flee
         away.

⁴ "In those days, at that time,"
      declares the LORD,
   "the people of Israel and the people
         of Judah together
   will go in tears to seek the LORD
      their God.
⁵ They will ask the way to Zion
      and turn their faces toward it.
   They will come and bind themselves
         to the LORD
      in an everlasting covenant
      that will not be forgotten.

⁶ "My people have been lost sheep;
      their shepherds have led them
         astray
      and caused them to roam on the
         mountains.
   They wandered over mountain and
         hill
      and forgot their own resting place.

> "THEY will come and bind themselves
>   to the LORD
> in an everlasting covenant
> that will not be forgotten."
>
> JEREMIAH 50:5

⁷ Whoever found them devoured them;
      their enemies said, 'We are not
         guilty,
   for they sinned against the LORD,
      their true pasture,
      the LORD, the hope of their
         fathers.'

⁸ "Flee out of Babylon;
      leave the land of the Babylonians,
      and be like the goats that lead
         the flock.
⁹ For I will stir up and bring against
         Babylon
      an alliance of great nations from
         the land of the north.
   They will take up their positions
         against her,
      and from the north she will
         be captured.
   Their arrows will be like skilled
         warriors
      who do not return empty-handed.
¹⁰ So Babylonia[b] will be plundered;
      all who plunder her will have
         their fill,"
            declares the LORD.

¹¹ "Because you rejoice and are glad,
      you who pillage my inheritance,
   because you frolic like a heifer
         threshing grain
      and neigh like stallions,
¹² your mother will be greatly
         ashamed;
      she who gave you birth will be
         disgraced.
   She will be the least of the nations—
      a wilderness, a dry land, a desert.
¹³ Because of the LORD's anger she will
         not be inhabited
      but will be completely desolate.
   All who pass Babylon will be horrified
         and scoff
      because of all her wounds.

---

[a]1 Or *Chaldeans*; also in verses 8, 25, 35 and 45
[b]10 Or *Chaldea*

¹⁴ "Take up your positions around
    Babylon,
  all you who draw the bow.
  Shoot at her! Spare no arrows,
    for she has sinned against the LORD.
¹⁵ Shout against her on every side!
  She surrenders, her towers fall,
    her walls are torn down.
  Since this is the vengeance of
    the LORD,
  take vengeance on her;
    do to her as she has done to others.
¹⁶ Cut off from Babylon the sower,
    and the reaper with his sickle
    at harvest.
  Because of the sword of the
    oppressor
  let everyone return to his own
    people,
  let everyone flee to his own land.

¹⁷ "Israel is a scattered flock
    that lions have chased away.
  The first to devour him
    was the king of Assyria;
  the last to crush his bones
    was Nebuchadnezzar king of
    Babylon."

¹⁸ Therefore this is what the LORD Almighty, the God of Israel, says:

  "I will punish the king of Babylon
    and his land
  as I punished the king of Assyria.
¹⁹ But I will bring Israel back to his own
    pasture
  and he will graze on Carmel and
    Bashan;
  his appetite will be satisfied
    on the hills of Ephraim and Gilead.
²⁰ In those days, at that time,"
    declares the LORD,
  "search will be made for Israel's guilt,
    but there will be none,
  and for the sins of Judah,
    but none will be found,
  for I will forgive the remnant
    I spare.

²¹ "Attack the land of Merathaim
    and those who live in Pekod.
  Pursue, kill and completely destroy*
    them,"
      declares the LORD.
  "Do everything I have commanded
    you.

²² The noise of battle is in the land,
    the noise of great destruction!
²³ How broken and shattered
    is the hammer of the whole earth!
  How desolate is Babylon
    among the nations!
²⁴ I set a trap for you, O Babylon,
    and you were caught before you
    knew it;
  you were found and captured
    because you opposed the LORD.
²⁵ The LORD has opened his arsenal
    and brought out the weapons of his
    wrath,
  for the Sovereign LORD Almighty has
    work to do
  in the land of the Babylonians.
²⁶ Come against her from afar.
  Break open her granaries;
    pile her up like heaps of grain.
  Completely destroy her
    and leave her no remnant.
²⁷ Kill all her young bulls;
    let them go down to the slaughter!
  Woe to them! For their day has come,
    the time for them to be punished.
²⁸ Listen to the fugitives and refugees
    from Babylon
  declaring in Zion
  how the LORD our God has taken
    vengeance,
  vengeance for his temple.

²⁹ "Summon archers against Babylon,
    all those who draw the bow.
  Encamp all around her;
    let no one escape.
  Repay her for her deeds;
    do to her as she has done.
  For she has defied the LORD,
    the Holy One of Israel.
³⁰ Therefore, her young men will fall in
    the streets;
  all her soldiers will be silenced in
    that day,"
      declares the LORD.
³¹ "See, I am against you, O arrogant
    one,"
    declares the Lord, the LORD
    Almighty,
  "for your day has come,
    the time for you to be punished.

---

a21 The Hebrew term refers to the irrevocable
giving over of things or persons to the LORD, often
by totally destroying them; also in verse 26.

³²The arrogant one will stumble
    and fall
  and no one will help her up;
I will kindle a fire in her towns
  that will consume all who are
    around her."

³³This is what the LORD Almighty says:

"The people of Israel are oppressed,
  and the people of Judah as well.
All their captors hold them fast,
  refusing to let them go.
³⁴Yet their Redeemer is strong;
  the LORD Almighty is his name.
He will vigorously defend their
    cause
  so that he may bring rest to
    their land,
  but unrest to those who live in
    Babylon.

³⁵"A sword against the Babylonians!"
    declares the LORD—
"against those who live in Babylon
  and against her officials and
    wise men!
³⁶A sword against her false prophets!
  They will become fools.
A sword against her warriors!
  They will be filled with terror.
³⁷A sword against her horses and
    chariots
  and all the foreigners in her
    ranks!
  They will become women.
A sword against her treasures!
  They will be plundered.
³⁸A drought on*ª* her waters!
  They will dry up.
For it is a land of idols,
  idols that will go mad with
    terror.

³⁹"So desert creatures and hyenas will
    live there,
  and there the owl will dwell.
It will never again be inhabited
  or lived in from generation to
    generation.
⁴⁰As God overthrew Sodom and
    Gomorrah
  along with their neighboring
    towns,"
            declares the LORD,
"so no one will live there;
  no man will dwell in it.

⁴¹"Look! An army is coming from
    the north;
  a great nation and many kings
    are being stirred up from the ends
    of the earth.
⁴²They are armed with bows and
    spears;
  they are cruel and without mercy.
They sound like the roaring sea
  as they ride on their horses;
they come like men in battle
    formation
  to attack you, O Daughter of
    Babylon.
⁴³The king of Babylon has heard
    reports about them,
  and his hands hang limp.
Anguish has gripped him,
  pain like that of a woman in labor.
⁴⁴Like a lion coming up from Jordan's
    thickets
  to a rich pastureland,
I will chase Babylon from its land in
    an instant.
  Who is the chosen one I will
    appoint for this?
Who is like me and who can
    challenge me?
  And what shepherd can stand
    against me?"
⁴⁵Therefore, hear what the LORD has
    planned against Babylon,
  what he has purposed against the
    land of the Babylonians:
The young of the flock will be
    dragged away;
  he will completely destroy their
    pasture because of them.
⁴⁶At the sound of Babylon's capture the
    earth will tremble;
  its cry will resound among the
    nations.

51 This is what the LORD says:

"See, I will stir up the spirit of a
    destroyer
  against Babylon and the people of
    Leb Kamai.*ᵇ*
²I will send foreigners to Babylon
  to winnow her and to devastate
    her land;

ª38 Or *A sword against*   *ᵇ1 Leb Kamai* is a
cryptogram for Chaldea, that is, Babylonia.

they will oppose her on every side
  in the day of her disaster.
³ Let not the archer string his bow,
  nor let him put on his armor.
Do not spare her young men;
  completely destroy[a] her army.
⁴ They will fall down slain in
      Babylon,[b]
  fatally wounded in her streets.
⁵ For Israel and Judah have not been
      forsaken
  by their God, the LORD Almighty,
though their land[c] is full of guilt
  before the Holy One of Israel.

⁶ "Flee from Babylon!
  Run for your lives!
  Do not be destroyed because of
      her sins.
It is time for the LORD's vengeance;
  he will pay her what she deserves.
⁷ Babylon was a gold cup in the LORD's
      hand;
  she made the whole earth drunk.
The nations drank her wine;
  therefore they have now gone mad.
⁸ Babylon will suddenly fall and be
      broken.
  Wail over her!
Get balm for her pain;
  perhaps she can be healed.

⁹ " 'We would have healed Babylon,
  but she cannot be healed;
let us leave her and each go to his
      own land,
  for her judgment reaches to the
      skies,
  it rises as high as the clouds.'

¹⁰ " 'The LORD has vindicated us;
  come, let us tell in Zion
  what the LORD our God has done.'

¹¹ "Sharpen the arrows,
  take up the shields!
The LORD has stirred up the kings of
      the Medes,
  because his purpose is to destroy
      Babylon.
The LORD will take vengeance,
  vengeance for his temple.
¹² Lift up a banner against the walls of
      Babylon!
Reinforce the guard,
  station the watchmen,
  prepare an ambush!

The LORD will carry out his
      purpose,
  his decree against the people of
      Babylon.
¹³ You who live by many waters
  and are rich in treasures,
your end has come,
  the time for you to be cut off.
¹⁴ The LORD Almighty has sworn by
      himself:
  I will surely fill you with men, as
      with a swarm of locusts,
  and they will shout in triumph
      over you.

¹⁵ "He made the earth by his power;
  he founded the world by his
      wisdom
  and stretched out the heavens by
      his understanding.
¹⁶ When he thunders, the waters in the
      heavens roar;
  he makes clouds rise from the ends
      of the earth.
He sends lightning with the rain
  and brings out the wind from his
      storehouses.

¹⁷ "Every man is senseless and without
      knowledge;
  every goldsmith is shamed by his
      idols.
His images are a fraud;
  they have no breath in them.
¹⁸ They are worthless, the objects of
      mockery;
  when their judgment comes, they
      will perish.
¹⁹ He who is the Portion of Jacob is not
      like these,
  for he is the Maker of all things,
including the tribe of his
      inheritance—
  the LORD Almighty is his name.

²⁰ "You are my war club,
  my weapon for battle—
with you I shatter nations,
  with you I destroy kingdoms,
²¹ with you I shatter horse and rider,
  with you I shatter chariot and
      driver,

ᵃ3 The Hebrew term refers to the irrevocable
giving over of things or persons to the LORD, often
by totally destroying them.   ᵇ4 Or Chaldea
ᶜ5 Or / and the land of the Babylonians

²² with you I shatter man and woman,
　with you I shatter old man and
　　youth,
　with you I shatter young man and
　　maiden,
²³ with you I shatter shepherd and
　　flock,
　with you I shatter farmer and
　　oxen,
　with you I shatter governors and
　　officials.

²⁴ "Before your eyes I will repay Babylon and all who live in Babylonia[a] for all the wrong they have done in Zion," declares the LORD.

²⁵ "I am against you, O destroying
　　mountain,
　you who destroy the whole earth,"
　　　　declares the LORD.
"I will stretch out my hand against
　　you,
　roll you off the cliffs,
　and make you a burned-out
　　mountain.
²⁶ No rock will be taken from you for a
　　cornerstone,
　nor any stone for a foundation,
　for you will be desolate forever,"
　　　　declares the LORD.

²⁷ "Lift up a banner in the land!
　Blow the trumpet among the
　　nations!
　Prepare the nations for battle against
　　her;
　summon against her these
　　kingdoms:
　Ararat, Minni and Ashkenaz.
　Appoint a commander against her;
　send up horses like a swarm of
　　locusts.
²⁸ Prepare the nations for battle against
　　her—
　the kings of the Medes,
　their governors and all their officials,
　and all the countries they rule.
²⁹ The land trembles and writhes,
　for the LORD's purposes against
　　Babylon stand—
　to lay waste the land of Babylon
　so that no one will live there.
³⁰ Babylon's warriors have stopped
　　fighting;
　they remain in their strongholds.

Their strength is exhausted;
　they have become like women.
Her dwellings are set on fire;
　the bars of her gates are broken.
³¹ One courier follows another
　and messenger follows messenger
to announce to the king of Babylon
　that his entire city is captured,
³² the river crossings seized,
　the marshes set on fire,
　and the soldiers terrified."

³³ This is what the LORD Almighty, the God of Israel, says:

"The Daughter of Babylon is like a
　　threshing floor
　at the time it is trampled;
　the time to harvest her will soon
　　come."

³⁴ "Nebuchadnezzar king of Babylon
　　has devoured us,
　he has thrown us into confusion,
　he has made us an empty jar.
Like a serpent he has swallowed us
　and filled his stomach with our
　　delicacies,
　and then has spewed us out.
³⁵ May the violence done to our flesh[b]
　　be upon Babylon,"
　say the inhabitants of Zion.
"May our blood be on those who live
　　in Babylonia,"
　says Jerusalem.

³⁶ Therefore, this is what the LORD says:

"See, I will defend your cause
　and avenge you;
I will dry up her sea
　and make her springs dry.
³⁷ Babylon will be a heap of ruins,
　a haunt of jackals,
　an object of horror and scorn,
　a place where no one lives.
³⁸ Her people all roar like young
　　lions,
　they growl like lion cubs.
³⁹ But while they are aroused,
　I will set out a feast for them
　and make them drunk,
so that they shout with laughter—
　then sleep forever and not awake,"
　　　　declares the LORD.

a24 Or Chaldea; also in verse 35　b35 Or done to us and to our children

⁴⁰ "I will bring them down
    like lambs to the slaughter,
    like rams and goats.

⁴¹ "How Sheshach*ᵃ* will be captured,
    the boast of the whole earth
        seized!
What a horror Babylon will be
    among the nations!
⁴² The sea will rise over Babylon;
    its roaring waves will cover her.
⁴³ Her towns will be desolate,
    a dry and desert land,
    a land where no one lives,
    through which no man travels.
⁴⁴ I will punish Bel in Babylon
    and make him spew out what he
        has swallowed.
The nations will no longer stream
    to him.
And the wall of Babylon will fall.

⁴⁵ "Come out of her, my people!
    Run for your lives!
    Run from the fierce anger of the
        LORD.
⁴⁶ Do not lose heart or be afraid
    when rumors are heard in the land;
one rumor comes this year, another
        the next,
    rumors of violence in the land
    and of ruler against ruler.
⁴⁷ For the time will surely come
    when I will punish the idols of
        Babylon;
    her whole land will be disgraced
    and her slain will all lie fallen
        within her.
⁴⁸ Then heaven and earth and all that is
        in them
    will shout for joy over Babylon,
for out of the north
    destroyers will attack her,"
            declares the LORD.

⁴⁹ "Babylon must fall because of Israel's
        slain,
    just as the slain in all the earth
    have fallen because of Babylon.
⁵⁰ You who have escaped the sword,
    leave and do not linger!
Remember the LORD in a distant land,
    and think on Jerusalem."

⁵¹ "We are disgraced,
    for we have been insulted
    and shame covers our faces,
because foreigners have entered
    the holy places of the LORD's
        house."

⁵² "But days are coming," declares
        the LORD,
    "when I will punish her idols,
and throughout her land
    the wounded will groan.
⁵³ Even if Babylon reaches the sky
    and fortifies her lofty stronghold,
    I will send destroyers against
        her,"
            declares the LORD.

⁵⁴ "The sound of a cry comes from
        Babylon,
    the sound of great destruction
    from the land of the Babylonians.*ᵇ*
⁵⁵ The LORD will destroy Babylon;
    he will silence her noisy din.
Waves ⌐of enemies⌐ will rage like
        great waters;
    the roar of their voices will
        resound.
⁵⁶ A destroyer will come against
        Babylon;
    her warriors will be captured,
    and their bows will be broken.
For the LORD is a God of retribution;
    he will repay in full.
⁵⁷ I will make her officials and wise
        men drunk,
    her governors, officers and
        warriors as well;
they will sleep forever and not
        awake,"
    declares the King, whose name is
        the LORD Almighty.

⁵⁸ This is what the LORD Almighty says:

"Babylon's thick wall will be
        leveled
    and her high gates set on fire;
the peoples exhaust themselves for
        nothing,
    the nations' labor is only fuel
        for the flames."

⁵⁹ This is the message Jeremiah gave to
the staff officer Seraiah son of Neriah,
the son of Mahseiah, when he went to
Babylon with Zedekiah king of Judah in
the fourth year of his reign. ⁶⁰ Jeremiah

ᵃ41 Sheshach is a cryptogram for Babylon.
ᵇ54 Or *Chaldeans*

had written on a scroll about all the disasters that would come upon Babylon—all that had been recorded concerning Babylon. 61He said to Seraiah, "When you get to Babylon, see that you read all these words aloud. 62Then say, 'O Lord, you have said you will destroy this place, so that neither man nor animal will live in it; it will be desolate forever.' 63When you finish reading this scroll, tie a stone to it and throw it into the Euphrates. 64Then say, 'So will Babylon sink to rise no more because of the disaster I will bring upon her. And her people will fall.'"

The words of Jeremiah end here.

The Fall of Jerusalem

52 Zedekiah was twenty-one years old when he became king, and he reigned in Jerusalem eleven years. His mother's name was Hamutal daughter of Jeremiah; she was from Libnah. 2He did evil in the eyes of the Lord, just as Jehoiakim had done. 3It was because of the Lord's anger that all this happened to Jerusalem and Judah, and in the end he thrust them from his presence.

Now Zedekiah rebelled against the king of Babylon.

4So in the ninth year of Zedekiah's reign, on the tenth day of the tenth month, Nebuchadnezzar king of Babylon marched against Jerusalem with his whole army. They camped outside the city and built siege works all around it. 5The city was kept under siege until the eleventh year of King Zedekiah.

6By the ninth day of the fourth month the famine in the city had become so severe that there was no food for the people to eat. 7Then the city wall was broken through, and the whole army fled. They left the city at night through the gate between the two walls near the king's garden, though the Babylonians*a* were surrounding the city. They fled toward the Arabah,*b* 8but the Babylonian*c* army pursued King Zedekiah and overtook him in the plains of Jericho. All his soldiers were separated from him and scattered, 9and he was captured.

He was taken to the king of Babylon at Riblah in the land of Hamath, where he

pronounced sentence on him. 10There at Riblah the king of Babylon slaughtered the sons of Zedekiah before his eyes; he also killed all the officials of Judah. 11Then he put out Zedekiah's eyes, bound him with bronze shackles and took him to Babylon, where he put him in prison till the day of his death.

12On the tenth day of the fifth month, in the nineteenth year of Nebuchadnezzar king of Babylon, Nebuzaradan commander of the imperial guard, who served the king of Babylon, came to Jerusalem. 13He set fire to the temple of the Lord, the royal palace and all the houses of Jerusalem. Every important building he burned down. 14The whole Babylonian army under the commander of the imperial guard broke down all the walls around Jerusalem. 15Nebuzaradan the commander of the guard carried into exile some of the poorest people and those who remained in the city, along with the rest of the craftsmen*d* and those who had gone over to the king of Babylon. 16But Nebuzaradan left behind the rest of the poorest people of the land to work the vineyards and fields.

17The Babylonians broke up the bronze pillars, the movable stands and the bronze Sea that were at the temple of the Lord and they carried all the bronze to Babylon. 18They also took away the pots, shovels, wick trimmers, sprinkling bowls, dishes and all the bronze articles used in the temple service. 19The commander of the imperial guard took away the basins, censers, sprinkling bowls, pots, lampstands, dishes and bowls used for drink offerings—all that were made of pure gold or silver.

20The bronze from the two pillars, the Sea and the twelve bronze bulls under it, and the movable stands, which King Solomon had made for the temple of the Lord, was more than could be weighed. 21Each of the pillars was eighteen cubits high and twelve cubits in circumference*e*; each was four fingers thick, and

---

*a*7 Or *Chaldeans*; also in verse 17   *b*7 Or *the Jordan Valley*   *c*8 Or *Chaldean*; also in verse 14   *d*15 Or *populace*   *e*21 That is, about 27 feet (about 8.1 meters) high and 18 feet (about 5.4 meters) in circumference

hollow. [22]The bronze capital on top of the one pillar was five cubits[a] high and was decorated with a network and pomegranates of bronze all around. The other pillar, with its pomegranates, was similar. [23]There were ninety-six pomegranates on the sides; the total number of pomegranates above the surrounding network was a hundred.

[24]The commander of the guard took as prisoners Seraiah the chief priest, Zephaniah the priest next in rank and the three doorkeepers. [25]Of those still in the city, he took the officer in charge of the fighting men, and seven royal advisers. He also took the secretary who was chief officer in charge of conscripting the people of the land and sixty of his men who were found in the city. [26]Nebuzaradan the commander took them all and brought them to the king of Babylon at Riblah. [27]There at Riblah, in the land of Hamath, the king had them executed.

So Judah went into captivity, away from her land. [28]This is the number of the people Nebuchadnezzar carried into exile:

in the seventh year, 3,023 Jews;
[29]in Nebuchadnezzar's eighteenth year, 832 people from Jerusalem;
[30]in his twenty-third year, 745 Jews taken into exile by Nebuzaradan the commander of the imperial guard.
There were 4,600 people in all.

Jehoiachin Released

[31]In the thirty-seventh year of the exile of Jehoiachin king of Judah, in the year Evil-Merodach[b] became king of Babylon, he released Jehoiachin king of Judah and freed him from prison on the twenty-fifth day of the twelfth month. [32]He spoke kindly to him and gave him a seat of honor higher than those of the other kings who were with him in Babylon. [33]So Jehoiachin put aside his prison clothes and for the rest of his life ate regularly at the king's table. [34]Day by day the king of Babylon gave Jehoiachin a regular allowance as long as he lived, till the day of his death.

[a]22 That is, about 7 1/2 feet (about 2.3 meters)
[b]31 Also called *Amel-Marduk*

Lamentations

THE GRAND CANYON makes the Colorado River appear beautiful and powerful. Further downstream, as the river flows along the Arizona and California borders toward Mexico, its banks become indistinct, and it gets shallow and lazy and dirty. But upstream, through the canyon, where the walls are high and the space narrow, the river is a glorious force. The boundaries and structures of the canyon make it a better river.

This is a metaphor that can be applied to the book of Lamentations, which is about the topic of grief. The book speaks of grief as water. To pray one's grief is to "pour out your heart like water in the presence of the Lord" (2:19). But grief, like pouring water, can be very messy.

There is nothing necessarily wrong with being messy. Childbirth is messy, surgeries are messy, life is messy. But good boundaries keep the mess from turning to chaos and sloppy shallowness. Like the walls of the Grand Canyon, boundaries deepen grief and make it a creative, healing and powerful force for prayer. Mere raw emotion has little value over time, but when disciplined and instructed by hope, it turns despair to praise and ashes to beauty (see Isaiah 61:3).

Lamentations is a book about grief within boundaries. The grief it expresses is horrific, but its structure is studied and poetic. There are five laments, each with twenty-two verses—except the third lament, which has sixty-six verses—arranged according to the twenty-two letters of the Hebrew alphabet. To learn to pray like Lamentations is to learn to grieve within life-giving boundaries. Even the progression of the book's themes teaches something. The book begins with lament, moves to hope (the center of the grieving process) and concludes with repentance. Grief can result in bad or good things. Bad grief is crippling, but good grief leads to repentance by way of hope, as Paul described in 2 Corinthians 7:8–10. Hope is the center; without hope, grief leads only to despair.

BECAUSE OF THE LORD'S GREAT LOVE WE ARE NOT CONSUMED, FOR HIS COMPASSIONS NEVER FAIL. (3:22)

1 ^a How deserted lies the city,
  once so full of people!
How like a widow is she,
  who once was great among the
    nations!
She who was queen among the
    provinces
  has now become a slave.

² Bitterly she weeps at night,
  tears are upon her cheeks.
Among all her lovers
  there is none to comfort her.
All her friends have betrayed her;
  they have become her enemies.

³ After affliction and harsh labor,
  Judah has gone into exile.
She dwells among the nations;
  she finds no resting place.
All who pursue her have overtaken
    her
  in the midst of her distress.

⁴ The roads to Zion mourn,
  for no one comes to her appointed
    feasts.
All her gateways are desolate,
  her priests groan,
her maidens grieve,
  and she is in bitter anguish.

⁵ Her foes have become her masters;
  her enemies are at ease.
The LORD has brought her grief
  because of her many sins.
Her children have gone into exile,
  captive before the foe.

⁶ All the splendor has departed
  from the Daughter of Zion.
Her princes are like deer
  that find no pasture;
in weakness they have fled
  before the pursuer.

⁷ In the days of her affliction and
    wandering
  Jerusalem remembers all the
    treasures
  that were hers in days of old.
When her people fell into enemy
    hands,
  there was no one to help her.
Her enemies looked at her
  and laughed at her destruction.

⁸ Jerusalem has sinned greatly
  and so has become unclean.

All who honored her despise her,
  for they have seen her nakedness;
she herself groans
  and turns away.

⁹ Her filthiness clung to her skirts;
  she did not consider her future.
Her fall was astounding;
  there was none to comfort her.
"Look, O LORD, on my affliction,
  for the enemy has triumphed."

¹⁰ The enemy laid hands
  on all her treasures;
she saw pagan nations
  enter her sanctuary—
those you had forbidden
  to enter your assembly.

¹¹ All her people groan
  as they search for bread;
they barter their treasures for food
  to keep themselves alive.
"Look, O LORD, and consider,
  for I am despised."

¹² "Is it nothing to you, all you who
    pass by?
  Look around and see.
Is any suffering like my suffering
  that was inflicted on me,
that the LORD brought on me
  in the day of his fierce anger?

¹³ "From on high he sent fire,
  sent it down into my bones.
He spread a net for my feet
  and turned me back.
He made me desolate,
  faint all the day long.

¹⁴ "My sins have been bound into
    a yoke^b;
  by his hands they were woven
    together.
They have come upon my neck
  and the Lord has sapped my
    strength.
He has handed me over
  to those I cannot withstand.

¹⁵ "The Lord has rejected
  all the warriors in my midst;

---

^aThis chapter is an acrostic poem, the verses of
which begin with the successive letters of the
Hebrew alphabet.   ^b14 Most Hebrew
manuscripts; Septuagint *He kept watch over my
sins*

he has summoned an army
    against me
    to[a] crush my young men.
In his winepress the Lord has
    trampled
    the Virgin Daughter of Judah.

16 "This is why I weep
    and my eyes overflow with tears.
No one is near to comfort me,
    no one to restore my spirit.
My children are destitute
    because the enemy has prevailed."

17 Zion stretches out her hands,
    but there is no one to comfort her.
The LORD has decreed for Jacob
    that his neighbors become his foes;
Jerusalem has become
    an unclean thing among them.

18 "The LORD is righteous,
    yet I rebelled against his command.
Listen, all you peoples;
    look upon my suffering.
My young men and maidens
    have gone into exile.

19 "I called to my allies
    but they betrayed me.
My priests and my elders
    perished in the city
while they searched for food
    to keep themselves alive.

20 "See, O LORD, how distressed I am!
    I am in torment within,
and in my heart I am disturbed,
    for I have been most rebellious.
Outside, the sword bereaves;
    inside, there is only death.

21 "People have heard my groaning,
    but there is no one to comfort me.
All my enemies have heard of my
    distress;
    they rejoice at what you have done.
May you bring the day you have
    announced
    so they may become like me.

22 "Let all their wickedness come
    before you;
    deal with them
as you have dealt with me
    because of all my sins.
My groans are many
    and my heart is faint."

2 [b] How the Lord has covered the
    Daughter of Zion
    with the cloud of his anger[c]!
He has hurled down the splendor
    of Israel
    from heaven to earth;
he has not remembered his footstool
    in the day of his anger.

2 Without pity the Lord has swallowed
    up
    all the dwellings of Jacob;
in his wrath he has torn down
    the strongholds of the Daughter
    of Judah.
He has brought her kingdom and its
    princes
    down to the ground in dishonor.

3 In fierce anger he has cut off
    every horn[d] of Israel.
He has withdrawn his right hand
    at the approach of the enemy.
He has burned in Jacob like a
    flaming fire
    that consumes everything around it.

4 Like an enemy he has strung his bow;
    his right hand is ready.
Like a foe he has slain
    all who were pleasing to the eye;
he has poured out his wrath like fire
    on the tent of the Daughter of Zion.

5 The Lord is like an enemy;
    he has swallowed up Israel.
He has swallowed up all her palaces
    and destroyed her strongholds.
He has multiplied mourning and
    lamentation
    for the Daughter of Judah.

6 He has laid waste his dwelling like
    a garden;
    he has destroyed his place of
    meeting.
The LORD has made Zion forget
    her appointed feasts and her
    Sabbaths;
in his fierce anger he has spurned
    both king and priest.

---

[a]15 Or has set a time for me / when he will
[b]This chapter is an acrostic poem, the verses of
which begin with the successive letters of the
Hebrew alphabet.   [c]1 Or How the Lord in his
anger / has treated the Daughter of Zion with
contempt   [d]3 Or / all the strength; or every
king; horn here symbolizes strength.

⁷The Lord has rejected his altar
and abandoned his sanctuary.
He has handed over to the enemy
the walls of her palaces;
they have raised a shout in the
house of the LORD
as on the day of an appointed
feast.

⁸The LORD determined to tear down
the wall around the Daughter
of Zion.
He stretched out a measuring line
and did not withhold his hand from
destroying.
He made ramparts and walls lament;
together they wasted away.

⁹Her gates have sunk into the ground;
their bars he has broken and
destroyed.
Her king and her princes are exiled
among the nations,
the law is no more,
and her prophets no longer find
visions from the LORD.

¹⁰The elders of the Daughter of Zion
sit on the ground in silence;
they have sprinkled dust on their
heads
and put on sackcloth.
The young women of Jerusalem
have bowed their heads to the
ground.

¹¹My eyes fail from weeping,
I am in torment within,
my heart is poured out on the ground
because my people are destroyed,
because children and infants faint
in the streets of the city.

¹²They say to their mothers,
"Where is bread and wine?"
as they faint like wounded men
in the streets of the city,
as their lives ebb away
in their mothers' arms.

¹³What can I say for you?
With what can I compare you,
O Daughter of Jerusalem?
To what can I liken you,
that I may comfort you,
O Virgin Daughter of Zion?
Your wound is as deep as the sea.
Who can heal you?

¹⁴The visions of your prophets
were false and worthless;
they did not expose your sin
to ward off your captivity.
The oracles they gave you
were false and misleading.

¹⁵All who pass your way
clap their hands at you;
they scoff and shake their heads
at the Daughter of Jerusalem:
"Is this the city that was called
the perfection of beauty,
the joy of the whole earth?"

¹⁶All your enemies open their mouths
wide against you;
they scoff and gnash their teeth
and say, "We have swallowed her
up.
This is the day we have waited for;
we have lived to see it."

¹⁷The LORD has done what he planned;
he has fulfilled his word,
which he decreed long ago.
He has overthrown you without pity,
he has let the enemy gloat
over you,
he has exalted the horn[a] of your
foes.

¹⁸The hearts of the people
cry out to the Lord.
O wall of the Daughter of Zion,
let your tears flow like a river
day and night;
give yourself no relief,
your eyes no rest.

¹⁹Arise, cry out in the night,
as the watches of the night begin;
pour out your heart like water
in the presence of the Lord.
Lift up your hands to him
for the lives of your children,
who faint from hunger
at the head of every street.

²⁰"Look, O LORD, and consider:
Whom have you ever treated
like this?
Should women eat their offspring,
the children they have cared for?
Should priest and prophet be killed
in the sanctuary of the Lord?

[a] *17* Horn here symbolizes strength.

> ARISE, cry out in the night,
>   as the watches of the night begin;
> pour out your heart like water
>   in the presence of the Lord.
> Lift up your hands to him
>   for the lives of your children,
> who faint from hunger
>   at the head of every street.
>
> LAMENTATIONS 2:19

21 "Young and old lie together
  in the dust of the streets;
my young men and maidens
  have fallen by the sword.
You have slain them in the day of
    your anger;
  you have slaughtered them without
    pity.

22 "As you summon to a feast day,
  so you summoned against me
    terrors on every side.
In the day of the LORD's anger
  no one escaped or survived;
those I cared for and reared,
  my enemy has destroyed."

3 a I am the man who has seen affliction
  by the rod of his wrath.
2 He has driven me away and made
    me walk
  in darkness rather than light;
3 indeed, he has turned his hand
    against me
  again and again, all day long.

4 He has made my skin and my flesh
    grow old
  and has broken my bones.
5 He has besieged me and surrounded
    me
  with bitterness and hardship.
6 He has made me dwell in darkness
  like those long dead.

7 He has walled me in so I cannot
    escape;
  he has weighed me down with
    chains.
8 Even when I call out or cry for help,
  he shuts out my prayer.
9 He has barred my way with blocks
    of stone;
  he has made my paths crooked.

10 Like a bear lying in wait,
  like a lion in hiding,
11 he dragged me from the path and
    mangled me
  and left me without help.
12 He drew his bow
  and made me the target for his
    arrows.

13 He pierced my heart
  with arrows from his quiver.
14 I became the laughingstock of all my
    people;
  they mock me in song all day long.
15 He has filled me with bitter herbs
  and sated me with gall.

16 He has broken my teeth with gravel;
  he has trampled me in the dust.
17 I have been deprived of peace;
  I have forgotten what prosperity is.
18 So I say, "My splendor is gone
  and all that I had hoped from the
    LORD."

19 I remember my affliction and my
    wandering,
  the bitterness and the gall.
20 I well remember them,
  and my soul is downcast within me.
21 Yet this I call to mind
  and therefore I have hope:

22 Because of the LORD's great love we
    are not consumed,
  for his compassions never fail.
23 They are new every morning;
  great is your faithfulness.
24 I say to myself, "The LORD is my
    portion;
  therefore I will wait for him."

25 The LORD is good to those whose hope
    is in him,
  to the one who seeks him;
26 it is good to wait quietly
  for the salvation of the LORD.
27 It is good for a man to bear the yoke
  while he is young.

28 Let him sit alone in silence,
  for the LORD has laid it on him.
29 Let him bury his face in the dust—
  there may yet be hope.

---

a This chapter is an acrostic poem; the verses of each stanza begin with the successive letters of the Hebrew alphabet, and the verses within each stanza begin with the same letter.

LAMENTATIONS 3:19-33

Make Memory a Good Servant

3:19,21 I REMEMBER MY AFFLICTION AND MY WANDERING, THE BITTERNESS AND THE GALL ... YET THIS I CALL TO MIND AND THEREFORE I HAVE HOPE.

The value of memory, like intellect, is determined by what it serves. Memory in the service of despair has the power to destroy, whereas memory in the service of hope has the power to save. In John Bunyan's *Pilgrim's Progress*, the main character, Christian, is locked up in Doubting Castle and beaten savagely with a club by Giant Despair. The giant's club is made of memory. As he is beaten, Christian is filled with memories of his sin and how many times he'd been warned not to sin but had anyway. As he's clubbed by memory, Christian sinks deeper and deeper into despair. But one night, the same memory that Despair had used for torture came to him and whispered something in his ear. Then Christian realized with joy that all along he had been carrying the key to unlock Doubting Castle. The key was in his heart, and it was Promise. He thrust it into the lock, and though it was hard to turn, the lock yielded and he was set free.[1]

Sometimes praying about things like loss, disappointment and failure can leave us more despondent after we pray than before. The memories, the recollection of these things even when spoken to God, are like Despair's club in Doubting Castle. The key is promise. Pray the promises of God into your despair. Make memory into a good servant. Remember God's love and faithfulness. "Yet this I call to mind and therefore I have hope: Because of the Lord's great love we are not consumed, for his compassions never fail" (3:21–22).

The Lord wants our suffering to refine us, not consume us. We may think that we are getting exactly what we deserve for the wrongs we have done, and we bow our heads in resignation. But we are wrong! We never get exactly what we deserve. Only one person got exactly what we deserve—he died on a cross and was raised from the dead for our justification (see Romans 4:25). Our sin and guilt is real. But God's love is greater than both. Where there was once condemnation, now there is discipline.

P R A Y :

Pray this prayer from Lamentations thankfully:
"Though he brings grief, he will show compassion,
so great is his unfailing love. For he does not willingly
bring affliction or grief to the children of men" (verses 32–33).

FOR YOUR NEXT DEVOTIONAL READING, GO TO PAGE 977.

³⁰ Let him offer his cheek to one who
would strike him,
and let him be filled with
disgrace.
³¹ For men are not cast off
by the Lord forever.
³² Though he brings grief, he will show
compassion,
so great is his unfailing love.
³³ For he does not willingly bring
affliction
or grief to the children of men.

³⁴ To crush underfoot
all prisoners in the land,
³⁵ to deny a man his rights
before the Most High,
³⁶ to deprive a man of justice—
would not the Lord see such
things?

³⁷ Who can speak and have it happen
if the Lord has not decreed it?
³⁸ Is it not from the mouth of the
Most High
that both calamities and good
things come?
³⁹ Why should any living man complain
when punished for his sins?

⁴⁰ Let us examine our ways and
test them,
and let us return to the LORD.
⁴¹ Let us lift up our hearts and our
hands
to God in heaven, and say:
⁴² "We have sinned and rebelled
and you have not forgiven.

⁴³ "You have covered yourself with
anger and pursued us;
you have slain without pity.
⁴⁴ You have covered yourself with
a cloud
so that no prayer can get through.
⁴⁵ You have made us scum and refuse
among the nations.

⁴⁶ "All our enemies have opened their
mouths
wide against us.

"YOU have covered yourself with a cloud
so that no prayer can get through."

LAMENTATIONS 3:44

⁴⁷ We have suffered terror and
pitfalls,
ruin and destruction."
⁴⁸ Streams of tears flow from my eyes
because my people are
destroyed.
⁴⁹ My eyes will flow unceasingly,
without relief,
⁵⁰ until the LORD looks down
from heaven and sees.
⁵¹ What I see brings grief to my soul
because of all the women of
my city.

⁵² Those who were my enemies
without cause
hunted me like a bird.
⁵³ They tried to end my life in a pit
and threw stones at me;
⁵⁴ the waters closed over my head,
and I thought I was about to be
cut off.

⁵⁵ I called on your name, O LORD,
from the depths of the pit.
⁵⁶ You heard my plea: "Do not close
your ears
to my cry for relief."
⁵⁷ You came near when I called you,
and you said, "Do not fear."

⁵⁸ O Lord, you took up my case;
you redeemed my life.
⁵⁹ You have seen, O LORD, the wrong
done to me.
Uphold my cause!
⁶⁰ You have seen the depth of their
vengeance,
all their plots against me.

⁶¹ O LORD, you have heard their insults,
all their plots against me—
⁶² what my enemies whisper and
mutter
against me all day long.
⁶³ Look at them! Sitting or standing,
they mock me in their songs.

⁶⁴ Pay them back what they deserve,
O LORD,
for what their hands have done.
⁶⁵ Put a veil over their hearts,
and may your curse be on them!
⁶⁶ Pursue them in anger and destroy
them
from under the heavens of the
LORD.

4 [a] How the gold has lost its luster,
    the fine gold become dull!
The sacred gems are scattered
    at the head of every street.

2 How the precious sons of Zion,
    once worth their weight in gold,
are now considered as pots of clay,
    the work of a potter's hands!

3 Even jackals offer their breasts
    to nurse their young,
but my people have become heartless
    like ostriches in the desert.

4 Because of thirst the infant's tongue
    sticks to the roof of its mouth;
the children beg for bread,
    but no one gives it to them.

5 Those who once ate delicacies
    are destitute in the streets.
Those nurtured in purple
    now lie on ash heaps.

6 The punishment of my people
    is greater than that of Sodom,
which was overthrown in a moment
    without a hand turned to help her.

7 Their princes were brighter than
    snow
    and whiter than milk,
their bodies more ruddy than rubies,
    their appearance like sapphires.[b]

8 But now they are blacker than soot;
    they are not recognized in the
    streets.
Their skin has shriveled on their
    bones;
    it has become as dry as a stick.

9 Those killed by the sword are
    better off
than those who die of famine;
    racked with hunger, they waste away
    for lack of food from the field.

10 With their own hands compassionate
    women
    have cooked their own children,
who became their food
    when my people were destroyed.

11 The LORD has given full vent to his
    wrath;
    he has poured out his fierce anger.
He kindled a fire in Zion
    that consumed her foundations.

12 The kings of the earth did not
    believe,
    nor did any of the world's people,
that enemies and foes could enter
    the gates of Jerusalem.

13 But it happened because of the sins
    of her prophets
    and the iniquities of her priests,
who shed within her
    the blood of the righteous.

14 Now they grope through the streets
    like men who are blind.
They are so defiled with blood
    that no one dares to touch their
    garments.

15 "Go away! You are unclean!" men
    cry to them.
    "Away! Away! Don't touch us!"
When they flee and wander about,
    people among the nations say,
    "They can stay here no longer."

16 The LORD himself has scattered
    them;
    he no longer watches over them.
The priests are shown no honor,
    the elders no favor.

17 Moreover, our eyes failed,
    looking in vain for help;
from our towers we watched
    for a nation that could not save us.

18 Men stalked us at every step,
    so we could not walk in our streets.
Our end was near, our days were
    numbered,
    for our end had come.

19 Our pursuers were swifter
    than eagles in the sky;
they chased us over the mountains
    and lay in wait for us in the desert.

20 The LORD's anointed, our very life
    breath,
    was caught in their traps.
We thought that under his shadow
    we would live among the nations.

21 Rejoice and be glad, O Daughter
    of Edom,
    you who live in the land of Uz.

[a]This chapter is an acrostic poem, the verses of
which begin with the successive letters of the
Hebrew alphabet.   [b]7 Or *lapis lazuli*

But to you also the cup will be
passed;
you will be drunk and stripped
naked.
²² O Daughter of Zion, your punishment
will end;
he will not prolong your exile.
But, O Daughter of Edom, he will
punish your sin
and expose your wickedness.

5 Remember, O LORD, what has
happened to us;
look, and see our disgrace.
² Our inheritance has been turned over
to aliens,
our homes to foreigners.
³ We have become orphans and
fatherless,
our mothers like widows.
⁴ We must buy the water we drink;
our wood can be had only at a
price.
⁵ Those who pursue us are at our
heels;
we are weary and find no rest.
⁶ We submitted to Egypt and Assyria
to get enough bread.
⁷ Our fathers sinned and are no more,
and we bear their punishment.
⁸ Slaves rule over us,
and there is none to free us from
their hands.
⁹ We get our bread at the risk of our
lives
because of the sword in the desert.
¹⁰ Our skin is hot as an oven,
feverish from hunger.

¹¹ Women have been ravished in Zion,
and virgins in the towns of Judah.
¹² Princes have been hung up by their
hands;
elders are shown no respect.
¹³ Young men toil at the millstones;
boys stagger under loads of wood.
¹⁴ The elders are gone from the city
gate;
the young men have stopped
their music.
¹⁵ Joy is gone from our hearts;
our dancing has turned to
mourning.
¹⁶ The crown has fallen from our head.
Woe to us, for we have sinned!
¹⁷ Because of this our hearts are faint,
because of these things our eyes
grow dim
¹⁸ for Mount Zion, which lies desolate,
with jackals prowling over it.

> I do not pray for success; I ask for
> faithfulness.
>
> MOTHER TERESA

¹⁹ You, O LORD, reign forever;
your throne endures from
generation to generation.
²⁰ Why do you always forget us?
Why do you forsake us so long?
²¹ Restore us to yourself, O LORD, that
we may return;
renew our days as of old
²² unless you have utterly rejected us
and are angry with us beyond
measure.

Ezekiel

WHY DOES there always seem to be more to talk with God about when things are going badly? Part of the answer to that question probably has something to do with how quickly we forget to be thankful. Humans have been described as the "ungrateful biped." We need to pray what George Herbert prayed: "Thou that hast given so much to me, give one thing more, a grateful heart." The second part of the answer is that God is usually speaking to us in new ways when things go badly. It's not that he isn't speaking when they go well, but that he has something new to say when they take a turn for the worse. When God takes something away from us, it's so he can give something better.

Like most of the other prophets, Ezekiel prophesied during dark days—perhaps the darkest in Israel's history—and among the most difficult people: a privileged upper class with a highly developed sense of entitlement and shallow optimism. They were in exile, having been deported to Babylon about ten years before the destruction of Jerusalem, but they didn't expect to be there for long. They were convinced that soon they would be back in Jerusalem, worshiping in the temple, their pride and joy. However, the reality was that most of the people would die before anyone would return to Jerusalem. And when the people would return, it would be to a city that had been razed and a temple that had been seriously compromised (see the books of Ezra and Nehemiah). When shallow optimism falls, it goes down hard and doesn't always grow into something stronger and deeper. So Ezekiel's task was to see that the people would grow in spite of their complacency.

God planned to give the Israelites something better to replace what had been taken away. Instead of the temple in Jerusalem, God would be the sanctuary and so would their hearts (see Ezekiel 11:16–25; 36:26–27). The future of this "temple's" ministry would be more glorious than the first. Ezekiel's vision showed a river flowing from the altar: first a trickle, then a stream and then a torrent of water giving life to everything around it, like the river in Eden (see Genesis 2:10; Ezekiel 47:1–12). The great opportunity for prayer in hard times is to try to discern the new things God is trying to do and to pray them into existence.

"THEY WILL KNOW THAT I AM THE LORD, WHEN I DISPERSE THEM AMONG THE NATIONS." (12:15)

The Living Creatures and the Glory of the LORD

1 In the[a] thirtieth year, in the fourth month on the fifth day, while I was among the exiles by the Kebar River, the heavens were opened and I saw visions of God.

2On the fifth of the month—it was the fifth year of the exile of King Jehoiachin— 3the word of the LORD came to Ezekiel the priest, the son of Buzi,[b] by the Kebar River in the land of the Babylonians.[c] There the hand of the LORD was upon him.

4I looked, and I saw a windstorm coming out of the north—an immense cloud with flashing lightning and surrounded by brilliant light. The center of the fire looked like glowing metal, 5and in the fire was what looked like four living creatures. In appearance their form was that of a man, 6but each of them had four faces and four wings. 7Their legs were straight; their feet were like those of a calf and gleamed like burnished bronze. 8Under their wings on their four sides they had the hands of a man. All four of them had faces and wings, 9and their wings touched one another. Each one went straight ahead; they did not turn as they moved.

10Their faces looked like this: Each of the four had the face of a man, and on the right side each had the face of a lion, and on the left the face of an ox; each also had the face of an eagle. 11Such were their faces. Their wings were spread out upward; each had two wings, one touching the wing of another creature on either side, and two wings covering its body. 12Each one went straight ahead. Wherever the spirit would go, they would go, without turning as they went. 13The appearance of the living creatures was like burning coals of fire or like torches. Fire moved back and forth among the creatures; it was bright, and lightning flashed out of it. 14The creatures sped back and forth like flashes of lightning.

15As I looked at the living creatures, I saw a wheel on the ground beside each creature with its four faces. 16This was the appearance and structure of the wheels: They sparkled like chrysolite, and all four looked alike. Each appeared to be made like a wheel intersecting a wheel. 17As they moved, they would go in any one of the four directions the creatures faced; the wheels did not turn about[d] as the creatures went. 18Their rims were high and awesome, and all four rims were full of eyes all around.

19When the living creatures moved, the wheels beside them moved; and when the living creatures rose from the ground, the wheels also rose. 20Wherever the spirit would go, they would go, and the wheels would rise along with them, because the spirit of the living creatures was in the wheels. 21When the creatures moved, they also moved; when the creatures stood still, they also stood still; and when the creatures rose from the ground, the wheels rose along with them, because the spirit of the living creatures was in the wheels.

22Spread out above the heads of the living creatures was what looked like an expanse, sparkling like ice, and awesome. 23Under the expanse their wings were stretched out one toward the other, and each had two wings covering its body. 24When the creatures moved, I heard the sound of their wings, like the roar of rushing waters, like the voice of the Almighty,[e] like the tumult of an army. When they stood still, they lowered their wings.

25Then there came a voice from above the expanse over their heads as they stood with lowered wings. 26Above the expanse over their heads was what looked like a throne of sapphire,[f] and high above on the throne was a figure like that of a man. 27I saw that from what appeared to be his waist up he looked like glowing metal, as if full of fire, and that from there down he looked like fire; and brilliant light surrounded him. 28Like the appearance of a rainbow in the clouds on a rainy day, so was the radiance around him.

This was the appearance of the likeness of the glory of the LORD. When I saw it, I fell facedown, and I heard the voice of one speaking.

[a]1 Or my,   [b]3 Or Ezekiel son of Buzi the priest   [c]3 Or Chaldeans   [d]17 Or aside   [e]24 Hebrew Shaddai   [f]26 Or lapis lazuli

Ezekiel's Call

2 He said to me, "Son of man, stand up on your feet and I will speak to you." [2]As he spoke, the Spirit came into me and raised me to my feet, and I heard him speaking to me.

[3]He said: "Son of man, I am sending you to the Israelites, to a rebellious nation that has rebelled against me; they and their fathers have been in revolt against me to this very day. [4]The people to whom I am sending you are obstinate and stubborn. Say to them, 'This is what the Sovereign LORD says.' [5]And whether they listen or fail to listen—for they are a rebellious house—they will know that a prophet has been among them. [6]And you, son of man, do not be afraid of them or their words. Do not be afraid, though briers and thorns are all around you and you live among scorpions. Do not be afraid of what they say or terrified by them, though they are a rebellious house. [7]You must speak my words to them, whether they listen or fail to listen, for they are rebellious. [8]But you, son of man, listen to what I say to you. Do not rebel like that rebellious house; open your mouth and eat what I give you."

[9]Then I looked, and I saw a hand stretched out to me. In it was a scroll, [10]which he unrolled before me. On both sides of it were written words of lament and mourning and woe.

3 And he said to me, "Son of man, eat what is before you, eat this scroll; then go and speak to the house of Israel." [2]So I opened my mouth, and he gave me the scroll to eat.

[3]Then he said to me, "Son of man, eat this scroll I am giving you and fill your stomach with it." So I ate it, and it tasted as sweet as honey in my mouth.

[4]He then said to me: "Son of man, go now to the house of Israel and speak my words to them. [5]You are not being sent to a people of obscure speech and difficult language, but to the house of Israel— [6]not to many peoples of obscure speech and difficult language, whose words you cannot understand. Surely if I had sent you to them, they would have listened to you. [7]But the house of Israel is not willing to listen to you because they are not willing to listen to me, for the whole house of Israel is hardened and obstinate. [8]But I will make you as unyielding and hardened as they are. [9]I will make your forehead like the hardest stone, harder than flint. Do not be afraid of them or terrified by them, though they are a rebellious house."

[10]And he said to me, "Son of man, listen carefully and take to heart all the words I speak to you. [11]Go now to your countrymen in exile and speak to them. Say to them, 'This is what the Sovereign LORD says,' whether they listen or fail to listen."

[12]Then the Spirit lifted me up, and I heard behind me a loud rumbling sound—May the glory of the LORD be praised in his dwelling place!— [13]the sound of the wings of the living creatures brushing against each other and the

> THEN the Spirit lifted me up, and I heard behind me a loud rumbling sound—May the glory of the LORD be praised in his dwelling place!
>
> EZEKIEL 3:12

sound of the wheels beside them, a loud rumbling sound. [14]The Spirit then lifted me up and took me away, and I went in bitterness and in the anger of my spirit, with the strong hand of the LORD upon me. [15]I came to the exiles who lived at Tel Abib near the Kebar River. And there, where they were living, I sat among them for seven days—overwhelmed.

Warning to Israel

[16]At the end of seven days the word of the LORD came to me: [17]"Son of man, I have made you a watchman for the house of Israel; so hear the word I speak and give them warning from me. [18]When I say to a wicked man, 'You will surely die,' and you do not warn him or speak out to dissuade him from his evil ways in order to save his life, that wicked man will die for[a] his sin, and I will hold you accountable for his blood. [19]But if you do warn the wicked man and he does not turn from his wickedness or from his evil

[a]18 Or *in*; also in verses 19 and 20

ways, he will die for his sin; but you will have saved yourself.

²⁰"Again, when a righteous man turns from his righteousness and does evil, and I put a stumbling block before him, he will die. Since you did not warn him, he will die for his sin. The righteous things he did will not be remembered, and I will hold you accountable for his blood. ²¹But if you do warn the righteous man not to sin and he does not sin, he will surely live because he took warning, and you will have saved yourself."

²²The hand of the LORD was upon me there, and he said to me, "Get up and go out to the plain, and there I will speak to you." ²³So I got up and went out to the plain. And the glory of the LORD was standing there, like the glory I had seen by the Kebar River, and I fell facedown. ²⁴Then the Spirit came into me and raised me to my feet. He spoke to me and said: "Go, shut yourself inside your house. ²⁵And you, son of man, they will tie with ropes; you will be bound so that you cannot go out among the people. ²⁶I will make your tongue stick to the roof of your mouth so that you will be silent and unable to rebuke them, though they are a rebellious house. ²⁷But when I speak to you, I will open your mouth and you shall say to them, 'This is what the Sovereign LORD says.' Whoever will listen let him listen, and whoever will refuse let him refuse; for they are a rebellious house.

Siege of Jerusalem Symbolized

4 "Now, son of man, take a clay tablet, put it in front of you and draw the city of Jerusalem on it. ²Then lay siege to it: Erect siege works against it, build a ramp up to it, set up camps against it and put battering rams around it. ³Then take an iron pan, place it as an iron wall between you and the city and turn your face toward it. It will be under siege, and you shall besiege it. This will be a sign to the house of Israel.

⁴"Then lie on your left side and put the sin of the house of Israel upon yourself.ᵃ You are to bear their sin for the number of days you lie on your side. ⁵I have assigned you the same number of days as the years of their sin. So for 390 days you will bear the sin of the house of Israel.

⁶"After you have finished this, lie down again, this time on your right side, and bear the sin of the house of Judah. I have assigned you 40 days, a day for each year. ⁷Turn your face toward the siege of Jerusalem and with bared arm prophesy against her. ⁸I will tie you up with ropes so that you cannot turn from one side to the other until you have finished the days of your siege.

⁹"Take wheat and barley, beans and lentils, millet and spelt; put them in a storage jar and use them to make bread for yourself. You are to eat it during the 390 days you lie on your side. ¹⁰Weigh out twenty shekelsᵇ of food to eat each day and eat it at set times. ¹¹Also measure out a sixth of a hinᶜ of water and drink it at set times. ¹²Eat the food as you would a barley cake; bake it in the sight of the people, using human excrement for fuel." ¹³The LORD said, "In this way the people of Israel will eat defiled food among the nations where I will drive them."

¹⁴Then I said, "Not so, Sovereign LORD! I have never defiled myself. From my youth until now I have never eaten anything found dead or torn by wild animals. No unclean meat has ever entered my mouth."

¹⁵"Very well," he said, "I will let you bake your bread over cow manure instead of human excrement."

¹⁶He then said to me: "Son of man, I will cut off the supply of food in Jerusalem. The people will eat rationed food in anxiety and drink rationed water in despair, ¹⁷for food and water will be scarce. They will be appalled at the sight of each other and will waste away because ofᵈ their sin.

5 "Now, son of man, take a sharp sword and use it as a barber's razor to shave your head and your beard. Then take a set of scales and divide up the

ᵃ4 Or your side   ᵇ10 That is, about 8 ounces (about 0.2 kilogram)   ᶜ11 That is, about 2/3 quart (about 0.6 liter)   ᵈ17 Or away in

hair. ²When the days of your siege come to an end, burn a third of the hair with fire inside the city. Take a third and strike it with the sword all around the city. And scatter a third to the wind. For I will pursue them with drawn sword. ³But take a few strands of hair and tuck them away in the folds of your garment. ⁴Again, take a few of these and throw them into the fire and burn them up. A fire will spread from there to the whole house of Israel.

⁵"This is what the Sovereign LORD says: This is Jerusalem, which I have set in the center of the nations, with countries all around her. ⁶Yet in her wickedness she has rebelled against my laws and decrees more than the nations and countries around her. She has rejected my laws and has not followed my decrees.

⁷"Therefore this is what the Sovereign LORD says: You have been more unruly than the nations around you and have not followed my decrees or kept my laws. You have not even*ᵃ* conformed to the standards of the nations around you.

⁸"Therefore this is what the Sovereign LORD says: I myself am against you, Jerusalem, and I will inflict punishment on you in the sight of the nations. ⁹Because of all your detestable idols, I will do to you what I have never done before and will never do again. ¹⁰Therefore in your midst fathers will eat their children, and children will eat their fathers. I will inflict punishment on you and will scatter all your survivors to the winds. ¹¹Therefore as surely as I live, declares the Sovereign LORD, because you have defiled my sanctuary with all your vile images and detestable practices, I myself will withdraw my favor; I will not look on you with pity or spare you. ¹²A third of your people will die of the plague or perish by famine inside you; a third will fall by the sword outside your walls; and a third I will scatter to the winds and pursue with drawn sword.

¹³"Then my anger will cease and my wrath against them will subside, and I will be avenged. And when I have spent my wrath upon them, they will know that I the LORD have spoken in my zeal.

¹⁴"I will make you a ruin and a reproach among the nations around you, in the sight of all who pass by. ¹⁵You will be a reproach and a taunt, a warning and an object of horror to the nations around you when I inflict punishment on you in anger and in wrath and with stinging rebuke. I the LORD have spoken. ¹⁶When I shoot at you with my deadly and destructive arrows of famine, I will shoot to destroy you. I will bring more and more famine upon you and cut off your supply of food. ¹⁷I will send famine and wild beasts against you, and they will leave you childless. Plague and bloodshed will sweep through you, and I will bring the sword against you. I the LORD have spoken."

A Prophecy Against the Mountains of Israel

6 The word of the LORD came to me: ²"Son of man, set your face against the mountains of Israel; prophesy against them ³and say: 'O mountains of Israel, hear the word of the Sovereign LORD. This is what the Sovereign LORD says to the mountains and hills, to the ravines and valleys: I am about to bring a sword against you, and I will destroy your high places. ⁴Your altars will be demolished and your incense altars will be smashed; and I will slay your people in front of your idols. ⁵I will lay the dead bodies of the Israelites in front of their idols, and I will scatter your bones around your altars. ⁶Wherever you live, the towns will be laid waste and the high places demolished, so that your altars will be laid waste and devastated, your idols smashed and ruined, your incense altars broken down, and what you have made wiped out. ⁷Your people will fall slain among you, and you will know that I am the LORD.

⁸"'But I will spare some, for some of you will escape the sword when you are scattered among the lands and nations. ⁹Then in the nations where they have been carried captive, those who escape will remember me—how I have been grieved by their adulterous hearts, which have turned away from me, and by their eyes, which have lusted after their idols. They will loathe themselves for the evil

ᵃ7 Most Hebrew manuscripts; some Hebrew manuscripts and Syriac *You have*

they have done and for all their detestable practices. [10]And they will know that I am the LORD; I did not threaten in vain to bring this calamity on them.

[11]" 'This is what the Sovereign LORD says: Strike your hands together and stamp your feet and cry out "Alas!" because of all the wicked and detestable practices of the house of Israel, for they will fall by the sword, famine and plague. [12]He that is far away will die of the plague, and he that is near will fall by the sword, and he that survives and is spared will die of famine. So will I spend my wrath upon them. [13]And they will know that I am the LORD, when their people lie slain among their idols around their altars, on every high hill and on all the mountaintops, under every spreading tree and every leafy oak—places where they offered fragrant incense to all their idols. [14]And I will stretch out my hand against them and make the land a desolate waste from the desert to Diblah[a]— wherever they live. Then they will know that I am the LORD.' "

The End Has Come

7 The word of the LORD came to me: [2]"Son of man, this is what the Sovereign LORD says to the land of Israel: The end! The end has come upon the four corners of the land. [3]The end is now upon you and I will unleash my anger against you. I will judge you according to your conduct and repay you for all your detestable practices. [4]I will not look on you with pity or spare you; I will surely repay you for your conduct and the detestable practices among you. Then you will know that I am the LORD.

[5]"This is what the Sovereign LORD says: Disaster! An unheard-of[b] disaster is coming. [6]The end has come! The end has come! It has roused itself against you. It has come! [7]Doom has come upon you— you who dwell in the land. The time has come, the day is near; there is panic, not joy, upon the mountains. [8]I am about to pour out my wrath on you and spend my anger against you; I will judge you according to your conduct and repay you for all your detestable practices. [9]I will not look on you with pity or spare you; I will repay you in accordance with your conduct and the detestable practices among you. Then you will know that it is I the LORD who strikes the blow.

[10]"The day is here! It has come! Doom has burst forth, the rod has budded, arrogance has blossomed! [11]Violence has grown into[c] a rod to punish wickedness; none of the people will be left, none of that crowd—no wealth, nothing of value. [12]The time has come, the day has arrived. Let not the buyer rejoice nor the seller grieve, for wrath is upon the whole crowd. [13]The seller will not recover the land he has sold as long as both of them live, for the vision concerning the whole crowd will not be reversed. Because of their sins, not one of them will preserve his life. [14]Though they blow the trumpet and get everything ready, no one will go into battle, for my wrath is upon the whole crowd.

[15]"Outside is the sword, inside are plague and famine; those in the country will die by the sword, and those in the city will be devoured by famine and plague. [16]All who survive and escape will be in the mountains, moaning like doves of the valleys, each because of his sins. [17]Every hand will go limp, and every knee will become as weak as water. [18]They will put on sackcloth and be clothed with terror. Their faces will be covered with shame and their heads will be shaved. [19]They will throw their silver into the streets, and their gold will be an unclean thing. Their silver and gold will not be able to save them in the day of the LORD's wrath. They will not satisfy their hunger or fill their stomachs with it, for it has made them stumble into sin. [20]They were proud of their beautiful jewelry and used it to make their detestable idols and vile images. Therefore I will turn these into an unclean thing for them. [21]I will hand it all over as plunder to foreigners and as loot to the wicked of the earth, and they will defile it. [22]I will turn my face away from them, and they will desecrate my treasured place; robbers will enter it and desecrate it.

[a]14 Most Hebrew manuscripts; a few Hebrew manuscripts *Riblah*   [b]5 Most Hebrew manuscripts; some Hebrew manuscripts and Syriac *Disaster after*   [c]11 Or *The violent one has become*

23"Prepare chains, because the land is full of bloodshed and the city is full of violence. 24I will bring the most wicked of the nations to take possession of their houses; I will put an end to the pride of the mighty, and their sanctuaries will be desecrated. 25When terror comes, they will seek peace, but there will be none. 26Calamity upon calamity will come, and rumor upon rumor. They will try to get a vision from the prophet; the teaching of the law by the priest will be lost, as will the counsel of the elders. 27The king will mourn, the prince will be clothed with despair, and the hands of the people of the land will tremble. I will deal with them according to their conduct, and by their own standards I will judge them. Then they will know that I am the LORD."

Idolatry in the Temple

8 In the sixth year, in the sixth month on the fifth day, while I was sitting in my house and the elders of Judah were sitting before me, the hand of the Sovereign LORD came upon me there. 2I looked, and I saw a figure like that of a man.ᵃ From what appeared to be his waist down he was like fire, and from there up his appearance was as bright as glowing metal. 3He stretched out what looked like a hand and took me by the hair of my head. The Spirit lifted me up between earth and heaven and in visions of God he took me to Jerusalem, to the entrance to the north gate of the inner court, where the idol that provokes to jealousy stood. 4And there before me was the glory of the God of Israel, as in the vision I had seen in the plain.

5Then he said to me, "Son of man, look toward the north." So I looked, and in the entrance north of the gate of the altar I saw this idol of jealousy.

6And he said to me, "Son of man, do you see what they are doing—the utterly detestable things the house of Israel is doing here, things that will drive me far

from my sanctuary? But you will see things that are even more detestable."

7Then he brought me to the entrance to the court. I looked, and I saw a hole in the wall. 8He said to me, "Son of man, now dig into the wall." So I dug into the wall and saw a doorway there.

9And he said to me, "Go in and see the wicked and detestable things they are doing here." 10So I went in and looked, and I saw portrayed all over the walls all kinds of crawling things and detestable animals and all the idols of the house of Israel. 11In front of them stood seventy elders of the house of Israel, and Jaazaniah son of Shaphan was standing among them. Each had a censer in his hand, and a fragrant cloud of incense was rising.

12He said to me, "Son of man, have you seen what the elders of the house of Israel are doing in the darkness, each at the shrine of his own idol? They say, 'The LORD does not see us; the LORD has forsaken the land.'" 13Again, he said, "You will see them doing things that are even more detestable."

14Then he brought me to the entrance to the north gate of the house of the LORD, and I saw women sitting there, mourning for Tammuz. 15He said to me, "Do you see this, son of man? You will see things that are even more detestable than this."

16He then brought me into the inner court of the house of the LORD, and there at the entrance to the temple, between the portico and the altar, were about twenty-five men. With their backs toward the temple of the LORD and their faces toward the east, they were bowing down to the sun in the east.

17He said to me, "Have you seen this, son of man? Is it a trivial matter for the house of Judah to do the detestable things they are doing here? Must they also fill the land with violence and continually provoke me to anger? Look at them putting the branch to their nose! 18Therefore I will deal with them in anger; I will not look on them with pity or spare them. Although they shout in my ears, I will not listen to them."

> *Never be afraid to trust an unknown future to a known God.*
>
> CORRIE TEN BOOM

ᵃ2 Or *saw a fiery figure*

Idolaters Killed

9 Then I heard him call out in a loud voice, "Bring the guards of the city here, each with a weapon in his hand." [2]And I saw six men coming from the direction of the upper gate, which faces north, each with a deadly weapon in his hand. With them was a man clothed in linen who had a writing kit at his side. They came in and stood beside the bronze altar.

[3]Now the glory of the God of Israel went up from above the cherubim, where it had been, and moved to the threshold of the temple. Then the LORD called to the man clothed in linen who had the writing kit at his side [4]and said to him, "Go throughout the city of Jerusalem and put a mark on the foreheads of those who grieve and lament over all the detestable things that are done in it."

[5]As I listened, he said to the others, "Follow him through the city and kill, without showing pity or compassion. [6]Slaughter old men, young men and maidens, women and children, but do not touch anyone who has the mark. Begin at my sanctuary." So they began with the elders who were in front of the temple.

[7]Then he said to them, "Defile the temple and fill the courts with the slain. Go!" So they went out and began killing throughout the city. [8]While they were killing and I was left alone, I fell facedown, crying out, "Ah, Sovereign LORD! Are you going to destroy the entire remnant of Israel in this outpouring of your wrath on Jerusalem?"

[9]He answered me, "The sin of the house of Israel and Judah is exceedingly great; the land is full of bloodshed and the city is full of injustice. They say, 'The LORD has forsaken the land; the LORD does not see.' [10]So I will not look on them with pity or spare them, but I will bring down on their own heads what they have done."

[11]Then the man in linen with the writing kit at his side brought back word, saying, "I have done as you commanded."

The Glory Departs From the Temple

10 I looked, and I saw the likeness of a throne of sapphire[a] above the expanse that was over the heads of the cherubim. [2]The LORD said to the man clothed in linen, "Go in among the wheels beneath the cherubim. Fill your hands with burning coals from among the cherubim and scatter them over the city." And as I watched, he went in.

[3]Now the cherubim were standing on the south side of the temple when the man went in, and a cloud filled the inner court. [4]Then the glory of the LORD rose from above the cherubim and moved to the threshold of the temple. The cloud filled the temple, and the court was full of the radiance of the glory of the LORD. [5]The sound of the wings of the cherubim could be heard as far away as the outer court, like the voice of God Almighty[b] when he speaks.

[6]When the LORD commanded the man in linen, "Take fire from among the wheels, from among the cherubim," the man went in and stood beside a wheel. [7]Then one of the cherubim reached out his hand to the fire that was among them. He took up some of it and put it into the hands of the man in linen, who took it and went out. [8](Under the wings of the cherubim could be seen what looked like the hands of a man.)

[9]I looked, and I saw beside the cherubim four wheels, one beside each of the cherubim; the wheels sparkled like chrysolite. [10]As for their appearance, the four of them looked alike; each was like a wheel intersecting a wheel. [11]As they moved, they would go in any one of the four directions the cherubim faced; the wheels did not turn about[c] as the cherubim went. The cherubim went in whatever direction the head faced, without turning as they went. [12]Their entire bodies, including their backs, their hands and their wings, were completely full of eyes, as were their four wheels. [13]I heard the wheels being called "the whirling wheels." [14]Each of the cherubim had four faces: One face was that of a cherub, the second the face of a man, the third the face of a lion, and the fourth the face of an eagle.

[15]Then the cherubim rose upward. These were the living creatures I had

[a]1 Or lapis lazuli   [b]5 Hebrew El-Shaddai
[c]11 Or aside

seen by the Kebar River. ¹⁶When the cherubim moved, the wheels beside them moved; and when the cherubim spread their wings to rise from the ground, the wheels did not leave their side. ¹⁷When the cherubim stood still, they also stood still; and when the cherubim rose, they rose with them, because the spirit of the living creatures was in them.

¹⁸Then the glory of the LORD departed from over the threshold of the temple and stopped above the cherubim. ¹⁹While I watched, the cherubim spread their wings and rose from the ground, and as they went, the wheels went with them. They stopped at the entrance to the east gate of the LORD's house, and the glory of the God of Israel was above them.

²⁰These were the living creatures I had seen beneath the God of Israel by the Kebar River, and I realized that they were cherubim. ²¹Each had four faces and four wings, and under their wings was what looked like the hands of a man. ²²Their faces had the same appearance as those I had seen by the Kebar River. Each one went straight ahead.

Judgment on Israel's Leaders

11 Then the Spirit lifted me up and brought me to the gate of the house of the LORD that faces east. There at the entrance to the gate were twenty-five men, and I saw among them Jaazaniah son of Azzur and Pelatiah son of Benaiah, leaders of the people. ²The LORD said to me, "Son of man, these are the men who are plotting evil and giving wicked advice in this city. ³They say, 'Will it not soon be time to build houses?ᵃ This city is a cooking pot, and we are the meat.' ⁴Therefore prophesy against them; prophesy, son of man."

⁵Then the Spirit of the LORD came upon me, and he told me to say: "This is what the LORD says: That is what you are saying, O house of Israel, but I know what is going through your mind. ⁶You have killed many people in this city and filled its streets with the dead.

⁷"Therefore this is what the Sovereign LORD says: The bodies you have thrown there are the meat and this city is the pot, but I will drive you out of it. ⁸You fear

the sword, and the sword is what I will bring against you, declares the Sovereign LORD. ⁹I will drive you out of the city and hand you over to foreigners and inflict punishment on you. ¹⁰You will fall by the sword, and I will execute judgment on you at the borders of Israel. Then you will know that I am the LORD. ¹¹This city will not be a pot for you, nor will you be the meat in it; I will execute judgment on you at the borders of Israel. ¹²And you will know that I am the LORD, for you have not followed my decrees or kept my laws but have conformed to the standards of the nations around you."

¹³Now as I was prophesying, Pelatiah son of Benaiah died. Then I fell facedown and cried out in a loud voice, "Ah, Sovereign LORD! Will you completely destroy the remnant of Israel?"

¹⁴The word of the LORD came to me: ¹⁵"Son of man, your brothers—your brothers who are your blood relativesᵇ and the whole house of Israel—are those of whom the people of Jerusalem have said, 'They areᶜ far away from the LORD; this land was given to us as our possession.'

Promised Return of Israel

¹⁶"Therefore say: 'This is what the Sovereign LORD says: Although I sent them far away among the nations and scattered them among the countries, yet for a little while I have been a sanctuary for them in the countries where they have gone.'

¹⁷"Therefore say: 'This is what the Sovereign LORD says: I will gather you from the nations and bring you back from the countries where you have been scattered, and I will give you back the land of Israel again.'

¹⁸"They will return to it and remove all its vile images and detestable idols. ¹⁹I will give them an undivided heart and put a new spirit in them; I will remove from them their heart of stone and give them a heart of flesh. ²⁰Then they will follow my decrees and be careful to keep my laws. They will be my people, and I

ᵃ3 Or *This is not the time to build houses.*
ᵇ15 Or *are in exile with you* (see Septuagint and Syriac)   ᶜ15 Or *those to whom the people of Jerusalem have said, 'Stay*

will be their God. ²¹But as for those whose hearts are devoted to their vile images and detestable idols, I will bring down on their own heads what they have done, declares the Sovereign LORD."

²²Then the cherubim, with the wheels beside them, spread their wings, and the glory of the God of Israel was above them. ²³The glory of the LORD went up from within the city and stopped above the mountain east of it. ²⁴The Spirit lifted me up and brought me to the exiles in

[FRIDAY]

He in You and You in Him

11:16 "YET FOR A LITTLE WHILE I HAVE BEEN A SANCTUARY FOR THEM IN THE COUNTRIES WHERE THEY HAVE GONE."

What God says here is so startlingly uncommon in the Old Testament that it might as well be a new concept. The sanctuary, the temple in Jerusalem, had been the symbol of God's presence among his people. Now the people are in exile in Babylon, the home of other gods. Where could they go to be with God? God's answer is, "I've come to meet with you. I'm not *in* the sanctuary, I *am* the sanctuary," and by inference, "You are in me." The people couldn't get to the temple, so the temple came to them! The gospel appears in the least expected places, doesn't it? It would be 600 years before the full implications of this statement would be known, when Jesus calls himself the new temple (see John 2:19–22). It took the tragedy of the exile and separation from the temple for God to make the point he had been trying to make all along: that he wanted to live among the people as their God.

But there was more that God wanted. He not only wanted *them* to be in *him* as their true sanctuary, *he* wanted to be in *them*, as his sanctuary. "I will give them an undivided heart and put a new spirit in them; I will remove from them their heart of stone and give them a heart of flesh" (Ezekiel 11:19). He is more explicit later in Ezekiel: "I will put my Spirit in you and move you to follow my decrees and be careful to keep my laws" (36:27). Again, it would be 600 years before the full implications were understood when Paul tells the Corinthians, "Do you not know that your body is a temple of the Holy Spirit, who is in you, whom you have received from God?" (1 Corinthians 6:19).

Stated philosophically, this is the ontological basis, the relationship proper, for prayer: In Christ, we are in God and God is in us. He is our sanctuary and we are his. As we enjoy spiritual blessings in Christ, the chief blessing is Christ in us; he is the hope of glory (see Ephesians 1:3; Colossians 1:27). To speak to him and be heard, we don't need to climb up to heaven or cross the sea. He is near to us, in our hearts and our mouths so we may speak (see Deuteronomy 30:11–14).

PRAY:

Precious Lord, how awesome that you are our sanctuary and we are yours! In you we live and move and have our being (see Acts 17:28). May this reality have its full impact on my prayer life.

FOR YOUR NEXT DEVOTIONAL READING, GO TO PAGE 984.

Babylonia[a] in the vision given by the Spirit of God.

Then the vision I had seen went up from me, ²⁵and I told the exiles everything the LORD had shown me.

The Exile Symbolized

12 The word of the LORD came to me: ²"Son of man, you are living among a rebellious people. They have eyes to see but do not see and ears to hear but do not hear, for they are a rebellious people.

³"Therefore, son of man, pack your belongings for exile and in the daytime, as they watch, set out and go from where you are to another place. Perhaps they will understand, though they are a rebellious house. ⁴During the daytime, while they watch, bring out your belongings packed for exile. Then in the evening, while they are watching, go out like those who go into exile. ⁵While they watch, dig through the wall and take your belongings out through it. ⁶Put them on your shoulder as they are watching and carry them out at dusk. Cover your face so that you cannot see the land, for I have made you a sign to the house of Israel."

⁷So I did as I was commanded. During the day I brought out my things packed for exile. Then in the evening I dug through the wall with my hands. I took my belongings out at dusk, carrying them on my shoulders while they watched.

⁸In the morning the word of the LORD came to me: ⁹"Son of man, did not that rebellious house of Israel ask you, 'What are you doing?'

¹⁰"Say to them, 'This is what the Sovereign LORD says: This oracle concerns the prince in Jerusalem and the whole house of Israel who are there.' ¹¹Say to them, 'I am a sign to you.'

"As I have done, so it will be done to them. They will go into exile as captives.

¹²"The prince among them will put his things on his shoulder at dusk and leave, and a hole will be dug in the wall for him to go through. He will cover his face so that he cannot see the land. ¹³I will spread my net for him, and he will be caught in my snare; I will bring him to Babylonia, the land of the Chaldeans,

but he will not see it, and there he will die. ¹⁴I will scatter to the winds all those around him—his staff and all his troops—and I will pursue them with drawn sword.

¹⁵"They will know that I am the LORD, when I disperse them among the nations and scatter them through the countries. ¹⁶But I will spare a few of them from the sword, famine and plague, so that in the nations where they go they may acknowledge all their detestable practices. Then they will know that I am the LORD."

¹⁷The word of the LORD came to me: ¹⁸"Son of man, tremble as you eat your food, and shudder in fear as you drink your water. ¹⁹Say to the people of the land: 'This is what the Sovereign LORD says about those living in Jerusalem and in the land of Israel: They will eat their food in anxiety and drink their water in despair, for their land will be stripped of everything in it because of the violence of all who live there. ²⁰The inhabited towns will be laid waste and the land will be desolate. Then you will know that I am the LORD.'"

²¹The word of the LORD came to me: ²²"Son of man, what is this proverb you have in the land of Israel: 'The days go by and every vision comes to nothing'? ²³Say to them, 'This is what the Sovereign LORD says: I am going to put an end to this proverb, and they will no longer quote it in Israel.' Say to them, 'The days are near when every vision will be fulfilled. ²⁴For there will be no more false visions or flattering divinations among the people of Israel. ²⁵But I the LORD will speak what I will, and it shall be fulfilled without delay. For in your days, you rebellious house, I will fulfill whatever I say, declares the Sovereign LORD.'"

²⁶The word of the LORD came to me: ²⁷"Son of man, the house of Israel is saying, 'The vision he sees is for many years from now, and he prophesies about the distant future.'

²⁸"Therefore say to them, 'This is what the Sovereign LORD says: None of my words will be delayed any longer; whatever I say will be fulfilled, declares the Sovereign LORD.'"

[a]24 Or *Chaldea*

False Prophets Condemned

13 The word of the LORD came to me: ²"Son of man, prophesy against the prophets of Israel who are now prophesying. Say to those who prophesy out of their own imagination: 'Hear the word of the LORD! ³This is what the Sovereign LORD says: Woe to the foolish[a] prophets who follow their own spirit and have seen nothing! ⁴Your prophets, O Israel, are like jackals among ruins. ⁵You have not gone up to the breaks in the wall to repair it for the house of Israel so that it will stand firm in the battle on the day of the LORD. ⁶Their visions are false and their divinations a lie. They say, "The LORD declares," when the LORD has not sent them; yet they expect their words to be fulfilled. ⁷Have you not seen false visions and uttered lying divinations when you say, "The LORD declares," though I have not spoken?

⁸" 'Therefore this is what the Sovereign LORD says: Because of your false words and lying visions, I am against you, declares the Sovereign LORD. ⁹My hand will be against the prophets who see false visions and utter lying divinations. They will not belong to the council of my people or be listed in the records of the house of Israel, nor will they enter the land of Israel. Then you will know that I am the Sovereign LORD.

¹⁰" 'Because they lead my people astray, saying, "Peace," when there is no peace, and because, when a flimsy wall is built, they cover it with whitewash, ¹¹therefore tell those who cover it with whitewash that it is going to fall. Rain will come in torrents, and I will send hailstones hurtling down, and violent winds will burst forth. ¹²When the wall collapses, will people not ask you, "Where is the whitewash you covered it with?"

¹³" 'Therefore this is what the Sovereign LORD says: In my wrath I will unleash a violent wind, and in my anger hailstones and torrents of rain will fall with destructive fury. ¹⁴I will tear down the wall you have covered with whitewash and will level it to the ground so that its foundation will be laid bare. When it[b] falls, you will be destroyed in it; and you will know that I am the LORD. ¹⁵So I will spend my wrath against the wall and against those who covered it with white-

wash. I will say to you, "The wall is gone and so are those who whitewashed it, ¹⁶those prophets of Israel who prophesied to Jerusalem and saw visions of peace for her when there was no peace, declares the Sovereign LORD." '

¹⁷"Now, son of man, set your face against the daughters of your people who prophesy out of their own imagination. Prophesy against them ¹⁸and say, 'This is what the Sovereign LORD says: Woe to the women who sew magic charms on all their wrists and make veils of various lengths for their heads in order to ensnare people. Will you ensnare the lives of my people but preserve your own? ¹⁹You have profaned me among my people for a few handfuls of barley and scraps of bread. By lying to my people, who listen to lies, you have killed those who should not have died and have spared those who should not live.

> The strength of your prayer lies in your faith in the promise which you pleaded before the Lord.
>
> C.H. SPURGEON

²⁰" 'Therefore this is what the Sovereign LORD says: I am against your magic charms with which you ensnare people like birds and I will tear them from your arms; I will set free the people that you ensnare like birds. ²¹I will tear off your veils and save my people from your hands, and they will no longer fall prey to your power. Then you will know that I am the LORD. ²²Because you disheartened the righteous with your lies, when I had brought them no grief, and because you encouraged the wicked not to turn from their evil ways and so save their lives, ²³therefore you will no longer see false visions or practice divination. I will save my people from your hands. And then you will know that I am the LORD.' "

Idolaters Condemned

14 Some of the elders of Israel came to me and sat down in front of me. ²Then the word of the LORD came to me: ³"Son of man, these men have set up idols

a 3 Or wicked   b 14 Or the city

in their hearts and put wicked stumbling blocks before their faces. Should I let them inquire of me at all? ⁴Therefore speak to them and tell them, 'This is what the Sovereign LORD says: When any Israelite sets up idols in his heart and puts a wicked stumbling block before his face and then goes to a prophet, I the LORD will answer him myself in keeping with his great idolatry. ⁵I will do this to recapture the hearts of the people of Israel, who have all deserted me for their idols.'

⁶"Therefore say to the house of Israel, 'This is what the Sovereign LORD says: Repent! Turn from your idols and renounce all your detestable practices!

⁷" 'When any Israelite or any alien living in Israel separates himself from me and sets up idols in his heart and puts a wicked stumbling block before his face and then goes to a prophet to inquire of me, I the LORD will answer him myself. ⁸I will set my face against that man and make him an example and a byword. I will cut him off from my people. Then you will know that I am the LORD.

⁹" 'And if the prophet is enticed to utter a prophecy, I the LORD have enticed that prophet, and I will stretch out my hand against him and destroy him from among my people Israel. ¹⁰They will bear their guilt—the prophet will be as guilty as the one who consults him. ¹¹Then the people of Israel will no longer stray from me, nor will they defile themselves anymore with all their sins. They will be my people, and I will be their God, declares the Sovereign LORD.' "

Judgment Inescapable

¹²The word of the LORD came to me: ¹³"Son of man, if a country sins against me by being unfaithful and I stretch out my hand against it to cut off its food supply and send famine upon it and kill its men and their animals, ¹⁴even if these three men—Noah, Daniel*a* and Job— were in it, they could save only themselves by their righteousness, declares the Sovereign LORD.

¹⁵"Or if I send wild beasts through that country and they leave it childless and it becomes desolate so that no one can pass through it because of the beasts, ¹⁶as surely as I live, declares the Sover-

eign LORD, even if these three men were in it, they could not save their own sons or daughters. They alone would be saved, but the land would be desolate.

¹⁷"Or if I bring a sword against that country and say, 'Let the sword pass throughout the land,' and I kill its men and their animals, ¹⁸as surely as I live, declares the Sovereign LORD, even if these three men were in it, they could not save their own sons or daughters. They alone would be saved.

¹⁹"Or if I send a plague into that land and pour out my wrath upon it through bloodshed, killing its men and their animals, ²⁰as surely as I live, declares the Sovereign LORD, even if Noah, Daniel and Job were in it, they could save neither son nor daughter. They would save only themselves by their righteousness.

²¹"For this is what the Sovereign LORD says: How much worse will it be when I send against Jerusalem my four dreadful judgments—sword and famine and wild beasts and plague—to kill its men and their animals! ²²Yet there will be some survivors—sons and daughters who will be brought out of it. They will come to you, and when you see their conduct and their actions, you will be consoled regarding the disaster I have brought upon Jerusalem—every disaster I have brought upon it. ²³You will be consoled when you see their conduct and their actions, for you will know that I have done nothing in it without cause, declares the Sovereign LORD."

Jerusalem, A Useless Vine

15 The word of the LORD came to me: ²"Son of man, how is the wood of a vine better than that of a branch on any of the trees in the forest? ³Is wood ever taken from it to make anything useful? Do they make pegs from it to hang things on? ⁴And after it is thrown on the fire as fuel and the fire burns both ends and chars the middle, is it then useful for anything? ⁵If it was not useful for anything when it was whole, how much less can it be made into something useful when the fire has burned it and it is charred?

---

a14 Or *Daniel*; the Hebrew spelling may suggest a person other than the prophet Daniel; also in verse 20.

6 "Therefore this is what the Sovereign Lord says: As I have given the wood of the vine among the trees of the forest as fuel for the fire, so will I treat the people living in Jerusalem. 7 I will set my face against them. Although they have come out of the fire, the fire will yet consume them. And when I set my face against them, you will know that I am the Lord. 8 I will make the land desolate because they have been unfaithful, declares the Sovereign Lord."

An Allegory of Unfaithful Jerusalem

16 The word of the Lord came to me: 2 "Son of man, confront Jerusalem with her detestable practices 3 and say, 'This is what the Sovereign Lord says to Jerusalem: Your ancestry and birth were in the land of the Canaanites; your father was an Amorite and your mother a Hittite. 4 On the day you were born your cord was not cut, nor were you washed with water to make you clean, nor were you rubbed with salt or wrapped in cloths. 5 No one looked on you with pity or had compassion enough to do any of these things for you. Rather, you were thrown out into the open field, for on the day you were born you were despised.

6 "'Then I passed by and saw you kicking about in your blood, and as you lay there in your blood I said to you, "Live!"a 7 I made you grow like a plant of the field. You grew up and developed and became the most beautiful of jewels.b Your breasts were formed and your hair grew, you who were naked and bare.

8 "'Later I passed by, and when I looked at you and saw that you were old enough for love, I spread the corner of my garment over you and covered your nakedness. I gave you my solemn oath and entered into a covenant with you, declares the Sovereign Lord, and you became mine.

9 "'I bathedc you with water and washed the blood from you and put ointments on you. 10 I clothed you with an embroidered dress and put leather sandals on you. I dressed you in fine linen and covered you with costly garments. 11 I adorned you with jewelry: I put bracelets on your arms and a necklace around your neck, 12 and I put a ring on your nose, earrings on your ears and a beautiful crown on your head. 13 So you were adorned with gold and silver; your clothes were of fine linen and costly fabric and embroidered cloth. Your food was fine flour, honey and olive oil. You became very beautiful and rose to be a queen. 14 And your fame spread among the nations on account of your beauty, because the splendor I had given you made your beauty perfect, declares the Sovereign Lord.

15 "'But you trusted in your beauty and used your fame to become a prostitute. You lavished your favors on anyone who passed by and your beauty became his.d 16 You took some of your garments to make gaudy high places, where you carried on your prostitution. Such things should not happen, nor should they ever occur. 17 You also took the fine jewelry I gave you, the jewelry made of my gold and silver, and you made for yourself male idols and engaged in prostitution with them. 18 And you took your embroidered clothes to put on them, and you offered my oil and incense before them. 19 Also the food I provided for you—the fine flour, olive oil and honey I gave you to eat—you offered as fragrant incense before them. That is what happened, declares the Sovereign Lord.

20 "'And you took your sons and daughters whom you bore to me and sacrificed them as food to the idols. Was your prostitution not enough? 21 You slaughtered my children and sacrificed theme to the idols. 22 In all your detestable practices and your prostitution you did not remember the days of your youth, when you were naked and bare, kicking about in your blood.

23 "'Woe! Woe to you, declares the Sovereign Lord. In addition to all your other wickedness, 24 you built a mound for yourself and made a lofty shrine in every public square. 25 At the head of every street you built your lofty shrines and degraded your beauty, offering your body

---

a6 A few Hebrew manuscripts, Septuagint and Syriac; most Hebrew manuscripts "Live!" And as you lay there in your blood I said to you, "Live!"
b7 Or became mature   c9 Or I had bathed
d15 Most Hebrew manuscripts; one Hebrew manuscript (see some Septuagint manuscripts) by. Such a thing should not happen   e21 Or and made them pass through the fire.

with increasing promiscuity to anyone who passed by. ²⁶You engaged in prostitution with the Egyptians, your lustful neighbors, and provoked me to anger with your increasing promiscuity. ²⁷So I stretched out my hand against you and reduced your territory; I gave you over to the greed of your enemies, the daughters of the Philistines, who were shocked by your lewd conduct. ²⁸You engaged in prostitution with the Assyrians too, because you were insatiable; and even after that, you still were not satisfied. ²⁹Then you increased your promiscuity to include Babylonia,ᵃ a land of merchants, but even with this you were not satisfied.

³⁰" 'How weak-willed you are, declares the Sovereign LORD, when you do all these things, acting like a brazen prostitute! ³¹When you built your mounds at the head of every street and made your lofty shrines in every public square, you were unlike a prostitute, because you scorned payment.

³²" 'You adulterous wife! You prefer strangers to your own husband! ³³Every prostitute receives a fee, but you give gifts to all your lovers, bribing them to come to you from everywhere for your illicit favors. ³⁴So in your prostitution you are the opposite of others; no one runs after you for your favors. You are the very opposite, for you give payment and none is given to you.

³⁵" 'Therefore, you prostitute, hear the word of the LORD! ³⁶This is what the Sovereign LORD says: Because you poured out your wealthᵇ and exposed your nakedness in your promiscuity with your lovers, and because of all your detestable idols, and because you gave them your children's blood, ³⁷therefore I am going to gather all your lovers, with whom you found pleasure, those you loved as well as those you hated. I will gather them against you from all around and will strip you in front of them, and they will see all your nakedness. ³⁸I will sentence you to the punishment of women who commit adultery and who shed blood; I will bring upon you the blood vengeance of my wrath and jealous anger. ³⁹Then I will hand you over to your lovers, and they will tear down your mounds and destroy your lofty shrines. They will strip you of

your clothes and take your fine jewelry and leave you naked and bare. ⁴⁰They will bring a mob against you, who will stone you and hack you to pieces with their swords. ⁴¹They will burn down your houses and inflict punishment on you in the sight of many women. I will put a stop to your prostitution, and you will no longer pay your lovers. ⁴²Then my wrath against you will subside and my jealous anger will turn away from you; I will be calm and no longer angry.

⁴³" 'Because you did not remember the days of your youth but enraged me with all these things, I will surely bring down on your head what you have done, declares the Sovereign LORD. Did you not add lewdness to all your other detestable practices?

⁴⁴" 'Everyone who quotes proverbs will quote this proverb about you: "Like mother, like daughter." ⁴⁵You are a true daughter of your mother, who despised her husband and her children; and you are a true sister of your sisters, who despised their husbands and their children. Your mother was a Hittite and your father an Amorite. ⁴⁶Your older sister was Samaria, who lived to the north of you with her daughters; and your younger sister, who lived to the south of you with her daughters, was Sodom. ⁴⁷You not only walked in their ways and copied their detestable practices, but in all your ways you soon became more depraved than they. ⁴⁸As surely as I live, declares the Sovereign LORD, your sister Sodom and her daughters never did what you and your daughters have done.

⁴⁹" 'Now this was the sin of your sister Sodom: She and her daughters were arrogant, overfed and unconcerned; they did not help the poor and needy. ⁵⁰They were haughty and did detestable things before me. Therefore I did away with them as you have seen. ⁵¹Samaria did not commit half the sins you did. You have done more detestable things than they, and have made your sisters seem righteous by all these things you have done. ⁵²Bear your disgrace, for you have furnished some justification for your sisters. Because your sins were more vile than

ᵃ29 Or Chaldea   ᵇ36 Or lust

theirs, they appear more righteous than you. So then, be ashamed and bear your disgrace, for you have made your sisters appear righteous.

⁵³ "However, I will restore the fortunes of Sodom and her daughters and of Samaria and her daughters, and your fortunes along with them, ⁵⁴so that you may bear your disgrace and be ashamed of all you have done in giving them comfort. ⁵⁵And your sisters, Sodom with her daughters and Samaria with her daughters, will return to what they were before; and you and your daughters will return to what you were before. ⁵⁶You would not even mention your sister Sodom in the day of your pride, ⁵⁷before your wickedness was uncovered. Even so, you are now scorned by the daughters of Edomᵃ and all her neighbors and the daughters of the Philistines—all those around you who despise you. ⁵⁸You will bear the consequences of your lewdness and your detestable practices, declares the LORD.

⁵⁹ "This is what the Sovereign LORD says: I will deal with you as you deserve, because you have despised my oath by breaking the covenant. ⁶⁰Yet I will remember the covenant I made with you in the days of your youth, and I will establish an everlasting covenant with you. ⁶¹Then you will remember your ways and be ashamed when you receive your sisters, both those who are older than you and those who are younger. I will give them to you as daughters, but not on the basis of my covenant with you. ⁶²So I will establish my covenant with you, and you will know that I am the LORD. ⁶³Then, when I make atonement for you for all you have done, you will remember and be ashamed and never again open your mouth because of your humiliation, declares the Sovereign LORD.' "

Two Eagles and a Vine

17 The word of the LORD came to me: ²"Son of man, set forth an allegory and tell the house of Israel a parable. ³Say to them, 'This is what the Sovereign LORD says: A great eagle with powerful wings, long feathers and full plumage of varied colors came to Lebanon. Taking hold of the top of a cedar, ⁴he broke off its topmost shoot and carried it away to a land of merchants, where he planted it in a city of traders.

⁵" 'He took some of the seed of your land and put it in fertile soil. He planted it like a willow by abundant water, ⁶and it sprouted and became a low, spreading vine. Its branches turned toward him, but its roots remained under it. So it became a vine and produced branches and put out leafy boughs.

⁷" 'But there was another great eagle with powerful wings and full plumage. The vine now sent out its roots toward him from the plot where it was planted and stretched out its branches to him for water. ⁸It had been planted in good soil by abundant water so that it would produce branches, bear fruit and become a splendid vine.'

⁹"Say to them, 'This is what the Sovereign LORD says: Will it thrive? Will it not be uprooted and stripped of its fruit so that it withers? All its new growth will wither. It will not take a strong arm or many people to pull it up by the roots. ¹⁰Even if it is transplanted, will it thrive? Will it not wither completely when the east wind strikes it—wither away in the plot where it grew?' "

¹¹Then the word of the LORD came to me: ¹²"Say to this rebellious house, 'Do you not know what these things mean?' Say to them: 'The king of Babylon went to Jerusalem and carried off her king and her nobles, bringing them back with him to Babylon. ¹³Then he took a member of the royal family and made a treaty with him, putting him under oath. He also carried away the leading men of the land, ¹⁴so that the kingdom would be brought low, unable to rise again, surviving only by keeping his treaty. ¹⁵But the king rebelled against him by sending his envoys to Egypt to get horses and a large army. Will he succeed? Will he who does such things escape? Will he break the treaty and yet escape?

¹⁶" 'As surely as I live, declares the Sovereign LORD, he shall die in Babylon, in the land of the king who put him on the throne, whose oath he despised and

ᵃ57 Many Hebrew manuscripts and Syriac; most Hebrew manuscripts, Septuagint and Vulgate Aram

God Plus One

MARY SLESSOR, missionary to the Sudan, once put herself directly between two tribal armies about to fight, demanding that they lay down their arms. At the end of the day the determined woman stood by a pile of weapons five feet high!

From childhood the odds were stacked against Mary Mitchell Slessor. Her mother worked long shifts as a weaver, while her alcoholic father drank away the money and terrified the children with his unstable lifestyle. At age 11 Slessor was forced to leave school and begin working 12-hour shifts in a factory. Yet the harsh conditions of her childhood didn't break her spirit. She volunteered her time teaching Sunday School in the slums, became active in the Presbyterian Church and secretly dreamed of becoming a missionary.

In 1874, the death of David Livingstone set off a wave of missionary zeal throughout Scotland, and Slessor seized the opportunity to volunteer for missionary service in the Sudan.

Twelve years into her service, Slessor discovered a traditional practice of the Okyong people. The Okyongs believed that if a woman gave birth to twins, one of them was the result of intercourse with a demon. It was common practice to leave newborns outside the village in clay pots to be eaten by ants or to die of neglect. Slessor decided there was only one thing to do: She built a hut for herself out of sticks and mud and immediately began caring for any abandoned children, sometimes pulling them from trash heaps outside the villages. Soon her hut became an orphanage, a tangled web of hammocks and cradles all connected with string, so she could rock the babies all at once while she prayed or read.

Slessor saved the lives of hundreds of orphans. She eventually became a district tribal judge and was awarded the "Order of the Hospital of St. John of Jerusalem." All the accolades mostly embarrassed her, and she dismissed it as a bunch of "blarney." Slessor died among her adopted children on January 13, 1915.

Among the many remarkable things in this remarkable woman's life was her attitude toward prayer. Though every inch an activist, she believed prayer was the foundation of all activity. She wrote, "My life is one long daily, hourly, record of answered prayer. For physical health, for mental health over strain, for guidance given marvelously, for errors and dangers averted, for enmity to the Gospel subdued, for food provided at the exact hour needed, for everything that goes to make up life and my poor service . . . I can testify with a full and often wonder-stricken awe that I . . . know God answers prayer . . . Prayer is the greatest power God has put into our hands for service. Praying is harder work than doing . . . but the dynamic lies that way to advance the kingdom . . . Pray on—power lies that way."[1]

P R A Y :

Make this prayer of Mary Slessor's your own: "God plus one are always a majority—let me know that thou art with me."

M E M O R I Z E :

The angel of the LORD encamps around those who fear him, and he delivers them. PSALM 34:7

FOR YOUR NEXT DEVOTIONAL READING, GO TO PAGE 993.

whose treaty he broke. ¹⁷Pharaoh with his mighty army and great horde will be of no help to him in war, when ramps are built and siege works erected to destroy many lives. ¹⁸He despised the oath by breaking the covenant. Because he had given his hand in pledge and yet did all these things, he shall not escape.

¹⁹ "'Therefore this is what the Sovereign LORD says: As surely as I live, I will bring down on his head my oath that he despised and my covenant that he broke. ²⁰I will spread my net for him, and he will be caught in my snare. I will bring him to Babylon and execute judgment upon him there because he was unfaithful to me. ²¹All his fleeing troops will fall by the sword, and the survivors will be scattered to the winds. Then you will know that I the LORD have spoken.

²² "'This is what the Sovereign LORD says: I myself will take a shoot from the very top of a cedar and plant it; I will break off a tender sprig from its topmost shoots and plant it on a high and lofty mountain. ²³On the mountain heights of Israel I will plant it; it will produce branches and bear fruit and become a splendid cedar. Birds of every kind will nest in it; they will find shelter in the shade of its branches. ²⁴All the trees of the field will know that I the LORD bring down the tall tree and make the low tree grow tall. I dry up the green tree and make the dry tree flourish.

"'I the LORD have spoken, and I will do it.'"

The Soul Who Sins Will Die

18 The word of the LORD came to me: ²"What do you people mean by quoting this proverb about the land of Israel:

" 'The fathers eat sour grapes,
    and the children's teeth are set
        on edge'?

³"As surely as I live, declares the Sovereign LORD, you will no longer quote this proverb in Israel. ⁴For every living soul belongs to me, the father as well as the son—both alike belong to me. The soul who sins is the one who will die.

⁵ "Suppose there is a righteous man
    who does what is just and right.

⁶He does not eat at the mountain
        shrines
    or look to the idols of the house of
        Israel.
He does not defile his neighbor's wife
    or lie with a woman during her
        period.
⁷He does not oppress anyone,
    but returns what he took in pledge
        for a loan.
He does not commit robbery
    but gives his food to the hungry
    and provides clothing for the naked.
⁸He does not lend at usury
    or take excessive interest.ᵃ
He withholds his hand from doing
        wrong
    and judges fairly between man
        and man.
⁹He follows my decrees
    and faithfully keeps my laws.
That man is righteous;
    he will surely live,
            declares the Sovereign LORD.

¹⁰"Suppose he has a violent son, who sheds blood or does any of these other thingsᵇ ¹¹(though the father has done none of them):

"He eats at the mountain shrines.
He defiles his neighbor's wife.
¹²He oppresses the poor and needy.
He commits robbery.
He does not return what he took in
        pledge.
He looks to the idols.
He does detestable things.
¹³He lends at usury and takes excessive
        interest.

Will such a man live? He will not! Because he has done all these detestable things, he will surely be put to death and his blood will be on his own head.

¹⁴"But suppose this son has a son who sees all the sins his father commits, and though he sees them, he does not do such things:

¹⁵ "He does not eat at the mountain
        shrines
    or look to the idols of the house of
        Israel.

ᵃ8 Or *take interest*; similarly in verses 13 and 17
ᵇ10 Or *things to a brother*

He does not defile his neighbor's
wife.
16 He does not oppress anyone
or require a pledge for a loan.
He does not commit robbery
but gives his food to the hungry
and provides clothing for the
naked.
17 He withholds his hand from sin[a]
and takes no usury or excessive
interest.
He keeps my laws and follows my
decrees.

He will not die for his father's sin; he will
surely live. 18 But his father will die for his
own sin, because he practiced extortion,
robbed his brother and did what was
wrong among his people.

19 "Yet you ask, 'Why does the son not
share the guilt of his father?' Since the
son has done what is just and right and
has been careful to keep all my decrees,
he will surely live. 20 The soul who sins is
the one who will die. The son will not
share the guilt of the father, nor will the
father share the guilt of the son. The righteousness of the righteous man will be
credited to him, and the wickedness of
the wicked will be charged against him.

21 "But if a wicked man turns away from
all the sins he has committed and keeps
all my decrees and does what is just and
right, he will surely live; he will not die.
22 None of the offenses he has committed
will be remembered against him. Because of the righteous things he has
done, he will live. 23 Do I take any pleasure in the death of the wicked? declares
the Sovereign LORD. Rather, am I not
pleased when they turn from their ways
and live?

24 "But if a righteous man turns from
his righteousness and commits sin and
does the same detestable things the
wicked man does, will he live? None of
the righteous things he has done will be
remembered. Because of the unfaithfulness he is guilty of and because of the
sins he has committed, he will die.

25 "Yet you say, 'The way of the Lord is
not just.' Hear, O house of Israel: Is my
way unjust? Is it not your ways that are
unjust? 26 If a righteous man turns from
his righteousness and commits sin, he

will die for it; because of the sin he has
committed he will die. 27 But if a wicked
man turns away from the wickedness he
has committed and does what is just
and right, he will save his life. 28 Because
he considers all the offenses he has
committed and turns away from them,
he will surely live; he will not die. 29 Yet
the house of Israel says, 'The way of the
Lord is not just.' Are my ways unjust,
O house of Israel? Is it not your ways
that are unjust?

30 "Therefore, O house of Israel, I will
judge you, each one according to his
ways, declares the Sovereign LORD. Repent! Turn away from all your offenses;
then sin will not be your downfall. 31 Rid
yourselves of all the offenses you have
committed, and get a new heart and a
new spirit. Why will you die, O house of
Israel? 32 For I take no pleasure in the
death of anyone, declares the Sovereign
LORD. Repent and live!

A Lament for Israel's Princes

19 "Take up a lament concerning the
princes of Israel 2 and say:

" 'What a lioness was your mother
among the lions!
She lay down among the young lions
and reared her cubs.
3 She brought up one of her cubs,
and he became a strong lion.
He learned to tear the prey
and he devoured men.
4 The nations heard about him,
and he was trapped in their pit.
They led him with hooks
to the land of Egypt.

5 " 'When she saw her hope unfulfilled,
her expectation gone,
she took another of her cubs
and made him a strong lion.
6 He prowled among the lions,
for he was now a strong lion.
He learned to tear the prey
and he devoured men.
7 He broke down[b] their strongholds
and devastated their towns.
The land and all who were in it
were terrified by his roaring.

[a] 17 Septuagint (see also verse 8); Hebrew *from
the poor*   [b] 7 Targum (see Septuagint); Hebrew
He knew

⁸ Then the nations came against him,
    those from regions round about.
They spread their net for him,
    and he was trapped in their pit.
⁹ With hooks they pulled him into a
    cage
    and brought him to the king of
    Babylon.
They put him in prison,
    so his roar was heard no longer
    on the mountains of Israel.

¹⁰ " 'Your mother was like a vine in your
    vineyard*^a*
    planted by the water;
it was fruitful and full of branches
    because of abundant water.
¹¹ Its branches were strong,
    fit for a ruler's scepter.
It towered high
    above the thick foliage,
conspicuous for its height
    and for its many branches.
¹² But it was uprooted in fury
    and thrown to the ground.
The east wind made it shrivel,
    it was stripped of its fruit;
its strong branches withered
    and fire consumed them.
¹³ Now it is planted in the desert,
    in a dry and thirsty land.
¹⁴ Fire spread from one of its main^b
    branches
    and consumed its fruit.
No strong branch is left on it
    fit for a ruler's scepter.'

This is a lament and is to be used as a lament."

Rebellious Israel

20 In the seventh year, in the fifth month on the tenth day, some of the elders of Israel came to inquire of the LORD, and they sat down in front of me.

²Then the word of the LORD came to me: ³"Son of man, speak to the elders of Israel and say to them, 'This is what the Sovereign LORD says: Have you come to inquire of me? As surely as I live, I will not let you inquire of me, declares the Sovereign LORD.'

⁴"Will you judge them? Will you judge them, son of man? Then confront them with the detestable practices of their fathers ⁵and say to them: 'This is what the Sovereign LORD says: On the day I chose Israel, I swore with uplifted hand to the descendants of the house of Jacob and revealed myself to them in Egypt. With uplifted hand I said to them, "I am the LORD your God." ⁶On that day I swore to them that I would bring them out of Egypt into a land I had searched out for them, a land flowing with milk and honey, the most beautiful of all lands. ⁷And I said to them, "Each of you, get rid of the vile images you have set your eyes on, and do not defile yourselves with the idols of Egypt. I am the LORD your God."

⁸" 'But they rebelled against me and would not listen to me; they did not get rid of the vile images they had set their eyes on, nor did they forsake the idols of Egypt. So I said I would pour out my wrath on them and spend my anger against them in Egypt. ⁹But for the sake of my name I did what would keep it from being profaned in the eyes of the nations they lived among and in whose sight I had revealed myself to the Israelites by bringing them out of Egypt. ¹⁰Therefore I led them out of Egypt and brought them into the desert. ¹¹I gave them my decrees and made known to them my laws, for the man who obeys them will live by them. ¹²Also I gave them my Sabbaths as a sign between us, so they would know that I the LORD made them holy.

¹³" 'Yet the people of Israel rebelled against me in the desert. They did not follow my decrees but rejected my laws—although the man who obeys them will live by them—and they utterly desecrated my Sabbaths. So I said I would pour out my wrath on them and destroy them in the desert. ¹⁴But for the sake of my name I did what would keep it from being profaned in the eyes of the nations in whose sight I had brought them out. ¹⁵Also with uplifted hand I swore to them in the desert that I would not bring them into the land I had given them—a land flowing with milk and honey, most beautiful of all lands— ¹⁶because they rejected my laws and did not follow my decrees and desecrated my Sabbaths.

^a*10* Two Hebrew manuscripts; most Hebrew manuscripts *your blood*   ^b*14* Or *from under its*

For their hearts were devoted to their idols. ¹⁷Yet I looked on them with pity and did not destroy them or put an end to them in the desert. ¹⁸I said to their children in the desert, "Do not follow the statutes of your fathers or keep their laws or defile yourselves with their idols. ¹⁹I am the LORD your God; follow my decrees and be careful to keep my laws. ²⁰Keep my Sabbaths holy, that they may be a sign between us. Then you will know that I am the LORD your God.'

²¹" 'But the children rebelled against me: They did not follow my decrees, they were not careful to keep my laws—although the man who obeys them will live by them—and they desecrated my Sabbaths. So I said I would pour out my wrath on them and spend my anger against them in the desert. ²²But I withheld my hand, and for the sake of my name I did what would keep it from being profaned in the eyes of the nations in whose sight I had brought them out. ²³Also with uplifted hand I swore to them in the desert that I would disperse them among the nations and scatter them through the countries, ²⁴because they had not obeyed my laws but had rejected my decrees and desecrated my Sabbaths, and their eyes ⸤lusted⸥ after their fathers' idols. ²⁵I also gave them over to statutes that were not good and laws they could not live by; ²⁶I let them become defiled through their gifts—the sacrifice of every firstborn*a*—that I might fill them with horror so they would know that I am the LORD.'

²⁷"Therefore, son of man, speak to the people of Israel and say to them, 'This is what the Sovereign LORD says: In this also your fathers blasphemed me by forsaking me: ²⁸When I brought them into the land I had sworn to give them and they saw any high hill or any leafy tree, there they offered their sacrifices, made offerings that provoked me to anger, presented their fragrant incense and poured out their drink offerings. ²⁹Then I said to them: What is this high place you go to?' " (It is called Bamah*b* to this day.)

Judgment and Restoration

³⁰"Therefore say to the house of Israel: 'This is what the Sovereign LORD says:

Will you defile yourselves the way your fathers did and lust after their vile images? ³¹When you offer your gifts—the sacrifice of your sons in*c* the fire—you continue to defile yourselves with all your idols to this day. Am I to let you inquire of me, O house of Israel? As surely as I live, declares the Sovereign LORD, I will not let you inquire of me.

³²" 'You say, "We want to be like the nations, like the peoples of the world, who serve wood and stone." But what you have in mind will never happen. ³³As surely as I live, declares the Sovereign LORD, I will rule over you with a mighty hand and an outstretched arm and with outpoured wrath. ³⁴I will bring you from the nations and gather you from the countries where you have been scattered—with a mighty hand and an outstretched arm and with outpoured wrath. ³⁵I will bring you into the desert of the nations and there, face to face, I will execute judgment upon you. ³⁶As I judged your fathers in the desert of the land of Egypt, so I will judge you, declares the Sovereign LORD. ³⁷I will take note of you as you pass under my rod, and I will bring you into the bond of the covenant. ³⁸I will purge you of those who revolt and rebel against me. Although I will bring them out of the land where they are living, yet they will not enter the land of Israel. Then you will know that I am the LORD.

³⁹" 'As for you, O house of Israel, this is what the Sovereign LORD says: Go and serve your idols, every one of you! But afterward you will surely listen to me and no longer profane my holy name with your gifts and idols. ⁴⁰For on my holy mountain, the high mountain of Israel, declares the Sovereign LORD, there in the land the entire house of Israel will serve me, and there I will accept them. There I will require your offerings and your choice gifts,*d* along with all your holy sacrifices. ⁴¹I will accept you as fragrant incense when I bring you out from the nations and gather you from the countries where you have been scattered, and

---

a26 Or *—making every firstborn pass through the fire,*   *b29* Bamah means high place.
c31 Or *—making your sons pass through*
d40 Or *and the gifts of your firstfruits*

I will show myself holy among you in the sight of the nations. ⁴²Then you will know that I am the LORD, when I bring you into the land of Israel, the land I had sworn with uplifted hand to give to your fathers. ⁴³There you will remember your conduct and all the actions by which you have defiled yourselves, and you will loathe yourselves for all the evil you have done. ⁴⁴You will know that I am the LORD, when I deal with you for my name's sake and not according to your evil ways and your corrupt practices, O house of Israel, declares the Sovereign LORD.'"

Prophecy Against the South

⁴⁵The word of the LORD came to me: ⁴⁶"Son of man, set your face toward the south; preach against the south and prophesy against the forest of the southland. ⁴⁷Say to the southern forest: 'Hear the word of the LORD. This is what the Sovereign LORD says: I am about to set fire to you, and it will consume all your trees, both green and dry. The blazing flame will not be quenched, and every face from south to north will be scorched by it. ⁴⁸Everyone will see that I the LORD have kindled it; it will not be quenched.'"

⁴⁹Then I said, "Ah, Sovereign LORD! They are saying of me, 'Isn't he just telling parables?'"

Babylon, God's Sword of Judgment

21 The word of the LORD came to me: ²"Son of man, set your face against Jerusalem and preach against the sanctuary. Prophesy against the land of Israel ³and say to her: 'This is what the LORD says: I am against you. I will draw my sword from its scabbard and cut off from you both the righteous and the wicked. ⁴Because I am going to cut off the righteous and the wicked, my sword will be unsheathed against everyone from south to north. ⁵Then all people will know that I the LORD have drawn my sword from its scabbard; it will not return again.'

⁶"Therefore groan, son of man! Groan before them with broken heart and bitter grief. ⁷And when they ask you, 'Why are you groaning?' you shall say, 'Because of the news that is coming. Every heart will melt and every hand go limp; every spirit will become faint and every knee be-

come as weak as water.' It is coming! It will surely take place, declares the Sovereign LORD."

⁸The word of the LORD came to me: ⁹"Son of man, prophesy and say, 'This is what the Lord says:

"'A sword, a sword,
    sharpened and polished—
¹⁰sharpened for the slaughter,
    polished to flash like lightning!

"'Shall we rejoice in the scepter of my son ˻Judah˼? The sword despises every such stick.

¹¹"'The sword is appointed to be
        polished,
    to be grasped with the hand;
it is sharpened and polished,
    made ready for the hand of the
        slayer.
¹²Cry out and wail, son of man,
    for it is against my people;
    it is against all the princes of Israel.
They are thrown to the sword
    along with my people.
Therefore beat your breast.

> "CRY OUT and wail, son of man,
>   for it is against my people;
>   it is against all the princes of Israel."
>
> EZEKIEL 21:12

¹³"'Testing will surely come. And what if the scepter ˻of Judah˼, which the sword despises, does not continue? declares the Sovereign LORD.'

¹⁴"So then, son of man, prophesy
    and strike your hands together.
Let the sword strike twice,
    even three times.
It is a sword for slaughter—
    a sword for great slaughter,
    closing in on them from every side.
¹⁵So that hearts may melt
    and the fallen be many,
I have stationed the sword for
        slaughterᵃ
    at all their gates.
Oh! It is made to flash like lightning,
    it is grasped for slaughter.

ᵃ15 Septuagint; the meaning of the Hebrew for this word is uncertain.

¹⁶O sword, slash to the right,
then to the left,
wherever your blade is turned.
¹⁷I too will strike my hands together,
and my wrath will subside.
I the LORD have spoken."

¹⁸The word of the LORD came to me:
¹⁹"Son of man, mark out two roads for
the sword of the king of Babylon to take,
both starting from the same country.
Make a signpost where the road branches off to the city. ²⁰Mark out one road for
the sword to come against Rabbah of the
Ammonites and another against Judah
and fortified Jerusalem. ²¹For the king of
Babylon will stop at the fork in the road,
at the junction of the two roads, to seek
an omen: He will cast lots with arrows,
he will consult his idols, he will examine
the liver. ²²Into his right hand will come
the lot for Jerusalem, where he is to set
up battering rams, to give the command
to slaughter, to sound the battle cry, to
set battering rams against the gates, to
build a ramp and to erect siege works.
²³It will seem like a false omen to those
who have sworn allegiance to him, but
he will remind them of their guilt and
take them captive.

²⁴"Therefore this is what the Sovereign
LORD says: 'Because you people have
brought to mind your guilt by your open
rebellion, revealing your sins in all that
you do—because you have done this,
you will be taken captive.

²⁵"'O profane and wicked prince of Israel, whose day has come, whose time of
punishment has reached its climax, ²⁶this
is what the Sovereign LORD says: Take off
the turban, remove the crown. It will not
be as it was: The lowly will be exalted
and the exalted will be brought low. ²⁷A
ruin! A ruin! I will make it a ruin! It will
not be restored until he comes to whom
it rightfully belongs; to him I will give it.'

²⁸"And you, son of man, prophesy and
say, 'This is what the Sovereign LORD says
about the Ammonites and their insults:

"'A sword, a sword,
drawn for the slaughter,
polished to consume
and to flash like lightning!
²⁹Despite false visions concerning you
and lying divinations about you,

it will be laid on the necks
of the wicked who are to be slain,
whose day has come,
whose time of punishment has
reached its climax.
³⁰Return the sword to its scabbard.
In the place where you were
created,
in the land of your ancestry,
I will judge you.
³¹I will pour out my wrath upon you
and breathe out my fiery anger
against you;
I will hand you over to brutal men,
men skilled in destruction.
³²You will be fuel for the fire,
your blood will be shed in your
land,
you will be remembered no more;
for I the LORD have spoken.'"

Jerusalem's Sins

22 The word of the LORD came to me:
²"Son of man, will you judge her?
Will you judge this city of bloodshed?
Then confront her with all her detestable
practices ³and say: 'This is what the Sovereign LORD says: O city that brings on
herself doom by shedding blood in her
midst and defiles herself by making idols,
⁴you have become guilty because of the
blood you have shed and have become
defiled by the idols you have made. You
have brought your days to a close, and
the end of your years has come. Therefore I will make you an object of scorn to
the nations and a laughingstock to all
the countries. ⁵Those who are near and
those who are far away will mock you,
O infamous city, full of turmoil.

⁶"'See how each of the princes of Israel who are in you uses his power to shed
blood. ⁷In you they have treated father
and mother with contempt; in you they
have oppressed the alien and mistreated
the fatherless and the widow. ⁸You have
despised my holy things and desecrated
my Sabbaths. ⁹In you are slanderous
men bent on shedding blood; in you are
those who eat at the mountain shrines
and commit lewd acts. ¹⁰In you are those
who dishonor their fathers' bed; in you
are those who violate women during
their period, when they are ceremonially unclean. ¹¹In you one man commits a

detestable offense with his neighbor's wife, another shamefully defiles his daughter-in-law, and another violates his sister, his own father's daughter. ¹²In you men accept bribes to shed blood; you take usury and excessive interest*ᵃ* and make unjust gain from your neighbors by extortion. And you have forgotten me, declares the Sovereign LORD.

¹³" 'I will surely strike my hands together at the unjust gain you have made and at the blood you have shed in your midst. ¹⁴Will your courage endure or your hands be strong in the day I deal with you? I the LORD have spoken, and I will do it. ¹⁵I will disperse you among the nations and scatter you through the countries; and I will put an end to your uncleanness. ¹⁶When you have been defiled*ᵇ* in the eyes of the nations, you will know that I am the LORD.' "

¹⁷Then the word of the LORD came to me: ¹⁸"Son of man, the house of Israel has become dross to me; all of them are the copper, tin, iron and lead left inside a furnace. They are but the dross of silver. ¹⁹Therefore this is what the Sovereign LORD says: 'Because you have all become dross, I will gather you into Jerusalem. ²⁰As men gather silver, copper, iron, lead and tin into a furnace to melt it with a fiery blast, so will I gather you in my anger and my wrath and put you inside the city and melt you. ²¹I will gather you and I will blow on you with my fiery wrath, and you will be melted inside her. ²²As silver is melted in a furnace, so you will be melted inside her, and you will know that I the LORD have poured out my wrath upon you.' "

²³Again the word of the LORD came to me: ²⁴"Son of man, say to the land, 'You are a land that has had no rain or showers*ᶜ* in the day of wrath.' ²⁵There is a conspiracy of her princes*ᵈ* within her like a roaring lion tearing its prey; they devour people, take treasures and precious things and make many widows within her. ²⁶Her priests do violence to my law and profane my holy things; they do not distinguish between the holy and the common; they teach that there is no difference between the unclean and the clean; and they shut their eyes to the keeping of my Sabbaths, so that I am profaned among them. ²⁷Her officials within her are like wolves tearing their prey; they shed blood and kill people to make unjust gain. ²⁸Her prophets whitewash these deeds for them by false visions and lying divinations. They say, 'This is what the Sovereign LORD says'— when the LORD has not spoken. ²⁹The people of the land practice extortion and commit robbery; they oppress the poor and needy and mistreat the alien, denying them justice.

³⁰"I looked for a man among them who would build up the wall and stand before me in the gap on behalf of the land so I would not have to destroy it, but I found none. ³¹So I will pour out my wrath on them and consume them with my fiery anger, bringing down on their own heads all they have done, declares the Sovereign LORD."

Two Adulterous Sisters

23 The word of the LORD came to me: ²"Son of man, there were two women, daughters of the same mother. ³They became prostitutes in Egypt, engaging in prostitution from their youth. In that land their breasts were fondled and their virgin bosoms caressed. ⁴The older was named Oholah, and her sister was Oholibah. They were mine and gave birth to sons and daughters. Oholah is Samaria, and Oholibah is Jerusalem.

⁵"Oholah engaged in prostitution while she was still mine; and she lusted after her lovers, the Assyrians—warriors ⁶clothed in blue, governors and commanders, all of them handsome young men, and mounted horsemen. ⁷She gave herself as a prostitute to all the elite of the Assyrians and defiled herself with all the idols of everyone she lusted after. ⁸She did not give up the prostitution she began in Egypt, when during her youth men slept with her, caressed her virgin bosom and poured out their lust upon her.

⁹"Therefore I handed her over to her lovers, the Assyrians, for whom she lusted. ¹⁰They stripped her naked, took away her sons and daughters and killed her

---

ᵃ12 Or *usury and interest*   *ᵇ16* Or *When I have allotted you your inheritance*   *ᶜ24* Septuagint; Hebrew *has not been cleansed or rained on*   *ᵈ25* Septuagint; Hebrew *prophets*

with the sword. She became a byword among women, and punishment was inflicted on her.

11 "Her sister Oholibah saw this, yet in her lust and prostitution she was more depraved than her sister. 12She too lusted after the Assyrians—governors and commanders, warriors in full dress, mounted horsemen, all handsome young men.

13I saw that she too defiled herself; both of them went the same way.

14 "But she carried her prostitution still further. She saw men portrayed on a wall, figures of Chaldeans*a* portrayed in red, 15with belts around their waists and flowing turbans on their heads; all of them

a14 Or Babylonians

[MONDAY]

EZEKIEL 22:30–31

In the Gap

22:30 "I LOOKED FOR A MAN AMONG THEM WHO WOULD BUILD UP THE WALL AND STAND BEFORE ME IN THE GAP."

Does God look for anything? Is there anything he seeks? Whenever the Bible speaks of God's searching, it usually has something to do with prayer. Three examples will suffice: When Asa forsook prayer for a military alliance with Aram, God said, "For the eyes of the LORD range throughout the earth to strengthen those whose hearts are fully committed to him" (2 Chronicles 16:9). He is on the hunt for people who will ask him for help. When Jesus discussed worship with the Samaritan woman, he said his Father seeks those who will worship him in spirit and in truth (see John 4:23). God is on a search, looking for true worshipers. Worship and prayer are integral to each other.

Then there is Ezekiel 22:30–31. The picture is of a crumbling wall around a city, with an enemy army poised to rush in and destroy everything in its path. The army is savage and heavily armed, shouting, with their swords drawn and bows bent. The gap is small enough for one man to defend but big enough for an army to rush through. Only a brave man would step into that breach to fight. God is looking for that kind of person. Moses was such a man; he stood in the breach for the Israelites (see Psalm 106:23). So was Jesus, who in his suffering and death made intercession for sinners (see Isaiah 53:12).

This passage in Ezekiel is one of the most vivid and dramatic pictures of intercessory prayer. It says the stakes are high in intercession: between life and death, heaven and hell. It says it takes great faith and courage to pray. It says God's call for us to intercede is a call to great dignity and responsibility; and that says prayer is a great mystery! We can only speculate as to why the sovereign, almighty God, who needs no help from anyone, would choose to depend upon our prayers. But the fact that he has is clearly noted in Scripture. If we don't intercede until we understand why, we will never intercede, and some will die (see Ezekiel 22:31). God is looking for people to stand in the gap.

PRAY:

Here I am, Lord. I will stand before you in the gap for the sake of your holy name, and for the lives of those I pray for.

FOR YOUR NEXT DEVOTIONAL READING, GO TO PAGE 1011.

looked like Babylonian chariot officers, natives of Chaldea.[a] 16As soon as she saw them, she lusted after them and sent messengers to them in Chaldea. 17Then the Babylonians came to her, to the bed of love, and in their lust they defiled her. After she had been defiled by them, she turned away from them in disgust. 18When she carried on her prostitution openly and exposed her nakedness, I turned away from her in disgust, just as I had turned away from her sister. 19Yet she became more and more promiscuous as she recalled the days of her youth, when she was a prostitute in Egypt. 20There she lusted after her lovers, whose genitals were like those of donkeys and whose emission was like that of horses. 21So you longed for the lewdness of your youth, when in Egypt your bosom was caressed and your young breasts fondled.[b]

22"Therefore, Oholibah, this is what the Sovereign LORD says: I will stir up your lovers against you, those you turned away from in disgust, and I will bring them against you from every side— 23the Babylonians and all the Chaldeans, the men of Pekod and Shoa and Koa, and all the Assyrians with them, handsome young men, all of them governors and commanders, chariot officers and men of high rank, all mounted on horses. 24They will come against you with weapons,[c] chariots and wagons and with a throng of people; they will take up positions against you on every side with large and small shields and with helmets. I will turn you over to them for punishment, and they will punish you according to their standards. 25I will direct my jealous anger against you, and they will deal with you in fury. They will cut off your noses and your ears, and those of you who are left will fall by the sword. They will take away your sons and daughters, and those of you who are left will be consumed by fire. 26They will also strip you of your clothes and take your fine jewelry. 27So I will put a stop to the lewdness and prostitution you began in Egypt. You will not look on these things with longing or remember Egypt anymore.

28"For this is what the Sovereign LORD says: I am about to hand you over to those you hate, to those you turned away from in disgust. 29They will deal with you in hatred and take away everything you have worked for. They will leave you naked and bare, and the shame of your prostitution will be exposed. Your lewdness and promiscuity 30have brought this upon you, because you lusted after the nations and defiled yourself with their idols. 31You have gone the way of your sister; so I will put her cup into your hand.

32"This is what the Sovereign LORD says:

"You will drink your sister's cup,
    a cup large and deep;
it will bring scorn and derision,
    for it holds so much.
33You will be filled with drunkenness
        and sorrow,
    the cup of ruin and desolation,
    the cup of your sister Samaria.
34You will drink it and drain it dry;
    you will dash it to pieces
    and tear your breasts.

I have spoken, declares the Sovereign LORD.

35"Therefore this is what the Sovereign LORD says: Since you have forgotten me and thrust me behind your back, you must bear the consequences of your lewdness and prostitution."

36The LORD said to me: "Son of man, will you judge Oholah and Oholibah? Then confront them with their detestable practices, 37for they have committed adultery and blood is on their hands. They committed adultery with their idols; they even sacrificed their children, whom they bore to me,[d] as food for them. 38They have also done this to me: At that same time they defiled my sanctuary and desecrated my Sabbaths. 39On the very day they sacrificed their children to their idols, they entered my sanctuary and desecrated it. That is what they did in my house.

40"They even sent messengers for men who came from far away, and when they arrived you bathed yourself for them,

a15 Or Babylonia; also in verse 16   b21 Syriac (see also verse 3); Hebrew caressed because of your young breasts   c24 The meaning of the Hebrew for this word is uncertain.   d37 Or even made the children they bore to me pass through the fire

painted your eyes and put on your jewelry. ⁴¹You sat on an elegant couch, with a table spread before it on which you had placed the incense and oil that belonged to me.

⁴²"The noise of a carefree crowd was around her; Sabeansᵃ were brought from the desert along with men from the rabble, and they put bracelets on the arms of the woman and her sister and beautiful crowns on their heads. ⁴³Then I said about the one worn out by adultery, 'Now let them use her as a prostitute, for that is all she is.' ⁴⁴And they slept with her. As men sleep with a prostitute, so they slept with those lewd women, Oholah and Oholibah. ⁴⁵But righteous men will sentence them to the punishment of women who commit adultery and shed blood, because they are adulterous and blood is on their hands.

⁴⁶"This is what the Sovereign LORD says: Bring a mob against them and give them over to terror and plunder. ⁴⁷The mob will stone them and cut them down with their swords; they will kill their sons and daughters and burn down their houses.

⁴⁸"So I will put an end to lewdness in the land, that all women may take warning and not imitate you. ⁴⁹You will suffer the penalty for your lewdness and bear the consequences of your sins of idolatry. Then you will know that I am the Sovereign LORD."

The Cooking Pot

24 In the ninth year, in the tenth month on the tenth day, the word of the LORD came to me: ²"Son of man, record this date, this very date, because the king of Babylon has laid siege to Jerusalem this very day. ³Tell this rebellious house a parable and say to them: 'This is what the Sovereign LORD says:

" 'Put on the cooking pot; put it on
    and pour water into it.
⁴ Put into it the pieces of meat,
    all the choice pieces—the leg and
        the shoulder.
Fill it with the best of these bones;
⁵   take the pick of the flock.
Pile wood beneath it for the bones;
    bring it to a boil
    and cook the bones in it.

⁶" 'For this is what the Sovereign LORD says:

" 'Woe to the city of bloodshed,
    to the pot now encrusted,
    whose deposit will not go away!
Empty it piece by piece
    without casting lots for them.

⁷ " 'For the blood she shed is in her
        midst:
She poured it on the bare rock;
she did not pour it on the ground,
    where the dust would cover it.
⁸ To stir up wrath and take revenge
    I put her blood on the bare rock,
    so that it would not be covered.

⁹ " 'Therefore this is what the Sovereign LORD says:

" 'Woe to the city of bloodshed!
    I, too, will pile the wood high.
¹⁰ So heap on the wood
    and kindle the fire.
Cook the meat well,
    mixing in the spices;
    and let the bones be charred.
¹¹ Then set the empty pot on the coals
    till it becomes hot and its
        copper glows
so its impurities may be melted
    and its deposit burned away.
¹² It has frustrated all efforts;
    its heavy deposit has not been
        removed,
    not even by fire.

¹³" 'Now your impurity is lewdness. Because I tried to cleanse you but you would not be cleansed from your impurity, you will not be clean again until my wrath against you has subsided.

¹⁴" 'I the LORD have spoken. The time has come for me to act. I will not hold back; I will not have pity, nor will I relent. You will be judged according to your conduct and your actions, declares the Sovereign LORD.' "

Ezekiel's Wife Dies

¹⁵The word of the LORD came to me: ¹⁶"Son of man, with one blow I am about to take away from you the delight of your

ᵃ42 Or drunkards

eyes. Yet do not lament or weep or shed any tears. ¹⁷Groan quietly; do not mourn for the dead. Keep your turban fastened and your sandals on your feet; do not cover the lower part of your face or eat the customary food ⌞of mourners⌟." ¹⁸So I spoke to the people in the morning, and in the evening my wife died. The next morning I did as I had been commanded.

¹⁹Then the people asked me, "Won't you tell us what these things have to do with us?"

²⁰So I said to them, "The word of the LORD came to me: ²¹Say to the house of Israel, 'This is what the Sovereign LORD says: I am about to desecrate my sanctuary—the stronghold in which you take pride, the delight of your eyes, the object of your affection. The sons and daughters you left behind will fall by the sword. ²²And you will do as I have done. You will not cover the lower part of your face or eat the customary food ⌞of mourners⌟. ²³You will keep your turbans on your heads and your sandals on your feet. You will not mourn or weep but will waste away because of[a] your sins and groan among yourselves. ²⁴Ezekiel will be a sign to you; you will do just as he has done. When this happens, you will know that I am the Sovereign LORD.'

²⁵"And you, son of man, on the day I take away their stronghold, their joy and glory, the delight of their eyes, their heart's desire, and their sons and daughters as well— ²⁶on that day a fugitive will come to tell you the news. ²⁷At that time your mouth will be opened; you will speak with him and will no longer be silent. So you will be a sign to them, and they will know that I am the LORD."

> 66 To know God as the sovereign disposer of all good, inviting us to present our requests, and yet not to approach or ask of him, were so far from availing us, that it were just as if one told of a treasure were to allow it to remain buried in the ground. 99
>
> JOHN CALVIN

A Prophecy Against Ammon

25 The word of the LORD came to me: ²"Son of man, set your face against the Ammonites and prophesy against them. ³Say to them, 'Hear the word of the Sovereign LORD. This is what the Sovereign LORD says: Because you said "Aha!" over my sanctuary when it was desecrated and over the land of Israel when it was laid waste and over the people of Judah when they went into exile, ⁴therefore I am going to give you to the people of the East as a possession. They will set up their camps and pitch their tents among you; they will eat your fruit and drink your milk. ⁵I will turn Rabbah into a pasture for camels and Ammon into a resting place for sheep. Then you will know that I am the LORD. ⁶For this is what the Sovereign LORD says: Because you have clapped your hands and stamped your feet, rejoicing with all the malice of your heart against the land of Israel, ⁷therefore I will stretch out my hand against you and give you as plunder to the nations. I will cut you off from the nations and exterminate you from the countries. I will destroy you, and you will know that I am the LORD.' "

A Prophecy Against Moab

⁸"This is what the Sovereign LORD says: 'Because Moab and Seir said, "Look, the house of Judah has become like all the other nations," ⁹therefore I will expose the flank of Moab, beginning at its frontier towns—Beth Jeshimoth, Baal Meon and Kiriathaim—the glory of that land. ¹⁰I will give Moab along with the Ammonites to the people of the East as a possession, so that the Ammonites will not be remembered among the nations; ¹¹and I will inflict punishment on Moab. Then they will know that I am the LORD.' "

A Prophecy Against Edom

¹²"This is what the Sovereign LORD says: 'Because Edom took revenge on the house of Judah and became very guilty by doing so, ¹³therefore this is what the Sovereign LORD says: I will stretch out my hand against Edom and kill its men and their animals. I will lay it waste, and from

---

[a] 23 Or *away in*

Teman to Dedan they will fall by the sword. [14]I will take vengeance on Edom by the hand of my people Israel, and they will deal with Edom in accordance with my anger and my wrath; they will know my vengeance, declares the Sovereign LORD.'"

A Prophecy Against Philistia

[15]"This is what the Sovereign LORD says: 'Because the Philistines acted in vengeance and took revenge with malice in their hearts, and with ancient hostility sought to destroy Judah, [16]therefore this is what the Sovereign LORD says: I am about to stretch out my hand against the Philistines, and I will cut off the Kerethites and destroy those remaining along the coast. [17]I will carry out great vengeance on them and punish them in my wrath. Then they will know that I am the LORD, when I take vengeance on them.'"

A Prophecy Against Tyre

26 In the eleventh year, on the first day of the month, the word of the LORD came to me: [2]"Son of man, because Tyre has said of Jerusalem, 'Aha! The gate to the nations is broken, and its doors have swung open to me; now that she lies in ruins I will prosper,' [3]therefore this is what the Sovereign LORD says: I am against you, O Tyre, and I will bring many nations against you, like the sea casting up its waves. [4]They will destroy the walls of Tyre and pull down her towers; I will scrape away her rubble and make her a bare rock. [5]Out in the sea she will become a place to spread fishnets, for I have spoken, declares the Sovereign LORD. She will become plunder for the nations, [6]and her settlements on the mainland will be ravaged by the sword. Then they will know that I am the LORD.

[7]"For this is what the Sovereign LORD says: From the north I am going to bring against Tyre Nebuchadnezzar[a] king of Babylon, king of kings, with horses and chariots, with horsemen and a great army. [8]He will ravage your settlements on the mainland with the sword; he will set up siege works against you, build a ramp up to your walls and raise his shields against you. [9]He will direct the blows of his battering rams against your walls and demolish your towers with his weapons. [10]His horses will be so many that they will cover you with dust. Your walls will tremble at the noise of the war horses, wagons and chariots when he enters your gates as men enter a city whose walls have been broken through. [11]The hoofs of his horses will trample all your streets; he will kill your people with the sword, and your strong pillars will fall to the ground. [12]They will plunder your wealth and loot your merchandise; they will break down your walls and demolish your fine houses and throw your stones, timber and rubble into the sea. [13]I will put an end to your noisy songs, and the music of your harps will be heard no more. [14]I will make you a bare rock, and you will become a place to spread fishnets. You will never be rebuilt, for I the LORD have spoken, declares the Sovereign LORD.

[15]"This is what the Sovereign LORD says to Tyre: Will not the coastlands tremble at the sound of your fall, when the wounded groan and the slaughter takes place in you? [16]Then all the princes of the coast will step down from their thrones and lay aside their robes and take off their embroidered garments. Clothed with terror, they will sit on the ground, trembling every moment, appalled at you. [17]Then they will take up a lament concerning you and say to you:

" 'How you are destroyed, O city of renown,
    peopled by men of the sea!
You were a power on the seas,
    you and your citizens;
you put your terror
    on all who lived there.
[18]Now the coastlands tremble
    on the day of your fall;
the islands in the sea
    are terrified at your collapse.'

[19]"This is what the Sovereign LORD says: When I make you a desolate city, like cities no longer inhabited, and when I bring the ocean depths over you and its vast waters cover you, [20]then I will bring you down with those who go down to the pit, to the people of long ago. I will make

[a]7 Hebrew *Nebuchadrezzar*, of which *Nebuchadnezzar* is a variant; here and often in Ezekiel and Jeremiah

you dwell in the earth below, as in ancient ruins, with those who go down to the pit, and you will not return or take your place[a] in the land of the living. ²¹I will bring you to a horrible end and you will be no more. You will be sought, but you will never again be found, declares the Sovereign LORD."

A Lament for Tyre

27 The word of the LORD came to me: ²"Son of man, take up a lament concerning Tyre. ³Say to Tyre, situated at the gateway to the sea, merchant of peoples on many coasts, 'This is what the Sovereign LORD says:

" 'You say, O Tyre,
  "I am perfect in beauty."
⁴Your domain was on the high seas;
  your builders brought your beauty
    to perfection.
⁵They made all your timbers
  of pine trees from Senir[b];
they took a cedar from Lebanon
  to make a mast for you.
⁶Of oaks from Bashan
  they made your oars;
of cypress wood[c] from the coasts
    of Cyprus[d]
they made your deck, inlaid
  with ivory.
⁷Fine embroidered linen from Egypt
    was your sail
  and served as your banner;
your awnings were of blue and purple
  from the coasts of Elishah.
⁸Men of Sidon and Arvad were your
    oarsmen;
  your skilled men, O Tyre, were
    aboard as your seamen.
⁹Veteran craftsmen of Gebal[e] were
    on board
  as shipwrights to caulk your seams.
All the ships of the sea and their
    sailors
  came alongside to trade for
    your wares.

¹⁰ " 'Men of Persia, Lydia and Put
  served as soldiers in your army.
They hung their shields and helmets
    on your walls,
  bringing you splendor.
¹¹Men of Arvad and Helech
  manned your walls on every side;

men of Gammad
  were in your towers.
They hung their shields around
    your walls;
  they brought your beauty to
    perfection.

¹² " 'Tarshish did business with you because of your great wealth of goods; they exchanged silver, iron, tin and lead for your merchandise.

¹³ " 'Greece, Tubal and Meshech traded with you; they exchanged slaves and articles of bronze for your wares.

¹⁴ " 'Men of Beth Togarmah exchanged work horses, war horses and mules for your merchandise.

¹⁵ " 'The men of Rhodes[f] traded with you, and many coastlands were your customers; they paid you with ivory tusks and ebony.

¹⁶ " 'Aram[g] did business with you because of your many products; they exchanged turquoise, purple fabric, embroidered work, fine linen, coral and rubies for your merchandise.

¹⁷ " 'Judah and Israel traded with you; they exchanged wheat from Minnith and confections,[h] honey, oil and balm for your wares.

¹⁸ " 'Damascus, because of your many products and great wealth of goods, did business with you in wine from Helbon and wool from Zahar.

¹⁹ " 'Danites and Greeks from Uzal bought your merchandise; they exchanged wrought iron, cassia and calamus for your wares.

²⁰ " 'Dedan traded in saddle blankets with you.

²¹ " 'Arabia and all the princes of Kedar were your customers; they did business with you in lambs, rams and goats.

²² " 'The merchants of Sheba and Raamah traded with you; for your merchandise they exchanged the finest of all kinds of spices and precious stones, and gold.

---

[a]20 Septuagint; Hebrew *return, and I will give glory*
[b]5 That is, Hermon   [c]6 Targum; the Masoretic Text has a different division of the consonants.
[d]6 Hebrew *Kittim*   [e]9 That is, Byblos
[f]15 Septuagint; Hebrew *Dedan*   [g]16 Most Hebrew manuscripts; some Hebrew manuscripts and Syriac *Edom*   [h]17 The meaning of the Hebrew for this word is uncertain.

²³ " 'Haran, Canneh and Eden and merchants of Sheba, Asshur and Kilmad traded with you. ²⁴In your marketplace they traded with you beautiful garments, blue fabric, embroidered work and multicolored rugs with cords twisted and tightly knotted.

²⁵ " 'The ships of Tarshish serve
as carriers for your wares.
You are filled with heavy cargo
in the heart of the sea.
²⁶ Your oarsmen take you
out to the high seas.
But the east wind will break you
to pieces
in the heart of the sea.
²⁷ Your wealth, merchandise and wares,
your mariners, seamen and
shipwrights,
your merchants and all your soldiers,
and everyone else on board
will sink into the heart of the sea
on the day of your shipwreck.
²⁸ The shorelands will quake
when your seamen cry out.
²⁹ All who handle the oars
will abandon their ships;
the mariners and all the seamen
will stand on the shore.
³⁰ They will raise their voice
and cry bitterly over you;
they will sprinkle dust on their heads
and roll in ashes.
³¹ They will shave their heads because
of you
and will put on sackcloth.
They will weep over you with anguish
of soul
and with bitter mourning.
³² As they wail and mourn over you,
they will take up a lament
concerning you:
"Who was ever silenced like Tyre,
surrounded by the sea?"
³³ When your merchandise went out on
the seas,
you satisfied many nations;
with your great wealth and your
wares
you enriched the kings of the earth.
³⁴ Now you are shattered by the sea
in the depths of the waters;
your wares and all your company
have gone down with you.

³⁵ All who live in the coastlands
are appalled at you;
their kings shudder with horror
and their faces are distorted with
fear.
³⁶ The merchants among the nations
hiss at you;
you have come to a horrible end
and will be no more.' "

> When a man is at his wits' end,
> it is not a cowardly thing to pray; it is
> the only way he can get in touch with
> Reality.
>
> OSWALD CHAMBERS

A Prophecy Against the King of Tyre

28 The word of the LORD came to me: ²"Son of man, say to the ruler of Tyre, 'This is what the Sovereign LORD says:

" 'In the pride of your heart
you say, "I am a god;
I sit on the throne of a god
in the heart of the seas."
But you are a man and not a god,
though you think you are as wise
as a god.
³ Are you wiser than Daniel[a]?
Is no secret hidden from you?
⁴ By your wisdom and understanding
you have gained wealth for yourself
and amassed gold and silver
in your treasuries.
⁵ By your great skill in trading
you have increased your wealth,
and because of your wealth
your heart has grown proud.

⁶ " 'Therefore this is what the Sovereign LORD says:

" 'Because you think you are wise,
as wise as a god,
⁷ I am going to bring foreigners against
you,
the most ruthless of nations;
they will draw their swords against
your beauty and wisdom
and pierce your shining splendor.

[a] 3 Or *Danel*; the Hebrew spelling may suggest a person other than the prophet Daniel.

⁸They will bring you down to the pit,
  and you will die a violent death
  in the heart of the seas.
⁹Will you then say, "I am a god,"
  in the presence of those who kill
    you?
You will be but a man, not a god,
  in the hands of those who slay you.
¹⁰You will die the death of the
    uncircumcised
  at the hands of foreigners.

I have spoken, declares the Sovereign
LORD.' "

¹¹The word of the LORD came to me:
¹²"Son of man, take up a lament concerning the king of Tyre and say to him: 'This is what the Sovereign LORD says:

" 'You were the model of perfection,
  full of wisdom and perfect in
    beauty.
¹³You were in Eden,
  the garden of God;
every precious stone adorned you:
  ruby, topaz and emerald,
  chrysolite, onyx and jasper,
  sapphire,ᵃ turquoise and beryl.ᵇ
Your settings and mountingsᶜ were
    made of gold;
  on the day you were created they
    were prepared.
¹⁴You were anointed as a guardian
    cherub,
  for so I ordained you.
You were on the holy mount of God;
  you walked among the fiery stones.
¹⁵You were blameless in your ways
  from the day you were created
  till wickedness was found in you.
¹⁶Through your widespread trade
  you were filled with violence,
    and you sinned.
So I drove you in disgrace from the
    mount of God,
  and I expelled you, O guardian
    cherub,
  from among the fiery stones.
¹⁷Your heart became proud
  on account of your beauty,
  and you corrupted your wisdom
    because of your splendor.
So I threw you to the earth;
  I made a spectacle of you before
    kings.

¹⁸By your many sins and dishonest
    trade
  you have desecrated your
    sanctuaries.
So I made a fire come out from you,
  and it consumed you,
  and I reduced you to ashes on the
    ground
  in the sight of all who were
    watching.
¹⁹All the nations who knew you
  are appalled at you;
you have come to a horrible end
  and will be no more.' "

A Prophecy Against Sidon

²⁰The word of the LORD came to me:
²¹"Son of man, set your face against Sidon; prophesy against her ²²and say: 'This is what the Sovereign LORD says:

" 'I am against you, O Sidon,
  and I will gain glory within you.
They will know that I am the LORD,
  when I inflict punishment on her
  and show myself holy within her.
²³I will send a plague upon her
  and make blood flow in her
    streets.
The slain will fall within her,
  with the sword against her
    on every side.
Then they will know that I am the
    LORD.

²⁴" 'No longer will the people of Israel have malicious neighbors who are painful briers and sharp thorns. Then they will know that I am the Sovereign LORD.

²⁵" 'This is what the Sovereign LORD says: When I gather the people of Israel from the nations where they have been scattered, I will show myself holy among them in the sight of the nations. Then they will live in their own land, which I gave to my servant Jacob. ²⁶They will live there in safety and will build houses and plant vineyards; they will live in safety when I inflict punishment on all their neighbors who maligned them. Then they will know that I am the LORD their God.' "

ᵃ13 Or *lapis lazuli*   ᵇ13 The precise
identification of some of these precious stones is
uncertain.   ᶜ13 The meaning of the Hebrew for
this phrase is uncertain.

A Prophecy Against Egypt

29 In the tenth year, in the tenth month on the twelfth day, the word of the LORD came to me: ²"Son of man, set your face against Pharaoh king of Egypt and prophesy against him and against all Egypt. ³Speak to him and say: 'This is what the Sovereign LORD says:

"'I am against you, Pharaoh king
    of Egypt,
  you great monster lying among
    your streams.
You say, "The Nile is mine;
  I made it for myself."
⁴But I will put hooks in your jaws
  and make the fish of your streams
    stick to your scales.
I will pull you out from among your
    streams,
  with all the fish sticking to your
    scales.
⁵I will leave you in the desert,
  you and all the fish of your streams.
You will fall on the open field
  and not be gathered or picked up.
I will give you as food
  to the beasts of the earth and the
    birds of the air.

⁶Then all who live in Egypt will know that I am the LORD.

"'You have been a staff of reed for the house of Israel. ⁷When they grasped you with their hands, you splintered and you tore open their shoulders; when they leaned on you, you broke and their backs were wrenched.ᵃ

⁸"'Therefore this is what the Sovereign LORD says: I will bring a sword against you and kill your men and their animals. ⁹Egypt will become a desolate wasteland. Then they will know that I am the LORD.

"'Because you said, "The Nile is mine; I made it," ¹⁰therefore I am against you and against your streams, and I will make the land of Egypt a ruin and a desolate waste from Migdol to Aswan, as far as the border of Cush.ᵇ ¹¹No foot of man or animal will pass through it; no one will live there for forty years. ¹²I will make the land of Egypt desolate among devastated lands, and her cities will lie desolate forty years among ruined cities. And I will disperse the Egyptians among the nations and scatter them through the countries.

¹³"'Yet this is what the Sovereign LORD says: At the end of forty years I will gather the Egyptians from the nations where they were scattered. ¹⁴I will bring them back from captivity and return them to Upper Egypt,ᶜ the land of their ancestry. There they will be a lowly kingdom. ¹⁵It will be the lowliest of kingdoms and will never again exalt itself above the other nations. I will make it so weak that it will never again rule over the nations. ¹⁶Egypt will no longer be a source of confidence for the people of Israel but will be a reminder of their sin in turning to her for help. Then they will know that I am the Sovereign LORD.'"

¹⁷In the twenty-seventh year, in the first month on the first day, the word of the LORD came to me: ¹⁸"Son of man, Nebuchadnezzar king of Babylon drove his army in a hard campaign against Tyre; every head was rubbed bare and every shoulder made raw. Yet he and his army got no reward from the campaign he led against Tyre. ¹⁹Therefore this is what the Sovereign LORD says: I am going to give Egypt to Nebuchadnezzar king of Babylon, and he will carry off its wealth. He will loot and plunder the land as pay for his army. ²⁰I have given him Egypt as a reward for his efforts because he and his army did it for me, declares the Sovereign LORD.

²¹"On that day I will make a hornᵈ grow for the house of Israel, and I will open your mouth among them. Then they will know that I am the LORD."

A Lament for Egypt

30 The word of the LORD came to me: ²"Son of man, prophesy and say: 'This is what the Sovereign LORD says:

"'Wail and say,
  "Alas for that day!"
³For the day is near,
  the day of the LORD is near—
a day of clouds,
  a time of doom for the nations.

ᵃ7 Syriac (see also Septuagint and Vulgate); Hebrew *and you caused their backs to stand* ᵇ10 That is, the upper Nile region ᶜ14 Hebrew *to Pathros* ᵈ21 *Horn* here symbolizes strength.

⁴A sword will come against Egypt,
  and anguish will come upon Cush.ᵃ
When the slain fall in Egypt,
  her wealth will be carried away
  and her foundations torn down.

⁵Cush and Put, Lydia and all Arabia, Libyaᵇ and the people of the covenant land will fall by the sword along with Egypt.

⁶" 'This is what the LORD says:

" 'The allies of Egypt will fall
  and her proud strength will fail.
From Migdol to Aswan
  they will fall by the sword
    within her,
      declares the Sovereign LORD.
⁷ " 'They will be desolate
  among desolate lands,
and their cities will lie
  among ruined cities.
⁸Then they will know that I am the
  LORD,
when I set fire to Egypt
  and all her helpers are crushed.

⁹" 'On that day messengers will go out from me in ships to frighten Cush out of her complacency. Anguish will take hold of them on the day of Egypt's doom, for it is sure to come.

¹⁰" 'This is what the Sovereign LORD says:

" 'I will put an end to the hordes of
  Egypt
by the hand of Nebuchadnezzar
  king of Babylon.
¹¹He and his army—the most ruthless
  of nations—
will be brought in to destroy the
  land.
They will draw their swords against
  Egypt
and fill the land with the slain.
¹²I will dry up the streams of the Nile
  and sell the land to evil men;
by the hand of foreigners
  I will lay waste the land and
  everything in it.

I the LORD have spoken.

¹³" 'This is what the Sovereign LORD says:

" 'I will destroy the idols
  and put an end to the images in
  Memphis.ᶜ

No longer will there be a prince in
  Egypt,
and I will spread fear throughout
  the land.
¹⁴I will lay waste Upper Egypt,ᵈ
  set fire to Zoan
and inflict punishment on Thebes.ᵉ
¹⁵I will pour out my wrath on
  Pelusium,ᶠ
the stronghold of Egypt,
  and cut off the hordes of Thebes.
¹⁶I will set fire to Egypt;
  Pelusium will writhe in agony.
Thebes will be taken by storm;
  Memphis will be in constant
  distress.
¹⁷The young men of Heliopolisᵍ and
  Bubastisʰ
will fall by the sword,
  and the cities themselves will go
  into captivity.
¹⁸Dark will be the day at Tahpanhes
  when I break the yoke of Egypt;
there her proud strength will come
  to an end.
She will be covered with clouds,
  and her villages will go into
  captivity.
¹⁹So I will inflict punishment on Egypt,
  and they will know that I am
  the LORD.' "

²⁰In the eleventh year, in the first month on the seventh day, the word of the LORD came to me: ²¹"Son of man, I have broken the arm of Pharaoh king of Egypt. It has not been bound up for healing or put in a splint so as to become strong enough to hold a sword. ²²Therefore this is what the Sovereign LORD says: I am against Pharaoh king of Egypt. I will break both his arms, the good arm as well as the broken one, and make the sword fall from his hand. ²³I will disperse the Egyptians among the nations and scatter them through the countries. ²⁴I will strengthen the arms of the king of Babylon and put my sword in his hand, but I will break the arms of Pharaoh, and he will groan before him like a mortally

ᵃ4 That is, the upper Nile region; also in verses 5 and 9   ᵇ5 Hebrew *Cub*   ᶜ13 Hebrew *Noph*; also in verse 16   ᵈ14 Hebrew *waste Pathros*   ᵉ14 Hebrew *No*; also in verses 15 and 16   ᶠ15 Hebrew *Sin*; also in verse 16   ᵍ17 Hebrew *Awen* (or *On*)   ʰ17 Hebrew *Pi Beseth*

wounded man. ²⁵I will strengthen the arms of the king of Babylon, but the arms of Pharaoh will fall limp. Then they will know that I am the LORD, when I put my sword into the hand of the king of Babylon and he brandishes it against Egypt. ²⁶I will disperse the Egyptians among the nations and scatter them through the countries. Then they will know that I am the LORD."

A Cedar in Lebanon

31 In the eleventh year, in the third month on the first day, the word of the LORD came to me: ²"Son of man, say to Pharaoh king of Egypt and to his hordes:

" 'Who can be compared with you
      in majesty?
³ Consider Assyria, once a cedar in
      Lebanon,
   with beautiful branches
      overshadowing the forest;
   it towered on high,
      its top above the thick foliage.
⁴ The waters nourished it,
      deep springs made it grow tall;
   their streams flowed
      all around its base
   and sent their channels
      to all the trees of the field.
⁵ So it towered higher
      than all the trees of the field;
   its boughs increased
      and its branches grew long,
      spreading because of abundant
         waters.
⁶ All the birds of the air
      nested in its boughs,
   all the beasts of the field
      gave birth under its branches;
   all the great nations
      lived in its shade.
⁷ It was majestic in beauty,
      with its spreading boughs,
   for its roots went down
      to abundant waters.
⁸ The cedars in the garden of God
      could not rival it,
   nor could the pine trees
      equal its boughs,
   nor could the plane trees
      compare with its branches—
   no tree in the garden of God
      could match its beauty.

⁹ I made it beautiful
      with abundant branches,
   the envy of all the trees of Eden
      in the garden of God.

¹⁰ " 'Therefore this is what the Sovereign LORD says: Because it towered on high, lifting its top above the thick foliage, and because it was proud of its height, ¹¹I handed it over to the ruler of the nations, for him to deal with according to its wickedness. I cast it aside, ¹²and the most ruthless of foreign nations cut it down and left it. Its boughs fell on the mountains and in all the valleys; its branches lay broken in all the ravines of the land. All the nations of the earth came out from under its shade and left it. ¹³All the birds of the air settled on the fallen tree, and all the beasts of the field were among its branches. ¹⁴Therefore no other trees by the waters are ever to tower proudly on high, lifting their tops above the thick foliage. No other trees so well-watered are ever to reach such a height; they are all destined for death, for the earth below, among mortal men, with those who go down to the pit.

¹⁵ " 'This is what the Sovereign LORD says: On the day it was brought down to the graveᵃ I covered the deep springs with mourning for it; I held back its streams, and its abundant waters were restrained. Because of it I clothed Lebanon with gloom, and all the trees of the field withered away. ¹⁶I made the nations tremble at the sound of its fall when I brought it down to the grave with those who go down to the pit. Then all the trees of Eden, the choicest and best of Lebanon, all the trees that were well-watered, were consoled in the earth below. ¹⁷Those who lived in its shade, its allies among the nations, had also gone down to the grave with it, joining those killed by the sword.

¹⁸ " 'Which of the trees of Eden can be compared with you in splendor and majesty? Yet you, too, will be brought down with the trees of Eden to the earth below; you will lie among the uncircumcised, with those killed by the sword.

" 'This is Pharaoh and all his hordes, declares the Sovereign LORD.' "

ᵃ15 Hebrew *Sheol*; also in verses 16 and 17

A Lament for Pharaoh

32 In the twelfth year, in the twelfth month on the first day, the word of the LORD came to me: ²"Son of man, take up a lament concerning Pharaoh king of Egypt and say to him:

"'You are like a lion among the
nations;
you are like a monster in the seas
thrashing about in your streams,
churning the water with your feet
and muddying the streams.

³"'This is what the Sovereign LORD says:

"'With a great throng of people
I will cast my net over you,
and they will haul you up in my net.
⁴ I will throw you on the land
and hurl you on the open field.
I will let all the birds of the air settle
on you
and all the beasts of the earth
gorge themselves on you.
⁵ I will spread your flesh on the
mountains
and fill the valleys with your
remains.
⁶ I will drench the land with your
flowing blood
all the way to the mountains,
and the ravines will be filled with
your flesh.
⁷ When I snuff you out, I will cover the
heavens
and darken their stars;
I will cover the sun with a cloud,
and the moon will not give its light.
⁸ All the shining lights in the heavens
I will darken over you;
I will bring darkness over your
land,
declares the Sovereign LORD.
⁹ I will trouble the hearts of many
peoples
when I bring about your
destruction among the nations,
among[a] lands you have not known.
¹⁰ I will cause many peoples to be
appalled at you,
and their kings will shudder with
horror because of you
when I brandish my sword before
them.

On the day of your downfall
each of them will tremble
every moment for his life.

¹¹"'For this is what the Sovereign LORD says:

"'The sword of the king of Babylon
will come against you.
¹² I will cause your hordes to fall
by the swords of mighty men—
the most ruthless of all nations.
They will shatter the pride of Egypt,
and all her hordes will be
overthrown.
¹³ I will destroy all her cattle
from beside abundant waters
no longer to be stirred by the foot of
man
or muddied by the hoofs of cattle.
¹⁴ Then I will let her waters settle
and make her streams flow like oil,
declares the Sovereign LORD.
¹⁵ When I make Egypt desolate
and strip the land of everything
in it,
when I strike down all who live there,
then they will know that I am the
LORD.'

¹⁶"This is the lament they will chant for her. The daughters of the nations will chant it; for Egypt and all her hordes they will chant it, declares the Sovereign LORD."

¹⁷In the twelfth year, on the fifteenth day of the month, the word of the LORD came to me: ¹⁸"Son of man, wail for the hordes of Egypt and consign to the earth below both her and the daughters of mighty nations, with those who go down to the pit. ¹⁹Say to them, 'Are you more favored than others? Go down and be laid among the uncircumcised.' ²⁰They will fall among those killed by the sword. The sword is drawn; let her be dragged off with all her hordes. ²¹From within the grave[b] the mighty leaders will say of Egypt and her allies, 'They have come down and they lie with the uncircumcised, with those killed by the sword.'

²²"Assyria is there with her whole army; she is surrounded by the graves of

---

a9 Hebrew; Septuagint *bring you into captivity among the nations, / to*   *b21* Hebrew *Sheol;* also in verse 27

all her slain, all who have fallen by the sword. 23Their graves are in the depths of the pit and her army lies around her grave. All who had spread terror in the land of the living are slain, fallen by the sword.

24"Elam is there, with all her hordes around her grave. All of them are slain, fallen by the sword. All who had spread terror in the land of the living went down uncircumcised to the earth below. They bear their shame with those who go down to the pit. 25A bed is made for her among the slain, with all her hordes around her grave. All of them are uncircumcised, killed by the sword. Because their terror had spread in the land of the living, they bear their shame with those who go down to the pit; they are laid among the slain.

26"Meshech and Tubal are there, with all their hordes around their graves. All of them are uncircumcised, killed by the sword because they spread their terror in the land of the living. 27Do they not lie with the other uncircumcised warriors who have fallen, who went down to the grave with their weapons of war, whose swords were placed under their heads? The punishment for their sins rested on their bones, though the terror of these warriors had stalked through the land of the living.

28"You too, O Pharaoh, will be broken and will lie among the uncircumcised, with those killed by the sword.

29"Edom is there, her kings and all her princes; despite their power, they are laid with those killed by the sword. They lie with the uncircumcised, with those who go down to the pit.

30"All the princes of the north and all the Sidonians are there; they went down with the slain in disgrace despite the terror caused by their power. They lie uncircumcised with those killed by the sword and bear their shame with those who go down to the pit.

31"Pharaoh—he and all his army—will see them and he will be consoled for all his hordes that were killed by the sword, declares the Sovereign LORD. 32Although I had him spread terror in the land of the living, Pharaoh and all his hordes will be laid among the uncircumcised, with

those killed by the sword, declares the Sovereign LORD."

Ezekiel a Watchman

33 The word of the LORD came to me: 2"Son of man, speak to your countrymen and say to them: 'When I bring the sword against a land, and the people of the land choose one of their men and make him their watchman, 3and he sees the sword coming against the land and blows the trumpet to warn the people, 4then if anyone hears the trumpet but does not take warning and the sword comes and takes his life, his blood will be on his own head. 5Since he heard the sound of the trumpet but did not take warning, his blood will be on his own head. If he had taken warning, he would have saved himself. 6But if the watchman sees the sword coming and does not blow the trumpet to warn the people and the sword comes and takes the life of one of them, that man will be taken away because of his sin, but I will hold the watchman accountable for his blood.'

7"Son of man, I have made you a watchman for the house of Israel; so hear the word I speak and give them warning from me. 8When I say to the wicked, 'O wicked man, you will surely die,' and you do not speak out to dissuade him from his ways, that wicked man will die for[a] his sin, and I will hold you accountable for his blood. 9But if you do warn the wicked man to turn from his ways and he does not do so, he will die for his sin, but you will have saved yourself.

> *Allow your dreams a place in your prayers and plans. God-given dreams can help you move into the future he is preparing for you.*
>
> BARBARA JOHNSON

10"Son of man, say to the house of Israel, 'This is what you are saying: "Our offenses and sins weigh us down, and we are wasting away because of[b] them. How then can we live?"' 11Say to them, 'As surely as I live, declares the Sovereign

[a]8 Or in; also in verse 9   [b]10 Or away in

LORD, I take no pleasure in the death of the wicked, but rather that they turn from their ways and live. Turn! Turn from your evil ways! Why will you die, O house of Israel?'

¹²"Therefore, son of man, say to your countrymen, 'The righteousness of the righteous man will not save him when he disobeys, and the wickedness of the wicked man will not cause him to fall when he turns from it. The righteous man, if he sins, will not be allowed to live because of his former righteousness.' ¹³If I tell the righteous man that he will surely live, but then he trusts in his righteousness and does evil, none of the righteous things he has done will be remembered; he will die for the evil he has done. ¹⁴And if I say to the wicked man, 'You will surely die,' but he then turns away from his sin and does what is just and right— ¹⁵if he gives back what he took in pledge for a loan, returns what he has stolen, follows the decrees that give life, and does no evil, he will surely live; he will not die. ¹⁶None of the sins he has committed will be remembered against him. He has done what is just and right; he will surely live.

¹⁷"Yet your countrymen say, 'The way of the Lord is not just.' But it is their way that is not just. ¹⁸If a righteous man turns from his righteousness and does evil, he will die for it. ¹⁹And if a wicked man turns away from his wickedness and does what is just and right, he will live by doing so. ²⁰Yet, O house of Israel, you say, 'The way of the Lord is not just.' But I will judge each of you according to his own ways."

Jerusalem's Fall Explained

²¹In the twelfth year of our exile, in the tenth month on the fifth day, a man who had escaped from Jerusalem came to me and said, "The city has fallen!" ²²Now the evening before the man arrived, the hand of the LORD was upon me, and he opened my mouth before the man came to me in the morning. So my mouth was opened and I was no longer silent.

²³Then the word of the LORD came to me: ²⁴"Son of man, the people living in those ruins in the land of Israel are saying, 'Abraham was only one man, yet he possessed the land. But we are many;

surely the land has been given to us as our possession.' ²⁵Therefore say to them, 'This is what the Sovereign LORD says: Since you eat meat with the blood still in it and look to your idols and shed blood, should you then possess the land? ²⁶You rely on your sword, you do detestable things, and each of you defiles his neighbor's wife. Should you then possess the land?'

²⁷"Say this to them: 'This is what the Sovereign LORD says: As surely as I live, those who are left in the ruins will fall by the sword, those out in the country I will give to the wild animals to be devoured, and those in strongholds and caves will die of a plague. ²⁸I will make the land a desolate waste, and her proud strength will come to an end, and the mountains of Israel will become desolate so that no one will cross them. ²⁹Then they will know that I am the LORD, when I have made the land a desolate waste because of all the detestable things they have done.'

³⁰"As for you, son of man, your countrymen are talking together about you by the walls and at the doors of the houses, saying to each other, 'Come and hear the message that has come from the LORD.' ³¹My people come to you, as they usually do, and sit before you to listen to your words, but they do not put them into practice. With their mouths they express devotion, but their hearts are greedy for unjust gain. ³²Indeed, to them you are nothing more than one who sings love songs with a beautiful voice and plays an instrument well, for they hear your words but do not put them into practice.

³³"When all this comes true—and it surely will—then they will know that a prophet has been among them."

Shepherds and Sheep

34 The word of the LORD came to me: ²"Son of man, prophesy against the shepherds of Israel; prophesy and say to them: 'This is what the Sovereign LORD says: Woe to the shepherds of Israel who only take care of themselves! Should not shepherds take care of the flock? ³You eat the curds, clothe yourselves with the wool and slaughter the choice animals, but you do not take care of the flock.

⁴You have not strengthened the weak or healed the sick or bound up the injured. You have not brought back the strays or searched for the lost. You have ruled them harshly and brutally. ⁵So they were scattered because there was no shepherd, and when they were scattered they became food for all the wild animals. ⁶My sheep wandered over all the mountains and on every high hill. They were scattered over the whole earth, and no one searched or looked for them.

⁷" 'Therefore, you shepherds, hear the word of the LORD: ⁸As surely as I live, declares the Sovereign LORD, because my flock lacks a shepherd and so has been plundered and has become food for all the wild animals, and because my shepherds did not search for my flock but cared for themselves rather than for my flock, ⁹therefore, O shepherds, hear the word of the LORD: ¹⁰This is what the Sovereign LORD says: I am against the shepherds and will hold them accountable for my flock. I will remove them from tending the flock so that the shepherds can no longer feed themselves. I will rescue my flock from their mouths, and it will no longer be food for them.

¹¹" 'For this is what the Sovereign LORD says: I myself will search for my sheep and look after them. ¹²As a shepherd looks after his scattered flock when he is with them, so will I look after my sheep. I will rescue them from all the places where they were scattered on a day of clouds and darkness. ¹³I will bring them out from the nations and gather them from the countries, and I will bring them into their own land. I will pasture them on the mountains of Israel, in the ravines and in all the settlements in the land. ¹⁴I will tend them in a good pasture, and the mountain heights of Israel will be their grazing land. There they will lie down in good grazing land, and there they will feed in a rich pasture on the mountains of Israel. ¹⁵I myself will tend my sheep and have them lie down, declares the Sovereign LORD. ¹⁶I will search for the lost and bring back the strays. I will bind up the injured and strengthen the weak, but the sleek and the strong I will destroy. I will shepherd the flock with justice.

¹⁷" 'As for you, my flock, this is what the Sovereign LORD says: I will judge between one sheep and another, and between rams and goats. ¹⁸Is it not enough for you to feed on the good pasture? Must you also trample the rest of your pasture with your feet? Is it not enough for you to drink clear water? Must you also muddy the rest with your feet? ¹⁹Must my flock feed on what you have trampled and drink what you have muddied with your feet?

²⁰" 'Therefore this is what the Sovereign LORD says to them: See, I myself will judge between the fat sheep and the lean sheep. ²¹Because you shove with flank and shoulder, butting all the weak sheep with your horns until you have driven them away, ²²I will save my flock, and they will no longer be plundered. I will judge between one sheep and another. ²³I will place over them one shepherd, my servant David, and he will tend them; he will tend them and be their shepherd. ²⁴I the LORD will be their God, and my servant David will be prince among them. I the LORD have spoken.

²⁵" 'I will make a covenant of peace with them and rid the land of wild beasts so that they may live in the desert and sleep in the forests in safety. ²⁶I will bless them and the places surrounding my hill.ᵃ I will send down showers in season; there will be showers of blessing. ²⁷The trees of the field will yield their fruit and the ground will yield its crops; the people will be secure in their land. They will know that I am the LORD, when I break the bars of their yoke and rescue them from the hands of those who enslaved them. ²⁸They will no longer be plundered by the nations, nor will wild animals devour them. They will live in safety, and no one will make them afraid. ²⁹I will provide for them a land renowned for its crops, and they will no longer be victims of famine in the land or bear the scorn of the nations. ³⁰Then they will know that I, the LORD their God, am with them and that they, the house of Israel, are my people, declares the Sovereign LORD. ³¹You my sheep, the sheep of my pasture, are people, and I am your God, declares the Sovereign LORD.' "

ᵃ26 Or I will make them and the places surrounding my hill a blessing

A Prophecy Against Edom

35 The word of the LORD came to me: ²"Son of man, set your face against Mount Seir; prophesy against it ³and say: 'This is what the Sovereign LORD says: I am against you, Mount Seir, and I will stretch out my hand against you and make you a desolate waste. ⁴I will turn your towns into ruins and you will be desolate. Then you will know that I am the LORD.

⁵ 'Because you harbored an ancient hostility and delivered the Israelites over to the sword at the time of their calamity, the time their punishment reached its climax, ⁶therefore as surely as I live, declares the Sovereign LORD, I will give you over to bloodshed and it will pursue you. Since you did not hate bloodshed, bloodshed will pursue you. ⁷I will make Mount Seir a desolate waste and cut off from it all who come and go. ⁸I will fill your mountains with the slain; those killed by the sword will fall on your hills and in your valleys and in all your ravines. ⁹I will make you desolate forever; your towns will not be inhabited. Then you will know that I am the LORD.

¹⁰ 'Because you have said, "These two nations and countries will be ours and we will take possession of them," even though I the LORD was there, ¹¹therefore as surely as I live, declares the Sovereign LORD, I will treat you in accordance with the anger and jealousy you showed in your hatred of them and I will make myself known among them when I judge you. ¹²Then you will know that I the LORD have heard all the contemptible things you have said against the mountains of Israel. You said, "They have been laid waste and have been given over to us to devour." ¹³You boasted against me and spoke against me without restraint, and I heard it. ¹⁴This is what the Sovereign LORD says: While the whole earth rejoices, I will make you desolate. ¹⁵Because you rejoiced when the inheritance of the house of Israel became desolate, that is how I will treat you. You will be desolate, O Mount Seir, you and all of Edom. Then they will know that I am the LORD.'"

A Prophecy to the Mountains of Israel

36 "Son of man, prophesy to the mountains of Israel and say, 'O mountains of Israel, hear the word of the LORD. ²This is what the Sovereign LORD says: The enemy said of you, "Aha! The ancient heights have become our possession."' ³Therefore prophesy and say, 'This is what the Sovereign LORD says: Because they ravaged and hounded you from every side so that you became the possession of the rest of the nations and the object of people's malicious talk and slander, ⁴therefore, O mountains of Israel, hear the word of the Sovereign LORD: This is what the Sovereign LORD says to the mountains and hills, to the ravines and valleys, to the desolate ruins and the deserted towns that have been plundered and ridiculed by the rest of the nations around you— ⁵this is what the Sovereign LORD says: In my burning zeal I have spoken against the rest of the nations, and against all Edom, for with glee and with malice in their hearts they made my land their own possession so that they might plunder its pastureland.' ⁶Therefore prophesy concerning the land of Israel and say to the mountains and hills, to the ravines and valleys: 'This is what the Sovereign LORD says: I speak in my jealous wrath because you have suffered the scorn of the nations. ⁷Therefore this is what the Sovereign LORD says: I swear with uplifted hand that the nations around you will also suffer scorn.

⁸ 'But you, O mountains of Israel, will produce branches and fruit for my people Israel, for they will soon come home. ⁹I am concerned for you and will look on you with favor; you will be plowed and sown, ¹⁰and I will multiply the number of people upon you, even the whole house of Israel. The towns will be inhabited and the ruins rebuilt. ¹¹I will increase the number of men and animals upon you, and they will be fruitful and become numerous. I will settle people on you as in the past and will make you prosper more than before. Then you will know that I am the LORD. ¹²I will cause people, my people Israel, to walk upon you. They will possess you, and you will be their inheritance; you will never again deprive them of their children.

¹³ 'This is what the Sovereign LORD says: Because people say to you, "You devour men and deprive your nation of

its children," ¹⁴therefore you will no longer devour men or make your nation childless, declares the Sovereign LORD. ¹⁵No longer will I make you hear the taunts of the nations, and no longer will you suffer the scorn of the peoples or cause your nation to fall, declares the Sovereign LORD.'"

¹⁶Again the word of the LORD came to me: ¹⁷"Son of man, when the people of Israel were living in their own land, they defiled it by their conduct and their actions. Their conduct was like a woman's monthly uncleanness in my sight. ¹⁸So I poured out my wrath on them because they had shed blood in the land and because they had defiled it with their idols. ¹⁹I dispersed them among the nations, and they were scattered through the countries; I judged them according to their conduct and their actions. ²⁰And wherever they went among the nations they profaned my holy name, for it was said of them, 'These are the LORD's people, and yet they had to leave his land.' ²¹I had concern for my holy name, which the house of Israel profaned among the nations where they had gone.

²²"Therefore say to the house of Israel, 'This is what the Sovereign LORD says: It is not for your sake, O house of Israel, that I am going to do these things, but for the sake of my holy name, which you have profaned among the nations where you have gone. ²³I will show the holiness of my great name, which has been profaned among the nations, the name you have profaned among them. Then the nations will know that I am the LORD, declares the Sovereign LORD, when I show myself holy through you before their eyes.

²⁴"'For I will take you out of the nations; I will gather you from all the countries and bring you back into your own land. ²⁵I will sprinkle clean water on you, and you will be clean; I will cleanse you from all your impurities and from all your idols. ²⁶I will give you a new heart and put a new spirit in you; I will remove from you your heart of stone and give you a heart of flesh. ²⁷And I will put my Spirit in you and move you to follow my decrees and be careful to keep my laws. ²⁸You will live in the land I gave your forefathers; you will be my people, and I

will be your God. ²⁹I will save you from all your uncleanness. I will call for the grain and make it plentiful and will not bring famine upon you. ³⁰I will increase the fruit of the trees and the crops of the field, so that you will no longer suffer disgrace among the nations because of famine. ³¹Then you will remember your evil ways and wicked deeds, and you will loathe yourselves for your sins and detestable practices. ³²I want you to know that I am not doing this for your sake, declares the Sovereign LORD. Be ashamed and disgraced for your conduct, O house of Israel!

³³"'This is what the Sovereign LORD says: On the day I cleanse you from all your sins, I will resettle your towns, and the ruins will be rebuilt. ³⁴The desolate land will be cultivated instead of lying desolate in the sight of all who pass through it. ³⁵They will say, "This land that was laid waste has become like the garden of Eden; the cities that were lying in ruins, desolate and destroyed, are now fortified and inhabited." ³⁶Then the nations around you that remain will know that I the LORD have rebuilt what was destroyed and have replanted what was desolate. I the LORD have spoken, and I will do it.'

³⁷"This is what the Sovereign LORD says: Once again I will yield to the plea of the house of Israel and do this for them: I will make their people as numerous as sheep, ³⁸as numerous as the flocks for offerings at Jerusalem during her appointed feasts. So will the ruined cities be filled with flocks of people. Then they will know that I am the LORD."

The Valley of Dry Bones

37 The hand of the LORD was upon me, and he brought me out by the Spirit of the LORD and set me in the middle of a valley; it was full of bones. ²He led me back and forth among them, and I saw a great many bones on the floor of the valley, bones that were very dry. ³He asked me, "Son of man, can these bones live?"

I said, "O Sovereign LORD, you alone know."

⁴Then he said to me, "Prophesy to these bones and say to them, 'Dry bones,

hear the word of the LORD! ⁵This is what the Sovereign LORD says to these bones: I will make breath*ᵃ* enter you, and you will come to life. ⁶I will attach tendons to you and make flesh come upon you and cover you with skin; I will put breath in you, and you will come to life. Then you will know that I am the LORD.'"

⁷So I prophesied as I was commanded. And as I was prophesying, there was a noise, a rattling sound, and the bones came together, bone to bone. ⁸I looked, and tendons and flesh appeared on them and skin covered them, but there was no breath in them.

⁹Then he said to me, "Prophesy to the breath; prophesy, son of man, and say to it, 'This is what the Sovereign LORD says: Come from the four winds, O breath, and breathe into these slain, that they may live.'" ¹⁰So I prophesied as he commanded me, and breath entered them; they came to life and stood up on their feet— a vast army.

¹¹Then he said to me: "Son of man, these bones are the whole house of Israel. They say, 'Our bones are dried up and our hope is gone; we are cut off.' ¹²Therefore prophesy and say to them: 'This is what the Sovereign LORD says: O my people, I am going to open your graves and bring you up from them; I will bring you back to the land of Israel. ¹³Then you, my people, will know that I am the LORD, when I open your graves and bring you up from them. ¹⁴I will put my Spirit in you and you will live, and I will settle you in your own land. Then you will know that I the LORD have spoken, and I have done it, declares the LORD.'"

One Nation Under One King

¹⁵The word of the LORD came to me: ¹⁶"Son of man, take a stick of wood and write on it, 'Belonging to Judah and the Israelites associated with him.' Then take another stick of wood, and write on it, 'Ephraim's stick, belonging to Joseph and all the house of Israel associated with him.' ¹⁷Join them together into one stick so that they will become one in your hand.

¹⁸"When your countrymen ask you, 'Won't you tell us what you mean by this?' ¹⁹say to them, 'This is what the Sov-

ereign LORD says: I am going to take the stick of Joseph—which is in Ephraim's hand—and of the Israelite tribes associated with him, and join it to Judah's stick, making them a single stick of wood, and they will become one in my hand.' ²⁰Hold before their eyes the sticks you have written on ²¹and say to them, 'This is what the Sovereign LORD says: I will take the Israelites out of the nations where they have gone. I will gather them from all around and bring them back into their own land. ²²I will make them one nation in the land, on the mountains of Israel. There will be one king over all of them and they will never again be two nations or be divided into two kingdoms. ²³They will no longer defile themselves with their idols and vile images or with any of their offenses, for I will save them from all their sinful backsliding,*ᵇ* and I will cleanse them. They will be my people, and I will be their God.

²⁴"'My servant David will be king over them, and they will all have one shepherd. They will follow my laws and be careful to keep my decrees. ²⁵They will live in the land I gave to my servant Jacob, the land where your fathers lived. They and their children and their children's children will live there forever, and David my servant will be their prince forever. ²⁶I will make a covenant of peace with them; it will be an everlasting covenant. I will establish them and increase their numbers, and I will put my sanctuary among them forever. ²⁷My dwelling place will be with them; I will be their God, and they will be my people. ²⁸Then the nations will know that I the LORD make Israel holy, when my sanctuary is among them forever.'"

A Prophecy Against Gog

38 The word of the LORD came to me: ²"Son of man, set your face against Gog, of the land of Magog, the chief prince of*ᶜ* Meshech and Tubal; prophesy against him ³and say: 'This is what the Sovereign LORD says: I am

---

ᵃ5 The Hebrew for this word can also mean *wind* or *spirit* (see verses 6–14). *ᵇ23* Many Hebrew manuscripts (see also Septuagint); most Hebrew manuscripts *all their dwelling places where they sinned* *ᶜ2* Or *the prince of Rosh,*

against you, O Gog, chief prince of[a] Meshech and Tubal. [4]I will turn you around, put hooks in your jaws and bring you out with your whole army—your horses, your horsemen fully armed, and a great horde with large and small shields, all of them brandishing their swords. [5]Persia, Cush[b] and Put will be with them, all with shields and helmets, [6]also Gomer with all its troops, and Beth Togarmah from the far north with all its troops—the many nations with you.

[7]"'Get ready; be prepared, you and all the hordes gathered about you, and take command of them. [8]After many days you will be called to arms. In future years you will invade a land that has recovered from war, whose people were gathered

[a]3 Or *Gog, prince of Rosh,*   [b]5 That is, the upper Nile region

---

EZEKIEL 37:1–14

[TUESDAY]

Can These Bones Live?

37:1 [HE] SET ME IN THE MIDDLE OF A VALLEY; IT WAS FULL OF BONES.

The scene was like the aftermath of the atrocities by the Khmer Rouge in Cambodia. The Lord took Ezekiel to a valley full of dry bones and asked him, "Son of man, can these bones live?" (37:3). God can do anything. The only question is: What does he want to do? And in this case, how does he want to do it?

God wants to raise the bones to life, as a symbol of what he wants to do for his people. How he intends to do it is very important for understanding how prayer, the Word of God and spiritual revival fit together. God tells Ezekiel, "Prophesy to these bones" (verse 4). That means to preach to them. The message Ezekiel is to preach is a message of hope from the Lord: "I will make breath enter you, and you will come to life" (verse 5). The message is powerful; the bones come together and are connected by tendons and covered by flesh. But the bodies are still dead; lifelike, but lifeless. Then God tells Ezekiel, "Prophesy to the breath" (verse 9). That means to pray for the Spirit to come into these corpses and give them life, the way God first breathed into Adam and he became a living being (see Genesis 2:7). Spiritual revival will come through preaching the gospel of hope and praying for the Spirit of life.

Preaching and praying: These are God's chief means for spiritual revival. Paul linked the two together when he told the Ephesians to take "the sword of the Spirit, which is the word of God," and to "pray in the Spirit on all occasions with all kinds of prayers and requests" (Ephesians 6:17–18). The text literally says to take the sword of the Spirit *by means* of all prayer and petition. The sword of the Spirit, the Word of God, is wielded by prayer. God is still asking, "Can these bones live? Can the bones of a corrupt culture and a lukewarm church yet come alive?" His means haven't changed. Preach the Word and pray.

PRAY:

O Holy Spirit, raise up a generation of "Ezekiels" for our times.
Make them—and me—powerful to preach and faithful to pray.

FOR YOUR NEXT DEVOTIONAL READING, GO TO PAGE 1034.

from many nations to the mountains of Israel, which had long been desolate. They had been brought out from the nations, and now all of them live in safety. ⁹You and all your troops and the many nations with you will go up, advancing like a storm; you will be like a cloud covering the land.

¹⁰" 'This is what the Sovereign LORD says: On that day thoughts will come into your mind and you will devise an evil scheme. ¹¹You will say, "I will invade a land of unwalled villages; I will attack a peaceful and unsuspecting people—all of them living without walls and without gates and bars. ¹²I will plunder and loot and turn my hand against the resettled ruins and the people gathered from the nations, rich in livestock and goods, living at the center of the land." ¹³Sheba and Dedan and the merchants of Tarshish and all her villages*ᵃ* will say to you, "Have you come to plunder? Have you gathered your hordes to loot, to carry off silver and gold, to take away livestock and goods and to seize much plunder?" '

¹⁴"Therefore, son of man, prophesy and say to Gog: 'This is what the Sovereign LORD says: In that day, when my people Israel are living in safety, will you not take notice of it? ¹⁵You will come from your place in the far north, you and many nations with you, all of them riding on horses, a great horde, a mighty army. ¹⁶You will advance against my people Israel like a cloud that covers the land. In days to come, O Gog, I will bring you against my land, so that the nations may know me when I show myself holy through you before their eyes.

¹⁷"'This is what the Sovereign LORD says: Are you not the one I spoke of in former days by my servants the prophets of Israel? At that time they prophesied for years that I would bring you against them. ¹⁸This is what will happen in that day: When Gog attacks the land of Israel, my hot anger will be aroused, declares the Sovereign LORD. ¹⁹In my zeal and fiery wrath I declare that at that time there shall be a great earthquake in the land of Israel. ²⁰The fish of the sea, the birds of the air, the beasts of the field, every creature that moves along the ground, and all the people on the face of the earth will tremble at my presence. The mountains will be overturned, the cliffs will crumble and every wall will fall to the ground. ²¹I will summon a sword against Gog on all my mountains, declares the Sovereign LORD. Every man's sword will be against his brother. ²²I will execute judgment upon him with plague and bloodshed; I will pour down torrents of rain, hailstones and burning sulfur on him and on his troops and on the many nations with him. ²³And so I will show my greatness and my holiness, and I will make myself known in the sight of many nations. Then they will know that I am the LORD.'

39 "Son of man, prophesy against Gog and say: 'This is what the Sovereign LORD says: I am against you, O Gog, chief prince of*ᵇ* Meshech and Tubal. ²I will turn you around and drag you along. I will bring you from the far north and send you against the mountains of Israel. ³Then I will strike your bow from your left hand and make your arrows drop from your right hand. ⁴On the mountains of Israel you will fall, you and all your troops and the nations with you. I will give you as food to all kinds of carrion birds and to the wild animals. ⁵You will fall in the open field, for I have spoken, declares the Sovereign LORD. ⁶I will send fire on Magog and on those who live in safety in the coastlands, and they will know that I am the LORD.

⁷" 'I will make known my holy name among my people Israel. I will no longer let my holy name be profaned, and the nations will know that I the LORD am the Holy One in Israel. ⁸It is coming! It will surely take place, declares the Sovereign LORD. This is the day I have spoken of.

⁹" 'Then those who live in the towns of Israel will go out and use the weapons for fuel and burn them up—the small and large shields, the bows and arrows, the war clubs and spears. For seven years they will use them for fuel. ¹⁰They will not need to gather wood from the fields or cut it from the forests, because they will use the weapons for fuel. And they will plunder those who plundered them and loot those who looted them, declares the Sovereign LORD.

ᵃ13 Or *her strong lions*   *ᵇ1* Or *Gog, prince of Rosh,*

¹¹ " 'On that day I will give Gog a burial place in Israel, in the valley of those who travel east toward[a] the Sea.[b] It will block the way of travelers, because Gog and all his hordes will be buried there. So it will be called the Valley of Hamon Gog.[c]

¹² " 'For seven months the house of Israel will be burying them in order to cleanse the land. ¹³All the people of the land will bury them, and the day I am glorified will be a memorable day for them, declares the Sovereign LORD.

¹⁴ " 'Men will be regularly employed to cleanse the land. Some will go throughout the land and, in addition to them, others will bury those that remain on the ground. At the end of the seven months they will begin their search. ¹⁵As they go through the land and one of them sees a human bone, he will set up a marker beside it until the gravediggers have buried it in the Valley of Hamon Gog. ¹⁶(Also a town called Hamonah[d] will be there.) And so they will cleanse the land.'

¹⁷"Son of man, this is what the Sovereign LORD says: Call out to every kind of bird and all the wild animals: 'Assemble and come together from all around to the sacrifice I am preparing for you, the great sacrifice on the mountains of Israel. There you will eat flesh and drink blood. ¹⁸You will eat the flesh of mighty men and drink the blood of the princes of the earth as if they were rams and lambs, goats and bulls—all of them fattened animals from Bashan. ¹⁹At the sacrifice I am preparing for you, you will eat fat till you are glutted and drink blood till you are drunk. ²⁰At my table you will eat your fill of horses and riders, mighty men and soldiers of every kind,' declares the Sovereign LORD.

²¹"I will display my glory among the nations, and all the nations will see the punishment I inflict and the hand I lay upon them. ²²From that day forward the house of Israel will know that I am the LORD their God. ²³And the nations will know that the people of Israel went into exile for their sin, because they were unfaithful to me. So I hid my face from them and handed them over to their enemies, and they all fell by the sword. ²⁴I dealt with them according to their uncleanness and their offenses, and I hid my face from them.

²⁵"Therefore this is what the Sovereign LORD says: I will now bring Jacob back from captivity[e] and will have compassion on all the people of Israel, and I will be zealous for my holy name. ²⁶They will forget their shame and all the unfaithfulness they showed toward me when they lived in safety in their land with no one to make them afraid. ²⁷When I have brought them back from the nations and have gathered them from the countries of their enemies, I will show myself holy through them in the sight of many nations. ²⁸Then they will know that I am the LORD their God, for though I sent them into exile among the nations, I will gather them to their own land, not leaving any behind. ²⁹I will no longer hide my face from them, for I will pour out my Spirit on the house of Israel, declares the Sovereign LORD."

The New Temple Area

40 In the twenty-fifth year of our exile, at the beginning of the year, on the tenth of the month, in the fourteenth year after the fall of the city—on that very day the hand of the LORD was upon me and he took me there. ²In visions of God he took me to the land of Israel and set me on a very high mountain, on whose south side were some buildings that looked like a city. ³He took me there, and I saw a man whose appearance was like bronze; he was standing in the gateway with a linen cord and a measuring rod in his hand. ⁴The man said to me, "Son of man, look with your eyes and hear with your ears and pay attention to everything I am going to show you, for that is why you have been brought here. Tell the house of Israel everything you see."

The East Gate to the Outer Court

⁵I saw a wall completely surrounding the temple area. The length of the measuring rod in the man's hand was six long cubits, each of which was a cubit[f] and a handbreadth.[g] He measured the

---

[a]11 Or of   [b]11 That is, the Dead Sea
[c]11 Hamon Gog means hordes of Gog.
[d]16 Hamonah means horde.   [e]25 Or now
restore the fortunes of Jacob   [f]5 The common
cubit was about 1 1/2 feet (about 0.5 meter).
[g]5 That is, about 3 inches (about 8 centimeters)

wall; it was one measuring rod thick and one rod high.

[6]Then he went to the gate facing east. He climbed its steps and measured the threshold of the gate; it was one rod deep.[a] [7]The alcoves for the guards were one rod long and one rod wide, and the projecting walls between the alcoves were five cubits thick. And the threshold of the gate next to the portico facing the temple was one rod deep.

[8]Then he measured the portico of the gateway; [9]it[b] was eight cubits deep and its jambs were two cubits thick. The portico of the gateway faced the temple.

[10]Inside the east gate were three alcoves on each side; the three had the same measurements, and the faces of the projecting walls on each side had the same measurements. [11]Then he measured the width of the entrance to the gateway; it was ten cubits and its length was thirteen cubits. [12]In front of each alcove was a wall one cubit high, and the alcoves were six cubits square. [13]Then he measured the gateway from the top of the rear wall of one alcove to the top of the opposite one; the distance was twenty-five cubits from one parapet opening to the opposite one. [14]He measured along the faces of the projecting walls all around the inside of the gateway—sixty cubits. The measurement was up to the portico[c] facing the courtyard.[d] [15]The distance from the entrance of the gateway to the far end of its portico was fifty cubits. [16]The alcoves and the projecting walls inside the gateway were surmounted by narrow parapet openings all around, as was the portico; the openings all around faced inward. The faces of the projecting walls were decorated with palm trees.

The Outer Court

[17]Then he brought me into the outer court. There I saw some rooms and a pavement that had been constructed all around the court; there were thirty rooms along the pavement. [18]It abutted the sides of the gateways and was as wide as they were long; this was the lower pavement. [19]Then he measured the distance from the inside of the lower gateway to the outside of the inner court;

it was a hundred cubits on the east side as well as on the north.

The North Gate

[20]Then he measured the length and width of the gate facing north, leading into the outer court. [21]Its alcoves—three on each side—its projecting walls and its portico had the same measurements as those of the first gateway. It was fifty cubits long and twenty-five cubits wide. [22]Its openings, its portico and its palm tree decorations had the same measurements as those of the gate facing east. Seven steps led up to it, with its portico opposite them. [23]There was a gate to the inner court facing the north gate, just as there was one on the east. He measured from one gate to the opposite one; it was a hundred cubits.

The South Gate

[24]Then he led me to the south side and I saw a gate facing south. He measured its jambs and its portico, and they had the same measurements as the others. [25]The gateway and its portico had narrow openings all around, like the openings of the others. It was fifty cubits long and twenty-five cubits wide. [26]Seven steps led up to it, with its portico opposite them; it had palm tree decorations on the faces of the projecting walls on each side. [27]The inner court also had a gate facing south, and he measured from this gate to the outer gate on the south side; it was a hundred cubits.

Gates to the Inner Court

[28]Then he brought me into the inner court through the south gate, and he measured the south gate; it had the same measurements as the others. [29]Its alcoves, its projecting walls and its portico had the same measurements as the others. The gateway and its portico had openings all around. It was fifty cubits long and twenty-five cubits wide. [30](The

---

[a]6 Septuagint; Hebrew *deep, the first threshold, one rod deep* [b]8,9 Many Hebrew manuscripts, Septuagint, Vulgate and Syriac; most Hebrew manuscripts *gateway facing the temple; it was one rod deep.* [9]*Then he measured the portico of the gateway; it* [c]14 Septuagint; Hebrew *projecting wall* [d]14 The meaning of the Hebrew for this verse is uncertain.

porticoes of the gateways around the inner court were twenty-five cubits wide and five cubits deep.) ³¹Its portico faced the outer court; palm trees decorated its jambs, and eight steps led up to it.

³²Then he brought me to the inner court on the east side, and he measured the gateway; it had the same measurements as the others. ³³Its alcoves, its projecting walls and its portico had the same measurements as the others. The gateway and its portico had openings all around. It was fifty cubits long and twenty-five cubits wide. ³⁴Its portico faced the outer court; palm trees decorated the jambs on either side, and eight steps led up to it.

³⁵Then he brought me to the north gate and measured it. It had the same measurements as the others, ³⁶as did its alcoves, its projecting walls and its portico, and it had openings all around. It was fifty cubits long and twenty-five cubits wide. ³⁷Its portico*a* faced the outer court; palm trees decorated the jambs on either side, and eight steps led up to it.

The Rooms for Preparing Sacrifices

³⁸A room with a doorway was by the portico in each of the inner gateways, where the burnt offerings were washed. ³⁹In the portico of the gateway were two tables on each side, on which the burnt offerings, sin offerings and guilt offerings were slaughtered. ⁴⁰By the outside wall of the portico of the gateway, near the steps at the entrance to the north gateway were two tables, and on the other side of the steps were two tables. ⁴¹So there were four tables on one side of the gateway and four on the other—eight tables in all—on which the sacrifices were slaughtered. ⁴²There were also four tables of dressed stone for the burnt offerings, each a cubit and a half long, a cubit and a half wide and a cubit high. On them were placed the utensils for slaughtering the burnt offerings and the other sacrifices. ⁴³And double-pronged hooks, each a handbreadth long, were attached to the wall all around. The tables were for the flesh of the offerings.

Rooms for the Priests

⁴⁴Outside the inner gate, within the inner court, were two rooms, one*b* at the

side of the north gate and facing south, and another at the side of the south*c* gate and facing north. ⁴⁵He said to me, "The room facing south is for the priests who have charge of the temple, ⁴⁶and the room facing north is for the priests who have charge of the altar. These are the sons of Zadok, who are the only Levites who may draw near to the LORD to minister before him."

⁴⁷Then he measured the court: It was square—a hundred cubits long and a hundred cubits wide. And the altar was in front of the temple.

The Temple

⁴⁸He brought me to the portico of the temple and measured the jambs of the portico; they were five cubits wide on either side. The width of the entrance was fourteen cubits and its projecting walls were*d* three cubits wide on either side. ⁴⁹The portico was twenty cubits wide, and twelve*e* cubits from front to back. It was reached by a flight of stairs,*f* and there were pillars on each side of the jambs.

41 Then the man brought me to the outer sanctuary and measured the jambs; the width of the jambs was six cubits*g* on each side.*h* ²The entrance was ten cubits wide, and the projecting walls on each side of it were five cubits wide. He also measured the outer sanctuary; it was forty cubits long and twenty cubits wide.

³Then he went into the inner sanctuary and measured the jambs of the entrance; each was two cubits wide. The entrance was six cubits wide, and the projecting walls on each side of it were seven cubits wide. ⁴And he measured the length of the inner sanctuary; it was twenty cubits, and its width was twenty cubits across the end of the outer sanctuary. He said to me, "This is the Most Holy Place."

*a*37 Septuagint (see also verses 31 and 34); Hebrew *jambs*   *b*44 Septuagint; Hebrew *were rooms for singers, which were*   *c*44 Septuagint; Hebrew *east*   *d*48 Septuagint; Hebrew *entrance was*   *e*49 Septuagint; Hebrew *eleven*   *f*49 Hebrew; Septuagint *Ten steps led up to it*   *g*1 The common cubit was about 1 1/2 feet (about 0.5 meter).   *h*1 One Hebrew manuscript and Septuagint; most Hebrew manuscripts *side, the width of the tent*

⁵Then he measured the wall of the temple; it was six cubits thick, and each side room around the temple was four cubits wide. ⁶The side rooms were on three levels, one above another, thirty on each level. There were ledges all around the wall of the temple to serve as supports for the side rooms, so that the supports were not inserted into the wall of the temple. ⁷The side rooms all around the temple were wider at each successive level. The structure surrounding the temple was built in ascending stages, so that the rooms widened as one went upward. A stairway went up from the lowest floor to the top floor through the middle floor.

⁸I saw that the temple had a raised base all around it, forming the foundation of the side rooms. It was the length of the rod, six long cubits. ⁹The outer wall of the side rooms was five cubits thick. The open area between the side rooms of the temple ¹⁰and the ‚priests'‚ rooms was twenty cubits wide all around the temple. ¹¹There were entrances to the side rooms from the open area, one on the north and another on the south; and the base adjoining the open area was five cubits wide all around.

¹²The building facing the temple courtyard on the west side was seventy cubits wide. The wall of the building was five cubits thick all around, and its length was ninety cubits.

¹³Then he measured the temple; it was a hundred cubits long, and the temple courtyard and the building with its walls were also a hundred cubits long. ¹⁴The width of the temple courtyard on the east, including the front of the temple, was a hundred cubits.

¹⁵Then he measured the length of the building facing the courtyard at the rear of the temple, including its galleries on each side; it was a hundred cubits.

The outer sanctuary, the inner sanctuary and the portico facing the court, ¹⁶as well as the thresholds and the narrow windows and galleries around the three of them—everything beyond and including the threshold was covered with wood. The floor, the wall up to the windows, and the windows were covered. ¹⁷In the space above the outside of the entrance to the inner sanctuary and on the walls at regular intervals all around the inner and outer sanctuary ¹⁸were carved cherubim and palm trees. Palm trees alternated with cherubim. Each cherub had two faces: ¹⁹the face of a man toward the palm tree on one side and the face of a lion toward the palm tree on the other. They were carved all around the whole temple. ²⁰From the floor to the area above the entrance, cherubim and palm trees were carved on the wall of the outer sanctuary.

²¹The outer sanctuary had a rectangular doorframe, and the one at the front of the Most Holy Place was similar. ²²There was a wooden altar three cubits high and two cubits square[a]; its corners, its base[b] and its sides were of wood. The man said to me, "This is the table that is before the LORD." ²³Both the outer sanctuary and the Most Holy Place had double doors. ²⁴Each door had two leaves— two hinged leaves for each door. ²⁵And on the doors of the outer sanctuary were carved cherubim and palm trees like those carved on the walls, and there was a wooden overhang on the front of the portico. ²⁶On the sidewalls of the portico were narrow windows with palm trees carved on each side. The side rooms of the temple also had overhangs.

Rooms for the Priests

42 Then the man led me northward into the outer court and brought me to the rooms opposite the temple courtyard and opposite the outer wall on the north side. ²The building whose door faced north was a hundred cubits[c] long and fifty cubits wide. ³Both in the section twenty cubits from the inner court and in the section opposite the pavement of the outer court, gallery faced gallery at the three levels. ⁴In front of the rooms was an inner passageway ten cubits wide and a hundred cubits[d] long. Their doors were on the north. ⁵Now the upper rooms were narrower, for the galleries took more space from them than from the rooms on the lower and middle floors

---

[a]22 Septuagint; Hebrew *long*   [b]22 Septuagint; Hebrew *length*   [c]2 The common cubit was about 1 1/2 feet (about 0.5 meter).
[d]4 Septuagint and Syriac; Hebrew *and one cubit*

of the building. ⁶The rooms on the third floor had no pillars, as the courts had; so they were smaller in floor space than those on the lower and middle floors. ⁷There was an outer wall parallel to the rooms and the outer court; it extended in front of the rooms for fifty cubits. ⁸While the row of rooms on the side next to the outer court was fifty cubits long, the row on the side nearest the sanctuary was a hundred cubits long. ⁹The lower rooms had an entrance on the east side as one enters them from the outer court.

¹⁰On the south side*a* along the length of the wall of the outer court, adjoining the temple courtyard and opposite the outer wall, were rooms ¹¹with a passageway in front of them. These were like the rooms on the north; they had the same length and width, with similar exits and dimensions. Similar to the doorways on the north ¹²were the doorways of the rooms on the south. There was a doorway at the beginning of the passageway that was parallel to the corresponding wall extending eastward, by which one enters the rooms.

¹³Then he said to me, "The north and south rooms facing the temple courtyard are the priests' rooms, where the priests who approach the LORD will eat the most holy offerings. There they will put the most holy offerings—the grain offerings, the sin offerings and the guilt offerings—for the place is holy. ¹⁴Once the priests enter the holy precincts, they are not to go into the outer court until they leave behind the garments in which they minister, for these are holy. They are to put on other clothes before they go near the places that are for the people."

¹⁵When he had finished measuring what was inside the temple area, he led me out by the east gate and measured the area all around: ¹⁶He measured the east side with the measuring rod; it was five hundred cubits.*b* ¹⁷He measured the north side; it was five hundred cubits*c* by the measuring rod. ¹⁸He measured the south side; it was five hundred cubits by the measuring rod. ¹⁹Then he turned to the west side and measured; it was five hundred cubits by the measuring rod. ²⁰So he measured the area on all four sides. It had a wall around it,

five hundred cubits long and five hundred cubits wide, to separate the holy from the common.

The Glory Returns to the Temple

43 Then the man brought me to the gate facing east, ²and I saw the glory of the God of Israel coming from the east. His voice was like the roar of rushing waters, and the land was radiant with his glory. ³The vision I saw was like the vision I had seen when he*d* came to destroy the city and like the visions I had seen by the Kebar River, and I fell facedown. ⁴The glory of the LORD entered the temple through the gate facing east. ⁵Then the Spirit lifted me up and brought me into the inner court, and the glory of the LORD filled the temple.

⁶While the man was standing beside me, I heard someone speaking to me from inside the temple. ⁷He said: "Son of man, this is the place of my throne and the place for the soles of my feet. This is where I will live among the Israelites forever. The house of Israel will never again defile my holy name—neither they nor their kings—by their prostitution*e* and the lifeless idols*f* of their kings at their high places. ⁸When they placed their threshold next to my threshold and their doorposts beside my doorposts, with only a wall between me and them, they defiled my holy name by their detestable practices. So I destroyed them in my anger. ⁹Now let them put away from me their prostitution and the lifeless idols of their kings, and I will live among them forever.

¹⁰"Son of man, describe the temple to the people of Israel, that they may be ashamed of their sins. Let them consider the plan, ¹¹and if they are ashamed of all they have done, make known to them the design of the temple—its arrangement, its exits and entrances—its whole design and all its regulations*g* and laws. Write

a 10 Septuagint; Hebrew *Eastward*   *b 16* See Septuagint of verse 17; Hebrew *rods*; also in verses 18 and 19.   *c 17* Septuagint; Hebrew *rods*
d 3 Some Hebrew manuscripts and Vulgate; most Hebrew manuscripts *I*   *e 7* Or *their spiritual adultery*; also in verse 9   *f 7* Or *the corpses*; also in verse 9   *g 11* Some Hebrew manuscripts and Septuagint; most Hebrew manuscripts *regulations and its whole design*

these down before them so that they may be faithful to its design and follow all its regulations. ¹²"This is the law of the temple: All the surrounding area on top of the mountain will be most holy. Such is the law of the temple.

The Altar

¹³"These are the measurements of the altar in long cubits, that cubit being a cubit[a] and a handbreadth[b]: Its gutter is a cubit deep and a cubit wide, with a rim of one span[c] around the edge. And this is the height of the altar: ¹⁴From the gutter on the ground up to the lower ledge it is two cubits high and a cubit wide, and from the smaller ledge up to the larger ledge it is four cubits high and a cubit wide. ¹⁵The altar hearth is four cubits high, and four horns project upward from the hearth. ¹⁶The altar hearth is square, twelve cubits long and twelve cubits wide. ¹⁷The upper ledge also is square, fourteen cubits long and fourteen cubits wide, with a rim of half a cubit and a gutter of a cubit all around. The steps of the altar face east."

¹⁸Then he said to me, "Son of man, this is what the Sovereign LORD says: These will be the regulations for sacrificing burnt offerings and sprinkling blood upon the altar when it is built: ¹⁹You are to give a young bull as a sin offering to the priests, who are Levites, of the family of Zadok, who come near to minister before me, declares the Sovereign LORD. ²⁰You are to take some of its blood and put it on the four horns of the altar and on the four corners of the upper ledge and all around the rim, and so purify the altar and make atonement for it. ²¹You are to take the bull for the sin offering and burn it in the designated part of the temple area outside the sanctuary. ²²"On the second day you are to offer a male goat without defect for a sin offering, and the altar is to be purified as it

was purified with the bull. ²³When you have finished purifying it, you are to offer a young bull and a ram from the flock, both without defect. ²⁴You are to offer them before the LORD, and the priests are to sprinkle salt on them and sacrifice them as a burnt offering to the LORD.

²⁵"For seven days you are to provide a male goat daily for a sin offering; you are also to provide a young bull and a ram from the flock, both without defect. ²⁶For seven days they are to make atonement for the altar and cleanse it; thus they will dedicate it. ²⁷At the end of these days, from the eighth day on, the priests are to present your burnt offerings and fellowship offerings[d] on the altar. Then I will accept you, declares the Sovereign LORD."

The Prince, the Levites, the Priests

44 Then the man brought me back to the outer gate of the sanctuary, the one facing east, and it was shut. ²The LORD said to me, "This gate is to remain shut. It must not be opened; no one may enter through it. It is to remain shut because the LORD, the God of Israel, has entered through it. ³The prince himself is the only one who may sit inside the gateway to eat in the presence of the LORD. He is to enter by way of the portico of the gateway and go out the same way."

⁴Then the man brought me by way of the north gate to the front of the temple. I looked and saw the glory of the LORD filling the temple of the LORD, and I fell facedown.

⁵The LORD said to me, "Son of man, look carefully, listen closely and give attention to everything I tell you concerning all the regulations regarding the temple of the LORD. Give attention to the entrance of the temple and all the exits of the sanctuary. ⁶Say to the rebellious house of Israel, 'This is what the Sovereign LORD says: Enough of your detestable practices, O house of Israel! ⁷In addition to all your other detestable practices, you brought foreigners uncircumcised in heart and flesh into my

---

[a]13 The common cubit was about 1 1/2 feet (about 0.5 meter).   [b]13 That is, about 3 inches (about 8 centimeters)   [c]13 That is, about 9 inches (about 22 centimeters)
[d]27 Traditionally *peace offerings*

sanctuary, desecrating my temple while you offered me food, fat and blood, and you broke my covenant. [8]Instead of carrying out your duty in regard to my holy things, you put others in charge of my sanctuary. [9]This is what the Sovereign LORD says: No foreigner uncircumcised in heart and flesh is to enter my sanctuary, not even the foreigners who live among the Israelites.

[10]" 'The Levites who went far from me when Israel went astray and who wandered from me after their idols must bear the consequences of their sin. [11]They may serve in my sanctuary, having charge of the gates of the temple and serving in it; they may slaughter the burnt offerings and sacrifices for the people and stand before the people and serve them. [12]But because they served them in the presence of their idols and made the house of Israel fall into sin, therefore I have sworn with uplifted hand that they must bear the consequences of their sin, declares the Sovereign LORD. [13]They are not to come near to serve me as priests or come near any of my holy things or my most holy offerings; they must bear the shame of their detestable practices. [14]Yet I will put them in charge of the duties of the temple and all the work that is to be done in it.

[15]" 'But the priests, who are Levites and descendants of Zadok and who faithfully carried out the duties of my sanctuary when the Israelites went astray from me, are to come near to minister before me; they are to stand before me to offer sacrifices of fat and blood, declares the Sovereign LORD. [16]They alone are to enter my sanctuary; they alone are to come near my table to minister before me and perform my service.

[17]" 'When they enter the gates of the inner court, they are to wear linen clothes; they must not wear any woolen garment while ministering at the gates of the inner court or inside the temple. [18]They are to wear linen turbans on their heads and linen undergarments around their waists. They must not wear anything that makes them perspire. [19]When they go out into the outer court where the people are, they are to take off the clothes they have been ministering in and are to leave them in the sacred rooms, and put on other clothes, so that they do not consecrate the people by means of their garments.

[20]" 'They must not shave their heads or let their hair grow long, but they are to keep the hair of their heads trimmed. [21]No priest is to drink wine when he enters the inner court. [22]They must not marry widows or divorced women; they may marry only virgins of Israelite descent or widows of priests. [23]They are to teach my people the difference between the holy and the common and show them how to distinguish between the unclean and the clean.

[24]" 'In any dispute, the priests are to serve as judges and decide it according to my ordinances. They are to keep my laws and my decrees for all my appointed feasts, and they are to keep my Sabbaths holy.

[25]" 'A priest must not defile himself by going near a dead person; however, if the dead person was his father or mother, son or daughter, brother or unmarried sister, then he may defile himself. [26]After he is cleansed, he must wait seven days. [27]On the day he goes into the inner court of the sanctuary to minister in the sanctuary, he is to offer a sin offering for himself, declares the Sovereign LORD.

[28]" 'I am to be the only inheritance the priests have. You are to give them no possession in Israel; I will be their possession. [29]They will eat the grain offerings, the sin offerings and the guilt offerings; and everything in Israel devoted[a] to the LORD will belong to them. [30]The best of all the firstfruits and of all your special gifts will belong to the priests. You are to give them the first portion of your ground meal so that a blessing may rest on your household. [31]The priests must not eat anything, bird or animal, found dead or torn by wild animals.

Division of the Land

45 " 'When you allot the land as an inheritance, you are to present to the LORD a portion of the land as a sacred district, 25,000 cubits long and 20,000[b] cubits wide; the entire area will be holy.

[a]29 The Hebrew term refers to the irrevocable giving over of things or persons to the LORD.
[b]1 Septuagint (see also verses 3 and 5 and 48:9); Hebrew 10,000

²Of this, a section 500 cubits square is to be for the sanctuary, with 50 cubits around it for open land. ³In the sacred district, measure off a section 25,000 cubits*a* long and 10,000 cubits*b* wide. In it will be the sanctuary, the Most Holy Place. ⁴It will be the sacred portion of the land for the priests, who minister in the sanctuary and who draw near to minister before the LORD. It will be a place for their houses as well as a holy place for the sanctuary. ⁵An area 25,000 cubits long and 10,000 cubits wide will belong to the Levites, who serve in the temple, as their possession for towns to live in.*c*

⁶" 'You are to give the city as its property an area 5,000 cubits wide and 25,000 cubits long, adjoining the sacred portion; it will belong to the whole house of Israel.

⁷" 'The prince will have the land bordering each side of the area formed by the sacred district and the property of the city. It will extend westward from the west side and eastward from the east side, running lengthwise from the western to the eastern border parallel to one of the tribal portions. ⁸This land will be his possession in Israel. And my princes will no longer oppress my people but will allow the house of Israel to possess the land according to their tribes.

⁹" 'This is what the Sovereign LORD says: You have gone far enough, O princes of Israel! Give up your violence and oppression and do what is just and right. Stop dispossessing my people, declares the Sovereign LORD. ¹⁰You are to use accurate scales, an accurate ephah*d* and an accurate bath.*e* ¹¹The ephah and the bath are to be the same size, the bath containing a tenth of a homer*f* and the ephah a tenth of a homer; the homer is to be the standard measure for both. ¹²The shekel*g* is to consist of twenty gerahs. Twenty shekels plus twenty-five shekels plus fifteen shekels equal one mina.*h*

Offerings and Holy Days

¹³" 'This is the special gift you are to offer: a sixth of an ephah from each homer of wheat and a sixth of an ephah from each homer of barley. ¹⁴The prescribed portion of oil, measured by the bath, is a tenth of a bath from each cor (which consists of ten baths or one homer, for ten baths are equivalent to a homer). ¹⁵Also one sheep is to be taken from every flock of two hundred from the well-watered pastures of Israel. These will be used for the grain offerings, burnt offerings and fellowship offerings*i* to make atonement for the people, declares the Sovereign LORD. ¹⁶All the people of the land will participate in this special gift for the use of the prince in Israel. ¹⁷It will be the duty of the prince to provide the burnt offerings, grain offerings and drink offerings at the festivals, the New Moons and the Sabbaths—at all the appointed feasts of the house of Israel. He will provide the sin offerings, grain offerings, burnt offerings and fellowship offerings to make atonement for the house of Israel.

¹⁸" 'This is what the Sovereign LORD says: In the first month on the first day you are to take a young bull without defect and purify the sanctuary. ¹⁹The priest is to take some of the blood of the sin offering and put it on the doorposts of the temple, on the four corners of the upper ledge of the altar and on the gateposts of the inner court. ²⁰You are to do the same on the seventh day of the month for anyone who sins unintentionally or through ignorance; so you are to make atonement for the temple.

²¹" 'In the first month on the fourteenth day you are to observe the Passover, a feast lasting seven days, during which you shall eat bread made without yeast. ²²On that day the prince is to provide a bull as a sin offering for himself and for all the people of the land. ²³Every day during the seven days of the Feast he is to provide seven bulls and seven rams without defect as a burnt offering to the LORD, and a male goat for a sin offering. ²⁴He is to provide as a grain offering an ephah for each bull and an ephah for each ram, along with a hin*j* of oil for each ephah.

---

a 3 That is, about 7 miles (about 12 kilometers)
b 3 That is, about 3 miles (about 5 kilometers)
c 5 Septuagint; Hebrew *temple; they will have as their possession 20 rooms*   *d 10* An ephah was a dry measure.   *e 10* A bath was a liquid measure.
f 11 A homer was a dry measure.   *g 12* A shekel weighed about 2/5 ounce (about 11.5 grams).
h 12 That is, 60 shekels; the common mina was 50 shekels.   *i 15* Traditionally *peace offerings*; also in verse 17   *j 24* That is, probably about 4 quarts (about 4 liters)

²⁵" 'During the seven days of the Feast, which begins in the seventh month on the fifteenth day, he is to make the same provision for sin offerings, burnt offerings, grain offerings and oil.

46 " 'This is what the Sovereign LORD says: The gate of the inner court facing east is to be shut on the six working days, but on the Sabbath day and on the day of the New Moon it is to be opened. ²The prince is to enter from the outside through the portico of the gateway and stand by the gatepost. The priests are to sacrifice his burnt offering and his fellowship offerings.ᵃ He is to worship at the threshold of the gateway and then go out, but the gate will not be shut until evening. ³On the Sabbaths and New Moons the people of the land are to worship in the presence of the LORD at the entrance to that gateway. ⁴The burnt offering the prince brings to the LORD on the Sabbath day is to be six male lambs and a ram, all without defect. ⁵The grain offering given with the ram is to be an ephah,ᵇ and the grain offering with the lambs is to be as much as he pleases, along with a hinᶜ of oil for each ephah. ⁶On the day of the New Moon he is to offer a young bull, six lambs and a ram, all without defect. ⁷He is to provide as a grain offering one ephah with the bull, one ephah with the ram, and with the lambs as much as he wants to give, along with a hin of oil with each ephah. ⁸When the prince enters, he is to go in through the portico of the gateway, and he is to come out the same way.

⁹" 'When the people of the land come before the LORD at the appointed feasts, whoever enters by the north gate to worship is to go out the south gate; and whoever enters by the south gate is to go out the north gate. No one is to return through the gate by which he entered, but each is to go out the opposite gate. ¹⁰The prince is to be among them, going in when they go in and going out when they go out.

¹¹" 'At the festivals and the appointed feasts, the grain offering is to be an ephah with a bull, an ephah with a ram, and with the lambs as much as one pleases, along with a hin of oil for each ephah. ¹²When the prince provides a freewill of-

fering to the LORD—whether a burnt offering or fellowship offerings—the gate facing east is to be opened for him. He shall offer his burnt offering or his fellowship offerings as he does on the Sabbath day. Then he shall go out, and after he has gone out, the gate will be shut.

¹³" 'Every day you are to provide a year-old lamb without defect for a burnt offering to the LORD; morning by morning you shall provide it. ¹⁴You are also to provide with it morning by morning a grain offering, consisting of a sixth of an ephah with a third of a hin of oil to moisten the flour. The presenting of this grain offering to the LORD is a lasting ordinance. ¹⁵So the lamb and the grain offering and the oil shall be provided morning by morning for a regular burnt offering.

¹⁶" 'This is what the Sovereign LORD says: If the prince makes a gift from his inheritance to one of his sons, it will also belong to his descendants; it is to be their property by inheritance. ¹⁷If, however, he makes a gift from his inheritance to one of his servants, the servant may keep it until the year of freedom; then it will revert to the prince. His inheritance belongs to his sons only; it is theirs. ¹⁸The prince must not take any of the inheritance of the people, driving them off their property. He is to give his sons their inheritance out of his own property, so that none of my people will be separated from his property.' "

¹⁹Then the man brought me through the entrance at the side of the gate to the sacred rooms facing north, which belonged to the priests, and showed me a place at the western end. ²⁰He said to me, "This is the place where the priests will cook the guilt offering and the sin offering and bake the grain offering, to avoid bringing them into the outer court and consecrating the people."

²¹He then brought me to the outer court and led me around to its four corners, and I saw in each corner another court. ²²In the four corners of the outer court were enclosedᵈ courts, forty cubits long and thirty cubits wide; each of the courts

ᵃ2 Traditionally peace offerings; also in verse 12 ᵇ5 That is, probably about 3/5 bushel (about 22 liters)   ᶜ5 That is, probably about 4 quarts (about 4 liters)   ᵈ22 The meaning of the Hebrew for this word is uncertain.

in the four corners was the same size. ²³Around the inside of each of the four courts was a ledge of stone, with places for fire built all around under the ledge. ²⁴He said to me, "These are the kitchens where those who minister at the temple will cook the sacrifices of the people."

The River From the Temple

47 The man brought me back to the entrance of the temple, and I saw water coming out from under the threshold of the temple toward the east (for the temple faced east). The water was coming down from under the south side of the temple, south of the altar. ²He then brought me out through the north gate and led me around the outside to the outer gate facing east, and the water was flowing from the south side.

³As the man went eastward with a measuring line in his hand, he measured off a thousand cubits[a] and then led me through water that was ankle-deep. ⁴He measured off another thousand cubits and led me through water that was knee-deep. He measured off another thousand and led me through water that was up to the waist. ⁵He measured off another thousand, but now it was a river that I could not cross, because the water had risen and was deep enough to swim in— a river that no one could cross. ⁶He asked me, "Son of man, do you see this?"

Then he led me back to the bank of the river. ⁷When I arrived there, I saw a great number of trees on each side of the river. ⁸He said to me, "This water flows toward the eastern region and goes down into the Arabah,[b] where it enters the Sea.[c] When it empties into the Sea,[c] the water there becomes fresh. ⁹Swarms of living creatures will live wherever the river flows. There will be large numbers of fish, because this water flows there and makes the salt water fresh; so where the river flows everything will live. ¹⁰Fishermen will stand along the shore; from En Gedi to En Eglaim there will be places for spreading nets. The fish will be of many kinds—like the fish of the Great Sea.[d] ¹¹But the swamps and marshes will not become fresh; they will be left for salt. ¹²Fruit trees of all kinds will grow on both banks of the river. Their leaves will not

wither, nor will their fruit fail. Every month they will bear, because the water from the sanctuary flows to them. Their fruit will serve for food and their leaves for healing."

The Boundaries of the Land

¹³This is what the Sovereign LORD says: "These are the boundaries by which you are to divide the land for an inheritance among the twelve tribes of Israel, with two portions for Joseph. ¹⁴You are to divide it equally among them. Because I swore with uplifted hand to give it to your forefathers, this land will become your inheritance.

¹⁵"This is to be the boundary of the land:

"On the north side it will run from the Great Sea by the Hethlon road past Lebo[e] Hamath to Zedad, ¹⁶Berothah[f] and Sibraim (which lies on the border between Damascus and Hamath), as far as Hazer Hatticon, which is on the border of Hauran. ¹⁷The boundary will extend from the sea to Hazar Enan,[g] along the northern border of Damascus, with the border of Hamath to the north. This will be the north boundary.

¹⁸"On the east side the boundary will run between Hauran and Damascus, along the Jordan between Gilead and the land of Israel, to the eastern sea and as far as Tamar.[h] This will be the east boundary.

¹⁹"On the south side it will run from Tamar as far as the waters of Meribah Kadesh, then along the Wadi ˌof Egyptˌ to the Great Sea. This will be the south boundary.

²⁰"On the west side, the Great Sea will be the boundary to a point opposite Lebo[i] Hamath. This will be the west boundary.

---

[a]3 That is, about 1,500 feet (about 450 meters)   [b]8 Or the Jordan Valley   [c]8 That is, the Dead Sea   [d]10 That is, the Mediterranean; also in verses 15, 19 and 20   [e]15 Or past the entrance to   [f]15,16 See Septuagint and Ezekiel 48:1; Hebrew road to go into Zedad, ¹⁶Hamath, Berothah   [g]17 Hebrew Enon, a variant of Enan   [h]18 Septuagint and Syriac; Hebrew Israel. You will measure to the eastern sea   [i]20 Or opposite the entrance to

²¹"You are to distribute this land among yourselves according to the tribes of Israel. ²²You are to allot it as an inheritance for yourselves and for the aliens who have settled among you and who have children. You are to consider them as native-born Israelites; along with you they are to be allotted an inheritance among the tribes of Israel. ²³In whatever tribe the alien settles, there you are to give him his inheritance," declares the Sovereign LORD.

The Division of the Land

48 "These are the tribes, listed by name: At the northern frontier, Dan will have one portion; it will follow the Hethlon road to Lebo*ᵃ* Hamath; Hazar Enan and the northern border of Damascus next to Hamath will be part of its border from the east side to the west side.

²"Asher will have one portion; it will border the territory of Dan from east to west.

³"Naphtali will have one portion; it will border the territory of Asher from east to west.

⁴"Manasseh will have one portion; it will border the territory of Naphtali from east to west.

⁵"Ephraim will have one portion; it will border the territory of Manasseh from east to west.

⁶"Reuben will have one portion; it will border the territory of Ephraim from east to west.

⁷"Judah will have one portion; it will border the territory of Reuben from east to west.

⁸"Bordering the territory of Judah from east to west will be the portion you are to present as a special gift. It will be 25,000 cubits*ᵇ* wide, and its length from east to west will equal one of the tribal portions; the sanctuary will be in the center of it.

⁹"The special portion you are to offer to the LORD will be 25,000 cubits long and 10,000 cubits*ᶜ* wide. ¹⁰This will be the sacred portion for the priests. It will be 25,000 cubits long on the north side, 10,000 cubits wide on the west side, 10,000 cubits wide on the east side and 25,000 cubits long on the south side. In the center of it will be the sanctuary of the LORD. ¹¹This will be for the consecrat-

ed priests, the Zadokites, who were faithful in serving me and did not go astray as the Levites did when the Israelites went astray. ¹²It will be a special gift to them from the sacred portion of the land, a most holy portion, bordering the territory of the Levites.

¹³"Alongside the territory of the priests, the Levites will have an allotment 25,000 cubits long and 10,000 cubits wide. Its total length will be 25,000 cubits and its width 10,000 cubits. ¹⁴They must not sell or exchange any of it. This is the best of the land and must not pass into other hands, because it is holy to the LORD.

¹⁵"The remaining area, 5,000 cubits wide and 25,000 cubits long, will be for the common use of the city, for houses and for pastureland. The city will be in the center of it ¹⁶and will have these measurements: the north side 4,500 cubits, the south side 4,500 cubits, the east side 4,500 cubits, and the west side 4,500 cubits. ¹⁷The pastureland for the city will be 250 cubits on the north, 250 cubits on the south, 250 cubits on the east, and 250 cubits on the west. ¹⁸What remains of the area, bordering on the sacred portion and running the length of it, will be 10,000 cubits on the east side and 10,000 cubits on the west side. Its produce will supply food for the workers of the city. ¹⁹The workers from the city who farm it will come from all the tribes of Israel. ²⁰The entire portion will be a square, 25,000 cubits on each side. As a special gift you will set aside the sacred portion, along with the property of the city.

²¹"What remains on both sides of the area formed by the sacred portion and the city property will belong to the prince. It will extend eastward from the 25,000 cubits of the sacred portion to the eastern border, and westward from the 25,000 cubits to the western border. Both these areas running the length of the tribal portions will belong to the prince, and the sacred portion with the temple sanctuary will be in the center of them. ²²So the property of the Levites and the

ᵃ1 Or *to the entrance to* *ᵇ8* That is, about 7 miles (about 12 kilometers) *ᶜ9* That is, about 3 miles (about 5 kilometers)

property of the city will lie in the center of the area that belongs to the prince. The area belonging to the prince will lie between the border of Judah and the border of Benjamin.

23 "As for the rest of the tribes: Benjamin will have one portion; it will extend from the east side to the west side.

24 "Simeon will have one portion; it will border the territory of Benjamin from east to west.

25 "Issachar will have one portion; it will border the territory of Simeon from east to west.

26 "Zebulun will have one portion; it will border the territory of Issachar from east to west.

27 "Gad will have one portion; it will border the territory of Zebulun from east to west.

28 "The southern boundary of Gad will run south from Tamar to the waters of Meribah Kadesh, then along the Wadi of Egypt to the Great Sea.ᵃ

29 "This is the land you are to allot as an inheritance to the tribes of Israel, and these will be their portions," declares the Sovereign LORD.

The Gates of the City

30 "These will be the exits of the city: Beginning on the north side, which is 4,500 cubits long, 31 the gates of the city will be named after the tribes of Israel. The three gates on the north side will be the gate of Reuben, the gate of Judah and the gate of Levi.

32 "On the east side, which is 4,500 cubits long, will be three gates: the gate of Joseph, the gate of Benjamin and the gate of Dan.

33 "On the south side, which measures 4,500 cubits, will be three gates: the gate of Simeon, the gate of Issachar and the gate of Zebulun.

34 "On the west side, which is 4,500 cubits long, will be three gates: the gate of Gad, the gate of Asher and the gate of Naphtali.

35 "The distance all around will be 18,000 cubits.

"And the name of the city from that time on will be:

THE LORD IS THERE."

ᵃ28 That is, the Mediterranean

Daniel

THE BOOK of Daniel can read like the greatest hits collection in a children's Sunday school curriculum: "Shadrach, Meshach and Abednego in the fiery furnace," "The writing on the wall," "Daniel in the lions' den." But this book deserves an "R-rating," not "G," because of violence. The nations of the earth are portrayed as monsters, predatory and grotesque, devouring weaker nations as prey and each other as competitors (see chapter 7). The drama of Daniel is set amid powerfully stubborn and callous forces of evil, as seen in nation-states and empires. The message is the sovereignty of God over these forces and the call for God's people to be humbly faithful as they wait for him to fulfill his purposes.

Therefore, the book of Daniel contains some of the most exciting, mind-stretching teaching on prayer in the entire Bible. The courage of Daniel's prayer life, his intercession for Israel and his collaboration with the angels in prayer, are remarkable for their vividness and the theology that underlies them. The book of Daniel is an extended version of the answer Psalm 11 gives to the question, "When the foundations are being destroyed, what can the righteous do?" (verse 3). The answer of the psalm—and of Daniel—is to know that "The LORD is in his holy temple; the LORD is on his heavenly throne" (Psalm 11:4) and to pray accordingly.

"O LORD, THE GREAT AND AWESOME GOD, WHO KEEPS HIS COVENANT OF LOVE WITH ALL WHO LOVE HIM AND OBEY HIS COMMANDS." (9:4)

Daniel's Training in Babylon

1 In the third year of the reign of Jehoiakim king of Judah, Nebuchadnezzar king of Babylon came to Jerusalem and besieged it. ²And the Lord delivered Jehoiakim king of Judah into his hand, along with some of the articles from the temple of God. These he carried off to the temple of his god in Babylonia*a* and put in the treasure house of his god.

³Then the king ordered Ashpenaz, chief of his court officials, to bring in some of the Israelites from the royal family and the nobility— ⁴young men without any physical defect, handsome, showing aptitude for every kind of learning, well informed, quick to understand, and qualified to serve in the king's palace. He was to teach them the language and literature of the Babylonians.*b* ⁵The king assigned them a daily amount of food and wine from the king's table. They were to be trained for three years, and after that they were to enter the king's service.

⁶Among these were some from Judah: Daniel, Hananiah, Mishael and Azariah. ⁷The chief official gave them new names: to Daniel, the name Belteshazzar; to Hananiah, Shadrach; to Mishael, Meshach; and to Azariah, Abednego.

⁸But Daniel resolved not to defile himself with the royal food and wine, and he asked the chief official for permission not to defile himself this way. ⁹Now God had caused the official to show favor and sympathy to Daniel, ¹⁰but the official told Daniel, "I am afraid of my lord the king, who has assigned your*c* food and drink. Why should he see you looking worse than the other young men your age? The king would then have my head because of you."

¹¹Daniel then said to the guard whom the chief official had appointed over Daniel, Hananiah, Mishael and Azariah, ¹²"Please test your servants for ten days: Give us nothing but vegetables to eat and water to drink. ¹³Then compare our appearance with that of the young men who eat the royal food, and treat your servants in accordance with what you see." ¹⁴So he agreed to this and tested them for ten days.

¹⁵At the end of the ten days they looked healthier and better nourished than any of the young men who ate the royal food. ¹⁶So the guard took away their choice food and the wine they were to drink and gave them vegetables instead.

¹⁷To these four young men God gave knowledge and understanding of all kinds of literature and learning. And Daniel could understand visions and dreams of all kinds.

¹⁸At the end of the time set by the king to bring them in, the chief official presented them to Nebuchadnezzar. ¹⁹The king talked with them, and he found none equal to Daniel, Hananiah, Mishael and Azariah; so they entered the king's service. ²⁰In every matter of wisdom and understanding about which the king questioned them, he found them ten times better than all the magicians and enchanters in his whole kingdom.

²¹And Daniel remained there until the first year of King Cyrus.

Nebuchadnezzar's Dream

2 In the second year of his reign, Nebuchadnezzar had dreams; his mind was troubled and he could not sleep. ²So the king summoned the magicians, enchanters, sorcerers and astrologers*d* to tell him what he had dreamed. When they came in and stood before the king, ³he said to them, "I have had a dream that troubles me and I want to know what it means.*e*"

⁴Then the astrologers answered the king in Aramaic,*f* "O king, live forever! Tell your servants the dream, and we will interpret it."

⁵The king replied to the astrologers, "This is what I have firmly decided: If you do not tell me what my dream was and interpret it, I will have you cut into pieces and your houses turned into piles of rubble. ⁶But if you tell me the dream and explain it, you will receive from me gifts and rewards and great honor. So tell me the dream and interpret it for me."

---

*a*2 Hebrew *Shinar*   *b*4 Or *Chaldeans*
*c*10 The Hebrew for *your* and *you* in this verse is plural.   *d*2 Or *Chaldeans*; also in verses 4, 5 and 10   *e*3 Or *was*   *f*4 The text from here through chapter 7 is in Aramaic.

⁷Once more they replied, "Let the king tell his servants the dream, and we will interpret it."

⁸Then the king answered, "I am certain that you are trying to gain time, because you realize that this is what I have firmly decided: ⁹If you do not tell me the dream, there is just one penalty for you. You have conspired to tell me misleading and wicked things, hoping the situation will change. So then, tell me the dream, and I will know that you can interpret it for me."

¹⁰The astrologers answered the king, "There is not a man on earth who can do what the king asks! No king, however great and mighty, has ever asked such a thing of any magician or enchanter or astrologer. ¹¹What the king asks is too difficult. No one can reveal it to the king except the gods, and they do not live among men."

¹²This made the king so angry and furious that he ordered the execution of all the wise men of Babylon. ¹³So the decree was issued to put the wise men to death, and men were sent to look for Daniel and his friends to put them to death.

¹⁴When Arioch, the commander of the king's guard, had gone out to put to death the wise men of Babylon, Daniel spoke to him with wisdom and tact. ¹⁵He asked the king's officer, "Why did the king issue such a harsh decree?" Arioch then explained the matter to Daniel. ¹⁶At this, Daniel went in to the king and asked for time, so that he might interpret the dream for him.

¹⁷Then Daniel returned to his house and explained the matter to his friends Hananiah, Mishael and Azariah. ¹⁸He urged them to plead for mercy from the God of heaven concerning this mystery, so that he and his friends might not be executed with the rest of the wise men of Babylon. ¹⁹During the night the mystery

> HE URGED them to plead for mercy from the God of heaven concerning this mystery, so that he and his friends might not be executed with the rest of the wise men of Babylon.
>
> DANIEL 2:18

was revealed to Daniel in a vision. Then Daniel praised the God of heaven ²⁰and said:

"Praise be to the name of God for
    ever and ever;
    wisdom and power are his.
²¹ He changes times and seasons;
    he sets up kings and deposes them.
He gives wisdom to the wise
    and knowledge to the discerning.
²² He reveals deep and hidden things;
    he knows what lies in darkness,
    and light dwells with him.
²³ I thank and praise you, O God of my
    fathers:
    You have given me wisdom and
        power,
    you have made known to me what we
        asked of you,
    you have made known to us the
        dream of the king."

Daniel Interprets the Dream

²⁴Then Daniel went to Arioch, whom the king had appointed to execute the wise men of Babylon, and said to him, "Do not execute the wise men of Babylon. Take me to the king, and I will interpret his dream for him."

²⁵Arioch took Daniel to the king at once and said, "I have found a man among the exiles from Judah who can tell the king what his dream means."

²⁶The king asked Daniel (also called Belteshazzar), "Are you able to tell me what I saw in my dream and interpret it?"

²⁷Daniel replied, "No wise man, enchanter, magician or diviner can explain to the king the mystery he has asked about, ²⁸but there is a God in heaven who reveals mysteries. He has shown King Nebuchadnezzar what will happen in days to come. Your dream and the visions that passed through your mind as you lay on your bed are these: ²⁹"As you were lying there, O king, your mind turned to things to come, and the revealer of mysteries showed you what is going to happen. ³⁰As for me, this mystery has been revealed to me, not because I have greater wisdom than other living men, but so that you, O king, may know the interpretation and that you may understand what went through your mind.

[31] "You looked, O king, and there before you stood a large statue—an enormous, dazzling statue, awesome in appearance. [32]The head of the statue was made of pure gold, its chest and arms of silver, its belly and thighs of bronze, [33]its legs of iron, its feet partly of iron and partly of baked clay. [34]While you were watching, a rock was cut out, but not by human hands. It struck the statue on its feet of iron and clay and smashed them. [35]Then the iron, the clay, the bronze, the silver and the gold were broken to pieces at the same time and became like chaff on a threshing floor in the summer. The wind swept them away without leaving a trace. But the rock that struck the statue became a huge mountain and filled the whole earth.

[36]"This was the dream, and now we will interpret it to the king. [37]You, O king, are the king of kings. The God of heaven has given you dominion and power and might and glory; [38]in your hands he has placed mankind and the beasts of the field and the birds of the air. Wherever they live, he has made you ruler over them all. You are that head of gold.

[39]"After you, another kingdom will rise, inferior to yours. Next, a third kingdom, one of bronze, will rule over the whole earth. [40]Finally, there will be a fourth kingdom, strong as iron—for iron breaks and smashes everything—and as iron breaks things to pieces, so it will crush and break all the others. [41]Just as you saw that the feet and toes were partly of baked clay and partly of iron, so this will be a divided kingdom; yet it will have some of the strength of iron in it, even as you saw iron mixed with clay. [42]As the toes were partly iron and partly clay, so this kingdom will be partly strong and partly brittle. [43]And just as you saw the iron mixed with baked clay, so the people will be a mixture and will not remain united, any more than iron mixes with clay.

[44]"In the time of those kings, the God of heaven will set up a kingdom that will never be destroyed, nor will it be left to another people. It will crush all those kingdoms and bring them to an end, but it will itself endure forever. [45]This is the meaning of the vision of the rock cut out of a mountain, but not by human hands—a rock that broke the iron, the bronze, the clay, the silver and the gold to pieces.

"The great God has shown the king what will take place in the future. The dream is true and the interpretation is trustworthy."

[46]Then King Nebuchadnezzar fell prostrate before Daniel and paid him honor and ordered that an offering and incense be presented to him. [47]The king said to Daniel, "Surely your God is the God of gods and the Lord of kings and a revealer of mysteries, for you were able to reveal this mystery."

[48]Then the king placed Daniel in a high position and lavished many gifts on him. He made him ruler over the entire province of Babylon and placed him in charge of all its wise men. [49]Moreover, at Daniel's request the king appointed Shadrach, Meshach and Abednego administrators over the province of Babylon, while Daniel himself remained at the royal court.

The Image of Gold and the Fiery Furnace

3 King Nebuchadnezzar made an image of gold, ninety feet high and nine feet[a] wide, and set it up on the plain of Dura in the province of Babylon. [2]He then summoned the satraps, prefects, governors, advisers, treasurers, judges, magistrates and all the other provincial officials to come to the dedication of the image he had set up. [3]So the satraps, prefects, governors, advisers, treasurers, judges, magistrates and all the other provincial officials assembled for the dedication of the image that King Nebuchadnezzar had set up, and they stood before it.

[4]Then the herald loudly proclaimed, "This is what you are commanded to do, O peoples, nations and men of every language: [5]As soon as you hear the sound of the horn, flute, zither, lyre, harp, pipes and all kinds of music, you must fall down and worship the image of gold that King Nebuchadnezzar has set up. [6]Whoever does not fall down and worship will immediately be thrown into a blazing furnace."

[7]Therefore, as soon as they heard the sound of the horn, flute, zither, lyre, harp

---

[a]1 Aramaic *sixty cubits high and six cubits wide* (about 27 meters high and 2.7 meters wide)

and all kinds of music, all the peoples, nations and men of every language fell down and worshiped the image of gold that King Nebuchadnezzar had set up.

⁸At this time some astrologers*a* came forward and denounced the Jews. ⁹They said to King Nebuchadnezzar, "O king, live forever! ¹⁰You have issued a decree, O king, that everyone who hears the sound of the horn, flute, zither, lyre, harp, pipes and all kinds of music must fall down and worship the image of gold, ¹¹and that whoever does not fall down and worship will be thrown into a blazing furnace. ¹²But there are some Jews whom you have set over the affairs of the province of Babylon—Shadrach, Meshach and Abednego—who pay no attention to you, O king. They neither serve your gods nor worship the image of gold you have set up."

> ❝ We must lay before him what is in us, not what ought to be in us.
>
> C . S . L E W I S

¹³Furious with rage, Nebuchadnezzar summoned Shadrach, Meshach and Abednego. So these men were brought before the king, ¹⁴and Nebuchadnezzar said to them, "Is it true, Shadrach, Meshach and Abednego, that you do not serve my gods or worship the image of gold I have set up? ¹⁵Now when you hear the sound of the horn, flute, zither, lyre, harp, pipes and all kinds of music, if you are ready to fall down and worship the image I made, very good. But if you do not worship it, you will be thrown immediately into a blazing furnace. Then what god will be able to rescue you from my hand?"

¹⁶Shadrach, Meshach and Abednego replied to the king, "O Nebuchadnezzar, we do not need to defend ourselves before you in this matter. ¹⁷If we are thrown into the blazing furnace, the God we serve is able to save us from it, and he will rescue us from your hand, O king. ¹⁸But even if he does not, we want you to know, O king, that we will not serve your gods or worship the image of gold you have set up."

¹⁹Then Nebuchadnezzar was furious with Shadrach, Meshach and Abednego, and his attitude toward them changed. He ordered the furnace heated seven times hotter than usual ²⁰and commanded some of the strongest soldiers in his army to tie up Shadrach, Meshach and Abednego and throw them into the blazing furnace. ²¹So these men, wearing their robes, trousers, turbans and other clothes, were bound and thrown into the blazing furnace. ²²The king's command was so urgent and the furnace so hot that the flames of the fire killed the soldiers who took up Shadrach, Meshach and Abednego, ²³and these three men, firmly tied, fell into the blazing furnace.

²⁴Then King Nebuchadnezzar leaped to his feet in amazement and asked his advisers, "Weren't there three men that we tied up and threw into the fire?"

They replied, "Certainly, O king."

²⁵He said, "Look! I see four men walking around in the fire, unbound and unharmed, and the fourth looks like a son of the gods."

²⁶Nebuchadnezzar then approached the opening of the blazing furnace and shouted, "Shadrach, Meshach and Abednego, servants of the Most High God, come out! Come here!"

So Shadrach, Meshach and Abednego came out of the fire, ²⁷and the satraps, prefects, governors and royal advisers crowded around them. They saw that the fire had not harmed their bodies, nor was a hair of their heads singed; their robes were not scorched, and there was no smell of fire on them.

²⁸Then Nebuchadnezzar said, "Praise be to the God of Shadrach, Meshach and Abednego, who has sent his angel and rescued his servants! They trusted in him and defied the king's command and were willing to give up their lives rather than serve or worship any god except their own God. ²⁹Therefore I decree that the people of any nation or language who say anything against the God of Shadrach, Meshach and Abednego be cut into pieces and their houses be turned into piles of rubble, for no other god can save in this way."

a8 Or *Chaldeans*

³⁰Then the king promoted Shadrach, Meshach and Abednego in the province of Babylon.

Nebuchadnezzar's Dream of a Tree

4 King Nebuchadnezzar,

To the peoples, nations and men of every language, who live in all the world:

May you prosper greatly!

²It is my pleasure to tell you about the miraculous signs and wonders that the Most High God has performed for me.

³ How great are his signs,
   how mighty his wonders!
His kingdom is an eternal
   kingdom;
   his dominion endures from
   generation to generation.

⁴I, Nebuchadnezzar, was at home in my palace, contented and prosperous. ⁵I had a dream that made me afraid. As I was lying in my bed, the images and visions that passed through my mind terrified me. ⁶So I commanded that all the wise men of Babylon be brought before me to interpret the dream for me. ⁷When the magicians, enchanters, astrologersᵃ and diviners came, I told them the dream, but they could not interpret it for me. ⁸Finally, Daniel came into my presence and I told him the dream. (He is called Belteshazzar, after the name of my god, and the spirit of the holy gods is in him.)

⁹I said, "Belteshazzar, chief of the magicians, I know that the spirit of the holy gods is in you, and no mystery is too difficult for you. Here is my dream; interpret it for me. ¹⁰These are the visions I saw while lying in my bed: I looked, and there before me stood a tree in the middle of the land. Its height was enormous. ¹¹The tree grew large and strong and its top touched the sky; it was visible to the ends of the earth. ¹²Its leaves were beautiful, its fruit abundant, and on it was food for all. Under it the beasts of the field found shelter, and the birds of the air lived in its branches; from it every creature was fed.

¹³"In the visions I saw while lying in my bed, I looked, and there before me was a messenger,ᵇ a holy one, coming down from heaven. ¹⁴He called in a loud voice: 'Cut down the tree and trim off its branches; strip off its leaves and scatter its fruit. Let the animals flee from under it and the birds from its branches. ¹⁵But let the stump and its roots, bound with iron and bronze, remain in the ground, in the grass of the field.

" 'Let him be drenched with the dew of heaven, and let him live with the animals among the plants of the earth. ¹⁶Let his mind be changed from that of a man and let him be given the mind of an animal, till seven timesᶜ pass by for him.

¹⁷" 'The decision is announced by messengers, the holy ones declare the verdict, so that the living may know that the Most High is sovereign over the kingdoms of men and gives them to anyone he wishes and sets over them the lowliest of men.'

¹⁸"This is the dream that I, King Nebuchadnezzar, had. Now, Belteshazzar, tell me what it means, for none of the wise men in my kingdom can interpret it for me. But you can, because the spirit of the holy gods is in you."

Daniel Interprets the Dream

¹⁹Then Daniel (also called Belteshazzar) was greatly perplexed for a time, and his thoughts terrified him. So the king said, "Belteshazzar, do not let the dream or its meaning alarm you."

Belteshazzar answered, "My lord, if only the dream applied to your enemies and its meaning to your adversaries! ²⁰The tree you saw, which grew large and strong, with its top touching the sky, visible to the whole earth, ²¹with beautiful leaves and abundant fruit, providing food

ᵃ7 Or *Chaldeans*   ᵇ13 Or *watchman*; also in verses 17 and 23   ᶜ16 Or *years*; also in verses 23, 25 and 32

for all, giving shelter to the beasts of the field, and having nesting places in its branches for the birds of the air— ²²you, O king, are that tree! You have become great and strong; your greatness has grown until it reaches the sky, and your dominion extends to distant parts of the earth.

²³"You, O king, saw a messenger, a holy one, coming down from heaven and saying, 'Cut down the tree and destroy it, but leave the stump, bound with iron and bronze, in the grass of the field, while its roots remain in the ground. Let him be drenched with the dew of heaven; let him live like the wild animals, until seven times pass by for him.'

²⁴"This is the interpretation, O king, and this is the decree the Most High has issued against my lord the king: ²⁵You will be driven away from people and will live with the wild animals; you will eat grass like cattle and be drenched with the dew of heaven. Seven times will pass by for you until you acknowledge that the Most High is sovereign over the kingdoms of men and gives them to anyone he wishes. ²⁶The command to leave the stump of the tree with its roots means that your kingdom will be restored to you when you acknowledge that Heaven rules. ²⁷Therefore, O king, be pleased to accept my advice: Renounce your sins by doing what is right, and your wickedness by being kind to the oppressed. It may be that then your prosperity will continue."

The Dream Is Fulfilled

²⁸All this happened to King Nebuchadnezzar. ²⁹Twelve months later, as the king was walking on the roof of the royal palace of Babylon, ³⁰he said, "Is not this the great Babylon I have built as the royal residence, by my mighty power and for the glory of my majesty?"

³¹The words were still on his lips when a voice came from heaven, "This is what is decreed for you, King Nebuchadnezzar: Your royal authority has been taken from you.

³²You will be driven away from people and will live with the wild animals; you will eat grass like cattle. Seven times will pass by for you until you acknowledge that the Most High is sovereign over the kingdoms of men and gives them to anyone he wishes."

³³Immediately what had been said about Nebuchadnezzar was fulfilled. He was driven away from people and ate grass like cattle. His body was drenched with the dew of heaven until his hair grew like the feathers of an eagle and his nails like the claws of a bird.

³⁴At the end of that time, I, Nebuchadnezzar, raised my eyes toward heaven, and my sanity was restored. Then I praised the Most High; I honored and glorified him who lives forever.

> ❝ Our real work is prayer. What good is the cold iron of our frantic little efforts unless first we heat it in the furnace of our prayer? Only heat will diffuse heat. ❞
>
> MOTHER MARIBEL

His dominion is an eternal dominion;
  his kingdom endures from
    generation to generation.
³⁵All the peoples of the earth
  are regarded as nothing.
He does as he pleases
  with the powers of heaven
  and the peoples of the earth.
No one can hold back his hand
  or say to him: "What have you
    done?"

³⁶At the same time that my sanity was restored, my honor and splendor were returned to me for the glory of my kingdom. My advisers and nobles sought me out, and I was restored to my throne and became even greater than before. ³⁷Now I, Nebuchadnezzar, praise and exalt and glorify the King of heaven, because everything he does is right and all his ways are just. And those who walk in pride he is able to humble.

The Writing on the Wall

5 King Belshazzar gave a great banquet for a thousand of his nobles and drank wine with them. [2]While Belshazzar was drinking his wine, he gave orders to bring in the gold and silver goblets that Nebuchadnezzar his father[a] had taken from the temple in Jerusalem, so that the king and his nobles, his wives and his concubines might drink from them. [3]So they brought in the gold goblets that had been taken from the temple of God in Jerusalem, and the king and his nobles, his wives and his concubines drank from them. [4]As they drank the wine, they praised the gods of gold and silver, of bronze, iron, wood and stone.

[5]Suddenly the fingers of a human hand appeared and wrote on the plaster of the wall, near the lampstand in the royal palace. The king watched the hand as it wrote. [6]His face turned pale and he was so frightened that his knees knocked together and his legs gave way.

[7]The king called out for the enchanters, astrologers[b] and diviners to be brought and said to these wise men of Babylon, "Whoever reads this writing and tells me what it means will be clothed in purple and have a gold chain placed around his neck, and he will be made the third highest ruler in the kingdom."

[8]Then all the king's wise men came in, but they could not read the writing or tell the king what it meant. [9]So King Belshazzar became even more terrified and his face grew more pale. His nobles were baffled.

[10]The queen,[c] hearing the voices of the king and his nobles, came into the banquet hall. "O king, live forever!" she said. "Don't be alarmed! Don't look so pale! [11]There is a man in your kingdom who has the spirit of the holy gods in him. In the time of your father he was found to have insight and intelligence and wisdom like that of the gods. King Nebuchadnezzar your father—your father the king, I say—appointed him chief of the magicians, enchanters, astrologers and diviners. [12]This man Daniel, whom the king called Belteshazzar, was found to have a keen mind and knowledge and understanding, and also the ability to interpret dreams, explain riddles and solve difficult problems. Call for Daniel, and he will tell you what the writing means."

[13]So Daniel was brought before the king, and the king said to him, "Are you Daniel, one of the exiles my father the king brought from Judah? [14]I have heard that the spirit of the gods is in you and that you have insight, intelligence and outstanding wisdom. [15]The wise men and enchanters were brought before me to read this writing and tell me what it means, but they could not explain it. [16]Now I have heard that you are able to give interpretations and to solve difficult problems. If you can read this writing and tell me what it means, you will be clothed in purple and have a gold chain placed around your neck, and you will be made the third highest ruler in the kingdom."

[17]Then Daniel answered the king, "You may keep your gifts for yourself and give your rewards to someone else. Nevertheless, I will read the writing for the king and tell him what it means.

[18]"O king, the Most High God gave your father Nebuchadnezzar sovereignty and greatness and glory and splendor. [19]Because of the high position he gave him, all the peoples and nations and men of every language dreaded and feared him. Those the king wanted to put to death, he put to death; those he wanted to spare, he spared; those he wanted to promote, he promoted; and those he wanted to humble, he humbled. [20]But when his heart became arrogant and hardened with pride, he was deposed from his royal throne and stripped of his glory. [21]He was driven away from people and given the mind of an animal; he lived with the wild donkeys and ate grass like cattle; and his body was drenched with the dew of heaven, until he acknowledged that the Most High God is sovereign over the kingdoms of men and sets over them anyone he wishes.

[22]"But you his son,[d] O Belshazzar, have not humbled yourself, though you knew all this. [23]Instead, you have set yourself up against the Lord of heaven. You had the

---

[a]2 Or *ancestor*; or *predecessor*; also in verses 11, 13 and 18   [b]7 Or *Chaldeans*; also in verse 11
[c]10 Or *queen mother*   [d]22 Or *descendant*; or *successor*

goblets from his temple brought to you, and you and your nobles, your wives and your concubines drank wine from them. You praised the gods of silver and gold, of bronze, iron, wood and stone, which cannot see or hear or understand. But you did not honor the God who holds in his hand your life and all your ways. ²⁴Therefore he sent the hand that wrote the inscription.

²⁵"This is the inscription that was written:

MENE, MENE, TEKEL, PARSIN*a*

²⁶"This is what these words mean:

Mene[b]: God has numbered the days of your reign and brought it to an end.
²⁷ *Tekel*[c]: You have been weighed on the scales and found wanting.
²⁸ *Peres*[d]: Your kingdom is divided and given to the Medes and Persians."

²⁹Then at Belshazzar's command, Daniel was clothed in purple, a gold chain was placed around his neck, and he was proclaimed the third highest ruler in the kingdom.

³⁰That very night Belshazzar, king of the Babylonians,[e] was slain, ³¹and Darius the Mede took over the kingdom, at the age of sixty-two.

Daniel in the Den of Lions

6 It pleased Darius to appoint 120 satraps to rule throughout the kingdom, ²with three administrators over them, one of whom was Daniel. The satraps were made accountable to them so that the king might not suffer loss. ³Now Daniel so distinguished himself among the administrators and the satraps by his exceptional qualities that the king planned to set him over the whole kingdom. ⁴At this, the administrators and the satraps tried to find grounds for charges against Daniel in his conduct of government affairs, but they were unable to do so. They could find no corruption in him, because he was trustworthy and neither corrupt nor negligent. ⁵Finally these men said, "We will never find any basis for charges against this man Daniel unless it has something to do with the law of his God."

⁶So the administrators and the satraps went as a group to the king and said: "O King Darius, live forever! ⁷The royal administrators, prefects, satraps, advisers and governors have all agreed that the king should issue an edict and enforce the decree that anyone who prays to any god or man during the next thirty days, except to you, O king, shall be thrown into the lions' den. ⁸Now, O king, issue the decree and put it in writing so that it cannot be altered—in accordance with the laws of the Medes and Persians, which cannot be repealed." ⁹So King Darius put the decree in writing.

¹⁰Now when Daniel learned that the decree had been published, he went home to his upstairs room where the windows opened toward Jerusalem. Three times a day he got down on his knees and prayed, giving thanks to his God, just as he had done before. ¹¹Then these men went as a group and found Daniel praying and asking God for help. ¹²So they went to the king and spoke to him about his royal decree: "Did you not publish a decree that during the next thirty days anyone who prays to any god or man except to you, O king, would be thrown into the lions' den?"

The king answered, "The decree stands—in accordance with the laws of the Medes and Persians, which cannot be repealed."

¹³Then they said to the king, "Daniel, who is one of the exiles from Judah, pays no attention to you, O king, or to the decree you put in writing. He still prays three times a day." ¹⁴When the king heard this, he was greatly distressed; he was determined to rescue Daniel and made every effort until sundown to save him.

¹⁵Then the men went as a group to the king and said to him, "Remember, O king, that according to the law of the Medes and Persians no decree or edict that the king issues can be changed."

¹⁶So the king gave the order, and they brought Daniel and threw him into the

---

*a*25 Aramaic *UPARSIN* (that is, *AND PARSIN*)
*b*26 *Mene* can mean *numbered* or *mina* (a unit of money).   *c*27 *Tekel* can mean *weighed* or *shekel*.   *d*28 *Peres* (the singular of *Parsin*) can mean *divided* or *Persia* or *a half mina* or *a half shekel.*   *e*30 Or *Chaldeans*

lions' den. The king said to Daniel, "May your God, whom you serve continually, rescue you!"

¹⁷A stone was brought and placed over the mouth of the den, and the king sealed it with his own signet ring and with the rings of his nobles, so that Daniel's situation might not be changed. ¹⁸Then the king returned to his palace and spent the night without eating and without any en-

---

[WEDNESDAY]

DANIEL 6:1–15

Publicly Innocuous?

6:10 THREE TIMES A DAY HE GOT DOWN ON HIS KNEES AND PRAYED.

It was quite a compliment. The king's administrators knew the only way they could get anything on Daniel would be because of his faith, not his morals (see 6:4–5). Of course the two are intertwined, but they can be separated. Too often it's the other way around: a leader's theology and religious practice will be sound, but his or her moral integrity will crack. So the king's administrators duped King Darius into passing a law forbidding prayer to any god or human but Darius for 30 days. The king was just enough of an egoist and a fool to pass such a law.

What would you do if such a law were passed? Pray "incognito"—in a way that no one could tell what you were doing? Take a break from spiritual discipline for a month? Surely God would understand if you obeyed the order of the king, wouldn't he? Daniel didn't think so. Without batting an eye, he continued his practice of praying on his knees to God, while facing Jerusalem, three times a day from his upstairs prayer room (see 2 Chronicles 6:38–39; Psalm 55:17). His prayers could not be merely inner dispositions. These prayers were a declaration of reverence and allegiance to a God whose name and kingdom were in direct conflict with Darius's pretensions. Evidently the jealous officials were well aware of Daniel's practice of prayer, so they were able to easily catch Daniel in the act of "praying and asking God for help" (verse 11). Daniel understood what we all must understand about prayer: It is a radically subversive act. Whether silent or spoken, public or private, prayer is the ultimate interference with the status quo. Darius's edict gave Daniel an opportunity to demonstrate that spiritual reality.

Some critics have deemed Western Christianity privately engaging but publicly innocuous, meaning we have compartmentalized our faith into the purely private realm—it feels good to pray in a small group or alone on a mountaintop. But many people don't think prayer has anything to do with our daily schedules, deadlines, business, politics and justice. Test yourself and ask, "Do the things I pray for affect what I do out in the world? Do I pray for things that have any meaning beyond my personal life?" Learn from and be encouraged by Daniel's prayer example.

PRAY:
Lord, teach me to pray for things that will make a difference in the hectic world of scheduling, deadlines, business, politics and justice. Give me the courage to live publicly what I pray privately.

FOR YOUR NEXT DEVOTIONAL READING, GO TO PAGE 1039.

tertainment being brought to him. And he could not sleep.

¹⁹At the first light of dawn, the king got up and hurried to the lions' den. ²⁰When he came near the den, he called to Daniel in an anguished voice, "Daniel, servant of the living God, has your God, whom you serve continually, been able to rescue you from the lions?" ²¹Daniel answered, "O king, live forever! ²²My God sent his angel, and he shut the mouths of the lions. They have not hurt me, because I was found innocent in his sight. Nor have I ever done any wrong before you, O king."

²³The king was overjoyed and gave orders to lift Daniel out of the den. And when Daniel was lifted from the den, no wound was found on him, because he had trusted in his God.

²⁴At the king's command, the men who had falsely accused Daniel were brought in and thrown into the lions' den, along with their wives and children. And before they reached the floor of the den, the lions overpowered them and crushed all their bones.

²⁵Then King Darius wrote to all the peoples, nations and men of every language throughout the land:

"May you prosper greatly!

²⁶"I issue a decree that in every part of my kingdom people must fear and reverence the God of Daniel.

"For he is the living God
and he endures forever;
his kingdom will not be destroyed,
his dominion will never end.
²⁷He rescues and he saves;
he performs signs and wonders
in the heavens and on the earth.
He has rescued Daniel
from the power of the lions."

²⁸So Daniel prospered during the reign of Darius and the reign of Cyrus*ª* the Persian.

Daniel's Dream of Four Beasts

7 In the first year of Belshazzar king of Babylon, Daniel had a dream, and visions passed through his mind as he was lying on his bed. He wrote down the substance of his dream.

²Daniel said: "In my vision at night I looked, and there before me were the four winds of heaven churning up the great sea. ³Four great beasts, each different from the others, came up out of the sea.

⁴"The first was like a lion, and it had the wings of an eagle. I watched until its wings were torn off and it was lifted from the ground so that it stood on two feet like a man, and the heart of a man was given to it.

⁵"And there before me was a second beast, which looked like a bear. It was raised up on one of its sides, and it had three ribs in its mouth between its teeth. It was told, 'Get up and eat your fill of flesh!'

⁶"After that, I looked, and there before me was another beast, one that looked like a leopard. And on its back it had four wings like those of a bird. This beast had four heads, and it was given authority to rule.

⁷"After that, in my vision at night I looked, and there before me was a fourth beast—terrifying and frightening and very powerful. It had large iron teeth; it crushed and devoured its victims and trampled underfoot whatever was left. It was different from all the former beasts, and it had ten horns.

⁸"While I was thinking about the horns, there before me was another horn, a little one, which came up among them; and three of the first horns were uprooted before it. This horn had eyes like the eyes of a man and a mouth that spoke boastfully.

⁹"As I looked,

"thrones were set in place,
and the Ancient of Days took his
seat.
His clothing was as white as snow;
the hair of his head was white
like wool.
His throne was flaming with fire,
and its wheels were all ablaze.
¹⁰A river of fire was flowing,
coming out from before him.
Thousands upon thousands attended
him;
ten thousand times ten thousand
stood before him.
The court was seated,
and the books were opened.

ª28 Or Darius, that is, the reign of Cyrus

¹¹"Then I continued to watch because of the boastful words the horn was speaking. I kept looking until the beast was slain and its body destroyed and thrown into the blazing fire. ¹²(The other beasts had been stripped of their authority, but were allowed to live for a period of time.)

¹³"In my vision at night I looked, and there before me was one like a son of man, coming with the clouds of heaven. He approached the Ancient of Days and was led into his presence. ¹⁴He was given authority, glory and sovereign power; all peoples, nations and men of every language worshiped him. His dominion is an everlasting dominion that will not pass away, and his kingdom is one that will never be destroyed.

The Interpretation of the Dream

¹⁵"I, Daniel, was troubled in spirit, and the visions that passed through my mind disturbed me. ¹⁶I approached one of those standing there and asked him the true meaning of all this.

"So he told me and gave me the interpretation of these things: ¹⁷'The four great beasts are four kingdoms that will rise from the earth. ¹⁸But the saints of the Most High will receive the kingdom and will possess it forever—yes, for ever and ever.'

¹⁹"Then I wanted to know the true meaning of the fourth beast, which was different from all the others and most terrifying, with its iron teeth and bronze claws—the beast that crushed and devoured its victims and trampled underfoot whatever was left. ²⁰I also wanted to know about the ten horns on its head and about the other horn that came up, before which three of them fell—the horn that looked more imposing than the others and that had eyes and a mouth that spoke boastfully. ²¹As I watched, this horn was waging war against the saints and defeating them, ²²until the Ancient of Days came and pronounced judgment in favor of the saints of the Most High, and the time came when they possessed the kingdom.

²³"He gave me this explanation: 'The fourth beast is a fourth kingdom that will appear on earth. It will be different from all the other kingdoms and will devour the whole earth, trampling it down and crushing it. ²⁴The ten horns are ten kings who will come from this kingdom. After them another king will arise, different from the earlier ones; he will subdue three kings. ²⁵He will speak against the Most High and oppress his saints and try to change the set times and the laws. The saints will be handed over to him for a time, times and half a time.ᵃ

²⁶" 'But the court will sit, and his power will be taken away and completely destroyed forever. ²⁷Then the sovereignty, power and greatness of the kingdoms under the whole heaven will be handed over to the saints, the people of the Most High. His kingdom will be an everlasting kingdom, and all rulers will worship and obey him.'

²⁸"This is the end of the matter. I, Daniel, was deeply troubled by my thoughts, and my face turned pale, but I kept the matter to myself."

Daniel's Vision of a Ram and a Goat

8 In the third year of King Belshazzar's reign, I, Daniel, had a vision, after the one that had already appeared to me. ²In my vision I saw myself in the citadel of Susa in the province of Elam; in the vision I was beside the Ulai Canal. ³I looked up, and there before me was a ram with two horns, standing beside the canal, and the horns were long. One of the horns was longer than the other but grew up later. ⁴I watched the ram as he charged toward the west and the north and the south. No animal could stand against him, and none could rescue from his power. He did as he pleased and became great.

⁵As I was thinking about this, suddenly a goat with a prominent horn between his eyes came from the west, crossing the whole earth without touching the ground. ⁶He came toward the two-horned ram I had seen standing beside the canal and charged at him in great rage. ⁷I saw him attack the ram furiously, striking the ram and shattering his two horns. The ram was powerless to stand against him; the goat knocked him to the ground and trampled on him, and none could rescue the ram from his power. ⁸The goat became very great, but at the

ᵃ25 Or for a year, two years and half a year

height of his power his large horn was broken off, and in its place four prominent horns grew up toward the four winds of heaven.

⁹Out of one of them came another horn, which started small but grew in power to the south and to the east and toward the Beautiful Land. ¹⁰It grew until it reached the host of the heavens, and it threw some of the starry host down to the earth and trampled on them. ¹¹It set itself up to be as great as the Prince of the host; it took away the daily sacrifice from him, and the place of his sanctuary was brought low. ¹²Because of rebellion, the host ₗof the saints₎ᵃ and the daily sacrifice were given over to it. It prospered in everything it did, and truth was thrown to the ground.

¹³Then I heard a holy one speaking, and another holy one said to him, "How long will it take for the vision to be fulfilled—the vision concerning the daily sacrifice, the rebellion that causes desolation, and the surrender of the sanctuary and of the host that will be trampled underfoot?"

¹⁴He said to me, "It will take 2,300 evenings and mornings; then the sanctuary will be reconsecrated."

The Interpretation of the Vision

¹⁵While I, Daniel, was watching the vision and trying to understand it, there before me stood one who looked like a man. ¹⁶And I heard a man's voice from the Ulai calling, "Gabriel, tell this man the meaning of the vision."

¹⁷As he came near the place where I was standing, I was terrified and fell prostrate. "Son of man," he said to me, "understand that the vision concerns the time of the end."

¹⁸While he was speaking to me, I was in a deep sleep, with my face to the ground. Then he touched me and raised me to my feet.

¹⁹He said: "I am going to tell you what will happen later in the time of wrath, because the vision concerns the appointed time of the end.ᵇ ²⁰The two-horned ram that you saw represents the kings of Media and Persia. ²¹The shaggy goat is the king of Greece, and the large horn between his eyes is the first king. ²²The four horns that replaced the one that was broken off represent four kingdoms that will emerge from his nation but will not have the same power.

²³"In the latter part of their reign, when rebels have become completely wicked, a stern-faced king, a master of intrigue, will arise. ²⁴He will become very strong, but not by his own power. He will cause astounding devastation and will succeed in whatever he does. He will destroy the mighty men and the holy people. ²⁵He will cause deceit to prosper, and he will consider himself superior. When they feel secure, he will destroy many and take his stand against the Prince of princes. Yet he will be destroyed, but not by human power.

²⁶"The vision of the evenings and mornings that has been given you is true, but seal up the vision, for it concerns the distant future."

²⁷I, Daniel, was exhausted and lay ill for several days. Then I got up and went about the king's business. I was appalled by the vision; it was beyond understanding.

Daniel's Prayer

9 In the first year of Darius son of Xerxesᶜ (a Mede by descent), who was made ruler over the Babylonianᵈ kingdom— ²in the first year of his reign, I, Daniel, understood from the Scriptures, according to the word of the LORD given to Jeremiah the prophet, that the desolation of Jerusalem would last seventy years. ³So I turned to the Lord God and pleaded with him in prayer and petition, in fasting, and in sackcloth and ashes.

> SO I TURNED to the Lord God and pleaded with him in prayer and petition, in fasting, and in sackcloth and ashes.
>
> DANIEL 9:3

⁴I prayed to the LORD my God and confessed:

"O Lord, the great and awesome God, who keeps his covenant of love with all who love him and obey his

---

ᵃ12 Or rebellion, the armies   ᵇ19 Or because the end will be at the appointed time
ᶜ1 Hebrew Ahasuerus   ᵈ1 Or Chaldean

commands, [5]we have sinned and done wrong. We have been wicked and have rebelled; we have turned away from your commands and laws. [6]We have not listened to your servants the prophets, who spoke in your name to our kings, our princes and our fathers, and to all the people of the land.

[7]"Lord, you are righteous, but this day we are covered with shame— the men of Judah and people of Jerusalem and all Israel, both near and far, in all the countries where you have scattered us because of our unfaithfulness to you. [8]O LORD, we and our kings, our princes and our fathers are covered with shame because we have sinned against you. [9]The Lord our God is merciful and forgiving, even though we have rebelled against him; [10]we have not obeyed the LORD our God or kept the laws he gave us through his servants the prophets. [11]All Israel has transgressed your law and turned away, refusing to obey you.

"Therefore the curses and sworn judgments written in the Law of Moses, the servant of God, have been poured out on us, because we have sinned against you. [12]You have fulfilled the words spoken against us and against our rulers by bringing upon us great disaster. Under the whole heaven nothing has ever been done like what has been done to Jerusalem. [13]Just as it is written in the Law of Moses, all this disaster has come upon us, yet we have not sought the favor of the LORD our God by turning from our sins and giving attention to your truth. [14]The LORD did not hesitate to bring the disaster upon us, for the LORD our God is righteous in everything he does; yet we have not obeyed him.

[15]"Now, O Lord our God, who brought your people out of Egypt with a mighty hand and who made for yourself a name that endures to this day, we have sinned, we have done wrong. [16]O Lord, in keeping with all your righteous acts, turn away your anger and your wrath from Jerusalem, your city, your holy hill. Our sins and the iniquities of our fathers have made Jerusalem and your people an object of scorn to all those around us.

[17]"Now, our God, hear the prayers and petitions of your servant. For your sake, O Lord, look with favor on your desolate sanctuary. [18]Give ear, O God, and hear; open your eyes and see the desolation of the city that bears your Name. We do not make requests of you because we are righteous, but because of your great mercy. [19]O Lord, listen! O Lord, forgive! O Lord, hear and act! For your sake, O my God, do not delay, because your city and your people bear your Name."

> "NOW, our God, hear the prayers and petitions of your servant."
>
> DANIEL 9:17

The Seventy "Sevens"

[20]While I was speaking and praying, confessing my sin and the sin of my people Israel and making my request to the LORD my God for his holy hill— [21]while I was still in prayer, Gabriel, the man I had seen in the earlier vision, came to me in swift flight about the time of the evening sacrifice. [22]He instructed me and said to me, "Daniel, I have now come to give you insight and understanding. [23]As soon as you began to pray, an answer was given, which I have come to tell you, for you are highly esteemed. Therefore, consider the message and understand the vision:

[24]"Seventy 'sevens'[a] are decreed for your people and your holy city to finish[b] transgression, to put an end to sin, to atone for wickedness, to bring in everlasting righteousness, to seal up vision and prophecy and to anoint the most holy.[c]

[25]"Know and understand this: From the issuing of the decree[d] to restore and rebuild Jerusalem until the Anointed One,[e] the ruler, comes, there will be sev-

[a]24 Or 'weeks'; also in verses 25 and 26   [b]24 Or restrain   [c]24 Or Most Holy Place; or most holy One   [d]25 Or word   [e]25 Or an anointed one; also in verse 26

DANIEL 9:1–19

From the Bible and From the Heart

9:4 I PRAYED TO THE LORD MY GOD.

Daniel's prayer is marvelous—truly a great prayer of Scripture. Its structure, content and method are timeless and worth imitating.

What makes Daniel's prayer so worthy of imitation? First, it is a Biblical prayer. A careful study of this prayer reveals Daniel's vast knowledge of the Hebrew Scriptures. His prayer is laced with references and allusions from the Bible he knew. This prayer shows that he doesn't just know the Scriptures, he breathes them in and out. George Herbert's great thought that prayer is "God's breath in man returning to its birth" is true of Daniel. When Daniel prayed, he breathed the same Spirit that Abraham, Moses and Jeremiah breathed. He prayed what they prayed, and he prayed with them. Daniel is sometimes thought of as a solitary man of prayer, but even when he was most alone, he wasn't. He was with the faithful people who came before him.

Also, this prayer is a liturgical prayer. The language of the prayer is overwhelmingly the language of the Bible, not necessarily the language of Babylonian exiles in the sixth century. This is not to imply that using contemporary language was something Daniel never did, or that it was less spiritual than the Bible's language. It's just that the Bible's language dominated the way Daniel prayed. The words of Scripture are not dead words; they are alive and active (see Hebrews 4:12–13). This kind of liturgical prayer can give new life and energy to our more spontaneous and extemporaneous prayers.

Finally, this is a heartfelt prayer. Daniel prayed with passion. The strong Biblical content and liturgical style of his prayer did not take away from his sincerity; they strengthened it. Heartfelt prayers come directly from the heart, but sometimes the heart needs to be carried along. That's where the Bible and liturgy can serve us so well. Powerful prayers come from a heart transformed by the Word of God and informed by the distilled wisdom of the church through the ages. James Gilmour, a pioneer missionary to Mongolia, wrote about the role of the Bible and liturgy in his prayer life:

> When I feel I cannot make headway in devotion, I open the Psalms and push my canoe and let myself be carried along on the stream of devotion that flows through the whole book. The current always sets toward God and in most places is strong and deep.[1]

Pray like Daniel, and you will pray with Christ (see Hebrews 7:25) and his people from the heart.

PRAY:

God, open my ears to your Word that I may open my mouth in heartfelt prayers that are pleasing to you; through Jesus Christ my Lord.

FOR YOUR NEXT DEVOTIONAL READING, GO TO PAGE 1041.

en 'sevens,' and sixty-two 'sevens.' It will be rebuilt with streets and a trench, but in times of trouble. ²⁶After the sixty-two 'sevens,' the Anointed One will be cut off and will have nothing.ᵃ The people of the ruler who will come will destroy the city and the sanctuary. The end will come like a flood: War will continue until the end, and desolations have been decreed. ²⁷He will confirm a covenant with many for one 'seven.'ᵇ In the middle of the 'seven'ᵇ he will put an end to sacrifice and offering. And on a wing ⌊of the temple⌋ he will set up an abomination that causes desolation, until the end that is decreed is poured out on him.ᶜᵈ

Daniel's Vision of a Man

10 In the third year of Cyrus king of Persia, a revelation was given to Daniel (who was called Belteshazzar). Its message was true and it concerned a great war.ᵉ The understanding of the message came to him in a vision.

²At that time I, Daniel, mourned for three weeks. ³I ate no choice food; no meat or wine touched my lips; and I used no lotions at all until the three weeks were over.

⁴On the twenty-fourth day of the first month, as I was standing on the bank of the great river, the Tigris, ⁵I looked up and there before me was a man dressed in linen, with a belt of the finest gold around his waist. ⁶His body was like chrysolite, his face like lightning, his eyes like flaming torches, his arms and legs like the gleam of burnished bronze, and his voice like the sound of a multitude.

⁷I, Daniel, was the only one who saw the vision; the men with me did not see it, but such terror overwhelmed them that they fled and hid themselves. ⁸So I was left alone, gazing at this great vision; I had no strength left, my face turned deathly pale and I was helpless. ⁹Then I heard him speaking, and as I listened to him, I fell into a deep sleep, my face to the ground.

¹⁰A hand touched me and set me trembling on my hands and knees. ¹¹He said, "Daniel, you who are highly esteemed, consider carefully the words I am about to speak to you, and stand up, for I have now been sent to you." And when he said this to me, I stood up trembling.

¹²Then he continued, "Do not be afraid, Daniel. Since the first day that you set your mind to gain understanding and to humble yourself before your God, your words were heard, and I have come in response to them. ¹³But the prince of the Persian kingdom resisted me twenty-one days. Then Michael, one of the chief princes, came to help me, because I was detained there with the king of Persia. ¹⁴Now I have come to explain to you what will happen to your people in the future, for the vision concerns a time yet to come."

¹⁵While he was saying this to me, I bowed with my face toward the ground and was speechless. ¹⁶Then one who looked like a manᶠ touched my lips, and I opened my mouth and began to speak. I said to the one standing before me, "I am overcome with anguish because of the vision, my lord, and I am helpless. ¹⁷How can I, your servant, talk with you, my lord? My strength is gone and I can hardly breathe."

¹⁸Again the one who looked like a man touched me and gave me strength. ¹⁹"Do not be afraid, O man highly esteemed," he said. "Peace! Be strong now; be strong."

When he spoke to me, I was strengthened and said, "Speak, my lord, since you have given me strength."

²⁰So he said, "Do you know why I have come to you? Soon I will return to fight against the prince of Persia, and when I go, the prince of Greece will come; ²¹but first I will tell you what is written in the Book of Truth. (No one supports me against them except Michael, your prince.

11 ¹And in the first year of Darius the Mede, I took my stand to support and protect him.)

The Kings of the South and the North

²"Now then, I tell you the truth: Three more kings will appear in Persia, and

---

ᵃ26 Or *off and will have no one;* or *off, but not for himself*   ᵇ27 Or *'week'*   ᶜ27 Or *it*
ᵈ27 Or *And one who causes desolation will come upon the pinnacle of the abominable* ⌊*temple*⌋, *until the end that is decreed is poured out on the desolated* ⌊*city*⌋   ᵉ1 Or *true and burdensome*
ᶠ16 Most manuscripts of the Masoretic Text; one manuscript of the Masoretic Text, Dead Sea Scrolls and Septuagint *Then something that looked like a man's hand*

then a fourth, who will be far richer than all the others. When he has gained power by his wealth, he will stir up everyone against the kingdom of Greece. ³Then a mighty king will appear, who will rule with great power and do as he pleases.

⁴After he has appeared, his empire will be broken up and parceled out toward the four winds of heaven. It will not go to his descendants, nor will it have the power he exercised, because his empire will be uprooted and given to others.

{ FRIDAY }

DANIEL 10:1 — 11:1

Prayer and the Powers

10:12 "YOUR WORDS WERE HEARD, AND I HAVE COME IN RESPONSE TO THEM."

The angel in this text could give our imaginations a makeover. True, some people have let their imaginations get a little too creative when it comes to angels, but we should not be so put off by others' excesses that we fall into our own. Echoing C. S. Lewis's comment about devils,² Old Testament scholar John Duncan said that beliefs about angels tend to bounce back and forth between "vulgar credulity" and "presumptuous incredulity."³ Angels are real and often play significant roles in God's dealings with his world. Maybe their role serves to remind us that God, though near, is also high and exalted (see Isaiah 57:15). Although God is our friend, he lives in unapproachable light and cannot be seen (see 1 Timothy 6:16). So when he sends a message to humans, he sends his servants, the angels.

The reality of angels points to the greater reality of war in the heavenly realms, also known as spiritual warfare. There is always more going on around us in the unseen realm than we ever know is happening. "For our struggle is not against flesh and blood, but against the rulers, against the authorities, against the powers of this dark world and against the spiritual forces of evil in the heavenly realms" (Ephesians 6:12). In Daniel's context, some of these rulers and authorities are "the prince of the Persian kingdom" and "the prince of Greece" (10:13,20).

Prayer plays a critical role in spiritual conflict. Daniel's earlier prayer in chapter 9 triggered the angel Gabriel's mission. Gabriel said to Daniel, "As soon as you began to pray, an answer was given, which I have come to tell you" (9:23). The fight involving the prince of Persia against Michael and the angel sent to Daniel took place as Daniel engaged in an intense time of prayer and fasting (see 10:3,13). It isn't only that our struggles on earth parallel cosmic struggles; our prayers actually participate in those unseen conflicts and affect their results. Great is the mystery of prayer! Our prayers matter to the angels, and can actually affect the outcome of spiritual conflicts. We may never see the effects of our prayers on this side of heaven, but until then we must walk and pray, not by sight, but by faith.

PRAY:

Praise the Lord, and fight the good fight, "you his angels,
you mighty ones who do his bidding, who obey his word" (Psalm 103:20).
Father in heaven, strengthen your servants in the heavenly realms.

FOR YOUR NEXT DEVOTIONAL READING, GO TO PAGE 1048.

⁵"The king of the South will become strong, but one of his commanders will become even stronger than he and will rule his own kingdom with great power. ⁶After some years, they will become allies. The daughter of the king of the South will go to the king of the North to make an alliance, but she will not retain her power, and he and his power*ᵃ* will not last. In those days she will be handed over, together with her royal escort and her father*ᵇ* and the one who supported her.

⁷"One from her family line will arise to take her place. He will attack the forces of the king of the North and enter his fortress; he will fight against them and be victorious. ⁸He will also seize their gods, their metal images and their valuable articles of silver and gold and carry them off to Egypt. For some years he will leave the king of the North alone. ⁹Then the king of the North will invade the realm of the king of the South but will retreat to his own country. ¹⁰His sons will prepare for war and assemble a great army, which will sweep on like an irresistible flood and carry the battle as far as his fortress.

¹¹"Then the king of the South will march out in a rage and fight against the king of the North, who will raise a large army, but it will be defeated. ¹²When the army is carried off, the king of the South will be filled with pride and will slaughter many thousands, yet he will not remain triumphant. ¹³For the king of the North will muster another army, larger than the first; and after several years, he will advance with a huge army fully equipped.

¹⁴"In those times many will rise against the king of the South. The violent men among your own people will rebel in fulfillment of the vision, but without success. ¹⁵Then the king of the North will come and build up siege ramps and will capture a fortified city. The forces of the South will be powerless to resist; even their best troops will not have the strength to stand. ¹⁶The invader will do as he pleases; no one will be able to stand against him. He will establish himself in the Beautiful Land and will have the power to destroy it. ¹⁷He will determine to come with the might of his entire kingdom and will make an alliance with the king of the South. And he will give him a daughter in marriage in order to overthrow the kingdom, but his plans*ᶜ* will not succeed or help him. ¹⁸Then he will turn his attention to the coastlands and will take many of them, but a commander will put an end to his insolence and will turn his insolence back upon him. ¹⁹After this, he will turn back toward the fortresses of his own country but will stumble and fall, to be seen no more.

²⁰"His successor will send out a tax collector to maintain the royal splendor. In a few years, however, he will be destroyed, yet not in anger or in battle.

²¹"He will be succeeded by a contemptible person who has not been given the honor of royalty. He will invade the kingdom when its people feel secure, and he will seize it through intrigue. ²²Then an overwhelming army will be swept away before him; both it and a prince of the covenant will be destroyed. ²³After coming to an agreement with him, he will act deceitfully, and with only a few people he will rise to power. ²⁴When the richest provinces feel secure, he will invade them and will achieve what neither his fathers nor his forefathers did. He will distribute plunder, loot and wealth among his followers. He will plot the overthrow of fortresses—but only for a time.

²⁵"With a large army he will stir up his strength and courage against the king of the South. The king of the South will wage war with a large and very powerful army, but he will not be able to stand because of the plots devised against him. ²⁶Those who eat from the king's provisions will try to destroy him; his army will be swept away, and many will fall in battle. ²⁷The two kings, with their hearts bent on evil, will sit at the same table and lie to each other, but to no avail, because an end will still come at the appointed time. ²⁸The king of the North will return to his own country with great wealth, but his heart will be set against the holy covenant. He will take action against it and then return to his own country.

ᵃ6 Or *offspring*   *ᵇ6* Or *child* (see Vulgate and Syriac)   *ᶜ17* Or *but she*

²⁹"At the appointed time he will invade the South again, but this time the outcome will be different from what it was before. ³⁰Ships of the western coastlands*a* will oppose him, and he will lose heart. Then he will turn back and vent his fury against the holy covenant. He will return and show favor to those who forsake the holy covenant.

³¹"His armed forces will rise up to desecrate the temple fortress and will abolish the daily sacrifice. Then they will set up the abomination that causes desolation. ³²With flattery he will corrupt those who have violated the covenant, but the people who know their God will firmly resist him.

³³"Those who are wise will instruct many, though for a time they will fall by the sword or be burned or captured or plundered. ³⁴When they fall, they will receive a little help, and many who are not sincere will join them. ³⁵Some of the wise will stumble, so that they may be refined, purified and made spotless until the time of the end, for it will still come at the appointed time.

The King Who Exalts Himself

³⁶"The king will do as he pleases. He will exalt and magnify himself above every god and will say unheard-of things against the God of gods. He will be successful until the time of wrath is completed, for what has been determined must take place. ³⁷He will show no regard for the gods of his fathers or for the one desired by women, nor will he regard any god, but will exalt himself above them all. ³⁸Instead of them, he will honor a god of fortresses; a god unknown to his fathers he will honor with gold and silver, with precious stones and costly gifts. ³⁹He will attack the mightiest fortresses with the help of a foreign god and will greatly honor those who acknowledge him. He will make them rulers over many people and will distribute the land at a price.*b*

⁴⁰"At the time of the end the king of the South will engage him in battle, and the king of the North will storm out against him with chariots and cavalry and a great fleet of ships. He will invade many countries and sweep through them like a flood. ⁴¹He will also invade the Beautiful Land. Many countries will fall, but Edom, Moab and the leaders of Ammon will be delivered from his hand. ⁴²He will extend his power over many countries; Egypt will not escape. ⁴³He will gain control of the treasures of gold and silver and all the riches of Egypt, with the Libyans and Nubians in submission. ⁴⁴But reports from the east and the north will alarm him, and he will set out in a great rage to destroy and annihilate many. ⁴⁵He will pitch his royal tents between the seas at*c* the beautiful holy mountain. Yet he will come to his end, and no one will help him.

> Practice in life whatever you pray for, and God will give it to you more abundantly.
>
> EDWARD BOUVERIE PUSEY

The End Times

12 "At that time Michael, the great prince who protects your people, will arise. There will be a time of distress such as has not happened from the beginning of nations until then. But at that time your people—everyone whose name is found written in the book—will be delivered. ²Multitudes who sleep in the dust of the earth will awake: some to everlasting life, others to shame and everlasting contempt. ³Those who are wise*d* will shine like the brightness of the heavens, and those who lead many to righteousness, like the stars for ever and ever. ⁴But you, Daniel, close up and seal the words of the scroll until the time of the end. Many will go here and there to increase knowledge."

⁵Then I, Daniel, looked, and there before me stood two others, one on this bank of the river and one on the opposite bank. ⁶One of them said to the man clothed in linen, who was above the waters of the river, "How long will it be before these astonishing things are fulfilled?"

---

a30 Hebrew of Kittim   *b39* Or *land for a reward*   *c45* Or *the sea and*   *d3* Or *who impart wisdom*

⁷The man clothed in linen, who was above the waters of the river, lifted his right hand and his left hand toward heaven, and I heard him swear by him who lives forever, saying, "It will be for a time, times and half a time.ᵃ When the power of the holy people has been finally broken, all these things will be completed."

⁸I heard, but I did not understand. So I asked, "My lord, what will the outcome of all this be?"

⁹He replied, "Go your way, Daniel, because the words are closed up and sealed until the time of the end. ¹⁰Many will be purified, made spotless and refined, but the wicked will continue to be wicked. None of the wicked will understand, but those who are wise will understand.

¹¹"From the time that the daily sacrifice is abolished and the abomination that causes desolation is set up, there will be 1,290 days. ¹²Blessed is the one who waits for and reaches the end of the 1,335 days.

¹³"As for you, go your way till the end. You will rest, and then at the end of the days you will rise to receive your allotted inheritance."

ᵃ 7 Or *a year, two years and half a year*

Hosea

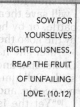

NOT ALL marriages made in heaven are happy. Just ask Hosea. God himself had arranged Hosea's marriage to Gomer, but it was a disaster from the beginning, thanks to her constant infidelity. But that was the point: Hosea's bad marriage was to be a living illustration of his prophetic message that God had a bad marriage to the nation of Israel. Israel, like Gomer, had a "spirit of prostitution" (5:4). Gomer just wouldn't stay out of bed with other men— and Israel just wouldn't keep away from other gods.

The point that the book of Hosea makes is that God's marriage to Israel originated and ended with God alone. This is how God loves. New Testament scholar Anders Nygren described God's love as "subject-centered" as opposed to "object-centered." Object-centered love flows because the object of love, the beloved, is so irresistibly wonderful. This kind of love is more a reflex than a choice. This kind of love leads one to "fall" in love. On the other hand, subject-centered love originates in the lover, not because the beloved is so lovable, but because the lover is. This kind of love is definitely a choice. But it does not mean it is any less passionate. God's love for Israel let them break his heart. God cried out about his people, "How can I give you up . . . How can I hand you over, Israel? . . . My heart is changed within me; all my compassion is aroused" (11:8).

> SOW FOR YOURSELVES RIGHTEOUSNESS, REAP THE FRUIT OF UNFAILING LOVE. (10:12)

Although academic sounding, the very notion of something called subject-centered love speaks of the gospel. For the gospel, the Good News, is not that we loved God, but that he loved us. We love him because he first loved us (see 1 John 4:19). This is also great news for prayer. We do not confess our sins to a God who loves us only when we are good; we confess our sins to a God who loves us all the time. Our prayers are preceded by his petition that we open our eyes and see his love that pursues us our whole lives. We don't have to get his attention; we already have it.

1 The word of the LORD that came to Hosea son of Beeri during the reigns of Uzziah, Jotham, Ahaz and Hezekiah, kings of Judah, and during the reign of Jeroboam son of Jehoash[a] king of Israel:

Hosea's Wife and Children

²When the LORD began to speak through Hosea, the LORD said to him, "Go, take to yourself an adulterous wife and children of unfaithfulness, because the land is guilty of the vilest adultery in departing from the LORD." ³So he married Gomer daughter of Diblaim, and she conceived and bore him a son.

⁴Then the LORD said to Hosea, "Call him Jezreel, because I will soon punish the house of Jehu for the massacre at Jezreel, and I will put an end to the kingdom of Israel. ⁵In that day I will break Israel's bow in the Valley of Jezreel."

⁶Gomer conceived again and gave birth to a daughter. Then the LORD said to Hosea, "Call her Lo-Ruhamah,[b] for I will no longer show love to the house of Israel, that I should at all forgive them. ⁷Yet I will show love to the house of Judah; and I will save them—not by bow, sword or battle, or by horses and horsemen, but by the LORD their God."

⁸After she had weaned Lo-Ruhamah, Gomer had another son. ⁹Then the LORD said, "Call him Lo-Ammi,[c] for you are not my people, and I am not your God.

¹⁰"Yet the Israelites will be like the sand on the seashore, which cannot be measured or counted. In the place where it was said to them, 'You are not my people,' they will be called 'sons of the living God.' ¹¹The people of Judah and the people of Israel will be reunited, and they will appoint one leader and will come up out of the land, for great will be the day of Jezreel.

2 "Say of your brothers, 'My people,' and of your sisters, 'My loved one.'

Israel Punished and Restored

² "Rebuke your mother, rebuke her,
 for she is not my wife,
 and I am not her husband.
Let her remove the adulterous look
 from her face
 and the unfaithfulness from
 between her breasts.

> *If you begin to live life looking for the God that is all around you, every moment becomes a prayer.*
>
> FRANK BIANCO

³Otherwise I will strip her naked
 and make her as bare as on the day
 she was born;
I will make her like a desert,
 turn her into a parched land,
 and slay her with thirst.
⁴I will not show my love to her
 children,
 because they are the children of
 adultery.
⁵Their mother has been unfaithful
 and has conceived them in
 disgrace.
She said, 'I will go after my lovers,
 who give me my food and my
 water,
 my wool and my linen, my oil and
 my drink.'
⁶Therefore I will block her path with
 thornbushes;
 I will wall her in so that she cannot
 find her way.
⁷She will chase after her lovers but not
 catch them;
 she will look for them but not find
 them.
Then she will say,
 'I will go back to my husband as at
 first,
 for then I was better off than now.'
⁸She has not acknowledged that I was
 the one
 who gave her the grain, the new
 wine and oil,
who lavished on her the silver and
 gold—
 which they used for Baal.
⁹ "Therefore I will take away my
 grain when it ripens,
 and my new wine when it is
 ready.
I will take back my wool and my
 linen,
 intended to cover her nakedness.

---

[a]1 Hebrew *Joash*, a variant of *Jehoash*.
[b]6 *Lo-Ruhamah* means *not loved*.
[c]9 *Lo-Ammi* means *not my people*.

¹⁰ So now I will expose her lewdness
   before the eyes of her lovers;
   no one will take her out of my
      hands.
¹¹ I will stop all her celebrations:
   her yearly festivals, her New
      Moons,
   her Sabbath days—all her
      appointed feasts.
¹² I will ruin her vines and her fig trees,
   which she said were her pay from
      her lovers;
   I will make them a thicket,
   and wild animals will devour them.
¹³ I will punish her for the days
   she burned incense to the Baals;
she decked herself with rings and
      jewelry,
   and went after her lovers,
   but me she forgot,"
                     declares the LORD.

¹⁴ "Therefore I am now going to
      allure her;
   I will lead her into the desert
   and speak tenderly to her.
¹⁵ There I will give her back her
      vineyards,
   and will make the Valley of Achor*ᵃ*
      a door of hope.
   There she will sing*ᵇ* as in the days of
      her youth,
   as in the day she came up out of
      Egypt.

¹⁶ "In that day," declares the LORD,
   "you will call me 'my husband';
   you will no longer call me 'my
      master.*ᶜ*'
¹⁷ I will remove the names of the Baals
      from her lips;
   no longer will their names be
      invoked.
¹⁸ In that day I will make a covenant for
      them
   with the beasts of the field and the
      birds of the air
   and the creatures that move along
      the ground.
Bow and sword and battle
   I will abolish from the land,
   so that all may lie down in safety.
¹⁹ I will betroth you to me forever;
   I will betroth you in*ᵈ* righteousness
      and justice,
   in*ᵉ* love and compassion.

²⁰ I will betroth you in faithfulness,
   and you will acknowledge the LORD.

²¹ "In that day I will respond,"
   declares the LORD—
   "I will respond to the skies,
   and they will respond to the earth;
²² and the earth will respond to the
      grain,
   the new wine and oil,
   and they will respond to Jezreel.*ᶠ*
²³ I will plant her for myself in the land;
   I will show my love to the one I
      called 'Not my loved one.*ᵍ*'
   I will say to those called 'Not my
      people,*ʰ*' 'You are my people';
   and they will say, 'You are my
      God.'"

Hosea's Reconciliation With His Wife

3 The LORD said to me, "Go, show your
love to your wife again, though she
is loved by another and is an adulteress.
Love her as the LORD loves the Israelites,
though they turn to other gods and love
the sacred raisin cakes."

²So I bought her for fifteen shekels*ⁱ* of
silver and about a homer and a lethek*ʲ* of
barley. ³Then I told her, "You are to live
with*ᵏ* me many days; you must not be a
prostitute or be intimate with any man,
and I will live with*ᵏ* you."

⁴For the Israelites will live many days
without king or prince, without sacrifice
or sacred stones, without ephod or idol.
⁵Afterward the Israelites will return and
seek the LORD their God and David their
king. They will come trembling to the
LORD and to his blessings in the last days.

The Charge Against Israel

4 Hear the word of the LORD, you
   Israelites,
   because the LORD has a charge to
      bring
   against you who live in the land:
"There is no faithfulness, no love,
   no acknowledgment of God in
      the land.

ᵃ15 Achor means *trouble.*   *ᵇ15* Or *respond*
ᶜ16 Hebrew *baal*   *ᵈ19* Or *with*; also in verse 20
ᵉ19 Or *with*   *ᶠ22* Jezreel means *God plants.*
ᵍ23 Hebrew *Lo-Ruhamah*   *ʰ23* Hebrew
Lo-Ammi   *ⁱ2* That is, about 6 ounces (about
170 grams)   *ʲ2* That is, probably about 10
bushels (about 330 liters)   *ᵏ3* Or *wait for*

JOHANN SEBASTIAN BACH (1685–1750)

SDG

JOHANN SEBASTIAN BACH was a musician of prodigious genius in every way. On one hand, the quality of his work has earned him universal admiration as one of the greatest composers of all time. On the other, the quantity of what he produced is breathtaking. In his lifetime he composed over 1,000 musical pieces, including nearly 200 cantatas and pieces for violin, cello, lute, organ, music box and timpani. He composed in relative obscurity, working mainly as a church organist. It wasn't until Mendelssohn "rediscovered" Bach's music a generation later that Bach became known throughout the world.

What is often overlooked about Bach's work is its theological and spiritual depth. Bach was a devout Lutheran and believed that the only legitimate reasons to write music were for the praise of God and what he called the "permissible" refreshment of the spirit. He strongly believed in creating "well-regulated church music to the glory of God." Bach was deeply affected by 1 Chronicles 25, which gives an account of the singers and musicians in charge of making music and prophesying in the Lord's temple. He penned in the margin of his Bible: "This chapter is the true foundation for all God-pleasing music."[1]

Among other things, Bach is known for his cantatas—musical pieces written for church services, which feature Biblical texts, hymns and Christian poetry. These works are not simply words arbitrarily put to music; the very structure and melody of the music expresses the themes of the lyrics. For example, in his St. Matthew Passion, Bach created a kind of halo around the words of Jesus on the cross by having the strings play long, quiet tones whenever his lines are sung. This ends abruptly with the line, "My God, my God, why have you forsaken me?" Here, at the moment of Christ's greatest cry of dereliction, the string halo is removed. The stark contrast creates a jarring emotional effect.

In a very real sense, Bach's works were bathed in prayer. He often penned the letters *JJ* near the beginning of a score and *SDG* at the end. JJ stands for *Jesu Juva*, Latin for "Help, O Jesus"; SDG stands for another Latin phrase, *Soli Deo Gloria*, "To God Alone Be the Glory." Bach was clearly influenced by the Reformation (and Biblical!) insight regarding vocation and work. Though the work we do as Christians takes many shapes, we all have the same calling: "Whatever you do, do it all for the glory of God" (1 Corinthians 10:31). God can be glorified as much in the writing of a cantata or the plowing of a field as in the serving of Holy Communion—for artists, farmers and clergy alike have the same call.

P R A Y :

God of all that is lovely, may I so pray that my fellowship with you will translate into refreshment for others and glory to you.

M E M O R I Z E :

Praise the LORD. Praise God in his sanctuary; praise him in his mighty heavens. Praise him for his acts of power; praise him for his surpassing greatness. Let everything that has breath praise the LORD. Praise the LORD. PSALM 150:1–2,6

FOR YOUR NEXT DEVOTIONAL READING, GO TO PAGE 1052.

2 There is only cursing,[a] lying and murder,
  stealing and adultery;
they break all bounds,
  and bloodshed follows bloodshed.
3 Because of this the land mourns,[b]
  and all who live in it waste away;
the beasts of the field and the birds of the air
  and the fish of the sea are dying.

4 "But let no man bring a charge,
  let no man accuse another,
for your people are like those
  who bring charges against a priest.
5 You stumble day and night,
  and the prophets stumble with you.
So I will destroy your mother—
6   my people are destroyed from lack of knowledge.

"Because you have rejected knowledge,
  I also reject you as my priests;
because you have ignored the law of your God,
  I also will ignore your children.
7 The more the priests increased,
  the more they sinned against me;
  they exchanged[c] their[d] Glory for something disgraceful.
8 They feed on the sins of my people
  and relish their wickedness.
9 And it will be: Like people, like priests.
  I will punish both of them for their ways
  and repay them for their deeds.

10 "They will eat but not have enough;
  they will engage in prostitution but not increase,
because they have deserted the LORD
  to give themselves 11 to prostitution,
to old wine and new,
  which take away the understanding 12 of my people.
They consult a wooden idol
  and are answered by a stick of wood.
A spirit of prostitution leads them astray;
  they are unfaithful to their God.
13 They sacrifice on the mountaintops
  and burn offerings on the hills,
under oak, poplar and terebinth,
  where the shade is pleasant.
Therefore your daughters turn to prostitution
  and your daughters-in-law to adultery.

14 "I will not punish your daughters
  when they turn to prostitution,
nor your daughters-in-law
  when they commit adultery,
because the men themselves consort with harlots
  and sacrifice with shrine prostitutes—
a people without understanding
  will come to ruin!

15 "Though you commit adultery, O Israel,
  let not Judah become guilty.

"Do not go to Gilgal;
  do not go up to Beth Aven.[e]
And do not swear, 'As surely as the LORD lives!'
16 The Israelites are stubborn,
  like a stubborn heifer.
How then can the LORD pasture them
  like lambs in a meadow?
17 Ephraim is joined to idols;
  leave him alone!
18 Even when their drinks are gone,
  they continue their prostitution;
  their rulers dearly love shameful ways.
19 A whirlwind will sweep them away,
  and their sacrifices will bring them shame.

Judgment Against Israel

5 "Hear this, you priests!
  Pay attention, you Israelites!
Listen, O royal house!
  This judgment is against you:
You have been a snare at Mizpah,
  a net spread out on Tabor.
2 The rebels are deep in slaughter.
  I will discipline all of them.
3 I know all about Ephraim;
  Israel is not hidden from me.

---

[a]2 That is, to pronounce a curse upon
[b]3 Or dries up   [c]7 Syriac and an ancient Hebrew scribal tradition; Masoretic Text I will exchange   [d]7 Masoretic Text; an ancient Hebrew scribal tradition my   [e]15 Beth Aven means house of wickedness (a name for Bethel, which means house of God).

Ephraim, you have now turned to
prostitution;
Israel is corrupt.

4 "Their deeds do not permit them
to return to their God.
A spirit of prostitution is in their
heart;
they do not acknowledge the LORD.
5 Israel's arrogance testifies against
them;
the Israelites, even Ephraim,
stumble in their sin;
Judah also stumbles with them.
6 When they go with their flocks and
herds
to seek the LORD,
they will not find him;
he has withdrawn himself from
them.
7 They are unfaithful to the LORD;
they give birth to illegitimate
children.
Now their New Moon festivals
will devour them and their fields.

8 "Sound the trumpet in Gibeah,
the horn in Ramah.
Raise the battle cry in Beth Aven[a];
lead on, O Benjamin.
9 Ephraim will be laid waste
on the day of reckoning.
Among the tribes of Israel
I proclaim what is certain.
10 Judah's leaders are like those
who move boundary stones.
I will pour out my wrath on them
like a flood of water.
11 Ephraim is oppressed,
trampled in judgment,
intent on pursuing idols.[b]
12 I am like a moth to Ephraim,
like rot to the people of Judah.

13 "When Ephraim saw his sickness,
and Judah his sores,
then Ephraim turned to Assyria,
and sent to the great king for help.
But he is not able to cure you,
not able to heal your sores.
14 For I will be like a lion to Ephraim,
like a great lion to Judah.
I will tear them to pieces and go
away;
I will carry them off, with no one
to rescue them.

15 Then I will go back to my place
until they admit their guilt.
And they will seek my face;
in their misery they will earnestly
seek me."

Israel Unrepentant

6 "Come, let us return to the LORD.
He has torn us to pieces
but he will heal us;
he has injured us
but he will bind up our wounds.
2 After two days he will revive us;
on the third day he will restore us,
that we may live in his presence.
3 Let us acknowledge the LORD;
let us press on to acknowledge
him.
As surely as the sun rises,
he will appear;
he will come to us like the winter
rains,
like the spring rains that water
the earth."

4 "What can I do with you, Ephraim?
What can I do with you, Judah?
Your love is like the morning mist,
like the early dew that disappears.
5 Therefore I cut you in pieces with my
prophets,
I killed you with the words of my
mouth;
my judgments flashed like
lightning upon you.
6 For I desire mercy, not sacrifice,
and acknowledgment of God rather
than burnt offerings.
7 Like Adam,[c] they have broken the
covenant—
they were unfaithful to me there.
8 Gilead is a city of wicked men,
stained with footprints of blood.
9 As marauders lie in ambush for a
man,
so do bands of priests;
they murder on the road to
Shechem,
committing shameful crimes.
10 I have seen a horrible thing
in the house of Israel.

---

a8 Beth Aven means house of wickedness (a name
for Bethel, which means house of God).
b11 The meaning of the Hebrew for this word is
uncertain.   c7 Or As at Adam; or Like men

Great, but Insincere

6:4 "YOUR LOVE IS LIKE THE MORNING MIST."

It is easy to pray more than we know and more than we mean. For instance, every time people pray the Lord's Prayer, they pray more than they know. Who can fully understand and appreciate the magnitude of praying for God's kingdom to come? Paul prayed that the Ephesians would know a love that was beyond knowing (see Ephesians 3:19), which presumably he didn't understand either. But he prayed for it anyway. When we pray the big prayers of Scripture, our reach always exceeds our grasp. But that's OK.

But what about praying for things we don't really mean? Didn't Jesus soundly condemn that sort of thing when he quoted and applied Isaiah 29:13 to some Pharisees and teachers of the law? "These people honor me with their lips, but their hearts are far from me" (Matthew 15:8). Why would anyone want to pray that way? Maybe to sound good to others, which can be done, or even to sound good to God, which is the most foolish thing in the world. This is apparently what the people of Israel were doing in this prayer in Hosea 6. It is a model prayer, beautiful and thoughtful, expressive of the highest and best. God does wound to heal; he does revive and restore; his mercy is as reliable and refreshing as the winter and spring rains. Therefore, "Come, let us return to the LORD" (verse 1). But God's response is less than enthusiastic. It is sad and grief-stricken. "What can I do with you, Ephraim? What can I do with you, Judah? Your love is like the morning mist, like the early dew that disappears" (verse 4). God looked past the great words and saw insincere hearts.

The Israelites' eloquent but shallow prayer is probably more common than we wish. The human heart is deceitful; can any of us know our real motives in anything we pray? David understood this well and prayed, "Who can discern his errors? Forgive my hidden faults" (Psalm 19:12). When we doubt the purity of our motives in the things we pray, we can do three things. First, we can confess our sin. Secondly, we can pray that God will purify our motives: "Give me an undivided heart, that I may fear your name" (Psalm 86:11). Finally, we can keep on praying good prayers until we mean them!

PRAY:

Father, you know all things. You know my heart better than I do.
Forgive my insincerity and form my motives according to your truth, that
I may honor you in my deeds, my words, my thoughts and my prayers.

FOR YOUR NEXT DEVOTIONAL READING, GO TO PAGE 1059.

There Ephraim is given to
prostitution
and Israel is defiled.

[11] "Also for you, Judah,
a harvest is appointed.

"Whenever I would restore the
fortunes of my people,

7 [1]whenever I would heal Israel,
the sins of Ephraim are exposed
and the crimes of Samaria
revealed.
They practice deceit,
thieves break into houses,
bandits rob in the streets;
[2]but they do not realize
that I remember all their evil
deeds.
Their sins engulf them;
they are always before me.

[3] "They delight the king with their
wickedness,
the princes with their lies.
[4]They are all adulterers,
burning like an oven
whose fire the baker need not stir
from the kneading of the dough
till it rises.
[5]On the day of the festival of our king
the princes become inflamed
with wine,
and he joins hands with the
mockers.
[6]Their hearts are like an oven;
they approach him with intrigue.
Their passion smolders all night;
in the morning it blazes like a
flaming fire.
[7]All of them are hot as an oven;
they devour their rulers.
All their kings fall,
and none of them calls on me.

[8] "Ephraim mixes with the nations;
Ephraim is a flat cake not turned
over.
[9]Foreigners sap his strength,
but he does not realize it.
His hair is sprinkled with gray,
but he does not notice.
[10]Israel's arrogance testifies against
him,
but despite all this
he does not return to the LORD his God
or search for him.

[11] "Ephraim is like a dove,
easily deceived and senseless—
now calling to Egypt,
now turning to Assyria.
[12]When they go, I will throw my net
over them;
I will pull them down like birds
of the air.
When I hear them flocking together,
I will catch them.
[13]Woe to them,
because they have strayed from me!
Destruction to them,
because they have rebelled
against me!
I long to redeem them
but they speak lies against me.
[14]They do not cry out to me from
their hearts
but wail upon their beds.
They gather together[a] for grain
and new wine
but turn away from me.

> "THEY do not cry out to me from their
> hearts."
>
> HOSEA 7:14

[15]I trained them and strengthened them,
but they plot evil against me.
[16]They do not turn to the Most High;
they are like a faulty bow.
Their leaders will fall by the sword
because of their insolent words.
For this they will be ridiculed
in the land of Egypt.

Israel to Reap the Whirlwind

8 "Put the trumpet to your lips!
An eagle is over the house of the
LORD
because the people have broken my
covenant
and rebelled against my law.
[2]Israel cries out to me,
'O our God, we acknowledge you!'

> "ISRAEL cries out to me,
> 'O our God, we acknowledge you!'"
>
> HOSEA 8:2

[a]14 Most Hebrew manuscripts; some Hebrew
manuscripts and Septuagint *They slash themselves*

3 But Israel has rejected what is
   good;
     an enemy will pursue him.
4 They set up kings without my
   consent;
     they choose princes without my
       approval.
With their silver and gold
   they make idols for themselves
   to their own destruction.
5 Throw out your calf-idol, O Samaria!
   My anger burns against them.
How long will they be incapable of
   purity?
6   They are from Israel!
This calf—a craftsman has made it;
   it is not God.
It will be broken in pieces,
   that calf of Samaria.

7 "They sow the wind
   and reap the whirlwind.
The stalk has no head;
   it will produce no flour.
Were it to yield grain,
   foreigners would swallow it up.
8 Israel is swallowed up;
   now she is among the nations
   like a worthless thing.
9 For they have gone up to Assyria
   like a wild donkey wandering
     alone.
Ephraim has sold herself to lovers.
10 Although they have sold themselves
   among the nations,
   I will now gather them together.
They will begin to waste away
   under the oppression of the
     mighty king.

11 "Though Ephraim built many altars
   for sin offerings,
   these have become altars for
     sinning.
12 I wrote for them the many things
   of my law,
   but they regarded them as
     something alien.
13 They offer sacrifices given to me
   and they eat the meat,
   but the LORD is not pleased with
     them.
Now he will remember their
   wickedness
   and punish their sins:
   They will return to Egypt.

14 Israel has forgotten his Maker
   and built palaces;
   Judah has fortified many towns.
But I will send fire upon their cities
   that will consume their fortresses."

Punishment for Israel

9 Do not rejoice, O Israel;
   do not be jubilant like the other
     nations.
For you have been unfaithful to
   your God;
   you love the wages of a prostitute
   at every threshing floor.
2 Threshing floors and winepresses will
   not feed the people;
   the new wine will fail them.
3 They will not remain in the LORD's
   land;
   Ephraim will return to Egypt
   and eat unclean[a] food in Assyria.
4 They will not pour out wine offerings
   to the LORD,
   nor will their sacrifices please him.
Such sacrifices will be to them like
   the bread of mourners;
   all who eat them will be unclean.
This food will be for themselves;
   it will not come into the temple of
     the LORD.

5 What will you do on the day of your
   appointed feasts,
   on the festival days of the LORD?
6 Even if they escape from destruction,
   Egypt will gather them,
   and Memphis will bury them.
Their treasures of silver will be taken
   over by briers,
   and thorns will overrun their tents.
7 The days of punishment are coming,
   the days of reckoning are at hand.
   Let Israel know this.
Because your sins are so many
   and your hostility so great,
   the prophet is considered a fool,
   the inspired man a maniac.
8 The prophet, along with my God,
   is the watchman over Ephraim,[b]
   yet snares await him on all his paths,
   and hostility in the house of his
     God.

---

[a]3 That is, ceremonially unclean   [b]8 Or The
prophet is the watchman over Ephraim, / the
people of my God

⁹They have sunk deep into corruption,
  as in the days of Gibeah.
God will remember their wickedness
  and punish them for their sins.

¹⁰ "When I found Israel,
  it was like finding grapes in the
    desert;
when I saw your fathers,
  it was like seeing the early fruit on
    the fig tree.
But when they came to Baal Peor,
  they consecrated themselves to
    that shameful idol
and became as vile as the thing
  they loved.
¹¹ Ephraim's glory will fly away like
    a bird—
  no birth, no pregnancy, no
    conception.
¹² Even if they rear children,
  I will bereave them of every one.
Woe to them
  when I turn away from them!
¹³ I have seen Ephraim, like Tyre,
  planted in a pleasant place.
But Ephraim will bring out
  their children to the slayer."

¹⁴ Give them, O LORD—
  what will you give them?
Give them wombs that miscarry
  and breasts that are dry.

¹⁵ "Because of all their wickedness
    in Gilgal,
  I hated them there.
Because of their sinful deeds,
  I will drive them out of my house.
I will no longer love them;
  all their leaders are rebellious.
¹⁶ Ephraim is blighted,
  their root is withered,
  they yield no fruit.
Even if they bear children,
  I will slay their cherished
    offspring."

¹⁷ My God will reject them
  because they have not obeyed him;
they will be wanderers among
  the nations.

10 Israel was a spreading vine;
     he brought forth fruit for himself.
As his fruit increased,
  he built more altars;

as his land prospered,
  he adorned his sacred stones.
²Their heart is deceitful,
  and now they must bear their
    guilt.
The LORD will demolish their altars
  and destroy their sacred stones.

³Then they will say, "We have no
    king
  because we did not revere the
    LORD.
But even if we had a king,
  what could he do for us?"
⁴They make many promises,
  take false oaths
and make agreements;
  therefore lawsuits spring up
like poisonous weeds in a plowed
    field.
⁵The people who live in Samaria
    fear
  for the calf-idol of Beth Aven.ᵃ
Its people will mourn over it,
  and so will its idolatrous priests,
those who had rejoiced over its
    splendor,
  because it is taken from them
    into exile.
⁶It will be carried to Assyria
  as tribute for the great king.
Ephraim will be disgraced;
  Israel will be ashamed of its
    wooden idols.ᵇ
⁷Samaria and its king will float away
  like a twig on the surface of the
    waters.
⁸The high places of wickednessᶜ will
    be destroyed—
  it is the sin of Israel.
Thorns and thistles will grow up
  and cover their altars.
Then they will say to the mountains,
    "Cover us!"
  and to the hills, "Fall on us!"

⁹ "Since the days of Gibeah, you have
    sinned, O Israel,
  and there you have remained.ᵈ
Did not war overtake
  the evildoers in Gibeah?

ᵃ5 *Beth Aven* means *house of wickedness* (a name
for Bethel, which means *house of God*).
ᵇ6 Or *its counsel*   ᶜ8 Hebrew *aven*, a reference
to Beth Aven (a derogatory name for Bethel)
ᵈ9 Or *there a stand was taken*

¹⁰ When I please, I will punish them;
    nations will be gathered against
      them
    to put them in bonds for their
      double sin.
¹¹ Ephraim is a trained heifer
    that loves to thresh;
  so I will put a yoke
    on her fair neck.
  I will drive Ephraim,
    Judah must plow,
    and Jacob must break up the ground.
¹² Sow for yourselves righteousness,
    reap the fruit of unfailing love,
  and break up your unplowed ground;
  for it is time to seek the LORD,
  until he comes
    and showers righteousness on you.
¹³ But you have planted wickedness,
    you have reaped evil,
    you have eaten the fruit of deception.
  Because you have depended on your
      own strength
    and on your many warriors,
¹⁴ the roar of battle will rise against
      your people,
    so that all your fortresses will be
      devastated—
  as Shalman devastated Beth Arbel on
      the day of battle,
    when mothers were dashed to the
      ground with their children.
¹⁵ Thus will it happen to you, O Bethel,
    because your wickedness is great.
  When that day dawns,
    the king of Israel will be completely
      destroyed.

> " Before we can pray 'Lord, Thy
> Kingdom come,' we must be willing to
> pray, 'My Kingdom go.'
>
> ALAN REDPATH

God's Love for Israel

11 "When Israel was a child, I loved
      him,
    and out of Egypt I called my son.
² But the more Iᵃ called Israel,
    the further they went from me.ᵇ
  They sacrificed to the Baals
    and they burned incense to images.
³ It was I who taught Ephraim to walk,
    taking them by the arms;

but they did not realize
    it was I who healed them.
⁴ I led them with cords of human
      kindness,
    with ties of love;
  I lifted the yoke from their neck
    and bent down to feed them.

⁵ "Will they not return to Egypt
    and will not Assyria rule over them
    because they refuse to repent?
⁶ Swords will flash in their cities,
    will destroy the bars of their gates
    and put an end to their plans.
⁷ My people are determined to turn
      from me.
    Even if they call to the Most High,
    he will by no means exalt them.

⁸ "How can I give you up, Ephraim?
    How can I hand you over, Israel?
  How can I treat you like Admah?
    How can I make you like Zeboiim?
  My heart is changed within me;
    all my compassion is aroused.
⁹ I will not carry out my fierce anger,
    nor will I turn and devastate
      Ephraim.
  For I am God, and not man—
    the Holy One among you.
  I will not come in wrath.ᶜ
¹⁰ They will follow the LORD;
    he will roar like a lion.
  When he roars,
    his children will come trembling
      from the west.
¹¹ They will come trembling
    like birds from Egypt,
    like doves from Assyria.
  I will settle them in their homes,"
    declares the LORD.

Israel's Sin

¹² Ephraim has surrounded me with
      lies,
    the house of Israel with deceit.
  And Judah is unruly against God,
    even against the faithful Holy One.

12 ¹ Ephraim feeds on the wind;
      he pursues the east wind all day
    and multiplies lies and violence.
  He makes a treaty with Assyria
    and sends olive oil to Egypt.

ᵃ2 Some Septuagint manuscripts; Hebrew *they*
ᵇ2 Septuagint; Hebrew *them*   ᶜ9 Or *come
against any city*

2 The LORD has a charge to bring
  against Judah;
  he will punish Jacob[a] according
    to his ways
  and repay him according to his
    deeds.
3 In the womb he grasped his brother's
    heel;
  as a man he struggled with God.
4 He struggled with the angel and
    overcame him;
  he wept and begged for his favor.
  He found him at Bethel
  and talked with him there—
5 the LORD God Almighty,
  the LORD is his name of renown!
6 But you must return to your God;
  maintain love and justice,
  and wait for your God always.

7 The merchant uses dishonest scales;
  he loves to defraud.
8 Ephraim boasts,
  "I am very rich; I have become
    wealthy.
  With all my wealth they will not find
    in me
  any iniquity or sin."

9 "I am the LORD your God,
  ⌞who brought you⌟ out of[b] Egypt;
  I will make you live in tents again,
  as in the days of your appointed
    feasts.
10 I spoke to the prophets,
  gave them many visions
  and told parables through them."

11 Is Gilead wicked?
  Its people are worthless!
  Do they sacrifice bulls in Gilgal?
  Their altars will be like piles of
    stones
  on a plowed field.
12 Jacob fled to the country of Aram[c];
  Israel served to get a wife,
  and to pay for her he tended sheep.
13 The LORD used a prophet to bring
    Israel up from Egypt,
  by a prophet he cared for him.
14 But Ephraim has bitterly provoked
    him to anger;
  his Lord will leave upon him the
    guilt of his bloodshed
  and will repay him for his
    contempt.

The LORD's Anger Against Israel

13 When Ephraim spoke, men
    trembled;
  he was exalted in Israel.
  But he became guilty of Baal
    worship and died.
2 Now they sin more and more;
  they make idols for themselves
    from their silver,
  cleverly fashioned images,
  all of them the work of craftsmen.
  It is said of these people,
  "They offer human sacrifice
  and kiss[d] the calf-idols."

> O brother, pray; in spite of Satan,
> pray; spend hours in prayer, rather neglect
> friends than not pray; rather fast, and lose
> breakfast, dinner, tea, and supper—and
> sleep too—than not pray.
>
> ANDREW A. BONAR

3 Therefore they will be like the
    morning mist,
  like the early dew that disappears,
  like chaff swirling from a threshing
    floor,
  like smoke escaping through
    a window.

4 "But I am the LORD your God,
  ⌞who brought you⌟ out of[b] Egypt.
  You shall acknowledge no God but
    me,
  no Savior except me.
5 I cared for you in the desert,
  in the land of burning heat.
6 When I fed them, they were
    satisfied;
  when they were satisfied, they
    became proud;
  then they forgot me.
7 So I will come upon them like a
    lion,
  like a leopard I will lurk by the
    path.
8 Like a bear robbed of her cubs,
  I will attack them and rip them
    open.

---

[a]2 *Jacob* means *he grasps the heel* (figuratively,
he deceives).   [b]9,4 Or *God / ever since you
were in*   [c]12 That is, Northwest Mesopotamia
[d]2 Or *"Men who sacrifice / kiss*

Like a lion I will devour them;
a wild animal will tear them
apart.

9 "You are destroyed, O Israel,
because you are against me,
against your helper.
10 Where is your king, that he may
save you?
Where are your rulers in all your
towns,
of whom you said,
'Give me a king and princes'?
11 So in my anger I gave you a king,
and in my wrath I took him
away.
12 The guilt of Ephraim is stored up,
his sins are kept on record.
13 Pains as of a woman in childbirth
come to him,
but he is a child without wisdom;
when the time arrives,
he does not come to the opening
of the womb.

14 "I will ransom them from the power
of the grave[a];
I will redeem them from death.
Where, O death, are your plagues?
Where, O grave,[a] is your
destruction?

"I will have no compassion,
15 even though he thrives among
his brothers.
An east wind from the LORD will
come,
blowing in from the desert;
his spring will fail
and his well dry up.
His storehouse will be plundered
of all its treasures.
16 The people of Samaria must bear
their guilt,
because they have rebelled against
their God.
They will fall by the sword;
their little ones will be dashed to
the ground,
their pregnant women ripped
open."

Repentance to Bring Blessing

14 Return, O Israel, to the LORD
your God.
Your sins have been your downfall!
2 Take words with you
and return to the LORD.
Say to him:
"Forgive all our sins
and receive us graciously,
that we may offer the fruit of our
lips.[b]
3 Assyria cannot save us;
we will not mount war-horses.
We will never again say 'Our gods'
to what our own hands have made,
for in you the fatherless find
compassion."

4 "I will heal their waywardness
and love them freely,
for my anger has turned away
from them.
5 I will be like the dew to Israel;
he will blossom like a lily.
Like a cedar of Lebanon
he will send down his roots;
6 his young shoots will grow.
His splendor will be like an olive tree,
his fragrance like a cedar of
Lebanon.
7 Men will dwell again in his shade.
He will flourish like the grain.
He will blossom like a vine,
and his fame will be like the wine
from Lebanon.
8 O Ephraim, what more have I[c] to do
with idols?
I will answer him and care for him.
I am like a green pine tree;
your fruitfulness comes from me."

9 Who is wise? He will realize these
things.
Who is discerning? He will
understand them.
The ways of the LORD are right;
the righteous walk in them,
but the rebellious stumble in them.

---

[a]14 Hebrew *Sheol*   [b]2 Or *offer our lips as*
sacrifices of bulls   [c]8 Or *What more has Ephraim*

HOSEA 14:1–9

Great and Sincere

14:1 RETURN, O ISRAEL, TO THE LORD YOUR GOD.

God wants his people back, the way a lover wants his beloved back. God's promises are rich and extravagant: "I will heal their waywardness and love them freely" (14:4). When the people of Israel return to God, they will have the splendor of an olive tree, the fragrance of a cedar, the fame of Lebanon's wine (verses 6–7). The language God uses in verse 5 to describe what he will be to Israel is strongly reminiscent of the language used in the Song of Songs. God will be like refreshing dew, causing Israel to "blossom like a lily."

In the Song of Songs, the concept of blossoming is used in the context of a lush, romantic setting for love (see Song of Songs 6:11; 7:12). The word "lily" is even more sensual, used to describe the amorous couple's physical attractiveness and intimate charms (see Song of Songs 2:1–2; 2:16; 4:5; 5:13; 6:3). This romantic language points to God's willingness to forgive and bless, which is always greater than our desire to be forgiven and blessed.

But God's promise to pour out forgiveness and healing is contingent upon the people of Israel praying a prayer Hosea told them to pray: "Take words with you and return to the LORD. Say to him: 'Forgive all our sins and receive us graciously, that we may offer the fruit of our lips'" (14:2). What makes this prayer so remarkable is that it is merely a shortened version of the beautiful but insincere prayer of 6:1–3—the prayer God rejected. But this prayer is based on true repentance, for it includes a renunciation of the false security of military power, the sin of idolatry, and a commitment to justice: "Assyria cannot save us; we will not mount war-horses. We will never again say 'Our gods' to what our own hands have made, for in you the fatherless find compassion" (14:3).

Repentance and prayer go together. It's not that God doesn't like our words; he just doesn't like our *empty* words. When our words are sincere and backed by our actions, they can even be a kind of sacrifice of praise offered to God. The writer of Hebrews alludes to this kind of prayer to make that very point: "Through Jesus, therefore, let us continually offer to God a sacrifice of praise—the fruit of lips that confess his name." The writer of Hebrews adds the same concern for justice that Hosea called for: "And do not forget to do good and to share with others, for with such sacrifices God is pleased" (Hebrews 13:15–16).

PRAY:
Lord, make my life a sacrifice of praise, so the fruit of my lips
will also please you. Forgive me and bless me and make me your own.

———

FOR YOUR NEXT DEVOTIONAL READING, GO TO PAGE 1064.

Joel

WHEN CALLED upon to explain the extraordinary events of Pentecost, Peter went to the book of Joel (see Acts 2:14–21). There were at least two good reasons for doing this. The obvious reason was the fulfillment of the prophecy in Joel 2:28–32; the not-so-obvious reason was the overall point of view of the book. Joel's prophecies were aimed in part at expanding Israel's sense of the scope of God's sovereignty in history, to help the people understand that God's interests weren't confined to his dealings with Israel but included all nations.

From the beginning, God's interest in Israel had been for the sake of everyone (see Genesis 12:1–3). During Joel's time the popular idea in Israel was that "the great and dreadful day of the LORD" (Joel 2:31) would mean only the punishment of other nations for their sins. But Joel includes Israel in this punishment, too. However, if the people repented, then restoration and blessing would come. And in the New Testament, from the vantage point of being able to look back and clearly see God's marvelous long-range plan, we see God's desire and intent to bless all nations. The book of Joel is part of a vital body of Old Testament prophecy that lays the foundation for the Great Commission of Jesus in the New Testament (see Matthew 28:19–20; Acts 1:8).

Exactly how universal judgment and blessing will happen is not entirely clear in the book of Joel. But what is clear is that it will hinge on an unprecedented outpouring of the Holy Spirit on all people. The New Testament admonition to "pray in the Spirit" (Ephesians 6:18) has its roots in Pentecost, and centuries before, in the prophecy of Joel. We pray for many reasons, including our own personal benefit and the good of those we love. We pray to the end that God will pour out his Spirit on all people, so that "everyone who calls on the name of the LORD will be saved" (Joel 2:32).

RETURN TO THE LORD YOUR GOD, FOR HE IS GRACIOUS AND COMPASSIONATE, SLOW TO ANGER AND ABOUNDING IN LOVE. (2:13)

1

The word of the LORD that came to Joel son of Pethuel.

An Invasion of Locusts

2 Hear this, you elders;
   listen, all who live in the land.
Has anything like this ever happened
   in your days
   or in the days of your forefathers?
3 Tell it to your children,
   and let your children tell it to their
      children,
   and their children to the next
      generation.
4 What the locust swarm has left
   the great locusts have eaten;
what the great locusts have left
   the young locusts have eaten;
what the young locusts have left
   other locusts*a* have eaten.

5 Wake up, you drunkards, and
      weep!
   Wail, all you drinkers of wine;
wail because of the new wine,
   for it has been snatched from
      your lips.
6 A nation has invaded my land,
   powerful and without number;
it has the teeth of a lion,
   the fangs of a lioness.
7 It has laid waste my vines
   and ruined my fig trees.
It has stripped off their bark
   and thrown it away,
   leaving their branches white.

8 Mourn like a virgin*b* in sackcloth
   grieving for the husband*c* of her
      youth.
9 Grain offerings and drink offerings
   are cut off from the house of
      the LORD.
The priests are in mourning,
   those who minister before the
      LORD.
10 The fields are ruined,
   the ground is dried up*d*;
the grain is destroyed,
   the new wine is dried up,
   the oil fails.
11 Despair, you farmers,
   wail, you vine growers;
grieve for the wheat and the barley,
   because the harvest of the field is
      destroyed.

12 The vine is dried up
   and the fig tree is withered;
the pomegranate, the palm and the
      apple tree—
   all the trees of the field—are
      dried up.
Surely the joy of mankind
   is withered away.

A Call to Repentance

13 Put on sackcloth, O priests, and
      mourn;
   wail, you who minister before
      the altar.
Come, spend the night in sackcloth,
   you who minister before my God;
for the grain offerings and drink
      offerings
   are withheld from the house of
      your God.
14 Declare a holy fast;
   call a sacred assembly.
Summon the elders
   and all who live in the land
to the house of the LORD your God,
   and cry out to the LORD.

> DECLARE *a holy fast;*
>   *call a sacred assembly.*
> *Summon the elders*
>   *and all who live in the land*
> *to the house of the LORD your God,*
>   *and cry out to the LORD.*
>
> JOEL 1:14

15 Alas for that day!
   For the day of the LORD is near;
   it will come like destruction from
      the Almighty.*e*

16 Has not the food been cut off
   before our very eyes—
joy and gladness
   from the house of our God?
17 The seeds are shriveled
   beneath the clods.*f*
The storehouses are in ruins,
   the granaries have been broken
      down,
   for the grain has dried up.

---

*a*4 The precise meaning of the four Hebrew words
used here for locusts is uncertain.   *b*8 Or *young
woman*   *c*8 Or *betrothed*   *d*10 Or *ground
mourns*   *e*15 Hebrew *Shaddai*   *f*17 The meaning
of the Hebrew for this word is uncertain.

18 How the cattle moan!
　　The herds mill about
because they have no pasture;
　　even the flocks of sheep are
　　　　suffering.

19 To you, O LORD, I call,
　　for fire has devoured the open
　　　　pastures
and flames have burned up all the
　　trees of the field.
20 Even the wild animals pant for you;
　　the streams of water have
　　　　dried up
and fire has devoured the open
　　pastures.

> *A generous prayer is never presented
> in vain; the petition may be refused, but
> the petitioner is always, I believe,
> rewarded by some gracious visitation.*
>
> ROBERT LOUIS STEVENSON

An Army of Locusts

2 Blow the trumpet in Zion;
　　sound the alarm on my holy hill.
Let all who live in the land tremble,
　　for the day of the LORD is coming.
It is close at hand—
　　2 　a day of darkness and gloom,
　　a day of clouds and blackness.
Like dawn spreading across the
　　　　mountains
　　a large and mighty army
　　　　comes,
such as never was of old
　　nor ever will be in ages to come.

3 Before them fire devours,
　　behind them a flame blazes.
Before them the land is like the
　　　　garden of Eden,
　　behind them, a desert waste—
　　nothing escapes them.
4 They have the appearance of
　　　　horses;
　　they gallop along like cavalry.
5 With a noise like that of chariots
　　they leap over the mountaintops,
　　like a crackling fire consuming
　　　　stubble,
　　like a mighty army drawn up for
　　　　battle.

6 At the sight of them, nations are in
　　　　anguish;
　　every face turns pale.
7 They charge like warriors;
　　they scale walls like soldiers.
They all march in line,
　　not swerving from their course.
8 They do not jostle each other;
　　each marches straight ahead.
They plunge through defenses
　　without breaking ranks.
9 They rush upon the city;
　　they run along the wall.
They climb into the houses;
　　like thieves they enter through the
　　　　windows.

10 Before them the earth shakes,
　　the sky trembles,
the sun and moon are darkened,
　　and the stars no longer shine.
11 The LORD thunders
　　at the head of his army;
his forces are beyond number,
　　and mighty are those who obey his
　　　　command.
The day of the LORD is great;
　　it is dreadful.
　　Who can endure it?

Rend Your Heart

12 "Even now," declares the LORD,
　　"return to me with all your heart,
　　with fasting and weeping and
　　　　mourning."

13 Rend your heart
　　and not your garments.
Return to the LORD your God,
　　for he is gracious and
　　　　compassionate,
slow to anger and abounding in love,
　　and he relents from sending
　　　　calamity.
14 Who knows? He may turn and have
　　　　pity
　　and leave behind a blessing—
grain offerings and drink offerings
　　for the LORD your God.

15 Blow the trumpet in Zion,
　　declare a holy fast,
　　call a sacred assembly.
16 Gather the people,
　　consecrate the assembly;
bring together the elders,

gather the children,
those nursing at the breast.
Let the bridegroom leave his room
and the bride her chamber.
¹⁷ Let the priests, who minister before
the LORD,
weep between the temple porch
and the altar.
Let them say, "Spare your people,
O LORD.
Do not make your inheritance an
object of scorn,
a byword among the nations.
Why should they say among the
peoples,
'Where is their God?' "

The LORD's Answer

¹⁸ Then the LORD will be jealous for his
land
and take pity on his people.

¹⁹ The LORD will reply[a] to them:

"I am sending you grain, new wine
and oil,
enough to satisfy you fully;
never again will I make you
an object of scorn to the nations.

²⁰ "I will drive the northern army far
from you,
pushing it into a parched and
barren land,
with its front columns going into the
eastern sea[b]
and those in the rear into the
western sea.[c]
And its stench will go up;
its smell will rise."

Surely he has done great things.[d]
²¹   Be not afraid, O land;
be glad and rejoice.
Surely the LORD has done great
things.
²²   Be not afraid, O wild animals,
for the open pastures are becoming
green.
The trees are bearing their fruit;
the fig tree and the vine yield their
riches.
²³ Be glad, O people of Zion,
rejoice in the LORD your God,
for he has given you
the autumn rains in
righteousness.[e]

He sends you abundant showers,
both autumn and spring rains, as
before.
²⁴ The threshing floors will be filled with
grain;
the vats will overflow with new
wine and oil.

²⁵ "I will repay you for the years the
locusts have eaten—
the great locust and the young
locust,
the other locusts and the locust
swarm[f]—
my great army that I sent among you.
²⁶ You will have plenty to eat, until you
are full,
and you will praise the name of the
LORD your God,
who has worked wonders for you;
never again will my people be
shamed.
²⁷ Then you will know that I am in
Israel,
that I am the LORD your God,
and that there is no other;
never again will my people be
shamed.

The Day of the LORD

²⁸ "And afterward,
I will pour out my Spirit on all
people.
Your sons and daughters will
prophesy,
your old men will dream dreams,
your young men will see visions.
²⁹ Even on my servants, both men and
women,
I will pour out my Spirit in those
days.
³⁰ I will show wonders in the heavens
and on the earth,
blood and fire and billows of
smoke.
³¹ The sun will be turned to darkness
and the moon to blood
before the coming of the great and
dreadful day of the LORD.

---

[a] 18,19 Or LORD was jealous… / and took pity… /
[a] ¹⁹The LORD replied   [b] 20 That is, the Dead Sea
[c] 20 That is, the Mediterranean   [d] 20 Or rise. /
Surely it has done great things."   [e] 23 Or / the
teacher for righteousness: [f] 25 The precise
meaning of the four Hebrew words used here for
locusts is uncertain.

³²And everyone who calls
    on the name of the LORD will be
        saved;
for on Mount Zion and in Jerusalem
    there will be deliverance,
    as the LORD has said,
among the survivors
    whom the LORD calls.

The Nations Judged

3 "In those days and at that time,
    when I restore the fortunes of
        Judah and Jerusalem,

²I will gather all nations
    and bring them down to the Valley
        of Jehoshaphat.ᵃ
There I will enter into judgment
    against them
    concerning my inheritance, my
        people Israel,
for they scattered my people among
        the nations
    and divided up my land.

ᵃ2 *Jehoshaphat* means *the LORD judges*; also in
verse 12.

JOEL 2:28–32

I Will Pour Out My Spirit

2:28 "I WILL POUR OUT MY SPIRIT."

This passage begins with a striking image. "I will pour out my Spirit" (2:28).
We don't just get a taste, not just a crumb or a bite, but *all* of the Spirit
poured out. How much of the Holy Spirit do you want? John the Baptist
promised that, although he baptized people with water, Jesus would baptize them with the Holy Spirit (see Matthew 3:11). What would that be
like—to be immersed in God, washed in him, drenched in his Spirit, brought
completely under his influence? Do you want God only in moderation under
your terms, or freely and entirely? People are inoculated against disease by
getting a small dose of the real thing. A little bit of the real thing keeps us
protected against the full-blown sickness.

   "On all people" (verse 28). The gift of the Spirit that Jesus brings will
be poured out to people regardless of gender or age, ethnic or national
background (see Acts 2:17–18,38–39). To be baptized in the Spirit means to
gain God's view of other people, for he comes to everyone equally. God's
Spirit poured out can be a very personal experience for those he touches,
but it is never private. The Spirit is given to the church, and the gift of the
Spirit is to build the church with living stones drawn from every nation (see
Ephesians 2:19–22; 1 Peter 2:4–5; Revelation 5:9–10). To pray in the Spirit
includes praying for the mystery of the gospel to be powerfully preached
and made known to everyone (see Ephesians 6:18–20).

   "And everyone who calls on the name of the LORD will be saved" (Joel
2:32). This promise of the Spirit creates a crisis, a call for decision. It is not an
indiscriminate, general pouring out; it must be prayed for. Does it not follow
that if "everyone who calls on the name of the LORD shall be saved," then
the greatest prayer we can pray is that everyone will?

PRAY:

*Holy Spirit, I don't want just a little of you; I want all of you. Pour yourself on
me and fill me. I plead with you to draw others to pray for this, too.*

FOR YOUR NEXT DEVOTIONAL READING, GO TO PAGE 1072.

³They cast lots for my people
   and traded boys for prostitutes;
they sold girls for wine
   that they might drink.

⁴"Now what have you against me, O Tyre and Sidon and all you regions of Philistia? Are you repaying me for something I have done? If you are paying me back, I will swiftly and speedily return on your own heads what you have done. ⁵For you took my silver and my gold and carried off my finest treasures to your temples. ⁶You sold the people of Judah and Jerusalem to the Greeks, that you might send them far from their homeland.

⁷"See, I am going to rouse them out of the places to which you sold them, and I will return on your own heads what you have done. ⁸I will sell your sons and daughters to the people of Judah, and they will sell them to the Sabeans, a nation far away." The LORD has spoken.

⁹Proclaim this among the nations:
   Prepare for war!
Rouse the warriors!
   Let all the fighting men draw near
      and attack.
¹⁰Beat your plowshares into swords
   and your pruning hooks into
      spears.
Let the weakling say,
   "I am strong!"
¹¹Come quickly, all you nations from
      every side,
   and assemble there.

Bring down your warriors, O LORD!

¹²"Let the nations be roused;
   let them advance into the Valley of
      Jehoshaphat,
for there I will sit
   to judge all the nations on every
      side.
¹³Swing the sickle,
   for the harvest is ripe.
Come, trample the grapes,
   for the winepress is full
   and the vats overflow—
so great is their wickedness!"

¹⁴Multitudes, multitudes
   in the valley of decision!

For the day of the LORD is near
   in the valley of decision.
¹⁵The sun and moon will be darkened,
   and the stars no longer shine.
¹⁶The LORD will roar from Zion
   and thunder from Jerusalem;
   the earth and the sky will tremble.
But the LORD will be a refuge for his
      people,
   a stronghold for the people of
      Israel.

Blessings for God's People

¹⁷"Then you will know that I, the LORD
      your God,
   dwell in Zion, my holy hill.
Jerusalem will be holy;
   never again will foreigners invade
      her.

¹⁸"In that day the mountains will drip
      new wine,
   and the hills will flow with milk;
all the ravines of Judah will run
      with water.
A fountain will flow out of the LORD's
      house
   and will water the valley of
      acacias.ᵃ
¹⁹But Egypt will be desolate,
   Edom a desert waste,
because of violence done to the
      people of Judah,
   in whose land they shed innocent
      blood.
²⁰Judah will be inhabited forever
   and Jerusalem through all
      generations.
²¹Their bloodguilt, which I have not
      pardoned,
   I will pardon."

The LORD dwells in Zion!

ᵃ18 Or Valley of Shittim

Amos

PROBABLY THE best-known line from the book of Amos is, "But let justice roll on like a river, righteousness like a never-failing stream!" (5:24). That was God speaking. To understand his great call to justice, we need to understand the enormous appeal of the religious alternatives that beckoned Israel on every side. The practice of Canaanite religion was basically the practice of sacred sex. The Canaanites believed that humanity was woven into a divine cosmos, that there was no qualitative difference between a human being and the earth. Therefore, to tap into the power of the universe one needed to get in touch with the energy of one's body. What more powerful urge was there than sex? Sociologist Peter Berger put it bluntly: "The gods were as close as one's own genitalia; to establish contact with them, when all was said mythologically and all was done ritually, one had only to do what, after all, one wanted to do anyway."[1] Prostitution wasn't legalized; it was solemnized. This was a religion of self-centered pleasure.

If the gods of Canaan were encountered in carnal ecstasy, the true and living God was encountered in a covenant and a law. Canaanite religion was about power and how to get it; the worship of the true God was about love and how to live it. The religion of Israel was inescapably ethical. The Ten Commandments were structured around how one was to treat God and other people.

Amos's message of social justice goes right to the heart of the difference between pagan religion and the religion of the living God. Our prayers should do the same. Every petition of the prayer Jesus taught (see Matthew 6:9–13) should be understood, especially the first three: God's holiness, God's kingdom and God's will. The scope of these petitions is not exhausted by the concerns of social justice, but it cannot be understood apart from them. It is a dangerous thing to pray the Lord's Prayer with our mouths in the right place but our hearts, money, time and priorities in another.

1 The words of Amos, one of the shepherds of Tekoa—what he saw concerning Israel two years before the earthquake, when Uzziah was king of Judah and Jeroboam son of Jehoash[a] was king of Israel.
²He said:

"The LORD roars from Zion
and thunders from Jerusalem;
the pastures of the shepherds dry up,[b]
and the top of Carmel withers."

Judgment on Israel's Neighbors

³This is what the LORD says:

"For three sins of Damascus,
even for four, I will not turn back
˻my wrath˼.
Because she threshed Gilead
with sledges having iron teeth,
⁴I will send fire upon the house of
Hazael
that will consume the fortresses of
Ben-Hadad.
⁵I will break down the gate of
Damascus;
I will destroy the king who is in[c] the
Valley of Aven[d]
and the one who holds the scepter in
Beth Eden.
The people of Aram will go into
exile to Kir,"
says the LORD.

⁶This is what the LORD says:

"For three sins of Gaza,
even for four, I will not turn back
˻my wrath˼.
Because she took captive whole
communities
and sold them to Edom,
⁷I will send fire upon the walls of Gaza
that will consume her fortresses.
⁸I will destroy the king[e] of Ashdod
and the one who holds the scepter
in Ashkelon.
I will turn my hand against Ekron,
till the last of the Philistines is
dead,"
says the Sovereign LORD.

⁹This is what the LORD says:

"For three sins of Tyre,
even for four, I will not turn back
˻my wrath˼.

Because she sold whole communities
of captives to Edom,
disregarding a treaty of
brotherhood,
¹⁰I will send fire upon the walls of
Tyre
that will consume her fortresses."

¹¹This is what the LORD says:

"For three sins of Edom,
even for four, I will not turn back
˻my wrath˼.
Because he pursued his brother with
a sword,
stifling all compassion,[f]
because his anger raged continually
and his fury flamed unchecked,
¹²I will send fire upon Teman
that will consume the fortresses of
Bozrah."

¹³This is what the LORD says:

"For three sins of Ammon,
even for four, I will not turn back
˻my wrath˼.
Because he ripped open the pregnant
women of Gilead
in order to extend his borders,
¹⁴I will set fire to the walls of Rabbah
that will consume her fortresses
amid war cries on the day of battle,
amid violent winds on a stormy
day.
¹⁵Her king[g] will go into exile,
he and his officials together,"
says the LORD.

2 This is what the LORD says:

"For three sins of Moab,
even for four, I will not turn back
˻my wrath˼.
Because he burned, as if to lime,
the bones of Edom's king,
²I will send fire upon Moab
that will consume the fortresses
of Kerioth.[h]
Moab will go down in great tumult
amid war cries and the blast of the
trumpet.

---

[a]1 Hebrew *Joash*, a variant of *Jehoash* [b]2 Or *shepherds mourn* [c]5 Or *the inhabitants of* [d]5 *Aven* means *wickedness*. [e]8 Or *inhabitants* [f]11 Or *sword / and destroyed his allies* [g]15 Or / *Molech*; Hebrew *malcam* [h]2 Or *of her cities*

> *God is not a cosmic bell-boy for whom we can press a button to get things.*
>
> H.E. FOSDICK

³ I will destroy her ruler
  and kill all her officials with him,"
                    says the LORD.

⁴This is what the LORD says:

"For three sins of Judah,
  even for four, I will not turn back
    ⌐my wrath⌐.
Because they have rejected the law of
    the LORD
  and have not kept his decrees,
because they have been led astray by
    false gods,*a*
  the gods*b* their ancestors followed,
⁵ I will send fire upon Judah
  that will consume the fortresses of
    Jerusalem."

Judgment on Israel

⁶This is what the LORD says:

"For three sins of Israel,
  even for four, I will not turn back
    ⌐my wrath⌐.
They sell the righteous for silver,
  and the needy for a pair of sandals.
⁷They trample on the heads of the
    poor
  as upon the dust of the ground
  and deny justice to the oppressed.
Father and son use the same girl
  and so profane my holy name.
⁸They lie down beside every altar
  on garments taken in pledge.
In the house of their god
  they drink wine taken as fines.

⁹ "I destroyed the Amorite before
    them,
  though he was tall as the cedars
  and strong as the oaks.
I destroyed his fruit above
  and his roots below.

¹⁰ "I brought you up out of Egypt,
  and I led you forty years in the
    desert
  to give you the land of the
    Amorites.

¹¹ I also raised up prophets from among
    your sons
  and Nazirites from among your
    young men.
Is this not true, people of Israel?"
                    declares the LORD.
¹² "But you made the Nazirites drink
    wine
  and commanded the prophets not
    to prophesy.

¹³ "Now then, I will crush you
  as a cart crushes when loaded with
    grain.
¹⁴ The swift will not escape,
  the strong will not muster their
    strength,
  and the warrior will not save his
    life.
¹⁵ The archer will not stand his ground,
  the fleet-footed soldier will not get
    away,
  and the horseman will not save his
    life.
¹⁶ Even the bravest warriors
  will flee naked on that day,"
                    declares the LORD.

Witnesses Summoned Against Israel

3 Hear this word the LORD has spoken
  against you, O people of Israel—
against the whole family I brought up out
of Egypt:

² "You only have I chosen
  of all the families of the earth;
therefore I will punish you
  for all your sins."

³ Do two walk together
  unless they have agreed to do so?
⁴ Does a lion roar in the thicket
  when he has no prey?
Does he growl in his den
  when he has caught nothing?
⁵ Does a bird fall into a trap on the
    ground
  where no snare has been set?
Does a trap spring up from the earth
  when there is nothing to catch?
⁶ When a trumpet sounds in a city,
  do not the people tremble?
When disaster comes to a city,
  has not the LORD caused it?

*a*4 Or *by lies*   *b*4 Or *lies*

7 Surely the Sovereign LORD does
  nothing
    without revealing his plan
    to his servants the prophets.

8 The lion has roared—
    who will not fear?
  The Sovereign LORD has spoken—
    who can but prophesy?

9 Proclaim to the fortresses of
    Ashdod
  and to the fortresses of Egypt:
  "Assemble yourselves on the
      mountains of Samaria;
    see the great unrest within her
    and the oppression among her
      people."

10 "They do not know how to do right,"
      declares the LORD,
  "who hoard plunder and loot in
      their fortresses."

11 Therefore this is what the Sovereign
  LORD says:

  "An enemy will overrun the land;
    he will pull down your strongholds
    and plunder your fortresses."

12 This is what the LORD says:

  "As a shepherd saves from the lion's
      mouth
    only two leg bones or a piece of an
      ear,
  so will the Israelites be saved,
    those who sit in Samaria
    on the edge of their beds
    and in Damascus on their
      couches.ᵃ"

13 "Hear this and testify against the
  house of Jacob," declares the Lord, the
  LORD God Almighty.

14 "On the day I punish Israel for her
      sins,
    I will destroy the altars of Bethel;
  the horns of the altar will be cut off
    and fall to the ground.
15 I will tear down the winter house
    along with the summer house;
  the houses adorned with ivory will be
      destroyed
    and the mansions will be
      demolished,"
        declares the LORD.

Israel Has Not Returned to God

4 Hear this word, you cows of Bashan
    on Mount Samaria,
  you women who oppress the poor
    and crush the needy
  and say to your husbands, "Bring
      us some drinks!"
2 The Sovereign LORD has sworn by his
      holiness:
  "The time will surely come
    when you will be taken away with
      hooks,
    the last of you with fishhooks.
3 You will each go straight out
    through breaks in the wall,
    and you will be cast out toward
      Harmon,ᵇ"
        declares the LORD.
4 "Go to Bethel and sin;
    go to Gilgal and sin yet more.
  Bring your sacrifices every morning,
    your tithes every three years.ᶜ
5 Burn leavened bread as a thank
      offering
    and brag about your freewill
      offerings—
  boast about them, you Israelites,
    for this is what you love to do,"
        declares the Sovereign LORD.

6 "I gave you empty stomachsᵈ in
      every city
    and lack of bread in every town,
  yet you have not returned to me,"
        declares the LORD.

7 "I also withheld rain from you
    when the harvest was still three
      months away.
  I sent rain on one town,
    but withheld it from another.
  One field had rain;
    another had none and dried up.
8 People staggered from town to town
      for water
    but did not get enough to drink,
  yet you have not returned to me,"
        declares the LORD.

9 "Many times I struck your gardens
      and vineyards,

ᵃ12 The meaning of the Hebrew for this line is
uncertain.   ᵇ3 Masoretic Text; with a different
word division of the Hebrew (see Septuagint) out,
O mountain of oppression   ᶜ4 Or tithes on the
third day   ᵈ6 Hebrew you cleanness of teeth

I struck them with blight and
   mildew.
Locusts devoured your fig and olive
   trees,
      yet you have not returned to me,"
            declares the LORD.

10 "I sent plagues among you
   as I did to Egypt.
I killed your young men with the
   sword,
   along with your captured horses.
I filled your nostrils with the stench of
   your camps,
      yet you have not returned to me,"
            declares the LORD.

11 "I overthrew some of you
   as I*a* overthrew Sodom and
      Gomorrah.
You were like a burning stick
   snatched from the fire,
      yet you have not returned to me,"
            declares the LORD.

12 "Therefore this is what I will do to
      you, Israel,
   and because I will do this to you,
   prepare to meet your God,
      O Israel."

13 He who forms the mountains,
   creates the wind,
   and reveals his thoughts to man,
he who turns dawn to darkness,
   and treads the high places of the
      earth—
   the LORD God Almighty is his name.

A Lament and Call to Repentance

5 Hear this word, O house of Israel,
   this lament I take up concerning you:

2 "Fallen is Virgin Israel,
   never to rise again,
deserted in her own land,
   with no one to lift her up."

3 This is what the Sovereign LORD says:

"The city that marches out a
      thousand strong for Israel
   will have only a hundred left;
the town that marches out a hundred
      strong
   will have only ten left."

4 This is what the LORD says to the
house of Israel:

"Seek me and live;
5   do not seek Bethel,
do not go to Gilgal,
   do not journey to Beersheba.
For Gilgal will surely go into exile,
   and Bethel will be reduced to
      nothing.*b*"
6 Seek the LORD and live,
   or he will sweep through the house
      of Joseph like a fire;
it will devour,
   and Bethel will have no one to
      quench it.

7 You who turn justice into bitterness
   and cast righteousness to the
      ground
8 (he who made the Pleiades and
      Orion,
   who turns blackness into dawn
   and darkens day into night,
who calls for the waters of the sea
   and pours them out over the face of
      the land—
   the LORD is his name—
9 he flashes destruction on the
      stronghold
   and brings the fortified city to
      ruin),
10 you hate the one who reproves in
      court
   and despise him who tells the
      truth.

11 You trample on the poor
   and force him to give you grain.
Therefore, though you have built
      stone mansions,
   you will not live in them;
though you have planted lush
      vineyards,
   you will not drink their wine.
12 For I know how many are your
      offenses
   and how great your sins.

You oppress the righteous and take
      bribes
   and you deprive the poor of justice
      in the courts.
13 Therefore the prudent man keeps
      quiet in such times,
   for the times are evil.

---

*a*11 Hebrew *God*   *b*5 Or *grief*; or *wickedness*;
Hebrew *aven*, a reference to Beth Aven (a
derogatory name for Bethel)

14 Seek good, not evil,
that you may live.
Then the LORD God Almighty will be
with you,
just as you say he is.
15 Hate evil, love good;
maintain justice in the courts.
Perhaps the LORD God Almighty will
have mercy
on the remnant of Joseph.

16 Therefore this is what the Lord, the
LORD God Almighty, says:

"There will be wailing in all the
streets
and cries of anguish in every public
square.
The farmers will be summoned to
weep
and the mourners to wail.
17 There will be wailing in all the
vineyards,
for I will pass through your midst,"
says the LORD.

The Day of the LORD

18 Woe to you who long
for the day of the LORD!
Why do you long for the day of the
LORD?
That day will be darkness, not
light.
19 It will be as though a man fled from a
lion
only to meet a bear,
as though he entered his house
and rested his hand on the wall
only to have a snake bite him.
20 Will not the day of the LORD be
darkness, not light—
pitch-dark, without a ray of
brightness?

21 "I hate, I despise your religious
feasts;
I cannot stand your assemblies.
22 Even though you bring me burnt
offerings and grain offerings,
I will not accept them.
Though you bring choice fellowship
offerings,ª
I will have no regard for them.
23 Away with the noise of your songs!
I will not listen to the music of your
harps.

24 But let justice roll on like a river,
righteousness like a never-failing
stream!
25 "Did you bring me sacrifices and
offerings
forty years in the desert, O house
of Israel?
26 You have lifted up the shrine of your
king,
the pedestal of your idols,
the star of your godᵇ—
which you made for yourselves.
27 Therefore I will send you into exile
beyond Damascus,"
says the LORD, whose name is God
Almighty.

Woe to the Complacent

6 Woe to you who are complacent
in Zion,
and to you who feel secure on
Mount Samaria,
you notable men of the foremost
nation,
to whom the people of Israel come!
2 Go to Calneh and look at it;
go from there to great Hamath,
and then go down to Gath in
Philistia.
Are they better off than your two
kingdoms?
Is their land larger than yours?
3 You put off the evil day
and bring near a reign of terror.
4 You lie on beds inlaid with ivory
and lounge on your couches.
You dine on choice lambs
and fattened calves.
5 You strum away on your harps like
David
and improvise on musical
instruments.
6 You drink wine by the bowlful
and use the finest lotions,
but you do not grieve over the ruin
of Joseph.
7 Therefore you will be among the first
to go into exile;
your feasting and lounging will
end.

ª 22 Traditionally *peace offerings*   ᵇ 26 Or *lifted
up Sakkuth your king / and Kaiwan your idols, /
your star-gods*; Septuagint *lifted up the shrine of
Molech / and the star of your god Rephan, / their
idols*

Let's Roll

5:24 LET JUSTICE ROLL ON LIKE A RIVER.

Human nature being what it is, it's easy to see why Israel was tempted to follow a few different directions. They could turn to Baalism altogether for religious fulfillment, or they could waffle a bit and customize their faith—mix Baal with God, selfish pleasure with a little love (see the Introduction to Amos). Most Israelites took this second route. If we had to guess which one God hated more, it was probably the latter. What so infuriated God wasn't the people's observance of appropriate religious practices but their duplicity. This is the background of the famous call for justice in Amos 5:24. It was preceded in verses 21 and 23 by God telling the people: "I despise your religious feasts . . . Away with all the noise of your songs!" Read that as, "You can't mix and match your faith."

Religious rituals and ceremonies are peculiar things; they can either delight God or disgust him. When they are ends unto themselves, they disgust him. When they are the means to a holy end, they delight him. As ends unto themselves, they are seen as religious compartmentalizing that dissatisfies God. The gist of this is that the worshiper can do what she pleases most of the time, do religious things some of the time, and get credit for being good all the time. Jeremiah's take on this was that it turned the house of the Lord into a place where people went to hide from God, not meet with him (see Jeremiah 7:9–11). Used as a means to a higher purpose, religion can express true love for God and impress his love upon us; it gives voice to what's already inside, and it speaks to our hearts. When religion is used as a means, it unifies believers.

The phrase "But let justice roll on like a river" (Amos 5:24) says a lot. God wants our spiritual lives to be a continuous flow of justice and righteousness, nurturing life the way rain nurtures a desert. People flourish in justice and righteousness, but they wither and die without these traits. God hates religious compartments because nothing flows out of them. They're like boxes of bottled water, sealed and unopened. He doesn't want to be sprinkled here and there or sipped and rationed. He wants his justice and righteousness to flow out of us like the living water Jesus promised would bubble up in those who believe in him (see John 4:14). Are your prayers ends or means? Do they delight or disgust God?

P R A Y :

Righteous Lord, may my life not be like bottled water, but like
a river. Teach me your justice that I may pray it and live
according to it, as a flowing, rolling river.

———

FOR YOUR NEXT DEVOTIONAL READING, GO TO PAGE 1074.

The Lord Abhors the Pride of Israel

8The Sovereign Lord has sworn by himself—the Lord God Almighty declares:

"I abhor the pride of Jacob
and detest his fortresses;
I will deliver up the city
and everything in it."

9If ten men are left in one house, they too will die. **10**And if a relative who is to burn the bodies comes to carry them out of the house and asks anyone still hiding there, "Is anyone with you?" and he says, "No," then he will say, "Hush! We must not mention the name of the Lord."

11 For the Lord has given the command,
and he will smash the great house
into pieces
and the small house into bits.

12 Do horses run on the rocky crags?
Does one plow there with oxen?
But you have turned justice into
poison
and the fruit of righteousness into
bitterness—
13 you who rejoice in the conquest of
Lo Debar*a*
and say, "Did we not take
Karnaim*b* by our own
strength?"

14 For the Lord God Almighty declares,
"I will stir up a nation against you,
O house of Israel,
that will oppress you all the way
from Lebo*c* Hamath to the valley of
the Arabah."

Locusts, Fire and a Plumb Line

7 This is what the Sovereign Lord showed me: He was preparing swarms of locusts after the king's share had been harvested and just as the second crop was coming up. **2**When they had stripped the land clean, I cried out, "Sovereign Lord, forgive! How can Jacob survive? He is so small!"

3So the Lord relented.

"This will not happen," the Lord said.

4This is what the Sovereign Lord showed me: The Sovereign Lord was calling for judgment by fire; it dried up the great deep and devoured the land. **5**Then I cried out, "Sovereign Lord, I beg you, stop! How can Jacob survive? He is so small!"

6So the Lord relented.

"This will not happen either," the Sovereign Lord said.

7This is what he showed me: The Lord was standing by a wall that had been built true to plumb, with a plumb line in his hand. **8**And the Lord asked me, "What do you see, Amos?"

"A plumb line," I replied.

Then the Lord said, "Look, I am setting a plumb line among my people Israel; I will spare them no longer.

9 "The high places of Isaac will be
destroyed
and the sanctuaries of Israel will be
ruined;
with my sword I will rise against
the house of Jeroboam."

Amos and Amaziah

10Then Amaziah the priest of Bethel sent a message to Jeroboam king of Israel: "Amos is raising a conspiracy against you in the very heart of Israel. The land cannot bear all his words. **11**For this is what Amos is saying:

" 'Jeroboam will die by the sword,
and Israel will surely go into exile,
away from their native land.' "

12Then Amaziah said to Amos, "Get out, you seer! Go back to the land of Judah. Earn your bread there and do your prophesying there. **13**Don't prophesy anymore at Bethel, because this is the king's sanctuary and the temple of the kingdom."

14Amos answered Amaziah, "I was neither a prophet nor a prophet's son, but I was a shepherd, and I also took care of sycamore-fig trees. **15**But the Lord took me from tending the flock and said to me, 'Go, prophesy to my people Israel.' **16**Now then, hear the word of the Lord. You say,

" 'Do not prophesy against Israel,
and stop preaching against the
house of Isaac.'

---

a13 Lo Debar means *nothing.*   *b13 Karnaim*
means *horns; horn* here symbolizes strength.
c14 Or *from the entrance to*

AMOS 7:1–6

The Mystery of Prayer

7:3 SO THE LORD RELENTED.

Here is the mystery of amazing grace: "So the LORD relented" (7:3,6). If we all got what we deserved, we would be dead. Two vivid pictures of what Israel deserved are in this text. One is of swarms of locusts that strip the land completely bare; the other is of a fire that devours even the "great deep," probably referring to the Mediterranean Sea. But the Lord relented! The thing that should mystify us is not that bad things seem sometimes to happen to good people, but that such a good thing as mercy should happen to bad people. Whenever we pray for God to give us mercy, we do two things. We acknowledge that we have done something terrible; and we plead that instead of responding in kind, God would do something wonderful.

The amazing mystery of prayer: "I cried out, 'Sovereign LORD, forgive!'" (verse 2). In order to draw Amos into prayer, the Lord showed him his will to destroy Israel. When Amos prayed, it then pleased God to relent. Destruction, prayer, mercy—all were dimensions of God's will. The mystery of prayer is great because of a greater mystery: how God's sovereign and immutable will interacts with human freedom. How can it be that "all things have their will, yet none but thine" (George Herbert)? It is beyond understanding, but it is clear that somehow the two coexist. God can both propose prayer and answer prayer; declare his mind and change his mind; and through it all, carry out his unchanging will through the prayers of the saints.

A key to this mystery, but only a key—for the mystery has many doors—is the perspective Amos brought to his prayer for mercy. Amos was a typical prophet, gloriously unbalanced in his zeal for God's glory, a magnifying glass who concentrated the blazing light of holy truth on sin (see the Introduction to Isaiah). But the light can set things on fire and destroy them. So Amos pled for mercy, not as one who had a casual attitude toward truth, but as one who had a reverent attitude. In the same way, Jesus taught us to pray that God's name be hallowed before we ask for mercy (see Matthew 6:9,12).

P R A Y :

Lord, because you call me to come, I enter into the mystery
of prayer. Give me the boldness and humility of Amos.
Give me your perspective on the things I pray for. Let me
pray always that your holy will be done, believing that somehow
my prayers are part of getting your will done.

FOR YOUR NEXT DEVOTIONAL READING, GO TO PAGE 1076.

17"Therefore this is what the LORD says:

" 'Your wife will become a prostitute
in the city,
and your sons and daughters will
fall by the sword.
Your land will be measured and
divided up,
and you yourself will die in a
pagan[a] country.
And Israel will certainly go into exile,
away from their native land.' "

A Basket of Ripe Fruit

8 This is what the Sovereign LORD
showed me: a basket of ripe fruit.
2"What do you see, Amos?" he asked.

"A basket of ripe fruit," I answered.

Then the LORD said to me, "The time is
ripe for my people Israel; I will spare
them no longer.

3"In that day," declares the Sovereign
LORD, "the songs in the temple will turn
to wailing.[b] Many, many bodies—flung
everywhere! Silence!"

4Hear this, you who trample the needy
and do away with the poor of the
land,

5saying,

"When will the New Moon be over
that we may sell grain,
and the Sabbath be ended
that we may market wheat?"—
skimping the measure,
boosting the price
and cheating with dishonest scales,
6buying the poor with silver
and the needy for a pair of sandals,
selling even the sweepings with the
wheat.

7The LORD has sworn by the Pride of Jacob: "I will never forget anything they
have done.

8"Will not the land tremble for this,
and all who live in it mourn?
The whole land will rise like the Nile;
it will be stirred up and then sink
like the river of Egypt.

9"In that day," declares the Sovereign
LORD,

"I will make the sun go down at noon
and darken the earth in broad
daylight.

10I will turn your religious feasts into
mourning
and all your singing into weeping.
I will make all of you wear sackcloth
and shave your heads.
I will make that time like mourning
for an only son
and the end of it like a bitter day.

11"The days are coming," declares the
Sovereign LORD,
"when I will send a famine through
the land—
not a famine of food or a thirst for
water,
but a famine of hearing the words
of the LORD.
12Men will stagger from sea to sea
and wander from north to east,
searching for the word of the LORD,
but they will not find it.

13"In that day

"the lovely young women and strong
young men
will faint because of thirst.
14They who swear by the shame[c] of
Samaria,
or say, 'As surely as your god lives,
O Dan,'
or, 'As surely as the god[d] of
Beersheba lives'—
they will fall,
never to rise again."

Israel to Be Destroyed

9 I saw the Lord standing by the altar,
and he said:

"Strike the tops of the pillars
so that the thresholds shake.
Bring them down on the heads of all
the people;
those who are left I will kill with
the sword.
Not one will get away,
none will escape.
2Though they dig down to the depths
of the grave,[e]
from there my hand will take them.
Though they climb up to the heavens,
from there I will bring them down.

---

a17 Hebrew an unclean   b3 Or "the temple
singers will wail   c14 Or by Ashima; or by the
idol   d14 Or power   e2 Hebrew to Sheol

BROTHER LAWRENCE (1611–1691)

The Redemption of Work

"THERE IS nothing more terrible than activity without insight." For many people, these words of Thomas Carlyle describe the miserable state of their daily work. For those of us who resonate with Carlyle's words, a 17th century monk known as Brother Lawrence has much to teach us.

Nicholas Herman was born in 1611 in Lorraine, France. He described himself as a "great awkward fellow who broke everything." After an unsuccessful career as a foot soldier and a brief stint as a hermit, Herman joined the Carmelite monastery as a lay member. He was given the name Brother Lawrence of the Resurrection and became a full member of the order in 1642.

From the beginning, Brother Lawrence was assigned kitchen duty, a job that no one wanted. For 40 years, his daily routine remained the same: rising early to slice vegetables; cooking soup and pouring wine; scrubbing pots and pans after each meal. For the first 10 years of his work Brother Lawrence struggled. Then one day, quite unexpectedly, he experienced a change. "I suddenly found myself changed," he wrote, "and my soul, which up till then was always disturbed, experienced a profound interior peace."[2]

What changed was that Brother Lawrence had begun to do his work "as working for the Lord" (Colossians 3:23), or as he put it famously, to "practice the presence of God." The dishes were still dirty, the kitchen still loud and frantic, yet he maintained an inner communion with God that made his work bearable, even joyful. "The time of business does not with me differ from the time of prayer, and in the noise and clatter of my kitchen while several persons are at the same time calling me for different things, I possess God in as great tranquility as if I were upon my knees at the blessed sacrament."[3] Lawrence enjoyed the practice of God's presence so much that at times he had to keep himself from laughing in front of others.

Brother Lawrence's simple message of bringing insight to activity through continuous prayer—practicing the presence of God—has helped to redeem the daily work of many who feel they labor at thankless tasks. "So think of God all the time—during the day, at night, in your daily work, even in your leisure time activities. He is always nearby. Don't ignore him. If you had a friend nearby, you would not ignore him when he came to visit. Why then would you neglect God? In short, do not forget him. Think of him often. Adore him continually. Live and die with him. As a Christian this is our job and calling. This is what we are here for. It is glorious!"[4]

PRAY:

Father, forgive my complaining. The lowliest work done in your
name is more than I deserve. Give me a renewed spirit of gratitude
and a sense of your presence to sustain me in my duties.

MEMORIZE:

Keep your lives free from the love of money and be
content with what you have, because God has said, "Never will
I leave you; never will I forsake you." HEBREWS 13:5

FOR YOUR NEXT DEVOTIONAL READING, GO TO PAGE 1081.

³ Though they hide themselves on the
top of Carmel,
there I will hunt them down and
seize them.
Though they hide from me at the
bottom of the sea,
there I will command the serpent
to bite them.
⁴ Though they are driven into exile by
their enemies,
there I will command the sword to
slay them.
I will fix my eyes upon them
for evil and not for good."

⁵ The Lord, the LORD Almighty,
he who touches the earth and it
melts,
and all who live in it mourn—
the whole land rises like the Nile,
then sinks like the river of Egypt—
⁶ he who builds his lofty palace^a in the
heavens
and sets its foundation^b on the
earth,
who calls for the waters of the sea
and pours them out over the face of
the land—
the LORD is his name.

⁷ "Are not you Israelites
the same to me as the Cushites^c?"
declares the LORD.
"Did I not bring Israel up from Egypt,
the Philistines from Caphtor^d
and the Arameans from Kir?

⁸ "Surely the eyes of the Sovereign LORD
are on the sinful kingdom.
I will destroy it
from the face of the earth—
yet I will not totally destroy
the house of Jacob,"
declares the LORD.
⁹ "For I will give the command,
and I will shake the house of Israel
among all the nations
as grain is shaken in a sieve,
and not a pebble will reach the
ground.

¹⁰ All the sinners among my people
will die by the sword,
all those who say,
'Disaster will not overtake or
meet us.'

Israel's Restoration

¹¹ "In that day I will restore
David's fallen tent.
I will repair its broken places,
restore its ruins,
and build it as it used to be,
¹² so that they may possess the remnant
of Edom
and all the nations that bear my
name,^{e}"
declares the LORD, who will
do these things.

¹³ "The days are coming," declares the
LORD,

"when the reaper will be overtaken
by the plowman
and the planter by the one treading
grapes.
New wine will drip from the
mountains
and flow from all the hills.
¹⁴ I will bring back my exiled^f people
Israel;
they will rebuild the ruined cities
and live in them.
They will plant vineyards and drink
their wine;
they will make gardens and eat
their fruit.
¹⁵ I will plant Israel in their own land,
never again to be uprooted
from the land I have given them,"

says the LORD your God.

---

^{a}6 The meaning of the Hebrew for this phrase is
uncertain. ^{b}6 The meaning of the Hebrew for
this word is uncertain. ^{c}7 That is, people from
the upper Nile region ^{d}7 That is, Crete
^{e}12 Hebrew; Septuagint *so that the remnant of
men / and all the nations that bear my name may
seek ⌊the Lord⌋* ^{f}14 Or *will restore the fortunes
of my*

Obadiah

THE FACT that Obadiah is the shortest book in the Old Testament in no way diminishes its importance. The bitter rivalry between Israel and Edom, both of whom descended from Abraham and Isaac, is more than a backdrop for a prophecy; it is a grim and vivid reminder that hatred and revenge only intensify over time. Centuries after this book was written, Herod the Great, an Idumean and descendant of Edom, sought to destroy Jesus at his birth (see Matthew 2:16). Only repentance heals the cancer of hatred. Obadiah's warnings to the people of Edom were ignored, and many people suffered for generations.

Obadiah also warns against the danger of smugness. "Famous last words" is a phrase we use to speak ironically of the way things can turn out opposite from the way we thought they would. Falsely secure in high mountain fortresses, Edom's famous last words were, "Who can bring me down to the ground?" (verse 3). God was unimpressed: "'Though you soar like the eagle and make your nest among the stars, from there I will bring you down,' declares the LORD" (verse 4). God hates smugness.

BECAUSE OF THE VIOLENCE AGAINST YOUR BROTHER JACOB, YOU WILL BE COVERED WITH SHAME. (10)

Smugness is deadly in prayer: Witness the two men in Jesus' parable who went to the temple to pray (see Luke 18:9–14). One was quite confident that God would hear his prayers appreciatively; the other was afraid to even look up—he was so sure he deserved judgment. The first man looked for confirmation; the second man cried out for mercy. Jesus said the first man prayed only about himself and was therefore heard only by himself. The second man, though low, was brought high, and "went home justified before God. For everyone who exalts himself will be humbled, and he who humbles himself will be exalted" (Luke 18:14). The book of Obadiah reminds us that Edom is more than a place and a nation; it is an attitude.

¹The vision of Obadiah.

This is what the Sovereign LORD says about Edom—

We have heard a message from the
LORD:
An envoy was sent to the nations to
say,
"Rise, and let us go against her for
battle"—

² "See, I will make you small among
the nations;
you will be utterly despised.
³ The pride of your heart has deceived
you,
you who live in the clefts of the
rocks*ᵃ*
and make your home on the
heights,
you who say to yourself,
'Who can bring me down to the
ground?'
⁴ Though you soar like the eagle
and make your nest among the
stars,
from there I will bring you down,"
declares the LORD.
⁵ "If thieves came to you,
if robbers in the night—
Oh, what a disaster awaits you—
would they not steal only as much
as they wanted?
If grape pickers came to you,
would they not leave a few
grapes?
⁶ But how Esau will be ransacked,
his hidden treasures pillaged!
⁷ All your allies will force you to the
border;
your friends will deceive and
overpower you;
those who eat your bread will set a
trap for you,*ᵇ*
but you will not detect it.

⁸ "In that day," declares the LORD,
"will I not destroy the wise men of
Edom,
men of understanding in the
mountains of Esau?
⁹ Your warriors, O Teman, will be
terrified,
and everyone in Esau's mountains
will be cut down in the slaughter.

¹⁰ Because of the violence against your
brother Jacob,
you will be covered with shame;
you will be destroyed forever.
¹¹ On the day you stood aloof
while strangers carried off his
wealth
and foreigners entered his gates
and cast lots for Jerusalem,
you were like one of them.
¹² You should not look down on your
brother
in the day of his misfortune,
nor rejoice over the people of Judah
in the day of their destruction,
nor boast so much
in the day of their trouble.
¹³ You should not march through the
gates of my people
in the day of their disaster,
nor look down on them in their
calamity
in the day of their disaster,
nor seize their wealth
in the day of their disaster.
¹⁴ You should not wait at the crossroads
to cut down their fugitives,
nor hand over their survivors
in the day of their trouble.

¹⁵ "The day of the LORD is near
for all nations.
As you have done, it will be done to
you;
your deeds will return upon your
own head.
¹⁶ Just as you drank on my holy hill,
so all the nations will drink
continually;
they will drink and drink
and be as if they had never been.
¹⁷ But on Mount Zion will be deliverance;
it will be holy,
and the house of Jacob
will possess its inheritance.
¹⁸ The house of Jacob will be a fire
and the house of Joseph a flame;
the house of Esau will be stubble,
and they will set it on fire and
consume it.
There will be no survivors
from the house of Esau."
The LORD has spoken.

ᵃ3 Or *of Sela*   *ᵇ7* The meaning of the Hebrew
for this clause is uncertain.

Family Feud

In William Shakespeare's famous play *Romeo and Juliet*, Juliet mourns the ancient hatred between her family and the family of her beloved Romeo. Mere family labels should mean nothing, especially if they keep earnest lovers apart: "What's in a name? That which we call a rose by any other name would smell as sweet."[1]

"Or as foul," an Edomite might add of an Israelite. The tragedy was that both Edomites and Israelites belonged to the same family. The rivalry between the two nations went back for centuries to the rivalry between the brothers Jacob and Esau; and over the years the hatred was embellished and inflamed countless ways by countless slurs, insults and acts of aggression. When Israel fell prey to foreign powers, Edom not only offered no help but gloated—and even heartlessly took advantage of their cousins' fall (see Obadiah 10–14). God would punish Edom for this. No doubt he saw again in Edom's hatred the same evil that caused Cain to strike down his brother Abel. As with Abel, God had chosen to uniquely bless the line of Jacob, not Esau. God saw through Edom's animosity toward Israel to its real source: animosity toward God.

Look past the names of Edom and Israel, and think of the names you know that are stained with bitterness in your own heart, especially in your own family. These hurts and hatreds can run deep. Their longevity can give them almost mythic power to shape perceptions. Obadiah's prophecy is a pointed reminder to repent of bitterness and callousness, for its source is not ultimately in what you think others have done to you, but in whether you respect the way God runs the world. The implications for prayer are profound: You can't love a God you can't see if you won't love a brother or sister that you can (see 1 John 4:20).

P R A Y :

O Spirit of God, cleanse my heart of all bitterness. Forgive me for
the ways I have grown hard toward others, especially family
members. May I forgive as I have been forgiven and be
an instrument of peace in the world.

FOR YOUR NEXT DEVOTIONAL READING, GO TO PAGE 1086.

¹⁹People from the Negev will occupy
the mountains of Esau,
and people from the foothills will
possess
the land of the Philistines.
They will occupy the fields of
Ephraim and Samaria,
and Benjamin will possess Gilead.
²⁰This company of Israelite exiles who
are in Canaan
will possess ⌞the land⌟ as far as
Zarephath;
the exiles from Jerusalem who are in
Sepharad

> 66 Work as if you were to live a hundred years. Pray as if you were to die tomorrow. 99
>
> BENJAMIN FRANKLIN

will possess the towns of the
Negev.
²¹Deliverers will go up on*ᵃ* Mount Zion
to govern the mountains of Esau.
And the kingdom will be the LORD's.

ᵃ21 Or *from*

Jonah

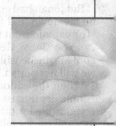

AT THE 1976 Urbana Student Mission Convention, Dr. John R. W. Stott spoke to 17,000 students gathered there about God's heart for missions. How much is mission work a part of God's character and will? The titles of Dr. Stott's addresses say it all:

1. The Lord God is a Missionary God
2. The Lord Christ is a Missionary Christ
3. The Holy Spirit is a Missionary Spirit
4. The Christian Church is a Missionary Church

Mission work is the very essence of who God has revealed himself to be. The eternal communion of Father, Son and Holy Spirit has always been directed toward the whole world, not just particular people. The church's mission is missions. In the words of theologian Emil Brunner, the church exists by missions as a fire exists by burning.

The story of Jonah is one of the most engaging and theologically significant stories in the Bible. It satirizes and indicts Israel for its refusal to live up to its calling to be a blessing to the world (see Genesis 12:1–3). Jonah, like the nation he represents, is frankly scandalized to learn that the God of Israel loves even their worst enemies. His story turns on his reluctance to line his affections up with God's. "Reluctance" is a weak description for how Jonah acted. "Intransigence" is a better word for this man, who never even prayed for the Ninevites, the people to whom he was sent to preach. Jonah the man has nothing to teach us about how to pray for the world God loves. But Jonah the book does, especially in God's answers to Jonah's complaints and self-pity.

> "O LORD, IS THIS NOT WHAT I SAID WHEN I WAS STILL AT HOME? THAT IS WHY I WAS SO QUICK TO FLEE TO TARSHISH. I KNEW THAT YOU ARE A GRACIOUS AND COMPASSIONATE GOD." (4:2)

Jonah Flees From the LORD

1 The word of the LORD came to Jonah son of Amittai: [2] "Go to the great city of Nineveh and preach against it, because its wickedness has come up before me."

[3] But Jonah ran away from the LORD and headed for Tarshish. He went down to Joppa, where he found a ship bound for that port. After paying the fare, he went aboard and sailed for Tarshish to flee from the LORD.

[4] Then the LORD sent a great wind on the sea, and such a violent storm arose that the ship threatened to break up. [5] All the sailors were afraid and each cried out to his own god. And they threw the cargo into the sea to lighten the ship.

But Jonah had gone below deck, where he lay down and fell into a deep sleep. [6] The captain went to him and said, "How can you sleep? Get up and call on your god! Maybe he will take notice of us, and we will not perish."

[7] Then the sailors said to each other, "Come, let us cast lots to find out who is responsible for this calamity." They cast lots and the lot fell on Jonah.

[8] So they asked him, "Tell us, who is responsible for making all this trouble for us? What do you do? Where do you come from? What is your country? From what people are you?"

[9] He answered, "I am a Hebrew and I worship the LORD, the God of heaven, who made the sea and the land."

[10] This terrified them and they asked, "What have you done?" (They knew he was running away from the LORD, because he had already told them so.)

> It is not well for a man to pray cream and live skim milk.
>
> HENRY WARD BEECHER

[11] The sea was getting rougher and rougher. So they asked him, "What should we do to you to make the sea calm down for us?"

[12] "Pick me up and throw me into the sea," he replied, "and it will become calm. I know that it is my fault that this great storm has come upon you."

[13] Instead, the men did their best to row back to land. But they could not, for the sea grew even wilder than before. [14] Then they cried to the LORD, "O LORD, please do not let us die for taking this man's life. Do not hold us accountable for killing an innocent man, for you, O LORD, have done as you pleased." [15] Then they took Jonah and threw him overboard, and the raging sea grew calm. [16] At this the men greatly feared the LORD, and they offered a sacrifice to the LORD and made vows to him.

[17] But the LORD provided a great fish to swallow Jonah, and Jonah was inside the fish three days and three nights.

Jonah's Prayer

2 From inside the fish Jonah prayed to the LORD his God. [2] He said:

"In my distress I called to the LORD,
  and he answered me.
From the depths of the grave[a] I called
    for help,
  and you listened to my cry.

> FROM inside the fish Jonah prayed to the LORD his God.
>
> JONAH 2:1

[3] You hurled me into the deep,
    into the very heart of the seas,
  and the currents swirled about me;
all your waves and breakers
    swept over me.
[4] I said, 'I have been banished
    from your sight;
  yet I will look again
    toward your holy temple.'
[5] The engulfing waters threatened
    me,[b]
  the deep surrounded me;
  seaweed was wrapped around my
    head.
[6] To the roots of the mountains I sank
    down;
  the earth beneath barred me in
    forever.
But you brought my life up from the
    pit,
  O LORD my God.

---

[a]2 Hebrew *Sheol*   [b]5 Or *waters were at my throat*

The Things That Break God's Heart

4:11 "SHOULD I NOT BE CONCERNED ABOUT THAT GREAT CITY?"

In 1947, Bob Pierce was touring mainland China as an evangelist. After one of his services, a distraught mother pushed her way through the surrounding crowd, carrying in her arms her starving infant daughter, White Jade. She thrust the baby into his arms and disappeared. Pierce dug into his own pockets and gave money to help a missionary buy food for the child. After that experience, he was never the same. Three years later he founded the organization known as World Vision, which is still helping millions of people worldwide. Later, in 1951, he wrote a prayer in his Bible, which he kept until his death in 1978: "Let my heart be broken with the things that break the heart of God."

God's rhetorical question to Jonah was an invitation to pray the same prayer as that of Bob Pierce: "Should I not be concerned about that great city?" (4:11). There were 120,000 people in Nineveh who didn't know left from right, right from wrong, up from down. They were utterly lost and confused, like sheep without a shepherd. And they were *people*—not an insignificant vine! God's rebuke to Jonah was an invitation to be moved by something more than Jonah's own personal peace and comfort. God wanted Jonah—and us—to share his great and expansive love with others, even through our prayers.

American newspapers have a formula to gauge reader interest in stories: 10,000 dead in Nepal = 100 dead in Wales = 10 dead on the other side of the country = 1 dead next door. God's invitation is to level the ground of our emotional playing field—or *praying* field—and pray for more than our own peace and satisfaction. What percent of your prayers are for the unreached peoples of the world?

God's drastic measures with Jonah fit his transgressions. The belly of a big fish is a dark and constricted place. So is a heart that can't love beyond one's neighborhood and family.

PRAY:

"Let my heart be broken with the things that break the heart of God." (Bob Pierce)

FOR YOUR NEXT DEVOTIONAL READING, GO TO PAGE 1091.

> *"WHEN my life was ebbing away,*
> *I remembered you, LORD,*
> *and my prayer rose to you,*
> *to your holy temple."*
>
> JONAH 2:7

⁷ "When my life was ebbing away,
    I remembered you, LORD,
and my prayer rose to you,
    to your holy temple.

⁸ "Those who cling to worthless idols
    forfeit the grace that could be
        theirs.
⁹ But I, with a song of thanksgiving,
    will sacrifice to you.
What I have vowed I will make good.
    Salvation comes from the LORD."

¹⁰And the LORD commanded the fish, and it vomited Jonah onto dry land.

Jonah Goes to Nineveh

3 Then the word of the LORD came to Jonah a second time: ²"Go to the great city of Nineveh and proclaim to it the message I give you."

³Jonah obeyed the word of the LORD and went to Nineveh. Now Nineveh was a very important city—a visit required three days. ⁴On the first day, Jonah started into the city. He proclaimed: "Forty more days and Nineveh will be overturned." ⁵The Ninevites believed God. They declared a fast, and all of them, from the greatest to the least, put on sackcloth.

⁶When the news reached the king of Nineveh, he rose from his throne, took off his royal robes, covered himself with sackcloth and sat down in the dust. ⁷Then he issued a proclamation in Nineveh:

"By the decree of the king and his nobles:

Do not let any man or beast, herd or flock, taste anything; do not let them eat or drink. ⁸But let man and beast be covered with sackcloth. Let everyone call urgently on God. Let them give up their evil ways and their violence. ⁹Who knows? God may yet relent and with compassion turn from his fierce anger so that we will not perish."

¹⁰When God saw what they did and how they turned from their evil ways, he had compassion and did not bring upon them the destruction he had threatened.

Jonah's Anger at the LORD's Compassion

4 But Jonah was greatly displeased and became angry. ²He prayed to the LORD, "O LORD, is this not what I said when I was still at home? That is why I was so quick to flee to Tarshish. I knew that you are a gracious and compassionate God, slow to anger and abounding in love, a God who relents from sending calamity. ³Now, O LORD, take away my life, for it is better for me to die than to live."

⁴But the LORD replied, "Have you any right to be angry?"

⁵Jonah went out and sat down at a place east of the city. There he made himself a shelter, sat in its shade and waited to see what would happen to the city. ⁶Then the LORD God provided a vine and made it grow up over Jonah to give shade for his head to ease his discomfort, and Jonah was very happy about the vine. ⁷But at dawn the next day God provided a worm, which chewed the vine so that it withered. ⁸When the sun rose, God provided a scorching east wind, and the sun blazed on Jonah's head so that he grew faint. He wanted to die, and said, "It would be better for me to die than to live."

⁹But God said to Jonah, "Do you have a right to be angry about the vine?"

"I do," he said. "I am angry enough to die."

¹⁰But the LORD said, "You have been concerned about this vine, though you did not tend it or make it grow. It sprang up overnight and died overnight. ¹¹But Nineveh has more than a hundred and twenty thousand people who cannot tell their right hand from their left, and many cattle as well. Should I not be concerned about that great city?"

Micah

GOD IS not vague. Although he is beyond us, he doesn't typically say things that are totally over our heads. He wants to be understood and known—not comprehensively, for that would be impossible for us—but enough that we know how he wants us to act. We may never know the depths of God's truth while we live on Earth, but God has allowed us to wade in the shallows. How deep we go is a matter of grace, time and desire. The book of Micah contains one of the most famous summary statements in the entire Bible of what God wants us to know.

Micah 6:8 has been memorized, preached and even sung for centuries: "He has showed you, O man, what is good. And what does the LORD require of you? To act justly and to love mercy and to walk humbly with your God." There is nothing vague about that. There are other things God is equally definite about. He hates—repeat, *hates*—idolatry, injustice, rebellion and empty formalism in religion. If we open the book of Micah to just about any page, we will find expressions of God's loathing of these things. But he is just as definite about how much he loves to forgive the repentant. He loves to restore those who do what he hates. Micah exults in this: "Who is a God like you, who pardons sin and forgives the transgression of the remnant of his inheritance? You do not stay angry forever but delight to show mercy" (7:18). What could be better than to know exactly what God hates, loves and expects of us?

God is not vague, but humans are. Part of what it means to be a sinner is to know how to complicate the simple, confuse the unmistakable and qualify the unqualified. God responds likewise; to the pure he shows himself pure, to the shrewd he shows himself shrewd (see Psalm 18:25–27) and to the vague he seems vague. Reading a book like Micah scrubs the ambiguity out of our brains. It works like a splash of cold water on the face, or a compass in a forest pointing to true north. Read Micah, and don't be vague. Heartily agree with what God hates and loves. Offer him your praise, thanksgiving, petition and confession.

I WAIT FOR GOD MY SAVIOR; MY GOD WILL HEAR ME. (7:7)

1 The word of the LORD that came to Micah of Moresheth during the reigns of Jotham, Ahaz and Hezekiah, kings of Judah—the vision he saw concerning Samaria and Jerusalem.

² Hear, O peoples, all of you,
  listen, O earth and all who are in it,
that the Sovereign LORD may witness
  against you,
  the Lord from his holy temple.

> *Any prayer on my part is a conscious response to what God is already doing in my life.*
>
> MALCOLM BOYD

Judgment Against Samaria and Jerusalem

³ Look! The LORD is coming from his
  dwelling place;
he comes down and treads the high
  places of the earth.
⁴ The mountains melt beneath him
  and the valleys split apart,
like wax before the fire,
  like water rushing down a slope.
⁵ All this is because of Jacob's
  transgression,
  because of the sins of the house of
    Israel.
What is Jacob's transgression?
  Is it not Samaria?
What is Judah's high place?
  Is it not Jerusalem?

⁶ "Therefore I will make Samaria a
  heap of rubble,
  a place for planting vineyards.
I will pour her stones into the valley
  and lay bare her foundations.
⁷ All her idols will be broken to pieces;
  all her temple gifts will be burned
    with fire;
  I will destroy all her images.
Since she gathered her gifts from the
  wages of prostitutes,
as the wages of prostitutes they will
  again be used."

Weeping and Mourning

⁸ Because of this I will weep and wail;
  I will go about barefoot and naked.

I will howl like a jackal
  and moan like an owl.
⁹ For her wound is incurable;
  it has come to Judah.
It*ᵃ* has reached the very gate of my
  people,
  even to Jerusalem itself.
¹⁰ Tell it not in Gath*ᵇ*;
  weep not at all.*ᶜ*
In Beth Ophrah*ᵈ*
  roll in the dust.
¹¹ Pass on in nakedness and shame,
  you who live in Shaphir.*ᵉ*
Those who live in Zaanan*ᶠ*
  will not come out.
Beth Ezel is in mourning;
  its protection is taken from you.
¹² Those who live in Maroth*ᵍ* writhe
    in pain,
  waiting for relief,
because disaster has come from the
  LORD,
  even to the gate of Jerusalem.
¹³ You who live in Lachish,*ʰ*
  harness the team to the chariot.
You were the beginning of sin
  to the Daughter of Zion,
for the transgressions of Israel
  were found in you.
¹⁴ Therefore you will give parting gifts
  to Moresheth Gath.
The town of Aczib*ⁱ* will prove
    deceptive
  to the kings of Israel.
¹⁵ I will bring a conqueror against you
  who live in Mareshah.*ʲ*
He who is the glory of Israel
  will come to Adullam.
¹⁶ Shave your heads in mourning
  for the children in whom you
    delight;
make yourselves as bald as the
    vulture,
  for they will go from you into exile.

ᵃ9 Or *He*   *ᵇ10 Gath* sounds like the Hebrew for *tell.*   *ᶜ10* Hebrew; Septuagint may suggest *not in Acco.* The Hebrew for *in Acco* sounds like the Hebrew for *weep.*   *ᵈ10 Beth Ophrah* means *house of dust.*   *ᵉ11 Shaphir* means *pleasant.*   *ᶠ11 Zaanan* sounds like the Hebrew for *come out.*   *ᵍ12 Maroth* sounds like the Hebrew for *bitter.*   *ʰ13 Lachish* sounds like the Hebrew for *team.*   *ⁱ14 Aczib* means *deception.*   *ʲ15 Mareshah* sounds like the Hebrew for *conqueror.*

Man's Plans and God's

2 Woe to those who plan iniquity,
  to those who plot evil on their
    beds!
At morning's light they carry it out
  because it is in their power to do it.
[2] They covet fields and seize them,
  and houses, and take them.
They defraud a man of his home,
  a fellowman of his inheritance.

[3] Therefore, the LORD says:

"I am planning disaster against this
    people,
  from which you cannot save
    yourselves.
You will no longer walk proudly,
  for it will be a time of calamity.
[4] In that day men will ridicule you;
  they will taunt you with this
    mournful song:
'We are utterly ruined;
  my people's possession is divided
    up.
He takes it from me!
  He assigns our fields to traitors.'"

[5] Therefore you will have no one in the
    assembly of the LORD
  to divide the land by lot.

False Prophets

[6] "Do not prophesy," their prophets
    say.
"Do not prophesy about these
    things;
  disgrace will not overtake us."
[7] Should it be said, O house of Jacob:
"Is the Spirit of the LORD angry?
  Does he do such things?"

"Do not my words do good
  to him whose ways are upright?
[8] Lately my people have risen up
  like an enemy.
You strip off the rich robe
  from those who pass by without a
    care,
  like men returning from battle.
[9] You drive the women of my people
  from their pleasant homes.
You take away my blessing
  from their children forever.
[10] Get up, go away!
  For this is not your resting place,

because it is defiled,
  it is ruined, beyond all remedy.
[11] If a liar and deceiver comes and
    says,
'I will prophesy for you plenty of
    wine and beer,'
  he would be just the prophet for
    this people!

Deliverance Promised

[12] "I will surely gather all of you,
    O Jacob;
  I will surely bring together the
    remnant of Israel.
I will bring them together like sheep
    in a pen,
  like a flock in its pasture;
  the place will throng with people.
[13] One who breaks open the way will go
    up before them;
  they will break through the gate
    and go out.
Their king will pass through before
    them,
  the LORD at their head."

Leaders and Prophets Rebuked

3 Then I said,

"Listen, you leaders of Jacob,
  you rulers of the house of Israel.
Should you not know justice,
[2] you who hate good and love evil;
who tear the skin from my people
  and the flesh from their bones;
[3] who eat my people's flesh,
  strip off their skin
  and break their bones in pieces;
who chop them up like meat for the
    pan,
  like flesh for the pot?"

[4] Then they will cry out to the LORD,
  but he will not answer them.
At that time he will hide his face
    from them
  because of the evil they have
    done.

> *We cannot ask in behalf of Christ
> what Christ would not ask himself if he
> were praying.*
>
> A.B. SIMPSON

[5]This is what the LORD says:

"As for the prophets
  who lead my people astray,
if one feeds them,
  they proclaim 'peace';
if he does not,
  they prepare to wage war against
    him.
[6]Therefore night will come over you,
  without visions,
and darkness, without divination.
The sun will set for the prophets,
  and the day will go dark for them.
[7]The seers will be ashamed
  and the diviners disgraced.
They will all cover their faces
  because there is no answer from
    God."

> "THE SEERS will be ashamed
> and the diviners disgraced.
> They will all cover their faces
> because there is no answer
> from God."
>
> MICAH 3:7

[8]But as for me, I am filled with
    power,
  with the Spirit of the LORD,
  and with justice and might,
to declare to Jacob his transgression,
  to Israel his sin.
[9]Hear this, you leaders of the house
    of Jacob,
  you rulers of the house of Israel,
who despise justice
  and distort all that is right;
[10]who build Zion with bloodshed,
  and Jerusalem with wickedness.
[11]Her leaders judge for a bribe,
  her priests teach for a price,
  and her prophets tell fortunes for
    money.
Yet they lean upon the LORD and say,
  "Is not the LORD among us?
  No disaster will come upon us."
[12]Therefore because of you,
  Zion will be plowed like a field,
Jerusalem will become a heap of
    rubble,
  the temple hill a mound overgrown
    with thickets.

The Mountain of the LORD

4 In the last days

the mountain of the LORD's temple
    will be established
  as chief among the mountains;
it will be raised above the hills,
  and peoples will stream to it.

[2]Many nations will come and say,

"Come, let us go up to the mountain
    of the LORD,
  to the house of the God of Jacob.
He will teach us his ways,
  so that we may walk in his paths."
The law will go out from Zion,
  the word of the LORD from
    Jerusalem.
[3]He will judge between many peoples
  and will settle disputes for strong
    nations far and wide.
They will beat their swords into
    plowshares
  and their spears into pruning
    hooks.
Nation will not take up sword against
    nation,
  nor will they train for war anymore.
[4]Every man will sit under his own vine
  and under his own fig tree,
and no one will make them afraid,
  for the LORD Almighty has spoken.
[5]All the nations may walk
  in the name of their gods;
we will walk in the name of the LORD
  our God for ever and ever.

The LORD's Plan

[6]"In that day," declares the LORD,

"I will gather the lame;
  I will assemble the exiles
  and those I have brought to grief.
[7]I will make the lame a remnant,
  those driven away a strong nation.
The LORD will rule over them in
    Mount Zion
  from that day and forever.
[8]As for you, O watchtower of the flock,
  O stronghold[a] of the Daughter of
    Zion,
the former dominion will be restored
    to you;

[a]8 Or *hill*

kingship will come to the Daughter
of Jerusalem."

⁹ Why do you now cry aloud—
have you no king?
Has your counselor perished,
that pain seizes you like that of a
woman in labor?
¹⁰ Writhe in agony, O Daughter of Zion,
like a woman in labor,
for now you must leave the city
to camp in the open field.
You will go to Babylon;
there you will be rescued.

There the LORD will redeem you
out of the hand of your enemies.
¹¹ But now many nations
are gathered against you.
They say, "Let her be defiled,
let our eyes gloat over Zion!"
¹² But they do not know
the thoughts of the LORD;
they do not understand his plan,
he who gathers them like sheaves
to the threshing floor.
¹³ "Rise and thresh, O Daughter of Zion,
for I will give you horns of iron;

{WEDNESDAY}

MICAH 4:1–5

A Sign on the Rubble

4:1 THE MOUNTAIN OF THE LORD'S TEMPLE WILL BE ESTABLISHED AS CHIEF AMONG THE
MOUNTAINS; IT WILL BE RAISED ABOVE THE HILLS, AND PEOPLES WILL STREAM TO IT.

Builders often post signs on construction sites telling passersby what they're
building—a future restaurant, market or office complex, perhaps. This verse
is like a sign on a building site, except the site will be a heap of rubble
before it is a building. God said that before Mount Zion is established as
chief among all mountains, "Zion will be plowed like a field, Jerusalem will
become a heap of rubble, the temple hill a mound overgrown with thickets"
(3:12). Other nations will do this to execute God's judgment on Israel. One
day those other nations will stream back to the place they once destroyed
so they can learn about the Lord. The place of tragedy will become the
place of joy.

God loves to turn ashes into beauty and mourning into happiness. He
makes things that *are* out of things that *aren't*. He raises the dead. He makes
the blind see, the lame walk and infertile couples have babies. In the end,
an old and denuded heaven and earth will make way for a new heaven and
earth. Where we see only rubble, God sees possibilities and building
material. If your life is a mess, ask yourself—and ask the Lord—what kind
of sign is posted on the rubble? What new thing is God building?

Take these thoughts back to the text and go one step further: How can
you pray for a world that has seen so much bloodshed and oppression? If
God indeed makes the place of tragedy a place of joy, will you pray that he
will do it for the ancient hostility between Jews and Arabs? For the deep
hurt and bitterness of racism? For tribal and ethnic hatred that has poisoned
lives for centuries?

PRAY:
*Come, Lord, and rule over us! Settle the disputes and discord among peoples;
bring in your kingdom of peace. May we train for war no longer.*

FOR YOUR NEXT DEVOTIONAL READING, GO TO PAGE 1094.

I will give you hoofs of bronze
and you will break to pieces many
nations."
You will devote their ill-gotten gains
to the LORD,
their wealth to the Lord of all the
earth.

A Promised Ruler From Bethlehem

5 Marshal your troops, O city of
troops,[a]
for a siege is laid against us.
They will strike Israel's ruler
on the cheek with a rod.

2 "But you, Bethlehem Ephrathah,
though you are small among the
clans[b] of Judah,
out of you will come for me
one who will be ruler over Israel,
whose origins[c] are from of old,
from ancient times.[d]"

3 Therefore Israel will be abandoned
until the time when she who is in
labor gives birth
and the rest of his brothers return
to join the Israelites.

4 He will stand and shepherd his flock
in the strength of the LORD,
in the majesty of the name of the
LORD his God.
And they will live securely, for then
his greatness
will reach to the ends of the earth.
5 And he will be their peace.

Deliverance and Destruction

When the Assyrian invades our land
and marches through our
fortresses,
we will raise against him seven
shepherds,
even eight leaders of men.
6 They will rule[e] the land of Assyria
with the sword,
the land of Nimrod with drawn
sword.[f]
He will deliver us from the Assyrian
when he invades our land
and marches into our borders.

7 The remnant of Jacob will be
in the midst of many peoples
like dew from the LORD,
like showers on the grass,

which do not wait for man
or linger for mankind.
8 The remnant of Jacob will be among
the nations,
in the midst of many peoples,
like a lion among the beasts of the
forest,
like a young lion among flocks of
sheep,
which mauls and mangles as it goes,
and no one can rescue.
9 Your hand will be lifted up in triumph
over your enemies,
and all your foes will be destroyed.

10 "In that day," declares the LORD,

"I will destroy your horses from
among you
and demolish your chariots.
11 I will destroy the cities of your land
and tear down all your strongholds.
12 I will destroy your witchcraft
and you will no longer cast spells.
13 I will destroy your carved images
and your sacred stones from
among you;
you will no longer bow down
to the work of your hands.
14 I will uproot from among you your
Asherah poles[g]
and demolish your cities.
15 I will take vengeance in anger and
wrath
upon the nations that have not
obeyed me."

The LORD's Case Against Israel

6 Listen to what the LORD says:

"Stand up, plead your case before the
mountains;
let the hills hear what you have to
say.
2 Hear, O mountains, the LORD's
accusation;
listen, you everlasting foundations
of the earth.
For the LORD has a case against his
people;
he is lodging a charge against
Israel.

---

a 1 Or *Strengthen your walls, O walled city*
b 2 Or *rulers*   *c 2* Hebrew *goings out*
d 2 Or *from days of eternity*   *e 6* Or *crush*
f 6 Or *Nimrod in its gates*   *g 14* That is, symbols
of the goddess Asherah

³ "My people, what have I done to you?
How have I burdened you? Answer
me.
⁴ I brought you up out of Egypt
and redeemed you from the land of
slavery.
I sent Moses to lead you,
also Aaron and Miriam.
⁵ My people, remember
what Balak king of Moab counseled
and what Balaam son of Beor
answered.
Remember ⌊your journey⌋ from
Shittim to Gilgal,
that you may know the righteous
acts of the LORD."

⁶ With what shall I come before the
LORD
and bow down before the exalted
God?
Shall I come before him with burnt
offerings,
with calves a year old?
⁷ Will the LORD be pleased with
thousands of rams,
with ten thousand rivers of oil?
Shall I offer my firstborn for my
transgression,
the fruit of my body for the sin of
my soul?
⁸ He has showed you, O man, what is
good.
And what does the LORD require
of you?
To act justly and to love mercy
and to walk humbly with your God.

Israel's Guilt and Punishment

⁹ Listen! The LORD is calling to the
city—
and to fear your name is wisdom—
"Heed the rod and the One who
appointed it.ᵃ
¹⁰ Am I still to forget, O wicked house,
your ill-gotten treasures
and the short ephah,ᵇ which is
accursed?
¹¹ Shall I acquit a man with dishonest
scales,
with a bag of false weights?
¹² Her rich men are violent;
her people are liars
and their tongues speak
deceitfully.

¹³ Therefore, I have begun to destroy
you,
to ruin you because of your sins.
¹⁴ You will eat but not be satisfied;
your stomach will still be empty.ᶜ
You will store up but save nothing,
because what you save I will give to
the sword.
¹⁵ You will plant but not harvest;
you will press olives but not use the
oil on yourselves,
you will crush grapes but not drink
the wine.
¹⁶ You have observed the statutes of
Omri
and all the practices of Ahab's
house,
and you have followed their
traditions.
Therefore I will give you over to ruin
and your people to derision;
you will bear the scorn of the
nations.ᵈ"

Israel's Misery

7 What misery is mine!
I am like one who gathers summer
fruit
at the gleaning of the vineyard;
there is no cluster of grapes to eat,
none of the early figs that I crave.
² The godly have been swept from the
land;
not one upright man remains.
All men lie in wait to shed blood;
each hunts his brother with a net.
³ Both hands are skilled in doing evil;
the ruler demands gifts,
the judge accepts bribes,
the powerful dictate what they
desire—
they all conspire together.
⁴ The best of them is like a brier,
the most upright worse than a
thorn hedge.
The day of your watchmen has come,
the day God visits you.
Now is the time of their confusion.
⁵ Do not trust a neighbor;
put no confidence in a friend.

ᵃ9 The meaning of the Hebrew for this line is
uncertain.   ᵇ10 An ephah was a dry measure.
ᶜ14 The meaning of the Hebrew for this word is
uncertain.   ᵈ16 Septuagint; Hebrew scorn due
my people

Even with her who lies in your
embrace
be careful of your words.
⁶ For a son dishonors his father,
a daughter rises up against her
mother,
a daughter-in-law against her
mother-in-law—
a man's enemies are the members
of his own household.

⁷ But as for me, I watch in hope for
the LORD,
I wait for God my Savior;
my God will hear me.

Israel Will Rise

⁸ Do not gloat over me, my enemy!
Though I have fallen, I will rise.
Though I sit in darkness,
the LORD will be my light.

[THURSDAY]

MICAH 6:8

Good in the Best Sense of the Word

6:8 AND WHAT DOES THE LORD REQUIRE OF YOU?

God works on us from inside and out. In the Ten Commandments, he starts with the deep things: No god but God; no idols; no dishonoring God's name; keep the Sabbath holy. These are the foundational principles, the building blocks for all the rest: Honor your parents; don't murder; don't commit adultery; don't steal; don't lie; don't covet (see Exodus 20:3–17). A right relationship with God is the basis for a right relationship with people. The greatest command is to love God with your whole being. The second greatest command is to love your neighbor as yourself (see Matthew 22:36–40).

Micah's famous summary of God's requirements starts on the outside and works inwardly. "To act justly" is essential morality, ethics, basic human decency, giving others their due. It's a good place to start, but not to end. These acts must not be only external; they must come from the heart. Merely to do the right thing without love and understanding, to borrow a phrase from Mark Twain, is to be a good person, but in the worst sense of the word. That's why Micah adds, "to love mercy." Justice done only because it is right is better than no justice at all. It's like taking out the trash in a household. The house will be a lot worse if it's not done, but not a lot better if it is. Trash taken out for love can be almost sacramental in its impact, just as justice done for love of mercy can heal whole societies. Good laws alone can't make good people, but love can make good laws work powerfully.

Love is a matter of the heart. What if our hearts don't love justice? How can we make our hearts be what they are not? Only God can do that. Micah's list ends with "to walk humbly with your God." Life with God enlivens life with others. "We love because he first loved us" (1 John 4:19) means that if we let God love us, we will love others too. To pray is to let God love us. Who we become in the presence of God will impact the world around us in love of mercy and acts of justice. It will make us good in the best sense of the word.

PRAY:

Righteous Father, work from the inside out to infect me with a humble
and intimate walk with you, with a love for mercy, and with acts of justice.

FOR YOUR NEXT DEVOTIONAL READING, GO TO PAGE 1098.

9 Because I have sinned against him,
  I will bear the LORD's wrath,
until he pleads my case
  and establishes my right.
He will bring me out into the light;
  I will see his righteousness.
10 Then my enemy will see it
  and will be covered with shame,
she who said to me,
  "Where is the LORD your God?"
My eyes will see her downfall;
  even now she will be trampled
    underfoot
  like mire in the streets.

11 The day for building your walls will
    come,
  the day for extending your
    boundaries.
12 In that day people will come to you
  from Assyria and the cities of Egypt,
even from Egypt to the Euphrates
  and from sea to sea
  and from mountain to mountain.
13 The earth will become desolate
    because of its inhabitants,
  as the result of their deeds.

Prayer and Praise

14 Shepherd your people with your staff,
  the flock of your inheritance,
which lives by itself in a forest,
  in fertile pasturelands.ᵃ
Let them feed in Bashan and Gilead
  as in days long ago.

15 "As in the days when you came out
    of Egypt,
  I will show them my wonders."

16 Nations will see and be ashamed,
  deprived of all their power.

They will lay their hands on their
    mouths
  and their ears will become deaf.
17 They will lick dust like a snake,
  like creatures that crawl on the
    ground.
They will come trembling out of their
    dens;
  they will turn in fear to the LORD
    our God
  and will be afraid of you.
18 Who is a God like you,
  who pardons sin and forgives the
    transgression
  of the remnant of his inheritance?
You do not stay angry forever
  but delight to show mercy.

> WHO is a God like you,
>   who pardons sin and forgives the
>   transgression
>   of the remnant of his inheritance?
> You do not stay angry forever
>   but delight to show mercy.
>
> MICAH 7:18

19 You will again have compassion
    on us;
  you will tread our sins underfoot
  and hurl all our iniquities into the
    depths of the sea.
20 You will be true to Jacob,
  and show mercy to Abraham,
as you pledged on oath to our
    fathers
  in days long ago.

ᵃ 14 Or *in the middle of Carmel*

Nahum

IT'S THE same God. Read the book of Jonah and hear of God's merciful pardon of the wicked people of Nineveh; then read the book of Nahum and hear of his plans to destroy them. The same God does both. God himself is infinite, but his patience is not. There comes a time when his holy love and wisdom deem it time to stop being patient. The message of Nahum is that this very time has come. Nineveh's unrepentant evil will bring God's righteous wrath to the city.

The Chinese word for "crisis" is made up of two characters: *way* and *gee*. Each of these forms half the word; the first means *danger*; the second indicates *opportunity*. A crisis by this definition is literally a "dangerous opportunity." As with any proclamation of God's word, Jonah's preaching to the city brought a crisis— a dangerous opportunity—to Nineveh. The opportunity was to live in God's favor; the danger was not to. Otherwise, one day the preaching of a Jonah will give way to the preaching of a Nahum.

All prayer for the lost is crisis praying. There should be urgency to our intercession, for one day time will run out. When that happens, there will be no more opportunity, only danger. "Now is the time of God's favor" (2 Corinthians 6:2) doesn't necessarily mean that tomorrow will be the same.

THE LORD IS SLOW TO ANGER AND GREAT IN POWER; THE LORD WILL NOT LEAVE THE GUILTY UNPUNISHED. (1:3)

1 An oracle concerning Nineveh. The book of the vision of Nahum the El-koshite.

The LORD's Anger Against Nineveh

2 The LORD is a jealous and avenging God;
  the LORD takes vengeance and is filled with wrath.
The LORD takes vengeance on his foes
  and maintains his wrath against his enemies.
3 The LORD is slow to anger and great in power;
  the LORD will not leave the guilty unpunished.
His way is in the whirlwind and the storm,
  and clouds are the dust of his feet.
4 He rebukes the sea and dries it up;
  he makes all the rivers run dry.
Bashan and Carmel wither
  and the blossoms of Lebanon fade.
5 The mountains quake before him
  and the hills melt away.
The earth trembles at his presence,
  the world and all who live in it.
6 Who can withstand his indignation?
  Who can endure his fierce anger?
His wrath is poured out like fire;
  the rocks are shattered before him.
7 The LORD is good,
  a refuge in times of trouble.
He cares for those who trust in him,
8   but with an overwhelming flood
he will make an end of ˌNinevehˌ;
  he will pursue his foes into darkness.

9 Whatever they plot against the LORD
  heª will bring to an end;
  trouble will not come a second time.
10 They will be entangled among thorns
  and drunk from their wine;
  they will be consumed like dry stubble.ᵇ

THE LORD is good,
  a refuge in times of trouble.
He cares for those who trust in him.

NAHUM 1:7

---

11 From you, ˌO Nineveh,ˌ has one come forth
  who plots evil against the LORD
  and counsels wickedness.

12 This is what the LORD says:

"Although they have allies and are numerous,
  they will be cut off and pass away.
Although I have afflicted you,
  ˌO Judah,ˌ
  I will afflict you no more.
13 Now I will break their yoke from your neck
  and tear your shackles away."

14 The LORD has given a command concerning you, ˌNinevehˌ:
"You will have no descendants to bear your name.
I will destroy the carved images and cast idols
  that are in the temple of your gods.
I will prepare your grave,
  for you are vile."

15 Look, there on the mountains,
  the feet of one who brings good news,
  who proclaims peace!
Celebrate your festivals, O Judah,
  and fulfill your vows.
No more will the wicked invade you;
  they will be completely destroyed.

Nineveh to Fall

2 An attacker advances against you, ˌNinevehˌ.
  Guard the fortress,
  watch the road,
  brace yourselves,
  marshal all your strength!

2 The LORD will restore the splendor of Jacob
  like the splendor of Israel,
though destroyers have laid them waste
  and have ruined their vines.

3 The shields of his soldiers are red;
  the warriors are clad in scarlet.

ª9 Or *What do you foes plot against the LORD? / He*
ᵇ10 The meaning of the Hebrew for this verse is uncertain.

NAHUM 1:1–8

Holy Jealousy

1:2 THE LORD IS A JEALOUS AND AVENGING GOD.

The "avenging" part of this verse is more palatable to our religious sensibilities than the "jealous" part. However, jealousy has gotten a bad name because it's been used indiscriminately. In fact, jealousy is more than a morally legitimate word in love's vocabulary—it is a necessity. If promises were made to be faithful and loyal forever, no matter what, not being jealous if those promises are broken is morally reprehensible. Picture this scenario between a married couple: "You say you're having an affair? All right; just let me know if you'll be in late tonight. I'll leave the porch light on for you." It doesn't work that way. In the same way, God's jealousy is his holy passion for his bride.

In the context of Nahum 1, God's passion for his people will show itself by avenging the evil the Assyrians (represented by Nineveh, the capital city) have wrought on Israel. There is an important principle at work here. Sometimes, when God's people are unfaithful to him, his jealousy for them stirs him to anger. When this happens, he will sometimes use other nations as his instruments of justice. Unwittingly, Assyria was one of these nations. God used their evil imperial schemes to conquer other nations to punish his people for their unfaithfulness. But Assyria's plans were still evil, so once God used them to punish the Israelites, he then punished the Assyrians themselves. In both cases it was his jealousy at work: in one case against his people with Assyria; in the other case against Assyria—*for* his people!

The point of this passage is that God is supremely good (see verse 7). He will accept no rivals and will leave no sin unpunished. He will love his chosen ones with a vengeance, and he will wound those he uses to do the wounding. God knows what he is doing! "Nothing in all creation is hidden from God's sight. Everything is uncovered and laid bare before the eyes of him to whom we must give account" (Hebrews 4:13).

Sometimes it is good to pause and consider this God to whom we often speak so glibly in prayer and to be moved to greater wonder and reverence for his holy love. "He is terribly tender and terribly demanding, terribly loving and terribly stern, terribly soft and terribly hard."[1] In other words, God loves us the way we all want and need to be loved.

PRAY:

Holy One, you are God and I am not. Your thoughts are not my thoughts,
and your ways are not my ways. I thank you that they are not.

FOR YOUR NEXT DEVOTIONAL READING, GO TO PAGE 1100.

The metal on the chariots flashes
on the day they are made ready;
the spears of pine are brandished.[a]
⁴ The chariots storm through the
streets,
rushing back and forth through the
squares.
They look like flaming torches;
they dart about like lightning.

⁵ He summons his picked troops,
yet they stumble on their way.
They dash to the city wall;
the protective shield is put in place.
⁶ The river gates are thrown open
and the palace collapses.
⁷ It is decreed[b] that ⌊the city⌋
be exiled and carried away.
Its slave girls moan like doves
and beat upon their breasts.
⁸ Nineveh is like a pool,
and its water is draining away.
"Stop! Stop!" they cry,
but no one turns back.
⁹ Plunder the silver!
Plunder the gold!
The supply is endless,
the wealth from all its treasures!
¹⁰ She is pillaged, plundered, stripped!
Hearts melt, knees give way,
bodies tremble, every face grows
pale.

> More tears are shed over answered
> prayers than unanswered ones.
>
> MOTHER TERESA

¹¹ Where now is the lions' den,
the place where they fed their
young,
where the lion and lioness went,
and the cubs, with nothing to fear?
¹² The lion killed enough for his cubs
and strangled the prey for his
mate,
filling his lairs with the kill
and his dens with the prey.
¹³ "I am against you,"
declares the LORD Almighty.
"I will burn up your chariots in
smoke,
and the sword will devour your
young lions.

I will leave you no prey on the earth.
The voices of your messengers
will no longer be heard."

Woe to Nineveh

3 Woe to the city of blood,
full of lies,
full of plunder,
never without victims!
² The crack of whips,
the clatter of wheels,
galloping horses
and jolting chariots!
³ Charging cavalry,
flashing swords
and glittering spears!
Many casualties,
piles of dead,
bodies without number,
people stumbling over the corpses—
⁴ all because of the wanton lust of a
harlot,
alluring, the mistress of sorceries,
who enslaved nations by her
prostitution
and peoples by her witchcraft.

⁵ "I am against you," declares the LORD
Almighty.
"I will lift your skirts over your face.
I will show the nations your
nakedness
and the kingdoms your shame.
⁶ I will pelt you with filth,
I will treat you with contempt
and make you a spectacle.
⁷ All who see you will flee from you
and say,
'Nineveh is in ruins—who will
mourn for her?'
Where can I find anyone to comfort
you?"

⁸ Are you better than Thebes,[c]
situated on the Nile,
with water around her?
The river was her defense,
the waters her wall.
⁹ Cush[d] and Egypt were her boundless
strength;
Put and Libya were among her
allies.

---

[a]3 Hebrew; Septuagint and Syriac / the horsemen
rush to and fro   [b]7 The meaning of the Hebrew
for this word is uncertain.   [c]8 Hebrew No
Amon   [d]9 That is, the upper Nile region

So That You May Know Me

THE OPPORTUNITY she had long prayed for and was sure would come
had finally arrived: Elisabeth Elliot could now enter the village of the people
that had murdered her husband two years before. Elisabeth Elliot's
husband, Jim, was one of five missionaries murdered by the Auca Indians
on the banks of the Curaray River deep in the Ecuadorian jungle. Elliot
wrote of this opportunity: "The decision to accept or not—ordinarily one I
would have made quickly and without much difficulty—struck me this time
as being rather an important one. I prayed about it … the answer was a
strong affirmative—I should go."[2]

Elisabeth Elliot journeyed to the Auca village with her young daughter
Valerie and Rachel Saint, the sister of Nate Saint, another of the murdered
missionaries. Elliot and her daughter lived among the Aucas for two years,
long enough to see many come to Christ. She tells her story in *The Savage
My Kinsman*. Today there is a thriving church among the Aucas.

During that time and afterward, Elliot asked herself, "What is a
missionary?" Her initial answer had to do with things that fall under the
general heading of philanthropy: things like preaching, teaching, church-
building, medical work, baptizing, catechizing and social work. But as she
reflected on her time with the Aucas, she realized that she couldn't do any
of these things for them. Her questions took her back to the Scriptures,
where the word missionary was nowhere to be found. However, what she
did find in many passages was the word "witness." One passage in particular
arrested her, Isaiah 43:10: "'You are my witnesses,' declares the LORD, 'and
my servant whom I have chosen, *so that you may know and believe me* and
understand that I am he'" (italics added). Here the purpose of a witness is

above all to know, understand and believe God. Everything a witness does is a means to this end.

"He will go to any lengths to teach us, and his manipulation of the movements of men—Aucas, missionaries, whomever—is never accidental. Those movements may be *incidental* to the one thing towards which he goads us: the recognition of Christ."[3] Elliot believed that her husband and his friends went into harm's way because they believed God wanted them to do it—and that in order to know God, one must obey God. It was the knowing that made the obeying worthwhile. They took literally the words of 1 John 2:17, "The world and its desires pass away, but the man who does the will of God lives forever."

Elliot's insight has profound implications for the meaning of prayer. Prayer is often thought of only as a means to an end: for guidance and healing, for evangelistic and missionary success. But if the ultimate meaning of these things is that Christ may be known, should we not also see the true end of prayer as the same thing? We pray that Christ may be known, and as we pray, we come to know him better. The greatest gift of prayer is not the answer but the Answerer.

PRAY:

Jesus, it is the pleasure of your company that makes prayer and service worthwhile. Make me aware of your sweet presence that I may serve you with gladness all my days.

MEMORIZE:

I want to know Christ and the power of his resurrection and the fellowship of sharing in his sufferings, becoming like him in his death, and so, somehow, to attain to the resurrection from the dead. PHILIPPIANS 3:10–11

FOR YOUR NEXT DEVOTIONAL READING, GO TO PAGE 1107.

¹⁰ Yet she was taken captive
and went into exile.
Her infants were dashed to pieces
at the head of every street.
Lots were cast for her nobles,
and all her great men were put in
chains.
¹¹ You too will become drunk;
you will go into hiding
and seek refuge from the enemy.

¹² All your fortresses are like fig trees
with their first ripe fruit;
when they are shaken,
the figs fall into the mouth of the
eater.
¹³ Look at your troops—
they are all women!
The gates of your land
are wide open to your enemies;
fire has consumed their bars.

¹⁴ Draw water for the siege,
strengthen your defenses!
Work the clay,
tread the mortar,
repair the brickwork!
¹⁵ There the fire will devour you;
the sword will cut you down
and, like grasshoppers, consume
you.

Multiply like grasshoppers,
multiply like locusts!
¹⁶ You have increased the number of
your merchants
till they are more than the stars of
the sky,
but like locusts they strip the land
and then fly away.
¹⁷ Your guards are like locusts,
your officials like swarms of locusts
that settle in the walls on a cold
day—
but when the sun appears they fly
away,
and no one knows where.

¹⁸ O king of Assyria, your shepherds*a*
slumber;
your nobles lie down to rest.
Your people are scattered on the
mountains
with no one to gather them.
¹⁹ Nothing can heal your wound;
your injury is fatal.
Everyone who hears the news about
you
claps his hands at your fall,
for who has not felt
your endless cruelty?

a 18 Or *rulers*

Habakkuk

THE TALMUD records the judgment of one rabbi who says, "Moses gave Israel 613 commandments, David reduced them to ten, Isaiah to two, Habakkuk to one: *the righteous shall live by his faith*" (see Habakkuk 2:4).[1] It could be argued that Martin Luther's understanding of this same verse as Paul used it in his Romans epistle (see Romans 1:17) sparked the Protestant Reformation and changed the history of the world. It was a God-given insight that came to Habakkuk in a great crisis of faith.

The very thought that God would use an evil nation like Babylon to punish Israel was unthinkable to Habakkuk.[2] But that was exactly what God was doing. He said, "Look at the nations and watch—and be utterly amazed. For I am going to do something in your days that you would not believe, even if you were told" (1:5). That was certainly true! All Habakkuk could think to say in reply was, "Your eyes are too pure to look on evil; you cannot tolerate wrong. Why then do you tolerate the treacherous?" (1:13). The Lord's reply was to wait and see what would happen. Judgment would come to Babylon, too: "For the revelation awaits an appointed time; it speaks of the end and will not prove false. Though it linger, wait for it; it will certainly come and will not delay" (2:3). It is after this that God tells Habakkuk and all his people that "the righteous will live by his faith" (2:4). In other words, "You don't see the whole picture, but I do, and I will do what is right. You're right: I cannot tolerate wrong. Trust me and wait, and you will see just how true that is."

The hardest part of prayer is the waiting. The faith of some has weakened and faltered because of it. But what was true for Habakkuk is true for us: "Though it linger, wait for it; it will certainly come and will not delay."

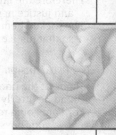

HIS GLORY COVERED THE HEAVENS AND HIS PRAISE FILLED THE EARTH. (3:3)

1 The oracle that Habakkuk the prophet received.

Habakkuk's Complaint

2 How long, O LORD, must I call for
help,
but you do not listen?
Or cry out to you, "Violence!"
but you do not save?
3 Why do you make me look at
injustice?
Why do you tolerate wrong?
Destruction and violence are before
me;
there is strife, and conflict
abounds.
4 Therefore the law is paralyzed,
and justice never prevails.
The wicked hem in the righteous,
so that justice is perverted.

The LORD's Answer

5 "Look at the nations and watch—
and be utterly amazed.
For I am going to do something in
your days
that you would not believe,
even if you were told.
6 I am raising up the Babylonians,[a]
that ruthless and impetuous
people,
who sweep across the whole earth
to seize dwelling places not their
own.
7 They are a feared and dreaded
people;
they are a law to themselves
and promote their own honor.
8 Their horses are swifter than
leopards,
fiercer than wolves at dusk.
Their cavalry gallops headlong;
their horsemen come from afar.
They fly like a vulture swooping to
devour;
9 they all come bent on violence.
Their hordes[b] advance like a desert
wind
and gather prisoners like sand.
10 They deride kings
and scoff at rulers.
They laugh at all fortified cities;
they build earthen ramps and
capture them.

11 Then they sweep past like the wind
and go on—
guilty men, whose own strength is
their god."

Habakkuk's Second Complaint

12 O LORD, are you not from everlasting?
My God, my Holy One, we will not
die.
O LORD, you have appointed them to
execute judgment;
O Rock, you have ordained them to
punish.
13 Your eyes are too pure to look
on evil;
you cannot tolerate wrong.
Why then do you tolerate the
treacherous?
Why are you silent while the
wicked
swallow up those more righteous
than themselves?
14 You have made men like fish in
the sea,
like sea creatures that have no
ruler.
15 The wicked foe pulls all of them up
with hooks,
he catches them in his net,
he gathers them up in his dragnet;
and so he rejoices and is glad.
16 Therefore he sacrifices to his net
and burns incense to his dragnet,
for by his net he lives in luxury
and enjoys the choicest food.
17 Is he to keep on emptying his net,
destroying nations without mercy?

> 66 *No man ever prayed heartily without
> learning something.* 99
>
> RALPH WALDO EMERSON

2 I will stand at my watch
and station myself on the
ramparts;
I will look to see what he will say
to me,
and what answer I am to give to
this complaint.[c]

---

[a]6 Or *Chaldeans*   [b]9 The meaning of the
Hebrew for this word is uncertain.   [c]1 Or *and
what to answer when I am rebuked*

The Lord's Answer

² Then the Lord replied:

"Write down the revelation
  and make it plain on tablets
  so that a herald[a] may run with it.
³ For the revelation awaits an
    appointed time;
  it speaks of the end
  and will not prove false.
Though it linger, wait for it;
  it[b] will certainly come and will not
    delay.

⁴ "See, he is puffed up;
  his desires are not upright—
  but the righteous will live by his
    faith[c]—
⁵ indeed, wine betrays him;
  he is arrogant and never at rest.
Because he is as greedy as the grave[d]
  and like death is never satisfied,
he gathers to himself all the nations
  and takes captive all the peoples.

⁶ "Will not all of them taunt him with
  ridicule and scorn, saying,

" 'Woe to him who piles up stolen
    goods
  and makes himself wealthy by
    extortion!
How long must this go on?'
⁷ Will not your debtors[e] suddenly arise?
  Will they not wake up and make
    you tremble?
  Then you will become their victim.
⁸ Because you have plundered many
    nations,
  the peoples who are left will
    plunder you.
For you have shed man's blood;
  you have destroyed lands and cities
  and everyone in them.

⁹ "Woe to him who builds his realm by
    unjust gain
  to set his nest on high,
  to escape the clutches of ruin!
¹⁰ You have plotted the ruin of many
    peoples,
  shaming your own house and
    forfeiting your life.
¹¹ The stones of the wall will cry out,
  and the beams of the woodwork
    will echo it.

¹² "Woe to him who builds a city with
    bloodshed
  and establishes a town by crime!
¹³ Has not the Lord Almighty
    determined
  that the people's labor is only fuel
    for the fire,
  that the nations exhaust
    themselves for nothing?
¹⁴ For the earth will be filled with the
    knowledge of the glory of the
    Lord,
  as the waters cover the sea.

¹⁵ "Woe to him who gives drink to his
    neighbors,
  pouring it from the wineskin till
    they are drunk,
  so that he can gaze on their naked
    bodies.
¹⁶ You will be filled with shame instead
    of glory.
  Now it is your turn! Drink and be
    exposed[f]!
The cup from the Lord's right hand is
    coming around to you,
  and disgrace will cover your glory.
¹⁷ The violence you have done to
    Lebanon will overwhelm you,
  and your destruction of animals
    will terrify you.
For you have shed man's blood;
  you have destroyed lands and cities
  and everyone in them.

¹⁸ "Of what value is an idol, since a man
    has carved it?
  Or an image that teaches lies?
For he who makes it trusts in his own
    creation;
  he makes idols that cannot speak.
¹⁹ Woe to him who says to wood, 'Come
    to life!'
  Or to lifeless stone, 'Wake up!'
Can it give guidance?
  It is covered with gold and silver;
  there is no breath in it.
²⁰ But the Lord is in his holy temple;
  let all the earth be silent before
    him."

---

a 2 Or *so that whoever reads it*   *b 3* Or *Though
he linger, wait for him; / he*   *c 4* Or *faithfulness*
d 5 Hebrew *Sheol*   *e 7* Or *creditors*
f 16 Masoretic Text; Dead Sea Scrolls, Aquila,
Vulgate and Syriac (see also Septuagint) *and
stagger*

Habakkuk's Prayer

3 A prayer of Habakkuk the prophet.
On *shigionoth*.[a]

[2] LORD, I have heard of your fame;
I stand in awe of your deeds, O LORD.
Renew them in our day,
in our time make them known;
in wrath remember mercy.

[3] God came from Teman,
the Holy One from Mount Paran.
Selah[b]

His glory covered the heavens
and his praise filled the earth.
[4] His splendor was like the sunrise;
rays flashed from his hand,
where his power was hidden.
[5] Plague went before him;
pestilence followed his steps.
[6] He stood, and shook the earth;
he looked, and made the nations
tremble.
The ancient mountains crumbled
and the age-old hills collapsed.
His ways are eternal.
[7] I saw the tents of Cushan in distress,
the dwellings of Midian in anguish.

[8] Were you angry with the rivers,
O LORD?
Was your wrath against the
streams?
Did you rage against the sea
when you rode with your horses
and your victorious chariots?
[9] You uncovered your bow,
you called for many arrows.   *Selah*
You split the earth with rivers;
[10] the mountains saw you and writhed.
Torrents of water swept by;
the deep roared
and lifted its waves on high.

[11] Sun and moon stood still in the
heavens
at the glint of your flying arrows,
at the lightning of your flashing
spear.
[12] In wrath you strode through the earth
and in anger you threshed the
nations.

[13] You came out to deliver your people,
to save your anointed one.
You crushed the leader of the land of
wickedness,
you stripped him from head
to foot.   *Selah*
[14] With his own spear you pierced his
head
when his warriors stormed out to
scatter us,
gloating as though about to devour
the wretched who were in hiding.
[15] You trampled the sea with your
horses,
churning the great waters.

[16] I heard and my heart pounded,
my lips quivered at the sound;
decay crept into my bones,
and my legs trembled.
Yet I will wait patiently for the day of
calamity
to come on the nation invading us.
[17] Though the fig tree does not bud
and there are no grapes on the
vines,
though the olive crop fails
and the fields produce no food,
though there are no sheep in the pen
and no cattle in the stalls,
[18] yet I will rejoice in the LORD,
I will be joyful in God my Savior.

[19] The Sovereign LORD is my strength;
he makes my feet like the feet of
a deer,
he enables me to go on the heights.

For the director of music. On my
stringed instruments.

> THE Sovereign LORD is my strength;
> he makes my feet like the feet
> of a deer,
> he enables me to go on the heights.
>
> HABAKKUK 3:19

[a]1 Probably a literary or musical term
[b]3 A word of uncertain meaning; possibly a
musical term; also in verses 9 and 13

Though ... Yet

3:18 YET I WILL REJOICE IN THE LORD.

It may be a little scary, but make a list of the worst things you can think of that could happen to you. Read each of them to God, with the preface, "Though ..." and the response, "Yet I will rejoice in the LORD, I will be joyful in God my Savior" (3:18). When you are through the list, end with verse 19: "The Sovereign LORD is my strength; he makes my feet like the feet of a deer, he enables me to go on the heights."

If you do this, you will do as Habakkuk did in this spectacular faith-text. In verse 17, he lists the kind of things that will probably come with a Babylonian invasion: no living plants, no crops, no livestock. Then he ends his worst-case scenario with "yet I will rejoice in the LORD" (verse 18).

The statement, "He makes my feet like the feet of a deer, he enables me to go on the heights" is likely more complex than it looks. Obviously, Habakkuk is praying that God will make him sure-footed, no matter what high and dangerous places he may have to tread in the future. He may also be saying more. "High places" in the Bible usually refers to places under the control of demonic forces, places of pagan worship. False prophets chose these places for worship because they symbolized power; those who have the high ground in a battle generally control the action. The faith of Habakkuk is that God may lead him to dangerous and dark places. But his feet will not slip; in fact, he will take the high ground and, with it, possession of the land!

This passage can be used with another great passage of faith, Romans 8:37–39. Pray these passages antiphonally as shown below.

"No, in all these things we are more than conquerors through him who loved us."

"He makes my feet like the feet of a deer, he enables me to go on the heights."

"For I am convinced that neither death nor life, neither angels nor demons, neither the present nor the future, nor any powers, neither height nor depth, nor anything else in all creation ..."

"Though the fig tree does not bud and there are no grapes on the vines, though the olive crop fails and the fields produce no food, though there are no sheep in the pen and no cattle in the stalls ..."

"will be able to separate us from the love of God that is in Christ Jesus our Lord."

"yet I will rejoice in the LORD."

This is the faith the righteous live by!

PRAY:
Try the prayer exercise suggested above.

FOR YOUR NEXT DEVOTIONAL READING, GO TO PAGE 1111.

Zephaniah

IN ZEPHANIAH 1:7, there is as grisly a picture of God's judgment as there is anywhere in the Bible: "The LORD has prepared a sacrifice; he has consecrated those he has invited." It's just one line, and there aren't any elaborate adjectives in it, but the picture is horrible. The "sacrifice" referred to the people of Israel; the consecrated guests would be their Babylonian conquerors. Every Jew knew what sacrificing entailed: slitting an animal's throat, butchering the carcass, eating a portion of the meat and burning the remains. That's what the pagan Babylonians, as God's consecrated ones, were going to do to the Israelites as they feasted on the plunder.

SEEK RIGHTEOUSNESS, SEEK HUMILITY; PERHAPS YOU WILL BE SHELTERED ON THE DAY OF THE LORD'S ANGER. (2:3)

Descriptions of ancient battles confirm the brutality of which these consecrated ones were capable. This type of judgment was shockingly pertinent to Israel's sin: Since they wouldn't offer themselves as living sacrifices to God in their actions, God himself would make a deadly sacrifice of them in judgment.

Zephaniah is absorbed by the theme of judgment, generally toward Israel and its enemies but really toward the whole world. He writes God's words, "I have decided to assemble the nations, to gather the kingdoms and to pour my wrath on them—all my fierce anger. The whole world will be consumed by the fire of my jealous anger" (3:8).

What does this mean for those who pray that God's kingdom will come? It means that one day time will run out, and those who refused to pray will suddenly pray for mountains and rocks to fall on them and hide them from the wrath of God (see Revelation 6:15–17). It means our prayers should be sober and urgent; for every prayer for Jesus to come implies a prayer for the great and final cosmic Day of the Lord, of which Zephaniah's prophecy was but a foretaste.

1 The word of the LORD that came to Zephaniah son of Cushi, the son of Gedaliah, the son of Amariah, the son of Hezekiah, during the reign of Josiah son of Amon king of Judah:

Warning of Coming Destruction

2 "I will sweep away everything
from the face of the earth,"
declares the LORD.
3 "I will sweep away both men and
animals;
I will sweep away the birds of the
air
and the fish of the sea.
The wicked will have only heaps of
rubble[a]
when I cut off man from the face
of the earth,"
declares the LORD.

Against Judah

4 "I will stretch out my hand against
Judah
and against all who live in
Jerusalem.
I will cut off from this place every
remnant of Baal,
the names of the pagan and the
idolatrous priests—
5 those who bow down on the roofs
to worship the starry host,
those who bow down and swear by
the LORD
and who also swear by Molech,[b]
6 those who turn back from following
the LORD
and neither seek the LORD nor
inquire of him.
7 Be silent before the Sovereign LORD,
for the day of the LORD is near.
The LORD has prepared a sacrifice;
he has consecrated those he has
invited.
8 On the day of the LORD's sacrifice
I will punish the princes
and the king's sons
and all those clad
in foreign clothes.
9 On that day I will punish
all who avoid stepping on the
threshold,[c]
who fill the temple of their gods
with violence and deceit.

10 "On that day," declares the LORD,
"a cry will go up from the Fish Gate,
wailing from the New Quarter,
and a loud crash from the hills.
11 Wail, you who live in the market
district[d];
all your merchants will be wiped out,
all who trade with[e] silver will be
ruined.
12 At that time I will search Jerusalem
with lamps
and punish those who are
complacent,
who are like wine left on its dregs,
who think, 'The LORD will do nothing,
either good or bad.'
13 Their wealth will be plundered,
their houses demolished.
They will build houses
but not live in them;
they will plant vineyards
but not drink the wine.

The Great Day of the LORD

14 "The great day of the LORD is near—
near and coming quickly.
Listen! The cry on the day of the LORD
will be bitter,
the shouting of the warrior there.
15 That day will be a day of wrath,
a day of distress and anguish,
a day of trouble and ruin,
a day of darkness and gloom,
a day of clouds and blackness,
16 a day of trumpet and battle cry
against the fortified cities
and against the corner towers.
17 I will bring distress on the people
and they will walk like blind men,
because they have sinned against
the LORD.
Their blood will be poured out like
dust
and their entrails like filth.
18 Neither their silver nor their gold
will be able to save them
on the day of the LORD's wrath.
In the fire of his jealousy
the whole world will be consumed,
for he will make a sudden end
of all who live in the earth."

a3 The meaning of the Hebrew for this line is
uncertain.   b5 Hebrew Malcam, that is,
Milcom   c9 See 1 Samuel 5:5.   d11 Or the
Mortar   e11 Or in

2 Gather together, gather together,
   O shameful nation,
² before the appointed time arrives
   and that day sweeps on like chaff,
before the fierce anger of the LORD
   comes upon you,
before the day of the LORD's wrath
   comes upon you.
³ Seek the LORD, all you humble of the
   land,
   you who do what he commands.
Seek righteousness, seek humility;
   perhaps you will be sheltered
   on the day of the LORD's anger.

Against Philistia

⁴ Gaza will be abandoned
   and Ashkelon left in ruins.
At midday Ashdod will be emptied
   and Ekron uprooted.
⁵ Woe to you who live by the sea,
   O Kerethite people;
the word of the LORD is against you,
   O Canaan, land of the Philistines.
   "I will destroy you,
   and none will be left."

⁶ The land by the sea, where the
   Kerethites*a* dwell,
will be a place for shepherds and
   sheep pens.
⁷ It will belong to the remnant of the
   house of Judah;
   there they will find pasture.
In the evening they will lie down
   in the houses of Ashkelon.
The LORD their God will care for them;
   he will restore their fortunes.*b*

Against Moab and Ammon

⁸ "I have heard the insults of Moab
   and the taunts of the Ammonites,
who insulted my people
   and made threats against their
   land.
⁹ Therefore, as surely as I live,"
   declares the LORD Almighty, the
   God of Israel,
"surely Moab will become like
   Sodom,
   the Ammonites like Gomorrah—
a place of weeds and salt pits,
   a wasteland forever.
The remnant of my people will
   plunder them;

the survivors of my nation will
   inherit their land."

¹⁰ This is what they will get in return for
   their pride,
   for insulting and mocking the
   people of the LORD Almighty.
¹¹ The LORD will be awesome to them
   when he destroys all the gods of
   the land.
The nations on every shore will
   worship him,
   every one in its own land.

> *THE LORD will be awesome to them
> when he destroys all the gods
> of the land.
> The nations on every shore will
> worship him,
> every one in its own land.*
>
> ZEPHANIAH 2:11

Against Cush

¹² "You too, O Cushites,*c*
   will be slain by my sword."

Against Assyria

¹³ He will stretch out his hand against
   the north
   and destroy Assyria,
leaving Nineveh utterly desolate
   and dry as the desert.
¹⁴ Flocks and herds will lie down there,
   creatures of every kind.
The desert owl and the screech owl
   will roost on her columns.
Their calls will echo through the
   windows,
   rubble will be in the doorways,
   the beams of cedar will be exposed.
¹⁵ This is the carefree city
   that lived in safety.
She said to herself,
   "I am, and there is none besides
   me."
What a ruin she has become,
   a lair for wild beasts!
All who pass by her scoff
   and shake their fists.

---

a6 The meaning of the Hebrew for this word is
uncertain.   *b7* Or *will bring back their captives*
c12 That is, people from the upper Nile region

ZEPHANIAH 1:1 – 7; 2:1 – 3; 3:9 – 20

Made Pure by Fire

3:9 "THEN WILL I PURIFY THE LIPS OF THE PEOPLES."

A wedding ring is a splendid symbol of the marriage between a man and woman, and between God and his people. It is a circle, a symbol of eternity. Human love is beautiful, like flowers in a wedding. But like the flowers in a wedding, it wilts and fades over time if it is uprooted from the soil of God's eternal love. To survive and flourish, our love must be planted in God.

A ring is also made of a precious metal. Precious metals are refined by fire; it is the fire that burns out the impurities. Marriages have their fires—turmoil and disappointment, tragedies and misunderstandings—but the fires need not destroy the marriage. They can help make it more pure and precious.

God is a husband to his people; he has married himself to us in covenant love. When we persist in sin like an unfaithful spouse, he brings the fire of judgment on us. Sometimes the fire is brutal and searing, like the Day of the Lord described in Zephaniah. But its purpose is for purity: "Then will I purify the lips of the peoples, that all of them may call on the name of the LORD" (3:9). The fire of judgment isn't God's last word; it's his next-to-last word. His last word is the redemption and restoration described at the end of Zephaniah's prophecy, and it is for the whole world, "that all of them may call on the name of the LORD."

God doesn't enjoy judgment. It is work he must do, but Isaiah calls it "his strange work . . . his alien task" (Isaiah 28:21). "As surely as I live, declares the Sovereign LORD, I take no pleasure in the death of the wicked, but rather that they turn from their ways and live. Turn! Turn from your evil ways!" (Ezekiel 33:11).

Understanding God's perspective gives us great hope to pray in the face of judgment. We pray to a God who is not wanting anyone to perish (see 2 Peter 3:9), and who wills to turn the fires of judgment into the fires of purification. Even in the midst of Zephaniah's harshest words, he says, "Seek the LORD, all you humble of the land, you who do what he commands. Seek righteousness, seek humility; perhaps you will be sheltered on the day of the LORD's anger" (2:3).

PRAY:

Holy and merciful Father, if we got what we deserved, we
would all die for our sins. In your justice, please remember
your mercy, and let your punishment be for our
purification, not our destruction.

FOR YOUR NEXT DEVOTIONAL READING, GO TO PAGE 1116.

The Future of Jerusalem

3 Woe to the city of oppressors,
  rebellious and defiled!
² She obeys no one,
    she accepts no correction.
  She does not trust in the LORD,
    she does not draw near to her God.
³ Her officials are roaring lions,
    her rulers are evening wolves,
    who leave nothing for the morning.
⁴ Her prophets are arrogant;
    they are treacherous men.
  Her priests profane the sanctuary
    and do violence to the law.
⁵ The LORD within her is righteous;
    he does no wrong.
  Morning by morning he dispenses his
      justice,
    and every new day he does not fail,
    yet the unrighteous know no
      shame.

⁶ "I have cut off nations;
    their strongholds are demolished.
  I have left their streets deserted,
    with no one passing through.
  Their cities are destroyed;
    no one will be left—no one at all.
⁷ I said to the city,
  'Surely you will fear me
    and accept correction!'
  Then her dwelling would not be
      cut off,
    nor all my punishments come
      upon her.
  But they were still eager
    to act corruptly in all they did.
⁸ Therefore wait for me," declares the
      LORD,
  "for the day I will stand up to
      testify.ᵃ
  I have decided to assemble the
      nations,
    to gather the kingdoms
  and to pour out my wrath on them—
    all my fierce anger.
  The whole world will be consumed
    by the fire of my jealous anger.

⁹ "Then will I purify the lips of the
      peoples,
    that all of them may call on the
      name of the LORD
    and serve him shoulder to
      shoulder.

> "THEN will I purify the lips of the
> peoples,
>   that all of them may call on the name
>   of the LORD
>   and serve him shoulder to shoulder."
>
> ZEPHANIAH 3:9

¹⁰ From beyond the rivers of Cushᵇ
    my worshipers, my scattered
      people,
    will bring me offerings.
¹¹ On that day you will not be put to
      shame
    for all the wrongs you have done to
      me,
  because I will remove from this city
    those who rejoice in their pride.
  Never again will you be haughty
    on my holy hill.
¹² But I will leave within you
    the meek and humble,
    who trust in the name of the LORD.
¹³ The remnant of Israel will do no
      wrong;
    they will speak no lies,
    nor will deceit be found in their
      mouths.
  They will eat and lie down
    and no one will make them afraid."

¹⁴ Sing, O Daughter of Zion;
    shout aloud, O Israel!
  Be glad and rejoice with all your
      heart,
    O Daughter of Jerusalem!
¹⁵ The LORD has taken away your
      punishment,
    he has turned back your enemy.
  The LORD, the King of Israel, is with
      you;
    never again will you fear any harm.
¹⁶ On that day they will say to
      Jerusalem,
  "Do not fear, O Zion;
    do not let your hands hang limp.
¹⁷ The LORD your God is with you,
    he is mighty to save.
  He will take great delight in you,
    he will quiet you with his love,
    he will rejoice over you with
      singing."

ᵃ8 Septuagint and Syriac; Hebrew *will rise up to
plunder*   ᵇ10 That is, the upper Nile region

18 "The sorrows for the appointed feasts
   I will remove from you;
   they are a burden and a reproach
      to you.*a*
19 At that time I will deal
   with all who oppressed you;
   I will rescue the lame
   and gather those who have been
      scattered.
   I will give them praise and honor
   in every land where they were put
      to shame.

20 At that time I will gather you;
   at that time I will bring you
      home.
   I will give you honor and praise
   among all the peoples of the
      earth
   when I restore your fortunes*b*
   before your very eyes,"
                              says the LORD.

a18 Or *"I will gather you who mourn for the
appointed feasts; / your reproach is a burden to
you*   *b20* Or *I bring back your captives*

Haggai

AND THE PEOPLE
FEARED THE LORD.
(1:12)

THE HARDEST part of a long distance race is the middle. The beginning is flushed with excitement; the end is animated by the hope of finishing and, for some, possibly winning. But the middle is in-between, where boredom and fatigue set in, and it can feel as if it will never end. The runner is only aware of weariness and effort. People can become self-absorbed when this long distance race is life. Changing the metaphor, they become prey to the sins of the afternoon. "There comes an hour in the afternoon," wrote G. K. Chesterton, "when the child is tired of 'pretending'; when he is weary of being a robber or a cowboy. It is then that he torments the cat ... The effect of this staleness is everywhere."[1] For Israel, after the exile and the return to Jerusalem, with all the hopes of a new beginning and the rebuilding of the temple, it is the middle of the race and the middle of the afternoon. They have turned toward purely selfish pursuits for personal peace and affluence.

This is the situation to which the prophets Haggai, Zechariah and Malachi spoke. Each had a message of hope, and a message of warning to the bored and slothful. Their prophecies anticipate the fulfillment of all hopes, with glimpses into God's good future when "the sun of righteousness will rise with healing in its wings" (Malachi 4:2); when "the desired of all nations will come" (Haggai 2:7); when "they will look on ... the one they have pierced, and they will mourn for him as one mourns for an only child" (Zechariah 12:10); and when at last, "a fountain will be opened ... to cleanse them from sin and impurity" (Zechariah 13:1).

Throughout the prophecies of these last three Old Testament prophets, a bright future invades Israel's pallid present. As Chesterton put it, right in the middle of the staleness of the afternoon, "stands up an enormous exception. It is quite unlike anything else. It is a thing final like the trumpet of doom, though it is also a piece of good news, or news that seems too good to be true. It is nothing less than the loud assertion that this mysterious maker of the world has visited his world in person."[2] If that hope doesn't spur us to eager, faithful prayer, nothing will!

A Call to Build the House of the LORD

1 In the second year of King Darius, on the first day of the sixth month, the word of the LORD came through the prophet Haggai to Zerubbabel son of Shealtiel, governor of Judah, and to Joshua[a] son of Jehozadak, the high priest:

²This is what the LORD Almighty says: "These people say, 'The time has not yet come for the LORD's house to be built.'"

³Then the word of the LORD came through the prophet Haggai: ⁴"Is it a time for you yourselves to be living in your paneled houses, while this house remains a ruin?"

> THEN the word of the LORD came through the prophet Haggai.
>
> HAGGAI 1:3

⁵Now this is what the LORD Almighty says: "Give careful thought to your ways. ⁶You have planted much, but have harvested little. You eat, but never have enough. You drink, but never have your fill. You put on clothes, but are not warm. You earn wages, only to put them in a purse with holes in it."

⁷This is what the LORD Almighty says: "Give careful thought to your ways. ⁸Go up into the mountains and bring down timber and build the house, so that I may take pleasure in it and be honored," says the LORD. ⁹"You expected much, but see, it turned out to be little. What you brought home, I blew away. Why?" declares the LORD Almighty. "Because of my house, which remains a ruin, while each of you is busy with his own house. ¹⁰Therefore, because of you the heavens have withheld their dew and the earth its crops. ¹¹I called for a drought on the fields and the mountains, on the grain, the new wine, the oil and whatever the ground produces, on men and cattle, and on the labor of your hands."

¹²Then Zerubbabel son of Shealtiel, Joshua son of Jehozadak, the high priest, and the whole remnant of the people obeyed the voice of the LORD their God and the message of the prophet Haggai, because the LORD their God had sent him. And the people feared the LORD.

¹³Then Haggai, the LORD's messenger, gave this message of the LORD to the people: "I am with you," declares the LORD. ¹⁴So the LORD stirred up the spirit of Zerubbabel son of Shealtiel, governor of Judah, and the spirit of Joshua son of Jehozadak, the high priest, and the spirit of the whole remnant of the people. They came and began to work on the house of the LORD Almighty, their God, ¹⁵on the twenty-fourth day of the sixth month in the second year of King Darius.

The Promised Glory of the New House

2 On the twenty-first day of the seventh month, the word of the LORD came through the prophet Haggai: ²"Speak to Zerubbabel son of Shealtiel, governor of Judah, to Joshua son of Jehozadak, the high priest, and to the remnant of the people. Ask them, ³'Who of you is left who saw this house in its former glory? How does it look to you now? Does it not seem to you like nothing? ⁴But now be strong, O Zerubbabel,' declares the LORD. 'Be strong, O Joshua son of Jehozadak, the high priest. Be strong, all you people of the land,' declares the LORD, 'and work. For I am with you,' declares the LORD Almighty. ⁵'This is what I covenanted with you when you came out of Egypt. And my Spirit remains among you. Do not fear.'

⁶"This is what the LORD Almighty says: 'In a little while I will once more shake the heavens and the earth, the sea and the dry land. ⁷I will shake all nations, and the desired of all nations will come, and I will fill this house with glory,' says the LORD Almighty. ⁸'The silver is mine and the gold is mine,' declares the LORD Almighty. ⁹'The glory of this present house will be greater than the glory of the former house,' says the LORD Almighty. 'And in this place I will grant peace,' declares the LORD Almighty."

Blessings for a Defiled People

¹⁰On the twenty-fourth day of the ninth month, in the second year of Darius, the word of the LORD came to the prophet Haggai: ¹¹"This is what the LORD Almighty says: 'Ask the priests what the

---

[a] 1 A variant of *Jeshua*; here and elsewhere in Haggai

HAGGAI 1:1–11

Misplaced Priorities

1:5 "GIVE CAREFUL THOUGHT TO YOUR WAYS."

After two years of falling profits, a management guru was called in to help a large corporation streamline its operations and become more productive. After in-depth interviews with people at all levels of the organization, he submitted his recommendations. Beginning with the president, he wanted each employee to make a list each day of the things that needed to be done. Then they were to assign numbers to each of the items on their lists: number one for the most important item, number two for the second most important item, and so on. In other words, to improve productivity they were to set priorities: Do first things first, and second things second.

Jesus said basically the same thing when he said, "But seek first [God's] kingdom and his righteousness, and all these things will be given to you as well" (Matthew 6:33). "These things" are food, clothing and shelter, the so-called basics, or necessities, of life. But there is something more basic than the basics, more necessary than the necessaries. That is seeking God's kingdom. No matter how good the superstructure, the building will collapse if the foundation is missing.

Haggai was preaching kingdom priorities when he asked, "Is it a time for you yourselves to be living in your paneled houses, while this house remains a ruin?" (1:4). The house in ruin was the temple, the place of worship. The "paneled houses" were the Israelites' homes, which they were building to look like palaces—cedar paneling was the preferred interior for king's dwellings. Clearly, the people's priorities were upside down, and as a result, so was everything else. The economy was failing, and every effort they made to fix it seemed to do the opposite: "You have planted much, but have harvested little ... You earn wages, only to put them in a purse with holes in it" (verse 6). The way to fix their problems was to stop trying to do things on their own, and instead to put God back in his proper place. The problem wasn't with work; it was a problem with worship.

How are your priorities in relation to your work and your worship? Andrew Murray spoke like Haggai when he wrote, "Our true aim must not be to work a great deal and pray just enough to keep the work right. We should pray a great deal and then work enough for the power and blessing obtained in prayer to find its way through us to men."[3]

P R A Y :

Father, forgive me for my misplaced priorities.
Help me to seek first your kingdom and your righteousness.

FOR YOUR NEXT DEVOTIONAL READING, GO TO PAGE 1127.

law says: [12]If a person carries consecrated meat in the fold of his garment, and that fold touches some bread or stew, some wine, oil or other food, does it become consecrated?'"

The priests answered, "No."

[13]Then Haggai said, "If a person defiled by contact with a dead body touches one of these things, does it become defiled?"

"Yes," the priests replied, "it becomes defiled."

[14]Then Haggai said, "'So it is with this people and this nation in my sight,' declares the LORD. 'Whatever they do and whatever they offer there is defiled.

[15]"'Now give careful thought to this from this day on[a]—consider how things were before one stone was laid on another in the LORD's temple. [16]When anyone came to a heap of twenty measures, there were only ten. When anyone went to a wine vat to draw fifty measures, there were only twenty. [17]I struck all the work of your hands with blight, mildew and hail, yet you did not turn to me,' declares the LORD. [18]'From this day on, from this twenty-fourth day of the ninth month, give careful thought to the day when the foundation of the LORD's temple was laid. Give careful thought: [19]Is there yet any seed left

in the barn? Until now, the vine and the fig tree, the pomegranate and the olive tree have not borne fruit.

"'From this day on I will bless you.'"

> ❝ I have been driven many times to my knees by the overwhelming conviction that I had nowhere else to go. ❞
>
> ABRAHAM LINCOLN

Zerubbabel the LORD's Signet Ring

[20]The word of the LORD came to Haggai a second time on the twenty-fourth day of the month: [21]"Tell Zerubbabel governor of Judah that I will shake the heavens and the earth. [22]I will overturn royal thrones and shatter the power of the foreign kingdoms. I will overthrow chariots and their drivers; horses and their riders will fall, each by the sword of his brother.

[23]"'On that day,' declares the LORD Almighty, 'I will take you, my servant Zerubbabel son of Shealtiel,' declares the LORD, 'and I will make you like my signet ring, for I have chosen you,' declares the LORD Almighty."

[a]15 Or to the days past

Zechariah

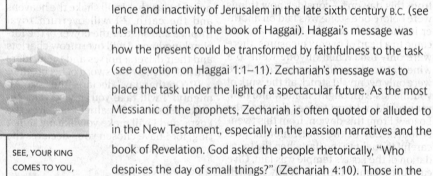

THE TASK at hand for the exiles was to finish rebuilding the temple. But work had stalled more than once. Like Haggai his contemporary, Zechariah declared his prophecies against the indolence and inactivity of Jerusalem in the late sixth century B.C. (see the Introduction to the book of Haggai). Haggai's message was how the present could be transformed by faithfulness to the task (see devotion on Haggai 1:1–11). Zechariah's message was to place the task under the light of a spectacular future. As the most Messianic of the prophets, Zechariah is often quoted or alluded to in the New Testament, especially in the passion narratives and the book of Revelation. God asked the people rhetorically, "Who despises the day of small things?" (Zechariah 4:10). Those in the nation who had the audacity to raise their hands should have put them back down. Paraphrased, the point was, "Things don't look great right now, but they will; work as though you believe it."

SEE, YOUR KING COMES TO YOU, RIGHTEOUS AND HAVING SALVATION, GENTLE AND RIDING ON A DONKEY. (9:9)

Jesus said the kingdom of God is like a mustard seed (see Mark 4:30–32). It starts tiny but grows into something huge. It's God's nature to start small, like yeast in dough, a seed in the soil, a word spoken into nothing. Hope sustains work and prayer like nothing else can. The key is to think like a farmer and wait for the harvest, always watering, feeding, cultivating and hoping. No one who waits on the Lord will be disappointed.

A Call to Return to the LORD

1 In the eighth month of the second year of Darius, the word of the LORD came to the prophet Zechariah son of Berekiah, the son of Iddo:

2 "The LORD was very angry with your forefathers. 3 Therefore tell the people: This is what the LORD Almighty says: 'Return to me,' declares the LORD Almighty, 'and I will return to you,' says the LORD Almighty. 4 Do not be like your forefathers, to whom the earlier prophets proclaimed: This is what the LORD Almighty says: 'Turn from your evil ways and your evil practices.' But they would not listen or pay attention to me, declares the LORD. 5 Where are your forefathers now? And the prophets, do they live forever? 6 But did not my words and my decrees, which I commanded my servants the prophets, overtake your forefathers?

> "THEREFORE tell the people: This is what the LORD Almighty says: 'Return to me,' declares the LORD Almighty, 'and I will return to you,' says the LORD Almighty."
>
> ZECHARIAH 1:3

"Then they repented and said, 'The LORD Almighty has done to us what our ways and practices deserve, just as he determined to do.'"

The Man Among the Myrtle Trees

7 On the twenty-fourth day of the eleventh month, the month of Shebat, in the second year of Darius, the word of the LORD came to the prophet Zechariah son of Berekiah, the son of Iddo.

8 During the night I had a vision—and there before me was a man riding a red horse! He was standing among the myrtle trees in a ravine. Behind him were red, brown and white horses.

9 I asked, "What are these, my lord?"

The angel who was talking with me answered, "I will show you what they are."

10 Then the man standing among the myrtle trees explained, "They are the ones the LORD has sent to go throughout the earth."

11 And they reported to the angel of the LORD, who was standing among the myrtle trees, "We have gone throughout the earth and found the whole world at rest and in peace."

12 Then the angel of the LORD said, "LORD Almighty, how long will you withhold mercy from Jerusalem and from the towns of Judah, which you have been angry with these seventy years?" 13 So the LORD spoke kind and comforting words to the angel who talked with me.

14 Then the angel who was speaking to me said, "Proclaim this word: This is what the LORD Almighty says: 'I am very jealous for Jerusalem and Zion, 15 but I am very angry with the nations that feel secure. I was only a little angry, but they added to the calamity.'

16 "Therefore, this is what the LORD says: 'I will return to Jerusalem with mercy, and there my house will be rebuilt. And the measuring line will be stretched out over Jerusalem,' declares the LORD Almighty.

17 "Proclaim further: This is what the LORD Almighty says: 'My towns will again overflow with prosperity, and the LORD will again comfort Zion and choose Jerusalem.'"

Four Horns and Four Craftsmen

18 Then I looked up—and there before me were four horns! 19 I asked the angel who was speaking to me, "What are these?"

He answered me, "These are the horns that scattered Judah, Israel and Jerusalem."

20 Then the LORD showed me four craftsmen. 21 I asked, "What are these coming to do?"

He answered, "These are the horns that scattered Judah so that no one could raise his head, but the craftsmen have come to terrify them and throw down these horns of the nations who lifted up their horns against the land of Judah to scatter its people."

A Man With a Measuring Line

2 Then I looked up—and there before me was a man with a measuring line in his hand! 2 I asked, "Where are you going?"

He answered me, "To measure Jerusalem, to find out how wide and how long it is."

³Then the angel who was speaking to me left, and another angel came to meet him ⁴and said to him: "Run, tell that young man, 'Jerusalem will be a city without walls because of the great number of men and livestock in it. ⁵And I myself will be a wall of fire around it,' declares the LORD, 'and I will be its glory within.'

⁶"Come! Come! Flee from the land of the north," declares the LORD, "for I have scattered you to the four winds of heaven," declares the LORD.

⁷"Come, O Zion! Escape, you who live in the Daughter of Babylon!" ⁸For this is what the LORD Almighty says: "After he has honored me and has sent me against the nations that have plundered you—for whoever touches you touches the apple of his eye— ⁹I will surely raise my hand against them so that their slaves will plunder them.ᵃ Then you will know that the LORD Almighty has sent me.

¹⁰"Shout and be glad, O Daughter of Zion. For I am coming, and I will live among you," declares the LORD. ¹¹"Many nations will be joined with the LORD in that day and will become my people. I will live among you and you will know that the LORD Almighty has sent me to you. ¹²The LORD will inherit Judah as his portion in the holy land and will again choose Jerusalem. ¹³Be still before the LORD, all mankind, because he has roused himself from his holy dwelling."

> "SHOUT and be glad, O Daughter of Zion. For I am coming, and I will live among you," declares the LORD.
>
> ZECHARIAH 2:10

Clean Garments for the High Priest

3 Then he showed me Joshuaᵇ the high priest standing before the angel of the LORD, and Satanᶜ standing at his right side to accuse him. ²The LORD said to Satan, "The LORD rebuke you, Satan! The LORD, who has chosen Jerusalem, rebuke you! Is not this man a burning stick snatched from the fire?"

³Now Joshua was dressed in filthy clothes as he stood before the angel. ⁴The angel said to those who were standing before him, "Take off his filthy clothes."

Then he said to Joshua, "See, I have taken away your sin, and I will put rich garments on you."

⁵Then I said, "Put a clean turban on his head." So they put a clean turban on his head and clothed him, while the angel of the LORD stood by.

⁶The angel of the LORD gave this charge to Joshua: ⁷"This is what the LORD Almighty says: 'If you will walk in my ways and keep my requirements, then you will govern my house and have charge of my courts, and I will give you a place among these standing here.

⁸"'Listen, O high priest Joshua and your associates seated before you, who are men symbolic of things to come: I am going to bring my servant, the Branch. ⁹See, the stone I have set in front of Joshua! There are seven eyesᵈ on that one stone, and I will engrave an inscription on it,' says the LORD Almighty, 'and I will remove the sin of this land in a single day.

¹⁰"'In that day each of you will invite his neighbor to sit under his vine and fig tree,' declares the LORD Almighty."

The Gold Lampstand and the Two Olive Trees

4 Then the angel who talked with me returned and wakened me, as a man is wakened from his sleep. ²He asked me, "What do you see?"

I answered, "I see a solid gold lampstand with a bowl at the top and seven lights on it, with seven channels to the lights. ³Also there are two olive trees by it, one on the right of the bowl and the other on its left."

⁴I asked the angel who talked with me, "What are these, my lord?"

⁵He answered, "Do you not know what these are?"

"No, my lord," I replied.

⁶So he said to me, "This is the word of the LORD to Zerubbabel: 'Not by might

---

ᵃ8,9 Or says after... eye; ⁹ "I... plunder them."
ᵇ1 A variant of Jeshua; here and elsewhere in Zechariah   ᶜ1 Satan means accuser.
ᵈ9 Or facets

nor by power, but by my Spirit,' says the LORD Almighty.

[7]"What[a] are you, O mighty mountain? Before Zerubbabel you will become level ground. Then he will bring out the capstone to shouts of 'God bless it! God bless it!' "

> 66 Whatever a man prays for, he prays for a miracle. Every prayer reduces itself to this: Great God, grant that twice two be not four. 99
>
> IVAN TURGENEV

[8]Then the word of the LORD came to me: [9]"The hands of Zerubbabel have laid the foundation of this temple; his hands will also complete it. Then you will know that the LORD Almighty has sent me to you.

[10]"Who despises the day of small things? Men will rejoice when they see the plumb line in the hand of Zerubbabel.

"(These seven are the eyes of the LORD, which range throughout the earth.)"

[11]Then I asked the angel, "What are these two olive trees on the right and the left of the lampstand?"

[12]Again I asked him, "What are these two olive branches beside the two gold pipes that pour out golden oil?"

[13]He replied, "Do you not know what these are?"

"No, my lord," I said.

[14]So he said, "These are the two who are anointed to[b] serve the Lord of all the earth."

The Flying Scroll

5 I looked again—and there before me was a flying scroll!

[2]He asked me, "What do you see?"

I answered, "I see a flying scroll, thirty feet long and fifteen feet wide.[c]"

[3]And he said to me, "This is the curse that is going out over the whole land; for according to what it says on one side, every thief will be banished, and according to what it says on the other, everyone who swears falsely will be banished. [4]The LORD Almighty declares, 'I will send it out, and it will enter the house of the thief and the house of him who swears falsely by my name. It will remain in his house and destroy it, both its timbers and its stones.' "

The Woman in a Basket

[5]Then the angel who was speaking to me came forward and said to me, "Look up and see what this is that is appearing."

[6]I asked, "What is it?"

He replied, "It is a measuring basket.[d]" And he added, "This is the iniquity[e] of the people throughout the land."

[7]Then the cover of lead was raised, and there in the basket sat a woman! [8]He said, "This is wickedness," and he pushed her back into the basket and pushed the lead cover down over its mouth.

[9]Then I looked up—and there before me were two women, with the wind in their wings! They had wings like those of a stork, and they lifted up the basket between heaven and earth.

[10]"Where are they taking the basket?" I asked the angel who was speaking to me.

[11]He replied, "To the country of Babylonia[f] to build a house for it. When it is ready, the basket will be set there in its place."

Four Chariots

6 I looked up again—and there before me were four chariots coming out from between two mountains—mountains of bronze! [2]The first chariot had red horses, the second black, [3]the third white, and the fourth dappled—all of them powerful. [4]I asked the angel who was speaking to me, "What are these, my lord?"

[5]The angel answered me, "These are the four spirits[g] of heaven, going out from standing in the presence of the Lord of the whole world. [6]The one with the black horses is going toward the north country, the one with the white horses toward the west,[h] and the one with the dappled horses toward the south."

[7]When the powerful horses went out, they were straining to go throughout the

---

[a]7 Or Who   [b]14 Or two who bring oil and
[c]2 Hebrew twenty cubits long and ten cubits wide (about 9 meters long and 4.5 meters wide)
[d]6 Hebrew an ephah; also in verses 7–11
[e]6 Or appearance   [f]11 Hebrew Shinar
[g]5 Or winds   [h]6 Or horses after them

earth. And he said, "Go throughout the earth!" So they went throughout the earth.

⁸Then he called to me, "Look, those going toward the north country have given my Spirit*ᵃ* rest in the land of the north."

A Crown for Joshua

⁹The word of the LORD came to me: ¹⁰"Take ˌsilver and goldˌ from the exiles Heldai, Tobijah and Jedaiah, who have arrived from Babylon. Go the same day to the house of Josiah son of Zephaniah. ¹¹Take the silver and gold and make a crown, and set it on the head of the high priest, Joshua son of Jehozadak. ¹²Tell him this is what the LORD Almighty says: 'Here is the man whose name is the Branch, and he will branch out from his place and build the temple of the LORD. ¹³It is he who will build the temple of the LORD, and he will be clothed with majesty and will sit and rule on his throne. And he will be a priest on his throne. And there will be harmony between the two.' ¹⁴The crown will be given to Heldai,*ᵇ* Tobijah, Jedaiah and Hen*ᶜ* son of Zephaniah as a memorial in the temple of the LORD. ¹⁵Those who are far away will come and help to build the temple of the LORD, and you will know that the LORD Almighty has sent me to you. This will happen if you diligently obey the LORD your God."

Justice and Mercy, Not Fasting

7 In the fourth year of King Darius, the word of the LORD came to Zechariah on the fourth day of the ninth month, the month of Kislev. ²The people of Bethel had sent Sharezer and Regem-Melech, together with their men, to entreat the LORD ³by asking the priests of the house of the LORD Almighty and the prophets, "Should I mourn and fast in the fifth month, as I have done for so many years?"

⁴Then the word of the LORD Almighty came to me: ⁵"Ask all the people of the land and the priests, 'When you fasted and mourned in the fifth and seventh months for the past seventy years, was it really for me that you fasted? ⁶And when you were eating and drinking, were you not just feasting for yourselves? ⁷Are these not the words the LORD proclaimed

through the earlier prophets when Jerusalem and its surrounding towns were at rest and prosperous, and the Negev and the western foothills were settled?' "

> 〝 Each time, before you intercede, be quiet first, and worship God in his glory. Think of what he can do, and how he delights to hear the prayers of his redeemed people. Think of your place and privilege in Christ, and expect great things! 〞
>
> ANDREW MURRAY

⁸And the word of the LORD came again to Zechariah: ⁹"This is what the LORD Almighty says: 'Administer true justice; show mercy and compassion to one another. ¹⁰Do not oppress the widow or the fatherless, the alien or the poor. In your hearts do not think evil of each other.'

¹¹"But they refused to pay attention; stubbornly they turned their backs and stopped up their ears. ¹²They made their hearts as hard as flint and would not listen to the law or to the words that the LORD Almighty had sent by his Spirit through the earlier prophets. So the LORD Almighty was very angry.

¹³" 'When I called, they did not listen; so when they called, I would not listen,' says the LORD Almighty. ¹⁴'I scattered them with a whirlwind among all the nations, where they were strangers. The land was left so desolate behind them that no one could come or go. This is how they made the pleasant land desolate.' "

The LORD Promises to Bless Jerusalem

8 Again the word of the LORD Almighty came to me. ²This is what the LORD Almighty says: "I am very jealous for Zion; I am burning with jealousy for her." ³This is what the LORD says: "I will return to Zion and dwell in Jerusalem. Then Jerusalem will be called the City of Truth, and the mountain of the LORD Almighty will be called the Holy Mountain." ⁴This is what the LORD Almighty says: "Once again men and women of ripe old

---

ᵃ8 Or *spirit*   *ᵇ14* Syriac; Hebrew *Helem*
ᶜ14 Or *and the gracious one, the*

age will sit in the streets of Jerusalem, each with cane in hand because of his age. [5]The city streets will be filled with boys and girls playing there."

[6]This is what the LORD Almighty says: "It may seem marvelous to the remnant of this people at that time, but will it seem marvelous to me?" declares the LORD Almighty.

[7]This is what the LORD Almighty says: "I will save my people from the countries of the east and the west. [8]I will bring them back to live in Jerusalem; they will be my people, and I will be faithful and righteous to them as their God."

[9]This is what the LORD Almighty says: "You who now hear these words spoken by the prophets who were there when the foundation was laid for the house of the LORD Almighty, let your hands be strong so that the temple may be built. [10]Before that time there were no wages for man or beast. No one could go about his business safely because of his enemy, for I had turned every man against his neighbor. [11]But now I will not deal with the remnant of this people as I did in the past," declares the LORD Almighty.

[12]"The seed will grow well, the vine will yield its fruit, the ground will produce its crops, and the heavens will drop their dew. I will give all these things as an inheritance to the remnant of this people. [13]As you have been an object of cursing among the nations, O Judah and Israel, so will I save you, and you will be a blessing. Do not be afraid, but let your hands be strong."

[14]This is what the LORD Almighty says: "Just as I had determined to bring disaster upon you and showed no pity when your fathers angered me," says the LORD Almighty, [15]"so now I have determined to do good again to Jerusalem and Judah. Do not be afraid. [16]These are the things you are to do: Speak the truth to each other, and render true and sound judgment in your courts; [17]do not plot evil against your neighbor, and do not love to swear falsely. I hate all this," declares the LORD.

[18]Again the word of the LORD Almighty came to me. [19]This is what the LORD Almighty says: "The fasts of the fourth, fifth, seventh and tenth months will be-

come joyful and glad occasions and happy festivals for Judah. Therefore love truth and peace."

[20]This is what the LORD Almighty says: "Many peoples and the inhabitants of many cities will yet come, [21]and the inhabitants of one city will go to another and say, 'Let us go at once to entreat the LORD and seek the LORD Almighty. I myself am going.' [22]And many peoples and powerful nations will come to Jerusalem to seek the LORD Almighty and to entreat him."

[23]This is what the LORD Almighty says: "In those days ten men from all languages and nations will take firm hold of one Jew by the hem of his robe and say, 'Let us go with you, because we have heard that God is with you.'"

Judgment on Israel's Enemies

An Oracle

9 The word of the LORD is against the
land of Hadrach
and will rest upon Damascus—
for the eyes of men and all the tribes
of Israel
are on the LORD—[a]
[2]and upon Hamath too, which borders
on it,
and upon Tyre and Sidon, though
they are very skillful.
[3]Tyre has built herself a stronghold;
she has heaped up silver like dust,
and gold like the dirt of the streets.
[4]But the Lord will take away her
possessions
and destroy her power on the sea,
and she will be consumed by fire.
[5]Ashkelon will see it and fear;
Gaza will writhe in agony,
and Ekron too, for her hope will
wither.
Gaza will lose her king
and Ashkelon will be deserted.
[6]Foreigners will occupy Ashdod,
and I will cut off the pride of the
Philistines.
[7]I will take the blood from their
mouths,
the forbidden food from between
their teeth.

[a]1 Or Damascus. / For the eye of the LORD is on all mankind, / as well as on the tribes of Israel,

Those who are left will belong to
  our God
and become leaders in Judah,
and Ekron will be like the Jebusites.
⁸ But I will defend my house
  against marauding forces.
Never again will an oppressor
  overrun my people,
  for now I am keeping watch.

The Coming of Zion's King

⁹ Rejoice greatly, O Daughter of Zion!
  Shout, Daughter of Jerusalem!
See, your king*ᵃ* comes to you,
  righteous and having salvation,
  gentle and riding on a donkey,
  on a colt, the foal of a donkey.

> *REJOICE greatly, O Daughter of Zion!*
> *Shout, Daughter of Jerusalem!*
> *See, your king comes to you,*
> *righteous and having salvation,*
> *gentle and riding on a donkey,*
> *on a colt, the foal of a donkey.*
>
> ZECHARIAH 9:9

¹⁰ I will take away the chariots from
  Ephraim
and the war-horses from
  Jerusalem,
and the battle bow will be broken.
He will proclaim peace to the nations.
His rule will extend from sea to sea
and from the River*ᵇ* to the ends of
  the earth.*ᶜ*
¹¹ As for you, because of the blood of
  my covenant with you,
I will free your prisoners from the
  waterless pit.
¹² Return to your fortress, O prisoners
  of hope;
even now I announce that I will
  restore twice as much to you.
¹³ I will bend Judah as I bend my bow
and fill it with Ephraim.
I will rouse your sons, O Zion,
  against your sons, O Greece,
and make you like a warrior's
  sword.

The LORD Will Appear

¹⁴ Then the LORD will appear over them;
  his arrow will flash like lightning.

The Sovereign LORD will sound the
  trumpet;
he will march in the storms of the
  south,
¹⁵ and the LORD Almighty will shield
  them.
They will destroy
  and overcome with slingstones.
They will drink and roar as with wine;
  they will be full like a bowl
  used for sprinkling*ᵈ* the corners of
  the altar.
¹⁶ The LORD their God will save them on
  that day
  as the flock of his people.
They will sparkle in his land
  like jewels in a crown.
¹⁷ How attractive and beautiful they
  will be!
Grain will make the young men
  thrive,
and new wine the young women.

The LORD Will Care for Judah

10 Ask the LORD for rain in the
  springtime;
it is the LORD who makes the storm
  clouds.
He gives showers of rain to men,
  and plants of the field to everyone.

> *ASK the LORD for rain in the springtime;*
> *it is the LORD who makes the storm*
> *clouds.*
> *He gives showers of rain to men,*
> *and plants of the field to everyone.*
>
> ZECHARIAH 10:1

² The idols speak deceit,
  diviners see visions that lie;
they tell dreams that are false,
  they give comfort in vain.
Therefore the people wander like
  sheep
  oppressed for lack of a shepherd.

³ "My anger burns against the
  shepherds,
  and I will punish the leaders;
for the LORD Almighty will care
  for his flock, the house of Judah,

ᵃ9 Or *King* *ᵇ10* That is, the Euphrates
ᶜ10 Or *the end of the land* *ᵈ15* Or *bowl, / like*

and make them like a proud horse
in battle.
⁴From Judah will come the
cornerstone,
from him the tent peg,
from him the battle bow,
from him every ruler.
⁵Together they*a* will be like mighty
men
trampling the muddy streets in
battle.
Because the LORD is with them,
they will fight and overthrow the
horsemen.

⁶ "I will strengthen the house of Judah
and save the house of Joseph.
I will restore them
because I have compassion on
them.
They will be as though
I had not rejected them,
for I am the LORD their God
and I will answer them.
⁷The Ephraimites will become like
mighty men,
and their hearts will be glad as
with wine.
Their children will see it and be
joyful;
their hearts will rejoice in the
LORD.
⁸I will signal for them
and gather them in.
Surely I will redeem them;
they will be as numerous as before.
⁹Though I scatter them among the
peoples,
yet in distant lands they will
remember me.
They and their children will survive,
and they will return.
¹⁰I will bring them back from Egypt
and gather them from Assyria.
I will bring them to Gilead and
Lebanon,
and there will not be room enough
for them.
¹¹They will pass through the sea of
trouble;
the surging sea will be subdued
and all the depths of the Nile will
dry up.
Assyria's pride will be brought down
and Egypt's scepter will pass away.

¹²I will strengthen them in the LORD
and in his name they will walk,"
declares the LORD.

11 Open your doors, O Lebanon,
so that fire may devour your
cedars!
²Wail, O pine tree, for the cedar has
fallen;
the stately trees are ruined!
Wail, oaks of Bashan;
the dense forest has been cut
down!
³Listen to the wail of the shepherds;
their rich pastures are destroyed!
Listen to the roar of the lions;
the lush thicket of the Jordan is
ruined!

Two Shepherds

⁴This is what the LORD my God says:
"Pasture the flock marked for slaughter.
⁵Their buyers slaughter them and go unpunished. Those who sell them say,
'Praise the LORD, I am rich!' Their own
shepherds do not spare them. ⁶For I will
no longer have pity on the people of the
land," declares the LORD. "I will hand everyone over to his neighbor and his king.
They will oppress the land, and I will not
rescue them from their hands."

⁷So I pastured the flock marked for
slaughter, particularly the oppressed of
the flock. Then I took two staffs and
called one Favor and the other Union,
and I pastured the flock. ⁸In one month I
got rid of the three shepherds.

The flock detested me, and I grew weary of them ⁹and said, "I will not be your
shepherd. Let the dying die, and the perishing perish. Let those who are left eat
one another's flesh."

¹⁰Then I took my staff called Favor and
broke it, revoking the covenant I had
made with all the nations. ¹¹It was revoked on that day, and so the afflicted of
the flock who were watching me knew it
was the word of the LORD.

¹²I told them, "If you think it best, give
me my pay; but if not, keep it." So they
paid me thirty pieces of silver.

¹³And the LORD said to me, "Throw it to
the potter"—the handsome price at
which they priced me! So I took the thirty

---

a4,5 Or ruler, all of them together. / ⁵They

pieces of silver and threw them into the house of the LORD to the potter.

¹⁴Then I broke my second staff called Union, breaking the brotherhood between Judah and Israel.

¹⁵Then the LORD said to me, "Take again the equipment of a foolish shepherd. ¹⁶For I am going to raise up a shepherd over the land who will not care for the lost, or seek the young, or heal the injured, or feed the healthy, but will eat the meat of the choice sheep, tearing off their hoofs.

¹⁷ "Woe to the worthless shepherd,
who deserts the flock!
May the sword strike his arm and his
right eye!
May his arm be completely
withered,
his right eye totally blinded!"

Jerusalem's Enemies to Be Destroyed

An Oracle

12 This is the word of the LORD concerning Israel. The LORD, who stretches out the heavens, who lays the foundation of the earth, and who forms the spirit of man within him, declares: ²"I am going to make Jerusalem a cup that sends all the surrounding peoples reeling. Judah will be besieged as well as Jerusalem. ³On that day, when all the nations of the earth are gathered against her, I will make Jerusalem an immovable rock for all the nations. All who try to move it will injure themselves. ⁴On that day I will strike every horse with panic and its rider with madness," declares the LORD. "I will keep a watchful eye over the house of Judah, but I will blind all the horses of the nations. ⁵Then the leaders of Judah will say in their hearts, 'The people of Jerusalem are strong, because the LORD Almighty is their God.'

⁶"On that day I will make the leaders of Judah like a firepot in a woodpile, like a flaming torch among sheaves. They will consume right and left all the surrounding peoples, but Jerusalem will remain intact in her place.

⁷"The LORD will save the dwellings of Judah first, so that the honor of the house of David and of Jerusalem's inhabitants may not be greater than that of Judah.

⁸On that day the LORD will shield those who live in Jerusalem, so that the feeblest among them will be like David, and the house of David will be like God, like the Angel of the LORD going before them. ⁹On that day I will set out to destroy all the nations that attack Jerusalem.

Mourning for the One They Pierced

¹⁰"And I will pour out on the house of David and the inhabitants of Jerusalem a spirit*ᵃ* of grace and supplication. They will look on*ᵇ* me, the one they have pierced, and they will mourn for him as one mourns for an only child, and grieve bitterly for him as one grieves for a firstborn son. ¹¹On that day the weeping in Jerusalem will be great, like the weeping of Hadad Rimmon in the plain of Megiddo. ¹²The land will mourn, each clan by itself, with their wives by themselves: the clan of the house of David and their wives, the clan of the house of Nathan and their wives, ¹³the clan of the house of Levi and their wives, the clan of Shimei and their wives, ¹⁴and all the rest of the clans and their wives.

Cleansing From Sin

13 "On that day a fountain will be opened to the house of David and the inhabitants of Jerusalem, to cleanse them from sin and impurity.

²"On that day, I will banish the names of the idols from the land, and they will be remembered no more," declares the LORD Almighty. "I will remove both the prophets and the spirit of impurity from the land. ³And if anyone still prophesies, his father and mother, to whom he was born, will say to him, 'You must die, because you have told lies in the LORD's name.' When he prophesies, his own parents will stab him.

⁴"On that day every prophet will be ashamed of his prophetic vision. He will not put on a prophet's garment of hair in order to deceive. ⁵He will say, 'I am not a prophet. I am a farmer; the land has been my livelihood since my youth.*ᶜ*' ⁶If someone asks him, 'What are these wounds on your body*ᵈ*?' he will answer, 'The wounds I was given at the house of my friends.'

---

*ᵃ*10 Or *the Spirit*   *ᵇ*10 Or *to*   *ᶜ*5 Or *farmer; a man sold me in my youth*   *ᵈ*6 Or *wounds between your hands*

ZECHARIAH 12:10 — 13:1

Good Grief

12:12 THE LAND WILL MOURN.

Sometimes we have to hurt before we can heal, just like we often have to mourn before we can rejoice. This is the good grief Paul spoke of to the Corinthians: "For you became sorrowful as God intended . . . Godly sorrow brings repentance that leads to salvation and leaves no regret" (2 Corinthians 7:9–10). The "spirit of grace and supplication" that Zechariah prophesied God would pour out is also good grief. Grace and supplication will come when people "look on me, the one they have pierced" (Zechariah 12:10). The one they have pierced is Christ! "And they will mourn for him as one mourns for an only child, and grieve bitterly for him as one grieves for a firstborn son." The supplication will be prayers of sorrowful repentance. Zechariah is truly the most Messianic of the prophets—he clearly tells of the coming Christ.

This piercing of God's Servant and Son by the very ones he loved runs deep in the Biblical witness to the Savior of Israel (see Isaiah 53:5; John 19:31–37; Revelation 1:7). Even Jesus' mother would feel the stab of pain (see Luke 2:35). To look to Jesus and mourn would be to acknowledge that the people were the perpetrators of his wounds. Zechariah's prophecy peeled the bandages off a very deep and festering wound in their relationship with God. It must do the same for all of us.

The heart of our darkness is that we have pierced the heart of God. The heart of his love is that he has allowed us to do it. "But he was pierced for our transgressions, he was crushed for our iniquities; the punishment that brought us peace was upon him, and by his wounds we are healed" (Isaiah 53:5). This healing cannot come unless we are smitten by the godly grief that leads to repentance and salvation.

"God, have mercy on me, a sinner!" (Luke 18:13) is the most essential of prayers. It is the grace and supplication the Spirit brings to anyone who will look on the one who was pierced, and mourn. When that prayer is prayed, "a fountain will be opened . . . to cleanse them from sin and impurity" (Zechariah 13:1).

P R A Y :

"What thou, my Lord, hast suffered, was all for sinners' gain;
Mine, mine was the transgression, but thine the deadly pain."[1]
God, have mercy on me, a sinner.

FOR YOUR NEXT DEVOTIONAL READING, GO TO PAGE 1133.

The Shepherd Struck, the Sheep Scattered

7 "Awake, O sword, against my
shepherd,
against the man who is close to me!"
declares the LORD Almighty.
"Strike the shepherd,
and the sheep will be scattered,
and I will turn my hand against the
little ones.
8 In the whole land," declares the
LORD,
"two-thirds will be struck down
and perish;
yet one-third will be left in it.
9 This third I will bring into the fire;
I will refine them like silver
and test them like gold.
They will call on my name
and I will answer them;
I will say, 'They are my people,'
and they will say, 'The LORD is
our God.' "

> "THIS third I will bring into the fire;
> I will refine them like silver
> and test them like gold.
> They will call on my name
> and I will answer them;
> I will say, 'They are my people,'
> and they will say, 'The LORD is
> our God.'"
>
> ZECHARIAH 13:9

The LORD Comes and Reigns

14 A day of the LORD is coming when
your plunder will be divided among
you. 2 I will gather all the nations to Jerusalem to fight against it; the city will be
captured, the houses ransacked, and the
women raped. Half of the city will go into
exile, but the rest of the people will not
be taken from the city. 3 Then the LORD will go out and fight
against those nations, as he fights in the
day of battle. 4 On that day his feet will
stand on the Mount of Olives, east of Jerusalem, and the Mount of Olives will be
split in two from east to west, forming a
great valley, with half of the mountain
moving north and half moving south.
5 You will flee by my mountain valley, for

it will extend to Azel. You will flee as you
fled from the earthquake[a] in the days of
Uzziah king of Judah. Then the LORD my
God will come, and all the holy ones with
him.
6 On that day there will be no light, no
cold or frost. 7 It will be a unique day,
without daytime or nighttime—a day
known to the LORD. When evening
comes, there will be light.
8 On that day living water will flow out
from Jerusalem, half to the eastern sea[b]
and half to the western sea,[c] in summer
and in winter.
9 The LORD will be king over the whole
earth. On that day there will be one LORD,
and his name the only name.
10 The whole land, from Geba to Rimmon, south of Jerusalem, will become
like the Arabah. But Jerusalem will be
raised up and remain in its place, from
the Benjamin Gate to the site of the First
Gate, to the Corner Gate, and from the
Tower of Hananel to the royal winepresses. 11 It will be inhabited; never again will
it be destroyed. Jerusalem will be secure.
12 This is the plague with which the
LORD will strike all the nations that
fought against Jerusalem: Their flesh will
rot while they are still standing on their
feet, their eyes will rot in their sockets,
and their tongues will rot in their
mouths. 13 On that day men will be strick-
en by the LORD with great panic. Each
man will seize the hand of another, and
they will attack each other. 14 Judah too
will fight at Jerusalem. The wealth of all
the surrounding nations will be collected—great quantities of gold and silver
and clothing. 15 A similar plague will
strike the horses and mules, the camels
and donkeys, and all the animals in
those camps.
16 Then the survivors from all the nations that have attacked Jerusalem will
go up year after year to worship the King,
the LORD Almighty, and to celebrate the
Feast of Tabernacles. 17 If any of the peoples of the earth do not go up to Jerusalem to worship the King, the LORD
Almighty, they will have no rain. 18 If the

---

a 5 Or 5 My mountain valley will be blocked and
will extend to Azel. It will be blocked as it was
blocked because of the earthquake   b 8 That is,
the Dead Sea   c 8 That is, the Mediterranean

Egyptian people do not go up and take part, they will have no rain. The Lord[a] will bring on them the plague he inflicts on the nations that do not go up to celebrate the Feast of Tabernacles. [19]This will be the punishment of Egypt and the punishment of all the nations that do not go up to celebrate the Feast of Tabernacles.

[20]On that day HOLY TO THE LORD will be inscribed on the bells of the horses, and the cooking pots in the Lord's house will be like the sacred bowls in front of the altar. [21]Every pot in Jerusalem and Judah will be holy to the Lord Almighty, and all who come to sacrifice will take some of the pots and cook in them. And on that day there will no longer be a Canaanite[b] in the house of the Lord Almighty.

[a]18 Or *part, then the* LORD   [b]21 Or *merchant*

Malachi

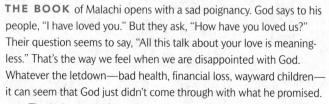

THE BOOK of Malachi opens with a sad poignancy. God says to his people, "I have loved you." But they ask, "How have you loved us?" Their question seems to say, "All this talk about your love is meaningless." That's the way we feel when we are disappointed with God. Whatever the letdown—bad health, financial loss, wayward children— it can seem that God just didn't come through with what he promised.

That's the state of Israel's psyche when Malachi delivers his prophecy. In a sense, the glorious prophecies of Haggai and Zechariah had come true: The exiles had returned to the land, rebuilt the temple and repaired the wall in Jerusalem as predicted. Israel was a nation again. But nothing about it seemed very glorious. Israel was still a third-rate power, a "nobody" on the margins of the Persian Empire. Jerusalem and the temple had once been "beautiful in its loftiness, the joy of the whole earth" (Psalm 48:2). What a joke those words seemed now, as the people looked at a city and temple that were bare sketches, little stick figures of what they once were.

Disappointment with God takes us to very predictable places. Bitterness sets in, and we think thoughts that were once unthinkable: "All who do evil are good in the eyes of the LORD" (Malachi 2:17). Worship becomes listless and disgusting to God: "Oh, that one of you would shut the temple doors, so that you would not light useless fires on my altar! I am not pleased with you" (1:10). We hold so tightly to whatever security we think we have, especially money, that we rob God: "Yet you rob me ... in tithes and offerings" (3:8). Even marriages suffer because of it. Hearts that grow cold toward God will soon grow cold to those nearest us: "You have broken faith with her, though she is your partner, the wife of your marriage covenant" (2:14).

Malachi provides an agenda for prayer in a time of disappointment with God. First, praise God for his faithfulness in the past and his promises for the future. Remember to "guard yourself in your spirit," and that "I the LORD do not change" (2:15; 3:6). Second, get back into conversation with God. Throughout this book, God structures his message in the form of an invitation to a dialogue (see 1:2,6–7; 2:17; 3:7–8,13–14). Talk to God more than you talk about him.

1
An oracle: The word of the Lord to Israel through Malachi.[a]

Jacob Loved, Esau Hated

2"I have loved you," says the Lord.

"But you ask, 'How have you loved us?'

"Was not Esau Jacob's brother?" the Lord says. "Yet I have loved Jacob, 3but Esau I have hated, and I have turned his mountains into a wasteland and left his inheritance to the desert jackals."

4Edom may say, "Though we have been crushed, we will rebuild the ruins."

But this is what the Lord Almighty says: "They may build, but I will demolish. They will be called the Wicked Land, a people always under the wrath of the Lord. 5You will see it with your own eyes and say, 'Great is the Lord—even beyond the borders of Israel!'

Blemished Sacrifices

6"A son honors his father, and a servant his master. If I am a father, where is the honor due me? If I am a master, where is the respect due me?" says the Lord Almighty. "It is you, O priests, who show contempt for my name.

"But you ask, 'How have we shown contempt for your name?'

7"You place defiled food on my altar.

"But you ask, 'How have we defiled you?'

"By saying that the Lord's table is contemptible. 8When you bring blind animals for sacrifice, is that not wrong? When you sacrifice crippled or diseased animals, is that not wrong? Try offering them to your governor! Would he be pleased with you? Would he accept you?" says the Lord Almighty.

9"Now implore God to be gracious to us. With such offerings from your hands, will he accept you?"—says the Lord Almighty.

10"Oh, that one of you would shut the temple doors, so that you would not light useless fires on my altar! I am not pleased with you," says the Lord Almighty, "and I will accept no offering from your hands. 11My name will be great among the nations, from the rising to the setting of the sun. In every place incense and pure offerings will be brought to my name, because my name

> "MY NAME will be great among the nations, from the rising to the setting of the sun. In every place incense and pure offerings will be brought to my name, because my name will be great among the nations," says the Lord Almighty.
>
> MALACHI 1:11

will be great among the nations," says the Lord Almighty.

12"But you profane it by saying of the Lord's table, 'It is defiled,' and of its food, 'It is contemptible.' 13And you say, 'What a burden!' and you sniff at it contemptuously," says the Lord Almighty.

"When you bring injured, crippled or diseased animals and offer them as sacrifices, should I accept them from your hands?" says the Lord. 14"Cursed is the cheat who has an acceptable male in his flock and vows to give it, but then sacrifices a blemished animal to the Lord. For I am a great king," says the Lord Almighty, "and my name is to be feared among the nations.

Admonition for the Priests

2
"And now this admonition is for you, O priests. 2If you do not listen, and if you do not set your heart to honor my name," says the Lord Almighty, "I will send a curse upon you, and I will curse your blessings. Yes, I have already cursed them, because you have not set your heart to honor me.

3"Because of you I will rebuke[b] your descendants[c]; I will spread on your faces the offal from your festival sacrifices, and you will be carried off with it. 4And you will know that I have sent you this admonition so that my covenant with Levi may continue," says the Lord Almighty. 5"My covenant was with him, a covenant of life and peace, and I gave them to him; this called for reverence and he revered me and stood in awe of my name. 6True instruction was in his mouth and nothing false was found on his lips. He walked with me in peace and uprightness, and turned many from sin.

---

[a]1 Malachi means my messenger. [b]3 Or cut off (see Septuagint) [c]3 Or will blight your grain

⁷"For the lips of a priest ought to preserve knowledge, and from his mouth men should seek instruction—because he is the messenger of the LORD Almighty. ⁸But you have turned from the way and by your teaching have caused many to stumble; you have violated the covenant with Levi," says the LORD Almighty. ⁹"So I have caused you to be despised and humiliated before all the people, because you have not followed my ways but have shown partiality in matters of the law."

Judah Unfaithful

¹⁰Have we not all one Father*a*? Did not one God create us? Why do we profane the covenant of our fathers by breaking faith with one another? ¹¹Judah has broken faith. A detestable thing has been committed in Israel and in Jerusalem: Judah has desecrated the sanctuary the LORD loves, by marrying the daughter of a foreign god. ¹²As for the man who does this, whoever he may be, may the LORD cut him off from the tents of Jacob*b*—even though he brings offerings to the LORD Almighty.

¹³Another thing you do: You flood the LORD's altar with tears. You weep and wail because he no longer pays attention to your offerings or accepts them with pleasure from your hands. ¹⁴You ask, "Why?" It is because the LORD is acting as the witness between you and the wife of your youth, because you have broken faith with her, though she is your partner, the wife of your marriage covenant.

> YOU *flood the* LORD's *altar with tears. You weep and wail because he no longer pays attention to your offerings or accepts them with pleasure from your hands.*
>
> MALACHI 2:13

¹⁵Has not ⌊the LORD⌋ made them one? In flesh and spirit they are his. And why one? Because he was seeking godly offspring.*c* So guard yourself in your spirit, and do not break faith with the wife of your youth.

¹⁶"I hate divorce," says the LORD God of Israel, "and I hate a man's covering himself*d* with violence as well as with his garment," says the LORD Almighty.

So guard yourself in your spirit, and do not break faith.

The Day of Judgment

¹⁷You have wearied the LORD with your words.

"How have we wearied him?" you ask.

By saying, "All who do evil are good in the eyes of the LORD, and he is pleased with them" or "Where is the God of justice?"

3 "See, I will send my messenger, who will prepare the way before me. Then suddenly the Lord you are seeking will come to his temple; the messenger of the covenant, whom you desire, will come," says the LORD Almighty. ²But who can endure the day of his coming? Who can stand when he appears? For he will be like a refiner's fire or a launderer's soap. ³He will sit as a refiner and purifier of silver; he will purify the Levites and refine them like gold and silver. Then the LORD will have men who will bring offerings in righteousness, ⁴and the offerings of Judah and Jerusalem will be acceptable to the LORD, as in days gone by, as in former years.

⁵"So I will come near to you for judgment. I will be quick to testify against sorcerers, adulterers and perjurers, against those who defraud laborers of their wages, who oppress the widows and the fatherless, and deprive aliens of justice, but do not fear me," says the LORD Almighty.

Robbing God

⁶"I the LORD do not change. So you, O descendants of Jacob, are not destroyed. ⁷Ever since the time of your forefathers you have turned away from my decrees and have not kept them. Return to me, and I will return to you," says the LORD Almighty.

"But you ask, 'How are we to return?'

---

a 10 Or *father*   *b* 12 Or *¹²May the* LORD *cut off from the tents of Jacob anyone who gives testimony in behalf of the man who does this*   *c* 15 Or *¹⁵But the one who is our father, did not do this, not as long as life remained in him. And what was he seeking? An offspring from God*   *d* 16 Or *his wife*

⁸"Will a man rob God? Yet you rob me. "But you ask, 'How do we rob you?' "In tithes and offerings. ⁹You are under a curse—the whole nation of you—because you are robbing me. ¹⁰Bring the whole tithe into the storehouse, that there may be food in my house. Test me in this," says the Lord Almighty, "and see if I will not throw open the floodgates of heaven and pour out so much blessing that you will not have room enough for it. ¹¹I will prevent pests from devouring your crops, and the vines in your fields will not cast their fruit," says the Lord Almighty. ¹²"Then all the nations will call you blessed, for yours will be a delightful land," says the Lord Almighty.

{ FRIDAY }

MALACHI 3:6–12

Prayer and Money

3:8 "WILL A MAN ROB GOD?"

The accusation that the people were robbing God had to grate on the conscience and patience of Malachi's listeners. Crops had been bad, cash was scarce, and now they were being pressured to give. But robbing God was a serious offense that could not be sloughed off by complaining about how little they had. They knew about the tithing laws, and they knew they hadn't been tithing. Malachi's prophecy would have sent them into angry despair if they didn't hear why God was so insistent about their giving. He wanted to bless them: "Test me in this . . . and see if I will not throw open the floodgates of heaven and pour out so much blessing that you will not have room enough for it" (3:10). Storing up their treasures in heaven (see Matthew 6:20) would actually increase their treasures on earth!

What we do with our finances has a direct bearing on our prayer life. Robbing God certainly puts a strain on the relationship. But there is a deeper reason for its importance: Jesus said giving was a form of investment, of storing up treasures in heaven, and added, "For where your treasure is, there your heart will be also" (Matthew 6:21).

This is where money and prayer intersect. Prayer is a matter of the heart; a bad heart makes for bad prayer, a good heart makes for good prayer. If our hearts are somewhere other than with the Lord, then our prayer life will suffer. If we put our treasure with God, then our hearts will be there too. It's that simple. "'Return to me, and I will return to you,' says the Lord Almighty" (Malachi 3:7). We can grow closer to God by what we do with our money. We don't truly give to God because what we have came from him in the first place. What happens is that when we give, we imitate God; we act like him, and thus form a deeper fellowship of love. We become a little more like his beloved Son. "For you know the grace of our Lord Jesus Christ, that though he was rich, yet for your sakes he became poor, so that you through his poverty might become rich" (2 Corinthians 8:9).

PRAY:

Gracious and generous God, you are my treasure; if giving you my money brings me closer to you, then no amount of giving is too much.

FOR YOUR NEXT DEVOTIONAL READING, GO TO PAGE 1134.

Through a Mighty Strength

MAGONUS SUCATUS PATRICIUS was just a boy at the time. The son of a prosperous Roman official, he lived in relative ease on a little farm on the western coast of the Roman Empire's territory today know as Britain. But one night everything in his life changed. Pirates ransacked the farm and shipped Patricius to Ireland as a slave.

Patricius spent the next six years as a slave, tending the flocks of a proud Irish territorial ruler named Milchu. Deprived of education, warm clothes and regular human contact, the heartbreak of his dismal situation would have finished him had he not begun to seek God in prayer. "I would pray constantly during the daylight hours," he wrote later. "The love of God and the fear of him surrounded me more and more—and faith grew and the Spirit was roused, so that in one day I would say as many as a hundred prayers and after dark nearly as many again … through snow, frost, rain."[1]

One night Patricius heard a mysterious voice speak to him: "Your hungers are rewarded: You are going home. Look, your ship is ready."[2] Shaken but excited, Patricius miraculously escaped his imprisonment and made the 200-mile journey to the sea. He found safe passage on a ship and returned home to an astonished family who received him as one brought back from the dead.

But for Patricius, home wasn't home anymore. He was haunted by a sense of restlessness, and he couldn't find a place to settle down. One night he had a disturbing dream. He saw an Irish man he knew holding many letters, one of them with the heading "The Voice of the Irish." Then he heard the sound of many Irish voices crying out, "We beg you to come and walk among us once more." Patricius woke up, "stabbed in the heart." He knew God was calling him back to Ireland.[3]

In 432, Patricius, the man we know as St. Patrick, sailed back to Ireland armed only with the gospel and prayer. He traveled the country in a chariot, spreading the gospel, calling for social reform, educating his converts and ultimately changing the culture of an entire people.

Patricius's work was always dangerous. The Irish were a warrior culture; their Druid priests held great power, and Patricius experienced many life-threatening confrontations. One account tells of how all the fires in Ireland were extinguished as a part of the Druid ritual of vernal equinox. When nightfall came, the Druids were enraged to find Patricius standing by a blazing fire in celebration of the resurrection of Christ. The Druids mobbed him and brought him before the authorities. He used the opportunity to speak boldly about the power of Christ and his resurrection. Some believed, but others swore to kill him.

Remarkable prayers came out of this missionary's experience of violent opposition and danger. Appropriately called "breastplate prayers," they are prayers for protection against the foes of the gospel—St. Patrick's efforts to put on the armor of God.

PRAY:

Pray this Breastplate Prayer of St. Patrick's:

"I arise today/Through a mighty strength, the invocation of the Trinity,/Through belief in the threeness,/Through confession of the oneness/Of the Creator of Creation . . . I arise today/Through God's strength to pilot me:/God's might to uphold me,/God's wisdom to guide me,/God's eye to look before me,/God's ear to hear me,/God's word to speak for me,/God's hand to guard me,/God's way to lie before me,/God's shield to protect me,/God's host to save me/From snares of devils,/From temptations of vices,/From everyone who shall wish me ill,/ Afar and anear,/Alone and in multitude."[4]

MEMORIZE:

It is God who arms me with strength and makes my way perfect.
He makes my feet like the feet of a deer;
he enables me to stand on the heights. PSALM 18:32–33

FOR YOUR NEXT DEVOTIONAL READING, GO TO PAGE 1141.

¹³"You have said harsh things against me," says the LORD.

"Yet you ask, 'What have we said against you?'

¹⁴"You have said, 'It is futile to serve God. What did we gain by carrying out his requirements and going about like mourners before the LORD Almighty? ¹⁵But now we call the arrogant blessed. Certainly the evildoers prosper, and even those who challenge God escape.'"

¹⁶Then those who feared the LORD talked with each other, and the LORD listened and heard. A scroll of remembrance was written in his presence concerning those who feared the LORD and honored his name.

¹⁷"They will be mine," says the LORD Almighty, "in the day when I make up my treasured possession.ᵃ I will spare them, just as in compassion a man spares his son who serves him. ¹⁸And you will again see the distinction between the righteous and the wicked, between those who serve God and those who do not.

The Day of the LORD

4 "Surely the day is coming; it will burn like a furnace. All the arrogant and every evildoer will be stubble, and that day that is coming will set them on fire," says the LORD Almighty. "Not a root or a branch will be left to them. ²But for you who revere my name, the sun of righteousness will rise with healing in its wings. And you will go out and leap like calves released from the stall. ³Then you will trample down the wicked; they will be ashes under the soles of your feet on the day when I do these things," says the LORD Almighty.

⁴"Remember the law of my servant Moses, the decrees and laws I gave him at Horeb for all Israel.

⁵"See, I will send you the prophet Elijah before that great and dreadful day of the LORD comes. ⁶He will turn the hearts of the fathers to their children, and the hearts of the children to their fathers; or else I will come and strike the land with a curse."

ᵃ17 Or Almighty, "my treasured possession, in the day when I act

The New Testament

Matthew

MANY SCHOLARS have recognized the book of Matthew as the most Jewish of the Gospels. Its first words are, "A record of the genealogy of Jesus Christ the son of David, the son of Abraham" (1:1). Matthew first and foremost wants to establish Jesus' credentials as the promised Jewish Messiah, the sum of the Jews' identity and hopes. Matthew's overriding passion is to show Jesus to be the fulfillment of all of God's Old Testament promises. Jesus fulfills all God did and said to his people throughout known history.

Although Matthew's Gospel begins by sounding as Jewish as can be, in the end his book delivers a message that is globally significant, a message for all generations. Along the way, hints of where Matthew is heading appear frequently. In Jesus' infancy, the Magi, men from other nations, come to worship the "king of the Jews" (2:2). Then the Gospel unfolds the story of John the Baptist, whose call to baptism in effect puts the entire Jewish nation on the same footing as every other nation (see 3:1–12).

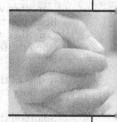

"YOUR FATHER KNOWS WHAT YOU NEED BEFORE YOU ASK HIM." (6:8)

Matthew tells how Jesus continues to widen the circle of God's grace. The exemplary faith of a Roman centurion earns Jesus' most glowing accolade, "I tell you the truth, I have not found anyone in Israel with such great faith" (8:10). In chapter 13, Jesus tells the parable of the weeds, in which the "field" represents the "world" (see 13:38). In chapter 15 we read the story of the faith of another non-Jew, a Canaanite woman (verses 21–28). By the end of his Gospel, Matthew leaves his readers with an identity and hope as big as the world. Jesus' parting words to his disciples are, "Go and make disciples of all nations" (28:19).

Surprisingly, it is the very Jewish nature of Matthew's perspective that serves as a bridge linking God's promises to a particular people with his intentions for all people. The son of David (1:1) is in truth the Son of God, the second person of the Trinity (see 28:19). He is the hope of all!

Just as God's vision for the nation of Israel was better and bigger than his people could imagine, so too is God's kingdom better and bigger than we can imagine. Even when we pray as Jesus taught, we always pray for more than we understand. The bread we are commanded to pray for (see 6:11) is but a sign of the "food that endures to eternal life" (John 6:27). God fulfills our hopes and our prayers in ways that no eye has seen, no ear has heard and no mind has conceived (see 1 Corinthians 2:9).

The Genealogy of Jesus

1 A record of the genealogy of Jesus Christ the son of David, the son of Abraham:

2 Abraham was the father of Isaac,
Isaac the father of Jacob,
Jacob the father of Judah and his brothers,
3 Judah the father of Perez and Zerah, whose mother was Tamar,
Perez the father of Hezron,
Hezron the father of Ram,
4 Ram the father of Amminadab,
Amminadab the father of Nahshon,
Nahshon the father of Salmon,
5 Salmon the father of Boaz, whose mother was Rahab,
Boaz the father of Obed, whose mother was Ruth,
Obed the father of Jesse,
6 and Jesse the father of King David.

David was the father of Solomon, whose mother had been Uriah's wife,
7 Solomon the father of Rehoboam,
Rehoboam the father of Abijah,
Abijah the father of Asa,
8 Asa the father of Jehoshaphat,
Jehoshaphat the father of Jehoram,
Jehoram the father of Uzziah,
9 Uzziah the father of Jotham,
Jotham the father of Ahaz,
Ahaz the father of Hezekiah,
10 Hezekiah the father of Manasseh,
Manasseh the father of Amon,
Amon the father of Josiah,
11 and Josiah the father of Jeconiah[a] and his brothers at the time of the exile to Babylon.

12 After the exile to Babylon:
Jeconiah was the father of Shealtiel,
Shealtiel the father of Zerubbabel,
13 Zerubbabel the father of Abiud,
Abiud the father of Eliakim,
Eliakim the father of Azor,
14 Azor the father of Zadok,
Zadok the father of Akim,
Akim the father of Eliud,
15 Eliud the father of Eleazar,
Eleazar the father of Matthan,
Matthan the father of Jacob,

16 and Jacob the father of Joseph, the husband of Mary, of whom was born Jesus, who is called Christ.

17 Thus there were fourteen generations in all from Abraham to David, fourteen from David to the exile to Babylon, and fourteen from the exile to the Christ.[b]

The Birth of Jesus Christ

18 This is how the birth of Jesus Christ came about: His mother Mary was pledged to be married to Joseph, but before they came together, she was found to be with child through the Holy Spirit. 19 Because Joseph her husband was a righteous man and did not want to expose her to public disgrace, he had in mind to divorce her quietly.

20 But after he had considered this, an angel of the Lord appeared to him in a dream and said, "Joseph son of David, do not be afraid to take Mary home as your wife, because what is conceived in her is from the Holy Spirit. 21 She will give birth to a son, and you are to give him the name Jesus,[c] because he will save his people from their sins."

22 All this took place to fulfill what the Lord had said through the prophet: 23 "The virgin will be with child and will give birth to a son, and they will call him Immanuel"[d]—which means, "God with us."

24 When Joseph woke up, he did what the angel of the Lord had commanded him and took Mary home as his wife. 25 But he had no union with her until she gave birth to a son. And he gave him the name Jesus.

The Visit of the Magi

2 After Jesus was born in Bethlehem in Judea, during the time of King Herod, Magi[e] from the east came to Jerusalem 2 and asked, "Where is the one who has been born king of the Jews? We saw his star in the east[f] and have come to worship him."

---

[a]11 That is, Jehoiachin; also in verse 12
[b]17 Or Messiah. "The Christ" (Greek) and "the Messiah" (Hebrew) both mean "the Anointed One."   [c]21 Jesus is the Greek form of Joshua, which means the LORD saves.   [d]23 Isaiah 7:14
[e]1 Traditionally Wise Men   [f]2 Or star when it rose

³When King Herod heard this he was disturbed, and all Jerusalem with him. ⁴When he had called together all the people's chief priests and teachers of the law, he asked them where the Christ*a* was to be born. ⁵"In Bethlehem in Judea," they replied, "for this is what the prophet has written:

⁶ " 'But you, Bethlehem, in the land of Judah,
    are by no means least among the rulers of Judah;

for out of you will come a ruler
    who will be the shepherd of my people Israel.'*b*"

⁷Then Herod called the Magi secretly and found out from them the exact time the star had appeared. ⁸He sent them to Bethlehem and said, "Go and make a careful search for the child. As soon as you find him, report to me, so that I too may go and worship him."

a4 Or *Messiah*   *b6* Micah 5:2

[MONDAY]

MATTHEW 1:1–17

He's Been Waiting for You

1:1 A RECORD OF THE GENEALOGY OF JESUS CHRIST.

This is one of two passages that many people skip over when reading the Gospels. The other is Luke 3:23–38. Both are genealogies, lists of obscure people with hard-to-pronounce names that serve as a kind of family tree or pedigree for Jesus. Both include names of people who can only be described as good, bad, ugly and surprising. Look up the names sometime; it's worth the effort.

When did God start thinking about Jesus? Matthew's list says it began at least with Abraham, 2000 years before Jesus was born. Luke's list goes back even further to Adam, the first human. Actually, the orthodox and correct answer is, God never *started* thinking about Jesus. God the Son was *always* with God the Father.

Maybe a better question is: When did God start thinking about us? The genealogies tell us that God has been thinking about saving us for a very long time. These names are like synapses in the mind of God, leading up to the great name he will speak in *Jesus*. The names in these genealogies are the connections in God's thoughts about his plan to save the world through his Son. Actually, his thoughts began before these people. "For he chose us in [Christ] before the creation of the world" (Ephesians 1:4).

Before you speak to God today, know that he has been speaking to you. To pray is to enter into the conversation. Jesus said your Father knows what you need before you ask him (see Matthew 6:8). That's because he knew you before you knew him. There is nothing you can say that can possibly surprise him—no sin you might confess, no need you might express. He has been waiting for you to talk with him for a very long time.

PRAY:

Father in Heaven! I come to you today knowing that you've been thinking about me for a long time now. Thank you for making me part of your eternal plan, and that I can join you in your grand purposes as I pray.

FOR YOUR NEXT DEVOTIONAL READING, GO TO PAGE 1146.

⁹After they had heard the king, they went on their way, and the star they had seen in the east^a went ahead of them until it stopped over the place where the child was. ¹⁰When they saw the star, they were overjoyed. ¹¹On coming to the house, they saw the child with his mother Mary, and they bowed down and worshiped him. Then they opened their treasures and presented him with gifts of gold and of incense and of myrrh. ¹²And having been warned in a dream not to go back to Herod, they returned to their country by another route.

The Escape to Egypt

¹³When they had gone, an angel of the Lord appeared to Joseph in a dream. "Get up," he said, "take the child and his mother and escape to Egypt. Stay there until I tell you, for Herod is going to search for the child to kill him."

¹⁴So he got up, took the child and his mother during the night and left for Egypt, ¹⁵where he stayed until the death of Herod. And so was fulfilled what the Lord had said through the prophet: "Out of Egypt I called my son."^{b}

¹⁶When Herod realized that he had been outwitted by the Magi, he was furious, and he gave orders to kill all the boys in Bethlehem and its vicinity who were two years old and under, in accordance with the time he had learned from the Magi. ¹⁷Then what was said through the prophet Jeremiah was fulfilled:

¹⁸ "A voice is heard in Ramah,
    weeping and great mourning,
Rachel weeping for her children
    and refusing to be comforted,
because they are no more."^{c}

The Return to Nazareth

¹⁹After Herod died, an angel of the Lord appeared in a dream to Joseph in Egypt ²⁰and said, "Get up, take the child and his mother and go to the land of Israel, for those who were trying to take the child's life are dead."

²¹So he got up, took the child and his mother and went to the land of Israel. ²²But when he heard that Archelaus was reigning in Judea in place of his father Herod, he was afraid to go there. Having

> *There is no way that Christians, in a private capacity, can do so much to promote the work of God and advance the kingdom of Christ as by prayer.*
>
> JONATHAN EDWARDS

been warned in a dream, he withdrew to the district of Galilee, ²³and he went and lived in a town called Nazareth. So was fulfilled what was said through the prophets: "He will be called a Nazarene."

John the Baptist Prepares the Way

3 In those days John the Baptist came, preaching in the Desert of Judea ²and saying, "Repent, for the kingdom of heaven is near." ³This is he who was spoken of through the prophet Isaiah:

"A voice of one calling in the desert,
'Prepare the way for the Lord,
    make straight paths for him.' "^{d}

⁴John's clothes were made of camel's hair, and he had a leather belt around his waist. His food was locusts and wild honey. ⁵People went out to him from Jerusalem and all Judea and the whole region of the Jordan. ⁶Confessing their sins, they were baptized by him in the Jordan River.

⁷But when he saw many of the Pharisees and Sadducees coming to where he was baptizing, he said to them: "You brood of vipers! Who warned you to flee from the coming wrath? ⁸Produce fruit in keeping with repentance. ⁹And do not think you can say to yourselves, 'We have Abraham as our father.' I tell you that out of these stones God can raise up children for Abraham. ¹⁰The ax is already at the root of the trees, and every tree that does not produce good fruit will be cut down and thrown into the fire.

¹¹ "I baptize you with^e water for repentance. But after me will come one who is more powerful than I, whose sandals I am not fit to carry. He will baptize you with the Holy Spirit and with fire. ¹²His winnowing fork is in his hand, and he will clear his threshing floor, gathering

^{a}9 Or *seen when it rose* ^{b}15 Hosea 11:1
^{c}18 Jer. 31:15 ^{d}3 Isaiah 40:3 ^{e}11 Or *in*

his wheat into the barn and burning up the chaff with unquenchable fire."

The Baptism of Jesus

¹³Then Jesus came from Galilee to the Jordan to be baptized by John. ¹⁴But John tried to deter him, saying, "I need to be baptized by you, and do you come to me?" ¹⁵Jesus replied, "Let it be so now; it is proper for us to do this to fulfill all righteousness." Then John consented.

¹⁶As soon as Jesus was baptized, he went up out of the water. At that moment heaven was opened, and he saw the Spirit of God descending like a dove and lighting on him. ¹⁷And a voice from heaven said, "This is my Son, whom I love; with him I am well pleased."

The Temptation of Jesus

4 Then Jesus was led by the Spirit into the desert to be tempted by the devil. ²After fasting forty days and forty nights, he was hungry. ³The tempter came to him and said, "If you are the Son of God, tell these stones to become bread."

⁴Jesus answered, "It is written: 'Man does not live on bread alone, but on every word that comes from the mouth of God.'ᵃ"

> JESUS answered, "It is written: 'Man does not live on bread alone, but on every word that comes from the mouth of God.'"
>
> MATTHEW 4:4

⁵Then the devil took him to the holy city and had him stand on the highest point of the temple. ⁶"If you are the Son of God," he said, "throw yourself down. For it is written:

"'He will command his angels
concerning you,
and they will lift you up in their
hands,
so that you will not strike your foot
against a stone.'ᵇ"

⁷Jesus answered him, "It is also written: 'Do not put the Lord your God to the test.'ᶜ"

⁸Again, the devil took him to a very high mountain and showed him all the kingdoms of the world and their splendor. ⁹"All this I will give you," he said, "if you will bow down and worship me."

¹⁰Jesus said to him, "Away from me, Satan! For it is written: 'Worship the Lord your God, and serve him only.'ᵈ"

¹¹Then the devil left him, and angels came and attended him.

Jesus Begins to Preach

¹²When Jesus heard that John had been put in prison, he returned to Galilee. ¹³Leaving Nazareth, he went and lived in Capernaum, which was by the lake in the area of Zebulun and Naphtali— ¹⁴to fulfill what was said through the prophet Isaiah:

¹⁵ "Land of Zebulun and land of
Naphtali,
the way to the sea, along the
Jordan,
Galilee of the Gentiles—
¹⁶ the people living in darkness
have seen a great light;
on those living in the land of the
shadow of death
a light has dawned."ᵉ

¹⁷From that time on Jesus began to preach, "Repent, for the kingdom of heaven is near."

The Calling of the First Disciples

¹⁸As Jesus was walking beside the Sea of Galilee, he saw two brothers, Simon called Peter and his brother Andrew. They were casting a net into the lake, for they were fishermen. ¹⁹"Come, follow me," Jesus said, "and I will make you fishers of men." ²⁰At once they left their nets and followed him.

²¹Going on from there, he saw two other brothers, James son of Zebedee and his brother John. They were in a boat with their father Zebedee, preparing their nets. Jesus called them, ²²and immediately they left the boat and their father and followed him.

Jesus Heals the Sick

²³Jesus went throughout Galilee, teaching in their synagogues, preaching the

ᵃ4 Deut. 8:3   ᵇ6 Psalm 91:11,12
ᶜ7 Deut. 6:16   ᵈ10 Deut. 6:13
ᵉ16 Isaiah 9:1,2

good news of the kingdom, and healing every disease and sickness among the people. ²⁴News about him spread all over Syria, and people brought to him all who were ill with various diseases, those suffering severe pain, the demon-possessed, those having seizures, and the paralyzed, and he healed them. ²⁵Large crowds from Galilee, the Decapolis,ᵃ Jerusalem, Judea and the region across the Jordan followed him.

The Beatitudes

5 Now when he saw the crowds, he went up on a mountainside and sat down. His disciples came to him, ²and he began to teach them, saying:

³ "Blessed are the poor in spirit,
   for theirs is the kingdom of heaven.
⁴ Blessed are those who mourn,
   for they will be comforted.
⁵ Blessed are the meek,
   for they will inherit the earth.
⁶ Blessed are those who hunger and
      thirst for righteousness,
   for they will be filled.
⁷ Blessed are the merciful,
   for they will be shown mercy.
⁸ Blessed are the pure in heart,
   for they will see God.
⁹ Blessed are the peacemakers,
   for they will be called sons of God.
¹⁰ Blessed are those who are persecuted
      because of righteousness,
   for theirs is the kingdom of heaven.

¹¹ "Blessed are you when people insult you, persecute you and falsely say all kinds of evil against you because of me. ¹²Rejoice and be glad, because great is your reward in heaven, for in the same way they persecuted the prophets who were before you.

Salt and Light

¹³ "You are the salt of the earth. But if the salt loses its saltiness, how can it be made salty again? It is no longer good for anything, except to be thrown out and trampled by men.

¹⁴ "You are the light of the world. A city on a hill cannot be hidden. ¹⁵Neither do people light a lamp and put it under a bowl. Instead they put it on its stand, and it gives light to everyone in the house. ¹⁶In the same way, let your light shine before men, that they may see your good deeds and praise your Father in heaven.

The Fulfillment of the Law

¹⁷ "Do not think that I have come to abolish the Law or the Prophets; I have not come to abolish them but to fulfill them. ¹⁸I tell you the truth, until heaven and earth disappear, not the smallest letter, not the least stroke of a pen, will by any means disappear from the Law until everything is accomplished. ¹⁹Anyone who breaks one of the least of these commandments and teaches others to do the same will be called least in the kingdom of heaven, but whoever practices and teaches these commands will be called great in the kingdom of heaven. ²⁰For I tell you that unless your righteousness surpasses that of the Pharisees and the teachers of the law, you will certainly not enter the kingdom of heaven.

Murder

²¹ "You have heard that it was said to the people long ago, 'Do not murder,ᵇ and anyone who murders will be subject to judgment.' ²²But I tell you that anyone who is angry with his brotherᶜ will be subject to judgment. Again, anyone who says to his brother, 'Raca,'ᵈ is answerable to the Sanhedrin. But anyone who says, 'You fool!' will be in danger of the fire of hell.

²³ "Therefore, if you are offering your gift at the altar and there remember that your brother has something against you, ²⁴leave your gift there in front of the altar. First go and be reconciled to your brother; then come and offer your gift.

²⁵ "Settle matters quickly with your adversary who is taking you to court. Do it while you are still with him on the way, or he may hand you over to the judge, and the judge may hand you over to the officer, and you may be thrown into prison. ²⁶I tell you the truth, you will not get out until you have paid the last penny.ᵉ

ᵃ25 That is, the Ten Cities   ᵇ21 Exodus 20:13
ᶜ22 Some manuscripts brother without cause
ᵈ22 An Aramaic term of contempt   ᵉ26 Greek kodrantes

Adultery

27"You have heard that it was said, 'Do not commit adultery.'[a] 28But I tell you that anyone who looks at a woman lustfully has already committed adultery with her in his heart. 29If your right eye causes you to sin, gouge it out and throw it away. It is better for you to lose one part of your body than for your whole body to be thrown into hell. 30And if your right hand causes you to sin, cut it off and throw it away. It is better for you to lose one part of your body than for your whole body to go into hell.

Divorce

31"It has been said, 'Anyone who divorces his wife must give her a certificate of divorce.'[b] 32But I tell you that anyone who divorces his wife, except for marital unfaithfulness, causes her to become an adulteress, and anyone who marries the divorced woman commits adultery.

Oaths

33"Again, you have heard that it was said to the people long ago, 'Do not break your oath, but keep the oaths you have made to the Lord.' 34But I tell you, Do not swear at all: either by heaven, for it is God's throne; 35or by the earth, for it is his footstool; or by Jerusalem, for it is the city of the Great King. 36And do not swear by your head, for you cannot make even one hair white or black. 37Simply let your 'Yes' be 'Yes,' and your 'No,' 'No'; anything beyond this comes from the evil one.

An Eye for an Eye

38"You have heard that it was said, 'Eye for eye, and tooth for tooth.'[c] 39But I tell you, Do not resist an evil person. If someone strikes you on the right cheek, turn to him the other also. 40And if someone wants to sue you and take your tunic, let him have your cloak as well. 41If someone forces you to go one mile, go with him two miles. 42Give to the one who asks you, and do not turn away from the one who wants to borrow from you.

Love for Enemies

43"You have heard that it was said, 'Love your neighbor[d] and hate your enemy.'

44But I tell you: Love your enemies[e] and pray for those who persecute you, 45that you may be sons of your Father in heaven. He causes his sun to rise on the evil and the good, and sends rain on the righteous and the unrighteous. 46If you love those who love you, what reward will you get? Are not even the tax collectors doing that? 47And if you greet only your brothers, what are you doing more than others? Do not even pagans do that? 48Be perfect, therefore, as your heavenly Father is perfect.

Giving to the Needy

6 "Be careful not to do your 'acts of righteousness' before men, to be seen by them. If you do, you will have no reward from your Father in heaven.

2"So when you give to the needy, do not announce it with trumpets, as the hypocrites do in the synagogues and on the streets, to be honored by men. I tell you the truth, they have received their reward in full. 3But when you give to the needy, do not let your left hand know what your right hand is doing, 4so that your giving may be in secret. Then your Father, who sees what is done in secret, will reward you.

Prayer

5"And when you pray, do not be like the hypocrites, for they love to pray standing in the synagogues and on the street corners to be seen by men. I tell you the truth, they have received their reward in full. 6But when you pray, go into your room, close the door and pray to your Father, who is unseen. Then your Father, who sees what is done in secret, will reward you. 7And when you pray, do not keep on babbling like pagans, for they think they will be heard because of their many words. 8Do not be like them, for your Father knows what you need before you ask him.

9"This, then, is how you should pray:

" 'Our Father in heaven,
hallowed be your name,

---

[a]27 Exodus 20:14   [b]31 Deut. 24:1
[c]38 Exodus 21:24; Lev. 24:20; Deut. 19:21
[d]43 Lev. 19:18   [e]44 Some late manuscripts
enemies, bless those who curse you, do good to
those who hate you

¹⁰your kingdom come,
  your will be done
    on earth as it is in heaven.
¹¹ Give us today our daily bread.
¹² Forgive us our debts,
  as we also have forgiven our
    debtors.
¹³ And lead us not into temptation,
  but deliver us from the evil one.^{a'}

¹⁴For if you forgive men when they sin against you, your heavenly Father will also forgive you. ¹⁵But if you do not forgive men their sins, your Father will not forgive your sins.

Fasting

¹⁶"When you fast, do not look somber as the hypocrites do, for they disfigure their faces to show men they are fasting. I tell you the truth, they have received their reward in full. ¹⁷But when you fast, put oil on your head and wash your face, ¹⁸so that it will not be obvious to men that you are fasting, but only to your Father, who is unseen; and your Father, who sees what is done in secret, will reward you.

^a13 Or from evil; some late manuscripts one, / for yours is the kingdom and the power and the glory forever. Amen.

[**TUESDAY**]

MATTHEW 6:5 – 8

At Ease With God

6:5 "AND WHEN YOU PRAY, DO NOT BE LIKE THE HYPOCRITES."

"Hypocrisy is the homage that vice pays to virtue," wrote La Rochefoucauld. With some cynicism he added, "Our virtues are frequently but vices disguised." The point, it seems, is that good is enormously attractive, even to those who are bad. If they won't be good, they at least try to look good.

The problem with praying as a hypocrite is that God can't be fooled. In God's eyes there is no exterior and interior person, no "public me" and "private me." There is only me. If I pray to look good to others and pull it off, Jesus said I will be rewarded all right; I will be well thought of by others. But that will be my only reward; I pray a spiritually impoverished prayer because I pray without God.

Pagans aren't unlike the hypocrites. Their repetitive babblings to a long list of gods may be sincere, but they are sincerely wrong in the same way hypocrites are insincerely "right": Both pray to false gods. The hypocrite thinks God doesn't see; the pagan doesn't know the true God. Jesus assures us that God both sees who we are on the inside, and knows what we need before we ask.

The good news is that we can be completely at ease with a God like this. There is no way we can surprise or shock him. He loves us as much before we confess our sins as he does after we confess them. He knows what we need before we do. We don't need to impress him with eloquence or theological depth in our prayers, and frankly, we can't anyway. The sincere lisp of a child's prayer means as much to him as a poet's greatest effort!

PRAY:

*Father, you know me inside and out. May that knowledge
encourage me to greater intimacy with you.*

FOR YOUR NEXT DEVOTIONAL READING, GO TO PAGE 1147.

The Sum of All Prayers

6:9 "THIS, THEN, IS HOW YOU SHOULD PRAY . . ."

Thomas Aquinas believed that everything we need to know is found in three documents: The Apostles' Creed tells us what to believe; the Ten Commandments tells us what to do; and the Lord's Prayer tells us what to pray.

The Lord's Prayer is like a compass. It points to our true north, God's heart, and when we know that, we can discern east, west and south. In other words, when we are clear on God's priorities, all other concerns fall into their proper place. The Lord's Prayer purifies our longings and desires, and gives them proper expression. Every area of our lives can be hung on the pegs of its petitions.

Clearly, Jesus meant for the Lord's Prayer to be repeated; not as meaning*less* repetitions (see 6:7), but as a meaning*ful* repetition. It can be like a Christmas tree, on which we hang our own "decorations," our own prayers. Or it can be like a map: The directions are there, but we must take the trouble to travel, to pray them.[1] Each direction, each guideline, says, "pray this way":

- That God's name be hallowed, revered, held in awe and adored. The beginning of wisdom, after all, is the fear of the Lord (see Psalm 111:10; Proverbs 1:7).

- That God's kingdom come, that he sovereignly bring about the glorious day when the earth will be as full of the knowledge of him as the waters that cover the sea (see Isaiah 11:9), that every knee will bow and every tongue confess that Jesus Christ is Lord (see Philippians 2:10–11).

- That God's will be our food and drink as we work and wait for his kingdom (see John 4:34).

- That God give us what we need in the meantime: our bread, our necessities, whatever we need to persevere (see Matthew 6:25–34).

- That God forgive our sins. Isn't it lovely that Jesus teaches us to wait before we talk to God about our sins—to speak first to God about *God* before we speak to God about *us*?

- That we be protected from every evil as we struggle in this spiritual warfare for God's rule on earth (see Ephesians 6:10–12).

PRAY:

Pray these petitions frequently. The variations are endless.

FOR YOUR NEXT DEVOTIONAL READING, GO TO PAGE 1148.

Forgive as You Have Been Forgiven

6:15 "BUT IF YOU DO NOT FORGIVE [OTHERS] THEIR SINS, YOUR FATHER WILL NOT FORGIVE YOUR SINS."

It is possible to pray and still be far from God. When Cain brought his offering to God, he was full of anger and hate. His heart was revealed by his actions toward his brother Abel when Abel's offering was accepted and Cain's was refused (see Genesis 4:1–8).

In the same way, the Pharisee praying alongside the tax collector was also far from God, though he imagined himself to standing in God's presence (see Luke 18:9–14). These two examples from Scripture indicate that there's a direct connection between our relationship to others and our relationship to God. If things aren't right between us and others, we can be sure they aren't right between us and God.

This powerful principle is especially true in the area of forgiveness. Jesus is alarmingly blunt. If you forgive others, God will forgive you. If you refuse others forgiveness, God will refuse you forgiveness. There is a profound logic here. It goes like this. Question: What do we most need from God? Answer: His mercy. Question: What do others most need from us? Answer: Our mercy. Question: How can we expect to receive what we most need from God if we refuse others the thing they most need from us?

What are we saying to God if we refuse to forgive others? Do we think their sin against us is so bad that it is beyond mercy? Or worse, do we think the sin God forgave us wasn't really so bad after all or that we in some way deserved his forgiveness? Either way, the cross is emptied of its power, God's mercy is trivialized and we make ourselves little gods.

To forgive requires humility and to be forgiven is very humbling. John Newton, the author of the hymn "Amazing Grace," was a slave trader and libertine before his conversion. He never forgot what it meant for God to forgive him, and what that forgiveness meant in his attitude toward others. He wrote, "A man, truly illuminated, will no more despise others, than Bartimaeus, after his own eyes were opened, would take a stick, and beat every blind man he met."

P R A Y :

As you pray, forgive those who have sinned against you.
If need be, ask God to forgive your lack of forgiveness.

FOR YOUR NEXT DEVOTIONAL READING, GO TO PAGE 1150.

Treasures in Heaven

19 "Do not store up for yourselves treasures on earth, where moth and rust destroy, and where thieves break in and steal. 20 But store up for yourselves treasures in heaven, where moth and rust do not destroy, and where thieves do not break in and steal. 21 For where your treasure is, there your heart will be also.

22 "The eye is the lamp of the body. If your eyes are good, your whole body will be full of light. 23 But if your eyes are bad, your whole body will be full of darkness. If then the light within you is darkness, how great is that darkness!

24 "No one can serve two masters. Either he will hate the one and love the other, or he will be devoted to the one and despise the other. You cannot serve both God and Money.

Do Not Worry

25 "Therefore I tell you, do not worry about your life, what you will eat or drink; or about your body, what you will wear. Is not life more important than food, and the body more important than clothes? 26 Look at the birds of the air; they do not sow or reap or store away in barns, and yet your heavenly Father feeds them. Are you not much more valuable than they? 27 Who of you by worrying can add a single hour to his life*a*? 28 "And why do you worry about clothes? See how the lilies of the field grow. They do not labor or spin. 29 Yet I tell you that not even Solomon in all his splendor was dressed like one of these. 30 If that is how God clothes the grass of the field, which is here today and tomorrow is thrown into the fire, will he not much more clothe you, O you of little faith? 31 So do not worry, saying, 'What shall we eat?' or 'What shall we drink?' or 'What shall we wear?' 32 For the pagans run after all these things, and your heavenly Father knows that you need them. 33 But seek first his kingdom and his righteousness, and all these things will be given to you as well. 34 Therefore do not worry about tomorrow, for tomorrow will worry about itself. Each day has enough trouble of its own.

Judging Others

7 "Do not judge, or you too will be judged. 2 For in the same way you judge others, you will be judged, and with the measure you use, it will be measured to you.

3 "Why do you look at the speck of sawdust in your brother's eye and pay no attention to the plank in your own eye? 4 How can you say to your brother, 'Let me take the speck out of your eye,' when all the time there is a plank in your own eye? 5 You hypocrite, first take the plank out of your own eye, and then you will see clearly to remove the speck from your brother's eye.

6 "Do not give dogs what is sacred; do not throw your pearls to pigs. If you do, they may trample them under their feet, and then turn and tear you to pieces.

Ask, Seek, Knock

7 "Ask and it will be given to you; seek and you will find; knock and the door will be opened to you. 8 For everyone who asks receives; he who seeks finds; and to him who knocks, the door will be opened.

9 "Which of you, if his son asks for bread, will give him a stone? 10 Or if he asks for a fish, will give him a snake? 11 If you, then, though you are evil, know how to give good gifts to your children, how much more will your Father in heaven give good gifts to those who ask him! 12 So in everything, do to others what you would have them do to you, for this sums up the Law and the Prophets.

The Narrow and Wide Gates

13 "Enter through the narrow gate. For wide is the gate and broad is the road that leads to destruction, and many enter through it. 14 But small is the gate and narrow the road that leads to life, and only a few find it.

A Tree and Its Fruit

15 "Watch out for false prophets. They come to you in sheep's clothing, but inwardly they are ferocious wolves. 16 By their fruit you will recognize them. Do people pick grapes from thornbushes, or figs from thistles? 17 Likewise every good tree bears

a27 Or single cubit to his height

good fruit, but a bad tree bears bad fruit. [18]A good tree cannot bear bad fruit, and a bad tree cannot bear good fruit. [19]Every tree that does not bear good fruit is cut down and thrown into the fire. [20]Thus, by their fruit you will recognize them.

[21]"Not everyone who says to me, 'Lord, Lord,' will enter the kingdom of heaven, but only he who does the will of my Father who is in heaven. [22]Many will say to me on that day, 'Lord, Lord, did we not prophesy in your name, and in your name drive out demons and perform many miracles?' [23]Then I will tell them plainly, 'I never knew you. Away from me, you evildoers!'

The Wise and Foolish Builders

[24]"Therefore everyone who hears these words of mine and puts them into practice is like a wise man who built his house on the rock. [25]The rain came

---

[FRIDAY]

MATTHEW 7:7–11

Always Ready to Listen

7:11 "HOW MUCH MORE WILL YOUR FATHER IN HEAVEN GIVE GOOD GIFTS TO THOSE WHO ASK HIM!"

Considering how much stock Jesus put in prayer, it's a little surprising how little he had to say about techniques or mechanics of prayer. Perhaps, since prayer is a heart matter, prayer is more about who we are than what we do. It's more about *communion,* or being with God, than it is about *communication,* or talking to God.

Other than his teaching in the Lord's Prayer (see Matthew 6:9–13), about all Jesus had to say about how to pray is to seek God and ask for what we need (see 7:7–8) and to keep at it, to persist and persevere (see Luke 18:1–8). But he had more to say about *why* we should pray. He reasoned this way: Even imperfect people can be pretty good parents because even people who don't have it all together know how to give good things to their kids. Everyone knows this. So how much more will our Father in heaven, of whom even the best parents are but rough copies, give good things to those who ask him? God is the very best parent, always ready to listen and incredibly generous with his gifts (verses 9–11).

Luke's version of this passage tells us that Jesus specified the Holy Spirit as God's good gift. "How much more will your Father in heaven give the Holy Spirit to those who ask him!" (Luke 11:13). Here is an even more profound reason to trust God's good intentions for us. Not only does God want to give us good gifts, he wants to give us himself in the person of the Holy Spirit.

So we persist and persevere in prayer, not because God is reluctant to give, but because he is so very ready to give! "Perseverance is the rope that ties the soul to the doorpost of heaven," wrote Francis Roberts. But we would not have the rope unless God had first thrown it down to us.

PRAY:
Father, you have commanded this: So I seek your good gifts,
I ask you to meet my needs and those of the world, but above all
I pray for your presence and seek your face.

FOR YOUR NEXT DEVOTIONAL READING, GO TO PAGE 1152.

down, the streams rose, and the winds blew and beat against that house; yet it did not fall, because it had its foundation on the rock. [26]But everyone who hears these words of mine and does not put them into practice is like a foolish man who built his house on sand. [27]The rain came down, the streams rose, and the winds blew and beat against that house, and it fell with a great crash."

[28]When Jesus had finished saying these things, the crowds were amazed at his teaching, [29]because he taught as one who had authority, and not as their teachers of the law.

The Man With Leprosy

8 When he came down from the mountainside, large crowds followed him. [2]A man with leprosy[a] came and knelt before him and said, "Lord, if you are willing, you can make me clean."

[3]Jesus reached out his hand and touched the man. "I am willing," he said. "Be clean!" Immediately he was cured[b] of his leprosy. [4]Then Jesus said to him, "See that you don't tell anyone. But go, show yourself to the priest and offer the gift Moses commanded, as a testimony to them."

The Faith of the Centurion

[5]When Jesus had entered Capernaum, a centurion came to him, asking for help. [6]"Lord," he said, "my servant lies at home paralyzed and in terrible suffering."

[7]Jesus said to him, "I will go and heal him."

[8]The centurion replied, "Lord, I do not deserve to have you come under my roof. But just say the word, and my servant will be healed. [9]For I myself am a man under authority, with soldiers under me. I tell this one, 'Go,' and he goes; and that one, 'Come,' and he comes. I say to my servant, 'Do this,' and he does it."

[10]When Jesus heard this, he was astonished and said to those following him, "I tell you the truth, I have not found anyone in Israel with such great faith. [11]I say to you that many will come from the east and the west, and will take their places at the feast with Abraham, Isaac and Jacob in the kingdom of heaven. [12]But the subjects of the kingdom will be thrown outside, into the darkness, where there will be weeping and gnashing of teeth." [13]Then Jesus said to the centurion, "Go! It will be done just as you believed it would." And his servant was healed at that very hour.

Jesus Heals Many

[14]When Jesus came into Peter's house, he saw Peter's mother-in-law lying in bed with a fever. [15]He touched her hand and the fever left her, and she got up and began to wait on him.

[16]When evening came, many who were demon-possessed were brought to him, and he drove out the spirits with a word and healed all the sick. [17]This was to fulfill what was spoken through the prophet Isaiah:

"He took up our infirmities
and carried our diseases."[c]

The Cost of Following Jesus

[18]When Jesus saw the crowd around him, he gave orders to cross to the other side of the lake. [19]Then a teacher of the law came to him and said, "Teacher, I will follow you wherever you go."

[20]Jesus replied, "Foxes have holes and birds of the air have nests, but the Son of Man has no place to lay his head." [21]Another disciple said to him, "Lord, first let me go and bury my father."

[22]But Jesus told him, "Follow me, and let the dead bury their own dead."

Jesus Calms the Storm

[23]Then he got into the boat and his disciples followed him. [24]Without warning, a furious storm came up on the lake, so that the waves swept over the boat. But Jesus was sleeping. [25]The disciples went and woke him, saying, "Lord, save us! We're going to drown!"

[26]He replied, "You of little faith, why are you so afraid?" Then he got up and rebuked the winds and the waves, and it was completely calm.

[27]The men were amazed and asked, "What kind of man is this? Even the winds and the waves obey him!"

---

[a]2 The Greek word was used for various diseases affecting the skin—not necessarily leprosy.
[b]3 Greek *made clean*   [c]17 Isaiah 53:4

Man of Prayer

E. M. BOUNDS never forgot the men who had fought and died under his care. While serving as a chaplain in the Confederate army, he won the respect of the men he served, traveling with them, leading them in prayer and worship, and braving the front lines in some of the bloodiest battles in American history. He served until 1864, when he and his men were soundly defeated and captured in Franklin, Tennessee. Exhausted and battle-weary, his battalion signed an oath of allegiance to the Union. The war was soon over.

For the rest of his days Bounds kept a list of the names of the soldiers from his battalion in his wallet so he could pray for their families. The postwar South was in shambles; its people defeated and dejected. The chilling evidence of war was everywhere, from charred barns and houses to the common sight of men without arms, legs or eyes. Bounds felt a deep love for the defeated people of Franklin and served as their faithful intercessor and preacher in a local pulpit.

Bounds strongly believed in the power of prayer. He gathered a group of men to pray with him every Tuesday night for revival, "until God answered by fire." A year passed, but the men continued praying. Finally, revival did come, and nearly 150 men and women "were gloriously converted." Soon afterward, Bounds moved on to ministry in Alabama and Missouri, and continued in his passion to pray for the revival of the American church.

Later, Bounds became editor of the *Christian Advocate,* the official publication of the Methodist Episcopal Church. He spent his years with the *Advocate* calling the church to pray for revival while fighting the rising invasion of theological liberalism in America. "It is not new truth that the world needs," wrote Bounds, "so much as the constant iteration of old truths, yet ever new truths, of the Bible."

For the last 17 years of his life, Bounds lived with his family in Washington, Georgia. His time was spent reading, writing and praying. His habit was to rise every morning at four o'clock for prayer, breaking at seven o'clock for breakfast and then spending the morning writing, only to return to prayer in the afternoon. His writings, many of them published posthumously, are considered to be classic works on prayer. On August 24, 1913, E. M. Bounds died—an old soldier of Jesus. A close friend received a postcard from Bounds written shortly before his death. It read: "Hold to the old truths—double distilled."

Bounds' writings on prayer are imminently quotable. He was at his best when speaking prophetically:

"We are constantly on a stretch, if not a strain, to devise new methods, new plans, new organizations to advance the church and secure enlargement and efficiency for the gospel. This trend of the day has a tendency to lose sight of the man or sink the man in the plan or the organization. God's plan is to make much of the man, far more of him than of anything else. Men are God's method. The church is looking for better methods; God is looking for better men ... What the church needs today is not more machinery or better, not new organizations or more and novel methods, but men whom the Holy Spirit can use— men of prayer, mighty in prayer. The Holy Spirit does not flow through methods, but through men. He does not come on machinery, but on men. He does not anoint plans, but men—men of prayer."[2]

PRAY:

Spirit of God, I want to be a person of prayer. Use me,
flow through me, anoint me—to be mighty in prayer.

MEMORIZE:

Be joyful always; pray continually; give thanks
in all circumstances, for this is God's will for
you in Christ Jesus. 1 THESSALONIANS 5:16–18

FOR YOUR NEXT DEVOTIONAL READING, GO TO PAGE 1154.

The Healing of Two Demon-possessed Men

²⁸When he arrived at the other side in the region of the Gadarenes,ᵃ two demon-possessed men coming from the tombs met him. They were so violent that no one could pass that way. ²⁹"What do you want with us, Son of God?" they shouted. "Have you come here to torture us before the appointed time?"

³⁰Some distance from them a large herd of pigs was feeding. ³¹The demons begged Jesus, "If you drive us out, send us into the herd of pigs."

³²He said to them, "Go!" So they came out and went into the pigs, and the whole herd rushed down the steep bank into the lake and died in the water.

ᵃ28 Some manuscripts *Gergesenes*; others *Gerasenes*

[MONDAY]

MATTHEW 8:5–13

How to Astonish Jesus

8:10 WHEN JESUS HEARD THIS, HE WAS ASTONISHED.

It would be very hard to impress the one who spoke the universe into existence (see Hebrews 1:1–3; 11:2), much less astonish him. But only once in the New Testament is it said that Jesus was actually astonished. This is that one occasion. What makes Jesus' astonishment even more astonishing is that it was not in reaction to the words of a Pharisee, one of the spiritual leaders of God's chosen people, but at the words of a Gentile, an outsider, an officer in the Roman army of occupation. And even more impressive is that Jesus is delighted and amazed at this man's *faith*.

Faith lets God be God as nothing else can. Faith is about receiving. It is God's nature to give to his children with overflowing grace. In faith we open our hands and let God give all that he wants to give us. Psalm 104 tells us how God rejoices to feed and water his creation: "He makes grass grow for the cattle, and plants for man to cultivate—bringing forth food from the earth: wine that gladdens the heart of man, oil to make his face shine, and bread that sustains his heart" (verses 14–15). The very pinnacle of God's giving of himself to us was in his Son Jesus, who broke bread and said, "Take and eat; this is my body" (Matthew 26:26). And God actually grieves when we *won't* receive his grace. He even pleads, "If you would but listen to me, O Israel ... Open wide your mouth and I will fill it ... If my people would but listen to me" (Psalm 81:8,10,13).

Jesus appreciated the centurion's faith because the man humbly and without reservation accepted the healing Jesus gave his servant. Hebrews 11:6 declares that without faith it is impossible to please God. With his great faith, the centurion surely pleased Jesus.

And with faith you, too, may astonish Jesus, and you will definitely please him. Tell him what you need today, and as you do, thank him that it is his pleasure to give it.

PRAY:
Thank you, dear Jesus, that it so pleases you when
I open my hand to receive your good gifts. I do so now.

FOR YOUR NEXT DEVOTIONAL READING, GO TO PAGE 1157.

33Those tending the pigs ran off, went into the town and reported all this, including what had happened to the demon-possessed men. 34Then the whole town went out to meet Jesus. And when they saw him, they pleaded with him to leave their region.

Jesus Heals a Paralytic

9 Jesus stepped into a boat, crossed over and came to his own town. 2Some men brought to him a paralytic, lying on a mat. When Jesus saw their faith, he said to the paralytic, "Take heart, son; your sins are forgiven."

3At this, some of the teachers of the law said to themselves, "This fellow is blaspheming!"

4Knowing their thoughts, Jesus said, "Why do you entertain evil thoughts in your hearts? 5Which is easier: to say, 'Your sins are forgiven,' or to say, 'Get up and walk'? 6But so that you may know that the Son of Man has authority on earth to forgive sins..." Then he said to the paralytic, "Get up, take your mat and go home." 7And the man got up and went home. 8When the crowd saw this, they were filled with awe; and they praised God, who had given such authority to men.

The Calling of Matthew

9As Jesus went on from there, he saw a man named Matthew sitting at the tax collector's booth. "Follow me," he told him, and Matthew got up and followed him.

10While Jesus was having dinner at Matthew's house, many tax collectors and "sinners" came and ate with him and his disciples. 11When the Pharisees saw this, they asked his disciples, "Why does your teacher eat with tax collectors and 'sinners'?"

12On hearing this, Jesus said, "It is not the healthy who need a doctor, but the sick. 13But go and learn what this means: 'I desire mercy, not sacrifice.'a For I have not come to call the righteous, but sinners."

Jesus Questioned About Fasting

14Then John's disciples came and asked him, "How is it that we and the Pharisees fast, but your disciples do not fast?"

15Jesus answered, "How can the guests of the bridegroom mourn while he is with them? The time will come when the bridegroom will be taken from them; then they will fast.

16"No one sews a patch of unshrunk cloth on an old garment, for the patch will pull away from the garment, making the tear worse. 17Neither do men pour new wine into old wineskins. If they do, the skins will burst, the wine will run out and the wineskins will be ruined. No, they pour new wine into new wineskins, and both are preserved."

A Dead Girl and a Sick Woman

18While he was saying this, a ruler came and knelt before him and said, "My daughter has just died. But come and put your hand on her, and she will live." 19Jesus got up and went with him, and so did his disciples.

20Just then a woman who had been subject to bleeding for twelve years came up behind him and touched the edge of his cloak. 21She said to herself, "If I only touch his cloak, I will be healed."

22Jesus turned and saw her. "Take heart, daughter," he said, "your faith has healed you." And the woman was healed from that moment.

23When Jesus entered the ruler's house and saw the flute players and the noisy crowd, 24he said, "Go away. The girl is not dead but asleep." But they laughed at him. 25After the crowd had been put outside, he went in and took the girl by the hand, and she got up. 26News of this spread through all that region.

Jesus Heals the Blind and Mute

27As Jesus went on from there, two blind men followed him, calling out, "Have mercy on us, Son of David!"

28When he had gone indoors, the blind men came to him, and he asked them, "Do you believe that I am able to do this?"

"Yes, Lord," they replied.

29Then he touched their eyes and said, "According to your faith will it be done to you"; 30and their sight was restored. Jesus warned them sternly, "See that no

a13 Hosea 6:6

one knows about this." ³¹But they went out and spread the news about him all over that region.

³²While they were going out, a man who was demon-possessed and could not talk was brought to Jesus. ³³And when the demon was driven out, the man who had been mute spoke. The crowd was amazed and said, "Nothing like this has ever been seen in Israel."

³⁴But the Pharisees said, "It is by the prince of demons that he drives out demons."

The Workers Are Few

³⁵Jesus went through all the towns and villages, teaching in their synagogues, preaching the good news of the kingdom and healing every disease and sickness. ³⁶When he saw the crowds, he had compassion on them, because they were harassed and helpless, like sheep without a shepherd. ³⁷Then he said to his disciples, "The harvest is plentiful but the workers are few. ³⁸Ask the Lord of the harvest, therefore, to send out workers into his harvest field."

Jesus Sends Out the Twelve

10 He called his twelve disciples to him and gave them authority to drive out evil*ᵃ* spirits and to heal every disease and sickness.

²These are the names of the twelve apostles: first, Simon (who is called Peter) and his brother Andrew; James son of Zebedee, and his brother John; ³Philip and Bartholomew; Thomas and Matthew the tax collector; James son of Alphaeus, and Thaddaeus; ⁴Simon the Zealot and Judas Iscariot, who betrayed him.

⁵These twelve Jesus sent out with the following instructions: "Do not go among the Gentiles or enter any town of the Samaritans. ⁶Go rather to the lost sheep of Israel. ⁷As you go, preach this message: 'The kingdom of heaven is near.' ⁸Heal the sick, raise the dead, cleanse those who have leprosy,*ᵇ* drive out demons. Freely you have received, freely give. ⁹Do not take along any gold or silver or copper in your belts; ¹⁰take no bag for the journey, or extra tunic, or sandals or a staff; for the worker is worth his keep.

¹¹"Whatever town or village you enter, search for some worthy person there and stay at his house until you leave. ¹²As you enter the home, give it your greeting. ¹³If the home is deserving, let your peace rest on it; if it is not, let your peace return to you. ¹⁴If anyone will not welcome you or listen to your words, shake the dust off your feet when you leave that home or town. ¹⁵I tell you the truth, it will be more bearable for Sodom and Gomorrah on the day of judgment than for that town. ¹⁶I am sending you out like sheep among wolves. Therefore be as shrewd as snakes and as innocent as doves.

¹⁷"Be on your guard against men; they will hand you over to the local councils and flog you in their synagogues. ¹⁸On my account you will be brought before governors and kings as witnesses to them and to the Gentiles. ¹⁹But when they arrest you, do not worry about what to say or how to say it. At that time you will be given what to say, ²⁰for it will not be you speaking, but the Spirit of your Father speaking through you.

²¹"Brother will betray brother to death, and a father his child; children will rebel against their parents and have them put to death. ²²All men will hate you because of me, but he who stands firm to the end will be saved. ²³When you are persecuted in one place, flee to another. I tell you the truth, you will not finish going through the cities of Israel before the Son of Man comes.

²⁴"A student is not above his teacher, nor a servant above his master. ²⁵It is enough for the student to be like his teacher, and the servant like his master. If the head of the house has been called Beelzebub,*ᶜ* how much more the members of his household!

²⁶"So do not be afraid of them. There is nothing concealed that will not be disclosed, or hidden that will not be made known. ²⁷What I tell you in the dark, speak in the daylight; what is whispered in your ear, proclaim from the roofs. ²⁸Do not be afraid of those who kill the body but cannot kill the soul. Rather, be afraid of the One who can destroy both soul

---

ᵃ1 Greek unclean   *ᵇ8 The Greek word was used for various diseases affecting the skin—not necessarily leprosy.*   *ᶜ25 Greek Beezeboul or Beelzeboul*

and body in hell. ²⁹Are not two sparrows sold for a penny*ᵃ*? Yet not one of them will fall to the ground apart from the will of your Father. ³⁰And even the very hairs of your head are all numbered. ³¹So don't be afraid; you are worth more than many sparrows.

³²"Whoever acknowledges me before men, I will also acknowledge him before my Father in heaven. ³³But whoever disowns me before men, I will disown him before my Father in heaven.

*ᵃ*29 Greek *an assarion*

MATTHEW 9:35–38

[**TUESDAY**]

Why Even Try?

9:38 "ASK THE LORD OF THE HARVEST, THEREFORE, TO SEND OUT WORKERS INTO HIS HARVEST FIELD."

So many people, so much need, so few resources. If you and I were faced with the crowds that Jesus saw before him, we probably would have given up. No amount of love and food would have been enough to meet their needs, so why even try?

But Jesus saw those crowds, harassed and helpless, and his first impulse was not hopelessness, but compassion, not just on the crowds before him, but also on all humanity. And the first thing he tells his disciples (and us) to do is pray.

Prayer is primary because only God is big enough to do the impossible. Only God, the Great Shepherd of the sheep, can marshal the resources and the people—especially the people—necessary to care for the helpless and harassed. Prayer is not the last resort; it is the first. It is not something to be done instead of compassion; it is the beginning of compassion. Jesus' heart goes out to these lost ones, so he prays.

Prayer is the beginning of compassion, but not the end of it. True prayer comes from love and leads to more love, active love. Those who pray authentically are always ready to be the answer to the prayer they have prayed. Jesus urged his disciples to pray for the Lord of the harvest to send out workers, and in the very next verse (10:1), he equipped them to go out and be the workers they prayed would come!

Prayer comes from compassion and leads to hope. It opens our eyes to see the possibilities. We see a multitude of lost and needy people. God sees a harvest of souls for eternal life. To pray with Jesus for the lost is to put our love and hope to work. Let your mind range far and wide around the world. There are neighbors and nations and peoples and tribes who don't know the Savior. The AIDS pandemic rages across Africa and Asia. Poverty saps the life out of helpless children. Oppression and injustice hold billions in their grip. Take heart, be strong, and ask the Lord of the harvest to send people—to send you!—to do his great work. There is a kingdom to build (Matthew 16:18–19) and harvests to reap.

PRAY:

Lord of the harvest, Shepherd of the sheep, because of your great love, send your people to love the harassed and helpless in your name. Send me.

FOR YOUR NEXT DEVOTIONAL READING, GO TO PAGE 1160.

³⁴"Do not suppose that I have come to bring peace to the earth. I did not come to bring peace, but a sword. ³⁵For I have come to turn

" 'a man against his father,
a daughter against her mother,
a daughter-in-law against her
mother-in-law—
³⁶ a man's enemies will be the
members of his own
household.'ᵃ

³⁷"Anyone who loves his father or mother more than me is not worthy of me; anyone who loves his son or daughter more than me is not worthy of me; ³⁸and anyone who does not take his cross and follow me is not worthy of me. ³⁹Whoever finds his life will lose it, and whoever loses his life for my sake will find it.

⁴⁰"He who receives you receives me, and he who receives me receives the one who sent me. ⁴¹Anyone who receives a prophet because he is a prophet will receive a prophet's reward, and anyone who receives a righteous man because he is a righteous man will receive a righteous man's reward. ⁴²And if anyone gives even a cup of cold water to one of these little ones because he is my disciple, I tell you the truth, he will certainly not lose his reward."

Jesus and John the Baptist

11 After Jesus had finished instructing his twelve disciples, he went on from there to teach and preach in the towns of Galilee.ᵇ

²When John heard in prison what Christ was doing, he sent his disciples ³to ask him, "Are you the one who was to come, or should we expect someone else?"

⁴Jesus replied, "Go back and report to John what you hear and see: ⁵The blind receive sight, the lame walk, those who have leprosyᶜ are cured, the deaf hear, the dead are raised, and the good news is preached to the poor. ⁶Blessed is the man who does not fall away on account of me."

⁷As John's disciples were leaving, Jesus began to speak to the crowd about John: "What did you go out into the desert to see? A reed swayed by the wind? ⁸If not, what did you go out to see? A man dressed in fine clothes? No, those who wear fine clothes are in kings' palaces. ⁹Then what did you go out to see? A prophet? Yes, I tell you, and more than a prophet. ¹⁰This is the one about whom it is written:

" 'I will send my messenger ahead of
you,
who will prepare your way before
you.'ᵈ

¹¹I tell you the truth: Among those born of women there has not risen anyone greater than John the Baptist; yet he who is least in the kingdom of heaven is greater than he. ¹²From the days of John the Baptist until now, the kingdom of heaven has been forcefully advancing, and forceful men lay hold of it. ¹³For all the Prophets and the Law prophesied until John. ¹⁴And if you are willing to accept it, he is the Elijah who was to come. ¹⁵He who has ears, let him hear.

¹⁶"To what can I compare this generation? They are like children sitting in the marketplaces and calling out to others:

¹⁷ " 'We played the flute for you,
and you did not dance;
we sang a dirge,
and you did not mourn.'

¹⁸For John came neither eating nor drinking, and they say, 'He has a demon.' ¹⁹The Son of Man came eating and drinking, and they say, 'Here is a glutton and a drunkard, a friend of tax collectors and "sinners." ' But wisdom is proved right by her actions."

Woe on Unrepentant Cities

²⁰Then Jesus began to denounce the cities in which most of his miracles had been performed, because they did not repent. ²¹"Woe to you, Korazin! Woe to you, Bethsaida! If the miracles that were performed in you had been performed in Tyre and Sidon, they would have repented long ago in sackcloth and ashes. ²²But I tell you, it will be more bearable for

---

ᵃ36 Micah 7:6   ᵇ1 Greek in their towns
ᶜ5 The Greek word was used for various diseases
affecting the skin—not necessarily leprosy.
ᵈ10 Mal. 3:1

Tyre and Sidon on the day of judgment than for you. ²³And you, Capernaum, will you be lifted up to the skies? No, you will go down to the depths.ᵃ If the miracles that were performed in you had been performed in Sodom, it would have remained to this day. ²⁴But I tell you that it will be more bearable for Sodom on the day of judgment than for you."

Rest for the Weary

²⁵At that time Jesus said, "I praise you, Father, Lord of heaven and earth, because you have hidden these things from the wise and learned, and revealed them to little children. ²⁶Yes, Father, for this was your good pleasure.

²⁷"All things have been committed to me by my Father. No one knows the Son except the Father, and no one knows the Father except the Son and those to whom the Son chooses to reveal him.

²⁸"Come to me, all you who are weary and burdened, and I will give you rest. ²⁹Take my yoke upon you and learn from me, for I am gentle and humble in heart, and you will find rest for your souls. ³⁰For my yoke is easy and my burden is light."

Lord of the Sabbath

12 At that time Jesus went through the grainfields on the Sabbath. His disciples were hungry and began to pick some heads of grain and eat them. ²When the Pharisees saw this, they said to him, "Look! Your disciples are doing what is unlawful on the Sabbath."

³He answered, "Haven't you read what David did when he and his companions were hungry? ⁴He entered the house of God, and he and his companions ate the consecrated bread—which was not lawful for them to do, but only for the priests. ⁵Or haven't you read in the Law that on the Sabbath the priests in the temple desecrate the day and yet are innocent? ⁶I tell you that oneᵇ greater than the temple is here. ⁷If you had known what these words mean, 'I desire mercy, not sacrifice,'ᶜ you would not have condemned the innocent. ⁸For the Son of Man is Lord of the Sabbath."

⁹Going on from that place, he went into their synagogue, ¹⁰and a man with a shriveled hand was there. Looking for a reason to accuse Jesus, they asked him, "Is it lawful to heal on the Sabbath?"

¹¹He said to them, "If any of you has a sheep and it falls into a pit on the Sabbath, will you not take hold of it and lift it out? ¹²How much more valuable is a man than a sheep! Therefore it is lawful to do good on the Sabbath."

¹³Then he said to the man, "Stretch out your hand." So he stretched it out and it was completely restored, just as sound as the other. ¹⁴But the Pharisees went out and plotted how they might kill Jesus.

God's Chosen Servant

¹⁵Aware of this, Jesus withdrew from that place. Many followed him, and he healed all their sick, ¹⁶warning them not to tell who he was. ¹⁷This was to fulfill what was spoken through the prophet Isaiah:

¹⁸ "Here is my servant whom I have
          chosen,
     the one I love, in whom I delight;
 I will put my Spirit on him,
     and he will proclaim justice to the
          nations.
¹⁹ He will not quarrel or cry out;
     no one will hear his voice in the
          streets.
²⁰ A bruised reed he will not break,
     and a smoldering wick he will not
          snuff out,
 till he leads justice to victory.
²¹   In his name the nations will put
          their hope."ᵈ

Jesus and Beelzebub

²²Then they brought him a demon-possessed man who was blind and mute, and Jesus healed him, so that he could both talk and see. ²³All the people were astonished and said, "Could this be the Son of David?"

²⁴But when the Pharisees heard this, they said, "It is only by Beelzebub,ᵉ the prince of demons, that this fellow drives out demons."

²⁵Jesus knew their thoughts and said to them, "Every kingdom divided against

---

ᵃ23 Greek *Hades*   ᵇ6 Or *something*; also in verses 41 and 42   ᶜ7 Hosea 6:6
ᵈ21 Isaiah 42:1–4   ᵉ24 Greek *Beezeboul* or *Beelzeboul*; also in verse 27

itself will be ruined, and every city or household divided against itself will not stand. ²⁶If Satan drives out Satan, he is divided against himself. How then can his kingdom stand? ²⁷And if I drive out demons by Beelzebub, by whom do your people drive them out? So then, they will be your judges. ²⁸But if I drive out demons by the Spirit of God, then the kingdom of God has come upon you.

²⁹"Or again, how can anyone enter a strong man's house and carry off his possessions unless he first ties up the strong man? Then he can rob his house.

MATTHEW 11:25–30

{WEDNESDAY}

Know Thyself

11:25 "I PRAISE YOU, FATHER ... BECAUSE YOU HAVE HIDDEN THESE THINGS FROM THE WISE AND LEARNED, AND REVEALED THEM TO LITTLE CHILDREN."

The 16th century theologian and reformer John Calvin began his monumental *Institutes of the Christian Religion* with an assertion that sounds startlingly modern, even psychological: "Without knowledge of self there is no knowledge of God ... Without knowledge of God there is no knowledge of self."[3] This certainly makes sense on a human level: A man cannot be a husband unless he has some idea of what a husband is, as well as an idea of what a wife is. Knowledge of the two goes together—of the self and the other. It is no different with God because our relationship with God is just that—a *relationship* between an I and a Thou, a self and an Other.

In order to pray, what do you need to know about yourself and God? Jesus tells you about both. Of himself, Jesus says that he is gentle and humble in heart, and that he offers rest for your soul. Notice what he is not: He is not a dictator or a slave driver, a project manager trying to get the most out of you. He doesn't want to burn you out. He won't add to the burdens you bring him in prayer. "A bruised reed he will not break, and a smoldering wick he will not snuff out" (Matthew 12:20). That's very good news about Jesus. It gives you confidence to go to him, doesn't it?

What do you need to know about yourself? In a word, Jesus says you need to know you are like a little child. In this context, being a child is the opposite of proud. The proud are those Jesus calls "wise and learned," whose confidence is in themselves, not in God or anybody else. The proud cannot really pray, because, as C. S. Lewis said, "A proud man is always looking down on things and people; and, of course, as long as you are looking down, you cannot see something that is above you." God resists the proud, but he gives grace to the humble (see 1 Peter 5:5)—the grace to know yourself and to know God.

That's good news about you too, very good news. You don't have to be anyone important or super-spiritual to come to Jesus. All you need to be is yourself—his child, in need of love and mercy. And doesn't that give you confidence to pray?

PRAY:
Father, dear Father, I happily renounce all my pretensions to strength. My only hope is in the gentle mercy of your Son. Teach me your way, Jesus.

FOR YOUR NEXT DEVOTIONAL READING, GO TO PAGE 1169.

³⁰"He who is not with me is against me, and he who does not gather with me scatters. ³¹And so I tell you, every sin and blasphemy will be forgiven men, but the blasphemy against the Spirit will not be forgiven. ³²Anyone who speaks a word against the Son of Man will be forgiven, but anyone who speaks against the Holy Spirit will not be forgiven, either in this age or in the age to come.

³³"Make a tree good and its fruit will be good, or make a tree bad and its fruit will be bad, for a tree is recognized by its fruit. ³⁴You brood of vipers, how can you who are evil say anything good? For out of the overflow of the heart the mouth speaks. ³⁵The good man brings good things out of the good stored up in him, and the evil man brings evil things out of the evil stored up in him. ³⁶But I tell you that men will have to give account on the day of judgment for every careless word they have spoken. ³⁷For by your words you will be acquitted, and by your words you will be condemned."

The Sign of Jonah

³⁸Then some of the Pharisees and teachers of the law said to him, "Teacher, we want to see a miraculous sign from you."

³⁹He answered, "A wicked and adulterous generation asks for a miraculous sign! But none will be given it except the sign of the prophet Jonah. ⁴⁰For as Jonah was three days and three nights in the belly of a huge fish, so the Son of Man will be three days and three nights in the heart of the earth. ⁴¹The men of Nineveh will stand up at the judgment with this generation and condemn it; for they repented at the preaching of Jonah, and now one*a* greater than Jonah is here. ⁴²The Queen of the South will rise at the judgment with this generation and condemn it; for she came from the ends of the earth to listen to Solomon's wisdom, and now one greater than Solomon is here.

⁴³"When an evil*b* spirit comes out of a man, it goes through arid places seeking rest and does not find it. ⁴⁴Then it says, 'I will return to the house I left.' When it arrives, it finds the house unoccupied, swept clean and put in order.

⁴⁵Then it goes and takes with it seven other spirits more wicked than itself, and they go in and live there. And the final condition of that man is worse than the first. That is how it will be with this wicked generation."

Jesus' Mother and Brothers

⁴⁶While Jesus was still talking to the crowd, his mother and brothers stood outside, wanting to speak to him. ⁴⁷Someone told him, "Your mother and brothers are standing outside, wanting to speak to you."*c*

⁴⁸He replied to him, "Who is my mother, and who are my brothers?" ⁴⁹Pointing to his disciples, he said, "Here are my mother and my brothers. ⁵⁰For whoever does the will of my Father in heaven is my brother and sister and mother."

The Parable of the Sower

13 That same day Jesus went out of the house and sat by the lake. ²Such large crowds gathered around him that he got into a boat and sat in it, while all the people stood on the shore. ³Then he told them many things in parables, saying: "A farmer went out to sow his seed. ⁴As he was scattering the seed, some fell along the path, and the birds came and ate it up. ⁵Some fell on rocky places, where it did not have much soil. It sprang up quickly, because the soil was shallow. ⁶But when the sun came up, the plants were scorched, and they withered because they had no root. ⁷Other seed fell among thorns, which grew up and choked the plants. ⁸Still other seed fell on good soil, where it produced a crop—a hundred, sixty or thirty times what was sown. ⁹He who has ears, let him hear."

¹⁰The disciples came to him and asked, "Why do you speak to the people in parables?"

¹¹He replied, "The knowledge of the secrets of the kingdom of heaven has been given to you, but not to them. ¹²Whoever has will be given more, and he will have an abundance. Whoever does not have, even what he has will be taken from him. ¹³This is why I speak to them in parables:

a41 Or something; also in verse 42   b43 Greek unclean   c47 Some manuscripts do not have verse 47.

"Though seeing, they do not see;
   though hearing, they do not hear
   or understand.

14In them is fulfilled the prophecy of Isaiah:

" 'You will be ever hearing but never
      understanding;
   you will be ever seeing but never
      perceiving.
15For this people's heart has become
      calloused;
   they hardly hear with their ears,
   and they have closed their eyes.
Otherwise they might see with their
      eyes,
   hear with their ears,
   understand with their hearts
and turn, and I would heal them.'a

16But blessed are your eyes because they see, and your ears because they hear. 17For I tell you the truth, many prophets and righteous men longed to see what you see but did not see it, and to hear what you hear but did not hear it.

> 66 *It is from prayer that the spirit's victory springs.* 99
>
> SCHILLERBUCH

18"Listen then to what the parable of the sower means: 19When anyone hears the message about the kingdom and does not understand it, the evil one comes and snatches away what was sown in his heart. This is the seed sown along the path. 20The one who received the seed that fell on rocky places is the man who hears the word and at once receives it with joy. 21But since he has no root, he lasts only a short time. When trouble or persecution comes because of the word, he quickly falls away. 22The one who received the seed that fell among the thorns is the man who hears the word, but the worries of this life and the deceitfulness of wealth choke it, making it unfruitful. 23But the one who received the seed that fell on good soil is the man who hears the word and understands it. He produces a crop, yielding a hundred, sixty or thirty times what was sown."

The Parable of the Weeds

24Jesus told them another parable: "The kingdom of heaven is like a man who sowed good seed in his field. 25But while everyone was sleeping, his enemy came and sowed weeds among the wheat, and went away. 26When the wheat sprouted and formed heads, then the weeds also appeared.

27"The owner's servants came to him and said, 'Sir, didn't you sow good seed in your field? Where then did the weeds come from?'

28" 'An enemy did this,' he replied.

"The servants asked him, 'Do you want us to go and pull them up?'

29" 'No,' he answered, 'because while you are pulling the weeds, you may root up the wheat with them. 30Let both grow together until the harvest. At that time I will tell the harvesters: First collect the weeds and tie them in bundles to be burned; then gather the wheat and bring it into my barn.' "

The Parables of the Mustard Seed and the Yeast

31He told them another parable: "The kingdom of heaven is like a mustard seed, which a man took and planted in his field. 32Though it is the smallest of all your seeds, yet when it grows, it is the largest of garden plants and becomes a tree, so that the birds of the air come and perch in its branches."

33He told them still another parable: "The kingdom of heaven is like yeast that a woman took and mixed into a large amountb of flour until it worked all through the dough."

34Jesus spoke all these things to the crowd in parables; he did not say anything to them without using a parable. 35So was fulfilled what was spoken through the prophet:

"I will open my mouth in parables,
   I will utter things hidden since the
      creation of the world."c

The Parable of the Weeds Explained

36Then he left the crowd and went into the house. His disciples came to him and

---

a15 Isaiah 6:9,10   b33 Greek three satas
(probably about 1/2 bushel or 22 liters)
c35 Psalm 78:2

said, "Explain to us the parable of the weeds in the field."

37He answered, "The one who sowed the good seed is the Son of Man. 38The field is the world, and the good seed stands for the sons of the kingdom. The weeds are the sons of the evil one, 39and the enemy who sows them is the devil. The harvest is the end of the age, and the harvesters are angels.

40"As the weeds are pulled up and burned in the fire, so it will be at the end of the age. 41The Son of Man will send out his angels, and they will weed out of his kingdom everything that causes sin and all who do evil. 42They will throw them into the fiery furnace, where there will be weeping and gnashing of teeth. 43Then the righteous will shine like the sun in the kingdom of their Father. He who has ears, let him hear.

The Parables of the Hidden Treasure and the Pearl

44"The kingdom of heaven is like treasure hidden in a field. When a man found it, he hid it again, and then in his joy went and sold all he had and bought that field.

45"Again, the kingdom of heaven is like a merchant looking for fine pearls. 46When he found one of great value, he went away and sold everything he had and bought it.

The Parable of the Net

47"Once again, the kingdom of heaven is like a net that was let down into the lake and caught all kinds of fish. 48When it was full, the fishermen pulled it up on the shore. Then they sat down and collected the good fish in baskets, but threw the bad away. 49This is how it will be at the end of the age. The angels will come and separate the wicked from the righteous 50and throw them into the fiery furnace, where there will be weeping and gnashing of teeth.

51"Have you understood all these things?" Jesus asked.

"Yes," they replied.

52He said to them, "Therefore every teacher of the law who has been instructed about the kingdom of heaven is like the owner of a house who brings out of his storeroom new treasures as well as old."

A Prophet Without Honor

53When Jesus had finished these parables, he moved on from there. 54Coming to his hometown, he began teaching the people in their synagogue, and they were amazed. "Where did this man get this wisdom and these miraculous powers?" they asked. 55"Isn't this the carpenter's son? Isn't his mother's name Mary, and aren't his brothers James, Joseph, Simon and Judas? 56Aren't all his sisters with us? Where then did this man get all these things?" 57And they took offense at him.

But Jesus said to them, "Only in his hometown and in his own house is a prophet without honor."

58And he did not do many miracles there because of their lack of faith.

John the Baptist Beheaded

14 At that time Herod the tetrarch heard the reports about Jesus, 2and he said to his attendants, "This is John the Baptist; he has risen from the dead! That is why miraculous powers are at work in him."

3Now Herod had arrested John and bound him and put him in prison because of Herodias, his brother Philip's wife, 4for John had been saying to him: "It is not lawful for you to have her." 5Herod wanted to kill John, but he was afraid of the people, because they considered him a prophet.

6On Herod's birthday the daughter of Herodias danced for them and pleased Herod so much 7that he promised with an oath to give her whatever she asked. 8Prompted by her mother, she said, "Give me here on a platter the head of John the Baptist." 9The king was distressed, but because of his oaths and his dinner guests, he ordered that her request be granted 10and had John beheaded in the prison. 11His head was brought in on a platter and given to the girl, who carried it to her mother. 12John's disciples came and took his body and buried it. Then they went and told Jesus.

Jesus Feeds the Five Thousand

13When Jesus heard what had happened, he withdrew by boat privately to a solitary place. Hearing of this, the crowds followed him on foot from the towns. ¹⁴When Jesus landed and saw a large crowd, he had compassion on them and healed their sick.

¹⁵As evening approached, the disciples came to him and said, "This is a remote place, and it's already getting late. Send the crowds away, so they can go to the villages and buy themselves some food."

¹⁶Jesus replied, "They do not need to go away. You give them something to eat."

¹⁷"We have here only five loaves of bread and two fish," they answered.

¹⁸"Bring them here to me," he said. ¹⁹And he directed the people to sit down on the grass. Taking the five loaves and the two fish and looking up to heaven, he gave thanks and broke the loaves. Then he gave them to the disciples, and the disciples gave them to the people. ²⁰They all ate and were satisfied, and the disciples picked up twelve basketfuls of broken pieces that were left over. ²¹The number of those who ate was about five thousand men, besides women and children.

Jesus Walks on the Water

²²Immediately Jesus made the disciples get into the boat and go on ahead of him to the other side, while he dismissed the crowd. ²³After he had dismissed them, he went up on a mountainside by himself to pray. When evening came, he was there alone, ²⁴but the boat was already a considerable distance[a] from land, buffeted by the waves because the wind was against it.

²⁵During the fourth watch of the night Jesus went out to them, walking on the lake. ²⁶When the disciples saw him walking on the lake, they were terrified. "It's a ghost," they said, and cried out in fear.

²⁷But Jesus immediately said to them: "Take courage! It is I. Don't be afraid."

²⁸"Lord, if it's you," Peter replied, "tell me to come to you on the water."

²⁹"Come," he said.

Then Peter got down out of the boat, walked on the water and came toward Jesus. ³⁰But when he saw the wind, he was afraid and, beginning to sink, cried out, "Lord, save me!"

³¹Immediately Jesus reached out his hand and caught him. "You of little faith," he said, "why did you doubt?"

³²And when they climbed into the boat, the wind died down. ³³Then those who were in the boat worshiped him, saying, "Truly you are the Son of God."

³⁴When they had crossed over, they landed at Gennesaret. ³⁵And when the men of that place recognized Jesus, they sent word to all the surrounding country. People brought all their sick to him ³⁶and begged him to let the sick just touch the edge of his cloak, and all who touched him were healed.

Clean and Unclean

15 Then some Pharisees and teachers of the law came to Jesus from Jerusalem and asked, ²"Why do your disciples break the tradition of the elders? They don't wash their hands before they eat!"

³Jesus replied, "And why do you break the command of God for the sake of your tradition? ⁴For God said, 'Honor your father and mother'[b] and 'Anyone who curses his father or mother must be put to death.'[c] ⁵But you say that if a man says to his father or mother, 'Whatever help you might otherwise have received from me is a gift devoted to God,' ⁶he is not to 'honor his father'[d] with it. Thus you nullify the word of God for the sake of your tradition. ⁷You hypocrites! Isaiah was right when he prophesied about you:

⁸ " 'These people honor me with their
       lips,
   but their hearts are far from me.
⁹They worship me in vain;
   their teachings are but rules taught
       by men.'[e]

¹⁰Jesus called the crowd to him and said, "Listen and understand. ¹¹What goes into a man's mouth does not make him 'unclean,' but what comes out of his mouth, that is what makes him 'unclean.'"

¹²Then the disciples came to him and asked, "Do you know that the Pharisees were offended when they heard this?"

¹³He replied, "Every plant that my heavenly Father has not planted will be pulled up by the roots. ¹⁴Leave them; they

---

[a]24 Greek *many stadia*   [b]4 Exodus 20:12;
Deut. 5:16   [c]4 Exodus 21:17; Lev. 20:9
[d]6 Some manuscripts *father or his mother*
[e]9 Isaiah 29:13

are blind guides.[a] If a blind man leads a blind man, both will fall into a pit."

[15]Peter said, "Explain the parable to us."

[16]"Are you still so dull?" Jesus asked them. [17]"Don't you see that whatever enters the mouth goes into the stomach and then out of the body? [18]But the things that come out of the mouth come from the heart, and these make a man 'unclean.' [19]For out of the heart come evil thoughts, murder, adultery, sexual immorality, theft, false testimony, slander. [20]These are what make a man 'unclean'; but eating with unwashed hands does not make him 'unclean.'"

The Faith of the Canaanite Woman

[21]Leaving that place, Jesus withdrew to the region of Tyre and Sidon. [22]A Canaanite woman from that vicinity came to him, crying out, "Lord, Son of David, have mercy on me! My daughter is suffering terribly from demon-possession."

[23]Jesus did not answer a word. So his disciples came to him and urged him, "Send her away, for she keeps crying out after us."

[24]He answered, "I was sent only to the lost sheep of Israel."

[25]The woman came and knelt before him. "Lord, help me!" she said.

[26]He replied, "It is not right to take the children's bread and toss it to their dogs."

[27]"Yes, Lord," she said, "but even the dogs eat the crumbs that fall from their masters' table."

[28]Then Jesus answered, "Woman, you have great faith! Your request is granted." And her daughter was healed from that very hour.

> THE woman came and knelt before him. "Lord, help me!" she said ... Then Jesus answered, "Woman, you have great faith! Your request is granted." And her daughter was healed from that very hour.
>
> MATTHEW 15:25 - 28

Jesus Feeds the Four Thousand

[29]Jesus left there and went along the Sea of Galilee. Then he went up on a mountainside and sat down. [30]Great crowds came to him, bringing the lame, the blind, the crippled, the mute and many others, and laid them at his feet; and he healed them. [31]The people were amazed when they saw the mute speaking, the crippled made well, the lame walking and the blind seeing. And they praised the God of Israel.

[32]Jesus called his disciples to him and said, "I have compassion for these people; they have already been with me three days and have nothing to eat. I do not want to send them away hungry, or they may collapse on the way."

[33]His disciples answered, "Where could we get enough bread in this remote place to feed such a crowd?"

[34]"How many loaves do you have?" Jesus asked.

"Seven," they replied, "and a few small fish."

[35]He told the crowd to sit down on the ground. [36]Then he took the seven loaves and the fish, and when he had given thanks, he broke them and gave them to the disciples, and they in turn to the people. [37]They all ate and were satisfied. Afterward the disciples picked up seven basketfuls of broken pieces that were left over. [38]The number of those who ate was four thousand, besides women and children. [39]After Jesus had sent the crowd away, he got into the boat and went to the vicinity of Magadan.

The Demand for a Sign

16 The Pharisees and Sadducees came to Jesus and tested him by asking him to show them a sign from heaven.

[2]He replied,[b] "When evening comes, you say, 'It will be fair weather, for the sky is red,' [3]and in the morning, 'Today it will be stormy, for the sky is red and overcast.' You know how to interpret the appearance of the sky, but you cannot interpret the signs of the times. [4]A wicked and adulterous generation looks for a miraculous sign, but none will be given it except the sign of Jonah." Jesus then left them and went away.

[a]14 Some manuscripts guides of the blind
[b]2 Some early manuscripts do not have the rest of verse 2 and all of verse 3.

The Yeast of the Pharisees and Sadducees

⁵When they went across the lake, the disciples forgot to take bread. ⁶"Be careful," Jesus said to them. "Be on your guard against the yeast of the Pharisees and Sadducees."

⁷They discussed this among themselves and said, "It is because we didn't bring any bread."

⁸Aware of their discussion, Jesus asked, "You of little faith, why are you talking among yourselves about having no bread? ⁹Do you still not understand? Don't you remember the five loaves for the five thousand, and how many basketfuls you gathered? ¹⁰Or the seven loaves for the four thousand, and how many basketfuls you gathered? ¹¹How is it you don't understand that I was not talking to you about bread? But be on your guard against the yeast of the Pharisees and Sadducees." ¹²Then they understood that he was not telling them to guard against the yeast used in bread, but against the teaching of the Pharisees and Sadducees.

Peter's Confession of Christ

¹³When Jesus came to the region of Caesarea Philippi, he asked his disciples, "Who do people say the Son of Man is?"

¹⁴They replied, "Some say John the Baptist; others say Elijah; and still others, Jeremiah or one of the prophets."

¹⁵"But what about you?" he asked. "Who do you say I am?"

¹⁶Simon Peter answered, "You are the Christ,ᵃ the Son of the living God."

¹⁷Jesus replied, "Blessed are you, Simon son of Jonah, for this was not revealed to you by man, but by my Father in heaven. ¹⁸And I tell you that you are Peter,ᵇ and on this rock I will build my church, and the gates of Hadesᶜ will not overcome it.ᵈ ¹⁹I will give you the keys of the kingdom of heaven; whatever you bind on earth will beᵉ bound in heaven, and whatever you loose on earth will beᵉ loosed in heaven." ²⁰Then he warned his disciples not to tell anyone that he was the Christ.

Jesus Predicts His Death

²¹From that time on Jesus began to explain to his disciples that he must go to Jerusalem and suffer many things at the hands of the elders, chief priests and teachers of the law, and that he must be killed and on the third day be raised to life.

²²Peter took him aside and began to rebuke him. "Never, Lord!" he said. "This shall never happen to you!"

²³Jesus turned and said to Peter, "Get behind me, Satan! You are a stumbling block to me; you do not have in mind the things of God, but the things of men."

²⁴Then Jesus said to his disciples, "If anyone would come after me, he must deny himself and take up his cross and follow me. ²⁵For whoever wants to save his lifeᶠ will lose it, but whoever loses his life for me will find it. ²⁶What good will it be for a man if he gains the whole world, yet forfeits his soul? Or what can a man give in exchange for his soul? ²⁷For the Son of Man is going to come in his Father's glory with his angels, and then he will reward each person according to what he has done. ²⁸I tell you the truth, some who are standing here will not taste death before they see the Son of Man coming in his kingdom."

The Transfiguration

17 After six days Jesus took with him Peter, James and John the brother of James, and led them up a high mountain by themselves. ²There he was transfigured before them. His face shone like the sun, and his clothes became as white as the light. ³Just then there appeared before them Moses and Elijah, talking with Jesus.

⁴Peter said to Jesus, "Lord, it is good for us to be here. If you wish, I will put up three shelters—one for you, one for Moses and one for Elijah."

⁵While he was still speaking, a bright cloud enveloped them, and a voice from the cloud said, "This is my Son, whom I love; with him I am well pleased. Listen to him!"

⁶When the disciples heard this, they fell facedown to the ground, terrified. ⁷But Jesus came and touched them. "Get up,"

ᵃ16 Or *Messiah*; also in verse 20   ᵇ18 *Peter* means *rock.*   ᶜ18 Or *hell*   ᵈ18 Or *not prove stronger than it*   ᵉ19 Or *have been*   ᶠ25 The Greek word means either *life* or *soul*; also in verse 26.

he said. "Don't be afraid." [8]When they looked up, they saw no one except Jesus.

[9]As they were coming down the mountain, Jesus instructed them, "Don't tell anyone what you have seen, until the Son of Man has been raised from the dead."

[10]The disciples asked him, "Why then do the teachers of the law say that Elijah must come first?"

[11]Jesus replied, "To be sure, Elijah comes and will restore all things. [12]But I tell you, Elijah has already come, and they did not recognize him, but have done to him everything they wished. In the same way the Son of Man is going to suffer at their hands." [13]Then the disciples understood that he was talking to them about John the Baptist.

The Healing of a Boy With a Demon

[14]When they came to the crowd, a man approached Jesus and knelt before him. [15]"Lord, have mercy on my son," he said. "He has seizures and is suffering greatly. He often falls into the fire or into the water. [16]I brought him to your disciples, but they could not heal him."

[17]"O unbelieving and perverse generation," Jesus replied, "how long shall I stay with you? How long shall I put up with you? Bring the boy here to me." [18]Jesus rebuked the demon, and it came out of the boy, and he was healed from that moment.

[19]Then the disciples came to Jesus in private and asked, "Why couldn't we drive it out?"

[20]He replied, "Because you have so little faith. I tell you the truth, if you have faith as small as a mustard seed, you can say to this mountain, 'Move from here to there' and it will move. Nothing will be impossible for you.[a]"

[22]When they came together in Galilee, he said to them, "The Son of Man is going to be betrayed into the hands of men. [23]They will kill him, and on the third day he will be raised to life." And the disciples were filled with grief.

The Temple Tax

[24]After Jesus and his disciples arrived in Capernaum, the collectors of the two-drachma tax came to Peter and asked, "Doesn't your teacher pay the temple tax[b]?"

[25]"Yes, he does," he replied.

When Peter came into the house, Jesus was the first to speak. "What do you think, Simon?" he asked. "From whom do the kings of the earth collect duty and taxes—from their own sons or from others?"

[26]"From others," Peter answered.

"Then the sons are exempt," Jesus said to him. [27]"But so that we may not offend them, go to the lake and throw out your line. Take the first fish you catch; open its mouth and you will find a four-drachma coin. Take it and give it to them for my tax and yours."

The Greatest in the Kingdom of Heaven

18 At that time the disciples came to Jesus and asked, "Who is the greatest in the kingdom of heaven?"

[2]He called a little child and had him stand among them. [3]And he said: "I tell you the truth, unless you change and become like little children, you will never enter the kingdom of heaven. [4]Therefore, whoever humbles himself like this child is the greatest in the kingdom of heaven.

[5]"And whoever welcomes a little child like this in my name welcomes me. [6]But if anyone causes one of these little ones who believe in me to sin, it would be better for him to have a large millstone hung around his neck and to be drowned in the depths of the sea.

[7]"Woe to the world because of the things that cause people to sin! Such things must come, but woe to the man through whom they come! [8]If your hand or your foot causes you to sin, cut it off and throw it away. It is better for you to enter life maimed or crippled than to have two hands or two feet and be thrown into eternal fire. [9]And if your eye causes you to sin, gouge it out and throw it away. It is better for you to enter life with one eye than to have two eyes and be thrown into the fire of hell.

The Parable of the Lost Sheep

[10]"See that you do not look down on one of these little ones. For I tell you that

---

[a]20 Some manuscripts you. [21]But this kind does not go out except by prayer and fasting.
[b]24 Greek the two drachmas

their angels in heaven always see the face of my Father in heaven.*ᵃ*

¹²"What do you think? If a man owns a hundred sheep, and one of them wanders away, will he not leave the ninety-nine on the hills and go to look for the one that wandered off? ¹³And if he finds it, I tell you the truth, he is happier about that one sheep than about the ninety-nine that did not wander off. ¹⁴In the same way your Father in heaven is not willing that any of these little ones should be lost.

A Brother Who Sins Against You

¹⁵"If your brother sins against you,*ᵇ* go and show him his fault, just between the two of you. If he listens to you, you have won your brother over. ¹⁶But if he will not listen, take one or two others along, so that 'every matter may be established by the testimony of two or three witnesses.'*ᶜ* ¹⁷If he refuses to listen to them, tell it to the church; and if he refuses to listen even to the church, treat him as you would a pagan or a tax collector.

¹⁸"I tell you the truth, whatever you bind on earth will be*ᵈ* bound in heaven, and whatever you loose on earth will be*ᵈ* loosed in heaven.

¹⁹"Again, I tell you that if two of you on earth agree about anything you ask for, it will be done for you by my Father in heaven. ²⁰For where two or three come together in my name, there am I with them."

The Parable of the Unmerciful Servant

²¹Then Peter came to Jesus and asked, "Lord, how many times shall I forgive my brother when he sins against me? Up to seven times?"

²²Jesus answered, "I tell you, not seven times, but seventy-seven times.*ᵉ*

²³"Therefore, the kingdom of heaven is like a king who wanted to settle accounts with his servants. ²⁴As he began the settlement, a man who owed him ten thousand talents*ᶠ* was brought to him. ²⁵Since he was not able to pay, the master ordered that he and his wife and his children and all that he had be sold to repay the debt.

²⁶"The servant fell on his knees before him. 'Be patient with me,' he begged,

'and I will pay back everything.' ²⁷The servant's master took pity on him, canceled the debt and let him go.

²⁸"But when that servant went out, he found one of his fellow servants who owed him a hundred denarii.*ᵍ* He grabbed him and began to choke him. 'Pay back what you owe me!' he demanded.

²⁹"His fellow servant fell to his knees and begged him, 'Be patient with me, and I will pay you back.'

³⁰"But he refused. Instead, he went off and had the man thrown into prison until he could pay the debt. ³¹When the other servants saw what had happened, they were greatly distressed and went and told their master everything that had happened.

³²"Then the master called the servant in. 'You wicked servant,' he said, 'I canceled all that debt of yours because you begged me to. ³³Shouldn't you have had mercy on your fellow servant just as I had on you?' ³⁴In anger his master turned him over to the jailers to be tortured, until he should pay back all he owed.

³⁵"This is how my heavenly Father will treat each of you unless you forgive your brother from your heart."

Divorce

19 When Jesus had finished saying these things, he left Galilee and went into the region of Judea to the other side of the Jordan. ²Large crowds followed him, and he healed them there.

³Some Pharisees came to him to test him. They asked, "Is it lawful for a man to divorce his wife for any and every reason?"

⁴"Haven't you read," he replied, "that at the beginning the Creator 'made them male and female,'*ʰ* ⁵and said, 'For this reason a man will leave his father and mother and be united to his wife, and the two will become one flesh'*ⁱ*? ⁶So they are no longer two, but one. Therefore what God has joined together, let man not separate."

⁷"Why then," they asked, "did Moses

ᵃ10 Some manuscripts *heaven.* *¹¹The Son of Man came to save what was lost.* *ᵇ15* Some manuscripts do not have *against you.* *ᶜ16* Deut. 19:15 *ᵈ18* Or *have been* *ᵉ22* Or *seventy times seven* *ᶠ24* That is, millions of dollars *ᵍ28* That is, a few dollars *ʰ4* Gen. 1:27 *ⁱ5* Gen. 2:24

command that a man give his wife a certificate of divorce and send her away?"

⁸Jesus replied, "Moses permitted you to divorce your wives because your hearts were hard. But it was not this way from the beginning. ⁹I tell you that anyone who divorces his wife, except for marital unfaithfulness, and marries another woman commits adultery."

¹⁰The disciples said to him, "If this is the situation between a husband and wife, it is better not to marry."

MATTHEW 18:19-20

[THURSDAY]

Strike Up the Band

18:19 "IF TWO OF YOU ON EARTH AGREE ABOUT ANYTHING YOU ASK FOR, IT WILL BE DONE FOR YOU BY MY FATHER IN HEAVEN."

It could be argued that, in a sense, these verses changed the course of American history. The imagination of the brilliant theologian Jonathan Edwards had been ignited by the word "agree" in the text. The Greek word is *sumphoneo*, from which we get our word "symphony." Taking his cue from this word, he wrote a long pamphlet calling the churches of New England to see prayer as a kind of concert in which they would pray in agreement for two things: the revival of religion in the church and the spread of God's kingdom in the world. Many churches prayed this way, and the Great Awakenings of the 18th and 19th centuries sprang from this kind of prayer. The spiritual renewal and profound social and political reform that came out of these revivals has been well documented. America was not the same after its churches prayed this concert.

In the context of the Scripture, these verses are not about prayer, per se, but church discipline. Jesus promises to be present with the church when its people gather in his name to discipline recalcitrant members. But the principle applies equally to prayer because Christ is present with his people in a special way when they are unified. John's Gospel tells us that a prayer for unity was Jesus' last prayer for the church before he was arrested. He asked his Father to make his people one, just as he and his Father are one. That way the world would believe in Jesus and know the church to be a uniquely blessed community (see John 17:23)—the very thing that happens in a spiritual awakening. When we agree in Jesus' name, the Maestro strikes up his band, and the music is beautiful.

Many of the prayers of the Bible were meant to be prayed in the congregation or community, not by individuals. It is the same for many of the Bible's instructions on prayer: God puts great stock in corporate prayer. We should too, for it requires and creates a level of Christian community that speaks powerfully to the world of the reality of God. If you haven't already done so, find people who will promise to pray with you in the symphonic way Jonathan Edwards called the churches in New England to pray. Christ has promised great things to those who pray this way.

PRAY:

Holy Spirit, you have made us one in Christ. Awaken us to that reality, and teach us to pray together, as one, for God's kingdom to come.

FOR YOUR NEXT DEVOTIONAL READING, GO TO PAGE 1179.

¹¹Jesus replied, "Not everyone can accept this word, but only those to whom it has been given. ¹²For some are eunuchs because they were born that way; others were made that way by men; and others have renounced marriage*ᵃ* because of the kingdom of heaven. The one who can accept this should accept it."

The Little Children and Jesus

¹³Then little children were brought to Jesus for him to place his hands on them and pray for them. But the disciples rebuked those who brought them.

> THEN little children were brought to Jesus for him to place his hands on them and pray for them.
>
> MATTHEW 19:13

¹⁴Jesus said, "Let the little children come to me, and do not hinder them, for the kingdom of heaven belongs to such as these." ¹⁵When he had placed his hands on them, he went on from there.

The Rich Young Man

¹⁶Now a man came up to Jesus and asked, "Teacher, what good thing must I do to get eternal life?"

¹⁷"Why do you ask me about what is good?" Jesus replied. "There is only One who is good. If you want to enter life, obey the commandments."

¹⁸"Which ones?" the man inquired.

Jesus replied, " 'Do not murder, do not commit adultery, do not steal, do not give false testimony, ¹⁹honor your father and mother,'*ᵇ* and 'love your neighbor as yourself.'*ᶜ*"

²⁰"All these I have kept," the young man said. "What do I still lack?"

²¹Jesus answered, "If you want to be perfect, go, sell your possessions and give to the poor, and you will have treasure in heaven. Then come, follow me."

²²When the young man heard this, he went away sad, because he had great wealth.

²³Then Jesus said to his disciples, "I tell you the truth, it is hard for a rich man to enter the kingdom of heaven. ²⁴Again I tell you, it is easier for a camel to go through the eye of a needle than for a rich man to enter the kingdom of God."

²⁵When the disciples heard this, they were greatly astonished and asked, "Who then can be saved?"

²⁶Jesus looked at them and said, "With man this is impossible, but with God all things are possible."

²⁷Peter answered him, "We have left everything to follow you! What then will there be for us?"

²⁸Jesus said to them, "I tell you the truth, at the renewal of all things, when the Son of Man sits on his glorious throne, you who have followed me will also sit on twelve thrones, judging the twelve tribes of Israel. ²⁹And everyone who has left houses or brothers or sisters or father or mother*ᵈ* or children or fields for my sake will receive a hundred times as much and will inherit eternal life. ³⁰But many who are first will be last, and many who are last will be first.

The Parable of the Workers in the Vineyard

20 "For the kingdom of heaven is like a landowner who went out early in the morning to hire men to work in his vineyard. ²He agreed to pay them a denarius for the day and sent them into his vineyard.

³"About the third hour he went out and saw others standing in the marketplace doing nothing. ⁴He told them, 'You also go and work in my vineyard, and I will pay you whatever is right.' ⁵So they went.

"He went out again about the sixth hour and the ninth hour and did the same thing. ⁶About the eleventh hour he went out and found still others standing around. He asked them, 'Why have you been standing here all day long doing nothing?'

⁷" 'Because no one has hired us,' they answered.

"He said to them, 'You also go and work in my vineyard.'

⁸"When evening came, the owner of the vineyard said to his foreman, 'Call the workers and pay them their wages,

---

ᵃ12 Or *have made themselves eunuchs*
ᵇ19 Exodus 20:12–16; Deut. 5:16–20
ᶜ19 Lev. 19:18   *ᵈ29* Some manuscripts *mother or wife*

beginning with the last ones hired and going on to the first.'

⁹"The workers who were hired about the eleventh hour came and each received a denarius. ¹⁰So when those came who were hired first, they expected to receive more. But each one of them also received a denarius. ¹¹When they received it, they began to grumble against the landowner. ¹²'These men who were hired last worked only one hour,' they said, 'and you have made them equal to us who have borne the burden of the work and the heat of the day.'

¹³"But he answered one of them, 'Friend, I am not being unfair to you. Didn't you agree to work for a denarius? ¹⁴Take your pay and go. I want to give the man who was hired last the same as I gave you. ¹⁵Don't I have the right to do what I want with my own money? Or are you envious because I am generous?'

¹⁶"So the last will be first, and the first will be last."

Jesus Again Predicts His Death

¹⁷Now as Jesus was going up to Jerusalem, he took the twelve disciples aside and said to them, ¹⁸"We are going up to Jerusalem, and the Son of Man will be betrayed to the chief priests and the teachers of the law. They will condemn him to death ¹⁹and will turn him over to the Gentiles to be mocked and flogged and crucified. On the third day he will be raised to life!"

A Mother's Request

²⁰Then the mother of Zebedee's sons came to Jesus with her sons and, kneeling down, asked a favor of him.

²¹"What is it you want?" he asked.

She said, "Grant that one of these two sons of mine may sit at your right and the other at your left in your kingdom."

²²"You don't know what you are asking," Jesus said to them. "Can you drink the cup I am going to drink?"

"We can," they answered.

²³Jesus said to them, "You will indeed drink from my cup, but to sit at my right or left is not for me to grant. These places belong to those for whom they have been prepared by my Father."

²⁴When the ten heard about this, they were indignant with the two brothers. ²⁵Jesus called them together and said, "You know that the rulers of the Gentiles lord it over them, and their high officials exercise authority over them. ²⁶Not so with you. Instead, whoever wants to become great among you must be your servant, ²⁷and whoever wants to be first must be your slave— ²⁸just as the Son of Man did not come to be served, but to serve, and to give his life as a ransom for many."

Two Blind Men Receive Sight

²⁹As Jesus and his disciples were leaving Jericho, a large crowd followed him. ³⁰Two blind men were sitting by the roadside, and when they heard that Jesus was going by, they shouted, "Lord, Son of David, have mercy on us!"

³¹The crowd rebuked them and told them to be quiet, but they shouted all the louder, "Lord, Son of David, have mercy on us!"

³²Jesus stopped and called them. "What do you want me to do for you?" he asked.

³³"Lord," they answered, "we want our sight."

³⁴Jesus had compassion on them and touched their eyes. Immediately they received their sight and followed him.

The Triumphal Entry

21 As they approached Jerusalem and came to Bethphage on the Mount of Olives, Jesus sent two disciples, ²saying to them, "Go to the village ahead of you, and at once you will find a donkey tied there, with her colt by her. Untie them and bring them to me. ³If anyone says anything to you, tell him that the Lord needs them, and he will send them right away."

⁴This took place to fulfill what was spoken through the prophet:

⁵ "Say to the Daughter of Zion,
    'See, your king comes to you,
gentle and riding on a donkey,
    on a colt, the foal of a donkey.'"ᵃ

⁶The disciples went and did as Jesus had instructed them. ⁷They brought the

ᵃ5 Zech. 9:9

donkey and the colt, placed their cloaks on them, and Jesus sat on them. [8]A very large crowd spread their cloaks on the road, while others cut branches from the trees and spread them on the road. [9]The crowds that went ahead of him and those that followed shouted,

"Hosanna[a] to the Son of David!"

"Blessed is he who comes in the
　　name of the Lord!"[b]

"Hosanna[a] in the highest!"

[10]When Jesus entered Jerusalem, the whole city was stirred and asked, "Who is this?"

[11]The crowds answered, "This is Jesus, the prophet from Nazareth in Galilee."

Jesus at the Temple

[12]Jesus entered the temple area and drove out all who were buying and selling there. He overturned the tables of the money changers and the benches of those selling doves. [13]"It is written," he said to them, "'My house will be called a house of prayer,'[c] but you are making it a 'den of robbers.'[d]"

[14]The blind and the lame came to him at the temple, and he healed them. [15]But when the chief priests and the teachers of the law saw the wonderful things he did and the children shouting in the temple area, "Hosanna to the Son of David," they were indignant.

[16]"Do you hear what these children are saying?" they asked him.

"Yes," replied Jesus, "have you never read,

"'From the lips of children and
　　infants
　you have ordained praise'[e]?"

[17]And he left them and went out of the city to Bethany, where he spent the night.

The Fig Tree Withers

[18]Early in the morning, as he was on his way back to the city, he was hungry. [19]Seeing a fig tree by the road, he went up to it but found nothing on it except leaves. Then he said to it, "May you never bear fruit again!" Immediately the tree withered.

[20]When the disciples saw this, they were amazed. "How did the fig tree wither so quickly?" they asked.

[21]Jesus replied, "I tell you the truth, if you have faith and do not doubt, not only can you do what was done to the fig tree, but also you can say to this mountain, 'Go, throw yourself into the sea,' and it will be done. [22]If you believe, you will receive whatever you ask for in prayer."

> "IF YOU believe, you will receive
> whatever you ask for in prayer."
>
> MATTHEW 21:22

The Authority of Jesus Questioned

[23]Jesus entered the temple courts, and, while he was teaching, the chief priests and the elders of the people came to him. "By what authority are you doing these things?" they asked. "And who gave you this authority?"

[24]Jesus replied, "I will also ask you one question. If you answer me, I will tell you by what authority I am doing these things. [25]John's baptism—where did it come from? Was it from heaven, or from men?"

They discussed it among themselves and said, "If we say, 'From heaven,' he will ask, 'Then why didn't you believe him?' [26]But if we say, 'From men'—we are afraid of the people, for they all hold that John was a prophet."

[27]So they answered Jesus, "We don't know."

Then he said, "Neither will I tell you by what authority I am doing these things.

The Parable of the Two Sons

[28]"What do you think? There was a man who had two sons. He went to the first and said, 'Son, go and work today in the vineyard.'

[29]"'I will not,' he answered, but later he changed his mind and went.

[30]"Then the father went to the other son and said the same thing. He answered, 'I will, sir,' but he did not go.

[a]9 A Hebrew expression meaning "Save!" which became an exclamation of praise; also in verse 15
[b]9 Psalm 118:26　　[c]13 Isaiah 56:7
[d]13 Jer. 7:11　　[e]16 Psalm 8:2

[31] "Which of the two did what his father wanted?"

"The first," they answered.

Jesus said to them, "I tell you the truth, the tax collectors and the prostitutes are entering the kingdom of God ahead of you. [32]For John came to you to show you the way of righteousness, and you did not believe him, but the tax collectors and the prostitutes did. And even after you saw this, you did not repent and believe him.

The Parable of the Tenants

[33]"Listen to another parable: There was a landowner who planted a vineyard. He put a wall around it, dug a winepress in it and built a watchtower. Then he rented the vineyard to some farmers and went away on a journey. [34]When the harvest time approached, he sent his servants to the tenants to collect his fruit.

[35]"The tenants seized his servants; they beat one, killed another, and stoned a third. [36]Then he sent other servants to them, more than the first time, and the tenants treated them the same way. [37]Last of all, he sent his son to them. 'They will respect my son,' he said.

[38]"But when the tenants saw the son, they said to each other, 'This is the heir. Come, let's kill him and take his inheritance.' [39]So they took him and threw him out of the vineyard and killed him.

[40]"Therefore, when the owner of the vineyard comes, what will he do to those tenants?"

[41]"He will bring those wretches to a wretched end," they replied, "and he will rent the vineyard to other tenants, who will give him his share of the crop at harvest time."

[42]Jesus said to them, "Have you never read in the Scriptures:

" 'The stone the builders rejected
    has become the capstone[a];
the Lord has done this,
    and it is marvelous in our eyes'[b]?

[43]"Therefore I tell you that the kingdom of God will be taken away from you and given to a people who will produce its fruit. [44]He who falls on this stone will be broken to pieces, but he on whom it falls will be crushed."[c]

[45]When the chief priests and the Pharisees heard Jesus' parables, they knew he was talking about them. [46]They looked for a way to arrest him, but they were afraid of the crowd because the people held that he was a prophet.

The Parable of the Wedding Banquet

22 Jesus spoke to them again in parables, saying: [2]"The kingdom of heaven is like a king who prepared a wedding banquet for his son. [3]He sent his servants to those who had been invited to the banquet to tell them to come, but they refused to come.

[4]"Then he sent some more servants and said, 'Tell those who have been invited that I have prepared my dinner: My oxen and fattened cattle have been butchered, and everything is ready. Come to the wedding banquet.'

[5]"But they paid no attention and went off—one to his field, another to his business. [6]The rest seized his servants, mistreated them and killed them. [7]The king was enraged. He sent his army and destroyed those murderers and burned their city.

[8]"Then he said to his servants, 'The wedding banquet is ready, but those I invited did not deserve to come. [9]Go to the street corners and invite to the banquet anyone you find.' [10]So the servants went out into the streets and gathered all the people they could find, both good and bad, and the wedding hall was filled with guests.

[11]"But when the king came in to see the guests, he noticed a man there who was not wearing wedding clothes. [12]'Friend,' he asked, 'how did you get in here without wedding clothes?' The man was speechless.

[13]"Then the king told the attendants, 'Tie him hand and foot, and throw him outside, into the darkness, where there will be weeping and gnashing of teeth.'

[14]"For many are invited, but few are chosen."

Paying Taxes to Caesar

[15]Then the Pharisees went out and laid plans to trap him in his words. [16]They sent

---

[a]42 Or cornerstone   [b]42 Psalm 118:22,23
[c]44 Some manuscripts do not have verse 44.

their disciples to him along with the Herodians. "Teacher," they said, "we know you are a man of integrity and that you teach the way of God in accordance with the truth. You aren't swayed by men, because you pay no attention to who they are. [17]Tell us then, what is your opinion? Is it right to pay taxes to Caesar or not?"

[18]But Jesus, knowing their evil intent, said, "You hypocrites, why are you trying to trap me? [19]Show me the coin used for paying the tax." They brought him a denarius, [20]and he asked them, "Whose portrait is this? And whose inscription?"

[21]"Caesar's," they replied.

Then he said to them, "Give to Caesar what is Caesar's, and to God what is God's."

[22]When they heard this, they were amazed. So they left him and went away.

Marriage at the Resurrection

[23]That same day the Sadducees, who say there is no resurrection, came to him with a question. [24]"Teacher," they said, "Moses told us that if a man dies without having children, his brother must marry the widow and have children for him. [25]Now there were seven brothers among us. The first one married and died, and since he had no children, he left his wife to his brother. [26]The same thing happened to the second and third brother, right on down to the seventh. [27]Finally, the woman died. [28]Now then, at the resurrection, whose wife will she be of the seven, since all of them were married to her?"

[29]Jesus replied, "You are in error because you do not know the Scriptures or the power of God. [30]At the resurrection people will neither marry nor be given in marriage; they will be like the angels in heaven. [31]But about the resurrection of the dead—have you not read what God said to you, [32]'I am the God of Abraham, the God of Isaac, and the God of Jacob'[a]? He is not the God of the dead but of the living."

[33]When the crowds heard this, they were astonished at his teaching.

The Greatest Commandment

[34]Hearing that Jesus had silenced the Sadducees, the Pharisees got together. [35]One of them, an expert in the law, tested him with this question: [36]"Teacher, which is the greatest commandment in the Law?"

[37]Jesus replied: " 'Love the Lord your God with all your heart and with all your soul and with all your mind.'[b] [38]This is the first and greatest commandment. [39]And the second is like it: 'Love your neighbor as yourself.'[c] [40]All the Law and the Prophets hang on these two commandments."

Whose Son Is the Christ?

[41]While the Pharisees were gathered together, Jesus asked them, [42]"What do you think about the Christ[d]? Whose son is he?"

"The son of David," they replied.

[43]He said to them, "How is it then that David, speaking by the Spirit, calls him 'Lord'? For he says,

[44] " 'The Lord said to my Lord:
"Sit at my right hand
until I put your enemies
under your feet." '[e]

[45]If then David calls him 'Lord,' how can he be his son?" [46]No one could say a word in reply, and from that day on no one dared to ask him any more questions.

Seven Woes

23 Then Jesus said to the crowds and to his disciples: [2]"The teachers of the law and the Pharisees sit in Moses' seat. [3]So you must obey them and do everything they tell you. But do not do what they do, for they do not practice what they preach. [4]They tie up heavy loads and put them on men's shoulders, but they themselves are not willing to lift a finger to move them.

[5]"Everything they do is done for men to see: They make their phylacteries[f] wide and the tassels on their garments long; [6]they love the place of honor at banquets and the most important seats in the synagogues; [7]they love to be greeted in the marketplaces and to have men call them 'Rabbi.'

[8]"But you are not to be called 'Rabbi,'

---

[a]32 Exodus 3:6   [b]37 Deut. 6:5
[c]39 Lev. 19:18   [d]42 Or Messiah
[e]44 Psalm 110:1   [f]5 That is, boxes containing Scripture verses, worn on forehead and arm

for you have only one Master and you are all brothers. ⁹And do not call anyone on earth 'father,' for you have one Father, and he is in heaven. ¹⁰Nor are you to be called 'teacher,' for you have one Teacher, the Christ.ᵃ ¹¹The greatest among you will be your servant. ¹²For whoever exalts himself will be humbled, and whoever humbles himself will be exalted.

¹³"Woe to you, teachers of the law and Pharisees, you hypocrites! You shut the kingdom of heaven in men's faces. You yourselves do not enter, nor will you let those enter who are trying to.ᵇ

¹⁵"Woe to you, teachers of the law and Pharisees, you hypocrites! You travel over land and sea to win a single convert, and when he becomes one, you make him twice as much a son of hell as you are.

¹⁶"Woe to you, blind guides! You say, 'If anyone swears by the temple, it means nothing; but if anyone swears by the gold of the temple, he is bound by his oath.' ¹⁷You blind fools! Which is greater: the gold, or the temple that makes the gold sacred? ¹⁸You also say, 'If anyone swears by the altar, it means nothing; but if anyone swears by the gift on it, he is bound by his oath.' ¹⁹You blind men! Which is greater: the gift, or the altar that makes the gift sacred? ²⁰Therefore, he who swears by the altar swears by it and by everything on it. ²¹And he who swears by the temple swears by it and by the one who dwells in it. ²²And he who swears by heaven swears by God's throne and by the one who sits on it.

²³"Woe to you, teachers of the law and Pharisees, you hypocrites! You give a tenth of your spices—mint, dill and cummin. But you have neglected the more important matters of the law—justice, mercy and faithfulness. You should have practiced the latter, without neglecting the former. ²⁴You blind guides! You strain out a gnat but swallow a camel.

²⁵"Woe to you, teachers of the law and Pharisees, you hypocrites! You clean the outside of the cup and dish, but inside they are full of greed and self-indulgence. ²⁶Blind Pharisee! First clean the inside of the cup and dish, and then the outside also will be clean.

²⁷"Woe to you, teachers of the law and Pharisees, you hypocrites! You are like whitewashed tombs, which look beautiful on the outside but on the inside are full of dead men's bones and everything unclean. ²⁸In the same way, on the outside you appear to people as righteous but on the inside you are full of hypocrisy and wickedness.

²⁹"Woe to you, teachers of the law and Pharisees, you hypocrites! You build tombs for the prophets and decorate the graves of the righteous. ³⁰And you say, 'If we had lived in the days of our forefathers, we would not have taken part with them in shedding the blood of the prophets.' ³¹So you testify against yourselves that you are the descendants of those who murdered the prophets. ³²Fill up, then, the measure of the sin of your forefathers!

³³"You snakes! You brood of vipers! How will you escape being condemned to hell? ³⁴Therefore I am sending you prophets and wise men and teachers. Some of them you will kill and crucify; others you will flog in your synagogues and pursue from town to town. ³⁵And so upon you will come all the righteous blood that has been shed on earth, from the blood of righteous Abel to the blood of Zechariah son of Berekiah, whom you murdered between the temple and the altar. ³⁶I tell you the truth, all this will come upon this generation.

> ❝ Grace isn't a little prayer you chant before receiving a meal. It's a way to live. ❞
>
> JACKIE WINDSPEAR

³⁷"O Jerusalem, Jerusalem, you who kill the prophets and stone those sent to you, how often I have longed to gather your children together, as a hen gathers her chicks under her wings, but you were not willing. ³⁸Look, your house is left to you desolate. ³⁹For I tell you, you will not see me again until you say, 'Blessed is he who comes in the name of the Lord.'ᶜ"

ᵃ10 Or Messiah   ᵇ13 Some manuscripts to.
¹⁴Woe to you, teachers of the law and Pharisees, you hypocrites! You devour widows' houses and for a show make lengthy prayers. Therefore you will be punished more severely.   ᶜ39 Psalm 118:26

Signs of the End of the Age

24 Jesus left the temple and was walking away when his disciples came up to him to call his attention to its buildings. [2]"Do you see all these things?" he asked. "I tell you the truth, not one stone here will be left on another; every one will be thrown down."

[3]As Jesus was sitting on the Mount of Olives, the disciples came to him privately. "Tell us," they said, "when will this happen, and what will be the sign of your coming and of the end of the age?"

[4]Jesus answered: "Watch out that no one deceives you. [5]For many will come in my name, claiming, 'I am the Christ,[a]' and will deceive many. [6]You will hear of wars and rumors of wars, but see to it that you are not alarmed. Such things must happen, but the end is still to come. [7]Nation will rise against nation, and kingdom against kingdom. There will be famines and earthquakes in various places. [8]All these are the beginning of birth pains.

[9]"Then you will be handed over to be persecuted and put to death, and you will be hated by all nations because of me. [10]At that time many will turn away from the faith and will betray and hate each other, [11]and many false prophets will appear and deceive many people. [12]Because of the increase of wickedness, the love of most will grow cold, [13]but he who stands firm to the end will be saved. [14]And this gospel of the kingdom will be preached in the whole world as a testimony to all nations, and then the end will come.

[15]"So when you see standing in the holy place 'the abomination that causes desolation,'[b] spoken of through the prophet Daniel—let the reader understand— [16]then let those who are in Judea flee to the mountains. [17]Let no one on the roof of his house go down to take anything out of the house. [18]Let no one in the field go back to get his cloak. [19]How dreadful it will be in those days for pregnant women and nursing mothers! [20]Pray that your flight will not take place in winter or on the Sabbath. [21]For then there will be great distress, unequaled from the beginning of the world until now—

and never to be equaled again. [22]If those days had not been cut short, no one would survive, but for the sake of the elect those days will be shortened. [23]At that time if anyone says to you, 'Look, here is the Christ!' or, 'There he is!' do not believe it. [24]For false Christs and false prophets will appear and perform great signs and miracles to deceive even the elect—if that were possible. [25]See, I have told you ahead of time.

[26]"So if anyone tells you, 'There he is, out in the desert,' do not go out; or, 'Here he is, in the inner rooms,' do not believe it. [27]For as lightning that comes from the east is visible even in the west, so will be the coming of the Son of Man. [28]Wherever there is a carcass, there the vultures will gather.

[29]"Immediately after the distress of those days

" 'the sun will be darkened,
and the moon will not give its light;
the stars will fall from the sky,
and the heavenly bodies will be
shaken.'[c]

[30]"At that time the sign of the Son of Man will appear in the sky, and all the nations of the earth will mourn. They will see the Son of Man coming on the clouds of the sky, with power and great glory. [31]And he will send his angels with a loud trumpet call, and they will gather his elect from the four winds, from one end of the heavens to the other.

[32]"Now learn this lesson from the fig tree: As soon as its twigs get tender and its leaves come out, you know that summer is near. [33]Even so, when you see all these things, you know that it[d] is near, right at the door. [34]I tell you the truth, this generation[e] will certainly not pass away until all these things have happened. [35]Heaven and earth will pass away, but my words will never pass away.

The Day and Hour Unknown

[36]"No one knows about that day or hour, not even the angels in heaven, nor

[a]5 Or Messiah; also in verse 23
[b]15 Daniel 9:27; 11:31; 12:11
[c]29 Isaiah 13:10; 34:4   [d]33 Or he
[e]34 Or race

the Son,[a] but only the Father. 37As it was in the days of Noah, so it will be at the coming of the Son of Man. 38For in the days before the flood, people were eating and drinking, marrying and giving in marriage, up to the day Noah entered the ark; 39and they knew nothing about what would happen until the flood came and took them all away. That is how it will be at the coming of the Son of Man. 40Two men will be in the field; one will be taken and the other left. 41Two women will be grinding with a hand mill; one will be taken and the other left.

42"Therefore keep watch, because you do not know on what day your Lord will come. 43But understand this: If the owner of the house had known at what time of night the thief was coming, he would have kept watch and would not have let his house be broken into. 44So you also must be ready, because the Son of Man will come at an hour when you do not expect him.

45"Who then is the faithful and wise servant, whom the master has put in charge of the servants in his household to give them their food at the proper time? 46It will be good for that servant whose master finds him doing so when he returns. 47I tell you the truth, he will put him in charge of all his possessions. 48But suppose that servant is wicked and says to himself, 'My master is staying away a long time,' 49and he then begins to beat his fellow servants and to eat and drink with drunkards. 50The master of that servant will come on a day when he does not expect him and at an hour he is not aware of. 51He will cut him to pieces and assign him a place with the hypocrites, where there will be weeping and gnashing of teeth.

The Parable of the Ten Virgins

25 "At that time the kingdom of heaven will be like ten virgins who took their lamps and went out to meet the bridegroom. 2Five of them were foolish and five were wise. 3The foolish ones took their lamps but did not take any oil with them. 4The wise, however, took oil in jars along with their lamps. 5The bridegroom was a long time in coming, and they all became drowsy and fell asleep.

6"At midnight the cry rang out: 'Here's the bridegroom! Come out to meet him!'

7"Then all the virgins woke up and trimmed their lamps. 8The foolish ones said to the wise, 'Give us some of your oil; our lamps are going out.'

9" 'No,' they replied, 'there may not be enough for both us and you. Instead, go to those who sell oil and buy some for yourselves.'

10"But while they were on their way to buy the oil, the bridegroom arrived. The virgins who were ready went in with him to the wedding banquet. And the door was shut.

11"Later the others also came. 'Sir! Sir!' they said. 'Open the door for us!'

12"But he replied, 'I tell you the truth, I don't know you.'

13"Therefore keep watch, because you do not know the day or the hour.

The Parable of the Talents

14"Again, it will be like a man going on a journey, who called his servants and entrusted his property to them. 15To one he gave five talents[b] of money, to another two talents, and to another one talent, each according to his ability. Then he went on his journey. 16The man who had received the five talents went at once and put his money to work and gained five more. 17So also, the one with the two talents gained two more. 18But the man who had received the one talent went off, dug a hole in the ground and hid his master's money.

19"After a long time the master of those servants returned and settled accounts with them. 20The man who had received the five talents brought the other five. 'Master,' he said, 'you entrusted me with five talents. See, I have gained five more.'

21"His master replied, 'Well done, good and faithful servant! You have been faithful with a few things; I will put you in charge of many things. Come and share your master's happiness!'

22"The man with the two talents also came. 'Master,' he said, 'you entrusted me with two talents; see, I have gained two more.'

a36 Some manuscripts do not have nor the Son.
b15 A talent was worth more than a thousand dollars.

23"His master replied, 'Well done, good and faithful servant! You have been faithful with a few things; I will put you in charge of many things. Come and share your master's happiness!'

24"Then the man who had received the one talent came. 'Master,' he said, 'I knew that you are a hard man, harvesting where you have not sown and gathering where you have not scattered seed. 25So I was afraid and went out and hid your talent in the ground. See, here is what belongs to you.'

26"His master replied, 'You wicked, lazy servant! So you knew that I harvest where I have not sown and gather where I have not scattered seed? 27Well then, you should have put my money on deposit with the bankers, so that when I returned I would have received it back with interest.

28"'Take the talent from him and give it to the one who has the ten talents. 29For everyone who has will be given more, and he will have an abundance. Whoever does not have, even what he has will be taken from him. 30And throw that worthless servant outside, into the darkness, where there will be weeping and gnashing of teeth.'

The Sheep and the Goats

31"When the Son of Man comes in his glory, and all the angels with him, he will sit on his throne in heavenly glory. 32All the nations will be gathered before him, and he will separate the people one from another as a shepherd separates the sheep from the goats. 33He will put the sheep on his right and the goats on his left.

34"Then the King will say to those on his right, 'Come, you who are blessed by my Father; take your inheritance, the kingdom prepared for you since the creation of the world. 35For I was hungry and you gave me something to eat, I was thirsty and you gave me something to drink, I was a stranger and you invited me in, 36I needed clothes and you clothed me, I was sick and you looked after me, I was in prison and you came to visit me.'

37"Then the righteous will answer him, 'Lord, when did we see you hungry and feed you, or thirsty and give you something to drink? 38When did we see you a stranger and invite you in, or needing clothes and clothe you? 39When did we see you sick or in prison and go to visit you?'

40"The King will reply, 'I tell you the truth, whatever you did for one of the least of these brothers of mine, you did for me.'

41"Then he will say to those on his left, 'Depart from me, you who are cursed, into the eternal fire prepared for the devil and his angels. 42For I was hungry and you gave me nothing to eat, I was thirsty and you gave me nothing to drink, 43I was a stranger and you did not invite me in, I needed clothes and you did not clothe me, I was sick and in prison and you did not look after me.'

44"They also will answer, 'Lord, when did we see you hungry or thirsty or a stranger or needing clothes or sick or in prison, and did not help you?'

45"He will reply, 'I tell you the truth, whatever you did not do for one of the least of these, you did not do for me.'

46"Then they will go away to eternal punishment, but the righteous to eternal life."

The Plot Against Jesus

26 When Jesus had finished saying all these things, he said to his disciples, 2"As you know, the Passover is two days away—and the Son of Man will be handed over to be crucified."

3Then the chief priests and the elders of the people assembled in the palace of the high priest, whose name was Caiaphas, 4and they plotted to arrest Jesus in some sly way and kill him. 5"But not during the Feast," they said, "or there may be a riot among the people."

Jesus Anointed at Bethany

6While Jesus was in Bethany in the home of a man known as Simon the Leper, 7a woman came to him with an alabaster jar of very expensive perfume, which she poured on his head as he was reclining at the table.

8When the disciples saw this, they were indignant. "Why this waste?" they asked. 9"This perfume could have been sold at a high price and the money given to the poor."

¹⁰Aware of this, Jesus said to them, "Why are you bothering this woman? She has done a beautiful thing to me. ¹¹The poor you will always have with you, but you will not always have me. ¹²When she poured this perfume on my body, she did it to prepare me for burial. ¹³I tell you the truth, wherever this gospel is preached throughout the world, what she has done will also be told, in memory of her."

Judas Agrees to Betray Jesus

¹⁴Then one of the Twelve—the one called Judas Iscariot—went to the chief priests ¹⁵and asked, "What are you willing

---

[FRIDAY]

MATTHEW 26:6–13

Something Beautiful for God

26:10 "SHE HAS DONE A BEAUTIFUL THING TO ME."

The woman crossed the line of social nicety and religious propriety when she entered a roomful of men and poured on Jesus' head a jar of very expensive perfume (worth a year's wages, according to the parallel account in Mark 14:5). The disciples certainly thought so. "Why this waste?" they asked. "This perfume could have been sold at a high price and the money given to the poor." Clearly this emotional creature had lost her perspective.

But Jesus didn't think so, and he defended her. What she did was entirely appropriate: "She has done a beautiful thing to me," he retorted. The Greek word translated "beautiful" also means fine, noble, elegant. In the Greek Old Testament, the Septuagint, it is a word used to describe the things that please and delight God. What makes Jesus' response so remarkable is that it is preceded, in chapter 25, by some of his strongest words about caring for the poor. He so identified with them that he said, "Whatever you did for one of the least of these brothers of mine, you did for me" (25:40).

Why then did he so willingly—even enthusiastically—accept for himself what could have been given to the poor? It is because the adoration of God is supreme and leads to every other kind of love. There can be good works without love for God, but never love for God without good works. Without love for God, even the best works will sputter and die. So when Paul commended the Macedonians for their generosity, he wrote, "They gave themselves first to the Lord and then to us in keeping with God's will" (2 Corinthians 8:5).

Martin Luther called worship the "bridal chamber." The qualities natural to the bridal chamber are extravagant passion, intimacy and exuberance. "How beautiful you are and how pleasing, O love, with your delights!" the Lover says in the Song of Songs (7:6). Dare we take those qualities to our worship of God? Dare we not? Have you ever abandoned yourself to the worship of God the way this woman did?

PRAY:
Precious Lord, how beautiful, how pleasing you are! You deserve my best and my all. May my worship be exuberant, passionate and extravagant.

FOR YOUR NEXT DEVOTIONAL READING, GO TO PAGE 1182.

to give me if I hand him over to you?" So they counted out for him thirty silver coins. ¹⁶From then on Judas watched for an opportunity to hand him over.

The Lord's Supper

¹⁷On the first day of the Feast of Unleavened Bread, the disciples came to Jesus and asked, "Where do you want us to make preparations for you to eat the Passover?"

¹⁸He replied, "Go into the city to a certain man and tell him, 'The Teacher says: My appointed time is near. I am going to celebrate the Passover with my disciples at your house.'" ¹⁹So the disciples did as Jesus had directed them and prepared the Passover.

²⁰When evening came, Jesus was reclining at the table with the Twelve. ²¹And while they were eating, he said, "I tell you the truth, one of you will betray me."

²²They were very sad and began to say to him one after the other, "Surely not I, Lord?"

²³Jesus replied, "The one who has dipped his hand into the bowl with me will betray me. ²⁴The Son of Man will go just as it is written about him. But woe to that man who betrays the Son of Man! It would be better for him if he had not been born."

²⁵Then Judas, the one who would betray him, said, "Surely not I, Rabbi?"

Jesus answered, "Yes, it is you."[a]

²⁶While they were eating, Jesus took bread, gave thanks and broke it, and gave it to his disciples, saying, "Take and eat; this is my body."

²⁷Then he took the cup, gave thanks and offered it to them, saying, "Drink from it, all of you. ²⁸This is my blood of the[b] covenant, which is poured out for many for the forgiveness of sins. ²⁹I tell you, I will not drink of this fruit of the vine from now on until that day when I drink it anew with you in my Father's kingdom."

³⁰When they had sung a hymn, they went out to the Mount of Olives.

Jesus Predicts Peter's Denial

³¹Then Jesus told them, "This very night you will all fall away on account of me, for it is written:

"'I will strike the shepherd,
    and the sheep of the flock will be
        scattered.'[c]

³²But after I have risen, I will go ahead of you into Galilee."

³³Peter replied, "Even if all fall away on account of you, I never will."

³⁴"I tell you the truth," Jesus answered, "this very night, before the rooster crows, you will disown me three times."

³⁵But Peter declared, "Even if I have to die with you, I will never disown you." And all the other disciples said the same.

Gethsemane

³⁶Then Jesus went with his disciples to a place called Gethsemane, and he said to them, "Sit here while I go over there and pray." ³⁷He took Peter and the two sons of Zebedee along with him, and he began to be sorrowful and troubled. ³⁸Then he said to them, "My soul is overwhelmed with sorrow to the point of death. Stay here and keep watch with me."

> **THEN** *Jesus went with his disciples to a place called Gethsemane, and he said to them, "Sit here while I go over there and pray."*
>
> MATTHEW 26:36

³⁹Going a little farther, he fell with his face to the ground and prayed, "My Father, if it is possible, may this cup be taken from me. Yet not as I will, but as you will."

⁴⁰Then he returned to his disciples and found them sleeping. "Could you men not keep watch with me for one hour?" he asked Peter. ⁴¹"Watch and pray so that you will not fall into temptation. The spirit is willing, but the body is weak."

⁴²He went away a second time and prayed, "My Father, if it is not possible for this cup to be taken away unless I drink it, may your will be done."

⁴³When he came back, he again found them sleeping, because their eyes were heavy. ⁴⁴So he left them and went away once more and prayed the third time, saying the same thing.

---

*a*25 Or *"You yourself have said it"*   *b*28 Some manuscripts *the new*   *c*31 Zech. 13:7

[45]Then he returned to the disciples and said to them, "Are you still sleeping and resting? Look, the hour is near, and the Son of Man is betrayed into the hands of sinners. [46]Rise, let us go! Here comes my betrayer!"

Jesus Arrested

[47]While he was still speaking, Judas, one of the Twelve, arrived. With him was a large crowd armed with swords and clubs, sent from the chief priests and the elders of the people. [48]Now the betrayer had arranged a signal with them: "The one I kiss is the man; arrest him." [49]Going at once to Jesus, Judas said, "Greetings, Rabbi!" and kissed him.

[50]Jesus replied, "Friend, do what you came for."[a]

Then the men stepped forward, seized Jesus and arrested him. [51]With that, one of Jesus' companions reached for his sword, drew it out and struck the servant of the high priest, cutting off his ear.

[52]"Put your sword back in its place," Jesus said to him, "for all who draw the sword will die by the sword. [53]Do you think I cannot call on my Father, and he will at once put at my disposal more than twelve legions of angels? [54]But how then would the Scriptures be fulfilled that say it must happen in this way?"

[55]At that time Jesus said to the crowd, "Am I leading a rebellion, that you have come out with swords and clubs to capture me? Every day I sat in the temple courts teaching, and you did not arrest me. [56]But this has all taken place that the writings of the prophets might be fulfilled." Then all the disciples deserted him and fled.

Before the Sanhedrin

[57]Those who had arrested Jesus took him to Caiaphas, the high priest, where the teachers of the law and the elders had assembled. [58]But Peter followed him at a distance, right up to the courtyard of the high priest. He entered and sat down with the guards to see the outcome.

[59]The chief priests and the whole Sanhedrin were looking for false evidence against Jesus so that they could put him to death. [60]But they did not find any, though many false witnesses came forward.

Finally two came forward [61]and declared, "This fellow said, 'I am able to destroy the temple of God and rebuild it in three days.'"

[62]Then the high priest stood up and said to Jesus, "Are you not going to answer? What is this testimony that these men are bringing against you?" [63]But Jesus remained silent.

The high priest said to him, "I charge you under oath by the living God: Tell us if you are the Christ,[b] the Son of God."

[64]"Yes, it is as you say," Jesus replied. "But I say to all of you: In the future you will see the Son of Man sitting at the right hand of the Mighty One and coming on the clouds of heaven."

[65]Then the high priest tore his clothes and said, "He has spoken blasphemy! Why do we need any more witnesses? Look, now you have heard the blasphemy. [66]What do you think?"

"He is worthy of death," they answered.

[67]Then they spit in his face and struck him with their fists. Others slapped him [68]and said, "Prophesy to us, Christ. Who hit you?"

Peter Disowns Jesus

[69]Now Peter was sitting out in the courtyard, and a servant girl came to him. "You also were with Jesus of Galilee," she said.

[70]But he denied it before them all. "I don't know what you're talking about," he said.

[71]Then he went out to the gateway, where another girl saw him and said to the people there, "This fellow was with Jesus of Nazareth."

[72]He denied it again, with an oath: "I don't know the man!"

[73]After a little while, those standing there went up to Peter and said, "Surely you are one of them, for your accent gives you away."

[74]Then he began to call down curses on himself and he swore to them, "I don't know the man!"

Immediately a rooster crowed. [75]Then Peter remembered the word Jesus had

[a]50 Or "Friend, why have you come?"
[b]63 Or Messiah; also in verse 68

THOMAS À KEMPIS (1379 or 1380–1471)
The Imitation of Christ

THE IMITATION OF CHRIST by Thomas à Kempis is considered by many to be second only to the Bible in its profound wisdom, clarity of thought and converting power. The spectrum of its admirers is as broad as the church of Christ: St. Thomas More, General Gordon, St. Ignatius Loyola, John Wesley and St. Francis Xavier, not to mention countless other lay people who have acknowledged their debt to his book, despite the fact that it was originally written by a monk for monks.

Thomas à Kempis was born Thomas Haemerken and raised in the town of Kempen in the Netherlands. He and his brother John were ordinary boys, but both would spend their lives in distinguished service to Christ—John as prior of the monastery of St. Agnes, and Thomas as Thomas à Kempis (named after his birthplace at Kempen), author of *The Imitation of Christ* and other works.

The common theme throughout the *Imitation* is our complete dependence on the love, mercy and holiness of God. Like Augustine, à Kempis believed that God made us for himself, "and our heart is restless until it repose in Thee." Therefore, our highest good and deepest happiness are to be found only in the knowledge and service of God.

> Nothing is sweeter than love, nothing stronger, nothing higher, nothing wider, nothing more pleasant, and nothing fuller or better in heaven or earth; for love is born of God, and can rest only in God, above all created things.[4]

Moreover, through the personal nature of his dialogues between man and God in the *Imitation*, à Kempis shows that Christ is not a static figure frozen in history but a living and present reality. The risen Christ shapes the spiritual lives of his disciples today as decisively as Christ shaped his disciples in the first century. Love is not an idea or abstract virtue but a person. Ever the pastor, à Kempis speaks as a mystic and scholar, but also as a guide to the practical issues of spiritual life. He tells us not only *why* we must imitate Christ but *how*.

The Imitation of Christ was finished in 1427, and hand-written copies were circulated. In 1472, a year after à Kempis's death, the *Imitation* was set in type. By 1779, over 1500 editions and translations had spread across Europe.

PRAY:

"O Lord, what can I trust in this life? And what is my greatest comfort on earth? It is you, O Lord, whose love is without limit. When have I ever done well without you? When have I ever been harmed when you are present? I would rather be poor with you, than rich without you. I would rather be a wanderer on the earth with you, than to be in heaven without you. For where you are, there is heaven. And where you are not, there is death and hell. You are everything that I long for; therefore I will earnestly pray to you. There is no one who can help me except you alone, O my God. For you are my hope, you are my assurance, you are my strength, you are my comfort, and my most faithful helper in every need."[5]

MEMORIZE:

Whom have I in heaven but you? And earth has nothing I desire besides you. My flesh and my heart may fail, but God is the strength of my heart and my portion forever. PSALM 73:25–26

FOR YOUR NEXT DEVOTIONAL READING, GO TO PAGE 1189.

spoken: "Before the rooster crows, you will disown me three times." And he went outside and wept bitterly.

Judas Hangs Himself

27 Early in the morning, all the chief priests and the elders of the people came to the decision to put Jesus to death. ²They bound him, led him away and handed him over to Pilate, the governor.

³When Judas, who had betrayed him, saw that Jesus was condemned, he was seized with remorse and returned the thirty silver coins to the chief priests and the elders. ⁴"I have sinned," he said, "for I have betrayed innocent blood."

"What is that to us?" they replied. "That's your responsibility."

⁵So Judas threw the money into the temple and left. Then he went away and hanged himself.

⁶The chief priests picked up the coins and said, "It is against the law to put this into the treasury, since it is blood money." ⁷So they decided to use the money to buy the potter's field as a burial place for foreigners. ⁸That is why it has been called the Field of Blood to this day. ⁹Then what was spoken by Jeremiah the prophet was fulfilled: "They took the thirty silver coins, the price set on him by the people of Israel, ¹⁰and they used them to buy the potter's field, as the Lord commanded me."*a*

Jesus Before Pilate

¹¹Meanwhile Jesus stood before the governor, and the governor asked him, "Are you the king of the Jews?"

"Yes, it is as you say," Jesus replied.

¹²When he was accused by the chief priests and the elders, he gave no answer. ¹³Then Pilate asked him, "Don't you hear the testimony they are bringing against you?" ¹⁴But Jesus made no reply, not even to a single charge—to the great amazement of the governor.

¹⁵Now it was the governor's custom at the Feast to release a prisoner chosen by the crowd. ¹⁶At that time they had a notorious prisoner, called Barabbas. ¹⁷So when the crowd had gathered, Pilate asked them, "Which one do you want me to release to you: Barabbas, or Jesus who

is called Christ?" ¹⁸For he knew it was out of envy that they had handed Jesus over to him.

¹⁹While Pilate was sitting on the judge's seat, his wife sent him this message: "Don't have anything to do with that innocent man, for I have suffered a great deal today in a dream because of him."

²⁰But the chief priests and the elders persuaded the crowd to ask for Barabbas and to have Jesus executed.

²¹"Which of the two do you want me to release to you?" asked the governor.

"Barabbas," they answered.

²²"What shall I do, then, with Jesus who is called Christ?" Pilate asked.

They all answered, "Crucify him!"

²³"Why? What crime has he committed?" asked Pilate.

But they shouted all the louder, "Crucify him!"

²⁴When Pilate saw that he was getting nowhere, but that instead an uproar was starting, he took water and washed his hands in front of the crowd. "I am innocent of this man's blood," he said. "It is your responsibility!"

²⁵All the people answered, "Let his blood be on us and on our children!"

²⁶Then he released Barabbas to them. But he had Jesus flogged, and handed him over to be crucified.

The Soldiers Mock Jesus

²⁷Then the governor's soldiers took Jesus into the Praetorium and gathered the whole company of soldiers around him. ²⁸They stripped him and put a scarlet robe on him, ²⁹and then twisted together a crown of thorns and set it on his head. They put a staff in his right hand and knelt in front of him and mocked him. "Hail, king of the Jews!" they said. ³⁰They spit on him, and took the staff and struck him on the head again and again. ³¹After they had mocked him, they took off the robe and put his own clothes on him. Then they led him away to crucify him.

The Crucifixion

³²As they were going out, they met a man from Cyrene, named Simon, and

a10 See Zech. 11:12,13; Jer. 19:1–13; 32:6–9.

they forced him to carry the cross. ³³They came to a place called Golgotha (which means The Place of the Skull). ³⁴There they offered Jesus wine to drink, mixed with gall; but after tasting it, he refused to drink it. ³⁵When they had crucified him, they divided up his clothes by casting lots.ᵃ ³⁶And sitting down, they kept watch over him there. ³⁷Above his head they placed the written charge against him: THIS IS JESUS, THE KING OF THE JEWS. ³⁸Two robbers were crucified with him, one on his right and one on his left. ³⁹Those who passed by hurled insults at him, shaking their heads ⁴⁰and saying, "You who are going to destroy the temple and build it in three days, save yourself! Come down from the cross, if you are the Son of God!"

⁴¹In the same way the chief priests, the teachers of the law and the elders mocked him. ⁴²"He saved others," they said, "but he can't save himself! He's the King of Israel! Let him come down now from the cross, and we will believe in him. ⁴³He trusts in God. Let God rescue him now if he wants him, for he said, 'I am the Son of God.'" ⁴⁴In the same way the robbers who were crucified with him also heaped insults on him.

The Death of Jesus

⁴⁵From the sixth hour until the ninth hour darkness came over all the land. ⁴⁶About the ninth hour Jesus cried out in a loud voice, *"Eloi, Eloi,ᵇ lama sabachthani?"*—which means, "My God, my God, why have you forsaken me?"ᶜ

> ABOUT the ninth hour Jesus cried out in a loud voice, "Eloi, Eloi, lama sabachthani?"—which means, "My God, my God, why have you forsaken me?"
>
> MATTHEW 27:46

⁴⁷When some of those standing there heard this, they said, "He's calling Elijah." ⁴⁸Immediately one of them ran and got a sponge. He filled it with wine vinegar, put it on a stick, and offered it to Jesus to drink. ⁴⁹The rest said, "Now leave him alone. Let's see if Elijah comes to save him."

⁵⁰And when Jesus had cried out again in a loud voice, he gave up his spirit.

⁵¹At that moment the curtain of the temple was torn in two from top to bottom. The earth shook and the rocks split. ⁵²The tombs broke open and the bodies of many holy people who had died were raised to life. ⁵³They came out of the tombs, and after Jesus' resurrection they went into the holy city and appeared to many people.

⁵⁴When the centurion and those with him who were guarding Jesus saw the earthquake and all that had happened, they were terrified, and exclaimed, "Surely he was the Sonᵈ of God!"

⁵⁵Many women were there, watching from a distance. They had followed Jesus from Galilee to care for his needs. ⁵⁶Among them were Mary Magdalene, Mary the mother of James and Joses, and the mother of Zebedee's sons.

The Burial of Jesus

⁵⁷As evening approached, there came a rich man from Arimathea, named Joseph, who had himself become a disciple of Jesus. ⁵⁸Going to Pilate, he asked for Jesus' body, and Pilate ordered that it be given to him. ⁵⁹Joseph took the body, wrapped it in a clean linen cloth, ⁶⁰and placed it in his own new tomb that he had cut out of the rock. He rolled a big stone in front of the entrance to the tomb and went away. ⁶¹Mary Magdalene and the other Mary were sitting there opposite the tomb.

The Guard at the Tomb

⁶²The next day, the one after Preparation Day, the chief priests and the Pharisees went to Pilate. ⁶³"Sir," they said, "we remember that while he was still alive that deceiver said, 'After three days I will rise again.' ⁶⁴So give the order for the tomb to be made secure until the third day. Otherwise, his disciples may come and steal the body and tell the people that he has been raised from the dead.

ᵃ35 A few late manuscripts *lots that the word spoken by the prophet might be fulfilled: "They divided my garments among themselves and cast lots for my clothing"* (Psalm 22:18)   ᵇ46 Some manuscripts *Eli, Eli*   ᶜ46 Psalm 22:1
ᵈ54 Or *a son*

This last deception will be worse than the first."

65"Take a guard," Pilate answered. "Go, make the tomb as secure as you know how." 66So they went and made the tomb secure by putting a seal on the stone and posting the guard.

The Resurrection

28 After the Sabbath, at dawn on the first day of the week, Mary Magdalene and the other Mary went to look at the tomb.

2There was a violent earthquake, for an angel of the Lord came down from heaven and, going to the tomb, rolled back the stone and sat on it. 3His appearance was like lightning, and his clothes were white as snow. 4The guards were so afraid of him that they shook and became like dead men.

5The angel said to the women, "Do not be afraid, for I know that you are looking for Jesus, who was crucified. 6He is not here; he has risen, just as he said. Come and see the place where he lay. 7Then go quickly and tell his disciples: 'He has risen from the dead and is going ahead of you into Galilee. There you will see him.' Now I have told you."

8So the women hurried away from the tomb, afraid yet filled with joy, and ran to tell his disciples. 9Suddenly Jesus met them. "Greetings," he said. They came to him, clasped his feet and worshiped him. 10Then Jesus said to them, "Do not be afraid. Go and tell my brothers to go to Galilee; there they will see me."

The Guards' Report

11While the women were on their way, some of the guards went into the city and reported to the chief priests everything that had happened. 12When the chief priests had met with the elders and devised a plan, they gave the soldiers a large sum of money, 13telling them, "You are to say, 'His disciples came during the night and stole him away while we were asleep.' 14If this report gets to the governor, we will satisfy him and keep you out of trouble." 15So the soldiers took the money and did as they were instructed. And this story has been widely circulated among the Jews to this very day.

The Great Commission

16Then the eleven disciples went to Galilee, to the mountain where Jesus had told them to go. 17When they saw him, they worshiped him; but some doubted. 18Then Jesus came to them and said, "All authority in heaven and on earth has been given to me. 19Therefore go and make disciples of all nations, baptizing them in*a* the name of the Father and of the Son and of the Holy Spirit, 20and teaching them to obey everything I have commanded you. And surely I am with you always, to the very end of the age."

a19 Or *into*; see Acts 8:16; 19:5; Romans 6:3; 1 Cor. 1:13; 10:2 and Gal. 3:27.

Mark

THE BOOK of Mark is the fastest paced of the four Gospels. Mark's narrative style is almost childlike in its breathlessness. Fond of the historical present, he tells past events as if they were happening in the present. His favorite words are "and" and "immediately." In the third chapter alone, 34 clauses or sentences are linked together by nothing more than a principle verb and the word "and."

Mark brings this fast-paced perspective to his portrait of Jesus as a strong man of great energy, constantly on the move. Stories of the miracles Jesus performs make up the bulk of the Gospel: exorcisms, healings, feeding crowds, walking on water. Words like "amazed" and "astonished" are the words Mark often uses to describe people's reactions to Jesus. Yet it is Jesus the activist, who in this respect lived a life not unlike our own, who Mark shows to be also a man of prayer. He rises very early to pray on the morning after an exhausting day, not in spite of his schedule, but because of it (see 1:35–39). To learn to pray from the Gospel of Mark is to learn to pray amid busyness and the tyranny of the urgent.

"ALL THINGS ARE POSSIBLE WITH GOD." (10:27)

The first words out of Jesus' mouth in this Gospel are, "The time has come. The kingdom of God is near. Repent and believe the good news!" (1:15). With those words, Mark establishes his Gospel's topic. True to his style, he not only tells us what Jesus actually *said* about the kingdom but also shows us what he *did* about it. What emerges is a picture of God's rule that is a mystery—present and future, already and not yet, a reality to be received and hoped for.

Mark's Gospel shows us that prayer, like the kingdom, is a mystery. We pray *for* the kingdom of God to come (see Matthew 6:10; Luke 11:2), and *in* the kingdom of God that has already come. Though for the time being we live by unseen realities, the day is coming when faith will become sight. All prayer is ultimately a kind of joyful yearning; we are glad for what is and hungry for what will be. By faith, prayer sows in apparent weakness and hopes for what will be raised in power (see 1 Corinthians 15:42–44).

Jesus lived by these unseen realities. Though he was God's strong man, the Messiah and Son of God, his mission was to die the death of a common criminal (see Mark 8:31–38). From the world's perspective, he was a failure. But his "failure" was in fact the liberation of many (see 10:45), and one day his triumph will be plain for all to see (see 14:61–62). To pray the Gospel of Mark is to pray with this Jesus.

John the Baptist Prepares the Way

1 The beginning of the gospel about Jesus Christ, the Son of God.[a]

²It is written in Isaiah the prophet:

"I will send my messenger ahead of you,
 who will prepare your way"[b]—
³ "a voice of one calling in the desert,
 'Prepare the way for the Lord,
 make straight paths for him.' "[c]

⁴And so John came, baptizing in the desert region and preaching a baptism of repentance for the forgiveness of sins. ⁵The whole Judean countryside and all the people of Jerusalem went out to him. Confessing their sins, they were baptized by him in the Jordan River. ⁶John wore clothing made of camel's hair, with a leather belt around his waist, and he ate locusts and wild honey. ⁷And this was his message: "After me will come one more powerful than I, the thongs of whose sandals I am not worthy to stoop down and untie. ⁸I baptize you with[d] water, but he will baptize you with the Holy Spirit."

The Baptism and Temptation of Jesus

⁹At that time Jesus came from Nazareth in Galilee and was baptized by John in the Jordan. ¹⁰As Jesus was coming up out of the water, he saw heaven being torn open and the Spirit descending on him like a dove. ¹¹And a voice came from heaven: "You are my Son, whom I love; with you I am well pleased."

¹²At once the Spirit sent him out into the desert, ¹³and he was in the desert forty days, being tempted by Satan. He was with the wild animals, and angels attended him.

The Calling of the First Disciples

¹⁴After John was put in prison, Jesus went into Galilee, proclaiming the good news of God. ¹⁵"The time has come," he said. "The kingdom of God is near. Repent and believe the good news!"

¹⁶As Jesus walked beside the Sea of Galilee, he saw Simon and his brother Andrew casting a net into the lake, for they were fishermen. ¹⁷"Come, follow me," Jesus said, "and I will make you fishers of men." ¹⁸At once they left their nets and followed him.

¹⁹When he had gone a little farther, he saw James son of Zebedee and his brother John in a boat, preparing their nets. ²⁰Without delay he called them, and they left their father Zebedee in the boat with the hired men and followed him.

Jesus Drives Out an Evil Spirit

²¹They went to Capernaum, and when the Sabbath came, Jesus went into the synagogue and began to teach. ²²The people were amazed at his teaching, because he taught them as one who had authority, not as the teachers of the law. ²³Just then a man in their synagogue who was possessed by an evil[e] spirit cried out, ²⁴"What do you want with us, Jesus of Nazareth? Have you come to destroy us? I know who you are—the Holy One of God!"

²⁵"Be quiet!" said Jesus sternly. "Come out of him!" ²⁶The evil spirit shook the man violently and came out of him with a shriek.

²⁷The people were all so amazed that they asked each other, "What is this? A new teaching—and with authority! He even gives orders to evil spirits and they obey him." ²⁸News about him spread quickly over the whole region of Galilee.

Jesus Heals Many

²⁹As soon as they left the synagogue, they went with James and John to the home of Simon and Andrew. ³⁰Simon's mother-in-law was in bed with a fever, and they told Jesus about her. ³¹So he went to her, took her hand and helped her up. The fever left her and she began to wait on them.

³²That evening after sunset the people brought to Jesus all the sick and demon-possessed. ³³The whole town gathered at the door, ³⁴and Jesus healed many who had various diseases. He also drove out many demons, but he would not let the demons speak because they knew who he was.

Jesus Prays in a Solitary Place

³⁵Very early in the morning, while it was still dark, Jesus got up, left the house

---

[a]1 Some manuscripts do not have *the Son of God*.
[b]2 Mal. 3:1   [c]3 Isaiah 40:3   [d]8 Or *in*
[e]23 Greek *unclean*; also in verses 26 and 27

and went off to a solitary place, where he prayed. 36Simon and his companions went to look for him, 37and when they found him, they exclaimed: "Everyone is looking for you!"

38Jesus replied, "Let us go somewhere else—to the nearby villages—so I can preach there also. That is why I have come." 39So he traveled throughout Galilee, preaching in their synagogues and driving out demons.

A Man With Leprosy

40A man with leprosy*a* came to him and begged him on his knees, "If you are willing, you can make me clean."

41Filled with compassion, Jesus reached out his hand and touched the man. "I am willing," he said. "Be clean!" 42Immediately the leprosy left him and he was cured.

a40 The Greek word was used for various diseases affecting the skin—not necessarily leprosy.

[MONDAY]

MARK 1:21–35

The First Thing

1:35 VERY EARLY IN THE MORNING, WHILE IT WAS STILL DARK, JESUS GOT UP, LEFT THE HOUSE AND WENT OFF TO A SOLITARY PLACE, WHERE HE PRAYED.

The day before this one (see 1:21–34) had been a full and demanding one for Jesus. He started off the day by teaching in the Capernaum synagogue. When a man with a demon interrupted his teaching, Jesus healed him. Then he went home with Peter and Andrew and healed Peter's mother-in-law, who was sick in bed with a fever. Word of his miraculous power spread throughout the region, and when the Sabbath ended that evening, people came from miles around to be healed. Jesus must have been exhausted when he finally went to bed late that night. But he was up very early the next morning to pray.

Was Jesus up early to pray *in spite* of what he had been doing the day before or *because* of what he had been doing? Clearly Jesus needed to speak with God because of what he had been doing. There was too much at stake for him to miss communion with his Father. To pray was to be restored and refocused. He had done his Father's will the day before. What was his Father's will for this day? In order to face another hectic day, he needed guidance from the Father.

What about you? Does your schedule determine your prayer life, or does your prayer life determine your schedule? Do you sometimes think you're too busy to pray—or too busy *not* to pray? Who sets your priorities? Jesus depended completely on the Father for direction (see John 5:19–20,30). On whom do you depend? If he, the sinless Son of God, found it necessary to be diligent in prayer, how much more should you and I? Make communion with your Father in heaven the first thing you do each day.

PRAY:

Jesus, sometimes I am pulled this way and that, from daylight to dusk.
There are so many voices asking, inviting, demanding and pleading
for my attention. Clear my mind, focus my thoughts and order
my priorities, for the sake of your kingdom. Amen.

FOR YOUR NEXT DEVOTIONAL READING, GO TO PAGE 1194.

43Jesus sent him away at once with a strong warning: 44"See that you don't tell this to anyone. But go, show yourself to the priest and offer the sacrifices that Moses commanded for your cleansing, as a testimony to them." 45Instead he went out and began to talk freely, spreading the news. As a result, Jesus could no longer enter a town openly but stayed outside in lonely places. Yet the people still came to him from everywhere.

Jesus Heals a Paralytic

2 A few days later, when Jesus again entered Capernaum, the people heard that he had come home. 2So many gathered that there was no room left, not even outside the door, and he preached the word to them. 3Some men came, bringing to him a paralytic, carried by four of them. 4Since they could not get him to Jesus because of the crowd, they made an opening in the roof above Jesus and, after digging through it, lowered the mat the paralyzed man was lying on. 5When Jesus saw their faith, he said to the paralytic, "Son, your sins are forgiven."

> WHEN Jesus saw their faith, he said to the paralytic, "Son, your sins are forgiven."
>
> MARK 2:5

6Now some teachers of the law were sitting there, thinking to themselves, 7"Why does this fellow talk like that? He's blaspheming! Who can forgive sins but God alone?"

8Immediately Jesus knew in his spirit that this was what they were thinking in their hearts, and he said to them, "Why are you thinking these things? 9Which is easier: to say to the paralytic, 'Your sins are forgiven,' or to say, 'Get up, take your mat and walk'? 10But that you may know that the Son of Man has authority on earth to forgive sins..." He said to the paralytic, 11"I tell you, get up, take your mat and go home." 12He got up, took his mat and walked out in full view of them all. This amazed everyone and they praised God, saying, "We have never seen anything like this!"

The Calling of Levi

13Once again Jesus went out beside the lake. A large crowd came to him, and he began to teach them. 14As he walked along, he saw Levi son of Alphaeus sitting at the tax collector's booth. "Follow me," Jesus told him, and Levi got up and followed him.

15While Jesus was having dinner at Levi's house, many tax collectors and "sinners" were eating with him and his disciples, for there were many who followed him. 16When the teachers of the law who were Pharisees saw him eating with the "sinners" and tax collectors, they asked his disciples: "Why does he eat with tax collectors and 'sinners'?"

17On hearing this, Jesus said to them, "It is not the healthy who need a doctor, but the sick. I have not come to call the righteous, but sinners."

Jesus Questioned About Fasting

18Now John's disciples and the Pharisees were fasting. Some people came and asked Jesus, "How is it that John's disciples and the disciples of the Pharisees are fasting, but yours are not?"

19Jesus answered, "How can the guests of the bridegroom fast while he is with them? They cannot, so long as they have him with them. 20But the time will come when the bridegroom will be taken from them, and on that day they will fast.

21"No one sews a patch of unshrunk cloth on an old garment. If he does, the new piece will pull away from the old, making the tear worse. 22And no one pours new wine into old wineskins. If he does, the wine will burst the skins, and both the wine and the wineskins will be ruined. No, he pours new wine into new wineskins."

Lord of the Sabbath

23One Sabbath Jesus was going through the grainfields, and as his disciples walked along, they began to pick some heads of grain. 24The Pharisees said to him, "Look, why are they doing what is unlawful on the Sabbath?"

25He answered, "Have you never read what David did when he and his companions were hungry and in need? 26In the days of Abiathar the high priest, he entered the house of God and ate the consecrated bread, which is lawful only for priests to eat. And he also gave some to his companions."

²⁷Then he said to them, "The Sabbath was made for man, not man for the Sabbath. ²⁸So the Son of Man is Lord even of the Sabbath."

3 Another time he went into the synagogue, and a man with a shriveled hand was there. ²Some of them were looking for a reason to accuse Jesus, so they watched him closely to see if he would heal him on the Sabbath. ³Jesus said to the man with the shriveled hand, "Stand up in front of everyone."

⁴Then Jesus asked them, "Which is lawful on the Sabbath: to do good or to do evil, to save life or to kill?" But they remained silent.

⁵He looked around at them in anger and, deeply distressed at their stubborn hearts, said to the man, "Stretch out your hand." He stretched it out, and his hand was completely restored. ⁶Then the Pharisees went out and began to plot with the Herodians how they might kill Jesus.

Crowds Follow Jesus

⁷Jesus withdrew with his disciples to the lake, and a large crowd from Galilee followed. ⁸When they heard all he was doing, many people came to him from Judea, Jerusalem, Idumea, and the regions across the Jordan and around Tyre and Sidon. ⁹Because of the crowd he told his disciples to have a small boat ready for him, to keep the people from crowding him. ¹⁰For he had healed many, so that those with diseases were pushing forward to touch him. ¹¹Whenever the evil*a* spirits saw him, they fell down before him and cried out, "You are the Son of God." ¹²But he gave them strict orders not to tell who he was.

The Appointing of the Twelve Apostles

¹³Jesus went up on a mountainside and called to him those he wanted, and they came to him. ¹⁴He appointed twelve— designating them apostles*b*—that they might be with him and that he might send them out to preach ¹⁵and to have authority to drive out demons. ¹⁶These

are the twelve he appointed: Simon (to whom he gave the name Peter); ¹⁷James son of Zebedee and his brother John (to them he gave the name Boanerges, which means Sons of Thunder); ¹⁸Andrew, Philip, Bartholomew, Matthew, Thomas, James son of Alphaeus, Thaddaeus, Simon the Zealot ¹⁹and Judas Iscariot, who betrayed him.

Jesus and Beelzebub

²⁰Then Jesus entered a house, and again a crowd gathered, so that he and his disciples were not even able to eat. ²¹When his family heard about this, they went to take charge of him, for they said, "He is out of his mind."

²²And the teachers of the law who came down from Jerusalem said, "He is possessed by Beelzebub*c*! By the prince of demons he is driving out demons."

²³So Jesus called them and spoke to them in parables: "How can Satan drive out Satan? ²⁴If a kingdom is divided against itself, that kingdom cannot stand. ²⁵If a house is divided against itself, that house cannot stand. ²⁶And if Satan opposes himself and is divided, he cannot stand; his end has come. ²⁷In fact, no one can enter a strong man's house and carry off his possessions unless he first ties up the strong man. Then he can rob his house. ²⁸I tell you the truth, all the sins and blasphemies of men will be forgiven them. ²⁹But whoever blasphemes against the Holy Spirit will never be forgiven; he is guilty of an eternal sin."

³⁰He said this because they were saying, "He has an evil spirit."

Jesus' Mother and Brothers

³¹Then Jesus' mother and brothers arrived. Standing outside, they sent someone in to call him. ³²A crowd was sitting around him, and they told him, "Your mother and brothers are outside looking for you."

³³"Who are my mother and my brothers?" he asked.

³⁴Then he looked at those seated in a circle around him and said, "Here are my

---

a11 Greek unclean; also in verse 30   b14 Some manuscripts do not have designating them apostles.   c22 Greek Beezeboul or Beelzeboul

mother and my brothers! [35]Whoever does God's will is my brother and sister and mother."

The Parable of the Sower

4 Again Jesus began to teach by the lake. The crowd that gathered around him was so large that he got into a boat and sat in it out on the lake, while all the people were along the shore at the water's edge. [2]He taught them many things by parables, and in his teaching said: [3]"Listen! A farmer went out to sow his seed. [4]As he was scattering the seed, some fell along the path, and the birds came and ate it up. [5]Some fell on rocky places, where it did not have much soil. It sprang up quickly, because the soil was shallow. [6]But when the sun came up, the plants were scorched, and they withered because they had no root. [7]Other seed fell among thorns, which grew up and choked the plants, so that they did not bear grain. [8]Still other seed fell on good soil. It came up, grew and produced a crop, multiplying thirty, sixty, or even a hundred times."

[9]Then Jesus said, "He who has ears to hear, let him hear."

[10]When he was alone, the Twelve and the others around him asked him about the parables. [11]He told them, "The secret of the kingdom of God has been given to you. But to those on the outside everything is said in parables [12]so that,

" 'they may be ever seeing but never perceiving,
and ever hearing but never understanding;
otherwise they might turn and be forgiven!'[a]"

[13]Then Jesus said to them, "Don't you understand this parable? How then will you understand any parable? [14]The farmer sows the word. [15]Some people are like seed along the path, where the word is sown. As soon as they hear it, Satan comes and takes away the word that was sown in them. [16]Others, like seed sown on rocky places, hear the word and at once receive it with joy. [17]But since they have no root, they last only a short time. When trouble or persecution comes because of the word, they quickly fall away.

[18]Still others, like seed sown among thorns, hear the word; [19]but the worries of this life, the deceitfulness of wealth and the desires for other things come in and choke the word, making it unfruitful. [20]Others, like seed sown on good soil, hear the word, accept it, and produce a crop—thirty, sixty or even a hundred times what was sown."

A Lamp on a Stand

[21]He said to them, "Do you bring in a lamp to put it under a bowl or a bed? Instead, don't you put it on its stand? [22]For whatever is hidden is meant to be disclosed, and whatever is concealed is meant to be brought out into the open. [23]If anyone has ears to hear, let him hear."

[24]"Consider carefully what you hear," he continued. "With the measure you use, it will be measured to you—and even more. [25]Whoever has will be given more; whoever does not have, even what he has will be taken from him."

The Parable of the Growing Seed

[26]He also said, "This is what the kingdom of God is like. A man scatters seed on the ground. [27]Night and day, whether he sleeps or gets up, the seed sprouts and grows, though he does not know how. [28]All by itself the soil produces grain—first the stalk, then the head, then the full kernel in the head. [29]As soon as the grain is ripe, he puts the sickle to it, because the harvest has come."

The Parable of the Mustard Seed

[30]Again he said, "What shall we say the kingdom of God is like, or what parable shall we use to describe it? [31]It is like a mustard seed, which is the smallest seed you plant in the ground. [32]Yet when planted, it grows and becomes the largest of all garden plants, with such big branches that the birds of the air can perch in its shade."

[33]With many similar parables Jesus spoke the word to them, as much as they could understand. [34]He did not say anything to them without using a parable. But when he was alone with his own disciples, he explained everything.

[a]12 Isaiah 6:9,10

Jesus Calms the Storm

35That day when evening came, he said to his disciples, "Let us go over to the other side." **36**Leaving the crowd behind, they took him along, just as he was, in the boat. There were also other boats with him. **37**A furious squall came up, and the waves broke over the boat, so that it was nearly swamped. **38**Jesus was in the stern, sleeping on a cushion. The disciples woke him and said to him, "Teacher, don't you care if we drown?"

39He got up, rebuked the wind and said to the waves, "Quiet! Be still!" Then the wind died down and it was completely calm.

40He said to his disciples, "Why are you so afraid? Do you still have no faith?"

41They were terrified and asked each other, "Who is this? Even the wind and the waves obey him!"

The Healing of a Demon-possessed Man

5 They went across the lake to the region of the Gerasenes.[a] **2**When Jesus got out of the boat, a man with an evil[b] spirit came from the tombs to meet him. **3**This man lived in the tombs, and no one could bind him any more, not even with a chain. **4**For he had often been chained hand and foot, but he tore the chains apart and broke the irons on his feet. No one was strong enough to subdue him. **5**Night and day among the tombs and in the hills he would cry out and cut himself with stones.

6When he saw Jesus from a distance, he ran and fell on his knees in front of him. **7**He shouted at the top of his voice, "What do you want with me, Jesus, Son of the Most High God? Swear to God that you won't torture me!" **8**For Jesus had said to him, "Come out of this man, you evil spirit!"

9Then Jesus asked him, "What is your name?"

"My name is Legion," he replied, "for we are many." **10**And he begged Jesus again and again not to send them out of the area.

11A large herd of pigs was feeding on the nearby hillside. **12**The demons begged Jesus, "Send us among the pigs; allow us to go into them." **13**He gave them permission, and the evil spirits came out and went into the pigs. The herd, about two thousand in number, rushed down the steep bank into the lake and were drowned.

14Those tending the pigs ran off and reported this in the town and countryside, and the people went out to see what had happened. **15**When they came to Jesus, they saw the man who had been possessed by the legion of demons, sitting there, dressed and in his right mind; and they were afraid. **16**Those who had seen it told the people what had happened to the demon-possessed man—and told about the pigs as well. **17**Then the people began to plead with Jesus to leave their region.

18As Jesus was getting into the boat, the man who had been demon-possessed begged to go with him. **19**Jesus did not let him, but said, "Go home to your family and tell them how much the Lord has done for you, and how he has had mercy on you." **20**So the man went away and began to tell in the Decapolis[c] how much Jesus had done for him. And all the people were amazed.

A Dead Girl and a Sick Woman

21When Jesus had again crossed over by boat to the other side of the lake, a large crowd gathered around him while he was by the lake. **22**Then one of the synagogue rulers, named Jairus, came there. Seeing Jesus, he fell at his feet **23**and pleaded earnestly with him, "My little daughter is dying. Please come and put your hands on her so that she will be healed and live." **24**So Jesus went with him.

A large crowd followed and pressed around him. **25**And a woman was there who had been subject to bleeding for twelve years. **26**She had suffered a great

---

a1 Some manuscripts Gadarenes; other manuscripts Gergesenes   *b2 Greek unclean; also in verses 8 and 13*   *c20 That is, the Ten Cities*

deal under the care of many doctors and had spent all she had, yet instead of getting better she grew worse. ²⁷When she heard about Jesus, she came up behind him in the crowd and touched his cloak, ²⁸because she thought, "If I just touch his clothes, I will be healed." ²⁹Immediately her bleeding stopped and she felt in her body that she was freed from her suffering.

³⁰At once Jesus realized that power had gone out from him. He turned around in the crowd and asked, "Who touched my clothes?"

³¹"You see the people crowding against you," his disciples answered, "and yet you can ask, 'Who touched me?'"

³²But Jesus kept looking around to see who had done it. ³³Then the woman, knowing what had happened to her, came and fell at his feet and, trembling with fear, told him the whole truth. ³⁴He

---

[TUESDAY]

MARK 5:21–43

Death, Be Not Proud

5:23 "MY LITTLE DAUGHTER IS DYING. PLEASE COME AND PUT YOUR HANDS ON HER SO THAT SHE WILL BE HEALED AND LIVE."

On the wall of a room in the cancer ward was taped a picture drawn by a dying child. Filling the paper was a giant tank, its big gun pointed down at a tiny little girl holding a tiny little sign with the barely discernible word, "stop."

No one can stand before death. It is a cold, remorseless monster with an insatiable appetite. It is the great leveler, swallowing up young and old, high and low alike (see Psalm 103:15–16). No one escapes it. The human mortality rate is 100%. We are all helpless before death.

And yet, here again is just a little girl! And here is her loving father, for whom all this helpless and hopeless talk about mortality is unacceptable. He will pray; he will argue his case before Jesus. And what a case he makes! He falls at the Master's feet and pleads earnestly for Jesus to put his hands on the little girl and heal her. And tender Jesus, who loves a broken and contrite heart, who lives with the lowly in spirit (see Isaiah 57:15), and who especially delights in faith (see Luke 7:9), moves to take a stand against death.

Death is helpless before Jesus. In him, death is swallowed up in victory (see 1 Corinthians 15:54–57). Faith is the victory that overcomes the world, not because faith is, in itself, so strong, but because the One in whom our faith rests is so powerful (see 1 John 5:4).

Bring your helpless hopelessness to Jesus as tenaciously and passionately as Jairus brought his daughter to Jesus. Bring the dying and those dead in sin to him. What Jesus did for this little girl and her father he has pledged to do for all who believe, whether now or when he returns. He will gather all his lambs to his great heart of love, and not one will be missing (see John 10:27–29).

PRAY:

Father in heaven! You have conquered our great enemy, death.
May this day be lived with hope and thankfulness that
nothing can separate us from your love.

FOR YOUR NEXT DEVOTIONAL READING, GO TO PAGE 1198.

said to her, "Daughter, your faith has healed you. Go in peace and be freed from your suffering."

³⁵While Jesus was still speaking, some men came from the house of Jairus, the synagogue ruler. "Your daughter is dead," they said. "Why bother the teacher any more?"

³⁶Ignoring what they said, Jesus told the synagogue ruler, "Don't be afraid; just believe."

³⁷He did not let anyone follow him except Peter, James and John the brother of James. ³⁸When they came to the home of the synagogue ruler, Jesus saw a commotion, with people crying and wailing loudly. ³⁹He went in and said to them, "Why all this commotion and wailing? The child is not dead but asleep." ⁴⁰But they laughed at him.

After he put them all out, he took the child's father and mother and the disciples who were with him, and went in where the child was. ⁴¹He took her by the hand and said to her, *"Talitha koum!"* (which means, "Little girl, I say to you, get up!"). ⁴²Immediately the girl stood up and walked around (she was twelve years old). At this they were completely astonished. ⁴³He gave strict orders not to let anyone know about this, and told them to give her something to eat.

A Prophet Without Honor

6 Jesus left there and went to his hometown, accompanied by his disciples. ²When the Sabbath came, he began to teach in the synagogue, and many who heard him were amazed.

"Where did this man get these things?" they asked. "What's this wisdom that has been given him, that he even does miracles! ³Isn't this the carpenter? Isn't this Mary's son and the brother of James, Joseph,ᵃ Judas and Simon? Aren't his sisters here with us?" And they took offense at him.

⁴Jesus said to them, "Only in his hometown, among his relatives and in his own house is a prophet without honor." ⁵He could not do any miracles there, except lay his hands on a few sick people and heal them. ⁶And he was amazed at their lack of faith.

Jesus Sends Out the Twelve

Then Jesus went around teaching from village to village. ⁷Calling the Twelve to him, he sent them out two by two and gave them authority over evilᵇ spirits.

⁸These were his instructions: "Take nothing for the journey except a staff—no bread, no bag, no money in your belts. ⁹Wear sandals but not an extra tunic. ¹⁰Whenever you enter a house, stay there until you leave that town. ¹¹And if any place will not welcome you or listen to you, shake the dust off your feet when you leave, as a testimony against them."

¹²They went out and preached that people should repent. ¹³They drove out many demons and anointed many sick people with oil and healed them.

John the Baptist Beheaded

¹⁴King Herod heard about this, for Jesus' name had become well known. Some were saying,ᶜ "John the Baptist has been raised from the dead, and that is why miraculous powers are at work in him."

¹⁵Others said, "He is Elijah."

And still others claimed, "He is a prophet, like one of the prophets of long ago."

¹⁶But when Herod heard this, he said, "John, the man I beheaded, has been raised from the dead!"

¹⁷For Herod himself had given orders to have John arrested, and he had him bound and put in prison. He did this because of Herodias, his brother Philip's wife, whom he had married. ¹⁸For John had been saying to Herod, "It is not lawful for you to have your brother's wife." ¹⁹So Herodias nursed a grudge against John and wanted to kill him. But she was not able to, ²⁰because Herod feared John and protected him, knowing him to be a righteous and holy man. When Herod heard John, he was greatly puzzledᵈ; yet he liked to listen to him.

²¹Finally the opportune time came. On his birthday Herod gave a banquet for his high officials and military commanders and the leading men of Galilee. ²²When

---

ᵃ3 Greek *Joses,* a variant of *Joseph*   ᵇ7 Greek *unclean*   ᶜ14 Some early manuscripts *He was saying*   ᵈ20 Some early manuscripts *he did many things*

the daughter of Herodias came in and danced, she pleased Herod and his dinner guests.

The king said to the girl, "Ask me for anything you want, and I'll give it to you." ²³And he promised her with an oath, "Whatever you ask I will give you, up to half my kingdom."

²⁴She went out and said to her mother, "What shall I ask for?"

"The head of John the Baptist," she answered.

²⁵At once the girl hurried in to the king with the request: "I want you to give me right now the head of John the Baptist on a platter."

²⁶The king was greatly distressed, but because of his oaths and his dinner guests, he did not want to refuse her. ²⁷So he immediately sent an executioner with orders to bring John's head. The man went, beheaded John in the prison, ²⁸and brought back his head on a platter. He presented it to the girl, and she gave it to her mother. ²⁹On hearing of this, John's disciples came and took his body and laid it in a tomb.

Jesus Feeds the Five Thousand

³⁰The apostles gathered around Jesus and reported to him all they had done and taught. ³¹Then, because so many people were coming and going that they did not even have a chance to eat, he said to them, "Come with me by yourselves to a quiet place and get some rest."

³²So they went away by themselves in a boat to a solitary place. ³³But many who saw them leaving recognized them and ran on foot from all the towns and got there ahead of them. ³⁴When Jesus landed and saw a large crowd, he had compassion on them, because they were like sheep without a shepherd. So he began teaching them many things.

³⁵By this time it was late in the day, so his disciples came to him. "This is a remote place," they said, "and it's already very late. ³⁶Send the people away so they can go to the surrounding countryside and villages and buy themselves something to eat."

³⁷But he answered, "You give them something to eat."

They said to him, "That would take eight months of a man's wages*! Are we to go and spend that much on bread and give it to them to eat?"

³⁸"How many loaves do you have?" he asked. "Go and see."

When they found out, they said, "Five—and two fish."

³⁹Then Jesus directed them to have all the people sit down in groups on the green grass. ⁴⁰So they sat down in groups of hundreds and fifties. ⁴¹Taking the five loaves and the two fish and looking up to heaven, he gave thanks and broke the loaves. Then he gave them to his disciples to set before the people. He also divided the two fish among them all. ⁴²They all ate and were satisfied, ⁴³and the disciples picked up twelve basketfuls of broken pieces of bread and fish. ⁴⁴The number of the men who had eaten was five thousand.

Jesus Walks on the Water

⁴⁵Immediately Jesus made his disciples get into the boat and go on ahead of him to Bethsaida, while he dismissed the crowd. ⁴⁶After leaving them, he went up on a mountainside to pray.

> AFTER leaving them, he went up on a mountainside to pray.
>
> MARK 6:46

⁴⁷When evening came, the boat was in the middle of the lake, and he was alone on land. ⁴⁸He saw the disciples straining at the oars, because the wind was against them. About the fourth watch of the night he went out to them, walking on the lake. He was about to pass by them, ⁴⁹but when they saw him walking on the lake, they thought he was a ghost. They cried out, ⁵⁰because they all saw him and were terrified.

Immediately he spoke to them and said, "Take courage! It is I. Don't be afraid." ⁵¹Then he climbed into the boat with them, and the wind died down. They were completely amazed, ⁵²for they had not understood about the loaves; their hearts were hardened.

---

*37 Greek *take two hundred denarii*

[53]When they had crossed over, they landed at Gennesaret and anchored there. [54]As soon as they got out of the boat, people recognized Jesus. [55]They ran throughout that whole region and carried the sick on mats to wherever they heard he was. [56]And wherever he went—into villages, towns or countryside—they placed the sick in the marketplaces. They begged him to let them touch even the edge of his cloak, and all who touched him were healed.

Clean and Unclean

7 The Pharisees and some of the teachers of the law who had come from Jerusalem gathered around Jesus and [2]saw some of his disciples eating food with hands that were "unclean," that is, unwashed. [3](The Pharisees and all the Jews do not eat unless they give their hands a ceremonial washing, holding to the tradition of the elders. [4]When they come from the marketplace they do not eat unless they wash. And they observe many other traditions, such as the washing of cups, pitchers and kettles.[a])

[5]So the Pharisees and teachers of the law asked Jesus, "Why don't your disciples live according to the tradition of the elders instead of eating their food with 'unclean' hands?"

[6]He replied, "Isaiah was right when he prophesied about you hypocrites; as it is written:

" 'These people honor me with their lips,
    but their hearts are far from me.
[7]They worship me in vain;
    their teachings are but rules taught by men.'[b]

[8]You have let go of the commands of God and are holding on to the traditions of men."

[9]And he said to them: "You have a fine way of setting aside the commands of God in order to observe[c] your own traditions! [10]For Moses said, 'Honor your father and your mother,'[d] and, 'Anyone who curses his father or mother must be put to death.'[e] [11]But you say that if a man says to his father or mother: 'Whatever help you might otherwise have received from me is Corban' (that is, a gift devoted to God), [12]then you no longer let him do anything for his father or mother. [13]Thus you nullify the word of God by your tradition that you have handed down. And you do many things like that."

[14]Again Jesus called the crowd to him and said, "Listen to me, everyone, and understand this. [15]Nothing outside a man can make him 'unclean' by going into him. Rather, it is what comes out of a man that makes him 'unclean.'[f]"

[17]After he had left the crowd and entered the house, his disciples asked him about this parable. [18]"Are you so dull?" he asked. "Don't you see that nothing that enters a man from the outside can make him 'unclean'? [19]For it doesn't go into his heart but into his stomach, and then out of his body." (In saying this, Jesus declared all foods "clean.")

[20]He went on: "What comes out of a man is what makes him 'unclean.' [21]For from within, out of men's hearts, come evil thoughts, sexual immorality, theft, murder, adultery, [22]greed, malice, deceit, lewdness, envy, slander, arrogance and folly. [23]All these evils come from inside and make a man 'unclean.' "

The Faith of a Syrophoenician Woman

[24]Jesus left that place and went to the vicinity of Tyre.[g] He entered a house and did not want anyone to know it; yet he could not keep his presence secret. [25]In fact, as soon as she heard about him, a woman whose little daughter was possessed by an evil[h] spirit came and fell at his feet. [26]The woman was a Greek, born in Syrian Phoenicia. She begged Jesus to drive the demon out of her daughter.

[27]"First let the children eat all they want," he told her, "for it is not right to take the children's bread and toss it to their dogs."

[28]"Yes, Lord," she replied, "but even the dogs under the table eat the children's crumbs."

[a]4 Some early manuscripts *pitchers, kettles and dining couches*   [b]6,7 Isaiah 29:13   [c]9 Some manuscripts *set up*   [d]10 Exodus 20:12; Deut. 5:16   [e]10 Exodus 21:17; Lev. 20:9   [f]15 Some early manuscripts *'unclean.'* [16]*If anyone has ears to hear, let him hear.*   [g]24 Many early manuscripts *Tyre and Sidon*   [h]25 Greek *unclean*

MARK 7:24–30

Chutzpah!

7:28 "YES, LORD," SHE REPLIED, "BUT EVEN THE DOGS UNDER THE TABLE EAT THE CHILDREN'S CRUMBS."

Coming from the Hebrew, *chutzpah* is a Yiddish word for the quality of nerve and brazen temerity that won't take no for an answer. Although the Syrophoenician woman in this story is most certainly not a Hebrew, she has plenty of *chutzpah*. Jesus came to her region to get away from the crowds and specifically did not want to have people know he was in the area. So what's the first thing this woman does when she discovers Jesus is in her neighborhood? She goes to see him! Not only that, but she falls at his feet and begs him to deliver her daughter from demon possession. No apologies from this woman for interrupting Jesus' plans.

In Matthew's account (15:21–28), we are told that, at first, Jesus answers the woman with silence. So what does she do? She keeps asking, keeps pestering, so much so that the disciples urge Jesus to send the annoying woman away. When Jesus finally does answer this woman, he lets her know that he has different priorities for the time being. The Greek for "dogs" is "little dogs," meaning a household pet. But the woman surely is also aware that Jews typically referred to Gentiles as "dogs." So Jesus was saying that the gospel must first be given to the Jews. Nevertheless, this Gentile woman doesn't relent. She says, "Yes Lord, but even the dogs under the table eat the children's crumbs." In other words, "Regardless of who I am, I intend to get from you what I need for my daughter, and I won't go away until I do."

And Jesus gives this "little dog" something he doesn't give to any of the "children." Not only does he deliver her daughter, but he says, "Woman, you have great faith!" (Matthew 15:28). The only other person to get this commendation was also a "dog," a Roman centurion (see Matthew 8:8–10). Content to receive from Jesus only "crumbs," this woman wins "best in show" for her faith.

This woman had tenacious faith. That's the kind of faith the Lord looks for in prayer. It is not only the capacity to believe God will do something, but also the persistence to keep coming to him until he does. Jesus loves a faith that will wrestle as much as he loves a faith that will rest. His greatest promises are for those who will keep on asking, seeking and knocking (see Luke 11:9–10). That's holy *chutzpah*.

PRAY:

Gracious Master! I know you love me in ways that woman didn't when she came to you. May I all the more come to you with persistence and the boldness of holy chutzpah.

———

FOR YOUR NEXT DEVOTIONAL READING, GO TO PAGE 1201.

²⁹Then he told her, "For such a reply, you may go; the demon has left your daughter."

³⁰She went home and found her child lying on the bed, and the demon gone.

The Healing of a Deaf and Mute Man

³¹Then Jesus left the vicinity of Tyre and went through Sidon, down to the Sea of Galilee and into the region of the Decapolis.ᵃ ³²There some people brought to him a man who was deaf and could hardly talk, and they begged him to place his hand on the man.

³³After he took him aside, away from the crowd, Jesus put his fingers into the man's ears. Then he spit and touched the man's tongue. ³⁴He looked up to heaven and with a deep sigh said to him, *"Eph-phatha!"* (which means, "Be opened!"). ³⁵At this, the man's ears were opened, his tongue was loosened and he began to speak plainly.

³⁶Jesus commanded them not to tell anyone. But the more he did so, the more they kept talking about it. ³⁷People were overwhelmed with amazement. "He has done everything well," they said. "He even makes the deaf hear and the mute speak."

Jesus Feeds the Four Thousand

8 During those days another large crowd gathered. Since they had nothing to eat, Jesus called his disciples to him and said, ²"I have compassion for these people; they have already been with me three days and have nothing to eat. ³If I send them home hungry, they will collapse on the way, because some of them have come a long distance."

⁴His disciples answered, "But where in this remote place can anyone get enough bread to feed them?"

⁵"How many loaves do you have?" Jesus asked.

"Seven," they replied.

⁶He told the crowd to sit down on the ground. When he had taken the seven loaves and given thanks, he broke them and gave them to his disciples to set before the people, and they did so. ⁷They had a few small fish as well; he gave thanks for them also and told the disciples to distribute them. ⁸The people ate and were satisfied. Afterward the disci-

> *Prayer does not change God, but it changes him who prays.*
>
> SØREN KIERKEGAARD

ples picked up seven basketfuls of broken pieces that were left over. ⁹About four thousand men were present. And having sent them away, ¹⁰he got into the boat with his disciples and went to the region of Dalmanutha.

¹¹The Pharisees came and began to question Jesus. To test him, they asked him for a sign from heaven. ¹²He sighed deeply and said, "Why does this generation ask for a miraculous sign? I tell you the truth, no sign will be given to it." ¹³Then he left them, got back into the boat and crossed to the other side.

The Yeast of the Pharisees and Herod

¹⁴The disciples had forgotten to bring bread, except for one loaf they had with them in the boat. ¹⁵"Be careful," Jesus warned them. "Watch out for the yeast of the Pharisees and that of Herod."

¹⁶They discussed this with one another and said, "It is because we have no bread."

¹⁷Aware of their discussion, Jesus asked them: "Why are you talking about having no bread? Do you still not see or understand? Are your hearts hardened? ¹⁸Do you have eyes but fail to see, and ears but fail to hear? And don't you remember? ¹⁹When I broke the five loaves for the five thousand, how many basketfuls of pieces did you pick up?"

"Twelve," they replied.

²⁰"And when I broke the seven loaves for the four thousand, how many basketfuls of pieces did you pick up?"

They answered, "Seven."

²¹He said to them, "Do you still not understand?"

The Healing of a Blind Man at Bethsaida

²²They came to Bethsaida, and some people brought a blind man and begged Jesus to touch him. ²³He took the blind man by the hand and led him outside the village. When he had spit on the man's eyes and put his hands on him, Jesus asked, "Do you see anything?"

ᵃ31 That is, the Ten Cities

24He looked up and said, "I see people; they look like trees walking around."

25Once more Jesus put his hands on the man's eyes. Then his eyes were opened, his sight was restored, and he saw everything clearly. 26Jesus sent him home, saying, "Don't go into the village."*ᵃ*

Peter's Confession of Christ

27Jesus and his disciples went on to the villages around Caesarea Philippi. On the way he asked them, "Who do people say I am?"

28They replied, "Some say John the Baptist; others say Elijah; and still others, one of the prophets."

29"But what about you?" he asked. "Who do you say I am?"

Peter answered, "You are the Christ."*ᵇ*

30Jesus warned them not to tell anyone about him.

Jesus Predicts His Death

31He then began to teach them that the Son of Man must suffer many things and be rejected by the elders, chief priests and teachers of the law, and that he must be killed and after three days rise again. 32He spoke plainly about this, and Peter took him aside and began to rebuke him.

33But when Jesus turned and looked at his disciples, he rebuked Peter. "Get behind me, Satan!" he said. "You do not have in mind the things of God, but the things of men."

34Then he called the crowd to him along with his disciples and said: "If anyone would come after me, he must deny himself and take up his cross and follow me. 35For whoever wants to save his life*ᶜ* will lose it, but whoever loses his life for me and for the gospel will save it. 36What good is it for a man to gain the whole world, yet forfeit his soul? 37Or what can a man give in exchange for his soul? 38If anyone is ashamed of me and my words in this adulterous and sinful generation, the Son of Man will be ashamed of him when he comes in his Father's glory with the holy angels.

9 And he said to them, "I tell you the truth, some who are standing here will not taste death before they see the kingdom of God come with power."

The Transfiguration

2After six days Jesus took Peter, James and John with him and led them up a high mountain, where they were all alone. There he was transfigured before them. 3His clothes became dazzling white, whiter than anyone in the world could bleach them. 4And there appeared before them Elijah and Moses, who were talking with Jesus.

5Peter said to Jesus, "Rabbi, it is good for us to be here. Let us put up three shelters—one for you, one for Moses and one for Elijah." 6(He did not know what to say, they were so frightened.)

7Then a cloud appeared and enveloped them, and a voice came from the cloud: "This is my Son, whom I love. Listen to him!"

8Suddenly, when they looked around, they no longer saw anyone with them except Jesus.

9As they were coming down the mountain, Jesus gave them orders not to tell anyone what they had seen until the Son of Man had risen from the dead. 10They kept the matter to themselves, discussing what "rising from the dead" meant.

11And they asked him, "Why do the teachers of the law say that Elijah must come first?"

12Jesus replied, "To be sure, Elijah does come first, and restores all things. Why then is it written that the Son of Man must suffer much and be rejected? 13But I tell you, Elijah has come, and they have done to him everything they wished, just as it is written about him."

The Healing of a Boy With an Evil Spirit

14When they came to the other disciples, they saw a large crowd around them and the teachers of the law arguing with them. 15As soon as all the people saw Jesus, they were overwhelmed with wonder and ran to greet him.

16"What are you arguing with them about?" he asked.

17A man in the crowd answered, "Teach-

ᵃ26 Some manuscripts *Don't go and tell anyone in the village*   *ᵇ29* Or *Messiah*. "The Christ" (Greek) and "the Messiah" (Hebrew) both mean "the Anointed One."   *ᶜ35* The Greek word means either *life* or *soul*; also in verse 36.

er, I brought you my son, who is possessed by a spirit that has robbed him of speech. ¹⁸Whenever it seizes him, it throws him to the ground. He foams at the mouth, gnashes his teeth and becomes rigid. I asked your disciples to drive out the spirit, but they could not."

¹⁹"O unbelieving generation," Jesus replied, "how long shall I stay with you? How long shall I put up with you? Bring the boy to me."

²⁰So they brought him. When the spirit saw Jesus, it immediately threw the boy into a convulsion. He fell to the ground and rolled around, foaming at the mouth.

²¹Jesus asked the boy's father, "How long has he been like this?"

"From childhood," he answered. ²²"It has often thrown him into fire or water to kill him. But if you can do anything, take pity on us and help us."

²³"'If you can'?" said Jesus. "Everything is possible for him who believes."

²⁴Immediately the boy's father exclaimed, "I do believe; help me overcome my unbelief!"

²⁵When Jesus saw that a crowd was running to the scene, he rebuked the evil[a]

[a]25 Greek *unclean*

[THURSDAY]

MARK 9:14-29

I Believe, Help My Unbelief!

9:24 "I DO BELIEVE; HELP ME OVERCOME MY UNBELIEF!"

How do you come to Jesus? What do you expect from him? Some of us come like this father, thinking Jesus is probably willing to help, but not sure he is able: "But if you can do anything . . ." (9:22). Others are like the leper who came to Jesus, thinking he was able, but wondering if he was willing: "If you are willing, you can make me clean" (1:40). Both kinds of people have an incomplete belief in God: Either they believe that God has lots of love but limited power, or they believe that God has plenty of power but limited love. But the God we pray to in the name of Jesus is perfect both in power and in love.

The Lord shows remarkable patience with those who have limited faith in him. To those like the father of the boy with a demon, Jesus laughs and says, "'If you can'? . . . Everything is possible for him who believes" (9:23). To those like the leper, he is "filled with compassion" and smiles as he says, "I am willing" (1:41).

Healing faith, or for that matter any kind of faith, is not necessarily an either/or. It is not that you either have it all or you have nothing. Both the father and the leper, with their puny little faith, come away from Jesus blessed. That's because our faith is not in faith itself, but in Jesus. He said it only takes a little bit of faith, a mustard seed-sized faith actually (see Matthew 17:20), for him to laugh or smile and do for us what we need. Thanks be to God, it is enough to say to him, "I do believe; help me overcome my unbelief!"

PRAY:

Blessed Father, I believe everything you have said is true—most of the time. Please be patient with me and grow my faith. I believe; help me when I don't.

FOR YOUR NEXT DEVOTIONAL READING, GO TO PAGE 1203.

spirit. "You deaf and mute spirit," he said, "I command you, come out of him and never enter him again."

²⁶The spirit shrieked, convulsed him violently and came out. The boy looked so much like a corpse that many said, "He's dead." ²⁷But Jesus took him by the hand and lifted him to his feet, and he stood up.

²⁸After Jesus had gone indoors, his disciples asked him privately, "Why couldn't we drive it out?"

²⁹He replied, "This kind can come out only by prayer.ᵃ"

³⁰They left that place and passed through Galilee. Jesus did not want anyone to know where they were, ³¹because he was teaching his disciples. He said to them, "The Son of Man is going to be betrayed into the hands of men. They will kill him, and after three days he will rise." ³²But they did not understand what he meant and were afraid to ask him about it.

Who Is the Greatest?

³³They came to Capernaum. When he was in the house, he asked them, "What were you arguing about on the road?" ³⁴But they kept quiet because on the way they had argued about who was the greatest.

³⁵Sitting down, Jesus called the Twelve and said, "If anyone wants to be first, he must be the very last, and the servant of all."

³⁶He took a little child and had him stand among them. Taking him in his arms, he said to them, ³⁷"Whoever welcomes one of these little children in my name welcomes me; and whoever welcomes me does not welcome me but the one who sent me."

Whoever Is Not Against Us Is for Us

³⁸"Teacher," said John, "we saw a man driving out demons in your name and we told him to stop, because he was not one of us."

³⁹"Do not stop him," Jesus said. "No one who does a miracle in my name can in the next moment say anything bad about me, ⁴⁰for whoever is not against us is for us. ⁴¹I tell you the truth, anyone who gives you a cup of water in my name because you belong to Christ will certainly not lose his reward.

Causing to Sin

⁴²"And if anyone causes one of these little ones who believe in me to sin, it would be better for him to be thrown into the sea with a large millstone tied around his neck. ⁴³If your hand causes you to sin, cut it off. It is better for you to enter life maimed than with two hands to go into hell, where the fire never goes out.ᵇ ⁴⁵And if your foot causes you to sin, cut it off. It is better for you to enter life crippled than to have two feet and be thrown into hell.ᶜ ⁴⁷And if your eye causes you to sin, pluck it out. It is better for you to enter the kingdom of God with one eye than to have two eyes and be thrown into hell, ⁴⁸where

> "'their worm does not die,
> and the fire is not quenched.'ᵈ

⁴⁹Everyone will be salted with fire.

⁵⁰"Salt is good, but if it loses its saltiness, how can you make it salty again? Have salt in yourselves, and be at peace with each other."

Divorce

10 Jesus then left that place and went into the region of Judea and across the Jordan. Again crowds of people came to him, and as was his custom, he taught them.

²Some Pharisees came and tested him by asking, "Is it lawful for a man to divorce his wife?"

³"What did Moses command you?" he replied.

⁴They said, "Moses permitted a man to write a certificate of divorce and send her away."

⁵"It was because your hearts were hard that Moses wrote you this law," Jesus replied. ⁶"But at the beginning of creation God 'made them male and female.'ᵉ ⁷'For this reason a man will leave his father and mother and be united to his wife,ᶠ ⁸and the two will become one flesh.'ᵍ So

---

ᵃ29 Some manuscripts *prayer and fasting*
ᵇ43 Some manuscripts *out, ⁴⁴where / "'their worm does not die, / and the fire is not quenched.'*
ᶜ45 Some manuscripts *hell, ⁴⁶where / "'their worm does not die, / and the fire is not quenched.'*
ᵈ48 Isaiah 66:24   ᵉ6 Gen. 1:27   ᶠ7 Some early manuscripts do not have *and be united to his wife.*   ᵍ8 Gen. 2:24

they are no longer two, but one. ⁹Therefore what God has joined together, let man not separate."

¹⁰When they were in the house again, the disciples asked Jesus about this. ¹¹He answered, "Anyone who divorces his wife and marries another woman commits adultery against her. ¹²And if she divorces her husband and marries another man, she commits adultery."

The Little Children and Jesus

¹³People were bringing little children to Jesus to have him touch them, but the disciples rebuked them. ¹⁴When Jesus saw this, he was indignant. He said to them, "Let the little children come to me, and do not hinder them, for the kingdom of God belongs to such as these. ¹⁵I tell you the truth, anyone who will not receive the kingdom of God like a little child will never enter it." ¹⁶And he took the children in his arms, put his hands on them and blessed them.

The Rich Young Man

¹⁷As Jesus started on his way, a man ran up to him and fell on his knees before him. "Good teacher," he asked, "what must I do to inherit eternal life?"

MARK 10:13–16

Pray for the Children, Pray Like the Children

10:16 AND HE TOOK THE CHILDREN IN HIS ARMS, PUT HIS HANDS ON THEM AND BLESSED THEM.

Jesus paid a lot of attention to children, and so should we. Jesus was indignant when his disciples tried to keep the children away from him. Perhaps they thought he had more important things to do than to pray for children. But Jesus didn't think so.

Trust and receptivity come naturally to children. Maybe that is why Jesus so wants us to bring children to him. It is their nature to trust. If they don't have him to trust, they will trust something else. How vulnerable they are to those whose only desire is to steal, kill and destroy them (see John 10:10)! Unless they are brought to Jesus, the very strength of their faith becomes their fatal weakness. Those who think children should be left alone to decide for themselves about Jesus don't understand children or Jesus. Children need his touch and blessing.

Not only should we pray for children, but we should pray like children. Jesus showed that children have a lot to teach us about prayer. He said the kingdom of God belongs to those such as children (Mark 10:14), and those who will not receive the kingdom like children will never enter it (verse 15). In prayer, we speak to God as Father. Who is better able to understand this concept than a child who has a loving father? Think of it. They give their hearts willingly and uncritically. Grace is a given. Love is expected. Nothing complicated here.

PRAY:

Kind and merciful Jesus, bless these children I know (say their names);
and bless me to know how to be like them in simple trust.

FOR YOUR NEXT DEVOTIONAL READING, GO TO PAGE 1204.

Not Typical

BY ANY standard, Pandita Ramabai was not a typical Indian woman. Born in 1858 into a wealthy Hindu Brahmin family, her father insisted that she be educated in classic Sanskrit literature. As a young woman, she so impressed the pundits (scholars) of Calcutta with her knowledge that they called her "Pandita," a feminized version of their title. She broke tradition by marrying a man who belonged to a caste lower than her own, and further rankled Indian custom by speaking out in favor of female emancipation. Her book, *The High-Caste Hindu Woman* (1887), was a pioneer work of its kind and prompted interest in her cause from the West. She founded a boarding school for girls and labored tirelessly for the education and welfare of widows and orphans. A tour of the United States in 1883 resulted in enough income for her to fund a program to educate high-caste widows. As if all this were not enough, she converted to Christianity, which sealed her rejection by the Hindus. After this, Ramabai became a passionate evangelist and social worker, leading many women to Christ.

The land in Kedgaon, near Poona, became the location for Ramabai's greatest life work. There she formed a center for orphans and widows called "Mukti," meaning "salvation" or "deliverance." At Mukti hundreds of women and girls were rescued from a famine that struck in 1896. Ramabai longed for Christ's transforming power to revive the helpless widows and orphans of India. This desire was intensified in December 1904 when she got word of the Welsh revival. Thrilled by reports of mass conversions in Wales, Ramabai organized the girls into prayer circles, urging them to pray for the salvation of people everywhere—not just in India. At first, 70 women prayed. Then Ramabai sent out a call for other prayer groups to be formed and gave each group a list of unsaved women to pray for. Within six months, 550 women gathered at Mukti to pray twice daily for revival.

On June 29, 1905, God answered their prayers, and the Holy Spirit fell on the Mukti community. Women and girls everywhere began to weep and confess their sins, crying out to God for empowerment. Classes were suspended, and many students spent hours in intercessory prayer for people they had never met. Some of the prayer meetings lasted for over ten hours. Twenty years later, to the surprise and delight of those who participated in the revival, they learned that those whose experiences of God were most emotional at the time were still living godly lives.

The Mukti Mission later grew to encompass 1300 women. After the revival, Ramabai threw herself into the translation of the Bible into Marathi, a project that took 18 years. Though Ramabai died in 1922, Mukti still had 649 students in 1971. A woman of prayer and great courage, Pandita Ramabai was not a typical Indian woman.

PRAY:

Lord, send me to proclaim freedom to captives,
good news to the poor, healing for the brokenhearted,
and the day of the Lord's favor! (see Isaiah 61:1–2).

MEMORIZE:

He has showed you, O man, what is good. And what does
the LORD require of you? To act justly and to love mercy
and to walk humbly with your God. MICAH 6:8

FOR YOUR NEXT DEVOTIONAL READING, GO TO PAGE 1208.

[18]"Why do you call me good?" Jesus answered. "No one is good—except God alone. [19]You know the commandments: 'Do not murder, do not commit adultery, do not steal, do not give false testimony, do not defraud, honor your father and mother.'[a]

[20]"Teacher," he declared, "all these I have kept since I was a boy."

[21]Jesus looked at him and loved him. "One thing you lack," he said. "Go, sell everything you have and give to the poor, and you will have treasure in heaven. Then come, follow me."

[22]At this the man's face fell. He went away sad, because he had great wealth.

[23]Jesus looked around and said to his disciples, "How hard it is for the rich to enter the kingdom of God!"

[24]The disciples were amazed at his words. But Jesus said again, "Children, how hard it is[b] to enter the kingdom of God! [25]It is easier for a camel to go through the eye of a needle than for a rich man to enter the kingdom of God."

[26]The disciples were even more amazed, and said to each other, "Who then can be saved?"

[27]Jesus looked at them and said, "With man this is impossible, but not with God; all things are possible with God."

[28]Peter said to him, "We have left everything to follow you!"

[29]"I tell you the truth," Jesus replied, "no one who has left home or brothers or sisters or mother or father or children or fields for me and the gospel [30]will fail to receive a hundred times as much in this present age (homes, brothers, sisters, mothers, children and fields—and with them, persecutions) and in the age to come, eternal life. [31]But many who are first will be last, and the last first."

Jesus Again Predicts His Death

[32]They were on their way up to Jerusalem, with Jesus leading the way, and the disciples were astonished, while those who followed were afraid. Again he took the Twelve aside and told them what was going to happen to him. [33]"We are going up to Jerusalem," he said, "and the Son of Man will be betrayed to the chief priests and teachers of the law. They will condemn him to death and will hand him

over to the Gentiles, [34]who will mock him and spit on him, flog him and kill him. Three days later he will rise."

The Request of James and John

[35]Then James and John, the sons of Zebedee, came to him. "Teacher," they said, "we want you to do for us whatever we ask."

[36]"What do you want me to do for you?" he asked.

[37]They replied, "Let one of us sit at your right and the other at your left in your glory."

[38]"You don't know what you are asking," Jesus said. "Can you drink the cup I drink or be baptized with the baptism I am baptized with?"

[39]"We can," they answered.

Jesus said to them, "You will drink the cup I drink and be baptized with the baptism I am baptized with, [40]but to sit at my right or left is not for me to grant. These places belong to those for whom they have been prepared."

[41]When the ten heard about this, they became indignant with James and John. [42]Jesus called them together and said, "You know that those who are regarded as rulers of the Gentiles lord it over them, and their high officials exercise authority over them. [43]Not so with you. Instead, whoever wants to become great among you must be your servant, [44]and whoever wants to be first must be slave of all. [45]For even the Son of Man did not come to be served, but to serve, and to give his life as a ransom for many."

Blind Bartimaeus Receives His Sight

[46]Then they came to Jericho. As Jesus and his disciples, together with a large crowd, were leaving the city, a blind man, Bartimaeus (that is, the Son of Timaeus), was sitting by the roadside begging. [47]When he heard that it was Jesus of Nazareth, he began to shout, "Jesus, Son of David, have mercy on me!"

[48]Many rebuked him and told him to be quiet, but he shouted all the more, "Son of David, have mercy on me!"

[49]Jesus stopped and said, "Call him."

So they called to the blind man, "Cheer

[a]19 Exodus 20:12–16; Deut. 5:16–20   [b]24 Some manuscripts is for those who trust in riches

up! On your feet! He's calling you."
⁵⁰Throwing his cloak aside, he jumped to his feet and came to Jesus.

⁵¹"What do you want me to do for you?" Jesus asked him.

The blind man said, "Rabbi, I want to see."

⁵²"Go," said Jesus, "your faith has healed you." Immediately he received his sight and followed Jesus along the road.

The Triumphal Entry

11 As they approached Jerusalem and came to Bethphage and Bethany at the Mount of Olives, Jesus sent two of his disciples, ²saying to them, "Go to the village ahead of you, and just as you enter it, you will find a colt tied there, which no one has ever ridden. Untie it and bring it here. ³If anyone asks you, 'Why are you doing this?' tell him, 'The Lord needs it and will send it back here shortly.'"

⁴They went and found a colt outside in the street, tied at a doorway. As they untied it, ⁵some people standing there asked, "What are you doing, untying that colt?" ⁶They answered as Jesus had told them to, and the people let them go. ⁷When they brought the colt to Jesus and threw their cloaks over it, he sat on it. ⁸Many people spread their cloaks on the road, while others spread branches they had cut in the fields. ⁹Those who went ahead and those who followed shouted,

"Hosanna!ᵃ"

"Blessed is he who comes in the
    name of the Lord!"ᵇ

¹⁰ "Blessed is the coming kingdom of
    our father David!"

"Hosanna in the highest!"

¹¹Jesus entered Jerusalem and went to the temple. He looked around at everything, but since it was already late, he went out to Bethany with the Twelve.

Jesus Clears the Temple

¹²The next day as they were leaving Bethany, Jesus was hungry. ¹³Seeing in the distance a fig tree in leaf, he went to find out if it had any fruit. When he reached it, he found nothing but leaves, because it was not the season for figs. ¹⁴Then he said to the tree, "May no one

ever eat fruit from you again." And his disciples heard him say it.

¹⁵On reaching Jerusalem, Jesus entered the temple area and began driving out those who were buying and selling there. He overturned the tables of the money changers and the benches of those selling doves, ¹⁶and would not allow anyone to carry merchandise through the temple courts. ¹⁷And as he taught them, he said, "Is it not written:

" 'My house will be called
    a house of prayer for all nations'ᶜ?

But you have made it 'a den of robbers.'ᵈ"

¹⁸The chief priests and the teachers of the law heard this and began looking for a way to kill him, for they feared him, because the whole crowd was amazed at his teaching.

¹⁹When evening came, theyᵉ went out of the city.

The Withered Fig Tree

²⁰In the morning, as they went along, they saw the fig tree withered from the roots. ²¹Peter remembered and said to Jesus, "Rabbi, look! The fig tree you cursed has withered!"

²²"Haveᶠ faith in God," Jesus answered. ²³"I tell you the truth, if anyone says to this mountain, 'Go, throw yourself into the sea,' and does not doubt in his heart but believes that what he says will happen, it will be done for him. ²⁴Therefore I tell you, whatever you ask for in prayer, believe that you have received it, and it will be yours. ²⁵And when you stand praying, if you hold anything against anyone, forgive him, so that your Father in heaven may forgive you your sins.ᵍ"

> "AND when you stand praying, if you hold anything against anyone, forgive him, so that your Father in heaven may forgive you your sins."
>
> MARK 11:25

ᵃ9 A Hebrew expression meaning "Save!" which became an exclamation of praise; also in verse 10
ᵇ9 Psalm 118:25,26   ᶜ17 Isaiah 56:7
ᵈ17 Jer. 7:11   ᵉ19 Some early manuscripts he
ᶠ22 Some early manuscripts If you have
ᵍ25 Some manuscripts sins. ²⁶But if you do not forgive, neither will your Father who is in heaven forgive your sins.

The Authority of Jesus Questioned

²⁷They arrived again in Jerusalem, and while Jesus was walking in the temple courts, the chief priests, the teachers of the law and the elders came to him. ²⁸"By what authority are you doing these things?" they asked. "And who gave you authority to do this?"

²⁹Jesus replied, "I will ask you one question. Answer me, and I will tell you by what authority I am doing these things. ³⁰John's baptism—was it from heaven, or from men? Tell me!"

³¹They discussed it among themselves and said, "If we say, 'From heaven,' he will ask, 'Then why didn't you believe him?' ³²But if we say, 'From men'…" (They feared the people, for everyone held that John really was a prophet.)

³³So they answered Jesus, "We don't know."

Jesus said, "Neither will I tell you by what authority I am doing these things."

MARK 11:12–25

[MONDAY]

Holy Excavation!

11:24 "WHATEVER YOU ASK FOR IN PRAYER, BELIEVE THAT YOU HAVE RECEIVED IT, AND IT WILL BE YOURS."

The setting for these words of Jesus probably made the scene much more dramatic for his disciples than it is for us. From the Mount of Olives, the Dead Sea can be clearly seen. Picture it. Perhaps the mountain towered over the group as Jesus looked toward it and said, "If anyone says to *this* mountain, 'Go, throw yourself into the sea,' and does not doubt in his heart but believes that what he says will happen, it will be done for him."

The incident may have been more dramatic for Jesus' disciples than for us, and it was probably less difficult for them to understand. As Jews, they were used to hearing their rabbis speak proverbially. Teachers would often use hyperbole to make a point. For instance, Jesus also said, "If anyone comes to me and does not hate his father and mother, his wife and children, his brothers and sisters—yes, even his own life—he cannot be my disciple" (Luke 14:26). The point is not that we should actually hate our families, but that our love for Jesus should be so much greater than our love for others that our love for them *looks* like hate. Jesus' Jewish audience understood what he meant about the mountain and the sea in the same way.

Prayer does work wonders, like throwing a mountain into the sea! Of course this proverb must be interpreted wisely and soberly. God is not like a cosmic vending machine: Put in a nickel of faith, and you get a nickel's worth of wonders; put in a million dollars, and you get a million dollars' worth. He knows what is best and will always do what is best.

Nevertheless, prayer is powerful, and Jesus wants us to pray with confidence. He wants us to pray as Andrew Murray urged us to pray, laying claim to "every promise God has made, in its largest and fullest meaning."

PRAY:

Almighty God, you are a great God; nothing is too hard for you.
Give me a faith worthy of your greatness.

FOR YOUR NEXT DEVOTIONAL READING, GO TO PAGE 1213.

The Parable of the Tenants

12 He then began to speak to them in parables: "A man planted a vineyard. He put a wall around it, dug a pit for the winepress and built a watchtower. Then he rented the vineyard to some farmers and went away on a journey. ²At harvest time he sent a servant to the tenants to collect from them some of the fruit of the vineyard. ³But they seized him, beat him and sent him away empty-handed. ⁴Then he sent another servant to them; they struck this man on the head and treated him shamefully. ⁵He sent still another, and that one they killed. He sent many others; some of them they beat, others they killed.

⁶"He had one left to send, a son, whom he loved. He sent him last of all, saying, 'They will respect my son.'

⁷"But the tenants said to one another, 'This is the heir. Come, let's kill him, and the inheritance will be ours.' ⁸So they took him and killed him, and threw him out of the vineyard.

⁹"What then will the owner of the vineyard do? He will come and kill those tenants and give the vineyard to others. ¹⁰Haven't you read this scripture:

" 'The stone the builders rejected
   has become the capstone[a];
¹¹ the Lord has done this,
   and it is marvelous in our eyes'[b]?"

¹²Then they looked for a way to arrest him because they knew he had spoken the parable against them. But they were afraid of the crowd; so they left him and went away.

Paying Taxes to Caesar

¹³Later they sent some of the Pharisees and Herodians to Jesus to catch him in his words. ¹⁴They came to him and said, "Teacher, we know you are a man of integrity. You aren't swayed by men, because you pay no attention to who they are; but you teach the way of God in accordance with the truth. Is it right to pay taxes to Caesar or not? ¹⁵Should we pay or shouldn't we?"

But Jesus knew their hypocrisy. "Why are you trying to trap me?" he asked. "Bring me a denarius and let me look at it." ¹⁶They brought the coin, and he asked them, "Whose portrait is this? And whose inscription?"

"Caesar's," they replied.

¹⁷Then Jesus said to them, "Give to Caesar what is Caesar's and to God what is God's."

And they were amazed at him.

Marriage at the Resurrection

¹⁸Then the Sadducees, who say there is no resurrection, came to him with a question. ¹⁹"Teacher," they said, "Moses wrote for us that if a man's brother dies and leaves a wife but no children, the man must marry the widow and have children for his brother. ²⁰Now there were seven brothers. The first one married and died without leaving any children. ²¹The second one married the widow, but he also died, leaving no child. It was the same with the third. ²²In fact, none of the seven left any children. Last of all, the woman died too. ²³At the resurrection[c] whose wife will she be, since the seven were married to her?"

²⁴Jesus replied, "Are you not in error because you do not know the Scriptures or the power of God? ²⁵When the dead rise, they will neither marry nor be given in marriage; they will be like the angels in heaven. ²⁶Now about the dead rising—have you not read in the book of Moses, in the account of the bush, how God said to him, 'I am the God of Abraham, the God of Isaac, and the God of Jacob'[d]? ²⁷He is not the God of the dead, but of the living. You are badly mistaken!"

The Greatest Commandment

²⁸One of the teachers of the law came and heard them debating. Noticing that Jesus had given them a good answer, he asked him, "Of all the commandments, which is the most important?"

²⁹"The most important one," answered Jesus, "is this: 'Hear, O Israel, the Lord our God, the Lord is one.[e] ³⁰Love the Lord your God with all your heart and with all your soul and with all your mind and with all your strength.'[f] ³¹The second is

---

[a]10 Or cornerstone   [b]11 Psalm 118:22,23
[c]23 Some manuscripts resurrection, when men rise from the dead,   [d]26 Exodus 3:6
[e]29 Or the Lord our God is one Lord
[f]30 Deut. 6:4,5

this: 'Love your neighbor as yourself.'[a] There is no commandment greater than these."

[32]"Well said, teacher," the man replied. "You are right in saying that God is one and there is no other but him. [33]To love him with all your heart, with all your understanding and with all your strength, and to love your neighbor as yourself is more important than all burnt offerings and sacrifices."

[34]When Jesus saw that he had answered wisely, he said to him, "You are not far from the kingdom of God." And from then on no one dared ask him any more questions.

Whose Son Is the Christ?

[35]While Jesus was teaching in the temple courts, he asked, "How is it that the teachers of the law say that the Christ[b] is the son of David? [36]David himself, speaking by the Holy Spirit, declared:

" 'The Lord said to my Lord:
"Sit at my right hand
until I put your enemies
under your feet." '[c]

[37]David himself calls him 'Lord.' How then can he be his son?"

The large crowd listened to him with delight.

[38]As he taught, Jesus said, "Watch out for the teachers of the law. They like to walk around in flowing robes and be greeted in the marketplaces, [39]and have the most important seats in the synagogues and the places of honor at banquets. [40]They devour widows' houses and for a show make lengthy prayers. Such men will be punished most severely."

The Widow's Offering

[41]Jesus sat down opposite the place where the offerings were put and watched the crowd putting their money into the temple treasury. Many rich people threw in large amounts. [42]But a poor widow came and put in two very small copper coins,[d] worth only a fraction of a penny.[e]

[43]Calling his disciples to him, Jesus said, "I tell you the truth, this poor widow has put more into the treasury than all the others. [44]They all gave out of their wealth; but she, out of her poverty, put in everything—all she had to live on."

Signs of the End of the Age

13 As he was leaving the temple, one of his disciples said to him, "Look, Teacher! What massive stones! What magnificent buildings!"

[2]"Do you see all these great buildings?" replied Jesus. "Not one stone here will be left on another; every one will be thrown down."

[3]As Jesus was sitting on the Mount of Olives opposite the temple, Peter, James, John and Andrew asked him privately, [4]"Tell us, when will these things happen? And what will be the sign that they are all about to be fulfilled?"

[5]Jesus said to them: "Watch out that no one deceives you. [6]Many will come in my name, claiming, 'I am he,' and will deceive many. [7]When you hear of wars and rumors of wars, do not be alarmed. Such things must happen, but the end is still to come. [8]Nation will rise against nation, and kingdom against kingdom. There will be earthquakes in various places, and famines. These are the beginning of birth pains.

[9]"You must be on your guard. You will be handed over to the local councils and flogged in the synagogues. On account of me you will stand before governors and kings as witnesses to them. [10]And the gospel must first be preached to all nations. [11]Whenever you are arrested and brought to trial, do not worry beforehand about what to say. Just say whatever is given you at the time, for it is not you speaking, but the Holy Spirit.

[12]"Brother will betray brother to death, and a father his child. Children will rebel against their parents and have them put to death. [13]All men will hate you because of me, but he who stands firm to the end will be saved.

[14]"When you see 'the abomination that causes desolation'[f] standing where it[g] does not belong—let the reader understand—then let those who are in Judea flee to the mountains. [15]Let no one on the

[a]31 Lev. 19:18   [b]35 Or Messiah
[c]36 Psalm 110:1   [d]42 Greek two lepta
[e]42 Greek kodrantes   [f]14 Daniel 9:27; 11:31;
12:11   [g]14 Or he; also in verse 29

roof of his house go down or enter the house to take anything out. ¹⁶Let no one in the field go back to get his cloak. ¹⁷How dreadful it will be in those days for pregnant women and nursing mothers! ¹⁸Pray that this will not take place in winter, ¹⁹because those will be days of distress unequaled from the beginning, when God created the world, until now—and never to be equaled again. ²⁰If the Lord had not cut short those days, no one would survive. But for the sake of the elect, whom he has chosen, he has shortened them. ²¹At that time if anyone says to you, 'Look, here is the Christ*ᵃ*!' or, 'Look, there he is!' do not believe it. ²²For false Christs and false prophets will appear and perform signs and miracles to deceive the elect—if that were possible. ²³So be on your guard; I have told you everything ahead of time.

²⁴"But in those days, following that distress,

" 'the sun will be darkened,
    and the moon will not give its light;
²⁵ the stars will fall from the sky,
    and the heavenly bodies will be
        shaken.'*ᵇ*

²⁶"At that time men will see the Son of Man coming in clouds with great power and glory. ²⁷And he will send his angels and gather his elect from the four winds, from the ends of the earth to the ends of the heavens.

²⁸"Now learn this lesson from the fig tree: As soon as its twigs get tender and its leaves come out, you know that summer is near. ²⁹Even so, when you see these things happening, you know that it is near, right at the door. ³⁰I tell you the truth, this generation*ᶜ* will certainly not pass away until all these things have happened. ³¹Heaven and earth will pass away, but my words will never pass away.

The Day and Hour Unknown

³²"No one knows about that day or hour, not even the angels in heaven, nor the Son, but only the Father. ³³Be on guard! Be alert*ᵈ*! You do not know when that time will come. ³⁴It's like a man going away: He leaves his house and puts his servants in charge, each with his as-

signed task, and tells the one at the door to keep watch.

³⁵"Therefore keep watch because you do not know when the owner of the house will come back—whether in the evening, or at midnight, or when the rooster crows, or at dawn. ³⁶If he comes suddenly, do not let him find you sleeping. ³⁷What I say to you, I say to everyone: 'Watch!' "

> " There are thoughts which are prayers. There are moments when, whatever the posture of the body, the soul is on its knees. "
>
> VICTOR HUGO

Jesus Anointed at Bethany

14 Now the Passover and the Feast of Unleavened Bread were only two days away, and the chief priests and the teachers of the law were looking for some sly way to arrest Jesus and kill him. ²"But not during the Feast," they said, "or the people may riot."

³While he was in Bethany, reclining at the table in the home of a man known as Simon the Leper, a woman came with an alabaster jar of very expensive perfume, made of pure nard. She broke the jar and poured the perfume on his head.

⁴Some of those present were saying indignantly to one another, "Why this waste of perfume? ⁵It could have been sold for more than a year's wages*ᵉ* and the money given to the poor." And they rebuked her harshly.

⁶"Leave her alone," said Jesus. "Why are you bothering her? She has done a beautiful thing to me. ⁷The poor you will always have with you, and you can help them any time you want. But you will not always have me. ⁸She did what she could. She poured perfume on my body beforehand to prepare for my burial. ⁹I tell you the truth, wherever the gospel is preached throughout the world, what she has done will also be told, in memory of her."

*ᵃ21 Or Messiah   ᵇ25 Isaiah 13:10; 34:4
ᶜ30 Or race   ᵈ33 Some manuscripts alert and pray   ᵉ5 Greek than three hundred denarii*

[10]Then Judas Iscariot, one of the Twelve, went to the chief priests to betray Jesus to them. [11]They were delighted to hear this and promised to give him money. So he watched for an opportunity to hand him over.

The Lord's Supper

[12]On the first day of the Feast of Unleavened Bread, when it was customary to sacrifice the Passover lamb, Jesus' disciples asked him, "Where do you want us to go and make preparations for you to eat the Passover?"

[13]So he sent two of his disciples, telling them, "Go into the city, and a man carrying a jar of water will meet you. Follow him. [14]Say to the owner of the house he enters, 'The Teacher asks: Where is my guest room, where I may eat the Passover with my disciples?' [15]He will show you a large upper room, furnished and ready. Make preparations for us there."

[16]The disciples left, went into the city and found things just as Jesus had told them. So they prepared the Passover.

[17]When evening came, Jesus arrived with the Twelve. [18]While they were reclining at the table eating, he said, "I tell you the truth, one of you will betray me—one who is eating with me."

[19]They were saddened, and one by one they said to him, "Surely not I?"

[20]"It is one of the Twelve," he replied, "one who dips bread into the bowl with me. [21]The Son of Man will go just as it is written about him. But woe to that man who betrays the Son of Man! It would be better for him if he had not been born."

[22]While they were eating, Jesus took bread, gave thanks and broke it, and gave it to his disciples, saying, "Take it; this is my body."

[23]Then he took the cup, gave thanks and offered it to them, and they all drank from it.

[24]"This is my blood of the[a] covenant, which is poured out for many," he said

to them. [25]"I tell you the truth, I will not drink again of the fruit of the vine until that day when I drink it anew in the kingdom of God."

[26]When they had sung a hymn, they went out to the Mount of Olives.

Jesus Predicts Peter's Denial

[27]"You will all fall away," Jesus told them, "for it is written:

> "'I will strike the shepherd,
>   and the sheep will be scattered.'[b]

[28]But after I have risen, I will go ahead of you into Galilee."

[29]Peter declared, "Even if all fall away, I will not."

[30]"I tell you the truth," Jesus answered, "today—yes, tonight—before the rooster crows twice[c] you yourself will disown me three times."

[31]But Peter insisted emphatically, "Even if I have to die with you, I will never disown you." And all the others said the same.

Gethsemane

[32]They went to a place called Gethsemane, and Jesus said to his disciples, "Sit here while I pray." [33]He took Peter, James and John along with him, and he began to be deeply distressed and troubled. [34]"My soul is overwhelmed with sorrow to the point of death," he said to them. "Stay here and keep watch."

[35]Going a little farther, he fell to the ground and prayed that if possible the hour might pass from him. [36]"Abba,[d] Father," he said, "everything is possible for you. Take this cup from me. Yet not what I will, but what you will."

[37]Then he returned to his disciples and found them sleeping. "Simon," he said to Peter, "are you asleep? Could you not keep watch for one hour? [38]Watch and pray so that you will not fall into temptation. The spirit is willing, but the body is weak."

[39]Once more he went away and prayed the same thing. [40]When he came back, he again found them sleeping, because their eyes were heavy. They did not know what to say to him.

THEN he took the cup, gave thanks and offered it to them, and they all drank from it.

[a]24 Some manuscripts *the new*   [b]27 Zech. 13:7   [c]30 Some early manuscripts do not have *twice.*   [d]36 Aramaic for *Father*

⁴¹Returning the third time, he said to them, "Are you still sleeping and resting? Enough! The hour has come. Look, the Son of Man is betrayed into the hands of sinners. ⁴²Rise! Let us go! Here comes my betrayer!"

Jesus Arrested

⁴³Just as he was speaking, Judas, one of the Twelve, appeared. With him was a crowd armed with swords and clubs, sent from the chief priests, the teachers of the law, and the elders. ⁴⁴Now the betrayer had arranged a signal with them: "The one I kiss is the man; arrest him and lead him away under guard." ⁴⁵Going at once to Jesus, Judas said, "Rabbi!" and kissed him. ⁴⁶The men seized Jesus and arrested him. ⁴⁷Then one of those standing near drew his

---

{ TUESDAY }

MARK 14:32–42

Please Take It Away, Papa

14:36 "ABBA, FATHER," HE SAID, "EVERYTHING IS POSSIBLE FOR YOU. TAKE THIS CUP FROM ME. YET NOT WHAT I WILL, BUT WHAT YOU WILL."

Jesus had his Father's full attention because nothing so seizes a father's attention like hearing his child cry out, "*Papa!*" That's a rough equivalent of the extraordinary intimacy and urgency implied by the words "*Abba,* Father." His son was in distress, and the Father could fix it. Everything is possible for him. Everything. He could have canceled the mission to the cross; he could have taken away the bitter cup. He could have done it, he really could. Jesus was prostrate, pleading, "Please take it away, Papa."

Gethsemane was the place. *Gethsemane* means "olive oil press," after the device by which olives are crushed under the weight of a big stone, their oil flowing into a receptacle, the way Jesus' sweat fell like drops of blood to the ground (see Luke 22:44). Jesus was being crushed by the weight of his Father's will for him: Jesus was to carry the load of our sins and sorrows.

Three times Jesus asked if he might be excused from his assignment. But three times he added, "Yet not what I will, but what you will." As hard as it was, his Father's will became Jesus' will too. Sometimes the only way for a cup to pass is to drink it to the dregs. Fully confident of God's power ("everything is possible for you") and love ("*Abba,* Father"), Jesus willingly submitted to his wisdom.

Thus, in his submission Jesus was never more powerful. His death on the cross looked like weakness, but it was in reality God's mighty strength to save. By the world's standards, a premature and ignominious death looked silly, but it was in reality God's profound wisdom (see 1 Corinthians 1:18–25). Because of this, every knee will bow and every tongue confess that Jesus Christ is Lord (see Philippians 2:10–11). What about you? The most powerful words you can ever say to God are the same as Jesus', "Yet not what I will, but what you will."

PRAY:

Dear Father! Not what I will, but what you will.
Make me your captive, and I will be free.

FOR YOUR NEXT DEVOTIONAL READING, GO TO PAGE 1216.

sword and struck the servant of the high priest, cutting off his ear.

⁴⁸"Am I leading a rebellion," said Jesus, "that you have come out with swords and clubs to capture me? ⁴⁹Every day I was with you, teaching in the temple courts, and you did not arrest me. But the Scriptures must be fulfilled." ⁵⁰Then everyone deserted him and fled.

⁵¹A young man, wearing nothing but a linen garment, was following Jesus. When they seized him, ⁵²he fled naked, leaving his garment behind.

Before the Sanhedrin

⁵³They took Jesus to the high priest, and all the chief priests, elders and teachers of the law came together. ⁵⁴Peter followed him at a distance, right into the courtyard of the high priest. There he sat with the guards and warmed himself at the fire.

⁵⁵The chief priests and the whole Sanhedrin were looking for evidence against Jesus so that they could put him to death, but they did not find any. ⁵⁶Many testified falsely against him, but their statements did not agree.

⁵⁷Then some stood up and gave this false testimony against him: ⁵⁸"We heard him say, 'I will destroy this man-made temple and in three days will build another, not made by man.'" ⁵⁹Yet even then their testimony did not agree.

⁶⁰Then the high priest stood up before them and asked Jesus, "Are you not going to answer? What is this testimony that these men are bringing against you?" ⁶¹But Jesus remained silent and gave no answer.

Again the high priest asked him, "Are you the Christ,ᵃ the Son of the Blessed One?"

⁶²"I am," said Jesus. "And you will see the Son of Man sitting at the right hand of the Mighty One and coming on the clouds of heaven."

⁶³The high priest tore his clothes. "Why do we need any more witnesses?" he asked. ⁶⁴"You have heard the blasphemy. What do you think?"

They all condemned him as worthy of death. ⁶⁵Then some began to spit at him; they blindfolded him, struck him with their fists, and said, "Prophesy!" And the guards took him and beat him.

Peter Disowns Jesus

⁶⁶While Peter was below in the courtyard, one of the servant girls of the high priest came by. ⁶⁷When she saw Peter warming himself, she looked closely at him.

"You also were with that Nazarene, Jesus," she said.

⁶⁸But he denied it. "I don't know or understand what you're talking about," he said, and went out into the entryway.ᵇ

⁶⁹When the servant girl saw him there, she said again to those standing around, "This fellow is one of them." ⁷⁰Again he denied it.

After a little while, those standing near said to Peter, "Surely you are one of them, for you are a Galilean."

⁷¹He began to call down curses on himself, and he swore to them, "I don't know this man you're talking about."

⁷²Immediately the rooster crowed the second time.ᶜ Then Peter remembered the word Jesus had spoken to him: "Before the rooster crows twiceᵈ you will disown me three times." And he broke down and wept.

Jesus Before Pilate

15 Very early in the morning, the chief priests, with the elders, the teachers of the law and the whole Sanhedrin, reached a decision. They bound Jesus, led him away and handed him over to Pilate.

²"Are you the king of the Jews?" asked Pilate.

"Yes, it is as you say," Jesus replied.

³The chief priests accused him of many things. ⁴So again Pilate asked him, "Aren't you going to answer? See how many things they are accusing you of."

⁵But Jesus still made no reply, and Pilate was amazed.

⁶Now it was the custom at the Feast to release a prisoner whom the people requested. ⁷A man called Barabbas was in prison with the insurrectionists who had committed murder in the uprising. ⁸The crowd came up and asked Pilate to do for them what he usually did.

ᵃ61 Or Messiah   ᵇ68 Some early manuscripts entryway and the rooster crowed   ᶜ72 Some early manuscripts do not have the second time.
ᵈ72 Some early manuscripts do not have twice.

⁹"Do you want me to release to you the king of the Jews?" asked Pilate, ¹⁰knowing it was out of envy that the chief priests had handed Jesus over to him. ¹¹But the chief priests stirred up the crowd to have Pilate release Barabbas instead.

¹²"What shall I do, then, with the one you call the king of the Jews?" Pilate asked them.

¹³"Crucify him!" they shouted.

¹⁴"Why? What crime has he committed?" asked Pilate.

But they shouted all the louder, "Crucify him!"

¹⁵Wanting to satisfy the crowd, Pilate released Barabbas to them. He had Jesus flogged, and handed him over to be crucified.

The Soldiers Mock Jesus

¹⁶The soldiers led Jesus away into the palace (that is, the Praetorium) and called together the whole company of soldiers. ¹⁷They put a purple robe on him, then twisted together a crown of thorns and set it on him. ¹⁸And they began to call out to him, "Hail, king of the Jews!" ¹⁹Again and again they struck him on the head with a staff and spit on him. Falling on their knees, they paid homage to him. ²⁰And when they had mocked him, they took off the purple robe and put his own clothes on him. Then they led him out to crucify him.

The Crucifixion

²¹A certain man from Cyrene, Simon, the father of Alexander and Rufus, was passing by on his way in from the country, and they forced him to carry the cross. ²²They brought Jesus to the place called Golgotha (which means The Place of the Skull). ²³Then they offered him wine mixed with myrrh, but he did not take it. ²⁴And they crucified him. Dividing up his clothes, they cast lots to see what each would get.

²⁵It was the third hour when they crucified him. ²⁶The written notice of the charge against him read: THE KING OF THE JEWS. ²⁷They crucified two robbers with him, one on his right and one on his left.ᵃ ²⁹Those who passed by hurled insults at him, shaking their heads and saying, "So! You who are going to destroy the

temple and build it in three days, ³⁰come down from the cross and save yourself!" ³¹In the same way the chief priests and the teachers of the law mocked him among themselves. "He saved others," they said, "but he can't save himself! ³²Let this Christ,ᵇ this King of Israel, come down now from the cross, that we may see and believe." Those crucified with him also heaped insults on him.

The Death of Jesus

³³At the sixth hour darkness came over the whole land until the ninth hour. ³⁴And at the ninth hour Jesus cried out in a loud voice, *"Eloi, Eloi, lama sabachthani?"*—which means, "My God, my God, why have you forsaken me?"ᶜ

³⁵When some of those standing near heard this, they said, "Listen, he's calling Elijah."

³⁶One man ran, filled a sponge with wine vinegar, put it on a stick, and offered it to Jesus to drink. "Now leave him alone. Let's see if Elijah comes to take him down," he said.

³⁷With a loud cry, Jesus breathed his last.

³⁸The curtain of the temple was torn in two from top to bottom. ³⁹And when the centurion, who stood there in front of Jesus, heard his cry andᵈ saw how he died, he said, "Surely this man was the Sonᵉ of God!"

⁴⁰Some women were watching from a distance. Among them were Mary Magdalene, Mary the mother of James the younger and of Joses, and Salome. ⁴¹In Galilee these women had followed him and cared for his needs. Many other women who had come up with him to Jerusalem were also there.

The Burial of Jesus

⁴²It was Preparation Day (that is, the day before the Sabbath). So as evening approached, ⁴³Joseph of Arimathea, a prominent member of the Council, who was himself waiting for the kingdom of God, went boldly to Pilate and asked for

---

ᵃ27 Some manuscripts *left, ²⁸and the scripture was fulfilled which says, "He was counted with the lawless ones"* (Isaiah 53:12)   ᵇ32 Or *Messiah*   ᶜ34 Psalm 22:1   ᵈ39 Some manuscripts do not have *heard his cry and*   ᵉ39 Or *a son*

Jesus' body. ⁴⁴Pilate was surprised to hear that he was already dead. Summoning the centurion, he asked him if Jesus had already died. ⁴⁵When he learned from the centurion that it was so, he gave the body to Joseph. ⁴⁶So Joseph bought some linen cloth, took down the body, wrapped it in the linen, and placed it in a tomb cut out of rock. Then he rolled a stone against the entrance of the tomb. ⁴⁷Mary Magdalene and Mary the mother of Joses saw where he was laid.

MARK 15:33–34

Why Have You Forsaken Me?

15:34 AND AT THE NINTH HOUR JESUS CRIED OUT IN A LOUD VOICE ... "MY GOD, MY GOD, WHY HAVE YOU FORSAKEN ME?"

It was suffering like this that moved Bernard of Clairvaux to write, "What language shall I borrow to thank Thee, dearest Friend, for this Thy dying sorrow, Thy pity without end?" Who indeed can understand, much less speak of, the suffering of the Son of God that made him feel such dereliction? Was he indeed abandoned by his Father at that moment of bearing and dying for the sins of the world? There is a profound mystery here that no one should dare to explain with confidence.

But there is something to be learned here about prayer. Jesus was quoting the first line of Psalm 22, a psalm that would become the most quoted psalm in the New Testament. Those Jews who heard him would have recognized the source and context of his words. First-century Jews were Biblically literate in a way that is hard for modern Christians to fathom. Jesus too, of course, knew the source and context of his words, and would not have torn a line of Scripture out of its context just to express his emotions at the moment. His cry of abandonment pointed beyond itself to something glorious and wonderful: Psalm 22 is a psalm that begins with despair but ends with soaring hope. In this psalm the sufferer (King David) will be so overwhelmingly vindicated by God that, "All the ends of the earth will remember and turn to the LORD, and all the families of the nations will bow down before him" (Psalm 22:27).

We too can pray like Jesus in our sufferings. We too can pray appropriate Scripture to give words to what we feel. We too may pour out our hearts in grief and anguish, as Jesus and the psalmist David did. There need be no reticence to our cries. But we must also affirm the hope we nevertheless have, even as we express that pain. For "when a man gets to despair, he knows that all his thinking will never get him out, he will only get out by the sheer, creative effort of God; consequently, he is in the right attitude to receive from God that which he cannot gain for himself" (Oswald Chambers).

P R A Y :

My God and my only hope, when I run out of options, you remain
with me, and you are all I need. When I seem to have many options,
you still are my only hope and all I really need.

FOR YOUR NEXT DEVOTIONAL READING, GO TO PAGE 1220.

The Resurrection

16 When the Sabbath was over, Mary Magdalene, Mary the mother of James, and Salome bought spices so that they might go to anoint Jesus' body. [2]Very early on the first day of the week, just after sunrise, they were on their way to the tomb [3]and they asked each other, "Who will roll the stone away from the entrance of the tomb?"

[4]But when they looked up, they saw that the stone, which was very large, had been rolled away. [5]As they entered the tomb, they saw a young man dressed in a white robe sitting on the right side, and they were alarmed.

[6]"Don't be alarmed," he said. "You are looking for Jesus the Nazarene, who was crucified. He has risen! He is not here. See the place where they laid him. [7]But go, tell his disciples and Peter, 'He is going ahead of you into Galilee. There you will see him, just as he told you.'"

[8]Trembling and bewildered, the women went out and fled from the tomb. They said nothing to anyone, because they were afraid.

[The earliest manuscripts and some other ancient witnesses do not have Mark 16:9–20.]

[9]When Jesus rose early on the first day of the week, he appeared first to Mary Magdalene, out of whom he had driven seven demons. [10]She went and told those who had been with him and who were mourning and weeping. [11]When they heard that Jesus was alive and that she had seen him, they did not believe it.

[12]Afterward Jesus appeared in a different form to two of them while they were walking in the country. [13]These returned and reported it to the rest; but they did not believe them either.

[14]Later Jesus appeared to the Eleven as they were eating; he rebuked them for their lack of faith and their stubborn refusal to believe those who had seen him after he had risen.

[15]He said to them, "Go into all the world and preach the good news to all creation. [16]Whoever believes and is baptized will be saved, but whoever does not believe will be condemned. [17]And these signs will accompany those who believe: In my name they will drive out demons; they will speak in new tongues; [18]they will pick up snakes with their hands; and when they drink deadly poison, it will not hurt them at all; they will place their hands on sick people, and they will get well."

[19]After the Lord Jesus had spoken to them, he was taken up into heaven and he sat at the right hand of God. [20]Then the disciples went out and preached everywhere, and the Lord worked with them and confirmed his word by the signs that accompanied it.

Luke

LUKE'S GOSPEL has been aptly labeled the Gospel of prayer. At every decisive moment of Jesus' life, Luke shows that he prayed. Jesus prays at his baptism, before his first great conflict with the Pharisees, before choosing the Twelve, before asking his disciples who they think he is and then predicting his death, and on the Mount of Transfiguration. The book of Luke also contains material on Jesus' prayer life and teaching on prayer that the other Gospel writers do not: Jesus' prayer for Peter's crisis of faith (22:32), and the parables of the midnight visit (11:5–10) and the persistent widow (18:1–8). The phrase "praising God" occurs more times in Luke's Gospel than in all the other New Testament books combined. The book of Luke contains four great hymns the church has sung for centuries (1:46–55; 1:68–79; 2:14; 2:29–32). To read this book thoughtfully is to have one's spiritual acuity sharpened and to be led to pray as Jesus did.

Luke's Gospel has also been called the universal gospel, and rightly so. Jesus is shown to be a man for all peoples, especially the outcast, the poor, the disenfranchised and non-Jews. The instances are too numerous to list them all, but one unique aspect of Luke's Gospel is the story we know as the parable of the Good Samaritan. For the typical Jew of Jesus' day, a "good Samaritan" was an oxymoron. Luke also shows the special place women have in Jesus' respect and affections, and he alone tells of the criminal's prayer on the cross (23:42). And only Luke tells the story of the traitor-tax collector Zacchaeus (19:1–10).

With his emphasis on prayer and the universality of the gospel, no other Gospel writer shows the scope and depth of intercessory prayer as Luke does. Bob Pierce, the founder of World Vision, once prayed that his heart would be broken with the things that break the heart of God. That is a good prayer, but Luke's Gospel takes a different approach. It simply invites us to have our hearts expanded and enriched to include in our love and our prayers all those whom God loves.

Introduction

1 Many have undertaken to draw up an account of the things that have been fulfilled[a] among us, [2]just as they were handed down to us by those who from the first were eyewitnesses and servants of the word. [3]Therefore, since I myself have carefully investigated everything from the beginning, it seemed good also to me to write an orderly account for you, most excellent Theophilus, [4]so that you may know the certainty of the things you have been taught.

The Birth of John the Baptist Foretold

[5]In the time of Herod king of Judea there was a priest named Zechariah, who belonged to the priestly division of Abijah; his wife Elizabeth was also a descendant of Aaron. [6]Both of them were upright in the sight of God, observing all the Lord's commandments and regulations blamelessly. [7]But they had no children, because Elizabeth was barren; and they were both well along in years.

[8]Once when Zechariah's division was on duty and he was serving as priest before God, [9]he was chosen by lot, according to the custom of the priesthood, to go into the temple of the Lord and burn incense. [10]And when the time for the burning of incense came, all the assembled worshipers were praying outside.

[11]Then an angel of the Lord appeared to him, standing at the right side of the altar of incense. [12]When Zechariah saw him, he was startled and was gripped with fear. [13]But the angel said to him: "Do not be afraid, Zechariah; your prayer has been heard. Your wife Elizabeth will bear you a son, and you are to give him the name John. [14]He will be a joy and delight to you, and many will rejoice because of his birth, [15]for he will be great in the sight of the Lord. He is never to take wine or other fermented drink, and he will be filled with the Holy Spirit even from birth.[b] [16]Many of the people of Israel will he bring back to the Lord their God. [17]And he will go on before the Lord, in the spirit and power of Elijah, to turn the hearts of the fathers to their children and the disobedient to the wisdom of the righteous—to make ready a people prepared for the Lord."

[18]Zechariah asked the angel, "How can I be sure of this? I am an old man and my wife is well along in years."

[19]The angel answered, "I am Gabriel. I stand in the presence of God, and I have been sent to speak to you and to tell you this good news. [20]And now you will be silent and not able to speak until the day this happens, because you did not believe my words, which will come true at their proper time."

[21]Meanwhile, the people were waiting for Zechariah and wondering why he stayed so long in the temple. [22]When he came out, he could not speak to them. They realized he had seen a vision in the temple, for he kept making signs to them but remained unable to speak.

[23]When his time of service was completed, he returned home. [24]After this his wife Elizabeth became pregnant and for five months remained in seclusion. [25]"The Lord has done this for me," she said. "In these days he has shown his favor and taken away my disgrace among the people."

The Birth of Jesus Foretold

[26]In the sixth month, God sent the angel Gabriel to Nazareth, a town in Galilee, [27]to a virgin pledged to be married to a man named Joseph, a descendant of David. The virgin's name was Mary. [28]The angel went to her and said, "Greetings, you who are highly favored! The Lord is with you."

[29]Mary was greatly troubled at his words and wondered what kind of greeting this might be. [30]But the angel said to her, "Do not be afraid, Mary, you have found favor with God. [31]You will be with child and give birth to a son, and you are to give him the name Jesus. [32]He will be great and will be called the Son of the Most High. The Lord God will give him the throne of his father David, [33]and he will reign over the house of Jacob forever; his kingdom will never end."

[34]"How will this be," Mary asked the angel, "since I am a virgin?"

[35]The angel answered, "The Holy Spirit will come upon you, and the power of

[a]1 Or been surely believed   [b]15 Or from his mother's womb

LUKE 1:5 – 20

Scars From an Old Wound

1:18 "HOW CAN I BE SURE OF THIS?"

It was the biggest day of his life. Many priests in Israel would live an entire lifetime and never get this opportunity. At long last he would enter the Holy Place. There he would burn incense on the altar in front of the Most Holy Place as the congregation waited outside to see the smoke rise. The smoke symbolized the prayers of the people; when they saw it, they would fall on their faces and offer up their prayers and thanksgivings. In a sense, Zechariah was standing as close to God as a man could in that day, leading his nation in prayer. So he shouldn't have been all that surprised when he saw an angel standing there with him.

Zechariah was surprised. He was not only surprised, but unbelieving; when he heard the angel speak those thrilling and comforting words, "Do not be afraid, Zechariah; your prayer has been heard," all the old man could muster was, "How can I be sure of this?" One who stood in the very presence of God had told this aging priest that he and his wife would finally have the son they had so long prayed for. But it wasn't enough.

We may be amazed that after all these years of serving God and praying, Zechariah was now doubting God's answer to his prayer. We may wonder why Zechariah would disbelieve an angel. How can this be? Sadly for Zechariah, his faith was suffering from scars from an old wound. The years of waiting for a child had taken their toll on Zechariah's faith. His fear of disappointment made him prefer the safety of doubt to the risk of believing.

Is this a description of you? Do you find yourself hanging back where you would most like to move forward, shrugging your shoulders when everything in you wants to embrace God's love for you? Is your prayer life stuck in a rut because of a frightened and weakened faith? Remember, the only difference between a rut and a grave is in their dimensions.

Jesus' greatest promises are for those who keep on seeking and asking in faith. But he is merciful even to those who are weak. Zechariah still got his longed-for child, even though he underwent a season of divine discipline. God's faithfulness is greater than your doubt and fear. Don't ask God, in unbelief, "How can it be?" Ask him, in wonder and gratitude, "Amazing love! How can it be?" (Charles Wesley).

PRAY:

Forgive me my fear, faithful Lord. Free me to
trust you with a whole heart. Be patient with my
doubt and lead me in your way.

FOR YOUR NEXT DEVOTIONAL READING, GO TO PAGE 1222.

the Most High will overshadow you. So the holy one to be born will be called[a] the Son of God. 36Even Elizabeth your relative is going to have a child in her old age, and she who was said to be barren is in her sixth month. 37For nothing is impossible with God."

38"I am the Lord's servant," Mary answered. "May it be to me as you have said." Then the angel left her.

Mary Visits Elizabeth

39At that time Mary got ready and hurried to a town in the hill country of Judea, 40where she entered Zechariah's home and greeted Elizabeth. 41When Elizabeth heard Mary's greeting, the baby leaped in her womb, and Elizabeth was filled with the Holy Spirit. 42In a loud voice she exclaimed: "Blessed are you among women, and blessed is the child you will bear! 43But why am I so favored, that the mother of my Lord should come to me? 44As soon as the sound of your greeting reached my ears, the baby in my womb leaped for joy. 45Blessed is she who has believed that what the Lord has said to her will be accomplished!"

Mary's Song

46And Mary said:

"My soul glorifies the Lord
47 and my spirit rejoices in God my Savior,
48for he has been mindful
of the humble state of his servant.
From now on all generations will call me blessed,
49 for the Mighty One has done great things for me—
holy is his name.
50His mercy extends to those who fear him,
from generation to generation.
51He has performed mighty deeds with his arm;
he has scattered those who are proud in their inmost thoughts.
52He has brought down rulers from their thrones
but has lifted up the humble.
53He has filled the hungry with good things
but has sent the rich away empty.

54He has helped his servant Israel,
remembering to be merciful
55to Abraham and his descendants forever,
even as he said to our fathers."

56Mary stayed with Elizabeth for about three months and then returned home.

The Birth of John the Baptist

57When it was time for Elizabeth to have her baby, she gave birth to a son. 58Her neighbors and relatives heard that the Lord had shown her great mercy, and they shared her joy.

59On the eighth day they came to circumcise the child, and they were going to name him after his father Zechariah, 60but his mother spoke up and said, "No! He is to be called John."

61They said to her, "There is no one among your relatives who has that name."

62Then they made signs to his father, to find out what he would like to name the child. 63He asked for a writing tablet, and to everyone's astonishment he wrote, "His name is John." 64Immediately his mouth was opened and his tongue was loosed, and he began to speak, praising God. 65The neighbors were all filled with awe, and throughout the hill country of Judea people were talking about all these things. 66Everyone who heard this wondered about it, asking, "What then is this child going to be?" For the Lord's hand was with him.

Zechariah's Song

67His father Zechariah was filled with the Holy Spirit and prophesied:

68"Praise be to the Lord, the God of Israel,
because he has come and has redeemed his people.
69He has raised up a horn[b] of salvation for us
in the house of his servant David
70(as he said through his holy prophets of long ago),
71 salvation from our enemies
and from the hand of all who hate us—

---

[a]35 Or So the child to be born will be called holy,
[b]69 Horn here symbolizes strength.

LUKE 1:39–55

Holy Exaggeration

1:46 "MY SOUL GLORIFIES THE LORD."

What do people do when they have an encounter with God? Whatever else they may do, they start moving. The angel Gabriel has just told Mary that she will be the mother of the Son of God. Mary surely has incredibly mixed feelings: She will be privileged to give birth to the Messiah; yet, being unmarried, she will undoubtedly become the object of skepticism and ridicule. But she is anxious to observe the sign the angel told her about regarding her relative Elizabeth's miraculous pregnancy (Luke 1:36), so instead of sitting still in Nazareth she packs up and makes the long journey to Elizabeth's house. When Mary arrives, the baby in Elizabeth's womb gets moving too, and leaps for joy.

When Mary's feelings find a voice, she sings a song the church has echoed for centuries. It is traditionally known as *The Magnificat*, from the Latin "to glorify," or "to magnify." "My soul glorifies (or magnifies) the Lord," Mary sings.

The word "glorify" in the NIV is perfectly accurate, but "magnify" offers some refreshment to the imagination. Think of it this way—there are two kinds of magnification: the kind that makes the small seem big, as in a microscope; and the kind that shows what seems small to actually *be* big, as in a telescope. This world's glories are of the microscopic variety; what is really tiny is made to look big. God's glory is of the telescopic variety. As with the pinpoints of light in the night sky, so with the embryo in Mary's womb; what seems small is discovered to be gigantic—when seen through the lens of faith.

G. K. Chesterton defined a saint as one who exaggerates what the world neglects. That is what Mary did the day she sang her praise to God. And it's clear from her song that God also exaggerates what the world neglects, and neglects what the world exaggerates. The lowly will be lifted up, and the high and mighty will be brought down. Praise is the great corrective lens of existence. To learn to glory in what God glories is to see things as they really are. Praise God, and be moved!

PRAY:

Open my mouth to praise you, God of wonders!
You are worthy of all praise.
Teach me to exaggerate what the world neglects,
to maximize what sin minimizes.

FOR YOUR NEXT DEVOTIONAL READING, GO TO PAGE 1224.

⁷² to show mercy to our fathers
and to remember his holy
covenant,
⁷³   the oath he swore to our father
Abraham:
⁷⁴ to rescue us from the hand of our
enemies,
and to enable us to serve him
without fear
⁷⁵   in holiness and righteousness
before him all our days.

⁷⁶ And you, my child, will be called a
prophet of the Most High;
for you will go on before the Lord
to prepare the way for him,
⁷⁷ to give his people the knowledge of
salvation
through the forgiveness of their
sins,
⁷⁸ because of the tender mercy of our
God,
by which the rising sun will come
to us from heaven
⁷⁹ to shine on those living in darkness
and in the shadow of death,
to guide our feet into the path of
peace."

⁸⁰And the child grew and became strong
in spirit; and he lived in the desert until
he appeared publicly to Israel.

The Birth of Jesus

2 In those days Caesar Augustus issued
a decree that a census should be tak-
en of the entire Roman world. ²(This was
the first census that took place while Qui-
rinius was governor of Syria.) ³And everyone went to his own town to register.

⁴So Joseph also went up from the town
of Nazareth in Galilee to Judea, to Bethlehem the town of David, because he be-
longed to the house and line of David. ⁵He
went there to register with Mary, who
was pledged to be married to him and
was expecting a child. ⁶While they were
there, the time came for the baby to be
born, ⁷and she gave birth to her firstborn,
a son. She wrapped him in cloths and
placed him in a manger, because there
was no room for them in the inn.

The Shepherds and the Angels

⁸And there were shepherds living out
in the fields nearby, keeping watch over

their flocks at night. ⁹An angel of the
Lord appeared to them, and the glory of
the Lord shone around them, and they
were terrified. ¹⁰But the angel said to
them, "Do not be afraid. I bring you good
news of great joy that will be for all the
people. ¹¹Today in the town of David a
Savior has been born to you; he is Christ^a
the Lord. ¹²This will be a sign to you: You
will find a baby wrapped in cloths and lying in a manger."

¹³Suddenly a great company of the
heavenly host appeared with the angel,
praising God and saying,

¹⁴ "Glory to God in the highest,
and on earth peace to men on
whom his favor rests."

¹⁵When the angels had left them and
gone into heaven, the shepherds said to
one another, "Let's go to Bethlehem and
see this thing that has happened, which
the Lord has told us about."

¹⁶So they hurried off and found Mary
and Joseph, and the baby, who was lying
in the manger. ¹⁷When they had seen him,
they spread the word concerning what
had been told them about this child, ¹⁸and
all who heard it were amazed at what the
shepherds said to them. ¹⁹But Mary treasured up all these things and pondered
them in her heart. ²⁰The shepherds returned, glorifying and praising God for all
the things they had heard and seen,
which were just as they had been told.

> THE shepherds returned, glorifying and
> praising God for all the things they had
> heard and seen, which were just as they
> had been told.
>
> LUKE 2:20

Jesus Presented in the Temple

²¹On the eighth day, when it was time
to circumcise him, he was named Jesus,
the name the angel had given him before
he had been conceived.

²²When the time of their purification
according to the Law of Moses had been
completed, Joseph and Mary took him to

^a11 Or *Messiah.* "The Christ" (Greek) and "the
Messiah" (Hebrew) both mean "the Anointed
One"; also in verse 26.

CORRIE TEN BOOM (1892–1983)

Then Help Me, Lord

HER PRAYER was a simple and desperate, "Lord Jesus, protect me!" It was all she could gasp out as the Gestapo beat her, demanding to know where her family had hidden the Jews. She kept her secret. That night, in jail, her father led the family in devotions from Psalm 91: "He who dwells in the shelter of the Most High will rest in the shadow of the Almighty." The ten Booms had hidden Jews from the Nazis; surely God would shelter and hide them, too. However, in the months that followed, Mr. ten Boom died in prison, and Corrie and her sister Betsie were sent to the infamous concentration camp Ravensbruck. There, Betsie also died after months of intense suffering.

Corrie ten Boom grew up in a family that was famous for its hospitality. After World War I, Germany was filled with thousands of deprived and malnourished people. Although the ten Booms lived in the Netherlands, Mr. ten Boom, as president of International Watchmakers, arranged for many needy Germans to be taken into the homes of the members of his organization. Four young children came to live with his family.

The ten Boom's also reached out to their community. Corrie ten Boom started a youth club. Its first law was "Seek Your Strength Through Prayer." She could not have known then how prophetic that law would be for her personally.

It was only natural that the ten Boom family would open their home to hide fugitive Jews during the beginnings of the Second World War. It was also only natural that Corrie ten Boom would find strength in prayer to endure the awful punishment the Nazis wreaked when they caught her and her family. The story of her struggles in Ravensbruck and the faithfulness and grace of God for such a time is a classic example of the power of prayer.

Years after the war, Corrie ten Boom spoke at a church in Germany, telling again of God's amazing faithfulness in dark places and the need to forgive enemies. After the service, to her surprise and profound discomfort, she saw a former Ravensbruck guard walking her way with his face beaming and his hand extended. "Thank you for the message," he said. "Isn't it wonderful that Jesus has washed my sins away?" His hand was still extended as hers hung limply at her side. He was the one who had stood by leering as she, Betsie and other prisoners were forced to strip naked to enter the showers. Rage rose up inside. "I can't do it, Lord. Don't ask me for this; it's too much."

Then she remembered the message of forgiveness she had preached all over the world and in that place just moments before. She also remembered the many times the Lord had answered her simple, desperate prayers. "Then help me, Lord," she prayed silently. She felt a power rush through her arm and a warmth enter her mind, as she extended her hand and shook his. Once more she had cried out for Jesus to help her, and once more he had given her strength.

PRAY:

"Keep me safe, O God, for in you I take refuge" (Psalm 16:1).

MEMORIZE:

Keep me as the apple of your eye; hide me
in the shadow of your wings. PSALM 17:8

FOR YOUR NEXT DEVOTIONAL READING, GO TO PAGE 1229.

Jerusalem to present him to the Lord ²³(as it is written in the Law of the Lord, "Every firstborn male is to be consecrated to the Lord"ᵃ), ²⁴and to offer a sacrifice in keeping with what is said in the Law of the Lord: "a pair of doves or two young pigeons."ᵇ

²⁵Now there was a man in Jerusalem called Simeon, who was righteous and devout. He was waiting for the consolation of Israel, and the Holy Spirit was upon him. ²⁶It had been revealed to him by the Holy Spirit that he would not die before he had seen the Lord's Christ. ²⁷Moved by the Spirit, he went into the temple courts. When the parents brought in the child Jesus to do for him what the custom of the Law required, ²⁸Simeon took him in his arms and praised God, saying:

²⁹ "Sovereign Lord, as you have
        promised,
    you now dismissᶜ your servant in
        peace.
³⁰ For my eyes have seen your salvation,
³¹   which you have prepared in the
        sight of all people,
³² a light for revelation to the Gentiles
    and for glory to your people Israel."

> *"SOVEREIGN Lord, as you have promised, you now dismiss your servant in peace."*
>
> LUKE 2:29

³³The child's father and mother marveled at what was said about him. ³⁴Then Simeon blessed them and said to Mary, his mother: "This child is destined to cause the falling and rising of many in Israel, and to be a sign that will be spoken against, ³⁵so that the thoughts of many hearts will be revealed. And a sword will pierce your own soul too."

³⁶There was also a prophetess, Anna, the daughter of Phanuel, of the tribe of Asher. She was very old; she had lived with her husband seven years after her marriage, ³⁷and then was a widow until she was eighty-four.ᵈ She never left the temple but worshiped night and day, fasting and praying. ³⁸Coming up to them

> *[ANNA] never left the temple but worshiped night and day, fasting and praying.*
>
> LUKE 2:37

at that very moment, she gave thanks to God and spoke about the child to all who were looking forward to the redemption of Jerusalem.

³⁹When Joseph and Mary had done everything required by the Law of the Lord, they returned to Galilee to their own town of Nazareth. ⁴⁰And the child grew and became strong; he was filled with wisdom, and the grace of God was upon him.

The Boy Jesus at the Temple

⁴¹Every year his parents went to Jerusalem for the Feast of the Passover. ⁴²When he was twelve years old, they went up to the Feast, according to the custom. ⁴³After the Feast was over, while his parents were returning home, the boy Jesus stayed behind in Jerusalem, but they were unaware of it. ⁴⁴Thinking he was in their company, they traveled on for a day. Then they began looking for him among their relatives and friends. ⁴⁵When they did not find him, they went back to Jerusalem to look for him. ⁴⁶After three days they found him in the temple courts, sitting among the teachers, listening to them and asking them questions. ⁴⁷Everyone who heard him was amazed at his understanding and his answers. ⁴⁸When his parents saw him, they were astonished. His mother said to him, "Son, why have you treated us like this? Your father and I have been anxiously searching for you."

⁴⁹"Why were you searching for me?" he asked. "Didn't you know I had to be in my Father's house?" ⁵⁰But they did not understand what he was saying to them. ⁵¹Then he went down to Nazareth with them and was obedient to them. But his mother treasured all these things in her heart. ⁵²And Jesus grew in wisdom and stature, and in favor with God and men.

ᵃ23 Exodus 13:2,12   ᵇ24 Lev. 12:8
ᶜ29 Or *promised, / now dismiss*   ᵈ37 Or *widow for eighty-four years*

John the Baptist Prepares the Way

3 In the fifteenth year of the reign of Tiberius Caesar—when Pontius Pilate was governor of Judea, Herod tetrarch of Galilee, his brother Philip tetrarch of Iturea and Traconitis, and Lysanias tetrarch of Abilene— ²during the high priesthood of Annas and Caiaphas, the word of God came to John son of Zechariah in the desert. ³He went into all the country around the Jordan, preaching a baptism of repentance for the forgiveness of sins. ⁴As is written in the book of the words of Isaiah the prophet:

"A voice of one calling in the desert,
'Prepare the way for the Lord,
    make straight paths for him.
⁵ Every valley shall be filled in,
    every mountain and hill made low.
The crooked roads shall become
    straight,
    the rough ways smooth.
⁶ And all mankind will see God's
    salvation.' "ᵃ

⁷John said to the crowds coming out to be baptized by him, "You brood of vipers! Who warned you to flee from the coming wrath? ⁸Produce fruit in keeping with repentance. And do not begin to say to yourselves, 'We have Abraham as our father.' For I tell you that out of these stones God can raise up children for Abraham. ⁹The ax is already at the root of the trees, and every tree that does not produce good fruit will be cut down and thrown into the fire."

¹⁰"What should we do then?" the crowd asked.

¹¹John answered, "The man with two tunics should share with him who has none, and the one who has food should do the same."

¹²Tax collectors also came to be baptized. "Teacher," they asked, "what should we do?"

¹³"Don't collect any more than you are required to," he told them.

¹⁴Then some soldiers asked him, "And what should we do?"

He replied, "Don't extort money and don't accuse people falsely—be content with your pay."

¹⁵The people were waiting expectantly and were all wondering in their hearts if John might possibly be the Christ.ᵇ ¹⁶John answered them all, "I baptize you withᶜ water. But one more powerful than I will come, the thongs of whose sandals I am not worthy to untie. He will baptize you with the Holy Spirit and with fire. ¹⁷His winnowing fork is in his hand to clear his threshing floor and to gather the wheat into his barn, but he will burn up the chaff with unquenchable fire." ¹⁸And with many other words John exhorted the people and preached the good news to them.

¹⁹But when John rebuked Herod the tetrarch because of Herodias, his brother's wife, and all the other evil things he had done, ²⁰Herod added this to them all: He locked John up in prison.

The Baptism and Genealogy of Jesus

²¹When all the people were being baptized, Jesus was baptized too. And as he was praying, heaven was opened ²²and the Holy Spirit descended on him in bodily form like a dove. And a voice came from heaven: "You are my Son, whom I love; with you I am well pleased."

²³Now Jesus himself was about thirty years old when he began his ministry. He was the son, so it was thought, of Joseph,

the son of Heli, ²⁴the son of Matthat,
the son of Levi, the son of Melki,
    the son of Jannai, the son of Joseph,
²⁵ the son of Mattathias, the son of
    Amos,
the son of Nahum, the son of Esli,
    the son of Naggai, ²⁶the son of Maath,
the son of Mattathias, the son of
    Semein,
the son of Josech, the son of Joda,
²⁷ the son of Joanan, the son of Rhesa,
the son of Zerubbabel, the son of
    Shealtiel,
the son of Neri, ²⁸the son of Melki,
the son of Addi, the son of Cosam,
    the son of Elmadam, the son of Er,
²⁹ the son of Joshua, the son of Eliezer,
the son of Jorim, the son of Matthat,
    the son of Levi, ³⁰the son of Simeon,
the son of Judah, the son of Joseph,
    the son of Jonam, the son of Eliakim,

ᵃ6 Isaiah 40:3–5   ᵇ15 Or Messiah
ᶜ16 Or in

³¹the son of Melea, the son of Menna,
the son of Mattatha, the son of Nathan,
the son of David, ³²the son of Jesse,
the son of Obed, the son of Boaz,
the son of Salmon,ᵃ the son of Nahshon,
³³the son of Amminadab, the son of
Ram,ᵇ
the son of Hezron, the son of Perez,
the son of Judah, ³⁴the son of Jacob,
the son of Isaac, the son of Abraham,
the son of Terah, the son of Nahor,
³⁵the son of Serug, the son of Reu,
the son of Peleg, the son of Eber,
the son of Shelah, ³⁶the son of Cainan,
the son of Arphaxad, the son of Shem,
the son of Noah, the son of Lamech,
³⁷the son of Methuselah, the son of
Enoch,
the son of Jared, the son of Mahalalel,
the son of Kenan, ³⁸the son of Enosh,
the son of Seth, the son of Adam,
the son of God.

The Temptation of Jesus

4 Jesus, full of the Holy Spirit, returned
from the Jordan and was led by the
Spirit in the desert, ²where for forty days
he was tempted by the devil. He ate nothing during those days, and at the end of
them he was hungry.

³The devil said to him, "If you are the
Son of God, tell this stone to become
bread."

⁴Jesus answered, "It is written: 'Man
does not live on bread alone.'ᶜ"

⁵The devil led him up to a high place
and showed him in an instant all the
kingdoms of the world. ⁶And he said to
him, "I will give you all their authority
and splendor, for it has been given to me,
and I can give it to anyone I want to. ⁷So
if you worship me, it will all be yours."

⁸Jesus answered, "It is written: 'Worship the Lord your God and serve him
only.'ᵈ"

⁹The devil led him to Jerusalem and
had him stand on the highest point of the
temple. "If you are the Son of God," he
said, "throw yourself down from here.
¹⁰For it is written:

" 'He will command his angels
concerning you
to guard you carefully;
¹¹they will lift you up in their hands,
so that you will not strike your foot
against a stone.'ᵉ"

¹²Jesus answered, "It says: 'Do not put
the Lord your God to the test.'ᶠ"

¹³When the devil had finished all this
tempting, he left him until an opportune
time.

Jesus Rejected at Nazareth

¹⁴Jesus returned to Galilee in the power of the Spirit, and news about him
spread through the whole countryside.
¹⁵He taught in their synagogues, and everyone praised him.

¹⁶He went to Nazareth, where he had
been brought up, and on the Sabbath
day he went into the synagogue, as was
his custom. And he stood up to read.
¹⁷The scroll of the prophet Isaiah was
handed to him. Unrolling it, he found the
place where it is written:

¹⁸ "The Spirit of the Lord is on me,
because he has anointed me
to preach good news to the poor.
He has sent me to proclaim freedom
for the prisoners
and recovery of sight for the blind,
to release the oppressed,
¹⁹   to proclaim the year of the Lord's
favor."ᵍ

²⁰Then he rolled up the scroll, gave it
back to the attendant and sat down. The
eyes of everyone in the synagogue were
fastened on him, ²¹and he began by saying to them, "Today this scripture is fulfilled in your hearing."

²²All spoke well of him and were
amazed at the gracious words that came
from his lips. "Isn't this Joseph's son?"
they asked.

²³Jesus said to them, "Surely you will
quote this proverb to me: 'Physician,
heal yourself! Do here in your hometown what we have heard that you did
in Capernaum.' "

ᵃ32 Some early manuscripts *Sala*   ᵇ33 Some
manuscripts *Amminadab, the son of Admin, the
son of Arni*; other manuscripts vary widely.
ᶜ4 Deut. 8:3   ᵈ8 Deut. 6:13   ᵉ11 Psalm 91:11,12
ᶠ12 Deut. 6:16   ᵍ19 Isaiah 61:1,2

To Know Who and Whose You Are

3:22 "YOU ARE MY SON, WHOM I LOVE; WITH YOU I AM WELL PLEASED."

This was undoubtedly an intensely personal and emotional moment for Jesus. As he prayed, he heard his Father say, "You are my Son, whom I love; with you I am well pleased." This experience was something he would have to cling to for dear life in the days ahead, for the meaning of his identity as God's Son would be tested severely in the desert and on his way to the cross. He must not forget who and whose he was. It was a matter of life or death.

What did it mean for Jesus to be God's Son? On the one hand it meant that he was—and is!—related to God as no one else can be. He was of the same stuff, the same nature, the same genetic endowment, if you will, as God the Father. He was "God of God, light of light, very God of very God" (The Nicene Creed). On the other hand, it meant that he was God's Son not only by his nature, but also by his obedience. "The Son can do nothing by himself; he can do only what he sees his Father doing, because whatever the Father does the Son also does" (John 5:19). Obedience is particularly what Jesus' water baptism is all about.

The Father was thrilled with Jesus at his baptism, for there he stood in the muddy waters of the river, among sinners, in perfect obedience to his Father's will. If he would lead them into his Father's kingdom, he would have to do it his Father's way: by becoming one of them and by suffering with them and for them. The cross must precede the crown. Jesus knew this; his Father knew he knew this; and God the Father was delighted with his Son.

In the wilderness, the devil would challenge the Father's will and test Jesus' identity at every point. The challenge, "If you are the Son of God . . ." was Satan's attempt to redefine Jesus' mission on his terms. He failed because Jesus knew who and whose he was.

Jesus told us to address his Father as our Father when we pray (Matthew 6:9). It's different for us, because who he is by nature, we become through faith, by adoption (John 1:12). But we share this with Jesus: Our identity is also revealed by our obedience. "We are yours by adoption," prayed Thomas Wilson, "make us yours by the choice of our will." To pray this way is to delight and please our Father.

P R A Y :

"We are yours by adoption; make us yours by the choice of our will." THOMAS WILSON

FOR YOUR NEXT DEVOTIONAL READING, GO TO PAGE 1232.

²⁴"I tell you the truth," he continued, "no prophet is accepted in his hometown. ²⁵I assure you that there were many widows in Israel in Elijah's time, when the sky was shut for three and a half years and there was a severe famine throughout the land. ²⁶Yet Elijah was not sent to any of them, but to a widow in Zarephath in the region of Sidon. ²⁷And there were many in Israel with leprosy[a] in the time of Elisha the prophet, yet not one of them was cleansed—only Naaman the Syrian."

²⁸All the people in the synagogue were furious when they heard this. ²⁹They got up, drove him out of the town, and took him to the brow of the hill on which the town was built, in order to throw him down the cliff. ³⁰But he walked right through the crowd and went on his way.

Jesus Drives Out an Evil Spirit

³¹Then he went down to Capernaum, a town in Galilee, and on the Sabbath began to teach the people. ³²They were amazed at his teaching, because his message had authority.

³³In the synagogue there was a man possessed by a demon, an evil[b] spirit. He cried out at the top of his voice, ³⁴"Ha! What do you want with us, Jesus of Nazareth? Have you come to destroy us? I know who you are—the Holy One of God!"

³⁵"Be quiet!" Jesus said sternly. "Come out of him!" Then the demon threw the man down before them all and came out without injuring him.

³⁶All the people were amazed and said to each other, "What is this teaching? With authority and power he gives orders to evil spirits and they come out!" ³⁷And the news about him spread throughout the surrounding area.

Jesus Heals Many

³⁸Jesus left the synagogue and went to the home of Simon. Now Simon's mother-in-law was suffering from a high fever, and they asked Jesus to help her. ³⁹So he bent over her and rebuked the fever, and it left her. She got up at once and began to wait on them.

⁴⁰When the sun was setting, the people brought to Jesus all who had various kinds of sickness, and laying his hands on each one, he healed them. ⁴¹Moreover, demons came out of many people, shouting, "You are the Son of God!" But he rebuked them and would not allow them to speak, because they knew he was the Christ.[c]

⁴²At daybreak Jesus went out to a solitary place. The people were looking for him and when they came to where he was, they tried to keep him from leaving them. ⁴³But he said, "I must preach the good news of the kingdom of God to the other towns also, because that is why I was sent." ⁴⁴And he kept on preaching in the synagogues of Judea.[d]

The Calling of the First Disciples

5 One day as Jesus was standing by the Lake of Gennesaret,[e] with the people crowding around him and listening to the word of God, ²he saw at the water's edge two boats, left there by the fishermen, who were washing their nets. ³He got into one of the boats, the one belonging to Simon, and asked him to put out a little from shore. Then he sat down and taught the people from the boat.

⁴When he had finished speaking, he said to Simon, "Put out into deep water, and let down[f] the nets for a catch."

⁵Simon answered, "Master, we've worked hard all night and haven't caught anything. But because you say so, I will let down the nets."

⁶When they had done so, they caught such a large number of fish that their nets began to break. ⁷So they signaled their partners in the other boat to come and help them, and they came and filled both boats so full that they began to sink.

⁸When Simon Peter saw this, he fell at Jesus' knees and said, "Go away from me, Lord; I am a sinful man!" ⁹For he and all his companions were astonished at the catch of fish they had taken, ¹⁰and so were James and John, the sons of Zebedee, Simon's partners.

Then Jesus said to Simon, "Don't be afraid; from now on you will catch men."

---

a27 The Greek word was used for various diseases affecting the skin—not necessarily leprosy. *b33* Greek *unclean*; also in verse 36 *c41* Or *Messiah* *d44* Or *the land of the Jews*; some manuscripts *Galilee* *e1* That is, Sea of Galilee *f4* The Greek verb is plural.

[11]So they pulled their boats up on shore, left everything and followed him.

The Man With Leprosy

[12]While Jesus was in one of the towns, a man came along who was covered with leprosy.[a] When he saw Jesus, he fell with his face to the ground and begged him, "Lord, if you are willing, you can make me clean."

[13]Jesus reached out his hand and touched the man. "I am willing," he said. "Be clean!" And immediately the leprosy left him.

[14]Then Jesus ordered him, "Don't tell anyone, but go, show yourself to the priest and offer the sacrifices that Moses commanded for your cleansing, as a testimony to them."

[15]Yet the news about him spread all the more, so that crowds of people came to hear him and to be healed of their sicknesses. [16]But Jesus often withdrew to lonely places and prayed.

> BUT *Jesus often withdrew to lonely places and prayed.*
>
> LUKE 5:16

Jesus Heals a Paralytic

[17]One day as he was teaching, Pharisees and teachers of the law, who had come from every village of Galilee and from Judea and Jerusalem, were sitting there. And the power of the Lord was present for him to heal the sick. [18]Some men came carrying a paralytic on a mat and tried to take him into the house to lay him before Jesus. [19]When they could not find a way to do this because of the crowd, they went up on the roof and lowered him on his mat through the tiles into the middle of the crowd, right in front of Jesus.

[20]When Jesus saw their faith, he said, "Friend, your sins are forgiven."

[21]The Pharisees and the teachers of the law began thinking to themselves, "Who is this fellow who speaks blasphemy? Who can forgive sins but God alone?"

[22]Jesus knew what they were thinking and asked, "Why are you thinking these things in your hearts? [23]Which is easier: to say, 'Your sins are forgiven,' or to say, 'Get up and walk'? [24]But that you may know that the Son of Man has authority on earth to forgive sins..." He said to the paralyzed man, "I tell you, get up, take your mat and go home." [25]Immediately he stood up in front of them, took what he had been lying on and went home praising God. [26]Everyone was amazed and gave praise to God. They were filled with awe and said, "We have seen remarkable things today."

The Calling of Levi

[27]After this, Jesus went out and saw a tax collector by the name of Levi sitting at his tax booth. "Follow me," Jesus said to him, [28]and Levi got up, left everything and followed him.

[29]Then Levi held a great banquet for Jesus at his house, and a large crowd of tax collectors and others were eating with them. [30]But the Pharisees and the teachers of the law who belonged to their sect complained to his disciples, "Why do you eat and drink with tax collectors and 'sinners'?"

[31]Jesus answered them, "It is not the healthy who need a doctor, but the sick. [32]I have not come to call the righteous, but sinners to repentance."

Jesus Questioned About Fasting

[33]They said to him, "John's disciples often fast and pray, and so do the disciples of the Pharisees, but yours go on eating and drinking."

[34]Jesus answered, "Can you make the guests of the bridegroom fast while he is with them? [35]But the time will come when the bridegroom will be taken from them; in those days they will fast."

[36]He told them this parable: "No one tears a patch from a new garment and sews it on an old one. If he does, he will have torn the new garment, and the patch from the new will not match the old. [37]And no one pours new wine into old wineskins. If he does, the new wine will burst the skins, the wine will run out and the wineskins will be ruined. [38]No, new wine must be poured into new

---

[a]12 The Greek word was used for various diseases affecting the skin—not necessarily leprosy.

If You Are Willing

5:12 "LORD, IF YOU ARE WILLING, YOU CAN MAKE ME CLEAN."

Some come to Jesus the way this leper did, convinced he is able to heal them, but afraid he doesn't want to. "Lord, if you are *willing*, you can make me clean." They believe in Jesus, but they don't think he believes in them. It's a terrible feeling to be powerfully drawn to someone you think may be repelled by you. Do you feel that way sometimes?

The word "leprosy" in the Bible actually included a number of skin diseases (see NIV text note). In severe cases, leprosy disfigures and cripples. Leprosy was also considered a source of spiritual and social contamination. Lepers were legally required stay away from healthy people and to issue this dire warning to all who approached: "Unclean! Unclean!" Just to approach Jesus, this leper had to break the law.

So this account of the leper is more than a story about the healing of a diseased man; it is also a metaphor. The disease of leprosy stands for all that separates people from God and makes them unfit to be in his presence. Note that Luke positioned the story of the leper just after the story of Peter and Jesus. When it dawned on Peter just how good Jesus was, he fell on his knees and said, "Go away from me, Lord; I am a sinful man!" (5:8). Peter realized that he was also a leper—on the inside.

To pray is to stand naked before God. We're all naked anyway, whether or not we pray, because God sees through pretense and deception into the depths of our hearts. But to pray is to really feel this unsettling truth. And if we think God is disgusted by what he sees inside, we're less likely to pray. If that's you, watch what Jesus does with this leper: He touched this untouchable and said, "I am willing. Be clean!" (5:13). To Peter he said, "Don't be afraid; from now on you will catch men" (5:10). In other words, "Not only am I not disgusted by you, I want you to be my partner."

Jesus touched the unclean because he came to be touched by the unclean. He came not to condemn sinners, but to bear their sin. Charles Spurgeon wrote, "The heart of Christ became like a reservoir in the midst of the mountains. All the tributary streams of iniquity, and every drop of the sins of his people, ran down and gathered into one vast lake, deep as hell and shoreless as eternity. All these met, as it were, in Christ's heart, and he endured them all." That's how much he wants us to come to him in prayer.

P R A Y :
Loving Father, you know me inside and out; to you my darkness is as day.
Yet you look with pity and forgiveness. I receive your love,
teach me to love you.

FOR YOUR NEXT DEVOTIONAL READING, GO TO PAGE 1234.

wineskins. ³⁹And no one after drinking old wine wants the new, for he says, 'The old is better.'"

Lord of the Sabbath

6 One Sabbath Jesus was going through the grainfields, and his disciples began to pick some heads of grain, rub them in their hands and eat the kernels. ²Some of the Pharisees asked, "Why are you doing what is unlawful on the Sabbath?"

³Jesus answered them, "Have you never read what David did when he and his companions were hungry? ⁴He entered the house of God, and taking the consecrated bread, he ate what is lawful only for priests to eat. And he also gave some to his companions." ⁵Then Jesus said to them, "The Son of Man is Lord of the Sabbath."

⁶On another Sabbath he went into the synagogue and was teaching, and a man was there whose right hand was shriveled. ⁷The Pharisees and the teachers of the law were looking for a reason to accuse Jesus, so they watched him closely to see if he would heal on the Sabbath. ⁸But Jesus knew what they were thinking and said to the man with the shriveled hand, "Get up and stand in front of everyone." So he got up and stood there.

⁹Then Jesus said to them, "I ask you, which is lawful on the Sabbath: to do good or to do evil, to save life or to destroy it?"

¹⁰He looked around at them all, and then said to the man, "Stretch out your hand." He did so, and his hand was completely restored. ¹¹But they were furious and began to discuss with one another what they might do to Jesus.

The Twelve Apostles

¹²One of those days Jesus went out to a mountainside to pray, and spent the night praying to God. ¹³When morning came, he called his disciples to him and chose twelve of them, whom he also designated apostles: ¹⁴Simon (whom he named Peter), his brother Andrew, James, John, Philip, Bartholomew, ¹⁵Matthew, Thomas, James son of Alphaeus, Simon who was called the Zealot, ¹⁶Judas son of James, and Judas Iscariot, who became a traitor.

Blessings and Woes

¹⁷He went down with them and stood on a level place. A large crowd of his disciples was there and a great number of people from all over Judea, from Jerusalem, and from the coast of Tyre and Sidon, ¹⁸who had come to hear him and to be healed of their diseases. Those troubled by evil*ᵃ* spirits were cured, ¹⁹and the people all tried to touch him, because power was coming from him and healing them all.

²⁰Looking at his disciples, he said:

"Blessed are you who are poor,
    for yours is the kingdom of God.
²¹ Blessed are you who hunger now,
    for you will be satisfied.
Blessed are you who weep now,
    for you will laugh.
²² Blessed are you when men hate you,
    when they exclude you and insult
        you
    and reject your name as evil,
        because of the Son of Man.

²³"Rejoice in that day and leap for joy, because great is your reward in heaven. For that is how their fathers treated the prophets.

²⁴ "But woe to you who are rich,
    for you have already received your
        comfort.
²⁵ Woe to you who are well fed now,
    for you will go hungry.
Woe to you who laugh now,
    for you will mourn and weep.
²⁶ Woe to you when all men speak well
        of you,
    for that is how their fathers treated
        the false prophets.

Love for Enemies

²⁷"But I tell you who hear me: Love your enemies, do good to those who hate you, ²⁸bless those who curse you, pray for those who mistreat you. ²⁹If someone strikes you on one cheek, turn to him the

> "BLESS those who curse you, pray for those who mistreat you."
>
> LUKE 6:28

ᵃ18 Greek *unclean*

other also. If someone takes your cloak, do not stop him from taking your tunic. ³⁰Give to everyone who asks you, and if anyone takes what belongs to you, do not demand it back. ³¹Do to others as you would have them do to you.

³²"If you love those who love you, what credit is that to you? Even 'sinners' love those who love them. ³³And if you do good to those who are good to you, what credit is that to you? Even 'sinners' do that. ³⁴And if you lend to those from

---

{WEDNESDAY}

LUKE 6:12–16

Prayer and Decision-Making

6:12 "AND SPENT THE NIGHT PRAYING"

All night is a long time to pray, especially if you're alone, as Jesus was. Why would he do such a thing? The obvious answer is that Jesus was making one of the biggest decisions of his life: The next day he would select the men who would be his apostles, the inner circle of leaders to whom he would entrust so much. A lot was riding on his choices, so of course he would want to consult his Father. From the time of his temptation and before, Jesus' guiding principle had always been, "I seek not to please myself but him who sent me" (John 5:30). Jesus took a lesson from history. He knew the Scriptures well: how badly things had gone with the Gibeonites when Joshua had not inquired of the Lord (see Joshua 9:1–27); how well things went for David when he did (see 2 Samuel 5:17–25).

The more pressing question for us is not why Jesus prayed all night, but how. It's not hard to imagine working all night, or watching movies all night, or even reading all night if the book is really fascinating—but *praying* all night? How does one do that? Did Jesus just ask, over and over again, "Who should be among the Twelve?" That's highly unlikely, not only because it would be incredibly boring, but because Jesus had spoken out against "babbling," or meaningless repetition (see Matthew 6:7).

Jesus probably spent the night doing the kind of thing David asked the Lord to let him do forever: "One thing I ask of the LORD, this is what I seek: that I may dwell in the house of the LORD all the days of my life, to gaze upon the beauty of the LORD and to seek him in his temple" (Psalm 27:4). Since God knows what we need before we ask, prayer is more about *communion* than *communication* (see Matthew 6:8). Jesus knew that, and therefore knew that what he needed most in order to make good decisions was not information but a refreshed fellowship with his Father. His night was spent doing all the things that genuine prayer is: asking and listening, inquiring and praising, thinking and thanking, meditating and singing, sitting in silence and speaking forth.

Making good, prayerful decisions is not about a moment's effort, but a lifelong relationship. God is more interested in us becoming the right people than in us merely making the right decisions.

PRAY:

Jesus, teach me to pray like you did: not just communicating
with the Father about the details and decisions of life,
but enjoying the refreshing gift of communion.

FOR YOUR NEXT DEVOTIONAL READING, GO TO PAGE 1243.

whom you expect repayment, what credit is that to you? Even 'sinners' lend to 'sinners,' expecting to be repaid in full. ³⁵But love your enemies, do good to them, and lend to them without expecting to get anything back. Then your reward will be great, and you will be sons of the Most High, because he is kind to the ungrateful and wicked. ³⁶Be merciful, just as your Father is merciful.

Judging Others

³⁷"Do not judge, and you will not be judged. Do not condemn, and you will not be condemned. Forgive, and you will be forgiven. ³⁸Give, and it will be given to you. A good measure, pressed down, shaken together and running over, will be poured into your lap. For with the measure you use, it will be measured to you."

³⁹He also told them this parable: "Can a blind man lead a blind man? Will they not both fall into a pit? ⁴⁰A student is not above his teacher, but everyone who is fully trained will be like his teacher.

⁴¹"Why do you look at the speck of sawdust in your brother's eye and pay no attention to the plank in your own eye? ⁴²How can you say to your brother, 'Brother, let me take the speck out of your eye,' when you yourself fail to see the plank in your own eye? You hypocrite, first take the plank out of your eye, and then you will see clearly to remove the speck from your brother's eye.

A Tree and Its Fruit

⁴³"No good tree bears bad fruit, nor does a bad tree bear good fruit. ⁴⁴Each tree is recognized by its own fruit. People do not pick figs from thornbushes, or grapes from briers. ⁴⁵The good man brings good things out of the good stored up in his heart, and the evil man brings evil things out of the evil stored up in his heart. For out of the overflow of his heart his mouth speaks.

The Wise and Foolish Builders

⁴⁶"Why do you call me, 'Lord, Lord,' and do not do what I say? ⁴⁷I will show you what he is like who comes to me and hears my words and puts them into practice. ⁴⁸He is like a man building a house, who dug down deep and laid the foundation on rock. When a flood came, the torrent struck that house but could not shake it, because it was well built. ⁴⁹But the one who hears my words and does not put them into practice is like a man who built a house on the ground without a foundation. The moment the torrent struck that house, it collapsed and its destruction was complete."

The Faith of the Centurion

7 When Jesus had finished saying all this in the hearing of the people, he entered Capernaum. ²There a centurion's servant, whom his master valued highly, was sick and about to die. ³The centurion heard of Jesus and sent some elders of the Jews to him, asking him to come and heal his servant. ⁴When they came to Jesus, they pleaded earnestly with him, "This man deserves to have you do this, ⁵because he loves our nation and has built our synagogue." ⁶So Jesus went with them.

He was not far from the house when the centurion sent friends to say to him: "Lord, don't trouble yourself, for I do not deserve to have you come under my roof. ⁷That is why I did not even consider myself worthy to come to you. But say the word, and my servant will be healed. ⁸For I myself am a man under authority, with soldiers under me. I tell this one, 'Go,' and he goes; and that one, 'Come,' and he comes. I say to my servant, 'Do this,' and he does it."

⁹When Jesus heard this, he was amazed at him, and turning to the crowd following him, he said, "I tell you, I have not found such great faith even in Israel." ¹⁰Then the men who had been sent returned to the house and found the servant well.

Jesus Raises a Widow's Son

¹¹Soon afterward, Jesus went to a town called Nain, and his disciples and a large crowd went along with him. ¹²As he approached the town gate, a dead person was being carried out—the only son of his mother, and she was a widow. And a large crowd from the town was with her. ¹³When the Lord saw her, his heart went out to her and he said, "Don't cry."

[14]Then he went up and touched the coffin, and those carrying it stood still. He said, "Young man, I say to you, get up!" [15]The dead man sat up and began to talk, and Jesus gave him back to his mother.

[16]They were all filled with awe and praised God. "A great prophet has appeared among us," they said. "God has come to help his people." [17]This news about Jesus spread throughout Judea[a] and the surrounding country.

Jesus and John the Baptist

[18]John's disciples told him about all these things. Calling two of them, [19]he sent them to the Lord to ask, "Are you the one who was to come, or should we expect someone else?"

[20]When the men came to Jesus, they said, "John the Baptist sent us to you to ask, 'Are you the one who was to come, or should we expect someone else?'"

[21]At that very time Jesus cured many who had diseases, sicknesses and evil spirits, and gave sight to many who were blind. [22]So he replied to the messengers, "Go back and report to John what you have seen and heard: The blind receive sight, the lame walk, those who have leprosy[b] are cured, the deaf hear, the dead are raised, and the good news is preached to the poor. [23]Blessed is the man who does not fall away on account of me."

[24]After John's messengers left, Jesus began to speak to the crowd about John: "What did you go out into the desert to see? A reed swayed by the wind? [25]If not, what did you go out to see? A man dressed in fine clothes? No, those who wear expensive clothes and indulge in luxury are in palaces. [26]But what did you go out to see? A prophet? Yes, I tell you, and more than a prophet. [27]This is the one about whom it is written:

> "'I will send my messenger ahead of
>   you,
>   who will prepare your way before
>   you.'[c]

[28]I tell you, among those born of women there is no one greater than John; yet the one who is least in the kingdom of God is greater than he."

[29](All the people, even the tax collectors, when they heard Jesus' words, acknowledged that God's way was right, because they had been baptized by John. [30]But the Pharisees and experts in the law rejected God's purpose for themselves, because they had not been baptized by John.)

[31]"To what, then, can I compare the people of this generation? What are they like? [32]They are like children sitting in the marketplace and calling out to each other:

> "'We played the flute for you,
>   and you did not dance;
> we sang a dirge,
>   and you did not cry.'

[33]For John the Baptist came neither eating bread nor drinking wine, and you say, 'He has a demon.' [34]The Son of Man came eating and drinking, and you say, 'Here is a glutton and a drunkard, a friend of tax collectors and "sinners."' [35]But wisdom is proved right by all her children."

Jesus Anointed by a Sinful Woman

[36]Now one of the Pharisees invited Jesus to have dinner with him, so he went to the Pharisee's house and reclined at the table. [37]When a woman who had lived a sinful life in that town learned that Jesus was eating at the Pharisee's house, she brought an alabaster jar of perfume, [38]and as she stood behind him at his feet weeping, she began to wet his feet with her tears. Then she wiped them with her hair, kissed them and poured perfume on them.

[39]When the Pharisee who had invited him saw this, he said to himself, "If this man were a prophet, he would know who is touching him and what kind of woman she is—that she is a sinner."

[40]Jesus answered him, "Simon, I have something to tell you."

"Tell me, teacher," he said.

[41]"Two men owed money to a certain moneylender. One owed him five hundred denarii,[d] and the other fifty. [42]Nei-

[a]17 Or *the land of the Jews*   [b]22 The Greek word was used for various diseases affecting the skin—not necessarily leprosy.   [c]27 Mal. 3:1 [d]41 A denarius was a coin worth about a day's wages.

ther of them had the money to pay him back, so he canceled the debts of both. Now which of them will love him more?" [43]Simon replied, "I suppose the one who had the bigger debt canceled."

"You have judged correctly," Jesus said.

[44]Then he turned toward the woman and said to Simon, "Do you see this woman? I came into your house. You did not give me any water for my feet, but she wet my feet with her tears and wiped them with her hair. [45]You did not give me a kiss, but this woman, from the time I entered, has not stopped kissing my feet. [46]You did not put oil on my head, but she has poured perfume on my feet. [47]Therefore, I tell you, her many sins have been forgiven—for she loved much. But he who has been forgiven little loves little."

[48]Then Jesus said to her, "Your sins are forgiven."

> 66 Our praying, however, needs to be pressed and pursued with an energy that never tires, a persistency which will not be denied, and a courage which never fails. 99
>
> E. M. BOUNDS

[49]The other guests began to say among themselves, "Who is this who even forgives sins?"

[50]Jesus said to the woman, "Your faith has saved you; go in peace."

The Parable of the Sower

8 After this, Jesus traveled about from one town and village to another, proclaiming the good news of the kingdom of God. The Twelve were with him, [2]and also some women who had been cured of evil spirits and diseases: Mary (called Magdalene) from whom seven demons had come out; [3]Joanna the wife of Cuza, the manager of Herod's household; Susanna; and many others. These women were helping to support them out of their own means.

[4]While a large crowd was gathering and people were coming to Jesus from town after town, he told this parable: [5]"A farmer went out to sow his seed. As he was scattering the seed, some fell along the path; it was trampled on, and the birds of the air ate it up. [6]Some fell on rock, and when it came up, the plants withered because they had no moisture. [7]Other seed fell among thorns, which grew up with it and choked the plants. [8]Still other seed fell on good soil. It came up and yielded a crop, a hundred times more than was sown."

When he said this, he called out, "He who has ears to hear, let him hear."

[9]His disciples asked him what this parable meant. [10]He said, "The knowledge of the secrets of the kingdom of God has been given to you, but to others I speak in parables, so that,

> " 'though seeing, they may not see;
>   though hearing, they may not
>   understand.'[a]

[11]"This is the meaning of the parable: The seed is the word of God. [12]Those along the path are the ones who hear, and then the devil comes and takes away the word from their hearts, so that they may not believe and be saved. [13]Those on the rock are the ones who receive the word with joy when they hear it, but they have no root. They believe for a while, but in the time of testing they fall away. [14]The seed that fell among thorns stands for those who hear, but as they go on their way they are choked by life's worries, riches and pleasures, and they do not mature. [15]But the seed on good soil stands for those with a noble and good heart, who hear the word, retain it, and by persevering produce a crop.

A Lamp on a Stand

[16]"No one lights a lamp and hides it in a jar or puts it under a bed. Instead, he puts it on a stand, so that those who come in can see the light. [17]For there is nothing hidden that will not be disclosed, and nothing concealed that will not be known or brought out into the open. [18]Therefore consider carefully how you listen. Whoever has will be given more; whoever does not have, even what he thinks he has will be taken from him."

[a]10 Isaiah 6:9

Jesus' Mother and Brothers

¹⁹Now Jesus' mother and brothers came to see him, but they were not able to get near him because of the crowd. ²⁰Someone told him, "Your mother and brothers are standing outside, wanting to see you."

²¹He replied, "My mother and brothers are those who hear God's word and put it into practice."

Jesus Calms the Storm

²²One day Jesus said to his disciples, "Let's go over to the other side of the lake." So they got into a boat and set out. ²³As they sailed, he fell asleep. A squall came down on the lake, so that the boat was being swamped, and they were in great danger.

²⁴The disciples went and woke him, saying, "Master, Master, we're going to drown!"

He got up and rebuked the wind and the raging waters; the storm subsided, and all was calm. ²⁵"Where is your faith?" he asked his disciples.

In fear and amazement they asked one another, "Who is this? He commands even the winds and the water, and they obey him."

The Healing of a Demon-possessed Man

²⁶They sailed to the region of the Gerasenes,ᵃ which is across the lake from Galilee. ²⁷When Jesus stepped ashore, he was met by a demon-possessed man from the town. For a long time this man had not worn clothes or lived in a house, but had lived in the tombs. ²⁸When he saw Jesus, he cried out and fell at his feet, shouting at the top of his voice, "What do you want with me, Jesus, Son of the Most High God? I beg you, don't torture me!" ²⁹For Jesus had commanded the evilᵇ spirit to come out of the man. Many times it had seized him, and though he was chained hand and foot and kept under guard, he had broken his chains and had been driven by the demon into solitary places.

³⁰Jesus asked him, "What is your name?"

"Legion," he replied, because many demons had gone into him. ³¹And they begged him repeatedly not to order them to go into the Abyss.

³²A large herd of pigs was feeding there on the hillside. The demons begged Jesus to let them go into them, and he gave them permission. ³³When the demons came out of the man, they went into the pigs, and the herd rushed down the steep bank into the lake and was drowned.

³⁴When those tending the pigs saw what had happened, they ran off and reported this in the town and countryside, ³⁵and the people went out to see what had happened. When they came to Jesus, they found the man from whom the demons had gone out, sitting at Jesus' feet, dressed and in his right mind; and they were afraid. ³⁶Those who had seen it told the people how the demon-possessed man had been cured. ³⁷Then all the people of the region of the Gerasenes asked Jesus to leave them, because they were overcome with fear. So he got into the boat and left.

³⁸The man from whom the demons had gone out begged to go with him, but Jesus sent him away, saying, ³⁹"Return home and tell how much God has done for you." So the man went away and told all over town how much Jesus had done for him.

A Dead Girl and a Sick Woman

⁴⁰Now when Jesus returned, a crowd welcomed him, for they were all expecting him. ⁴¹Then a man named Jairus, a ruler of the synagogue, came and fell at Jesus' feet, pleading with him to come to his house ⁴²because his only daughter, a girl of about twelve, was dying.

As Jesus was on his way, the crowds almost crushed him. ⁴³And a woman was there who had been subject to bleeding for twelve years,ᶜ but no one could heal her. ⁴⁴She came up behind him and touched the edge of his cloak, and immediately her bleeding stopped.

⁴⁵"Who touched me?" Jesus asked.

When they all denied it, Peter said, "Master, the people are crowding and pressing against you."

⁴⁶But Jesus said, "Someone touched me; I know that power has gone out from me."

ᵃ26 Some manuscripts *Gadarenes*; other manuscripts *Gergesenes*; also in verse 37   ᵇ29 Greek *unclean*   ᶜ43 Many manuscripts *years, and she had spent all she had on doctors*

⁴⁷Then the woman, seeing that she could not go unnoticed, came trembling and fell at his feet. In the presence of all the people, she told why she had touched him and how she had been instantly healed. ⁴⁸Then he said to her, "Daughter, your faith has healed you. Go in peace."

⁴⁹While Jesus was still speaking, someone came from the house of Jairus, the synagogue ruler. "Your daughter is dead," he said. "Don't bother the teacher any more."

⁵⁰Hearing this, Jesus said to Jairus, "Don't be afraid; just believe, and she will be healed."

⁵¹When he arrived at the house of Jairus, he did not let anyone go in with him except Peter, John and James, and the child's father and mother. ⁵²Meanwhile, all the people were wailing and mourning for her. "Stop wailing," Jesus said. "She is not dead but asleep."

> **Be thankful that God's answers are wiser than your answers.**
>
> WILLIAM CULBERTSON

⁵³They laughed at him, knowing that she was dead. ⁵⁴But he took her by the hand and said, "My child, get up!" ⁵⁵Her spirit returned, and at once she stood up. Then Jesus told them to give her something to eat. ⁵⁶Her parents were astonished, but he ordered them not to tell anyone what had happened.

Jesus Sends Out the Twelve

9 When Jesus had called the Twelve together, he gave them power and authority to drive out all demons and to cure diseases, ²and he sent them out to preach the kingdom of God and to heal the sick. ³He told them: "Take nothing for the journey—no staff, no bag, no bread, no money, no extra tunic. ⁴Whatever house you enter, stay there until you leave that town. ⁵If people do not welcome you, shake the dust off your feet when you leave their town, as a testimony against them." ⁶So they set out and went from village to village, preaching the gospel and healing people everywhere.

⁷Now Herod the tetrarch heard about all that was going on. And he was perplexed, because some were saying that John had been raised from the dead, ⁸others that Elijah had appeared, and still others that one of the prophets of long ago had come back to life. ⁹But Herod said, "I beheaded John. Who, then, is this I hear such things about?" And he tried to see him.

Jesus Feeds the Five Thousand

¹⁰When the apostles returned, they reported to Jesus what they had done. Then he took them with him and they withdrew by themselves to a town called Bethsaida, ¹¹but the crowds learned about it and followed him. He welcomed them and spoke to them about the kingdom of God, and healed those who needed healing.

¹²Late in the afternoon the Twelve came to him and said, "Send the crowd away so they can go to the surrounding villages and countryside and find food and lodging, because we are in a remote place here."

¹³He replied, "You give them something to eat."

They answered, "We have only five loaves of bread and two fish—unless we go and buy food for all this crowd." ¹⁴(About five thousand men were there.)

But he said to his disciples, "Have them sit down in groups of about fifty each." ¹⁵The disciples did so, and everybody sat down. ¹⁶Taking the five loaves and the two fish and looking up to heaven, he gave thanks and broke them. Then he gave them to the disciples to set before the people. ¹⁷They all ate and were satisfied, and the disciples picked up twelve basketfuls of broken pieces that were left over.

Peter's Confession of Christ

¹⁸Once when Jesus was praying in private and his disciples were with him, he asked them, "Who do the crowds say I am?"

> ONCE when Jesus was praying in private and his disciples were with him, he asked them, "Who do the crowds say I am?"
>
> LUKE 9:18

¹⁹They replied, "Some say John the Baptist; others say Elijah; and still others, that one of the prophets of long ago has come back to life."

²⁰"But what about you?" he asked. "Who do you say I am?"

Peter answered, "The Christ[a] of God." ²¹Jesus strictly warned them not to tell this to anyone. ²²And he said, "The Son of Man must suffer many things and be rejected by the elders, chief priests and teachers of the law, and he must be killed and on the third day be raised to life."

²³Then he said to them all: "If anyone would come after me, he must deny himself and take up his cross daily and follow me. ²⁴For whoever wants to save his life will lose it, but whoever loses his life for me will save it. ²⁵What good is it for a man to gain the whole world, and yet lose or forfeit his very self? ²⁶If anyone is ashamed of me and my words, the Son of Man will be ashamed of him when he comes in his glory and in the glory of the Father and of the holy angels. ²⁷I tell you the truth, some who are standing here will not taste death before they see the kingdom of God."

The Transfiguration

²⁸About eight days after Jesus said this, he took Peter, John and James with him and went up onto a mountain to pray. ²⁹As he was praying, the appearance of his face changed, and his clothes became as bright as a flash of lightning. ³⁰Two men, Moses and Elijah, ³¹appeared in

> AS HE was praying, the appearance of his face changed, and his clothes became as bright as a flash of lightning.
>
> LUKE 9:29

glorious splendor, talking with Jesus. They spoke about his departure, which he was about to bring to fulfillment at Jerusalem. ³²Peter and his companions were very sleepy, but when they became fully awake, they saw his glory and the two men standing with him. ³³As the men were leaving Jesus, Peter said to him, "Master, it is good for us to be here. Let us put up three shelters—one for you,

one for Moses and one for Elijah." (He did not know what he was saying.)

³⁴While he was speaking, a cloud appeared and enveloped them, and they were afraid as they entered the cloud. ³⁵A voice came from the cloud, saying, "This is my Son, whom I have chosen; listen to him." ³⁶When the voice had spoken, they found that Jesus was alone. The disciples kept this to themselves, and told no one at that time what they had seen.

The Healing of a Boy With an Evil Spirit

³⁷The next day, when they came down from the mountain, a large crowd met him. ³⁸A man in the crowd called out, "Teacher, I beg you to look at my son, for he is my only child. ³⁹A spirit seizes him and he suddenly screams; it throws him into convulsions so that he foams at the mouth. It scarcely ever leaves him and is destroying him. ⁴⁰I begged your disciples to drive it out, but they could not."

⁴¹"O unbelieving and perverse generation," Jesus replied, "how long shall I stay with you and put up with you? Bring your son here."

⁴²Even while the boy was coming, the demon threw him to the ground in a convulsion. But Jesus rebuked the evil[b] spirit, healed the boy and gave him back to his father. ⁴³And they were all amazed at the greatness of God.

While everyone was marveling at all that Jesus did, he said to his disciples, ⁴⁴"Listen carefully to what I am about to tell you: The Son of Man is going to be betrayed into the hands of men." ⁴⁵But they did not understand what this meant. It was hidden from them, so that they did not grasp it, and they were afraid to ask him about it.

Who Will Be the Greatest?

⁴⁶An argument started among the disciples as to which of them would be the greatest. ⁴⁷Jesus, knowing their thoughts, took a little child and had him stand beside him. ⁴⁸Then he said to them, "Whoever welcomes this little child in my name welcomes me; and whoever welcomes me welcomes the one who sent

[a]20 Or Messiah   [b]42 Greek unclean

me. For he who is least among you all—he is the greatest."

⁴⁹"Master," said John, "we saw a man driving out demons in your name and we tried to stop him, because he is not one of us."

⁵⁰"Do not stop him," Jesus said, "for whoever is not against you is for you."

Samaritan Opposition

⁵¹As the time approached for him to be taken up to heaven, Jesus resolutely set out for Jerusalem. ⁵²And he sent messengers on ahead, who went into a Samaritan village to get things ready for him; ⁵³but the people there did not welcome him, because he was heading for Jerusalem. ⁵⁴When the disciples James and John saw this, they asked, "Lord, do you want us to call fire down from heaven to destroy them*ᵃ*?" ⁵⁵But Jesus turned and rebuked them, ⁵⁶and*ᵇ* they went to another village.

The Cost of Following Jesus

⁵⁷As they were walking along the road, a man said to him, "I will follow you wherever you go."

⁵⁸Jesus replied, "Foxes have holes and birds of the air have nests, but the Son of Man has no place to lay his head."

⁵⁹He said to another man, "Follow me."

But the man replied, "Lord, first let me go and bury my father."

⁶⁰Jesus said to him, "Let the dead bury their own dead, but you go and proclaim the kingdom of God."

⁶¹Still another said, "I will follow you, Lord; but first let me go back and say good-by to my family."

⁶²Jesus replied, "No one who puts his hand to the plow and looks back is fit for service in the kingdom of God."

Jesus Sends Out the Seventy-two

10 After this the Lord appointed seventy-two*ᶜ* others and sent them two by two ahead of him to every town and place where he was about to go. ²He told them, "The harvest is plentiful, but the workers are few. Ask the Lord of the harvest, therefore, to send out workers into his harvest field. ³Go! I am sending you out like lambs among wolves. ⁴Do not take a purse or bag or sandals; and do not greet anyone on the road.

⁵"When you enter a house, first say, 'Peace to this house.' ⁶If a man of peace is there, your peace will rest on him; if not, it will return to you. ⁷Stay in that house, eating and drinking whatever they give you, for the worker deserves his wages. Do not move around from house to house.

⁸"When you enter a town and are welcomed, eat what is set before you. ⁹Heal the sick who are there and tell them, 'The kingdom of God is near you.' ¹⁰But when you enter a town and are not welcomed, go into its streets and say, ¹¹'Even the dust of your town that sticks to our feet we wipe off against you. Yet be sure of this: The kingdom of God is near.' ¹²I tell you, it will be more bearable on that day for Sodom than for that town.

¹³"Woe to you, Korazin! Woe to you, Bethsaida! For if the miracles that were performed in you had been performed in Tyre and Sidon, they would have repented long ago, sitting in sackcloth and ashes. ¹⁴But it will be more bearable for Tyre and Sidon at the judgment than for you. ¹⁵And you, Capernaum, will you be lifted up to the skies? No, you will go down to the depths.*ᵈ*

¹⁶"He who listens to you listens to me; he who rejects you rejects me; but he who rejects me rejects him who sent me."

¹⁷The seventy-two returned with joy and said, "Lord, even the demons submit to us in your name."

¹⁸He replied, "I saw Satan fall like lightning from heaven. ¹⁹I have given you authority to trample on snakes and scorpions and to overcome all the power of the enemy; nothing will harm you. ²⁰However, do not rejoice that the spirits submit to you, but rejoice that your names are written in heaven."

²¹At that time Jesus, full of joy through the Holy Spirit, said, "I praise you, Father, Lord of heaven and earth, because you have hidden these things from the wise and learned, and revealed them to little children. Yes, Father, for this was your good pleasure.

ᵃ54 Some manuscripts *them, even as Elijah did*
ᵇ55,56 Some manuscripts *them. And he said,*
"You do not know what kind of spirit you are of, for the Son of Man did not come to destroy men's lives, but to save them." ⁵⁶And   *ᶜ1* Some manuscripts *seventy;* also in verse 17
ᵈ15 Greek *Hades*

> AT THAT time Jesus, full of joy through the Holy Spirit, said, "I praise you, Father, Lord of heaven and earth, because you have hidden these things from the wise and learned, and revealed them to little children. Yes, Father, for this was your good pleasure."
>
> LUKE 10:21

22"All things have been committed to me by my Father. No one knows who the Son is except the Father, and no one knows who the Father is except the Son and those to whom the Son chooses to reveal him."

23Then he turned to his disciples and said privately, "Blessed are the eyes that see what you see. 24For I tell you that many prophets and kings wanted to see what you see but did not see it, and to hear what you hear but did not hear it."

The Parable of the Good Samaritan

25On one occasion an expert in the law stood up to test Jesus. "Teacher," he asked, "what must I do to inherit eternal life?"

26"What is written in the Law?" he replied. "How do you read it?"

27He answered: " 'Love the Lord your God with all your heart and with all your soul and with all your strength and with all your mind'*a*; and, 'Love your neighbor as yourself.'*b*"

28"You have answered correctly," Jesus replied. "Do this and you will live."

29But he wanted to justify himself, so he asked Jesus, "And who is my neighbor?"

30In reply Jesus said: "A man was going down from Jerusalem to Jericho, when he fell into the hands of robbers. They stripped him of his clothes, beat him and went away, leaving him half dead. 31A priest happened to be going down the same road, and when he saw the man, he passed by on the other side. 32So too, a Levite, when he came to the place and saw him, passed by on the other side. 33But a Samaritan, as he traveled, came where the man was; and when he saw him, he took pity on him. 34He went to him and bandaged his wounds, pouring on oil and wine. Then he put the man on his own donkey, took him to an inn and took care of him. 35The next day he took out two silver coins*c* and gave them to the innkeeper. 'Look after him,' he said, 'and when I return, I will reimburse you for any extra expense you may have.'

36"Which of these three do you think was a neighbor to the man who fell into the hands of robbers?"

37The expert in the law replied, "The one who had mercy on him."

Jesus told him, "Go and do likewise."

At the Home of Martha and Mary

38As Jesus and his disciples were on their way, he came to a village where a woman named Martha opened her home to him. 39She had a sister called Mary, who sat at the Lord's feet listening to what he said. 40But Martha was distracted by all the preparations that had to be made. She came to him and asked, "Lord, don't you care that my sister has left me to do the work by myself? Tell her to help me!"

41"Martha, Martha," the Lord answered, "you are worried and upset about many things, 42but only one thing is needed.*d* Mary has chosen what is better, and it will not be taken away from her."

Jesus' Teaching on Prayer

11 One day Jesus was praying in a certain place. When he finished, one of his disciples said to him, "Lord, teach us to pray, just as John taught his disciples."

> ONE day Jesus was praying in a certain place. When he finished, one of his disciples said to him, "Lord, teach us to pray, just as John taught his disciples."
>
> LUKE 11:1

2He said to them, "When you pray, say:

" 'Father,*e*
hallowed be your name,
your kingdom come.*f*

---

*a*27 Deut. 6:5   *b*27 Lev. 19:18   *c*35 Greek two denarii   *d*42 Some manuscripts but few things are needed—or only one   *e*2 Some manuscripts Our Father in heaven   *f*2 Some manuscripts come. May your will be done on earth as it is in heaven.

³Give us each day our daily bread.
⁴Forgive us our sins,
  for we also forgive everyone who
    sins against us.ᵃ
And lead us not into temptation.ᵇ'"

⁵Then he said to them, "Suppose one of you has a friend, and he goes to him at midnight and says, 'Friend, lend me three loaves of bread, ⁶because a friend of mine on a journey has come to me, and I have nothing to set before him.'

⁷"Then the one inside answers, 'Don't bother me. The door is already locked,

ᵃ4 Greek *everyone who is indebted to us*
ᵇ4 Some manuscripts *temptation but deliver us from the evil one*

LUKE 10:38–42

Being and Doing

10:42 "BUT ONLY ONE THING IS NEEDED."

Martha may be one of the most "modern" of all the characters in the Bible. The reason? She is so busy. Other times and cultures have had their own besetting sins; one of ours today is undoubtedly our busy-ness. And the thing that makes it so subtly pernicious is that we are often busy doing good things. For many of us, the great enemy of God's best is not the bad—the classically venal sins like lust, greed and gluttony—but the good.

Luke describes Martha's busy-ness as distraction. There's the irony. Martha thinks she is attending to what is important, but she has been drawn away from what is *truly* important. Jesus expanded on this and said, "Martha, Martha, you are worried and upset about many things, but only one thing is needed" (10:41–42). Martha's distraction is her confusion over the distinction between the many and the One, the good and the Best. She's lost her bearings on the sea of possibilities. She's buried in the details.

Jesus leads Martha out of her muddle by pointing to Mary. The way out is listening at the feet of Jesus in obedient attentiveness. He says his purpose is not to add work to our lives but to show us how to carry the burdens that we have. He is gentle and humble in heart; his yoke is easy, and his burden is light (see Matthew 11:28–30).

It isn't that God's against *doing*, it's that he wants us to understand that *being* always precedes *doing*, and that who we are with him is more important than what we do. Take care of the being, and the doing will take care of itself. Let Mary's posture at Jesus' feet be a picture of prayer and work, being and doing. "You can do more than pray, after you have prayed," wrote A. J. Gordon, "but you can never do more than pray until you have prayed."

PRAY:

I confess, Lord, that I am easily distracted—even as I pray.
Make me like Mary; teach me to sit at your feet and
listen, to be so I may do, to be your child so I may be your servant.

FOR YOUR NEXT DEVOTIONAL READING, GO TO PAGE 1250.

and my children are with me in bed. I can't get up and give you anything.' [8]I tell you, though he will not get up and give him the bread because he is his friend, yet because of the man's boldness[a] he will get up and give him as much as he needs.

[9]"So I say to you: Ask and it will be given to you; seek and you will find; knock and the door will be opened to you. [10]For everyone who asks receives; he who seeks finds; and to him who knocks, the door will be opened.

> "SO I SAY to you: Ask and it will be given to you; seek and you will find; knock and the door will be opened to you."
>
> LUKE 11:9

[11]"Which of you fathers, if your son asks for[b] a fish, will give him a snake instead? [12]Or if he asks for an egg, will give him a scorpion? [13]If you then, though you are evil, know how to give good gifts to your children, how much more will your Father in heaven give the Holy Spirit to those who ask him!"

Jesus and Beelzebub

[14]Jesus was driving out a demon that was mute. When the demon left, the man who had been mute spoke, and the crowd was amazed. [15]But some of them said, "By Beelzebub,[c] the prince of demons, he is driving out demons." [16]Others tested him by asking for a sign from heaven.

[17]Jesus knew their thoughts and said to them: "Any kingdom divided against itself will be ruined, and a house divided against itself will fall. [18]If Satan is divided against himself, how can his kingdom stand? I say this because you claim that I drive out demons by Beelzebub. [19]Now if I drive out demons by Beelzebub, by whom do your followers drive them out? So then, they will be your judges. [20]But if I drive out demons by the finger of God, then the kingdom of God has come to you.

[21]"When a strong man, fully armed, guards his own house, his possessions are safe. [22]But when someone stronger attacks and overpowers him, he takes away the armor in which the man trusted and divides up the spoils.

[23]"He who is not with me is against me, and he who does not gather with me, scatters.

[24]"When an evil[d] spirit comes out of a man, it goes through arid places seeking rest and does not find it. Then it says, 'I will return to the house I left.' [25]When it arrives, it finds the house swept clean and put in order. [26]Then it goes and takes seven other spirits more wicked than itself, and they go in and live there. And the final condition of that man is worse than the first."

[27]As Jesus was saying these things, a woman in the crowd called out, "Blessed is the mother who gave you birth and nursed you."

[28]He replied, "Blessed rather are those who hear the word of God and obey it."

The Sign of Jonah

[29]As the crowds increased, Jesus said, "This is a wicked generation. It asks for a miraculous sign, but none will be given it except the sign of Jonah. [30]For as Jonah was a sign to the Ninevites, so also will the Son of Man be to this generation. [31]The Queen of the South will rise at the judgment with the men of this generation and condemn them; for she came from the ends of the earth to listen to Solomon's wisdom, and now one[e] greater than Solomon is here. [32]The men of Nineveh will stand up at the judgment with this generation and condemn it; for they repented at the preaching of Jonah, and now one greater than Jonah is here.

The Lamp of the Body

[33]"No one lights a lamp and puts it in a place where it will be hidden, or under a bowl. Instead he puts it on its stand, so that those who come in may see the light. [34]Your eye is the lamp of your body. When your eyes are good, your whole body also is full of light. But when they are bad, your body also is full of darkness. [35]See to it, then, that the light within you is not

---

[a]8 Or persistence   [b]11 Some manuscripts for bread, will give him a stone; or if he asks for
[c]15 Greek Beezeboul or Beelzeboul; also in verses 18 and 19   [d]24 Greek unclean
[e]31 Or something; also in verse 32

darkness. [36]Therefore, if your whole body is full of light, and no part of it dark, it will be completely lighted, as when the light of a lamp shines on you."

Six Woes

[37]When Jesus had finished speaking, a Pharisee invited him to eat with him; so he went in and reclined at the table. [38]But the Pharisee, noticing that Jesus did not first wash before the meal, was surprised.

[39]Then the Lord said to him, "Now then, you Pharisees clean the outside of the cup and dish, but inside you are full of greed and wickedness. [40]You foolish people! Did not the one who made the outside make the inside also? [41]But give what is inside the dish[a] to the poor, and everything will be clean for you.

[42]"Woe to you Pharisees, because you give God a tenth of your mint, rue and all other kinds of garden herbs, but you neglect justice and the love of God. You should have practiced the latter without leaving the former undone.

[43]"Woe to you Pharisees, because you love the most important seats in the synagogues and greetings in the marketplaces.

[44]"Woe to you, because you are like unmarked graves, which men walk over without knowing it."

[45]One of the experts in the law answered him, "Teacher, when you say these things, you insult us also."

[46]Jesus replied, "And you experts in the law, woe to you, because you load people down with burdens they can hardly carry, and you yourselves will not lift one finger to help them.

[47]"Woe to you, because you build tombs for the prophets, and it was your forefathers who killed them. [48]So you testify that you approve of what your forefathers did; they killed the prophets, and you build their tombs. [49]Because of this, God in his wisdom said, 'I will send them prophets and apostles, some of whom they will kill and others they will persecute.' [50]Therefore this generation will be held responsible for the blood of all the prophets that has been shed since the beginning of the world, [51]from the blood of Abel to the blood of Zechariah, who was killed between the altar and the sanctuary. Yes, I tell you, this generation will be held responsible for it all.

[52]"Woe to you experts in the law, because you have taken away the key to knowledge. You yourselves have not entered, and you have hindered those who were entering."

[53]When Jesus left there, the Pharisees and the teachers of the law began to oppose him fiercely and to besiege him with questions, [54]waiting to catch him in something he might say.

Warnings and Encouragements

12 Meanwhile, when a crowd of many thousands had gathered, so that they were trampling on one another, Jesus began to speak first to his disciples, saying: "Be on your guard against the yeast of the Pharisees, which is hypocrisy. [2]There is nothing concealed that will not be disclosed, or hidden that will not be made known. [3]What you have said in the dark will be heard in the daylight, and what you have whispered in the ear in the inner rooms will be proclaimed from the roofs.

[4]"I tell you, my friends, do not be afraid of those who kill the body and after that can do no more. [5]But I will show you whom you should fear: Fear him who, after the killing of the body, has power to throw you into hell. Yes, I tell you, fear him. [6]Are not five sparrows sold for two pennies[b]? Yet not one of them is forgotten by God. [7]Indeed, the very hairs of your head are all numbered. Don't be afraid; you are worth more than many sparrows.

[8]"I tell you, whoever acknowledges me before men, the Son of Man will also acknowledge him before the angels of God. [9]But he who disowns me before men will be disowned before the angels of God. [10]And everyone who speaks a word against the Son of Man will be forgiven, but anyone who blasphemes against the Holy Spirit will not be forgiven.

[11]"When you are brought before synagogues, rulers and authorities, do not worry about how you will defend yourselves or what you will say, [12]for the Holy Spirit will teach you at that time what you should say."

[a]41 Or what you have   [b]6 Greek two assaria

The Parable of the Rich Fool

¹³Someone in the crowd said to him, "Teacher, tell my brother to divide the inheritance with me."

¹⁴Jesus replied, "Man, who appointed me a judge or an arbiter between you?" ¹⁵Then he said to them, "Watch out! Be on your guard against all kinds of greed; a man's life does not consist in the abundance of his possessions."

¹⁶And he told them this parable: "The ground of a certain rich man produced a good crop. ¹⁷He thought to himself, 'What shall I do? I have no place to store my crops.'

¹⁸"Then he said, 'This is what I'll do. I will tear down my barns and build bigger ones, and there I will store all my grain and my goods. ¹⁹And I'll say to myself, "You have plenty of good things laid up for many years. Take life easy; eat, drink and be merry."'

²⁰"But God said to him, 'You fool! This very night your life will be demanded from you. Then who will get what you have prepared for yourself?'

²¹"This is how it will be with anyone who stores up things for himself but is not rich toward God."

Do Not Worry

²²Then Jesus said to his disciples: "Therefore I tell you, do not worry about your life, what you will eat; or about your body, what you will wear. ²³Life is more than food, and the body more than clothes. ²⁴Consider the ravens: They do not sow or reap, they have no storeroom or barn; yet God feeds them. And how much more valuable you are than birds! ²⁵Who of you by worrying can add a single hour to his life*? ²⁶Since you cannot do this very little thing, why do you worry about the rest?

²⁷"Consider how the lilies grow. They do not labor or spin. Yet I tell you, not even Solomon in all his splendor was dressed like one of these. ²⁸If that is how God clothes the grass of the field, which is here today, and tomorrow is thrown into the fire, how much more will he clothe you, O you of little faith! ²⁹And do not set your heart on what you will eat or drink; do not worry about it. ³⁰For the pagan world runs after all such things, and your Father knows that you need them. ³¹But seek his kingdom, and these things will be given to you as well.

³²"Do not be afraid, little flock, for your Father has been pleased to give you the kingdom. ³³Sell your possessions and give to the poor. Provide purses for yourselves that will not wear out, a treasure in heaven that will not be exhausted, where no thief comes near and no moth destroys. ³⁴For where your treasure is, there your heart will be also.

Watchfulness

³⁵"Be dressed ready for service and keep your lamps burning, ³⁶like men waiting for their master to return from a wedding banquet, so that when he comes and knocks they can immediately open the door for him. ³⁷It will be good for those servants whose master finds them watching when he comes. I tell you the truth, he will dress himself to serve, will have them recline at the table and will come and wait on them. ³⁸It will be good for those servants whose master finds them ready, even if he comes in the second or third watch of the night. ³⁹But understand this: If the owner of the house had known at what hour the thief was coming, he would not have let his house be broken into. ⁴⁰You also must be ready, because the Son of Man will come at an hour when you do not expect him."

⁴¹Peter asked, "Lord, are you telling this parable to us, or to everyone?"

⁴²The Lord answered, "Who then is the faithful and wise manager, whom the master puts in charge of his servants to give them their food allowance at the proper time? ⁴³It will be good for that servant whom the master finds doing so when he returns. ⁴⁴I tell you the truth, he will put him in charge of all his possessions. ⁴⁵But suppose the servant says to himself, 'My master is taking a long time in coming,' and he then begins to beat the menservants and maidservants and to eat and drink and get drunk. ⁴⁶The master of that servant will come on a day when he does not expect him and at an hour he is not aware of. He will cut him

---

*25 Or *single cubit to his height*

to pieces and assign him a place with the unbelievers.

⁴⁷"That servant who knows his master's will and does not get ready or does not do what his master wants will be beaten with many blows. ⁴⁸But the one who does not know and does things deserving punishment will be beaten with few blows. From everyone who has been given much, much will be demanded; and from the one who has been entrusted with much, much more will be asked.

> *When you pray, rather let your heart be without words than your words be without heart.*
>
> JOHN BUNYAN

Not Peace but Division

⁴⁹"I have come to bring fire on the earth, and how I wish it were already kindled! ⁵⁰But I have a baptism to undergo, and how distressed I am until it is completed! ⁵¹Do you think I came to bring peace on earth? No, I tell you, but division. ⁵²From now on there will be five in one family divided against each other, three against two and two against three. ⁵³They will be divided, father against son and son against father, mother against daughter and daughter against mother, mother-in-law against daughter-in-law and daughter-in-law against mother-in-law."

Interpreting the Times

⁵⁴He said to the crowd: "When you see a cloud rising in the west, immediately you say, 'It's going to rain,' and it does. ⁵⁵And when the south wind blows, you say, 'It's going to be hot,' and it is. ⁵⁶Hypocrites! You know how to interpret the appearance of the earth and the sky. How is it that you don't know how to interpret this present time?

⁵⁷"Why don't you judge for yourselves what is right? ⁵⁸As you are going with your adversary to the magistrate, try hard to be reconciled to him on the way, or he may drag you off to the judge, and the judge turn you over to the officer, and the officer throw you into prison. ⁵⁹I tell you, you will not get out until you have paid the last penny.ᵃ"

Repent or Perish

13 Now there were some present at that time who told Jesus about the Galileans whose blood Pilate had mixed with their sacrifices. ²Jesus answered, "Do you think that these Galileans were worse sinners than all the other Galileans because they suffered this way? ³I tell you, no! But unless you repent, you too will all perish. ⁴Or those eighteen who died when the tower in Siloam fell on them—do you think they were more guilty than all the others living in Jerusalem? ⁵I tell you, no! But unless you repent, you too will all perish."

⁶Then he told this parable: "A man had a fig tree, planted in his vineyard, and he went to look for fruit on it, but did not find any. ⁷So he said to the man who took care of the vineyard, 'For three years now I've been coming to look for fruit on this fig tree and haven't found any. Cut it down! Why should it use up the soil?'

⁸"'Sir,' the man replied, 'leave it alone for one more year, and I'll dig around it and fertilize it. ⁹If it bears fruit next year, fine! If not, then cut it down.'"

A Crippled Woman Healed on the Sabbath

¹⁰On a Sabbath Jesus was teaching in one of the synagogues, ¹¹and a woman was there who had been crippled by a spirit for eighteen years. She was bent over and could not straighten up at all. ¹²When Jesus saw her, he called her forward and said to her, "Woman, you are set free from your infirmity." ¹³Then he put his hands on her, and immediately she straightened up and praised God.

¹⁴Indignant because Jesus had healed on the Sabbath, the synagogue ruler said to the people, "There are six days for work. So come and be healed on those days, not on the Sabbath."

¹⁵The Lord answered him, "You hypocrites! Doesn't each of you on the Sabbath untie his ox or donkey from the stall and lead it out to give it water? ¹⁶Then should not this woman, a daughter of Abraham, whom Satan has kept bound for eighteen long years, be set free on the Sabbath day from what bound her?"

ᵃ59 Greek *lepton*

> *The devil is aware that one hour of close fellowship, hearty converse with God in prayer, is able to pull down what he hath been contriving and building many a year.*
>
> JOHN FLAVEL

[17]When he said this, all his opponents were humiliated, but the people were delighted with all the wonderful things he was doing.

The Parables of the Mustard Seed and the Yeast

[18]Then Jesus asked, "What is the kingdom of God like? What shall I compare it to? [19]It is like a mustard seed, which a man took and planted in his garden. It grew and became a tree, and the birds of the air perched in its branches."

[20]Again he asked, "What shall I compare the kingdom of God to? [21]It is like yeast that a woman took and mixed into a large amount[a] of flour until it worked all through the dough."

The Narrow Door

[22]Then Jesus went through the towns and villages, teaching as he made his way to Jerusalem. [23]Someone asked him, "Lord, are only a few people going to be saved?"

He said to them, [24]"Make every effort to enter through the narrow door, because many, I tell you, will try to enter and will not be able to. [25]Once the owner of the house gets up and closes the door, you will stand outside knocking and pleading, 'Sir, open the door for us.'

"But he will answer, 'I don't know you or where you come from.'

[26]"Then you will say, 'We ate and drank with you, and you taught in our streets.'

[27]"But he will reply, 'I don't know you or where you come from. Away from me, all you evildoers!'

[28]"There will be weeping there, and gnashing of teeth, when you see Abraham, Isaac and Jacob and all the prophets in the kingdom of God, but you yourselves thrown out. [29]People will come from east and west and north and south, and will take their places at the feast in the kingdom of God. [30]Indeed there are those who are last who will be first, and first who will be last."

Jesus' Sorrow for Jerusalem

[31]At that time some Pharisees came to Jesus and said to him, "Leave this place and go somewhere else. Herod wants to kill you."

[32]He replied, "Go tell that fox, 'I will drive out demons and heal people today and tomorrow, and on the third day I will reach my goal.' [33]In any case, I must keep going today and tomorrow and the next day—for surely no prophet can die outside Jerusalem!

[34]"O Jerusalem, Jerusalem, you who kill the prophets and stone those sent to you, how often I have longed to gather your children together, as a hen gathers her chicks under her wings, but you were not willing! [35]Look, your house is left to you desolate. I tell you, you will not see me again until you say, 'Blessed is he who comes in the name of the Lord.'[b]"

Jesus at a Pharisee's House

14 One Sabbath, when Jesus went to eat in the house of a prominent Pharisee, he was being carefully watched. [2]There in front of him was a man suffering from dropsy. [3]Jesus asked the Pharisees and experts in the law, "Is it lawful to heal on the Sabbath or not?" [4]But they remained silent. So taking hold of the man, he healed him and sent him away.

[5]Then he asked them, "If one of you has a son[c] or an ox that falls into a well on the Sabbath day, will you not immediately pull him out?" [6]And they had nothing to say.

[7]When he noticed how the guests picked the places of honor at the table, he told them this parable: [8]"When someone invites you to a wedding feast, do not take the place of honor, for a person more distinguished than you may have been invited. [9]If so, the host who invited both of you will come and say to you, 'Give this man your seat.' Then, humiliated, you will have to take the least impor-

---

[a]21 Greek *three satas* (probably about 1/2 bushel or 22 liters)   [b]35 Psalm 118:26   [c]5 Some manuscripts *donkey*

tant place. ¹⁰But when you are invited, take the lowest place, so that when your host comes, he will say to you, 'Friend, move up to a better place.' Then you will be honored in the presence of all your fellow guests. ¹¹For everyone who exalts himself will be humbled, and he who humbles himself will be exalted."

¹²Then Jesus said to his host, "When you give a luncheon or dinner, do not invite your friends, your brothers or relatives, or your rich neighbors; if you do, they may invite you back and so you will be repaid. ¹³But when you give a banquet, invite the poor, the crippled, the lame, the blind, ¹⁴and you will be blessed. Although they cannot repay you, you will be repaid at the resurrection of the righteous."

The Parable of the Great Banquet

¹⁵When one of those at the table with him heard this, he said to Jesus, "Blessed is the man who will eat at the feast in the kingdom of God."

¹⁶Jesus replied: "A certain man was preparing a great banquet and invited many guests. ¹⁷At the time of the banquet he sent his servant to tell those who had been invited, 'Come, for everything is now ready.'

¹⁸"But they all alike began to make excuses. The first said, 'I have just bought a field, and I must go and see it. Please excuse me.'

¹⁹"Another said, 'I have just bought five yoke of oxen, and I'm on my way to try them out. Please excuse me.'

²⁰"Still another said, 'I just got married, so I can't come.'

²¹"The servant came back and reported this to his master. Then the owner of the house became angry and ordered his servant, 'Go out quickly into the streets and alleys of the town and bring in the poor, the crippled, the blind and the lame.'

²²"'Sir,' the servant said, 'what you ordered has been done, but there is still room.'

²³"Then the master told his servant, 'Go out to the roads and country lanes and make them come in, so that my house will be full. ²⁴I tell you, not one of those men who were invited will get a taste of my banquet.'"

The Cost of Being a Disciple

²⁵Large crowds were traveling with Jesus, and turning to them he said: ²⁶"If anyone comes to me and does not hate his father and mother, his wife and children, his brothers and sisters—yes, even his own life—he cannot be my disciple. ²⁷And anyone who does not carry his cross and follow me cannot be my disciple.

²⁸"Suppose one of you wants to build a tower. Will he not first sit down and estimate the cost to see if he has enough money to complete it? ²⁹For if he lays the foundation and is not able to finish it, everyone who sees it will ridicule him, ³⁰saying, 'This fellow began to build and was not able to finish.'

³¹"Or suppose a king is about to go to war against another king. Will he not first sit down and consider whether he is able with ten thousand men to oppose the one coming against him with twenty thousand? ³²If he is not able, he will send a delegation while the other is still a long way off and will ask for terms of peace. ³³In the same way, any of you who does not give up everything he has cannot be my disciple.

³⁴"Salt is good, but if it loses its saltiness, how can it be made salty again? ³⁵It is fit neither for the soil nor for the manure pile; it is thrown out.

"He who has ears to hear, let him hear."

The Parable of the Lost Sheep

15 Now the tax collectors and "sinners" were all gathering around to hear him. ²But the Pharisees and the teachers of the law muttered, "This man welcomes sinners and eats with them."

³Then Jesus told them this parable: ⁴"Suppose one of you has a hundred sheep and loses one of them. Does he not leave the ninety-nine in the open country and go after the lost sheep until he finds it? ⁵And when he finds it, he joyfully puts it on his shoulders ⁶and goes home. Then he calls his friends and neighbors together and says, 'Rejoice with me; I have found my lost sheep.' ⁷I tell you that in the same way there will be more rejoicing in heaven over one sinner who repents than over ninety-nine righteous persons who do not need to repent.

The Parable of the Lost Coin

⁸"Or suppose a woman has ten silver coins[a] and loses one. Does she not light a lamp, sweep the house and search carefully until she finds it? ⁹And when she finds it, she calls her friends and neighbors together and says, 'Rejoice with me; I have found my lost coin.' ¹⁰In the same way, I tell you, there is rejoicing in the presence of the angels of God over one sinner who repents."

The Parable of the Lost Son

¹¹Jesus continued: "There was a man who had two sons. ¹²The younger one said to his father, 'Father, give me my

[a]8 Greek ten drachmas, each worth about a day's wages

[FRIDAY]

LUKE 15

Heaven's Joy

15:10 "IN THE SAME WAY, I TELL YOU, THERE IS REJOICING IN THE PRESENCE OF THE ANGELS OF GOD OVER ONE SINNER WHO REPENTS."

One of the Bible's most compelling descriptions of what it means to pray is to stand before God in "the Most Holy Place by the blood of Jesus" (Hebrews 10:19). What do we find in the presence of the Holy One? Truth? Mystery? Blinding light? Ineffable goodness? A party? All of the above! But it's the party part we need to get our minds around now because Jesus said there is a party going on in heaven whenever a sinner repents and comes home.

Luke 15 has been called the "gospel in the gospel." In three short stories, Jesus describes God's attitude toward sinners. First he describes what it means to be a sinner. It's like being a lost sheep, who, for sheer stupidity, wanders from patch of grass to patch of grass, living for the moment, easy prey for wolves. Or it's like being a lost coin in a dark house, as helpless as an inanimate object. Or it's like a rebellious son, with only himself to blame, deliberately taking the fast track to destruction, never looking back, laughing all the way. Stupid, helpless and bullheaded—that's how God sees sinners. The one word that describes them all is *lost*.

Jesus also points out God's love for sinners. Quite simply, he shamelessly loves them all, even in their stupidity, helplessness and rebellion. And when one is found or comes home, his joy is so great there has to be a party. As the waiting father told the callous and unforgiving older son, "we *had* to celebrate and be glad, because this brother of yours was dead and is alive again; he was lost and is found" (15:32, italics added). Joy is a divine necessity.

Thank God that you were once lost and are found; helpless and now recovered; a rebel that has come home. If the joy has left you, pray that he will restore in you the joy of his salvation. Do your prayers for the lost match God's passion for them? Pray that his Spirit will expand your compassion. Enter the Most Holy Place; come into the joy of heaven.

PRAY:

"I thank thee, who hast overthrown my foes and healed my wounded mind: I thank thee whose enlivening voice bids my freed heart in thee rejoice."

JOHANN SCHLEFFER (TR. JOHN WESLEY)

FOR YOUR NEXT DEVOTIONAL READING, GO TO PAGE 1252.

share of the estate.' So he divided his property between them.

¹³"Not long after that, the younger son got together all he had, set off for a distant country and there squandered his wealth in wild living. ¹⁴After he had spent everything, there was a severe famine in that whole country, and he began to be in need. ¹⁵So he went and hired himself out to a citizen of that country, who sent him to his fields to feed pigs. ¹⁶He longed to fill his stomach with the pods that the pigs were eating, but no one gave him anything.

¹⁷"When he came to his senses, he said, 'How many of my father's hired men have food to spare, and here I am starving to death! ¹⁸I will set out and go back to my father and say to him: Father, I have sinned against heaven and against you. ¹⁹I am no longer worthy to be called your son; make me like one of your hired men.' ²⁰So he got up and went to his father.

"But while he was still a long way off, his father saw him and was filled with compassion for him; he ran to his son, threw his arms around him and kissed him.

²¹"The son said to him, 'Father, I have sinned against heaven and against you. I am no longer worthy to be called your son.ᵃ'

²²"But the father said to his servants, 'Quick! Bring the best robe and put it on him. Put a ring on his finger and sandals on his feet. ²³Bring the fattened calf and kill it. Let's have a feast and celebrate. ²⁴For this son of mine was dead and is alive again; he was lost and is found.' So they began to celebrate.

²⁵"Meanwhile, the older son was in the field. When he came near the house, he heard music and dancing. ²⁶So he called one of the servants and asked him what was going on. ²⁷'Your brother has come,' he replied, 'and your father has killed the fattened calf because he has him back safe and sound.'

²⁸"The older brother became angry and refused to go in. So his father went out and pleaded with him. ²⁹But he answered his father, 'Look! All these years I've been slaving for you and never disobeyed your orders. Yet you never gave me even a young goat so I could celebrate with my friends. ³⁰But when this

son of yours who has squandered your property with prostitutes comes home, you kill the fattened calf for him!'

³¹" 'My son,' the father said, 'you are always with me, and everything I have is yours. ³²But we had to celebrate and be glad, because this brother of yours was dead and is alive again; he was lost and is found.' "

The Parable of the Shrewd Manager

16 Jesus told his disciples: "There was a rich man whose manager was accused of wasting his possessions. ²So he called him in and asked him, 'What is this I hear about you? Give an account of your management, because you cannot be manager any longer.'

³"The manager said to himself, 'What shall I do now? My master is taking away my job. I'm not strong enough to dig, and I'm ashamed to beg— ⁴I know what I'll do so that, when I lose my job here, people will welcome me into their houses.'

⁵"So he called in each one of his master's debtors. He asked the first, 'How much do you owe my master?'

⁶" 'Eight hundred gallonsᵇ of olive oil,' he replied.

"The manager told him, 'Take your bill, sit down quickly, and make it four hundred.'

⁷"Then he asked the second, 'And how much do you owe?'

" 'A thousand bushelsᶜ of wheat,' he replied.

"He told him, 'Take your bill and make it eight hundred.'

⁸"The master commended the dishonest manager because he had acted shrewdly. For the people of this world are more shrewd in dealing with their own kind than are the people of the light. ⁹I tell you, use worldly wealth to gain friends for yourselves, so that when it is gone, you will be welcomed into eternal dwellings.

¹⁰"Whoever can be trusted with very little can also be trusted with much, and whoever is dishonest with very little will

ᵃ21 Some early manuscripts son. Make me like one of your hired men.   ᵇ6 Greek one hundred batous (probably about 3 kiloliters)
ᶜ7 Greek one hundred korous (probably about 35 kiloliters)

By Prayer Alone

HUDSON TAYLOR made a vow before he left England as a missionary to China: "When I get out to China I shall have no claim on anyone for anything. My only claim will be on God. How important to learn … to move man through God by prayer alone." The enormity of what Taylor saw when he stepped off the boat in Shanghai made it clear that his vow would be tested severely, many times over.

Shanghai was a war zone, under siege from the North. Taylor watched in horror as stretchers of wounded men were bought into the marketplace. From his tiny bedroom window, he witnessed the torture and execution of many prisoners and the casual attitude of the people toward death and suffering. He felt as never before the staggering burden of people without the hope of the gospel. His work would be evangelizing "a parish of a million." Who was equal to such a task? Certainly no mere human effort would ever be sufficient to open their eyes.

Then there were Taylor's personal limitations. He had no social standing, only a tenuous grasp of the language, and barely enough money to afford the lowest living quarters. He did not fit in socially with the missionary community and disagreed with the way they lived in European-style colonies, complete with servants and afternoon tea. His decision to dress, eat and wear his hair like the Chinese was a scandal to them all, and further isolated him.

But he pressed on "by prayer alone," and saw the power of God amidst war, death threats and the loss of his wife and two children to disease. A Chinese businessman once heard Taylor speak about Jesus. He approached

Taylor and said, "I have long sought the Truth, as did my father before me, but without finding it out. In Confucianism, Buddhism, Taoism, I have found no rest, but I do find rest in what we have heard tonight. Henceforward I am a believer in Jesus." The businessman then asked Taylor how long England had the light of Christ. Taylor replied that it had been several hundred years. "What?" cried the businessman. "Several hundreds of years! Is it possible that you have known about Jesus so long, and only now have come to tell us? My father sought the truth for more than twenty years and died without finding it. Oh, why did you not come sooner?"

When Hudson Taylor first arrived in Shanghai, the founder of the China Inland Mission knew of only 300 believers in the whole country. By the time of his death in 1905, that number had grown to 100,000. He prayed for God to send more missionaries—100 was his request, but 600 came. Taylor once described his work: "Envied of some, despised by many, hated perhaps by others; often blamed for things I never heard of, or had nothing to do with . . . often sick in body as well as perplexed in mind and embarrassed by circumstances . . . but the battle is the Lord's and He will conquer." By prayer alone.

PRAY:

Faithful Savior, you are everything I will ever need.
Teach me to pray and live in that truth.

MEMORIZE:

"Not by might nor by power, but by my Spirit,"
says the LORD Almighty. ZECHARIAH 4:6B

FOR YOUR NEXT DEVOTIONAL READING, GO TO PAGE 1257.

also be dishonest with much. ¹¹So if you have not been trustworthy in handling worldly wealth, who will trust you with true riches? ¹²And if you have not been trustworthy with someone else's property, who will give you property of your own?

¹³"No servant can serve two masters. Either he will hate the one and love the other, or he will be devoted to the one and despise the other. You cannot serve both God and Money."

¹⁴The Pharisees, who loved money, heard all this and were sneering at Jesus. ¹⁵He said to them, "You are the ones who justify yourselves in the eyes of men, but God knows your hearts. What is highly valued among men is detestable in God's sight.

Additional Teachings

¹⁶"The Law and the Prophets were proclaimed until John. Since that time, the good news of the kingdom of God is being preached, and everyone is forcing his way into it. ¹⁷It is easier for heaven and earth to disappear than for the least stroke of a pen to drop out of the Law.

¹⁸"Anyone who divorces his wife and marries another woman commits adultery, and the man who marries a divorced woman commits adultery.

The Rich Man and Lazarus

¹⁹"There was a rich man who was dressed in purple and fine linen and lived in luxury every day. ²⁰At his gate was laid a beggar named Lazarus, covered with sores ²¹and longing to eat what fell from the rich man's table. Even the dogs came and licked his sores.

²²"The time came when the beggar died and the angels carried him to Abraham's side. The rich man also died and was buried. ²³In hell,ᵃ where he was in torment, he looked up and saw Abraham far away, with Lazarus by his side. ²⁴So he called to him, 'Father Abraham, have pity on me and send Lazarus to dip the tip of his finger in water and cool my tongue, because I am in agony in this fire.'

²⁵"But Abraham replied, 'Son, remember that in your lifetime you received your good things, while Lazarus received bad things, but now he is comforted here and you are in agony. ²⁶And besides all

this, between us and you a great chasm has been fixed, so that those who want to go from here to you cannot, nor can anyone cross over from there to us.'

²⁷"He answered, 'Then I beg you, father, send Lazarus to my father's house, ²⁸for I have five brothers. Let him warn them, so that they will not also come to this place of torment.'

²⁹"Abraham replied, 'They have Moses and the Prophets; let them listen to them.'

³⁰"'No, father Abraham,' he said, 'but if someone from the dead goes to them, they will repent.'

³¹"He said to him, 'If they do not listen to Moses and the Prophets, they will not be convinced even if someone rises from the dead.'"

Sin, Faith, Duty

17 Jesus said to his disciples: "Things that cause people to sin are bound to come, but woe to that person through whom they come. ²It would be better for him to be thrown into the sea with a millstone tied around his neck than for him to cause one of these little ones to sin. ³So watch yourselves.

"If your brother sins, rebuke him, and if he repents, forgive him. ⁴If he sins against you seven times in a day, and seven times comes back to you and says, 'I repent,' forgive him."

⁵The apostles said to the Lord, "Increase our faith!"

⁶He replied, "If you have faith as small as a mustard seed, you can say to this mulberry tree, 'Be uprooted and planted in the sea,' and it will obey you.

⁷"Suppose one of you had a servant plowing or looking after the sheep. Would he say to the servant when he comes in from the field, 'Come along now and sit down to eat'? ⁸Would he not rather say, 'Prepare my supper, get yourself ready and wait on me while I eat and drink; after that you may eat and drink'? ⁹Would he thank the servant because he did what he was told to do? ¹⁰So you also, when you have done everything you were told to do, should say, 'We are unworthy servants; we have only done our duty.'"

ᵃ23 Greek *Hades*

Ten Healed of Leprosy

[11]Now on his way to Jerusalem, Jesus traveled along the border between Samaria and Galilee. [12]As he was going into a village, ten men who had leprosy[a] met him. They stood at a distance [13]and called out in a loud voice, "Jesus, Master, have pity on us!"

[14]When he saw them, he said, "Go, show yourselves to the priests." And as they went, they were cleansed.

[15]One of them, when he saw he was healed, came back, praising God in a loud voice. [16]He threw himself at Jesus' feet and thanked him—and he was a Samaritan.

[17]Jesus asked, "Were not all ten cleansed? Where are the other nine? [18]Was no one found to return and give praise to God except this foreigner?" [19]Then he said to him, "Rise and go; your faith has made you well."

The Coming of the Kingdom of God

[20]Once, having been asked by the Pharisees when the kingdom of God would come, Jesus replied, "The kingdom of God does not come with your careful observation, [21]nor will people say, 'Here it is,' or 'There it is,' because the kingdom of God is within[b] you."

[22]Then he said to his disciples, "The time is coming when you will long to see one of the days of the Son of Man, but you will not see it. [23]Men will tell you, 'There he is!' or 'Here he is!' Do not go running off after them. [24]For the Son of Man in his day[c] will be like the lightning, which flashes and lights up the sky from one end to the other. [25]But first he must suffer many things and be rejected by this generation.

[26]"Just as it was in the days of Noah, so also will it be in the days of the Son of Man. [27]People were eating, drinking, marrying and being given in marriage up to the day Noah entered the ark. Then the flood came and destroyed them all.

[28]"It was the same in the days of Lot. People were eating and drinking, buying and selling, planting and building. [29]But the day Lot left Sodom, fire and sulfur rained down from heaven and destroyed them all.

[30]"It will be just like this on the day the Son of Man is revealed. [31]On that day no one who is on the roof of his house, with his goods inside, should go down to get them. Likewise, no one in the field should go back for anything. [32]Remember Lot's wife! [33]Whoever tries to keep his life will lose it, and whoever loses his life will preserve it. [34]I tell you, on that night two people will be in one bed; one will be taken and the other left. [35]Two women will be grinding grain together; one will be taken and the other left.[d]"

[37]"Where, Lord?" they asked.

He replied, "Where there is a dead body, there the vultures will gather."

The Parable of the Persistent Widow

18 Then Jesus told his disciples a parable to show them that they should always pray and not give up. [2]He said: "In a certain town there was a judge who neither feared God nor cared about men. [3]And there was a widow in that town who kept coming to him with the plea, 'Grant me justice against my adversary.'

[4]"For some time he refused. But finally he said to himself, 'Even though I don't fear God or care about men, [5]yet because this widow keeps bothering me, I will see that she gets justice, so that she won't eventually wear me out with her coming!' "

[6]And the Lord said, "Listen to what the unjust judge says. [7]And will not God bring about justice for his chosen ones, who cry out to him day and night? Will he keep putting them off? [8]I tell you, he will see that they get justice, and quickly. However, when the Son of Man comes, will he find faith on the earth?"

The Parable of the Pharisee and the Tax Collector

[9]To some who were confident of their own righteousness and looked down on everybody else, Jesus told this parable: [10]"Two men went up to the temple to pray, one a Pharisee and the other a tax collector. [11]The Pharisee stood up and

[a]12 The Greek word was used for various diseases affecting the skin—not necessarily leprosy.
[b]21 Or among   [c]24 Some manuscripts do not have in his day.   [d]35 Some manuscripts left.
[36]Two men will be in the field; one will be taken and the other left.

prayed about*ᵃ* himself: 'God, I thank you that I am not like other men—robbers, evildoers, adulterers—or even like this tax collector. ¹²I fast twice a week and give a tenth of all I get.'

¹³"But the tax collector stood at a distance. He would not even look up to heaven, but beat his breast and said, 'God, have mercy on me, a sinner.'

¹⁴"I tell you that this man, rather than the other, went home justified before God. For everyone who exalts himself will be humbled, and he who humbles himself will be exalted."

The Little Children and Jesus

¹⁵People were also bringing babies to Jesus to have him touch them. When the disciples saw this, they rebuked them. ¹⁶But Jesus called the children to him and said, "Let the little children come to me, and do not hinder them, for the kingdom of God belongs to such as these. ¹⁷I tell you the truth, anyone who will not receive the kingdom of God like a little child will never enter it."

The Rich Ruler

¹⁸A certain ruler asked him, "Good teacher, what must I do to inherit eternal life?"

¹⁹"Why do you call me good?" Jesus answered. "No one is good—except God alone. ²⁰You know the commandments: 'Do not commit adultery, do not murder, do not steal, do not give false testimony, honor your father and mother.'*ᵇ*"

²¹"All these I have kept since I was a boy," he said.

²²When Jesus heard this, he said to him, "You still lack one thing. Sell everything you have and give to the poor, and you will have treasure in heaven. Then come, follow me."

²³When he heard this, he became very sad, because he was a man of great wealth. ²⁴Jesus looked at him and said, "How hard it is for the rich to enter the kingdom of God! ²⁵Indeed, it is easier for a camel to go through the eye of a needle than for a rich man to enter the kingdom of God."

²⁶Those who heard this asked, "Who then can be saved?"

²⁷Jesus replied, "What is impossible with men is possible with God."

²⁸Peter said to him, "We have left all we had to follow you!"

²⁹"I tell you the truth," Jesus said to them, "no one who has left home or wife or brothers or parents or children for the sake of the kingdom of God ³⁰will fail to receive many times as much in this age and, in the age to come, eternal life."

Jesus Again Predicts His Death

³¹Jesus took the Twelve aside and told them, "We are going up to Jerusalem, and everything that is written by the prophets about the Son of Man will be fulfilled. ³²He will be handed over to the Gentiles. They will mock him, insult him, spit on him, flog him and kill him. ³³On the third day he will rise again."

³⁴The disciples did not understand any of this. Its meaning was hidden from them, and they did not know what he was talking about.

A Blind Beggar Receives His Sight

³⁵As Jesus approached Jericho, a blind man was sitting by the roadside begging. ³⁶When he heard the crowd going by, he asked what was happening. ³⁷They told him, "Jesus of Nazareth is passing by."

> 66 *Most men pray for power, the strength to do things. Few people pray for love, the quality to be someone.* 99
>
> ROBERT D. FOSTER

³⁸He called out, "Jesus, Son of David, have mercy on me!"

³⁹Those who led the way rebuked him and told him to be quiet, but he shouted all the more, "Son of David, have mercy on me!"

⁴⁰Jesus stopped and ordered the man to be brought to him. When he came near, Jesus asked him, ⁴¹"What do you want me to do for you?"

"Lord, I want to see," he replied.

⁴²Jesus said to him, "Receive your sight; your faith has healed you." ⁴³Immediately he received his sight and followed Jesus, praising God. When all the people saw it, they also praised God.

ᵃ11 Or to *ᵇ20 Exodus 20:12–16; Deut. 5:16–20*

LUKE 18:1–14

Persistence and Humility in Prayer

18:1 "ALWAYS PRAY AND NOT GIVE UP."

Martin Luther is credited with two word pictures of prayer that capture what Jesus was teaching in these two parables. The first was what he said as he watched his dog beg for food, eyes burning, ears perked, tail wagging: "If only I would pray that way." That's what Jesus meant when he taught his disciples to pray and not give up (see 18:1). In Jesus' parable, the widow was doggedly persistent, like a dog who knows where the food is.

Luther's second picture was of a beggar. He said: "God fills up only empty hands." That's what Jesus meant when he said, "For everyone who exalts himself will be humbled, and he who humbles himself will be exalted" (18:14). Pray to God like the tax collector in this parable. He understood his position before God.

These prayer parables gain strength if seen against the background of what precedes them in Luke's Gospel. In chapters 16–17, Jesus challenged his followers to live their lives with eternity in view. In the story of the shrewd manager (see 16:1–15), he urged them to invest in heaven by the way they handle money on earth. In the parable of the rich man and Lazarus (see 16:19–31), he did essentially the same thing: this time with the sober reminder that what is at stake is life and death, heaven and hell. Then comes a lengthy teaching about the coming of the end (see 17:20–37). Through all of these teachings runs this warning: Things aren't what they appear to be—what you now see is temporary, what you don't yet see is eternal. The temporary is passing away; the eternal is coming. Stay alert, and be prepared. Everything depends on it.

But how do we live wisely and alertly in these deceptive and unstable times? Jesus' answer is in the two prayer parables in chapter 18: Stay closely connected to God through persistent, humble prayer. Ninety percent of prayer is just showing up, persistently, day in and day out. We are like children crossing a busy highway; we need to hold on to our Father's hand to keep safe. One hundred percent of prayer is knowing our deep need for God. Of course, it only follows that if we know how much we need God, we won't find it hard to persist in prayer. Humility is the root of persistence.

PRAY:

Keep before me my need, Father. Don't let anything
distract me from the absolute necessity of staying
closely connected to you. Teach me to pray and not give up.

FOR YOUR NEXT DEVOTIONAL READING, GO TO PAGE 1260.

Zacchaeus the Tax Collector

19 Jesus entered Jericho and was passing through. ²A man was there by the name of Zacchaeus; he was a chief tax collector and was wealthy. ³He wanted to see who Jesus was, but being a short man he could not, because of the crowd. ⁴So he ran ahead and climbed a sycamore-fig tree to see him, since Jesus was coming that way.

⁵When Jesus reached the spot, he looked up and said to him, "Zacchaeus, come down immediately. I must stay at your house today." ⁶So he came down at once and welcomed him gladly.

⁷All the people saw this and began to mutter, "He has gone to be the guest of a 'sinner.'"

⁸But Zacchaeus stood up and said to the Lord, "Look, Lord! Here and now I give half of my possessions to the poor, and if I have cheated anybody out of anything, I will pay back four times the amount."

⁹Jesus said to him, "Today salvation has come to this house, because this man, too, is a son of Abraham. ¹⁰For the Son of Man came to seek and to save what was lost."

The Parable of the Ten Minas

¹¹While they were listening to this, he went on to tell them a parable, because he was near Jerusalem and the people thought that the kingdom of God was going to appear at once. ¹²He said: "A man of noble birth went to a distant country to have himself appointed king and then to return. ¹³So he called ten of his servants and gave them ten minas.ᵃ 'Put this money to work,' he said, 'until I come back.'

¹⁴"But his subjects hated him and sent a delegation after him to say, 'We don't want this man to be our king.'

¹⁵"He was made king, however, and returned home. Then he sent for the servants to whom he had given the money, in order to find out what they had gained with it.

¹⁶"The first one came and said, 'Sir, your mina has earned ten more.'

¹⁷"'Well done, my good servant!' his master replied. 'Because you have been trustworthy in a very small matter, take charge of ten cities.'

¹⁸"The second came and said, 'Sir, your mina has earned five more.'

¹⁹"His master answered, 'You take charge of five cities.'

²⁰"Then another servant came and said, 'Sir, here is your mina; I have kept it laid away in a piece of cloth. ²¹I was afraid of you, because you are a hard man. You take out what you did not put in and reap what you did not sow.'

²²"His master replied, 'I will judge you by your own words, you wicked servant! You knew, did you, that I am a hard man, taking out what I did not put in, and reaping what I did not sow? ²³Why then didn't you put my money on deposit, so that when I came back, I could have collected it with interest?'

²⁴"Then he said to those standing by, 'Take his mina away from him and give it to the one who has ten minas.'

²⁵"'Sir,' they said, 'he already has ten!'

²⁶"He replied, 'I tell you that to everyone who has, more will be given, but as for the one who has nothing, even what he has will be taken away. ²⁷But those enemies of mine who did not want me to be king over them—bring them here and kill them in front of me.'"

The Triumphal Entry

²⁸After Jesus had said this, he went on ahead, going up to Jerusalem. ²⁹As he approached Bethphage and Bethany at the hill called the Mount of Olives, he sent two of his disciples, saying to them, ³⁰"Go to the village ahead of you, and as you enter it, you will find a colt tied there, which no one has ever ridden. Untie it and bring it here. ³¹If anyone asks you, 'Why are you untying it?' tell him, 'The Lord needs it.'"

³²Those who were sent ahead went and found it just as he had told them. ³³As they were untying the colt, its owners asked them, "Why are you untying the colt?"

³⁴They replied, "The Lord needs it."

³⁵They brought it to Jesus, threw their cloaks on the colt and put Jesus on it. ³⁶As he went along, people spread their cloaks on the road.

ᵃ13 A mina was about three months' wages.

³⁷When he came near the place where the road goes down the Mount of Olives, the whole crowd of disciples began joyfully to praise God in loud voices for all the miracles they had seen:

³⁸ "Blessed is the king who comes in the name of the Lord!"ᵃ

"Peace in heaven and glory in the highest!"

³⁹Some of the Pharisees in the crowd said to Jesus, "Teacher, rebuke your disciples!"

⁴⁰"I tell you," he replied, "if they keep quiet, the stones will cry out."

⁴¹As he approached Jerusalem and saw the city, he wept over it ⁴²and said, "If you, even you, had only known on this day what would bring you peace—but now it is hidden from your eyes. ⁴³The days will come upon you when your enemies will build an embankment against you and encircle you and hem you in on every side. ⁴⁴They will dash you to the ground, you and the children within your walls. They will not leave one stone on another, because you did not recognize the time of God's coming to you."

Jesus at the Temple

⁴⁵Then he entered the temple area and began driving out those who were selling. ⁴⁶"It is written," he said to them, "'My house will be a house of prayer'ᵇ; but you have made it 'a den of robbers.'ᶜ"

⁴⁷Every day he was teaching at the temple. But the chief priests, the teachers of the law and the leaders among the people were trying to kill him. ⁴⁸Yet they could not find any way to do it, because all the people hung on his words.

The Authority of Jesus Questioned

20 One day as he was teaching the people in the temple courts and preaching the gospel, the chief priests and the teachers of the law, together with the elders, came up to him. ²"Tell us by what authority you are doing these things," they said. "Who gave you this authority?"

³He replied, "I will also ask you a question. Tell me, ⁴John's baptism—was it from heaven, or from men?"

⁵They discussed it among themselves and said, "If we say, 'From heaven,' he will ask, 'Why didn't you believe him?' ⁶But if we say, 'From men,' all the people will stone us, because they are persuaded that John was a prophet."

⁷So they answered, "We don't know where it was from."

⁸Jesus said, "Neither will I tell you by what authority I am doing these things."

The Parable of the Tenants

⁹He went on to tell the people this parable: "A man planted a vineyard, rented it to some farmers and went away for a long time. ¹⁰At harvest time he sent a servant to the tenants so they would give him some of the fruit of the vineyard. But the tenants beat him and sent him away empty-handed. ¹¹He sent another servant, but that one also they beat and treated shamefully and sent away empty-handed. ¹²He sent still a third, and they wounded him and threw him out.

¹³"Then the owner of the vineyard said, 'What shall I do? I will send my son, whom I love; perhaps they will respect him.'

¹⁴"But when the tenants saw him, they talked the matter over. 'This is the heir,' they said. 'Let's kill him, and the inheritance will be ours.' ¹⁵So they threw him out of the vineyard and killed him.

"What then will the owner of the vineyard do to them? ¹⁶He will come and kill those tenants and give the vineyard to others."

When the people heard this, they said, "May this never be!"

¹⁷Jesus looked directly at them and asked, "Then what is the meaning of that which is written:

"'The stone the builders rejected has become the capstoneᵈ'ᵉ?

¹⁸Everyone who falls on that stone will be broken to pieces, but he on whom it falls will be crushed."

¹⁹The teachers of the law and the chief priests looked for a way to arrest him immediately, because they knew he had spoken this parable against them. But they were afraid of the people.

ᵃ38 Psalm 118:26   ᵇ46 Isaiah 56:7
ᶜ46 Jer. 7:11   ᵈ17 Or cornerstone
ᵉ17 Psalm 118:22

For the Sake of its Non-Members

19:46 "MY HOUSE WILL BE A HOUSE OF PRAYER."

What Jesus saw that day sent him into a fury. We don't have many accounts of Jesus' anger, so we would do well to pay close attention to whatever it was that led him to knock over tables, kick over benches and generally wreck a place that should evoke peace and communion with God.

Let's be clear about what upset him. It wasn't simply that business was being conducted in the temple; what was being done there was official temple business. Worshipers needed to purchase animals to sacrifice, and many of them also needed to be able to exchange their money into the local currency to pay the annual temple tax. Jesus objected to the way that the merchants "robbed" the people with unfair prices. He also objected to where the business was being done—in the outer court, the Court of the Gentiles. The place reserved for non-Jews to come and pray had become a noisy, smelly marketplace. There was no room for prayer anymore! Jesus wasn't just angry about what *was* happening there, but also about what *wasn't* happening.

The temple was meant to be, above all else, a place to pray, to meet God. It was to be a place for all the peoples of the earth, not just the "chosen." Jesus cited Isaiah 56:7, "My house will be called a house of prayer." Mark, in his Gospel, completed the quotation from Isaiah with the phrase, "for all nations." Jesus was furious that the very place reserved for all peoples to encounter God was shut off from them. The "business" of the temple was keeping the temple from its true business.

The church, the community of Christ, is the new temple (see Ephesians 2:19–22). How much more might Jesus be upset if his church, which he also calls his body, forgets its true business? William Temple said the church is the only institution in the world that exists for the sake of its nonmembers. The future of the church lies in a great celebration in which people from east and west, north and south will come and sit at God's table in his kingdom (see Luke 13:29). Woe to his people if they forget that!

Pray for your church. Pray that its business will be God's business, not ecclesiastical clutter. Pray that your church will be a place where all peoples can feel welcome, and where all peoples are lifted up to God in prayer.

P R A Y :

"May the peoples praise you, O God;
may all the peoples praise you" (Psalm 67:5).

FOR YOUR NEXT DEVOTIONAL READING, GO TO PAGE 1264.

Paying Taxes to Caesar

²⁰Keeping a close watch on him, they sent spies, who pretended to be honest. They hoped to catch Jesus in something he said so that they might hand him over to the power and authority of the governor. ²¹So the spies questioned him: "Teacher, we know that you speak and teach what is right, and that you do not show partiality but teach the way of God in accordance with the truth. ²²Is it right for us to pay taxes to Caesar or not?"

²³He saw through their duplicity and said to them, ²⁴"Show me a denarius. Whose portrait and inscription are on it?"

²⁵"Caesar's," they replied.

He said to them, "Then give to Caesar what is Caesar's, and to God what is God's."

²⁶They were unable to trap him in what he had said there in public. And astonished by his answer, they became silent.

The Resurrection and Marriage

²⁷Some of the Sadducees, who say there is no resurrection, came to Jesus with a question. ²⁸"Teacher," they said, "Moses wrote for us that if a man's brother dies and leaves a wife but no children, the man must marry the widow and have children for his brother. ²⁹Now there were seven brothers. The first one married a woman and died childless. ³⁰The second ³¹and then the third married her, and in the same way the seven died, leaving no children. ³²Finally, the woman died too. ³³Now then, at the resurrection whose wife will she be, since the seven were married to her?"

³⁴Jesus replied, "The people of this age marry and are given in marriage. ³⁵But those who are considered worthy of taking part in that age and in the resurrection from the dead will neither marry nor be given in marriage, ³⁶and they can no longer die; for they are like the angels. They are God's children, since they are children of the resurrection. ³⁷But in the account of the bush, even Moses showed that the dead rise, for he calls the Lord 'the God of Abraham, and the God of Isaac, and the God of Jacob.'ᵃ ³⁸He is not the God of the dead, but of the living, for to him all are alive."

³⁹Some of the teachers of the law responded, "Well said, teacher!" ⁴⁰And no one dared to ask him any more questions.

Whose Son Is the Christ?

⁴¹Then Jesus said to them, "How is it that they say the Christᵇ is the Son of David? ⁴²David himself declares in the Book of Psalms:

" 'The Lord said to my Lord:
  "Sit at my right hand
⁴³until I make your enemies
  a footstool for your feet." 'ᶜ

⁴⁴David calls him 'Lord.' How then can he be his son?"

⁴⁵While all the people were listening, Jesus said to his disciples, ⁴⁶"Beware of the teachers of the law. They like to walk around in flowing robes and love to be greeted in the marketplaces and have the most important seats in the synagogues and the places of honor at banquets. ⁴⁷They devour widows' houses and for a show make lengthy prayers. Such men will be punished most severely."

The Widow's Offering

21 As he looked up, Jesus saw the rich putting their gifts into the temple treasury. ²He also saw a poor widow put in two very small copper coins.ᵈ ³"I tell you the truth," he said, "this poor widow has put in more than all the others. ⁴All these people gave their gifts out of their wealth; but she out of her poverty put in all she had to live on."

Signs of the End of the Age

⁵Some of his disciples were remarking about how the temple was adorned with beautiful stones and with gifts dedicated to God. But Jesus said, ⁶"As for what you see here, the time will come when not one stone will be left on another; every one of them will be thrown down."

⁷"Teacher," they asked, "when will these things happen? And what will be the sign that they are about to take place?"

⁸He replied: "Watch out that you are not deceived. For many will come in my name, claiming, 'I am he,' and, 'The time is near.'

ᵃ37 Exodus 3:6   ᵇ41 Or Messiah
ᶜ43 Psalm 110:1   ᵈ2 Greek two lepta

Do not follow them. ⁹When you hear of wars and revolutions, do not be frightened. These things must happen first, but the end will not come right away."

¹⁰Then he said to them: "Nation will rise against nation, and kingdom against kingdom. ¹¹There will be great earthquakes, famines and pestilences in various places, and fearful events and great signs from heaven.

¹²"But before all this, they will lay hands on you and persecute you. They will deliver you to synagogues and prisons, and you will be brought before kings and governors, and all on account of my name. ¹³This will result in your being witnesses to them. ¹⁴But make up your mind not to worry beforehand how you will defend yourselves. ¹⁵For I will give you words and wisdom that none of your adversaries will be able to resist or contradict. ¹⁶You will be betrayed even by parents, brothers, relatives and friends, and they will put some of you to death. ¹⁷All men will hate you because of me. ¹⁸But not a hair of your head will perish. ¹⁹By standing firm you will gain life.

²⁰"When you see Jerusalem being surrounded by armies, you will know that its desolation is near. ²¹Then let those who are in Judea flee to the mountains, let those in the city get out, and let those in the country not enter the city. ²²For this is the time of punishment in fulfillment of all that has been written. ²³How dreadful it will be in those days for pregnant women and nursing mothers! There will be great distress in the land and wrath against this people. ²⁴They will fall by the sword and will be taken as prisoners to all the nations. Jerusalem will be trampled on by the Gentiles until the times of the Gentiles are fulfilled.

²⁵"There will be signs in the sun, moon and stars. On the earth, nations will be in anguish and perplexity at the roaring and tossing of the sea. ²⁶Men will faint from terror, apprehensive of what is coming on the world, for the heavenly bodies will be shaken. ²⁷At that time they will see the Son of Man coming in a cloud with power and great glory. ²⁸When these things begin to take place, stand up and lift up your heads, because your redemption is drawing near."

²⁹He told them this parable: "Look at the fig tree and all the trees. ³⁰When they sprout leaves, you can see for yourselves and know that summer is near. ³¹Even so, when you see these things happening, you know that the kingdom of God is near.

³²"I tell you the truth, this generation*a* will certainly not pass away until all these things have happened. ³³Heaven and earth will pass away, but my words will never pass away.

³⁴"Be careful, or your hearts will be weighed down with dissipation, drunkenness and the anxieties of life, and that day will close on you unexpectedly like a trap. ³⁵For it will come upon all those who live on the face of the whole earth. ³⁶Be always on the watch, and pray that you may be able to escape all that is about to happen, and that you may be able to stand before the Son of Man."

> "BE ALWAYS on the watch, and pray that you may be able to escape all that is about to happen, and that you may be able to stand before the Son of Man."
>
> LUKE 21:36

³⁷Each day Jesus was teaching at the temple, and each evening he went out to spend the night on the hill called the Mount of Olives, ³⁸and all the people came early in the morning to hear him at the temple.

Judas Agrees to Betray Jesus

22 Now the Feast of Unleavened Bread, called the Passover, was approaching, ²and the chief priests and the teachers of the law were looking for some way to get rid of Jesus, for they were afraid of the people. ³Then Satan entered Judas, called Iscariot, one of the Twelve. ⁴And Judas went to the chief priests and the officers of the temple guard and discussed with them how he might betray Jesus. ⁵They were delighted and agreed to give him money. ⁶He consented, and watched for an opportunity to hand Jesus over to them when no crowd was present.

a 32 Or race

The Last Supper

⁷Then came the day of Unleavened Bread on which the Passover lamb had to be sacrificed. ⁸Jesus sent Peter and John, saying, "Go and make preparations for us to eat the Passover."

⁹"Where do you want us to prepare for it?" they asked.

¹⁰He replied, "As you enter the city, a man carrying a jar of water will meet you. Follow him to the house that he enters, ¹¹and say to the owner of the house, 'The Teacher asks: Where is the guest room, where I may eat the Passover with my disciples?' ¹²He will show you a large upper room, all furnished. Make preparations there."

¹³They left and found things just as Jesus had told them. So they prepared the Passover.

¹⁴When the hour came, Jesus and his apostles reclined at the table. ¹⁵And he said to them, "I have eagerly desired to eat this Passover with you before I suffer. ¹⁶For I tell you, I will not eat it again until it finds fulfillment in the kingdom of God."

¹⁷After taking the cup, he gave thanks and said, "Take this and divide it among you. ¹⁸For I tell you I will not drink again of the fruit of the vine until the kingdom of God comes."

¹⁹And he took bread, gave thanks and broke it, and gave it to them, saying, "This is my body given for you; do this in remembrance of me."

²⁰In the same way, after the supper he took the cup, saying, "This cup is the new covenant in my blood, which is poured out for you. ²¹But the hand of him who is going to betray me is with mine on the table. ²²The Son of Man will go as it has been decreed, but woe to that man who betrays him." ²³They began to question among themselves which of them it might be who would do this.

²⁴Also a dispute arose among them as to which of them was considered to be greatest. ²⁵Jesus said to them, "The kings of the Gentiles lord it over them; and those who exercise authority over them call themselves Benefactors. ²⁶But you are not to be like that. Instead, the greatest among you should be like the youngest, and the one who rules like the one who serves. ²⁷For who is greater, the one who is at the table or the one who serves? Is it not the one who is at the table? But I am among you as one who serves. ²⁸You are those who have stood by me in my trials. ²⁹And I confer on you a kingdom, just as my Father conferred one on me, ³⁰so that you may eat and drink at my table in my kingdom and sit on thrones, judging the twelve tribes of Israel.

³¹"Simon, Simon, Satan has asked to sift you*a* as wheat. ³²But I have prayed for you, Simon, that your faith may not fail. And when you have turned back, strengthen your brothers."

³³But he replied, "Lord, I am ready to go with you to prison and to death."

³⁴Jesus answered, "I tell you, Peter, before the rooster crows today, you will deny three times that you know me."

³⁵Then Jesus asked them, "When I sent you without purse, bag or sandals, did you lack anything?"

"Nothing," they answered.

³⁶He said to them, "But now if you have a purse, take it, and also a bag; and if you don't have a sword, sell your cloak and buy one. ³⁷It is written: 'And he was numbered with the transgressors'*b*; and I tell you that this must be fulfilled in me. Yes, what is written about me is reaching its fulfillment."

³⁸The disciples said, "See, Lord, here are two swords."

"That is enough," he replied.

Jesus Prays on the Mount of Olives

³⁹Jesus went out as usual to the Mount of Olives, and his disciples followed him. ⁴⁰On reaching the place, he said to them, "Pray that you will not fall into temptation." ⁴¹He withdrew about a stone's throw beyond them, knelt down and prayed, ⁴²"Father, if you are willing, take this cup from me; yet not my will, but yours be done." ⁴³An angel from heaven appeared to him and strengthened him.

> HE withdrew about a stone's throw beyond them, knelt down and prayed.
>
> LUKE 22:41

a31 The Greek is plural.   *b37* Isaiah 53:12

LUKE 22:31–32

"But I Have Prayed for You"

22:32 "BUT I HAVE PRAYED FOR YOU, SIMON, THAT YOUR FAITH MAY NOT FAIL."

Satan already has Judas in his hip pocket (see Luke 22:3); now he wants the rest of the disciples. "Satan has asked to sift you as wheat," Jesus told them. The "you" is plural, referring to all the disciples, and the picture is of sheep scattered by fear, disillusionment and disunity, to be picked off one by one by the Predator. This is the very thing that will happen to them: In Matthew's Gospel Jesus speaks of the aftermath of his arrest and crucifixion, and he quotes the prophet Zechariah: "I will strike the shepherd, and the sheep of the flock will be scattered" (Matthew 26:31).

Significantly, Jesus' prayer zeroes in specifically on Simon Peter, to whom he says, "But I have prayed for you." Here the "you" is singular. Note the Lord's priorities. When the sheep are scattered, he prays first for the leader of the sheep, the undershepherd, as it were. Satan has particularly targeted this central disciple, and Peter's leadership role will be critical in the restoration of the disciples. When he is restored, he must strengthen his brothers (see verse 32). Jesus knows how important shepherds are for his sheep because he is the great and good shepherd (see John 10:11). When the shepherd is lost, the sheep suffer. Jesus saw what was coming—the very next day.

What a vivid picture of Jesus' love for his church, and for its shepherds and pastors. Even on the eve of his execution, he was thinking of their welfare—no, *especially* on the eve of his execution, for after all, his death was for the sake of the church (see Ephesians 5:25).

We should pray for pastors and leaders with the same tender compassion that Jesus prayed for Peter. When they fail in their calling to care for the sheep, our response should not be to scorn them or become cynical in response. We need to pray for their restoration and the restoration of the sheep scattered by their fall. We may imagine Jesus interceding for his church right now, at the right hand of the Father (see Hebrews 7:25; 8:1). We may also picture him praying especially for the leaders of his church. Let us join Jesus in our prayers.

PRAY:

Lord Jesus, you are the great Shepherd of the sheep.
You have appointed some to be your undershepherds
to serve you by serving your people.
Bless them and keep them, Lord; restore them when
they sin, and strengthen them to be faithful.
I pray especially for _____.

FOR YOUR NEXT DEVOTIONAL READING, GO TO PAGE 1267.

[44]And being in anguish, he prayed more earnestly, and his sweat was like drops of blood falling to the ground.[a]

> AND being in anguish, he prayed more earnestly, and his sweat was like drops of blood falling to the ground.
>
> LUKE 22:44

[45]When he rose from prayer and went back to the disciples, he found them asleep, exhausted from sorrow. [46]"Why are you sleeping?" he asked them. "Get up and pray so that you will not fall into temptation."

Jesus Arrested

[47]While he was still speaking a crowd came up, and the man who was called Judas, one of the Twelve, was leading them. He approached Jesus to kiss him, [48]but Jesus asked him, "Judas, are you betraying the Son of Man with a kiss?"

[49]When Jesus' followers saw what was going to happen, they said, "Lord, should we strike with our swords?" [50]And one of them struck the servant of the high priest, cutting off his right ear.

[51]But Jesus answered, "No more of this!" And he touched the man's ear and healed him.

[52]Then Jesus said to the chief priests, the officers of the temple guard, and the elders, who had come for him, "Am I leading a rebellion, that you have come with swords and clubs? [53]Every day I was with you in the temple courts, and you did not lay a hand on me. But this is your hour—when darkness reigns."

Peter Disowns Jesus

[54]Then seizing him, they led him away and took him into the house of the high priest. Peter followed at a distance. [55]But when they had kindled a fire in the middle of the courtyard and had sat down together, Peter sat down with them. [56]A servant girl saw him seated there in the firelight. She looked closely at him and said, "This man was with him."

[57]But he denied it. "Woman, I don't know him," he said.

[58]A little later someone else saw him and said, "You also are one of them."

"Man, I am not!" Peter replied.

[59]About an hour later another asserted, "Certainly this fellow was with him, for he is a Galilean."

[60]Peter replied, "Man, I don't know what you're talking about!" Just as he was speaking, the rooster crowed. [61]The Lord turned and looked straight at Peter. Then Peter remembered the word the Lord had spoken to him: "Before the rooster crows today, you will disown me three times." [62]And he went outside and wept bitterly.

The Guards Mock Jesus

[63]The men who were guarding Jesus began mocking and beating him. [64]They blindfolded him and demanded, "Prophesy! Who hit you?" [65]And they said many other insulting things to him.

Jesus Before Pilate and Herod

[66]At daybreak the council of the elders of the people, both the chief priests and teachers of the law, met together, and Jesus was led before them. [67]"If you are the Christ,[b]" they said, "tell us."

Jesus answered, "If I tell you, you will not believe me, [68]and if I asked you, you would not answer. [69]But from now on, the Son of Man will be seated at the right hand of the mighty God."

[70]They all asked, "Are you then the Son of God?"

He replied, "You are right in saying I am."

[71]Then they said, "Why do we need any more testimony? We have heard it from his own lips."

23 Then the whole assembly rose and led him off to Pilate. [2]And they began to accuse him, saying, "We have found this man subverting our nation. He opposes payment of taxes to Caesar and claims to be Christ,[c] a king."

[3]So Pilate asked Jesus, "Are you the king of the Jews?"

"Yes, it is as you say," Jesus replied.

[4]Then Pilate announced to the chief priests and the crowd, "I find no basis for a charge against this man."

---

[a]44 Some early manuscripts do not have verses 43 and 44.   [b]67 Or Messiah   [c]2 Or Messiah; also in verses 35 and 39

[5]But they insisted, "He stirs up the people all over Judea[a] by his teaching. He started in Galilee and has come all the way here."

[6]On hearing this, Pilate asked if the man was a Galilean. [7]When he learned that Jesus was under Herod's jurisdiction, he sent him to Herod, who was also in Jerusalem at that time.

[8]When Herod saw Jesus, he was greatly pleased, because for a long time he had been wanting to see him. From what he had heard about him, he hoped to see him perform some miracle. [9]He plied him with many questions, but Jesus gave him no answer. [10]The chief priests and the teachers of the law were standing there, vehemently accusing him. [11]Then Herod and his soldiers ridiculed and mocked him. Dressing him in an elegant robe, they sent him back to Pilate. [12]That day Herod and Pilate became friends—before this they had been enemies.

[13]Pilate called together the chief priests, the rulers and the people, [14]and said to them, "You brought me this man as one who was inciting the people to rebellion. I have examined him in your presence and have found no basis for your charges against him. [15]Neither has Herod, for he sent him back to us; as you can see, he has done nothing to deserve death. [16]Therefore, I will punish him and then release him.[b]"

[18]With one voice they cried out, "Away with this man! Release Barabbas to us!" [19](Barabbas had been thrown into prison for an insurrection in the city, and for murder.)

[20]Wanting to release Jesus, Pilate appealed to them again. [21]But they kept shouting, "Crucify him! Crucify him!"

[22]For the third time he spoke to them: "Why? What crime has this man committed? I have found in him no grounds for the death penalty. Therefore I will have him punished and then release him."

[23]But with loud shouts they insistently demanded that he be crucified, and their shouts prevailed. [24]So Pilate decided to grant their demand. [25]He released the man who had been thrown into prison for insurrection and murder, the one they asked for, and surrendered Jesus to their will.

The Crucifixion

[26]As they led him away, they seized Simon from Cyrene, who was on his way in from the country, and put the cross on him and made him carry it behind Jesus. [27]A large number of people followed him, including women who mourned and wailed for him. [28]Jesus turned and said to them, "Daughters of Jerusalem, do not weep for me; weep for yourselves and for your children. [29]For the time will come when you will say, 'Blessed are the barren women, the wombs that never bore and the breasts that never nursed!' [30]Then

> "'they will say to the mountains,
>   "Fall on us!"
> and to the hills, "Cover us!"'[c]

[31]For if men do these things when the tree is green, what will happen when it is dry?"

[32]Two other men, both criminals, were also led out with him to be executed. [33]When they came to the place called the Skull, there they crucified him, along with the criminals—one on his right, the other on his left. [34]Jesus said, "Father, forgive them, for they do not know what they are doing."[d] And they divided up his clothes by casting lots.

> JESUS said, "Father, forgive them, for they do not know what they are doing." And they divided up his clothes by casting lots.
>
> LUKE 23:34

[35]The people stood watching, and the rulers even sneered at him. They said, "He saved others; let him save himself if he is the Christ of God, the Chosen One."

[36]The soldiers also came up and mocked him. They offered him wine vinegar [37]and said, "If you are the king of the Jews, save yourself."

[38]There was a written notice above him, which read: THIS IS THE KING OF THE JEWS.

[39]One of the criminals who hung there hurled insults at him: "Aren't you the Christ? Save yourself and us!"

---

[a]5 Or *over the land of the Jews*   [b]16 Some manuscripts *him."* [17]*Now he was obliged to release one man to them at the Feast.*
[c]30 Hosea 10:8   [d]34 Some early manuscripts do not have this sentence.

LUKE 23:32–43

It's Never Too Late
or Too Simplistic

23:42 "JESUS, REMEMBER ME WHEN YOU COME INTO YOUR KINGDOM."

Two lives were lived badly, but one ended well. One man went to his death cursing Christ; the other reached out to him in faith. That's one way to read this brief encounter between Jesus and the criminals as they hung dying on their crosses. There is great hope here for all who feel they have wasted their lives and who wonder late in life if there is any hope for them. Be assured that there is—according to this story.

The latecomer who spoke to Jesus and asked for pardon was given an insight into Jesus that even the disciples didn't have. When the man requested, "Jesus, remember me when you come into your kingdom," he confessed a faith in Jesus' victory that the apostles were despairing of at the moment. The criminal is very much like the workers in Jesus' parable who get a full day's wages for an hour's work (see Matthew 20:1–16).

This man's prayer was a model of simplicity. The criminal prayed, "Remember me!" What could be more elemental? The two irreducible minimums of all true prayer are: You must know your need, and you must know the only one who can meet your need. All genuine prayer is rooted in humility and hope: humility about yourself and hope in the Savior who "was numbered with the transgressors . . . and made intercession for the transgressors" (Isaiah 53:12; see also Luke 22:37).

Jesus' answer to the criminal was a paradigm of God's eagerness to answer prayer. It was immediate—"today you will be with me in paradise." And it was gracious. One might even say Jesus over-answered when he added, "in paradise." The criminal wanted simply to be remembered; Jesus promised that the man would be by his side in paradise. The word "paradise" is synonymous with "Abraham's side" or "bosom," the place reserved for people the quality of Abraham (see Luke 16:22–23). The Persian root word referred to a king's walled, private garden, the place of special honor, reserved for a favored servant or subject to be with the king. Jesus gives more than we ask and better than we ask.

Know this: It is never too late or too simplistic to cry out, "Remember me!" Know also that God is more ready to hear your prayer than you are to pray it.

PRAY:

*Dear Jesus, you know my folly and my guilt. You know the time
I've wasted. Please be merciful to me, for I pray with that
dying criminal, "Remember me!"*

FOR YOUR NEXT DEVOTIONAL READING, GO TO PAGE 1268.

⁴⁰But the other criminal rebuked him. "Don't you fear God," he said, "since you are under the same sentence? ⁴¹We are punished justly, for we are getting what our deeds deserve. But this man has done nothing wrong."

⁴²Then he said, "Jesus, remember me when you come into your kingdom.ᵃ"

⁴³Jesus answered him, "I tell you the truth, today you will be with me in paradise."

Jesus' Death

⁴⁴It was now about the sixth hour, and darkness came over the whole land until the ninth hour, ⁴⁵for the sun stopped shining. And the curtain of the temple was torn in two. ⁴⁶Jesus called out with a loud voice, "Father, into your hands I commit my spirit." When he had said this, he breathed his last.

ᵃ42 Some manuscripts *come with your kingly power*

{ FRIDAY }

LUKE 23:46

Into Your Hands

23:46 "FATHER, INTO YOUR HANDS I COMMIT MY SPIRIT."

What a way to go. What a way to pray as you go: "Father, into your hands I commit my spirit." The prayer is taken from Psalm 31:5. Some scholars believe that "Into your hands I commit my spirit" was the first prayer every Jewish mother taught her child to pray before going to sleep at night. When Jesus prayed this prayer, he added "Father" to it. Jesus died, then, the way a child falls to sleep in his Father's arms.[1]

Right up to the very end of his life, Jesus drew on the Scriptures to shape his prayers. Charles Spurgeon remarked with admiration how even the incarnate Son of God, the grand original thinker, prayed from the Scriptures:

> How instructive is this great truth that the Incarnate Word lived on the Inspired Word! It was food to him, as it is to us; and ... if Christ thus lived upon the Word of God, should not you and I do the same? ... Oh, that you and I might get into the very heart of the word of God and get that word into ourselves! As I have seen the silkworm eat into the leaf, and consume it, so ought we do to the Word of the Lord—not crawl over its surface, but eat right into it till we have taken it into our inmost parts. It is idle merely to let the eye glance over the words ... But it is blessed to eat into the very soul of the Bible until, you come to talk in Scriptural language, and your very style is fashioned with Scriptural models ... [as with] John Bunyan ... Prick him anywhere; his blood is Bibline ... I think it well worthy of your constant remembrance that, even in death, our blessed Master showed the ruling passion of his spirit, so that his last words were a quotation from Scripture.[2]

If this is the way Jesus prayed, how much more should we? May it be said of us, "Prick them anywhere; their blood is Bibline."

P R A Y :

Lord Jesus, teach me to pray as you taught your disciples, and as you taught us on the cross. Let your word find a home in my heart, mind and mouth. Teach me to pray as you did, from and through Holy Scripture.

FOR YOUR NEXT DEVOTIONAL READING, GO TO PAGE 1270.

47The centurion, seeing what had happened, praised God and said, "Surely this was a righteous man." 48When all the people who had gathered to witness this sight saw what took place, they beat their breasts and went away. 49But all those who knew him, including the women who had followed him from Galilee, stood at a distance, watching these things.

Jesus' Burial

50Now there was a man named Joseph, a member of the Council, a good and upright man, 51who had not consented to their decision and action. He came from the Judean town of Arimathea and he was waiting for the kingdom of God. 52Going to Pilate, he asked for Jesus' body. 53Then he took it down, wrapped it in linen cloth and placed it in a tomb cut in the rock, one in which no one had yet been laid. 54It was Preparation Day, and the Sabbath was about to begin.

55The women who had come with Jesus from Galilee followed Joseph and saw the tomb and how his body was laid in it. 56Then they went home and prepared spices and perfumes. But they rested on the Sabbath in obedience to the commandment.

The Resurrection

24 On the first day of the week, very early in the morning, the women took the spices they had prepared and went to the tomb. 2They found the stone rolled away from the tomb, 3but when they entered, they did not find the body of the Lord Jesus. 4While they were wondering about this, suddenly two men in clothes that gleamed like lightning stood beside them. 5In their fright the women bowed down with their faces to the ground, but the men said to them, "Why do you look for the living among the dead? 6He is not here; he has risen! Remember how he told you, while he was still with you in Galilee: 7'The Son of Man must be delivered into the hands of sinful men, be crucified and on the third day be raised again.'" 8Then they remembered his words.

9When they came back from the tomb, they told all these things to the Eleven and to all the others. 10It was Mary Magdalene, Joanna, Mary the mother of James, and the others with them who told this to the apostles. 11But they did not believe the women, because their words seemed to them like nonsense. 12Peter, however, got up and ran to the tomb. Bending over, he saw the strips of linen lying by themselves, and he went away, wondering to himself what had happened.

On the Road to Emmaus

13Now that same day two of them were going to a village called Emmaus, about seven miles[a] from Jerusalem. 14They were talking with each other about everything that had happened. 15As they talked and discussed these things with each other, Jesus himself came up and walked along with them; 16but they were kept from recognizing him.

17He asked them, "What are you discussing together as you walk along?"

They stood still, their faces downcast. 18One of them, named Cleopas, asked him, "Are you only a visitor to Jerusalem and do not know the things that have happened there in these days?"

19"What things?" he asked.

"About Jesus of Nazareth," they replied. "He was a prophet, powerful in word and deed before God and all the people. 20The chief priests and our rulers handed him over to be sentenced to death, and they crucified him; 21but we had hoped that he was the one who was going to redeem Israel. And what is more, it is the third day since all this took place. 22In addition, some of our women amazed us. They went to the tomb early this morning 23but didn't find his body. They came and told us that they had seen a vision of angels, who said he was alive. 24Then some of our companions went to the tomb and found it just as the women had said, but him they did not see."

25He said to them, "How foolish you are, and how slow of heart to believe all that the prophets have spoken! 26Did not the Christ[b] have to suffer these things and then enter his glory?" 27And beginning

a13 Greek sixty stadia (about 11 kilometers)
b26 Or Messiah; also in verse 46

Prayer and Obedience

NEARLY 300 PEOPLE were waiting in line at the dispensary at Nala, in the Belgian Congo (now Democratic Republic of Congo). But it was the leper at the end of the line that had Edith Patton's attention. He had the worst case of leprosy she had ever seen; his skin was rotted and his fingers and toes ravaged by the disease. Judging from his appearance, she guessed that he had traveled eighty miles to get to the hospital. Her first response was visceral. She found the disease so repugnant that she wanted nothing to do with him. She said later that it was "the biggest crisis in my missionary life." Rationalizations flooded her mind: She didn't have the medicines he needed; she might catch the disease; once she treated one leper many more would follow, and she didn't have the money to carry out a full-blown leper ministry.

Hoping he would leave on his own, she didn't treat the man for four days. She prayed a lot, arguing with God—telling him that yes, she felt sorry for lepers; yes, she knew she couldn't close her heart to him, but that he had not called her to treat lepers—that it wasn't her job. The Holy Spirit kept pressing her heart until she came to the realization that if she wouldn't obey God, he didn't want to hear any more of her prayers. After days of intense struggle, she was utterly exhausted, and wilted in submission to God's will. Victory came with her surrender.

The next morning, Patton went to the leper and confessed to him that God had spoken to her about his great need, that she had intentionally shunned him, and that she needed God's help to assist him. She also invited the man to stay permanently and promised that she would do her best to help him. She explained to the man that he would have to look to God for help because she did not have any medicine to give him nor a place to house him.

Confident that God would meet their needs, they knelt in prayer together. Thus began a thriving leper ministry through which many souls were saved.

From 1929 to 1931 the hospital compound grew, and the dispensary treated nearly 17,000 people a year. Through it all, Patton kept the spiritual ministry in the foreground, and conversions abounded. She also began a leper settlement where over 60 lepers lived. Many came to know the Lord and began preaching the Good News to others. By 1932, the ministry Patton had so resisted was thriving, and due to medical advances, the once incurable disease of leprosy became curable.

Patton suffered many hardships throughout her ministry, including the death of her husband, Percy Moules, after only being married three years. Prayer sustained her. Her ministry to lepers drove her to prayer for long hours. The lepers often complained and were lacking in discipline, but she would always take them to God. Through her wrestling with God over these "least of Christ's brethren," she came to the profound understanding that if Christ died for us, we must also be willing to lay down our lives for others.

PRAY:
Lord Jesus, you did not cling to your rights as God's equal but laid down your life for me. May your love compel me to see people as you see them and to no longer live for myself, but for you and others.

MEMORIZE:
For Christ's love compels us, because we are convinced that one died for all, and therefore all died. And he died for all, that those who live should no longer live for themselves but for him who died for them and was raised again. 2 CORINTHIANS 5:14–15

FOR YOUR NEXT DEVOTIONAL READING, GO TO PAGE 1272.

with Moses and all the Prophets, he explained to them what was said in all the Scriptures concerning himself.

²⁸As they approached the village to which they were going, Jesus acted as if he were going farther. ²⁹But they urged him strongly, "Stay with us, for it is nearly evening; the day is almost over." So he went in to stay with them.

³⁰When he was at the table with them, he took bread, gave thanks, broke it and began to give it to them. ³¹Then their eyes were opened and they recognized him, and he disappeared from their sight. ³²They asked each other, "Were not our hearts burning within us while he talked with us on the road and opened the Scriptures to us?"

[MONDAY]

LUKE 24:13–32

The Fellowship of the Burning Heart

24:32 "WERE NOT OUR HEARTS BURNING WITHIN US WHILE HE TALKED WITH US ON THE ROAD AND OPENED THE SCRIPTURES TO US?"

We all need a companion, a guide, when we read the Bible. These two disciples had a companion on their way to the village of Emmaus on resurrection Sunday. They were confused about a lot of things. Then Jesus came along and explained the Scriptures to them, and their lives made sense again. He demonstrated how he was both the subject of the whole Bible and its authoritative interpreter. "Beginning with Moses and all the Prophets, he explained to them what was said in all the Scriptures concerning himself" (verse 27). When he finished, they looked at each other and exclaimed, "Were not our hearts burning within us while he talked with us on the road and opened the Scriptures to us?" (verse 32).

Nothing could be better than a personal Bible study with Jesus! What would it be like to have Jesus himself at your side whenever you read the Bible, explaining its meaning as you read it? He promised something like that when he promised the gift of his Holy Spirit, whom he appropriately called the Counselor. "But the Counselor, the Holy Spirit, whom the Father will send in my name, will teach you all things and will remind you of everything I have said to you" (John 14:26). Just as Christ revealed Scripture to these two disciples, his Spirit reveals its truth to us. This doesn't guarantee theological precision to a prayerful reader or make every Christian an infallible interpreter of the Bible. But it does assure us that God will reveal its truth to us if we ask him to. He never disappoints those who earnestly seek him the way Jesus said to pray: asking, seeking and knocking—continually (Luke 11:9–10; Hebrews 11:6).

The Bible has been called God's love letter to us. But it's even better than that because the Lover himself breathed into the Book (see 2 Timothy 3:16). Happy are those whose hearts burn within them as they find, through the Bible, not only God's expression, but also his very presence.

PRAY:

"Open my eyes that I may see wonderful things in your law" (Psalm 119:18).

FOR YOUR NEXT DEVOTIONAL READING, GO TO PAGE 1276.

> *Prayer is the spirit speaking truth to Truth.*
>
> PHILIP JAMES BAILEY

³³They got up and returned at once to Jerusalem. There they found the Eleven and those with them, assembled together ³⁴and saying, "It is true! The Lord has risen and has appeared to Simon." ³⁵Then the two told what had happened on the way, and how Jesus was recognized by them when he broke the bread.

Jesus Appears to the Disciples

³⁶While they were still talking about this, Jesus himself stood among them and said to them, "Peace be with you."

³⁷They were startled and frightened, thinking they saw a ghost. ³⁸He said to them, "Why are you troubled, and why do doubts rise in your minds? ³⁹Look at my hands and my feet. It is I myself! Touch me and see; a ghost does not have flesh and bones, as you see I have."

⁴⁰When he had said this, he showed them his hands and feet. ⁴¹And while they still did not believe it because of joy and amazement, he asked them, "Do you have anything here to eat?" ⁴²They gave him a piece of broiled fish, ⁴³and he took it and ate it in their presence.

⁴⁴He said to them, "This is what I told you while I was still with you: Everything must be fulfilled that is written about me in the Law of Moses, the Prophets and the Psalms."

⁴⁵Then he opened their minds so they could understand the Scriptures. ⁴⁶He told them, "This is what is written: The Christ will suffer and rise from the dead on the third day, ⁴⁷and repentance and forgiveness of sins will be preached in his name to all nations, beginning at Jerusalem. ⁴⁸You are witnesses of these things. ⁴⁹I am going to send you what my Father has promised; but stay in the city until you have been clothed with power from on high."

The Ascension

⁵⁰When he had led them out to the vicinity of Bethany, he lifted up his hands and blessed them. ⁵¹While he was blessing them, he left them and was taken up into heaven. ⁵²Then they worshiped him and returned to Jerusalem with great joy. ⁵³And they stayed continually at the temple, praising God.

> *AND they stayed continually at the temple, praising God.*
>
> LUKE 24:53

John

WILLIAM BARCLAY[1] thought each of the four Gospels could be symbolized by one of the four marvelous and mysterious creatures that surround the throne of God in the book of Revelation (see Revelation 4:7). Stained glass windows in many churches follow the same idea. The *man* stands for Mark because his is the most human of the Gospels. The *lion* stands for Matthew because his Gospel shows Jesus as the Messiah, the Lion of the tribe of Judah. The *ox* stands for Luke because Luke shows Jesus, like the ox, to be the universal sacrifice and servant of humankind. The *eagle* stands for John because it was believed that the eagle is the only creature that can look directly into the sun and not be blinded. John's Gospel is like the eagle because it looks deep into the heart of Jesus and leaves the reader illuminated, but not blinded. For this reason it has been called the intimate Gospel.[2] Even John's own self-description is "the disciple whom Jesus loved," who reclined at the table beside Jesus at the place of intimacy (see 13:23; 19:26).

"I WILL DO WHAT-
EVER YOU ASK IN
MY NAME, SO THAT
THE SON MAY
BRING GLORY TO
THE FATHER." (14:13)

There is no better picture of the purpose and pleasure of prayer than this: communion with the Savior, seeking his face as we would a friend's (see Exodus 33:11; 2 Corinthians 3:18). The book of John is the product of a lifetime of unity and reflection on Jesus, recording fewer events than the other three Gospels, but giving much more commentary on what Jesus thought, felt and said about them. In this sense, the very content of this Gospel is like prayer.

Perhaps John's greatest contribution to the life of prayer is what he records Jesus saying about the tender and loving relationship of the Father and the Son (see 5:19–20). Jesus regularly spoke of God as "my Father," and he tells us to address God as "our Father" (Matthew 6:9; see John 20:17). What Jesus is "naturally" by birth, we may become by new birth through faith in him (see John 1:12–13; 3:3–8). The result is that we share in the rights and blessings of the Father's Son when we become his Father's children.

Because of our status as God's children, we have great confidence and expectation in prayer. Jesus prayed that we would actually enter into the same fellowship of love he has with God (see 17:20–21,23). To pray from such a privileged position of love and inclusion—to actually be part of the Father and the Son—is to be sure that whatever we ask in the Son's name will be given us (see 14:13–14; 16:24). To believe this is to breathe the atmosphere of prayer.

The Word Became Flesh

1 In the beginning was the Word, and the Word was with God, and the Word was God. [2]He was with God in the beginning.

[3]Through him all things were made; without him nothing was made that has been made. [4]In him was life, and that life was the light of men. [5]The light shines in the darkness, but the darkness has not understood[a] it.

[6]There came a man who was sent from God; his name was John. [7]He came as a witness to testify concerning that light, so that through him all men might believe. [8]He himself was not the light; he came only as a witness to the light. [9]The true light that gives light to every man was coming into the world.[b]

[10]He was in the world, and though the world was made through him, the world did not recognize him. [11]He came to that which was his own, but his own did not receive him. [12]Yet to all who received him, to those who believed in his name, he gave the right to become children of God— [13]children born not of natural descent,[c] nor of human decision or a husband's will, but born of God.

[14]The Word became flesh and made his dwelling among us. We have seen his glory, the glory of the One and Only,[d] who came from the Father, full of grace and truth.

[15]John testifies concerning him. He cries out, saying, "This was he of whom I said, 'He who comes after me has surpassed me because he was before me.'" [16]From the fullness of his grace we have all received one blessing after another. [17]For the law was given through Moses; grace and truth came through Jesus Christ. [18]No one has ever seen God, but God the One and Only,[e,f] who is at the Father's side, has made him known.

John the Baptist Denies Being the Christ

[19]Now this was John's testimony when the Jews of Jerusalem sent priests and Levites to ask him who he was. [20]He did not fail to confess, but confessed freely, "I am not the Christ.[g]"

[21]They asked him, "Then who are you? Are you Elijah?"

He said, "I am not."

"Are you the Prophet?"

He answered, "No."

[22]Finally they said, "Who are you? Give us an answer to take back to those who sent us. What do you say about yourself?"

[23]John replied in the words of Isaiah the prophet, "I am the voice of one calling in the desert, 'Make straight the way for the Lord.'"[h]

[24]Now some Pharisees who had been sent [25]questioned him, "Why then do you baptize if you are not the Christ, nor Elijah, nor the Prophet?"

[26]"I baptize with[i] water," John replied, "but among you stands one you do not know. [27]He is the one who comes after me, the thongs of whose sandals I am not worthy to untie."

[28]This all happened at Bethany on the other side of the Jordan, where John was baptizing.

Jesus the Lamb of God

[29]The next day John saw Jesus coming toward him and said, "Look, the Lamb of God, who takes away the sin of the world! [30]This is the one I meant when I said, 'A man who comes after me has surpassed me because he was before me.' [31]I myself did not know him, but the reason I came baptizing with water was that he might be revealed to Israel."

[32]Then John gave this testimony: "I saw the Spirit come down from heaven as a dove and remain on him. [33]I would not have known him, except that the one who sent me to baptize with water told me, 'The man on whom you see the Spirit come down and remain is he who will baptize with the Holy Spirit.' [34]I have seen and I testify that this is the Son of God."

Jesus' First Disciples

[35]The next day John was there again with two of his disciples. [36]When he saw

---

[a]5 Or darkness, and the darkness has not overcome   [b]9 Or This was the true light that gives light to every man who comes into the world   [c]13 Greek of bloods   [d]14 Or the Only Begotten   [e]18 Or the Only Begotten   [f]18 Some manuscripts but the only (or only begotten) Son   [g]20 Or Messiah. "The Christ" (Greek) and "the Messiah" (Hebrew) both mean "the Anointed One"; also in verse 25.   [h]23 Isaiah 40:3   [i]26 Or in; also in verses 31 and 33

Jesus passing by, he said, "Look, the Lamb of God!"

[37]When the two disciples heard him say this, they followed Jesus. [38]Turning around, Jesus saw them following and asked, "What do you want?"

They said, "Rabbi" (which means Teacher), "where are you staying?"

[39]"Come," he replied, "and you will see."

So they went and saw where he was staying, and spent that day with him. It was about the tenth hour.

[40]Andrew, Simon Peter's brother, was one of the two who heard what John had said and who had followed Jesus. [41]The

---

[TUESDAY]

JOHN 1:10–13

It's All in the Family

1:13 BORN OF GOD.

Jesus taught his disciples to start their prayers with "Our Father" (Matthew 6:9). What a wonderful place to begin! To pray to the true and living God is not to address a vague and distant deity but to speak as a child to one's Father.

But wait—how can any mere human presume to be called a child of God? There are some sentimental—and blasphemous—views of God that try to reduce him a bit, to make him more like us and make us all his children. But the God that John speaks of is the Holy One of Israel, whom no one can see and live (see John 1:18; Exodus 33:20), and who lives in unapproachable light (see 1 Timothy 6:16). A miracle must take place, a gracious gift must be given to our humanity, for any of us to speak to God as Father. The miracle and the gift are spoken of in these stunning words: "Yet to all who received him, to those who believed in his name, he gave the right to become children of God—children born not of natural descent, nor of human decision or a husband's will, but born of God" (John 1:12–13).

We may become God's children, not by natural birth, but by new birth; or to use one of Paul's concepts, by the miracle of adoption. This is God's gift to us in Christ, to be received by faith—not achieved by human effort but received by simply trusting in his promise that all who believe will receive the gift and the miracle.

How should we then pray? Start with the most sublime of all relationships. Say "Father." Or if you have never asked God to become your Father through faith in Christ, start there. Ask him; trust him; receive the gift and miracle of new birth. Then say "Father." Say it over and over again, and let it sink into the depths of your soul and thrill you with its possibilities. St. Teresa of Avila said she found it difficult when she prayed to get past the word "Father." It was to her like a beautiful land that she wanted to live in forever. She *will* live there forever, you know, and so will we.

PRAY:

"Our Father, who art in heaven—In whom we live, and move, and have our being; grant that I and all Christians may live worthy of this glorious relation, and that we may not sin, knowing that we are accounted as yours. We are yours by adoption; make us yours by choice of our will."[3]

FOR YOUR NEXT DEVOTIONAL READING, GO TO PAGE 1281.

first thing Andrew did was to find his brother Simon and tell him, "We have found the Messiah" (that is, the Christ). [42]And he brought him to Jesus.

Jesus looked at him and said, "You are Simon son of John. You will be called Cephas" (which, when translated, is Peter[a]).

Jesus Calls Philip and Nathanael

[43]The next day Jesus decided to leave for Galilee. Finding Philip, he said to him, "Follow me."

[44]Philip, like Andrew and Peter, was from the town of Bethsaida. [45]Philip found Nathanael and told him, "We have found the one Moses wrote about in the Law, and about whom the prophets also wrote—Jesus of Nazareth, the son of Joseph."

[46]"Nazareth! Can anything good come from there?" Nathanael asked.

"Come and see," said Philip.

[47]When Jesus saw Nathanael approaching, he said of him, "Here is a true Israelite, in whom there is nothing false."

[48]"How do you know me?" Nathanael asked.

Jesus answered, "I saw you while you were still under the fig tree before Philip called you."

[49]Then Nathanael declared, "Rabbi, you are the Son of God; you are the King of Israel."

[50]Jesus said, "You believe[b] because I told you I saw you under the fig tree. You shall see greater things than that." [51]He then added, "I tell you[c] the truth, you[c] shall see heaven open, and the angels of God ascending and descending on the Son of Man."

Jesus Changes Water to Wine

2 On the third day a wedding took place at Cana in Galilee. Jesus' mother was there, [2]and Jesus and his disciples had also been invited to the wedding. [3]When the wine was gone, Jesus' mother said to him, "They have no more wine."

[4]"Dear woman, why do you involve me?" Jesus replied. "My time has not yet come."

[5]His mother said to the servants, "Do whatever he tells you."

[6]Nearby stood six stone water jars, the kind used by the Jews for ceremonial washing, each holding from twenty to thirty gallons.[d]

[7]Jesus said to the servants, "Fill the jars with water"; so they filled them to the brim.

[8]Then he told them, "Now draw some out and take it to the master of the banquet."

They did so, [9]and the master of the banquet tasted the water that had been turned into wine. He did not realize where it had come from, though the servants who had drawn the water knew. Then he called the bridegroom aside [10]and said, "Everyone brings out the choice wine first and then the cheaper wine after the guests have had too much to drink; but you have saved the best till now."

[11]This, the first of his miraculous signs, Jesus performed at Cana in Galilee. He thus revealed his glory, and his disciples put their faith in him.

Jesus Clears the Temple

[12]After this he went down to Capernaum with his mother and brothers and his disciples. There they stayed for a few days.

[13]When it was almost time for the Jewish Passover, Jesus went up to Jerusalem. [14]In the temple courts he found men selling cattle, sheep and doves, and others sitting at tables exchanging money. [15]So he made a whip out of cords, and drove all from the temple area, both sheep and cattle; he scattered the coins of the money changers and overturned their tables. [16]To those who sold doves he said, "Get these out of here! How dare you turn my Father's house into a market!"

[17]His disciples remembered that it is written: "Zeal for your house will consume me."[e]

[18]Then the Jews demanded of him, "What miraculous sign can you show us to prove your authority to do all this?"

[19]Jesus answered them, "Destroy this temple, and I will raise it again in three days."

---

[a]42 Both Cephas (Aramaic) and Peter (Greek) mean rock.   [b]50 Or Do you believe...?
[c]51 The Greek is plural.   [d]6 Greek two to three metretes (probably about 75 to 115 liters)
[e]17 Psalm 69:9

20The Jews replied, "It has taken forty-six years to build this temple, and you are going to raise it in three days?" 21But the temple he had spoken of was his body. 22After he was raised from the dead, his disciples recalled what he had said. Then they believed the Scripture and the words that Jesus had spoken.

23Now while he was in Jerusalem at the Passover Feast, many people saw the miraculous signs he was doing and believed in his name.*a* 24But Jesus would not entrust himself to them, for he knew all men. 25He did not need man's testimony about man, for he knew what was in a man.

Jesus Teaches Nicodemus

3 Now there was a man of the Pharisees named Nicodemus, a member of the Jewish ruling council. 2He came to Jesus at night and said, "Rabbi, we know you are a teacher who has come from God. For no one could perform the miraculous signs you are doing if God were not with him."

> *The man who says his evening prayer is a captain posting sentinels. He can sleep.*
>
> CHARLES BAUDELAIRE

3In reply Jesus declared, "I tell you the truth, no one can see the kingdom of God unless he is born again.*b*"

4"How can a man be born when he is old?" Nicodemus asked. "Surely he cannot enter a second time into his mother's womb to be born!"

5Jesus answered, "I tell you the truth, no one can enter the kingdom of God unless he is born of water and the Spirit. 6Flesh gives birth to flesh, but the Spirit*c* gives birth to spirit. 7You should not be surprised at my saying, 'You*d* must be born again.' 8The wind blows wherever it pleases. You hear its sound, but you cannot tell where it comes from or where it is going. So it is with everyone born of the Spirit."

9"How can this be?" Nicodemus asked.

10"You are Israel's teacher," said Jesus, "and do you not understand these things? 11I tell you the truth, we speak of what we know, and we testify to what we have seen, but still you people do not accept our testimony. 12I have spoken to you of earthly things and you do not believe; how then will you believe if I speak of heavenly things? 13No one has ever gone into heaven except the one who came from heaven—the Son of Man.*e* 14Just as Moses lifted up the snake in the desert, so the Son of Man must be lifted up, 15that everyone who believes in him may have eternal life.*f*

16"For God so loved the world that he gave his one and only Son,*g* that whoever believes in him shall not perish but have eternal life. 17For God did not send his Son into the world to condemn the world, but to save the world through him. 18Whoever believes in him is not condemned, but whoever does not believe stands condemned already because he has not believed in the name of God's one and only Son.*h* 19This is the verdict: Light has come into the world, but men loved darkness instead of light because their deeds were evil. 20Everyone who does evil hates the light, and will not come into the light for fear that his deeds will be exposed. 21But whoever lives by the truth comes into the light, so that it may be seen plainly that what he has done has been done through God."*i*

John the Baptist's Testimony About Jesus

22After this, Jesus and his disciples went out into the Judean countryside, where he spent some time with them, and baptized. 23Now John also was baptizing at Aenon near Salim, because there was plenty of water, and people were constantly coming to be baptized. 24(This was before John was put in prison.) 25An argument developed between some of John's disciples and a certain Jew*j* over the matter of ceremonial washing. 26They came to John and said to him, "Rabbi, that man who was with you on the other side of the Jordan—the one

---

*a*23 Or *and believed in him*   *b*3 Or *born from above*; also in verse 7   *c*6 Or *but spirit*
*d*7 The Greek is plural.   *e*13 Some manuscripts *Man, who is in heaven*   *f*15 Or *believes may have eternal life in him*   *g*16 Or *his only begotten Son*   *h*18 Or *God's only begotten Son*
*i*21 Some interpreters end the quotation after verse 15.   *j*25 Some manuscripts *and certain Jews*

you testified about—well, he is baptizing, and everyone is going to him."

²⁷To this John replied, "A man can receive only what is given him from heaven. ²⁸You yourselves can testify that I said, 'I am not the Christ[a] but am sent ahead of him.' ²⁹The bride belongs to the bridegroom. The friend who attends the bridegroom waits and listens for him, and is full of joy when he hears the bridegroom's voice. That joy is mine, and it is now complete. ³⁰He must become greater; I must become less.

³¹"The one who comes from above is above all; the one who is from the earth belongs to the earth, and speaks as one from the earth. The one who comes from heaven is above all. ³²He testifies to what he has seen and heard, but no one accepts his testimony. ³³The man who has accepted it has certified that God is truthful. ³⁴For the one whom God has sent speaks the words of God, for God[b] gives the Spirit without limit. ³⁵The Father loves the Son and has placed everything in his hands. ³⁶Whoever believes in the Son has eternal life, but whoever rejects the Son will not see life, for God's wrath remains on him."[c]

Jesus Talks With a Samaritan Woman

4 The Pharisees heard that Jesus was gaining and baptizing more disciples than John, ²although in fact it was not Jesus who baptized, but his disciples. ³When the Lord learned of this, he left Judea and went back once more to Galilee. ⁴Now he had to go through Samaria. ⁵So he came to a town in Samaria called Sychar, near the plot of ground Jacob had given to his son Joseph. ⁶Jacob's well was there, and Jesus, tired as he was from the journey, sat down by the well. It was about the sixth hour.

⁷When a Samaritan woman came to draw water, Jesus said to her, "Will you give me a drink?" ⁸(His disciples had gone into the town to buy food.)

⁹The Samaritan woman said to him, "You are a Jew and I am a Samaritan woman. How can you ask me for a drink?" (For Jews do not associate with Samaritans.[d])

¹⁰Jesus answered her, "If you knew the gift of God and who it is that asks you for

> JESUS answered her, "If you knew the gift of God and who it is that asks you for a drink, you would have asked him and he would have given you living water."
>
> JOHN 4:10

a drink, you would have asked him and he would have given you living water."

¹¹"Sir," the woman said, "you have nothing to draw with and the well is deep. Where can you get this living water? ¹²Are you greater than our father Jacob, who gave us the well and drank from it himself, as did also his sons and his flocks and herds?"

¹³Jesus answered, "Everyone who drinks this water will be thirsty again, ¹⁴but whoever drinks the water I give him will never thirst. Indeed, the water I give him will become in him a spring of water welling up to eternal life."

¹⁵The woman said to him, "Sir, give me this water so that I won't get thirsty and have to keep coming here to draw water."

¹⁶He told her, "Go, call your husband and come back."

¹⁷"I have no husband," she replied.

Jesus said to her, "You are right when you say you have no husband. ¹⁸The fact is, you have had five husbands, and the man you now have is not your husband. What you have just said is quite true."

¹⁹"Sir," the woman said, "I can see that you are a prophet. ²⁰Our fathers worshiped on this mountain, but you Jews claim that the place where we must worship is in Jerusalem."

²¹Jesus declared, "Believe me, woman, a time is coming when you will worship the Father neither on this mountain nor in Jerusalem. ²²You Samaritans worship what you do not know; we worship what we do know, for salvation is from the Jews. ²³Yet a time is coming and has now come when the true worshipers will worship the Father in spirit and truth, for they are the kind of worshipers the Father seeks. ²⁴God is spirit, and his worshipers must worship in spirit and in truth."

a28 Or Messiah   b34 Greek he   c36 Some interpreters end the quotation after verse 30.
d9 Or do not use dishes Samaritans have used

25The woman said, "I know that Messiah" (called Christ) "is coming. When he comes, he will explain everything to us." 26Then Jesus declared, "I who speak to you am he."

The Disciples Rejoin Jesus

27Just then his disciples returned and were surprised to find him talking with a woman. But no one asked, "What do you want?" or "Why are you talking with her?" 28Then, leaving her water jar, the woman went back to the town and said to the people, 29"Come, see a man who told me everything I ever did. Could this be the Christ*a*?" 30They came out of the town and made their way toward him.

31Meanwhile his disciples urged him, "Rabbi, eat something."

32But he said to them, "I have food to eat that you know nothing about."

33Then his disciples said to each other, "Could someone have brought him food?"

34"My food," said Jesus, "is to do the will of him who sent me and to finish his work. 35Do you not say, 'Four months more and then the harvest'? I tell you, open your eyes and look at the fields! They are ripe for harvest. 36Even now the reaper draws his wages, even now he harvests the crop for eternal life, so that the sower and the reaper may be glad together. 37Thus the saying 'One sows and another reaps' is true. 38I sent you to reap what you have not worked for. Others have done the hard work, and you have reaped the benefits of their labor."

Many Samaritans Believe

39Many of the Samaritans from that town believed in him because of the woman's testimony, "He told me everything I ever did." 40So when the Samaritans came to him, they urged him to stay with them, and he stayed two days. 41And because of his words many more became believers.

42They said to the woman, "We no longer believe just because of what you said; now we have heard for ourselves, and we know that this man really is the Savior of the world."

Jesus Heals the Official's Son

43After the two days he left for Galilee. 44(Now Jesus himself had pointed out that a prophet has no honor in his own country.) 45When he arrived in Galilee, the Galileans welcomed him. They had seen all that he had done in Jerusalem at the Passover Feast, for they also had been there.

46Once more he visited Cana in Galilee, where he had turned the water into wine. And there was a certain royal official whose son lay sick at Capernaum. 47When this man heard that Jesus had arrived in Galilee from Judea, he went to him and begged him to come and heal his son, who was close to death.

48"Unless you people see miraculous signs and wonders," Jesus told him, "you will never believe."

49The royal official said, "Sir, come down before my child dies."

50Jesus replied, "You may go. Your son will live."

The man took Jesus at his word and departed. 51While he was still on the way, his servants met him with the news that his boy was living. 52When he inquired as to the time when his son got better, they said to him, "The fever left him yesterday at the seventh hour."

53Then the father realized that this was the exact time at which Jesus had said to him, "Your son will live." So he and all his household believed.

54This was the second miraculous sign that Jesus performed, having come from Judea to Galilee.

The Healing at the Pool

5 Some time later, Jesus went up to Jerusalem for a feast of the Jews. 2Now there is in Jerusalem near the Sheep Gate a pool, which in Aramaic is called Bethesda*b* and which is surrounded by five covered colonnades. 3Here a great number of disabled people used to lie—the blind, the lame, the paralyzed.*c* 5One who was there had been an invalid for thirty-eight years. 6When Jesus saw him lying there and learned that he had been in

a29 Or *Messiah*   *b2* Some manuscripts *Bethzatha*; other manuscripts *Bethsaida*
c3 Some less important manuscripts *paralyzed—and they waited for the moving of the waters.* *4From time to time an angel of the Lord would come down and stir up the waters. The first one into the pool after each such disturbance would be cured of whatever disease he had.*

Praying When Jesus Perplexes

4:47 HE WENT TO HIM AND BEGGED HIM TO COME AND HEAL HIS SON, WHO WAS CLOSE TO DEATH.

This is Jesus' second miraculous sign as recorded in John's Gospel. The first happened in the same town in Galilee, Cana, and involved the rescue of a wedding party. The wine had run out, and Jesus provided more wine—over 120 gallons more—and better wine than they had before (see John 2:1–11). The second sign, involves the healing of an official's son.

Both signs in Cana were homey and personal, sharp contrasts with Jesus' massive acts of mercy, such as miraculously feeding the crowds. With these signs, only a limited number of people were involved, and if these miracles were all Jesus ever did, they may have been all but forgotten within a couple of generations—like the people they touched. That fact alone is blessing enough for those who pray. Most of us are average citizens, of no significance in the world's grand schemes. Yet the Father hears our prayers. Our weddings and children, hopes and dreams, lives and deaths may be negligible in the world's eyes, but not in our Father's.

As small as we are, it is our Father's good pleasure to teach us great lessons about prayer (see Luke 10:21). There are two lessons to be learned here. The first is about our credentials. What do we possess that we can bring to Jesus to recommend ourselves and our need to him? Our need is our only credential. In the story of the official's son, the boy's father begs; he doesn't demand (see John 4:47). It's not that he thinks Jesus wants him to grovel; it's that he knows Jesus is all he has. He is poor in spirit, a blessed and basic condition for prayer (see Matthew 5:3). If Jesus doesn't hear and act, the man's son will die. The only credential we need to bring to Jesus in prayer is our need.

The second great lesson about prayer here is that Jesus often responds to our prayers in ways we find perplexing, even discouraging. Jesus initially responds to the father with a rebuke, though his remark is probably directed more to the Galileans, in general, who are listening: "Unless you people see miraculous signs and wonders, you will never believe" (verse 48). Then he refuses the father's request for him to come to his son's bedside (see verses 49–50). But what Jesus does, he does out of his great wisdom and love. The rebuke focuses the father's faith on higher things than even his son's recovery. The refusal shows Jesus to be even more powerful than the man thought; Jesus doesn't need to be physically present to be powerfully present. Through it all, the father clings tenaciously and tremblingly to Jesus, despite what he doesn't understand. In the end his faith is rewarded and strengthened.

PRAY:

Other refuge have I none; hangs my helpless soul on Thee; leave, ah! leave me not alone, still support and comfort me. All my trust on Thee is stayed, all my help from Thee I bring; cover my defenseless head with the shadow of Thy wing. CHARLES WESLEY

FOR YOUR NEXT DEVOTIONAL READING, GO TO PAGE 1285.

this condition for a long time, he asked him, "Do you want to get well?"

⁷"Sir," the invalid replied, "I have no one to help me into the pool when the water is stirred. While I am trying to get in, someone else goes down ahead of me."

⁸Then Jesus said to him, "Get up! Pick up your mat and walk." ⁹At once the man was cured; he picked up his mat and walked.

The day on which this took place was a Sabbath, ¹⁰and so the Jews said to the man who had been healed, "It is the Sabbath; the law forbids you to carry your mat."

¹¹But he replied, "The man who made me well said to me, 'Pick up your mat and walk.'"

¹²So they asked him, "Who is this fellow who told you to pick it up and walk?"

¹³The man who was healed had no idea who it was, for Jesus had slipped away into the crowd that was there.

¹⁴Later Jesus found him at the temple and said to him, "See, you are well again. Stop sinning or something worse may happen to you." ¹⁵The man went away and told the Jews that it was Jesus who had made him well.

> ❝ Faith is putting all your eggs in God's basket, then counting your blessings before they hatch. ❞
>
> RAMONA C. CARROLL

Life Through the Son

¹⁶So, because Jesus was doing these things on the Sabbath, the Jews persecuted him. ¹⁷Jesus said to them, "My Father is always at his work to this very day, and I, too, am working." ¹⁸For this reason the Jews tried all the harder to kill him; not only was he breaking the Sabbath, but he was even calling God his own Father, making himself equal with God.

¹⁹Jesus gave them this answer: "I tell you the truth, the Son can do nothing by himself; he can do only what he sees his Father doing, because whatever the Father does the Son also does. ²⁰For the Father loves the Son and shows him all he does. Yes, to your amazement he will show him even greater things than these.

²¹For just as the Father raises the dead and gives them life, even so the Son gives life to whom he is pleased to give it. ²²Moreover, the Father judges no one, but has entrusted all judgment to the Son, ²³that all may honor the Son just as they honor the Father. He who does not honor the Son does not honor the Father, who sent him.

²⁴"I tell you the truth, whoever hears my word and believes him who sent me has eternal life and will not be condemned; he has crossed over from death to life. ²⁵I tell you the truth, a time is coming and has now come when the dead will hear the voice of the Son of God and those who hear will live. ²⁶For as the Father has life in himself, so he has granted the Son to have life in himself. ²⁷And he has given him authority to judge because he is the Son of Man.

²⁸"Do not be amazed at this, for a time is coming when all who are in their graves will hear his voice ²⁹and come out—those who have done good will rise to live, and those who have done evil will rise to be condemned. ³⁰By myself I can do nothing; I judge only as I hear, and my judgment is just, for I seek not to please myself but him who sent me.

Testimonies About Jesus

³¹"If I testify about myself, my testimony is not valid. ³²There is another who testifies in my favor, and I know that his testimony about me is valid.

³³"You have sent to John and he has testified to the truth. ³⁴Not that I accept human testimony; but I mention it that you may be saved. ³⁵John was a lamp that burned and gave light, and you chose for a time to enjoy his light.

³⁶"I have testimony weightier than that of John. For the very work that the Father has given me to finish, and which I am doing, testifies that the Father has sent me. ³⁷And the Father who sent me has himself testified concerning me. You have never heard his voice nor seen his form, ³⁸nor does his word dwell in you, for you do not believe the one he sent. ³⁹You diligently study[a] the Scriptures because you think that by them you possess

---

a39 Or *Study diligently* (the imperative)

eternal life. These are the Scriptures that testify about me, 40yet you refuse to come to me to have life.

41"I do not accept praise from men, 42but I know you. I know that you do not have the love of God in your hearts. 43I have come in my Father's name, and you do not accept me; but if someone else comes in his own name, you will accept him. 44How can you believe if you accept praise from one another, yet make no effort to obtain the praise that comes from the only God*a*?

45"But do not think I will accuse you before the Father. Your accuser is Moses, on whom your hopes are set. 46If you believed Moses, you would believe me, for he wrote about me. 47But since you do not believe what he wrote, how are you going to believe what I say?"

Jesus Feeds the Five Thousand

6 Some time after this, Jesus crossed to the far shore of the Sea of Galilee (that is, the Sea of Tiberias), 2and a great crowd of people followed him because they saw the miraculous signs he had performed on the sick. 3Then Jesus went up on a mountainside and sat down with his disciples. 4The Jewish Passover Feast was near.

5When Jesus looked up and saw a great crowd coming toward him, he said to Philip, "Where shall we buy bread for these people to eat?" 6He asked this only to test him, for he already had in mind what he was going to do.

7Philip answered him, "Eight months' wages*b* would not buy enough bread for each one to have a bite!"

8Another of his disciples, Andrew, Simon Peter's brother, spoke up, 9"Here is a boy with five small barley loaves and two small fish, but how far will they go among so many?"

10Jesus said, "Have the people sit down." There was plenty of grass in that place, and the men sat down, about five thousand of them. 11Jesus then took the loaves, gave thanks, and distributed to those who were seated as much as they wanted. He did the same with the fish.

12When they had all had enough to eat, he said to his disciples, "Gather the pieces that are left over. Let nothing be wast-

ed." 13So they gathered them and filled twelve baskets with the pieces of the five barley loaves left over by those who had eaten.

14After the people saw the miraculous sign that Jesus did, they began to say, "Surely this is the Prophet who is to come into the world." 15Jesus, knowing that they intended to come and make him king by force, withdrew again to a mountain by himself.

Jesus Walks on the Water

16When evening came, his disciples went down to the lake, 17where they got into a boat and set off across the lake for Capernaum. By now it was dark, and Jesus had not yet joined them. 18A strong wind was blowing and the waters grew rough. 19When they had rowed three or three and a half miles,*c* they saw Jesus approaching the boat, walking on the water; and they were terrified. 20But he said to them, "It is I; don't be afraid." 21Then they were willing to take him into the boat, and immediately the boat reached the shore where they were heading.

22The next day the crowd that had stayed on the opposite shore of the lake realized that only one boat had been there, and that Jesus had not entered it with his disciples, but that they had gone away alone. 23Then some boats from Tiberias landed near the place where the people had eaten the bread after the Lord had given thanks. 24Once the crowd realized that neither Jesus nor his disciples were there, they got into the boats and went to Capernaum in search of Jesus.

Jesus the Bread of Life

25When they found him on the other side of the lake, they asked him, "Rabbi, when did you get here?"

26Jesus answered, "I tell you the truth, you are looking for me, not because you saw miraculous signs but because you ate the loaves and had your fill. 27Do not work for food that spoils, but for food that endures to eternal life, which the

a44 Some early manuscripts *the Only One*
b7 Greek *two hundred denarii*   *c19* Greek *rowed twenty-five or thirty stadia* (about 5 or 6 kilometers)

Son of Man will give you. On him God the Father has placed his seal of approval."

²⁸Then they asked him, "What must we do to do the works God requires?"

²⁹Jesus answered, "The work of God is this: to believe in the one he has sent."

³⁰So they asked him, "What miraculous sign then will you give that we may see it and believe you? What will you do? ³¹Our forefathers ate the manna in the desert; as it is written: 'He gave them bread from heaven to eat.'^a"

³²Jesus said to them, "I tell you the truth, it is not Moses who has given you the bread from heaven, but it is my Father who gives you the true bread from heaven. ³³For the bread of God is he who comes down from heaven and gives life to the world."

³⁴"Sir," they said, "from now on give us this bread."

³⁵Then Jesus declared, "I am the bread of life. He who comes to me will never go hungry, and he who believes in me will never be thirsty. ³⁶But as I told you, you have seen me and still you do not believe. ³⁷All that the Father gives me will come to me, and whoever comes to me I will never drive away. ³⁸For I have come down from heaven not to do my will but to do the will of him who sent me. ³⁹And this is the will of him who sent me, that I shall lose none of all that he has given me, but raise them up at the last day. ⁴⁰For my Father's will is that everyone who looks to the Son and believes in him shall have eternal life, and I will raise him up at the last day."

⁴¹At this the Jews began to grumble about him because he said, "I am the bread that came down from heaven." ⁴²They said, "Is this not Jesus, the son of Joseph, whose father and mother we know? How can he now say, 'I came down from heaven'?"

⁴³"Stop grumbling among yourselves," Jesus answered. ⁴⁴"No one can come to me unless the Father who sent me draws him, and I will raise him up at the last day. ⁴⁵It is written in the Prophets: 'They will all be taught by God.'^b Everyone who listens to the Father and learns from him comes to me. ⁴⁶No one has seen the Father except the one who is from God; only he has seen the Father. ⁴⁷I tell you

the truth, he who believes has everlasting life. ⁴⁸I am the bread of life. ⁴⁹Your forefathers ate the manna in the desert, yet they died. ⁵⁰But here is the bread that comes down from heaven, which a man may eat and not die. ⁵¹I am the living bread that came down from heaven. If anyone eats of this bread, he will live forever. This bread is my flesh, which I will give for the life of the world."

⁵²Then the Jews began to argue sharply among themselves, "How can this man give us his flesh to eat?"

⁵³Jesus said to them, "I tell you the truth, unless you eat the flesh of the Son of Man and drink his blood, you have no life in you. ⁵⁴Whoever eats my flesh and drinks my blood has eternal life, and I will raise him up at the last day. ⁵⁵For my flesh is real food and my blood is real drink. ⁵⁶Whoever eats my flesh and drinks my blood remains in me, and I in him. ⁵⁷Just as the living Father sent me and I live because of the Father, so the one who feeds on me will live because of me. ⁵⁸This is the bread that came down from heaven. Your forefathers ate manna and died, but he who feeds on this bread will live forever." ⁵⁹He said this while teaching in the synagogue in Capernaum.

Many Disciples Desert Jesus

⁶⁰On hearing it, many of his disciples said, "This is a hard teaching. Who can accept it?"

⁶¹Aware that his disciples were grumbling about this, Jesus said to them, "Does this offend you? ⁶²What if you see the Son of Man ascend to where he was before! ⁶³The Spirit gives life; the flesh counts for nothing. The words I have spoken to you are spirit^c and they are life. ⁶⁴Yet there are some of you who do not believe." For Jesus had known from the beginning which of them did not believe and who would betray him. ⁶⁵He went on to say, "This is why I told you that no one can come to me unless the Father has enabled him."

⁶⁶From this time many of his disciples turned back and no longer followed him.

⁶⁷"You do not want to leave too, do you?" Jesus asked the Twelve.

^a31 Exodus 16:4; Neh. 9:15; Psalm 78:24,25
^b45 Isaiah 54:13   ^c63 Or Spirit

⁶⁸Simon Peter answered him, "Lord, to whom shall we go? You have the words of eternal life. ⁶⁹We believe and know that you are the Holy One of God."

⁷⁰Then Jesus replied, "Have I not chosen you, the Twelve? Yet one of you is a devil!" ⁷¹(He meant Judas, the son of Simon Iscariot, who, though one of the Twelve, was later to betray him.)

Jesus Goes to the Feast of Tabernacles

7 After this, Jesus went around in Galilee, purposely staying away from Judea because the Jews there were waiting to take his life. ²But when the Jewish Feast of Tabernacles was near, ³Jesus' brothers said to him, "You ought to leave here and go to Judea, so that your disciples may see the miracles you do. ⁴No

---

[THURSDAY]

JOHN 6:25–69

We Are More Than Our Bellies

6:35 "I AM THE BREAD OF LIFE."

The crowd prayed a good prayer, although they didn't realize they were voicing a prayer: "Sir, from now on give us this bread" (6:34). Who wouldn't make this kind of request? Jesus had just said that this "true bread from heaven . . . gives life to the world" (verses 32–33).

But the crowd prayed for far more than they knew. They were still thinking that what Jesus offered was some kind of super-bread, a new manna (see Numbers 11:7–9) that would cure forever an empty stomach. But the bread Jesus was offering was himself, and the satisfaction was eternal. "I am the bread of life. He who comes to me will never go hungry" (John 6:35). They were looking for less than they actually asked. That's usually the way it is with God and us. We ask for silver, said Luther, and God gives gold. And he pays us a great compliment as he does: He tells us we are more than our bellies and fleshly appetites. We were made for eternity, for God.

But sometimes the "more" God gives seems to us like less. In John 6, we see that many were deeply offended by Jesus' offer. Wasn't he just Joseph's boy, one of the locals? How can he make such an incredible offer (see verse 42)? You can see their eyes rolling as they speak. Then their offense turned to disgust: "How can this man give us his flesh to eat?" (verse 52). When all was said and done, Jesus' "hard teaching" (see verse 60) marked a mass defection of disciples: "From this time many of his disciples turned back and no longer followed him" (verse 66). Beware! Don't get so focused on what you ask of God that you no longer see God. The Giver is always better than the gift—infinitely better. In order to give you the very best, he may have to refuse you the merely good you ask for.

After his amazing offer of himself, Jesus found himself standing rejected, looking at a greatly diminished following and asking the Twelve, "You do not want to leave too, do you?" (verse 67). May Peter's answer be ours: "Lord, to whom shall we go? You have the words of eternal life. We believe and know that you are the Holy One of God" (verses 68–69).

PRAY:

Jesus, *"From the best bliss that life imparts,*
we turn unfilled to Thee again." BERNARD OF CLAIRVAUX

FOR YOUR NEXT DEVOTIONAL READING, GO TO PAGE 1287.

one who wants to become a public figure acts in secret. Since you are doing these things, show yourself to the world." ⁵For even his own brothers did not believe in him.

⁶Therefore Jesus told them, "The right time for me has not yet come; for you any time is right. ⁷The world cannot hate you, but it hates me because I testify that what it does is evil. ⁸You go to the Feast. I am not yet*ᵃ* going up to this Feast, because for me the right time has not yet come." ⁹Having said this, he stayed in Galilee.

¹⁰However, after his brothers had left for the Feast, he went also, not publicly, but in secret. ¹¹Now at the Feast the Jews were watching for him and asking, "Where is that man?"

¹²Among the crowds there was widespread whispering about him. Some said, "He is a good man."

Others replied, "No, he deceives the people." ¹³But no one would say anything publicly about him for fear of the Jews.

Jesus Teaches at the Feast

¹⁴Not until halfway through the Feast did Jesus go up to the temple courts and begin to teach. ¹⁵The Jews were amazed and asked, "How did this man get such learning without having studied?"

¹⁶Jesus answered, "My teaching is not my own. It comes from him who sent me. ¹⁷If anyone chooses to do God's will, he will find out whether my teaching comes from God or whether I speak on my own. ¹⁸He who speaks on his own does so to gain honor for himself, but he who works for the honor of the one who sent him is a man of truth; there is nothing false about him. ¹⁹Has not Moses given you the law? Yet not one of you keeps the law. Why are you trying to kill me?"

²⁰"You are demon-possessed," the crowd answered. "Who is trying to kill you?"

²¹Jesus said to them, "I did one miracle, and you are all astonished. ²²Yet, because Moses gave you circumcision (though actually it did not come from Moses, but from the patriarchs), you circumcise a child on the Sabbath. ²³Now if a child can be circumcised on the Sabbath so that the law of Moses may not be broken, why are you angry with me for healing the whole man on the Sabbath? ²⁴Stop judging by mere appearances, and make a right judgment."

Is Jesus the Christ?

²⁵At that point some of the people of Jerusalem began to ask, "Isn't this the man they are trying to kill? ²⁶Here he is, speaking publicly, and they are not saying a word to him. Have the authorities really concluded that he is the Christ*ᵇ*? ²⁷But we know where this man is from; when the Christ comes, no one will know where he is from."

²⁸Then Jesus, still teaching in the temple courts, cried out, "Yes, you know me, and you know where I am from. I am not here on my own, but he who sent me is true. You do not know him, ²⁹but I know him because I am from him and he sent me."

³⁰At this they tried to seize him, but no one laid a hand on him, because his time had not yet come. ³¹Still, many in the crowd put their faith in him. They said, "When the Christ comes, will he do more miraculous signs than this man?"

³²The Pharisees heard the crowd whispering such things about him. Then the chief priests and the Pharisees sent temple guards to arrest him.

³³Jesus said, "I am with you for only a short time, and then I go to the one who sent me. ³⁴You will look for me, but you will not find me; and where I am, you cannot come."

³⁵The Jews said to one another, "Where does this man intend to go that we cannot find him? Will he go where our people live scattered among the Greeks, and teach the Greeks? ³⁶What did he mean when he said, 'You will look for me, but you will not find me,' and 'Where I am, you cannot come'?"

³⁷On the last and greatest day of the Feast, Jesus stood and said in a loud voice, "If anyone is thirsty, let him come to me and drink. ³⁸Whoever believes in me, as*ᶜ* the Scripture has said, streams of living water will flow from within him." ³⁹By this he meant the Spirit, whom those

---

ᵃ8 Some early manuscripts do not have *yet.*
ᵇ26 Or *Messiah*; also in verses 27, 31, 41 and 42
ᶜ37,38 Or / *If anyone is thirsty, let him come to me. / And let him drink,* *³⁸who believes in me. / As*

who believed in him were later to receive. Up to that time the Spirit had not been given, since Jesus had not yet been glorified.

⁴⁰On hearing his words, some of the people said, "Surely this man is the Prophet."

⁴¹Others said, "He is the Christ."

Still others asked, "How can the Christ come from Galilee? ⁴²Does not the Scripture say that the Christ will come from David's family*a* and from Bethlehem, the

a42 Greek *seed*

JOHN 7:37–39

Drinkable Light

7:37 "IF ANYONE IS THIRSTY, LET HIM COME TO ME AND DRINK."

In C. S. Lewis's story *The Voyage of the Dawn Treader*, the pilgrims have sailed to the very edge of the world, to the utter East, and discovered that the water there is no longer salty, but sweet. More amazing is the effect the water has on all who drink it. When Caspian drank it, "His face was changed. Not only his eyes but everything about him seemed to be brighter." He said the water was more like light than anything else. "That is what it is," said the mouse Reepicheep, "drinkable light." In the days that followed, everyone on the ship "drew buckets of dazzling water from the sea, stronger than wine and somehow wetter, more liquid, than ordinary water ... And one or two of the sailors who had been oldish men when the voyage began now grew younger everyday."⁴

On the last and greatest day of the Feast of Tabernacles, Jesus loudly invited all who heard to come to him and drink water like that described in Lewis's story. John added that this living water was the Holy Spirit (see 7:39). The occasion made the offer even more dramatic. The Feast of Tabernacles celebrated God's gracious provision for Israel in its wilderness wanderings, including the provision of water. For each of the seven days of the Feast, water was carried from the pool of Siloam to the temple to remind the people of how God had never failed to quench their thirst during those long years in the desert. It was on the last of these days that Jesus made his announcement, saying in effect, "I am the greater water, the fulfillment of all God has ever done to satisfy your thirst."

There may be another layer of meaning in Jesus' words. The Feast was marked by a lot of feasting, or partying, as we might say. A lot of food and wine had been consumed by this time. Jesus' words may have been intended to sound like, "Are you still thirsty after all that? Then come to me and be satisfied."

Like his teachings about bread in chapter 6, the Lord is again offering to fill us with something better than food and water, something our other hungers and thirsts can only point to. He is offering himself, the Holy Spirit. Of all the good gifts God gives us in prayer, he is the greatest (see Luke 11:13). He is "drinkable light."

PRAY:

Christ, you are the light of the world and the water of life. Fill me till I thirst no more. Give to me what you promised: the fullness of your Spirit.

FOR YOUR NEXT DEVOTIONAL READING, GO TO PAGE 1290.

town where David lived?" ⁴³Thus the people were divided because of Jesus. ⁴⁴Some wanted to seize him, but no one laid a hand on him.

Unbelief of the Jewish Leaders

⁴⁵Finally the temple guards went back to the chief priests and Pharisees, who asked them, "Why didn't you bring him in?"

⁴⁶"No one ever spoke the way this man does," the guards declared.

⁴⁷"You mean he has deceived you also?" the Pharisees retorted. ⁴⁸"Has any of the rulers or of the Pharisees believed in him? ⁴⁹No! But this mob that knows nothing of the law—there is a curse on them."

⁵⁰Nicodemus, who had gone to Jesus earlier and who was one of their own number, asked, ⁵¹"Does our law condemn anyone without first hearing him to find out what he is doing?"

⁵²They replied, "Are you from Galilee, too? Look into it, and you will find that a prophet*a* does not come out of Galilee."

[The earliest manuscripts and many other ancient witnesses do not have John 7:53–8:11.]

⁵³Then each went to his own home. ⁸But Jesus went to the Mount of Olives. ²At dawn he appeared again in the temple courts, where all the people gathered around him, and he sat down to teach them. ³The teachers of the law and the Pharisees brought in a woman caught in adultery. They made her stand before the group ⁴and said to Jesus, "Teacher, this woman was caught in the act of adultery. ⁵In the Law Moses commanded us to stone such women. Now what do you say?" ⁶They were using this question as a trap, in order to have a basis for accusing him.

But Jesus bent down and started to write on the ground with his finger. ⁷When they kept on questioning him, he straightened up and said to them, "If any one of you is without sin, let him be the first to throw a stone at her." ⁸Again he stooped down and wrote on the ground.

⁹At this, those who heard began to go away one at a time, the older ones first, until only Jesus was left, with the woman still standing there. ¹⁰Jesus straightened up and asked her, "Woman, where are they? Has no one condemned you?"

¹¹"No one, sir," she said.

"Then neither do I condemn you," Jesus declared. "Go now and leave your life of sin."

The Validity of Jesus' Testimony

¹²When Jesus spoke again to the people, he said, "I am the light of the world. Whoever follows me will never walk in darkness, but will have the light of life."

¹³The Pharisees challenged him, "Here you are, appearing as your own witness; your testimony is not valid."

¹⁴Jesus answered, "Even if I testify on my own behalf, my testimony is valid, for I know where I came from and where I am going. But you have no idea where I come from or where I am going. ¹⁵You judge by human standards; I pass judgment on no one. ¹⁶But if I do judge, my decisions are right, because I am not alone. I stand with the Father, who sent me. ¹⁷In your own Law it is written that the testimony of two men is valid. ¹⁸I am one who testifies for myself; my other witness is the Father, who sent me."

¹⁹Then they asked him, "Where is your father?"

"You do not know me or my Father," Jesus replied. "If you knew me, you would know my Father also." ²⁰He spoke these words while teaching in the temple area near the place where the offerings were put. Yet no one seized him, because his time had not yet come.

²¹Once more Jesus said to them, "I am going away, and you will look for me, and you will die in your sin. Where I go, you cannot come."

²²This made the Jews ask, "Will he kill himself? Is that why he says, 'Where I go, you cannot come'?"

²³But he continued, "You are from below; I am from above. You are of this world; I am not of this world. ²⁴I told you

a52 Two early manuscripts *the Prophet*

that you would die in your sins; if you do not believe that I am ⌐the one I claim to be⌐,[a] you will indeed die in your sins."

25 "Who are you?" they asked.

"Just what I have been claiming all along," Jesus replied. 26 "I have much to say in judgment of you. But he who sent me is reliable, and what I have heard from him I tell the world."

27 They did not understand that he was telling them about his Father. 28 So Jesus said, "When you have lifted up the Son of Man, then you will know that I am ⌐the one I claim to be⌐ and that I do nothing on my own but speak just what the Father has taught me. 29 The one who sent me is with me; he has not left me alone, for I always do what pleases him." 30 Even as he spoke, many put their faith in him.

The Children of Abraham

31 To the Jews who had believed him, Jesus said, "If you hold to my teaching, you are really my disciples. 32 Then you will know the truth, and the truth will set you free."

33 They answered him, "We are Abraham's descendants[b] and have never been slaves of anyone. How can you say that we shall be set free?"

34 Jesus replied, "I tell you the truth, everyone who sins is a slave to sin. 35 Now a slave has no permanent place in the family, but a son belongs to it forever. 36 So if the Son sets you free, you will be free indeed. 37 I know you are Abraham's descendants. Yet you are ready to kill me, because you have no room for my word. 38 I am telling you what I have seen in the Father's presence, and you do what you have heard from your father.[c]"

39 "Abraham is our father," they answered.

"If you were Abraham's children," said Jesus, "then you would[d] do the things Abraham did. 40 As it is, you are determined to kill me, a man who has told you the truth that I heard from God. Abraham did not do such things. 41 You are doing the things your own father does."

"We are not illegitimate children," they protested. "The only Father we have is God himself."

The Children of the Devil

42 Jesus said to them, "If God were your Father, you would love me, for I came from God and now am here. I have not come on my own; but he sent me. 43 Why is my language not clear to you? Because you are unable to hear what I say. 44 You belong to your father, the devil, and you want to carry out your father's desire. He was a murderer from the beginning, not holding to the truth, for there is no truth in him. When he lies, he speaks his native language, for he is a liar and the father of lies. 45 Yet because I tell the truth, you do not believe me! 46 Can any of you prove me guilty of sin? If I am telling the truth, why don't you believe me? 47 He who belongs to God hears what God says. The reason you do not hear is that you do not belong to God."

The Claims of Jesus About Himself

48 The Jews answered him, "Aren't we right in saying that you are a Samaritan and demon-possessed?"

49 "I am not possessed by a demon," said Jesus, "but I honor my Father and you dishonor me. 50 I am not seeking glory for myself; but there is one who seeks it, and he is the judge. 51 I tell you the truth, if anyone keeps my word, he will never see death."

52 At this the Jews exclaimed, "Now we know that you are demon-possessed! Abraham died and so did the prophets, yet you say that if anyone keeps your word, he will never taste death. 53 Are you greater than our father Abraham? He died, and so did the prophets. Who do you think you are?"

54 Jesus replied, "If I glorify myself, my glory means nothing. My Father, whom you claim as your God, is the one who glorifies me. 55 Though you do not know him, I know him. If I said I did not, I would be a liar like you, but I do know him and keep his word. 56 Your father Abraham rejoiced at the thought of seeing my day; he saw it and was glad."

---

[a]24 Or I am he; also in verse 28   [b]33 Greek seed; also in verse 37   [c]38 Or presence. Therefore do what you have heard from the Father.   [d]39 Some early manuscripts "If you are Abraham's children," said Jesus, "then

Batter My Heart

NO ANTHOLOGY of English literature is complete without selections from the poetry and sermons of John Donne. Though better known now as a poet than as a preacher, Donne was considered the most eloquent preacher of his time. He served as dean of St. Paul's Cathedral and chaplain to James I, King of England. One of his most famous sermons was the one he preached for his own funeral, entitled "Death's Duel." He left his sickbed to preach it, returned home to pose for a portrait in a funeral shroud, and died a few weeks later.

Imminently quotable, some of Donne's lines—such as "No man is an island" and "Death, be not proud"—have become part of common discourse even to the present. The *Oxford Dictionary of Quotations* has 79 entries from Donne's writings. His work is a brilliant example of the power of a "baptized imagination." When called into the service of God, a vivid imagination and a powerful intellect can produce works of beauty that are powerful to both commend and illumine the truth of the gospel. The following are examples of the power of Donne's craft to encourage and enlighten.

Donne knew well the struggle of prayer amid the distractions of everyday life. He wondered what kind of creatures we are that the trivial so easily crowds out the eternal. "I throw myself down in my chamber, and I call in, and invite God, and his angels thither, and when they are there, I neglect God and his angels, for the noise of a fly, for the rattling of a coach, for the whining of a door."[5] Our treasures are in heaven, but our instincts and appetites are so often only of the earth. So, "A memory of yesterday's pleasures, a fear of tomorrow's dangers, a straw under my knee, a noise in mine ear, a light in mine eye, an anything, a nothing, a fancy, a chimera in my brain, troubles me in my prayer. So certainly is there nothing, nothing in spiritual things, perfect in this world."[6]

Like Jacob and the apostle Paul, Donne agonized over the surrender of his will to God's will and prayed for God to do whatever it took to bring him to submission:

> Batter my heart, three person'd God; for, you
> As yet but knock, breathe, shine, and seek to mend;
> That I may rise, and stand, overthrow me, and bend
> Your force, to break, blow, burn and make me new.

Donne cried out that he was like a walled city held by God's enemy, or worse, a bride betrothed to God's enemy! Would God divorce him from their common foe?

> I, like a usurped town, to another due,
> Labor to admit you, but O, to no end,
> Reason, your viceroy in me, me should defend,
> But is captive, and proves weak or untrue.
> Yet dearly I love you, and would be loved fain,
> But am betrothed unto your enemy:
> Divorce me, untie, or break that knot again.

Donne prayed that God would work in him the paradox of true freedom (see Luke 9:24):

> Take me to you, imprison me, for I
> Except you enthrall me, never shall be free,
> Nor ever chaste, except you ravish me.[7]

PRAY:

Lord, take me to yourself and imprison me! For if you do not enthrall me, I will never be free; nor will I ever be chaste unless you ravish me.

MEMORIZE:

No discipline seems pleasant at the time, but painful. Later on, however, it produces a harvest of righteousness and peace for those who have been trained by it. HEBREWS 12:11

FOR YOUR NEXT DEVOTIONAL READING, GO TO PAGE 1294.

⁵⁷"You are not yet fifty years old," the Jews said to him, "and you have seen Abraham!"

⁵⁸"I tell you the truth," Jesus answered, "before Abraham was born, I am!" ⁵⁹At this, they picked up stones to stone him, but Jesus hid himself, slipping away from the temple grounds.

Jesus Heals a Man Born Blind

9 As he went along, he saw a man blind from birth. ²His disciples asked him, "Rabbi, who sinned, this man or his parents, that he was born blind?"

³"Neither this man nor his parents sinned," said Jesus, "but this happened so that the work of God might be displayed in his life. ⁴As long as it is day, we must do the work of him who sent me. Night is coming, when no one can work. ⁵While I am in the world, I am the light of the world."

⁶Having said this, he spit on the ground, made some mud with the saliva, and put it on the man's eyes. ⁷"Go," he told him, "wash in the Pool of Siloam" (this word means Sent). So the man went and washed, and came home seeing.

⁸His neighbors and those who had formerly seen him begging asked, "Isn't this the same man who used to sit and beg?" ⁹Some claimed that he was.

Others said, "No, he only looks like him."

But he himself insisted, "I am the man."

¹⁰"How then were your eyes opened?" they demanded.

¹¹He replied, "The man they call Jesus made some mud and put it on my eyes. He told me to go to Siloam and wash. So I went and washed, and then I could see."

¹²"Where is this man?" they asked him.

"I don't know," he said.

The Pharisees Investigate the Healing

¹³They brought to the Pharisees the man who had been blind. ¹⁴Now the day on which Jesus had made the mud and opened the man's eyes was a Sabbath. ¹⁵Therefore the Pharisees also asked him how he had received his sight. "He put mud on my eyes," the man replied, "and I washed, and now I see."

¹⁶Some of the Pharisees said, "This man is not from God, for he does not keep the Sabbath."

But others asked, "How can a sinner do such miraculous signs?" So they were divided.

¹⁷Finally they turned again to the blind man, "What have you to say about him? It was your eyes he opened."

The man replied, "He is a prophet."

¹⁸The Jews still did not believe that he had been blind and had received his sight until they sent for the man's parents. ¹⁹"Is this your son?" they asked. "Is this the one you say was born blind? How is it that now he can see?"

²⁰"We know he is our son," the parents answered, "and we know he was born blind. ²¹But how he can see now, or who opened his eyes, we don't know. Ask him. He is of age; he will speak for himself." ²²His parents said this because they were afraid of the Jews, for already the Jews had decided that anyone who acknowledged that Jesus was the Christ[a] would be put out of the synagogue. ²³That was why his parents said, "He is of age; ask him."

²⁴A second time they summoned the man who had been blind. "Give glory to God,[b]" they said. "We know this man is a sinner."

²⁵He replied, "Whether he is a sinner or not, I don't know. One thing I do know. I was blind but now I see!"

²⁶Then they asked him, "What did he do to you? How did he open your eyes?"

²⁷He answered, "I have told you already and you did not listen. Why do you want to hear it again? Do you want to become his disciples, too?"

²⁸Then they hurled insults at him and said, "You are this fellow's disciple! We are disciples of Moses! ²⁹We know that God spoke to Moses, but as for this fellow, we don't even know where he comes from."

³⁰The man answered, "Now that is remarkable! You don't know where he comes from, yet he opened my eyes. ³¹We know that God does not listen to sinners. He listens to the godly man who does his

*a*22 Or *Messiah*   *b*24 A solemn charge to tell the truth (see Joshua 7:19) will. [32]Nobody has ever heard of opening the eyes of a man born blind. [33]If this man were not from God, he could do nothing."

[34]To this they replied, "You were steeped in sin at birth; how dare you lecture us!" And they threw him out.

Spiritual Blindness

[35]Jesus heard that they had thrown him out, and when he found him, he said, "Do you believe in the Son of Man?"

[36]"Who is he, sir?" the man asked. "Tell me so that I may believe in him."

[37]Jesus said, "You have now seen him; in fact, he is the one speaking with you."

[38]Then the man said, "Lord, I believe," and he worshiped him.

[39]Jesus said, "For judgment I have come into this world, so that the blind will see and those who see will become blind."

[40]Some Pharisees who were with him heard him say this and asked, "What? Are we blind too?"

[41]Jesus said, "If you were blind, you would not be guilty of sin; but now that you claim you can see, your guilt remains.

The Shepherd and His Flock

10 "I tell you the truth, the man who does not enter the sheep pen by the gate, but climbs in by some other way, is a thief and a robber. [2]The man who enters by the gate is the shepherd of his sheep. [3]The watchman opens the gate for him, and the sheep listen to his voice. He calls his own sheep by name and leads them out. [4]When he has brought out all his own, he goes on ahead of them, and his sheep follow him because they know his voice. [5]But they will never follow a stranger; in fact, they will run away from him because they do not recognize a stranger's voice." [6]Jesus used this figure of speech, but they did not understand what he was telling them.

[7]Therefore Jesus said again, "I tell you the truth, I am the gate for the sheep. [8]All who ever came before me were thieves and robbers, but the sheep did not listen to them. [9]I am the gate; whoever enters through me will be saved.[a] He will come in and go out, and find pasture. [10]The thief comes only to steal and kill and destroy; I have come that they may have life, and have it to the full.

[11]"I am the good shepherd. The good shepherd lays down his life for the sheep. [12]The hired hand is not the shepherd who owns the sheep. So when he sees the wolf coming, he abandons the sheep and runs away. Then the wolf attacks the flock and scatters it. [13]The man runs away because he is a hired hand and cares nothing for the sheep.

[14]"I am the good shepherd; I know my sheep and my sheep know me— [15]just as the Father knows me and I know the Father—and I lay down my life for the sheep. [16]I have other sheep that are not of this sheep pen. I must bring them also. They too will listen to my voice, and there shall be one flock and one shepherd. [17]The reason my Father loves me is that I lay down my life—only to take it up again. [18]No one takes it from me, but I lay it down of my own accord. I have authority to lay it down and authority to take it up again. This command I received from my Father."

[19]At these words the Jews were again divided. [20]Many of them said, "He is demon-possessed and raving mad. Why listen to him?"

[21]But others said, "These are not the sayings of a man possessed by a demon. Can a demon open the eyes of the blind?"

The Unbelief of the Jews

[22]Then came the Feast of Dedication[b] at Jerusalem. It was winter, [23]and Jesus was in the temple area walking in Solomon's Colonnade. [24]The Jews gathered around him, saying, "How long will you keep us in suspense? If you are the Christ,[c] tell us plainly."

[25]Jesus answered, "I did tell you, but you do not believe. The miracles I do in my Father's name speak for me, [26]but you do not believe because you are not my sheep. [27]My sheep listen to my voice; I know them, and they follow me. [28]I give them eternal life, and they shall never perish; no one can snatch them out of my hand. [29]My Father, who has given them

---

[a]9 Or kept safe   [b]22 That is, Hanukkah
[c]24 Or Messiah

to me, is greater than all[a]; no one can snatch them out of my Father's hand. ³⁰I and the Father are one."

³¹Again the Jews picked up stones to stone him, ³²but Jesus said to them, "I have shown you many great miracles from the Father. For which of these do you stone me?"

³³"We are not stoning you for any of these," replied the Jews, "but for blasphemy, because you, a mere man, claim to be God."

³⁴Jesus answered them, "Is it not written in your Law, 'I have said you are gods'[b]? ³⁵If he called them 'gods,' to whom the word of God came—and the Scripture cannot be broken— ³⁶what about the one whom the Father set apart as his very own and sent into the world? Why then do you accuse me of blasphemy because I said, 'I am God's Son'? ³⁷Do

[a]29 Many early manuscripts *What my Father has given me is greater than all*   [b]34 Psalm 82:6

JOHN 10:1–18,27–30

Everything Depends on the One to Whom You Pray

10:11 "I AM THE GOOD SHEPHERD."

If you are a sheep, everything depends on whom you have for a shepherd. There are the hired hands who are in it only for the money, and the moment being a shepherd gets a little inconvenient or dangerous, they resign, and the sheep are left to wolves and thieves. A question worth asking is: Which is worse—hired hands or wolves? Wolves are "honest"; they only do what comes naturally. Hired hands are profoundly dishonest, pretending to do what they don't. God hates the pretenders (see Isaiah 56:9–12; Ezekiel 34). There can be any number of wolves licking their chops, wanting to eat the sheep, but if the shepherd is good, the sheep will be safe. If the shepherd is bad, it only takes one wolf to destroy the whole flock.

Jesus is the Good Shepherd—in every way the opposite of the hired hand. He is the gate. He keeps the sheep secure; no one can get to them except through him. He makes the sheep free, so they can "come in and go out, and find pasture" (John 10:9). The Good Shepherd knows the sheep by name, each one of them; everyone matters (see verse 14). Above all, Jesus is good because he lays down his life for the sheep (see verses 11,15).

When you pray, everything depends on the One to whom you pray. What is God like? Can you trust him? Will your life be safe in his hands? Does he love you? Put him to the test: Does God listen? He does, for he is the Good Shepherd who knows your name! Does God care about you? He does, for he laid down his life for you! Does God have good plans for you? He does, for his purpose is to give you life in its fullness (see verse 10)! God is no pretender; he hates pretenders. He is the real thing. Come to him with confidence and joy.

PRAY:

Protect and guide me, Good Shepherd. Forgive my sins, heal my wounds and refresh me, not because I deserve it, but because you are the Good Shepherd.

FOR YOUR NEXT DEVOTIONAL READING, GO TO PAGE 1297.

> " *Where there is much prayer, there will be much of the Spirit; where there is much of the Spirit, there will be ever-increasing prayer.* "
>
> ANDREW MURRAY

not believe me unless I do what my Father does. ³⁸But if I do it, even though you do not believe me, believe the miracles, that you may know and understand that the Father is in me, and I in the Father." ³⁹Again they tried to seize him, but he escaped their grasp.

⁴⁰Then Jesus went back across the Jordan to the place where John had been baptizing in the early days. Here he stayed ⁴¹and many people came to him. They said, "Though John never performed a miraculous sign, all that John said about this man was true." ⁴²And in that place many believed in Jesus.

The Death of Lazarus

11 Now a man named Lazarus was sick. He was from Bethany, the village of Mary and her sister Martha. ²This Mary, whose brother Lazarus now lay sick, was the same one who poured perfume on the Lord and wiped his feet with her hair. ³So the sisters sent word to Jesus, "Lord, the one you love is sick."

⁴When he heard this, Jesus said, "This sickness will not end in death. No, it is for God's glory so that God's Son may be glorified through it." ⁵Jesus loved Martha and her sister and Lazarus. ⁶Yet when he heard that Lazarus was sick, he stayed where he was two more days.

⁷Then he said to his disciples, "Let us go back to Judea."

⁸"But Rabbi," they said, "a short while ago the Jews tried to stone you, and yet you are going back there?"

⁹Jesus answered, "Are there not twelve hours of daylight? A man who walks by day will not stumble, for he sees by this world's light. ¹⁰It is when he walks by night that he stumbles, for he has no light."

¹¹After he had said this, he went on to tell them, "Our friend Lazarus has fallen asleep; but I am going there to wake him up."

¹²His disciples replied, "Lord, if he sleeps, he will get better." ¹³Jesus had been speaking of his death, but his disciples thought he meant natural sleep.

¹⁴So then he told them plainly, "Lazarus is dead, ¹⁵and for your sake I am glad I was not there, so that you may believe. But let us go to him."

¹⁶Then Thomas (called Didymus) said to the rest of the disciples, "Let us also go, that we may die with him."

Jesus Comforts the Sisters

¹⁷On his arrival, Jesus found that Lazarus had already been in the tomb for four days. ¹⁸Bethany was less than two miles*ᵃ* from Jerusalem, ¹⁹and many Jews had come to Martha and Mary to comfort them in the loss of their brother. ²⁰When Martha heard that Jesus was coming, she went out to meet him, but Mary stayed at home.

²¹"Lord," Martha said to Jesus, "if you had been here, my brother would not have died. ²²But I know that even now God will give you whatever you ask."

²³Jesus said to her, "Your brother will rise again."

²⁴Martha answered, "I know he will rise again in the resurrection at the last day."

²⁵Jesus said to her, "I am the resurrection and the life. He who believes in me will live, even though he dies; ²⁶and whoever lives and believes in me will never die. Do you believe this?"

²⁷"Yes, Lord," she told him, "I believe that you are the Christ,*ᵇ* the Son of God, who was to come into the world."

²⁸And after she had said this, she went back and called her sister Mary aside. "The Teacher is here," she said, "and is asking for you." ²⁹When Mary heard this, she got up quickly and went to him. ³⁰Now Jesus had not yet entered the village, but was still at the place where Martha had met him. ³¹When the Jews who had been with Mary in the house, comforting her, noticed how quickly she got up and went out, they followed her, supposing she was going to the tomb to mourn there.

ᵃ18 Greek *fifteen stadia* (about 3 kilometers)
ᵇ27 Or *Messiah*

³²When Mary reached the place where Jesus was and saw him, she fell at his feet and said, "Lord, if you had been here, my brother would not have died."

³³When Jesus saw her weeping, and the Jews who had come along with her also weeping, he was deeply moved in spirit and troubled. ³⁴"Where have you laid him?" he asked.

"Come and see, Lord," they replied.

³⁵Jesus wept.

³⁶Then the Jews said, "See how he loved him!"

³⁷But some of them said, "Could not he who opened the eyes of the blind man have kept this man from dying?"

Jesus Raises Lazarus From the Dead

³⁸Jesus, once more deeply moved, came to the tomb. It was a cave with a stone laid across the entrance. ³⁹"Take away the stone," he said.

"But, Lord," said Martha, the sister of the dead man, "by this time there is a bad odor, for he has been there four days."

⁴⁰Then Jesus said, "Did I not tell you that if you believed, you would see the glory of God?"

⁴¹So they took away the stone. Then Jesus looked up and said, "Father, I thank you that you have heard me. ⁴²I knew that you always hear me, but I said this for the benefit of the people standing here, that they may believe that you sent me."

> SO they took away the stone. Then Jesus looked up and said, "Father, I thank you that you have heard me."
>
> JOHN 11:41

⁴³When he had said this, Jesus called in a loud voice, "Lazarus, come out!" ⁴⁴The dead man came out, his hands and feet wrapped with strips of linen, and a cloth around his face.

Jesus said to them, "Take off the grave clothes and let him go."

The Plot to Kill Jesus

⁴⁵Therefore many of the Jews who had come to visit Mary, and had seen what Jesus did, put their faith in him. ⁴⁶But some of them went to the Pharisees and told them what Jesus had done. ⁴⁷Then the chief priests and the Pharisees called a meeting of the Sanhedrin.

"What are we accomplishing?" they asked. "Here is this man performing many miraculous signs. ⁴⁸If we let him go on like this, everyone will believe in him, and then the Romans will come and take away both our place*ᵃ* and our nation."

⁴⁹Then one of them, named Caiaphas, who was high priest that year, spoke up, "You know nothing at all! ⁵⁰You do not realize that it is better for you that one man die for the people than that the whole nation perish."

⁵¹He did not say this on his own, but as high priest that year he prophesied that Jesus would die for the Jewish nation, ⁵²and not only for that nation but also for the scattered children of God, to bring them together and make them one. ⁵³So from that day on they plotted to take his life.

⁵⁴Therefore Jesus no longer moved about publicly among the Jews. Instead he withdrew to a region near the desert, to a village called Ephraim, where he stayed with his disciples.

⁵⁵When it was almost time for the Jewish Passover, many went up from the country to Jerusalem for their ceremonial cleansing before the Passover. ⁵⁶They kept looking for Jesus, and as they stood in the temple area they asked one another, "What do you think? Isn't he coming to the Feast at all?" ⁵⁷But the chief priests and Pharisees had given orders that if anyone found out where Jesus was, he should report it so that they might arrest him.

Jesus Anointed at Bethany

12 Six days before the Passover, Jesus arrived at Bethany, where Lazarus lived, whom Jesus had raised from the dead. ²Here a dinner was given in Jesus' honor. Martha served, while Lazarus was among those reclining at the table with him. ³Then Mary took about a pint*ᵇ* of pure nard, an expensive perfume; she poured it on Jesus' feet

---

ᵃ48 Or *temple*   *ᵇ3* Greek *a litra* (probably about 0.5 liter)

JOHN 11:1–44

Because He Loves Us So

11:33 HE WAS DEEPLY MOVED IN SPIRIT AND TROUBLED.

This story has a spectacular ending: A dead man gets raised, and later his sister pours out her love for Jesus in a way that Jesus said will never be forgotten (see John 11:2; 12:1–8; Matthew 26:13). The road to the ending is short, only about four days, but packed with meaning. It is a case study in how death can affect us—and how our prayers affect God.

Our prayers always affect God, and he always responds—not according to our power, wisdom and love, but according to his. When Jesus received the message from Mary and Martha that his friend Lazarus was sick, instead of leaving immediately to be by his side, Jesus waited two more days, even though he knew Lazarus was dead (see John 11:11–15). Either Jesus was negligent or divinely in charge. Either he let things get out of control, or he was so in control that no turn of circumstances could thwart his purpose. Clearly it was the latter, and this story encourages us to pray with our eyes not on our frightening and discouraging circumstances, but on his unseen power.

Jesus' power served his wisdom. He saw that it would be better for all involved for Lazarus to die, because God would get greater glory from raising Lazarus from the dead than from healing him (see verse 4). And when God gets glory, everything else gets glorious—like people's faith: "Lazarus is dead, and for your sake I am glad I was not there, so that you may believe" (verses 14–15).

The range of loving emotions Jesus expresses in this story is amazing, especially given the fact that he was so confident of his power and wisdom. He was "deeply moved in spirit and troubled," and he "wept" (see verses 33,35,38). The word translated "troubled" is used two other times of Jesus in John's Gospel: when he spoke of his impending death (see 12:27) and when he announced that one of the disciples was going to betray him (see 13:21). But why should Jesus be upset about anything at all since he knew everything would all turn out so wonderfully? Because God's children were suffering, and it is his nature to suffer with them. Our prayers affect God because he loves us so. When we grieve, he grieves too—not because he is helpless, but because he loves.

PRAY:

Thank you, dear Jesus, that you are moved by my tears, but unmoved by anything I might ask that would be less than your perfect will. Give me faith to trust you when you seem unresponsive.

FOR YOUR NEXT DEVOTIONAL READING, GO TO PAGE 1299.

and wiped his feet with her hair. And the house was filled with the fragrance of the perfume.

⁴But one of his disciples, Judas Iscariot, who was later to betray him, objected, ⁵"Why wasn't this perfume sold and the money given to the poor? It was worth a year's wages.ᵃ" ⁶He did not say this because he cared about the poor but because he was a thief; as keeper of the money bag, he used to help himself to what was put into it.

⁷"Leave her alone," Jesus replied. "It was intended that she should save this perfume for the day of my burial. ⁸You will always have the poor among you, but you will not always have me."

⁹Meanwhile a large crowd of Jews found out that Jesus was there and came, not only because of him but also to see Lazarus, whom he had raised from the dead. ¹⁰So the chief priests made plans to kill Lazarus as well, ¹¹for on account of him many of the Jews were going over to Jesus and putting their faith in him.

The Triumphal Entry

¹²The next day the great crowd that had come for the Feast heard that Jesus was on his way to Jerusalem. ¹³They took palm branches and went out to meet him, shouting,

"Hosanna!ᵇ"

"Blessed is he who comes in the name of the Lord!"ᶜ

"Blessed is the King of Israel!"

¹⁴Jesus found a young donkey and sat upon it, as it is written,

¹⁵ "Do not be afraid, O Daughter of Zion;
see, your king is coming,
seated on a donkey's colt."ᵈ

¹⁶At first his disciples did not understand all this. Only after Jesus was glorified did they realize that these things had been written about him and that they had done these things to him.

¹⁷Now the crowd that was with him when he called Lazarus from the tomb and raised him from the dead continued to spread the word. ¹⁸Many people, because they had heard that he had given this miraculous sign, went out to meet him. ¹⁹So the Pharisees said to one another, "See, this is getting us nowhere. Look how the whole world has gone after him!"

Jesus Predicts His Death

²⁰Now there were some Greeks among those who went up to worship at the Feast. ²¹They came to Philip, who was from Bethsaida in Galilee, with a request. "Sir," they said, "we would like to see Jesus." ²²Philip went to tell Andrew; Andrew and Philip in turn told Jesus.

²³Jesus replied, "The hour has come for the Son of Man to be glorified. ²⁴I tell you the truth, unless a kernel of wheat falls to the ground and dies, it remains only a single seed. But if it dies, it produces many seeds. ²⁵The man who loves his life will lose it, while the man who hates his life in this world will keep it for eternal life. ²⁶Whoever serves me must follow me; and where I am, my servant also will be. My Father will honor the one who serves me.

²⁷"Now my heart is troubled, and what shall I say? 'Father, save me from this hour'? No, it was for this very reason I came to this hour. ²⁸Father, glorify your name!"

Then a voice came from heaven, "I have glorified it, and will glorify it again." ²⁹The crowd that was there and heard it said it had thundered; others said an angel had spoken to him.

³⁰Jesus said, "This voice was for your benefit, not mine. ³¹Now is the time for judgment on this world; now the prince of this world will be driven out. ³²But I, when I am lifted up from the earth, will draw all men to myself." ³³He said this to show the kind of death he was going to die.

³⁴The crowd spoke up, "We have heard from the Law that the Christᵉ will remain forever, so how can you say, 'The Son of Man must be lifted up'? Who is this 'Son of Man'?"

ᵃ5 Greek *three hundred denarii*
ᵇ13 A Hebrew expression meaning "Save!"
which became an exclamation of praise
ᶜ13 Psalm 118:25,26   ᵈ15 Zech. 9:9
ᵉ34 Or *Messiah*

³⁵Then Jesus told them, "You are going to have the light just a little while longer. Walk while you have the light, before darkness overtakes you. The man who walks in the dark does not know where he is going. ³⁶Put your trust in the light while you have it, so that you may become sons of light." When he had finished speaking, Jesus left and hid himself from them.

JOHN 12:23–28

[WEDNESDAY]

Father, Glorify Your Name!

12:23 "THE HOUR HAS COME FOR THE SON OF MAN TO BE GLORIFIED."

What do you pray when you are in trouble? You pray, "Help!"—right? It's instinctive and reflexive, the most natural thing in the world, to want to get away and get out of trouble; that is, unless you are being guided by some other principle, some higher purpose, like Jesus was. That is the only way to understand his words: "Now my heart is troubled, and what shall I say? 'Father, save me from this hour'? No, it was for this very reason I came to this hour. Father, glorify your name!" (12:28). Greater than avoiding his own pain was gaining his Father's glory, so Jesus prayed, "Father, glorify your name!"

Yet Jesus' glory was involved too. In verse 23 he says, "The hour has come for the Son of Man to be glorified." Jesus, too, will be glorified, but by a strange route: by renouncing his own glory and seeking another's glory. Jesus' glory will come through his death. Jesus' heart was troubled because he was in big trouble from a worldly perspective. But it was the kind of "trouble" a seed is in when it is buried in the soil. "Kill" the seed, and it will come back better and stronger than it was before.

God's glory is his infinite, inestimable worth—his "weight," as the Hebrew word for glory, *kabod*, suggests. The heavens declare his glory. God made us in his image, in part, to show his glory. Our glory is a borrowed glory and is fading away. God's glory is eternal. When we make his glory our goal, we will share in it forever. There is no higher prayer to pray, no prayer more beneficial to our own good, in trouble or out of trouble, than to pray that God's name be glorified. In the prayer that Jesus taught his disciples, it is the first thing to pray for: "Hallowed be your name" (see Matthew 6:9).

Missionary Helen Roseveare saved hundreds of lives by her faithful service in the Belgian Congo. During the Simba rebellion, however, she was captured by the rebels and beaten and raped repeatedly. Later she was asked if her accomplishments offset the pain she suffered. Her answer was an unsentimental, "No." Then the Lord spoke to her and said, "Helen, the question is not, 'Was *it* worth it?' but 'Am *I* worthy?'" She answered, "Of course you are, Lord." Her glory, her accomplishments, were not enough to satisfy her. But God's glory was—through the saving of many lives.

PRAY:

Father in heaven! Your glory is my greatest good. Whether by dying
or by living, may your glory be my highest goal.

FOR YOUR NEXT DEVOTIONAL READING, GO TO PAGE 1301.

The Jews Continue in Their Unbelief

37Even after Jesus had done all these miraculous signs in their presence, they still would not believe in him. 38This was to fulfill the word of Isaiah the prophet:

"Lord, who has believed our message
    and to whom has the arm of the
    Lord been revealed?"*a*

39For this reason they could not believe, because, as Isaiah says elsewhere:

40 "He has blinded their eyes
    and deadened their hearts,
so they can neither see with their eyes,
    nor understand with their hearts,
    nor turn—and I would heal them."*b*

41Isaiah said this because he saw Jesus' glory and spoke about him.

42Yet at the same time many even among the leaders believed in him. But because of the Pharisees they would not confess their faith for fear they would be put out of the synagogue; 43for they loved praise from men more than praise from God.

44Then Jesus cried out, "When a man believes in me, he does not believe in me only, but in the one who sent me. 45When he looks at me, he sees the one who sent me. 46I have come into the world as a light, so that no one who believes in me should stay in darkness.

47"As for the person who hears my words but does not keep them, I do not judge him. For I did not come to judge the world, but to save it. 48There is a judge for the one who rejects me and does not accept my words; that very word which I spoke will condemn him at the last day. 49For I did not speak of my own accord, but the Father who sent me commanded me what to say and how to say it. 50I know that his command leads to eternal life. So whatever I say is just what the Father has told me to say."

Jesus Washes His Disciples' Feet

13 It was just before the Passover Feast. Jesus knew that the time had come for him to leave this world and go to the Father. Having loved his own who were in the world, he now showed them the full extent of his love.*c*

2The evening meal was being served, and the devil had already prompted Judas Iscariot, son of Simon, to betray Jesus. 3Jesus knew that the Father had put all things under his power, and that he had come from God and was returning to God; 4so he got up from the meal, took off his outer clothing, and wrapped a towel around his waist. 5After that, he poured water into a basin and began to wash his disciples' feet, drying them with the towel that was wrapped around him.

6He came to Simon Peter, who said to him, "Lord, are you going to wash my feet?"

7Jesus replied, "You do not realize now what I am doing, but later you will understand."

8"No," said Peter, "you shall never wash my feet."

Jesus answered, "Unless I wash you, you have no part with me."

9"Then, Lord," Simon Peter replied, "not just my feet but my hands and my head as well!"

10Jesus answered, "A person who has had a bath needs only to wash his feet; his whole body is clean. And you are clean, though not every one of you." 11For he knew who was going to betray him, and that was why he said not every one was clean.

12When he had finished washing their feet, he put on his clothes and returned to his place. "Do you understand what I have done for you?" he asked them. 13"You call me 'Teacher' and 'Lord,' and rightly so, for that is what I am. 14Now that I, your Lord and Teacher, have washed your feet, you also should wash one another's feet. 15I have set you an example that you should do as I have done for you. 16I tell you the truth, no servant is greater than his master, nor is a messenger greater than the one who sent him. 17Now that you know these things, you will be blessed if you do them.

Jesus Predicts His Betrayal

18"I am not referring to all of you; I know those I have chosen. But this is to fulfill the scripture: 'He who shares my bread has lifted up his heel against me.'*d*

a38 Isaiah 53:1   *b40* Isaiah 6:10   *c1* Or *he loved them to the last*   *d18* Psalm 41:9

¹⁹"I am telling you now before it happens, so that when it does happen you will believe that I am He. ²⁰I tell you the truth, whoever accepts anyone I send accepts me; and whoever accepts me accepts the one who sent me."

²¹After he had said this, Jesus was troubled in spirit and testified, "I tell you the truth, one of you is going to betray me."

²²His disciples stared at one another, at a loss to know which of them he meant. ²³One of them, the disciple whom Jesus

---

JOHN 13:1–17

[THURSDAY]

Maximum Love, Not Minimum Love

13:1 HAVING LOVED HIS OWN WHO WERE IN THE WORLD, HE NOW SHOWED THEM THE FULL EXTENT OF HIS LOVE.

The disciples were in no mood for what Jesus did at dinner that night. Their mood was competitive. Still glowing from the enthusiastic reception the crowds gave them the Sunday before, they were arguing with each other, preoccupied with the rank they would get when their master's kingdom was established (see Luke 22:24).

Jesus' mood was very different. He was absolutely clear on what lay ahead. He would soon die. There was glory and a kingdom ahead, but the path was one of suffering. As the disciples chattered, he looked at how dirty their feet were. They had no clue—no idea what was going on. And he loved them.

According to some ancient Jewish sources, the task of footwashing was regarded as so menial that slaves couldn't be forced to do such demeaning service. It was up to the individual slave's discretion whether to wash the guests' feet, which appears to be the point here. In the room was a collection of mere individuals, men arguing about what belonged to them, relating to each other in a minimal way.⁸ There was no breach of etiquette, nor was there any love. They weren't brothers; they were associates.

And Jesus loved them. So he sought them out. Without fanfare, he got up and began to relate to his men in a *maximal* way; and as he washed their feet, he practiced the opposite of what they were practicing. They weren't in the mood for this sort of thing, and Peter's response summed up their feelings: "No! Never!" But it was too late, for Jesus had already penetrated their defenses. When Jesus said, "Unless I wash you, you have no part with me," Peter could only reply, "Then, Lord, not just my feet but my hands and my head as well!" (John 13:8–9).

Jesus had made his point visually, but lest they miss it, he made it verbally: "I have set you an example that you should do as I have done for you" (verse 15). A little later he said that this kind of love will inform and enlighten the world (see 13:34–35). In other words, you must seek each other out as I have sought you. You dare not be mere individuals, getting along politely and minimally. The world must see clearly that you belong to me; and the only way it will know that is if you belong to each other in the same way you belong to me.

PRAY:

Jesus, you have commanded it, so we pray it:
May we love one another as you have loved us.

FOR YOUR NEXT DEVOTIONAL READING, GO TO PAGE 1303.

loved, was reclining next to him. [24]Simon Peter motioned to this disciple and said, "Ask him which one he means."

[25]Leaning back against Jesus, he asked him, "Lord, who is it?"

[26]Jesus answered, "It is the one to whom I will give this piece of bread when I have dipped it in the dish." Then, dipping the piece of bread, he gave it to Judas Iscariot, son of Simon. [27]As soon as Judas took the bread, Satan entered into him.

"What you are about to do, do quickly," Jesus told him, [28]but no one at the meal understood why Jesus said this to him. [29]Since Judas had charge of the money, some thought Jesus was telling him to buy what was needed for the Feast, or to give something to the poor. [30]As soon as Judas had taken the bread, he went out. And it was night.

Jesus Predicts Peter's Denial

[31]When he was gone, Jesus said, "Now is the Son of Man glorified and God is glorified in him. [32]If God is glorified in him,[a] God will glorify the Son in himself, and will glorify him at once.

[33]"My children, I will be with you only a little longer. You will look for me, and just as I told the Jews, so I tell you now: Where I am going, you cannot come.

[34]"A new command I give you: Love one another. As I have loved you, so you must love one another. [35]By this all men will know that you are my disciples, if you love one another."

[36]Simon Peter asked him, "Lord, where are you going?"

Jesus replied, "Where I am going, you cannot follow now, but you will follow later."

[37]Peter asked, "Lord, why can't I follow you now? I will lay down my life for you."

[38]Then Jesus answered, "Will you really lay down your life for me? I tell you the truth, before the rooster crows, you will disown me three times!

Jesus Comforts His Disciples

14 "Do not let your hearts be troubled. Trust in God[b]; trust also in me. [2]In my Father's house are many rooms; if it were not so, I would have told you. I am going there to prepare a place for you.

[3]And if I go and prepare a place for you, I will come back and take you to be with me that you also may be where I am. [4]You know the way to the place where I am going."

Jesus the Way to the Father

[5]Thomas said to him, "Lord, we don't know where you are going, so how can we know the way?"

[6]Jesus answered, "I am the way and the truth and the life. No one comes to the Father except through me. [7]If you really knew me, you would know[c] my Father as well. From now on, you do know him and have seen him."

> JESUS answered, "I am the way and the truth and the life. No one comes to the Father except through me."
>
> JOHN 14:6

[8]Philip said, "Lord, show us the Father and that will be enough for us."

[9]Jesus answered: "Don't you know me, Philip, even after I have been among you such a long time? Anyone who has seen me has seen the Father. How can you say, 'Show us the Father'? [10]Don't you believe that I am in the Father, and that the Father is in me? The words I say to you are not just my own. Rather, it is the Father, living in me, who is doing his work. [11]Believe me when I say that I am in the Father and the Father is in me; or at least believe on the evidence of the miracles themselves. [12]I tell you the truth, anyone who has faith in me will do what I have been doing. He will do even greater things than these, because I am going to the Father. [13]And I will do whatever you ask in my name, so that the Son may bring glory to the Father. [14]You may ask me for anything in my name, and I will do it.

Jesus Promises the Holy Spirit

[15]"If you love me, you will obey what I command. [16]And I will ask the Father, and he will give you another Counselor to be with you forever— [17]the Spirit of

---

[a]32 Many early manuscripts do not have *If God is glorified in him.*   [b]1 Or *You trust in God*
[c]7 Some early manuscripts *If you really have known me, you will know*

truth. The world cannot accept him, because it neither sees him nor knows him. But you know him, for he lives with you and will be[a] in you. 18I will not leave you as orphans; I will come to you. 19Before long, the world will not see me anymore, but you will see me. Because I live, you also will live. 20On that day you will real-

ize that I am in my Father, and you are in me, and I am in you. 21Whoever has my commands and obeys them, he is the one who loves me. He who loves me will be loved by my Father, and I too will love him and show myself to him."

a17 Some early manuscripts *and is*

{ FRIDAY }

JOHN 14:12–14; 15:7,16; 16:23–24

The Power of the Name

14:14 "YOU MAY ASK ME FOR ANYTHING IN MY NAME, AND I WILL DO IT."

There is something here that Jesus absolutely does not want us to miss; so he says it six times over three chapters, the first in John 14:13, "I will do whatever you ask in my name." Then he says it five more times (see 14:14; 15:7,16; 16:23,24). Read them all, and be duly impressed with how strongly the Lord wants us to remember the power of praying in his name. Not only will he and his Father do what we ask in his name, but praying this way will give God great glory and us great joy (see 15:8; 16:24).

"What a deal," some have thought, "just use his name, and he'll do whatever you ask." They say that because they don't understand the significance of the name. A lot of materialistic self-promotion has been justified by this kind of misunderstanding. And the faith of many has been damaged when the use of the name did not achieve the desired results.

In the Bible a name is not a label; it is a person, a character. To pray in the name of Jesus is not to use his name as a mantra, but to submit to his will as one would to a master. Jesus is saying, "Whatever you ask according to who I am and what I will, *it will be done for you*." The "whatever" is conditioned by the "name," not the other way around. To pray in the name of Jesus is just another way of saying, "Your will be done on earth as it is in heaven" (see Matthew 6:10).

Should we be encouraged or discouraged by this qualification? Will our prayers shrink or expand according to this knowledge? They must get bigger and better! What Jesus desires and wills is glorious and beautiful. In contrast to his, all our desires are cheap and tawdry. When our prayers are aligned with his name, we are better people, and our prayers take on divine power in a way very much like what Dante described as what happened to him when he looked into the face of God: "But now my desire and will were revolved, like a wheel which is moved evenly, by the Love which moves the sun and the other stars."9 Now that is power in prayer!

PRAY:
Holy Jesus, teach me your ways, that I may I revere your name.
Teach me the power of wanting what you want,
that I may have the joy of answered prayer in your name.

FOR YOUR NEXT DEVOTIONAL READING, GO TO PAGE 1304.

Blessed Are the Peacemakers

WHEN HE was a boy, Elias Chacour prayed a prayer that changed his life forever. Chacour was born into a Palestinian Christian family in 1939. When he was eight, he and his family were displaced by the Israelis to the village of Gish. While there, Chacour was awakened one night by the sound of angry voices blaring over loudspeakers: "Come out of your houses. We want all men to come out and give themselves up. You are leaving here at once." That night Elias' father and brothers were arrested and taken away.

In the months that followed, something peculiar began to stir in the young boy. He began to crave solitude. Sometimes while playing a game, his eyes would gaze off into the surrounding hills, and he would wander away to be alone. One hot day as he sat under an olive tree, aching for his father and brothers, he remembered words of Jesus he had heard his mother recite as he lay in her lap: "Blessed are those who mourn, for they will be comforted." Then he imagined Jesus walking toward him, saying those words. For the first time, the words made sense. Chacour began to pray. "Almost without thinking, I began innocently pouring out my heart. 'Mother has your comfort. I can see that. But can't you just speak a word and make all this trouble go away? Do you want us to be your lips and hands and feet—as Mother prays—to bring peace again? If that's true, you can use my hands and feet. Even my tongue,' I added, thinking of my usually fiery words." He also prayed that the Lord would bring his father and brothers home. Three months later, they were reunited. But there was much more to come.

Not long afterward, Israeli soldiers roared into Gish again, looking for a thief they believed had cut a piece of telephone wire from the new kibbutz they were building. They grabbed any children who were nearby and began to beat them, accusing them of the crime. Chacour was among the victims. As he was being beaten, he could hear their words: "You are worth nothing ... thieves ... dirty Palestinians." But he heard another voice too, speaking more of the words of Jesus he had heard from his mother: "Peace, be still," and "Blessed are you when people falsely say all kinds of evil against you ... for in the same way they persecuted the prophets who were before you." A few days later the wire was found. It had been cut accidentally by a wagon wheel on the hard ground. Chacour remembered his prayer under the olive tree: "You can use my hands and feet. Even my tongue."

As an adult, Elias Chacour became an ordained Melkite priest and served Christ for years in a little church in Ibillin, Galilee. He is the recipient of many international peace awards, and he has traveled the world, preaching the gospel and speaking on peace and justice, leading non-violent demonstrations and working for reconciliation between Palestinians and Israelis. He refers to Israelis as "brothers and sisters."

P R A Y :

My Creator and Savior: You have given me everything I am
and have. I belong to you, body and soul, in life and in death.
You can use my hands and feet. Even my tongue.

M E M O R I Z E :

Blessed are the peacemakers, for they
will be called sons of God. MATTHEW 5:9

FOR YOUR NEXT DEVOTIONAL READING, GO TO PAGE 1307.

22Then Judas (not Judas Iscariot) said, "But, Lord, why do you intend to show yourself to us and not to the world?"

23Jesus replied, "If anyone loves me, he will obey my teaching. My Father will love him, and we will come to him and make our home with him. 24He who does not love me will not obey my teaching. These words you hear are not my own; they belong to the Father who sent me.

25"All this I have spoken while still with you. 26But the Counselor, the Holy Spirit, whom the Father will send in my name, will teach you all things and will remind you of everything I have said to you. 27Peace I leave with you; my peace I give you. I do not give to you as the world gives. Do not let your hearts be troubled and do not be afraid.

28"You heard me say, 'I am going away and I am coming back to you.' If you loved me, you would be glad that I am going to the Father, for the Father is greater than I. 29I have told you now before it happens, so that when it does happen you will believe. 30I will not speak with you much longer, for the prince of this world is coming. He has no hold on me, 31but the world must learn that I love the Father and that I do exactly what my Father has commanded me.

"Come now; let us leave.

The Vine and the Branches

15 "I am the true vine, and my Father is the gardener. 2He cuts off every branch in me that bears no fruit, while every branch that does bear fruit he prunes*a* so that it will be even more fruitful. 3You are already clean because of the word I have spoken to you. 4Remain in me, and I will remain in you. No branch can bear fruit by itself; it must remain in the vine. Neither can you bear fruit unless you remain in me.

5"I am the vine; you are the branches. If a man remains in me and I in him, he will bear much fruit; apart from me you can do nothing. 6If anyone does not remain in me, he is like a branch that is thrown away and withers; such branches are picked up, thrown into the fire and burned. 7If you remain in me and my words remain in you, ask whatever you wish, and it will be given you. 8This is to my Father's glory, that you bear much fruit, showing yourselves to be my disciples.

9"As the Father has loved me, so have I loved you. Now remain in my love. 10If you obey my commands, you will remain in my love, just as I have obeyed my Father's commands and remain in his love. 11I have told you this so that my joy may be in you and that your joy may be complete. 12My command is this: Love each other as I have loved you. 13Greater love has no one than this, that he lay down his life for his friends. 14You are my friends if you do what I command. 15I no longer call you servants, because a servant does not know his master's business. Instead, I have called you friends, for everything that I learned from my Father I have made known to you. 16You did not choose me, but I chose you and appointed you to go and bear fruit—fruit that will last. Then the Father will give you whatever you ask in my name. 17This is my command: Love each other.

The World Hates the Disciples

18"If the world hates you, keep in mind that it hated me first. 19If you belonged to the world, it would love you as its own. As it is, you do not belong to the world, but I have chosen you out of the world. That is why the world hates you. 20Remember the words I spoke to you: 'No servant is greater than his master.'*b* If they persecuted me, they will persecute you also. If they obeyed my teaching, they will obey yours also. 21They will treat you this way because of my name, for they do not know the One who sent me. 22If I had not come and spoken to them, they would not be guilty of sin. Now, however, they have no excuse for their sin. 23He who hates me hates my Father as well. 24If I had not done among them what no one else did, they would not be guilty of sin. But now they have seen these miracles, and yet they have hated both me and my Father. 25But this is to fulfill what is written in their Law: 'They hated me without reason.'*c*

26"When the Counselor comes, whom I will send to you from the Father, the Spirit of truth who goes out from the Father,

---

a2 The Greek for *prunes* also means *cleans.*
b20 John 13:16   *c25* Psalms 35:19; 69:4

JOHN 15:1–17

Of Fruit and of Prayer

15:1 "I AM THE TRUE VINE."

Some scholars believe that Jesus' words in John 14:31 signal that he and the disciples left the upper room at that point. In that case, the group was now walking as Jesus spoke to them. Their walk that night would likely have taken them by the temple, on which was a golden vine and clusters of grapes. The historian Josephus said the clusters were "as large as a man."[10] The moment was perfect for the point Jesus wanted to make: He is the vine; his disciples are his branches. The goal of the disciples' lives, as with a branch, is to be fruitful; the way to be fruitful is to be a branch that is vitally connected to the vine.

What is the fruit? It is the fruit of the Spirit (see Galatians 5:22–23), of which Jesus singles out joy and love for special mention (see John 15:11,17). Pause and let that sink in. God's great purpose for your life is not to make you more productive, as in achievements and getting a lot of work done—but more fruitful, as in the delight and pleasure of living and loving in the intimate relationship of branch to vine, of disciple to God and others. Jesus gives us a powerfully inviting image of the Christian life: It's like a cluster of juicy, sweet grapes! The productivity will come not as a cause but as an effect. Jesus really did come that we may have life to the full (see John 10:10).

The place of prayer in this economy is very interesting—and thrilling. We may think prayer will make us fruitful. Jesus thinks it is the other way around: being fruitful will lead us to prayer. "You did not choose me, but I chose you and appointed you to go and bear fruit—fruit that will last. *Then* the Father will give you whatever you ask in my name" (John 15:16, italics added). The source of all prayer is not in the branch, but in the Vine; it is the life of Jesus coursing in us, leading us to cry out, "*Abba*, Father" (see Romans 8:15–16). To be sure, prayer that originates in Jesus will soon die if it is not expressed back to Jesus. But the critical truth here is that prayer is a gift, not an achievement. We pray for the same reason we love: because he first loved us (see 1 John 4:19). Prayer is so much more than a duty—it is the life of Jesus flowing through us. We *must* pray because, as branches in the Vine, we *may* pray.

PRAY:

Jesus, you are the vine, and I am but a branch—
but a grateful branch! Make me fruitful so that I may
pray more, and cause me to pray more
that I may be more fruitful.

FOR YOUR NEXT DEVOTIONAL READING, GO TO PAGE 1310.

he will testify about me. 27And you also must testify, for you have been with me from the beginning.

16 "All this I have told you so that you will not go astray. 2They will put you out of the synagogue; in fact, a time is coming when anyone who kills you will think he is offering a service to God. 3They will do such things because they have not known the Father or me. 4I have told you this, so that when the time comes you will remember that I warned you. I did not tell you this at first because I was with you.

The Work of the Holy Spirit

5"Now I am going to him who sent me, yet none of you asks me, 'Where are you going?' 6Because I have said these things, you are filled with grief. 7But I tell you the truth: It is for your good that I am going away. Unless I go away, the Counselor will not come to you; but if I go, I will send him to you. 8When he comes, he will convict the world of guilt*a* in regard to sin and righteousness and judgment: 9in regard to sin, because men do not believe in me; 10in regard to righteousness, because I am going to the Father, where you can see me no longer; 11and in regard to judgment, because the prince of this world now stands condemned.

12"I have much more to say to you, more than you can now bear. 13But when he, the Spirit of truth, comes, he will guide you into all truth. He will not speak on his own; he will speak only what he hears, and he will tell you what is yet to come. 14He will bring glory to me by taking from what is mine and making it known to you. 15All that belongs to the Father is mine. That is why I said the Spirit will take from what is mine and make it known to you.

16"In a little while you will see me no more, and then after a little while you will see me."

The Disciples' Grief Will Turn to Joy

17Some of his disciples said to one another, "What does he mean by saying, 'In a little while you will see me no more, and then after a little while you will see me,' and 'Because I am going to the Father'?" 18They kept asking, "What does he mean

> *Next to the wonder of seeing my Savior will be, I think, the wonder that I made so little use of the power of prayer.*
>
> D.L. MOODY

by 'a little while'? We don't understand what he is saying."

19Jesus saw that they wanted to ask him about this, so he said to them, "Are you asking one another what I meant when I said, 'In a little while you will see me no more, and then after a little while you will see me'? 20I tell you the truth, you will weep and mourn while the world rejoices. You will grieve, but your grief will turn to joy. 21A woman giving birth to a child has pain because her time has come; but when her baby is born she forgets the anguish because of her joy that a child is born into the world. 22So with you: Now is your time of grief, but I will see you again and you will rejoice, and no one will take away your joy. 23In that day you will no longer ask me anything. I tell you the truth, my Father will give you whatever you ask in my name. 24Until now you have not asked for anything in my name. Ask and you will receive, and your joy will be complete.

25"Though I have been speaking figuratively, a time is coming when I will no longer use this kind of language but will tell you plainly about my Father. 26In that day you will ask in my name. I am not saying that I will ask the Father on your behalf. 27No, the Father himself loves you because you have loved me and have believed that I came from God. 28I came from the Father and entered the world; now I am leaving the world and going back to the Father."

29Then Jesus' disciples said, "Now you are speaking clearly and without figures of speech. 30Now we can see that you know all things and that you do not even need to have anyone ask you questions. This makes us believe that you came from God."

31"You believe at last!"*b* Jesus answered. 32"But a time is coming, and has come, when you will be scattered, each to his

a8 Or *will expose the guilt of the world*
b31 Or *"Do you now believe?"*

own home. You will leave me all alone. Yet I am not alone, for my Father is with me. ³³"I have told you these things, so that in me you may have peace. In this world you will have trouble. But take heart! I have overcome the world."

Jesus Prays for Himself

17 After Jesus said this, he looked toward heaven and prayed:

"Father, the time has come. Glorify your Son, that your Son may glorify you. ²For you granted him authority over all people that he might give eternal life to all those you have given him. ³Now this is eternal life: that they may know you, the only true God, and Jesus Christ, whom you have sent. ⁴I have brought you glory on earth by completing the work you gave me to do. ⁵And now, Father, glorify me in your presence with the glory I had with you before the world began.

Jesus Prays for His Disciples

⁶"I have revealed you[a] to those whom you gave me out of the world. They were yours; you gave them to me and they have obeyed your word. ⁷Now they know that everything you have given me comes from you. ⁸For I gave them the words you gave me and they accepted them. They knew with certainty that I came from you, and they believed that you sent me. ⁹I pray for them. I am not praying for the world, but for those you have given me, for they are yours. ¹⁰All I have is yours, and all you have is mine. And glory has come to me through them. ¹¹I will remain in the world no longer, but they are still in the world, and I am coming to you. Holy Father, protect them by the power of your name—the name you gave me—so that they may be one as we are one. ¹²While I was with them, I protected them and kept them safe by that name you gave me. None has been lost except the one doomed to destruction so that Scripture would be fulfilled.

¹³"I am coming to you now, but I say these things while I am still in the world, so that they may have the full measure of my joy within them. ¹⁴I have given them your word and the world has hated them, for they are not of the world any more than I am of the world. ¹⁵My prayer is not that you take them out of the world but that you protect them from the evil one. ¹⁶They are not of the world, even as I am not of it. ¹⁷Sanctify[b] them by the truth; your word is truth. ¹⁸As you sent me into the world, I have sent them into the world. ¹⁹For them I sanctify myself, that they too may be truly sanctified.

> "I PRAY for them. I am not praying for the world, but for those you have given me, for they are yours."
>
> JOHN 17:9

Jesus Prays for All Believers

²⁰"My prayer is not for them alone. I pray also for those who will believe in me through their message, ²¹that all of them may be one, Father, just as you are in me and I am in you. May they also be in us so that the world may believe that you have sent me. ²²I have given them the glory that you gave me, that they may be one as we are one: ²³I in them and you in me. May they be brought to complete unity to let the world know that you sent me and have loved them even as you have loved me.

²⁴"Father, I want those you have given me to be with me where I am, and to see my glory, the glory you have given me because you loved me before the creation of the world.

²⁵"Righteous Father, though the world does not know you, I know you, and they know that you have sent me. ²⁶I have made you known to them, and will continue to make you known in order that the love you have for me may be in them and that I myself may be in them."

[a]6 Greek your name; also in verse 26
[b]17 Greek hagiazo (set apart for sacred use or make holy); also in verse 19

Jesus Arrested

18 When he had finished praying, Jesus left with his disciples and crossed the Kidron Valley. On the other side there was an olive grove, and he and his disciples went into it.

²Now Judas, who betrayed him, knew the place, because Jesus had often met there with his disciples. ³So Judas came to the grove, guiding a detachment of soldiers and some officials from the chief priests and Pharisees. They were carrying torches, lanterns and weapons.

⁴Jesus, knowing all that was going to happen to him, went out and asked them, "Who is it you want?"

⎡**TUESDAY**⎤

JOHN 17

The "Real" Lord's Prayer

17:23 "I IN THEM AND YOU IN ME. MAY THEY BE BROUGHT TO COMPLETE UNITY."

People lean close to hear the words of a dying person. Last words can carry great weight. When it is all said and done, what was most important to this person? The last things said and prayed can be an important clue to what his or her life was all about.

How important was it to Jesus that Christians get along with each other? It was one of the last things he prayed for before he was arrested and crucified.

But greater than the timing of his prayer was the depth of the unity for which Jesus prayed. His passion for Christian unity was so intense that he asked his Father to make us one as he and his Father are one (see 17:21,23). He wanted his church to be a living demonstration of the love and oneness of the Godhead—the Three in One and the One in Three!

There is more: The claim Jesus made for the power of Christian unity is unparalleled in all his teachings. He said it would convince the world that he was sent by God (see verse 23). Jesus believed that the greatest argument for the truth of his unique and divine identity would come not from theologians and philosophers, but from simple believers living together in the kind of love he prayed for that night. He said this of nothing else. This is the Lord's great prayer. Clearly, Christian unity mattered greatly to him.

Does it matter that much to you? Christ died for individuals, but the New Testament's favorite way of speaking of individuals is as God's people, his body, his bride, the temple of the Holy Spirit (see 1 Corinthians 12:27; Ephesians 5:25–33; 1 Corinthians 3:16–17). There can be no place for individualism in the church, for "The man who seeks God in isolation from his fellows," wrote R. H. Tawney, "is likely to find, not God, but the devil, who will bear an embarrassing resemblance to himself." Pray the "real" Lord's Prayer, pray that we will be one as he and his Father are one. Pray that you will be an answer to his prayer in the care you give to his body, the church.

PRAY:

Heavenly Father, as Jesus prayed, so I pray: Bring us as believers to complete unity, that the world may know that Jesus came from you, and that you love us as you love your Son.

FOR YOUR NEXT DEVOTIONAL READING, GO TO PAGE 1318.

⁵"Jesus of Nazareth," they replied.

"I am he," Jesus said. (And Judas the traitor was standing there with them.) ⁶When Jesus said, "I am he," they drew back and fell to the ground.

⁷Again he asked them, "Who is it you want?"

And they said, "Jesus of Nazareth."

⁸"I told you that I am he," Jesus answered. "If you are looking for me, then let these men go." ⁹This happened so that the words he had spoken would be fulfilled: "I have not lost one of those you gave me."ᵃ

¹⁰Then Simon Peter, who had a sword, drew it and struck the high priest's servant, cutting off his right ear. (The servant's name was Malchus.)

¹¹Jesus commanded Peter, "Put your sword away! Shall I not drink the cup the Father has given me?"

Jesus Taken to Annas

¹²Then the detachment of soldiers with its commander and the Jewish officials arrested Jesus. They bound him ¹³and brought him first to Annas, who was the father-in-law of Caiaphas, the high priest that year. ¹⁴Caiaphas was the one who had advised the Jews that it would be good if one man died for the people.

Peter's First Denial

¹⁵Simon Peter and another disciple were following Jesus. Because this disciple was known to the high priest, he went with Jesus into the high priest's courtyard, ¹⁶but Peter had to wait outside at the door. The other disciple, who was known to the high priest, came back, spoke to the girl on duty there and brought Peter in.

¹⁷"You are not one of his disciples, are you?" the girl at the door asked Peter.

He replied, "I am not."

¹⁸It was cold, and the servants and officials stood around a fire they had made to keep warm. Peter also was standing with them, warming himself.

The High Priest Questions Jesus

¹⁹Meanwhile, the high priest questioned Jesus about his disciples and his teaching.

²⁰"I have spoken openly to the world," Jesus replied. "I always taught in synagogues or at the temple, where all the Jews come together. I said nothing in secret. ²¹Why question me? Ask those who heard me. Surely they know what I said."

²²When Jesus said this, one of the officials nearby struck him in the face. "Is this the way you answer the high priest?" he demanded.

²³"If I said something wrong," Jesus replied, "testify as to what is wrong. But if I spoke the truth, why did you strike me?" ²⁴Then Annas sent him, still bound, to Caiaphas the high priest.ᵇ

Peter's Second and Third Denials

²⁵As Simon Peter stood warming himself, he was asked, "You are not one of his disciples, are you?"

He denied it, saying, "I am not."

²⁶One of the high priest's servants, a relative of the man whose ear Peter had cut off, challenged him, "Didn't I see you with him in the olive grove?" ²⁷Again Peter denied it, and at that moment a rooster began to crow.

Jesus Before Pilate

²⁸Then the Jews led Jesus from Caiaphas to the palace of the Roman governor. By now it was early morning, and to avoid ceremonial uncleanness the Jews did not enter the palace; they wanted to be able to eat the Passover. ²⁹So Pilate came out to them and asked, "What charges are you bringing against this man?"

³⁰"If he were not a criminal," they replied, "we would not have handed him over to you."

³¹Pilate said, "Take him yourselves and judge him by your own law."

"But we have no right to execute anyone," the Jews objected. ³²This happened so that the words Jesus had spoken indicating the kind of death he was going to die would be fulfilled.

³³Pilate then went back inside the palace, summoned Jesus and asked him, "Are you the king of the Jews?"

³⁴"Is that your own idea," Jesus asked, "or did others talk to you about me?"

ᵃ9 John 6:39   ᵇ24 Or (Now Annas had sent him, still bound, to Caiaphas the high priest.)

35"Am I a Jew?" Pilate replied. "It was your people and your chief priests who handed you over to me. What is it you have done?"

36Jesus said, "My kingdom is not of this world. If it were, my servants would fight to prevent my arrest by the Jews. But now my kingdom is from another place."

37"You are a king, then!" said Pilate.

Jesus answered, "You are right in saying I am a king. In fact, for this reason I was born, and for this I came into the world, to testify to the truth. Everyone on the side of truth listens to me."

38"What is truth?" Pilate asked. With this he went out again to the Jews and said, "I find no basis for a charge against him. 39But it is your custom for me to release to you one prisoner at the time of the Passover. Do you want me to release 'the king of the Jews'?"

40They shouted back, "No, not him! Give us Barabbas!" Now Barabbas had taken part in a rebellion.

Jesus Sentenced to Be Crucified

19 Then Pilate took Jesus and had him flogged. 2The soldiers twisted together a crown of thorns and put it on his head. They clothed him in a purple robe 3and went up to him again and again, saying, "Hail, king of the Jews!" And they struck him in the face.

4Once more Pilate came out and said to the Jews, "Look, I am bringing him out to you to let you know that I find no basis for a charge against him." 5When Jesus came out wearing the crown of thorns and the purple robe, Pilate said to them, "Here is the man!"

6As soon as the chief priests and their officials saw him, they shouted, "Crucify! Crucify!"

But Pilate answered, "You take him and crucify him. As for me, I find no basis for a charge against him."

7The Jews insisted, "We have a law, and according to that law he must die, because he claimed to be the Son of God."

8When Pilate heard this, he was even more afraid, 9and he went back inside the palace. "Where do you come from?" he asked Jesus, but Jesus gave him no answer. 10"Do you refuse to speak to me?"

Pilate said. "Don't you realize I have power either to free you or to crucify you?"

11Jesus answered, "You would have no power over me if it were not given to you from above. Therefore the one who handed me over to you is guilty of a greater sin."

12From then on, Pilate tried to set Jesus free, but the Jews kept shouting, "If you let this man go, you are no friend of Caesar. Anyone who claims to be a king opposes Caesar."

13When Pilate heard this, he brought Jesus out and sat down on the judge's seat at a place known as the Stone Pavement (which in Aramaic is Gabbatha). 14It was the day of Preparation of Passover Week, about the sixth hour.

"Here is your king," Pilate said to the Jews.

15But they shouted, "Take him away! Take him away! Crucify him!"

"Shall I crucify your king?" Pilate asked.

"We have no king but Caesar," the chief priests answered.

16Finally Pilate handed him over to them to be crucified.

The Crucifixion

So the soldiers took charge of Jesus. 17Carrying his own cross, he went out to the place of the Skull (which in Aramaic is called Golgotha). 18Here they crucified him, and with him two others—one on each side and Jesus in the middle.

19Pilate had a notice prepared and fastened to the cross. It read: JESUS OF NAZARETH, THE KING OF THE JEWS. 20Many of the Jews read this sign, for the place where Jesus was crucified was near the city, and the sign was written in Aramaic, Latin and Greek. 21The chief priests of the Jews protested to Pilate, "Do not write 'The King of the Jews,' but that this man claimed to be king of the Jews."

22Pilate answered, "What I have written, I have written."

23When the soldiers crucified Jesus, they took his clothes, dividing them into four shares, one for each of them, with the undergarment remaining. This garment was seamless, woven in one piece from top to bottom.

24"Let's not tear it," they said to one another. "Let's decide by lot who will get it."

This happened that the scripture might be fulfilled which said,

> "They divided my garments among them
> and cast lots for my clothing."[a]

So this is what the soldiers did.

²⁵Near the cross of Jesus stood his mother, his mother's sister, Mary the wife of Clopas, and Mary Magdalene. ²⁶When Jesus saw his mother there, and the disciple whom he loved standing nearby, he said to his mother, "Dear woman, here is your son," ²⁷and to the disciple, "Here is your mother." From that time on, this disciple took her into his home.

The Death of Jesus

²⁸Later, knowing that all was now completed, and so that the Scripture would be fulfilled, Jesus said, "I am thirsty." ²⁹A jar of wine vinegar was there, so they soaked a sponge in it, put the sponge on a stalk of the hyssop plant, and lifted it to Jesus' lips. ³⁰When he had received the drink, Jesus said, "It is finished." With that, he bowed his head and gave up his spirit.

³¹Now it was the day of Preparation, and the next day was to be a special Sabbath. Because the Jews did not want the bodies left on the crosses during the Sabbath, they asked Pilate to have the legs broken and the bodies taken down. ³²The soldiers therefore came and broke the legs of the first man who had been crucified with Jesus, and then those of the other. ³³But when they came to Jesus and found that he was already dead, they did not break his legs. ³⁴Instead, one of the soldiers pierced Jesus' side with a spear, bringing a sudden flow of blood and water. ³⁵The man who saw it has given testimony, and his testimony is true. He knows that he tells the truth, and he testifies so that you also may believe. ³⁶These things happened so that the scripture would be fulfilled: "Not one of his bones will be broken,"[b] ³⁷and, as another scripture says, "They will look on the one they have pierced."[c]

The Burial of Jesus

³⁸Later, Joseph of Arimathea asked Pilate for the body of Jesus. Now Joseph was a disciple of Jesus, but secretly because he feared the Jews. With Pilate's permission, he came and took the body away. ³⁹He was accompanied by Nicodemus, the man who earlier had visited Jesus at night. Nicodemus brought a mixture of myrrh and aloes, about seventy-five pounds.[d] ⁴⁰Taking Jesus' body, the two of them wrapped it, with the spices, in strips of linen. This was in accordance with Jewish burial customs. ⁴¹At the place where Jesus was crucified, there was a garden, and in the garden a new tomb, in which no one had ever been laid. ⁴²Because it was the Jewish day of Preparation and since the tomb was nearby, they laid Jesus there.

The Empty Tomb

20 Early on the first day of the week, while it was still dark, Mary Magdalene went to the tomb and saw that the stone had been removed from the entrance. ²So she came running to Simon Peter and the other disciple, the one Jesus loved, and said, "They have taken the Lord out of the tomb, and we don't know where they have put him!"

³So Peter and the other disciple started for the tomb. ⁴Both were running, but the other disciple outran Peter and reached the tomb first. ⁵He bent over and looked in at the strips of linen lying there but did not go in. ⁶Then Simon Peter, who was behind him, arrived and went into the tomb. He saw the strips of linen lying there, ⁷as well as the burial cloth that had been around Jesus' head. The cloth was folded up by itself, separate from the linen. ⁸Finally the other disciple, who had reached the tomb first, also went inside. He saw and believed. ⁹(They still did not understand from Scripture that Jesus had to rise from the dead.)

Jesus Appears to Mary Magdalene

¹⁰Then the disciples went back to their homes, ¹¹but Mary stood outside the tomb crying. As she wept, she bent over to look into the tomb ¹²and saw two angels in white, seated where Jesus' body had been, one at the head and the other at the foot.

---

[a]24 Psalm 22:18 [b]36 Exodus 12:46; Num. 9:12; Psalm 34:20 [c]37 Zech. 12:10
[d]39 Greek a hundred litrai (about 34 kilograms)

¹³They asked her, "Woman, why are you crying?"

"They have taken my Lord away," she said, "and I don't know where they have put him." ¹⁴At this, she turned around and saw Jesus standing there, but she did not realize that it was Jesus.

¹⁵"Woman," he said, "why are you crying? Who is it you are looking for?"

Thinking he was the gardener, she said, "Sir, if you have carried him away, tell me where you have put him, and I will get him."

¹⁶Jesus said to her, "Mary."

She turned toward him and cried out in Aramaic, "Rabboni!" (which means Teacher).

¹⁷Jesus said, "Do not hold on to me, for I have not yet returned to the Father. Go instead to my brothers and tell them, 'I am returning to my Father and your Father, to my God and your God.'"

¹⁸Mary Magdalene went to the disciples with the news: "I have seen the Lord!" And she told them that he had said these things to her.

Jesus Appears to His Disciples

¹⁹On the evening of that first day of the week, when the disciples were together, with the doors locked for fear of the Jews, Jesus came and stood among them and said, "Peace be with you!" ²⁰After he said this, he showed them his hands and side. The disciples were overjoyed when they saw the Lord.

²¹Again Jesus said, "Peace be with you! As the Father has sent me, I am sending you." ²²And with that he breathed on them and said, "Receive the Holy Spirit. ²³If you forgive anyone his sins, they are forgiven; if you do not forgive them, they are not forgiven."

Jesus Appears to Thomas

²⁴Now Thomas (called Didymus), one of the Twelve, was not with the disciples when Jesus came. ²⁵So the other disciples told him, "We have seen the Lord!"

But he said to them, "Unless I see the nail marks in his hands and put my finger where the nails were, and put my hand into his side, I will not believe it."

²⁶A week later his disciples were in the house again, and Thomas was with them.

Though the doors were locked, Jesus came and stood among them and said, "Peace be with you!" ²⁷Then he said to Thomas, "Put your finger here; see my hands. Reach out your hand and put it into my side. Stop doubting and believe."

²⁸Thomas said to him, "My Lord and my God!"

²⁹Then Jesus told him, "Because you have seen me, you have believed; blessed are those who have not seen and yet have believed."

> THEN Jesus told him, "Because you have seen me, you have believed; blessed are those who have not seen and yet have believed."
>
> JOHN 20:29

³⁰Jesus did many other miraculous signs in the presence of his disciples, which are not recorded in this book. ³¹But these are written that you may*ᵃ* believe that Jesus is the Christ, the Son of God, and that by believing you may have life in his name.

Jesus and the Miraculous Catch of Fish

21 Afterward Jesus appeared again to his disciples, by the Sea of Tiberias.*ᵇ* It happened this way: ²Simon Peter, Thomas (called Didymus), Nathanael from Cana in Galilee, the sons of Zebedee, and two other disciples were together. ³"I'm going out to fish," Simon Peter told them, and they said, "We'll go with you." So they went out and got into the boat, but that night they caught nothing.

⁴Early in the morning, Jesus stood on the shore, but the disciples did not realize that it was Jesus.

⁵He called out to them, "Friends, haven't you any fish?"

"No," they answered.

⁶He said, "Throw your net on the right side of the boat and you will find some." When they did, they were unable to haul the net in because of the large number of fish.

⁷Then the disciple whom Jesus loved said to Peter, "It is the Lord!" As soon as

---

ᵃ31 Some manuscripts *may continue to*
ᵇ1 That is, Sea of Galilee

Simon Peter heard him say, "It is the Lord," he wrapped his outer garment around him (for he had taken it off) and jumped into the water. ⁸The other disciples followed in the boat, towing the net full of fish, for they were not far from shore, about a hundred yards.ᵃ ⁹When they landed, they saw a fire of burning coals there with fish on it, and some bread.

¹⁰Jesus said to them, "Bring some of the fish you have just caught."

¹¹Simon Peter climbed aboard and dragged the net ashore. It was full of large fish, 153, but even with so many the net was not torn. ¹²Jesus said to them, "Come and have breakfast." None of the disciples dared ask him, "Who are you?" They knew it was the Lord. ¹³Jesus came, took the bread and gave it to them, and did the same with the fish. ¹⁴This was now the third time Jesus appeared to his disciples after he was raised from the dead.

> ❝ Prayer does not fit us for the greater work; prayer is the greater work. ❞
>
> OSWALD CHAMBERS

Jesus Reinstates Peter

¹⁵When they had finished eating, Jesus said to Simon Peter, "Simon son of John, do you truly love me more than these?"

"Yes, Lord," he said, "you know that I love you."

Jesus said, "Feed my lambs."

¹⁶Again Jesus said, "Simon son of John, do you truly love me?"

He answered, "Yes, Lord, you know that I love you."

Jesus said, "Take care of my sheep."

¹⁷The third time he said to him, "Simon son of John, do you love me?"

Peter was hurt because Jesus asked him the third time, "Do you love me?" He said, "Lord, you know all things; you know that I love you."

Jesus said, "Feed my sheep. ¹⁸I tell you the truth, when you were younger you dressed yourself and went where you wanted; but when you are old you will stretch out your hands, and someone else will dress you and lead you where you do not want to go." ¹⁹Jesus said this to indicate the kind of death by which Peter would glorify God. Then he said to him, "Follow me!"

²⁰Peter turned and saw that the disciple whom Jesus loved was following them. (This was the one who had leaned back against Jesus at the supper and had said, "Lord, who is going to betray you?") ²¹When Peter saw him, he asked, "Lord, what about him?"

²²Jesus answered, "If I want him to remain alive until I return, what is that to you? You must follow me." ²³Because of this, the rumor spread among the brothers that this disciple would not die. But Jesus did not say that he would not die; he only said, "If I want him to remain alive until I return, what is that to you?"

²⁴This is the disciple who testifies to these things and who wrote them down. We know that his testimony is true.

²⁵Jesus did many other things as well. If every one of them were written down, I suppose that even the whole world would not have room for the books that would be written.

ᵃ8 Greek *about two hundred cubits* (about 90 meters)

Acts

THE REAL ACTION in the book of Acts is not exactly the acts of the apostles, as commonly thought. The apostles are very busy, surely, but the interest of the book is who is working through them. Luke opens the second book of his two-volume work (started in the Gospel of Luke) by saying, "In my former book, Theophilus, I wrote about all that Jesus began to do and to teach until the day he was taken up to heaven, after giving instructions through the Holy Spirit to the apostles he had chosen" (1:1–2). The clear implication is that Luke wants his readers to understand that his book was a continuing record of the things Jesus was doing before his ascension and now would continue to do by his Spirit through his apostles. John Stott proposes that a more accurate, though cumbersome, title of the book would be "The Continuing Words and Deeds of Jesus by his Spirit through his Apostles."[1]

So much depends, then, on the church obeying Jesus' command to "wait for the gift my Father promised"—the gift of the Holy Spirit (1:4). One way to read this exciting book is from the perspective of how the church waits on God, receiving his power and doing his will. Repeatedly, the church waits in prayer (see 1:14; 2:42–47; 4:23–31; 12:5; 13:2–3). Repeatedly, the mission of Christ is advanced as they do. The book of Acts calls and encourages us to do Jesus' work Jesus' way, through prayer and the Word of God (see 6:1–7).

Jesus Taken Up Into Heaven

1 In my former book, Theophilus, I wrote about all that Jesus began to do and to teach ²until the day he was taken up to heaven, after giving instructions through the Holy Spirit to the apostles he had chosen. ³After his suffering, he showed himself to these men and gave many convincing proofs that he was alive. He appeared to them over a period of forty days and spoke about the kingdom of God. ⁴On one occasion, while he was eating with them, he gave them this command: "Do not leave Jerusalem, but wait for the gift my Father promised, which you have heard me speak about. ⁵For John baptized with*ᵃ* water, but in a few days you will be baptized with the Holy Spirit."

⁶So when they met together, they asked him, "Lord, are you at this time going to restore the kingdom to Israel?"

⁷He said to them: "It is not for you to know the times or dates the Father has set by his own authority. ⁸But you will receive power when the Holy Spirit comes on you; and you will be my witnesses in Jerusalem, and in all Judea and Samaria, and to the ends of the earth."

⁹After he said this, he was taken up before their very eyes, and a cloud hid him from their sight.

¹⁰They were looking intently up into the sky as he was going, when suddenly two men dressed in white stood beside them. ¹¹"Men of Galilee," they said, "why do you stand here looking into the sky? This same Jesus, who has been taken from you into heaven, will come back in the same way you have seen him go into heaven."

Matthias Chosen to Replace Judas

¹²Then they returned to Jerusalem from the hill called the Mount of Olives, a Sabbath day's walk*ᵇ* from the city. ¹³When they arrived, they went upstairs to the room where they were staying. Those present were Peter, John, James and Andrew; Philip and Thomas, Bartholomew and Matthew; James son of Alphaeus and Simon the Zealot, and Judas son of James. ¹⁴They all joined together constantly in prayer, along with the women and Mary the mother of Jesus, and with his brothers.

¹⁵In those days Peter stood up among the believers*ᶜ* (a group numbering about a hundred and twenty) ¹⁶and said, "Brothers, the Scripture had to be fulfilled which the Holy Spirit spoke long ago through the mouth of David concerning Judas, who served as guide for those who arrested Jesus— ¹⁷he was one of our number and shared in this ministry."

¹⁸(With the reward he got for his wickedness, Judas bought a field; there he fell headlong, his body burst open and all his intestines spilled out. ¹⁹Everyone in Jerusalem heard about this, so they called that field in their language Akeldama, that is, Field of Blood.)

²⁰"For," said Peter, "it is written in the book of Psalms,

> " 'May his place be deserted;
>   let there be no one to dwell in it,'*ᵈ*

and,

> " 'May another take his place of
>   leadership.'*ᵉ*

²¹Therefore it is necessary to choose one of the men who have been with us the whole time the Lord Jesus went in and out among us, ²²beginning from John's baptism to the time when Jesus was taken up from us. For one of these must become a witness with us of his resurrection."

²³So they proposed two men: Joseph called Barsabbas (also known as Justus) and Matthias. ²⁴Then they prayed, "Lord, you know everyone's heart. Show us which of these two you have chosen ²⁵to take over this apostolic ministry, which Judas left to go where he belongs." ²⁶Then they cast lots, and the lot fell to Matthias; so he was added to the eleven apostles.

The Holy Spirit Comes at Pentecost

2 When the day of Pentecost came, they were all together in one place. ²Suddenly a sound like the blowing of a

> 66 *Prayer is exhaling the spirit of man and inhaling the spirit of God.* 99
>
> EDWIN KEITH

ᵃ5 Or *in*   *ᵇ12* That is, about 3/4 mile (about 1,100 meters)   *ᶜ15* Greek *brothers*
ᵈ20 Psalm 69:25   *ᵉ20* Psalm 109:8

violent wind came from heaven and filled the whole house where they were sitting. ³They saw what seemed to be tongues of fire that separated and came to rest on each of them. ⁴All of them were filled with the Holy Spirit and began to speak in other tongues[a] as the Spirit enabled them.

⁵Now there were staying in Jerusalem God-fearing Jews from every nation under heaven. ⁶When they heard this sound, a crowd came together in bewilderment, because each one heard them speaking in his own language. ⁷Utterly amazed, they asked: "Are not all these men who are speaking Galileans? ⁸Then how is it that each of us hears them in his own native language? ⁹Parthians, Medes and Elamites; residents of Mesopotamia, Judea and Cappadocia, Pontus and Asia, ¹⁰Phrygia and Pamphylia, Egypt and the parts of Libya near Cyrene; visitors from Rome ¹¹(both Jews and converts to Judaism); Cretans and Arabs—we hear them declaring the wonders of God in our own tongues!" ¹²Amazed and perplexed, they asked one another, "What does this mean?"

¹³Some, however, made fun of them and said, "They have had too much wine.[b]"

[a]4 Or languages; also in verse 11
[b]13 Or sweet wine

ACTS 1:1–14

Being a Prayer Meeting

1:14 THEY ALL JOINED TOGETHER CONSTANTLY IN PRAYER.

"The early church didn't *have* a prayer meeting," said Armin Gesswein, "the church *was* a prayer meeting." Prayer wasn't a specialized ministry for the first Christians; it was their life. They joined together in prayer "constantly" (1:14); prayer was their devotion (see 2:42).

Why was this so? It was their direct response to the Lord's direct command to "wait for the gift my Father promised" (see 1:4–5,8). To wait was to pray, to pray was to wait. Waiting is not passively allowing time to pass until the promise comes; it is a vigorous laying hold of what is promised, a living into the future. That is what prayer is. To pray is to do what watchmen do as they wait for the morning, eyes fixed on the horizon, straining to see the sun: "My soul waits for the Lord more than watchmen wait for the morning" (Psalm 130:6).

Prayer is fueled by hope. We don't pray to get God's attention; we pray because he has ours. His promises are wonderful and sure. He commands us to wait for them, actively, prayerfully. We have not because we ask not, or ask badly, with base motives, says James (see James 4:2–3). But there is another reason: We have not because we wait not, as opposed to these Jerusalem believers. Those who wait receive, and are strengthened as they wait. "Wait for the LORD; be strong and take heart and wait for the LORD" (Psalm 27:14). Let the church stop having prayer meetings and start *being* a prayer meeting! That is where the power lies.

PRAY:
You have my attention, Lord! May I, and all those in your church,
wait upon you and your good promises.

───────

FOR YOUR NEXT DEVOTIONAL READING, GO TO PAGE 1320.

Peter Addresses the Crowd

¹⁴Then Peter stood up with the Eleven, raised his voice and addressed the crowd: "Fellow Jews and all of you who live in Jerusalem, let me explain this to you; listen carefully to what I say. ¹⁵These men are not drunk, as you suppose. It's only nine in the morning! ¹⁶No, this is what was spoken by the prophet Joel:

¹⁷ " 'In the last days, God says,
    I will pour out my Spirit on all
        people.
Your sons and daughters will
        prophesy,
    your young men will see
        visions,
    your old men will dream dreams.
¹⁸ Even on my servants, both men and
        women,
    I will pour out my Spirit in those
        days,
    and they will prophesy.
¹⁹ I will show wonders in the heaven
        above
    and signs on the earth below,
    blood and fire and billows of
        smoke.
²⁰ The sun will be turned to darkness
    and the moon to blood
    before the coming of the great and
        glorious day of the Lord.
²¹ And everyone who calls
    on the name of the Lord will be
        saved.' ᵃ

²²"Men of Israel, listen to this: Jesus of Nazareth was a man accredited by God to you by miracles, wonders and signs, which God did among you through him, as you yourselves know. ²³This man was handed over to you by God's set purpose and foreknowledge; and you, with the help of wicked men,ᵇ put him to death by nailing him to the cross. ²⁴But God raised him from the dead, freeing him from the agony of death, because it was impossible for death to keep its hold on him. ²⁵David said about him:

" 'I saw the Lord always before me.
    Because he is at my right hand,
    I will not be shaken.
²⁶ Therefore my heart is glad and my
        tongue rejoices;
    my body also will live in hope,
²⁷ because you will not abandon me to
        the grave,
    nor will you let your Holy One see
        decay.
²⁸ You have made known to me the
        paths of life;
    you will fill me with joy in your
        presence.' ᶜ

²⁹"Brothers, I can tell you confidently that the patriarch David died and was buried, and his tomb is here to this day. ³⁰But he was a prophet and knew that God had promised him on oath that he would place one of his descendants on his throne. ³¹Seeing what was ahead, he spoke of the resurrection of the Christ,ᵈ that he was not abandoned to the grave, nor did his body see decay. ³²God has raised this Jesus to life, and we are all witnesses of the fact. ³³Exalted to the right hand of God, he has received from the Father the promised Holy Spirit and has poured out what you now see and hear. ³⁴For David did not ascend to heaven, and yet he said,

" 'The Lord said to my Lord:
    "Sit at my right hand
³⁵ until I make your enemies
    a footstool for your feet." ' ᵉ

³⁶"Therefore let all Israel be assured of this: God has made this Jesus, whom you crucified, both Lord and Christ."

³⁷When the people heard this, they were cut to the heart and said to Peter and the other apostles, "Brothers, what shall we do?"

³⁸Peter replied, "Repent and be baptized, every one of you, in the name of Jesus Christ for the forgiveness of your sins. And you will receive the gift of the Holy Spirit. ³⁹The promise is for you and your children and for all who are far off— for all whom the Lord our God will call."

⁴⁰With many other words he warned them; and he pleaded with them, "Save yourselves from this corrupt generation." ⁴¹Those who accepted his message were baptized, and about three thousand were added to their number that day.

ᵃ21 Joel 2:28–32   ᵇ23 Or of those not having the law (that is, Gentiles)   ᶜ28 Psalm 16:8–11   ᵈ31 Or Messiah. "The Christ" (Greek) and "the Messiah" (Hebrew) both mean "the Anointed One"; also in verse 36.   ᵉ35 Psalm 110:1

The Fellowship of the Believers

⁴²They devoted themselves to the apostles' teaching and to the fellowship, to the breaking of bread and to prayer. ⁴³Everyone was filled with awe, and many wonders and miraculous signs were done by the apostles. ⁴⁴All the believers were together and had everything in common. ⁴⁵Selling their possessions and goods, they gave to anyone as he had need. ⁴⁶Every day they continued to meet together in the temple courts. They broke bread in their homes and ate together with glad and sincere hearts, ⁴⁷praising God and enjoying the favor of all the people. And the Lord added to their number daily those who were being saved.

Peter Heals the Crippled Beggar

3 One day Peter and John were going up to the temple at the time of prayer—at three in the afternoon. ²Now a man crippled from birth was being carried to the temple gate called Beautiful, where he was put every day to beg from those going into the temple courts. ³When he saw Peter and John about to enter, he asked them for money. ⁴Peter looked straight at him, as did John. Then Peter said, "Look at us!" ⁵So the man

---

ACTS 2:42–47

Vital Signs

2:42 THEY DEVOTED THEMSELVES TO THE APOSTLES' TEACHING AND TO THE FELLOWSHIP, TO THE BREAKING OF BREAD AND TO PRAYER.

The church waited for Christ's extraordinary promise, the baptism of the Holy Spirit. The waiting was rewarded, the extraordinary came, and Christ's community was immersed in the very life of God. What was next? More waiting, more praying. Luke says the church was devoted to four things: teaching, fellowship, the breaking of bread and *prayer*. The extraordinary was to be lived out in the ordinary patterns of life. The church continued the way it began: waiting. Waiting was becoming a habit.

Prayer is one of the four vital signs of a healthy church—like a heartbeat. If the pulse is weak and erratic, the body is sick. If it is strong and steady, the body is healthy and strong. Look at the health of the Jerusalem church: There was a pervasive sense of awe as the people saw wonders and miraculous signs. There was great joy as they shared their money, their time and their homes. Outsiders wanted to be on the inside, as "the Lord added to their number daily those who were being saved" (2:47).

What the church needs today is what it has needed from the beginning: more and more of the presence of Jesus. Our greatest need isn't for more programs and meetings; our greatest need is for more of Jesus. Look again at what was happening in the Jerusalem church. God comes to churches and individuals who wait for him. To wait is to pray, to pray is to wait—not as an occasional, extraordinary thing, but as a pattern, a habit of life.

P R A Y :

Lord Jesus, we need you so desperately! Form within me,
and my church, a devoted habit of waiting on you in prayer.

FOR YOUR NEXT DEVOTIONAL READING, GO TO PAGE 1323.

gave them his attention, expecting to get something from them.

[6]Then Peter said, "Silver or gold I do not have, but what I have I give you. In the name of Jesus Christ of Nazareth, walk." [7]Taking him by the right hand, he helped him up, and instantly the man's feet and ankles became strong. [8]He jumped to his feet and began to walk. Then he went with them into the temple courts, walking and jumping, and praising God. [9]When all the people saw him walking and praising God, [10]they recognized him as the same man who used to sit begging at the temple gate called Beautiful, and they were filled with wonder and amazement at what had happened to him.

Peter Speaks to the Onlookers

[11]While the beggar held on to Peter and John, all the people were astonished and came running to them in the place called Solomon's Colonnade. [12]When Peter saw this, he said to them: "Men of Israel, why does this surprise you? Why do you stare at us as if by our own power or godliness we had made this man walk? [13]The God of Abraham, Isaac and Jacob, the God of our fathers, has glorified his servant Jesus. You handed him over to be killed, and you disowned him before Pilate, though he had decided to let him go. [14]You disowned the Holy and Righteous One and asked that a murderer be released to you. [15]You killed the author of life, but God raised him from the dead. We are witnesses of this. [16]By faith in the name of Jesus, this man whom you see and know was made strong. It is Jesus' name and the faith that comes through him that has given this complete healing to him, as you can all see.

[17]"Now, brothers, I know that you acted in ignorance, as did your leaders. [18]But this is how God fulfilled what he had foretold through all the prophets, saying that his Christ[a] would suffer. [19]Repent, then, and turn to God, so that your sins may be wiped out, that times of refreshing may come from the Lord, [20]and that he may send the Christ, who has been appointed for you—even Jesus. [21]He must remain in heaven until the time comes for God to restore everything, as he promised long ago through his holy prophets. [22]For Moses said, 'The Lord your God will raise up for you a prophet like me from among your own people; you must listen to everything he tells you. [23]Anyone who does not listen to him will be completely cut off from among his people.'[b]

[24]"Indeed, all the prophets from Samuel on, as many as have spoken, have foretold these days. [25]And you are heirs of the prophets and of the covenant God made with your fathers. He said to Abraham, 'Through your offspring all peoples on earth will be blessed.'[c] [26]When God raised up his servant, he sent him first to you to bless you by turning each of you from your wicked ways."

Peter and John Before the Sanhedrin

4 The priests and the captain of the temple guard and the Sadducees came up to Peter and John while they were speaking to the people. [2]They were greatly disturbed because the apostles were teaching the people and proclaiming in Jesus the resurrection of the dead. [3]They seized Peter and John, and because it was evening, they put them in jail until the next day. [4]But many who heard the message believed, and the number of men grew to about five thousand.

[5]The next day the rulers, elders and teachers of the law met in Jerusalem. [6]Annas the high priest was there, and so were Caiaphas, John, Alexander and the other men of the high priest's family. [7]They had Peter and John brought before them and began to question them: "By what power or what name did you do this?"

[8]Then Peter, filled with the Holy Spirit, said to them: "Rulers and elders of the people! [9]If we are being called to account today for an act of kindness shown to a cripple and are asked how he was healed, [10]then know this, you and all the people of Israel: It is by the name of Jesus Christ of Nazareth, whom you crucified but whom God raised from the dead, that this man stands before you healed. [11]He is

" 'the stone you builders rejected,
  which has become the capstone.[d]'[e]

---

[a]18 Or *Messiah*; also in verse 20
[b]23 Deut. 18:15,18,19   [c]25 Gen. 22:18; 26:4
[d]11 Or *cornerstone*   [e]11 Psalm 118:22

¹²Salvation is found in no one else, for there is no other name under heaven given to men by which we must be saved."

¹³When they saw the courage of Peter and John and realized that they were unschooled, ordinary men, they were astonished and they took note that these men had been with Jesus. ¹⁴But since they could see the man who had been healed standing there with them, there was nothing they could say. ¹⁵So they ordered them to withdraw from the Sanhedrin and then conferred together. ¹⁶"What are we going to do with these men?" they asked. "Everybody living in Jerusalem knows they have done an outstanding miracle, and we cannot deny it. ¹⁷But to stop this thing from spreading any further among the people, we must warn these men to speak no longer to anyone in this name."

¹⁸Then they called them in again and commanded them not to speak or teach at all in the name of Jesus. ¹⁹But Peter and John replied, "Judge for yourselves whether it is right in God's sight to obey you rather than God. ²⁰For we cannot help speaking about what we have seen and heard."

²¹After further threats they let them go. They could not decide how to punish them, because all the people were praising God for what had happened. ²²For the man who was miraculously healed was over forty years old.

The Believers' Prayer

²³On their release, Peter and John went back to their own people and reported all that the chief priests and elders had said to them. ²⁴When they heard this, they raised their voices together in prayer to God. "Sovereign Lord," they said, "you made the heaven and the earth and the sea, and everything in them. ²⁵You spoke by the Holy Spirit through the mouth of your servant, our father David:

" 'Why do the nations rage
    and the peoples plot in vain?
²⁶ The kings of the earth take their
        stand
    and the rulers gather together
against the Lord
    and against his Anointed One.ᵃᵇ

²⁷Indeed Herod and Pontius Pilate met together with the Gentiles and the peopleᶜ of Israel in this city to conspire against your holy servant Jesus, whom you anointed. ²⁸They did what your power and will had decided beforehand should happen. ²⁹Now, Lord, consider their threats and enable your servants to speak your word with great boldness. ³⁰Stretch out your hand to heal and perform miraculous signs and wonders through the name of your holy servant Jesus."

³¹After they prayed, the place where they were meeting was shaken. And they were all filled with the Holy Spirit and spoke the word of God boldly.

> AFTER they prayed, the place where they were meeting was shaken. And they were all filled with the Holy Spirit and spoke the word of God boldly.
>
> ACTS 4:31

The Believers Share Their Possessions

³²All the believers were one in heart and mind. No one claimed that any of his possessions was his own, but they shared everything they had. ³³With great power the apostles continued to testify to the resurrection of the Lord Jesus, and much grace was upon them all. ³⁴There were no needy persons among them. For from time to time those who owned lands or houses sold them, brought the money from the sales ³⁵and put it at the apostles' feet, and it was distributed to anyone as he had need.

³⁶Joseph, a Levite from Cyprus, whom the apostles called Barnabas (which means Son of Encouragement), ³⁷sold a field he owned and brought the money and put it at the apostles' feet.

Ananias and Sapphira

5 Now a man named Ananias, together with his wife Sapphira, also sold a piece of property. ²With his wife's full knowledge he kept back part of the money for himself, but brought the rest and put it at the apostles' feet.

ᵃ26 That is, Christ or Messiah
ᵇ26 Psalm 2:1,2   ᶜ27 The Greek is plural.

ACTS 4:23–31

Earthshaking Prayer

4:24 WHEN THEY HEARD THIS, THEY RAISED THEIR VOICES TOGETHER IN PRAYER
TO GOD.

Peter and John had just been detained, and then released, by the Sanhedrin
on account of their bold proclamation of the gospel. After their release, the
believers immediately entered into prayer. Their prayer time ended with a
kind of earthquake. How did that happen? It began with the church praying
a classically Biblical prayer, which is to say they proceeded the way so many
of the psalms and other great prayers of Scripture do. It is a prayer worthy
of imitation.

1. They rehearsed before God a summary of what he had done and
   said in history. He had always been the Sovereign Lord, creator of
   heaven and earth, King of kings and ruler of the nations. Read—or
   better, pray—this prayer thoughtfully, and you will get a crash
   course in a sound Biblical theology of creation, revelation and history, all summed up in the verbs used of God: He made; he spoke;
   he decided beforehand what would happen.
2. In the light of the past, they recounted what was going on in the
   present. God already knew everything that happened, of course, but
   it is a key part of the communion of prayer for God's people to lay it
   all out before God anyway. According to Jesus, God's comprehensive knowledge of all things gives us greater reason to speak our
   needs, not less (see Matthew 6:8).
3. Then they made their requests. The order of the prayer is important.
   First the rehearsal of God's past goodness, then the requests; for the
   requests come a lot easier when we are reminded of who we are
   speaking to! We are speaking to the Almighty, and nothing is too
   hard for him. From God, they asked that he do what only God can
   do: heal and perform miracles. For themselves, they asked that God
   help them do what they were supposed to do: be bold in their
   speaking. It's a great arrangement. May God be who he is, powerful
   and wise; may his people be who they are supposed to be, bold and
   faithful witnesses.

This kind of prayer moves the earth, not usually as in the shaking these
believers experienced, but in more important ways. Kingdoms rise and fall,
and history unfolds as the prayers of the saints are presented before the
throne of God (see Revelation 8:1–5).

PRAY:

Sovereign Lord, you are the God of creation,
revelation and history. I know that nothing is too hard for you,
so do what you desire to do in and through my life.

───────

FOR YOUR NEXT DEVOTIONAL READING, GO TO PAGE 1324.

Earthshaking Prayer

BLIND CHANG (DIED 1900)
With His Dying Breath

THIRTY-TWO THOUSAND Chinese Christians, along with 188 missionaries and their children, died in the Boxer Rebellion of 1900. Among them was a powerful evangelist known as Blind Chang. His death was no more remarkable than the many others who sealed their testimonies for Christ by laying down their lives. What is remarkable is the privilege granted him of publicly praising God even to his very last breath.

Before his conversion, Chang was so reprobate a sinner that he was nicknamed "Wu so pu wei te," which means "one without a particle of good within him." One day in a rage, this thief, gambler and womanizer even threw his wife and daughter out of their home. When he suddenly lost his eyesight at age 30, many of his neighbors were sure it was God's judgment that made him blind.

Chang heard of a missionary hospital, hundreds of miles from his home, where surgeries were being performed that could restore his sight. Somehow he got to the hospital, only to be told that all the beds were filled and that he could not be admitted as a patient. But when the hospital evangelist gave him a bed and Chang's sight was partially restored, he received the gospel with great joy and expressed a fervent desire to be baptized and follow Christ. James Webster, one of the missionaries at the hospital, told Chang he would not baptize him until he showed evidence of the genuineness of his faith by returning to his village and living his faith with the people who had given him his nickname. When Webster later visited his village, he was thrilled to see that Chang's testimony had led over 400 people to faith in Christ.

Though Chang eventually lost his sight again due to a botched medical procedure, his faith wasn't lost, and he became a powerful evangelist.

Chang memorized most of the New Testament and large portions of the Old. When the Boxers tried to stamp out Christianity in China, he became their prime target. To capture him, they held 50 Chinese Christians prisoner and threatened to kill them all if someone did not tell them of Chang's whereabouts. When Chang heard of this, he turned himself in.

Blind Chang was to be executed by decapitation. Unafraid, he sang the first Christian song he had ever learned as his captors took him to the place of execution. "Wu so pu wei te" had made peace with his Judge and Maker, and he knew Jesus' face would be the first thing he would see.

> Jesus loves me! he who died
> Heaven's gate to open wide;
> He will wash away my sin,
> Let his little child come in.
> Jesus loves me! he will stay
> Close beside me all the way;
> If I love him when I die,
> He will take me home on high.[2]

As the executioner's sword flashed in the sun and came down, Chang prayed, "Heavenly Father, receive my spirit."

P R A Y :

*Almighty and merciful Father, grant me the joy and the
privilege to praise you as long as I have breath, even to
the moment I don't. Let me glorify you in life and death.*

M E M O R I Z E :

*I will sing to the LORD all my life; I will sing praise
to my God as long as I live.* PSALM 104:33

FOR YOUR NEXT DEVOTIONAL READING, GO TO PAGE 1328.

[3]Then Peter said, "Ananias, how is it that Satan has so filled your heart that you have lied to the Holy Spirit and have kept for yourself some of the money you received for the land? [4]Didn't it belong to you before it was sold? And after it was sold, wasn't the money at your disposal? What made you think of doing such a thing? You have not lied to men but to God."

[5]When Ananias heard this, he fell down and died. And great fear seized all who heard what had happened. [6]Then the young men came forward, wrapped up his body, and carried him out and buried him.

[7]About three hours later his wife came in, not knowing what had happened. [8]Peter asked her, "Tell me, is this the price you and Ananias got for the land?"

"Yes," she said, "that is the price."

[9]Peter said to her, "How could you agree to test the Spirit of the Lord? Look! The feet of the men who buried your husband are at the door, and they will carry you out also."

[10]At that moment she fell down at his feet and died. Then the young men came in and, finding her dead, carried her out and buried her beside her husband. [11]Great fear seized the whole church and all who heard about these events.

The Apostles Heal Many

[12]The apostles performed many miraculous signs and wonders among the people. And all the believers used to meet together in Solomon's Colonnade. [13]No one else dared join them, even though they were highly regarded by the people. [14]Nevertheless, more and more men and women believed in the Lord and were added to their number. [15]As a result, people brought the sick into the streets and laid them on beds and mats so that at least Peter's shadow might fall on some of them as he passed by. [16]Crowds gathered also from the towns around Jerusalem, bringing their sick and those tormented by evil[a] spirits, and all of them were healed.

The Apostles Persecuted

[17]Then the high priest and all his associates, who were members of the party of the Sadducees, were filled with jealousy.

[18]They arrested the apostles and put them in the public jail. [19]But during the night an angel of the Lord opened the doors of the jail and brought them out. [20]"Go, stand in the temple courts," he said, "and tell the people the full message of this new life."

[21]At daybreak they entered the temple courts, as they had been told, and began to teach the people.

When the high priest and his associates arrived, they called together the Sanhedrin—the full assembly of the elders of Israel—and sent to the jail for the apostles. [22]But on arriving at the jail, the officers did not find them there. So they went back and reported, [23]"We found the jail securely locked, with the guards standing at the doors; but when we opened them, we found no one inside." [24]On hearing this report, the captain of the temple guard and the chief priests were puzzled, wondering what would come of this.

[25]Then someone came and said, "Look! The men you put in jail are standing in the temple courts teaching the people." [26]At that, the captain went with his officers and brought the apostles. They did not use force, because they feared that the people would stone them.

[27]Having brought the apostles, they made them appear before the Sanhedrin to be questioned by the high priest. [28]"We gave you strict orders not to teach in this name," he said. "Yet you have filled Jerusalem with your teaching and are determined to make us guilty of this man's blood."

[29]Peter and the other apostles replied: "We must obey God rather than men! [30]The God of our fathers raised Jesus from the dead—whom you had killed by hanging him on a tree. [31]God exalted him to his own right hand as Prince and Savior that he might give repentance and forgiveness of sins to Israel. [32]We are witnesses of these things, and so is the Holy Spirit, whom God has given to those who obey him."

[33]When they heard this, they were furious and wanted to put them to death. [34]But a Pharisee named Gamaliel, a teacher of the law, who was honored by all the

[a]16 Greek *unclean*

people, stood up in the Sanhedrin and ordered that the men be put outside for a little while. 35Then he addressed them: "Men of Israel, consider carefully what you intend to do to these men. 36Some time ago Theudas appeared, claiming to be somebody, and about four hundred men rallied to him. He was killed, all his followers were dispersed, and it all came to nothing. 37After him, Judas the Galilean appeared in the days of the census and led a band of people in revolt. He too was killed, and all his followers were scattered. 38Therefore, in the present case I advise you: Leave these men alone! Let them go! For if their purpose or activity is of human origin, it will fail. 39But if it is from God, you will not be able to stop these men; you will only find yourselves fighting against God."

40His speech persuaded them. They called the apostles in and had them flogged. Then they ordered them not to speak in the name of Jesus, and let them go.

41The apostles left the Sanhedrin, rejoicing because they had been counted worthy of suffering disgrace for the Name. 42Day after day, in the temple courts and from house to house, they never stopped teaching and proclaiming the good news that Jesus is the Christ.ᵃ

The Choosing of the Seven

6 In those days when the number of disciples was increasing, the Grecian Jews among them complained against the Hebraic Jews because their widows were being overlooked in the daily distribution of food. 2So the Twelve gathered all the disciples together and said, "It would not be right for us to neglect the ministry of the word of God in order to wait on tables. 3Brothers, choose seven men from among you who are known to be full of the Spirit and wisdom. We will turn this responsibility over to them 4and will give our attention to prayer and the ministry of the word."

5This proposal pleased the whole group. They chose Stephen, a man full of faith and of the Holy Spirit; also Philip, Procorus, Nicanor, Timon, Parmenas, and Nicolas from Antioch, a convert to Judaism. 6They presented these men to

the apostles, who prayed and laid their hands on them.

7So the word of God spread. The number of disciples in Jerusalem increased rapidly, and a large number of priests became obedient to the faith.

Stephen Seized

8Now Stephen, a man full of God's grace and power, did great wonders and miraculous signs among the people. 9Opposition arose, however, from members of the Synagogue of the Freedmen (as it was called)—Jews of Cyrene and Alexandria as well as the provinces of Cilicia and Asia. These men began to argue with Stephen, 10but they could not stand up against his wisdom or the Spirit by whom he spoke.

11Then they secretly persuaded some men to say, "We have heard Stephen speak words of blasphemy against Moses and against God."

12So they stirred up the people and the elders and the teachers of the law. They seized Stephen and brought him before the Sanhedrin. 13They produced false witnesses, who testified, "This fellow never stops speaking against this holy place and against the law. 14For we have heard him say that this Jesus of Nazareth will destroy this place and change the customs Moses handed down to us."

15All who were sitting in the Sanhedrin looked intently at Stephen, and they saw that his face was like the face of an angel.

Stephen's Speech to the Sanhedrin

7 Then the high priest asked him, "Are these charges true?"

2To this he replied: "Brothers and fathers, listen to me! The God of glory appeared to our father Abraham while he was still in Mesopotamia, before he lived in Haran. 3'Leave your country and your people,' God said, 'and go to the land I will show you.'ᵇ

4"So he left the land of the Chaldeans and settled in Haran. After the death of his father, God sent him to this land where you are now living. 5He gave him no inheritance here, not even a foot of ground. But God promised him that he

ᵃ42 Or Messiah   ᵇ3 Gen. 12:1

and his descendants after him would possess the land, even though at that time Abraham had no child. ⁶God spoke to him in this way: 'Your descendants will be strangers in a country not their own, and they will be enslaved and mistreated four hundred years. ⁷But I will punish the nation they serve as slaves,' God said, 'and afterward they will come out of that country and worship me in this place.'ᵃ ⁸Then he gave Abraham the covenant of circumcision. And Abraham became the

ᵃ7 Gen. 15:13,14

ACTS 6:1–7

Priorities

6:3–4 "WE WILL TURN THIS RESPONSIBILITY OVER TO THEM AND WILL GIVE OUR ATTENTION TO PRAYER AND THE MINISTRY OF THE WORD."

It took a crisis for the church to realign its priorities. It usually does. A spiritual euphoria had carried the young Christian community along up to this point. The church was growing everywhere: in conversions, in favor with the people—and in those who needed help. In that day there was no governmental safety net to help widows. It was up to the church to obey God's clear mandate to care for these people (see James 1:27; see also Deuteronomy 26:12).

But it was a huge job, and there were complaints—serious complaints. Some were accusing the church of prejudice, of giving preferential treatment to the "Hebraic Jews," whose language and cultural roots were in Israel, over the "Grecian Jews," whose language and cultural roots were from outside the Holy Land. Something had to be done. The apostles were involved in the controversy, so much so that they were spending less time in prayer and the ministry of the word. They were in a quandary: The widows must be cared for, prejudice (if the charge was true) must be eradicated, and they must tend to the ministry of prayer and the word. "It would not be right for us to neglect the ministry of the word of God in order to wait on tables" (6:2). But the tables still needed waiting, and it was clear they couldn't do everything.

So the church leaders delegated some of the work. Some people were set apart to be table-waiters. The Greek word used for their job is the word behind our English word *deacon*. Significantly, all the names of the deacons were Greek: There could be no room for prejudice in the church.

Two things precious to the integrity of the church were preserved in the church leaders' wise decision. The widows got what they needed, and the church got what it needed—leadership that was devoted to prayer and ministering the word of God. These two priorities were not seen as either/or choices, but as both/ands. If the church loses either of these—prayer and teaching the word on the one hand, or caring for the poor on the other—both will soon be gone.

PRAY:

I pray for my church, Father, that we may all do our part so that both spiritual and material needs are met. Lead us as we lay our priorities before you.

FOR YOUR NEXT DEVOTIONAL READING, GO TO PAGE 1331.

father of Isaac and circumcised him eight days after his birth. Later Isaac became the father of Jacob, and Jacob became the father of the twelve patriarchs.

⁹"Because the patriarchs were jealous of Joseph, they sold him as a slave into Egypt. But God was with him ¹⁰and rescued him from all his troubles. He gave Joseph wisdom and enabled him to gain the goodwill of Pharaoh king of Egypt; so he made him ruler over Egypt and all his palace.

¹¹"Then a famine struck all Egypt and Canaan, bringing great suffering, and our fathers could not find food. ¹²When Jacob heard that there was grain in Egypt, he sent our fathers on their first visit. ¹³On their second visit, Joseph told his brothers who he was, and Pharaoh learned about Joseph's family. ¹⁴After this, Joseph sent for his father Jacob and his whole family, seventy-five in all. ¹⁵Then Jacob went down to Egypt, where he and our fathers died. ¹⁶Their bodies were brought back to Shechem and placed in the tomb that Abraham had bought from the sons of Hamor at Shechem for a certain sum of money.

¹⁷"As the time drew near for God to fulfill his promise to Abraham, the number of our people in Egypt greatly increased. ¹⁸Then another king, who knew nothing about Joseph, became ruler of Egypt. ¹⁹He dealt treacherously with our people and oppressed our forefathers by forcing them to throw out their newborn babies so that they would die.

²⁰"At that time Moses was born, and he was no ordinary child.ᵃ For three months he was cared for in his father's house. ²¹When he was placed outside, Pharaoh's daughter took him and brought him up as her own son. ²²Moses was educated in all the wisdom of the Egyptians and was powerful in speech and action.

²³"When Moses was forty years old, he decided to visit his fellow Israelites. ²⁴He saw one of them being mistreated by an Egyptian, so he went to his defense and avenged him by killing the Egyptian. ²⁵Moses thought that his own people would realize that God was using him to rescue them, but they did not. ²⁶The next day Moses came upon two Israelites who were fighting. He tried to reconcile them

by saying, 'Men, you are brothers; why do you want to hurt each other?'

²⁷"But the man who was mistreating the other pushed Moses aside and said, 'Who made you ruler and judge over us? ²⁸Do you want to kill me as you killed the Egyptian yesterday?'ᵇ ²⁹When Moses heard this, he fled to Midian, where he settled as a foreigner and had two sons.

³⁰"After forty years had passed, an angel appeared to Moses in the flames of a burning bush in the desert near Mount Sinai. ³¹When he saw this, he was amazed at the sight. As he went over to look more closely, he heard the Lord's voice: ³²'I am the God of your fathers, the God of Abraham, Isaac and Jacob.'ᶜ Moses trembled with fear and did not dare to look.

³³"Then the Lord said to him, 'Take off your sandals; the place where you are standing is holy ground. ³⁴I have indeed seen the oppression of my people in Egypt. I have heard their groaning and have come down to set them free. Now come, I will send you back to Egypt.'ᵈ

³⁵"This is the same Moses whom they had rejected with the words, 'Who made you ruler and judge?' He was sent to be their ruler and deliverer by God himself, through the angel who appeared to him in the bush. ³⁶He led them out of Egypt and did wonders and miraculous signs in Egypt, at the Red Seaᵉ and for forty years in the desert.

³⁷"This is that Moses who told the Israelites, 'God will send you a prophet like me from your own people.'ᶠ ³⁸He was in the assembly in the desert, with the angel who spoke to him on Mount Sinai, and with our fathers; and he received living words to pass on to us.

³⁹"But our fathers refused to obey him. Instead, they rejected him and in their hearts turned back to Egypt. ⁴⁰They told Aaron, 'Make us gods who will go before us. As for this fellow Moses who led us out of Egypt—we don't know what has happened to him!'ᵍ ⁴¹That was the time they made an idol in the form of a calf. They brought sacrifices to it and held a celebration in honor of what their hands

ᵃ20 Or *was fair in the sight of God*
ᵇ28 Exodus 2:14   ᶜ32 Exodus 3:6
ᵈ34 Exodus 3:5,7,8,10   ᵉ36 That is, Sea of Reeds   ᶠ37 Deut. 18:15   ᵍ40 Exodus 32:1

had made. ⁴²But God turned away and gave them over to the worship of the heavenly bodies. This agrees with what is written in the book of the prophets:

> " 'Did you bring me sacrifices and offerings
>   forty years in the desert, O house of Israel?
> ⁴³You have lifted up the shrine of Molech
>   and the star of your god Rephan,
>   the idols you made to worship.
> Therefore I will send you into exile'ᵃ beyond Babylon.

⁴⁴"Our forefathers had the tabernacle of the Testimony with them in the desert. It had been made as God directed Moses, according to the pattern he had seen. ⁴⁵Having received the tabernacle, our fathers under Joshua brought it with them when they took the land from the nations God drove out before them. It remained in the land until the time of David, ⁴⁶who enjoyed God's favor and asked that he might provide a dwelling place for the God of Jacob.ᵇ ⁴⁷But it was Solomon who built the house for him.

⁴⁸"However, the Most High does not live in houses made by men. As the prophet says:

> ⁴⁹" 'Heaven is my throne,
>   and the earth is my footstool.
> What kind of house will you build for me?
>   says the Lord.
> Or where will my resting place be?
> ⁵⁰Has not my hand made all these things?'ᶜ

⁵¹"You stiff-necked people, with uncircumcised hearts and ears! You are just like your fathers: You always resist the Holy Spirit! ⁵²Was there ever a prophet your fathers did not persecute? They even killed those who predicted the coming of the Righteous One. And now you have betrayed and murdered him— ⁵³you who have received the law that was put into effect through angels but have not obeyed it."

The Stoning of Stephen

⁵⁴When they heard this, they were furious and gnashed their teeth at him. ⁵⁵But Stephen, full of the Holy Spirit, looked up to heaven and saw the glory of God, and Jesus standing at the right hand of God. ⁵⁶"Look," he said, "I see heaven open and the Son of Man standing at the right hand of God."

⁵⁷At this they covered their ears and, yelling at the top of their voices, they all rushed at him, ⁵⁸dragged him out of the city and began to stone him. Meanwhile, the witnesses laid their clothes at the feet of a young man named Saul.

⁵⁹While they were stoning him, Stephen prayed, "Lord Jesus, receive my spirit." ⁶⁰Then he fell on his knees and cried out, "Lord, do not hold this sin against them." When he had said this, he fell asleep.

8 And Saul was there, giving approval to his death.

The Church Persecuted and Scattered

On that day a great persecution broke out against the church at Jerusalem, and all except the apostles were scattered throughout Judea and Samaria. ²Godly men buried Stephen and mourned deeply for him. ³But Saul began to destroy the church. Going from house to house, he dragged off men and women and put them in prison.

Philip in Samaria

⁴Those who had been scattered preached the word wherever they went. ⁵Philip went down to a city in Samaria and proclaimed the Christᵈ there. ⁶When the crowds heard Philip and saw the miraculous signs he did, they all paid close attention to what he said. ⁷With shrieks, evilᵉ spirits came out of many, and many paralytics and cripples were healed. ⁸So there was great joy in that city.

Simon the Sorcerer

⁹Now for some time a man named Simon had practiced sorcery in the city and amazed all the people of Samaria. He boasted that he was someone great, ¹⁰and all the people, both high and low, gave him their attention and exclaimed,

---

ᵃ43 Amos 5:25-27   ᵇ46 Some early manuscripts *the house of Jacob*
ᶜ50 Isaiah 66:1,2   ᵈ5 Or *Messiah*
ᵉ7 Greek *unclean*

"This man is the divine power known as the Great Power." [11]They followed him because he had amazed them for a long time with his magic. [12]But when they believed Philip as he preached the good news of the kingdom of God and the name of Jesus Christ, they were baptized, both men and women. [13]Simon himself believed and was baptized. And he followed Philip everywhere, astonished by the great signs and miracles he saw.

[14]When the apostles in Jerusalem heard that Samaria had accepted the word of God, they sent Peter and John to them. [15]When they arrived, they prayed for them that they might receive the Holy Spirit, [16]because the Holy Spirit had not yet come upon any of them; they had

---

{ TUESDAY }

ACTS 7:54–60

The Breath of the Soul

7:59 WHILE THEY WERE STONING HIM, STEPHEN PRAYED.

Execution by stoning, though quicker than crucifixion, is still a ghastly way to die. Typically, the victim was stripped, then knocked off a 9-foot-high scaffold by one of the witnesses to the crime. If the person survived the fall, another witness would drop a stone on his chest. If he survived that, others would pelt him with stones until he was dead. Stephen's death was probably not as deliberate—it had all the markings of a lynching in its spontaneity.

While all this was going on, Stephen, the church's first martyr, prayed. It has been said that prayer is the breath of the soul. How fitting: The first thing we do when we come into the world is breathe; the last thing we do as we depart is breathe. In between, the Bible says, "Let everything that has breath praise the LORD" (Psalm 150:6). Stephen's last breath, like his Lord's, was the breath of his very soul. He prayed for himself, "Lord Jesus, receive my spirit"; and he prayed for his murderers, "Lord, do not hold this sin against them."

How could Stephen breathe such a prayer in this horrific moment? No doubt it was because he was allowed to see something of the glory of God and of Jesus standing at his right hand (see 7:55–56). Although Stephen's exclamation at what he saw probably pushed the angry crowd over the edge, it only hastened what was inevitable. But the glorious immensity of what he saw made the inevitable, grisly as it was, seem small in comparison. This has been the experience of many martyrs over the centuries. Often, but not always, their troubles are made to seem light and momentary in the light of God's glory (see 2 Corinthians 4:16–18).

We can learn from Stephen's prayer that we can be ready for eternity now. "Lord Jesus, receive my spirit—I'm not in control, but you are; I leave myself in your hands." We can pray now, "Lord, do not hold this sin against them—Let me live forgiven and forgiving, without bitterness." Good living makes for good dying.

PRAY:

Lord Jesus, I'm not in control, but you are; I leave myself in your hands.
Let me live forgiven and forgiving, without bitterness.

FOR YOUR NEXT DEVOTIONAL READING, GO TO PAGE 1333.

simply been baptized into[a] the name of the Lord Jesus. [17]Then Peter and John placed their hands on them, and they received the Holy Spirit.

[18]When Simon saw that the Spirit was given at the laying on of the apostles' hands, he offered them money [19]and said, "Give me also this ability so that everyone on whom I lay my hands may receive the Holy Spirit."

[20]Peter answered: "May your money perish with you, because you thought you could buy the gift of God with money! [21]You have no part or share in this ministry, because your heart is not right before God. [22]Repent of this wickedness and pray to the Lord. Perhaps he will forgive you for having such a thought in your heart. [23]For I see that you are full of bitterness and captive to sin."

[24]Then Simon answered, "Pray to the Lord for me so that nothing you have said may happen to me."

[25]When they had testified and proclaimed the word of the Lord, Peter and John returned to Jerusalem, preaching the gospel in many Samaritan villages.

Philip and the Ethiopian

[26]Now an angel of the Lord said to Philip, "Go south to the road—the desert road—that goes down from Jerusalem to Gaza." [27]So he started out, and on his way he met an Ethiopian[b] eunuch, an important official in charge of all the treasury of Candace, queen of the Ethiopians. This man had gone to Jerusalem to worship, [28]and on his way home was sitting in his chariot reading the book of Isaiah the prophet. [29]The Spirit told Philip, "Go to that chariot and stay near it."

[30]Then Philip ran up to the chariot and heard the man reading Isaiah the prophet. "Do you understand what you are reading?" Philip asked.

[31]"How can I," he said, "unless someone explains it to me?" So he invited Philip to come up and sit with him.

[32]The eunuch was reading this passage of Scripture:

"He was led like a sheep to the
    slaughter,
and as a lamb before the shearer is
    silent,
so he did not open his mouth.

[33]In his humiliation he was deprived of
    justice.
Who can speak of his descendants?
    For his life was taken from the
    earth."[c]

[34]The eunuch asked Philip, "Tell me, please, who is the prophet talking about, himself or someone else?" [35]Then Philip began with that very passage of Scripture and told him the good news about Jesus.

[36]As they traveled along the road, they came to some water and the eunuch said, "Look, here is water. Why shouldn't I be baptized?"[d] [38]And he gave orders to stop the chariot. Then both Philip and the eunuch went down into the water and Philip baptized him. [39]When they came up out of the water, the Spirit of the Lord suddenly took Philip away, and the eunuch did not see him again, but went on his way rejoicing. [40]Philip, however, appeared at Azotus and traveled about, preaching the gospel in all the towns until he reached Caesarea.

Saul's Conversion

9 Meanwhile, Saul was still breathing out murderous threats against the Lord's disciples. He went to the high priest [2]and asked him for letters to the synagogues in Damascus, so that if he found any there who belonged to the Way, whether men or women, he might take them as prisoners to Jerusalem. [3]As he neared Damascus on his journey, suddenly a light from heaven flashed around him. [4]He fell to the ground and heard a voice say to him, "Saul, Saul, why do you persecute me?"

[5]"Who are you, Lord?" Saul asked.

"I am Jesus, whom you are persecuting," he replied. [6]"Now get up and go into the city, and you will be told what you must do."

[7]The men traveling with Saul stood there speechless; they heard the sound but did not see anyone. [8]Saul got up from the ground, but when he opened his eyes he could see nothing. So they led him by

[a]16 Or in   [b]27 That is, from the upper Nile region   [c]33 Isaiah 53:7,8   [d]36 Some late manuscripts baptized?" [37]Philip said, "If you believe with all your heart, you may." The eunuch answered, "I believe that Jesus Christ is the Son of God."

the hand into Damascus. ⁹For three days he was blind, and did not eat or drink anything.

¹⁰In Damascus there was a disciple named Ananias. The Lord called to him in a vision, "Ananias!"

"Yes, Lord," he answered.

¹¹The Lord told him, "Go to the house of Judas on Straight Street and ask for a man from Tarsus named Saul, for he is praying. ¹²In a vision he has seen a man

named Ananias come and place his hands on him to restore his sight."

¹³"Lord," Ananias answered, "I have heard many reports about this man and all the harm he has done to your saints in Jerusalem. ¹⁴And he has come here with authority from the chief priests to arrest all who call on your name."

¹⁵But the Lord said to Ananias, "Go! This man is my chosen instrument to carry my name before the Gentiles and their

---

ACTS 9:1–19

[WEDNESDAY]

Brought in Kicking

9:4 HE FELL TO THE GROUND AND HEARD A VOICE SAY TO HIM, "SAUL, SAUL, WHY DO YOU PERSECUTE ME?"

C. S. Lewis described himself at his conversion as "the most dejected and reluctant convert in all England."³ Paul was no doubt the most surprised and surprising convert in all history. On his way to imprison and kill Christians, he became one.

Blinded by the light, Saul asked, "Who are you, Lord?" It was a prayer, truly! The answer Paul got was the last he expected. The voice from the light was Jesus, the very one whose name he despised and had devoted his life to destroying. How could he possibly have known that one day he would say, "I consider my life worth nothing to me, if only I may finish the race and complete the task the Lord Jesus has given me" (Acts 20:24)?

The life of prayer is filled with many such surprises. Sometimes the circumstances and events of life come at us with the force of a blinding light, and the God we thought we knew is really very different than we imagined. Very different. Unsettlingly different. And we kick against the light, as God told Saul he did: "Saul, Saul, why do you persecute me? It is hard for you to kick against the goads" (26:14). His mercy is severe, but it is still mercy. His hardness is really his kindness.

In later years, Lewis's memory of his reluctant conversion, like Saul's, had served to underline for him the amazing grace of God: "The Prodigal Son at least walked home on his own feet. But who can truly adore that love which will open the high gates to a prodigal who is brought in kicking, struggling, resentful, and darting his eyes in every direction for a chance of escape? . . . The hardness of God is kinder than the softness of men, and his compulsion is our liberation."⁴

PRAY:

Your grace truly is amazing, God!
Thank you for your everlasting mercy and kindness—
even when it comes in surprising and severe ways.

FOR YOUR NEXT DEVOTIONAL READING, GO TO PAGE 1338.

kings and before the people of Israel. ¹⁶I will show him how much he must suffer for my name."

¹⁷Then Ananias went to the house and entered it. Placing his hands on Saul, he said, "Brother Saul, the Lord—Jesus, who appeared to you on the road as you were coming here—has sent me so that you may see again and be filled with the Holy Spirit." ¹⁸Immediately, something like scales fell from Saul's eyes, and he could see again. He got up and was baptized, ¹⁹and after taking some food, he regained his strength.

Saul in Damascus and Jerusalem

Saul spent several days with the disciples in Damascus. ²⁰At once he began to preach in the synagogues that Jesus is the Son of God. ²¹All those who heard him were astonished and asked, "Isn't he the man who raised havoc in Jerusalem among those who call on this name? And hasn't he come here to take them as prisoners to the chief priests?" ²²Yet Saul grew more and more powerful and baffled the Jews living in Damascus by proving that Jesus is the Christ.ᵃ

²³After many days had gone by, the Jews conspired to kill him, ²⁴but Saul learned of their plan. Day and night they kept close watch on the city gates in order to kill him. ²⁵But his followers took him by night and lowered him in a basket through an opening in the wall.

²⁶When he came to Jerusalem, he tried to join the disciples, but they were all afraid of him, not believing that he really was a disciple. ²⁷But Barnabas took him and brought him to the apostles. He told them how Saul on his journey had seen the Lord and that the Lord had spoken to him, and how in Damascus he had preached fearlessly in the name of Jesus. ²⁸So Saul stayed with them and moved about freely in Jerusalem, speaking boldly in the name of the Lord. ²⁹He talked and debated with the Grecian Jews, but they tried to kill him. ³⁰When the brothers learned of this, they took him down to Caesarea and sent him off to Tarsus.

³¹Then the church throughout Judea, Galilee and Samaria enjoyed a time of peace. It was strengthened; and encouraged by the Holy Spirit, it grew in numbers, living in the fear of the Lord.

Aeneas and Dorcas

³²As Peter traveled about the country, he went to visit the saints in Lydda. ³³There he found a man named Aeneas, a paralytic who had been bedridden for eight years. ³⁴"Aeneas," Peter said to him, "Jesus Christ heals you. Get up and take care of your mat." Immediately Aeneas got up. ³⁵All those who lived in Lydda and Sharon saw him and turned to the Lord.

³⁶In Joppa there was a disciple named Tabitha (which, when translated, is Dorcasᵇ), who was always doing good and helping the poor. ³⁷About that time she became sick and died, and her body was washed and placed in an upstairs room. ³⁸Lydda was near Joppa; so when the disciples heard that Peter was in Lydda, they sent two men to him and urged him, "Please come at once!"

³⁹Peter went with them, and when he arrived he was taken upstairs to the room. All the widows stood around him, crying and showing him the robes and other clothing that Dorcas had made while she was still with them.

⁴⁰Peter sent them all out of the room; then he got down on his knees and prayed. Turning toward the dead woman, he said, "Tabitha, get up." She opened her eyes, and seeing Peter she sat up. ⁴¹He took her by the hand and helped her to her feet. Then he called the believers and the widows and presented her to them alive. ⁴²This became known all over Joppa, and many people believed in the Lord. ⁴³Peter stayed in Joppa for some time with a tanner named Simon.

Cornelius Calls for Peter

10 At Caesarea there was a man named Cornelius, a centurion in what was known as the Italian Regiment. ²He and all his family were devout and God-fearing; he gave generously to those in need and prayed to God regularly. ³One day at about three in the afternoon he had a vision. He distinctly

---

ᵃ22 Or *Messiah*   ᵇ36 Both *Tabitha* (Aramaic) and *Dorcas* (Greek) mean *gazelle*.

saw an angel of God, who came to him and said, "Cornelius!"

⁴Cornelius stared at him in fear. "What is it, Lord?" he asked.

The angel answered, "Your prayers and gifts to the poor have come up as a memorial offering before God. ⁵Now send men to Joppa to bring back a man named Simon who is called Peter. ⁶He is staying with Simon the tanner, whose house is by the sea."

⁷When the angel who spoke to him had gone, Cornelius called two of his servants and a devout soldier who was one of his attendants. ⁸He told them everything that had happened and sent them to Joppa.

Peter's Vision

⁹About noon the following day as they were on their journey and approaching the city, Peter went up on the roof to pray. ¹⁰He became hungry and wanted something to eat, and while the meal was being prepared, he fell into a trance.

> ABOUT noon the following day as they were on their journey and approaching the city, Peter went up on the roof to pray.
>
> ACTS 10:9

¹¹He saw heaven opened and something like a large sheet being let down to earth by its four corners. ¹²It contained all kinds of four-footed animals, as well as reptiles of the earth and birds of the air. ¹³Then a voice told him, "Get up, Peter. Kill and eat."

¹⁴"Surely not, Lord!" Peter replied. "I have never eaten anything impure or unclean."

¹⁵The voice spoke to him a second time, "Do not call anything impure that God has made clean."

¹⁶This happened three times, and immediately the sheet was taken back to heaven.

¹⁷While Peter was wondering about the meaning of the vision, the men sent by Cornelius found out where Simon's house was and stopped at the gate. ¹⁸They called out, asking if Simon who was known as Peter was staying there.

¹⁹While Peter was still thinking about the vision, the Spirit said to him, "Simon, three*ᵃ* men are looking for you. ²⁰So get up and go downstairs. Do not hesitate to go with them, for I have sent them."

²¹Peter went down and said to the men, "I'm the one you're looking for. Why have you come?"

²²The men replied, "We have come from Cornelius the centurion. He is a righteous and God-fearing man, who is respected by all the Jewish people. A holy angel told him to have you come to his house so that he could hear what you have to say." ²³Then Peter invited the men into the house to be his guests.

Peter at Cornelius's House

The next day Peter started out with them, and some of the brothers from Joppa went along. ²⁴The following day he arrived in Caesarea. Cornelius was expecting them and had called together his relatives and close friends. ²⁵As Peter entered the house, Cornelius met him and fell at his feet in reverence. ²⁶But Peter made him get up. "Stand up," he said, "I am only a man myself."

²⁷Talking with him, Peter went inside and found a large gathering of people. ²⁸He said to them: "You are well aware that it is against our law for a Jew to associate with a Gentile or visit him. But God has shown me that I should not call any man impure or unclean. ²⁹So when I was sent for, I came without raising any objection. May I ask why you sent for me?"

³⁰Cornelius answered: "Four days ago I was in my house praying at this hour, at three in the afternoon. Suddenly a man in shining clothes stood before me ³¹and said, 'Cornelius, God has heard your prayer and remembered your gifts to the poor. ³²Send to Joppa for Simon who is called Peter. He is a guest in the home of Simon the tanner, who lives by the sea.' ³³So I sent for you immediately, and it was good of you to come. Now we are all here in the presence of God to listen to everything the Lord has commanded you to tell us."

³⁴Then Peter began to speak: "I now realize how true it is that God does not

---

ᵃ19 One early manuscript *two*; other manuscripts do not have the number.

show favoritism ³⁵but accepts men from every nation who fear him and do what is right. ³⁶You know the message God sent to the people of Israel, telling the good news of peace through Jesus Christ, who is Lord of all. ³⁷You know what has happened throughout Judea, beginning in Galilee after the baptism that John preached— ³⁸how God anointed Jesus of Nazareth with the Holy Spirit and power, and how he went around doing good and healing all who were under the power of the devil, because God was with him.

³⁹"We are witnesses of everything he did in the country of the Jews and in Jerusalem. They killed him by hanging him on a tree, ⁴⁰but God raised him from the dead on the third day and caused him to be seen. ⁴¹He was not seen by all the people, but by witnesses whom God had already chosen—by us who ate and drank with him after he rose from the dead. ⁴²He commanded us to preach to the people and to testify that he is the one whom God appointed as judge of the living and the dead. ⁴³All the prophets testify about him that everyone who believes in him receives forgiveness of sins through his name."

⁴⁴While Peter was still speaking these words, the Holy Spirit came on all who heard the message. ⁴⁵The circumcised believers who had come with Peter were astonished that the gift of the Holy Spirit had been poured out even on the Gentiles. ⁴⁶For they heard them speaking in tongues[a] and praising God.

Then Peter said, ⁴⁷"Can anyone keep these people from being baptized with water? They have received the Holy Spirit just as we have." ⁴⁸So he ordered that they be baptized in the name of Jesus Christ. Then they asked Peter to stay with them for a few days.

Peter Explains His Actions

11 The apostles and the brothers throughout Judea heard that the Gentiles also had received the word of God. ²So when Peter went up to Jerusalem, the circumcised believers criticized him ³and said, "You went into the house of uncircumcised men and ate with them."

⁴Peter began and explained everything to them precisely as it had happened: ⁵"I was in the city of Joppa praying, and in a trance I saw a vision. I saw something like a large sheet being let down from heaven by its four corners, and it came down to where I was. ⁶I looked into it and saw four-footed animals of the earth, wild beasts, reptiles, and birds of the air. ⁷Then I heard a voice telling me, 'Get up, Peter. Kill and eat.'

⁸"I replied, 'Surely not, Lord! Nothing impure or unclean has ever entered my mouth.'

⁹"The voice spoke from heaven a second time, 'Do not call anything impure that God has made clean.' ¹⁰This happened three times, and then it was all pulled up to heaven again.

¹¹"Right then three men who had been sent to me from Caesarea stopped at the house where I was staying. ¹²The Spirit told me to have no hesitation about going with them. These six brothers also went with me, and we entered the man's house. ¹³He told us how he had seen an angel appear in his house and say, 'Send to Joppa for Simon who is called Peter. ¹⁴He will bring you a message through which you and all your household will be saved.'

¹⁵"As I began to speak, the Holy Spirit came on them as he had come on us at the beginning. ¹⁶Then I remembered what the Lord had said: 'John baptized with[b] water, but you will be baptized with the Holy Spirit.' ¹⁷So if God gave them the same gift as he gave us, who believed in the Lord Jesus Christ, who was I to think that I could oppose God?"

¹⁸When they heard this, they had no further objections and praised God, saying, "So then, God has granted even the Gentiles repentance unto life."

The Church in Antioch

¹⁹Now those who had been scattered by the persecution in connection with Stephen traveled as far as Phoenicia, Cyprus and Antioch, telling the message only to Jews. ²⁰Some of them, however, men from Cyprus and Cyrene, went to Antioch and began to speak to Greeks

---

[a]46 Or other languages   [b]16 Or in

> 'Give us this day our daily bread' is probably the most perfectly constructed and useful sentence ever set down in the English language.

also, telling them the good news about the Lord Jesus. ²¹The Lord's hand was with them, and a great number of people believed and turned to the Lord.

²²News of this reached the ears of the church at Jerusalem, and they sent Barnabas to Antioch. ²³When he arrived and saw the evidence of the grace of God, he was glad and encouraged them all to remain true to the Lord with all their hearts. ²⁴He was a good man, full of the Holy Spirit and faith, and a great number of people were brought to the Lord.

²⁵Then Barnabas went to Tarsus to look for Saul, ²⁶and when he found him, he brought him to Antioch. So for a whole year Barnabas and Saul met with the church and taught great numbers of people. The disciples were called Christians first at Antioch.

²⁷During this time some prophets came down from Jerusalem to Antioch. ²⁸One of them, named Agabus, stood up and through the Spirit predicted that a severe famine would spread over the entire Roman world. (This happened during the reign of Claudius.) ²⁹The disciples, each according to his ability, decided to provide help for the brothers living in Judea. ³⁰This they did, sending their gift to the elders by Barnabas and Saul.

Peter's Miraculous Escape From Prison

12 It was about this time that King Herod arrested some who belonged to the church, intending to persecute them. ²He had James, the brother of John, put to death with the sword. ³When he saw that this pleased the Jews, he proceeded to seize Peter also. This happened during the Feast of Unleavened Bread. ⁴After arresting him, he put him in prison, handing him over to be guarded by four squads of four soldiers each. Herod intended to bring him out for public trial after the Passover.

⁵So Peter was kept in prison, but the church was earnestly praying to God for him.

⁶The night before Herod was to bring him to trial, Peter was sleeping between two soldiers, bound with two chains, and sentries stood guard at the entrance. ⁷Suddenly an angel of the Lord appeared and a light shone in the cell. He struck Peter on the side and woke him up. "Quick, get up!" he said, and the chains fell off Peter's wrists.

⁸Then the angel said to him, "Put on your clothes and sandals." And Peter did so. "Wrap your cloak around you and follow me," the angel told him. ⁹Peter followed him out of the prison, but he had no idea that what the angel was doing was really happening; he thought he was seeing a vision. ¹⁰They passed the first and second guards and came to the iron gate leading to the city. It opened for them by itself, and they went through it. When they had walked the length of one street, suddenly the angel left him.

¹¹Then Peter came to himself and said, "Now I know without a doubt that the Lord sent his angel and rescued me from Herod's clutches and from everything the Jewish people were anticipating."

¹²When this had dawned on him, he went to the house of Mary the mother of John, also called Mark, where many people had gathered and were praying. ¹³Peter knocked at the outer entrance, and a servant girl named Rhoda came to answer the door. ¹⁴When she recognized Peter's voice, she was so overjoyed she ran back without opening it and exclaimed, "Peter is at the door!"

¹⁵"You're out of your mind," they told her. When she kept insisting that it was so, they said, "It must be his angel."

¹⁶But Peter kept on knocking, and when they opened the door and saw him, they were astonished. ¹⁷Peter motioned with his hand for them to be quiet and described how the Lord had brought him out of prison. "Tell James and the brothers about this," he said, and then he left for another place.

¹⁸In the morning, there was no small commotion among the soldiers as to what had become of Peter. ¹⁹After Herod had a thorough search made for him

and did not find him, he cross-examined the guards and ordered that they be executed.

Herod's Death

Then Herod went from Judea to Caesarea and stayed there a while. ²⁰He had been quarreling with the people of Tyre and Sidon; they now joined together and sought an audience with him. Having secured the support of Blastus, a trusted personal servant of the king, they asked for peace, because they depended on the king's country for their food supply.

²¹On the appointed day Herod, wearing his royal robes, sat on his throne and delivered a public address to the people. ²²They shouted, "This is the voice of a

---

[THURSDAY]

ACTS 12:1–24

God's Weakness Is Stronger Than Human Strength

12:24 BUT THE WORD OF GOD CONTINUED TO INCREASE AND SPREAD.

Acts 12 begins with a sword coming down on the neck of James (see verse 2) and ends with Herod, the man who ordered it, being eaten by worms (see verse 23). There is a beheading and a consumption—a study in grisly contrasts.

More elegant and instructive is the contrast between methods and audiences. Herod's audience is the Jewish leaders who were pleased with his execution of James. His method is more of the same: Arrest another apostle, Peter this time, and kill him. If one execution advanced his power that much, then a second execution will double it (see verses 3–4). His audience is the humanly powerful, his method is coercion and intimidation—the tried and true in a world hostile to God. The church, on the other hand, has God as its audience and prayer as its method (see verse 5). Prayer is all it has because all it has is God. If bets were placed on the outcome, the worldly wise of that time and any time would put their money on Herod. Compared to Herod, the church looks weak and silly.

But God's weakness is stronger than human strength, and his foolishness wiser than human wisdom (see 1 Corinthians 1:25). The outcome is almost comedic. Herod is dead; the church is stunned with amazement and joy. Herod can't keep Peter in jail, and the church can't believe he's out. Peter has to knock on the door a long time before the little prayer meeting will believe its prayers are really answered. Instead of being squelched, "the word of God continued to increase and spread."

Prayer can look rather foolish and weak to some, even the people of God. But it moves mountains and kingdoms, to the laughter of heaven. God loves it when his people pray, and the powers of darkness tremble.

PRAY:

Forgive me, God, for the times when I doubt the power and effectiveness of my prayers. Keep reminding me that true strength and wisdom reside with you and are unleashed when your people pray.

FOR YOUR NEXT DEVOTIONAL READING, GO TO PAGE 1340.

god, not of a man." ²³Immediately, because Herod did not give praise to God, an angel of the Lord struck him down, and he was eaten by worms and died.

²⁴But the word of God continued to increase and spread.

²⁵When Barnabas and Saul had finished their mission, they returned from[a] Jerusalem, taking with them John, also called Mark.

Barnabas and Saul Sent Off

13 In the church at Antioch there were prophets and teachers: Barnabas, Simeon called Niger, Lucius of Cyrene, Manaen (who had been brought up with Herod the tetrarch) and Saul. ²While they were worshiping the Lord and fasting, the Holy Spirit said, "Set apart for me Barnabas and Saul for the work to which I have called them." ³So after they had fasted and prayed, they placed their hands on them and sent them off.

On Cyprus

⁴The two of them, sent on their way by the Holy Spirit, went down to Seleucia and sailed from there to Cyprus. ⁵When they arrived at Salamis, they proclaimed the word of God in the Jewish synagogues. John was with them as their helper.

⁶They traveled through the whole island until they came to Paphos. There they met a Jewish sorcerer and false prophet named Bar-Jesus, ⁷who was an attendant of the proconsul, Sergius Paulus. The proconsul, an intelligent man, sent for Barnabas and Saul because he wanted to hear the word of God. ⁸But Elymas the sorcerer (for that is what his name means) opposed them and tried to turn the proconsul from the faith. ⁹Then Saul, who was also called Paul, filled with the Holy Spirit, looked straight at Elymas and said, ¹⁰"You are a child of the devil and an enemy of everything that is right! You are full of all kinds of deceit and trickery. Will you never stop perverting the right ways of the Lord? ¹¹Now the hand of the Lord is against you. You are going to be blind, and for a time you will be unable to see the light of the sun."

Immediately mist and darkness came over him, and he groped about, seeking someone to lead him by the hand. ¹²When the proconsul saw what had happened, he believed, for he was amazed at the teaching about the Lord.

In Pisidian Antioch

¹³From Paphos, Paul and his companions sailed to Perga in Pamphylia, where John left them to return to Jerusalem. ¹⁴From Perga they went on to Pisidian Antioch. On the Sabbath they entered the synagogue and sat down. ¹⁵After the reading from the Law and the Prophets, the synagogue rulers sent word to them, saying, "Brothers, if you have a message of encouragement for the people, please speak."

¹⁶Standing up, Paul motioned with his hand and said: "Men of Israel and you Gentiles who worship God, listen to me! ¹⁷The God of the people of Israel chose our fathers; he made the people prosper during their stay in Egypt, with mighty power he led them out of that country, ¹⁸he endured their conduct[b] for about forty years in the desert, ¹⁹he overthrew seven nations in Canaan and gave their land to his people as their inheritance. ²⁰All this took about 450 years.

"After this, God gave them judges until the time of Samuel the prophet. ²¹Then the people asked for a king, and he gave them Saul son of Kish, of the tribe of Benjamin, who ruled forty years. ²²After removing Saul, he made David their king. He testified concerning him: 'I have found David son of Jesse a man after my own heart; he will do everything I want him to do.'

²³"From this man's descendants God has brought to Israel the Savior Jesus, as he promised. ²⁴Before the coming of Jesus, John preached repentance and baptism to all the people of Israel. ²⁵As John was completing his work, he said: 'Who do you think I am? I am not that one. No, but he is coming after me, whose sandals I am not worthy to untie.'

²⁶"Brothers, children of Abraham, and you God-fearing Gentiles, it is to us that this message of salvation has been sent. ²⁷The people of Jerusalem and their rulers

a25 Some manuscripts to   b18 Some manuscripts and cared for them

did not recognize Jesus, yet in condemning him they fulfilled the words of the prophets that are read every Sabbath. ²⁸Though they found no proper ground for a death sentence, they asked Pilate to have him executed. ²⁹When they had carried out all that was written about him,

they took him down from the tree and laid him in a tomb. ³⁰But God raised him from the dead, ³¹and for many days he was seen by those who had traveled with him from Galilee to Jerusalem. They are now his witnesses to our people.

³²"We tell you the good news: What

[FRIDAY]

ACTS 13:1–3

The Fuel and the Goal of Missions

13:3 SO AFTER THEY HAD FASTED AND PRAYED, THEY PLACED THEIR HANDS ON THEM AND SENT THEM OFF.

Herod's death marks also the demise of Jerusalem as the center of action in the book of Acts. There is a saying, "he who marries the spirit of the age will be a widow in the next." Jerusalem's leaders had committed themselves to the likes of Herod and what he stood for. When Herod's time was up, so was theirs: The catastrophe Jesus had wept over (see Luke 19:41–44) was coming. Jerusalem will no longer play a significant role in the advancement of the kingdom of God. The center of kingdom activity has moved to Gentile cities like Antioch.

Once again, the real action happens in a prayer meeting: "While they were worshiping the Lord and fasting, the Holy Spirit said, 'Set apart for me Barnabas and Saul for the work to which I have called them.'" The work is to take the gospel to the peoples of the earth, beginning with an evangelistic outreach on the island of Cyprus. World missions are launched, not in Jerusalem, but in a Gentile city, as believers worship and pray. That it should begin in a service of prayer and worship is highly significant. Why? The missionary movement of the church must begin as the church does what missions are ultimately for: the worship of God. "Missions is not the ultimate goal of the church. Worship is," writes John Piper.

"Missions exist because worship doesn't . . . When this age is over, and the countless millions of the redeemed fall on their faces before the throne of God, missions will be no more. It is a temporary necessity. But worship abides forever . . . Worship, therefore, is the fuel and goal of missions. It's the goal of missions because in missions we simply aim to bring the nations into the white-hot enjoyment of God's glory . . . But worship is also the fuel of missions. Passion for God in worship precedes the offer of God in preaching. You can't commend what you do not cherish."⁵

The better we learn to cherish God in prayer, the more passionate and empowered we will be to commend him in missions. After Antioch, the rest is history.

PRAY:

"Sing to the LORD, all the earth; proclaim his salvation day after day. Declare his glory among the nations, his marvelous deeds among all peoples" (1 Chronicles 16:23–24).

FOR YOUR NEXT DEVOTIONAL READING, GO TO PAGE 1342.

God promised our fathers ³³he has fulfilled for us, their children, by raising up Jesus. As it is written in the second Psalm:

" 'You are my Son;
today I have become your Father.'ᵃʾᵇ

³⁴The fact that God raised him from the dead, never to decay, is stated in these words:

" 'I will give you the holy and sure blessings promised to David.'ᶜ

³⁵So it is stated elsewhere:

" 'You will not let your Holy One see decay.'ᵈ

³⁶"For when David had served God's purpose in his own generation, he fell asleep; he was buried with his fathers and his body decayed. ³⁷But the one whom God raised from the dead did not see decay.

³⁸"Therefore, my brothers, I want you to know that through Jesus the forgiveness of sins is proclaimed to you. ³⁹Through him everyone who believes is justified from everything you could not be justified from by the law of Moses. ⁴⁰Take care that what the prophets have said does not happen to you:

⁴¹ " 'Look, you scoffers,
wonder and perish,
for I am going to do something in
your days
that you would never believe,
even if someone told you.'ᵉ"

⁴²As Paul and Barnabas were leaving the synagogue, the people invited them to speak further about these things on the next Sabbath. ⁴³When the congregation was dismissed, many of the Jews and devout converts to Judaism followed Paul and Barnabas, who talked with them and urged them to continue in the grace of God.

⁴⁴On the next Sabbath almost the whole city gathered to hear the word of the Lord. ⁴⁵When the Jews saw the crowds, they were filled with jealousy and talked abusively against what Paul was saying.

⁴⁶Then Paul and Barnabas answered them boldly: "We had to speak the word of God to you first. Since you reject it and do not consider yourselves worthy of eternal life, we now turn to the Gentiles. ⁴⁷For this is what the Lord has commanded us:

" 'I have made youᶠ a light for the
Gentiles,
that youᶠ may bring salvation to the
ends of the earth.'ᵍ"

⁴⁸When the Gentiles heard this, they were glad and honored the word of the Lord; and all who were appointed for eternal life believed.

⁴⁹The word of the Lord spread through the whole region. ⁵⁰But the Jews incited the God-fearing women of high standing and the leading men of the city. They stirred up persecution against Paul and Barnabas, and expelled them from their region. ⁵¹So they shook the dust from their feet in protest against them and went to Iconium. ⁵²And the disciples were filled with joy and with the Holy Spirit.

In Iconium

14 At Iconium Paul and Barnabas went as usual into the Jewish synagogue. There they spoke so effectively that a great number of Jews and Gentiles believed. ²But the Jews who refused to believe stirred up the Gentiles and poisoned their minds against the brothers. ³So Paul and Barnabas spent considerable time there, speaking boldly for the Lord, who confirmed the message of his grace by enabling them to do miraculous signs and wonders. ⁴The people of the city were divided; some sided with the Jews, others with the apostles. ⁵There was a plot afoot among the Gentiles and Jews, together with their leaders, to mistreat them and stone them. ⁶But they found out about it and fled to the Lycaonian cities of Lystra and Derbe and to the surrounding country, ⁷where they continued to preach the good news.

In Lystra and Derbe

⁸In Lystra there sat a man crippled in his feet, who was lame from birth and had never walked. ⁹He listened to Paul as

ᵃ33 Or *have begotten you*   ᵇ33 Psalm 2:7
ᶜ34 Isaiah 55:3   ᵈ35 Psalm 16:10
ᵉ41 Hab. 1:5   ᶠ47 The Greek is singular.
ᵍ47 Isaiah 49:6

TERESA OF AVILA (1512–1582)
A Castle and a Garden

TERESA OF AVILA was a woman who possessed plenty of what we would today call "grit." She, and others like her (among them her friend St. John of the Cross), needed a lot of grit to navigate their way spiritually through the tumultuous years of 16th century Europe. The Protestant Reformation had ushered in a new age of religious freedom with an emphasis on Biblical, personal faith—an idea embraced by many. People like Teresa agreed with some of the Reformers' critique of the Roman Catholic church. But she remained within the church as a Carmelite nun to work for internal renewal.

Teresa's major work began when she was over 40 years old. One day, while deep in prayer, she had the first of many heavenly visions, in which an angel pierced her heart with a flame-tipped spear, leaving her pierced with a great love for God and a renewed passion to serve Christ. She wrote a prayer:

> Thine am I, I was born for Thee,
> What wouldst Thou, Master, make of me? . . .
> 'Tis Thou alone dost live in me.
> What wilt Thou I should do for Thee?[6]

Teresa's best-known work is *The Interior Castle*, an allegory in which the soul moves from the outer courtyard to the innermost sanctuary of the castle's seven mansions. Along the way, prowling beasts, symbolizing the hindrances to prayer, seek to waylay the pilgrim. Each mansion is a stage along the way to union with Christ, which is beautifully pictured as the emergence of a silkworm from a cocoon to the life of a white butterfly. Beyond the mansion of union with Christ is the dark night of the soul, and finally that of spiritual marriage to Christ.

Though a mystic, Teresa was very practical and uncomplicated in her advice about prayer. She compared the cultivation of prayer to the cultivation of a garden in which Christ himself pulls the weeds, and we, with his help, water the flowers so they will delight our Lord with their fragrance. "Pray as you can," she advised, "for prayer doesn't consist in thinking a great deal, but of loving a great deal." She believed God could lead the simplest Christian, using only the words of the Lord's Prayer, into the heights of contemplation. For her, the bottom line was that we must "never, for any reason whatever, neglect to pray."[7]

By the time of her death, Teresa had founded 20 new Carmelite convents and had spread mysticism as a practical method of reform throughout Spain. She and her friend St. John of the Cross were criticized and even imprisoned by the church they loved for their reform efforts. Today they are considered by many Christians of diverse traditions to be the preeminent authorities of the theology of spiritual life.

PRAY:

Pray this prayer of Teresa's:

Govern all by your wisdom, O Lord, so that my soul may always be serving you according to your will, and now as I desire. Do not punish me, I pray, by granting what I want and ask, if it offends your love, which would always live in me. Let me die to myself, that I may serve you, let me live to you, who in yourself are the true life.[8]

MEMORIZE:

How lovely is your dwelling place, O LORD Almighty!
My soul yearns, even faints, for the courts of the LORD;
my heart and my flesh cry out for the living God. PSALM 84:1–2

FOR YOUR NEXT DEVOTIONAL READING, GO TO PAGE 1347.

he was speaking. Paul looked directly at him, saw that he had faith to be healed [10]and called out, "Stand up on your feet!" At that, the man jumped up and began to walk.

[11]When the crowd saw what Paul had done, they shouted in the Lycaonian language, "The gods have come down to us in human form!" [12]Barnabas they called Zeus, and Paul they called Hermes because he was the chief speaker. [13]The priest of Zeus, whose temple was just outside the city, brought bulls and wreaths to the city gates because he and the crowd wanted to offer sacrifices to them.

[14]But when the apostles Barnabas and Paul heard of this, they tore their clothes and rushed out into the crowd, shouting: [15]"Men, why are you doing this? We too are only men, human like you. We are bringing you good news, telling you to turn from these worthless things to the living God, who made heaven and earth and sea and everything in them. [16]In the past, he let all nations go their own way. [17]Yet he has not left himself without testimony: He has shown kindness by giving you rain from heaven and crops in their seasons; he provides you with plenty of food and fills your hearts with joy." [18]Even with these words, they had difficulty keeping the crowd from sacrificing to them.

[19]Then some Jews came from Antioch and Iconium and won the crowd over. They stoned Paul and dragged him outside the city, thinking he was dead. [20]But after the disciples had gathered around him, he got up and went back into the city. The next day he and Barnabas left for Derbe.

The Return to Antioch in Syria

[21]They preached the good news in that city and won a large number of disciples. Then they returned to Lystra, Iconium and Antioch, [22]strengthening the disciples and encouraging them to remain true to the faith. "We must go through many hardships to enter the kingdom of God," they said. [23]Paul and Barnabas appointed elders[a] for them in each church and, with prayer and fasting, committed them to the Lord, in whom they had put their trust. [24]After going through Pisidia,

> PAUL and Barnabas appointed elders for them in each church and, with prayer and fasting, committed them to the Lord, in whom they had put their trust.
>
> ACTS 14:23

they came into Pamphylia, [25]and when they had preached the word in Perga, they went down to Attalia.

[26]From Attalia they sailed back to Antioch, where they had been committed to the grace of God for the work they had now completed. [27]On arriving there, they gathered the church together and reported all that God had done through them and how he had opened the door of faith to the Gentiles. [28]And they stayed there a long time with the disciples.

The Council at Jerusalem

15 Some men came down from Judea to Antioch and were teaching the brothers: "Unless you are circumcised, according to the custom taught by Moses, you cannot be saved." [2]This brought Paul and Barnabas into sharp dispute and debate with them. So Paul and Barnabas were appointed, along with some other believers, to go up to Jerusalem to see the apostles and elders about this question. [3]The church sent them on their way, and as they traveled through Phoenicia and Samaria, they told how the Gentiles had been converted. This news made all the brothers very glad. [4]When they came to Jerusalem, they were welcomed by the church and the apostles and elders, to whom they reported everything God had done through them.

[5]Then some of the believers who belonged to the party of the Pharisees stood up and said, "The Gentiles must be circumcised and required to obey the law of Moses."

[6]The apostles and elders met to consider this question. [7]After much discussion, Peter got up and addressed them: "Brothers, you know that some time ago God made a choice among you that the Gentiles might hear from my lips the

---

[a]23 Or Barnabas ordained elders; or Barnabas had elders elected

message of the gospel and believe. ⁸God, who knows the heart, showed that he accepted them by giving the Holy Spirit to them, just as he did to us. ⁹He made no distinction between us and them, for he purified their hearts by faith. ¹⁰Now then, why do you try to test God by putting on the necks of the disciples a yoke that neither we nor our fathers have been able to bear? ¹¹No! We believe it is through the grace of our Lord Jesus that we are saved, just as they are."

¹²The whole assembly became silent as they listened to Barnabas and Paul telling about the miraculous signs and wonders God had done among the Gentiles through them. ¹³When they finished, James spoke up: "Brothers, listen to me. ¹⁴Simonᵃ has described to us how God at first showed his concern by taking from the Gentiles a people for himself. ¹⁵The words of the prophets are in agreement with this, as it is written:

¹⁶ " 'After this I will return
    and rebuild David's fallen tent.
  Its ruins I will rebuild,
    and I will restore it,
¹⁷ that the remnant of men may seek
      the Lord,
    and all the Gentiles who bear my
      name,
  says the Lord, who does these
      things'ᵇ
¹⁸ that have been known for ages.ᶜ

¹⁹"It is my judgment, therefore, that we should not make it difficult for the Gentiles who are turning to God. ²⁰Instead we should write to them, telling them to abstain from food polluted by idols, from sexual immorality, from the meat of strangled animals and from blood. ²¹For Moses has been preached in every city from the earliest times and is read in the synagogues on every Sabbath."

The Council's Letter to Gentile Believers

²²Then the apostles and elders, with the whole church, decided to choose some of their own men and send them to Antioch with Paul and Barnabas. They chose Judas (called Barsabbas) and Silas, two men who were leaders among the brothers. ²³With them they sent the following letter:

The apostles and elders, your brothers,

To the Gentile believers in Antioch, Syria and Cilicia:

Greetings.

²⁴We have heard that some went out from us without our authorization and disturbed you, troubling your minds by what they said. ²⁵So we all agreed to choose some men and send them to you with our dear friends Barnabas and Paul— ²⁶men who have risked their lives for the name of our Lord Jesus Christ. ²⁷Therefore we are sending Judas and Silas to confirm by word of mouth what we are writing. ²⁸It seemed good to the Holy Spirit and to us not to burden you with anything beyond the following requirements: ²⁹You are to abstain from food sacrificed to idols, from blood, from the meat of strangled animals and from sexual immorality. You will do well to avoid these things.

Farewell.

³⁰The men were sent off and went down to Antioch, where they gathered the church together and delivered the letter. ³¹The people read it and were glad for its encouraging message. ³²Judas and Silas, who themselves were prophets, said much to encourage and strengthen the brothers. ³³After spending some time there, they were sent off by the brothers with the blessing of peace to return to those who had sent them.ᵈ ³⁵But Paul and Barnabas remained in Antioch, where they and many others taught and preached the word of the Lord.

Disagreement Between Paul and Barnabas

³⁶Some time later Paul said to Barnabas, "Let us go back and visit the brothers in all the towns where we preached the word of the Lord and see how they

ᵃ14 Greek Simeon, a variant of Simon; that is, Peter   ᵇ17 Amos 9:11,12   ᶜ17,18 Some manuscripts things'— /¹⁸known to the Lord for ages is his work   ᵈ33 Some manuscripts them, ³⁴but Silas decided to remain there

are doing." [37]Barnabas wanted to take John, also called Mark, with them, [38]but Paul did not think it wise to take him, because he had deserted them in Pamphylia and had not continued with them in the work. [39]They had such a sharp disagreement that they parted company. Barnabas took Mark and sailed for Cyprus, [40]but Paul chose Silas and left, commended by the brothers to the grace of the Lord. [41]He went through Syria and Cilicia, strengthening the churches.

Timothy Joins Paul and Silas

16 He came to Derbe and then to Lystra, where a disciple named Timothy lived, whose mother was a Jewess and a believer, but whose father was a Greek. [2]The brothers at Lystra and Iconium spoke well of him. [3]Paul wanted to take him along on the journey, so he circumcised him because of the Jews who lived in that area, for they all knew that his father was a Greek. [4]As they traveled from town to town, they delivered the decisions reached by the apostles and elders in Jerusalem for the people to obey. [5]So the churches were strengthened in the faith and grew daily in numbers.

Paul's Vision of the Man of Macedonia

[6]Paul and his companions traveled throughout the region of Phrygia and Galatia, having been kept by the Holy Spirit from preaching the word in the province of Asia. [7]When they came to the border of Mysia, they tried to enter Bithynia, but the Spirit of Jesus would not allow them to. [8]So they passed by Mysia and went down to Troas. [9]During the night Paul had a vision of a man of Macedonia standing and begging him, "Come over to Macedonia and help us." [10]After Paul had seen the vision, we got ready at once to leave for Macedonia, concluding that God had called us to preach the gospel to them.

Lydia's Conversion in Philippi

[11]From Troas we put out to sea and sailed straight for Samothrace, and the next day on to Neapolis. [12]From there we traveled to Philippi, a Roman colony and the leading city of that district of Macedonia. And we stayed there several days.

[13]On the Sabbath we went outside the city gate to the river, where we expected to find a place of prayer. We sat down and began to speak to the women who had gathered there. [14]One of those listening was a woman named Lydia, a dealer in purple cloth from the city of Thyatira, who was a worshiper of God. The Lord opened her heart to respond to Paul's message. [15]When she and the members of her household were baptized, she invited us to her home. "If you consider me a believer in the Lord," she said, "come and stay at my house." And she persuaded us.

Paul and Silas in Prison

[16]Once when we were going to the place of prayer, we were met by a slave girl who had a spirit by which she predicted the future. She earned a great deal of money for her owners by fortune-telling. [17]This girl followed Paul and the rest of us, shouting, "These men are servants of the Most High God, who are telling you the way to be saved." [18]She kept this up for many days. Finally Paul became so troubled that he turned around and said to the spirit, "In the name of Jesus Christ I command you to come out of her!" At that moment the spirit left her.

[19]When the owners of the slave girl realized that their hope of making money was gone, they seized Paul and Silas and dragged them into the marketplace to face the authorities. [20]They brought them before the magistrates and said, "These men are Jews, and are throwing our city into an uproar [21]by advocating customs unlawful for us Romans to accept or practice."

[22]The crowd joined in the attack against Paul and Silas, and the magistrates ordered them to be stripped and beaten. [23]After they had been severely flogged, they were thrown into prison, and the jailer was commanded to guard them carefully. [24]Upon receiving such orders, he put them in the inner cell and fastened their feet in the stocks.

[25]About midnight Paul and Silas were praying and singing hymns to God, and the other prisoners were listening to them. [26]Suddenly there was such a violent earthquake that the foundations of the prison were shaken. At once all the

prison doors flew open, and everybody's chains came loose. ²⁷The jailer woke up, and when he saw the prison doors open, he drew his sword and was about to kill himself because he thought the prisoners had escaped. ²⁸But Paul shouted, "Don't harm yourself! We are all here!"

²⁹The jailer called for lights, rushed in and fell trembling before Paul and Silas.

³⁰He then brought them out and asked, "Sirs, what must I do to be saved?"

³¹They replied, "Believe in the Lord Jesus, and you will be saved—you and your household." ³²Then they spoke the word of the Lord to him and to all the others in his house. ³³At that hour of the night the jailer took them and washed their wounds; then immediately he and

---

[MONDAY]

ACTS 16:16–40

Unstoppable Joy

16:25 ABOUT MIDNIGHT PAUL AND SILAS WERE PRAYING AND SINGING HYMNS TO GOD.

The whole idea of flogging was to beat a person to within an inch of his or her life, and to stop just before the victim expired. Presumably, the purpose of being "*severely* flogged," as Paul and Silas were, was to beat them to within a half-inch of their lives. Whatever the level of torture, it was a horrible experience made worse by having their feet fastened in stocks; it was therefore impossible for them to lie on their stomachs, which was the only way a flogging victim would want to lie.

But there they staunchly sat, backs raw, praying and singing hymns at midnight. Luke adds dryly, "and the other prisoners were listening to them." No mystery that! Of course they were listening—you can be sure the prisoners had never heard flogging victims in stocks singing at midnight. What kind of joy is that?!

It was a joy grounded not in the present moment but in the big picture. Clearly the present moment was terrible, but it was temporary. What would last would be everlasting joy for a moment's misery on earth. Everything that mattered was guaranteed for Paul and Silas: Their sins were forgiven, and they were assured of an eternity with God. Everything was fundamentally sound, just a few passing details were askew.

Paul and Silas's joy was nurtured by rejoicing, that is, by praying and singing. *Joy* is a noun, what we experience when our lives are fundamentally sound. *Rejoice* is a verb. It is what we do when we express our gratitude. It is declaring to ourselves, and to others, but above all to God, that we are glad everything is so ultimately good. To not rejoice is to stifle joy. To rejoice is to open once again the soul's perception of how fundamentally great things really are. Paul spoke with great authority when he later commanded the church he had founded in Philippi to "Rejoice in the Lord always. I will say it again: Rejoice!" (Philippians 4:4).

PRAY:

I do rejoice in you, Lord! Free me from the trap of having my joy hinged to my circumstances. Thank you for your provision for what really matters—for my eternal needs.

FOR YOUR NEXT DEVOTIONAL READING, GO TO PAGE 1365.

all his family were baptized. ³⁴The jailer brought them into his house and set a meal before them; he was filled with joy because he had come to believe in God— he and his whole family.

³⁵When it was daylight, the magistrates sent their officers to the jailer with the order: "Release those men." ³⁶The jailer told Paul, "The magistrates have ordered that you and Silas be released. Now you can leave. Go in peace."

³⁷But Paul said to the officers: "They beat us publicly without a trial, even though we are Roman citizens, and threw us into prison. And now do they want to get rid of us quietly? No! Let them come themselves and escort us out."

³⁸The officers reported this to the magistrates, and when they heard that Paul and Silas were Roman citizens, they were alarmed. ³⁹They came to appease them and escorted them from the prison, requesting them to leave the city. ⁴⁰After Paul and Silas came out of the prison, they went to Lydia's house, where they met with the brothers and encouraged them. Then they left.

In Thessalonica

17 When they had passed through Amphipolis and Apollonia, they came to Thessalonica, where there was a Jewish synagogue. ²As his custom was, Paul went into the synagogue, and on three Sabbath days he reasoned with them from the Scriptures, ³explaining and proving that the Christ*ᵃ* had to suffer and rise from the dead. "This Jesus I am proclaiming to you is the Christ,*ᵃ*" he said. ⁴Some of the Jews were persuaded and joined Paul and Silas, as did a large number of God-fearing Greeks and not a few prominent women.

⁵But the Jews were jealous; so they rounded up some bad characters from the marketplace, formed a mob and started a riot in the city. They rushed to Jason's house in search of Paul and Silas in order to bring them out to the crowd.*ᵇ* ⁶But when they did not find them, they dragged Jason and some other brothers before the city officials, shouting: "These men who have caused trouble all over the world have now come here, ⁷and Jason has welcomed them into his house.

They are all defying Caesar's decrees, saying that there is another king, one called Jesus." ⁸When they heard this, the crowd and the city officials were thrown into turmoil. ⁹Then they made Jason and the others post bond and let them go.

In Berea

¹⁰As soon as it was night, the brothers sent Paul and Silas away to Berea. On arriving there, they went to the Jewish synagogue. ¹¹Now the Bereans were of more noble character than the Thessalonians, for they received the message with great eagerness and examined the Scriptures every day to see if what Paul said was true. ¹²Many of the Jews believed, as did also a number of prominent Greek women and many Greek men.

¹³When the Jews in Thessalonica learned that Paul was preaching the word of God at Berea, they went there too, agitating the crowds and stirring them up. ¹⁴The brothers immediately sent Paul to the coast, but Silas and Timothy stayed at Berea. ¹⁵The men who escorted Paul brought him to Athens and then left with instructions for Silas and Timothy to join him as soon as possible.

In Athens

¹⁶While Paul was waiting for them in Athens, he was greatly distressed to see that the city was full of idols. ¹⁷So he reasoned in the synagogue with the Jews and the God-fearing Greeks, as well as in the marketplace day by day with those who happened to be there. ¹⁸A group of Epicurean and Stoic philosophers began to dispute with him. Some of them asked, "What is this babbler trying to say?" Others remarked, "He seems to be advocating foreign gods." They said this because Paul was preaching the good news about Jesus and the resurrection. ¹⁹Then they took him and brought him to a meeting of the Areopagus, where they said to him, "May we know what this new teaching is that you are presenting? ²⁰You are bringing some strange ideas to our ears, and we want to know what they mean." ²¹(All the Athenians and the foreigners

---

ᵃ3 Or *Messiah*   *ᵇ5* Or *the assembly of the people*

who lived there spent their time doing nothing but talking about and listening to the latest ideas.) ²²Paul then stood up in the meeting of the Areopagus and said: "Men of Athens! I see that in every way you are very religious. ²³For as I walked around and looked carefully at your objects of worship, I even found an altar with this inscription: TO AN UNKNOWN GOD. Now what you worship as something unknown I am going to proclaim to you.

²⁴"The God who made the world and everything in it is the Lord of heaven and earth and does not live in temples built by hands. ²⁵And he is not served by human hands, as if he needed anything, because he himself gives all men life and breath and everything else. ²⁶From one man he made every nation of men, that they should inhabit the whole earth; and he determined the times set for them and the exact places where they should live. ²⁷God did this so that men would seek him and perhaps reach out for him and find him, though he is not far from each one of us. ²⁸'For in him we live and move and have our being.' As some of your own poets have said, 'We are his offspring.'

²⁹"Therefore since we are God's offspring, we should not think that the divine being is like gold or silver or stone—an image made by man's design and skill. ³⁰In the past God overlooked such ignorance, but now he commands all people everywhere to repent. ³¹For he has set a day when he will judge the world with justice by the man he has appointed. He has given proof of this to all men by raising him from the dead."

³²When they heard about the resurrection of the dead, some of them sneered, but others said, "We want to hear you again on this subject." ³³At that, Paul left the Council. ³⁴A few men became followers of Paul and believed. Among them was Dionysius, a member of the Areopagus, also a woman named Damaris, and a number of others.

In Corinth

18 After this, Paul left Athens and went to Corinth. ²There he met a Jew named Aquila, a native of Pontus, who had recently come from Italy with his wife Priscilla, because Claudius had ordered all the Jews to leave Rome. Paul went to see them, ³and because he was a tentmaker as they were, he stayed and worked with them. ⁴Every Sabbath he reasoned in the synagogue, trying to persuade Jews and Greeks.

⁵When Silas and Timothy came from Macedonia, Paul devoted himself exclusively to preaching, testifying to the Jews that Jesus was the Christ.ᵃ ⁶But when the Jews opposed Paul and became abusive, he shook out his clothes in protest and said to them, "Your blood be on your own heads! I am clear of my responsibility. From now on I will go to the Gentiles."

⁷Then Paul left the synagogue and went next door to the house of Titius Justus, a worshiper of God. ⁸Crispus, the synagogue ruler, and his entire household believed in the Lord; and many of the Corinthians who heard him believed and were baptized.

⁹One night the Lord spoke to Paul in a vision: "Do not be afraid; keep on speaking, do not be silent. ¹⁰For I am with you, and no one is going to attack and harm you, because I have many people in this city." ¹¹So Paul stayed for a year and a half, teaching them the word of God.

> 66 Any concern too small to be turned into a prayer is too small to be made into a burden. 99
>
> CORRIE TEN BOOM

¹²While Gallio was proconsul of Achaia, the Jews made a united attack on Paul and brought him into court. ¹³"This man," they charged, "is persuading the people to worship God in ways contrary to the law."

¹⁴Just as Paul was about to speak, Gallio said to the Jews, "If you Jews were making a complaint about some misdemeanor or serious crime, it would be reasonable for me to listen to you. ¹⁵But since it involves questions about words and names and your own law—settle the matter yourselves. I will not be a judge of such things." ¹⁶So he had them ejected from the court. ¹⁷Then they all turned on

ᵃ5 Or Messiah; also in verse 28

Sosthenes the synagogue ruler and beat him in front of the court. But Gallio showed no concern whatever.

Priscilla, Aquila and Apollos

18Paul stayed on in Corinth for some time. Then he left the brothers and sailed for Syria, accompanied by Priscilla and Aquila. Before he sailed, he had his hair cut off at Cenchrea because of a vow he had taken. 19They arrived at Ephesus, where Paul left Priscilla and Aquila. He himself went into the synagogue and reasoned with the Jews. 20When they asked him to spend more time with them, he declined. 21But as he left, he promised, "I will come back if it is God's will." Then he set sail from Ephesus. 22When he landed at Caesarea, he went up and greeted the church and then went down to Antioch.

23After spending some time in Antioch, Paul set out from there and traveled from place to place throughout the region of Galatia and Phrygia, strengthening all the disciples.

24Meanwhile a Jew named Apollos, a native of Alexandria, came to Ephesus. He was a learned man, with a thorough knowledge of the Scriptures. 25He had been instructed in the way of the Lord, and he spoke with great fervor*d* and taught about Jesus accurately, though he knew only the baptism of John. 26He began to speak boldly in the synagogue. When Priscilla and Aquila heard him, they invited him to their home and explained to him the way of God more adequately.

27When Apollos wanted to go to Achaia, the brothers encouraged him and wrote to the disciples there to welcome him. On arriving, he was a great help to those who by grace had believed. 28For he vigorously refuted the Jews in public debate, proving from the Scriptures that Jesus was the Christ.

Paul in Ephesus

19 While Apollos was at Corinth, Paul took the road through the interior and arrived at Ephesus. There he found some disciples 2and asked them, "Did you receive the Holy Spirit when*b* you believed?"

They answered, "No, we have not even heard that there is a Holy Spirit."

3So Paul asked, "Then what baptism did you receive?"

"John's baptism," they replied.

4Paul said, "John's baptism was a baptism of repentance. He told the people to believe in the one coming after him, that is, in Jesus." 5On hearing this, they were baptized into*c* the name of the Lord Jesus. 6When Paul placed his hands on them, the Holy Spirit came on them, and they spoke in tongues*d* and prophesied. 7There were about twelve men in all.

8Paul entered the synagogue and spoke boldly there for three months, arguing persuasively about the kingdom of God. 9But some of them became obstinate; they refused to believe and publicly maligned the Way. So Paul left them. He took the disciples with him and had discussions daily in the lecture hall of Tyrannus. 10This went on for two years, so that all the Jews and Greeks who lived in the province of Asia heard the word of the Lord.

11God did extraordinary miracles through Paul, 12so that even handkerchiefs and aprons that had touched him were taken to the sick, and their illnesses were cured and the evil spirits left them.

13Some Jews who went around driving out evil spirits tried to invoke the name of the Lord Jesus over those who were demon-possessed. They would say, "In the name of Jesus, whom Paul preaches, I command you to come out." 14Seven sons of Sceva, a Jewish chief priest, were doing this. 15⌐One day⌐ the evil spirit answered them, "Jesus I know, and I know about Paul, but who are you?" 16Then the man who had the evil spirit jumped on them and overpowered them all. He gave them such a beating that they ran out of the house naked and bleeding.

17When this became known to the Jews and Greeks living in Ephesus, they were all seized with fear, and the name of the Lord Jesus was held in high honor. 18Many of those who believed now came and openly confessed their evil deeds. 19A number who had practiced sorcery brought their scrolls together and burned them publicly. When they calculated the value of the scrolls, the total came to fifty thou-

*a*25 Or with fervor in the Spirit   *b*2 Or after   *c*5 Or in   *d*6 Or other languages

sand drachmas.*a* ²⁰In this way the word of the Lord spread widely and grew in power.

²¹After all this had happened, Paul decided to go to Jerusalem, passing through Macedonia and Achaia. "After I have been there," he said, "I must visit Rome also." ²²He sent two of his helpers, Timothy and Erastus, to Macedonia, while he stayed in the province of Asia a little longer.

The Riot in Ephesus

²³About that time there arose a great disturbance about the Way. ²⁴A silversmith named Demetrius, who made silver shrines of Artemis, brought in no little business for the craftsmen. ²⁵He called them together, along with the workmen in related trades, and said: "Men, you know we receive a good income from this business. ²⁶And you see and hear how this fellow Paul has convinced and led astray large numbers of people here in Ephesus and in practically the whole province of Asia. He says that man-made gods are no gods at all. ²⁷There is danger not only that our trade will lose its good name, but also that the temple of the great goddess Artemis will be discredited, and the goddess herself, who is worshiped throughout the province of Asia and the world, will be robbed of her divine majesty."

²⁸When they heard this, they were furious and began shouting: "Great is Artemis of the Ephesians!" ²⁹Soon the whole city was in an uproar. The people seized Gaius and Aristarchus, Paul's traveling companions from Macedonia, and rushed as one man into the theater. ³⁰Paul wanted to appear before the crowd, but the disciples would not let him. ³¹Even some of the officials of the province, friends of Paul, sent him a message begging him not to venture into the theater.

³²The assembly was in confusion: Some were shouting one thing, some another. Most of the people did not even know why they were there. ³³The Jews pushed Alexander to the front, and some of the crowd shouted instructions to him. He motioned for silence in order to make a defense before the people. ³⁴But when they realized he was a Jew, they all shouted in unison for about two hours: "Great is Artemis of the Ephesians!"

³⁵The city clerk quieted the crowd and said: "Men of Ephesus, doesn't all the world know that the city of Ephesus is the guardian of the temple of the great Artemis and of her image, which fell from heaven? ³⁶Therefore, since these facts are undeniable, you ought to be quiet and not do anything rash. ³⁷You have brought these men here, though they have neither robbed temples nor blasphemed our goddess. ³⁸If, then, Demetrius and his fellow craftsmen have a grievance against anybody, the courts are open and there are proconsuls. They can press charges. ³⁹If there is anything further you want to bring up, it must be settled in a legal assembly. ⁴⁰As it is, we are in danger of being charged with rioting because of today's events. In that case we would not be able to account for this commotion, since there is no reason for it." ⁴¹After he had said this, he dismissed the assembly.

Through Macedonia and Greece

20 When the uproar had ended, Paul sent for the disciples and, after encouraging them, said good-by and set out for Macedonia. ²He traveled through that area, speaking many words of encouragement to the people, and finally arrived in Greece, ³where he stayed three months. Because the Jews made a plot against him just as he was about to sail for Syria, he decided to go back through Macedonia. ⁴He was accompanied by Sopater son of Pyrrhus from Berea, Aristarchus and Secundus from Thessalonica, Gaius from Derbe, Timothy also, and Tychicus and Trophimus from the province of Asia. ⁵These men went on ahead and waited for us at Troas. ⁶But we sailed from Philippi after the Feast of Unleavened Bread, and five days later joined the others at Troas, where we stayed seven days.

Eutychus Raised From the Dead at Troas

⁷On the first day of the week we came together to break bread. Paul spoke to the people and, because he intended to leave the next day, kept on talking until midnight. ⁸There were many lamps in the

---

a 19 A drachma was a silver coin worth about a day's wages.

upstairs room where we were meeting. ⁹Seated in a window was a young man named Eutychus, who was sinking into a deep sleep as Paul talked on and on. When he was sound asleep, he fell to the ground from the third story and was picked up dead. ¹⁰Paul went down, threw himself on the young man and put his arms around him. "Don't be alarmed," he said. "He's alive!" ¹¹Then he went upstairs again and broke bread and ate. After talking until daylight, he left. ¹²The people took the young man home alive and were greatly comforted.

Paul's Farewell to the Ephesian Elders

¹³We went on ahead to the ship and sailed for Assos, where we were going to take Paul aboard. He had made this arrangement because he was going there on foot. ¹⁴When he met us at Assos, we took him aboard and went on to Mitylene. ¹⁵The next day we set sail from there and arrived off Kios. The day after that we crossed over to Samos, and on the following day arrived at Miletus. ¹⁶Paul had decided to sail past Ephesus to avoid spending time in the province of Asia, for he was in a hurry to reach Jerusalem, if possible, by the day of Pentecost.

¹⁷From Miletus, Paul sent to Ephesus for the elders of the church. ¹⁸When they arrived, he said to them: "You know how I lived the whole time I was with you, from the first day I came into the province of Asia. ¹⁹I served the Lord with great humility and with tears, although I was severely tested by the plots of the Jews. ²⁰You know that I have not hesitated to preach anything that would be helpful to you but have taught you publicly and from house to house. ²¹I have declared to both Jews and Greeks that they must turn to God in repentance and have faith in our Lord Jesus.

²²"And now, compelled by the Spirit, I am going to Jerusalem, not knowing what will happen to me there. ²³I only know that in every city the Holy Spirit warns me that prison and hardships are facing me. ²⁴However, I consider my life worth nothing to me, if only I may finish the race and complete the task the Lord Jesus has given me—the task of testifying to the gospel of God's grace.

²⁵"Now I know that none of you among whom I have gone about preaching the kingdom will ever see me again. ²⁶Therefore, I declare to you today that I am innocent of the blood of all men. ²⁷For I have not hesitated to proclaim to you the whole will of God. ²⁸Keep watch over yourselves and all the flock of which the Holy Spirit has made you overseers.ᵃ Be shepherds of the church of God,ᵇ which he bought with his own blood. ²⁹I know that after I leave, savage wolves will come in among you and will not spare the flock. ³⁰Even from your own number men will arise and distort the truth in order to draw away disciples after them. ³¹So be on your guard! Remember that for three years I never stopped warning each of you night and day with tears.

³²"Now I commit you to God and to the word of his grace, which can build you up and give you an inheritance among all those who are sanctified. ³³I have not coveted anyone's silver or gold or clothing. ³⁴You yourselves know that these hands of mine have supplied my own needs and the needs of my companions. ³⁵In everything I did, I showed you that by this kind of hard work we must help the weak, remembering the words the Lord Jesus himself said: 'It is more blessed to give than to receive.'"

³⁶When he had said this, he knelt down with all of them and prayed. ³⁷They all wept as they embraced him and kissed him. ³⁸What grieved them most was his statement that they would never see his face again. Then they accompanied him to the ship.

> WHEN he had said this, he knelt down with all of them and prayed.
>
> ACTS 20:36

On to Jerusalem

21 After we had torn ourselves away from them, we put out to sea and sailed straight to Cos. The next day we went to Rhodes and from there to Patara. ²We found a ship crossing over to Phoe-

ᵃ28 Traditionally *bishops*   ᵇ28 Many manuscripts *of the Lord*

nicia, went on board and set sail. ³After sighting Cyprus and passing to the south of it, we sailed on to Syria. We landed at Tyre, where our ship was to unload its cargo. ⁴Finding the disciples there, we stayed with them seven days. Through the Spirit they urged Paul not to go on to Jerusalem. ⁵But when our time was up, we left and continued on our way. All the disciples and their wives and children accompanied us out of the city, and there on the beach we knelt to pray. ⁶After saying good-by to each other, we went aboard the ship, and they returned home.

> BUT *when our time was up, we left and continued on our way. All the disciples and their wives and children accompanied us out of the city, and there on the beach we knelt to pray.*
>
> ACTS 21:5

⁷We continued our voyage from Tyre and landed at Ptolemais, where we greeted the brothers and stayed with them for a day. ⁸Leaving the next day, we reached Caesarea and stayed at the house of Philip the evangelist, one of the Seven. ⁹He had four unmarried daughters who prophesied.

¹⁰After we had been there a number of days, a prophet named Agabus came down from Judea. ¹¹Coming over to us, he took Paul's belt, tied his own hands and feet with it and said, "The Holy Spirit says, 'In this way the Jews of Jerusalem will bind the owner of this belt and will hand him over to the Gentiles.'"

¹²When we heard this, we and the people there pleaded with Paul not to go up to Jerusalem. ¹³Then Paul answered, "Why are you weeping and breaking my heart? I am ready not only to be bound, but also to die in Jerusalem for the name of the Lord Jesus." ¹⁴When he would not be dissuaded, we gave up and said, "The Lord's will be done."

¹⁵After this, we got ready and went up to Jerusalem. ¹⁶Some of the disciples from Caesarea accompanied us and brought us to the home of Mnason, where we were to stay. He was a man from Cyprus and one of the early disciples.

Paul's Arrival at Jerusalem

¹⁷When we arrived at Jerusalem, the brothers received us warmly. ¹⁸The next day Paul and the rest of us went to see James, and all the elders were present. ¹⁹Paul greeted them and reported in detail what God had done among the Gentiles through his ministry.

²⁰When they heard this, they praised God. Then they said to Paul: "You see, brother, how many thousands of Jews have believed, and all of them are zealous for the law. ²¹They have been informed that you teach all the Jews who live among the Gentiles to turn away from Moses, telling them not to circumcise their children or live according to our customs. ²²What shall we do? They will certainly hear that you have come, ²³so do what we tell you. There are four men with us who have made a vow. ²⁴Take these men, join in their purification rites and pay their expenses, so that they can have their heads shaved. Then everybody will know there is no truth in these reports about you, but that you yourself are living in obedience to the law. ²⁵As for the Gentile believers, we have written to them our decision that they should abstain from food sacrificed to idols, from blood, from the meat of strangled animals and from sexual immorality."

²⁶The next day Paul took the men and purified himself along with them. Then he went to the temple to give notice of the date when the days of purification would end and the offering would be made for each of them.

Paul Arrested

²⁷When the seven days were nearly over, some Jews from the province of Asia saw Paul at the temple. They stirred up the whole crowd and seized him, ²⁸shouting, "Men of Israel, help us! This is the man who teaches all men everywhere against our people and our law and this place. And besides, he has brought Greeks into the temple area and defiled this holy place." ²⁹(They had previously seen Trophimus the Ephesian in the city with Paul and assumed that Paul had brought him into the temple area.)

³⁰The whole city was aroused, and the people came running from all directions. Seizing Paul, they dragged him from the temple, and immediately the gates were shut. ³¹While they were trying to kill him, news reached the commander of the Roman troops that the whole city of Jerusalem was in an uproar. ³²He at once took some officers and soldiers and ran down to the crowd. When the rioters saw the commander and his soldiers, they stopped beating Paul.

³³The commander came up and arrested him and ordered him to be bound with two chains. Then he asked who he was and what he had done. ³⁴Some in the crowd shouted one thing and some another, and since the commander could not get at the truth because of the uproar, he ordered that Paul be taken into the barracks. ³⁵When Paul reached the steps, the violence of the mob was so great he had to be carried by the soldiers. ³⁶The crowd that followed kept shouting, "Away with him!"

Paul Speaks to the Crowd

³⁷As the soldiers were about to take Paul into the barracks, he asked the commander, "May I say something to you?"

"Do you speak Greek?" he replied. ³⁸"Aren't you the Egyptian who started a revolt and led four thousand terrorists out into the desert some time ago?"

³⁹Paul answered, "I am a Jew, from Tarsus in Cilicia, a citizen of no ordinary city. Please let me speak to the people."

⁴⁰Having received the commander's permission, Paul stood on the steps and motioned to the crowd. When they were all silent, he said to them in Aramaic[a]:

22 ¹"Brothers and fathers, listen now to my defense."

²When they heard him speak to them in Aramaic, they became very quiet.

Then Paul said: ³"I am a Jew, born in Tarsus of Cilicia, but brought up in this city. Under Gamaliel I was thoroughly trained in the law of our fathers and was just as zealous for God as any of you are today. ⁴I persecuted the followers of this Way to their death, arresting both men and women and throwing them into prison, ⁵as also the high priest and all the Council can testify. I even obtained letters from them to their brothers in Damascus, and went there to bring these people as prisoners to Jerusalem to be punished.

⁶"About noon as I came near Damascus, suddenly a bright light from heaven flashed around me. ⁷I fell to the ground and heard a voice say to me, 'Saul! Saul! Why do you persecute me?'

⁸"'Who are you, Lord?' I asked.

"'I am Jesus of Nazareth, whom you are persecuting,' he replied. ⁹My companions saw the light, but they did not understand the voice of him who was speaking to me.

¹⁰"'What shall I do, Lord?' I asked.

"'Get up,' the Lord said, 'and go into Damascus. There you will be told all that you have been assigned to do.' ¹¹My companions led me by the hand into Damascus, because the brilliance of the light had blinded me.

¹²"A man named Ananias came to see me. He was a devout observer of the law and highly respected by all the Jews living there. ¹³He stood beside me and said, 'Brother Saul, receive your sight!' And at that very moment I was able to see him.

¹⁴"Then he said: 'The God of our fathers has chosen you to know his will and to see the Righteous One and to hear words from his mouth. ¹⁵You will be his witness to all men of what you have seen and heard. ¹⁶And now what are you waiting for? Get up, be baptized and wash your sins away, calling on his name.'

¹⁷"When I returned to Jerusalem and was praying at the temple, I fell into a trance ¹⁸and saw the Lord speaking. 'Quick!' he said to me. 'Leave Jerusalem immediately, because they will not accept your testimony about me.'

¹⁹"'Lord,' I replied, 'these men know that I went from one synagogue to another to imprison and beat those who believe in you. ²⁰And when the blood of your martyr[b] Stephen was shed, I stood there giving my approval and guarding the clothes of those who were killing him.'

²¹"Then the Lord said to me, 'Go; I will send you far away to the Gentiles.'"

---

[a]40 Or possibly *Hebrew*; also in 22:2
[b]20 Or *witness*

Paul the Roman Citizen

²²The crowd listened to Paul until he said this. Then they raised their voices and shouted, "Rid the earth of him! He's not fit to live!"

²³As they were shouting and throwing off their cloaks and flinging dust into the air, ²⁴the commander ordered Paul to be taken into the barracks. He directed that he be flogged and questioned in order to find out why the people were shouting at him like this. ²⁵As they stretched him out to flog him, Paul said to the centurion standing there, "Is it legal for you to flog a Roman citizen who hasn't even been found guilty?"

²⁶When the centurion heard this, he went to the commander and reported it. "What are you going to do?" he asked. "This man is a Roman citizen."

²⁷The commander went to Paul and asked, "Tell me, are you a Roman citizen?"

"Yes, I am," he answered.

²⁸Then the commander said, "I had to pay a big price for my citizenship."

"But I was born a citizen," Paul replied.

²⁹Those who were about to question him withdrew immediately. The commander himself was alarmed when he realized that he had put Paul, a Roman citizen, in chains.

Before the Sanhedrin

³⁰The next day, since the commander wanted to find out exactly why Paul was being accused by the Jews, he released him and ordered the chief priests and all the Sanhedrin to assemble. Then he brought Paul and had him stand before them.

23 Paul looked straight at the Sanhedrin and said, "My brothers, I have fulfilled my duty to God in all good conscience to this day." ²At this the high priest Ananias ordered those standing near Paul to strike him on the mouth. ³Then Paul said to him, "God will strike you, you whitewashed wall! You sit there to judge me according to the law, yet you yourself violate the law by commanding that I be struck!"

⁴Those who were standing near Paul said, "You dare to insult God's high priest?"

⁵Paul replied, "Brothers, I did not realize that he was the high priest; for it is written: 'Do not speak evil about the ruler of your people.'ᵃ"

⁶Then Paul, knowing that some of them were Sadducees and the others Pharisees, called out in the Sanhedrin, "My brothers, I am a Pharisee, the son of a Pharisee. I stand on trial because of my hope in the resurrection of the dead." ⁷When he said this, a dispute broke out between the Pharisees and the Sadducees, and the assembly was divided. ⁸(The Sadducees say that there is no resurrection, and that there are neither angels nor spirits, but the Pharisees acknowledge them all.)

> " Prayer may not change things for you, but it sure changes you for things. "
>
> SAMUEL M. SHOEMAKER

⁹There was a great uproar, and some of the teachers of the law who were Pharisees stood up and argued vigorously. "We find nothing wrong with this man," they said. "What if a spirit or an angel has spoken to him?" ¹⁰The dispute became so violent that the commander was afraid Paul would be torn to pieces by them. He ordered the troops to go down and take him away from them by force and bring him into the barracks.

¹¹The following night the Lord stood near Paul and said, "Take courage! As you have testified about me in Jerusalem, so you must also testify in Rome."

The Plot to Kill Paul

¹²The next morning the Jews formed a conspiracy and bound themselves with an oath not to eat or drink until they had killed Paul. ¹³More than forty men were involved in this plot. ¹⁴They went to the chief priests and elders and said, "We have taken a solemn oath not to eat anything until we have killed Paul. ¹⁵Now then, you and the Sanhedrin petition the commander to bring him before you on the pretext of wanting more accurate information about his case. We are ready to kill him before he gets here."

ᵃ5 Exodus 22:28

¹⁶But when the son of Paul's sister heard of this plot, he went into the barracks and told Paul.

¹⁷Then Paul called one of the centurions and said, "Take this young man to the commander; he has something to tell him." ¹⁸So he took him to the commander.

The centurion said, "Paul, the prisoner, sent for me and asked me to bring this young man to you because he has something to tell you."

¹⁹The commander took the young man by the hand, drew him aside and asked, "What is it you want to tell me?"

²⁰He said: "The Jews have agreed to ask you to bring Paul before the Sanhedrin tomorrow on the pretext of wanting more accurate information about him. ²¹Don't give in to them, because more than forty of them are waiting in ambush for him. They have taken an oath not to eat or drink until they have killed him. They are ready now, waiting for your consent to their request."

²²The commander dismissed the young man and cautioned him, "Don't tell anyone that you have reported this to me."

Paul Transferred to Caesarea

²³Then he called two of his centurions and ordered them, "Get ready a detachment of two hundred soldiers, seventy horsemen and two hundred spearmen[a] to go to Caesarea at nine tonight. ²⁴Provide mounts for Paul so that he may be taken safely to Governor Felix."

²⁵He wrote a letter as follows:

²⁶Claudius Lysias,

To His Excellency, Governor Felix:

Greetings.

²⁷This man was seized by the Jews and they were about to kill him, but I came with my troops and rescued him, for I had learned that he is a Roman citizen. ²⁸I wanted to know why they were accusing him, so I brought him to their Sanhedrin. ²⁹I found that the accusation had to do with questions about their law, but there was no charge against him that deserved death or imprisonment. ³⁰When I was informed of a plot to be carried out against the man, I sent him to you at once. I also ordered his accusers to present to you their case against him.

³¹So the soldiers, carrying out their orders, took Paul with them during the night and brought him as far as Antipatris. ³²The next day they let the cavalry go on with him, while they returned to the barracks. ³³When the cavalry arrived in Caesarea, they delivered the letter to the governor and handed Paul over to him. ³⁴The governor read the letter and asked what province he was from. Learning that he was from Cilicia, ³⁵he said, "I will hear your case when your accusers get here." Then he ordered that Paul be kept under guard in Herod's palace.

The Trial Before Felix

24 Five days later the high priest Ananias went down to Caesarea with some of the elders and a lawyer named Tertullus, and they brought their charges against Paul before the governor. ²When Paul was called in, Tertullus presented his case before Felix: "We have enjoyed a long period of peace under you, and your foresight has brought about reforms in this nation. ³Everywhere and in every way, most excellent Felix, we acknowledge this with profound gratitude. ⁴But in order not to weary you further, I would request that you be kind enough to hear us briefly.

⁵"We have found this man to be a troublemaker, stirring up riots among the Jews all over the world. He is a ringleader of the Nazarene sect ⁶and even tried to desecrate the temple; so we seized him. ⁸By[b] examining him yourself you will be able to learn the truth about all these charges we are bringing against him."

⁹The Jews joined in the accusation, asserting that these things were true.

¹⁰When the governor motioned for him to speak, Paul replied: "I know that for a number of years you have been a judge

---

a 23 The meaning of the Greek for this word is uncertain.   *b 6-8* Some manuscripts *him and wanted to judge him according to our law.* ⁷*But the commander, Lysias, came and with the use of much force snatched him from our hands* ⁸*and ordered his accusers to come before you. By*

over this nation; so I gladly make my defense. ¹¹You can easily verify that no more than twelve days ago I went up to Jerusalem to worship. ¹²My accusers did not find me arguing with anyone at the temple, or stirring up a crowd in the synagogues or anywhere else in the city. ¹³And they cannot prove to you the charges they are now making against me. ¹⁴However, I admit that I worship the God of our fathers as a follower of the Way, which they call a sect. I believe everything that agrees with the Law and that is written in the Prophets, ¹⁵and I have the same hope in God as these men, that there will be a resurrection of both the righteous and the wicked. ¹⁶So I strive always to keep my conscience clear before God and man.

¹⁷"After an absence of several years, I came to Jerusalem to bring my people gifts for the poor and to present offerings. ¹⁸I was ceremonially clean when they found me in the temple courts doing this. There was no crowd with me, nor was I involved in any disturbance. ¹⁹But there are some Jews from the province of Asia, who ought to be here before you and bring charges if they have anything against me. ²⁰Or these who are here should state what crime they found in me when I stood before the Sanhedrin— ²¹unless it was this one thing I shouted as I stood in their presence: 'It is concerning the resurrection of the dead that I am on trial before you today.'"

²²Then Felix, who was well acquainted with the Way, adjourned the proceedings. "When Lysias the commander comes," he said, "I will decide your case." ²³He ordered the centurion to keep Paul under guard but to give him some freedom and permit his friends to take care of his needs.

²⁴Several days later Felix came with his wife Drusilla, who was a Jewess. He sent for Paul and listened to him as he spoke about faith in Christ Jesus. ²⁵As Paul discoursed on righteousness, self-control and the judgment to come, Felix was afraid and said, "That's enough for now! You may leave. When I find it convenient, I will send for you." ²⁶At the same time he was hoping that Paul would offer him a bribe, so he sent for him frequently and talked with him.

²⁷When two years had passed, Felix was succeeded by Porcius Festus, but because Felix wanted to grant a favor to the Jews, he left Paul in prison.

The Trial Before Festus

25 Three days after arriving in the province, Festus went up from Caesarea to Jerusalem, ²where the chief priests and Jewish leaders appeared before him and presented the charges against Paul. ³They urgently requested Festus, as a favor to them, to have Paul transferred to Jerusalem, for they were preparing an ambush to kill him along the way. ⁴Festus answered, "Paul is being held at Caesarea, and I myself am going there soon. ⁵Let some of your leaders come with me and press charges against the man there, if he has done anything wrong."

⁶After spending eight or ten days with them, he went down to Caesarea, and the next day he convened the court and ordered that Paul be brought before him. ⁷When Paul appeared, the Jews who had come down from Jerusalem stood around him, bringing many serious charges against him, which they could not prove.

⁸Then Paul made his defense: "I have done nothing wrong against the law of the Jews or against the temple or against Caesar."

⁹Festus, wishing to do the Jews a favor, said to Paul, "Are you willing to go up to Jerusalem and stand trial before me there on these charges?"

¹⁰Paul answered: "I am now standing before Caesar's court, where I ought to be tried. I have not done any wrong to the Jews, as you yourself know very well. ¹¹If, however, I am guilty of doing anything deserving death, I do not refuse to die. But if the charges brought against me by these Jews are not true, no one has the right to hand me over to them. I appeal to Caesar!"

¹²After Festus had conferred with his council, he declared: "You have appealed to Caesar. To Caesar you will go!"

Festus Consults King Agrippa

¹³A few days later King Agrippa and Bernice arrived at Caesarea to pay their

respects to Festus. [14]Since they were spending many days there, Festus discussed Paul's case with the king. He said: "There is a man here whom Felix left as a prisoner. [15]When I went to Jerusalem, the chief priests and elders of the Jews brought charges against him and asked that he be condemned.

[16]"I told them that it is not the Roman custom to hand over any man before he has faced his accusers and has had an opportunity to defend himself against their charges. [17]When they came here with me, I did not delay the case, but convened the court the next day and ordered the man to be brought in. [18]When his accusers got up to speak, they did not charge him with any of the crimes I had expected. [19]Instead, they had some points of dispute with him about their own religion and about a dead man named Jesus who Paul claimed was alive. [20]I was at a loss how to investigate such matters; so I asked if he would be willing to go to Jerusalem and stand trial there on these charges. [21]When Paul made his appeal to be held over for the Emperor's decision, I ordered him held until I could send him to Caesar."

[22]Then Agrippa said to Festus, "I would like to hear this man myself."

He replied, "Tomorrow you will hear him."

Paul Before Agrippa

[23]The next day Agrippa and Bernice came with great pomp and entered the audience room with the high ranking officers and the leading men of the city. At the command of Festus, Paul was brought in. [24]Festus said: "King Agrippa,

> " Every great movement of God can be traced to a kneeling figure. "
>
> D. L. MOODY

and all who are present with us, you see this man! The whole Jewish community has petitioned me about him in Jerusalem and here in Caesarea, shouting that he ought not to live any longer. [25]I found he had done nothing deserving of death, but because he made his appeal to the Emperor I decided to send him to Rome.

[26]But I have nothing definite to write to His Majesty about him. Therefore I have brought him before all of you, and especially before you, King Agrippa, so that as a result of this investigation I may have something to write. [27]For I think it is unreasonable to send on a prisoner without specifying the charges against him."

26 Then Agrippa said to Paul, "You have permission to speak for yourself."

So Paul motioned with his hand and began his defense: [2]"King Agrippa, I consider myself fortunate to stand before you today as I make my defense against all the accusations of the Jews, [3]and especially so because you are well acquainted with all the Jewish customs and controversies. Therefore, I beg you to listen to me patiently.

[4]"The Jews all know the way I have lived ever since I was a child, from the beginning of my life in my own country, and also in Jerusalem. [5]They have known me for a long time and can testify, if they are willing, that according to the strictest sect of our religion, I lived as a Pharisee. [6]And now it is because of my hope in what God has promised our fathers that I am on trial today. [7]This is the promise our twelve tribes are hoping to see fulfilled as they earnestly serve God day and night. O king, it is because of this hope that the Jews are accusing me. [8]Why should any of you consider it incredible that God raises the dead?

[9]"I too was convinced that I ought to do all that was possible to oppose the name of Jesus of Nazareth. [10]And that is just what I did in Jerusalem. On the authority of the chief priests I put many of the saints in prison, and when they were put to death, I cast my vote against them. [11]Many a time I went from one synagogue to another to have them punished, and I tried to force them to blaspheme. In my obsession against them, I even went to foreign cities to persecute them.

[12]"On one of these journeys I was going to Damascus with the authority and commission of the chief priests. [13]About noon, O king, as I was on the road, I saw a light from heaven, brighter than the sun, blazing around me and my companions. [14]We all fell to the ground, and I

heard a voice saying to me in Aramaic,[a] 'Saul, Saul, why do you persecute me? It is hard for you to kick against the goads.'

[15]"Then I asked, 'Who are you, Lord?'

"'I am Jesus, whom you are persecuting,' the Lord replied. [16]'Now get up and stand on your feet. I have appeared to you to appoint you as a servant and as a witness of what you have seen of me and what I will show you. [17]I will rescue you from your own people and from the Gentiles. I am sending you to them [18]to open their eyes and turn them from darkness to light, and from the power of Satan to God, so that they may receive forgiveness of sins and a place among those who are sanctified by faith in me.'

[19]"So then, King Agrippa, I was not disobedient to the vision from heaven. [20]First to those in Damascus, then to those in Jerusalem and in all Judea, and to the Gentiles also, I preached that they should repent and turn to God and prove their repentance by their deeds. [21]That is why the Jews seized me in the temple courts and tried to kill me. [22]But I have had God's help to this very day, and so I stand here and testify to small and great alike. I am saying nothing beyond what the prophets and Moses said would happen— [23]that the Christ[b] would suffer and, as the first to rise from the dead, would proclaim light to his own people and to the Gentiles."

[24]At this point Festus interrupted Paul's defense. "You are out of your mind, Paul!" he shouted. "Your great learning is driving you insane."

[25]"I am not insane, most excellent Festus," Paul replied. "What I am saying is true and reasonable. [26]The king is familiar with these things, and I can speak freely to him. I am convinced that none of this has escaped his notice, because it was not done in a corner. [27]King Agrippa, do you believe the prophets? I know you do."

[28]Then Agrippa said to Paul, "Do you think that in such a short time you can persuade me to be a Christian?"

[29]Paul replied, "Short time or long—I pray God that not only you but all who are listening to me today may become what I am, except for these chains."

[30]The king rose, and with him the gov-

> PAUL replied, "Short time or long—I pray God that not only you but all who are listening to me today may become what I am, except for these chains."
>
> ACTS 26:29

ernor and Bernice and those sitting with them. [31]They left the room, and while talking with one another, they said, "This man is not doing anything that deserves death or imprisonment."

[32]Agrippa said to Festus, "This man could have been set free if he had not appealed to Caesar."

Paul Sails for Rome

27 When it was decided that we would sail for Italy, Paul and some other prisoners were handed over to a centurion named Julius, who belonged to the Imperial Regiment. [2]We boarded a ship from Adramyttium about to sail for ports along the coast of the province of Asia, and we put out to sea. Aristarchus, a Macedonian from Thessalonica, was with us.

[3]The next day we landed at Sidon; and Julius, in kindness to Paul, allowed him to go to his friends so they might provide for his needs. [4]From there we put out to sea again and passed to the lee of Cyprus because the winds were against us. [5]When we had sailed across the open sea off the coast of Cilicia and Pamphylia, we landed at Myra in Lycia. [6]There the centurion found an Alexandrian ship sailing for Italy and put us on board. [7]We made slow headway for many days and had difficulty arriving off Cnidus. When the wind did not allow us to hold our course, we sailed to the lee of Crete, opposite Salmone. [8]We moved along the coast with difficulty and came to a place called Fair Havens, near the town of Lasea.

[9]Much time had been lost, and sailing had already become dangerous because by now it was after the Fast.[c] So Paul warned them, [10]"Men, I can see that our voyage is going to be disastrous and bring great loss to ship and cargo, and to

[a]14 Or Hebrew   [b]23 Or Messiah   [c]9 That is, the Day of Atonement (Yom Kippur)

our own lives also." [11]But the centurion, instead of listening to what Paul said, followed the advice of the pilot and of the owner of the ship. [12]Since the harbor was unsuitable to winter in, the majority decided that we should sail on, hoping to reach Phoenix and winter there. This was a harbor in Crete, facing both southwest and northwest.

The Storm

[13]When a gentle south wind began to blow, they thought they had obtained what they wanted; so they weighed anchor and sailed along the shore of Crete. [14]Before very long, a wind of hurricane force, called the "northeaster," swept down from the island. [15]The ship was caught by the storm and could not head into the wind; so we gave way to it and were driven along. [16]As we passed to the lee of a small island called Cauda, we were hardly able to make the lifeboat secure. [17]When the men had hoisted it aboard, they passed ropes under the ship itself to hold it together. Fearing that they would run aground on the sandbars of Syrtis, they lowered the sea anchor and let the ship be driven along. [18]We took such a violent battering from the storm that the next day they began to throw the cargo overboard. [19]On the third day, they threw the ship's tackle overboard with their own hands. [20]When neither sun nor stars appeared for many days and the storm continued raging, we finally gave up all hope of being saved.

[21]After the men had gone a long time without food, Paul stood up before them and said: "Men, you should have taken my advice not to sail from Crete; then you would have spared yourselves this damage and loss. [22]But now I urge you to keep up your courage, because not one of you will be lost; only the ship will be destroyed. [23]Last night an angel of the God whose I am and whom I serve stood beside me [24]and said, 'Do not be afraid, Paul. You must stand trial before Caesar; and God has graciously given you the lives of all who sail with you.' [25]So keep up your courage, men, for I have faith in God that it will happen just as he told me. [26]Nevertheless, we must run aground on some island."

The Shipwreck

[27]On the fourteenth night we were still being driven across the Adriatic[a] Sea, when about midnight the sailors sensed they were approaching land. [28]They took soundings and found that the water was a hundred and twenty feet[b] deep. A short time later they took soundings again and found it was ninety feet[c] deep. [29]Fearing that we would be dashed against the rocks, they dropped four anchors from the stern and prayed for daylight. [30]In an attempt to escape from the ship, the sailors let the lifeboat down into the sea, pretending they were going to lower some anchors from the bow. [31]Then Paul said to the centurion and the soldiers, "Unless these men stay with the ship, you cannot be saved." [32]So the soldiers cut the ropes that held the lifeboat and let it fall away.

[33]Just before dawn Paul urged them all to eat. "For the last fourteen days," he said, "you have been in constant suspense and have gone without food—you haven't eaten anything. [34]Now I urge you to take some food. You need it to survive. Not one of you will lose a single hair from his head." [35]After he said this, he took some bread and gave thanks to God in front of them all. Then he broke it and began to eat. [36]They were all encouraged and ate some food themselves. [37]Altogether there were 276 of us on board. [38]When they had eaten as much as they wanted, they lightened the ship by throwing the grain into the sea.

[39]When daylight came, they did not recognize the land, but they saw a bay with a sandy beach, where they decided to run the ship aground if they could. [40]Cutting loose the anchors, they left them in the sea and at the same time untied the ropes that held the rudders. Then they hoisted the foresail to the wind and made for the beach. [41]But the ship struck a sandbar and ran aground. The bow stuck fast and would not move, and the stern was broken to pieces by the pounding of the surf.

[42]The soldiers planned to kill the pris-

---

[a]27 In ancient times the name referred to an area extending well south of Italy.   [b]28 Greek *twenty orguias* (about 37 meters)   [c]28 Greek *fifteen orguias* (about 27 meters)

oners to prevent any of them from swimming away and escaping. ⁴³But the centurion wanted to spare Paul's life and kept them from carrying out their plan. He ordered those who could swim to jump overboard first and get to land. ⁴⁴The rest were to get there on planks or on pieces of the ship. In this way everyone reached land in safety.

Ashore on Malta

28 Once safely on shore, we found out that the island was called Malta. ²The islanders showed us unusual kindness. They built a fire and welcomed us all because it was raining and cold. ³Paul gathered a pile of brushwood and, as he put it on the fire, a viper, driven out by the heat, fastened itself on his hand. ⁴When the islanders saw the snake hanging from his hand, they said to each other, "This man must be a murderer; for though he escaped from the sea, Justice has not allowed him to live." ⁵But Paul shook the snake off into the fire and suffered no ill effects. ⁶The people expected him to swell up or suddenly fall dead, but after waiting a long time and seeing nothing unusual happen to him, they changed their minds and said he was a god.

⁷There was an estate nearby that belonged to Publius, the chief official of the island. He welcomed us to his home and for three days entertained us hospitably. ⁸His father was sick in bed, suffering from fever and dysentery. Paul went in to see him and, after prayer, placed his hands on him and healed him. ⁹When

> HIS father was sick in bed, suffering from fever and dysentery. Paul went in to see him and, after prayer, placed his hands on him and healed him.
>
> ACTS 28:8

this had happened, the rest of the sick on the island came and were cured. ¹⁰They honored us in many ways and when we were ready to sail, they furnished us with the supplies we needed.

Arrival at Rome

¹¹After three months we put out to sea in a ship that had wintered in the island. It was an Alexandrian ship with the figurehead of the twin gods Castor and Pollux. ¹²We put in at Syracuse and stayed there three days. ¹³From there we set sail and arrived at Rhegium. The next day the south wind came up, and on the following day we reached Puteoli. ¹⁴There we found some brothers who invited us to spend a week with them. And so we came to Rome. ¹⁵The brothers there had heard that we were coming, and they traveled as far as the Forum of Appius and the Three Taverns to meet us. At the sight of these men Paul thanked God and was encouraged. ¹⁶When we got to Rome, Paul was allowed to live by himself, with a soldier to guard him.

Paul Preaches at Rome Under Guard

¹⁷Three days later he called together the leaders of the Jews. When they had assembled, Paul said to them: "My brothers, although I have done nothing against our people or against the customs of our ancestors, I was arrested in Jerusalem and handed over to the Romans. ¹⁸They examined me and wanted to release me, because I was not guilty of any crime deserving death. ¹⁹But when the Jews objected, I was compelled to appeal to Caesar—not that I had any charge to bring against my own people. ²⁰For this reason I have asked to see you and talk with you. It is because of the hope of Israel that I am bound with this chain."

²¹They replied, "We have not received any letters from Judea concerning you, and none of the brothers who have come from there has reported or said anything bad about you. ²²But we want to hear what your views are, for we know that people everywhere are talking against this sect."

²³They arranged to meet Paul on a certain day, and came in even larger numbers to the place where he was staying. From morning till evening he explained and declared to them the kingdom of God and tried to convince them about Jesus from the Law of Moses and from the Prophets. ²⁴Some were convinced by what he said, but others would not believe. ²⁵They disagreed among themselves and began to leave after Paul had

made this final statement: "The Holy Spirit spoke the truth to your forefathers when he said through Isaiah the prophet:

26 " 'Go to this people and say,
  "You will be ever hearing but never understanding;
    you will be ever seeing but never perceiving."
27 For this people's heart has become calloused;
    they hardly hear with their ears,
    and they have closed their eyes.
  Otherwise they might see with their eyes,
    hear with their ears,
    understand with their hearts
  and turn, and I would heal them.'[a]

> ❝ *And help us, this and every day, to live more nearly as we pray.* ❞
>
> JOHN KEBLE

28 "Therefore I want you to know that God's salvation has been sent to the Gentiles, and they will listen!"[b]

30 For two whole years Paul stayed there in his own rented house and welcomed all who came to see him. 31 Boldly and without hindrance he preached the kingdom of God and taught about the Lord Jesus Christ.

[a]27 Isaiah 6:9,10 [b]28 Some manuscripts listen!" 29 After he said this, the Jews left, arguing vigorously among themselves.

Romans

SOME OF the most spectacular views in all of the Rocky Mountains are in the Grand Teton range in Wyoming. At a point just south of the Grand Teton itself—the great peak that gives the mountains their name—one can look east down into the city of Jackson Hole, Wyoming, and west down into the town of Pierre's Hole, Idaho. Straight north is the great peak, usually shrouded in clouds and mystery, terrifying in its splendor. Other peaks and ranges stretch out in every direction. To stand there on a clear day is to have the sensation of being on top of it all, seeing everything worthwhile in God's creation.

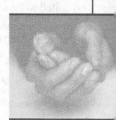

"THE SPIRIT HIMSELF INTERCEDES FOR US WITH GROANS THAT WORDS CANNOT EXPRESS." (8:26)

Paul's letter to the Romans has a similar effect related to the rest of the Bible. "If we have gained a true understanding of this Epistle," wrote John Calvin, "we have an open door to all the most profound treasures of Scripture." No other book in the Bible states so coherently and profoundly the meaning of the gospel and its implications. Martin Luther believed it to be the "chief part of the New Testament, and . . . truly the purest gospel." He preached that every Christian should "know it word for word, by heart," and "occupy himself with it every day, as the daily bread of the soul."[1] To know this book is to know the great themes of Scripture—and therefore how to pray with understanding the great things Jesus told us to pray for: the hallowing of God's name, the coming of his kingdom and the doing of his will. Moreover, to read Romans 8 in particular is to begin to probe the mystery and miracle of prayer *to* God and *in* and *through* God—Father, Son and Holy Spirit.

Though Romans is grand in its sweep, it is also very practical. The movement in thought from Romans 11:33–36 to 12:1–2 is a model of how much earthly good can come from being heavenly minded. In just six verses, Paul explains how to move from contemplation to action, from prayer to work, from singing the "depth of the riches of the wisdom and knowledge of God" to offering our "bodies as living sacrifices." Instructions follow that provide insights on how to pray for everything from governments and taxes to eating and evangelization. To understand and pray the letter to the Romans is to have your mind in heaven and your feet planted firmly on the earth.

1 Paul, a servant of Christ Jesus, called to be an apostle and set apart for the gospel of God— ²the gospel he promised beforehand through his prophets in the Holy Scriptures ³regarding his Son, who as to his human nature was a descendant of David, ⁴and who through the Spirit*ᵃ* of holiness was declared with power to be the Son of God*ᵇ* by his resurrection from the dead: Jesus Christ our Lord. ⁵Through him and for his name's sake, we received grace and apostleship to call people from among all the Gentiles to the obedience that comes from faith. ⁶And you also are among those who are called to belong to Jesus Christ.

⁷To all in Rome who are loved by God and called to be saints:

Grace and peace to you from God our Father and from the Lord Jesus Christ.

Paul's Longing to Visit Rome

⁸First, I thank my God through Jesus Christ for all of you, because your faith is being reported all over the world. ⁹God, whom I serve with my whole heart in preaching the gospel of his Son, is my witness how constantly I remember you ¹⁰in my prayers at all times; and I pray that now at last by God's will the way may be opened for me to come to you.

¹¹I long to see you so that I may impart to you some spiritual gift to make you strong— ¹²that is, that you and I may be mutually encouraged by each other's faith. ¹³I do not want you to be unaware, brothers, that I planned many times to come to you (but have been prevented from doing so until now) in order that I might have a harvest among you, just as I have had among the other Gentiles.

¹⁴I am obligated both to Greeks and non-Greeks, both to the wise and the foolish. ¹⁵That is why I am so eager to preach the gospel also to you who are at Rome.

¹⁶I am not ashamed of the gospel, because it is the power of God for the salvation of everyone who believes: first for the Jew, then for the Gentile. ¹⁷For in the gospel a righteousness from God is revealed, a righteousness that is by faith from first to last,*ᶜ* just as it is written: "The righteous will live by faith."*ᵈ*

God's Wrath Against Mankind

¹⁸The wrath of God is being revealed from heaven against all the godlessness and wickedness of men who suppress the truth by their wickedness, ¹⁹since what may be known about God is plain to them, because God has made it plain to them. ²⁰For since the creation of the world God's invisible qualities—his eternal power and divine nature—have been clearly seen, being understood from what has been made, so that men are without excuse.

²¹For although they knew God, they neither glorified him as God nor gave thanks to him, but their thinking became futile and their foolish hearts were darkened. ²²Although they claimed to be wise, they became fools ²³and exchanged the glory of the immortal God for images made to look like mortal man and birds and animals and reptiles.

²⁴Therefore God gave them over in the sinful desires of their hearts to sexual impurity for the degrading of their bodies with one another. ²⁵They exchanged the truth of God for a lie, and worshiped and served created things rather than the Creator—who is forever praised. Amen.

²⁶Because of this, God gave them over to shameful lusts. Even their women exchanged natural relations for unnatural ones. ²⁷In the same way the men also abandoned natural relations with women and were inflamed with lust for one another. Men committed indecent acts with other men, and received in themselves the due penalty for their perversion.

²⁸Furthermore, since they did not think it worthwhile to retain the knowledge of God, he gave them over to a depraved mind, to do what ought not to be done. ²⁹They have become filled with every kind of wickedness, evil, greed and depravity. They are full of envy, murder, strife, deceit and malice. They are gossips, ³⁰slanderers, God-haters, insolent, arrogant and boastful; they invent ways of doing evil; they disobey their parents; ³¹they are senseless, faithless, heartless, ruthless. ³²Although they know God's righteous decree that those who do such

ᵃ4 Or *who as to his spirit*   *ᵇ4* Or *was appointed to be the Son of God with power*   *ᶜ17* Or *is from faith to faith*   *ᵈ17* Hab. 2:4

A Model Prayer

1:8 "I THANK MY GOD THROUGH JESUS CHRIST FOR ALL OF YOU."

To learn to pray well, we don't need manuals; we need models. We need to pray with the great people of prayer more than we need to read about another formula for prayer. This prayer of Paul's is a wonderful model. Try praying for others the way he prayed for the Romans.

Pray as Paul did—thankfully (see 1:8). Thankful intercession does good things for the intercessor—you! It can keep you from condescension in your prayers for others. Sometimes when we pray, a little superiority can creep in, especially if the ones we pray for have wandered far from God. We feel like we are the doctors and they are the patients. To thank God for the ones we pray for is to acknowledge that the Lord is already at work in their lives, that we tell him nothing he doesn't already know and that they are beloved of the Father. It's impressive how often Paul's prayers for others are thankful prayers, even if the people he prays for are in trouble spiritually (see 1 Corinthians 1:4; Ephesians 1:16; Philippians 1:3; Colossians 1:3; 1 Thessalonians 1:2; 2 Thessalonians 1:3; 2 Timothy 1:3; Philemon 4).

Pray as Paul did—constantly (see Romans 1:9–10a). This may seem impossible, but it isn't. The sense of the Greek is that Paul's prayers were repeated and frequent. Paul probably turned his every thought and memory of others into short "bullet" prayers—expressions of longing and love to God for their blessing and peace. Sometimes his prayers were long discourses; more often they probably were phrases. You can pray as Paul did as you go about your daily activities. A prayer can be simply a mental image of God's light and truth flooding into the person prayed for.

Pray as Paul did—that somehow you might be an answer to your prayers (see verses 10b–12). Paul wanted to be with his fellow believers to encourage them and for them to encourage him. Always be willing to let God use you to do the thing you ask him to do. "Prayer and labor ought to go together. To pray without laboring is to mock God; to labor without prayer is to rob God of his glory. Until these things are conjoined, the gospel will not be extensively successful."

P R A Y :

As an exercise in following Paul's model of prayer, list the names
of people you pray for, and simply give thanks to God for
each one. As you do, ask God how you may be the answer
to the prayers you have been praying for them.

FOR YOUR NEXT DEVOTIONAL READING, GO TO PAGE 1366.

things deserve death, they not only continue to do these very things but also approve of those who practice them.

God's Righteous Judgment

2 You, therefore, have no excuse, you who pass judgment on someone else, for at whatever point you judge the other, you are condemning yourself, because you who pass judgment do the same things. ²Now we know that God's judgment against those who do such things is based on truth. ³So when you, a mere man, pass judgment on them and yet do the same things, do you think you will escape God's judgment? ⁴Or do you show contempt for the riches of his kindness, tolerance and patience, not realizing that God's kindness leads you toward repentance?

⁵But because of your stubbornness and your unrepentant heart, you are storing up wrath against yourself for the day of God's wrath, when his righteous judg-

---

{WEDNESDAY}

ROMANS 1:18-32

Fatal Omission

1:21 ALTHOUGH THEY KNEW GOD, THEY NEITHER GLORIFED HIM AS GOD NOR GAVE THANKS TO HIM.

Sin has a history with a beginning, a middle and an end. The end is death (see Romans 6:23a), the middle is the history of humankind, and the beginning is described here in these verses. It is the fatal omission of refusing to give God his due: "For although they knew God, they neither glorified him as God nor gave thanks to him" (1:21). The essence of sin is ingratitude and the deliberate debasing of God's glory that goes with it. What follows is devastating: Thinking becomes futile; the heart is darkened; and worst of all, God steps back and lets the process take its course. Three times Paul says that God "gave them over" (verses 24,26,28). To what? To the things that inevitably come from refusing to reverently and joyfully acknowledge that God is God. Ingratitude has a trajectory that leads to all the awful and sordid things detailed in verses 24-32. Fatal omission leads to fatal commissions.

Sin has a history in the world and also in your personal history. Here Paul describes sin's birth and growth along certain fairly predictable lines. It moves from ingratitude to a confused mind and a darkened heart, and then to immoral and appalling behavior. Other passages in Scripture describe the same process (see Genesis 3; James 1:13-15). A good exercise in self-awareness and confession is to examine a particular personal sin. Go back over the "history" of what you did wrong, letting this passage in Romans ask you some hard questions. Where did my fatal omission begin? When did I fail to be grateful and give God glory? What influenced me to forget God? How did my thinking get confused? In what ways was my heart blinded?

To do this once or twice is not to remove the possibility of repeating the same sin in the future. But to do it repeatedly over a lifetime is to begin to cut off sin at its source and take many practical steps on the sacred journey of holiness.

PRAY:

For your prayer time, do the exercise in self-awareness and confession.

FOR YOUR NEXT DEVOTIONAL READING, GO TO PAGE 1373.

ment will be revealed. ⁶God "will give to each person according to what he has done."ᵃ ⁷To those who by persistence in doing good seek glory, honor and immortality, he will give eternal life. ⁸But for those who are self-seeking and who reject the truth and follow evil, there will be wrath and anger. ⁹There will be trouble and distress for every human being who does evil: first for the Jew, then for the Gentile; ¹⁰but glory, honor and peace for everyone who does good: first for the Jew, then for the Gentile. ¹¹For God does not show favoritism.

¹²All who sin apart from the law will also perish apart from the law, and all who sin under the law will be judged by the law. ¹³For it is not those who hear the law who are righteous in God's sight, but it is those who obey the law who will be declared righteous. ¹⁴(Indeed, when Gentiles, who do not have the law, do by nature things required by the law, they are a law for themselves, even though they do not have the law, ¹⁵since they show that the requirements of the law are written on their hearts, their consciences also bearing witness, and their thoughts now accusing, now even defending them.) ¹⁶This will take place on the day when God will judge men's secrets through Jesus Christ, as my gospel declares.

The Jews and the Law

¹⁷Now you, if you call yourself a Jew; if you rely on the law and brag about your relationship to God; ¹⁸if you know his will and approve of what is superior because you are instructed by the law; ¹⁹if you are convinced that you are a guide for the blind, a light for those who are in the dark, ²⁰an instructor of the foolish, a teacher of infants, because you have in the law the embodiment of knowledge and truth— ²¹you, then, who teach others, do you not teach yourself? You who preach against stealing, do you steal? ²²You who say that people should not

commit adultery, do you commit adultery? You who abhor idols, do you rob temples? ²³You who brag about the law, do you dishonor God by breaking the law? ²⁴As it is written: "God's name is blasphemed among the Gentiles because of you."ᵇ

²⁵Circumcision has value if you observe the law, but if you break the law, you have become as though you had not been circumcised. ²⁶If those who are not circumcised keep the law's requirements, will they not be regarded as though they were circumcised? ²⁷The one who is not circumcised physically and yet obeys the law will condemn you who, even though you have theᶜ written code and circumcision, are a lawbreaker.

²⁸A man is not a Jew if he is only one outwardly, nor is circumcision merely outward and physical. ²⁹No, a man is a Jew if he is one inwardly; and circumcision is circumcision of the heart, by the Spirit, not by the written code. Such a man's praise is not from men, but from God.

God's Faithfulness

3 What advantage, then, is there in being a Jew, or what value is there in circumcision? ²Much in every way! First of all, they have been entrusted with the very words of God.

³What if some did not have faith? Will their lack of faith nullify God's faithfulness? ⁴Not at all! Let God be true, and every man a liar. As it is written:

"So that you may be proved right
    when you speak
and prevail when you judge."ᵈ

⁵But if our unrighteousness brings out God's righteousness more clearly, what shall we say? That God is unjust in bringing his wrath on us? (I am using a human argument.) ⁶Certainly not! If that were so, how could God judge the world? ⁷Someone might argue, "If my falsehood enhances God's truthfulness and so increases his glory, why am I still condemned as a sinner?" ⁸Why not say—as we are being slanderously reported as

ᵃ6 Psalm 62:12; Prov. 24:12   ᵇ24 Isaiah 52:5; Ezek. 36:22   ᶜ27 Or who, by means of a   ᵈ4 Psalm 51:4

saying and as some claim that we say—"Let us do evil that good may result"? Their condemnation is deserved.

> 66 *Prayer is not asking. Prayer is putting oneself in the hands of God, at his disposition, and listening to his voice in the depths of our hearts.* 99
>
> MOTHER TERESA

No One Is Righteous

⁹What shall we conclude then? Are we any better[a]? Not at all! We have already made the charge that Jews and Gentiles alike are all under sin. ¹⁰As it is written:

"There is no one righteous, not even one;
¹¹ there is no one who understands,
no one who seeks God.
¹²All have turned away,
they have together become worthless;
there is no one who does good,
not even one."[b]
¹³ "Their throats are open graves;
their tongues practice deceit."[c]
"The poison of vipers is on their lips."[d]
¹⁴ "Their mouths are full of cursing and bitterness."[e]
¹⁵ "Their feet are swift to shed blood;
¹⁶ ruin and misery mark their ways,
¹⁷ and the way of peace they do not know."[f]
¹⁸ "There is no fear of God before their eyes."[g]

¹⁹Now we know that whatever the law says, it says to those who are under the law, so that every mouth may be silenced and the whole world held accountable to God. ²⁰Therefore no one will be declared righteous in his sight by observing the law; rather, through the law we become conscious of sin.

Righteousness Through Faith

²¹But now a righteousness from God, apart from law, has been made known, to which the Law and the Prophets testify. ²²This righteousness from God comes through faith in Jesus Christ to all who believe. There is no difference, ²³for all have sinned and fall short of the glory of God, ²⁴and are justified freely by his grace through the redemption that came by Christ Jesus. ²⁵God presented him as a sacrifice of atonement,[h] through faith in his blood. He did this to demonstrate his justice, because in his forbearance he had left the sins committed beforehand unpunished— ²⁶he did it to demonstrate his justice at the present time, so as to be just and the one who justifies those who have faith in Jesus.

²⁷Where, then, is boasting? It is excluded. On what principle? On that of observing the law? No, but on that of faith. ²⁸For we maintain that a man is justified by faith apart from observing the law. ²⁹Is God the God of Jews only? Is he not the God of Gentiles too? Yes, of Gentiles too, ³⁰since there is only one God, who will justify the circumcised by faith and the uncircumcised through that same faith. ³¹Do we, then, nullify the law by this faith? Not at all! Rather, we uphold the law.

Abraham Justified by Faith

4 What then shall we say that Abraham, our forefather, discovered in this matter? ²If, in fact, Abraham was justified by works, he had something to boast about—but not before God. ³What does the Scripture say? "Abraham believed God, and it was credited to him as righteousness."[i]

⁴Now when a man works, his wages are not credited to him as a gift, but as an obligation. ⁵However, to the man who does not work but trusts God who justifies the wicked, his faith is credited as righteousness. ⁶David says the same thing when he speaks of the blessedness of the man to whom God credits righteousness apart from works:

⁷ "Blessed are they
whose transgressions are forgiven,
whose sins are covered.
⁸ Blessed is the man
whose sin the Lord will never count against him."[j]

---

a9 Or *worse*   *b12* Psalms 14:1–3; 53:1–3; Eccles. 7:20   *c13* Psalm 5:9
d13 Psalm 140:3   *e14* Psalm 10:7
f17 Isaiah 59:7,8   *g18* Psalm 36:1
h25 Or *as the one who would turn aside his wrath, taking away sin*   *i3* Gen. 15:6; also in verse 22   *j8* Psalm 32:1,2

[9]Is this blessedness only for the circumcised, or also for the uncircumcised? We have been saying that Abraham's faith was credited to him as righteousness. [10]Under what circumstances was it credited? Was it after he was circumcised, or before? It was not after, but before! [11]And he received the sign of circumcision, a seal of the righteousness that he had by faith while he was still uncircumcised. So then, he is the father of all who believe but have not been circumcised, in order that righteousness might be credited to them. [12]And he is also the father of the circumcised who not only are circumcised but who also walk in the footsteps of the faith that our father Abraham had before he was circumcised.

[13]It was not through law that Abraham and his offspring received the promise that he would be heir of the world, but through the righteousness that comes by faith. [14]For if those who live by law are heirs, faith has no value and the promise is worthless, [15]because law brings wrath. And where there is no law there is no transgression.

[16]Therefore, the promise comes by faith, so that it may be by grace and may be guaranteed to all Abraham's offspring—not only to those who are of the law but also to those who are of the faith of Abraham. He is the father of us all. [17]As it is written: "I have made you a father of many nations."[a] He is our father in the sight of God, in whom he believed—the God who gives life to the dead and calls things that are not as though they were.

> 66 I throw myself down in my chamber, and I call in, and invite God, and his Angels thither, and when they are there, I neglect God and his Angels, for the noise of a fly, for the rattling of a coach, for the whining of a door. 99
>
> JOHN DONNE

[18]Against all hope, Abraham in hope believed and so became the father of many nations, just as it had been said to him, "So shall your offspring be."[b] [19]Without weakening in his faith, he faced the fact that his body was as good as dead—since he was about a hundred years old—and that Sarah's womb was also dead. [20]Yet he did not waver through unbelief regarding the promise of God, but was strengthened in his faith and gave glory to God, [21]being fully persuaded that God had power to do what he had promised. [22]This is why "it was credited to him as righteousness." [23]The words "it was credited to him" were written not for him alone, [24]but also for us, to whom God will credit righteousness—for us who believe in him who raised Jesus our Lord from the dead. [25]He was delivered over to death for our sins and was raised to life for our justification.

Peace and Joy

5 Therefore, since we have been justified through faith, we[c] have peace with God through our Lord Jesus Christ, [2]through whom we have gained access by faith into this grace in which we now stand. And we[c] rejoice in the hope of the glory of God. [3]Not only so, but we[c] also rejoice in our sufferings, because we know that suffering produces perseverance; [4]perseverance, character; and character, hope. [5]And hope does not disappoint us, because God has poured out his love into our hearts by the Holy Spirit, whom he has given us.

[6]You see, at just the right time, when we were still powerless, Christ died for the ungodly. [7]Very rarely will anyone die for a righteous man, though for a good man someone might possibly dare to die. [8]But God demonstrates his own love for us in this: While we were still sinners, Christ died for us.

[9]Since we have now been justified by his blood, how much more shall we be saved from God's wrath through him! [10]For if, when we were God's enemies, we were reconciled to him through the death of his Son, how much more, having been reconciled, shall we be saved through his life! [11]Not only is this so, but we also rejoice in God through our Lord Jesus Christ, through whom we have now received reconciliation.

[a]17 Gen. 17:5   [b]18 Gen. 15:5
[c]1,2,3 Or let us

Death Through Adam, Life Through Christ

¹²Therefore, just as sin entered the world through one man, and death through sin, and in this way death came to all men, because all sinned— ¹³for before the law was given, sin was in the world. But sin is not taken into account when there is no law. ¹⁴Nevertheless, death reigned from the time of Adam to the time of Moses, even over those who did not sin by breaking a command, as did Adam, who was a pattern of the one to come.

¹⁵But the gift is not like the trespass. For if the many died by the trespass of the one man, how much more did God's grace and the gift that came by the grace of the one man, Jesus Christ, overflow to the many! ¹⁶Again, the gift of God is not like the result of the one man's sin: The judgment followed one sin and brought condemnation, but the gift followed many trespasses and brought justification. ¹⁷For if, by the trespass of the one man, death reigned through that one man, how much more will those who receive God's abundant provision of grace and of the gift of righteousness reign in life through the one man, Jesus Christ.

¹⁸Consequently, just as the result of one trespass was condemnation for all men, so also the result of one act of righteousness was justification that brings life for all men. ¹⁹For just as through the disobedience of the one man the many were made sinners, so also through the obedience of the one man the many will be made righteous.

²⁰The law was added so that the trespass might increase. But where sin increased, grace increased all the more, ²¹so that, just as sin reigned in death, so also grace might reign through righteousness to bring eternal life through Jesus Christ our Lord.

Dead to Sin, Alive in Christ

6 What shall we say, then? Shall we go on sinning so that grace may increase? ²By no means! We died to sin; how can we live in it any longer? ³Or don't you know that all of us who were baptized into Christ Jesus were baptized into his death? ⁴We were therefore buried with him through baptism into death in order that, just as Christ was raised from the dead through the glory of the Father, we too may live a new life.

⁵If we have been united with him like this in his death, we will certainly also be united with him in his resurrection. ⁶For we know that our old self was crucified with him so that the body of sin might be done away with,ᵃ that we should no longer be slaves to sin— ⁷because anyone who has died has been freed from sin.

⁸Now if we died with Christ, we believe that we will also live with him. ⁹For we know that since Christ was raised from the dead, he cannot die again; death no longer has mastery over him. ¹⁰The death he died, he died to sin once for all; but the life he lives, he lives to God.

¹¹In the same way, count yourselves dead to sin but alive to God in Christ Jesus. ¹²Therefore do not let sin reign in your mortal body so that you obey its evil desires. ¹³Do not offer the parts of your body to sin, as instruments of wickedness, but rather offer yourselves to God, as those who have been brought from death to life; and offer the parts of your body to him as instruments of righteousness. ¹⁴For sin shall not be your master, because you are not under law, but under grace.

Slaves to Righteousness

¹⁵What then? Shall we sin because we are not under law but under grace? By no means! ¹⁶Don't you know that when you offer yourselves to someone to obey him as slaves, you are slaves to the one whom you obey—whether you are slaves to sin, which leads to death, or to obedience, which leads to righteousness? ¹⁷But thanks

> BUT thanks be to God that, though you used to be slaves to sin, you wholeheartedly obeyed the form of teaching to which you were entrusted.
>
> ROMANS 6:17

be to God that, though you used to be slaves to sin, you wholeheartedly obeyed the form of teaching to which you were entrusted. ¹⁸You have been set free from sin and have become slaves to righteousness.

ᵃ6 Or *be rendered powerless*

[19]I put this in human terms because you are weak in your natural selves. Just as you used to offer the parts of your body in slavery to impurity and to ever-increasing wickedness, so now offer them in slavery to righteousness leading to holiness. [20]When you were slaves to sin, you were free from the control of righteousness. [21]What benefit did you reap at that time from the things you are now ashamed of? Those things result in death! [22]But now that you have been set free from sin and have become slaves to God, the benefit you reap leads to holiness, and the result is eternal life. [23]For the wages of sin is death, but the gift of God is eternal life in[a] Christ Jesus our Lord.

An Illustration From Marriage

7 Do you not know, brothers—for I am speaking to men who know the law—that the law has authority over a man only as long as he lives? [2]For example, by law a married woman is bound to her husband as long as he is alive, but if her husband dies, she is released from the law of marriage. [3]So then, if she marries another man while her husband is still alive, she is called an adulteress. But if her husband dies, she is released from that law and is not an adulteress, even though she marries another man.

[4]So, my brothers, you also died to the law through the body of Christ, that you might belong to another, to him who was raised from the dead, in order that we might bear fruit to God. [5]For when we were controlled by the sinful nature,[b] the sinful passions aroused by the law were at work in our bodies, so that we bore fruit for death. [6]But now, by dying to what once bound us, we have been released from the law so that we serve in the new way of the Spirit, and not in the old way of the written code.

Struggling With Sin

[7]What shall we say, then? Is the law sin? Certainly not! Indeed I would not have known what sin was except through the law. For I would not have known what coveting really was if the law had not said, "Do not covet."[c] [8]But sin, seizing the opportunity afforded by the commandment, produced in me every kind of covetous desire. For apart from law, sin is dead. [9]Once I was alive apart from law; but when the commandment came, sin sprang to life and I died. [10]I found that the very commandment that was intended to bring life actually brought death. [11]For sin, seizing the opportunity afforded by the commandment, deceived me, and through the commandment put me to death. [12]So then, the law is holy, and the commandment is holy, righteous and good.

[13]Did that which is good, then, become death to me? By no means! But in order that sin might be recognized as sin, it produced death in me through what was good, so that through the commandment sin might become utterly sinful. [14]We know that the law is spiritual; but I am unspiritual, sold as a slave to sin. [15]I do not understand what I do. For what I want to do I do not do, but what I hate I do. [16]And if I do what I do not want to do, I agree that the law is good. [17]As it is, it is no longer I myself who do it, but it is sin living in me. [18]I know that nothing good lives in me, that is, in my sinful nature.[d] For I have the desire to do what is good, but I cannot carry it out. [19]For what I do is not the good I want to do; no, the evil I do not want to do—this I keep on doing. [20]Now if I do what I do not want to do, it is no longer I who do it, but it is sin living in me that does it.

[21]So I find this law at work: When I want to do good, evil is right there with me. [22]For in my inner being I delight in God's law; [23]but I see another law at work in the members of my body, waging war against the law of my mind and making me a prisoner of the law of sin at work within my members. [24]What a wretched man I am! Who will rescue me from this body of death? [25]Thanks be to God—through Jesus Christ our Lord!

> THANKS be to God—through Jesus Christ our Lord!
>
> ROMANS 7:25

[a]23 Or through [b]5 Or the flesh; also in verse 25 [c]7 Exodus 20:17; Deut. 5:21 [d]18 Or my flesh

So then, I myself in my mind am a slave to God's law, but in the sinful nature a slave to the law of sin.

Life Through the Spirit

8 Therefore, there is now no condemnation for those who are in Christ Jesus,[a] [2]because through Christ Jesus the law of the Spirit of life set me free from the law of sin and death. [3]For what the law was powerless to do in that it was weakened by the sinful nature,[b] God did by sending his own Son in the likeness of sinful man to be a sin offering.[c] And so he condemned sin in sinful man,[d] [4]in order that the righteous requirements of the law might be fully met in us, who do not live according to the sinful nature but according to the Spirit.

[5]Those who live according to the sinful nature have their minds set on what that nature desires; but those who live in accordance with the Spirit have their minds set on what the Spirit desires. [6]The mind of sinful man[e] is death, but the mind controlled by the Spirit is life and peace; [7]the sinful mind[f] is hostile to God. It does not submit to God's law, nor can it do so. [8]Those controlled by the sinful nature cannot please God.

[9]You, however, are controlled not by the sinful nature but by the Spirit, if the Spirit of God lives in you. And if anyone does not have the Spirit of Christ, he does not belong to Christ. [10]But if Christ is in you, your body is dead because of sin, yet your spirit is alive because of righteousness. [11]And if the Spirit of him who raised Jesus from the dead is living in you, he who raised Christ from the dead will also give life to your mortal bodies through his Spirit, who lives in you.

[12]Therefore, brothers, we have an obligation—but it is not to the sinful nature, to live according to it. [13]For if you live according to the sinful nature, you will die; but if by the Spirit you put to death the misdeeds of the body, you will live, [14]because those who are led by the Spirit of God are sons of God. [15]For you did not receive a spirit that makes you a slave again to fear, but you received the Spirit of sonship.[g] And by him we cry, "Abba,[h] Father." [16]The Spirit himself testifies with our spirit that we are God's children.

[17]Now if we are children, then we are heirs—heirs of God and co-heirs with Christ, if indeed we share in his sufferings in order that we may also share in his glory.

Future Glory

[18]I consider that our present sufferings are not worth comparing with the glory that will be revealed in us. [19]The creation waits in eager expectation for the sons of God to be revealed. [20]For the creation was subjected to frustration, not by its own choice, but by the will of the one who subjected it, in hope [21]that[i] the creation itself will be liberated from its bondage to decay and brought into the glorious freedom of the children of God.

[22]We know that the whole creation has been groaning as in the pains of childbirth right up to the present time. [23]Not only so, but we ourselves, who have the firstfruits of the Spirit, groan inwardly as we wait eagerly for our adoption as sons, the redemption of our bodies. [24]For in this hope we were saved. But hope that is seen is no hope at all. Who hopes for what he already has? [25]But if we hope for what we do not yet have, we wait for it patiently.

[26]In the same way, the Spirit helps us in our weakness. We do not know what we ought to pray for, but the Spirit himself intercedes for us with groans that words cannot express. [27]And he who searches our hearts knows the mind of the Spirit, because the Spirit intercedes for the saints in accordance with God's will.

More Than Conquerors

[28]And we know that in all things God works for the good of those who love him,[j] who[k] have been called according to his purpose. [29]For those God foreknew he

[a]1 Some later manuscripts *Jesus, who do not live according to the sinful nature but according to the Spirit,* [b]3 Or *the flesh;* also in verses 4, 5, 8, 9, 12 and 13 [c]3 Or *man, for sin* [d]3 Or *in the flesh* [e]6 Or *mind set on the flesh* [f]7 Or *the mind set on the flesh* [g]15 Or *adoption* [h]15 Aramaic for *Father* [i]20,21 Or *subjected it in hope.* [21]For [j]28 Some manuscripts *And we know that all things work together for good to those who love God* [k]28 Or *works together with those who love him to bring about what is good—with those who*

also predestined to be conformed to the likeness of his Son, that he might be the firstborn among many brothers. ³⁰And those he predestined, he also called; those he called, he also justified; those he justified, he also glorified.

³¹What, then, shall we say in response to this? If God is for us, who can be against us? ³²He who did not spare his own Son, but gave him up for us all—how will he not also, along with him, graciously give us all things? ³³Who will

---

ROMANS 8:15–27

[THURSDAY]

Crying and Groaning and Learning to Pray

8:26 WE DO NOT KNOW WHAT WE OUGHT TO PRAY FOR, BUT THE SPIRIT HIMSELF INTERCEDES FOR US WITH GROANS THAT WORDS CANNOT EXPRESS.

For a Christian to pray is to do the most natural thing in the world. It is as natural as a baby yearning and learning to say "Daddy" or "Mommy." That's what prayer is at its core—simply crying out to God as a child would to a trusted and loving parent (see 8:15). It is a thrilling privilege, made even more remarkable by the fact that God goes out of his way to assure us that this wonderful reality is true: He gives us his Spirit to testify with our spirit that it is true (see verse 16).

Prayer is natural for Christians, but it doesn't always come easy. Sometimes the problem is that our understanding of God's purposes is too limited, and we just don't know what to pray for (see verse 26). Sometimes the difficulty is part of a much larger struggle—the groaning of the created order as it waits to be "brought into the glorious freedom of the children of God" (see verses 20–21). The creation groans, and we do too as we wait for our freedom. Paul says the pain we both feel is like the pain of childbirth, and the best prayers we can utter are no more than inarticulate groans. Again, the Holy Spirit is our helper, translating, as it were, our prayers to the Father (see verses 22–23,26–27).

James Boice says learning to pray with the help of the Holy Spirit is a little like a man learning to play the violin with virtuosos. No instrument sounds worse in the beginning stages of learning; it's all screech and scratch. But the student is determined to play well, so he checks the program guide for the classical music station and notes when the violin concertos will be aired. He buys the music for each concerto and does his best to play along with the orchestra. At first he sounds terrible. But as time passes, he begins little by little to sound more and more like the orchestra. But all along, as he groans on his instrument, the orchestra plays the music beautifully—his poor performance is caught up and completed in the music of the masters.

Praying with the help of the Holy Spirit is like that. As God conducts the orchestra flawlessly, his Spirit patiently teaches us—until one day we play with the Master himself.[2]

PRAY:

Abba, Father! Thank you for giving me your Spirit to pray for me and through me when I don't know how to pray.

FOR YOUR NEXT DEVOTIONAL READING, GO TO PAGE 1375.

bring any charge against those whom God has chosen? It is God who justifies. [34]Who is he that condemns? Christ Jesus, who died—more than that, who was raised to life—is at the right hand of God and is also interceding for us. [35]Who shall separate us from the love of Christ? Shall trouble or hardship or persecution or famine or nakedness or danger or sword? [36]As it is written:

> "For your sake we face death all day long;
> we are considered as sheep to be slaughtered."[a]

[37]No, in all these things we are more than conquerors through him who loved us. [38]For I am convinced that neither death nor life, neither angels nor demons,[b] neither the present nor the future, nor any powers, [39]neither height nor depth, nor anything else in all creation, will be able to separate us from the love of God that is in Christ Jesus our Lord.

God's Sovereign Choice

9 I speak the truth in Christ—I am not lying, my conscience confirms it in the Holy Spirit— [2]I have great sorrow and unceasing anguish in my heart. [3]For I could wish that I myself were cursed and cut off from Christ for the sake of my brothers, those of my own race, [4]the people of Israel. Theirs is the adoption as sons; theirs the divine glory, the covenants, the receiving of the law, the temple worship and the promises. [5]Theirs are the patriarchs, and from them is traced the human ancestry of Christ, who is God over all, forever praised![c] Amen.

[6]It is not as though God's word had failed. For not all who are descended from Israel are Israel. [7]Nor because they are his descendants are they all Abraham's children. On the contrary, "It is through Isaac that your offspring will be reckoned."[d] [8]In other words, it is not the natural children who are God's children, but it is the children of the promise who are regarded as Abraham's offspring. [9]For this was how the promise was stated: "At the appointed time I will return, and Sarah will have a son."[e]

[10]Not only that, but Rebekah's children had one and the same father, our father Isaac. [11]Yet, before the twins were born or had done anything good or bad—in order that God's purpose in election might stand: [12]not by works but by him who calls—she was told, "The older will serve the younger."[f] [13]Just as it is written: "Jacob I loved, but Esau I hated."[g]

[14]What then shall we say? Is God unjust? Not at all! [15]For he says to Moses,

> "I will have mercy on whom I have mercy,
> and I will have compassion on whom I have compassion."[h]

[16]It does not, therefore, depend on man's desire or effort, but on God's mercy. [17]For the Scripture says to Pharaoh: "I raised you up for this very purpose, that I might display my power in you and that my name might be proclaimed in all the earth."[i] [18]Therefore God has mercy on whom he wants to have mercy, and he hardens whom he wants to harden.

> THEREFORE God has mercy on whom he wants to have mercy.
>
> ROMANS 9:18

[19]One of you will say to me: "Then why does God still blame us? For who resists his will?" [20]But who are you, O man, to talk back to God? "Shall what is formed say to him who formed it, 'Why did you make me like this?'"[j] [21]Does not the potter have the right to make out of the same lump of clay some pottery for noble purposes and some for common use?

[22]What if God, choosing to show his wrath and make his power known, bore with great patience the objects of his wrath—prepared for destruction? [23]What if he did this to make the riches of his glory known to the objects of his mercy, whom he prepared in advance for glory— [24]even us, whom he also called, not only from the Jews but also from the Gentiles? [25]As he says in Hosea:

---

[a]36 Psalm 44:22   [b]38 Or nor heavenly rulers
[c]5 Or Christ, who is over all. God be forever praised! Or Christ. God who is over all be forever praised!   [d]7 Gen. 21:12   [e]9 Gen. 18:10,14
[f]12 Gen. 25:23   [g]13 Mal. 1:2,3
[h]15 Exodus 33:19   [i]17 Exodus 9:16
[j]20 Isaiah 29:16; 45:9

"I will call them 'my people' who are
  not my people;
  and I will call her 'my loved one'
  who is not my loved one,"[a]

[26]and,

"It will happen that in the very place
  where it was said to them,
'You are not my people,'
they will be called 'sons of the living
  God.'"[b]

[27]Isaiah cries out concerning Israel:

"Though the number of the
  Israelites be like the sand by
  the sea,
only the remnant will be saved.
[28]For the Lord will carry out
  his sentence on earth with speed
  and finality."[c]

[a]25 Hosea 2:23   [b]26 Hosea 1:10
[c]28 Isaiah 10:22,23

{ FRIDAY }

ROMANS 9:1–5; 10:1

Passion for One's People

10:1 MY HEART'S DESIRE AND PRAYER TO GOD FOR THE ISRAELITES IS THAT THEY MAY BE SAVED.

Here is love of unimaginable proportions! So great is his love for his people, Paul would be eternally removed from the Christ he loves if it would mean his people would love the Christ he loves (see Romans 9:3). The Greek for the word "cursed" is *anathema*, which means to be given over to God's wrath for eternal destruction. Only one other person in Scripture prayed with this kind of love: Moses, who prayed that if God would not forgive the sin of his people, "then blot me out of the book you have written" (Exodus 32:32).

It's not exactly accurate to mention only Moses and Paul in the list of great, self-sacrificing leaders. One other person prayed and acted with even greater love than these two: Jesus Christ was actually given over to God's wrath for the sake of the whole world. His words on the cross, "My God, my God, why have you forsaken me?" (Matthew 27:46), were more than mere emotional expressions. They were descriptions of fact. He who knew no sin actually *became* sin for our sakes and was, in fact, cut off from the presence of God (see 2 Corinthians 5:21). "Amazing love! how can it be that thou, my God, shouldst die for me?" (Charles Wesley)

Love like Christ's can be hard to receive because it is so vast, so unimaginable. It is even harder to identify with and to practice. Who can love this way but Jesus and perhaps a chosen few super-saints? There is a way—the only way. Through the power of his Spirit, Christ can live in our hearts through faith, and so root and establish us in his love that we can actually "know this love that surpasses knowledge" (Ephesians 3:16–19).

It's not an overnight process, this miracle of being made like Jesus. It takes place over a lifetime of spending time with him and gazing at his love through the eyes of faith.

PRAY:

*Dear Jesus, through your Spirit strengthen me with your love, that
I may know this love that surpasses knowledge. Then may my heart
be broken in loving intercession for the salvation of my people.*

FOR YOUR NEXT DEVOTIONAL READING, GO TO PAGE 1376.

The True Seminary

JOHN SUNG'S zeal for Christ landed him in a mental hospital because the authorities of New York's Union Theological Seminary didn't know what to do with a student who became so joyful in his faith that he would sometimes weep and shout for joy on campus. Since his behavior didn't fit their theology, they had him committed. Incarcerated for 193 days with only a Bible and a fountain pen, he devoted himself to Scripture and prayer, reading his Bible front to back 40 times. Sung referred to his time of quiet solitude in the asylum as his "true seminary," for it prepared him for the role he would play in one of the mightiest revivals of the 20th century.

A native of China, Sung came to Union Seminary with impressive academic credentials, having completed three degrees in just over five years: a Bachelor of Science, a Master of Science and a Doctor of Philosophy. But his immersion in the world of academia had left him empty spiritually. He had backslidden and began doubting everything he believed. Seminary made matters worse until he experienced the dramatic renewal of his faith that got him into so much trouble.

After his discharge from the mental hospital, Sung boarded a ship and returned to China. All his honors would have given him much prestige in his homeland, but as he neared Shanghai he took literally the words of Paul in Philippians 3:7—"Whatever was to my profit I now consider loss"—and dumped his diplomas and honors overboard, except for his doctoral diploma. He kept that for his father's sake.

In the years that followed, Sung organized an apostolic team he named the "Bethel Evangelistic Band" and preached all over China. Wherever the team went, people responded to their message in droves, weeping openly and often publicly confessing their sins. Though quiet personally, Sung would transform in the pulpit, preaching fiery sermons proclaiming the tender mercy of God and the need for complete repentance from sins and full restitution where it was at all possible.

Sung urged people to give themselves to prayer as the first priority of the believer's life. He let nothing hinder his prayer life and rose every morning at five o'clock to pray for two or three hours. He liked to have small pictures of the people he interceded for, so he could pray for them with a "deeper burden." Many people were healed and converted through his prayers. It was said of Sung that he talked least, preached more, and prayed most.

John Sung died at age 43 of intestinal tuberculosis. But his ministry continued long afterward, with some of the evangelistic groups he founded still in operation 50 years later. Not bad for a man who got his seminary education by being kicked out of seminary.

PRAY:

Lord Jesus, like your servant John Sung, I want to know you,
the power of your resurrection, and the fellowship of sharing
in your sufferings, becoming like you in your death, that I may
attain the resurrection from the dead (see Philippians 3:10–11).

MEMORIZE:

But whatever was to my profit I now consider loss
for the sake of Christ. PHILIPPIANS 3:7

FOR YOUR NEXT DEVOTIONAL READING, GO TO PAGE 1379.

²⁹It is just as Isaiah said previously:

"Unless the Lord Almighty
  had left us descendants,
we would have become like Sodom,
  we would have been like
    Gomorrah."ᵃ

Israel's Unbelief

³⁰What then shall we say? That the Gentiles, who did not pursue righteousness, have obtained it, a righteousness that is by faith; ³¹but Israel, who pursued a law of righteousness, has not attained it. ³²Why not? Because they pursued it not by faith but as if it were by works. They stumbled over the "stumbling stone." ³³As it is written:

"See, I lay in Zion a stone that causes
    men to stumble
  and a rock that makes them fall,
  and the one who trusts in him will
    never be put to shame."ᵇ

> ❝ Effective prayer is prayer that attains what it seeks. It is prayer that moves God, effecting its end. ❞
>
> CHARLES G. FINNEY

10 Brothers, my heart's desire and prayer to God for the Israelites is that they may be saved. ²For I can testify about them that they are zealous for God, but their zeal is not based on knowledge. ³Since they did not know the righteousness that comes from God and sought to establish their own, they did not submit to God's righteousness. ⁴Christ is the end of the law so that there may be righteousness for everyone who believes.

⁵Moses describes in this way the righteousness that is by the law: "The man who does these things will live by them."ᶜ ⁶But the righteousness that is by faith says: "Do not say in your heart, 'Who will ascend into heaven?'ᵈ" (that is, to bring Christ down) ⁷"or 'Who will descend into the deep?'ᵉ" (that is, to bring Christ up from the dead). ⁸But what does it say? "The word is near you; it is in your mouth and in your heart,"ᶠ that is, the word of faith we are proclaiming: ⁹That if you confess with your mouth, "Jesus is Lord,"

and believe in your heart that God raised him from the dead, you will be saved. ¹⁰For it is with your heart that you believe and are justified, and it is with your mouth that you confess and are saved. ¹¹As the Scripture says, "Anyone who trusts in him will never be put to shame."ᵍ ¹²For there is no difference between Jew and Gentile—the same Lord is Lord of all and richly blesses all who call on him, ¹³for, "Everyone who calls on the name of the Lord will be saved."ʰ

¹⁴How, then, can they call on the one they have not believed in? And how can they believe in the one of whom they have not heard? And how can they hear without someone preaching to them? ¹⁵And how can they preach unless they are sent? As it is written, "How beautiful are the feet of those who bring good news!"ⁱ

¹⁶But not all the Israelites accepted the good news. For Isaiah says, "Lord, who has believed our message?"ʲ ¹⁷Consequently, faith comes from hearing the message, and the message is heard through the word of Christ. ¹⁸But I ask: Did they not hear? Of course they did:

"Their voice has gone out into all
    the earth,
  their words to the ends of the
    world."ᵏ

¹⁹Again I ask: Did Israel not understand? First, Moses says,

"I will make you envious by those
    who are not a nation;
  I will make you angry by a nation
    that has no understanding."ˡ

²⁰And Isaiah boldly says,

"I was found by those who did not
    seek me;
  I revealed myself to those who did
    not ask for me."ᵐ

²¹But concerning Israel he says,

"All day long I have held out my hands
    to a disobedient and obstinate
    people."ⁿ

ᵃ29 Isaiah 1:9   ᵇ33 Isaiah 8:14; 28:16
ᶜ5 Lev. 18:5   ᵈ6 Deut. 30:12   ᵉ7 Deut. 30:13
ᶠ8 Deut. 30:14   ᵍ11 Isaiah 28:16
ʰ13 Joel 2:32   ⁱ15 Isaiah 52:7   ʲ16 Isaiah 53:1
ᵏ18 Psalm 19:4   ˡ19 Deut. 32:21
ᵐ20 Isaiah 65:1   ⁿ21 Isaiah 65:2

The Remnant of Israel

11 I ask then: Did God reject his people? By no means! I am an Israelite myself, a descendant of Abraham, from the tribe of Benjamin. ²God did not reject his people, whom he foreknew. Don't you know what the Scripture says in the passage about Elijah—how he appealed to God against Israel: ³"Lord, they have killed your prophets and torn down your altars; I am the only one left, and they are trying to kill me"ᵃ? ⁴And what was God's answer to him? "I have reserved for myself seven thousand who have not bowed the knee to Baal."ᵇ ⁵So too, at the present time there is a remnant chosen by grace. ⁶And if by grace, then it is no longer by works; if it were, grace would no longer be grace.ᶜ

⁷What then? What Israel sought so earnestly it did not obtain, but the elect did. The others were hardened, ⁸as it is written:

"God gave them a spirit of stupor,
    eyes so that they could not see
    and ears so that they could not
        hear,
to this very day."ᵈ

ᵃ3 1 Kings 19:10,14   ᵇ4 1 Kings 19:18
ᶜ6 Some manuscripts *be grace. But if by works,
then it is no longer grace; if it were, work would
no longer be work.*   ᵈ8 Deut. 29:4;
Isaiah 29:10

[MONDAY]

ROMANS 10:8–13

Open Your Mouth

10:10 IT IS WITH YOUR MOUTH THAT YOU CONFESS AND ARE SAVED.

Open your mouth. Go ahead—just do it. Open your mouth and simply say, "Jesus is Lord!" Whisper it; say it out loud; try shouting it sometime. For "it is with your mouth that you confess and are saved," and "Everyone who calls on the name of the Lord will be saved" (10:10,13). Your salvation depends on it. So does your prayer life.

Salvation and prayer are both inward and outward experiences. Both involve heart and mouth, inward belief and outward confession. What you are on the inside and what you do on the outside are flip sides of the same coin. Both involve your whole being, spiritual and physical. Each depends on the other and is incomplete without its counterpart. To have a mouth without a heart is to be a hypocrite. To have a heart without a way to express its feelings is death to what is inside. It is like having a baby without a birth. Prayer is more than what you express, but it is not less.

Sometimes the hardest part of prayer is just starting the dialogue with God. Strong feelings and longings may well up inside the heart but get stuck there. So open your mouth and begin to speak. Don't worry about the spiritual depth of your words or whether they are worthy of what is inside you. The Holy Spirit will dress and translate them to the Father (see 8:26–27). God promises wonderful things for those who will simply begin to communicate with him. He says, "Open wide your mouth and I will fill it" (Psalm 81:10).

PRAY:

Jesus, you are risen from the dead, and you are my Lord.
Be my Lord in all I think, say and do.

FOR YOUR NEXT DEVOTIONAL READING, GO TO PAGE 1381.

⁹And David says:

"May their table become a snare and
a trap,
a stumbling block and a retribution
for them.
¹⁰May their eyes be darkened so they
cannot see,
and their backs be bent forever."ᵃ

Ingrafted Branches

¹¹Again I ask: Did they stumble so as to
fall beyond recovery? Not at all! Rather,
because of their transgression, salvation
has come to the Gentiles to make Israel
envious. ¹²But if their transgression
means riches for the world, and their loss
means riches for the Gentiles, how much
greater riches will their fullness bring!

¹³I am talking to you Gentiles. Inasmuch as I am the apostle to the Gentiles,
I make much of my ministry ¹⁴in the hope
that I may somehow arouse my own people to envy and save some of them. ¹⁵For
if their rejection is the reconciliation of
the world, what will their acceptance be
but life from the dead? ¹⁶If the part of the
dough offered as firstfruits is holy, then
the whole batch is holy; if the root is
holy, so are the branches.

¹⁷If some of the branches have been
broken off, and you, though a wild olive
shoot, have been grafted in among the
others and now share in the nourishing
sap from the olive root, ¹⁸do not boast
over those branches. If you do, consider
this: You do not support the root, but the
root supports you. ¹⁹You will say then,
"Branches were broken off so that I
could be grafted in." ²⁰Granted. But they
were broken off because of unbelief, and
you stand by faith. Do not be arrogant,
but be afraid. ²¹For if God did not spare
the natural branches, he will not spare
you either.

²²Consider therefore the kindness and
sternness of God: sternness to those who
fell, but kindness to you, provided that
you continue in his kindness. Otherwise,
you also will be cut off. ²³And if they do
not persist in unbelief, they will be grafted in, for God is able to graft them in
again. ²⁴After all, if you were cut out of
an olive tree that is wild by nature, and
contrary to nature were grafted into a
cultivated olive tree, how much more
readily will these, the natural branches,
be grafted into their own olive tree!

All Israel Will Be Saved

²⁵I do not want you to be ignorant of
this mystery, brothers, so that you may
not be conceited: Israel has experienced
a hardening in part until the full number
of the Gentiles has come in. ²⁶And so all
Israel will be saved, as it is written:

"The deliverer will come from Zion;
he will turn godlessness away from
Jacob.
²⁷And this isᵇ my covenant with them
when I take away their sins."ᶜ

²⁸As far as the gospel is concerned, they
are enemies on your account; but as far
as election is concerned, they are loved
on account of the patriarchs, ²⁹for God's
gifts and his call are irrevocable. ³⁰Just as
you who were at one time disobedient to
God have now received mercy as a result
of their disobedience, ³¹so they too have
now become disobedient in order that
they too may nowᵈ receive mercy as a result of God's mercy to you. ³²For God has
bound all men over to disobedience so
that he may have mercy on them all.

Doxology

³³Oh, the depth of the riches of the
wisdom andᵉ knowledge of
God!
How unsearchable his judgments,
and his paths beyond tracing out!
³⁴"Who has known the mind of the
Lord?
Or who has been his counselor?"ᶠ
³⁵"Who has ever given to God,
that God should repay him?"ᵍ
³⁶For from him and through him and to
him are all things.
To him be the glory forever! Amen.

Living Sacrifices

12 Therefore, I urge you, brothers, in
view of God's mercy, to offer your
bodies as living sacrifices, holy and

ᵃ10 Psalm 69:22,23   ᵇ27 Or will be
ᶜ27 Isaiah 59:20,21; 27:9; Jer. 31:33,34
ᵈ31 Some manuscripts do not have now.
ᵉ33 Or riches and the wisdom and the
ᶠ34 Isaiah 40:13   ᵍ35 Job 41:11

pleasing to God—this is your spiritual[a] act of worship. ²Do not conform any longer to the pattern of this world, but be transformed by the renewing of your mind. Then you will be able to test and approve what God's will is—his good, pleasing and perfect will.

³For by the grace given me I say to every one of you: Do not think of yourself more highly than you ought, but rather think of yourself with sober judgment, in accordance with the measure of faith God

[a] *1 Or reasonable*

[TUESDAY]

With Our Lives and Our Lips

11:36 FROM HIM AND THROUGH HIM AND TO HIM ARE ALL THINGS.

In the book of Romans, chapters 9–11 is one of the most wondrously amazing passages, capping off eight other chapters that set forth the essence and global implications of the Christian message as does no other Scripture portion. This section of Scripture is also one of the thorniest and hardest to understand in the Bible. Subjects like divine election and predestination, God's sovereignty and human freedom, the destiny of Israel and the peoples of the world all appear in their bewildering and breathtaking glory. Coming to the end of chapter 11, it's hard to know whether to gasp or to sing.

Paul chooses to sing. We are but flecks of foam on the ocean of God's grandeur. No one can give to, advise or second-guess God. Everything, all there is, comes from him and through him and to him. As awesome and intimidating as a God like this can be, there is a deep comfort in his greatness. Who really wants a God who is easily understood and manageable? If God is only a human writ large, then there is cause for great worry in this chaotic drama we know as human history. In the final analysis, a God we can "relate to" is in the same mess we are in. Thank God that the God of the Bible is not a God we can "relate to."

But there is even greater cause for comfort and joy in this awesome and frightening God. He has chosen to relate to us! He so loves the world that he gave his only Son for our salvation (see John 3:16). Though we are nothing before his awesome glory, he has counted the hairs on our heads (see Matthew 10:30), and we may call on his name and be heard and saved (see Romans 10:13).

There is nothing left to do but sing, not only with our lips, but also with our lives by offering them as living sacrifices. The command of Romans 12:1–2 is matched by the old prayer from the *Book of Common Prayer*: "And, we pray, give us such an awareness of your mercies, that our hearts may be sincerely thankful, and that we may show forth your praise not only with our lips, but in our lives, by giving up ourselves to your service, and by walking before you in holiness and righteousness all our days; through Jesus Christ our Lord ... Amen."

PRAY:
Pray the lines from the Book of Common Prayer.

FOR YOUR NEXT DEVOTIONAL READING, GO TO PAGE 1383.

has given you. ⁴Just as each of us has one body with many members, and these members do not all have the same function, ⁵so in Christ we who are many form one body, and each member belongs to all the others. ⁶We have different gifts, according to the grace given us. If a man's gift is prophesying, let him use it in proportion to his*ᵃ* faith. ⁷If it is serving, let him serve; if it is teaching, let him teach; ⁸if it is encouraging, let him encourage; if it is contributing to the needs of others, let him give generously; if it is leadership, let him govern diligently; if it is showing mercy, let him do it cheerfully.

Love

⁹Love must be sincere. Hate what is evil; cling to what is good. ¹⁰Be devoted to one another in brotherly love. Honor one another above yourselves. ¹¹Never be lacking in zeal, but keep your spiritual fervor, serving the Lord. ¹²Be joyful in hope, patient in affliction, faithful in prayer. ¹³Share with God's people who are in need. Practice hospitality.

¹⁴Bless those who persecute you; bless and do not curse. ¹⁵Rejoice with those who rejoice; mourn with those who mourn. ¹⁶Live in harmony with one another. Do not be proud, but be willing to associate with people of low position.*ᵇ* Do not be conceited.

¹⁷Do not repay anyone evil for evil. Be careful to do what is right in the eyes of everybody. ¹⁸If it is possible, as far as it depends on you, live at peace with everyone. ¹⁹Do not take revenge, my friends, but leave room for God's wrath, for it is written: "It is mine to avenge; I will repay,"*ᶜ* says the Lord. ²⁰On the contrary:

"If your enemy is hungry, feed him;
    if he is thirsty, give him something
        to drink.
In doing this, you will heap burning
    coals on his head."*ᵈ*

²¹Do not be overcome by evil, but overcome evil with good.

Submission to the Authorities

13 Everyone must submit himself to the governing authorities, for there is no authority except that which God has established. The authorities that ex-

ist have been established by God. ²Consequently, he who rebels against the authority is rebelling against what God has instituted, and those who do so will bring judgment on themselves. ³For rulers hold no terror for those who do right, but for those who do wrong. Do you want to be free from fear of the one in authority? Then do what is right and he will commend you. ⁴For he is God's servant to do you good. But if you do wrong, be afraid, for he does not bear the sword for nothing. He is God's servant, an agent of wrath to bring punishment on the wrongdoer. ⁵Therefore, it is necessary to submit to the authorities, not only because of possible punishment but also because of conscience.

⁶This is also why you pay taxes, for the authorities are God's servants, who give their full time to governing. ⁷Give everyone what you owe him: If you owe taxes, pay taxes; if revenue, then revenue; if respect, then respect; if honor, then honor.

> ❝ Pray for "all men." We usually pray more for things than we do for men. Our prayers should be thrown across their pathways as they rush in their downward course to a lost eternity. ❞
>
> E.M. BOUNDS

Love, for the Day Is Near

⁸Let no debt remain outstanding, except the continuing debt to love one another, for he who loves his fellowman has fulfilled the law. ⁹The commandments, "Do not commit adultery," "Do not murder," "Do not steal," "Do not covet,"*ᵉ* and whatever other commandment there may be, are summed up in this one rule: "Love your neighbor as yourself."*ᶠ* ¹⁰Love does no harm to its neighbor. Therefore love is the fulfillment of the law.

¹¹And do this, understanding the present time. The hour has come for you to wake up from your slumber, because our salvation is nearer now than when we

---

*ᵃ*6 Or *in agreement with the*   *ᵇ*16 Or *willing to do menial work*   *ᶜ*19 Deut. 32:35   *ᵈ*20 Prov. 25:21,22   *ᵉ*9 Exodus 20:13–15,17; Deut. 5:17–19,21   *ᶠ*9 Lev. 19:18

first believed. ¹²The night is nearly over; the day is almost here. So let us put aside the deeds of darkness and put on the armor of light. ¹³Let us behave decently, as in the daytime, not in orgies and drunkenness, not in sexual immorality and debauchery, not in dissension and jealousy. ¹⁴Rather, clothe yourselves with the Lord Jesus Christ, and do not think about how to gratify the desires of the sinful nature.ᵃ

The Weak and the Strong

14 Accept him whose faith is weak, without passing judgment on disputable matters. ²One man's faith allows him to eat everything, but another man, whose faith is weak, eats only vegetables. ³The man who eats everything must not look down on him who does not, and the

ᵃ14 Or *the flesh*

ROMANS 12:12

Dancing to the Music of the Future

12:12 BE JOYFUL IN HOPE, PATIENT IN AFFLICTION, FAITHFUL IN PRAYER.

Joy, hope, patience and faithfulness: Taken together, these constitute a powerful prescription for spiritual health in hard times. Joy is an obvious ingredient. What could be better in a difficult marriage or a terminal illness or an oppressive job than somehow being fundamentally glad despite it all and through it all! Joy is linked with hope, something Reubem Alves said is the music of the future. He wrote, "Hope is hearing the music of the future, faith is to dance to it." The joy is in the believing, the dancing. To know that God's good promises for the future are sure is to be set free to be glad in the midst of a suffering present.

Patience in affliction is possible only if there is hope. Without hope, there is only despair. With hope there is the confidence, the dancing confidence, that whatever we may have to go through now is less than nothing compared to the glorious future God has planned for us (see Romans 8:18). We can wait patiently because our wait, no matter how hard and long, is light and momentary when compared to eternity (see 2 Corinthians 4:17–18).

Prayer plays a pivotal role in the prescription. On one hand, hope nurtures prayer. No one will pray without it—what's the point if there is no possibility of things ever being better? But on the other hand, prayer nurtures hope because hope is a miracle that the Holy Spirit produces in our heart. We cannot will hope into being. So Paul prayed for the Ephesians that the eyes of their heart would be opened, in order that they would know the hope to which God had called them (see Ephesians 1:18). There is a symbiotic relationship between prayer and hope; we pray because of hope, and we have hope because of prayer. Each is the cause and the effect of the other.

Ask God to open your spiritual eyes to see the hope to which he has called you. Pray the promises of Scripture as you do. Don't be surprised to feel your spirit start to dance.

PRAY:
God of all hope, tune my ears to hear the music of your future;
strengthen my faith to dance to it now.

FOR YOUR NEXT DEVOTIONAL READING, GO TO PAGE 1385.

man who does not eat everything must not condemn the man who does, for God has accepted him. [4]Who are you to judge someone else's servant? To his own master he stands or falls. And he will stand, for the Lord is able to make him stand.

[5]One man considers one day more sacred than another; another man considers every day alike. Each one should be fully convinced in his own mind. [6]He who regards one day as special, does so to the Lord. He who eats meat, eats to the Lord, for he gives thanks to God; and he who abstains, does so to the Lord and gives thanks to God. [7]For none of us lives to himself alone and none of us dies to himself alone. [8]If we live, we live to the Lord; and if we die, we die to the Lord. So, whether we live or die, we belong to the Lord.

> HE who regards one day as special, does so to the Lord. He who eats meat, eats to the Lord, for he gives thanks to God; and he who abstains, does so to the Lord and gives thanks to God.
>
> ROMANS 14:6

[9]For this very reason, Christ died and returned to life so that he might be the Lord of both the dead and the living. [10]You, then, why do you judge your brother? Or why do you look down on your brother? For we will all stand before God's judgment seat. [11]It is written:

" 'As surely as I live,' says the Lord,
'every knee will bow before me;
every tongue will confess to God.' "[a]

[12]So then, each of us will give an account of himself to God.

[13]Therefore let us stop passing judgment on one another. Instead, make up your mind not to put any stumbling block or obstacle in your brother's way. [14]As one who is in the Lord Jesus, I am fully convinced that no food[b] is unclean in itself. But if anyone regards something as unclean, then for him it is unclean. [15]If your brother is distressed because of what you eat, you are no longer acting in love. Do not by your eating destroy your brother for whom Christ died. [16]Do not allow what you consider good to be spoken of as evil. [17]For the kingdom of God is not a matter of eating and drinking, but of righteousness, peace and joy in the Holy Spirit, [18]because anyone who serves Christ in this way is pleasing to God and approved by men.

[19]Let us therefore make every effort to do what leads to peace and to mutual edification. [20]Do not destroy the work of God for the sake of food. All food is clean, but it is wrong for a man to eat anything that causes someone else to stumble. [21]It is better not to eat meat or drink wine or to do anything else that will cause your brother to fall.

[22]So whatever you believe about these things keep between yourself and God. Blessed is the man who does not condemn himself by what he approves. [23]But the man who has doubts is condemned if he eats, because his eating is not from faith; and everything that does not come from faith is sin.

15 We who are strong ought to bear with the failings of the weak and not to please ourselves. [2]Each of us should please his neighbor for his good, to build him up. [3]For even Christ did not please himself but, as it is written: "The insults of those who insult you have fallen on me."[c] [4]For everything that was written in the past was written to teach us, so that through endurance and the encouragement of the Scriptures we might have hope.

[5]May the God who gives endurance and encouragement give you a spirit of unity among yourselves as you follow Christ Jesus, [6]so that with one heart and mouth you may glorify the God and Father of our Lord Jesus Christ.

[7]Accept one another, then, just as Christ accepted you, in order to bring praise to God. [8]For I tell you that Christ has become a servant of the Jews[d] on behalf of God's truth, to confirm the promises made to the patriarchs [9]so that the Gentiles may glorify God for his mercy, as it is written:

"Therefore I will praise you among
the Gentiles;
I will sing hymns to your name."[e]

[a]11 Isaiah 45:23   [b]14 Or that nothing
[c]3 Psalm 69:9   [d]8 Greek circumcision
[e]9 2 Samuel 22:50; Psalm 18:49

ROMANS 15:5–6

Unity, Not Uniformity

15:5 "MAY THE GOD WHO GIVES ENDURANCE AND ENCOURAGMENT GIVE YOU A SPIRIT OF UNITY."

The Puritan Richard Baxter summarized the intent of this prayer of Paul's in a grand way. Paraphrased, it was unity in essentials, freedom in nonessentials and love in all things. Essentials are the things all Christians must agree on to be Christians in the first place: things like the divinity of Christ, the triune God, salvation by grace through faith, and the resurrection. Nonessentials are the things Christians may legitimately disagree about. In this passage the nonessentials had to do with dietary practices that separated Jewish and Greek Christians. Love in all things is the attitude Christians must always take toward one another, especially in those matters about which they disagree.

Paul's prayer that God give the Romans "a spirit of unity" is in regard to this last category, "love in all things." Paul is not saying the believers had to agree on everything, but he's saying that they should lovingly make allowances for each other in the areas where they disagree. In a section extending back to the beginning of chapter 14, Paul repeatedly urges the believers at Rome to accept each other and not to judge, despise or offend each other over matters of individual conscience. He summarizes his teaching in the words found just before this prayer: "We who are strong ought to bear with the failings of the weak and not to please ourselves. Each of us should please his neighbor for his good, to build him up. For even Christ did not please himself" (15:1–3).

Paul's prayer is not that all Christians think the same, but that they have the mind of Christ (see Philippians 2:1–11). Absolute uniformity of thought belongs to cults where doctrines and opinions become more important than love. Unity belongs to the mind of Christ because it springs from a love that seeks the good of others. Uniformity is a dull, deadening thing. Unity is lively and life-giving. Uniformity is easy to achieve; all that is required is that the standards for membership be narrowed to exclude all who disagree. Unity is hard because it requires that people lay down their "rights" in order to serve others. God gets great glory when his people lay down their rights. When they do, they imitate Christ. "Accept one another, then, just as Christ accepted you, in order to bring praise to God" (Romans 15:7).

As you pray for unity in your church, ask God in what areas he may be asking you to make allowance for those with whom you disagree.

PRAY:

God, you are three in one and one in three; Father, Son and Holy Spirit.
Make us one as you are one and remove from me any action or
attitude that disturbs the unity of your body, the church.

FOR YOUR NEXT DEVOTIONAL READING, GO TO PAGE 1387.

¹⁰Again, it says,

> "Rejoice, O Gentiles, with his
> people."ᵃ

¹¹And again,

> "Praise the Lord, all you Gentiles,
> and sing praises to him, all you
> peoples."ᵇ

¹²And again, Isaiah says,

> "The Root of Jesse will spring up,
> one who will arise to rule over the
> nations;
> the Gentiles will hope in him."ᶜ

¹³May the God of hope fill you with all joy and peace as you trust in him, so that you may overflow with hope by the power of the Holy Spirit.

Paul the Minister to the Gentiles

¹⁴I myself am convinced, my brothers, that you yourselves are full of goodness, complete in knowledge and competent to instruct one another. ¹⁵I have written you quite boldly on some points, as if to remind you of them again, because of the grace God gave me ¹⁶to be a minister of Christ Jesus to the Gentiles with the priestly duty of proclaiming the gospel of God, so that the Gentiles might become an offering acceptable to God, sanctified by the Holy Spirit.

¹⁷Therefore I glory in Christ Jesus in my service to God. ¹⁸I will not venture to speak of anything except what Christ has accomplished through me in leading the Gentiles to obey God by what I have said and done— ¹⁹by the power of signs and miracles, through the power of the Spirit. So from Jerusalem all the way around to Illyricum, I have fully proclaimed the gospel of Christ. ²⁰It has always been my ambition to preach the gospel where Christ was not known, so that I would not be building on someone else's foundation. ²¹Rather, as it is written:

> "Those who were not told about him
> will see,
> and those who have not heard will
> understand."ᵈ

²²This is why I have often been hindered from coming to you.

Paul's Plan to Visit Rome

²³But now that there is no more place for me to work in these regions, and since I have been longing for many years to see you, ²⁴I plan to do so when I go to Spain. I hope to visit you while passing through and to have you assist me on my journey there, after I have enjoyed your company for a while. ²⁵Now, however, I am on my way to Jerusalem in the service of the saints there. ²⁶For Macedonia and Achaia were pleased to make a contribution for the poor among the saints in Jerusalem. ²⁷They were pleased to do it, and indeed they owe it to them. For if the Gentiles have shared in the Jews' spiritual blessings, they owe it to the Jews to share with them their material blessings. ²⁸So after I have completed this task and have made sure that they have received this fruit, I will go to Spain and visit you on the way. ²⁹I know that when I come to you, I will come in the full measure of the blessing of Christ.

³⁰I urge you, brothers, by our Lord Jesus Christ and by the love of the Spirit, to join me in my struggle by praying to God for me. ³¹Pray that I may be rescued

> I URGE you, brothers, by our Lord Jesus Christ and by the love of the Spirit, to join me in my struggle by praying to God for me.
>
> ROMANS 15:30

from the unbelievers in Judea and that my service in Jerusalem may be acceptable to the saints there, ³²so that by God's will I may come to you with joy and together with you be refreshed. ³³The God of peace be with you all. Amen.

Personal Greetings

16 I commend to you our sister Phoebe, a servantᵉ of the church in Cenchrea. ²I ask you to receive her in the Lord in a way worthy of the saints and to give her any help she may need from you, for she has been a great help to many people, including me.

ᵃ10 Deut. 32:43   ᵇ11 Psalm 117:1
ᶜ12 Isaiah 11:10   ᵈ21 Isaiah 52:15
ᵉ1 Or deaconess

ROMANS 15:30–33

Yes; Yes and No; and Yes, But[3]

15:30 I URGE YOU ... TO JOIN ME IN MY STRUGGLE BY PRAYING TO GOD FOR ME.

To be a Christian is to take sides in a cosmic conflict, a spiritual struggle that engages everything we are—body, mind and spirit—in a fight for the kingdom of God. Eternity hangs in the balance for all involved, and all are involved, whether they know it or not.

Knowing the struggle is spiritual, Paul asks the Romans to join him by praying for him and his work. Spiritual warfare requires spiritual weapons (see Ephesians 6:10–20). Prayer is a critical weapon in this battle, not because prayer is so powerful in itself, but because prayer calls upon the name of the God who is powerful and can make us strong in the strength of his Spirit.

Prayer is also a fellowship in the fight. That's why Paul asks the Romans to join him in his struggle by praying for him. God wills not only that we need him, but also each other, in order to stand and fight. We pray for each other, not as a substitute for other forms of help, but as the fount of help, the foundation. The kingdom and the power and the glory are all God's; but he gives his kingdom and power and glory to his church when it asks for them in the unity of the Holy Spirit.

To pray is to fight in a fellowship of love, but finally, it is to surrender—to God. When we pray, we do not bend God's will to ours; we rather align our wills with his. We cannot conquer in his name unless he first conquers us. Paul's requests are very specific: that he be rescued from unbelievers when he travels to Jerusalem, that his service of presenting an offering to the believers there would be acceptable to them (see Romans 15:25–27), and that he be able to visit the Romans. As for the Jerusalem Christians' acceptance of his service, God's answer was probably "yes." What about rescue? The answer was more like "yes and no": He was arrested, tried and imprisoned in Jerusalem; but he was also rescued three times from lynching, once from a plot to kill him and once from flogging. The trip to Rome? That was more like "yes, but." When he did finally get to Rome it was as a prisoner!

We may ask God to do things in a way we think best, but he always reserves the right to be God and do them in the way he thinks best. His "yes and no" and his "yes, but" are as wise and good as his "yes."

PRAY:

Lord Jesus, I surrender to your perfect and creative will,
whether it is yes, no, yes and no, or yes, but.

FOR YOUR NEXT DEVOTIONAL READING, GO TO PAGE 1388.

The Joy of a Melancholy Man

THOUGH FIRST in his class, David Brainerd was kicked out of Yale in 1743. Just four years later, he died of tuberculosis at age 29, after preaching alone among the Mohican and Delaware Indians in the dangerous wilderness that was then the western frontier of the American colonies. Brainerd was melancholy in the extreme, and his diaries are filled with references to dejection and self-doubt. Yet his diaries are still in print and have exerted enormous influence throughout the years. Often discouraged, Brainerd's personal testimony to God's grace has nevertheless encouraged people of the stature of Jonathan Edwards, who edited his diaries, Henry Martyn, William Carey and Adoniram Judson.

Brainerd's natural bent was toward depression, but his delight in God and faith in prayer sustained him supernaturally during his arduous years on the frontier. On his first assignment among the Mohicans, he was secretly tracked by hostile warriors. As the moment to kill him drew near, the warriors were suddenly held back at the sight of a rattlesnake coiled on the ground beside Brainerd, ready to strike him. But the snake miraculously uncoiled and slithered away. Astonished, the warriors took this as a sign that the Great Spirit was with him, so they left him unharmed.

To read Brainerd's diaries is to long to know the God he knew:

> "Tuesday, July 3 [1744]. Was still very weak. This morning, was enabled
> to pray under a feeling sense of my need of help from God, and, I trust,
> had some faith in exercise. Blessed be God, was enabled to plead with
> him a considerable time. Truly God is good to me. But my soul
> mourned and was grieved at my sinfulness and barrenness, and longed

to be more engaged for God. Near nine, withdrew again for prayer and through divine goodness had the blessed spirit of prayer. My soul loved the duty and longed for God in it. Oh, it is sweet to be the Lord's, to be sensibly devoted to him! What a blessed portion is God! How glorious, how lovely in himself! Oh, my soul longed to improve time wholly for God! Spent most of the day in translating prayers into Indian. In the evening, was enabled again to wrestle with God in prayer with fervency. Was enabled to maintain a self-diffident and watchful frame of spirit in the evening, and was jealous and afraid lest I should admit carelessness and self-confidence."[4]

PRAY:

Pray this prayer of David Brainerd's:
"Lord, to thee I dedicate myself! Oh, accept of me and let
me be thine forever. Lord, I desire nothing else; I desire
nothing more. Oh, come, come, Lord, accept a poor worm.
'Whom have I in heaven but thee? and there is none
upon earth, that I desire besides thee.'"

MEMORIZE:

Why are you downcast, O my soul? Why so disturbed
within me? Put your hope in God, for I will yet
praise him, my Savior. PSALM 42:5

FOR YOUR NEXT DEVOTIONAL READING, GO TO PAGE 1393.

³Greet Priscilla[a] and Aquila, my fellow workers in Christ Jesus. ⁴They risked their lives for me. Not only I but all the churches of the Gentiles are grateful to them.

⁵Greet also the church that meets at their house.

Greet my dear friend Epenetus, who was the first convert to Christ in the province of Asia.

⁶Greet Mary, who worked very hard for you.

⁷Greet Andronicus and Junias, my relatives who have been in prison with me. They are outstanding among the apostles, and they were in Christ before I was.

⁸Greet Ampliatus, whom I love in the Lord.

⁹Greet Urbanus, our fellow worker in Christ, and my dear friend Stachys.

¹⁰Greet Apelles, tested and approved in Christ.

Greet those who belong to the household of Aristobulus.

¹¹Greet Herodion, my relative.

Greet those in the household of Narcissus who are in the Lord.

¹²Greet Tryphena and Tryphosa, those women who work hard in the Lord.

Greet my dear friend Persis, another woman who has worked very hard in the Lord.

¹³Greet Rufus, chosen in the Lord, and his mother, who has been a mother to me, too.

¹⁴Greet Asyncritus, Phlegon, Hermes, Patrobas, Hermas and the brothers with them.

¹⁵Greet Philologus, Julia, Nereus and his sister, and Olympas and all the saints with them.

¹⁶Greet one another with a holy kiss.

All the churches of Christ send greetings.

¹⁷I urge you, brothers, to watch out for those who cause divisions and put obstacles in your way that are contrary to the teaching you have learned. Keep away from them. ¹⁸For such people are not serving our Lord Christ, but their own appetites. By smooth talk and flattery they deceive the minds of naive people. ¹⁹Everyone has heard about your obedience, so I am full of joy over you; but I want you to be wise about what is good, and innocent about what is evil.

²⁰The God of peace will soon crush Satan under your feet.

The grace of our Lord Jesus be with you.

²¹Timothy, my fellow worker, sends his greetings to you, as do Lucius, Jason and Sosipater, my relatives.

²²I, Tertius, who wrote down this letter, greet you in the Lord.

²³Gaius, whose hospitality I and the whole church here enjoy, sends you his greetings.

Erastus, who is the city's director of public works, and our brother Quartus send you their greetings.[b]

²⁵Now to him who is able to establish you by my gospel and the proclamation of Jesus Christ, according to the revelation of the mystery hidden for long ages past, ²⁶but now revealed and made known through the prophetic writings by the command of the eternal God, so that all nations might believe and obey him— ²⁷to the only wise God be glory forever through Jesus Christ! Amen.

[a]3 Greek *Prisca*, a variant of *Priscilla*
[b]23 Some manuscripts *their greetings.* ²⁴*May the grace of our Lord Jesus Christ be with all of you. Amen.*

1 Corinthians

IF PAUL kept a prayer list for the Corinthians in his journals and we could peek at it, we might be surprised to discover how very contemporary it looked. His concerns for these people included things like quarreling and cliques, lawsuits and sexual immorality, false teaching and narcissistic religious experience, resistance to authority on one hand and a cult of leadership on the other. The church was a mess. Its people were shallow, arrogant and self-absorbed.

Yet the Corinthians were a people holy to God and called by God to be holy: "sanctified in Christ Jesus and called to be holy" (1:2). They were also a people of prayer, part of the worldwide communion of those "who call on the name of our Lord Jesus Christ" (1:2). Paul prayed for the Corinthians with fear and trembling (see 2:1–5). The alternative was despair. He couldn't rely on personal charisma to persuade them to do the right thing because many in the church thought he was a pretty unimpressive apostle. His singular hope and only boast was in the power of Christ (see 2:4–5).

"THE GREATEST OF THESE IS LOVE." (13:13)

The Corinthian correspondence is a great encouragement to obey Jesus' command to pray and not give up (see Luke 18:1). In spite of the Corinthians' immaturity and resistance to the Holy Spirit, out of Paul's struggle with them came two of the greatest chapters in the Bible: the hymn of love in chapter 13 and the resurrection manifesto in chapter 15.

1 Paul, called to be an apostle of Christ Jesus by the will of God, and our brother Sosthenes,

2 To the church of God in Corinth, to those sanctified in Christ Jesus and called to be holy, together with all those everywhere who call on the name of our Lord Jesus Christ—their Lord and ours:

3 Grace and peace to you from God our Father and the Lord Jesus Christ.

Thanksgiving

4 I always thank God for you because of his grace given you in Christ Jesus. 5 For in him you have been enriched in every way—in all your speaking and in all your knowledge— 6 because our testimony about Christ was confirmed in you. 7 Therefore you do not lack any spiritual gift as you eagerly wait for our Lord Jesus Christ to be revealed. 8 He will keep you strong to the end, so that you will be blameless on the day of our Lord Jesus Christ. 9 God, who has called you into fellowship with his Son Jesus Christ our Lord, is faithful.

Divisions in the Church

10 I appeal to you, brothers, in the name of our Lord Jesus Christ, that all of you agree with one another so that there may be no divisions among you and that you may be perfectly united in mind and thought. 11 My brothers, some from Chloe's household have informed me that there are quarrels among you. 12 What I mean is this: One of you says, "I follow Paul"; another, "I follow Apollos"; another, "I follow Cephas[a]"; still another, "I follow Christ."

13 Is Christ divided? Was Paul crucified for you? Were you baptized into[b] the name of Paul? 14 I am thankful that I did not baptize any of you except Crispus and Gaius, 15 so no one can say that you were baptized into my name. 16 (Yes, I also baptized the household of Stephanas; beyond that, I don't remember if I baptized anyone else.) 17 For Christ did not send me to baptize, but to preach the gospel—not with words of human wisdom, lest the cross of Christ be emptied of its power.

Christ the Wisdom and Power of God

18 For the message of the cross is foolishness to those who are perishing, but to us who are being saved it is the power of God. 19 For it is written:

"I will destroy the wisdom of the
    wise;
  the intelligence of the intelligent
    I will frustrate."[c]

20 Where is the wise man? Where is the scholar? Where is the philosopher of this age? Has not God made foolish the wisdom of the world? 21 For since in the wisdom of God the world through its wisdom did not know him, God was pleased through the foolishness of what was preached to save those who believe. 22 Jews demand miraculous signs and Greeks look for wisdom, 23 but we preach Christ crucified: a stumbling block to Jews and foolishness to Gentiles, 24 but to those whom God has called, both Jews and Greeks, Christ the power of God and the wisdom of God. 25 For the foolishness of God is wiser than man's wisdom, and the weakness of God is stronger than man's strength.

26 Brothers, think of what you were when you were called. Not many of you were wise by human standards; not many were influential; not many were of noble birth. 27 But God chose the foolish things of the world to shame the wise; God chose the weak things of the world to shame the strong. 28 He chose the lowly things of this world and the despised things—and the things that are not—to nullify the things that are, 29 so that no one may boast before him. 30 It is because of him that you are in Christ Jesus, who has become for us wisdom from God— that is, our righteousness, holiness and redemption. 31 Therefore, as it is written: "Let him who boasts boast in the Lord."[d]

2 When I came to you, brothers, I did not come with eloquence or superior wisdom as I proclaimed to you the testimony about God.[e] 2 For I resolved to know nothing while I was with you except Jesus Christ and him crucified. 3 I came to you in

---

[a]12 That is, Peter   [b]13 Or in; also in verse 15
[c]19 Isaiah 29:14   [d]31 Jer. 9:24   [e]1 Some
manuscripts as I proclaimed to you God's mystery

weakness and fear, and with much trembling. ⁴My message and my preaching were not with wise and persuasive words, but with a demonstration of the Spirit's power, ⁵so that your faith might not rest on men's wisdom, but on God's power.

Wisdom From the Spirit

⁶We do, however, speak a message of wisdom among the mature, but not the wisdom of this age or of the rulers of this age, who are coming to nothing. ⁷No, we speak of God's secret wisdom, a wisdom

---

[**MONDAY**]

1 CORINTHIANS 2:1–5

"I'd Rather Learn How to Pray"

2:1 "I DID NOT COME WITH ELOQUENCE OR SUPERIOR WISDOM AS I PROCLAIMED TO YOU THE TESTIMONY ABOUT GOD."

It's not hard to guess why Paul would have felt so weak and fearful as he first went to Corinth and began preaching to the Corinthians. He knew the message and the messenger were not tailor-made to the tastes of these Greek city dwellers. Quite the contrary. The message of a crucified Savior radically cut across the grain of Greek intellectualism and Corinthian Greek ideas of success. As for the messenger, Paul's speaking abilities did not match the Greek ideals of the orator. The most powerful and influential people in that culture were those who could use words with dramatic and rhetorical flair. Later on, even after the Corinthian church was established, there were some in the church who complained that Paul's speaking "amount[ed] to nothing" (2 Corinthians 10:10).

From a human perspective, it was impossible for these people to be impressed with this unimpressive apostle and his bizarre message. So Paul didn't try to convince his audience. He knew it would be a miracle if they believed him. But then, it's always a miracle when anyone believes, for, "The god of this age has blinded the minds of unbelievers, so that they cannot see the light of the gospel of the glory of Christ" (2 Corinthians 4:4). Paul's only hope for success would be the empowerment of the Holy Spirit. So Paul preached with great simplicity and humble reliance on the power of God to open the eyes of these nonbelievers. And God answered his prayer.

Which is harder, anyway? To dazzle the ears and eyes and impress the mind, or to see human hearts changed? No argument or orator has ever changed a heart. Only God can do that. So Paul rejoiced that the Corinthians' faith could be real, since his preaching was "not with wise and persuasive words, but with a demonstration of the Spirit's power, so that your faith might not rest on men's wisdom, but on God's power" (1 Corinthians 2:4–5).

That is why prayer is so important for the advancement of the kingdom. When we pray, we are asking God to do what only God can do—open eyes and change hearts. And that is why the great evangelist D. L. Moody, impressive preacher that he was, said, "I'd rather learn how to pray than preach. Jesus' disciples never asked him to teach them how to preach, but how to pray."

PRAY:
Almighty God, the things we most need are the things only you can give: forgiveness and understanding, faith, hope and love. So I cry out to you to give us these things, for in ourselves we can do nothing.

FOR YOUR NEXT DEVOTIONAL READING, GO TO PAGE 1395.

that has been hidden and that God destined for our glory before time began. [8]None of the rulers of this age understood it, for if they had, they would not have crucified the Lord of glory. [9]However, as it is written:

"No eye has seen,
no ear has heard,
no mind has conceived
what God has prepared for those
who love him"[a]—

[10]but God has revealed it to us by his Spirit.

The Spirit searches all things, even the deep things of God. [11]For who among men knows the thoughts of a man except the man's spirit within him? In the same way no one knows the thoughts of God except the Spirit of God. [12]We have not received the spirit of the world but the Spirit who is from God, that we may understand what God has freely given us. [13]This is what we speak, not in words taught us by human wisdom but in words taught by the Spirit, expressing spiritual truths in spiritual words.[b] [14]The man without the Spirit does not accept the things that come from the Spirit of God, for they are foolishness to him, and he cannot understand them, because they are spiritually discerned. [15]The spiritual man makes judgments about all things, but he himself is not subject to any man's judgment:

[16] "For who has known the mind of
the Lord
that he may instruct him?"[c]

But we have the mind of Christ.

On Divisions in the Church

3 Brothers, I could not address you as spiritual but as worldly—mere infants in Christ. [2]I gave you milk, not solid food, for you were not yet ready for it. Indeed, you are still not ready. [3]You are still worldly. For since there is jealousy and quarreling among you, are you not worldly? Are you not acting like mere men? [4]For when one says, "I follow Paul," and another, "I follow Apollos," are you not mere men?

[5]What, after all, is Apollos? And what is Paul? Only servants, through whom you came to believe—as the Lord has as-

signed to each his task. [6]I planted the seed, Apollos watered it, but God made it grow. [7]So neither he who plants nor he who waters is anything, but only God, who makes things grow. [8]The man who plants and the man who waters have one purpose, and each will be rewarded according to his own labor. [9]For we are God's fellow workers; you are God's field, God's building.

[10]By the grace God has given me, I laid a foundation as an expert builder, and someone else is building on it. But each one should be careful how he builds. [11]For no one can lay any foundation other than the one already laid, which is Jesus Christ. [12]If any man builds on this foundation using gold, silver, costly stones, wood, hay or straw, [13]his work will be shown for what it is, because the Day will bring it to light. It will be revealed with fire, and the fire will test the quality of each man's work. [14]If what he has built survives, he will receive his reward. [15]If it is burned up, he will suffer loss; he himself will be saved, but only as one escaping through the flames.

[16]Don't you know that you yourselves are God's temple and that God's Spirit lives in you? [17]If anyone destroys God's temple, God will destroy him; for God's temple is sacred, and you are that temple.

[18]Do not deceive yourselves. If any one of you thinks he is wise by the standards of this age, he should become a "fool" so that he may become wise. [19]For the wisdom of this world is foolishness in God's sight. As it is written: "He catches the wise in their craftiness"[d]; [20]and again, "The Lord knows that the thoughts of the wise are futile."[e] [21]So then, no more boasting about men! All things are yours, [22]whether Paul or Apollos or Cephas[f] or the world or life or death or the present or the future—all are yours, [23]and you are of Christ, and Christ is of God.

Apostles of Christ

4 So then, men ought to regard us as servants of Christ and as those entrusted with the secret things of God.

[a]9 Isaiah 64:4   [b]13 Or *Spirit, interpreting spiritual truths to spiritual men*
[c]16 Isaiah 40:13   [d]19 Job 5:13
[e]20 Psalm 94:11   [f]22 That is, Peter

²Now it is required that those who have been given a trust must prove faithful. ³I care very little if I am judged by you or by any human court; indeed, I do not even judge myself. ⁴My conscience is clear, but that does not make me innocent. It is the Lord who judges me. ⁵Therefore judge nothing before the appointed time; wait till the Lord comes. He will bring to light what is hidden in darkness and will expose the motives of men's hearts. At that time each will receive his praise from God.

⁶Now, brothers, I have applied these things to myself and Apollos for your benefit, so that you may learn from us

[TUESDAY]

1 CORINTHIANS 3:1–17

You Are God's Temple

3:9 "YOU ARE GOD'S FIELD, GOD'S BUILDING."

Paul says something here that would have stunned King Solomon and the architects and builders of the great Jerusalem temple. In all of its grandeur and glory, there was a greater glory yet to come when the people of God would be the temple of God. One can never say of any precious stone, fine wood or beautiful design that it was made in the image of God. Not even the brightest star can be spoken of this way. Only *people* are made in God's image. Human beings reflect the glory of God as nothing else in creation can. So the church is made of the very finest materials, constructed in the very finest design.

The church must have a very lofty purpose in God's economy. The first temple was built to be a house of communion with God, or as Jesus put it, "a house of prayer for all nations" (Mark 11:17). The first temple was a *place* of prayer. The new temple is not a place, but a *community* of prayer: a fellowship of pray-ers who, by their life together in the world, invite the peoples of the earth into that glorious communion.

Paul's great concern here is that both he, as an apostle, and the people themselves, build the church well, with the finest materials. Specifically, it matters greatly to him that the people of the church not damage what is being built. The Corinthians were damaging the church with their divisions, a serious crime indeed, for, "If anyone destroys God's temple, God will destroy him; for God's temple is sacred, and you are that temple" (1 Corinthians 3:17).

The implications for prayer are direct and devastating. How can the Corinthian believers have fellowship with God if they can't have fellowship with each other? How can they pray to God for others if they won't pray with each other? The church can't be a house of prayer for all nations if it can't be a community of prayer in the neighborhood or city in which it meets. Pray for your church. Pray that it be united in the Spirit, and that its people may unite in prayer for the peoples of the earth.

PRAY:

Father in heaven, thank you for including me in your church,
your holy temple! Unite your people in the Spirit, that we may
be united in prayer for the peoples of the earth.

FOR YOUR NEXT DEVOTIONAL READING, GO TO PAGE 1401.

> 66 *A wish for prayer is a prayer in itself.* 99

GEORGE BERNANOS

the meaning of the saying, "Do not go beyond what is written." Then you will not take pride in one man over against another. [7]For who makes you different from anyone else? What do you have that you did not receive? And if you did receive it, why do you boast as though you did not?

[8]Already you have all you want! Already you have become rich! You have become kings—and that without us! How I wish that you really had become kings so that we might be kings with you! [9]For it seems to me that God has put us apostles on display at the end of the procession, like men condemned to die in the arena. We have been made a spectacle to the whole universe, to angels as well as to men. [10]We are fools for Christ, but you are so wise in Christ! We are weak, but you are strong! You are honored, we are dishonored! [11]To this very hour we go hungry and thirsty, we are in rags, we are brutally treated, we are homeless. [12]We work hard with our own hands. When we are cursed, we bless; when we are persecuted, we endure it; [13]when we are slandered, we answer kindly. Up to this moment we have become the scum of the earth, the refuse of the world.

[14]I am not writing this to shame you, but to warn you, as my dear children. [15]Even though you have ten thousand guardians in Christ, you do not have many fathers, for in Christ Jesus I became your father through the gospel. [16]Therefore I urge you to imitate me. [17]For this reason I am sending to you Timothy, my son whom I love, who is faithful in the Lord. He will remind you of my way of life in Christ Jesus, which agrees with what I teach everywhere in every church.

[18]Some of you have become arrogant, as if I were not coming to you. [19]But I will come to you very soon, if the Lord is willing, and then I will find out not only how these arrogant people are talking, but what power they have. [20]For the kingdom of God is not a matter of talk but of power. [21]What do you prefer? Shall I come to you with a whip, or in love and with a gentle spirit?

Expel the Immoral Brother!

5 It is actually reported that there is sexual immorality among you, and of a kind that does not occur even among pagans: A man has his father's wife. [2]And you are proud! Shouldn't you rather have been filled with grief and have put out of your fellowship the man who did this? [3]Even though I am not physically present, I am with you in spirit. And I have already passed judgment on the one who did this, just as if I were present. [4]When you are assembled in the name of our Lord Jesus and I am with you in spirit, and the power of our Lord Jesus is present, [5]hand this man over to Satan, so that the sinful nature[a] may be destroyed and his spirit saved on the day of the Lord.

[6]Your boasting is not good. Don't you know that a little yeast works through the whole batch of dough? [7]Get rid of the old yeast that you may be a new batch without yeast—as you really are. For Christ, our Passover lamb, has been sacrificed. [8]Therefore let us keep the Festival, not with the old yeast, the yeast of malice and wickedness, but with bread without yeast, the bread of sincerity and truth.

[9]I have written you in my letter not to associate with sexually immoral people— [10]not at all meaning the people of this world who are immoral, or the greedy and swindlers, or idolaters. In that case you would have to leave this world. [11]But now I am writing you that you must not associate with anyone who calls himself a brother but is sexually immoral or greedy, an idolater or a slanderer, a drunkard or a swindler. With such a man do not even eat.

[12]What business is it of mine to judge those outside the church? Are you not to judge those inside? [13]God will judge those outside. "Expel the wicked man from among you."[b]

[a]5 Or *that his body*; or *that the flesh*
[b]13 Deut. 17:7; 19:19; 21:21; 22:21,24; 24:7

Lawsuits Among Believers

6 If any of you has a dispute with another, dare he take it before the ungodly for judgment instead of before the saints? [2]Do you not know that the saints will judge the world? And if you are to judge the world, are you not competent to judge trivial cases? [3]Do you not know that we will judge angels? How much more the things of this life! [4]Therefore, if you have disputes about such matters, appoint as judges even men of little account in the church![a] [5]I say this to shame you. Is it possible that there is nobody among you wise enough to judge a dispute between believers? [6]But instead, one brother goes to law against another—and this in front of unbelievers!

[7]The very fact that you have lawsuits among you means you have been completely defeated already. Why not rather be wronged? Why not rather be cheated? [8]Instead, you yourselves cheat and do wrong, and you do this to your brothers.

[9]Do you not know that the wicked will not inherit the kingdom of God? Do not be deceived: Neither the sexually immoral nor idolaters nor adulterers nor male prostitutes nor homosexual offenders [10]nor thieves nor the greedy nor drunkards nor slanderers nor swindlers will inherit the kingdom of God. [11]And that is what some of you were. But you were washed, you were sanctified, you were justified in the name of the Lord Jesus Christ and by the Spirit of our God.

Sexual Immorality

[12]"Everything is permissible for me"—but not everything is beneficial. "Everything is permissible for me"—but I will not be mastered by anything. [13]"Food for the stomach and the stomach for food"—but God will destroy them both. The body is not meant for sexual immorality, but for the Lord, and the Lord for the body. [14]By his power God raised the Lord from the dead, and he will raise us also. [15]Do you not know that your bodies are members of Christ himself? Shall I then take the members of Christ and unite them with a prostitute? Never! [16]Do you not know that he who unites himself with a prostitute is one with her in body? For it is said, "The two will become one flesh."[b]

[17]But he who unites himself with the Lord is one with him in spirit.

[18]Flee from sexual immorality. All other sins a man commits are outside his body, but he who sins sexually sins against his own body. [19]Do you not know that your body is a temple of the Holy Spirit, who is in you, whom you have received from God? You are not your own; [20]you were bought at a price. Therefore honor God with your body.

> **❝** In our home there was always prayer—aloud, proud, and unapologetic. **❞**
>
> LYNDON B. JOHNSON

Marriage

7 Now for the matters you wrote about: It is good for a man not to marry.[c] [2]But since there is so much immorality, each man should have his own wife, and each woman her own husband. [3]The husband should fulfill his marital duty to his wife, and likewise the wife to her husband. [4]The wife's body does not belong to her alone but also to her husband. In the same way, the husband's body does not belong to him alone but also to his wife. [5]Do not deprive each other except by mutual consent and for a time, so that you may devote yourselves to prayer. Then come together again so that Satan will not tempt you because of your lack of self-control. [6]I say this as a concession, not as a command. [7]I wish that all men were as I am. But each man has his own gift from God; one has this gift, another has that.

> DO NOT deprive each other except by mutual consent and for a time, so that you may devote yourselves to prayer.
>
> 1 CORINTHIANS 7:5

[8]Now to the unmarried and the widows I say: It is good for them to stay unmarried, as I am. [9]But if they cannot control themselves, they should marry, for it is better to marry than to burn with passion.

[a]4 Or matters, do you appoint as judges men of little account in the church?   [b]16 Gen. 2:24
[c]1 Or "It is good for a man not to have sexual relations with a woman."

¹⁰To the married I give this command (not I, but the Lord): A wife must not separate from her husband. ¹¹But if she does, she must remain unmarried or else be reconciled to her husband. And a husband must not divorce his wife.

¹²To the rest I say this (I, not the Lord): If any brother has a wife who is not a believer and she is willing to live with him, he must not divorce her. ¹³And if a woman has a husband who is not a believer and he is willing to live with her, she must not divorce him. ¹⁴For the unbelieving husband has been sanctified through his wife, and the unbelieving wife has been sanctified through her believing husband. Otherwise your children would be unclean, but as it is, they are holy.

¹⁵But if the unbeliever leaves, let him do so. A believing man or woman is not bound in such circumstances; God has called us to live in peace. ¹⁶How do you know, wife, whether you will save your husband? Or, how do you know, husband, whether you will save your wife?

¹⁷Nevertheless, each one should retain the place in life that the Lord assigned to him and to which God has called him. This is the rule I lay down in all the churches. ¹⁸Was a man already circumcised when he was called? He should not become uncircumcised. Was a man uncircumcised when he was called? He should not be circumcised. ¹⁹Circumcision is nothing and uncircumcision is nothing. Keeping God's commands is what counts. ²⁰Each one should remain in the situation which he was in when God called him. ²¹Were you a slave when you were called? Don't let it trouble you—although if you can gain your freedom, do so. ²²For he who was a slave when he was called by the Lord is the Lord's freedman; similarly, he who was a free man when he was called is Christ's slave. ²³You were bought at a price; do not become slaves of men. ²⁴Brothers, each man, as responsible to God, should remain in the situation God called him to.

²⁵Now about virgins: I have no command from the Lord, but I give a judgment as one who by the Lord's mercy is trustworthy. ²⁶Because of the present crisis, I think that it is good for you to remain as you are. ²⁷Are you married? Do not seek a divorce. Are you unmarried? Do not look for a wife. ²⁸But if you do marry, you have not sinned; and if a virgin marries, she has not sinned. But those who marry will face many troubles in this life, and I want to spare you this.

²⁹What I mean, brothers, is that the time is short. From now on those who have wives should live as if they had none; ³⁰those who mourn, as if they did not; those who are happy, as if they were not; those who buy something, as if it were not theirs to keep; ³¹those who use the things of the world, as if not engrossed in them. For this world in its present form is passing away.

³²I would like you to be free from concern. An unmarried man is concerned about the Lord's affairs—how he can please the Lord. ³³But a married man is concerned about the affairs of this world—how he can please his wife— ³⁴and his interests are divided. An unmarried woman or virgin is concerned about the Lord's affairs: Her aim is to be devoted to the Lord in both body and spirit. But a married woman is concerned about the affairs of this world—how she can please her husband. ³⁵I am saying this for your own good, not to restrict you, but that you may live in a right way in undivided devotion to the Lord.

³⁶If anyone thinks he is acting improperly toward the virgin he is engaged to, and if she is getting along in years and he feels he ought to marry, he should do as he wants. He is not sinning. They should get married. ³⁷But the man who has settled the matter in his own mind, who is under no compulsion but has control over his own will, and who has made up his mind not to marry the virgin—this man also does the right thing. ³⁸So then, he who marries the virgin does right, but he who does not marry her does even better.ᵃ

ᵃ *36–38* Or ³⁶*If anyone thinks he is not treating his daughter properly, and if she is getting along in years, and he feels she ought to marry, he should do as he wants. He is not sinning. He should let her get married. ³⁷But the man who has settled the matter in his own mind, who is under no compulsion but has control over his own will, and who has made up his mind to keep the virgin unmarried—this man also does the right thing. ³⁸So then, he who gives his virgin in marriage does right, but he who does not give her in marriage does even better.*

³⁹A woman is bound to her husband as long as he lives. But if her husband dies, she is free to marry anyone she wishes, but he must belong to the Lord. ⁴⁰In my judgment, she is happier if she stays as she is—and I think that I too have the Spirit of God.

Food Sacrificed to Idols

8 Now about food sacrificed to idols: We know that we all possess knowledge.ᵃ Knowledge puffs up, but love builds up. ²The man who thinks he knows something does not yet know as he ought to know. ³But the man who loves God is known by God.

> " The Lord's Prayer may be committed to memory quickly, but it slowly learnt by heart. "
>
> FREDRICK DENISON MAURICE

⁴So then, about eating food sacrificed to idols: We know that an idol is nothing at all in the world and that there is no God but one. ⁵For even if there are so-called gods, whether in heaven or on earth (as indeed there are many "gods" and many "lords"), ⁶yet for us there is but one God, the Father, from whom all things came and for whom we live; and there is but one Lord, Jesus Christ, through whom all things came and through whom we live.

⁷But not everyone knows this. Some people are still so accustomed to idols that when they eat such food they think of it as having been sacrificed to an idol, and since their conscience is weak, it is defiled. ⁸But food does not bring us near to God; we are no worse if we do not eat, and no better if we do.

⁹Be careful, however, that the exercise of your freedom does not become a stumbling block to the weak. ¹⁰For if anyone with a weak conscience sees you who have this knowledge eating in an idol's temple, won't he be emboldened to eat what has been sacrificed to idols? ¹¹So this weak brother, for whom Christ died, is destroyed by your knowledge. ¹²When you sin against your brothers in this way and wound their weak conscience, you sin against Christ. ¹³Therefore, if what I eat causes my brother to fall into sin, I will never eat meat again, so that I will not cause him to fall.

The Rights of an Apostle

9 Am I not free? Am I not an apostle? Have I not seen Jesus our Lord? Are you not the result of my work in the Lord? ²Even though I may not be an apostle to others, surely I am to you! For you are the seal of my apostleship in the Lord.

³This is my defense to those who sit in judgment on me. ⁴Don't we have the right to food and drink? ⁵Don't we have the right to take a believing wife along with us, as do the other apostles and the Lord's brothers and Cephasᵇ? ⁶Or is it only I and Barnabas who must work for a living?

⁷Who serves as a soldier at his own expense? Who plants a vineyard and does not eat of its grapes? Who tends a flock and does not drink of the milk? ⁸Do I say this merely from a human point of view? Doesn't the Law say the same thing? ⁹For it is written in the Law of Moses: "Do not muzzle an ox while it is treading out the grain."ᶜ Is it about oxen that God is concerned? ¹⁰Surely he says this for us, doesn't he? Yes, this was written for us, because when the plowman plows and the thresher threshes, they ought to do so in the hope of sharing in the harvest. ¹¹If we have sown spiritual seed among you, is it too much if we reap a material harvest from you? ¹²If others have this right of support from you, shouldn't we have it all the more?

But we did not use this right. On the contrary, we put up with anything rather than hinder the gospel of Christ. ¹³Don't you know that those who work in the temple get their food from the temple, and those who serve at the altar share in what is offered on the altar? ¹⁴In the same way, the Lord has commanded that those who preach the gospel should receive their living from the gospel.

¹⁵But I have not used any of these rights. And I am not writing this in the hope that you will do such things for

---

ᵃ1 Or "We all possess knowledge," as you say ᵇ5 That is, Peter ᶜ9 Deut. 25:4

me. I would rather die than have anyone deprive me of this boast. ¹⁶Yet when I preach the gospel, I cannot boast, for I am compelled to preach. Woe to me if I do not preach the gospel! ¹⁷If I preach voluntarily, I have a reward; if not voluntarily, I am simply discharging the trust committed to me. ¹⁸What then is my reward? Just this: that in preaching the gospel I may offer it free of charge, and so not make use of my rights in preaching it.

¹⁹Though I am free and belong to no man, I make myself a slave to everyone, to win as many as possible. ²⁰To the Jews I became like a Jew, to win the Jews. To those under the law I became like one under the law (though I myself am not under the law), so as to win those under the law. ²¹To those not having the law I became like one not having the law (though I am not free from God's law but am under Christ's law), so as to win those not having the law. ²²To the weak I became weak, to win the weak. I have become all things to all men so that by all possible means I might save some. ²³I do all this for the sake of the gospel, that I may share in its blessings.

²⁴Do you not know that in a race all the runners run, but only one gets the prize? Run in such a way as to get the prize. ²⁵Everyone who competes in the games goes into strict training. They do it to get a crown that will not last; but we do it to get a crown that will last forever. ²⁶Therefore I do not run like a man running aimlessly; I do not fight like a man beating the air. ²⁷No, I beat my body and make it my slave so that after I have preached to others, I myself will not be disqualified for the prize.

Warnings From Israel's History

10 For I do not want you to be ignorant of the fact, brothers, that our forefathers were all under the cloud and that they all passed through the sea. ²They were all baptized into Moses in the cloud and in the sea. ³They all ate the same spiritual food ⁴and drank the same spiritual drink; for they drank from the spiritual rock that accompanied them, and that rock was Christ. ⁵Nevertheless, God was not pleased

with most of them; their bodies were scattered over the desert.

⁶Now these things occurred as examples*ᵃ* to keep us from setting our hearts on evil things as they did. ⁷Do not be idolaters, as some of them were; as it is written: "The people sat down to eat and drink and got up to indulge in pagan revelry."*ᵇ* ⁸We should not commit sexual immorality, as some of them did—and in one day twenty-three thousand of them died. ⁹We should not test the Lord, as some of them did—and were killed by snakes. ¹⁰And do not grumble, as some of them did—and were killed by the destroying angel.

¹¹These things happened to them as examples and were written down as warnings for us, on whom the fulfillment of the ages has come. ¹²So, if you think you are standing firm, be careful that you don't fall! ¹³No temptation has seized you except what is common to man. And God is faithful; he will not let you be tempted beyond what you can bear. But when you are tempted, he will also provide a way out so that you can stand up under it.

Idol Feasts and the Lord's Supper

¹⁴Therefore, my dear friends, flee from idolatry. ¹⁵I speak to sensible people; judge for yourselves what I say. ¹⁶Is not the cup of thanksgiving for which we give thanks a participation in the blood of Christ? And is not the bread that we break a participation in the body of Christ? ¹⁷Because there is one loaf, we, who are many, are one body, for we all partake of the one loaf.

¹⁸Consider the people of Israel: Do not those who eat the sacrifices participate in the altar? ¹⁹Do I mean then that a sacrifice offered to an idol is anything, or that an idol is anything? ²⁰No, but the sacrifices of pagans are offered to demons, not to God, and I do not want you to be participants with demons. ²¹You cannot drink the cup of the Lord and the cup of demons too; you cannot have a part in both the Lord's table and the table of demons. ²²Are we trying to arouse the Lord's jealousy? Are we stronger than he?

ᵃ6 Or *types*; also in verse 11   *ᵇ7* Exodus 32:6

The Believer's Freedom

23 "Everything is permissible"—but not everything is beneficial. "Everything is permissible"—but not everything is constructive. **24** Nobody should seek his own good, but the good of others.

25 Eat anything sold in the meat market without raising questions of conscience,

26 for, "The earth is the Lord's, and everything in it."ᵃ

27 If some unbeliever invites you to a meal and you want to go, eat whatever is put before you without raising questions of conscience. **28** But if anyone says to you, "This has been offered in sacrifice," then

ᵃ26 Psalm 24:1

---

1 CORINTHIANS 9:24–27

Spiritual Discipline

9:25 "EVERYONE WHO COMPETES IN THE GAMES GOES INTO STRICT TRAINING."

There is a poster of a wrestler working out with weights, his face wrinkled in a sweaty grimace, veins bulging in his neck and biceps. It is a picture of pain and determination. The caption of the poster reads, "There are two kinds of pain; the pain of discipline and the pain of regrets." To be alive is to experience pain; we have no choice in the matter. But when it comes to discipline, we can choose the kind of pain we want. Discipline hurts, but so does the lack of discipline. The wrestler was in pain, but it was a good pain; better by far than the pain of regrets, the pain of losing to his next opponent.

This was clearly the apostle Paul's take on the discipline of living the Christian life. He forced his body to cooperate with his great goal of winning the prize for which God called him heavenward in Christ Jesus (see Philippians 3:14). Sure, it was unpleasant at times, but that was nothing compared to missing the prize—and the added irony of having taught others to run for it. Dallas Willard was thinking like Paul when he wrote about the costs of "nondiscipleship":

> Nondiscipleship costs abiding peace, a life penetrated throughout by love, faith that sees everything in the light of God's overriding governance for good, hopefulness that stands firm in the most discouraging of circumstances, power to do what is right and withstands the forces of evil. In short, it costs exactly that abundance of life Jesus said he came to bring (see John 10:10).[1]

But discipline is not so much a negative quality as a positive refusal: saying no to something lesser in order to say yes to something greater. Cultivating a life of prayer can be costly and inconvenient, but how much greater the value! And as with all disciplines, when pursued over time the duty will become delight.

PRAY:

Father, help me to see the big picture of my life,
to look beyond momentary little pleasures to the
really great pleasures, to say no in order to say
a greater yes to the abundant life you promised. Amen.

FOR YOUR NEXT DEVOTIONAL READING, GO TO PAGE 1403.

do not eat it, both for the sake of the man who told you and for conscience' sake[a]— [29]the other man's conscience, I mean, not yours. For why should my freedom be judged by another's conscience? [30]If I take part in the meal with thankfulness, why am I denounced because of something I thank God for?

[31]So whether you eat or drink or whatever you do, do it all for the glory of God. [32]Do not cause anyone to stumble, whether Jews, Greeks or the church of God— [33]even as I try to please everybody in every way. For I am not seeking my own good but the good of many, so that they may be saved. [1]Follow my example, as I follow the example of Christ.

Propriety in Worship

[2]I praise you for remembering me in everything and for holding to the teachings,[b] just as I passed them on to you.

[3]Now I want you to realize that the head of every man is Christ, and the head of the woman is man, and the head of Christ is God. [4]Every man who prays or prophesies with his head covered dishonors his head. [5]And every woman who prays or prophesies with her head uncovered dishonors her head—it is just as though her head were shaved. [6]If a woman does not cover her head, she should have her hair cut off; and if it is a disgrace for a woman to have her hair cut or shaved off, she should cover her head. [7]A man ought not to cover his head,[c] since he is the image and glory of God; but the woman is the glory of man. [8]For man did not come from woman, but woman from man; [9]neither was man created for woman, but woman for man. [10]For this reason, and because of the angels, the woman ought to have a sign of authority on her head. [11]In the Lord, however, woman is not independent of man, nor is man independent of woman. [12]For as woman came from man, so also man is born of woman. But everything comes from God. [13]Judge for yourselves: Is it proper for a woman to pray to God with her head uncovered? [14]Does not the very nature of things teach you that if a man has long hair, it is a disgrace to him, [15]but that if a woman has long hair, it is her glory? For long hair is given to her as a covering. [16]If anyone wants to be contentious about this, we have no other practice—nor do the churches of God.

The Lord's Supper

[17]In the following directives I have no praise for you, for your meetings do more harm than good. [18]In the first place, I hear that when you come together as a church, there are divisions among you, and to some extent I believe it. [19]No doubt there have to be differences among you to show which of you have God's approval. [20]When you come together, it is not the Lord's Supper you eat, [21]for as you eat, each of you goes ahead without waiting for anybody else. One remains hungry, another gets drunk. [22]Don't you have homes to eat and drink in? Or do you despise the church of God and humiliate those who have nothing? What shall I say to you? Shall I praise you for this? Certainly not!

[23]For I received from the Lord what I also passed on to you: The Lord Jesus, on the night he was betrayed, took bread, [24]and when he had given thanks, he broke it and said, "This is my body, which is for you; do this in remembrance of me." [25]In the same way, after supper he took the cup, saying, "This cup is the new covenant in my blood; do this, whenever you drink it, in remembrance of me." [26]For whenever you eat this bread and drink this cup, you proclaim the Lord's death until he comes.

[27]Therefore, whoever eats the bread or drinks the cup of the Lord in an unworthy manner will be guilty of sinning against the body and blood of the Lord. [28]A man ought to examine himself before he eats of the bread and drinks of the cup. [29]For anyone who eats and drinks without recognizing the body of the Lord eats and drinks judgment on himself.

[a]28 Some manuscripts *conscience' sake, for "the earth is the Lord's and everything in it"*
[b]2 Or *traditions*   [c]4–7 Or *4Every man who prays or prophesies with long hair dishonors his head. 5And every woman who prays or prophesies with no covering ⌊of hair⌋ on her head dishonors her head—she is just like one of the "shorn women." 6If a woman has no covering, let her be for now with short hair, but since it is a disgrace for a woman to have her hair shorn or shaved, she should grow it again. 7A man ought not to have long hair*

30That is why many among you are weak and sick, and a number of you have fallen asleep. 31But if we judged ourselves, we would not come under judgment. 32When we are judged by the Lord, we are being disciplined so that we will not be condemned with the world.

33So then, my brothers, when you come together to eat, wait for each other. 34If anyone is hungry, he should eat at home, so that when you meet together it may not result in judgment.

And when I come I will give further directions.

{THURSDAY}

1 CORINTHIANS 10:31 — 11:16

A Difficult Passage on Prayer

10:31 WHATEVER YOU DO, DO IT ALL FOR THE GLORY OF GOD.

Paul's words about head coverings and men and women in prayer are one of his more difficult teachings. There have been four broad ways to read this passage:

1. Skip over it, put it out of your mind and move on to things that are easier to understand and seem more relevant to our times.
2. Be offended by it, conclude that Paul was displaying a kind of male chauvinist cultural myopia and read no further.
3. Take Paul's words about head coverings as timeless divine truths to be followed today.
4. Assume that what he said about head coverings had relevance for that time and place, but only for that time and place.

As important as it may be, one doesn't have to consider and critique the merits of these four approaches to appreciate the important truth that lies behind Paul's instructions. His reason for giving them was to help the Corinthians apply the truly timeless principle of doing all for the glory of God. This principle, stated in 10:31, is critical for what Paul writes both before and after it: "So whether you eat or drink or whatever you do, do it all for the glory of God." Paul then uses his own life to underline the principle, and he urges the Corinthians to follow his example: "even as I try to please everybody in every way. For I am not seeking my own good but the good of many, so that they may be saved. Follow my example, as I follow the example of Christ" (10:33—11:1).

The principle is simply, "Glorify God in all you do." The flipside of the principle is, "Don't seek to please yourself, but please God by pleasing others." Fit into the norms of your culture (whether timeless or not) so the attention will be on God when you pray, not on how you are dressed when you pray. Remember that all prayer, especially public prayer, is not about self-expression, but about the glory of God. Surely this is one thing all four positions can agree on! It's not about us; it's about God.

PRAY:
Dear God, unite your people in worship. Help us to lay aside
all arguments about externals and seek to glorify you with one voice.

FOR YOUR NEXT DEVOTIONAL READING, GO TO PAGE 1405.

Spiritual Gifts

12 Now about spiritual gifts, brothers, I do not want you to be ignorant. ²You know that when you were pagans, somehow or other you were influenced and led astray to mute idols. ³Therefore I tell you that no one who is speaking by the Spirit of God says, "Jesus be cursed," and no one can say, "Jesus is Lord," except by the Holy Spirit.

⁴There are different kinds of gifts, but the same Spirit. ⁵There are different kinds of service, but the same Lord. ⁶There are different kinds of working, but the same God works all of them in all men.

⁷Now to each one the manifestation of the Spirit is given for the common good. ⁸To one there is given through the Spirit the message of wisdom, to another the message of knowledge by means of the same Spirit, ⁹to another faith by the same Spirit, to another gifts of healing by that one Spirit, ¹⁰to another miraculous powers, to another prophecy, to another distinguishing between spirits, to another speaking in different kinds of tongues,ᵃ and to still another the interpretation of tongues.ᵃ ¹¹All these are the work of one and the same Spirit, and he gives them to each one, just as he determines.

One Body, Many Parts

¹²The body is a unit, though it is made up of many parts; and though all its parts are many, they form one body. So it is with Christ. ¹³For we were all baptized byᵇ one Spirit into one body—whether Jews or Greeks, slave or free—and we were all given the one Spirit to drink.

¹⁴Now the body is not made up of one part but of many. ¹⁵If the foot should say, "Because I am not a hand, I do not belong to the body," it would not for that reason cease to be part of the body. ¹⁶And if the ear should say, "Because I am not an eye, I do not belong to the body," it would not for that reason cease to be part of the body. ¹⁷If the whole body were an eye, where would the sense of hearing be? If the whole body were an ear, where would the sense of smell be? ¹⁸But in fact God has arranged the parts in the body, every one of them, just as he wanted them to be. ¹⁹If they were all one part, where would the body be? ²⁰As it is, there are many parts, but one body.

²¹The eye cannot say to the hand, "I don't need you!" And the head cannot say to the feet, "I don't need you!" ²²On the contrary, those parts of the body that seem to be weaker are indispensable, ²³and the parts that we think are less honorable we treat with special honor. And the parts that are unpresentable are treated with special modesty, ²⁴while our presentable parts need no special treatment. But God has combined the members of the body and has given greater honor to the parts that lacked it, ²⁵so that there should be no division in the body, but that its parts should have equal concern for each other. ²⁶If one part suffers, every part suffers with it; if one part is honored, every part rejoices with it.

²⁷Now you are the body of Christ, and each one of you is a part of it. ²⁸And in the church God has appointed first of all apostles, second prophets, third teachers, then workers of miracles, also those having gifts of healing, those able to help others, those with gifts of administration, and those speaking in different kinds of tongues. ²⁹Are all apostles? Are all prophets? Are all teachers? Do all work miracles? ³⁰Do all have gifts of healing? Do all speak in tonguesᶜ? Do all interpret? ³¹But eagerly desireᵈ the greater gifts.

Love

And now I will show you the most excellent way.

13 If I speak in the tonguesᵉ of men and of angels, but have not love, I am only a resounding gong or a clanging cymbal. ²If I have the gift of prophecy and can fathom all mysteries and all knowledge, and if I have a faith that can move mountains, but have not love, I am nothing. ³If I give all I possess to the poor and surrender my body to the flames,ᶠ but have not love, I gain nothing.

ᵃ10 Or languages; also in verse 28
ᵇ13 Or with; or in   ᶜ30 Or other languages
ᵈ31 Or But you are eagerly desiring
ᵉ1 Or languages   ᶠ3 Some early manuscripts body that I may boast

1 CORINTHIANS 12:1 – 3

Prayer, Experience and the Truth

12:3 NO ONE WHO IS SPEAKING BY THE SPIRIT OF GOD SAYS, "JESUS BE CURSED."

Of course, no one could ever say by the Spirit of God, "Jesus be cursed." It's ridiculous. Why state the obvious? Because Paul wants to use the obvious to make a not-so-obvious point.

First, a brief word about the pagan religious background of many of the Corinthian believers. They were surrounded by a variety of Greek mystery religions that placed a premium on religious experience as the test of being touched by God. They assumed that the practice of a religion would cause them to be "moved" by the deity being worshiped. Ecstasy and trances were the rule, and everybody expected them. The Greek word translated "influenced" in our text can also be translated "moved." Paul here is reminding the Corinthians that they were once "moved" in bad directions, "influenced and led astray to mute idols" (12:2). To be "moved" is not necessarily a good thing.

The not-so-obvious point for the Corinthians is, "Be careful that you do not infuse your old pagan assumptions into your newfound faith in Christ." Just because you feel something strongly in your heart does not mean God is speaking to you. Simply being "moved" in prayer is not self-authenticating. So Paul states the obvious: You may be "moved" very strongly to say something really foolish or evil, like "Jesus be cursed." But that would not make it true! The real test of authentic prayer is not "Is it moving?" but "Is it in spirit and in truth?" (see John 4:24).

Christian spirituality embraces both objective truth and subjective experience. But truth must govern experience. The apostles understood this when they insisted that they must be devoted not only to prayer, but also to the Word of God (see Acts 6:2–4).

It is also significant that Paul makes this critical point before he launches into a discussion of spiritual gifts. The overarching theme will be the purpose of spiritual gifts, which is the common good of the church (see 1 Corinthians 12:7). God doesn't give a Christian a spiritual gift so he or she can have a great religious experience. He gives the gift so all the people in the church can have a great experience—of encouragement and ministry. The real test of prayer, as with all God's gifts, is faithfulness to the truth and the building up of the church.

P R A Y :

Lord, be Lord of my experience.
Teach me to care more about you and your truth
when I pray than about how I feel when I pray.
Be the center of all my experience.

FOR YOUR NEXT DEVOTIONAL READING, GO TO PAGE 1406.

A Diary of Private Prayer

JOHN BAILLIE was one of the leading theologians of his time, holding teaching posts in Edinburgh, Toronto and at Union and Auburn Theological Seminaries in the United States. His two most important theological works are *The Knowledge of God* (1939) and *The Sense of the Presence of God* (published posthumously in 1962). But what he is more likely to be remembered for is his little *Diary of Private Prayer* (1936), which is said to have set up a chain of prayer around the globe. *Diary* is a 20th century devotional classic.

Baillie said there was never a time, from his childhood in Northern Scotland on, when he did not know the presence of God. Indeed, even the titles of his academic works show the impact of this lifelong gift. As a result, Baillie was one of those rare persons who combined faith and reason with grace and ease. His facility with the English language also made him an eminently quotable author:

> The evidence for Christian truth is not exhaustive, but it is sufficient. Too often, Christianity has not been tried and found wanting—it has been found demanding, and not tried.[2]

> The final reality, and the ultimate fact of our total situation to which we need to be adjusted, is God. That indeed would be my definition of God: God is he with whom we have ultimately to do, the final reality to which we have to face up, and with whom we have, in the last resort, to reckon.[3]

The following prayer is taken from *Diary*, which is arranged in pairs of prayers, one for morning and one for evening, each day for thirty-one days. This is the prayer for the morning of the fifth day. Read it slowly, and pray it as though it were your own.

PRAY:

God of my forefathers, I cry unto thee. Thou hast been the refuge
of good and wise men in every generation ... Through
all ages thou hast been the Lord and giver of life, the source
of all knowledge, the fountain of all goodness.
The patriarchs trusted thee and were not put to shame:
The prophets sought thee and thou didst commit thy word to their lips:
The psalmists rejoiced in thee and thou wert present in their song:
The apostles waited upon thee and they were filled
with thy Holy Spirit:
The martyrs called upon thee and thou wert with
them in the midst of the flame:
This poor man cried, and the Lord heard him, and
saved him out of all his troubles ...
Forbid it, Holy Lord, that I should fail to profit by these
great memories of the ages that are gone by, or to enter
into the glorious inheritance which thou hast prepared for me;
through Jesus Christ my Lord. Amen.[4]

MEMORIZE:

Therefore, since we are surrounded by such a great
cloud of witnesses, let us throw off everything that hinders
and the sin that so easily entangles, and let us run with
perseverance the race marked out for us. Let us fix our eyes
on Jesus, the author and perfecter of our faith, who for the joy set
before him endured the cross, scorning its shame, and sat down
at the right hand of the throne of God. HEBREWS 12:1–2

FOR YOUR NEXT DEVOTIONAL READING, GO TO PAGE 1408.

1 CORINTHIANS 13

Love: the Fuel and Goal of Prayer

13:13 "THE GREATEST OF THESE IS LOVE."

If Scripture were the Himalayas, this chapter could qualify as Mt. Everest. By any reckoning, it is one of the highest points in the entire Bible, a place to stand and understand all the rest. What Paul said is true: There are "three great lasting qualities"[5] in this life—faith, hope and love—but the greatest of these is love.

Some scholars believe 1 Corinthians 13 was originally a song that Paul inserted in his letter to move his readers to sing it. It has been put to music, and if you know a tune to sing it to, thank God that you do, because singing can be another way to pray. For love is the fuel and goal of prayer.

Prayer is fueled by appreciation for the God to whom we speak. Try reading this chapter aloud, substituting "God" for "love." Windows and doors can fly open in your mind as you do. You may find yourself exclaiming, "So this is the God I'm speaking to! How wonderful he is! Who wouldn't be delighted to speak with him for hours?" Our minds can do funny things with God, imagining him to an abstraction or a peevish old man. Neither view inspires prayer. First Corinthians 13 is the antidote to a shrunken imagination.

Or take this chapter a step further: Add the phrase "with me" or "to me." For instance, instead of praying, "Love is patient," pray, "God is patient with me." Do you sometimes come to prayer feeling dull and cold inside, fearful and apprehensive? God is patient with you. He is not irritated that you are dull and lifeless. Let him love you for a while. Don't try to speak until you've let his love warm your heart and banish your fear. God is patient with you. He is not easily angered. He keeps no record of wrongs.

Love is the goal of all prayer. Jesus told us to pray that God's name be hallowed and that his rule be established on earth. How do we hallow his name? By loving him with our whole being and loving our neighbors as ourselves. First Corinthians 13 describes what that looks like. What does God's kingdom look like? And what is his will for all the earth? Again, 1 Corinthians 13 will tell you how to pray for those things.

Open this chapter and use it as a prayer agenda. Pray the qualities of love into the people you pray for, into your church, your neighbors and the world. Ask God to work in those for whom you pray the greatest thing in the world—love.

PRAY:

Gracious Father, warm my heart to your tender love.
Work your love in me. Let your love reign over all the earth.

———

FOR YOUR NEXT DEVOTIONAL READING, GO TO PAGE 1410.

[4]Love is patient, love is kind. It does not envy, it does not boast, it is not proud. [5]It is not rude, it is not self-seeking, it is not easily angered, it keeps no record of wrongs. [6]Love does not delight in evil but rejoices with the truth. [7]It always protects, always trusts, always hopes, always perseveres.

[8]Love never fails. But where there are prophecies, they will cease; where there are tongues, they will be stilled; where there is knowledge, it will pass away. [9]For we know in part and we prophesy in part, [10]but when perfection comes, the imperfect disappears. [11]When I was a child, I talked like a child, I thought like a child, I reasoned like a child. When I became a man, I put childish ways behind me. [12]Now we see but a poor reflection as in a mirror; then we shall see face to face. Now I know in part; then I shall know fully, even as I am fully known.

[13]And now these three remain: faith, hope and love. But the greatest of these is love.

Gifts of Prophecy and Tongues

14 Follow the way of love and eagerly desire spiritual gifts, especially the gift of prophecy. [2]For anyone who speaks in a tongue[a] does not speak to men but to God. Indeed, no one understands him; he utters mysteries with his spirit.[b] [3]But everyone who prophesies speaks to men for their strengthening, encouragement and comfort. [4]He who speaks in a tongue edifies himself, but he who prophesies edifies the church. [5]I would like every one of you to speak in tongues,[c] but I would rather have you prophesy. He who prophesies is greater than one who speaks in tongues,[c] unless he interprets, so that the church may be edified.

[6]Now, brothers, if I come to you and speak in tongues, what good will I be to you, unless I bring you some revelation or knowledge or prophecy or word of instruction? [7]Even in the case of lifeless things that make sounds, such as the flute or harp, how will anyone know what tune is being played unless there is a distinction in the notes? [8]Again, if the trumpet does not sound a clear call, who will get ready for battle? [9]So it is with you. Unless you speak intelligible words

with your tongue, how will anyone know what you are saying? You will just be speaking into the air. [10]Undoubtedly there are all sorts of languages in the world, yet none of them is without meaning. [11]If then I do not grasp the meaning of what someone is saying, I am a foreigner to the speaker, and he is a foreigner to me. [12]So it is with you. Since you are eager to have spiritual gifts, try to excel in gifts that build up the church.

[13]For this reason anyone who speaks in a tongue should pray that he may interpret what he says. [14]For if I pray in a

> FOR this reason anyone who speaks in a tongue should pray that he may interpret what he says.
>
> 1 CORINTHIANS 14:13

tongue, my spirit prays, but my mind is unfruitful. [15]So what shall I do? I will pray with my spirit, but I will also pray with my mind; I will sing with my spirit, but I will also sing with my mind. [16]If you are praising God with your spirit, how can one who finds himself among those who do not understand[d] say "Amen" to your thanksgiving, since he does not know what you are saying? [17]You may be giving thanks well enough, but the other man is not edified. [18]I thank God that I speak in tongues more than all of you. [19]But in the church I would rather speak five intelligible words to instruct others than ten thousand words in a tongue.

[20]Brothers, stop thinking like children. In regard to evil be infants, but in your thinking be adults. [21]In the Law it is written:

"Through men of strange tongues
    and through the lips of foreigners
I will speak to this people,
    but even then they will not listen
        to me,"[e]

says the Lord.

[22]Tongues, then, are a sign, not for believers but for unbelievers; prophecy,

[a]2 Or another language; also in verses 4, 13, 14, 19, 26 and 27   [b]2 Or by the Spirit
[c]5 Or other languages; also in verses 6, 18, 22, 23 and 39   [d]16 Or among the inquirers
[e]21 Isaiah 28:11,12

however, is for believers, not for unbelievers. ²³So if the whole church comes together and everyone speaks in tongues, and some who do not understand*ᵃ* or some unbelievers come in, will they not say that you are out of your mind? ²⁴But if an unbeliever or someone who does not understand*ᵇ* comes in while everybody is

prophesying, he will be convinced by all that he is a sinner and will be judged by all, ²⁵and the secrets of his heart will be laid bare. So he will fall down and worship God, exclaiming, "God is really among you!"

ᵃ23 Or *some inquirers*   *ᵇ24* Or *or some inquirer*

---

1 CORINTHIANS 14:13–17

Pray With Your Mind, Too

14:15 I WILL PRAY WITH MY SPIRIT, BUT I WILL ALSO PRAY WITH MY MIND.

Bertrand Russell, the atheist philosopher, said, "Most Christians would rather be caught dead than thinking, and most are." That's unfair, but there is enough truth in it to cause us to pause and consider what Paul meant when he wrote, "So what shall I do? I will pray with my spirit, but I will also pray with my mind; I will sing with my spirit, but I will also sing with my mind" (14:15).

What was the apostle driving at? At the very least, he was trying to be obedient to the Lord Jesus' command to love God with all his heart, soul and *mind* (see Matthew 22:37). A mind is a terrible thing to waste by restricting its use to the things of this earth. Employ it in the greatest of uses—the worship of the God who made the mind!

Paul was also addressing the Corinthians' over-emphasis on the ecstatic and non-rational in worship. Some of this was a holdover from their pagan past in the Greek mystery cults (see devotion on 1 Corinthians 12:1–3). But some of it was just plain selfishness and laziness.

The selfish part was their absorption in private subjective experience. In a service of worship, a few individuals might be experiencing profoundly moving intimations of the presence of God. But the church is not a collection of individuals; it is the body of Christ. If the private experience of an individual doesn't ultimately go public and build up others, then it is selfish experience; and perhaps it is not of God at all, or it's an abuse of God's gifts.

This is where the mind is so important. Good thinking leads to clear communication. If private experience is going to go public and encourage others, it must be spoken. Language means logic and syntax, words and ideas. Paul said what he said about praying and singing with his mind in the context of public worship (see 14:5,12,19,26); so one of the ways we can love our neighbor is to think well about our faith, so we can speak well about our faith. Anything less is laziness and not love at all.

PRAY:

Father in heaven! I will praise you with my mind, too. Teach me
to think well so I can speak well to your greater glory and
the encouragement of your people.

———

FOR YOUR NEXT DEVOTIONAL READING, GO TO PAGE 1416.

Orderly Worship

²⁶What then shall we say, brothers? When you come together, everyone has a hymn, or a word of instruction, a revelation, a tongue or an interpretation. All of these must be done for the strengthening of the church. ²⁷If anyone speaks in a tongue, two—or at the most three—should speak, one at a time, and someone must interpret. ²⁸If there is no interpreter, the speaker should keep quiet in the church and speak to himself and God.

²⁹Two or three prophets should speak, and the others should weigh carefully what is said. ³⁰And if a revelation comes to someone who is sitting down, the first speaker should stop. ³¹For you can all prophesy in turn so that everyone may be instructed and encouraged. ³²The spirits of prophets are subject to the control of prophets. ³³For God is not a God of disorder but of peace.

As in all the congregations of the saints, ³⁴women should remain silent in the churches. They are not allowed to speak, but must be in submission, as the Law says. ³⁵If they want to inquire about something, they should ask their own husbands at home; for it is disgraceful for a woman to speak in the church.

³⁶Did the word of God originate with you? Or are you the only people it has reached? ³⁷If anybody thinks he is a prophet or spiritually gifted, let him acknowledge that what I am writing to you is the Lord's command. ³⁸If he ignores this, he himself will be ignored.^a

³⁹Therefore, my brothers, be eager to prophesy, and do not forbid speaking in tongues. ⁴⁰But everything should be done in a fitting and orderly way.

The Resurrection of Christ

15 Now, brothers, I want to remind you of the gospel I preached to you, which you received and on which you have taken your stand. ²By this gospel you are saved, if you hold firmly to the word I preached to you. Otherwise, you have believed in vain.

³For what I received I passed on to you as of first importance^b: that Christ died for our sins according to the Scriptures, ⁴that he was buried, that he was raised on the third day according to the Scriptures, ⁵and that he appeared to Peter,^c and then to the Twelve. ⁶After that, he appeared to more than five hundred of the brothers at the same time, most of whom are still living, though some have fallen asleep. ⁷Then he appeared to James, then to all the apostles, ⁸and last of all he appeared to me also, as to one abnormally born.

⁹For I am the least of the apostles and do not even deserve to be called an apostle, because I persecuted the church of God. ¹⁰But by the grace of God I am what I am, and his grace to me was not without effect. No, I worked harder than all of them—yet not I, but the grace of God that was with me. ¹¹Whether, then, it was I or they, this is what we preach, and this is what you believed.

The Resurrection of the Dead

¹²But if it is preached that Christ has been raised from the dead, how can some of you say that there is no resurrection of the dead? ¹³If there is no resurrection of the dead, then not even Christ has been raised. ¹⁴And if Christ has not been raised, our preaching is useless and so is your faith. ¹⁵More than that, we are then found to be false witnesses about God, for we have testified about God that he raised Christ from the dead. But he did not raise him if in fact the dead are not raised. ¹⁶For if the dead are not raised, then Christ has not been raised either. ¹⁷And if Christ has not been raised, your faith is futile; you are still in your sins. ¹⁸Then those also who have fallen asleep in Christ are lost. ¹⁹If only for this life we have hope in Christ, we are to be pitied more than all men.

²⁰But Christ has indeed been raised from the dead, the firstfruits of those who have fallen asleep. ²¹For since death came through a man, the resurrection of the dead comes also through a man. ²²For as in Adam all die, so in Christ all will be made alive. ²³But each in his own turn: Christ, the firstfruits; then, when he comes, those who belong to him. ²⁴Then the end will come, when he hands over

^a38 Some manuscripts *If he is ignorant of this, let him be ignorant*   ^b3 Or *you at the first*   ^c5 Greek *Cephas*

the kingdom to God the Father after he has destroyed all dominion, authority and power. 25For he must reign until he has put all his enemies under his feet. 26The last enemy to be destroyed is death. 27For he "has put everything under his feet."[a] Now when it says that "everything" has been put under him, it is clear that this does not include God himself, who put everything under Christ. 28When he has done this, then the Son himself will be made subject to him who put everything under him, so that God may be all in all.

29Now if there is no resurrection, what will those do who are baptized for the dead? If the dead are not raised at all, why are people baptized for them? 30And as for us, why do we endanger ourselves every hour? 31I die every day—I mean that, brothers—just as surely as I glory over you in Christ Jesus our Lord. 32If I fought wild beasts in Ephesus for merely human reasons, what have I gained? If the dead are not raised,

"Let us eat and drink,
    for tomorrow we die."[b]

33Do not be misled: "Bad company corrupts good character." 34Come back to your senses as you ought, and stop sinning; for there are some who are ignorant of God—I say this to your shame.

The Resurrection Body

35But someone may ask, "How are the dead raised? With what kind of body will they come?" 36How foolish! What you sow does not come to life unless it dies. 37When you sow, you do not plant the body that will be, but just a seed, perhaps of wheat or of something else. 38But God gives it a body as he has determined, and to each kind of seed he gives its own body. 39All flesh is not the same: Men have one kind of flesh, animals have another, birds another and fish another. 40There are also heavenly bodies and there are earthly bodies; but the splendor of the heavenly bodies is one kind, and the splendor of the earthly bodies is another. 41The sun has one kind of splendor, the moon another and the stars another; and star differs from star in splendor.

42So will it be with the resurrection of the dead. The body that is sown is perishable, it is raised imperishable; 43it is sown in dishonor, it is raised in glory; it is sown in weakness, it is raised in power; 44it is sown a natural body, it is raised a spiritual body.

If there is a natural body, there is also a spiritual body. 45So it is written: "The first man Adam became a living being"[c]; the last Adam, a life-giving spirit. 46The spiritual did not come first, but the natural, and after that the spiritual. 47The first man was of the dust of the earth, the second man from heaven. 48As was the earthly man, so are those who are of the earth; and as is the man from heaven, so also are those who are of heaven. 49And just as we have borne the likeness of the earthly man, so shall we[d] bear the likeness of the man from heaven.

50I declare to you, brothers, that flesh and blood cannot inherit the kingdom of God, nor does the perishable inherit the imperishable. 51Listen, I tell you a mystery: We will not all sleep, but we will all be changed— 52in a flash, in the twinkling of an eye, at the last trumpet. For the trumpet will sound, the dead will be raised imperishable, and we will be changed. 53For the perishable must clothe itself with the imperishable, and the mortal with immortality. 54When the perishable has been clothed with the imperishable, and the mortal with immortality, then the saying that is written will come true: "Death has been swallowed up in victory."[e]

55 "Where, O death, is your victory?
    Where, O death, is your sting?"[f]

56The sting of death is sin, and the power of sin is the law. 57But thanks be to God! He gives us the victory through our Lord Jesus Christ.

58Therefore, my dear brothers, stand firm. Let nothing move you. Always give

> BUT thanks be to God! He gives us the
> victory through our Lord Jesus Christ.
>
> 1 CORINTHIANS 15:57

[a]27 Psalm 8:6   [b]32 Isaiah 22:13
[c]45 Gen. 2:7   [d]49 Some early manuscripts so
let us   [e]54 Isaiah 25:8   [f]55 Hosea 13:14

yourselves fully to the work of the Lord, because you know that your labor in the Lord is not in vain.

The Collection for God's People

16 Now about the collection for God's people: Do what I told the Galatian churches to do. [2]On the first day of every week, each one of you should set aside a sum of money in keeping with his income, saving it up, so that when I come no collections will have to be made. [3]Then, when I arrive, I will give letters of introduction to the men you approve and send them with your gift to Jerusalem. [4]If it seems advisable for me to go also, they will accompany me.

Personal Requests

[5]After I go through Macedonia, I will come to you—for I will be going through Macedonia. [6]Perhaps I will stay with you awhile, or even spend the winter, so that you can help me on my journey, wherever I go. [7]I do not want to see you now and make only a passing visit; I hope to spend some time with you, if the Lord permits. [8]But I will stay on at Ephesus until Pentecost, [9]because a great door for effective work has opened to me, and there are many who oppose me.

> *Just pray for a tough hide and a tender heart.*
>
> RUTH GRAHAM

[10]If Timothy comes, see to it that he has nothing to fear while he is with you, for he is carrying on the work of the Lord, just as I am. [11]No one, then, should refuse to accept him. Send him on his way in peace so that he may return to me. I am expecting him along with the brothers.

[12]Now about our brother Apollos: I strongly urged him to go to you with the brothers. He was quite unwilling to go now, but he will go when he has the opportunity.

[13]Be on your guard; stand firm in the faith; be men of courage; be strong. [14]Do everything in love.

[15]You know that the household of Stephanas were the first converts in Achaia, and they have devoted themselves to the service of the saints. I urge you, brothers, [16]to submit to such as these and to everyone who joins in the work, and labors at it. [17]I was glad when Stephanas, Fortunatus and Achaicus arrived, because they have supplied what was lacking from you. [18]For they refreshed my spirit and yours also. Such men deserve recognition.

Final Greetings

[19]The churches in the province of Asia send you greetings. Aquila and Priscilla[a] greet you warmly in the Lord, and so does the church that meets at their house. [20]All the brothers here send you greetings. Greet one another with a holy kiss.

[21]I, Paul, write this greeting in my own hand.

[22]If anyone does not love the Lord—a curse be on him. Come, O Lord[b]!

[23]The grace of the Lord Jesus be with you.

[24]My love to all of you in Christ Jesus. Amen.[c]

---

[a]19 Greek *Prisca*, a variant of *Priscilla*
[b]22 In Aramaic the expression *Come, O Lord* is *Marana tha.*   [c]24 Some manuscripts do not have *Amen.*

2 Corinthians

THIS SECOND letter to the Corinthians is further evidence of Paul's love and concern for the Corinthian church. As noted in the Introduction to 1 Corinthians, Paul had his hands full with a variety of problems related to the Corinthian church. Yet Paul persevered in prayer for the Corinthians.

Paul's difficult relationship with the Corinthians mirrors the difficulties he faced in ministry to all the churches. In chapter 6 he describes the struggles he has endured in the service of God (see 6:3–13). Yet Paul continued to be encouraged by any growth or triumph he could find in the lives of the church members: "I have great confidence in you; I take great pride in you. I am greatly encouraged; in all our troubles my joy knows no bounds ... Godly sorrow brings repentance that leads to salvation" (7:4,10). Paul found joy in the midst of the struggles in his own life and the challenges faced by his need to discipline the Corinthians. Out of his deep hurt and discouragement in ministry came a witness to the power of God perfected in human weakness (see 12:7–10).

"MY GRACE IS SUFFICIENT FOR YOU, FOR MY POWER IS MADE PERFECT IN WEAKNESS." (12:9)

1 Paul, an apostle of Christ Jesus by the will of God, and Timothy our brother,

To the church of God in Corinth, together with all the saints throughout Achaia:

[2]Grace and peace to you from God our Father and the Lord Jesus Christ.

The God of All Comfort

[3]Praise be to the God and Father of our Lord Jesus Christ, the Father of compassion and the God of all comfort, [4]who comforts us in all our troubles, so that we can comfort those in any trouble with the comfort we ourselves have received from God. [5]For just as the sufferings of Christ flow over into our lives, so also through Christ our comfort overflows. [6]If we are distressed, it is for your comfort and salvation; if we are comforted, it is for your comfort, which produces in you patient endurance of the same sufferings we suffer. [7]And our hope for you is firm, because we know that just as you share in our sufferings, so also you share in our comfort.

[8]We do not want you to be uninformed, brothers, about the hardships we suffered in the province of Asia. We were under great pressure, far beyond our ability to endure, so that we despaired even of life. [9]Indeed, in our hearts we felt the sentence of death. But this happened that we might not rely on ourselves but on God, who raises the dead. [10]He has delivered us from such a deadly peril, and he will deliver us. On him we have set our hope that he will continue to deliver us, [11]as you help us by your prayers. Then many will give thanks on our[a] behalf for the gracious favor granted us in answer to the prayers of many.

Paul's Change of Plans

[12]Now this is our boast: Our conscience testifies that we have conducted ourselves in the world, and especially in our relations with you, in the holiness and sincerity that are from God. We have done so not according to worldly wisdom but according to God's grace. [13]For we do not write you anything you cannot read or understand. And I hope that, [14]as you have understood us in part, you will come to understand fully that you can boast of us just as we will boast of you in the day of the Lord Jesus.

[15]Because I was confident of this, I planned to visit you first so that you might benefit twice. [16]I planned to visit you on my way to Macedonia and to come back to you from Macedonia, and then to have you send me on my way to Judea. [17]When I planned this, did I do it lightly? Or do I make my plans in a worldly manner so that in the same breath I say, "Yes, yes" and "No, no"?

[18]But as surely as God is faithful, our message to you is not "Yes" and "No." [19]For the Son of God, Jesus Christ, who was preached among you by me and Silas[b] and Timothy, was not "Yes" and "No," but in him it has always been "Yes." [20]For no matter how many promises God has made, they are "Yes" in Christ. And so through him the "Amen" is spoken by us to the glory of God. [21]Now it is God who makes both us and you stand firm in Christ. He anointed us, [22]set his seal of ownership on us, and put his Spirit in our hearts as a deposit, guaranteeing what is to come.

[23]I call God as my witness that it was in order to spare you that I did not return to Corinth. [24]Not that we lord it over your faith, but we work with you for your joy, because it is by faith you stand firm.

2 [1]So I made up my mind that I would not make another painful visit to you. [2]For if I grieve you, who is left to make me glad but you whom I have grieved? [3]I wrote as I did so that when I came I should not be distressed by those who ought to make me rejoice. I had confidence in all of you, that you would all share my joy. [4]For I wrote you out of great distress and anguish of heart and with many tears, not to grieve you but to let you know the depth of my love for you.

> ❝ Courage is fear that has said its prayers. ❞
>
> DOROTHY BERNARD

[a]11 Many manuscripts your   [b]19 Greek Silvanus, a variant of Silas

The God of All Comfort

1:5 "FOR JUST AS THE SUFFERINGS OF CHRIST FLOW OVER INTO OUR LIVES, SO ALSO THROUGH CHRIST OUR COMFORT OVERFLOWS."

> What a friend we have in Jesus,
> All our sins and griefs to bear!
> What a privilege to carry
> Everything to God in prayer!

Take all your troubles to God, for he is the "Father of compassion and the God of all comfort" (1:3). Compassion is God's nature; to comfort is his pleasure. And know, as you pour out your heart, what he will do with your troubles. Sometimes he will take them away, but that is not usually the case. He has a greater purpose: He will redeem your suffering from meaninglessness by making it useful for others "so that we can comfort those in any trouble with the comfort we ourselves have received from God" (verse 4). The worst thing that suffering can do is isolate us. God's comfort turns the suffering into a bond with others who suffer.

> O what peace we often forfeit,
> O what needless pain we bear,
> All because we do not carry
> Everything to God in prayer.

What is needless pain? It is unnecessary pain. It is burden enough to carry the trouble of life; that is a given. But the burden becomes intolerably heavy when we add to it the needless pain of isolation. Take your troubles to God; he will turn your suffering into a fellowship by leading you to comfort others with the comfort he has given you. You probably already know this is true. Have you ever gone to comfort someone only to be comforted by that person instead? God had been there ahead of you.

Let God work with your troubles and behold a miracle: Within your pain emerges an inexplicable joy. Your suffering isn't just yours anymore—it is Christ's, too! "For just as the sufferings of Christ flow over into our lives, so also through Christ our comfort overflows" (verse 5). Let your trouble forge a bond with Jesus.

> Can we find a friend so faithful
> Who will all our sorrows share?
> Jesus knows our every weakness,
> Take it to the Lord in prayer.[1]

PRAY:

Father of compassion and God of all comfort—thank you
for the bond with you that comes from the sufferings and
comfort of Christ in my life, and for the bond that comes with
others when I share with them the gift of your comfort.

FOR YOUR NEXT DEVOTIONAL READING, GO TO PAGE 1418.

Forgiveness for the Sinner

[5] If anyone has caused grief, he has not so much grieved me as he has grieved all of you, to some extent—not to put it too severely. [6] The punishment inflicted on him by the majority is sufficient for him. [7] Now instead, you ought to forgive and comfort him, so that he will not be overwhelmed by excessive sorrow. [8] I urge you, therefore, to reaffirm your love for him. [9] The reason I wrote you was to see if you would stand the test and be obedient in everything. [10] If you forgive anyone, I also forgive him. And what I have forgiven—if there was anything to forgive—I have forgiven in the sight of Christ for your sake, [11] in order that Satan might not outwit us. For we are not unaware of his schemes.

Ministers of the New Covenant

[12] Now when I went to Troas to preach the gospel of Christ and found that the Lord had opened a door for me, [13] I still had no peace of mind, because I did not find my brother Titus there. So I said good-by to them and went on to Macedonia.

[14] But thanks be to God, who always leads us in triumphal procession in Christ and through us spreads everywhere the fragrance of the knowledge of him. [15] For we are to God the aroma of Christ among those who are being saved and those who are perishing. [16] To the one we are the smell of death; to the other, the fragrance of life. And who is equal to such a task? [17] Unlike so many, we do not peddle the word of God for profit. On the contrary, in Christ we speak before God with sincerity, like men sent from God.

3 Are we beginning to commend ourselves again? Or do we need, like some people, letters of recommendation to you or from you? [2] You yourselves are our letter, written on our hearts, known and read by everybody. [3] You show that you are a letter from Christ, the result of our ministry, written not with ink but with the Spirit of the living God, not on tablets of stone but on tablets of human hearts.

[4] Such confidence as this is ours through Christ before God. [5] Not that we are competent in ourselves to claim anything for ourselves, but our competence comes from God. [6] He has made us competent as ministers of a new covenant—not of the letter but of the Spirit; for the letter kills, but the Spirit gives life.

The Glory of the New Covenant

[7] Now if the ministry that brought death, which was engraved in letters on stone, came with glory, so that the Israelites could not look steadily at the face of Moses because of its glory, fading though it was, [8] will not the ministry of the Spirit be even more glorious? [9] If the ministry that condemns men is glorious, how much more glorious is the ministry that brings righteousness! [10] For what was glorious has no glory now in comparison with the surpassing glory. [11] And if what was fading away came with glory, how much greater is the glory of that which lasts!

[12] Therefore, since we have such a hope, we are very bold. [13] We are not like Moses, who would put a veil over his face to keep the Israelites from gazing at it while the radiance was fading away. [14] But their minds were made dull, for to this day the same veil remains when the old covenant is read. It has not been removed, because only in Christ is it taken away. [15] Even to this day when Moses is read, a veil covers their hearts. [16] But whenever anyone turns to the Lord, the veil is taken away. [17] Now the Lord is the Spirit, and where the Spirit of the Lord is, there is freedom. [18] And we, who with unveiled faces all reflect[a] the Lord's glory, are being transformed into his likeness with ever-increasing glory, which comes from the Lord, who is the Spirit.

Treasures in Jars of Clay

4 Therefore, since through God's mercy we have this ministry, we do not lose heart. [2] Rather, we have renounced secret and shameful ways; we do not use deception, nor do we distort the word of God. On the contrary, by setting forth the truth plainly we commend ourselves to every man's conscience in the sight of

[a] 18 Or contemplate

God. ³And even if our gospel is veiled, it is veiled to those who are perishing. ⁴The god of this age has blinded the minds of unbelievers, so that they cannot see the light of the gospel of the glory of Christ, who is the image of God. ⁵For we do not preach ourselves, but Jesus Christ as Lord, and ourselves as your servants for Jesus' sake. ⁶For God, who said, "Let light shine out of darkness,"ᵃ made his light shine in our hearts to give us the light of the knowledge of the glory of God in the face of Christ.

⁷But we have this treasure in jars of

ᵃ6 Gen. 1:3

---

2 CORINTHIANS 3:4–6

Our True Confidence in Prayer

3:4 "SUCH CONFIDENCE AS THIS IS OURS THROUGH CHRIST BEFORE GOD."

"Who do you think you are?" That was the kind of mocking question implicit in the words of Paul's critics at Corinth. Paul has spoken to them as though he thought he was somebody, but he seemed like nobody. But it's not a bad question. Who do any of us think we are who claim to have a message from God that will change human lives? "Who do I think I am?" That is the question every Christian should ask. Do we really believe we have any authority or power to speak so confidently about God?

Paul was very clear about this issue. He had no confidence in himself but every confidence "through Christ before God" (3:4). As for competence, the question of whether he had any was irrelevant because whatever competence anyone has comes from God alone (see verse 5). In his first letter, Paul put the question of competence back in the lap of his critics: "For who makes you different from anyone else? What do you have that you did not receive? And if you did receive it, why do you boast as though you did not?" (1 Corinthians 4:7). Everything we have comes from God; every ability, every gift. We came into the world naked; we will leave the world naked. The Lord gave, and we will have to give it back, all of it; may the name of the Lord be praised (see Job 1:21). Yes, praise the name of the *Lord*, not some apostle, evangelist or religious authority.

That's why we pray. Our confidence and competence come from God alone. Even the gifts and abilities we were given at birth or through education and life experience are of no use without God's blessing. Again, that's why we pray—because life comes, not from us, but from the Spirit (see 2 Corinthians 3:6). Spiritual realities being what they are, we have no cause for confidence in ourselves on one hand and no cause for fear on the other. But we have every cause to pray because our confidence and competence come from God alone.

PRAY:

Almighty God, yours alone is the kingdom and the power
and the glory. My confidence and competence are in you alone.
May it always be, so that you, not I, should receive all the glory
for the great things you have done through me.

FOR YOUR NEXT DEVOTIONAL READING, GO TO PAGE 1419.

clay to show that this all-surpassing power is from God and not from us. ⁸We are hard pressed on every side, but not crushed; perplexed, but not in despair; ⁹persecuted, but not abandoned; struck down, but not destroyed. ¹⁰We always carry around in our body the death of Jesus, so that the life of Jesus may also be revealed in our body. ¹¹For we who are alive are always being given over to death for Jesus' sake, so that his life may be revealed in our mortal body. ¹²So then, death is at work in us, but life is at work in you.

{FRIDAY}

2 CORINTHIANS 3:7–18

The Glory of Prayer

3:18 "WE ... ALL REFLECT THE LORD'S GLORY."

There is an old children's Sunday school song that goes, "Climb, climb up sunshine mountain, faces all aglow." The theology of the song was better than anyone knew or even intended. For that was exactly what happened to Moses whenever he climbed up Mount Sinai to meet with God. When he came back down the mountain into the Israelite camp, "his face was radiant because he had spoken with the LORD" (Exodus 34:29). To prevent the people from seeing the radiance fade away, Moses put a veil over his face (see Exodus 34:33–35; 2 Corinthians 3:13). That was the way it was in the days of the Old Covenant, before Christ.

Now the veil is off! And not just off the face of Moses but off the face of every believer. Through Jesus, we all have the privilege of standing in the presence of the living God. And we who stand in God's presence both reflect his glory and "are being transformed into his likeness with ever-increasing glory" (2 Corinthians 3:18). Our "glow" is better than Moses' because his faded and ours won't.

This is a great passage on prayer, even though the actual word "prayer" doesn't appear in it. The Bible says that when Moses went up Sinai, "he entered the LORD's presence to speak with him" (Exodus 34:34). In comparing our experience of the Holy Spirit with Moses' experience on Sinai, Paul makes a powerful connection with prayer and its effects on those who pray.

What are the effects of prayer? In the words of John Piper, "seeing is becoming." We become what we attentively and lovingly gaze at. When what we gaze at is someone as brightly glorious and splendid as God, we cannot help but be changed by what we see. This is the secret of prayer and of Christian growth: Ninety percent is just showing up. To simply come into God's presence in the name of his Son is to be deeply affected. Archimedes said, "Give me a place to stand, and I will move the world." This is the place to stand! The world is changed by those who will reflect and be transformed by the glory of God.

PRAY:

"My heart says of you, 'Seek his face!' Your face, LORD,
I will seek" (Psalm 27:8). Make your face shine on me. Change me,
with ever-increasing glory, to be more like your Son.

FOR YOUR NEXT DEVOTIONAL READING, GO TO PAGE 1420.

Pour Out Your Heart

"POUR OUT your heart like water in the presence of the Lord. Lift up your hands to him for the lives of your children, who faint from hunger at the head of every street" (Lamentations 2:19). The original context of these words was the terrible siege and destruction of Jerusalem in the sixth century B.C., which saw, among many other horrors, starving children and their starving mothers reduced to cannibalism. But the call to "pour out your heart like water ... for the lives of your children" has a certain universality to it. Parents in every time and place have been moved to pour out their hearts like water and cry out to God for the sake of their children's lives.

Fern Nichols was moved to pray in the fall of 1984 when her two oldest children were about to go off to what she called the "jaws of junior high peer pressure" in Abbotsford, British Columbia. She asked a friend to pray with her, but soon five other mothers were gathered around her kitchen table to pray. They prayed that God would protect their children spiritually and physically. They prayed for their children's teachers. They also prayed that anyone trying to sell drugs on campus would be caught. Three months later three men were arrested for selling marijuana, and a house only a block from the school was found to be a main distribution center for marijuana in the area.

Word got out about the dramatic answers to their prayers, and by the end of the year there was a group of mothers pouring out their hearts for the lives of their children for every school in the district. The ministry took on a name, "Moms in Touch," and when the Nichols moved to Poway, California, the next year the movement spread to the high school there.

Since then, Moms in Touch has added the word "International" and can be found in 90 countries. In North America there are at least 150,000 moms in 25,000 groups praying for children in 34,000 schools. Without political agitation or public confrontation, the lives of thousands in schools have been quietly and gently changed—as have many of their schools.

Nichols' vision for each prayer meeting includes a simple format and a strong grounding in Scripture. Each MITI prayer meeting is to start promptly on time and to last an hour. These meetings are to be for prayer only; no refreshments are to be served to distract the participants from the precious time allotted for prayer. The pray-ers learn to pray Scripture into the lives of their children and their schools.

So many prayer meetings founder because there is no vision, no clear sense of purpose and therefore no strong motivation to pray. Who could be more motivated, passionate and visionary than mothers are for the well-being of their children?

PRAY:

Holy Father! We love because you first loved us; and whatever
love we have for the children in our lives is but an imperfect
reflection of your love. So we cry out for you to keep them safe from
all evil and to make them secure in your powerful, saving love.

MEMORIZE:

Arise, cry out in the night, as the watches of the night begin;
pour out your heart like water in the presence of the Lord. Lift up
your hands to him for the lives of your children, who faint from
hunger at the head of every street. LAMENTATIONS 2:19

FOR YOUR NEXT DEVOTIONAL READING, GO TO PAGE 1423.

[13]It is written: "I believed; therefore I have spoken."[a] With that same spirit of faith we also believe and therefore speak, [14]because we know that the one who raised the Lord Jesus from the dead will also raise us with Jesus and present us with you in his presence. [15]All this is for your benefit, so that the grace that is reaching more and more people may cause thanksgiving to overflow to the glory of God.

[16]Therefore we do not lose heart. Though outwardly we are wasting away, yet inwardly we are being renewed day by day. [17]For our light and momentary troubles are achieving for us an eternal glory that far outweighs them all. [18]So we fix our eyes not on what is seen, but on what is unseen. For what is seen is temporary, but what is unseen is eternal.

Our Heavenly Dwelling

5 Now we know that if the earthly tent we live in is destroyed, we have a building from God, an eternal house in heaven, not built by human hands. [2]Meanwhile we groan, longing to be clothed with our heavenly dwelling, [3]because when we are clothed, we will not be found naked. [4]For while we are in this tent, we groan and are burdened, because we do not wish to be unclothed but to be clothed with our heavenly dwelling, so that what is mortal may be swallowed up by life. [5]Now it is God who has made us for this very purpose and has given us the Spirit as a deposit, guaranteeing what is to come.

[6]Therefore we are always confident and know that as long as we are at home in the body we are away from the Lord. [7]We live by faith, not by sight. [8]We are confident, I say, and would prefer to be away from the body and at home with the Lord. [9]So we make it our goal to please him, whether we are at home in the body or away from it. [10]For we must all appear before the judgment seat of Christ, that each one may receive what is due him for the things done while in the body, whether good or bad.

The Ministry of Reconciliation

[11]Since, then, we know what it is to fear the Lord, we try to persuade men. What we are is plain to God, and I hope it is also plain to your conscience. [12]We are not trying to commend ourselves to you again, but are giving you an opportunity to take pride in us, so that you can answer those who take pride in what is seen rather than in what is in the heart. [13]If we are out of our mind, it is for the sake of God; if we are in our right mind, it is for you. [14]For Christ's love compels us, because we are convinced that one died for all, and therefore all died. [15]And he died for all, that those who live should no longer live for themselves but for him who died for them and was raised again.

[16]So from now on we regard no one from a worldly point of view. Though we once regarded Christ in this way, we do so no longer. [17]Therefore, if anyone is in Christ, he is a new creation; the old has gone, the new has come! [18]All this is from God, who reconciled us to himself through Christ and gave us the ministry of reconciliation: [19]that God was reconciling the world to himself in Christ, not counting men's sins against them. And he has committed to us the message of reconciliation. [20]We are therefore Christ's ambassadors, as though God were making his appeal through us. We implore you on Christ's behalf: Be reconciled to God. [21]God made him who had no sin to be sin[b] for us, so that in him we might become the righteousness of God.

6 As God's fellow workers we urge you not to receive God's grace in vain. [2]For he says,

"In the time of my favor I heard you,
    and in the day of salvation I helped
    you."[c]

I tell you, now is the time of God's favor, now is the day of salvation.

Paul's Hardships

[3]We put no stumbling block in anyone's path, so that our ministry will not be discredited. [4]Rather, as servants of God we commend ourselves in every way: in great endurance; in troubles, hardships and distresses; [5]in beatings, imprisonments and riots; in hard work,

---

[a]13 Psalm 116:10   [b]21 Or be a sin offering
[c]2 Isaiah 49:8

sleepless nights and hunger; ⁶in purity, understanding, patience and kindness; in the Holy Spirit and in sincere love; ⁷in truthful speech and in the power of God; with weapons of righteousness in the right hand and in the left; ⁸through glory and dishonor, bad report and good report; genuine, yet regarded as impostors; ⁹known, yet regarded as unknown; dying, and yet we live on; beaten, and yet not killed; ¹⁰sorrowful, yet always rejoicing; poor, yet making many rich; having nothing, and yet possessing everything.

¹¹We have spoken freely to you, Corinthians, and opened wide our hearts to you. ¹²We are not withholding our affection from you, but you are withholding yours from us. ¹³As a fair exchange—I speak as to my children—open wide your hearts also.

{ MONDAY }

2 CORINTHIANS 4:16–18

The Worldview of Prayer

4:18 FOR WHAT IS SEEN IS TEMPORARY, BUT WHAT IS UNSEEN IS ETERNAL.

G. K. Chesterton wrote a parable about what it means to be converted. He said the unconverted are like a man born with his head stuck in the earth. He is upside down: The earth seems to be the only solid thing, and the heavens feel airy, insubstantial. When he is converted, he gets set right side up: His feet are placed on the ground, where they belong; and his head is in the heavens, where it belongs. Now he can walk the earth and not stumble because he sees where he is going. Have you heard the saying, "too heavenly minded to be any earthly good"? Don't believe it. The only way to be any earthly good is to be heavenly minded.

That is the worldview of prayer. There are two realities—earthly and heavenly. Both are real, but the heavenly reality is much larger than the earthly; it is determinative and permanent, while the earthly is not. We pray because we know this to be the case—to pray is to keep one's head in heaven. Prayer is conversation with the King of Heaven. And no matter how badly things may be going presently, we keep praying and don't give up, just as Jesus taught (see Luke 18:1). Paul's words in 2 Corinthians 4:16–18 are his way of saying the same thing: "Therefore we do not lose heart. Though outwardly we are wasting away, yet inwardly we are being renewed day by day. For our light and momentary troubles are achieving for us an eternal glory that far outweighs them all. So we fix our eyes not on what is seen, but on what is unseen. For what is seen is temporary, but what is unseen is eternal."

For many of us, our problem with prayer is a worldview problem. On some deep level of our consciousness, we have become secularized and no longer believe that heavenly realities have anything to do with earthly matters. Nothing could be further from the truth.

P R A Y :

Open my eyes to see things as they are, Lord. Strengthen my heart
to pray and not give up, until the world of the seen has passed away and
the kingdom of the unseen is here to stay. Come, Lord Jesus.

FOR YOUR NEXT DEVOTIONAL READING, GO TO PAGE 1427.

Do Not Be Yoked With Unbelievers

[14]Do not be yoked together with unbelievers. For what do righteousness and wickedness have in common? Or what fellowship can light have with darkness? [15]What harmony is there between Christ and Belial[a]? What does a believer have in common with an unbeliever? [16]What agreement is there between the temple of God and idols? For we are the temple of the living God. As God has said: "I will live with them and walk among them, and I will be their God, and they will be my people."[b]

[17] "Therefore come out from them
and be separate,
says the Lord.
Touch no unclean thing,
and I will receive you."[c]
[18] "I will be a Father to you,
and you will be my sons and
daughters,
says the Lord Almighty."[d]

7 Since we have these promises, dear friends, let us purify ourselves from everything that contaminates body and spirit, perfecting holiness out of reverence for God.

Paul's Joy

[2]Make room for us in your hearts. We have wronged no one, we have corrupted no one, we have exploited no one. [3]I do not say this to condemn you; I have said before that you have such a place in our hearts that we would live or die with you. [4]I have great confidence in you; I take great pride in you. I am greatly encouraged; in all our troubles my joy knows no bounds.

[5]For when we came into Macedonia, this body of ours had no rest, but we were harassed at every turn—conflicts on the outside, fears within. [6]But God, who comforts the downcast, comforted us by the coming of Titus, [7]and not only by his coming but also by the comfort you had given him. He told us about your longing for me, your deep sorrow, your ardent concern for me, so that my joy was greater than ever.

[8]Even if I caused you sorrow by my letter, I do not regret it. Though I did regret it—I see that my letter hurt you, but only for a little while— [9]yet now I am happy, not because you were made sorry, but because your sorrow led you to repentance. For you became sorrowful as God intended and so were not harmed in any way by us. [10]Godly sorrow brings repentance that leads to salvation and leaves no regret, but worldly sorrow brings death. [11]See what this godly sorrow has produced in you: what earnestness, what eagerness to clear yourselves, what indignation, what alarm, what longing, what concern, what readiness to see justice done. At every point you have proved yourselves to be innocent in this matter. [12]So even though I wrote to you, it was not on account of the one who did the wrong or of the injured party, but rather that before God you could see for yourselves how devoted to us you are. [13]By all this we are encouraged.

In addition to our own encouragement, we were especially delighted to see how happy Titus was, because his spirit has been refreshed by all of you. [14]I had boasted to him about you, and you have not embarrassed me. But just as everything we said to you was true, so our boasting about you to Titus has proved to be true as well. [15]And his affection for you is all the greater when he remembers that you were all obedient, receiving him with fear and trembling. [16]I am glad I can have complete confidence in you.

[a]15 Greek *Beliar*, a variant of *Belial*
[b]16 Lev. 26:12; Jer. 32:38; Ezek. 37:27
[c]17 Isaiah 52:11; Ezek. 20:34,41
[d]18 2 Samuel 7:14; 7:8

Generosity Encouraged

8 And now, brothers, we want you to know about the grace that God has given the Macedonian churches. [2]Out of the most severe trial, their overflowing joy and their extreme poverty welled up in rich generosity. [3]For I testify that they gave as much as they were able, and even beyond their ability. Entirely on their own, [4]they urgently pleaded with us for the privilege of sharing in this service to the saints. [5]And they did not do as we expected, but they gave themselves first to the Lord and then to us in keeping with God's will. [6]So we urged Titus, since he had earlier made a beginning, to bring also to completion this act of grace on your part. [7]But just as you excel in everything—in faith, in speech, in knowledge, in complete earnestness and in your love for us[a]—see that you also excel in this grace of giving.

[8]I am not commanding you, but I want to test the sincerity of your love by comparing it with the earnestness of others. [9]For you know the grace of our Lord Jesus Christ, that though he was rich, yet for your sakes he became poor, so that you through his poverty might become rich.

[10]And here is my advice about what is best for you in this matter: Last year you were the first not only to give but also to have the desire to do so. [11]Now finish the work, so that your eager willingness to do it may be matched by your completion of it, according to your means. [12]For if the willingness is there, the gift is acceptable according to what one has, not according to what he does not have.

> You pray in your distress and in your need; would that you might also pray in the fullness of your joy and in your days of abundance.
>
> KAHLIL GIBRAN

[13]Our desire is not that others might be relieved while you are hard pressed, but that there might be equality. [14]At the present time your plenty will supply what they need, so that in turn their plenty will supply what you need. Then there will be equality, [15]as it is written: "He who gathered much did not have too much, and he who gathered little did not have too little."[b]

Titus Sent to Corinth

[16]I thank God, who put into the heart of Titus the same concern I have for you. [17]For Titus not only welcomed our appeal, but he is coming to you with much enthusiasm and on his own initiative. [18]And we are sending along with him the brother who is praised by all the churches for his service to the gospel. [19]What is more, he was chosen by the churches to accompany us as we carry the offering, which we administer in order to honor the Lord himself and to show our eagerness to help. [20]We want to avoid any criticism of the way we administer this liberal gift. [21]For we are taking pains to do what is right, not only in the eyes of the Lord but also in the eyes of men.

[22]In addition, we are sending with them our brother who has often proved to us in many ways that he is zealous, and now even more so because of his great confidence in you. [23]As for Titus, he is my partner and fellow worker among you; as for our brothers, they are representatives of the churches and an honor to Christ. [24]Therefore show these men the proof of your love and the reason for our pride in you, so that the churches can see it.

9 There is no need for me to write to you about this service to the saints. [2]For I know your eagerness to help, and I have been boasting about it to the Macedonians, telling them that since last year you in Achaia were ready to give; and your enthusiasm has stirred most of them to action. [3]But I am sending the brothers in order that our boasting about you in this matter should not prove hollow, but that you may be ready, as I said you would be. [4]For if any Macedonians come with me and find you unprepared, we—not to say anything about you—would be ashamed of having been so confident. [5]So I thought it necessary to urge the brothers to visit you in advance and finish the arrangements for the generous gift you had

---

[a]7 Some manuscripts in our love for you
[b]15 Exodus 16:18

promised. Then it will be ready as a generous gift, not as one grudgingly given.

Sowing Generously

⁶Remember this: Whoever sows sparingly will also reap sparingly, and whoever sows generously will also reap generously. ⁷Each man should give what he has decided in his heart to give, not reluctantly or under compulsion, for God loves a cheerful giver. ⁸And God is able to make all grace abound to you, so that in all things at all times, having all that you need, you will abound in every good work. ⁹As it is written:

"He has scattered abroad his gifts to
    the poor;
his righteousness endures
    forever."ᵃ

¹⁰Now he who supplies seed to the sower and bread for food will also supply and increase your store of seed and will enlarge the harvest of your righteousness. ¹¹You will be made rich in every way so that you can be generous on every occasion, and through us your generosity will result in thanksgiving to God.

¹²This service that you perform is not only supplying the needs of God's people but is also overflowing in many expressions of thanks to God. ¹³Because of the service by which you have proved yourselves, men will praise God for the obedience that accompanies your confession of the gospel of Christ, and for your generosity in sharing with them and with everyone else. ¹⁴And in their prayers for you their hearts will go out to you, because of the surpassing grace God has given you. ¹⁵Thanks be to God for his indescribable gift!

> AND in their prayers for you their hearts will go out to you, because of the surpassing grace God has given you.
>
> 2 CORINTHIANS 9:14

Paul's Defense of His Ministry

10 By the meekness and gentleness of Christ, I appeal to you—I, Paul, who am "timid" when face to face with you, but "bold" when away! ²I beg you that when I come I may not have to be as bold as I expect to be toward some people who think that we live by the standards of this world. ³For though we live in the world, we do not wage war as the world does. ⁴The weapons we fight with are not the weapons of the world. On the contrary, they have divine power to demolish strongholds. ⁵We demolish arguments and every pretension that sets itself up against the knowledge of God, and we take captive every thought to make it obedient to Christ. ⁶And we will be ready to punish every act of disobedience, once your obedience is complete.

⁷You are looking only on the surface of things.ᵇ If anyone is confident that he belongs to Christ, he should consider again that we belong to Christ just as much as he. ⁸For even if I boast somewhat freely about the authority the Lord gave us for building you up rather than pulling you down, I will not be ashamed of it. ⁹I do not want to seem to be trying to frighten you with my letters. ¹⁰For some say, "His letters are weighty and forceful, but in person he is unimpressive and his speaking amounts to nothing." ¹¹Such people should realize that what we are in our letters when we are absent, we will be in our actions when we are present.

¹²We do not dare to classify or compare ourselves with some who commend themselves. When they measure themselves by themselves and compare themselves with themselves, they are not wise. ¹³We, however, will not boast beyond proper limits, but will confine our boasting to the field God has assigned to us, a field that reaches even to you. ¹⁴We are not going too far in our boasting, as would be the case if we had not come to you, for we did get as far as you with the gospel of Christ. ¹⁵Neither do we go beyond our limits by boasting of work done by others.ᶜ Our hope is that, as your faith continues to grow, our area of activity among you will greatly expand, ¹⁶so that

ᵃ9 Psalm 112:9   ᵇ7 Or Look at the obvious facts   ᶜ13–15 Or ¹³We, however, will not boast about things that cannot be measured, but we will boast according to the standard of measurement that the God of measure has assigned us—a measurement that relates even to you. ¹⁴. . . ¹⁵Neither do we boast about things that cannot be measured in regard to the work done by others.

we can preach the gospel in the regions beyond you. For we do not want to boast about work already done in another man's territory. [17]But, "Let him who boasts boast in the Lord."[a] [18]For it is not the one who commends himself who is approved, but the one whom the Lord commends.

Paul and the False Apostles

11 I hope you will put up with a little of my foolishness; but you are already doing that. [2]I am jealous for you with a godly jealousy. I promised you to one husband, to Christ, so that I might present

[a]17 Jer. 9:24

[**TUESDAY**]

2 CORINTHIANS 10:1–6

Spiritual Warfare

10:3 "FOR THOUGH WE LIVE IN THE WORLD, WE DO NOT WAGE WAR AS THE WORLD DOES."

God often has to tear things down before he can build them up. Paul calls these things "strongholds . . . arguments and every pretension that sets itself up against the knowledge of God" (10:4–5). These things must be demolished, for they are the very essence of evil: deeply entrenched attitudes and ways of thinking that keep us from God, "the spring of living water" (Jeremiah 2:13). These strongholds don't exist "out there," independent and detached, but inside us, in our minds and our thoughts. The mere thought of their existence should give us a chill. But it won't if they have a strong place in our minds.

That's the point: Part of what it means to be in a spiritual stronghold is not to know you are. We cannot set ourselves free, nor can anyone else. It takes "divine power" to "demolish strongholds" (2 Corinthians 10:4). That is what spiritual warfare is all about. It is calling on God's power to set ourselves and others free, using what Paul calls the "weapons of righteousness" (6:7). The list of these weapons is expanded in Ephesians 6:10–20 (see the devotion there). Prayer is not the only weapon of righteousness, but it is by prayer that the others are wielded, including the Word of God. We are at war in this world, but our weapons are not the weapons of this world.

One more very important point: It is no fun bringing down a stronghold, especially if the stronghold is in you. The very nature of a spiritual stronghold is that it is a "pretension" set up against the knowledge of God. That word suggests it has to do with pride, self-sufficiency and ignorance, none of which go down willingly or quietly. But before God can build, he must destroy. "No man will ever reach the heights to which Christ can lift him," wrote Alexander Maclaren, "who does not begin his upward course by descending to the depth into which Christ's Gospel begins its work by plunging him."[2] Pray earnestly for God to tear down the strongholds of others, as you plead for him to do the same with you.

PRAY:

Holy Spirit, do your powerful work to bring down the strongholds in my life and in the lives of others. Bring down my pride and self-sufficiency; help me take captive every thought and make it obedient to Christ.

FOR YOUR NEXT DEVOTIONAL READING, GO TO PAGE 1430.

you as a pure virgin to him. ³But I am afraid that just as Eve was deceived by the serpent's cunning, your minds may somehow be led astray from your sincere and pure devotion to Christ. ⁴For if someone comes to you and preaches a Jesus other than the Jesus we preached, or if you receive a different spirit from the one you received, or a different gospel from the one you accepted, you put up with it easily enough. ⁵But I do not think I am in the least inferior to those "super-apostles." ⁶I may not be a trained speaker, but I do have knowledge. We have made this perfectly clear to you in every way.

⁷Was it a sin for me to lower myself in order to elevate you by preaching the gospel of God to you free of charge? ⁸I robbed other churches by receiving support from them so as to serve you. ⁹And when I was with you and needed something, I was not a burden to anyone, for the brothers who came from Macedonia supplied what I needed. I have kept myself from being a burden to you in any way, and will continue to do so. ¹⁰As surely as the truth of Christ is in me, nobody in the regions of Achaia will stop this boasting of mine. ¹¹Why? Because I do not love you? God knows I do! ¹²And I will keep on doing what I am doing in order to cut the ground from under those who want an opportunity to be considered equal with us in the things they boast about.

¹³For such men are false apostles, deceitful workmen, masquerading as apostles of Christ. ¹⁴And no wonder, for Satan himself masquerades as an angel of light. ¹⁵It is not surprising, then, if his servants masquerade as servants of righteousness. Their end will be what their actions deserve.

Paul Boasts About His Sufferings

¹⁶I repeat: Let no one take me for a fool. But if you do, then receive me just as you would a fool, so that I may do a little boasting. ¹⁷In this self-confident boasting I am not talking as the Lord would, but as a fool. ¹⁸Since many are boasting in the way the world does, I too will boast. ¹⁹You gladly put up with fools since you are so wise! ²⁰In fact, you even put up with anyone who enslaves you or exploits you or takes advantage of you or

pushes himself forward or slaps you in the face. ²¹To my shame I admit that we were too weak for that!

What anyone else dares to boast about—I am speaking as a fool—I also dare to boast about. ²²Are they Hebrews? So am I. Are they Israelites? So am I. Are they Abraham's descendants? So am I. ²³Are they servants of Christ? (I am out of my mind to talk like this.) I am more. I have worked much harder, been in prison more frequently, been flogged more severely, and been exposed to death again and again. ²⁴Five times I received from the Jews the forty lashes minus one. ²⁵Three times I was beaten with rods, once I was stoned, three times I was shipwrecked, I spent a night and a day in the open sea, ²⁶I have been constantly on the move. I have been in danger from rivers, in danger from bandits, in danger from my own countrymen, in danger from Gentiles; in danger in the city, in danger in the country, in danger at sea; and in danger from false brothers. ²⁷I have labored and toiled and have often gone without sleep; I have known hunger and thirst and have often gone without food; I have been cold and naked. ²⁸Besides everything else, I face daily the pressure of my concern for all the churches. ²⁹Who is weak, and I do not feel weak? Who is led into sin, and I do not inwardly burn?

> 66 *A simple grateful thought turned heavenwards is the most perfect prayer.* 99
>
> DORIS LESSING

³⁰If I must boast, I will boast of the things that show my weakness. ³¹The God and Father of the Lord Jesus, who is to be praised forever, knows that I am not lying. ³²In Damascus the governor under King Aretas had the city of the Damascenes guarded in order to arrest me. ³³But I was lowered in a basket from a window in the wall and slipped through his hands.

Paul's Vision and His Thorn

12 I must go on boasting. Although there is nothing to be gained, I will go on to visions and revelations from the

Lord. [2]I know a man in Christ who fourteen years ago was caught up to the third heaven. Whether it was in the body or out of the body I do not know—God knows. [3]And I know that this man— whether in the body or apart from the body I do not know, but God knows— [4]was caught up to paradise. He heard inexpressible things, things that man is not permitted to tell. [5]I will boast about a man like that, but I will not boast about myself, except about my weaknesses. [6]Even if I should choose to boast, I would not be a fool, because I would be speaking the truth. But I refrain, so no one will think more of me than is warranted by what I do or say.

[7]To keep me from becoming conceited because of these surpassingly great revelations, there was given me a thorn in my flesh, a messenger of Satan, to torment me. [8]Three times I pleaded with the Lord to take it away from me. [9]But he said to me, "My grace is sufficient for you, for my power is made perfect in weakness." Therefore I will boast all the more gladly about my weaknesses, so that Christ's power may rest on me. [10]That is why, for Christ's sake, I delight in weaknesses, in insults, in hardships, in persecutions, in difficulties. For when I am weak, then I am strong.

Paul's Concern for the Corinthians

[11]I have made a fool of myself, but you drove me to it. I ought to have been commended by you, for I am not in the least inferior to the "super-apostles," even though I am nothing. [12]The things that mark an apostle—signs, wonders and miracles—were done among you with great perseverance. [13]How were you inferior to the other churches, except that I was never a burden to you? Forgive me this wrong!

[14]Now I am ready to visit you for the third time, and I will not be a burden to you, because what I want is not your possessions but you. After all, children should not have to save up for their parents, but parents for their children. [15]So I will very gladly spend for you everything I have and expend myself as well. If I love you more, will you love me less? [16]Be that as it may, I have not been a burden to

you. Yet, crafty fellow that I am, I caught you by trickery! [17]Did I exploit you through any of the men I sent you? [18]I urged Titus to go to you and I sent our brother with him. Titus did not exploit you, did he? Did we not act in the same spirit and follow the same course?

[19]Have you been thinking all along that we have been defending ourselves to you? We have been speaking in the sight of God as those in Christ; and everything we do, dear friends, is for your strengthening. [20]For I am afraid that when I come I may not find you as I want you to be, and you may not find me as you want me to be. I fear that there may be quarreling, jealousy, outbursts of anger, factions, slander, gossip, arrogance and disorder. [21]I am afraid that when I come again my God will humble me before you, and I will be grieved over many who have sinned earlier and have not repented of the impurity, sexual sin and debauchery in which they have indulged.

Final Warnings

13 This will be my third visit to you. "Every matter must be established by the testimony of two or three witnesses."[a] [2]I already gave you a warning when I was with you the second time. I now repeat it while absent: On my return I will not spare those who sinned earlier or any of the others, [3]since you are demanding proof that Christ is speaking through me. He is not weak in dealing with you, but is powerful among you. [4]For to be sure, he was crucified in weakness, yet he lives by God's power. Likewise, we are weak in him, yet by God's power we will live with him to serve you.

[5]Examine yourselves to see whether you are in the faith; test yourselves. Do you not realize that Christ Jesus is in you—unless, of course, you fail the test? [6]And I trust that you will discover that we have not failed the test. [7]Now we pray to God that you will not do anything wrong. Not that people will see that we have stood the test but that you will do what is right even though we may seem to have failed. [8]For we cannot do anything against the truth, but only for the truth.

[a]1 Deut. 19:15

God's Gracious Refusal

12:9 "MY GRACE IS SUFFICIENT FOR YOU, FOR MY POWER IS MADE PERFECT IN WEAKNESS."

Like Jesus prayed in Gethsemane, three times Paul pleaded with God to take away the "thorn in [his] flesh." And three times he got the same answer Jesus got: "No" (see Mark 14:32–42). The fact that neither was finally disappointed in God's refusal is one of the greatest lessons we can learn about prayer, especially prayer for the things we want the most.

What did Paul ask for God to take away? No one knows what it was exactly; all we know for sure is his acceptance of why God refused it. It was to keep him humble and dependent on God's grace and power. God had given him a vision that could only be described as "inexpressible" (2 Corinthians 12:4). This religious experience of his was very valuable to Paul's ministry in Corinth because the Corinthians were very impressed with visions and those who had them. And those who had visions tended to be very impressed with themselves. In Corinth, supernatural manifestations and experiences were regarded as validations of an apostle's authority. Apparently some in Corinth saw themselves as so heavily "validated" that Paul sarcastically called them "super-apostles" (11:5). Their pride in their religious experiences had taken the focus off God and his glory and put it on themselves. Pride is a terrible thing, an aggressive and terminal cancer in the soul, something to be avoided at all costs because God opposes the proud but gives grace to the humble (see 1 Peter 5:5).

So Paul welcomed anything that kept him from robbing God of his glory. If a frustrating and debilitating "thorn" was what it took, then it was just fine with him. If less for him meant more—of God—for him, then let there be less! Weaknesses, hardships, insults and persecutions are transformed into delight, "For when I am weak, then I am strong" (2 Corinthians 12:10).

There's a great lesson in prayer here: Learn to trust and appreciate the wisdom of God's gracious refusals. If he says "No" it is because he wants to say a greater "Yes." John Calvin pointed out that God may sometimes grant the end we desire but not the means we think necessary to achieve it. Paul desired God's glory, a good end, and for awhile thought the best means to that end was through removal of his thorn. He got nothing he asked for but everything he hoped for.

P R A Y :

Dear Father, if your "Yes" to my request
would mean less of you, then say "No."
Your love is better than life.

———

FOR YOUR NEXT DEVOTIONAL READING, GO TO PAGE 1436.

⁹We are glad whenever we are weak but you are strong; and our prayer is for your perfection. ¹⁰This is why I write these things when I am absent, that when I come I may not have to be harsh in my use of authority—the authority the Lord gave me for building you up, not for tearing you down.

Final Greetings

¹¹Finally, brothers, good-by. Aim for perfection, listen to my appeal, be of one mind, live in peace. And the God of love and peace will be with you.

¹²Greet one another with a holy kiss. ¹³All the saints send their greetings.

¹⁴May the grace of the Lord Jesus Christ, and the love of God, and the fellowship of the Holy Spirit be with you all.

> WE ARE glad whenever we are weak but you are strong; and our prayer is for your perfection.
>
> 2 CORINTHIANS 13:9

Galatians

"THE RIGHTEOUS
WILL LIVE BY FAITH."
(3:11)

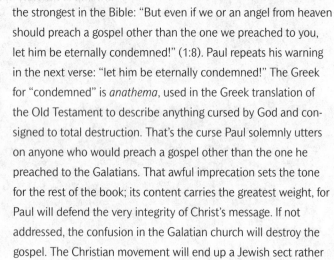

PAUL'S LANGUAGE in his letter to the Galatians is among
the strongest in the Bible: "But even if we or an angel from heaven
should preach a gospel other than the one we preached to you,
let him be eternally condemned!" (1:8). Paul repeats his warning
in the next verse: "let him be eternally condemned!" The Greek
for "condemned" is *anathema*, used in the Greek translation of
the Old Testament to describe anything cursed by God and con-
signed to total destruction. That's the curse Paul solemnly utters
on anyone who would preach a gospel other than the one he
preached to the Galatians. That awful imprecation sets the tone
for the rest of the book; its content carries the greatest weight, for
Paul will defend the very integrity of Christ's message. If not
addressed, the confusion in the Galatian church will destroy the
gospel. The Christian movement will end up a Jewish sect rather
than a world religion; the fulfillment of God's covenant with Israel
will be aborted.

Paul's letter to the Galatians bids us pray for matters of the
utmost importance. So much is at stake. Jesus said, "I will build
my church, and the gates of Hades will not overcome it"
(Matthew 16:18). The ultimate outcome of the struggle is guaranteed, but there can be many casualties along the way. Christ will
build his church and his kingdom will come, but what will happen
to the Galatians and those their heresy affects? Will they be lost?
What will happen in your church? Pray with Paul and with Jesus
that his church will be built successfully in your congregation.

1 Paul, an apostle—sent not from men nor by man, but by Jesus Christ and God the Father, who raised him from the dead— ²and all the brothers with me,

To the churches in Galatia:

³Grace and peace to you from God our Father and the Lord Jesus Christ, ⁴who gave himself for our sins to rescue us from the present evil age, according to the will of our God and Father, ⁵to whom be glory for ever and ever. Amen.

No Other Gospel

⁶I am astonished that you are so quickly deserting the one who called you by the grace of Christ and are turning to a different gospel— ⁷which is really no gospel at all. Evidently some people are throwing you into confusion and are trying to pervert the gospel of Christ. ⁸But even if we or an angel from heaven should preach a gospel other than the one we preached to you, let him be eternally condemned! ⁹As we have already said, so now I say again: If anybody is preaching to you a gospel other than what you accepted, let him be eternally condemned!

¹⁰Am I now trying to win the approval of men, or of God? Or am I trying to please men? If I were still trying to please men, I would not be a servant of Christ.

Paul Called by God

¹¹I want you to know, brothers, that the gospel I preached is not something that man made up. ¹²I did not receive it from any man, nor was I taught it; rather, I received it by revelation from Jesus Christ.

¹³For you have heard of my previous way of life in Judaism, how intensely I persecuted the church of God and tried to destroy it. ¹⁴I was advancing in Judaism beyond many Jews of my own age and was extremely zealous for the traditions of my fathers. ¹⁵But when God, who set me apart from birth[a] and called me by his grace, was pleased ¹⁶to reveal his Son in me so that I might preach him among the Gentiles, I did not consult any man, ¹⁷nor did I go up to Jerusalem to see those who were apostles before I was, but I went immediately into Arabia and later returned to Damascus.

¹⁸Then after three years, I went up to Jerusalem to get acquainted with Peter[b] and stayed with him fifteen days. ¹⁹I saw none of the other apostles—only James, the Lord's brother. ²⁰I assure you before God that what I am writing you is no lie. ²¹Later I went to Syria and Cilicia. ²²I was personally unknown to the churches of Judea that are in Christ. ²³They only heard the report: "The man who formerly persecuted us is now preaching the faith he once tried to destroy." ²⁴And they praised God because of me.

> *AND* they praised God because of me.
>
> GALATIANS 1:24

Paul Accepted by the Apostles

2 Fourteen years later I went up again to Jerusalem, this time with Barnabas. I took Titus along also. ²I went in response to a revelation and set before them the gospel that I preach among the Gentiles. But I did this privately to those who seemed to be leaders, for fear that I was running or had run my race in vain. ³Yet not even Titus, who was with me, was compelled to be circumcised, even though he was a Greek. ⁴This matter arose, because some false brothers had infiltrated our ranks to spy on the freedom we have in Christ Jesus and to make us slaves. ⁵We did not give in to them for a moment, so that the truth of the gospel might remain with you.

⁶As for those who seemed to be important—whatever they were makes no difference to me; God does not judge by external appearance—those men added nothing to my message. ⁷On the contrary, they saw that I had been entrusted with the task of preaching the gospel to the Gentiles,[c] just as Peter had been to the Jews.[d] ⁸For God, who was at work in the ministry of Peter as an apostle to the Jews, was also at work in my ministry as an apostle to the Gentiles. ⁹James, Peter[e] and John, those reputed to be pillars, gave me and Barnabas the right hand of

---

[a]15 Or *from my mother's womb*   [b]18 Greek *Cephas*   [c]7 Greek *uncircumcised*   [d]7 Greek *circumcised*; also in verses 8 and 9   [e]9 Greek *Cephas*; also in verses 11 and 14

fellowship when they recognized the grace given to me. They agreed that we should go to the Gentiles, and they to the Jews. [10]All they asked was that we should continue to remember the poor, the very thing I was eager to do.

Paul Opposes Peter

[11]When Peter came to Antioch, I opposed him to his face, because he was clearly in the wrong. [12]Before certain men came from James, he used to eat with the Gentiles. But when they arrived, he began to draw back and separate himself from the Gentiles because he was afraid of those who belonged to the circumcision group. [13]The other Jews joined him in his hypocrisy, so that by their hypocrisy even Barnabas was led astray.

[14]When I saw that they were not acting in line with the truth of the gospel, I said to Peter in front of them all, "You are a Jew, yet you live like a Gentile and not like a Jew. How is it, then, that you force Gentiles to follow Jewish customs?

[15]"We who are Jews by birth and not 'Gentile sinners' [16]know that a man is not justified by observing the law, but by faith in Jesus Christ. So we, too, have put our faith in Christ Jesus that we may be justified by faith in Christ and not by observing the law, because by observing the law no one will be justified.

[17]"If, while we seek to be justified in Christ, it becomes evident that we ourselves are sinners, does that mean that Christ promotes sin? Absolutely not! [18]If I rebuild what I destroyed, I prove that I am a lawbreaker. [19]For through the law I died to the law so that I might live for God. [20]I have been crucified with Christ and I no longer live, but Christ lives in me. The life I live in the body, I live by faith in the Son of God, who loved me and gave himself for me. [21]I do not set aside the grace of God, for if righteousness could be gained through the law, Christ died for nothing!"[a]

Faith or Observance of the Law

3 You foolish Galatians! Who has bewitched you? Before your very eyes Jesus Christ was clearly portrayed as crucified. [2]I would like to learn just one thing from you: Did you receive the Spirit by observing the law, or by believing what you heard? [3]Are you so foolish? After beginning with the Spirit, are you now trying to attain your goal by human effort? [4]Have you suffered so much for nothing—if it really was for nothing? [5]Does God give you his Spirit and work miracles among you because you observe the law, or because you believe what you heard?

[6]Consider Abraham: "He believed God, and it was credited to him as righteousness."[b] [7]Understand, then, that those who believe are children of Abraham. [8]The Scripture foresaw that God would justify the Gentiles by faith, and announced the gospel in advance to Abraham: "All nations will be blessed through you."[c] [9]So those who have faith are blessed along with Abraham, the man of faith.

[10]All who rely on observing the law are under a curse, for it is written: "Cursed is everyone who does not continue to do everything written in the Book of the Law."[d] [11]Clearly no one is justified before God by the law, because, "The righteous will live by faith."[e] [12]The law is not based on faith; on the contrary, "The man who does these things will live by them."[f] [13]Christ redeemed us from the curse of the law by becoming a curse for us, for it is written: "Cursed is everyone who is hung on a tree."[g] [14]He redeemed us in order that the

[a]21 Some interpreters end the quotation after verse 14.   [b]6 Gen. 15:6   [c]8 Gen. 12:3; 18:18; 22:18   [d]10 Deut. 27:26   [e]11 Hab. 2:4   [f]12 Lev. 18:5   [g]13 Deut. 21:23

blessing given to Abraham might come to the Gentiles through Christ Jesus, so that by faith we might receive the promise of the Spirit.

The Law and the Promise

[15]Brothers, let me take an example from everyday life. Just as no one can set aside or add to a human covenant that has been duly established, so it is in this case. [16]The promises were spoken to Abraham and to his seed. The Scripture does not say "and to seeds," meaning many people, but "and to your seed,"[a] meaning one person, who is Christ. [17]What I mean is this: The law, introduced 430 years later, does not set aside the covenant previously established by God and thus do away with the promise. [18]For if the inheritance depends on the law, then it no longer depends on a promise; but God in his grace gave it to Abraham through a promise.

[19]What, then, was the purpose of the law? It was added because of transgressions until the Seed to whom the promise referred had come. The law was put into effect through angels by a mediator. [20]A mediator, however, does not represent just one party; but God is one.

[21]Is the law, therefore, opposed to the promises of God? Absolutely not! For if a law had been given that could impart life, then righteousness would certainly have come by the law. [22]But the Scripture declares that the whole world is a prisoner of sin, so that what was promised, being given through faith in Jesus Christ, might be given to those who believe.

[23]Before this faith came, we were held prisoners by the law, locked up until faith should be revealed. [24]So the law was put in charge to lead us to Christ[b] that we might be justified by faith. [25]Now that faith has come, we are no longer under the supervision of the law.

Sons of God

[26]You are all sons of God through faith in Christ Jesus, [27]for all of you who were baptized into Christ have clothed yourselves with Christ. [28]There is neither Jew nor Greek, slave nor free, male nor female, for you are all one in Christ Jesus. [29]If you belong to Christ, then you are Abraham's seed, and heirs according to the promise.

4 What I am saying is that as long as the heir is a child, he is no different from a slave, although he owns the whole estate. [2]He is subject to guardians and trustees until the time set by his father. [3]So also, when we were children, we were in slavery under the basic principles of the world. [4]But when the time had fully come, God sent his Son, born of a woman, born under law, [5]to redeem those under law, that we might receive the full rights of sons. [6]Because you are sons, God sent the Spirit of his Son into our hearts, the Spirit who calls out, "Abba,[c] Father." [7]So you are no longer a slave, but a son; and since you are a son, God has made you also an heir.

Paul's Concern for the Galatians

[8]Formerly, when you did not know God, you were slaves to those who by nature are not gods. [9]But now that you know God—or rather are known by God—how is it that you are turning back to those weak and miserable principles? Do you wish to be enslaved by them all over again? [10]You are observing special days and months and seasons and years! [11]I fear for you, that somehow I have wasted my efforts on you.

[12]I plead with you, brothers, become like me, for I became like you. You have done me no wrong. [13]As you know, it was because of an illness that I first preached the gospel to you. [14]Even though my illness was a trial to you, you did not treat me with contempt or scorn. Instead, you welcomed me as if I were an angel of God, as if I were Christ Jesus himself. [15]What has happened to all your joy? I can testify that, if you could have done so, you would have torn out your eyes and given them to me. [16]Have I now become your enemy by telling you the truth?

[17]Those people are zealous to win you over, but for no good. What they want is to alienate you ⌐from us⌐, so that you may be zealous for them. [18]It is fine to be zealous, provided the purpose is good, and

[a]16 Gen. 12:7; 13:15; 24:7   [b]24 Or charge until Christ came   [c]6 Aramaic for Father

to be so always and not just when I am with you. ¹⁹My dear children, for whom I am again in the pains of childbirth until Christ is formed in you, ²⁰how I wish I could be with you now and change my tone, because I am perplexed about you!

Hagar and Sarah

²¹Tell me, you who want to be under the law, are you not aware of what the law says? ²²For it is written that Abraham had two sons, one by the slave woman and the other by the free woman. ²³His son by the

---

[THURSDAY]

GALATIANS 4:1–10

Abba!

4:6 "BECAUSE YOU ARE SONS, GOD SENT THE SPIRIT OF HIS SON INTO OUR HEARTS."

"Daaaa . . . da! Maaa . . . ma!" It doesn't usually come out smoothly the first time, but there's great celebration when an infant first says "Mommy" or "Daddy." For it means that, with the coming of language, the relationship between parent and child has entered a new phase; the two can communicate on a new level; there's a heightened awareness and delight in each other. Now the child can call for the parent when afraid or excited or lonely. There is nothing that gets a parent's attention like the sound of a child calling out, "Daddy!" or "Mommy!" God is the same way.

That language is exactly what Paul says the Holy Spirit gives the believer. The noun *Abba* comes close to our "Dad," an intimate word of affection and confidence—and also of awe and respect. The verb "calls out" is a word for strong emotion or a stammering cry. It is as primal and elementary as a child's cry for Mommy or Daddy. This is where all prayer begins: with the witness of God's Spirit prompting and releasing our hearts to cry out, "Abba!" This is also stunning and hard to believe—that the Holy One of Israel, the Creator of heaven and earth, should have us call him "Father!" Whether whispered or shouted, spoken quietly or sung, an exclamation point always belongs with "Father!" No matter how long you've had a relationship with God, are you still amazed and grateful to be able to relate to him in that way?

All the things that precede this unprecedented privilege are "basic principles of the world" (4:3). These are the fundamental principles of all religion, whether Jewish or pagan (see verses 8–10). At best, they serve only as preparation for the real thing. At worst, they are substitutes for the real thing. The real thing is a relationship of awe, love and trust embodied in the cry, "Abba!" Ultimately, that is what all spiritual disciplines are for, even the disciplines of reading Scripture and prayer: to lead us to a face-to-face encounter with our Father, God. Has the practice of your faith led you closer to the Father or farther away?

PRAY:

*Father in Heaven! I both tremble and am at peace when
I speak to you that way. Thank you that one as great and awesome,
as worthy of fear and reverence, as you are should bid me
to cry out as a child, "Father, Dear Father!"*

FOR YOUR NEXT DEVOTIONAL READING, GO TO PAGE 1437.

slave woman was born in the ordinary way; but his son by the free woman was born as the result of a promise.

²⁴These things may be taken figuratively, for the women represent two covenants. One covenant is from Mount Sinai and bears children who are to be slaves: This is Hagar. ²⁵Now Hagar stands for Mount Sinai in Arabia and corresponds to the present city of Jerusalem, because she is in slavery with her children. ²⁶But the Jerusalem that is above is

[FRIDAY]

GALATIANS 4:19–20

Intercession Is Like Childbirth

4:19 MY DEAR CHILDREN.

Out of his frustration with the Galatian believers, Paul used a remarkable metaphor to describe the nature of his work among them: He said he was like a mother "again" in labor for the birth of her child. In other words, he thought the child was birthed, but it is still in the birth canal and the outcome is still in question. This is supreme frustration but profound insight into the nature of intercessory prayer for difficult things and hard-hearted people.

There is the love that moves one to intercede. Like a pregnant mother's expectant love for her unborn child, a love coming from her very insides, "It always protects, always trusts, always hopes, always perseveres" (1 Corinthians 13:7). No one is more hopeful and passionate for the future than a pregnant woman. No one is more submitted to her task—her body no longer her own, pressed into the service of another. What love! And what a way to pray.

There is the work of intercession. It can be like childbirth: difficult, exhausting, but full of hope. Some see prayer primarily as a path to relaxation and inner quiet. It can be that way, but serious intercession is anything but calming. This type of prayer will end in the joy of birth, but the process is never relaxing. Paul told the Romans that to pray this way is to be part of a cosmic effort he described as "groaning" (Romans 8:22–26).

There is the end of intercession. Its purpose: nothing less than a fully functioning, healthy child. This goes way beyond the moment of birth—it extends to the end of life. No good mother is content with merely a baby, as delightful as a baby is. She wants her child to grow up into maturity. The idea of childbirth echoes in Paul's statement of his goal in ministry, which is "to present everyone perfect in Christ." He said, "To this end I labor" (Colossians 1:28–29). Paul's labor was more than intercession, but it was never less; his labor of love was a labor of intercession for those whose lives God had entrusted him.

PRAY:

*Lord, teach me to pray the way
a mother gives birth to her child: passionately,
determinedly, unselfishly—with the same love,
the same labor and the same goal.*

FOR YOUR NEXT DEVOTIONAL READING, GO TO PAGE 1438.

A Demonstration of the Spirit's Power

SAMUEL CHADWICK'S preaching took on a supernatural power after he set all of his sermons on fire. One night as he prayed, Chadwick became conscience stricken about his self-reliance. For months he had labored day and night preparing catchy, exciting and pertinent sermons, but the congregation remained unmoved. "[There was a] false aim in my work," Chadwick later recalled. "I lived and labored for my sermons, and was unfortunately more concerned about their excellence and reputation than the repentance of the people."[1] Revivals were happening in the surrounding villages of the Rossendale Valley in England, but his small congregation of workers and beer brewers in Stacksteads, Lancashire, remained untouched. Lack of success slowly wore down Chadwick's confidence in himself. "The demands of the impossible task [of converting the congregation] awakened me to a sense of need. I had neither power nor might in either service or prayer."[2]

So it was with trembling hands that he pulled out his precious collection of sermons and set them on fire. Almost immediately he experienced an inner change: "I could not explain what had happened, but it was a bigger thing than I had ever known. There came into my soul a deep peace, a thrilling joy, and a new sense of power."[3]

The next Sunday seven people were converted. Revitalized, Chadwick called the entire congregation to prayer. Soon afterward the church at Stacksteads experienced a revival that spread into the surrounding villages. Hundreds were converted, including Robert Hamer, a.k.a. "Bury Bob," a man notorious for his drunken violence and brawling. "God led us to Pentecost," Chadwick later wrote. "It awakened my mind as well as cleansed my heart. It gave me a new job and a new power, a new love and a new compassion. It gave me a new Bible and a new message. Above all else, it gave me a new understanding and a new intimacy in the communion and ministry of prayer, it taught me to pray in the Spirit."[4]

For the rest of his life Chadwick preached the necessity of the power of the Spirit through prayer. "Prayer is the test of faith and the secret of power ... The energy of the flesh can run bazaars, organize amusements, and raise millions, but it is the presence of the Holy Spirit that makes a temple of the Living God."[5] Chadwick also wrote, "We are never really men of prayer in the best sense, until we are filled with the Holy Ghost. Therefore, Lord, teach us to pray in the Spirit!"[6]

Chadwick later became principal of Cliff College in Calver and editor of the "Joyful News" magazine. He also served as chairman of Sheffield District and president of the Methodist Conference, while going on sporadic preaching tours of the United States and South Africa. He is still remembered for his powerful and simple writings, including "The Path of Prayer" and "The Way to Pentecost." These were written, he said, not for "critics nor for scholars, but for plain people who are deeply religious and sincerely simple in their trust."[7]

PRAY:
Come, Holy Spirit! Better one word spoken in your power than a thousand spoken with mere human eloquence. Teach me to be slow to speak, and quick to pray before I do.

MEMORIZE:
My message and my preaching were not with wise and persuasive words, but with a demonstration of the Spirit's power, so that your faith might not rest on men's wisdom, but on God's power. 1 CORINTHIANS 2:4–5

FOR YOUR NEXT DEVOTIONAL READING, GO TO PAGE 1441.

free, and she is our mother. [27]For it is written:

"Be glad, O barren woman,
  who bears no children;
break forth and cry aloud,
  you who have no labor pains;
because more are the children of
    the desolate woman
  than of her who has a husband."[a]

[28]Now you, brothers, like Isaac, are children of promise. [29]At that time the son born in the ordinary way persecuted the son born by the power of the Spirit. It is the same now. [30]But what does the Scripture say? "Get rid of the slave woman and her son, for the slave woman's son will never share in the inheritance with the free woman's son."[b] [31]Therefore, brothers, we are not children of the slave woman, but of the free woman.

Freedom in Christ

5 It is for freedom that Christ has set us free. Stand firm, then, and do not let yourselves be burdened again by a yoke of slavery.

[2]Mark my words! I, Paul, tell you that if you let yourselves be circumcised, Christ will be of no value to you at all. [3]Again I declare to every man who lets himself be circumcised that he is obligated to obey the whole law. [4]You who are trying to be justified by law have been alienated from Christ; you have fallen away from grace. [5]But by faith we eagerly await through the Spirit the righteousness for which we hope. [6]For in Christ Jesus neither circumcision nor uncircumcision has any value. The only thing that counts is faith expressing itself through love.

[7]You were running a good race. Who cut in on you and kept you from obeying the truth? [8]That kind of persuasion does not come from the one who calls you. [9]"A little yeast works through the whole batch of dough." [10]I am confident in the Lord that you will take no other view. The one who is throwing you into confusion will pay the penalty, whoever he may be. [11]Brothers, if I am still preaching circumcision, why am I still being persecuted? In that case the offense of the cross has been abolished. [12]As for those

agitators, I wish they would go the whole way and emasculate themselves!

[13]You, my brothers, were called to be free. But do not use your freedom to indulge the sinful nature[c]; rather, serve one another in love. [14]The entire law is summed up in a single command: "Love your neighbor as yourself."[d] [15]If you keep on biting and devouring each other, watch out or you will be destroyed by each other.

Life by the Spirit

[16]So I say, live by the Spirit, and you will not gratify the desires of the sinful nature. [17]For the sinful nature desires what is contrary to the Spirit, and the Spirit what is contrary to the sinful nature. They are in conflict with each other, so that you do not do what you want. [18]But if you are led by the Spirit, you are not under law.

[19]The acts of the sinful nature are obvious: sexual immorality, impurity and debauchery; [20]idolatry and witchcraft; hatred, discord, jealousy, fits of rage, selfish ambition, dissensions, factions [21]and envy; drunkenness, orgies, and the like. I warn you, as I did before, that those who live like this will not inherit the kingdom of God.

[22]But the fruit of the Spirit is love, joy, peace, patience, kindness, goodness, faithfulness, [23]gentleness and self-control. Against such things there is no law. [24]Those who belong to Christ Jesus have crucified the sinful nature with its passions and desires. [25]Since we live by the Spirit, let us keep in step with the Spirit. [26]Let us not become conceited, provoking and envying each other.

Doing Good to All

6 Brothers, if someone is caught in a sin, you who are spiritual should restore him gently. But watch yourself, or you also may be tempted. [2]Carry each other's burdens, and in this way you will fulfill the law of Christ. [3]If anyone thinks he is something when he is nothing, he deceives himself. [4]Each one should test

---

[a]27 Isaiah 54:1   [b]30 Gen. 21:10
[c]13 Or the flesh; also in verses 16, 17, 19 and 24
[d]14 Lev. 19:18

GALATIANS 5:22–23

Praying for the Fruit of the Spirit

5:22–23 BUT THE FRUIT OF THE SPIRIT IS LOVE, JOY, PEACE, PATIENCE, KINDNESS, GOODNESS, FAITHFULNESS, GENTLENESS AND SELF-CONTROL.

This little list of nine fruit makes a wonderful prayer list—nine things to pray for yourself and others. Since there are nine, one is tempted to say "fruits," but the word is singular in the text and for good reason: The source is singular. The source is the Holy Spirit. Think of these nine attributes as descriptions of the qualities that emerge in the character of a man or woman filled with the Spirit. Or think of them as the fruit of the same Spirit that moves us to pray (see Romans 8:15; Galatians 4:6). Or think of them as the fulfillment of Jesus' promise: "I am the vine; you are the branches. If a man remains in me and I in him, he will bear much fruit" (John 15:5).

Or think of these nine fruit as love in all its glory. Love is the greatest of Christian virtues, "the most excellent way" of all (1 Corinthians 12:31). Dr. Kenneth Moynagh has summarized the glory of love in the fruit of the Spirit:

> Joy is love exulting, and peace is love at rest;
> Patience, love enduring in every trial and test.
> Gentleness, love yielding to all that is not sin,
> Goodness, love in actions that flow from Christ within.
> Faith is love's eyes opened the living Christ to see;
> Meekness, love not fighting, but bowed at Calvary.
> Temperance, love in harness and under Christ's control,
> For Christ is love in person, and love, Christ in the soul.[8]

That last line is the best of all: Think of the fruit of the Spirit as a sketch of Jesus' character. The more we look like these fruit, the more we look like our Lord. *And the more we look at our Lord, the more we will look like these fruit.* What is prayer but gazing at the glory of Jesus through the lens of Scripture, and becoming what we behold (see devotion on 2 Corinthians 3:7–18)? Spiritual growth comes by letting the light into our souls the way a shutter lets light into a camera. The image will be impressed on the light-sensitive heart, the picture taken, and we will begin to look like Jesus. Memorize the list, and pray daily for each of these fruit to be evident in your own life.

PRAY:

Lord, I want to be like Jesus. Grant that I show
today, in all I think, say and do, love,
joy, peace, patience, kindness, goodness,
faithfulness, gentleness and self-control.

FOR YOUR NEXT DEVOTIONAL READING, GO TO PAGE 1445.

his own actions. Then he can take pride in himself, without comparing himself to somebody else, [5]for each one should carry his own load.

[6]Anyone who receives instruction in the word must share all good things with his instructor.

> *Simple acts of love and prayer keep the light of Christ burning.*
>
> MOTHER TERESA

[7]Do not be deceived: God cannot be mocked. A man reaps what he sows. [8]The one who sows to please his sinful nature, from that nature[a] will reap destruction; the one who sows to please the Spirit, from the Spirit will reap eternal life. [9]Let us not become weary in doing good, for at the proper time we will reap a harvest if we do not give up. [10]Therefore, as we have opportunity, let us do good to all people, especially to those who belong to the family of believers.

Not Circumcision but a New Creation

[11]See what large letters I use as I write to you with my own hand!

[12]Those who want to make a good impression outwardly are trying to compel you to be circumcised. The only reason they do this is to avoid being persecuted for the cross of Christ. [13]Not even those who are circumcised obey the law, yet they want you to be circumcised that they may boast about your flesh. [14]May I never boast except in the cross of our Lord Jesus Christ, through which[b] the world has been crucified to me, and I to the world. [15]Neither circumcision nor uncircumcision means anything; what counts is a new creation. [16]Peace and mercy to all who follow this rule, even to the Israel of God.

[17]Finally, let no one cause me trouble, for I bear on my body the marks of Jesus.

[18]The grace of our Lord Jesus Christ be with your spirit, brothers. Amen.

[a]8 Or *his flesh, from the flesh*   [b]14 Or *whom*

Ephesians

HER FATHER wanted to read the newspaper, but the five-year-old girl wanted him to read to her from a book. She kept pestering him until he came up with a plan to put her off a little longer. To keep her busy, he devised a puzzle from a full-page picture of the earth in the newspaper. Thinking her ignorance of the world would make it impossible to do, he cut it up into little pieces and said to her, "As soon as you put the world together, Honey, I'll read to you." She looked at the heap of newspaper pieces on the floor, groaned with frustration, and dove into the project. Pleased with himself, the father smiled and settled into his chair to read the rest of the paper. Not more than five minutes later he heard her squeal with delight and shout, "I'm done, Daddy!" He looked down, and to his astonishment saw that she was.

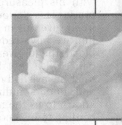

"How could you do such a hard puzzle so quickly?" he asked her.

"It was easy," she replied. "There was a big picture of a man's face on the back of the world. When his face came together, the world came together."

We may not be able to see it now, but one day the world, and all its bloodstained history, will look like the face of Christ. That is the heart of the message of Ephesians. God's purpose in Christ is "to bring all things in heaven and on earth together under one head, even Christ" (1:10). All the divisions and warring factions will one day be united in Christ, with the church as the prototype of what this will look like. "God placed all things under [Christ's] feet and appointed him to be head over everything for the church" (1:22). For the church? Yes! Ephesians is the premier book on the church in the New Testament.

In this letter, Paul's prayers for the church are unparalleled in their depth, elegance and eloquence. Ephesians 1:15–23 and 3:14–21 should set the prayer agenda for any church that seriously wants to fulfill God's purpose for it. Pray with Paul for the church, for your church, and you may discover that your perception of "the church" was far too small. It is Christ's "body, the fullness of him who fills everything in every way" (1:23).

> "I PRAY THAT OUT OF HIS GLORIOUS RICHES HE MAY STRENGTHEN YOU WITH POWER THROUGH HIS SPIRIT IN YOUR INNER BEING." (3:16)

1

Paul, an apostle of Christ Jesus by the will of God,

To the saints in Ephesus,[a] the faithful[b] in Christ Jesus:

[2]Grace and peace to you from God our Father and the Lord Jesus Christ.

Spiritual Blessings in Christ

[3]Praise be to the God and Father of our Lord Jesus Christ, who has blessed us in the heavenly realms with every spiritual blessing in Christ. [4]For he chose us in him before the creation of the world to be holy and blameless in his sight. In love [5]he[c] predestined us to be adopted as his sons through Jesus Christ, in accordance with his pleasure and will— [6]to the praise of his glorious grace, which he has freely given us in the One he loves. [7]In him we have redemption through his blood, the forgiveness of sins, in accordance with the riches of God's grace [8]that he lavished on us with all wisdom and understanding. [9]And he[d] made known to us the mystery of his will according to his good pleasure, which he purposed in Christ, [10]to be put into effect when the times will have reached their fulfillment—to bring all things in heaven and on earth together under one head, even Christ.

[11]In him we were also chosen,[e] having been predestined according to the plan of him who works out everything in conformity with the purpose of his will, [12]in order that we, who were the first to hope in Christ, might be for the praise of his glory. [13]And you also were included in Christ when you heard the word of truth, the gospel of your salvation. Having believed, you were marked in him with a seal, the promised Holy Spirit, [14]who is a deposit guaranteeing our inheritance until the redemption of those who are God's possession—to the praise of his glory.

Thanksgiving and Prayer

[15]For this reason, ever since I heard about your faith in the Lord Jesus and your love for all the saints, [16]I have not stopped giving thanks for you, remembering you in my prayers. [17]I keep asking that the God of our Lord Jesus Christ, the glorious Father, may give you the Spirit[f]

> *I HAVE not stopped giving thanks for you, remembering you in my prayers.*
>
> EPHESIANS 1:16

of wisdom and revelation, so that you may know him better. [18]I pray also that the eyes of your heart may be enlightened in order that you may know the hope to which he has called you, the riches of his glorious inheritance in the saints, [19]and his incomparably great power for us who believe. That power is like the working of his mighty strength, [20]which he exerted in Christ when he raised him from the dead and seated him at his right hand in the heavenly realms, [21]far above all rule and authority, power and dominion, and every title that can be given, not only in the present age but also in the one to come. [22]And God placed all things under his feet and appointed him to be head over everything for the church, [23]which is his body, the fullness of him who fills everything in every way.

Made Alive in Christ

2

As for you, you were dead in your transgressions and sins, [2]in which you used to live when you followed the ways of this world and of the ruler of the kingdom of the air, the spirit who is now at work in those who are disobedient. [3]All of us also lived among them at one time, gratifying the cravings of our sinful nature[g] and following its desires and thoughts. Like the rest, we were by nature objects of wrath. [4]But because of his great love for us, God, who is rich in mercy, [5]made us alive with Christ even when we were dead in transgressions—it is by

> 66 *To be a Christian without prayer is no more possible than to be alive without breathing.* 99
>
> MARTIN LUTHER

[a]1 Some early manuscripts do not have *in Ephesus.* [b]1 Or *believers who are* [c]4,5 Or *sight in love.* [5]He [d]8,9 Or *us. With all wisdom and understanding,* [9]*he* [e]11 Or *were made heirs* [f]17 Or *a spirit* [g]3 Or *our flesh*

grace you have been saved. ⁶And God raised us up with Christ and seated us with him in the heavenly realms in Christ Jesus, ⁷in order that in the coming ages he might show the incomparable riches of his grace, expressed in his kindness to us in Christ Jesus. ⁸For it is by grace you have been saved, through faith—and this not from yourselves, it is the gift of God— ⁹not by works, so that no one can boast. ¹⁰For we are God's workmanship, created in Christ Jesus to do good works, which God prepared in advance for us to do.

EPHESIANS 1:3–14

Every Spiritual Blessing in Christ: A Psalm

1:3 PRAISE BE TO THE GOD AND FATHER OF OUR LORD JESUS CHRIST.

It is one long, breathless sentence in the Greek, verses 3–14 of the first chapter of Paul's letter to the Ephesians. It reads like a psalm, worthy of comparison with the great psalms like Psalms 23, 103, 139 and 145. And it is packed theologically. Densely. The reality of the Trinity is there implicitly but strongly, along with some of the great ideas of the gospel: chosen, predestined, adopted, forgiven, redeemed.

This is definitely a psalm to personalize. Read it through slowly and prayerfully, substituting the first-person singular for all the second person plurals. For instance, instead of "us" say, "who has blessed *me* in the heavenly realms." Do this repeatedly, over a week or a month, until you really mean what you read and the apostle Paul's words become your own. Expect your outlook to brighten as you do.

Personalize this passage with understanding. Get a commentary on Ephesians or a Bible dictionary and familiarize yourself with the big theological concepts. With every increase in your understanding will come a corresponding increase in wonder and praise for our great God. That, after all, is the purpose of the gospel celebrated by this New Testament psalm, "that we, who . . . hope in Christ, might be for the praise of his glory" (verse 12).

Let your understanding give you a new perspective on your life. Paul says we who know Christ know something no one else does: the meaning of history, God's purpose, "to bring all things in heaven and on earth together under one head, even Christ" (verse 10). In other words, a child, a person from a third-world culture or an illiterate farmer in Appalachia can know the secret of history—while a Ph.D. in history may not! The point is that our little lives are part of something unimaginably great. We can rest secure in the present because we know the one who holds the future. And he who holds the last hour is in control of the next moment—"to the praise of his glory."

PRAY:

You are the God and Father of my Lord Jesus Christ! Praise be to you for blessing me with every spiritual blessing in Christ.

FOR YOUR NEXT DEVOTIONAL READING, GO TO PAGE 1446.

One in Christ

¹¹Therefore, remember that formerly you who are Gentiles by birth and called "uncircumcised" by those who call themselves "the circumcision" (that done in the body by the hands of men)— ¹²remember that at that time you were separate from Christ, excluded from citizenship in Israel and foreigners to the covenants of the promise, without hope and without God in the world. ¹³But now in Christ Jesus you who once were far

---

EPHESIANS 1:15–23

A Prayer for Illumination

1:18 | I PRAY ALSO THAT THE EYES OF YOUR HEART MAY BE ENLIGHTENED.

Søren Kierkegaard told a parable about a poor peasant who could never afford to buy a pair of shoes. One day the peasant went to the city and earned enough money to not only buy shoes but also to get drunk. That night the man got drunk and passed out on the street. The next morning as he slept, a wagon drove up, and the driver shouted at him to move or he would run over his legs. The badly hungover peasant woke up, raised his head and looked at his legs. But he didn't recognize them because he was wearing shoes and stockings. He laid his head back, closed his eyes, and shouted back to the driver, "Drive on; they're not my legs."

Lest we suffer the same thing spiritually, Paul prays, "I pray also that the eyes of your heart may be enlightened" (1:18). The magnitude of the spiritual blessings described in verses 3–14 are to our spiritual consciousness what shoes were to that poor peasant—except multiplied by 10,000! The gap between what we were apart from Christ and what we are in Christ is too great for our little minds to comprehend (see 2:1–7). We need more than data and information about the transformation; we need enlightenment. That's what Paul prays for the Ephesians and what we must pray for ourselves and others—that we may:

Know God better. "I keep asking that the God of our Lord Jesus Christ, the glorious Father, may give you the Spirit of wisdom and revelation, so that you may know him better" (1:17).

Know our hope. "I pray also that the eyes of your heart may be enlightened in order that you may know the hope to which he has called you, the riches of his glorious inheritance in the saints" (verse 18).

Know God's power. "And his incomparably great power for us who believe. That power is like the working of his mighty strength, which he exerted in Christ when he raised him from the dead and seated him at his right hand in the heavenly realms" (verses 19–20).

These are stunning things to pray, much less to experience and understand. But they are nevertheless things we may—and must—ask God for, or we will be like the peasant who didn't recognize his own legs.

PRAY:

Father in heaven: Open the eyes of my heart!
I want to know you and the hope and power I have in Christ.

FOR YOUR NEXT DEVOTIONAL READING, GO TO PAGE 1448.

away have been brought near through the blood of Christ.

¹⁴For he himself is our peace, who has made the two one and has destroyed the barrier, the dividing wall of hostility, ¹⁵by abolishing in his flesh the law with its commandments and regulations. His purpose was to create in himself one new man out of the two, thus making peace, ¹⁶and in this one body to reconcile both of them to God through the cross, by which he put to death their hostility. ¹⁷He came and preached peace to you who were far away and peace to those who were near. ¹⁸For through him we both have access to the Father by one Spirit.

¹⁹Consequently, you are no longer foreigners and aliens, but fellow citizens with God's people and members of God's household, ²⁰built on the foundation of the apostles and prophets, with Christ Jesus himself as the chief cornerstone. ²¹In him the whole building is joined together and rises to become a holy temple in the Lord. ²²And in him you too are being built together to become a dwelling in which God lives by his Spirit.

Paul the Preacher to the Gentiles

3 For this reason I, Paul, the prisoner of Christ Jesus for the sake of you Gentiles—

²Surely you have heard about the administration of God's grace that was given to me for you, ³that is, the mystery made known to me by revelation, as I have already written briefly. ⁴In reading this, then, you will be able to understand my insight into the mystery of Christ, ⁵which was not made known to men in other generations as it has now been revealed by the Spirit to God's holy apostles and prophets. ⁶This mystery is that through the gospel the Gentiles are heirs together with Israel, members together of one body, and sharers together in the promise in Christ Jesus.

⁷I became a servant of this gospel by the gift of God's grace given me through the working of his power. ⁸Although I am less than the least of all God's people, this grace was given me: to preach to the Gentiles the unsearchable riches of Christ, ⁹and to make plain to everyone the administration of this mystery, which

for ages past was kept hidden in God, who created all things. ¹⁰His intent was that now, through the church, the manifold wisdom of God should be made known to the rulers and authorities in the heavenly realms, ¹¹according to his eternal purpose which he accomplished in Christ Jesus our Lord. ¹²In him and through faith in him we may approach God with freedom and confidence. ¹³I ask you, therefore, not to be discouraged because of my sufferings for you, which are your glory.

A Prayer for the Ephesians

¹⁴For this reason I kneel before the Father, ¹⁵from whom his whole family*a* in heaven and on earth derives its name. ¹⁶I pray that out of his glorious riches he may strengthen you with power through his Spirit in your inner being, ¹⁷so that Christ may dwell in your hearts through faith. And I pray that you, being rooted and established in love, ¹⁸may have power, together with all the saints, to grasp how wide and long and high and deep is the love of Christ, ¹⁹and to know this love that surpasses knowledge—that you may be filled to the measure of all the fullness of God.

²⁰Now to him who is able to do immeasurably more than all we ask or imagine, according to his power that is at work within us, ²¹to him be glory in the church and in Christ Jesus throughout all generations, for ever and ever! Amen.

Unity in the Body of Christ

4 As a prisoner for the Lord, then, I urge you to live a life worthy of the calling you have received. ²Be completely humble and gentle; be patient, bearing with one another in love. ³Make every effort to keep the unity of the Spirit through the bond of peace. ⁴There is one body and one Spirit—just as you were called to one hope when you were called— ⁵one Lord, one faith, one baptism; ⁶one God and Father of all, who is over all and through all and in all.

⁷But to each one of us grace has been given as Christ apportioned it. ⁸This is why it*b* says:

---

a15 Or whom all fatherhood   *b8 Or God*

EPHESIANS 3:14–21

Making Mud Pies in a Slum

3:16 "I PRAY THAT OUT OF HIS GLORIOUS RICHES HE MAY STRENGTHEN YOU WITH POWER."

Question: Does God think you want too much or are satisfied with too little? Before you answer that question, do two things. First, hear the answer C. S. Lewis gave:

> Indeed, if we consider the unblushing promises of reward and the staggering nature of the rewards promised in the Gospels, it would seem that our Lord finds our desires, not too strong, but too weak. We are half-hearted creatures, fooling about with drink and sex and ambition when infinite joy is offered us, like an ignorant child who wants to go on making mud pies in a slum because he cannot imagine what is meant by the offer of a holiday at the sea. We are far too easily pleased.[1]

That's one way to answer the question. Now do the second thing: Measure your desires for yourself against the prayer Paul prays here for the Ephesians—which, as part of Holy Scripture, is also relevant for you. Do you desire anything like …

Christ actually making his home and setting up permanent residence in your inner being? "That Christ may dwell in your hearts through faith" (3:17).

Knowing the full dimensions of Christ's love—knowing, in a sense, the unknowable? "To grasp how wide and long and high and deep is the love of Christ, and to know this love that surpasses knowledge" (verses 18–19a).

Being as full of God as you can be and still be you? "That you may be filled to the measure of all the fullness of God" (verse 19b).

Can anyone ever really pray for these things and fully understand what they mean? Probably not even the apostle Paul fully comprehended what he was praying. But no matter—we should pray for these things anyway. It's OK if our reach exceeds our grasp. For "what's a heaven for" if not for that? (Robert Browning)

PRAY:
My heart is narrow, my vision shortsighted, Lord.
Expand me, open me, fill me to the measure of yourself.

———

FOR YOUR NEXT DEVOTIONAL READING, GO TO PAGE 1451.

"When he ascended on high,
he led captives in his train
and gave gifts to men."[a]

[9](What does "he ascended" mean except that he also descended to the lower, earthly regions[b]? [10]He who descended is the very one who ascended higher than all the heavens, in order to fill the whole universe.) [11]It was he who gave some to be apostles, some to be prophets, some to be evangelists, and some to be pastors and teachers, [12]to prepare God's people for works of service, so that the body of Christ may be built up [13]until we all reach unity in the faith and in the knowledge of the Son of God and become mature, attaining to the whole measure of the fullness of Christ.

[14]Then we will no longer be infants, tossed back and forth by the waves, and blown here and there by every wind of teaching and by the cunning and craftiness of men in their deceitful scheming. [15]Instead, speaking the truth in love, we will in all things grow up into him who is the Head, that is, Christ. [16]From him the whole body, joined and held together by every supporting ligament, grows and builds itself up in love, as each part does its work.

Living as Children of Light

[17]So I tell you this, and insist on it in the Lord, that you must no longer live as the Gentiles do, in the futility of their thinking. [18]They are darkened in their understanding and separated from the life of God because of the ignorance that is in them due to the hardening of their hearts. [19]Having lost all sensitivity, they have given themselves over to sensuality so as to indulge in every kind of impurity, with a continual lust for more.

[20]You, however, did not come to know Christ that way. [21]Surely you heard of him and were taught in him in accordance with the truth that is in Jesus. [22]You were taught, with regard to your former way of life, to put off your old self, which is being corrupted by its deceitful desires; [23]to be made new in the attitude of your minds; [24]and to put on the new self, created to be like God in true righteousness and holiness.

[25]Therefore each of you must put off falsehood and speak truthfully to his neighbor, for we are all members of one body. [26]"In your anger do not sin"[c]: Do not let the sun go down while you are still angry, [27]and do not give the devil a foothold. [28]He who has been stealing must steal no longer, but must work, doing something useful with his own hands, that he may have something to share with those in need.

[29]Do not let any unwholesome talk come out of your mouths, but only what is helpful for building others up according to their needs, that it may benefit those who listen. [30]And do not grieve the Holy Spirit of God, with whom you were sealed for the day of redemption. [31]Get rid of all bitterness, rage and anger, brawling and slander, along with every form of malice. [32]Be kind and compassionate to one another, forgiving each other, just as in Christ God forgave you.

> BE KIND and compassionate to one another, forgiving each other, just as in Christ God forgave you.
>
> EPHESIANS 4:32

5 Be imitators of God, therefore, as dearly loved children [2]and live a life of love, just as Christ loved us and gave himself up for us as a fragrant offering and sacrifice to God.

[3]But among you there must not be even a hint of sexual immorality, or of any kind of impurity, or of greed, because these are improper for God's holy people. [4]Nor should there be obscenity, foolish talk or coarse joking, which are out of place, but rather thanksgiving. [5]For of this you can be sure: No immoral, impure or greedy person—such a man is an idolater—has any inheritance in the kingdom of Christ and of God.[d] [6]Let no one deceive you with empty words, for because of such things God's wrath comes on those who are disobedient. [7]Therefore do not be partners with them. [8]For you were once darkness, but now you are light in the Lord. Live as children

---

[a]8 Psalm 68:18   [b]9 Or *the depths of the earth*
[c]26 Psalm 4:4   [d]5 Or *kingdom of the Christ and God*

of light ⁹(for the fruit of the light consists in all goodness, righteousness and truth) ¹⁰and find out what pleases the Lord. ¹¹Have nothing to do with the fruitless deeds of darkness, but rather expose them. ¹²For it is shameful even to mention what the disobedient do in secret. ¹³But everything exposed by the light becomes visible, ¹⁴for it is light that makes everything visible. This is why it is said:

"Wake up, O sleeper,
  rise from the dead,
and Christ will shine on you."

¹⁵Be very careful, then, how you live—not as unwise but as wise, ¹⁶making the most of every opportunity, because the days are evil. ¹⁷Therefore do not be foolish, but understand what the Lord's will is. ¹⁸Do not get drunk on wine, which leads to debauchery. Instead, be filled with the Spirit. ¹⁹Speak to one another with psalms, hymns and spiritual songs. Sing and make music in your heart to the Lord, ²⁰always giving thanks to God the Father for everything, in the name of our Lord Jesus Christ.

²¹Submit to one another out of reverence for Christ.

Wives and Husbands

²²Wives, submit to your husbands as to the Lord. ²³For the husband is the head of the wife as Christ is the head of the church, his body, of which he is the Savior. ²⁴Now as the church submits to Christ, so also wives should submit to their husbands in everything.

²⁵Husbands, love your wives, just as Christ loved the church and gave himself up for her ²⁶to make her holy, cleansing[a] her by the washing with water through the word, ²⁷and to present her to himself as a radiant church, without stain or wrinkle or any other blemish, but holy and blameless. ²⁸In this same way, husbands ought to love their wives as their own bodies. He who loves his wife loves himself. ²⁹After all, no one ever hated his own body, but he feeds and cares for it, just as Christ does the church— ³⁰for we are members of his body. ³¹"For this reason a man will leave his father and mother and be united to his wife, and the two will become one flesh."[b] ³²This is a profound mystery—but I am

> *Prayer should be short, without giving God Almighty reasons why he should grant this or that; he knows best what is good for us.*
>
> JOHN SELDEN

talking about Christ and the church. ³³However, each one of you also must love his wife as he loves himself, and the wife must respect her husband.

Children and Parents

6 Children, obey your parents in the Lord, for this is right. ²"Honor your father and mother"—which is the first commandment with a promise— ³"that it may go well with you and that you may enjoy long life on the earth."[c]

⁴Fathers, do not exasperate your children; instead, bring them up in the training and instruction of the Lord.

Slaves and Masters

⁵Slaves, obey your earthly masters with respect and fear, and with sincerity of heart, just as you would obey Christ. ⁶Obey them not only to win their favor when their eye is on you, but like slaves of Christ, doing the will of God from your heart. ⁷Serve wholeheartedly, as if you were serving the Lord, not men, ⁸because you know that the Lord will reward everyone for whatever good he does, whether he is slave or free.

⁹And masters, treat your slaves in the same way. Do not threaten them, since you know that he who is both their Master and yours is in heaven, and there is no favoritism with him.

The Armor of God

¹⁰Finally, be strong in the Lord and in his mighty power. ¹¹Put on the full armor of God so that you can take your stand against the devil's schemes. ¹²For our struggle is not against flesh and blood, but against the rulers, against the authorities, against the powers of this dark world and against the spiritual forces of evil in the heavenly realms. ¹³Therefore

---

[a]26 Or *having cleansed*   [b]31 Gen. 2:24
[c]3 Deut. 5:16

put on the full armor of God, so that when the day of evil comes, you may be able to stand your ground, and after you have done everything, to stand. ¹⁴Stand firm then, with the belt of truth buckled around your waist, with the breastplate of righteousness in place, ¹⁵and with your feet fitted with the readiness that comes from the gospel of peace. ¹⁶In addition to all this, take up the shield of faith, with which you can extinguish all the flaming arrows of the evil one. ¹⁷Take the helmet

---

{ FRIDAY }

EPHESIANS 5:19–20

A Culture of Prayer and Praise

5:19 SPEAK TO ONE ANOTHER WITH PSALMS, HYMNS AND SPIRITUAL SONGS.

Cultures have tremendous influence on how people grow, think and behave. A violent culture tends to produce violent people. A culture of peace tends to produce peaceful people. The word *culture* comes from the Latin, *colere*, which means "to cultivate." A culture is to people what soil, sun, water and fertilizer are to a garden. A good garden is well-cultivated; a bad garden is poorly cultivated.

In the same way, a family, Christian community, even a workplace can become cultures of prayer and praise. That's what Paul is recommending in Ephesians 5:19–20: "Speak to one another with psalms, hymns and spiritual songs. Sing and make music in your heart to the Lord, always giving thanks to God the Father for everything, in the name of our Lord Jesus Christ." Prayer and praise don't automatically flourish in a church any more than a flower automatically grows in a garden. It requires planting and cultivation. The growth and health of prayer and praise must be intentional.

What's the kind of discourse that typically takes place during your church gatherings? Someone said that there is more to life than news, weather and sports. But one might never know that by the level of conversation that takes place in many churches before and after a worship service. It's not that topics like these are unworthy of Christians; it's just that other things are so much more worthy. It's not that the only things we should do when we get together is speak with psalms, hymns and spiritual songs; it's just that these should characterize what we do. Without being stilted or mechanical about it, we can be more intentional about the things we talk about in Christian fellowship. A culture of praise and thanksgiving grows faithful, wise and happy people.

Maybe Paul gives us a clue in verse 18 as to how it should be in a culture of prayer and praise. He says, "Do not get drunk on wine, which leads to debauchery." Alcohol is a powerful and pervasive influence. It leads people in certain very definite directions. "Instead, be filled with the Spirit." The Holy Spirit should be the most powerful and pervasive influence in a Christian fellowship. He leads people in very definite directions, too. They tend toward "psalms, hymns and spiritual songs."

PRAY:

Father God: May my fellowship with others be a culture of prayer and praise. Fill us, pervade us, with your Holy Spirit.

FOR YOUR NEXT DEVOTIONAL READING, GO TO PAGE 1452.

BEN PATTERSON
Of Sparrows and Stuffed Animals

I REGRETTED praying the prayer the moment I prayed it; but it seemed to jump out of my mouth. After tucking in my eight-year-old son Andy, I said a goodnight prayer at his bedside. He had been disconsolate for a week over the loss of his little stuffed animal, a gray wolf he named "Wolfie." His grief would escalate at bedtime since Wolfie was his sleeping companion. Seeing his furrowed little brow and moist eyes every night broke my heart. I had prayed for God to comfort him, and I had prayed that we would find Wolfie; but tonight my spontaneous, non-premeditated bedside prayer was, "Father, please show us where Wolfie is *so that Andy will know how much you love him.*" My first thought after the "Amen" was, *What if I just wrote a check God won't sign?* What if we don't find Wolfie—will Andy now conclude that God doesn't love him? I resisted the urge to throw in a caveat and add to the prayer, "But if we don't find Wolfie, help Andy to know you still love him anyway."

I got up from my knees and walked out Andy's bedroom door. At that moment a pictured popped into my mind: It was Wolfie in a sleeping bag in a box in our attic. Andy had been invited to a sleepover at a friend's house last week; it was possible that Andy left Wolfie in his sleeping bag. I climbed up into the attic and crawled through the dust to the box with the sleeping bags. I pulled one out, opened it, and there was Wolfie! I scrambled out of the attic and ran to Andy's room with the proof of God's love in my hand. Though he didn't appear to be in the mood for theological reflection on the event, Andy was very grateful and held Wolfie to his chest as we thanked God for his goodness.

Actually, had I engaged in a little theological reflection before my prayer, I probably wouldn't have prayed it. I probably would have dismissed it as trivial and narcissistic. I would have wanted to hedge my bets and not put God on trial, lest the Almighty come up short in Andy's eyes. But having prayed the prayer, quite by accident—no, not by accident—I have engaged in theological reflection of this sort: If the Father notices sparrows and counts hairs, he knows where the "Wolfies" of our lives can be found. If God became a human to show us his face, he certainly must care about a child's face creased with sadness. Nothing is too hard, too big, or too small for his love.

PRAY:

Gracious and tender Father in heaven!
You know how we are formed; you understand that
we are little and afraid and confused. Show us your
tender mercy; stoop down Almighty One,
take us by the hand and take us home.

MEMORIZE:

"Are not five sparrows sold for two pennies? Yet not one
of them is forgotten by God. Indeed, the very hairs of your head
are all numbered. Don't be afraid; you are worth more
than many sparrows." LUKE 12:6–7

FOR YOUR NEXT DEVOTIONAL READING, GO TO PAGE 1454.

EPHESIANS 6:10–20

God's Armor

6:11 PUT ON THE FULL ARMOR OF GOD.

"Don't take it personally." That was the advice a retired older pastor gave to a young pastor. "Don't take what personally?" the younger man asked. "Don't take it personally when you are attacked and opposed in the ministry. It's not about you. You're in a battle; it goes with the territory." That advice is relevant for all believers. A soldier in a war gets shot at. His feelings don't get hurt when that happens; he doesn't take it personally; he knows it comes with being in combat.

Paul assumed his readers knew about the battle part, that every believer is a soldier. He wanted to remind the believers of the nature of the battle, that it was spiritual. The battle wasn't against the things that physical senses can perceive, the things we can taste, touch, hear, smell and see. It was against the powers of the unseen realm, things seen only through the eyes of faith. Spiritual warfare calls for spiritual weapons. Worldly weapons are useless in a spiritual conflict (see devotion on 2 Corinthians 10:1–6); to use them is like hunting a lion with a squirt gun. Spiritual armor and spiritual weapons are essential: things like the helmet of salvation, the breastplate of righteousness and the shield of faith.

But how does one put on a "helmet of salvation," for instance? We put it on, and put on all the rest, by prayer. At the end of the list of spiritual armor comes the "sword of the Spirit, which is the word of God" (Ephesians 6:17). The next verse reads, "And pray in the Spirit." The Greek is literally something like, "by means of prayer." The idea is that the armor is donned by prayer, and the sword of the Spirit is wielded by prayer.

Paul makes prayer comprehensive in its application with four "alls": We are to pray on all occasions, with all kinds of prayers, with all perseverance and for all the saints. Prayer is the one thing that fits all the circumstances of spiritual warfare. It is always appropriate. Just as significant is the way we are to pray in spiritual warfare. Paul wants the Ephesians to pray that he would be fearless and wise ("that . . . words may be given me"). These are the classically essential qualities of any good soldier: courage and good judgment. It isn't enough to have the heart to charge the enemy; we also need the head to know when and how.

Paul's instructions to the Ephesians are essential briefing for any soldier of Christ fighting the good fight.

PRAY:

Father, give me the heart and the head I need
to fight the good fight. Give me courage and teach me wisdom.

FOR YOUR NEXT DEVOTIONAL READING, GO TO PAGE 1458.

of salvation and the sword of the Spirit, which is the word of God. [18]And pray in the Spirit on all occasions with all kinds of prayers and requests. With this in mind, be alert and always keep on praying for all the saints.

[19]Pray also for me, that whenever I open my mouth, words may be given me so that I will fearlessly make known the mystery of the gospel, [20]for which I am an ambassador in chains. Pray that I may declare it fearlessly, as I should.

Final Greetings

[21]Tychicus, the dear brother and faithful servant in the Lord, will tell you everything, so that you also may know how I am and what I am doing. [22]I am sending him to you for this very purpose, that you may know how we are, and that he may encourage you.

[23]Peace to the brothers, and love with faith from God the Father and the Lord Jesus Christ. [24]Grace to all who love our Lord Jesus Christ with an undying love.

Philippians

ONE WAY to look at Paul's remarkable letter is to see it as a missionary update and thank-you note to his supporters (see 4:10–19). That alone is a delightful thought—within the canon of Holy Scripture is a thank-you letter!

Of course, the letter to the Philippians is much more than that. As Paul writes his thanks, he delivers one of the classic formulations of Christian doctrine regarding the incarnation of Christ (see 2:6–11). Scholars call these verses the *kenosis* passage, from the Greek verb in 2:7 translated "made himself nothing" but which literally means "he emptied himself."

This letter is also known for its emphasis on joy; the words "joy" or "rejoice" or related ideas appear again and again. The emphasis on joy is not incidental to the letter's thanksgiving purpose. Joy is what one experiences when thankful for the grace that has been given. Theologian Karl Barth said grace evokes gratitude like the voice of an echo; gratitude follows grace like thunder follows lightning. That construct is everywhere in Philippians. Are the people fighting amongst themselves? Paul's appeal is to gratitude and joy. Should not their experience of God's grace in the incarnation and union with Christ motivate them to get along? Because of all that grace, couldn't they make his joy complete by being like-minded and having the same love (see 2:1–11)? It isn't that the Philippians are forced to live in love or be punished. There's more to it than that. How can they do anything else, knowing what they know of God's goodness? It is their joy to do so, is it not?

Maybe Philippians isn't much more than a thank-you note after all. Joyful gratitude sustains the prisoner (see 1:12–26), unifies congregations (2:1–11), calms the worrier (4:4–7), and makes a poor man content (4:10–13). We can never pay God back for his goodness to us. What we can do is pray and live joyfully (see Psalm 116:12–14). Is there any other way to be thankful?

1 Paul and Timothy, servants of Christ Jesus,

To all the saints in Christ Jesus at Philippi, together with the overseers[a] and deacons:

[2]Grace and peace to you from God our Father and the Lord Jesus Christ.

Thanksgiving and Prayer

[3]I thank my God every time I remember you. [4]In all my prayers for all of you, I always pray with joy [5]because of your partnership in the gospel from the first day until now, [6]being confident of this, that he who began a good work in you will carry it on to completion until the day of Christ Jesus.

[7]It is right for me to feel this way about all of you, since I have you in my heart; for whether I am in chains or defending and confirming the gospel, all of you share in God's grace with me. [8]God can testify how I long for all of you with the affection of Christ Jesus.

[9]And this is my prayer: that your love may abound more and more in knowledge and depth of insight, [10]so that you may be able to discern what is best and may be pure and blameless until the day of Christ, [11]filled with the fruit of righteousness that comes through Jesus Christ—to the glory and praise of God.

Paul's Chains Advance the Gospel

[12]Now I want you to know, brothers, that what has happened to me has really served to advance the gospel. [13]As a result, it has become clear throughout the whole palace guard[b] and to everyone else that I am in chains for Christ. [14]Because of my chains, most of the brothers in the Lord have been encouraged to speak the word of God more courageously and fearlessly.

[15]It is true that some preach Christ out of envy and rivalry, but others out of goodwill. [16]The latter do so in love, knowing that I am put here for the defense of the gospel. [17]The former preach Christ out of selfish ambition, not sincerely, supposing that they can stir up trouble for me while I am in chains.[c] [18]But what does it matter? The important thing is that in every way, whether from false motives or true, Christ is preached. And because of this I rejoice.

Yes, and I will continue to rejoice, [19]for I know that through your prayers and the help given by the Spirit of Jesus Christ, what has happened to me will turn out for my deliverance.[d] [20]I eagerly expect and

> FOR *I know that through your prayers and the help given by the Spirit of Jesus Christ, what has happened to me will turn out for my deliverance.*
>
> PHILIPPIANS 1:19

hope that I will in no way be ashamed, but will have sufficient courage so that now as always Christ will be exalted in my body, whether by life or by death. [21]For to me, to live is Christ and to die is gain. [22]If I am to go on living in the body, this will mean fruitful labor for me. Yet what shall I choose? I do not know! [23]I am torn between the two: I desire to depart and be with Christ, which is better by far; [24]but it is more necessary for you that I remain in the body. [25]Convinced of this, I know that I will remain, and I will continue with all of you for your progress and joy in the faith, [26]so that through my being with you again your joy in Christ Jesus will overflow on account of me.

[27]Whatever happens, conduct yourselves in a manner worthy of the gospel of Christ. Then, whether I come and see you or only hear about you in my absence, I will know that you stand firm in one spirit, contending as one man for the faith of the gospel [28]without being frightened in any way by those who oppose you. This is a sign to them that they will be destroyed, but that you will be saved—and that by God. [29]For it has been granted to you on behalf of Christ not only to believe on him, but also to suffer for him, [30]since you are going through the same struggle you saw I had, and now hear that I still have.

Imitating Christ's Humility

2 If you have any encouragement from being united with Christ, if any comfort from his love, if any fellowship with

---

[a]1 Traditionally *bishops*   [b]13 Or *whole palace*
[c]16,17 Some late manuscripts have verses 16 and 17 in reverse order.   [d]19 Or *salvation*

PHILIPPIANS 1:3–11

Joyful, Thankful, Confident Prayer

1:3 "I THANK MY GOD EVERY TIME I REMEMBER YOU."

The problem with prayer is not that it is boring but that our methods for it are—at least sometimes. Paul's prayer for the Philippians is a great prayer in its own right and worth repeating, but it is also a model of how to revitalize prayer.

First, note that Paul prayed for the Philippians joyfully (see 1:4). His joy came from two things: his memory of the past and his confident hope in the future. The past was full of thankful memories of the Philippians' "partnership in the gospel" and the ways they had shared in God's grace with him. All that added up to a longing in his heart for them "with the affection of Christ Jesus" (verse 8). When you pray for those you love, take the time to remember the good and happy history you have had with them. Some find it helpful to keep photos nearby as a way to add color to their intercession. It helps to pray for others when your memory of them is warmly vivid and loving.

Paul's prayers were also joyful because he was confident that he need not worry about the Philippians as he prayed for them. Sometimes intercession becomes heavy, even depressing, because of our concern. Joy and a certain lightness come when we remember that "he who began a good work in you will carry it on to completion" (verse 6). We are not praying upstream or against the grain, but with a God whose purposes for those we love will be fulfilled. God is more willing to answer prayer than we are willing to pray.

Second, look at *what* Paul prayed for the Philippians: love (see verses 9–11). But not just emotional love. He prayed for a wise love, a love that is filled with knowledge and depth of insight, a love that can sort out from many options the one thing needed. In loving others, love always wants what is best for the beloved. In loving God, love always wants to do what God thinks best. In both cases, love is happiest when it knows what is best. Prayer for what makes love happiest is happy prayer. When God answers this prayer in those we love, the possibilities in life multiply. There is simply no telling what wonderful surprises lay ahead. And we can be sure that God most assuredly will answer this kind of prayer for wise love (see James 1:5).

PRAY:

Faithful God, strengthen my hope and awaken
my memory that I may pray for others with
confidence and joy. Give me, and those I pray for,
a wise and discerning love.

FOR YOUR NEXT DEVOTIONAL READING, GO TO PAGE 1461.

the Spirit, if any tenderness and compassion, ²then make my joy complete by being like-minded, having the same love, being one in spirit and purpose. ³Do nothing out of selfish ambition or vain conceit, but in humility consider others better than yourselves. ⁴Each of you should look not only to your own interests, but also to the interests of others.

⁵Your attitude should be the same as that of Christ Jesus:

⁶ Who, being in very nature*ᵃ* God,
did not consider equality with God
something to be grasped,
⁷ but made himself nothing,
taking the very nature*ᵇ* of a
servant,
being made in human likeness.
⁸ And being found in appearance as a
man,
he humbled himself
and became obedient to death—
even death on a cross!
⁹ Therefore God exalted him to the
highest place
and gave him the name that is
above every name,
¹⁰ that at the name of Jesus every knee
should bow,
in heaven and on earth and under
the earth,
¹¹ and every tongue confess that Jesus
Christ is Lord,
to the glory of God the Father.

Shining as Stars

¹²Therefore, my dear friends, as you have always obeyed—not only in my presence, but now much more in my absence—continue to work out your salvation with fear and trembling, ¹³for it is God who works in you to will and to act according to his good purpose.

¹⁴Do everything without complaining or arguing, ¹⁵so that you may become blameless and pure, children of God without fault in a crooked and depraved generation, in which you shine like stars in the universe ¹⁶as you hold out*ᶜ* the word of life—in order that I may boast on the day of Christ that I did not run or labor for nothing. ¹⁷But even if I am being poured out like a drink offering on the sacrifice and service coming from your faith, I am glad and rejoice with all of you. ¹⁸So you too should be glad and rejoice with me.

Timothy and Epaphroditus

¹⁹I hope in the Lord Jesus to send Timothy to you soon, that I also may be cheered when I receive news about you. ²⁰I have no one else like him, who takes a genuine interest in your welfare. ²¹For everyone looks out for his own interests, not those of Jesus Christ. ²²But you know that Timothy has proved himself, because as a son with his father he has served with me in the work of the gospel. ²³I hope, therefore, to send him as soon as I see how things go with me. ²⁴And I am confident in the Lord that I myself will come soon.

²⁵But I think it is necessary to send back to you Epaphroditus, my brother, fellow worker and fellow soldier, who is also your messenger, whom you sent to take care of my needs. ²⁶For he longs for all of you and is distressed because you heard he was ill. ²⁷Indeed he was ill, and almost died. But God had mercy on him, and not on him only but also on me, to spare me sorrow upon sorrow. ²⁸Therefore I am all the more eager to send him, so that when you see him again you may be glad and I may have less anxiety. ²⁹Welcome him in the Lord with great joy, and honor men like him, ³⁰because he almost died for the work of Christ, risking his life to make up for the help you could not give me.

No Confidence in the Flesh

3 Finally, my brothers, rejoice in the Lord! It is no trouble for me to write the same things to you again, and it is a safeguard for you.

ᵃ6 Or in the form of   *ᵇ7 Or the form*
ᶜ16 Or hold on to

²Watch out for those dogs, those men who do evil, those mutilators of the flesh. ³For it is we who are the circumcision, we who worship by the Spirit of God, who glory in Christ Jesus, and who put no confidence in the flesh— ⁴though I myself have reasons for such confidence.

If anyone else thinks he has reasons to put confidence in the flesh, I have more: ⁵circumcised on the eighth day, of the people of Israel, of the tribe of Benjamin, a Hebrew of Hebrews; in regard to the law, a Pharisee; ⁶as for zeal, persecuting the church; as for legalistic righteousness, faultless.

⁷But whatever was to my profit I now consider loss for the sake of Christ. ⁸What is more, I consider everything a loss compared to the surpassing greatness of knowing Christ Jesus my Lord, for whose sake I have lost all things. I consider them rubbish, that I may gain Christ ⁹and be found in him, not having a righteousness of my own that comes from the law, but that which is through faith in Christ—the righteousness that comes from God and is by faith. ¹⁰I want to know Christ and the power of his resurrection and the fellowship of sharing in his sufferings, becoming like him in his death, ¹¹and so, somehow, to attain to the resurrection from the dead.

Pressing on Toward the Goal

¹²Not that I have already obtained all this, or have already been made perfect, but I press on to take hold of that for which Christ Jesus took hold of me. ¹³Brothers, I do not consider myself yet to have taken hold of it. But one thing I do: Forgetting what is behind and straining toward what is ahead, ¹⁴I press on toward the goal to win the prize for which God has called me heavenward in Christ Jesus.

¹⁵All of us who are mature should take such a view of things. And if on some point you think differently, that too God will make clear to you. ¹⁶Only let us live up to what we have already attained.

¹⁷Join with others in following my example, brothers, and take note of those who live according to the pattern we gave you. ¹⁸For, as I have often told you before and now say again even with tears, many live as enemies of the cross of Christ.

¹⁹Their destiny is destruction, their god is their stomach, and their glory is in their shame. Their mind is on earthly things. ²⁰But our citizenship is in heaven. And we eagerly await a Savior from there, the Lord Jesus Christ, ²¹who, by the power that enables him to bring everything under his control, will transform our lowly bodies so that they will be like his glorious body.

> " Do we sing as much as the birds do? Yet what have birds to sing about, compared with us? Do we sing as much as the angels do? Yet they were never redeemed by the blood of Christ. Birds of the air, shall you excel me? Angels, shall you exceed me? You have done so, but I intend to emulate you, and day by day, and night by night, pour forth my soul in sacred song. "
>
> CHARLES SPURGEON

4 Therefore, my brothers, you whom I love and long for, my joy and crown, that is how you should stand firm in the Lord, dear friends!

Exhortations

²I plead with Euodia and I plead with Syntyche to agree with each other in the Lord. ³Yes, and I ask you, loyal yokefellow,ᵃ help these women who have contended at my side in the cause of the gospel, along with Clement and the rest of my fellow workers, whose names are in the book of life.

⁴Rejoice in the Lord always. I will say it again: Rejoice! ⁵Let your gentleness be evident to all. The Lord is near. ⁶Do not be anxious about anything, but in everything, by prayer and petition, with thanksgiving, present your requests to God. ⁷And the peace of God, which transcends all understanding, will guard your hearts and your minds in Christ Jesus.

⁸Finally, brothers, whatever is true, whatever is noble, whatever is right, whatever is pure, whatever is lovely, whatever is admirable—if anything is excellent or praiseworthy—think about such things.

ᵃ3 Or loyal Syzygus

Longing

3:7 "WHATEVER WAS TO MY PROFIT I NOW CONSIDER LOSS FOR THE SAKE OF CHRIST."

Prayer, as in all the life of the Spirit, has a beginning, a road and a goal. It begins with a vision of something—or better, of *someone* of inestimable worth. Jesus said the kingdom of God is like a man who found a treasure buried in a field. He hid it and joyfully went off and sold all he owned to buy the field and get the treasure (see Matthew 13:44). Some might watch the man liquidate his assets and wonder about his sanity in betting everything he owned on a field. But the man knows better. Paul was like that man. When he saw Christ, he looked at everything he had ever gained and saw it as loss compared to knowing him. It was worse than loss; it was rubbish, actually (see 3:7–8). The desire to pray is directly proportionate to our sense of the preciousness of Christ.

The road of the spiritual life is strenuous and hard. Paul said, "I press on to take hold of that for which Christ Jesus took hold of me" (verse 12). The sense of the Greek for "press on" is of a hunter pursuing a quarry or a runner running for the gold medal. "Take hold," a wrestling term, is even more vigorous. The Greek is literally, "I grasp, inasmuch as I was grasped by Christ." Picture Paul's conversion on the road to Damascus this way: He was on a mission to persecute disciples of Jesus, "breathing out murderous threats" against them (Acts 9:1). Jesus met him on the way and "grasped him"—he wrestled him to the ground and pinned him. Everything changed for Paul that day, and from then on the purpose for which Christ wrestled him to the ground and pinned him was the purpose for which Paul will wrestle to the ground and pin any and every obstacle to knowing Christ. The same qualities that make for a great athlete make for a great pray-er: a vision of glory and a sober estimate of what it will take to get there.

The goal of prayer is the same as its beginning. What makes us want to pray in the first place is a vision of the inestimable worth of Christ. The goal then is to know him and the power of his resurrection, to share even in his sufferings—if it means fellowship with the one we so desperately want to know.

P R A Y :

*Dear Jesus, I want to know you and the power of your
resurrection, to share even in your sufferings
and become like you in your death—
if it means fellowship with you.*

FOR YOUR NEXT DEVOTIONAL READING, GO TO PAGE 1462.

[9]Whatever you have learned or received or heard from me, or seen in me—put it into practice. And the God of peace will be with you.

Thanks for Their Gifts

[10]I rejoice greatly in the Lord that at last you have renewed your concern for me. Indeed, you have been concerned, but you had no opportunity to show it. [11]I am not saying this because I am in need, for I have learned to be content whatever the circumstances. [12]I know what it is to be in need, and I know what it is to have plenty. I have learned the secret of being content in any and every situation, whether well fed or hungry, whether living in plenty or in want. [13]I

[THURSDAY]

PHILIPPIANS 4:4–9

Peace of Mind Praying

4:6 "DO NOT BE ANXIOUS ABOUT ANYTHING."

Have you ever tried to stop worrying by stopping worry? It doesn't work, does it? It's like deciding not to think about something; the more you think about not thinking, the more thinking you do.

The best way not to worry is by indirection; do something else, preferably something that is the opposite of worry. The opposite of worry is thankful prayer: "Do not be anxious about anything, but in everything, by prayer and petition, with thanksgiving, present your requests to God. And the peace of God, which transcends all understanding, will guard your hearts and your minds in Christ Jesus" (4:6–7). What is it about prayer that is so effective against worry?

The Latin words for *prayer* and *anxiety* offer a good picture of how it works. The Latin word for "anxiety" is *curare*, a word used also to name a poison some South American tribes would put on the tips of their arrows. The poison works like anxiety; it so constricts the muscles of the body, especially the throat, that the victim suffocates. Isn't that the way worry feels? It is like hands around the throat, a weight on the chest. The Latin word for "prayer" is *orare*, which means essentially to open the mouth and speak. *Orare* works against *curare* by opening us up and letting in the oxygen.

That's a picture of how it works conceptually. Here is how it works practically: Tell God everything you're worried about, but as you tell him, give thanks. Give thanks that he hears you and answers prayer. Give thanks that your sins are forgiven and you will spend eternity in heaven. Give thanks that nothing can separate you from the love of Christ. In short, give thanks that everything that really matters has already been taken care of; all the rest are details—like the things you're worrying about as you pray.

And try this little spiritual discipline: When you're worried and someone asks you how you are, say something like, "I'm fundamentally sound." Or if you want a little laugh, say, "Other than the fact that my sins are forgiven, and I will spend an eternity of joy with God, I'm not doing too well."

PRAY:
Dear Father! Thank you that all the things that nag at
my peace of mind have no power to separate me from your love.

FOR YOUR NEXT DEVOTIONAL READING, GO TO PAGE 1466.

can do everything through him who gives me strength.

[14]Yet it was good of you to share in my troubles. [15]Moreover, as you Philippians know, in the early days of your acquaintance with the gospel, when I set out from Macedonia, not one church shared with me in the matter of giving and receiving, except you only; [16]for even when I was in Thessalonica, you sent me aid again and again when I was in need. [17]Not that I am looking for a gift, but I am looking for what may be credited to your account. [18]I have received full payment and even more; I am amply supplied, now that I have received from Epaphroditus the gifts you sent. They are a fra-

grant offering, an acceptable sacrifice, pleasing to God. [19]And my God will meet all your needs according to his glorious riches in Christ Jesus.

[20]To our God and Father be glory for ever and ever. Amen.

Final Greetings

[21]Greet all the saints in Christ Jesus. The brothers who are with me send greetings. [22]All the saints send you greetings, especially those who belong to Caesar's household.

[23]The grace of the Lord Jesus Christ be with your spirit. Amen.[a]

[a]23 Some manuscripts do not have *Amen*.

Colossians

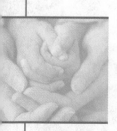

"WHY DO people climb mountains?" The most famous answer to that question is Sir George Mallory's. When asked why he climbed the Matterhorn, he replied, "Because it was there!" Willy Unsoeld, a mountaineer and a philosopher, didn't like that answer. He thought there was a deeper reason: "People climb mountains because of a universal desire to find the point of convergence."[1] That is what it feels like on a mountaintop. Looking at the complexity of all the geography below, the cities and forests and rivers and hills, one has the sensation that all lines come together and converge at the peak. If only there were a place to stand where all the complexity of life truly came together the way it feels on a mountaintop!

But there is a point like this: in the person of Jesus Christ. He is, in his own words, "the First and the Last," the beginning and the end (Revelation 1:17). No other book in the Bible states this concept more powerfully than Colossians. "He is the image of the invisible God, the firstborn over all creation . . . all things were created by him and for him. He is before all things, and in him all things hold together" (1:15–17). A. T. Robertson said Colossians gives a "full length portrait of Christ." In doing so, it shows Christ to be the point of convergence we all long for.

The church in Colosse was in danger of losing its grasp of Christ's supremacy. Instead of being the integrator of all things, Christ was being integrated into the Colossians' schemes. Instead of Christ alone, they wanted Christ plus—Christ with supplements. Paul wanted the Colossians to know that Jesus isn't one of the treasures of wisdom and knowledge. He isn't even the greatest of the treasures of wisdom and knowledge. He is the one "in whom are hidden all the treasures of wisdom and knowledge" (2:3).

The letter to the Colossians calls us to pray and to do everything in the name of our great Christ (see 3:17). Paul's prayer for these people is a model of pastoral concern coupled with theological acuity (see 1:9–14). Paul knows that ideas have far-reaching consequences for good or for bad; there is no idea more determinative of everything else than our understanding of Christ. Our faith, and our prayers, will be as big or as small as our grasp of his greatness.

1 Paul, an apostle of Christ Jesus by the will of God, and Timothy our brother,

²To the holy and faithful[a] brothers in Christ at Colosse:

Grace and peace to you from God our Father.[b]

Thanksgiving and Prayer

³We always thank God, the Father of our Lord Jesus Christ, when we pray for you, ⁴because we have heard of your faith in Christ Jesus and of the love you have for all the saints— ⁵the faith and love that spring from the hope that is stored up for you in heaven and that you have already heard about in the word of truth, the gospel ⁶that has come to you. All over the world this gospel is bearing fruit and growing, just as it has been doing among you since the day you heard it and understood God's grace in all its truth. ⁷You learned it from Epaphras, our dear fellow servant, who is a faithful minister of Christ on our[c] behalf, ⁸and who also told us of your love in the Spirit.

⁹For this reason, since the day we heard about you, we have not stopped praying for you and asking God to fill you with the knowledge of his will through all spiritual wisdom and understanding. ¹⁰And we pray this in order that you may live a life worthy of the Lord and may please him in every way: bearing fruit in every good work, growing in the knowledge of God, ¹¹being strengthened with all power according to his glorious might so that you may have great endurance and patience, and joyfully ¹²giving thanks to the Father, who has qualified you[d] to share in the inheritance of the saints in the kingdom of light. ¹³For he has rescued us from the dominion of darkness and brought us into the kingdom of the Son he loves, ¹⁴in whom we have redemption,[e] the forgiveness of sins.

The Supremacy of Christ

¹⁵He is the image of the invisible God, the firstborn over all creation. ¹⁶For by him all things were created: things in heaven and on earth, visible and invisible, whether thrones or powers or rulers or authorities; all things were created by him and for him. ¹⁷He is before all things, and in him all things hold together. ¹⁸And he is the head of the body, the church; he is the beginning and the firstborn from among the dead, so that in everything he might have the supremacy. ¹⁹For God was pleased to have all his fullness dwell in him, ²⁰and through him to reconcile to himself all things, whether things on earth or things in heaven, by making peace through his blood, shed on the cross.

²¹Once you were alienated from God and were enemies in your minds because of[f] your evil behavior. ²²But now he has reconciled you by Christ's physical body through death to present you holy in his sight, without blemish and free from accusation— ²³if you continue in your faith, established and firm, not moved from the

> 66 *The time to pray is not when we are in a tight spot but just as soon as we get out of it.* 99
>
> JOSH BILLINGS

hope held out in the gospel. This is the gospel that you heard and that has been proclaimed to every creature under heaven, and of which I, Paul, have become a servant.

Paul's Labor for the Church

²⁴Now I rejoice in what was suffered for you, and I fill up in my flesh what is still lacking in regard to Christ's afflictions, for the sake of his body, which is the church. ²⁵I have become its servant by the commission God gave me to present to you the word of God in its fullness— ²⁶the mystery that has been kept hidden for ages and generations, but is now disclosed to the saints. ²⁷To them God has chosen to make known among the Gentiles the glorious riches of this mystery, which is Christ in you, the hope of glory. ²⁸We proclaim him, admonishing and teaching everyone with all wisdom, so that we may present everyone perfect in Christ. ²⁹To this end I labor, struggling with all his energy, which so powerfully works in me.

[a]2 Or *believing*   [b]2 Some manuscripts *Father and the Lord Jesus Christ*   [c]7 Some manuscripts *your*   [d]12 Some manuscripts *us*   [e]14 A few late manuscripts *redemption through his blood*   [f]21 Or *minds, as shown by*

Pleasing God

1:9 WE HAVE NOT STOPPED PRAYING FOR YOU.

Ever since Charles Sheldon's bestseller *In His Steps*, Christians have had their imaginations fired by the question, "What would Jesus do?" It can be helpful to project Jesus into a situation we are faced with and imagine how he would act. But if we are not careful, it can also be limiting. We can easily attribute to the Jesus we imagine in the situation all kinds of things that Jesus isn't and never was. The Jesus of our imaginations may have nothing to do with the real Jesus.

A better approach is to pray the way Paul prayed for the Colossians: "asking God to fill you with the knowledge of his will through all spiritual wisdom and understanding" (1:9). This request goes far beyond imitating what you think Jesus might do. It asks God to give you the mind and attitude of Jesus. It's more than accurate information and good behavior; it is a living, breathing knowledge of God's will. It's like what happens to an athlete when all the techniques have been mastered and performance becomes art.

The purpose for Paul's prayer gives an important clue as to how this knowledge comes about. He prayed that the Colossians would know God's will so they could "live a life worthy of the Lord and . . . please him in every way" (verse 10). The sense of the Greek word translated "please" is to anticipate every wish, the way a slave anticipates his or her master's every wish. In classical Greek, this attitude was never considered a good thing. The desire to please connoted servility and cringing submissiveness. It lacked dignity; it belonged to the weak. It was the attitude of a slave, and no free person would want to be *that*. Precisely. Only those who want to be God's slave will know God's will. "Obedience is the opener of eyes," wrote George Macdonald. We will know only what we will to do. Better, we will not only know the will of God; we will have the mind of God, "through all spiritual wisdom and understanding."

As you pray for this marvelous revelation, pay close attention to the ways it shows itself:

- bearing fruit in every good work,
- growing in the knowledge of God,
- being strengthened with all power according to his glorious might so that you may have great endurance and patience,
- joyfully giving thanks to the Father (verses 10b–12a).

PRAY:

*Dear God, in the name of your Son, I ask you to fill me
with the knowledge of your will through all spiritual insight
and understanding—that I may live a life worthy
of your name and please you in every way.*

FOR YOUR NEXT DEVOTIONAL READING, GO TO PAGE 1468.

2 I want you to know how much I am struggling for you and for those at Laodicea, and for all who have not met me personally. ²My purpose is that they may be encouraged in heart and united in love, so that they may have the full riches of complete understanding, in order that they may know the mystery of God, namely, Christ, ³in whom are hidden all the treasures of wisdom and knowledge. ⁴I tell you this so that no one may deceive you by fine-sounding arguments. ⁵For though I am absent from you in body, I am present with you in spirit and delight to see how orderly you are and how firm your faith in Christ is.

Freedom From Human Regulations Through Life With Christ

⁶So then, just as you received Christ Jesus as Lord, continue to live in him, ⁷rooted and built up in him, strengthened in the faith as you were taught, and overflowing with thankfulness.

> 66 Were there no God, we would be in this glorious world with grateful hearts and no one to thank. 99
>
> CHRISTINA ROSSETTI

⁸See to it that no one takes you captive through hollow and deceptive philosophy, which depends on human tradition and the basic principles of this world rather than on Christ.

⁹For in Christ all the fullness of the Deity lives in bodily form, ¹⁰and you have been given fullness in Christ, who is the head over every power and authority. ¹¹In him you were also circumcised, in the putting off of the sinful nature,ᵃ not with a circumcision done by the hands of men but with the circumcision done by Christ, ¹²having been buried with him in baptism and raised with him through your faith in the power of God, who raised him from the dead.

¹³When you were dead in your sins and in the uncircumcision of your sinful nature,ᵇ God made youᶜ alive with Christ. He forgave us all our sins, ¹⁴having canceled the written code, with its regulations, that was against us and that stood opposed to us; he took it away, nailing it to the cross. ¹⁵And having disarmed the powers and authorities, he made a public spectacle of them, triumphing over them by the cross.ᵈ

¹⁶Therefore do not let anyone judge you by what you eat or drink, or with regard to a religious festival, a New Moon celebration or a Sabbath day. ¹⁷These are a shadow of the things that were to come; the reality, however, is found in Christ. ¹⁸Do not let anyone who delights in false humility and the worship of angels disqualify you for the prize. Such a person goes into great detail about what he has seen, and his unspiritual mind puffs him up with idle notions. ¹⁹He has lost connection with the Head, from whom the whole body, supported and held together by its ligaments and sinews, grows as God causes it to grow.

²⁰Since you died with Christ to the basic principles of this world, why, as though you still belonged to it, do you submit to its rules: ²¹"Do not handle! Do not taste! Do not touch!"? ²²These are all destined to perish with use, because they are based on human commands and teachings. ²³Such regulations indeed have an appearance of wisdom, with their self-imposed worship, their false humility and their harsh treatment of the body, but they lack any value in restraining sensual indulgence.

Rules for Holy Living

3 Since, then, you have been raised with Christ, set your hearts on things above, where Christ is seated at the right hand of God. ²Set your minds on things above, not on earthly things. ³For you died, and your life is now hidden with Christ in God. ⁴When Christ, who is yourᵉ life, appears, then you also will appear with him in glory.

⁵Put to death, therefore, whatever belongs to your earthly nature: sexual immorality, impurity, lust, evil desires and greed, which is idolatry. ⁶Because of these, the wrath of God is coming.ᶠ ⁷You

ᵃ11 Or the flesh   ᵇ13 Or your flesh
ᶜ13 Some manuscripts us   ᵈ15 Or them in him   ᵉ4 Some manuscripts our   ᶠ6 Some early manuscripts coming on those who are disobedient

SAMUEL JOHNSON (1709–1784)
A Great Mind and a Greater God

WHEN A MAN who had been very unhappy in marriage immediately remarried after the death of his wife, Samuel Johnson, the great lexicographer and man of letters, described his act as "the triumph of hope over experience."[2]

Johnson was easily amused or inflamed by his own and others' foibles, and he could express either sentiment with elegance, biting wit and devastating sarcasm. He was greatly to be feared as an opponent in an argument. Once when insulted, he replied, "A fly, Sir, may sting a stately horse and make him wince; but one is but an insect, and the other a horse still."[3] After an evening of conversation marked by spirited debate and repartee, Johnson remarked to Boswell, his biographer, that the conversation had been good. Boswell agreed, and said, "Yes, Sir; you tossed and gored several persons."[4]

But Johnson's sharpest jabs were directed at those skeptics who ridiculed the Christian faith he so cherished. The 18th century, like the 20th, was a time when intellectuals and aesthetes treated the faith with contempt. Joseph Butler said it was "an agreed point among people of discernment" that the faith was worthy only "as a principle subject of mirth and ridicule, as it were by way of reprisals, for so long having interrupted the pleasures of the world."[5] Of these skeptics, Johnson wrote, "Truth . . . is a cow, which will yield such people no more milk, and so they are gone to milk the bull."[6]

But the man with the proud and formidable intellect before people was a child before God. His great mind was humble before a greater God.

Johnson's prayers reveal a man with a deep, even tortured, sense of his own sinfulness. Trust in God's mercy did not come easily to Johnson, but it came, and he seemed never to be less than grateful and humbled that it did.

PRAY:

Pray this prayer of Samuel Johnson's: O merciful God,
full of compassion, long-suffering, and of great pity,
who sparest when we deserve punishment, and in thy wrath
thinkest upon mercy; make me earnestly to repent, and heartily
to be sorry for all my misdoings; make the remembrance
so burdensome and painful, that I may flee to thee with
a troubled spirit and a contrite heart; and, O merciful Lord,
visit, comfort, and relieve me; cast me not out from thy presence,
and take not thy Holy Spirit from me, but excite in me
true repentance; give me in this world knowledge of thy truth,
and confidence in thy mercy, and in the world to
come life everlasting, for the sake of our Lord and savior,
thy Son Jesus Christ. Amen[7]

MEMORIZE:

For since in the wisdom of God the world through its wisdom
did not know him, God was pleased through the foolishness
of what was preached to save those who believe . . .

For the foolishness of God is wiser than man's wisdom,
and the weakness of God is stronger than
man's strength. 1 CORINTHIANS 1:21,25

FOR YOUR NEXT DEVOTIONAL READING, GO TO PAGE 1470.

used to walk in these ways, in the life you once lived. ⁸But now you must rid yourselves of all such things as these: anger, rage, malice, slander, and filthy language from your lips. ⁹Do not lie to each other, since you have taken off your old self with its practices ¹⁰and have put on the new self, which is being renewed in knowledge in the image of its Creator. ¹¹Here there is no Greek or Jew, circumcised or uncircumcised, barbarian, Scythian, slave or free, but Christ is all, and is in all.

¹²Therefore, as God's chosen people, holy and dearly loved, clothe yourselves with compassion, kindness, humility, gentleness and patience. ¹³Bear with

[MONDAY]

COLOSSIANS 3:1–4

The Still Point of the Turning World

3:2 SET YOUR MINDS ON THINGS ABOVE, NOT ON EARTHLY THINGS.

There is such a thing as a praying imagination. This passage is a prime example. Picture yourself walking through a shopping mall fashioned after John Bunyan's Vanity Fair, the town given over completely to worldly pursuits and pleasures. All around you are shopkeepers and street vendors hawking their wares: drink, sex, ambition, wealth, power, beauty. Lights flash, music blares and a loud calliope plays crazily. Hands reach for you, strangers whisper in your ears. But your heart is still fixed on Christ, "the still point of the turning world" (T. S. Eliot, *East Coker*). You are not touched by what clutches at you. Your heart and mind is set on things above, "where Christ is seated at the right hand of God . . . on things above, not on earthly things" (3:1–2).⁸

There is no getting through Vanity Fair without prayer. To be sure, praying is not all there is to be done, but you won't get to other things until you pray. To pray is to set your compass on heaven and stay on track through the trackless wastes of the world.

It's not an easy journey, walking through this world with your heart and mind set on heaven. But it's not as hard as it looks, either. In this text Paul uses one of his classic formulations, known by scholars as the indicative and imperative. The *indicative* is an objective truth, what *is*. The *imperative* is what must and can be done, based on the indicative. In these verses the indicative is: You died with Christ; you are raised with Christ; and your true life is hidden with Christ in God. Therefore, the imperative: Set your heart and mind on things above, not on earthly things. The indicative makes the imperative possible. The point is that you can live your life differently in the world because your true life is hidden with Christ in heaven. The journey may be hard, but it can be done; it may stretch you, but it is a stretching toward—not away from—your true self. Prayer can feel unnatural on earth, but it is the most natural thing in heaven; and that is where you belong.

PRAY:

Father in heaven! Give me a praying imagination.
Open my eyes to heaven's realities and close them
to the pretensions of the world.

FOR YOUR NEXT DEVOTIONAL READING, GO TO PAGE 1472.

each other and forgive whatever grievances you may have against one another. Forgive as the Lord forgave you. [14]And over all these virtues put on love, which binds them all together in perfect unity.

[15]Let the peace of Christ rule in your hearts, since as members of one body you were called to peace. And be thankful. [16]Let the word of Christ dwell in you richly as you teach and admonish one another with all wisdom, and as you sing psalms, hymns and spiritual songs with gratitude in your hearts to God. [17]And whatever you do, whether in word or deed, do it all in the name of the Lord Jesus, giving thanks to God the Father through him.

> AND whatever you do, whether in word or deed, do it all in the name of the Lord Jesus, giving thanks to God the Father through him.
>
> COLOSSIANS 3:17

Rules for Christian Households

[18]Wives, submit to your husbands, as is fitting in the Lord.

[19]Husbands, love your wives and do not be harsh with them.

[20]Children, obey your parents in everything, for this pleases the Lord.

[21]Fathers, do not embitter your children, or they will become discouraged.

[22]Slaves, obey your earthly masters in everything; and do it, not only when their eye is on you and to win their favor, but with sincerity of heart and reverence for the Lord. [23]Whatever you do, work at it with all your heart, as working for the Lord, not for men, [24]since you know that you will receive an inheritance from the Lord as a reward. It is the Lord Christ you are serving. [25]Anyone who does wrong will be repaid for his wrong, and there is no favoritism.

4 Masters, provide your slaves with what is right and fair, because you know that you also have a Master in heaven.

Further Instructions

[2]Devote yourselves to prayer, being watchful and thankful. [3]And pray for us, too, that God may open a door for our message, so that we may proclaim the mystery of Christ, for which I am in chains. [4]Pray that I may proclaim it clearly, as I should. [5]Be wise in the way you act toward outsiders; make the most of every opportunity. [6]Let your conversation be always full of grace, seasoned with salt, so that you may know how to answer everyone.

Final Greetings

[7]Tychicus will tell you all the news about me. He is a dear brother, a faithful minister and fellow servant in the Lord. [8]I am sending him to you for the express purpose that you may know about our[a] circumstances and that he may encourage your hearts. [9]He is coming with Onesimus, our faithful and dear brother, who is one of you. They will tell you everything that is happening here.

[10]My fellow prisoner Aristarchus sends you his greetings, as does Mark, the cousin of Barnabas. (You have received instructions about him; if he comes to you, welcome him.) [11]Jesus, who is called Justus, also sends greetings. These are the only Jews among my fellow workers for the kingdom of God, and they have proved a comfort to me. [12]Epaphras, who is one of you and a servant of Christ Jesus, sends greetings. He is always wrestling in prayer for you, that you may stand firm in all the will of God, mature and fully assured. [13]I vouch for him that he is working hard for you and for those at Laodicea and Hierapolis. [14]Our dear friend Luke, the doctor, and Demas send greetings. [15]Give my greetings to the brothers at Laodicea, and to Nympha and the church in her house.

[16]After this letter has been read to you, see that it is also read in the church of the Laodiceans and that you in turn read the letter from Laodicea.

[17]Tell Archippus: "See to it that you complete the work you have received in the Lord."

[18]I, Paul, write this greeting in my own hand. Remember my chains. Grace be with you.

---

[a]8 Some manuscripts *that he may know about your*

COLOSSIANS 4:2–4,12–13

Muscular Prayer

4:12 HE IS ALWAYS WRESTLING IN PRAYER FOR YOU.

Epaphras prayed like a fighter. The Greek for "wrestling" is the word behind our English word "agony." Originally it was a noun, referring to the place where people went to watch wrestlers and boxers. Then it came to mean not only where they went, but also what they went to watch. By Jesus' day it was also used to describe the activity of attorneys in court! It is a muscular word, a vigorous word. That's how Epaphras prayed. He went to the mat for the church at Colosse, as well as at Laodicea and Hierapolis.

Concentration is essential in any athletic endeavor. But it is critical in boxing and wrestling. Lose your focus and you may get a black eye or pinned to the mat. That image gives a particular vividness to Paul's words about prayer earlier in the chapter: "Devote yourselves to prayer, being watchful and thankful" (4:2). A lot depends on watchful, muscular prayer: for example, the effectiveness of gospel preaching. Paul wants the message to go out to an unbelieving world with clarity, vigor and supernatural power (see verses 3–4). So he urges us to wrestle with God in prayer, to speak to God about people before we speak to people about God.

Thankfulness in this intense kind of prayer keeps it from becoming exhausting. When you wrestle in prayer for souls, give thanks for them, and repeatedly express gratitude for the glorious gospel—doing so will keep the duty of prayer delightful.

This is a high calling, more worthy of concentrated devotion than the Olympic games. Why do we hold back? "What makes us Christians shrug our shoulders when we ought to be flexing our muscles?" asked Billy Graham. "What makes us apathetic in a day when there are loads to lift, a world to be won and captives to be set free? Why are so many bored when the times demand action?"

Pray like Epaphras. Why not start a prayer group and name it "The Epaphras Fellowship"?

P R A Y :

Heavenly Father: Your Son wrestled in Gethsemane
for the sake of our salvation. Teach us
to wrestle in prayer for the salvation of others.

FOR YOUR NEXT DEVOTIONAL READING, GO TO PAGE 1475.

INTRODUCTION

1 Thessalonians

IF YOU KNOW how a book or movie is going to end, it makes a great deal of difference how you interpret any scene or episode that precedes the ending. The future has a way of invading and altering the present in a way the past never can.

If you knew that Christ were returning tomorrow, would you live any differently? Stated another way—Since you don't know whether he is or isn't, should that in any way affect your living? Actually both questions should have the same answer: We should live every day in the light of the possibility of the Lord's return. Knowing that he will return should keep us on our toes. Not knowing when he is coming should keep us on our toes even more. That future should invade and alter our present.

Paul's first letter to the Thessalonians was written to a people keenly aware that the Lord was going to come back—today, tomorrow or next year; it didn't matter. Everything they did was to be done in that light: evangelism, ministry, behavior, community life. Paul wrote to urge them to live out, in very practical ways, that ethic of hope.

What could be more encouraging to our prayers than to know the things we pray for will one day come to pass: that God's name will be hallowed, his kingdom will come and all that is wrong will be set right? How happy we will be if, when the Lord returns, he finds us crying out for him to come (see Luke 18:1–8).

"AND SO WE WILL BE WITH THE LORD FOREVER." (4:17)

1

Paul, Silas[a] and Timothy,

To the church of the Thessalonians in God the Father and the Lord Jesus Christ:

Grace and peace to you.[b]

Thanksgiving for the Thessalonians' Faith

[2]We always thank God for all of you, mentioning you in our prayers. [3]We continually remember before our God and Father your work produced by faith, your labor prompted by love, and your endurance inspired by hope in our Lord Jesus Christ.

> 66 *Prayer makes your heart bigger, until it is capable of containing the gift of God himself.* 99
>
> MOTHER TERESA

[4]For we know, brothers loved by God, that he has chosen you, [5]because our gospel came to you not simply with words, but also with power, with the Holy Spirit and with deep conviction. You know how we lived among you for your sake. [6]You became imitators of us and of the Lord; in spite of severe suffering, you welcomed the message with the joy given by the Holy Spirit. [7]And so you became a model to all the believers in Macedonia and Achaia. [8]The Lord's message rang out from you not only in Macedonia and Achaia—your faith in God has become known everywhere. Therefore we do not need to say anything about it, [9]for they themselves report what kind of reception you gave us. They tell how you turned to God from idols to serve the living and true God, [10]and to wait for his Son from heaven, whom he raised from the dead—Jesus, who rescues us from the coming wrath.

Paul's Ministry in Thessalonica

2

You know, brothers, that our visit to you was not a failure. [2]We had previously suffered and been insulted in Philippi, as you know, but with the help of our God we dared to tell you his gospel in spite of strong opposition. [3]For the appeal we make does not spring from error or impure motives, nor are we trying to trick you. [4]On the contrary, we speak as men approved by God to be entrusted with the gospel. We are not trying to please men but God, who tests our hearts. [5]You know we never used flattery, nor did we put on a mask to cover up greed—God is our witness. [6]We were not looking for praise from men, not from you or anyone else.

As apostles of Christ we could have been a burden to you, [7]but we were gentle among you, like a mother caring for her little children. [8]We loved you so much that we were delighted to share with you not only the gospel of God but our lives as well, because you had become so dear to us. [9]Surely you remember, brothers, our toil and hardship; we worked night and day in order not to be a burden to anyone while we preached the gospel of God to you.

[10]You are witnesses, and so is God, of how holy, righteous and blameless we were among you who believed. [11]For you know that we dealt with each of you as a father deals with his own children, [12]encouraging, comforting and urging you to live lives worthy of God, who calls you into his kingdom and glory.

[13]And we also thank God continually because, when you received the word of God, which you heard from us, you accepted it not as the word of men, but as it actually is, the word of God, which is at work in you who believe. [14]For you, brothers,

> AND we also thank God continually because, when you received the word of God, which you heard from us, you accepted it not as the word of men, but as it actually is, the word of God, which is at work in you who believe.
>
> 1 THESSALONIANS 2:13

became imitators of God's churches in Judea, which are in Christ Jesus: You suffered from your own countrymen the same things those churches suffered from the Jews, [15]who killed the Lord Jesus and

---

[a]1 Greek *Silvanus*, a variant of *Silas*   [b]1 Some early manuscripts *you from God our Father and the Lord Jesus Christ*

the prophets and also drove us out. They displease God and are hostile to all men [16]in their effort to keep us from speaking to the Gentiles so that they may be saved. In this way they always heap up their sins to the limit. The wrath of God has come upon them at last.[a]

Paul's Longing to See the Thessalonians

[17]But, brothers, when we were torn away from you for a short time (in person, not in thought), out of our intense longing we made every effort to see you.

[a]16 Or *them fully*

---

1 THESSALONIANS 1:2–3

The Causes of Happy Effects

1:2 WE ALWAYS THANK GOD FOR ALL OF YOU.

Good roots make for healthy trees and good fruit. They are the cause of a happy effect. As Paul prayed for the Thessalonians, he thanked God for their good roots and excellent fruit. Their roots were faith, hope and love, what theologians have called the three theological virtues. These are to moral virtues what roots are to fruit.

The Thessalonians' faith produced work. One could say their faith worked, as faith always does. Faith without works is dead. It appears that with the Thessalonians, the work was their accomplishments, the things they had done because of their trust in the Lord. William Carey said we should believe great things of God and attempt great things for God. The two go together.

Their love prompted labor. Love makes people work hard. Faith that believes a great thing must have a love that will work hard for it. The old adage that genius is one percent inspiration and ninety-nine percent perspiration is another way of saying it takes love to get the job done. The work of the Thessalonian church was people. People can be notoriously difficult and ungrateful even while they are being served. Only love will put up with that.

Their hope inspired endurance. One of the devil's greatest weapons is discouragement. Fatigue is soil for discouragement. The weary are prone to think there is no hope: "Why bother? What difference does it make anyway?" Hope inspires endurance because it assures us that what we do will make a difference if we just keep at it.

We can pray for others and ourselves that we would attempt great things for God, work hard at them and keep at it. That would be good. Or we might pray that God would build our faith, hope and love. That might be better, for then we would be cultivating the roots of good fruit, the cause of a happy effect. We wouldn't just *do* good, we would *be* good.

PRAY:

Holy Spirit of God! Strengthen my faith, deepen my love and broaden my hope that I might attempt great things, labor in love and persevere in hope.

FOR YOUR NEXT DEVOTIONAL READING, GO TO PAGE 1477.

¹⁸For we wanted to come to you—certainly I, Paul, did, again and again—but Satan stopped us. ¹⁹For what is our hope, our joy, or the crown in which we will glory in the presence of our Lord Jesus when he comes? Is it not you? ²⁰Indeed, you are our glory and joy.

3 So when we could stand it no longer, we thought it best to be left by ourselves in Athens. ²We sent Timothy, who is our brother and God's fellow worker*a* in spreading the gospel of Christ, to strengthen and encourage you in your faith, ³so that no one would be unsettled by these trials. You know quite well that we were destined for them. ⁴In fact, when we were with you, we kept telling you that we would be persecuted. And it turned out that way, as you well know. ⁵For this reason, when I could stand it no longer, I sent to find out about your faith. I was afraid that in some way the tempter might have tempted you and our efforts might have been useless.

Timothy's Encouraging Report

⁶But Timothy has just now come to us from you and has brought good news about your faith and love. He has told us that you always have pleasant memories of us and that you long to see us, just as we also long to see you. ⁷Therefore, brothers, in all our distress and persecution we were encouraged about you because of your faith. ⁸For now we really live, since you are standing firm in the Lord. ⁹How can we thank God enough for you in return for all the joy we have in the presence of our God because of you? ¹⁰Night and day we pray most earnestly that we may see you again and supply what is lacking in your faith.

> *NIGHT and day we pray most earnestly that we may see you again and supply what is lacking in your faith.*
>
> 1 THESSALONIANS 3:10

¹¹Now may our God and Father himself and our Lord Jesus clear the way for us to come to you. ¹²May the Lord make your love increase and overflow for each other and for everyone else, just as ours does for you. ¹³May he strengthen your hearts so that you will be blameless and holy in the presence of our God and Father when our Lord Jesus comes with all his holy ones.

Living to Please God

4 Finally, brothers, we instructed you how to live in order to please God, as in fact you are living. Now we ask you and urge you in the Lord Jesus to do this more and more. ²For you know what instructions we gave you by the authority of the Lord Jesus.

³It is God's will that you should be sanctified: that you should avoid sexual immorality; ⁴that each of you should learn to control his own body*b* in a way

> *Prayer is talking with God and telling him you love him, conversing with God about all the things that are important in life, both large and small, and being assured that he is listening.*
>
> C. NEIL STRAIT

that is holy and honorable, ⁵not in passionate lust like the heathen, who do not know God; ⁶and that in this matter no one should wrong his brother or take advantage of him. The Lord will punish men for all such sins, as we have already told you and warned you. ⁷For God did not call us to be impure, but to live a holy life. ⁸Therefore, he who rejects this instruction does not reject man but God, who gives you his Holy Spirit.

⁹Now about brotherly love we do not need to write to you, for you yourselves have been taught by God to love each other. ¹⁰And in fact, you do love all the brothers throughout Macedonia. Yet we urge you, brothers, to do so more and more. ¹¹Make it your ambition to lead a quiet life, to mind your own business and to work with your hands, just as we told you, ¹²so that your daily life may win the respect of outsiders and so that you will not be dependent on anybody.

a2 Some manuscripts brother and fellow worker; other manuscripts *brother and God's servant*
b4 Or learn to live with his own wife; or *learn to acquire a wife*

1 THESSALONIANS 5:16 – 18, 23 – 24

Prayer, Praise and Perfection

5:16–18 BE JOYFUL ALWAYS; PRAY CONTINUALLY; GIVE THANKS IN ALL CIRCUMSTANCES.

Paul gave three short commands—to be joyful always, pray continually and give thanks in all circumstances. William Law spoke from the heart of these when he wrote, "Would you know who is the greatest saint in the world? It is not he who prays most or fasts most; it is not he who gives most alms or is most eminent for temperance, chastity or justice; but it is he who is always thankful to God, who wills everything that God wills, who receives everything as an instance of God's goodness and has a heart always ready to praise God for it ... Could you therefore work miracles, you could not do more for yourself than by this thankful spirit, for it ... turns all that it touches into happiness."[1]

These are extravagant claims, but true. Why is continual thanksgiving so important to spiritual health? Because it comes from an attitude toward God that is so healthy: God is perfect in love, wisdom and power. He always wills what is best, always knows what is best and is powerful enough to always effect what is best. Continual thanksgiving practices this life-giving perspective. It says, "Father, even though I can't see your love, wisdom and power in these circumstances, I believe you are bigger than what I can see. I will praise you that you are God and that you are good in every circumstance of my life."

Thanksgiving is a spiritual discipline. So thank God for all you see (which usually isn't very much!). Then, when you run out of things to thank him for, thank him for what you cannot see (which is infinitely greater than what you can see!).

Thanksgiving should be indiscriminate; and if it is, it will lead to indefatigable joy. As Law says, it "turns all that it touches into happiness." Nothing can stop our God! He will sanctify us through and through, no matter what. He will present us blameless at Christ's return, no matter what. He is faithful, and he will do it (see verses 23–24), no matter what. So thank him, no matter what.

PRAY:

Father, even though I can't see your love,
wisdom and power in all circumstances,
I believe you are bigger than what I can see.
I will praise you that you are God
and that you are good in every
circumstance of my life.

———

FOR YOUR NEXT DEVOTIONAL READING, GO TO PAGE 1481.

The Coming of the Lord

¹³Brothers, we do not want you to be ignorant about those who fall asleep, or to grieve like the rest of men, who have no hope. ¹⁴We believe that Jesus died and rose again and so we believe that God will bring with Jesus those who have fallen asleep in him. ¹⁵According to the Lord's own word, we tell you that we who are still alive, who are left till the coming of the Lord, will certainly not precede those who have fallen asleep. ¹⁶For the Lord himself will come down from heaven, with a loud command, with the voice of the archangel and with the trumpet call of God, and the dead in Christ will rise first. ¹⁷After that, we who are still alive and are left will be caught up together with them in the clouds to meet the Lord in the air. And so we will be with the Lord forever. ¹⁸Therefore encourage each other with these words.

5 Now, brothers, about times and dates we do not need to write to you, ²for you know very well that the day of the Lord will come like a thief in the night. ³While people are saying, "Peace and safety," destruction will come on them suddenly, as labor pains on a pregnant woman, and they will not escape.

⁴But you, brothers, are not in darkness so that this day should surprise you like a thief. ⁵You are all sons of the light and sons of the day. We do not belong to the night or to the darkness. ⁶So then, let us not be like others, who are asleep, but let us be alert and self-controlled. ⁷For those who sleep, sleep at night, and those who get drunk, get drunk at night. ⁸But since we belong to the day, let us be self-controlled, putting on faith and love as a breastplate, and the hope of salvation as a helmet. ⁹For God did not appoint us to suffer wrath but to receive salvation through our Lord Jesus Christ. ¹⁰He died for us so that, whether we are awake or asleep, we may live together with him. ¹¹Therefore encourage one another and build each other up, just as in fact you are doing.

Final Instructions

¹²Now we ask you, brothers, to respect those who work hard among you, who are over you in the Lord and who admonish you. ¹³Hold them in the highest regard in love because of their work. Live in peace with each other. ¹⁴And we urge you, brothers, warn those who are idle, encourage the timid, help the weak, be patient with everyone. ¹⁵Make sure that nobody pays back wrong for wrong, but always try to be kind to each other and to everyone else.

¹⁶Be joyful always; ¹⁷pray continually; ¹⁸give thanks in all circumstances, for this is God's will for you in Christ Jesus.

¹⁹Do not put out the Spirit's fire; ²⁰do not treat prophecies with contempt. ²¹Test everything. Hold on to the good. ²²Avoid every kind of evil.

²³May God himself, the God of peace, sanctify you through and through. May your whole spirit, soul and body be kept blameless at the coming of our Lord Jesus Christ. ²⁴The one who calls you is faithful and he will do it.

²⁵Brothers, pray for us. ²⁶Greet all the brothers with a holy kiss. ²⁷I charge you before the Lord to have this letter read to all the brothers.

²⁸The grace of our Lord Jesus Christ be with you.

2 Thessalonians

THE FIRST letter that Paul wrote to the Thessalonians dealt with the Lord's return. This second letter continues on the subject of eschatology. The situation in the Thessalonian church has not changed much. The people are still under tremendous persecution, and they long for the return of Christ. Paul writes to the believers to encourage them and give them hope.

Today in our lives, we may not be facing persecution from outside sources hostile to Christianity. However, we are not necessarily immune to struggle or adversity. Daily we face loss, temptations and hurt. We suffer injustice or face unasked-for pain. That's why Paul's message to the Thessalonians can support us in whatever hardship we face. He tells the Thessalonians that Jesus Christ and God our Father had given them the hope they need: "eternal encouragement and good hope" (2:16).

When we bring our requests to God in prayer, we can know that the same comfort that kept the Thessalonians firm in their sufferings is available to us in our hour of need.

"MAY THE LORD DIRECT YOUR HEARTS INTO GOD'S LOVE AND CHRIST'S PERSEVERANCE."
(3:5)

1 Paul, Silas[a] and Timothy,

To the church of the Thessalonians in God our Father and the Lord Jesus Christ:

[2]Grace and peace to you from God the Father and the Lord Jesus Christ.

Thanksgiving and Prayer

[3]We ought always to thank God for you, brothers, and rightly so, because your faith is growing more and more, and the love every one of you has for each other is increasing. [4]Therefore, among God's churches we boast about your perseverance and faith in all the persecutions and trials you are enduring.

[5]All this is evidence that God's judgment is right, and as a result you will be counted worthy of the kingdom of God, for which you are suffering. [6]God is just: He will pay back trouble to those who trouble you [7]and give relief to you who are troubled, and to us as well. This will happen when the Lord Jesus is revealed from heaven in blazing fire with his powerful angels. [8]He will punish those who do not know God and do not obey the gospel of our Lord Jesus. [9]They will be punished with everlasting destruction and shut out from the presence of the Lord and from the majesty of his power [10]on the day he comes to be glorified in his holy people and to be marveled at among all those who have believed. This includes you, because you believed our testimony to you.

[11]With this in mind, we constantly pray for you, that our God may count you worthy of his calling, and that by his power he may fulfill every good purpose of yours and every act prompted by your faith. [12]We pray this so that the name of our Lord Jesus may be glorified in you, and you in him, according to the grace of our God and the Lord Jesus Christ.[b]

The Man of Lawlessness

2 Concerning the coming of our Lord Jesus Christ and our being gathered to him, we ask you, brothers, [2]not to become easily unsettled or alarmed by some prophecy, report or letter supposed to have come from us, saying that the day of the Lord has already come. [3]Don't

> " Great praying is the sign and seal of God's great leaders. "
>
> E.M. BOUNDS

let anyone deceive you in any way, for ⌊that day will not come⌋ until the rebellion occurs and the man of lawlessness[c] is revealed, the man doomed to destruction. [4]He will oppose and will exalt himself over everything that is called God or is worshiped, so that he sets himself up in God's temple, proclaiming himself to be God.

[5]Don't you remember that when I was with you I used to tell you these things? [6]And now you know what is holding him back, so that he may be revealed at the proper time. [7]For the secret power of lawlessness is already at work; but the one who now holds it back will continue to do so till he is taken out of the way. [8]And then the lawless one will be revealed, whom the Lord Jesus will overthrow with the breath of his mouth and destroy by the splendor of his coming. [9]The coming of the lawless one will be in accordance with the work of Satan displayed in all kinds of counterfeit miracles, signs and wonders, [10]and in every sort of evil that deceives those who are perishing. They perish because they refused to love the truth and so be saved. [11]For this reason God sends them a powerful delusion so that they will believe the lie [12]and so that all will be condemned who have not believed the truth but have delighted in wickedness.

Stand Firm

[13]But we ought always to thank God for you, brothers loved by the Lord, because

> BUT we ought always to thank God for you, brothers loved by the Lord, because from the beginning God chose you to be saved through the sanctifying work of the Spirit and through belief in the truth.
>
> 2 THESSALONIANS 2:13

[a]1 Greek *Silvanus*, a variant of *Silas*   [b]12 Or *God and Lord, Jesus Christ*   [c]3 Some manuscripts *sin*

2 THESSALONIANS 3:1–5

Prayer for Success of the Gospel

3:1 BROTHERS, PRAY FOR US.

Napoleon said, "An army marches on its stomach." He knew the chow line was the backbone of the front line. The church, however, advances on its knees, by prayer. We stoop to conquer. With this in mind, Paul asked the Thessalonians to pray three things for his work as a church-planting apostle, the first two for the message (see 3:1) and the third for him as the messenger (see verse 2). Praying Paul's prayer is a great way to pray for every missionary, preacher and teacher you know. No, wait—it is a great way for you to pray for all *your* efforts to speak the "message of the Lord" (verse 1) into others' lives.

1. Pray that the message will spread rapidly. The image Paul uses here is athletic and robust. The Greek word translated "spread rapidly" is literally "run." Paul does not ask that the gospel be listened to and considered or that it be given a fair hearing in the marketplace of ideas among many other options. He says to pray that the Good News will bound into the minds of hearers like a runner sprinting down a track, and that it will leave all the others in the dust (see Psalms 19:4–6; 147:15)!

2. Pray that the message will be honored. The Greek is literally "glorified": "Pray for us that the message of the Lord may run and be glorified, just as it was with you." Maybe the picture here is of a victorious runner being crowned on the victor stand. It certainly is a prayer for continuation. When the believers in Thessalonica heard the Gospel themselves, they accepted it: "You accepted it not as the word of men, but as it actually is, the word of God, which is at work in you who believe" (1 Thessalonians 2:13). And Paul prays that this reaction will happen again and again.

3. Pray that you, and other messengers, will be delivered from "wicked and evil men" (verse 2). The sad truth is that sometimes those most in need of a doctor are those who least want one. And they will not only resist the gospel themselves but also will work to keep others from hearing it. Paul knew what he was talking about from personal experience (see 2 Corinthians 11:23–26). Along with a prayer that the message spread rapidly and be honored, we need to pray that its messengers be protected from evil people and the evil one (see verse 3).

PRAY:

Dear Holy Spirit, anoint your message that it
might run and be victorious; and protect
your messengers from all sources of evil.

FOR YOUR NEXT DEVOTIONAL READING, GO TO PAGE 1482.

CHARLES WESLEY (1707–1788)
And Can It Be?

ON MAY 21, 1738, through the ministry of the Moravian Peter Bohler, Charles Wesley came to a profound sense of assurance that he really belonged to Christ and was truly saved from his sins through the atoning death of Christ. The hymn below was written a year after that transforming event and expressed his newfound confidence.

But it stood for much more. Along with his older brother John, and George Whitfield, he believed hymns played a key role in the evangelical renewal of the 18th century. Wesley was convinced that thoughtful hymns not only gave expression to spiritual experience but brought impression as well—that good hymns could teach good theology enjoyably. In all, Charles Wesley wrote some 6500 hymns, often employing the tunes of the popular songs and folk traditions of his times. "And Can It Be?" was originally titled, "Free Grace." It masterfully weaves together the powerful Biblical themes of salvation, liberation and enlightenment.

> And can it be that I should gain
> An int'rest in the Savior's blood?
> Died He for me, who caused His pain?
> For me, who Him to death pursued?
> Amazing love! how can it be
> That Thou, my God, shouldst die for me?
> 'Tis mystery all! Th'Immortal dies!
> Who can explore His strange design?
> In vain the first-born seraph tries
> To sound the depths of love divine!

'Tis mercy all! let earth adore,
Let angel minds inquire no more.
He left His Father's throne above,
So free, so infinite His grace!
Emptied Himself of all but love,
And bled for Adam's helpless race;
'Tis mercy all, immense and free,
For, O my God, it found out me.
Long my imprisoned spirit lay
Fast bound in sin and nature's night.
Thine eye diffused a quick'ning ray,
I woke, the dungeon flamed with light;
My chains fell off, my heart was free,
I rose, went forth, and followed Thee.
No condemnation now I dread;
Jesus, and all in Him, is mine!
Alive in Him, my living Head,
And clothed in righteousness divine,
Bold I approach th'eternal throne,
And claim the crown, through Christ my own.[1]

PRAY:

Make Wesley's hymn your own prayer of gratitude
and an instruction in the theology of grace.

MEMORIZE:

But God demonstrates his own love for us in this:
While we were still sinners, Christ died for us. ROMANS 5:8

FOR YOUR NEXT DEVOTIONAL READING, GO TO PAGE 1487.

from the beginning God chose you[a] to be saved through the sanctifying work of the Spirit and through belief in the truth. [14]He called you to this through our gospel, that you might share in the glory of our Lord Jesus Christ. [15]So then, brothers, stand firm and hold to the teachings[b] we passed on to you, whether by word of mouth or by letter.

[16]May our Lord Jesus Christ himself and God our Father, who loved us and by his grace gave us eternal encouragement and good hope, [17]encourage your hearts and strengthen you in every good deed and word.

Request for Prayer

3 Finally, brothers, pray for us that the message of the Lord may spread rapidly and be honored, just as it was with you. [2]And pray that we may be delivered from wicked and evil men, for not everyone has faith. [3]But the Lord is faithful, and he will strengthen and protect you from the evil one. [4]We have confidence in the Lord that you are doing and will continue to do the things we command. [5]May the Lord direct your hearts into God's love and Christ's perseverance.

Warning Against Idleness

[6]In the name of the Lord Jesus Christ, we command you, brothers, to keep away from every brother who is idle and does not live according to the teaching[c] you received from us. [7]For you yourselves know how you ought to follow our example. We were not idle when we were with you, [8]nor did we eat anyone's food without paying for it. On the contrary, we worked night and day, laboring and toil-

> 66 *Never be entirely idle; but either be reading, or writing, or praying or meditating or endeavoring something for the public good.* 99
>
> THOMAS À KEMPIS

ing so that we would not be a burden to any of you. [9]We did this, not because we do not have the right to such help, but in order to make ourselves a model for you to follow. [10]For even when we were with you, we gave you this rule: "If a man will not work, he shall not eat."

[11]We hear that some among you are idle. They are not busy; they are busybodies. [12]Such people we command and urge in the Lord Jesus Christ to settle down and earn the bread they eat. [13]And as for you, brothers, never tire of doing what is right.

[14]If anyone does not obey our instruction in this letter, take special note of him. Do not associate with him, in order that he may feel ashamed. [15]Yet do not regard him as an enemy, but warn him as a brother.

Final Greetings

[16]Now may the Lord of peace himself give you peace at all times and in every way. The Lord be with all of you.

[17]I, Paul, write this greeting in my own hand, which is the distinguishing mark in all my letters. This is how I write.

[18]The grace of our Lord Jesus Christ be with you all.

[a]13 Some manuscripts *because God chose you as his firstfruits*   [b]15 Or *traditions*   [c]6 Or *tradition*

1 Timothy

A MAN'S office has a wall covered with pictures of the likes of Martin Luther, C. S. Lewis, Flannery O'Connor, Dietrich Bonhoeffer and Francis Schaeffer. He calls it his wall of "Those Who Have Finished Strong." A friend was looking at the wall and joked, "Why isn't my picture there?" "You have to be dead to get there," the man replied. The race isn't over until it's over. We won't know how well we've finished until we finish.

The drama of Paul's letters to Timothy is that he is near the end of his life, and Timothy is closer to the beginning of his. Athletic and military metaphors abound as Paul strives to finish well and to encourage Timothy to do the same. They have a fight to engage in, a race to run, a prize to take hold of. Paul knew that to finish well would involve not only how he finished but also how Timothy finished. The race is a relay; its success depends on how well we pass the baton to the next runner. None of us is really finished until everyone is (see Hebrews 11:39—12:1).

"FIGHT THE GOOD
FIGHT OF THE
FAITH." (6:12)

1 Paul, an apostle of Christ Jesus by the command of God our Savior and of Christ Jesus our hope,

²To Timothy my true son in the faith:

Grace, mercy and peace from God the Father and Christ Jesus our Lord.

Warning Against False Teachers of the Law

³As I urged you when I went into Macedonia, stay there in Ephesus so that you may command certain men not to teach false doctrines any longer ⁴nor to devote themselves to myths and endless genealogies. These promote controversies rather than God's work—which is by faith. ⁵The goal of this command is love, which comes from a pure heart and a good conscience and a sincere faith. ⁶Some have wandered away from these and turned to meaningless talk. ⁷They want to be teachers of the law, but they do not know what they are talking about or what they so confidently affirm.

⁸We know that the law is good if one uses it properly. ⁹We also know that law*ᵃ* is made not for the righteous but for lawbreakers and rebels, the ungodly and sinful, the unholy and irreligious; for those who kill their fathers or mothers, for murderers, ¹⁰for adulterers and perverts, for slave traders and liars and perjurers—and for whatever else is contrary to the sound doctrine ¹¹that conforms to the glorious gospel of the blessed God, which he entrusted to me.

The Lord's Grace to Paul

¹²I thank Christ Jesus our Lord, who has given me strength, that he considered me faithful, appointing me to his service. ¹³Even though I was once a blasphemer and a persecutor and a violent man, I was shown mercy because I acted in ignorance and unbelief. ¹⁴The grace of our Lord was poured out on me abundantly, along with the faith and love that are in Christ Jesus.

¹⁵Here is a trustworthy saying that deserves full acceptance: Christ Jesus came into the world to save sinners—of whom I am the worst. ¹⁶But for that very reason I was shown mercy so that in me, the worst of sinners, Christ Jesus might display his unlimited patience as an example for those who would believe on him and receive eternal life. ¹⁷Now to the King eternal, immortal, invisible, the only God, be honor and glory for ever and ever. Amen.

¹⁸Timothy, my son, I give you this instruction in keeping with the prophecies once made about you, so that by following them you may fight the good fight, ¹⁹holding on to faith and a good conscience. Some have rejected these and so have shipwrecked their faith. ²⁰Among them are Hymenaeus and Alexander, whom I have handed over to Satan to be taught not to blaspheme.

Instructions on Worship

2 I urge, then, first of all, that requests, prayers, intercession and thanksgiving be made for everyone— ²for kings and all those in authority, that we may live peaceful and quiet lives in all godliness and holiness. ³This is good, and pleases God our Savior, ⁴who wants all men to be saved and to come to a knowledge of the truth. ⁵For there is one God and one mediator between God and men, the man Christ Jesus, ⁶who gave himself as a ransom for all men—the testimony given in its proper time. ⁷And for this purpose I was appointed a herald and an apostle—I am telling the truth, I am not lying—and a teacher of the true faith to the Gentiles.

⁸I want men everywhere to lift up holy hands in prayer, without anger or disputing.

⁹I also want women to dress modestly, with decency and propriety, not with braided hair or gold or pearls or expensive clothes, ¹⁰but with good deeds, appropriate for women who profess to worship God.

¹¹A woman should learn in quietness and full submission. ¹²I do not permit a woman to teach or to have authority over a man; she must be silent. ¹³For Adam

> ❝ We know little of the things for which we pray. ❞
>
> GEOFFREY CHAUCER

ᵃ9 Or *that the law*

1 TIMOTHY 1:12–17

Guilt, Grace and Gratitude

1:15 "CHRIST JESUS CAME INTO THE WORLD TO SAVE SINNERS—OF WHOM I AM THE WORST."

Just how bad a sinner was Paul before his conversion? Wrong question. Paul spoke in the present tense when he said to Timothy, "Here is a trustworthy saying that deserves full acceptance: Christ Jesus came into the world to save sinners—of whom I *am* the worst" (1:15, italics added). It's true; there was a past tense to Paul's sinfulness. He describes himself as having once been a blasphemer, a persecutor and a violent man (see verse 13). The word "violent" is particularly shameful. It is a word that described one who took a sadistic pleasure in humiliating and inflicting pain on wrongdoers. That part of Paul's life was over, but he still believed himself to be a great sinner. Paul's attitude toward himself is not unique among the great men and women of God over the centuries. The closer they come to God, the more vividly they become aware of their sinfulness.

There is a great value in this perspective, despite what we may think of its effect on self-esteem. As few things can, it can serve to keep us humble. A Russian proverb says that nothing ages faster than memory. If we lose our memory of what we were, we lose our gratitude for what God has forgiven. Then our humility will erode, and what is left is a kind of amnesic pride. Then we reason subconsciously that we are not all that bad. Such an attitude is fatal to the life of the Spirit because the implication is that Christ didn't really have to be beaten and tortured and die nailed naked to a cross to secure our freedom. All we ever needed was some good advice, not radical redemption. That last line is the creed of the lukewarm church.

Instead of making us morose, a good memory of what Christ forgave keeps joy alive. John Newton, who wrote the hymn "Amazing Grace," had been a slave trader before his conversion. Throughout his life he never forgot that fact. Yet he was the most gentle and cheerful of men, not in spite of his memory, but because of it. He wrote his own epitaph: "John Newton . . . once an Infidel and Libertine . . . was by the Mercy of our Lord and Savior Jesus Christ, Preserved, Restored, Pardoned and Appointed to Preach the faith he had so long labored to destroy."

PRAY:

Pray this prayer of Søren Kierkegaard: "Father in Heaven!
Hold not our sins up against us but hold us up against our sins,
so that the thought of thee when it wakens in our soul,
and each time it wakens, should not remind us of
what we have committed but of what thou didst forgive,
not of how we went astray but of how thou didst save us!"

FOR YOUR NEXT DEVOTIONAL READING, GO TO PAGE 1488.

1 TIMOTHY 2:1 – 8

First Priority

2:1 I URGE, THEN, FIRST OF ALL, THAT REQUESTS, PRAYERS, INTERCESSION AND THANKSGIVING BE MADE FOR EVERYONE.

One New Year's Day, the whole Tournament of Roses Parade ground to a halt when a large, beautiful float sputtered and came to a stop. It had run out of gas, and the whole parade had to wait until it was refueled. The amusing part of the incident was that the float represented the Standard Oil Company! As large as its oil resources were, they were of no use whatsoever to the float unless someone remembered to put some fuel into it. That huge, lovely, stalled float on Colorado Boulevard in Pasadena is a picture of a prayerless church: blessed with all God's vast resources but going nowhere, stalled in its mission. Paul urged Timothy to not let that kind of thing happen to Timothy's church by reminding him of four things about prayer:

1. Prayer is of urgent and primary importance: "I urge, then, first of all" (2:1). Prayer should demand our immediate and frequent attention.
2. Prayer is all-inclusive. There are seven Greek words for prayer used in the New Testament; four of them are used here in verse 1. We are to pray in all ways, always, for all people. Praying for "kings and all those in authority" (verse 2) means praying even for rulers like the godless Nero, the Roman emperor at the time Paul wrote this letter. Prayer is one of the great multi-purpose "alls" of Scripture.
3. Prayer is founded on God's great passion to save people. The God we address in prayer "wants all men to be saved" (verse 4), so we must pray to him for their salvation.
4. Prayer is intimately linked to Jesus' great prayer for the church to be one so that the world will know God sent him (see devotion on John 17). Paul's desire for "men everywhere to lift up holy hands in prayer, without anger or disputing" (verse 8) is a connection to this prayer and principle.

The fourth point raises a very important issue: It is significant that Paul's concern in this passage was for the prayer life of the gathered church, or corporate prayer. The recovery of this vital practice may be the greatest single need in the modern church. When most people think of prayer, they think of individual, private prayer. As valuable as that is, references to corporate prayer also permeate the Scriptures. For it is as Jesus said it would be, "where two or three come together in my name, there am I with them" (Matthew 18:20).

PRAY:

Lord, teach us to always pray, as of first importance,
in all ways, for all people. And may we, as your body, respond to
your call to unite in strong corporate prayer.

FOR YOUR NEXT DEVOTIONAL READING, GO TO PAGE 1491.

was formed first, then Eve. [14]And Adam was not the one deceived; it was the woman who was deceived and became a sinner. [15]But women[a] will be saved[b] through childbearing—if they continue in faith, love and holiness with propriety.

Overseers and Deacons

3 Here is a trustworthy saying: If anyone sets his heart on being an overseer,[c] he desires a noble task. [2]Now the overseer must be above reproach, the husband of but one wife, temperate, self-controlled, respectable, hospitable, able to teach, [3]not given to drunkenness, not violent but gentle, not quarrelsome, not a lover of money. [4]He must manage his own family well and see that his children obey him with proper respect. [5](If anyone does not know how to manage his own family, how can he take care of God's church?) [6]He must not be a recent convert, or he may become conceited and fall under the same judgment as the devil. [7]He must also have a good reputation with outsiders, so that he will not fall into disgrace and into the devil's trap.

[8]Deacons, likewise, are to be men worthy of respect, sincere, not indulging in much wine, and not pursuing dishonest gain. [9]They must keep hold of the deep truths of the faith with a clear conscience. [10]They must first be tested; and then if there is nothing against them, let them serve as deacons.

[11]In the same way, their wives[d] are to be women worthy of respect, not malicious talkers but temperate and trustworthy in everything.

> *Prayer is the slender nerve that moves the muscle of omnipotence.*
>
> MARTIN TUPPER

[12]A deacon must be the husband of but one wife and must manage his children and his household well. [13]Those who have served well gain an excellent standing and great assurance in their faith in Christ Jesus.

[14]Although I hope to come to you soon, I am writing you these instructions so that, [15]if I am delayed, you will know how people ought to conduct themselves in God's household, which is the church of the living God, the pillar and foundation of the truth. [16]Beyond all question, the mystery of godliness is great:

He[e] appeared in a body,[f]
was vindicated by the Spirit,
was seen by angels,
was preached among the nations,
was believed on in the world,
was taken up in glory.

Instructions to Timothy

4 The Spirit clearly says that in later times some will abandon the faith and follow deceiving spirits and things taught by demons. [2]Such teachings come through hypocritical liars, whose consciences have been seared as with a hot iron. [3]They forbid people to marry and order them to abstain from certain foods, which God created to be received with thanksgiving by those who believe and who know the truth. [4]For everything God created is good, and nothing is to be rejected if it is received with thanksgiving, [5]because it is consecrated by the word of God and prayer.

> FOR everything God created is good, and nothing is to be rejected if it is received with thanksgiving, because it is consecrated by the word of God and prayer.
>
> 1 TIMOTHY 4:4-5

[6]If you point these things out to the brothers, you will be a good minister of Christ Jesus, brought up in the truths of the faith and of the good teaching that you have followed. [7]Have nothing to do with godless myths and old wives' tales; rather, train yourself to be godly. [8]For physical training is of some value, but godliness has value for all things, holding promise for both the present life and the life to come.

[9]This is a trustworthy saying that deserves full acceptance [10](and for this we labor and strive), that we have put our

---

[a]15 Greek *she*   [b]15 Or *restored*
[c]1 Traditionally *bishop*; also in verse 2
[d]11 Or *way, deaconesses*   [e]16 Some manuscripts *God*   [f]16 Or *in the flesh*

hope in the living God, who is the Savior of all men, and especially of those who believe.

[11]Command and teach these things. [12]Don't let anyone look down on you because you are young, but set an example for the believers in speech, in life, in love, in faith and in purity. [13]Until I come, devote yourself to the public reading of Scripture, to preaching and to teaching. [14]Do not neglect your gift, which was given you through a prophetic message when the body of elders laid their hands on you.

[15]Be diligent in these matters; give yourself wholly to them, so that everyone may see your progress. [16]Watch your life and doctrine closely. Persevere in them, because if you do, you will save both yourself and your hearers.

Advice About Widows, Elders and Slaves

5 Do not rebuke an older man harshly, but exhort him as if he were your father. Treat younger men as brothers, [2]older women as mothers, and younger women as sisters, with absolute purity.

[3]Give proper recognition to those widows who are really in need. [4]But if a widow has children or grandchildren, these should learn first of all to put their religion into practice by caring for their own family and so repaying their parents and grandparents, for this is pleasing to God. [5]The widow who is really in need and left all alone puts her hope in God and continues night and day to pray and to ask God for help. [6]But the widow who lives for pleasure is dead even while she lives. [7]Give the people these instructions, too,

> THE widow who is really in need and left all alone puts her hope in God and continues night and day to pray and to ask God for help.
>
> 1 TIMOTHY 5:5

so that no one may be open to blame. [8]If anyone does not provide for his relatives, and especially for his immediate family, he has denied the faith and is worse than an unbeliever.

[9]No widow may be put on the list of widows unless she is over sixty, has been faithful to her husband,[a] [10]and is well known for her good deeds, such as bringing up children, showing hospitality, washing the feet of the saints, helping those in trouble and devoting herself to all kinds of good deeds.

[11]As for younger widows, do not put them on such a list. For when their sensual desires overcome their dedication to Christ, they want to marry. [12]Thus they bring judgment on themselves, because they have broken their first pledge. [13]Besides, they get into the habit of being idle and going about from house to house. And not only do they become idlers, but also gossips and busybodies, saying things they ought not to. [14]So I counsel younger widows to marry, to have children, to manage their homes and to give the enemy no opportunity for slander. [15]Some have in fact already turned away to follow Satan.

[16]If any woman who is a believer has widows in her family, she should help them and not let the church be burdened with them, so that the church can help those widows who are really in need.

[17]The elders who direct the affairs of the church well are worthy of double honor, especially those whose work is preaching and teaching. [18]For the Scripture says, "Do not muzzle the ox while it is treading out the grain,"[b] and "The worker deserves his wages."[c] [19]Do not entertain an accusation against an elder unless it is brought by two or three witnesses. [20]Those who sin are to be rebuked publicly, so that the others may take warning.

[21]I charge you, in the sight of God and Christ Jesus and the elect angels, to keep these instructions without partiality, and to do nothing out of favoritism.

[22]Do not be hasty in the laying on of hands, and do not share in the sins of others. Keep yourself pure.

[23]Stop drinking only water, and use a little wine because of your stomach and your frequent illnesses.

[24]The sins of some men are obvious, reaching the place of judgment ahead of them; the sins of others trail behind

[a]9 Or *has had but one husband*
[b]18 Deut. 25:4   [c]18 Luke 10:7

1 TIMOTHY 6:11–16

Pray for a Muscular Faith!

6:12 FIGHT THE GOOD FIGHT OF THE FAITH.

The language in this passage calls for strong exertion, what some have called a "muscular faith": "flee," "pursue," "fight the good fight," "take hold," "I charge you." Jesus was clear that we have no strength in ourselves (see John 15:1–5). But that doesn't mean we are to think of ourselves as power-less. Quite the opposite. We are to be strong in the grace of God, exerting ourselves in the strength of the Holy Spirit, living and praying with the focused aggressiveness and passion of a fighter (see devotion on Colossians 4:2–4; 12–13; see also Colossians 1:29).

Why must we pray so strongly? We are faced with a great and challeng-ing choice, an "either/or." On the one hand, there could be great loss—on the other, great gain (see 1 Timothy 6:6–12). There is something to fear greatly and something to desire greatly. The choice is literally between "ruin and destruction" (1 Timothy 6:9) and "eternal life" (verse 12). To make mat-ters worse, the enemy of our souls would deceive us into fearing what we shouldn't fear and not fearing what we should. The gravity of the choice is not always apparent to us.

We need prayers to match the choice because we need a God great enough to make us strong enough to see it for what it is—and to make it. He is "God, the blessed and only Ruler, the King of kings and Lord of lords, who alone is immortal and who lives in unapproachable light" (verses 15–16). We need to cultivate a vision of this God in adoring prayer: powerful enough to make us to flee what obscures his glory and to pursue what reveals it. We need to delight in God the way an athlete delights to run a race.

It is not enough to fear evil; we must develop what Thomas Chalmers called "the expulsive power of a new affection." In the Greek myth, when Ulysses passed the Isle of the Sirens, he tied himself to the mast and stopped his ears with wax that he might not hear their song, follow it and be destroyed. His was a negative goodness. Orpheus, however, sat on the deck and survived by playing his own music, a music far more beautiful than the Sirens.' His was a positive goodness—a muscular faith.

PRAY:

Father in Heaven! Take away anything that dims
my vision of your glory or dulls my appetite
for the Scriptures or distracts me from prayer:
so that I may fight the good fight
and take hold of eternal life.

———

FOR YOUR NEXT DEVOTIONAL READING, GO TO PAGE 1495.

> *It is a tremendously hard thing to pray aright; yea, it is verily the science of all sciences.*
>
> MARTIN LUTHER

them. ²⁵In the same way, good deeds are obvious, and even those that are not cannot be hidden.

6 All who are under the yoke of slavery should consider their masters worthy of full respect, so that God's name and our teaching may not be slandered. ²Those who have believing masters are not to show less respect for them because they are brothers. Instead, they are to serve them even better, because those who benefit from their service are believers, and dear to them. These are the things you are to teach and urge on them.

Love of Money

³If anyone teaches false doctrines and does not agree to the sound instruction of our Lord Jesus Christ and to godly teaching, ⁴he is conceited and understands nothing. He has an unhealthy interest in controversies and quarrels about words that result in envy, strife, malicious talk, evil suspicions ⁵and constant friction between men of corrupt mind, who have been robbed of the truth and who think that godliness is a means to financial gain.

⁶But godliness with contentment is great gain. ⁷For we brought nothing into the world, and we can take nothing out of it. ⁸But if we have food and clothing, we will be content with that. ⁹People who want to get rich fall into temptation and a trap and into many foolish and harmful desires that plunge men into ruin and destruction. ¹⁰For the love of money is a root of all kinds of evil. Some people, ea-

ger for money, have wandered from the faith and pierced themselves with many griefs.

Paul's Charge to Timothy

¹¹But you, man of God, flee from all this, and pursue righteousness, godliness, faith, love, endurance and gentleness. ¹²Fight the good fight of the faith. Take hold of the eternal life to which you were called when you made your good confession in the presence of many witnesses. ¹³In the sight of God, who gives life to everything, and of Christ Jesus, who while testifying before Pontius Pilate made the good confession, I charge you ¹⁴to keep this command without spot or blame until the appearing of our Lord Jesus Christ, ¹⁵which God will bring about in his own time—God, the blessed and only Ruler, the King of kings and Lord of lords, ¹⁶who alone is immortal and who lives in unapproachable light, whom no one has seen or can see. To him be honor and might forever. Amen.

¹⁷Command those who are rich in this present world not to be arrogant nor to put their hope in wealth, which is so uncertain, but to put their hope in God, who richly provides us with everything for our enjoyment. ¹⁸Command them to do good, to be rich in good deeds, and to be generous and willing to share. ¹⁹In this way they will lay up treasure for themselves as a firm foundation for the coming age, so that they may take hold of the life that is truly life.

²⁰Timothy, guard what has been entrusted to your care. Turn away from godless chatter and the opposing ideas of what is falsely called knowledge, ²¹which some have professed and in so doing have wandered from the faith.

Grace be with you.

2 Timothy

PAUL WROTE his final letter to Timothy while he was in prison.
In contrast to the time when he wrote 1 Timothy, Paul was now in
an actual prison cell. He was in chains like a common criminal
(see 2:9). The letter is permeated with a sense from Paul that his
work on earth was almost over (see 4:6–8).

Throughout Paul's letter, in the lines and between them, is
the passionate prayer of a faithful soldier of Christ to see the next
generation take up the same cross and be found faithful. Paul's
prayer might well have been the prayer of another old man in the
Bible: "Even when I am old and gray, do not forsake me, O God,
till I declare your power to the next generation, your might to all
who are to come" (Psalm 71:18). Paul knew his time was about
up, so he encourages Timothy to carry on and stand firm.

Read 2 Timothy and pray with Paul for the next generation.

"I HAVE FOUGHT
THE GOOD FIGHT,
I HAVE FINISHED
THE RACE,
I HAVE KEPT THE
FAITH." (4:7)

1 Paul, an apostle of Christ Jesus by the will of God, according to the promise of life that is in Christ Jesus,

²To Timothy, my dear son:

Grace, mercy and peace from God the Father and Christ Jesus our Lord.

Encouragement to Be Faithful

³I thank God, whom I serve, as my forefathers did, with a clear conscience, as night and day I constantly remember you in my prayers. ⁴Recalling your tears, I long to see you, so that I may be filled with joy. ⁵I have been reminded of your sincere faith, which first lived in your grandmother Lois and in your mother Eunice and, I am persuaded, now lives in you also. ⁶For this reason I remind you to fan into flame the gift of God, which is in you through the laying on of my hands. ⁷For God did not give us a spirit of timidity, but a spirit of power, of love and of self-discipline.

⁸So do not be ashamed to testify about our Lord, or ashamed of me his prisoner. But join with me in suffering for the gospel, by the power of God, ⁹who has saved us and called us to a holy life—not because of anything we have done but because of his own purpose and grace. This grace was given us in Christ Jesus before the beginning of time, ¹⁰but it has now been revealed through the appearing of our Savior, Christ Jesus, who has destroyed death and has brought life and immortality to light through the gospel. ¹¹And of this gospel I was appointed a herald and an apostle and a teacher. ¹²That is why I am suffering as I am. Yet I am not ashamed, because I know whom I have believed, and am convinced that he is able to guard what I have entrusted to him for that day.

¹³What you heard from me, keep as the pattern of sound teaching, with faith and love in Christ Jesus. ¹⁴Guard the good deposit that was entrusted to you—guard it with the help of the Holy Spirit who lives in us.

¹⁵You know that everyone in the province of Asia has deserted me, including Phygelus and Hermogenes.

¹⁶May the Lord show mercy to the household of Onesiphorus, because he often refreshed me and was not ashamed of my chains. ¹⁷On the contrary, when he was in Rome, he searched hard for me until he found me. ¹⁸May the Lord grant that he will find mercy from the Lord on that day! You know very well in how many ways he helped me in Ephesus.

> MAY the Lord grant that he will find mercy from the Lord on that day! You know very well in how many ways he helped me in Ephesus.
>
> 2 TIMOTHY 1:18

2 You then, my son, be strong in the grace that is in Christ Jesus. ²And the things you have heard me say in the presence of many witnesses entrust to reliable men who will also be qualified to teach others. ³Endure hardship with us like a good soldier of Christ Jesus. ⁴No one serving as a soldier gets involved in civilian affairs—he wants to please his commanding officer. ⁵Similarly, if anyone competes as an athlete, he does not receive the victor's crown unless he competes according to the rules. ⁶The hardworking farmer should be the first to receive a share of the crops. ⁷Reflect on what I am saying, for the Lord will give you insight into all this.

⁸Remember Jesus Christ, raised from the dead, descended from David. This is my gospel, ⁹for which I am suffering even to the point of being chained like a criminal. But God's word is not chained. ¹⁰Therefore I endure everything for the sake of the elect, that they too may obtain the salvation that is in Christ Jesus, with eternal glory.

¹¹Here is a trustworthy saying:

If we died with him,
    we will also live with him;
¹²if we endure,
    we will also reign with him.
If we disown him,
    he will also disown us;
¹³if we are faithless,
    he will remain faithful,
    for he cannot disown himself.

A Workman Approved by God

¹⁴Keep reminding them of these things. Warn them before God against quarrel-

Fan the Flame

1:6 FAN INTO FLAME THE GIFT OF GOD.

Service to Christ is carried out in a way similar to someone starting a fire: by building it, lighting it, feeding it, poking it, stirring it and fanning it. Paul told Timothy to "fan into flame the gift of God" (1:6) by reminding him of how the fire was first built in his heart. He said, "I have been reminded of your sincere faith, which first lived in your grandmother Lois and in your mother Eunice and . . . now lives in you also" (verse 5). Lois's and Eunice's sincere faith had been passed on to Timothy. Theologian Karl Barth was once asked a series of serious questions by a group of doctoral students in the United States. They were surprised at his answer:

> Q. How do you know the Bible is true?
>
> A. Because my mother told me.

Barth's answer wasn't flippant. The power of parents to build a fire in a man or woman is inestimable—as is the power of trusted and wise mentors. Paul reminded Timothy of how the wood was stacked and arranged in Timothy's heart by Paul's example (see verses 8,13). There is a saying worth putting into practice: Everyone needs a Timothy, a Paul and a Barnabas in his or her life: someone to mentor, someone to be mentored by, and someone to walk with as a peer. They keep the fire burning.

But a fire must be lit to burn. That is the meaning of the reference to the laying on of Paul's hands (see verse 6) and the kind of spirit God gave Timothy: not "of timidity, but a spirit of power, of love and of self-discipline" (verse 7). Like stacking wood for a fire, the bones can be assembled in the valley of dry bones, but the Spirit must be blown into them for them to live (see Ezekiel 37:1–14). So Paul also reminded Timothy of the kind of man God had made him through his Spirit.

A fire must be fed. That's the importance of knowing the Word of God (see next devotion, on 2 Timothy 3). Christ's servants must remember what the Word of God has made them and is continuing to make them. Then the fire must be poked and stirred and fanned again and again. Left alone, a fire will die; it must be continually cultivated by the Scriptures and the memory of what God and others have made us.

PRAY:

*Dear Lord, you have given me your Spirit
and the Holy Scriptures; give me also a love
for your Word, and the people and memory
I need to keep the fire burning in my heart.*

FOR YOUR NEXT DEVOTIONAL READING, GO TO PAGE 1497.

ing about words; it is of no value, and only ruins those who listen. [15]Do your best to present yourself to God as one approved, a workman who does not need to be ashamed and who correctly handles the word of truth. [16]Avoid godless chatter, because those who indulge in it will become more and more ungodly. [17]Their teaching will spread like gangrene. Among them are Hymenaeus and Philetus, [18]who have wandered away from the truth. They say that the resurrection has already taken place, and they destroy the faith of some. [19]Nevertheless, God's solid foundation stands firm, sealed with this inscription: "The Lord knows those who are his,"[a] and, "Everyone who confesses the name of the Lord must turn away from wickedness."

[20]In a large house there are articles not only of gold and silver, but also of wood and clay; some are for noble purposes and some for ignoble. [21]If a man cleanses himself from the latter, he will be an instrument for noble purposes, made holy, useful to the Master and prepared to do any good work.

> **❝** When we pray to God we must be seeking nothing—nothing. **❞**
>
> ST. FRANCIS OF ASSISI

[22]Flee the evil desires of youth, and pursue righteousness, faith, love and peace, along with those who call on the Lord out of a pure heart. [23]Don't have anything to do with foolish and stupid arguments, because you know they produce quarrels. [24]And the Lord's servant must not quarrel; instead, he must be kind to everyone, able to teach, not resentful. [25]Those who oppose him he must gently instruct, in the hope that God will grant them repentance leading them to a knowledge of the truth, [26]and that they will come to their senses and escape from the trap of the devil, who has taken them captive to do his will.

Godlessness in the Last Days

3 But mark this: There will be terrible times in the last days. [2]People will be lovers of themselves, lovers of money, boastful, proud, abusive, disobedient to their parents, ungrateful, unholy, [3]without love, unforgiving, slanderous, without self-control, brutal, not lovers of the good, [4]treacherous, rash, conceited, lovers of pleasure rather than lovers of God— [5]having a form of godliness but denying its power. Have nothing to do with them.

> **❝** No one is a firmer believer in the power of prayer than the devil; not that he practices it, but he suffers from it. **❞**
>
> GUY H. KING

[6]They are the kind who worm their way into homes and gain control over weak-willed women, who are loaded down with sins and are swayed by all kinds of evil desires, [7]always learning but never able to acknowledge the truth. [8]Just as Jannes and Jambres opposed Moses, so also these men oppose the truth—men of depraved minds, who, as far as the faith is concerned, are rejected. [9]But they will not get very far because, as in the case of those men, their folly will be clear to everyone.

Paul's Charge to Timothy

[10]You, however, know all about my teaching, my way of life, my purpose, faith, patience, love, endurance, [11]persecutions, sufferings—what kinds of things happened to me in Antioch, Iconium and Lystra, the persecutions I endured. Yet the Lord rescued me from all of them. [12]In fact, everyone who wants to live a godly life in Christ Jesus will be persecuted, [13]while evil men and impostors will go from bad to worse, deceiving and being deceived. [14]But as for you, continue in what you have learned and have become convinced of, because you know those from whom you learned it, [15]and how from infancy you have known the holy Scriptures, which are able to make you wise for salvation through faith in Christ Jesus. [16]All Scripture is God-breathed and is useful for teaching, rebuking, correcting and training in righteousness, [17]so that the man of God may be thoroughly equipped for every good work.

[a]*19* Num. 16:5 (see Septuagint)

God's Breath in Man Returning . . .

3:16 ALL SCRIPTURE IS GOD-BREATHED.

The 29 words that comprise 2 Timothy 3:16–17 are nothing short of remarkable. They are the most carefully considered, precise, authoritative and balanced statement of the origin, use and purpose of the Bible that is in the Bible. Paul even coined a word to describe his take on the Bible: "God-breathed."

These verses also give the best rationale in Scripture for praying Scripture. Part of that rationale is in their context: persecution (see verses 10–12) and apostasy (see verses 1–9,13). Paul's assessment of the world is sobering: "In fact, everyone who wants to live a godly life in Christ Jesus will be persecuted, while evil men and impostors will go from bad to worse, deceiving and being deceived" (verses 12–13). It's not easy to be a follower of Jesus; there is pressure on all sides to go the world's way. We need the strength of God to stay faithful; or as P. T. Forsyth put it, "If we find nothing over us, we succumb to what is around us." The Scriptures give us strength to resist that which is around us. But this strength doesn't come from merely knowing the facts of Scripture; it comes from knowing the God who breathes his breath into them.

The word Paul coined, "God-breathed," gives a beautiful picture of what it means to pray the Word of God. George Herbert's poem, "Prayer (I)," describes prayer as "God's breath in man returning to his birth."[1] In other words, the breath of God that gives us life (see Genesis 2:7) we breathe back to him in prayer. Paul's word suggests that in the Bible we meet God again, as in creation, and are renewed and revived—breathing in his life and breathing it back in prayer. In God-breathed Scripture we encounter afresh the breath of God, and when we pray Scripture, we breathe back what is breathed into us!

Paul used four precisely chosen words to describe Scripture. He said the Bible is useful for teaching, rebuking, correcting and training in righteousness. Paraphrased, the Bible teaches us what is true, rebukes us for what is false, sets us on the right path when we've strayed away and conditions our spiritual muscles to stay on the right path. Pray the Word of God! Pray to understand it; pray back to God what you understand; and pray for more understanding.

PRAY:
*"Breathe on me, Breath of God,
Fill me with life anew,
that I may love what thou dost love,
And do what thou wouldst do."* EDWIN HATCH

FOR YOUR NEXT DEVOTIONAL READING, GO TO PAGE 1498.

Take My Life

BY MOST standards, young Miss Frances Havergal was an exceptional Christian. By age 22, she had memorized large tracts of Scripture: all four Gospels, all the epistles, the books of Revelation, Psalms and Isaiah. In later years she also learned all the Minor Prophets by heart. It was common for her to pray three times a day.

Havergal was gifted with a lovely voice, and she often sang before large audiences. She was also a talented poet and hymn writer. At age nine she was composing long letters to her friends in perfect rhyme.

But there was something missing in her life. She so longed to know more of Christ and to be more fully consecrated to him that she was restless in spirit and often disconsolate. A hymn she wrote at age 22 touched on the source of her yearning. In it Jesus questioned her:

> I gave my life for thee,
> My precious blood I shed,
> That thou might'st ransomed be,
> And quickened from the dead;
> I gave, I gave my life for thee,
> What hast thou given for me?[2]

It seemed to Havergal that such immense love on Christ's part pointed to an experience of consecration on her part that was commensurate with his great love, a deeper knowledge of the dimensions of a love that surpasses knowledge (see Ephesians 3:18–19).

The experience came to her on Advent Sunday, December 2, 1873. She described it to her sister Maria as the day "I first saw clearly the blessings of true consecration. I saw it as a flash of electric light, and what you see, you can never unsee. There must be full surrender before there can be full blessedness."[3] Her famous hymn, "Take My Life and Let It Be," grew out of that defining spiritual experience. It was her lifelong prayer, and has been the prayer of all those who know that surrender is the path to blessedness.

PRAY:

Take my life and let it be / Consecrated, Lord, to thee;
Take my moments and my days— / Let them flow in ceaseless praise,
Let them flow in ceaseless praise. / Take my voice and let me sing
Always, only, for my King; / Take my lips and let them be
Filled with messages from thee, / Filled with messages from thee.
Take my love—my Lord, I pour / At thy feet its treasure store;
Take myself and I will be / Ever, only, all for thee, / Ever, only, all for thee.[4]

MEMORIZE:

Therefore, I urge you, brothers, in view of God's mercy,
to offer your bodies as living sacrifices, holy and pleasing to God—
this is your spiritual act of worship. Do not conform any longer to
the pattern of this world, but be transformed by the renewing
of your mind. Then you will be able to test and approve what
God's will is—his good, pleasing and perfect will. ROMANS 12:1–2

FOR YOUR NEXT DEVOTIONAL READING, GO TO PAGE 1500.

2 TIMOTHY 4:1–8

Finishing Strong

4:7 I HAVE FOUGHT THE GOOD FIGHT, I HAVE FINISHED THE RACE, I HAVE KEPT THE FAITH.

"The whole trouble in life today is that people only look at the beginning," wrote Martyn Lloyd-Jones.[5] He called this the "cinema" or "film" view of life. We could add that it is also the celebrity and glamour magazine view of life. Everybody looks so young and fresh and beautiful and cool. It's easy to think that this is *la dolce vita*, the good life. But the real question for people is not "Where are they now?" but "Where will they be?" The pressing concern should be not their beginning but their end: What is the trajectory of their lives? Will they finish strong? Charles Wesley boasted of the early Methodists, "Our people die well." Will people today? Will you?

This is a tender passage: An old man, a father in the faith, near death, is giving some parting words of encouragement to a young man, his son in the faith. Paul's words to Timothy are stirring and "muscular" in their impact (see also the devotion on 1 Timothy 6:11–16): "In the presence of God and of Christ Jesus, who will judge the living and the dead, and in view of his appearing and his kingdom, I give you this charge . . . keep your head in all situations, endure hardship, do the work of an evangelist, discharge all the duties of your ministry" (verses 1,5). Paul seals his encouragement to courage and faithfulness in the strongest possible way: his own example. "For I am already being poured out like a drink offering, and the time has come for my departure. I have fought the good fight, I have finished the race, I have kept the faith" (verses 6–7).

Timothy is still in the early years of his life; Paul is near the end of his. Will Timothy finish well, finish strong, like Paul? Will you? The only way to finish strong is to do now what you want to be found doing at the end. The road before Timothy, and us all, calls for "a long obedience in the same direction" (Nietzsche). The Christian life is a marathon, not a sprint; the crown of righteousness belongs to those who persevere. Persevere in prayer, so that you may persevere in life.

PRAY:

O Righteous Judge, may I, by your grace, finish well.
Strengthen me to live in such a way now
that at the end of my life I can say,
"I have fought the good fight,
I have finished the race, I have kept the faith."

FOR YOUR NEXT DEVOTIONAL READING, GO TO PAGE 1504.

4 In the presence of God and of Christ Jesus, who will judge the living and the dead, and in view of his appearing and his kingdom, I give you this charge: [2]Preach the Word; be prepared in season and out of season; correct, rebuke and encourage—with great patience and careful instruction. [3]For the time will come when men will not put up with sound doctrine. Instead, to suit their own desires, they will gather around them a great number of teachers to say what their itching ears want to hear. [4]They will turn their ears away from the truth and turn aside to myths. [5]But you, keep your head in all situations, endure hardship, do the work of an evangelist, discharge all the duties of your ministry.

[6]For I am already being poured out like a drink offering, and the time has come for my departure. [7]I have fought the good fight, I have finished the race, I have kept the faith. [8]Now there is in store for me the crown of righteousness, which the Lord, the righteous Judge, will award to me on that day—and not only to me, but also to all who have longed for his appearing.

Personal Remarks

[9]Do your best to come to me quickly, [10]for Demas, because he loved this world, has deserted me and has gone to Thessalonica. Crescens has gone to Galatia, and Titus to Dalmatia. [11]Only Luke is with me. Get Mark and bring him with you, because he is helpful to me in my ministry. [12]I sent Tychicus to Ephesus. [13]When you come, bring the cloak that I left with Carpus at Troas, and my scrolls, especially the parchments.

[14]Alexander the metalworker did me a great deal of harm. The Lord will repay him for what he has done. [15]You too should be on your guard against him, because he strongly opposed our message.

[16]At my first defense, no one came to my support, but everyone deserted me. May it not be held against them. [17]But the Lord stood at my side and gave me strength, so that through me the message might be fully proclaimed and all the Gentiles might hear it. And I was delivered from the lion's mouth. [18]The Lord will rescue me from every evil attack and will bring me safely to his heavenly kingdom. To him be glory for ever and ever. Amen.

Final Greetings

[19]Greet Priscilla[a] and Aquila and the household of Onesiphorus. [20]Erastus stayed in Corinth, and I left Trophimus sick in Miletus. [21]Do your best to get here before winter. Eubulus greets you, and so do Pudens, Linus, Claudia and all the brothers.

[22]The Lord be with your spirit. Grace be with you.

> " Prayer should be the key of the day and the lock of the night. "
>
> GEORGE HERBERT

[a]19 Greek *Prisca*, a variant of *Priscilla*

Titus

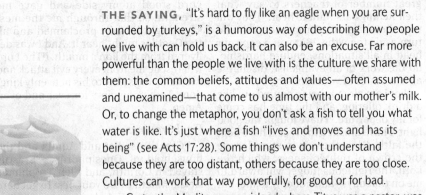

THE SAYING, "It's hard to fly like an eagle when you are surrounded by turkeys," is a humorous way of describing how people we live with can hold us back. It can also be an excuse. Far more powerful than the people we live with is the culture we share with them: the common beliefs, attitudes and values—often assumed and unexamined—that come to us almost with our mother's milk. Or, to change the metaphor, you don't ask a fish to tell you what water is like. It's just where a fish "lives and moves and has its being" (see Acts 17:28). Some things we don't understand because they are too distant, others because they are too close. Cultures can work that way powerfully, for good or for bad.

Crete, the Mediterranean island where Titus was a pastor, was world-renowned for its culture of avarice and greed. The Greek poet Epimenides, a native Cretan whom Paul quoted in this letter, expressed a widely held opinion when he wrote, "Cretans are always liars, evil brutes, lazy gluttons" (1:12). To "Cretanize" or "cretize" meant to lie and cheat. According to William Barclay, the proverbial phrase "to cretize against a Cretan" meant to match lies with lies. The very phrase "Cretan church" is almost an oxymoron.

If that was the culture of the Cretan church, how could the church both be in the world but not of it? Paul's letter to Titus proposed a strategy for how to do this, and with it a way to pray for any church, especially a church planted in a culture as virulent as Crete's.

1. Pray for the leaders of the church (see 1:5–9). A church will go no further spiritually than its leaders have gone.
2. Pray for the church to know and do what is good. Paul underlined the need for this kind of moral vision (see 1:16; 2:7,14; 3:1,8,14).
3. Pray for the church to understand the distinctiveness of the faith it professes. Compared to other books of the New Testament, Titus has a disproportionate number of classic creedal summaries. Each one is crystalline in clarity and beauty (see 1:1–3; 2:11–14; 3:3–7).

1 Paul, a servant of God and an apostle of Jesus Christ for the faith of God's elect and the knowledge of the truth that leads to godliness— ²a faith and knowledge resting on the hope of eternal life, which God, who does not lie, promised before the beginning of time, ³and at his appointed season he brought his word to light through the preaching entrusted to me by the command of God our Savior,

⁴To Titus, my true son in our common faith:

Grace and peace from God the Father and Christ Jesus our Savior.

Titus's Task on Crete

⁵The reason I left you in Crete was that you might straighten out what was left unfinished and appoint*ᵃ* elders in every town, as I directed you. ⁶An elder must be blameless, the husband of but one wife, a man whose children believe and are not open to the charge of being wild and disobedient. ⁷Since an overseer*ᵇ* is entrusted with God's work, he must be blameless—not overbearing, not quick-tempered, not given to drunkenness, not violent, not pursuing dishonest gain. ⁸Rather he must be hospitable, one who loves what is good, who is self-controlled, upright, holy and disciplined. ⁹He must hold firmly to the trustworthy message as it has been taught, so that he can encourage others by sound doctrine and refute those who oppose it.

> 66 When we fail to wait prayerfully for God's guidance and strength, we are saying with our actions if not our lips that we do not need him. 99
>
> CHARLES HUMMEL

¹⁰For there are many rebellious people, mere talkers and deceivers, especially those of the circumcision group. ¹¹They must be silenced, because they are ruining whole households by teaching things they ought not to teach—and that for the sake of dishonest gain. ¹²Even one of their own prophets has said, "Cretans are always liars, evil brutes, lazy gluttons." ¹³This testimony is true. Therefore, rebuke them sharply, so that they will be sound in the faith ¹⁴and will pay no attention to Jewish myths or to the commands of those who reject the truth. ¹⁵To the pure, all things are pure, but to those who are corrupted and do not believe, nothing is pure. In fact, both their minds and consciences are corrupted. ¹⁶They claim to know God, but by their actions they deny him. They are detestable, disobedient and unfit for doing anything good.

What Must Be Taught to Various Groups

2 You must teach what is in accord with sound doctrine. ²Teach the older men to be temperate, worthy of respect, self-controlled, and sound in faith, in love and in endurance.

³Likewise, teach the older women to be reverent in the way they live, not to be slanderers or addicted to much wine, but to teach what is good. ⁴Then they can train the younger women to love their husbands and children, ⁵to be self-controlled and pure, to be busy at home, to be kind, and to be subject to their husbands, so that no one will malign the word of God.

⁶Similarly, encourage the young men to be self-controlled. ⁷In everything set them an example by doing what is good. In your teaching show integrity, seriousness ⁸and soundness of speech that cannot be condemned, so that those who oppose you may be ashamed because they have nothing bad to say about us.

⁹Teach slaves to be subject to their masters in everything, to try to please them, not to talk back to them, ¹⁰and not to steal from them, but to show that they can be fully trusted, so that in every way they will make the teaching about God our Savior attractive.

¹¹For the grace of God that brings salvation has appeared to all men. ¹²It teaches us to say "No" to ungodliness and worldly passions, and to live self-controlled, upright and godly lives in this

> FOR the grace of God that brings salvation has appeared to all men.
>
> TITUS 2:11

*ᵃ*5 Or *ordain*   *ᵇ*7 Traditionally *bishop*

present age, ¹³while we wait for the blessed hope—the glorious appearing of our great God and Savior, Jesus Christ, ¹⁴who gave himself for us to redeem us from all wickedness and to purify for himself a people that are his very own, eager to do what is good.

¹⁵These, then, are the things you should teach. Encourage and rebuke with all authority. Do not let anyone despise you.

[**TUESDAY**]

TITUS 1:5–9

Good Shepherds

1:5 APPOINT ELDERS IN EVERY TOWN.

No one is surprised when a wolf behaves like a wolf. It's a different matter altogether when a shepherd doesn't act the way a shepherd is supposed to act. Wolves naturally want to eat sheep; they are carnivores—it's the way they are made. Shepherds are appointed to protect sheep, but it's not their nature; it's their choice, their responsibility. Wolves can be wolves, but as long as a shepherd chooses to be a shepherd, the sheep will be safe. Jesus had some pretty strong opinions about how this ought to be (see John 10:11–15).

Paul advised his friend and coworker Titus on the qualities and choices a shepherd or elder must make to be a good elder. It's a total package, involving family (see Titus 1:6), personal and social qualities (see verses 7–8) and belief (see verse 9). Family, personal and social qualities are as important as belief. But we should keep in mind that belief plays a pivotal role in the mix. Most people are worse than their principles; but that reflects on the people, not the principles. The principles should get the credit for the goodness, the people for the badness. The point is that the elders' confession of faith should be as orthodox and pure as the church expects their lives to be. It is significant that this short letter has three summaries of Christian theology that are gems of gospel truth (see 1:1–3; 2:11–14; 3:3–7). Paul meant the connection to be vital between faith and morality.

A good elder should then both think and behave like Jesus, the Good Shepherd. In the early days of telescopes, the image of the heavenly body being observed came through the lens to a mirror, which reflected the image to the eye of the astronomer. The leaders of the church have the great duty and privilege of reflecting the image of Christ to the people of the church. They, along with all believers, have the awesome responsibility of making "the teaching about God our Savior attractive" (Titus 2:10). The job is everyone's in the church, but if the elders fail at it, the chances that the others will succeed are greatly diminished. Do you pray for your leaders according to the Bible's profile of their character and faith?

PRAY:

Make Titus 1:6–9 a prayer for your church's leadership.
Pray something like, "Dear Lord, may _____ be faithful
in marriage, blameless in public life, not overbearing,
not quick-tempered . . ." and so on,

FOR YOUR NEXT DEVOTIONAL READING, GO TO PAGE 1505.

Doing What Is Good

3 Remind the people to be subject to rulers and authorities, to be obedient, to be ready to do whatever is good, [2]to slander no one, to be peaceable and considerate, and to show true humility toward all men.

[3]At one time we too were foolish, disobedient, deceived and enslaved by all kinds of passions and pleasures. We lived in malice and envy, being hated and hating one another. [4]But when the kindness and love of God our Savior appeared, [5]he saved us, not because of righteous things

---

TITUS 3:3 – 8

From Slaves to Children

3:5 HE SAVED US, NOT BECAUSE OF RIGHTEOUS THINGS WE HAD DONE, BUT BECAUSE OF HIS MERCY.

Jesus said no one can serve two masters; we will always hate one and love the other. That's the way God made us. We are congenital monotheists. No matter how many gods we think we have, it finally comes down to the true and living God or some substitute god, an idol. The great German theologian Helmut Thielicke added a bit of commentary to this idea when he said everyone must serve one of two masters; the choice is not *whether* but *who*. One master, however, will make us slaves; the other will make us children. God's servants are his children who serve him freely, out of love and gratitude. Actually, Thielicke was only summarizing things Jesus and the apostles had already said (see Matthew 6:24; Romans 8:15).

The structure of Paul's confession of faith here follows Jesus' view of things in a kind of before and after picture. Before, we were "enslaved by all kinds of passions and pleasures," including things like foolishness, disobedience, deception, malice, envy and hatred (see Titus 3:3–4). Paradoxically, we were enslaved to pleasures; we couldn't stop having "fun." What was touted as freedom was really slavery. We were like the depressed woman back in the 60s who came to a New York psychiatrist complaining of the effects her lifestyle of sex, drugs and rock and roll was having on her. When the psychiatrist asked her why she didn't just stop living that way, she looked puzzled and said, "You mean I don't have to keep doing what I want to do?"

After all this—after we were saved, washed, reborn, renewed, justified and made heirs of eternal life—What a list (see verses 5–7)!—a new relationship was established. Where formerly we were slaves, we are now devoted "to doing what is good" (verse 8). Devotion is a love word. Good is, well, good, "excellent and profitable for everyone" (verse 8). Devotion to good is for beloved children, men and women made glad and grateful for the grace of God that set them free.

Enslaved or devoted; take your pick. But if you have been set free, let your devotion begin with frequent prayers of praise and thanksgiving. Recite this passage using singular pronouns ("I," "my" and "me") instead of plural pronouns ("we," "our" and "us"). Be amazed again at God's goodness to you. Let the redeemed of the Lord say so (see Psalm 107:1–2, KJV)!

PRAY:
"O for a thousand tongues to sing my great Redeemer's praise,
The glories of my God and King, The triumphs of his grace." CHARLES WESLEY

FOR YOUR NEXT DEVOTIONAL READING, GO TO PAGE 1508.

we had done, but because of his mercy. He saved us through the washing of rebirth and renewal by the Holy Spirit, ⁶whom he poured out on us generously through Jesus Christ our Savior, ⁷so that, having been justified by his grace, we might become heirs having the hope of eternal life. ⁸This is a trustworthy saying. And I want you to stress these things, so that those who have trusted in God may be careful to devote themselves to doing what is good. These things are excellent and profitable for everyone.

⁹But avoid foolish controversies and genealogies and arguments and quarrels about the law, because these are unprofitable and useless. ¹⁰Warn a divisive person once, and then warn him a second time. After that, have nothing to do with him. ¹¹You may be sure that such a man is warped and sinful; he is self-condemned.

Final Remarks

¹²As soon as I send Artemas or Tychicus to you, do your best to come to me at Nicopolis, because I have decided to winter there. ¹³Do everything you can to help Zenas the lawyer and Apollos on their way and see that they have everything they need. ¹⁴Our people must learn to devote themselves to doing what is good, in order that they may provide for daily necessities and not live unproductive lives.

¹⁵Everyone with me sends you greetings. Greet those who love us in the faith.

Grace be with you all.

> 66 Meanwhile continue in earnest prayer, knowing that with God no word is impossible; and that he will either in due time take the temptation away, or make it a blessing to your soul. 99
>
> JOHN WESLEY

Philemon

RECOGNITION OF who others are in the sight of God is the foundation of true justice. As valuable as they can be, no amount of laws and social programs can substitute for this transformingly fundamental shift in human consciousness. Paul urged Philemon to forgive and receive his runaway slave, Onesimus, "no longer as a slave, but better than a slave, as a dear brother" (verse 16). Then Paul added that he was confident Philemon would "do even more than I ask" (verse 21)—perhaps intimating that Philemon set Onesimus free. At any rate, Paul sowed a seed that would ulti-mately destroy the very basis of slavery. To call for the abolition of slavery in that time would have been to perform a radical act— and to fail. But to invite a Christian slave owner to see his slave as a brother was to do something even more radical and subversive. For Philemon to do this would mean a change in his heart, and the human heart is the wellspring of life (see Proverbs 4:23). This is the place where the most radical of changes begin.

"I APPEAL TO YOU ON THE BASIS OF LOVE." (9)

Prayer for justice and reconciliation is a radical act too. It takes a changed heart to pray for these things; and as Paul's prayer for Philemon shows, it looks for a changed heart in others.

¹Paul, a prisoner of Christ Jesus, and Timothy our brother,

To Philemon our dear friend and fellow worker, ²to Apphia our sister, to Archippus our fellow soldier and to the church that meets in your home:

³Grace to you and peace from God our Father and the Lord Jesus Christ.

Thanksgiving and Prayer

⁴I always thank my God as I remember you in my prayers, ⁵because I hear about your faith in the Lord Jesus and your love for all the saints. ⁶I pray that you may be active in sharing your faith, so that you will have a full understanding of every good thing we have in Christ. ⁷Your love has given me great joy and encourage-

---

[THURSDAY]

PHILEMON

Do What Is Good to Know What Is Good

6 I PRAY THAT YOU MAY BE ACTIVE IN SHARING YOUR FAITH.

The expert in the Law of Moses wanted to know how to get eternal life. Jesus told him to love God with his whole being and love his neighbor as himself. Insincerely, the scholar then asked Jesus who his neighbor was. Jesus told him who his neighbor was—or more precisely, how to *be* a "neighbor"—and added, "Go and do likewise" (Luke 10:25–37). That's the usual sequence: Find out what is good, then do what is good; know the truth, then do the truth.

But sometimes it works the other way: *Do the truth so you can know the truth.* That's what Paul was driving at when he prayed for Philemon: "I pray that you may be active in sharing your faith, so that you will have a full understanding of every good thing we have in Christ" (verse 6). Philemon already knew a lot about the faith. But there were things he could know only by doing, like forgiving his runaway slave and receiving him back as a brother in Christ. The greatest intellectual grasp of that simple request of Paul's could not amount to one percent of the knowledge that could be had by simply doing it. In the Bible, knowledge involves so much more than the mind. It involves one's whole being. The Hebrew in Genesis 4:1 is literally, "Adam *knew* his wife Eve, and she became pregnant." Their knowledge consisted in getting their bodies together, not just their brains. Like the legal expert in his encounter with Jesus, Philemon needed to do the truth so he could really know the truth. He had to get involved with a most unlikely neighbor, Onesimus.

We can pray that way for others: that their eyes would be opened to know the truth and that their bodies would get involved so their eyes can be opened. We can pray that way for ourselves, too. Nothing is more critical for the growth of justice in a society than that people begin to see others as God sees them. There is no better view than the view you get when you serve and are reconciled to those you have hurt and who have hurt you.

PRAY:
Holy Spirit, unite my heart, mind and body. May I know the truth
so that I can do the truth; and may I do the truth so that I can know the truth.

FOR YOUR NEXT DEVOTIONAL READING, GO TO PAGE 1512.

ment, because you, brother, have refreshed the hearts of the saints.

Paul's Plea for Onesimus

⁸Therefore, although in Christ I could be bold and order you to do what you ought to do, ⁹yet I appeal to you on the basis of love. I then, as Paul—an old man and now also a prisoner of Christ Jesus— ¹⁰I appeal to you for my son Onesimus,ᵃ who became my son while I was in chains. ¹¹Formerly he was useless to you, but now he has become useful both to you and to me.

¹²I am sending him—who is my very heart—back to you. ¹³I would have liked to keep him with me so that he could take your place in helping me while I am in chains for the gospel. ¹⁴But I did not want to do anything without your consent, so that any favor you do will be spontaneous and not forced. ¹⁵Perhaps

the reason he was separated from you for a little while was that you might have him back for good— ¹⁶no longer as a slave, but better than a slave, as a dear brother. He is very dear to me but even dearer to you, both as a man and as a brother in the Lord.

¹⁷So if you consider me a partner, welcome him as you would welcome me. ¹⁸If he has done you any wrong or owes you anything, charge it to me. ¹⁹I, Paul, am writing this with my own hand. I will pay it back—not to mention that you owe me your very self. ²⁰I do wish, brother, that I may have some benefit from you in the Lord; refresh my heart in Christ. ²¹Confident of your obedience, I write to you, knowing that you will do even more than I ask.

²²And one thing more: Prepare a guest room for me, because I hope to be restored to you in answer to your prayers.

²³Epaphras, my fellow prisoner in Christ Jesus, sends you greetings. ²⁴And so do Mark, Aristarchus, Demas and Luke, my fellow workers.

²⁵The grace of the Lord Jesus Christ be with your spirit.

ᵃ10 Onesimus means useful.

Hebrews

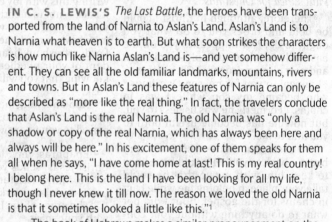

IN C. S. LEWIS'S *The Last Battle*, the heroes have been transported from the land of Narnia to Aslan's Land. Aslan's Land is to Narnia what heaven is to earth. But what soon strikes the characters is how much like Narnia Aslan's Land is—and yet somehow different. They can see all the old familiar landmarks, mountains, rivers and towns. But in Aslan's Land these features of Narnia can only be described as "more like the real thing." In fact, the travelers conclude that Aslan's Land is the real Narnia. The old Narnia was "only a shadow or copy of the real Narnia, which has always been here and always will be here." In his excitement, one of them speaks for them all when he says, "I have come home at last! This is my real country! I belong here. This is the land I have been looking for all my life, though I never knew it till now. The reason we loved the old Narnia is that it sometimes looked a little like this."[1]

The book of Hebrews makes a similar pronouncement on the relation of Christ to the laws, sacrifices and prophets of the Old Testament. Two Greek words for "better" and "superior" occur 15 times in the book—all used in relation to Jesus. All that came before him was a copy or shadow of the real thing. Jesus is the real thing, the fulfillment of the old. The reason the old was so good was that it was a little like the new. "In the past God spoke to our forefathers through the prophets at many times and in various ways, but in these last days he has spoken to us by his Son, whom he appointed heir of all things, and through whom he made the universe. The Son is the radiance of God's glory and the exact representation of his being" (1:1–3).

The portrayal of Jesus as the perfect high priest makes the book of Hebrews perhaps the most important book on prayer in the New Testament. The supreme issue of Biblical faith has always been access to God. How can sinful people come into the presence of a holy God? The answer, under the Old Covenant, was through sacrifice and the ministrations of the priesthood. The message of Hebrews is that these things were only copies and shadows of Jesus: He is the perfect priest and sacrifice. He opened the way to God, and because he still lives to intercede for us, we may come into God's presence with confidence (see 2:17–18; 4:14–16; 6:19–20; 7:25; 10:19–25).

The Son Superior to Angels

1 In the past God spoke to our forefathers through the prophets at many times and in various ways, ²but in these last days he has spoken to us by his Son, whom he appointed heir of all things, and through whom he made the universe. ³The Son is the radiance of God's glory and the exact representation of his being, sustaining all things by his powerful word. After he had provided purification for sins, he sat down at the right hand of the Majesty in heaven. ⁴So he became as much superior to the angels as the name he has inherited is superior to theirs.

⁵For to which of the angels did God ever say,

"You are my Son;
  today I have become your
    Father"ᵃˮᵇ?

Or again,

"I will be his Father,
  and he will be my Son"ᶜ?

⁶And again, when God brings his first-born into the world, he says,

"Let all God's angels worship him."ᵈ

⁷In speaking of the angels he says,

"He makes his angels winds,
  his servants flames of fire."ᵉ

⁸But about the Son he says,

"Your throne, O God, will last for ever
    and ever,
  and righteousness will be the
    scepter of your kingdom.
⁹ You have loved righteousness and
    hated wickedness;
  therefore God, your God, has set
    you above your companions
  by anointing you with the oil of
    joy."ᶠ

¹⁰He also says,

"In the beginning, O Lord, you laid
    the foundations of the earth,
  and the heavens are the work of
    your hands.
¹¹ They will perish, but you remain;
  they will all wear out like a
    garment.

¹² You will roll them up like a robe;
  like a garment they will be
    changed.
But you remain the same,
  and your years will never end."ᵍ

¹³To which of the angels did God ever say,

"Sit at my right hand
until I make your enemies
  a footstool for your feet"ʰ?

¹⁴Are not all angels ministering spirits sent to serve those who will inherit salvation?

Warning to Pay Attention

2 We must pay more careful attention, therefore, to what we have heard, so that we do not drift away. ²For if the message spoken by angels was binding, and every violation and disobedience received its just punishment, ³how shall we escape if we ignore such a great salvation? This salvation, which was first announced by the Lord, was confirmed to us by those who heard him. ⁴God also testified to it by signs, wonders and various miracles, and gifts of the Holy Spirit distributed according to his will.

Jesus Made Like His Brothers

⁵It is not to angels that he has subjected the world to come, about which we are speaking. ⁶But there is a place where someone has testified:

"What is man that you are mindful
    of him,
  the son of man that you care for
    him?
⁷ You made him a littleⁱ lower than the
    angels;
  you crowned him with glory and
    honor
⁸   and put everything under his feet."ʲ

ᵃ5 Or *have begotten you*   ᵇ5 Psalm 2:7
ᶜ5 2 Samuel 7:14; 1 Chron. 17:13
ᵈ6 Deut. 32:43 (see Dead Sea Scrolls and Septuagint)   ᵉ7 Psalm 104:4
ᶠ9 Psalm 45:6,7   ᵍ12 Psalm 102:25–27
ʰ13 Psalm 110:1   ⁱ7 Or *him for a little while*; also in verse 9   ʲ8 Psalm 8:4–6

In putting everything under him, God left nothing that is not subject to him. Yet at present we do not see everything subject to him. ⁹But we see Jesus, who was made a little lower than the angels, now crowned with glory and honor because he suffered death, so that by the grace of God he might taste death for everyone.

¹⁰In bringing many sons to glory, it was fitting that God, for whom and through whom everything exists, should make the author of their salvation perfect through suffering. ¹¹Both the one who makes men holy and those who are made holy are of the same family. So Jesus is not ashamed to call them brothers. ¹²He says,

[FRIDAY]

HEBREWS 2:5–18

He Was One of Us

2:17 FOR THIS REASON HE HAD TO BE MADE LIKE HIS BROTHERS IN EVERY WAY.

One way to approach this marvelous text is by opening a book on baby and child care and reading the index. Try reading the list of childhood diseases and behavior issues, prefacing each reference with something like, "Jesus was susceptible to . . ." and read whooping cough, colic, measles, mumps, colds; or, "Jesus may very well have . . ." sucked his thumb, been anxious when separated from his mother at eighteen months or contrary when two years old. The purpose of this suggestion is not to be irreverent but to open up the rich meaning in the phrase, "He had to be made like his brothers in every way" (2:17). True, the writer is speaking of much more than childhood issues. He has in mind the whole range of things that make up what it means to be a human being. Jesus was one of us.

The point is, if you find it difficult to pray because of shame or fear of judgment, this passage is good news for you. Jesus is your brother. He knows what it means to be a human being (see verse 14). He knows what it's like to be afraid and tempted and weak. Because he was made like you in every way, he is inclined toward mercy, not censure.

Jesus is also your high priest. In Old Testament times, the high priest was the one who went into the Most Holy Place, stood before God on behalf of the people, and interceded for them. As a priest Jesus was divinely sanctioned for the purpose; as a human he was emotionally suited for the purpose, for he was one of the people he represented. Jesus was, quite literally, a "bridge" between the people and God, one who could pray for humanity with great sympathy. This is Jesus, but there's more! As God's Son, he is divinely sanctioned to speak to God on your behalf as no earthly high priest could ever be. As a human, he understands your humanity as one who was human, from the inside out.

Put away shame and fear when you come to Jesus. He knows all there is to know about you, from the inside; and he will be merciful.

PRAY:
Jesus, you know me inside and out;
and you still love me and sympathize
with my weaknesses. Thank you!

FOR YOUR NEXT DEVOTIONAL READING, GO TO PAGE 1514.

"I will declare your name to my
 brothers;
 in the presence of the congregation
 I will sing your praises."[a]

[13]And again,

"I will put my trust in him."[b]

And again he says,

"Here am I, and the children God has
 given me."[c]

[14]Since the children have flesh and blood, he too shared in their humanity so that by his death he might destroy him who holds the power of death—that is, the devil— [15]and free those who all their lives were held in slavery by their fear of death. [16]For surely it is not angels he helps, but Abraham's descendants. [17]For this reason he had to be made like his brothers in every way, in order that he might become a merciful and faithful high priest in service to God, and that he might make atonement for[d] the sins of the people. [18]Because he himself suffered when he was tempted, he is able to help those who are being tempted.

Jesus Greater Than Moses

3 Therefore, holy brothers, who share in the heavenly calling, fix your thoughts on Jesus, the apostle and high priest whom we confess. [2]He was faithful to the one who appointed him, just as Moses was faithful in all God's house. [3]Jesus has been found worthy of greater honor than Moses, just as the builder of a house has greater honor than the house itself. [4]For every house is built by someone, but God is the builder of everything. [5]Moses was faithful as a servant in all God's house, testifying to what would be said in the future. [6]But Christ is faithful as a son over God's house. And we are his house, if we hold on to our courage and the hope of which we boast.

Warning Against Unbelief

[7]So, as the Holy Spirit says:

"Today, if you hear his voice,
[8] do not harden your hearts
 as you did in the rebellion,
  during the time of testing in the
   desert,

[9]where your fathers tested and tried
  me
 and for forty years saw what I did.
[10]That is why I was angry with that
  generation,
 and I said, 'Their hearts are always
  going astray,
 and they have not known my ways.'
[11]So I declared on oath in my anger,
 'They shall never enter my rest.' "[e]

> **Real knowledge, like everything else of value, is not to be obtained easily. It must be worked for, studied for, and, more than all, must be prayed for.**
>
> THOMAS ARNOLD

[12]See to it, brothers, that none of you has a sinful, unbelieving heart that turns away from the living God. [13]But encourage one another daily, as long as it is called Today, so that none of you may be hardened by sin's deceitfulness. [14]We have come to share in Christ if we hold firmly till the end the confidence we had at first. [15]As has just been said:

"Today, if you hear his voice,
 do not harden your hearts
 as you did in the rebellion."[f]

[16]Who were they who heard and rebelled? Were they not all those Moses led out of Egypt? [17]And with whom was he angry for forty years? Was it not with those who sinned, whose bodies fell in the desert? [18]And to whom did God swear that they would never enter his rest if not to those who disobeyed[g]? [19]So we see that they were not able to enter, because of their unbelief.

A Sabbath-Rest for the People of God

4 Therefore, since the promise of entering his rest still stands, let us be careful that none of you be found to have fallen short of it. [2]For we also have had the gospel preached to us, just as they did; but the message they heard was of no value to them, because those who

---

[a]12 Psalm 22:22   [b]13 Isaiah 8:17
[c]13 Isaiah 8:18   [d]17 Or and that he might turn aside God's wrath, taking away
[e]11 Psalm 95:7–11   [f]15 Psalm 95:7,8
[g]18 Or disbelieved

The Small Woman

WHEN A Hollywood movie is based on the life of a woman who was an English parlor maid, it's usually a rags-to-riches Cinderella tale. Gladys Aylward went from poverty and obscurity to international fame, and a movie was made about her life: *The Inn of the Sixth Happiness*, starring the renowned actress Ingrid Bergman. But "rags-to-riches" hardly describes her story. "Miracle of God's sovereign grace" comes closer.

Gladys Aylward heard God's call to go to China as a young woman. But her poor educational background had not prepared her for the rigors of the China Inland Mission's missionary training classes, and she flunked her exams. Deemed unqualified for service, she went back to her life as a parlor maid. But her passion for China and the gospel wouldn't go away, and when she heard that Jeannie Lawson, an elderly missionary in China, needed help, she wrote and asked her if she could come and assist her. Lawson answered that she was welcome to come, but that she couldn't pay any travel expenses. With no money and no backing, Aylward felt herself slipping into depression. She returned to her empty bedroom in the servants' quarters and emptied the contents of her pocketbook upon her Bible. Three copper coins fell out. She prayed, "Oh, God, here's my Bible! Here's my money! Here's me! Use me, God!"[2]

The events that followed that desperate and powerful prayer are nothing less than extraordinary. With only her meager savings, Gladys booked passage to China by the most dangerous route possible. As an undeclared war between Russia and China raged, she rode the Trans-Siberian Railway across Russia to Vladivostock. She then boarded a boat to Japan, and from Japan sailed to Tientsin, China. To make a very long and wonderful story short, Gladys Aylward lived a life of such unbelievable courage and miraculous providence that when a *Newsweek* film critic reviewed the movie about her life, some readers thought it was a work of fiction. A letter to the editor complained, "In order for a movie to be good, the story should be believable!"[3]

Aylward's life was characterized by one extreme and impossible situation after another, amazingly overcome by humble dependence on God. One of the most amazing events happened during the Japanese invasion of China in 1938. With a price on her head by the invaders, this little woman led 100 Chinese orphans on a perilous 27-day journey across the mountains to safety. But at the end of her life all she could say about herself was, "My heart is full of praise that one so insignificant, uneducated, and ordinary in every way could be used to his glory for the blessing of his people in poor persecuted China."[4] Aylward's judgment was echoed in the title of Alan Burgess's 1957 biography: *The Small Woman*.

PRAY:
*With your Bible open, and believing that all that is in it is
your hope, your guide and your command, place your wallet
or pocketbook on its pages and pray the powerful prayer
of Gladys Aylward: "Oh, God, here's my Bible!
Here's my money! Here's me! Use me, God!"*

MEMORIZE:
*But by the grace of God I am what I am, and his grace to me
was not without effect. No, I worked harder than all of them—
yet not I, but the grace of God that was with me.* 1 CORINTHIANS 15:10

FOR YOUR NEXT DEVOTIONAL READING, GO TO PAGE 1516.

heard did not combine it with faith.[a] ³Now we who have believed enter that rest, just as God has said,

"So I declared on oath in my anger,
  'They shall never enter my rest.'"[b]

And yet his work has been finished since the creation of the world. ⁴For some-

where he has spoken about the seventh day in these words: "And on the seventh day God rested from all his work."[c] ⁵And again in the passage above he says, "They shall never enter my rest."

[a]2 Many manuscripts *because they did not share in the faith of those who obeyed* [b]3 Psalm 95:11; also in verse 5 [c]4 Gen. 2:2

HEBREWS 4:14–16

[MONDAY]

Stunned Confidence

4:16 LET US THEN APPROACH THE THRONE OF GRACE WITH CONFIDENCE.

There are different kinds of confidence. There is the cocksure confidence of the athlete who has never been challenged or the daredevil who is thrilled by the heights and the danger. There is the foolish confidence of one who just doesn't get it, who is blissfully ignorant of what is at stake, like the toddler blithely waddling into rush hour traffic on a four-lane highway. Then there is the rare and wonderful confidence of one stunned, amazed and trembling at what she is doing, like the novice fighter pilot on her first solo flight. Or like the man or woman who realizes the miraculous and utterly undeserved privilege of entering the presence of God. That's the confidence spoken of in verse 16: "Let us then approach the throne of grace with confidence, so that we may receive mercy and find grace to help us in our time of need."

This is the second time the author of the book of Hebrews has spoken of Jesus' great sympathy with our weaknesses (see Friday's devotion on Hebrews 2:5–18). He does it to encourage fearful believers to approach God with confidence. In response, ask yourself, "Do I need that reminder? Or does it seem self-evident to me? Am I so accustomed to the gift that it seems no longer a gift but an entitlement? Is my confidence cocksure or foolish?" It is a wonderful privilege to enter the presence of the holy God and address him as Father. Philosopher Peter Kreeft speaks a corrective to the cocksure and foolish:

> We appreciate how incredible this intimacy is only after we have learned the opposite lesson, God's awesomeness and infinite otherness, the distinctively Jewish revelation of God as transcendent Creator. Only after we are Jews can we be Christians; only after we know God in awe can we know God in intimacy. "The fear [awe] of the Lord is the beginning of wisdom" and filial intimacy is the end.[5]

When you pray, pray boldly—as one stunned and amazed at the privilege.

PRAY:

O Holy One! How kind of you to open wide the doors of communion
with you through the precious blood of Jesus. May I never tire
of thanking you or grow callous to the gift.

FOR YOUR NEXT DEVOTIONAL READING, GO TO PAGE 1518.

⁶It still remains that some will enter that rest, and those who formerly had the gospel preached to them did not go in, because of their disobedience. ⁷Therefore God again set a certain day, calling it Today, when a long time later he spoke through David, as was said before:

"Today, if you hear his voice,
  do not harden your hearts."ᵃ

⁸For if Joshua had given them rest, God would not have spoken later about another day. ⁹There remains, then, a Sabbath-rest for the people of God; ¹⁰for anyone who enters God's rest also rests from his own work, just as God did from his. ¹¹Let us, therefore, make every effort to enter that rest, so that no one will fall by following their example of disobedience.

¹²For the word of God is living and active. Sharper than any double-edged sword, it penetrates even to dividing soul and spirit, joints and marrow; it judges the thoughts and attitudes of the heart. ¹³Nothing in all creation is hidden from God's sight. Everything is uncovered and laid bare before the eyes of him to whom we must give account.

Jesus the Great High Priest

¹⁴Therefore, since we have a great high priest who has gone through the heavens,ᵇ Jesus the Son of God, let us hold firmly to the faith we profess. ¹⁵For we do not have a high priest who is unable to sympathize with our weaknesses, but we have one who has been tempted in every way, just as we are—yet was without sin. ¹⁶Let us then approach the throne of grace with confidence, so that we may receive mercy and find grace to help us in our time of need.

5 Every high priest is selected from among men and is appointed to represent them in matters related to God, to offer gifts and sacrifices for sins. ²He is able to deal gently with those who are ignorant and are going astray, since he himself is subject to weakness. ³This is why he has to offer sacrifices for his own sins, as well as for the sins of the people. ⁴No one takes this honor upon himself; he must be called by God, just as Aaron was. ⁵So Christ also did not take upon himself the glory of becoming a high priest. But God said to him,

"You are my Son;
  today I have become your
    Father."ᶜ ᵈ

⁶And he says in another place,

"You are a priest forever,
  in the order of Melchizedek."ᵉ

⁷During the days of Jesus' life on earth, he offered up prayers and petitions with loud cries and tears to the one who could save him from death, and he was heard because of his reverent submission. ⁸Although he was a son, he learned obedience from what he suffered ⁹and, once made perfect, he became the source of eternal salvation for all who obey him ¹⁰and was designated by God to be high priest in the order of Melchizedek.

Warning Against Falling Away

¹¹We have much to say about this, but it is hard to explain because you are slow to learn. ¹²In fact, though by this time you ought to be teachers, you need someone to teach you the elementary truths of God's word all over again. You need milk, not solid food! ¹³Anyone who lives on milk, being still an infant, is not acquainted with the teaching about righteousness. ¹⁴But solid food is for the mature, who by constant use have trained themselves to distinguish good from evil.

6 Therefore let us leave the elementary teachings about Christ and go on to maturity, not laying again the foundation of repentance from acts that lead to death,ᶠ and of faith in God, ²instruction about baptisms, the laying on of hands, the resurrection of the dead, and eternal judgment. ³And God permitting, we will do so.

⁴It is impossible for those who have once been enlightened, who have tasted the heavenly gift, who have shared in the Holy Spirit, ⁵who have tasted the goodness of the word of God and the powers of the coming age, ⁶if they fall away, to be brought back to repentance, becauseᵍ to

ᵃ7 Psalm 95:7,8   ᵇ14 Or gone into heaven
ᶜ5 Or have begotten you   ᵈ5 Psalm 2:7
ᵉ6 Psalm 110:4   ᶠ1 Or from useless rituals
ᵍ6 Or repentance while

their loss they are crucifying the Son of God all over again and subjecting him to public disgrace.

⁷Land that drinks in the rain often falling on it and that produces a crop useful to those for whom it is farmed receives the blessing of God. ⁸But land that produces thorns and thistles is worthless and is in danger of being cursed. In the end it will be burned.

⁹Even though we speak like this, dear friends, we are confident of better things

---

HEBREWS 5:7–10

Loud Cries and Tears

5:7 DURING THE DAYS OF JESUS' LIFE ON EARTH, HE OFFERED UP PRAYERS AND PETITIONS WITH LOUD CRIES AND TEARS.

When Jesus' disciples asked him to teach them to pray, they probably didn't have this part in mind: "During the days of Jesus' life on earth, he offered up prayers and petitions with loud cries and tears" (5:7). Whether or not the disciples realized what Jesus would teach them, they eventually began to learn that prayer includes loud cries and tears, as all learn who enter Christ's school of prayer. Gethsemane and the cross still lay ahead, as they do in their many forms for all believers.

But what on earth does it mean that Jesus "learned obedience from what he suffered" (verse 8)? Was Jesus imperfect here on earth? Was he a little disobedient when he arrived here but got that straightened out before he left? No, not at all. The writer of the book of Hebrews is telling us that Jesus' obedience was completed, that he carried his mission to the full extent. Jesus didn't "learn" to obey; he learned where his obedience would take him, experientially. He made himself nothing, humbled himself and became obedient to death, even death on a cross (see Philippians 2:7–8). He knew what would happen before he came to earth, and he was committed to it. In this sense he had no obedience to learn. But in another sense he had much to learn, in the same way a traveler learns what is on a map by actually traveling the roads. We, of course, have much more to learn. And learn it we will in Christ's school of prayer; for where our Master is, so will we be.

"He was heard because of his reverent submission" (Hebrews 5:7). Though Jesus was God's Son, he learned obedience. Because he was God's Son and submitted to the Father, he was heard—and saved from eternal death, through resurrection. Our Lord's Sonship involved more than his unique ontological relationship with God; it included his reverent submission to the will of God. That is what it means to pray in the name of Jesus. It is to wrap all our petitions in adoration and reverent submission to our Father, in the same way our Savior and brother (see devotion on Hebrews 2:5–18) did. This is what it means to pray like Jesus.

PRAY:

Lord Jesus, blessed Savior and brother! Thank you for the way you prayed and obeyed. Teach me to pray that way—confident in my relationship to the Father, deeply dependent, reverent and obedient.

FOR YOUR NEXT DEVOTIONAL READING, GO TO PAGE 1520.

in your case—things that accompany salvation. ¹⁰God is not unjust; he will not forget your work and the love you have shown him as you have helped his people and continue to help them. ¹¹We want each of you to show this same diligence to the very end, in order to make your hope sure. ¹²We do not want you to become lazy, but to imitate those who through faith and patience inherit what has been promised.

> GOD is not unjust; he will not forget your work and the love you have shown him as you have helped his people and continue to help them.
>
> HEBREWS 6:10

The Certainty of God's Promise

¹³When God made his promise to Abraham, since there was no one greater for him to swear by, he swore by himself, ¹⁴saying, "I will surely bless you and give you many descendants."[a] ¹⁵And so after waiting patiently, Abraham received what was promised.

¹⁶Men swear by someone greater than themselves, and the oath confirms what is said and puts an end to all argument. ¹⁷Because God wanted to make the unchanging nature of his purpose very clear to the heirs of what was promised, he confirmed it with an oath. ¹⁸God did this so that, by two unchangeable things in which it is impossible for God to lie, we who have fled to take hold of the hope offered to us may be greatly encouraged. ¹⁹We have this hope as an anchor for the soul, firm and secure. It enters the inner sanctuary behind the curtain, ²⁰where Jesus, who went before us, has entered on our behalf. He has become a high priest forever, in the order of Melchizedek.

Melchizedek the Priest

7 This Melchizedek was king of Salem and priest of God Most High. He met Abraham returning from the defeat of the kings and blessed him, ²and Abraham gave him a tenth of everything. First, his name means "king of righteousness"; then also, "king of Salem" means "king of peace." ³Without father or mother, without genealogy, without beginning of days or end of life, like the Son of God he remains a priest forever.

⁴Just think how great he was: Even the patriarch Abraham gave him a tenth of the plunder! ⁵Now the law requires the descendants of Levi who become priests to collect a tenth from the people—that is, their brothers—even though their brothers are descended from Abraham. ⁶This man, however, did not trace his descent from Levi, yet he collected a tenth from Abraham and blessed him who had the promises. ⁷And without doubt the lesser person is blessed by the greater. ⁸In the one case, the tenth is collected by men who die; but in the other case, by him who is declared to be living. ⁹One might even say that Levi, who collects the tenth, paid the tenth through Abraham, ¹⁰because when Melchizedek met Abraham, Levi was still in the body of his ancestor.

Jesus Like Melchizedek

¹¹If perfection could have been attained through the Levitical priesthood (for on the basis of it the law was given to the people), why was there still need for another priest to come—one in the order of Melchizedek, not in the order of Aaron? ¹²For when there is a change of the priesthood, there must also be a change of the law. ¹³He of whom these things are said belonged to a different tribe, and no one from that tribe has ever served at the altar. ¹⁴For it is clear that our Lord descended from Judah, and in regard to that tribe Moses said nothing about priests. ¹⁵And what we have said is even more clear if another priest like Melchizedek appears, ¹⁶one who has become a priest not on the basis of a regulation as to his ancestry but on the basis of the power of an indestructible life. ¹⁷For it is declared:

> "You are a priest forever,
>   in the order of Melchizedek."[b]

¹⁸The former regulation is set aside because it was weak and useless ¹⁹(for the law made nothing perfect), and a better

[a]14 Gen. 22:17   [b]17 Psalm 110:4

hope is introduced, by which we draw near to God.

²⁰And it was not without an oath! Others became priests without any oath, ²¹but he became a priest with an oath when God said to him:

"The Lord has sworn
and will not change his mind:
'You are a priest forever.' "ᵃ

²²Because of this oath, Jesus has become the guarantee of a better covenant.

²³Now there have been many of those priests, since death prevented them from continuing in office; ²⁴but because Jesus lives forever, he has a permanent priesthood. ²⁵Therefore he is able to save completelyᵇ those who come to God through

ᵃ21 Psalm 110:4   ᵇ25 Or forever

HEBREWS 6:13–20

The Anchor

6:19 WE HAVE THIS HOPE AS AN ANCHOR FOR THE SOUL.

There are some things that will never change. Jesus "has become a high priest forever, in the order of Melchizedek" (6:20). Do you know what Jesus is doing right now, this very moment, and will be doing forever? Hint: Read Hebrews 7:25. "He always lives to intercede for them." Right now Jesus is praying for you. These things will never change. God will never lie; Jesus will never leave his side; Jesus will never stop praying for his people. Better start praying; for if you do, you will answer what Jesus is praying for you to do!

The Melchizedek of Genesis 14:18–20 is seen here as a prefiguration of Jesus. Without mention of parents, children, birth or death, Melchizedek appeared out of nowhere, from heaven as it were. Like Melchizedek, Jesus is both king and priest; he will stand as king and priest forever (see Hebrews 7:1–3,15–17).

This hope—that Jesus stands as king and priest forever—serves as "an anchor for the soul" (Hebrews 6:19). It's probably a little confusing to visualize, but as an anchor is thrown out to secure a ship in its place, Jesus has gone behind the curtain of the Most Holy Place and stands there as high priest for us. Nothing can move him from that place; therefore, nothing can move us from that hope (see Romans 8:38–39). Early Christians appreciated this symbolism so much that the anchor, along with the fish and a ship, was one of their favorite symbols of the church.

There is great comfort in this anchor and great encouragement to pray. We may feel tossed about by life's storms, but we are anchored. We may be distracted and anxious in prayer, but we are anchored. We may lose all speech and lie mute in grief, but our anchor holds. Our high priest lives to pray for us, and we are anchored.

PRAY:

Son of God and great High Priest! You are my anchor
in heaven, my confidence and my hope. Hear my prayers
and answer me according to your mercy.

FOR YOUR NEXT DEVOTIONAL READING, GO TO PAGE 1524.

> *Prayer obtains fresh and continued outpourings of the Spirit. He alone begins the work of grace in a man's heart. He alone can carry it forward and make it prosper. But the good Spirit loves to be entreated. And those who ask most will have most of his influence.*
>
> J.C. RYLE

him, because he always lives to intercede for them.

26Such a high priest meets our need— one who is holy, blameless, pure, set apart from sinners, exalted above the heavens. 27Unlike the other high priests, he does not need to offer sacrifices day after day, first for his own sins, and then for the sins of the people. He sacrificed for their sins once for all when he offered himself. 28For the law appoints as high priests men who are weak; but the oath, which came after the law, appointed the Son, who has been made perfect forever.

The High Priest of a New Covenant

8 The point of what we are saying is this: We do have such a high priest, who sat down at the right hand of the throne of the Majesty in heaven, 2and who serves in the sanctuary, the true tabernacle set up by the Lord, not by man.

3Every high priest is appointed to offer both gifts and sacrifices, and so it was necessary for this one also to have something to offer. 4If he were on earth, he would not be a priest, for there are already men who offer the gifts prescribed by the law. 5They serve at a sanctuary that is a copy and shadow of what is in heaven. This is why Moses was warned when he was about to build the tabernacle: "See to it that you make everything according to the pattern shown you on the mountain."[a] 6But the ministry Jesus has received is as superior to theirs as the covenant of which he is mediator is superior to the old one, and it is founded on better promises.

7For if there had been nothing wrong with that first covenant, no place would have been sought for another. 8But God found fault with the people and said[b]:

"The time is coming, declares the Lord,
    when I will make a new covenant
  with the house of Israel
    and with the house of Judah.
9It will not be like the covenant
    I made with their forefathers
  when I took them by the hand
    to lead them out of Egypt,
  because they did not remain faithful
    to my covenant,
  and I turned away from them,
            declares the Lord.
10This is the covenant I will make with
        the house of Israel
  after that time, declares the Lord.
  I will put my laws in their minds
    and write them on their hearts.
  I will be their God,
    and they will be my people.
11No longer will a man teach his
        neighbor,
    or a man his brother, saying,
        'Know the Lord,'
  because they will all know me,
    from the least of them to the
        greatest.
12For I will forgive their wickedness
    and will remember their sins no
        more."[c]

> *"FOR I will forgive their wickedness and will remember their sins no more."*
>
> HEBREWS 8:12

13By calling this covenant "new," he has made the first one obsolete; and what is obsolete and aging will soon disappear.

Worship in the Earthly Tabernacle

9 Now the first covenant had regulations for worship and also an earthly sanctuary. 2A tabernacle was set up. In its first room were the lampstand, the table and the consecrated bread; this was called the Holy Place. 3Behind the second curtain was a room called the Most Holy Place, 4which had the golden

[a]5 Exodus 25:40   [b]8 Some manuscripts may be translated *fault and said to the people.*
[c]12 Jer. 31:31–34

altar of incense and the gold-covered ark of the covenant. This ark contained the gold jar of manna, Aaron's staff that had budded, and the stone tablets of the covenant. [5]Above the ark were the cherubim of the Glory, overshadowing the atonement cover.[a] But we cannot discuss these things in detail now.

[6]When everything had been arranged like this, the priests entered regularly into the outer room to carry on their ministry. [7]But only the high priest entered the inner room, and that only once a year, and never without blood, which he offered for himself and for the sins the people had committed in ignorance. [8]The Holy Spirit was showing by this that the way into the Most Holy Place had not yet been disclosed as long as the first tabernacle was still standing. [9]This is an illustration for the present time, indicating that the gifts and sacrifices being offered were not able to clear the conscience of the worshiper. [10]They are only a matter of food and drink and various ceremonial washings—external regulations applying until the time of the new order.

The Blood of Christ

[11]When Christ came as high priest of the good things that are already here,[b] he went through the greater and more perfect tabernacle that is not manmade, that is to say, not a part of this creation. [12]He did not enter by means of the blood of goats and calves; but he entered the Most Holy Place once for all by his own blood, having obtained eternal redemption. [13]The blood of goats and bulls and the ashes of a heifer sprinkled on those who are ceremonially unclean sanctify them so that they are outwardly clean. [14]How much more, then, will the blood of Christ, who through the eternal Spirit offered himself unblemished to God, cleanse our consciences from acts that lead to death,[c] so that we may serve the living God!

[15]For this reason Christ is the mediator of a new covenant, that those who are called may receive the promised eternal inheritance—now that he has died as a ransom to set them free from the sins committed under the first covenant.

[16]In the case of a will,[d] it is necessary to prove the death of the one who made it, [17]because a will is in force only when somebody has died; it never takes effect while the one who made it is living. [18]This is why even the first covenant was not put into effect without blood. [19]When Moses had proclaimed every commandment of the law to all the people, he took the blood of calves, together with water, scarlet wool and branches of hyssop, and sprinkled the scroll and all the people. [20]He said, "This is the blood of the covenant, which God has commanded you to keep."[e] [21]In the same way, he sprinkled with the blood both the tabernacle and everything used in its ceremonies. [22]In fact, the law requires that nearly everything be cleansed with blood, and without the shedding of blood there is no forgiveness.

[23]It was necessary, then, for the copies of the heavenly things to be purified with these sacrifices, but the heavenly things themselves with better sacrifices than these. [24]For Christ did not enter a manmade sanctuary that was only a copy of the true one; he entered heaven itself, now to appear for us in God's presence. [25]Nor did he enter heaven to offer himself again and again, the way the high priest enters the Most Holy Place every year with blood that is not his own. [26]Then Christ would have had to suffer many times since the creation of the

> 66 Pray: v. To ask that the laws of the universe be annulled in behalf of a single petitioner confessedly unworthy. 99
>
> AMBROSE BIERCE

world. But now he has appeared once for all at the end of the ages to do away with sin by the sacrifice of himself. [27]Just as man is destined to die once, and after that to face judgment, [28]so Christ was sacrificed once to take away the sins of many people; and he will appear a second time, not to bear sin, but to bring salvation to those who are waiting for him.

[a]5 Traditionally *the mercy seat*   [b]11 Some early manuscripts *are to come*   [c]14 Or *from useless rituals*   [d]16 Same Greek word as *covenant*; also in verse 17   [e]20 Exodus 24:8

Christ's Sacrifice Once for All

10 The law is only a shadow of the good things that are coming—not the realities themselves. For this reason it can never, by the same sacrifices repeated endlessly year after year, make perfect those who draw near to worship. ²If it could, would they not have stopped being offered? For the worshipers would have been cleansed once for all, and would no longer have felt guilty for their sins. ³But those sacrifices are an annual reminder of sins, ⁴because it is impossible for the blood of bulls and goats to take away sins.

⁵Therefore, when Christ came into the world, he said:

"Sacrifice and offering you did not
    desire,
    but a body you prepared for me;
⁶with burnt offerings and sin
    offerings
    you were not pleased.
⁷Then I said, 'Here I am—it is written
    about me in the scroll—
    I have come to do your will,
    O God.' "[a]

⁸First he said, "Sacrifices and offerings, burnt offerings and sin offerings you did not desire, nor were you pleased with them" (although the law required them to be made). ⁹Then he said, "Here I am, I have come to do your will." He sets aside the first to establish the second. ¹⁰And by that will, we have been made holy through the sacrifice of the body of Jesus Christ once for all.

¹¹Day after day every priest stands and performs his religious duties; again and again he offers the same sacrifices, which can never take away sins. ¹²But when this priest had offered for all time one sacrifice for sins, he sat down at the right hand of God. ¹³Since that time he waits for his enemies to be made his footstool, ¹⁴because by one sacrifice he has made perfect forever those who are being made holy.

¹⁵The Holy Spirit also testifies to us about this. First he says:

¹⁶ "This is the covenant I will make with
    them
    after that time, says the Lord.

I will put my laws in their hearts,
    and I will write them on their
    minds."[b]

¹⁷Then he adds:

"Their sins and lawless acts
    I will remember no more."[c]

¹⁸And where these have been forgiven, there is no longer any sacrifice for sin.

A Call to Persevere

¹⁹Therefore, brothers, since we have confidence to enter the Most Holy Place by the blood of Jesus, ²⁰by a new and living way opened for us through the curtain, that is, his body, ²¹and since we have a great priest over the house of God, ²²let us draw near to God with a sincere heart in full assurance of faith, having our hearts sprinkled to cleanse us from a guilty conscience and having our bodies washed with pure water. ²³Let us hold unswervingly to the hope we profess, for he who promised is faithful. ²⁴And let us consider how we may spur one another on toward love and good deeds. ²⁵Let us not give up meeting together, as some are in the habit of doing, but let us encourage one another—and all the more as you see the Day approaching.

²⁶If we deliberately keep on sinning after we have received the knowledge of the truth, no sacrifice for sins is left, ²⁷but only a fearful expectation of judgment and of raging fire that will consume the enemies of God. ²⁸Anyone who rejected the law of Moses died without mercy on the testimony of two or three witnesses. ²⁹How much more severely do you think a man deserves to be punished who has trampled the Son of God under foot, who has treated as an unholy thing the blood of the covenant that sanctified him, and who has insulted the Spirit of grace? ³⁰For we know him who said, "It is mine to avenge; I will repay,"[d] and again, "The Lord will judge his people."[e] ³¹It is a dreadful thing to fall into the hands of the living God.

³²Remember those earlier days after you had received the light, when you

---

[a]7 Psalm 40:6–8 (see Septuagint)   [b]16 Jer. 31:33
[c]17 Jer. 31:34   [d]30 Deut. 32:35
[e]30 Deut. 32:36; Psalm 135:14

stood your ground in a great contest in the face of suffering. ³³Sometimes you were publicly exposed to insult and persecution; at other times you stood side by side with those who were so treated. ³⁴You sympathized with those in prison

and joyfully accepted the confiscation of your property, because you knew that you yourselves had better and lasting possessions.

³⁵So do not throw away your confidence; it will be richly rewarded. ³⁶You

---

HEBREWS 10:19–25

Prayer, Encouragement and the Family of God

10:25 LET US ENCOURAGE ONE ANOTHER.

Prayer is decidedly a family matter, a community activity. It is so much more than "me and God." It is, above all, "we and God." "No Christian is an only child."⁶ Count the plurals in this text, the number of times words like "we," "you," "us," "our," "one another" and "brothers" appear. There are 17 occurrences in only four sentences (plus the corporate concept of the "house" or "household" of God). What follows in chapters 11 and 12 reminds us that this family is very, very, big—stretching out over space, but also back in time. All we do now happens before "a great cloud of witnesses" (Hebrews 12:1) who came before. The Apostles' Creed calls the life of this family "the communion of saints."

There is a direct link between the privilege of prayer and the responsibility of living together as a family. It's based on the word "therefore" in 10:19: "Therefore, brothers, since we have confidence to enter the Most Holy Place by the blood of Jesus ... and since we have a great high priest over the house of God" (verses 19,21). To come into the presence of the living God is always to come with all those other people who, like you, have been given the same privilege. To ignore them is to reject the gift. "Prayer is an act, indeed *the* act of fellowship," wrote Peter Taylor Forsyth. "We cannot truly pray for ourselves without passing beyond ourselves and our individual experience ... Even private prayer is common prayer."⁷

A healthy church has a culture of encouragement and prayer. People consider how they may "spur one another on toward love and good deeds" (verse 24). The word translated "spur" is used usually in a negative sense, as in goading someone to fight. But here it refers to positive, proactive efforts we should make to produce love and goodness in one another. Since the privilege of prayer is the basis of the communion of saints, the encouragement to pray should sustain the communion. Tell a brother or sister in Christ that you are praying for them. Better, ask a fellow believer to pray with you.

PRAY:

Dear Lord, I am thrilled and encouraged to know that I pray to the God of Abraham, Isaac and Jacob; the God of Paul, Augustine and Luther; the God who unites me with all believers everywhere. Make me an encourager to all in your family and a force for united prayer.

FOR YOUR NEXT DEVOTIONAL READING, GO TO PAGE 1527.

need to persevere so that when you have done the will of God, you will receive what he has promised. [37]For in just a very little while,

"He who is coming will come and will not delay.

[38]   But my righteous one[a] will live by faith.
And if he shrinks back,
    I will not be pleased with him."[b]

[39]But we are not of those who shrink back and are destroyed, but of those who believe and are saved.

By Faith

11 Now faith is being sure of what we hope for and certain of what we do not see. [2]This is what the ancients were commended for.

> 66 *Prayer is as natural an expression of faith as breathing is of life.* 99
>
> JONATHAN EDWARDS

[3]By faith we understand that the universe was formed at God's command, so that what is seen was not made out of what was visible.

[4]By faith Abel offered God a better sacrifice than Cain did. By faith he was commended as a righteous man, when God spoke well of his offerings. And by faith he still speaks, even though he is dead.

[5]By faith Enoch was taken from this life, so that he did not experience death; he could not be found, because God had taken him away. For before he was taken, he was commended as one who pleased God. [6]And without faith it is impossible to please God, because anyone who comes to him must believe that he exists and that he rewards those who earnestly seek him.

[7]By faith Noah, when warned about things not yet seen, in holy fear built an ark to save his family. By his faith he condemned the world and became heir of the righteousness that comes by faith.

[8]By faith Abraham, when called to go to a place he would later receive as his inheritance, obeyed and went, even though he did not know where he was going. [9]By faith he made his home in the promised land like a stranger in a foreign country; he lived in tents, as did Isaac and Jacob, who were heirs with him of the same promise. [10]For he was looking forward to the city with foundations, whose architect and builder is God.

[11]By faith Abraham, even though he was past age—and Sarah herself was barren—was enabled to become a father because he[c] considered him faithful who had made the promise. [12]And so from this one man, and he as good as dead, came descendants as numerous as the stars in the sky and as countless as the sand on the seashore.

[13]All these people were still living by faith when they died. They did not receive the things promised; they only saw them and welcomed them from a distance. And they admitted that they were aliens and strangers on earth. [14]People who say such things show that they are looking for a country of their own. [15]If they had been thinking of the country they had left, they would have had opportunity to return. [16]Instead, they were longing for a better country—a heavenly one. Therefore God is not ashamed to be called their God, for he has prepared a city for them.

[17]By faith Abraham, when God tested him, offered Isaac as a sacrifice. He who had received the promises was about to sacrifice his one and only son, [18]even though God had said to him, "It is through Isaac that your offspring[d] will be reckoned."[e] [19]Abraham reasoned that God could raise the dead, and figuratively speaking, he did receive Isaac back from death.

[20]By faith Isaac blessed Jacob and Esau in regard to their future.

[21]By faith Jacob, when he was dying, blessed each of Joseph's sons, and worshiped as he leaned on the top of his staff.

[22]By faith Joseph, when his end was near, spoke about the exodus of the Israelites from Egypt and gave instructions about his bones.

---

[a]38 One early manuscript *But the righteous*   [b]38 Hab. 2:3,4   [c]11 Or *By faith even Sarah, who was past age, was enabled to bear children because she*   [d]18 Greek *seed*   [e]18 Gen. 21:12

[23]By faith Moses' parents hid him for three months after he was born, because they saw he was no ordinary child, and they were not afraid of the king's edict.

[24]By faith Moses, when he had grown up, refused to be known as the son of Pharaoh's daughter. [25]He chose to be mistreated along with the people of God rather than to enjoy the pleasures of sin for a short time. [26]He regarded disgrace for the sake of Christ as of greater value than the treasures of Egypt, because he was looking ahead to his reward. [27]By faith he left Egypt, not fearing the king's anger; he persevered because he saw him who is invisible. [28]By faith he kept the Passover and the sprinkling of blood, so that the destroyer of the firstborn would not touch the firstborn of Israel.

[29]By faith the people passed through the Red Sea[a] as on dry land; but when the Egyptians tried to do so, they were drowned.

[30]By faith the walls of Jericho fell, after the people had marched around them for seven days.

[31]By faith the prostitute Rahab, because she welcomed the spies, was not killed with those who were disobedient.[b]

[32]And what more shall I say? I do not have time to tell about Gideon, Barak, Samson, Jephthah, David, Samuel and the prophets, [33]who through faith conquered kingdoms, administered justice, and gained what was promised; who shut the mouths of lions, [34]quenched the fury of the flames, and escaped the edge of the sword; whose weakness was turned to strength; and who became powerful in battle and routed foreign armies. [35]Women received back their dead, raised to life again. Others were tortured and refused to be released, so that they might gain a better resurrection. [36]Some faced jeers and flogging, while still others were chained and put in prison. [37]They were stoned[c]; they were sawed in two; they were put to death by the sword. They went about in sheepskins and goatskins, destitute, persecuted and mistreated— [38]the world was not worthy of them. They wandered in deserts and mountains, and in caves and holes in the ground.

[39]These were all commended for their faith, yet none of them received what had been promised. [40]God had planned something better for us so that only together with us would they be made perfect.

God Disciplines His Sons

12 Therefore, since we are surrounded by such a great cloud of witnesses, let us throw off everything that hinders and the sin that so easily entangles, and let us run with perseverance the race marked out for us. [2]Let us fix our eyes on Jesus, the author and perfecter of our faith, who for the joy set before him endured the cross, scorning its shame, and sat down at the right hand of the throne of God. [3]Consider him who endured such opposition from sinful men, so that you will not grow weary and lose heart.

> 66 In Gethsemane the holiest of all petitioners prayed three times that a certain cup might pass from him. It did not. After that the idea that prayer is recommended to use as a sort of infallible gimmick may be dismissed. 99
>
> C.S. LEWIS

[4]In your struggle against sin, you have not yet resisted to the point of shedding your blood. [5]And you have forgotten that word of encouragement that addresses you as sons:

"My son, do not make light of the
  Lord's discipline,
and do not lose heart when he
  rebukes you,
[6]because the Lord disciplines those
  he loves,
and he punishes everyone he
  accepts as a son."[d]

[7]Endure hardship as discipline; God is treating you as sons. For what son is not disciplined by his father? [8]If you are not disciplined (and everyone undergoes discipline), then you are illegitimate children and not true sons. [9]Moreover, we have all had human fathers who disciplined us and we respected them for it. How much more should we submit to the Father of our spirits and live! [10]Our fathers disci-

[a]29 That is, Sea of Reeds   [b]31 Or unbelieving
[c]37 Some early manuscripts stoned; they were put to the test;   [d]6 Prov. 3:11,12

plined us for a little while as they thought best; but God disciplines us for our good, that we may share in his holiness. ¹¹No discipline seems pleasant at the time, but painful. Later on, however, it produces a harvest of righteousness and peace for those who have been trained by it.

¹²Therefore, strengthen your feeble arms and weak knees. ¹³"Make level paths for your feet,"ᵃ so that the lame may not be disabled, but rather healed.

Warning Against Refusing God

¹⁴Make every effort to live in peace with all men and to be holy; without holiness no one will see the Lord. ¹⁵See to it that

ᵃ13 Prov. 4:26

{ FRIDAY }

HEBREWS 12:25–29

Prayer and Awe

12:29 OUR "GOD IS A CONSUMING FIRE."

Here is a sobering item in the Biblical view of time: One day, everything that can be shaken will be shaken, and that "everything" is all things in heaven and earth (see 12:26–27). All that can be shaken will be removed, and all that will remain is what cannot be shaken. God is a consuming fire. The only unshakeable reality is the kingdom of God. Another way of saying this is: "The world and its desires pass away, but the man who does the will of God lives forever" (1 John 2:17). To be in this unshakeable kingdom is to be "part of the permanent."[8]

So what things keep you from prayer? Know this: Whatever they are, they are always shakable things that will pass away. Don't let the temporary keep you away from the permanent. Instead, be thankful and filled with reverence and awe that you can pray. That is part of what it means to "worship God acceptably" (Hebrews 12:28). Gratitude is what must follow grace— like thunder follows lightning. What an incredible grace we have been given to be in a kingdom that is eternal. Neither death nor calamity nor demons can separate us from our King and our place in his kingdom (see Romans 8:31–39). So be grateful and pray, for prayer is the first and most important act of gratitude.[9]

Awe and reverence are what you feel when you know the enormity of the stakes involved. The kingdom is a matter of life and death, heaven and hell. You have been saved as one snatched from certain death. Pray as one who knows this. The way to God has been opened to you; enter boldly, but don't swagger in or saunter as one who has forgotten the gravity and greatness of the gift. And pray for others to be rescued from their attachment and slavery to the things that will be shaken, that they may be brought into the kingdom that cannot be shaken (see Colossians 1:13–14). When you gather to worship, remind others that God is the lover of our souls, a tender Father, but also a consuming fire—not a God to trifle with.

PRAY:

Holy Father! Give us such a vision of your holiness and tenderness that we will see no conflict between love and fear, but only a trembling joy that we belong to a God as great as you.

FOR YOUR NEXT DEVOTIONAL READING, GO TO PAGE 1528.

Sweet Delight in God

AS A YOUNG MAN, Jonathan Edwards had a profound experience of the goodness of God that shaped his ministry and spirituality for the rest of his life:

> The first instance I remember of that sort of inward, sweet delight in God and in divine things, that I have lived much in since, was on reading these words, 1 Timothy 1:17: "Now unto the King eternal, immortal, invisible, the only wise God, be honor and glory for ever and ever. Amen." As I read the words, there came into my soul, and was as it were diffused through it, a sense of the glory of the Divine Being; a new sense, quite different from any thing I ever experienced before. Never any words of scripture seemed to me as these words did. I thought with myself, how excellent a Being that was, and how happy I should be, if I might enjoy that God, and be rapt up to him in heaven, and be as it were swallowed up in him for ever![10]

Jonathan Edwards is considered by many to be the greatest theologian and philosopher America has produced. Brilliant and versatile, his gifts were multifaceted. Before his premature death in 1758 from the ill effects of a smallpox vaccination, Edwards served as a pastor, revivalist, preacher, educator, controversialist and author. Beneath and above all these gifts, giving them coherence, was his piety: a warm and intense devotional life rooted in his "sweet delight in God." Were it not for his love for God, Lyman Beecher, a great preacher of a later generation, believed Edwards' powerful intellect might have been tempted to do evil. In 1830, Beecher wrote his son George:

[Edwards'] vigor of intellect, compass of thought, patience of investigation, accuracy of discrimination, power of argument, knowledge of the Bible, and strength of holiness, stand unrivalled. But for his piety, he might have been a skeptic more dangerous than Hume or Voltaire . . . But the attractions of his heart to God kept him in orbit.[11]

Edwards' marriage to Sarah Pierrepont, a woman also of deep mystical piety, strengthened "the attractions of his heart to God." In his classic work, *Religious Affections*, Edwards' powerful intellect combined with his "sweet delight in God" to interpret and defend the revival known as the Great Awakening that swept through the American colonies in the mid 1730s. In his *An Humble Attempt*[12], he proposed a plan for strategic, synchronized prayer that transcended denominations—a true "Concert of Prayer." *An Humble Attempt* was widely circulated in America and had a profound effect on the hundreds of "prayer societies" in both England and America.

PRAY:

Holy and blessed God! In your Son are hidden all the treasures of wisdom and knowledge. Send your Spirit to so kindle in me a delight in your perfections that I may love you passionately with my whole being: heart, soul and mind.

MEMORIZE:

Now to the King eternal, immortal, invisible, the only God, be honor and glory for ever and ever. Amen. 1 TIMOTHY 1:17

FOR YOUR NEXT DEVOTIONAL READING, GO TO PAGE 1531.

no one misses the grace of God and that no bitter root grows up to cause trouble and defile many. [16]See that no one is sexually immoral, or is godless like Esau, who for a single meal sold his inheritance rights as the oldest son. [17]Afterward, as you know, when he wanted to inherit this blessing, he was rejected. He could bring about no change of mind, though he sought the blessing with tears.

[18]You have not come to a mountain that can be touched and that is burning with fire; to darkness, gloom and storm; [19]to a trumpet blast or to such a voice speaking words that those who heard it begged that no further word be spoken to them, [20]because they could not bear what was commanded: "If even an animal touches the mountain, it must be stoned."[a] [21]The sight was so terrifying that Moses said, "I am trembling with fear."[b]

[22]But you have come to Mount Zion, to the heavenly Jerusalem, the city of the living God. You have come to thousands upon thousands of angels in joyful assembly, [23]to the church of the firstborn, whose names are written in heaven. You have come to God, the judge of all men, to the spirits of righteous men made perfect, [24]to Jesus the mediator of a new covenant, and to the sprinkled blood that speaks a better word than the blood of Abel.

[25]See to it that you do not refuse him who speaks. If they did not escape when they refused him who warned them on earth, how much less will we, if we turn away from him who warns us from heaven? [26]At that time his voice shook the earth, but now he has promised, "Once more I will shake not only the earth but also the heavens."[c] [27]The words "once more" indicate the removing of what can be shaken—that is, created things—so that what cannot be shaken may remain.

[28]Therefore, since we are receiving a kingdom that cannot be shaken, let us be thankful, and so worship God acceptably with reverence and awe, [29]for our "God is a consuming fire."[d]

Concluding Exhortations

13 Keep on loving each other as brothers. [2]Do not forget to entertain strangers, for by so doing some people have entertained angels without knowing it. [3]Remember those in prison as if you were their fellow prisoners, and those who are mistreated as if you yourselves were suffering.

[4]Marriage should be honored by all, and the marriage bed kept pure, for God will judge the adulterer and all the sexually immoral. [5]Keep your lives free from the love of money and be content with what you have, because God has said,

"Never will I leave you;
    never will I forsake you."[e]

[6]So we say with confidence,

"The Lord is my helper; I will not be afraid.
    What can man do to me?"[f]

[7]Remember your leaders, who spoke the word of God to you. Consider the outcome of their way of life and imitate their faith. [8]Jesus Christ is the same yesterday and today and forever.

[9]Do not be carried away by all kinds of strange teachings. It is good for our hearts to be strengthened by grace, not by ceremonial foods, which are of no value to those who eat them. [10]We have an altar from which those who minister at the tabernacle have no right to eat.

[11]The high priest carries the blood of animals into the Most Holy Place as a sin offering, but the bodies are burned outside the camp. [12]And so Jesus also suffered outside the city gate to make the people holy through his own blood. [13]Let us, then, go to him outside the camp, bearing the disgrace he bore. [14]For here we do not have an enduring city, but we are looking for the city that is to come.

[15]Through Jesus, therefore, let us continually offer to God a sacrifice of praise—the fruit of lips that confess his name. [16]And do not forget to do good and to share with others, for with such sacrifices God is pleased.

[17]Obey your leaders and submit to their authority. They keep watch over you as men who must give an account. Obey them so that their work will be a joy, not a burden, for that would be of no advantage to you.

[a]20 Exodus 19:12,13   [b]21 Deut. 9:19
[c]26 Haggai 2:6   [d]29 Deut. 4:24
[e]5 Deut. 31:6   [f]6 Psalm 118:6,7

¹⁸Pray for us. We are sure that we have a clear conscience and desire to live honorably in every way. ¹⁹I particularly urge you to pray so that I may be restored to you soon.

²⁰May the God of peace, who through the blood of the eternal covenant brought back from the dead our Lord Jesus, that great Shepherd of the sheep,

> *PRAY for us. We are sure that we have a clear conscience and desire to live honorably in every way.*
>
> HEBREWS 13:18

²¹equip you with everything good for doing his will, and may he work in us what

---

HEBREWS 13:15

A Sacrifice of Praise

13:15 THROUGH JESUS, THEREFORE, LET US CONTINUALLY OFFER TO GOD A SACRIFICE OF PRAISE—THE FRUIT OF LIPS THAT CONFESS HIS NAME.

This simple sentence tells us a lot about who we are and how we are to live. If you are a Christian—that is, if you confess the name of Christ—then you are a member of what the Bible elsewhere calls a holy priesthood: "You also, like living stones, are being built into a spiritual house to be a holy priesthood, offering spiritual sacrifices acceptable to God through Jesus Christ" (1 Peter 2:5). In the Old Testament, priests were to reflect God's holiness, intercede for people before God and represent God before people.

But what priests were most known for was the offering of sacrifices. The sacrifices were usually animals like lambs or goats, and they had three things in common. First, the sacrifice was to be precious, the best that one had. Second, the sacrifice was to be total because death is total. Nothing could be held back. A sacrifice was, by definition, given in total abandon. Third, the sacrifice was to give life, symbolically. The point of a sacrifice was not death but life released through death. "For the life of a creature is in the blood" (Leviticus 17:11). When blood was spilled, life was given symbolically.

Because Christ is the complete sacrifice, the perfect atonement for our sins, the only sacrifice that can now have any legitimacy is a living sacrifice of praise on our part (see Romans 12:1–2). This is the sacrifice that pleases God. This is the fruit of lips that confess his name.

Try to imagine giving praise as sacrifice. Do you hold anything back? Of course not! Is your whole self involved—spirit, soul, mind and body? Absolutely! Does God get your best? Is your mind engaged? Are your emotions free? Is your attention total? Is your sacrifice of praise precious, total and life-giving—like Christ's sacrifice? Such extravagant grace calls for extravagant praise.

Poet George Herbert said humankind is the world's high priest. We can offer what no other creature can: eloquence of words, clarity of thought and depth of feeling unparalleled in the creation. How tragic if we refuse to offer what only we can offer, and the stones must cry out by default (see Luke 19:40).

PRAY:

Holy Spirit! Summon from my heart, mind and body the best I have, that I may truly offer a sacrifice of praise.

FOR YOUR NEXT DEVOTIONAL READING, GO TO PAGE 1532.

is pleasing to him, through Jesus Christ, to whom be glory for ever and ever. Amen.

²²Brothers, I urge you to bear with my word of exhortation, for I have written you only a short letter.

²³I want you to know that our brother Timothy has been released. If he arrives soon, I will come with him to see you.

²⁴Greet all your leaders and all God's people. Those from Italy send you their greetings.

²⁵Grace be with you all.

HEBREWS 13:20–21

Prayer for All We Really Need

13:20–21 MAY THE GOD OF PEACE . . . EQUIP YOU WITH EVERYTHING GOOD FOR DOING HIS WILL.

It is all here in these two short verses. All you ever really need to desire and to ask for is in verse 21: "everything good for doing his will." The only one you ever need to ask is described in verse 20: "the God of peace, who through the blood of the eternal covenant brought back from the dead our Lord Jesus, that great Shepherd of the sheep."

Start with the only one you ever need to ask. Have you ever stood at the construction site of a giant building and watched the builders dig the foundation? Deep holes are dug for massive pilings of concrete and steel upon which the great structure will be secured. The bigger and stronger the foundation, the greater the building will be. Spiritually speaking, great hopes for great things are guaranteed in great foundations. We have the greatest of foundations for the greatest of prayers in these three things:

1. The name of God: He is the God of peace, the one who has forgiven us and reconciled us to himself in Christ. Will he not also give us everything else that we need (see Romans 8:32)?
2. The risen Shepherd: Jesus Christ is the Good Shepherd who laid down his life for the sheep, and whom God raised from the dead. Nothing can separate us from his love (see Romans 8:37–39).
3. The everlasting covenant: God has placed himself under major obligations and guaranteed his promise with his Son's blood. He will do nothing less than give us new hearts (see Jeremiah 31:31–34; Ezekiel 36:26–27).

To change the metaphor, a threefold cord is not easily broken (see Ecclesiastes 4:12): the name of God, the risen Shepherd and the blood of the eternal covenant. Give God thanks! Praise his name!

Now ask God for what you need according to who he is. Ask him to give you and others "everything good for doing his will." Everything. Don't be timid; ask him to work in you everything good for doing his will. Let your aspirations be as high as his purposes. Don't insult him by praying only little prayers. Pray the big prayers.

PRAY:

"My hope is built on nothing less than Jesus' blood and righteousness. I dare not trust the sweetest frame, but wholly lean on Jesus' name. On Christ the solid rock I stand, all other ground is sinking sand." EDWARD MOTE

FOR YOUR NEXT DEVOTIONAL READING, GO TO PAGE 1535.

James

THE BOOK of James is known for its espousal of "practical Christianity." The epigram "faith without deeds is dead" (2:26) is a poignant rejoinder to those who would divide faith and action. Truly, we are saved by faith, not by deeds. But real faith *acts*. With biting sarcasm, James says faith without deeds is the faith of the devil, whose knowledge of the facts about God is thoroughly orthodox. But of course he wants nothing to do with *doing* what that knowledge demands. "You believe that there is one God. Good! Even the demons believe that—and shudder" (2:19).

How significant that a book so practically minded and action-oriented should have such strong passages about prayer. The wisdom we need to survive the rigors of the Christian life is found through prayer (see 1:5–8). Prayer is the one thing that fits all sizes and situations in life: trouble, joy, sickness and reconciliation (see 5:13–18). The secularization of our culture may have us acting as though prayer has little practical power, but James knows better. Faith without works is dead; prayer is one of the chief works of a robust faith. Prayer is practical, the basis of all action under God.

"THE PRAYER OF A RIGHTEOUS MAN IS POWERFUL AND EFFECTIVE." (5:16)

1 James, a servant of God and of the Lord Jesus Christ,

To the twelve tribes scattered among the nations:

Greetings.

Trials and Temptations

[2]Consider it pure joy, my brothers, whenever you face trials of many kinds, [3]because you know that the testing of your faith develops perseverance. [4]Perseverance must finish its work so that you may be mature and complete, not lacking anything. [5]If any of you lacks wisdom, he should ask God, who gives generously to all without finding fault, and it will be given to him. [6]But when he asks,

> IF ANY of you lacks wisdom, he should ask God, who gives generously to all without finding fault, and it will be given to him.
>
> JAMES 1:5

he must believe and not doubt, because he who doubts is like a wave of the sea, blown and tossed by the wind. [7]That man should not think he will receive anything from the Lord; [8]he is a double-minded man, unstable in all he does.

[9]The brother in humble circumstances ought to take pride in his high position. [10]But the one who is rich should take pride in his low position, because he will pass away like a wild flower. [11]For the sun rises with scorching heat and withers the plant; its blossom falls and its beauty is destroyed. In the same way, the rich man will fade away even while he goes about his business.

[12]Blessed is the man who perseveres under trial, because when he has stood the test, he will receive the crown of life that God has promised to those who love him.

[13]When tempted, no one should say, "God is tempting me." For God cannot be tempted by evil, nor does he tempt anyone; [14]but each one is tempted when, by his own evil desire, he is dragged away and enticed. [15]Then, after desire has conceived, it gives birth to sin; and sin, when it is full-grown, gives birth to death.

[16]Don't be deceived, my dear brothers. [17]Every good and perfect gift is from above, coming down from the Father of the heavenly lights, who does not change like shifting shadows. [18]He chose to give us birth through the word of truth, that we might be a kind of firstfruits of all he created.

Listening and Doing

[19]My dear brothers, take note of this: Everyone should be quick to listen, slow to speak and slow to become angry, [20]for man's anger does not bring about the righteous life that God desires. [21]Therefore, get rid of all moral filth and the evil that is so prevalent and humbly accept the word planted in you, which can save you.

[22]Do not merely listen to the word, and so deceive yourselves. Do what it says. [23]Anyone who listens to the word but does not do what it says is like a man who looks at his face in a mirror [24]and, after looking at himself, goes away and immediately forgets what he looks like. [25]But the man who looks intently into the perfect law that gives freedom, and continues to do this, not forgetting what he has heard, but doing it—he will be blessed in what he does.

[26]If anyone considers himself religious and yet does not keep a tight rein on his tongue, he deceives himself and his religion is worthless. [27]Religion that God our Father accepts as pure and faultless is this: to look after orphans and widows in their distress and to keep oneself from being polluted by the world.

Favoritism Forbidden

2 My brothers, as believers in our glorious Lord Jesus Christ, don't show favoritism. [2]Suppose a man comes into your meeting wearing a gold ring and fine clothes, and a poor man in shabby clothes also comes in. [3]If you show special attention to the man wearing fine clothes and say, "Here's a good seat for you," but say to the poor man, "You stand there" or "Sit on the floor by my feet," [4]have you not discriminated among yourselves and become judges with evil thoughts?

[5]Listen, my dear brothers: Has not God chosen those who are poor in the eyes of

Wisdom: Do You Really Want It?

1:5 IF ANY OF YOU LACKS WISDOM, HE SHOULD ASK GOD.

The Christian life is hard. You'll need a lot of help from God to live it, and he will give generously. But take note—the help you want may not be the kind of help he'll give.

The hard part is that the road to heaven is uphill. There will be trials along the way, guaranteed (see Acts 14:22; 2 Timothy 3:12). The harder part is that you should regard the trials with "pure joy" because of the wonderful things they will do for your character—"because you know that the testing of your faith develops perseverance. Perseverance must finish its work so that you may be mature and complete, not lacking anything" (James 1:3–4). The way the Lord wants us to respond to our trials can be harder than going through the trials themselves! Most of us would be glad to just be able to get through our trials. But God wants us to get through them with pure joy and emerge from them "mature and complete, not lacking anything." For that we will need wisdom.

What is this wisdom? It is not so much knowing what to do, as how to be. It is described in some detail in James 3:17 as qualities of character and perspective: "pure ... peace-loving, considerate, submissive, full of mercy and good fruit, impartial and sincere." This is the wisdom God gives to get us through trials with pure joy. To understand the strength of this wisdom, think of its opposites—impurity, combativeness, inconsiderateness, rebelliousness, vindictiveness, partiality and insincerity. People with such qualities will never get through trials with pure joy—pure rage and resentment maybe, but not joy. The wisdom God gives makes us teachable. It gives us a mind and a heart that will be shaped into the image of Christ. God is more concerned about what we become as we suffer than he is that we be free from suffering.

Pray for wisdom, but ask yourself, "Do I really want this kind of wisdom in my trials? Or do I just want to get out of my trials?" God will give wisdom generously but only to those who do not doubt, to those who do not continually waver in their spiritual confidence and commitment. The idea is that you need to be of one mind about God's wisdom to receive it. Do you really want it or just sort of want it? Ambivalence and a divided heart will not make you wise.

PRAY:
"Have thine own way, Lord!
Have thine own way!
Thou art the Potter, I am the clay.
Mold me and make me after thy will,
While I am waiting, yielded and still."[1]

FOR YOUR NEXT DEVOTIONAL READING, GO TO PAGE 1537.

the world to be rich in faith and to inherit the kingdom he promised those who love him? [6]But you have insulted the poor. Is it not the rich who are exploiting you? Are they not the ones who are dragging you into court? [7]Are they not the ones who are slandering the noble name of him to whom you belong?

> " *Pray that your loneliness may spur you into finding something to live for, great enough to die for.* "
>
> DAG HAMMARSKJOLD

[8]If you really keep the royal law found in Scripture, "Love your neighbor as yourself,"[a] you are doing right. [9]But if you show favoritism, you sin and are convicted by the law as lawbreakers. [10]For whoever keeps the whole law and yet stumbles at just one point is guilty of breaking all of it. [11]For he who said, "Do not commit adultery,"[b] also said, "Do not murder."[c] If you do not commit adultery but do commit murder, you have become a lawbreaker.

[12]Speak and act as those who are going to be judged by the law that gives freedom, [13]because judgment without mercy will be shown to anyone who has not been merciful. Mercy triumphs over judgment!

Faith and Deeds

[14]What good is it, my brothers, if a man claims to have faith but has no deeds? Can such faith save him? [15]Suppose a brother or sister is without clothes and daily food. [16]If one of you says to him, "Go, I wish you well; keep warm and well fed," but does nothing about his physical needs, what good is it? [17]In the same way, faith by itself, if it is not accompanied by action, is dead.

[18]But someone will say, "You have faith; I have deeds."

Show me your faith without deeds, and I will show you my faith by what I do. [19]You believe that there is one God. Good! Even the demons believe that—and shudder.

[20]You foolish man, do you want evidence that faith without deeds is useless[d]? [21]Was not our ancestor Abraham considered righteous for what he did when he offered his son Isaac on the altar? [22]You see that his faith and his actions were working together, and his faith was made complete by what he did. [23]And the scripture was fulfilled that says, "Abraham believed God, and it was credited to him as righteousness,"[e] and he was called God's friend. [24]You see that a person is justified by what he does and not by faith alone.

[25]In the same way, was not even Rahab the prostitute considered righteous for what she did when she gave lodging to the spies and sent them off in a different direction? [26]As the body without the spirit is dead, so faith without deeds is dead.

Taming the Tongue

3 Not many of you should presume to be teachers, my brothers, because you know that we who teach will be judged more strictly. [2]We all stumble in many ways. If anyone is never at fault in what he says, he is a perfect man, able to keep his whole body in check.

[3]When we put bits into the mouths of horses to make them obey us, we can turn the whole animal. [4]Or take ships as an example. Although they are so large and are driven by strong winds, they are steered by a very small rudder wherever the pilot wants to go. [5]Likewise the tongue is a small part of the body, but it makes great boasts. Consider what a great forest is set on fire by a small spark. [6]The tongue also is a fire, a world of evil among the parts of the body. It corrupts the whole person, sets the whole course of his life on fire, and is itself set on fire by hell.

[7]All kinds of animals, birds, reptiles and creatures of the sea are being tamed and have been tamed by man, [8]but no man can tame the tongue. It is a restless evil, full of deadly poison.

[9]With the tongue we praise our Lord and Father, and with it we curse men, who have been made in God's likeness. [10]Out of the same mouth come praise and cursing. My brothers, this should not be. [11]Can both fresh water and salt[f] water

---

[a]8 Lev. 19:18   [b]11 Exodus 20:14; Deut. 5:18
[c]11 Exodus 20:13; Deut. 5:17   [d]20 Some early manuscripts *dead*   [e]23 Gen. 15:6
[f]11 Greek *bitter* (see also verse 14)

flow from the same spring? ¹²My brothers, can a fig tree bear olives, or a grapevine bear figs? Neither can a salt spring produce fresh water.

> WITH the tongue we praise our Lord and Father, and with it we curse men, who have been made in God's likeness . . . My brothers, this should not be.
>
> JAMES 3:9,11

JAMES 4:1–3

Two Kinds of Wisdom

¹³Who is wise and understanding among you? Let him show it by his good life, by deeds done in the humility that comes from wisdom. ¹⁴But if you harbor bitter envy and selfish ambition in your hearts, do not boast about it or deny the truth. ¹⁵Such "wisdom" does not come down from heaven but is earthly, unspiritual, of the devil. ¹⁶For where you have envy and selfish ambition, there you find disorder and every evil practice.

[THURSDAY]

Pure Motives, Loving Community and Prayer

4:2 YOU DO NOT HAVE, BECAUSE YOU DO NOT ASK GOD.

As it stands, taken by itself, the line "You do not have, because you do not ask God" is one of the most encouraging thoughts for prayer in all of Scripture. The only thing standing between you and receiving what you need is your failure to ask. It's taken right out of the Sermon on the Mount (see Matthew 7:7–8). And as far as it goes, it's good advice; so ask that you may receive.

But there's more to it than just asking in prayer. Your motives in asking are all-important: "When you ask, you do not receive, because you ask with wrong motives, that you may spend what you get on your pleasures" (James 4:3). The first three petitions of the Lord's Prayer—"hallowed be your name, your kingdom come, your will be done"—are there to bathe your requests in the holy water of God's kingdom and will. Without them, your desires can easily be the kind of desires condemned by James: hedonistic and self-centered. In fact, the Greek word for "desires" in verse 1 (as well as for "pleasures" in verse 3) is the very word behind our English word *hedonism*.

There is something else we must not miss about proper asking: We must pray in a loving community. A church of individuals driven by selfish desires will be a church whose members are at war with each other (see verses 1–2). Right relationships in the church are one of the fundamentals of answered prayer. Jesus prayed that we would be one as he and his Father are one (see John 17:20–23). How can we expect our prayers to be heard by the Father if we are, in our relationships with one other, working against the prayer his Son prayed for us? There is a one-to-one relationship between our motives in prayer and answered prayer, and between our relationships with one another and answered prayer.

PRAY:

"Thee will I love with all my power in all my works and thee alone, thee will I love till sacred fire fills my whole soul with pure desire."²

FOR YOUR NEXT DEVOTIONAL READING, GO TO PAGE 1539.

[17]But the wisdom that comes from heaven is first of all pure; then peace-loving, considerate, submissive, full of mercy and good fruit, impartial and sincere. [18]Peacemakers who sow in peace raise a harvest of righteousness.

Submit Yourselves to God

4 What causes fights and quarrels among you? Don't they come from your desires that battle within you? [2]You want something but don't get it. You kill and covet, but you cannot have what you want. You quarrel and fight. You do not have, because you do not ask God. [3]When you ask, you do not receive, because you ask with wrong motives, that you may spend what you get on your pleasures.

[4]You adulterous people, don't you know that friendship with the world is hatred toward God? Anyone who chooses to be a friend of the world becomes an enemy of God. [5]Or do you think Scripture says without reason that the spirit he caused to live in us envies intensely?[a] [6]But he gives us more grace. That is why Scripture says:

> "God opposes the proud
>   but gives grace to the humble."[b]

[7]Submit yourselves, then, to God. Resist the devil, and he will flee from you. [8]Come near to God and he will come near to you. Wash your hands, you sinners, and purify your hearts, you double-minded. [9]Grieve, mourn and wail. Change your laughter to mourning and your joy to gloom. [10]Humble yourselves before the Lord, and he will lift you up.

[11]Brothers, do not slander one another. Anyone who speaks against his brother or judges him speaks against the law and judges it. When you judge the law, you are not keeping it, but sitting in judgment on it. [12]There is only one Lawgiver and Judge, the one who is able to save and destroy. But you—who are you to judge your neighbor?

Boasting About Tomorrow

[13]Now listen, you who say, "Today or tomorrow we will go to this or that city, spend a year there, carry on business and make money." [14]Why, you do not

> 66 *What we usually pray to God is not that his will be done, but that he approve ours.* 99
>
> HELGA BERGOLD GROSS

even know what will happen tomorrow. What is your life? You are a mist that appears for a little while and then vanishes. [15]Instead, you ought to say, "If it is the Lord's will, we will live and do this or that." [16]As it is, you boast and brag. All such boasting is evil. [17]Anyone, then, who knows the good he ought to do and doesn't do it, sins.

Warning to Rich Oppressors

5 Now listen, you rich people, weep and wail because of the misery that is coming upon you. [2]Your wealth has rotted, and moths have eaten your clothes. [3]Your gold and silver are corroded. Their corrosion will testify against you and eat your flesh like fire. You have hoarded wealth in the last days. [4]Look! The wages you failed to pay the workmen who mowed your fields are crying out against you. The cries of the harvesters have reached the ears of the Lord Almighty. [5]You have lived on earth in luxury and self-indulgence. You have fattened yourselves in the day of slaughter.[c] [6]You have condemned and murdered innocent men, who were not opposing you.

Patience in Suffering

[7]Be patient, then, brothers, until the Lord's coming. See how the farmer waits for the land to yield its valuable crop and how patient he is for the autumn and spring rains. [8]You too, be patient and stand firm, because the Lord's coming is near. [9]Don't grumble against each other, brothers, or you will be judged. The Judge is standing at the door!

[10]Brothers, as an example of patience in the face of suffering, take the prophets who spoke in the name of the Lord. [11]As you know, we consider blessed those who have persevered. You have heard of

---

[a]5 Or *that God jealously longs for the spirit that he made to live in us; or that the Spirit he caused to live in us longs jealously* [b]6 Prov. 3:34 [c]5 Or *yourselves as in a day of feasting*

Job's perseverance and have seen what the Lord finally brought about. The Lord is full of compassion and mercy.

¹²Above all, my brothers, do not swear—not by heaven or by earth or by anything else. Let your "Yes" be yes, and your "No," no, or you will be condemned.

The Prayer of Faith

¹³Is any one of you in trouble? He should pray. Is anyone happy? Let him sing songs of praise. ¹⁴Is any one of you sick? He should call the elders of the church to pray over him and anoint him with oil in the name of the Lord. ¹⁵And

JAMES 5:13-18

Always Appropriate

5:16 THE PRAYER OF A RIGHTEOUS MAN IS POWERFUL AND EFFECTIVE.

In the United States, most people tend to stay away from church services when they are sick. In Africa and other parts of the Third World, church is the first place Christians want to be when they are sick. Western Christians think of containing a disease; most other Christians think of healing a disease, largely because of this passage from the book of James. "Is any one of you sick? He should call the elders of the church to pray over him and anoint him with oil in the name of the Lord. And the prayer offered in faith will make the sick person well; the Lord will raise him up" (5:14–15).

There is also a hint here of the relationship between prayer and medical care. The oil of anointing was probably more than a symbolic gesture pointing to the presence of the Holy Spirit. It was ancient practice to use oil medicinally. The picture here appears to be one of prayer *and* medicine, not prayer *or* medicine. Both, under God, are legitimate collaborators in working his mercy in the world.

There are other wonderful things this passage touches on about prayer. It is always appropriate to pray. Are you in trouble? Pray. Are you happy? Pray. Are you sick? Pray. It is never rude or inappropriate or uncouth to pray. God is the God of all situations and seasons—"For from him and through him and to him are all things" (Romans 11:36). Since God is the God of all seasons, prayer is the act for all seasons. Because all of life is lived under God, all of life is enriched and transformed by prayer. Prayer affects everything. It enhances joy, lightens trouble, heals sickness and aids reconciliation and forgiveness.

The book of James begins with the assertion that hardship is a big part of the Christian pilgrimage and immediately calls the church to pray for the special wisdom God gives in hardship. The book ends the same way: There will be suffering; we must be patient (see 5:7–12); and we must pray, pray, pray.

PRAY:

Father, there is so much to do each day and there are so many different situations; remind me to pray in all of them! Help me to acknowledge you in all my ways, that you may direct my steps.

FOR YOUR NEXT DEVOTIONAL READING, GO TO PAGE 1540.

Enfolded in Love

HER TIMES were as bloody and sordid as any in human history. From 1337 to 1453, England and France were locked in the so-called "Hundred Years War," a catastrophe that wracked medieval society top to bottom. The bubonic plague struck twice: 1348–1349 and 1361, cutting the population of Europe by a third to as much as a half. Yet at a time when God's love might have been seriously in question, this medieval mystic is remembered for her "Revelations of Divine Love."

No one knows her baptismal name; she is called Julian because of the years she spent in solitude in her cell at the church of St. Julian and St. Edward at Carrow, England. The "revelations," or "shewings," as she called them, 16 in all, came to her on May 8, 1373; her writings on these revelations are the result of her 20-year meditation on them.

Julian's revelation of the immense and sovereign love of God strengthened her faith. She focused on the truth that nothing can separate us from the love of God (see Romans 8:35–39). Even though we may not see that now, we will in heaven. She wrote:

> When judgment is given and we are brought up above, then we shall see clearly the secrets now hidden from us. In that day not one of us will want to say, "Lord, if it had been done this way, it would have been well done." But we shall all say with one voice, "Lord, blessed may you be, for it is so, and it is well. And now we see truly that all things were done as it was ordained before anything was made."[3]

Indeed, as she said poetically, "All shall be well and all shall be well, and all manner of things shall be well."[4] Because God does all things well, in spite of appearances, Julian counseled praise as the way to strengthen the heart when spiritually dry or apathetic or assaulted by temptation, doubt and fear. She believed that praise and thanksgiving were powerful acts of faith that teach the heart to joyfully beat with God's great heart of love. Through them we are assured that:

We are enfolded in the Father, and we are enfolded in the Son, and we are enfolded in the Holy Spirit. And the Father is enfolded in us, and the Son is enfolded in us, and the Holy Spirit is enfolded in us: almightiness, all wisdom, all goodness: one God, one Lord.[5]

PRAY:

"God, of your goodness, give me yourself,
for you are sufficient for me. I may not ask for anything less,
to be worthy of you. If I were to ask anything less I should
always be in need, for in you alone do I have all."[6]

MEMORIZE:

For I am convinced that neither death nor life,
neither angels nor demons, neither the present nor the future,
nor any powers, neither height nor depth, nor anything else in all
creation, will be able to separate us from the love of God that
is in Christ Jesus our Lord. ROMANS 8:38–39

FOR YOUR NEXT DEVOTIONAL READING, GO TO PAGE 1545.

the prayer offered in faith will make the sick person well; the Lord will raise him up. If he has sinned, he will be forgiven. ¹⁶Therefore confess your sins to each other and pray for each other so that you may be healed. The prayer of a righteous man is powerful and effective.

¹⁷Elijah was a man just like us. He prayed earnestly that it would not rain, and it did not rain on the land for three and a half years. ¹⁸Again he prayed, and the heavens gave rain, and the earth produced its crops.

¹⁹My brothers, if one of you should wander from the truth and someone should bring him back, ²⁰remember this: Whoever turns a sinner from the error of his way will save him from death and cover over a multitude of sins.

> *AND the prayer offered in faith will make the sick person well; the Lord will raise him up. If he has sinned, he will be forgiven.*
>
> JAMES 5:15

1 Peter

CLARENCE JORDAN, a remarkable man who founded the first interracial community in the deep South, was visiting a church. The pastor gave him a red-carpet tour of the church's new sanctuary, pointing with pride at the rich wood of the imported pews and the elegance of the decorations. He saved the best for last. Darkness was falling as he led Jordan outside to the front lawn of the church. A spotlight illumined a huge cross, perched atop the church steeple. Beaming, the pastor said to Jordan, "That cross alone cost us $10,000."

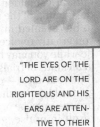

"You got cheated," said Jordan. "Times were when Christians could get them for free."

There was indeed a time when Christians quite literally got their crosses for free—they were nailed to them like Jesus because of their faith in him. Persecution still happens today. But where there are no literal crosses, there are cross-equivalents. Some analysts believe that in the 20th century more Christians died because of their faith than in all other centuries combined. But then, as now, the persecution did not destroy the church. In fact, in some ways it made the church stronger. As someone said, "Christians are like nails; the harder you hit them, the deeper they go."

This reality is the backdrop against which Peter wrote his two epistles. Much of what he said was to encourage believers to live faithfully in a hostile world. Add to this external pressure the internal threat of heresy addressed in 2 Peter, and Peter the pastor-shepherd had his hands full as he wrote. But he was carrying out to the letter his Master's command to feed his sheep (see John 21:15–17). Peter's two letters provide a wealth of material to help us pray through the pressures and enticements of a world that is no less hostile today.

> "THE EYES OF THE LORD ARE ON THE RIGHTEOUS AND HIS EARS ARE ATTENTIVE TO THEIR PRAYER." (3:12)

1 Peter, an apostle of Jesus Christ,

To God's elect, strangers in the world, scattered throughout Pontus, Galatia, Cappadocia, Asia and Bithynia, 2who have been chosen according to the foreknowledge of God the Father, through the sanctifying work of the Spirit, for obedience to Jesus Christ and sprinkling by his blood:

Grace and peace be yours in abundance.

Praise to God for a Living Hope

3Praise be to the God and Father of our Lord Jesus Christ! In his great mercy he has given us new birth into a living hope through the resurrection of Jesus Christ from the dead, 4and into an inheritance that can never perish, spoil or fade—kept in heaven for you, 5who through faith are shielded by God's power until the coming of the salvation that is ready to be revealed in the last time. 6In this you greatly rejoice, though now for a little while you may have had to suffer grief in all kinds of trials. 7These have come so that your faith—of greater worth than gold, which perishes even though refined by fire—may be proved genuine and may result in praise, glory and honor when Jesus Christ is revealed. 8Though you have not seen him, you love him; and even though you do not see him now, you believe in him and are filled with an inexpressible and glorious joy, 9for you are receiving the goal of your faith, the salvation of your souls.

10Concerning this salvation, the prophets, who spoke of the grace that was to come to you, searched intently and with the greatest care, 11trying to find out the time and circumstances to which the Spirit of Christ in them was pointing when he predicted the sufferings of Christ and the glories that would follow. 12It was revealed to them that they were not serving themselves but you, when they spoke of the things that have now been told you by those who have preached the gospel to you by the Holy Spirit sent from heaven. Even angels long to look into these things.

Be Holy

13Therefore, prepare your minds for action; be self-controlled; set your hope fully on the grace to be given you when Jesus Christ is revealed. 14As obedient children, do not conform to the evil desires you had when you lived in ignorance. 15But just as he who called you is holy, so be holy in all you do; 16for it is written: "Be holy, because I am holy."[a]

17Since you call on a Father who judges each man's work impartially, live your lives as strangers here in reverent fear. 18For you know that it was not with perishable things such as silver or gold that you were redeemed from the empty way of life handed down to you from your forefathers, 19but with the precious blood of Christ, a lamb without blemish or defect. 20He was chosen before the creation of the world, but was revealed in these last times for your sake. 21Through him you believe in God, who raised him from the dead and glorified him, and so your faith and hope are in God.

22Now that you have purified yourselves by obeying the truth so that you have sincere love for your brothers, love one another deeply, from the heart.[b] 23For you have been born again, not of perishable seed, but of imperishable, through the living and enduring word of God. 24For,

"All men are like grass,
    and all their glory is like the
        flowers of the field;
the grass withers and the flowers fall,
25   but the word of the Lord stands
        forever."[c]

And this is the word that was preached to you.

2 Therefore, rid yourselves of all malice and all deceit, hypocrisy, envy, and slander of every kind. 2Like newborn babies, crave pure spiritual milk, so that by it you may grow up in your salvation, 3now that you have tasted that the Lord is good.

The Living Stone and a Chosen People

4As you come to him, the living Stone—rejected by men but chosen by God and

---

a16 Lev. 11:44,45; 19:2   *b22* Some early manuscripts *from a pure heart*
c25 Isaiah 40:6–8

precious to him—⁵you also, like living stones, are being built into a spiritual house to be a holy priesthood, offering spiritual sacrifices acceptable to God through Jesus Christ. ⁶For in Scripture it says:

"See, I lay a stone in Zion,
a chosen and precious cornerstone,
and the one who trusts in him
will never be put to shame."ᵃ

ᵃ6 Isaiah 28:16

[MONDAY]

1 PETER 1:3–9

The Gigantic Secret

1:6 IN THIS YOU GREATLY REJOICE.

G. K. Chesterton wrote, "Joy, which was the small publicity of the pagan, is the gigantic secret of the Christian."¹ What Chesterton meant was that the mass of people in the world without Christ can only be happy about the little things in life and be sad about the really big things. For example, death and eternity—the big things—are terrors to be denied or faced stoically. All there is to be happy about are the little things like health, money, friends, houses and vacations. The best the unbeliever can do in this miserable state of affairs is to make much ado about nothing and create a publicity of the small and insignificant. Worthless things carry big price tags and command big advertising campaigns.

The Christian, on the other hand, may have much to be sad about, for persecution and death may be at hand, as they were for Peter's readers. But these are small things compared to the forgiveness of sins and the prospect of an eternity of joy in the presence of God. Joy is indeed "the gigantic secret of the Christian." How gigantic? It is so big that it filled Peter's audience of believers "with an inexpressible and glorious joy" (1:8). This is truly amazing because their joy came from love and faith in someone they had not seen. Peter must have been delighted in these believers since he had seen the Lord and they had not.

Are you a Christian? Does your faith bring you the kind of joy Peter describes? If it doesn't, you need to dig deeper channels in your soul for the joy to flow into. There is no better way to do this than to pray this great passage and others like it, and pray often. Make it personal; change the pronouns to "I," "me" and "my." Get a commentary on 1 Peter or a Bible dictionary and soak in the meaning of Peter's theological vocabulary. Words and phrases like "new birth," "living hope," "resurrection" and "an inheritance that can never perish" will make room in your heart and mind for more truth, and with it "an inexpressible and glorious joy."

PRAY:

My heart is narrow and my capacity for joy is too small.
Dear Lord, open my eyes to see your gigantic goodness
and expand my heart to sing your praise
with inexpressible and glorious joy.

FOR YOUR NEXT DEVOTIONAL READING, GO TO PAGE 1546.

[7]Now to you who believe, this stone is precious. But to those who do not believe,

> "The stone the builders rejected
>   has become the capstone,"[a][b]

[8]and,

> "A stone that causes men to stumble
>   and a rock that makes them fall."[c]

They stumble because they disobey the message—which is also what they were destined for.

[9]But you are a chosen people, a royal priesthood, a holy nation, a people belonging to God, that you may declare the praises of him who called you out of

[a]7 Or *cornerstone* [b]7 Psalm 118:22
[c]8 Isaiah 8:14

{ TUESDAY }

1 PETER 2:4–12

Pray for Your Church

2:9 YOU ARE A CHOSEN PEOPLE.

How does your experience of church square with Peter's description of the church in this text? His language couldn't be loftier—and perhaps sound more unrealistic to some. The church is a spiritual house, a holy priesthood, a holy nation and a chosen people. The church is central to God's purposes in the world. Is that what you think of when you go to church and look at those with whom you sit in worship?

In C. S. Lewis's *The Screwtape Letters*, the senior devil Screwtape urges the junior devil Wormwood to weaken the faith of a new Christian by highlighting the disparity between what the church can actually look like and what the Bible says it is.

> When he gets to his pew and looks around him he sees just that selection of his neighbors whom he has hitherto avoided. You want to lean pretty heavily on those neighbors. Make his mind flit to and fro between an expression like the "body of Christ" and the actual faces in the next pew. It matters very little, of course, what kind of people that next pew really contains . . . Provided that any of those neighbors sing out of tune, or have boots that squeak, or double chins, or odd clothes, the patient will quite easily believe that their religion must therefore be somehow ridiculous.[2]

The devil has great insight here. It is but a small step from thinking the church to be ridiculous to believing the faith of the church to be ridiculous—and though unstated, Jesus, as head of the church, to be foolish. This text in 1 Peter gives us much to pray for a local church and its members. Begin by praising God for the church. Celebrate, with gratitude and wonder, that somehow in his infinite wisdom, he chose to create a community comprised of weak and foolish people like us to offer "spiritual sacrifices acceptable to God through Jesus Christ" (2:5). Intercede for the church, your church, that it would faithfully "declare the praises of him who called you out of darkness into his wonderful light" (verse 9).

PRAY:
Pray for your church, following the ideas suggested in the above paragraph.

FOR YOUR NEXT DEVOTIONAL READING, GO TO PAGE 1549.

darkness into his wonderful light. [10]Once you were not a people, but now you are the people of God; once you had not received mercy, but now you have received mercy.

[11]Dear friends, I urge you, as aliens and strangers in the world, to abstain from sinful desires, which war against your soul. [12]Live such good lives among the pagans that, though they accuse you of doing wrong, they may see your good deeds and glorify God on the day he visits us.

Submission to Rulers and Masters

[13]Submit yourselves for the Lord's sake to every authority instituted among men: whether to the king, as the supreme authority, [14]or to governors, who are sent by him to punish those who do wrong and to commend those who do right. [15]For it is God's will that by doing good you should silence the ignorant talk of foolish men. [16]Live as free men, but do not use your freedom as a cover-up for evil; live as servants of God. [17]Show proper respect to everyone: Love the brotherhood of believers, fear God, honor the king.

> 66 Is prayer your steering wheel or your spare tire? 99
>
> CORRIE TEN BOOM

[18]Slaves, submit yourselves to your masters with all respect, not only to those who are good and considerate, but also to those who are harsh. [19]For it is commendable if a man bears up under the pain of unjust suffering because he is conscious of God. [20]But how is it to your credit if you receive a beating for doing wrong and endure it? But if you suffer for doing good and you endure it, this is commendable before God. [21]To this you were called, because Christ suffered for you, leaving you an example, that you should follow in his steps.

[22] "He committed no sin,
    and no deceit was found in his
        mouth."[a]

[23]When they hurled their insults at him, he did not retaliate; when he suffered, he made no threats. Instead, he entrusted himself to him who judges justly. [24]He himself bore our sins in his body on the tree, so that we might die to sins and live for righteousness; by his wounds you have been healed. [25]For you were like sheep going astray, but now you have returned to the Shepherd and Overseer of your souls.

Wives and Husbands

3 Wives, in the same way be submissive to your husbands so that, if any of them do not believe the word, they may be won over without words by the behavior of their wives, [2]when they see the purity and reverence of your lives. [3]Your beauty should not come from outward adornment, such as braided hair and the wearing of gold jewelry and fine clothes. [4]Instead, it should be that of your inner self, the unfading beauty of a gentle and quiet spirit, which is of great worth in God's sight. [5]For this is the way the holy women of the past who put their hope in God used to make themselves beautiful. They were submissive to their own husbands, [6]like Sarah, who obeyed Abraham and called him her master. You are her daughters if you do what is right and do not give way to fear.

[7]Husbands, in the same way be considerate as you live with your wives, and treat them with respect as the weaker partner and as heirs with you of the gracious gift of life, so that nothing will hinder your prayers.

Suffering for Doing Good

[8]Finally, all of you, live in harmony with one another; be sympathetic, love as brothers, be compassionate and humble. [9]Do not repay evil with evil or insult with insult, but with blessing, because to this you were called so that you may inherit a blessing. [10]For,

"Whoever would love life
    and see good days
must keep his tongue from evil
    and his lips from deceitful speech.
[11] He must turn from evil and do good;
    he must seek peace and pursue it.

[a]22 Isaiah 53:9

> "FOR the eyes of the Lord are on the
> righteous
> and his ears are attentive to their
> prayer,
> but the face of the Lord is against
> those who do evil."
>
> 1 PETER 3:12

¹²For the eyes of the Lord are on the
righteous
and his ears are attentive to their
prayer,
but the face of the Lord is against
those who do evil."ᵃ

¹³Who is going to harm you if you are eager to do good? ¹⁴But even if you should
suffer for what is right, you are blessed.
"Do not fear what they fearᵇ; do not be
frightened."ᶜ ¹⁵But in your hearts set apart
Christ as Lord. Always be prepared to give
an answer to everyone who asks you to
give the reason for the hope that you have.
But do this with gentleness and respect,
¹⁶keeping a clear conscience, so that those
who speak maliciously against your good
behavior in Christ may be ashamed of
their slander. ¹⁷It is better, if it is God's will,
to suffer for doing good than for doing evil.
¹⁸For Christ died for sins once for all, the
righteous for the unrighteous, to bring you
to God. He was put to death in the body
but made alive by the Spirit, ¹⁹through
whomᵈ also he went and preached to the
spirits in prison ²⁰who disobeyed long ago
when God waited patiently in the days of
Noah while the ark was being built. In it
only a few people, eight in all, were saved
through water, ²¹and this water symbolizes baptism that now saves you also—not
the removal of dirt from the body but the
pledgeᵉ of a good conscience toward God.
It saves you by the resurrection of Jesus
Christ, ²²who has gone into heaven and is
at God's right hand—with angels, authorities and powers in submission to him.

Living for God

4 Therefore, since Christ suffered in his
body, arm yourselves also with the
same attitude, because he who has suffered in his body is done with sin. ²As a
result, he does not live the rest of his

earthly life for evil human desires, but
rather for the will of God. ³For you have
spent enough time in the past doing what
pagans choose to do—living in debauchery, lust, drunkenness, orgies, carousing
and detestable idolatry. ⁴They think it
strange that you do not plunge with them
into the same flood of dissipation, and
they heap abuse on you. ⁵But they will
have to give account to him who is ready
to judge the living and the dead. ⁶For this
is the reason the gospel was preached
even to those who are now dead, so that
they might be judged according to men
in regard to the body, but live according
to God in regard to the spirit.

⁷The end of all things is near. Therefore be clear minded and self-controlled
so that you can pray. ⁸Above all, love
each other deeply, because love covers
over a multitude of sins. ⁹Offer hospitality to one another without grumbling.
¹⁰Each one should use whatever gift he
has received to serve others, faithfully
administering God's grace in its various
forms. ¹¹If anyone speaks, he should do it
as one speaking the very words of God. If
anyone serves, he should do it with the
strength God provides, so that in all
things God may be praised through Jesus
Christ. To him be the glory and the power for ever and ever. Amen.

> IF ANYONE speaks, he should do it as
> one speaking the very words of God. If
> anyone serves, he should do it with the
> strength God provides, so that in all
> things God may be praised through Jesus
> Christ. To him be the glory and the
> power for ever and ever. Amen.
>
> 1 PETER 4:11

Suffering for Being a Christian

¹²Dear friends, do not be surprised at
the painful trial you are suffering, as
though something strange were happening to you. ¹³But rejoice that you participate in the sufferings of Christ, so that
you may be overjoyed when his glory is
revealed. ¹⁴If you are insulted because of

ᵃ12 Psalm 34:12–16   ᵇ14 Or not fear their
threats   ᶜ14 Isaiah 8:12   ᵈ18,19 Or alive in
the spirit, ¹⁹through which   ᵉ21 Or response

the name of Christ, you are blessed, for the Spirit of glory and of God rests on you. ¹⁵If you suffer, it should not be as a murderer or thief or any other kind of criminal, or even as a meddler. ¹⁶Howeverer, if you suffer as a Christian, do not be ashamed, but praise God that you bear that name. ¹⁷For it is time for judgment to begin with the family of God; and if it begins with us, what will the outcome be for those who do not obey the gospel of God? ¹⁸And,

---

[WEDNESDAY]

1 PETER 3:7

A Marriage that Can Pray

3:7 SO THAT NOTHING WILL HINDER YOUR PRAYERS.

It is one thing to pray to have a good marriage. It is another thing, equally important, to have a marriage that can pray. That's what Peter means when he tells husbands to relate to their wives in such a way "so that nothing will hinder your prayers" (3:7). How one treats a spouse has a lot to do with how God hears prayer. We must pray to have good and godly marriages. We must pray that marriages will be good and godly so we can pray!

This touches on a profound reality, developed more fully by Paul in his letter to the Ephesians (see Ephesians 5:21–33). Marriage, for the Christian, is defined christologically, that is, in terms of our relationship to the Lord Jesus. The relationship of Christ to his church is pictured in marriage. Wives are to submit to their husbands as the church submits to Christ. Moreover, husbands are to love their wives as Christ loved the church. The upshot of this is that there is more going on in a marriage than the mere coming together of two people to love and cherish each other. As important and wonderful as that is, the significance of marriage is much greater. In God's miraculous calculus, two become one and multiply love exponentially. One of the ways this shows itself is in the ability of a husband and wife to pray.

Marriage is therefore yet another arena in which Christians must live out their vocation to serve Christ. Dietrich Bonhoeffer once spoke to a love-struck couple in a marriage homily: "In your love you see only the heaven of your happiness, but in marriage you are placed at a post of responsibility towards the world and mankind." What greater way to stand at that post and live out that responsibility than to have the kind of marriage that can pray powerfully? We do nothing in this life unto ourselves alone. Even a happy marriage is not only for the happiness of husbands, wives and children; it is for God's glory in the world.

PRAY:

*Pray for your marriage, or if you are single,
pray for the marriages of those close to you . . .*

*Dear God, you created marriage for our happiness
and to display your glory. Strengthen our love for each other so that we
can better pray and stand at our post of responsibility in the world.*

FOR YOUR NEXT DEVOTIONAL READING, GO TO PAGE 1553.

"If it is hard for the righteous to be
saved,
what will become of the ungodly
and the sinner?"[a]

[19]So then, those who suffer according to God's will should commit themselves to their faithful Creator and continue to do good.

> ❝ Whatsoever we beg of God, let us also work for it. ❞
>
> JEREMY TAYLOR

To Elders and Young Men

5 To the elders among you, I appeal as a fellow elder, a witness of Christ's sufferings and one who also will share in the glory to be revealed: [2]Be shepherds of God's flock that is under your care, serving as overseers—not because you must, but because you are willing, as God wants you to be; not greedy for money, but eager to serve; [3]not lording it over those entrusted to you, but being examples to the flock. [4]And when the Chief Shepherd appears, you will receive the crown of glory that will never fade away.

[5]Young men, in the same way be submissive to those who are older. All of you, clothe yourselves with humility toward one another, because,

"God opposes the proud
but gives grace to the humble."[b]

[6]Humble yourselves, therefore, under God's mighty hand, that he may lift you up in due time. [7]Cast all your anxiety on him because he cares for you.

> CAST all your anxiety on [God] because he cares for you.
>
> 1 PETER 5:7

[8]Be self-controlled and alert. Your enemy the devil prowls around like a roaring lion looking for someone to devour. [9]Resist him, standing firm in the faith, because you know that your brothers throughout the world are undergoing the same kind of sufferings.

[10]And the God of all grace, who called you to his eternal glory in Christ, after you have suffered a little while, will himself restore you and make you strong, firm and steadfast. [11]To him be the power for ever and ever. Amen.

Final Greetings

[12]With the help of Silas,[c] whom I regard as a faithful brother, I have written to you briefly, encouraging you and testifying that this is the true grace of God. Stand fast in it.

[13]She who is in Babylon, chosen together with you, sends you her greetings, and so does my son Mark. [14]Greet one another with a kiss of love.

Peace to all of you who are in Christ.

[a]18 Prov. 11:31 [b]5 Prov. 3:34 [c]12 Greek *Silvanus*, a variant of *Silas*

2 Peter

PETER SPENDS time in this his second letter reminding the believers of things they already knew. His readers were Christians, and they apparently knew the basic message of salvation and discipleship. However, Peter wants the truth to be deeply embedded in their hearts: "I will always remind you of these things, even though you know them and are firmly established in the truth you now have" (1:12).

The readers of 2 Peter were undergoing persecution. In his first letter to them, Peter helps them deal with the issue of remaining strong in the faith. In this second letter, Peter addresses the danger of false teachers (see 2:1–3). In both instances, knowing the truth and living the truth are central to Peter's message. He encourages his readers to add to their faith goodness, godliness, self-control and love (see 1:5–7). Such qualities will ensure for his readers a strong foundation and a rich reward (see 1:10–11).

"HIS DIVINE POWER HAS GIVEN US EVERYTHING WE NEED FOR LIFE AND GODLINESS." (1:3)

1 Simon Peter, a servant and apostle of Jesus Christ,

To those who through the righteousness of our God and Savior Jesus Christ have received a faith as precious as ours:

[2]Grace and peace be yours in abundance through the knowledge of God and of Jesus our Lord.

Making One's Calling and Election Sure

[3]His divine power has given us everything we need for life and godliness through our knowledge of him who called us by his own glory and goodness. [4]Through these he has given us his very great and precious promises, so that through them you may participate in the divine nature and escape the corruption in the world caused by evil desires.

[5]For this very reason, make every effort to add to your faith goodness; and to goodness, knowledge; [6]and to knowledge, self-control; and to self-control, perseverance; and to perseverance, godliness; [7]and to godliness, brotherly kindness; and to brotherly kindness, love. [8]For if you possess these qualities in increasing measure, they will keep you from being ineffective and unproductive in your knowledge of our Lord Jesus Christ. [9]But if anyone does not have them, he is nearsighted and blind, and has forgotten that he has been cleansed from his past sins.

[10]Therefore, my brothers, be all the more eager to make your calling and election sure. For if you do these things, you will never fall, [11]and you will receive a rich welcome into the eternal kingdom of our Lord and Savior Jesus Christ.

Prophecy of Scripture

[12]So I will always remind you of these things, even though you know them and are firmly established in the truth you now have. [13]I think it is right to refresh your memory as long as I live in the tent of this body, [14]because I know that I will soon put it aside, as our Lord Jesus Christ has made clear to me. [15]And I will make every effort to see that after my departure you will always be able to remember these things.

[16]We did not follow cleverly invented stories when we told you about the power and coming of our Lord Jesus Christ, but we were eyewitnesses of his majesty. [17]For he received honor and glory from God the Father when the voice came to him from the Majestic Glory, saying, "This is my Son, whom I love; with him I am well pleased."[a] [18]We ourselves heard this voice that came from heaven when we were with him on the sacred mountain.

> WE ourselves heard this voice that came from heaven when we were with him on the sacred mountain.
>
> 2 PETER 1:18

[19]And we have the word of the prophets made more certain, and you will do well to pay attention to it, as to a light shining in a dark place, until the day dawns and the morning star rises in your hearts. [20]Above all, you must understand that no prophecy of Scripture came about by the prophet's own interpretation. [21]For prophecy never had its origin in the will of man, but men spoke from God as they were carried along by the Holy Spirit.

False Teachers and Their Destruction

2 But there were also false prophets among the people, just as there will be false teachers among you. They will secretly introduce destructive heresies, even denying the sovereign Lord who bought them—bringing swift destruction on themselves. [2]Many will follow their shameful ways and will bring the way of truth into disrepute. [3]In their greed these teachers will exploit you with stories they have made up. Their condemnation has long been hanging over them, and their destruction has not been sleeping.

[4]For if God did not spare angels when they sinned, but sent them to hell,[b] putting them into gloomy dungeons[c] to be held for judgment; [5]if he did not spare the ancient world when he brought the flood on its ungodly people, but protected Noah, a preacher of righteousness,

---

[a]17 Matt. 17:5; Mark 9:7; Luke 9:35   [b]4 Greek *Tartarus*   [c]4 Some manuscripts *into chains of darkness*

and seven others; ⁶if he condemned the cities of Sodom and Gomorrah by burning them to ashes, and made them an example of what is going to happen to the ungodly; ⁷and if he rescued Lot, a righteous man, who was distressed by the filthy lives of lawless men ⁸(for that righteous man, living among them day after day, was tormented in his righteous soul by the lawless deeds he saw and heard)— ⁹if this is so, then the Lord knows how to rescue godly men from trials and to hold the unrighteous for the day of judgment, while continuing their

[**THURSDAY**]

2 PETER 1:3–11

Praying to Participate in the Divine Nature

1:4 HE HAS GIVEN US HIS GREAT AND PRECIOUS PROMISES.

Peter says you have everything you need to participate in the divine nature (see 1:3–4). To get your mind around this staggering declaration—and to pray for it—start with something small. What would you like to be on a lesser scale? Perhaps a great athlete or an artist or a musician? Imagine if God told you he had given you everything you need to be just what you've always wanted, and he guaranteed you would become it. If your desire was athletic, say to be a great distance runner, would you then think, "Good, I'll be a great distance runner. It's in me. Since it is a given, I'll spend all my time watching television and eating fatty foods"? That would be ridiculous and unthinkable. If you really wanted to be what God had given and promised, then you'd "make every effort" (verse 5) and "be all the more eager" (verse 10) to pursue it. The guarantee would stimulate effort, not smother it.

What does it mean to participate in the divine nature? It means to be as full of God and in God as a human can be and still be a human. It is to be what Paul prayed the Ephesians would be: "filled to the measure of all the fullness of God" (Ephesians 3:19). Does that appeal to you? Read the list of the fruit of the Spirit in Galatians 5:22–23. Is God's love perfect and infinite? Would you like to participate in this kind of love as fully as a human being can? Or his joy? Or his peace and patience and kindness?

The possibilities are breathtaking. Do you perceive the glory of the promise of 2 Peter 1:3–4? It is a promise to become divinely human or humanly divine. It is the restoration and fulfillment of what was short-circuited in the fall—to be all God made you to be when he made you in his image. Pray for the promise by praying for the things you are told to make every effort to have in verses 5–7: faith, goodness, knowledge, self-control, perseverance, godliness, brotherly kindness and love.

Because God has given us such "great and precious promises . . . be all the more eager to make your calling and election sure" (verses 4,10).

PRAY:

Strengthen me, O Lord, by your Spirit, to grow in faith, goodness, knowledge, self-control, perseverance, godliness, brotherly kindness and love. Fill me to the measure of all the fullness of God.

FOR YOUR NEXT DEVOTIONAL READING, GO TO PAGE 1555.

punishment.*a* 10This is especially true of those who follow the corrupt desire of the sinful nature*b* and despise authority.

Bold and arrogant, these men are not afraid to slander celestial beings; 11yet even angels, although they are stronger and more powerful, do not bring slanderous accusations against such beings in the presence of the Lord. 12But these men blaspheme in matters they do not understand. They are like brute beasts, creatures of instinct, born only to be caught and destroyed, and like beasts they too will perish.

13They will be paid back with harm for the harm they have done. Their idea of pleasure is to carouse in broad daylight. They are blots and blemishes, reveling in their pleasures while they feast with you.*c* 14With eyes full of adultery, they never stop sinning; they seduce the unstable; they are experts in greed—an accursed brood! 15They have left the straight way and wandered off to follow the way of Balaam son of Beor, who loved the wages of wickedness. 16But he was rebuked for his wrongdoing by a donkey—a beast without speech—who spoke with a man's voice and restrained the prophet's madness.

> *If thou shouldst never see my face again, pray for my soul. More things are wrought by prayer than this world dreams.*
>
> ALFRED, LORD TENNYSON

17These men are springs without water and mists driven by a storm. Blackest darkness is reserved for them. 18For they mouth empty, boastful words and, by appealing to the lustful desires of sinful human nature, they entice people who are just escaping from those who live in error. 19They promise them freedom, while they themselves are slaves of depravity—for a man is a slave to whatever has mastered him. 20If they have escaped the corruption of the world by knowing our Lord and Savior Jesus Christ and are again entangled in it and overcome, they are worse off at the end than they were at the beginning. 21It would have been better for them not to have known the way of righteousness, than to have known it and then to turn their backs on the sacred command that was passed on to them. 22Of them the proverbs are true: "A dog returns to its vomit,"*d* and, "A sow that is washed goes back to her wallowing in the mud."

The Day of the Lord

3 Dear friends, this is now my second letter to you. I have written both of them as reminders to stimulate you to wholesome thinking. 2I want you to recall the words spoken in the past by the holy prophets and the command given by our Lord and Savior through your apostles.

3First of all, you must understand that in the last days scoffers will come, scoffing and following their own evil desires. 4They will say, "Where is this 'coming' he promised? Ever since our fathers died, everything goes on as it has since the beginning of creation." 5But they deliberately forget that long ago by God's word the heavens existed and the earth was formed out of water and by water. 6By these waters also the world of that time was deluged and destroyed. 7By the same word the present heavens and earth are reserved for fire, being kept for the day of judgment and destruction of ungodly men.

8But do not forget this one thing, dear friends: With the Lord a day is like a thousand years, and a thousand years are like a day. 9The Lord is not slow in keeping his promise, as some understand slowness. He is patient with you, not wanting anyone to perish, but everyone to come to repentance.

10But the day of the Lord will come like a thief. The heavens will disappear with a roar; the elements will be destroyed by

> *O God, forgive the poverty and the pettiness of our prayers. Listen not to our words but to the yearnings of our hearts. Hear beneath our petitions the crying of our need.*
>
> PETER MARSHALL

*a*9 Or *unrighteous for punishment until the day of judgment*   *b*10 Or *the flesh*   *c*13 Some manuscripts *in their love feasts*   *d*22 Prov. 26:11

Prayer for the Coming of the Lord

3:11–12 YOU OUGHT TO LIVE HOLY AND GODLY LIVES AS YOU LOOK FORWARD TO THE DAY OF GOD AND SPEED ITS COMING.

At the entrance of the fossil museum at the La Brea tar pits in Los Angeles, California, is a painting of a ribbon 85 feet long. It represents five billion years of the earth's assumed history. Guess how much space on that ribbon belongs to the supposed history of humanity, from caveman to astronaut . . . less than one-half inch! Looking at that ribbon, one wonders what God was doing with the other 84 feet and 11½ inches. What were all those bizarre and extinct creatures who roamed the earth for 100 million years? What was God thinking? Only he knows. One thing we do know is the truth of what Peter wrote: "With the Lord a day is like a thousand years, and a thousand years are like a day" (3:8).

But Peter didn't write this to speculate about the mysteries of God's sense of time. Those are implicit. The point was to encourage his readers to keep their focus and conviction concerning the coming of the day of the Lord. During the early years of the church, Christians were very animated by thoughts about the end of things as we know them. They were eager for the day when the old order would disappear and "a new heaven and a new earth, the home of righteousness" would appear (verse 13). As time passed, persecution increased and false teachers gained influence, and some were tempted to lose heart and wondered if that day would ever arrive. Peter wrote to strengthen their hope by reminding them not only that God's sense of time is not like ours, but also, more importantly, that whatever may seem like a delay to us is really his mercy and patience at work. He does not want "anyone to perish, but everyone to come to repentance" (verse 9).

But here is the really encouraging thing: "You ought to live holy and godly lives as you look forward to the day of God and speed its coming" (verses 11–12). We don't know when that day will come, but we can have an effect on how soon! The way Christians live and pray in this world has a direct impact on the history of the world (see devotions on Revelation 8:1–5 and 22:20). One of the Christian community's earliest calls to worship was the prayer, "Maranatha!" It meant, "Come, Lord!" Hope in the coming of Christ will make us live holy and godly lives and pray holy and godly prayers.

PRAY:

Maranatha! Come, Lord Jesus!
And until you do, work in us by your Spirit
the will and the power to live holy and godly lives.

———

FOR YOUR NEXT DEVOTIONAL READING, GO TO PAGE 1556.

YAH

We Thank You, O God, for Your Faithfulness

YOU PROBABLY haven't heard of Yah. That's OK because God has. He's heard from her many thousands of times. The little Saturday night prayer group that met with her and her pastor-husband, Sei, during the winter of 1995 in Holland, Michigan, will never forget her.

When she joined the group, Yah and her four children had been reunited with Sei after many months of separation. A nightmarish civil war was sucking the life out of their beloved Liberia. Throughout the country, there was mayhem, murder and rape. Children with assault rifles were swaggering through streets and villages. The family fled their homeland to seek sanctuary, first in neighboring Sierra Leone and then in Kenya. When the opportunity presented itself for Sei to come to Western Seminary in Michigan for theological training, they prayerfully decided that it was a door opened by God and that he should go, even though they didn't know how the rest of the family could join him. The war had already separated Yah from her mother, and now she had to say goodbye to her husband and find her way as a mother of four and a refugee in a foreign country. It was a great day of rejoicing when she and the children arrived at the Grand Rapids airport in the frigid winter of 1995.

How to describe her? Picture a short woman with a round, richly black face, from which dazzling white teeth explode whenever she smiles or laughs, which is often. Picture her in prayer. Picture the layers of clothing she has to wear *indoors* for her West African body to be comfortable in a Michigan winter. Look at her sweet ebony face, barely above the wool turtleneck, and see it glow as you hear her say to the Lord, "We *fank* you, O God, for your faithfulness."

The English "th" sound doesn't come easily in her language, so *thank* becomes *fank* as it merges with the easier "f" of *faithful*. The merger was heard over and over again in those prayer meetings. It was used almost as punctuation, as comma and semi-colon. It was a sound theological merger, too—spiritually profound and edifying and full of hope. For "we thank you" is the most natural response in any language to the goodness of a faithful God.

Picture Yah as standing for so many others, a representative of the millions who are displaced, oppressed and persecuted, but who have put their hope in the living God. See especially a humble faith that can give thanks in every circumstance.

Pray with her in eager expectation for the day when her prayers and the prayers of so many others will be answered, and they return to their native land. Cry out, day and night for God's justice (see Luke 18:1–8). Believe that God is faithful, and there will again be laughter in the "Liberias" of this life. We thank you, O God, for your faithfulness.

PRAY:

"Restore our fortunes, O LORD, like streams in the Negev.
Those who sow in tears will reap with songs of joy. He who goes
out weeping, carrying seed to sow, will return with songs of joy,
carrying sheaves with him" (Psalm 126:4–6).

MEMORIZE:

"Do not be afraid, little flock, for your Father has been
pleased to give you the kingdom." LUKE 12:32

FOR YOUR NEXT DEVOTIONAL READING, GO TO PAGE 1561.

fire, and the earth and everything in it will be laid bare.[a]

[11]Since everything will be destroyed in this way, what kind of people ought you to be? You ought to live holy and godly lives [12]as you look forward to the day of God and speed its coming.[b] That day will bring about the destruction of the heavens by fire, and the elements will melt in the heat. [13]But in keeping with his promise we are looking forward to a new heaven and a new earth, the home of righteousness.

[14]So then, dear friends, since you are looking forward to this, make every effort to be found spotless, blameless and at peace with him. [15]Bear in mind that our Lord's patience means salvation, just as our dear brother Paul also wrote you with the wisdom that God gave him. [16]He writes the same way in all his letters, speaking in them of these matters. His letters contain some things that are hard to understand, which ignorant and unstable people distort, as they do the other Scriptures, to their own destruction.

[17]Therefore, dear friends, since you already know this, be on your guard so that you may not be carried away by the error of lawless men and fall from your secure position. [18]But grow in the grace and knowledge of our Lord and Savior Jesus Christ. To him be glory both now and forever! Amen.

[a]10 Some manuscripts *be burned up*
[b]12 Or *as you wait eagerly for the day of God to come*

1 John

MARY AND DON were both very old and very senile. Life had definitely whittled them down to their core; what was left was what had been essentially "them" through their whole life. Mary couldn't remember names, or what day it was, but when asked to pray, her face beamed beatifically, and her prayer was the prayer of one who had long known Jesus and was conversing with him in that moment. She ended the way she had always been. Don, on the other hand, had chased money his whole life. It was sad and pathetic to hear this old man drone and babble about the money he had made. It was worthless to him now, but what he had always been he now was.

John was perhaps the youngest of the disciples when we first met him in the Gospels, and he was something of an ambitious firebrand (see Mark 10:35–45; Luke 9:54). But he described himself as the one Jesus loved (see John 20:2; 21:7). As we meet him now through his epistles, he is a very old man near the end of his life, and probably the only disciple who will die of natural causes. What is left of him are the effects of having been loved by Jesus all those years. It is touching to read his repeated grandfatherly encouragements for his people to love one another (1 John 3:11–16,23). John's Gospel is an intimate look at Jesus; his epistles give an intimate look at what Jesus made of John. He was the apostle of love. The best thing we will ever have to give to others will be what we became in time we spent with Jesus in prayer, letting him love us.

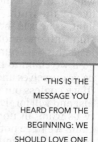

"THIS IS THE MESSAGE YOU HEARD FROM THE BEGINNING: WE SHOULD LOVE ONE ANOTHER." (3:11)

The Word of Life

1 That which was from the beginning, which we have heard, which we have seen with our eyes, which we have looked at and our hands have touched— this we proclaim concerning the Word of life. ²The life appeared; we have seen it and testify to it, and we proclaim to you the eternal life, which was with the Father and has appeared to us. ³We proclaim to you what we have seen and heard, so that you also may have fellowship with us. And our fellowship is with the Father and with his Son, Jesus Christ. ⁴We write this to make our*ᵃ* joy complete.

Walking in the Light

⁵This is the message we have heard from him and declare to you: God is light; in him there is no darkness at all. ⁶If we claim to have fellowship with him yet walk in the darkness, we lie and do not live by the truth. ⁷But if we walk in the light, as he is in the light, we have fellowship with one another, and the blood of Jesus, his Son, purifies us from all*ᵇ* sin.

⁸If we claim to be without sin, we deceive ourselves and the truth is not in us. ⁹If we confess our sins, he is faithful and just and will forgive us our sins and purify us from all unrighteousness. ¹⁰If we claim we have not sinned, we make him out to be a liar and his word has no place in our lives.

> IF WE *confess our sins, he is faithful and just and will forgive us our sins and purify us from all unrighteousness.*
>
> 1 JOHN 1:9

2 My dear children, I write this to you so that you will not sin. But if anybody does sin, we have one who speaks to the Father in our defense—Jesus Christ, the Righteous One. ²He is the atoning sacrifice for our sins, and not only for ours but also for*ᶜ* the sins of the whole world.

³We know that we have come to know him if we obey his commands. ⁴The man who says, "I know him," but does not do what he commands is a liar, and the truth is not in him. ⁵But if anyone obeys his word, God's love*ᵈ* is truly made complete in him. This is how we know we are in him: ⁶Whoever claims to live in him must walk as Jesus did.

⁷Dear friends, I am not writing you a new command but an old one, which you have had since the beginning. This old command is the message you have heard. ⁸Yet I am writing you a new command; its truth is seen in him and you, because the darkness is passing and the true light is already shining.

⁹Anyone who claims to be in the light but hates his brother is still in the darkness. ¹⁰Whoever loves his brother lives in the light, and there is nothing in him*ᵉ* to make him stumble. ¹¹But whoever hates his brother is in the darkness and walks around in the darkness; he does not know where he is going, because the darkness has blinded him.

¹² I write to you, dear children,
    because your sins have been
        forgiven on account of his
        name.
¹³ I write to you, fathers,
    because you have known him who
        is from the beginning.
  I write to you, young men,
    because you have overcome the
        evil one.
  I write to you, dear children,
    because you have known the
        Father.
¹⁴ I write to you, fathers,
    because you have known him who
        is from the beginning.
  I write to you, young men,
    because you are strong,
    and the word of God lives in you,
    and you have overcome the evil
        one.

Do Not Love the World

¹⁵Do not love the world or anything in the world. If anyone loves the world, the love of the Father is not in him. ¹⁶For everything in the world—the cravings of sinful man, the lust of his eyes and the boasting of what he has and does— comes not from the Father but from the

---

ᵃ4 Some manuscripts *your*   *ᵇ7* Or *every*
ᶜ2 Or *He is the one who turns aside God's wrath, taking away our sins, and not only ours but also*
ᵈ5 Or *word, love for God*   *ᵉ10* Or *it*

1 JOHN 1:5 — 2:2

Good for the Soul and the Cell

1:9 IF WE CONFESS OUR SINS, HE IS FAITHFUL AND JUST AND WILL FORGIVE US OUR SINS.

A writer invented a creative and illuminating title for a meditation on this text. It was, "Confession is good for the cell." The word "cell" sounds just enough like the word "soul" in the older, more familiar saying to catch the attention. Both are true; confession is good for the soul and for the cell. The cell is the darkness that imprisons our soul if we do not confess. And that's the message here: God is light; sin is darkness—the two cannot coexist. But sin's greatest darkness is the refusal to admit its own existence. God forgives sin, but he will not forgive sin that is denied. Denial deceives and imprisons us and insults God: "If we claim to be without sin, we deceive ourselves and the truth is not in us ... If we claim we have not sinned, we make him out to be a liar and his word has no place in our lives" (1:8,10).

Confession of sin is a "must" and a "may." We *must* confess or lose fellowship with God—and each other (see verses 6–7). If we say we have no sin, we say Christ died for nothing. The good news, however, is that we *may* confess without fear of condemnation: "If we confess our sins, he is faithful and just and will forgive us our sins and purify us from all unrighteousness" (verse 9). There are few prayers more liberating than honest prayers of confession. This is because confession takes us straight to the heart of the gospel.

> When Satan tempts me to despair,
> And tells me of the guilt within,
> Upward I look and see him there
> Who made an end to all my sin.
> Because the sinless Savior died,
> My sinful soul is counted free;
> For God, the just, is satisfied
> To look on him and pardon me.[1]

P R A Y :

Holy One, I have chosen darkness over light;
I have not loved you with my whole being
or my neighbor as myself.
I have left undone things I should do,
and I have done things I shouldn't do.
Forgive me and restore me,
that I may live in the light as you are in the light.

———

FOR YOUR NEXT DEVOTIONAL READING, GO TO PAGE 1564.

world. [17]The world and its desires pass away, but the man who does the will of God lives forever.

Warning Against Antichrists

[18]Dear children, this is the last hour; and as you have heard that the antichrist is coming, even now many antichrists have come. This is how we know it is the last hour. [19]They went out from us, but they did not really belong to us. For if they had belonged to us, they would have remained with us; but their going showed that none of them belonged to us.

[20]But you have an anointing from the Holy One, and all of you know the truth.[a] [21]I do not write to you because you do not know the truth, but because you do know it and because no lie comes from the truth. [22]Who is the liar? It is the man who denies that Jesus is the Christ. Such a man is the antichrist—he denies the Father and the Son. [23]No one who denies the Son has the Father; whoever acknowledges the Son has the Father also.

[24]See that what you have heard from the beginning remains in you. If it does, you also will remain in the Son and in the Father. [25]And this is what he promised us—even eternal life.

> ❝ The greatest and best talent that God gives to any man or woman in this world is the talent of prayer. ❞
>
> ALEXANDER WHYTE

[26]I am writing these things to you about those who are trying to lead you astray. [27]As for you, the anointing you received from him remains in you, and you do not need anyone to teach you. But as his anointing teaches you about all things and as that anointing is real, not counterfeit—just as it has taught you, remain in him.

Children of God

[28]And now, dear children, continue in him, so that when he appears we may be confident and unashamed before him at his coming.

[29]If you know that he is righteous, you know that everyone who does what is right has been born of him.

3 How great is the love the Father has lavished on us, that we should be called children of God! And that is what we are! The reason the world does not know us is that it did not know him. [2]Dear friends, now we are children of God, and what we will be has not yet been made known. But we know that when he appears,[b] we shall be like him, for we shall see him as he is. [3]Everyone who has this hope in him purifies himself, just as he is pure.

[4]Everyone who sins breaks the law; in fact, sin is lawlessness. [5]But you know that he appeared so that he might take away our sins. And in him is no sin. [6]No one who lives in him keeps on sinning. No one who continues to sin has either seen him or known him.

[7]Dear children, do not let anyone lead you astray. He who does what is right is righteous, just as he is righteous. [8]He who does what is sinful is of the devil, because the devil has been sinning from the beginning. The reason the Son of God appeared was to destroy the devil's work. [9]No one who is born of God will continue to sin, because God's seed remains in him; he cannot go on sinning, because he has been born of God. [10]This is how we know who the children of God are and who the children of the devil are: Anyone who does not do what is right is not a child of God; nor is anyone who does not love his brother.

Love One Another

[11]This is the message you heard from the beginning: We should love one another. [12]Do not be like Cain, who belonged to the evil one and murdered his brother. And why did he murder him? Because his own actions were evil and his brother's were righteous. [13]Do not be surprised, my brothers, if the world hates you. [14]We know that we have passed from death to life, because we love our brothers. Anyone who does not love remains in death. [15]Anyone who hates his brother is a murderer, and you know that no murderer has eternal life in him. [16]This is how we know what love is:

[a]20 Some manuscripts *and you know all things*
[b]2 Or *when it is made known*

Jesus Christ laid down his life for us. And we ought to lay down our lives for our brothers. [17]If anyone has material possessions and sees his brother in need but has no pity on him, how can the love of God be in him? [18]Dear children, let us not love with words or tongue but with actions and in truth. [19]This then is how we know that we belong to the truth, and how we set our hearts at rest in his presence [20]whenever our hearts condemn us. For God is greater than our hearts, and he knows everything.

> *Prayer is thinking, in which we ask to be open to strange answers.*
>
> RISTO NIVARI

[21]Dear friends, if our hearts do not condemn us, we have confidence before God [22]and receive from him anything we ask, because we obey his commands and do what pleases him. [23]And this is his command: to believe in the name of his Son, Jesus Christ, and to love one another as he commanded us. [24]Those who obey his commands live in him, and he in them. And this is how we know that he lives in us: We know it by the Spirit he gave us.

Test the Spirits

4 Dear friends, do not believe every spirit, but test the spirits to see whether they are from God, because many false prophets have gone out into the world. [2]This is how you can recognize the Spirit of God: Every spirit that acknowledges that Jesus Christ has come in the flesh is from God, [3]but every spirit that does not acknowledge Jesus is not from God. This is the spirit of the antichrist, which you have heard is coming and even now is already in the world.

[4]You, dear children, are from God and have overcome them, because the one who is in you is greater than the one who is in the world. [5]They are from the world and therefore speak from the viewpoint of the world, and the world listens to them. [6]We are from God, and whoever knows God listens to us; but whoever is not from God does not listen to us. This is how we recognize the Spirit[a] of truth and the spirit of falsehood.

God's Love and Ours

[7]Dear friends, let us love one another, for love comes from God. Everyone who loves has been born of God and knows God. [8]Whoever does not love does not know God, because God is love. [9]This is how God showed his love among us: He sent his one and only Son[b] into the world that we might live through him. [10]This is love: not that we loved God, but that he loved us and sent his Son as an atoning sacrifice for[c] our sins. [11]Dear friends, since God so loved us, we also ought to love one another. [12]No one has ever seen God; but if we love one another, God lives in us and his love is made complete in us.

[13]We know that we live in him and he in us, because he has given us of his Spirit. [14]And we have seen and testify that the Father has sent his Son to be the Savior of the world. [15]If anyone acknowledges that Jesus is the Son of God, God lives in him and he in God. [16]And so we know and rely on the love God has for us.

God is love. Whoever lives in love lives in God, and God in him. [17]In this way, love is made complete among us so that we will have confidence on the day of judgment, because in this world we are like him. [18]There is no fear in love. But perfect love drives out fear, because fear has to do with punishment. The one who fears is not made perfect in love.

> *Prayer is not the moment when God and humans are in relationship, for that is always. Prayer is taking initiative to intentionally respond to God's presence.*
>
> L. ROBERT KECK

[19]We love because he first loved us. [20]If anyone says, "I love God," yet hates his brother, he is a liar. For anyone who does not love his brother, whom he has seen, cannot love God, whom he has not seen. [21]And he has given us this command: Whoever loves God must also love his brother.

---

[a]6 Or *spirit*   [b]9 Or *his only begotten Son*
[c]10 Or *as the one who would turn aside his wrath, taking away*

1 JOHN 5:14–15

Praying According to God's Will

5:14 THIS IS THE CONFIDENCE WE HAVE IN APPROACHING GOD: THAT IF WE ASK ANYTHING ACCORDING TO HIS WILL, HE HEARS US.

This sounds simple enough: Ask God for what he already wants to give, and he will hear and answer. But what's the point? Why ask at all? Two reasons: What God wants to give is wonderful, and we become wonderful when we pray for what he wants to give. Consider what God wants to give. The petitions of the Lord's Prayer alone take one's breath away. To ask that God's kingdom come and that he rule the world in peace, justice and love is to ask for the fulfillment of the dreams of billions of people, regardless of their religious convictions. Most people would follow after any leader at all if they were sure he could deliver these things. God not only wants to give us these things, but he is able and promises to bring them about if we ask. Our pulse rate should go up every time we pray for the things God wants to give.

Consider what we become when we pray for the things God wants to give. Jesus said he will give the Holy Spirit to those who ask him (see Luke 11:13). What could be better than to "be filled to the measure of all the fullness of God" (Ephesians 3:19)? Can anything match the beauty and power of the fruit of the Holy Spirit—love, joy, peace, patience, kindness, goodness, faithfulness, gentleness and self-control (see Galatians 5:22–23)? The greatness of what John promises in this passage is not that we may convince God to give us what we want, but that we can come to want what he wants. Just as we become what we worship, we become what we pray to the one we worship.

It stretches the imagination to even begin to appreciate what is being offered here. This may help: In May, 1982, astronomers saw a solar flare shoot out from the sun so powerful that their instruments couldn't measure it. They estimated that in 20 minutes it released more energy than is produced by the entire earth in one year. To be anywhere near that flare would result in combustion. Imagine that light compared to a candle. Then imagine a love so rich and deep that it is to all human love what that solar flare was to that candle—or a joy that is to all earthly joys what that solar flare was to a flashlight. Get the picture? No eye has seen, no ear has heard, no mind can imagine the glory of what God wills to give to those who ask for what he wants to give!

P R A Y :

Come, thou fount of every blessing, tune my heart to sing
and pray for your grace. Give us your Spirit, make us like Christ,
and so rule over us that in us you are all in all.

FOR YOUR NEXT DEVOTIONAL READING, GO TO PAGE 1567.

Faith in the Son of God

5 Everyone who believes that Jesus is the Christ is born of God, and everyone who loves the father loves his child as well. ²This is how we know that we love the children of God: by loving God and carrying out his commands. ³This is love for God: to obey his commands. And his commands are not burdensome, ⁴for everyone born of God overcomes the world. This is the victory that has overcome the world, even our faith. ⁵Who is it that overcomes the world? Only he who believes that Jesus is the Son of God.

⁶This is the one who came by water and blood—Jesus Christ. He did not come by water only, but by water and blood. And it is the Spirit who testifies, because the Spirit is the truth. ⁷For there are three that testify: ⁸the*ª* Spirit, the water and the blood; and the three are in agreement. ⁹We accept man's testimony, but God's testimony is greater because it is the testimony of God, which he has given about his Son. ¹⁰Anyone who believes in the Son of God has this testimony in his heart. Anyone who does not believe God has made him out to be a liar, because he has not believed the testimony God has given about his Son. ¹¹And this is the testimony: God has given us eternal life, and this life is in his Son. ¹²He who has the Son has life; he who does not have the Son of God does not have life.

Concluding Remarks

¹³I write these things to you who believe in the name of the Son of God so that you may know that you have eternal life. ¹⁴This is the confidence we have in approaching God: that if we ask anything according to his will, he hears us. ¹⁵And if we know that he hears us—whatever we ask—we know that we have what we asked of him.

> AND if we know that he hears us—whatever we ask—we know that we have what we asked of him.
>
> 1 JOHN 5:15

¹⁶If anyone sees his brother commit a sin that does not lead to death, he should pray and God will give him life. I refer to those whose sin does not lead to death. There is a sin that leads to death. I am not saying that he should pray about that. ¹⁷All wrongdoing is sin, and there is sin that does not lead to death.

¹⁸We know that anyone born of God does not continue to sin; the one who was born of God keeps him safe, and the evil one cannot harm him. ¹⁹We know that we are children of God, and that the whole world is under the control of the evil one. ²⁰We know also that the Son of God has come and has given us understanding, so that we may know him who is true. And we are in him who is true—even in his Son Jesus Christ. He is the true God and eternal life.

²¹Dear children, keep yourselves from idols.

ª 7,8 Late manuscripts of the Vulgate *testify in heaven: the Father, the Word and the Holy Spirit, and these three are one. ⁸And there are three that testify on earth: the* (not found in any Greek manuscript before the fourteenth century)

2 John

THE AUTHOR John is now an old man (see the Introduction to 1 John). As in 1 John, he reminds his readers of the importance of loving each other. This little letter strikes a balance between the priority of love and the necessity of truth. Rather than weakening one at the expense of the other, John urges that both of these powerful elements of the Christian life be strengthened.

John addresses his letter to those "whom I love in the truth" (verse 1). The elderly apostle expresses great joy "to find some of your children walking in the truth" (verse 4). But walking in the truth also means "that you walk in love" (verse 6).

Genuine truth embodies love and compassion. John reminds us all that the two are elements that we as Christians must have.

"GRACE, MERCY AND PEACE ... WILL BE WITH US IN TRUTH AND LOVE." (3)

¹The elder,

To the chosen lady and her children, whom I love in the truth—and not I only, but also all who know the truth— ²because of the truth, which lives in us and will be with us forever:

³Grace, mercy and peace from God the Father and from Jesus Christ, the Father's Son, will be with us in truth and love.

> GRACE, mercy and peace from God the Father and from Jesus Christ, the Father's Son, will be with us in truth and love.
>
> 2 JOHN 3

⁴It has given me great joy to find some of your children walking in the truth, just as the Father commanded us. ⁵And now, dear lady, I am not writing you a new

[WEDNESDAY]

2 JOHN

Praying for an Old Man's Joy

5 I ASK THAT WE LOVE ONE ANOTHER.

This letter and the next are first century equivalents of office memos and e-mail. Of course, no communication traveled with that kind of speed in those days. But the situation called for a brief note from the aged apostle to address troubling situations—itinerant heretics in the first, a despotic pastor (Diotrephes) in the second. The people he wrote to—"the chosen lady and her children" (verse 1) and Gaius (see 3 John 1)—are trustworthy, and John is confident they will follow through on what needs to be done.

Regarding prayer, the kind of man who wrote these notes becomes visible almost between the lines. His overriding concern for "the chosen lady and her children" is that they have a love that honors the truth. "It has given me great joy to find some of your children walking in the truth, just as the Father commanded us" (2 John 4). For love to truly desire and affect what is best for those it loves, it must be true. Blind love is not love at all. What good is the love of a parent for a child if the parent doesn't understand that eating rat poison is bad for the child? If the child dies, there will be no comfort in the thought that the parent meant well. Paul showed the same concern in his prayer for the Philippians, that their love would "abound more and more in knowledge and depth of insight, so that you may be able to discern what is best and may be pure and blameless until the day of Christ" (Philippians 1:9–10).

Think of those you love and for whom you pray and the ways you pray for them. What could be better than to ask the Holy Spirit to give them love that is wise and faithful to the truth? A person with a tender heart, a keen mind and a strong backbone of integrity is a beautiful person to behold. The world needs more people like that.

PRAY:

Father, give us a love that is wise and faithful to the truth; give us tender hearts, keen minds and genuine integrity, to the praise of your glory.

FOR YOUR NEXT DEVOTIONAL READING, GO TO PAGE 1570.

command but one we have had from the beginning. I ask that we love one another. [6]And this is love: that we walk in obedience to his commands. As you have heard from the beginning, his command is that you walk in love.

[7]Many deceivers, who do not acknowledge Jesus Christ as coming in the flesh, have gone out into the world. Any such person is the deceiver and the antichrist. [8]Watch out that you do not lose what you have worked for, but that you may be rewarded fully. [9]Anyone who runs ahead and does not continue in the teaching of Christ does not have God; whoever continues in the teaching has both the Father and the Son. [10]If anyone comes to you and does not bring this teaching, do not take him into your house or welcome him. [11]Anyone who welcomes him shares in his wicked work.

[12]I have much to write to you, but I do not want to use paper and ink. Instead, I hope to visit you and talk with you face to face, so that our joy may be complete.

[13]The children of your chosen sister send their greetings.

3 John

IN JOHN'S DAY, itinerant teachers relied on the hospitality of church members for room and board. If the travelers did not meet up with hospitable people, they would have to endure the discomfort and danger of staying in less than ideal situations. This letter was written to praise one hospitable person, Gaius, for helping out the missionaries, and to warn Diotrephes, who was not welcoming those sent by John.

John commends Gaius with these words: "Dear friend, you are faithful in what you are doing for the brothers, even though they are strangers to you" (5). Gaius's kindness, especially in the face of detractors, showed that Gaius was dedicated to the truth, and that he was putting his faith into action. John honors this kind of faith, and we can learn from it.

"I HAVE NO GREATER JOY THAN TO HEAR THAT MY CHILDREN ARE WALKING IN THE TRUTH." (4)

¹The elder,

To my dear friend Gaius, whom I love in the truth.

²Dear friend, I pray that you may enjoy good health and that all may go well with you, even as your soul is getting along well. ³It gave me great joy to have some brothers come and tell about your faithfulness to the truth and how you continue to walk in the truth. ⁴I have no greater joy than to hear that my children are walking in the truth.

⁵Dear friend, you are faithful in what you are doing for the brothers, even though they are strangers to you. ⁶They have told the church about your love. You will do well to send them on their way in a manner worthy of God. ⁷It was for the sake of the Name that they went out, receiving no help from the pagans. ⁸We ought therefore to show hospitality

> DEAR friend, I pray that you may enjoy good health and that all may go well with you, even as your soul is getting along well.
>
> 3 JOHN 2

Fellowship With God and With Others in the Church

11 DO NOT IMITATE WHAT IS EVIL BUT WHAT IS GOOD.

Love needs truth to have a backbone (see the devotion in 2 John). A concern for the truth will determine the proper boundaries between what is faith and what is not. Love needs the support of sound doctrine to be effective. By itself, mere passion can be foolish or destructive. The proper order in the life of the church is "ready, aim, fire," not "ready, *fire*, aim."

But truth needs love, too. John's concern in this memo is that the church be loving and hospitable, "so that we may work together for the truth" (verse 8). Let the emphasis here fall on the word "together." Jesus said the greatest argument for the truth of the gospel would be the unity of his people (see John 17:23). Note that he didn't say the greatest argument for the truth would be an argument! Beyond words and powerful rhetoric, as important as they are, is the love of Christ manifest in Christ's people. The truth is credible only when we proclaim it in the way we live together. That's why Diotrephes is such a dangerous man. He "loves to be first," gossips maliciously, refuses to welcome other Christian leaders, and even goes to great lengths to prevent others from doing so (see verses 9–10). That means he is more than an irritant in the church; he is an enemy of the truth.

Pray for your church. Pray that the truth of Christ will be commended to outsiders by the way you live together. Shun absolutely gossip and slander, backbiting and competition, so you can pray and work *together*.

PRAY:

Father, grant that we will commend the truth to outsiders by the way we live together. Save us from gossip, backbiting and competition; show us how to work together for your glory.

FOR YOUR NEXT DEVOTIONAL READING, GO TO PAGE 1573.

to such men so that we may work together for the truth.

⁹I wrote to the church, but Diotrephes, who loves to be first, will have nothing to do with us. ¹⁰So if I come, I will call attention to what he is doing, gossiping maliciously about us. Not satisfied with that, he refuses to welcome the brothers. He also stops those who want to do so and puts them out of the church.

¹¹Dear friend, do not imitate what is evil but what is good. Anyone who does what is good is from God. Anyone who does what is evil has not seen God. ¹²Demetrius is well spoken of by everyone— and even by the truth itself. We also speak well of him, and you know that our testimony is true.

¹³I have much to write you, but I do not want to do so with pen and ink. ¹⁴I hope to see you soon, and we will talk face to face.

Peace to you. The friends here send their greetings. Greet the friends there by name.

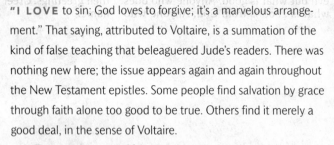

Jude

"I LOVE to sin; God loves to forgive; it's a marvelous arrangement." That saying, attributed to Voltaire, is a summation of the kind of false teaching that beleaguered Jude's readers. There was nothing new here; the issue appears again and again throughout the New Testament epistles. Some people find salvation by grace through faith alone too good to be true. Others find it merely a good deal, in the sense of Voltaire.

The practitioners of false teaching likely managed to sound very "spiritual" as they exploited God's grace. They were the forerunners of a yet more virulent Gnostic heresy to come later, who reasoned that the spirit was good and the body was bad, or of no account. So what one did with one's body had no bearing on the state of one's spirit. True spiritual religion is spiritual, not physical, they postulated. Sexual behavior is physical, and irrelevant to the spiritual life—so do whatever you want. Jude's approach is to roundly condemn this heresy and to give his readers some very good advice. "But you, dear friends, build yourselves up in your most holy faith and pray in the Holy Spirit" (20). Prayer again is a key element in walking the straight and narrow in a crooked world.

¹Jude, a servant of Jesus Christ and a brother of James,

To those who have been called, who are loved by God the Father and kept by*ᵃ* Jesus Christ:

²Mercy, peace and love be yours in abundance.

The Sin and Doom of Godless Men

³Dear friends, although I was very eager to write to you about the salvation we share, I felt I had to write and urge you to contend for the faith that was once for all entrusted to the saints. ⁴For certain men

ᵃ1 Or for; or in

[FRIDAY]

JUDE 20

Praying in the Holy Spirit

20 BUILD YOURSELVES UP IN YOUR MOST HOLY FAITH AND PRAY IN THE HOLY SPIRIT.

The strength of slogans is that they are easy to remember. The weakness of slogans is that they are easy to remember because they oversimplify things. But as slogans go, verse 20 would make a good one. The Christian life comes down to two things: "Build Yourself Up in the Faith and Pray in the Holy Spirit." It is worthy of calligraphy on parchment or a laminated card.

"Build Yourself Up in the Faith." By alluding to "your most holy faith," Jude doesn't mean the subjective sense of trust in Christ by which we stake our lives on his faithfulness. That kind of faith is, of course, critical; but what Jude has in mind is its flipside. He means faith in an objective sense—as a body of doctrine, a set of propositions, as in the "Christian faith" as opposed to, say, the Muslim faith or Hindu faith. Such is the faith mentioned in verse 3, "that was once for all entrusted to the saints," for which we are to contend. This sort of faith is also critical. It reminds us that our subjective faith is not built on something we have made up but on something we have received; it was there before we came on the scene and will be there after we leave the scene. Further, it has been entrusted to us. We are stewards of something that we adhere to, but which we do not own as a private possession to do with whatever we wish. We must give an account for what we do with the body of truth that was entrusted to us.

"Pray in the Holy Spirit." This is prayer prompted and empowered by the Holy Spirit. Prayer in the Holy Spirit is related to the faith, the way breath and blood and the central nervous system is to a skeleton. There can be no body without a skeleton (objective faith), but the body can have no life without the Spirit (subjective, personal faith). We can be right theologically—but dead right, nonetheless, unless the life of God courses through our veins. Doctrines can stay locked up in the head unless the Holy Spirit writes them on the heart (see Ezekiel 36:26–27). If we are to have desires and behavior worthy of the great doctrines we hold to, we need the Holy Spirit to blow in and through us the way a smoldering fire is fanned into flame by fresh air.

PRAY:

Holy Spirit, make us courageous to hold to the most holy faith. Give us desires and behavior and promptings to pray that are worthy of that great faith.

FOR YOUR NEXT DEVOTIONAL READING, GO TO PAGE 1574.

Wrestling With God

THE ROMAN Catholic writer Carlo Carretto said he did not trust theologians who do not pray, presumably because the great temptation of theological inquiry is to reduce Almighty God to an object for study. Prayer is the great antidote to this presumption because true prayer is loving, humble communion with a person.

In this sense, Peter Taylor Forsyth was the ideal theologian, for he was a theologian who loved to pray, and he wrote lovingly and wisely about prayer. He began his little classic, *The Soul of Prayer*, with fear and trembling: "It is a difficult and even formidable thing to write on prayer, and one fears to touch the Ark. Perhaps no one ought to undertake it unless he has spent more toil in the practice of prayer than on its principle."[1] But Forsyth prayed that God would nevertheless regard his efforts as a theologian of prayer "as a prayer to know better how to pray."[2]

Forsyth believed prayer was so central to the health of the Christian life that "the worst sin is prayerlessness. Overt sin ... [is] the effect of this, or its punishment. We are left by God for lack of seeking him."[3]

Forsyth was also a pastor. He believed that one had to spend time with people in order to know their problems and to spend time with God in order to solve them. It is this combination of Forsyth as pastor and theologian that makes *The Soul of Prayer* so helpful. As theologian, Forsyth writes thoughtfully on the mysteries of prayer; as pastor, he speaks to our hearts.

Only a pastor/theologian could have written as creatively as Forsyth did about what it means to wrestle with God in prayer. Forsyth hated resignation and fatalism in prayer, believing that sometimes to resist the permissive will of God is to do the perfect will of God—if what we resist is what God only temporarily wills to be (e.g., poor health, a bad job, a difficult marriage). It may be God's will that we be in a difficult circumstance but not necessarily that we stay in that situation. "He has a lower will and a higher, a prior and a posterior. And the purpose of the lower will is that it be resisted and struggled through to the higher"[4] Wrestling in prayer from the lower to the higher is one of God's chief means of educating our spirits.

Resist God, in the sense of rejecting God, and you will not be able to resist any evil. But resist God in the sense of closing with God, cling to him with all your strength, not your weakness only, with your active and not only your passive faith, and he will give you strength. Cast yourself into his arms not to be caressed but to wrestle with him. He loves that holy war. He may be too many for you, and lift you from your feet. But it will be to lift you from earth, and set you in the heavenly places which are theirs who fight the good fight and lay hold of God as their eternal life.[5]

PRAY:

*Dear Father, you are my only hope; I have no place to go
but to you. Your Son said to pray and not give up. Jacob would not
let go of you until you blessed him. Strengthen me to pray this
way—with tenacity, grit and strong faith!*

MEMORIZE:

*Then the man said, "Your name will no longer be Jacob,
but Israel, because you have struggled with God and
with men and have overcome."* GENESIS 32:28

FOR YOUR NEXT DEVOTIONAL READING, GO TO PAGE 1582.

whose condemnation was written about[a] long ago have secretly slipped in among you. They are godless men, who change the grace of our God into a license for immorality and deny Jesus Christ our only Sovereign and Lord.

[5]Though you already know all this, I want to remind you that the Lord[b] delivered his people out of Egypt, but later destroyed those who did not believe. [6]And the angels who did not keep their positions of authority but abandoned their own home—these he has kept in darkness, bound with everlasting chains for judgment on the great Day. [7]In a similar way, Sodom and Gomorrah and the surrounding towns gave themselves up to sexual immorality and perversion. They serve as an example of those who suffer the punishment of eternal fire.

[8]In the very same way, these dreamers pollute their own bodies, reject authority and slander celestial beings. [9]But even the archangel Michael, when he was disputing with the devil about the body of Moses, did not dare to bring a slanderous accusation against him, but said, "The Lord rebuke you!" [10]Yet these men speak abusively against whatever they do not understand; and what things they do understand by instinct, like unreasoning animals—these are the very things that destroy them.

> 66 If our petitions are in accordance with his will, and if we seek his glory in the asking, the answers will come in ways that will astonish us and fill our hearts with songs of thanksgiving. 99
>
> J.K. MACLEAN

[11]Woe to them! They have taken the way of Cain; they have rushed for profit into Balaam's error; they have been destroyed in Korah's rebellion.

[12]These men are blemishes at your love feasts, eating with you without the slightest qualm—shepherds who feed only themselves. They are clouds without rain, blown along by the wind; autumn trees, without fruit and uprooted—twice dead. [13]They are wild waves of the sea, foaming up their shame; wandering stars,

for whom blackest darkness has been reserved forever.

[14]Enoch, the seventh from Adam, prophesied about these men: "See, the Lord is coming with thousands upon thousands of his holy ones [15]to judge everyone, and to convict all the ungodly of all the ungodly acts they have done in the ungodly way, and of all the harsh words ungodly sinners have spoken against him." [16]These men are grumblers and faultfinders; they follow their own evil desires; they boast about themselves and flatter others for their own advantage.

A Call to Persevere

[17]But, dear friends, remember what the apostles of our Lord Jesus Christ foretold. [18]They said to you, "In the last times there will be scoffers who will follow their own ungodly desires." [19]These are the men who divide you, who follow mere natural instincts and do not have the Spirit.

[20]But you, dear friends, build yourselves up in your most holy faith and pray in the Holy Spirit. [21]Keep yourselves in God's love as you wait for the mercy of our Lord Jesus Christ to bring you to eternal life.

[22]Be merciful to those who doubt; [23]snatch others from the fire and save them; to others show mercy, mixed with fear—hating even the clothing stained by corrupted flesh.

Doxology

[24]To him who is able to keep you from falling and to present you before his glorious presence without fault and with great joy— [25]to the only God our Savior be glory, majesty, power and authority, through Jesus Christ our Lord, before all ages, now and forevermore! Amen.

> TO the only God our Savior be glory, majesty, power and authority, through Jesus Christ our Lord, before all ages, now and forevermore! Amen.
>
> JUDE 25

[a]4 Or *men who were marked out for condemnation*   [b]5 Some early manuscripts *Jesus*

INTRODUCTION

Revelation

THERE IS an apocryphal story about an evening when seminary students were playing basketball in a church gym. As they played, the night custodian sat on the sidelines and read his Bible. On this particular evening, one of the students noticed that the custodian was reading the book of Revelation. Knowing the many difficulties of the book, he asked the custodian, "Do you understand what you are reading?"

The custodian surprised him and said, "Yes, I do."

The student arched his brows and replied, "What do you think it means?"

"It means Jesus is gonna win," the custodian answered.

Whether or not the story is true, the point is. Amid all the controversies that have surrounded the interpretation of this wonderful and puzzling book, there remains the central truth: "Jesus is gonna win," or more accurately, "Jesus already won and will continue to win." He is introduced in the book like this: "I am the First and the Last. I am the Living One; I was dead, and behold I am alive for ever and ever! And I hold the keys of death and Hades" (1:17–18). This is the one to whom we pray!

Great praying requires a great imagination[1]—not in the sense of fantasy or wishful thinking, but in the sense of seeing with the heart the burning realities that lay beyond our five senses. John's visions may tax our minds, but they will inspire our hearts to pray with fervor and faith to the One who has conquered, to the "Lord God Almighty, who was, and is, and is to come" (4:8).

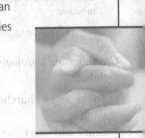

"THE SMOKE OF THE INCENSE, TOGETHER WITH THE PRAYERS OF THE SAINTS, WENT UP BEFORE GOD FROM THE ANGEL'S HAND." (8:4)

Prologue

1 The revelation of Jesus Christ, which God gave him to show his servants what must soon take place. He made it known by sending his angel to his servant John, ²who testifies to everything he saw—that is, the word of God and the testimony of Jesus Christ. ³Blessed is the one who reads the words of this prophecy, and blessed are those who hear it and take to heart what is written in it, because the time is near.

> *Prayer is translation. A man translates himself into a child asking for all there is in a language he has barely mastered.*
>
> LEONARD COHEN

Greetings and Doxology

⁴John,

To the seven churches in the province of Asia:

Grace and peace to you from him who is, and who was, and who is to come, and from the seven spirits*a* before his throne, ⁵and from Jesus Christ, who is the faithful witness, the firstborn from the dead, and the ruler of the kings of the earth.

To him who loves us and has freed us from our sins by his blood, ⁶and has made us to be a kingdom and priests to serve his God and Father—to him be glory and power for ever and ever! Amen.

⁷Look, he is coming with the clouds,
  and every eye will see him,
  even those who pierced him;
  and all the peoples of the earth will
    mourn because of him.
      So shall it be! Amen.

⁸"I am the Alpha and the Omega," says the Lord God, "who is, and who was, and who is to come, the Almighty."

One Like a Son of Man

⁹I, John, your brother and companion in the suffering and kingdom and patient endurance that are ours in Jesus, was on the island of Patmos because of the word of God and the testimony of Jesus. ¹⁰On the Lord's Day I was in the Spirit, and I heard behind me a loud voice like a trumpet, ¹¹which said: "Write on a scroll what you see and send it to the seven churches: to Ephesus, Smyrna, Pergamum, Thyatira, Sardis, Philadelphia and Laodicea."

¹²I turned around to see the voice that was speaking to me. And when I turned I saw seven golden lampstands, ¹³and among the lampstands was someone "like a son of man,"*b* dressed in a robe reaching down to his feet and with a golden sash around his chest. ¹⁴His head and hair were white like wool, as white as snow, and his eyes were like blazing fire. ¹⁵His feet were like bronze glowing in a furnace, and his voice was like the sound of rushing waters. ¹⁶In his right hand he held seven stars, and out of his mouth came a sharp double-edged sword. His face was like the sun shining in all its brilliance.

¹⁷When I saw him, I fell at his feet as though dead. Then he placed his right hand on me and said: "Do not be afraid. I am the First and the Last. ¹⁸I am the Living One; I was dead, and behold I am alive for ever and ever! And I hold the keys of death and Hades.

¹⁹"Write, therefore, what you have seen, what is now and what will take place later. ²⁰The mystery of the seven stars that you saw in my right hand and of the seven golden lampstands is this: The seven stars are the angels*c* of the seven churches, and the seven lampstands are the seven churches.

To the Church in Ephesus

2 "To the angel*d* of the church in Ephesus write:

These are the words of him who holds the seven stars in his right hand and walks among the seven golden lampstands: ²I know your deeds, your hard work and your perseverance. I know that you cannot tolerate wicked men, that you have tested those who claim to be apos-

---

*a*4 Or *the sevenfold Spirit*   *b*13 Daniel 7:13
*c*20 Or *messengers*   *d*1 Or *messenger*; also in verses 8, 12 and 18

tles but are not, and have found them false. ³You have persevered and have endured hardships for my name, and have not grown weary.

⁴Yet I hold this against you: You have forsaken your first love. ⁵Remember the height from which you have fallen! Repent and do the things you did at first. If you do not repent, I will come to you and remove your lampstand from its place. ⁶But you have this in your favor: You hate the practices of the Nicolaitans, which I also hate.

⁷He who has an ear, let him hear what the Spirit says to the churches. To him who overcomes, I will give the right to eat from the tree of life, which is in the paradise of God.

To the Church in Smyrna

⁸"To the angel of the church in Smyrna write:

These are the words of him who is the First and the Last, who died and came to life again. ⁹I know your afflictions and your poverty—yet you are rich! I know the slander of those who say they are Jews and are not, but are a synagogue of Satan. ¹⁰Do not be afraid of what you are about to suffer. I tell you, the devil will put some of you in prison to test you, and you will suffer persecution for ten days. Be faithful, even to the point of death, and I will give you the crown of life.

¹¹He who has an ear, let him hear what the Spirit says to the churches. He who overcomes will not be hurt at all by the second death.

To the Church in Pergamum

¹²"To the angel of the church in Pergamum write:

These are the words of him who has the sharp, double-edged sword. ¹³I know where you live—where Satan has his throne. Yet you remain true to my name. You did not renounce your faith in me, even in the days of Antipas, my faithful witness, who was put to death in your city— where Satan lives.

¹⁴Nevertheless, I have a few things against you: You have people there who hold to the teaching of Balaam, who taught Balak to entice the Israelites to sin by eating food sacrificed to idols and by committing sexual immorality. ¹⁵Likewise you also have those who hold to the teaching of the Nicolaitans. ¹⁶Repent therefore! Otherwise, I will soon come to you and will fight against them with the sword of my mouth.

¹⁷He who has an ear, let him hear what the Spirit says to the churches. To him who overcomes, I will give some of the hidden manna. I will also give him a white stone with a new name written on it, known only to him who receives it.

To the Church in Thyatira

¹⁸"To the angel of the church in Thyatira write:

These are the words of the Son of God, whose eyes are like blazing fire and whose feet are like burnished bronze. ¹⁹I know your deeds, your love and faith, your service and perseverance, and that you are now doing more than you did at first.

²⁰Nevertheless, I have this against you: You tolerate that woman Jezebel, who calls herself a prophetess. By her teaching she misleads my servants into sexual immorality and the eating of food sacrificed to idols. ²¹I have given her time to repent of her immorality, but she is unwilling. ²²So I will cast her on a bed of suffering, and I will make those who commit adultery with her suffer intensely, unless they repent of her ways. ²³I will strike her children dead. Then all the churches will know that I am he who searches hearts and minds, and I will repay each of you according to your deeds. ²⁴Now I say to the rest of you in Thyatira, to you who do not hold to her teaching and have not learned Satan's so-called deep secrets (I will not impose any other burden on you): ²⁵Only hold on to what you have until I come.

²⁶To him who overcomes and does my will to the end, I will give authority over the nations—

²⁷ 'He will rule them with an iron
   scepter;
   he will dash them to pieces
   like pottery'ᵃ—

just as I have received authority from my Father. ²⁸I will also give him the morning star. ²⁹He who has an ear, let him hear what the Spirit says to the churches.

To the Church in Sardis

3 "To the angelᵇ of the church in Sardis write:

These are the words of him who holds the seven spiritsᶜ of God and the seven stars. I know your deeds; you have a reputation of being alive, but you are dead. ²Wake up! Strengthen what remains and is about to die, for I have not found your deeds complete in the sight of my God. ³Remember, therefore, what you have received and heard; obey it, and repent. But if you do not wake up, I will come like a thief, and you will not know at what time I will come to you.

⁴Yet you have a few people in Sardis who have not soiled their clothes. They will walk with me, dressed in white, for they are worthy. ⁵He who overcomes will, like them, be dressed in white. I will never blot out his name from the book of life, but will acknowledge his name before my Father and his angels. ⁶He who has an

A grandfather was walking through his yard when he heard his granddaughter repeating the alphabet in a tone of voice that sounded like a prayer. He asked her what she was doing. The little girl explained: "I'm praying, but I can't think of exactly the right words, so I'm just saying all the letters, and God will put them together for me, because he knows what I'm thinking."

CHARLES B. VAUGHAN

ear, let him hear what the Spirit says to the churches.

To the Church in Philadelphia

⁷"To the angel of the church in Philadelphia write:

These are the words of him who is holy and true, who holds the key of David. What he opens no one can shut, and what he shuts no one can open. ⁸I know your deeds. See, I have placed before you an open door that no one can shut. I know that you have little strength, yet you have kept my word and have not denied my name. ⁹I will make those who are of the synagogue of Satan, who claim to be Jews though they are not, but are liars—I will make them come and fall down at your feet and acknowledge that I have loved you. ¹⁰Since you have kept my command to endure patiently, I will also keep you from the hour of trial that is going to come upon the whole world to test those who live on the earth.

¹¹I am coming soon. Hold on to what you have, so that no one will take your crown. ¹²Him who overcomes I will make a pillar in the temple of my God. Never again will he leave it. I will write on him the name of my God and the name of the city of my God, the new Jerusalem, which is coming down out of heaven from my God; and I will also write on him my new name. ¹³He who has an ear, let him hear what the Spirit says to the churches.

To the Church in Laodicea

¹⁴"To the angel of the church in Laodicea write:

These are the words of the Amen, the faithful and true witness, the ruler of God's creation. ¹⁵I know your deeds, that you are neither cold nor hot. I wish you were either one or the other! ¹⁶So, because you are lukewarm—neither hot nor cold—I am

ᵃ27 Psalm 2:9   ᵇ1 Or *messenger*; also in verses 7 and 14   ᶜ1 Or *the sevenfold Spirit*

about to spit you out of my mouth. [17]You say, 'I am rich; I have acquired wealth and do not need a thing.' But you do not realize that you are wretched, pitiful, poor, blind and naked. [18]I counsel you to buy from me gold refined in the fire, so you can become rich; and white clothes to wear, so you can cover your shameful nakedness; and salve to put on your eyes, so you can see.

[19]Those whom I love I rebuke and discipline. So be earnest, and repent. [20]Here I am! I stand at the door and knock. If anyone hears my voice and opens the door, I will come in and eat with him, and he with me.

[21]To him who overcomes, I will give the right to sit with me on my throne, just as I overcame and sat down with my Father on his throne. [22]He who has an ear, let him hear what the Spirit says to the churches."

The Throne in Heaven

4 After this I looked, and there before me was a door standing open in heaven. And the voice I had first heard speaking to me like a trumpet said, "Come up here, and I will show you what must take place after this." [2]At once I was in the Spirit, and there before me was a throne in heaven with someone sitting on it. [3]And the one who sat there had the appearance of jasper and carnelian. A rainbow, resembling an emerald, encircled the throne. [4]Surrounding the throne were twenty-four other thrones, and seated on them were twenty-four elders. They were dressed in white and had crowns of gold on their heads. [5]From the throne came flashes of lightning, rumblings and peals of thunder. Before the throne, seven lamps were blazing. These are the seven spirits[a] of God. [6]Also before the throne there was what looked like a sea of glass, clear as crystal.

In the center, around the throne, were four living creatures, and they were covered with eyes, in front and in back. [7]The first living creature was like a lion, the second was like an ox, the third had a face like a man, the fourth was like a flying eagle. [8]Each of the four living creatures had six wings and was covered with eyes all around, even under his wings. Day and night they never stop saying:

"Holy, holy, holy
is the Lord God Almighty,
who was, and is, and is to come."

[9]Whenever the living creatures give glory, honor and thanks to him who sits on the throne and who lives for ever and ever, [10]the twenty-four elders fall down before him who sits on the throne, and worship him who lives for ever and ever. They lay their crowns before the throne and say:

[11] "You are worthy, our Lord and God,
to receive glory and honor and
power,
for you created all things,
and by your will they were created
and have their being."

> WHENEVER the living creatures give glory, honor and thanks to him who sits on the throne and who lives for ever and ever, the twenty-four elders fall down before him who sits on the throne, and worship him who lives for ever and ever.
>
> REVELATION 4:9–10

The Scroll and the Lamb

5 Then I saw in the right hand of him who sat on the throne a scroll with writing on both sides and sealed with seven seals. [2]And I saw a mighty angel proclaiming in a loud voice, "Who is worthy to break the seals and open the scroll?" [3]But no one in heaven or on earth or under the earth could open the scroll or even look inside it. [4]I wept and wept because no one was found who was worthy to open the scroll or look inside. [5]Then one of the elders said to me, "Do not weep! See, the Lion of the tribe of Judah, the Root of David, has triumphed. He is able to open the scroll and its seven seals."

[6]Then I saw a Lamb, looking as if it had been slain, standing in the center of the throne, encircled by the four living creatures and the elders. He had seven horns and seven eyes, which are the seven

---

[a]5 Or the sevenfold Spirit

spirits[a] of God sent out into all the earth. [7]He came and took the scroll from the right hand of him who sat on the throne. [8]And when he had taken it, the four living creatures and the twenty-four elders fell down before the Lamb. Each one had a harp and they were holding golden bowls full of incense, which are the prayers of the saints. [9]And they sang a new song:

"You are worthy to take the scroll
    and to open its seals,
because you were slain,
    and with your blood you purchased
        men for God
    from every tribe and language and
        people and nation.

[a]6 Or *the sevenfold Spirit*

[MONDAY]

REVELATION 4

Praise to the Creator-Sustainer

4:8 "HOLY, HOLY, HOLY IS THE LORD GOD ALMIGHTY."

When John says he stepped through a door opened in heaven, he means he has stepped into the control room of history and the entire cosmos. What he sees there is of immense comfort: a throne. The word for "throne" is used in the New Testament some 60 times, and John is responsible for over 40 of those instances. His readers are familiar with earthly thrones, particularly Caesar's. Earthly thrones and powers were often threats to the church in John's day. The comfort is that in the control room of history there is a throne above all others, and it is occupied by the King of kings and Lord of lords. Earthly powers do not have the last word—God does.

There is more: Encircling the throne is a rainbow, the sign of God's covenant to preserve his creation (see Genesis 9:12–16). No matter how bad things may seem on earth, God is still in control; he still remembers his promise, and he still loves the world. That is how he is worshiped. Nothing has changed; he is the still the Creator God. He is the same yesterday, today and forever: "Holy, holy, holy is the Lord God Almighty, who was, and is, and is to come . . . You are worthy, our Lord and God, to receive glory and honor and power, for you created all things, and by your will they were created and have their being" (Revelation 4:8,11). The last book of the Bible reaffirms and celebrates what the first book celebrates (see Genesis 1:1–31).

These verses are great to pray. They have been sung and prayed throughout the church's history. As when they were first written, they still bring peace and comfort to troubled hearts. You could pray these verses right now, and it would honor God and be good for your soul. As you do, note this: Praise is going on in heaven right now, day and night (see 4:8). Whenever you praise God, you never do it alone. Join the citizens of heaven in something that never changes. Sing along.

PRAY:
"Holy, holy, holy is the Lord God Almighty, who was, and is,
and is to come . . . You are worthy, our Lord and God, to receive glory and
honor and power, for you created all things, and by your will
they were created and have their being" (4:8,11).

FOR YOUR NEXT DEVOTIONAL READING, GO TO PAGE 1583.

REVELATION 5

Praise to the Lamb

5:6 THEN I SAW A LAMB, LOOKING AS IF IT HAD BEEN SLAIN.

A new player is added to the ensemble around the throne of God. God holds in his right hand a sealed scroll. In it are written his decrees, purposes and judgments in history—what he will do to save and redeem his world. But someone needs to open the scroll for these to be carried out, someone who is "worthy" to do so (see 5:2). John wept bitterly because no one could be found to open the scroll. Then, in a moment of high drama, one of the elders of heaven announces that there is one who is worthy: "the Lion of the tribe of Judah, the Root of David" (verse 5). All heaven stands on tiptoe to see the Lion appear, but what they see is a Lamb, "looking as if it had been slain" (verse 6)! The creature that symbolizes regality, ferocity and strength is embodied in a creature that denotes meekness, vulnerability and sacrifice. The Lion is a Lamb; the Lamb is a Lion.

Jesus is the Lamb of God who takes away the sin of the world (see John 1:29). The Lamb will be the controlling image of Christ throughout the remainder of the book of Revelation. He stands at the position of equality, on the throne at God's right hand.

The Creator (see previous devotion) is also worshiped as Savior:

> You are worthy to take the scroll and to open its seals, because you were slain, and with your blood you purchased men for God from every tribe and language and people and nation. You have made them to be a kingdom and priests to serve our God, and they will reign on the earth . . . Worthy is the Lamb, who was slain, to receive power and wealth and wisdom and strength and honor and glory and praise! (Revelation 5:9–10,12).

The church has sung and prayed these words for centuries—much to God's glory and to its own comfort and encouragement. You may sing these words, too, remembering again to never do so alone; you join all the citizens of heaven (see verses 8,11,13–14). Be thrilled to know this: "You have come to thousands upon thousands of angels in joyful assembly, to the church of the firstborn, whose names are written in heaven. You have come to God, the judge of all men, to the spirits of righteous men made perfect, to Jesus the mediator of a new covenant" (Hebrews 12:22–24).

P R A Y :

Worship with the multitudes of heaven, and change the pronouns
in Revelation 5:9–10,12 to personally involve you and your church:
"You are worthy to take the scroll and open its seals, because you
were slain, and with your blood you purchased us for God . . ."

FOR YOUR NEXT DEVOTIONAL READING, GO TO PAGE 1585.

¹⁰You have made them to be a kingdom
and priests to serve our God,
and they will reign on the earth."

¹¹Then I looked and heard the voice of
many angels, numbering thousands
upon thousands, and ten thousand times
ten thousand. They encircled the throne
and the living creatures and the elders.
¹²In a loud voice they sang:

"Worthy is the Lamb, who was slain,
to receive power and wealth and
wisdom and strength
and honor and glory and praise!"

¹³Then I heard every creature in heaven
and on earth and under the earth and on
the sea, and all that is in them, singing:

"To him who sits on the throne and
to the Lamb
be praise and honor and glory and
power,
for ever and ever!"

¹⁴The four living creatures said, "Amen,"
and the elders fell down and worshiped.

The Seals

6 I watched as the Lamb opened the
first of the seven seals. Then I heard
one of the four living creatures say in a
voice like thunder, "Come!" ²I looked,
and there before me was a white horse!
Its rider held a bow, and he was given a
crown, and he rode out as a conqueror
bent on conquest.

³When the Lamb opened the second
seal, I heard the second living creature
say, "Come!" ⁴Then another horse came
out, a fiery red one. Its rider was given
power to take peace from the earth and
to make men slay each other. To him was
given a large sword.

⁵When the Lamb opened the third seal,
I heard the third living creature say,
"Come!" I looked, and there before me
was a black horse! Its rider was holding a
pair of scales in his hand. ⁶Then I heard
what sounded like a voice among the
four living creatures, saying, "A quart*ᵃ* of
wheat for a day's wages,*ᵇ* and three
quarts of barley for a day's wages,*ᵇ* and
do not damage the oil and the wine!"

⁷When the Lamb opened the fourth
seal, I heard the voice of the fourth living creature say, "Come!" ⁸I looked, and
there before me was a pale horse! Its rider was named Death, and Hades was following close behind him. They were
given power over a fourth of the earth to
kill by sword, famine and plague, and by
the wild beasts of the earth.

⁹When he opened the fifth seal, I saw
under the altar the souls of those who
had been slain because of the word of
God and the testimony they had maintained. ¹⁰They called out in a loud voice,
"How long, Sovereign Lord, holy and
true, until you judge the inhabitants of
the earth and avenge our blood?" ¹¹Then
each of them was given a white robe, and
they were told to wait a little longer, until the number of their fellow servants
and brothers who were to be killed as
they had been was completed.

¹²I watched as he opened the sixth seal.
There was a great earthquake. The sun
turned black like sackcloth made of goat
hair, the whole moon turned blood red,
¹³and the stars in the sky fell to earth, as
late figs drop from a fig tree when shaken
by a strong wind. ¹⁴The sky receded like a
scroll, rolling up, and every mountain
and island was removed from its place.

¹⁵Then the kings of the earth, the
princes, the generals, the rich, the
mighty, and every slave and every free
man hid in caves and among the rocks of
the mountains. ¹⁶They called to the
mountains and the rocks, "Fall on us and
hide us from the face of him who sits on
the throne and from the wrath of the
Lamb! ¹⁷For the great day of their wrath
has come, and who can stand?"

144,000 Sealed

7 After this I saw four angels standing
at the four corners of the earth, holding back the four winds of the earth to
prevent any wind from blowing on the
land or on the sea or on any tree. ²Then I
saw another angel coming up from the
east, having the seal of the living God. He
called out in a loud voice to the four angels who had been given power to harm
the land and the sea: ³"Do not harm the
land or the sea or the trees until we put a

ᵃ6 Greek *a choinix* (probably about a liter)
ᵇ6 Greek *a denarius*

REVELATION 6:9–11

Pray for the Persecuted Church

6:9 I SAW UNDER THE ALTAR THE SOULS OF THOSE WHO HAD BEEN SLAIN BECAUSE OF THE WORD OF GOD.

This is a jarring passage. For one thing, the kind of prayer being prayed here is not what one would expect in heaven. The prayers come from the souls of martyrs crying out from under the altar, the place where the blood of slaughtered, sacrificial animals was poured in the Old Testament temple. They plead, "How long, Sovereign Lord, holy and true, until you judge the inhabitants of the earth and avenge our blood?" (6:10). Even in heaven the martyrs are longing for justice.

Furthermore, God's answer is equally unsettling: "They were told to wait a little longer, until the number of their fellow servants and brothers who were to be killed as they had been was completed" (verse 11). More have to die to "complete" what they have started. The victory comes through sacrifice. Satan, the accuser of God's people, is hurled down and overcome by the blood of the Lamb and his martyrs: "They overcame him by the blood of the Lamb and by the word of their testimony; they did not love their lives so much as to shrink from death" (Revelation 12:11).

Vernard Eller, in his commentary on Revelation, underlines the significance of God's answer to the martyrs' prayer:

> As clearly as can be stated, we are told that *the* human activity upon which the outcome of history depends, the action by which progress toward the kingdom is marked, is not the piling up of good deeds, not our winning of men to Christ, not our consolidating of power for the Good, not our chasing out and cleaning up Evil, not our taking over or building up anything. No, we contribute to the coming of the kingdom by making like the Lamb, being willing, in love, to *give* ourselves, even to the slaughter.[2]

How should we pray for the persecuted church? We should pray as the persecuted church in heaven prays—for justice! We should pray knowing that God's chief method of doing his work is by the blood of the Lamb and that the Greek word for *witness* and *martyr* is one and the same. We should also pray, therefore, for the church to remain faithful, courageous and full of the hope that one day all will be well, not in spite of its sufferings, but through them.

P R A Y :

As you pray, say the names of the countries in the world where you know the church is suffering persecution: Sovereign Lord, you are holy and true. Do not delay! Act swiftly to bring justice in _____. Strengthen my brothers and sisters there with hope, so that they will remain faithful and courageous until the day of Christ.

_____

FOR YOUR NEXT DEVOTIONAL READING, GO TO PAGE 1587.

seal on the foreheads of the servants of our God." ⁴Then I heard the number of those who were sealed: 144,000 from all the tribes of Israel.

⁵ From the tribe of Judah 12,000 were
    sealed,
  from the tribe of Reuben 12,000,
  from the tribe of Gad 12,000,
⁶ from the tribe of Asher 12,000,
  from the tribe of Naphtali 12,000,
  from the tribe of Manasseh 12,000,
⁷ from the tribe of Simeon 12,000,
  from the tribe of Levi 12,000,
  from the tribe of Issachar 12,000,
⁸ from the tribe of Zebulun 12,000,
  from the tribe of Joseph 12,000,
  from the tribe of Benjamin 12,000.

The Great Multitude in White Robes

⁹After this I looked and there before me was a great multitude that no one could count, from every nation, tribe, people and language, standing before the throne and in front of the Lamb. They were wearing white robes and were holding palm branches in their hands. ¹⁰And they cried out in a loud voice:

"Salvation belongs to our God,
  who sits on the throne,
  and to the Lamb."

¹¹All the angels were standing around the throne and around the elders and the four living creatures. They fell down on their faces before the throne and worshiped God, ¹²saying:

"Amen!
Praise and glory
and wisdom and thanks and honor
and power and strength
be to our God for ever and ever.
Amen!"

¹³Then one of the elders asked me, "These in white robes—who are they, and where did they come from?"

> ALL the angels were standing around the throne and around the elders and the four living creatures. They fell down on their faces before the throne and worshiped God.
>
> REVELATION 7:11

¹⁴I answered, "Sir, you know."

And he said, "These are they who have come out of the great tribulation; they have washed their robes and made them white in the blood of the Lamb. ¹⁵Therefore,

"they are before the throne of God
  and serve him day and night in his
    temple;
and he who sits on the throne will
  spread his tent over them.
¹⁶ Never again will they hunger;
  never again will they thirst.
The sun will not beat upon them,
  nor any scorching heat.
¹⁷ For the Lamb at the center of the
  throne will be their shepherd;
  he will lead them to springs of
    living water.
And God will wipe away every tear
  from their eyes."

The Seventh Seal and the Golden Censer

8 When he opened the seventh seal, there was silence in heaven for about half an hour.

²And I saw the seven angels who stand before God, and to them were given seven trumpets.

³Another angel, who had a golden censer, came and stood at the altar. He was given much incense to offer, with the prayers of all the saints, on the golden altar before the throne. ⁴The smoke of the

> THE smoke of the incense, together with the prayers of all the saints, went up before God from the angel's hand.
>
> REVELATION 8:4

incense, together with the prayers of the saints, went up before God from the angel's hand. ⁵Then the angel took the censer, filled it with fire from the altar, and hurled it on the earth; and there came peals of thunder, rumblings, flashes of lightning and an earthquake.

The Trumpets

⁶Then the seven angels who had the seven trumpets prepared to sound them.

⁷The first angel sounded his trumpet, and there came hail and fire mixed with

blood, and it was hurled down upon the earth. A third of the earth was burned up, a third of the trees were burned up, and all the green grass was burned up.

⁸The second angel sounded his trumpet, and something like a huge mountain, all ablaze, was thrown into the sea. A third of the sea turned into blood, ⁹a third of the living creatures in the sea died, and a third of the ships were destroyed.

¹⁰The third angel sounded his trumpet, and a great star, blazing like a torch, fell from the sky on a third of the rivers and on the springs of water— ¹¹the name of

---

{ **THURSDAY** }

REVELATION 8:1–5

Heaven's View of Prayer

8:4 THE SMOKE OF THE INCENSE, TOGETHER WITH THE PRAYERS OF THE SAINTS, WENT UP BEFORE GOD.

Try asking a group, perhaps a congregation on Sunday morning, to be silent for half an hour. Or try it yourself at home. It's not only difficult to do, but it creates a tremendous sense of expectancy. Ears and eyes begin to strain, to lean into whatever will be next. That is the scene in heaven. There has been silence for about half an hour, and all heaven is eager to hear what will come next. Then seven angels are given seven trumpets. Watch out! Hands move to cover ears; people move to the edges of their seats; the first sound will be a trumpet blast! Anticipation becomes electric as another angel, with a golden censer, moves to the altar before the throne of God. In the censer, mixed with the incense, are the prayers of God's people. The smoke of their prayers goes up before God. Then the angel scoops, with the censer, fire from the altar, and hurls it down to earth. The first sound heaven hears is louder and more startling than trumpets: "There came peals of thunder, rumblings, flashes of lightning and an earthquake" (8:5).

Sometimes prayer can feel so impotent. Have your words ever seemed to dribble off your tongue and pool on the floor? That is an earthly view of prayer. Heaven's view is that prayer is powerful! There is thunder, lightning, earthquakes; the prayers of God's people move the whole earth. The future belongs to the intercessors, says New Testament scholar Walter Wink. It pleases God to give prayer this power for the same reason it pleased him to save the world through the "foolishness" of the cross and to perfect his strength through human weakness—"so that no one may boast before him" (1 Corinthians 1:18–29; see 2 Corinthians 12:9–10). When we pray, God gets all the glory, and we get the joy of seeing him work wonders. Prayer truly changes things: Kings and those in authority are affected, unknowingly, and churches stand firm and mature in hope (see 1 Timothy 2:1–2; Colossians 4:12).

PRAY:

Take time to pray about things that seem to be the really frightening and intractable issues in the world. Declare them to the Lord, one at a time, and pray: Come Lord; save us, Lord! May the kingdoms of this world become the kingdom of Christ. May your will be done on earth as fully as it is done in heaven.

FOR YOUR NEXT DEVOTIONAL READING, GO TO PAGE 1599.

the star is Wormwood.[a] A third of the waters turned bitter, and many people died from the waters that had become bitter.

[12] The fourth angel sounded his trumpet, and a third of the sun was struck, a third of the moon, and a third of the stars, so that a third of them turned dark. A third of the day was without light, and also a third of the night.

[13] As I watched, I heard an eagle that was flying in midair call out in a loud voice: "Woe! Woe! Woe to the inhabitants of the earth, because of the trumpet blasts about to be sounded by the other three angels!"

9 The fifth angel sounded his trumpet, and I saw a star that had fallen from the sky to the earth. The star was given the key to the shaft of the Abyss. [2] When he opened the Abyss, smoke rose from it like the smoke from a gigantic furnace. The sun and sky were darkened by the smoke from the Abyss. [3] And out of the smoke locusts came down upon the earth and were given power like that of scorpions of the earth. [4] They were told not to harm the grass of the earth or any plant or tree, but only those people who did not have the seal of God on their foreheads. [5] They were not given power to kill them, but only to torture them for five months. And the agony they suffered was like that of the sting of a scorpion when it strikes a man. [6] During those days men will seek death, but will not find it; they will long to die, but death will elude them.

[7] The locusts looked like horses prepared for battle. On their heads they wore something like crowns of gold, and their faces resembled human faces. [8] Their hair was like women's hair, and their teeth were like lions' teeth. [9] They had breastplates like breastplates of iron, and the sound of their wings was like the thundering of many horses and chariots rushing into battle. [10] They had tails and stings like scorpions, and in their tails they had power to torment people for five months. [11] They had as king over them the angel of the Abyss, whose name in Hebrew is Abaddon, and in Greek, Apollyon.[b]

[12] The first woe is past; two other woes are yet to come.

[13] The sixth angel sounded his trumpet, and I heard a voice coming from the horns[c] of the golden altar that is before God. [14] It said to the sixth angel who had the trumpet, "Release the four angels who are bound at the great river Euphrates." [15] And the four angels who had been kept ready for this very hour and day and month and year were released to kill a third of mankind. [16] The number of the mounted troops was two hundred million. I heard their number.

[17] The horses and riders I saw in my vision looked like this: Their breastplates were fiery red, dark blue, and yellow as sulfur. The heads of the horses resembled the heads of lions, and out of their mouths came fire, smoke and sulfur. [18] A third of mankind was killed by the three plagues of fire, smoke and sulfur that came out of their mouths. [19] The power of the horses was in their mouths and in their tails; for their tails were like snakes, having heads with which they inflict injury.

> " I have not placed reading before praying because I regard it more important, but because, in order to pray aright, we must understand what we are praying for. "
>
> ANGELINA GRIMKE

[20] The rest of mankind that were not killed by these plagues still did not repent of the work of their hands; they did not stop worshiping demons, and idols of gold, silver, bronze, stone and wood—idols that cannot see or hear or walk. [21] Nor did they repent of their murders, their magic arts, their sexual immorality or their thefts.

The Angel and the Little Scroll

10 Then I saw another mighty angel coming down from heaven. He was robed in a cloud, with a rainbow above his head; his face was like the sun, and his legs were like fiery pillars. [2] He was holding a little scroll, which lay open in his hand. He planted his right foot on the sea and his left foot on the land, [3] and he

[a] 11 That is, Bitterness   [b] 11 Abaddon and Apollyon mean Destroyer.   [c] 13 That is, projections

gave a loud shout like the roar of a lion. When he shouted, the voices of the seven thunders spoke. 4And when the seven thunders spoke, I was about to write; but I heard a voice from heaven say, "Seal up what the seven thunders have said and do not write it down."

5Then the angel I had seen standing on the sea and on the land raised his right hand to heaven. 6And he swore by him who lives for ever and ever, who created the heavens and all that is in them, the earth and all that is in it, and the sea and all that is in it, and said, "There will be no more delay! 7But in the days when the seventh angel is about to sound his trumpet, the mystery of God will be accomplished, just as he announced to his servants the prophets."

8Then the voice that I had heard from heaven spoke to me once more: "Go, take the scroll that lies open in the hand of the angel who is standing on the sea and on the land."

9So I went to the angel and asked him to give me the little scroll. He said to me, "Take it and eat it. It will turn your stomach sour, but in your mouth it will be as sweet as honey." 10I took the little scroll from the angel's hand and ate it. It tasted as sweet as honey in my mouth, but when I had eaten it, my stomach turned sour. 11Then I was told, "You must prophesy again about many peoples, nations, languages and kings."

The Two Witnesses

11 I was given a reed like a measuring rod and was told, "Go and measure the temple of God and the altar, and count the worshipers there. 2But exclude the outer court; do not measure it, because it has been given to the Gentiles. They will trample on the holy city for 42 months. 3And I will give power to my two witnesses, and they will prophesy for 1,260 days, clothed in sackcloth." 4These are the two olive trees and the two lampstands that stand before the Lord of the earth. 5If anyone tries to harm them, fire comes from their mouths and devours their enemies. This is how anyone who wants to harm them must die. 6These men have power to shut up the sky so that it will not rain during the time

they are prophesying; and they have power to turn the waters into blood and to strike the earth with every kind of plague as often as they want.

7Now when they have finished their testimony, the beast that comes up from the Abyss will attack them, and overpower and kill them. 8Their bodies will lie in the street of the great city, which is figuratively called Sodom and Egypt, where also their Lord was crucified. 9For three and a half days men from every people, tribe, language and nation will gaze on their bodies and refuse them burial. 10The inhabitants of the earth will gloat over them and will celebrate by sending each other gifts, because these two prophets had tormented those who live on the earth.

11But after the three and a half days a breath of life from God entered them, and they stood on their feet, and terror struck those who saw them. 12Then they heard a loud voice from heaven saying to them, "Come up here." And they went up to heaven in a cloud, while their enemies looked on.

13At that very hour there was a severe earthquake and a tenth of the city collapsed. Seven thousand people were killed in the earthquake, and the survivors were terrified and gave glory to the God of heaven.

14The second woe has passed; the third woe is coming soon.

The Seventh Trumpet

15The seventh angel sounded his trumpet, and there were loud voices in heaven, which said:

"The kingdom of the world has
    become the kingdom of our
    Lord and of his Christ,
and he will reign for ever and ever."

16And the twenty-four elders, who were seated on their thrones before God, fell on their faces and worshiped God, 17saying:

"We give thanks to you, Lord God
    Almighty,
the One who is and who was,
because you have taken your great
    power
and have begun to reign.

> *AND the twenty-four elders, who were seated on their thrones before God, fell on their faces and worshiped God, saying:*
>
> *"We give thanks to you, Lord God Almighty,*
> *the One who is and who was,*
> *because you have taken your great power*
> *and have begun to reign."*
>
> REVELATION 11:16–17

¹⁸ The nations were angry;
    and your wrath has come.
The time has come for judging the dead,
    and for rewarding your servants
        the prophets
and your saints and those who
        reverence your name,
    both small and great—
and for destroying those who destroy
        the earth."

¹⁹ Then God's temple in heaven was opened, and within his temple was seen the ark of his covenant. And there came flashes of lightning, rumblings, peals of thunder, an earthquake and a great hailstorm.

The Woman and the Dragon

12 A great and wondrous sign appeared in heaven: a woman clothed with the sun, with the moon under her feet and a crown of twelve stars on her head. ²She was pregnant and cried out in pain as she was about to give birth. ³Then another sign appeared in heaven: an enormous red dragon with seven heads and ten horns and seven crowns on his heads. ⁴His tail swept a third of the stars out of the sky and flung them to the earth. The dragon stood in front of the woman who was about to give birth, so that he might devour her child the moment it was born. ⁵She gave birth to a son, a male child, who will rule all the nations with an iron scepter. And her child was snatched up to God and to his throne. ⁶The woman fled into the desert to a place prepared for her by God, where she might be taken care of for 1,260 days.

⁷And there was war in heaven. Michael and his angels fought against the dragon, and the dragon and his angels fought back. ⁸But he was not strong enough, and they lost their place in heaven. ⁹The great dragon was hurled down—that ancient serpent called the devil, or Satan, who leads the whole world astray. He was hurled to the earth, and his angels with him.

¹⁰Then I heard a loud voice in heaven say:

"Now have come the salvation and
        the power and the kingdom of
        our God,
    and the authority of his Christ.
For the accuser of our brothers,
    who accuses them before our God
        day and night,
    has been hurled down.
¹¹ They overcame him
    by the blood of the Lamb
    and by the word of their testimony;
they did not love their lives so much
    as to shrink from death.
¹² Therefore rejoice, you heavens
    and you who dwell in them!
But woe to the earth and the sea,
    because the devil has gone down
        to you!
He is filled with fury,
    because he knows that his time is
        short."

> ❝ *God can pick sense out of a confused prayer.* ❞
>
> RICHARD SIBBES

¹³When the dragon saw that he had been hurled to the earth, he pursued the woman who had given birth to the male child. ¹⁴The woman was given the two wings of a great eagle, so that she might fly to the place prepared for her in the desert, where she would be taken care of for a time, times and half a time, out of the serpent's reach. ¹⁵Then from his mouth the serpent spewed water like a river, to overtake the woman and sweep her away with the torrent. ¹⁶But the earth helped the woman by opening its mouth and swallowing the river that the dragon had spewed out of his mouth. ¹⁷Then the drag-

on was enraged at the woman and went off to make war against the rest of her offspring—those who obey God's commandments and hold to the testimony of Jesus.

13 ¹And the dragon[a] stood on the shore of the sea.

The Beast out of the Sea

And I saw a beast coming out of the sea. He had ten horns and seven heads, with ten crowns on his horns, and on each head a blasphemous name. ²The beast I saw resembled a leopard, but had feet like those of a bear and a mouth like that of a lion. The dragon gave the beast his power and his throne and great authority. ³One of the heads of the beast seemed to have had a fatal wound, but the fatal wound had been healed. The whole world was astonished and followed the beast. ⁴Men worshiped the dragon because he had given authority to the beast, and they also worshiped the beast and asked, "Who is like the beast? Who can make war against him?"

⁵The beast was given a mouth to utter proud words and blasphemies and to exercise his authority for forty-two months. ⁶He opened his mouth to blaspheme God, and to slander his name and his dwelling place and those who live in heaven. ⁷He was given power to make war against the saints and to conquer them. And he was given authority over every tribe, people, language and nation. ⁸All inhabitants of the earth will worship the beast—all whose names have not been written in the book of life belonging to the Lamb that was slain from the creation of the world.[b]

⁹He who has an ear, let him hear.

¹⁰If anyone is to go into captivity,
  into captivity he will go.
If anyone is to be killed[c] with the
    sword,
  with the sword he will be killed.

This calls for patient endurance and faithfulness on the part of the saints.

The Beast out of the Earth

¹¹Then I saw another beast, coming out of the earth. He had two horns like a lamb, but he spoke like a dragon. ¹²He exercised all the authority of the first beast on his behalf, and made the earth and its inhabitants worship the first beast, whose fatal wound had been healed. ¹³And he performed great and miraculous signs, even causing fire to come down from heaven to earth in full view of men. ¹⁴Because of the signs he was given power to do on behalf of the first beast, he deceived the inhabitants of the earth. He ordered them to set up an image in honor of the beast who was wounded by the sword and yet lived. ¹⁵He was given power to give breath to the image of the first beast, so that it could speak and cause all who refused to worship the image to be killed. ¹⁶He also forced everyone, small and great, rich and poor, free and slave, to receive a mark on his right hand or on his forehead, ¹⁷so that no one could buy or sell unless he had the mark, which is the name of the beast or the number of his name.

¹⁸This calls for wisdom. If anyone has insight, let him calculate the number of the beast, for it is man's number. His number is 666.

The Lamb and the 144,000

14 Then I looked, and there before me was the Lamb, standing on Mount Zion, and with him 144,000 who had his name and his Father's name written on their foreheads. ²And I heard a sound from heaven like the roar of rushing waters and like a loud peal of thunder. The sound I heard was like that of harpists playing their harps. ³And they sang a new song before the throne and before the four living creatures and the elders. No one could learn the song except the 144,000 who had been redeemed from the earth. ⁴These are those who did not defile themselves with women, for they kept themselves pure. They follow the Lamb wherever he goes. They were purchased from among men and offered as firstfruits to God and the Lamb. ⁵No lie was found in their mouths; they are blameless.

---

[a]1 Some late manuscripts *And I*   [b]8 Or *written from the creation of the world in the book of life belonging to the Lamb that was slain*
[c]10 Some manuscripts *anyone kills*

The Three Angels

[6]Then I saw another angel flying in midair, and he had the eternal gospel to proclaim to those who live on the earth—to every nation, tribe, language and people. [7]He said in a loud voice, "Fear God and give him glory, because the hour of his judgment has come. Worship him who made the heavens, the earth, the sea and the springs of water."

> THEN *I saw another angel flying in midair, and he had the eternal gospel to proclaim to those who live on the earth—to every nation, tribe, language and people. He said in a loud voice, "Fear God and give him glory, because the hour of his judgment has come. Worship him who made the heavens, the earth, the sea and the springs of water."*
>
> REVELATION 14:6-7

[8]A second angel followed and said, "Fallen! Fallen is Babylon the Great, which made all the nations drink the maddening wine of her adulteries."

[9]A third angel followed them and said in a loud voice: "If anyone worships the beast and his image and receives his mark on the forehead or on the hand, [10]he, too, will drink of the wine of God's fury, which has been poured full strength into the cup of his wrath. He will be tormented with burning sulfur in the presence of the holy angels and of the Lamb. [11]And the smoke of their torment rises for ever and ever. There is no rest day or night for those who worship the beast and his image, or for anyone who receives the mark of his name." [12]This calls for patient endurance on the part of the saints who obey God's commandments and remain faithful to Jesus.

[13]Then I heard a voice from heaven say, "Write: Blessed are the dead who die in the Lord from now on."

"Yes," says the Spirit, "they will rest from their labor, for their deeds will follow them."

The Harvest of the Earth

[14]I looked, and there before me was a white cloud, and seated on the cloud was one "like a son of man"[a] with a crown of gold on his head and a sharp sickle in his hand. [15]Then another angel came out of the temple and called in a loud voice to him who was sitting on the cloud, "Take your sickle and reap, because the time to reap has come, for the harvest of the earth is ripe." [16]So he who was seated on the cloud swung his sickle over the earth, and the earth was harvested.

[17]Another angel came out of the temple in heaven, and he too had a sharp sickle. [18]Still another angel, who had charge of the fire, came from the altar and called in a loud voice to him who had the sharp sickle, "Take your sharp sickle and gather the clusters of grapes from the earth's vine, because its grapes are ripe." [19]The angel swung his sickle on the earth, gathered its grapes and threw them into the great winepress of God's wrath. [20]They were trampled in the winepress outside the city, and blood flowed out of the press, rising as high as the horses' bridles for a distance of 1,600 stadia.[b]

> 66 *Prayer is not a collection of balanced phrases; it is the pouring out of the soul.* 99
>
> SAMUEL CHADWICK

Seven Angels With Seven Plagues

15 I saw in heaven another great and marvelous sign: seven angels with the seven last plagues—last, because with them God's wrath is completed. [2]And I saw what looked like a sea of glass mixed with fire and, standing beside the sea, those who had been victorious over the beast and his image and over the number of his name. They held harps given them by God [3]and sang the song of Moses the servant of God and the song of the Lamb:

"Great and marvelous are your
    deeds,
  Lord God Almighty.
Just and true are your ways,
  King of the ages.

[a]14 Daniel 7:13 [b]20 That is, about 180 miles (about 300 kilometers)

> WHO will not fear you, O Lord,
> and bring glory to your name?
> For you alone are holy.
> All nations will come
> and worship before you,
> for your righteous acts have been
> revealed.
>
> REVELATION 15:4

[4]Who will not fear you, O Lord,
and bring glory to your name?
For you alone are holy.
All nations will come
and worship before you,
for your righteous acts have been
revealed."

[5]After this I looked and in heaven the temple, that is, the tabernacle of the Testimony, was opened. [6]Out of the temple came the seven angels with the seven plagues. They were dressed in clean, shining linen and wore golden sashes around their chests. [7]Then one of the four living creatures gave to the seven angels seven golden bowls filled with the wrath of God, who lives for ever and ever. [8]And the temple was filled with smoke from the glory of God and from his power, and no one could enter the temple until the seven plagues of the seven angels were completed.

The Seven Bowls of God's Wrath

16 Then I heard a loud voice from the temple saying to the seven angels, "Go, pour out the seven bowls of God's wrath on the earth."

[2]The first angel went and poured out his bowl on the land, and ugly and painful sores broke out on the people who had the mark of the beast and worshiped his image.

> 66 A prayer in its simplest definition is merely a wish turned Godward. 99
>
> PHILLIP BROOKS

[3]The second angel poured out his bowl on the sea, and it turned into blood like that of a dead man, and every living thing in the sea died.

[4]The third angel poured out his bowl on the rivers and springs of water, and they became blood. [5]Then I heard the angel in charge of the waters say:

"You are just in these judgments,
you who are and who were, the
Holy One,
because you have so judged;
[6]for they have shed the blood of your
saints and prophets,
and you have given them blood to
drink as they deserve."

[7]And I heard the altar respond:

"Yes, Lord God Almighty,
true and just are your judgments."

[8]The fourth angel poured out his bowl on the sun, and the sun was given power to scorch people with fire. [9]They were seared by the intense heat and they cursed the name of God, who had control over these plagues, but they refused to repent and glorify him.

[10]The fifth angel poured out his bowl on the throne of the beast, and his kingdom was plunged into darkness. Men gnawed their tongues in agony [11]and cursed the God of heaven because of their pains and their sores, but they refused to repent of what they had done.

[12]The sixth angel poured out his bowl on the great river Euphrates, and its water was dried up to prepare the way for the kings from the East. [13]Then I saw three evil[a] spirits that looked like frogs; they came out of the mouth of the dragon, out of the mouth of the beast and out of the mouth of the false prophet. [14]They are spirits of demons performing miraculous signs, and they go out to the kings of the whole world, to gather them for the battle on the great day of God Almighty.

[15]"Behold, I come like a thief! Blessed is he who stays awake and keeps his clothes with him, so that he may not go naked and be shamefully exposed."

[16]Then they gathered the kings together to the place that in Hebrew is called Armageddon.

[17]The seventh angel poured out his bowl into the air, and out of the temple came a loud voice from the throne, saying,

[a]13 Greek *unclean*

"It is done!" [18]Then there came flashes of lightning, rumblings, peals of thunder and a severe earthquake. No earthquake like it has ever occurred since man has been on earth, so tremendous was the quake. [19]The great city split into three parts, and the cities of the nations collapsed. God remembered Babylon the Great and gave her the cup filled with the wine of the fury of his wrath. [20]Every island fled away and the mountains could not be found. [21]From the sky huge hailstones of about a hundred pounds each fell upon men. And they cursed God on account of the plague of hail, because the plague was so terrible.

The Woman on the Beast

17 One of the seven angels who had the seven bowls came and said to me, "Come, I will show you the punishment of the great prostitute, who sits on many waters. [2]With her the kings of the earth committed adultery and the inhabitants of the earth were intoxicated with the wine of her adulteries."

[3]Then the angel carried me away in the Spirit into a desert. There I saw a woman sitting on a scarlet beast that was covered with blasphemous names and had seven heads and ten horns. [4]The woman was dressed in purple and scarlet, and was glittering with gold, precious stones and pearls. She held a golden cup in her hand, filled with abominable things and the filth of her adulteries. [5]This title was written on her forehead:

MYSTERY
BABYLON THE GREAT
THE MOTHER OF PROSTITUTES
AND OF THE ABOMINATIONS OF THE EARTH.

[6]I saw that the woman was drunk with the blood of the saints, the blood of those who bore testimony to Jesus.

When I saw her, I was greatly astonished. [7]Then the angel said to me: "Why are you astonished? I will explain to you the mystery of the woman and of the beast she rides, which has the seven heads and ten horns. [8]The beast, which you saw, once was, now is not, and will come up out of the Abyss and go to his destruction. The inhabitants of the earth whose names have not been written in the book of life from the creation of the world will be astonished when they see the beast, because he once was, now is not, and yet will come.

[9]"This calls for a mind with wisdom. The seven heads are seven hills on which the woman sits. [10]They are also seven kings. Five have fallen, one is, the other has not yet come; but when he does come, he must remain for a little while. [11]The beast who once was, and now is not, is an eighth king. He belongs to the seven and is going to his destruction.

[12]"The ten horns you saw are ten kings who have not yet received a kingdom, but who for one hour will receive authority as kings along with the beast. [13]They have one purpose and will give their power and authority to the beast. [14]They will make war against the Lamb, but the Lamb will overcome them because he is Lord of lords and King of kings—and with him will be his called, chosen and faithful followers."

> 66 The fewer the words, the better the prayer. 99
>
> MARTIN LUTHER

[15]Then the angel said to me, "The waters you saw, where the prostitute sits, are peoples, multitudes, nations and languages. [16]The beast and the ten horns you saw will hate the prostitute. They will bring her to ruin and leave her naked; they will eat her flesh and burn her with fire. [17]For God has put it into their hearts to accomplish his purpose by agreeing to give the beast their power to rule, until God's words are fulfilled. [18]The woman you saw is the great city that rules over the kings of the earth."

The Fall of Babylon

18 After this I saw another angel coming down from heaven. He had great authority, and the earth was illuminated by his splendor. [2]With a mighty voice he shouted:

"Fallen! Fallen is Babylon the Great!
    She has become a home for
        demons

and a haunt for every evil[a] spirit,
a haunt for every unclean and
detestable bird.
³For all the nations have drunk
the maddening wine of her
adulteries.
The kings of the earth committed
adultery with her,
and the merchants of the earth
grew rich from her excessive
luxuries."

⁴Then I heard another voice from heaven say:

"Come out of her, my people,
so that you will not share in her
sins,
so that you will not receive any of
her plagues;
⁵for her sins are piled up to heaven,
and God has remembered her
crimes.
⁶Give back to her as she has given;
pay her back double for what she
has done.
Mix her a double portion from her
own cup.
⁷Give her as much torture and grief
as the glory and luxury she gave
herself.
In her heart she boasts,
'I sit as queen; I am not a widow,
and I will never mourn.'
⁸Therefore in one day her plagues will
overtake her:
death, mourning and famine.
She will be consumed by fire,
for mighty is the Lord God who
judges her.

⁹"When the kings of the earth who committed adultery with her and shared her luxury see the smoke of her burning, they will weep and mourn over her. ¹⁰Terrified at her torment, they will stand far off and cry:

"'Woe! Woe, O great city,
O Babylon, city of power!
In one hour your doom has come!'

¹¹"The merchants of the earth will weep and mourn over her because no one buys their cargoes any more— ¹²cargoes of gold, silver, precious stones and pearls; fine linen, purple, silk and scarlet cloth; every sort of citron wood, and articles of every kind made of ivory, costly wood, bronze, iron and marble; ¹³cargoes of cinnamon and spice, of incense, myrrh and frankincense, of wine and olive oil, of fine flour and wheat; cattle and sheep; horses and carriages; and bodies and souls of men.

¹⁴"They will say, 'The fruit you longed for is gone from you. All your riches and splendor have vanished, never to be recovered.' ¹⁵The merchants who sold these things and gained their wealth from her will stand far off, terrified at her torment. They will weep and mourn ¹⁶and cry out:

"'Woe! Woe, O great city,
dressed in fine linen, purple and
scarlet,
and glittering with gold, precious
stones and pearls!
¹⁷In one hour such great wealth has
been brought to ruin!'

"Every sea captain, and all who travel by ship, the sailors, and all who earn their living from the sea, will stand far off. ¹⁸When they see the smoke of her burning, they will exclaim, 'Was there ever a city like this great city?' ¹⁹They will throw dust on their heads, and with weeping and mourning cry out:

"'Woe! Woe, O great city,
where all who had ships on the
sea
became rich through her wealth!
In one hour she has been brought
to ruin!
²⁰Rejoice over her, O heaven!
Rejoice, saints and apostles and
prophets!
God has judged her for the way she
treated you.'"

²¹Then a mighty angel picked up a boulder the size of a large millstone and threw it into the sea, and said:

"With such violence
the great city of Babylon will be
thrown down,
never to be found again.
²²The music of harpists and musicians,
flute players and trumpeters,
will never be heard in you again.

---

[a]2 Greek unclean

No workman of any trade
will ever be found in you again.
The sound of a millstone
will never be heard in you again.
23 The light of a lamp
will never shine in you again.
The voice of bridegroom and bride
will never be heard in you again.
Your merchants were the world's
great men.
By your magic spell all the nations
were led astray.
24 In her was found the blood of
prophets and of the saints,
and of all who have been killed on
the earth."

> The trouble with our praying is we
> just do it as a means of last resort.
>
> WILL ROGERS

Hallelujah!

19 After this I heard what sounded
like the roar of a great multitude in
heaven shouting:

"Hallelujah!
Salvation and glory and power
belong to our God,
2   for true and just are his judgments.
He has condemned the great
prostitute
who corrupted the earth by her
adulteries.
He has avenged on her the blood of
his servants."

3 And again they shouted:

"Hallelujah!
The smoke from her goes up for ever
and ever."

4 The twenty-four elders and the four
living creatures fell down and worshiped
God, who was seated on the throne. And
they cried:

"Amen, Hallelujah!"

5 Then a voice came from the throne,
saying:

"Praise our God,
all you his servants,
you who fear him,
both small and great!"

> THE twenty-four elders and the four
> living creatures fell down and worshiped
> God, who was seated on the throne. And
> they cried:
>
> "Amen, Hallelujah!"
>
> REVELATION 19:4

6 Then I heard what sounded like a great
multitude, like the roar of rushing waters
and like loud peals of thunder, shouting:

"Hallelujah!
For our Lord God Almighty reigns.
7 Let us rejoice and be glad
and give him glory!
For the wedding of the Lamb has
come,
and his bride has made herself
ready.
8 Fine linen, bright and clean,
was given her to wear."

(Fine linen stands for the righteous acts
of the saints.)

9 Then the angel said to me, "Write:
'Blessed are those who are invited to
the wedding supper of the Lamb!' " And
he added, "These are the true words of
God."

10 At this I fell at his feet to worship him.
But he said to me, "Do not do it! I am a
fellow servant with you and with your
brothers who hold to the testimony of
Jesus. Worship God! For the testimony of
Jesus is the spirit of prophecy."

The Rider on the White Horse

11 I saw heaven standing open and
there before me was a white horse,
whose rider is called Faithful and True.
With justice he judges and makes war.
12 His eyes are like blazing fire, and on his
head are many crowns. He has a name
written on him that no one knows but he
himself. 13 He is dressed in a robe dipped
in blood, and his name is the Word of
God. 14 The armies of heaven were following him, riding on white horses and
dressed in fine linen, white and clean.
15 Out of his mouth comes a sharp sword
with which to strike down the nations.
"He will rule them with an iron scepter."[a]

a 15 Psalm 2:9

He treads the winepress of the fury of the wrath of God Almighty. ¹⁶On his robe and on his thigh he has this name written:

KING OF KINGS AND LORD OF LORDS.

¹⁷And I saw an angel standing in the sun, who cried in a loud voice to all the birds flying in midair, "Come, gather together for the great supper of God, ¹⁸so that you may eat the flesh of kings, generals, and mighty men, of horses and their riders, and the flesh of all people, free and slave, small and great."

¹⁹Then I saw the beast and the kings of the earth and their armies gathered together to make war against the rider on the horse and his army. ²⁰But the beast was captured, and with him the false prophet who had performed the miraculous signs on his behalf. With these signs he had deluded those who had received the mark of the beast and worshiped his image. The two of them were thrown alive into the fiery lake of burning sulfur. ²¹The rest of them were killed with the sword that came out of the mouth of the rider on the horse, and all the birds gorged themselves on their flesh.

The Thousand Years

20 And I saw an angel coming down out of heaven, having the key to the Abyss and holding in his hand a great chain. ²He seized the dragon, that ancient serpent, who is the devil, or Satan, and bound him for a thousand years. ³He threw him into the Abyss, and locked and sealed it over him, to keep him from deceiving the nations anymore until the thousand years were ended. After that, he must be set free for a short time.

⁴I saw thrones on which were seated those who had been given authority to judge. And I saw the souls of those who had been beheaded because of their testimony for Jesus and because of the word of God. They had not worshiped the beast or his image and had not received his mark on their foreheads or their hands. They came to life and reigned with Christ a thousand years. ⁵(The rest of the dead did not come to life until the thousand years were ended.) This is the first resurrection. ⁶Blessed and holy are those who have part in the first resurrec-

tion. The second death has no power over them, but they will be priests of God and of Christ and will reign with him for a thousand years.

Satan's Doom

⁷When the thousand years are over, Satan will be released from his prison ⁸and will go out to deceive the nations in the four corners of the earth—Gog and Magog—to gather them for battle. In number they are like the sand on the seashore. ⁹They marched across the breadth of the earth and surrounded the camp of God's people, the city he loves. But fire came down from heaven and devoured them. ¹⁰And the devil, who deceived them, was thrown into the lake of burning sulfur, where the beast and the false prophet had been thrown. They will be tormented day and night for ever and ever.

The Dead Are Judged

¹¹Then I saw a great white throne and him who was seated on it. Earth and sky fled from his presence, and there was no place for them. ¹²And I saw the dead, great and small, standing before the throne, and books were opened. Another book was opened, which is the book of life. The dead were judged according to what they had done as recorded in the books. ¹³The sea gave up the dead that were in it, and death and Hades gave up the dead that were in them, and each person was judged according to what he had done. ¹⁴Then death and Hades were thrown into the lake of fire. The lake of fire is the second death. ¹⁵If anyone's name was not found written in the book of life, he was thrown into the lake of fire.

The New Jerusalem

21 Then I saw a new heaven and a new earth, for the first heaven and the first earth had passed away, and there was no longer any sea. ²I saw the Holy City, the new Jerusalem, coming down out of heaven from God, prepared as a bride beautifully dressed for her husband. ³And I heard a loud voice from the throne saying, "Now the dwelling of God is with men, and he will live with them. They will be his people, and God himself

will be with them and be their God. [4]He will wipe every tear from their eyes. There will be no more death or mourning or crying or pain, for the old order of things has passed away."

> "*HE will wipe every tear from their eyes. There will be no more death or mourning or crying or pain, for the old order of things has passed away.*"
>
> REVELATION 21:4

[5]He who was seated on the throne said, "I am making everything new!" Then he said, "Write this down, for these words are trustworthy and true."

[6]He said to me: "It is done. I am the Alpha and the Omega, the Beginning and the End. To him who is thirsty I will give to drink without cost from the spring of the water of life. [7]He who overcomes will inherit all this, and I will be his God and he will be my son. [8]But the cowardly, the unbelieving, the vile, the murderers, the sexually immoral, those who practice magic arts, the idolaters and all liars—their place will be in the fiery lake of burning sulfur. This is the second death."

[9]One of the seven angels who had the seven bowls full of the seven last plagues came and said to me, "Come, I will show you the bride, the wife of the Lamb." [10]And he carried me away in the Spirit to a mountain great and high, and showed me the Holy City, Jerusalem, coming down out of heaven from God. [11]It shone with the glory of God, and its brilliance was like that of a very precious jewel, like a jasper, clear as crystal. [12]It had a great, high wall with twelve gates, and with twelve angels at the gates. On the gates were written the names of the twelve tribes of Israel. [13]There were three gates on the east, three on the north, three on the south and three on the west. [14]The wall of the city had twelve foundations, and on them were the names of the twelve apostles of the Lamb.

[15]The angel who talked with me had a measuring rod of gold to measure the city, its gates and its walls. [16]The city was laid out like a square, as long as it was wide. He measured the city with the rod and found it to be 12,000 stadia[a] in length, and as wide and high as it is long. [17]He measured its wall and it was 144 cubits[b] thick,[c] by man's measurement, which the angel was using. [18]The wall was made of jasper, and the city of pure gold, as pure as glass. [19]The foundations of the city walls were decorated with every kind of precious stone. The first foundation was jasper, the second sapphire, the third chalcedony, the fourth emerald, [20]the fifth sardonyx, the sixth carnelian, the seventh chrysolite, the eighth beryl, the ninth topaz, the tenth chrysoprase, the eleventh jacinth, and the twelfth amethyst.[d] [21]The twelve gates were twelve pearls, each gate made of a single pearl. The great street of the city was of pure gold, like transparent glass.

[22]I did not see a temple in the city, because the Lord God Almighty and the Lamb are its temple. [23]The city does not need the sun or the moon to shine on it, for the glory of God gives it light, and the Lamb is its lamp. [24]The nations will walk by its light, and the kings of the earth will bring their splendor into it. [25]On no day will its gates ever be shut, for there will be no night there. [26]The glory and honor of the nations will be brought into it. [27]Nothing impure will ever enter it, nor will anyone who does what is shameful or deceitful, but only those whose names are written in the Lamb's book of life.

The River of Life

22 Then the angel showed me the river of the water of life, as clear as crystal, flowing from the throne of God and of the Lamb [2]down the middle of the great street of the city. On each side of the river stood the tree of life, bearing twelve crops of fruit, yielding its fruit every month. And the leaves of the tree are for the healing of the nations. [3]No longer will there be any curse. The throne of God and of the Lamb will be in the city, and his servants will serve him. [4]They will see his face, and his name will be on their foreheads. [5]There will be no more night. They will not need the light of a

---

[a]16 That is, about 1,400 miles (about 2,200 kilometers) [b]17 That is, about 200 feet (about 65 meters) [c]17 Or *high* [d]20 The precise identification of some of these precious stones is uncertain.

REVELATION 22:7 – 21

Maranatha!

22:17 WHOEVER IS THIRSTY, LET HIM COME.

The first and last words of the Bible are of grace. At the end of the Bible, the words come in the form of a benediction: "The grace of the Lord Jesus be with God's people. Amen" (22:21). In the beginning of the Bible, the words weren't actual words; they were an awesome *act* of grace. Freely and sovereignly, entirely on his own initiative, God spoke the universe into existence. No one made him do it; no one asked him to do it; he did it simply because it was his gracious pleasure. It pleased him to create in the same way it later pleased him to save—freely, by grace.

The first and last words of the Bible are of blessing: "Whoever is thirsty, let him come; and whoever wishes, let him take the free gift of the water of life" (verse 17). In the beginning, God was delighting in everything he made, pronouncing it all very good and blessing humankind with the command to be fruitful (see Genesis 1:28,31). Why did God bless? Why does he bless? Not because he must, for he is free, but because it is who he is. It pleases him.

Between the first and last words of the Bible is the story of the Bible. On one hand there is the human debacle: our irrational and inexplicable refusal to be graced and blessed. But on the other hand there remains the divine freedom to grace and bless: God's dogged determination to say "Nevertheless" to our sin. So the Bible ends with another promise and appeal: Three times Jesus says, "I am coming soon" (Revelation 22:7,12,20). In between, an open invitation is given to the world: "Whoever is thirsty, let him come" (verse 17). The message is, "I am coming. Will you come, too? Everything depends on it—life or death, heaven or hell."

What is there left for us to do but pray, "Amen. Come, Lord Jesus" (verse 20)? The early church made this prayer a standard call to worship with an Aramaic word that has found its way into our vocabulary: "Maranatha!" When it was prayed, the church sincerely believed the prayer would be answered and Jesus would come, if not physically, then spiritually. Will you pray it now—with the church throughout the ages, one more time or for the first time? "Amen. Maranatha!" He will come because he is coming.

PRAY:

Amen. Come, Lord Jesus. We are thirsty;
we crave the water of life. So come and save us
and gather us to yourself, in the name of the Father
and the Son and the Holy Spirit.

———

FOR YOUR NEXT DEVOTIONAL READING, GO TO PAGE 1600.

WILLIAM CAREY AND ROBERT MORRISON
Plodding Tenacity

JESUS ONCE told a parable for the express purpose of encouraging his disciples to "always pray and not give up" (see Luke 18:1–8). Two faithful men, whose missionary careers spanned the late 18th and early 19th centuries, had those words of Jesus embedded in their spiritual DNA.

William Carey was born in England in 1761, and from his boyhood he wanted nothing more than to be a professional gardener. However, a skin disease foiled his plans. He had to stay out of the sun, so he took an apprenticeship with a local shoemaker. But Carey's love of plants and gardening sensitized him to a crucial dimension of ministry and prayer: It takes time and patience to plant and cultivate until the harvest comes.

When Carey announced that he wanted to be a missionary, his father tried to dissuade him from his calling. He harshly attacked the boy's self-esteem and listed his deficiencies, intellectually and emotionally. Carey's humble response was, "But I can plod." And so he sailed to India.

Robert Morrison was born into an agricultural family in Scotland 19 years after Carey was born. He was considered an average student but a very hard worker. After his conversion at age 15, Morrison set up his bed in a corner of his father's workshop so he could pray and study his Bible through the night. When he discovered that he had a gift in languages, he decided to become a missionary. His invalid mother was heartbroken and begged him to stay home. After her death a year later, he joined the London Missionary Society and sailed to China as the first Protestant missionary to that nation.

Thus Carey the horticulturalist and Morrison the agriculturalist offered their gifts for plodding tenacity to the service of the kingdom of God. In

India, Carey set about translating the Bible into as many languages as he had energy for. In 1812, a fire swept through the printing building and destroyed his entire library—all his dictionaries and lexicons, along with 10 translations of the Bible, a completed Sanskrit dictionary and all his printing presses. Shocked and dismayed, Carey wept, but said, "The Lord has laid me low, that I may look simply to him ... The loss is heavy, but as traveling a road the second time is usually done with greater ease than the first time ... We are not discouraged; indeed the work is already begun in every language. We are cast down but not in despair."[3]

Morrison labored in China for seven years before baptizing his first convert. Only a dozen Chinese came to Christ over the next eighteen years. When Morrison died, there was little to show for a lifetime of service. But he paved the way for missionaries like James Hudson Taylor and the China Inland Mission. Today the believers in China number in the hundreds of millions.

Carey and Morrison were living illustrations that the work of the kingdom is like farming and gardening; some plant, some water and some harvest—but it is God who makes everything grow (see 1 Corinthians 3:5–9). Our responsibility is always to persevere in faithfulness.

PRAY:

Father, forgive me for how easily I am discouraged.
Strengthen me by your Spirit to be patient with you and your eternal
purposes, and to not lose heart in prayer and service.

MEMORIZE:

"And will not God bring about justice for his chosen ones,
who cry out to him day and night? Will he keep putting them off?
I tell you, he will see that they get justice, and quickly." LUKE 18:7–8

lamp or the light of the sun, for the Lord God will give them light. And they will reign for ever and ever.

⁶The angel said to me, "These words are trustworthy and true. The Lord, the God of the spirits of the prophets, sent his angel to show his servants the things that must soon take place."

Jesus Is Coming

⁷"Behold, I am coming soon! Blessed is he who keeps the words of the prophecy in this book."

⁸I, John, am the one who heard and saw these things. And when I had heard and seen them, I fell down to worship at the feet of the angel who had been showing them to me. ⁹But he said to me, "Do not do it! I am a fellow servant with you and with your brothers the prophets and of all who keep the words of this book. Worship God!"

¹⁰Then he told me, "Do not seal up the words of the prophecy of this book, because the time is near. ¹¹Let him who does wrong continue to do wrong; let him who is vile continue to be vile; let him who does right continue to do right; and let him who is holy continue to be holy."

¹²"Behold, I am coming soon! My reward is with me, and I will give to everyone according to what he has done. ¹³I am the Alpha and the Omega, the First and the Last, the Beginning and the End.

¹⁴"Blessed are those who wash their robes, that they may have the right to the tree of life and may go through the gates

> *Sincere prayer is the heart of a happy and productive life. Prayer strengthens faith. Prayer is the preparation for miracles.*
>
> H. BURKE PETERSON

into the city. ¹⁵Outside are the dogs, those who practice magic arts, the sexually immoral, the murderers, the idolaters and everyone who loves and practices falsehood.

¹⁶"I, Jesus, have sent my angel to give you[a] this testimony for the churches. I am the Root and the Offspring of David, and the bright Morning Star."

¹⁷The Spirit and the bride say, "Come!" And let him who hears say, "Come!" Whoever is thirsty, let him come; and whoever wishes, let him take the free gift of the water of life.

¹⁸I warn everyone who hears the words of the prophecy of this book: If anyone adds anything to them, God will add to him the plagues described in this book. ¹⁹And if anyone takes words away from this book of prophecy, God will take away from him his share in the tree of life and in the holy city, which are described in this book.

²⁰He who testifies to these things says, "Yes, I am coming soon."

Amen. Come, Lord Jesus.

²¹The grace of the Lord Jesus be with God's people. Amen.

---

[a]16 The Greek is plural.

Table of Weights and Measures

	BIBLICAL UNIT	APPROXIMATE AMERICAN EQUIVALENT	APPROXIMATE METRIC EQUIVALENT
Weights	talent (60 minas)	75 pounds	34 kilograms
	mina (50 shekels)	1¼ pounds	0.6 kilogram
	shekel (2 bekas)	⅖ ounce	11.5 grams
	pim (⅔ shekel)	⅓ ounce	7.6 grams
	beka (10 gerahs)	⅕ ounce	5.5 grams
	gerah	⅟₅₀ ounce	0.6 gram
Length	cubit	18 inches	0.5 meter
	span	9 inches	23 centimeters
	handbreadth	3 inches	8 centimeters
Capacity	DRY MEASURE		
	cor [homer] (10 ephahs)	6 bushels	220 liters
	lethek (5 ephahs)	3 bushels	110 liters
	ephah (10 omers)	⅗ bushel	22 liters
	seah (⅓ ephah)	7 quarts	7.3 liters
	omer (⅟₁₀ ephah)	2 quarts	2 liters
	cab (⅟₁₈ ephah)	1 quart	1 liter
	LIQUID MEASURE		
	bath (1 ephah)	6 gallons	22 liters
	hin (⅙ bath)	4 quarts	4 liters
	log (⅟₇₂ bath)	⅓ quart	0.3 liter

The figures of the table are calculated on the basis of a shekel equaling 11.5 grams, a cubit equaling 18 inches and an ephah equaling 22 liters. The quart referred to is either a dry quart (slightly larger than a liter) or a liquid quart (slightly smaller than a liter), whichever is applicable. The ton referred to in the footnotes is the American ton of 2,000 pounds.

This table is based upon the best available information, but it is not intended to be mathematically precise; like the measurement equivalents in the footnotes, it merely gives approximate amounts and distances. Weights and measures differed somewhat at various times and places in the ancient world. There is uncertainty particularly about the ephah and the bath; further discoveries may shed more light on these units of capacity.

Topical Index

Index of Names

Prayers of the Bible

Prayers of the Old Testament

Abraham's prayer for Sodom	Genesis 18:22–33
Abraham's servant prays for guidance	Genesis 24:12–14
Isaac's blessing	Genesis 27
Jacob's vow at Bethel	Genesis 28
Jacob's desperate prayer at Peniel	Genesis 32
Jacob blesses his sons	Genesis 48—49
Moses' song of thanksgiving for deliverance from Egypt	Exodus 15
Moses' plea for Israel when they had worshiped the golden calf	Exodus 32; Deuteronomy 9
Moses asks to see God's glory	Exodus 33
Aaron's blessing	Numbers 6
Moses pleads with God to forgive his rebellious people	Numbers 14
Balaam, on God's instruction, blesses Israel	Numbers 22—24
Moses' song. God and his people	Deuteronomy 32
Moses blesses the people of Israel	Deuteronomy 33
Joshua's prayer after defeat at Ai	Joshua 7
Joshua prays for time to complete his victory	Joshua 10
Deborah's song of thanksgiving for victory	Judges 5

Prayers of the Old Testament (CONTINUED)

Gideon's prayer for signs	Judges 6
Hannah's prayer for a son her thanksgiving	1 Samuel 1; 1 Samuel 2
Samuel's prayer for the nation	1 Samuel 7
David's prayer following God's promise of a lasting succession	2 Samuel 7; 1 Chronicles 17
David's song of thanksgiving for deliverance	2 Samuel 22; Psalm 18
Solomon's prayer for wisdom	1 Kings 3; 2 Chronicles 1
Solomon's prayer at the dedication of the temple	1 Kings 8; 2 Chronicles 6
Elijah's prayer on Mt Carmel	1 Kings 18
Elijah and the gentle voice	1 Kings 19
Hezekiah's prayer at the time of Sennacherib's siege	2 Kings 19; Isaiah 37
Thanksgiving as the covenant box is brought to Jerusalem	1 Chronicles 16
David's prayer for Solomon	2 Chronicles 29
Ezra's confession of the nation's sin	Ezra 9
Nehemiah's prayer for his people	Nehemiah 1
The public confession led by Ezra	Nehemiah 9
Job seeks the reason for his suffering	Job 10
Job pleads his case	Job 13—14
Job's confession	Job 42

Some Prayers from the Psalms

Evening prayer	Psalm 4
Morning prayer	Psalm 5
The shepherd psalm	Psalm 23
Praise and worship	Psalm 24; 67; 92; 95—98; 100; 113; 145; 148; 150
Guidance	Psalm 25
Trust	Psalm 37; 62
Deliverance	Psalm 40; 116
Longing for God	Psalm 27; 42; 63; 84
Forgiveness	Psalm 51; 130
Thanksgiving	Psalm 65; 111; 136
Help in trouble	Psalm 66; 69; 86; 88; 102; 140; 143
God's constant love and care	Psalm 89; 103; 107; 146
God's majesty and glory	Psalm 8; 29; 93; 104
God's knowledge and presence	Psalm 139
God's word	Psalm 19; 119
God's protection	Psalm 46; 91; 125

Prayers from the Prophets

Prayers of Isaiah	Isaiah 25; 33; 63—64
Hezekiah's prayer in his illness	Isaiah 38
Jeremiah's prayers	Jeremiah 11; 14; 20; 32
Laments for the fall of Jerusalem	Lamentations 1—4
Prayer for restoration	Lamentations 5
The king's dream; Daniel's prayer	Daniel 2
Nebuchadnezzar praises God	Daniel 4
Daniel's prayer at the end of the exile	Daniel 9
Jonah's prayer	Jonah 2
Habakkuk questions God	Habakkuk 1
Habakkuk's prayer	Habakkuk 3

Prayers of Jesus

The Lord's Prayer	Matthew 6:9–13; Luke 11:2–4
Praise that God reveals himself to simple people	Matthew 11:25–26; Luke 10:21
In the garden of Gethsemane	Matthew 26:36–44; Mark 14:32–39; Luke 22:46
From the cross	Matthew 27:46; Mark 15:34; Luke 23:34,46
At the raising of Lazarus	John 11:41–42
Facing death	John 12:27–28
For his followers	John 17

Prayers of the New Testament

Mary's thanksgiving	Luke 1:46–55
Zechariah's prayer	Luke 1:68–79
Simeon's prayer	Luke 2:29–35
Prayers of the Pharisee and the tax collector	Luke 18:10–13
The church's prayer in the face of threats	Acts 4:24–30
Stephen's prayer at his death	Acts 7:59–60
Peter's thanksgiving	1 Peter 1:3–5
John's prayer for Gaius	3 John 1:2

Prayers of Paul

For the Christians at Rome	Romans 1:8–10
For Israel	Romans 10:1
For the church at Corinth	I Corinthians 1:4–9; 2 Corinthians 13:7–9
Thanksgiving for God's comfort in trouble	2 Corinthians 1:3–4
Thanksgiving for spiritual riches in Christ	Ephesians 1:8–14
For the Ephesian Christians	Ephesians 1:16–23; 3:14–19
For the Philippian Christians	Philippians 1:8–11
For the church at Colossae	Colossians 1:3–14
For the Thessalonian Christians	1 Thessalonians 1:2–3; 2:13; 3:9–13; 5:23; 2 Thessalonians 1:3; 2:13,16–17; 3:16
For Timothy	2 Timothy 1:3–4
For Philemon	Philemon 1:4–6

Prayers of Praise to God (DOXOLOGIES) **and Prayers for Blessing** (BENEDICTIONS)

Romans 16:25–27	Hebrews 13:20–21
Ephesians 3:20–211	Peter 5:10–11
Philippians 4:20	2 Peter 3:18
1 Thessalonians 3:11–13	Jude 1:24–25

Notes

Welcome
1. Bingham Hunter, *The God Who Hears* (Downers Grove, IL: InterVarsity Press, 1986), 12.
2. Charles Spurgeon, *Spurgeon's Expository Encyclopedia*, vol. 4 (Grand Rapids, MI: Baker Book House, 1978), 329.
3. P. T. Forsyth, *The Soul of Prayer* (London: Independent Press Ltd., 1954), 14.
4. Source unknown.

Genesis
1. Frederick Buechner, *Wishful Thinking* (New York: Harper and Row Publishers, 1973), 88.
2. Luci Shaw, "The Foolishness of God," from *A Widening Light*, ed. Luci Shaw (Wheaton, IL: Harold Shaw, 1984), 134.
3. P. T. Forsyth, *The Soul of Prayer* (London: Independent Press, Ltd., 1954), 92.
4. Karl Barth, *Church Dogmatics 3:4*, ed. G. W. Bromiley and T. F. Torrance (Edinburgh: T & T Clark, 1978), 615.
5. *The Heidelberg Catechism* (Grand Rapids, MI: CRC Publications, 1988), questions 27 and 28.

Exodus
1. The question mark, exclamation point metaphor comes from Old Testament scholar, Tremper Longman.
2. Told by Peter Kreeft in *Three Philosophies of Life* (San Francisco: Ignatius Press, 1989), 94–95.

Leviticus
1. John Newton, "Approach, My Soul, the Mercy Seat," *Hymns II* (Downers Grove, IL: InterVarsity Press, 1976), 141.

Numbers
1. "Confessions, VII, XXI," quoted by C. S. Lewis in *Surprised by Joy* (New York: Harcourt, Brace and World, 1955), 230.
2. Robert Robinson, "Come, Thou Fount of Every Blessing," *The Hymnal for Worship and Celebration* (Waco, TX: Word Inc., 1986), 2.
3. Owen Collins, ed. *2000 Years of Classic Christian Prayers* (Maryknoll, NY: Orbis Books, 1999), 185–186.

Deuteronomy
1. *The Heidelberg Catechism* (Grand Rapids, MI: CRC Publications, 1988), questions 2 and 116.
2. Daniel Iverson, "O Spirit Divine" (Birdwing Music & BMG, 1935, 1965).

Joshua
1. Betty and Lewis Drummond, *Women of Awakenings: The Historic Contribution of Women to Revival Movements* (Grand Rapids, MI: Kregel Publications, 1997), 69–70.
2. Richard Foster and James Bryan Smith, eds. *Devotional Classics* (San Francisco: Harper Collins, 1993), 323.
3. Drummond, 77.

Judges
1. Earle Cairns, *An Endless Line of Splendor* (Wheaton, IL: Tyndale House Publishers, 1986), 19.
2. John White, *The Fight* (Downers Grove, IL: InterVarsity Press, 1976), 165–167.
3. Elisabeth Elliot, *Shadow of the Almighty* (New York: Harper and Brothers, 1958), 53, 247–249.

Ruth
1. Virginia Stem Owens, "Prayer—Into the Lion's Jaws," *Christianity Today* (November 1976): 17–21.

1 Samuel
1. C. S. Lewis, *Surprised by Joy* (New York: Harcourt, Brace and World, Inc., 1955), 229.
2. From a summary of the essay, "Work and Prayer," from *God in the Dock* (Grand Rapids, MI: William B. Eerdmans, 1970), 104–107.

2 Samuel
1. Annie Dillard, *Pilgrim at Tinker Creek* (New York: Harper's Magazine Press, 1974), 11–12
2. "The Elixir," George Herbert, *The Complete English Works*, Ann Pasternak Slater, ed. (London: Everyman's Library, David Campbell Publishers, Ltd., 1974), 180.
3. C. S. Lewis, *Mere Christianity* (New York: Macmillan Publishing Company, 1960), 94,96.
4. Ibid., 96–97.

1 Kings
1. *The Prayers of Susanna Wesley*, edited and arranged by W. L. Doughty (Grand Rapids, MI: Clarion Classics, Zondervan Publishing House, 1984), x.
2. Ibid., vii.
3. Betty and Lewis Drummond, *Women of Awakenings: The Historic Contribution of Women to Revival Movements* (Grand Rapids, MI: Kregel Publications, 1997), 80.
4. Doughty, *Prayers* 17.
5. C. S. Lewis, *The Weight of Glory* (New York: The Macmillan Company, 1965), 2.

2 Kings
1. Basil Mitchell, *George Mueller, Man of Faith* (Minneapolis: Bethany House, 1972), 9.
2. Ibid., 11.
3. Ibid., 3.

1 Chronicles
1. *The Trees Clap Their Hands*, quoted in *Disciplines for the Inner Life*, by Bob Benson and Michael W. Benson (Waco, TX: Word, Incorporated, 1985), 334.
2. "Gratefulness," George Herbert, *The Complete English Works*, Ann Pasternak Slater, ed. (London: Everyman's Library, David Campbell Publishers, Ltd, 1974), 120.

2 Chronicles
1. Norman Grubb, *Rees Howells, Intercessor* (Fort Washington, PN: Christian Literataure Crusade), 41.
2. Ibid., 256.
3. Ibid., 255.

Nehemiah
1. John Donne, "Meditation XVII," in *John Donne, Selections from Divine Poems, Sermons, Devotions and Prayers*, John Booty, ed., *Classics of Western Spirituality* (New York: Paulist Press, 1990), 270.
2. Simone Weil, "Reflections on the Right Use of School Studies with a View to the Love of God," quoted in *A Passion for Learning*, ed. Bruce Lockerbie (Chicago: Moody Press, 1994), 388.
3. Ibid., 387.

Esther
1. See the chapter on Esther in *An Introduction to the Old Testament*, Raymond B. Dillard and Tremper Longman III (Grand Rapids, MI: Zondervan Publishing House, 1994), 189–198.
2. See devotion on Genesis 1:1–31.

Job
1. Søren Kierkegaard, *Edifying Discourses* (London: Collins Publishers, 1958), 78–80.
2. Eusebius, "History of the Church IV 15," quoted in *Eerdman's Handbook to the History of Christianity*, ed. Tim Dowley (Grand Rapids, MI: Eerdmans, 1977), 81.
3. Karl Barth, *Church Dogmatics vol. 3/4*, ed. G.W. Bromiley and T. F. Torrance (Edinburgh: T & T Clark, 1978), 615.
4. Eusebuis, 81.

Psalms
1. Quoted by Phillip E. Howard in his introduction to *The Life and Diary of David Brainerd*, Jonathan Edwards, ed. (Grand Rapids, MI: Baker Book House, 1989), 14.
2. E. Michael and Sharon Rusten, *The One Year Book of Christian History* (Wheaton, IL: Tyndale, 2003), 154.
3. John Cowart, *People Whose Faith Got Them in Trouble* (Downers Grove, IL: InterVarsity Press, 1990), 63.
4. Ibid.
5. Owen Collins, ed., *2000 Years of Classic Christian Prayers* (Maryknoll, NY: Orbis Press, 1999), 193.
6. *The Poems of George Herbert*, Ann Pasternak Slater, ed. (London: Everyman's Library, David Campbell Publishers, Ltd, 1974), 156.
7. Frederick Buechner, *Wishful Thinking* (New York: Harper and Row Publishers, 1973), 2.
8. Alexander Maclaren, *Expositions of Holy Scripture*, *Psalm 73* (Grand Rapids, MI: Baker Book House, 1977), 104.
9. "Providence," *George Herbert, The Complete English Works*, Ann Pasternak Slater, ed. (London: Random House, Everyman's Library, 1974), 113.
10. Saint Augustine, *The Confessions*, translated by R. S. Pine-Coffin (New York: Penguin Books, 1961), 69–70.
11. From the Gelasian Sacramentary, based on a prayer by Augustine, quoted in *2000 Years of Classic Christian Prayers*, Owen Collins, ed. (Maryknoll, NY: Orbis Books, 1999), 27.
12. Frederick M. Lehman, "The Love of God" in *Songs That Are Different*, vol. 2, (1919).
13. The themes in the following list are taken from Eugene Peterson's *A Long Obedience in the Same Direction* (Downers Grove, IL: InterVarsity Press, 1980).
14. Saint Augustine, *The Confessions*, translated by R. S. Pine-Coffin (New York: Penguin Books, 1961), 100–101.

Proverbs
1. Blaise Pascal, *Penseés*, translated by A. J. Krailsheimer (New York: Penguin Books, 1966), nos. 434, 133.
2. Robert O. Bakke, *The Power of Extraordinary Prayer* (Wheaton, IL: Crossway Books, 2000), 76.

Ecclesiastes
1. Quoted in Robert Raines, *Creative Brooding* (London: The Macmillan Company, 1969), 76.
2. Quoted in Ben Patterson, *Deepening Your Conversation with God* (Minneapolis, MN: Bethany House, 1999), 20.
3. Andrew Murray, *With Christ in the School of Prayer* (New Kensington, PA: Whitaker House, 1981), 236.

4. Peter Kreeft, *Love Is Stronger Than Death* (San Francisco: Harper and Row, 1979), 104–105.
5. J. B. Phillips, *The New Testament in Modern English* (London: Geoffrey Bles, 1960), 502.
6. Quoted by Derek Kidner, *The Message of Ecclesiastes* (Downers Grove, IL: InterVarsity Press, 1976), 110.

Songs of Songs
1. David Hubbard, *The Communicator's Commentary, Ecclesiastes, Song of Solomon* (Dallas, TX: Word Books, 1991), 267–270.

Isaiah
1. David Smithers, "Andrew Murray: He Almost Stopped a True Revival!" (http://www.watchword.org/smithers/andrew_murray ww53a.htm).
2. "Andrew Murray: The Apostle of Abiding Love!" (http://www.intouch.org/myintouch/mighty/ortraits/andrew_murray_213652.htm).
3. Andrew Murray, quoted at *Daily Christian Quote* (http://psalm121.ca/quotes/dcqmurray.html).
4. C. S. Lewis, *The Problem of Pain* (New York: Touchstone Books, 1996), 45,41.
5. John Piper, *Let the Nations Be Glad* (Grand Rapids, MI: Baker Book House, 1993),11.
6. Sir Herbert Grierson, ed., *John Donne Poems* (Franklin Center, PA: The Franklin Library, 1982), 356.
7. Mary Geegh, *God Guides* (Wausau, WI: Color Vision Printing, 2000), 2–3.
8. Ibid., 1.
9. A paraphrase of a statement by theologian Donald Bloesch.
10. Blaise Pascal's description of why God lets us act on him in prayer.
11. Clyde E. Fant, Jr. and William M. Pinson, Jr., *Robert Murray McCheyne Twenty Centuries of Great Preaching* (Waco, TX: Word Books, 1971), 262.
12. Iain H. Murray, "Robert Murray McCheyne" (http://web.ukonline.co.uk/d.haslam/mccheyne/ihmurray.htm).
13. "Robert Murray McCheyne, 1813–1843" (http://bsrich.tripod.com/scottish/mccheye.html).

Jeremiah
1. C. S. Lewis, *The Lion, the Witch and the Wardrobe* (New York: The Macmillan Publishing Company, 1950), 64.
2. *Chapters into Verse, Poetry in English Inspired by the Bible*, assembled and edited by Robert Atwan and Laurance Wieder (Oxford: Oxford University Press, 1993), 412.
3. See devotion on Romans 15:30–33
4. Quoted in Donald Bloesch, *The Struggle of Prayer* (New York: Harper and Row, 1960), 93.
5. Ibid., 93.
6. Ibid., 91.
7. Ibid., 90.
8. Quoted in *2000 Years of Classic Christian Prayers*, Owen Collins, ed. (Maryknoll, NY: Orbis Press, 1999), 96.

Lamentations
1. John Bunyan, *Pilgrim's Progress* (http://calvarychapel.com/library/Bunyan_John/PilgrimsProgress/PilgrimsProgress.htm#010), 283–293.

Ezekiel
1. Quoted in Basil Miller, *Mary Slessor* (Minneapolis: Bethany House Publishers, 1974), 130,138.

Daniel
1. Quoted by Ronald Wallace, *The Message of Daniel* (Downers Grove, IL: InterVarsity Press, 1979), 155. This devotion owes much to Wallace's insights.
2. "There are two equal and opposite errors into which our race can fall about the devils. One is to disbelieve in their existence. The other is to

believe, and to feel an excessive and unhealthy interest in them. They themselves are pleased by both errors and hail a materialist or a magician with the same delight." From the preface of *The Screwtape Letters* by C. S. Lewis.

3. Cited by Ronald Wallace, *The Message of Daniel*, 160.

Hosea

1. Quoted by Robert J. Morgan, *On This Day: 365 Amazing and Inspiring Stories About Saints, Martyrs, & Heroes* (Nashville: Thomas Nelson, 1997).

Amos

1. Peter Berger, "Cakes for the Queen of Heaven: 2,500 Years of Religious Ecstasy," *Christian Century* (December 25, 1974): 1217–1223.
2. Brother Lawrence, quoted in *"Brother Lawrence, The Practice of the Presence of God."* http://www.homechurch.com/spirituality/brother_lawrence.html.
3. Quoted by Elliott Wright, *Holy Company* (New York: MacMillan Publishing Co., 1980), 87.
4. Gary Thomas, "Historical Profile: Brother Lawrence," 2000. http://www.garythomas.com/resources/classics/lawrence.html.

Obadiah

1. *Romeo and Juliet* in *The Complete Works of William Shakespeare* by W. G. Clark and W. Aldis Wright, eds. (Garden City, NY: Nelson Doubleday, Inc.), 256.

Nahum

1. Peter Kreeft, *Fundamentals of the Faith* (San Francisco: Ignatius Press, 1988), 194.
2. Elisabeth Elliot, *The Savange My Kinsman* (Ann Arbor, MI: Servant Publications, 1996), 18.
3. Ibid., 12.

Habakkuk

1. Raymond B. Dillard and Tremper Longman III, *An Introduction to the Old Testament* (Grand Rapids, MI: Zondervan, 1994), 409.
2. See devotion on Nahum 1:1–8.

Haggai

1. Quoted by Earl Palmer, *Alive from the Center* (Waco, TX: Word, Incorporated, 1982), 7.
2. Ibid.
3. Andrew Murray, *With Christ in the School of Prayer* (New Kensington, PA: Whitaker House, 1981), 236.

Zechariah

1. Bernard of Clairvaux, "O Sacred Head, Now Wounded." http://www.cyberhymnal.org/htm/o/s/osacredh.htm.

Malachi

1. John Cowart, *People Whose Faith Got Them in Trouble* (Downers Grove, IL: InterVarsity Press, 1990), 33.
2. Ibid., 34.
3. Ibid.
4. Translation taken from Thomas Cahill, *How the Irish Saved Civilization* (New York: Doubleday, 1995), 212.

Matthew

1. These wonderful metaphors come from Peter Kreeft, *Fundamentals of the Faith* (San Francisco: Ignatius Press, 1988), 190–191.
2. E. M. Bounds, *Power Through Prayer*, in *The Complete Works of E. M. Bounds on Prayer* (Grand Rapids, MI: Baker Book House, 1990), 447.
3. John Calvin, *Institutes of the Christian Religion*, vol. 1 (Philadelphia: The Westminster Press, 1977), 35,37.
4. Thomas à Kempis, *The Imitation of Christ*. Leo Sherley-Price, trans. (New York: Penguin Classics, 1952), 98.

5. Ronald Klug, ed. *Prayers from the Imitation of Christ* (Minneapolis: Augsburg, 1996), 24.

Luke

1. William Barclay, *The Gospel of Luke* (Philadelphia: The Westminster Press, 1956), 301–302.
2. Charles Spurgeon, *Spurgeon's Expository Encyclopedia*, vol. 4 (Grand Rapids, MI: Baker Book House, 1978), 329.

John

1. William Barclay, *The Gospel of John*, vol. 1 (Philadelphia: The Westminster Press,1955), xv.
2. Earl Palmer, *The Intimate Gospel* (Waco, TX: Word Books, 1978).
3. Thomas Wilson, quoted in *2000 Years of Classic Christian Prayers*, Owen Collins, ed. (Maryknoll, NY: Orbis Books, 1999), 126.
4. C. S. Lewis, *The Voyage of the Dawn Treader* (New York: The Macmillan Company, 1952), 193,196.
5. "At The Funeral of Sir William Cockayne," *Great Thoughts*, 191:1, LXXX, 12 December 1626.
6. "XXVI Sermons," *Great Thoughts*, 191:2, (1660), x. 29 February 1627/8.
7. John Donne, *Selections from Divine Poems, Sermons, Devotions, and Prayers*, John Booty, ed. (New York: Paulist Press, 1990), 82.
8. See Palmer, *The Intimate Gospel*, for an excellent discussion of the scene, 115–118.
9. Dante Alighieri, *The Divine Comedy*, Charles Eliot Norton, trans. (Chicago: Encyclopedia Britannica, 1952), 157.
10. Quoted in Earl Palmer, *The Intimate Gospel*, 129.

Acts

1. John Stott, *The Spirit, The Church and the World, The Message of Acts* (Downers Grove, IL: InterVarsity Press, 1990), 34.
2. Anna B. Warner and David Rutherford McGuire, "Jesus Loves Me." Public Domain.
3. C. S. Lewis, *Surprised by Joy* (New York: Harcourt and Brace, 1955), 228–229.
4. Ibid, 229.
5. John Piper, *Let the Nations Be Glad* (Grand Rapids, MI: Baker Book House, 1993), 11.
6. Elliott Wright, *Holy Company* (New York: Macmillan Publishing Co., Inc., 1980), 28.
7. *The Study of Spirituality*, edited by Cheslyn Jones, Geoffrey Wainwright, Edward Yarnold, S.J. (New York: Oxford University Press, 1986), 366.
8. Owen Collins, ed. *2000 Years of Classic Christian Prayers* (Maryknoll, NY: Orbis Books, 1999), 71.

Romans

1. Quoted in John Stott, *Romans, God's Good News for the World* (Downers Grove, IL: InterVarsity Press, 1994), 19.
2. James Boice, *Romans*, vol. 2, "The Reign of Grace," Romans 5–8 (Grand Rapids, MI: Baker Book House, 1992), 892.
3. I am indebted to John Stott for these categories taken from his commentary *Romans, God's Good News for the World* (Downers Grove, IL: InterVarsity Press, 1994), 390.
4. *The Diaries of David Brainerd*, Jonathan Edwards, ed. (Grand Rapids, MI: Baker Book House, 1989), 170.

1 Corinthians

1. Quoted in *Devotional Classics*, A RENOVARE Resource for Spiritual Renewal, Richard J. Foster and James Bryan Smith, eds. (HarperSanFrancisco: 1993), 16.
2. http://www.hamline.edu/~dkrueger/jbaillie.html.
3. http://www.familychristian.com/shop/product.asp?ProdID=5680.

4. John Baillie, *A Diary of Private Prayer* (New York: Charles Scribner's Sons, 1949), 25.

5. 1 Corinthians 13:13, Phillip's paraphrase.

2 Corinthians 1. Joseph Scriven, "What a Friend We Have in Jesus," *The Hymnal* (Waco, TX: Word, Inc., 1986), 435.

2. Sermon on 2 Corinthians 10:4–5 by Alexander Maclaren, *Expositions of Holy Scripture*, vol. 14 (Grand Rapids, MI: Baker Book House, 1977), 61.

Galatians 1. http://www.jesus.org.uk/ja/mag_revivalfires_chadwick.shtml.

2. Samuel Chadwick, *Praying in the Spirit* (April 2000). http://www.heraldofhiscoming.com.

3. http://www.jesus.org.uk/ja/mag_revivalfires_chadwick.shtml/other/home_htm.

4. Chadwick, *Praying in the Spirit.*

5. Samuel Chadwick, *The Way to Pentecost*, http://www.heraldofhiscoming.com.

6. Samuel Chadwick, *The Path of Prayer*, http://www.heraldofhiscoming.com.

7. Chadwick, *The Path of Prayer.*

8. Quoted in John Stott, *The Contemporary Christian* (Downers Grove, IL: InterVarsity Press, 1992), 156.

Ephesians 1. C. S. Lewis, *The Weight of Glory* (Grand Rapids, MI: Eerdmans, 1977), 1–2.

Colossians 1. Story told by Earl Palmer, *Alive From the Center* (Waco, TX: Word Incorporated, 1982), 19.

2. *The Oxford Dictionary of Quotations* (Oxford: Oxford University Press, 1980), 275:36.

3. Ibid., 274:8.

4. Ibid., 90:15.

5. *Dr. Johnson's Prayers*, Elton Trueblood, ed. (New York: Harper and Brothers, 1947), x–xi.

6. *The Oxford Dictionary*, 275:3.

7. Trueblood, *Dr. Johnson's Prayers*, 5.

8. See also the devotion on 2 Corinthians 4:16–18.

1 Thessalonians 1. Quoted by Robert Llewelyn, *Our Duty and Our Joy* (London: Darton, Longman and Todd, Ltd, 1993), p. 1; from chapter 15 of William Law's, *A Serious Call to a Devout and Holy Life.*

2 Thessalonians 1. Charles Wesley, *Psalms and Hymns*, 1738.

2 Timothy 1. George Herbert, "Prayer (I)." http://eir.library.utoronto.ca/rpo/display/poem983.html.

2. "I Gave My Life for Thee," *The Hymnal for Worship and Celebration*, Tom Fettke, ed. (Waco, TX: Word Music, 1986), 453

3. J. Gilchrist Lawson, *Deeper Experiences of Famous Christians* (Uhrichsville, OH: Barbour Publishing, Inc., 1999), 268.

4. Frances R. Havergal, "Take My Life and Let It Be," *The Hymnal*, 379.

5. Martyn Lloyd-Jones, *Twenty Centuries of Great Preaching*, vol. 11, Maier to Sangster (Waco, TX: Word, Inc., 1971), 296.

Hebrews 1. C. S. Lewis, *The Last Battle* (New York: The Macmillan Company, 1956), 160, 162.

2. Catharine Swift, *Gladys Aylward* (Minneapolis, MN: Bethany House Publishers, 1989), 15.

3. *Biographical Sketches of Memorable Christians of the Past, 3 January, 1970.* http://justus.anglican.org/resources/bio/73.html.
4. *Glimpses Issue #6:* "Gladys Aylward's 'Impossible Mission' to China", http://www.gospelcom.net/chi/GLIMPSEF/Glimpses/glmps006.shtml.
5. Peter Kreeft, *Fundamentals of the Faith, Essays in Christian Apologetics* (San Francisco: Ignatius Press, 1988), 193.
6. Eugene Peterson, *A Long Obedience in the Same Direction* (Downers Grove, IL: InterVarsity Press, 2000), 175.
7. P. T. Forsyth, *The Soul of Prayer* (London: Independent Press, 1954), 11.
8. J. B. Phillips, *The New Testament in Modern English* (London: Geoffrey Bles, 1960), 502.
9. *The Heidelberg Catechism* (Grand Rapids, MI: CRC Publications, 1988), question 116.
10. Quoted in *The Life and Diary of David Brainerd*, Jonathan Edwards, ed. (Grand Rapids, MI: Baker Book House, 1989), 14.
11. Quoted in *The Study of Spirituality*, Cheslyn Jones, Geoffrey Wainwright, Edward Yarnold, SJ, eds. (Oxford: Oxford University Press, 1986), 474.
12. This is an abbreviation of the full title, *An Humble Attempt to Promote Explicit Agreement and Visible Union Among God's People, in Extraordinary Prayer for the Revival of Religion, and the Advancement of Christ's Kingdom on Earth, Pursuant to Scripture Promises and Prophecies Concerning the Last Times.*

James
1. Adelaide A. Pollard, "Have Thine Own Way, Lord," *The Hymnal for Worship and Celebration* (Waco, TX: Word Music, 1986), 371.
2. Johann Scheffler, translated by John Wesley, "Thee Will I Love, My Strength," *Hymns II* (Downers Grove, IL: Intervarsity Press, 1976), 117.
3. Quoted by Robert Llewelyn, *Our Duty and Our Joy* (London: Darton, Longman and Todd, Ltd, 1993), 25.
4. Quoted in *Devotional Classics*, Richard J. Foster and James Bryan Smith, eds. (San Francisco: HarperSanFrancisco, 1993), 68.
5. *2000 Years of Classic Christian Prayers*, Owen Collins, ed. (Maryknoll, NY: Orbis Books, 1999), 44.
6. Ibid., 67.

1 Peter
1. G. K. Chesterton, *Orthodoxy* (San Francisco: Ignatius Press, 1986), 365.
2. C. S. Lewis, *The Screwtape Letters* (New York: The Macmillan Company, 1944), 16.

1 John
1. "Before the Throne of God Above," by Charitie Lees Bancroft, quoted by David Jackman, *The Message of John's Letters* (Downers Grove, IL: InterVarsity Press, 1988), 40.

Jude
1. P. T. Forsyth, *The Soul of Prayer* (London: Independent Press, 1954), 11.
2. Ibid.
3. Ibid.
4. Ibid., 88.
5. Ibid., 92.

Revelation
1. See Eugene Peterson, *Reversed Thunder, The Revelation of John and the Praying Imagination* (San Francisco: Harper and Row, 1988).
2. Vernard Eller, *The Most Revealing Book of the Bible: Making Sense Out of Revelation* (Grand Rapids, MI: Eerdmans, 1974), 93.
3. Quoted by E. Michael and Sharon Rusten, *The One Year Book of Christian History* (Wheaton, IL: Tyndale House Publishers, 2003), 142–143.

DATE

REQUEST

GOD'S RESPONSE

DATE

REQUEST

GOD'S RESPONSE

PRAYER REQUESTS

DATE

REQUEST

GOD'S RESPONSE

DATE

REQUEST

GOD'S RESPONSE

DATE

REQUEST

GOD'S RESPONSE

DATE

REQUEST

GOD'S RESPONSE

PRAYER REQUESTS

DATE

REQUEST

GOD'S RESPONSE

DATE

REQUEST

GOD'S RESPONSE

PRAYER REQUESTS

DATE

REQUEST

GOD'S RESPONSE

DATE

REQUEST

GOD'S RESPONSE

PRAYER REQUESTS

DATE

REQUEST

GOD'S RESPONSE

DATE

REQUEST

GOD'S RESPONSE

PRAYER REQUESTS

DATE

REQUEST

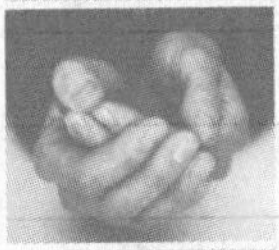

GOD'S RESPONSE

DATE

REQUEST

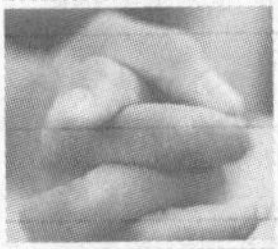

GOD'S RESPONSE

PRAYER REQUESTS

DATE

REQUEST

GOD'S RESPONSE

DATE

REQUEST

GOD'S RESPONSE

DATE

REQUEST

GOD'S RESPONSE

DATE

REQUEST

GOD'S RESPONSE

PRAYER REQUESTS

DATE

REQUEST

GOD'S RESPONSE

DATE

REQUEST

GOD'S RESPONSE

DATE

REQUEST

_____

_____

_____

_____

GOD'S RESPONSE

_____

_____

_____

_____

_____

DATE

REQUEST

_____

_____

_____

_____

GOD'S RESPONSE

_____

_____

_____

_____

_____

PRAYER REQUESTS

DATE

REQUEST

GOD'S RESPONSE

DATE

REQUEST

GOD'S RESPONSE

DATE

REQUEST

GOD'S RESPONSE

DATE

REQUEST

GOD'S RESPONSE

PRAYER REQUESTS

DATE

REQUEST

GOD'S RESPONSE

DATE

REQUEST

GOD'S RESPONSE

DATE

REQUEST

GOD'S RESPONSE

DATE

REQUEST

GOD'S RESPONSE

Prayer Devotional Bible

GENERAL EDITOR:
Ben Patterson

PROJECT MANAGEMENT AND EDITORIAL:
Shari Vanden Berg

EDITORIAL ASSISTANCE:
Julie Zahm; Kathryn Jesse

THEOLOGICAL REVIEWER:
Andrew Sloan, M. Div., Oral Roberts University

PRODUCTION MANAGEMENT:
Phil Herich

COVER DESIGN:
Jamie DeBruyn

INTERIOR DESIGN:
Sharon VanLoozenoord, Belmont, MI

PROOFREADING:
Peachtree Editorial and Proofreading Service, Peachtree, GA

INTERIOR TYPESETTING:
Nancy Wilson

Guarantee

Care